Submarine Periscopes

There is over half a century of experience in the design and manufacture of Barr & Stroud periscopes. In service with the Royal Navy and many other navies. In all classes of submarine, from midget to nuclear. Optical system achieves maximum light transmission and image quality. Periscope design tailored to individual specification.

- ☐ Diameters 180mm, 240mm and 254mm.
- ☐ Dual Magnification.
- ☐ Anti vibration.
- ☐ Sextant – natural or artificial horizon.
- ☐ Photography – standard or motorised 35mm.
- ☐ Low light television.
- ☐ Image intensifier.
- ☐ Electronic support measures.
- ☐ Laser rangefinder.

Masts for medium and large submarines supplied for radar navigation, wide band radar warning, direction finding and vhf communication. Also snort induction and exhaust masts.

For further details contact Barr & Stroud Limited, 1 Pall Mall East, London SW1Y 5AU, England. Telephone: 01-930 1541. Telex: 261877.

Barr & Stroud

RANK NIGHTSIGHTS STAR IN ALL THEATRES OF WAR.

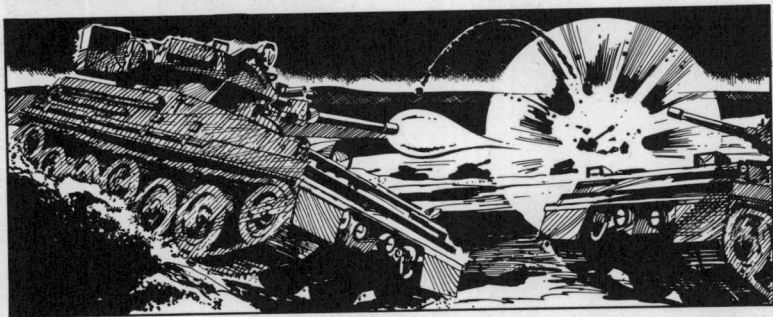

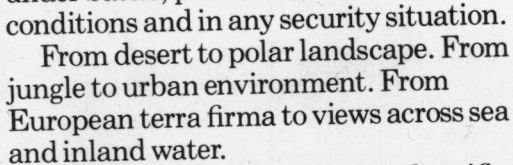

Each Rank nightsight is fully effective under battle, patrol or surveillance conditions and in any security situation.

From desert to polar landscape. From jungle to urban environment. From European terra firma to views across sea and inland water.

Rank nightsights can be fitted to rifles, machine guns, rocket launchers, light field artillery and armoured fighting vehicles, including main battle tanks.

The range also includes four different types for surveillance or directing action.

Rank nightsights out perform any others. For instance, the latest AFV sight combines day and night viewing, injects ballistic information, incorporates laser range finding, detects infra red and searches up to 360°.

Rank nightsights have been proven in action in major wars, guerilla warfare and general security throughout the world.

Rank sights are rugged, soldier proof, easy to operate, simple to maintain and last at least ten years. Each Rank sight has been subject to the fullest environment and approval testing.

Because they're a complete family of nightsights, many parts are interchangeable. You have a single source for spares and service back up. And technician training is part of the Rank service.

RANK PRECISION INDUSTRIES
RANK PULLIN CONTROLS
Langston Road, Debden, Loughton, Essex, England.
Tel.: 01-508 5522. Telex: 23855. Cables: Survey, Loughton.

JANE'S FIGHTING SHIPS
1978/79

When they join the Services, will your trainers and simulators still resemble the real thing?

Buying training equipment is an investment in the future.

Face the fact that your needs are going to change year by year, and think of this when you choose.

Ferranti trainers and simulators are designed to be expandable and versatile. They need to be, whether they're for training crews, or command teams, or operator teams, or individual operators. (Which reminds us to tell you that Ferranti make trainers for all these).

Ask us about our Action Speed Tactical Trainer for command teams, our Radar Operator Trainer, our operations room models, our team trainers for ASW helicopters, frigates and submarines. All give you the benefits of advanced Ferranti technology, and all are adaptable to changing needs.

Choose Ferranti and have training equipment you can build on as well as depend on.

Ferranti Limited,
Digital Systems Division, Bracknell,
Berkshire RG12 1RA
Telephone: 0344 3232
Military Systems Division, Wythenshawe,
Manchester M22 5LA
Telephone: 061-437 5291

FERRANTI
Computer Systems

DSD 74

LM 2500:
Facts - not a fisherman's tale

From the pathways of the sky to the routes of the oceans. Jointly built by Fiat and General Electric, the LM 2500 is the only turbine of the new generation to have been developed from aircraft engines with technical specifications ensuring its safe use in the propulsion of ships, namely low size-to-power and weight-to-power ratios, a high standard of performance permitting a low level of fuel consumption, and power outputs ranging from 16,000 to 27,000 horsepower. In the wake of the success enjoyed by the LM 2500 on the U.S.S. Callaghan, the U.S. Navy has made provision for the adoption of more than 300 such units as the standard power plant of her new ships. And the Navies of Italy, West Germany, Peru, Venezuela, Australia, Iran, Indonesia, and Saudi Arabia have followed suit by choosing this outstanding turbine for carrying their latest ships over the seven seas. Of great interest is also the possibility of using the LM 2500 on merchant vessels, especially container ships and liquid oil tankers. This is sound technological fact - not a fisherman's tale.

Fiat Aviazione
the history of aviation

Alphabetical list of advertisers

A

ABMTM Ltd
Marine Division, 20 Park Street,
London W1Y 4NA, England .... [112]

Aerimpianti SpA
Via Bergamo 21, 20135 Milan, Italy .... [83]

Aermarelli
Viale V. Lancetti 43, 20158 Milan, Italy .... [110]

Aérospatiale
37 boulevard de Montmorency,
75781 Paris Cedex 16, France .... [128]

Agusta
Cascina Costa, 20151 Gallarate, Italy .... [78]

Ailsa Shipbuilding Co Ltd
Harbour Road, Troon, Ayrshire, Scotland .... [114]

Alsthom-Atlantique
2 quai de Seine, 93 St Denis, France .... [134]

Ameeco (Hydrospace) Ltd
Bilton Road, Manor Road, Erith, Kent, England .. [82]

Ateliers & Chantiers C Auroux
7 boulevard Chanzy,
33120 Arcachon, France .... [90]

Avco Lycoming
550 South Main Street, Stratford,
Connecticut 06479, USA .... [19]

B

Barr & Stroud Ltd
Kinnaird House, 1 Pall Mall East, London
SW1Y 5AU, England .... *facing inside front cover*

Blohm & Voss AG
PO Box 10 07 20, D-2000 Hamburg 1,
Federal Republic of Germany .... [51]

Bofors AB
Ordnance Division, Box 500,
S-690 20, Bofors, Sweden .... [132]

Borletti Fratelli SpA
Defence Products Division, Via Washington 70,
20146 Milan, Italy .... [85]

Breda Meccanica Bresciana SpA
Via Lunga 2, 25100 Brescia, Italy .... [91]

Bremer Vulkan
Lindenstrasse, D-2820 Bremen 70,
Federal Republic of Germany .... [109]

British Aerospace Aircraft Group
Richmond Road, Kingston upon Thames,
Surrey KT2 5QS, England .... [72] & [73]

British Aerospace Dynamics Group
Six Hills Way, Stevenage,
Hertfordshire SG1 2DA, England .... [21]

British Hovercraft Corporation
East Cowes, Isle of Wight, England .... [23]

Brooke Marine Ltd
Heath Road, Lowestoft, Suffolk NR33 9LZ,
England .... [56] & [57]

SG Brown Communications Ltd
King George's Avenue, Watford,
Hertfordshire WD1 7QP, England .... [35]

C

Cantiere Navale Breda SpA
Via Delle Industrie 18,
Venice Marghera, Italy .... [66] & [67]

Cantiere Navaltecnica SpA
22 Via S Raineri, 98100 Messina, Italy .... [117]

Cantieri Baglietto SpA
Piazza Stefano Baglietto 3,
17019 Varozze, Italy .... [88] & [89]

Cantieri Navali Riuniti SpA
Via Cipro 11, 16129 Genoa, Italy .... [46] & [47]

Castoldi SpA
Viale Mazzini 161, 20081 Abbiategrosse,
Milan, Italy .... [63]

Chantiers & Atelier de la Perriere
8 boulevard Abbé le Cam,
56100 Lorient, France .... [43]

Chantiers Navals de L'Esterel
BP 10, 06321 Cannes-La-Bocca, France .... [62]

CIT Alcatel
Marine Division, 1 avenue Aristidue-Briand,
49117 Arcue 1, Paris, France .... [60]

CNIM
50 avenue des Champs-Elysées,
75008 Paris, France .... [82]

Crestitalia SpA
Via Gallarate 36, 20151 Milan, Italy .... [52]

CRM SrL
Via Manzoni 12, 20100 Milan, Italy ...... [118] & [119]

D

The Decca Navigator Co Ltd
Decca Radar Ltd, 9 Albert Embankment,
London SE1 7SW, England .... [103]

De Vries Shipyards
PO Box 258, Aalsmeer, The Netherlands .... [68]

DMS Inc
DMS Building, 100 Northfield Street,
Greenwich, Connecticut 06830, USA .... [62]

DMS Inc
31 Station Road, Henley-on-Thames, Oxfordshire,
England .... [62]

Dravo Steelship Corporation
Route 4, Box 167, Pine Bluff, Arkansas 71602,
USA .... [43]

DTCN
2 rue Royale, 75008 Paris, France .... [122]

Dubigeon-Normandie
24 avenue de la Grande Armée,
75016 Paris, France .... [114]

E

Edo Corporation
13-10 111th Street, College Point,
New York 11356, USA .... [84]

Elettronica San Georgio SpA (ELSAG)
Via Hermada 6, 16154 Genoa/Sestri, Italy .. [40] & [41]

Graseby

Principal suppliers of Sonar to the Royal Navy

Sonars for
**Anti-Submarine Carriers
Destroyers
Frigates
Corvettes
Submarines**

Supplied World-wide

GRASEBY INSTRUMENTS LIMITED
Kingston-By-Pass, Surbiton, Surrey, Great Britain, KT6 7LR.   Telephone: 01-397 5311.   Telex: 262795

ALPHABETICAL LIST OF ADVERTISERS

Elettronica SpA
Via Tiburtina Valeria km 13.700,
Rome, Italy .... [61]

Elmer Montadel SpA
PO Box 189, Viale dell'Industria 4,
00040 Pomezia, Rome, Italy .... [115]

F

Fairey Marine Ltd
School Lane, Hamble, Southampton,
Hampshire SO3 5NB, England .... [29]

Ferranti Ltd
Digital Systems Division, Bracknell,
Berkshire RG12 1DA, England .... [2]

Fiat Aviazione
Via Nizza 312, Caselle Postale 1389,
10100 Turin, Italy .... [3]

Fincantieri
Via Sardegna n.40, Rome 00187, Italy .... [38]

G

Grandi Motori Trieste
PO Box 497, 34100 Trieste, Italy .... [44]

Graseby Instruments Ltd
Kingston-by-Pass, Surbiton,
Surrey KT6 7LR, England .... [5]

H

Halter Marine Services Inc
PO Box 29266, New Orleans,
Louisiana 70189, USA .... [15]

Hatch & Kirk Export Co Inc
5111 Leary Avenue NW, Seattle,
Washington 98107, USA .... [39]

Hollandse Signaalapparaten BV
PO Box 42, Henglo, The Netherlands .... [124]

Howaldtswerke-Deutsche Werft AG
PO Box 146309, D-2300 Kiel 14,
Federal Republic of Germany .... [64]

Hycor Inc
North Woburn Industrial Park, Woburn,
Massachusetts 01801, USA .... [142]

I

Ingenieurkontor Lübeck
PO Box 1690, Niels-Bohr-Ring 5, D-2400
Lübeck 1, Federal Republic of Germany .... [64]

INMA SpA
Viale S Bartolomeo 362, 19100 La Spezia,
Italy .... [94]

Isotta Fraschini Motori Breda
Via Milan 7, 21047 Saronno, Varese, Italy .... [59]

Israel Aircraft Industries
Ben Gurion International Airport, Israel .... [13]

Italcantieri SpA
Corso Cavour 1, 54132 Trieste, Italy .... [93]

Italsider SpA
Piazza Dante 7, 16121 Genoa, Italy .... [49]

Italtel SpA
12 Piazzale Zavattari, 20149 Milan, Italy .... [140]

K

Kaeser Klimatechnik
Schnackemburgallee 47-51, 2000 Hamburg 54,
Federal Republic of Germany .... [9]

K

Kollmorgen Corporation
Electro-Optical Division, Northampton,
Massachusetts 01060, USA .... [35]

Korody-Colyer Corporation
112 North Avalon Boulevard, Wilmington,
California 90744, USA .... [130]

Fried. Krupp GmbH
Krupp Atlas-Elektronik, Sebaldsbrucker
Herrstr. 235, POB 448545, 2800 Bremen 44,
Federal Republic of Germany .... [70]

L

Lips BV
Lipsstraat 52, Drunen, The Netherlands
inside back cover

Lürssen Werft
Friedrick-Klippert Strasse 1, PO Box 70 00 30,
D-2820 Bremen 70, Federal Republic of
Germany .... [100] & [101]

M

MacTaggart Scott & Co Ltd
PO Box 1, Hunter Avenue, Loanhead,
Midlothian EH20 9SP, Scotland .... [77]

Marconi Communications Systems Ltd
Marconi House, New Street, Chelmsford,
Essex CH1 19L, England .... *inside front cover*

Marconi Space & Defence Systems Ltd
The Grove, Warren Lane, Stanmore,
Middlesex HA7 4LY, England .... [11]

Melara Club
c/o Elettronica San Giorgio (ELSAG), Via Hermada 6,
16153 Genoa/Sestri, Italy .... [96] & [97]

Misar SpA
Via Gavardo 6, 25016 Ghedi (Brescia), Italy ..... [102]

Montedison Group
Head Office, Via GB Morgagni 31,
00161 Rome, Italy .... [71]

Motoren-und Turbinen-Union GmbH (MTU)
Olgastrasse 75, D-7990 Friedrichshafen 1,
Federal Republic of Germany .... [17]

N

Nevesbu
PO Box 289-2501 CG, The Hague,
The Netherlands .... [111]

O

Oerlikon-Bührle/Contraves
PO Box 888, CH-8050 Zurich, Switzerland .... [136]

Officine Galileo
Montedison Group, Via Carlo Bini 44,
50134 Florence, Italy .... [76]

Officine Panerai SrL
2 Piazza G Ferraris, 50131 Florence, Italy .... [43]

OTO Melara SpA
Via Valdilocchi 15, 19100 La Spezia, Italy .... [27]

P

Paxman Diesels Ltd
PO Box 8, Paxman Works, Colchester,
Essex CO1 2HW, England .... [24] & [25]

Philips Elektronikindustrier AB
Defense Elektronics, S-17520 Järfälla 1,
Sweden .... [75]

Plessey Marine is the principal sonar contractor to the Royal Navy —and to navies around the world.

- ☐ Frigate and Corvette sonars
- ☐ Submarine sonars
- ☐ Helicopter sonars
- ☐ Minehunting sonars
- ☐ Passive sonars

PLESSEY
electronic systems

PLESSEY MARINE
Ilford Essex United Kingdom IG2 6BB
Telephone: London (01) 478 3040

ALPHABETICAL LIST OF ADVERTISERS

Philips Usfa BV
Meerenakkerweg 1, Eindhoven,
The Netherlands .... [58]

Plessey Avionics & Communications
Ilford, Essex IG1 4AQ, England .... [95]

Plessey Marine
Uppark Drive, Ilford, Essex IG1 4AQ, England ... [7]

Plessey Radar
Addlestone, Weybridge, Surrey KT15 2PW,
England .... [50]

R

Rank Pullin Controls
Langston Road, Debden, Loughton, Essex,
England .... *front endpaper iv*

Raytheon Corporation
141 Spring Street, Lexington,
Massachusetts 02173, USA .... [104] & [105]

Rhine-Schelde-Verolme
BV kon Mij "de Schelde", Glacisstraat 165,
PO Box 16, Vlissingen, The Netherlands .... [54]

Rinaldo Piaggio SpA
Viale Brigata Bisagno 14, 16129 Genoa, Italy .... [98]

Riva Calzoni SpA
Via Emilia Ponente, 72 Bologna, Italy .... [31]

S

SACM
BP 1210, 1 rue de la Fonderie, F-68054
Mulhouse Cedex, France .... [92]

Safare-Crouzet
BP 171, 06005 Nice Cedex, France .... [90]

SEPA SpA
Lungo Stura Lazio 45, 10156 Turin, Italy .... [106]

Selenia SpA
Marine Division, Via Tiburtina km 12.400,
00131 Rome, Italy .... [80]

Selenia SpA
Special Equipment & Systems Sivision, PO Box 7083,
Via Tiburtina km 12.400, 00131 Rome, Italy ..... [87]

SFCN
66 quai Alfred Sisley,
92390 Villeneuve la Garenne, France .... [86]

Sillinger
150 rue de Lyon, 75012 Paris, France .... [76]

The Sippican Corporation
Oceanographic Systems Division, 7 Barnabas Road,
Massachusetts 02738, USA .... [36] & [37]

Sistel-Sistemi Elettronica SpA
The Montedison Group, Via Tiburtina 1210,
Rome, Italy .... [113]

SMA SpA
Via del Ferrone 5, Casella Postale 200, 50100 Florence,
Italy .... *facing inside back cover*

Snia Viscosa SpA
Defence & Space Division, Via Sicilia 162,
00187 Rome, Italy .... [65]

Sofrexan
30 rue d'Astorg, 75008 Paris, France .... [68]

Sperry Gyroscope
Downshire Way, Bracknell,
Berkshire RG12 1QL, England .... [126]

T

Termomeccanica Italiana SpA
Via del Molo 1, 19100 La Spezia, Italy .... [108]

Thomson CSF/ASM
23 rue de Courcelles, 75008 Paris, France .... [53]

Thomson CFS/AVS
23 rue de Courcelles, 75008 Paris, France .... [48]

Thomson CSF/DRS
23 rue de Courcelles, 75008 Paris, France .... [79]

Thyssen Nordseewerke GmbH
D-2970 Emden, Federal Republic of Germany ... [42]

Trieste Club
c/o Selenia, Via Tiburtina km 12.400,
00131 Rome, Italy .... [74]

U

USEA SpA
Corso G. Matteotti 63, 19030
Pugliola di Lerici, Italy .... [82]

V

Valtec Italiana SrL
Via Valtellina 65, Milan, Italy .... [69]

Vickers Shipbuilding Ltd
PO Box 6, Barrow-in-Furness,
Cumbria LA14 1AB, England .... [107]

Vitro Selenia
Via Tiburtina 1020, 00156 Rome, Italy .... [55]

Vosper Singapore Ltd
200 Tanjong Rhu Road, Singapore 15,
Singapore .... [33]

Vosper Thornycroft (UK) Ltd
Vosper House, Southampton Road, Paulsgrove,
Portsmouth, Hampshire PO6 4QA, England ..... [45]

W

Whipp & Bourne (1975) Ltd
Castleton, Nr Rochdale, Lancashire, England .... [99]

Y

Yarrow (Shipbuilders) Ltd
Scotstoun, Glasgow G14 0XN, Scotland .... [138]

Z

Zahnradfabrik Friedrichshafen AG
PO Box 2520, D-7990 Friedrichshafen 1,
Federal Republic of Germany .... [81]

airconditioned by Kaeser

We produce and supply airconditioning systems for destroyers, frigates, corvettes, minehunters, fast patrol boats, minesweepers, submarines and hydrofoils.

Our reputation as experts in the field of marine airconditioning is world-wide. Our extensive experience and our ability to adapt to individual conditions enable us to develop and install airconditioning systems designed to meet specific demands (for instance, spacesaving units, lightweight units, shock and vibration proof units or intermagnetic models of our airconditioning equipment and systems).

In this respect we have up to now installed airconditioning for 371 navy-vessels for over 50 different international customers.

Our airconditioning experts are ready for a new challenge. Contact us personally or ask for our brochure "Marine Airconditioning".

KAESER KLIMATECHNIK: Partner of shipyards all over the world.
As examples, some of the shipyards, with whom we cooperate, are mentioned below:
Abeking & Rasmussen
Blohm & Voss AG
Boeing Corporation
Boelwerf
Cantieri Navali Fratelli Benetti
S/A Cockerill Yards
Constructions Mécaniques de Normandie
Empresa Nacional Bazan
Gruman Aircraft Corporation
Hellenic Shipyards Co.
Hong Leong Lürssen Shipyard
Howaldtswerke Deutsche Werft AG
Karlskrona Varvet AB
Korea Tacoma Marine Industries
Krögerwerft GmbH
Lürssen Werft
Lindenau
Orenstein-Koppel und Lübecker Maschinenbau
Rheinstahl Nordseewerke Emden GmbH
Schichau AG
Schlichting Werft
Supramar Pacific Shipbuilding Co. Ltd.
Singapore Shipbuilding & Engineering Ltd.
Vosper Thornycroft Ltd.
Vickers Limited Barrow Shipbuilding Works
Westermoen Hydrofoil AS

KAESER KLIMATECHNIK

marine division
Kaeser Klimatechnik
Schnackenburgallee 47-51
2000 Hamburg 54
Tel.: 040/85441
Telex: 02 13177

Classified list of advertisers

The companies advertising in this publication have informed us that they are involved in the fields of manufacture indicated below:

Acoustic sweeps
Sperry Gyroscope

Acoustic transducers
Graseby instruments

Action information systems
Decca Navigator

Active information systems
Ferranti
Plessey Radar
SMA
Vickers

Active information trainers
DTCN
Ferranti

Air compressors
CIT Alcatel
Fincantieri

Aircraft, anti-submarine patrol
British Aerospace Aircraft Group
Rinaldo Piaggio

Aircraft arresting gear
Aérospatiale
MacTaggart Scott

Aircraft carriers
Cantieri Navali Riuniti
DTCN
Fincantieri
Vickers
Vosper Thornycroft

Aircraft countermeasure dispenser systems
Hycor

Aircraft instruments
Decca Navigator
DTCN
Edo Corporation
Ferranti
Sperry Gyroscope
Thomson CSF

Aircraft, maritime reconnaissance
British Aerospace Aircraft Group
DTCN
Rinaldo Piaggio

Air cushion vehicles
British Hovercraft Corporation
DTCN
Halter Marine
Vosper Thornycroft

Airframe manufacturers
Aérospatiale
Agusta
British Aerospace Aircraft Group
British Hovercraft Corporation
Rinaldo Piaggio

Alignment equipment
British Aerospace Dynamics Group

Alternators
DTCN

Ammunition
Bofors
DTCN
Oerlikon-Bührle
Snia Viscosa

Ammunition fuses
Borletti
DTCN
Oerlikon-Bührle
Snia Viscosa
Thomson CSF

Ammunition hoists
Blohm & Voss
DTCN
MacTaggart Scott
OTO Melara
Vickers

Antennae
British Aerospace Dynamics Group
SG Brown Communications
Decca Navigator
Hollandse Signaalapparaten
Marconi
Philips Elektronikindustrier
Plessey Radar
Selenia
Thomson CSF

Anti-ship missile defence systems
Hycor

Anti-submarine launchers
Brooke Marine
DTCN
Plessey Marine
Vickers
Yarrow (Shipbuilders)

Anti-submarine rocket launchers
Bofors
DTCN
Vickers

Anti-submarine rockets
Bofors
CIT Alcatel
DTCN

Anti-submarine weapon systems, long range
British Aerospace Dynamics Group

Assault craft
Ailsa Shipbuilding
Blohm & Voss
British Hovercraft Corporation
Brooke Marine
Cantieri Baglietto
Crestitalia
Dravo Steelship
Fairey Marine
Fincantieri
Halter Marine
SFCN
Supramar
Vosper Singapore
Vosper Thornycroft

Assault ships
Blohm & Voss
Brooke Marine
Cantieri Navali Riuniti
Dravo Steelship
DTCN
Fincantieri
SFCN
Vickers
Vosper Singapore
Vosper Thornycroft
Yarrow (Shipbuilders)

ASW weapon control systems
DTCN
Ferranti
Graseby Instruments
Hollandse Signaalapparaten
Philips Elektronikindustrier
Plessey Radar
Selenia
Thomson CSF

Audio ancillary test sets
SG Brown Communications
Safare-Crouzet

Automatic control systems
CIT Alcatel
DTCN
Ferranti
MTU
Selenia
Sperry Gyroscope
Thomson CSF

Automatic steering
Decca Navigator
Sperry Gyroscope

Auxiliary machinery
Blohm & Voss
DTCN
Fincantieri
MTU

Binoculars
Barr & Stroud
British Aerospace Dynamics Group
DTCN
Kollmorgen
Montedison Group
Officine Galileo

Binnacles, compass
Decca Navigator

Boilers
Blohm & Voss
Bremer Vulkan
DTCN
Howaldtswerke-Deutsche Werft
Paxman Diesels
Yarrow (Shipbuilders)

Books, naval
Vosper Thornycroft

MSDS—
weapons for the 1980s and beyond

Marconi Space and Defence Systems is the nominated prime contractor for all current torpedo programmes in the United Kingdom, for both submarine-launched and air-launched weapons.

To meet defence needs in the 1980s and beyond, the MSDS Tigerfish wire-guided and acoustic-homing torpedo is in full production for the Royal Navy; and the new and very advanced MSDS Sting Ray lighweight torpedo, which can be launched from aircraft, surface ships or pilotless carriers, is in the late stages of development.

MSDS capability and experience in underwater weapons covers every aspect of research, development, manufacture and in-service support, including torpedo handling and ATE equipment, ancillary instrumentation packages and pre-setters, complex instrumentation systems for underwater test ranges, acoustic targets and facsimile weapons for exercise use.

Marconi Space and Defence Systems Limited
A GEC-Marconi Electronics Company
Marketing Department, The Grove, Warren Lane, Stanmore, Middlesex HA7 4LY, England
Telephone: 01-954 2311 Telex: 22616
Telegrams: SPADEF Stanmore

MSDS *underwater weapons*
TECHNOLOGY IN DEPTH

CLASSIFIED LIST OF ADVERTISERS

Bulk carriers
Ailsa Shipbuilding
Blohm & Voss
Bremer Vulkan
Cantieri Navali Riuniti
Dubigeon-Normandie
Fincantieri
Howaldtswerke-Deutsche Werft
Italcantieri
Lürssen Werft
Sippican Corporation
Thyssen Nordseewerke
Vickers

B-OSS in sternframe
Italsider

Cable glands
Graseby instruments

Cable looms (with or without caissons)
DTCN

Capstans and windlasses
MacTaggart Scott
Riva Calzoni
Thyssen Nordseewerke

Car ferries
Ailsa Shipbuilding
Blohm & Voss
Bremer Vulkan
British Hovercraft Corporation
Brooke Marine
Cantieri Navali Riuniti
Chantiers de la Perriere
CNIM
DTCN
Dubigeon-Normandie
Fincantieri
Halter Marine
Italcantieri
Lürssen Werft
Thyssen Nordseewerke
Vickers
Yarrow (Shipbuilders)

Cargo handling equipment
Blohm & Voss
Bremer Vulkan
Fincantieri
MacTaggart Scott
Thyssen Nordseewerke

Cargo ships
Ailsa Shipbuilding
Blohm & Voss
Bremer Vulkan
Brooke Marine
Cantieri Navali Riuniti
Chantiers de la Perriere
Dubigeon-Normandie
Fincantieri
Halter Marine
Howaldtswerke-Deutsche Werft
Italcantieri
Lürssen WERFT
Rhine-Schelde-Verolme
Thyssen Nordseewerke
Vickers

Castings, aluminium-bronze
Barr & Stroud
DTCN
Lips
Vickers

Castings, high duty iron
Bremer Vulkan
DTCN

Castings, non-ferrous
DTCN
Vickers

Castings, shell moulded
Bremer Vulkan
DTCN
Ferranti

Castings, sg iron
Bremer Vulkan
DTCN
Ferranti

Castings, steel
Bremer Vulkan
DTCN
Italsider

Cathodic protection equipment
Marconi
Thomson CSF
Vickers

Centralised and automatic control
CIT Alcatel
Selenia
Thomson CSF
Vosper Thornycroft

Chaff
Hycor

Charts, nautical and aeronautical
Decca Navigator

Clear view screens
Decca Navigator

Coastal and inshore minesweepers
Ailsa Shipbuilding
British Hovercraft Corporation
Brooke Marine
Cantieri Baglietto
Cantieri Navali Riuniti
DTCN
Fincantieri
Halter Marine
Italcantieri
Nevesbu
Rhine-Schelde-Verolme
Vickers
Vosper Thornycroft
Yarrow (Shipbuilders)

Command/control/communications systems
DTCN
Ferranti
Graseby Instruments
Hollandse Signaalapparaten
Marconi
Oerlikon-Bührle
Philips Elektronikindustrier
Plessey Radar
Selenia
Sippican Corporation
Thomson CSF
Vosper Thornycroft

Command/control real-time displays
Ferranti
Hollandse Signaalapparaten
Philips Elektronikindustrier
Plessey Radar
Selenia
Thomson CSF

Communications systems
SG Brown Communications

Compressed air starters for gas turbines and diesel engines
DTCN
Hatch & Kirk

Compressors
CIT Alcatel
DTCN
Fincantieri

Computer guidance
Raytheon

Computer services
British Aerospace Dynamics Group
Ferranti
Plessey Radar
Thomson CSF
Vickers
Yarrow (Shipbuilders)

Computers
CIT Alcatel
Decca Navigator
Ferranti
Hollandse Signaalapparaten
Montedison Group
OTO Melara
Philips Elektronikindustrier
Selenia
Sperry Gyroscope
Thomson CSF

Condenser tubes
Fincantieri
Rhine-Schelde-Verolme

Condensers
Blohm & Voss
Bremer Vulkan
Fincantieri
Howaldtswerke-Deutsche Werft
Rhine-Schelde-Verolme
Thomson CSF

Container ships
Ailsa Shipbuilding
Blohm & Voss
Bremer Vulkan
Brooke Marine
Cantieri Navali Riuniti
DTCN
Dubigeon-Normandie
Fincantieri
Halter Marine
Howaldtswerke-Deutsche Werft
Italcantieri
Rhine-Schelde-Verolme
Thyssen Nordseewerke
Vickers

Control desks, electric
Lürssen Werft
Thomson CSF
Vosper Thornycroft
Whipp & Bourne

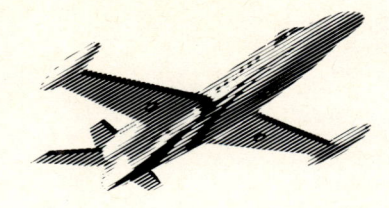

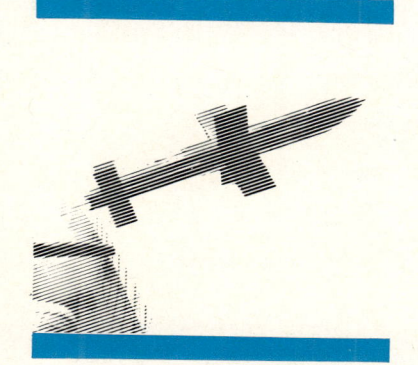

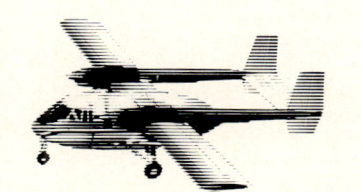

Your requirement: a modern navy. Your choice: IAI

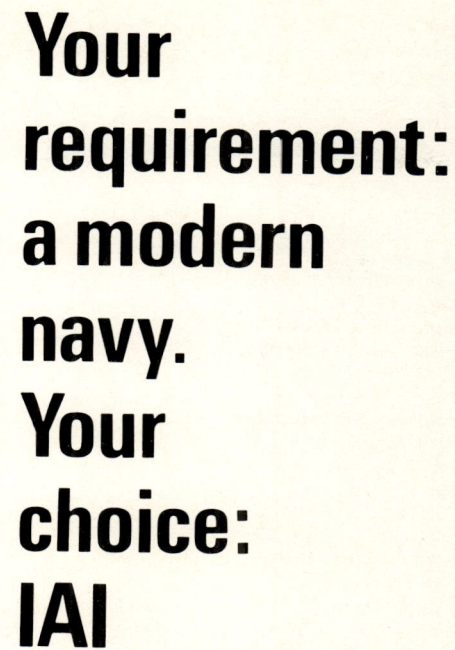

Ben Gurion International Airport, Israel
Tel: 973111. Telex: ISRAVIA 031102, 031114.
Cables: ISRAELAVIA.
New York:
Israel Aircraft Industries International Inc.,
50 West 23rd Street, N.Y. 10010. Tel: (212) 620-4400.
Brussels:
50, Ave des Arts. Tel: 5131455.

Israel Aircraft Industries
presents a complete naval package: Dvora missile boats and Dabur patrol vessels, Gabriel Mark I and II weapon systems; sea-to-sea missiles and launchers, EW capability, for both new and in-service vessels. Shipborne and coastal radar. Broad coverage communication systems. Sea Scan and Arava tactical naval support aircraft. Weapon trainer simulators. Even an electronic security fence. And most important of all, total operational training and logistic support, to bring your Navy to full readiness.
Your Navy. Your Nation.
They can depend on IAI's combat proven equipment and tri-space experience.
Call, write or telex:

IAI
Israel Aircraft Industries

a foundation to build on.

CLASSIFIED LIST OF ADVERTISERS

Control gear
Philips Elektronikindustrier
Paxman Diesels
Vosper Thornycroft

Corvettes
Blohm & Voss
Bremer Vulkan
Brooke Marine
Cantieri Navali Riuniti
Crestitalia
DTCN
Dubigeon-Normandie
Fincantieri
Halter Marine
Howaldtswerke-Deutsche Werft
INMA
Italcantieri
Lürssen Werft
Nevesbu
Rhine-Schelde-Verolme
Sofrexan
Thyssen Nordseewerke
Vickers
Vosper Singapore
Vosper Thornycroft
Yarrow (Shipbuilders)

Cranes, ships
DTCN
Dubigeon-Normandie
Howaldtswerke-Deutsche Werft
Rhine-Schelde-Verolme

Crankshafts for low-speed diesel engines
Italsider

Crankshafts in continuous-grain-flow for medium speed engines
Italsider

Cruisers
Brooke Marine
Cantieri Navali Riuniti
Crestitalia
Dubigeon-Normandie
Fincantieri
Nevesbu
Rhine-Schelde-Verolme
Vickers
Vosper Thornycroft
Yarrow (Shipbuilders)

Cylinder covers, forged and cast
Italsider

Data recording systems
British Aerospace Dynamics Group
SG Brown Communications
Decca Navigator
Plessey Radar
Sperry Gyroscope
Thomson CSF

Deck machinery
Cantieri Navali Riunti
DTCN
Fincantieri
Graseby Instruments
MacTaggart Scott
Thyssen Nordseewerke

Design-systems study and management services
Decca Navigator

Destroyers
Blohm & Voss
Brooke Marine
Cantieri Navali Riuniti
DTCN
Dubigeon-Normandie
Fincantieri
Italcantieri
Nevesbu
Rhine-Schelde-Verolme
Sofrexan
Thyssen Nordseewerke
Vickers
Vosper Thornycroft
Yarrow (Shipbuilders)

Diesel engines, auxiliary
Blohm & Voss
Bremer Vulkan
CRM
DTCN
Fincantieri
Grandi Motori Trieste
Isotta Fraschini
Korody-Colyer
MTU
Paxman Diesels
SACM
Vickers

Diesel engines, main propulsion
Alsthom Atlantique
Blohm & Voss
Bremer Vulkan
CRM
DTCN
Fincantieri
Grandi Motori Trieste
Isotta Fraschini
Korody-Colyer
MTU
Paxman Diesels
Rhine-Schelde-Verolme
SACM
Vickers

Diesel engine spare parts
Blohm & Voss
Bremer Vulkan
Cantieri Navali Riuniti
CRM
DTCN
Grandi Motori Trieste
Fincantieri
Hatch & Kirk
Korody-Colyer
MTU
Paxman Diesels
Rhine-Schelde-Verolme
Vickers

Diesel, fuel injection equipment
DTCN
Hatch & Kirk
Korody-Colyer
Rhine-Schelde-Verolme

Display systems
Decca Navigator
Graseby Instruments
Hollandse Signaalapparaten
Philips Elektronikindustrier
Plessey Radar
Selenia
Thomson CSF

Diving equipment
DTCN
Graseby Instruments
Officine Panerai
Safare-Crouzet
Sillinger

Diving vessels
Chantiers de la Perriere

Dock gates
Bremer Vulkan
DTCN
Dubigeon-Normandie
Fincantieri
Rhine-Schelde-Verolme
Thyssen Nordseewerke
Vickers

Doppler aircraft navigation systems
Decca Navigator

Dredgers
Ailsa Shipbuilding
Brooke Marine
DTCN
Dubigeon-Normandie
Fincantieri
Rhine-Schelde-Verolme
SFCN
Thyssen Nordseewerke

Dry cargo vessels
Ailsa Shipbuilding
Blohm & Voss
Bremer Vulkan
Brooke Marine
Cantieri Navali Riuniti
Dubigeon-Normandie
Fincantieri
Halter Marine
Howaldtswerke-Deutsche Werft
Italcantieri
Lürssen Werft
Rhine-Schelde-Verolme
Thyssen Nordseewerke
Vickers

Dry dock proprietors
Ailsa Shipbuilding
Blohm & Voss
CIT Alcatel
Fincantieri
Thyssen Nordseewerke

Dynamic positioning
British Hovercraft Corporation
DTCN
Lips
Thomson CSF
Vosper Thornycroft

Early warning systems
Raytheon

Echo sounders
DTCN
Edo Corporation
Graseby Instruments
Marconi
Thomson CSF

Electric cables
British Hovercraft Corporation

Electric countermeasures
Bofors
Decca Navigator
DTCN
Sperry Gyroscope
Thomson CSF

Electrical auxiliaries
DTCN
Paxman Diesels

Electrical equipment
DTCN
Officine Panerai

We build high speed patrol vessels.

Halter builds reliable, high speed craft for coastal, harbor and river patrol, fisheries surveillance, inland waterways security, air/sea rescue, fast attack, customs duties, perimeter defense, or whatever your mission.

Behind each Halter patrol boat is more than twenty years of shipbuilding experience and over 700 vessels delivered. This heritage brings a new dimension of operational reliability and maintenance simplicity while providing a platform for modern, sophisticated weaponry.

The Halmar patrol classes include 20 models ranging in size from 32 feet (9.7m.) to 188 feet (57m.). Their high performance hull forms contribute to exceptional speed, stability and seakeeping capabilities. Built of steel or aluminum, a great variety of propulsion systems are available for optimum efficiency.

Our service goes beyond the design and production of vessels to meet your specific requirements. We also provide crew training · in your nation and in your language and complete logistical support.

For complete information, please write or call us. We will be pleased to discuss your requirements.

Halter Marine Services, Inc.
Executive Plaza
Dept. AJR/NP Tel. (504)254-1222
10001 Lake Forest Blvd.
New Orleans, La. 70127
International Telex— 6821246
Domestic Telex— 58-4200
Cable: HALMAR

HALTER MARINE SERVICES INC.

The Total Shipbuilding Group

CLASSIFIED LIST OF ADVERTISERS

Electrical fittings
DTCN

Electrical installations and repairs
Bremer Vulkan
DTCN
Fincantieri
Vickers
Vosper Singapore
Vosper Thornycroft

Electrical switchgear
DTCN
Lürssen Werft
Thomson CSF
Vosper Singapore
Vosper Thornycroft
Whipp & Bourne

Electro-hydraulic auxiliaries
DTCN
Fincantieri
MacTaggart Scott
Vosper Thornycroft

Electronic countermeasures
Decca Navigator
DTCN
Hollandse Signaalapparaten
Philips Elektronikindustrier
Plessey Radar
Raytheon
Selenia
Thomson CSF

Electronic engine room telegraph
Officine Panerai
Vosper Thornycroft

Electronic equipment
SG Brown Communications
CIT Alcatel
Decca Navigator
DTCN
Ferranti
Marconi
Montedel
MTU
OTO Melara
Plessey Marine
Plessey Radar
Philips Elektronikindustrier
Raytheon
Selenia
Sippican Corporation
SMA
Sperry Gyroscope
Thomson CSF
USEA
Vickers
Vosper Thornycroft

Electronic equipment refits
Edo Corporation
DTCN
Ferranti
Marconi
Philips Elektronikindustrier
Plessey Marine
Plessey Radar
Sperry Gyroscope
Thomson CSF
Vosper Thornycroft

Engine monitors and data loggers
Decca Navigator
Vosper Thornycroft

Engine parts, diesel
Bremer Vulkan
CRM
DTCN
Fincantieri
Grandi Motori Trieste
Hatch & Kirk
Paxman Diesels
Rhine-Schelde-Verolme
Vickers

Engine speed controls
DTCN
Vosper Thornycroft

Engine start and shut-down controls
DTCN
Vosper Thornycroft

Engines, aircraft
Avo Lycoming
Fiat
MTU
Rinaldo Piaggio

Engines, diesel
Alsthom Atlantique
Blohm & Voss
Bremer Vulkan
Chantiers de L'Atlantique
CRM
DTCN
Fincantieri
Isotta Fraschini
MTU
Paxman Diesels
SACM

Engines, gas turbine
Avco Lycoming
CIT Alcatel
DTCN
Fiat
MTU
Rhine-Schelde-Verolme
Rinaldo Piaggio
SACM
Yarrow (Shipbuilders)

Engines, steam turbine
Blohm & Voss
Bremer Vulkan
Cantieri Navali Riuniti
Fincantieri
Yarrow (Shipbuilders)

Epicyclic gears
British Hovercraft Corporation
Vickers

Equipment for helicopter night deck landing
DTCN
Officine Panerai

Escort vessels
Blohm & Voss
Bremer Vulkan
Brooke Marine
Cantieri Navali Riuniti
DTCN
Fairey Marine
Fincantieri
Halter Marine
Italcantieri
Lürssen Werft
Nevesbu
Rhine-Schelde-Verolme
SFCN
Sofrexan
Thyssen Nordseewerke
Vickers

Fast patrol craft
Ailsa Shipbuilding
British Hovercraft Corporation
Brooke Marine
Cantieri Baglietto
Cantieri Navali Riuniti
Chantiers de la Perriere
Crestitalia
Dravo Steelship
DTCN
Fairey Marine
Fincantieri
Halter Marine
INMA
Lürssen Werft
Nevesbu
SFCN
Sillinger
Sofrexan
Supramar
Vosper Singapore
Vosper Thornycroft
Yarrow (Shipbuilders)

Fast warship design service
British Hovercraft Corporation
Brooke Marine
Cantieri Navali Riuniti
DTCN
Lürssen Werft
Rhine-Schelde-Verolme
Supramar
Vickers
Vosper Singapore
Vosper Thornycroft

Feed water heaters
Blohm & Voss
Fincantieri

Ferries
Ailsa Shipbuilding
Bremer Vulkan
British Hovercraft Corporation
Brooke Marine
Cantieri Navali Riuniti
DTCN
Dubigeon-Normandie
Fincantieri
Halter Marine
Howaldtswerke-Deutsche Werft
Italcantieri
Rhine-Schelde-Verolme
SFCN
Thyssen Nordseewerke
Vickers
Yarrow (Shipbuilders)

Fibre optics
Barr & Stroud
DTCN
Plessey Radar

Fibreglass vessels and other products
Crestitalia
DTCN
Fairey Marine
Halter Marine
Lürssen Werft
Vickers
Vosper Singapore
Vosper Thornycroft

Filters
DTCN

Filters, electronic
Barr & Stroud

Portrait of a Corporate Enterprise

Name

The MTU Group is formed by two companies, namely Motoren- und Turbinen-Union München GmbH and Motoren- und Turbinen-Union Friedrichshafen GmbH.

Headquarters

The main plants are located in Munich and Friedrichshafen, with a branch factory in Peißenberg/Obb.

Workforce

11,000 people on the payroll.
Service mechanics and engineers, lathe operators and data processors, toolmakers and salesmen, and a multitude of other vocations for a large variety of important tasks.

Turnover

More than 1 billion DM – Proof of the prominent position of leadership maintained by the MTU Group.

Products

Whether railroad or marine, vehicular or special-purpose, stationary or mobile applications – MTU Friedrichshafen's high-performance diesels are well known and highly appreciated throughout the world.

MTU München excels in the development, production and technical support of aircraft propulsion systems: Gas turbines for helicopters, turboprop engines, jet engines for commercial and military aircraft.

History

MTU is closely related to the beginning of motorization. Diesel, Daimler, Benz, and Maybach are the big names behind MTU. Daimler-Benz, Maybach, BMW, and M.A.N. are the technical and organizational roots of the MTU Group which was established in 1969.

Peculiarities

Through consistent engineering advancement and development of the high-performance diesel into an economical, ecology-oriented and powerful prime mover, MTU Friedrichshafen has set an example of modern technology usage.

Intensive research and testing in the development of advanced jet engines, use of up-to-date production and quality control techniques, and handling of materials technology tasks are featured functions of MTU München.

---

mtu
MOTOREN- UND TURBINEN-UNION GESELLSCHAFTEN
MÜNCHEN UND FRIEDRICHSHAFEN

CLASSIFIED LIST OF ADVERTISERS

Fire and salvage vessels
Brooke Marine
Cantieri Navali Riuniti
Chantiers de la Perriere
Crestitalia
Fincantieri
Halter Marine
Rhine-Schelde-Verolme
SFCN

Fire control
Raytheon

Fire control and gunnery equipment
Bofors
Ferranti
Hollandse Signaalapparaten
Kollmorgen
Montedison Group
Oerlikon-Bührle
OTO Melara
Philips Elektronikindustrier
Plessey Marine
Plessey Radar
Sperry Gyroscope
Thomson CSF
Vickers

Fittings, ships
DTCN
Fincantieri
Rhine-Schelde-Verolme
Vosper Singapore

Flares
Hycor

Forgings, steel
Italsider

Frigates
Blohm & Voss
Bremer Vulkan
Brooke Marine
Cantieri
Navali Riuniti
DTCN
Dubigeon-Normandie
Fincantieri
Italcantieri
Nevesbu
Rhine-Schelde-Verolme
Sofrexen
Thyssen Nordseewerke
Vickers
Vosper Thornycroft
Yarrow (Shipbuilders)

Fuel filtration equipment
DTCN
Fincantieri
Vickers

Fuel injectors, oil
DTCN

Gas turbine boats
Avco Lycoming
Blohm & Voss
Cantieri Baglietto
Cantieri Navali Riuniti
DTCN
Halter Marine
Vickers
Vosper Thornycroft
Yarrow (Shipbuilders)

Gas turbines
Avco Lycoming
CIT Alcatel
DTCN
Fiat
MTU
Rhine-Schelde-Verolme
SACM

Gear casings
Bremer Vulkan
Fincantieri
Rhine-Schelde-Verolme
Vickers

Gears
Isotta Fraschini

Gears and gearing
Bremer Vulkan
British Hovercraft Corporation
Fiat
Fincantieri
Howaldtswerke-Deutsche Werft
Vickers
Vosper Thornycroft

Gears, hypoid
Rhine-Schelde-Verolme

Gears, spiral bevel
Rhine-Schelde-Verolme

Gears, reverse-reduction
CRM
Isotta Fraschini
MTU
Rhine-Schelde-Verolme
Vickers
Vosper Thornycroft
Zahnradfabrik

Gears, spur
Rhine-Schelde-Verolme

Gears, vee drive
CRM
Rhine-Schelde-Verolme
Vosper Thornycroft
Isotta Fraschini
Zahnradfabrik

Generators, electric
Avco Lycoming
DTCN
Ferranti
Paxman Diesels

Governors
DTCN
Fincantieri
Hatch & Kirk

Governors, engine speed
DTCN
Hatch & Kirk

Guided missile servicing equipment
Aérospatiale
British Aerospace Dynamics Group
Fincantieri
OTO Melara
Rhine-Schelde-Verolme
Selenia
Thomson
CSF

Guided missile ships
Blohm & Voss
Bremer Vulkan
Brooke Marine
Cantieri Navali Riuniti
Dravo Steelship
DTCN
Fincantieri
Halter Marine
Italcantieri
Lürssen Werft
Montedison Group
Nevesbu
Rhine-Schelde-Verolme
Selenia
SFCN
Supramar
Thyssen Nordseewerke
Vickers
Vosper Thornycroft
Yarrow (Shipbuilders)

Guided missiles
Aérospatiale
Bofors
British Aerospace Dynamics Group
DTCN
Montedison Group
OTO Melara
Sistel-Sistemi
SMA
Sperry Gyroscope

Gun boats
Ailsa Shipbuilding
Brooke Marine
Cantieri Baglietto
Cantieri Navali Riuniti
Crestitalia
DTCN
Fairey Marine
Fincantieri
Halter Marine
INMA
Nevesbu
SFCN
Vosper Singapore
Vosper Thornycroft
Yarrow (Shipbuilders)

Guns and mountings
Bofors
Breda Meccanica
DTCN
Oerlikon-Bührle
OTO Melara
Vickers

Gun mounts
Bofors
Breda Meccanica
DTCN
Oerlikon-Bührle
OTO Melara
Vickers

Gun-sighting apparatus and height finders
DTCN
Montedison Group
Oerlikon-Burhle
Officine Galileo
Philips Elektronikindustrier
Thomson CSF
Vickers

Gyroscopic compasses
Decca Navigator
DTCN
Sperry Gyroscope
Thomson CSF

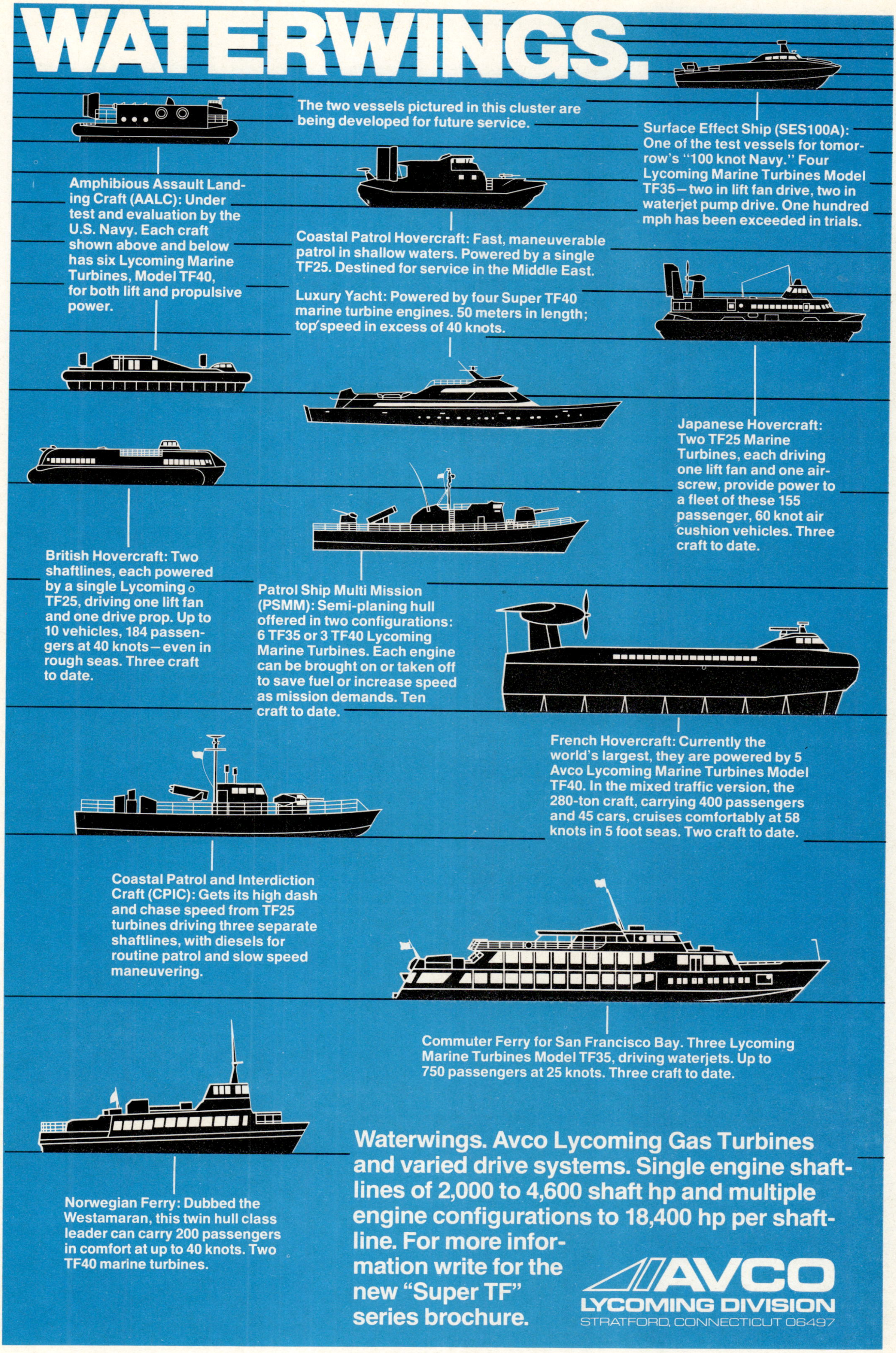

WATERWINGS.

Amphibious Assault Landing Craft (AALC): Under test and evaluation by the U.S. Navy. Each craft shown above and below has six Lycoming Marine Turbines, Model TF40, for both lift and propulsive power.

The two vessels pictured in this cluster are being developed for future service.

Coastal Patrol Hovercraft: Fast, maneuverable patrol in shallow waters. Powered by a single TF25. Destined for service in the Middle East.

Luxury Yacht: Powered by four Super TF40 marine turbine engines. 50 meters in length; top speed in excess of 40 knots.

Surface Effect Ship (SES100A): One of the test vessels for tomorrow's "100 knot Navy." Four Lycoming Marine Turbines Model TF35—two in lift fan drive, two in waterjet pump drive. One hundred mph has been exceeded in trials.

Japanese Hovercraft: Two TF25 Marine Turbines, each driving one lift fan and one airscrew, provide power to a fleet of these 155 passenger, 60 knot air cushion vehicles. Three craft to date.

British Hovercraft: Two shaftlines, each powered by a single Lycoming TF25, driving one lift fan and one drive prop. Up to 10 vehicles, 184 passengers at 40 knots—even in rough seas. Three craft to date.

Patrol Ship Multi Mission (PSMM): Semi-planing hull offered in two configurations: 6 TF35 or 3 TF40 Lycoming Marine Turbines. Each engine can be brought on or taken off to save fuel or increase speed as mission demands. Ten craft to date.

French Hovercraft: Currently the world's largest, they are powered by 5 Avco Lycoming Marine Turbines Model TF40. In the mixed traffic version, the 280-ton craft, carrying 400 passengers and 45 cars, cruises comfortably at 58 knots in 5 foot seas. Two craft to date.

Coastal Patrol and Interdiction Craft (CPIC): Gets its high dash and chase speed from TF25 turbines driving three separate shaftlines, with diesels for routine patrol and slow speed maneuvering.

Commuter Ferry for San Francisco Bay. Three Lycoming Marine Turbines Model TF35, driving waterjets. Up to 750 passengers at 25 knots. Three craft to date.

Norwegian Ferry: Dubbed the Westamaran, this twin hull class leader can carry 200 passengers in comfort at up to 40 knots. Two TF40 marine turbines.

Waterwings. Avco Lycoming Gas Turbines and varied drive systems. Single engine shaftlines of 2,000 to 4,600 shaft hp and multiple engine configurations to 18,400 hp per shaftline. For more information write for the new "Super TF" series brochure.

AVCO LYCOMING DIVISION
STRATFORD, CONNECTICUT 06497

CLASSIFIED LIST OF ADVERTISERS

Gyroscopic compasses, aircraft
Sperry Gyroscope

Gyroscopic compasses, land vehicles
Sperry Gyroscope

Gyroscopic compasses, ships
Sperry Gyroscope

Handsets
SG Brown Communications
Thomson CSF

Headphones
SG Brown Communications
DTCN
Marconi
Thomson CSF

Headsets
SG Brown Communications
Thomson CSF

Heat exchangers
Blohm & Voss
Bremer Vulkan
Hatch & Kirk
Howaldtswerke-Deutsche Werft
Yarrow (Shipbuilders)

Heavy duty mooring motorboats
Chantiers de la Perriere
DTCN
Fairey Marine

Helicopter, anti-submarine patrol
Agusta

Helicopter, maritime reconnaissance
Agusta

High level liquid alarm systems
Officine Panerai

Hovercraft
Aérospatiale
British Hovercraft Corporation
DTCN
Halter Marine
Vosper Thornycroft

Hydraulic equipment
DTCN
Fincantieri
MacTaggart Scott
Officine Galileo
OTO Melara
Riva Calzoni
Vickers
Vosper Thornycroft

Hydraulic machinery
Cantieri Navali Riuniti
DTCN
Fincantieri
MacTaggart Scott
Riva Calzoni
Thyssen Nordseewerke
Vickers
Vosper Thornycroft

Hydraulic plant
Aerimpianti
Fincantieri
DTCN
MacTaggart Scott
Riva Calzoni
Vosper Thornycroft

Hydrofoils
Aérospatiale
Blohm & Voss
Cantiere Navaltecnica
Cantieri Navali Riuniti
DTCN
Fincantieri
Supramar
Vosper Thornycroft

Hydrographic survey equipment
DTCN
Edo Corporation

Hydrophones
Graseby Instruments

IFF radar
DTCN
Hollandse Signaalapparaten
Philips Elektronikindustrier
Plessey Radar
Thomson CSF

IFF Mk 10 systems
DTCN
Plessey RADAR
Thomson CSF

Indicators, electric
DTCN
Thomson CSF
Vosper Thornycroft

Inertial gyro calibration equipment
Graseby Instruments

Inertial navigation systems
British Aerospace Dynamics Group
DTCN
Ferranti
Sperry Gyroscope

Infra-red countermeasure systems
Hycor

Infra-red materials
Barr & Stroud
DTCN
Philips Usfa

Infra-red systems
Barr & Stroud
British Aerospace Dynamics Group
DTCN
Hollandse Signaalapparaten
Montedison Group
Officine Galileo
Philips Usfa
Selenia
Thomson CSF
Vickers

Injectors, fuel
Hatch & Kirk

Instrument calibration services
British Aerospace Dynamics Group
Vickers

Instrument components, mechanical
British Aerospace Dynamics Group
Thomson CSF

Instruments, electronic
Bofors
SG Brown Communications
Decca Navigator
Ferranti
Howaldtswerke-Deutsche Werft
Safare-Crouzet
Sperry Gyroscope
Thomson CSF

Instruments, nautical
DTCN
Sippican Corporation
Sperry Gyroscope

Instrument panels
Ferranti
Decca Navigator
Lürssen Werft
Thomson CSF
Vosper Thornycroft

Instruments, precision
British Aerospace Dynamics Group
DTCN
Ferranti
Sperry Gyroscope

Instruments, test equipment
British Hovercraft Corporation
SG Brown Communications
DTCN
Ferranti
Hatch & Kirk
Sperry Gyroscope
Thomson CSF
Vickers

Interior design and furnishing for ships
Blohm & Voss
Bremer Vulkan
Brooke Marine
DTCN
Vickers
Vosper Thornycroft

Inverters and battery chargers
Ferranti

Landing craft
Ailsa Shipbuilding
Bremer Vulkan
British Hovercraft Corporation
Brooke Marine
Cantieri Baglietto
Chantiers de la Perriere
CNIM
DTCN
Halter Marine
Howaldtswerke-Deutsche Werft
INMA
Lürssen Werft
Nevesbu
Rhine-Schelde-Verolme
SFCN
Sillinger
Vosper Singapore
Vosper Thornycroft
Yarrow (Shipbuilders)

Two unique Royal Navy answers to missile attack on warships

...at close range

Seawolf is the only ship-borne point defence missile system with proven anti-missile as well as anti-aircraft capability – and missiles, not aircraft, are the real threat to today's warships. No comparable system has demonstrated the ability to intercept and destroy small, supersonic, anti-ship missiles. Successful sea trials on the British frigate HMS Penelope have cleared the way for Seawolf's service with entry into the Royal Navy in the late 1970s. The standard version is fully automatic and all-weather. Lighter-weight "blindfire", "darkfire" and "visual-only" variants are suitable for ships from 400–2,000 tons.

...at long range

Sea Skua is the only helicopter launched lightweight weapon which has been developed to counter the threat from missile-carrying fast patrol craft, launching their attacks from over the horizon. The combination of the wide radius of action of modern helicopters and Sea Skua's own considerable range ensures that the threat can be neutralised before the attacking craft can approach within effective missile-launching distance. Already at an advanced stage of development, Sea Skua will be widely used on frigate-borne Lynx helicopters of the Royal Navy from the late 1970s onwards.

Seawolf
Ship-borne anti-missile and anti-aircraft system

Sea Skua
Lightweight helicopter borne anti-ship system

BRITISH AEROSPACE DYNAMICS GROUP
Stevenage Herts England

A World Leader in Missile Defence Systems, Space Satellites and related technologies

GWN 12B

CLASSIFIED LIST OF ADVERTISERS

Laser rangefinders
Barr & Stroud
Bofors
DTCN
Ferranti
Hollandse Signaalapparaten
Selenia
Thomson CSF

Laser systems
Barr & Stroud
DTCN
Ferranti
Montedison Group
Officine Galileo
Selenia
Thomson CSF
Vickers

Lifeboats
Brooke Marine
Crestitalia
DTCN
Fairey Marine
SFCN
Sillinger
Vosper Thornycroft

Lifts, hydraulic
MacTaggart Scott

Lights and lighting
Officine Panerai

Liquid petroleum gas carriers
Bremer Vulkan
CNIM
DTCN
Dubigeon-Normandie
Fincantieri
Howaldtswerke-Deutsche Werft
Italcantieri
SFCN
Vickers

Loudspeaker equipment
Safare-Crouzet
Thomson CSF

Machined parts, ferrous
Blohm & Voss
Bremer Vulkan
DTCN
Vickers

Machined parts, non-ferrous
Blohm & Voss
Bremer Vulkan
DTCN
Vickers

Maintenance and repair ships
Bremer Vulkan
Brooke Marine
Cantiere Navaltecnica
DTCN
Dubigeon-Normandie
Fincantieri
Vickers
Vosper Singapore
Vosper Thornycroft

Marine architects
ABMTM
Bremer Vulkan
British Hovercraft Corporation
Brooke Marine
DTCN
Fincantieri
Ingenieurkontor Lübeck
Lürssen Werft
Nevesbu
Rhine-Schelde-Verolme
Vickers
Vosper Singapore
Vosper Thornycroft

Marine consultants
ABMTM

Marine engine monitoring and data recording systems
Decca Navigator
DTCN
Hatch & Kirk
Vosper Thornycroft

Marine management
ABMTM

Marine radar
Decca Navigator
DTCN
Ferranti
Hollandse Signaalapparaten
Graseby Instruments
Marconi
Oerlikon-Bührle
Philips Elektronikindustrier
Plessey Radar
Selenia
SMA
Thomson CSF

Materials handling equipment
DTCN
MacTaggart Scott

Market intelligence reports
DMS

Memory storage systems for military vehicles
Sperry Gyroscope

Merchant ships
Ailsa Shipbuilding
Blohm & Voss
Bremer Vulkan
Brooke Marine
Cantieri Navali Riuniti
Chantiers de la Perriere
Dubigeon-Normandie
Fincantieri
Halter Marine
Italcantieri
Lürssen Werft
Rhine-Schelde-Verolme
SFCN
Thyssen Nordseewerke
Vickers

Message processing systems
Sperry Gyroscope

Microphone equipment
SG Brown Communications
DTCN
Thomson CSF

Microwave systems
Kollmorgen

Mine countermeasures
British Hovercraft Corporation
CIT Alcatel
Decca Navigator
DTCN
Edo Corporation
Fairey Marine
Fried. Krupp
Philips Elektronikindustrier
Plessey Marine
SMA
Sperry Gyroscope

Mine hunting equipment
Sperry Gyroscope

Minelayers
Blohm & Voss
Bremer Vulkan
British Hovercraft Corporation
Brooke Marine
Cantieri Navali Riuniti
DTCN
Dubigeon-Normandie
Fincantieri
Halter Marine
Nevesbu
Rhine-Schelde-Verolme
Vickers
Vosper Thornycroft
Yarrow (Shipbuilders)

Minesweepers
Ailsa Shipbuilding
Blohm & Voss
British Hovercraft Corporation
Brooke Marine
Cantieri Baglietto
Cantieri Navali Riuniti
DTCN
Dubigeon-Normandie
Edo Corporation
Fincantieri
Halter Marine
Italcantieri
Nevesbu
Rhine-Schelde-Verolme
Thomson CSF
Vickers
Vosper Thornycroft
Yarrow (Shipbuilders)

Minesweeping equipment
Sperry Gyroscope

Missile control systems
Aérospatiale
British Aerospace Dynamics Group
CIT Alcatel
DTCN
Ferranti
Oerlikon-Bührle
Montedison Group
Officine Galileo
OTO Melara
Philips Elektronikindustrier
Plessey Radar
Raytheon
Selenia
Sistel-Sistemi
Sperry Gyroscope
Thomson CSF
Vickers

Minefields

Move in fast.
Sweep in safety. Moored mines can't reach you. Your very low acoustic and magnetic signatures below the surface provide maximum immunity.
No submerged hull, no propellers – just a shock-absorbing air cushion.
The perfect minesweeper –
British Hovercraft.

British Hovercraft Corporation
East Cowes, Isle of Wight, England
Telephone Cowes 4101. Telex 86761-2

A Westland Company

The Queen's Award to Industry has been won 7 times by Companies in the Westland Group

CLASSIFIED LIST OF ADVERTISERS

Missile installations
Aérospatiale
British Aerospace Dynamics Group
DTCN
Montedison Group
OTO Melara
Selenia
Sistel-Sistemi
Thomson CSF
Vickers
Vosper Singapore

Missile launching systems
Aérospatiale
British Aerospace Dynamics Group
British Hovercraft Corporation
CIT Alcatel
DTCN
Ferranti
Montedison Group
OTO Melara
Selenia
Sistel-Sistemi
Vickers

Missile ships
Blohm & Voss
Bremer Vulkan
British Hovercraft Corporation
Brooke Marine
Cantiere Navaltecnica
Cantieri Baglietto
Cantieri Navali Riuniti
Dravo Steelship
DTCN
Fincantieri
Italcantieri
Lürssen Werft
Montedison Group
Nevesbu
Sofrexen
Vickers
Vosper Singapore
Vosper Thornycroft
Yarrow (Shipbuilders)

Model makers and designers
Ailsa Shipbuilding
British Hovercraft Corporation
Fincantieri
Ingenieurkontor Lübeck
Nevesbu
Vickers
Vosper Thornycroft
Yarrow (Shipbuilders)

Model test towing tank service
British Hovercraft Corporation
Vickers

Motor control gear
Bremer Vulkan
Thomson CSF
Vosper Singapore

Motor starters
Thomson CSF
Vosper Singapore

Motor torpedo boats
Brooke Marine
Cantieri Baglietto
Cantieri Navali Riuniti
DTCN
Dubigeon-Normandie
Halter Marine
INMA
Lürssen Werft
Nevesbu
Rhine-Schelde-Verolme
SFCN
Thomson CSF
Vosper Thornycroft
Yarrow (Shipbuilders)

Motors, electric
Thomson CSF

Naval guns
Bofors
Breda Meccanica
DTCN
Oerlikon-Bührle
OTO Melara
Vickers

Naval radar
Decca Navigator
DTCN
Ferranti
Hollandse Signaalapparaten
Oerlikon-Bührle
Marconi
Philips Elektronikindustrier
Plessey Radar
Selenia
SMA
Sperry Gyroscope
Thomson CSF

Navigation aids
Decca Navigator
DTCN
Marconi
Sperry Gyroscope
Thomson CSF
USEA

Night vision systems
Barr & Stroud
DTCN
Kollmorgen
Montedison Group
Officine Galileo
Philips Usfa
Thomson CSF

HMS Invincible by Vickers...

Invincible

Model by John Glossop

Paxman Diesels Limited

Paxman Works, Colchester, CO1 2HW, Essex, England. Telephone 0206 5151 Telex: 98151

Holding Company — The General Electric Company Limited
A management company of GEC Diesels Limited

GEC DIESELS

CLASSIFIED LIST OF ADVERTISERS

Non-magnetic minesweepers
British Hovercraft Corporation
Cantieri Baglietto
DTCN
Dubigeon-Normandie
Fincantieri
Nevesbu
Rhine-Schelde-Verolme
Sperry Gyroscope
Vickers
Vosper Thornycroft

Oceanographic electronic systems
Decca Navigator
DTCN
Safare-Crouzet
Sippican Corporation
Thomson CSF

Oceanographic survey ships
Bremer Vulkan
Brooke Marine
Cantieri Navali Riuniti
Chantiers de la Perriere
DTCN
Fairey Marine
Fincantieri
Halter Marine
Lürssen Werft
Nevesbu
Rhine-Schelde-Verolme
SFCN
Thyssen Nordseewerke
Vickers
Yarrow (Shipbuilders)

Offshore countermeasures
DTCN
Dubigeon-Normandie

Oil drilling rigs
Bremer Vulkan
CIT Alcatel
Fincantieri
Howaldtswerke-Deutsche Werft
Vickers

Oil fuel heaters
Blohm & Voss
Fincantieri

Oil rig supply vessels and work boats
Brooke Marine
Cantieri Navali Riuniti
Chantiers de la Perriere
Crestitalia
Dubigeon-Normandie
Fairey Marine
Fincantieri
Halter Marine
Supramar
Vosper Singapore
Yarrow (Shipbuilders)

Optical equipment
Barr & Stroud
British Aerospace Dynamics Group
DTCN
Kollmorgen
Montedison Group
Officine Panerai
Vickers

Optical filters
Barr & Stroud
DTCN

Optronics
Hollandse Signaalapparaten

Ordnance
Bofors
Borletti
OTO Melara
Oerlikon-Bührle
Vickers

Oropesa sweeps
Sperry Gyroscope

Parts for diesel engines
Blohm & Voss
Bremer Vulkan
CRM
DTCN
Fincantieri
Grandi Motori Trieste
Hatch & Kirk
Italsider
Paxman Diesels
Rhine-Schelde-Verolme
Vickers

Passenger ships
Ailsa Shipbuilding
Blohm & Voss
Bremer Vulkan
Brooke Marine
Cantiere Navaltecnica
Cantieri Navali Riuniti
Chantiers de la Perriere
Crestitalia
DTCN
Fincantieri
Howaldtswerke-Deutsche Werft
Rhine-Schelde-Verolme
SFCN
Supramar
Thyssen Nordseewerke
Vickers

Patrol boats
Dravo Steelship
Vosper Thornycroft

Auxiliary Power by Paxman

HMS Invincible, the Royal Navy's new through-deck cruiser, relies on the award winning Paxman Valenta diesel engine for its essential auxiliary services. A total of eight Paxman 16RP200 Valenta generating sets (each with a potential output of 1.75 mW) are installed in Invincible. Six of these sets are contained in specially sound-proofed and shock-proof enclosures which include all necessary services. For the modern fighting ship, where the requirement for reliability and efficiency is paramount, Paxman diesels offer most. Send for full technical specifications and literature.

16 cylinder RP 200 Valenta

CLASSIFIED LIST OF ADVERTISERS

Patrol boats: launches, tenders and pinnaces
Ailsa Shipbuilding
British Hovercraft Corporation
Brooke Marine
Cantiere Navaltecnica
Cantieri Baglietto
Cantieri Navali Riuniti
Chantiers de la Perriere
Chantiers Navals de L'Esterel
Crestitalia
DTCN
Dubigeon-Normandie
Fairey Marine
Lürssen Werft
Nevesbu
SFCN
Sillinger
Valtec
Vosper Thornycroft

Penetrators
Graseby Instruments

Periscope fairings
DTCN
Edo Corporation
MacTaggart Scott

Periscopes
Barr & Stroud
DTCN
Kollmorgen
Sofrexan

Pipes, copper and brass
Fincantieri
Vickers

Pipes, sea water
Fincantieri
Vickers

Piston heads
Italsider

Pistons, piston rings and gudgeon pins
Bremer Vulkan
Hatch & Kirk

Plotting tables
Philips Elektronikindustrier
Plessey Radar
SMA
Sofrexan
Thomson CSF

Plugs and sockets
Thomson CSF

Pontoons, self propelled
Bremer Vulkan
Brooke Marine
Chantiers de la Perriere
CNIM
DTCN
SFCN
Thyssen Nordseewerke

Portable equipment for aircraft landing
Officine Panerai

Pressure vessels
Bremer Vulkan
Vickers
Yarrow (Shipbuilders)

Propellants
Bofors
Snia Viscosa

Propeller shaft couplings, flexible
DTCN
Vickers

Propeller shafts and intermediate shafts
Italsider

Propellers, hovercraft
British Aerospace Dynamics Group

Propellers, ships
DTCN
Fincantieri
Lips
Vickers
Vosper Thornycroft

Propellers, ship research
DTCN
Fincantieri
Lips
Vosper Thornycroft

Propulsion machinery
Avco Lycoming
Blohm & Voss
Bremer Vulkan
Cantieri Navali Riuniti
DTCN
Fincantieri
MTU
Paxman Diesels
Rhine-Schelde-Verolme
SACM
Vickers

Publishers
DMS
Macdonald & Jane's

Pumps
CIT Alcatel
DTCN
Fincantieri
MacTaggart Scott
Termomeccanica
Thomson CSF
Vickers

Radar aerials
British Aerospace Dynamics Group
Decca Navigator
DTCN
Hollandse Signaalapparaten
Marconi
Philips Elektronikindustrier
Plessey Radar
Raytheon
Selenia
SMA
Thomson CSF

Radar countermeasures
Hycor

Radar for fire control
DTCN
Ferranti
Hollandse Signaalapparaten
Marconi
Oerlikon-Bührle
Philips Elektronikindustrier
Plessey Radar
Raytheon
Selenia
SMA
Sperry Gyroscope
Thomson CSF

Radar for harbour supervision
Decca Navigator
DTCN
Hollandse Signaalapparaten
Plessey Radar Raytheon
SMA
Thomson CSF

Radar for navigation warning interception
Decca Navigator
DTCN
Hollandse Signaalapparaten
Marconi
Philips Elektronikindustrier
Plessey Radar
Raytheon
Selenia
SMA
Thomson CSF

Radar transponders
DTCN
Plessey Radar
Raytheon
Thomson CSF

Radio, air
Thomson CSF

Radio, direction finding
Marconi

Radio equipment
SG Brown Communications
Marconi
Montedel
Montedison Group
Thomson CSF

Radio transmitters and receivers
SG Brown Communications
Ferranti
Marconi
Montedel
Montedison Group
Philips Elektronikindustrier
Thomson CSF

Radomes
British Aerospace Dynamics Group
British Hovercraft Corporation
DTCN
Hollandse Signaalapparaten
Lürssen Werft
Plessey Radar
Raytheon
Thomson CSF
Vickers

Ramjets
Aérospatiale

Rangefinders
Barr & Stroud
SMA
Thomson CSF

Relocalisation device
CIT Alcatel
DTCN

Remote Controls
Decca Navigator
Lips
Oerlikon-Bührle
OTO Melara
Thomson CSF
Vosper Thornycroft

OTO MELARA
WORLD LEADER FOR NAVAL GUNS AND MISSILE SYSTEMS

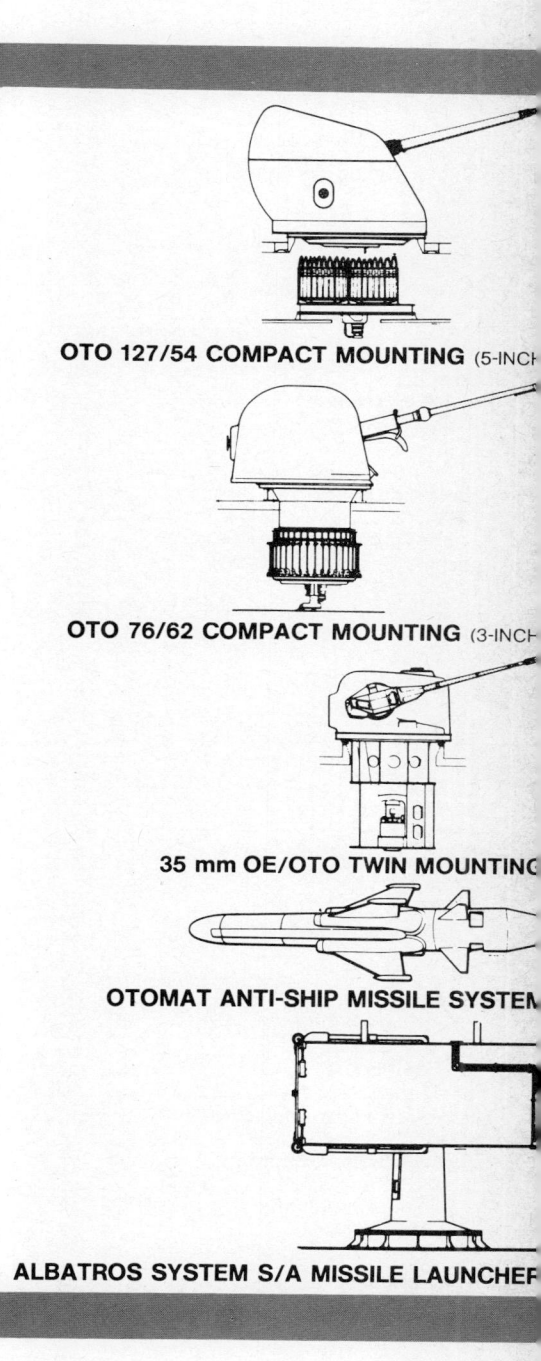

OTO 127/54 COMPACT MOUNTING (5-INCH)

OTO 76/62 COMPACT MOUNTING (3-INCH)

35 mm OE/OTO TWIN MOUNTING

OTOMAT ANTI-SHIP MISSILE SYSTEM

ALBATROS SYSTEM S/A MISSILE LAUNCHER

OTO MELARA S.p.A
19100 - La Spezia (Italy)
15, Via Valdilocchi
Tel. 504041 - TELEX 27368 OTO

CLASSIFIED LIST OF ADVERTISERS

Remote level indicator equipment for submarine trim tanks
DTCN
Officine Panerai

Replacement parts for diesel engines
Blohm & Voss
Bremer Vulkan
DRM
DTCN
Fincantieri
MacTaggart Scott
Vickers

Research ships
Ailsa Shipbuilding
Bremer Vulkan
Brooke Marine
Cantieri Navali Riuniti
Chantiers de la Perriere
DTCN
Dubigeon-Normandie
Fincantieri
Halter Marine
Lürssen Werft
Nevesbu
Rhine-Schelde-Verolme
SFCN
Sillinger
Thyssen Nordseewerke
Vickers
Yarrow (Shipbuilders)

Reverse reduction gears, oil operated
CRM
Isotta Fraschini
Vickers

Reversing gears
CRM
Isotta Fraschini
Vickers

Rocket launchers
Bofors
Breda Meccanica
CNIM
DTCN
OTO Melara
Snia Viscosa
Vickers

Roll damping fins
Blohm & Voss
Vickers
Vosper Thornycroft

Rudders
Ailsa Shipbuilding
Bremer Vulkan
Brooke Marine
Fincantieri
Howaldtswerke-Deutsche Werft
Italsider
Rhine-Schelde-Verolme
Vosper Thornycroft
Yarrow (Shipbuilders)

Rudderstocks
Italsider

Running gears/forgings
Italsider

Salvage vessels
Ailsa Shipbuilding
Brooke Marine
Crestitalia
Fincantieri
Halter Marine
INMA
SFCN

Salvage and boom vessels
Ailsa Shipbuilding
Bremer Vulkan
Brooke Marine
Cantiere Navaltecnica
Cantieri Navali Riuniti
Crestitalia
Fincantieri
Halter Marine
Nevesbu
Yarrow (Shipbuilders)

Scientific instruments
DTCN
Ferranti
Thomson CSF
Vickers

Screen wipers
Decca Navigator

Self homing torpedo guidance head
Selenia

Ship defence systems
Hycor

Ship and submarine design
Ailsa Shipbuilding
Cantieri Navali Riuniti
DTCN
Dubigeon-Normandie
Fincantieri
Halter Marine
Howaldtswerke-Deutsche Werft
Ingenieurkontor Lübeck
Nevesbu
Rhine-Schelde-Verolme
Thyssen Nordseewerke
Vickers
Vosper Thornycroft
Yarrow (Shipbuilders)

Ship machinery
Alsthom Atlantique
Blohm & Voss
Bremer Vulkan
Cantieri Navali Riuniti
DTCN
Fincantieri
MTU
Paxman Diesels
Rhine-Schelde-Verolme
Vickers
Yarrow (Shipbuilders)

Ship stabilisers
Blohm & Voss
Cantieri Navali Riuniti
DTCN
Fincantieri
Howaldtswerke-Deutsche Werft
Supramar
Vickers
Vosper Thornycroft

Ship systems engineering
Bremer Vulkan
British Aerospace Dynamics Group
Cantiere Navaltecnica
Cantieri Navali Riuniti
DTCN
Lips
Nevesbu
Rhine-Schelde-Verolme
Vickers
Vosper Thornycroft

Shipboard air-conditioning and ventilating plant
Aerimpianti
Kaesar Klimatechnik

Ship brass foundry for sonar and radar
DTCN

Shipbuilders and ship repairers
Ailsa Shipbuilding
Blohm & Voss
Bremer Vulkan
Brooke Marine
Cantiere Navaltecnica
Cantieri Navali Riuniti
Chantiers de la Perriere
DTCN
Dubigeon-Normandie
Fairey Marine
Fincantieri
Halter Marine
Howaldtswerke-Deutsche Werft
Italcantieri
Lürssen Werft
Nevesbu
Rhine-Schelde-Verolme
SFCN
Sofrexan
Thyssen Nordseewerke
Vickers
Vosper Singapore
Vosper Thornycroft
Yarrow (Shipbuilders)

Ships magnetic compass test tables
Barr & Stroud
DTCN

Signals
Hycor

Simulators
DTCN
Ferranti
Fried. Krupp
Philips Elektronikindustrier
Vickers

Smoke indicators
Barr & Stroud

Sonar equipment
CIT Alcatel
DTCN
Edo Corporation
Ferranti
Fried. Krupp
Graseby Instruments
Hollandse Signaalapparaten
Marconi
Plessey Marine
Raytheon
Safare-Crouzet
Selenia
Sippican Corporation
Thomson CSF
USEA

Sonar equipment (passive active-intercept)
CIT Alcatel
DTCN
Edo Corporation
Fried. Krupp
Graseby Instruments
Hollandse Signaalapparaten
Plessey Marine
Safare-Crouzet
Selenia
Thomson CSF
USEA

Where the action's fast and the going's rough

FAIREY MARINE

Coastguard, Police, Commercial and Rescue Craft

Fairey Marine Limited, Hamble, Southampton SO3 5NB, England.
Telephone: 0421-22-2661   Cable: Airily Hamble
Telex: 47546 A/B Fairey

- LANCE PILOT
- COMBAT SUPPORT BOAT
- 13·7m G.P.
- BULLDOG
- LANCE F.P.B.
- SWORD
- SPEAR
- LANCE F.G.B.
- MEDINA
- INTERCEPTOR F.R.R.C.
- TRACKER
- HAMBLE

CLASSIFIED LIST OF ADVERTISERS

Sonar equipment, hull fittings and hydraulics
CIT Alcatel
DTCN
Edo Corporation
Fried. Krupp
Graseby Instruments
Hollandse Signaalapparaten
Plessey Marine
Safare-Crouzet
Thomson CSF
USEA

Sonar interceptor, direct finder
Safare-Crouzet

Sonar ranges (design and installation)
DTCN
Graseby Instruments
Raytheon
Safare-Crouzet
Thomson CSF

Spare parts for diesel engines
Blohm & Voss
Bremer Vulkan
CRM
Grandi Motori Trieste
Hatch & Kirk
Vickers

Speed boats
Cantieri Baglietto
Chantiers Navals de L'Esterel
Crestitalia
DTCN
Fairey Marine
Halter Marine
SFCN
Sillinger
Vosper Thornycroft

Stabilising equipment
Blohm & Voss
British Aerospace Dynamics Group
DTCN
Ferranti
Hollandse Signaalapparaten
Vickers
Vosper Thornycroft

Stabilising equipment for fire control
DTCN
Ferranti
Sperry Gyroscope
Vickers

Steam-raising plant, conventional
Blohm & Voss
Bremer Vulkan
Yarrow (Shipbuilders)

Steam-raising plant, nuclear
DTCN
Vickers
Yarrow (Shipbuilders)

Steam turbines
Blohm & Voss
Bremer Vulkan
Cantieri Navali Riuniti
DTCN
Fincantieri
Howaldtswerke-Deutsche Werft

Steel-alloy and special steel forgings, plates and sections, stampings
Bofors
DTCN

Steel manganese, wear-resisting
Bofors

Steering gear
Decca Navigator
Vickers
Vosper Thornycroft

Sternframes
Italsider

Stress relieving
Bremer Vulkan
Fincantieri
Vickers
Yarrow (Shipbuilders)

Submarine distress buoy
Barr & Stroud
DTCN
Safare-Crouzet
Sofrexan
Thomson CSF

Submarine fire control
CIT Alcatel
DTCN
Ferranti
Hollandse Signaalapparaten
Philips Elektronikindustrier
Sperry Gyroscope
Vickers

Submarine-launched buoy systems
Sippican Corporation

Submarine periscopes
Barr & Stroud
DTCN
Kollmorgen
Thomson CSF

Submarines
DTCN
Fincantieri
Howaldtswerke-Deutsche Werft
Ingenieurkontor Lübeck
Italcantieri
Nevesbu
Rhine-Schelde Verolme
Thyssen Nordseewerke
Vickers

Submarines, conventional
DTCN
Dubigeon-Normandie
Fincantieri
Howaldtswerke-Deutsche Werft
Ingenieurkontor Lübeck
Nevesbu
Rhine-Schelde-Verolme
Vickers

Submarines, wet
DTCN
Rhine-Schelde-Verolme
Vickers
Yarrow (Shipbuilders)

Submarines, unmanned submersibles
British Aerospace Dynamics Group

Superheaters
Bremer Vulkan
DTCN
Fincantieri

Superstructure and cavitation noise detector
Safare-Crouzet

Support services
Blohm & Voss
Bremer Vulkan
Brooke Marine
DTCN
Fincantieri
Halter Marine
Vickers
Vosper Singapore
Vosper Thornycroft

Support service vessels
Chantiers de la Perriere

Survey equipment
DTCN
Sillinger

Surveys/market intellingence
DMS

Switchboards
Blohm & Voss
SG Brown Communications
Lürssen Werft
Thomson CSF
Vosper Singapore
Vosper Thornycroft
Whipp & Bourne

Switchboards and switchgear
Lürssen Werft
Thomson CSF
Vosper Singapore
Vosper Thornycroft
Whipp & Bourne

Tactical training simulators
British Aerospace Dynamics Group
British Hovercraft Corporation
DTCN
Ferranti
Marconi
Oerlikon-Bührle
Selenia
Sofrexan
Thomson CSF
Vickers

Tankers
Blohm & Voss
Bremer Vulkan
Cantieri Navali Riuniti
DTCN
Fincantieri
Howaldtswerke-Deutsche Werft
Italcantieri
Nevesbu
Rhine-Schelde-Verolme
SFCN
Vickers
Yarrow (Shipbuilders)

Tankers, small
Bremer Vulkan
Cantieri Navali Riuniti
DTCN
Dubigeon-Normandie
Fincantieri
Halter Marine
Italcantieri
Lürssen Werft
Yarrow (Shipbuilders)

Tanks, oil and water storage
Bremer Vulkan
DTCN
Howaldtswerke-Deutsche Werft
Sillinger

CALZONI

Special oil hydro-mechanical devices and complete systems for submarines and other warships

- extra noiseless pumps
- steering and diving gears
- antenna and periscope hoisting devices
- m.t.b. flood and vent valve controls
- remotely controlled hull valves
- windlass and capstan gears
- torpedo handling systems
- trim manifold (remote controlled)
- induction and exhaust snorkel
- etc.

- **noiseless**
- **compact**
- **tailor-made**
- **high shock resistant devices**

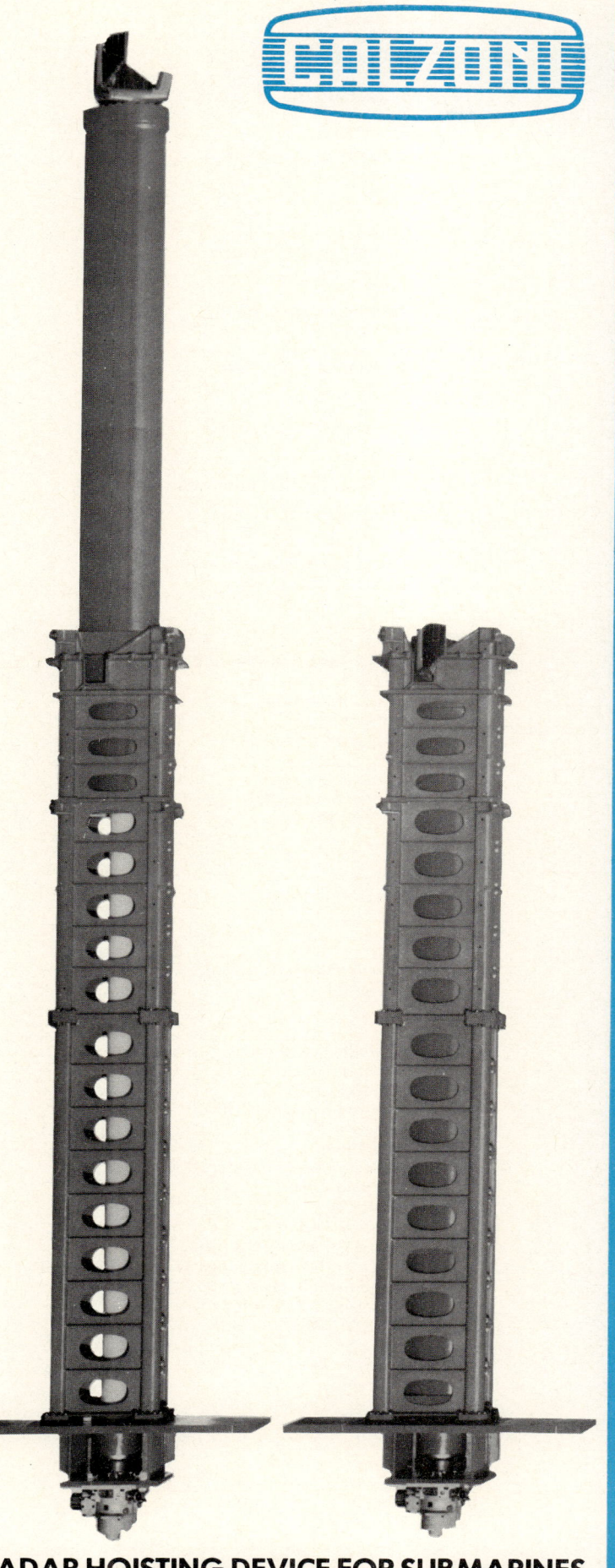

RADAR HOISTING DEVICE FOR SUBMARINES
RAISED   LOWERED

The device, as the other hoisting devices (ECM, VHF), is extremely compact and does not pass through the control room.

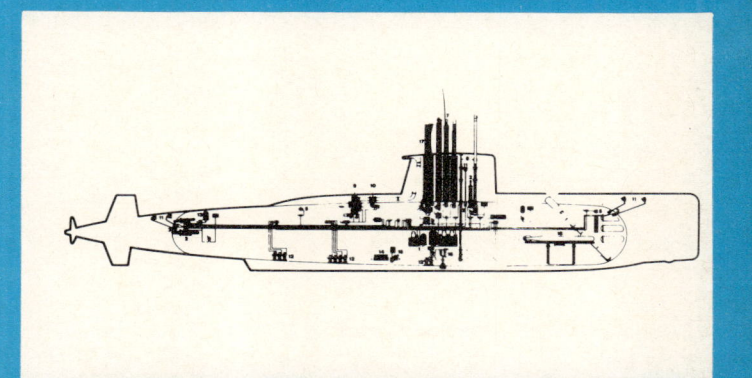

RIVA CALZONI S.p.A. — Via Emilia Ponente, 72-Bologna-Italy-Telex 51156

CLASSIFIED LIST OF ADVERTISERS

Technical publications
Vickers
Vosper Thornycroft

Telecommunication equipment
SG Brown Communications
CIT Alcatel
Ferranti
Marconi
Montedel
Montedison Group
Safare-Crouzet
Thomson CSF

Telegraph systems
Montedel
Thomson CSF

Telemotors
MacTaggart Scott

Tenders
Ailsa Shipbuilding
Blohm & Voss
Bremer Vulkan
Brooke Marine
Fairey Marine
Halter Marine
Howaldtswerke-Deutsche Werft
Nevesbu
Sillinger
Yarrow (Shipbuilders)

Test equipment for fire control systems
CIT Alcatel
DTCN
Hollandse Signaalapparaten
Philips Elektronikindustrier
Selenia
Thomson CSF

Textile fibres
DTCN

Thermal imaging systems
Barr & Stroud

Throughwater communications
Graseby Instruments

Timers
Borletti

Torpedo control systems
CIT Alcatel
DTCN
Ferranti
Hollandse Signaalapparaten
Philips Elektronikindustrier
Plessey Marine
Sperry Gyroscope
Thomson CSF
Vickers

Torpedo decoys
Graseby Instruments

Torpedo depth and roll recorders
DTCN

Torpedo order and reflection control
CIT Alcatel
DTCN
Vickers

Torpedo side-launchers
Crestitalia
DTCN

Torpedoes and torpedo tubes
CIT Alcatel
DTCN
Plessey Marine
Vickers

Training equipment
ABMTM
CIT Alcatel
Decca Navigator
DTCN
Ferranti
Graseby Instruments
Oerlikon-Bührle
Philips Elektronikindustrier
Sillinger
Vickers

Training programmes
ABMTM

Training services
Decca Navigator

Transmitting magnetic compasses
Decca Navigator

Trawlers
Brooke Marine
Crestitalia
Dubigeon-Normandie
Fincantieri
Halter Marine
Howaldtswerke-Deutsche Werft
SFCN
Yarrow (Shipbuilders)

Tugs
Ailsa Shipbuilding
Ameeco (Hydrospace)
Brooke Marine
Crestitalia
Dubigeon-Normandie
Fincantieri
Halter Marine
SFCN
Yarrow (Shipbuilders)

Turbine gears
Bremer Vulkan
Cantieri Navali Riuniti
CIT Alcatel
DTCN
Fiat
Fincantieri
Rhine-Schelde-Verolme
Vickers

Turbines
Blohm & Voss
Bremer Vulkan
Cantieri Navali Riuniti
DTCN
Fiat
Fincantieri
Hatch & Kirk
Howaldtswerke-Deutsche Werft
SACM
Yarrow (Shipbuilders)

Turbines, exhaust
Avco Lycoming
Cantieri
Navali Riuniti
DTCN
Fincantieri

Turbines, gas marine
Avco Lycoming
DTCN
Fiat
SACM
Yarrow (Shipbuilders)

Turbines, steam marine
Blohm & Voss
Bremer Vulkan
Cantieri Navali Riuniti
DTCN
Fincantieri
Yarrow (Shipbuilders)

Underwater communication
Marconi

Underwater lights
DTCN
Officine Panerai

Underwater television equipment
DTCN
Edo Corporation
Sofrexan
Thomson CSF

Valves and cocks
Riva Calzoni

Valves and cocks, hydraulic
MacTaggart Scott
Riva Calzoni

Voltage regulators, automatic
Ferranti

Warship repairers
Bremer Vulkan
Brooke Marine
Cantieri Navali Riuniti
DTCN
Fincantieri
Howaldtswerke-Deutsche Werft
Lürssen Werft
Nevesbu
Plessey Radar
Rhine-Schelde-Verolme
Thyssen Nordseewerke
Vosper Singapore
Vosper Thornycroft
Yarrow (Shipbuilders)

Warships
Blohm & Voss
Bremer Vulkan
Brooke Marine
Cantieri Navali Riuniti
DTCN
Dubigeon-Normandie
Fincantieri
Halter Marine
Howaldtswerke-Deutsche Werft
Lürssen Werft
Nevesbu
Rhine-Schelde-Verolme
SFCN
Sofrexan
Thyssen Nordseewerke
Vosper Singapore
Vosper Thornycroft
Yarrow (Shipbuilders)

We design — fast patrol craft . . . . .

We are ideally based in Singapore . . . .

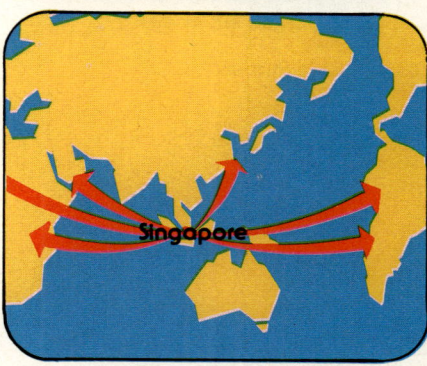

We build to the highest standards at the most competitive cost . . . . .

We are the only shipbuilder in S.E. Asia that can design as well as build fast patrol craft and other high speed vessels for navies, police, customs and other special government departments. Since our inception in 1923 we have gained wide experience in this field.

We are based in Singapore, where there is a highly trained, low cost labour force, which makes Singapore an ideal location for the Vosper shipyard. This benefit, together with the high qualifications of Vosper's technical personnel means that we can design and build to the highest standards at the most competitive cost.

And we can deliver on time.

We are . . . . . .

VOSPER SINGAPORE

VOSPER PRIVATE LIMITED 200 Tanjong Rhu Road, Singapore 15.
Tel: 4467144 Telex: RS21219 Cable: VOSPER SINGAPORE

uspneedham vs/15/7

CLASSIFIED LIST OF ADVERTISERS

Water tube boilers
Bremer Vulkan
DTCN
Fincantieri
Rhine-Schelde-Verolme
Yarrow (Shipbuilders)

Weapon systems
Aérospatiale
Bofors
British Aerospace Aircraft Group
British Aerospace Dynamics Group
CNIM
DTCN
Ferranti
Montedison Group
Oerlikon-Bührle
Officine Galileo
OTO Melara
Philips Elektronikindustrier
Plessey Marine
Plessey Radar
Selenia
Sippican Corporation
Sistel-Sistemi
Snia Viscosa
Sofrexan
Sperry Gyroscope
Thomson CSF
Vickers
Vosper Singapore
Vosper Thornycroft

Weapon systems, sonar components
CIT Alcatel
DTCN
Edo Corporation
Graseby Instruments
Oerlikon-Bührle
Plessey Marine
Raytheon
Selenia
Thomson CSF
Vosper Thornycroft

Welding: arc, argon arc or gas
Bremer Vulkan
Chantiers de la Perriere
DTCN
Lürssen Werft
Rhine-Schelde-Verolme
Vickers
Yarrow (Shipbuilders)

Winches
DTCN
Thyssen Nordseewerke
Vickers

Wrist compasses and depth meters for underwater operators
DTCN
Officine Panerai

X-ray work
Bremer Vulkan
DTCN
Lürssen Werft
Vickers

Yachts, powered
Ailsa Shipbuilding
Brooke Marine
Cantiere Navaltecnica
Cantieri Baglietto
Chantiers Navals de L'Esterel
Crestitalia
DTCN
Dubigeon-Normandie
Fairey Marine
Halter Marine
Lürssen Werft
Vosper Thornycroft
Yarrow (Shipbuilders)

Detect
Inspect
Protect...

KOLLMORGEN MODEL **76** Submarine Periscope System

For more information about the new Model 76 Periscope System and for information concerning Retrofit, write

Electro-Optical Division
KOLLMORGEN CORPORATION
Northampton, Massachusetts 01060
Telephone: (413) 586-2330
TWX: 510-290-2001

Search – Attack – Combined

The designer of submarine periscopes for the U.S. Navy offers for domestic and foreign navies a modern and integrated periscope, suitable for installation in small or large submarines. Common modules and compatible subsystems permit selection in a variety of characteristics, to be specified or planned for future growth.

- Biocular visual observation
- Magnification to 12×
- Reflex photography – 35 mm with exposure control
- Television
- Target bearing display and transmission – relative and true bearing
- Stadimetric ranging
- Radar and communication receiving system

Kollmorgen... Tomorrow's Insight Into Today's Problems

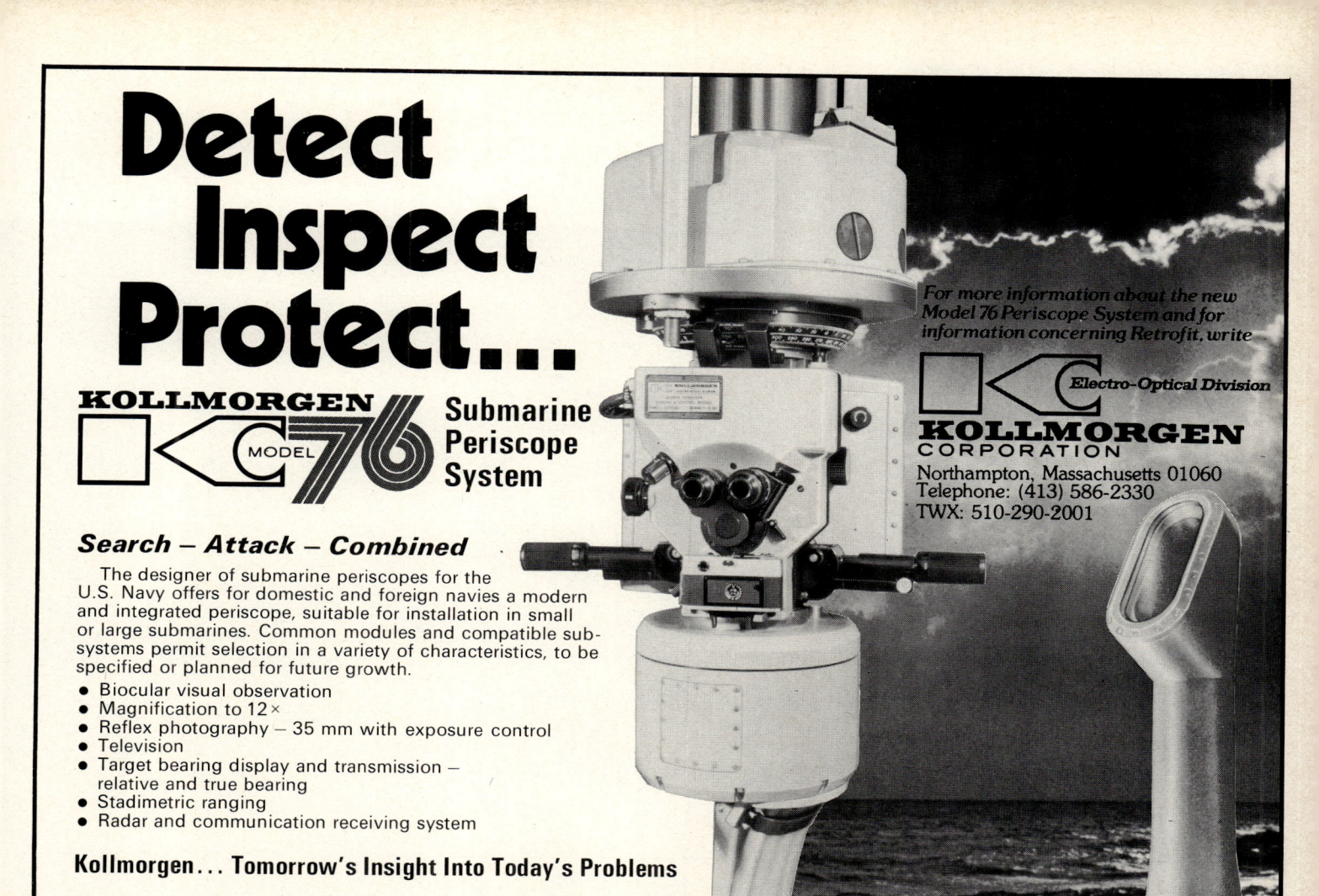

CAPABILITY BROWN

S.G. Brown Communications Limited has played a pioneering role in the development and manufacture of acoustic ancillaries for defence communications.

For over fifty years we have supplied equipment to Navies worldwide and are also heavily committed in commercial marine, civil and military aviation activities.

Headsets ● Communications Systems ● Microphones & earphones ● Field telephones

S.G. BROWN
Communications Limited,
King George's Avenue, Watford,
Hertfordshire, England, WD1 7QP

Telephone: Watford (0923) 35311
Telex: 23412

RACAL

..for excel

XSV

expendable sound velocimeter

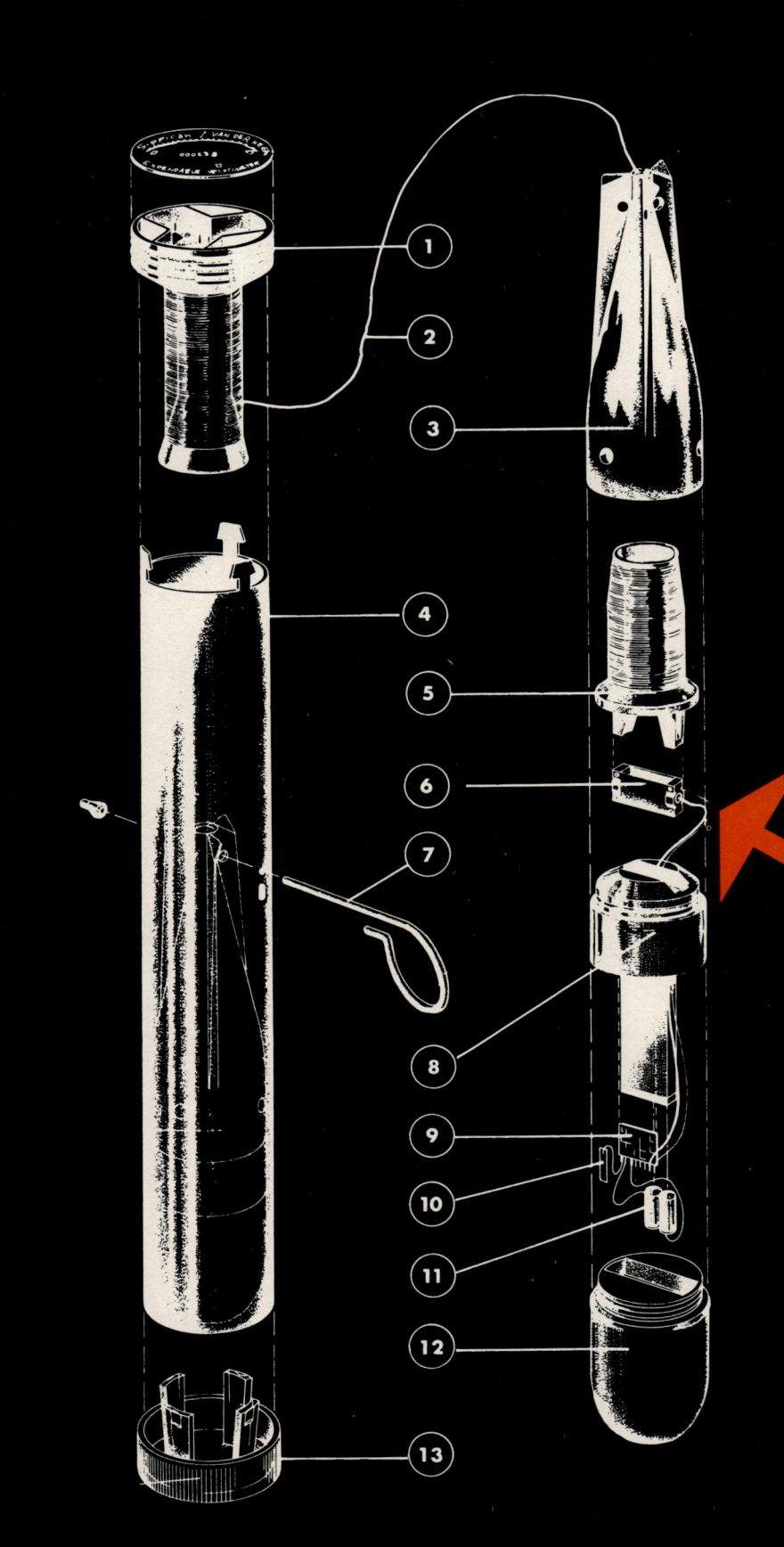

XSV EXPLODED VIEW

1 SHIPBOARD SPOOL
2 SIGNAL WIRE
3 AFTERBODY
4 CANISTER
5 PROBE SPOOL
6 SOUND VELOCITY SENSOR
7 RETAINING PIN
8 ELECTRONICS HOUSING
9 INTEGRATED CIRCUIT
10 STARTING CONTACT
11 BATTERIES
12 ZINC NOSE
13 SHIPPING CAP

lence in ASW

Sippican helps you sample a changing ocean.

SING-AROUND SOUND VELOCIMETER SENSOR

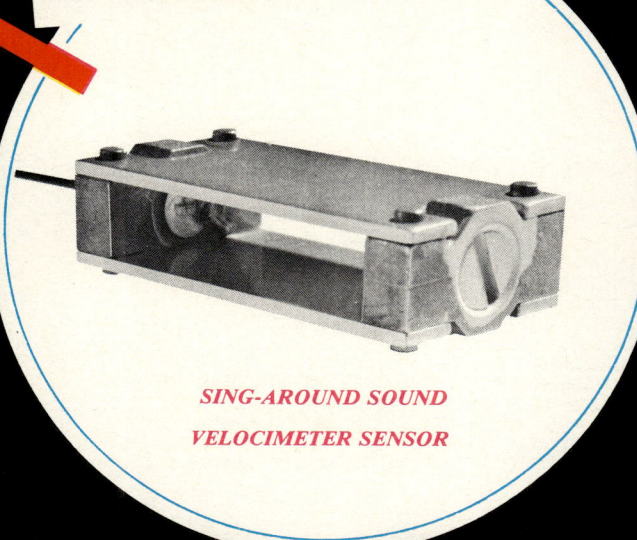

One of the key innovations in the design of the XSV has been the development of a tiny, high-accuracy sing-around sensor capable of production at the low costs essential for expendable instrumentation. The five-millimeter diameter transducer is a PZT-5 ceramic separated by 26 millimeters from a brass reflector. The reflector itself is of a modified spherical design in order to eliminate multiple reflections. The transducer/reflector spacing is hand-calibrated during production and is held constant during use by the selection of materials and construction techniques which eliminate path length alterations caused by thermal expansion effects.

If you are really interested in the sound velocity profile, why not measure it?

Most modern naval vessels involved in antisubmarine warfare (ASW) have a critical need for real-time knowledge of the sound velocity profile. Such information is essential to ensure the most effective employment of today's complex ASW sensors.

For want of a simple, cost-effective means of measuring sound velocity directly, ASW tacticians have relied on temperature profiles to compute the sound velocity. This procedure ignores the influence of salinity on sound velocity and can introduce important errors which are particularly significant in near-coastal regions, in the vicinity of open-ocean fronts and in close proximity to ice formations.

In order to solve the problem of measuring sound velocity at sea, Sippican has developed the Expendable Sound Velocimeter (XSV). The XSV is capable of sound velocity profile measurement to an accuracy of ± 0.25 meters/second with the same ease afforded by the Expendable Bathythermograph (XBT).

The XSV consists of a ballistically-shaped probe and wire link similar to the XBT, a sing-around sound velocimeter sensor, a battery power supply and a custom integrated circuit. The probe, as configured on the left, has undergone extensive at-sea testing and is now being sold worldwide.

sippican

Ocean Systems   Marion, Massachusetts

Distributors: Plessey Marine, The Plessey Co., Ltd., Ilford, Essex, England   Tsurumi Seiki Co., Ltd., Yokohama, Japan
TRT - Telecommunications Radioelectriques et Telephoniques, Paris, France

THE LARGEST SHIPBUILDING AND SHIPREPAIRING GROUP IN THE MEDITERRANEAN

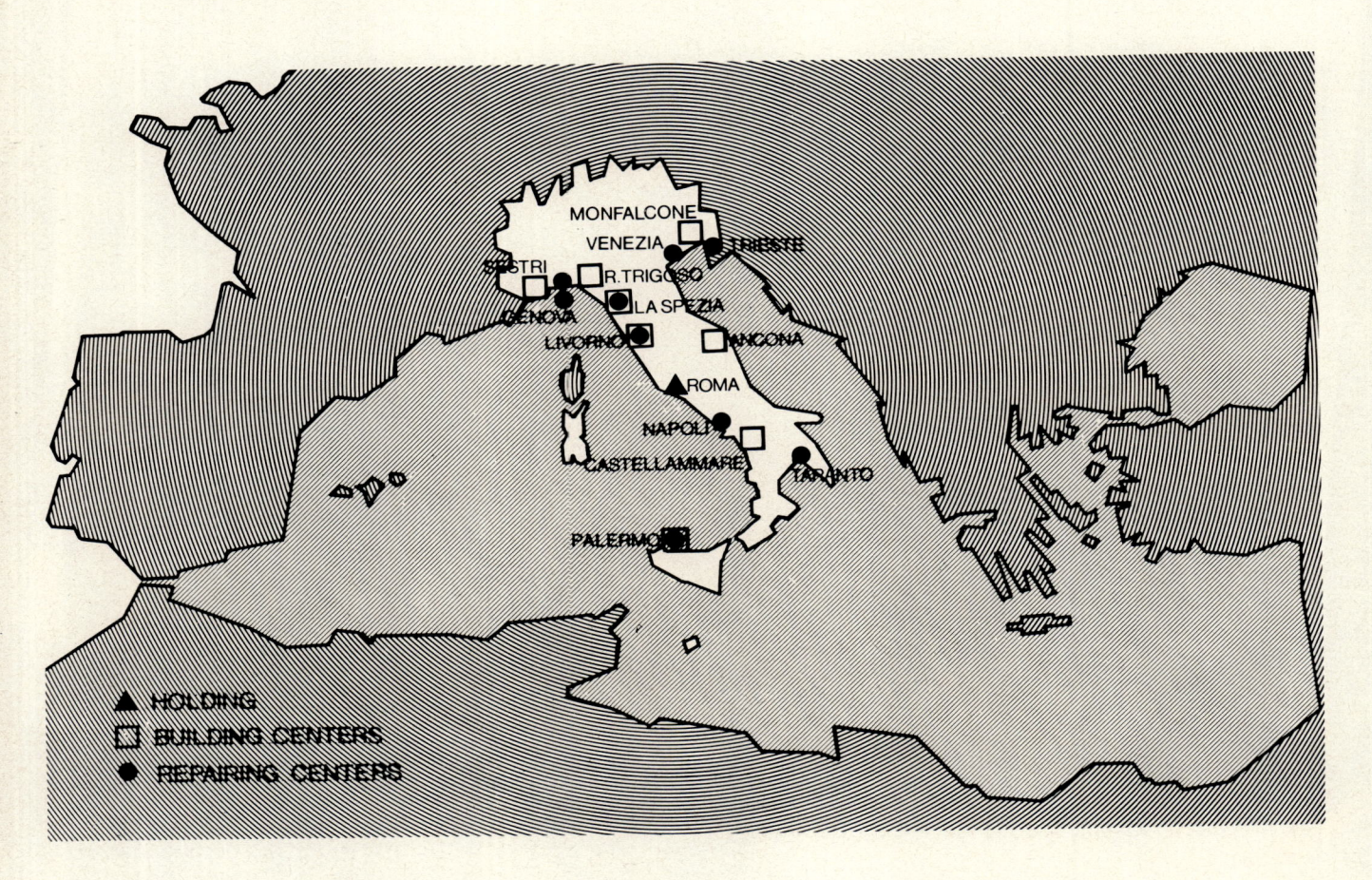

▲ HOLDING
□ BUILDING CENTERS
● REPAIRING CENTERS

Shipbuilding system
8 yards with an annual production capacity of about 1 million grt. for any kind of ship up to over 300,000 dwt. Each yard is specialized in building the ships most suitable for its own lay-out, equipment, skills and traditions.

Shiprepairing system
9 yards with 26 graving docks for ships up to 350,000 dwt. (3 new graving docks for v.l.c.c. up to 400,000 dwt. under construction), 10 floating docks for ships up to 160,000 dwt. and about 15 kilometres of outfitting quays.

Mechanical products
3 factories for the production of main and auxiliary Diesel engines, main and auxiliary turbines, deck and E.R. machinery and marine propellers.

GROUP'S COMPANIES

ITALCANTIERI (Trieste)
CANTIERI NAVALI RIUNITI "C.N.R." (Genova)
CANTIERE NAVALE MUGGIANO (La Spezia)
CANTIERE NAVALE LUIGI ORLANDO "C.N.L.O."(Livorno)
OFFICINE ALLESTIMENTO E RIPARAZIONE NAVI "O.A.R.N." (Genova)
SOCIETÀ ESERCIZIO BACINI NAPOLETANI "S.E.B.N." (Napoli)
STABILIMENTI NAVALI (Taranto)
CANTIERI NAVALI E OFFICINE MECCANICHE DI VENEZIA "C.N.O.M.V." (Venezia)
ARSENALE TRIESTINO S. MARCO (Trieste)
LIPS ITALIANA (Livorno)
GRANDI MOTORI TRIESTE "G.M.T." (Trieste)

FINCANTIERI
Società Finanziaria Cantieri Navali
via Sardegna n. 40 Roma
phone (06) 482241
telex 61180 FINCANT.

HK
Hatch & Kirk Export Co., Inc.

5111 Leary Avenue N.W.
Seattle, Washington 98107

LARGEST INVENTORY OF DIESEL ENGINE PARTS AND ACCESSORIES IN THE WORLD

ALCO	ENTERPRISE
ATLAS	FAIRBANKS MORSE
ALLIS CHALMERS (BUDA)	GM CLEVELAND 268A-278A
BALDWIN	GM DETROIT
COOPER BESSEMER	HERCULES
CUMMINS	NORDBERG
ELECTROMOTIVE	WHITE - SUPERIOR

AMERICAN BOSCH-BENDIX-ROOSAMASTER FUEL SYSTEMS
BACHARACH TEST EQUIPMENT AND TOOLS
DeLAVAL AND SHARPLES OIL SEPARATORS
HYDRAULIC AND AIR STARTING SYSTEMS
HYDRAULIC AND ELECTRIC GOVERNORS
MARINE REVERSE AND REDUCTION GEARS
TURBOCHARGER ASSEMBLIES AND PARTS

SERVING NAVAL AND COMMERCIAL ACCOUNTS THROUGHOUT THE WORLD

TELEX 32-8714   TELEPHONE (206) 783-2766

DARDO

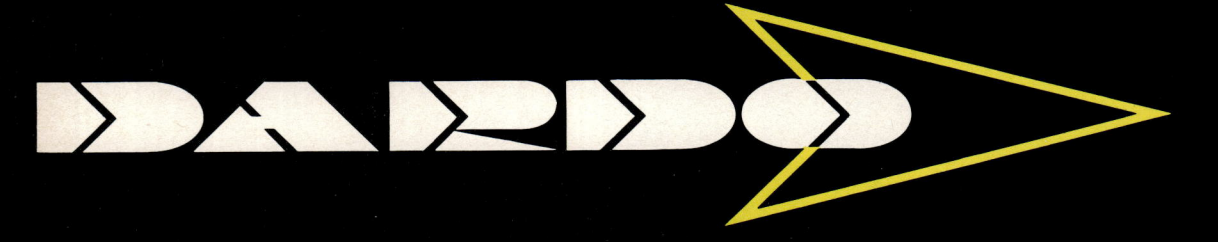

DARDO SYSTEM FOR SHORT RANGE DEFENSE

This System has been developed for ensuring maximum kill probability against various types of missile targets (sea-skimmer, divers) and it forms the last line of defence against the anti-ship missile threat.

The salient features of this system are:

- fully automatic operation from start of search to opening of fire
- very short reaction time
- high kill probability even in case of multiple-target threat.

The System utilizes a fully automatic weapon, the BREDA Compact 40/70 twin mount, firing specialized proximity-fuze projectiles at very high rates.

The threat under consideration :

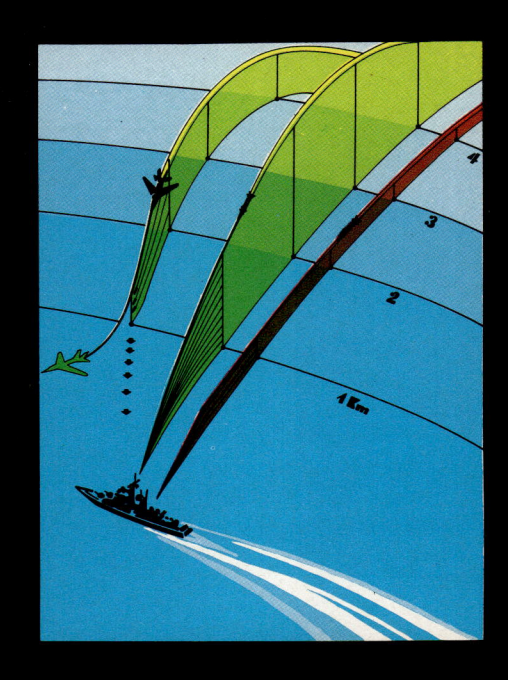

SELENIA
INDUSTRIE ELETTRONICHE ASSOCIATE
S.p.A.
via Tiburtina km 12,400
00131 ROMA (Italy)

ELETTRONICA SAN GIORGIO
ELSAG   S.p.A.
via Hermada, 6
16154 GENOVA-SESTRI (Italy)

NAVAL SYSTEMS DIVISION

SELENIA
Elsag

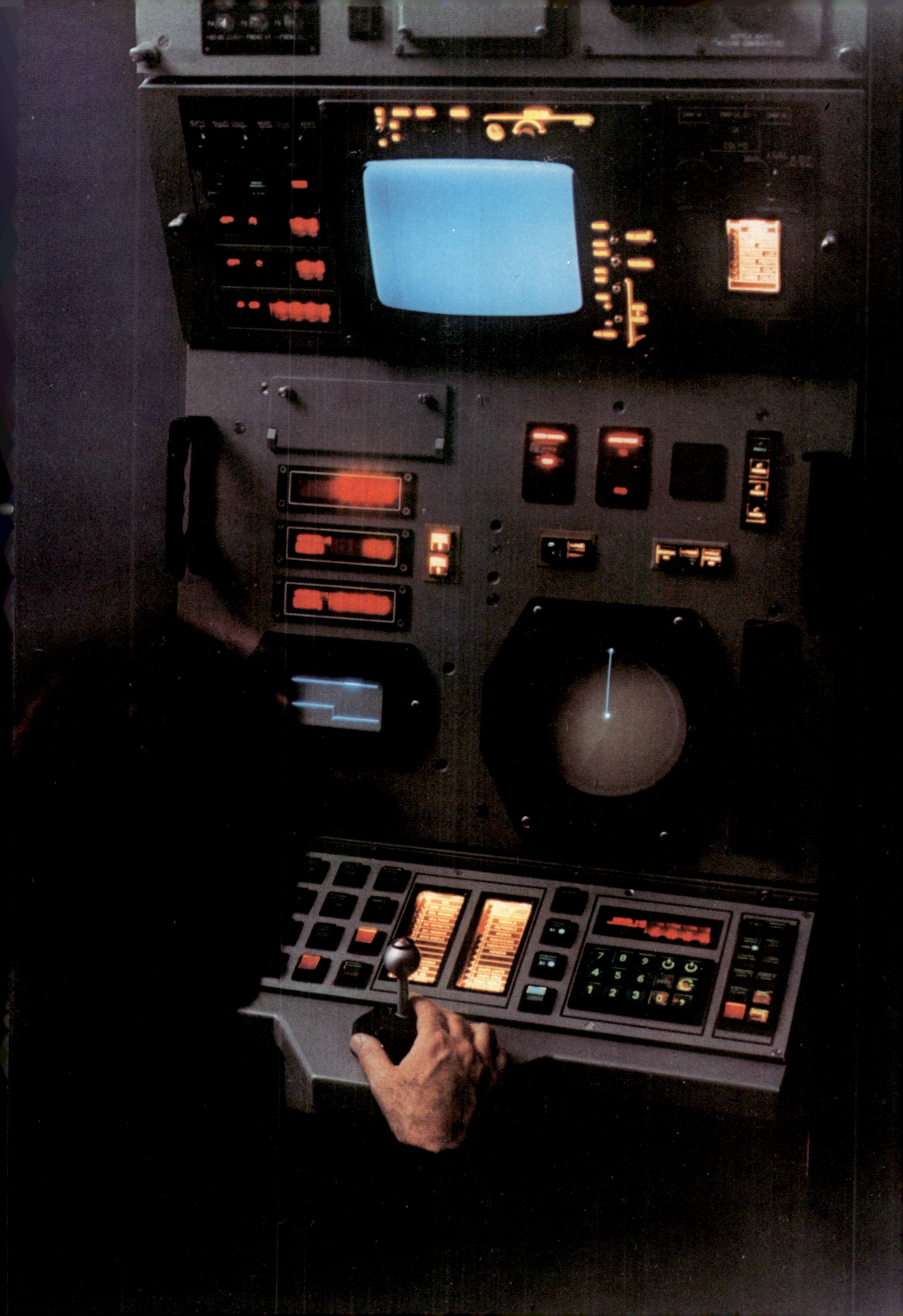

THYSSEN

Know How
Quality
Reliability

THYSSEN NORDSEEWERKE GMBH

D-2970 Emden, Am Zungenkai,
Tel. (04921) 8 51 — Telex 027 802

CHANTIERS DE LA PERRIERE

8 Blvd. Abbé Le Cam—56100 LORIENT—France
Tel: 37 23 11
Telex: 730 653

Regional Support Vessel

New class of multi-purpose district ship for the French Navy

EVERY TYPE OF SHIP UP TO 65 METRES L.O.A.

Aluminium Alloy and Steel Shipbuilding

Tugs - Pushers — Fast Launches — Passenger Ships etc.

The Navy's after us...

...so are the Marines, the Customs and the Coastguards. And who can blame them? Because Dravo SteelShip make the toughest, fastest and most advanced military craft in the world. From a 36ft. assault craft to a 185ft. missile-launching patrol vessel. And everything in between.
Want a standard vessel modified? Dravo SteelShip can do that too. Or custom design a craft for a specific military operation. Dravo SteelShip Corporation. The name with a world-wide reputation for quality, delivery and price.

Dravo

Dravo SteelShip Corporation
Route 4, Box 167, Pine Bluff,
Arkansas 71602 TWX 910-729-2919
Tel: 501-536-0362

OFFICINE PANERAI SRL

has elaborated for over a century an activity of research, design and production of optical, mechanical and electronic equipment, apparatus and devices.
Panerai precision devices, such as compasses, pressure gauges, depth-meters, watches, depth-recorders and watertight flashlights were used underwater by the first frog-men, honour and pride of the Italian Navy.
The main headline of this activity has always been the quality of produced materials, made in small and medium series for special uses. Herein are some characteristic items of the present, non-classified production of the company, in use by the Italian Armed Forces:
- Equipment for helicopters night deck landing
- Portable equipment for aircraft landing
- Remote level indicator equipment for submarines trim tanks
- High level water (or liquid in general) alarm systems
- Electronic engine room telegraph
- Fixed and portable optical apparatus, for naval and land uses
- Wrist compasses and depth-meters for underwater operators.

The production and studies of the company include also the field of weapons, devices and fixtures for special troops, which, owing to their top secret nature, cannot be disclosed to the public, but for which the company may give direct and exact information to parties concerned, except when, in very particular productions, the release of these information requires the permission of the Italian Navy.
The accurate performance and high reliability of Panerai production have always obtained the widest acknowledgement and also the personal and warm thanks of many Commanders for whom the availability of Panerai equipment, at the right place and time, has been the resolutive factor in the aims achievement.

OFFICINE PANERAI S.R.L.
2 Piazza G. Ferraris
50131 FIRENZE

Phone: 055/579304
Cable: PANERAI FIRENZE

G.M.T. high-performance naval diesel engines for propulsive and auxiliary duty

Grandi Motori Trieste
FIAT-ANSALDO-C.R.D.A.-S.p.A.

34100 Trieste - Italy - P.O. box 497 - Tel.: (040) 8991 - Telegr.: Grandimotori Trieste - Telex: GMT 46274/5

ON TRIALS – The first of the Mark 10 General Purpose frigates armed with Exocet SSM and two 4.5-inch guns.

COMPLETED – One of three 60ft patrol craft for the Bahamas.

COMPLETED – One of two 103ft patrol craft for Tunisia.

MULTI-PURPOSE – The VT2 hovercraft can be operated without a conventional harbour and in any depth of water. In its multi-purpose form it can carry out many duties – coastal patrol, assault landings, firefighting, disaster relief, air sea rescue and containment of oil pollution – which otherwise requires specialised vessels.

Vosper Thornycroft today

Major extensions are being made to our shipyard at Portchester to cater for orders valued at some hundreds of millions of pounds for fast patrol boats of advanced design.

Successful trials of Lynx helicopters have been carried out in a Mark 10 frigate.
The second Mark 9 Corvette for Nigeria has been launched.

VOSPER THORNYCROFT

Vosper Thornycroft (UK) Limited, Vosper House, Southampton Road, Paulsgrove, Portsmouth PO6 4QA.
Telephone: Cosham 79481. Telex: 86115. Cables: Repsov, Portsmouth.
A Member of British Shipbuilders

Italy is surrounded by sea. And of the sea, we are the most important experts in Italy.

CNR CANTIERI NAVALI RIUNITI IR GROUP
NAVAL SHIPBUILDERS & REFITTERS

- DESTROYERS
- FRIGATES
- CORVETTES
- FAST PATROL BOATS
- HYDROFOILS
- AUXILIARY SHIPS
- SUPPORT VESSELS
- TRAINING SHIPS
- HYDROGRAPHIC RESEARCH SHIPS
- LANDING CRAFTS

LUPO CLASS FRIGATE

COMPACT
SPEEDY

CONFIRMED 14 TIMES
(UNTIL NOW)

BEFORE THE FIRST LUPO CLASS FRIGATE LAUNCHED FROM OUR SHIPYARDS
HAD COMPLETED HER SEA TRIALS,
WE WERE ALREADY RECEIVING UNANIMOUS TRIBUTES
FROM NAVIES ALL OVER THE WORLD.

FRANKLY, THAT WAS WHAT WE WERE EXPECTING.

BECAUSE IN THINKING ABOUT HER, PROJECTING AND BUILDING HER,
WE AIMED AT TECHNOLOGICAL SUCCESS.

THE 14 ORDERS RECEIVED HAVE CONVINCED US
THAT WE HAVE SUCCEEDED.

LUPO CLASS FRIGATE, 2400 TONS OF POWER.

CNR CANTIERI NAVALI RIUNITI
FINCANTIERI GROUP

HEAD OFFICE: GENOA (Italy) ☐ Via Cipro 11 ☐ Telephone 59951 ☐ Telex 27168
SHIPYARDS: Riva Trigoso ☐ Ancona ☐ Palermo ☐ La Spezia ☐ Genoa

AR.CO adv

Photo : E.C.P. Armées

ALARM !

Against low-flying attacks:
THOMSON-CSF proximity fuzes for navy shells
are available in all calibres.

Unaffected by weather conditions.

THOMSON-CSF

DIVISION ÉQUIPEMENTS AVIONIQUES
178, BD GABRIEL PERI / 92240 MALAKOFF / FRANCE / TEL. (1) 655 44.22

60 years of experience at the service of Engine Builder

italsider products over the 7 seas

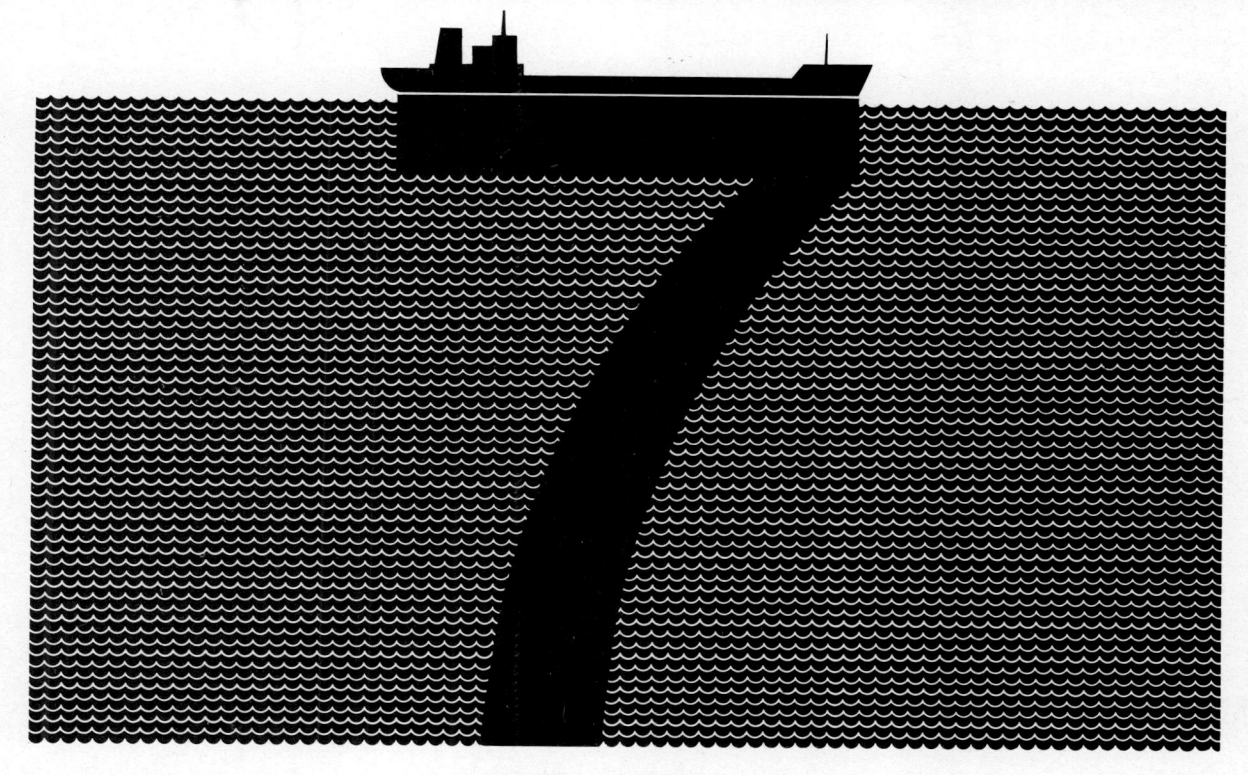

steel forgings and castings for the marine industry

crankshafts, running gear forgings and castings, hull castings, shaftings and rudder stocks

Italsider produces the largest crankshafts required in the world with weights in excess of 220 tons

Sales office
ITALSIDER s.p.a.
16121 GENOVA - Italy
piazza Dante 7
phone (010) 59.99
telex 27.690 Italsid

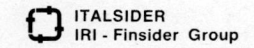

ITALSIDER
IRI - Finsider Group

Coastal radar systems for area defence or control of artillery and missile batteries.

Displays for action information and tactical control.

Modular Radar Systems for Navies of the eighties

As Naval tactics increasingly depend on the adaptability of sensor and control systems, Plessey technology has an increasing part to play in the development of warship and coastal defence capability.

The specialist skills that Plessey Radar has perfected in surveillance and detection of missile and other targets, and in weapon control have given it an unrivalled place as a supplier of advanced electronic systems to many of the world's navies.

Plessey Radar has a deep understanding of how to translate operational requirements into practical and cost-effective hardware. Modular designs and adaptive control enable Plessey to match the needs of a wide range of ship sizes and roles.

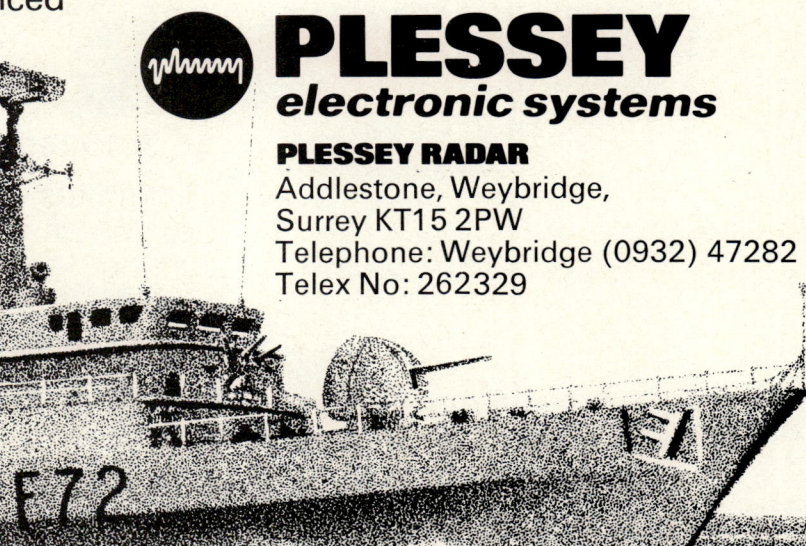

PLESSEY
electronic systems

PLESSEY RADAR
Addlestone, Weybridge,
Surrey KT15 2PW
Telephone: Weybridge (0932) 47282
Telex No: 262329

603 P272

Blohm+Voss

100 Years Blohm+Voss

1892	Small Cruiser "Condor"
to	3 Cruisers
1918	9 Heavy Cruisers and Battle Ships a. o. "Goeben", "Seydlitz", "Derfflinger"
	6 Torpedo Boats
	100 Submarines

1918	3 Training Sail Ships and 1 Aviso
to	6 Frigates and Destroyers
1945	1 Heavy Cruiser "Admiral Hipper"
	1 Battle Ship "Bismarck"
	230 Submarines

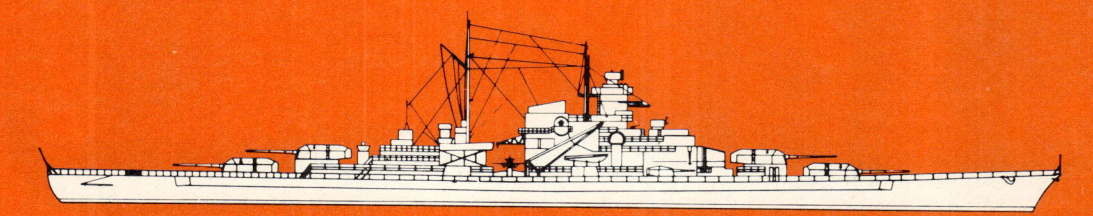

80 Years Naval Construction

1958	1 Training Sail Ship
to	4 Destroyers of the "Hamburg Class"
1971	6 Frigates of the "Köln Class"
	3 Escorts
	3 Supply Ships and 2 Mine Carriers
	2 Landing Craft
	3 Corvettes

| 1972 | Modernisation of the "Hamburg Class" |
| to 1977 | destroyers |

| 1977 | General Management for "General Purpose Frigate" (MEKO 300) |

Blohm+Voss AG · P.O. Box 10 07 20 · D-2000 Hamburg 1 · Phone 40-3061

Crestitalia S.p.A.

21 METRES HIGH-SPEED PATROL BOAT

CRESTITALIA builds a wide selection of g.r.p. fast patrol boats ranging from 7 to 21 metres.
The high speed patrol boat shown above is one of the most modern, efficient and rational boats yet built in the field of open sea planing hulls. The main features of the vessel are the hydrodynamic hull shape, the robustness of the hull and its proportions as well as the proportions and the reliability of the essential equipment (In particular the power plant and the control equipment) the stability, the safety, the manoeuvrability and, finally, the combination of the logistic, styling and functional characteristics.

The Deep-Vee hull has been developed from the well proven "CLIPPER 37" and "SENECA" line of power boats.

Open sea tests carried out on the prototype only served to confirm the parameters characteristic of this series and high-lighted the low water resistance, the very best performance in heavy seas even at low speed and when in a displacement condition, the excellent qualities of manoeuvrability and directional stability.

MAIN SPECIFICATION

LOA overall lenght	mts.	21
LWL stationary width	mts.	5,3
displacement, unloaded and dry	tons.	32,6
maximum speed, at full power with full load plus four (4) persons, in still water and calm air	Knots	35
cruising speed	Knots	30
engines: Isotta Fraschini Breda mod. ID 36 SS 12 V	HP	2x1.400

This boat can be equipped also with diesel engines: CRM, GM, Caterpillar, M.T.U.

CRESTITALIA S.p.A. - Head office: 20151 Milano - Via Gallarate, 36 - tel. 3271873 - telegr. Crestitalia-Milano
Yard: 19031 Ameglia (La Spezia) tel. 65746 - 65583 - 65584 - telex: Savid 38201

IBIS

A remarkable mine detection and identification SONAR, designed and constructed by THOMSON-CSF in collaboration with Services Techniques des Constructions et Armes Navales (French Naval Weapons and Constructions Establishment).

This sonar, of reduced size, can equip not only newly constructed vessels specialized in the detection and destruction of mines, but also minesweepers refurbished as minehunters.

In addition to the IBIS SONAR, THOMSON-CSF also supplies all related component parts of the mine "detection, identification, destruction" weapon system.

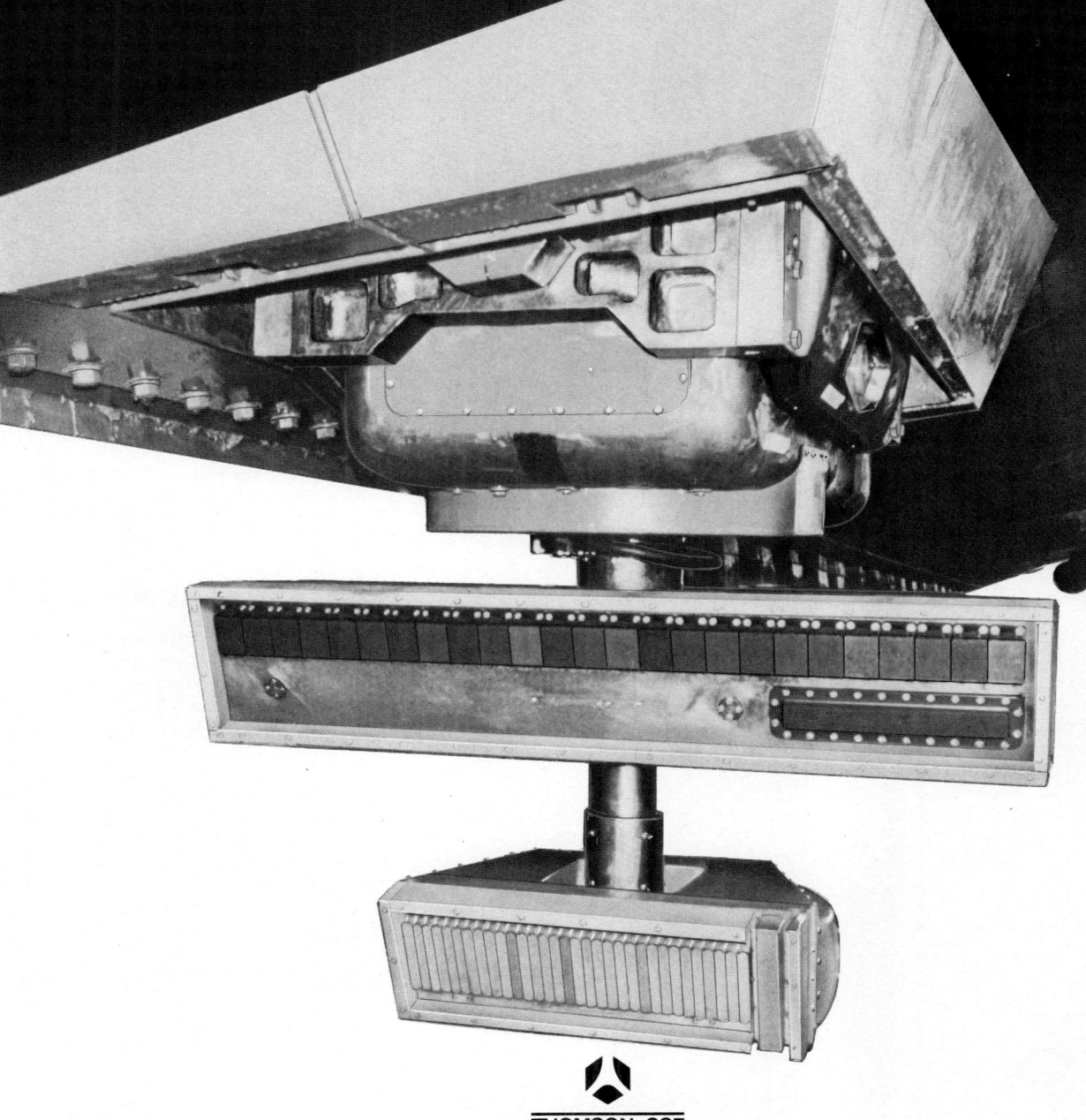

THOMSON-CSF
DIVISION ACTIVITES SOUS-MARINES
ROUTE DU CONQUET / 29283 BREST / FRANCE / TEL (98) 45.38.20

Better ships and better delivery times:

you'd better come to RSV

You know us

RSV is the largest shipbuilding group in The Netherlands, with over one hundred years' experience in the construction of naval vessels. Yards for naval shipbuilding in RSV are:

Royal Schelde Vlissingen
Wilton Fijenoord Schiedam
Rotterdam Dockyard Company Rotterdam

Naval shipbuilding is our business

Frigate, corvette, submarine, replenishment ship, fast attack craft, any type of naval vessel - you name it, we'll make it. Standard or custom-made. Task and mission taken into account, the result will be not just a ship but a comprehensive, integrated system of platform, sensors, weapons, communication and navigation equipment, together with all follow-up support services. Recent orders for the Royal Netherlands Navy and other navies include ships of the Tromp, Kortenaer, Zwaardvis and Zuider-kruis classes.

What's your problem?

If your naval program calls for new vessels to meet specific operational requirements - consult RSV. A specialized briefing team will be pleased to discuss possibilities. Excellent yard facilities are also available for repairs, conversions and modernisations.
And, count on it, delivery time means delivery time. That's our way at RSV. We invite you to contact us for further information.

RSV/ Naval Engineering

P.O. Box 1425 - Rotterdam - Holland
Telephone: (+31 10) 14 28 11 -
Telex: 23652

Rhine-Schelde-Verolme
Engineers and Shipbuilders/The Netherlands

√S

VITROSELENIA USUAL REFITTING ACTIVITIES IN THE NAVAL ELECTRONICS AND SYSTEM ENGINEERING:

- INSTALLATION OF TERRIER, TARTAR, ASROC AND SEA SPARROW MISSILE SYSTEM EQUIPMENT
- SEARCH AND NAVAL RADAR SYSTEM (SIOC) INSTALLATION
- FUNCTIONAL TEST AND ELECTRICAL ALIGNMENTS
- INSTALLATION OF FIRE CONTROL SYSTEMS
- DESIGN, SUPPLY AND INSTALLATION OF AUXILIARY SYSTEMS AND INTEGRATION THEREOF
- DESIGN, SUPPLY AND INSTALLATION OF WEAPON SYSTEM INTERFACE EQUIPMENT
- CABLING AND WIRING OF ALL EQUIPMENT MENTIONED ABOVE
- DESIGN, SUPPLY AND INSTALLATION OF WAVEGUIDES AND EQUIPMENT FOR PRESSURIZATION AND REFRIGERATION
- PREPARATION AND SUPPLY OF TECHNICAL DOCUMENTATION

AS PERFORMED ON ITALIAN AND FOREIGN NAVIES UNITS.

VitroSelenia

Via Tiburtina 1020 - 00156 Rome, ITALY
P.O.Box 7119 - 00162 Rome
Phone: 416641 - 415251
Cables: VITROSELENIA ROMA
Telex: 62309 VITROSEL

Brooke Marine

SHIPBUILDERS · ENGINEERS AND CONSULTING NAVAL AR[CHITECTS]

Designers and builders of specialised ships and naval vessels for British, Commonwealth and Foreign navies

Now building Logistic Support Ship for the Sultanate of Oman

37.5 metre Fast Patrol Craft for the Sultanate of Oman

Lowestoft · Suffolk · England A MEMBER OF BRITISH SHIPBUILDERS
TELEPHONE: LOWESTOFT 65221 · TELEX 97145 ·
CABLES BROOKCRAFT LOWESTOFT.

...imited
...ITECTS
ESTABLISHED 1874

100 YEARS OF ENGINEERING & SHIPBUILDING

42 metre Fast Patrol now building similar craft for the Royal Australian Navy

Landing Craft Logistic for the British Ministry of Defence (Army)

Image Intensification and Thermal Imaging equipment from Philips Usfa B.V.

Driver's Universal Passive Periscope
adaptable for all types of armoured vehicle, by the use of easily exchangeable top prisms. A range of these prisms is available, tailored according to vehicle type.

Military Mini Cooler 80 K
a compact cryogenerator for cooling detectors in the thermal imaging equipment of armoured vehicles, ships and aircraft.
Cool-down time approx. 10 minutes.
MTBF over 2000 hours.

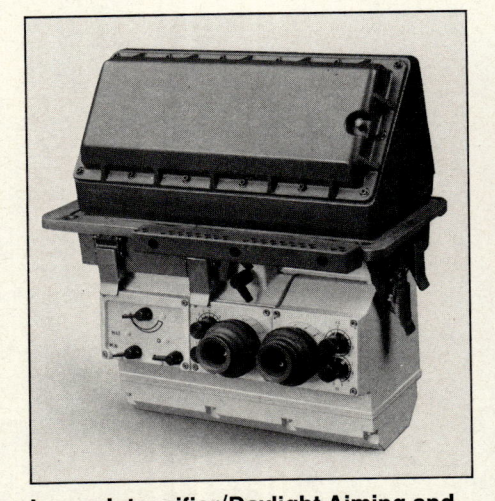

Image Intensifier/Daylight Aiming and Observation Periscopic System
(including vision block) designed and tested for day and night use under specific operational conditions.

Infrared Camera
for integration into weapon control systems, enabling the passive automatic tracking of air targets.

Remember, for Reliability in Defence

A leading supplier of defence equipment since 1954

Philips Usfa B.V.
Meerenakkerweg 1
Eindhoven
The Netherlands
Telex 51732 USFAE NL

PHILIPS

isotta fraschini
marine diesel

propulsion units for military or civil crafts, pleasure boats
from **200** up to **2000** hp

if you are looking for a dependable marine diesel engine...

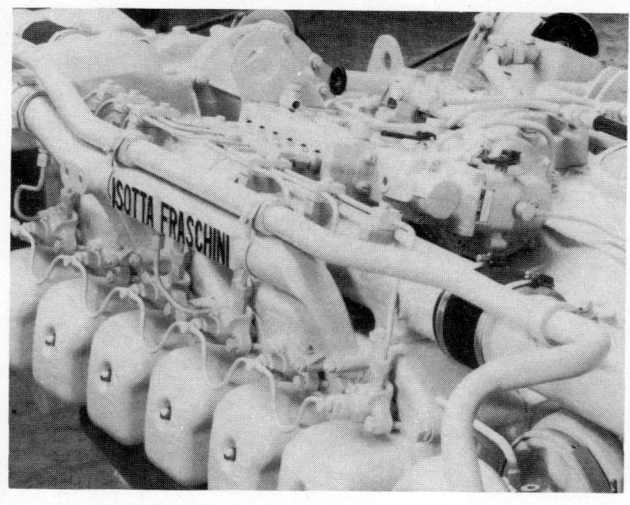

f.a. isotta fraschini e motori breda s.p.a.
21047 saronno (va), italy, via milano 7
phone (02) 960.3251/2/3 · cable brif. · telex 39403 brif

a.s.w.

CIT-ALCATEL
DIVISION MARINE

Anti-submarine warfare
French specialist

systems • equipment • armaments
for surface ships • submarines
and aircrafts

CIT Alcatel
GROUPE CGE

DIVISION MARINE
1, avenue Aristide - Briand, 94117 Arcueil (Paris) - France
Tél: (1) 657.11.70 - Télex 260 675 F

ELETTRONICA SPA
ROMA

**FULL EW AND IR CAPABILITY
FOR AIR, NAVAL AND LAND FORCES**

- passive electronic warfare equipment for search, detection, analysis and identification of e.m. emissions (esm-elint)
- electronic countermeasures equipment (ecm)
- esm/ecm integrated systems
- infrared warfare equipment
- travelling wave tubes (twt)
- special microwave and optoelectronic components
- microwave landing systems (mls)

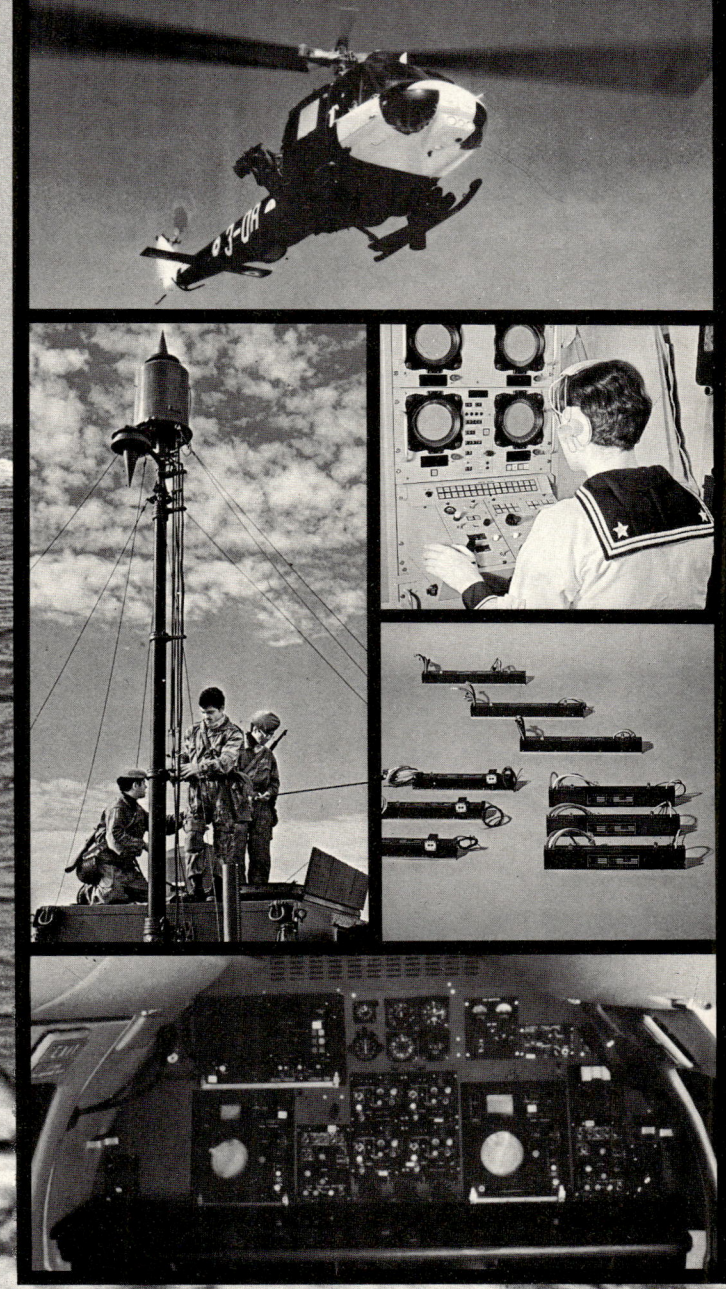

ELETTRONICA SPA
VIA TIBURTINA VALERIA KM. 13,700
ROME ITALY PH. 43641 TELEX 61024 ELT

CHANTIERS NAVALS DE L'ESTEREL S.A.
B. P. 10 — 06321 CANNES-LA BOCCA — FRANCE
Tél. (93) 47 04 27   Câble : Esterel-Cannes   Télex 470.876 F Esterel

HIGH PERFORMANCES FAST PATROL AND COST GUARD BOATS

MISSILE LAUNCHER FAST PATROL BOAT
42 m.   40 or 35 knots
In service in 1 country

COAST GUARD BOAT
28 m   35 knots
In service in 2 countries

FAST PATROL BOAT
37 m.   35 or 30 knots
In service in 1 country

COAST GUARD BOAT
27 m.   30 or 25 knots
In service in 3 countries

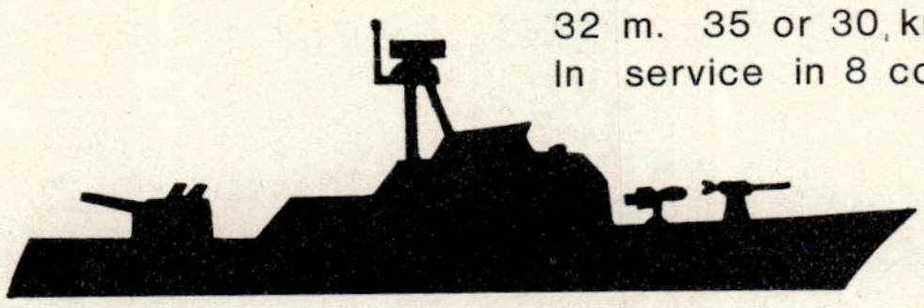

FAST PATROL BOAT
32 m.   35 or 30 knots
In service in 8 countries

- BUILDING'S QUALITY
- HIGH SPEEDS
- VERY SEAWORTHY
- HIGH MANŒUVRABILITY
- MAINTENANCE EASINESS
- LONG LIFE

MORE THAN 150 BOATS IN SERVICE, IN MORE THAN 20 COUNTRIES, SOME OF THEM FOR 25 YEARS IN ALL LATITUDES

DMS MARKET INTELLIGENCE REPORTS

AEROSPACE AGENCIES • AEROSPACE COMPANIES • "AN" EQUIPMENT
CIVIL AIRCRAFT • CONTRACT QUARTERLY • DEFENSE MARKET

ELECTRONIC SYSTEMS • ENVIRONMENTAL & CIVIL PROGRAMS
GAS TURBINE ENGINES • MILITARY AIRCRAFT • MISSILES/SPACECRAFT

SHIPS/VEHICLES/ORDNANCE • DEFENSE RESEARCH & DEVELOPMENT MARKETS
DMS INTELLIGENCE • RESEARCH STUDIES

FOREIGN MILITARY MARKETS
NATO / EUROPE • MIDDLE EAST / AFRICA • SOUTH AMERICA / AUSTRALASIA

FOR MORE INFORMATION CONTACT:
DMS INC., 100 NORTHFIELD ST., GREENWICH, CT 06830 USA - TEL (203) 661-7800, TX 131526
DMS INC., 500 CHESHAM HOUSE, 150 REGENT ST., LONDON, ENGLAND - TEL 01-734-5351, TX 261-426

CASTOLDI Jet

THE MARINE PROPULSION OF THE MODERN AGE

WATER-JET UNITS

JET 04
20 - 110 HP

JET 05
30 - 200 HP

JET 06
100 - 400 HP

MARINE JET ENGINES

900/04 - 46 HP

1600/04 - 89 HP

2000/05 - 108 HP

3000/05 - 141 HP

2400-D/05 - 62 HP

3500-D/05 - 93 HP

ALL OVER THE WATERS, COMMERCIAL AND MILITARY CRAFTS (NAVY, MARINE CORPS, ARMY, COAST GUARD, FIRE FIGHTING UNITS, POLICE, RED CROSS) ARE POWERED BY CASTOLDI JET

CASTOLDI S.p.A. - V.le Mazzini 161 - Tel. 02/949341 - Telex 36236 - 20081 Abbiategrasso MILANO - ITALY

All submarines built in the Federal Republic of Germany after World War II for the Federal German Navy as well as for foreign navies, were designed by INGENIEURKONTOR LÜBECK

In compliance with our drawings the following submarines were built and/or ordered till 1977:

- 3 Submarines class 201
- 2 Submarines class 202
- 5 Submarines class 205
- 8 Submarines class 205 mod.
- 18 Submarines class 206
- 15 Submarines class 207
- 28 Submarines class 209
- 3 Submarines type 540
- 2 Complete conversions
- 2 Work submersibles TOURS

Totally 86 Submarines for 14 countries

Our program comprises:

- Type 100
- Type 450
- Type 540
- Type 600
- Type 1000 with variants
- Type 2000

We are working at the enlargement of our program for our navy and foreign ones

INGENIEURKONTOR LÜBECK

Prof. Dipl.-Ing. Ulrich Gabler
P. O. Box 1690 · Niels-Bohr-Ring 5
D-2400 Lübeck 1
Telephone 04 51/31 07-1, Telex 26 768

HDW

HOWALDTSWERKE-DEUTSCHE WERFT
AKTIENGESELLSCHAFT HAMBURG UND KIEL
A Company of the Salzgitter Group

SUBMARINES

of a standard displacement between 100 and 2000 tons

P.O. BOX 146309 · D-2300 KIEL 14 · TELEPHONE: (0431) 7021 · TELEX: 292 428 hdwk d · TELEGRAMS: HOWALDTDEUTSCH

SNIA

DEFENCE AND SPACE DIVISION

00187 ROMA, V. SICILIA 162 - TEL. 4680 - TX. 61114

CONVENTIONAL AMMUNITION
- COMPLETE ROUNDS FOR ARTILLERY & MORTARS
- CARTRIDGES FOR SMALL ARMS
- PROPELLING POWDERS AND BURSTING EXPLOSIVES

ADVANCED AMMUNITION
- AIR TO GROUND ROCKETS
- SURFACE TO SURFACE ROCKETS
- FIELD SATURATION ROCKETS
- ROCKET AND MISSILE WARHEADS
- SOLID PROPELLANT MOTORS
- DOUBLE BASE AND COMPOSITE PROPELLANTS

SPACE ACTIVITIES
- APOGEE MOTORS
- STAGE SEPARATION MOTORS
- ORBITAL TRANSFER SYSTEMS
- SPACE LAUNCH VEHICLE MOTORS

RESEARCH AND DEVELOPMENT
- ANALYSIS AND DEVELOPMENT OF DEFENCE SYSTEMS
- DEVELOPMENT OF NEW WEAPON SYSTEMS
- TECHNICAL ASSISTANCE AND TRAINING FOR PLANTS INSTALLATION
- « TURN KEY » PLANTS OPERATION

cantiere navale breda

construction of: tankers up to 250.000 tdw; ore-oil carriers and bulkcarriers up to 175.000 tdw; ore-bulk-oil carriers, completely double-skinned, up to 150.000 tdw; product carriers up to 80.000 tdw; liquid gas carriers up to 80.000 tdw; container-ships of all types and dimensions; general dry cargo and multipurpose vessels of all types and dimensions; merchant and/or passenger/merchant ferry boats.

missile fast strike crafts, minesweepers, support ships, landing ships, corvettes, landing and assault crafts, special crafts, minisubmarines

3000 T
Rescue ship
Italian Navy

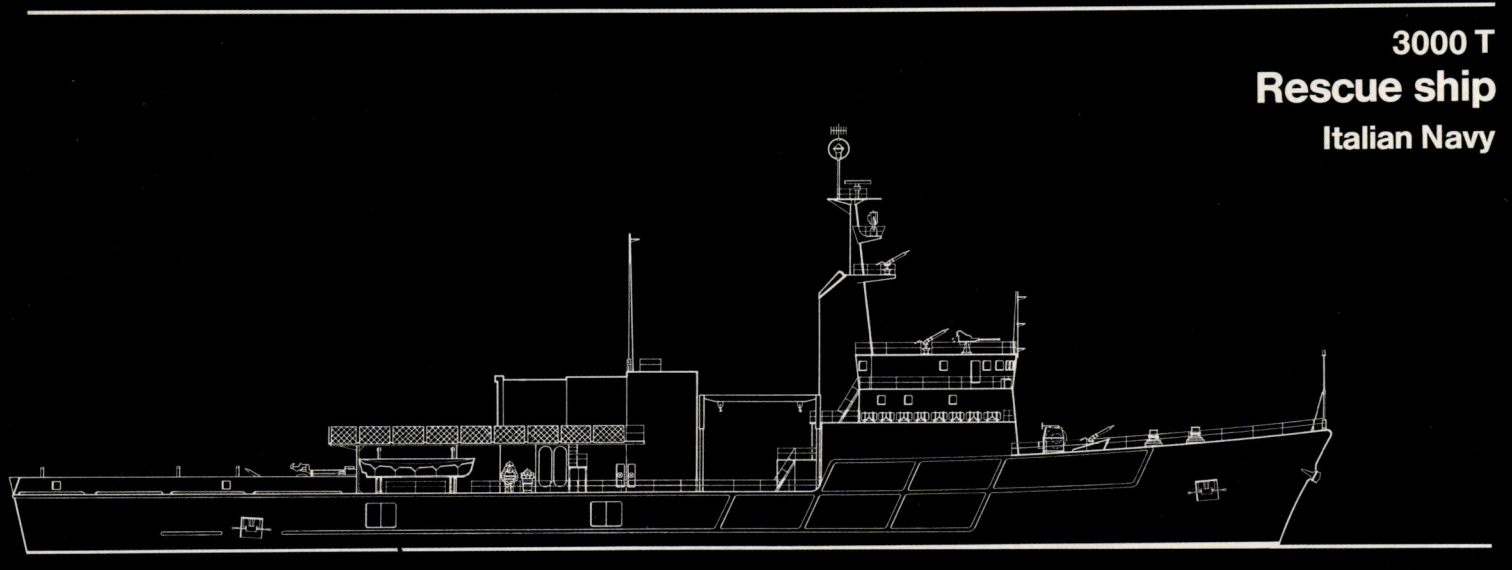

MV 400
Missiles fast strike craft

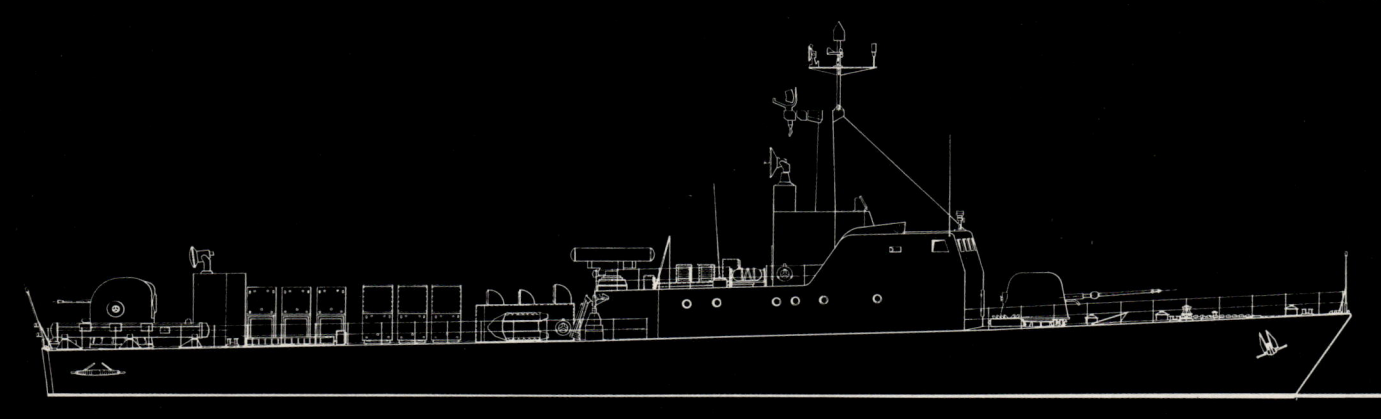

MV 400 H
Missiles fast strike craft helicopter carrier

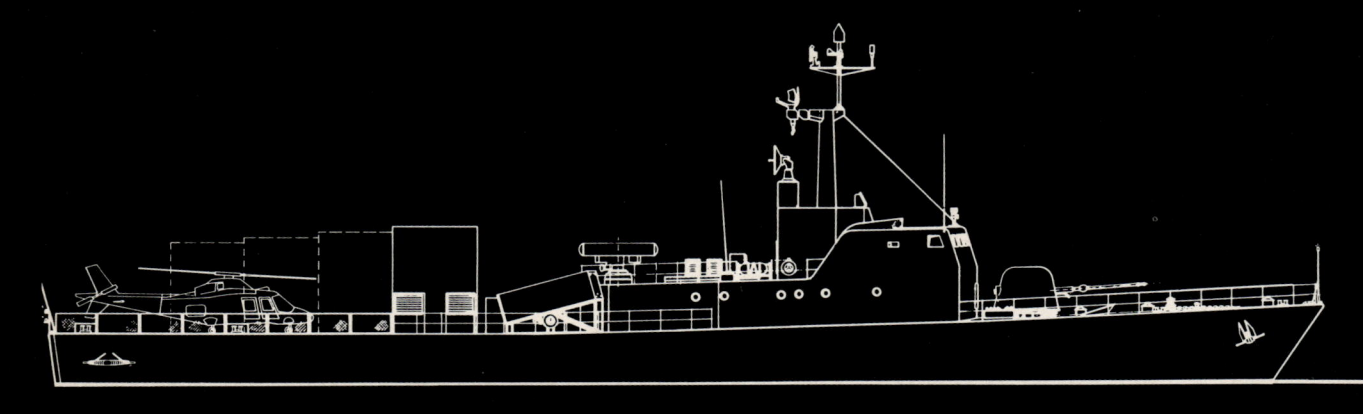

MV 250 S
Missiles fast strike craft standard

MV 250 T
Missiles fast strike craft
Royal Thai Navy

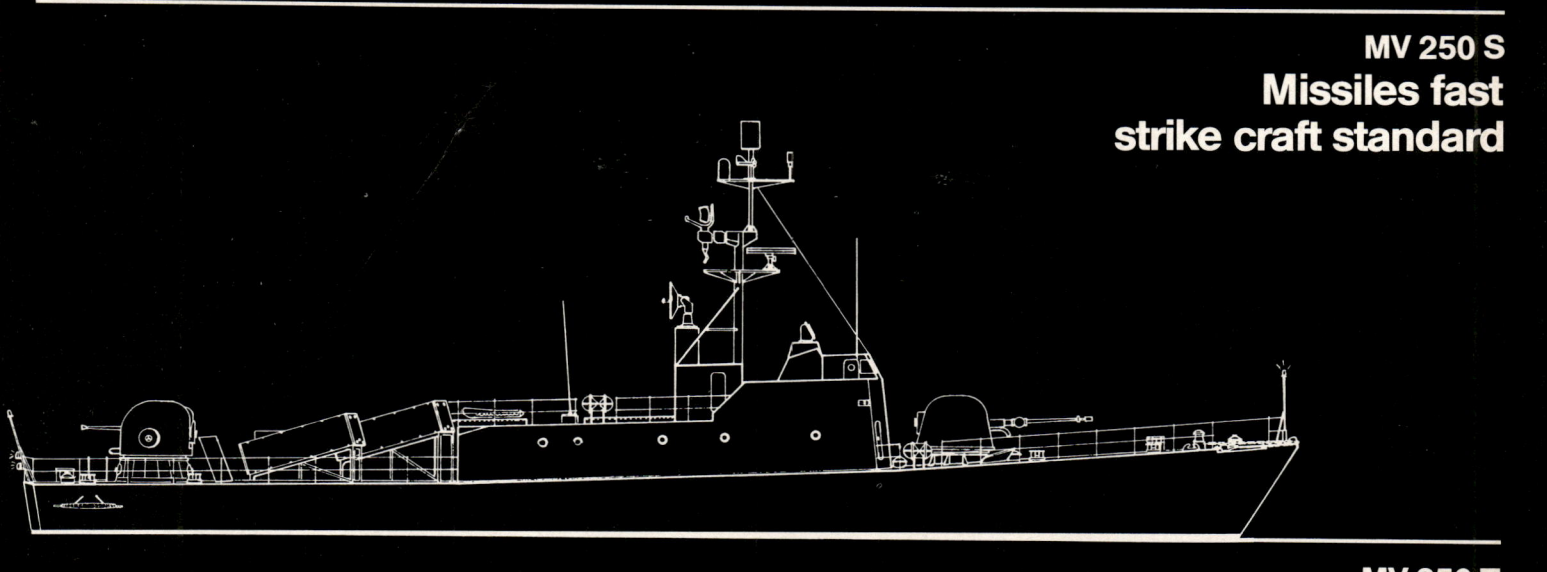

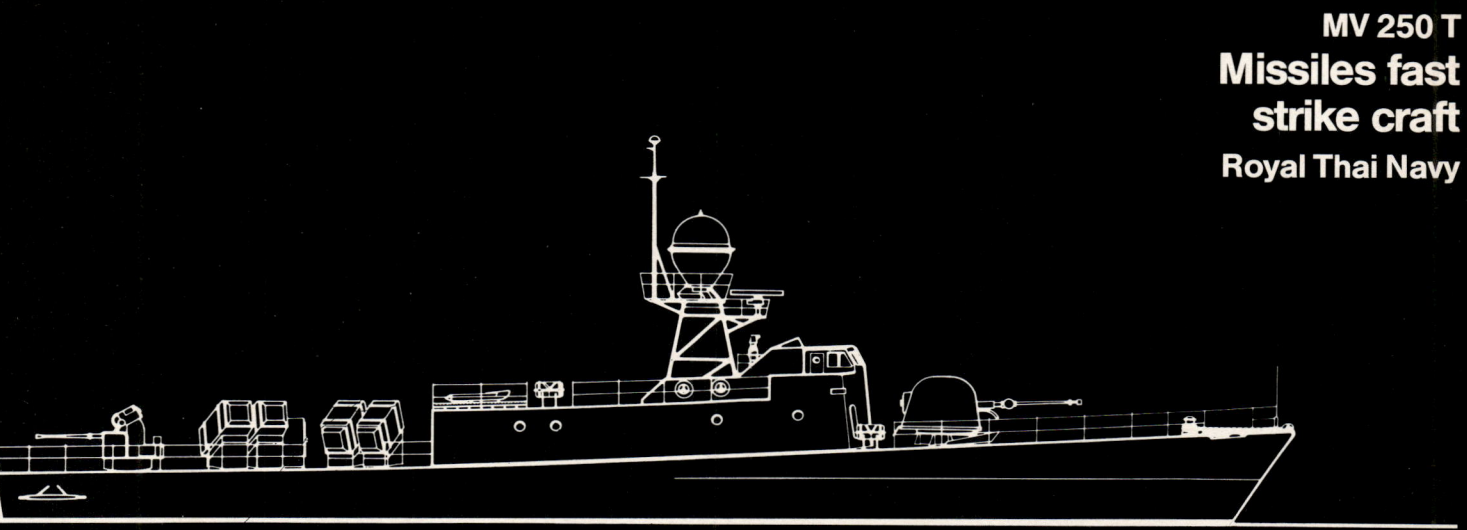

MV 150
Missiles fast strike craft

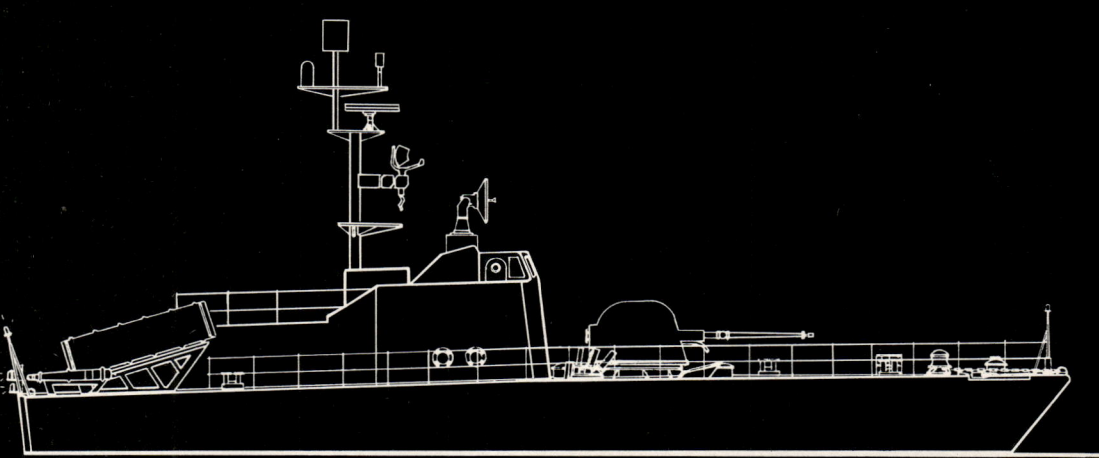

cantiere
navale breda spa

venice marghera italy
via delle industrie, 18
phone (041) 59860
telex 41106 bredanav
cables cantbreda venice

postal address
p.o.b. 1043 (succ. 1) 30170 mestre
capit. soc. 5.000.000.000 int. vers.
iscritta al n. 5181 trib. di venezia
iscritta al n. 49929 cciaa venezia

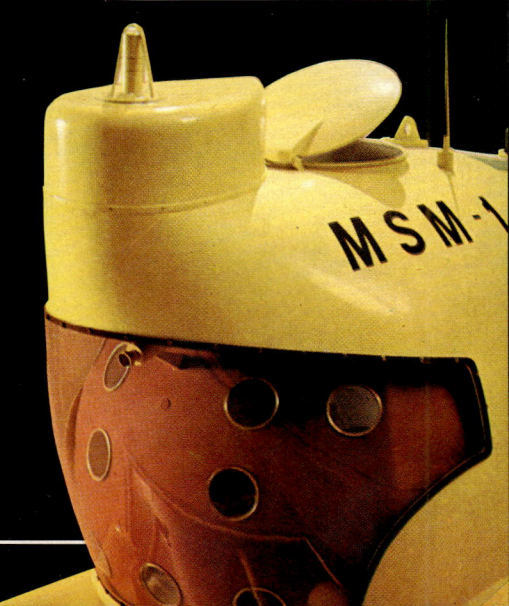

for all naval vessels and weapon-systems, new constructions, modernization, engineering, technical assistance

Shareholders:
Marine Française
Dubigeon-Normandie
Constructions Mécaniques de Normandie
Société Française de Constructions Navales
Chantiers Navals de l'Estérel
Thomson-CSF
Creusot-Loire
Société Nationale Industrielle Aérospatiale
Compagnie Industrielle des Télécommunications CIT-Alcatel
Compagnie de Signaux et d'Entreprises Electriques
Electronique Marcel Dassault

sofrexan

SOCIETE FRANCAISE D'EXPORTATION DE MATERIELS NAVALS MILITAIRES
créée en 1969 sous l'égide et avec la participation de l'Etat Français
30, rue d'Astorg, F - 75008 Paris, Tel. 265.47.47 / 265.12.11, Telex 640670 F

32 M (105') STEEL PATROL BOAT

for navy, police and customs patrol duties in open sea and coastal waters

cruising range 1000 naut. miles

2 diesel engines of 2600 hp each, speed 29 knots

accomodation for a crew of 19

De Vries: We, as shipbuilders, fulfil your every demand!

We have for seven decades been specializing in building all types and kinds of special purpose vessels, made of steel or aluminium, with lengths ranging from 40 to 200 feet. Quite a record for a small yard.

The de Vries building range includes a series of "customized" vessels, such as patrol and police boats, customs and harbour launches, pilot boats, crew and utility boats, inspection vessels, fire fighting boats. You can deal directly with one of the five members, of our Management team, who are all called de Vries, shipbuilders since 1907.

You can rely on them to provide the solution for your specific demands and requirements. Without any loss of time, without excessive costs, without any misunderstanding.

For details about the vessel you wish to buy contact:

de vries shipyards

DE VRIES SHIPYARDS, P.O. BOX 258,
AALSMEER/HOLLAND. TELEPHONE: (02977) 21551.
CABLES: VRIESYARDS, TELEX: 14256.

MOTOMAR
CANTIERI NAVALI S.p.A.

16003 Lavagna (Italy) – Via dei Devoto 169/171 – Tel. 303.636

CURRENTLY IN USE WITH THE ITALIAN NAVY POLICE HARBOUR AND PILOT AUTHORITIES OVERSEAS OIL COMPANIES.

Belonging to a standard range of hulls up to 64'.
Armament from 7.62 NATO to 30 mm. light gun.
Specially equipped for rescue duties.
More than one hundred
units operative in Italy and overseas.

MOTOMAR 40' Patrol Boat in G.R.P. & Steel

SALES ORGANIZATION:

Valtec Italiana s.r.l.
Milano, Via Valtellina 65
Telephone: 6882412-6887445
Cables: Valseltec-Roma
Telex: 36464 Motomar

⊕ KRUPP

Are your problems under the surface?

We'll solve them with

SONAR

Our experience is based on more than 70 years
in research, development and production.

KRUPP ATLAS-ELEKTRONIK
Naval Defence Systems Simulation Systems

FRIED. KRUPP GMBH
KRUPP ATLAS-ELEKTRONIK BREMEN
SEBALDSBRÜCKER HEERSTR. 235 · P.O.B. 44 85 45 · D 2800 BREMEN 44
PHONE (04 21) 4 58 31 · TELEX 02 44 890 · CABLE ADDRESS ATLASELEKT

on target with systems

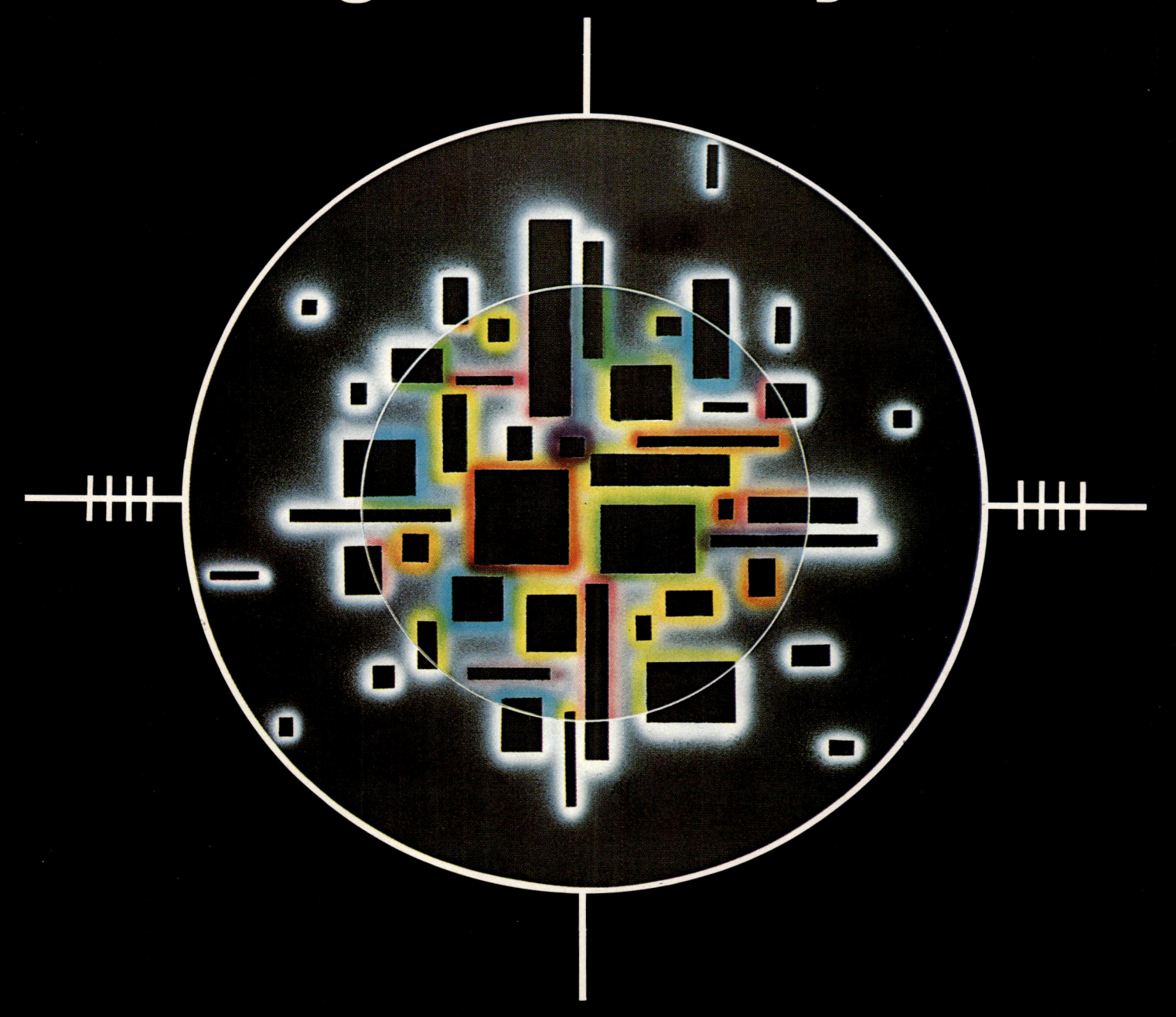

the most advanced defence systems

Fire Control and Weapon Guidance
- OFFICINE GALILEO 50134 Florence · via C. Bini, 44 · Tel. (055) 47.96

Missiles and Guided Weapons
- SISTEL 00131 Rome · via Tiburtina, 1210 · Tel. (06) 41.58.41

Space
- LABEN 20133 Milan · via Bassini, 15 · Tel. (02) 23.65.551

Telecommunications
- ELMER 00040 Pomezia (Rome) · viale dell'Industria, 4 · Tel. (06) 91.21.706/7
- OTE 50127 Florence · via E. Barsanti, 8 · Tel. (055) 410.921/413.171

Head Office
00161 Rome Italy · via G. B. Morgagni, 31 · Tel. (06) 86.01.51

MONTEDISON GROUP

MONTEDISON SISTEMI

creativity and experience

You don't push the boat until you're sure

out for V/STOL at sea of its potency.

Look who has.

Kiev is at sea. Minsk is afloat. Others are on the stocks.

So we're behind on ships. HMS Invincible enters RN service in 1979. Illustrious and Indomitable – her sister Command Cruisers – won't appear until the 1980's.

But we're way ahead with the V/STOL Sea Harrier.

A major advance on the version in RAF and USMC service, it joins the Fleet Air Arm in 1979.

Its V/STOL capability suits it for a wide range of warships – carriers, cruisers, helicopter flat-tops, aft-platform vessels: even support ships and merchantmen.

Jet airpower is the most flexible and powerful weapon available to a Command at sea.

Economical tactical air cover can be restored to the navies of the free world today only by the Sea Harrier.

The enemy at present is time. The longer the choice is delayed, the more catching up there will be to do.

HS SEA HARRIER

BRITISH AEROSPACE
AIRCRAFT GROUP
Kingston upon Thames, England.

a modern concept of integrated activity of italian companies cooperating in the underwater ordnance sector

**ANSALDO
GRANDI MOTORI TRIESTE
ITALCANTIERI
ERCOLE MARELLI
RIVA CALZONI
SELENIA
WHITEHEAD-MOTOFIDES**

TRIESTE CLUB

9 LV 100 Low cost, light weight fire control system

The 9 LV 100 is a complete, integrated optronic and radar fire control system for either very small warships, from 75 tons up, or larger paramilitary ships, such as Off-shore Inspection Boats, with limited armament and wartime duties. It is also well suited as a secondary, or back-up, independent fire control channel on board larger ships, of any size.

The 9 LV 100 will control:
- 1 dual purpose gun, optional extension to two guns.
- Surface-to-surface missiles.

The heart of the 9 LV 100 is a high speed, general purpose military minicomputer, of the same type as in the wellknown 9 LV 200 Mk 2.

The 9 LV 100 allows for:
- Search for air and surface targets using a lightweight S-band search radar with a 16″ PPI.
- Automatic trackning in fair weather of one air or surface target with the Director (see figures below).
- Automatic trackning in all weather conditions of one surface target with radar track-while-scan.
- Gun and missile control using Director or TWS data.

Philips Elektronikindustrier AB
Defence Electronics
Fack
S-175 20 JÄRFÄLLA 1, Sweden
Tel. Nat. 0758/100 00
Tel. Int. +46758 100 00
Telex: 115 05 peab S

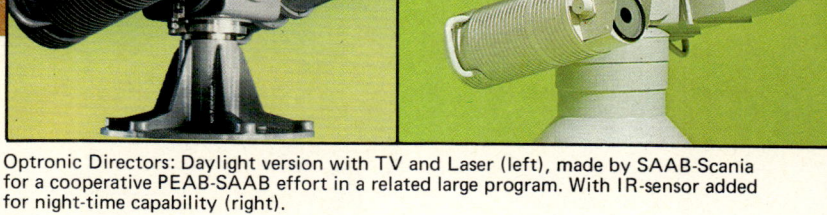

Optronic Directors: Daylight version with TV and Laser (left), made by SAAB-Scania for a cooperative PEAB-SAAB effort in a related large program. With IR-sensor added for night-time capability (right).

Control and Display console with 12″ TV monitor and control panel with pushbuttons and a joystick.

Philips Elektronikindustrier AB

PHILIPS

PEAB D 027 77 10

OFFICINE GALILEO

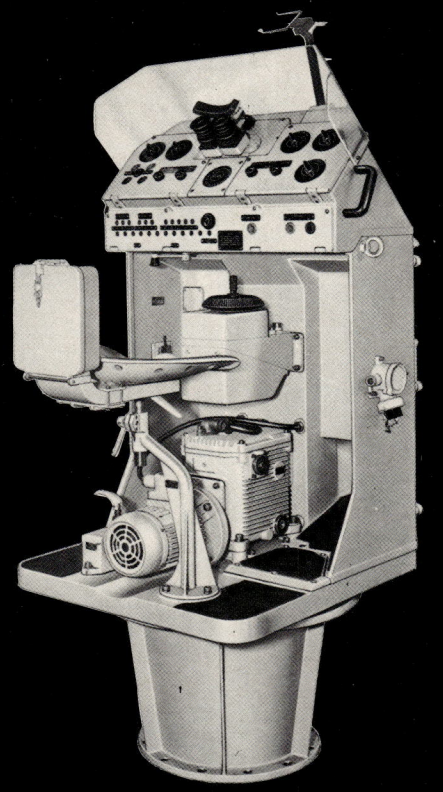

**the best experience for the sea defence:
electronics, infrared, laser, optics, with accuracy
and high performance**

Since 1950 fully transistorized fire control systems have been produced by Officine Galileo against air and surface targets

A new generation of acquisition, tracking and fire control equipments has been so far developped, which combines high performance and reliability with low cost maintenance and versatility:

OGR7/2 for 40/70 rapid fire guns
OGR7/3 for 76/62 battery with independent gun parallax processing
OGR7 "sea cat" for missile guidance
OG20 for weapons centralized control

Belong also to Officine Galileo naval production:
Stabilized pedestals for any type of sensors
Acquisition and tracking naval systems based on laser and IR technique, also integrated by iposcopical-optical sights

MONTEDISON GROUP

OFFICINE GALILEO
DIVISIONE SISTEMI
50134 FIRENZE - VIA C. BINI, 44
TEL. (055)4796 - TELEX 57126 GALILEO

T.R.S. SYSTEM

T.R. Sillinger has now an experience of 16 years in the field of inflatable boats and is considered as one of the worldwide leaders.

Because of their performances, their qualities and their reliability, T.R. Sillinger inflatable boats have been adopted by a majority of International Security Organizations, Civilian Protection, Fire Protection, but also by very numerous Armies and Navies all over the world.

T.R.S. SYSTEM

In order to answer the many demands from professionals, T.R. Sillinger has developped the U.M. Program (Maximum Use or Military Use) which is not simply a new range of strengthened conventional inflatable boats but "shock" boats completely built in a new fabric (1680 deniers) which outdistance by far anything that has existed up to now on the world market, 4 models in the U.M. Range from 4,20 m up to 6,30 m with a useful load from 945 to 2200 kilos. (For example: Average speed for 630 U.M. fully loaded with 115 H.P.: 55 km/h or 33 m.p.h.!).

Very numerous experts are unanimous on the performances of the U.M. Range:
– High reliability:
● Insubmersibility thanks to the hull designed in several compartments with inside reinforcments (1680 deniers material with incorporated Hypalon).
● Rigid keel which lends T.R. Sillinger crafts greater load capacity (men and equipments), stability and manœuvrability even by a rough sea.
– Specificity
● very simple and unexpensive maintenance,
● small bulk allowing quick transports (by helicopter and cargo) and easy storage,
● radar-undetectable,
● etc.
– Applications
(with conventional and sophisticated weapons)
● special missions for commando units,
● mine clearance operations
● survey and rescue missions
● assault landing operations (men and equipments),
● logistical and tactical support,
● etc.
T.R. SILLINGER: the only one manufacturer in the world of the revolutionary inflatable boat with hydrojet propulsion system.

	630 UM	500 UM	465 UM	420 UM
Length - Width	6,30 x 2,50 m	5 x 2 m	4,65 x 1,85 m	4,20 x 1,73 m
Occupancy	20/22 H	10/12 H	8/10 H	6/8 H
Useful Load	2200 kg	1350 kg	1150 kg	945 kg
Total Weight	240 kg	130 kg	110 kg	90 kg

T R S ILLINGER
BATEAUX PNEUMATIQUES

Special catalogues on request
T.R. SILLINGER - 150, rue de Lyon
75012 PARIS
Tel. 307.21.55 et 343.17.41
Telex: 680917 F TERSILL

Hydraulic Deck Machinery

Complete Systems for all class of ships

Motors · Pumps · Winches · Capstans
Anchor Gear · Boat Davits · R.A.S. Masts
Helicopter Handling · Lifts

MacTaggart Scott

P.O. Box No 1, Hunter Avenue, Loanhead,
Midlothian · EH20 9SP · Scotland.
Tele · 031·440·0311   Telex 72478

More and more Navies fly Agusta wings

Since ever Agusta is a Navy contractor.
This collaboration has brought experience to continuous improvements of naval helicopters.
Today Agusta has the most complete production line of Navy copters to fit any naval requirement.
"A family of twins" from the Agusta 109 light multi-purpose utility, through the Agusta-Bell 212 for ASW/ASMD roles to the Agusta-Sikorsky SH-3D long range missiles carrier.
Each helicopter is an integrated modular weapon system, carrying MAD, sonar, radar, missile guidance or electronic warfare equipment in order to be a self-sufficient hunter-killer, based either on ship or land.

AGUSTA helicopters are mission-ready NOW

Costruzioni Aeronautiche
GIOVANNI AGUSTA
Telex 25280 - Milan, Italy

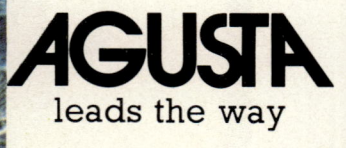

AGUSTA
leads the way

VEGA 80

The philosophy of the VEGA allied to the latest state of technology has led to a system which copes with the threat of the most modern weapons in the worst environmental conditions.

THOMSON-CSF
DIVISION RADARS DE SURFACE
1, RUE DES MATHURINS / B.P. 10 / 92222 BAGNEUX / FRANCE / TEL. (1) 657 13.65

SEA-TIGER
surveillance radar antenna
for the VEGA System.

SELENIA MARINE DIVISION

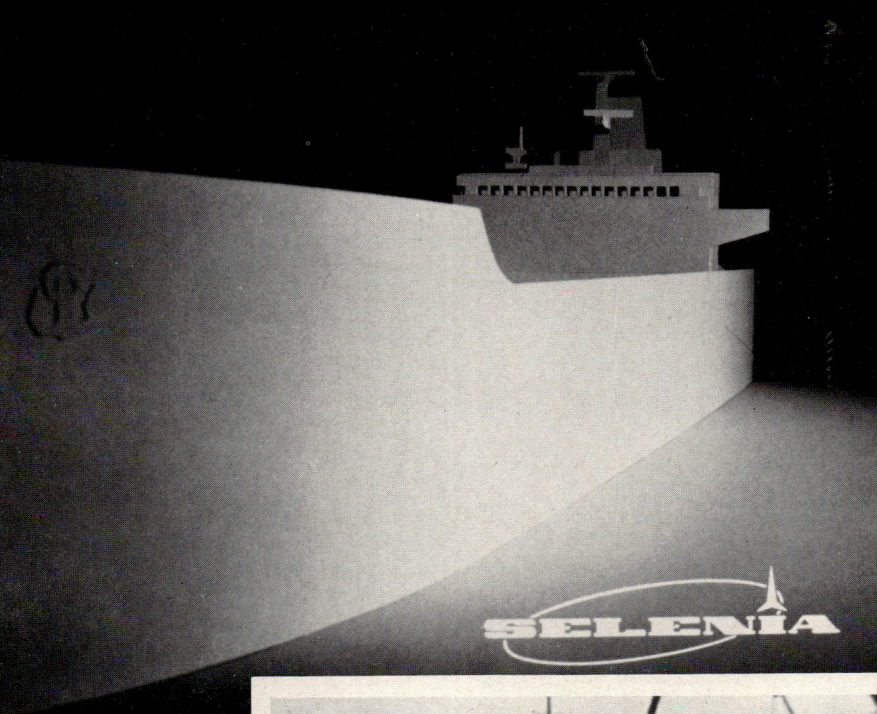

SELENIA S.p.A. is a leading Electronic Company well established internationally as a supplier of advanced systems for many applications, Air Traffic Control, Naval Communications, Data Handling and Missile Control.
SELENIA has from the beginning had a strong marine involvment and today there are more than 10.000 marine radars of Selenia design and manufacture in service worldwide, supported by an international network of more than 250 service organisations.
SELENIA MARINE DIVISION now offers specialist marine radar expertise directly to the end user and exploits the latest technology in the service of seafarers. A new line of accessories which improve the existing Product Line to state of the art are now available. These comprise:
MULTISCAN - A superb multilevel system of Video Processing producing a very Bright Display.
ELEPLOTTER - An electronic plotter giving fast and precise readout of selected targets dynamic data.
RADAR ALARM UNIT; providing an audible and visible alert of approaching targets.
RADAR PERFORMANCE MONITOR, offers accurate measurement of individual radar parameters.
Please contact your local **SELENIA DISTRIBUTOR** for details or write to:

SELENIA, Industrie Elettroniche Associate S.p.A.
MARINE DIVISION - Via Tiburtina Km. 12.400 / 00131 ROME, ITALY

ZF gearboxes...
big on performance – small in size.

ZF – Europe's No.1 gearbox specialist – is also taking the lead in the marine industry. More and more top designers are showing a preference for ZF drive units.

Marine quality and performance standards are among the most exacting. As with every other piece of equipment used on board, the utmost operational reliability is demanded of the reversing gearbox – coupled with quiet running and long life. The gearbox must not only match the performance of the high speed diesel engines, but not take up too much valuable space in the process.

ZF gearboxes meet the requirement precisely. They are compact, surprisingly light – give outstanding performance in ratings up to 5000 hp. Which is why they are being so widely chosen... on land, on sea and in the air.

If you have a driving problem you only have to say. ZF's gearbox specialists almost certainly have the answer.

ZF – the sign of progress

ZAHNRADFABRIK FRIEDRICHSHAFEN AG
D-7990 Friedrichshafen 1
P. O. Box 2520 W.-Germany

CNIM

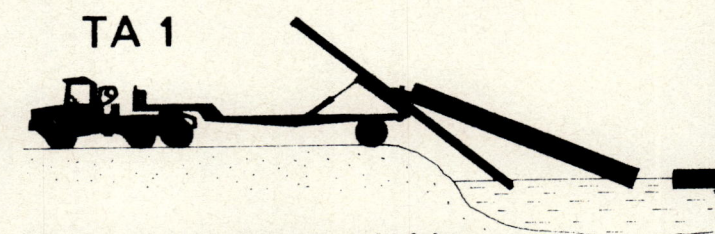

PS 700 — Landing ship for tanks

TA 1 — Motorised pontoon bridge

RAP 14 — Multiple rocket launcher

PS 774 — Multi-purpose logistic support ship

CONSTRUCTIONS NAVALES ET INDUSTRIELLES DE LA MEDITERRANEE

SIEGE SOCIAL
50, Avenue des champs Elysées, Paris 8°
Téléphone : (1) 225.74.23 + 225.86.57 +
TELEX N° 280 119VASCO- PARIS   CABLE VASCO-PARIS

DIRECTION GENERALE,
CHANTIERS ET ATELIERS :
83501-La Seyne-sur-Mer - FRANCE.

USEA

STUDY AND DESIGN IN THE AREA OF UNDERWATER ACOUSTIC SUBMARINE DETECTION EQUIPMENTS AND ELECTROMECHANIC AND ELECTRONIC AUXILIARIES

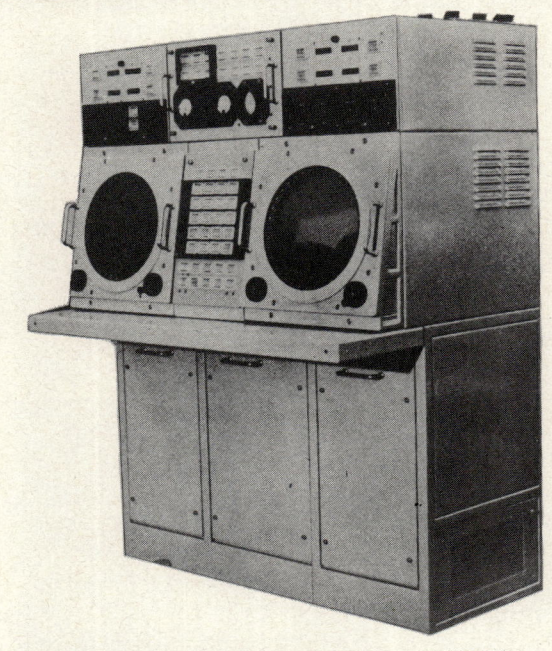

HEAD OFFICE AND RESEARCH LABORATORY
19030 Pugliola di Lerici (LA SPEZIA) - Italy - via G. Matteotti, 63
Tel. (0187) 967.125 / 968.605

REGISTERED OFFICE
00197 ROMA - Italy - viale Maresciallo Pilsudski, 92
Tel. (06) 874.450

We are specialists in the design, production and installation of underwater and marine equipment.

The Company's products include the following:-

Cable Penetrators and Connectors for Pressure Hull and Equipment Applications

Umbilical Cable Terminations

Cable Jointing Equipment

Hydrophones

Towed Seismic Arrays

Torsionmeters for propulsion Shafts

Complete Underwater Electrical and Electroacoustic Systems

Designed and manufactured to the highest standards of reliability for all underwater and marine applications.

ameeco
(Hydrospace Limited)

Bilton Road, Erith, Kent
Telephone: Erith 46821 Telex: 896230

SHIPBOARD AIRCONDITIONING

AERIMPIANTI

THE HIGHEST STANDARD IN EQUIPMENTS – DESIGN – ERECTION

TECHNICAL ASSISTANCE IN THE SHIPYARD AND DURING NAVIGATION

Address
20135 Milano—Italy ■ Via Bergamo, 21 ■ Tel. (02) 5497
Telex 33211 AERIMP ■ 61593 AERIMPRO ■ 77123 AERIMPNA
Milan　　　　　　　Rome　　　　　　　Naples

A mark of ASW superiority...

TACTAS AN/SQR-18

A mark of engineering excellence...

EDO

SQR-18... a new dimension in Surface Navy ASW. Its long range detection provides the Surface/Sub/Air Team with the tactical means to meet the modern submarine threat... a capability critical to national defense.

From conceptual in-house research and development to the fleet in only four years. That's just what the Navy-EDO SQR-18 team accomplished.

Record performance... in record time. It's one reason that EDO Sonar equipment is seen in more and more navies all over the free world.

EDO

For more information on Sonar Systems contact:

Mr. John Devine
President
EDO International Division
14-04 111th Street
College Point, New York 11356
(212) 445-6000/Telex 423094

TB 76 PROXIMITY FUZE

The TB 76 Proximity fuze, specially developed for the Oto Melara 76/62 naval gun system, is provided with proximity, percussion and self-destruction functions and incorporates antiwave circuits. Its burst area complies with the optimum fragmentation effect of the OS shell.

BORLETTI
DEFENCE PRODUCTS DIVISION
VIA WASHINGTON 70 - MILANO - ITALY
PHONE 4389 - TELEX 39067

SOCIÉTÉ FRANÇAISE DE CONSTRUCTIONS NAVALES | FOR HIGH SPEED MISSILED LONG RANGE STRIKE CRAFTS

sfcn

Société Française de
Constructions Navales
66, quai Alfred Sisley
92390 Villeneuve-la-Garenne
Tél. 794.64.46
Télex: 610998 F FRACONA

SELENIA ELECTRONIC WARFARE

ESM & ECM require:
Technical skill and operational experience
We have got them working in this area since 1962
Knowledge of existing and foreseeable threats
We design and produce sophisticated radars incorporating the threat technologies of tomorrow
Full integration with command and control systems
We are system integration experts for optimal operational effectiveness
Selenia electronic warfare production line includes the RQN and TQN series of advanced radar and IR detection and warning receivers, as well as active jammers and associated peripherals

they boast their radars cannot be blinded or deceived. we are sure they can and we know how.

Industrie Elettroniche
Associate S.p.A.
SPECIAL EQUIPMENT AND SYSTEMS DIVISION
00131, Rome ITALY
Via Tiburtina Km 12.400
P.O. Box 7083
00100 Rome
Cables: **SELENIA ROMA**
Telex: **61106 SELENIAT**
Phone: **(06) 413702**

SELENIA

BAGL

MANGUSTA 30

20 GC

ETTO
SINCE 1854

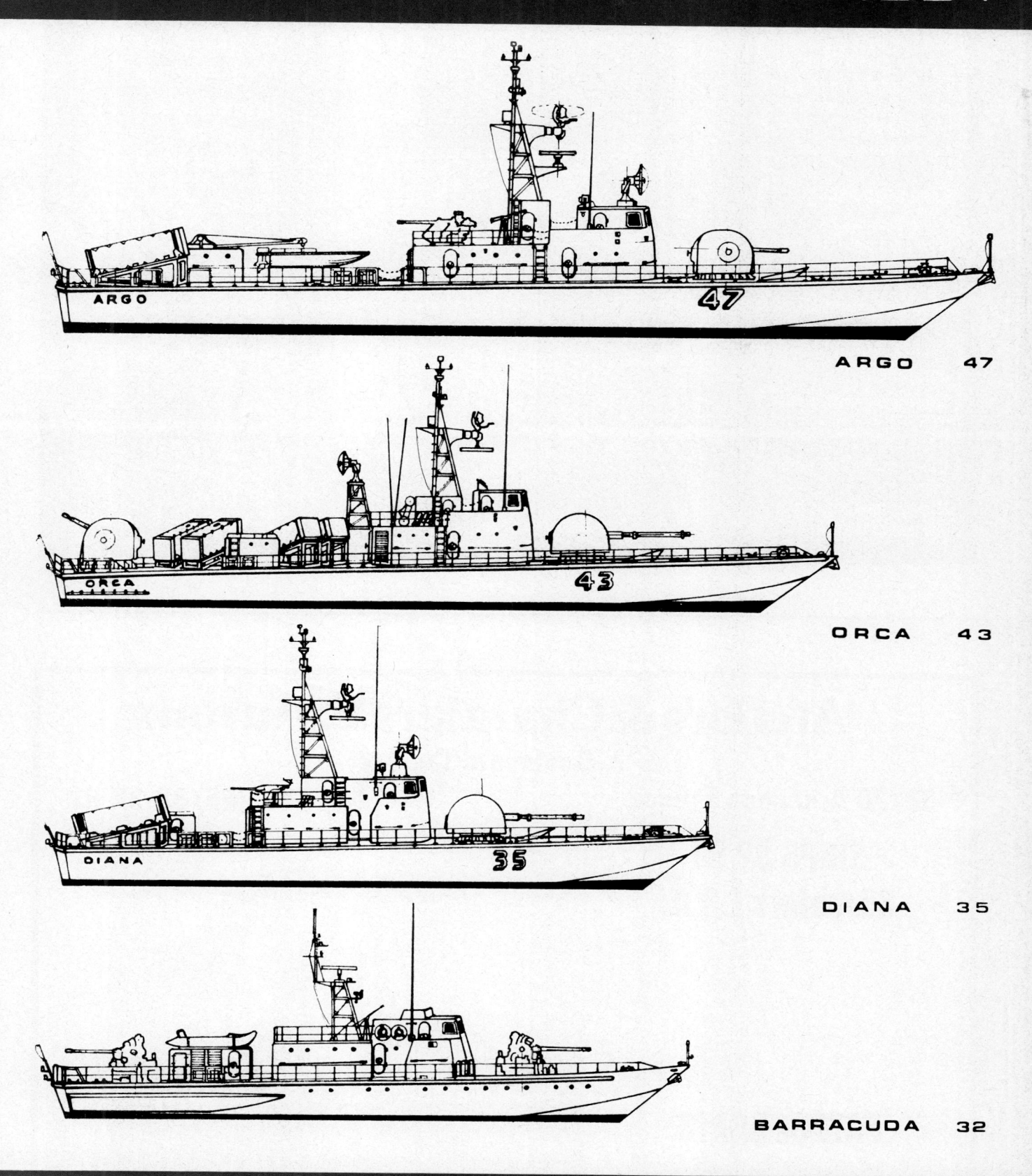

ARGO 47

ORCA 43

DIANA 35

BARRACUDA 32

CANTIERI BAGLIETTO S.p.A.
17019 VARAZZE ITALY

✠ BAGLIETTO VARAZZE
☎ (019) 95901 — 95902 — 95903
TX 28214 CANABAG

30 of the world's navies use Safare equipment

Underwater and surface detection

Sonar interceptor, analyser, direction-finder. Cavitation and superstructure noise detector. Test equipment for active and passive Sonars (transducer directivity checks, recording of ship's self-noise).

Echo-sounding

Navigation sounders for surface ships and submarines.
Watertight forward and vertical sounder.
Atmospheric sounder.

Divers' communication equipment

Telephones : wired systems, ultrasonic, and cable-attached telephones.
Coded telephone for extreme depths.
Homing : transmitting beacon and telephone receiver.

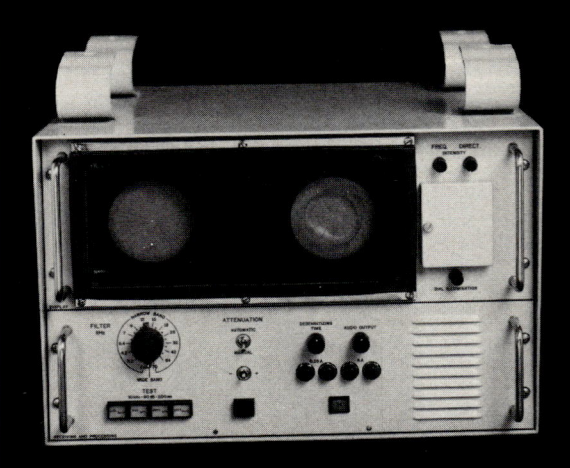

Sonar interceptor, direction finder, analyser equipment VELOX. M

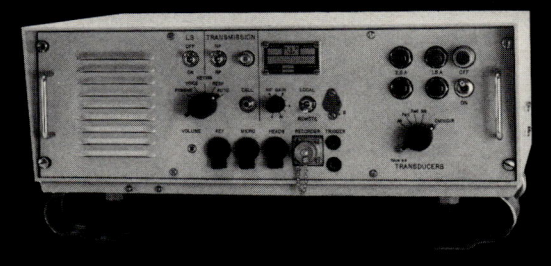

Long range ultrasonic telephone : TUUM-2 A

Underwater telephony

Long-range ultrasonic telephones, for surface craft and for submarines.
Responding beacons.
Acoustic transducers.

Oceanographic equipment

Meteorological telemetering network with drifting buoys.
Oceanographic telemetering network with fixed buoys.
Ultrasonic equipment for remote measurement of swell and tides.
Oceanographic and meteorological data sensors.
Autonomous submerged monitoring stations.

SAFARE-CROUZET
Tel. (93) 84.72.79
Telex 460 813
B.P. 171
06005 Nice Cedex France

Ateliers & Chantiers C. Auroux
7, Boulevard Chanzy

33120 Arcachon France   Tel : (56) 83-32-62

SHIPS UP TO 65 meters L.O.A.

PATROL BOATS

STEEL SHIPBUILDING

Fast Patrol Boat Delivered in 1976 to the French Navy.

[90]

ANTI-
MISSILE
and
ANTI-AIRCRAFT
DEFENCE

BREDA

40 L 70 TWIN MOUNTING

- *600 rds/min*
- *proximity fuse ammunition*
- *736 ready-use rounds*
- *above or below deck installation*

| BREDA NAVAL ROCKET LAUNCHER | 40 L 70 SINGLE NAVAL GUN with 144 round AFD | BREDA ANTI TANK WEAPON 'FOLGORE' | BREDA SHOTGUNS |

BREDA MECCANICA BRESCIANA S.p.A.
2, VIA LUNGA (25100) BRESCIA ITALY - TEL. (030) 31 40 61 - TELEX 30 056 BREDARMI

NEW ENGINES FOR NEW NAVAL REQUIREMENTS
propulsion and on-board generating sets

Engines from 90 to 6200 kW (120 to 8400 hp)
DIESEL POYAUD 135 and 150 mm bore / **DIESEL SACM** 175, 195 and 240 mm bore

1	2	3
4	5	6

1. 2 X 2200 hp SACM main engines
2. 4 X 3300 hp SACM main engines
   3 X 140 kW POYAUD generating sets
3. 3 X 4000 hp SACM main engines
   (40 knot patrol boat)
4. 2 X 1800 hp SACM main engines
   2 X 180 kW POYAUD generating sets
5. 3 X 480 kW SACM generating sets
6. 6 X 480 kW SACM generating sets

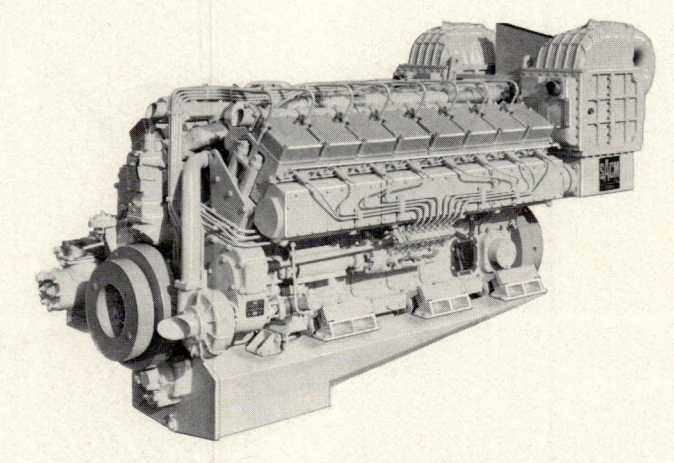

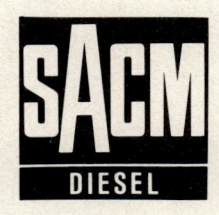

Photos : SACM - SKYFOTO - MARIUS BAR.

SACM DIESEL

SALES OFFICE FOR ENGINES UP TO 1000 kW :   SOCIETE *grossol*
14, RUE CHAPTAL – BP 104 – F 92303 LEVALLOIS CEDEX
TEL. : (1) 757.82.90 – TELEX : GROSSOL LVALL 620207 F

SALES OFFICE FOR ENGINES OVER 1000 kW :
SOCIÉTÉ ALSACIENNE DE CONSTRUCTIONS MÉCANIQUES DE MULHOUSE
1, RUE DE LA FONDERIE – BP 1210 – F 68054 MULHOUSE CEDEX
TEL. : (89) 46.01.08 – TELEX : SACMM 881699 F

H+H Conseil

ITALCANTIERI
A LARGE SHIPBUILDING CONCERN FOR ALL TYPES OF VESSELS

HEAD OFFICE: TRIESTE, Corso Cavour 1 • Tel. 7367 • Telex 46041 Italcant • Cables Italcant Trieste

SHIPYARDS: CASTELLAMMARE DI STABIA, GENOA SESTRI – MONFALCONE

IRI-FINCANTIERI GROUP

4.400 SHIPS BUILT FOR ALL FLAGS of which 1.870 naval vessels

13,250 ton. SEA CONTROL – HELICOPTER CARRIER

SUBMARINE 1081 TYPE SAURO CLASS
SURFACE DISPLACEMENT 1,450 TONS

SUBMARINE 1077 TYPE
500-TON CLASS

INMA

INDUSTRIE NAVALI MECCANICHE AFFINI

technical, administrative and commercial
management and shipyard
362, **viale S. Bartolomeo** 19100 **La Spezia**
p.o. box 346 **telephone** (0187) 504000
telex 27297 **INMA**
telegraphic add. INMA La Spezia

CONSTRUCTIONS OF:
training ship
landing ship
fleet support ship

fast patrol boats	up to 230	tons
fast missile boats	225	tons
vedette escorteur	130	tons
fast patrol craft	27,90	tons
fast corvette	690	tons
fast strike craft	290	tons
missile boat	153	tons

[94]

Plessey the communicators

Advanced electronic systems and communications equipment for ground, air and naval defence forces.

On the ground - A full capability in combat net radios based on HF, VHF, and UHF transceivers for vehicle, manpack, and helicopter use. The range includes the Plessey PRC 320 hf ssb manpack - one of the British Army's Clansman Range of combat radios designed for use worldwide under all climatic conditions. Another key product is the Plessey Gun Sound Ranging System for accurate location of hostile artillery in the battlefield.

In the air - A cost effective family of UHF, VHF, U/VHF transceivers is available as well as weapon control and IFF/SSR systems.

On the sea - A comprehensive range of UHF, VHF and U/VHF transceivers and IFF/SSR systems are available to equip vessels from fast patrol craft through to present generation cruisers.

For full information please contact:
The Military Product Manager

PLESSEY AVIONICS & COMMUNICATIONS
Ilford Essex United Kingdom IG1 4AQ
Tel: London (01) 478 3040

PLESSEY
electronic systems

607 P092

Plessey UK/PRC 320

CANTIERI NAVALI RIUNITI	GENOVA via Cipro 11	telex 27168
GRANDI MOTORI TRIESTE	TRIESTE via Cavour 1	telex 46274
FIAT AVIAZIONE SEPA	TORINO via Nizza 312 TORINO lungo Stura Lazio 45	telex 23320 telex
OTO MELARA	LA SPEZIA via Valdilocchi 15	telex 27368
BREDA MECCANICA BRESCIANA	BRESCIA via Lunga 2	telex 30056
SELENIA ELETTRONICA SAN GIORGIO NAVAL SYSTEMS DIVISION	ROMA via Tiburtina Km 12.400 GENOVA-SESTRI via Hermada 6	telex 61106 telex 27660
ELETTRONICA	ROMA via Tiburtina Km 13.700	telex 62024
MONTEDEL ELMER DIVISION	POMEZIA (ROMA) viale Industria 4	telex 61112

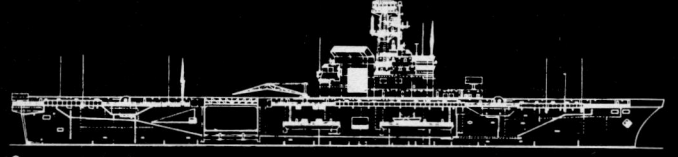

Sea control and assault ship

Training command and assault ship

Fleet support ship

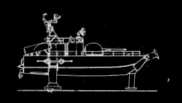

Missile Hydrofoil

2400 ton guided missile frigate

Hydrographic survey ship

1000 ton Corvette

550 ton guided missile Corvette

280 ton missile fast patrol boat

MELARA CLUB

·MELARA CLUB· MAY BE IDENTIFIED AS A GROUP OF FIRMS FORMING THE BACKBONE OF THE ITALIAN SHIPBUILDING INDUSTRY FOR THE NAVY.

WITH THE DIRECT POSITIVE AID OF THE ITALIAN NAVY, THIS GROUP CAN, ON A WORLDWIDE SCALE, PROVIDE FOR COMPLETE SHIPS, ITALIAN-MADE THROUGHOUT, AS WELL AS REFITTING PROJECTS AND CONNECTED LOGISTIC SUPPORT

P.166-DL3 : the versatile round-the-clock performer

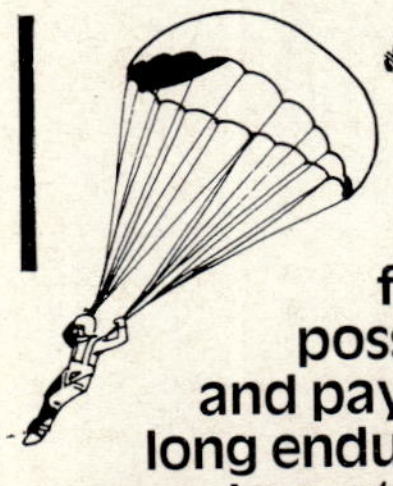

Powered by two Avco Lycoming LTP-101-600, the P.166-DL3 is the new turboprop model of the well known P.166 family. Specifically designed for airwork, the -DL3 possesses better performance and payload, while retaining long endurance, rough field capability, rugged construction, ease of maintenance and built-in operational flexibility. This higly cost-effective and reliable aircraft is an ideal tool for a variety of military and commercial missions. Maritime patrol SAR, light tactical transport, air command post, paratroop-dropping and ambulance are just a few of the various tasks which have been field-proven by the P.166 family and which will be even better performed by this new turboprop.

RINALDO PIAGGIO
Via Brigata Bisagno 14 - Genova - Italy - Telex 27695

Trust Whipp & Bourne Switchgear – they do.

Whipp & Bourne Switchgear and Switchboards have been chosen for 2 Shell Production Platforms at Brent.

In challenging projects like North Sea drilling where reliability is essential, we believe our reputation stands supreme. Rigorous quality control at every stage ensures that Whipp & Bourne Switchgear, Switchboards and Circuit Breakers are specified with confidence for application in oil, power, chemicals, traction, water, shipping and indeed, throughout the whole of industry.

Write for technical literature:-

Whipp & Bourne (1975) ltd

Castleton, Rochdale, England. Tel: Rochdale 32051 (10 lines)
Telex: 63442 (Whipps.G.)
Member of Babcock & Wilcox Ltd. (Electrical Engineering Group).

TNC 45

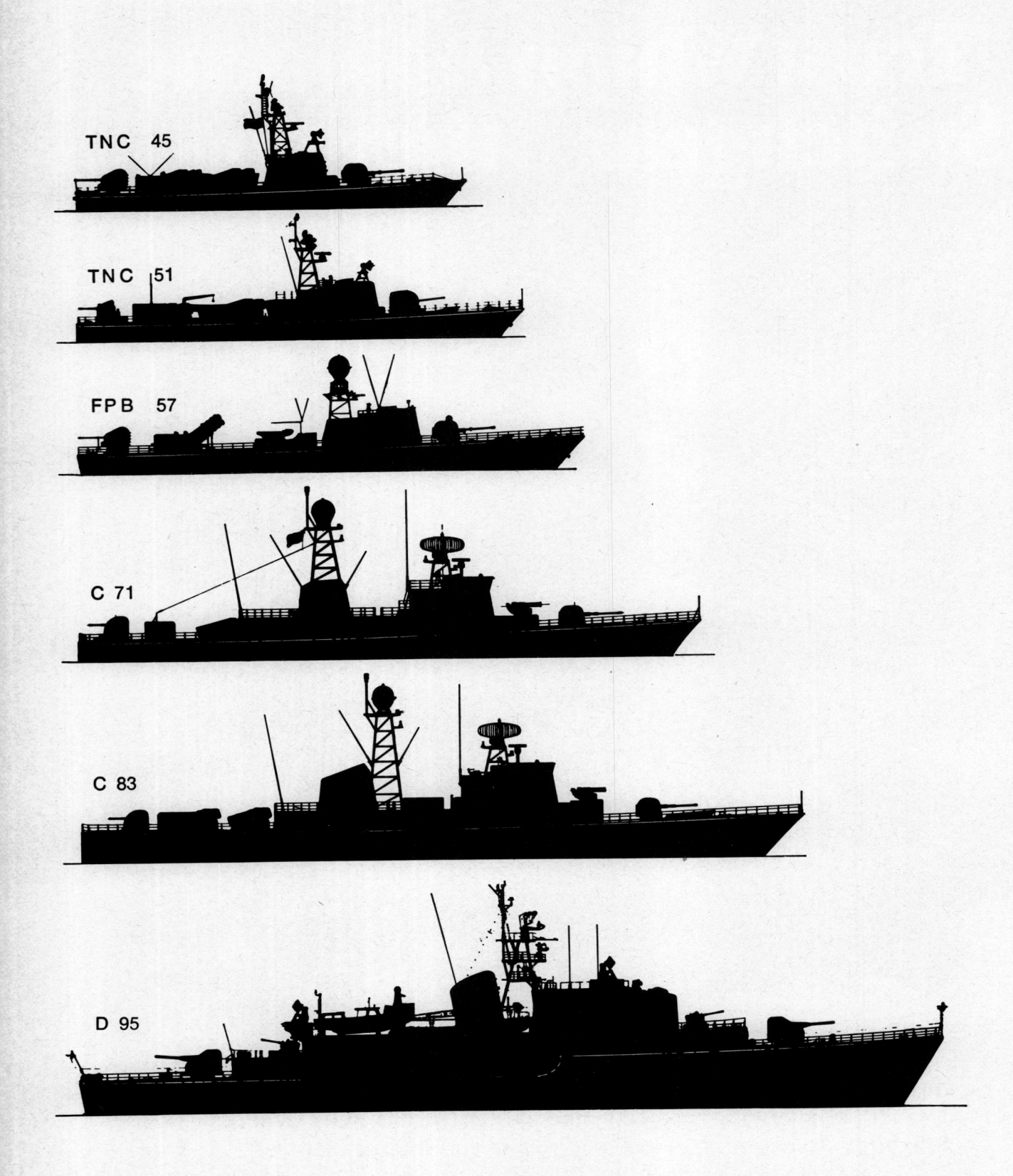

TNC 51

FPB 57

C 71

C 83

D 95

**DESIGNERS & BUILDERS
OF SOPHISTICATED
NAVAL CRAFT**

FR. LÜRSSEN WERFT

FED. REPUBLIC OF GERMANY

2820 BREMEN 70
P.O. BOX 70 00 30
TELEPHONE 04 21 / 6 60 41
TELEX 02 44 484

MISAR means mines

SEA MINE MR-80

The newest general purpose ground influence mine presently produced.

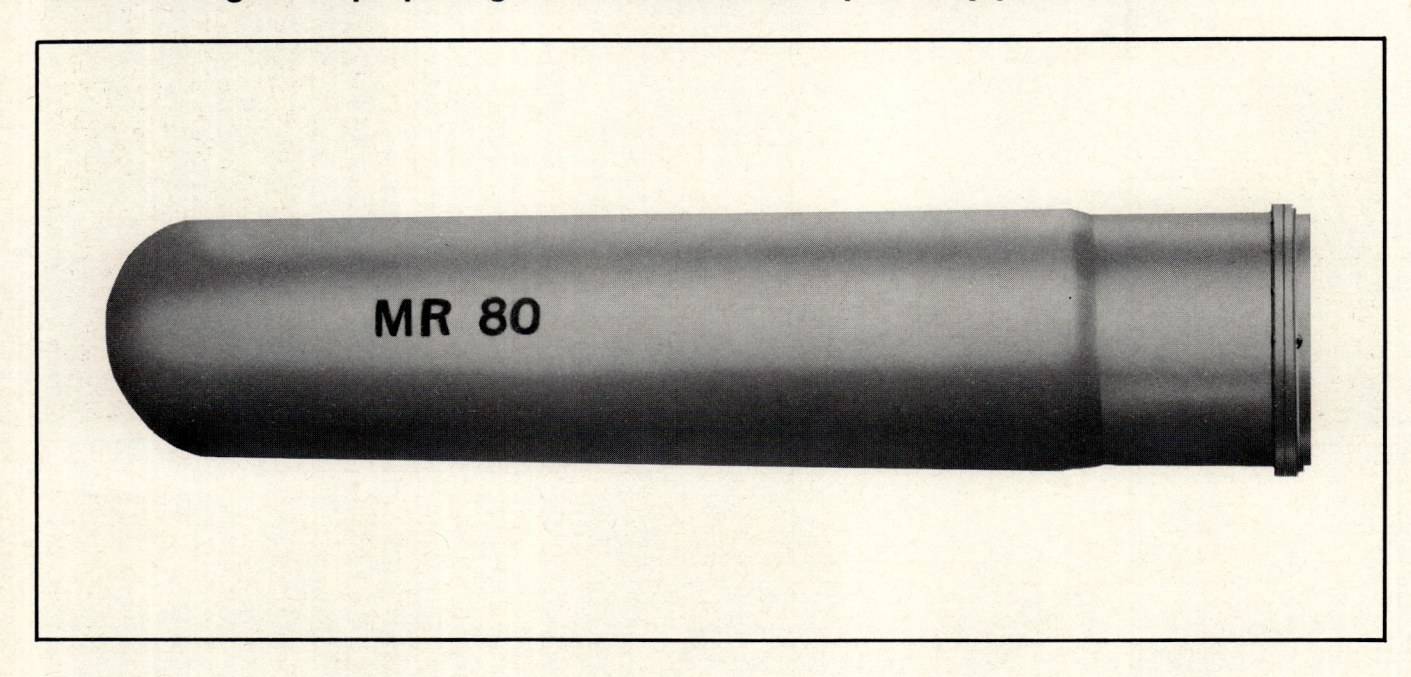

It can be laid by surface vessels, by submarines and it is launchable from aircrafts.
The MR-80 is equipped with the devices for the processing and the combination of the following target signals: pressure, magnetic, low frequency acoustic, audiofrequency acoustic.
It is laid at a variable depth between 8 and 300 meters and it remains effective in water also for over two years.
It can be remote-controlled.
The MR-80 is available in three war versions containing different quantity of explosive and in one drill version with possibility to record on land the working of the mine and of every influence channel.

MISAR S.p.A. ENTERTAINS POSSIBILITY TO MANUFACTURE SEA MINES WITH DIFFERENT CHARACTERISTICS ACCORDING TO THE CLIENT'S REQUIREMENTS.

MISAR S.P.A.

Via Gavardo 6 - 25016 GHEDI (Brescia) Italy - Tel. 030/901864-901865 - Telex 30489.

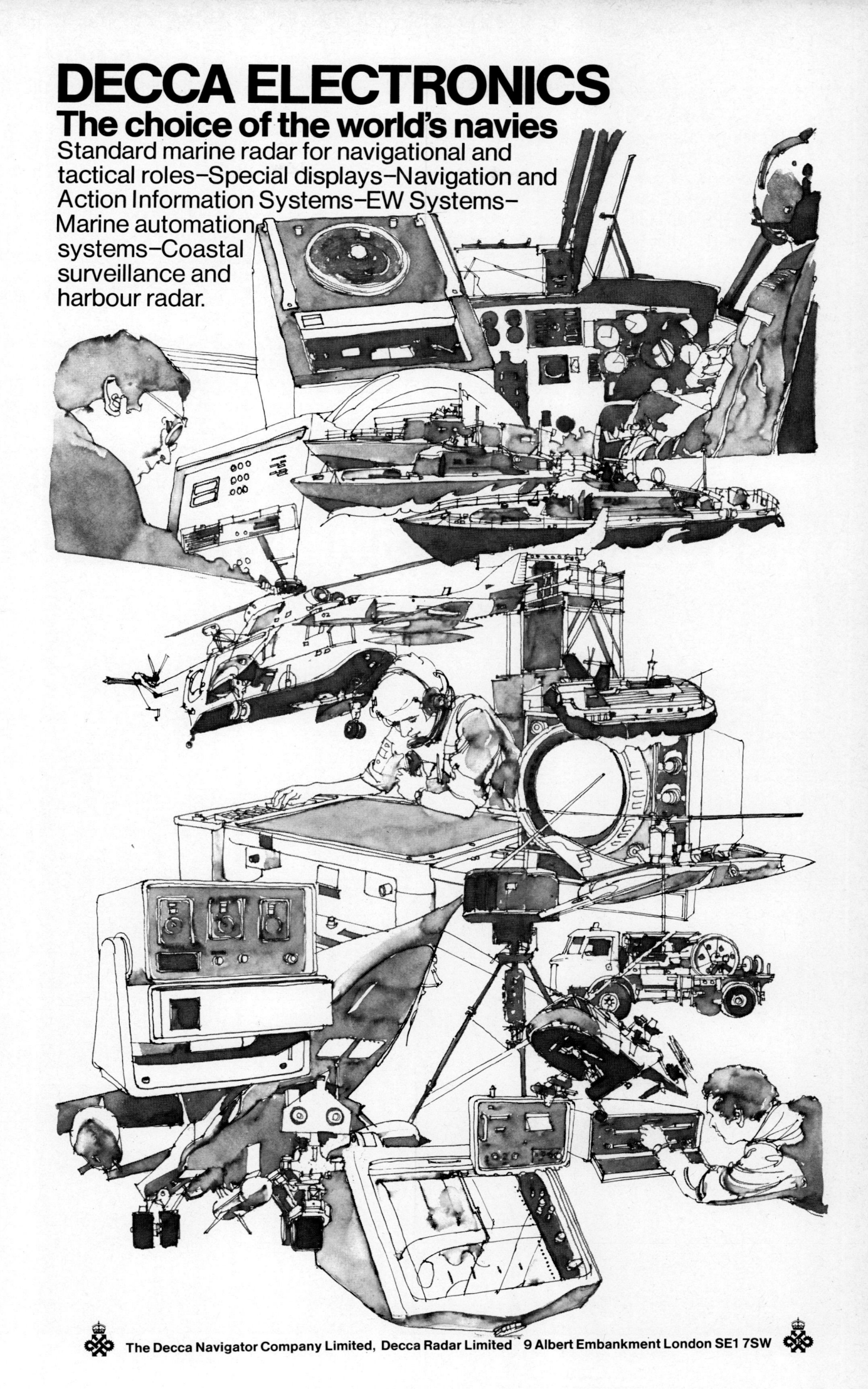

DECCA ELECTRONICS
The choice of the world's navies
Standard marine radar for navigational and tactical roles–Special displays–Navigation and Action Information Systems–EW Systems–Marine automation systems–Coastal surveillance and harbour radar.

The Decca Navigator Company Limited, Decca Radar Limited 9 Albert Embankment London SE1 7SW

The USS *Oliver Hazard Perry*—first of the Navy's new FFG-7 class of guided missile frigates—is built for rugged action. And versatility. Three major systems from Raytheon will help the *Oliver Hazard Perry*—and the more than 60 frigates to follow—carry out a wide range of escort missions.

- AN/SPS-49. This long-range, air-search radar—developed and now being produced by Raytheon—acquires fast targets at all altitudes in clutter, bad weather, and in the presence of active and passive countermeasures. The radar features solid-state electronics, digital design, and an antenna stabilized to the horizon.
- AN/SQS-56. This Raytheon-developed sonar provides directional as well as omni-directional active and passive detection, and determines precise range and bearing for weapons control and guidance.
- AN/SLQ-32(V). This just-developed, advanced shipboard EW system—to be installed on the *Oliver Hazard Perry*—utilizes Raytheon's unique, lens-fed, multiple beam array. AN/SLQ-32(V) will provide rapid signal intercept, analysis, identification, ECM response, and alerting signals to other shipboard weapons.

In addition, Raytheon-produced continuous-wave illuminators and signal data converters contribute to the speed and reliability of the *Oliver Hazard Perry*'s missile fire control system.

These systems on board the *Oliver Hazard Perry* typify Raytheon's capabilities in shipboard defense. Other examples include the systems man-

Fast, versatile—and loaded with electronics from

agement and production of the NATO Seasparrow Surface Missile System, supplying the computer and guidance electronics for the TRIDENT missile, and production of the TARTAR-D shipboard fire control system.

For more specific information on the AN/SPS-49 radar, the AN/SQS-56 surface sonar, or the AN/SLQ-32(V) EW system, please write Raytheon Company, Government Marketing, 141 Spring Street, Lexington, Massachusetts 02173.

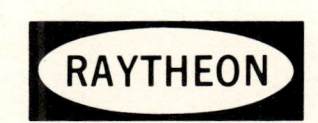

RAYTHEON

Raytheon.

Nowadays manoeuvring a warship can be as easy as pressing a button...

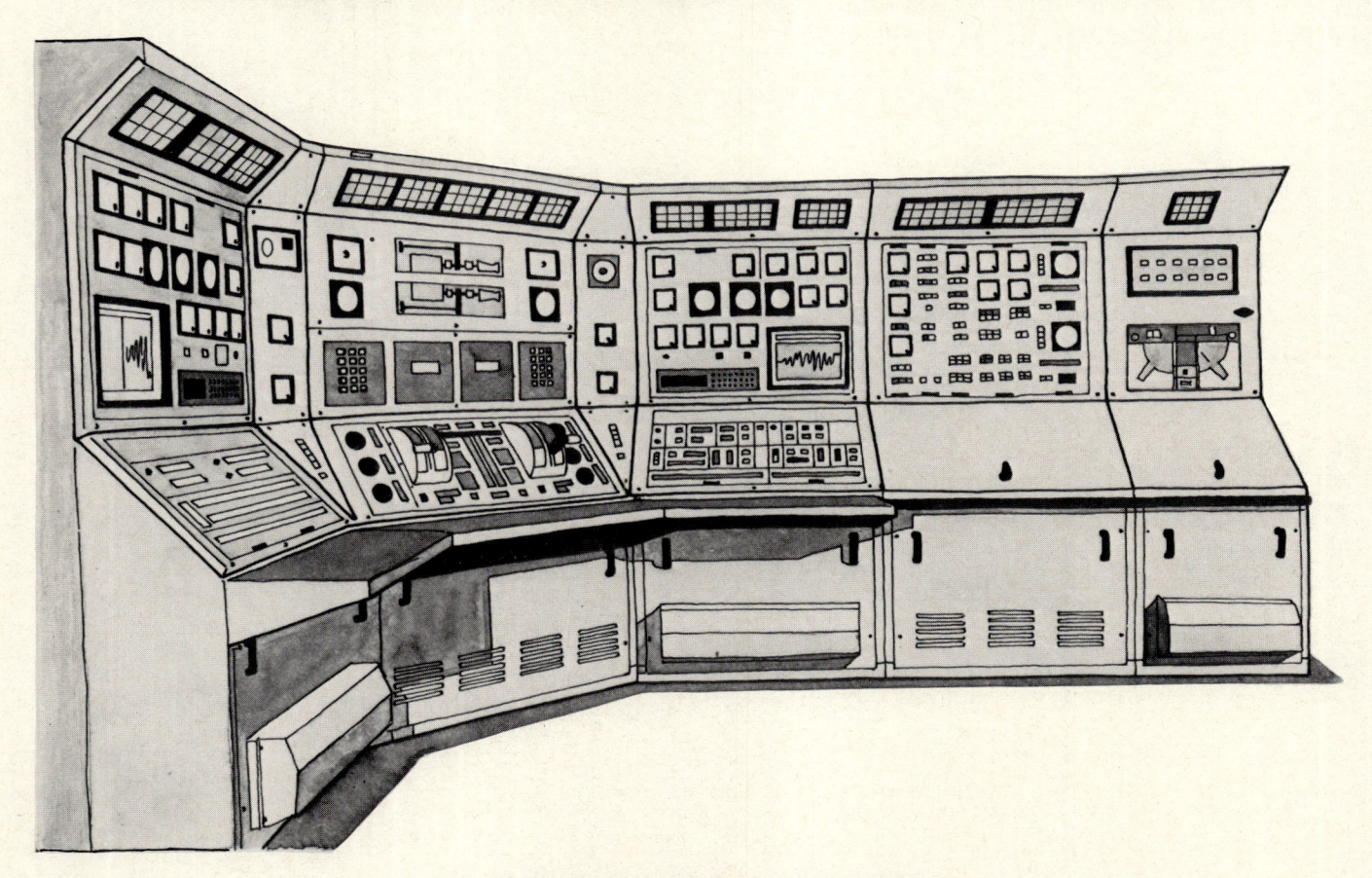

...with SEPA military systems

- Entirely electronic, making wide use of militarized original SEPA mini and microcomputers
- Simple to be operated and maintained
- Modular in construction easily adaptable to any propulsion configuration
- Highly reliable with great availability factor

Our experience covers

- Propulsion plant automation including gas turbine, diesel and mixed
- Electrical generation and distribution automation
- Control systems for special purpose military vessels
- Governor units and instrumentation for gas turbines
- Hydrofoils automatic depth and attitude control
- Torpedo guidance and home controls
- Multiple fire stations controls
- Shipborne system trainers
- Mathematical simulation of ship systems
- Automatic test equipments

Società di Elettronica per l'Automazione S.p.A.
Lungo Stura Lazio 45 - 10156 Torino (Italy)
Tel. (011) 262.3333 (5 linee r.a.) Telex: 23527 Sepa

SEPA
User size electronics

Vickers make another addition to their submarine fleet.

Piranha

500 class

1100 class

Vickers have made another important addition to their range of smaller submarines – the Piranha Class Coastal Submarine.

The Piranha, with a submerged displacement of about 140 tonnes, is small – only a tenth of the size of the Type 1100, but it is large in attacking power. It has a tactical range of up to 1,000 miles from base and has the capacity to release divers or carry landing parties. Its normal complement of 7 can be augmented with about 10 other personnel, and its armament can include 6 mines plus limpet mines, 2 torpedoes plus limpet mines, or two 2-man chariots.

Vickers patrol submarines also include the Type 500 with an advanced design and construction which enable it to carry extremely powerful armament, sonars and batteries for its size, and the 1100 with even greater range, speed and diving depth.

All these designs incorporate advanced technology of the kind derived from the Vickers 'Polaris' pedigree.

For more information on these submarines and their related weapon systems contact the Vickers Shipbuilding Group.

Vickers Shipbuilding Group Limited, Barrow-in-Furness, Cumbria, England.
Telephone: 0229 20351. Telex: 65171 VICVSB G
A member company of British Shipbuilders.

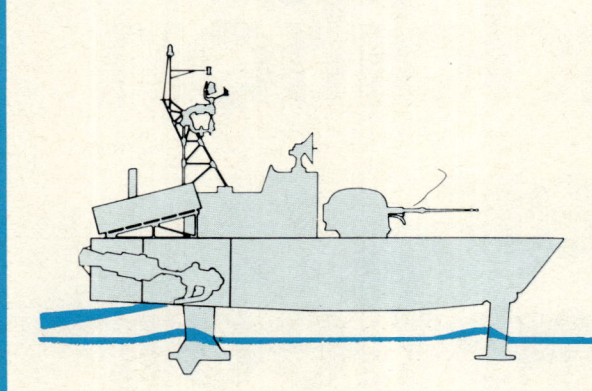

idrogetti per propulsione navale

marine propulsion water jets

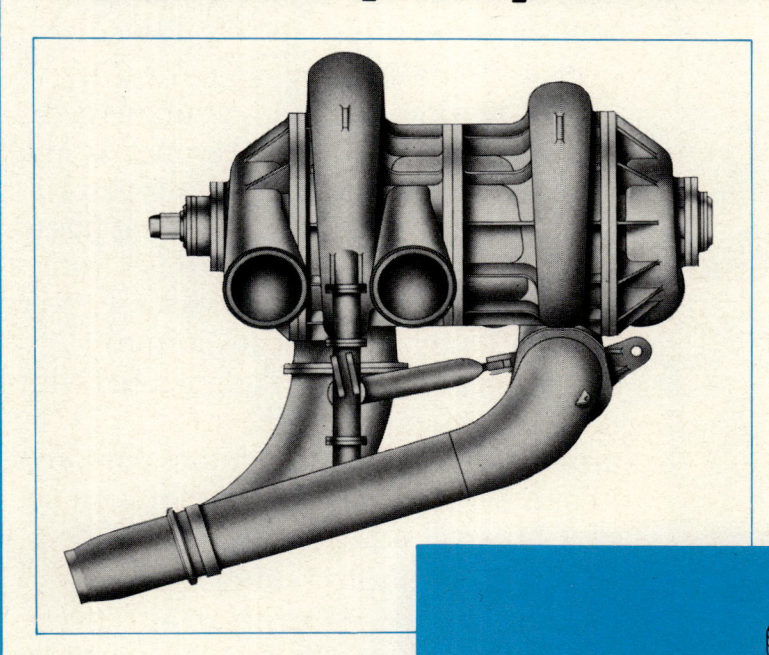

S.P.A. TERMOMECCANICA ITALIANA
ITALY - 19100 LA SPEZIA - VIA DEL MOLO, 1
P.O. BOX 341 - TEL. (0187) 503151 - TX 27171 TERMO SP

Modern Ships for Modern Navies

Prime Contractor
NATO Frigate Class 122

BREMER Ⓥ VULKAN
SCHIFFBAU UND   MASCHINENFABRIK

Lindenstraße, 2820 Bremen 70, Fed. Rep. Germ., Tel.: (04 21) 6 60 31

engineers and contractors for fighting ships

Aermarelli

1. systems for civil buildings
   - educational centers
   - medical centers
   - business centers
   - residential centers
   - airports

2. industrial air conditioning
   - textile industry
   - chemical pharmaceutical industry
   - food industry
   - manufacturing industry
   - nuclear plants
   - services

3. marine air conditioning and special military systems
   - passengers ships
   - cargo ships
   - drilling ships
   - navy vessels
   - special military systems

4. refrigeration systems
   - cold storages
   - food industry
   - chemical industry
   - sports facilities

The Italian Navy's new Sauro class submarines are fitted with high performance and reliable AERMARELLI air conditioning equipment and systems

'Nazario Sauro'   launched 9 oct. 76

'Fecia di Cossato'   launched 16 nov. 77

The air filtration and ventilation so as two indipendent air conditioning systems including a special refrigerating station are of AERMARELLI original design and make with changeover facility

Machineries and equipment have the Italian Navy antishock "A class" homologation

Ercole Marelli Group

Aermarelli
Viale V. Lancetti, 43 - 20158 Milan - Italy
Tel. (02) 6998 - Telex: Aermarel 36004

[110]

Tomorrow we'll be facing a different sea.

Our image of the sea may change any moment. This requires alertness and possibly action, which means a need of new ships. Here we come in to help find the best solution.

The first step is to produce the design and specifications, to make a contract for the delivery of ships and their main systems.

The next step is to provide the drawings for the actual construction, assembly and outfitting as well as the technical preparations for the purchase of materials and components.

And finally we can advise on supervision, training of personnel and logistic support.

Don't hesitate to contact Nevesbu when you want to anticipate at new naval tasks. We have a briefing team available at short notice.

Nevesbu

P.O. Box 289 – 2501 CG – The Hague – The Netherlands
Telephone (+31 70) 602813 – Telex 31640 genuf nl.

Providing expertise in every aspect of marine projects

Field Studies – Designs –
Specifications – Construction –
Commissioning – Training – Servicing –
Maintenance – Project Management

ABMTM Marine Division

backed by the 60 years of home and export
engineering experience of the ABMTM Group,
is at the service of international
government and commercial organisations.

ABMTM Ltd., 20 Park Street, London, W1Y 4NA
Tel.: 01-492 1161 / 6. Telex: 21611. Cables: Britoolmak, London W1

MARTE

SELECTED BY THE ITALIAN NAVY TO DESTROY OR DISABLE HOSTILE NAVAL UNITS BY SEA KILLER MK2 MISSILES LAUNCHED IN "ALL WEATHER" CONDITIONS FROM SH-3D HELICOPTERS IN STAND-OFF POSITIONS.

- 4 hrs/200 nm surface strike (and anti-submarine) mission
- Armament: 2 Sea Killer MK2 missiles
- Unique TWS radar for navigation, search, tracking, guidance
- Electronic warfare equipment

SEA KILLER MK2 MISSILE (MARTE AND MARINER)

- Speed: 250 m/sec
- Warhead: 70 Kg, HE, semi-armour piercing
- Range: 20 Km
- Guidance system: Command to line-of-sight (radar or optical) Radio altimeter
- Guided up to the impact.
- Sea-skimming flight profile.

MARINER

THE SHIPBORNE VERSION OF MARTE SYSTEM ENDOWING VERY SMALL NAVAL UNITS WITH A MISSILE STRIKE CAPABILITY.

Total installation (2 missiles in launching containers)
- Weight: less than 1600 Kg.
- Power: ~ 6kW

WE GUARANTEE LIFE TIME PRODUCT SUPPORT AND TRAINING OF PERSONNEL

SISTEL
SISTEL — Sistemi Elettronici S.p.A.
00131 ROME — Via Tiburtina, 1210
Phone 415841 — Telex 68112 SISTELRO

One of eleven vessels of a twenty one vessel programme of Fast Patrol Craft for the Federal Mexican Government built by Ailsa Shipbuilding Co. Ltd.

At the Ailsa yard at Troon on the Clyde Estuary facilities exist to design and build defence craft up to 114 metres overall. The yard has wide experience to British Ministry of Defence standards and considerable familiarity with high speed machinery. Fabrication in non-ferrous materials and close liaison with armament suppliers plus easy access to open water give this Scottish yard considerable advantages in the international defence markets.

AILSA

AILSA SHIPBUILDING CO. LTD. · Harbour Road · Troon · Ayrshire · Tel: 0292 311311 · Telex 778027

DUBIGEON-NORMANDIE

FRANCE

Shipbuilding of naval surface ships and submarines.

Modernization and conversion of naval ships.

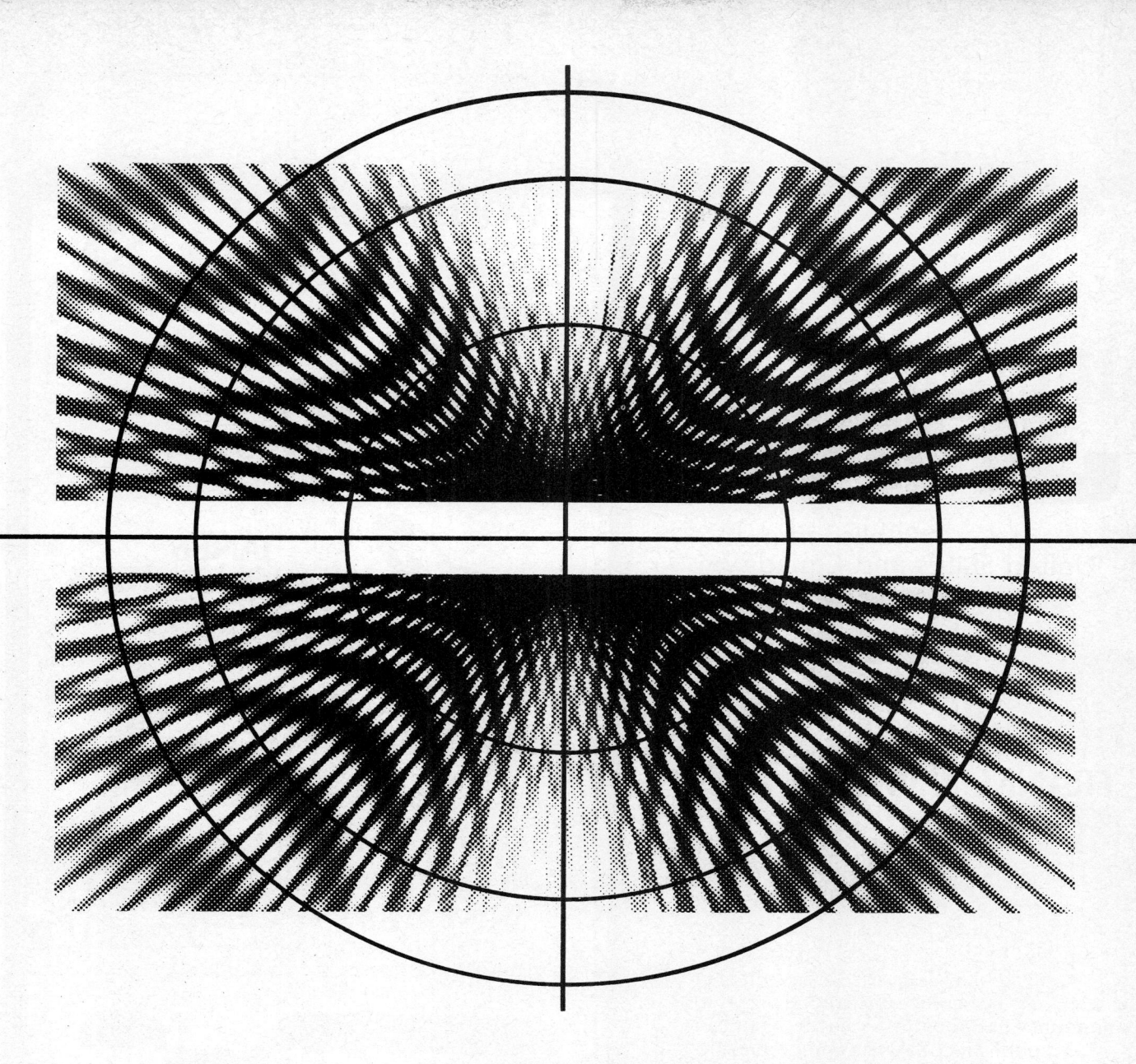

confidence through ELMER radiocommunication systems

The most comprehensive range of multi-purpose radiocommunication equipment integrated in very advanced radiocommunication systems

MONTEDISON GROUP
MONTEDISON SISTEMI

ELMER
DIVISION OF **MONTEDEL**
Viale dell'Industria, 4 - 00040 Pomezia (Italy)
P.O. Box 189 - Telex 61112 ELMER
Phone (06) 9121706

Cantiere Navaltecnica S.p.A. - 22, Via S. Raineri, 98100 Messina, Italy.
Telephone: (090) 774862 (6 lines) - Cable: Navaltecnica Messina - Tlx: 98030 Rodrikez.

JANE'S ALL THE

Is the engine or the hull more

1 DIESEL ENGINE for Tehi hydrofoil	 2 DIESEL ENGINES for Idell M/Y	 2 DIESEL ENGINES for Moc 201	 4 DIESEL ENGINES for MTB 205 Class P6	 2 DIESEL ENGINES for Riomar M/Y
 2 DIESEL ENGINES for GL 432	 2 DIESEL ENGINES for Inzucchi CV Dark Class	 2 DIESEL ENGINES for Atzeis CV	 4 DIESEL ENGINES for Mau Mau III M/Y	 2 DIESEL ENGINES for Corsara M/Y
 2 DIESEL ENGINES for Sciuto CV	 4 DIESEL ENGINES for MTB 209 Class P6	 3 DIESEL ENGINES for Saharet M/Y	 2 DIESEL ENGINES for Mandorlo MSO	 3 DIESEL ENGINES for Bagheera M/Y
 2 DIESEL ENGINES for Kylebhan III M/Y	 2 DIESEL ENGINES for Cochise M/Y	 2 DIESEL ENGINES for Nuvoletta CV	 2 DIESEL ENGINES for Stefanini CV	 2 DIESEL ENGINES for Previte CV
 3 DIESEL ENGINES for Grasso CV	 2 DIESEL ENGINES for Laspina CV Dark Class	 2 DIESEL ENGINES for GL 433	 2 DIESEL ENGINES for Bold Daniel M/Y	 2 DIESEL ENGINES for Nautilus M/Y
 2 DIESEL ENGINES for Sidone CV	 2 DIESEL ENGINES for Colombina CV	 4 DIESEL ENGINES for MTB 207 Class P6	 3 DIESEL ENGINES for Gabriele CV	 2 DIESEL ENGINES for Darida CV

If a boat's going to be excellent it must have an excellent engine and an excellent hull. We put the engine in it, a 12 cylinder diesel for example. The type? That depends. If you need a 700 - 900 Hp output you can opt for our V-type 12 cylinder engine, the one used by the Italian coastguards.
The engine has undergone trials of every sort, and is now the power unit in hundreds of small-and medium-sized boats used by both civilians and the forces. In short an engine you can be sure of, one that will face up to any sea.
Should, however, your boat be required to work in special magnetic fields, then our 12 cylinder non-magnetic engine's the one for you. Here again its technical features will leave you in no doubt. It's not that we say so: it's proved by the punishing trials it was subjected to before being installed on the Italian navy's minesweepers.

If, lastly, you fancy a slim, swift boat (really slim and swift) then there are no doubts: the compact version of the new 12D/S-3 is the engine for you. When it was displayed at the Italian boat show the most important names in the boat engine business came and complimented us on the splendid achievement of our study and research centre. Just think that first, without altering its weight, its output was increased to 1350 Hp

important? In our case the hull.

2 DIESEL ENGINES for Tavormina CV	2 DIESEL ENGINES for Laganà CV Dark Class	2 DIESEL ENGINES for Mistere III M/Y	3 DIESEL ENGINES for Lady Ship M/Y	2 DIESEL ENGINES for Sanna CV Dark Class
2 DIESEL ENGINES for Sguazzin CV	2 DIESEL ENGINES for Contenta M/Y	2 DIESEL ENGINES for Cristiana IV M/Y	4 DIESEL ENGINES for MTB 206 Class P6	2 DIESEL ENGINES for Urso CV Dark Class
2 DIESEL ENGINES for Lissen M/Y	2 DIESEL ENGINES for Denaro CV	2 DIESEL ENGINES for Barreca CV	2 DIESEL ENGINES for RD 36 CV	2 DIESEL ENGINES for Amici CV
2 DIESEL ENGINES for Cohete M/Y	2 DIESEL ENGINES for Socargio M/Y	2 DIESEL ENGINES for Esposito CV	2 DIESEL ENGINES for Calabrese CV Dark Class	4 DIESEL ENGINES for 208 MTB Class P6
2 DIESEL ENGINES for Fazio CV	2 DIESEL ENGINES for Genna CV Dark Class	2 DIESEL ENGINES for Cicalé CV	2 DIESEL ENGINES for Vitali CV Dark Class	2 DIESEL ENGINES for Silanos CV
2 DIESEL ENGINES for Pizzighella CV	2 DIESEL ENGINES for Tridenti CV			

at 2075 revs a minute. Then its size was reduced and all the components were incorporated in the engine group (before they were spread outside). This resulted in an engine weighing only 1800 Kgs with a weight-power ratio of 1.42 Kgs/Hp. It can be installed on extremely slim craft, a feat that would be impossible with other engines of the same weight. At this point, faced as we are with such sophisticated, highly-developed engines, is it clear why in our case the hull is more important when the boat must be excellent?

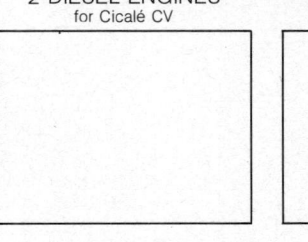

CRM

making seafaring history

CRM. Via Manzoni, 12 - MILANO - phone 02/708326 ● 784118 - telex 26382 CREMME

French Destroyer **Duguay Trouin** *Dr. Giorgio Arra*

JANE'S FIGHTING SHIPS

FOUNDED IN 1897 BY FRED T. JANE

EDITED BY
CAPTAIN JOHN E. MOORE RN, FRGS

1978-79

ISBN 531 03297 3

LC 75-18766

JANE'S YEARBOOKS

FRANKLIN WATTS INC., NEW YORK

"Jane's" is a registered trade mark

Copyright © 1978 by Macdonald and Jane's Publishers Limited, Paulton House, 8 Shepherdess Walk, London N1 7LW, England

First published in the United Kingdom 1978 by Jane's Yearbooks
First American publication 1978 by Franklin Watts Inc.

For copyright reasons this edition is available for sale only in Canada, the Philippines and the USA and its dependencies.

Leading european builder of surface ships

Landing ships for the transport of personnel and vehicles.

Fast attack craft of the 130 t PATRA class.

Minehunters.

5090 t guided missile frigates.

"Aviso" 1200 t for ASW and the protection of offshore zones of economic areas.

Fast attack craft designed for interception missions at sea and long endurance maritime surveillance.

Design and construction
of surface ships, submarines and weapons systems.

**Shipyards at Cherbourg, Brest, Lorient, Toulon, Dakar, Papeete.
Offices at Paris, Indret, Ruelle, St-Tropez.**

DTCN

Direction Technique des Constructions Navales - 2, rue Royale 75200 Paris Naval - tél. 260.33.30

CONTENTS

Alphabetical List of Advertisers	[4]	France	144	Poland	390
		Gabon	179	Portugal	395
		Gambia	179	Qatar	399
Classified List of Advertisers	[10]	Germany (Democratic Republic)	180	Romania	400
				Sabah	403
Use of Jane's Fighting Ships	[125]	Germany (Federal Republic)	186	St. Kitts	403
		Ghana	201	St. Lucia	403
Foreword	[127]	Greece	203	St. Vincent	403
		Grenada	214	Saudi Arabia	404
Major Matters	[137]	Guatemala	214	Senegal	406
		Guinea	215	Sierra Leone	407
Acknowledgements	[141]	Guinea Bissau	215	Singapore	408
		Guyana	216	Somalia	410
Major Surface Ships Pennant List	[143]	Haiti	216	South Africa	411
		Honduras	217	Spain	416
		Hong Kong	217	Sri Lanka	432
Recognition Silhouettes	1	Hungary	219	Sudan	434
		Iceland	220	Surinam	435
Ship Reference Section	17	India	222	Sweden	436
Ship Designations	18	Indonesia	231	Switzerland	449
		Iran	240	Syria	449
Albania	19	Iraq	247	Taiwan	451
Algeria	21	Ireland (Republic)	249	Tanzania	460, 758
Angola	22	Israel	251	Thailand	461
Anguilla	23	Italy	255	Togo	467
Argentina	23	Ivory Coast	273	Tonga	467
Australia	34	Jamaica	274	Trinidad and Tobago	468
Austria	46	Japan, Navy	275	Tunisia	469
Bahamas	47	Maritime Safety Agency	291	Turkey	471
Bahrain	47	Jordan	301	Union of Soviet Socialist Republics	483
Bangladesh	48	Kampuchea	301		
Barbados	49	Kenya	303	United Arab Emirates	557
Belgium	50	Korea (North)	304	United Kingdom	559
Belize	53	Korea (South)	310	United States of America, Navy	603
Bermuda	53	Kuwait	317		
Bolivia	53	Laos	318	Coast Guard	723
Brazil	54	Lebanon	318	Uruguay	736
Brunei	64	Liberia	319	Venezuela	740
Bulgaria	65	Libya	319	Viet-Nam	746
Burma	67	Madagascar	323	Virgin Islands	750
Cameroon	69	Malawi	324	Yemen (North)	751
Cambodia see Kampuchea		Malaysia	324	Yemen (South)	751
Canada, Navy	70	Maldives	328	Yugoslavia	752
Coast Guard	80	Mali	328	Zaire	758
Chile	87	Malta	328	Zanzibar	758
China, People's Republic	95	Mauritania	330		
Colombia	105	Mauritius	331		
Comoro Islands	110	Mexico	331	**Appendices**	759
Congo	111	Montserrat	336	Naval Strengths	759
Costa Rica	111	Morocco	336	Naval Equipment	763
Cuba	111	Netherlands	339	Aircraft	764
Cyprus	114	New Zealand	349	Guns	774
Czechoslovakia	114	Nicaragua	351	Missiles	778
Denmark	114	Nigeria	352	Radar	782
Dominican Republic	122	Norway	355	Sonar Equipment	786
Ecuador	126	Oman	361	Torpedoes	788
Egypt	130	Pakistan	364		
El Salvador	135	Panama	369	**Addenda**	791
Equatorial Guinea	135	Papua New Guinea	370		
Ethiopia	136	Paraguay	371	**Indexes**	795
Fiji	137	Peru	372	Named Ships	797
Finland	138	Philippines	382	Classes	811

SIGNAAL

Mini Combat System.
Compact Control Ability.

Up to now, 27 navies picked Signaal's M20 mini combat system for radar and weapon control.
Since no other accurate combat control system proves to be so compact and flexible that it provides small craft not only with large ship capabilities, but also with a high kill potential. Watch out for any ship with the typical Signaal-dome on top!

The shape of ultimate control.

Weapon control systems: Hollandse Signaalapparaten B.V. Hengelo - The Netherlands.

USE OF JANE'S FIGHTING SHIPS

Current information on the world's navies appears under the following headings:

Major Matters: summaries by country of the significant naval events between March 1977 and March 1978.

Pennant List of Major Surface Ships: lists in numerical order of pennant numbers of the larger surface ships, indicating their type and the country to whose fleet they belong. Soviet ships are not included as their pennant numbers change frequently.

Recognition Silhouettes: are grouped according to similarity of shape to aid visual identification and are not all to the same scale.

Ship Designations: explains the formula used throughout the book for categorising different classes of ship.

Ship Refence Section: contains detailed information and illustrations of naval forces alphabetically by country. Within each country information is presented where available as follows:

At the beginning appears data including listings of Naval Boards, Diplomatic Representatives, details of personnel, strength and composition of the fleet and the mercantile marine. Following are details of deletions from the fleet during the last five years. Pennant lists are provided for major navies with drawings at a scale of 1:1200 unless specified otherwise.

The detailed information about the fleet's ships follows this general section in an order which varies according to the size and variety of the fleet concerned. Generally, submarines head this main section followed by aircraft carriers, cruisers, destroyers, frigates, corvettes, amphibious forces, light forces, mine warfare forces, survey vessels, service forces, tenders and tugs. A miscellaneous section may include training ships, royal yachts, floating docks, hovercraft and such like, although craft listed will depend on the size of the fleet concerned.

Within the main information section of each navy tonnages are included in both standard and full-load displacements—that of standard because it is used in international documents (eg. The London Treaty of March 1936 and the Montreux Convention of July 1936) and is defined as "the displacement of the vessel, complete, fully manned, engined and equipped ready for sea—but without fuel or reserve feed-water on board". Unless otherwise stated the lengths given are overall.

Appendices: present statistical summaries on comparative strengths and composition of major fleets and types of associated equipment—naval aircraft, guns, missiles, radar, sonar and torpedoes held by the principal navies.

Addenda: covers information received after the main reference section has gone to press.

Indexes: give page references for all ships in alphabetical order of name and class.

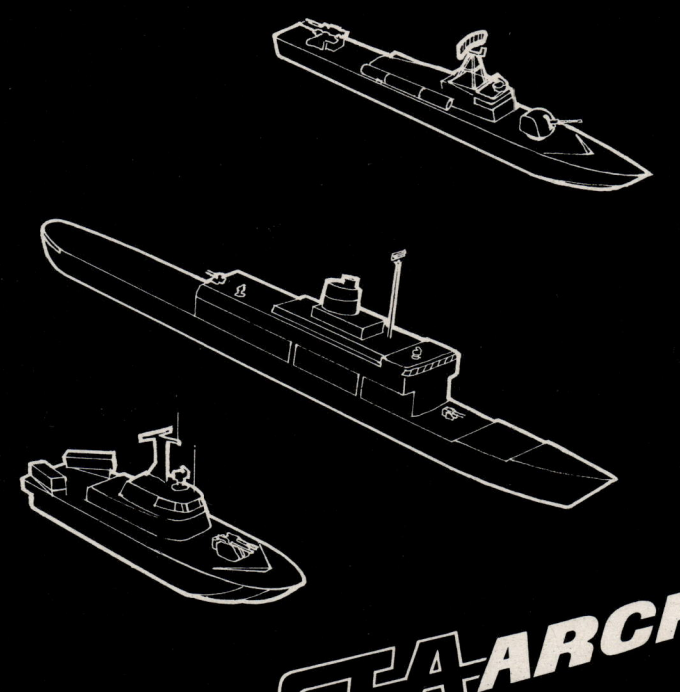

SEA-ARCHER
FOR EFFECTIVE GUNNERY

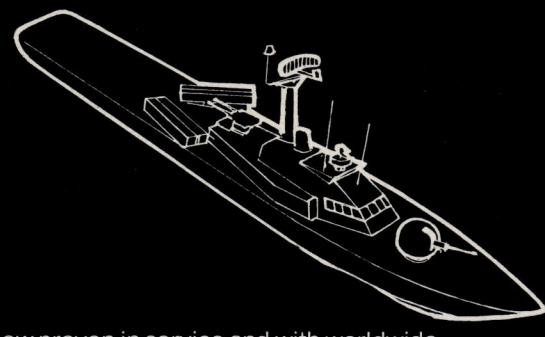

The SEA ARCHER digital fire control system now proven in service and with worldwide orders maintains earlier Sperry achievements in the field of advanced technology naval systems. Computer prediction ensures high accuracy fire against air, surface or shore targets, and gives the improved weapon performance which until now has only been available with radar fire control systems.

- ☐ **EASE OF INSTALLATION, OPERATION AND MAINTENANCE**
- ☐ **HIGH RELIABILITY** ☐ **COMPACT AND LIGHTWEIGHT EQUIPMENTS**
- ☐ **HIGH EFFECTIVENESS FOR LOW-COST**
- ☐ **A CHOICE OF IR, TV, RADAR AND LASER SENSORS**

SPERRY
GYROSCOPE
DOWNSHIRE WAY BRACKNELL
BERKSHIRE ENGLAND RG12 1QL
TELEPHONE: BRACKNELL 0344 3222
TELEX: No. 848129

SPERRY GYROSCOPE IS A DIVISION OF SPERRY RAND LIMITED

FOREWORD

It is rare during the preparation of this book to find one salient change occurring world-wide. This year, however, despite the failure of the Sixth Session of the Law of the Sea negotiations to produce any overall agreement, the adoption of a 200-mile Exclusive Economic Zone (EEZ) by many countries is illustrated by the dramatic increase in the number of ships clearly intended to patrol an area suddenly expanded by 98.5 per cent. Available budgets have obviously influenced the choice of vessels in all cases and what is equally clear, in some instances, is that insufficient consideration has been given to the role intended for these craft. In basic terms, if the role is to intercept illegal immigrants in fast canoes all that is needed is faster canoes with some form of communication and minimal armament. If the role is to intercept and board fast trawlers poaching in the outer fringes of a 200-mile EEZ then many other considerations must come into play. Should there be an aggressive neighbour who must be deterred and if this task is to be combined with patrolling the EEZ more complicated factors are clearly involved. Variations in the apprehended tasks of a naval force make it both practically and financially imperative that a clear appreciation of those tasks be made and that certain basic parameters which can be achieved at minimum expense be agreed. In a normal (if there is such a thing) democracy this programme must then be put into phrases of an adequacy and clarity to satisfy both the administration and the voting public that the need really exists and that the proposed solution is the best possible.

During a recent discussion on the vagaries of public taste with regard to contemporary music of the more serious kind a wise old musician answered an infuriated young man who complained that the public did not appreciate his compositions, 'The listeners who, after all, provide our financial support have been brought up to understand a musical language which may vary slightly with their age,' he said. 'If you wish to express yourself in totally different musical jargon you cannot expect them to buckle down to learning a new language every time you see fit to change.' This is as true in the realms of defence as it is in those of music—if you want support the surest way of receiving it is to provide a well-considered argument in terms sufficiently simple and straightforward to explain your requirements to those who control your finances. Jargon may be necessary for intra-mural exchange—it butters no parsnips for those beyond the walls. Dean Swift meant much the same thing when he wrote of a

'Barren superfluity of words—
Proper words in proper places.'

The roles of navies are by no means cut and dried. The definition of 'sea power' is still a matter of semantics between those concerned with maritime affairs. What is clear, however, is that geographical situation and self-sufficiency, or otherwise, in raw materials combine with the state of a country's industrial and financial base to cause widely varying approaches to the problem. To provide a fleet which is solely reactive to a current threat which may alter with a change in emphasis or government is the result of a basic failure to appreciate not only the form but the longevity of the principles of sea power. A state that is dependent on the sea for its living, on sea transport, on fisheries and on all that lies beneath the surface must view the whole scope of that dependence with objectivity. History has proved too often that those who live by the sword shall likewise die—he who depends on the sea may also die should it be denied him. The briefest survey of today's trade figures shows that the greatest proportion of the world's countries depend on free use of the oceans for their existence. Anyone wishing to dominate the world need only achieve control of certain nodal areas of these oceans to fulfil his aim. In vast areas of the threequarters of the world which is water-covered, far from national boundaries and from the land where population may be put at risk, great conflicts may occur and then recede attended by little understanding and minimum reaction from governments not immediately concerned. Across the seas huge quantities of trade flow to countries which possess neither the finances nor the ability to protect those ships on whom their future depends. These states must rely on neutrality or alliances to ensure their continued existence yet, in a world where the imperfections of modern politics put such compacts at daily risk, it is not hard to appreciate the successive dilemmas of Western politicians. Faced without by a vast authoritarian structure backed by all the power of modern forces and within by schisms in their own parties, bloody terrorists and apathy their problems may seem insoluble. However, amid all the diverse characters of their complaints they have one prime duty, the succour and the welfare of their people which, in every Western case, depends on the free use of the sea and, therefore, adequate arrangements for the protection of maritime interests.

These invocations are based not on emotion but on the undeniable facts of this last year. The increase in inter-dependence is shown by the steady augmentation of the world's merchant-ship tonnage. The 11 982 major vessels registered by Lloyds in 1977 represented a six per cent increase on the previous year following advances of nine per cent and ten per cent in preceding years. Of the total, 44 per cent are oil-tankers and 25 per cent ore- and bulk-carriers while the leading shipping countries are Liberia, Japan, the United Kingdom, Norway and Greece. Of these, none is able to defend its own fleet on the whole stretch of the world's seaways. Close on their heels, with a steady annual increase, is the merchant fleet of the USSR, now sixth in overall tonnage, having overhauled the USA. The chief value of this fleet to the USSR is in the gathering of hard currency and the weakening of Western trade facilities by vigorous undercutting of tariffs. As this trade is valuable in peacetime it is also unnecessary in war for a country which relies little on external sources of raw materials. Of the American merchant fleet, about one tenth is currently in reserve and a high proportion of trade is carried in foreign bottoms or under flags of convenience. As this trade includes a considerable percentage of the increasing American dependence on external oil supplies political problems would arise were there interference with the latter two types of transport.

Although the pattern of world merchant shipping covers all oceans and seas it is more convenient and accurate to consider naval affairs in various geographical areas after discussing the overall situation of the two major powers, the USA and the USSR.

The Superpowers (USA and USSR)

Although many correspondents ask for a numerical assessment of the 'placing' of these two fleets this remains as impossible now as it has been for the last five or ten years. Each has its strengths and weaknesses and it is far more productive to consider these than it is to seek out some maritime Olympic standard with awful awards of Gold and Silver.

Firstly, ships' value depends on their geographical situation in the event of conflict. In the early part of this century Admiral Fisher concentrated his main force in British home waters to oppose the growing strength of Germany, which was drawn up along a North Sea coastline of little more than 200 miles. Today geographical factors are of just as great importance. The Soviet navy is split into four fleets, each of which has to emerge through narrow defiles. The Northern fleet must make passage through the four main openings in the Greenland-United Kingdom gap, the Baltic fleet must make use of Danish waters or the White Sea canal, the Black Sea fleet is forced to move through the Turkish straits or north through the Volga canal chain while the Pacific fleet is hedged about, except in the very north, by the mainland of Japan.

The US Navy, as well, faces geographical problems of deployment. With a not dissimilar pattern of assignment, with the exception of ballistic-missile submarines, between the Pacific and the Atlantic any concentration of forces must involve long passages. From San Diego in the Pacific to Norfolk, Virginia in the Atlantic is 4 500 miles through the Panama Canal. For those carriers and other ships too large to transit the Canal the closest route is via Cape Horn, a passage of 12 000 miles. Even at 30 knots this means 17 days of straight steaming—in the event of a crisis such a deployment might be too late. At the same time trade figures show that about 43 per cent of US traffic crosses the Pacific while 57 per cent is carried on the Atlantic, posing a major problem to the naval staff should it be faced with a threat on both eastern and western seaboards while, at the same time, operating a fleet halved in numbers in the last ten years. One must see some justification for an ex-Chairman of the US Joint Chiefs of Staff Committee who recently asked, 'Have we truly a two-ocean navy?'

One of the Soviet navy's strengths is, therefore, that, provided its passage to the open oceans has been unimpeded, it can concentrate where national policies dictate, unhampered by any trade defence requirements. With a fleet in which embarked aircraft are at last becoming more numerous this freedom of action is providing increased options for the Soviets while stretching the areas where reaction from the West may be needed. The recent operations of the Soviet task-force off Eritrea, a form of employment frequently forecast here in the last five years, is a sinister case in point.

From the material point of view the gap between the more conventional forces of the two navies is now beginning to close with the increasing introduction of Harpoon, Phalanx and Standard missiles into the US Navy. If both the strategic and tactical versions of the cruise-missile Tomahawk are also included in the US Navy's inventory the balance will be considerably tilted in their favour. No Soviet

EXOCET

a family of long range missiles
FOR SEA POWER

The MM 38 uses the full detection range of the launcher's radars.

The AM 39 can be launched at all altitudes.

Quadruple launcher MM 40.
MM 40 has an over-the-horizon capability.

☐ They can be:
- Surface-launched (MM 38 - MM 40) from ships of all tonnages, or from fixed or mobile coastal batteries.
- Air-launched (AM 39) from helicopters, strike aircraft or maritime patrol aircraft.
- Sub-launched (under development).

☐ They have basically the same principle of operation and the same maintenance equipment.

☐ They are FIRE AND FORGET and SEA SKIMMING, which makes them practically INVULNERABLE to all enemy defences.

☐ They provide SUPERIORITY in anti-surface warfare to those countries which adopt them, owing to their range, speed, accuracy and killing power.

22 countries have chosen the EXOCET.
More than 1.150 EXOCET missiles have been ordered.

aerospatiale
division engins tactiques
2, rue Béranger - Châtillon 92320 FRANCE

AEROSPATIALE MISSILES Ltd.,
178 Piccadilly, LONDON W1V OBA

FOREWORD

surface ships at present carry any form of strategic weapon and it would be to the great benefit of the USSR were they to forestall the introduction of the strategic Tomahawk by the processes of SALT II.

The present situation with regard to naval ballistic missiles is definitely on the side of the USSR. Both the submarine-borne SS-N-17 and 18 have materially increased the range at which strategic bombardment could take place and, therefore, have greatly widened the search areas of any hunting force. As the SS-N-18 can be fired to any point in the northern hemisphere from the Soviet coastal zone it will be seen that the problem of countering these monsters is formidable, but by 1980 the Soviet fleet will have a similar task when the American Trident I missile is at sea in the 'Ohio' class. It is significant that a new base for these submarines is in the north-west of the USA in the state of Washington giving access to the nearest part of Soviet territory across the great depths of the Pacific Ocean, an area from which Trident I could reach all points in the USSR. Thus in the next couple of years this balance in the Soviet's favour will be partly redressed and the proposed introduction of Trident II with a 6 000 mile range would further ensure the invulnerability of the submarines carrying it.

In the world of naval aviation the US Navy continues to retain a position of overwhelming superiority. With over half-a-century of experience the carriers now constituting that strength have probably reached the ultimate in this form of shipbuilding although their modernisation and replacement are of extreme importance. The greatest compliment to this type of naval strength is the long-delayed decision of the USSR to follow suit, but *Kiev* and her sisters, while of the same family, are of a different genus, designed for very varying operations. Their surface-to-surface missiles, torpedo tubes, guns and sonar show this to be a class with considerable fighting qualities apart from the aircraft they carry, a very different approach from American practice. *Kiev* may well have problems with her comparatively low freeboard and bluff-ended flight deck, her aircraft may yet need improvement in design and handling, but she is the first carrier of her size designed to operate V/STOL aircraft in any navy. As the focal point of a task-force deployed to enhance 'wars of national liberation,' to deter uprisings or to demolish political moves inimical to the USSR this is a very potent and important class of ship.

In the often misunderstood world of the submariners certain important things have been happening in the field of attack submarines which tend to alter previously calculated balances. The US Navy, with 68 nuclear-propelled attack submarines in service and 28 building, have a minimal edge over their Soviet opposite numbers with 87 operational and eight on the slips. The later submarines of the two navies are probably very similar in performance although the new 'Los Angeles' class is proving a more silent craft than the Soviet 'Charlies' and 'Victors'. When the submarine-launched Harpoon with a range of 60 miles is included in her armament, *Los Angeles* and her sisters will retrieve a position of advantage which was lost when the Soviet navy introduced a family of cruise-missiles, originally surface-launched, into their submarines. The dived-launched 25 mile range SS-N-7 missile was introduced into service in the Soviet 'Charlie' class in 1967. During the Harpoon development period the Soviets have evolved another weapon which has much the same capabilities as the American Subroc, the SS-N-15, a tube-launched missile able to carry a torpedo or a nuclear head to a range of 20 miles. However, no range advantage will be achieved as this weapon is put to sea in the newer attack submarines, of which four to six are completed every year.

The anti-submarine struggle would be a desperate affair should hostilities ever be joined. The USA has a very considerable geographical advantage so far as the laying-out and use of underwater detection devices such as the SOSUS chain are concerned. The great distances involved, should the USSR choose such a system, would, with present technology, make it either appallingly expensive or grossly inefficient. So the use of buoys, of intelligence ships off Allied ports and long-range aircraft are currently relied on for early warning—a position of inferiority for the USSR. However, the combined operations of weather and reconnaissance satellites and the huge fleet of Soviet research and survey ships, nearly 50 per cent of the world's total, are providing the essential knowledge of weather and oceanic conditions without which submarine hunting becomes a game of blind-man's-buff. The oceanographer is a key figure in the understanding of the submarine's environment and, while NATO countries are parsimonious in funding such studies, they are handing the initiative to the potential opposition.

Thus, in the sphere of material matters, the USSR has made great strides which are now being overtaken by the USA despite a very vocal opposition skilled in turning figures to fit their argument. The advantages held for so long by the US Navy by its possession of an unchallenged carrier force are not likely to be eroded in the immediate future although progressive cuts in building programmes can only weaken the overall balance. The advantage accruing from the education and training of the all-volunteer US Navy, with its emphasis on initiative, must, however, provide a position of strength compared with a navy manned by conscripted junior ratings, no matter how detailed the technical training of their superiors.

In all these considerations the first question must be whether the fleet, as it exists and is planned to exist, is adequate for the purposes of its masters, the politicians. The nation with great strength and an aggressive policy will always call the tune if facing a country or alliance whose aims are peaceful. At present the strength of the Soviet armed forces is clear for all to see and recent events such as the bombardment of Massawa and the search for ever more havens for their ships in foreign ports speak more eloquently of their policies of aggression, expansion and meddling in others' affairs than ten thousand words from Admiral Gorshkov, their naval Commander-in-Chief.

On the American side the political aims of the USA's foreign policy, strategy and security were put with unusual clarity by President Carter in March when he was apparently giving a public rendering of Presidential Directive No 18 of August 1977. The USA will, the President said, maintain the strategic nuclear balance, work for the strengthening of Europe with NATO and build up sufficient strength 'to counter any threats to the vital interests' of the USA and its friends in the Middle East, Asia and other areas. The world-wide commitments of the US Navy which are implicit in this statement are certainly not reflected in the comments of other US politicians or in the drastic cuts made to the naval programme as listed in the Addenda to this book. The deletion of six submarines and 20 major warships, the erasure of 13 important conversions and the reduction of the Naval Reserve by nearly a half can only have a weakening effect on material readiness and morale. It seems possible that some programme analysis, based on the Central Front syndrome and 'what can be afforded' rather than 'what is necessary', has produced this result which, if agreed by Congress, could only result in politicians entering discussions with a weakened backing. Theodore Roosevelt's 1910 recommendation to 'speak softly and carry a big stick' did not endear him to many of his peace-loving compatriots but the disasters of 1914-18 were not then contemplated. Today aggression is once again abroad, and no matter how much a display of strength is abhorrent, it is, regrettably, often the only way, even if expensive, of out-facing those who rely on threats to promote their policies. At the same time as active strength is essential in these circumstances, the sound condition of a country's Reserves is also most necessary. What Rear-Admiral A. T. Mahan wrote—'The place of a reserve in a system of preparation for war must be admitted because it is inevitable'—has been proved only too true over the last 80 years.

With the overall world situation dominated by the difference between two major power groups there exists, more than ever, a series of independent areas of strife where local rivalries, if undeterred, could very easily result in wide repercussions. As the declared policy of the USSR is to support 'wars of national liberation' it is logical to consider certain geographical areas and the impact which naval forces could have in them, as it is in these distant parts that NATO could well be outflanked, eventually encircled and separated from its sources of supply and its overseas markets.

The NATO area

This must be dealt with first as it will remain for the foreseeable future the primary objective of Soviet advances. While the Central Front in Europe continues to present a reasonably united show of NATO force the nibbling will probably be at the fringes and, although the main Soviet aim is presumably the political subjugation of these peripheral countries through the well-entrenched Fifth Column, activity at sea would also be expected. NATO's northern and southern flanks are areas where sea-borne operations would be needed and here we find a significant weakness in the North Cape area. The Norwegian fleet's major strength lies in submarines and fast attack craft. Reinforcement from without is becoming increasingly difficult as the Soviets' northern maritime frontier is pushed further forward towards the Greenland-United Kingdom barrier as the capabilities of their ships and aircraft increase. In the south political problems could well offset the growing abilities of the Turkish and Greek navies.

Within the Baltic the three Scandinavian navies and that of West Germany face a Warsaw Pact concentration of amphibious and minewarfare forces which can be reinforced or transferred through the White Sea canal route. Finland has concentrated largely on Light Forces and a large coast guard while Sweden backs up her fast attack craft and submarines with a considerable amphibious group and strong minewarfare forces for both minelaying and clearance. All her larger ships are reaching the end of their hull lives and replacement is

DIESEL SERVICE
our specialty

Our long experience in serving the free world's Navies, operating U.S.-made Diesel Equipment, is at your complete disposal, including:

- Supply of Spares
- Technical Assistance
- Instruction and Parts Book Library
- Special Tools and Test Equipment
- Preserving, Packaging and Packing to U.S. Navy Specifications
- Yearly Maintenance Contracts
- Complete Replacement and Exchange Engines, Transmissions and other Major Components
- Cut-Away Instruction Models

SERVING THE NAVIES OF THE FREE WORLD

WESTERN EUROPEAN BRANCH WAREHOUSE AT HAVAM, HERUNGERWEG, VENLO, HOLLAND

ADDRESS ALL CORRESPONDENCE TO:

KORODY-COLYER CORPORATION
112 NORTH AVALON BOULEVARD, WILMINGTON, CALIFORNIA
TELEPHONE (213) 830-0330.   CABLE: KORODIESEL

out of the question while the Government keeps the Defence Vote heavily pared. West Germany has fewer financial problems and although her navy is of generally similar form to that of Sweden her major ships are being reinforced by the Type 122 frigate programme. This is a navy of increasing capabilities and undoubted efficiency whose earlier preoccupation with Baltic problems has given way to a twofront attitude in which the North Sea is given greater attention than before.

Denmark, too, has this problem of two sea areas to consider but, in her case, the threat of invasion from the east must take prior place. For this task submarines, fast attack craft and minelayers are available with some of the larger ships and major patrol craft intended for the protection of her interests and fisheries in the Faeroes and Greenland.

The North Sea has always been a centre for European naval struggles but its varying depths make it unsuitable for the operation of nuclear submarines although diesel boats armed with cruise missiles could well patrol there. At present its importance lies in the multitude of sea routes which cross it and the increasing network of oil lines and routes which, for the rest of the century, will be of the greatest importance to the United Kingdom and Norway as well as to the rest of Western Europe in the event of interruption of supplies from the Persian Gulf. Protection of the rigs and the routes has become a subject of heated discussion and Norway has started a special force for this purpose. The British rely on the Royal Navy which has been reinforced by five (later, seven) 16 knot offshore patrol craft to be backed up if necessary by frigates from the fleet.

On the western flank of the North Sea the 'green and greedy land' of Britain has continued a naval building programme despite the increasing incidence of unofficial strikes, the opposition of the Government's left wing and consequential delays. The evidence of 'under-spend' continues, not through inadequate budgeting, but through the perennial problem of completion dates 'sliding to the right'. Thus the Royal Navy gets less for the allocated funds than it should; funds which are desperately needed as some of the 'Leander' class frigates pass their fifteenth birthday, as the 'Porpoise' class submarines reach the end of their years and over twenty other frigates move towards retirement or deletion. Not only is this need shown amongst the major fighting ships—only two of the Royal Navy's minesweepers are under twenty years old—while the Hydrographer of the Navy, with over four-fifths of the oil-rich North Sea alone needing adequate survey, has retained a quarter of his meagre force of eight ships (an eighth of those declared by the USSR and, in fact, a sixteenth of that country's total of major survey and research ships) only by making them pensioners of the Shah of Iran for service in the Gulf.

Meanwhile, despite the changes of mind of the politicians and the shipyard workers which hold back the building programme, the men of the fleet have reached an advanced pitch of professional ability as new training ideas bear fruit. The resultant efficiency can only be impaired by a sag in morale as these splendidly prepared and competent young men find their families suffering from pay anomalies and while they reflect on the fact that the whole structure of the fleet depends not only upon governmental support but also on the industrial efficiency and willingness to work of their countrymen ashore.

Across the Channel lies part of the fleet of a second country which has dual-frontier problems, France. This year the main striking force of her increasingly capable fleet lies in the Mediterranean, an outpost of NATO in technical terms but part of one of the two strongest fleets in Europe and of one of the world's three overseas navies. The steadily improving condition of the French navy is a tribute to her designers and her naval staff; it would probably be even more effective were it not for the incursion of political problems. At the same time this is the only navy, apart from those of the USA and USSR, which has a regular presence in the Atlantic, Mediterranean, the Indian Ocean, the West Indies and the Pacific. Also, with decree Number 78-272 of 9 March 1978, the French Navy has, through the authority of the three Prefets Maritimes, an over-riding interest and responsibility around French coasts and throughout their 200-mile EEZ 'pour le plus grand bien des usagers de mer et des intérêts de la nation.' The *Amoco Cadiz* disaster came only seven days after the promulgation of this decree. The sea-gods are very fickle and remarkably demanding.

Spanish armadas and treasure fleets are a part of history but the new fleet of King Carlos is growing into a significant contribution to current world naval strengths. New designs, both Spanish and foreign, are taking their place in the build-up of this navy and, with one of the fastest improving shipbuilding industries in the West, the yards of Spain are well-placed to support this advance. The situation in Italy is very similar. An integration of the production of Italian hulls, machinery and weapon systems are not only placing their fleet in a very strong position in the Mediterranean but also in the foreign export market. With an increase in on-board helicopter strength and afloat support this is becoming a long-range navy capable of deepwater operations.

Sandwiched between Italy and the two somewhat reluctant NATO partners, Greece and Turkey, lies Yugoslavia whose own naval programme shows a dependence on both Western and Soviet sources. With weapons and missiles from the USSR and radar and Rolls-Royce gas turbines from Western Europe the Yugoslavs are building a considerable naval force on the Adriatic, the Danube and the frontier lakes. It remains to be seen how much they will be needed in the upheavals which could follow Marshal Tito's death. Further differences in this area are centred on the problems arising between Greece and Turkey over Cyprus and the Aegean continental shelf. Both are building up navies on the classic pattern of the world's smaller fleets: submarines and fast attack craft. Both have in the past relied on Western Europe and the USA for their vessels although now each has an expanding indigenous shipbuilding industry. Weapon systems, nevertheless, must come from abroad and with the long-standing American embargo on arms' shipments to Turkey it would be simple for her to turn to nearer neighbours for assistance. Turkish pride and independence are not to be treated with cavalier disregard.

The Southern Mediterranean
The President of Syria has shown his capability for taking his own line both with his Arab neighbours and with the USSR. His naval needs have until now been met by imports from the Soviet navy, which uses his ports in an area where Egyptian bases are now denied to them. Now, with the possibility of disruption to this source, Syria has made moves into the Western market. If President Assad is worried about possible opposition, his view must be directed towards Israel. This country has clearly learned the lessons of the war of 1973. While the 'Reshef' class have been rearmed with a mix of Harpoon and Gabriel missiles the problem of controlling the former beyond the visual horizon has become a matter of increasing importance. The new helicopter-armed corvettes, a necessary adjunct while shore-based aircraft are in minimal numbers, could give the necessary direction for the new American missiles.

The provision of new equipment also faces President Sadat and his naval advisers in Egypt. The Soviet Union has never been well-known for providing spares and handbooks to its client countries and now that Egypt has left the Soviet arena she must place a greater dependence on Western sources. The funding for spares and replacements is probably by Saudi Arabia and Kuwait but speed is the need and the United Kingdom may have lost its chance owing to labour problems and resultant delays. The chances for other West European countries must therefore appear bright. New frigates from Italy, new submarines from West Germany, new weapon systems from those countries able to ensure delivery are highest on Egyptian shopping lists.

To the west, Libya is more than capable of financing her purchases from her own oil wealth. New submarines and missile craft from the USSR will, when training problems permit, be amalgamated with missile corvettes from Italy and fast attack craft from France to form a potent naval force in the gut of the Mediterranean. Should Mr Mintoff of Malta remain in power and offer facilities to President Ghadaffi and his Soviet supporters in 1979 the passage from the West to the eastern Mediterranean, including Turkey, Greece and the Suez Canal, will be at grave risk. NATO's southern flank will be at peril with little chance of reinforcement.

Further west still Tunisia and Algeria lean towards the East while Morocco, despite her recent orders from Spain, is now inclining to the Soviets with expectations of ship deliveries in the near future. Overall, the northern coasts of Africa and the interests of its littoral countries give little cause for satisfaction in the West. Soviet reinforcements for a combined Arab push against Israel could well be made easier by a Turkey rebuffed by the USA and the Western build-up in support of Israel disturbed by Libyan intervention.

Sub-Saharan Africa
The north-west and western coasts of Africa could soon become a Soviet paradise. With a major naval and air base at Conakry and Soviet naval exports to several West African countries providing an area wide open to military and naval advisers as well as so-called 'fisheries experts,' overall pressure can be exerted with little effort. Whatever the reaction of Nigeria with her new orders placed in Western Europe the Soviet position in the countries to her north and west could well frustrate any aims she may have for Western support or independent action. The same is true for the Ivory Coast, Togo, Cameroon and Gabon—any Westward leaning could swiftly be snuf-

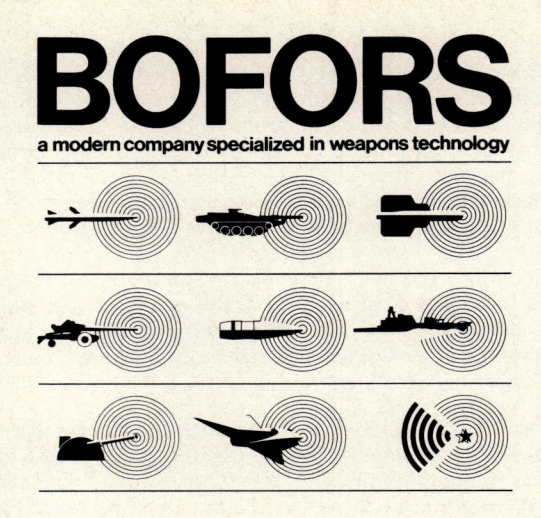

BOFORS
a modern company specialized in weapons technology

57 mm All-purpose Naval Gun

- The Bofors 57 mm all-purpose gun is specially intended for installation on small and medium-sized ships.

- With its proximity-fuzed ammunition, the gun can be used for combatting all kinds of aerial targets, with the same effect as guns intended strictly for anti-aircraft use.

- The penetrating shell with delayed burst gives an effect in surface targets comparable to that of guns with considerably larger calibres.

- Low weight, high rate of fire, and alternative types of ammunition for aerial and surface targets, make the Bofors 57 mm gun system a highly effective weapon.

BOFORS ORDNANCE

AB BOFORS Ordnance Division   Box 500   S-690 20 BOFORS, Sweden
Telephone: 0586-360 00   Cables: Boforsco, Bofors Telex: 73210 bofors s

fed out. Zaire, primarily dependent on Western supplies, and the Congo where China has staked her claim, also lie at risk. Guinea stands to the north and to the south, Angola, where the savage massacres by the surrogate Cubans have ensured a temporary Soviet claim to harbour rights in Luanda, Lobito and Mocamedes, a classic case of encirclement by sea and air power. Further south the future success of SWAPO in Namibia could open the excellent harbour of Walfish Bay to the Soviet fleet, a valuable adjunct as Western vacillations and double standards put the whole of the Republic of South Africa in jeopardy. The bloody internecine wars which appear to be the outcome expected by certain influential Americans could finally result in the black and coloured populations being placed under a yoke of a severity previously unknown and the splendid deep-water ports of the Cape Province and Natal being handed to those whose interests are best served by the disruption of the Cape route between Asia and Western Europe.

On the east coast of Africa Mozambique is, in addition to offering tacit acknowledgement of British Government support, providing deep-water harbour facilities to the USSR at a point where both the Mozambique Channel route and that outside Madagascar can most conveniently be reached. While her northern neighbour, Tanzania, is hitched to the red star of China from the naval point of view, Kenya remains Western-orientated. Somalia's fleet is Soviet-supplied but no longer supported from the same source, a classic condition in which deterioration soon sets in. Djibouti has an alliance with France, South Yemen provides ample airport and harbour space for the Soviets, North Yemen inclines towards Moscow in a dilatory fashion and the Eritrean coast remains a battleground fought over by Cubans, Soviets, Ethiopians and Eritrean guerillas. Navies have little part in this war as the Soviets have sufficient control of the sea to permit bombardment and reinforcement at will but the outcome of the war could be vital to Western shipping, to Saudi Arabia, to Sudan and to all those who revere the principles of free passage of the world's seas and oceans. With Massawa and the Dahlak Archipelago in Soviet hands entrance to and exit from the Suez Canal could be cut with no difficulty.

This is only part of the African state of affairs, the resolution of the whole being vital, as it always has been, to naval affairs around that continent's coasts. A Soviet presence in Libya, cutting the Mediterranean in two, could be linked via Chad and the southern areas of Sudan with Ethiopia and the closing of the Red Sea. A separate area of naval threat would be provided by the junction of Mozambique and Angola through Rhodesia and Zambia, giving an overland rail and road route for stores and personnel before the subjugation of the South African Republic. The increasing Soviet strength in West Africa, supported by hireling troops and naval task forces, could put all the vital Western trade routes around the continent at risk.

The Arabian Peninsula Area

No segment of the world, except the Polar regions, can be considered in isolation and this is more true of the Arabian Peninsula than most. With the enormously important strategic position of Turkey to the north, an area no doubt alluring to the Soviets, and with Syria and the Soviet tributary Iraq as buffers to the north and north-east the line of a second Soviet pincer, aligned with that through Africa, is clearly defined. The distance from the Caucasian border of the USSR through the Lake Van area of eastern Turkey to Mosul is 200 miles of inhospitable and difficult country, passable to determined troops. From Mosul to the Soviet naval installations on the Shatt-al-Arab near Basra is another 500 miles but these distances are nothing to modern aircraft and, with the growing strength of Soviet-supplied and supported ships in the Iraqi navy, much mischief could be wrought with mines and missiles in the vital oil exporting area from Abadan to the Straits of Hormuz.

It is hardly surprising, therefore, that Iran and Saudi Arabia are making great strides in building up considerable naval forces to restrain any impediment to the free flow of their enormously valuable oil trade. Both, however, are faced with the problem of training ships' companies which are, on entry, of a basically low educational standard. This may have been at the root of Iran's reduction of her order for 'Spruance' class destroyers in the USA but it has not deterred a plan, mentioned in the Addenda, for very large increases of major classes of ships in the future. The Saudis also, with two coasts to care for, are busily procuring increasing numbers of ships from the USA while the United Arab Emirates, Qatar, Bahrain and Kuwait are all candidates for inclusion in Western order books. Where these orders will eventually germinate is dependent on many factors not least of which are industrial cohesion resulting in the keeping of delivery dates, the stability or instability of the dollar affecting oil prices and trust engendered by strong and realistic foreign policies.

The Indian Ocean

Any understanding of the maritime situation in the Indian Ocean must start with a realisation of the immense distances involved and the fact that very few island areas exist as compared with the Pacific. From Durban to Fremantle is 4 200 miles, nearly twice the haul from San Diego to Hawaii and Fremantle is nearly 5 000 miles from Aden, further than the run from Hawaii to Hong Kong. The east coast of Africa bounding this ocean is some 4 000 miles long and it is these huge stretches which must affect the choice of ships required to operate further off shore than the 200-mile EEZ. The importance of this consideration is added to by the uncertainty of events in the north-western portion of the ocean. Not only does the Gulf traffic and that from the Suez Canal join here but also the political rivalries are more intense than elsewhere. The two bordering countries of the Indian Ocean possessing fleet air arms, Australia and India, must soon decide on the form of replacements for their ageing carriers and these could very sensibly be small ships with a mixed V/STOL/helicopter complement. Both these fleets are accelerating programmes for the deep-water and coastal ships needed to replace their elderly predecessors. Australia prefers to expand her own ship-building and this wise policy has been adopted in India, where submarine construction is planned. Pakistan has received ships from the USA and China while her larger Indian neighbour has preferred to accept help from the USSR and the United Kingdom. Whether 'Kashin' class destroyers are transferred or not, the Indian fleet will remain the main naval power in this area for many years ahead.

South-west Pacific

Included here are the northern and eastern interests of Australia, New Zealand and the problems of South-east Asia. Australia has to face an essential fact—50 per cent of her overseas trade is with the Asiatic countries from Singapore eastward and with North America. It is to the advantage of all involved to ensure the free passage of the ships involved in this commerce.

Both Australia and New Zealand have the 200-mile EEZ problem to face and both rely on harbours vulnerable to mines. They have extreme weather conditions to face and neither has the financial resources to provide a fleet of adequate size to meet all its needs. It is not surprising, therefore, to note a fair measure of co-operation with other Pacific powers in the naval exercises carried out in this area.

In South-east Asia the stark political divisions prevent any general form of co-operation but it is noticeable that Malaysia, Singapore, Indonesia and Thailand are developing short-range navies of very similar capabilities except for Indonesia's new submarines. One cannot believe that the large numbers of ships credited to Viet-Nam and Kampuchea (Cambodia) represent any great threat to their neighbours. They are both lacking in fuel supplies and training while the wholesale slaughter of all those experienced in any form of command pursued in Kampuchea must have demolished any chance of successful naval operations. The problems in the Philippines are very different. The build-up of this navy has been so rapid that the training organisation must be stretched to its limits although, with the main emphasis on coastal operations, this may have less impact than otherwise.

North-west Pacific

The possible upsurge in Sino-Japanese trade and relations is of considerable naval importance in this area. Japan's sea routes, which provide nearly all the raw materials needed for her industries, would be notably reduced and be more within the compass of the Maritime Self-Defence Force (MSDF) to protect were she to use Chinese resources. Of her major imports of crude oil and petroleum, ores, timber, coal, chemicals, textiles, cereals and machinery a growing quantity is likely to be available from China in the future and with routes of only 500 miles in a sea area which could be virtually sealed off from outside interference such a course of action must have considerable attractions.

The MSDF itself is steadily improving in its capabilities and with more helicopters joining the fleet and the new AOE 421 programme showing the first move towards afloat support this is becoming a far better balanced fleet than before. In the same context the 500 ships and craft of the Maritime Safety Agency cannot be ignored. Although under the wing of the Ministry of Transport this force is armed and highly skilled in such diverse trades as coast guard and rescue work, hydrography, oil pollution clearance, in all of which it has a full inventory of specialised vessels and its own air arm.

Japan's vast neighbour, China, still shows no signs of predatory ambitions, a point borne out by the composition of her naval building programme. New submarines, frigates and fast attack craft are increasing her self-defence capability. With no embarked aircraft

Same concept for 3 modern engines: PC2-PC3-PC4
(Ranging from 3000 to 27000 hp.)

PC2
PC3
PC4

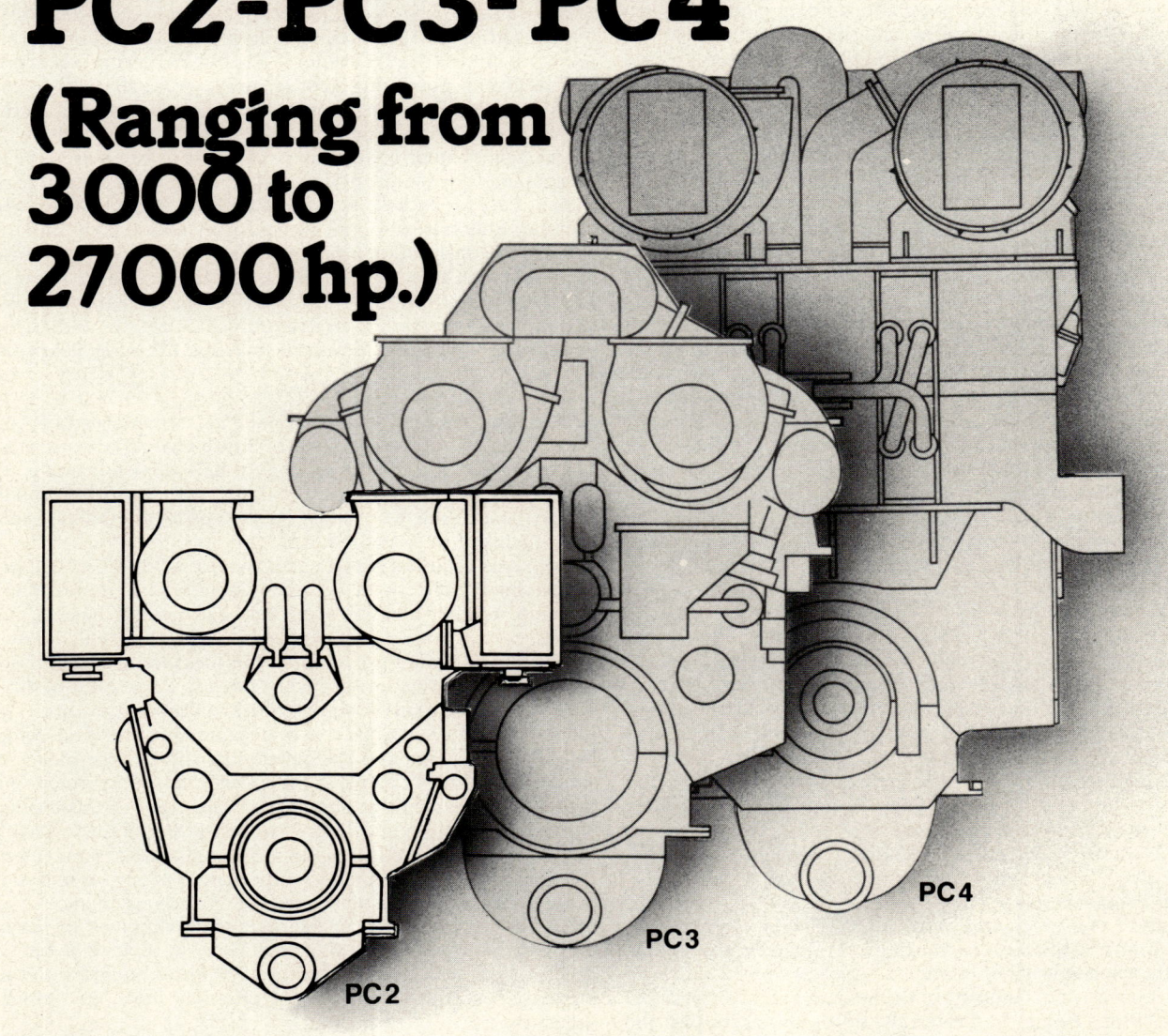

Welded frame - Water jacket
Two-part connecting rods - Compactness
Easy maintenance - Low consumption

ALSTHOM-ATLANTIQUE DÉPARTEMENT MOTEURS
2, quai de Seine, 93203 Saint-Denis - France - 820.61.91 - Télex 620333 F Motla

and no afloat support capability worth noting this is clearly not a navy intended to operate beyond the range of shore support. Chinese survey and research ships are now probing further afield but in a country where scientific studies have been the rule for more than 2 000 years and in which science is being restored to its rightful place this is hardly surprising. What is of transcending importance is the condition of Sino-Soviet relations now that the USSR's expectation of a major domestic upheaval in the wake of Mao's death has been proved false. The hope of a compromise with Mao's successors appears unlikely as do any immediate plans for a sharing of communist hegemony. With this situation the Soviet Pacific Fleet regains a position of maximum importance. With all forms of missile armament from short-range cruise missiles to 4 000-mile ballistic missiles available as well as normal artillery this is a force capable of use as a pressure group should relations be further exacerbated.

Points of difference exist in plenty—would the Soviets support Viet-Nam in disputes over off-shore rights in the South China Sea?—would China support Japanese claims over the Sakhalin Islands?—would the Soviets support operations by Taiwan?—which way would loyalties fall in the event of another Korean conflict? These are all valid questions and with the two Koreas pressing forward with their home-based shipyards and armament industries and with Taiwan an armed camp the chances of a conflict which could well spread its tentacles must be borne firmly in mind. A Soviet pre-emptive strike against China now appears less likely but her manipulation of local differences could well precipitate major hostilities which the USA would find difficult to evade.

North-east Pacific and the Arctic

In this area lies the main bulk of American warning lines for any sudden nuclear attack. The Canadians, now aiming to reinforce their naval and maritime air forces, are in the forefront of this zone whose frozen vastnesses are little known to those not involved. But this is an area where much could be attempted in the early phases leading to hostilities. Soviet submarine deployments through Baffin Bay, the use of the raucous ice-edge as cover for ballistic-missile and attack submarines must be part of any appreciation of future struggles. The popular misconception that submarines can leap at will through the Polar pack-ice is very wrong but navigation beneath the ice and use of the fringes as a cover from sonar detection are both well-tried and proved.

South America

A responsible figure who recently denied the strategic importance of South America was probably thinking only of the immediate future. The Soviet Union has two valuable entrepôts to the continent—Mexico City and Cuba. The former is the centre of the intelligence operators, the second of the activists. While the first remains fully-manned Cuba has been drained of over 40 000 troops to act in Africa in the Soviet's interest, leaving their home island's defence as the responsibility of others. There are therefore fewer Cubans available to follow the example of Che Guevara but the states of South America are preparing against invasion. This is a word improperly understood; one man can invade as well as ten thousand and cause greater devastation in the long run. The South American navies are split between the larger ships and submarines designed for protection against a neighbour's attack and the Light Forces and river craft, all available and being produced in increasing numbers as a barrier to incursion from without. Small raids can lead to mighty revolutions and it is here, on the coasts and up the great rivers, on the great lakes and the vast tributaries that defence against insidious penetration must be mounted. No matter how much the suppression of human rights may raise anger and protests in other countries, if these navies fail to protect their homelands against invasion all form of individual freedom will be at risk.

Current developments

Modern requirements and standards in Western countries ensure that minimal funds are made available for defence. A distinguished US Chief of Naval Operations once said, 'If my cash is cut give me an increase in Intelligence.' He meant it on a selective basis but, with the cash cut every effort must be made to ensure that the intelligence of designers and planners is combined in an attempt to use the available finances to the best advantage. Hog-tied by endless committees and mounting bumf, by continual demands for long-term evaluations, the process of improving the West's defensive capability against an advancing tide of tyranny is liable to deteriorate. It is only 40 years ago that politicians and the public, with a few noble exceptions, called for peace through patience. Today the situation is very little different. Wherever we look the glove has been thrown down and few have the courage to accept the fact. The West has reached a point where the pious calls of Helsinki have been ignored and where detente has been twisted to the Soviet's advantage.

The understanding of a country's defence needs depends on an appreciation of its history, its ideals and the policies rooted in those factors. No two countries are alike—each has its own pride and tradition which will not take kindly to foreign ideas or ways of life. This does not debar the integration of abilities and resources resulting in an overall saving and mutual assistance. The 'two-way street' agreement to ensure a greater equality in the sale of equipment between the USA and European NATO has now been in existence for some three years. As the present financial balance rests at about eight to one in favour of the USA there is clearly a long way to go. Nevertheless without such agreements the waste resulting from lack of standardisation and compatibility must gravely weaken the whole effort of deterrence. In this the navies stand in the forefront—long-range, long-endurance forces which can occupy an area without aggression and promote peaceful solutions. Many people, saddened by the evidence of tyranny and the vacillations of their leaders have turned their attention inwards as a barrier to the evil without. But understanding, wisdom and determination can still win—and not lose the victory.

J. E. MOORE, CAPT. RN
April 1978

Oerlikon

Modern and efficient automatic naval guns with appropriate ammunition against air-and surface-targets.

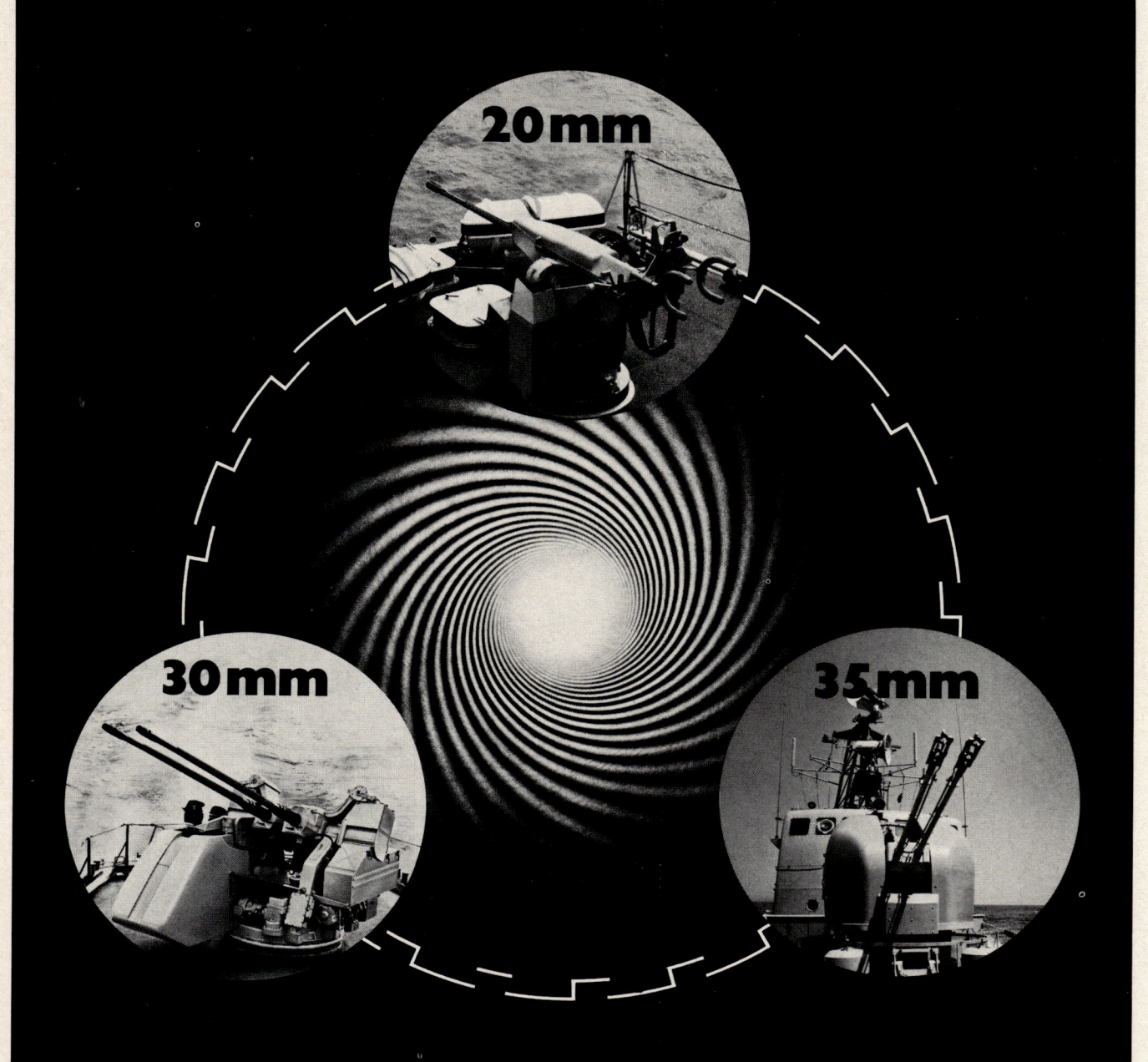

20 mm

30 mm

35 mm

Machine Tool Works Oerlikon-Bührle Ltd., Zurich/Switzerland
British Manufacture and Research Co. Ltd., Grantham/Great Britain
Oerlikon Italiana S.I.p.A., Milan/Italy
Members of the Oerlikon-Bührle Group

30-198

MAJOR MATTERS

Abu Dhabi
All forces now under UAE command.

Albania
One 'Whiskey' class submarine deleted. Four Chinese 'Hoku' class missile craft and two 'Shanghai' class added.

Algeria
Three 'Osa II' missile craft, one 'Polnocny' class LCT added to the fleet. Ten Baglietto patrol craft delivered to the Coast Guard.

Argentina
New frigate programme being discussed.

Australia
Replacement for *Melbourne* under discussion with a number of foreign builders. Fifteen patrol craft of Brooke PCF 420 Type to be built. *Tobruk* laid down. Third FFG ordered in USA. *Cook* launched. New survey ships and launches to be ordered. Plans for replacement of *Supply*—possibly by French 'Durance' class.

Belgium
E21 frigate programme completed. Fifteen new MCMV to be built.

Brazil
'Niteroi' class—two remain to be completed. Possibility of new corvette programme.

Canada
Order for new destroyers being put out to tender (Addenda).

Denmark
'Nils Juel' class frigates to complete 1979-80. 'Peder Skram' class to receive eight Harpoon missiles which are also to be fitted in 'Willemoes' class.

Dominican Republic
Three 'Cohoes' class now act as patrol ships.

Ecuador
'Gearing' class transferred from USA. Two Type 209 submarines now in service. Possibility of new construction programme of frigates and corvettes.

Egypt
Possible new construction—two 'Lupo' class frigates, two Type 209 submarines and 52 metre fast attack craft. 'Osas' to be re-engined and rearmed.

Ethiopia
Four 105 ft Sewart fast attack craft delivered.

Finland
New minelayer/training ship ordered. Plans for two frigates, five missile craft and four minesweepers.

France
SNA 72 continuing. PA75 delayed. Sixth SSBN delayed. New class of minehunter started. Deletion of several of 'E50' Type and 'Le Fougeux' class. Extra 'Durance' class to be built.

Germany (Federal Republic)
Continuation of Type 122 frigate programme. Details of Troika MCM programme (Addenda).

Greece
Confirmation of new submarine orders and indigenous fast attack craft programme.

Guatemala
New deliveries of Halter craft.

India
New Fleet Air Arm possibilities. Possible new 'Kashin' class frigate transfers. 'Nanuchka' class deliveries. Continuing programmes at Garden Reach, Calcutta.

Indonesia
New frigate programme in the Netherlands. New type 209 submarines from West Germany.

Iran
Possible new Western European orders (Addenda).

Ireland (Republic)
New Corvette (*Emer*) commissioned.

Israel
New helicopter-corvettes under construction. Three new submarines in commission. New order for 'Flagstaff' Hydrofoils from USA. Start of new 'Dvora' class (small FAC-missile).

Italy
Order for new helicopter-cruiser (*Giuseppe Garibaldi*) New 'Maestrale' class frigates and new helicopters.

Japan
New 'Improved Uzushio' class submarine building. New construction 'DD122' class approved. Second 'Tachikaze' destroyer launched. First 'Improved Haruna' class destroyer to be launched September 1978. New 1200 ton frigate class planned as well as new fleet support ship, new surveying ship and cable layer. One new and three projected large patrol vessels for Maritime Safety Agency.

Kenya
Reports of transfer from Israel.

Korea (North)
Building programme continues.

Kuwait
Ten fast attack craft to be ordered.

Libya
Completion of Italian corvettes continues. More 'Foxtrot' class submarines and 'Osa' class fast attack craft received.

Malaysia
Frigate *Mermaid* transferred from Royal Navy, July 1978 as *Hang Tuah*.

Mexico
Considerable building programmes under consideration.

Morocco
'Descubierta' class frigate and 'Lazaga' class fast attack craft on order from Spain. Deliveries of Soviet fast attack craft expected.

Netherlands
Holland transferred to Peru. First 'Kortenaer' class at sea. Order for first new submarine allocated (Addenda).

Nigeria
Orders placed for Blöhm and Voss frigate, three West German Type 143 and three French 'La Combattante III' class fast attack craft.

Norway
New ships taken up by charter for Coast Guard while seven new ships are building.

Pakistan
Two ex-US destroyers transferred.

Peru
Four helicopter-carriers ordered from Italy. *Aguirre* (ex-*De Zeven Provincien*) commissioned in the Netherlands after refit as a helicopter cruiser on 24 February 1978 as well as *Garcia y Garcia* (ex-*Holland*).

Saudi Arabia
The large programme of new construction in the USA is now listed by class and name.

South Africa
The purchase of two type A69 frigates and two 'Agosta' class submarines has been suspended by United Nations' resolution.

Spain
New helicopter-carrier ordered from Bazan to US Sea-Control Ship design.

Sri Lanka
New patrol craft delivered from the United Kingdom.

Surinam
Considerable orders from the Netherlands now listed.

YARROW
Naval Shipbuilders to the World for over 100 years

1. *HMS 'ARDENT'—Completed 1977. One of five Type 21 Frigates built for the British Royal Navy.*
2. *LOGISTIC SUPPORT SHIP—Capable of beach landing heavy military vehicles and troops and fitted with extensive Helicopter facilities.*
3. *Typical CORVETTE/LIGHT FRIGATE—Armed with an extensive range of Weapon and Sensor equipments.*
4. *Typical PATROL VESSEL—Armed with medium and small calibre guns and surface to surface missiles.*

Yarrow design and build most types of surface Naval Ships including Fast Attack Craft, Patrol Vessels, Corvettes, Frigates, Survey Ships and Support Ships.

YARROW
SHIPBUILDERS LTD

SCOTSTOUN, GLASGOW G14 0XN, SCOTLAND
Tel: 041-959 1207. Telex: 77357

A member of British Shipbuilders

Sweden
Continuing Government cuts in defence spending are preventing replacement of older ships.

Taiwan
Order for extra thirteen PSMM5 missile craft cancelled—to be replaced by Taiwan-designed patrol craft.

Thailand
Three missile craft ordered from CN Breda (Venezia).

Tunisia
Second ex-US 'Adjutant' class MSC transferred by France. Two Vosper Thornycroft 103 ft fast attack craft—patrol commissioned.

Turkey
Second pair of Type 209 submarines to commission in 1979-80. Last three of Lürssen fast attack craft due to commission. First of Abeking and Rasmussen SAR33 Type completed successful trials—presumed that next 13 are to be built.

Union of Soviet Socialist Republics
Second 'Kiev' class due to commission. Building of SSBNs now confined to 'Delta II' and 'III' classes at rate of six per year. 'Victor II', 'Charlie II' and 'Tango' class submarines building at rate of two per class per year. 'Kara' class cruisers and 'Krivak' class destroyers in continuing programme. New 'Koni' class frigate programme started. New radio-controlled minesweepers building. More tankers being converted for abeam refuelling.

United Kingdom
Ark Royal to pay off late-1978 and *Bulwark* to recommission. Third 'Invincible' class planned. Further orders for Type 42 destroyers planned. Fifth Type 22 frigate to be ordered in 1978. Further orders for MCM Vessels ('Hunt' class) planned. Two more 'Island' class off-shore patrol vessels ordered. *Andromeda*, first of the 'Broad-beamed Leander' class, has started conversion to carry Exocet and Sea Wolf missiles.

United States of America
Latest Five Year Programme is contained in the Addenda.

Yugoslavia
First of Yugoslav built missile craft now commissioned.

microwave tubes
ELTEL LINE

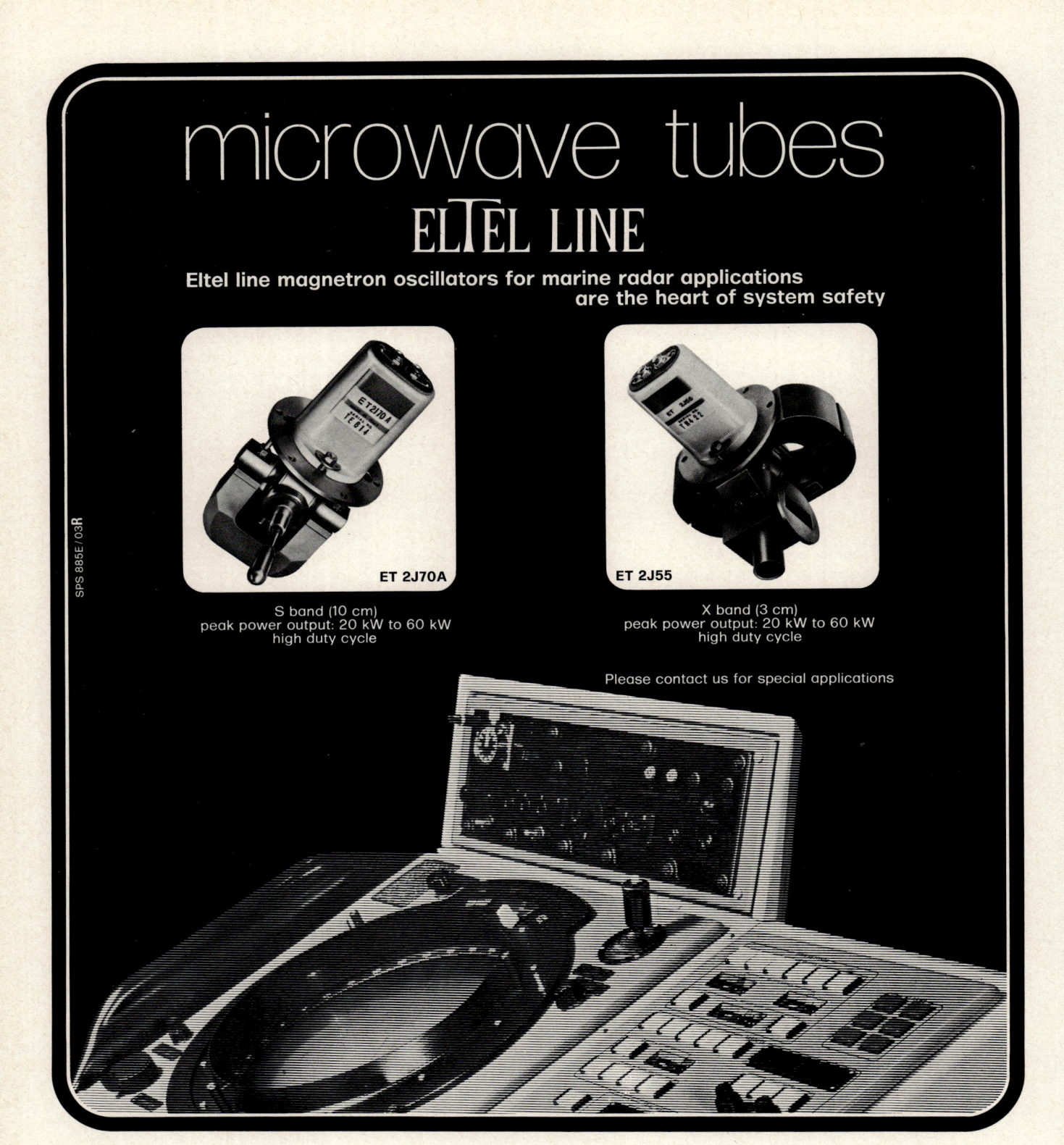

Eltel line magnetron oscillators for marine radar applications are the heart of system safety

ET 2J70A
S band (10 cm)
peak power output: 20 kW to 60 kW
high duty cycle

ET 2J55
X band (3 cm)
peak power output: 20 kW to 60 kW
high duty cycle

Please contact us for special applications

ITALTEL
SOCIETA' ITALIANA TELECOMUNICAZIONI
20149 Milan (Italy) - 12, Piazzale Zavattari - phone 4388.1

☐ Telephone exchanges ☐ Telex exchanges ☐ Private automatic branch exchanges ☐ Telephone sets and decorator phones ☐ Data transmission systems and data terminals ☐ FDM and PCM multiplex systems ☐ Microwave radio links and earth stations ☐ Line carrier transmission equipment ☐ Power line carrier systems ☐ Remote control systems ☐ Equipment for radio and TV studios ☐ Avionics equipment ☐ Audio and video intercom systems ☐ Power plants for telecommunications installations ☐ Test equipment ☐ Microwave tubes

ACKNOWLEDGEMENTS

Once again the growing band of correspondents has provided that essential assistance without which it would be very difficult to achieve the accuracy which is essential in a book of this type. Their names are too numerous to list here but, as usual, there are certain people who have given continued and unstinted help: Contre-Admiral M. J. Adam CVO CBE, Dr Ian Buxton, Mr Adrian English, Commander A. Fraccaroli, Lt-Cdr A. Hague VRD, Mr Bradley Hahn, Mr G. K. Jacobs, Mr John Mortimer, Mr A. J. R. Risseeuw, Mr C. W. E. Richardson, Senor X. Taibo, Mr R. Winfield and Mr John Young are among these. Of the regular consultants, the following have been responsible for a great deal of invaluable help: Mr Graeme Andrews with the Australian and New Zealand section, Captain F. de Blocq van Kuffeler and Dr Robert Scheina. Mr Samuel L. Morison has once again been entirely responsible for all the information for the USA section and has also been instrumental in organising the new sections therein as well as providing a great deal of help in the layout of that section. He would like to thank the following for their invaluable assistance: Rear-Admiral David M. Cooney, USN, Chief, Office of Naval Information, Captain William Blanchard, Mr Robert Carlisle, Petty Officer William Lane and Lieutenant Ed Zesk of his staff; Commander David Rogers, Security Assistance Division, Office of Chief of Naval Operations, Captain R. E. Groder, Lieutenant F. R. Robbins and Mr Walt Dailey of the Ships Maintenance and Logistics Division, Office of Chief of Naval Operations, Mr Stanley Krol of the Navy Shipbuilding Scheduling Office, Naval Sea Systems Command, Mr Christopher Wright, Naval Systems Division, Pentagon; Mrs Jeanne Koontz, Miss Barbara Gilmore and Mr Charles Haberlain of the Naval Historical Center; Captain R. E. Larson, Public Affairs Officer, US Coast Guard, Dr Robert L. Scheina, Coast Guard Historian, Miss Elizabeth Segedi, Head, Photo Branch, US Coast Guard, Mr R. D. Weir of the Coast Guard Operations Division and finally Commander J. Edgemond, USN, Naval Sea Systems Command. Mr Morison would especially like to acknowledge the following people whose contributions to this edition have been especially noteworthy: Captain Gerard M. Sturm, Jr and Captain William Test, both of the Ships Maintenance and Logistics Division and Mr Larry Manning, Legislative/Public Affairs Officer, Military Sealift Command, US Navy.

To the editors of the other major naval reference books I send my thanks for the part they have played: *Almanacco Navale* edited by Dr Giorgio Giorgerini and Signor Augusto Nani, *Flottentaschenbuch* edited by Herr Gerhard Albrecht, *Flottes de Combat,* edited by M. J. Labayle-Couhat, and *Marinkalender* edited by Captain Allan Kull.

The illustrations are a vital part of this publication and in the sphere of photography the continual assistance of Dr Giorgio Arra, Mr Robert Carlisle, Mr R. Forrest of Wright and Logan, Mr Michael Lennon and Mr and Mrs (C. and S.) Taylor as well as too many others to be individually noted has allowed nearly a third of the illustrations to be replaced this year. The line drawings have also been updated and here I thank Mr A. D. Baker III, Lieutenant-Commander Erminio Bagnasco, Herr Siegfried Breyer, Mr John Humphrey and the team of Mr Jack Wood and Mr Euslin Bruce.

In the preparation of the special sections I must once again acknowledge my debt to Mr Robert Abernethy and his staff for the basis of the silhouettes and major pennant list, to Mr John Taylor, editor of *Jane's all the World's Aircraft,* for not only putting the Aircraft section straight but for reading its galleys and to Senor X. Taibo, Commander Roy Corlett and Dr Robert Scheina for their specialised advice.

Finally, on the personal side, my wife, despite health problems, has given me her unstinting aid and advice while David Parsons has put in many unsung hours and his wife Jean has been responsible not only for the indexing but also for my correspondence when she has been able to pin me down. At the publishers, Stuart Bannerman, Valerie Passmore, Hope Cohen and Glynis Long (who has the responsibility for pasting-up the whole book) have been both very helpful and long-suffering while the printers at Netherwood Dalton of Huddersfield have shown their usual uncanny prescience and acumen in interpreting my copy—no more, it should be said, than is the normal for any well-organised Yorkshire firm.

From the governmental side the Naval Public Relations team of the Ministry of Defence in London under Captain D. R. Blacker have been continually helpful and the same is true for my many friends among the Naval Attachés in the same city. Some governments have, however, been less co-operative and it has proved necessary at times to complete certain sections without official aid. This is necessary for a book which is used not only by navies, governments and the public but also by senior legal courts throughout the world.

Information and photographs are invaluable and, quite obviously, the book could not continue without them. As preparation of material starts in mid-November and continues at the rate of seventy pages a week from then on, if data and pictures arrive after a particular country's section has been passed to the printer, they can be included only at the proof stage, an expensive form of correction. So, please, if you wish to help and save my ageing ulcers do not delay in passing on what you have available. We have started next year's edition and any contributions will be most gratefully received. The address is:

Captain J. E. Moore, RN
Elmhurst
Rickney
Hailsham
Sussex BN27 1SF
England

No illustration from this book may be reproduced without the publishers' permission but the Press may reproduce information and governmental photographs provided *Jane's Fighting Ships* is acknowledged as the source. Photographs credited to other than official organisations must not be reproduced without permission from the originator.

Ship Defense

from the world's leader in
ship countermeasure systems

CHAFFROC   HIRAM

RBOC *   NATO SEA GNAT

SUPER RBOC *   GEMINI

Suppliers of rapid bloom chaff and
infrared systems to the U.S. Navy
and other friendly fleets.

* Rapid Bloom Offboard Chaff

HYCOR

TEN GILL STREET
WOBURN, MASSACHUSETTS 01801 USA
Tel (617)935-5950 TWX 710-393-6345
Cable HYCOR

MAJOR SURFACE SHIPS
PENNANT LIST

Albania	Alb	Guatemala	Gua	Papua New Guinea	PNG
Algeria	Alg	Guinea	Gn	Paraguay	Par
Angola	Ang	Guinea Bissau	GB	Peru	Per
Anguilla	Ana	Guyana	Guy	Philippines	Plp
Argentina	Arg	Haiti	Hai	Poland	Pol
Australia	Aust	Honduras	Hon	Portugal	Por
Austria	Aus	Hong Kong	HK	Qatar	Qat
Bahamas	Bhm	Hungary	Hun	Romania	Rom
Bahrain	Bhr	Iceland	Ice	St Kitts	StK
Bangladesh	Ban	India	Ind	St Lucia	StL
Barbados	Bar	Indonesia	Indo	St Vincent	StV
Belgium	Bel	Iran	Iran	Saudi Arabia	SAr
Belize	Blz	Iraq	Iraq	Senegal	Sen
Bolivia	Bol	Ireland	Ire	Sierra Leone	SL
Brazil	Brz	Israel	Isr	Singapore	Sin
Brunei	Bru	Italy	Ita	Somalia	Som
Bulgaria	Bul	Ivory Coast	IC	South Africa	SA
Burma	Bur	Jamaica	Jam	Spain	Spn
Cameroon	Cam	Japan	Jap	Sri Lanka	Sri
Canada	Can	Jordon	Jor	Sudan	Sud
Chile	Chi	Kampuchea	Kam	Sweden	Swe
China, People's Republic	CPR	Keňya	Ken	Surinam	Sur
Colombia	Col	Korea, Democratic People's Republic (North)	DPRK	Syria	Syr
Comoro Islands	Com	Korea (Republic) (South)	RoK	Taiwan	RoC
Congo	Con	Kuwait	Kwt	Tanzania	Tan
Costa Rica	CR	Laos	Lao	Thailand	Tld
Cuba	Cub	Lebanon	Leb	Togo	Tog
Cyprus	Cyp	Liberia	Lbr	Tonga	Ton
Czechoslovakia	Cz	Libya	Lby	Trinidad and Tobago	TT
Denmark	Den	Madagascar	Mad	Tunisia	Tun
Dominican Republic	DR	Malawi	Mlw	Turkey	Tur
Ecuador	Ecu	Malaysia	Mly	Union of Soviet Socialist Republics	USSR
Egypt	Egy	Malta	Mlt	United Arab Emirates	UAE
Equatorial Guinea	EqG	Mauritania	Mtn	United Kingdom	UK
El Salvador	ElS	Mauritius	Mrt	United States of America	USA
Ethiopia	Eth	Mexico	Mex	Uganda	Uga
Fiji	Fij	Montserrat	Mnt	Uruguay	Uru
Finland	Fin	Morocco	Mor	Venezuela	Ven
France	Fra	Netherlands	Nld	Viet-Nam	Vtn
Gabon	Gab	New Zealand	NZ	Virgin Isles	VI
Gambia	Gam	Nicaragua	Nic	Yemen Arab Republic (North)	YAR
Germany, Democratic Republic	GDR	Nigeria	Nig	Yemen, People's Democratic Republic (South)	YPDR
Germany, Federal Republic	GFR	Norway	Nor	Yugoslavia	Yug
Ghana	Gha	Oman	Omn	Zaire	Zai
Greece	Gre	Pakistan	Pak	Zambia	Zam
Grenada	Gra	Panama	Pan	Zanzibar	Zan

Pennant No.	Ship Name	Type	Country	Pennant No.	Ship Name	Type	Country
1	Tahchin	FF	Tld	D 03	Santander	DD	Col
1	Brooke	FFG	USA	D 03	Presidente Velasco Ibarra	FF	Ecu
1	Glover	AGFF	USA	4	General Belgrano	CL	Arg
1	Raleigh	LPD	USA	4	Nassau	LHA	USA
1	Tarawa	LHA	USA	4	Austin	LPD	USA
B 1	Durango	FF	Mex	4	Talbot	FFG	USA
D 1	Hercules	DD	Arg	4	Lawrence	DDG	USA
DD 1	Hsiang Yang	DD	RoC	LHA4	Nassau	LHA	USA
D 1	25 De Julio	FF	Ecu	PS 4	Rajah Lakandula	FF	Plp
DE 1	Uruguay	FF	Uru	04	Latorre	CL	Chi
PF 1	Montevideo	PF	Uru	5	Nueve de Julio	CL	Arg
A 01	Ethiopia	FF	Eth	5	Tapi	FF	Tld
01	Aetos	FF	Gre	5	Da Nang	LHA	USA
01	Adelaide	FFG	Aust	5	Ogden	LPD	USA
D 01	Moran Valverde	FF	Ecu	5	Richard L. Page	FFG	USA
F 01	Dat Assawari	FFG	Lby	5	Claude V. Ricketts	DDG	USA
IE 01	Cuauthemoc	DD	Mex	5	Oklahoma City	CG	USA
PA 01	Dedalo	CVH	Spn	5	Da Nang	LHA	USA
2	Prasae	FF	Tld	D 5	Artemiz	DDGS	Iran
2	Ramsey	FFG	USA	DD 5	Yuen Yang	DD	RoC
2	Charles F. Adams	DDG	USA	05	Veinte De Julio	DD	Col
2	Iwo Jima	LPH	USA	IB 05	Tehuantepec	FF	Mex
2	Vancouver	LPD	USA	6	Khirirat	FF	Tld
2	Saipan	LHA	USA	6	Duluth	LPD	USA
D 2	Santissima Trinidad	DD	Arg	6	Julius A. Furer	FFG	USA
DD 2	Heng Yang	DD	RoC	6	Barney	DDG	USA
V 2	25 De Mayo	CVS	Arg	6	Providence	CG	USA
D 2	Presidente Alfaro	FF	Ecu	DD 6	Huei Yang	DD	RoC
DE 2	Artigas	FF	Uru	06	Condell	FFG	Chi
02	Canberra	FFG	Aust	06	Siete De Agosto	DD	Col
D 02	Presidente Alfaro	FF	Ecu	06	Aspis	DD	Gre
02	O'Higgins	CL	Chi	IB 06	Usumacinta	FF	Mex
D 02	Caldas	DD	Col	IA 06	Como Manuel Azueta	FF	Mex
D 02	Devonshire	DLGH	UK	7	Makut Rajakumarn	FF	Tld
IB 02	Coahuila	PF	Mex	7	Cleveland	LPD	USA
IE 02	Cuitlahuac	DD	Mex	7	Henry B. Wilson	DDG	USA
3	Pin Klao	FF	Tld	7	Springfield	CG	USA
3	Schofield	FFG	USA	7	Guadalcanal	LPH	USA
3	John King	DDG	USA	7	Oliver Hazard Perry	FFG	USA
3	Belleau Wood	LHA	USA	DD 7	Fu Yang	DD	RoC
3	Okinawa	LPH	USA	E 7	President Bourguiba	FF	Tur
D 3	Pres. Velasco Ibarra	FF	Ecu	PS 7	Andres Bonifacio	FF	Plp
DD 3	Hua Yang	DD	RoC	O7	Lynch	FFG	Chi
DE 3	18 De Julio	FF	Uru	8	McInerney	FFG	USA
LHA3	Belleau Wood	LHA	USA	8	Dubuque	LPD	USA
03	Prat	CL	Chi	8	Lynde McCormick	DDG	USA

Pennant No.	Ship Name	Type	Country	Pennant No.	Ship Name	Type	Country
DD 8	Kwei Yang	DD	RoC	J 18	Halland	DD	Swe
IB 08	Chihuahua	FF	Mex	19	Almirante Williams	DDG	Chi
PS 8	Gregorio de Pilar	FF	Plp	19	Blue Ridge	LCC	USA
R 08	Bulwark	LPH	UK	19	Tattnall	DDG	USA
08	Vendetta	DD	Aust	19	Dale	CG	USA
9	Guam	LPH	USA	D 19	Glamorgan	DLGH	UK
9	Denver	LPD	USA	DD 19	Kuen Yang	DD	RoC
9	Towers	DDG	USA	J 19	Småland	DD	Swe
9	Long Beach	CGN	USA	20	Almirante Brown	DD	Arg
DD 9	Chiang Yang	DD	RoC	20	Bennington	CVS	USA
PS 9	Diego Silang	FF	Plp	20	Mount Whitney	LCC	USA
R 09	Ark Royal	CV	UK	20	Donner	LSD	USA
10	Albany	CG	USA	20	Goldsborough	DDG	USA
10	Juneau	LPD	USA	20	Richmond K. Turner	CG	USA
10	Sampson	DDG	USA	C 20	Tiger	CL	UK
10	Duncan	FFG	USA	D 20	Almirante Brown	DD	Arg
10	Tripoli	LPH	USA	DD 20	Lao Yang	DD	RoC
DD 10	Po Yang	DD	RoC	D 20	Fife	DLGH	UK
F 10	Aurora	FFGH	UK	J 20	Ostergotland	DD	Swe
L 10	Fearless	LPD	UK	21	Espora	DD	Arg
PS 10	Francisco Dagahoy	FF	Plp	21	Melbourne	CVS	Aust
11	Vampire	DD	Aust	21	Cochrane	DDG	USA
11	Port Said	FF	Egy	21	Gridley	CG	USA
11	Intrepid	CVS	USA	D 21	Espora	DD	Arg
11	Chicago	CG	USA	D 21	Inhauma	DD	Brz
11	Coronado	LPD	USA	D 21	Lepanto	DD	Spn
11	Sellers	DDG	USA	D 21	Norfolk	DLGH	UK
11	New Orleans	LPH	USA	D 21	Falcon	DD	Ven
11	Split	DD	Yug	D 21	Carabobo	DD	Ven
A 11	Minas Gerais	CVS	Brz	DD 21	Liao Yang	DD	RoC
D 11	Nueva Esparta	DD	Ven	J 21	Södermanland	DD	Swe
DD 11	Dang Yang	DD	RoC	22	Rosales	DD	Arg
F 11	Jamuna	FF (survey)	Ind	22	Benjamin Stoddert	DDG	USA
F 11	Visby	DD	Swe	22	England	CG	USA
F 11	Almirante Clemente	FF	Ven	D 22	Rosales	DD	Arg
L 11	Intrepid	LPD	UK	D 22	Jaceguay	DD	Brz
R 11	Vikrant	CVS	Ind	D 22	Almirante Ferrandiz	DD	Spn
12	Shreveport	LPD	USA	D 22	Falcon	DD	Ven
12	Robison	DDG	USA	J 22	Gästrikland	DD	Swe
12	Inchon	LPH	USA	23	Almirante Domecq Garcia	DD	Arg
D 12	Kent	DLGH	UK	23	Richard E. Byrd	DDG	USA
D 12	Zulia	DD	Ven	23	Halsey	CG	USA
DD 12	Chien Yang	DD	RoC	D 23	Almirante Domecq Garcia	DD	Arg
F 12	Sundsval	DD	Swe	D 23	Frontin	DD	Brz
F 12	Achilles	FFGH	UK	D 23	Almirante Valdes	DD	Spn
F 12	Gen. José Trinidad Moran	FF	Ven	D 23	Bristol	DLG	UK
R 12	Hermes	LPH	UK	J 23	Halsingland	DD	Swe
13	Nashville	LPD	USA	24	Almirante Storni	DD	Arg
13	Hoel	DDG	USA	24	Waddell	DDG	USA
D 13	Gen. Juan Jose Flores	FF	Ven	24	Reeves	CG	USA
F 13	Halsingborg	FF	Swe	D 24	Almirante Storni	DD	Arg
14	Blanco Encalada	DD	Chi	D 24	Alcala Galiano	DD	Spn
14	Trenton	LPD	USA	F 24	Rahmat	FF	Mly
14	Buchanan	DDG	USA	25	Bainbridge	CGN	USA
DD 14	Lo Yang	DD	RoC	D 25	Segui	DD	Arg
F 14	Kalmar	FF	Swe	D 25	Marcilio Diaz	DD	Brz
F 14	Leopard	FF	UK	D 25	Jorge Juan	DD	Spn
F 14	Almirante Brion	FF	Ven	F 25	Bayandor	PF	Iran
15	Cochrane	DD	Chi	26	Bouchard	DD	Arg
15	Cordoba	DT	Col	26	Serrano	PF	Chi
15	Ponce	LPD	USA	26	Belknap	CG	USA
15	Berkeley	DDG	USA	26	Tortuga	LSD	USA
DD 15	Lao Yang	DD	RoC	D 26	Bouchard	DD	Arg
DT 15	Cordoba	FF	Col	D 26	Mariz E. Barros	DD	Brz
F 15	Euryalus	FFGH	UK	F 26	Naghdi	PF	Iran
16	Ministero Zenteno	DD	Chi	27	Py	DD	Arg
16	Boyaca	FF	Col	27	Orella	PF	Chi
16	Velos	DD	Gre	27	Josephus Daniels	CG	USA
16	Cabildo	LSD	USA	27	Whetstone	LSD	USA
16	Joseph Strauss	DDG	USA	D 27	Py	DD	Arg
16	Lexington	CVT	USA	D 27	Para	DD	Brz
16	Leahy	CG	USA	F 27	Lynx	FF	UK
D 16	London	DLGH	UK	PF 27	Tai Yuan	DD	RoC
DE 16	Boyaca	FF	Col	28	Thyella	DD	Gre
F 16	Diomede	FFGH	UK	28	Wainwright	CG	USA
F 16	Umar Farooq	FF	Ban	28	Thomaston	LSD	USA
F 16	Oland	FF	Swe	D 28	Paraiba	DD	Brz
17	Ministero Portales	DD	Chi	F 28	Kahnamuie	PF	Iran
17	Conyngham	DDG	USA	28	Cleopatra	FFGH	UK
17	Harry E. Yarnell	CG	USA	29	Uribe	PF	Chi
DD 17	Nan Yang	DD	RoC	29	Jouett	CG	USA
F 17	Uppland	FF	Swe	29	Plymouth Rock	LSD	USA
18	Almirante Riveros	DDG	Chi	D 29	Buena Piedra	DD	Arg
18	Colonial	LSD	USA	D 29	Parana	DD	Brz
18	Semmes	DDG	USA	30	Horne	CG	USA
18	Worden	CG	USA	30	Fort Snelling	LSD	USA
D 18	Antrim	DLGH	UK	D 30	Pernambuco	DD	Brz
DD 18	An Yang	DD	RoC	31	Ierax	FF	Gre
F 18	Galatea	FFGH	UK	31	Galicia	LSD	Spn

Pennant No.	Ship Name	Type	Country	Pennant No.	Ship Name	Type	Country
31	Bon Homme Richard	CVA	USA	F 43	Liberal	DDH	Brz
31	Sterett	CG	USA	F 43	Torquay	FF	UK
31	Decatur	DDG	USA	PF 43	Chung Shan	FF	RoC
31	Point Defiance	LSD	USA	44	William V. Pratt	DDG	USA
D 31	Piaui	DD	Brz	F 44	Independencia	DDH	Brz
F 31	Descubierta	FF	Spn	45	Yarra	FF	Aust
F 31	Brahamaputra	FF	Ind	45	Dewey	DDG	USA
D 32	Santa Catarina	DD	Brz	F 45	União	DDH	Brz
32	William H. Standley	CG	USA	F 45	Minerva	FFGH	UK
32	John Paul Jones	DDG	USA	46	Parramatta	FF	Aust
32	Spiegel Grove	LSD	USA	46	Preble	DDG	USA
D 32	General Jose De Austria	FF	Ven	F 46	Kistna	FF	Ind
F 32	Nilgiri	FF	Ind	F 47	Danae	FFGH	UK
F 32	Diana	FF	Spn	48	Stuart	FF	Aust
F 32	Salisbury	FF	UK	49	Derwent	FF	Aust
PF 32	Yu Shan	FF	RoC	50	Swan	FF	Aust
33	Fox	CG	USA	51	Artemiz	DD	Iran
33	Parsons	DDG	USA	51	Meliton Carvajal	FF	Per
33	Alamo	LSD	USA	D 51	Liniers	DD	Spn
D 33	Maranhao	DD	Brz	D 52	Alava	DD	Spn
D 33	Almirante Jose Garcia	FF	Ven	F 52	Juno	FFGH	UK
F 33	Himgiri	FF	Ind	53	Torrens	FF	Aust
F 33	Infanta Elena	FF	Spn	54	Leon	FF	Gre
PF 33	Hua Shau	FF	RoC	F 54	Hardy	FF	UK
34	Biddle	CG	USA	F 55	Waikato	FFGH	NZ
34	Somers	DDG	USA	56	Lonchi	DD	Gre
34	Oriskany	CV	USA	F 56	Argonaut	FFGH	UK
34	Hermitage	LSD	USA	F 57	Andromeda	FFGH	UK
D 34	Mato Grosso	DD	Brz	F 58	Hermione	FFGH	UK
F 34	Udaygiri	FF	Ind	59	Forrestal	CV	USA
F 34	Infanta Cristina	FF	Spn	A 59	Deutschland	CLT	GFR
F 34	Wen Shan	FF	RoC	F 59	Chichester	FF	UK
35	Mitscher	DDG	USA	60	Saratoga	CV	USA
35	Monticello	LSD	USA	C 60	Mysore	CL	Ind
35	Truxtun	CGN	USA	F 60	Jupiter	FFGH	UK
D 35	Alagoas	DD	Brz	61	Castilla	FF	Per
D 36	Sergipe	DD	Brz	61	Iowa	BB	USA
F 35	Dunagiri	FF	Ind	61	Ranger	CV	USA
PF 35	Fu Shan	FF	RoC	61	Babr	DDG	Iran
36	Anchorage	LSD	USA	D 61	Churruca	DD	Spn
36	California	CGN	USA	F 61	Atrevida	FF	Spn
36	John S. McCain	DDG	USA	62	Independence	CV	USA
F 36	Taragiri	FF	Ind	62	New Jersey	BB	USA
F 36	Whitby	FF	UK	62	Palang	DDG	Iran
PF 36	Lu Shan	FF	RoC	D 62	Gravina	DD	Spn
37	Portland	LSD	USA	F 62	Princesa	FF	Spn
37	South Carolina	CGN	USA	63	Navarinon	DD	Gre
37	Farragut	DDG	USA	63	Rodriquez	FF	Per
D 37	Rio Grande Do Norte	DD	Brz	63	Kitty Hawk	CV	USA
F 37	Vindhyagiri	FF	Ind	63	Missouri	BB	USA
F 37	Jaguar	FF	UK	D 63	Mendez Nuñez	DD	Spn
PF 37	Shoa Shan	FF	RoC	64	Constellation	CV	USA
38	Perth	DDG	Aust	64	Wisconsin	BB	USA
38	Shangri-La	CVS	USA	D 64	Langara	DD	Spn
38	Pensacola	LSD	USA	F 64	Nautilus	FF	Spn
38	Luce	DDG	USA	65	Enterprise	CVN	USA
38	Virginia	CGN	USA	D 65	Blas De Lezo	DD	Spn
D 38	Espirito Santo	DD	Brz	F 65	Villa Bilbao	FF	Spn
D 38	Intrepido	FF	Spn	66	America	CV	USA
F 38	Arethusa	FFGH	UK	67	Panthir	FF	Gre
PF 38	Tai Shan	FF	RoC	67	John F. Kennedy	CV	USA
39	Hobart	DDG	Aust	68	Nimitz	CVN	USA
39	Mount Vernon	LSD	USA	P 68	Arnala	FFL	Ind
39	Macdonough	DDG	USA	69	Dwight D. Eisenhower	CVN	USA
39	Texas	CGN	USA	F 69	Bacchante	FFGH	UK
F 39	Naiad	FFGH	UK	P 69	Androth	FFL	Ind
40	Mississippi	CGN	USA	70	Carl Vinson	CVN	USA
40	Fort Fisher	LSD	USA	70	Canberra	CA	USA
40	Coontz	DDG	USA	F 70	Apollo	FFGH	UK
40	Mississippi	CGN	USA	71	Villar	DD	Per
F 40	Niteroi	DDH	Brz	71	Saam	FF	Iran
F 40	Sirius	FFGH	UK	F 71	Baleares	FFG	Spn
41	Brisbane	DDG	Aust	F 71	Scylla	FFGH	UK
41	Arkansas	CGN	USA	72	Zaal	FF	Iran
41	King	DDG	USA	72	Guise	DD	Per
41	Midway	CV	USA	F 72	Andalucia	FFG	Spn
D 41	Oquendo	DD	Spn	F 72	Ariadne	FFGH	UK
F 41	Defensora	DDH	Brz	73	Rostam	FF	Iran
F 41	Vincent Yanez Pinzon	FF	Spn	73	Chung Nam	FF	RoK
42	Mahan	DDG	USA	73	St Paul	CA	USA
D 42	Roger De Lauria	DD	Spn	73	Palacios	DDGS	Per
F 42	Constituição	DDH	Brz	F 73	Cataluña	FFG	Spn
F 42	Legazpi	FF	Spn	P 73	Anjadip	FFL	Ind
F 42	Phoebe	FFGH	UK	74	Ferré	DDGS	Per
PF 42	Kang Shan	FF	RoC	74	Faramaz	FF	Iran
43	Rashid	FF	Egy	C 74	Delhi	CL	Ind
43	Dahlgren	DDG	USA	F 74	Asturias	FFG	Spn
43	Coral Sea	CV	USA	P 74	Andaman	FFL	Ind
D 43	Marques De La Ensenada	DD	Spn	F 75	Extremadura	FFG	Spn

Pennant No.	Ship Name	Type	Country	Pennant No.	Ship Name	Type	Country
F 75	Charybdis	FFGH	UK	134	Des Moines	CA	USA
P 75	Amini	FFL	Ind	F 137	Beas	FF	Ind
76	Datu Kalantiaw	FF	Plp	139	Salem	CA	USA
F 76	Hang Tuah	FF	Mly	F 139	Betwa	FF	Ind
P 77	Kamorta	FF	Ind	F 140	Talwar	FF	Ind
P 78	Kadmath	FF	Ind	141	Haruna	DDH	Jap
P 79	Kiltan	FF	Ind	142	Hiei	DDH	Jap
D 80	Sheffield	DDGH	UK	F 143	Trishul	FF	Ind
P 80	Kavaratti	FF	Ind	F 144	Kirpan	FF	Ind
81	Kyong Nam	PF	RoK	F 145	President Pretorius	FF	SA
81	Almirante Grau	CL	Per	F 146	Kuthar	FF	Ind
F 81	Descubierta	FF	Spn	F 147	President Steyn	FF	SA
P 81	Katchal	FF	Ind	148	Newport News	CA	USA
82	Ah San	PF	RoK	F 148	Taranaki	FF	NZ
82	Coronel Bolognesi	CL	Per	F 150	President Kruger	FF	SA
P 82	Kanjar	FF	Ind	L 153	Nafkratoussa	LSD	Gre
83	Ung Po	PF	RoK	160	Alamgir	DD	Pak
83	Capitan Quiñones	CL	Per	161	Akizuki	DD	Jap
P 83	Amindivi	FF	Ind	161	Badr	DD	Pak
84	Babur	CL	Pak	162	Teruzuki	DD	Jap
84	Aguirre	CL	Per	162	Jahangir	DD	Pak
85	Sfendoni	DD	Gre	163	Amatsukaze	DDG	Jap
85	Kyong Puk	PF	RoK	164	Takatsuki	DD	Jap
F 85	Keppel	FF	UK	164	Shah Jahan	DD	Pak
86	Jonnam	PF	RoK	165	Kikuzuki	DD	Jap
D 86	Birmingham	DDGH	UK	D 165	Tariq	DD	Pak
87	Chi Ju	PF	RoK	166	Mochizuki	DD	Jap
D 87	Newcastle	DDGH	UK	D 166	Taimur	DD	Pak
F 87	Nigeria	FF	Nig	167	Nagatsuki	DD	Jap
F 88	Broadsword	FFG	UK	168	Tachikaze	DDG	Jap
D 88	Glasgow	DDGH	UK	169	Asakaze	DDG	Jap
90	Kwang Ju	DD	RoK	F 169	Amazon	FFGH	UK
91	Chung Mu	DD	RoK	F 170	Antelope	FFGH	UK
92	Seoul	DD	RoK	D 171	Z 2	DD	GFR
D 92	Godavari	FF	Ind	F 171	Active	FFGH	UK
93	Pusan	DD	RoK	D 172	Z 3	DD	GFR
95	Chung Buk	DD	RoK	F 172	Ambuscade	FFGH	UK
F 95	Sutlej	FF (survey)	Ind	F 173	Arrow	FFGH	UK
96	Jeong Buk	DD	RoK	F 174	Alacrity	FFGH	UK
97	Dae Gu	DD	RoK	F 176	Avenger	FFGH	UK
R 97	Jeanne D'Arc	CHV	Fra	F 177	Kamorta	FF	Ind
98	In Cheon	DD	RoK	D 178	Z 4	DD	GFR
R 98	Clemenceau	CVS	Fra	P 179	Z 5	DD	GFR
99	Taejon	DD	RoK	D 181	Hamburg	DD	GFR
C 99	Blake	CL	UK	D 182	Schleswig Holstein	DD	GFR
F 99	Lincoln	FF	UK	D 183	Bayern	DD	GFR
R 99	Foch	CVS	Fra	D 184	Hessen	DD	GFR
F 101	Yarmouth	FFH	UK	F 184	Ardent	FFGH	UK
101	Harukaze	DD	Jap	D 185	Lütjens	DDG	GFR
102	Yukikaze	DD	Jap	F 185	Avenger	FFGH	UK
103	Ayanami	DD	Jap	D 186	Mölders	DDG	GFR
F 103	Lowestoft	FFH	UK	D 187	Rommel	DDG	GFR
104	Isonami	DD	Jap	202	Ikazuchi	FF	Jap
F 104	Dido	FFGH	UK	203	Inazuma	FF	Jap
105	Uranami	DD	Jap	204	"Riga" Class	FF	CPR
106	Shikinami	DD	Jap	205	"Riga" Class	FF	CPR
F 106	Brighton	FFH	UK	205	St. Laurent	DDH	Can
107	Murasame	DD	Jap	206	"Riga" Class	FF	CPR
F 107	Rothesay	FFH	UK	206	Saguenay	DDH	Can
108	Yudachi	DD	Jap	207	"Riga" Class	FF	CPR
D 108	Cardiff	DDGH	UK	207	Skeena	DDH	Can
F 108	Londonderry	FFH	UK	209	Kiangnan	FF	CPR
109	Harusame	DD	Jap	210	Themistocles	DD	Gre
F 109	Leander	FFGH	UK	211	Miaoulis	DD	Gre
110	Takanami	DD	Jap	211	Isuzu	FF	Jap
F 110	Kaveri	FF	Ind	212	Kanaris	DD	Gre
111	Oonami	DD	Jap	212	Mogami	FF	Jap
111	Otago	FF	NZ	213	Kontouriotis	DD	Gre
112	Makinami	DD	Jap	213	Kitakami	FF	Jap
113	Yamagumo	DD	Jap	214	Sachtouris	DD	Gre
F 113	Falmouth	FFH	UK	214	Ooi	FF	Jap
114	Makigumo	DD	Jap	215	Chikugo	FF	Jap
F 114	Ajax	FFGH	UK	APD 215	Tien Shan	FF	RoC
115	Asagumo	DD	Jap	216	Ayase	FF	Jap
F 115	Berwick	FFH	UK	217	Mikuma	FF	Jap
116	Minegumo	DD	Jap	F 217	Milanian	PF	Iran
117	Natsugumo	DD	Jap	218	Tokachi	FF	Jap
F 117	Ashanti	FFH	UK	219	Iwase	FF	Jap
118	Murakumo	DD	Jap	220	Chitose	FF	Jap
D 118	Coventry	DDGH	UK	F 220	Köln	FF	GFR
119	Aokumo	DD	Jap	221	Niyodo	FF	Jap
F 119	Eskimo	FFH	UK	F 221	Emden	FF	GFR
120	Akigumo	DD	Jap	222	Teshio	FF	Jap
F 122	Gurkha	FFH	UK	F 222	Augsburg	FF	GFR
F 124	Zulu	FFH	UK	223	Yoshino	FF	Jap
F 125	Mohawk	FFH	UK	F 223	Karlsrühe	FF	GFR
F 126	Plymouth	FFH	UK	224	Kumano	FF	Jap
F 127	Penelope	FFGH	UK	F 224	Lübek	FF	GFR
F 129	Rhyl	FFH	UK	225	Noshiro	FF	Jap
F 131	Nubian	FFH	UK	F 225	Braunschweig	FF	GFR
F 133	Tartar	FFH	UK				

Pennant No.	Ship Name	Type	Country	Pennant No.	Ship Name	Type	Country
229	Ottawa	DDH	Can	F 482	Com Roberto Ivens	FF	Por
230	Margaree	DDH	Can	F 483	Com Sacadura Cabral	FF	Por
231	"Kiangnan" class	FF	CPR	F 484	Augusto De Castilho	FF	Por
232	"Kiangnan" class	FF	CPR	F 485	Honorio Barreto	FF	Por
233	"Kiangnan" class	FF	CPR	525	Port Said	FF	Egy
233	Fraser	DDH	Can	F 540	Pietro De Cristofaro	PF	Ita
F 233	Nilgiri	FFGH	Ind	F 541	Umberto Grosso	PF	Ita
234	Assiniboine	DDH	Can	F 542	Aquila	PF	Ita
F 234	Himgiri	FFGH	Ind	F 543	Albatros	PF	Ita
236	Gatineau	DD	Can	F 544	Alcione	PF	Ita
240-246	"Luta" Class	DD	CPR	F 545	Airone	PF	Ita
250	Iman Bondjol	PF	Indo	F 546	Licio Visintini	PF	Ita
251	Surapati	PF	Indo	C 550	Vittorio Veneto	CGH	Ita
252	Pattimura	PF	Indo	D 550	Ardito	DDG	Ita
253	Sultan Hasanudin	PF	Indo	D 551	Audace	DDG	Ita
257	Restigouche	DD	Can	F 551	Canopo	FF	Ita
258	Kootenay	DD	Can	C 553	Andrea Doria	DLGH	Ita
259	Terra Nova	DD	Can	F 553	Castore	FF	Ita
260	Tippu Sultan	FF	Pak	C 554	Caio Duilio	DLGH	Ita
261	Mackenzie	DD	Can	F 554	Centauro	FF	Ita
261	Tughril	FF	Pak	555	Tariq	FF	Egy
262	Saskatchewan	DD	Can	D 555	Geniere	DD	Ita
263	Yukon	DD	Can	F 555	Cigno	FF	Ita
264	Qu'Appelle	DD	Can	D 558	Impetuoso	DD	Ita
265	Annapolis	DDH	Can	D 559	Indomito	DD	Ita
266	Nipigon	DDH	Can	D 562	San Giorgio	DD	Ita
275	Warszawa	DDG	Pol	F 564	Lupo	FF	Ita
D 278	Jan Van Riebeeck	FF	SA	F 565	Sagittario	FF	Ita
280	Iroquois	DDH	Can	F 566	Perseo	FF	Ita
281	Huron	DDH	Can	F 567	Orsa	FF	Ita
282	Athabaskan	DDH	Can	D 570	Impavido	DDG	Ita
283	Algonquin	DDH	Can	F 570	Maestrale	FF	Ita
F 300	Oslo	FF	Nor	D 571	Intrepido	DDG	Ita
F 301	Bergen	FF	Nor	F 571	Grecale	FF	Ita
F 302	Trondheim	FF	Nor	F 572	Libeccio	FF	Ita
F 303	Stavanger	FF	Nor	F 573	Scirocco	FF	Ita
F 304	Narvik	FF	Nor	F 574	Alisco	FF	Ita
F 310	Sleipner	FF	Nor	F 575	Euro	FF	Ita
F 311	Aeger	FF	Nor	F 580	Alpino	FF	Ita
D 340	Istanbul	DD	Tur	F 581	Carabiniere	FF	Ita
F 340	Beskytteren	FFH	Den	F 590	Aldebaran	FF	Ita
341	Samadikun	FF	Indo	F 593	Carlo Bergamini	FF	Ita
D 341	Izmir	DD	Tur	F 594	Virginio Fasan	FF	Ita
342	Martadinata	FF	Indo	F 595	Carlo Margottini	FF	Ita
D 342	Izmit	DD	Tur	F 596	Luigi Rizzo	FF	Ita
343	Ngurah Rai	FF	Indo	D 602	Suffren	DLG	Fra
D 343	Iskenderun	DD	Tur	D 603	Duquesne	DLG	Fra
344	Monginsidi	FF	Indo	D 609	Aconit	DD	Fra
D 344	Içel	DD	Tur	D 610	Tourville	DDG	Fra
F 344	Bellona	PF	Den	C 611	Colbert	CLG	Fra
F 345	Diana	PF	Den	D 611	Duguay-Trouin	DDG	Fra
F 346	Flora	PF	Den	D 612	De Grasse	DDG	Fra
F 347	Triton	PF	Den	D 622	Kersaint	DDG	Fra
F 348	Hvidbjornen	FFH	Den	D 624	Bouvet	DDG	Fra
F 349	Vaedderen	FFH	Den	D 625	Dupetit Thouars	DDG	Fra
F 350	Ingolf	FFH	Den	D 627	Maille Brezé	DDG	Fra
351	Jos Sudarso	FF	Indo	D 628	Vauquelin	DDG	Fra
F 351	Fylla	FFH	Den	D 629	D'Estrées	DDG	Fra
D 352	Gayret	DD	Tur	D 630	Du Chayla	DDG	Fra
F 352	Peder Skram	FF	Den	D 631	Casabianca	DDG	Fra
D 353	Adatepe	DD	RoC	D 632	Guépratte	DDG	Fra
F 353	Herluf Trolle	FF	Den	D 633	Duperré	DDG	Fra
D 354	Kocatepe	DD	Tur	D 634	La Bourdonnais	DDG	Fra
F 354	Niels Juel	FF	Den	D 635	Forbin	DDG	Fra
355	Iman Bondjol	FF	Indo	D 636	Tartu	DDG	Fra
D 355	Tinaztepe	DD	Tur	D 638	La Galissonière	DD	Fra
F 355	Olfert Fischer	FF	Den	D 640	Georges Leygues	DDGH	Fra
356	Surapati	FF	Indo	D 641	Dupleix	DDGH	Fra
D 356	Zafer	DD	Tur	D 642	Montcalm	DDGH	Fra
F 356	Peter Tordenskjold	FF	Den	D 643	Jean de Vienne	DDGH	Fra
357	Lambung Makurat	FF	Indo	714	William R. Rush	DD	USA
D 357	Muavenet	DD	Tur	715	Willian McWood	DD	USA
D 358	Berk	FF	Tur	718	Hamner	DD	USA
D 359	Peyk	FF	Tur	F 725	Victor Schoelcher	FF	Fra
360	Nuku	FF	Indo	F 726	Commandant Bory	FF	Fra
F 421	Canterbury	FFGH	NZ	F 727	Admiral Charner	FF	Fra
451	Mella	FF	DR	F 728	Doudart de Lagrée	FF	Fra
452	Gregorio Luperon	FF	DR	F 729	Balny	FF	Fra
453	Pedro Santana	FF	DR	F 733	Commandant Riviére	FF	Fra
462	Hayase	AM	Jap	F 740	Commandant Bourdais	FF	Fra
F 471	Antonio Enes	FF	Por	743	Southerland	DD	USA
F 472	Alm Pereira Da Silva	FF	Por	F 748	Protet	FF	Fra
F 473	Alm Gago Coutinho	FF	Por	F 749	Enseigne de Vaisseau Henry	FF	Fra
F 474	Alm Magalhaes Correia	FF	Por	763	William C. Lawe	DD	USA
F 475	Joao Coutinho	FF	Por	F 763	Le Boulonnais	FF	Fra
F 476	Jacinto Candido	FF	Por	F 765	Le Normand	FF	Fra
F 477	Gen. Pereira D'Eca	FF	Por	F 766	Le Picard	FF	Fra
F 480	Com Joao Belo	FF	Por	F 767	Le Gascon	FF	Fra
F 481	Com Hermenegildo Capelo	FF	Por	F 771	Le Savoyard	FF	Fra

Pennant No.	Ship Name	Type	Country
F 773	Le Basque	FF	Fra
F 774	L'Agenais	FF	Fra
F 775	Le Béarnais	FF	Fra
F 776	L'Alsacien	FF	Fra
F 777	Le Provencal	FF	Fra
F 778	Le Vendeen	FF	Fra
F 781	D'Estienne D'Orves	FF	Fra
F 782	Amyot D'Inville	FF	Fra
F 783	Drogou	FF	Fra
784	McKean	DD	USA
F 784	Detroyat	FF	Fra
785	Henderson	DD	USA
F 785	Jean Moulin	FF	Fra
F 786	Quartier Maitre Anquetil	FF	Fra
F 787	Commandant De Pimodan	FF	Fra
788	Hollister	DD	USA
F 788	Seconde Maitre Le Bihan	FF	Fra
F 790	Lieutenant de Vaisseau Lavallée	FF	Fra
F 792	Premier Maitre L'Her	FF	Fra
F 793	Commandant Blaison	FF	Fra
F 794	Enseigne de Vaisseau Jacoubet	FF	Fra
801	Pattimura	FF	Indo
F 801	Tromp	DDG	Nld
802	Sultan Hasanudin	FF	Indo
F 802	Van Speijk	FFGH	Nld
F 803	Van Galen	FFGH	Nld
F 804	Tjerk Hiddes	FFGH	Nld
F 805	Van Nes	FFGH	Nld
806	Higbee	DD	USA
F 806	De Ruyter	DDG	Nld
D 808	Holland	DDH	Nld
D 809	Zeeland	DDH	Nld
D 812	Friesland	DD	Nld
D 813	Gröningen	DD	Nld
D 814	Limburg	DD	Nld
F 814	Isaac Sweers	FFGH	Nld
D 815	Overijssel	DD	Nld
F 815	Evertsen	FFGH	Nld
D 816	Drenthe	DD	Nld
817	Corry	DD	USA
D 817	Utrecht	DD	Nld
D 818	Rotterdam	DD	Nld
D 819	Amsterdam	DD	Nld
821	Johnston	DD	USA
822	Robert H. McCard	DD	USA
825	Carpenter	DD	USA
826	Agerholm	DD	USA
827	Robert A. Owens	DD	USA
829	Myles C. Fox	DD	USA
835	Charles P. Cecil	DD	USA
842	Fiske	DD	USA
845	Baussell	DD	USA
862	Vogelgesang	DD	USA
863	Steinaker	DD	USA
864	Harold J. Ellison	DD	USA
866	Cone	DD	USA
871	Damato	DD	USA
873	Hawkins	DD	USA
876	Rogers	DD	USA
880	Dyess	DD	USA
883	Newman K. Perry	DD	USA
885	John R. Craig	DD	USA
886	Orleck	DD	USA
890	Meredith	DD	USA
F 910	Wielingen	FF	Bel
F 911	Westdiep	FF	Bel
F 912	Wanderlaar	FF	Bel
F 913	Westhinder	FF	Bel
931	Forrest Sherman	DD	USA
933	Barry	DD	USA
937	George F. Davis	DD	USA
938	Jonas Ingram	DD	USA
940	Manley	DD	USA
941	Du Pont	DD	USA
942	Bigelow	DD	USA
943	Blandy	DD	USA
944	Mullinnix	DD	USA
945	Hull	DD	USA
946	Edson	DD	USA
948	Morton	DD	USA
950	Richard S. Edwards	DD	USA
951	Turner Joy	DD	USA
951	Souya	ML	Jap
963	Spruance	DD	USA
964	Paul F. Foster	DD	USA
965	Kincaid	DD	USA
966	Hewitt	DD	USA
967	Elliott	DD	USA
968	Arthur W. Radford	DD	USA
969	Peterson	DD	USA
970	Caron	DD	USA
971	David R. Ray	DD	USA
972	Oldendorf	DD	USA
973	John Young	DD	USA
974	Comte De Grasse	DD	USA
975	O'Brien	DD	USA
976	Merrill	DD	USA
977	Brisco	DD	USA
978	Stump	DD	USA
979	Connolly	DD	USA
980	Moosburgger	DD	USA
981	John Hancock	DD	USA
982	Nicholson	DD	USA
983	John Rogers	DD	USA
984	Leftwich	DD	USA
985	Cushing	DD	USA
986	Harry W. Hill	DD	USA
987	O'Bannon	DD	USA
988	Thorn	DD	USA
989	Deyo	DD	USA
990	Ingersoll	DD	USA
991	Fife	DD	USA
992	Fletcher	DD	USA
1037	Bronstein	FF	USA
1038	McCloy	FF	USA
1040	Garcia	FF	USA
1041	Bradley	FF	USA
1043	Edward McDonnell	FF	USA
1044	Brumby	FF	USA
1045	Davidson	FF	USA
1047	Voge	FF	USA
1048	Sample	FF	USA
1049	Koelsch	FF	USA
1050	Albert David	FF	USA
1051	O'Callahan	FF	USA
1052	Knox	FF	USA
1053	Roark	FF	USA
1054	Gray	FF	USA
1055	Hepburn	FF	USA
1056	Connole	FF	USA
1057	Rathburne	FF	USA
1058	Meyerkord	FF	USA
1059	W. S. Sims	FF	USA
1060	Lang	FF	USA
1061	Patterson	FF	USA
1062	Whipple	FF	USA
1063	Reasoner	FF	USA
1064	Lockwood	FF	USA
1065	Stein	FF	USA
1066	Marvin Shields	FF	USA
1067	Francis Hammond	FF	USA
1068	Vreeland	FF	USA
1069	Bagley	FF	USA
1070	Downes	FF	USA
1071	Badger	FF	USA
1072	Blakely	FF	USA
1073	Robert E. Peary	FF	USA
1074	Harold E. Holt	FF	USA
1075	Trippe	FF	USA
1076	Fanning	FF	USA
1077	Ouellet	FF	USA
1078	Joseph Hewes	FF	USA
1079	Bowen	FF	USA
1080	Paul	FF	USA
1081	Aylwin	FF	USA
1082	Elmer Montgomery	FF	USA
1083	Cook	FF	USA
1084	McCandless	FF	USA
1085	Donald B. Beary	FF	USA
1086	Brewton	FF	USA
1087	Kirk	FF	USA
1088	Barbey	FF	USA
1089	Jesse L. Brown	FF	USA
1090	Ainsworth	FF	USA
1091	Miller	FF	USA
1092	Thomas S. Hart	FF	USA
1093	Capodanno	FF	USA
1094	Pharris	FF	USA
1095	Truett	FF	USA
1096	Valdez	FF	USA
1097	Moinester	FF	USA
1179	Newport	LST	USA
1180	Manitowoc	LST	USA
1181	Sumter	LST	USA
1182	Fresno	LST	USA
1183	Peoria	LST	USA

Pennant No.	Ship Name	Type	Country	Pennant No.	Ship Name	Type	Country
1184	Frederick	LST	USA	1193	Fairfax County	LST	USA
1185	Schenectady	LST	USA	1194	La Moure County	LST	USA
1186	Cayuga	LST	USA	1195	Barbour County	LST	USA
1187	Tuscaloosa	LST	USA	1196	Harlan County	LST	USA
1188	Saginaw	LST	USA	1197	Barnstable County	LST	USA
1189	San Bernardino	LST	USA	1198	Bristol County	LST	USA
1190	Boulder	LST	USA	3501	Katori	AGDE	Jap
1191	Racine	LST	USA	4201	Azuma	ATS	Jap
1192	Spartanburg County	LST	USA				

RECOGNITION SILHOUETTES

The following silhouettes are not to scale but are arranged in an order which is designed to make it easier to differentiate between the various classes; eg. ships with two funnels, ships with an island and no visible funnels, ships with one funnel and massive bridge-structure.

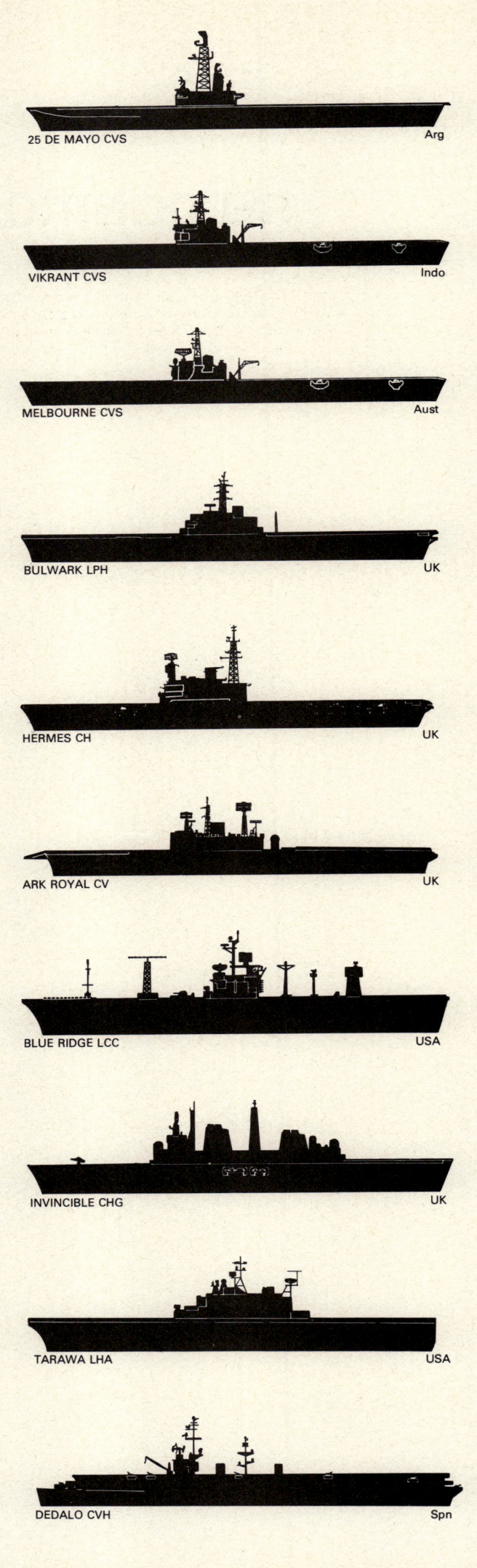

2 RECOGNITION SILHOUETTES

NIMITZ CVN — USA	25 DE MAYO CVS — Arg
ENTERPRISE CVN — USA	VIKRANT CVS — Indo
JOHN F. KENNEDY CV — USA	MELBOURNE CVS — Aust
KITTY HAWK CV — USA	BULWARK LPH — UK
SARATOGA CV — USA	HERMES CH — UK
FORRESTAL CV — USA	ARK ROYAL CV — UK
CORAL SEA CV — USA	BLUE RIDGE LCC — USA
CLEMENCEAU CVA — Fra	INVINCIBLE CHG — UK
IWO JIMA LPH — USA	TARAWA LHA — USA
MINAS GERAIS CVS — Brz	DEDALO CVH — Spn

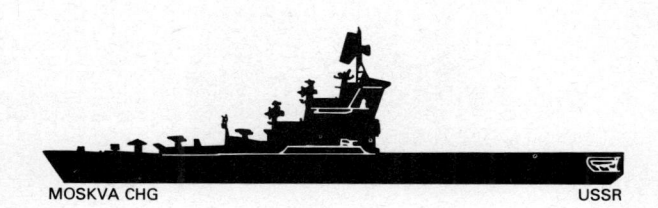

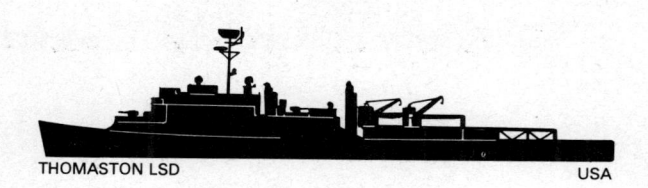

RECOGNITION SILHOUETTES 3

KIEV CVSG — USSR

MOSKVA CHG — USSR

VITTORIO VENETO CHG — Ita

NEWPORT LST — USA

THOMASTON LSD — USA

AUSTIN LPD — USA

ASHLAND LSD — RoC

JEANNE D'ARC CVH — Fra

CASA GRANDE/CABILDO LSD — Gre, RoC, Spa, USA

FEARLESS LPD — UK

ANCHORAGE LSD — USA

RALEIGH LPD — USA

4 RECOGNITION SILHOUETTES

LONG BEACH CGN — USA	TRUXTUN CGN — USA
KRESTA II CLG — USSR	GEORGE LEYGUES DDG — Fra
KRESTA I CLG — USSR	ALBANY CG — USA
VIRGINIA CGN — USA	WAINWRIGHT CG — USA
CALIFORNIA CGN — USA	BELKNAP CG — USA
TOURVILLE DDG — Fra	LEAHY CG — USA
SUFFREN DLG — Fra	TAKATSUKI DD — Jap
KNOX FF (unmodified) — USA	AUDACE DDG — Ita
ACONIT FF — Fra	
BAINBRIDGE CGN — USA	LUTJENS DDG — GFR

RECOGNITION SILHOUETTES 5

SALISBURY FF UK
Chichester has no main radar.

HALLAND DDG Swe

ALMIRANTE WILLIAMS DDG Chi

TIGER CLH UK

FERRE DDG Per

COLONY MOD CL Ind, Per

FRIESLAND DD Nld

ZEELAND DD Nld

TYPE 47 (ASW) DD Fra

PROVIDENCE CG USA

OKLAHOMA CITY CG USA

HALLAND MOD DD Col

GEARING FRAM II DD Tur

DANG YANG DD RoC

ALLEN M. SUMNER FRAM DDG Iran

ALLEN M. SUMNER FRAM DD, DDG Arg, Brz, Col, Gre, RoC, RoK, Tur, Ven

GEARING FRAM I DD Brz, Gre, RoC, Spn, Tur

GEARING FRAM I DD Brz, Spn, Tur, USA

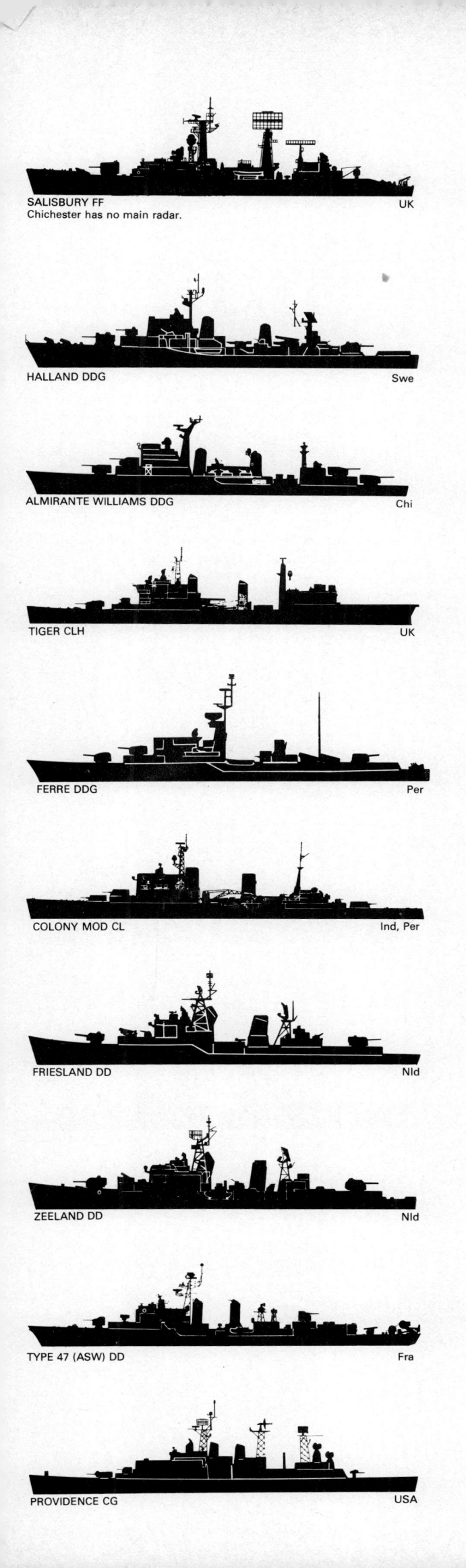

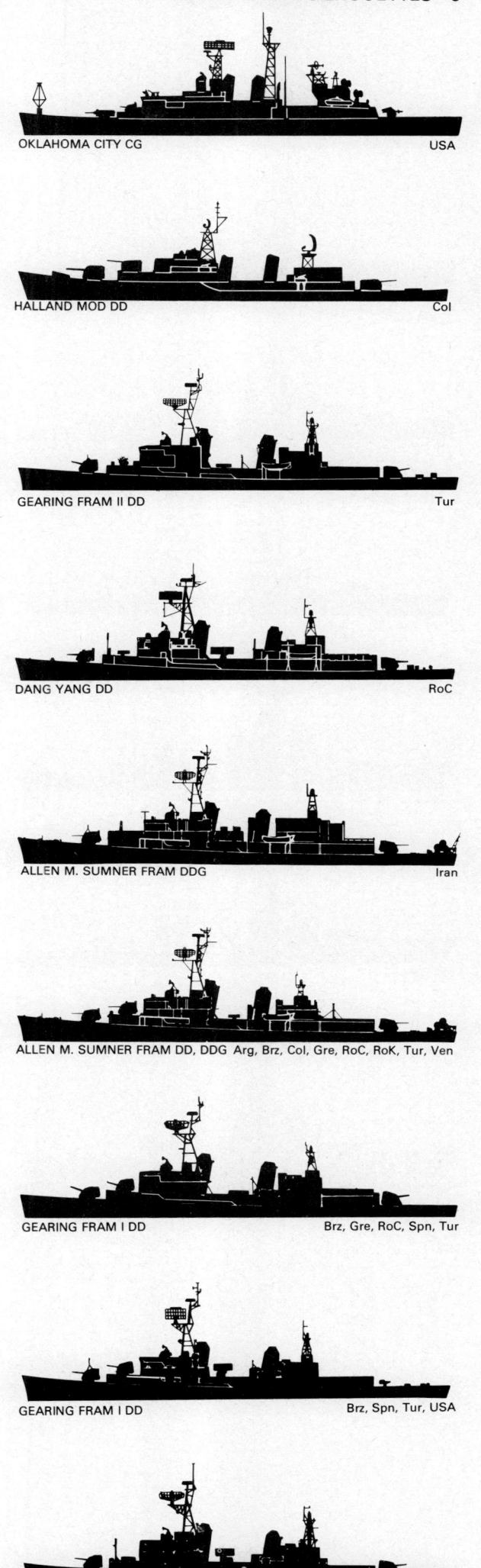

GEARING FRAM II DD (some have no Asroc) Arg, Gre, RoK

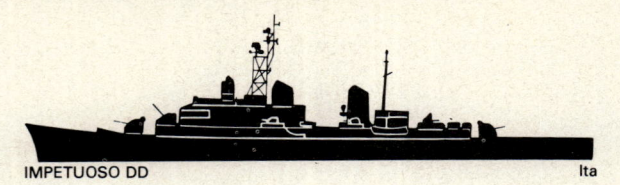

6 RECOGNITION SILHOUETTES

IMPETUOSO DD — Ita

BROOKLYN CL — Arg, Chi

DIDO MOD CL — Pak

AYANAMI DD — Jap

SAMADIKUN FF — Indo

KYNDA CLG — USSR

ANDREA DORIA DLG — Ita

BRISTOL DLG — UK

COUNTY DLGH — UK

COUNTY DLGH — UK

PEDER SKRAM FF — Den

OSTERGOTLAND DD — Swe

KANIN DDG — USSR

KOTLIN DDG — Pol, USSR

KRUPNY DDG — USSR

RECOGNITION SILHOUETTES 7

FARRAGUT DDG — USA

DECATUR DDG — USA

MITSCHER DDG — USA

MAHAN DDG — USA

KASHIN DLG — USSR

YAMAGUMO DD — Jap

KASHIN DLG — USSR

KILDIN MOD DDG — USSR

TYPE 47 DDG — Fra

KILDIN DDG — USSR

SPRUANCE DD — USA

DARING DD — Aust

HAMBURG DD — GFR

BARRY DD — USA

TYPE 53 DDG — Fra

KOTLIN DD — USSR

MURASAME DD — Jap

KOTLIN MOD DD — USSR

8 RECOGNITION SILHOUETTES

IMPAVIDO DDG — Ita	KOLA FF — USSR
ALMIRANTE GRAU CL (*Aguirre* differs) — Per	ALMIRANTE LATORRE CL — Chi
AKIZUKI DD — Jap	SAN GIORGIO DL — Ita
SVERDLOV CL — USSR	MANLEY DD — USA
SVERDLOV CLG — USSR	JONAS INGRAHAM DD — USA
SVERDLOV CLC — USSR	CARPENTER DD — USA
GEARING FRAM II DD — GFR, RoC	LUTA DDG — CPR
SKORY DD — Egy, Fin, Pol, USSR	SKORY MOD DD — Egy, USSR

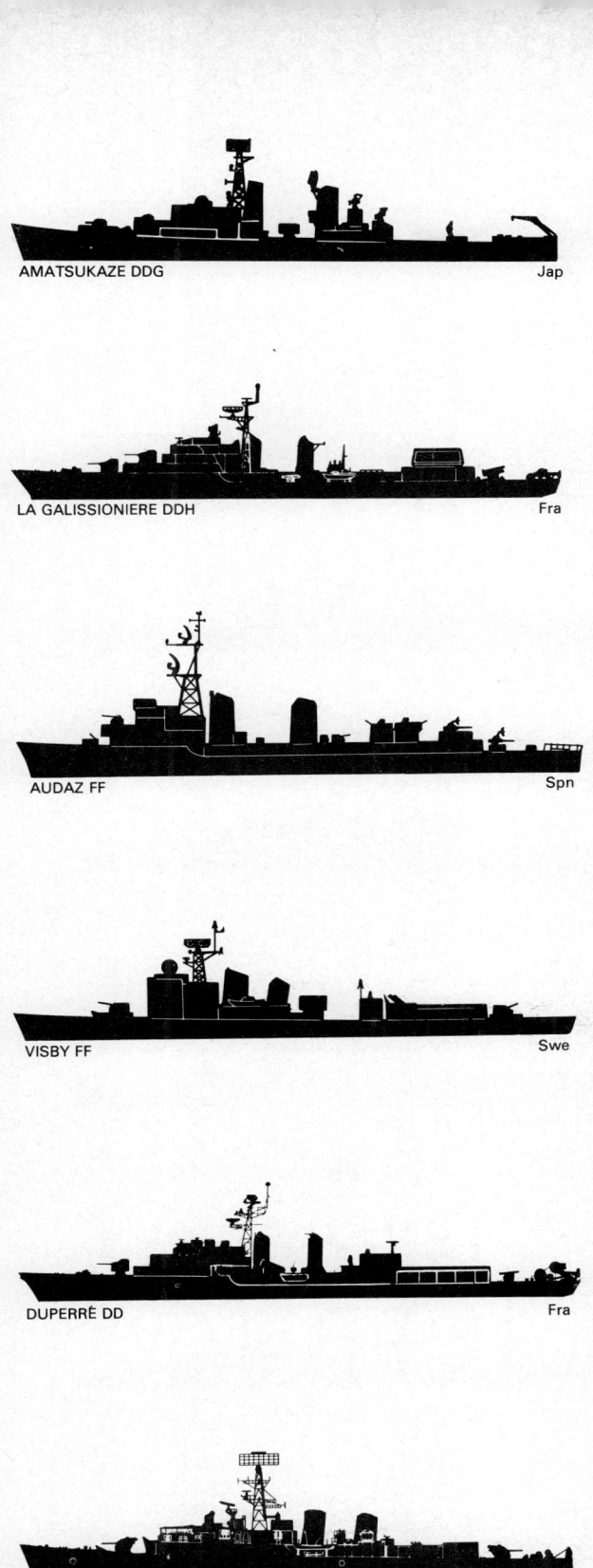

RECOGNITION SILHOUETTES 9

AMATSUKAZE DDG — Jap

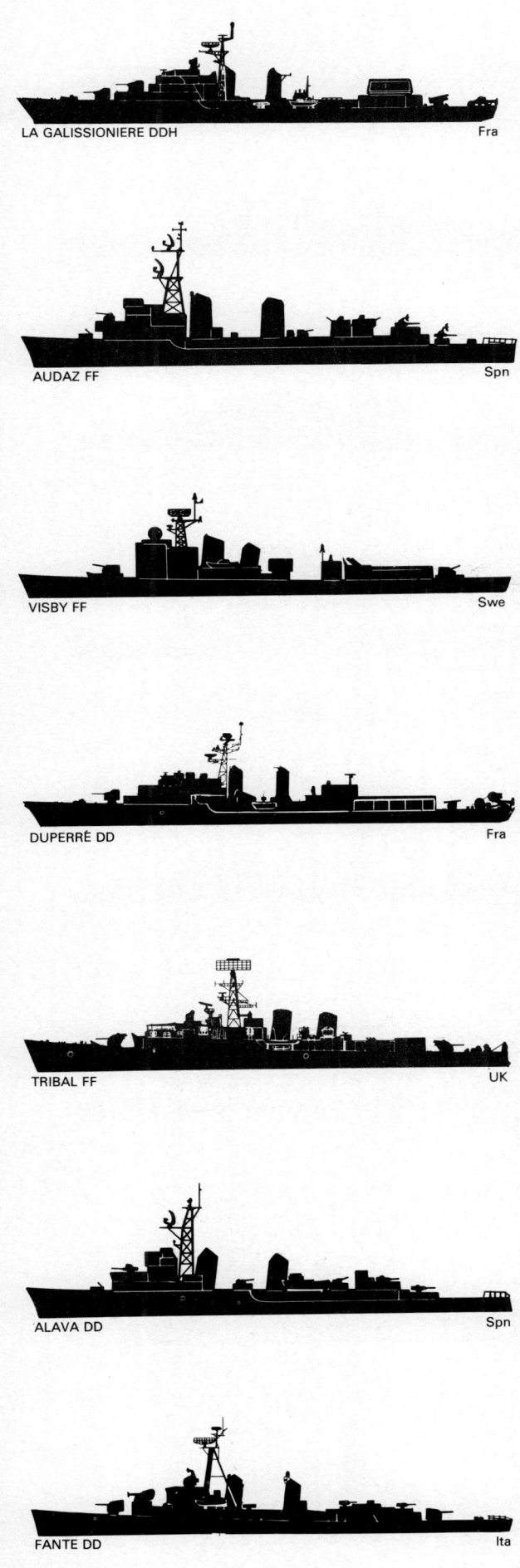

LA GALISSIONIERE DDH — Fra

AUDAZ FF — Spn

VISBY FF — Swe

DUPERRÉ DD — Fra

TRIBAL FF — UK

ALAVA DD — Spn

FANTE DD — Ita

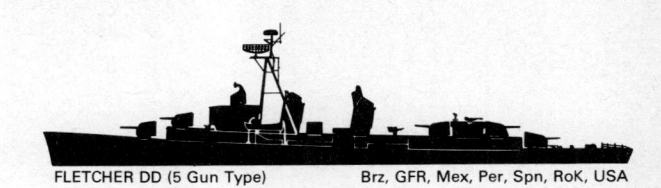

FLETCHER DD (5 Gun Type) — Brz, GFR, Mex, Per, Spn, RoK, USA

FLETCHER DD (4 Gun Type) — Arg, Brz, Chi, Col, Ita, GFR, Gre, Per, Spn, USA

ALLEN M. SUMNER DD — Arg, Brz, Col, RoC, Tur, Ven

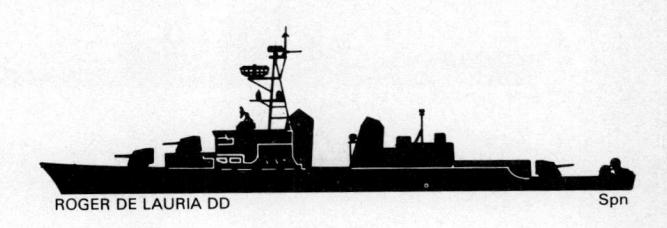

ROGER DE LAURIA DD — Spn

HARUKAZE DD — Jap

CENTAURO FF — Ita

CHARLES F. ADAMS DDG — Aus, USA

10 RECOGNITION SILHOUETTES

TROMP DDGH — Nld

ARTEMIZ DDGSP — Iran

KATORI AGFF — Jap

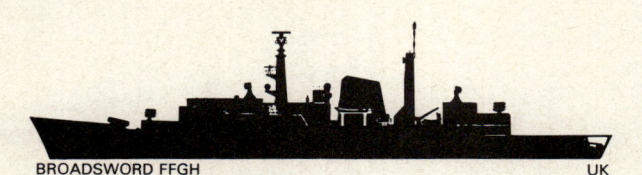

BROADSWORD FFGH — UK

HANG TUAH FF — Mly

LEANDER FF, FFG — UK

NITEROI DDH (GP version) — Brz

LEANDER FFGH — UK

DAT-ASSAWARI FF — Lbr

LEANDER FFGH — UK

RAHMAT FF — Mly

ALMIRANTE CONDELL FFG — Chi

MAKUT RAJAKUMARN FF — Tld

SWAN FF — Aust

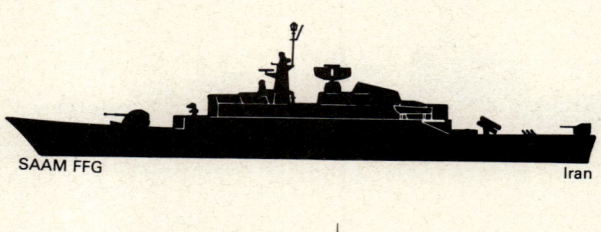

SAAM FFG — Iran

SHEFFIELD DDGH — Arg, UK

AMAZON FFG — UK

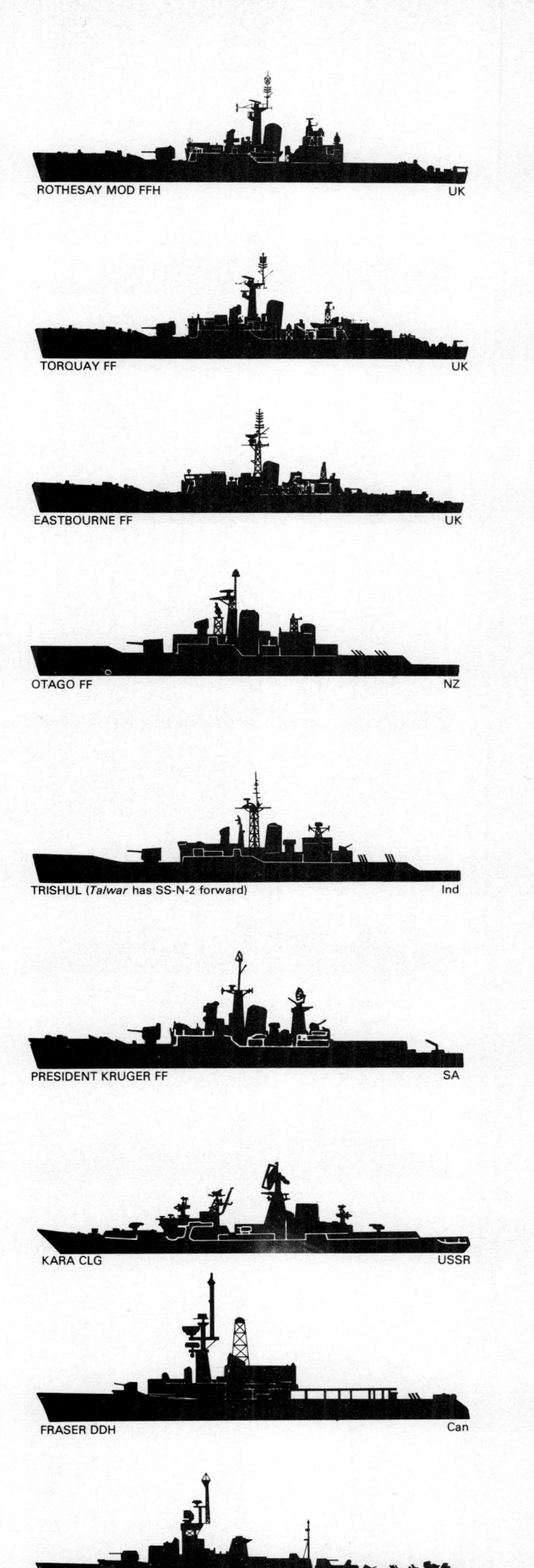

RECOGNITION SILHOUETTES

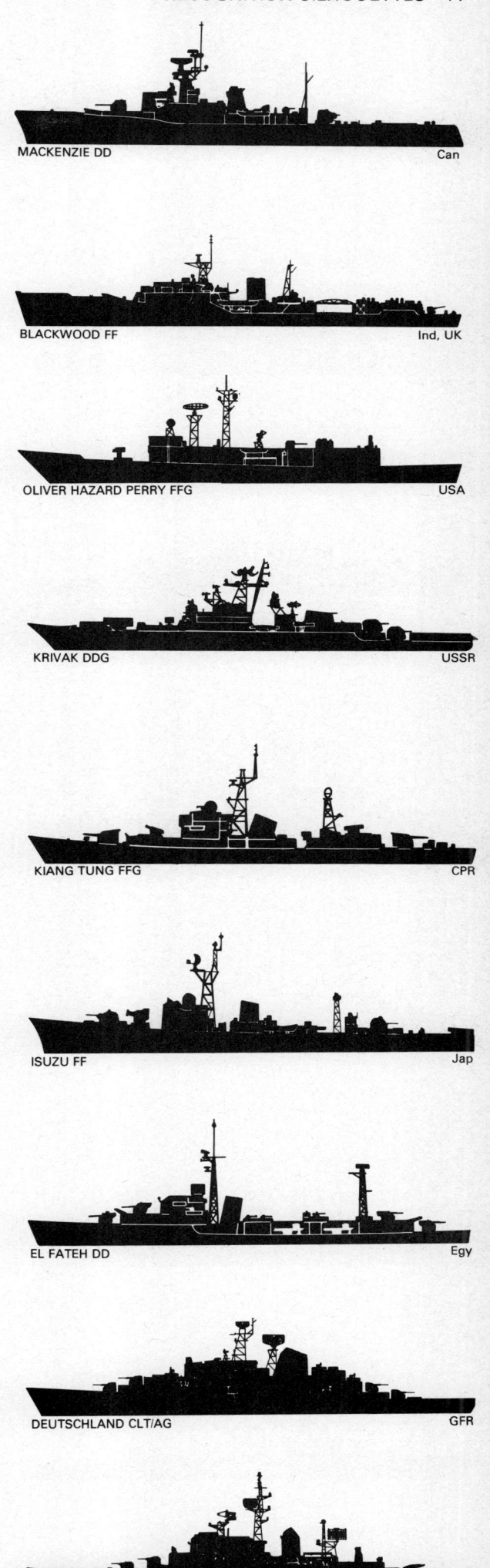

ROTHESAY MOD FFH — UK	MACKENZIE DD — Can
TORQUAY FF — UK	BLACKWOOD FF — Ind, UK
EASTBOURNE FF — UK	OLIVER HAZARD PERRY FFG — USA
OTAGO FF — NZ	KRIVAK DDG — USSR
TRISHUL (*Talwar* has SS-N-2 forward) — Ind	KIANG TUNG FFG — CPR
PRESIDENT KRUGER FF — SA	ISUZU FF — Jap
KARA CLG — USSR	EL FATEH DD — Egy
FRASER DDH — Can	DEUTSCHLAND CLT/AG — GFR
CHAUDIERE DD — Can	COLBERT CLG — Fra

12 RECOGNITION SILHOUETTES

LEOPARD FF — Ind, UK

STUART FF — Aust

Note: Other RIVER Class units differ in main mast configuration

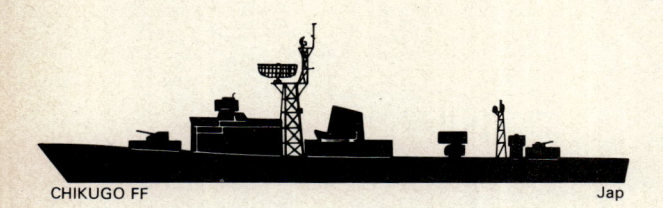

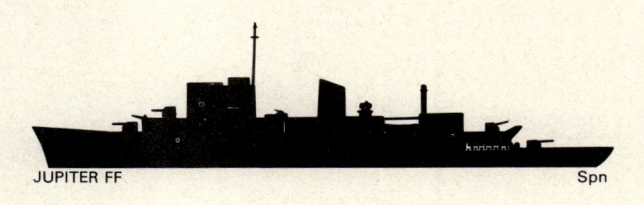

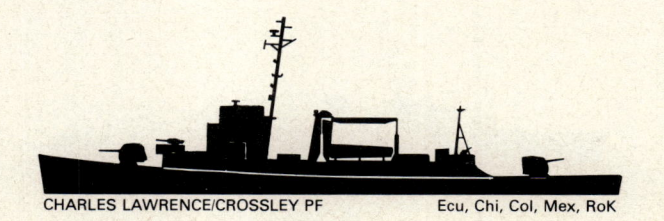

MINEGUMO DD — Jap

CHIKUGO FF — Jap

AM SHAN DDG — CPR

NIGERIA FF — Nig

SPLIT DD — Yug

SAVAGE FF/FFR — Mex, Tun, USA

JUPITER FF — Spn

DELHI CL — Ind

LE NORMAND FF — Fra

LE CORSE FF — Fra

CROSSLEY PF — Col, Mex, RoC, RoK

CHARLES LAWRENCE/CROSSLEY PF — Ecu, Chi, Col, Mex, RoK

RECOGNITION SILHOUETTES 13

GARCIA FF — USA

GARCIA FF (with Lamps) — USA

GLOVER AGFF — USA

BROOKE FFG — USA

BRONSTEIN FF — USA

MIRKA FF — USSR

KNOX FF — USA

KNOX FF (Improved) — USA

BALEARES FFG — Spn

BERGAMINI FF — Ita

HARUNA DDH — Jap

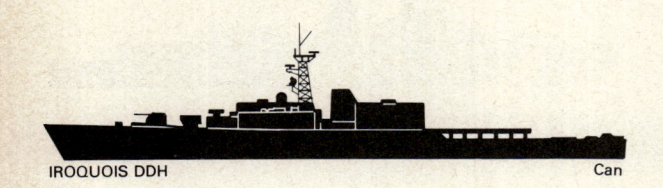

14 RECOGNITION SILHOUETTES

ALPINO FF — Ita	 PETYA 1 FF — Ind, USSR
KOLN FF — GFR	 PETYA II FF — USSR
PIETRO DE CRISTOFARO PF — Ita	 PETYA IA FF — Uru
ÖLAND DD — Swe	 COMMANDANTE RIVIERE FF — Por
IROQUOIS DDH — Can	 RIGA FF — Bul, CPR, GFR, Indo, USSR
SAGUENAY DDH — Can	 RIGA FF — Fin
ANNAPOLIS DDH — Can	 NUEVA ESPARTA DD, DDP — Ven

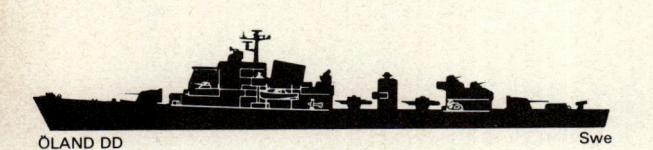

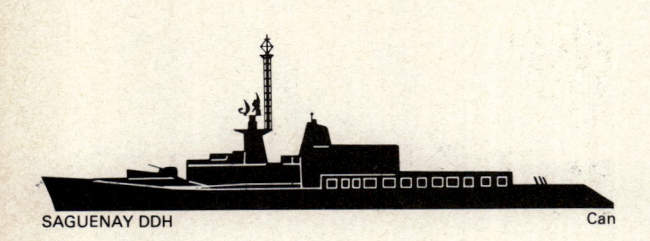

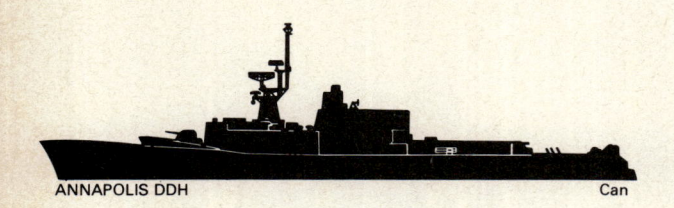

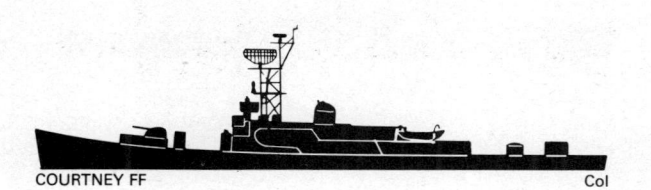

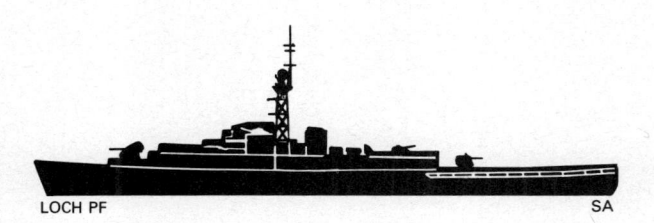

RECOGNITION SILHOUETTES 15

ALAMGIR DD — Pak
TIPPU SULTAN FF — Pak 
TARIK FF — Egy
PIZARRO MOD FF — Spn 
KISTNA FF — Ind
ATREVIDA FF — Spn 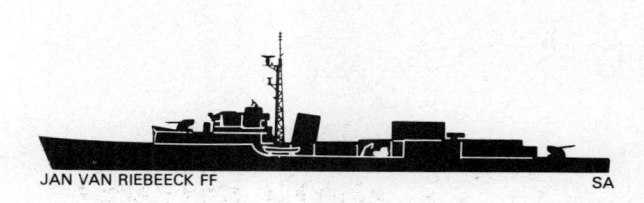
SHAH JAHAN DD — Pak
JAN VAN RIEBEECK FF — SA 
COURTNEY FF — Col
DEALEY FF — Por, Uru 
LOCH PF — SA
ALMIRANTE CLEMENTE FF — Ven 
GATINEAU DD — Can
JOAO COUNTINHO FF — Por

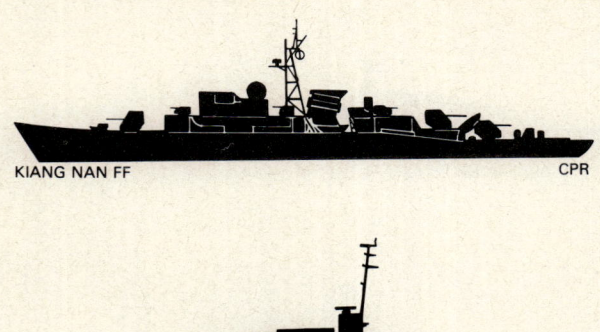

16 RECOGNITION SILHOUETTES

KIANG NAN FF — CPR

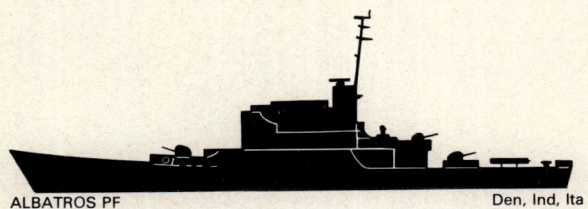

ALBATROS PF — Den, Ind, Ita

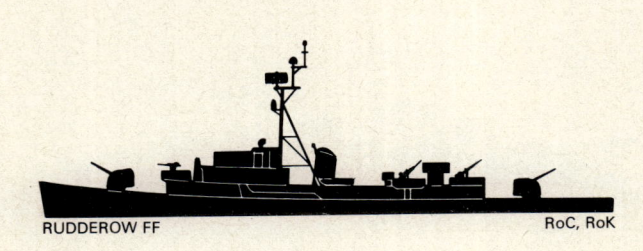

RUDDEROW FF — RoC, RoK

OSLO FF/FFG — Nor

HUNT FF — Ecu, Egy, Ind

BERK FF — Tur

BAYANDOR PF — Iran

CANNON FF — Gre, Per, Plp, RoK, Tld, Uru

IKAZUCHI FF — Jap

SHIP REFERENCE SECTION

SHIP DESIGNATIONS

In an effort to standardise the type designations in the various navies, despite somewhat idiosyncratic listing in some fleets, a regular formula has been used wherever possible in the majority of sections. This has caused some queries and comments, therefore a list is given below.

SUBMARINES
    Strategic Missile — Nuclear propelled and conventionally propelled
    Cruise Missile — Nuclear propelled and conventionally propelled
    Fleet Submarines — Nuclear propelled
    Patrol Submarines — Conventionally propelled

AIRCRAFT CARRIERS
    Attack Aircraft Carriers (Nuclear) — US "Nimitz" and "Enterprise" classes
    Attack Aircraft Carriers
    ASW Aircraft Carriers

MAJOR SURFACE SHIPS
    A/S Cruisers — "Invincible" class, "Moskva" class
    Cruisers — Over 10 000 tons, including missile conversions
    Light Cruisers — 5 000 tons—10 000 tons
    Destroyers — 3 000 to 5 000 tons, plus original conventional destroyers
    Frigates — 1 100 to 3 000 tons
    Corvettes — 500 to 1 100 tons

LIGHT FORCES
    Fast Attack Craft (FAC) (25 knots and above)
        FAC (Missile)
        FAC (Gun)
        FAC (Torpedo)
        FAC (Patrol)

    Patrol Craft (below 25 knots)
        Large Patrol Craft (100 to 500 tons)
        Coastal Patrol Craft (below 100 tons)

AMPHIBIOUS FORCES
    Command Ships
    Assault Ships
    Landing Ships
    Landing Craft
    Transports

MINE WARFARE FORCES
    Mine Layers
    MCM Support Ships
    Mine Sweepers (Ocean)
    Mine Hunters
    Mine Sweepers (Coastal)
    Mine Sweepers (Inshore)
    Mine Sweeping Boats

SURVEYING VESSELS
    Surveying Ships
    Coastal Surveying Craft
    Inshore Surveying Craft

ABU DHABI
(see United Arab Emirates)

ALBANIA

Ministerial

Minister of Defence:
  Mehmet Shehu

Personnel

(a) 1978: Total 3 000 including 300 coastal frontier guards.
(b) Ratings on 3 years military service.

Bases

Durazzo (Durresi) and Valona (Vlora)

General

Since the break with USSR the remaining Soviet craft must have been decreasing in efficiency due to lack of spares. The transfer of Chinese craft since 1965 (including missile craft in 1976) has provided a small nucleus of new and effective vessels. Future needs—probably submarines and MCM vessels.

Strength of the Fleet

Submarines	3
Large Patrol Craft	4
Fast Attack Craft (Missile)	4
Fast Attack Craft (Torpedo)	38
Fast Attack Craft (Gun)	6
Minesweepers—Ocean	2
Minesweepers—Inshore	6
MSB	11
Tankers	4
Small Auxiliaries	approx 20

Mercantile Marine

Lloyd's Register of Shipping:
  20 vessels of 55 870 tons gross.

DELETIONS

Submarines

1976 1 "Whiskey" class

Light Forces

1976 6 "P 4" class

SUBMARINES
3 Ex-SOVIET "WHISKEY" CLASS

Displacement, tons: 1 030 surfaced; 1 350 dived
Length, feet (metres): 249·3 *(76)*
Beam, feet (metres): 22·0 *(6·7)*
Draught, feet (metres): 15·0 *(4·6)*
Torpedo tubes: 6—21 in (4 bow, 2 stern); 14 torpedoes or 40 mines
Main machinery: Diesels; 4 000 bhp; 2 shafts = 17 knots surfaced; electric motors; 2 500 hp = 15 knots dived
Range, miles: 13 000 at 8 knots surfaced
Complement: 60

Two of these are operational and one is now used as a harbour training boat. All are based at Vlora. Two were transferred from the USSR in 1960, and two others were reportedly seized from the USSR in mid-1961 upon the withdrawal of Soviet ships from their Albanian base.

Radar: Snoop Plate.

"WHISKEY" Class

LIGHT FORCES
4 Ex-SOVIET "KRONSHTADT" CLASS (LARGE PATROL CRAFT)

150   151   340   341

Displacement, tons: 310 standard; 380 full load
Dimensions, feet (metres): 170·6 × 21·5 × 9·0 *(52·0 × 6·5 × 2·7)*
Guns: 1—3·5 in *(85 mm)*; 2—37 mm (single); 6—12·7 MG (3 vertical twin)
A/S weapons: 2 depth charge projectors; 2 DC rails; 2—5-tube rocket launchers
Main engines: 3 diesels; 3 shafts; 3 300 bhp = 24 knots
Range, miles: 1 500 at 12 knots
Complement: 65

Equipped for minelaying; 2 rails; about 8 mines. Four were transferred from the USSR in 1958. Albania sent two for A/S updating in 1960 and two others in 1961

Radar: Surface search: Ball Gun. Navigation: Neptune. IFF: High Pole.

"KRONSHTADT" Class

4 Ex-CHINESE "HOKU" CLASS (FAST ATTACK CRAFT—MISSILE)

Displacement, tons: 70 standard; 80 full load
Dimensions, feet (metres): 83·7 × 19·8 × 5 *(25·5 × 6 × 1·5)*
Missiles: 2—SS-N-2 type
Guns: 2—25 mm (twin, forward)
Main engines: 2 diesels; 2 shafts; 4 800 bhp = 40 knots
Range, miles: 400 at 30 knots
Complement: 20

Transferred by China 1976-77. Steel hulls.

"KOMAR" Class ("HOKU" similar but with pole mast and launchers further inboard)   1970, USN

32 Ex-CHINESE "HU CHWAN" CLASS
(FAST ATTACK HYDROFOIL—TORPEDO)

Displacement, tons: 45
Dimensions, feet (metres): 71 × 14·5 × 3·1 *(21·8 × 4·5 × 0·9)*
Guns: 2—14·5 mm (twin vertical)
Torpedo tubes: 2—21 inch
Main engines: 3 M50 diesels; 2 shafts; 3 600 hp = 55 knots
Built in Shanghai and transferred as follows; 6 in 1968, 15 in 1969, 2 in 1970, 7 in 1971 and 2 in June 1974.
Construction: Have foils forward while the stern planes on the surface.
Radar: Skinhead.

HU CHWAN

ALBANIA

6 Ex-CHINESE "SHANGHAI II" CLASS (FAST ATTACK CRAFT—GUN)

Displacement, tons: 120 standard; 155 full load
Dimensions, feet (metres): 128 × 18 × 5·6 (39 × 5·5 × 1·7)
Guns: 4—37 mm (twins); 4—25 mm (twins)
A/S armament: 8 DCs
Mines: Minerails can be fitted; probably only 10 mines
Main engines: 4 diesels; 4 800 bhp = 30 knots
Complement: 25

Four transferred in mid-1974 and two in 1975.

Radar: Skinhead.

"SHANGHAI II" Class

6 Ex-CHINESE "P 4" CLASS (FAST ATTACK CRAFT—TORPEDO)

111   115   304   +3

Displacement, tons: 22
Dimensions, feet (metres): 62·3 × 11·5 × 5·6 (19·0 × 3·5 × 1·7)
Guns: (See notes)
Torpedo tubes: 2—18 in (450 mm)
Main engines: 2 M50 diesels; 2 shafts; 2 200 bhp = 50 knots

Six were transferred from the USSR in 1956 (with radar and 2-12·7 mm MG) and six from China, three in April 1965 and three in Sep 1965, without radar and with 4—12·7 mm MG (2 twin). Radar now fitted. The ex-Soviet craft now believed deleted.

MINE WARFARE FORCES

2 Ex-SOVIET "T 43" CLASS (MINESWEEPERS—OCEAN)

152   342

Displacement, tons: 500 standard; 610 full load
Dimensions, feet (metres): 190·2 × 28·2 × 6·9 (58·0 × 8·6 × 2·1)
Guns: 4—37 mm (2 twin); 8—12·7 mm MG
A/S weapons: 2 DCT
Main engines: 2 Type 9D diesels; 2 shafts; 2 000 bhp = 17 knots
Range, miles: 1 600 at 10 knots
Complement: 40

Transferred in Aug 1960.

"T 43" Class

6 Ex-SOVIET "T 301" CLASS (MINESWEEPERS—INSHORE)

343   344   +4

Displacement, tons: 150 standard; 180 full load
Dimensions, feet (metres): 128·0 × 18·0 × 4·9 (39·0 × 5·5 × 1·5)
Guns: 2—37 mm; 4—12·7 mm (twins)
Main engines: 3 diesels; 3 shafts; 1 440 bhp = 9 knots
Range, miles: 2 200 at 9 knots
Complement: 25

Transferred from USSR—two in 1957, two in 1959 and two in 1960.

11 Ex-SOVIET "PO 2" CLASS (MSB)

Displacement, tons: 40 to 45 standard; 45 to 50 full load
Dimensions, feet (metres): 70·0 × 16·7 × 5·6 (21·3 × 5·1 × 1·7)
Gun: 1—12·7 mm MG
Main engines: Diesels = 9 knots

There are reports of some 11 "PO 2" class in service and possibly 3 ex-Italian "MS 501" class. The "PO 2" class, though primarily minesweeping boats, are also general utility craft. They were transferred as follows: 3 in 1957, 3 in 1958-59, 5 in 1960.

TANKERS

2 Ex-SOVIET "KHOBI" CLASS (PETROL TANKERS)

PATOS   SEMANI

Displacement, tons: 2 200
Measurement, tons: 1 600 deadweight; 1 500 oil
Dimensions, feet (metres): 220·0 × 33·0 × 15·0 (67·1 × 10·1 × 4·6)
Main engines: 2 diesels; 1 600 bhp = 12 knots

Launched in 1956. Transferred from the USSR in Sep 1958 and Feb 1959. *Semani* may be ex-Soviet M/V *Linda*.

Radar: Neptun.

1 Ex-SOVIET "TOPLIVO 1" CLASS (YARD TANKER)

Displacement, tons: 425
Dimensions, feet (metres): 115 × 22 × 9·6 (34·5 × 6·5 × 3)
Main engines: 1 diesel; 1 shaft = 10 knots
Range, miles: 400 at 7 knots
Complement: 16

Transferred from the USSR in March 1960. Similar to "Khobi" class in appearance though smaller. Oil fuel capacity about 200 tons.

1 Ex-SOVIET "TOPLIVO 3" CLASS (YARD TANKER)

Displacement, tons: 425

Transferred from the USSR in 1960. Generally similar to "Toplivo 1" class.

MISCELLANEOUS

TUGS

Several small tugs are employed in local duties or harbour service.

There are reported to be a dozen or so harbour and port tenders including a water carrier and two small transports. The "Atrek" class submarine tender transferred from USSR in 1961 as a depot ship was converted into a merchant ship. With large lakes on both the Yugoslav and Greek borders a number of small patrol craft is stationed on these lakes.

2 Ex-SOVIET "POLUCHAT 1" CLASS

SKENDERBEU A641   +1

Displacement, tons: 86 standard; 91 full load
Dimensions, feet (metres): 98·0 pp × 15·0 × 4·8 (29·9 × 4·6 × 1·5)
Guns: 2—14·5 mm
Main engines: 2 M50 diesels; 2 shafts; 2 400 bhp = 18 knots
Range, miles: 460 at 17 knots
Complement: 16

Probably used for torpedo recovery. Transferred in 1968.

AUXILIARIES

1 Ex-SOVIET "SEKSTAN" CLASS (DEGAUSSING SHIP)

354

Dimensions, feet (metres): 134·0 × 40·8 × 14·0 (40·8 × 12·2 × 4·3)
Main engines: Diesels; 400 bhp = 11 knots
Complement: 35

Built in Finland in 1956. Transferred from the USSR in 1960.

2 Ex-SOVIET "NYRYAT" CLASS (DIVING TENDERS)

ALGERIA

Ministerial

Minister of Defence:
Colonel Houari Boumediene (President)

General

Although up to now Algeria has relied on Soviet support, which is still continuing, the Italian order with Baglietto suggests a diversification which could be important with her patrol and fast attack craft and her minesweepers reaching well into the second half of their lives.

Personnel

(a) 1978: Total 3 800 (300 officers and cadets and 3 500 men)
(b) Voluntary service

Bases

Algiers, Annaba, Mers el Kebir

Mercantile Marine

Lloyd's Register of Shipping:
112 vessels of 1 050 962 tons gross

Strength of the Fleet

Large Patrol Craft	6
Fast Attack Craft (Missile)	12
Fast Attack Craft (Torpedo)	10
Fast Attack Craft (Gun)	10
Minesweepers—Ocean	2
LCT	1
Miscellaneous	5

Aircraft

12 Fokker F27 are operated by the Algerian Air Force (AAF) in a maritime role.

Deletion

1976   *Sidi Fradj* (training ship)

LIGHT FORCES

6 Ex-SOVIET "SO I" CLASS (LARGE PATROL CRAFT)

P651-656

Displacement, tons: 215 light; 250 full load
Dimensions, feet (metres): 138·6 × 20·0 × 9·2 *(42·3 × 6·1 × 2·8)*
Guns: 4—25 mm (2 twin mounts)
Torpedo tubes: 2—21 inch *(533 mm)* (in three craft)
A/S weapons: 4 MBU 1800 rocket launchers
Main engines: 3 diesels; 6 000 bhp = 29 knots
Range, miles: 1 100 at 13 knots
Complement: 30

Delivered by USSR between Oct 1965 and 8 Oct 1967, the torpedo tubes used were removed from P6 Fast Attack Craft.

"SO I" Class

3 Ex-SOVIET "OSA II" AND 3 "OSA I" CLASS (FAST ATTACK CRAFT—MISSILE)

R167   R267   R367   +3

Displacement, tons: 165 standard; 200 full load
Dimensions, feet (metres): 128·7 × 25·1 × 5·9 *(39·3 × 7·7 × 1·8)*
Missiles: 4 SS-N-2 (Styx)
Guns: 4—30 mm (2 twin)
Main engines: 3 diesels, 13 000 bhp = 32 knots
Range, miles: 800 at 25 knots
Complement: 25

One Osa I was delivered by USSR on 7 Oct 1967. Two others transferred later in same year.
Osa IIs transferred 1976-77.

"OSA I" Class

6 Ex-SOVIET "KOMAR" CLASS (FAST ATTACK CRAFT—MISSILE)

671-676

Displacement, tons: 70 standard; 80 full load
Dimensions, feet (metres): 84·2 × 21·1 × 5·0 *(25·7 × 6·4 × 1·5)*
Missiles: 2 SS-N-2 (Styx)
Guns: 2—25 mm (twin)
Main engines: 4 diesels, 4 shafts, 4 800 bhp = 40 knots
Range, miles: 400 at 30 knots
Complement: 20

Acquired in 1966 from USSR.

10 Ex-SOVIET "P6" CLASS (FAST ATTACK CRAFT—TORPEDO)

623-626, 629-634

Displacement, tons: 66 standard; 75 full load
Dimensions, feet (metres): 84·2 × 20·0 × 5·0 *(25·7 × 6·1 × 1·5)*
Guns: 4—25 mm (twin)
Torpedo tubes: 2—21 inch (or mines or depth charges) (see notes)
Main engines: 4 diesels, 4 shafts, 4 800 bhp = 43 knots
Range, miles: 450 at 30 knots
Complement: 25

Acquired from the USSR between 1963 and 1968. Four retain their original armament whilst the remainder, with tubes removed, are used for coast-guard and instructional duties. Two deleted 1975.

10 BAGLIETTO TYPE (FAST ATTACK CRAFT—GUN)

235   236   +8

Displacement, tons: 44 full load
Dimensions, feet (metres): 66·9 × 17·1 × 5·5 *(20·4 × 5·2 × 1·7)*
Guns: 2—20 mm
Main engines: 2 diesels; 2 660 bhp = 35 knots
Complement: 11

The first pair delivered by Baglietto, Varazze in Aug 1976 and the remainder in pairs at two monthly intervals.

AMPHIBIOUS FORCES

1 Ex-SOVIET "POLNOCNY" CLASS (LCT)

Displacement, tons: 870 standard; 1 000 full load
Dimensions, feet (metres): 239·4 × 29·5 × 9·8 *(75 × 9 × 3)*
Guns: 2—30 mm
Main engines: 2 diesels; 5 000 bhp = 18 knots
Complement: 40

Transferred in Aug 1976.

"POLNOCNY" Class

22 ALGERIA / ANGOLA

MINE WARFARE FORCES
2 Ex-SOVIET "T 43" CLASS (MINESWEEPERS—OCEAN)

M221 M222

Displacement, tons: 500 standard; 610 full load
Dimensions, feet (metres): 190·2 × 28·2 × 6·9 (58·0 × 8·6 × 2·1)
Guns: 4—37 mm (twins); 8—12·7 mm (twins)
A/S weapons: 2 DCT
Main engines: 2 Type 9D diesels; 2 shafts; 2 200 bhp = 17 knots
Range, miles: 1 600 at 10 knots
Complement: 40

Transferred in 1968.

1 Ex-SOVIET "POLUCHAT" CLASS
A641

Operates as TRV.

1 Ex-SOVIET "SEKSTAN" CLASS
VASOUYA A640

Transferred in 1964. Operates as survey ship.

MISCELLANEOUS
1 HARBOUR TUG
YAVDEZAN VP650

Completed in 1965 used as diving tender.

2 FISHERY PROTECTION CRAFT
JEBEL ANTAR   JEBEL HONDA

ANGOLA

Ministerial

Minister of Defence:
  Major Enrique Carreira

General

A number of Portuguese ships were transferred at independence, in 1975, and it is reported that these have been reinforced by ex-Soviet landing craft and ships taken up from trade. Angolan names are not known—the details given are in all cases Portuguese. In the confused state of affairs existing in Angola it is impossible to assess the availability of the craft listed.

Personnel

(a) 1978: Approx 600
(b) Voluntary service

Ports and Bases

Luanda, Lobito, Moçamedes. (A number of other good harbours is available on the 1 000 mile coastline).

Strength of the Fleet

Large Patrol Craft	4
Coastal Patrol Craft	6
LCTs	2
LCUs	5
Auxiliaries	?8

Mercantile Marine

Lloyds Register of Shipping:
  22 vessels of 22 043 tons gross.

LIGHT FORCES
4 Ex-PORTUGUESE "ARGOS" CLASS (LARGE PATROL CRAFT)

Name	No.	Builders	Commissioned (Portugal)
Ex-LIRA	P 361	Estaleiros Navais de Viano do Castelo	1963
Ex-PEGASO	P 362	Estaleiros Navais de Viano do Castelo	1963
Ex-ESCORPIAO	P 375	Arsenal do Alfeite, Lisbon	1964
Ex-CENTAURO	P1130	Arsenal do Alfeite, Lisbon	1965

Displacement, tons: 180 standard; 210 full load
Dimensions, feet (metres): 136·8 oa × 20·5 × 7 (41·6 × 6·2 × 2·2)
Guns: 2—40 mm
Main engines: 2 Maybach (MTU) diesels; 1 200 bhp = 17 knots
Oil fuel, tons: 16
Complement: 24

Argos, Dragao and *Orion* of same class transferred, reportedly, for spares.

"ARGOS" Class   *Portuguese Navy*

2 Ex-PORTUGUESE "JUPITER" CLASS (COASTAL PATROL CRAFT)

Name	No.	Builders	Commissioned (Portugal)
Ex-JUPITER	P 1132	Estaleiros Navais do Mondego	1964
Ex-VENUS	P 1133	Estaleiros Navais do Mondego	1965

Displacement, tons: 32 standard; 43·5 full load
Dimensions, feet (metres): 69 oa × 16·5 × 4·3 (21 × 5 × 1·3)
Gun: 1—20 mm Oerlikon
Main engines: 2 Cummins diesels; 1 270 bhp = 20 knots
Complement: 8

Ex-JUPITER   *Portuguese Navy*

4 Ex-PORTUGUESE "BELLATRIX" CLASS (COASTAL PATROL CRAFT)

Name	No.	Builders	Commissioned (Portugal)
Ex-ESPIGA	P 366	Beyerische Schiffbaugesellschaft	1961
Ex-POLLUX	P 368	Beyerische Schiffbaugesellschaft	1961
Ex-ALTAIR	P 377	Beyerische Schiffbaugesellschaft	1962
Ex-RIGEL	P 378	Beyerische Schiffbaugesellschaft	1962

Displacement, tons: 23 standard; 27·6 full load
Dimensions, feet (metres): 68 oa × 16·2 × 4 (20·7 × 5·1 × 1·2)
Gun: 1—20 mm Oerlikon
Main engines: 2 Cummins diesels; 470 bhp = 15 knots
Complement: 7

"BELLATRIX" Class   *Portuguese Navy*

AMPHIBIOUS FORCES

Note: In addition to those below 5 ex-Soviet LCUs reported transferred in 1976.

2 Ex-PORTUGUESE "ALFANGE" CLASS (LCT)

Name	No.	Builders	Commissioned (Portugal)
Ex-**ALFANGE**	LDG 101	Estaleiros Navais do Mondego	1965
Ex-**ARIETE**(?)	LDG 102	Estaleiros Navais do Mondego	1965

Displacement, tons: 500
Dimensions, feet (metres): 187 × 39 × 6·2 *(57 × 12 × 1·9)*
Main engines: 2 diesels; 1 000 bhp = 11 knots
Complement: 20

Ex-ALFANGE *Portuguese Navy*

MISCELLANEOUS

Also reported that up to 8 merchant ships have been acquired from local shipping.

ANGUILLA

1 FAIREY MARINE "HUNTSMAN" CLASS

A 28 ft launch supplied in 1974. She is unarmed and used for anti-smuggling operations and for Air-Sea Rescue. Belongs to the Royal St. Kitts, Nevis and Anguilla Police Force being based at Basseterre, St. Kitts under the supervision of Superintendent W. Galloway. There are also one or two smaller police launches.

ARGENTINA

Headquarters Appointments

Commander of the Navy and Chief of Naval Operations:
  Rear-Admiral E. E. Massera
Chief of Naval Staff:
  Rear-Admiral A. Lambruschini

Diplomatic Representation

Head of Argentinian Naval Mission Asunción, Paraguay:
  Captain Federico L. A. Roussillion
Naval Attaché in Asuncion, Paraguay:
  Captain Alex N. Richmond
Naval Attaché in Bogota:
  Captain Luis Santiago Martella
Naval Attaché in Brasilia:
  Captain Walter J. Colombo
Naval Attaché in Cape Town:
  Captain Enrique A. Garret
Naval Attaché in Caracas:
  Captain Edgardo N. Acuña
Naval Attaché in La Paz:
  Captain Jorge A. Echavarria
Head of Naval Mission, La Paz:
  Captain Guillermo M. Obiglio
Naval Attaché in London and The Hague and Head of the Argentine Naval Mission in Europe:
  Rear-Admiral Edgardo J. Segura
Naval Attaché in Lima:
  Captain Jorge A. Goulu
Naval Attaché in Madrid:
  Captain Hector A. Terranova
Naval Attaché in Montevideo:
  Captain Jose A. Suppicich
Naval Attaché in Paris:
  Captain Eduardo M. Girling
Naval Attaché in Quito:
  Captain Ernesto M. Lopez Fabre
Naval Attaché in Rome:
  Captain Roberto A. Day
Naval Attaché in Santiago:
  Captain Jorge C. G. Vallarino
Naval Attaché in Tokyo:
  Captain Juan M. H. Zabalet
Naval Attaché in Washington:
  Rear-Admiral Raul, A. Fitte

Personnel

(a) 1978: 32 900 (2 890 officers, 18 010 petty officers and ratings and 12 000 conscripts)
  Marine Corps: 6 000 officers and men
(b) Volunteers plus 14 months national service

Note. Cuerpo de Infanteria de Marina (Marine Corps)
1st Marine Force: 3 Infantry Battalions
1st Marine Brigade: 3 Infantry Battalions; 1 Field Artillery Battalion; 1 Service Battalion; 1 Command Battalion.
Amphibious Support Force: 1 Air Defence Battalion; 1 Communications Battalion; Amphibious craft units.
Based at or near naval bases and installations. Equipped with 20 LVTP-7, 15 LARC-5, 10 "Tigercat" SAM, 105 mm how., "Bantam" A-T missiles, 88 mm AA guns, 106 and 120 mm mortars, 75 mm and 105 mm recoilless rifles.

Naval Bases

Buenos Aires (Darsena Norte): Dockyard, 2 Dry Docks, 3 Floating Docks, 1 Floating Crane, Schools.
Rio Santiago (La Plata): Naval Base, Schools, Naval shipbuilding yard (AFNE), 1 Slipway, 1 Floating Crane.
Mar de Plata: Submarine base with slipway, 1 Floating Crane.
Puerto Belgrano: Main Naval Base, Schools, 2 Dry Docks, 1 Floating Dock, 1 Floating Crane.
Ushaia: Small naval base.

Naval Aviation

- 15 A-4Q Skyhawk*
- 12 Aermacchi MB 326 GB
- 6 S-2A Tracker*

- 3 HU-16B Albatross maritime patrol
- 4 P2-H Neptune
- — PBY-5A Catalina

- 4 Alouette III Helicopter
- 6 Bell 47 (Sioux) (2 with PNA)
- 6 Hughes 500M (Cayuse) (PNA)
- 4 Sikorsky S-61D (Sea King)
- 2 Sikorsky S-61 NR
- 2 Sea Lynx
- 5 Sikorsky S-55 (Chickasaw)

- 3 DHC Beaver Transport
- 8 C-47 Dakota/Skytrain
- 3 C-54 Skymaster
- 1 FMA IA 50 GII
- 1 HS 125 Srs. 400A
- 3 Lockheed L-188 Electra
- 5 Short Skyvan (PNA)
- 30 T-28 Fennec Trainer
- 1 DHC-6 Twin Otter
- 2 Beech Super King Air 200
- 3 Fairchild-Hiller Porter
- 6 Beech C45-H/AT 11
- 10 North American SNJ-5C/T-6

*Carrier-based.

Naval Air Bases

Punta Indio, Puerto Belgrano, Commandante Espora, Ezeiza (Buenos Aires), Trelew, Ushuaia.

General

With their one carrier over 30 years old, both cruisers of pre-war vintage, eight destroyers with a hull life of 32 or years more and all their corvettes over 30 years old the proposed increase in Type 42 destroyers and the reported frigate programme present no surprises. The production of more submarines, a new Harrier-Carrier programme and a new class of offshore patrol craft would seem sensible additions to the new construction plans.

Prefectura Naval Argentina (PNA)

PNA is responsible for coastguard and rescue duties. It also administers the Merchant Navy School at Buenos Aires.

Prefix to Ships' Names

ARA

Strength of the Fleet

Type	Active	Building
Attack Carrier (Medium)	1	—
Cruisers	2	—
Destroyers	9	1
Frigates	—	(?8)*
Corvettes	9	—
Patrol Submarines	4	(2)**
Landing Ships (Tank)	4	1
Landing Craft (Tank)	1	—
Minor Landing Craft	27	—
Fast Attack Craft (Missile)	—	2
Fast Attack Craft (Gun)	2	—
Fast Attack Craft (Torpedo)	2	—
Large Patrol Craft	6	—
Minesweepers (Coastal)	4	—
Minehunters	2	—
Survey/Oceanographic Ships	6	2
Survey Launches	2	—
Transports	2	3
Tankers (Fleet Support)	3	—
Icebreaker	1	1
Training Ship	1	—
Tugs	16	—

*See Frigate section for details.
**2 Type 209 projected for building in Argentine yards.

Mercantile Marine

Lloyd's Register of Shipping:
  401 vessels of 1 677 169 tons gross

24 ARGENTINA

DELETIONS

Attack Carrier (medium)

1971 *Independencia*

Cruiser

1973 *La Argentina*

Destroyers

1971 *Buenos Aires, Misiones, San Luis*
1973 *Entre Rios, San Juan, Santa Cruz*
1977 *Espora*

Frigates

1973 *Juan B Azopardo* **(PNA)**, *Piedrabuena, Azopardo*

Patrol Craft

1971 *Anzoategui* **(PNA)**

Corvette

1976 *Commandante General Zapiola* grounded and lost (Nov)

Minesweeper Support Ship

1971 *Corrientes* (to Paraguay)

Submarines

1972 *Santa Fe (ex-Lamprey) Santiago del Estero (ex-Macabi)*, scrapped for spares

Amphibious Forces

1971 *BDI 4, BDI 15, BDM 1, Cabo San Bartolome*
1973 *EDVP 4, 5, 6, 11, 20, 22, 27*

Survey Ships

1970 *Commodoro Augusto Lasserre*
1972 *Capitan Canepa* (scrap)
1973 *Ushuia* sunk in collision

Transports

1971 *La Pataia* (sold)
1973 *Bahia Thetis*
1975 *San Julian*

Tankers

1971 *Punta Rasa, Punta Lara*

Salvage Ship

1974 *Guardiamarina Zicari*

Tugs

1971 *Querendi*
1974 *Mataco*

PENNANT LIST

Aircraft Carrier

V2	25 de Mayo

Cruisers

C4	Belgrano
C5	9 de Julio

Destroyers

D1	Hercules
D2	Santissima Trinidad
D20	Almirante Brown
D21	Espora
D22	Rosales
D23	Almirante Domecq Garcia
D24	Almirante Storni
D25	Segui
D26	Bouchard
D27	Py

Corvettes

P20	Murature
P21	King
A1	Com. G. Irigoyen
A2	Com. G. Zapiola
A3	Francisco de Churruca
A4	Thompson
A5	Diaguita
A6	Yamana
A7	Chiriguano
A8	Sanavirón
A9	Alferez Sobral
A10	Comodoro Somellera

Submarines

S21	Santa Fe
S22	Santiago del Estero
S31	Salta
S32	San Luis

Mine Warfare Forces

M1	Neuquen
M2	Rio Negro
M3	Chubut
M4	Tierra del Fuego
M5	Chaco
M6	Formosa

Light Forces

P55	Surubi
P82	Alakush
P84	Towara
ELPR1	Intrepida
ELPR2	Indomita
GC13	Delfin
GC21	Lynch
GC22	Toll
GC23	Erezcano
GC31	—
GC46	Pacu

Amphibious Forces

Q42	Cabo San Antonio
Q43	Candido De Lasala
Q44	Cabo San Gonzalo
Q46	Cabo San Isidro
Q50	Cabo San Pio
Q56	BDI

Miscellaneous

B2	Bahia Aguirre
B6	Bahia Buen Suceso
B12	Punta Alta
B16	Punta Delgada
B18	Punta Médanos
Q2	Libertad
Q4	General San Martin
Q7	El Austral
Q9	Islas Orcadas
Q11	Comodoro Rivadavia
Q15	Cormoran
Q17	Goyena
R3	Mataco
R4	Toba
R5	Mocovi
R6	Calchaqui
R10	Huarpe
R12	Huarpe
R16	Capayan
R18	Chiquillan
R19	Morcoyan
R29	Pehuenche
R30	Tonocote
R32	Quilmes
R33	Guaycuru

VEINTICINCO DE MAYO

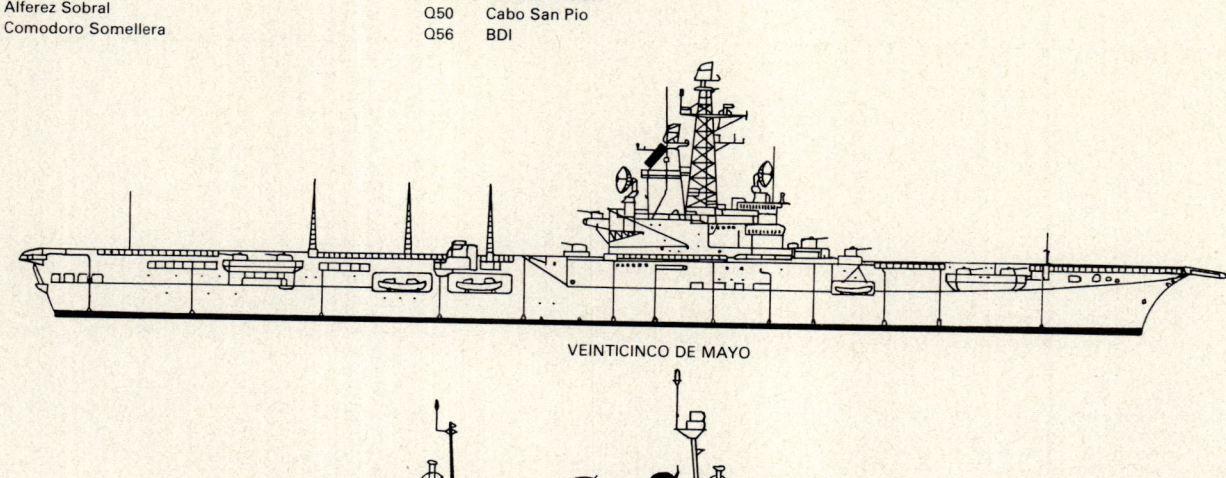

"BROOKLYN" Class

ARGENTINA

SUBMARINES

2 +(2) "SALTA" CLASS (TYPE 209)

Name	No.	Builders	Laid down	Launched	Commissioned
SALTA	S 31	Howaldtswerke, Kiel	—	22 Nov 1972	May 1974
SAN LUIS	S 32	Howaldtswerke, Kiel	—	2 May 1973	May 1974

Displacement, tons: 1 180 surfaced; 1 230 dived
Length, feet (metres): 183·4 *(55·9)*
Beam, feet (metres): 20·5 *(6·25)*
Draught, feet (metres): 17·9 *(5·5)*
Torpedo tubes: 8—21 in; bow tubes (with reloads)
Main machinery: Diesel-electric; MTU diesels, 4 generators; 1 shaft; 5 000 hp
Speed knots: 10 surfaced, 22 dived
Complement: 32

Built in sections by Howaldtswerke Deutsche Werft AG, Kiel from the IK 68 design of Ingenieurkontor, Lübeck. Sections were shipped to Argentina for assembly at Tandanor, Buenos Aires.

Future Programme: Two more projected for building in Argentina.

SALTA   1973, Argentine Navy

2 "GUPPY (IA and II)" CLASS

Name	No.	Builders	Laid down	Launched	Commissioned
SANTE FE (ex-USS *Catfish* SS 339)	S 21	Electric Boat Co.	—	19 Nov 1944	19 Mar 1945
SANTIAGO DEL ESTERO (ex-USS *Chivo* SS 341)	S 22	Electric Boat Co.	—	14 Jan 1945	28 Apr 1945

Displacement, tons: 1 870 surfaced; 2 420 *(Santa Fe)*; 2 540 *(Santiago)* dived
Length, feet (metres): 307·5 *(93·7)* oa
Beam, feet (metres): 27·2 *(8·3)*
Draught, feet (metres): 18·0 *(5·5) (Santa Fe)*; 17·0 *(5·2) (Santiago)*
Torpedo tubes: 10—21 in *(533 mm)*; 6 fwd, 4 aft
Main machinery: 3 diesels; 4 800 shp; 2 electric motors; 5 400 shp; 2 shafts
Speed, knots: 18 surfaced; 15 dived
Oil fuel, tons: 300
Range, miles: 12 000 at 10 knots
Complement: 82-84

Both of the "Balao" class. *Catfish* was modified under the Guppy II programme (1948-50) and *Chivo* under the Guppy 1A programme (1951). Both transferred to Argentina at Mare Island on 7 Jan 1971 by sale.

SANTA FE   1972, Argentine Navy

AIRCRAFT CARRIER

1 Ex-BRITISH "COLOSSUS" CLASS

Name	No.	Builders	Laid down	Launched	Commissioned
VEINTICINCO DE MAYO (ex-HNMS *Karel Doorman*, ex-HMS *Venerable*)	V 2	Cammell Laird & Co Ltd, Birkenhead	3 Dec 1942	30 Dec 1943	17 Jan 1945

Displacement, tons: 15 892 standard; 19 896 full load
Length, feet (metres): 630 *(192·0)* pp 693·2 *(211·3)* oa
Beam, feet (metres): 80 *(24·4)*
Draught, feet (metres): 25 *(7·6)*
Width, feet (metres): 121·3 *(37·0)* oa
Hangar:
  Length, feet (metres): 455 *(138·7)*
  Width, feet (metres): 52 *(15·8)*
  Height, feet (metres): 17·5 *(5·3)*
Aircraft: Operates with variable complement of S-2A Trackers, A-4Q Skyhawks, S-61D Sea King ASW helicopters and A103 Alouette helicopters
Guns: 9—40 mm (single Bofors 40/70)
Main engines: Parsons geared turbines; 40 000 shp; 2 shafts
Boilers: 4 three-drum; working pressure 400 psi *(28·1 kg/cm²)*; Superheat 700°F *(371°C)*
Speed, knots: 24·25
Oil fuel, tons: 3 200
Range, miles: 12 000 at 14 knots, 6 200 at 23 knots
Complement: 1 500

Purchased from the United Kingdom on 1 Apr 1948 and commissioned in the Royal Netherlands Navy on 28 May 1948. Damaged by boiler fire on 29 Apr 1968. Sold to Argentina on 15 Oct 1968 and refitted at Rotterdam by N. V. Dok en Werf Mij Wilton Fijenoord. Commissioned in the Argentine Navy on 12 Mar 1969. Completed refit on 22 Aug 1969 and sailed for Argentina on 1 Sep 1969. With modified island superstructure and bridge lattice tripod radar mast, and tall raked funnel, she differs considerably from her former appearance and from her original sister ships in the British, Australian, Brazilian and Indian navies.

Electronics: Fitted with Ferranti CAAIS with Plessey Super-CAAIS displays. The system has been modified to provide control of carrier based aircraft and will be capable of direct computer-to-computer radio data links with the new Type 42 destroyers.

Engineering: The turbine sets and boilers are arranged *en echelon*, the two propelling-machinery spaces having two boilers and one set of turbines in each space, on the unit system. She was reboilered in 1965-1966 with boilers removed from HMS *Leviathan*. During refit for Argentina in 1968-1969 she received new turbines, also from HMS *Leviathan*.

Radar: Air surveillance: One LW-01, one LW-08.
Height finders: Two VI series.
Target Indicator and Tactical: One DA-02.
Surface Warning and Navigation: One ZW Series.

Reconstruction: Underwent extensive refit modernisation in 1955-1958 including angled flight deck and steam catapult, rebuilt island, mirror sight landing system, and new anti-aircraft battery of ten 40 mm guns, at the Wilton-Fijenoord Shipyard, at a cost of 25 million guilders. Conversion completed in July 1958.

25 DE MAYO   1969, Argentine Navy

ARGENTINA

CRUISERS
2 Ex-US "BROOKLYN" CLASS

Name	No.	Builders	Laid down	Launched	Commissioned
GENERAL BELGRANO (ex-*17 de Octubre*, ex-*Phoenix*, CL 46)	C 4	New York S.B. Corp, Camden	15 Apr 1935	12 Mar 1938	18 Mar 1939
NUEVE DE JULIO (ex-*Boise*, CL 47)	C 5	Newport News S.B. & D.D. Co.	1 Apr 1935	3 Dec 1936	1 Feb 1939

Displacement, tons: Gen. Belgrano: 10 800 standard; 13 645 full load. Nueve de Julio: 10 500 standard; 13 645 full load
Length, feet (metres): 608·3 *(185·4)* oa
Beam, feet (metres): 69 *(21·0)*
Draught, feet (metres): 24 *(7·3)*
Aircraft: 2 helicopters
Missiles: 2 quadruple Sea Cat launchers *(General Belgrano only)*
Guns: *Gen. Belgrano:* 15—6 in *(153 mm)* 47 cal; 8—5 in *(127 mm)* 25 cal; 2 twin—40 mm; 4—47 mm (saluting)
Nueve de Julio: 15—6 in *(153 mm)* 47 cal; 6—5 in *(127 mm)* 25 cal; 4 twin—40 mm; 4—47 mm (saluting)
Armour:
  Belt 4 in—1½ in *(102–38 mm)*
  Decks 3 in—2 in *(76–51 mm)*
  Turrets 5 in—3 in *(127–76 mm)*
  Conning Tower 8 in *(203 mm)*
Main engines: Parsons geared turbines; 100 000 shp; 4 shafts
Boilers: 8 Babcock & Wilcox Express type
Speed, knots: 32·5 (when new)
Range, miles: 7 600 at 15 knots
Oil fuel, tons: 2 200
Complement: 1 200

GENERAL BELGRANO   *1973, Argentine Navy*

Superstructure was reduced, bulges added, beam increased, and mainmast derricks and catapults removed before transfer. Purchased from the United States in 1951 at a cost of $7·8 million and transferred to the Argentine Navy on 12 April 1951. *General Belgrano* was commissioned under the name *17 de Octubre* at Philadelphia on 17 Oct 1951. *9 de Julio* was commissioned into the Argentine Navy at Philadelphia on 11 Mar 1952. *9 de Julio* refers to 9 July 1816, when the Argentine provinces signed the Declaration of Independence. *17 de Octubre* was renamed *General Belgrano* in 1956 following the overthrow of President Peron the year before.

Gunnery: FCS 33 (2) (1 in *Belgrano*), FCS 34 (1), FCS 57 (2), FCS 63 (2), FCS NA9-D1 (1 in *Belgrano*), TDS (1)

Hangar: The hangar in the hull right aft accommodates two helicopters together with engine spares and duplicate parts, though 4 aircraft was the original complement.

Radar: Search: LWO and DA Series (Signaal).

9 DE JULIO   *1971, Argentine Navy*

DESTROYERS
1 + 1 BRITISH TYPE 42

Name	No.	Builders	Laid down	Launched	Commissioned
HERCULES	D 1	Vickers, Barrow-in-Furness	16 June 1971	24 Oct 1972	12 July 1976
SANTISSIMA TRINIDAD	D 2	AFNE, Rio Santiago	11 Oct 1971	9 Nov 1974	1978

Displacement, tons: 3 150 standard; 3 500 full load
Length, feet (metres): 392·0 *(119·5)* wl; 410·0 *(125·0)* oa
Beam, feet (metres): 48 *(14·6)*
Draught, feet (metres): 17 *(5·2)*
Missile launchers: 1 Sea Dart (twin)
Aircraft: 1 Lynx helicopter
Guns: 1—4·5 in automatic; 2—20 mm Oerlikon
A/S weapons: 6—Mk 32 (2 triple) torpedo tubes
Main engines: Rolls-Royce Olympus gas turbines for full power; Rolls-Royce Tyne gas turbines for cruising; 2 shafts; 50 000 shp
Speed, knots: 30
Range, miles: 4 000 at 18 knots
Complement: 300

These two destroyers are of the British Type 42. On 18 May 1970 the signing of a contract between the Argentine Government and Vickers Ltd, Barrow-in-Furness was announced. This provided for the construction of these two ships, one to be built at Barrow-in-Furness and the second at Rio Santiago with British assistance and overseeing. *Santissima Trinidad* was sabotaged on 22 Aug 1975 whilst fitting-out and subsequently placed in floating-dock at AFNE. Completion date remains uncertain. *Hercules* was completed 10 May 1976 and arrived in Argentina 20 Aug 1977 after trials and work-up in the United Kingdom.
There is a possibility of further ships of this class being ordered.

Electronics: ADAWS-4 for co-ordination of action information by Plessey-Ferranti.

Radar: Search: One Type 965 with double AKE2 array and IFF Surveillance and Target Indication: One Type 992Q.
Sea Dart fire control: Two Type 909.
Navigation, HDWS and helicopter control: One Type 1006.

Sonar: Type 184 hull-mounted. Type 162 classification.

HERCULES   *6/1977, Dr. Giorgio Arra*

HERCULES   *6/1977, Dr. Giorgio Arra*

ARGENTINA

4 Ex-US "FLETCHER" CLASS

Name	No.	Builders	Laid down	Launched	Commissioned
ALMIRANTE BROWN (ex-USS *Heermann*, DD 532)	D 20	Bethlehem Steel Co, San Francisco	8 May 1942	5 Dec 1942	6 July 1943
ROSALES (ex-USS *Stembel*, DD 644)	D 22	Bath Iron Works Corporation, Bath, Maine	21 Dec 1942	8 May 1943	16 July 1943
ALMIRANTE DOMECQ GARCIA (ex-USS *Braine*, DD 630)	D 23	Bath Iron Works Corporation, Bath, Maine	12 Oct 1942	7 Mar 1943	11 May 1943
ALMIRANTE STORNI (ex-USS *Cowell*, DD 547)	D 24	Bethlehem Steel Co, San Pedro	7 Sep 1942	18 Mar 1943	23 Aug 1943

Displacement, tons: 2 050 standard; 3 050 full load
Length, feet (metres): 376·5 *(114·8)* oa
Beam, feet (metres): 39·5 *(12·0)*
Draught, feet (metres): 18 *(5·5)*
Guns: 4—5 in *(127 mm)* 38 cal; 6—3 in *(76 mm)* 50 cal; 2—40 mm (D20-22)
Torpedo tubes: 4—21 in *(533 mm)* quad (20, 21, 22)
A/S weapons: 2 fixed Hedgehogs; 1 DC rack (Mk 3); 6 (2 triple) Mk 32 torpedo tubes; 2 side-launching torpedo racks (D20-22)
Main engines: 2 sets GE or AC geared turbines 60 000 shp; 2 shafts
Boilers: 4 Babcock & Wilcox
Speed, knots: 35
Range, miles: 6 000 at 15 knots
Oil fuel, tons: 650
Complement: 300

First two transferred on loan to the Argentine Navy on 1 Aug 1961 and purchased 14 Jan 1977. Last pair transferred 17 Aug 1971.

A/S: All fitted with FCS 105.

Radar: Search: SPS 6.
Tactical: SPS 10.
Fire Control: Mk 37 director with Mk 25 radar; Mk 56 director with Mk 35 radar; Mk 63 director with Mk 34 radar (40 mm).

Sonar: 1 SQS 4.

"FLETCHER" Class   1974, Argentine Navy

3 Ex-US "ALLEN M. SUMNER" CLASS

Name	No.	Builders	Laid down	Launched	Commissioned
SEGUI (ex-USS *Hank* DD 702)	D 25	Federal SB & DD Co.	Dec 1943	21 May 1944	28 Aug 1944
BOUCHARD (ex-USS *Borie* DD 704)	D 26	Federal SB & DD Co.	Jan 1944	4 July 1944	21 Sep 1944
BUENA PIEDRA (ex-USS *Collett* DD 730)	D 29	Bath Iron Works Corp.	1943	5 Mar 1944	16 May 1944

Displacement, tons: 2 200 standard; 3 320 full load
Length, feet (metres): 376·5 *(114·8)* oa
Beam, feet (metres): 40·9 *(12·5)*
Draught, feet (metres): 19 *(5·8)*
Guns: 6—5 in *(127 mm)* 38 cal; (twin); 4—3 in *(Segui* only)
A/S weapons: 6—(2 triple) Mk 32 torpedo tubes; 2 ahead-firing Hedgehogs; Facilities for small helicopter
Main engines: 2 geared turbines; 60 000 shp; 2 shafts
Boilers: 4
Speed, knots: 34
Range, miles: 4 600 at 15 knots; 990 at 31 knots
Complement: *Bouchard* 291; *Segui* 331

First pair transferred to Argentina 1 July 1972. *Bouchard* has been modernised with VDS, helicopter facilities and hangar. Two units, ex-USS *Mansfield* DD 728 and ex-USS *Collet* DD 730, transferred June 1974 and Apr 1974 respectively for spares. DD 730 was recommissioned in 1977 as *Buena Piedra* to replace *Espora* D 21 when she was scrapped.

A/S: Fitted with FCS 105.

Missiles: To be fitted with Exocet.

Radar: Search: SPS 6.
Tactical: SPS 10.

BOUCHARD (as USS BORIE)

Fire control: Mk 37 director with Mk 25 radar. Mk 56 director with Mk 35 radar *(Segui)*.

Sonar: *(Bouchard).* SQS 30, SQA 10 (VDS). *(Segui)* SQS 30.

1 Ex-US "GEARING" CLASS (FRAM II)

Name	No.	Builders	Laid down	Launched	Commissioned
PY (ex-USS *Perkins* DD 877)	D 27	Consolidated Steel Corpn.	7 Dec 1944	Mar 1945	5 Apr 1945

Displacement, tons: 2 425 standard; approx 3 500 full load
Length, feet (metres): 390·5 *(119·0)*
Beam, feet (metres): 40·9 *(12·5)*
Draught, feet (metres): 19·0 *(5·8)*
Guns: 6—5 in *(127 mm)*, 38 cal (twins)
A/S weapons: 2 fixed Hedgehogs; 6 (2 triple) Mk 32 torpedo tubes; facilities for small helicopter
Main engines: 2 geared Westinghouse turbines
Boilers: 4 Babcock & Wilcox
Speed, knots: 31·5
Range, miles: 6 150 at 11 knots; 1 475 at 30 knots
Complement: 275

Transferred by sale 15 Jan 1973.

A/S: Fitted with FCS 105.

Gunnery: FCS 37 (1).

Missiles: To be fitted with Exocet.

Radar: SPS 37.

Sonar: SQS 29.

PY (as USS PERKINS)

FRIGATES

A design contract was signed with Vosper Thornycroft on 19 May 1975 which resulted in plans for a ship similar to the British Type 21 but 200 tons larger with one 4.5 in Mk 8 gun, 4 Exocet missiles and some form of PDMS. Anything from four to eight ships was mentioned. In August 1977 Vosper Thornycroft were reported as announcing a contract for seven ships (? plus one to be built at Woolston) and in the same month a British Liaison Officer (Argentine Frigate Project) was appointed.

CORVETTES

2 Ex-US "CHEROKEE" CLASS

Name	No.	Builders	Commissioned
COMMANDANTE GENERAL IRIGOYEN (ex-USS Cahuilla ATF 152)	A 1	Charleston SB and DD Co.	10 Mar 1945
FRANCISCO DE GURRUCHAGA (ex-USS Luiseno ATF 156)	A 3	Charleston SB and DD Co.	17 Mar 1945 (launched)

Displacement, tons: 1 235 standard; 1 675 full load
Dimensions, feet (metres): 195 wl; 205 oa × 38.2 × 15.3 (62.5 × 11.6 × 4.7)
Guns: 6—40/60 mm (2 twin; 2 single)
Main engines: 4 sets diesels with electric drive; 3 000 bhp = 16 knots
Complement: 85

Fitted with powerful pumps and other salvage equipment. *Commandante General Irigoyen* transferred to Argentina at San Diego, California, in 1961. Classified as a tug until 1966 when she was re-rated as patrol vessel. *Francisco De Gurruchaga* transferred 1 July 1975 by sale.

Loss: *Commandante General Zapiola* ran aground in Nov 1976 off Falkland Islands and was lost.

FRANCISCO DE GURRUCHAGA (as LUISENO)   USN

2 "KING" CLASS

Name	No.	Builders	Commissioned
MURATURE	P 20	Base Nav. Rio Santiago	April 1945
KING	P 21	Base Nav. Rio Santiago	Nov 1946

Displacement, tons: 913 standard; 1 000 normal; 1 032 full load
Length, feet (metres): 252.7 (77.0)
Beam, feet (metres): 29 (8.8)
Draught, feet (metres): 7.5 (2.3)
Guns: 4—40 mm Bofors; 5—MG
Main engines: 2—Werkspoor 4-stroke diesels; 2 500 bhp; 2 shafts
Speed, knots: 18
Oil fuel (tons): 90
Range, miles: 6 000 at 12 knots
Complement: 100

Named after Captain John King, an Irish follower of Admiral Brown, who distinguished himself in the war with Brazil, 1826-28; and Captain Murature, who performed conspicuous service against the Paraguayans at the Battle of Cuevas on Aug 6 1865. Used for cadet training.
King laid down June 1938, launched Nov 1943. *Murature* laid down Mar 1940, launched July 1943.

MURATURE   1974, Argentine Navy

4 Ex-US "SOTOYOMO" CLASS

Name	No.	Builders	Commissioned
DIAGUITA (ex-US ATA 124)	A 5	Levingstone Sb Co, Orange	24 July 1943
YAMANA (ex-USS Maricopa ATA 146)	A 6	Levingstone Sb Co, Orange	20 Jan 1943
ALFEREZ SOBRAL (ex-USS Catawba, ATA 210)	A 9	Levingstone Sb Co, Orange	18 April 1945
COMODORO SOMELLERA (ex-USS Salish ATA 187)	A 10	Levingstone Sb Co, Orange	7 Dec 1944

Displacement, tons: 689 standard; 800 full load
Dimensions, feet (metres): 134.5 wl; 143 oa × 34 × 12 (43.6 × 10.4 × 3.7)
Gun: 1—40/60 mm
Main engines: Diesel-electric; 1 500 bhp = 12.5 knots
Oil fuel (tons): 154
Range, miles: 16 500 at 8 knots
Complement: 49

Former US auxiliary ocean tugs. A 5 and A 6 are fitted as rescue ships and were acquired in 1947. They bear names of South American Indian tribes. Classified as ocean salvage tugs until 1966 when they were re-rated as patrol vessels. A 9 and A 10 were transferred on 10 Feb 1972. A 10 operated by the Coast Guard.

Reclassification: *Chiriguano* (ex-US ATA 227) and *Sanaviron* (ex-US ATA 228) now operate as tugs.

YAMANA   1969, Argentine Navy

1 "BOUCHARD" CLASS

Name	No.	Builders	Commissioned
SPIRO	GC 12	Rio Santiago	1938

Displacement, tons: 560 normal; 650 full load
Dimensions, feet (metres): 197 oa × 24 × 11.5 (60.0 × 7.3 × 3.5)
Guns: 4—40 mm
Main engines: 2 MAN diesels; 2 000 bhp = 13 knots
Range, miles: 3 000 at 10 knots
Complement: 77

Former minesweeper of the "Bouchard" class, now operated by the Prefectura Naval Argentina. Sister ships *Bouchard*, *Py*, *Parker* and *Seaver* were transferred to the Paraguayan Navy in 1964-67. This class, originally of 9, were the first warships built in Argentine yards.

SPIRO   1969, Argentine Navy

ARGENTINA 29

AMPHIBIOUS FORCES

1 Ex-US LANDING SHIP (DOCK)

Name	No.	Builders	Commissioned
CANDIDO DE LASALA	Q 43	Moor Dry Dock Co, Oakland	10 Nov 1943
(ex-USS *Gunston Hall* LSD 5)			

Displacement, tons: 5 480 standard; 9 375 full load
Dimensions, feet (metres): 457·8 oa × 72·2 × 18·0 *(139·6 × 22 × 5·5)*
Guns: 12—40 mm
Main engines: 2 Skinner Unaflow; 2 shafts; 7 400 shp = 15·4 knots
Boilers: 2 Two drum
Range, miles: 8 000 at 15 knots
Complement: Accommodation for 326 (17 officers and 309 men)

Arcticized in 1948/9. Transferred from the US Navy on 1 May 1970. Carries 14 LCA and has helicopter facilities. Used as light forces tender.

CANDIDO DE LASALA (Type TNC 45 in well)   *1976, Michael D. J. Lennon*

1 LANDING SHIP (TANK)

Name	No.	Builders	Commissioned
CABO SAN ANTONIO	Q 42	AFNE, Rio Santiago	1978

Displacement, tons: 4 300 light; 8 000 full load
Dimensions, feet (metres): 445 oa × 62 × 16·5 *(135·6 × 18·9 × 5)*
Guns: 12—40/60 mm (3 quad)
Main engines: Diesels; 2 shafts; 13 700 bhp = 16 knots
Complement: 124

Designed to carry a helicopter and two landing craft. Launched 1968. Completion delayed—fitting out continuing 1977. Modified US "De Soto County" Class—principal difference being the fitting of Stülcken heavy-lift gear.

Radar: Plessey AWS-1.

CABO SAN ANTONIO   *1974, Argentine Navy*

3 Ex-US LST TYPE

Name	No.	Builders	Commissioned
CABO SAN GONZALO	Q 44	Jefferson B & M Co, Indiana, USA	22 Jan 1945
(ex-USS LST 872)			
CABO SAN ISIDRO	Q 46	Bethlehem Steel Co, Hingham, Mass, USA	31 May 1944
(ex-USS LST 919)			
CABO SAN PIO	Q 50	Dravo Corpn, Neville Is, Pa, USA	2 Mar 1945
(ex-USS LST 1044)			

Displacement, tons: 2 366 beaching; 4 080 full load
Dimensions, feet (metres): 328 oa × 50 × 14 *(100 × 15·3 × 4·3)*
Main engines: 2 diesels; 2 shafts; 1 800 bhp = 11 knots
Oil fuel, tons: 700
Range, miles: 9 500 at 9 knots
Complement: 80

Transferred 1946-47. Being used commercially.

1 Ex-US LCT TYPE

BDI-1 (ex-USS *LSIL* 583) Q 54

Displacement, tons: 230 light; 387 full load
Dimensions, feet (metres): 159 oa × 23·2 × 5 *(48·5 × 7·1 × 1·5)*
Guns: 2—20 mm
Main engines: 8 sets diesels; 3 200 bhp = 14 knots. Two reversible propellers
Oil fuel, tons: 110
Range, miles: 6 000 at 12 knots
Complement: 30

Used for training.

19 Ex-US LCVPs

EDM 1, 2, 3, 4

Displacement, tons: 28
Dimensions, feet (metres): 56 × 14 × ?
Main engines: 2 Gray diesels; 450 bhp = 11 knots

Acquired in USA June 1971.

EDVP 1, 3, 7, 8, 9, 10, 12, 13, 17, 19, 21, 24, 28, 29, 30

Displacement, tons: 12
Dimensions, feet (metres): 39·5 × 10·5 × 5·5 *(12·1 × 3·2 × 1·7)*
Main engines: Diesels, 9 knots

Ex-USN LCVPs. Transferred 1946.

8 Ex-US LCVPs

Dimensions, feet (metres): 63 × 14·1 × —*(19·2 × 4·3 ×—)*
Main engine: 1 diesel; approx 250 hp

Incorporated in May 1970. Numbers not known.

LIGHT FORCES

2 MOD-TYPE 148 (FAST ATTACK CRAFT—MISSILE)

Displacement, tons: 234 standard; 265 full load
Dimensions, feet (metres): 147·3 × 23 × 6·9 *(44·9 × 7·0 × 2·1)*
Missiles: 5 launchers for Gabriel missiles (triple and twin)
Guns: 1—57 mm; 1—40 mm; 2—12·5 mm
Torpedo tubes: 2—21 in (or 8 mines)
Main engines: 4 MD16V diesels; 14 400 shp = 38 knots
Range, miles: 600 at 30 knots
Complement: 30

Building in Argentina. Similar to TNC 48 class of Singapore.

Radar: Signaal type for weapon control.

TNC 48 Class   *Lürssen Werft*

30 ARGENTINA

2 TYPE TNC 45 (FAST ATTACK CRAFT—GUN)

Name	No.	Builders	Commissioned
INTREPIDA	ELPR 1	Lürssen, Bremen	20 July 1974
INDOMITA	ELPR 2	Lürssen, Bremen	Dec 1974

Displacement, tons: 268 full load
Dimensions, feet (metres): 149 × 24·3 × 7·5 (45·4 × 7·4 × 2·3)
Guns: 1—3 in (76 mm) OTO Melara; 2—40 mm L70-350
Rocket launcher: 2 Oerlikon 81 mm
Torpedo tubes: 2—21 in for wire-guided torpedoes
Main engines: 4 diesels; 4 shafts; 12 000 hp = 40 knots
Complement: 37

These two vessels were ordered in 1970. *Intrepida* launched 12 Dec 1973, *Indomita* 8 Apr 1974.

Radar: Fire control: Hollandse Signaal WM20 for guns; M11 for torpedoes.

INDOMITA *Lürssen Werft*

3 "LYNCH" CLASS (LARGE PATROL CRAFT)

Name	No.	Builders	Commissioned
LYNCH	GC 21	AFNE Rio Santiago	1964
TOLL	GC 22	AFNE Rio Santiago	1965
EREZCANO	GC 23	AFNE Rio Santiago	1967

Displacement, tons: 100 normal; 117 full load
Dimensions, feet (metres): 90 × 19 × 6 (27·4 × 5·8 × 1·8)
Gun: 1—20 mm
Main engines: 2 Maybach diesels; 2 700 bhp = 22 knots
Complement: 16

Patrol craft operated by the Prefectura Naval Argentina.

LYNCH *1969, Argentine Navy*

1 LARGE PATROL CRAFT

Name	No.	Builders	Commissioned
SURUBI	P 55	Ast. Nav. del Estero	1951

Displacement, tons: 100
Guns: 2—20 mm
Speed, knots: 20

1 Ex-US 63 ft AVR (LARGE PATROL CRAFT)

GC 31

Dimensions as for US 63 ft AVR class but of slightly different silhouette.

1 LARGE PATROL CRAFT

Name	No.	Builders	Commissioned
DELFIN	GC 13	?	1957

Measurement, tons: 518 gross
Dimensions, feet (metres): 196·8 × 29·5 × 15·4 (60 × 9 × 4·7)
Main engines: 2 300 hp = 15 knots
Complement: 32

Trawler type acquired for PNA in 1970.

2 EX-US "HIGGINS" CLASS (FAST ATTACK CRAFT—TORPEDO)

Name	No.	Builders	Commissioned
ALAKUSH	P 82	New Orleans SB	1946
TOWWORA	P 84	New Orleans SB	1946

Displacement, tons: 45 standard; 50 full load
Dimensions, feet (metres): 78·7 × 9·8 × 4·6 (24 × 3 × 1·4)
Guns: 2—40/60 mm; 4—MG
Torpedo launchers: 4—21 in racks
Rocket launchers: 2 octuple sets 12·7 cm
Main engines: 3 Packard (petrol); 4 500 hp = 42 knots
Range, miles: 1 000 at 20 knots
Complement: 12

The last of a class of nine. Given names in 1972.

Note. In addition the following are listed as operated by PNA: Robalo, Mandubi, Adhara, Albatross, Dorado, LT 1 and 8, PAV 1, 2 and 3. PAM 1, 2 and 3, V 2 and 6, GN 1, 4, 38 and 42, PF 17, P 2, 5, 13, 22, 26, 39 and 41. A further craft *Pacu* GC 46 is listed.

MINE WARFARE FORCES

6 Ex-BRITISH "TON" CLASS
(MINESWEEPERS—COASTAL and MINEHUNTERS)

Name	No.	Builders	Launched
NEUQUEN (ex-HMS *Hickleton*)	M 1	Thornycroft	26 Jan 1955
RIO NEGRO (ex-HMS *Tarlton*)	M 2	Doig	10 Nov 1954
CHUBUT (ex-HMS *Santon*)	M 3	Fleetlands	18 Aug 1955
TIERRA DEL FUEGO (ex- HMS *Bevington*)	M 4	Whites	17 Mar 1953
CHACO (ex-HMS *Rennington*)	M 5	Richards	27 Nov 1958
FORMOSA (ex-HMS *Ilmington*)	M 6	Camper, Nicholson	8 Mar 1954

Displacement, tons: 360 standard; 425 full load
Dimensions, feet (metres): 140 pp; 153 oa × 28·8 × 8·2 (46·3 × 8·8 × 2·5)
Gun: 1—40/60 mm
Main engines: 2 diesels; 2 shafts; 3 000 bhp = 15 knots
Oil fuel, tons: 45
Range, miles: 2 300 at 13 knots; 3 000 at 8 knots
Complement: Minesweepers 27; Minehunters 36

Former British coastal minesweepers of the "Ton" class. Of composite wooden and non-magnetic metal construction. Purchased in 1967. In 1968 *Chaco* and *Formosa* were converted into minehunters in HM Dockyard, Portsmouth, and the other four were refitted and modernised as minesweepers by the Vosper Thornycroft Group with Vosper activated-fin stabiliser equipment.

NEUQUEN (SWEEPER) *1974, Argentine Navy*

SURVEY AND OCEANOGRAPHICAL SHIPS

1 NEW CONSTRUCTION OCEANOGRAPHICAL SHIP

Displacement, tons: 1 960 standard

Ordered from Alianza, Avellaneda in 1974(?).

ARGENTINA 31

1 + 1 RESEARCH SHIPS

Name	No.	Builders	Commissioned	
PUERTO DESEADO	—	Astarsa, San Fernando	1977	Laid down in 1974 for Consejo Nacional de Investigaciones Tecnicas y Scientificas. Civilian manned. Launched 4 Dec 1976. Second of class ordered May 1976.

Displacement, tons: 2 100 standard
Dimensions, feet (metres): 249 × 43·4 × 14·9 (75·9 × 13·2 × 4·5)
Main engine: 1 diesel; 2 600 hp = 12 knots

2 Ex-US TYPE V4 TUGS

Name	No.	Builders	Commissioned
GOYENA (ex-USS *Dry Tortuga*)	Q 17 (ex-A 3)	Pendleton SY, New Orleans	1943
THOMPSON (ex-USS *Sombrero Key*)	A 4	Pendleton SY, New Orleans	1943

Displacement, tons: 1 863 full load
Dimensions, feet (metres): 191·3 × 37 × 18 (58·3 × 11·3 × 5·5)
Guns: 2—40 mm Bofors (twin); 2—20 mm (single)
Main engines: 2 Enterprise diesels; 2 250 bhp = 12 knots
Oil fuel, tons: 532
Complement: 62

Leased to Argentina in 1965. Temporarily used as survey ships.

THOMPSON 1973, Argentine Navy

Name	No.	Builders	Commissioned
ISLAS ORCADAS (ex-USS *Eltanin*, T-AGOR 8—AK 270)	Q 9	Avondale, New Orleans	2 Aug 1957

Displacement, tons: 2 036 light; 4 942 full load
Dimensions, feet (metres): 262·2 oa × 51·5 × 18·7 (80 × 15·7 × 5·7)
Main engines: Diesel-electric; 3 200 bhp; 2 shafts = 12 knots
Complement: 12 officers, 36 men, 38 scientists

Converted for Antarctic Research 1961. Operated in conjunction by Argentine Navy, US National Science Foundation and Argentine National Directorate of the Antarctic. Transferred 15 Nov 1972.

Name	No.	Builders	Commissioned
COMODORO RIVADAVIA	Q 11	Mestrina, Tigre	6 Dec 1976

Displacement, tons: 609 standard; 667 full load
Dimensions, feet (metres): 167 × 28·9 × 8·5 (50·9 × 8·8 × 2·6)
Main engines: 2 Werkspoor diesels; 1 160 hp = 12 knots
Range, miles: 6 000 at 12 knots
Complement: 27

Laid down 17 July 1971, launched 2 Dec 1972. Completion ex-trials Dec 1974.

CORMORAN Q 15

Coastal survey launch of 102 tons with complement of 19, built in 1963. Speed 13 knots. Commissioned Feb 1964.

1 AUXILIARY SAILING SHIP

Name	No.	Builders	Commissioned
EL AUSTRAL (ex-*Atlantis*)	Q 7	Burmeister and Wain, Copenhagen	1931

Displacement, tons: 571
Dimensions, feet (metres): 110 pp; 141 oa × 27 × 20 (33·5; 43 × 8·2 × 6·1)
Main engines: Diesels; 400 bhp
Oil fuel, tons: 22
Complement: 19

PETREL

Coastal survey launch of 50 tons with complement of 9, built in 1965.

Incorporated into the Argentine Navy on 30 April, 1966. Acquired from USA. (Wood's Hole Institute).

TRANSPORTS

Name	No.	Builders	Commissioned
BAHIA AGUIRRE	B 2	Canadian Vickers, Halifax	1950
BAHIA BUEN SUCESO	B 6	Canadian Vickers, Halifax	June 1950

Displacement, tons: 3 100 standard; 5 000 full load
Dimensions, feet (metres): 334·7 × 47 × 13·8 (102 × 14·3 × 4·2)
Main engines: 2 sets Nordberg diesels; 2 shafts; 3 750 bhp = 16 knots
Oil fuel, tons: 442 (B 6); 355 (B 2)
Complement: 100

Survivors of class of three.

BAHIA AGUIRRE 8/1976, Michael D. J. Lennon

3 "COSTA SUR" CLASS

Name	No.	Builders	Commissioned	
CANAL BEAGLE	—	A. P. Menghi y Penco	1978	Ordered Dec 1975 from Ast. Principe Menghi y Penco Ga, Avellaneda. To replace 3 ex-US LSTs (*Cabo San Gonzalo*, *San Isidro* and *San Pio*). To be used commercially. First two laid down 1977.
BAHIA SAN BLAS	—	A. P. Menghi y Penco	1978	
BAHIA CAMARONES	—	A. P. Menghi y Penco	1979	

Measurement, tons: 4 600 gross; 5 800 deadweight
Dimensions, feet (metres): 390·3 × 57·4 × 21 (119 × 17·5 × 6·4)
Main engines: 2 diesels; 6 400 hp = 15 knots

32 ARGENTINA

TANKERS
1 LARGE FLEET TANKER (FLEET SUPPORT)

Name	No.	Builders	Commissioned
PUNTA MEDANOS	B 18	Swan Hunter	10 Oct 1950

Displacement, tons: 14 352 standard; 16 331 full load
Measurement, tons: 8 250 deadweight
Dimensions, feet (metres): 470 pp; 502 oa × 62 × 28·5 *(143·4; 153·1 × 18·9 × 8·7)*
Main engines: Double reduction geared turbines. 2 shafts; 9 500 shp = 18 knots
Boilers: 2 Babcock & Wilcox two-drum integral furnace water-tube
Oil fuel, tons: 1 500
Range, miles: 13 700 at 15 knots
Complement: 99

Available as a training vessel. Boilers built under licence by the Wallsend Slipway & Engineering Company. Steam conditions of 400 psi pressure and 750°F.

PUNTA MEDANOS *1973, Argentine Navy*

1 Ex-US "KUCKITAT" CLASS (FLEET SUPPORT)

Name	No.	Builders	Commissioned
PUNTA DELGADA (ex-SS *Sugarland*, ex-*Nanticoke* AOG 66)	B 16	St. Johns River SB, Jacksonville	1945

Displacement, tons: 5 930 standard; 6 090 full load
Dimensions, feet (metres): 325 × 48·2 × 20 *(99·1 × 14·7 × 6·1)*
Main engines: Westinghouse diesel; 1 shaft; 1 400 bhp = 11·5 knots
Oil fuel, tons: 150
Range, miles: 9 000 at 11 knots
Complement: 72

USMS type T1-M-BT1. Launched on 7 April 1945. Used commercially.

1 TANKER (FLEET SUPPORT)

Name	No.	Builder	Commissioned
PUNTA ALTA	B 12	Puerto Belgrano	1938

Displacement, tons: 1 600 standard; 1 900 full load
Measurement, tons: 800 deadweight
Dimensions, feet (metres): 210 × 33·8 × 12·5 *(64 × 10·3 × 3·8)*
Main engines: Diesel; 1 shaft; 1 850 bhp = 8 knots
Oil fuel, tons: 146
Complement: 40

TRAINING SHIP

Name	No.	Builders	Commissioned
LIBERTAD	Q 2	AFNE, Rio Santiago	1962

Displacement, tons: 3 025 standard; 3 765 full load
Dimensions, feet (metres): 262 wl; 301 oa × 47 × 21·8 *(79·9, 91·7 × 14·3 × 6·6)*
Guns: 1—3 in; 4—40 mm; 4—47 mm saluting
Main engines: 2 Sulzer diesels; 2 400 bhp = 13·5 knots
Complement: 370 (crew) plus 150 cadets

Launched on 20 June 1956. She is the largest sail training ship in the world and set up the fastest crossing of the N. Atlantic under sail in 1966, a record which still stands.

ICEBREAKERS
1 NEW CONSTRUCTION WÄRTSILA TYPE

Name	No.	Builders	Commissioned
ALMIRANTE IRIZAR	—	Wärtsila (Helsinki)	late 1978

Dimensions, feet (metres): 392 × 82 × 31·2 *(119·5 × 25 × 9·5)*
Main engines: Diesel-electric; 16 200 shp (4 Wärtsila-SEMT Pielstick 8PC2-5L diesels); 2 shafts
Speed, knots: 16·5
Complement: 133 ship's company; 100 passengers

Contract signed on 17 Dec 1975. The ship is designed for Antarctic support operations and will be able to remain in the polar regions throughout the winter with 210 people aboard. Fitted for helicopters and landing craft with two 16 ton cranes. Will have fin stabilisers, Wärtsila bubbling system and a 60 ton towing winch.

Radar: Search: AWS-2. Navigation: 2 Decca.

ALMIRANTE IRIZAR *1975, Wärtsila*

Name	No.	Builders	Commissioned
GENERAL SAN MARTIN	Q 4	Seebeck Yd-Weser AG	Oct 1954

Displacement, tons: 4 854 standard; 5 301 full load
Measurement, tons: 1 600 deadweight
Dimensions, feet (metres): 279 × 61 × 21 *(85·1 × 18·6 × 6·4)*
Aircraft: 1 reconnaissance aircraft and 1 helicopter
Guns: 2—40 mm Bofors
Main engines: 4 diesel-electric; 2 shafts; 7 100 hp = 16 knots
Oil fuel, tons: 1 100
Range, miles: 35 000 at 10 knots
Complement: 160

Launched on 24 June 1954. Fitted for research. New second radar mast fitted on after end of the hangar in late 1972.

GENERAL SAN MARTIN *1970, Argentine Navy*
(2nd radar mast now fitted and 4 in gun removed)

MISCELLANEOUS

TUGS

2 Ex-US "SOTOYOMO" CLASS

Name	No.	Builders	Commissioned
CHIRIGUANO (ex-US ATA 227)	—	Levingstone SB Co	1945
SANAVIRON (ex-US ATA 228)	—	Levingstone SB Co	1945

Details as for "Sotoyomo" class under "Corvettes" except that gun has been removed.

2 "QUILMES" CLASS

Name	No.	Builders	Commissioned
QUILMES	R 32	Rio Santiago	30 Mar 1960
GUAYCURU	R 33	Rio Santiago	29 July 1960

Displacement, tons: 368 full load
Dimensions, feet (metres): 107·2 × 24·4 × 12·5 (32·7 × 7·4 × 3·8)
Main engines: Skinner Unaflow engines; 645 hp = 9 knots
Boilers: Cylindrical
Oil fuel, tons: 52
Range, miles: 2 200 at 7 knots
Complement: 14

Laid down on 23 Aug and 15 Mar 1956 respectively, launched on 27 Dec 1959 and 8 July 1957.

Name	No.	Builders	Commissioned
PEHUENCHE	R 29	Rio Santiago	1954
TONOCOTE	R 30	Rio Santiago	1954

Displacement, tons: 330
Dimensions, feet (metres): 105 × 24·7 × 12·5 (32 × 7·5 × 3·8)
Main engines: Triple expansion; 600 ihp = 11 knots
Boilers: 2
Oil fuel, tons: 36
Range, miles: 1 200 at 9 knots
Complement: 13

Name	No.	Builders	Commissioned
TOBA	R 4	Hawthorn Leslie Ltd	Mar 1928

Displacement, tons: 600
Measurement, tons: 339 gross
Dimensions, feet (metres): 139 oa × 28·5 × 11·5 (42·4 × 8·7 × 3·5)
Main engines: Triple expansion; 2 shafts; 1 200 ihp = 12 knots
Boilers: 2
Oil fuel, tons: 95
Range, miles: 3 900 at 10 knots
Complement: 34

Launched on 23 Dec 1927.

Name	No.	Builders	Commissioned
QUERANDI	—	As. Vicente Forte	1977
TEHUELCHE	—	As. Vicente Forte	1977

Displacement, tons: 370
Dimensions, feet (metres): 110·2 × 27·6 × 9·8 (33·6 × 8·4 × 3·0)
Main engines: 2 MAN diesels; 1 200 bhp = 12 knots

Name	No.	Builders	Commissioned
HUARPE	R 12	Howaldtwerke	1927

Displacement, tons: 370
Dimensions, feet (metres): 107 × 27·2 × 12 (32·6 × 8·3 × 3·7)
Main engines: Triple expansion; 800 ihp
Boilers: 1 cylindrical (Howaldtwerke)
Oil fuel, tons: 58
Complement: 13

Entered service in the Argentine Navy in 1942.

MOCOVI	R 5 (ex-US YTL 441)	CAPAYAN	R 16 (ex-US YTL 443)
CALCHAQUI	R 6 (ex-US YTL 445)	CHIQUILLAN	R 18 (ex-US YTL 444)
CHULUPI	R 10 (ex-US YTL 426)	MORCOYAN	R 19 (ex-US YTL 448)

Displacement, tons: 70
Dimensions, feet (metres): 67 × 14 × 13 (20·4 × 4·3 × 4)
Main engines: Diesel; 310 bhp = 10 knots
Oil fuel, tons: 8·7
Complement: 5

YTL Type built in USA and transferred on lease in Mar 1965 (R 16, 18, 19), remainder in Mar 1969. All purchased 16 June 1977.

Note. Two harbour tugs built by Vicente Forte entered service in 1974.

FLOATING DOCKS

Number	Dimensions, feet (metres)	Capacity, tons
Y 1 (ex-ARD 23)	492 × 88·6 × 56 (150 × 27 × 17·1)	3 500
2	300·1 × 60 × 41 (91·5 × 18·3 × 12·5)	1 000
ASD 40	215·8 × 46 × 45·5 (65·8 × 14 × 13·7)	750
—	215·8 × 46 × 45·5 (65·8 × 14 × 13·7)	750

First three are at Darsena Norte, Buenos Aires and the fourth at Puerto Belgrano.

AUXILIARIES

Two naval sail-training ships, *Fortuna* and *Juana* built by Tandanor, Buenos Aires.
Two auxiliaries, *E 6*, and *Itati* listed.
The ex-training ship *Presidente Sarmiento* is retained at Buenos Aires as a museum ship, as also is the 1874 Corvette *Uruguay*.
Auxiliary EM6 launched by T.A.R. in 1976.

FLOATING CRANES

At least four—at Darsena Norte, Rio Santiago, Mar de Plata and Puerto Belgrano.

AUSTRALIA

Administration

Minister for Defence (and Navy):
  Hon D. J. Killen, MP
Chief of Defence Force Staff:
  General A. L. MacDonald CB, OBE

Headquarters Appointments

Chief of Naval Staff:
  Vice-Admiral A. M. Synnot, AO, CBE
Deputy Chief of the Naval Staff:
  Rear-Admiral B. S. Murray
Chief of Naval Personnel:
  Rear-Admiral G. R. Griffiths, DSO, DSC
Chief of Naval Technical Services:
  Rear-Admiral M. P. Reed, AO
Chief of Naval Materiel:
  Rear-Admiral P. H. Doyle, OBE
Chief of Naval Operational Requirements and Plans:
  Rear-Admiral A. A. Willis, OBE

Senior Appointments

Flag Officer Commanding Australian Fleet:
  Rear-Admiral N. E. McDonald, AO
Flag Officer Commanding East Australian Area:
  Rear-Admiral J. Davidson

Diplomatic Representation

Naval Attaché in Jakarta:
  Captain R. J. Whitten
Naval Representative in London:
  Commodore G. J. H. Woolrych
Naval Attaché in Tokyo:
  Captain P. E. M. Holloway
Naval Attaché in Washington:
  Commodore R. G. Loosli, CBE

Personnel

1 January 1973: 17 128 officers and sailors
1 January 1974: 16 743 officers and sailors
1 January 1975: 15 811 officers and sailors
1 January 1976: 15 909 officers and sailors
1 January 1977: 16 390 officers and sailors (app)
(including 850 WRANS)
1 June 1978: 16 380 officers and sailors
(target strength including 900 WRANS)

Navy Estimates
              $A
1972-73: 293 094 000*
1973-74: 319 994 000*
1974-75: 375 014 000
1975-76: 428 879 000
1976-77: 539 808 000
1977-78: 565 172 000
(*Includes United States Credits)

Naval Bases

FOCEA—Sydney and Jervis Bay
NOC Queensland—Brisbane and Cairns (PCs and LCHs)
NOC Northern Territory—Darwin (PCs)
NOC W. Australia—HMAS *Stirling* Cockburn Sound (estimated commissioning mid 1978)

Naval Shipyards

Building at Williamstown (Melbourne) and Cockatoo Island (Sydney). Refits at both and Garden Island (Sydney).

Fleet Air Arm

Squadron	Aircraft
HC-723	Iroquois, Wessex 31B (Utility) and Bell 206B-1 helos (Utility, SAR and FRU)
VC-724	A4G and TA4G Skyhawks, Macchi Trainers (Training, FRU and Trials)
VF-805	A4G Skyhawks (Front line fighter/strike)
VS-816	S2G Trackers (Front line A/S)
HS-817	Sea King Mk 50 helos (Front line A/S)
VC-851	S2G/S2E Trackers, HS 748 (Training, communications and FRU)

Note: The Royal Australian Air Force (RAAF) has 21 P3C (Orion) maritime patrol aircraft with 2 more ordered late 1976. 15 reconnaissance aircraft (without ASW equipment) are also planned.

Prefix to Ships' Names

HMAS. Her Majesty's Australian Ship

Mercantile Marine

Lloyd's Register of Shipping:
  424 vessels of 1 374 197 tons gross

Strength of the Fleet

Type	Active	Building
Attack Carrier (Medium)	1	—
Destroyers	5 (3DDG)	—
Frigates (GM)	—	3
Frigates	6	—
Patrol Submarines	6	—
MCM Vessels	3	—
Large Patrol Craft	12	(15)
Survey Ships	4	1 (2)
Fleet Tanker	1	—
Destroyer Tender	1	—
Landing Craft (Heavy)	6	—
Landing Ship (Heavy)	—	1
Training Ship	1	—

Naval Procurement and Modernisation

In February 1976 the Australian Government accepted a letter of offer from the US Navy for two guided missile frigates of the "Oliver Hazard Perry" (FFG7) class. These ships will enter service in the Royal Australian Navy (RAN) in 1981. In November 1977 the government announced its decision to acquire a third ship of this class. The acquisition of this ship will raise the strength of the destroyer fleet from 11 to 12. The White Paper also stated that investigations were being made into the concepts, characteristics, and cost of "follow-on" destroyers, preferably for construction in Australia. These investigations would be in conjunction with those of missile armed patrol boats.
In September 1977 the Defence Minister announced that an invitation would be issued to Australian and overseas companies to register interest in investigating possible aircraft carrier designs for the RAN. Studies of alternative capabilities which might possibly meet Australia's requirements on the retirement of HMAS *Melbourne* would continue concurrently.
The Invitation to Register Interest (ITR) lists five "illustrative ship options" as a guide to interested organisations. These range from 10 000 tonne helicopter-only ship to a ship of 25 000 tonnes or more operating V/STOL aircraft and helicopters. A decision on whether to proceed to a funded investigation will be made on completion of examination of responses to ITR.
A decision to acquire 15 Brooke Marine PCF420 patrol craft also was announced in September 1977. The lead craft is being built in the United Kingdom, and the remainder in Australia by North Queensland Engineers and Agents Pty Ltd of Cairns.
In November 1977 a contract was let to Carrington Slipways Pty Ltd for construction of a new Amphibious Heavy Lift Ship, to be named HMAS *Tobruk*.
The RAN plans to replace HMAS *Supply* with a new underway replenishment ship in 1980. Early in 1977 a contract was let to DTCN of France for project definition of a ship of the "Durance" class.
Plans to acquire a purpose-built training ship were dropped after the acquisition of the former roll-on roll-off ship MV *Australian Trader* in 1977. The ship is now commissioned as HMAS *Jervis Bay*.
The RAN is proceeding with initial prototype design and acquisition of long-lead items for two prototype mine-hunters. These ships, which will be the first of a class intended to replace the ageing "Ton" class ships now in service, will feature a GRP catamaran hull. The new class is due to enter service in the first half of the 1980s.
A new oceanographic ship, HMAS *Cook*, is being constructed to replace HMAS *Diamantina*, and a new trials and research ship to replace HMAS *Kimbla* in the mid 1980s is also contemplated. The 1976 Defence White Paper announced an intention to construct a further two hydrographic ships and six large survey launches. The new ships probably would be similar to HMAS *Flinders*.
Two new "Oberon" class submarines, HMAS *Orion* and HMAS *Otama*, were commissioned in the United Kingdom in 1977 and early 1978 respectively. The RAN's submarine squadron is being modernised by the fitting of new attack sonar and an advanced fire control system. Fitting of a new passive range-finding sonar is proceeding. The acquisition of an initial outfit of Mk 48 torpedoes from the USA was announced in October 1977.
Other procurement and modernisation plans include:
limited acquisition of anti-shipping missiles (e.g. Harpoon, Exocet) for destroyers and submarines.
"Perth" class DDGs are being progressively modernised by installation of new gun mounts, naval combat data systems, and "Standard" SAM systems.
Three of the older "River" class DEs will be modernised, and a fourth, HMAS *Yarra* completed a half-life refit in 1977. When this work is completed in 1982 it is planned to start modernisation of HMAS *Swan* and HMAS *Torrens*.
A study will be undertaken of the feasibility of modernising the RAN's Wessex utility helicopters to extend their effective operational life. The useful life of the Macchi jet trainer aircraft will be extended by an equipment and structural refurbishment programme to be carried out within the Australian aircraft industry.
A contract to supply 22 12 m aluminium workboats to the RAN and the Army was announced in September 1977.

Other Service Craft

(a) Australian Army
    11 Ex-US LCM (8)
    6 LCVPs
    2 Coastal Tugs
    1 Cargo Boat
(b) RAAF:
    1 76 ft ASR (Townsville)
    1 63 ft ASR (Newcastle)

DELETIONS

Ex-Carrier

Sydney	For disposal 20.7.73. Left Sydney for South Korean breakers 23.12.75

Destroyers

Arunta	Sank under tow to breaker 13.2.69
Tobruk	Left Sydney for Taiwan 10.4.72
Anzac	Left Sydney for Hong Kong 30.12.75
Duchess	Decommissioned 24.10.77 At Athol Bight

Frigates

Barcoo	Left Sydney for Taiwan 17.3.72
Culgoa	Left Sydney for Taiwan 17.3.72
Quickmatch	Left Sydney for Japan 10.4.72
Quiberon	Left Sydney for Japan 6.7.72
Gascoyne	Left Sydney for Taiwan 6.7.72
Queenborough	Left Sydney for Hong Kong 12.5.75

Landing Craft (Heavy)

Buna	To Papua New Guinea
Salamaua	Defence Force 14.11.74

MCM Vessels

Hawk	Sold 1975. Removed 1977
Gull	Sold 1975—Rebuilding as private rescue ship
Teal	Awaiting Disposal

Large Patrol Craft

Archer and Bandolier	To Indonesia 21.10.74 & 16.11.73
Arrow	Sunk Darwin (Cyclone Tracy) 25.12.74
Aitape, Ladava, Lae, Madang, Samarai	To Papua New Guinea Defence Force 16.9.75

Miscellaneous

SDB 1321	1972
Kara Kara	Base Ship sunk as target 30.1.73
Paluma	Sold Commercial 1974
Otter	Sold as fishing boat 1974
Tortoise and Turtle	Sold Commercial 1975
Bronzewing (tug)	Sold Commercial 3.6.77
Tug 503	To PNGDF 1974

PENNANT LIST

Aircraft Carrier

21 Melbourne

Submarines

57 Oxley
59 Otway
60 Onslow
61 Orion
62 Otama
70 Ovens

Destroyers

08 Vendetta
11 Vampire
38 Perth
39 Hobart
41 Brisbane

AUSTRALIA 35

Frigates

01 Adelaide
02 Canberra
45 Yarra
46 Parramatta
48 Stuart
49 Derwent
50 Swan
53 Torrens

Minehunters

1102 Snipe
1121 Curlew

Minesweeper (Coastal)

1183 Ibis

Training Ship

GT 203 Jervis Bay

Large Patrol Craft

81 Acute
82 Adroit
83 Advance
87 Ardent
89 Assail
90 Attack
91 Aware
97 Barbette
98 Barricade
99 Bombard
100 Buccaneer
101 Bayonet

Amphibious Heavy Lift Ship

L50 Tobruk

Landing Craft

L126 Balikpapan
L127 Brunei
L128 Labuan
L129 Tarakan
L130 Wewak
L133 Betano

General Purpose Ships

A244 Banks
A247 Bass

Survey Ships

A219 Cook
GOR266 Diamantina
GOR314 Kimbla
GS73 Moresby
GS312 Flinders

Fleet Tanker

O195 Supply

Destroyer Tender

D215 Stalwart

MELBOURNE

"PERTH" Class

VAMPIRE and VENDETTA

PARRAMATTA and YARRA

SWAN and TORRENS

MORESBY

STALWART

SUPPLY

AUSTRALIA

SUBMARINES

6 "OXLEY" CLASS (BRITISH "OBERON" CLASS)

Name	No.	Builders	Laid down	Launched	Commissioned
OXLEY	57	Scotts' Shipbuilding & Eng Co Ltd, Greenock	2 July 1964	24 Sep 1965	18 Apr 1967
OTWAY	59	Scotts' Shipbuilding & Eng Co Ltd, Greenock	29 June 1965	29 Nov 1966	23 Apr 1968
ONSLOW	60	Scotts' Shipbuilding & Eng Co Ltd, Greenock	4 Dec 1967	3 Dec 1968	22 Dec 1969
ORION	61	Scotts' Shipbuilding & Eng Co Ltd, Greenock	6 Oct 1972	16 Sep 1974	15 June 1977
OTAMA	62	Scotts' Shipbuilding & Eng Co Ltd, Greenock	25 May 1973	3 Dec 1975	early 1978
OVENS	70	Scotts' Shipbuilding & Eng Co Ltd, Greenock	17 June 1966	4 Dec 1967	18 Apr 1969

Displacement, tons: 1 610 standard; 2 196 surfaced; 2 417 dived
Length, feet (metres): 241 *(73·5)* pp; 295·5 *(90·1)* oa
Beam, feet (metres): 26·5 *(8·1)*
Draught, feet (metres): 18 *(5·5)*
Torpedo tubes: 8—21 in *(533 mm)* (6 bow, 2 stern)
Main machinery: 2 Admiralty Standard Range diesels; 3 600 bhp; 2 shafts; 2 electric motors; 6 000 shp; electric drive
Speed, knots: 16 surfaced; 18 dived
Oil fuel, tons: 300
Range, miles: 12 000 at 10 knots
Complement: 62 (7 officers, 55 sailors)

It was announced by the Minister for the Navy on 22 Jan 1963 that four submarines of the "Oberon" class were to be built in British shipyards under Admiralty supervision at an overall cost of £A5 million each. These were to constitute the 1st Submarine Squadron RAN based at HMAS Platypus, Neutral Bay, Sydney. Subsequently two more were ordered in October 1971 for delivery in 1975-76 later extended to 1977.

Dock: Slave Dock (Sydney) was first used in 1974, allowing submarine dockings to be carried out without occupying graving docks.

Modernisation: All submarines will be fitted with a new attack sonar from Krupp Atlas of Germany and an advanced fire control system being developed with Singer-Librascope Corporation. They are also being fitted with a new passive ranging sonar built by Sperry Corporation. Mk 48 torpedoes are to be acquired from the US and, possibly, Harpoon anti-ship guided missiles.

Names: *Oxley* and *Otway* are named after two earlier RAN submarines, completed in 1927. *Otama* is the Queensland aboriginal word for Dolphin, *Onslow* is a town in Western Australia, *Ovens* was an early explorer and *Orion* is named after the constellation.

Radar: Type 1006

Sonar: Attack: Type 187C.
Intercept: Type 197.
Torpedo warning: Type 719—being removed
Long range Passive Search: Type 2007
Passive Range Finding: AN/BQG

ORION
1977, Royal Australian Navy

OVENS
1976, John Mortimer

OTWAY
1976, John Mortimer

AUSTRALIA 37

AIRCRAFT CARRIER

1 MODIFIED "MAJESTIC" CLASS

Name	No.	Builders	Laid down	Launched	Commissioned
MELBOURNE (ex-Majestic)	21	Vickers-Armstrong, Barrow-in-Furness	15 Apr 1943	28 Feb 1945	28 Oct 1955

Displacement, tons: 16 000 standard; 19 966 full load
Length, feet (metres): 650·0 (198·1) wl; 701·5 (213·8) oa
Beam, feet (metres): 80·2 (24·4) hull
Draught, feet (metres): 25·5 (7·8)
Width, feet (metres): 80·0 (24·4) flight deck
126·0 (38·4) oa including 6 degree angled deck and mirrors
Hangar, feet (metres): 444 × 52 × 17·5 (135·3 × 15·8 × 5·3)
Aircraft: A mix of A4G Skyhawk jet fighters, S2E Tracker A/S aircraft and Sea King Mk 50 A/S helicopters (see Aircraft notes)
Guns: 12—40 mm (4 twin, 4 single) Bofors
Boilers: 4 Admiralty 3-drum type
Main engines: Parsons single reduction geared turbines; 2 shafts; 42 000 shp
Speed, knots: 23
Range, miles: 12 000 at 14 knots; 6 200 at 23 knots
Complement: 1 335 (includes 347 Carrier Air Group personnel); 1 070 (75 officers and 995 sailors) as Flagship

At the end of the Second World War, when she was still incomplete, work on this ship was brought to a standstill pending a decision as to future naval requirements. When full-scale work was resumed during 1949-55, and after her design had been re-cast several times, she underwent reconstruction and modernisation in the United Kingdom, including the fitting of the angled deck, steam catapult and mirror deck landing sights, and was transferred to the RAN on completion. She was commissioned and renamed at Barrow-in-Furness on 28 Oct 1955, sailed from Portsmouth on 5 Mar 1956, and arrived at Fremantle, Australia, on 23 April 1956. She became flagship of the Royal Australian Navy at Sydney on 14 May 1956. She cost £A8 309 000.

Aircraft: The aircraft complement formerly comprised 8 Sea Venom Mk 53 jet fighters, 16 Gannet Mk 1 turbo-prop A/S aircraft and 2 Sycamore helicopters. The complement changed twice before 1967 to 10 Sea Venoms, 10 Gannets, 2 Sycamores and finally 4 Sea Venoms, 6 Gannets and 10 Wessex Mk 31 A/S helicopters. Fourteen S2E Tracker A/S aircraft, eight A4G Skyhawk fighter/strike aircraft and two TA4G Skyhawk trainer aircraft were delivered from the USA in 1967 at a cost of about $A46,000,000. Squadrons first embarked in Melbourne in 1969. Another 8 A4G and 2 TA4G Skyhawk aircraft were delivered in 1971. HS-817 Squadron recommissioned in February 1976 with Sea King Mk 50 A/S helicopters. A general purpose complement embarked in Melbourne is 8 Skyhawks, 4 Trackers and 5 Sea Kings which can be varied to meet various other roles. Following a hangar fire at NAS Nowra in December 1976 in which all but 3 S2E Trackers were destroyed 16 ex-USN S2G Trackers were purchased and delivered in April 1977.

Electronics: Plessey tactical displays. URN-20 Tacan pod on masthead; Electronic intercept fitted.

Modernisation: Melbourne completed her extended refit during 1969 at a cost of over $A8 750 000 to enable her to operate with S2E Tracker and A4G Skyhawk aircraft, and to improve habitability. In 1971 the catapult was rebuilt and a bridle-catcher fitted, and the flight deck was strengthened. Under refit from November 1972 to July 1973.
On completion of a major refit in 1976 it was announced that Melbourne could remain operational until 1985.

Radar: Air surveillance: LW-02 (Type 944/954 IFF Mk 10 integrated).
Surface search: Type 293.
Carrier-controlled approach: SPN-35.
Navigation: Type 978.

MELBOURNE — Oct 1977, Graeme Andrews

MELBOURNE — June 1977, Dr. Giorgio Arra

MELBOURNE (with launch from Jubilee Review) — Oct 1977, John Mortimer

AUSTRALIA

DESTROYERS

3 "PERTH" CLASS (DDGs)

Name	No.	Builders	Laid down	Launched	Commissioned
PERTH	38	Defoe Shipbuilding Co, Bay City, Mich.	21 Sep 1962	26 Sep 1963	17 July 1965
HOBART	39	Defoe Shipbuilding Co, Bay City, Mich.	26 Oct 1962	9 Jan 1964	18 Dec 1965
BRISBANE	41	Defoe Shipbuilding Co, Bay City, Mich.	15 Feb 1965	5 May 1966	16 Dec 1967

Displacement, tons: 3 370 standard; 4 618 full load
Length, feet (metres): 440·8 *(134·3)*
Beam, feet (metres): 47·1 *(14·3)*
Draught, feet (metres): 20·1 *(6·1)*
Missile launchers: 1 single for Tartar (see Modernisation note)
Guns: 2—5 in *(127 mm)* 54 cal. Mk 42 mod 10, single-mount
A/S weapons: 2 single launchers for Ikara system
Torpedo tubes: 6 (2 triple) Mk 32 mod 5 for A/S torpedoes
Main engines: 2 GE double reduction turbines, 2 shafts; 70 000 shp
Boilers: 4 Foster Wheeler "D" type, 1 200 psi; 950°F
Speed, knots: 30+
Range, miles: 4 500 at 15 knots; 2 000 at 30 knots
Complement: 333 (21 officers, 312 sailors)

On 6 Jan 1962, in Washington, US defence representatives and Australian military officials (on behalf of the Royal Australian Navy) and executives of the Defoe Shipbuilding Company, of Bay City, Michigan, signed a $A25 726 700 contract for the construction of two guided-missile destroyers (shipbuilding cost only). On 22 Jan 1963 it was announced by the Navy Minister in Canberra, Australia, that a third guided-missile destroyer was to be built in USA for Australia. The first of their kind for the Australian Navy, they constitute the 1st Destroyer Squadron, RAN. All three ships saw action off Vietnam where they served with the US 7th fleet.
Brisbane is 1st DS loader.

Cost: Original estimate $A12·8 million to $A14 million each (with missiles and electronics $A40 million each). The total cost of *Perth* was reported to be $A50 million.

Design: Generally similar to the US "Charles F. Adams" class, but they differ by the addition of a broad deckhouse between the funnels enclosing the Ikara anti-submarine torpedo-carrying missile system.

Electronics: URN-20 Tacan pod; intercept equipment fitted; URD-4, UHFD/F; Enhanced JPTDS combat data system with UYK-7 computer and Link 11 exchange equipment.

Fire Control: Gunnery: GFCS Mk 68 with SPG53A radar.
Missiles: Mk 74 with SPG51C radar and single Mk 13 launcher.

Modernisation: *Perth* started a modernisation at the Long Beach Naval Shipyard on 3 Sep 1974, completing 2 Jan 1975. The work included the installation of a Naval Combat Data System, updating of the Tartar missile fire control system, replacing 5-inch gun mounts and modernising radars. *Hobart* and *Brisbane* will receive similar modernisations in Australia at Garden Island Dockyard. *Hobart's* modernisation started in Nov 1976 and *Brisbane's* will start late-1977. *Hobart's* gun mounts were replaced in the USA in 1972 and *Brisbane's* replacement was completed at Garden Island in Oct 1976. This gunnery alteration includes deletion of local surface fire control with increased reliability.

Radar: Three dimensional: SPS 52.
Air search: SPS 40.
Surface search: SPS 10.
Navigation: Type 975.

Sonar: SQS 23F; AN/UQC 1D; UQN 1.

BRISBANE *Oct 1977, Graeme Andrews*

HOBART *1976, John Mortimer*

PERTH *Oct, 1977, John Mortimer*

AUSTRALIA 39

2 "DARING" CLASS (DD)

Name	No.	Builders	Laid down	Launched	Commissioned
VENDETTA	08	HMA Naval Dockyard, Williamstown	4 July 1949	3 May 1954	26 Nov 1958
VAMPIRE	11	Cockatoo Island Dockyard, Sydney	1 July 1952	27 Oct 1956	23 June 1959

Displacement, tons: 2 800 standard; 3 600 full load
Length, feet (metres): 366 *(111·6)* pp; 388·5 *(118·4)* oa
Beam, feet (metres): 43 *(13·1)*
Draught, feet (metres): 12·8 *(3·9)*
Guns: 6—4·5 in *(115 mm)* in 3 twin turrets, two forward and one aft; 6—40 mm
A/S weapons: 1—3-barrelled Limbo mortar (see Design notes)
Main engines: English Electric geared turbines; 2 shafts; 54 000 shp
Boilers: 2 Foster Wheeler; 650 psi; 850°F
Speed, knots: 30·5
Range, miles: 3 700 at 20 knots
Oil fuel, tons: 584
Complement: 320 (14 officers, 306 sailors)

Vampire and *Vendetta,* constitute the 2nd Destroyer Squadron, RAN, and are the largest destroyers ever built in Australia. They were ordered in 1946. Their sister ship, *Voyager,* the prototype of the class, collided with the aircraft carrier *Melbourne* and sank off the southern coast of New South Wales on the night of 10 Feb 1964. She was replaced by the British destroyer *Duchess,* lent to Australia by the United Kingdom for four years on 8 May 1964, later extended to 1971, purchased by RAN in 1972 and decommissioned in 1977.

Four large destroyers of this type were originally projected, to have been named after the Royal Australian Navy's famous "Scrap Iron Flotilla" of destroyers during the Second World War, but *Waterhen* was cancelled in 1954. *Vampire* is 2nd DS leader.

Design: *Vampire* and *Vendetta* were of similar design, including all welded construction, to that of the "Daring" class, built in the United Kingdom, but were modified to suit Australian conditions and have "Limbo" instead of "Squid" anti-submarine mortars. The superstructure is of light alloy, instead of steel, to reduce weight.

Modernisation: *Vampire* completed in Dec 1971. *Vendetta* completed May 1973. The $A20 million programme for both ships included new Mk 22 fire-control systems, new LW-02 air-warning and navigation radars, new action-information centre, modernised communications, fitting modernised turrets, improved habitability, the fitting of an enclosed bridge and new funnels. The work was carried out by Williamstown Dockyard. These alterations afford an interesting comparison with the Peruvian "Darings" (ex-*Decoy* and *Diana)* with their eight Exocet SSMs, rebuilt forefunnel and radar and helicopter deck.

Radar: Air surveillance: LW-02.
Surface-search, target indication and fire-control: M22 series.
Surface-search and navigation: 8GR-301A.

Sonar: Types 162, 170, 174 and 185.

VENDETTA   Sept 1977, Dr. Giorgio Arra

VAMPIRE   Oct 1977, Graeme Andrews

VAMPIRE   Oct 1977, John Mortimer

VENDETTA   1977, Royal Australian Navy

40 AUSTRALIA

FRIGATES

0 + 2 + 1 US "FFG 7" CLASS

Name	No.	Builders	Laid down	Launched	Commissioned
ADELAIDE	01	Todd Pacific Shipyard Corpn, USA	29 July 1977	Aug 1978*	1980*
CANBERRA	02	Todd Pacific Shipyard Corpn, USA	Mar 1978	Dec 1978*	1981*

*planned dates

Displacement, tons: 3 605 full load
Length, feet (metres): 445 *(135·6)*
Beam, feet (metres): 45 *(13·7)*
Draught, feet (metres): 24·5 *(7·5)*
Missile launcher: 1 Mk 13 Mod 4 (US) for Standard/Harpoon missiles
Gun: 1—76 mm OTO-Melara; provision for point defence weapon system
A/S weapons: 2 helicopters (to be selected); 6 (2 triple) Mk 32 torpedo tubes
Main engines: 2 GE LM 2 500 gas turbines; 40 000 shp; 1 shaft (cp propeller)
Speed: 28+
Range, miles: 4 500 at 20 knots
Complement: 185/190

Two ordered from USA in Feb 1976 for delivery 1980-81. Consideration being given to order for a third. Space and weight reserved for CIWS. US Numbers—*Adelaide* FFG-17, *Canberra* FFG-18.

Fire Control: Mk 92/STIR gun and missile control.

Radar: Long range air search and early warning: AN SPS 49.
Search and navigation: AN SPS 55.

Sonar: SQS-56.

"FFG 7" Class
1977, RAN Model

6 "RIVER" CLASS

Name	No.	Builders	Laid down	Launched	Commissioned
YARRA	45	Williamstown Naval Dockyard, Melbourne	9 Apr 1957	30 Sep 1958	27 July 1961
PARRAMATTA	46	Cockatoo Island Dockyard, Sydney	3 Jan 1957	31 Jan 1959	4 July 1961
STUART	48	Cockatoo Island Dockyard, Sydney	20 Mar 1959	8 Apr 1961	28 June 1963
DERWENT	49	Williamstown Naval Dockyard, Melbourne	16 June 1958	17 Apr 1961	30 Apr 1964
SWAN	50	Williamstown Naval Dockyard, Melbourne	18 Aug 1965	16 Dec 1967	20 Jan 1970
TORRENS	53	Cockatoo Island Dockyard, Sydney	18 Aug 1965	28 Sep 1968	19 Jan 1971

Displacement, tons: 2 100 standard; 2 700 full load
Length, feet (metres): 360·0 *(109·7)* pp; 370·0 *(112·8)* oa
Beam, feet (metres): 41·0 *(12·5)*
Draught, feet (metres): 17·3 *(5·3)*
Missile launchers: 1 quadruple for Seacat
Guns: 2—4·5 in *(115 mm)*
A/S weapons: 1 launcher for Ikara system; 1 Limbo 3-barrelled DC mortar (not *Yarra*)
Main engines: 2 double reduction geared turbines; 2 shafts; 30 000 shp
Boilers: 2 Babcock & Wilcox; 550 psi; 850°F
Speed, knots: 30
Range, miles: 3 400 at 12 knots
Complement: 247 (13 officers, 234 sailors) in *Swan* and *Torrens;* 250 (13 officers, 237 sailors) in other four ships

The design of the first four is basically similar to that of British "Type 12", the last pair to that of the "Leander" frigates. All are modified by the RAN to incorporate improvements in equipment and habitability. *Stuart* was the first ship fitted with the Ikara anti-submarine guided missile; (trial ship for the system). *Derwent* was the first RAN ship to be fitted with Seacat. The variable depth sonar has been removed from *Derwent* and *Stuart*. Note difference in silhouette between *Swan* and *Torrens* and the earlier ships of the class, the former pair having a straight-run upper deck. *Torrens* is leader for the frigate squadron.

Modernisation: *Parramatta, Stuart* and *Derwent* will undergo half-life modernisation at Williamstown; work on *Parramatta* began in 1977 (paid off 10 May). This programme includes improved accommodation consequent on reduction in complement, installation of M22 gunnery direction system, the fitting of Australian Mulloka sonar (provided the set goes into production), the conversion of the boilers to burn diesel fuel, installation of Mk 32 torpedo tubes in lieu of Limbo mortar and new navigation radar. *Yarra* has been fitted with Mulloka sonar, trials beginning in April 1975. In Oct 1976 she started a half-life refit at Cockatoo Island Dockyard and rejoined the Fleet in Dec 1977. Her Limbo mortar was removed during refit. The whole modernisation programme is due to be completed by 1981.

PARRAMATTA and YARRA after half-life conversion
1977, Royal Australian Navy

STUART (DERWENT similar)
10/1977, Dr. Giorgio Arra

Radar: Air surveillance: LW-02 (all ships) (with Type 944/954 IFF Mk 10).
Surface search: Type 293 (first four).
Navigation: Type 978 (first four).
Surface search, target indication and fire-control: M22 (last pair).

Surface search and navigation: 8GR-301 (last pair).

Note: Type 293 to be replaced by SPS-55 at half-life modernisation and Type 293 and MRS3 by M22 at same time.

Sonar: Types 162, 170, 177M, 185.

SWAN (TORRENS similar)
Oct 1977, John Mortimer

AUSTRALIA 41

MINE WARFARE SHIPS

Note: The RAN is examining a new concept in minehunting vessels which should provide a more flexible and effective minehunting capability. This envisages an Australian-designed and developed glass-reinforced plastic catamaran fitted with modern minehunting and mine disposal equipment.
The Government has decided to proceed with the initial prototype design and acquisition of long lead items for two prototype vessels. The objective is to have new operational minehunting craft entering service during the first half of the 1980s.

3 BRITISH "TON" CLASS (MODIFIED)

Name	No.	Builders	Laid down	Launched	Commissioned
SNIPE (ex-HMS *Alcaston*)	1102	Thornycroft	1952	5 Jan 1953	1953
CURLEW (ex-HMS *Chediston*)	1121	Montrose SY	1952	6 Oct 1953	1954
IBIS (ex-HMS *Singleton*)	1183	Montrose SY	1952	23 Nov 1955	1956

Displacement, tons: 375 standard; 445 full load
Dimensions, feet (metres): 140 pp; 153 oa × 28·8 × 8·2 *(42·7; 46·6 × 8·8 × 2·5)*
Guns: *Ibis* 2—40 mm; *Curlew* and *Snipe* 1—40 mm
Main engines: Napier Deltic diesels; 2 shafts = 14 knots
Range, miles: 2 300 at 13 knots; 3 500 at 8 knots
Complement: *Ibis* 34 (4 officers; 30 sailors); *Curlew* and *Snipe* 38 (3 officers, 35 sailors)

"Ton" class coastal minesweepers. Six purchased from the United Kingdom in 1961, and modified in British Dockyards to suit Australian conditions. Turned over to the RAN, commissioned and re-named on 21 Aug, 7 Sep and 11 Sep 1962, respectively. Mirlees diesels were replaced by Napier Deltic, and ships air-conditioned and fitted with stabilisers. Sailed from Portsmouth to Australia on 1 Oct 1962. Constitute the 1st Mine Countermeasures Squadron. *Curlew* and *Snipe* have been converted into minehunters—*Curlew* 26 June 1967 to 13 Dec 1968 and *Snipe* 10 April 1969 to 18 Dec 1970.

Radar: Type 975 I-band.

Sonar: Type 193 (except *Ibis*)

SNIPE   *1976, John Mortimer*

LIGHT FORCES

0 + 15 "BROOKE PCF 420" CLASS (LARGE PATROL CRAFT)

Displacement, tons: 220
Dimensions, feet (metres): 137·8 × 23·3 × 5·9 *(42 × 7·1 × 1·8)*
Main engines: 2 MTU Series 538 diesels = approx 30 knots
Complement: 22

The decision to buy these new patrol craft was announced in Sept 1977. The design is by Brooke Marine Ltd, Lowestoft who will build the lead ship, the remainder being built by North Queensland Engineers and Agents Pty Ltd, Cairns. Delivery of lead ship planned for June 1979.

Armament: Temporarily 40/60 Bofors.

"PCF 420" Class   *1977, RAN Drawing*

12 "ATTACK" CLASS (LARGE PATROL CRAFT)

Name	No.	Builders	Laid down	Launched	Commissioned
ACUTE	81	Evans Deakin Ltd.	April 1967	26 Aug 1967	26 April 1968
ADROIT	82	Evans Deakin Ltd.	Aug 1967	3 Feb 1968	17 Aug 1968
ADVANCE	83	Walkers Ltd.	Mar 1967	16 Aug 1967	24 Jan 1968
ARDENT	87	Evans Deakin Ltd.	Oct 1967	27 April 1968	26 Oct 1968
ASSAIL	89	Evans Deakin Ltd.	Aug 1967	18 Nov 1967	12 July 1968
ATTACK	90	Evans Deakin Ltd.	Sep 1966	8 April 1967	17 Nov 1967
AWARE	91	Evans Deakin Ltd.	July 1967	7 Oct 1967	21 June 1968
BARBETTE	97	Walkers Ltd.	Nov 1967	10 April 1968	16 Aug 1968
BARRICADE	98	Evans Deakin Ltd.	Dec 1967	29 June 1968	26 Oct 1968
BOMBARD	99	Walkers Ltd.	April 1968	6 July 1968	5 Nov 1968
BUCCANEER	100	Evans Deakin Ltd.	June 1968	14 Sep 1968	11 Jan 1969
BAYONET	101	Walkers Ltd.	Oct 1968	6 Nov 1968	22 Feb 1969

Displacement, tons: 146 full load
Dimensions, feet (metres): 107·5 oa × 20 × 7·3 *(32·8 × 6·1 × 2·2)*
Guns: 1—40 mm; 2 medium MG
Main engines: Paxman 16 YJCM diesels; 3 500 hp; 2 shafts = 21-24 knots
Range, miles: 1 220 at 13 knots
Complement: 19 (3 officers, 16 sailors)

Steel construction. Ordered in Nov 1965. First vessel was originally scheduled for delivery in Aug 1966, but was not launched until Mar 1967. Cost $A800 000 each. All have been employed in fishery protection and search and rescue off North Australia.

Disposals: *Bandolier* transferred to Indonesia after refit 16 Nov 1973. *Archer* transferred 21 Oct 1974. *Aitape, Ladava, Lae, Madang, Samarai* transferred to Papua New Guinea Defence Force 16 Sept 1975.

Darwin Cyclone: On 25 Dec 1974 *Arrow* was lost during Cyclone Tracy at Darwin. *Attack* was beached and badly damaged at the same time but was salved and towed to Cairns for repairs.

Radar: Type 975 I band being replaced by RM916

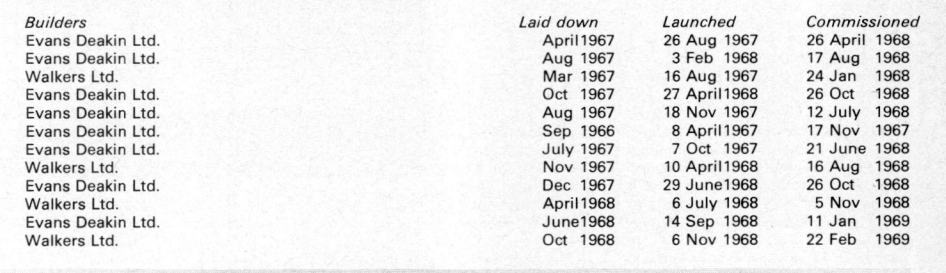

ARDENT   *1977, Graeme Andrews*

42 AUSTRALIA

OCEANOGRAPHIC AND SURVEY SHIPS

Note: The 1976 Defence White Paper stated plans to build two more survey ships and six large survey launches. One of the ships will probably be of the "Flinders" class.

Name	No.	Builders	Laid down	Launched	Commissioned
COOK	A 219	Williamstown Naval DY	30 Sep 1974	27 Aug 1977	mid-1979

Displacement, tons: 1 900 standard; 2 450 full load
Length, feet (metres): 316·7 (96·6)
Beam, feet (metres): 44·0 (13·4)
Draught, feet (metres): 15·1 (4·6)
Main engines: Diesels; 2 shafts; 3 400 bhp
Speed, knots: 17
Oil fuel, tons: 640
Range, miles: 11 000 at 14 knots
Complement: 150 including 13 scientists

Intended to replace HMAS *Diamantina*. She will have dual hydrographic and oceanographic roles. The after part of the ship will contain research equipment and facilities. Accommodation for 13 scientists. One survey launch. Specialised oceanographic gear will include a data logger, 3 oceanographic winches, wet laboratory, dry laboratory, magnetometer and gravimeter. No helicopter.

Radar: TM 829.

Sonar: Simrad SU2.

Surveying Equipment: Hi-Fix 6; Mini-Ranger MRS3; Atlas Deso 10 and Harris Narrow-Beam echo-sounders.

COOK on launching   *Aug 1977, Royal Australian Navy*

Name	No.	Builders	Laid down	Launched	Commissioned
MORESBY	GS 73	State Dockyard, Newcastle NSW	June 1961	7 Sep 1963	6 Mar 1964

Displacement, tons: 1 714 standard; 2 351 full load
Length, feet (metres): 284·5 (86·7) pp; 314·0 (95·7) oa
Beam, feet (metres): 42·0 (12·8)
Draught, feet (metres): 15·0 (4·6)
Aircraft: 1 Bell 206B-1 (Kiowa) helicopter
Guns: 2—40 mm Bofors (single) (removed)
Main engines: Diesel-electric; 3 diesels; 3 990 bhp; 2 electric motors; 2 shafts = 19 knots
Complement: 135

The RAN's first specifically designed survey ship. Built at a cost of £A2 million ($A4 million). Guns are not currently embarked.

Refit: During refit from 13 Aug 1973 to 18 Jan 1974 *Moresby's* funnel was heightened, her 40 mm guns removed and an exhaust outlet fitted on her forecastle.

Radar: TM 829

Sonar: Simrad SU2.

MORESBY   *1977, Royal Australian Navy*

Name	No.	Builders	Laid down	Launched	Commissioned
DIAMANTINA	GOR 266 (ex-F 377)	Walkers Ltd, Maryborough, Queensland	12 Apr 1943	6 Apr 1944	27 Apr 1945

Displacement, tons: 1 340 standard; 2 127 full load
Length, feet (metres): 283 (86·3) pp; 301·3 (91·8) oa
Beam, feet (metres): 36·7 (11·2)
Draught, feet (metres): 12·5 (3·8)
Gun: 1—40 mm
Main engines: Triple expansion 5 500 ihp; 2 shafts
Boilers: 2 Admiralty 3-drum
Speed, knots: 19·5
Range, miles: 7 700 at 12 knots
Complement: 125 (6 officers, 119 sailors)

Frigate converted in 1959-60 for survey and completed conversion for oceanographic research in June 1969. The conversion included the provision of special laboratories. Sister ship *Lachlan* was sold to the Royal New Zealand Navy (RNZN), and was finally paid off in 1975. *Diamantina* is to be replaced by *Cook* who is due to commission in 1979.

Armament: The two 4-inch guns and two "Squid" A/S mortars in "B" position were removed.

DIAMANTINA   *1974, John Mortimer*

Radar: Type 975   **Sonar:** Type 144

Name	No.	Builders	Laid down	Launched	Commissioned
FLINDERS	GS 312	Williamstown Naval Dockyard	11 June 1971	29 July 1972	27 Apr 1973

Displacement, tons: 750
Dimensions, feet (metres): 161 × 33 × 12 (49·1 × 10 × 3·7)
Main engines: 2 Paxman Ventura diesels; 1 680 bhp
Speed, knots: 13·5
Range, miles: 5 000 at 9 knots
Complement: 38 (4 officers, 34 sailors)

Similar in design to *Atyimba* built for the Philippines. *Flinders* is based at Cairns, with her primary responsibility in the Barrier Reef area.

Radar: TM 829.

Sonar: Simrad SU2.

FLINDERS   *1976, Royal Australian Navy*

AUSTRALIA

Name	No.	Builders	Laid down	Launched	Commissioned
KIMBLA	GOR 314	Walkers Ltd, Maryborough, Queensland	4 Nov 1953	23 Mar 1955	26 Mar 1956

Displacement, tons: 762 standard; 1 021 full load
Dimensions, feet (metres): 150 pp; 179 oa × 32 × 12 *(45·7; 54·6 × 9·8 × 3·7)*
Main engines: Triple expansion; 1 shaft; 350 ihp
Speed, knots: 9·5
Complement: 40 (4 officers, 36 sailors)

Built as a boom defence vessel. Converted to trials vessel in 1959. Guns were removed (1—40 mm; 2—20 mm). She is due for replacement about 1980, possibly by one of the "Flinders" class.

Appearance: Enclosed bridge fitted mid-1977.

Radar: Type 975.

Sonar: Simrad SU2.

KIMBLA *Aug 1977, Royal Australian Navy*

SERVICE FORCES

1 DESTROYER TENDER

Name	No.	Builders	Laid down	Launched	Commissioned
STALWART	D 215	Cockatoo Island DY, Sydney	June 1964	7 Oct 1966	9 Feb 1968

Displacement, tons: 10 000 standard; 15 500 full load
Length, feet (metres): 515·5 *(157·1)* oa
Beam, feet (metres): 67·5 *(20·6)*
Draught, feet (metres): 29·5 *(9·0)*
Missiles: Provision for Seacat
Guns: 4—40 mm (2 twin)
Main engines: 2 Scott-Sulzer 6-cyl diesels, 2 shafts; 14 400 bhp
Speed, knots: 20+
Range, miles: 12 000 at 12 knots
Complement: 396 (23 officers and 373 sailors)

Largest naval vessel designed and built in Australia. Ordered on 11 Sep 1963. Designed to maintain destroyers and frigates, and advanced weapons systems, including guided missiles. She has a helicopter flight deck and a hangar, being capable of operating two Wessex 31B or two Sea King Mk 50 helicopters. High standard of habitability. Formerly rated as Escort Maintenance Ship. Redesignated Destroyer Tender in 1968. Cost officially estimated at just under $A15 million.

STALWART *Oct 1977, John Mortimer*

1 FLEET TANKER

Name	No.	Builders	Laid down	Launched	Commissioned
SUPPLY (ex-*Tide Austral*)	O 195	Harland and Wolff, Belfast	5 Aug 1952	1 Sep 1954	Mar 1955

Displacement, tons: 15 000 standard; 25 941 full load
Measurement, tons: 17 600 deadweight; 11 200 gross
Dimensions, feet (metres): 550 pp; 583 oa × 71 × 32 *(167·6; 177·8 × 21·7 × 9·8)*
Guns: 6—40 mm (2 twin, 2 single)
Main engines: Double reduction geared turbines; 15 000 shp
Speed, knots: 17·25
Range, miles: 8 500 at 13 knots
Complement: 205

British "Tide" Class. Lent to the United Kingdom until 1 Sep 1962, when *Tide Austral* was re-named HMAS *Supply* and commissioned in the RAN at Portsmouth 15 Aug 1962. Sailed for Australia 1 Oct 1962. Bridge was rebuilt in 1973-74.

Radar: Type 975 (to be replaced by RM 16).

Replacement: An underway replenishment ship of a new class is planned for 1980. A contract was awarded to DTCN, France in early 1977 for a project definition of a "Durance" class ship.

SUPPLY *Oct 1977, Graeme Andrews*

44 AUSTRALIA

TRAINING SHIP

Name	No.	Builders	Laid down	Launched	Commissioned
JERVIS BAY (ex-*Australian Trader*)	GT 203	State Dockyard, Newcastle, NSW	18 Aug 1967	17 Feb 1969	17 June 1969 (completion)

Displacement, tons: 8 770; 8 915 full load
Length, feet (metres): 445·1 *(135·7)*
Beam, feet (metres): 70·6 *(21·5)*
Draught, feet (metres): 20·1 *(6·1)*
Main engines: 2—16PC 2V 400 Crossley Pielstick diesels; 2 shafts; 6 500 bhp *(4 875 kW)*
Speed, knots: 17
Fuel: 820·3 tons *(833·5 tonnes)*
Complement: 111 plus 40+ trainees

The former roll-on roll-off ship MV *Australian Trader* purchased in 1977 for $A5·07 million from the Australian National Line and commissioned in the RAN on 25 Aug 1977. A contract for $A720 000 for conversion of the ship to its new role was let to the Sydney firm of Storey and Keers (Ship Repairs) Pty Ltd in Oct 1977. Conversion work included the construction of a navigation training bridge on top of the existing bridge, and conversion of some cabins into a classroom. Fitted with bow thruster *Jervis Bay* was scheduled to make her first cruise as a training ship in Jan 1978. The ship's primary role is navigation training for the RAN, although her vehicle and cargo carrying capability have been retained.

JERVIS BAY   Oct 1977, Royal Australian Navy

AMPHIBIOUS FORCES
0 + 1 HEAVY LIFT SHIP

Name	No.	Builders	Laid down	Launched	Commissioned
TOBRUK	L 50	Carrington Slipways Pty Ltd	1978	1979	1980

Displacement, tonnes: 5 800
Dimensions, feet (metres): 425 × 60 × — *(129·6 × 18·3 × —)*
Aircraft: Wessex 31B helicopters
Landing craft: 2 LCVP at davits; 2 LCM8 can be carried on deck
Guns: 2—40 mm
Main engines: 2 diesels = 17 knots (?)
Complement: 130
Troops: 350-550

A contract to build an Amphibious Heavy Lift Ship in Australia was let in November 1977. The design is an update of the British "Sir Bedivere" class and will provide facilities for the operation of helicopters, landing craft, amphibians or side carried pontoons for ship-to-shore movement. A special feature will be the ship's heavy lift derrick system for handling heavy loads. The LSH will be able to embark a squadron of Leopard tanks plus a number of wheeled vehicles and artillery in addition to its troop lift. A comprehensive communication fit and minor hospital facilities will also be provided.

TOBRUK   1976, Royal Australian Navy Drawing

6 LANDING CRAFT (HEAVY) (LCH)

Name	No.	Builders	Laid down	Launched	Commissioned
BALIKPAPAN	L 126	Walkers Ltd	May 1971	15 Aug 1971	8 Dec 1971
BRUNEI	L 127	Walkers Ltd	July 1971	15 Oct 1971	5 Jan 1973
LABUAN	L 128	Walkers Ltd	Oct 1971	29 Dec 1971	9 Mar 1973
TARAKAN	L 129	Walkers Ltd	Dec 1971	16 Mar 1972	15 June 1973
WEWAK	L 130	Walkers Ltd	Mar 1972	18 May 1972	10 Aug 1973
BETANO	L 133	Walkers Ltd	Sep 1972	5 Dec 1972	8 Feb 1974

Displacement, tons: 310 light; 503 full load
Dimensions, feet (metres): 146 × 33 × 6·5 *(44·5 × 10·1 × 2)*
Guns: 2—0·5 in MG
Main engines: 2 GM diesels; twin screw = 10 knots
Range, miles: 3 000 at 10 knots
Complement: 13 (2 officers, 11 sailors)

Originally this class was ordered for the Army with whom *Balikpapan* remained until June 1974 being commissioned for naval service on 27 Sep 1974. All now transferred to RAN. Can carry three medium tanks.

PNGDF: *Buna* and *Salamaua* transferred to Papua New Guinea Defence Force in Nov 1974.

Radar: Decca 101 (to be replaced by RM 916).

BALIKPAPAN   1976, Royal Australian Navy

AUSTRALIA 45

MISCELLANEOUS

GENERAL PURPOSE VESSELS

Name	No.	Builders	Commissioned
BANKS	G 244	Walkers, Maryborough	16 Feb 1960
BASS	G 247	Walkers, Maryborough	25 May 1960

Displacement, tons: 207 standard; 255 and 260 full load respectively
Dimensions, feet (metres): 90 pp; 101 oa × 22 × 8 (27.5; 30.8 × 6.7 × 2.4)
Main engines: Diesels; speed = 10 knots
Complement: 14 (2 officers, 12 sailors)

"Explorer" class. Of all steel construction. *Banks* was fitted for fishery surveillance and *Bass* for surveying, but both are used for other duties, including reserve training. *Banks* based in Port Adelaide, *Bass* in Hobart. Minor differences—*Bass* has a higher flying bridge with consequent raising of her radar pedestal. Ventilators differ.

BASS *1977, Graeme Andrews*

GPV 958

75 ft (22.9 m) General purpose vessel based at HMAS *Leeuwin*, WA.

SDB 1324

80 ft (24.4 m) Seaward defence boat based at HMAS *Lonsdale*, Victoria.

SDB 1325

80 ft (24.4 m) Seaward defence boat based at HMAS *Leeuwin*, WA.

DIVING TENDERS

Name	No.	Builders	Launched
SEAL (ex-HMS *Wintringham*)	DTV 1001	White, Cowes	24 May 1955
PORPOISE (ex-HMS *Neasham*)	DTV 1002	White, Cowes	14 Mar 1956

Displacement, tons: 120 standard; 159 full load
Dimensions, feet (metres): 100 pp × 22 × 5.8 (30.5 × 6.7 × 1.8)
Main engines: 2 Paxman diesels; 1 100 bhp = 14 knots
Range, miles: 2 000 at 9 knots; 1 500 at 12 knots
Complement: 7 (can accommodate 14 divers)

Purchased from the Royal Navy in 1966-67, these ex-inshore Minesweepers were converted to Diving Tenders and attached to the Diving School at Sydney. HMS *Popham* (Vospers, launched 11 Jan 1955) also purchased and renamed *Otter* but not converted and was sold in 1974. Carry recompression chambers.

Status: *Seal* entered service in Dec 1968 and *Porpoise* in 1973. Neither is a commissioned ship but both are tenders to HMAS *Penguin*, Sydney, working from there as operational diving training vessels.

SEAL *Mar 1977, John Mortimer*

TORPEDO RECOVERY VESSELS

TRV 801 802 803

Displacement, tons: 91.6
Dimensions, feet (metres): 88.5 × 20.9 × 4.5 (27 × 6.4 × 1.4)
Main engines: 3 GM diesels; 890 hp; triple screws = 13 knots.
Complement: 9 (1 officer, 8 men)

All built at Williamstown—completed between Jan 1970 and Apr 1971. TRV 802 used as diving tender.

TRV 803 *11/1976, Graeme Andrews*

TUGS

501 502 504

Displacement, tons: 47.5
Dimensions, feet (metres): 50 × 15 × — (15.2 × 4.6 × —)
Main engines: 2 GM diesels; 340 bhp = 8-9 knots
Complement: 3

First pair with bipod mast funnel built by Stannard Bros, Sydney in 1969 and second pair with conventional funnel by Perrin Engineering, Brisbane in 1972.

Transfer: Tug 503 transferred to Papua New Guinea in 1974.

2 Ex-US ARMY TYPE

SARDIUS TB9, — TB1536

Of 29 tons GRT (approx 60 tons, full load), 45 ft long with 240 hp Hercules diesel, capable of 10 knots. Complement 4. *Sardius* employed in Sydney as ammunition-lighter tug, TB1536 at HMAS *Cerberus* (Victoria). Wooden hulled.

AUXILIARIES

1 TANK CLEANING VESSEL

Name	No.	Builders	Launched
COLAC	—	Mort's Dock Sydney	13 Aug 1941

Originally 1 025 ton "Bathurst" class minesweeper. Now a dumb craft, painted black, based in Sydney. Sister ship *Castlemaine*, given by D of D as museum ship to Melbourne in 1973.

1 AIR SEA RESCUE CRAFT

Name	No.	Builders	Commissioned
AIR SPRITE	Y256	Halvorsen, Sydney	1960

Displacement, tons: 23.5 standard
Dimensions, feet (metres): 63 × 15.5 × 3.3 (19.2 × 4.7 × 1)
Main engines: Two Scott Hall Defender (Petrol) = 25 knots
Complement: Up to 8

Used as reserve training and general purpose vessel in Sydney. Other similar craft are operated by the RAAF.

4 MOTOR WATER LIGHTERS

GAYUNDAH (MRL 253), **MWL 254, 256, 257**

Displacement, tons: 300 standard; 600 (app) full load.
Draught, feet (metres): 120 × 24 × — (36.6 × 7.3 × —).
Main engines: 2 Ruston and Hornsby diesels; 440 bhp=9.5 knots

Sisters of the earlier survey ship *Paluma*; used for carrying water and stores.

1 AIRCRAFT LIGHTER—CATAMARAN

AWL 304

Dimensions, feet (metres): 77.8 × 32 × 6.6 (23.7 × 9.8 × 2)

Built at Cockatoo Dockyard 1967-68. Coastal craft. Capacity one S2E Tracker or two A4G Skyhawks.

46 AUSTRALIA / AUSTRIA

3 CRANE STORES LIGHTERS

CSL 01   02   03

Based on design of AWL 304 but with crane and after superstructure. Built from 1972.

2 Ex-ASR CRAFT

38101   38102

38 ft Bertram craft of little value except in harbour.

WORK BOATS

AM 400-415 +5

More than 20 are in use all built to a basic 40 ft *(12·2 m)* design.

ARMY WATERCRAFT

11 Ex-US LCM(8) CLASS

AB 1050-1053   1055-1061

Displacement, tons: 116 full load
Dimensions, feet (metres): 73·5 × 21 × 3·3 *(22·4 × 6·4 × 1)*
Main engines: 2 GM diesels; 600 hp = 9 knots
Range, miles: 140 at 9 knots

Can carry 60 tons of cargo.

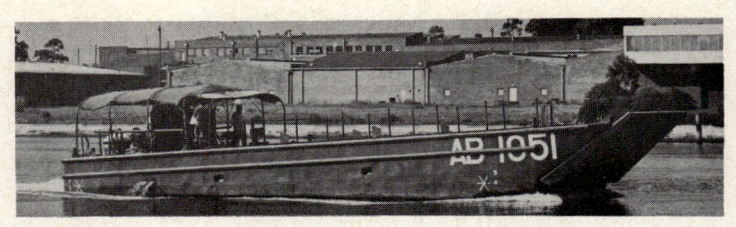

AB 1051   *Oct 1977, Graeme Andrews*

6 LCVP

AB 751   752   755   756   758   759

Of 56 ft. Can carry 120 people.

2 TUGS

JOE MANN   THE LUKE

Built in 1964. Of 60 tons with a range of 700 miles and fitted for firefighting, the first at Sydney, the second at Brisbane.

1 CARGO SHIP

LERIDA AS 3050

Of 22 tons with wooden hull. 66 × 17 ft, capable of 8 knots.

RAAF

1 76 ft ASR at Townsville.
1 63 ft ASR at Newcastle.

AUSTRIA

Commanding Officer

Major Walter Slovacek

Diplomatic Representation

Defence Attaché in London:
  Colonel L. Brosch-Fohraheim

Personnel

(a) 1978: 1 officer, 13 NCOs, 13 ratings (cadre personnel and national service), plus a small shipyard unit
(b) 6 months national service plus 2 months a year for 12 years

Base

Marinekaserne Tegetthof, Wien-Kuchelau (under command of Austrian School of Military Engineering)

Mercantile Marine

Lloyd's Register of Shipping:
  11 vessels of 53 284 tons gross

RIVERINE PATROL CRAFT

Name	No.	Builders	Commissioned
NIEDERÖSTERREICH	A 604	Korneuburg Werft AG	April 1970

Displacement, tons: 75
Dimensions, feet (metres): 96·8 × 17·8 × 3·6 *(29·4 × 5·4 × 1·1)*
Guns: 1—20 mm SPz Mk 66 Oerlikon in a turret; 1—12·7 mm MG; 1—Mk 42 MG;
  2—8·4 cm PAR 66 "Carl Gustav" AT rifles
Main engines: 2 V 16 diesels (turbo engines); 1 600 hp = 22 knots
Complement: 9

Fully welded. Only one built of a projected class of twelve. Engines by MWM, Munich.

NIEDERÖSTERREICH   *1975, Austrian Government*

Name	No.	Builders	Commissioned
OBERST BRECHT	A 601	Korneuburg Werft AG	—

Displacement, tons: 10
Dimensions, feet (metres): 40·3 × 8·2 × 2·5 *(12·3 × 2·5 × 0·75)*
Gun: 1—12·7 mm MG
Main engines: 2 diesels; 214 bhp = 10 knots
Complement: 5

Welded hull. Engines by Gräf and Stift, Vienna.

OBERST BRECHT   *1974, Heeres Film*

10 Ex-US "M3" PATROL CRAFT

	No.	Builders	Commissioned
4 M3B Type	—	Highway Products and Marine Corp USA	1965
6 M3D Type	—	Aluminium Co of America	1976

Displacement, tons: 2·9
Dimensions, feet (metres): 27·2 × 8·2 × 6·5 *(8·3 × 2·5 × 2)*
Main engines: M3B—2 Gray Patrol (petrol); 204 hp = 18 knots
  M3D—2 GM diesels; 184 hp = 18 knots

Unarmed, they form part of the military floating bridge equipment.

"M3" Class   *1976, Heeres Film*

BAHAMAS

Senior Officers

Assistant Commissioner:
  L. W. Major
Deputy Superintendent:
  Leon L. Smith
Assistant Superintendent:
  E. K. Andrews

Base

Bay Shore Marina, Nassau

Mercantile Marine

Lloyd's Register of Shipping:
  109 vessels of 106 317 tons gross

PATROL CRAFT
2 103 ft VOSPER THORNYCROFT

Name	No.	Builders	Commissioned
MARLIN	—	Vosper Thornycroft	1978
FLAMINGO (?)	—	Vosper Thornycroft	1978

Displacement, tons: 96 standard; 109 full load
Dimensions, feet (metres): 103 × 19.8 × 5.5 *(31.4 × 6 × 1.7)*
Guns: 2—40 mm
Main engines: 2 diesels; 3 500 bhp = 27 knots
Complement: 22

Marlin launched 20 June 1977. Part of a £5 million order placed in 1975 which also included three 60 ft craft below.

MARLIN
10/1977, Michael D. J. Lennon

7 60 ft GRP TYPE

Name	No.	Builders	Commissioned
ACKLINS	4	Vosper Thornycroft	5 Mar 1971
ANDROS	—	Vosper Thornycroft	5 Mar 1971
ELEVTHERA	—	Vosper Thornycroft	5 Mar 1971
SAN SALVADOR	—	Vosper Thornycroft	5 Mar 1971
—	—	Vosper Thornycroft	1978
—	—	Vosper Thornycroft	1978
—	—	Vosper Thornycroft	1978

Displacement, tons: 30 standard
Dimensions, feet (metres): 62.0 × 15.8 × 4.6 *(18.9 × 4.8 × 1.4)*
Guns: 1—20 mm forward; 2 LMG on bridge
Main engines: 2 Caterpillar diesels = 20 knots
Complement: 11

ACKLINS
1976, Bahamas Police, Marine Division

"60 ft" Keith Nelson patrol craft in glass reinforced plastic—the first four were the original units of the Bahamas Police Marine Division. With air-conditioned living spaces, these craft are designed for patrol amongst the many islands of the Bahamas Group. The foredeck is specially strengthened for a 20 mm MG with light MGs in sockets either side of the bridge.

BAHRAIN

Ministerial

Minister of the Interior:
  Shaikh Mohamad Bin Khalifa Al Khalifa

Personnel

(a) 1978: About 200.
(b) Voluntary service.

Coastguard

This unit is under the direction of the Ministry of the Interior and not Defence. The two "Interceptor" class listed last year have been sold.

Mercantile Marine

Lloyd's Register of Shipping:
  15 vessels of 3 670 tons

1 "TRACKER" CLASS

Name	No.	Builders	Commissioned
BAHRAIN I	—	Fairey Marine Ltd	1975

Displacement, tons: 26
Dimensions, feet (metres): 64 × 16 × 5 *(19.5 × 4.9 × 1.5)*
Gun: 1—20 mm
Main engines: 2 diesels; 1 120 bhp = 28 knots

Purchased 1974.

2 "SPEAR" CLASS

Name	No.	Builders	Commissioned
SAHAM	4	Fairey Marine Ltd	1975
KHATAF	5	Fairey Marine Ltd	1975

Dimensions, feet (metres): 29.8 × 9.2 × 2.6 *(9.1 × 2.8 × 0.8)*
Guns: 2 MG
Main engines: 2 Perkins diesels, 290 hp = 26 knots
Complement: 3

Purchased 1974 from Fairey (Marine) Ltd.

2 PATROL CRAFT

JIDA 2   HOWAR 3

Displacement, tons: 15
Dimensions, feet (metres): 45.5 × 12 × 3 *(13.9 × 3.7 × 0.9)*
Main engines: 2 diesels; 1 080 bhp = 23 knots

Completed Feb 1974 by Thornycroft, (Singapore).

1 50 ft CHEVERTON TYPE (COASTAL PATROL CRAFT)

Name	No.	Builders	Commissioned
MASHTAN	6	Cheverton	1976

Displacement, tons: 09
Dimensions, feet (metres): 50 × 14 × 4.5 *(15.2 × 4.3 × 1.4)*
Main engines: 2 Perkins diesels = 12 knots

GRP hull.

3 27 ft CHEVERTON TYPE (COASTAL PATROL CRAFT)

Name	No.	Builders	Commissioned
NOON	15	Cheverton	1977
ASKAR	16	Cheverton	1977
SUWAD	17	Cheverton	1977

Displacement, tons: 3.5
Dimensions, feet (metres): 27 × 9 × 2.8 *(8.2 × 2.7 × 0.8)*
Main engines: Twin diesels = 15 knots

Purchased 1976. In addition 10 Dhows are used for patrol duties.

AMPHIBIOUS CRAFT
1 60 ft "LOADMASTER"

Name	No.	Builders	Commissioned
SAFRA	7	Chevertons	1976

Measurement, tons: 60 deadweight
Dimensions, feet (metres): 60 oa × 20 × 3.5 *(18.3 × 6.1 × 1.1)*
Main engines: 2 diesels 120 hp = 8.5 knots

Note: In addition to the above are:

1 Hovercraft from Tropimire Ltd (UK) (1977);
1 60 ft Landing Craft from H.N. Development (Singapore) (1977);
2 56 ft launches from Vosper, (Singapore) (1977);
3 36 ft launches from Vosper, (Singapore) (1977).

48 BANGLADESH

BANGLADESH

Headquarters Appointments

Chief of Naval Staff:
 Rear-Admiral Mosharraf Hussain Khan psn
Assistant Chief of Naval Staff (Ops) and Administrative Authority, Dacca:
 Commodore Mahbub Ali Khan psn
Assistant Chief of Naval Staff (Material):
 Captain K. M. J. Akbar
Assistant Chief of Naval Staff (Logistics):
 Captain F. Ahmed

Senior Appointments

Commodore Chittagong:
 Captain Sultan Ahmad
NOIC Khulna:
 Captain Mujibur Rahman

Naval Bases

Chittagong (BNS Issa Khan), Dacca (BNS Haji Mohsin), Khulna (BNS Titumir), Kaptai (BNS Shaheed Moazzam), Juldia, Chittagong (Marine Academy)

Prefix to Ships' Names

BNS

Personnel:

a) 1978: 3 500 (200 officers, 3 300 ratings)
b) Voluntary service

Strength of the Fleet

Frigates	2
Large Patrol Craft	4
Riverine Patrol Craft	5
Training Ship	1

Mercantile Marine

Lloyd's Register of Shipping:
 120 vessels of 133 016 tons gross

FRIGATES

1 Ex-BRITISH "SALISBURY" CLASS (TYPE 61)

Name	No.	Builders	Laid down	Launched	Commissioned
UMAR FAROOQ (ex- HMS *Llandaff*)	F 16	Hawthorn Leslie Ltd, Hebburn-on-Tyne	27 Aug 1953	30 Nov 1955	11 Apr 1958

Displacement, tons: 2 170 standard; 2 408 full load
Length, feet (metres): 320 *(97.5)* pp; 339.8 *(103.6)* oa
Beam, feet (metres): 40 *(12.2)*
Draught, feet (metres): 15.5 *(4.7)*
Guns: 2—4.5 in *(115 mm)*; 2—40 mm
A/S weapons: 1 Squid triple-barrelled DC mortar
Main engines: 8 ASR 1 diesels in three engine rooms; 2 shafts; 14 400 bhp
Speed, knots: 24
Oil fuel, tons: 230
Range, miles: 2 300 at full power; 7 500 at 16 knots
Complement: 237 (14 officers, 223 ratings)

Ordered by RN on 28 June 1951. All welded. Transferred to Bangladesh at Royal Albert Dock, London on 10 Dec 1976 for work-up and passage.

Radar: Long-range surveillance: One Type 965 with double AKE 2 array.
Combined warning: One Type 993.
Height finder: One Type 277Q.
Target Indication: One Type 982.
Fire Control; Mk 6m director with Type 275.
Navigation: One Type 975.

Sonar: Types 174 and 170B.

UMAR FAROOQ   1977, Michael E. G. Lennon

1 Ex-BRITISH "LEOPARD" CLASS (TYPE 41)

Name	No.	Builders	Laid down	Launched	Commissioned
ALI HYDER (ex-HMS *Jaguar*)	—	Wm. Denny & Bros Ltd, Dumbarton	2 Nov 1953	30 July 1957	12 Dec 1959

Displacement, tons: 2 300 standard; 2 520 full load
Length, feet (metres): 320 *(97.5)* pp; 330 *(100.6)* wl; 339.8 *(103.6)* oa
Beam, feet (metres): 40 *(12.2)*
Draught, feet (metres): 16 *(4.9)*
Guns: 4—4.5 in *(115 mm)* (twin turrets); 1—40 mm
A/S weapons: 1 Squid 3-barrelled DC mortar
Main engines: 8 ASR 1 diesels in three engine rooms; 14 400 bhp; 2 shafts; 4 engines geared to each shaft
Speed, knots: 24
Oil fuel, tons: 220
Range, miles: 2 300 at full power; 7 500 at 16 knots
Complement: 235 (15 officers, 220 ratings)

Designed primarily for anti-aircraft protection. All welded. Ordered on 28 June 1951. Fitted with stabilisers. Transferred July 1978. Cost £2 million.

Electronics: ECM and D/F.

Engineering: Fitted with controllable pitch propellers, 12 ft diameter 200 rpm. The fuel tanks have a compensating system.

Radar: Air Search: One Type 965 with single AKE 1 array and IFF.
Fire Control: Mk 6 M I-band. Type 275.
Navigation: One Type 975.

Reconstruction: Refitted in 1966-7 with new mainmast and in 1977 before transfer.

Sonar: Types 164 and 174.

Transfer: Another ship of this class, *Panther*, was transferred to India while building and renamed *Brahmaputra*.

JAGUAR (with wooden bow sheathing for Cod War)   7/1976, MOD(N)

LIGHT FORCES

5 "PABNA" CLASS (RIVERINE PATROL CRAFT)

Name	No.	Builders	Commissioned
PABNA	P101	DEW Narayangonj, Dacca	12 June 1972
NOAKHALI	P102	DEW Narayangonj, Dacca	8 July 1972
PATUAKHALI	P103	DEW Narayangonj, Dacca	7 Nov 1974
BOGRA	P104	DEW Narayangonj, Dacca	June 1977
RANGAMATI	P105	DEW Narayangonj, Dacca	June 1977

Displacement, tons: 69.5
Dimensions, feet (metres): 75 × 20 × 3.5 *(22.9 × 6.1 × 1.1)*
Gun: 1—40/60 Bofors
Main engines: Cummins diesel = 10.8 knots
Range, miles: 700
Complement: 33 (3 officers, 30 ratings)

The first indigenous naval craft built in Bangladesh.

Radar: Decca Navigational.

PATUAKHALI   1975, Bangladesh Navy

BANGLADESH / BARBADOS 49

2 Ex-YUGOSLAV "KRALJEVICA" CLASS (LARGE PATROL CRAFT)

Name	No.	Builders	Commissioned
KARNAPHULI (ex-*PBR 502*)	P301	Yugoslavia	1956
TISTA (ex-*PBR 505*)	P302	Yugoslavia	1956

Displacement, tons: 190 standard; 202 full load
Dimensions, feet (metres): 134·5 × 20·7 × 7·2 *(41 × 6·3 × 2·2)*
Guns: 1—128 mm rocket launcher; 1—40/60 mm
Main engines: MAN W8V 30/38 diesels; 2 shafts; 3 300 bhp = 18 knots
Range, miles: 1 000 at 12 knots
Complement: 44 (4 officers, 40 ratings)

Transferred and commissioned on 6 June 1975.

Radar: Decca-45.

Sonar: QCU-2.

TISTA *1976, A. G. Burgoyne*

2 Ex-INDIAN "AKSHAY" CLASS (LARGE PATROL CRAFT)

Name	No.	Builders	Commissioned
PADMA (ex-*INS Akshay*)	P 201	Hooghly D & E Co, Calcutta	1962
SURMA (ex-*INS Ajay*)	P 202	Hooghly D & E Co, Calcutta	1962

Displacement, tons: 120 standard; 150 full load
Dimensions, feet (metres): 117·2 × 20 × 5·5 *(35·7 × 6·1 × 1·7)*
Gun: 1—40/60 mm
Main engines: 2 Paxman diesels = 12·5 knots
Range, miles: 5 000 at 10 knots
Complement: 35 (3 officers, 32 ratings)

Generally similar to Royal Navy's "Ford" class. Transferred and commissioned on 12 April 1973 and 26 July 1974 respectively.

SURMA *1975, Bangladesh Navy*

TRAINING SHIP

SHAHEED RUHUL AMIN (ex-*MV Anticosti*)

Displacement, tons: 710 full load
Dimensions, feet (metres): 155·8 × 36·5 × 10 *(47·5 × 11·1 × 3·1)*
Gun: 1—40/60 mm Bofors
Main engines: Caterpillar diesel; 1 shaft = 11·5 knots
Range, miles: 4 000
Complement: 80 (8 officers, 72 ratings)

Built in Dartmouth, Nova Scotia 1967. Sold to India as MV *Anticosti*. After use in relief work was handed over to BN in 1972, modified at Khulna and commissioned 10 Dec 1974.

SHAHEED RUHUL AMIN *1976, Bangladesh Navy*

BARBADOS

Senior Officer

CO Barbados Coast Guard:
 Major C. A. McConney

Personnel

(a) 1978: 61 (4 officers, 57 other ranks).
(b) Voluntary service

Coastguard

This was formed early in 1973.

Base

Christ Church, Barbados

Prefix to Ships' Names

BCGS

Mercantile Marine

Lloyd's Register of Shipping:
 30 vessels of 3 897 tons gross

1 20 Metre "GUARDIAN" CLASS (COASTAL PATROL CRAFT)

Name	No.	Builders	Commissioned
GEORGE FERGUSON	CG 601	Halmatic/Aquarius UK	Dec 1974

Displacement, tons: 30
Dimensions, feet (metres): 65·6 × 17·4 × 4·3 *(20 × 5·3 × 1·3)*
Guns: 2—·76 mm MG (provision for—not fitted)
Main engines: 2 GM 12V 71 TI diesels; 1 300 hp = 24 knots
Range, miles: 560 at 18 knots
Complement: 10

GRP hull. Air conditioned and designed for coastguard/SAR duties. Launched 16 Oct 1974 for delivery in December.

3 12 Metre "GUARDIAN" CLASS (COASTAL PATROL CRAFT)

Name	No.	Builders	Commissioned
COMMANDER MARSHALL	CG 402	Halmatic/Aquarius UK	Dec 1973
J. T. C. RAMSEY	CG 404	Halmatic/Aquarius UK	Nov 1974
T. T. LEWIS	CG 403	Halmatic/Aquarius UK	Feb 1974

Displacement, tons: 11
Dimensions, feet (metres): 41 × 12·1 × 3·3 *(12·5 × 3·7 × 1)*
Gun: 1—·76 mm MG (Provision for—not fitted)
Main engines: 2 Caterpillar diesels; 580 hp = 24 knots
Complement: 4

GRP Hulls. Designed for coastal patrol/SAR duties.

MISCELLANEOUS

The ex-US LST *Kemper County* was transferred to Barbadian commerical interests 6 Jan 1976.

BELGIUM

Headquarters Appointment

Chief of Naval Staff:
Vice-Admiral J. P. L. van Dyck

Diplomatic Representation

Naval, Military and Air Attaché in Bonn:
Colonel AF Derille (Army)
Naval, Military and Air Attaché in The Hague:
Lieutenant-Colonel de Brouchoven de Bergeyck
Naval, Military and Air Attaché in London:
Colonel K. De Wulf (Army)
Naval, Military and Air Attaché in Paris:
Colonel J. A. L. Joseph (Air Force)
Naval, Military and Air Attaché in Washington:
Brigadier-General CA de Wilde

Personnel

(a) 1978 4 220 (520 National Service)
(b) 10 months national service

General

The Belgian Navy has now moved its interests further to sea with its new frigates but the replacement programme of MCMVs mentioned below will probably absorb the majority of its new construction budget for several years to come.

New Construction

It is planned to build 15 new minehunters to replace ex-US MSOs and MSCs, the first unit to be completed in 1981 from an order to be placed in 1978. Two groups of shipyards have tendered for this programme—it is reported that one group will build the whole class.

Strength of the Fleet

Type	Active	Building
Frigates	4	—
Minehunters (Ocean)	7	—
Minehunters (Coastal)	2	—
Minesweepers (Coastal)	4	—
Minesweepers (Inshore)	14	—
Support Ships	2	—
River Patrol Boats	6	—
Research Ships	2	—
Auxiliary and Service Craft	14	—

Deletion

1976 *Knokke* (MSC)

Naval Aviation

3 Alouette III helicopters
1 Sikorsky S58 helicopter

Base

Ostend: 1 MSO Squadron, 1 MSC Squadron.
Nieuwpoort: 1 MSI Squadron, reserve MSCs.
Kallo: River patrol boats, 1 MSI Squadron, reserve MSIs.
Zeebrugge: Frigates, command and support ships.
Koksijde: Naval aviation.

Mercantile Marine

Lloyd's Register of Shipping:
258 vessels of 1 499 431 tons gross

PENNANT LIST

Minewarfare Forces

M 478	Herstal
M 479	Huy
M 480	Seraing
M 482	Vise
M 483	Ougrée
M 484	Dinant
M 485	Andenne
M 902	Haverbeke
M 903	Dufour
M 904	De Brouwer
M 906	Breydel
M 907	Artevelde
M 908	Truffaut
M 909	Bovesse
M 928	Stavelot
M 930	Rochefort
M 932	Nieuwport
M 933	Koksijde
M 934	Verviers
M 935	Veurne

Support Ships and Auxiliaries

A 950	Valcke
A 951	Hommel
A 952	Wesp
A 953	Bij
A 956	Krekel
A 958	Zenobe Gramme
A 959	Mier
A 960	Godetia
A 961	Zinnia
A 962	Mechelen
A 963	Spa
A 964	Heist

River Patrol Boats

P 901	Leie
P 902	Liberation
P 903	Meuse
P 904	Sambre
P 905	Schelde
P 906	Semois

Frigates

F 910	Wielingen
F 911	Westdiep
F 912	Wandelaar
F 913	Westhinder

Minewarfare Forces

M 471	Hasselt
M 472	Kortrijk
M 473	Lokeren
M 474	Turnhout
M 475	Tongeren
M 476	Merksem
M 477	Oudenaarde

FRIGATES

4 "E-71" CLASS

Name	No.	Builders	Laid down	Launched	Commissioned
WIELINGEN	F 910	Boelwerf, Temse	5 Mar 1974	30 Mar 1976	Sep 1977
WESTDIEP	F 911	Cockerill, Hoboken	2 Sep 1974	8 Dec 1975	Sep 1977
WANDELAAR	F 912	Boelwerf, Temse	1 April 1975	21 June 1977	1978
WESTHINDER	F 913	Cockerill, Hoboken	8 Dec 1975	1 Mar 1977	1978

Displacement, tons: 1 940 light; 2 430 full load
Length, feet (metres): 347·7 *(106)*
Beam, feet (metres): 40·3 *(12·3)*
Draught, feet (metres): 18·8 *(5·7)*
Guns: 1—3·9 in *(100 mm)* 1 CIWS
Missiles: 1 NATO Sea Sparrow SAM, (8 cells); 4 Exocet SSM
Torpedo launchers: 2 for L-5 torpedos
A/S rocket launchers: 1—6 × 375 mm LR Bofors
Rocket launchers: 2—8 barrelled Corvus dual-purpose Chaff/flare launchers
Main engines: CODOG—1 Rolls-Royce Olympus TM3 gas turbine; 28 000 bhp; 2 Cockerill CO-240 diesels; 6 000 bhp. Twin vp propellers
Speed, knots: 28 (15 on 1 diesel, 18 on 2 diesels)
Range, miles: 4 500 at 18 knots
Complement: 14 officers; 146 men

This compact, well-armed class of frigate is the first class fully designed by the Belgian Navy and built in Belgian yards. All to be fitted with hull-mounted sonar and fin stabilisers.
The programme was approved 23 June 1971 and design studies completed July 1973. A firm order was placed in October 1973 and *Wielingen* was laid down on time. Completion has, however, been delayed by strikes in Belgian yards.

Electronics: Fully integrated and automated weapons command and control system of HSA (SEWACO 4). ECM capability.

Missiles: Sea Sparrow RIM 7H-2. Exocet MM 38.

Radar: Air and surface warning and target indication radar with Control System (HSA). Navigation radar by Raytheon.

Sonar: SQS 505A (Westinghouse).

Transfers: It has been reported, though not confirmed, that Chile has an interest in acquiring two of this class.

WIELINGEN   1977, *Royal Belgian Navy*

WIELINGEN   1977, *Royal Belgian Navy*

BELGIUM

MINE WARFARE FORCES

7 Ex-US MSO (Ex-AM) TYPE 498 (MINEHUNTERS)

Name	No.	Builders	Laid down	Launched	Commissioned
J. E. VAN HAVERBEKE (ex-MSO 522)	M 902	Peterson Builders Inc, Sturgeon Bay, Wisc.	2 Mar 1959	25 Oct 1959	7 Nov 1960
A. F. DUFOUR (ex-*Lagen* M 950, ex-MSO 498, ex-AM 498)	M 903	Bellingham Shipyard Inc, Wash.	11 Feb 1954	13 Aug 1954	27 Sep 1955
DE BROUWER (ex-*Nansen*, M 951, ex-MSO 499, ex-AM 499)	M 904	Bellingham Shipyard Inc, Wash.	25 April 1954	15 Oct 1954	1 Nov 1955
BREYDEL (ex-MSO 504, ex-AM 504)	M 906	Tacoma Boatbuilding Co, Tacoma, Wash.	25 Nov 1954	25 Mar 1955	24 Jan 1956
ARTEVELDE (ex-MSO 503, ex-AM 503)	M 907	Tacoma Boatbuilding Co, Tacoma, Wash.	15 Oct 1953	19 June 1954	15 Dec 1955
G. TRUFFAUT (ex-MSO 515, ex-AM 515)	M 908	Tampa Shipbuilding Co, Inc, Tampa, Fla.	1 Feb 1955	1 Nov 1955	21 Sep 1956
F. BOVESSE (ex-MSO 516, ex-AM 516)	M 909	Tampa Shipbuilding Co, Inc. Tampa, Fla.	1 April 1954	8 Feb 1956	21 Dec 1956

Displacement, tons: 720 standard; 780 full load
Length, feet (metres): 165·0 *(50·3)* wl; 172·5 *(52·6)* oa
Beam, feet (metres): 35·0 *(10·7)*
Draught, feet (metres): 11·0 *(3·4)*
Gun: 1—40 mm (only *Artevelde*)
Main engines: 2 GM diesels; 2 shafts; 1 600 bhp
Speed, knots: 14
Oil fuel, tons: 50
Range, miles: 2 400 at 12 knots; 3 000 at 20 knots
Complement: 72 (5 officers, 67 men)

Wooden hulls and non-magnetic structure. Capable of sweeping mines of all types. Diesels of non-magnetic stainless steel alloy. Controllable pitch propellers.

Dufour and *De Brouwer* originally served in Royal Norwegian Navy (1955-66). *Artevelde* converted to Diving Vessel in 1972 but retains minehunting capability. 1974 fitted with Siebe Gorman recompression chamber.

Sonar: SQQ 14 (GE) (except *Artevelde*).

Transfer dates: M902 9 Dec 1960, M903 14 April 1966, M904 14 April 1966, M906 15 Feb 1956, M907 16 Dec 1955, M908 12 Oct 1956, M909 25 Jan 1957.

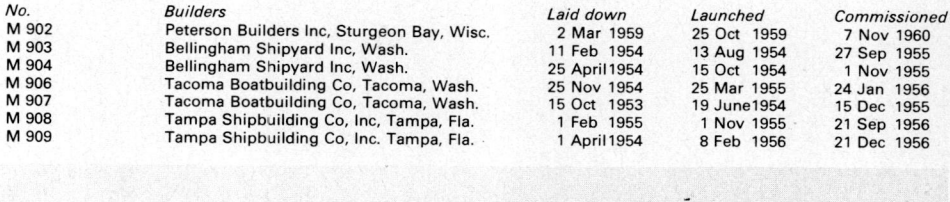

DE BROUWER 11/1976, Michael D. J. Lennon

6 Ex-US MSC (ex-AMS) TYPE 60 (MINESWEEPERS/HUNTERS—COASTAL)

Name	No.	Builders	Commissioned
STAVELOT	M 928	Boelwerf, Temse	21 Feb 1956
ROCHEFORT	M 930	Beliard, Ostend	28 Nov 1955
NIEUWPOORT	M 932	Beliard, Ostend	9 Jan 1956
KOKSIJDE	M 933	Beliard, Ostend	29 Nov 1955
VERVIERS (ex-*MSC 259*)	M 934	Boston, USA	19 June 1956
VEURNE (ex-*MSC 260*)	M 935	Boston, USA	7 Sep 1956

Displacement, tons: 330 light; 390 full load
Dimensions, feet (metres): 139 pp; 144 oa × 27·9 × 8 *(42·4; 44·0 × 8·5 × 2·4)*
Gun: 1—40 mm
Main engines: 2 GM diesels; 2 shafts (Voigt-Schneider propellers); 880 bhp = 13·5 knots
Oil fuel, tons: 28
Range, miles: 3 000 at economical speed (10·5 knots)
Complement: 39

Wooden hulls and constructed throughout of materials with the lowest possible magnetic signature. M 934 and 935 were built the in USA, under MDAP, the others were built in Belgium with machinery and equipment transferred from USA. M 934 (ex-*MSC 259*) transferred 19 June 1956, M 935 (ex-*MSC 260*) was transferred on 7 Sep 1956. *Verviers* (in 1972) and *Veurne* (in 1969) converted to minehunters with Voith-Schneider propellers. *Veurne* used for survey work since Oct 1970.

Names: This class was known only by numbers until 1958 when present names were given.

Reclassification: *Mechelen*, A 926 (ex-M 926): research ship since 1964.
Spa A 963 (ex-M 927): conversion to ammunition transport ship started in 1978.
Heist A 964 (ex-M 929): conversion to degaussing ship started in 1978.

KOKSIJDE 10/1976, Wright and Logan

Sonar: Type 193 (Plessey).

Transfers: 3 MSC to Norway—1966; 5 MSC to Greece—1969; 8 MSC to Taiwan—1969.

14 "HERSTAL" CLASS (MINESWEEPERS—INSHORE)

Name	No.	Builders	Commissioned
HASSELT	M 471	Mercantile Marine Yard, Kruibeke	24 April 1958
KORTRYK	M 472	Mercantile Marine Yard, Kruibeke	13 June 1958
LOKEREN	M 473	Mercantile Marine Yard, Kruibeke	8 Aug 1958
TURNHOUT	M 474	Mercantile Marine Yard, Kruibeke	29 Sep 1958
TONGEREN	M 475	Mercantile Marine Yard, Kruibeke	9 Dec 1958
MERKSEM	M 476	Mercantile Marine Yard, Kruibeke	6 Feb 1959
OUDENAARDE	M 477	Mercantile Marine Yard, Kruibeke	25 April 1959
HERSTAL	M 478 (ex-MSI 90)	Mercantile Marine Yard, Kruibeke	14 Oct 1957
HUY	M 479 (ex-MSI 91)	Mercantile Marine Yard, Kruibeke	24 Mar 1958
SERAING	M 480 (ex-MSI 92)	Mercantile Marine Yard, Kruibeke	3 June 1958
VISE	M 482 (ex-MSI 94)	Mercantile Marine Yard, Kruibeke	11 Sep 1958
OUGREE	M 483 (ex-MSI 95)	Mercantile Marine Yard, Kruibeke	10 Nov 1958
DINANT	M 484 (ex-MSI 96)	Mercantile Marine Yard, Kruibeke	14 Jan 1959
ANDENNE	M 485 (ex-MSI 97)	Mercantile Marine Yard, Kruibeke	20 April 1959

Displacement, tons: 160 light; 190 full load
Dimensions, feet (metres): 106·7 pp × 113·2 oa × 22·3 × 6 *(32·5; 34·5 × 6·8 × 1·8)*
Guns: 2—0·5 (twin)
Main engines: 2 diesels; 2 shafts; 1 260 bhp = 15 knots
Oil fuel, tons: 18
Range, miles: 2 300 at 10 knots
Complement: 17

Modified AMI "100-foot" class. Originally a class of sixteen.

The first group of eight (M 478 to 485) was a United States "off shore order", the remaining eight (M 470 to 477) being financed under the Belgian Navy Estimates.

Transfers: 2 MSI to Korea(S)—1970.

HUY 6/1977, C. and S. Taylor

52 BELGIUM

SUPPORT SHIPS

Name	No.	Builders	Commissioned
ZINNIA	A 961	Cockerill, Hoboken	5 Sep 1967

Displacement, tons: 1 705 light; 2 685 full load
Dimensions, feet (metres): 309 wl; 326·4 oa × 49·9 × 11·8 (94·2; 99·5 × 15·2 × 3·6)
Guns: 3—40 mm (single)
Aircraft: 1 helicopter
Main engines: 2 Cockerill V 12 RT 240 CO diesels; 5 000 bhp; 1 shaft
Speed, knots: 20
Oil fuel, tons: 500
Range, miles: 14 000 at 12·5 knots
Complement: 125

Laid down 8 Nov 1966, launched on 6 May 1967. Controllable pitch propeller. Design includes a platform and a retractable hangar for one light liaison-helicopter normally carried on board. Rated as Command and Logistic Support Ship.

ZINNIA   6/1977, Dr. Giorgio Arra

Name	No.	Builders	Commissioned
GODETIA	A 960	Boelwerf, Temse	23 May 1966

Displacement, tons: 1 700 light; 2 500 full load
Dimensions, feet (metres): 289 wl; 301 oa × 46 × 11·5 (88·0; 91·8 × 14 × 3·5)
Guns: 2—40 mm (twin)
Main engines: 4 ACEC—MAN diesels; 2 shafts; 5 400 bhp = 19 knots
Oil fuel, tons: 294
Range, miles: 8 700 at 12·5 knots
Complement: 100 plus 35 spare billets

Laid down on 15 Feb 1965, launched on 7 Dec 1965. Controllable pitch propellers. Provided with a platform which can take a light liaison-helicopter. Rated as Command and Logistic Support Ship.

GODETIA   2/1976, Dr. Giorgio Arra

MISCELLANEOUS

RIVER PATROL BOATS

LEIE	P 901	MEUSE	P 903	SCHELDE	P 905
LIBERATION	P 902	SAMBRE	P 904	SEMOIS	P 906

Displacement, tons: 25 light; 27·5 full load
Dimensions, feet (metres): 75·5 pp; 82 oa × 12·5 × 3 (23·0; 25·0 × 3·8 × 0·9)
  Liberation 85·5 × 13·1 × 3·2 (26·0 × 4·0 × 1·0)
Guns: 2—13 mm (0·50) MG
Main engines: 2 diesels; 2 shafts; 440 bhp = 19 knots
Complement: 7

Built by Hitzler, Regensburg, Germany, in 1953, except Liberation in 1954. Sister craft Rupel, deleted 1964, still operating as training craft for cadets—B30 Tresignes.

RIVER PATROL BOAT   1974, Belgian Navy

AUXILIARIES

Name	No.	Builders	Commissioned
SPA	A 963 (ex-M 927)	Boelwerf, Temse	1 Jan 1956
HEIST	A 964 (ex-M 929)	Boelwerf, Temse	4 Apr 1956

Ex-MSCs (details under Mine Warfare Forces) converted in 1978 to ammunition Transport and Degaussing Ship respectively.

Harbour craft: There are three tanker barges, namely **FN 4**, **FN 5** and **FN 6**, displacement 300 tons, length 105 feet, built by Plaquet, Peronne-lez-Antoing in 1957; the ammunition ship Ekster, displacement 140 tons, length 118 feet, built at Niel (Germany) in 1953; a diving cutter **ZM 4**, displacement 8 tons, length 33 feet, built by Panesi at Ostend in 1954; and the harbour transport cutter Spin, displacement 32 tons, length 47·8 feet, with 250 bhp diesels = 8 knots and Voith-Schneider propeller, built in the Netherlands in 1958.

RESEARCH SHIPS

Name	No.	Builders	Commissioned
ZENOBE GRAMME	A 958	Boelwerf, Temse	1962

Displacement, tons: 149
Dimensions, feet (metres): 92 × 22·5 × 7 (28·0 × 6·8 × 2·1)
Main engines: 1 MWM diesel; 1 shaft; 200 bhp = 10 knots
Complement: 14

Auxiliary sail ketch. Laid down 17 Oct 1960, launched 23 Oct 1961. Designed for scientific research.

Name	No.	Builders	Commissioned
MECHELEN	A 962 (ex-M 926)	Boelwerf, Temse	2 Dec 1954

Displacement, tons: 330 light; 390 full load
Dimensions, feet (metres): 139 pp; 144 oa × 27·9 × 7·5 (42·4; 44·0 × 8·5 × 2·6)
Main engines: 2 GM diesels; 2 shafts; 880 bhp = 13·5 knots
Oil fuel, tons: 28
Range, miles: 3 000 at economical speed (10·5 knots)
Complement: 26

Former coastal minesweeper of Type 60. Used as a research ship since 1964 being renumbered as A 962 in 1966. Similar to photograph under Mine Warfare Forces with longer bridge and additional deck house by mainmast.

TUGS

O/Lt VALCKE (ex-AT 1 Elis) A 950

Displacement, tons: 110
Dimensions, feet (metres): 78·8 pp; 95 oa × 21 × 5·5 (24·0; 29·0 × 6·4 × 1·7)
Main engines: 1 diesel; 1 shaft; 600 bhp = 12 knots
Complement: 14

Built by Holland Nautic NV, Haarlem, Netherlands in 1951 and served as Dutch mercantile tug Elis until purchased by Belgian Navy in 1953. Serves as diving tender.

BIJ A 953   **KREKEL** A 956

Harbour tugs with fire-fighting facilities. Of 71 tons and twin shafts; 400 hp with Voith-Schneider propellers. Bij built by Akerboom 1959, Krekel by Ch. Navals de Rupelmonde 1961.

HOMMEL A 951   **WESP** A 952

Harbour tugs of 22 tons, 300 bhp diesels with Voith-Schneider propellers. Both built by Voith, Heidenheim in 1953.

MIER A 959

Harbour tug of 17·5 tons with 90 bhp diesel. Built Liége 1962.

BELIZE

Personnel

(a) 50 approx
(b) Voluntary service

Base

Belize

Mercantile Marine

Lloyd's Register of Shipping:
3 vessels of 620 tons gross

2 COASTAL PATROL CRAFT

Name	No.	Builders	Commissioned
BELIZE	PBM 01	Brooke Marine, Lowestoft	1972
BELMOPAN	PBM 02	Brooke Marine, Lowestoft	1972

Displacement, tons: 15
Dimensions, feet (metres): 40 × 12 × 2 (12·2 × 3·6 × 0·6)
Guns: 3 MG
Main engines: 2 diesels; 370 hp × 22 knots

BERMUDA

Royal Navy

The RN retains a base facility in Bermuda.

Base

Hamilton.

Mercantile Marine

Lloyd's Register of Shipping:
69 vessels of 1 562 483 tons gross

Several 20ft coastal patrol craft are operated by the Bermuda Police.

BOLIVIA

Headquarters Appointment

Commander-in-Chief:
Rear-Admiral Gutemberg Barroso Hurtado

Personnel

(a) 1978: 1 500 officers and men (including marines)
(b) 12 months selective military service

A small navy used for patrolling Lake Titicaca and the Beni River system. Most of the training of officers and senior ratings is carried out in Argentina.

Bases

Tiquina.
Loma Suarez (building yard)

Prefix to Ships' Names

FNB

Name	No.	Tonnage	Dimensions (ft-m)	Notes
ALMIRANTE GRAU	M 01	52	44·3 × 10·5 × 4·8 (13·5 × 3·2 × 1·5)	Training and Transport. Diesel.
NICOLAS SUAREZ	M 02	26·5	57·6 × 11·2 × 6·4 (18 × 3·5 × 2)	Built 1963. Iron hull. Diesel.
MARISCAL SANTA CRUZ	M 03	52	44·3 × 10·5 × 4·8 (13·5 × 3·5 × 2)	Training and Transport. Diesel.
PRESIDENTE BUSCH	M 04	52	60·8 × 11·2 × 4·2 (19 × 3·5 × 1·3)	Wooden hull. Diesel.
COMANDANTE ARANDIA	M 05	82	72·3 × 12·8 × 4·5 (22·6 × 4 × 1·4)	Iron hull. Diesel. Rebuilt 1970.
TOPATER	M 06	—	—	—
BRUNO RACUA	M 07	17	57·6 × 13·1 × 3·8 (18 × 4·1 × 1·2)	Wooden-hull. Diesel.
CORONEL EDUARDO AVAROA	M 08	82	80 × 27·8 × 4·8 (25 × 8·7 × 1·5)	Built 1965.
PRESIDENTE KENNEDY	—	12	38·4 × 11·4 × 3·3 (12 × 3·5 × 1)	Wooden hull. Diesel. Ex-US PB Mk 1. Survivor of three transferred 1963.

YACUMA A-3-02, ITENEZ A-3-03, MADERA A-3-04, IBARE A-3-05, CHAPARE A-3-06, ICHILO A-3-07, MUCHULA A-3-08, TORIBIO A-3-09, LITORAL A-3-10, INDEPENDENCIA, MAYTA KAPAC, LADISLAO CABREA, MAPIRI, TAHUAMANU V-01 are all borne on the nominal list although details are not available.
In addition one river craft of 112 tons (built in Bolivia 1970) one of 55 tons (built in Bolivia 1971-72), eight smaller river craft (built in Bolivia 1973-76), two ex-US PBR Mark II of 8·5 tons (transferred April 1974) and one Lake Patrol Boat of 12 tons are in service although details, names and pennant numbers are not available.

BRAZIL

Headquarters Appointments

Chief of Naval Staff:
  Admiral Gualter Maria Menezes de Magalhães
Chief of Naval Material:
  Admiral Sylvio de Magalhães Figueiredo
Chief of Naval Personnel:
  Admiral Eddy Sampaio Espellet

Diplomatic Representation

Naval Attaché in Asunción:
  Captain Luiz Fernando da Silva e Souza
Naval and Defence Attaché in Athens:
  Captain Gerson Fleischauer
Naval and Defence Attaché in Buenos Aires:
  Captain Odilon Lima Cardoso
Naval and Defence Attaché in Lima:
  Captain Luis Carlos de Freitas
Naval Attaché in La Paz:
  Captain Paulo Demaria Seróa da Motta
Naval and Defence Attaché in Lisbon and Madrid:
  Captain Valbert Lisieux Medeiros de Figueiredo
Naval Attaché in London:
  Captain Lysias Ruland Kerr
Naval Attaché in Paris:
  Captain Henrique Octávio Aché Pillar
Naval and Defence Attaché in Santiago:
  Captain Francisco Lafayette de Moraes
Naval and Defence Attaché in Tokyo:
  Captain Luiz Augusto Paraguassu de Sá
Naval Attaché in Washington:
  Rear-Admiral Rafael de Azevedo Branco
Head of the Brazilian Naval Commission in Europe:
  Vice-Admiral José G. T. A. de Aratanha

General

With a coastline of 4 655 miles Brazil has a considerable problem even to patrol the more important areas in peacetime. The new "Niteroi" class will bring a considerable addition to the present strength which includes an aircraft-carrier, ten destroyers and seven submarines of World War II construction. While the patrol and river forces are probably adequate a considerable programme of replacement is needed amongst the larger ships.

Personnel

(a)
  1972: 42 125 (3 264 officers and 38 861 men)
  1973: 44 337 (3 591 officers and 40 746 men)
  1974: 49 600 (3 887 officers and 45 713 men)
  1975: 43 100 (3 800 officers and 39 300 men)
  1976: 45 300 (3 800 officers and 41 500 men)
  1977: 45 300 (3 800 officers and 41 500 men)
  1978: 45 500 (3 900 officers and 41 600 men)
Figures include marines and auxiliary corps

(b) 1 years national service

Naval Bases

Rio de Janeiro (main base with 3 dry docks and 1 floating dock)
Aratu (Bahia) (major naval yard with 1 dry dock and 1 floating dock)
Belém (naval base and repair yard with 1 dry dock)
Recife (naval base and repair yard)
Natal (small naval base and repair yard with 1 floating dock — being rebuilt as major base)
Ladario (river base of *Mato Grosso* flotilla)
Sao Pedro (naval air station)

Maritime Aviation

A Fleet Air Arm was formed on 26 Jan 1965.

Navy

  6 Sikorsky SH-3D
  3 Westland Whirlwind (UH-5)
  3 Westland Wasp HAS-1 (UH-2)
  18 Bell 206B Jetrangers
  9 Westland Lynx WG 13 to be provided for "Niteroi" class

Air Force (Comando Costeira)

  8 Grumman S-2E Trackers (ASW).
  12 Grumman HU-16A Albatross (SAR)
  5 Grumman S-2E Trackers (Transport and Training)
  3 Lockheed RC-130E Hercules (SAR/PR)
  6 Convair PBY-5A Catalinas (Transport)
  16 EMB-111 (on order—delivery from 1978)
  4 EMB-110B (PR)
  15 Neiva T25 Universal I (liaison)
  5 Bell SH-1D (SAR helicopters)
  2 Bell 47G (SAR helicopters)

Prefix to Ship' Names

These vary, indicating the type of ship e.g. N Ae L = Aircraft Carrier; CT = Destroyer.

Strength of the Fleet

Type	Active	Building
Attack Carrier (medium)	1	—
Destroyers	20	—
Submarines (Patrol)	9	1
Corvettes	10	—
Landing Ships	2	—
Landing Craft	48	—
Monitor	1	—
River Patrol Ships	5	—
Large Patrol Craft	6	—
River Patrol Craft	10	—
Minesweepers (Coastal)	6	—
Survey Ships	8	—
Survey Launches	6	—
Light Tenders	6	—
S/M Rescue Ships	1	—
Repair and Support ships	2	(1)
Large Tanker	1	—
Small Tankers	2	—
Transports	15	—
Tugs	6	(1)
Floating Docks	3	—

New Construction

A revised plan is being developed

Mercantile Marine

Lloyd's Register of Shipping:
  520 vessels of 3 096 293 tons gross

DELETIONS

Cruisers

1973 *Barroso*
1975 *Tamandaré* offered for auction (September)
  (both ex-US "St Louis" class)

Destroyers

1973 *Amazonas, Mariz E. Barros*
1974 *Acre, Araguaia, Araguari*—(auction July for scrap)
  (All Brazilian built 1949-51)

Frigates

1973 *Baependi, Bracui*
1975 *Benevente, Bocaina* (auction Feb for scrap)
  (All ex-US "Bostwick" class)

Submarines

1972 *Rio Grande do Sul* (ex-*Sandlance*) sold for scrap June 1975
  Bahia (ex-*Plaice*) sold to Brazilian Museum of Naval Technology, Santos by USA as a memorial

Mine Warfare Forces

1974 *Jutai, Juruena* (paid off in Aug)
  (ex-US AMS)

Patrol Forces

1971 *Piraju, Piranha*
1972 *Paraguaçu*
1973 *Pirague*

Auxiliaries

1976 *Javari* and *Jurua*

PENNANT LIST

Aircraft Carrier

A11	Minas Gerais

Destroyers

F40	Niteroi
F41	Defensora
F42	Independencia
F43	União
F44	Constituição
F45	Liberal
D25	Marcilio Dias
D26	Mariz E. Barros
D27	Para
D28	Paraiba
D29	Parana
D30	Pernambuco
D31	Piaui
D32	Santa Catarina
D33	Maranhão
D34	Mato Grosso
D35	Sergipe
D36	Alagoas
D37	Rio Grande do Norte
D38	Espirito Santo

Submarines

S10	Guanabara
S11	Rio Grande Do Sul
S12	Bahia
S13	Rio De Janeiro
S14	Ceara
S15	Goiaz
S16	Amazonas
S20	Humaita
S21	Tonelero
S22	Riachuelo

Amphibious Forces

G26	Duque De Caxias
G28	Garcia D'Avila

Patrol Forces

P20	Pedro Teixeira
P21	Raposo Tavares
P30	Roraima
P31	Rondonia
P32	Amapa
U17	Parnaiba
V15	Imperial Marinheiro
V16	Iguatemi
V17	Ipiranga
V18	Forte De Coimbra
V19	Cabocla
V20	Angostura
V21	Baiana
V22	Mearim
V23	Purus
V24	Solimoes

Light Forces

P10	Piratini
P11	Piraja
P12	Pampeiro
P13	Parati
P14	Penedo
P15	Poti
R54	Anchova
R55	Arenque
R56	Atum
R57	Acara
R58	Agulha
R59	Aruana

Mine Warfare Forces

M15	Aratu
M16	Anhatomirim
M17	Atalaia
M18	Aracatuba
M19	Abrolhos
M20	Albardão

Survey Vessels and Tenders

H11	Paraibano
H12	Rio Branco
H13	Mestre João dos Santos
H14	Nogueira da Gama
H15	Itacurussa
H16	Camocim
H17	Caravelas
H21	Sirius
H22	Canopus
H24	Castelhanos
H27	Faroleiro Areas
H28	Faroleiro Santana
H30	Faroleiro Nascimento
H31	Argus
H32	Orion
H33	Taurus
H34	Graça Aranha
H41	Almirante Camara
U10	Almirante Saldanha

Miscellaneous

G15	Paraguassu
G16	Barroso Pereira
G17	Potengi
G21	Ary Parreiras
G22	Soares Dutra
G24	Belmonte
G25	Afonso Pena
G26	Am. Jeronimo Gonçalves
G27	Marajó
K10	Gastao Moutinho
R21	Tritão
R22	Tridente
R23	Triunfo
U20	Rio Doce
U21	Rio das Contas
U22	Rio Formoso
U23	Rio Real
U24	Rio Turvo
U25	Rio Verde
U26	Custodio de Mello
U40	Rio Pardo
U41	Rio Negro
U42	Rio Chui
U43	Rio Oiapoque

BRAZIL 55

SUBMARINES

2 + 1 BRITISH "OBERON" CLASS

Name	No.	Builders	Laid down	Launched	Commissioned
HUMAITA	S 20	Vickers, Barrow	3 Nov 1970	5 Oct 1971	18 June 1973
TONELERO	S 21	Vickers, Barrow	18 Nov 1971	22 Nov 1972	? 1977
RIACHUELO	S 22	Vickers, Barrow	26 May 1973	6 Sep 1975	12 Mar 1977

Displacement, tons: 1 610 standard; 2 030 surfaced; 2 410 dived
Length, feet (metres): 295·5 (90·1) oa
Beam, feet (metres): 26·5 (8·1)
Draught, feet (metres): 18·0 (5·5)
Tubes: 8—21 in (533 mm) (6 bow and 2 stern)
Main machinery: 2 Admiralty Standard Range 1 16-cyl diesels; 3 680 bhp; 2 electric motors; 6 000 shp; 2 shafts; electric drive
Speed, knots: 12 surfaced, 17 dived
Complement: 70 (6 officers and 64 men)

In 1969 it was announced that two submarines of the British "Oberon" class were ordered from Vickers, Barrow. The third boat was ordered in 1972. Completion of *Tonelero* has been much delayed by a serious fire on board originating in the cabling. She spent a period in Chatham Dockyard, having been towed from Barrow, returning in January 1976. Completion unlikely before early 1978. It was this fire which resulted in re-cabling of all "Oberons" under construction. Whilst in Chatham the centre 60 ft was replaced. Diesels by Vickers Shipbuilding Group. Electric motors by AEI-English Electric. Sonar, modern navigational aids and provision for modern fire control system developed by Vickers.

HUMAITA   1977, Brazilian Navy

2 Ex-US GUPPY III TYPE

Name	No.	Builders	Laid down	Launched	Commissioned
GOIÁZ (ex-USS *Trumpetfish* SS 425)	S 15	Cramp SB Co	23 Aug 1943	13 May 1945	29 Jan 1946
AMAZONAS (ex-USS *Greenfish* SS 351)	S 16	Electric Boat Co	29 June 1944	21 Dec 1945	7 June 1946

Displacement, tons: 1 975 standard; 2 450 dived
Length, feet (metres): 326·5 (99·5)
Beam, feet (metres): 27 (8·2)
Draught, feet (metres): 17 (5·2)
Torpedo tubes: 10—21 in; 6 bow 4 stern
Main machinery: 4 diesels; 6 400 hp; 2 electric motors; 5 400 hp; 2 shafts
Speed, knots: 20 surfaced; 15 dived
Complement: 85

Converted in 1960-62. *Goiáz* transferred by sale 15 Oct 1973 and *Amazonas* by sale 19 Dec 1973.

Sonar: BQR-2 array, BQG-4 (PUFFS) fire control sonar (fins on casing).

AMAZONAS   1977, Brazilian Navy

5 Ex-US GUPPY II TYPE

Name	No.	Builders	Laid down	Launched	Commissioned
GUANABARA (ex-USS *Dogfish* SS 350)	S 10	Electric Boat Co	22 June 1944	27 Oct 1945	29 Apr 1946
RIO GRANDE DO SUL (ex-USS *Grampus* SS 523)	S 11	Boston Navy Yard	8 Feb 1944	15 Dec 1944	26 Oct 1946
BAHIA (ex-USS *Sea Leopard* SS 483)	S 12	Portsmouth Navy Yard	7 Nov 1944	2 Mar 1945	11 June 1945
RIO DE JANEIRO (ex-*Guanabara*, ex-USS *Odax* SS 484)	S 13	Portsmouth Navy Yard	4 Dec 1944	10 Apr 1945	11 July 1945
CEARÁ (ex-USS *Amberjack* SS 522)	S 14	Boston Navy Yard	8 Feb 1944	15 Dec 1944	4 Mar 1946

Displacement, tons: 1 870 standard; 2 420 dived
Length, feet (metres): 307·5 (93·7)
Beam, feet (metres): 27·2 (8·3)
Draught, feet (metres): 18 (5·5)
Torpedo tubes: 10—21 in (6 bow, 4 stern)
Main machinery: 3 diesels, 4 800 shp; 2 motors; 5 400 shp; 2 shafts
Speed, knots: 18 surfaced; 15 dived
Range, miles: 12 000 at 10 knots (surfaced)
Complement: 82

Modernised under Guppy II programme 1948-50 except *Rio de Janeiro* which was first modernised to Guppy I standards and later to Guppy II. Transferred 13 May 1972 (*Rio Grande do Sul*), 8 July 1972 (*Rio de Janeiro*), 28 July 1972 (*Guanabara*), 27 Mar 1973 (*Bahia*), 17 Oct 1973 (*Ceara*). All by sale.

RIO DE JANEIRO   1977, Brazilian Navy

56 BRAZIL

AIRCRAFT CARRIER
1 Ex-BRITISH "COLOSSUS" CLASS

Name	No.	Builders	Laid down	Launched	Commissioned
MINAS GERAIS (ex-HMS *Vengeance*)	A 11	Swan, Hunter & Wigham Richardson, Ltd, Wallsend on Tyne	16 Nov 1942	23 Feb 1944	15 Jan 1945

Displacement, tons: 15 890 standard; 17 500 normal; 19 890 full load (see *Displacement* note)
Length, feet (metres): 630 *(192·0)* pp; 695 *(211·8)* oa
Beam, feet (metres): 80 *(24·4)*
Draught, feet (metres): 24·5 *(7·5)*
Flight deck,
  Length, feet (metres): 690 *(210·3)*
  Width, feet (metres): 121 *(37·0)* oa as reconstructed
  Height, feet (metres): 39 *(11·9)* above water line
Catapults: 1 steam
Aircraft: 20 aircraft including 7 S2A Trackers, 4 Sea Kings
Guns: 10—40 mm (2 quadruple, 1 twin), 2—47 mm (saluting)
Main engines: Parsons geared turbines; 2 shafts; 40 000 shp
Boilers: 4 Admiralty 3-drum type; Working pressure 400 psi *(28 kg/cm²)*; max superheat 700°F *(371°C)*
Speed, knots: 24; 25·3 on trials after reconstruction
Oil fuel, tons: 3 200
Range, miles: 12 000 at 14 knots; 6 200 at 23 knots
Complement: 1 000 (1 300 with air group)

Served in the Royal Navy from 1945 onwards. Fitted out in late 1948 to early 1949 for experimental cruise to the Arctic. Lent to the RAN early in 1953, returned to the Royal Navy in Aug 1955. Purchased by the Brazilian Government on 14 Dec 1956. Reconstructed at Verolme Dock, Rotterdam from summer 1957 to Dec 1960. The conversion and overhaul included the installation of the angled deck, steam catapult, mirror-sight deck landing system, armament fire control and radar equipment. The ship was purchased for $9 million and the reconstruction cost $27 million. Commissioned in the Brazilian Navy at Rotterdam on 6 Dec 1960. Left Rotterdam for Rio de Janeiro on 13 Jan 1961. Used primarily for anti-submarine aircraft and helicopters. Currently under refit 1976-78.

Displacement: Before reconstruction: 13 190 tons standard; 18 010 tons full load.

Engineering: The two units each have one set of turbines and two boilers installed side by side. Maximum speed at 120 rpm. Steam capacity was increased when the boilers were retubed during reconstruction in 1957-60.

MINAS GERAIS   1971, Brazilian Navy

Electrical: During reconstruction an alternating current system was installed with a total of 2 500 kW supplied by four turbo-generators and one diesel generator.

Hangar: Dimensions: length, 445 feet; width, 52 feet; clear depth, 17·5 feet. Aircraft lifts: 45 feet by 34 feet. During reconstruction in 1957-60 new lifts replaced the original units.

Radar: Air Surveillance: SPS 12.

Surface Search: SPS 4.
Fighter Direction: SPS 8B.
Air Control: SPS 8A.
Fire Control: SPG 34.
Navigation: MP 1402.

Operational: Single track catapult for launching, and arrester wires for recovering, 30 000 lb aircraft at 60 knots. Catapult accelerator gear port side forward.

MINAS GERAIS   9/1972, USN

MINAS GERAIS   1972, Brazilian Navy

BRAZIL 57

DESTROYERS

6 "NITEROI" CLASS

Name	No.	Builders	Laid down	Launched	Commissioned
NITEROI	F 40	Vosper Thornycroft Ltd.	8 June 1972	8 Feb 1974	20 Nov 1976
DEFENSORA	F 41	Vosper Thornycroft Ltd.	14 Dec 1972	27 Mar 1975	5 Mar 1977
INDEPENDENCIA	F 42	Arsenal de Marinho, Rio de Janeiro	11 June 1972	2 Sep 1974	Mar 1978
UNIÃO	F 43	Arsenal de Marinho, Rio de Janeiro	11 June 1972	14 Mar 1975	Oct 1978
CONSTITUIÇÃO	F 44	Vosper Thornycroft Ltd.	13 Mar 1974	April 1976	Feb 1978
LIBERAL	F 45	Vosper Thornycroft Ltd.	2 May 1975	7 Feb 1977	Aug 1978

Displacement, tons: 3 200 standard; 3 800 full load
Length, feet (metres): 400 *(121·9)* wl; 424 *(129·2)* oa
Beam, feet (metres): 44·2 *(13·5)*
Draught, feet (metres): 18·2 *(5·5)*
Aircraft: One WG 13 Lynx helicopter
Missile launchers: 2 twin Exocet MM 38 surface-to-surface in General Purpose version; 2 triple Seacat; Ikara in Anti-Submarine version
Guns: 2—4·5 in Mark 8 in General Purpose version; 1—4·5 in Mark 8 in Anti-Submarine version; 2—40 mm
A/S weapons: One Bofors 375 mm twin tube A/S rocket launcher; Two triple Mark 32 torpedo tubes; 1 DC rail
Main engines: CODOG system; 2 Rolls-Royce Olympus gas turbines = 56 000 bhp; 4 MTU diesels = 18 000 shp
Speed, knots: 30 on gas turbines; 22 on diesels
Range, miles: 5 300 at 17 knots (2 diesels); 4 200 at 19 knots (4 diesels); 1 300 at 28 knots (gas turbine)
Endurance: 45 days stores; 60 days provisions
Complement: 200

A very interesting design of handsome appearance—Vosper Thornycroft Mark 10. The moulded depth is 28·5 feet *(8·8 metres)*. Exceptionally economical in personnel, amounting to a 50 per cent reduction of manpower in relation to previous warships of this size and complexity. Require 100 fewer men than the British Type 42 of approximately similar characteristics. *Niteroi* started trials in Jan 1976. *Defensora* started trials Oct 1976.

Class: F 40, 41, 44 and 45 are of the A/S configuration. F 42 and 43 are General Purpose design.

Contract: A contract announced on 29 Sep 1970, valued at about £100 million, was signed between the Brazilian Government and Vosper Thornycroft Ltd, Portsmouth, England for the design and building of these six Vosper Thornycroft Mark 10 frigates comparable with the British Type 42 guided missile destroyers being built for the Royal Navy.

Construction: Materials, equipment and lead-yard services supplied by Vosper Thornycroft at Arsenal de Marinho.

Electronics: CAAIS equipment by Ferranti (FM 1600B computers). ECM by Decca.

Names: The names of the six ships as originally allocated in 1971 were: *Campista, Constituição, Defensora, Imperatriz, Isabel* and *Niteroi*.

Radar:
Air Warning: 1 Plessey AWS-2 with Mk 10 IFF.
Surface Warning: 1 Signaal ZW-06.
Weapon Control and Tracking: 2 Selenia RTN-10X.
Ikara Tracker: 1 set in A/S ships only.

Sonar: 1 EDO 610E medium range.
1 EDO 700E VDS (A/S ships only).

NITEROI 1/1976, Michael D. J. Lennon

DEFENSORA 6/1977, C. and S. Taylor

NITEROI 2/1976, Michael D. J. Lennon

BRAZIL

7 Ex-US "FLETCHER" CLASS

Name	No.	Builders	Laid down	Launched	Commissioned
PARA (ex-USS *Guest*, DD 472)	D 27	Boston Navy Yard	27 Sep 1941	20 Feb 1942	15 Dec 1942
PARAIBA (ex-USS *Bennett*, DD 473)	D 28	Boston Navy Yard	10 Dec 1941	16 April 1942	9 Feb 1943
PARAÑA (ex-USS *Cushing*, DD 797)	D 29	Bethlehem Steel Co (Staten Island)	3 May 1943	30 Sep 1943	17 Jan 1944
PERNAMBUCO (ex-USS *Hailey*, DD 556)	D 30	Seattle-Tacoma SB Corp, (Seattle)	1 April 1942	9 Mar 1943	30 Sep 1943
PIAUI (ex-USS *Lewis Hancock*, DD 675)	D 31	Federal SB and DD Co	1943	1 Aug 1943	29 Sep 1943
SANTA CATARINA (ex-USS *Irwin*, DD 794)	D 32	Bethlehem Steel Co (San Pedro)	1943	31 Oct 1943	14 Feb 1944
MARANHAO (ex-USS *Shields*, DD 596)	D 33	Puget Sound Navy Yard	10 Aug 1943	25 Sep 1944	8 Feb 1945

Displacement, tons: 2 050 standard; 3 050 full load
Length, feet (metres): 376·5 (114·8) oa
Beam, feet (metres): 39·3 (12·0)
Draught, feet (metres): 18 (5·5)
Missiles: 1 quadruple Seacat (*Maranhao* only)
Guns: 5—5 in (127 mm) 38 cal (except *Pernambuco*: 4—5 in);
10—40 mm (2 quad, 1 twin) (*Paraiba, Paraña* and *Maranhão*);
6—40 mm (3 twin) (*Para*)
Torpedo tubes: 5—21 in (533 mm) (not in *Maranhao*)
A/S weapons: 2 Hedgehogs;
1 DC rack;
2 side launching torpedo racks (not in *Maranhao*);
2 triple Mk 32 torpedo tubes
Main engines: 2 GE geared turbines; 2 shafts; 60 000 shp
Boilers: 4 Babcock & Wilcox
Speed, knots: 35
Oil fuel, tons: 650
Range, miles: 5 000 at 15 knots; 1 260 at 30 knots
Complement: 260

Para was transferred on loan 5 June 1959; *Paraiba* on loan 15 Dec 1959 and subsequently by sale 1 Aug 1973. *Parana* on loan 20 July 1961 and subsequently by sale 8 Jan 1973; *Pernambuco* on loan 20 July 1961 and *Maranhao* by sale 1 July 1972. *Piaui* was transferred on loan 2 Aug 1967 whilst *Santa Catarina* was transferred on loan 10 May 1968, and both by sale 11 April 1973.

PIAUI   1977, Brazilian Navy

Radar: Search: SPS 6. Tactical: SPS 10. Fire Control: I Band.

1 Ex-US "ALLEN M. SUMNER" and 4 Ex-US "ALLEN M. SUMNER FRAM II" CLASSES

Name	No.	Builders	Laid down	Launched	Commissioned
MATO GROSSO (ex-USS *Compton*, DD 705)	D 34	Federal SB & DD Co.	28 Mar 1944	17 Sep 1944	4 Nov 1944
SERGIPE (ex-USS *James C. Owens* DD 776)	D 35	Bethlehem (San Pedro)	9 April 1944	1 Oct 1944	17 Feb 1945
ALAGOAS (ex-USS *Buck* DD 761)	D 36	Bethlehem (San Francisco)	1 Feb 1944	11 Mar 1945	28 June 1946
RIO GRANDE DO NORTE (ex-USS *Strong* DD 758)	D 37	Bethlehem (San Francisco)	25 July 1943	23 April 1944	8 Mar 1945
ESPIRITO SANTO (ex-USS *Lowry* DD 770)	D 38	Bethlehem (San Pedro)	1 Aug 1943	6 Feb 1944	23 July 1944

Displacement, tons: 2 200 standard; 3 320 full load
Length, feet (metres): 376·5 (114·8) oa
Beam, feet (metres): 40·9 (12·5)
Draught, feet (metres): 19 (5·8)
Missiles: Sea Cat system (*Mato Grosso* only)
Guns: 6—5 in (127 mm) 38 cal (twins)
A/S weapons: 2 triple torpedo launchers; 2 ahead-firing Hedgehogs; facilities for small helicopter (Fram II).
Depth charges (*Mato Grosso*)
Main engines: 2 geared turbines; 60 000 shp; 2 shafts
Boilers: 4
Speed, knots: 34
Range, miles: 4 600 at 15 knots, 1 260 at 30 knots
Complement: 274

Transferred to Brazil as follows: *Mato Grosso* 27 Sep 1972, *Sergipe* and *Alagoas* 16 July 1973, *Espirito Santo* 29 Oct 1973, *Rio Grande do Norte* 31 Oct 1973, the last four being FRAM II conversions, *Mato Grosso* being of the original "Sumner" class.

Gunnery: 3 inch guns in *Mato Grosso* removed before transfer.

Missiles: Sea Cat system transferred to *Mato Grosso* from deleted *Mariz E Barros* of "Marcilio Dias" class.
Radar: SPS 6 and 10 and Mk 20 director (*Mato Grosso*). SPS 10 and 37 (*Espirito Santo*). SPS 10 and 40 (remainder).

MATO GROSSO   1977, Brazilian Navy

Sonar: SQS 31 (*Mato Grosso*). SQA 10 and SQS 40 (remainder).

2 Ex-US "GEARING" (FRAM I) CLASS

Name	No.	Builders	Laid down	Launched	Commissioned
MARCILIO DIAS (ex-USS *Henry W. Tucker* DD 875)	D 25	Consolidated Steel	1944	8 Nov 1944	12 Mar 1945
MARIZ E. BARROS (ex-USS *Brinkley Bass* D 887)	D 26	Consolidated Steel	1944	26 May 1945	1 Oct 1945

Displacement, tons: 2 425 standard; 3 500 full load
Length, feet (metres): 390·5 (119·0)
Beam, feet (metres): 40·9 (12·4)
Draught, feet (metres): 19 (5·8)
Guns: 4—5 in (127 mm) 38 cal (twin)
A/S weapons: 1 Asroc 8-tube launcher; 2 triple Mk 32 torpedo launchers; facilities for small helicopter
Main engines: 2 GE geared turbines; 60 000 shp; 2 shafts
Boilers: 4 Babcock & Wilcox
Speed, knots: 34
Range, miles: 5 800 at 15 knots
Complement: 274 (14 officers, 260 men)

Enlarged "Allen M. Sumner" class—14 feet longer. Transferred 3 Dec 1973.

Radar: SPS-10 and SPS-40.

Sonar: SQS-23 and VDS.

MARIZ E. BARROS   1977, Brazilian Navy

BRAZIL 59

AMPHIBIOUS FORCES
1 Ex-US TANK LANDING SHIP

Name	No.	Builders	Commissioned
GARCIA D'AVILA (ex-USS *Outagamie County* LST 1073)	G 28	Bethlehem Steel Co Higham, Mass	17 April 1945

Displacement, tons: 1 653 standard; 2 366 beaching; 4 080 full load
Dimensions, feet (metres): 328 oa × 50 × 14 *(100 × 15·3 × 4·3)*
Guns: 8—40 mm (2 twin, 4 single)
Main engines: GM diesels; 2 shafts; 1 700 bhp = 11·6 knots
Complement: 119
Troops: 147

Of LST 511-1152 Series. Transferred on loan to Brazil by USN 21 May 1971, purchased 1 Dec 1973.

GARCIA D'AVILA   1977, Brazilian Navy

1 Ex-US TANK LANDING SHIP

Name	No.	Builders	Commissioned
DUQUE DE CAXAIS (ex-USS *Grant County* LST 1174)	G 26	Avondale, New Orleans	8 Nov 1957

Displacement, tons: 3 828 light; 7 804 full load
Dimensions, feet (metres): 445 oa × 62 × 16·9 *(135·7 × 18·9 × 5·2)*
Guns: 2—3 in 50 cal (twins)
Main engines: Diesels; 13 700 shp; 2 shafts; CP propellers = 17·2 knots
Complement: 175 (11 officers, 164 men)
Troops: App. 575

"De Soto County" Class. Launched 12 Oct 1956 and transferred 15 Jan 1973. On lease. Now has Stuċcken heavy-lift gear fitted.

28 LCV (P)

Built in Japan 1959-60.

7 EDVP

Fitted with Saab-Skania Diesels of 153 hp. 37 ft long and with glass-fibre hulls. Built in Brazil in 1971-73. Can carry 36 men or equivalent amount of equipment.

4 LCU TYPE

CAMBORIÁ   GUARAPARI   TIMBAN   TRAMANDAI

Built in Rio de Janeiro 1974-75 by Arsenal de Marinha.

9 LCM (6)

Also reported but not confirmed.

PATROL FORCES

Note: 6-12 750 ton corvettes are projected.

10 "IMPERIAL MARINHEIRO" CLASS

Name	No.	Builders	Commissioned
IMPERIAL MARINHEIRO	V 15	Netherlands	1954
IGUATEMI	V 16	Netherlands	1954
IPIRANGA	V 17	Netherlands	1954
FORTE DE COIMBRA	V 18	Netherlands	1954
CABACLA	V 19	Netherlands	1954
ANGOSTURA	V 20	Netherlands	1955
BAIANA	V 21	Netherlands	1955
MEARIM	V 22	Netherlands	1955
PURUS	V 23	Netherlands	1955
SOLIMOES	V 24	Netherlands	1955

Displacement, tons: 911 standard
Dimensions, feet (metres): 184 × 30·5 × 11·7 *(56 × 9·3 × 3·6)*
Guns: 1—3 in 50 cal; 4—20 mm
Main engines: 2 Sulzer diesels; 2 160 bhp = 16 knots
Oil fuel, tons: 135
Complement: 60

Actually fleet tugs classed as corvettes. Equipped for fire fighting. *Imperial Marinheiro* employed as submarine support ship.

IGUATEMI   1977, Brazilian Navy

2 "PEDRO TEIXEIRA" CLASS (RIVER PATROL SHIPS)

Name	No.	Builders	Commissioned
PEDRO TEIXEIRA	P 20	Arsenal de Marinha, Rio de Janeiro	17 Dec 1973
RAPOSO TAVARES	P 21	Arsenal de Marinha, Rio de Janeiro	17 Dec 1973

Displacement, tons: 700 standard
Dimensions, feet (metres): 203·4 × 30·7 × 6·3 *(62 × 9·4 × 1·9)*
Guns: 1—40 mm; 2—81 mm mortars 6—·50 cal MG
Main engines: 4 diesels; 2 shafts = 16 knots

Helicopter platform and hangar fitted. Carry one LCVP. *Pedro Teixeira* launched 14 Oct 1970—*Raposo Tavares* 11 June 1972. Belong to Amazon Flotilla.

PEDRO TEIXEIRA   1974, Brazilian Navy

1 THORNYCROFT TYPE (RIVER MONITOR)

Name	No.	Builders	Commissioned
PARNAIBA	U 17 (ex-P 2)	Arsenal de Marinha, Rio de Janeiro	Nov 1937

Displacement, tons: 620 standard; 720 full load
Dimensions, feet (metres): 180·5 oa × 33·3 × 5·1 *(55 × 10·1 × 1·6)*
Guns: 1—3 in, 50 cal; 2—47 mm; 6—20 mm
Armour: 3 in side and partial deck protection
Main engines: 2 Thornycroft triple expansion; 2 shafts; 1 300 ihp = 12 knots
Boilers: 2 three drum type, working pressure 250 psi
Oil fuel, tons: 70
Range, miles: 1 350 at 10 knots
Complement: 90

Laid down on 11 June 1936. Launched on 2 Sep 1937. In Mato Grosso Flotilla. Rearmed with the above guns in 1960.

PARNAIBA   1971, Brazilian Navy

60 BRAZIL

3 "RORAIMA" CLASS (RIVER PATROL SHIPS)

Name	No	Builders	Commissioned
RORAIMA	P 30	Maclaren, Niteroi	Mar 1974
RONDONIA	P 31	Maclaren, Niteroi	1974
AMAPA	P 32	Maclaren, Niteroi	Jan 1976

Displacement, tons: 340 standard; 365 full load
Dimensions, feet (metres): 147·6 × 27·7 × 4·2 *(45 × 8·4 × 1·3)*
Guns: 1—40 mm; 2—81 mm mortars; 6—·50 cal MGs
Main engines: Diesels; 2 shafts; 1 814 shp = 14·5 knots
Complement: 54

Rondonia launched 10 Jan 1973, *Amapa* 9 Mar 1973. Belong to Amazon Flotilla.

RONDONIA   *1977, Brazilian Navy*

LIGHT FORCES
Note: A new class of Fast Attack Craft is projected.

6 "PIRATINI" CLASS (LARGE PATROL CRAFT)

Name	No.	Builders	Commissioned
PIRATINI (ex-PGM 109)	P 10	Arsenal de Marinha, Rio de Janeiro	Nov 1970
PIRAJA (ex-PGM 110)	P 11	Arsenal de Marinha, Rio de Janeiro	Mar 1971
PAMPEIRO (ex-PGM 118)	P 12	Arsenal de Marinha, Rio de Janeiro	May 1971
PARATI (ex-PGM 119)	P 13	Arsenal de Marinha, Rio de Janeiro	July 1971
PENEDO (ex-PGM 120)	P 14	Arsenal de Marinha, Rio de Janeiro	Sept 1971
POTI (ex-PGM 121)	P 15	Arsenal de Marinha, Rio de Janeiro	Oct 1971

Displacement, tons: 105 standard
Dimensions, feet (metres): 95 × 19 × 6·5 *(29 × 5·8 × 2)*
Guns: 3—·50 cal MG; 1—81 mm mortar
Main engines: 4 diesels; 1 100 bhp = 17 knots
Range, miles: 1 700 at 12 knots
Complement: 15 officers and men

Built under offshore agreement with the USA.

PIRAJA   *1977, Brazilian Navy*

6 "ANCHOVA" CLASS (RIVER PATROL CRAFT)

Name	No.	Builders	Commissioned
ANCHOVA	R 54	Brazil	1965
ARENQUE	R 55	Brazil	1965
ATUM	R 56	Brazil	1966
ACARA	R 57	Brazil	1966
AGULHA	R 58	Brazil	1967
ARUANA	R 59	Brazil	1967

Displacement, tons: 11
Dimensions, feet (metres): 42·6 × 12·5 × 3·9 *(13 × 3·8 ×1·2)*
Main engines: 2 diesels; 280 hp = 25 knots
Range, miles: 400 at 20 knots
Complement: 3 plus 12 passengers

4 RIVER PATROL CRAFT

Built in 1968. Of about 30 tons and 45 ft *(13·7 m)* in length. Capable of 17 knots and with a range of 1 400 miles at 10 knots. Operate on the Upper Amazon.

MINE WARFARE FORCES

6 "SCHÜTZE" CLASS (MINESWEEPERS—COASTAL)

Name	No.	Builders	Commissioned
ARATU	M 15	Abeking and Rasmussen	5 May 1971
ANHATOMIRIM	M 16	Abeking and Rasmussen	30 Nov 1971
ATALAIA	M 17	Abeking and Rasmussen	13 Dec 1972
ARACATUBA	M 18	Abeking and Rasmussen	13 Dec 1972
ABROLHOS	M 19	Abeking and Rasmussen	16 April 1975
ALBARDÃO	M 20	Abeking and Rasmussen	21 July 1975

Displacement, tons: 230 standard; 280 full load
Dimensions, feet (metres): 154·9 × 23·6 × 6·9 *(47·2 × 7·2 × 2·1)*
Gun: 1—40 mm
Main engines: 4 Maybach diesels; 2 shafts; 4 500 bhp = 24 knots
Range, miles: 710 at 20 knots
Complement: 39

Wooden hulled. First four ordered in April 1969 and another pair in Nov 1973. Same design as W. German "Schütze" class.

ARATU   *1977, Brazilian Navy*

SURVEY SHIPS

ALVARO ALBERTO

Dimensions, feet (metres): 196·8 × 3·7 × 14·1 *(60 × 12 × 4·3)*
Speed, knots: 13
Complement: 26 plus 17 scientists

A new oceanographic research ship ordered in 1973.

BRAZIL 61

1 Ex-US "CONRAD" CLASS

Name	No.	Builders	Commissioned
ALMIRANTE CÂMARA (ex-USNS Sands T-AGOR 6)	H 41	Marietta Co, Point Pleasant West Va.	8 Feb 1965

Displacement, tons: 1 200 standard; 1 380 full load
Dimensions, feet (metres): 208·9 oa × 37·4 × 15·3 *(63·7 × 11·4 × 4·7)*
Main engines: Diesel-electric; Caterpillar Tractor Co diesels; 10 000 bhp; 1 shaft = 13·5 knots
Range, miles: 12 000 at 12 knots
Complement: 26 (+15 scientists)

Built specifically for oceanographic research. Equipped for gravimetric, magnetic and geological research. Has bow thruster, 10 ton crane and 620 hp gas turbine for providing "quiet power". Transferred 1 July 1974.

ALMIRANTE CAMARA (as USNS *Sands*) USN

2 "SIRIUS" CLASS

Name	No.	Builders	Commissioned
SIRIUS	H 21	Ishikawajima Co Ltd, Tokyo	1 Jan 1958
CANOPUS	H 22	Ishikawajima Co Ltd, Tokyo	15 Mar 1958

Displacement, tons: 1 463 standard; 1 800 full load
Dimensions, feet (metres): 255·7 oa × 39·3 × 12·2 *(78 × 12·1 × 3·7)*
Guns: 1—3 in; 4—20 mm MG
Main engines: 2 Sulzer diesels; 2 shafts; 2 700 bhp = 15·75 knots
Range, miles: 12 000 at cruising speed of 11 knots
Complement: 116

Laid down 1955-56. Helicopter platform aft. Special surveying apparatus, echo sounders, Raydist equipment, sounding machines installed, and helicopter, landing craft (LCVP), jeep, and survey launches carried. All living and working spaces are air-conditioned. Controllable pitch propellers.

CANOPUS 1977, Brazilian Navy

3 "ARGUS" CLASS

Name	No.	Builders	Commissioned
ARGUS	H 31	Arsenal da Marinha, Rio de Janeiro	29 Jan 1959
ORION	H 32	Arsenal da Marinha, Rio de Janeiro	11 June1959
TAURUS	H 33	Arsenal da Marinha, Rio de Janeiro	23 April1959

Displacement, tons: 250 standard; 343 full load
Dimensions, feet (metres): 147·7 oa × 20 × 6·6 *(45 × 6·1 × 2)*
Guns: 2—20 mm
Main engines: 2 diesels coupled to two shafts; 1 200 bhp = 15 knots
Oil fuel, tons: 35
Range, miles: 1 200 at 15 knots
Complement: 42

All laid down in 1955 and launched Dec 1957—Feb 1958.

ORION 1977, Brazilian Navy

Name	No.	Builders	Launched
ALMIRANTE SALDANHA	U 10 (ex-NE I)	Vickers Armstrong Ltd	19 Dec 1933

Displacement, tons: 3 325 standard; 3 825 full load
Dimensions, feet (metres): 307·2 oa × 52 × 18·2 *(93·6 × 15·8 × 5·5)*
Main engine: Diesel; 1 400 bhp = 11 knots
Range, miles: 12 000 at 10 knots
Complement: 218

Former training ship with a total sail area of 25 990 sq ft and armed with four 4-inch guns, one 3-inch AA gun and four 3-pounders. Cost £314 500. Instructional minelaying gear was included in equipment. The single 21-inch torpedo tube was removed. Re-classified as an Oceanographic Ship (NOc) Aug 1959, and completely remodelled by 1964. A photograph as sailing ship appears in the 1952-53 to 1959-60 editions.

ALMIRANTE SALDANHA 1977, Brazilian Navy

SURVEY LAUNCHES

PARAIBANO H 11
RIO BRANCO H 12
NOGUEIRA DA GAMA (ex-*Jaceguai*) H 14
ITACURUSSA H 15
CAMOCIM H 16
CARAVELAS H 17

Displacement, tons: 32 standard; 50 full load
Dimensions, feet (metres): 52·5 × 15·1 × 4·3 *(16 × 4·6 × 1·3)*
Main engine: 1 diesel; 165 bhp = 11 knots
Range, miles: 600 at 11 knots
Complement: 11

First pair launched 1968—last pair in 1972. Built by Bormann, Rio de Janeiro.

CARAVELAS 1977, Brazilian Navy

1 LIGHTHOUSE TENDER

Name	No.	Builders	Commissioned
GRAÇA ARANHA	H 34	Elbin, Niteroi	9 Sep 1976

Displacement, tons: 2 300
Dimensions, feet (metres): 247·6 × 42·6 × 12·1 *(75·5 × 13 × 3·7)*
Aircraft: 1 Helicopter
Main engines: 1 diesel; 2 000 hp; 1 shaft = 14 knots
Complement: 95

Laid down in 1971 and launched 23 May 1974. Fitted with collapsible helo-hangar.

5 BUOY TENDERS

MESTRE JOÃO DOS SANTOS H 13
CASTELHANOS H 24
FAROLEIRO NASCIMENTO H 25
FAROLEIRO AREAS H 27
FAROLEIRO SANTANA H 28

Taken over 1973.

62 BRAZIL

SUBMARINE RESCUE SHIP

Name	No.	Builders	Launched
GASTÃO MOUTINHO (ex-USS *Skylark* ASR 20)	K 10	Charleston SB & DD Co.	19 Mar 1946

Displacement, tons: 1 235 standard; 1 740 full load
Dimensions, feet (metres): 205 oa × 38·5 × 15·3 *(62·5 × 11·7 × 4·7)*
Main engines: Diesel-electric; 1 shaft; 3 000 bhp = 14 knots
Complement: 85

Converted to present form in 1947. Fitted with special pumps, compressors and submarine rescue chamber. Fitted for oxy-helium diving. Transferred 30 June 1973.

GASTÃO MOUTINHO   1975, Brazilian Navy

REPAIR AND SUPPORT SHIPS

Name	No.	Builders	Commissioned
BELMONTE (ex-USS *Helios* ARB 12, ex-LST 1127)	G 24	Maryland DD Co, Baltimore	26 Feb 1945

Displacement, tons: 1 625 light; 2 030 standard; 4 100 full load
Dimensions, feet (metres): 328 × 50 × 11 *(100 × 15·2 × 3·4)*
Guns: 8—40 mm
Main engines: GM diesels; 2 shafts; 1 800 bhp = 11·6 knots
Oil fuel, tons: 1 000
Range, miles: 6 000 at 9 knots

Former United States battle damage repair ship (ex-LST). Laid down on 23 Nov 1944. Launched on 14 Feb 1945. Loaned to Brazil by USA in Jan 1962 under MAP.

BAURU (ex-USS *McAnn* DE 179) U 28

An ex-US "Bostwick" class DE, last of eight transferred in 1944. Of 1 900 tons full load used as support vessel in Guanabara Bay.

1 NEW CONSTRUCTION

Projected river support ship. No further details.

TANKERS

Name	No.	Builders	Commissioned
MARAJO	G 27	Ishikawajima do Brasil-Estaleisos SA	22 Oct 1968

Measurements, tons: 10 500 deadweight
Dimensions, feet (metres): 440·7 × 63·3 × 24 *(134·4 × 19·3 × 7·3)*
Main engine: Diesel; 1 shaft = 13·6 knots
Capacity, (cu metres): 14 200
Range, miles: 9 200 at 13 knots
Complement: 80

Laid down on 13 Dec 1966 and launched on 31 Jan 1968.

MARAJÓ   1975, Brazilian Navy

Name	No.	Builders	Launched
POTENGI	G 17	Papendrecht, Netherlands	16 Mar 1938

Displacement, tons: 600
Dimensions, feet (metres): 178·8 oa × 24·5 × 6 *(54·5 × 7·5 × 1·8)*
Main engines: Diesels; 2 shafts; 550 bhp = 10 knots
Oil fuel, tons: 450
Complement: 19

Employed in the Mato Grosso Flotilla on river service.

MARTINS DE OLIVEIRA (Ex-*Gastao Moutinho*) R 11

Displacement, tons: 588
Dimensions, feet (metres): 162 × 23·1 × 7·9 *(49·4 × 7 × 2·4)*
Speed, knots: 10·3

Taken over 1973.

TRANSPORTS

Note: A new Training Ship is projected—to have helicopter and hangar.

4 "BARROSO PEREIRA" CLASS

Name	No.	Builders	Commissioned
BARROSO PEREIRA	G 16	Ishikawajima Co Ltd, Tokyo	1 Dec 1954
ARY PARREIRAS	G 21	Ishikawajima Co Ltd, Tokyo	29 Dec 1956
SOARES DUTRA	G 22	Ishikawajima Co Ltd, Tokyo	23 Mar 1957
CUSTÓDIO DE MELLO	U 26	Ishikawajima Co Ltd, Tokyo	30 Dec 1954

Displacement, tons: 4 800 standard; 7 300 full load
Measurement, tons: 4 200 deadweight; 4 879 gross (Panama)
Dimensions, feet (metres): 362 pp; 391·8 oa × 52·5 × 20·5 *(110·4; 119·5 × 16 × 6·3)*
Guns: 4—3 in (U 26); 2—3 in (others); 2/4—20 mm
Main engines: Ishikawajima double reduction geared turbines; 2 shafts; 4 800 shp = 17·67 knots (sea speed 15 knots)
Boilers: 2 Ishikawajima two drum water tube type, oil fuel
Complement: 127 (Troop capacity 497)

Transports and cargo vessels. Helicopter landing platform aft except in U26. Troop carrying capacity for 497, with commensurate medical, hospital and dental facilities. Working and living quarters are mechanically ventilated with partial air conditioning. Refrigerated cargo space 15 500 cubic feet. Can carry 4 000 tons of cargo. *Custódio de Mello* has been classified as a training ship since July 1961 with additional deckhouses. The other three operate commercially from time to time.

CUSTODIO DE MELLO   5/1975, C. and S. Taylor

6 "RIO DOCE" CLASS (HARBOUR TRANSPORTS)

Name	No.	Builders	Commissioned
RIO DOCE	U 20	Netherlands	1954
RIO DAS CONTAS	U 21	Netherlands	1954
RIO FORMOSO	U 22	Netherlands	1954
RIO REAL	U 23	Netherlands	1955
RIO TURVO	U 24	Netherlands	1955
RIO VERDE	U 25	Netherlands	1955

Displacement, tons: 150
Dimensions, feet (metres): 120 oa × 21·3 × 6·2 *(36·6 oa × 6·5 × 1·9)*
Main engines: 2 Sulzer 6-TD24; 900 bhp = 14 knots

Can carry 600 passengers.

BRAZIL 63

PARAGUASSU (ex-*Guarapunava*) G 15 (RIVER TRANSPORT)

Displacement, tons: 285
Dimensions, feet (metres): 131·2 × 23 × 3·9 *(40 × 7 × 1·2)*
Speed knots: 12
Range, miles: 2 500 at 10 knots

Acquired 1971. In Mato Grosso flotilla.

FLOATING DOCKS

CIDADE DE NATAL (ex-AFDL 39)

Displacement, tons: 7 600
Length, feet (metres): 390·3 *(119)*
Beam, feet (metres): 86·9 *(26·5)*
Capacity, tons: 2 800

Concrete floating dock loaned to Brazil by USN, 10 Nov 1966.

ALMIRANTE JERONIMO GONÇALVES
(ex-*Goiaz* AFDL 4 ex-G 26)

Displacement, tons: 3 000
Length, feet (metres): 200 *(61)*
Beam, feet (metres): 44 *(13·4)*
Capacity, tons: 1 000

Steel floating dock sold to Brazil by USN, 10 Nov 1966.

AFONSO PENA (ex-*Ceara*, ex-ARD 14) G 25

Displacement, tons: 5 200
Dimensions, feet (metres): 402·0 × 81·0 *(122·6 × 24·7)*

Transferred from the US Navy to the Brazilian Navy in 1963.

TUGS
Note: One fleet tug projected.

3 Ex-US "SOTOYOMO" CLASS

TRITÃO (ex-ATA 234) R 21 **TRIDENTE** (ex-ATA 235) R 22 **TRIUNFO** (ex-ATA 236) R 23

Displacement, tons: 534 standard; 835 full load
Dimensions, feet (metres): 143 oa × 33 × 13·2 *(43·6 × 10 × 4)*
Guns: 2—20 mm
Main engines: GM diesel-electric; 1 500 hp = 13 knots

All built by Gulfport Boiler & Welding Works, Inc, Port Arthur, Texas, and launched in 1944. Sold to Brazil 1947.

ISLAS DE NORONHA

Of 200 tons. Built 1972.

2 COASTAL TUGS

DNOG **LAHMEYER**

Of 100 tons and 105 ft long, built in Brazil in 1972. Based at Aratu.

LAURINDO PITTA R 14

514 tons. Vickers 1910. Reconstructed 1969.

WANDENKOLK R 20

350 tons. UK 1910.

ANTONIO JOA R 26

80 tons. Built Rio. Mato Grosso flotilla.

4 "RIO PARDO" (HARBOUR TRANSPORTS)

RIO PARDO U 40 **RIO NEGRO** U 41 **RIO CHUI** U 42 **RIO OIAPOQUE** U 43

Displacement, tons: 150
Dimensions, feet (metres): 116·8 × 21·3 × 6·2 *(35·6 × 6·5 × 1·9)*
Main engines: 2 diesels = 14 knots

Capable of carrying 600 passengers. Completed by Inconav de Niteroi 1975-76.

MISCELLANEOUS

AUDAZ R 31	**LAMEGO** R 34
CENTAURO R 32	**PASSO da PATRIA** R 35
GUARANI R 33	**VOLUNTARIO** R 36

Displacement, tons: 130 tons
Dimensions, feet (metres): 90·5 oa × 23·6 × 10·2 *(27·6 × 7·2 × 3·1)*
Main engines: Womag diesel of 765 hp = 11 knots
Complement: 12

Built by Holland Nautic Yard, Netherlands in 1953.

RAIMUNDO NONATO   **ETCHBARNE** R 28   **GRUMETE** (1961)

STORE TRANSPORTS

TENENTE FABIO   **TENENTE RAUL**

Displacement, tons: 55 tons
Dimensions, feet (metres): 66·6 × 16·7 × 3·9 *(20·3 × 5·1 × 1·2)*
Main engines: Diesel; 135 hp = 10 knots

1969. 2 ton derrick.

MUNITIONS TRANSPORTS

SAN FRANCISCO DOS SANTOS

1964.

UBIRAJARA DOS SANTOS   **OPERARIO LUIS LEAL**

1968.

TORPEDO TRANSPORTS

MIGUEL DOS SANTOS   **APRENDIZ LEDIO CONCEIÇAO**

1968.

TANKER

ANITA GARIBALDI

WATER BOATS

ITAPURA R 42   **PAULO AFONSO** R 43

Displacement, tons: 485·3
Dimensions, feet (metres): 140·5 × 23 × 8 *(42·8 × 7 × 2·5)*
Main engines: Diesel

Capacity 389 tons. Launched 1957.

FLOATING CRANES

At least two in service at Rio de Janeiro—1 of 100 tons capacity, 1 of 30 tons.

BUOY TENDERS/SURVEY CRAFT

GETULIO LIMA H 23   **FAROLEIRO WANDERLEY** H 29
PRATICO JUVENCIO H 26   **FAROL. N. SANTOS** H 30

AUXILIARIES

ALMIRANTE BRASIL R 13	**DR. GONDIM** R 38
TONELEROS R 18 Renamed or deleted	**GUAIRIA** R 40
A. BARBOSA R 27	**IGUASSU** R 41
RIO PARDO R 30 Renamed or deleted	**MARIA QUITERIA** R 44
RIO NEGRO R 37 Renamed or deleted	**MARISCO**
	TENENTE CLAUDIO
	DHN-225

BRUNEI

(Askar Melayu Diraja Brunei (Royal Brunei Malay Regiment) Flotilla)

Commanding Officer:
Commander David Wright RN

Personnel
(a) 1978: 350 (25 officers and 325 ratings)
(b) Voluntary service

Base
Muara Marine Base

Prefix to Ships' Names
KDB (Kapal Di-Raja Brunei)

Mercantile Marine
Lloyd's Register of Shipping:
2 vessels of 899 tons gross

Deletion
1977 Pahlawan

3 "PERWIRA" CLASS (COASTAL PATROL CRAFT)

Name	No.	Builders	Commissioned
PERWIRA	P 14	Vosper Thornycroft (Singapore)	9 Sept 1974
PEMBURU	P 15	Vosper Thornycroft (Singapore)	17 June 1975
PENYARANG	P 16	Vosper Thornycroft (Singapore)	24 June 1975

Displacement, tons: 30
Dimensions, feet (metres): 71 × 20 × 5 *(21·7 × 6·1 × 1·2)*
Guns: 2—20 mm Hispano Suiza, 2—7·62 MG
Main engines: 2 MTU MB 12V 331 TC81 diesels; 2 450 bhp
Speed, knots: 32
Range, miles: 600 at 22 knots; 1 000 at 16 knots
Complement: 12

Perwira launched 9 May 1974. Other two ordered June 1974. Of all wooden construction on laminated frames. Fitted with enclosed bridges—modified July 1976.

Radar: Decca 916.

PERWIRA 1974, Royal Brunei Malay Regiment

3 COASTAL PATROL CRAFT

Name	No.	Builders	Commissioned
SALEHA	P 11	Vosper Thornycroft (Singapore)	1972
MASNA	P 12	Vosper Thornycroft (Singapore)	1972
NORAIN	P 13	Vosper Thornycroft (Singapore)	Aug 1972

Displacement, tons: 25
Dimensions, feet (metres): 62·0 × 16·0 × 4·5 *(18·9 × 4·8 × 1·4)*
Guns: 2—20 mm Hispano-Suiza; 2 MG
Main engines: 2 GM 71 16 cyl diesels; 1 250 bhp = 26 knots
Range, miles: 600 at 23 knots
Complement: 8

Fitted with Decca 202 radar. Named after Brunei princesses.

NORAIN 1974, Royal Brunei Malay Regiment

3 PATROL CRAFT (RIVERINE)

Name	No.	Conversion
BENDAHARA	P 21	1974
MAHARAJALELA	P 22	1975
KEMAINDERA	P 23	1975

Displacement, tons: 10
Dimensions, feet (metres): 47·0 × 12·0 × 3·0 *(14·3 × 3·6 × 0·9)*
Guns: 2 twin MG 42, 7·62 cal
Main engines: 2 GM diesels; 334 bhp = 20 knots
Range, miles: 200
Complement: 6

Fitted with Decca 202 radar.

Conversion: *Kemaindera* was converted in July 1974 for riverine duties. Other pair were similarly converted during 1975.

BENDAHARA 1976, Royal Brunei Malay Regiment

AMPHIBIOUS FORCES

2 CHEVERTON "LOADMASTERS"

Name	No.	Builders	Commissioned
DAMUAN	L 31	Chevertons	May 1976
PUNI	L 32	Chevertons	Feb 1977

Displacement, tons: 60
Dimensions, feet (metres): 65 × 20 × 3·6 *(19·8 × 6·1 × 1·1)*
Main engines: 2 GM V 71 6 cyl diesels = 9 knots
Range, miles: 1 000
Complement: 13

Radar: Decca RM 1216.

DAMUAN 1976, Royal Brunei Malay Regiment

24 FAST ASSAULT BOATS

Rigid Raider type with 1 MG and two 50 hp outboards.

BULGARIA

Ministerial

Minister of National Defence:
General Dobri Dzhurov

Headquarters Appointment

Commander-in-Chief, Navy:
Vice-Admiral VG Yanakiev

Diplomatic Representation

Naval, Military and Air Attaché in London:
Colonel Dimitar Toskov

Personnel

(a) 1978: 10 000 officers and ratings
(b) 3 years national service (6 000)

Bases

Varna, Burgas, Sozopol

Naval Aviation

2 Mi1 Helicopters
6 Mi4 (Hound) Helicopters

Strength of the Fleet

No building programme available

Type	Active
Frigates	2
Corvettes	3
Patrol Submarines	2
Fast Attack Craft (Missile)	4
Fast Attack Craft (Torpedo)	10
Large Patrol Craft	6
Minesweepers (Ocean)	2
Minesweepers (Coastal)	4
Minesweeping Boats	12
Landing Craft	20
Surveying Ships	3
Tugs	8
Tankers Small	3
Salvage Craft	2
Auxiliaries	app 12

Mercantile Marine

Lloyd's Register of Shipping:
176 vessels of 933 361 tons gross

DELETIONS

Submarines

1972 2 "Whiskey" Class (names transferred to "Romeo" class)

Light Forces

1975 2 "Kronshstadt" class (numbers transferred to "Poti" class)
1975 4 "P4" class

Minewarfare Forces

1974 3 "T 301" class
1975 1 "T 301" class
1976 12 "P 02" class

SUBMARINES (PATROL)

2 Ex-SOVIET "ROMEO" CLASS

POBEDA   SLAVA

Displacement, tons: 1 000 surfaced; 1 600 dived
Length, feet (metres): 252 *(76·8)*
Beam, feet (metres): 23 *(7)*
Draught, feet (metres): 18 *(5·5)*
Torpedo tubes: 8—21 in *(533 mm)* (6 bow; 2 stern)
Main machinery: 2 diesels; 4 000 hp; 2 main motors; 4 000 hp; 2 shafts
Speed, knots: 17 surfaced, 14 dived
Range, miles: 16 000 at 10 knots (surfaced)
Complement: 60

Transferred in 1972-73 as replacements for "Whiskey", whose names they took over.

Radar. Snoop Plate.

"ROMEO" Class   1974

FRIGATES

2 Ex-SOVIET "RIGA" CLASS

DRUZKI 31   **SMELI** 32

Displacement, tons: 1 200 standard; 1 600 full load
Length, feet (metres): 298·8 *(91·0)*
Beam, feet (metres): 33·7 *(10·2)*
Draught, feet (metres): 11·0 *(3·4)*
Guns: 3—3·9 in *(100 mm);* 4—37 mm
A/S Weapons: 4 MBU 1 800 (5 tubed), 4 DCT
Torpedo tubes: 3—21 in *(533 mm)*
Main engines: Geared turbines; 2 shafts; 25 000 shp
Speed, knots: 28
Range, miles: 2 500 at 15 knots
Complement: 150

Transferred from USSR in 1957-8.

Radar: Search; Slim Net. Navigation; Neptune.
IFF; Highpole A. Fire Control; Wasphead/Sunvisor A.

"RIGA" Class

CORVETTES

3 Ex-SOVIET "POTI" CLASS

33   34   35

Displacement, tons: 550 standard; 600 full load
Dimensions, feet (metres): 193·5 × 26·2 × 9·2 *(59 × 8 × 2·8)*
Guns: 2—57 mm (twin)
Torpedo tubes: 4—16 in A/S
A/S weapons: 2 MBU 2 500 A
Main engines: 2 gas turbines; 16 000 hp; 2 M503A diesels; 4 000 shp; 4 shafts; = 28 knots

Transferred Dec 1975. Built 1961-68.

Radar: Strut curve, Muff Cob and Don.

Sonar: 1 hull-mounted.

Soviet "POTI" Class   1975

BULGARIA

LIGHT FORCES

Note: It is reported, but not confirmed, that 3 Ex-Soviet "Stenka" class have been transferred.

6 Ex-SOVIET "SO 1" CLASS (LARGE PATROL CRAFT)

41 to 46

Displacement, tons: 215 light; 250 full load
Length, feet (metres): 138·6 *(42·3)*
Beam, feet (metres): 20 *(6·1)*
Draught, feet (metres): 9·2 *(2·8)*
Guns: 4—25 mm (2 twin)
A/S weapons: 4 five-barrelled MBU 1800 launchers; DCs
Main engines: 3 diesels; 6 000 bhp = 26 knots
Range, miles: 1 100 at 13 knots
Complement: 30

Steel hulled vessels transferred from USSR in 1963.

Radar: Pot Head.

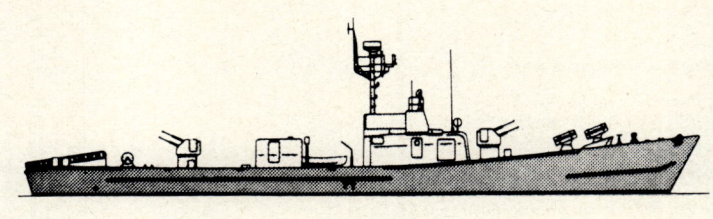

"SO 1" Class

4 Ex-SOVIET "OSA 1" CLASS (FAST ATTACK CRAFT—MISSILE)

21   22   23   24

Displacement, tons: 165 standard; 200 full load
Dimensions, feet (metres): 128·7 × 25·1 × 5·9 *(39·3 × 7·7 × 1·8)*
Missile launchers: 4 in two pairs abreast for SSN-2 system
Guns: 4—30 mm (2 twin, 1 forward, 1 aft)
Main engines: 3 diesels; 13 000 bhp = 36 knots
Range, miles: 800 at 25 knots
Complement: 25

Reported to have been transferred from USSR in 1970-71.

Radar: Drum Tilt and Square Tie.

"OSA 1" Class

6 Ex-SOVIET "SHERSHEN" CLASS (FAST ATTACK CRAFT—TORPEDO)

27   28   29   30   +2

Displacement, tons: 150 standard; 160 full load
Dimensions, feet (metres): 115·5 × 23·1 × 5·0 *(35·2 × 7·0 × 1·5)*
Guns: 4—30 mm (2 twin)
Torpedo tubes: 4—21 in (single)
A/S armament: 12 DCs
Main engines: 3 diesels; 3 shafts; 13 000 bhp = 41 knots
Range, miles: 700 at 20 knots
Complement: 25

Transferred from USSR in 1970.

Radar: Pot Drum, Drum Tilt. IFF; High Pole A.

4 Ex-SOVIET "P 4" CLASS (FAST ATTACK CRAFT—TORPEDO)

Displacement, tons: 22 full load
Dimensions, feet (metres): 62·7 × 11·6 × 5·6 *(19·1 × 3·5 × 1·7)*
Guns: 2—15 mm
Torpedo tubes: 2—18 in
Main engines: 2 diesels; 2 shafts; 2 200 bhp = 50 knots
Complement: 12

Transferred from USSR in 1956. Will soon be deleted.

MINE WARFARE FORCES

2 Ex-SOVIET "T 43" CLASS (MINESWEEPERS—OCEAN)

Displacement, tons: 500 standard; 610 full load
Dimensions, feet (metres): 190·2 × 28·2 × 6·9 *(58·0 × 8·6 × 2·1)*
Guns: 4—37 mm (twin); 4—12·7 mm
Main engines: 2 diesels; 2 shafts; 2 000 hp = 17 knots
Range, miles: 1 600 at 10 knots
Complement: 40

Three were transferred from USSR in 1953—One scrapped for spares. These are the only short-hulled, low bridge, tripod mast T43s in existance.

4 Ex-SOVIET "VANYA" CLASS (MINESWEEPERS—COASTAL)

36   37   38   39

Displacement, tons: 250 standard; 275 full load
Dimensions, feet (metres): 130·7 × 24 × 6·9 *(39·9 × 7·3 × 2·1)*
Guns: 2—30 mm (twin)
Main engines: 2 diesels; 2 200 bhp = 18 knots
Complement: 30

Transferred from USSR—two in 1970 and two in 1971.

12 "PO 2" CLASS (MSB)

Built in Bulgaria—first units completed in early 1950s and last in early 1960s. Originally a class of 24—some reports suggest there may be only 4 remaining.

AMPHIBIOUS FORCES

10 Ex-SOVIET "VYDRA" CLASS

Displacement, tons: 300 standard; 500 full load
Dimensions, feet (metres): 157·4 × 24·6 × 7·2 *(48 × 7·5 × 2·2)*
Main engines: 2 diesels; 2 shafts; 400 bhp = 15 knots

Transferred from USSR in 1970.

10 MFP D-3 TYPE

Dimensions, feet (metres): 164·0 oa × 20·0 × 6·6 *(50 × 6·1 × 2·0)*
Gun: 1—37 mm or none

Built in Bulgaria in 1954. Based on a German Second World War MFP design.

MISCELLANEOUS

VLADIMIR ZAIMOV 350 +1

"Varna" class survey ships built in Bulgaria in 1959.

1 "MOMA" CLASS

JUPITER

Survey ship transferred by USSR.

324, 441

Degaussing ships transferred by USSR in 1958 and 1962.

3 COASTAL TANKERS

2 SALVAGE CRAFT

1 FLEET TUG

7 COASTAL TUGS

10 or more other auxiliaries probably including diving craft and water boats.

BURMA

Ministerial

Minister of Defence:
Kyaw Htin

Headquarters Appointment

Vice-Chief of Staff, Defence Services (Navy):
Commodore Thaung Tin

Diplomatic Representation

Naval, Military and Air Attaché in London:
Lieutenant-Colonel Than Lwin

Naval, Military and Air Attaché in Washington:
Colonel Tin Htut

Light Forces

1975   T201-205—Saunders-Roe convertibles

Strength of the Fleet

Type	Active	Building
Frigates	2	—
Corvettes	4	—
River Patrol Craft	35	—
Gunboats	36	—
Survey Vessels	2	—
Auxiliaries	10	—

Aircraft

The Air Force operates a number of Alouette III, Husky and Sioux helicopters which work with the navy when needed.

Bases

Bassein, Mergui, Moulmein, Seikyi, Sinmalaik, Sittwo.

DELETIONS

Gunboats

1976   Indaw sold commercially.

General

This is an ageing fleet in dire need of replacements which, under the present financial circumstances seems unlikely.

Personnel

(a) 1978: 6 300 including 800 marines
(b) Voluntary service

Mercantile Marine

Lloyd's Register of Shipping:
39 vessels of 68 867 tons gross

Transport

1971   Pyi Daw Aye scrapped.

FRIGATES
1 Ex-BRITISH "RIVER" CLASS

Name	No.	Builders	Laid down	Launched	Commissioned
MAYU (ex-HMS Fal)	—	Smiths Dock Co Ltd, South Bank-on-Tees, Middlesbrough, England	20 May 1942	9 Nov 1942	2 July 1943

Displacement, tons: 1 460 standard; 2 170 full load
Length, feet (metres): 283 (86·3) pp; 301·3 (91·8) oa
Beam, feet (metres): 36·7 (11·2)
Draught, feet (metres): 12 (3·7)
Guns: 1—4 in (102 mm); 4—40 mm
Main engines: Triple expansion 5 500 ihp; 2 shafts
Boilers: 2—three drum type
Speed, knots: 19
Oil fuel, tons: 440
Range, miles: 4 200 at 12 knots
Complement: 140

"River" class frigate. Acquired from the United Kingdom and renamed in March 1948.

Radar: British Type 974.

MAYU   Burmese Navy

1 Ex-BRITISH "ALGERINE" CLASS

Name	No.	Builders	Laid down	Launched	Commissioned
YAN MYO AUNG (ex-HMS Mariner, ex-Kincardine)	—	Port Arthur Shipyards, Canada	26 Aug 1943	9 May 1944	23 May 1945

Displacement, tons: 1 040 standard; 1 335 full load
Length, feet (metres): 225 (68·6) pp; 235 (71·6) oa
Beam, feet (metres): 35·5 (10·8)
Draught, feet (metres): 11·5 (3·5)
Guns: 1—4 in (102 mm); 4—40 mm
Main engines: Triple expansion; 2 000 ihp; 2 shafts
Boilers: 2 three-drum type
Speed, knots: 16·5
Range, miles: 4 000 at 12 knots
Complement: 140

Former ocean minesweeper in the British Navy, used as escort vessel. Handed over to Burma in London and renamed Yan Myo Aung, on 18 April 1958. Fitted for minelaying and can carry 16 mines, eight on each side.

Radar: Decca Type 202.

Sonar: British Type 144.

YAN MYO AUNG   1964, Burmese Navy

CORVETTES
1 Ex-US "PCE 827" CLASS

Name	No.	Builders	Commissioned
YAN TAING AUNG (ex-USS Farmington PCE 894)	PCE 41	Willamette Iron & Steel Co, Portland, Oregon	10 Aug 1943

Displacement, tons: 640 standard; 903 full load
Dimensions, feet (metres): 180 wl; 184 oa × 33 × 9·5 (56 × 10·1 × 2·9)
Guns: 1—3 in 50 cal dp; 2—40 mm (1 twin); 8—20 mm (4 twin)
A/S weapons: 1 Hedgehog; 2 DCT; 2 DC racks
Main engines: GM diesels; 2 shafts; 1 800 bhp = 15 knots

Laid down on 7 Dec 1942, launched on 15 May 1943. Transferred on 18 June 1965.

1 Ex-US "ADMIRABLE" CLASS

Name	No.	Builders	Commissioned
YAN GYI AUNG (ex-USS Creddock MSF 356)	PCE 42	Willamette Iron & Steel Co, Portland, Oregon	1944

Displacement, tons: 650 standard; 945 full load
Dimensions, feet (metres): 180 wl; 184·5 oa × 33 × 9·8 (56·2 × 10·1 × 3·0)
Guns: 1—3 in 50 cal single forward; 4—40 mm (2 twin); 4—20 mm (2 twin)
A/S weapons: 1 US Hedgehog; 2 DCT; 2 DC Racks
Main engines: Diesels; 2 shafts; 1 710 shp = 14·8 knots
Range, miles: 4 300 at 10 knots

Laid down on 10 Nov 1943 and launched on 22 July 1944.
Transferred at San Diego on 31 Mar 1967.

68 BURMA

2 "NAWARAT" CLASS

Name	No.	Builders	Commissioned
NAGAKYAY	—	Government Dockyard, Dawbon, Rangoon	3 Dec 1960
NAWARAT	—	Government Dockyard, Dawbon, Rangoon	26 April 1960

Displacement, tons: 400 standard; 450 full load
Dimensions, feet (metres): 163 × 26·8 × 5·8 (49·7 × 8·2 × 1·8)
Guns: 2—25 pdr QF; 2—40 mm
Main engines: 2 Paxman-Ricardo turbo-charged diesels; 2 shafts; 1 160 bhp = 12 knots
Complement: 43

LIGHT FORCES

10 BURMESE-BUILT RIVER PATROL CRAFT

Small craft, 50 feet long, built in Burma in 1951-52.

25 YUGOSLAV-BUILT RIVER PATROL CRAFT

Small craft, 52 feet long, acquired from Yugoslavia in 1965.

GUNBOATS

3 Ex-BRITISH LCG (M) TYPE

INLAY   INMA   INYA

Displacement, tons: 381
Dimensions, feet (metres): 154 oa × 22·5 × 7·8 (46·9 × 6·9 × 2·4)
Guns: 2—25 pdr; 2—2 pdr
Main engines: Paxman Ricardo diesels; 2 shafts; 1 000 bhp = 13 knots
Complement: 39

Former British landing craft, gun (medium) LCG (M). Employed as gunboats.

Radar: British Type 974.

10 "Y 301" CLASS

Y 301 Y 302 Y 303 Y 304 Y 305 Y 306 Y 307 Y 308 Y 309 Y 310

Displacement, tons: 120
Dimensions, feet (metres): 100 pp; 104·8 oa × 24 × 3 (32 × 7·3 × 0·9)
Guns: 2—40 mm; 1—2 pdr
Main engines: 2 Mercedes-Benz (MTU) diesels; 2 shafts; 1 000 bhp = 13 knots
Complement: 29

All ten of these boats were completed in 1958 at the Uljanik Shipyard, Pula, Yugoslavia.

2 IMPROVED "Y 301" CLASS

Y 311   Y 312

Guns: 2—40 mm (single); 4—20 mm (single).

Dimensions approximately as "Y 301" Class. Built in Burma 1969.

8 GUNBOATS (Ex-TRANSPORTS)

| SABAN | SEINDA | SETYAHAT | SHWETHIDA |
| SAGU | SETKAYA | SHWEPAZUN | SINMIN |

Displacement, tons: 98
Dimensions, feet (metres): 94·5 × 22 × 4·5 (28·8 × 6·7 × 1·4)
Guns: 1—40 mm, 3—20 mm
Main engines: Crossley ERL—6 diesel; 160 bhp = 12 knots
Complement: 32

6 Ex-US PGM TYPE

PGM 401   PGM 402   PGM 403   PGM 404   PGM 405   PGM 406

Displacement, tons: 141
Dimensions, feet (metres): 101 × 21·1 × 7·5 (30·8 × 6·4 × 2·3)
Guns: 1—40 mm 2—20 mm (twin); 2—·50 Cal MG
Main engines: 8 GM 6-71 diesels; 2 shafts; 2 040 bhp = 17 knots
Range, miles: 1 000 cruising
Complement: 17

Built by the Marinette Marine Corporation, USA. Ex-US PGM 43-46, 51 and 52 respectively. Machinery comprises 2-stroke, 6-cyl, tandem geared twin diesel propulsion unit—1 LH and 1 RH; 500 bhp per unit.

Radar: Raytheon 1 500 in PGM 405-6; EDO 320 in PGM 401-4.

7 Ex-US CGC TYPE

MGB 101   MGB 102   MGB 104   MGB 105   MGB 106   MGB 108   MGB 110

Displacement, tons: 49 standard; 66 full load
Dimensions, feet (metres): 78 pp; 83 oa × 16 × 5·5 (25·3 × 4·9 × 1·7)
Guns: 1—40 mm; 1—20 mm
Main engines: 4 GM diesels; 2 shafts; 800 bhp = 11 knots
Complement: 16

Ex-USCG 83-ft type cutters with new hulls built in Burma. Completed in 1960. Three of this class are reported to have been sunk.

SURVEY VESSELS

1 OCEAN SURVEY SHIP

Name	No.	Builders	Commissioned
THU TAY THI	—	Yugoslavia	1965

Displacement, tons: 1 059
Length, feet (metres): 204 oa (62·2)
Complement: 99

Fitted with helicopter platform.

1 COASTAL SURVEY SHIP

Name	No.	Builders	Commissioned
YAY BO	UBHL 807	Netherlands	1957

Displacement, tons: 108
Complement: 25

SUPPORT SHIP

YAN LON AUNG

Light forces support ship of 520 tons, acquired from Japan in 1967.

TRANSPORTS

1 Ex-US LCU TYPE

AIYAR LULIN (ex-USS LCU 1626) 603

Displacement, tons: 200 light; 342 full load
Dimensions, feet (metres): 135·2 oa × 29 × 5·5 (41·2 × 8·8 × 1·7)
Main engines: 4 GM 12007 T diesels; 2 shafts (Kort nozzles); 1 000 bhp = 11 knots

US type utility landing craft 603 completed in Rangoon 1966. Two transferred as Grant aid in Oct 1967. Used as transport. Cargo capacity 168 tons.

8 Ex-US LCM 3 TYPE

LCM 701   LCM 702   LCM 703   LCM 704   LCM 705   LCM 706   LCM 707   LCM 708

Displacement, tons: 52 tons full load
Dimensions, feet (metres): 50 × 14 × 4 (15·2 × 4·3 × 1·2)
Guns: 2—20 mm single
Main engines: 2 Gray Marine diesels; 450 bhp = 9 knots

US-built LCM type landing craft. Used as local transports for stores and personnel. Cargo capacity 30 tons.

CAMEROON

Ministerial

Minister of Armed Forces:
Daoudou Sadou

Personnel

1978: 600 officers and men

Base

Douala

Mercantile Marine

Lloyd's Register of Shipping:
23 vessels of 19 045 tons gross

DELETIONS

1975 French VC Type—*Vigilant* (ex-VC 6), *Audacieux* (ex VC-8)

LIGHT FORCES
2 Ex-CHINESE "SHANGHAI" CLASS (FAST ATTACK CRAFT—GUN)

Displacement, tons: 120 standard; 155 full load
Dimensions, feet (metres): 115 × 18 × 5·5 *(35·1 × 5·5 × 1·7)*
Guns: 1—57 mm; 2—37 mm
A/S weapons: 8 DC
Minerails: Can be fitted for up to 10 mines
Main engines: 4 diesels; 4 800 bhp = 28 knots
Complement: 25

Transferred July 1976.

Radar: Skinhead.

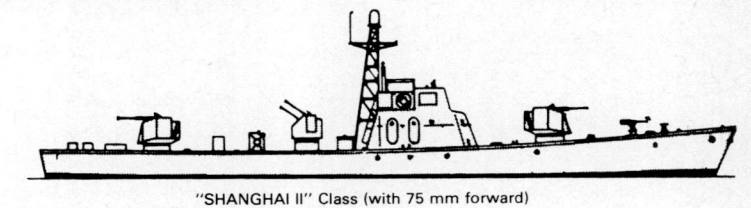

"SHANGHAI II" Class (with 75 mm forward)

1 PR 48 TYPE (LARGE PATROL CRAFT)

Name	No.	Builders	Commissioned
L'AUDACIEUX	—	Soc Français de Construction Naval	11 May 1976

Displacement, tons: 250 full load
Dimensions, feet (metres): 157·5 × 23·3 × 7·5 *(48 × 7·1 × 2·3)*
Missiles: Fitted for 8 SS-12
Guns: 2—40 mm
Main engines: 2 MGO diesels; 2 400 hp = 18·5 knots
Range, miles: 2 000 at 15 knots
Complement: 25

Ordered in Sep 1974. Laid down 10 Feb 1975, launched 31 Oct 1975. Similar to "Bizerte" class in Tunisia.

PR 48 Type

Name	No.	Builders	Commissioned
QUARTIER MAÎTRE ALFRED MOTTO	—	At. et Ch. de l'Afrique Equatoriale Libreville, Gabon	1974

Displacement, tons: 96
Dimensions, feet (metres): 95·4 × 20·3 × 6·3 *(29·1 × 6·2 × 1·9)*
Guns: 2—20 mm; 2 MG
Main engines: 2 Baudoin diesels; 1 290 bhp = 15·5 knots
Complement: 17

Name	No.	Builders	Commissioned
BRIGADIER M'BONGA TOUNDA	—	Ch. Navals d l'Esterel	1967

Displacement, tons: 20 full load
Dimensions, feet (metres): 60 × 13·5 × 4 *(18·3 × 4·1 × 1·2)*
Gun: 1—12·7 mm MG
Main engines: Caterpillar diesel; 2 shafts; 540 bhp = 22·5 knots
Complement: 8

Customs duties. Sister of Mauritanian *Imrag 'ni*.

Name	No.	Builders	Commissioned
LE VALEUREUX	—	Ch. Navals de l'Esterel	1970

Displacement, tons: 45 full load
Dimensions, feet (metres): 78·1 × 16·3 × 5·1 *(26·8 × 5·0 ×. 1·6)*
Guns: 2—20 mm
Main engines: 2 diesels; 2 shafts; 960 hp = 25 knots
Complement: 9

MISCELLANEOUS

1 FAIREY MARINE "INTERCEPTOR" CLASS

25 feet *(7·6 metres)* craft with catamaran hull. Can carry a platoon of soldiers or 8 life-rafts. Twin 135 hp outboard motors = 30 knots. Delivered 1 Dec 1976.

2 HARBOUR LAUNCHES

SANAGA   BIMBIA

Of 10 tons.

1 LCM

BAKASI

Built by Carena, Abidjan, Ivory Coast. Of 57 tons and 56 feet long. 9 knots on 2 Baudoin diesels.

5 LCVP

INDÉPENDANCE   REUNIFICATION   SOUELLABA   MACHTIGAL   MANOKA

Built by Ateliers et Chantiers de l'Afrique Equatoriale, Libreville, Gabon. Of 11 tons and 10 knots.

AUXILIARIES

Tornade and *Ouragan*—Built in 1966. *St. Sylvestre*—Built in 1967.
Four small outboard craft.
Mungo operated by Transport Ministry. *Dr. Jamot* operated by Health Ministry.

CANADA

Ministerial

Minister of National Defence:
Hon. Barney Danson, MP

Headquarters Appointments

Chief of Maritime Doctrine and Operations:
Rear-Admiral D. N. Mainguy CD

Senior Appointments

Commander, Maritime Command:
Vice-Admiral A. L. Collier, DSC, CD
Commander, Maritime Forces, Pacific:
Rear-Admiral M. A. Martin, CD

Diplomatic Representation

Senior Liaison Officer (Maritime) London:
Captain (N) H. O. Arnsdorf, CD
Canadian Forces Attaché and Maritime Liaison Officer, Washington:
Canadian Forces Attaché (Naval) Moscow:
Commander H. R. Waddell, CD

Personnel

(a) 1971: 16 906 (2 379 officers, 14 527 men and women)
    1972: 15 223 (2 590 officers, 12 633 men and women)
    1973: 16 003 (1 985 officers, 14 018 men and women)
    1974: 14 000 (2 000 officers, 12 000 men and women)
    Note: Canada no longer accounts for separate services in a unified command. Total armed forces 78 000
(b) Voluntary service

Defence Estimates (Naval)

1971-72: $348 000 000
1972-73: $363 000 000
1973-74: $394 300 000
1975-76: $472 268 000
1976-77: $712 000 000

Note: Canada no longer accounts for separate services in a unified command.

Bases

Halifax and Esquimalt

Air Arm

In an integrated force there is no specific Fleet Air Arm, but two squadrons of Sea King helicopters provide for ships' needs. The Argus maritime patrol aircraft are due to be replaced by Auroras, a special Canadian version of the Lockheed Orion.

Prefix to Ships' Names

HMCS

Establishment

The Royal Canadian Navy (RCN) was officially established on 4 May 1910, when Royal Assent was given to the Naval Service Act. On 1 February 1968 the Canadian Forces Reorganisation Act unified the three branches of the Canadian Forces and the title "Royal Canadian Navy" was dropped.

Strength of the Fleet

Type	Active	Building
Destroyers (DDH)	4	—
Frigates (some with helicopters)	16	—
Patrol Submarines	3	—
Replenishment Ships	3	—
Small Tankers	2	—
Patrol Escorts (Small)	7	—
Patrol Craft	6	—
Research Ships	4	—
Diving Support Ships and Tenders	3	—
Gate Vessels	5	—
Tugs: Ocean	2	—
Large	1	—
Medium	2	—
Coastal	5	—
Small	5	—
	(6 NRU)	
Police Patrol Vessels	32	—

Reserve (Cat. C)

Frigates

1974 Columbia, St. Croix, Chaudiere

Hydrofoil

1971 Bras D'Or

Mercantile Marine

Lloyd's Register of Shipping:
1 269 vessels of 2 638 692 tons gross

General

Because there has been no major surface ship construction since the last DD 280 was completed in 1973 there are now twelve ships of the "Restigouche" and "St Laurent" classes which are (1978) 19-21 years old. Even if the reported decision to build up to 8 replacements is taken in 1978 these are unlikely to be in service until the mid-1980s. By this time the two classes above will be long over the normal hull-life for such a type of ship or the Canadian naval forces will be much below the minimum strength needed even for peace-time duties.

Aircraft Carrier

1970 Bonaventure paid off 1 April, towed to Taiwan for scrap, leaving Halifax 27 October.

Destroyers

1971 Algonquin left Victoria BC for Taiwan 21 April,
Crescent left Victoria BC for Taiwan 21 May

DELETIONS

Frigates

1974 Granby
1975 St. Laurent. Break-up at Halifax

Submarine

1976 Rainbow broken up at Esquimalt

Maintenance Ships

1972 Cape Breton and Cape Scott decommissioned but in alongside service
1977 Cape Scott on sales list

TRANSFERS

Gate Vessels

1974 Porte Dauphine from MOT to DND

Research Vessels

1972 Fort Frances scrapped in Spain
1976 Kapuskasing
1977 Laymore on sales list

Tugs

1975 Glendyne sunk for diver training, Heatherton transferred to DPW (Canada)
1976 Clifton, Glenbrook, Glenlivet, Mannville, Parksville, Merrickville

Patrol Escorts (Small)

1973 Fort Steele from RCMP to DND
1975 PBLs 191, 192, 193, 194, 195 from RCMP to DND
1976 PBL 196 from RCMP to DND

PENNANT NUMBERS

Destroyers

280	Iroquois
281	Huron
282	Athabaskan
283	Algonquin

Frigates

206	Saguenay
207	Skeena
229	Ottawa
230	Margaree
233	Fraser
234	Assiniboine
235	*Chaudiere
236	Gatineau
256	*St. Croix
257	Restigouche
258	Kootenay
259	Terra Nova
260	*Columbia
261	Mackenzie
262	Saskatchewan
263	Yukon
264	Qu'Appelle
265	Annapolis
266	Nipigon

Submarines

72	Ojibwa
73	Onondaga
74	Okanagan

*Cat C Reserve 1974.

Replenishment Ships

AOR 508	Provider
AOR 509	Protecteur
AOR 510	Preserver
AOC 501	Dundalk
AOC 502	Dundurn

Research Vessels

AGOR 113	Sackville
AGOR 114	Bluethroat
AGOR 171	Endeavour
AGOR 172	Quest
ASXL 20	Cormorant

Patrol Escort (PFL)

140	Fort Steele
159	Fundy
160	Chignecto
161	Thunder
162	Cowichan
163	Miramichi
164	Chaleur

Gate Vessels

180	Porte St. Jean
183	Porte St. Louis
184	Porte de la Reine
185	Porte Quebec
186	Porte Dauphine

Patrol Craft (PBLs ex-RCMP)

191	Adversus
192	Detector
193	Captor
194	Acadian
195	Sidney
196	Nicholson

Tugs

ATA 528	Riverton
ATA 531	St. Anthony
ATA 533	St. Charles
ATA 640	Glendyne
ATA 641	Glendale
ATA 642	Glenevis
ATA 643	Glenbrook
ATA 644	Glenside
YMT 550	Eastwood
YMT 553	Wildwood
YTS 582	Burrard
YTS 583	Beamsville
YTS 584	Cree
YTS 586	Queensville
YTS 587	Plainsville
YTS 588	Youville
YTS 589	Loganville
YTS 590	Lawrenceville
YTS 591	Parksville
YTS 592	Listerville
YTS 593	Merrickville
YTS 594	Marysville

CANADA 71

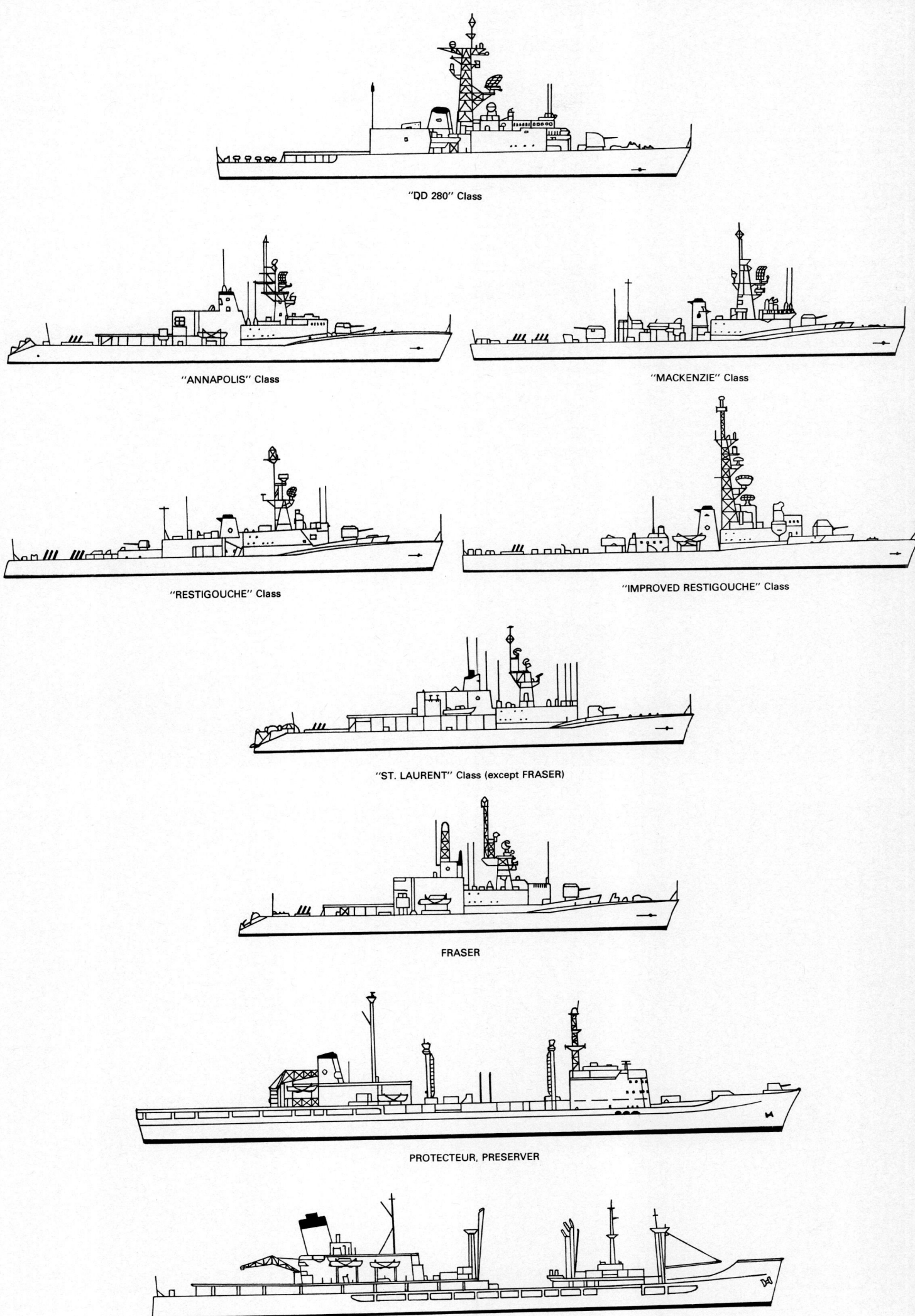

"DD 280" Class

"ANNAPOLIS" Class

"MACKENZIE" Class

"RESTIGOUCHE" Class

"IMPROVED RESTIGOUCHE" Class

"ST. LAURENT" Class (except FRASER)

FRASER

PROTECTEUR, PRESERVER

PROVIDER

CANADA

SUBMARINES

3 "OBERON" CLASS (PATROL SUBMARINES)

Name	No.	Builders	Laid down	Launched	Commissioned
OJIBWA (ex-Onyx)	72	HM Dockyard, Chatham	27 Sep 1962	29 Feb 1964	23 Sep 1965
ONONDAGA	73	HM Dockyard, Chatham	18 June 1964	25 Sep 1965	22 June 1967
OKANAGAN	74	HM Dockyard, Chatham	25 Mar 1965	17 Sep 1966	22 June 1968

Displacement, tons: 2 060 full bouyancy surface; 2 200 normal surfaced; 2 420 dived
Length, feet (metres): 294·2 *(89·7)*
Beam, feet (metres): 26·5 *(8·1)*
Draught, feet (metres): 18 *(5·5)*
Torpedo tubes: 8—21 in *(533 mm)*, 6 bow and 2 stern
Main machinery: 2 Admiralty Standard Range diesels; 3 680 bhp; 2 shafts; 2 electric motors; 6 000 hp
Speed, knots: 12 surfaced; 17 dived
Complement: 65 (7 officers, 58 ratings)

On 11 April 1962 the Ministry of National Defence announced that Canada was to buy three "Oberon" class submarines in the United Kingdom. The first of these patrol submarines was obtained by the Canadian Government from the Royal Navy construction programme. She was laid down as *Onyx* but launched as *Ojibwa*. The other two were specific Canadian orders. There were some design changes to meet specific new needs including installation of RCN communications equipment and increase of air-conditioning capacity to meet the wide extremes of climate encountered in Canadian operating areas.

Nomenclature: The name *Ojibwa* is that of a tribe of North American Indians now widely dispersed in Canada and the USA and one of the largest remnants of aboriginal population. *Okanagan* and *Onondaga* are also Canadian Indian tribes.

Radar: Type 1006.

Sonar: Attack: Type 187.
Intercept: Type 197.
Torpedo Warning: Type 719
Long Range Passive Search: Type 2007.

OKANAGAN   6/1973, Wright and Logan

OJIBWA   10/1975, Dr. Giorgio Arra

OKANAGAN   1976, Michael D. J. Lennon

CANADA 73

DESTROYERS

Note: It is reported that plans are in hand to build up to 8 new destroyers of some 3 500 tons with missiles, helicopter and A/S torpedoes and a complement of 175 or less. The first of class it is hoped would be laid down in 1980 for completion of the first group in 1985-1988. Up to 20 are eventually projected to replace the ageing surface force

4 "DD 280" CLASS (DDH)

Name	No.	Builders	Laid down	Launched	Commissioned
IROQUOIS	280	Marine Industries Ltd, Sorel	15 Jan 1969	28 Nov 1970	29 July 1972
HURON	281	Marine Industries Ltd, Sorel	15 Jan 1969	3 April 1971	16 Dec 1972
ATHABASKAN	282	Davie SB Co, Lauzon	1 June 1969	27 Nov 1970	30 Nov 1972
ALGONQUIN	283	Davie SB Co, Lauzon	1 Sep 1969	23 April 1971	30 Sep 1973

Displacement, tons: 4 200 full load
Length, feet (metres): 398 *(121·3)* pp; 426 *(129·8)* oa
Beam, feet (metres): 50 *(15·2)*
Draught, feet (metres): 14·5 *(4·4)*
Aircraft: 2 "Sea King" CHSS-2 A/S Helicopters
Missiles: (see note)
Gun: 1—5 in *(127 mm)* 54 cal single OTO-Melara
A/S weapons: 1 Mk 10 Limbo; 2 triple Mk 32 torpedo tubes
Main engines: Gas turbine; 2 Pratt & Whitney FT4A2 50 000 shp; 2 Pratt & Whitney FT12AH3 7 400 shp for cruising; 2 shafts
Speed, knots: 29 +
Range, miles: 4 500 at 20 knots
Complement: 245 (20 officers, 225 men) plus air unit, (7 officers + 33 men)

These ships have the same hull design, dimensions and basic characteristics as the large general purpose frigates cancelled at the end of 1963 (see particulars and illustration in the 1963-64 edition). Designed as anti-submarine ships, they are fitted with variable depth and hull sonar, landing deck equipped with double hauldown and Beartrap, flume type anti-rolling tanks to stabilise the ships at low speed, pre-wetting system to counter radio-active fallout, enclosed citadel, and bridge control of machinery.

Engineering: The gas turbines feed through a Swiss double reduction gearbox to two five bladed CP propellers.

Electronics: Mk 22 Weapon System Control by Hollandse Signaal. CSS 280.

Missiles: Launch system (GMLS) by Raytheon for Mk III Sea Sparrow missiles. Two quadruple launchers in forward end of the superstructure, retracting into deck-house.

Radar: Surface warning and navigation: SPQ 2D.
Long range warning: SPS 501 (SPS 12). Fire control: M 22.

Sonar: Hull mounted; SQS 505 in 14 ft dome. VDS; SQS 505, 18 ft towed body aft. Bottomed target classification; SQS 501.

Torpedoes: The Mk 32 tubes are to be used with Mk 46 torpedoes.

HURON   6/1977, Dr. Giorgio Arra

HURON   6/1977, Dr. Giorgio Arra

IROQUOIS   7/1976, A. D. Baker III

74 CANADA

FRIGATES
2 "ANNAPOLIS" CLASS

Name	No.
ANNAPOLIS	265
NIPIGON	266

Builders	Laid down	Launched	Commissioned
Halifax Shipyards Ltd, Halifax	July 1960	27 April 1963	19 Dec 1964
Marine Industries Ltd, Sorel	April 1960	10 Dec 1961	30 May 1964

Displacement, tons: 2 400 standard; 3 000 full load
Length, feet (metres): 371·0 (113·1) oa
Beam, feet (metres): 42·0 (12·8)
Draught, feet (metres): 14·4 (4·4)
Aircraft: 1 CHSS-2 Sea King helicopter
Guns: 2—3 in (76 mm) 50 cal (1 twin)
A/S weapons: 1 Mk 10 Limbo in after well; 6 (2 triple) Mk 32 A/S torpedo tubes
Main engines: Geared turbines; 2 shafts; 30 000 shp
Boilers: 2 water tube
Speed, knots: 28 (30 on trials)
Range, miles: 4 570 at 14 knots
Complement: 210 (11 0fficers, 199 ratings)

These two ships represented the logical development of the original "St. Laurent" class, through the "Restigouche" and "Mackenzie" designs. Due to the erection of a helicopter hangar and flight deck, and Variable Depth Sonar only one Limbo mounting could be installed. Also the 50 cal 3 inch mounting had to be moved forward to replace the 70 cal mounting in the original design.

Classification: Officially classified as DDH.

Construction: As these are largely prefabricated no firm laying down date is officially given. Work on hull units started under cover long before components were laid on the slip.

Electronics: Tacan (AN/URN-22) aerial fitted above funnel.

Radar: Search: SPS 12. Tactical: SPS 10. Fire Control: SPG 48.

Refit: *Nipigon* undergoing major refit 1977-78.

Sonar: Types 501, 502, 503, 504, SQS 10/11.

ANNAPOLIS   10/1977, C. and S. Taylor

4 "MACKENZIE" CLASS

Name	No.
MACKENZIE	261
*SASKATCHEWAN	262
YUKON	263
QU'APPELLE	264

Builders	Laid down	Launched	Commissioned
Canadian Vickers Ltd, Montreal	15 Dec 1958	25 May 1961	6 Oct 1962
Victoria Machinery (and Yarrow)	16 July 1959	1 Feb 1961	16 Feb 1963
Burrard DD & Shipbuilding	25 Oct 1959	27 July 1961	25 May 1963
Davie Shipbuilding & Repairing	14 Jan 1960	2 May 1962	14 Sep 1963

Displacement, tons: 2 380 standard; 2 880 full load
Length, feet (metres): 366·0 (111·6) oa
Beam, feet (metres): 42·0 (12·8)
Draught, feet (metres): 13·5 (4·1)
Guns: 4—3 in (76 mm) (2 twin) (UK 70 cal forward, US Mk 33 50 cal aft); (*Qu'Appelle* 2—3 in 50 cal (twin))
A/S weapons: 2 Mk 10 Limbo in well aft; side launchers for Mk 43 torpedoes
Main engines: Geared turbines; 2 shafts; 30 000 shp
Boilers: 2 water tube
Speed, knots: 28
Range, miles: 4 750 at 14 knots
Complement: 210 (11 officers, 199 ratings)

Classification: Officially classified as DDE.

Fire Control: GFCS Mk 69.

Radar: Search: SPS 12. Tactical: SPS 10. Fire Control: I Band.

Sonar: 501, 502, 503, SQS 10/11.

Saskatchewan was launched by Victoria Machinery Depot Co Ltd, but completed by Yarrow's Ltd.

SASKATCHEWAN   10/1977, Dr. Giorgio Arra

3 "RESTIGOUCHE" CLASS

Name	No.
CHAUDIERE	235
ST. CROIX	256
COLUMBIA	260

Builders	Laid down	Launched	Commissioned
Halifax Shipyards Ltd	30 July 1953	13 Nov 1957	14 Nov 1959
Marine Industries Ltd, Sorel	15 Oct 1954	17 Oct 1957	4 Oct 1958
Burrard DD and Shipbuilding	11 June 1953	1 Nov 1956	7 Nov 1959

Displacement, tons: 2 370 standard; 2 880 full load
Length, feet (metres): 366·0 (111·6) oa
Beam, feet (metres): 42·0 (12·8)
Draught, feet (metres): 13·5 (4·1)
Guns: 4—3 in (76 mm) (2 twin)
A/S weapons: 2 Mk 10 Limbo in well aft; side launchers for Mk 43 torpedoes
Main engines: Geared turbines; 2 shafts; 30 000 shp
Boilers: 2 water tube
Speed, knots: 28
Range, miles: 4 750 at 14 knots
Complement: 248 (12 officers, 236 ratings)

All three declared surplus and paid off into Category C Reserve in 1974.

Classification: Officially classified as DDE.

Radar: Search: SPS 12. Tactical: SPS 10. Fire Control: SPG 48.

Sonar: 501, 502, 503, SQS 10/11.

CHAUDIERE   1970, Canadian Forces

CANADA

4 "IMPROVED RESTIGOUCHE"

Name	No.
GATINEAU	236
RESTIGOUCHE	257
KOOTENAY	258
TERRA NOVA	259

Builders	Laid down	Launched	Commissioned
Davie Shipbuilding & Repairing	30 April 1953	3 June 1957	17 Feb 1959
Canadian Vickers, Montreal	15 July 1953	22 Nov 1954	7 June 1958
Burrard DD & Shipbuilding	21 Aug 1952	15 June 1954	7 Mar 1959
Victoria Machinery Depot Co.	14 Nov 1952	21 June 1955	6 June 1959

Displacement, tons: 2 390 standard; 2 900 full load
Length, feet (metres): 371·0 *(113·1)*
Beam, feet (metres): 42·0 *(12·8)*
Draught, feet (metres): 14·1 *(4·3)*
Missiles: Sea Sparrow
Guns: 2—3 in *(76 mm)* 70 cal (twin forward)
A/S weapons: ASROC aft and 1 Mk 10 Limbo in after well
Main engines: Geared turbines; 2 shafts; 30 000 shp
Boilers: 2 water tube
Speed, knots: 28 plus
Range, miles: 4 750 at 14 knots
Complement: 214 (13 officers, 201 ratings)

Classification: Officially classified as DDE.

Conversion: These four ships were refitted with ASROC aft and lattice foremast. Work included removing the after 3 inch 50 cal twin gun mounting and one Limbo A/S Mk 10 triple mortar, to make way for ASROC and Variable Depth Sonar. Dates of refits *Terra Nova* was completed on 18 Oct 1968: *Gatineau* completed in 1972, *Kootenay* and *Restigouche* in 1973. Refit also included improvements to communications fit and fitting of Sea Sparrow.

Radar: Search: SPS 12. Tactical: SPS 10. Fire Control: SPG 48. Navigation: Sperry Mk II.

Sonar: 501, 505, 505 VDS.

GATINEAU *1972, Canadian Forces*

6 "ST. LAURENT" CLASS

Name	No.
SAGUENAY	206
SKEENA	207
OTTAWA	229
MARGAREE	230
*FRASER	233
ASSINIBOINE	234

Builders	Laid down	Launched	Commissioned
Halifax Shipyards Ltd, Halifax	4 April 1951	30 July 1953	15 Dec 1956
Burrard Dry Dock & Shipbuilding	1 June 1951	19 Aug 1952	30 Mar 1957
Canadian Vickers Ltd, Montreal	8 June 1951	29 April 1953	10 Nov 1956
Halifax Shipyards Ltd, Halifax	12 Sep 1951	29 Mar 1956	5 Oct 1957
Yarrows Ltd, Esquimalt, BC	11 Dec 1951	19 Feb 1953	28 June 1957
Marine Industries Ltd, Sorel, Quebec	19 May 1952	12 Feb 1954	16 Aug 1956

Displacement, tons: 2 260 standard; 2 858 full load
Length, feet (metres): 366·0 *(111·6)* oa
Beam, feet (metres): 42·0 *(12·8)*
Draught, feet (metres): 13·2 *(4·0)*
Aircraft: 1 CHSS-2 "Sea King" helicopter
Guns: 2—3 in *(76 mm)* 50 cal (1 twin)
A/S weapons: 1 Mk 10 Limbo in after well; 2 triple Mk 32 torpedo tubes
Main engines: English Electric geared turbines; 2 shafts; 30 000 shp
Boilers: 2 water tube
Speed, knots: 28·5
Range, miles: 4 570 at 12 knots
Complement: 208 (11 officers, 197 ratings) (plus air unit of 7 officers and 13 ratings)

The first major warships to be designed in Canada. In design, much assistance was received from the Royal Navy (propelling machinery of British design) and the US Navy.
St. Laurent declared surplus in 1974.

*Fraser was launched by Burrard Dry Dock & Shipbuilding but completed by Yarrows Ltd.

Classification: Officially classified as DDH.

Gunnery: Original armament was 4—3 in, 50 cal (2 twin), 2—40 mm (single), and 2 Limbo mortars.

OTTAWA *10/1976, Wright and Logan*

Radars: Search: SPS 12. Tactical: SPS 10.
Navigation: Sperry Mk II. Fire control: SPG 48.

Reconstruction: All have helicopter platforms and VDS. Twin funnels were fitted to permit forward extension of the helicopter hangar.
Gunhouses are of glass fibre. In providing helicopter platforms and hangars it was possible to retain only one three barrelled Limbo mortar and only one twin 3-in gun mounting. Dates of recommissioning after conversion: *Assiniboine* 28 June 1963, *St. Laurent* 4 Oct 1963, *Ottawa* 21 Oct 1964, *Saguenay* 14 May 1965, *Skeena* 15 Aug 1965, *Margaree* 15 Oct 1965, *Fraser* 14 Oct 1966.

Fraser has lattice radar-mast between the funnels for Tacan aerial. All other ships have this aerial on a pole mast.

Refits: *Fraser*, *Ottawa* and *Skeena* undergoing major refit 1977-78.

Sonar: 501, 502, SQS 502, 503, 504.

SAGUENAY *10/1977, C. and S. Taylor*

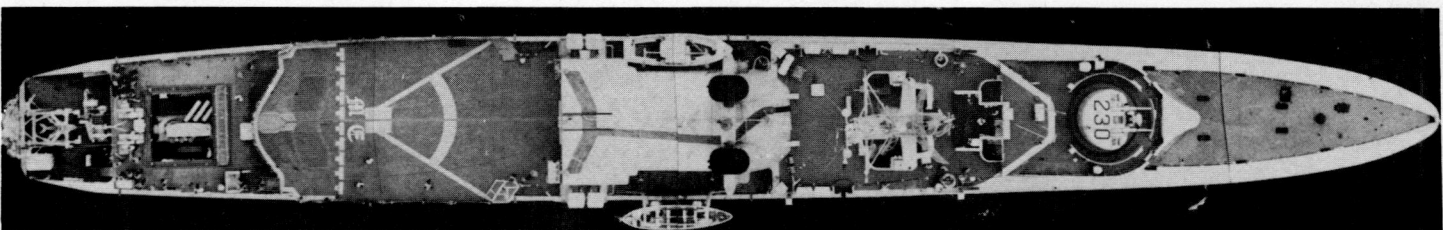

MARGAREE *1975, Commander R. E. George*

76 CANADA

REPLENISHMENT SHIPS

Name	No.	Builders	Laid down	Launched	Commissioned
PROTECTEUR	AOR 509	St John Dry Dock Co Ltd, NB	17 Oct 1967	18 July 1968	30 Aug 1969
PRESERVER	AOR 510	St John Dry Dock Co Ltd, NB	17 Oct 1967	29 May 1969	30 July 1970

Displacement, tons: 8 380 light; 24 700 full load
Measurement, tons: 22 100 gross; 13 250 deadweight
Length, feet (metres): 564 *(171·9)* oa
Beam, feet (metres): 76 *(23·2)*
Draught, feet (metres): 30 *(9·1)*
Aircraft: 3 CHSS-2 "Sea King" helicopters
Guns: 2—3 in *(76 mm)* (twin)
Main engines: Geared turbine; 21 000 shp; 1 shaft
Boilers: 2 forced draught water tube
Speed, knots: 21
Range, miles: 4 100 at 20, 7 500 at 11·5 knots
Complement: 227 (15 officers, 212 ratings)

Contract price $47·5 million for both ships. In design they are an improvement on that of the prototype *Provider*. They could carry spare anti-submarine helicopters, military vehicles and bulk equipment for sealift purposes. 13 100 tons FFO, 600 tons diesel, 400 tons aviation fuel, 1 048 tons dry cargo and 1 250 tons of ammunition.

Electronics: Tacan aerial.

Radar: Decca 969, Sperry Mk II.

Sonar: SQS 505.

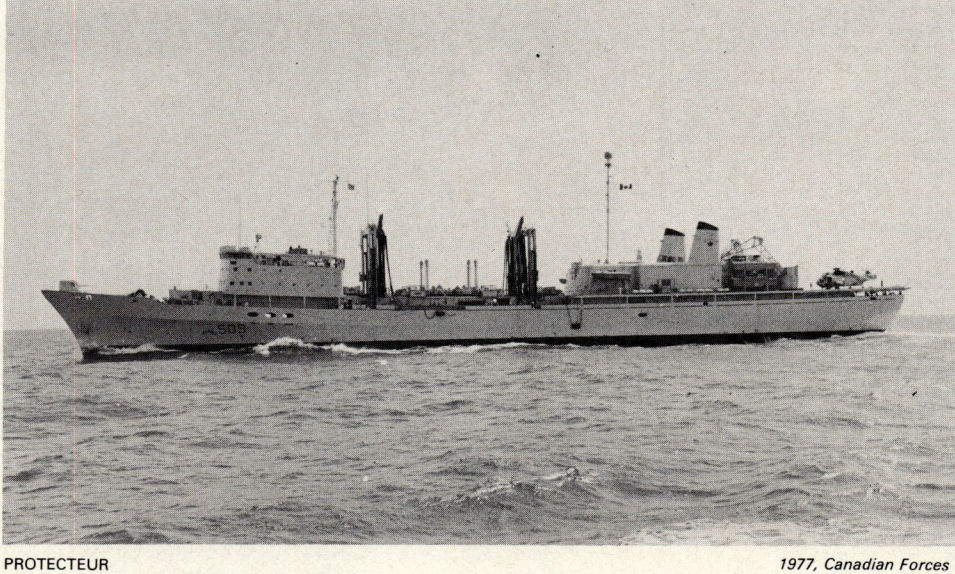

PROTECTEUR   *1977, Canadian Forces*

Name	No.	Builders	Laid down	Launched	Commissioned
PROVIDER	AOR 508	Davie Shipbuilding Ltd, Lauzon	1 May 1961	5 July 1962	28 Sep 1963

Displacement, tons: 7 300 light; 22 000 full load
Measurement, tons: 20 000 gross; 14 700 deadweight
Length, feet (metres): 523 *(159·4)* pp; 555 *(169·2)* oa
Beam, feet (metres): 76 *(23·2)*
Draught, feet (metres): 32 *(9·8)*
Aircraft: 3 CHSS-2 "Sea King" helicopters
Main engines: Double reduction geared turbine 21 000 shp; 1 shaft
Boilers: 2 water tube
Speed, knots: 20
Oil fuel, tons: 12 000
Range, miles: 3 600 at 20 knots
Complement: 166 (15 officers, 151 ratings)

Preliminary construction work was begun in September 1960. Cost $15·7 million.
The helicopter flight deck is aft with the hangar at the same level and immediately below the funnel. The flight deck can receive the largest and heaviest helicopters. A total of 20 electro-hydraulic winches are fitted on deck for ship-to-ship movements of cargo and supplies, as well as shore-to-ship requirements when alongside.

PROVIDER   *1975, Canadian Forces*

2 "DUN" CLASS TANKERS

DUNDALK AOC 501   **DUNDURN** AOC 502

Displacement, tons: 950
Dimensions, feet (metres): 178·8 × 32·2 × 13 *(54·5 × 9·8 × 3·9)*
Main engines: Diesel; 700 bhp = 10 knots
Complement: 24.

Small tankers, classed as fleet auxiliaries.

DUNDURN   *1969*

MAINTENANCE SHIP

1 "CAPE" CLASS

Name	No.	Builders	Laid down	Launched	Commissioned
CAPE BRETON	100	Burrard Dry Dock Co, Vancouver, BC	5 July 1944	7 Oct 1944	25 Apr 1945

Displacement, tons: 8 580 standard; 10 000 full load
Dimensions, feet (metres): 441·5 × 57 × 20 *(134·7 × 17·4 × 6·1)*

Alongside Base Ship for FMUs. Decommissioned and no further operational role is planned. This large class was originally built in Canada for the RN. Purchased back 1951.

CANADA 77

RESEARCH VESSELS

Name	No.	Builders	Commissioned
BLUETHROAT	AGOR 114	Geo. T. Davie & Sons Ltd, Lauzon	28 Nov 1955

Displacement, tons: 785 standard; 870 full load
Dimensions, feet (metres): 157 oa × 33 × 10 *(47 × 9·9 × 3)*
Main engines: Diesel; 2 shafts; 1 200 bhp = 13 knots

Authorised under 1951 Programme. Laid down on 31 Oct 1952. Launched on 15 Sep 1955. Completed on 28 Nov 1955 as Mine and Loop Layer. In 1957 she was rated Controlled Minelayer, NPC 114. Redesignated as Cable Layer (ALC) in 1959, and as Research Vessel (AGOR) and GP craft in 1964.

BLUETHROAT   1975, Canadian Forces

Name	No.	Builders	Commissioned
SACKVILLE	AGOR 113	St John Dry Dock Co.	30 Dec 1941

Displacement, tons: 1 085 standard; 1 350 full load
Dimensions, feet (metres): 205 oa × 33 × 14·5 *(62·5 × 10·1 × 6·4)*
Main engines: Triple expansion; 2 750 ihp = 16 knots
Boilers: 2 SE

Ex-"Flower" class corvette completed 30 Dec 1941. Later converted to loop layer. Designated AN 113—rated cable layer in 1959 (ALC). Redesignated as research vessel 1964. Employed by Naval Research Laboratories for oceanographic work.

SACKVILLE   1976, Michael D. J. Lemon

Name	No.	Builders	Commissioned
QUEST	AGOR 172	Burrard Dry Dock Co, Vancouver	21 Aug 1969

Displacement, tons: 2 130
Dimensions, feet (metres): 235 oa × 42 × 15·5 *(77·2 × 12·8 × 4·6)*
Aircraft: Light helicopter
Main engines: Diesel-electric; 2 shafts; 2 950 shp = 16 knots; bow thruster propeller
Range, miles: 10 000 at 12 knots
Complement: 55

Built for the Naval Research Establishment of the Defence Research Board for acoustic, hydrographic and general oceanographic work. Capable of operating in heavy ice in the company of an icebreaker. Construction began in 1967. Launched on 9 July 1968. Based at Halifax.

QUEST   1972, Canadian Maritime Command

Name	No.	Builders	Commissioned
ENDEAVOUR	AGOR 171	Yarrows Ltd, Esquimalt, BC	9 Mar 1965

Displacement, tons: 1 560
Dimensions, feet (metres): 236 oa × 38·5 × 13 *(71·9 × 11·7 × 4)*
Aircraft: 1 light helicopter
Main engines: Diesel-electric; 2 shafts; 2 960 shp = 16 knots
Range, miles: 10 000 at 12 knots
Complement: 50 (10 officers, 13 scientists, 25 ratings plus helicopter pilot and engineer)

A naval research ship designed primarily for anti-submarine research. Flight deck 48 by 31 feet. Stiffened for operating in ice-covered areas. She is able to turn in 2·5 times her own length. Two 9-ton Austin-Weston telescopic cranes are fitted. There are two oceanographical winches each holding 5 000 fathoms of wire, two bathythermograph winches and a deep-sea anchoring and coring winch. She has acoustic insulation in her machinery spaces.

ENDEAVOUR   1970, Canadian Maritime Command

1 ANTI-SUBMARINE HYDROFOIL (FHE)

BRAS D'OR FHE 400

Displacement, tons: 180
Dimensions, feet (metres): 150·8 × 21·5 × 15 (hull depth) *(46 × 6·6 × 5·1)* = *(7·5 (2·3)* (60 knots) draught on foils) Foil base 90
Main engines: Pratt & Whitney FT4A-2 gas turbine on foils; 22 000 shp = 50-60 knots
 Davey Paxman diesel when hull borne; 2 000 shp = 12-15 knots
 Pratt and Whitney ST 6A gas-turbine for hull-borne boost and foil-borne auxiliary power— 390 shp

A prototype craft designed by De Havilland Aircraft (Canada). After very successful trials she was laid up in Category C reserve, ashore at Halifax in 1971 for five years, a period now extended.

BRAS D'OR   1971, Canadian Forces

PATROL CRAFT

ADVERSUS	PBL 191	ACADIAN	PBL 194
DETECTOR	PBL 192	NICHOLSON	PBL 195
CAPTOR	PBL 193	SIDNEY	PBL 196

All transferred from RCMP in 1975, except *Nicholson* (75 feet) in 1976.

78 CANADA

TRAINING SHIPS

6 "BAY" CLASS Ex-MSC (PFL)

Name	No.	Builders	Commissioned
FUNDY	159	Davie Shipbuilding Co, Lauzon	27 Nov 1956
CHIGNECTO	160	Davie Shipbuilding Co, Lauzon	1 Aug 1957
THUNDER	161	Port Arthur SB Co	3 Oct 1957
COWICHAN	162	Yarrows Ltd, Esquimalt	19 Dec 1957
MIRAMICHI	163	Victoria Machinery Depot Co	28 Oct 1957
CHALEUR	164	Marine Industries Ltd, Sorel	12 Sep 1957

Displacement, tons: 390 standard; 464 full load
Dimensions, feet (metres): 152·0 oa × 28·0 × 7·0 (50 × 9·2 × 2·8)
Main engines: 2 GM V-12 diesels; 2 shafts; 2 400 bhp = 16 knots
Oil fuel, tons: 52
Range, miles: 3 290 at 12 knots
Complement: 18+ (2 officers, 16 ratings + trainees)

Extensively built of aluminium, including frames and decks. There were originally 20 vessels of this class of which six were transferred to France, four to Turkey and four sold commercially. Named after Canadian straits and bays. Designation changed from AMC to MCB in 1954. They were redesignated as Patrol Escorts (small) (PFL) in 1972 being used as training ships.

MIRAMICHI 1975, Canadian Forces

1 "FORT" CLASS PATROL ESCORT (PFL)

Name	No.	Builders	Commissioned
FORT STEELE	AGOR 140	Canadian SB and Eng. Co	Nov 1955

Displacement, tons: 85
Dimensions, feet (metres): 118 oa × 21 × 7 (36 × 6·4 × 2·1)
Main engines: 2 Paxman Ventura 12 YJCM diesels; 2 shafts; Kamewa cp propellers; 2 800 bhp = 18 knots
Complement: 16

Steel hull aluminium superstructure. Twin rudders. Acquired by DND in 1973 from RCMP—acts as Reserve Training ship based on Halifax.

FORT STEELE 1975, Canadian Forces

5 "PORTE" CLASS (GATE VESSELS)

Name	No.	Builders	Commissioned
PORTE ST. JEAN	180	Geo T. Davie	4 June 1952
PORTE ST. LOUIS	183	Geo T. Davie	28 Aug 1952
PORTE DE LA REINE	184	Victoria Machinery	19 Sep 1952
PORTE QUEBEC	185	Burrard Dry Dock	7 Oct 1952
PORTE DAUPHINE	186	Ferguson Ind.	12 Dec 1952

Displacement, tons: 429 full load
Dimensions, feet (metres): 125·5 × 26·3 × 13 (38·3 × 8·0 × 4·0)
Main engines: Diesel; AC electric; 1 shaft; 600 bhp = 11 knots
Complement: 23 (3 officers, 20 ratings)

Of trawler design. Multi-purpose vessels used for operating gates in A/S booms, fleet auxiliaries, anti-submarine netlayers for entrances to defended harbours. Can be fitted for minesweeping. Designation changed from YNG to YMG in 1954. First four used during summer for training Reserves. *Porte Dauphine* was reacquired from MOT in 1974 and employed in Reserve Training in Great Lakes area.

Note: Ex-Diving Tender YMT2 of 46 feet is used for sea-cadet training and the yacht *Oriole* QW3 has been used for officer cadet training since 1953.

PORTE ST. LOUIS 1972, Canadian Forces

DIVING SHIP

1 FLEET DIVING SUPPORT SHIP

CORMORANT (ex-*Aspa Quarto*) ASXL 20

Displacement, tons: 2 500
Dimensions, feet (metres): 236 × 39 × 16·5 (72 × 11·9 × 5)
Main engines: Diesel-electric = 14 knots

Ex-Italian stern trawler bought in 1975 for conversion. When operational she will carry, launch and recover the Canadian submersible SDL/1, and support saturation diving operations.

CORMORANT 1977, Canadian Forces

CANADA 79

MISCELLANEOUS

2 DIVING TENDERS

Name	No.	Builders	Commissioned
YMT 11	—	Ferguson, Picton, NS	Jan 1962
YMT 12	—	Ferguson, Picton, NS	7 Aug 1963

Displacement, tons: 110
Main engines: GM diesels; 228 bhp = 10·75 knots
Complement: 23 (3 officers, 20 ratings)

Can operate 4 divers at a time to 250 feet. Recompression chamber.

2 TORPEDO RECOVERY VESSELS

Name	No.	Builders	Commissioned
SONGHEE	YMR 1	Falconer Marine	1944
NIMPKISH	YMR 120	Falconer Marine	1944

Displacement, tons: 162
Length, feet (metres): 94·5 *(22·8)*
Main engines: 400 bhp
Complement: 7

7 "VILLE" CLASS (OLD)

Name	No.	Builders	Commissioned
BURRARD (ex-*Lawrenceville*)	YTS 582	Russell Bros	1944
BEAMSVILLE	YTS 583	Russell Bros	1944
CREE (ex-*Adamsville*)	YTS 584	Russell Bros	1944
QUEENSVILLE	YTS 586	Russell Bros	1944
PLAINSVILLE	YTS 587	Russell Bros	1944
YOUVILLE	YTS 588	Russell Bros	1944
LOGANVILLE	YTS 589	Russell Bros	1944

Dimensions, feet (metres): 40 × 10·5 × 4·8 *(12·2 × 3·2 × 1·5)*
Main engines: Diesel; 1 shaft; 150 bhp

Small harbour tugs now used for Reserve training.

There are small diving tenders YMT 6, YMT 8, YMT 9 and YMT 10, 70 tons, 75 × 18·5 × 8·5 feet, 2 diesels 165 bhp. YMT 1 (46 feet) was transferred to the Naval Research Establishment as a yard craft. Two new diving tenders, YSD 1 and YSD 2, entered service in 1965.

TUGS

2 "SAINT" CLASS

Name	No.	Builders	Commissioned
SAINT ANTHONY	ATA 531	St. John Dry Dock Co.	22 Feb 1957
SAINT CHARLES	ATA 533	St. John Dry Dock Co.	7 June 1957

Displacement, tons: 840 full load
Dimensions, feet (metres): 151·5 × 33 × 17 *(46·2 × 10 × 5·2)*
Main engines: Diesel; 1 shaft; 1 920 bhp = 14 knots
Complement: 21

Ocean tugs. Authorised under the 1951 Programme. Originally class of three.

1 "NORTON" CLASS

Name	No.	Builders	Commissioned
RIVERTON	ATA 528	—	Late 1944

Displacement, tons: 462
Dimensions, feet (metres): 111·2 oa × 28 × 11 *(33·9 × 8·5 × 3·4)*
Main engine: Dominion Sulzer diesel; 1 000 bhp = 11 knots
Complement: 17

Large harbour tug.

5 "GLEN" CLASS (HARBOUR/COASTAL)

Name	No.	Builders	Commissioned
GLENDYNE	ATA 640	Yarrows, Esquimalt	1975
GLENDALE	ATA 641	Yarrows, Esquimalt	1975
GLENEVIS	ATA 642	Georgetown Sy. PEI	1976
GLENBROOK	ATA 643	Georgetown Sy. PEI	16 Dec 1976
GLENSIDE	ATA 644	Georgetown Sy. PEI	1977

Displacement, tons: 255
Dimensions, feet (metres): 92·5 × 28 × 14·5 *(28·2 × 8·5 × 4·4)*
Main engines: 2 diesels with Voith-Schneider propellers; 1 300 hp = 11·5 knots
Complement: 6

2 "WOOD" CLASS

Name	No.	Builders	Commissioned
EASTWOOD	YMT 550	Le Blanc SB	1944
WILDWOOD	YMT 553	Falconer Marine	1944

Displacement, tons: 65
Dimensions, feet (metres): 60 oa × 16 × 5 *(18·3 × 4·9 × 1·5)*
Main engines: Diesel; 250 hp = 10 knots
Complement: 3

Medium harbour tugs. Used as A/S Target Towing Vessels.

Other medium harbour tugs are:
FT1, FT2. Employed as fire tugs, hull numbers YMT 556 and 557 respectively.

5 "VILLE" CLASS (NEW)

Name	No.	Builders	Commissioned
LAWRENCEVILLE	YTS 590	Vito Steel & Barge Co.	1974
PARKSVILLE	YTS 591	Vito Steel & Barge Co.	1974
LISTERVILLE	YTS 592	Georgetown SY PEI	1974
MERRICKVILLE	YTS 593	Georgetown SY PEI	1974
MARYSVILLE	YTS 594	Georgetown SY PEI	1974

Dimensions, feet (metres): 64 × 15·5 × 9 *(19·5 × 4·7 × 2·7)*
Main engines: Diesel; 1 shaft; 365 bhp = 9·8 knots

Small harbour tugs employed at Esquimalt and Halifax.

R.C.M.P. MARINE DIVISION

2 75 ft "DETACHMENT" CLASS

STAND OFF   CENTENNIAL

Displacement, tons: 69
Dimensions, feet (metres): 75 oa × 17 × 6·5 *(22·9 × 5·2 × 2)*
Main engines: 2 diesels; 1 018 bhp = 16 knots
Complement: 5

Of wood construction. *Stand Off* built by Smith and Rhuland Shipyard of Lunenburg, NS and completed in 1967. *Centennial* built by A. F. Therault and Sons Meteghan River NS. Intended for service on the Atlantic coast.

2 65 ft "DETACHMENT" CLASS

TOFINO   GANGES

Displacement, tons: 48
Dimensions, feet (metres): 65 × 15 × 4 *(19·8 × 4·6 × 1·2)*
Main engines: 1 Cummins diesel; 1 shaft; 410 bhp = 12 knots

Coastal patrol police boats for service on the east and west coasts.

2 52 ft PATROL VESSELS

RIVETT-CARNAC   PEARKES

Displacement, tons: 34
Dimensions, feet (metres): 52 × 14·75 × 3 *(15·8 × 4·5 × 0·9)*
Main engines: 2 Cummins 903 (320 hp each); twin shafts = 20 knots

1 50 ft "DETACHMENT" CLASS

MOOSOMIN II

Dimensions, feet (metres): 50 × 13 × 3 *(15·3 × 4·1 × 0·9)*
Main engines: 2 diesels; 600 bhp = over 17 knots

In service on the Great Lakes.

Valleyfield II, Outlook, Whitehorse, Yellowknife, Fort MacLeod and *Brule*, patrol craft varying from 26 to 41 feet in length, operate on the Great Lakes. *Advance, McLennan, Harvison* and *Mayberries* are located on the West coast together with *Duncan* (28 feet), *Dufferin* (41 feet) and *Regina* (41 feet).

80 CANADA

CANADIAN COAST GUARD

Administration

Minister of Transport:
  Rt Hon Otto Lang PC, MP
Deputy Minister of Transport:
  Mr. Sylvain Cloutier
Administrator, Marine Transportation Administration:
  Mr. R. Illing
Commissioner Canadian Coast Guard:
  Mr. W. A. O'Neil

Ships

The Canadian Coast Guard comprises 146 ships and craft of all types (including 63 barges). They operate in Canadian waters from the Great Lakes to the northernmost reaches of the Arctic Archipelago.
There are heavy icebreakers, icebreaking ships for tending buoys and lighthouses, marine survey craft, weather-oceanographic ships, and many specialised vessels for tasks such as search and rescue, cable lifting and repair, marine research and shallow-draft operations in areas such as the Mackenzie River system and some parts of the Arctic.
The Ship Building and Heavy Equipment Branch of the Department of Defence Productions arranges for the design, construction and repair of Coast Guard ships and also provides this service for a number of other Canadian Government departments.
Principal bases for the ships are the department's 11 District offices, located at— St. John's, Newfoundland; Dartmouth, NS; Saint John, NB; Charlottetown, PEI; Quebec and Sorel, Que; Prescott and Parry Sound, Ont.; Victoria and Prince Rupert, BC; and at Hay River, on Great Slave Lake.

Establishment

In January 1962 all ships owned and operated by the Federal Department of Transport with the exception of pilotage and canal craft, were amalgamated into the Canadian Coast Guard, a civilian service.

Flag

The Canadian Coast Guard has its own distinctive jack, a red maple leaf on a white ground at the hoist and two gold dolphins on a blue ground at the fly.
Canadian Coast Guard vessels have white funnels with a red band at the top and the red maple leaf against the white.

Missions

The Canadian Coast Guard carries out the following missions:
1. Icebreaking and Escort. Icebreaking is carried out in the Gulf of St. Lawrence and River St. Lawrence and the Great Lakes in winter to assist shipping and for flood control, and in Arctic waters in summer.
2. Icebreaker-Aids to Navigation Tenders. Installation, supply and maintenance of fixed and floating aids-to-navigation in Canadian waters.
3. Organise and provide icebreaker support and some cargo vessels for the annual Northern sealift which supplies bases and settlements in the Canadian Arctic and Hudson Bay.
4. Provide and operate special patrol cutters and lifeboats for marine search and rescue.
5. Provide and operate survey and sounding vessels for the St. Lawrence River Ship Channel.
6. Provide and operate weatherships for Ocean Station "Papa" in the Pacific.
7. Provide and operate vessel for the repairing of undersea cables.
8. Provide and operate vessel for Marine Traffic Control on the St. Lawrence river.
9. Operate a small fleet of aircraft primarily for aids to navigation, ice reconnaissance, and pollution control work.

Fleet Strength

Weather ships	2
Cable ship	1
Heavy Icebreakers	5 (+2)
Medium Icebreaking aid-to-navigation vessels	9
Light Icebreaking aid-to-navigation vessels	7
Ice strengthened aid-to-navigation vessels	4
Aid-to-navigation vessels	7
Offshore patrol cutters	6
Great Lakes Patrol Cutters	3
R Class cutters	6
Lifeboats	14
Hovercraft	1
Launches	6
St. Lawrence River vessels	4
Training vessels	2
Survey and sounding vessels	6
Mackenzie River navigation craft	5
Total	88

Aircraft

Fixed wing	1
Helicopters	33

New Construction

A new class of large icebreakers is under construction by Burrards, the first being launched in June 1977. There are discussions under way concerning a 33 000 ton icebreaker.

WEATHER SHIPS

Name	No.	Builders	Commissioned
QUADRA	—	Burrard Dry Dock Co Ltd	Mar 1967
VANCOUVER	—	Burrard Dry Dock Co Ltd	4 July 1966

Displacement, tons: 5 600 full load
Dimensions, feet (metres): 404·2 oa × 50 × 17·5 (123·2 × 15·2 × 5·3)
Aircraft: 1 helicopter
Main engines: Turbo-electric; 2 shafts; 7 500 shp = 18 knots
Boilers: 2 automatic Babcock & Wilcox D type
Range, miles: 10 400 at 14 knots
Complement: 96

Turbo-electric twin screw weather and oceanographic vessels for Pacific Ocean service. *Quadra* laid down Feb 1965, launched 4 July 1966. *Vancouver* laid down Mar 1964, launched 29 June 1965. They have bow water jet reaction system to assist steering at slow speeds. Flume stabilisation systems are fitted. They are turbo-electric powered, with oil-fired boilers to provide the quiet operation needed for vessels housing much scientific equipment. Their complement includes 15 technical officers such as meteorologists, oceanographers and electronics technicians.

VANCOUVER

1975, Canadian Ministry of Transport

CABLE SHIP

Name	No.	Builders	Commissioned
JOHN CABOT	—	Canadian Vickers Ltd, Montreal	July 1965

Displacement, tons: 6 375 full load
Dimensions, feet (metres): 313·3 × 60 × 21·5 (95·6 × 18·3 × 6·6)
Aircraft: 1 helicopter
Main engines: Diesel-electric; 2 shafts; 9 000 shp = 15 knots
Range, miles: 10 000 at 12 knots
Complement: 85 officers and men

Laid down May 1963 and launched 15 April 1964. Combination cable repair ship and icebreaker. Designed to repair and lay cable over the bow only. For use in East Coast and Arctic waters. Bow water jet reaction manoeuvring system, heeling tanks and Flume stabilisation system. Three circular storage holds handle a total of 400 miles of submarine cable. Personnel include technicians and helicopter pilots.

JOHN CABOT 1975, Canadian Ministry of Transport

ICEBREAKERS

Note: Design study in hand for 33 000 ton icebreaker (630 × 150·5 × 40 feet) capable of 20 knots on 90 000 hp and able to deal with 7 feet ice. Complement 118 plus 56 extra billets.

2 NEW CONSTRUCTION

Name	No.	Builders	Commissioned
PIERRE RADISSON	—	Burrard DD Co Ltd	1979
—	—	Burrard DD Co Ltd	?

Displacement, tons: 6 400 standard; 7 594 full load
Dimensions, feet (metres): 323 × 63·5 × 23 (98·5 × 19·4 × 7)
Aircraft: 1 helicopter
Main engines: Diesel-electric; 13 600 hp; 2 shafts = 13·5 knots
Oil fuel, tons: 2 240
Complement: 64 (11 spare billets)

Ordered 1 May 1975. *Pierre Radisson* laid down 16 Feb 1976 and launched 3 June 1977.

Name	No.	Builders	Commissioned
LOUIS ST. LAURENT	—	Canadian Vickers Ltd, Montreal	Oct 1969

Displacement, tons: 13 800 full load
Dimensions, feet (metres): 366·5 oa × 80 × 31 (111·7 × 24·4 × 9·5)
Aircraft: 2 helicopters
Main engines: Turbo-electric; 3 shafts; 24 000 shp = 17·75 knots
Range, miles: 16 000 miles at 13 knots cruising speed
Complement: Total accommodation for 216

She is larger than any of the former Coast Guard icebreakers. She has a helicopter hangar below the flight deck, with an elevator to raise the two helicopters to the deck when required. She was launched on 3 Dec 1966. She is officially rated as a heavy icebreaker.

LOUIS ST. LAURENT 1971, Canadian Coast Guard

Name	No.	Builders	Commissioned
NORMAN McLEOD ROGERS	—	Canadian Vickers Ltd, Montreal	Oct 1969

Displacement, tons: 6 320 full load
Dimensions, feet (metres): 295 oa × 62·5 × 20 (90 × 19·1 × 6·1)
Aircraft: 1 helicopter
Landing craft: 2
Main engines: 4 diesels and 2 gas turbines powering 2 electric motors; 2 shafts; 12 000 shp = 15 knots
Complement: 55

Built for use in the Gulf of St. Lawrence and East Coast waters. This is the world's first application of gas turbine/electric propulsion in an icebreaker. Officially rated as a heavy icebreaker.

NORMAN McLEOD ROGERS 1975, Canadian Coastguard

Name	No.	Builders	Commissioned
JOHN A. MACDONALD	—	Davie Shipbuilding Ltd, Lauzon	Sep 1960

Displacement, tons: 9 160 full load
Measurement, tons: 6 186 gross
Dimensions, feet (metres): 315 × 70 × 28 (96 × 21·3 × 8·5)
Aircraft: 2 helicopters
Main engines: Diesel-electric; 15 000 shp = 15·5 knots

Officially rated as a heavy icebreaker. Launched 3 Oct 1959.

JOHN A. MACDONALD 1975, Canadian Coastguard

82 CANADA

Name	No.	Builders	Commissioned
LABRADOR	—	Marine Industries Ltd, Sorel	8 July 1954

Displacement, tons: 6 490 full load
Measurement, tons: 3 823 gross
Dimensions, feet (metres): 290·0 oa × 63·5 × 29·0 (88·4 × 19·4 × 8·8)
Aircraft: 2 helicopters
Main engines: Diesel-electric; 10 000 shp = 16 knots

Ordered in Feb 1949, laid down on 18 Nov 1949, launched on 14 Dec 1951 and completed for the Royal Canadian Navy but transferred to the Department of Transport in Feb 1958. Officially rated as a Heavy Icebreaker. She was the first naval vessel to traverse the North West passage and circumnavigate North America, when she was Canada's largest and most modern icebreaker.

LABRADOR 1975, Dept. of Transport

Name	No.	Builders	Commissioned
d'IBERVILLE	—	Davie Shipbuilding Ltd, Lauzon	May 1953

Displacement, tons: 9 930 full load
Measurement, tons: 5 678 gross
Dimensions, feet (metres): 310 × 66·5 × 30·2 (94·5 × 20·3 × 9·2)
Aircraft: 1 helicopter
Main engines: Steam reciprocating; 10 800 ihp = 15 knots

Officially rated as a Heavy Icebreaker.

d'IBERVILLE 1975, Canadian Coast Guard

AID TO NAVIGATION VESSELS

Name	No.	Builders	Commissioned
GRIFFON	—	Davie Shipbuilding Ltd, Lauzon	Dec 1970

Displacement, tons: 3 096
Dimensions, feet (metres): 234 × 49 × 15·5 (71·4 × 14·9 × 4·7)
Aircraft: 1 helicopter
Main engines: Diesel; 4 000 bhp; 13·5 knots

Officially rated as Medium Icebreaking Aid to Navigation Vessel.

GRIFFON 1975, Canadian Coast Guard

Name	No.	Builders	Commissioned
J. E. BERNIER	—	Davie Shipbuilding Ltd, Lauzon	Aug 1967

Displacement, tons: 3 096
Dimensions, feet (metres): 231 × 49 × 16 (70·5 × 14·9 × 4·9)
Aircraft: 1 helicopter
Main engines: Diesel-electric; 4 250 bhp = 13·5 knots (trial speed)

Officially rated as Medium Icebreaking Aid to Navigation Vessel.

J. E. BERNIER 1975, Ministry of Transport

Name	No.	Builders	Commissioned
CAMSELL	—	Burrard Dry Dock Co Ltd	Oct 1959

Displacement, tons: 3 072 full load
Measurement, tons: 2 020 gross
Dimensions, feet (metres): 223·5 × 48 × 16 (68·2 × 14·6 × 4·9)
Aircraft: 1 helicopter
Main engines: Diesel-electric; 4 250 shp = 13 knots

Launched 17 Feb 1959. Officially rated as Medium Icebreaking Aid to Navigation Vessel.

CAMSELL 1975, Canadian Coast Guard

CANADA 83

Name	No.	Builders	Commissioned
MONTCALM	—	Davie Shipbuilding Ltd, Lauzon	June 1957
WOLFE	—	Canadian Vickers Ltd, Montreal	Nov 1959

Displacement, tons: 3 005 full load
Measurement, tons: 2 022 gross
Dimensions, feet (metres): 220 × 48 × 16 *(67·1 × 14·6 × 4·9)*
Aircraft: 1 helicopter
Main engines: Steam reciprocating; 4 000 ihp = 13 knots

Montcalm launched 23 Oct 1956. Officially rated as Medium Icebreaking Aid to Navigation Vessels.

WOLFE 1975, Canadian Coastguard

Name	No.	Builders	Commissioned
ALEXANDER HENRY	—	Port Arthur SB Ltd	July 1959

Displacement, tons: 2 497 full load
Measurements, tons: 1 647 gross
Dimensions, feet (metres): 210 × 43·5 × 16 *(64 × 13·3 × 4·9)*
Main engines: Diesel; 3 550 bhp = 13 knots

Launched 18 July 1958. Officially rated as a Medium Icebreaking Aid to Navigation Vessel.

Name	No.	Builders	Commissioned
SIR HUMPHREY GILBERT	—	Davie Shipbuilding Ltd, Lauzon	June 1959

Displacement, tons: 3 000 full load
Measurement, tons: 1 930 gross
Dimensions, feet (metres): 220 × 48 × 16·3 *(67 × 14·6 × 5·0)*
Aircraft: 1 helicopter
Main engines: Diesel-electric; 4 250 shp = 13 knots

SIR HUMPHREY GILBERT 1970, Canadian Coast Guard

Name	No.	Builders	Commissioned
SIR WILLIAM ALEXANDER	—	Halifax Shipyards Ltd	June 1959

Displacement, tons: 3 555 full load
Measurements, tons: 2 153 gross
Dimensions, feet (metres): 227·5 × 45 × 17·5 *(69·4 × 13·7 × 5·3)*
Main engines: Diesel-electric; 4 250 shp = 15 knots

Launched 13 Dec 1958. Equipped with Flume Stabilisation System. Officially rated as a Medium Icebreaking Aid to Navigation Vessel.

SIR WILLIAM ALEXANDER 1975, Dept. of Transport

Name	No.	Builders	Commissioned
ERNEST LAPOINTE	—	Davie Shipbuilding Ltd, Lauzon	Feb 1941

Displacement, tons: 1 675 full load
Measurement, tons: 1 179 gross
Dimensions, feet (metres): 184 × 36 × 15·5 *(56·1 × 11 × 4·7)*
Main engines: Steam reciprocating; 2 000 ihp = 13 knots

Officially rated as St. Lawrence Ship Channel Icebreaking Survey and Sounding Vessel.

Name	No.	Builders	Commissioned
TRACY	—	Port Weller Drydocks	1968

Displacement, tons: 1 300
Dimensions, feet (metres): 251·5 × 42 × 12 *(76·7 × 12·8 × 3·7)*
Main engines: Diesel; 2 000 bhp = 11 knots

Officially rated as Light Icebreaking Aid to Navigation Vessel.

Name	No.	Builders	Commissioned
NARWHAL	—	Canadian Vickers Ltd, Montreal	July 1963

Measurement, tons: 2 064 gross
Dimensions, feet (metres): 251·5 × 42·0 × 12·0 *(76·7 × 12·8 × 3·7)*
Main engines: Diesel; 2 000 bhp
Range, miles: 9 200 cruising
Complement: 32

Originally rated as Sealift Stevedore Depot Vessel, now re-rated as Light Icebreaking Aid to Navigation Vessel.

Name	No.	Builders	Commissioned
N. B. McLEAN	—	Halifax S.Y. Ltd	1930

Displacement, tons: 5 034 full load
Measurements, tons: 3 254 gross
Dimensions, feet (metres): 277 × 60·5 × 24·0 *(90 × 19·5 × 6·1)*
Main engines: Steam reciprocating; 6 500 ihp = 13 knots

Officially rated as Medium Icebreaker.

NARWHAL 1975, Canadian Coast Guard

84 CANADA

Name	No.	Builders	Commissioned
SIMON FRASER	—	Burrard D. Y. Co Ltd	Feb 1960
TUPPER	—	Marine Industries Ltd	Dec 1959

Displacement, tons: 1 876 full load
Measurements, tons: 1 357 gross
Dimensions, feet (metres): 204·5 × 42 × 14 *(62·4 × 12·8 × 4·3)*
Main engines: Diesel-electric; 2 900 shp = 13·5 knots

Simon Fraser was launched 18 Aug 1959. Both officially rated as Light Icebreaking Aid to Navigation Vessels.

Name	No.	Builders	Commissioned
WALTER E. FOSTER	—	Canadian Vickers Ltd, Montreal	Dec 1954

Displacement, tons: 2 715 full load
Measurement, tons: 1 672 gross
Dimensions, feet (metres): 229·2 × 42·5 × 16 *(69·9 × 12·9 × 4·9)*
Main engines: Steam reciprocating; 2 000 ihp = 12·5 knots

Officially rated as a Light Icebreaking Aid to Navigation Vessel.

Name	No.	Builder	Commissioned
EDWARD CORNWALLIS	—	Canadian Vickers Ltd, Montreal	Dec 1949

Displacement, tons: 3 700 full load
Measurement, tons: 1 965 gross
Dimensions, feet (metres): 259 × 43·5 × 18 *(79 × 13·3 × 5·5)*
Main engines: Steam reciprocating; 2 800 ihp = 13·5 knots

Launched 5 Aug 1949. In reserve. Officially rated as a Light Icebreaking Aid to Navigation Vessel.

Name	No.	Builders	Commissioned
BARTLETT	—	—	1970
PROVO WALLIS	—	—	1970

Displacement, tons: 1 620
Dimensions, feet (metres): 189·3 × 42·5 × 12·5 *(57·7 × 13 × 3·8)*
Main engines: Diesel; 1 760 bhp = 12 knots

Classed as Ice Strengthened Aid to Navigation Vessels.

Name	No.	Builders	Commissioned
SIMCOE	—	Canadian Vickers Ltd, Montreal	1962

Displacement, tons: 1 300 full load
Dimensions, feet (metres): 179·5 × 38 × 12 *(54·7 × 11·6 × 3·7)*
Main engines: Diesel-electric; 2 000 shp = 12 knots

Officially rated as Ice Strengthened Aid to Navigation Vessel.

Name	No.	Builders	Commissioned
MONTMORENCY	—	Davie Shipbuilding Ltd, Lauzon	Aug 1957

Displacement, tons: 1 006 full load
Measurement, tons: 750 gross
Dimensions, feet (metres): 163 × 34 × 11 *(49·7 × 10·2 × 3·4)*
Main engines: Diesel; 1 200 bhp

Officially rated as an Ice Strengthened Aid to Navigation Vessel.

Name	No.	Builders	Commissioned
THOMAS CARLETON	—	St. John Dry Dock Ltd	1960

Displacement, tons: 1 532 full load
Dimensions, feet (metres): 180 × 42 × 13 *(54·9 × 12·8 × 4)*
Main engines: Diesel; 2 000 bhp = 12 knots

Officially rated as Light Icebreaking Aid to Navigation Vessel.

WALTER E. FOSTER   1975, Canadian Coast Guard

EDWARD CORNWALLIS   1971, Canadian Coast Guard

BARTLETT   1975, Ministry of Transport

MONTMORENCY   1975, Canadian Coast Guard

CANADA 85

Name	No.	Builders	Commissioned
NAMAO	—	Coastguard Yard, Selkirk	1977

Displacement, tons: 370
Dimensions, feet (metres): 110 × 28 × 7 *(33.5 × 8.5 × 2.1)*
Main engines: 2 diesels; 540 shp = 11.5 knots
Range, miles: 2 000 at 11 knots

Launched 22 July 1976. Buoy tender for Lake Winnipeg.

Name	No.	Builders	Commissioned
MONTMAGNY	—	Russel Bros, Owen Sound	May 1963

Displacement, tons: 565 full load
Dimensions, feet (metres): 148.0 × 29.0 × 8.0 *(45.1 × 10.2 × 2.4)*
Main engines: Diesel; 1 000 bhp

Officially rated as Aid to Navigation Tender.

Name	No.	Builders	Commissioned
VERENDRYE	—	Davie Shipbuilding Ltd, Lauzon	Oct 1959

Displacement, tons: 400 full load
Dimensions, feet (metres): 125.0 × 26.0 × 7.0 *(38.1 × 7.9 × 2.1)*
Main engines: Diesel; 760 bhp

Officially rated as Aid to Navigation Tender.

KENOKI

Displacement, tons: 270
Dimensions, feet (metres): 108 × 36 × 5 *(32.9 × 11 × 1.5)*
Main engines: Diesel; 940 bhp = 10 knots

Officially rated as Aid to Navigation Tender.

Name	No.	Builders	Commissioned
ROBERT FOULIS	—	St. John Drydock	1969

Displacement, tons: 260
Dimensions, feet (metres): 104 × 25 × 7 *(31.7 × 7.6 × 2.1)*
Main engines: Diesel; 960 bhp = 10 knots

Officially rated as Aid to Navigation Tender.

MONTMAGNY   1970, Canadian Coast Guard

Name	No.	Builders	Commissioned
ALEXANDER MACKENZIE	—	Burrard Dry Dock Ltd	1950
SIR JAMES DOUGLAS	—	Burrard Dry Dock Ltd	Nov 1956

Displacement, tons: 720 full load
Dimensions, feet (metres): 150.0 × 30.0 × 10.3 *(45.7 × 9 × 3.1)*
Main engines: Diesel; 1 000 bhp

Officially rated as Aid to Navigation Tenders.

NOKOMIS

Displacement, tons: 64
Dimensions, feet (metres): 66 × 17 × 7 *(20.1 × 5.2 × 2.1)*
Main engines: Diesel; 120 bhp

Officially rated as Aid to Navigation Tender.

PATROL CUTTERS

3 NEW CONSTRUCTION

Name	No.	Builders	Commissioned
CAPE HARRISON	—	Breton Industrial and Marine	Jan 1977
CAPE —	—	Breton Industrial and Marine	1977
CAPE —	—	Breton Industrial and Marine	1978

Displacement, tons: 120
Length, feet (metres): 122 *(37.2)*
Main engines: 2 diesels; 4 500 shp(?) = 20 knots

Built at Port Hawkesbury.

Name	No.	Builders	Commissioned
ALERT	—	Davie Shipbuilding Ltd, Lauzon	Dec 1969

Displacement, tons: 2 025
Dimensions, feet (metres): 234.3 × 39.9 × 15.1 *(71.4 × 12.2 × 4.6)*
Aircraft: 1 helicopter
Main engines: Diesel-electric; 7 716 hp = 18.75 knots
Range, miles: 6 000

Officially rated as Offshore Patrol Cutter.

Name	No.	Builders	Commissioned
DARING (ex-*Wood*, MP 17)	—	Davie Shipbuilding Ltd, Lauzon	July 1958

Displacement, tons: 600 standard
Dimensions, feet (metres): 178 oa × 29 × 9.8 *(54.3 × 8.8 × 3.0)*
Main engines: 2 Fairbanks-Morse diesels; 2 shafts; 2 660 bhp = 16 knots

Used for patrol on the east coast of Canada, this ship is built of steel, strengthened against ice, with aluminium superstructure. Transferred from the Royal Canadian Mounted Police Marine Division to the Ministry of Transport in 1971, and renamed *Daring*. Offshore Patrol Cutter.

CG 101-109   CG 114-118

Displacement, tons: 18
Dimensions, feet (metres): 44 × 12 × 3 *(13.4 × 3.7 × 0.9)*
Main engines: Diesel; 294 bhp = 14 knots
Range, miles: 150

Lifeboats shore-based at Coast Guard Stations on both coasts.

1 NEW CONSTRUCTION

Name	No.	Builders	Commissioned
CAPE ROGERS	—	Ferguson (Picton)	Late 1976

Displacement, tons: 1 400
Dimensions, feet (metres): 205 × 40 × 13.3 *(62.5 × 12.2 × 4.1)*
Main engines: 2 diesels, 2 200 hp; 1 shaft = 16.5 knots
Range, miles: 7 000 at 13 knots
Complement: 42

Laid down 13 Nov 1975, launched 12 June 1976. Fishery protection vessel.

DARING (as *Wood*)   1966, Director of Marine Services

Name	No.	Builders	Commissioned
RACER	—	Yarrows Ltd, Esquimalt	1963
RALLY	—	Davie Shipbuilding Ltd	1963
RAPID	—	Ferguson Industries, Picton	1963
READY	—	Burrard Dry Dock	1963
RELAY	—	Kingston Shipyard	1963
RIDER	—	—	1963

Measurement, tons: 153 gross
Dimensions, feet (metres): 95.2 × 20 × 6.5 *(29 × 6.1 × 2)*
Main engines: Diesel; 2 400 bhp = 20 knots designed

Rider, completed for the Dept. of Fisheries, was taken over by the Coast Guard in Mar 1969.
Relay rerated as St. Lawrence River Marine Traffic Control Vessel.

86 CANADA

Name	No.	Builders	Commissioned
SPINDRIFT	—	Cliff Richardson Ltd, Meaford	1963
SPRAY	—	J. J. Taylor & Sons Ltd, Toronto	1963
SPUME	—	Grew Ltd, Penetanguishene	1964

Measurement, tons: 57 gross
Dimensions, feet (metres): 70 × 16·8 × 4·7 (21·4 × 5·1 × 1·4)
Main engines: 2 diesels; 1 050 bhp = 19 knots

Employed on Great Lakes Patrol.

Note. For search and rescue and patrol duties: six launches (*Mallard, Moorhen,* CG 110-113) and one Hovercraft (CG 021).

NORTHERN SUPPLY VESSELS

2 FORMER TANK LANDING CRAFT (LCT 8)

Name	No.	Builders	Commissioned
EIDER	—	Sir Wm Arrol & Co	1946
SKUA	—	Harland & Wolff	1946

Measurement, tons: 1 083 to 1 104 gross
Dimensions, feet (metres): 231·2 oa × 38 × 7 (70·5 × 11·6 × 2·1)
Main engines: Diesel; 1 000 shp = 9 knots

Converted LCT (8)s, acquired from the United Kingdom in 1957-61.

1 FORMER TANK LANDING CRAFT (LCT 4)

Name	No.	Builders	Commissioned
MINK	—	—	1944

Displacement, tons: 586 full load
Dimensions, feet (metres): 187·2 × 33·8 × 4 (57·1 × 10·3 × 1·2)
Main engines: Diesel; 920 shp = 8 knots

Converted LCT (4) acquired from the United Kingdom in 1958. Formerly officially rated as Steel Landing Craft for Northern Service, now re-rated as Aids to Navigation Tender, in reserve.

SHORE-BASED CRAFT

DUMIT   ECKALOO   MISKANAW   TEMBAH   NAHIDIK

Assist navigation in Mackenzie River operations. Small tug/buoy tender type.

1 HOVERCRAFT

One BH-6H-9009 was completed at Cowes by BHC Ltd on 3 March 1977.

SURVEY AND SOUNDING VESSELS

BEAUPORT

Displacement, tons: 767 full load
Dimensions, feet (metres): 167·5 × 24·0 × 9·0 (51·1 × 7·3 × 2·7)
Main engines: Diesels; 1 280 bhp

Completed in 1960.

DETECTOR

Displacement, tons: 584 full load
Dimensions, feet (metres): 140·0 × 35·0 × 10·0 (42·7 × 10·7 × 3·1)
Main engines: Steam reciprocating

NICOLET

Displacement, tons: 935 full load
Dimensions, feet (metres): 166·5 × 35·0 × 9·6 (50·8 × 10·7 × 2·9)
Main engines: Diesels; 1 350 bhp

VILLE MARIE

Displacement, tons: 493 full load
Dimensions, feet (metres): 134·0 × 28·0 × 9·5 (40·9 × 8·5 × 2·9)
Main engines: Diesel-electric; 1 000 hp

Completed in 1960.

There are also two smaller vessels *Glendada* and *Jean Bourdon* for the St. Lawrence Ship Channel.

TRAINING SHIPS

MIKULA

Displacement, tons: 617
Dimensions, feet (metres): 128 × 30 × 11 (39 × 9·2 × 3·4)
Main engines: Diesel; 150 bhp = 9 knots

Converted Light Vessel.

SKIDEGATE

Displacement, tons: 200
Dimensions, feet (metres): 87 × 22 × 8 (26·5 × 6·7 × 2·4)
Main engines: Diesel; 640 bhp = 11 knots

Formerly an Aid to Navigation Tender.

CHILE

Ministerial

Minister of National Defence:
 Major General H. J. Brady Roche

Headquarters Appointments

Commander-in-Chief of the Navy:
 Admiral José Toribio Merino Castro
Chief of the Naval Staff:
 Vice-Admiral Carlos A. Le May Délano

Diplomatic Representation

Naval Attaché in Brasilia:
 Captain Reinaldo Rivas
Naval Attaché in Buenos Aires, Montevideo and Asunción:
 Captain Fernando Camus
Naval Attaché in Lima:
 Captain Jorge Contreras
Naval Attaché in London, Paris, The Hague and Stockholm:
 Rear-Admiral Maurice Poisson
Naval Attaché in Madrid:
 Captain Pedro Romero
Naval Attaché in Quito and Bogota:
 Captain Franklin Gonzalez
Naval Attaché in Tokyo:
 Commander Enrique La Luz
Naval Attaché in Washington:
 Rear-Admiral Jorge Hess

General

Except for the 2 "Leander" Class, the 2 "Oberon" Class, 1 LPC and 4 "Lürssen" FAC the main units of the fleet are all reaching advanced age, even the "Almirante" Class, being 17 years old. With the remainder having hull-lives of 30-40 years a replacement programme is clearly needed if the 4 000 miles of coastline is to be patrolled to a 200 mile limit. The current problems of acquiring US vessels must make any future purchases more likely to be of European construction.

Personnel

(a) 1978: 23 000 (1 320 officers, 19 000 ratings, 3 680 marines)
(b) 1 year's national service

Naval Bases

Talcahuano. Main Naval Base, Schools, major repair yard, (2 dry docks, 2 floating docks) 2 floating cranes.
Valparaiso. Naval Base, Schools, major repair yard.
Puerto Monti. Small naval base.
Punta Arenas. Small naval base. Repair yard with slipway.
Puerto Williams. Small naval base.

Maritime Air

Personnel—500

 4 Bell 206 A JetRangers
 2 Bell 47
 5 Grumman HU-16B Albatross (Air force)
 6 EMB-111 ordered—delivery 1977-78
 5 Douglas C 47
 5 Beech C-45/D18s
 1 Piper PA-31-310 Navajo
 6 Beech T-34B Mentor
 3 EMB-110 Bandeirante

Infanteria de Marina

1 Brigade and Coast Defence units (2 680 marines). Four bases at Iquique, Punta Arenas, Talcahuano and Valparaiso in addition to an embarked battalion.

Strength of the Fleet

Type	Active	Building
Cruisers	3	—
Destroyers	6	—
Frigates	5	—
Patrol ships	3	—
Patrol Submarines	2	—
Landing Ships (Tank)	4	—
Landing Craft	7	—
Fast Attack Craft (Torpedo)	3	—
Large Patrol Craft	3	—
Coastal Patrol Craft	2	—
Survey Ship	1	—
Sail Training Ship	1	—
Transports	2	—
Tankers	2	1
Floating Docks	2	—
Tugs	6	—
Submarine Support Ship	1	—

Mercantile Marine

Lloyd's Register of Shipping:
 143 vessels of 405 971 tons gross

DELETIONS

Submarine

1973 *Thomson* (ex-US "Balao" Class)

Frigate

1973 *Riquelme* (ex-US "Charles Lawrence" Class)

Landing Craft

1971 *Bolados* (LCU 95)
1973 *Grumete Tellez* (withdrawn from service)
1977 *Aspirante Morel, Grumete Diaz, Comandante Toro*

Light Forces

1977 *Contramaestre Ortiz*

Tanker

1977 *Jorge Montt*

Tugs

1971 *Cabrales, Ugarte*
1977 *S. Aldea*

PENNANT LIST

Cruisers

02 O'Higgins
03 Prat
04 Latorre

Destroyers/Frigates

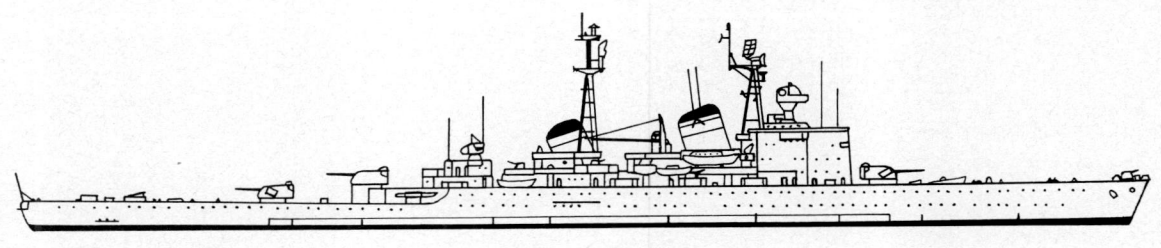

06 Condell
07 Lynch
14 Blanco Encalada
15 Cochrane
16 Ministero Zenteno
17 Ministero Portales
18 Almirante Riveros
19 Almirante Williams
26 Serrano
27 Orella
29 Uribe

Submarines

21 Simpson
22 O'Brien
23 Hyatt

Patrol Forces

60 Lientul
62 Lautaro
63 Sergento Aldea

Light Forces

37 Papudo
75 Marinero Fuentealba
76 Cabo Odger
80 Guacolda
81 Fresia
82 Quidora
83 Tegualda

Survey Ship

64 Yelcho

Training Ship

43 Esmeralda

Amphibious Forces

86 Valdivia
88 Comandante Hemmerdinger
89 Comandante Araya
90 Elicura
91 Aguila
94 Orompello

Transports

45 Piloto Pardo
47 Aquiles
110 Meteoro
111 Cirujano Videla

Submarine Support Ship

70 Angamos

Tankers

53 Araucano
54 Beagle

Tugs

73 Colocolo
104 Ancud
105 Monreal
120 Reyes
127 Caupolican
128 Cortez

LATORRE

88 CHILE

"BROOKLYN" Class

"ALMIRANTE" Class

"FLETCHER" Class

"ALLEN M. SUMNER" Class

"LEANDER" Class

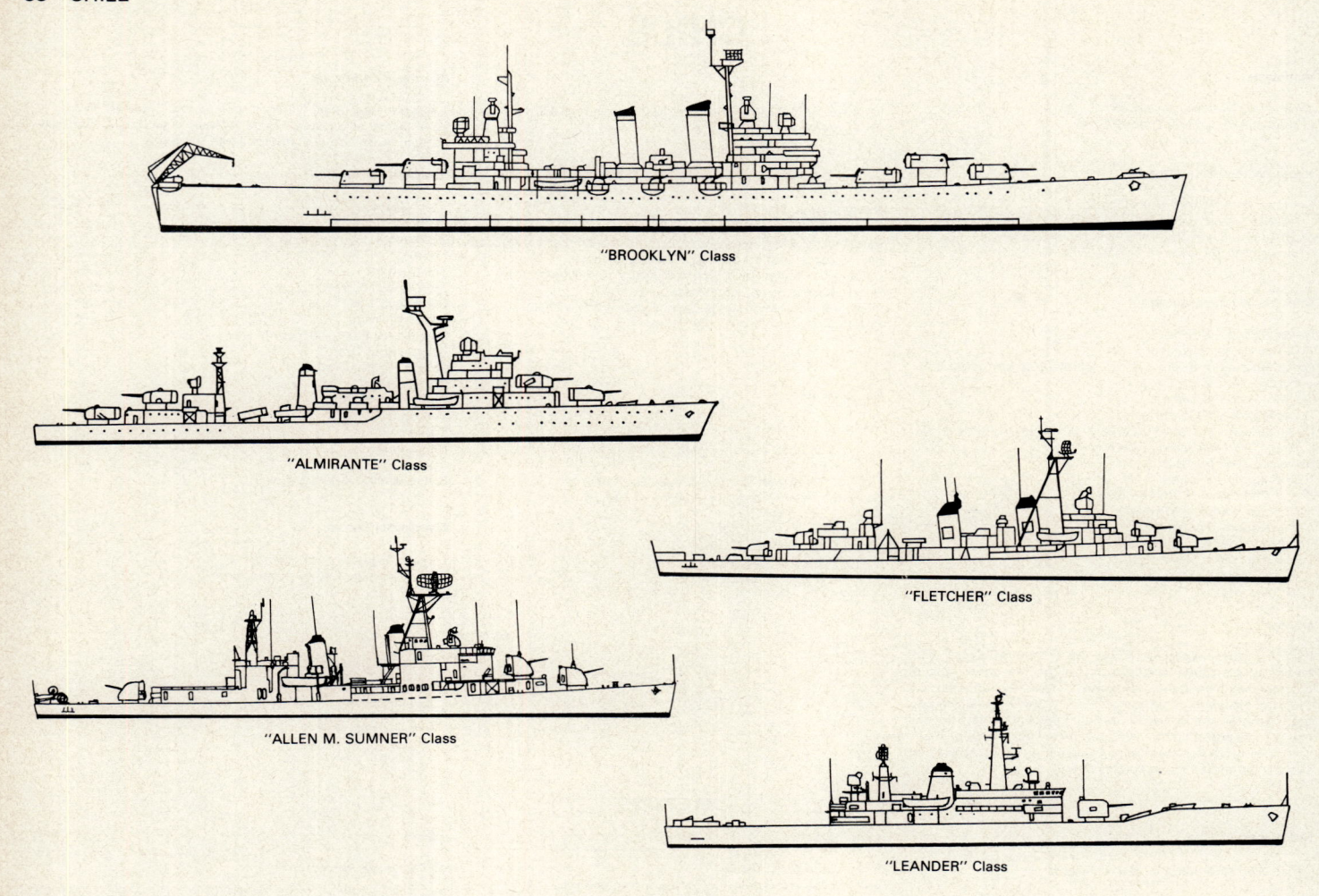

SUBMARINES

2 BRITISH "OBERON" CLASS

Name	No.	Builders	Laid down	Launched	Commissioned
O'BRIEN	22	Scott-Lithgow	17 Jan 1971	21 Dec 1972	April 1976
HYATT (ex-Condell)	23	Scott-Lithgow	10 Jan 1972	26 Sep 1973	27 Sep 1976

Displacement, tons: 1 610 standard; 2 030 surfaced; 2 410 dived
Length, feet (metres): 241·0 (73·5) pp; 295·2 (90·0) oa
Beam, feet (metres): 26·5 (8·1)
Draught, feet (metres): 18·1 (5·5)
Torpedo tubes: 8—21 in (533 mm)
Main machinery: 2 diesels 3 680 bhp; 2 electric motors 6 000 shp; 2 shafts, electric drive
Speed, knots: 12 surfaced; 17 dived

Ordered from Scott's Shipbuilding & Engineering Co Ltd, Greenock, late 1969. Both have suffered delays in fitting out due to re-cabling and a minor explosion in Hyatt in Jan 1976. Original completion was due in July 1974 and April 1975 (see new commissioning dates above). O'Brien arrived in Chile July 1976, Hyatt Feb 1977. Hyatt completed 31 Aug 1976.

O'BRIEN   1974, W. Ralston

1 Ex-US "BALAO" CLASS

Name	No.	Builders	Laid down	Launched	Commissioned
SIMPSON (ex-USS Spot, SS 413)	21	Mare Island Navy Yard	1943	20 May 1944	3 Aug 1944

Displacement, tons: 1 816 surfaced; 2 425 dived
Length, feet (metres): 311·6 (95)
Beam, feet (metres): 27 (8·2)
Draught, feet (metres): 17 (5·2)
Torpedo tubes: 10—21 in (533 mm) (6 bow, 4 stern)
Main machinery: 4 GM diesels; 6 500 hp; 2 electric motors; 4 610 bhp
Speed, knots: 20 surfaced; 10 dived
Complement: 80

Transferred end of 1961. Paid off 1975. Reactivated 1977.

SIMPSON   1972, Chilean Navy

CHILE

CRUISERS
1 Ex-SWEDISH "GOTA LEJON" CLASS

Name	No.	Builders	Laid down	Launched	Commissioned
LATORRE (ex-*Göta Lejon*)	04	Eriksberg Mekaniska Verkstad, Göteborg	27 Sep 1943	17 Nov 1945	15 Dec 1947

Displacement, tons: 8 200 standard; 9 200 full load
Length, feet (metres): 590·5 *(180·0)* wl; 597 *(182·0)* oa
Beam, feet (metres): 54 *(16·5)*
Draught, feet (metres): 21·5 *(6·6)*
Guns: 7—6 in *(150 mm)* 53 cal. (1 triple forward, 2 twin aft) 4—57 mm; 11—40 mm
Torpedo tubes: 6—21 in
Armour: 3 in—5 in *(75—125 mm)*
Main engines: 2 sets De Laval geared turbines; 100 000 shp; 2 shafts
Boilers: 4 Swedish 4-drum type
Speed, knots: 33
Complement: 610

Radar control arrangements were installed for 6-inch guns. Fitted for minelaying with a capacity of 120 mines. Reconstructed in 1951-52, modernised in 1958, with new radar, 57 mm guns etc.

Gunnery: The 6 inch guns are automatic weapons with an elevation of 70 degrees.

Radar: Search: LW-03, Type 227. Tactical: Type 293. Fire control: I band.

Transfer: Purchased by Chile from Sweden July 1971. Commissioned in Chilean Navy 18 Sep 1971.

LATORRE   1973, Chilean Navy

2 Ex-US "BROOKLYN" CLASS

Name	No.	Builders	Laid down	Launched	Commissioned
O'HIGGINS (ex-USS *Brooklyn* CL 40)	02	New York Navy Yard	12 Mar 1935	30 Nov 1936	18 July 1938
PRAT (ex-USS *Nashville* CL 43)	03	New York S.B. Corp.	24 Jan 1935	2 Oct 1937	25 Nov 1938

Displacement, tons: 10 000 standard; 13 500 full load
Length, feet (metres): 608·3 *(185·4)* oa
Beam, feet (metres): 69 *(21·0)*
Draught, feet (metres): 24 *(7·3)*
Aircraft: 1 Bell helicopter
Guns: 15—6 in *(153 mm)* 47 cal (5 triple); 8—5 in *(127 mm)* 25 cal (single); 28—40 mm; 24—20 mm
Armour, inches (mm):
  Belt 4—1½ *(102—38)*;
  Decks 3—2 *(76—51)*;
  Turrets 5—3 *(127—76)*; C.T. 8 in *(203)*
Main engines: Parsons geared turbines 100 000 shp; 4 shafts
Boilers: 8 Babcock & Wilcox Express type
Oil fuel, tons: 2 100
Speed, knots: 32·5
Range, miles: 14 500 at 15 knots
Complement: 888 to 975 (peace)

Former cruisers of the US "Brooklyn" Class. Purchased from the United States in 1951 at a price representing 10 per cent of original cost ($37 million) plus the expense of reconditioning. Again refitted in USA 1957-58.

Hangar: The hangar in the hull right aft could accommodate 6 aircraft if necessary together with engine spares and duplicate parts, though 4 aircraft was the normal capacity. Above the hangar two catapults were mounted as far outboard as possible, and a revolving crane was placed at the stern extremity overhanging the aircraft hatch.

Radar: Search: SPS 12. Tactical: SPS 10.

PRAT   1974, Chilean Navy

DESTROYERS
2 Ex-US "FLETCHER" CLASS

Name	No.	Builders	Laid down	Launched	Commissioned
BLANCO ENCALADA (ex-USS *Wadleigh* DD 689)	14	Bath Iron Works Corp, Bath	Mar 1943	7 Aug 1943	19 Oct 1943
COCHRANE (ex-USS *Rooks* DD 804)	15	Todd Pacific Shipyards	Jan 1944	6 June 1944	2 Sep 1944

Displacement, tons: 2 100 standard; 2 750 full load
Length, feet (metres): 376·5 *(110·5)* oa
Beam, feet (metres): 39·5 *(12·0)*
Draught, feet (metres): 18 *(5·5)*
Guns: 4—5 in *(127 mm)* 38 cal; 6—3 in *(76 mm)* 50 cal
Torpedo tubes: 5—21 in (quintupled)
A/S weapons: 2 Hedgehogs; 2 side launching torpedo racks; 1 DC rack; 6 "K" DCT
Main engines: 2 Westinghouse geared turbines; 60 000 shp; 2 shafts
Boilers: 4 Babcock & Wilcox
Speed, knots: 35
Oil fuel, tons: 650
Range, miles: 5 000 at 15 knots; 1 260 at 30 knots
Complement: 250 (14 officers, 236 men). Accommodation for 324 (24 officers, 300 men)

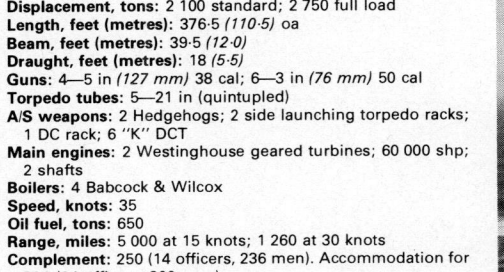

Transferred to Chile under the Military Aid Programme in 1963. Three more destroyers were scheduled for transfer from the United States Navy to the Chilean Navy under a new transfer law signed by the President of the United States in 1966. The ships were to have been refitted and modernised and adapted to Chilean requirements before transfer to the new flag, but the four frigates of the US "Charles Lawrence" Class were transferred instead.

Radar: Search: SPS 6. Tactical: SPS 10. Fire control: I Band.

COCHRANE   1972, Chilean Navy

CHILE

2 "ALMIRANTE" CLASS

Name	No.	Builders	Laid down	Launched	Commissioned
ALMIRANTE RIVEROS	18	Vickers-Armstrong Ltd, Barrow	12 April 1957	12 Dec 1958	31 Dec 1960
ALMIRANTE WILLIAMS	19	Vickers-Armstrong Ltd, Barrow	20 June 1956	5 May 1958	26 Mar 1960

Displacement, tons: 2 730 standard; 3 300 full load
Length, feet (metres): 402 *(122·5)* oa
Beam, feet (metres): 43 *(13·1)*
Draught, feet (metres): 13·3 *(4·0)*
Missiles: 4 Exocet MM 38 Launchers;
  2 Quadruple launchers for Seacat
Guns: 4—4 in *(102 mm)*; 4—40 mm (singles)
A/S weapons: 2 Squid 3-barrelled DC mortars;
  6 (2 triple) Mk 32 torpedo tubes (Mk 44 torpedoes)
Main engines: Parsons Pametrada geared turbines;
  54 000 shp; 2 shafts
Boilers: 2 Babcock & Wilcox
Speed, knots: 34·5
Range, miles: 6 000 at 16 knots
Complement: 266

Ordered in May 1955. Layout and general arrangements are conventional. Bunks fitted for entire crew. Both modernised by Swan Hunter, *Almirante Williams* in 1971-74 and *Almirante Riveros* in 1973-75.

Electrical: The electrical system is on alternating current. Galleys are all electric. There is widespread use of fluorescent lighting. Degaussing cables are fitted.

Gunnery: The 4 in guns are in four single mountings, two superimposed forward and two aft. They are automatic with a range of 12 500 yards *(11 400 metres)* and an elevation of 75 degrees.

Missiles: British Seacat surface-to-air installations were fitted at the Chilean Navy Yard at Talcahuano in 1964. Exocet MM 38 fitted during modernisations.

Operational: The operations room and similar spaces are air-conditioned. Twin rudders. Ventilation and heating system designed to suit Chilean conditions, extending from the tropics to the Antarctic.

Radar: Plessey AWS-I and Target Indication radar with AIO autonomous displays being fitted at refits.

ALMIRANTE RIVEROS *1976, Swan Hunter*

ALMIRANTE WILLIAMS *1977, Chilean Navy*

2 Ex-US "ALLEN M. SUMNER FRAM II" CLASS

Name	No.	Builders	Laid down	Launched	Commissioned
MINISTRO ZENTENO (ex-USS *Charles S. Sperry*, DD 697)	16	Todd (Pacific) Shipyards	1944	30 Sep 1944	26 Dec 1944
MINISTRO PORTALES (ex-USS *Douglas H. Fox*, DD 779)	17	Federal SB and DD Co.	1943	13 Mar 1944	17 May 1944

Displacement, tons: 2 200 standard; 3 320 full load
Length, feet (metres): 376·5 *(114·8)* oa
Beam, feet (metres): 40·9 *(12·4)*
Draught, feet (metres): 19 *(5·8)*
Aircraft: 1 helicopter
Guns: 6—5 in *(127 mm)* 38 cal
A/S weapons: 2 triple Mk 32 launchers; 2 Hedgehogs
Main engines: 2 geared turbines; 60 000 shp; 2 shafts
Boilers: 4
Speed, knots: 34
Range, miles: 4 600 at 15 knots
Complement: 274

Transferred 8 Jan 1974.

Radar: Search: SPS 37 *(Zenteno)*, SPS 40 *(Portales)*.
Tactical: SPS 10.

Sonar: SQS 40. VDS.

MINISTRO ZENTENO *1976, Chilean Navy*

MINISTRO PORTALES *1975*

CHILE 91

FRIGATES

2 BRITISH "LEANDER" CLASS

Name	No.	Builders	Laid down	Launched	Commissioned
CONDELL	06	Yarrow & Co Ltd	5 June 1971	12 June 1972	21 Dec 1973
ALMIRANTE LYNCH	07	Yarrow & Co Ltd	6 Dec 1971	6 Dec 1972	25 May 1974

Displacement, tons: 2 500 standard; 2 962 full load
Length, feet (metres): 360·0 *(109·7)* wl; 372·0 *(113·4)* oa
Beam, feet (metres): 43·0 *(13·1)*
Draught, feet (metres): 18·0 *(5·5)*
Aircraft: 1 light helicopter
Missiles: 4 Exocet launchers; 1 quadruple Seacat
Guns: 2—4·5 in (1 twin); 2—20 mm
A/S weapons: 6 (2 triple) Mk 32 torpedo tubes
Main engines: 2 geared turbines; 30 000 shp
Boilers: 2
Speed, knots: 30
Range, miles: 4 500 at 12 knots
Complement: 263

Ordered from Yarrow & Co Ltd, Scotstoun in the modernisation programme of the Chilean Navy. Until the Swedish cruiser was acquired, *Condell*, laid down on 5 June 1971, was to have been named *Latorre*. Renamed 1971. Both arrived in Chilean waters by February 1975.

Appearance: Have slightly taller foremasts than British "Leanders". No Limbo or VDS.

Missiles: The Exocet launchers are placed on the quarter-deck thus, as opposed to the British conversion, allowing the retention of the 4·5 in turret.

Radar: Surveillance, Target Indication; Type 992Q.
Air search; Type 965.
Navigation; Type 975.
Seacat/Gunnery; GWS 22/MRS3.

Sonar: Type 162, 170 and 177.

ALMIRANTE LYNCH   10/1974, C. and S. Taylor

3 Ex-US "CHARLES LAWRENCE" CLASS

Name	No.	Builders	Laid down	Launched	Commissioned
SERRANO (ex-USS *Odum*, APD 71, ex-DE 670)	26	Consolidated Steel, Orange	15 Oct 1943	19 Jan 1944	12 Jan 1945
ORELLA (ex-USS *Jack C. Robinson*, APD 72, ex-DE 671)	27	Consolidated Steel, Orange	10 Nov 1943	8 Jan 1944	2 Feb 1945
URIBE (ex-USS *Daniel Griffin*, APD 38, ex-DE 54)	29	Bethlehem, Hingham	7 Sep 1942	25 Feb 1943	9 June 1943

Displacement, tons: 1 400 standard; 2 130 full load
Length, feet (metres): 300·0 *(91·4)* wl; 306·0 *(93·3)* oa
Beam, feet (metres): 37·0 *(11·3)*
Draught, feet (metres): 12·6 *(3·8)*
Guns: 1—5 in 38 cal; 6—40 mm
A/S weapons: 2 Hedgehogs (some); 2 DC racks
Main engines: GE turbo-electric; 2 shafts; 12 000 shp = 23·6 knots; 2 turbines 6 000 hp each; 2 generators 4 500 kW each
Boilers: 2 Foster Wheeler "D" type
Range, miles: 5 000 at 15 knots; 2 000 at 23 knots
Complement: 209

These former high speed transports (APD) were purchased from the USA, transferred at Orange, Texas 25 Nov 1966 (first two) and Norfolk Va 1 Dec 1966 *(Uribe)*. They have been modernised, *Riquelme* was also transferred but was used for provision of spare parts. Deleted 1973.

Radar: Combined search; AN/SPS-4.
Navigation; commercial (no gunnery control by radar).

ORELLA   1974, Chilean Navy

PATROL FORCES

2 Ex-US "SOTOYOMO" CLASS

Name	No.	Builders	Commissioned
LIENTUR (ex-USS *ATA 177*)	60	Levingstone SB Co, Orange	1944
LAUTARO (ex-USS *ATA 122*)	62	Levingstone SB Co, Orange	1943

Displacement, tons: 534 standard; 835 full load
Dimensions, feet (metres): 134·5 wl; 143 oa × 33 × 13·2 *(43·6 × 10·1 × 4)*
Guns: 1—3 in; 2—20 mm
Main engines: GM diesel-electric; 1 500 shp = 12·5 knots
Oil fuel, tons: 187
Complement: 33

Launched—*Lautaro* 27 Nov 1942, *Lientur* 5 June 1944. Originally ocean rescue tugs (ATRs), transferred to the Chilean Navy and reclassified as patrol vessels.

LAUTARO   1969, Chilean Navy

1 Ex-US "CHEROKEE" CLASS

Name	No.	Builders	Commissioned
SERGENTO ALDEA (ex-USS *Arikara*, ATF 98)	63	Charleston SB & DD Co	5 Jan 1944

Displacement, tons: 1 235 standard; 1 675 full load
Dimensions, feet (metres): 195·0 wl; 205·0 oa × 38·5 × 15·5 *(62·5 × 11·7 × 4·7)*
Gun: 1—3 in 50 cal
Main engines: Diesel-electric; 1 shaft; 3 000 bhp = 15 knots
Complement: 85

Launched on 22 June 1943. Transferred on 1 July 1971.

SERGENTO ALDEA   1976, Chilean Navy

92 CHILE

LIGHT FORCES
4 LÜRSSEN TYPE (FAST ATTACK CRAFT—TORPEDO)

Name	No.	Builders	Commissioned
GUACOLDA	80	Bazan, Cadiz	30 July 1965
FRESIA	81	Bazan, Cadiz	9 Dec 1965
QUIDORA	82	Bazan, Cadiz	1966
TEGUALDA	83	Bazan, Cadiz	1966

Displacement, tons: 134
Dimensions, feet (metres): 118·1 × 18·4 × 7·2 (36 × 5·6 × 2·2)
Guns: 2—40 mm
Torpedo tubes: 4—21 in
Main engines: Diesels; 2 shafts; 4 800 bhp = 32 knots
Range, miles: 1 500 at 15 knots
Complement: 20

Built to German Lürssen design.

QUIDORA (*Tegualda* and *Guacolda* behind)   1976, Chilean Navy

1 US "PC-1638" CLASS (LARGE PATROL CRAFT)

Name	No.	Builders	Commissioned
PAPUDO (ex-US *PC 1646*)	37	Asmar, Talcahuano	27 Nov 1971

Displacement, tons: 450 full load
Dimensions, feet (metres): 173·0 × 23·0 × 10·2 (52·7 × 7 × 3·1)
Guns: 1—40 mm; 4—20 mm (twins)
A/S weapons: 1 Mk 15 Trainable Hedgehog; 2 "K" DCT; 4 DC racks
Main engines: 2 diesels; 2 shafts; 2 800 bhp = 19 knots
Complement: 69 (4 officers, 65 men)

Of similar design to the Turkish "Hisar" class built to the US PC plan.

PAPUDO   1976, Chilean Navy

2 LARGE PATROL CRAFT

Name	No.	Builders	Commissioned
MARINERO FUENTEALBA	75	Asmar, Talcahuano	22 July 1966
CABO ODGER	76	Asmar, Talcahuano	21 April 1967

Displacement, tons: 215
Dimensions, feet (metres): 80 × 21 × 9 (24·4 × 6·4 × 2·7)
Guns: 1—20 mm; 3—12·7 mm MG
Main engines: 1 Cummins diesel 340 hp = 9 knots
Range, miles: 2 600 at 9 knots
Complement: 19

Cabo Odger damaged in collision with Chilean M/V *Condor* 26 Jan 1977.

MARINERO FUENTEALBA   1972, Chilean Navy

2 COASTAL PATROL CRAFT

Two 32 ft Equity Standard Craft delivered in 1968. Diesel; 400 hp = 35 knots.

AMPHIBIOUS FORCES
3 Ex-US "LST 1-510" and "511-1152" SERIES

Name	No.	Builders	Commissioned
COMANDANTE HEMMERDINGER (ex-USS *New London County*, LST 1066)	88	Bethlehem Steel, Hingham, Mass	20 Mar 1945
COMANDANTE ARAYA (ex-USS *Nye County*, LST 1067)	89	Bethlehem Steel, Hingham, Mass	24 Mar 1945
AGUILA (ex-USS *Aventinus ARVE 3*, ex-LST 1092)	91	American Bridge Co, Ambridge	19 May 1945

Displacement, tons: 1 653 standard; 4 080 full load
Dimensions, feet (metres): 328 × 50 × 14 (100 × 15·3 × 4·3)
Guns: Fitted for 8—40 mm
Main engines: GM diesels; 1 700 shp; 2 shafts = 11·6 knots
Complement: approx 110

Nos 88 and 89 transferred 29 Aug 1973. No 91 was a conversion to Aircraft Repair Ship and was transferred to Chile in 1963 under MAP. After various employments all are now available for amphibious duties.

CHILE 93

1 Ex-US LCM

VALDIVIA 86

Survivor of three transferred in 1960 (*Pisagua* 85 and *Junin* 87 deleted).

6 Ex-US LCVPs

Transferred in 1960.

2 CHILEAN LANDING CRAFT

Name	No.	Builders	Commissioned
ELICURA	90	Talcahuano	10 Dec 1968
OROMPELLO	94	Dade Dry Dock Co, Miami	15 Sep 1964

Displacement, tons: 290 light; 750 full load
Dimensions, feet (metres): 138 wl; 145 oa × 34 × 12·8 *(44·2 × 10·4 × 3·9)*
Guns: 3—20 mm *(Elicura)*
Main engines: Diesels; 2 shafts; 900 bhp = 10·5 knots
Oil fuel (tons): 77
Range, miles: 2 900 at 9 knots
Complement: 20

Orompello was built for the Chilean Government in Miami, *Elicura* was launched on 21 April 1967.

OROMPELLO   1971, Chilean Navy

SUBMARINE DEPOT SHIP

Name	No.	Builders	Commissioned
ANGAMOS (ex-M/V *Puerto Montt,*— ex-M/V *Kobenhavn*)		Orenst & Koppel, Germany	1966

Measurement, tons: 4 616 gross
Dimensions, feet (metres): 308·2 × 53·2 × 13·6 *(93·92 × 16·20 × 4·15)*
Main engines: 2 Lind-Pielstick diesels; 6 500 hp = 17 knots

Acquired from Chilean state shipping company early 1977 for conversion to submarine depot ship.
Former Chilean and Danish ferryboat.

SURVEY SHIP

1 Ex-US "CHEROKEE" CLASS

Name	No.	Builders	Commissioned
YELCHO (ex-USS *Tekesta,* ATF 93)	64	Commercial Iron Works, Portland, Oregon	16 Aug 1943

Displacement, tons: 1 235 standard; 1 675 full load
Dimensions, feet (metres): 195 wl; 205 oa × 38·5 × 15·5 *(62·5 × 11·7 × 4·7)*
Guns: 2—40 mm
Main engines: 4 diesels/diesel-electric; 1 shaft; 3 000 bhp = 15 knots
Complement: 85

Fitted with powerful pumps and other salvage equipment. *Yelcho* was laid down on 7 Sep 1942, launched on 20 Mar 1943 and loaned to Chile by the USA on 15 May 1960, having since been employed as Antarctic research ship and surveying vessel.

YELCHO   1972, Chilean Navy

TRAINING SHIP

Name	No.	Builders	Commissioned
ESMERALDA (ex-*Don John de Austria*)	43	Echevarietta, Cadiz	1952

Displacement, tons: 3 040 standard; 3 673 full load
Dimensions, feet (metres): 308·8 oa × 43 × 23 *(94·1 × 13·1 ×7)*
Guns: 2—57 mm (saluting)
Sail area: Total 26 910 sq feet
Main engines: 1 Fiat auxiliary diesel; 1 shaft; 1 400 bhp = 11 knots
Range, miles: 8 000 at 8 knots
Complement: 271 plus 80 cadets

Four-masted schooner originally intended for the Spanish Navy. Transferred to Chile on 12 May 1953. Near sister ship of *Juan Sebastian de Elcano* in the Spanish Navy. Replaced transport *Presidente Pinto* as training ship. Refitted Saldanha Bay, South Africa, 1977.

ESMERALDA   1974, Chilean Navy

TRANSPORTS

Name	No.	Builders	Commissioned
AQUILES (ex-*Tjaldur*)	47	Aalborg Vaerft, Denmark	1953

Measurement, tons: 2 660 registered; 1 462 net; 1 395 deadweight
Dimensions, feet (metres): 288 × 44 × 17 *(87·8 × 13·4 × 5·2)*
Gun: 1—?40 mm
Main engines: 1 Slow Burmeister & Wain diesel; 3 600 bhp = 16 knots
Range, miles: 5 500 at 16 knots
Complement: 60 crew plus 447 troops

Ex-Danish M/V *Tjaldur* bought by Chile in 1967.

AQUILES   1976, Chilean Navy

94 CHILE

Name	No.	Builders	Commissioned
PILOTO PARDO	45	Haarlemsche Scheepsbouw, Netherlands	1959

Displacement, tons: 1 250 light; 2 000 standard; 3 000 full load
Dimensions, feet (metres): 269 × 39 × 15 (82 × 11·9 × 4·6)
Aircraft: 1 helicopter
Guns: 1—101 mm 50 cal; 2—20 mm
Main engines: 2 diesel-electric; 2 000 hp = 14 knots
Range, miles: 6 000 at 10 knots
Complement: 44 (plus 24 passengers)

Antarctic patrol ship, transport and research vessel with reinforced hull to navigate in ice. Launched 11 June 1958.

PILOTO PARDO   1974, Chilean Navy

Name	No.	Builders	Commissioned
METEORO	110	Asmar, Talcahuano	1967

Displacement, tons: 205
Main engines: Diesel = 8 knots

Ferry—capacity 220.

Name	No.	Builders	Commissioned
CIRUJANO VIDELA	111	Asmar, Talcahuano	1964

Displacement, tons: 140
Dimensions, feet (metres): 101·7 × 21·3 × 6·6 (31 × 6·5 × 2)
Main engines: Diesel; 700 hp = 14 knots

Hospital and dental facilities are fitted. A modified version of US PGM 59 design with larger superstructure and less power.

TANKERS

Name	No.	Builders	Commissioned
ARAUCANO	53	Burmeister & Wain, Copenhagen	10 Jan 1967

Displacement, tons: 17 300
Measurement, tons: 18 030 deadweight
Dimensions, feet (metres): 497·6 × 74·9 × 28·8 (151·7 × 22·8 × 8·8)
Guns: 8—40 mm (twin)
Main engines: B and W diesels; 10 800 bhp = 15·5 knots (17 on trial)
Range, miles: 12 000 at 15·5 knots

Launched on 21 June 1966.

ARAUCANO   1972, US Navy

1 Ex-US "PATAPSCO" CLASS

Name	No.	Builders	Commissioned
BEAGLE (ex-USS *Genesee*, AOG 8)	54	Cargill Inc, Savage, Minn.	27 May 1944

Displacement, tons: 4 240 standard
Dimensions, feet (metres): 310 × 48·7 × 16 (94·5 × 14·9 × 4·9)
Guns: 2—3 inch 50 cal; 4—20 mm
Range, miles: 6 690 at 10 knots

Transferred on loan 5 July 1972.

BEAGLE   1972, Chilean Navy

MISCELLANEOUS

TUGS

Name	No.	Builders	Commissioned
COLOCOLO	73	Bow, McLachlan & Co, Paisley	1930

Displacement, tons: 790
Dimensions, feet (metres): 126·5 × 27·0 × 12·0 (38·6 × 8·2 × 3·7)
Main engines: Triple expansion; 1 050 ihp = 11 knots
Oil fuel, tons: 155

Formerly classed as coastguard vessel. Rebuilt in 1962-63. Last of class of five.

Name	No.	Builders	Commissioned
GALVEZ	—	Southern Shipbuilders Ltd, Faversham, England	June 1975

Measurement, tons: 112 gross
Dimensions, feet (metres): 83·6 × 24 × 9·2 (25·5 × 7·3 × 2·8)

Dockyard tug in Talcahuano.

ANCUD 104   CAUPOLICAN 127
MONREAL 105   CORTEZ 128
         REYES 120

Note: Tug HMS *Samson* was reported sold to Chile in 1974 but is still laid up in Portsmouth.

FLOATING DOCKS

2 Ex-US ARD

INGENIERO MERY (ex-US *ARD 25*) 131
MUTILLA (ex-US *ARD 32*) 132

Displacement, tons: 5 200
Capacity, tons: 3 000
Dimensions, feet (metres): 492 × 84 × 5·7 to 33·2 (150·0 × 25·6 × 1·7 to 10·1)

Mutilla leased to Chile 15 Dec 1960. *Ingeniero Mery* transferred 20 Aug 1973.

2 Floating Cranes of 30 and 180 tons lift are at Talcahuano.

AUXILIARIES

Notes: (a) *Huascar*, completed 1865, previously Peruvian, now harbour flagship at Talcahuano.
(b) Two new ships, *Castor* and *Sobenes*, now listed.

CHINA (People's Republic)

Administration

Minister of National Defence:
  Yeh Chien-ying

Headquarters Appointments

Commander-in-Chief of the Navy:
  Hsiao Ching Kuang
Deputy Commander-in-Chief and 1st Political Commissar:
  Su Chen-Hua
2nd Political Commissar:
  Wang Hung-K'un
Chief of Staff:
  P'an Yen

Fleet Commanders

North Sea Fleet:
  Ma Chung-Ch'uan
East Sea Fleet:
  Mei Chia-Sheng
South Sea Fleet:
  Kuei Shao-Pin

Diplomatic Representation

Defence and Naval Attaché in London:
  Fang Wen

Personnel

(a) 1978: 192 000 officers and men, plus 30 000 naval air force and 28 000 marines.
(b) 6 years national service.

Training

Carried out at following schools/academies:
Shanghai:
  Officer Training School
  Naval Aviation School
  Coastal Artillery School
  Supply School
  Radar School
  School of Naval Architecture
  Fleet Training Centre (Ratings)
Dairen:
  Naval Academy
  Mining School
Nanking:
  War College
  Ratings Training School
Tsingtao:
  Naval Aviation School
  Main Ratings Training School
  Submarine School
Lushua:
  Submarine School
Yulin:
  Submarine School

Minor ratings' schools at Wei Hai Wee, An' Ching, Foochow, Chusan and Hangchow.

Bases

North Sea Fleet: Tsingtao (HQ), Lu Shun, Wei Hai Hui, Ching San, Luta, Hu Lu Tao, Hsiao Ping Tao
East Sea Fleet: Shanghai (HQ), Chusan, Tai Shan, Ta Hsieh Tao, Hsia Men, Wen Chou, Hai Men, Ma Wei, Fu Chou
South Sea Fleet: Chan Chiang (HQ), Yu Lin, Hai Kou, Huang Pu/Canton, Shan Tou, Pei Hai
(The fleet is split with the main emphasis on the North Sea Fleet).

Strength of the Fleet

Type	Active	Building
Fleet Submarines	1	?
Missile Firing Submarine	1	—
Patrol Submarines	75	6
Destroyers (DDG)	9	2
Frigates	14	4?
Fast Attack Craft (Missile)	162	20
Fast Attack Craft (Gun)	404	10?
Fast Attack Craft (Torpedo)	200	10?
Fast Attack Craft (Patrol)	23	4
Large Patrol Craft	21	—
Coastal Patrol Craft	100+	?
Minesweepers (Ocean)	17	—
Landing Ships (LST)	15	—
LSMs	14	?
LSILs	15	—
LCTs	17	—
LCMs—LCUs	450	—
Survey & Research Ships	20	—
Supply Ships	24 (+12?)	—
Tankers (small)	18	—
Boom Defence Vessels	6	—
Escorts (old)	15	—
Repair Ship	1	—
Misc. Small Craft	375	—

General

While studying this section it must be remembered that not only is there a steady building programme of all classes in the modernised Chinese Yards but also the Chinese have an advanced nuclear and missile capability. This combination will make the Chinese navy, already more than twice as strong in manpower as the Royal Navy, an important element in the future balance of power East of Suez.
Recently there has been evidence of delays in all the new building programmes except Submarines and Light Forces. Whether this is due to problems of weapon production, faults discovered in new construction ships or a straight political decision is not known. It is of interest that these delays appear to date from 1972, shortly after the flight and death of Lin Piao, the Defence Minister under whom the programmes were presumably generated. This may be coincidence but the plain fact is that the main emphasis today is on defensive units rather than the long-range forces whose design must have started in the mid or early 1960s.
Recent changes in government policy on foreign purchases have been reflected in interest being shown in European markets. This is believed to include equipment for ships of up to 10 000 tons.

Naval Air Force

With 30 000 officers and men and over 600 aircraft, this is a considerable land-based naval air force. Equipped with about 200-300 MIG 17 and 19 (and possibly MIG 21) fighter aircraft and SA2-SAM, with 150 IL 28 Torpedo bombers, Tu-2 bombers, Madge flying boats, Hound M14 helicopters and transport and communication aircraft this is primarily a defensive force.

Mercantile Marine

Lloyd's Register of Shipping:
  622 vessels of 4 245 446 tons gross

Naval Radars

Code Name	Frequency	Function	Fitting
Ball End	E/F	Surface Warning	Kaibokan and other escorts
Ball Gun	E/F	Surface Warning	Kronshtadt, T 43, Kiangnan
Cross Bird	G	Early Warning	Gordy
Cross Slot		Early Warning	Luta, Chang Ch'iang
Decca 707	I	Surface Search	Corvettes, Light Forces
Drum Tilt	I	Armament Control	Osa
High Pole A	G	IFF	General
Mina	I	Fire Control	Gordy 130mm
Neptun	I	Navigation	General
Post Lamp	I	Fire Control	Luta
Pot Head	I	Surface Search	Hai Nan, Kronshtadt, Light Forces
Skinhead	I	Surface Search	Light Forces
Ski Pole	G	IFF	Gordy
Slim Net	E/F	Surface Warning	Riga
Square Tie	I	Fire Control	Gordy, Luta, Riga, Osa
Sun Visor	I	Fire Control	Riga
Wok Won	I	Fire Control	Kiangnan

DELETIONS

1976 10 "P4" class, 1 "Shantung" class, 10 "Swatow" class, 5 "Whampoa" class, 4 ex-US YMS, 2 ex-Japanese AMS.
1977 20 "P4" class, 10 "Swatow" class, 10 "Whampoa" class.
(Where other alterations of numbers occur this is as a result of more up-to-date information).

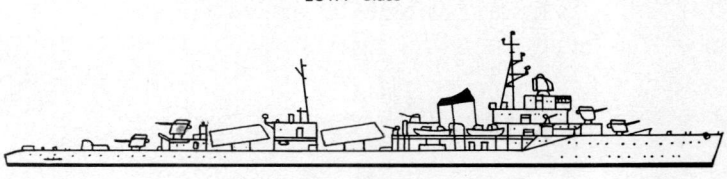

"LUTA" Class

"ANSHAN" Class

"KIANG NAN" Class

"CH'ENG TU" Class

"KRONSHTADT" Class

96 CHINA

SUBMARINES

Reports suggest the construction of at least one nuclear submarine. This combined with the known Chinese capability to build liquid-fuelled rockets of the MRBM, IRBM and ICBM types and the completion of a solid-propellant factory, suggests that the forecast of a Chinese ballistic-missile nuclear submarine in the early 1980s may not be out of the question.

1 "HAN" CLASS

This is the first possible Chinese nuclear submarine. With an Albacore hull the first of this class was probably laid down in 1971-72. Her construction may have been delayed if problems were encountered with the power plant, but she appears to have run trials in 1974. Existence of second "Han" class is reported but not confirmed. Built at Luta.

Displacement, tons: Possibly about 1 500 tons standard
Length, feet: Possibly about 250 feet
Armament: Possibly 6—21 in tubes
Main machinery: Probably diesels and main motors

2 "MING" CLASS

First believed to have been laid down in 1971-72 which would give an operational date around late 1974 or 1975.

1 SOVIET "GOLF" CLASS (BALLISTIC MISSILE TYPE)

Displacement, tons: 2 350 surfaced; 2 800 dived
Length, feet (metres): 320·0 (97·5)
Beam, feet (metres): 25·1 (7·6)
Draught, feet (metres): 22·0 (6·7)
Missile launchers: 3 vertical tubes
Torpedo tubes: 10—21 in (533 mm) bow
Main machinery: 3 diesels, total 6 000 hp; 3 shafts
    3 electric motors, total 6 000 hp
Speed, knots: 20 surfaced; 17 dived
Range, miles: 22 700 surfaced; cruising
Complement: 86 (1 officers, 74 men)

Ballistic missile submarine similar to the Soviet "Golf" class. Built at Dairen in 1964. The missile tubes are fitted in the conning tower. It is not known whether this boat has been fitted with missiles, although it is possible in the future and well within Chinese technical capability (see note above concerning SLBMs).

"GOLF" Class   1972

51 Ex-SOVIET AND CHINESE "ROMEO" CLASS (PATROL TYPE)

Displacement, tons: 1 100 surfaced; 1 600 dived
Length, feet (metres): 246·0 (75·0)
Beam, feet (metres): 24 (7·3)
Draught, feet (metres): 14·5 (4·4)
Torpedo tubes: 6—21 in (bow) 18 torpedoes
Main machinery: 2 diesels; total 4 000 hp; 2 electric motors;
    total 4 000 hp; 2 shafts
Speed, knots: 17 surfaced; 14 dived
Complement: 65

The Chinese are now building their own Soviet designed "Romeo" class submarines possibly at a rate of 6 a year at Kuang Chou/Canton, Kiangnan/Shanghai and Wu Chang. Above details are for Soviet "Romeo" of which possibly four were transferred in early 1960. It is reliably reported that the Chinese variant is larger—1 400 tons surfaced/1 800 dived, 6 feet longer, armed with 8 torpedo tubes and capable of carrying 36 mines in lieu of torpedoes.

"ROMEO" Class   1975

21 SOVIET "WHISKEY" CLASS (PATROL TYPE)

Displacement, tons: 1 030 surfaced; 1 180 dived
Length, feet (metres): 240 (73·2)
Beam, feet (metres): 22 (6·7)
Draught, feet (metres): 15 (4·6)
Guns: 2—25 mm (twin) in some at base of fin
Torpedo tubes: 6—21 in (533 mm); 4 bow 2 stern (20 torpedoes or 40 mines)
Main machinery: Diesel-electric; 2 shafts; 4 000 bhp diesels; 2 500 hp electric motors
Speed, knots: 17 surfaced; 15 dived
Range, miles: 13 000 at 8 knots surfaced
Complement: 60

Equipped with snort. Assembled from Soviet components in Chinese yards between 1956 and 1964.

"WHISKEY" Class   1974

1 Ex-SOVIET "S-1" CLASS (PATROL TYPE)

Displacement, tons: 840 surfaced; 1 050 dived
Torpedo tubes: 6—21 in (533 mm)
Main machinery: 4 200 hp diesels; 2 200 hp electric motors

Launched in 1939. Transferred from the USSR in 1955. One deleted. Last of class now harbour training boat.

CHINA 97

DESTROYERS

5 + 2 "LUTA" CLASS (DDG)

Name	No.	Builders	Laid down	Launched	Commissioned
—	240	Dairen (Luta)	—	—	1971
—	241	Dairen (Luta)	—	—	1972
—	242	Dairen (Luta)	—	—	1972
—	243	Dairen (Luta)	—	—	1973
—	244	Dairen (Luta)	—	—	1975
—	245	Dairen (Luta)	—	—	—
—	246	Dairen (Luta)	—	—	—

Displacement, tons: 3 250 standard; 3 750 full load
Dimensions, feet (metres): 430 × 45 × 15 *(131 × 13·7 × 4·6)*
Missile launchers: 2 Triple SS-N-2 type
Guns: 4—130 mm (2 twins) 4—57 mm; 8—25 mm
A/S weapons: 2—A/S rocket launchers
Main engines: Geared turbines; 60 000 shp
Speed: 32+
Range, miles (estimated): 4 000 at 15 knots
Complement (approx): 300

The first Chinese-designed destroyers of such a capability to be built. Of similarity to Soviet "Kotlin" class. The programme has been much retarded since 1971 which, possibly coincidentally, marked the death of Lin Piao. Although capable of foreign deployment none so far reported. Three of this class serve in the South Sea Fleet.

Radar: Air search: Cross Slot.
Fire control, guns: Wasphead, Post Lamp.
Fire control, missiles: Square Tie.
Navigation: Neptun.

"LUTA" Class   *1972, Chinese*

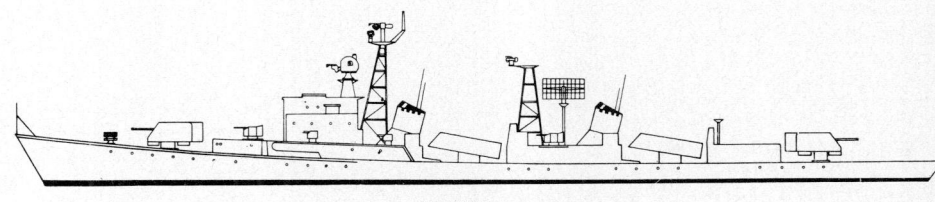

"LUTA" Class

"LUTA" Class   *1973*

4 "ANSHAN" (Ex-SOVIET "GORDY") CLASS

Name	No.	Builders	Laid down	Launched	Commissioned
ANSHAN	—	USSR	—	1936-41	1939-43
CHANG CHUN	—	USSR	—	1936-41	1939-43
CHI LIN	—	USSR	—	1936-41	1939-43
FU CHUN	—	USSR	—	1936-41	1939-43

Displacement, tons: 1 657 standard; 2 040 full load
Length, feet (metres): 357·7 *(109·0)* pp; 370 *(112·8)* oa
Beam, feet (metres): 33·5 *(10·2)*
Draught, feet (metres): 13 *(4·0)*
Missile launchers: 2 twin SS-N-2 type
Guns: 4—5·1 in *(130 mm)*; 8—37 mm (twins)
A/S weapons: 2 DC racks
Main engines: Tosi geared turbines; 48 000 shp; 2 shafts
Boilers: 3-drum type
Speed, knots: 32
Oil fuel, tons: 540
Range, miles: 2 600 at 19 knots
Complement: 200

Gordy Type 7 of Odero-Terni-Orlando design. Fitted for minelaying. Two transferred in Dec 1954 and two in July 1955.

Conversion: All converted between 1971 and 1974. The alterations consist of the replacement of the torpedo tubes by a pair of twin SS-N-2 launchers and the fitting of twin 37 mm mounts in place of the original singles.

Radar: Air search: Cross Bird.
Fire control: Square Tie.
Navigation: Neptun.
IFF: Ski Pole.

CHANG CHUN (before conversion)   *Hajime Fukaya*

"ANSHAN" Class (after conversion)

98 CHINA

FRIGATES

3 + 2 "KIANG HU" CLASS

Builders	Laid down	Launched	Commissioned
Shanghai	1974	1975	1976
Shanghai	1974	1975	1976
Shanghai	1975	1976	1977

Name	No.
—	521
—	525
—	—

Displacement, tons: 1 800 approx
Dimensions, feet (metres): 350 × 40 approx *(106 × 21)*
Missiles: 2 twin SS-N-2 type
Guns: 4—3·9 in *(100 mm)* (twins); 8—37 mm

Appears to be a modification of "Kiang Tung" class.

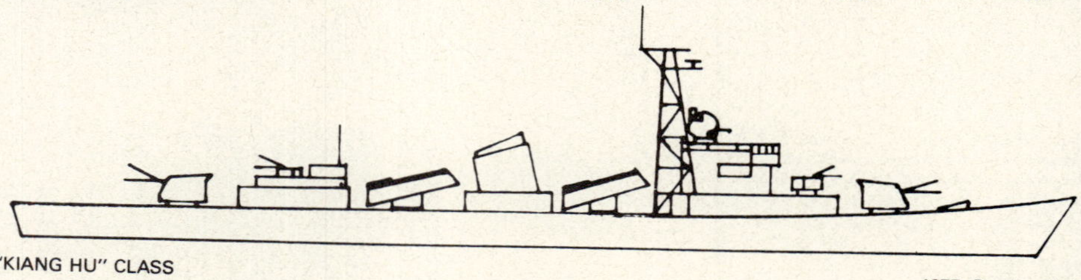

"KIANG HU" CLASS   1977, Bradley Hahn

2 + 2(?) "KIANG TUNG" CLASS

Builders	Laid down	Launched	Commissioned
Hutang-Shanghai	1971	1973	1977
Hutang-Shanghai	1972	1974	?

Name	No.
CHUNG TUNG	—
—	—

Displacement, tons: 1 800 tons standard
Dimensions, feet (metres): 350 × 40 approx *(106 × 12)*
Missiles: 2 twin SAM
Guns: 4—3·9 in *(100 mm)* twin; 8—37 mm (twins)
A/S weapons: 2 MBU 1 800; 2 DCT
Main engines: Diesel = ? 28 knots

There have apparently been no further additions to this class—further evidence of the delays in new construction of major surface ships. First SAM armed Chinese ships, a missile which may have caused problems when first introduced.

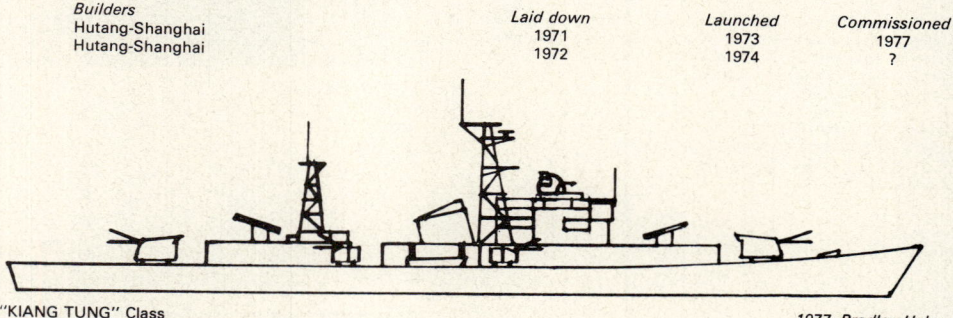

"KIANG TUNG" Class   1977, Bradley Hahn

5 "KIANG NAN" CLASS

Builders	Laid down	Launched	Commissioned
Kuang-Chou, Canton	1965	Jan 1966	1967
Kuang-Chou, Canton	1965	—	1967
Kuang-Chou, Canton	1966	—	1968
Kuang-Chou, Canton	1966	—	1968
Kuang-Chou, Canton	1967	—	1969

Name	No.
—	209
—	214
—	231
—	232
—	233

Displacement, tons: 1 350 standard; 1 600 full load
Length, feet (metres): 298 *(90·8)*
Beam, feet (metres): 33·5 *(10·2)*
Draught, feet (metres): 11 *(3·4)*
Guns: 3—3·9 in *(100 mm)* 56 cal, 1 forward, 2 aft;
  6—37 mm (twin); 4—12·7 mm (twin)
A/S weapons: 2 MBU 1 800; 4 DCT; 2 DC racks
Main engines: Diesels; 24 000 shp
Speed, knots: 28
Complement: 175

The Chinese Navy embarked on a new building programme in 1965 of which this class was the first. One of this class was reported as engaged with South Viet-Nam forces on 19-20 January 1974.

Mines: Reported to have a minelaying capability.

"KIANG NAN" Class   1973

Radar: Surface warning: Ball Gun.
Navigation: Neptun.
Fire control: Wok Won.

4 "CH'ENG TU" (Ex-SOVIET "RIGA") CLASS

Builders	Laid down	Launched	Commissioned
—	—	—	1958
Hutang, Shanghai	1955	26 Sept 1956	1959
—	—	1957	1959
Hutang, Shanghai	1955	28 April 1956	1958

Name	No.
KUEI LIN	204
KUEI YANG	205
K'UN MING	206
CH'ENG TU	207

Displacement, tons: 1 200 standard; 1 600 full load
Length, feet (metres): 298·8 *(91)* oa
Beam, feet (metres): 33·7 *(10·2)*
Draught, feet (metres): 10 *(3·0)*
Missile launchers: 1 twin SS-N-2 type
Guns: 3—3·9 in *(100 mm)* (single); 4—37 mm
A/S weapons: 4 DC projectors
Mines: 50 capacity, fitted with rails
Main engines: Geared turbines; 2 shafts; 25 000 shp
Boilers: 2
Speed, knots: 28
Oil fuel, tons: 300
Range, miles: 2 000 at 10 knots
Complement: 150

Assembled from Soviet components.
All had light tripod mast and high superstructure, but later converted with heavier mast and larger bridge. Similar to the Soviet "Riga" class frigates. Two were redesigned with modified superstructure.

Conversion: Two started conversion in 1971 for the replacement of the torpedo tubes by a twin SS-N-2 launcher. All now converted.

Radar: Surface warning: Slim Net.
Fire control: Sun Visor for Guns, Square Tie for missiles.
Navigation: Neptun.

"RIGA" Class (before conversion)   1971

ESCORTS

Note: It is reported that the majority of these escorts are, in fact, not only still in commission but have been refitted and rearmed.

Class	Total	Names	No.	Displacement tons, standard	Speed (knots)	Guns	Launched	Range, miles	Complement
Ex-Japanese "Kamishima"	1	—	391	766	16	2—3 in 6—37 mm	1945	2 400 at 11 knots	130 (est)
Ex-Japanese "Ukuru"	1	HUI AN (ex-*Shisaka*)	218	940	19·5	3—3·9 in 6—37 mm	1943	5 000 at 16 knots	—
Ex-Japanese "Etorofu"	1	CHANG PI (ex-*Oki*)	—	870	19	3—3·9 in 3—37 mm	1942	8 000 at 16 knots	—
Ex-Japanese "Hashidate"	1	NAN CHANG (ex-*Uji II*)	—	999	19·5	2—5·1 in 6—37 mm	1940	3 460 at 14 knots	—
Ex-Japanese "C"/Kaibokan I	2	— (ex-*Shen Yang*) — (ex-*Chi-An*)	— —	745	15·5	2—3·9 in 6—37 mm (single) 4/8—25 mm	1945	6 500 at 14 knots	145
Ex-Japanese "D"/Kaibokan II	5	TUNG AN (ex-*Jap 192*) CHIANG SHA (ex-*Chieh 12*) CHI NAN (ex-*Chieh 6*) HSI AN (ex-*Chieh 14*) WU CHANG (ex-*Chieh 5*)	215 216 217 219 220	740	17·5	2—3 in or 8—37 mm (single) 4/8—25 mm	1944 to 1945	4 500 at 14 knots	145
Ex-British "Castle"	1	KUANG CHOU (ex-HMS *Hever Castle*, ex-HMCS *Koppercliff*)	602	1 100	16·5	2—3·9 in 10—37 mm	1944	5 400 at 9·5 knots	120
Ex-British "Flower"	1	LIN I (ex-HMS *Heliotrope*)	213	1 020	16	2—3·9 inch 4—37 mm	1941	—	—
Ex-Australian "Bathurst"	1	LOYANG (ex-HMAS *Bendigo*)	—	815	15	2—3·9 in 4—37 mm	1941	4 300 at 10 knots	100
—	1	CHANG CHIANG (ex-*Hsien Nin*)	53/219	418	16	4—37 mm (twin)	1928	—	50?

HUI AN   1974

LIGHT FORCES

?2 "HAI DAU" CLASS

Displacement, tons: 300(?)
Dimensions, feet (metres): 155 × 23 × 6·5 *(47 × 7 × 2)*
Missiles: 6 SS-N-2 type
Guns: 4—57 mm (twins)
Main engines: Possibly 1 gas turbine and 2 diesels; 3 shafts = ?35 knots
Complement: possibly 40

First seen in a film sequence. Has an air intake some 15 feet high as well as radar, EW and communication aerials. If this is a new design, rather than an experimental class or film prop it is a radical departure and might have top-weight problems.

HAI DAU   1975, Bradley Hahn

80 SOVIET and CHINESE "OSA" CLASS
(FAST ATTACK CRAFT—MISSILE)

Displacement, tons: 165 standard; 200 full load
Dimensions, feet (metres): 128·7 × 25·1 × 5·9 *(39·3 × 7·7 × 1·8)*
Missiles: 4 SS-N-2 system launchers in two pairs abreast aft
Guns: 4—25 mm (2 twin, 1 forward and 1 aft) (30 mm in first four)
Main engines: 3 diesels; 13 000 bhp = 32 knots
Range, miles: 800 at 25 knots
Complement: 25

It was reported in Jan 1965 that one "Osa" class guided missile patrol boat had joined the Navy from the USSR. Four more were acquired in 1966-67, and two in 1968. A building programme of 10 boats a year in China is assumed. The only boat of the "Hola" class, a Chinese variant of the "Osa", has now joined the fleet. The chief differences are the fitting of a radome aft, (this may be a prototype for new missile guidance radar), no guns, slightly larger dimensions, and a folding mast.

Radar: Square Tie and Drum Tilt in "Osas".

"OSA" Class   1972

100 CHINA

4 + 76 SOVIET "KOMAR" and CHINESE "HOKU" CLASS
(FAST ATTACK CRAFT—MISSILE)

Displacement, tons: 70 standard; 80 full load
Dimensions, feet (metres): 83·7 oa × 19·8 × 5 (25·5 × 6 × 1·5)
Missiles: 2 SS-N-2 system launchers
Guns: 2—25 mm (1 twin forward)
Main engines: Diesels; 2 shafts; 4 800 bhp = 40 knots

One "Komar" class was reported as joining the fleet from the USSR in 1965. Two or three more were delivered in 1967. A building programme of 10 a year is assumed of the "Hoku" class a Chinese variant of the "Komar" with a steel hull instead of wooden. The chief external difference is the siting of the launchers clear of the bridge and further inboard, eliminating sponsons and use of pole instead of lattice mast. A hydrofoil variant has also been reported "Homa".

Transfers: 4 to Albania, 1976.

"KOMAR" Class   1972

20 "KRONSHTADT" CLASS (LARGE PATROL CRAFT)

Nos 251 252 253 261 262 263 264 265 266 286 + 10

Displacement, tons: 310 standard; 380 full load
Dimensions, feet (metres): 170·6 × 21·5 × 9 (52 × 6·5 × 2·7)
Guns: 1—3·5 in; 2—37 mm; 6—12·7 mm
A/S weapons: 2 rocket launchers; 2 DC racks
Mines: 2 rails for 8-10 mines
Main engines: Diesels; 2 shafts; 3 300 shp = 24 knots
Range, miles: 1 500 at 12 knots
Complement: 65

Six built in 1950-53 were received from USSR in 1956-57. Remainder were built at Shanghai and Canton, with 12 completed in 1956. The last was completed in 1957. A number of these may now be non-operational.

Radar: Ball Gun.

"KRONSHTADT" Class firing Rocket Launchers   1972

23 "HAINAN" CLASS (FAST ATTACK CRAFT—PATROL)

Nos 267—285 +4

Displacement, tons: 360 standard, 400 full load
Dimensions, feet (metres): 197 oa × 24 × 6·1 (60 × 7·4 × 2·1)
Guns: 2—3 in (fore and aft); 4—25 mm (twins)
A/S weapons: 4—MBU 1 800; 2 DCT; 2 DC racks
Mines: Rails fitted
Main engines: Diesels; 8 000 shp
Speed, knots: 28
Range, miles: 1 000 at 10 knots (est)
Complement: 60 (est)

Chinese built. Low freeboard. The 25 mm guns are abaft the bridge. Programme started 1963-64 and continues—probably 4 per year.

Radar: Pot Head in most ships, Skin Head in others.

"HAI NAN" Class   1976

1 Ex-US 170 ft TYPE (LARGE PATROL CRAFT)

Displacement, tons: 280 standard; 450 full load
Dimensions, feet (metres): 173·5 × 23 × 10·8 (52·9 × 7 × 3·3)
Guns: 2—3 in (76 mm) (single); 3—37 mm (single)
A/S weapons: 2 DC racks; 1 DC rail
Main engines: 2 diesels; 2 880 bhp; 2 shafts = 20 knots
Range, miles: 3 000 at 15 knots
Complement: 70

Transferred 1947. Partially rearmed in 1950s. Used for training in South Sea Fleet.

25 "SHANGHAI" CLASS TYPE I (FAST ATTACK CRAFT—GUN)

Displacement, tons: 100 full load
Dimensions, feet (metres): 115 × 18 × 5·5 (35·1 × 5·5 × 1·7)
Guns: 1—57 mm (forward); 2—37 mm (twin, aft)
Torpedo tubes: Twin 18 in (originally in some—now removed)
A/S armament: 8 DCs
Mines: Minerails can be fitted
Main engines: 4 diesels; 4 800 bhp = 28 knots
Complement: 25

The prototype of these boats appeared in 1959. Main difference from successors is lack of midships guns.

Radar: Skin Head.

6 "HAI KOU" CLASS (FAST ATTACK CRAFT—GUN)

Displacement, tons: 160 standard; 175 full load (est)
Dimensions, feet (metres): 150 × 21 × 7 (est) (45·7 × 6·4 × 2·1)
Guns: 4—37 mm (twin); 4—25 mm (twin, vertical)
Main engines: Diesel = 30 knots (?)
Range, miles: 850 at 20 knots (est)

Believed built in 1960s on enlarged "Shanghai" hull.

"HAI KOU" Class   1976

CHINA 101

340 "SHANGHAI" CLASS TYPE II (FAST ATTACK CRAFT—GUN)

Displacement, tons: 120 standard; 155 full load
Dimensions, feet (metres): 128 × 18 × 5·6 *(39 × 5·5 × 1·7)*
Guns: 4—37 mm (twin); 4—25 mm (twin)
   Note: In some boats a twin 75 mm recoilless rifle is mounted forward
A/S weapons: 8 DCs
Mines: Minerails can be fitted but probably for no more than 10 mines
Main engines: 4 diesels; 4 800 bhp = 30 knots
Complement: 25

Construction continues at Shanghai and other yards at rate of about 10 a year.

Appearance: The three types vary slightly in the outline of their bridges.

Radar: Skin Head.

Transfers: 6 to Albania, 2 to Cameroon in 1976, 3 to Congo, 4 to Guinea, 15 to North Korea, 12 to Pakistan, 5 to Sri Lanka in 1972, 2 to Sierra Leone in 1973, 6 to Tanzania in 1970-71, 4 to North Viet Nam in May 1966, + Romanian craft of indigenous construction.

"SHANGHAI II" Class   *1974, Bradley Hahn*

"SHANGHAI II" Class   *1970*

30 "SWATOW" CLASS (FAST ATTACK CRAFT—GUN)

Displacement, tons: 80 full load
Dimensions, feet (metres): 83·5 × 19 × 6·5 *(25·5 × 5·8 × 2)*
Guns: 4—37 mm, in twin mountings; 2—12·7 mm (some boats mount a twin 75 mm recoilless rifle forward)
A/S weapons: 8 DC
Main engines: 4 diesels; 3 000 bhp = 28 knots
Range, miles: 500 at 28 knots; 750 at 15 knots
Complement: 17

From 1958 constructed at Dairen, Canton, and Shanghai. Now obsolescent and being deleted.

Transfers: 12 to North Viet-Nam.

120 "HU CHWAN" CLASS (FAST ATTACK CRAFT—TORPEDO)

Displacement, tons: 45
Dimensions, feet (metres): 70 × 16·6 oa × 7·9 (hullborne) *(21·3 × 5 × 2·5)*
Guns: 4—12·7 mm (2 twins)
Torpedo tubes: 2—21 inch
Main engines: 3 M50 12 cyl diesels; 2 shafts; 3 600 hp = 50+ knots in calm conditions
Range, miles: 500 cruising

Hydrofoils designed and built by China, in the Hutang yard, Shanghai. Construction started in 1956. At least 25 hydrofoils were reported to be in the South China Fleet in 1968. Of all-metal construction with a bridge well forward and a low super-structure extending aft. The guns are mounted one pair on the main deck and one on the superstructure. Forward pair of foils can apparently be withdrawn into recesses in the hull. A continuing programme at possibly 10 per year.

"HU CHWAN" Class

Transfers: 32 to Albania, 4 to Pakistan, + Romanian craft of indigenous construction.

70 "P 6" CLASS (FAST ATTACK CRAFT—TORPEDO)

Displacement, tons: 66 standard; 75 full load
Dimensions, feet (metres): 84 × 20 × 6 *(25·7 × 6·1 × 1·8)*
Guns: 4—25 mm
Torpedo tubes: 2—21 in (or mines or DCs)
Main engines: 4 M50 diesels; 4 800 bhp = 43 knots
Range, miles: 450 at 30 knots
Complement: 25

This class has wooden hulls. Some were constructed in Chinese yards. Most built prior to 1966.

Radar: Pot Head or Skin Head.

Transfers: 6 to North Viet-Nam in 1967.

"P 6" Class

30 "P 4" CLASS (FAST ATTACK CRAFT—TORPEDO)

Displacement, tons: 25
Dimensions, feet (metres): 62·7 × 11·6 × 5·6 *(19·1 × 3·5 × 1·7)*
Guns: 2—14·5 mm
Torpedo tubes: 2—18 in
Main engines: 2 diesels; 2 200 bhp; 2 shafts = 50 knots

This class has aluminium hulls. Numbers decreasing.

"P 4" Class

102 CHINA

25 "WHAMPOA" CLASS (RIVER PATROL CRAFT)

Displacement, tons: 42 standard; 50 full load
Length, feet (metres): 75·5 × 13 × 5 *(23·0 × 4 × 1·5)*
Guns: 4—25 mm (twins) (rearmed)
Main engines: 2 diesels; 600 hp = 14 knots
Range, miles: 400 at 9 knots
Complement: 25

Built in Canton and Shanghai 1950-55 probably for riverine duties. Underpowered with low freeboard. Now probably decreasing in numbers.

"WHAMPOA" Class 1975, Bradley Hahn

2 "SHANTUNG" CLASS (FAST ATTACK HYDROFOIL—GUN)

Displacement, tons: 75-85
Dimensions, feet (metres): 80 × 16 × 6 *(24·4 × 4·9 × 1·8)*
Guns: 4—37 mm (twins)
Speed, knots: 40

An unsuccessful hydrofoil design. Numbers decreasing.

40 "YU LIN" CLASS (COASTAL PATROL CRAFT)

Displacement, tons: 10
Dimensions, feet (metres): 40 × 9·5 × 3·5 *(12·2 × 2·9 × 1·1)*
Guns: 2—14·5 mm (twin); 2—12·7 mm
Main engines: 1 diesel; 300 bhp; 1 shaft = 20-24 knots
Complement: 10

Built in Shanghai 1964-68.

Transfers: 4 to Congo (1966), 3 to Khmer, 4 to Tanzania.

Possible "YU LIN" Class 1975, Bradley Hahn

1 "FUKIEN" CLASS (FAST ATTACK CRAFT—GUN)

4 "TAI SHAN" CLASS (COASTAL PATROL CRAFT)

"YING KOU" CLASS (COASTAL PATROL CRAFT)

30 "WU HSI/PEI HAI" CLASS (COASTAL PATROL CRAFT)

Displacement, tons: 20 (est)
Dimensions, feet (metres): 70 × 12 × 3 *(21·3 × 3·7 × 0·8)*
Guns: 2—12·7 mm (single)
Main engines: 1 diesel; 300 bhp; 1 shaft = 16 knots

Built in early 1960s.

MINE WARFARE FORCES

Note: (a) 1 ship of "Wu Sung" class (MSC) built in 1970-72. Apparently unsuccessful. Reported transferred to North Viet-Nam 1974.
(b) There are also some 60 auxiliary minesweepers of various types including trawlers.
(c) 20 MSC of "Fushun" class also reported.

17 SOVIET "T 43" CLASS (MINESWEEPERS—OCEAN)

Nos 377, 386, 396 + 14

Displacement, tons: 500 standard; 610 full load
Dimensions, feet (metres): 196·8 × 28·2 × 6·9 *(60 × 8·6 × 2·1)*
Guns: 4—37 mm (2 twin); 4—25 mm (2 twin); 4—14·5 mm (twin—in most ships)
A/S weapons: 2 DCT
Main engines: 2 diesels; 2 shafts; 2 000 bhp = 17 knots
Range, miles: 1 600 at 10 knots
Complement: 40

Four were acquired from USSR in 1954-55. Two being returned 1960. Twenty-one more were built in Chinese shipyards, the first two in 1956. The construction of "T 43" class fleet minesweepers was stopped at Wuchang, but continued at Canton. 3 converted for surveying 3 transferred as civilian research ships. Most of the Chinese variant are of the 60 m "Long hull' design.

Radar: Ballgun.

"T 43" Class 1972

AMPHIBIOUS WARFARE FORCES

13 Ex-US LSM TYPE

Ex-**HUA 201** (ex-US *LSM 112*)
Ex-**HUA 202** (ex-US *LSM 248*)
Ex-**HUA 204** (ex-US *LSM 430*)
Ex-**HUA 205** (ex-US *LSM 336*)
Ex-**HUA 207** (ex-US *LSM 282*)
Ex-**HUA 208** (ex-US *LSM 42*)
Ex-**HUA 209** (ex-US *LSM 153*)
Ex-**HUA 211**
Ex-**HUA 212**
Ex-**CHUAN SHIH SHUI**
Ex-**HUAI HO** (ex-Chinese *Wan Fu*)
Ex-**HUANG HO** (ex-Chinese *Mei Sheng* ex-US *LSM 433*)
Ex-**YUN HO** (ex-Chinese *Wang Chung*)

Displacement, tons: 743 beaching; 1 095 full load
Dimensions, feet (metres): 196·5 wl; 203·5 oa × 34·5 × 8·8 *(59·9; 62·1 × 10·5 × 2·7)*
Guns: 4—37 mm (twins)
Main engines: Diesel; 2 shafts; 2 800 hp = 12 knots

Built in USA in 1944-45. Some were converted for minelaying and as support ships. Armament varies. Up to ten of these may be transferred temporarily to commercial operations.

CHINA 103

15 Ex-US LST 511-1152 SERIES

CHANG PAI SHAN
CH'ING KANG SHAN
I MENG SHAN (ex-*Chung 106*, ex-US *LST 589*)
TA PIEH SHAN
TAI HSING SHAN
SZU CH'ING SHAN
Ex-CHUNG 100 (ex-US *LST 355*)
Ex-CHUNG 101 (ex-US *LST 804*)
Ex-CHUNG 102
Ex-CHUNG 107 (ex-US *LST 1027*)
Ex-CHUNG 110
Ex-CHUNG 111 (ex-US *LST 805*)
Ex-CHUNG 116 (ex-US *LST 406*)
Ex-CHUNG 122 (ex-*Ch'ing Ling*)
Ex-CHUNG 125

Displacement, tons: 1 653 standard; 4 080 full load
Dimensions, feet (metres): 316 wl; 328 oa × 50 × x4 *(96·4; 100 × 15·3 × 4·4)*
Guns: 2/3—76·2 mm; 6/8—40 mm
Mines: All capable of minelaying
Main engines: Diesel; 2 shafts; 1 700 bhp = 11 knots

Two transferred to North Viet-Nam as tankers. Some other ex-US LSTs are in the merchant service.

US LST   *1968, USN*

15 Ex-US LSIL TYPE

MIN 301	306	312	319	
303	311	313	321	+7

Displacement, tons: 230 light; 387 full load
Dimensions, feet (metres): 159 × 23·7 × 5·7 *(48·5 × 7·2 × 1·7)*
Guns: 4—20 or 25 mm
Main engines: Diesel; 2 shafts; 1 320 bhp = 14 knots

Built in USA in 1943-45. Reported to be fitted with rocket launchers. Some are fitted as minesweepers. Armament varies.

1 "YU LING" CLASS (LSM)

250 feet *(76·3 metres)*—1 500 ton LSM built in China since 1971. Continuing programme.

300 "YUNNAN" CLASS (LCUs)

Built in China 1968-72.

17 Ex-US or BRITISH LCU (ex-LCT) TYPE

Displacement, tons: 160 light; 320 full load
Dimensions, feet (metres): 119 oa × 33 × 5 *(36·3 × 10 × 1·5)*
Main engines: Diesel; 3 shafts; 475 bhp = 10 knots
Oil fuel (tons): 80

Former United States Navy Tank Landing Craft later reclassified as Utility Landing Craft. There are reported to be eleven utility landing craft comprising two of the ex-British LCT (3) class and eight of the ex-US LCT (5) and LCT (6) class. Used for logistic support and carry auxiliary pennants.

About 150 Ex-BRITISH/US LCMs

MISCELLANEOUS

SUBMARINE SUPPORT SHIP

TA CHIH

Displacement, tons: 5 to 6 000
Dimensions, feet (metres): 350 × 50 × 20 *(106·7 × 15·3 × 6·1)*
Guns: 4—37 mm (twins); 4—25 mm (twins)

Reported in 1973.

REPAIR SHIP

TAKU SHAN (ex-*Hsing An*, ex-USS *Achilles*, ARL 41, ex-*LST 455*)

Displacement, tons: 1 625 light; 4 100 full load
Dimensions, feet (metres): 328 oa × 50 × 11 *(100 × 15·3 × 3·4)*
Guns: 12—37 mm (twins)
Main engines: Diesel-electric; 2 shafts; 1 800 bhp = 11 knots

Launched on 17 Oct 1942. Burned and grounded in 1949, salvaged and refitted. Reportedly operates from Shanghai.

SURVEY AND RESEARCH SHIPS

2 "SHIH JIAN" CLASS (AGOR)

SHIH JIAN   TUNG FAN HUNG 02

Displacement, tons: 3 750
Dimensions, feet (metres): 311·6 × 46 × 16·4 *(95 × 14 × 5)*
Guns: 8—14·5 mm (twins)
Main engines: Diesels; 2 shafts
Range, miles: 8 000
Complement: 125 approx

Completed Aug 1968.

Radar: Decca 707.

SHIH JIAN   *1973*

1 "YEN HSI" CLASS

HSIANG YANG HUNG WU

Displacement, tons: 14 000
Dimensions, feet (metres): 500 × 64 × 28·9 *(152·5 × 19·5 × 8·8)*
Main engines: 2 diesels; 7 250 shp = 16 knots
Range, miles: 12-15 000

Built as Polish B41 Type *(Francesco Nullo)* in 1967. Purchased by China and rebuilt 1970-72 at Kuanchou (Canton). Stationed at Canton. Possibly civilian manned. Acts as environmental research ship. Four sister ships in Chinese mercantile fleet.

HSIANG YANG HUNG SAN +2 others, maybe more

These ships, of varying tonnage but all of an ocean-going size, operate in conjunction with the Academy of Science.

2 "HA T'SE" CLASS (AGS)

HAI SHENG 701   HAI SHENG 702

Displacement, tons: 400 standard
Dimensions, feet (metres): 125 × 25 × 11 (est) *(38 × 7·6 × 3·4)*
Guns: 4—25 mm (vertical twins)
Main engines: 1 diesel; 4 600 bhp = 12 knots (est)

Possibly built in 1960s. Certainly operational in 1971 off Paraul Islands.

1 "YEN LUN" CLASS (AGOR)

YEN LUN

Completed in 1965, possibly at Shanghai. Similar to Soviet 3 000-ton "Zubov" class.

1 Ex-JAPANESE "KAIBOKAN" CLASS (AGS)

Displacement, tons: 740
Speed, knots: 17·5

Believed built in 1945.

104 CHINA

3 "SHU KUANG" CLASS (ex T-43) (AGOR)

SHU KUANG 1, 2 and 3   Nos 377, 386, 396

For details see under Mine Warfare Forces. Converted from Minesweepers in late 1960s. All painted white.

2-3 "YEN LAI" CLASS (AGS)

HAIT'SE 629   HAIT'SE 512

Displacement, tons: 1 100
Dimensions, feet (metres): 229.6 × 32.1 × 9.7 *(70 × 9.8 × 3)*
Guns: 4—37 mm (twin)
Main engines: Probably diesel; 1 shaft = 16 knots
Range, miles: 2 000 approx
Complement: 100

Probably built in Shanghai in early 1970s. Prominent square bridge and funnel amidships.

1 "KAN-CHU" CLASS (AGS)

K 420

Displacement, tons: 1 000
Dimensions, feet (metres): 213.2 × 29.5 × 9.7 *(65 × 9 × 3)*
Guns: 4—37 mm (twin); 4—25 mm (twin)
Main engines: Diesel; approx 5 000 shp = 20 knots
Complement: 125 (est)

Built at Changchou (Canton) 2971-73. Frigate-type bridge. Prominent raked funnel. Worked in Hong Kong area 1975.

1 Ex-BRITISH "FLOWER" CLASS (AGS)

KAI FENG (ex-*Clover*)

Displacement, tons: 1 160
Main engines: Steam reciprocating, 2 750 ihp

Built by Fleming and Ferguson in 1941. Sold commercially and acquired by China. Served as escort and reported as disarmed for survey duties in 1974-5.

1 COASTAL SURVEY CRAFT

Ex-CHUNG NING (ex-Japanese *Takebu Maru*)

Displacement, tons: 200 standard
Dimensions, feet (metres): 115 × 16 × 6 *(35 × 4.9 × 1.8)*
Speed, knots: 10

Former Japanese. Employed for hydrographic and general purpose duties.

1 COASTAL SURVEY CRAFT

Ex-FUTING

Displacement, tons: 160 standard
Dimensions, feet (metres): 90 × 20 × 8 *(27 × 6.1 × 2.4)*
Speed, knots: 11

BOOM DEFENCE VESSELS

Note: Probably now used as service vessels.

1 Ex-BRITISH "BAR" CLASS

— (Ex-Japanese No 101, ex-HMS *Barlight*)

Displacement, tons: 750 standard; 1 000 full load
Dimensions, feet (metres): 173.8 oa × 32.2 × 9.5 *(53 × 9.8 × 2.9)*
Guns: 1—3 in; 6 MG
Main engines: Triple expansion; 850 ihp = 11.75 knots
Boilers: 2 single-ended

Built by Lobnitz & Co Ltd, Renfrew. Launched on 10 Sep 1938. Captured by Japanese in 1941. Acquired by China in 1945.

5 Ex-US "TREE" CLASS

Displacement, tons: 560 standard; 805 full load
Dimensions, feet (metres): 163 oa × 30.5 × 11.8 *(49.7 × 9.3 × 3.6)*
Gun: 1—3 in
Main engines: Diesel-electric; 800 bhp = 13 knots

SUPPLY SHIPS

5 Ex-US ARMY FS 330 TYPE

Ex-US Army FS 146 (ex-*Clover*)
Ex-US Army FS 155 (ex-*Violet*)   +3

Displacement, tons: 1 000 standard
Dimensions, feet (metres): 175 oa × 32 × 10 *(53.4 × 9.9 × 2)*
Main engines: GM diesels; 1 000 bhp = 12 knots

Built in USA in 1944-45. Two are reported to be employed as support ships for fast attack craft.

2 "GALATI" CLASS (AK)

HAI YUN 318   HAI CHIU 600

Displacement, tons: 5 300
Dimensions, feet (metres): 328 × 47.9 × 21.6 *(100 × 14 × 6.6)*
Main engines: Diesel; 1 shaft = 12.5 knots
Oil fuel: 250 tons
Range, miles: 4—5 000
Complement: 50

Built at Santiereal Shipyard, Calati, Romania in 1960s. 9 ships purchased of which these two were converted to AKs in early 1970s. Cargo capacity approx 3 750 tons with 10 crane/booms for handling. Both reported operating in South Sea Fleet.

1 "CHAN TOU" CLASS (AK)

Displacement, tons: 4 500
Dimensions, feet (metres): 311.6 × 41 × 18 *(95 × 12.5 × 5.5)*
Main engines: 1 diesel; 1 shaft = 12.5 knots approx
Range, miles: 3—4 000
Complement: 50 approx

A class of 15-20 merchant ships was built in Shanghai 1959-65 of which one or maybe more transferred to the navy. Have prominent bridge and funnel aft.

1 "AN TUNG" CLASS (AF)

Chinese built.

2 or 3 "TAN LIN" CLASS (AK)

Displacement, tons: 1 500

There may be another 12 coastal merchant ships operating under naval control.

5 "LEI CHOU" CLASS (AOTL)

Displacement, tons: 900
Dimensions, feet (metres): 157.4 × 28.9 × 9.7 *(48 × 8.8 × 3)*
Main engines: Diesel; 1 shaft = 10-12 knots
Range, miles: 1 200
Complement: 25-30

Built in late 1960s probably at Ching Tao or Wutung.

3-4 "LEI CHOU" CLASS (WTL)

4-5 "FU CHOU" CLASS (WTL)

LEI CHOU   FOU CHOU   +2 or 3

Large water carriers of 1 100 tons. Details under same class in Tanker section.

TANKERS

14 + "FU CHOU" CLASS

Displacement, tons: 1 100
Dimensions, feet (metres): 164 × 29.5 × 11.5 *(50 × 9 × 3.5)*
Main engines: 1 diesel; 1 shaft = 12 knots
Range, miles: 1 500
Complement: 30-35

Reported as built in Shanghai 1964-70. Some may carry twin 25 mm or 37 mm mounts. Cargo capacity 650-700 tons. Prominent bridge and funnel aft.

2 Ex-US "MATTAWEE" CLASS (AOG)

Originally petrol tankers.

1 Ex-JAPANESE "TM" CLASS (AO)

HAI YU 401

Displacement, tons: 4 500
Dimensions, feet (metres): 308.3 × 44.3 × 19 *(94 × 13.5 × 5.8)*
Main engines: Turbo-electric; 1 shaft = 11 knots
Fuel: 250 tons
Range, miles: 3 750 at 7.5 knots
Complement: 35 (est)

Cargo capacity 3 750 tons FFO. Bridge and funnel aft. An emergency Japanese class handed to USSR in 1945 and to China in Shanghai 1945. Modernisation in 1960s changed appearance somewhat.

CHINA / COLOMBIA

ICEBREAKERS

2 "HAI PING" CLASS

101 102

Displacement, tons: 3 000
Dimensions, feet (metres): 275 × 50 × 16 (83·8 × 15·3 × 4·9)
Guns: 8—37 mm (twins)
Main engines: 3 000 hp; 1 shaft = 15 knots

Built in 1969-73 at Shanghai. Employed as icebreaking tugs in Po Hai Gulf for port clearance.

REPAIR SHIPS

1 Ex-US ARL TYPE

TAKU SHAN

1 "GALATI" CLASS

Converted AK.

SERVICE CRAFT

There are also reported to be 125 armed motor junks, 100 armed motor launches and 150 service craft and miscellaneous boats.

TUGS

16 "GROMOVOY" CLASS (ARS)

Chinese built.

3 "TING HAI" CLASS (ARS)

4 "YEN TENG" CLASS (ARS)

1 Ex-SOVIET "ROSLAVL" CLASS (ARS)
3 CHINESE "ROSLAVL" CLASS (ARS)

Displacement, tons: 670 full load
Dimensions, feet (metres): 145 × 31 × 11·4 (44·2 × 9·5 × 3·5)
Main engines: Diesel; 1 shaft; 1 500 shp = 12 knots
Fuel: 100 tons
Range, miles: 6 000 at 11 knots
Complement: 28

First ship transferred by USSR late-1950s. Remainder built in China in mid 1960s.

2 Ex-US 149' ATA
2 Ex-US 143' ATA
5 Ex-US ARMY 75' YTL
3 FT-14 CLASS (ARS)

COLOMBIA

Ministerial

Minister of National Defence:
 General Abraham Varon Valencia

Headquarters Appointments

Fleet Commander:
 Admiral Jaime Barrera Larrarte
Chief of Naval Operations:
 Vice-Admiral Alfonso Diaz Osorio
Chief of Naval Staff:
 Rear-Admiral Héctor Calderón Salazar

Diplomatic Representative

Naval Attaché in Washington:
 Captain Rafael Grau Arano

Personnel

(a) 1978: 700 officers and 6 500 men and 1 500 marines
(b) 2 years national service

Bases

Cartagena. Main naval base (floating dock, 1 slipway) synchrolift, schools.
Buenaventura. Small Pacific base.

Maritime Air Force

The Colombian Air Force with 50 helicopters and a number of attack/reconnaissance aircraft provides any support required by the navy.

Naval Infantry

Corpo de Infanteria de Marina is one battalion based at Cartagena, Buenaventura and Barranquilla.

Prefix to Ships' Names

ARC (Armada Republica de Colombia)

Strength of the Fleet

Type	Active	Building
Destroyers	3	—
Frigates	9	—
Submarines	2 + 4 (70 tons)	—
Large Patrol Craft	6	—
Coastal Patrol Craft	13	—
Gunboats	4	—
Survey Vessels	3	—
Transports	4	—
Tanker	1	—
Repair Ship	1	—
Training Ship	1	—
Tugs	10	—
Floating Docks	3	—
Floating Workshop	1	—
LST	1	—

Mercantile Marine

Lloyd's Register of Shipping:
 52 vessels of 247 240 tons gross

DELETIONS

Destroyers

1973 Antioquia ("Fletcher" class) (paid off 20 Dec)
1977 Caldes ("Allen M. Sumner" class)

Frigates

1972 Almirante Brion (ex-US APD type)
1973 Almirante Padilla (ex-US APD type)
1977 Almirante Tono (ex-US APD type)

Light Forces

1974 Gen. Rafael Reyes, Alberto Restrepo, Independiente, Palace, Tormentosa, Triunfante, Valerosa, Voladora

Survey Ship

1974 Bocas de Ceniza

Transport

1974 Bell Salter, Rafael Martinez

Tankers

1970 Tumaco, Barran Cabermeja
1974 Covenas, Mamonal, Sancho Jimeno

Tug

1975 Bahia Honda (grounded and scrapped 13 Feb)

SUBMARINES

2 TYPE 209 PATROL SUBMARINES

Name	No.	Builders	Commissioned
PIJAO	SS 28	Howaldtswerke, Kiel	17 April 1975
TAYRONA	SS 29	Howaldtswerke, Kiel	18 July 1975

Displacement, tons: 1 000 surfaced; 1 290 dived
Length, feet (metres): 183·4 (55·9)
Beam, feet (metres): 20·5 (6·25)
Torpedo tubes: 8—21 in bow with reloads
Main machinery: Diesel-electric; 1 shaft; 5 000 hp
Speed, knots: 22 dived

Ordered in 1971.

PIJAO

1975, Dhr. J. van der Woude

COLOMBIA

4 TYPE SX-506 SUBMARINES

Name	No.	Builders	Commissioned
INTREPIDO	SS 20	Cosmos Livorno	1972
INDOMABLE	SS 21	Cosmos Livorno	1972
RONCADOR	SS 23	Cosmos Livorno	1974
QUITA SUENO	SS 24	Cosmos Livorno	1974

Displacement, tons: 58 surfaced; 70 dived
Dimensions, feet (metres): 75·4 × 6·6 × 13·2 *(23 × 2 × 4)*
Main machinery: Diesel-electric; 300 bhp
Speed, knots: 8 surfaced; 6 dived; 7 snorting
Range, miles: 1 200 at 7 knots
Complement: 5

Delivered in sections for assembly in Cartagena. Can carry 8 attack swimmers with 2 tons of explosives, as well as two swimmer-delivery-vehicles (SDVs). Diving depth 330 ft *(100 m)*.

DESTROYERS

2 MODIFIED "HALLAND" CLASS

Name	No.
VEINTE DE JULIO	D 05
SIETE DE AGOSTO	D 06

Builders	Laid down	Launched	Commissioned
Kockums Mek Verkstads A/B, Malmo	Oct 1955	26 June 1956	15 June 1958
Götaverken, Göteborg	Nov 1955	19 June 1956	31 Oct 1958

Displacement, tons: 2 650 standard; 3 300 full load
Length, feet (metres): 380·5 *(116·0)* pp; 397·2 *(121·1)* oa
Beam, feet (metres): 40·7 *(12·4)*
Draught, feet (metres): 15·4 *(4·7)*
Guns: 6—4·7 in *(120 mm)* (3 twin turrets); 4—40 mm (single)
Torpedo tubes: 4—21 in *(533 mm)*
A/S weapons: 1 Bofors 375 mm A/S rocket launcher
Main engines: De Laval double reduction geared turbines; 2 shafts; 55 000 shp
Boilers: 2 Penhöet, Motala Verkstad; 568 psi; 840°F
Speed, knots: 25 (16 economical)
Oil fuel, tons: 524
Range, miles: 445 at full power
Complement: 260 (20 officers, 240 men)

Ordered in 1954. The hull and machinery are similar to the Swedish class but they have different armament (six 4·7 in instead of four, no 57 mm guns, four 40 mm guns instead of six, and four torpedo tubes instead of eight) and different accommodation arrangements. They have an anti-submarine rocket projector, more radar and communication equipment, and air-conditioned living spaces, having been designed for the tropics. *Veinte de Julio* due for deletion in 1978.

Engineering: Although the designed speed was 35 knots, it is officially stated that the maximum sustained speed does not exceed 25 knots.

Radar: Search: HSA, LW-03/SGR 114.
Tactical: HSA DA-02/SGR 105.
Fire control: I band, probably HSA M20 series.

Refit: *Siete de Agosto* returned to Colombia in 1975 after a lengthy refit in USA during which her engines were extensively overhauled.

VEINTE DE JULIO *1975, Dhr. J. van der Woude*

SIETE DE AGOSTO *1975, Dhr. J. van der Woude*

1 Ex-US "ALLEN M. SUMNER FRAM II" CLASS

Name	No.	Builders	Laid down	Launched	Commissioned
SANTANDER (ex-USS *Waldron*, DD 699)	D 03	Federal SB Co	—	26 Mar 1944	8 June 1944

Displacement, tons: 2 200 standard; 3 320 full load
Length, feet (metres): 376 *(114·6)* oa
Beam, feet (metres): 40·9 *(12·5)*
Draught, feet (metres): 19 *(5·8)*
Guns: 6—5 in *(127 mm)* 38 cal (twins)
A/S weapons: 2 fixed Hedgehogs; 2 triple torpedo tubes (Mk 32); Facilities for small helicopter
Main engines: 2 geared turbines; 2 shafts; 60 000 shp
Boilers: 4
Speed, knots: 34
Range, miles: 2 400 at 25 knots; 4 600 at 15 knots
Complement: 274

Santander was modernised under the Fram II programme and transferred by sale on 30 Oct 1973.

Fire control: Mk 37 director with Mk 25 radar.

Radar: Search: SPS 10 and 40.

Sonar: VDS removed before transfer.

SANTANDER *1975, Dhr. J. van der Woude*

COLOMBIA 107

FRIGATES

4 Ex-PORTUGUESE "JOAO COUTINHO" CLASS

Name	No.	Builders	Laid down	Launched	Commissioned
— (ex-*Alfonso Cerqueira*, F 488)	—	Empresa Nacional Bazan, Spain	1973	6 Oct 1973	26 June 1975
— (ex-*Baptiste de Andrade*, F 486)	—	Empresa Nacional Bazan, Spain	1972	Mar 1973	19 Nov 1974
— (ex-*Joao Roby*, F 487)	—	Empresa Nacional Bazan, Spain	1972	3 June 1973	18 Mar 1975
— (ex-*Oliveira E. Carmo*, F 489)	—	Empresa Nacional Bazan, Spain	1972	Feb 1974	Feb 1975

Displacement, tons: 1 250 standard; 1 380 full load
Dimensions, feet (metres): 277·5 × 33·8 × 11·8 *(84·6 × 10·3 × 3·6)*
Missiles: 2 Exocet MM 38
Guns: 1—3·9 in *(100 mm)*; 2—40 mm Bofors
A/S weapons: 2 triple Mk 32 torpedo tubes
Main engines: 2 OEW 12 cyl Pielstick diesels; 11 000 bhp = 23·5 knots
Range, miles: 5 900 at 18 knots
Complement: 107, plus marine detachment

Acquired from Portuguese navy in 1977.

Radar: Air search: Plessey AWS-2.
Navigation: Decca TM 626.
Fire control: Thomson SCF Pollux.

Sonar: Diodon.

OLIVEIRA E. CARMO 3/1976, Michael D. J. Lennon

1 Ex-US APD TYPE

Name	No.	Builders	Commissioned
CORDOBA (ex-USS *Ruchamkin* LPR 89, ex-*APD 89*, ex-*DE 228*)	DT 15	Philadelphia Navy Yard	June 1945

Displacement, tons: 1 400 standard; 2 130 full load
Dimensions, feet (metres): 306 oa × 37 × 12·6 *(93·3 × 11·3 × 3·8)*
Guns: 1—5 in 38 cal; 4—40 mm
A/S weapons: 2 Mk 32 launchers
Main engines: GEC turbines with electric drive; 2 shafts; 12 000 shp = 23 knots
Boilers: 2 "D" Express
Range, miles: 5 500 at 15 knots
Complement: 204 (plus accommodation for 162 troops)

Cordoba was laid down on 14 Feb 1944, launched on 15 June 1944 and transferred on 24 Nov 1969. Modernised to Fram II standards.

CORDOBA 1974

1 Ex-US "COURTNEY" CLASS

Name	No.	Builders	Commissioned
BOYACA (ex-USS *Hartley* DE 1029)	DE 16	New York SB Corp	26 Jan 1957

Displacement, tons: 1 450 standard; 1 914 full load
Dimensions, feet (metres): 314·5 oa × 36·8 × 13·6 *(95·9 × 11·2 × 4·1)*
Guns: 2—3 in; 50 cal (twin)
A/S weapons: 2 triple Mk 32 torpedo tubes; 1 DC rack
Main engines: 1 De Laval geared turbine; 20 000 shp; 1 shaft
Boilers: 2 Foster Wheeler
Speed, knots: 25
Complement: 165

Transferred 8 July 1972, by sale. Helicopter platform in X position.

Radar: SPS 6 and 10.

BOYACA 1974

3 Ex-US "CHEROKEE" CLASS

Name	No.	Builders	Commissioned
— (ex-USS *Carib*, ATF 82)	—	United Engineering Co. Alameda	1943
— (ex-USS *Hidatsa*, ATF 102)	—	Charleston SB and DD Co	1944
— (ex-USS *Jicarilla*, ATF 104)	—	Charleston SB and DD Co	1944

Displacement, tons: 1 235 standard; 1 640 full load
Dimensions, feet (metres): 205 × 38·5 × 15·5 *(62·5 × 11·7 × 4·7)*
Gun: 1—3 in *(76 mm)* 50 cal (Mk 22)
Main engines: Diesel-electric; 1 shaft; 3 000 bhp = 15 knots
Complement: 75

Built as fleet tugs. Launched 7 Feb 1943, 29 Dec 1943 and 25 Feb 1944 respectively. All three placed in reserve July 1963. Transferred in 1977 for duties as patrol frigates.

Appearance: See photo of *Pedro de Heredia* in Tugs section.

LIGHT FORCES

2 Ex-US "ASHEVILLE" CLASS (PG—LARGE PATROL CRAFT)

Name	No.	Builders	Commissioned
— (ex-USS *Gallup*, PG 85)	—	Tacoma Boatbuilding	22 Oct 1966
— (ex-USS *Canon*, PG 90)	—	Tacoma Boatbuilding	26 July 1968

Displacement, tons: 225 standard; 235 full load
Dimensions, feet (metres): 164·5 × 32·8 × 9·5 *(50·1 × 7·3 × 2·9)*
Guns: 1—3 in *(76 mm)* 50 cal; 1—40 mm; 4—50 cal MG
Main engines: 2 Cummins diesels; 1 450 shp = 16 knots; 1 GE LM 2500 gas turbine; 13 300 shp; 2 shafts = 40 knots
Range, miles: 1 700 at 16 knots; 325 at 37 knots
Complement: 24

To US reserve 1976—transferred to Colombia 1978.

"ASHEVILLE" Class 7/1976, Dr. Giorgio Arra

108 COLOMBIA

Name	No.	Builders	Commissioned
GENERAL VASQUES COBO	AN 202	Lürssen	1955

Displacement, tons: 146
Dimensions, feet (metres): 124·7 oa × 23 × 5 *(38 × 7 × 1·5)*
Gun: 1—40 mm
Main engines: 2 Maybach (MTU) diesels; 2 500 bhp = 18 knots
Complement: 20

Launched on 27 Sep 1955.

Name	No.	Builders	Commissioned
CARLOS ALBAN	—	Finland	1971
JORGE SOTO DEL CORVAL	—	Finland	1971
NITO RESTREPO	—	Finland	1971

Displacement, tons: 100
Dimensions, feet (metres): 108 × 18 × 6 *(33 × 5·5 × 1·8)*
Guns: 2—20 mm
Main engines: 2 (MTU) diesels; 2 450 bhp = 17 knots

Near sisters to Finnish "Ruissalo" class.

CARLOS ALBAN   1971, Colombian Navy

3 "ARAUCA" CLASS GUNBOATS

Name	No.	Builders	Commissioned
RIOHACHA	CF 35	Union Industrial de Barranquilla	1956
LETICIA	CF 36	Union Industrial de Barranquilla	1956
ARAUCA	CF 37	Union Industrial de Barranquilla	1956

Displacement, tons: 184 full load
Dimensions, feet (metres): 163·5 oa × 23·5 × 2·8 *(49·9 × 7·2 × 0·9)*
Guns: 2—3 in, 50 cal; 4—20 mm
Main engines: 2 Caterpillar diesels; 916 bhp = 14 knots
Range, miles: 1 890 at 14 knots
Complement: 43 *(Leticia 39 and 6 orderlies)*

Launched in 1955. *Leticia* has been equipped as a hospital ship with 6 beds.

RIOHACHA   1966, Colombian Navy

1 "BARRANQUILLA" CLASS GUNBOAT

Name	No.	Builders	Commissioned
CARTAGENA	CF 33	Yarrow & Co Ltd, Scotstoun	1930

Displacement, tons: 142
Dimensions, feet (metres): 137·8 oa × 23·5 × 2·8 *(42 × 7·2 × 0·9)*
Guns: 2—3 in; 1—20 mm; 4 MG
Main engines: 2 Gardner semi-diesels; 2 shafts working in tunnels; 600 hp = 15·5 knots
Oil fuel (tons): 24
Complement: 39

Launched on 22 Mar 1930. Sister ships *Santa Marta*, CF 32, withdrawn from service in Dec 1962, and *Barranquilla* in 1970.

CARTAGENA   1971, Colombian Navy

Name	No.	Builders	Commissioned
PEDRO GUAL	AN 204	Schurenstedt KG Barden Fleth	1964
ESTEBAN JARAMILLO	AN 205	Schurenstedt KG Barden Fleth	1964
CARLOS E. RESTREPO	AN 206	Schurenstedt KG Barden Fleth	1964

Displacement, tons: 85
Dimensions, feet (metres): 107·8 pp × 18 × 6 *(32·9 × 5·5 × 1·8)*
Gun: 1—20 mm
Main engines: 2 Maybach (MTU) diesels; 2 450 bhp = 26 knots

PEDRO GUAL   1965, Colombian Navy

Name	No.	Builders	Commissioned
OLAYA HERRERA	AN 203	Ast. Magdalena Barranquilla	1960

Displacement, tons: 40
Dimensions, feet (metres): 68·8 pp × 12·8 × 3·5 *(21 × 3·9 × 1·1)*
Gun: 1—50 mm Browning
Main engines: 2 Merbens diesels; 570 bhp = 20 knots

Name	No.	Builders	Commissioned
ESPARTANA	GC 100	Ast. Naval, Cartagena	1950

Displacement, tons: 50
Dimensions, feet (metres): 96 oa × 13·5 × 4 *(29·3 × 4·1 × 1·2)*
Gun: 1—20 mm
Main engines: 2 diesels; 300 bhp = 13·5 knots

Name	No.	Builders	Commissioned
CAPITAN R. D. BINNEY	GC 101	Ast. Naval, Cartagena	1947

Displacement, tons: 23
Dimensions, feet (metres): 67 × 10·7 × 3·5 *(20·4 × 3·3 × 1·1)*
Main engines: Diesels; 115 bhp = 13 knots

CALIBIO LR 127

Buoy and lighthouse inspection boat. Named after first head of Colombian Naval Academy, Lt-Commander Ralph Douglas Binney, RN.

Name	No.	Builders	Commissioned
JUAN LUCIO	LR 122	Ast. Naval, Cartagena	1953
ALFONSO VARGAS	LR 123	Ast. Naval, Cartagena	1952
FRITZ HAGALE	LR 124	Ast. Naval, Cartagena	1952
HUMBERTO CORTES	LR 126	Ast. Naval, Cartagena	1953
CARLOS GALINDO	LR 128	Ast. Naval, Cartagena	1954

Name	No.	Builders	Commissioned
DILIGENTE	LR 138	Ast. Naval, Cartagena	1952
VENGADORA	LR 139	Ast. Naval, Cartagena	1954

Originally a class of eight.

Displacement, tons: 33
Dimensions, feet (metres): 76 oa × 12 × 2·8 *(23·2 × 3·7 × 0·8)*
Guns: 1—20 mm; 4 MG
Main engines: 2 GM diesels 280 bhp = 13 knots
Complement: 10

Name	No.	Builders	Commissioned
RODRIGUEZ	AN 1	—	—

Designed for operations on rivers. Named after naval officers.

40 ft CGB.

AMPHIBIOUS SHIP

1 Ex-US "511-1152 SERIES" (LST)

Name	No.	Builders	Commissioned
— (ex-USS *Duval County*, LST 758)	—	—	19 Aug 1944

Displacement, tons: 1 653 standard; 4 080 full load
Dimensions, feet (metres): 328 × 50 × 14 *(100 × 15·2 × 4·3)*
Guns: 6—40 mm
Main engines: 2 GM diesels; 2 shafts; 1 700 bhp = 11·6 knots
Complement: 119
Troops: 147

Transferred 1977. She was the last World War II LST serving in the USN.

SURVEY VESSELS

Name	No.	Builders	Commissioned
SAN ANDRES (ex-USS *Rockville*, PCER 851)	BO 151	Pullman Standard Car Co, Chicago	15 May 1944

Displacement, tons: 674 standard; 968 full load
Dimensions, feet (metres): 184·5 oa × 33·6 × 7·0 *(56·2 × 10·2 × 2·1)*
Main engines: 2 diesels; 2 shafts; 1 800 bhp = 15 knots
Complement: 50

Former US patrol rescue escort vessel. Laid down on 18 Oct 1943, launched on 22 Feb 1944. Acquired on 5 June 1969 for conversion to a surveying vessel.

Name	No.	Builders	Commissioned
GORGONA	FB 161	Lidingoverken, Sweden	1955

Displacement, tons: 574
Dimensions, feet (metres): 135 × 29·5 × 9·3 *(41·2 × 9 × 2·8)*
Main engines: 2 Nohab diesels; 910 bhp = 13 knots
Complement: 45

Formerly classified as a tender.

GORGONA *1971, Colombian Navy*

Name	No.	Builders	Commissioned
QUINDIO (ex-US *YFR 443*)	BO 153	—	1943

Displacement, tons: 380 light; 600 full load
Dimensions, feet (metres): 131 × 29·8 × 9 *(40 × 9·1 × 2·7)*
Main engines: 2 diesels; 300 hp = 10 knots
Complement: 17

Transferred by lease July 1964.

TANKER

1 Ex-US "PATAPSCO" CLASS (AOG)

Name	No.	Builders	Commissioned
TUMACO (ex-USS *Chewaucan*, AOG 50)	BT 67	Cargill Inc, Savage, Minn.	19 Feb 1945

Displacement, tons: 1 850 light; 4 570
Dimensions, feet (metres): 310·8 × 48·5 × 16 *(94·8 × 14·8 × 4·9)*
Guns: 2—3 in *(76 mm)*
Main engines: Diesel-electric; 2 shafts; 3 840 bhp = 15 knots
Range, miles: 4 740 at 15 knots; 8 350 at 11·5 knots
Complement: 95

Transferred 1 July 1975 by sale.

TUMACO (As USS *Chewaucan*) *1970, A. and J. Pavia*

REPAIR SHIP

1 Ex-US "ARISTAEUS" CLASS

Name	No.	Builders	Commissioned
— (ex-USS *Midas*, ARB 5)	—	—	23 May 1944

Displacement, tons: 1 625 standard; 3 455 full load
Dimensions, feet (metres): 328 × 50 × 11 *(100 × 15·2 × 4·3)*
Guns: 8—40 mm
Main engines: Diesels; 1 800 bhp; 2 shafts = 11·6 knots
Complement: 190

Converted from LST hull. Transferred 1977.

"ARISTAEUS" Class

COLOMBIA / COMORO ISLANDS

TRANSPORTS

Name	No.	Builders	Commissioned
CIUDAD DE QUIBDO (ex-*Shamrock*)	TM 43	Gebr Sander Deltzijl	1953 (see note)

Displacement, tons: 633
Dimensions, feet (metres): 165 × 23·5 × 9 *(50·3 × 7·2 × 2·7)*
Main engines: 1 MAN diesel; 1 shaft; 390 bhp = 11 knots
Oil fuel, tons: 32
Complement: 12

Ex-Dutch coaster *Shamrock* sold to Colombia by commercial firm in Mar 1953.

Name	No.	Builders	Commissioned
MARIO SERPA	TF 51	Ast. Naval Cartagena	1954
HERNANDO GUTIERREZ	TF 52	Ast. Naval Cartagena	1955
SOCORRO (ex-*Alberto Gomez*)	BD 33	Ast. Naval Cartagena	1956

Displacement, tons: 70
Dimensions, feet (metres): 82 × 18 × 2·8 *(25 × 5·5 × 0·9)*
Main engines: 2 GM diesels; 260 bhp = 9 knots
Oil fuel, tons: 4
Range, miles: 650 at 9 knots
Complement: 12 (berths for 48 troops and medical staff)

River transports. Named after Army officers. *Socorro* was converted in July 1967 into a floating surgery. *Hernando Gutierrez* and *Mario Serpa* were converted into dispensary ships in 1970.

TRAINING SHIP

Name	No.	Builders	Commissioned
GLORIA	—	Bilbao	1968

Displacement, tons: 1 300
Dimensions, feet (metres): 212 × 34·8 × 21·7 *(64·7 × 10·6 × 6·6)*
Main engines: Auxiliary diesel; 500 bhp = 10·5 knots

Sail training ship. Barque rigged. Hull is entirely welded.
Sail area: 1 675 sq yards *(1 400 sq metres)*.

GLORIA   7/1976, USN

TUGS

PEDRO DE HEREDIA (ex-USS *Choctaw*, ATF 70) RM 72

Displacement, tons: 1 235 standard; 1 764 full load
Dimensions, feet (metres): 205 oa × 38·5 × 15·5 *(62·5 × 11·7 × 4·7)*
Main engines: 4 diesels; electric drive; 3 000 bhp = 15 knots
Complement: 75

Former United States ocean tug of the "Cherokee" class. Launched on 18 Oct 1942. Transferred 1961.

BAHIA UTRIA (ex-USS *Kalmia* ATA 184) RM 75

Displacement, tons: 534 standard; 858 full load
Dimensions, feet (metres): 143·0 oa × 33·9 × 8·0 *(43·6 × 10·3 × 2·4)*
Gun: 1—3 in
Main engines: 2 GM diesel-electric; 1 shaft; 1 500 bhp = 13 knots
Complement: 45

Launched 29 Aug 1944. Transferred from the United States Navy on 1 July 1971 on lease.

ANDAGOYA RM 71

Measurement, tons: 117 gross
Dimensions, feet (metres): 92·6 × 20 × 10 *(28·2 × 6·1 × 3·05)*
Main engines: Caterpillar diesel; 400 bhp = 10 knots

Launched in 1928. Re-engined in 1955.

CAPITAN CASTRO RR 81   **CAPITAN RIGOBERTO GIRALDO** RR 86
CANDIDO LEGUIZAMO RR 82   **TENIENTE LUIS BERNAL** RR 88
CAPITAN ALVARO RUIZ RR 84   **JOVES FIALLO** RR 90

Displacement, tons: 50
Dimensions, feet (metres): 63 × 14 × 2·5 *(19·2 × 4·3 × 0·8)*
Main engines: 2 GM diesels; 260 bhp = 9 knots

TENIENTE SORZANO RM 73

Displacement, tons: 54
Dimensions, feet (metres): 65·7 oa × 17·5 × 9 *(20 × 5·3 × 2·7)*
Main engines: 6 cyl diesel; 240 bhp

Former US tug.

FLOATING DOCK

MAYOR ARIAS

Displacement, tons: 700
Capacity, tons: 165
Length, feet (metres): 140 *(42·7)*

Note: It is reported that the 6 700 ton *Rodriguez Zamora* (ex-ARD 28), the small floating dock *Manuel Lara*, the floating workshop *Mantilla* (ex-YR 66) and the repair craft *Victor Cubillos* are probably under civil contract.

COMORO ISLANDS

Three of the four islands of this group joined in a unilateral declaration of independence in July 1975. This is being legitimised by France who has provided the following ship. The only port of any pretensions is Moroni.

Mercantile Marine

Lloyds Register of Shipping:
3 vessels of 765 tons gross

1 Ex-BRITISH LCT(8)

Ex-LCT 9061 (Ex-HMS *Buttress*, 4099)

Displacement, tons: 657 standard; 1 000 full load
Dimensions, feet (metres): 231·2 × 39 × 5·9 *(70·5 × 11·9 × 1·8)*
Guns: 2—20 mm; 1—120 mm mortar
Main engines: 4 Paxman diesels; 2 shafts; 1 840 bhp = 9 knots
Complement: 29

Bought by France in July 1965. Transferred 1976. Built in the United Kingdom in 1943.

CONGO

The People's Republic of Congo, which became independent on 15 Aug 1960, formed a naval service, but the patrol vessel *Reine N' Galifourou* (ex-French P 754) which was transferred 16 Nov 1962 was returned to France on 18 Feb 1965 and then re-transferred to Senegal as *Siné Saloum*.

Ministerial

Minister of Defence:
 Major Marien N'gouabi

Personnel

(a) 1978: 200 officers and men
(b) Voluntary service

Base

Pointe-Noire.

Mercantile Marine

Lloyd's Register of Shipping:
 14 vessels of 4 172 tons gross

3 Ex-CHINESE "SHANGHAI" CLASS

Displacement, tons: 120 standard; 155 full load
Dimensions, feet (metres): 128 × 18 × 5·6 *(39 × 5·5 × 1·7)*
Guns: 4—37 mm (twin); 4—25 mm (twin)
A/S armament: 8 DCs (may be removed)
Mines: Mine rails can be fitted for up to 10 mines
Main engines: 4 diesels; 4 800 hp = 30 knots
Complement: 25

Probably transferred in 1974.

"SHANGHAI" Class

4 RIVER PATROL CRAFT

Reported as about 10 tons, transferred by China.

MISCELLANEOUS

It is reported that up to 12 small craft with outboard motors are employed on river patrol.

COSTA RICA

Personnel

(a) 1978: 50 officers and men
(b) Voluntary service

Ports

Limon, Golfito, Puntarenas, Puerto Simon

Mercantile Marine

Lloyd's Register of Shipping:
 14 vessels of 6 811 tons gross

3 COASTAL PATROL CRAFT

401   402   403

Displacement, tons: 10
Dimensions, feet (metres): 41× 10 × 2·3 *(12·5 × 3·1 × 0·7)*
Gun: 1 MG

Built in mid-1950s. Of US Coastguard 40 ft type. Of 14 tons with 1 MG.

An armed tug is also reported.

CUBA

Ministerial

Minister of the Revolutionary Armed Forces:
 Raul Castro Ruz

Senior Appointment

Commander-in-Chief:
 Commodore Aldo Santamaria

Personnel

(a) 1978: 6 000 (380 officers, 220 petty officers and 5 400 men)
(b) 3 years national service

Standard of Efficiency

The US embargo on exports to Cuba has been running for over a decade. As a result all ex-USN ships in the Cuban Navy must be suffering from lack of spares, though some may have been stripped to provide for others. Cuba has the highest estimated defence expenditure in Central America and the Caribbean at about £120 million, a fair proportion of this being on Soviet aid. The navy is the smallest of the three services but, with an adequate budget and Soviet assistance in training, must be assessed as having a reasonable level of tactical and material efficiency.

Naval Establishments

Naval Academy:
 At Mariel, for officers and cadets

Naval School:
 At Morro Castle, for petty officers and men

Naval Bases:
 Cabanas, Cienfuegos, Havana, Mariel, Varadero plus at least four more in preparation.

Maritime Airforce

A helicopter force of 25 Mi-4 (Hound) and 30 Mi-1 (Hare) from USSR is in existence although these are probably all operated by the Air Force.

Strength of the Fleet

	Active	Building or (Reserve)
Frigates	—	(1)
Large Patrol Craft	18	—
Fast Attack Craft (Missile)	26	—
Fast Attack Craft (Torpedo)	24	—
Fast Attack Craft (Patrol)	5	—
Coastal Patrol Craft	12	—
LCMs	7	—
Survey Vessels	6	—
Miscellaneous	8	—
Frontier Guard	15	—

Mercantile Marine

Lloyd's Register of Shipping:
 315 vessels of 667 518 tons gross

DELETIONS

Cruiser (so called)

1972 *Cuba* (built 1911—of 2 000 tons)

Frigates

1975 *Antonio Maceo, Jose Marti* (ex-US PF Type) sunk as targets.

Corvettes

1973 *Sibony* (ex-US PCER)
1976 *Caribe* (ex-US PCER)

Light Forces

1973 *Donotivo, Matanzas*
1976 *Habana, Las Villas, Oriente, Pinar del Rio, Leoncio, Prado, GC 32, GC 33, GC 34, GC 11, GC 13, GC 14, R 41, R 42*

Tug

1976 *Diez de Octubre*

FRIGATES

One of the three ex-US frigates of the PF type—believed to be *Maximo Gomez*—which was completed in 1944 and acquired in 1947 is still in existence as harbour hulk but has no operational value.

112 CUBA

LIGHT FORCES

12 Ex-SOVIET "SO I" CLASS

Displacement, tons: 215 standard; 250 full load
Dimensions, feet (metres): 138·6 × 20 × 9·2 *(42·3 × 6·1 × 2·8)*
Guns: 4—25 mm (2 twin)
A/S weapons: 4 five-barrelled rocket launchers
Main engines: 3 diesels; 6 000 bhp = 29 knots
Range, miles: 1 100 at 13 knots
Complement: 30

Six were transferred from the USSR by Sep 1964, and six more in 1967.

"SO I" Class   1970, USN

6 Ex-SOVIET "KRONSHTADT" CLASS

Displacement, tons: 310 standard; 380 full load
Dimensions, feet (metres): 170·6 × 21·3 × 9 *(52·0 × 6·5 × 2·7)*
Guns: 1—3·5 in; 2—37 mm; 6—12·7 mm (twins)
A/S weapons: 2 MBU 1800A; 2 DCT; 2 DC racks
Mines: 6 on two racks at the stern
Main engines: 3 diesels; 3 shafts; 3 030 hp = 24 knots
Range, miles: 1 500 at 12 knots
Complement: 65

Transferred from the USSR in 1962.

Radar: Surface: Ballgun. Navigation: Don. IFF: High Pole A.

Soviet "KRONSHTADT" Class

5 Ex-SOVIET "OSA I" AND 3 "OSA II" CLASS
(FAST ATTACK CRAFT—MISSILE)

Displacement, tons: 165 standard; 200 full load
Dimensions, feet (metres): 128·7 × 25·1 × 5·9 *(39·3 × 7·7 × 1·8)*
Missiles: 4 SS-N-2 launchers in two pairs
Guns: 4—30 mm (2 twin, 1 forward, 1 aft)
Main engines: 3 diesels; 13 000 bhp = 35 knots
Range, miles: 800 at 25 knots
Complement: 25

Two boats of this class were transferred to Cuba from the USSR in January 1972 and three in 1973. These were followed by two "Osa II" in mid 1976 and one in Dec 1976. With the obvious rundown of the ex-USN ships in the Cuban Navy and the determination of the Cuban Government to maintain an independent Naval presence in the Caribbean, these could be the forerunners of further reinforcements. With the "Komar" class units there are now 26 hulls mounting 68 of the proven and effective Styx missiles in a highly sensitive area.

"OSA I" Class

18 Ex-SOVIET "KOMAR" CLASS (FAST ATTACK CRAFT—MISSILE)

Displacement, tons: 70 standard; 80 full load
Dimensions, feet (metres): 83·4 × 21·1 × 5·0 *(25·4 × 6·4 × 1·5)*
Missiles: 2 SS-N-2 launchers
Guns: 2—25 mm
Main engines: 4 diesels; 4 shafts; 4 800 bhp = 40 knots
Range, miles: 400 at 30 knots

First 12 transferred in 1962. Last pair arrived in Dec 1966.

"KOMAR" Class   1970, USN

CUBA 113

12 Ex-SOVIET "P 6" CLASS (FAST ATTACK CRAFT—TORPEDO)

Nos. 80-92

Displacement, tons: 66 standard; 75 full load
Dimensions, feet (metres): 83·4 × 20 × 6 *(25·4 × 6·1 × 1·5)*
Guns: 4—25 mm (two twin)
Torpedo tubes: 2—21 in (two single)
Main engines: 4 diesels; 4 shafts; 4 800 hp = 43 knots
Range, miles: 450 at 30 knots
Complement: 25

Transferred in 1962. Can carry mines or depth charges in place of torpedo tubes.

Radar: Pot Head or Skin Head.

"P 6" Class   1970, USN

12 Ex-SOVIET "P 4" CLASS (FAST ATTACK CRAFT—TORPEDO)

Displacement, tons: 25
Dimensions, feet (metres): 62·7 × 11·6 × 5·6 *(19·1 × 3·5 × 1·7)*
Guns: 2—25 mm
Torpedo tubes: 2—18 in
Main engines: 2 diesels; 2 200 bhp; 2 shafts = 50 knots
Complement: 12

Transferred from the USSR in 1962-64.

"P 4" Class   1971

5 Ex-SOVIET "ZHUK" CLASS (FAST ATTACK CRAFT—PATROL)

Displacement, tons: 60
Dimensions, feet (metres): 75 × 16 × 5 *(22·9 × 4·9 × 1·5)*
Guns: 4—14·5 mm (twin)
Main engines: Diesels = 34 knots (28 knots normal)
Complement: 18?

Transferred 1975.

"ZHUK" Class

6 COASTAL PATROL CRAFT

| SV 7 | SV 8 | SV 9 | SV 10 | SV 12 | SV 14 |

Length, feet (metres): 40 *(12·2)*
Gun: 1—50 cal MG
Main engines: 2 GM diesels = 25 knots

Later boats of the SV type equipped with radar. Completed 1958.

6 COASTAL PATROL CRAFT

| SV 1 | SV 2 | SV 3 | SV 4 | SV 5 | SV 6 |

Displacement, tons: 6·15
Dimensions, feet (metres): 32 × 10 × 2·8 *(9·8 × 3·1 × 0·8)*
Main engines: 2 Chrysler Crown, 230 bhp = 18 knots

Auxiliary patrol boats for port patrol, launched in 1953.

AMPHIBIOUS FORCES

7 "T4" CLASS LCMs

Obtained 1967-74. Mainly employed as Harbour Craft.

SURVEY VESSELS

6 Ex-Soviet "NYRYAT 1" CLASS

| H 91 | H 92 | H 93 | H 94 | H 95 | H 96 |

Displacement, tons: 145
Main engines: Diesels = 12·5 knots
Complement: 15

All-purpose craft reportedly used for surveying.

5 MOTOR LAUNCHES

No details available but all used for surveying.

MISCELLANEOUS

1 TRAINING SHIP

H 101

Measurement, tons: 530

An ex-fishing trawler/buoy tender now used for cadet training.

2 LIGHTHOUSE TENDERS

ENRIQUE COLLAZO (ex-*Joaquin Godoy*)

Displacement, tons: 815
Dimensions, feet (metres): 211 × 24 × 9 *(64·3 × 7·3 × 2·7)*
Main engines: Triple expansion; 2 shafts; 672 ihp = 8 knots

Built at Paisley, Scotland. Launched in 1906. Acquired in 1950 from Cuban Mercantile Marine.

114 CUBA / DENMARK

BERTHA SF 10

Displacement, tons: 98
Dimensions, feet (metres): 104 × 19 × 11 *(31·7 × 5·8 × 3·4)*
Main engines: 2 Gray Marine diesels; 450 bhp = 10 knots

Launched in 1944.

1 Ex-SOVIET "OKHTENSKY" CLASS (OCEAN TUG)

CARIBE

Displacement, tons: 835
Dimensions, feet (metres): 143 oa × 34 × 15 *(43·6 × 10·4 × 4·6)*
Guns: 1—3 in *(76 mm)*; 2—20 mm.
Main engines: 2 BM diesels; 2 electric motors; 2 shafts; 1 875 bhp = 14 knots
Oil fuel, tons: 187
Complement: 34

Transferred in 1976 to replace *Diez de Octubre*. Name taken from deleted corvette.

GRANMA A 11

Yacht which reached Cuba on 2 Dec 1956 with Dr Fidel Castro and the men who began the liberation war. Historic vessel incorporated into the Navy as an Auxiliary.

3 HARBOUR AUXILIARIES

A1   A2   A3

Displacement, tons: 60
Dimensions, feet (metres): 74 × 15 × 5 *(22·6 × 4·6 × 1·5)*
Gun: 1 MG
Main engines: 2 diesels

Built in USA 1949.

FRONTIER GUARD

A number of small craft operate under the direction of the Ministry of the Interior. Names and numbers available—*Marti, Camilo Cienfuegos, Maceo, Finlay, Escambray, Cuartel Moncada, Guanabacoa, GF 101, 102, 528, 701, 720, 725, 825.*

CYPRUS

General

For a considerable period 6 ex-Soviet "P 4" class and 2 ex-German "R" boats served in Cypriot waters. However the majority were sunk during the Turkish operations of July 1974 and one was stranded and lost. There is therefore no craft to be listed this year.

Mercantile Marine

Lloyd's Register of Shipping:
800 vessels of 2 787 908 tons gross

New Construction

Two Fast Attack Craft (Missile) ordered from Chantiers Navals de l'Esterel were not taken up and were transferred to Greece as *Kelefstis Stamou* and *Diopos Antionio*.

CZECHOSLOVAKIA

Although a navy as such does not exist there is a river patrol force, the personnel of which wear naval-type uniforms. About 1 200 strong with some 20 river patrol craft.

Mercantile Marine

Lloyds Register of Shipping:
14 vessels of 148 689 tons gross

DENMARK

Ministerial

Minister of Defence:
P. Søgaard

Headquarters Appointment

Commander-in-Chief:
Vice-Admiral S. Thostrup
Flag Officer Denmark:
Rear-Admiral H. M. Petersen

Diplomatic Representation

Defence Attaché, Bonn
Colonel P. E. M. O. Gruner
Defence Attaché, London:
Colonel H. H. Prince Georg of Denmark, KCVO
Assistant Defence Attaché, London:
Commander B. O. Sørensen
Defence Attaché, Washington:
Colonel P. B. Nissen

Personnel

(a) 1978: 5 300 officers and men
(Reserves of 3 100 Naval Home Guard)
(b) 9 months national service

Navy Estimates

1973-74: 583 600 000 Kr.
1974-75: 638 500 000 Kr.
1975-76: 729 900 000 Kr.
1976-77: 846 300 000 Kr.
1977-78: 775 700 000 Kr (Apr '76 level).

Naval Bases

Copenhagen, Korsør, Frederikshavn, Grønnedal (Greenland)

Farvands Direktoratet

This Directorate of Waters (under the MOD) now controls the Pilot Service, Lighthouse Service, and Lifeboat Service.

Naval Air Arm

8 Alouette III helicopters

Prefix to Ships' Names

HDMS

Strength of the Fleet

Type	Active	Building or Projected
Frigates	7	3
Corvettes	3	—
Submarines (Patrol)	6	—
Fast Attack Craft (Missile)	10	—
Fast Attack Craft (Torpedo)	6	—
Large Patrol Craft	23	—
Coastal Patrol Craft	23	—
Minelayers	7	—
Minesweepers (Coastal)	8	—
Tankers (Small)	2	—
Icebreakers	3	—
Royal Yacht	1	—

Mercantile Marine

Lloyd's Register of Shipping:
1 407 vessels of 5 331 165 tons gross

New Construction

Programme includes 2 Minelayers, 3 Fast Attack Craft.

DELETIONS

Corvette

1974 *Diana* ("Triton" class)

Fast Attack Craft

1974 6 "Flyvefisken" Class (scrapped May 1976)
1977 4 "Falken" Class

Large Patrol Craft

1972 *Alholm*

Coastal Patrol Craft

1975 Y 354, Y 359, *Ertholm, Lindholm*
1976 *Faeno*

Mine Warfare Forces

1974 2 "Lougen" Class Minelayers
      4 "Vig" Class Inshore Minesweepers

Tenders

1970 *Hollaenderdybet, Kongedybet*
1973 *Hjaelperen* (laid up)
1974 *Henrik Gerner*

Icebreakers

1972 *Lillebjørn*
1975 *Storebjørn*

DENMARK 115

PENNANT LIST

Frigates and Corvettes

F	340	Beskytteren
F	344	Bellona
F	346	Flora
F	347	Triton
F	348	Hvidbjørnen
F	349	Vaedderen
F	350	Ingolf
F	351	Fylla
F	352	Peder Skram
F	353	Herluf Trolle
F	354	Niels Juel
F	355	Olfert Fischer
F	356	Peter Tordenskjold

Submarines

S	320	Nahrvalen
S	321	Nordkaperen
S	326	Delfinen
S	327	Spaekhuggeren
S	328	Tumleren
S	329	Springeren

Light Forces

P	510	Søløven
P	511	Søridderen
P	512	Søbjørnen
P	513	Søhesten
P	514	Søhunden
P	515	Søulven
P	530	Daphne
P	531	Dryaden
P	532	Havmanden
P	533	Havfruen
P	534	Najaden
P	535	Nymfen
P	536	Neptun
P	537	Ran
P	538	Rota
P	540	Bille
P	541	Bredal
P	542	Hammer
P	543	Huitfeldt
P	544	Krieger
P	545	Norby
P	546	Rodsteen
P	547	Sehested

Light Forces

P	548	Suenson
P	549	Willemoes
Y	300	Barsø
Y	301	Drejø
Y	302	Romsø
Y	303	Samsø
Y	304	Thurø
Y	305	Vejrø
Y	306	Farø
Y	307	Laesø
Y	308	Rømø
Y	383	Tejsten
Y	384	Maagen
Y	385	Mallemukken
Y	386	Agdleq
Y	387	Agpa

Minewarfare Forces

N	80	Falster
N	81	Fyen
N	82	Møen
N	83	Sjaelland
M	571	Aarøsund
M	572	Alssund
M	573	Egernsund
M	574	Grønsund
M	575	Guldborgsund
M	576	Omøsund
M	577	Ulvsund
M	578	Wilsund

Auxiliaries

A	540	Dannebrog
A	568	Rimfaxe
A	569	Skinfaxe

Naval Home Guard

MHV 53
MHV 64
MHV 70
MHV 71
MHV 72
MHV 81 Askø
MHV 82 Enø
MHV 83 Manø
MHV 84 Baagø
MHV 85 Hjortø
MHV 86 Lyø
MHV 90
MHV 91
MHV 92
MHV 93
MHV 94
MHV 95

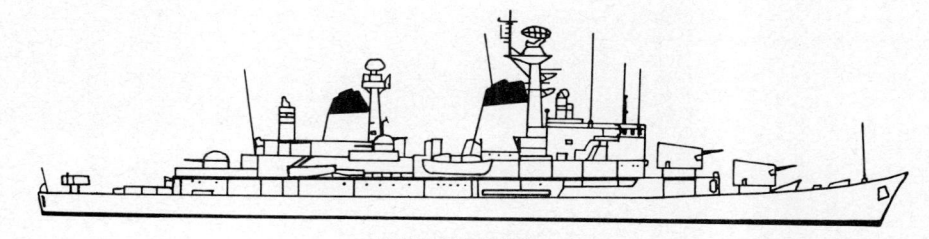

"PEDER SKRAM" Class

BESKYTTEREN

"FALSTER" Class

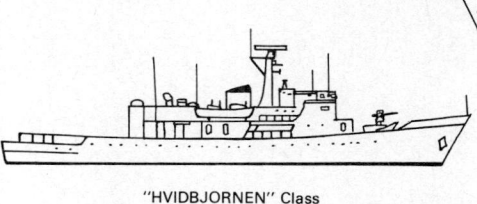

"HVIDBJORNEN" Class

SUBMARINES

Note: Denmark is planning to build six new submarines. It is likely that these will eventually be of the same design as the German/Norwegian Type 210 of about 750 tons. First informal contacts have already been made.

2 "NARHVALEN" CLASS

Name	No.	Builders	Laid down	Launched	Commissioned
NARHVALEN	S 320	Royal Dockyard, Copenhagen	16 Feb 1965	10 Sep 1968	27 Feb 1970
NORDKAPEREN	S 321	Royal Dockyard, Copenhagen	20 Jan 1966	18 Dec 1969	22 Dec 1970

Displacement, tons: 370 surfaced; 450 dived
Length, feet (metres): 144·4 *(44·0)*
Beam, feet (metres): 15 *(4·6)*
Draught, feet (metres): 12·5 *(3·8)*
Torpedo tubes: 8—21 in *(533 mm)* bow
Main machinery: 2 MB diesels; 1 500 bhp surfaced; 2 electric motors; 1 500 bhp dived
Speed, knots: 12 surfaced; 17 dived
Complement: 22

These coastal submarines are similar to the German Improved Type 205 and were built under licence at the Royal Dockyard, Copenhagen with modifications for Danish needs. Active and passive sonar.

NARHVALEN   *1974, Royal Danish Navy*

4 "DELFINEN" CLASS

Name	No.	Builders	Laid down	Launched	Commissioned
DELFINEN	S 326	Royal Dockyard, Copenhagen	1 July 1954	4 May 1956	16 Sep 1958
SPAEKHUGGEREN	S 327	Royal Dockyard, Copenhagen	1 Dec 1954	20 Feb 1957	27 June1959
TUMLEREN	S 328	Royal Dockyard, Copenhagen	22 May 1956	22 May 1958	15 Jan 1960
SPRINGEREN	S 329	Royal Dockyard, Copenhagen	3 Jan 1961	26 April1963	22 Oct 1964

Displacement, tons: 550 standard; 595 surfaced; 643 dived
Length, feet (metres): 177·2 *(54·0)*
Beam, feet (metres): 15·4 *(4·7)*
Draught, feet (metres): 13·1 *(4·0)*
Torpedo tubes: 4—21 in *(533 mm)*
Main machinery: 2 Burmeister & Wain diesels; 1 200 bhp surfaced; electric motors; 1 200 hp dived
Speed, knots: 15 surfaced and dived
Range, miles: 4 000 at 8 knots
Complement: 33

Active and passive sonar.

TUMLEREN   *1975, Royal Danish Navy*

DENMARK

FRIGATES

2 "PEDER SKRAM" CLASS

Name	No.	Builders	Laid down	Launched	Commissioned
PEDER SKRAM	F 352	Helsingörs J. & M.	25 Sep 1964	20 May 1965	30 June 1966
HERLUF TROLLE	F 353	Helsingörs J. & M.	18 Dec 1964	8 Sep 1965	16 April 1967

Displacement, tons: 2 030 standard; 2 720 full load
Length, feet (metres): 354·3 *(108)* pp; 396·5 *(112·6)* oa
Beam, feet (metres): 39·5 *(12)*
Draught, feet (metres): 11·8 *(3·6)*
Missiles: 1 Sea Sparrow (4 cell) on quarter-deck; 2—4 cell Harpoon launchers
Guns: 2—5 in *(127 mm)* 38 cal (twin); 4—40 mm
Torpedo tubes: 4—21 in for wire-guided and A/S torpedoes
A/S weapons: DCs
Main engines: CODOG:—2 GM 16-567 D diesels; 4 800 hp; 2 Pratt & Whitney PWA GG 4A-3 gas turbines; 44 000 hp total output; 2 shafts
Speed, knots: 30, 18 economical
Complement: 190

Danish design. In addition to other armament they were originally designed for three 21 inch torpedo tubes and the Terne anti-submarine weapon. But the latter has been dropped in favour of Sea Sparrow and two twin 21 in mountings fitted on the beams.

Conversion: Mid-life conversion in 1976-77. *Peder Skram* paid off 1977.

Radar: Combined warning: Two CWS 3.
Fire control: Three CGS-1.
Tactical: One NWS-1.
Navigation: One NWS-2.

Sonar: PMS 26.

HERLUF TROLLE   1977, Royal Danish Navy

3 "NIELS JUEL" CLASS

Name	No.	Builders	Laid down	Launched	Commissioned
NIELS JUEL	F 354	Aalborg Vaerft	1977	—	?1979
OLFERT FISCHER	F 355	Aalborg Vaerft	1977	—	?1979
PETER TORDENSKJOLD	F 356	Aalborg Vaerft	1977	—	?1980

Displacement, tons: 1 320 full load
Length, feet (metres): 275 oa *(84)*
Beam, feet (metres): 33·8 *(10·3)*
Draught, feet (metres): 10·1 *(3·1)*
Missiles: Sea Sparrow; (8 cell); 8 Harpoon (2 quad by funnel)
Gun: 1—76 mm OTO Melara
A/S weapons: Uncertain
Mines: Have laying capability
Rocket Projectors: 2 for illumination, Chaff and HE rockets
Main engines: CODOG 1 Rolls-Royce Olympus; 25 400 hp; 2 MTU 20 V—956 diesels; 4 800 hp at 1 500 revs, 6 000 for short periods; SSS clutches; GEC gearbox; 2 shafts
Speed, knots: 28
Complement: 90

First of a class which is planned eventually to reach a total of 6. Designed to replace "Triton" class and, possibly, "Peder Skram" class.
YARD Glasgow designed the class to Danish order. Three Danish shipyards were asked to tender in early 1975 (Helsingør, Lindø and Aalborg). On 5 Dec 1975 announced that first three would be built by Aalborg Vaerft.

Radar: Plessey AWS 5.

"NIELS JUEL" Class

1 MODIFIED "HVIDBJØRNEN" CLASS

Name	No.	Builders	Laid down	Launched	Commissioned
BESKYTTEREN	F 340	Aalborg Vaerft	15 Dec 1974	27 May 1975	27 Feb 1976

Displacement, tons: 1 970 full load
Length, feet (metres): 244 *(74·4)* oa
Beam, feet (metres): 39 *(11·8)*
Draught, feet (metres): 15 *(4·5)*
Aircraft: 1 Alouette III helicopter
Gun: 1—3 in *(76 mm)*
Main engines: 3 B.W. Alpha diesels; 7 440 bhp; 1 shaft
Speed, knots: 18
Range, miles: 4 500 at 16 knots on 2 engines; 6 000 at 13 knots on 1 engine
Complement: 60

Cost approx £5 million. Strengthened for navigation in ice. Designed for similar duties as *Hvidbjørnen*.

Radar: Search; One AWS 1/CWS 2.
Tactical: One NWS 1.
Navigation: One NWS 2.

Sonar: PMS 26.

BESKYTTEREN   1976, Royal Danish Navy

4 "HVIDBJØRNEN" CLASS

Name	No.	Builders	Laid down	Launched	Commissioned
HVIDBJØRNEN	F 348	Aarhus Flydedok	4 June 1961	23 Nov 1961	15 Dec 1962
VAEDDEREN	F 349	Aalborg Vaerft	30 Oct 1961	6 April 1962	19 Mar 1963
INGOLF	F 350	Svendborg Vaerft	5 Dec 1961	27 July 1962	27 July 1963
FYLLA	F 351	Aalborg Vaerft	27 June 1962	18 Dec 1962	10 July 1963

Displacement, tons: 1 345 standard; 1 650 full load
Length, feet (metres): 219·8 *(67·0)* pp; 238·2 *(72·6)* oa
Beam, feet (metres): 38·0 *(11·6)*
Draught, feet (metres): 16 *(4·9)*
Aircraft: 1 Alouette III helicopter
Gun: 1—3 in *(76 mm)*
Main engines: 4 GM 16—567C diesels; 6 400 bhp; 1 shaft
Speed, knots: 18
Range, miles: 6 000 at 13 knots
Complement: 75

Ordered in 1960-61. Of frigate type for fishery protection and surveying duties in the North Sea, Faroe Islands and Greenland waters. They are equipped with a helicopter platform aft.

Radar: Search: One AWS 1/CWS 2.
Tactical: One NWS 1.

Sonar: PMS 26.

INGOLF   1974, Royal Danish Navy

CORVETTES

3 "TRITON" CLASS

Name	No.	Builders	Laid down	Launched	Commissioned
BELLONA	F 344	Naval Meccanica, Castellammare	1954	9 Jan 1955	31 Jan 1957
FLORA	F 346	Cantiere del Tirreno, Riva Trigoso	1953	25 June 1955	28 Aug 1956
TRITON	F 347	Cantiere Navali di Taranto	1953	12 Sep 1954	10 Aug 1955

Displacement, tons: 760 standard; 873 full load
Length, feet (metres): 242·8 *(74·0)* pp; 250·3 *(76·3)* oa
Beam, feet (metres): 31·5 *(9·6)*
Draught, feet (metres): 9 *(2·7)*
Guns: 2—3 in *(76 mm)*; 1—40 mm
A/S: 2 Hedgehogs; 4 DCT
Main engines: 2 Ansaldo Fiat 409T diesels, 4 400 bhp; 2 shafts
Speed, knots: 20
Range, miles: 3 000 at 18 knots
Complement: 110

These were built in Italy for the Danish Navy under the United States "offshore" account. Sisters of the Italian "Albatros" class. *Diana* deleted 1974.

Classification: Officially classified as corvettes in 1954, but have "F" pennant numbers.

Radar: Search: Plessey AWS 1. Navigation: E Band.

Sonar: QCU-2.

FLORA   1974, Royal Danish Navy

LIGHT FORCES

10 "WILLEMOES" CLASS (FAST ATTACK CRAFT—MISSILE)

Name	No.	Builders	Commissioned
BILLE	P 540	Frederikshavn V and F	Oct 1976
BREDAL	P 541	Frederikshavn V and F	Jan 1977
HAMMER	P 542	Frederikshavn V and F	Mar 1977
HUITFELDE	P 543	Frederikshavn V and F	June 1977
KRIEGER	P 544	Frederikshavn V and F	Sep 1977
NORBY	P 545	Frederikshavn V and F	Nov 1977
RODSTEEN	P 546	Frederikshavn V and F	Jan 1978
SEHESTED	P 547	Frederikshavn V and F	Mar 1978
SUENSON	P 548	Frederikshavn V and F	June 1978
WILLEMOES	P 549	Frederikshavn V and F	June 1976 (trials)

Displacement, tons: 260 full load
Dimensions, feet (metres): 151 × 24 × 8 *(46 × 7·4 × 2·4)*
Missiles: 4 or 8 Harpoon (in place of after torpedo tubes)
Gun: 1—76 mm OTO Melara
Torpedo tubes: 2 or 4—21 in (see notes)
Main engines: CODOG arrangement of 3 Rolls-Royce Proteus gas turbines; 12 000 hp; diesels for cruising on wing shafts; 800 hp; cp propellers.
Speed, knots: 40 (12 on diesels).
Complement: 25 (6 officers, 19 ratings).

Designed by Lürssen to Danish order. Very similar to Swedish "Spica II" class (also Lürssen). Original order to Frederikshavn for 4 boats, increased to 8 and finally 10.
Building dates: *Willemoes* (prototype) laid down 20 July 1974, launched 5 Oct 1974 and completed for trials (with 4 torpedo tubes and no missiles) in 7 Oct 1975. Series production with *Bille* in 1974. She was launched 26 Mar 1976. Further boats laid down 12 Oct 1974, 14 Dec 1974 and 17 Feb 1975.

Armament: From the 6th boat all are being fitted with two torpedo tubes and Harpoon. The rest are to be similarly retrofitted.

Radar: Warning combined: One.
Fire control: One.
Navigation: One NWS 3.

WILLEMOES   1977, Royal Danish Navy

118   DENMARK

6 "SØLØVEN" CLASS (FAST ATTACK CRAFT—TORPEDO)

Name	No.	Builders	Commissioned
SØLØVEN	P 510	Vosper	12 Feb 1965
SØRIDDEREN	P 511	Vosper	10 Feb 1965
SØBJORNEN	P 512	R. Dockyard, Copenhagen	Sep 1965
SØHESTEN	P 513	R. Dockyard, Copenhagen	June 1966
SØHUNDEN	P 514	R. Dockyard, Copenhagen	Dec 1966
SØULVEN	P 515	R. Dockyard, Copenhagen	Mar 1967

Displacement, tons: 95 standard; 120 full load
Dimensions, feet (metres): 90 pp; 96 wl; 99 oa × 25·5 × 7 *(30·3 × 7·3 × 2·2)*
Guns: 2—40 mm Bofors
Torpedo tubes: 4—21 in
Main engines: 3 Bristol Siddeley Proteus gas turbines; 3 shafts; 12 750 bhp = 54 knots
  GM diesels on wing shafts for cruising = 10 knots
Range, miles: 400 at 46 knots
Complement: 29

The design is a combination of the Vosper "Brave" class hull form and "Ferocity" type construction. *Søløven* and *Søridderen* were both completed in June 1964 and handed over to the RDN after 6 month's trials.

Radar: One NWS 1.

SØHUNDEN   1974, Royal Danish Navy

9 "DAPHNE" CLASS (LARGE PATROL CRAFT)

Name	No.	Builders	Commissioned
DAPHNE	P 530	R. Dockyard, Copenhagen	19 Dec 1961
DRYADEN	P 531	R. Dockyard, Copenhagen	4 April 1962
HAVMANDEN	P 532	R. Dockyard, Copenhagen	30 Aug 1962
HAVFRUEN	P 533	R. Dockyard, Copenhagen	20 Dec 1962
NAJADEN	P 534	R. Dockyard, Copenhagen	26 April 1963
NYMFEN	P 535	R. Dockyard, Copenhagen	4 Oct 1963
NEPTUN	P 536	R. Dockyard, Copenhagen	18 Dec 1963
RAN	P 537	R. Dockyard, Copenhagen	15 May 1964
ROTA	P 538	R. Dockyard, Copenhagen	20 Jan 1965

Displacement, tons: 170
Dimensions, feet (metres): 121·3 × 20 × 6·5 *(37 × 6·8 × 2)* (P 530-533)
Gun: 1—40 mm plus 2—51 mm flare launchers
A/S weapons: DCs
Main engines: 2 FD6 Foden diesels; 2 shafts; 2 600 bhp = 20 knots
  (plus 1 cruising engine; 100 bhp)
Complement: 23

4 were built under US offshore programme. Some have been disarmed.

Design: P 530-533 have a rounded stern and P 534-538 have a straight stern.

Radar: One NWS 3.

Sonar: PMS 26.

NEPTUN   1974, Royal Danish Navy

2 "AGDLEQ" CLASS (LARGE PATROL CRAFT)

Name	No.	Builders	Commissioned
AGDLEQ	Y 386	Svendborg Vaerft	12 Mar 1974
AGPA	Y 387	Svendborg Vaerft	14 May 1974

Displacement, tons: 300
Dimensions, feet (metres): 101·7 × 25·3 × 10·9 *(31 × 7·7 × 3·3)*
Guns: 2—20 mm
Speed, knots: 12
Complement: 15

Designed for service off Greenland.

Radar: Navigation: Two NWS 3.

AGDLEQ   1974, Royal Danish Navy

2 "MAAGEN" CLASS (LARGE PATROL CRAFT)

Name	No.	Builders	Commissioned
MAAGEN	Y 384	Helsingør Dockyard	May 1960
MALLEMUKKEN	Y 385	Helsingør Dockyard	May 1960

Displacement, tons: 190
Dimensions, feet (metres): 88·5 × 21·7 × 9·5 *(27 × 6·6 × 2·9)*
Gun: 1—40 mm
Main engines: 385 hp; 1 shaft = 11 knots

Of steel construction. Laid down 15 Jan 1960.

Radar: Two NWS 3.

MAAGEN   1976, Royal Danish Navy

DENMARK 119

9 "BARSØ" CLASS (LARGE PATROL CRAFT)

Name	No.	Builders	Commissioned
BARSØ	Y 300	Svendborg Vaerft	1969
DREJØ	Y 301	Svendborg Vaerft	1969
ROMSØ	Y 302	Svendborg Vaerft	1969
SAMSØ	Y 303	Svendborg Vaerft	1969
THURØ	Y 304	Svendborg Vaerft	1969
VEJRØ	Y 305	Svendborg Vaerft	1969
FARØ	Y 306	Svendborg Vaerft	1972
LAESØ	Y 307	Svendborg Vaerft	1973
ROMØ	Y 308	Svendborg Vaerft	1973

Displacement, tons: 155
Dimensions, feet (metres): 83·7 × 19·7 × 9·8 *(25·5 × 6 × 2·8)*
Guns: 2—20 mm
Speed: 11 knots

Rated as patrol cutters.

Radar: One NWS 3.

DREJØ *1974, Royal Danish Navy*

1 "TEJSTEN" CLASS (LARGE PATROL CRAFT)

Name	No.	Builders	Commissioned
TEJSTEN	Y 383	Holbaek Skibsbyggeri	1951

Displacement, tons: 130
Dimensions, feet (metres): 82 × 20·7 × 9·4 *(25 × 6·1 × 2·9)*
Main engines: Alfa diesel; 180 bhp = 9 knots

Auxiliary ketch of wooden construction. Based in Faeroe Is.

2 LARGE BOTVED TYPE (COASTAL PATROL CRAFT)

Y 375   Y 376

Displacement, tons: 12
Dimensions, feet (metres): 42·9 × 14·8 × 3·7 *(13·1 × 4·5 × 1·1)*
Main engines: Diesel; 2 shafts; 680 hp = 26 knots

Built in 1974 by Botved Boats

Radar: One NWS 3.

Y 376 *1975, Royal Danish Navy*

3 SMALL BOTVED TYPE (COASTAL PATROL CRAFT)

Y 377   Y 378   Y 379

Displacement, tons: 9
Dimensions, feet (metres): 32·1 × 10·4 × 3·1 *(9·8 × 3·3 × 0·9)*
Main engines: Diesels; 2 shafts; 500 hp = 27 knots

Built in 1975 by Botved Boats.

Radar: One NWS 3.

Small BOTVED Type *1975, Royal Danish Navy*

3 Y TYPE (COASTAL PATROL CRAFT)

Y 338   Y 339   Y 343

Miscellaneous patrol cutters (ex-fishing vessels) all built in 1944-45.

6 "MHV 90" CLASS (COASTAL PATROL CRAFT)

MHV 90   MHV 91   MHV 92   MHV 93   MHV 94   MHV 95

Displacement, tons: 90
Dimensions, feet (metres): 64·9 × 18·7 × 8·2 *(19·8 × 5·7 × 2·5)*
Gun: 1—20 mm
Main engines: Diesel; 1 shaft = 10 knots

Built in 1975. Manned by Naval Home Guard.

Radar: One NWS 3.

MHV 93 *1975, Royal Danish Navy*

120 DENMARK

6 "MHV 80" CLASS (COASTAL PATROL CRAFT)

Name	No.	Builders	Commissioned
ASKØ (ex-Y 386, ex-M 560, ex-MS 2)	MHV 81	Denmark	1941
ENØ (ex-Y 388, ex-M 562, ex-MS 5)	MHV 82	Denmark	1941
MANØ (ex-Y 391, ex-M 566, ex-MS 9)	MHV 83	Denmark	1941
BAAGØ (ex-Y 387, ex-M 561, ex-MS 3)	MHV 84	Denmark	1941
HJORTØ (ex-Y 389, ex-M 564, ex- MS 7)	MHV 85	Denmark	1941
LYØ (ex-Y 390, ex-M 565, ex-MS 8)	MHV 86	Denmark	1941

Displacement, tons: 74
Dimensions, feet (metres): 78·8 × 21 × 5 *(24·0 × 6·4 × 1·5)*
Gun: 1—20 mm
Main engines: Diesel; 1 shaft; 350 bhp = 11 knots

Of wooden construction. All launched in 1941. Former inshore minesweepers. Manned by the Naval Home Guard.

Radar: One NWS. 3.

"MHV 80" Class   1974, Royal Danish Navy

3 "MHV 70" CLASS (COASTAL PATROL CRAFT)

Name	No.	Builders	Commissioned
MHV 70	—	R. Dockyard, Copenhagen	1958
MHV 71	—	R. Dockyard, Copenhagen	1958
MHV 72	—	R. Dockyard, Copenhagen	1958

Displacement, tons: 76
Dimensions, feet (metres): 65·9 × 16·7 × 8·2 *(20·1 × 5·1 × 2·5)*
Gun: 1—20 mm
Main engines: 200 bhp = 10 knots

Patrol boats and training craft for the Naval Home Guard. Formerly designated DMH, but allocated MHV numbers in 1969.

Radar: One NWS 3.

In addition there are some 20 small vessels of the trawler and other types—including MHV 53 and 64.

MHV 71   1974, Royal Danish Navy

MINE WARFARE FORCES

4 "FALSTER" CLASS (MINELAYERS)

Name	No.	Builders	Commissioned
FALSTER	N 80	Nakskov Skibsvaerft	7 Nov 1963
FYEN	N 81	Frederikshavn Vaerft	18 Sep 1963
MØEN	N 82	Frederikshavn Vaerft	29 April 1964
SJAELLAND	N 83	Nakskov Skibsvaerft	7 July 1964

Displacement, tons: 1 900 full load
Length, feet (metres): 238 *(72·5)* pp; 252·6 *(77·0)* oa
Beam, feet (metres): 41 *(12·5)*
Draught, feet (metres): 10 *(3·0)*
Missiles: Seasparrow
Guns: 4—3 in *(76 mm)*, (twin US Mk 35)
Mines: 400
Main engines: 2 GM—567D 3 diesels; 4 800 shp; 2 shafts
Speed, knots: 17
Complement: 120

Ordered in 1960-61 and launched 1962-63. All are named after Danish islands. The steel hull is flush-decked with a raking stem, a full stern and a prominent knuckle forward. The hull has been specially strengthened for ice navigation. Similar to Turkish *Nusret*. *Møen* employed on midshipmen's training.

Conversion: *Sjaelland* converted in 1976 to act as depôt ship for submarines and FAC in place of *Henrik Gerner*.

Gunnery: All mountings now fitted with shields.

FYEN (aerials on foremast differ in *Falster*)   1977, Royal Danish Navy

Radar: Warning Combined: One CWS 2.
Fire Control: One CGS 1.
Tactical: One NWS 1.
Navigation: One NWS 2.

2 "LINDORMEN" CLASS (MINELAYERS)

Name	No.	Builders	Commissioned
LINDORMEN	N 43	Svendborg Vaerft	1978
LOSSEN	N 44	Svendborg Vaerft	1978

Displacement, tons: 570
Dimensions, feet (metres): 147·6 × 29·5 × 8·9 *(45 × 9 × 2·7)*
Guns: 2—20 mm
Main engines: Diesels; 1 600 hp = 14 knots
Complement: 27

Replacements for "Lougen" Class. Controlled Minelayers. *Lindormen* laid down Jan 1977 and *Lossen* in Feb 1977.

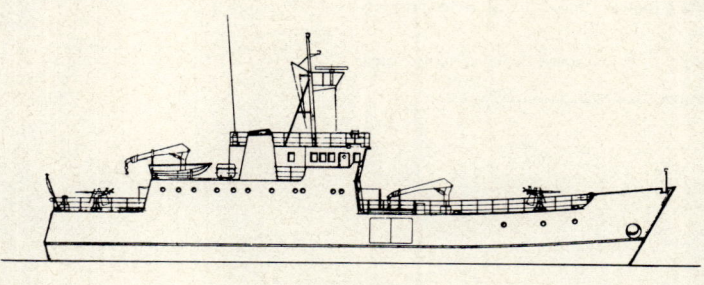

"LINDORMEN" Class

DENMARK 121

1 "LANGELAND" CLASS (COASTAL MINELAYER)

Name	No.	Builders	Commissioned
LANGELAND	N 42	Royal Dockyard, Copenhagen	1951

Displacement, tons: 310 standard; 332 full load
Dimensions, feet (metres): 133·5 oa; 128·2 pp × 23·7 × 7·2 *(40·7; 39·1 × 7·2 × 2·1)*
Guns: 2—40 mm; 2—20 mm Madsen
Main engines: Diesel; 2 shafts; 385 bhp = 11·6 knots
Complement: 37

Laid down in 1950. Launched on 17 May 1950.

LANGELAND 1973, Royal Danish Navy

8 Ex-US MSC (ex-AMS) TYPE 60 CLASS (MINESWEEPERS—COASTAL)

AARØSUND (ex-*MSC* 127) M 571 GULDBORGSUND (ex-*MSC* 257) M 575
ALSSUND (ex-*MSC* 128) M 572 OMØSUND (ex-*MSC* 221) M 576
EGERNSUND (ex-*MSC* 129) M 573 ULVSUND (ex-*MSC* 263) M 577
GRØNSUND (ex-*MSC* 256) M 574 VILSUND (ex-*MSC* 264) M 578

Displacement, tons: 350 standard; 376 full load
Dimensions, feet (metres): 138 pp; 144 oa × 27 × 8·5 *(42·1; 43·9 × 8·2 × 2·6)*
Guns: 1—40 mm or 2—20 mm
Main engines: Diesels; 2 shafts; 1 200 bhp = 13 knots
Range, miles: 2 500 at 10 knots
Complement: 35

MSC (ex-AMS) 60 class NATO coastal minesweepers all built in USA. Completed in 1954-56. *Aarøsund* was transferred on 24 Jan 1955, *Alssund* on 5 April 1955, *Egernsund* on 3 Aug 1955, *Grønsund* on 21 Sep 1956, *Guldborgsund* on 11 Nov 1956, *Omøsund* on 20 June 1956, *Ulvsund* on 20 Sep 1956 and *Vilsund* on 15 Nov 1956, *Guldborgsund* has been fitted with a charthouse between bridge and funnel and is employed on surveying duties.

Radar: One NWS 3.

ULVSUND 1975, Reiner Nerlich

SLEIPNER A 558

A 200 ton torpedo recovery/transporter.

SERVICE FORCES

TANKERS

Name	No.	Builders	Commissioned
RIMFAXE (ex-US *YO 226*)	A 568	USA	1945
SKINFAXE (ex-US *YO 229*)	A 569	USA	1945

Displacement, tons: 422 light; 1 390 full load
Dimensions, feet (metres): 174 oa × 32 × 13·2 *(53·1 × 9·8 × 4)*
Main engines: 1 GM diesel; 560 bhp = 10 knots
Complement: 23

Transferred to the Royal Danish Navy from the USA on 2 Aug 1962.

RIMFAXE 1971, Royal Danish Navy

ICEBREAKERS

Note: Icebreakers are controlled by the Ministry of Trade and Shipping, but are maintained by RDN at Frederikshavn in summer.

Name	No.	Builders	Commissioned
DANBJØRN	—	Lindø Vaerft	1965
ISBJØRN	—	Lindø Vaerft	1966

Displacement, tons: 3 685
Dimensions, feet (metres): 252 × 56 × 20 *(76·8 × 17·1 × 6·1)*
Main engines: Diesels; electric drive; 10 500 shp = 14 knots
Complement: 34

DANBJØRN 1976, Royal Danish Navy

Name	No.	Builders	Commissioned
ELBJØRN	—	Frederikshavn Vaerft	1966

Displacement, tons: 893 standard; 1 400 full load
Dimensions, feet (metres): 156·5 × 40·3 × 14·5 *(47 × 12·1 × 4·4)*
Main engines: Diesels; electric drive; 3 600 bhp = 12 knots

Recently used by RDN for surveying in summer.

122 DENMARK / DOMINICAN REPUBLIC

ROYAL YACHT

Name	No.	Builders	Commissioned
DANNEBROG	A 540	R. Dockyard, Copenhagen	1932

Displacement, tons: 1 130
Dimensions, feet (metres): 246 oa × 34 × 11·2 (75 × 10·4 × 3·4)
Guns: 2—37 mm
Main engines: 2 sets Burmeister & Wain 8 cyl; 2 cycle diesels; 1 800 bhp = 14 knots
Complement: 57

Launched on 10 Oct 1931.

DANNEBROG   1976, Royal Danish Navy

DOMINICAN REPUBLIC

Ministerial
Minister of the Armed Forces:
   Juan Rene Beauchamps Javier

Headquarters Appointments
Chief of Naval Staff:
   Vice-Admiral Francisco J. Rivera Caminero
Vice-Chief of Naval Staff:
   Captain Francisco A. Marte Victoria

Personnel
(a) 1978: 4 051 officers and men
(b) Selective military service

Mercantile Marine
Lloyd's Register of Shipping:
   20 vessels of 8 469 tons gross

Maritime Air
(All operated by Dominican Air Force)

2 PBY-5A Catalinas
3 Alouette II/III helicopters
2 H-19 Chickasaws
7 OH-6A Cayuse
2 Hiller 12-E Ravens

Naval Bases

"27 de Febrero", Santo Domingo Naval, Staff HQ.
"Las Calderas": Las Calderas, Bani. Naval dockyard and Training centre. 900 ton synchrolift.

Strength of the Fleet

Type	Active (Reserve)
Frigates	1 (2)
Corvettes	3 (2)
Minesweepers (Ocean)	2
Large Patrol Craft	5
Coastal Patrol Craft	10
LSM	1
LCUs	2
Survey Vessels	2
Tankers (Small)	2
Tugs (Large)	2
Tugs (Harbour)	6
Training Ship	1

Note: Although listed as "Active" several of the major units are reported as non-operational.

DELETIONS

Destroyer
1972 Duarte (ex-HMS Hotspur)

Corvettes
1972 Gerardo Jansen, Juan Bautista Cambiaso, Juan Bautista Maggiola (all ex-Canadian "Flower" class)

Light Forces
1975 Maymyon, Puerto Hemosa
1977 Albacora, Bonito

Amphibious Craft
1975 Enriquillo

Survey Craft
1972 Caonobo

Tugs
1975 Consuelo, Haina, Santana

FRIGATES
1 Ex-CANADIAN "RIVER" CLASS

Name	No.	Builders	Laid down	Launched	Commissioned
MELLA (ex-Presidente Trujillo, ex-HMCS Carlplace)	451	Davies SB & Repairing Co, Lauzon, Canada	—	6 July 1944	1944

Displacement, tons: 1 400 standard; 2 125 full load
Length, feet (metres): 301·5 (91·9)
Beam, feet (metres): 36·7 (11·2)
Draught, feet (metres): 12·0 (3·7)
Guns: 1—3 in; 2—47 mm; 1—40 mm; 4—20 mm (2 twin)
Main engines: Triple expansion; 2 shafts; 5 500 ihp
Boilers: 2 of three-drum type
Speed, knots: 20
Oil fuel, tons: 645
Range, miles: 4 200 at 12 knots
Complement: 195 (15 officers, 130 ratings, 50 midshipmen)

Transferred to the Dominican Navy in 1946. Modified for use as Presidential yacht with extra accommodation and deck-houses built up aft. Pennant number as a frigate was F 101, but as the Presidential yacht it was no longer worn. Now carries pennant number 451 as flagship of Dominican naval forces. Used by the staff in naval operations. Renamed Mella in 1962.

MELLA   1972, Dominican Navy

2 Ex-US "TACOMA" CLASS

Name
GREGORIO LUPERÓN (ex-Presidente Troncoso, ex-USS Pueblo, PF 13)
PEDRO SANTANA (ex-Presidente Peynado, ex-USS Knoxville, PF 64)

No.	Builders	Laid down	Launched	Commissioned
452 (ex-F 103)	Leatham D. Smith SB Co Wis.	15 April 1943	10 July 1943	29 April 1944
453 (ex-F 104)	Kaiser SY Richmond, Cal.	14 Nov 1943	20 Jan 1944	27 May 1944

Displacement, tons: 1 430 standard; 2 415 full load
Length, feet (metres): 298·0 (90·8) wl; 304·0 (92·7) oa
Beam, feet (metres): 37·5 (11·4)
Draught, feet (metres): 13·7 (4·2)
Guns: 3—3 in (76 mm) single; 4—40 mm (2 twin); 6—20 mm; 4—0·5 in (12·7 mm) MG (2 twin)
Main engines: Triple expansion; 2 shafts; 5 500 ihp
Boilers: 2 of three-drum type
Speed, knots: 19
Oil fuel, tons: 760
Range, miles: 9 500 at 12 knots
Complement: 140

Formerly United States patrol frigates, PF of the "Tacoma" class similar to the contemporary British frigates of the "River" class. Transferred from the US Navy to the Dominican Republic Navy in July 1946 (453) and Sept 1947 (452). Renamed in 1962. Both in reserve.

GREGORIO LUPERON   1972, Dominican Navy

DOMINICAN REPUBLIC 123

CORVETTES

3 Ex-US "COHOES" CLASS

Name	No.	Builders	Commissioned
CAMBIASO (ex-USS *Etlah*, AN 79)	P 207	Commercial Ironworks	1945
SEPARACION (ex-USS *Passaconaway*, AN 86)	P 208	Marine SB Co	1944
CALDERAS (ex-USS *Passaic*, AN 87)	P 209	Leatham D Smith SB Co	1944

Displacement, tons: 650 standard; 785 full load
Dimensions, feet (metres): 168·5 × 33 × 10·8 *(51·4 × 10 × 3·3)*
Guns: 1—3 in *(76 mm)*; 3—20 in
Main engines: Busch Sulzer diesel-electric; 1 200 shp = 12 knots
Complement: 48

Ex-netlayers in reserve in USA since 1963. Transferred by sale 29 Sep 1976. Now used for patrol duties.

SEPARACION 1977, Dominican Navy

2 Ex-CANADIAN "FLOWER" CLASS

Name
CRISTÓBAL COLÓN (ex-HMCS *Lachute*)
JUAN ALEJANDRO ACOSTA (ex-HMCS *Louisburg*)

No.	Builders	Laid down	Launched	Commissioned
401 (ex-C 101)	Morton Ltd, Quebec City	—	9 June 1944	24 Oct 1944
402 (ex-C 102)	Morton Ltd, Quebec City	—	13 July 1943	13 Dec 1943

Displacement, tons: 1 060 standard; 1 350 full load
Length, feet (metres): 193·0 *(58·8)* pp; 208·0 *(63·4)* oa
Beam, feet (metres): 33·0 *(10·0)*
Draught, feet (metres): 13·3 *(4·0)*
Guns: 1—4 in *(102 mm)*
 C. Colon: 1—40 mm; 6—20 mm; 4—0·5 in MG (2 twin)
 J. A. Acosta: 1—40 mm; 6—20 mm; 2—0·5 in MG
Main engines: Triple expansion; 2 750 ihp
Boilers: 2 of three-drum type
Speed, knots: 16
Oil fuel, tons: 282
Range, miles: 2 900 at 15 knots
Complement: 53

Built in Canadian shipyards under the emergency construction programme during the Second World War. Five were transferred to the Dominican Navy in 1947. Pennant numbers were changed in 1968. Both in reserve.

JUAN ALEJANDRO ACOSTA 1972, Dominican Navy

MINEWARFARE FORCES

2 Ex-US "ADMIRABLE" CLASS

Name	No.	Builders	Commissioned
PRESTOL BOTELLO (ex-*Separacion*, ex-USS *Skirmish*, MSF 303)	BM 454	Associated SB	16 Aug 1943
TORTUGUERO (ex-USS *Signet*, MSF 302)	BM 455	Associated SB	16 Aug 1943

Displacement, tons: 650 standard; 900 full load
Dimensions, feet (metres): 180·0 wl; 184·5 oa × 33·0 × 14·5 *(56·3 × 9·9 × 4·4)*
Guns: 1—3 in; 2—40 mm; 6—20 mm
A/S weapons: 1 Hedgehog
Main engines: 2 diesels; 2 shafts; 1 710 bhp = 14 knots
Range, miles: 5 600 at 9 knots
Complement: 90 (8 officers, 82 men)

Former US fleet minesweepers. Purchased on 13 Jan 1965. *Prestol Botello* renamed early 1976. Sweepgear removed. Hedgehog fitted.

PRESTOL BOTELLO 7/1976, Norman Friedman

LIGHT FORCES

3 Ex-USCG "ARGO" CLASS (LARGE PATROL CRAFT)

Name	No.	Builders	Commissioned
INDEPENDENCIA (ex-USCGC *Icarus*)	204 (ex-P 105)	Bath Ironworks	1932
LIBERTAD (ex-*Rafael Atoa*, ex-USCGC *Thetis*)	205 (ex-P 106)	—	—
RESTAURACION (ex-USCGC *Galathea*)	206 (ex-P 104)	John H. Machis & Co, Camden, NJ	1933

Displacement, tons: 337 standard
Dimensions, feet (metres): 165·0 × 25·2 × 9·5 *(50·3 × 7·7 × 2·9)*
Guns: 1—3 in; 1—40 mm; 1—20 mm
Main engines: 2 diesels; 1 280 bhp = 15 knots
Range, miles: 1 300 at 15 knots
Complement: 49 (5 officers, 44 men)

Ex-US Coastguard Cutters. Rebuilt in 1975.

RESTAURACION 1977, Dominican Navy

124 DOMINICAN REPUBLIC

1 US "PGM 71" CLASS (LARGE PATROL CRAFT)

Name	No.	Builders	Commissioned
BETELGEUSE (ex-US PGM 77)	GC 102	Peterson, USA	1966

Displacement, tons: 130 standard; 145·5 full load
Dimensions, feet (metres): 101·5 × 21·0 × 5·0 (30·9 × 6·4 × 1·5)
Guns: 1—40 mm; 4—20 mm (2 twin); 2—0·5 in 50 cal MG
Main engines: 8 GM6-71 diesels; 2 shafts; 2 200 bhp = 21 knots
Range, miles: 1 500 at 10 knots
Complement: 20

Built in the USA and transferred to the Dominican Republic under the Military Aid Programme on 14 Jan 1966.

BETELGEUSE   1972, Dominican Navy

1 LARGE PATROL CRAFT

Name	No.	Builders	Commissioned
CAPITAN ALSINA (ex-RL 101)	GC 105	—	1944

Displacement, tons: 100 standard
Dimensions, feet (metres): 92·0 wl; 104·8 oa × 19·2 × 5·8 (32 × 5·9 × 1·8)
Guns: 2—20 mm
Main engines: 2 GM diesels; 2 shafts; 1 000 hp = 17 knots
Complement: 20

Of wooden construction. Launched in 1944. Named as above in 1957. Rebuilt 1977.

CAPITAN ALSINA

1 "ATLANTIDA" CLASS (COASTAL PATROL CRAFT)

ATLANTIDA BA 8

Probably employed on surveying duties.

4 "BELLATRIX" CLASS (COASTAL PATROL CRAFT)

Name	No.	Builders	Commissioned
PROCION	GC 103	Sewart Seacraft Inc, Berwick, La.	1967
ALDEBARÁN	GC 104	Sewart Seacraft Inc, Berwick, La.	1972
BELLATRIX	GC 106	Sewart Seacraft Inc, Berwick, La.	1967
CAPELLA	GC 108	Sewart Seacraft Inc, Berwick, La.	1968

Displacement, tons: 60
Dimensions, feet (metres): 85 × 18 × 5 (25·9 × 5·5 × 1·5)
Guns: 3—0·5 MG
Main engines: 2 GM diesels; 500 bhp = 18·7 knots
Complement: 12

Transferred to the Dominican Navy by USA, *Bellatrix* on 18 Aug 1967, *Procion* on 1 May 1967, *Capella* on 15 Oct 1968 and *Aldebarán* in May 1972.

BELLATRIX   1970, Dominican Navy

1 COASTAL PATROL CRAFT

Name	No.	Builders	Commissioned
RIGEL (ex-US AVR)	GC 101	—	1953

Displacement, tons: 27 standard; 32·2 full load
Dimensions, feet (metres): 63·0 × 15·5 × 5·0 (19·2 × 4·7 × 1·5)
Guns: 2—50 cal MG
Main engines: General Motors V8—71 diesels = 18·5 knots
Complement: 9

Originally built in 1953. Reconditioned by NAUSTA, Key West, USA. Rebuilt 1976.

4 COASTAL PATROL CRAFT

Name	No.	Builders	Commissioned
CARITE	BA 3	Ast. Navales Dominicanos	1975
ATÚN	BA 6	Ast. Navales Dominicanos	1975
PICÚA	BA 9	Ast. Navales Dominicanas	1975
JUREL	BA 15	Ast. Navales Dominicanos	1975

Displacement, tons: 24
Dimensions, feet (metres): 45 × 13 × 6·6 (13·7 × 4 × 1·9)
Main engines: 1 GM diesel; 101 hp = 9 knots
Complement: 4

Auxiliary sailing craft with a sail area of 750 sq feet and a cargo capacity of 7 tons.

AMPHIBIOUS FORCES

1 LCU

Name	No.	Builders	Commissioned
SAMANA (ex-LA 2)	LDM 302	Ast. Navales Dominicanos	1958

Displacement, tons: 150 standard; 310 full load
Dimensions, feet (metres): 105 wl; 119·5 oa × 36 × 3 (36·4 × 11 × 0·9)
Gun: 1—0·5 cal MG
Main engines: 3 General Motors diesels; 441 bhp = 8 knots
Oil fuel, tons: 80
Complement: 17

Similar characteristics to US LCT 5 Type although slightly larger.

SAMANA   1972, Dominican Navy

1 LCU

Name	No.	Builders	Commissioned
OCOA	LDM 303	Ast. Navales Dominicanos	1976

Displacement, tons: 36·8
Dimensions, feet (metres): 56·2 × 14 × 3·9 (17·1 × 4·3 × 1·2)
Main engines: 2—6 cyl diesels; 225 bhp = 6 knots
Complement: 5

Capacity about 30 tons.

DOMINICAN REPUBLIC / DUBAI 125

MISCELLANEOUS

SURVEY VESSELS

(See also *Atlantida* under Light Forces)

Name	No.	Builders	Commissioned
CAPOTILLO (ex-*Camillia*)	FB 1	—	—

Displacement, tons: 337
Dimensions, feet (metres): 117 × 24 × 7·8 *(35·7 × 7·3 × 2·4)*
Main engines: 2 diesels; 880 bhp = 10 knots
Complement: 29

Built in the United States in 1911. Acquired from the United States Coast Guard in 1949. Underwent a major refit in Dominican Republic in 1970. Buoy Tender.

Name	No.	Builders	Commissioned
NEPTUNO (ex-*Toro*)	BA 10	John H. Mathis Co, New Jersey	Feb 1954

Displacement, tons: 72·2
Dimensions, feet (metres): 64 × 18·1 × 8 *(19·5 × 5·7 × 2·4)*
Main engines: 1 GM diesel = 10 knots
Complement: 7

NEPTUNO   1975, Dominican Navy

TANKERS

2 Ex-US OIL BARGES

Name	No.	Builders	Commissioned
CAPITAN W. ARVELO (ex-US *YO 213*)	BT 4	Ira S. Bushey Inc, Brooklyn	1943
CAPITAN BEOTEGUI (ex-US *YO 215*)	BT 5	Ira S. Bushey Inc, Brooklyn	1945

Displacement, tons: 370 light; 1 400 full load
Dimensions, feet (metres): 174 × 32 × 13·0 *(53 × 9·8 × 4)*
Gun: 1—20 mm
Main engines: 1 Fairbanks-Morse diesel; 285 hp = 8 knots
Capacity: 6 570 barrels
Complement: 27

Former United States self-propelled fuel oil barges. Lent by the USA in April 1964.

CAPITAN W. ARVELO   1977, Dominican Navy

AUXILIARY

1 Ex-US LSM

Name	No.	Builders	Commissioned
SIRIO (ex-US *LSM 483*)	BDM 301 (ex-*BA 104*)	Brown SB Co, Houston	13 April 1945

Displacement, tons: 734 standard; 1 100 full load
Dimensions, feet (metres): 196 wl; 203·5 oa × 34 × 10 *(62·1 × 10·4 × 3·1)*
Main engines: 2 General Motors diesels; 2 shafts; 1 800 bhp = 14 knots
Oil fuel, tons: 164
Complement: 30

Laid down on 17 Feb 1945, launched on 10 March 1945. Transferred to the Dominican Navy in March 1958. Refitted in Dominican Republic in 1970. Now decked over and used for commercial logistic service. Included because of capability in emergency.

SIRIO   1968, Dominican Navy

TUGS

1 Ex-US "CHEROKEE" CLASS

Name	No.	Builders	Commissioned
MACORIX (ex-USS *Kiowa* ATF 72)	RM 21	Charleston SB and DD Co	7 June 1943

Displacement, tons: 1 235 standard; 1 675 full load
Dimensions, feet (metres): 195 wl; 205 oa × 38·5 × 15·5 *(62·5 × 11·7 × 4·7)*
Gun: 1—3 in 50 cal
Main engines: Diesel-electric; 1 shaft; 3 000 bhp = 15 knots
Complement: 85

Carries additional salvage equipment. Transferred 16 Oct 1972.

Radar: AN/SPS-5D.

MACORIX   1975, Dominican Navy

1 Ex-US "SOTOYOMO" CLASS

Name	No.	Builders	Commissioned
CAONABO (ex-USS *Sagamore* ATA 208)	RM 18	Gulfport Boiler and Welding Works	1944

Displacement, tons: 534 standard; 835 full load
Dimensions, feet (metres): 143 oa × 33·9 × 13 *(43·6 × 10·3 × 4)*
Main engines: 2 GM diesel-electric; 1 shaft; 1 500 bhp = 13 knots

Transferred 1 Feb 1972.

Radar: AN/SPS-5D.

CAONABO   1975, Dominican Navy

2 "HERCULES" CLASS

Name	No.	Builders	Commissioned
HERCULES (ex-*R 2*)	RP 12	Ast. Navales Dominicanos	1960
GUACANAGARIX (ex-*R 5*)	RP 13	Ast. Navales Dominicanos	1960

Displacement, tons: 200 (approx)
Dimensions, feet (metres): 70·0 × 15·6 × 9·0 *(21·4 × 4·8 × 2·7)*
Main engines: 1 Caterpillar motor; 500 hp; 1 225 rpm
Complement: 8

4 HARBOUR TUGS

MAGUANA (ex-*R 10*) RP 14   CALDERAS RP 19
BOHECHIO RP 16   ISABELA (ex-*R 1*) RP 20

Small tugs for harbour and coastal use. Not all of uniform type and dimensions. *Bohechio* of US YTL 600 type, transferred Jan 1971.

TRAINING SHIP

DUARTE

Displacement, tons: 60
Dimensions, feet (metres): 75 × 18 × 7 *(22·9 × 5·7 × 2·1)*
Main engines: GM diesel; 325 hp; 1 shaft
Complement: 30

DUBAI

(see United Arab Emirates)

126 ECUADOR

ECUADOR

Ministerial

Minister of Defence:
  General Andres Arrata Macias

Headquarters Appointment

Commander-in-Chief of the Navy:
  Vice-Admiral Alfredo Poveda Burbano

Diplomatic Representation

Naval Attaché in Bonn:
  Captain Ethiel Rodriguez
Naval and Air Attaché in London:
  Colonel Alfonso Villagomez
Naval Attaché in Washington:
  Captain Fausto Cevallos V

Personnel

(a) 1978. Total 3 800 (300 officers and 3 500 men)
(b) Two years selective national service

Naval Bases

Guayaquil (main naval base).
San Lorenzo and Galapagos Island (small bases).

Establishments

The Naval Academy is in Guayaquil

Maritime Air

Air Force planes working with the Navy.

2 Alouette III helicopters
1 IAI Arava
1 Cessna 320E
1 Cessna 177
2 Cessna T 337 F/G
2 Cessna T-41D/172H

Naval Infantry

A small force of naval infantry (700 men) exists of which a detachment is based on the Galapagos Islands and in the Eastern area.

Prefix to Ships' Names

BAE

Mercantile Marine

Lloyd's Register of Shipping:
  55 vessels of 197 244 tons gross

Strength of the Fleet

Type	Active	Building
Destroyer	1	—
Frigates	3	—
Corvettes	2	—
Patrol Submarines	2	—
Fast Attack Craft (Missile)	3	—
Fast Attack Craft (Torpedo)	3	—
Large Patrol Craft	2	—
Coastal Patrol Craft	5	—
LST	1	—
LSMs	2	—
Survey Vessels	2	—
Tugs	5	—
Supply Ship (Small)	1	—
Floating Dock	1	—
Miscellaneous	4	—
Sail Training Ship	1	—

New Construction

The Ecuadorian Navy, is now investigating new construction frigates or corvettes. Whatever order is confirmed is likely to go to a European yard.

DELETIONS

Light Forces

1976   LSP 4, 5 and 6

PENNANT LIST

Light Forces

LC 61	24 De Mayo
LC 62	25 De Julio
LM 31	Quito
LM 32	Guayaquil
LM 33	Cuenca
LP 81	10 De Agosto
LP 82	9 De Octubre
LP 83	3 De Noviembre
LT 41	Manta
LT 42	Tulcan
LT 43	Nuevo Rocafuerte

Amphibious Forces

T 51	Jambeli
T 52	Tarqui

Survey Vessels

O 111	Orion
O 112	Rigel

Tugs

R 101	Cayambe
R 102	Sangay
R 103	Cotopaxi
R 104	Antizana

Miscellaneous

BE 01	Guayas
BT 123	Putumayo
DF 121	Amazonas
T 53	Calicuchima
T 62	Atahualpa
UT 111	Isla de la Plata
UT 112	Isla Puná

Frigate

1972 Guayas (ex-US PF Type)

Frigates

D 01	Morán Valverde
D 02	Presidente Alfaro
D 03	Presidente Velasco Ibarra

Corvettes

P 22	Esmeraldas
P 23	Manabi

Submarines

S 11	Shyri
S 12	Huancavilca

SUBMARINES

2 TYPE 209

Name	No.	Builders	Laid down	Launched	Commissioned
SHYRI	S 11	Howaldtswerke, Kiel	1975	8 Oct 1976	1978
HUANCAVILCA	S 12	Howaldtswerke, Kiel	1975	18 Mar 1977	1978

Displacement, tons: 980 surfaced; 1 356 dived
Dimensions, feet (metres): 183·4 × 20·5 × 17·9 *(55·9 × 6·3 × 5·4)*
Torpedo tubes: 8—21 in (bow) with reloads
Main machinery: Diesel-electric; MTU diesels; 4 generators; 1 shaft; 5 000 shp
Speed, knots: 10 surfaced; 22 dived
Complement: 32

Ordered in 1974.

DESTROYER

1 Ex-US "GEARING FRAM I" CLASS

Name	No.	Builders	Laid down	Launched	Commissioned
— (ex-USS *Holder*, DD 819)	—	Consolidated Steel Corp	1945	25 Aug 1945	18 May 1946

Displacement, tons: 2 425 standard; 3 425 full load
Dimensions, feet (metres): 390·5 × 40·9 × 19 *(119 × 12·4 × 5·8)*
Guns: 4—5 in *(127 mm)* 38 cal
A/S weapons: 2 triple Mk 32 torpedo tubes
Main engines: 2 geared turbines; 60 000 shp; 2 shafts = 34 knots
Boilers: 4
Complement: 274

An enlarged version of the "Allen M. Sumner" class. Served in the Naval Reserve Force until transferred in 1976.

ECUADOR 127

FRIGATES

1 Ex-US "CHARLES LAWRENCE" CLASS

Name	No.	Builders	Laid down	Launched	Commissioned
MORAN VALVERDE (ex-*Veinticinco de Julio*, ex-USS *Enright*, APD 66, ex-*DE 216*)	D 01 (ex-E 12)	Philadelphia Navy Yard	22 Feb 1943	29 May 1943	21 Sep 1943

Displacement, tons: 1 400 standard; 2 130 full load
Dimensions, feet (metres): 306·0 oa × 37·0 × 12·6 (93·3 × 11·3 × 3·8)
Guns: 1—5 in 38 cal; 4—40 mm
A/S weapons: DC racks
Main engines: GE geared turbines with electric drive; 2 shafts; 12 000 shp = 23 knots
Boilers: 2 "D" Express
Range, miles: 2 000 at 23 knots
Complement: 204

Former US high speed transport (APD, modified destroyer escort). Transferred to Ecuador on 14 July 1967 under MAP. Can carry 162 troops. To be modernised.

Radar: AN/SPS 6 and SPS 10.

MORAN VALVERDE (Now D 01) *1968, Ecuadorian Navy*

2 Ex-BRITISH "HUNT" CLASS (TYPE 1)

Name	No.	Builders	Laid down	Launched	Commissioned
PRESIDENTE ALFARO (ex-HMS *Quantock*)	D 02 (ex-D 01)	Scotts SB & Eng Co Ltd, Greenock	26 July 1939	22 April 1940	6 Feb 1941
PRESIDENTE VELASCO IBARRA (ex-HMS *Meynell*)	D 03 (ex-D 02)	Swan Hunter & Wigham Richardson, Wallsend	10 Aug 1939	7 June 1940	30 Dec 1940

Displacement, tons: 1 000 standard; 1 490 full load
Length, feet (metres): 272·3 *(83·0)* pp; 280 *(85·3)* oa
Beam, feet (metres): 29 *(8·8)*
Draught, feet (metres): 14 *(4·3)*
Guns: 4—4 in *(102 mm)*; 2—40 mm (twin); 2—20 mm
A/S weapons: DC throwers, DC racks
Main engines: Parsons geared turbines (by Wallsend Slipway in *Presidente Velasco Ibarra*); 19 000 shp; 2 shafts
Boilers: 2 Admiralty 3-drum
Speed, knots: 23
Oil fuel, tons: 280
Range, miles: 2 000 at 12 knots
Complement: 146

"Hunt" class. Type 1, purchased by Ecuador from the United Kingdom on 18 Oct 1954, and refitted by J. Samuel White & Co Ltd, Cowes, Isle of Wight. *Quantock* was taken over by the Ecuadorian Navy in Portsmouth Dockyard on 16 Aug 1955, when she was renamed *Presidente Alfaro*. Sister ship *Meynell* was transferred to the Ecuadorian Navy and renamed *Presidente Velasco Ibarra* in Aug 1955.
Due for disposal

PRESIDENTE ALFARO (now D 02) *1970, Ecuadorian Navy*

CORVETTES

2 Ex-US "PCE 827" CLASS

Name	No.	Builders	Laid down	Launched	Commissioned
ESMERALDAS (ex-USS *Eunice*, PCE 846)	P 22 (ex-E 22, ex-E 03)	USA	—	—	4 Mar 1944
MANABI (ex-USS *Pascagoula*, PCE 874)	P 23 (ex-E 23, ex-E 02)	USA	—	—	31 Dec 1943

Displacement, tons: 640 standard; 903 full load
Dimensions, feet (metres): 180 wl; 184·5 oa × 33 × 9·5 (56·3 × 10 × 2·9)
Guns: 1—3 in; 6—40 mm
A/S weapons: 4 DCT; 2 DC Racks; Hedgehog
Main engines: GM diesels; 2 shafts; 1 800 bhp = 15·4 knots
Range, miles: 4 300 at 10 knots
Complement: 100 officers and men

Former United States patrol vessels (180 ft Escorts). Transferred on 29 Nov and 5 Dec 1960 respectively.

MANABI *1974*

LIGHT FORCES

2 US "PGM-71" CLASS (LARGE PATROL CRAFT)

Name	No.	Builders	Commissioned
24 DE MAYO (ex-*Quito* ex-US PGM 75)	LC 61	Peterson, USA	1965
25 DE JULIO (ex-*Guayaquil*, ex-US PGM 76)	LC 62	Peterson, USA	1965

Displacement, tons: 130 standard; 145·5 full load
Dimensions, feet (metres): 101·5 oa × 21 × 5 *(30·9 × 6·4 × 1·5)*
Guns: 1—40 mm; 4—20 mm (twin); 2—0·5 cal MGs
Main engines: 8 GM 6-71 diesels; 2 shafts; 2 200 bhp = 21 knots
Range, miles: 1 500 at cruising speed
Complement: 15

Transferred to the Ecuadorian Navy under MAP on 30 Nov 1965. Original names transferred to missile craft

25 DE JULIO (old Pennant number) *1967, Ecuadorian Navy*

128 ECUADOR

3 LÜRSSEN TYPE (FAST ATTACK CRAFT—MISSILE)

Name	No.	Builders	Commissioned
QUITO	LM 31	Lürssen, Vegesack	13 July 1976
GUAYAQUIL	LM 32	Lürssen, Vegesack	early 1977
CUENCA	LM 33	Lürssen, Vegesack	July 1977

Displacement, tons: 255
Dimensions, feet (metres): 147·6 × 23 × 12·8 *(45 × 7 × 3·9)*
Missiles: 4—MM 38 Exocet
Guns: 1—76 mm; 2—35 mm
Main engines: 4 MTU diesels; 14 000 hp; 4 shafts = 40 knots
Range, miles: 700 at 40 knots; 1 800 at 16 knots
Complement: 35

Launched—*Quito*, 20 Nov 1975; *Guayaquil* 5 April 1976. *Cuenca* Dec 1976. *Cuenca* started trials in July 1977.

QUITO   1976, Lürssen Werft

3 "MANTA" CLASS (FAST ATTACK CRAFT—TORPEDO)

Name	No.	Builders	Commissioned
MANTA	LT 41	Lürssen, Vegesack	11 June 1971
TULCAN	LT 42	Lürssen, Vegesack	2 April 1971
NUEVO ROCAFUERTE	LT 43	Lürssen, Vegesack	23 June 1971

Displacement, tons: 119 standard; 134 full load
Dimensions, feet (metres): 119·4 × 19·1 × 6·0 *(36·4 × 5·8 × 1·8)*
Guns: 1—40 mm; 1—twin Oerlikon unguided rocket launcher
Torpedo tubes: 2—21 in
Main engines: 3 MTU diesels; 3 shafts; 9 000 bhp = 35 knots
Range, miles: 700 at 30 knots; 1 500 at 15 knots
Complement: 19

Similar design to the Chilean "Guacoida" Class with an extra diesel—3 knots faster. *Manta* launched 8 Sep 1970.

MANTA (old Pennant number)   1972, Ecuadorian Navy

3 COASTAL PATROL CRAFT

Name	No.	Builders	Commissioned
10 DE AGOSTO	LP 81	Schurenstedt, Bardenfleth	Aug 1954
9 DE OCTUBRE	LP 82	Schurenstedt, Bardenfleth	Aug 1954
3 DE NOVIEMBRE	LP 83	Schurenstedt, Bardenfleth	1955

Displacement, tons: 45 standard; 64 full load
Dimensions, feet (metres): 76·8 × 13·5 × 6·3 *(23·4 × 4·6 × 1·8)*
Guns: Light MGs
Main engines: 2 Bohn & Kähler diesels; 2 shafts; 1 200 bhp = 22 knots
Range, miles: 550 at 16 knots
Complement: 9

Ordered in 1954.

LP Class   1963, Ecuadorian Navy

1 US 65 ft COASTAL PATROL CRAFT

Built by Halter Marine, New Orleans. Delivered 1976.

1 US 40 ft COASTAL PATROL CRAFT

Transferred 1971.

AMPHIBIOUS SHIPS

1 Ex-US "512-1152 SERIES" (LST)

Name	No.	Builders	Commissioned
— (ex-USS *Summit County*, LST 1146)	T 55	Hualcopo	1945

Displacement, tons: 1 653 standard; 4 080 full load
Dimensions, feet (metres): 328 × 50 × 14 *(100 × 16·1 × 4·3)*
Guns: 6—40 mm
Main engines: 2 GM diesels; 1 700 bhp; 2 shafts = 11·6 knots
Complement: 119
Troops: 147

Transferred 14 Feb 1977.

2 Ex-US "LSM-1" CLASS

Name	No.	Builders	Commissioned
JAMBELI (ex-USS *LSM 539*)	T 51	Brown SB Co, Houston	1945
TARQUI (ex-USS *LSM 555*)	T 52	Charleston Navy Yard	1945

Displacement, tons: 743 beaching; 1 095 full load
Dimensions, feet (metres): 196·5 wl; 203·0 oa × 34·0 × 7·9 *(61·9 × 10·3 × 2·4)*
Guns: 2—40 mm
Range, miles: 2 500 at 12 knots
Main engines: Diesels; 2 shafts; 2 800 bhp = 12·5 knots

Jambeli was laid down on 10 May 1945, *Tarqui* was laid down on 3 March 1945 and launched on 22 March 1945. Transferred to the Ecuadorian Navy at Green Cove Springs, Florida in Nov 1958.

JAMBELI (old Pennant number)   1967, Ecuadorian Navy

ECUADOR

SURVEY VESSELS

1 Ex-US "ALOE" CLASS

Name	No.	Builders	Commissioned
ORION	O 111	American SB Co,	Nov 1941
(ex-USS *Mulberry*, AN 27)	(ex-*A 101*)	Cleveland, Ohio	

Displacement, tons: 560 standard; 805 full load
Dimensions, feet (metres): 146 wl; 163 oa × 30·5 × 11·8 *(49·7 × 9·3 × 3·6)*
Gun: 1—3 in
Main engines: Diesel-electric; 800 bhp = 13 knots
Complement: 35

Former United States netlayer. Launched on 26 March 1941. Transferred to Ecuador in Nov 1965 as loan.

RIGEL O 112

Of 50 tons, launched in 1975. Complement 10.

TUGS

2 Ex-US "CHEROKEE" CLASS

Name	No.	Builders	Commissioned
CAYAMBE	R 101	Charleston SB & DD Co	1945
(ex-USS *Cusabo*, ATF 155)	(ex-*R 51*, ex-*R 01*)		
— (ex-USS *Chowanoc* ATF 100)	—	—	1945

Displacement, tons: 1 235 standard; 1 675 full load
Dimensions, feet (metres): 195 wl; 205 oa × 38·5 × 15·5 *(62·5 × 11·7 × 4·7)*
Guns: 1—3 in; 2—40 mm; 2—20 mm
Main engines: 4 diesels with electric drive; 3 000 bhp = 16·5 knots
Complement: 85

Cayambe launched on 26 Feb 1945. Fitted with powerful pumps and other salvage equipment. Transferred to Ecuador by lease on 2 Nov 1960 and renamed *Los Rios*. Again renamed *Cayambe* in 1966. *Chowanoc* transferred 1977.

CAYAMBE (old Pennant number)   *1970, Ecuadorian Navy*

Name	No.	Builders	Commissioned
SANGAY (ex-*Loja*)	R 102 (ex-*R 53*)	—	1952

Displacement, tons: 295 light; 390 full load
Dimensions, feet (metres): 107 × 26 × 14 *(32·6 × 7·9 × 4·3)*
Main engines: Fairbanks Morse diesel; speed = 12 knots

Acquired by the Ecuadorian Navy in 1964. Renamed in 1966.

Name	No.	Builders	Commissioned
COTOPAXI (ex-USS *R. T. Ellis*)	R 103 (ex-*R 52*)	Equitable Building Corp	1945

Displacement, tons: 150
Dimensions, feet (metres): 82 × 21 × 8 *(25 × 6·4 × 2·4)*
Main engines: Diesel; 1 shaft; 650 bhp = 9 knots

Purchased from the United States in 1947.

ANTIZANA R 104

MISCELLANEOUS

TRAINING SHIP

Name	No.	Builders	Commissioned
GUAYAS	BE 01	Ast. Celaya, Spain	Mar 1977

Measurement, tons: 934 gross
Dimensions, feet (metres): 249·9 × 34·8 × 13·4 *(76·2 × 10·6 × 4·2)*
Main engines: General Motors; 700 bhp = 10 knots

Sail training ship. Launched 23 Sep 1976.

1 Ex-US SUPPLY SHIP

Name	No.	Builders	Commissioned
CALICUCHIMA (ex-US *FS 525*)	T 53 (ex-*T 34*, ex-*T 42*)	USA	1944

Displacement, tons: 650 light; 950 full load
Dimensions, feet (metres): 176 × 32 × 14 *(53·7 × 9·8 × 4·3)*
Main engines: Diesels; 2 shafts; 500 bhp = 11 knots

Former United States small cargo ship of the Army FS type. Leased to Ecuador on 8 April 1963 and purchased in April 1969. Provides service to the Galapagos Islands.

2 Ex-US YP TYPE

Name	No.	Builders	Commissioned
ISLA DE LA PLATA	UT 111	USA	—
ISLA PUNA	UT 112	USA	—

Displacement, tons: 650 light
Dimensions, feet (metres): 42 *(12·8)*
Main engines: 1 diesel

Transferred 1962. Coastguard utility boats.

1 Ex-US YR TYPE

Name	No.	Builders	Commissioned
PUTUMAYO (ex-US *YR 34*)	BT 123 (ex-*BT 62*)	USA	—

Repair barge leased July 1962.

1 Ex-US "YW" CLASS WATER CARRIER

Name	No.	Builders	Commissioned
ATAHUALPA	T 62	Leatham D. Smith SB Co.	1945
(ex-US *YW 131*)	(ex-*T 33*, ex-*T 41*, ex-*A 01*)		

Displacement, tons: 415 light; 1 235 full load
Dimensions, feet (metres): 174·0 × 32·0 × 15·0 *(53·1 × 9·8 × 4·6)*
Main engines: GM diesels; 750 bhp = 11·5 knots

Acquired by the Ecuadorian Navy on 2 May 1963.

1 Ex-US "ARD 12" CLASS FLOATING DOCK

Name	No.	Builders	Commissioned
AMAZONAS (ex-US *ARD 17*)	DF 121	USA	1944

Measurement, tons: 3 500 lifting capacity
Dimensions, feet (metres): 491·7 oa × 81·0 oa × 32·9 *(149·9 × 24·7 × 10)*

Transferred on loan on 7 Jan 1961. Suitable for docking destroyers and landing ships. Dry dock companion craft YFND 20 was leased on 2 Nov 1961.

EGYPT

Ministerial

Minister of War:
Muhammad Abd al-Ghani Jamasi

Administrative

Armed Forces Chief of Staff:
General Mohammad Ali Fahmi

Headquarters Appointment

Commander of Naval Forces:
Rear-Admiral Ashraf Mohammed Rifaat

Diplomatic Representation

Defence Attaché in London:
Brigadier M. Lotfy Abou el Kheir

Strength of the Fleet

Type	Active	Building (Projected)
Destroyers	5	—
Frigates	3	(2)
Submarines (Patrol)	12	(2)
Fast Attack Craft (Missile)	16	—
Fast Attack Craft (Torpedo)	26	—
Fast Attack Craft (Gun)	4	(6)
Large Patrol Craft	15	—
Coastal Patrol Craft	20	—
LCTs	4	—
LCUs	14	—
Minesweepers (Ocean)	10	—
Minesweepers (Inshore)	4	—
Training Ships	2	—
Tugs	2	—
Hovercraft	3	—
Miscellaneous	5	—

New Construction and Refits

The rupture of relations with the USSR has meant a greater reliance by Egypt on Western shipbuilders and repairers. So far reported—although not officially confirmed either in Egypt or by the contractors—are the following:

(a) Refit of "Osa" class in UK.
(b) Construction of 6—52 metre Fast Attack Craft by Vosper Thornycroft.
(c) Construction of 2 "Agosta" class submarines in France.
(d) Construction of 2 "Lupo" class frigates in Italy.
(e) Transfer of one "Porpoise" class submarine from United Kingdom

Personnel

(a) 1978: 17 500 officers and men, including the Coast Guard. (Reserves of about 12 000)
(b) 3 years national service

Bases

Alexandria, Port Said, Mersa Matru, Port Tewfik, Hurghada and Safaqa on the Red Sea.
Naval Academy; Abu Quir.

Coastal Defences

The Samlet missiles employed for Coastal Defence are Naval-manned.

Mercantile Marine

Lloyd's Register of Shipping:
176 vessels of 407 818 tons gross

DELETIONS

Auxiliary

1972(?)   *Nasr* (ex-HMS *Bude*) sunk as Styx target

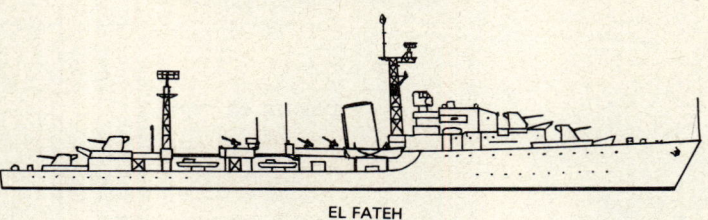

EL FATEH

SUBMARINES

Note: See New Construction section at head of entry.

6 Ex-SOVIET "ROMEO" CLASS

744   745   765   766   +2

Displacement, tons: 1 000 surfaced; 1 600 dived
Length, feet (metres): 249·3 *(76·0)*
Beam, feet (metres): 24·0 *(7·3)*
Draught, feet (metres): 18 *(5·5)*
Torpedo tubes: 6—21 in *(533 mm)* (bow); 2—21 in (stern)
Main machinery: 2 diesels; 4 000 bhp; 2 electric motors; 4 000 hp; 2 shafts
Speed, knots: 17 surfaced; 14 dived
Range, miles: 16 000 at 10 knots surfaced
Complement: 65

One "Romeo" was transferred to Egypt in Feb 1966. Two more replaced "Whiskeys" in May 1966 and another pair was delivered later that year. The sixth boat joined in 1969.
Unconfirmed reports suggest two of this class have been used for spares.

"ROMEO" Class   1968, Skyfotos

Light Forces

1975   4 "P 6" Class
       4 "108" Class

6 Ex-SOVIET "WHISKEY" CLASS

415   418   421   455   +2

Displacement, tons: 1 030 surface; 1 350 dived
Length, feet (metres): 249·6 *(76)* oa
Beam, feet (metres): 22 *(6·7)*
Draught, feet (metres): 15 *(4·6)*
Torpedo tubes: 6—21 in *(533 mm)*; 4 bow, 2 stern; 18 torpedoes or 40 mines
Main machinery: 2 diesels; 4 000 bhp; 2 electric motors; 2 500 hp
Speed, knots: 17 surfaced; 15 dived
Range, miles: 13 000 at 8 knots surfaced
Complement: 60

The first four "Whiskey" class were transferred from the Soviet Navy to the Egyptian Navy in June 1957. Three more arrived at Alexandria on 24 Jan 1958. Another was transferred to Egypt at Alexandria in Jan 1962. Two were replaced by "Romeos" in Feb 1966.
Two "Whiskey" class sailed from Alexandria to Leningrad in late 1971 under escort, being replaced the following year.

"WHISKEY" Class   1974

EGYPT 131

DESTROYERS

4 Ex-SOVIET "SKORY" CLASS

SUEZ	DIAMIETTE
AL ZAFFER	6 OCTOBER (ex-*Al Nasser*)

Displacement, tons: 2 600 standard; 3 500 full load
Length, feet (metres): 395·2 *(120·5)*
Beam, feet (metres): 38·7 *(11·8)*
Draught, feet (metres): 15·1 *(4·6)*
Guns: 4—5·1 in *(130 mm)* 50 cal; 2—3·4 in *(88 mm)*;
  8—37 mm; 4—25 mm (twins) (unmodified);
  4—57 mm (quad); 4—37 mm (twins);
  4—25 mm (twins) (modified)
A/S weapons: 2 DCT; 2 DC racks (unmodified)
  2—12 barrelled RBU 2500;
  2 DCT; 2 DC racks (modified)
Torpedo tubes: 10—21 in *(533 mm)* (quins)
Mines: 80 can be carried
Main engines: Geared turbines; 2 shafts; 60 000 shp
Boilers: 3
Speed, knots: 35
Range, miles: 4 000 at 15 knots
Complement: 260

"SKORY" Class   1966

Launched in 1951. *Al Nasser* and *Al Zaffer* were delivered to the Egyptian Navy on 11 June 1956 at Alexandria. *Damiette* and *Suez* were delivered at Alexandria in Jan 1962. In April 1967 the original *Al Nasser* and *Damiette* were exchanged for ships with modified secondary and A/S armament which took the same names. *Al Nasser* was later renamed *6 October* to commemorate the Egyptian crossing of the Suez Canal in the 1973 Israeli war.

Radar: Search: Probably E/F Band.
Tactical: Probably G Band.
Fire control: Hawk Screech.

1 Ex-BRITISH "Z" CLASS

Name	No.
EL FATEH (ex-HMS *Zenith*)	—

Displacement, tons: 1 730 standard; 2 575 full load
Length, feet (metres): 350 *(106·8)* wl; 362·8 *(110·6)* oa
Beam, feet (metres): 35·7 *(10·9)*
Draught, feet (metres): 17·1 *(5·2)*
Guns: 4—4·5 in *(115 mm)*; 6—40 mm
A/S weapons: 4 DCT
Main engines: Parsons geared turbines; 2 shafts; 40 000 shp
Boilers: 2 Admiralty three-drum
Speed, knots: 31
Oil fuel, tons: 580
Range, miles: 2 800 at 20 knots
Complement: 250

Builders	Laid down	Launched	Commissioned
Wm. Denny & Bros, Dumbarton	19 May 1942	5 June 1944	22 Dec 1944

Purchased from the United Kingdom in 1955. Before being taken over by Egypt, *El Fateh* was refitted by John I. Thornycroft & Co Ltd, Woolston, Southampton in July 1956, subsequently modernised by J. S. White & Co Ltd, Cowes, completing July 1964.

Radar: Search: Type 960 Metric wavelength.
Tactical: Type 293. E/F Band. Fire control: I Band.

EL FATEH

FRIGATES

Note: See New Construction section at head of entry.

1 Ex-BRITISH "BLACK SWAN" CLASS

Name
TARIQ (ex-*Malek Farouq*, ex-HMS *Whimbrel*)

Displacement, tons: 1 490 standard; 1 925 full load
Length, feet (metres): 283 *(86·3)* pp; 299·5 *(91·3)* oa
Beam, feet (metres): 38·5 *(11·7)*
Draught, feet (metres): 14·0 *(4·3)*
Guns: 6—4 in *(102 mm)*; 4—40 mm; 2—20 mm
A/S weapons: 4 DCT
Main engines: Geared turbines; 2 shafts; 4 300 shp
Boilers: 2 three-drum type
Speed, knots: 19·75
Oil fuel, tons: 370
Range, miles: 4 500 at 12 knots
Complement: 180

No.	Builders	Laid down	Launched	Commissioned
555 (ex-42)	Yarrow & Co Ltd, Glasgow	31 Oct 1941	25 Aug 1942	13 Jan 1943

Transferred from the United Kingdom in Nov 1949. Was recently to have been converted as a submarine tender—decision deferred.

TARIQ   1976, Michael D. J. Lennon

132 EGYPT

1 Ex-BRITISH "RIVER" CLASS

Name	No.	Builders	Laid down	Launched	Commissioned
RASHID (ex-HMS *Spey*)	43	Smith's Dock Co Ltd	18 July 1941	10 Dec 1941	19 May 1942

Displacement, tons: 1 490 standard; 2 216 full load
Length, feet (metres): 283 *(86·3)* pp; 301·5 *(91·9)* oa
Beam, feet (metres): 36·7 *(11·2)*
Draught, feet (metres): 14·1 *(4·3)*
Guns: 1—4 in *(102 mm)*; 2—40 mm; 6—20 mm
A/S weapons: 4 DCT
Main engines: Triple expansion; 2 shafts; 5 500 ihp
Boilers: 2 Admiralty three-drum type
Speed, knots: 18
Range, miles: 7 700 at 12 knots
Oil fuel, tons: 640
Complement: 180

Purchased in Dec 1949. Has been operated as Submarine Support Ship.

Appearance: Was fitted with large deck-house aft.

RASHID

1 Ex-BRITISH "HUNT" CLASS

Name	No.	Builders	Laid down	Launched	Commissioned
PORT SAID (ex-*Mohamed Ali*, ex-*Ibrahim el Awal*, ex-HMS *Cottesmore*)	525 (ex-11)	Yarrow & Co Ltd, Glasgow	12 Dec 1939	5 Sep 1940	29 Dec 1940

Displacement, tons: 1 000 standard; 1 490 full load
Length, feet (metres): 273 *(83·2)* wl; 280 *(85·3)* oa
Beam, feet (metres): 29 *(8·8)*
Draught, feet (metres): 14·1 *(4·3)*
Guns: 4—4 in *(103 mm)* 2—37 mm; 2—25 mm (twin); 2—0·50 cal MG (twin)
A/S weapons: 2DCT
Main engines: Parsons geared turbines; 2 shafts; 19 000 shp
Boilers: 2 three-drum type
Speed, knots: 25
Range, miles: 2 000 at 12 knots
Oil fuel, tons: 280
Complement: 146

Transferred from the Royal Navy to the Egyptian Navy in July 1950: sailed for Egypt in April 1951, after a nine months refit by J. Samuel White & Co Ltd, Cowes.

PORT SAID (ex-*Mohamed Ali*) (old pennant number)

LIGHT FORCES

Note: See New Construction section at head of entry.

6 Ex-SOVIET "OSA I" CLASS (FAST ATTACK CRAFT—MISSILE)

312 324 356 378 +2

Displacement, tons: 165 standard; 200 full load
Dimensions, feet (metres): 128·7 × 25·1 × 5·9 *(39·2 × 7·7 × 1·8)*
Missiles: 4 launchers in two pairs abreast for SS-N-2 system (see notes)
Guns: 4—30 mm (2 twin, 1 forward, 1 aft) (+2 MG in refitted craft)
Main engines: 3 diesels (MTU in refitted boats); 13 000 bhp = 35 knots
Complement: 25

Ten reported to have been delivered to Egypt by the Soviet Navy in 1966. Four reported sunk during the Israeli War October 1973. At least four have been refitted as above.

Missiles: All carry SA-7 Grail.
Radar: Recently refitted craft carry a new Kelvin Hughes 1006 surveillance radar and a Decca navigation radar.
Before refit: Search: Pot Drum.
Fire control: Drum Tilt.
IFF: High Pole.

"OSA I" Class   1974, USN

4 Ex-SOVIET "KOMAR" CLASS (FAST ATTACK CRAFT—MISSILE)

Displacement, tons: 70 standard; 80 full load
Dimensions, feet (metres): 83·7 × 19·8 × 5·0 *(25·5 × 6 × 1·5)*
Missiles: 2 launchers for SS-N-2 system
Guns: 2—25 mm (twin); 2—7·62 mm (single)
Main engines: 4 diesels; 4 shafts; 4 800 hp = 40 knots
Range, miles: 400 at 30 knots
Complement: 20

Transferred from the USSR in 1962 to 1967. One of this type was sunk by Israeli jets on 16 May 1970. Two reported sunk in Israeli War October 1973.

Radar: Search: Square Tie.
IFF: High Pole.

"KOMAR" Class   1966, Colonel Bjorn Borg

EGYPT 133

6 EGYPTIAN "OCTOBER 6" CLASS
(FAST ATTACK CRAFT—MISSILE)

Displacement, tons: 80 full load
Dimensions, feet (metres): 84 × 20 × 5 (25·6 × 6 × 1·5)
Missiles: Otomat (French version)
Guns: 2—30 mm British A 32
Main engines: 4 diesels; 4 shafts; 4 800 hp = 40 knots
Range, miles: 400 at 30 knots
Complement: ? 20

Built in Alexandria 1975—76. Hull of same design as Soviet "Komar" class and fitted with Soviet diesels although now reported that these have been replaced with MTU. The armament is of West European manufacture including British electronics.

6 Ex-SOVIET "SHERSHEN" CLASS
(2 FAST ATTACK CRAFT—TORPEDO, 4 FAST ATTACK CRAFT—GUN)

332   343   354   365   +2

Displacement, tons: 150 standard; 160 full load
Dimensions, feet (metres): 115·5 × 23 × 5 (35·2 × 7·1 × 1·5)
Guns: 4—30 mm (2 twin)
Rocket launchers: 40 tube; 122 mm (see notes)
Torpedo tubes: 4—21 in (single)
A/S weapons: 12 DC
Main engines: 3 diesels; 3 shafts; 13 000 hp = 41 knots
Complement: 16

One delivered from USSR in Feb 1967, two more in Oct 1967, and three since. Four have had their guns and tubes removed to make way for multiple BM21 rocket-launchers and one SA-7 Grail.

Radar: Search: Pot Drum.
Fire control: Drum Tilt.
IFF: High Pole.

"SHERSHEN" Class   1974, USN

20 Ex-SOVIET "P 6" CLASS (FAST ATTACK CRAFT—TORPEDO)

Displacement, tons: 66 standard; 75 full load
Dimensions, feet (metres): 84·2 × 20 × 6 (25·7 × 6·1 × 1·8)
Guns: 2 or 4—25 mm (some have forward guns replaced by 122 mm 8-barrelled rocket launcher)
Torpedo tubes: 2—21 in (4—21 in in two boats)
Main engines: 4 diesels; 4 shafts; 4 800 hp = 43 knots
Range, miles: 450 at 30 knots
Complement: 25

The first 12 boats arrived at Alexandria on 19 April 1956 six more in 1960. Two were destroyed by British naval aircraft on 4 Nov 1956, two were sunk by the Israeli destroyer *Elath* off Sinai on 12 July 1967, two by Israeli MTBs off Sinai coast on 11 July 1967, two by Israeli air attacks in 1969, and two in the Red Sea on 22 Jan 1970.
Further reinforcements have been sent by USSR—none since Oct 1973. Several have been built at Alexandria.

Radar: Decca in most craft.

"P 4" Class with 8-barrelled rocket launcher   10/1974

3 LARGE PATROL CRAFT

NISR 1, 2 and 3

Displacement, tons: 110
Gun: 1—20 mm

4 Ex-SOVIET/SYRIAN "P 4" CLASS
(FAST ATTACK CRAFT—TORPEDO)

Transferred by Syria in 1970. Now armed with 8-barrelled 122 mm rocket launcher forward and twin 14·5 mm aft as well as two torpedo tubes. Decca radar is now fitted.

12 Ex-SOVIET "SO I" CLASS (LARGE PATROL CRAFT)

211   217   222   229   233   236   244   255   +4

Displacement, tons: 215 light; 250 full load
Dimensions, feet (metres): 138·6 × 20 × 9·2 (42·3 × 6·1 × 2·8)
Guns: 4—25 mm (2 twin mountings)
A/S weapons: 4 five-barrelled MBU 1800
Main engines: 3 diesel; 6 000 bhp = 29 knots
Range, miles: 1 100 at 13 knots
Complement: 30

Eight reported to have been transferred by the USSR to Egypt in 1962 to 1967 and four others later.
Some craft carry SA-7 Grail missiles and others 2—21 in torpedo tubes.

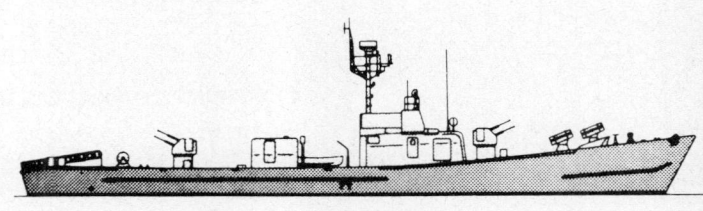

Built by Castro, Port Said and launched in May 1963.

"SO I" Class

20 BERTRAM TYPE (COASTAL PATROL CRAFT)

Displacement, tons: 8 approx
Length, feet (metres): 28 (8·5)
Guns: 2—12·7 mm MG
Rocket launchers: 4—122 mm

GRP hulls. Built in Miami, Florida

Now in service probably with the coastguard.

BERTRAM Type   10/1974

134 EGYPT

2 Ex-YUGOSLAVIAN "108" CLASS (FAST TARGET CRAFT)

Displacement, tons: 55 standard; 60 full load
Dimensions, feet (metres): 69 pp; 78 oa × 21·3 × 7·8 *(23·8 oa × 6·5 × 2·4)*
Main engines: 3 Packard motors; 3 shafts; 5 000 bhp = 36 knots
Complement: 14

Purchased from Yugoslavia in 1956. Similar to the boats of the US "Higgins" class. Originally a class of six. Remaining pair now fitted with reflectors and used as targets.

AMPHIBIOUS FORCES

3 Ex-SOVIET "POLNOCNY" CLASS (LCT)

Displacement, tons: 800 full load
Dimensions, feet (metres): 239·4 × 29·5 × 9·8 *(73 × 9 × 3)*
Guns: 2—25 mm (twin)
Rocket launchers: 2—18 barrelled 140 mm launchers
Main engines: 2 diesels; 5 000 bhp = 18 knots

Can carry 6 tanks. Transferred early 1970s.

Soviet "POLNOCNY" Class

1 SOVIET "MP 4" CLASS (LCT)

Displacement, tons: 780 full load
Dimensions, feet (metres): 183·7 × 26·2 × 8·9 *(56 × 8 × 2·7)*
Guns: 4—25 mm
Main engines: Diesel; 1 shaft; 1 100 bhp = 10 knots

Built in Egypt in 1970.

10 Ex-SOVIET "VYDRA" CLASS (LCU)

Displacement, tons: 300 standard; 500 full load
Dimensions, feet (metres): 157·4 × 24·6 × 7·2 *(48 × 7·5 × 2·2)*
Main engines: 2 3D 12 diesels; 2 shafts; 600 bhp = 15 knots

Can carry and land up to 250 tons of military equipment and stores. For a period after the "October War" several were fitted with rocket launchers and 2—37 or 40 mm guns all of which have now been removed.

4 Ex-SOVIET "SMB 1" CLASS (LCU)

Displacement, tons: 200 standard; 420 full load
Dimensions, feet (metres): 157·5 × 21·3 × 5·6 *(48 × 6·5 × 1·7)*
Main engines: 2 diesels; 2 shafts; 400 hp = 11 knots

Delivered to the Egyptian Navy in 1965. Can carry 150 tons of military equipment.

10 LCMs

Generally used as harbour-craft.

MINEWARFARE FORCES

6 Ex-SOVIET "T 43" CLASS (MINESWEEPERS—OCEAN)

ASSIUT   CHARKIEH   GHARBIA
BAHAIRA DAKHLA   SINAI

Displacement, tons: 500 standard; 610 full load
Dimensions, feet (metres): 190·2 × 28·2 × 6·9 *(58·0 × 8·6 × 2·1)*
Guns: 4—37 mm (twins); 8—14·5 mm (twins)
Main engines: 2 diesels; 2 shafts; 2 000 hp = 17 knots
Range, miles: 1 600 at 10 knots
Complement: 40

Three were transferred from the Soviet Navy and delivered to Egypt 1956-59, and three since 1970. *Miniya* was sunk by Israeli air attack in the Gulf of Suez on 6 Feb 1970 but was later replaced.

Soviet "T 43" Class   1967, USN

4 Ex-SOVIET "YURKA" CLASS (MINESWEEPERS—OCEAN)

GIZA 690   ASWAN 695   QENA 696   SOHAG 699

Displacement, tons: 500 standard; 550 full load
Dimensions, feet (metres): 172 × 31 × 8·9 *(52·5 × 9·5 × 2·7)*
Guns: 4—30 mm (2 twin)
Main engines: 2 diesels; 4 000 bhp = 18 knots

Steel-hulled minesweepers transferred from USSR 1970-71.

Appearance: Egyptian "Yurka" class do not carry Drum Tilt radar and have a number of ship's-side scuttles.

Soviet "YURKA" Class   S. Breyer

2 Ex-SOVIET "T 301" CLASS (MINESWEEPERS—INSHORE)

EL FAYOUD   EL MANUFIEH

Displacement, tons: 130 standard; 180 full load
Dimensions, feet (metres): 124·6 × 19·7 × 4·9 *(39 × 5·5 × 1·5)*
Guns: 2—37 mm; 2—MG
Main engines: 3 diesels; 1 440 hp = 9 knots
Complement: 30

Reported to have been transferred by the USSR to Egypt in 1962; a third ship may have been transferred later.

2 Ex-SOVIET "K 8" CLASS (MINESWEEPERS—INSHORE)

Displacement, tons: 50 standard; 70 full load
Dimensions, feet (metres): 92 × 13·5 × 2·3 *(28· × 4·1 × 0·7)*
Guns: 2—12·7 mm
Main engines: Diesels; 600 shp = 14 knots

Several transferred but survivors used mainly as harbour craft.

EGYPT / EQUATORIAL GUINEA 135

MISCELLANEOUS

3 WINCHESTER (SR.N6) HOVERCRAFT

Displacement, tons: 10 normal gross weight
Dimensions, feet (metres): 48·4 × 25·3 × 15·9 (height) *(14·8 × 7·7 × 4·8)*
Main engines: 1 Gnome Model 1050 gas turbine = 58 knots

Purchased in 1975 as refitted second-hand craft. Reportedly converted into minelayers

2 TRAINING SHIPS

EL HORRIYA (ex-*Mahroussa*)

Of 4 560 tons, built by Sanuda, Poplar in 1865 and once the Egyptian Royal Yacht, has been completely refitted and is used as a training ship.

EL HORRIYA   1976, USN

INTISHAT

A smaller training ship.

2 Ex-SOVIET "NYRYAT" CLASS

Diving support ships transferred in 1964.

2 Ex-SOVIET "POLUCHAT II" CLASS

Torpedo recovery craft.

2 Ex-SOVIET "OKHTENSKY" CLASS TUGS

AL MAKAS   ANTAR

Two transferred to the Egyptian Navy in 1966—assembled in Egypt.

1 Ex-SOVIET "SEKSTAN" CLASS

160

Used as cadet training ship.

SWIMMER DELIVERY VEHICLES

There is a strong underwater team in the Egyptian navy who use, amongst other equipment, the 2-man SDVs shown here. Range could be 4 hours at 3-4 knots.

SDV   10·1974

EL SALVADOR

Personnel
(a) 1978: 130 officers and men
(b) Voluntary service

Ports
Acajutla, La Libertad, La Union

Mercantile Marine
Lloyd's Register of Shipping:
2 vessels of 1 987 tons gross

DELETION

1975 GC 1

PATROL BOATS

1 Ex-BRITISH HDML

Name	No.	Builders	Commissioned
GC 2 (ex-*Nohaba*)	—	UK	1942

Displacement, tons: 46
Dimensions, feet (metres): 72 oa × 16 × 5·5 *(21·9 × 4·9 × 1·7)*
Gun: 1—20 mm
Main engines: 2 diesels; 2 shafts = 12 knots
Complement: 16

Purchased from commercial sources in 1959.

2 Ex-US CG TYPE

Name	No.	Builders	Commissioned
GC 3	—	USA	1950
GC 4	—	USA	1950

Displacement, tons: 14

1 SEWART 65 ft TYPE

Name	No.	Builders	Commissioned
GC 5	—	Sewart, USA	1967

Displacement, tons: 33
Dimensions, feet (metres): 65 × 16·3 × 5·0 *(19·8 × 4·9 × 1·5)*
Guns: 3 MG
Main engines: GM diesels; 1 600 hp = 25 knots

Transferred Sep 1967.

EQUATORIAL GUINEA

Ministerial

President and Minister of People's Armed Forces:
Francisco Macías Nguema

Ports
Santa Isabel (Macías Nguema Biyogo), Bata (Rio Muni).

Mercantile Marine
Lloyds Register of Shipping:
1 vessel of 3 070 tons gross

LIGHT FORCES

1 Ex-SOVIET "P6" CLASS (FAST ATTACK CRAFT—TORPEDO)

Displacement, tons: 66 standard; 75 full load
Dimensions, feet (metres): 84·2 × 20 × 6 *(25·7 × 6·1 × 1·8)*
Guns: 4—25 mm
Torpedo tubes: 2—21 in
Main engines: 4 diesels; 4 shafts; 4 800 hp = 43 knots
Range, miles: 450 at 30 knots
Complement: 25

Doubtful if the torpedo armament is operational. Up to four of this class reported but unconfirmed.

1 Ex-SOVIET "POLUCHAT" CLASS

Displacement, tons: 86 standard; 91 full load
Dimensions, feet (metres): 98 pp × 15 × 4·8 *(29·9 × 4·6 × 1·5)*
Guns: 2—14·5 mm (twin)
Main engines: 2 diesels; 2 shafts; 1 200 bhp = 18 knots
Range, miles: 460 at 17 knots
Complement: 16

ETHIOPIA

Personnel

(a) 1978: 1 500 officers and men
(b) Voluntary service

Naval Establishments

Massawa: Naval Base and College, established in 1956.
Embaticalla: Marine Commando Training School.
Assab: Naval Base, expanding to include a ship repair facility.

Mercantile Marine

Lloyd's Register of Shipping:
18 vessels of 23 989 tons gross

New Construction and Acquisitions

(a) Two French EDICs (LCTs) were ordered from SFCN Villeneuve la Garenne for delivery in 1977. Present status unknown
(b) Reported that 5 "Osa II" class have been or are being delivered by USSR. Unconfirmed report.

DELETION

1977 PC 12 sunk

FRIGATE

1 Ex-US "BARNEGAT" CLASS

Name	No.	Builders	Commissioned
ETHIOPIA (ex-USS *Orca*, AVP 49)	A 01	Lake Washington SY	23 Jan 1944

Displacement, tons: 1 766 standard; 2 800 full load
Dimensions, feet (metres): 310·8 oa × 41 × 13·5 *(94·7 × 12·5 × 3·7)*
Guns: 1—5 in 38 cal; 5—40 mm
Main engines: 2 sets diesels; 2 shafts; 6 080 bhp = 18·2 knots
Complement: 215

Former United States small seaplane tender of "Barnegat" class. Laid down 13 July 1942, launched on 4 Oct 1942. Transferred from the US Navy in Jan 1962.

ETHIOPIA   *1972, Imperial Ethiopian Navy*

EX-MINESWEEPER (COASTAL)

1 Ex-NETHERLANDS "WILDERVANK" CLASS

Name	No.	Builders	Commissioned
MS 41 (ex-*Elst*, M 829)	—	Netherlands	1956

Displacement, tons: 373 standard; 417 full load
Dimensions, feet (metres): 149·8 oa × 28·0 × 7·5 *(45·7 × 8·5 × 2·3)*
Guns: 2—40 mm
Main engines: 2 Werkspoor diesels; 2 shafts; 2 500 bhp = 14 knots
Oil fuel, tons: 25 tons
Range, miles: 2 500 at 10 knots
Complement: 38

Launched 21 Mar 1956. Purchased by Ethiopia and transferred from the Royal Netherlands Navy in 1971.

Missiles: It has been reported that MS 41 has been fitted for launching SS-12 missiles.

MS 41 (as *Elst*)

LIGHT FORCES

4 SEWART 105 ft TYPE (LARGE PATROL CRAFT)

Displacement, tons: 118
Dimensions, feet (metres): 105 × 20 × 6·5 *(32 × 6·1 × 2)*
Guns: 4 Emerlec 30 mm (twins); 1—20 mm
Main engines: 2 diesels = 30 knots
Complement: 21

Eight ordered in 1976 of which four were delivered in April 1977 before the cessation of US arms sales with Ethiopia.

SEWART 105 ft Type   *1977*

ETHIOPIA / FIJI 137

4 "PGM 53" AND USCG "CAPE" CLASSES (LARGE PATROL CRAFT)

Name	No.	Builders	Commissioned
PC 11 (ex-US CG WVP 95304)	—	Peterson, USA	1958
PC 13 (ex-USN PGM 53)	—	Peterson, USA	1961
PC 14 (ex-USN PGM 54)	—	Peterson, USA	1961
PC 15 (ex-USN PGM 58)	—	Peterson, USA	1962

Displacement, tons: 145·5 full load
Dimensions, feet (metres): 95 × 19 × 5·2 *(29·0 × 5·8 × 1·6)*
Guns: 1—40 mm; 1—50 cal MG
A/S weapons: 1 Mousetrap
Main engines: 4 diesels; 2 shafts; 2 200 bhp = 21 knots
Range, miles: 1 500 at cruising speed
Complement: 20

Loss: PC 12 sunk by Ethiopian Air Force in 1977 while trying to defect.

"PGM 53" Class   1970, Imperial Ethiopian Navy

1 Ex-YUGOSLAV "KRALJEVICA" CLASS (LARGE PATROL CRAFT)

Name	No.	Builders	Commissioned
— (ex-507)	—	Yugoslavia	1953

Displacement, tons: 190·5 standard; 202 full load
Dimensions, feet (metres): 134·5 × 20·7 × 7·2 *(41 × 6·3 × 2·2)*
Guns: 1—3 in; 1—40 mm; 4—20 mm
A/S weapons: DCs
Main engines: 2 MAN diesels; 2 shafts; 3 300 bhp = 18 knots

Transferred 1975.

4 "SEWART" CLASS (COASTAL PATROL CRAFT)

Name	No.	Builders	Commissioned
GB 21	—	Sewart Inc, Berwick	1966
GB 22	—	Sewart Inc, Berwick	1966
GB 23	—	Sewart Inc, Berwick	1967
GB 24	—	Sewart Inc, Berwick	1967

Displacement, tons: 15
Length, feet (metres): 40 *(12·2)*
Guns: 2—·50 calibre machine guns
Speed, knots: 20
Complement: 7

GB 21   1970, Imperial Ethiopian Navy

LANDING CRAFT

There are 2 of the US LCM type and 2 of the US LCVP type. Two were bought in 1962 and two in 1971.

FIJI

On 12 June 1974 the Royal Fiji Military Forces were authorised to raise a Naval Squadron to carry out Fishery Protection, Surveillance, Hydrographic Surveying and Coastguard duties. The RFMF is under the authority of the Minister for Home Affairs. In addition to its normal tasks the Naval Squadron runs an all-conquering Rugby Team.

Commanding Officers

RFMF:
Colonel P. F. Manueli OBE

Naval Squadron:
Commander S. B. Brown MBE VRD

Ministerial

Minister for Home Affairs:
Ratu Sir Penaia Ganilau KBE CMG CVO DSO

Prefix to Ships' Names

HMFS.

Personnel

1978: 159 (19 officers, 140 sailors)

Base

HMFS *Viti*, Suva.

Mercantile Marine

Lloyds Register of Shipping:
33 vessels of 10 879 tons gross

3 Ex-US "REDWING" CLASS (MINESWEEPERS—COASTAL)

Name	No.	Builders	Commissioned
KIKAU (ex-USS *Woodpecker*, MSC 209)	204	Bellingham SY, USA	3 Feb 1956
KULA (ex-USS *Vireo*, MSC 205)	205	Bellingham SY, USA	7 June 1955
KIRO (ex-USS *Warbler*, MSC 206)	206	Bellingham SY, USA	23 July 1955

Displacement, tons: 370 full load
Dimensions, feet (metres): 144 oa × 28 × 8·5 *(43·9 × 8·5 × 2·6)*
Guns: 1—20 mm; 2—0·5 MG
Main engines: 2 GM diesels; 2 shafts; 880 bhp = 13 knots
Range, miles: 2 500 at 10 knots
Complement: 39

First pair transferred 14 Oct 1975 and the third in June 1976. *Kiro* and *Kula* have been refitted for removal of magnetic MS equipment.

KIRO   1976, RFMF

RUVE (ex-*Volasiga*, ex-*Marinetta*)

Displacement, tons: 100
Dimensions, feet (metres): 94 oa × 17·5 × 7·5 *(28·7 × 5·3 × 2·3)*
Complement: 14

Transferred from Fiji Marine Department, June 1976. Used for Surveying.
Built in 1929. Replacement of 30 metres length, laid down at Suva April 1978 for completion April 1979.

FINLAND

Headquarters Appointment
Commander-in-Chief Finnish Navy:
  Rear-Admiral Bo Klenberg

Diplomatic Representation
Naval Attaché in London:
  Lieutenant-Colonel Pertti E. Nykänen

Naval Attaché in Moscow:
  Colonel E. Pallasvirta

Naval Attaché in Paris:
  Lieutenant-Colonel Sami Sihvo

Naval Attaché in Washington:
  Colonel Erkki Kaira

Treaty Limitations
The Finnish Navy is limited by the Treaty of Paris (1947) to 10 000 tons of ships and 4 500 personnel. Submarines and motor torpedo boats are prohibited.

Personnel
(a) 1972: 2 000 (150 officers and 1 850 ratings)
    1973: 2 500 (200 officers and 2 300 ratings)
    1974: 2 500 (200 officers and 2 300 ratings)
    1975: 2 500 (200 officers and 2 300 ratings)
    1976: 2 500 (200 officers and 2 300 ratings)
    1977: 2 500 (200 officers and 2 300 ratings)
    1978: 2 500 (200 officers and 2 300 ratings)
(b) 8-11 months national service

Hydrographic Department
This office and the survey ships come under the Ministry of Trade and Industry.

Frontier Guard
All Frontier Guard vessels come under the Ministry of the Interior.

Icebreakers
All these ships work for the Board of Navigation.

Mercantile Marine
Lloyd's Register of Shipping:
  337 vessels of 2 262 095 tons gross

Strength of the Fleet

Type	Active	Building (Planned)
Frigates	2	(2)
Corvettes	2	—
Fast Attack Craft (Missile)	4+1	(5)
Fast Attack Craft (Gun)	14	—
Large Patrol Craft	5	—
Minelayer	1	1
Minesweepers, Inshore	6	(8)
HQ Ships	2	—
Transports (LCUs)	13	—
Tugs	3	—
Support Ships	3	—
Transport Craft	57	—
Cable Ship	1	—
Icebreakers	9	—

Frontier Guard

Large Patrol Craft	5	3
Training Ship	1	—
Supply Ship	1	—
Coastal Patrol Craft	99	—

New Construction
Staff studies begun on two new frigates. Additional Fast Attack Craft (Missile) to bring total up to nine by addition of five "Tuima" class. New minelayer to commission in 1979—also to act as training ship.
Eight more "Kuha" class minesweepers to be built. Three more patrol craft, first ordered 24 June 1975, of improved "Valpas" class for Frontier Guard.

DELETIONS

Frigates
1975 *Matti Kurki* (ex-British "Bay" Class)

Light Forces
1975 *Tursas* (Large Patrol Craft)
1977 *Vasama I* (Fast Attack Craft)

Minewarfare Forces
1975 *Ruotsinsalmi*

Coastguard Vessels
1970 VMV 11, 13, 19 and 20
1971 *Aura*

"UUSIMAA" Class

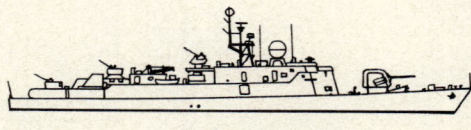

"TURUNMAA" Class

FRIGATES

2 Ex-SOVIET "RIGA" CLASS

HÄMEENMAA   UUSIMAA

Displacement, tons: 1 200 standard; 1 600 full load
Length, feet (metres): 298·8 *(91)*
Beam, feet (metres): 33·7 *(10·2)*
Draught, feet (metres): 11 *(3·4)*
Guns: 3—3·9 in *(100 mm)* single; 2—40 mm; 2—30 mm (twin) (in bow)
A/S weapons: 1 Hedgehog; 4 DC projectors
Torpedo tubes: 3—21 in *(533 mm)*
Mines: 50 (capacity)
Main engines: Geared turbines; 2 shafts; 25 000 shp
Speed, knots: 28
Boilers: 2
Range, miles: 2 000 at 10 knots
Complement: 150

Built in USSR—*Uusimaa* in 1955 and *Hämeenmaa* in 1957. Purchased from the USSR and transferred to the Finnish Navy on 29 April 1964 and 14 May 1964, respectively. Armament modified in 1971 with extra 30 mm.

Radar: Search: Slim Net.
Fire control: Sun Visor A (with Wasphead fire control system).
Navigation: Decca.
IFF: Ski Pole and Yard Rake.

UUSIMAA   1974, Finnish Navy–SA Kuva

Sonar: Hull mounted.

CORVETTES

2 "TURUNMAA" CLASS

Name	No.	Builders	Laid down	Launched	Commissioned
KARJALA	—	Wärtsilä, Helsinki	Mar 1967	16 Aug 1967	21 Oct 1968
TURUNMAA	—	Wärtsilä, Helsinki	Mar 1967	11 July 1967	29 Aug 1968

Displacement, tons: 660 standard; 770 full load
Dimensions, feet (metres): 243·1 × 25·6 × 7·9 *(74·1 × 7·8 × 2·4)*
Guns: 1—4·7 in *(120 mm)* Bofors forward; 2—40 mm; 2—30 mm (1 twin) aft
A/S weapons: 2 DCT; 2 DC racks
Main engines: CODOG. 3 Mercedes-Benz (MTU) diesels; 3 000 bhp; 1 Rolls-Royce Olympus gas turbine; 22 000 hp = 35 knots. On diesels = 17 knots
Complement: 70

Ordered on 18 Feb 1965 from Wärtsilä, Helsinki. Flush decked. Rocket flare guide rails on sides of 4·7 in turret. Fitted with Vosper Thornycroft fin stabiliser equipment.

Radar: Search and Tactical: H/I Band. (HSA).

KARJALA   1975, Finnish Navy

LIGHT FORCES

4 "TUIMA" CLASS (FAST ATTACK CRAFT—MISSILE)

TUIMA   TUULI   TUISKU   TYRSKY

Displacement, tons: 165 standard; 200 full load
Dimensions, feet (metres): 128·7 × 25·1 × 5·9 *(39·3 × 7·7 × 1·8)*
Missiles: 4—SS-N-2 system launchers
Guns: 4—30 mm (twin)
Main engines: 3 diesels; 13 000 hp
Speed, knots: 36
Range, miles: 800 at 25 knots
Complement: 25

Ex-Soviet "Osa" class purchased from USSR. 1974—75. New construction but with Finnish electronics. Five more planned.

TUIMA   *1975, Finnish Navy*

1 EXPERIMENTAL CRAFT—MISSILE

Name	No.	Builders	Commissioned
ISKU	—	Reposaaron, Konepaja	1970

Displacement, tons: 140 full load
Dimensions, feet (metres): 86·5 × 28·6 × 6·4 *(26·4 × 8·7 × 1·8)*
Missile launchers: 4 SS-N-2 system launchers
Guns: 2—30 mm (1 twin)
Main engines: 4 Soviet M50 diesels; 3 600 bhp = 15 knots
Complement: 25

Guided missile craft of novel design built for training and experimental work. The construction combines a missile boat armament on a landing craft hull. Laid down Nov 1968 and launched 4 Dec 1969.

ISKU   *1976, Finnish Navy*

13 "NUOLI" CLASS (FAST ATTACK CRAFT—GUN)

Name	No.	Builders	Commissioned
NUOLI 1—13	1—13	Laivateollisuus, Turku	1961—6

Displacement, tons: 40 standard
Dimensions, feet (metres): 72·2 × 21·7 × 5·0 *(22 × 6·6 × 1·5)*
Guns: 1—40 mm; 1—20 mm
A/S weapons: 4 DCs
Main engines: 3 Soviet M50 diesels; 2 700 bhp = 40 knots
Complement: 15

Designed by Laivateollisuus, Turku. Delivery dates— 14 Sep 1961, 19 Oct 1961, 1 Nov 1961, 21 Nov 1961, 6 July 1962, 3 Aug 1962, 22 Aug 1962, 10 Oct 1962, 27 Oct 1963, 5 May 1964, 5 May 1964, 30 Nov 1964, 12 Oct 1966. This class is split into two: Nuoli 1 (1-9) and Nuoli 2 (10-13). The main difference is a lower superstructure in Nuoli 2.

Radar: I-band Decca.

"NUOLI" Class   *1976, Finnish Navy*

1 "VASAMA" CLASS (FAST ATTACK CRAFT—GUN)

Name	No.	Builders	Commissioned
VASAMA 2	2	Saunders Roe (Anglesey) Ltd	1 May 1957

Displacement, tons: 50 standard; 70 full load
Dimensions, feet (metres): 67·0 pp; 71·5 oa × 19·8 × 6·1 *(21·8 oa × 5·9 × 1·8)*
Guns: 2—40 mm
A/S weapons: 4 DCT
Main engines: 2 Napier Deltic diesels; 5 000 bhp = 40 knots
Complement: 20

British "Dark" class.

VASAMA 2   *1976, Finnish Navy*

140 FINLAND

3 "RUISSALO" CLASS (LARGE PATROL CRAFT)

Name	No.	Builders	Commissioned
RUISSALO	3	Laivatteollisuus, Turku	11 Aug 1959
RAISIO	4	Laivatteollisuus, Turku	12 Sep 1959
RÖYTTA	5	Laivatteollisuus, Turku	14 Oct 1959

Displacement, tons: 110 standard; 130 full load
Dimensions, feet (metres): 111·5 × 19·8 × 5·9 *(34 × 6 × 1·8)*
Guns: 1—40 mm; 1—20 mm; 2 MG
A/S weapons: 1 Squid mortar
Mines: Can lay mines
Main engines: 2 Mercedes-Benz (MTU) diesels; 2 500 bhp = 18 knots
Complement: 20

Ordered in Jan 1958. Launched on 16 June, 2 July and 2 June 1959.

Radar: Decca.

Sonar: One hull-mounted.

RAISIO *1975, Finnish Navy*

2 "RIHTNIEMI" CLASS (LARGE PATROL CRAFT)

Name	No.	Builders	Commissioned
RIHTNIEMI	1	Rauma-Repola, Rauma	21 Feb 1957
RYMÄTTYLÄ	2	Rauma-Repola, Rauma	20 May 1957

Displacement, tons: 90 standard; 110 full load
Dimensions, feet (metres): 101·7 × 18·7 × 5·9 *(31 × 5·6 × 1·8)*
Guns: 1—40 mm; 1—20 mm; 2 MG
A/S weapons: 2 DC racks
Mines: Can lay mines
Main engines: 2 Mercedes-Benz (MTU) diesels; 1 400 bhp = 15 knots
Complement: 20

Ordered in June 1955, launched in 1956. Controllable pitch propellers.

RIHTNIEMI *1976, Finnish Navy*

MINE WARFARE FORCES

1 NEW CONSTRUCTION

Name	No.	Builders	Commissioned
—	—	Wärtsila, Helsinki	1979

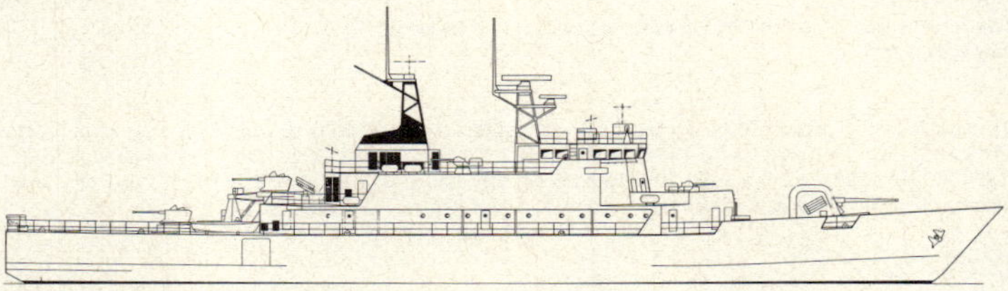

Displacement, tons: 1 100
Dimensions, feet (metres): 255·8 × 37·7 × 9·8 *(78 × 11·5 × 3)*
Guns: 1—120 mm Bofors (forward); 2—40 mm; 4—23 mm (twin)
A/S weapons: 2 DCT
Mines: ?
Main engines: 2 Wärtsila Vasa 16V22 diesels; 5 800 bhp; 2 shafts (cp propellers)
Complement: 77

Design completed 1976. Also to serve as training ship.

NEW WÄRTSILA MINELAYER *1977, Wärtsila*

1 MINELAYER

Name	No.	Builders	Commissioned
KEIHÄSSALMI	—	Valmet, Helsinki	1957

Displacement, tons: 360
Dimensions, feet (metres): 168 × 23 × 6 *(51·2 × 7 × 1·8)*
Guns: 4—30 mm (twins); 2—20 mm
Mines: Up to 100 capacity
Main engines: 2 Wärtsilä diesels; 2 shafts; 2 000 bhp = 15 knots
Complement: 60

Of improved "Ruotsinsalmi" Class. Contract dated June 1955. Launched on 16 Mar 1957. Armament modified in 1972.

Radar: Search and Tactical; I band. Decca.

KEIHÄSSALMI *1974, Finnish Navy*

6 "KUHA" CLASS (MINESWEEPERS—INSHORE)

Name	No.	Builders	Commissioned
KUHA 21—26	21—26	Laivatteollisuus, Turku	1974—75

Displacement, tons: 90
Dimensions, feet (metres): 87·2 × 23 *(26·6 × 7)*
Guns: 1 or 2—20 mm
Main engines: 2 diesels; 600 shp; 1 shaft (cp) = 12 knots
Complement: 15

All ordered 1972. Fitted for magnetic, acoustic and pressure-mine sweeping. Have active rudders.
Kuha 21 completed 28 June 1974. *Kuha 26* in late 1975. Hulls are of GRP. Funds for further 8 craft provided.

Radar: Decca.

KUHA 22 *1974, Finnish Navy—SA Kuva*

FINLAND 141

ICEBREAKERS

Controlled by Board of Navigation.

2 "URHO" CLASS

Name	No.	Builders	Commissioned
URHO	—	Wärtsilä, Helsinki	5 Mar 1975
SISU	—	Wärtsilä, Helsinki	28 Jan 1976

Displacement, tons: 7 800 *(Urho);* 7 900 *(Sisu)* standard; 9 500 full load
Dimensions, feet (metres): 343·1 × 78·1 × 23·9 *(104·6 × 23·8 × 8·3)*
Aircraft: 1 helicopter
Main engines: Diesel-electric; 5 Wärtsilä-SEMT Pielstick diesels 25 000 bhp. electric motors; 22 000 shp; 2 shafts forward, 2 aft; = 18 knots
Complement: 57

Ordered on 11 Dec 1970 and 10 May 1971 respectively. Fitted with two screws aft, taking 60 per cent of available power and two forward, taking the remainder. Sisters to Swedish "Atle" class.

SISU   1977, Wärtsila

3 "TARMO" CLASS

Name	No.	Builders	Commissioned
TARMO	—	Wärtsilä, Helsinki	1963
VARMA	—	Wärtsilä, Helsinki	1968
APU	—	Wärtsilä, Helsinki	25 Nov 1970

Displacement, tons: 4 890
Dimensions, feet (metres): 281·0 × 71·0 × 22·5 *(85·7 × 21·7 × 6·8)*
Aircraft: 1 helicopter
Main engines: Wärtsilä-Sulzer diesels; electric drive; 4 shafts (2 screws forward 2 screws aft); 12 000 shp = 17 knots

APU   1977, Finnish Navy

3 "KARHU" CLASS

Name	No.	Builders	Commissioned
KARHU	—	Wärtsilä, Helsinki	Dec 1958
MURTAJA	—	Wärtsilä, Helsinki	1959
SAMPO	—	Wärtsilä, Helsinki	1960

Displacement, tons: 3 540
Dimensions, feet (metres): 243·2 × 57 × 21 *(74·2 × 17·4 × 6·4)*
Main engines: Diesel-electric; 4 shafts; 7 500 bhp = 16 knots

Karhu was launched on 22 Oct 1957, *Murtaja* was launched on 23 Sep 1958. Both these ships have tripod foremasts.

SAMPO   1977, Finnish Navy

1 "VOIMA" CLASS

Name	No.	Builders	Commissioned
VOIMA	—	Wärtsilä, Helsinki	1954

Displacement, tons: 4 415
Dimensions, feet (metres): 274 oa × 63·7 × 22·5 *(83·6 × 19·4 × 6·8)*
Main engines: Diesels with electric drive; 4 shafts; 10 500 shp = 16·5 knots
Oil fuel, tons: 740

Launched in 1953. Two propellers forward and aft.

There is also the West German owned, Finnish manned, icebreaker *Hansa,* of the "Karhu" class, completed on 25 Nov 1966, which operates off Germany in winter and off Finland at other times.

VOIMA   1975, Finnish Navy

MISCELLANEOUS
1 Ex-ICEBREAKER (HQ SHIP)

Name	No.	Builders	Commissioned
LOUHI (ex-*Sisu*)	—	Wärtsilä, Helsinki	1939

Displacement, tons: 2 075
Dimensions, feet (metres): 210·2 oa × 46·5 × 16·8 *(64·1 × 14·2 × 5·1)*
Guns: 2—3·9 in
Main engines: 2 sets Atlas Polar diesels with electric drive; 2 shafts and a bow propeller; 4 000 hp = 16 knots
Complement: 28

Launched on 24 Sep 1938. Used as submarine depot ship 1939—45. Converted 1975 to be HQ and Logistics ship.

LOUHI   1977, Finnish Navy

142 FINLAND

1 HEADQUARTERS SHIP

KORSHOLM (ex-*Korsholm III,* ex-*Öland*)

Displacement, tons: 650
Dimensions, feet (metres): 157·4 × 27·9 × 9·5 *(48 × 8·5 × 2·9)*
Guns: 2—20 mm
Main engines: Steam; 865 hp = 11 knots

Converted car ferry. Built in 1931 in Sweden. Bought by Rederi Ab Vaasa-Umea in 1958. Sold to Navy in 1967.

2 "KAMPELA" CLASS (LCU TRANSPORTS)

Name	No.	Builders	Commissioned
KAMPELA 1	—	—	July 1977
KAMPELA 2	—	—	Oct 1977

Displacement, tons: 90
Dimensions, feet (metres): 106·6 × 26·2 × 4·9 *(32·5 × 8·0 × 1·5)*
Guns: 2—20 mm
Mines: ?
Main engines: 2 Scania diesels; 460 bhp = 9 knots
Complement: 10

Can be used as amphibious craft, transports, minelayers or for shore support. Armament can be changed to suit role.

"KAMPELA" Class   1977, Finnish Navy

6 "KALA" CLASS (LCU TRANSPORTS)

KALA 1—6

Displacement, tons: 60
Dimensions, feet (metres): 88·6 × 26·2 × 6 *(27 × 8 × 1·8)*
Gun: 1—20 mm
Mines: 34
Main engines: 2 Valmet diesels; 360 bhp = 9 knots
Complement: 10

Completed between 20 June 1956 *(Kala 1)* and 4 Dec 1959 *(Kala 6)*. Can be used as transports, amphibious craft, minelayers or for shore support. Armament can be changed to suit role.

KALA 2   7/1974, Dittmair

5 "KAVE" CLASS (LCU TRANSPORTS)

KAVE 1—4 and 6

Displacement, tons: 27
Dimensions, feet (metres): 59 × 16·4 × 4·3 *(18 × 5 × 1·3)*
Gun: 1—20 mm
Main engines: 2 Valmet diesels; 360 hp = 9 knots
Complement: 3

Completed between 16 Nov 1956 *(Kave 1)* and 1960 *(Kave 6* on 19 Dec 1960). Built by Haminan Konepaja Oy *(Kave 1)* remainder by F. W. Hollming, Rauma. *Kave 5* lost in tow 15 Dec 1960.

KAVE 4   1961, Finnish Navy

3 "PUKKIO" CLASS (SUPPORT SHIPS)

PANSIO   **PORKKALA**   **PUKKIO**

Displacement, tons: 162 standard
Dimensions, feet (metres): 93·4 × 19·2 × 9·0 *(28·5 × 6·0 × 2·7)*
Guns: 1—40 mm; 1—20 mm
Mines: 20
Main engines: Diesels; 300 bhp = 9 knots

Built by Valmet, Turku. Delivered 25 May 1947, 1940 and 1939 respectively. Vessels of the tug type used as transports, minesweeping tenders, minelayers and patrol vessels.

3 "PIRTTISAARI" CLASS

PIRTTISAARI (ex-DR 7)   **PURHA** (ex-DR 10)   **PYHTÄÄ** (ex-DR 2)

Displacement, tons: 150
Dimensions, feet (metres): 69 × 20 × 8·5 *(21 × 6·1 × 2·6)*
Guns: 1—20 mm
Main engines: 1 diesel; 400 bhp = 8 knots
Complement: 10

Former US Army Tugs. Launched in 1943-44. General purpose vessels used as minesweepers, minelayers, patrol vessels, tenders, tugs or personnel transports. *Pyhtää* belongs to the Coast Artillery.

PIRTTISAARI   1970, Finnish Navy

PUTSAARI (CABLE SHIP)

Displacement, tons: 430
Dimensions, feet (metres): 149·2 × 29·2 × 7·5 *(45·5 × 8·9 × 2·3)*
Main engines: 1 Wärtsilä diesel; 450 bhp = 10 knots
Complement: 10

Built by Rauma Repola, Rauma. Ordered 11 Nov 1963. Launched in Dec 1965. Fitted with bow-thruster and active rudder, two 10 ton cable winches and accommodation for 20. Strengthened for ice operations.

TRANSPORT CRAFT

Class	Nos.	Tonnage	Speed	Commissioned
K	1-24	16	9	1957-66
Fabian Wrede	2	20	10	1915
Y	1-10	8	7	1960
L	1-7	1·5	11	1960-68
YM 1	1&2	0·7 (GRP)	7	1970-71
YM 4	4 & 5	2	7	1947
YM 22	22	2	11	—
YM 55	55, 60, 63	6·5	8	1942-57
H	1-6	34	10	1960

FRONTIER GUARD

Controlled by Ministry of the Interior.

1 LARGE PATROL CRAFT

Name	No.	Builders	Commissioned
VALPAS	—	Laivateollisuus, Turku	21 July 1971

Displacement, tons: 545
Dimensions, feet (metres): 159·1 × 27·9 × 12·5 *(48·5 × 8·5 × 3·8)*
Gun: 1—20 mm
Main engines: 1 Werkspoor diesel; 2 000 bhp = 15 knots
Complement: 22

An improvement on the *Silmä* design. Ordered 14 July 1969, launched 22 Dec 1970. First frontier guard ship with sonar. Ice strengthened.

Sonar: Hull mounted set.

VALPAS   1975, Finnish Navy

FINLAND 143

3 NEW CONSTRUCTION

Displacement, tons: 550 approx
Dimensions, feet (metres): 159·1 × 28 × 14 *(48·5 × 8·6 × 3·9)*
Main engines: 2 diesels; one shaft; 2 000 shp = 16 knots

First laid down 17 Dec 1976. Two to follow. Builders, Laivatollisuus.

1 LARGE PATROL CRAFT

Name	No.	Builders	Commissioned
SILMÄ	—	Laivateollisuus, Turku	19 Aug 1963

Displacement, tons: 530
Dimensions, feet (metres): 158·5 × 27·2 × 14·1 *(48·3 × 8·3 × 4·3)*
Gun: 1—20 mm
Main engines: 1 Werkspoor diesel; 1 800 hp = 15 knots
Complement: 22

Improved *Uisko* design. Ordered 21 Feb 1962, launched 25 Mar 1963.

SILMÄ 1975, Finnish Navy

1 LARGE PATROL CRAFT

Name	No.	Builders	Commissioned
UISKO	—	Valmet, Helsinki	1959

Displacement, tons: 370
Dimensions, feet (metres): 141 × 24 × 12·8 *(43 × 7·3 × 3·9)*
Gun: 1—20 mm
Main engines: 1 Werkspoor diesel; 1 800 hp = 15 knots
Complement: 21

Launched in 1958.

UISKO 1975, Finnish Navy

1 LARGE PATROL CRAFT

Name	No.	Builders	Commissioned
VIIMA	—	Laivatteollisuus, Turku	1964

Displacement, tons: 135
Dimensions, feet (metres): 118·1 × 21·7 × 7·5 *(36 × 6·6 × 2·3)*
Gun: 1—20 mm
Main engines: 3 Mercedes-Benz diesels; 4 050 bhp = 25 knots
Complement: 13

Launched 20 July 1964.

VIIMA 1974, Finnish Navy

1 LARGE PATROL CRAFT

Name	No.	Builders	Commissioned
TURSAS	—	Tensche, Belgium	1938

Displacement, tons: 380
Dimensions, feet (metres): 133·5 × 23·6 × 14·4 *(40·7 × 7·2 × 4·4)*
Gun: 1—20 mm
Main engines: 950 hp = 13 knots
Complement: 20

Was bought from Belgium in 1939 with her sister *Uisko* who was lost by enemy action in 1943.

1 TRAINING SHIP

Name	No.	Builders	Commissioned
OCKERO	—	Kone and Silta	1954

Displacement, tons: 55
Dimensions, feet (metres): 70·2 × 13·1 × 6·2 *(21·4 × 4 × 1·9)*
Main engines: Mercedes-Benz diesel; 445 hp = 10 knots

Former customs vessel now used for coastguard training.

1 SUPPLY SHIP

Name	No.	Builders	Commissioned
TURJA	—	Hietalahden, Helsinki	1928

Displacement, tons: 65
Dimensions, feet (metres): 74·1 × 14·8 × 8·2 *(22·6 × 4·5 × 2·5)*
Main engines: Mercedes-Benz diesel; 225 hp = 11 knots

Former coastal patrol ship at Petsamo 1929-45. Then a customs vessel. Converted as supply ship in 1973.

8 "TELKKA/KOSKELO" CLASS (COASTAL PATROL CRAFT)

KAAKKURI**   KOSKELO*   KUIKKA**   TAVI*
KIISLA*   KUOVI*   KURKI*   TELKKA

(*"Koskelo" class, **Unmodified craft)

Displacement, tons: 92 *(Telkka)*; 95 *(Koskelo)* full load
Dimensions, feet (metres): 95·1 × 16·4 × 4·9 *(29 × 5 × 1·5)*
Guns: 1—20 mm (see notes)
Main engines: 2 Mercedes-Benz (MTU) diesels; 2 shafts; 2 700 bhp = 23 knots (modified).
2 Mercedes-Benz diesels; 1 000 hp = 15 knots (unmodified)
Complement: 9 *(Telkka)*, 11 *(Koskelo)*

Built of steel and strengthened against ice. Between 1955 *(Koskelo)* and 1960 *(Tavi)*. Originally of much lower horsepower. *Telkka* modernised in 1970 and "Koskelo"s in 1972-74 by Laivatteollisuus. New internal arrangements, new decking and new engines increasing their speed by 8 knots. Can all mount a 40 mm on quarter-deck.

2 COASTAL PATROL CRAFT

Dimensions, feet (metres): 46·9 × 11·8 × 5·2 *(14·3 × 3·6 × 1·6)*
Main engines: 1 diesel; 1 shaft = 12 knots

Built by Hollming Oy, Rauma. Both completed Jan 1978. For patrol, towing and salvage.

COASTAL PATROL CRAFT

Class	Nos.	Tonnage	Speed	Commissioned
RV 1	1	10	9	1933
RV 4	4 & 5	12	9	1951
RV 6	6 & 7	15	9	1953
RV 8	8	10	10	1958
RV 9	9-17	12	10	1959-60
RV 10	18-28	18	10	1961-63
RV 30	30-36	19	10	1973-74
RV 41	41	17	10	1965
RV 97	97, 102-105, 108, 121, 144, 145, 160, 162	10	9	1934-49
NV 11	11-12	3	35	1966
NV 13	13-14	4	33	1969
NV 15	15-22	4	34	1972-74
NV 24	24	1·6	45	1960
NV 30	30-35	1·1	35	1974
NV 101	Hydrofoil 101	1·8	33	1972 from USSR
PV 1	1, 3, 4-7, 9	2	19	1957-59
PV 11	11-12	2 (GRP)	13	1959
PV 21	21-26	4 (GRP)	21	1963
PV 27	27-34	4	21	1965-66
PV 32	32	4	26	1965
PV 51	51	5	21	1966
KR 3 (ice-riders)	3-9	1	?	1972-74

FRANCE

Ministerial

Minister of Defence:
  M. Yvon Bourges

Headquarters Appointments

Conseil Supérieur de la Marine:
  Amiraux Lannuzel and Le Franc
  Vice-Amiraux d'Escadre, Banuls, Tardy
  Vice-Amiraux Wacrenier and Sabarvin

Senior Appointments

Préfet Maritime de la Première Région (PREMAR UN):
  Vice-Amiral Wacrenier
C in C Atlantic Theatre (CECLANT) and Préfet Maritime de la Deuxième Région (PREMAR DEUX):
  Vice-Amiral d'Escadre Coulondier
C in C Mediterranean Theatre (CECMED) and Préfet Maritime de la Troisième Région (PREMAR TROIS):
  Vice-Amiral d'Escadre Tardy
C in C French Naval Forces, Polynesia:
  Contre-Amiral de Castelbajac
C in C Atlantic Fleet:
  Vice-Amiral de Gaulle
C in C Mediterranean Fleet:
  Vice-Amiral de Bigault de Cazanove

Diplomatic Representation

Naval Attaché in Algiers:
  Capitaine de Vaisseau Le Bars
Naval Attaché in Bonn:
  Capitaine de Frégate Faivre
Naval Attaché in Brasilia:
  Capitaine de Corvette de Gentile Duquesne
Naval Attaché in the Hague:
  Capitaine de Vaisseau Fabre
Naval Attaché in Lisbon:
  Capitaine de Frégate Rambourg
Naval Attaché in London (& Defence Attaché):
  Contre-Amiral Frances Queyler
Naval Attaché in Madrid:
  Capitaine de Vaisseau d'Illices
Naval Attaché in Moscow:
  Capitaine de Vaisseau Large
Naval Attaché in Oslo:
  Capitaine de Vaisseau Bigot
Naval Attaché in Rome:
  Capitaine de Vaisseau de Seynes
Naval Attaché in Santiago:
  Capitaine de Frégate Tourrel
Naval Attaché in Tokyo:
  Capitaine de Vaisseau Lemaire
Naval Attaché in Washington:
  Contre-Amiral Chaline
Naval Attaché in Wellington:
  Capitaine de Frégate Bouver

Personnel

(a) 1971: 68 586 (4 732 officers, 63 854 ratings)
    1972: 68 308 (4 604 officers, 63 704 ratings)
    1973: 67 600 (4 400 officers, 63 200 ratings)
    1974: 67 700 (4 500 officers, 63 200 ratings)
    1975: 68 000 (4 550 officers, 63 450 ratings)
    1976: 68 315 (4 550 officers, 63 765 ratings)
    1977: 68 285 (including 17 438 national service)

(personnel to be increased by 5 000 under the 15-year re-equipment plan)

(b) National service 12 months

Bases

Cherbourg: Atlantic Fleet base. Prémar Un
Brest: Main Atlantic base. SSBN base. Prémar Deux
Lorient: Atlantic submarine base
Toulon: Main Mediterranean Fleet base. Prémar Trois

Fleet Dispositions

Mediterranean Fleet: *Colbert* (Flag), 2 aircraft carriers, 12 submarines, 6 destroyers, 7 frigates, 4 large patrol craft, 6 MCM vessels, 3 survey ships, 4 support ships.
Atlantic Fleet: 11 destroyers, 4 frigates, 4 SSBNs, 6 submarines, 1 tanker.
Indian Ocean: *La Charente* (Flag), 1 destroyer, 4 frigates, 5 patrol craft, 3 support ships.
West Indies: 2 ships.
Training Squadron: *Jeanne d'Arc, Forbin.*

Mercantile Marine

Lloyd's Register of Shipping:
  1 327 vessels of 11 613 859 tons gross

Strength of the Fleet

Type	Active (Reserve)	Building or (Projected)
Attack Carriers (Medium)	2	—
Helicopter VSTOL Carrier (Nuclear)	—	(1)
Cruisers	2	—
Destroyers	22	1 (1)
Frigates	24 (3)	7
Submarines (Strat Missile)	4	1 (1)
	1 (Diesel powered)	
Submarines (Fleet)	—	1 (4)
Submarines (Patrol)	23	—
Fast Attack Craft (Missile)	5	— (6)
Large Patrol Craft	24	—
Coastal Patrol Craft	6	—
LPD	2	—
LST	7	—
LCT	13	—
LCM	36	—
Minesweepers (Ocean)	6	—
Minesweepers (Coastal)	22	—
Minehunters	12	1 (14)
Surveying Ships	5	—
Coastal Survey Ships	3	—
Inshore Survey Craft	1	—
Tankers (UR)	4	1 (1)
Tankers (Support)	5	—
Maintenance Ships	2	—
Depot Ships	5	—
Repair Ships (ex-LCT)	2	—
Trials Ships	9	—
Boom Defence Vessels	14	—
Torpedo Recovery Vessels	3	—
Victualling Stores Ship	1	—
Stores Ship	1	—
Supply Tenders	4	—
Small Transports	13	2
Tenders	17	—
Tugs	88	10
Training Ships	8	—

Naval Air Stations

St. Raphael, Lann Bihoue, Nimes Garon, Lanveox Poulmic, Dax, Aspretto, Landvisiau, Hyères, St. Mandrier.

Shipyards (Naval)

Cherbourg: Submarines and Fast Attack Craft
Brest: Major warships and refitting
Lorient: Destroyers, frigates and avisos

Submarine Service

Known as Force Océanique Stratégique (FOST) with HQ at Houilles near Paris. SSBN *(SNLE)* force based at Ile Longue Brest with a training base at Roche-Douvres and VLFW/T station at Rosay. Patrol submarines are based at Lorient and Toulon. Plans for nuclear fleet submarines are included in the 15 year plan, with the first being laid down in 1976.

15-Year Re-equipment Plan

Note: All submarines laid down after 1976 are nuclear-powered.

This programme ("Plan Bleu") was approved by l'Assemblé on 29 Feb 1972 and provided for the following fleet by 1985 and reduced to figures in brackets in 1977:

  2 Aircraft Carriers }
  2 Helicopter Carriers } (total 3)
  30 Frigates or Corvettes
  35 Avisos (27 Avisos)
  6 SSBN
  20 Patrol Submarines (or Fleet) (12 Fleet submarines)
  30 Fast Attack Craft
  36 MHC and MSC
  5 Replenishment Tankers
    Logistic Support and Maintenance Ships
    (total of 85 000 tons)
  2 Assault Ships
    Landing Ships and Craft
    Transports
  50 LRMP aircraft
    Carrier borne aircraft
    Helicopters

1971-75 New Construction Plan

Financial problems have necessitated the addition of an extra year to this plan. Financial allowance made for construction of ships listed below although this Plan and the 1977-81 Plan combined will not achieve the Plan Bleu strength.

  1 Helicopter Carrier (PH 75) (postponed to next Plan)
  3 Guided Missile Destroyers ("Corvettes") "C 70" Type
  3 Guided Missile Destroyers ("Corvettes") "C 67" Type
  14 Escorts (officially rated as *Avisos*) "A 69" Type (one delayed)
  3 Nuclear Powered Ballistic Missile Submarines (one delayed)
  4 Patrol Submarines
  4 Patrol Boats (for overseas service)
  1 Fleet Support & Repair Ship (major conversion)
  1 Fleet Replenishment Ship (one added—total two)
  2 Medium Landing Ships (Transports)
  1 Fleet Submarine added
  1 Minehunter added

1977-81 New Construction Plan

This plan allows for:
  1 Nuclear-propelled carrier (PA 75) (to be laid down 1981)
  3 "C 70" ASM destroyers ("Georges Leygues" class)
  3 "C 70" AA destroyers ("Georges Leygues" class) (at end of period)
  4 SSN Fleet submarines (3 sisters to SNA 72 and 1 advanced type)
  1 SSBN (*L'Inflexible*) postponed until 1982
  12 Minehunters (in collaboration with Belgium and Netherlands) (for total of 13—2 more to follow later)
  6 Large Patrol Vessels (250-350 tons)
  1 Fleet Replenishment ship added

DELETIONS

Helicopter Carrier
1974 *Arromanches*

Cruiser
1973 *De Grasse*

Destroyers
1974 *Chevalier Paul, Cassard*
1976 *La Bourdonnais*
1977 *Jaureguiberry*

Frigates
1974 *Le Bordelais, Le Corse* (Type E 50)
1975 *Le Brestois* (Type E 50)
1977 *Le Lorrain, Le Bourguignon, Le Champenois, Le Breton* (Type E 50)

Light Forces
1974 M 691, VC 2, VC 10, P 9785, P 9786
1975 *Le Fougueux, L'Opiniatre* and *L'Agile* ("Le Fougueux" class)
1977 *L'Intrepide, L'Étourdi, L'Effronté, Le Frondeur, L'Alerte, L'Attentif, L'Enjoué, Le Hardi* ("Le Fougueux" class)

Minewarfare Forces
1974 *Begonia,* and *Glaieul* deleted; *Aries* ("Sirius" class) (To Morocco)
1975 *Bellatrix, Dénébola, Pégase* ("Sirius" class) deleted; *Jacinthe, Liseron* and *Magnolia* ("Adjutant" class) as diving base ships.
1976 *Bleuér* and *Chrysanthéme* ("Adjutant" class)
1977 *Algol, Cassiopée* ("Sirius" class); *Giroflée* ("Adjutant" class)

Amphibious Forces
1974 LCT 9099 deleted; LCT 9095 to Senegal
1976 LCT 9061 to Comoro Is.

Survey Ships
1973 *La Coquille*
1975 *La Découverte* (for use as target)
1976 *Alidade*

BDV
1972 *Tarantule*
1974 *Scorpion, Locuste, Persistante*
1976 *Araignée*
1977 *Libellule, Luciole*

Service Forces
1972 *Lac Chambon, Lac Tchad* (small Tankers)
1973 *Médoc* (Supply Ship)
1974 *Oasis* (Water Carrier)
1975 *Maurienne* (Fleet Support Ship)
    L 9082 and 9083 (Repair Ships)
    Trébéron (ex-German Transport)
    Cataracte (Water Carrier)
1976 *La Seine*

Trials Ship
1975 *Arago*

Miscellaneous
1974 M691 (ex-*SC 525*), FNRS 3
1975 *Belier, Pachyderme, Infatigable, Peuplier* (Tugs)
1975 *Belouga* (Tender)
1977 *Commandant Robert Giraud* (mooring vessel); *Bambou, Canari, Délange, Fontaine, Forméne, Giens, Grive, Hanneton, Haut Barr, Hirondelle, Jonque, Tupa, Moule, Murène, Ondeé, Oursin, Rascasse, Rossignol, Marronier* (Tugs)

Transport
1976 *Falleron* (Jan)

PENNANT LIST

Aircraft and Helicopter Carriers

R	97	Jeanne d'Arc
R	98	Clemenceau
R	99	Foch

Cruiser

C	611	Colbert

Destroyers

D	602	Suffren
D	603	Duquesne
D	609	Aconit
D	610	Tourville
D	611	Duguay-Trouin
D	612	De Grasse
D	622	Kersaint
D	624	Bouvet
D	625	Dupetit Thouars
D	627	Maillé Brézé
D	628	Vauquelin
D	629	D'Estrées
D	630	Du Chayla
D	631	Casablanca
D	632	Guépratte
D	633	Duperré
D	635	Forbin
D	636	Tartu
D	638	La Galissonnière
D	640	Georges Leygues
D	641	Dupleix
D	642	Montcalm
D	643	Jean de Vienne

Submarines

S	610	Le Foudroyant
S	611	Le Redoutable
S	612	Le Terrible
S	613	L'Indomptable
S	614	Le Tonnant
S	616	SNA 72
S	620	Agosta
S	621	Bévéziers
S	622	La Praya
S	623	Ouessant
S	631	Narval
S	632	Marsouin
S	633	Dauphin
S	634	Requin
S	635	Aréthuse
S	636	Argonaute
S	637	Espadon
S	638	Morse
S	639	Amazone
S	640	Ariane
S	641	Daphné
S	642	Diane
S	643	Doris
S	645	Flore
S	646	Galatée
S	648	Junon
S	649	Venus
S	650	Psyche
S	651	Sirène
S	655	Gymnote

Frigates and Corvettes

F	725	Victor Schoelcher
F	726	Commandant Bory
F	727	Amiral Charner
F	728	Doudart de Lagrée
F	729	Balny
F	733	Commandant Rivière
F	740	Commandant Bourdais
F	748	Protet
F	749	Enseigne de Vaisseau Henry
F	763	Le Boulonnais
F	765	Le Normand
F	766	Le Picard
F	767	Le Gascon
F	771	Le Savoyard
F	773	Le Basque
F	774	L'Agenais
F	775	Le Béarnais
F	776	L'Alsacien
F	777	Le Provençal
F	778	Le Vendéen
F	781	D'Estienne d'Orves
F	782	Amyot d'Inville
F	783	Drogou
F	784	Detroyat
F	785	Jean Moulin
F	786	Quartier Maitre Anquetil
F	787	Commandant de Pimodan
F	788	Seconde Maitre Le Bihan
F	789	Lieutenant de Vaisseau le Henaff
F	790	Lieutenant de Vaisseau Lavallée
F	791	Commandant l'Herminier
F	792	Premier Maitre l'Her
F	793	Commandant Blaison
F	794	Enseigne de Vaisseau Jacoubet

Minewarfare Forces

M	609	Narvik
M	610	Ouistreham
M	612	Alençon
M	613	Berneval
M	615	Cantho
M	616	Dompaire
M	617	Garigliano
M	618	Mytho
M	619	Vinh-long
M	620	Berlaimont
M	622	Autun
M	623	Baccarat
M	624	Colmar
M	632	Pervenche
M	633	Pivoine
M	635	Réséda
M	638	Acacia
M	639	Acanthe
M	640	Marjolaine
M	668	Azalée
M	671	Camélia
M	674	Cyclamen
M	675	Eglantine
M	679	Glycine
M	681	Laurier
M	682	Lilas
M	684	Lobelia
M	687	Mimosa
M	688	Muguet
M	703	Antares
M	707	Véga
M	712	Cybele
M	713	Calliope
M	714	Clio
M	715	Circe
M	716	Ceres
M	737	Capricorne
M	741	Eridan
M	743	Sagittaire
M	747	Bételgeuse
M	749	Phénix
M	755	Capella
M	756	Céphée
M	757	Verseau
M	765	Mercure

Light Forces

P	635	L'Ardent
P	640	Le Fringant
P	644	L'Adroit
P	650	Arcturus
P	651	La Malouine
P	652	La Lorientaise
P	653	La Dunkerquoise
P	654	La Bayonnaise
P	655	La Dieppoise
P	656	Altair
P	657	La Paimpolaise
P	658	Croix du Sud
P	659	Canopus
P	660	Etoile Polaire
P	661	Jasmin
P	662	Petunia
P	670	Trident
P	671	Glaive
P	672	Epée
P	673	Pertuisane
P	703	Antares
P	707	Vega
P	730	La Combattante
P	741	Eridan
P	743	Sagittaire
P	759	Lyre
P	770	PB
P	771	PB
P	772	PB
P	774	PB
P	784	Geranium
P	787	Jonquille
P	789	Paquerette

Amphibious Forces

L	9003	Argens
L	9004	Bidassoa
L	9007	Trieux
L	9008	Dives
L	9009	Blavet
L	9021	Ouragan
L	9022	Orage
L	9030	Champlain
L	9031	Francis Garnier
L	9070	LCT
L	9071	LCT
L	9072	LCT
L	9073	LCT
L	9074	LCT

Amphibious Forces

L	9081	Workshop
L	9082	LCT
L	9083	LCT
L	9084	Workshop
L	9091	LCT
L	9092	LCT
L	9093	LCT
L	9094	LCT
L	9096	LCT

(CTM LCMs 1-16)

Auxiliaries Survey and Support Ships

A	603	Henry Poincaré
A	607	Meuse
A	608	Moselle
A	610	Ile d'Oléron
A	615	Loire
A	617	Garonne
A	618	Rance
A	619	Aber Wrach
A	620	Jules Verne
A	621	Rhin
A	622	Rhône
A	625	Papenoo
A	626	La Charente
A	627	La Seine
A	628	La Saône
A	629	La Durance
A	630	Lac Tonlé Sap
A	632	Punaruu
A	638	Sahel
A	640	Origny
A	643	Aunis
A	644	Berry
A	646	Triton
A	648	Archimède
A	649	L'Etoile
A	650	La Belle Poule
A	652	Mutin
A	653	La Grande Hermine
A	660	Hippopotame
A	664	Malabar
A	665	Goliath
A	666	Eléphant
A	667	Hercules
A	668	Rhinocéros
A	669	Tenace
A	671	Le Fort
A	672	Utile
A	673	Lutteur
A	674	Centaure
A	675	Isère
A	683	Octant
A	684	Coolie
A	685	Robuste
A	686	Actif
A	687	Laborieux
A	688	Valeureux
A	692	Travailleur
A	694	Efficace
A	695	Acharne
A	698	Petrel
A	699	Pelican
A	701	Ajonc
A	702	Girelle
A	706	Courageux
A	710	Myosotis
A	711	Gardénia
A	714	Tourmaline
A	716	Oiseau des Iles
A	722	Poseidon
A	723	Liseron
A	731	Tianée
A	733	Saintonge
A	735	Hibiscus
A	736	Dahlia
A	737	Tulipe
A	738	Capucine
A	739	Oeillet
A	740	Hortensia
A	741	Armoise
A	742	Violette
A	756	Espérance
A	757	D'Entrecasteaux
A	758	La Recherche
A	759	Gustave Zedé
A	760	Cigale
A	761	Criquet
A	762	Fourmi
A	763	Grillon
A	764	Scarabée
A	766	Estafette
A	767	Chamois
A	768	Elan
A	770	Magnolia
A	772	Engageante
A	773	Vigilante
A	774	Chevreuil
A	775	Gazelle
A	780	L'Astrolabe
A	781	Boussole
A	789	Archéonaute
A	794	Corail

Auxiliaries

Y	601	Acajou
Y	602	Aigrette
Y	604	Ariel
Y	607	Balsa
Y	611	Bengali
Y	612	Bouleau
Y	613	Faune
Y	617	Mouette
Y	618	Cascade
Y	620	Chataigner
Y	621	Mésange
Y	623	Charme
Y	624	Chêne
Y	628	Colibri
Y	629	Cormier
Y	630	Bonite
Y	631	Courlis
Y	632	Cygne
Y	634	Rouget
Y	635	Equeurdibille
Y	636	Martinet
Y	637	Fauvette
Y	644	Fréne
Y	645	Gave
Y	646	Geyser
Y	648	Goeland
Y	653	Heron
Y	654	Hêtre
Y	655	Hévéat
Y	661	Korrigan
Y	662	Dryade
Y	663	Latanier
Y	664	Lutin
Y	666	Manguier
Y	668	Méléze
Y	669	Merisier
Y	670	Merle
Y	671	Morgane
Y	673	Moineau
Y	675	Martin Pecheur
Y	682	Okoume
Y	684	Oued
Y	686	Palétuvier
Y	687	Passereau
Y	688	Peuplier
Y	689	Pin
Y	690	Pingouin
Y	691	Pinson
Y	694	Pivert
Y	695	Platane
Y	696	Alphée
Y	699	Poulpé
Y	704	Sycomore
Y	706	Chimère
Y	708	Saule
Y	710	Sylphe
Y	711	Farfadet
Y	717	Ebene
Y	718	Erable
Y	719	Olivier
Y	720	Santal
Y	721	Alouette
Y	722	Vauneau
Y	723	Engoulevent
Y	724	Surcelle
Y	725	Marabout
Y	726	Toucan
Y	727	Macreuse
Y	728	Grand Duc
Y	729	Eider
Y	730	Ara
Y	735	Merlin
Y	736	Mélusine
Y	739	Noyer
Y	740	Papayer
Y	741	Elfe
Y	743	Palangrin
Y	745	Aiguière
Y	746	Embrun
Y	747	Loriot
Y	748	Gelinotte
Y	749	La Prudente
Y	750	La Persévérante
Y	751	La Fidèle
Y	760	PB

146 FRANCE

NAVAL AIR ARM
Note: Crusaders and Etendards to be replaced in 1978 by Super Etendards

NAVAL AIR ARM

Squadron Number	Base	Aircraft	Task
Embarked Squadrons			
4F	Lann Bihoue	BR1050 "Alize"	Patrol & A/S
6F	Nimes Garons	BR1050 "Alize"	Patrol & A/S
11F	Landivisiau	ETD IV M	Fighter Bomber
12F	Landivisiau	F8E "Crusader"	Interceptors
14F	Landivisiau	F8E "Crusader"	Interceptors
16F	Landivisiau	ETD IV P	Reconnaissance
17F	Hyeres	ETD IV M	Fighter Bomber
31F	St. Mandrier	HSS 1	A/S
32F	Lanveoc Poulmic	Super-Frelon	A/S
33F	St. Mandrier	HSS 1	Assault
J. d'Arc	J. d'Arc or St. Mandrier	HSS 1	Training
SRL	Landivisiau	MS 760 "Paris"	Support

Squadron Number	Base	Aircraft	Task
Support Squadrons			
2S	Lann Bihoue	Navajo, Nord 262	Support 1st & 2nd Region
3S	Hyeres	Navajo, Nord 262	Support 3rd Region
10S	St. Raphael	Nord 2504, BR1050 Navajo, MS 733	Trials CEPA
20S	St. Raphael	AL 11, AL 111 AL 111 ASM HSS 1, Super Frelon	Trials CEPA
22S	Lanveoc Poulmic	AL 11, AL 111 AL 111 VSV	Support 2nd Region, SAR
23S	St. Mandrier	AL 11, AL 111	Support 3rd Region, SAR
SSD	Dugny	C 54, Nord 262 Navajo	Support

Squadron Number	Base	Aircraft	Task
Maritime Patrol Squadrons			
21F	Nimes Garons	BR 1150 "Atlantic"	MP
22F	Nimes Garons	BR 1150 "Atlantic"	MP
23F	Lann Bihoue	BR 1150 "Atlantic"	MP
24F	Lann Bihoue	BR 1150 "Atlantic"	MP
25F	Lann Bihoue	Neptune P2H	MP
Training Squadrons			
55S	Aspretto	Nord 262, SNB 5	Twin-engine conversion
56S	Nimes Garons	C 47	Flying School
59S	Hyeres	ET IV, BR 1050 CM 175 "Zephyr"	Fighter School
SVS	Lanveoc Poulmic	MS 733	Naval School Recreational
Esalat Dax	Dax	AL 11	Helicopter School
Overseas Detachments			
New Caledonia	Tontouta	C 54, C 47	Support and Liaison
Malagasy	Diego Suarez	C 47	Support and Liaison
CEP Formations			
Sectal Pac.	Hao	AL 111	Support
27S	Hao	Super-Frelon	Support
12S	Papeete	Neptune P2H	MP

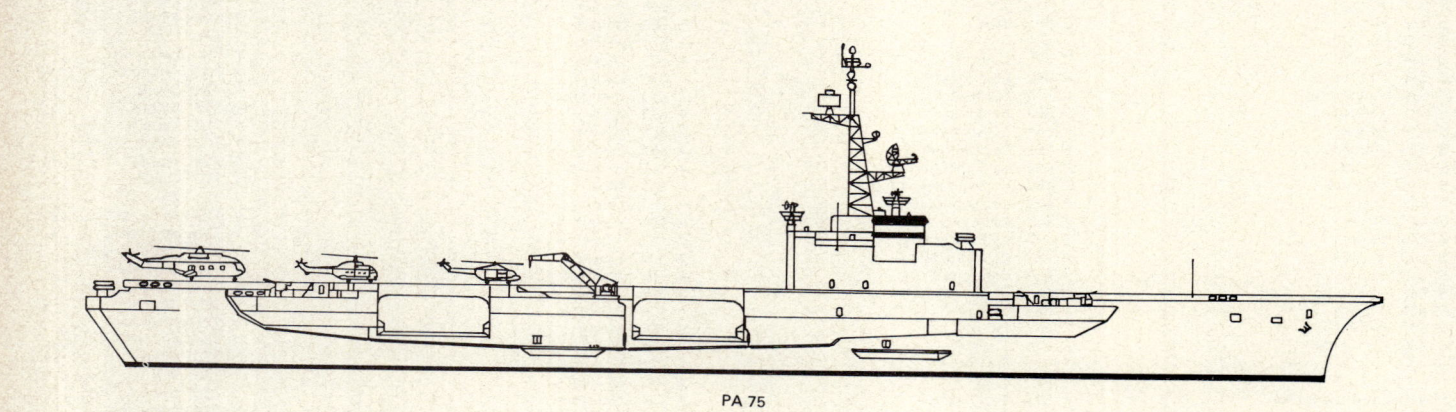

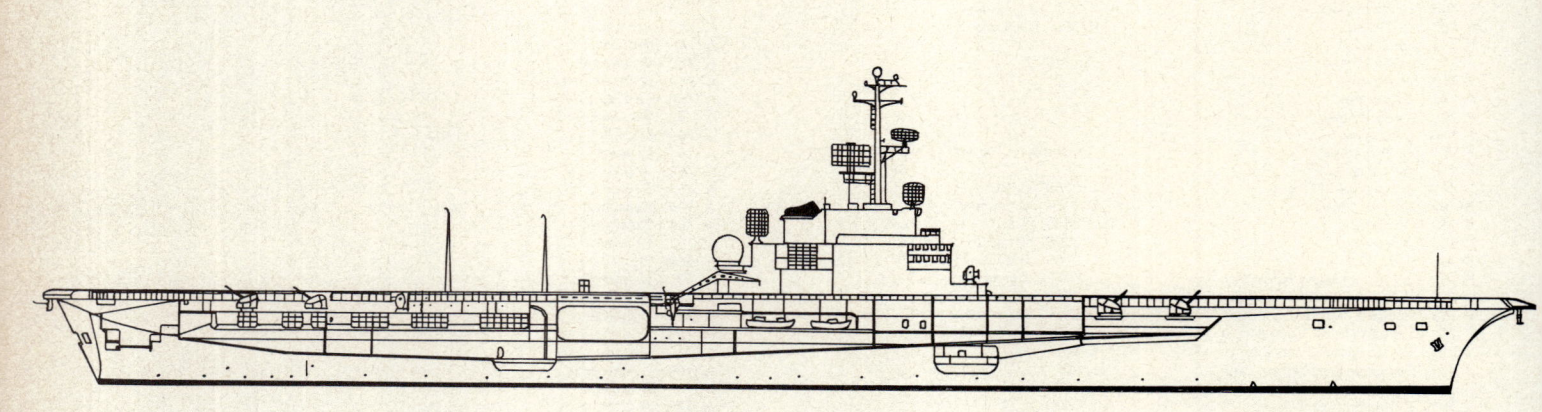

PA 75

"CLEMENCEAU" Class

FRANCE 147

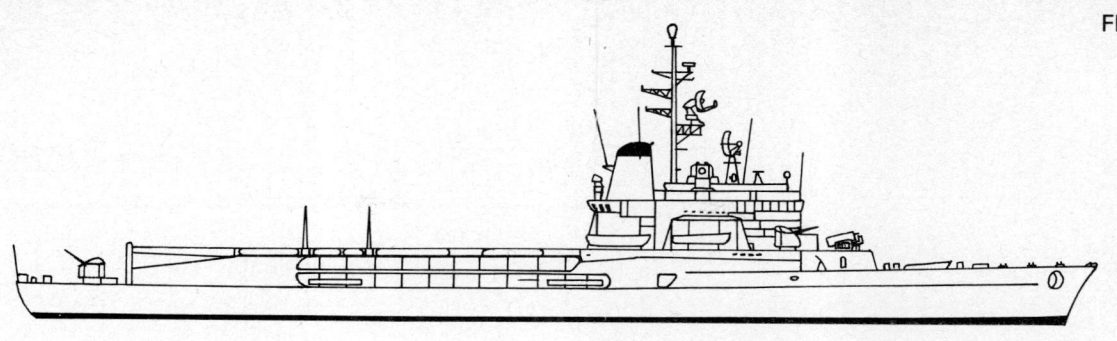

JEANNE D'ARC

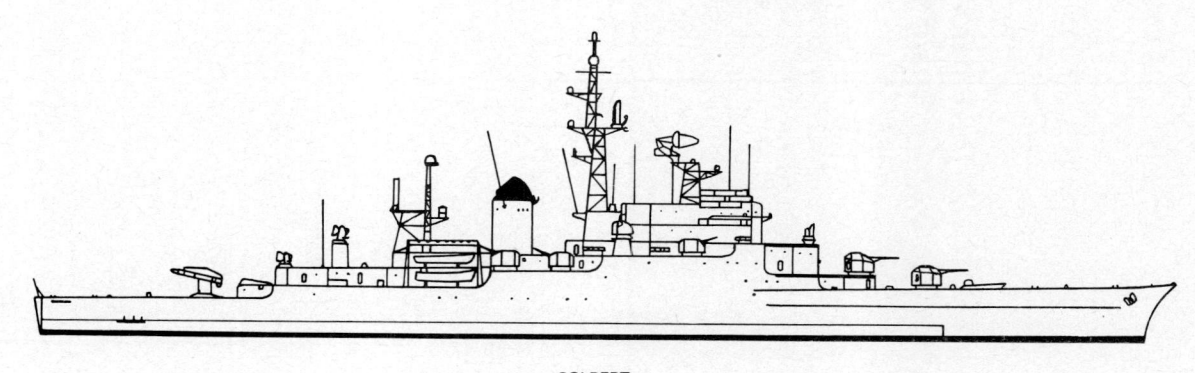

COLBERT

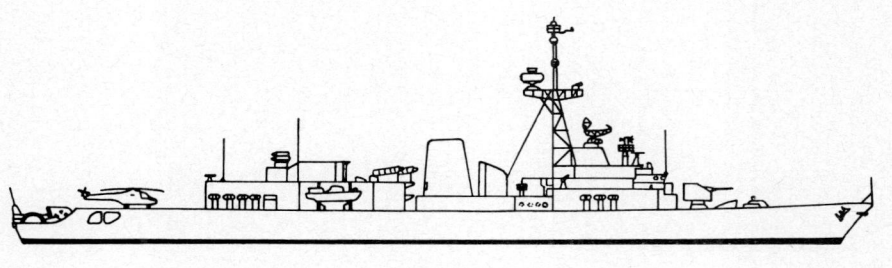

TYPE C70

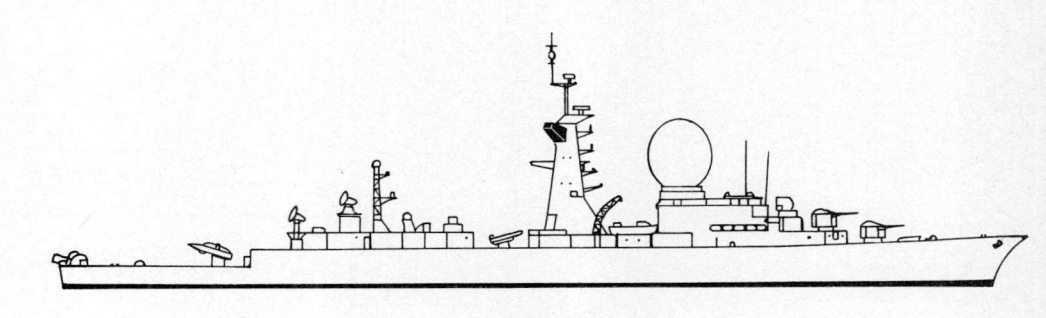

"SUFFREN" Class

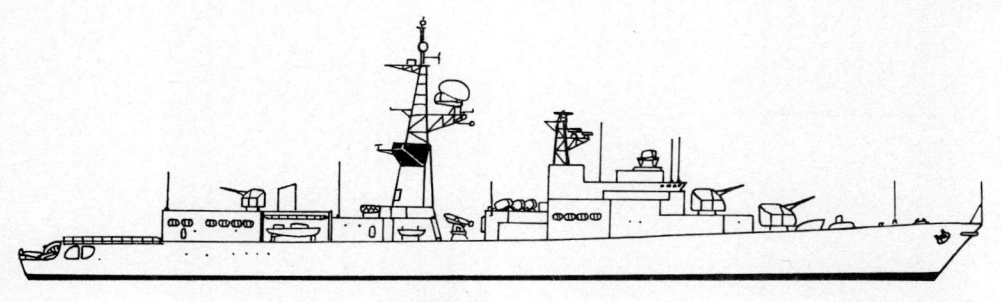

TYPE F67

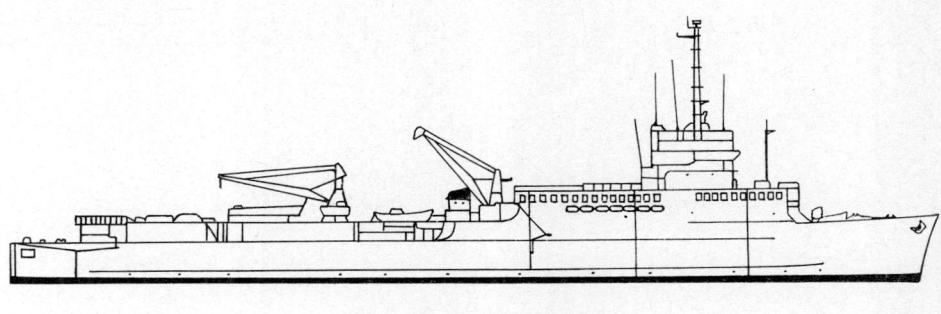

OURAGAN and ORAGE

148 FRANCE

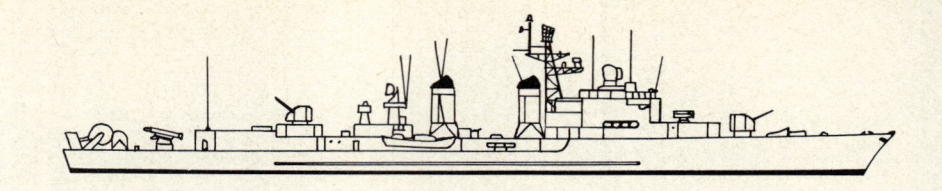

TYPE 47 (DDG)

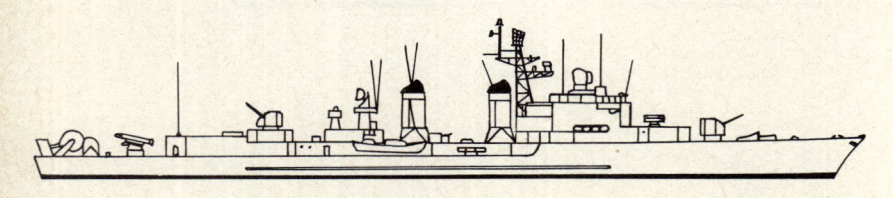

TYPE 47 (ASW)

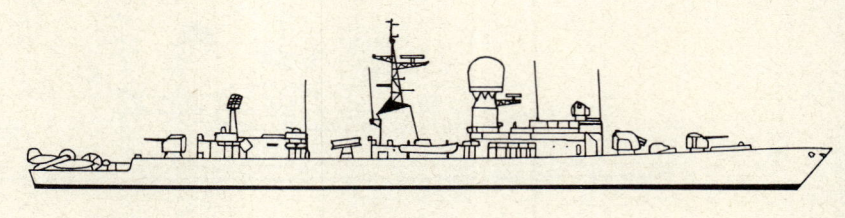

ACONIT

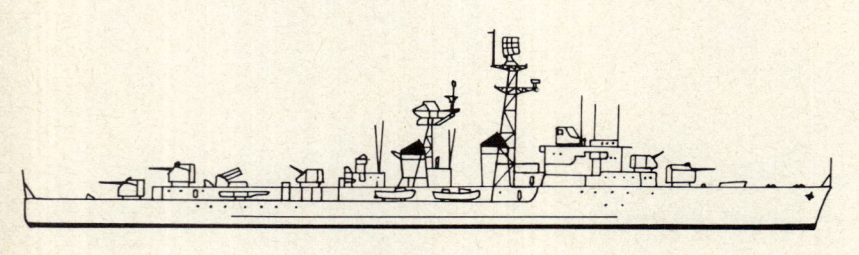

TYPE 53

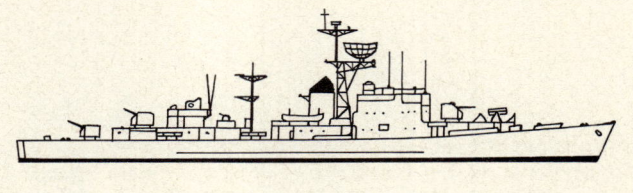

E52 TYPE

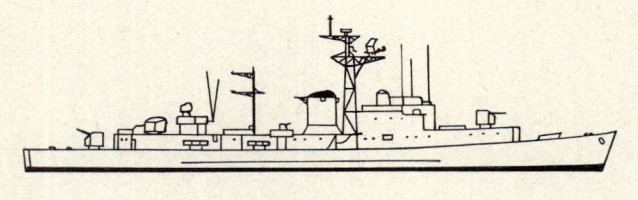

E52B TYPE

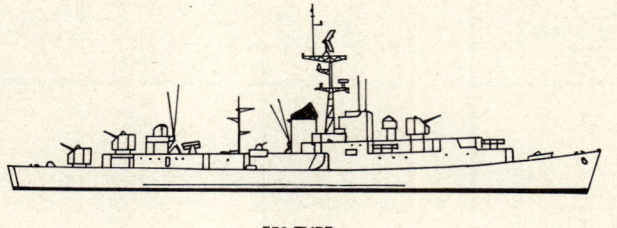

E50 TYPE

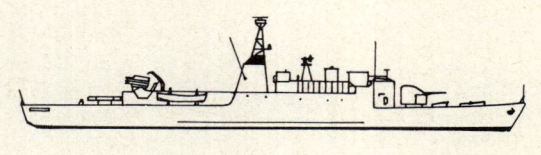

A69 TYPE

SUBMARINES

5 + 1 NUCLEAR POWERED BALLISTIC MISSILE TYPE (SNLE)

Name	No.	Builders	Laid down	Launched	Trials	Operational
LE FOUDROYANT	S 610	Cherbourg Naval Dockyard	12 Dec 1969	4 Dec 1971	May 1973	6 July 1974
LE REDOUTABLE	S 611	Cherbourg Naval Dockyard	30 Mar 1964	29 Mar 1967	July 1969	1 Dec 1971
LE TERRIBLE	S 612	Cherbourg Naval Dockyard	24 June 1967	12 Dec 1969	1971	1 Jan 1973
L'INDOMPTABLE	S 613	Cherbourg Naval Dockyard	4 Dec 1971	17 Aug 1974	Dec 1975	23 Dec 1976
LE TONNANT	S 614	Cherbourg Naval Dockyard	Oct 1974	17 Sep 1977	May 1979	May 1980
L'INFLEXIBLE (see note)	— (Q 260)	Cherbourg Naval Dockyard	—	—	—	—

Displacement, tons: 7 500 surfaced; 9 000 dived
Length, feet (metres): 420 *(128.0)*
Beam, feet (metres): 34.8 *(10.6)*
Draught, feet (metres): 32.8 *(10.0)*
Missile launchers: 16 tubes amidships for MSBS M-2 (M-20 in *L'Indomptable*)
Torpedo tubes: 4—21.7 in (18 torpedoes)
Nuclear reactor: 1 pressurised water-cooled
Main machinery: 2 turbo-alternators; 1 electric motor; 15 000 hp; 1 shaft
Auxiliary propulsion: 1 diesel; 2 670 hp; fuel for 5 000 miles
Speed, knots: 20 surfaced; 25 dived
Complement: Two alternating crews each of 135 (15 officers, 120 men)
Diving depth: Over 700 ft *(213.36 m)*

Le Redoutable was the first French nuclear-powered, ballistic missile armed submarine and the prototype of the *"Force de dissuasion"* of five such vessels. The decision to build a fourth unit of this class was announced on 7 Dec 1967, the fifth in Feb 1972 and the sixth on 30 April 1974. The construction of *L'Inflexible*, the sixth boat, delayed by 4th 5 Year Plan until 1982. She will then be lead-ship of an improved class, with an improved reactor, better navigation systems, a deeper diving depth and up-dated armament.

Missiles: Originally armed with MSBS M-1 of 18 tons launch weight. Now carry MSBS M-2 of 19.9 tons with a 1 300 n. mile range carrying a 500 KT head. *Le Redoutable* was fitted with M-2 at her first refit (started early 1976). *L'Indomptable* has the M-20 system with 1 500 n. mile range missiles carrying a megaton reinforced head. All of this class will later receive the M-4 system with a range reportedly in the 3 000 mile bracket and carrying MIRV warheads, *Le Terrible* being the first during her refit which started in 1977, *Le Tonnant* will receive M-20 system.

Radar: *Le Redoutable* is equipped with Calypso I Band radar for navigation and attack. Has passive ECM and DF systems.

Reactor: The reactor is a natural-water-cooled type running on enriched uranium, feeding twin turbines and two turbo-alternators.

Subroc: Possibility of acquisition being investigated.

LE REDOUTABLE   1975, French Navy

LE REDOUTABLE, LE TERRIBLE, LE FOUDROYANT   1973, French Navy

150 FRANCE

1 EXPERIMENTAL MISSILE TYPE

Name	No.	Builders	Laid down	Launched	Commissioned
GYMNOTE	S 655	Cherbourg Naval Dockyard	17 Mar 1963 (see **Hull** Note)	17 Mar 1964	17 Oct 1966

Displacement, tons: 3 000 surfaced; 3 250 dived
Length, feet (metres): 275·6 *(84·0)*
Beam, feet (metres): 34·7 *(10·6)*
Draught, feet (metres): 25 *(7·6)*
Missile launchers: 2 tubes for MSBS
Main machinery: 4 sets 620 kW diesel-electric; 2 electric motors; 2 shafts; 2 600 hp
Speed, knots: 11 surfaced; 10 dived
Complement: 78 (8 officers, 70 men)

An experimental submarine for testing ballistic missiles for the French nuclear-powered SSBNs, and for use as an underwater laboratory to prove equipment and arms for nuclear-powered submarines.
Started conversion in early 1977 (completion early 1978) for trial firings of M-4 Missiles. These will require tubes of greater diameter.

Hull: *Gymnote* was the hull laid down in 1958 as the nuclear-powered submarine Q 244 which was cancelled in 1959. The hull was still available when a trials vessel for the French MSBS type missiles was required and was completed as *Gymnote*. Has fixed bow-planes.

GYMNOTE *1970, French Navy*

FLEET SUBMARINES

1 + 4 TYPE SNA 72

Name	No.	Builders	Laid down	Launched	Commissioned
—	S 616	Cherbourg Naval Dockyard	10 Dec 1976	—	1981

Displacement, tons: 2 385 surfaced; 2 670 dived
Dimensions, feet (metres): 236·5 × 24·9 × 21 *(72·1 × 7·6 × 6·4)*
Torpedo tubes: 4—21 in *(533 mm)*·(14 torpedoes or mines)
Main machinery: 1 nuclear reactor; 48 MW; 2 turbo alternators; 1 main motor; 1 shaft; 6 400 hp (?)
Auxiliary machinery: 1 set diesel-electric
Speed, knots: 25
Complement: 66 (9 officers, 35 petty officers, 22 junior ratings)

A prototype for a new class of fleet-submarines included in the 1974 programme. The armament, sonar and fire control equipment will be similar to the "Agosta" class. Four more of this class are included in the 1977-82 building programme. Second boat ordered 1977.

Future: Two squadrons of these submarines are forecast, one to be stationed at Brest and the other at Toulon.

Machinery: Studies of the machinery are continuing at Cadarache. As this is the smallest class of SSNs ever designed except for the 400 ton NR-1 of the USN there has clearly been a great reduction in the size of the reactor compared with that of the "Le Redoutable" class.

Name: The well-known name "Rubis" has been mentioned as a possible choice.

PATROL SUBMARINES

4 "AGOSTA" CLASS

Name	No.	Builders	Laid down (see note)	Launched	Commissioned
AGOSTA	S 620	Cherbourg Naval Dockyard	1 Nov 1972	19 Oct 1974	Mar 1977
BÈVÈZIERS	S 621	Cherbourg Naval Dockyard	17 May 1973	14 June 1975	Oct 1977
LA PRAYA	S 622	Cherbourg Naval Dockyard	1974	15 May 1976	1978
OUESSANT	S 623	Cherbourg Naval Dockyard	1974	23 Oct 1976	1978

Displacement, tons: 1 200 standard; 1 450 surfaced; 1 725 dived
Length, feet (metres): 221·7 *(67·6)*
Beam, feet (metres): 22·3 *(6·8)*
Draught, feet (metres): 17·7 *(5·4)*
Torpedo tubes: 4—21·7 in *(550 mm)* (20 reload torpedoes)
Main machinery: Diesel-electric; 2 SEMT Pielstick 16 PA4 diesels 3 600 hp; 1 main motor (3 500 kW) 4 600 hp; 1 cruising motor (23 kW); 1 shaft
Speed, knots: 12 surfaced; 20 dived
Range, miles: 8 500 at 9 knots (snorting); 350 at 3·5 knots (dived)
Endurance: 45 days
Complement: 54 (7 officers, 47 men)

Building of this class was announced in 1970 under the third five-year new construction plan 1971-75. Considerable efforts have been made to improve the silencing of this class, including a clean casing and the damping of internal noise.

Laid down dates: Those given are for the placing of the first prefabricated section in the building dock. Prefabrication of *Agosta* started 7 Feb 1972 and of *Bevéziers* Dec 1972.

Radar: Possibly I Band Calypso Th D 1030 or 1031 for search/navigation.

Sonar: DUUA 2 active sonar with transducers forward and aft; DSUV passive sonar with 36 hydrophones; passive ranging; intercept set.

Trials: *Bèvèziers* Oct 1976, *La Praya* April 1977, *Ouessant* Oct 1977.

Torpedo tubes: A new design allowing for torpedo discharge at all speeds and down to full diving depth. Rapid reloading fitted.

Foreign orders: Four to be built at Cartagena for Spanish Navy and two for South Africa by Dubigeon.

AGOSTA *1977, French Navy*

FRANCE 151

9 "DAPHNÉ" CLASS

Name	No.	Builders	Laid down	Launched	Commissioned
DAPHNÉ	S 641	Dubigeon	Mar 1958	20 June1959	1 June 1964
DIANE	S 642	Dubigeon	July 1958	4 Oct 1960	20 June 1964
DORIS	S 643	Cherbourg Naval Dockyard	Sep 1958	14 May 1960	26 Aug 1964
FLORE	S 645	Cherbourg Naval Dockyard	Sep 1958	21 Dec 1960	21 May 1964
GALATÉE	S 646	Cherbourg Naval Dockyard	Sep 1958	22 Sep 1961	25 July 1964
JUNON	S 648	Cherbourg Naval Dockyard	July 1961	11 May 1964	25 Feb 1966
VENUS	S 649	Cherbourg Naval Dockyard	Aug 1961	24 Sep 1964	1 Jan 1966
PSYCHÉ	S 650	Brest Naval Dockyard	May 1965	28 June1967	1 July 1969
SIRÈNE	S 651	Brest Naval Dockyard	May 1965	28 June1967	1 Mar 1970

Displacement, tons: 869 surfaced; 1 043 dived
Length, feet (metres): 189·6 *(57·8)*
Beam, feet (metres): 22·3 *(6·8)*
Draught, feet (metres): 15·1 *(4·6)*
Torpedo tubes: 12—21·7 in *(550 mm)* 8 bow 4 stern
Main machinery: SEMT-Pielstick diesel-electric;
    1 300 bhp surfaced; 1 600 bhp motors dived; 2 shafts
Range, miles: 2 700 at 12·5 knots (surfaced); 4 500 at 5 knots
    (snorting); 3000 at 7 knots (snorting)
Speed, knots: 13·5 surfaced; 16 dived
Complement: 45 (6 officers, 39 men)

Improved "Aréthuse" class with diving depth about 1 000 feet *(300 metres)*. *Siréne* sank at Lorient in 1972, and was subsequently salved.

Diving depth: About 1 000 feet *(300 metres)*

Modernisation: In hand from 1971 to improve sonar and armament.

Radar: I Band Calypso II for search/navigation.

Sonar: DUUA 2 active sonar with transducers forward and aft; passive ranging; intercept set.

Foreign orders: South Africa (1967) (3), Pakistan (1966) (3), Portugal (1964) (4), Spain (built in Spain) (1965) (4), Libya (built in Spain) (1976 on) (4).

DAPHNÉ   7/1976, Dr. Giorgio Arra

SIRÈNE   10/1977, Leo van Ginderen

4 "ARÉTHUSE" CLASS

Name	No.	Builders	Laid down	Launched	Commissioned
ARÉTHUSE	S 635	Cherbourg Naval Dockyard	Mar 1955	9 Nov 1957	23 Oct 1958
ARGONAUTE	S 636	Cherbourg Naval Dockyard	Mar 1955	29 June1957	11 Feb 1959
AMAZONE	S 639	Cherbourg Naval Dockyard	Dec 1955	3 April1958	1 July 1959
ARIANE	S 640	Cherbourg Naval Dockyard	Dec 1955	12 Sep 1958	16 Mar 1960

Displacement, tons: 400 standard; 543 surfaced;
    669 dived
Length, feet (metres): 162·7 *(49·6)*
Beam, feet (metres): 19 *(5·8)*
Draught, feet (metres): 13·1 *(4·0)*
Torpedo tubes: 4—21·7 in *(550 mm)* bow, 4 reloads
Main machinery: 12-cyl SEMT-Pielstick diesel-electric;
    1 060 bhp surfaced; 1 300 hp motors dived; 1 shaft
Speed, knots: 12·5 surfaced; 16 dived
Complement: 40 (6 officers, 34 men)

An excellent class of small submarines with a minimum number of ballast tanks and a diving depth of about 600 feet *(182·8 metres)*.

Sonar: DUUA 2.

ARÉTHUSE   6/1976, Dr. Giorgio Arra

6 "NARVAL" CLASS

Name	No.	Builders	Laid down	Launched	Commissioned
NARVAL	S 631	Cherbourg Naval Dockyard	June 1951	11 Dec 1954	1 Dec 1957
MARSOUIN	S 632	Cherbourg Naval Dockyard	Sep 1951	21 May 1955	1 Oct 1957
DAUPHIN	S 633	Cherbourg Naval Dockyard	May 1952	17 Sep 1955	1 Aug 1958
REQUIN	S 634	Cherbourg Naval Dockyard	June 1952	3 Dec 1955	1 Aug 1958
ESPADON	S 637	Normand	Dec 1955	15 Sep 1958	2 April 1960
MORSE	S 638	Seine Maritime	Feb 1956	10 Dec 1958	2 May 1960

Displacement, tons: 1 320 standard; 1 635 surfaced; 1 910 dived
Length, feet (metres): 254·6 *(77·6)*
Beam, feet (metres): 25·6 *(7·8)*
Draught, feet (metres): 17·7 *(5·4)*
Torpedo tubes: 6—21·7 in *(550 mm)* bow; 14 reload torpedoes; capable of minelaying
Main machinery: Diesel-electric, 3 12-cyl SEMT-Pielstick diesels; 2 2 400 hp electric motors; 2 shafts
Speed, knots: 15 surfaced; 18 dived
Range, miles: 15 000 at 8 knots (snorting)
Endurance: 45 days
Complement: 63 (7 officers, 56 men)

Improved versions based on the German Type XXI. *Dauphin, Marsouin, Narval* and *Requin* were built in seven prefabricated parts each of 10 metres in length.

Engineering: New main propelling machinery installed on reconstruction during 1965 to 1970 includes diesel-electric drive on the surface with SEMT-Pielstick diesels. The original main machinery was Schneider 4 000 bhp 7 cyl 2 stroke diesels for surface propulsion and 5 000 hp electric motors dived.

Reconstruction: During a five-year reconstruction programme, announced in 1965 and completed by the end of 1970, these submarines, *Requin* in Spring 1967 and *Espadon* and *Morse* in succession at Lorient followed by the other three, were given a new diesel-electric power plant as well as new weapon and detection equipment.

Sonar: DUUA 1.

REQUIN   11/1976, Michael D. J. Lennon

152 FRANCE

AIRCRAFT CARRIERS
2 "CLEMENCEAU" CLASS

Name	No.	Builders	Laid down	Launched	Commissioned
CLEMENCEAU	R 98	Brest Naval Dockyard	Nov 1955	21 Dec 1957	22 Nov 1961
FOCH	R 99	Chantiers de l'Atlantique	Feb 1957	28 July 1960	15 July 1963

Displacement, tons: 27 307 normal; 32 780 full load
Length, feet (metres): 780·8 *(238·0)* pp; 869·4 *(265·0)* oa
Beam, feet (metres): 104·1 *(31·7)* hull (with bulges)
Width, feet (metres): 168·0 *(51·2)* oa (flight deck and sponsons)
Draught, feet (metres): 28·2 *(8·6)*
Aircraft: Capacity 40. Each carries 3 Flights—1 of Etendard IV, 1 of Crusader, 1 of Breguet Alizé (see note)
Catapults: 2 Mitchell-Brown steam, Mk BS 5
Guns: 8—3·9 in *(100 mm)* automatic in single turrets
Armour Flight deck, island superstructure and bridges, hull (over machinery spaces and magazines)
Main engines: 2 sets Parsons geared turbines; 2 shafts; 126 000 shp
Boilers: 6; steam pressure 640 psi *(45 kg/cm²)*, superheat 842°F *(450°C)*
Speed, knots: 32
Oil fuel, tons: 3 720
Range, miles: 7 500 at 18 knots; 4 800 at 24 knots; 3 500 at full power
Complement: 1 338 (64 officers, 1 274 men) (fixed wing) 984 (45 officers, 939 men) (helo)

First aircraft carriers designed as such and built from the keel to be completed in France. Authorised in 1953 and 1955, respectively. *Clemenceau* ordered from Brest Dockyard on 28 May 1954 and begun in Nov 1955. *Foch* begun at Chantiers de l'Atlantique at St. Nazaire, Penhoet-Loire, in a special dry dock (contract provided for the construction of the hull and propelling machinery) and completed by Brest Dockyard.

Aircraft: Each flight has 10 aircraft. In addition 2 Super Frelon and 2 Alouette III helicopters are carried. As a peacetime economy only one operates fixed wing aircraft, the other carrying out A/S duties with a reduced complement, all helicopters. See "Complement" for resultant changes.

Bulges: *Foch* was completed with bulges. These having proved successful, *Clemenceau* was modified similarly on first refit, increasing her beam by 6 feet *(1·83 metres)*.

Electronics: Comprehensive DF and ECM equipment. Both fitted with SENIT 4 Tactical data automation system.

Flight Deck: Angled deck, two lifts, measuring 52·5 × 36 feet *(16·00 × 10·97 metres)*, one on the starboard deck edge, two steam catapults and two mirror landing aids. The flight deck measures 543 × 96·8 feet *(165·50 × 29·50 metres)* and is angled at 8 degrees.
Flight deck letters: F = *Foch*, U = *Clemenceau*.

Gunnery: Originally to have been armed with 24—2·25 *(57 mm)* in guns in twin mountings, but the armament was revised to 12—3·9 in *(100 mm)* in 1956 and to 8—3·9 inch *(100 mm)* in 1958. Rate of fire 60 rounds per minute.

Hangar: Dimensions of the hangar are 590·6 × 78·7 × 23·0 feet *(180 × 24 × 7 metres)*

Radar: One DRBV 20C; one DRBV 23B; two DRBI 10; one DRBV 50; one DRBC 31.

Sonar: One SQS 505.

CLEMENCEAU 7/1976, Dr. Giorgio Arra

FOCH 1974, Dr. Giorgio Arra

CLEMENCEAU 7/1976, Dr. Giorgio Arra

1 PA 75 (NUCLEAR-PROPELLED AIRCRAFT CARRIER)

Name	No.	Builders	Laid down	Launched	Commissioning
—	PA 75	DCAN, Brest	1981	—	—

Displacement, tons: 16 400 trials; 18 400 full load
Length, feet (metres): 682·2 oa *(208)*
Length, feet (metres): 662·6 flight deck *(202)*
Beam, feet (metres): 86·6 wl *(26·4)*
Beam, feet (metres): 157·4 flight deck *(46)*
Draught, feet (metres): 21·3 *(6·5)*
Aircraft: 25 WG 13 Lynx or 10 Super Frelon or 15 Puma helicopters
Missiles: 2 Crotale SAM systems; 4 SAM systems with a sea-skimming capability for anti-missile defence are eventually to replace the guns
Guns: 2—100 mm (singles—forward); 2—40 mm Breda-Bofors
Main engines: 1—CAS 230 reactor to two turbines; 65 000 bhp; 2 emergency AGO diesels
Speed, knots: 28
Range, miles: Unlimited on reactor; 3 000 at 18 knots (diesels)
Endurance: Stores for 45 days; 30 days for passengers
Complement: 890 (840 ship, 50 staff) plus 1 500 passengers

Coming at a time of financial stringency, this is a bold design showing the French Navy's appreciation of the great and universal value of helicopters in both peace and war. While her wartime role in a force composed of both A/S and A/A ships is clear, she has been designed with an intervention role in mind as well. For peacetime duties in the event of natural disasters, her large passenger and hospital capacity will be of immense value. Although the original plan allowed for her completion in 1980 the new 1977-81 plan states that she will not be laid down until 1981, being the first of a class of three ships. However some long-lead items have already been ordered.

Accommodation: A crew of 840 plus 50 staff and Ground Intervention Staff is provided for. Passenger accommodation is available for 1 000, with more austere conditions on portable bunks for an extra 500 in the garage (forward of the hangar).

Aircraft: Although designed primarily for helicopter operations the possibility of VTOL operations was also taken into account.

Electrical supply: A total of 9 400 kW from two turbines each driving a pair of 1 500 kW alternators and four diesel alternators of 850 kW each.

Flight deck: The flight deck, 662 feet *(201·77 metres)* long, is 157 feet *(47·85 metres)* wide at its maximum and 102 feet *(31·09 metres)* at the island. Four spots are provided for Super Frelon helicopters and eight for Lynx or Puma.

Hangar: One hangar, 275 × 69 × 21 feet *(83·82 × 21·03 × 6·40 metres)*, is provided with two lateral lifts to starboard at the rear of the island. Storage for 1 000 cubic metres of TR5 fuel in tanks is available. One fixed crane and one mobile crane are provided.

Hospital: 3 main wards, 1 X-ray ward, 1 intensive care ward, 1 infectious diseases ward, 2 dental surgeries and a laboratory.

Main engines: The CAS 230 reactor of 230 megawatts is being constructed under the supervision of l'Etablissement des Constructions et Armes Navales d'Indret.

Operations rooms: Normal Operations Room, ASW centre and Communication Offices are supplemented by an Operations Centre with facilities for Ground Intervention Forces and Air Intervention Forces. These include a Warfare Coordinating Centre, an Air Intervention Command Centre and a Helicopter Command Station.

Radar: Air search: one DRBV 26
Combined search: one DRBV 51C
Missile guidance: one DRBC 32
Navigation: two Decca

Replenishment: 1 250 tons of fuel is carried for replenishment of Escorts.

Type: Although originally classified as PH (Porte helicoptères) this has been changed to PA (Porte aeronefs) signifying her V/STOL capability.

Sonar: one DUBA 25.

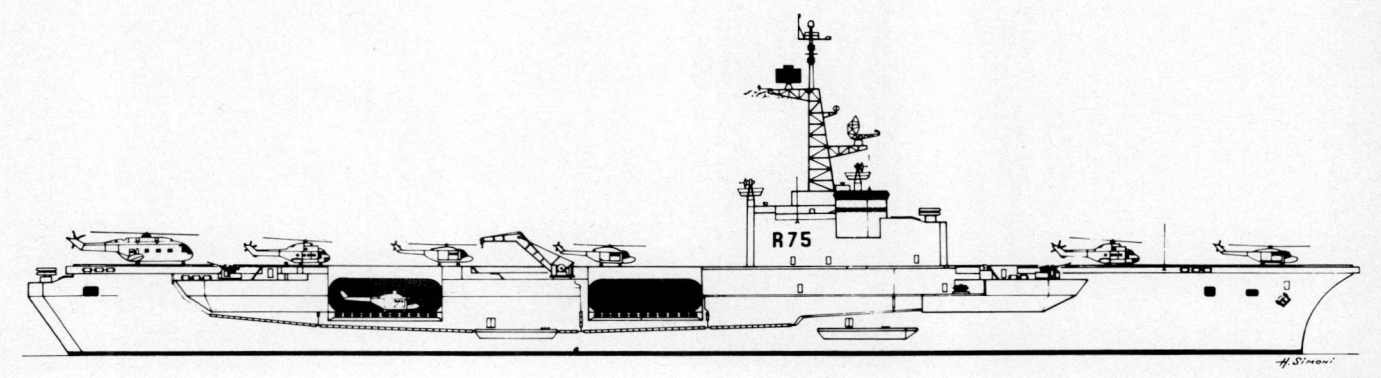

PA 75 1974, French Navy

FRANCE

CRUISERS

Name	No.	Builders	Laid down	Launched	Commissioned
JEANNE D'ARC (ex-*La Résolue*)	R 97	Brest Naval Dockyard	7 July 1960	30 Sep 1961	1 July 1963 (trials) 30 June 1964 (service)

Displacement, tons: 10 000 standard; 12 365 full load
Length, feet *(metres)*: 564·2 *(172)* pp; 597·1 *(182·0)* oa
Beam, feet *(metres)*: 78·7 *(24·0)* hull
Draught, feet *(metres)*: 24·0 *(7·3)*
Flight deck, feet *(metres)*: 203·4 × 68·9 *(62·0 × 21·0)*
Aircraft: Heavy A/S helicopters (4 in peace-time as training ship; 8 in wartime)
Missiles: 6—MM38 Exocet
Guns: 4—3·9 in *(100 mm)* single
Main engines: Rateau-Bretagne geared turbines; 2 shafts; 40 000 shp
Boilers: 4; working pressure 640 psi *(45 kg/cm²); 842°F (450°C)*
Speed, knots: 26·5
Oil fuel, tons: 1 360
Range, miles: 6 000 at 15 knots
Complement: 809 (30 officers, 587 ratings and 192 cadets)

Authorised under the 1957 estimates. Used for training officer cadets in peacetime. In wartime, after rapid modification, she would be used as a commando ship, helicopter carrier or troop transport with commando equipment and a battalion of 700 men. The lift has a capacity of 12 tons. The ship is almost entirely air-conditioned.

Electronics: 2 Syllex systems.

Missiles: Due to be fitted with Crotale.

Modifications: Between first steaming trials and completion for operational service the ship was modified with a taller funnel to clear the superstructure and prevent the smoke and exhaust gases swirling on to the bridges.

Radar: One DRBV 22D; one DRBV 50; one DRBN 32; one DRBI 10.

Sonar: One SQS 503.

JEANNE D'ARC   3/1977, Dr. Giorgio Arra

JEANNE D'ARC   3/1977, Dr. Giorgio Arra

JEANNE D'ARC   3/1977, Dr. Giorgio Arra

FRANCE 155

Name	No.	Builders	Laid down	Launched	Commissioned
COLBERT	C 611	Brest Dockyard	Dec 1953	24 Mar 1956 (floated out of dry dock)	5 May 1959 (trials late 1957)

Displacement, tons: 8 500 standard; 11 300 full load
Length, feet (metres): 593·2 *(180·8)*
Beam, feet (metres): 66·1 *(20·2)*
Draught, feet (metres): 25·2 *(7·7)*
Missile launchers: 1 twin Masurca surface-to-air aft. 4 MM38 Exocet to be fitted
Guns: 2—3·9 in *(100 mm)* single automatic; 12—57 mm in 6 twin mountings, 3 on each side
Armour: 50—80 mm belt and 50 mm deck
Main engines: 2 sets CEM-Parsons geared turbines; 2 shafts; 86 000 shp
Boilers: 4 Indret multitubular; 640 psi *(45 kg/cm²)*; 842°F *(450°C)*
Speed, knots: 31·5
Oil fuel, tons: 1 492
Range, miles: 4 000 at 25 knots
Complement: 560 (24 officers, 536 men)

She was equipped as command ship and for radar control of air strikes. Serves as Flagship of the Mediterranean Fleet.

Electronics: Senit data automation system; radar intercept equipment; wireless intercept equipment; two Knebworth Corvus dual-purpose launchers for CHAFF. 2 Syllex.

Gunnery: Priot to April 1970 the armament comprised 16 5 in *(127 mm)* dual purpose guns in 8 twin mountings, and 20 57 mm Bofors anti-aircraft guns in 10 twin mountings.

Missiles: *Colbert* carries 48 Masurca missiles (Mk 2 Mod 3 semi-active radar homing version). 4 Exocet to be shipped at a later refit.

Radar: Navigation: one Decca RM416.
Surveillance: one DRBV 50.
Air surveillance: one DRBV 23C
Warning: one DRBV 20.
Fire control: two DRBR 51; one DRBR 32C; two DRBC 31.
Height finder: one DRBI 10D.

Reconstruction: Between April 1970 and October 1972 she underwent a complete reconstruction and rearmament. The gunnery systems were altered to those given above, the Masurca surface-to-air missile system was fitted and helicopter facilities were installed on the quarter-deck. Reductions in the original armament schedule saved 80 million francs from the original refit cost of 350 million francs.

Sonar: Hull mounted set.

COLBERT   7/1976, Dr. Giorgio Arra

COLBERT   3/1976, Reinhard Nerlich

COLBERT   7/1976, Dr. Giorgio Arra

156 FRANCE

DESTROYERS

4 + 2 TYPE C 70

Name	No.	Builders	Laid down	Launched	Commissioned
GEORGES LEYGUES	D 640	Brest Naval Dockyard	June 1974	6 Sep 1975	April 1979
DUPLEIX	D 641	Brest Naval Dockyard	17 Oct 1975	—	1979
MONTCALM	D 642	Brest Naval Dockyard	Dec 1975	—	1979
JEAN DE VIENNE	D 643	Brest Naval Dockyard	1977	—	—

Displacement, tons: 3 800 standard; 4 100 full load
Length, feet (metres): 455·9 oa *(139)*
Beam, feet (metres): 45·9 *(14)*
Draught, feet (metres): 18·7 *(5·7)*
Aircraft: 2WG 13 Lynx helicopters with Mk 44 or 46 torpedoes
Missile launchers: 4—MM 38 Exocet; 1 Crotale (A/S version)
  4—MM 38 Exocet; 1—SM1 (SAM with 40 missiles) (AA version)
Guns: 1—3·9 in *(100 mm)*; 2—20 mm (A/S version)
  2—3·9 in *(100 mm)*; 2—20 mm (AA version)
Torpedo tubes: 10 tubes in 2 mountings for Mk L5
Main engines: CODOG; 2 Rolls-Royce Olympus gas turbines 42 000 bhp; 2 SEMT-Pielstick 16PA6 diesels 10 000 bhp; 2 shafts; vp screws
Speed, knots: 29·75 (19·5 on diesels)
Range, miles: 9 500 at 18 knots on diesels
Complement: 271 (21 officers, 250 men) (billets)

A new C 70 type of so-called "corvette".
A total of at least 24 is planned, 18 being of an A/S version like *G. Leygues* and 6 of an A/A version. Three more of the A/S version are to be built under the 4th Five Year Plan (1977-81). Three of the Air Defence version are also to be ordered under the same plan, the first to be laid down in 1978.

Electronics: Senit action data automation system. 2 Dagaie systems.

Helicopter: The Lynx, as well as its A/S role, can have an anti-surface role when armed with 4 AS 12 missiles.

Missiles: AA version to carry Standard SM2 system.

Radar: Surface/air surveillance: one DRBV 51
Air search: one DRBV 26
Fire control: one DRBV 32E
Navigation: two Decca 1226 (A/S version).
one DRBV 26; one DRBJ 11; two SPG 51C (AA version).

Sonar: One DUBV 23 (hull-mounted); one DUBV 43 (VDS) (A/S version).
One DUBV 25 or 26 (AA version).

Trials: *Georges Leygues* completed 23 June 1977; trials began Oct 1977.

GEORGES LEYGUES *1977, French Navy*

TYPE C 70 *1976, French Navy*

FRANCE 157

2 "SUFFREN" CLASS

Name	No.	Builders	Laid down	Launched	Commissioned
SUFFREN	D 602	Lorient Naval Dockyard	Dec 1962	15 May 1965	July 1967
DUQUESNE	D 603	Brest Naval Dockyard	Nov 1964	12 Feb 1966	April 1970

Displacement, tons: 5 090 standard; 6 090 full load
Length, feet (metres): 517·1 *(157·6)* oa
Beam, feet (metres): 50·9 *(15·5)*
Draught, feet (metres): 20·0 *(6·1)*
Missile launchers: Twin Masurca surface-air (see notes)
Guns: 2—3·9 in *(100 mm)* (automatic, single)
  2—20 mm (single)
A/S weapons: Malafon single launcher with 13 missiles; 4 launchers (2 each side) for L5 A/S homing torpedoes
Main engines: Double reduction Rateau geared turbines; 2 shafts; 72 500 shp
Boilers: 4 automatic; working pressure 640 psi *(45 kg/cm²)*; superheat 842°F *(450°C)*
Speed, knots: 34
Range, miles: 5 100 at 18 knots; 2 400 at 29 knots
Complement: 355 (23 officers, 332 men)

Ordered under the 1960 Programme. Equipped with gyro controlled stabilisers controlling three pairs of non-retractable fins. Air-conditioning of accommodation and operational areas. Excellent sea-boats and weapon platforms.

Electronics: Senit I action data automatic system. Two Syllex.

Missiles: Carry 48 Masurca missiles, a mix of Mk 2 Mod 2 beam riders and Mk 2 Mod 3 semi-active homers. During their 1977 refit 4 Exocet launchers replaced the 30 mm gun mountings. *Duquesne* completed Feb 1977, *Suffren* 1978.

Radar: Search and navigation: one DRBN 32.
Air surveillance and target designator (radome): one DRBI 23.
Surface surveillance: one DRBV 50.
Masurca fire-control: two DRBR 51.
Gun fire-control: one DRBC 32A.

Sonar: One DUBV 23 hull-mounted set and one DUBV 43 VDS.

SUFFREN 9/1976, Dr. Giorgio Arra

DUQUESNE 6/1977, Dr. Giorgio Arra

DUQUESNE 6/1977, C. and S. Taylor

158 FRANCE

3 TYPE F 67 (ex-C-67A)

Name	No.	Builders	Laid down	Launched	Commissioned
TOURVILLE	D 610	Lorient Naval Dockyard	16 Mar 1970	13 May 1972	21 June 1974
DUGUAY-TROUIN	D 611	Lorient Naval Dockyard	25 Feb 1971	1 June 1973	17 Sep 1975
DE GRASSE	D 612	Lorient Naval Dockyard	1972	30 Nov 1974	July 1976

Displacement, tons: 4 580 standard; 5 745 full load
Length, feet (metres): 501·3 (152·8) oa
Beam, feet (metres): 50·2 (15·3)
Draught, feet (metres): 18·7 (5·7)
Aircraft: 2 WG 13 Lynx ASW helicopters
Missile launchers: 6 MM 38 Exocet;
 1—Crotale SAM (De Grasse) (see note)
Guns: 2—3·9 in (100 mm)
A/S weapons: 1 Malafon rocket/homing torpedo (13 missiles); 2 mountings for Mk L5 torpedoes
Main engines: Rateau geared turbines; 2 shafts; 54 400 shp
Boilers: 4 automatic
Speed, knots: 31
Range, miles: 5 000 at 18 knots
Complement: 303 (25 officers, 278 men)

Developed from the "Aconit" design. Originally rated as "Corvettes" but reclassified as "Frigates" on 8 July 1971 and given "D" pennant numbers like destroyers.

Electronics: Senit action data automatic system. Two Syllex.

Missiles: Octuple Crotale now fitted in place of after 100 mm gun.

Radar: Surface/air surveillance: one DRBV 51
Fire control: one DRBC 32D
Navigation: two Decca type 1226
Air search: one DRBV 26

Sonars: One DUBV 23 hull-mounted; one DUBV 43 VDS.

TOURVILLE (see Missile note) — 7/1976, Dr. Giorgio Arra

DUGUAY-TROUIN (after 100 m removed) — 10/1977, C. and S. Taylor

1 TYPE T 56

Name	No.	Builders	Laid down	Launched	Commissioned
LA GALISSONNIÈRE	D 638	Lorient Naval Dockyard	Nov 1958	12 Mar 1960	July 1962

Displacement, tons: 2 750 standard; 3 740 full load
Length, feet (metres): 435·7 (132·8) oa
Beam, feet (metres): 41·7 (12·7)
Draught, feet (metres): 21·4 (6·3)
Aircraft: 1 A/S helicopter
A/S weapons: 1 Malafon rocket/homing torpedo launcher
Guns: 2—3·9 in (100 mm) automatic, single
Torpedo tubes: 6—21·7 in (550 mm) ASM, 2 triple for Mks K2 and L3
Main engines: 2 sets Rateau geared turbines; 2 shafts; 63 000 shp
Boilers: 4 A & C de B Indret; 500 psi (35 kg/cm²); 617°F (380°C)
Speed, knots: 32
Oil fuel, tons: 800
Range, miles: 5 000 at 18 knots
Complement: 270 (15 officers, 255 men)

Same characteristics as regards hull and machinery as T 47 and T 53 types, but different armament. She has a hangar which hinges outwards and a platform for landing a helicopter. When first commissioned she was used as an experimental ship for new sonars and anti-submarine weapons.

Armament: First French combatant ship to be armed with Malafon. This is the reason for the two 3·9 in (100 mm) guns instead of the 3 or 4 previously planned. France's first operational guided missile ship.

Electronics: Tacan beacon and full DF and ECM fit.

Radar: Surface/air surveillance: one DRBV 50
Navigation: one DRBN 32
Air search: one DRBV 22
Gun fire-control: one DRBC 32A

Sonar: One hull mounted DUBV 23; one DUBV 43 VDS.

LA GALISSONIÈRE — 7/1976, Dr. Giorgio Arra

FRANCE 159

1 TYPE T 53 (MODIFIED—ASW)

Name	No.	Builders	Laid down	Launched	Commissioned
DUPERRÉ	D 633	Lorient Naval Dockyard	Nov 1954	23 June 1956	8 Oct 1957

Displacement, tons: 2 800 standard; 3 900 full load
Length, feet (metres): 435·7 *(132·8)* oa
Beam, feet (metres): 41·7 *(12·7)*
Draught, feet (metres): 20 *(6·1)*
Aircraft: 1 WG 13 Lynx helicopter
Missiles: 4 MM 38 Exocet
Gun: 1—3·9 in *(100 mm)*
A/S weapons: Launcher for 8 torpedoes (Mk L5)
Main engines: 2 sets Rateau geared turbines; 2 shafts; 63 000 shp
Boilers: 4 A & C de B Indret; 500 psi *(35 kg/cm²)*; 617°F *(380°C)*
Speed, knots: 32
Oil fuel, tons: 800
Range, miles: 5 000 at 18 knots
Complement: 272 (15 officers, 257 men)

Originally built with 6—5 in guns.
After serving as trial ship from 1967-71, she was converted at Brest to her present state in 1972-74. Recommissioned 21 May 1974.

Electronics: One Senit automatic data system; two Syllex.

Gunnery: Appears to lack radar fire-control for 100 mm gun.

Radar: Air search: one DRBV 22A
Navigation: one Decca
Helicopter: one Decca
Fire control: one DRBC 32E
Surface/air surveillance: one DRBV 51

Sonar: DUBV 23 hull-mounted; DUBV 43 VDS.

DUPERRÉ 6/1975, Dr. Giorgio Arra

2 TYPE T 53

Name	No.	Builders	Laid down	Launched	Commissioned
FORBIN	D 635	Brest Naval Dockyard	Aug 1954	15 Oct 1955	1 Feb 1958
TARTU	D 636	At. Chantiers de Bretagne	Nov 1954	2 Dec 1955	5 Feb 1958

Displacement, tons: 2 750 standard; 3 740 full load
Length, feet (metres): 421·9 *(128·6)*
Beam, feet (metres): 41·7 *(12·7)*
Draught, feet (metres): 18·0 *(5·5)*
Guns: 6—5 in *(127 mm)* (twins); (Forbin 4—5 in); 6—57 mm (twins); 2—20 mm
A/S weapons: 2 triple mountings *(550 mm)* for Mk K2 and L3; 375 mm Mk 54 projector
Main engines: 2 geared turbines; 63 000 shp; 2 shafts
Boilers: 4 A & C de B Indret
Speed, knots: 32
Oil fuel, tons: 800
Range, miles: 5 000 at 18 knots
Complement: 276 (15 officers, 261 men)

Air-direction ships—*Forbin* has helicopter platform aft in place of Y mount.
Forbin acts as a training ship for l'École d'Application des Enseignes de Vaisseau, being part of the *Jeanne d'Arc* group. *Jaureguiberry* paid off 27 June 1977, *Tartu* to reserve 1978.

Electronics: Senit automatic data system.
Tacan Beacon.

Radar: Three dimensional air search: DRBI 10A
Air search: DRBV 22A
Navigation: DRBV 31

Sonar: One DUBA 1; one DUBV 24.

TARTU 7/1976, Dr. Giorgio Arra

FORBIN 3/1977, Dr. Giorgio Arra

FRANCE

4 TYPE T 47 (DDG)

Name	No.	Builders	Laid down	Launched	Commissioned
KERSAINT	D 622	Lorient Naval Dockyard	June 1951	3 Oct 1953	20 Mar 1956
BOUVET	D 624	Lorient Naval Dockyard	Nov 1951	3 Oct 1953	13 May 1956
DUPETIT THOUARS	D 625	Brest Naval Dockyard	Mar 1952	4 Mar 1954	15 Sep 1956
DU CHAYLA	D 630	Brest Naval Dockyard	July 1953	27 Nov 1954	4 June 1957

Displacement, tons: 2 750 standard; 3 740 full load
Length, feet (metres): 421·9 *(128·6)*
Beam, feet (metres): 41·7 *(12·7)*
Draught, feet (metres): 21·4 *(6·3)*
Missiles: Single Mk 13 Tartar launcher (40 missiles—SM-I or SM-IA)
Guns: 6—57 mm (twins)
A/S weapons: 2 triple mountings *(550 mm)* for Mk K2 and L3; 1—375 mm Mk 54 projector
Main engines: 2 geared turbines; 63 000 shp; 2 shafts
Boilers: 4 A & C de B Indret
Speed, knots: 32
Oil fuel, tons: 800
Range, miles: 5 000 at 18 knots
Complement: 277 (17 officers, 260 men) (peace); 320 (war)

Originally built as all-gun destroyers with 6—5 in guns. Converted into DDGs 1961-65.

Electronics: Senit automatic data system.

Radar: Air-search: one DRBV 20 A
Tartar search (3D): one SPS 39A or B
Tartar control: two SPG 51B
Navigation: one DRBV 31

Sonars: One DUBA 1; one DUBV 24.

KERSAINT
1976, Michael D. J. Lennon

KERSAINT
7/1976, Reinhard Nerlich

5 TYPE T 47 (ASW)

Name	No.	Builders	Laid down	Launched	Commissioned
MAILLE BRÉZÉ	D 627	Lorient Naval Dockyard	Oct 1953	26 Sep 1954	4 May 1957
VAUQUELIN	D 628	Lorient Naval Dockyard	Mar 1953	26 Sep 1954	3 Nov 1956
D'ESTRÉES	D 629	Brest Naval Dockyard	May 1953	27 Nov 1954	19 Mar 1957
CASABIANCA	D 631	F. C. Gironde	Oct 1953	13 Nov 1954	4 May 1957
GUÉPRATTE	D 632	A. C. Bretagne	Aug 1953	8 Nov 1954	6 June 1957

Displacement, tons: 2 750 standard; 3 900 full load
Length, feet (metres): 434·6 *(132·5)*
Beam, feet (metres): 41·7 *(12·7)*
Draught, feet (metres): 21·4 *(6·3)*
Guns: 2—3·9 in *(100 mm)* (singles); 2—20 mm
A/S weapons: 1 Malafon; 1—375 mm Mk 54 projector; 2 triple mountings *(550 mm)* for Mk K2 and L3
Main engines: 2 geared turbines; 63 000 shp; 2 shafts
Boilers: 4 A & C de B Indret
Speed, knots: 32
Oil fuel, tons: 800
Range, miles: 5 000 at 18 knots
Complement: 260 (15 officers, 245 men)

Originally with 6—5 in guns.
Converted between 1968-71 including air-conditioning of living spaces, replacement of electronic equipment and updating of damage control equipment.

Electronics: Senit data handling.

Radar: Navigation: one DRBN 32
Air surveillance: one DRBV 23A
Air/surface search: one DRBV 50
Gun fire control: two DRBC 32A

Sonars: One DUBV 23 hull mounted; one DUBV 43 VDS.

D'ESTRÉES (after last refit with new aerial outfit)
7/1976, Dr. Giorgio Arra

MAILLE BRÉZÉ
6/1975, Dr. Giorgio Arra

FRANCE 161

1 TYPE C 65

Name	No.	Builders	Laid down	Launched	Commissioned
ACONIT	D 609 (ex-F 703)	Lorient Naval Dockyard	Jan 1966	7 Mar 1970	30 Mar 1973 (trials 15 May 1971)

Displacement, tons: 3 500 standard; 3 900 full load
Length, feet (metres): 416·7 *(127·0)* oa
Beam, feet (metres): 44·0 *(13·4)*
Draught, feet (metres): 18·9 *(5·8)*
Missiles: Malafon rocket/homing torpedo;
    MM 38 Exocet to be fitted
Guns: 2—3·9 in *(100 mm)*
A/S weapons: 1 quadruple 12 in *(305 mm)* mortar;
    2 launchers for Mk L5 torpedoes
Main engines: 1 Rateau geared turbine; 1 shaft; 28 650 shp
Boilers: 2 automatic (450°C)
Speed, knots: 27
Range, miles: 5 000 at 18 knots
Complement: 228 (15 officers, 213 men)

Forerunner of the F67 Type. A one-off class ordered under 1965 programme. Has no helicopter or facilities for such.

Electronics: An early form of centralised data analysis. Two Syllex.

Radar: Pulse Doppler (E/F band surveillance): one DRBV 13
Air surveillance: one DRBV 22A.
100 mm guns fire-control: one DRBC 32B
Navigation: one DRBN 32

Sonar: One hull-mounted DUBV 23; one DUBV 43 VDS.

ACONIT   2/1977, Michael D. J. Lennon

FRIGATES

9 "COMMANDANT RIVIÈRE" CLASS

Name	No.	Builders	Laid down	Launched	Commissioned
VICTOR SCHOELCHER	F 725	Lorient Naval Dockyard	Oct 1957	Oct 1958	Dec 1962
COMMANDANT BORY	F 726	Lorient Naval Dockyard	Mar 1958	Oct 1958	Mar 1964
AMIRAL CHARNER	F 727	Lorient Naval Dockyard	Nov 1958	Mar 1960	Dec 1962
DOUDART DE LAGRÉE	F 728	Lorient Naval Dockyard	Mar 1960	April 1961	Mar 1963
BALNY	F 729	Lorient Naval Dockyard	Mar 1960	Mar 1962	Feb 1971
COMMANDANT RIVIÈRE	F 733	Lorient Naval Dockyard	April 1957	Oct 1958	Dec 1962
COMMANDANT BOURDAIS	F 740	Lorient Naval Dockyard	April 1959	April 1961	Mar 1963
PROTET	F 748	Lorient Naval Dockyard	Sep 1961	Dec 1962	May 1964
ENSEIGNE DE VAISSEAU HENRY	F 749	Lorient Naval Dockyard	Sep 1962	Dec 1963	Jan 1965

Displacement, tons: 1 750 standard; 2 250 full load
    (*Balny* 1 650 standard; 1 950 full load)
Length, feet (metres): 321·5 *(98·0)* pp; 340·3 *(103·7)* oa
Beam, feet (metres): 38·4 *(11·7)*
Draught, feet (metres): 15·7 *(4·8)*
Aircraft: 1 light helicopter can land aft
Missiles: 4—MM 38 Exocet (except *Balny*)
Guns: 2—3·9 in *(100 mm)* automatic, singles; 2—30 mm
A/S weapons: 1—12 in *(305 mm)* quadruple mortar;
    6—21 in *(533 mm)* (triple) for Mk K2 and L3
Main engines: 4 SEMT-Pielstick diesels; 16 000 bhp; 2 shafts;
    (except *Balny*: CODAG; 2 diesels (16 cyl); one TG Turboméca M38; 1 shaft; vp screw)
Speed, knots: 25
Range, miles: 7 500 at 15 knots (*Balny* 8 000 at 12 knots)
Complement: 167 (10 officers, 157 men)

Built for world-wide operations—air-conditioned.

Accommodation: Can carry a senior officer and staff. If necessary a force of 80 soldiers can be carried as well as two 30 ft *(9 m)* LCPs with a capacity of 25 men at 11 knots.

Engines: Experimental CODAG arrangement in *Balny*. *Commandant Bory* was fitted with experimental machinery which was replaced with SEMT-Pielstick diesels in 1974-75.

Helicopter: In 1973 the after 100 mm mounting in *Commandant Bourdais* and *Enseigne Henry* was removed to make way for a helicopter platform. *Amiral Charner* retained her gun and had a helicopter platform fitted. (See "Missile" note).

Missiles: All of this class except *Balny* have been fitted with 4—MM 38 Exocet in place of X gun. *Bory* was the first to be fitted followed by *Doudart de Lagrée*. At the same time the 100 mm gun is replaced in Y position.

Radar: Navigation: one DRBN 32
Fire control: one DRBC 32A
Air search: one DRBV 22A
Surface/air search: one DRBV 50
Exocet ships: one DRBC 32C.

Sonar: One DUBA 3; one SQS 17.

ENSEIGNE DE VAISSEAU HENRY   10/1977, Dr. Giorgio Arra

BALNY   9/1976, Dr. Giorgio Arra

162 FRANCE

7 TYPE E 52 and 3 TYPE E 52B

Name	No.	Builders	Laid down	Launched	Commissioned
LE NORMAND	F 765	F. Ch. de la Mediterranée	July 1953	13 Feb 1954	3 Nov 1956
LE PICARD	F 766	A. C. Loire	Nov 1953	31 May 1954	20 Sep 1956
LE GASCON	F 767	A. C. Loire	Feb 1954	23 Oct 1954	29 Mar 1957
LE SAVOYARD	F 771	F. Ch. de la Mediterranée	Nov 1953	7 May 1955	14 June1956
LE BASQUE	F 773	Lorient Naval Dockyard	Dec 1954	25 Feb 1956	18 Oct 1957
L'AGENAIS	F 774	Lorient Naval Dockyard	Aug 1955	23 June1956	14 May 1958
LE BÉARNAIS	F 775	Lorient Naval Dockyard	Dec 1955	23 June1956	18 Oct 1958
L'ALSACIEN	F 776	Lorient Naval Dockyard	July 1956	26 Jan 1957	27 Aug 1960
LE PROVENÇAL	F 777	Lorient Naval Dockyard	Feb 1957	5 Oct 1957	6 Nov 1959
LE VENDÉEN	F 778	F. Ch. de la Mediterranée	Mar 1957	27 July 1957	1 Oct 1960

Displacement, tons: 1 250 standard; 1 702 full load
Length, feet (metres): 311·7 *(95·0)* pp; 327·4 *(99·8)* oa
Beam, feet (metres): 33·8 *(10·3)*
Draught, feet (metres): 13·5 *(4·1)*
Guns: 6—2·25 in *(57 mm)* in twin mountings (4 only in F 771, 772, 773); 2—20 mm
A/S weapons: Sextuple Bofors ASM mortar forward (except F 776, 777, 778 with 1—12 in *(305 mm)* quadruple mortar; 2 DC mortars; 1 DC rack; 12 ASM (4 triple mountings aft) for Mk K2 and L3
Main engines: Parsons or Rateau geared turbines; 20 000 shp
Boilers: 2 Indret; pressure 500 psi *(35·2 kg/cm²)*; superheat 725°F *(385°C)*
Speed, knots: 27
Range, miles: 4 500 at 15 knots
Oil fuel, tons: 310
Complement: 205 (13 officers, 192 men)

L'Agenais, L'Alsacien, Le Basque, Le Béarnais, Le Provençal and *Le Vendéen* have a different arrangement of bridges from the remainder. *L'Alsacien, Le Provencal* and *Le Vendéen* are of the E 52B type and have the Strombos-Velensi modified funnel cap.

Class: *L'Agenais* and *Le Picard* to reserve in 1977 for disposal. *Le Gascon* to special reserve at Brest 16 Sep 1977.

Radar: Navigation: one DRBV 31
Air search: one DRBV 22A
Fire control: one DRBC 31

Sonar: One DUBV 24; (one DUBV 1 in 771, 772, 773); one DUBA 1

Trials: *Le Basque* carries experimental fire-control equipment in place of third mounting.
Le Savoyard carries large electronic missile guidance equipment in place of after gun-mounting.

LE SAVOYARD   1976, Michael D. J. Lennon

L'ALSACIEN   9/1976, Dr. Giorgio Arra

1 TYPE E 50

Name	No.	Builders	Laid down	Launched	Commissioned
LE BOULONNAIS	F 763	A. C. Loire	Mar 1952	12 May 1953	5 Aug 1955

Displacement, tons: 1 250 standard; 1 528 for trials; 1 702 full load
Length, feet (metres): 311·7 *(95·0)* pp; 327·4 *(99·8)* oa
Beam, feet (metres): 33·8 *(10·3)*
Draught, feet (metres): 13·5 *(4·1)*
Guns: 6—2·25 in *(57 mm)* (twins); 2—20 mm
A/S weapons: 1—375 mm Mk 54 rocket launcher;
Torpedo tubes: 12 tubes (4 triple mounts forward) for Mk K2 and L3
Main engines: 2 Rateau A & C de B geared turbines; 20 000 shp; 2 shafts
Speed, knots: 27 (29 on trials); economical speed 14
Oil fuel, tons: 292
Range, miles: 4 500 at 15 knots
Complement: 205 (13 officers, 192 men)

Last survivor of a class of four

Radar: Air search: one DRBV 20
Navigation: one DRBN 32
Fire control: one DRBC 31

Sonar: One DUBV 1; one DUBA 1.

LE BOULONNAIS

7 + 7 TYPE A 69

Name	No.	Builders	Laid down	Launched	Commissioned
D'ESTIENNE D'ORVES*	F 781	Lorient Naval Dockyard	1 Sep 1972	1 June 1973	10 Sep 1976
AMYOT D'INVILLE	F 782	Lorient Naval Dockyard	Sep 1973	30 July 1974	30 July 1976
DROGOU*	F 783	Lorient Naval Dockyard	1 Oct 1973	30 Nov 1974	30 Sep 1976
DÉTROYAT	F 784	Lorient Naval Dockyard	15 Dec 1974	31 Jan 1976	24 Mar 1977
JEAN MOULIN	F 785	Lorient Naval Dockyard	15 Jan 1975	31 Jan 1976	May 1977
QUARTIER MAITRE ANQUETIL	F 786	Lorient Naval Dockyard	1 Aug 1975	7 Aug 1976	Jan 1978
COMMANDANT DE PIMODAN*	F 787	Lorient Naval Dockyard	1 Sep 1975	7 Aug 1976	Mar 1978
SECOND MAITRE LE BIHAN	F 788	Lorient Naval Dockyard	15 Feb 1976	Sep 1977	Dec 1978
LIEUTENANT DE VAISSEAU LE HENAFF	F 789	Lorient Naval Dockyard	15 Mar 1976	Mar 1977	Mar 1978
LIEUTENANT DE VAISSEAU LAVALLÉE	F 790	Lorient Naval Dockyard	1 Sep 1976	Apr 1979	Feb 1980
COMMANDANT L'HERMINIER	F 791	Lorient Naval Dockyard	1 Oct 1976	Sep 1977	Nov 1978
PREMIER MAITRE L'HER	F 792	Lorient Naval Dockyard	July 1978	Dec 1979	Nov 1980
COMMANDANT BLAISON	F 793	Lorient Naval Dockyard	Sep 1978	Dec 1979	Feb 1981
ENSEIGNE DE VAISSEAU JACOUBET	F 794	Lorient Naval Dockyard	Apr 1979	June 1980	Sep 1981

*Exocet fitted

Displacement, tons: 950 standard; 1 170 full load
Length, feet (metres): 262·5 *(80·0)* oa
Beam, feet (metres): 33·8 *(10·3)*
Draught, feet (metres): 9·8 *(3·0)*
Missiles: 2—MM 38 Exocet (see *Missile* note)
Guns: 1—3·9 in *(100 mm)*; 2—20 mm
A/S weapons: 1—375 mm Mk 54 Rocket launcher; 4 fixed tubes for Mk L3 and L5 torpedoes
Main engines: 2 SEMT-Pielstick PC2V diesels; 2 shafts; controllable pitch propellers; 11 000 bhp
Speed, knots: 24
Range, miles: 4 500 at 15 knots
Endurance, days: 15
Complement: 79 (5 officers, 74 men)

Primarily intended for coastal A/S operations—officially classified as "Avisos". Also available for overseas patrols and can carry an extra detachment of 1 officer and 17 men. *D'Estienne d'Orves* commissioned for trials 26 Oct 1974. Construction of *Ens. de V. Jacoubet* has been delayed for financial reasons. *Commandant Blaison* and *Enseigne Jacoubet* will be fitted to receive a platform and light helicopter.

Appearance: *Jean Moulin* F 785 has a modified funnel, a feature in all ships in due course.

Missiles: 2—MM 38 Exocet will be fitted in those ships earmarked for the Mediterranean—either side of the funnel. The remainder will be fitted "for but not with".

Radar: Surface/air search: one DRBV 51
Fire control: one DRBC 32E
Navigation: one Decca Type 202; one DRBN 32

Sonar: One hull mounted sonar DUBA 25.

Trials: *Second Maitre Le Bihan* F 788 ready for trials April 1978.

Transfers: *Lieutenant de Vaisseau Le Henaff* (F 789) and *Commandant l'Herminier* (F 791) sold to South Africa in 1976 whilst under construction. As a result of the UN embargo on arms sales to South Africa. So the present situation of these ships is uncertain. They have therefore been replaced in the above list. South African names—*Good Hope* and *Transvaal* respectively.

D'ESTIENNE D'ORVES 9/1976, Dr. Giorgio Arra

D'ESTIENNE D'ORVES 4/1976, Dr. Giorgio Arra

AMYOT D'INVILLE 6/1976, French Navy

NEW CONSTRUCTION TYPE A 70

Although this was originally planned as a separate class with missiles the fitting of Exocet in type A 69 has removed the major difference.

164 FRANCE

AMPHIBIOUS FORCES

2 LANDING SHIPS (DOCK) (TCD)

Name	No.	Builders	Laid down	Launched	Commissioned
OURAGAN	L 9021	Brest Naval Dockyard	June 1962	9 Nov 1963	June 1965
ORAGE	L 9022	Brest Naval Dockyard	June 1966	22 April 1967	Mar 1968

Displacement, tons: 5 800 light; 8 500 full load; 15 000 when fully immersed
Length, feet (metres): 488·9 (149·0)
Beam, feet (metres): 75·4 (23)
Draught, feet (metres): 17·7 (5·4); 28·5 (8·7) (flooded)
Aircraft: Main helo deck; 3 Super Frelon or 10 Alouette helicopters.
Portable platform; 1 Super Frelon or 3 Alouette helicopters.
Guns: 2—4·7 in (120 mm) mortars; 6—30 mm
Main engines: 2 diesels; 2 shafts; (cp propellers); 8 600 bhp
Speed, knots: 17
Range, miles: 9 000 at 15 knots
Complement: 238; 343 troops; 129 passengers (short haul)

Ouragan was completed for trials in 1964. Bridge is on the starboard side. Fitted with a platform for helicopters and portable platform aft. Able to carry two EDICs loaded with eleven light tanks each, or 18 loaded LCMs Type VI. In the logistic role 1 500 tons of material and equipment can be carried and handled by two 35 ton cranes. *Orage* is allocated to the Pacific Nuclear Experimental Centre. Have command facilities for directing amphibious and helicopter operations. Carry 3 LCVPs.

Docking: Can dock a 400 ton ship.

Loading: Typical loads—18 Super Frelon or 80 Alouette helicopters or 120 AMX 13 tanks or 84 DUKWs or 340 Jeeps or 12—50 ton barges.

Radar: Navigational set.

Repair Facilities: Carry main, hull, engine, carpenters, electrical and ordnance workshops.

Sonar: One SQS-17 in *Ouragan*.

OURAGAN   1975, Wright and Logan

ORAGE   1969, French Navy

2 BATRAL TYPE (LIGHT TRANSPORTS)

Name	No.	Builders	Commissioned
CHAMPLAIN	L 9030	Brest Naval Dockyard	5 Oct 1974
FRANCIS GARNIER	L 9031	Brest Naval Dockyard	21 June 1974

Displacement, tons: 750 standard; 1 409 full load
Dimensions, feet (metres): 262·4 × 42·6 × 7·9 (80 × 13 × 2·4)
Guns: 2—40 mm; 1—81 mm mortar
Main engines: 2 diesels; 2 shafts; (cp propellers); 3 600 hp = 16 knots
Range, miles: 4 500 at 13 knots
Complement: 47

Fitted with bow doors, and stowage for vehicles above and below decks. Helicopter landing platform. Can carry a landing company (Guépard) of 4 officers and 175 men with 12 vehicles. Both launched 17 Nov 1973.
Total load 380 tons. One LCVP carried and one LCPS. Ten ton derrick fitted.

Radar: Decca navigation.

Sonar: One hull mounted.

CHAMPLAIN   1974, DCAN Brest

5 LANDING SHIPS (TANK) (BDC)

Name	No.	Builders	Commissioned
ARGENS	L 9003	Ch. de Bretagne	1960
BIDASSOA	L 9004	Ch. Seine Maritime	1961
TRIEUX	L 9007	Ch. de Bretagne	1960
DIVES	L 9008	Ch. Seine Maritime	1961
BLAVET	L 9009	Ch. de Bretagne	1960

Displacement, tons: 1 400 standard; 1 765 normal; 4 225 full load
Dimensions, feet (metres): 335 oa × 50·9 × 10·5 (102·1 × 15·5 × 3·2)
Guns: 3—40 mm; 1—20 mm; 1—4·7 in (120 mm) mortar
Main engines: SEMT-Pielstick diesels; 2 shafts; 2 000 bhp = 11 knots
Range, miles: 18 500 at 10 knots
Complement: 75 (6 officers and 69 men). Plus 170 troops (normal)

Launched on 7 April 1959, 30 Dec 1960, 15 Jan 1960, 29 June 1960 and 6 Dec 1958, respectively. Can carry: 4 LCVPs, 1 800 tons of freight, 335 troops under austere conditions (up to 807 in a brief emergency). *Blavet* and *Trieux* are fitted as light helicopter carriers with a hangar before the bridge and can carry two Alouette III.

ARGENS   11/1975, Dr. Giorgio Arra

FRANCE 165

12 LANDING CRAFT (TANK) (EDIC)

L 9070 (30 Mar 1967)	L 9082 (1964)	L 9092 (2 Dec 1958)
L 9072 (1968)	L 9083 (1964)	L 9093 (17 April 1958)
L 9073 (1968)	L 9084	L 9094 (24 July 1958)
L 9074 (22 July 1969)	L 9091 (7 Jan 1958)	L 9096 (11 Oct 1958)

Displacement, tons: 250 standard; 670 full load
Dimensions, feet (metres): 193·5 × 39·2 × 4·5 *(59 × 12 × 1·3)*
Guns: 2—20 mm
Main engines: MGO diesels; 2 shafts; 1 000 bhp = 8 knots
Range, miles: 1 800 at 8 knots
Complement: 16 (1 officer, and 15 men)

EDIC L 9092   1973, Dr. Giorgio Arra

Seven were built by C. N. Franco Belges, three by Toulon Dockyard, two by La Perrière. Launch dates above. Can carry 11 lorries or 5 Light Fighting Vehicles.

Transfer: L 9095 transferred to Senegal 1 July 1974 as *La Falence*.

ISSOLE A 734

Displacement, tons: 610 full load
Dimensions, feet (metres): 160·8 × 32 × 7·2 *(49 × 9·7 × 2·2)*
Main engines: 2 diesels; 1 000 bhp = 12 knots

Built at Toulon in 1957-58. LCT type with bow doors and ramp.

ISSOLE   1974, Michael D. J. Lennon

16 LCMs

CTM 1 to 16

Displacement, tons: 56 standard; 150 full load
Dimensions, feet (metres): 92·8 × 21 × 3·9 *(28·3 × 6·4 × 1·2)*
Main engines: Hispano diesels; 2 shafts; 225 hp = 9·5 knots
Complement: 6

Can carry up to 90 tons in coastal or protected waters. Built 1966-67. Bow ramp.

20 LCMs

Of varying displacements between 26 and 52 tons.

LIGHT FORCES

4 "TRIDENT" CLASS (FAST ATTACK CRAFT—MISSILE)

Note: Six more of a larger class (250-350 tons) to be built under 1977-81 programme.

Name	No.	Builders	Commissioned
TRIDENT	P 670	Auroux, Arcachon	17 Dec 1976
GLAIVE	P 671	Auroux, Arcachon	Mar 1977
EPÉE	P 672	C.M.N. Cherbourg	9 Oct 1976
PERTUISANE	P 673	C.M.N. Cherbourg	20 Jan 1977

Displacement, tons: 115 standard; 130 full load
Dimensions, feet (metres): 121·4 × 18 × 5·2 *(37 × 5·5 × 1·6)*
Missiles: 6—SS 12
Guns: 1—40 mm; 1—12·7 mm
Main engines: 2 AGO diesels; 2 shafts (cp propellers); 4 000 hp = 26 knots
Range, miles: 1 750 at 10 knots; 750 at 20 knots
Complement: 18 (1 officer and 17 men)

Trident laid down 3 Dec 1974, launched 31 May 1976; *Glaive*, 16 Jan 1975 and 27 Aug 1976; *Epée* 10 April 1975, 31 March 1976; *Pertuisane*, 26 Aug 1975 and 2 June 1976. These were intended as lead boats for a class of 30 in "Plan Bleu" of which 16 were to be adapted for overseas service. Like other craft of similar size they have proved too small for their intended role.
Trials for *Trident* started 1 Oct 1975.

PERTUISANE   6/1976, Contre-Amiral M. Adam

1 LA COMBATTANTE I TYPE (FAST ATTACK CRAFT—MISSILE)

Name	No.	Builders	Commissioned
LA COMBATTANTE	P 730	C.M.N. Cherbourg	1 Mar 1964

Displacement, tons: 180 standard; 202 full load
Dimensions, feet (metres): 147·8 × 24·2 × 6·5 *(45 × 7·4 × 2·5)*
Missiles: 1 quadruple launcher for SS 11
Guns: 2—40 mm
Main engines: 2 SEMT-Pielstick diesels; 2 shafts; controllable pitch propellers; 3 200 bhp = 23 knots
Range, miles: 2 000 at 12 knots
Complement: 25 (3 officers, 22 men)

LA COMBATTANTE   1974, Dr. Giorgio Arra

Authorised under the 1960 Programme. Laid down in April 1962, launched on 20 June 1963. Of wooden and plastic laminated non-magnetic construction. Can carry a raiding force of 80 for a very short run.

Gunnery. Flare launcher aft replaced by 40 mm Mk 3 gun before she left for Indian Ocean in 1975.

166 FRANCE

10 "SIRIUS" CLASS (LARGE PATROL CRAFT)

Name	No	Builder	Commissioned
ARCTURUS	P 650	C.N. Caen	1954
ALTAIR	P 656	C.M.N.	1956
CROIX DU SUD	P 658	Seine Maritime	1956
CANOPUS	P 659	Normand	1956
ÉTOILE POLAIRE	P 660	Seine Maritime	1957
ANTARES	P 703	C.M.N.	1954
VEGA	P 707	Penhoët	1953
ERIDAN	P 741	Penhoët	1955
SAGITTAIRE	P 743	Seine Maritime	1955
LYRE	P 759	Penhoët	1956

All of "Sirius" class minesweepers (see Minewarfare Section for details) transferred for coastal patrol operations 1973. Minesweeping gear removed. P 703, 707, 741, 743 in reserve.

CANOPUS 1975, J. van der Woude

3 "LE FOUGUEUX" CLASS (LARGE PATROL CRAFT)

Name	No	Builder	Commissioned
L'ARDENT	P 635	Normand	1959
LE FRINGANT	P 640	F. C. Mediterranée	1960
L'ADROIT	P 644	Lorient	1958

Displacement, tons: 325 standard; 400 full load
Dimensions, feet (metres): 173·9 × 24 × 10·2 *(53 × 7·3 × 3·1)*
Guns: 2—40 mm Bofors
A/S weapons: 1—120 mm A/S mortar; 2 DC mortars; 2 DC racks
Main engines: 4 SEMT-Pielstick diesel engines coupled 2 by 2; 3 240 bhp = 18·6 knots
Range, miles: 3 000 at 12 knots; 2 000 at 15 knots
Complement: 46 (4 officers, 42 men)

Originally class of 17.

Radar: One set Decca.

Sonar: One QCU2.

Similar classes: "Boavista" class (Portugal), one in Yugoslavia, one in W. Germany, one in Italy.

L'ADROIT 11/1977, Leo van Ginderen

6 Ex-CANADIAN "LA DUNKERQUOISE" CLASS (LARGE PATROL CRAFT)

Name	No.	Builders	Commissioned
LA MALOUINE (ex-HMCS *Cowichan*)	P 651	Davie SB	1952
LA LORIENTAISE (ex-HMCS *Miramichi*)	P 652	St John DD	1953
LA DUNKERQUOISE (ex-HMCS *Fundy*)	P 653	St John DD	1952
LA BAYONNAISE (ex-HMCS *Chignecto*)	P 654	Marine Industries	1954
LA DIEPPOISE (ex-HMCS *Chaleur*)	P 655	P. Arthur SY	1952
LA PAIMPOLAISE (ex-HMCS *Thunder*)	P 657	Vickers	1953

Displacement, tons: 370 full load; 470 standard
Dimensions, feet (metres): 164 × 30·2 × 9·2 *(50 × 9·2 × 2·8)*
Gun: 1—40 mm
Main engines: General Motors diesels; 2 shafts; 2 500 bhp = 15 knots
Oil fuel, tons: 52
Range, miles: 4 500 at 11 knots
Complement: 35 (4 officers, 31 men)

LA DIEPPOISE (old pennant number) 1971, French Navy

La Malouine (launched 12 Nov 1951) and *La Paimpolaise* (launched 17 July 1953) were transferred to the French flag at Halifax on 1 April 1954, *Dunkerquoise* (launched 17 July 1953) on 30 April 1954, and *La Dieppoise* (launched 21 June 1952) and *La Lorientaise* (launched in 1953) on 10 Oct 1954. All similar to the "Bay" class in the Canadian Forces. All transferred from minesweeping to overseas patrol operations 1973. They have been air conditioned.

Reserve: *La Malouine* and *La Bayonnaise* to reserve 1976.

5 Ex-BRITISH "HAM" CLASS (LARGE PATROL CRAFT)

Name	No.	Builders	Commissioned
JASMIN (ex-HMS *Stedham*, ex-M 776)	P 661	Blackmore, Bideford	1955
PETUNIA (ex-HMS *Pineham*, ex-M 789)	P 662	McLean, Renfrew	1956
GÉRANIUM (ex-HMS *Tibenham* ex-M 784)	P 784	McGruer	1955
JONQUILLE (ex-HMS *Sulham*, ex-M 787)	P 787	Fairlie Yacht Co	1955
PAQUERETTE (ex-HMS *Kingham*, ex-M 775)	P 789	J. S. White	1955

Displacement, tons: 140 standard; 170 full load
Dimensions, feet (metres): 100 pp; 106·5 oa × 21·2 × 5·5 *(32·4 × 6·5 × 1·7)*
Gun: 1—20 mm Oerlikon forward
Main engines: 2 Paxman diesels; 550 bhp = 14 knots
Oil fuel, tons: 15
Complement: 12 (2 officers, 10 men)

Former British inshore minesweepers of the "Ham" class transferred to France under the US "off-shore" procurement programme in 1955. Now used as patrol craft, *Geranium*, *Jonquille* and *Paquerette* by Gendarmerie Maritime. *Violette* replaced *Paquerette* A 742 in 1976, taking her place as a tender and assuming her number.

GERANIUM 1976, Michael D. J. Lennon

1 FAIRMILE ML TYPE (LARGE PATROL CRAFT)

OISEAU DES ILES A 716

Displacement, tons: 140 full load
Dimensions, feet (metres): 111·5 × 18·4 × 4·3 *(34 × 5·6 × 1·3)*
Speed, knots: 11·5

Former Fairmile motor launch used for training frogmen.

4 TECIMAR TYPE (COASTAL PATROL CRAFT)

| P 770 | P 771 | P 772 | P 774 |

Displacement, tons: 30
Dimensions, feet (metres): 43·6 × 13·4 × 3·5 *(13·3 × 4·1 × 1·1)*
Guns: 1—12·7 mm MG; 1—7·5 mm MG
Main engines: 2 GM diesels; 480 bhp = 25 knots

Hulls of moulded polyester. Built for gendarmerie in 1974.

FRANCE 167

1 COASTAL PATROL CRAFT

TOURMALINE A 714

Displacement, tons: 45
Dimensions, feet (metres): 88 × 16.8 × 4.8 *(26.8 × 5.1 × 1.5)*
Gun: 1—20 mm
Main engines: 2 diesels; 1 120 hp = 27 knots
Complement: 9

Completed 1974 by Ch. Navals de L'Esterel for training duties.

1 COASTAL PATROL CRAFT

Y 760 (ex-*P 9786*)

Displacement, tons: 45
Dimensions, feet (metres): 79.3 × 14.8 × 4.2 *(24.2 × 4.5 × 1.3)*
Guns: 8—0.5 MG (4 twin mountings)
Main engines: 2 Daimler-Benz (MTU) diesels; 2 shafts; 1 000 bhp = 18 knots

Built by Bodenwerft-Kressbronn. Completed in 1954.

MINE WARFARE FORCES

1 + 14 MODIFIED "CIRCÉ" CLASS (MINEHUNTERS)

Displacement, tons: 510 standard; 544 full load
Dimensions, feet (metres): 161 × 29.2 × 8.2 *(49.1 × 8.9 × 2.5)*
Gun: 1—20mm
Main engines: 1 Werkspoor diesel; 1 shaft (single anti-clockwise vp screw by LIPS); 2 280 bhp; 2 active rudders
Speed, knots: 15
Range, miles: 3 000 at 12 knots
Complement: 22 to 45 (see note)

Belgium, France and the Netherlands have agreed to build 15 of this design each with a joint bureau de programme in Paris. Each country will build its own GRP hulls to a central design. Belgium will provide all the electrical installations, France all the minehunting gear and some electronics and the Netherlands the propulsion systems. Netherlands ships classified as "Alkmaak" class.
The French ships will be built at Lorient where the prototype was laid down in 1976 for completion for trials in 1979. Twelve more to be built under 1977-81 Plan and two later.

Complement: For simple tasks a crew of 22 will be adequate, increasing to 45 for major minehunting operations.

Electronics and Navigation: Auto pilot and hovering; automatic radar navigation; Nav-aids by Loran and Syledis; Evec data system.

Minehunting and sweeping: 2 French PAP 104; Medium depth mechanical sweep gear.

Propulsion: Bow thruster and auxiliary system of 2-88 kw Wullocks = 7 knots.

Radar: One Decca 1229.

Sonar: One DUBM 21A

Tasks: Minehunting, minesweeping, patrol, training, directing ship for unmanned mine sweeping, HQ ship for diving operations and pollution control. Pre-packed 5 ton modules of equipment to be embarked for separate tasks.

5 "CIRCÉ" CLASS (MINEHUNTERS)

Name	No.	Builders	Commissioned
CYBÈLE	M 712	C.M. de Normandie	28 Sep 1972
CALLIOPE	M 713	C.M. de Normandie	28 Sep 1972
CLIO	M 714	C.M. de Normandie	18 May 1972
CIRCÉ	M 715	C.M. de Normandie	18 May 1972
CERES	M 716	C.M. de Normandie	8 Mar 1973

Displacement, tons: 460 standard; 495 normal; 510 full load
Dimensions, feet (metres): 167 oa × 29.2 × 11.15 *(50.9 × 8.9 × 3.4)*
Gun: 1—20 mm
Main engines: 1 MTU diesel; single axial screw; 1 800 bhp = 15 knots (2 active rudders)
Range, miles: 3 000 at 12 knots
Complement: 48 (4 officers, 44 men)

Ordered in 1968. *Circé* launched 15 Dec 1970; *Clio* launched 10 June 1971; *Calliope* launched 21 Nov 1971; *Cybèle* launched Jan 1972; *Ceres* launched 10 Aug 1972.

Minehunting: All ships are fitted with DUBM 20 minehunting sonar. The 9 foot *(2.74 metres)* long PAP is propelled by two electric motors at 6 knots and is wire-guided to a maximum range of 500 m. Fitted with a television camera, this machine detects the mine and lays its 100 kgm charge nearby. This is then detonated by an ultra-sonic signal.

Minesweeping: These ships carry no normal minesweeping equipment.

CYBELE 6/1975, Dr. Giorgio Arra

13 Ex-US "AGGRESSIVE" and "MSO-498" CLASS
(MINESWEEPERS—OCEAN and MINEHUNTERS)

NARVIK (ex-*MSO 512*) M 609
OUISTREHAM (ex-*MSO 513*) M 610
ALENCON (ex-*MSO 453*) M 612
BERNEVAL (ex-*MSO 450*) M 613
CANTHO (ex-*MSO 476*) M 615
DOMPAIRE (ex-*MSO 454*) M 616
GARIGLIANO (ex-*MSO 452*) M 617
MYTHO (ex-*MSO 475*) M 618
VINH LONG (ex-*MSO 477*) M 619
BERLAIMONT (ex-*MSO 500*) M 620
AUTUN (ex-*MSO 502*) M 622
BACCARAT (ex-*MSO 505*) M 623
COLMAR (ex-*MSO 514*) M 624

Displacement, tons: 700 standard; 780 full load
Dimensions, feet (metres): 165 wl; 171 oa × 35 × 10.3 *(50.3; 52.1 × 10.7 × 3.2)*
Gun: 1—40 mm
Main engines: 2 GM diesels; 2 shafts; vp propellers; 1 600 bhp = 13.5 knots
Oil fuel, tons: 47
Range, miles: 3 000 at 10 knots
Complement: 58 (5 officers, 53 men)

The USA transferred these MSOs to France in three batches during 1953. *Bir Hacheim* M 614 (ex-*MSO 451*) was returned to the US Navy at Brest on 4 Sep 1970 and transferred to Uruguayan navy, being renamed *Maldonado*. *Origny* converted for survey duties in 1960.

Appearance: *Autun, Baccarat, Berlaimont, Colmar, Narvik* and *Ouistreham* have a taller funnel.

Minehunters: *Cantho, Dompaire, Garigliano, Mytho* and *Vinh Long* converted for minehunting between 1975 and 1977. *Dompaire* commissioned as minehunter Jan 1976.
Autun, Baccarat, Berlaimont, Colmar and *Ouistreham* being converted as from 1976 to complete between 1 May 1977—Jan 1979. Considerable change in appearance results.
Berneval and *Alençon* will be converted when the above are completed.

Trials: *Narvik* engaged in trials of AP 4 sweep and lenticular sonar.

OUISTREHAM (tall funnel) 1976, Michael D. J. Lennon

GARIGLIANO (squat funnel) 1976, Michael D. J. Lennon

168 FRANCE

6 "SIRIUS" CLASS (MINESWEEPERS—COASTAL)

CAPRICORNE (8 Aug 1956) M 737
BETELGEUSE (12 July 1954) M 747
PHÉNIX (23 May 1955) M 749
CAPELLA (6 Sep 1955) M 755
CÉPHÉE (3 Jan 1956) M 756
VERSEAU (26 April 1956) M 757

Displacement, tons: 400 standard; 440 full load
Dimensions, feet (metres): 140 pp; 152 oa × 28 × 8·2 (42·7; 46·4 × 8·6 × 2·5)
Guns: 1—40 mm Bofors; 1—20 mm Oerlikon (several have 2—20 mm)
Main engines: SIGMA free piston generators and Alsthom or Rateau-Bretagne gas turbines or SEMT-Pielstick 16-cyl diesels; 2 shafts; 2 000 bhp = 15 knots (11·5 knots when sweeping)
Oil fuel, tons: 48
Range, miles: 3 000 at 10 knots
Complement: 38 (3 officers, 35 men)

Of wooden and aluminium alloy construction. Of same general characteristics as the British "Ton" class, Bételgeuse, Capella, Capricorne, Céphée, Lyre, Phénix and Verseau have SEMT-Pielstick diesels. Launch dates above. Built by CMN, Cherbourg.

Reserve: Antares, Lyre, Eridan, Sagittaire and Vega to reserve as patrol craft 1977.

Transfers: Three of this class, built in France and originally numbered D 25, 26 and 27 (now called Hrabri, Smeli and Slobodni), were joined by Snazni (built in Yugoslavia) after their transfer to Yugoslavia in 1957. Fomalhaut, Orion, Pollux and Procyon were returned to the USN in 1970, Achernar and Centaure in 1971. Aries (M 758) loaned to Morocco for four years 1974.

CAPRICORNE (20 mm guns)   1976, Michael D. J. Lennon

15 Ex-US "ADJUTANT" CLASS (MINESWEEPERS—COASTAL)

PERVENCHE (ex-MSC 141) M 632
PIVOINE (ex-MSC 125) M 633
RÉSÉDA (ex-MSC 126) M 635*
ACACIA (ex-MSC 69) M 638*
ACANTHE (ex-MSC 70) M 639
AZALÉE (ex-MSC 67) M 668*
CAMÉLIA (ex-MSC 68) M 671
CYCLAMEN (ex-MSC 119) M 674*
EGLANTINE (ex-MSC 117) M 675*
GLYCINE (ex-MSC 118) M 679
LAURIER (ex-MSC 86) M 681
LILAS (ex-MSC 93) M 682
LOBÉLIA (ex-MSC 96) M 684*
MIMOSA (ex-MSC 99) M 687
MUGUET (ex-MSC 97) M 688

*See Status notes

Displacement, tons: 300 standard; 372 full load
Dimensions, feet (metres): 136·2 pp; 141 oa × 26 × 8·3 (43 × 8 × 2·6)
Guns: 2—20 mm
Main engines: 2 GM diesels; 2 shafts; 1 200 bhp = 13 knots (8 sweeping)
Oil fuel, tons: 40
Range, miles: 2 500 at 10 knots
Complement: 38 (3 officers, 35 men)

The USA agreed in Sep 1952 to allocate to France in 1953, 36 new AMS (later redesignated MSC) under the Mutual Defence Assistance Programme, but only 30 were finally transferred to France in 1953.

Deletions:
Bleuét and Chrysanthème cannibalized for spares—1976 onwards.

Status: Réséda, Acacia, Azalée, Cyclamen, Eglantine and Lobelia no longer maintained in anti-magnetic state.

Transfers:
(a) Six of the class were not taken up by France—two (MSC 139 and 143) to Spain; two to Japan (MSC 95, 144) and two retained by USA.
(b) Marguerite (ex-MSC 94) M 686 returned to USA and transferred to Uruguay as Rio Negro 10 Nov 1969.
(c) Pavot (ex-MSC 124) M 631 and Renoncule (ex-MSC 142) M 634 returned to USA and transferred to Turkey on 24 Mar 1970 and 19 Nov 1970 respectively.
(d) Coquelicot (ex-MSC 84) M 673 to Tunisia in 1973.
(e) Bégonia (ex-MSC 83) M 669 and Glaieul (ex-MSC 120) M 678 returned to USA 1974.
(f) Marjolaine to Tunisia 26 July 1977.

LAURIER   7/1976, Dr. Giorgio Arra

Change of Task:
(a) Ajonc (ex-M 667) A 701 to diving training ship—1974.
(b) Liseron (ex-M 683) A 723 and Gardénia (ex-M 676) A 711 to clearance-diving base ship. Magnolia M 685 to join this task in 1976.
(c) Jacinthe M 680 to minelaying duties in 1968.
(d) Acacia M 638, Azalée M 668 and Lobélia M 684 to reserve 1976.
(e) Réséda M 635, Cyclamen M 674 and Eglantine M 675 to reserve 1977.

1 SPECIAL TYPE DB 1 (MINESWEEPER—COASTAL)

Name	No.	Builders	Commissioned
MERCURE	M 765	Mecaniques de Normandie	Dec 1958

Displacement, tons: 333 light; 365 normal; 400 full load
Dimensions, feet (metres): 137·8 pp; 145·5 oa × 27 × 8·5 (44·4 × 8·3 × 4)
Guns: 2—20 mm
Main engines: 2 Mercedes-Benz (MTU) diesels; 2 shafts; Kamewa variable pitch propellers; 4 000 bhp = 15 knots
Oil fuel, tons: 48
Range, miles: 3 000 at 15 knots
Complement: 48

Ordered in France under the "off-shore" programme. Laid down in Jan 1955. Launched on 21 Dec 1957. Will be fitted as fishery protection vessel. Currently in reserve.

Foreign sales: Six built for West Germany, five of which were later transferred to Turkey, the sixth now being a research ship.

MERCURE   1968, French Navy

OCEANOGRAPHIC AND SURVEY SHIPS

Note: (a) These ships are painted white. (b) A total of 20 officers and 74 technicians with oceanographic and hydrographic training is employed in addition to the ships' companies listed here. They occupy the extra billets marked as "scientists".

Name	No.	Builders	Commissioned
D'ENTRECASTEAUX	A 757	Brest Naval Dockyard	10 Oct 1970

Displacement, tons: 2 400 full load
Dimensions, feet (metres): 292 × 42·7 × 14·4 (89 × 13 × 4·4)
Main engines: 2 diesel-electric; 1 000 kW; 2 controllable pitch propellers; speed: 15 knots
Auxiliary engines: 2 Schottel trainable and retractable
Aircraft: 1 helicopter
Range, miles: 10 000 at 12 knots
Complement: 79 (6 officers, 73 men plus 38 scientific staff)

This ship was specially designed for oceanographic surveys capable of working to 6 000 metres. Accommodation for 38 scientists. Hangar for Alouette II helicopter. Carries one LCPS and three survey launches.

Radar: Two sets.
Sonar: Two sets.

D'ENTRECASTEAUX   1975, Wright and Logan

FRANCE 169

Name	No.	Builders	Commissioned
ESPÉRANCE (ex-*Jacques Coeur*)	A 756	Gdynia	see note
ESTAFETTE (ex-*Jacques Cartier*)	A 766	Gdynia	see note

Displacement, tons: 956 standard; 1 360 full load
Dimensions, feet (metres): 208·3 × 32·1 × 19·4 *(63·5 × 9·8 × 5·9)*
Main engines: MAN diesels; 1 850 bhp = 15 knots
Range, miles: 7 500 at 13 knots
Complement: 32 (3 officers, 29 men plus scientists)

Former trawlers built in 1962 at Gdynia and purchased in 1968-69. Adapted as survey ships commissioning in 1969 and 1972. Can carry 14 scientists.

ESPÉRANCE   10/1977, Leo van Ginderen

Name	No.	Builders	Commissioned
LA RECHERCHE (ex-*Guyane*)	A 758	Chantiers Ziegler, Dunkirk	see note

Displacement, tons: 810 standard; 910 full load
Dimensions, feet (metres): 221·5 oa × 34·2 × 13 *(67·5 × 10·4 × 4·5)*
Main engines: 1 Werkspoor diesel; 1 535 bhp = 13·5 knots
Range, miles: 3 100 at 10 knots
Complement: 23 (2 officers, 21 men) (plus 43 scientists)

Former passenger motor vessel. Launched in April 1951. Purchased in 1960 and converted by Cherbourg Dockyard into a surveying ship. Commissioned into the French Navy in March 1961 and her name changed from *Guyane* to *La Recherche*. To improve stability she was fitted with bulges. Now comes under the Ministry for Overseas Affairs.

LA RECHERCHE   1975, Dr. Giorgio Arra

1 "BERNEVAL" CLASS

ORIGNY A 640

Displacement, tons: 700 standard; 780 full load
Dimensions, feet (metres): 171 × 35 × 10·5 *(52·2 × 10·7 × 3·2)*
Gun: 1—40 mm
Main engines: 2 GM diesels; 2 shafts; 1 600 bhp = 13·5 knots
Range, miles: 3 000 at 10 knots
Complement: 52

Launched Feb 1955 as a Minesweeper—Ocean of "Berneval" class. Converted for Oceanographic research 1961-62.

ORIGNY   1974, Wright and Logan

Name	No.	Builders	Commissioned
L'ASTROLABE	A 780	Chantiers de la Seine Maritime, Le Trait	1964
BOUSSOLE	A 781	Chantiers de la Seine Maritime, Le Trait	1964

Displacement, tons: 330 standard; 440 full load
Dimensions, feet (metres): 140 × 27·9 × 9·5 *(42·7 × 8·5 × 2·9)*
Guns: 1—40 mm; 2 MG *(L'Astrolabe* only)
Main engines: 2 Baudoin DV.8 diesels; 1 shaft; variable pitch propeller; 800 bhp = 13 knots
Range, miles: 4 000 at 12 knots
Complement: 33 (1 officer, 32 men)

Authorised under the 1961 Programme. Specially designed for surveys in tropical waters. Laid down in 1962, launched on 27 May and 11 April 1963 respectively. Each ship carries a crane on either side of the funnel and has two 4·5 ton wireless-equipped survey craft.

L'ASTROLABE   3/1976, Michael D. J. Lennon

OCTANT (ex-*Michel Marie*) A 683

Displacement, tons: 128 standard; 133 full load
Dimensions, feet (metres): 78·7 × 20 × 10·5 *(24 × 6·1 × 3·2)*
Main engines: 2 diesels; 1 shaft; vp propeller; 200 bhp = 9 knots
Range, miles: 2 000 at 7 knots
Endurance: 12 days
Complement: 13 (12 men)

Small fishing trawler purchased by the Navy and converted into survey craft by the Constructions Mécaniques de Normandie at Cherbourg as tender to *La Recherche*. Wooden hull and steel upperworks. Conversion completed on 20 Dec 1962. Commissioned in 1963. Sister *Alidade* deleted April 1977.

OCTANT   6/1975, Dr. Giorgio Arra

170 FRANCE

1 INSHORE SURVEY CRAFT

Name	No.	Builders	Commissioned
CORAIL (ex-Marc Joly)	A 794	Thuin, Belgium	1967

Displacement, tons: 54·8 light
Dimensions, feet (metres): 58·4 × 16·1 × 5·9 (17·8 × 4·9 × 1·8)
Main engines: 1 Caterpillar diesel; 250 bhp = 10·3 knots
Complement: 7

Operating in New Caledonia from 1974.

SERVICE FORCES

2 + 1 "DURANCE" CLASS
(UNDERWAY REPLENISHMENT TANKERS)

Name	No.	Builders	Commissioned
MEUSE	A 607	Brest Naval Dockyard	—
DURANCE	A 629	Brest Naval Dockyard	Dec 1976

Displacement, tons: 17 800 full load
Dimensions, feet (metres): 515·9 × 69·5 × 28·5 (157·3 × 21·2 × 8·7)
Aircraft: 1 WG 13 Lynx helicopter
Guns: 2—40 mm
Main engines: 2 diesels SEMT-Pielstick 16 PC 2·5; 2 shafts; vp propellers 20 000 hp = 19 knots
Oil fuel, tons: 750
Range, miles: 9 000 at 15 knots
Complement: 150 (45 passengers)

Durance laid down 1973, launched 6 Sep 1975. Helicopter hangar. Classed as PRE (Pétrolier Ravitailleur d'Escadre). A second of this class, *Meuse* is in the 1976 Estimates and a third is to follow. *Meuse* laid down 1977 for launching in 1978 when third ship will be laid down.

Capacity: *Durance* can carry a total of 10 000 tonnes (7 500 FFO, 1 500 diesel, 500 TR5 Avcat, 130 distilled water, 170 victuals, 150 munitions, 50 naval stores). *Meuse* to carry 5 000 FFO, 3 200 diesel, 1 800 TR5 Avcat and the rest as in *Durance*.

Transfer: Four beam positions and one astern, two of the beam positions having heavy transfer capability.

DURANCE   1976, French Navy

1 UNDERWAY REPLENISHMENT TANKER and COMMAND SHIP

Name	No.	Builders	Commissioned
LA CHARENTE (ex-*Beaufort*)	A 626	Holdens Mek Verksted, Tönsberg	1957

Displacement, tons: 7 440 light; 26 000 full load
Dimensions, feet (metres): 587·2 × 72 × 34·1 (179 × 21·9 × 10·4)
Guns: 4—40 mm
Main engines: 1 General Electric geared turbine; 1 screw = 17·5 knots
Boilers: 2
Complement: 100 (6 officers, 94 men)

Former Norwegian tanker. Purchased by the French Navy in May 1964. Now converted for service as flagship of the Flag Officer commanding Indian Ocean forces. Fitted with helicopter platform and hangar and carries LCVP. Stern transfer position.

LA CHARENTE (after conversion)   1974, French Navy

1 UNDERWAY REPLENISHMENT TANKER

Name	No.	Builders	Commissioned
ISÈRE (ex-*La Mayenne*, ex-*Caltex Strasbourg*)	A 675	Ch. Seine Maritime	see note

Displacement, tons: 7 440 standard; 26 700 full load
Dimensions, feet (metres): 559 × 71·2 × 30·3 (170·4 × 21·7 × 9·3)
Main engines: 1 single geared Parsons turbine; 8 260 shp = 16 knots
Boilers: 2
Complement: 92 (6 officers, 86 men)

Launched on 22 June 1959. Former French tanker. Purchased in 1965. Fitted for two beam fuelling positions as well as stern rig.

ISÈRE   11/1975, Dr. Giorgio Arra

1 UNDERWAY REPLENISHMENT TANKER

Name	No.	Builders	Commissioned
LA SAÔNE	A 628	A. C. France	1948

Displacement, tons: 8 550 light; 24 200 full load
Dimensions, feet (metres): 525 × 72·5 × 33 (160 × 22·1 × 10)
Guns: 3—40 mm
Main engines: Parsons geared turbines; 2 shafts; 15 800 shp = 18 knots
Boilers: 3 Penhoet
Complement: 177 (9 officers, 168 men)

Ordered as fleet tanker. Completed as merchant tanker in 1948. Returned to the French Navy from charter company in Sep 1953. *La Saône* was fitted as a fleet replenishment ship in 1961. Carries 9 100 tons of fuel, 730 tons of diesel fuel, 200 tons of fresh provisions and wine tanks holding 82 000 litres. Fitted with automatic tensioning. Two heavy transfer positions abeam and two positions aft.
La Seine paid off 13 Oct 1976. *La Saône* due for replacement 1980.

LA SAÔNE   3/1976, Reinhard Nerlich

FRANCE 171

1 SUPPORT TANKER

Name	No.	Builders	Commissioned
ABER WRACH (ex-CA 1)	A 619	Cherbourg	1966

Displacement, tons: 1 220 standard; 3 500 full load
Dimensions, feet (metres): 284 oa × 40 × 19 (86·6 × 12·2 × 5·8)
Gun: 1—40 mm
Main engines: 1 diesel; vp propeller; 3 000 bhp = 12 knots
Range, miles: 5 000 at 12 knots
Complement: 48 (3 officers, 45 men)

Authorised in 1956. Ordered in 1959. Laid down in 1961. The after part with engine room was launched on 24 April 1963. The fore part was built on the vacated slip, launched and welded to the after part. Complete hull floated up on 21 Nov 1963. Carries white oil, lubricating oil and petrol—2 220 tons.

ABER WRACH   1977, Michael D. J. Lennon

2 SUPPORT TANKERS

PAPENOO (ex-Norwegian *Bow Queen*) A 625
PUNARUU (ex-Norwegian *Bow Cecil*) A 632

Displacement, tons: 1 195 standard; 2 927 full load
Dimensions, feet (metres): 272·2 × 45·6 × 19·0 (83 × 13·9 × 5·8)
Main engines: 2 diesels; 1 vp screw; 2 050 hp = 12 knots (bow screw in addition)

Two small Norwegian built tankers added to the navy in late 1969. Capacity 2 500 cu. m. (ten tanks). Have replenishment at sea facility astern.

PUNARUU   1975, French Navy

1 SUPPORT TANKER

LAC TONLÉ SAP A 630

Displacement, tons: 800 light; 2 700 full load
Dimensions, feet (metres): 235 × 37 × 15·8 (71·7 × 11·3 × 4·8)
Guns: 3—20 mm
Main engines: 2 Fairbanks-Morse diesels; 1 150 bhp = 11 knots
Range, miles: 6 300 at 11 knots
Complement: 37 (2 officers, 35 men)

Ex-US Oil Barge acquired in 1945. Due to stay in service until 1981. Has replenishment at sea facility abeam.

LAC TONLÉ SAP   1973, French Navy

1 SUPPORT TANKER

Name	No.	Builders	Commissioned
SAHEL	A 638	Chantiers Naval de Caen	Aug 1951

Displacement, tons: 630 light; 1 450 full load
Measurement, tons: 650 deadweight
Dimensions, feet (metres): 176·2 × 29·5 × 14·5 (53·7 × 9 × 4·5)
Guns: 2—20 mm
Main engines: 2 diesels; 1 400 bhp = 12 knots

SAHEL   1972, Dr. Giorgio Arra

5 "RHIN" CLASS (DEPOT SHIPS)

Name	No.	Builders	Commissioned
LOIRE	A 615	Lorient Naval Dockyard	10 Oct 1967
GARONNE	A 617	Lorient Naval Dockyard	1 Sep 1965
RANCE	A 618	Lorient Naval Dockyard	5 Feb 1966
RHIN	A 621	Lorient Naval Dockyard	1 Mar 1964
RHÔNE	A 622	Lorient Naval Dockyard	1 Dec 1964

Displacement, tons: 2 075 standard; 2 445 full load (*Rhin, Rance* and *Rhône*) 2 320 standard (*Garonne* and *Loire*)
Dimensions, feet (metres): 302·0 pp; 331·5 oa × 43·0 × 12·1 (92·1; 101·1 × 13·1 × 3·7)
Guns: 3—40 mm; 1—40 mm (*Garonne*)
Aircraft: 1 to 3 Alouette helicopters (except *Garonne* and *Loire*)
Landing craft: 2 LCP
Main engines: 2 SEMT-Pielstick diesels (16PA2V in *Rhin* and *Rhône*, 12PA4 in *Rance, Loire* and *Garonne*); 1 shaft; 3 300 bhp = 16·5 knots
Range, miles: 13 000 at 13 knots
Complement: *Rhin* and *Rhône* 148 (6 officers, 142 men); *Rance* 150 (10 officers, 140 men) and about 118 passengers; *Garonne* 221 (10 officers, 211 men); *Loire* 140 (9 officers, 131 men)

Designed for supporting various classes of ships. Have a 5 ton crane, carry two LCPs and have a helicopter platform (except *Garonne*). *Rhin* and *Rhône* have a hangar and carry an Alouette helicopter. *Rance* carries three in her hangar and *Loire* has only the helicopter platform. *Garonne* is designed as a Repair Workshop, *Loire* for minesweeper support, *Rance* for laboratory and radiological services, *Rhin* for electronic maintenance and *Rhône* for submarines.

Radar: One DRBV 50 (in *Rhin* and *Rhône*).

LOIRE (RHIN and RHÔNE similar)   10/1977, Michael D. J. Lennon

RANCE   11/1975, Dr. Giorgio Arra

172 FRANCE

1 MAINTENANCE SHIP

Name	No.	Builders	Commissioned
MOSELLE (ex-*Foucauld*)	A 608	Swan, Hunter & Wigham Richardson Ltd, Wallsend-on-Tyne	1948

Displacement, tons: 8 200 standard; 8 700 full load
Dimensions, feet (metres): 480 oa × 62 × 22·3 *(146·3 × 18·9 × 6·9)*
Main engines: 2 Doxford diesels; 2 shafts; 8 800 bhp = 15 knots
Complement: 177 (7 officers, 170 men)

Former motor passenger ship of the Chargeurs Réunis (West Africa Coast Service). Launched on 17 July 1947. *Moselle* was converted in 1967. Used as Base Ship in Pacific Trial Centre. Can carry 500 passengers.

MOSELLE 1976, Michael D. J. Lennon

1 MAINTENANCE and REPAIR SHIP

Name	No.	Builders	Commissioned
JULES VERNE (ex-*Achéron*)	A 620	Brest Naval Dockyard	1 June 1976

Displacement, tons: 6 485 standard; 10 250 full load
Dimensions, feet (metres): 482·2 × 70·5 × 21·3 *(147 × 21·5 × 6·5)*
Aircraft: 2 Helicopters
Guns: 2—40 mm
Main engines: 2 diesels SEMT-Pielstick; 1 shaft; 21 500 hp = 18 knots
Range, miles: 9 500 at 18 knots
Complement: 323 (20 officers, 303 men)

Ordered in 1961 budget, originally as an Armament Supply Ship. Role and design changed whilst building—now rated as Engineering and Electrical Maintenance Ship. Launched 30 May 1970. Currently serving in Indian Ocean. Carries stocks of torpedoes and ammunition.

JULES VERNE 3/1976, J. van der Woude

2 REPAIR SHIPS (Ex-LCT)

L 9081   L9084

Displacement, tons: 310 standard; 685 full load
Dimensions, feet (metres): 193·5 × 39 × 5 *(59 × 11·9 × 1·6)*
Main engines: 2 diesels MGO; 1 000 bhp = 8 knots
Range, miles: 1 800 at 8 knots
Complement: 15

Built in 1964-65 by Ch. N. Franco-Belge. Repair facilities grafted onto LCT hulls. 9081 is fitted with mechanical workshops, and 9084 is primarily an electrical stores ship.

Ex-LCT 1972, Dr. Giorgio Arra

4 SUPPLY TENDERS

Name	No.	Builders	Commissioned
CHAMOIS	A 767	La Perrière, Lorient	30 April 1976
ELAN	A 768	La Perrière, Lorient	1977
CHEVREUIL	A 774	La Perrière, Lorient	1977
GAZELLE	A 775	La Perrière, Lorient	1978

Displacement, tons: 495 full load
Dimensions, feet (metres): 136·1 × 24·6 × 10·5 *(41·5 × 7·5 × 3·2)*
Main engines: 2 diesels SACM AGO V-16; 2 vp propellers; 2 200 hp = 15 knots
Complement: 10 (10 spare berths)

Similar to the standard FISH oil rig support ships. Fitted with one 30 ton crane and one hydraulic crane (5·6 tons at 5 metres). Can act as tugs, oil pollution vessels, salvage craft (2—30 ton and 2—5 ton winches), coastal and harbour controlled minelaying, torpedo recovery, diving tenders and a variety of other tasks. Bow thruster of 80 hp and twin rudders. Can carry 100 tons of stores on deck or 125 tons of fuel and 40 tons of water or 65 tons of fuel and 120 tons of water. Five more planned.
Elan laid down 16 Mar 1977; *Chevreuil* laid down 15 Sep 1976, launched 4 Mar 1977; *Gazelle* laid down 30 Dec 1976, launched 7 June 1977.

1 VICTUALLING STORES SHIP

SAINTONGE (ex-*Santa Maria*) A 733

Measurement, tons: 300 standard; 990 full load
Dimensions, feet (metres): 177 × 28 × 10·5 *(54 × 8·5 × 3·2)*
Main engines: 1 diesel; 1 shaft; 760 bhp = 10 knots
Complement: 15

Built by Chantiers Duchesne et Bossière, Le Havre, for a Norwegian owner under the name of *Sven Germa*. Launched on 12 July 1956. Purchased in April 1965 from the firm of H. Beal & Co, Fort de France for the Pacific Nuclear Experimental Centre. Now serves in Indian Ocean.

FRANCE 173

TRIALS/RESEARCH SHIPS

Name	No.	Builders	Commissioned
HENRI POINCARÉ (ex-*Maina Marasso*)	A 603	Cantieri Riuniti de Adriaticos, Monfalcone	—

Displacement, tons: 24 000 full load
Dimensions, feet (metres): 565·0 pp; 590·6 oa × 72·8 × 28·9 *(180 × 22·2 × 9·4)*
Guns: 2—20 mm
Main engines: 1 Parsons geared turbine; 1 shaft; 10 000 shp = 15 knots
Boilers: 2 Foster Wheeler high pressure water tube
Range, miles: 11 800 at 13·5 knots
Complement: 214 + 9 (11 officers, 9 civilians, 203 men)

Launched in Oct 1960. Former Italian tanker. Purchased in Sep 1964. Converted in Brest dockyard from 1 Oct 1964 to 1967. To work with the experimental guided missile station in the Landes (SW France). Named after the mathematician and scientist.

Aircraft: Can land heavy helicopters and has space for two large or five light helicopters in her hangar.

Operations: She is primarily a missile-range-ship and acts as Flagship of Force M, the trials squadron of the French Navy. To enable her to plot the trajectory etc of missiles fired from land or sea she is equipped with three tracking radars, a telemetry station, transit nav-aid, cinetheodolite, infra-red tracking as well as an up-to-date fit of hull-mounted sonar, meteorological and oceanographic equipment.

Radar: One Savoie, two Bearn, one DRBV 22D.

HENRI POINCARÉ   7/1976, Michael D. J. Lennon

ILE D'OLÉRON (ex-*Munchen*, ex-*Mur*) A 610

Displacement, tons: 5 500 standard; 6 500 full load
Dimensions, feet (metres): 350·0 pp; 378 × 50·0 × 21·3 *(106·7 pp; 115·2 oa × 15·2 × 6·5)*
Main engines: MAN 6-cyl diesels; 1 shaft; 3 500 bhp
Speed, knots: 14·5
Oil fuel, tons: 340
Range, miles: 7 200 at 12 knots
Complement: 195 (12 officers, 183 men)

Launched in Germany in 1939. Taken as a war prize. Formerly rated as a transport. Converted to experimental guided missile ship in 1957-58 by Chantiers de Provence and l'Arsenal de Toulon. Commissioned early in 1959. Equipped with stabilisers.

Experimental: When converted, was designed for experiments with two launchers for ship-to-air missiles, the medium range Masurca and the long range Masalca, and one launcher for ship to shore missiles, the Malaface. Latterly fitted with one launcher for target planes. Now fitted for trials on MM 38 Exocet and for Crotale trials from 1977.

Radar: One DRBV 22C, one DRBV 50, one DRBI 10.
The missile system tracking radar operates in G band.

ILE D'OLÉRON   9/1976, Dr. Giorgio Arra

1 TRIALS SHIP

Name	No.	Builders	Commissioned
AUNIS (ex-*Regina Pacis*)	A 643	Roland Werft, Bremen	see note

Displacement, tons: 2 900 full load
Dimensions, feet (metres): 283·8 × 38 × 15 *(86·5 × 11·6 × 4·6)*
Main engines: MAN diesels geared to 1 shaft; 2 400 bhp = 12 knots
Range, miles: 4 500 at 12 knots

Launched on 3 July 1956. Purchased in Nov 1966 from Scotto Ambrosino & Pugliese and converted in Toulon 1972-73. Employed as trials ship in Operation Cormoran with deep sonar. Sonar transferred from *Duperré*.

AUNIS   1975, Wright and Logan

1 TRIALS SHIP

BERRY (ex-M/S *Médoc*) A 644

Displacement, tons: 1 148 standard; 2 700 full load
Dimensions, feet (metres): 284·5 oa × 38 × 15 *(86·7 × 11·6 × 4·6)*
Main engines: 2 MWM diesels coupled on one shaft; 2 400 bhp = 15 knots
Range, miles: 7 000 at 15 knots

Built by Roland Werft, Bremen. Launched on 10 May 1958. Purchased in Oct 1964 and refitted in 1964-66. In 1976-77 converted at Toulon from victualling stores ship to Mediterranean electronic trials ship. Recommissioned Feb 1977.

BERRY (before conversion)   1969, French Navy

174 FRANCE

1 TRIALS SHIP

Name	No.	Builders	Commissioned
TRITON	A 646	Lorient	1972

Displacement, tons: 1 410 standard; 1 510 full load
Dimensions, feet (metres): 242·7 × 38·9 × 12 *(74 × 11·8 × 3·7)*
Main engines: 2 MGO V diesels driving a Voith Schneider screw aft; 2 electric motors driving a Voith Schneider forward
Speed, knots: 13
Range, miles: 4 000 at 13 knots
Complement: 65 (4 officers, 44 men + 5 officers and 12 men for diving)

Under sea recovery and trials ship. Equipped with a helicopter platform. Launched on 7 Mar 1970. Support ship for the 2-man submarine *Griffon*. Painted white.

Operations: Operated by GISMER (Groupe d'Intervention sous la mer) for trials of submarines and deep-sea diving equipment. Underwater TV, recompression chamber, 4 man diving bell of 13·5 tons and laboratories are fitted. Available as submarine rescue ship. Also carries a number of diving saucers.

Radar: Navigational.

Sonar: Special equipment for deep operations.

Submarine: The submarine *Griffon* is carried amidships on the starboard side of *Triton*. She is 25 feet *(7·8 metres)* long, displaces 16 tons and is driven by an electric motor. Her diving depth is 2 000 feet *(600 metres)* and her endurance 24 miles at 4 knots. Can be used for deep recovery operations. Fitted with manipulating arm.

TRITON (with *Griffon* amidships)   6/1975, Dr. Giorgio Arra

1 TRIALS SHIP

Name	No.	Builders	Commissioned
GUSTAV ZEDÈ (ex-*Marcel Le Bihan*, ex-*Grief*)	A 759	Stettiner Oderwerke AG	1937

Displacement, tons: 800 standard; 1 250 full load
Dimensions, feet (metres): 236·2 × 34·8 × 10·5 *(72 × 10·6 × 3·2)*
Guns: 4—20 mm (twins)
Main engines: 2 GM diesels; 2 shafts; 4 400 bhp = 13 knots
Range, miles: 2 500 at 13 knots
Complement: 50 (3 officers, 47 men), accommodation for 22 extra hands

Former German aircraft tender. Launched in 1936. Transferred by USA in Feb 1948. 4·1 in gun and 2—40 mm removed. Tender for DSV *Archimède*. Renamed 1977 to avoid confusion with Type A 69 frigate.

GUSTAV ZEDÈ   7/1976, Dr. Giorgio Arra

1 DEEP SUBMERGENCE VEHICLE

ARCHIMÈDE A 648

Built in Toulon. 68·9 feet *(20·39 metres)* long with surface displacement of 60 tons. Diving depth 36 000 feet *(11 000 metres)*. *Gustav Zedé* acts as tender. FNRS 3 deleted 1974.

ARCHIMÈDE   1974, Wright and Logan

1 ARCHAEOLOGICAL RESEARCH CRAFT

L'ARCHÉONAUTE A 789

Built by Auroux, Arcachon August 1967. 120 tons full load and 96 feet long *(29·3 metres)* with two Baudoin diesels; 600 hp; twin vp propellers; 12 knots. For underwater archaeological research carries a complement of 2 officers, 4 men, 3 archaeologists and 6 divers.

L'ARCHÉONAUTE   1975, Wright and Logan

1 RADIOLOGICAL RESEARCH CRAFT

PALANGRIN Y 743

Acquired 1969. Of 44 tons with single diesel of 220 hp.

FRANCE 175

BOOM AND MOORING VESSELS

Name	No.	Builders	Commissioned
LA PRUDENTE	Y 749	AC Manche	1969
LA PERSÉVÉRANTE	Y 750	AC La Rochelle	1969
LA FIDÈLE	Y 751	AC Manche	1969

Displacement, tons: 446 standard; 626 full load
Dimensions, feet (metres): 142·8 × 32·8 × 9·2 *(43·5 × 10 × 2·8)*
Main engines: 2 Baudoin diesels; diesel-electric; 1 shaft; 620 bhp=10 knots
Range, miles: 4 000 at 10 knots
Complement: 30 (1 officer, 29 men)

Net layers and tenders. Launched on 26 Aug 1968 *(La Fidèle)*, 14 May 1968 *(La Persévérante)* and 13 May 1968 *(La Prudente)*. 25 ton lift.

LA PERSÉVÉRANTE   2/1977, J. A. Verhoog

Name	No.	Builders	Commissioned
TIANÉE	A 731	Brest	1975

Displacement, tons: 842 standard; 905 full load
Dimensions, feet (metres): 178·1 × 34·8 *(54·3 × 10·6)*
Main engines: Diesel-electric; 2 diesels; 1 shaft = 12 knots
Range, miles: 5 200 at 12 knots
Complement: 37 (1 officer, 36 men)

Launched 17 Nov 1973. For service in the Pacific. Fitted with lateral screws in bow tunnel.

TIANÉE   1974, French Navy

Name	No	Builders	Commissioned
CIGALE	A 760	CN La Pallice	1955
CRIQUET	A 761	AC Seine Maritime	1955
FOURMI	A 762	AC Seine Maritime	1955
GRILLON	A 763	Penhoët	1955
SCARABÉE	A 764	Penhoët	1954

Displacement, tons: 770 standard; 850 full load
Dimensions, feet (metres): 151·9 oa × 33·5 × 10·5 *(46·3 × 10·2 × 3·2)*
Guns: 1—40 mm Bofors; 4—20 mm
Main engines: 2, 4-stroke diesels, electric drive, 1 shaft; 1 600 bhp = 12 knots
Range, miles: 5 200 at 12 knots
Complement: 37 (1 officer, 36 men)

US off-shore order. Sister ship G 6 was allocated to Spain. *Cerberus* transferred to Netherlands and subsequently to Turkey as AG 6. *Criquet* was launched on 3 June 1954, *Cigale* on 23 Sep 1954, *Fourmi* on 6 July 1954, *Grillon* on 18 Feb 1954 and *Scarabée* on 21 Nov 1953. *Scarabée* has square upper bridge.

FOURMI   6/1975, Dr. Giorgio Arra

2 MOORING VESSELS

TUPA Y 667

292 tons with 210 hp diesel.

CALMAR Y 688

270 tons full load with Baudoin diesel = 9·5 knots. Complement 11. Converted for raising moorings.

TORPEDO RECOVERY VESSELS

PÉLICAN (ex-*Kerfany*) A 699

Displacement, tons: 362 standard; 425 full load
Dimensions, feet (metres): 121·4 × 28·0 × 13·1 *(37 × 8·6 × 4)*
Torpedo tube: 1
Main engines: 1 Burmeister & Wain diesel; 1 shaft; 650 bhp = 11 knots
Complement: 19

Built in USA in 1951. Purchased in 1965 and converted from tunny fisher into torpedo recovery craft in 1966.

PÉLICAN   11/1975, Dr. Giorgio Arra

176 FRANCE

PÉTREL (ex-*Cap Lopez*, ex-*Yvon Loic II*) A 698

Displacement, tons: 277 standard; 318 full load
Dimensions, feet (metres): 98·4 × 25·6 × 11·5 *(30 × 7·8 × 3·5)*
Main engines: 2 Baudoin diesels; 1 vp screw; 600 bhp = 10 knots
Complement: 19

Built by Dubigeon 1960. Purchased 1965 and converted from tunny fisher to torpedo recovery craft.

PEGASE

Catamaran TRV with 2 440 hp diesels completed by SFCN in 1975.

TRANSPORTS

8 SMALL TRANSPORTS

ARIEL Y 604	DRYADE Y 662	NEREIDE Y —
FAUNE Y 613	ALPHÉE Y 696	ONDINE Y —
KORRIGAN Y 661	ELFE Y 741	

Displacement, tons: 195 standard; 225 full load
Dimensions, feet (metres): 132·8 × 24·5 × 10·8 *(40·5 × 7·5 × 3·3)*
Main engines: 2 MGO or Poyaud diesels; 2 shafts; 1 640 bhp/1 730 bhp = 15 knots
Complement: 9

Ariel was launched on 27 April 1964. *Korrigan* on 6 March 1964. *Alphée* on 10 June 1969. *Elfe* on 14 April 1970, *Faune* on 8 Sept 1971, *Dryade* in 1973 and *Nereide* on 17 Feb 1977. All built by Societe Française de Construction Naval (ex-Franco-Belge) except for *Nereide* and *Ondine* by DCAN Brest. Can carry 400 passengers (250 seated).

ALPHÉE — 1972, Admiral M. Adam

5 SMALL TRANSPORTS

SYLPHE Y 710

Displacement, tons: 171 standard; 189 full load
Dimensions, feet (metres): 126·5 × 22·7 × 8·2 *(38·5 × 6·9 × 2·5)*
Main engines: One MGO diesel; 1 shaft; 425 bhp = 12 knots
Complement: 9

Small transport for passengers, built by Chantiers Franco-Belge in 1959-60. Based at Toulon.

LUTIN (ex-*Georges Clemenceau*) Y 664

Displacement, tons: 68
Main engines: 400 hp = 10 knots

Purchased in 1965. Ex-vedette. Detection school, Toulon.

MORGANE Y 671   **MERLIN** Y 735   **MÉLUSINE** Y 736

Displacement, tons: 170
Dimensions, feet (metres): 103·3 × 23·2 × 7·9 *(31·5 × 7·1 × 2·4)*
Main engines: MGO diesels; 2 shafts; 960 bhp = 11 knots

Small transports for 400 passengers built by Chantiers Navals Franco-Belge at Chalon sur Saône (*Mélusine* and *Merlin*) and Ars. de Mourillon (*Morgane*). Laid down in Dec 1966 and accepted June 1968. Their home port is Toulon.

MORGANE — 1975, Wright and Logan

DIVING TENDERS

4 Ex-US "ADJUTANT" CLASS (MSC)

AJONC (ex-*M 667*) A 701
GARDÉNIA (ex-*M 676*) A 711
LISERON (ex-*M683*) A 723
MAGNOLIA (ex-*M 685*) A 770

Details as in same class under Minewarfare Forces except for complement, now 11. *Ajonc* employed as diving training ship, remainder as clearance-diving base ships. *Magnolia* transferred 1976.

GARDÉNIA — 1977, Leo van Ginderen

1 Ex-BRITISH "HAM" CLASS (MSI)

MYOSOTIS (ex-*M 788*) A 710

Details as in same class under Light Forces. Employed as diving-tender.

TENDERS

8 Ex-BRITISH "HAM" CLASS (MSI)

HIBISCUS (ex-HMS *Sparham*, ex-*M 785*) A 735
DAHLIA (ex-HMS *Whippingham*, ex-*M 786*) A 736
TULIPE (ex-HMS *Frettenham*, ex-*M 771*) A 737
CAPUCINE (ex-HMS *Petersham*, ex-*M 782*) A 738
OEILLET (ex-HMS *Isham*, ex-*M 774*) A 739
HORTENSIA (ex-HMS *Mileham*, ex-*M 783*) A 740
ARMOISE (ex-HMS *Vexham*, ex-*M 772*) A 741
VIOLETTE (ex-HMS *Mersham*, ex-*M 773*) A 742

Details as in same class under Light Forces. Now general purpose tenders.

ARMOISE   11/1975, Dr. Giorgio Arra

POSEIDON A 722

Displacement, tons: 220
Dimensions, feet (metres): 132·9 × 23·6 × 7·3 *(40·5 × 7·2 × 2·2)*
Main engines: 1 diesel; 600 bhp = 13 knots
Endurance: 8 days
Complement: 42

Base ships for assault swimmers. Completed 6 Aug 1975.

POSEIDON   1975, French Navy

GIRELLE A 722

Patrol launch with twin davits aft.

TRAINING SHIPS

CHIMÈRE Y 706   **FARFADET** Y 711

Displacement, tons: 100
Main engine: 1 diesel; 200 hp = 11 knots

Auxiliary sail training ships built at Bayonne in 1971. Tenders to the Naval School.

LA GRANDE HERMINE (ex-*La Route Est Belle*, ex-*Ménestral*) A 653

Ex-sailing fishing boat built in 1932. Purchased in 1964 in replacement for *Dolphin* (ex-*Simone Marcelle*) as the Navigation School (E.O.R.) Training ship. Length 46 feet *(14·02 metres)*.

ENGAGEANTE (ex-*Cayolle*) A 772   **VIGILANTE** (ex-*Iseran*) A 773

Displacement, tons: 286
Dimensions, feet (metres): 98·4 × 22 × 12·5 *(30 × 6·7 × 3·8)*
Main engine: 1 Deutz diesel; 560 hp; 1 shaft = 11 knots

Ex-motor trawlers built by At. et Ch. de la Rochelle-Pallice in 1964. Bought in 1975 for conversion as training ships for the Petty Officers Navigation School. Decca radar.

L'ÉTOILE A 649   **LA BELLE POULE** A 650

Displacement, tons: 227
Dimensions, feet (metres): 128 oa × 23·7 × 11·8 *(32·3 × 7 × 3·2)*
Main engines: Sulzer diesels; 125 bhp = 6 knots

Auxiliary sail vessels. Built by Chantiers de Normandie (Fécamp) in 1932. Accommodation for 3 officers, 30 cadets, 5 petty officers, 12 men. Attached to Naval School.

MUTIN A 652

A 57 ton coastal tender built in 1927 by Chaffeteau, Les Sables. Auxiliary diesel and sails. Attached to the Navigation School.

TUGS

3 OCEAN TUGS

MALABAR A 664   **TENACE** A 669   **CENTAURE** A 674

Displacement, tons: 1 080 light; 1 454 full load
Dimensions, feet (metres): 167·3 oa × 37·8 × 18·6 *(51 × 11·5 × 5·7)*
Main engines: 2 diesels; Kort engines 4 600 hp; 1 shaft = 15 knots
Range, miles: 9 500 at 15 knots
Complement: 42

Malabar and *Tenace* built by J. Oelkers, Hamburg, *Centaure* built at La Pallice 1972-74. *Malabar* commissioned 7 Oct 1975.

TENACE   1973, Reiner Nerlich

178   FRANCE

1 OCEAN TUG

ÉLÉPHANT (ex-*Bar*) A 666

Displacement, tons: 880 standard; 1 180 full load
Main engines: Triple expansion 2 000 ihp = 11 knots

2 OCEAN TUGS

HIPPOPOTAME (ex-*Utrecht*) A 660   **RHINOCEROS** A 668

Displacement, tons: 640 standard; 940 full load
Main engines: Diesel-electric; 1 850 shp = 12 knots

Hippopotame built as USN ATA of "Sotoyomo" class. Former Netherlands civilian ocean tug. Built in 1943. Purchased by the French Navy in Jan 1964 to be used at the Experimental Base in the Pacific. *Rhinoceros* purchased direct from USN.

RHINOCEROS   7/1976, Dr. Giorgio Arra

1 COASTAL TUG

GOLIATH A 665

Displacement, tons: 380
Main engines: 900 hp

1 COASTAL TUG

COOLIE A 684

Displacement, tons: 300
Main engines: 1 000 hp

12 COASTAL TUGS

HERCULE A 667	ROBUSTE A 685	TRAVAILLEUR A 692
LE FORT A 671	ACTIF A 686	ACHARNÉ A 693
UTILE A 672	LABORIEUX A 687	EFFICACE A 694
LUTTEUR A 673	VALEUREUX A 688	COURAGEUX A 706

Displacement, tons: 230
Dimensions, feet (metres): 92 × 26 × 13 *(28·1 × 7·9 × 4)*
Main engines: 1 MGO diesel; 1 050 bhp = 11 knots
Range, miles: 2 400
Complement: 15

Courageux, Hercule, Robuste and *Valeureux* were completed in 1960, four more in 1962-63, two more in late 1960s and *Acharné* and *Efficace* in 1974.

HERCULE   11/1975, Dr. Giorgio Arra

62 HARBOUR TUGS

29 105 TON TYPE

Acajou Y601, *Balsa* Y607, *Bouleau* Y612, *Chataigner* Y620, *Charme* Y623, *Chene* Y624, *Cormier* Y629, *Equeurdeville* Y635, *Maronnier* Y638, *Frene* Y644, *Hêtre* Y654, *Hevea* Y655, *Latanier* Y663, *Manquier* Y666, *Meleze* Y668, *Merisier* Y669, *Okoume* Y682, *Paletuvier* Y686, *Peieplier* Y688, *Pin* Y689, *Platana* Y695, *Sycomore* Y704, *Saule* Y708, *Ebène* Y717, *Erable* Y718, *Olivier* Y719, *Santal* Y720, *Noyer* Y739, *Papayer* Y740.

Of 105 tons. 10 ton bollard pull with 700 bhp diesel and max speed of 11 knots.

2 93 TON TYPE

BONITE Y630   **ROUGET** Y634

Of 93 tons. 7 ton bollard pull with 380 bhp and max speed of 10 knots.

31 56 TON TYPE

Aigrette Y602, *Bengali* Y611, *Mouette* Y617, *Mesange* Y621, *Cigogne* Y625, *Colibri* Y628, *Cygne* Y632, *Martinet* Y636, *Fauvette* Y637, *Tourterelle* Y643, *Goeland* Y648, *Héron* Y653, *Merle* Y670, *Moineau* Y673, *Martin Pecheur* Y675, *Passereau* Y687, *Pingouin* Y690, *Pinson* Y691, *Pivert* Y694, *Alouette* Y721, *Vanneau* Y722, *Engoulevent* Y723, *Sarcelle* Y724, *Marabout* Y725, *Toucan* Y726, *Macreuse* Y727, *Grand Duc* Y728, *Eider* Y729, *Ara* Y730, *Loriot* Y747, *Gelinotte* Y748.

Of 56 tons 3·5 ton bollard pull with 250 bhp diesel and max speed of 9 knots. *Ibis* Y 658 loaned to Senegal.

Note: Reported that 10 Water Tractors are under construction. One additional Tug *Murene* Y 680 listed.

6 PUMP-TUGS

Aiguière Y 745, *Cascade* Y 618, *Embrun* Y 746, *Gave* Y 645, *Geyser* Y 646, *Oued* Y 684.

GOVERNMENT MARITIME FORCES

GENDARMERIE

A number of naval vessels and others are operated by the Gendarmerie.

LA DOUANE

The French customs service has a number of tasks not normally associated with such an organisation. In addition to the usual duties of dealing with ships entering either their coastal area of ports La Douane also has certain responsibilities for rescue at sea, control of navigation, fishery protection and pollution protection. For these purposes 650 officers and men operate a number of craft of various dimensions; Class I of 30 metres, 24 knots and a range of 1 200 miles—Class II of 27 metres, 24 knots and with a range of 900 miles—Class III of 17-20 metres, 24 knots and a range of 400 miles—Class IV of 12-17 metres, 24 knots and a range of 400 miles. In addition La Douane operates a number of helicopters and fixed wing aircraft.

GABON

Ministerial

Minister of National Defence:
President Albert Bernard Bongo

Bases

Libreville, Port Gentil

Personnel

(a) 1978: 100 officers and men
(b) Voluntary service

Mercantile Marine

Lloyd's Register of Shipping:
15 vessels of 98 645 tons gross

DELETION

1975 *Bouet-Willaumez* (ex-HDML 102)

LIGHT FORCES

1 FAST ATTACK CRAFT (MISSILE)

Name	No.	Builders	Commissioned
N'GOLO	GC-04	Chantiers Navals de l'Esterel	1977

Displacement, tons: 155
Dimensions, feet (metres): 137·8 × 25·6 × 6·2 *(42 × 7·8 × 1·9)*
Missiles: 4—SS 12
Guns: 2—40 mm Bofors
Main engines: 2 MTU 16 V 538 TB 91 diesels; 7 200 hp = 33 knots
Range, miles: 1 000 at 18 knots
Complement: 25

Laid down June 1976. Launched Dec 1976.

3 FAST ATTACK CRAFT (GUN)

Name	No	Builders	Commissioned
—	—	Intermarine (Italy)	1978
—	—	Intermarine (Italy)	1978
—	—	Intermarine (Italy)	1978

Displacement, tons: 165
Dimensions, feet (metres): 89·5 × 28·8 × 6·8 *(37·3 × 8·8 × 1·5)*
Guns: 1—40 mm; 2—20 mm (twin)
Main engines: 2 MTU diesels; 2 shafts; 9 000 hp = 35 knots
Range, miles: 1 000 at 35 knots
Complement: 13

Standard Intermarine Mk 4 design, ordered 1976. GRP hulls.

1 LARGE PATROL CRAFT

Name	No.	Builders	Commissioned
PRESIDENT ALBERT BERNARD BONGO	GC-02	Chantiers Navals de l'Esterel	Mar 1972

Displacement, tons: 80
Dimensions, feet (metres): 104 × 19 × 5 *(32 × 5·8 × 1·5)*
Guns: 2—20 mm
Main engines: 2 MTU diesels; 2 700 hp = 30 knots
Range, miles: 1 500 at 15 knots
Complement: 17 (3 officers, 14 ratings)

Fitted with radar and echo sounder.

2 LARGE PATROL CRAFT

Name	No.	Builders	Commissioned
PRESIDENT LEON M'BA	GC-01	Gabon	1968
N'GUENE	GC-03	Swiftships, USA	April 1975

PRESIDENT LEON M'BA
Displacement, tons: 85 standard
Dimensions, feet (metres): 92 × 20·5 × 5 *(28 × 6·3 × 1·5)*
Guns: 1—75 mm; 1—12·7 mm MG
Main engines: Diesel = 12·5 knots
Complement: 16

Launched on 16 Jan 1968.

N'GUENE
Displacement, tons: 118
Dimensions, feet (metres): 105·6 × — × 7·5 *(32·2 × — × 2·3)*
Guns: 2—40 mm (twin); 2—20 mm (twin); 2—12·7 mm MG
Main engines: 3 diesels; 3 shafts = 27 knots
Range, miles: 825 at 25 knots
Complement: 21

COASTGUARD

6 ARCOA COASTAL PATROL CRAFT

Capable of 15 knots.

1 ARCOA 960 COASTAL PATROL CRAFT

Capable of 25 knots.

2 COASTAL PATROL CRAFT

40 ft craft ordered from SFCN Oct 1976.

1 LAUNCH

Of 55·3 ft ordered from SFCN Oct 1976.

THE GAMBIA

Mercantile Marine

Lloyd's Register of Shipping:
5 vessels of 1 608 tons

Port

Banjul

MANSA KILA IV

Displacement, tons: 40
Dimensions, feet (metres): 74·5 × 19·7 × 5·0 *(22·7 × 6·0 × 1·5)*
Main engines: 2 Cummins diesels; 750 bhp = 20 knots

Built by Camper and Nicholson Ltd. Gosport, England to Keith Nelson 75 ft design for a private order—eventually purchased by The Gambia in 1974.

1 FAIREY MARINE "LANCE" CLASS (COASTAL PATROL CRAFT)

SEA DOG PI

Displacement, tons: 17
Dimensions, feet (metres): 48·7 × 15·3 × 4·3 *(14·8 × 4·7 × 1·3)*
Guns: 2—7·62 mm
Main engines: 2 GM 8 V 71 T1; 850 hp = 23 knots
Complement: 9

Delivered 28 Oct 1976 for the Customs service.

SEADOG   1976, Fairey Marine

180 GERMANY (DEMOCRATIC)

GERMANY (Democratic Republic)

Ministerial

Minister of National Defence:
General Heinz Hoffmann

Headquarters Appointments

Commander-in-Chief, Volksmarine:
Vice-Admiral Willi Ehm
Chief of Naval Staff:
Rear-Admiral Gustav Hesse

Personnel

(a) 1974: 1 750 officers and 15 300 men (including GBK)
    1975: 1 800 officers and 15 500 men (including GBK)
    1976: 1 850 officers and 16 000 men (including GBK)
    1977: 1 800 officers and 15 200 men (including GBK)
    1978: 1 800 officers and 15 200 men (including GBK)

(b) 18 months national service

Bases

Rostock/Gehlsdorf: Navy Headquarters;
Peenemunde: HQ 1st Flotilla;
Warnemunde: HQ 4th Flotilla;
Dranske-Bug: HQ 6th Flotilla;
Sassuitz: Minor base;
Wolgast: Minor base;
Tarnewitz: Minor base.

Naval Air

1 squadron with 8 Mi-4 helicopters

Grenzbrigade Kuste (GBK)

The seaborne branch of the Frontier Guards, this is a force of about 3 000 men. Their various craft are difficult to disentangle from those of the Navy, many being taken from that list. Where possible, mention of this is made in the notes.

Mercantile Marine

Lloyd's Register of Shipping:
447 vessels of 1 486 838 tons gross

Strength of the Fleet

Type	Active	Building
Frigate	1	—
Large Patrol Craft	18	—
Fast Attack Craft—Missile	15	—
Fast Attack Craft—Torpedo	65	—
Fast Attack Craft—Patrol	4 (GBK)	—
Coastal Patrol Craft	18	—
Landing Ships and Craft	20	—
Minesweepers—Coastal	52	3
Intelligence Ships	3	—
Survey Ships	4	—
Supply Ships	4	—
Support Tankers	4	—
Buoy Tenders	17	—
Ice Breakers	3	—
Tugs	13	—
Tenders	4	—
Training Ships and Craft	10	—
Cable Layer	1	—
Torpedo Recovery Vessels	2	—

New Construction and Acquisitions

It is reported that the Navy of the GDR is to receive a number of "Mirka" class frigates from the USSR to replace the "Riga" class.

DELETION

Frigate

1976 *Karl Marx* ("Riga" Class)

"HAI" Class

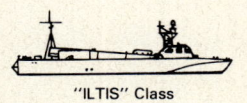

"ILTIS" Class

FRIGATE

1 Ex-SOVIET "RIGA" CLASS

ERNEST THÄLMANN 141

Displacement, tons: 1 200 standard; 1 600 full load
Dimensions, feet (metres): 298·8 × 33·7 × 11 *(91 × 10·2 × 3·4)*
Guns: 3—3·9 in (single); 4—37 mm (twin)
Torpedo tubes: 2—21 in (twin)
A/S weapons: 4 depth charge projectors; 4 RBU 1800
Mines: Can carry 50
Main engines: Geared turbines; 2 shafts; 25 000 shp = 28 knots
Oil fuel, tons: 300
Range, miles: 2 500 at 15 knots
Complement: 150

Sister ships *Friedrich Engels* 124 and *Karl Liebknecht* 123 were paid off in 1971. A fifth ship of this type was burnt out at the end of 1959 and became a total wreck. Two of these hulks are beached at Warnemünde. *Karl Marx* 142 deleted late 1976.

Radar: Slim Net; Sun Visor; Neptun.

"RIGA" Class   1965, Werner Kähling

LIGHT FORCES

4 Ex-SOVIET "SO-I" CLASS (LARGE PATROL CRAFT)

421   422   423   424

Displacement, tons: 215 standard; 250 full load
Dimensions, feet (metres): 138 × 20 × 9·2 *(42·3 × 6·1 × 2·8)*
Guns: 4—25 mm (2 twin mounts)
A/S weapons: 4 MBU 1 800 5-barrelled launchers; 2 DCT
Main engines: 3 diesels; 6 000 bhp = 29 knots
Range, miles: 1 100 at 13 knots
Complement: 30

Fitted with mine rails. These vessels belonged to the coast guard (GBK) but have now been returned to the navy.

"SO-I" Class   1970, Niels Gartig

GERMANY (DEMOCRATIC)

14 "HAI" CLASS (LARGE PATROL CRAFT)

BAD DOBERAN LÜBZ RIBNITZ-DAMGARTEN
BÜTZOW LUDWIGSLUST STERNBERG
GREVESMÜHLEN PARCHIM TETEROW
GADEBUSCH PERLEBERG WISMAR + 2

Displacement, tons: 300 standard; 370 full load
Dimensions, feet (metres): 174 pp; 187 oa × 19 × 10 *(53·1, 57 × 5·8 × 3·1)*
Guns: 4—30 mm (2 twin)
A/S weapons: 4 RBU 1 800 5-barrelled launchers
Main engines: 2 gas turbines; diesels; 8 000 bhp = 25 knots
Complement: 45

Built by Peenewerft, Wolgast. The prototype vessel was completed in 1963. All were in service by the end of 1969, and the programme is now completed.
Pennant numbers are: 411-414, 431-434, 451-454, V 81 and 1 unknown.

"HAI" Class 1974

"HAI" Class 1974

12 Ex-SOVIET "OSA I" CLASS — 3 "OSA II" CLASS
(FAST ATTACK CRAFT—MISSILE)

ARVID HARNACK MAX REICHPIETSCH
AUGUST LUTTGENS OTTO TOST
FRITZ GAST PAUL EISENSCHNEIDER
HEINRICH DORRENBACH PAUL WIECZOREK
JOSEF SCHARES RICHARD SORGE
KARL MESEBERG RUDOLF EGELHOFER +3

Displacement, tons: 165 standard; 200 full load
Dimensions, feet (metres): 128·7 × 25·1 × 5·9 *(39·3 × 7·7 × 1·8)*
Missiles: 4 mountings in 2 pairs for SS-N-2 system
Guns: 4—30 mm (2 twin, 1 forward, 1 aft)
Main engines: 3 diesels; 13 000 hp = 36 knots

Pennant numbers: 531, 711-714, 731-734, 751-754. 3 "Osa II" transferred 1976.

"OSA I" Class 1965, Reinecke

18 Ex-SOVIET "SHERSHEN" CLASS
(FAST ATTACK CRAFT—TORPEDO)

ADAM KUCKHOFF FIETE SCHULZE
ANTON SAEFKOW FRITZ BEHN
ARTHUR BECKER FRITZ HECKERT
BERNHARD BÄSTLEIN HANS COPPI
BRUNO KÜHN HEINZ KAPELLE
EDGAR ANDRÉ RUDOLF BREITSCHEID
ERNST GRUBE WILLI BANSCH
ERNST SCHNELLER +3

Displacement, tons: 150 standard; 160 full load
Dimensions, feet (metres): 115·5 × 23·1 × 5 *(35·2 × 7·1 × 1·5)*
Guns: 4—30 mm (2 twin)
A/S weapons: 12 DC
Torpedo tubes: 4—21 in (single)
Main engines: 3 diesels; 13 000 bhp; 3 shafts = 41 knots
Complement: 16

Acquired from the USSR. Four were delivered in 1968-69, the first installment of a flotilla. The last three transferred 1976. They do not differ from the Soviet boats of the class.
Pennant numbers 738, 811-5, 831-5, 842, 844, 845, 851-5.

"SHERSHEN" Class

7 "LIBELLE" CLASS (FAST ATTACK CRAFT—TORPEDO)

Displacement, tons: 30
Dimensions, feet (metres): 59 × 16·4 × 3·3 *(18 × 5 × 1)*
Guns: 2—23 mm (twin)
Torpedo tubes: 2—21 in (stern launching)
Main engines: 2 diesels; 2 400 hp = 40 knots

A new class first reported in 1975. An improved "Iltis" class. Can be used for minelaying and commando operations. Conversion for new tasks is a speedy job. In series production. Pennant number 992 known.

GERMANY (DEMOCRATIC)

40 "ILTIS" CLASS (FAST ATTACK CRAFT—TORPEDO)

Displacement, tons: 20
Dimensions, feet (metres): 55·8 × 10·5 × 2·5 *(17 × 3·2 × 0·8)*
Torpedo tubes: 2—21 in (torpedoes fired over stern). Some have 3 tubes (Type 3)
  Mines can be carried in place of torpedo tubes
Main engines: Diesels; 3 000 bhp = 30 knots

No guns. Several different types of this class exist, varying in hull material and silhouette, eg Type 1 are flush-decked and Type 2 have a raised forecastle. With the torpedo tubes removed these boats are used to land frogmen and raiding parties. Displacement and dimensions given are for Type 2. Others vary slightly. Built by Mitteldeutschland, starting in 1962. Some pennant numbers 912, 914, 915, 916 and in 970, 980, 990 series.

"ILTIS" Class 1971, S. Breyer

4 Ex-SOVIET "P 6" CLASS (FAST ATTACK CRAFT—PATROL)

Displacement, tons: 66 standard; 75 full load
Dimensions, feet (metres): 84·2 × 20 × 6 *(25·7 × 6·1 × 1·8)*
Guns: 4—25 mm (2 twin mountings) (removed in target boats)
Main engines: 4 diesels; 4 800 bhp; 4 shafts = 43 knots
Range, miles: 450 at 30 knots
Complement: 25

Acquired in 1957-60 from the USSR. Originally there were 27. Wooden hull. Most of this class has been scrapped or converted. Four have had their tubes removed and been transferred to the GBK.

"P 6" as target boat

18 "KB 123" CLASS (COASTAL PATROL CRAFT)

Displacement, tons: about 25
Dimensions, feet (metres): 74 × 16·4 × — *(23 × 5 × —)*
Main engines: 2 diesels = 14 knots

This class (total uncertain) was introduced in 1971 for operations on rivers and inland waterways by the GBK. It appears to be unarmed, though small arms are certainly carried. Pennant numbers: G 91, G 92 known.

"KB 123" Class 1972

AMPHIBIOUS FORCES

3 +1 "FRÖSCH" CLASS (LST)

Displacement, tons: 1 950
Length, feet (metres): 298·4 × 38·7 × 9·2 *(91 × 11·8 × 2·8)*
Guns: 4—57 mm (twins); 4—30 mm (twins)
Main engines: 2 diesels; 2 shafts = 18 knots

A new class similar but not identical to Soviet "Ropuchka" class building by Peene Werft, Wolgast. First seen in Baltic in 1976. Continuing programme—third ship completed Dec 1976.

Armament: Space provided for rocket launcher between forward 57 mm mounting and bridge. Not yet fitted. Fitted for minelaying with stern ports.

Radar: Muff Cob, Strut Curve, Square Head, Don, High Pole IFF.

10 "ROBBE" CLASS (LST)

EBERSWALDE GRIMMEN LÜBBEN
ELSENHÜTTENSTADT HOYERSWERDA SCHWEDT +4

Displacement, tons: 600 standard; 800 full load
Dimensions, feet (metres): 196·8 × 32·8 × 6·6 *(60 × 10 × 2·0)*
Guns: 2—57 mm (1 twin); 4—25 mm (2 twin)
Main engines: Diesels = 12 knots

Launched in 1962-64. Can carry 500 tons stores and vehicles. Pennant numbers—513-516, 611-616.

"ROBBE" Class 1971, S. Breyer

GERMANY (DEMOCRATIC) 183

12 "LABO" CLASS (LCT)

GERHARD PRENZLER   HEINZ WILKOWSKI   ROLF PETERS   + 9

Displacement, tons: 150 standard; 200 full load
Dimensions, feet (metres): 131·2 × 27·9 × 5·9 *(40·0 × 8·5 × 1·8)*
Guns: 4—25 mm (2 twin)
Main engines: Diesels = 10 knots

Built by Peenewerft, Wolgast. Launched in 1961-63.
Pennant numbers: 606, 607, 633, 635, 651, 654.

"LABO" Class   *1969, S. Breyer*

MINE WARFARE FORCES

52 "KONDOR I" and "II" CLASS (MINESWEEPERS—COASTAL)

AHRENSHOOP	GUBEN	ROSSLAU
ALTENTREPTOW	GREIFSWALD	SCHÖNEBECK
ANKLAM	KAMENZ	SÖMMERA
BANSIN	KLÜTZ	STRALSUND
BERGEN	KUHLUNGSBORN	STRASBURG
BITTERFELD	KYRITZ	TANGERHÜTTE
BERNAU	NEURUPPIN	TEMPLIN
BOLTENHAGEN	NEUSTRELITZ	UCKERMÜNDE
DEMMIN	ORANIENBURG	VITTE
DESSAU	PASEWALK	WARNEMÜNDE
EILENBURG	PREROW	WEISSWASSER
EISLEBEN	PRITZWALK	WILHELM PIECKSTADT
GENTHIN	RATHENOW	WITTSTOCK
GRAAL-MÜRITZ	RIESA	WOLGAST
GRIMMA	ROBEL	ZEITZ
		ZERBST
		ZINGST
		+5

Displacement, tons: 245 standard; 280 full load
Dimensions, feet (metres): 154·2 × 23·0 × 6·6 *(47 × 7 × 2)* ("Kondor II" plus 2 metres)
Guns: 2—25 mm ("Kondor I"); 6—25 mm (twins) ("Kondor II")
Main engines: 2 diesels; 2 shafts; 4 000 bhp = 21 knots

Built by Peenewerft Wolgast. Five units were operational in 1970 and 15 by the end of 1971. They replace the small minesweepers of the "Schwalbe" class. Type II has additional length and extra MGs. First appeared in 1971. Production continues.

"KONDOR II" Class   *9/1976*

PENNANT NUMBERS

These have been changed with some frequency. At present the following is as near as can be offered;

Type I (Total 22)   Prototype-V31. S24-26. Attached to GBK; G11-16. G21-26. G41-46.
                    Conversion for torpedo recovery—B73 and B74.
                    Conversion to AGIs Meteor and Komet.

Type II (Total 30) Prototype—V32. Active minesweepers 311-316, 321-327, 331-336, 341-347. S21-23.

"KONDOR I" Class   *9/1976*

INTELLIGENCE SHIPS

2 "KONDOR I" CLASS

METEOR   KOMET

Displacement, tons: 245 standard; 280 full load
Dimensions, feet (metres): 154·2 × 23·0 × 6·6 *(47 × 7 × 2)*
Guns: 2—25 mm
Main engines: 2 diesels; 2 shafts; 4 000 bhp
Speed, knots: 21

Conversions from standard "Kondor" I class Coastal Minesweepers with sweepgear removed and deckhouse fitted aft.

HYDROGRAPH

Displacement, tons: 500
Dimensions, feet (metres): 167 × 28·8 × — *(50·9 × 8·7 ×—)*
Main engines: Diesel; 540 hp = 11 knots

Built in 1960 by Volkswerft, Stralsund.

SURVEY SHIPS

KARL F. GAUS

Built on a 280 ton "Kondor" hull in 1976. Unarmed. Carries 4 small survey launches. Naval manned.

PROFESSOR KRÜMMEL

Built in 1954. Of 135 tons and 10 knots.
Civilian Research Ship.

JORDAN

Of 100 tons and 9 knots.

FLAGGTIEF

Built in 1953. Of 50 tons and 8 knots.

GERMANY (DEMOCRATIC)

SERVICE FORCES

1 "BASKUNCHAK" CLASS (SUPPLY SHIP)

USEDOM

Displacement, tons: 2 500
Dimensions, feet (metres): 227 × 29 × 12·3 (70 × 8·9 × 3·8)
Speed, knots: 13

Tanker converted to act as supply ship.

USEDOM 1973, S. Breyer

3 TYPE 600 (SUPPORT TANKERS)

C 37 (ex- *Hiddensee*)   C 76 (ex-*Riems*)   C — (ex-*Poel*)

Displacement, tons: 1 000
Dimensions, feet (metres): 195 oa × 29·5 × 12·5 (59·5 × 9·0 × 3·8)
Guns: 4—25 mm (twin)
Main engines: 2 diesels; 2 800 bhp = 14 knots
Complement: 26

Built by Peenewerft, Wolgast, in 1960-61. Civilian manned. Oil capacity 645 tons.

Ex-POEL 1971, S. Breyer

3 "KUMO" CLASS

RUDEN E 18   RUGEN V 71   VILM E 44

Displacement, tons: 550
Dimensions, feet (metres): 118 × 24 × 8·9 (36 × 7·3 × 2·7)
Main engines: Diesel = 10 knots

Built in mid-1950s by Mathias Thesen, Wismar. *Rugen* is a torpedo Trials Ship, *Vilm* a tanker and *Ruden* employed as Supply Ship.

1 Ex-SOVIET "KAMENKA" CLASS (BUOY LAYER)

BUK

Displacement, tons: 1 000 standard
Dimensions, feet (metres): 180·5 × 31·2 × 11·5 (55 × 9·5 × 3·4)
Main engines: Diesels = 16 knots

BUK 1970

1 CABLE LAYER

DORNBUSCH

Cable layer of 700 tons with bow rollers.

DORNBUSCH 1967

1 SALVAGE SHIP

Name	No	Builders	Commissioned
OTTO VON GUERICKE	—	Danzig North	1977

Displacement, tons: 1 560 standard; 1 732 full load
Dimensions, feet (metres): 240 × 32·8 × 13·1 (73·2 × 10 × 4)
Guns: 8—25 mm (4 twin)
Main engines: 2 diesels; 3 800 bhp; 2 shafts = 16·5 knots
Range, miles: 3 000 at 12 knots

Basically a "Moma" class hull; sister to Polish "Piast" class. Carries extensive towing and fire-fighting equipment as well as a bargee diving-bell stowed on port side forward of bridge.

2 "KONDOR I" CLASS (TRVs)

B 73   B 74

Details under Minewarfare Forces. Converted for Torpedo Recovery.

LUMME

Small diving tender. Tug type.

FREESENDORF

Built in 1963. Buoy-layer.

4 "TAUCHER" CLASS (DIVING TENDERS)

SATZHAFF (?) +3

Displacement, tons: 310 full load
Dimensions, feet (metres): 98·4 × 21·3 × 9 (30 × 6·5 × 3)
Main engines: 2 diesels = 12 knots

Small diving tenders with recompression chamber.

8 BUOY TENDERS

BREITLING   GOLWITZ   LANDTIEFF   RAMZOW
ESPER ORT   GRASS ORT   PALMER ORT   ROSEN ORT

Displacement, tons: 158
Dimensions, feet (metres): 97 × 20·3 × 6·2 (29·6 × 6·2 × 1·9)
Main engine: 1 diesel; 580 hp = 11·5 knots

Delivered 1970-72. Civilian manned under the Naval Hydrographic Service.

BREITLING 1972

3 BUOY TENDERS

ARKONA   DASSER ORT   STUBBENKAMMER

Built in 1956. Of 55 tons and 10 knots.

TRAINING SHIPS

Name	No.	Builders	Commissioned
WILHELM PIECK	561	Naval Yard, Gdynia	6 July 1976

Displacement, tons: 2 000
Dimensions, feet (metres): 239·4 × 39·4 × — (73 × 12 × —)
Guns: 2—30 mm (twin); 4—25 mm (twin)
Main engines: 2 diesels = 17 knots
Complement: 100

Cadets' training ship. Sister ship to Polish "Wodnik" class training ships.

NEW CONSTRUCTION

A new sailing ship is under consideration. USSR discussing such a programme with Blohm and Voss, Hamburg but it is not known if such an approach covers this ship.

6 "KONDOR I" CLASS

Details in Minewarfare Forces, being part of that total.

GERMANY (DEMOCRATIC) 185

3 "KRAKE" CLASS (ex-MINESWEEPERS—OCEAN)

BERLIN   POTSDAM   ROSTOCK

Displacement, tons: 650 standard
Dimensions, feet (metres): 229·7 × 26·5 × 12·2 *(70 × 8·1 × 3·7)*
Guns: 1—3·4 in; 10—25 mm (vertical twins)
A/S weapons: 4 DCT
Mines: Can carry 30
Main engines: Diesels; 2 shafts; 3 400 bhp = 18 knots
Complement: 90

Built in 1956-58 by Peenewerft, Wolgast. Of the original ten, four completed in 1958, were originally for Poland. Appearance is different compared with the first type, the squat wide funnel being close to the bridge with lattice mast and radar. Fitted for minelaying. On 1 May 1961 they were given the names of the capitals of districts etc of East Germany. Pennant numbers are S11-13. All used for training and will probably be deleted before long.

"KRAKE" Class   *1970, Niels Gartig*

ICEBREAKERS

STEPHAN JANTZEN

Of 2 500 tons and 13 knots built in 1965. Of Soviet "Dobrynya Nikitch" class. Civilian manned.

EISBAR   EISVOGEL

Of 550 tons and 12 knots built in 1957. Civilian manned.

TUGS

A 14

Of 800 tons and 12 knots.

11 HARBOUR TUGS

Of varying classes.

Note: Gesellschaft für Sport und Technik (GST) (Association for Sport and Technical Science) controls several training ships—*Ernst Thälman,* a retired "Habicht I" Class minesweeper; *Ernst Schneller,* "Tummler" class; *Partisan,* and *Pionier* of 80 tons; *Freundschaft* of 200 tons; *F. L. Jahn* of 100 tons; and the sail training ships *Seid Bereil, Jonny Scheer, Max Reichpietsch II* and *Knechtsand II.*

WISMAR

Of 700 tons and 14 knots. Possibly civilian manned.

GERMANY (Federal Republic)

Headquarters Appointment

Chief of Naval Staff, Federal German Navy:
  Vice-Admiral Gunter Luther

Senior Appointment

Commander-in-Chief of the Fleet:
  Vice-Admiral H. H. Klose

Diplomatic Representation

Naval Attaché in The Hague:
  Commander H. Grande
Defence Attaché in Lisbon:
  Commander K. Perlich
Naval Attaché in London:
  Captain K. Reichert
Naval Attaché in Oslo (and Stockholm):
  Commander H. Komatowsky
Naval Attaché in Paris:
  Captain W. Koever
Naval Attaché in Rome:
  Commander W. D. Fischer-Mühlen
Naval Attaché in Washington:
  Captain K-J. Steindorff

Personnel

(a) 1973: 36 000 (4 550 officers, 31 450 men)
    1974: 36 000 (4 550 officers, 31 450 men)
    1975: 35 900 (4 775 officers, 31 125 men)
    1976: 35 900 (5 100 officers, 30 800 men)
    1977: 38 275 (5 600 officers, 32 675 men)

        (Includes Naval Air Arm)

(b) 15 months national service

Bases

Flensburg, Wilhelmshaven, Kiel, Olpenitz.
The administration of these bases is vested in the Naval Support Command at Wilhelmshaven (Rear-Admiral Feindt)

Naval Air Arm

(See Future Developments)

  6 000 men total
  1 LRMP squadron (15 Breguet Atlantic), MFG 3
  2 Fighter bomber squadrons (60 F104G—conversion to Tornados to start May 1981), MFG 1 and 2
  1 Helicopter squadron (re-equipping with 22 Sea King Mk 41 for SAR.), MFG 4
  20 Liaison aircraft (DO28), MFG 5
  (MFG = Marine Flieger Geschwader)

Prefix to Ships' Names

Not normally used but in British waters prefix FGS is used.

Future Development

Interest is being shown by the Naval Staff in various and varied projects.
(a) Development of more powerful ship-to-ship missiles.
(b) Development of SAMs and ASMs with the Franco German Kormoran ASM
(c) New frigates of 2 500 tons standard, 3 800 tons full load with guided weapons to replace "Köln" Class—12 are planned, first batch similar to Netherlands "Kortenaer" class. 6 ordered.
(d) Replacement of F104G aircraft by MRCAs—Tornados.
(e) Replacement of Breguet Atlantics (originally meant to be Vikings S3A—these have proved as expensive as larger more suitable aircraft. Decision awaited).
(f) Minewarfare forces to be improved by conversion of 12 MSCs to Minehunters and replacement of "Schütze" class by remotely controlled unmanned systems.
(g) Development of new 750 ton submarine.
(h) Development of new FACs.

Hydrographic Service

This service is under the direction of the Ministry of Transport, is civilian manned with HQ at Hamburg. Survey ships are listed at the end of the section.

Strength of the Fleet

Type	Active	Building (Projected)
Destroyers	11	—
Frigates	6	6 (6)
Corvettes	6	—
Submarines—Patrol	24	—
Fast Attack Craft (Missile)	30	10
Fast Attack Craft (Torpedo)	10	—
LCUs	22	—
LCMs	19	—
Minesweepers— Coastal and Minehunter	40	—
Minesweepers—Inshore	18	—
Depot Ships	11	—
Repair Ships	3 (1 small)	—
Replenishment Tankers	6	—
Support Tankers	5	—
Support Ships	8	—
Ammunition Transports	2	—
Mine Transports	2	—
Training Ship	1	—
Sail Training Ships	2	—
Survey Ship	1	—
TRVs	13	—
SAR Launch	1	—
Coastal Patrol Craft	7	—
Auxiliaries (some non-naval)	28	—
Tugs—Ocean	8	—
Tugs—Harbour/Coastal	18	—
*Icebreakers	3	—
*Coastguard Craft	8+	—
*Survey Ships	6	—
*Fishery Protection Ships	10	—

  *Non-naval

Mercantile Marine

Lloyd's Register of Shipping:
  1 975 vessels of 9 592 314 tons gross

DELETIONS

Destroyers

1972 Z1

Frigates

1972 Scharnhorst and Gneisenau

Submarines

1974 U4, 5, 6, 7, 8, (Type 205)

Fast Attack Craft (Torpedo)

1972 Marder
1973 Jaguar, Kranich, Leopard, Luchs, Panther
1974 Dommel, Elster
1975 20 "Jaguar" class transferred (Alk, Fuchs, Häher, Löwe, Pelikan, Pinguin, Reiher, Storch, Tiger and Wolf to Turkey and Albatros, Bussard, Falke, Geier, Greif, Habicht, Kondor, Kormoran, Seeadler and Sperber to Greece).

Coastal Patrol Craft

1974 TM 1, KW 2, KW 8, FW 2, FW 3

Minelayers

1972 Bochum, Bottrop transferred to Turkey.

Minesweepers Coastal

1972 Algol ("Schütze" class) scrapped.
1973 Capella, Krebs, Mira, Orion, Pegasus, Steinbock, Uranus ("Schütze" class) (5 to Greece)
1975 Vegesack, Hampeln, Siegen, Detmold, Worms ("Vegesack" class) transferred to Turkey, Sept)

Depot Ships

1975 Weser transferred to Greece.
1976 Ruhr (transferred to Turkey)

Supply Ships

1972 Angeln transferred to Turkey.
1974 Schwarzwald
1976 Dithmarschen (transferred to Turkey)
1977 Frankenland, Emsland, Münsterland, Bodensee (last to Turkey)

Auxiliaries

1975 FW 6 to Turkey, Karl Kolls (sold).

PENNANT LIST

Destroyers

D	171	Z 2
D	172	Z 3
D	178	Z 4
D	179	Z 5
D	181	Hamburg
D	182	Schleswig-Holstein
D	183	Bayern
D	184	Hessen
D	185	Lütjens
D	186	Mölders
D	187	Rommel

Frigates

F	220	Köln
F	221	Emden
F	222	Augsburg
F	223	Karlsrühe
F	224	Lübeck
F	225	Braunschweig

Submarines

S	170	U 21	S	188	U 9
S	171	U 22	S	189	U 10
S	172	U 23	S	190	U 11
S	173	U 24	S	191	U 12
S	174	U 25	S	192	U 13
S	175	U 26	S	193	U 14
S	176	U 27	S	194	U 15
S	177	U 28	S	195	U 16
S	178	U 29	S	196	U 17
S	179	U 30	S	197	U 18
S	180	U 1	S	198	U 19
S	181	U 2	S	199	U 20

Light Forces

6092	Zobel	6141	S 41
6093	Wiesel	6142	S 42
6094	Dachs	6143	S 43
6095	Hermelin	6144	S 44
6096	Nerz	6145	S 45
6097	Puma	6146	S 46
6098	Gepard	6147	S 47
6099	Hyäne	6148	S 48
6100	Frettchen	6149	S 49
6101	Ozelot	6150	S 50
6111	S 61	6151	S 51
6112	S 62	6152	S 52
6113	S 63	6153	S 53
6114	S 64	6154	S 54
6115	S 65	6155	S 55
6116	S 66	6156	S 56
6117	S 67	6157	S 57
6118	S 68	6158	S 58
6119	S 69	6159	S 59
6120	S 70	6160	S 60

GERMANY (FEDERAL) 187

Minewarfare Forces

1051	Castor
1054	Pollux
1055	Sirius
1056	Rigel
1057	Regulus
1058	Mars
1059	Spica
1060	Skorpion
1062	Schütze
1063	Waage
1064	Deneb
1065	Jupiter
1067	Atair
1069	Wega
1070	Göttingen
1071	Koblenz
1072	Lindau
1073	Schleswig
1074	Tübingen
1075	Wetzlar
1076	Paderborn
1077	Weilheim
1078	Cuxhaven
1079	Düren
1080	Marburg
1081	Konstanz
1082	Wolfburg
1083	Ulm
1084	Flensburg
1085	Minden
1086	Fulda
1087	Völklingen
1090	Perseus
1092	Pluto
1093	Neptun
1094	Widder
1095	Herkilles
1096	Fischer
1097	Gemma
1099	Uranus
2650	Ariadne
2651	Freya
2652	Vineta
2653	Hertha
2654	Nymphe
2655	Nixe
2656	Amazone
2657	Gazelle
2658	Frauenlob
2659	Nautilus
2660	Gefion
2661	Medusa
2662	Undine
2663	Minerva
2664	Diana
2665	Loreley
2666	Atlantis
2667	Acheron

Patrol Craft

P	6052	Thetis
P	6053	Hermes
P	6054	Najade
P	6055	Triton
P	6056	Theseus

Amphibious Forces

L	760	Flunder
L	761	Karpfen
L	762	Lachs
L	763	Plötze
L	764	Rochen
L	765	Schleie
L	766	Stör
L	767	Tümmler
L	768	Wels
L	769	Zander
L	788	Butt
L	789	Brasse
L	790	Barbe
L	791	Delphin
L	792	Dorsch
L	793	Felchen
L	794	Forelle
L	795	Inger
L	796	Makrele
L	797	Mürane
L	798	Renke
L	799	Salm

Support Ships and Auxiliaries

A	50	Alster
A	52	Oste
A	53	Oker
A	54	Isar
A	55	Lahn
A	56	Lech
A	58	Rhein
A	59	Deutschland
A	60	Gorch Fock
A	61	Elbe
A	63	Main
A	65	Saar
A	66	Neckar
A	67	Mosel
A	68	Werra
A	69	Donau
A	512	Odin
A	513	Wotan
A	1401	Eisvogel
A	1402	Eisbär
A	1406	Bodensee
A	1407	Wittensee
A	1411	Lüneburg
A	1412	Coburg
A	1413	Freiburg
A	1414	Glücksburg
A	1415	Saarburg
A	1416	Nienburg
A	1417	Offenburg
A	1418	Meersburg
A	1424	Walchensee
A	1425	Ammersee
A	1426	Tegernsee
A	1427	Westensee
A	1428	Harz
A	1429	Eifel
A	1435	Westerwald
A	1436	Odenwald
A	1437	Sachsenwald
A	1438	Steigerwald
A	1439	Frankenland
A	1440	Emsland
A	1441	Münsterland
A	1442	Spessart
A	1443	Rhön
A	1449	Hans Bürkner
A	1450	Planet
A	1451	Wangerooge
A	1452	Spiekeroog
A	1453	Langeoog
A	1454	Baltrum
A	1455	Norderney
A	1456	Juist
A	1457	Helgoland
A	1458	Fehmarn
Y	801	Pellworm
Y	802	Plon
Y	803	Blauort
Y	804	Wieland
Y	805	Memmert
Y	806	Hansa
Y	809	Arcona
Y	811	Knurrhahn
Y	812	Lütje Hörn
Y	813	Mellum
Y	814	Knechtsand
Y	815	Schärhorn
Y	816	Vogelsand
Y	817	Nordstrant
Y	818	Trischen
Y	819	Langeness
Y	820	Sylt
Y	821	Föhr
Y	822	Amrum
Y	823	Neuwerk
Y	827	KW 15
Y	829	KW 3
Y	830	KW 16
Y	832	KW 18
Y	833	KW 19
Y	834	Nordwind
Y	836	Holnis
Y	837	SP 1
Y	838	Wilhelm Pullwer
Y	841	Walther van Ledebur
Y	845	KW 17
Y	846	KW 20
Y	847	OT 2
Y	849	Stier
Y	851-56	TF 101-106
Y	857-859	FL 5-7
Y	862	FL 10
Y	863	FL 11
Y	864-69	FW 1-6
Y	871	Heinz Roggenkamp
Y	872-74	TF 106-108
Y	877	H.C. Oersted
Y	878	H. von Helmholtz
Y	880	Wilhelm Bauer
Y	881	Adolf Bestelmeyer
Y	882	Otto Meycke
Y	887	Karl Kolls
Y	888	Friedrich Voge
Y	889	Rudolf Diesel
Y	1641	Förde
Y	1642	Jade
Y	1643	Niobe
Y	1662	Ems
Y	1663	Eider

Coastguard

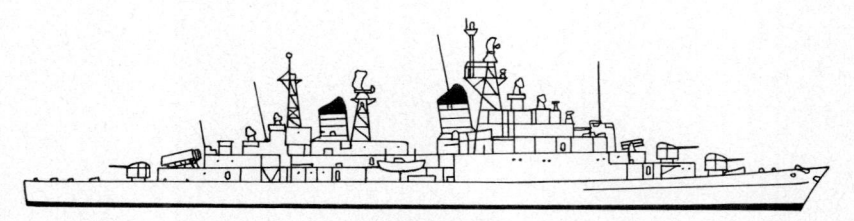

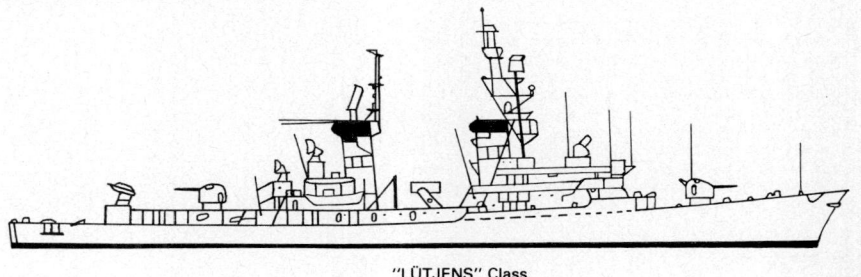

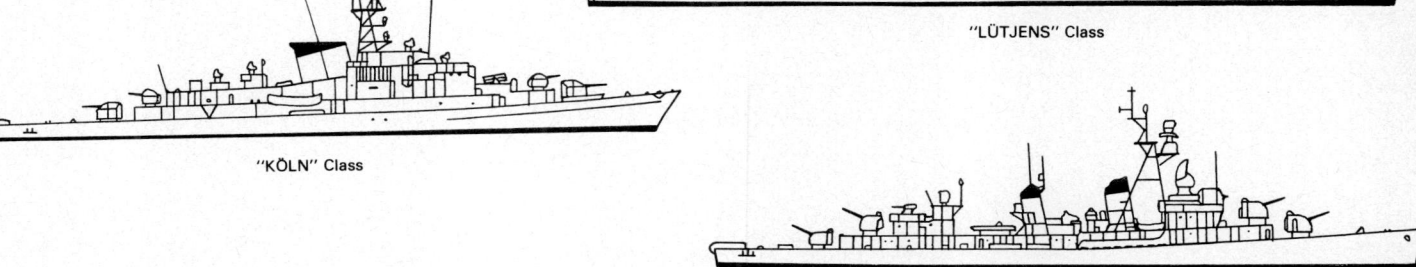

BG 11	Neustadt
BG 12	Bad Bramstedt
BG 13	Uelzen
BG 14	Duderstadt
BG 15	Eschwege
BG 16	Alsfeld
BG 17	Bayreuth
BG 18	Rosenheim

"HAMBURG" Class

"LÜTJENS" Class

"KÖLN" Class

"THETIS" Class

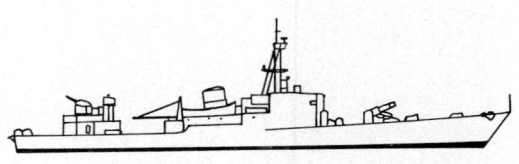

"Z 1" Class

188 GERMANY (FEDERAL)

SUBMARINES

TYPE 210

A development project is in hand by the Norwegian and Federal German navies for a 750 ton class to replace the Type 205 (FGN) and Type 207 (Norway) in the 1980s.

18 TYPE 206

Name	No.	Builders	Laid down	Launched	Commissioned
U 13	S 192	Howaldtswerke, Kiel	24 Nov 1969	28 Oct 1971	1973
U 14	S 193	Reinstahl Nordseewerke, Emden	21 Apr 1970	1 Mar 1972	1973
U 15	S 194	Howaldtswerke, Kiel	29 May 1970	15 June 1972	1973
U 16	S 195	Reinstahl Nordseewerke, Emden	15 Dec 1970	29 Aug 1972	1973
U 17	S 196	Howaldtswerke, Kiel	19 Oct 1970	10 Oct 1972	1973
U 18	S 197	Reinstahl Nordseewerke, Emden	16 Mar 1971	31 Oct 1972	1973
U 19	S 198	Howaldtswerke, Kiel	15 Jan 1971	15 Dec 1972	1973
U 20	S 199	Reinstahl Nordseewerke, Emden	7 May 1971	16 Jan 1973	1974
U 21	S 170	Howaldtswerke, Kiel	14 Apr 1971	9 Mar 1973	1974
U 22	S 171	Reinstahl Nordseewerke, Emden	7 July 1971	27 Mar 1973	1974
U 23	S 172	Reinstahl Nordseewerke, Emden	26 Apr 1972	22 May 1974	1975
U 24	S 173	Reinstahl Nordseewerke, Emden	1 Sep 1971	24 June 1973	1974
U 25	S 174	Howaldtswerke, Kiel	30 June 1971	23 May 1973	1974
U 26	S 175	Reinstahl Nordseewerke, Emden	28 Oct 1971	20 Nov 1973	1975
U 27	S 176	Howaldtswerke, Kiel	6 Oct 1971	21 Aug 1973	1975
U 28	S 177	Reinstahl Nordseewerke, Emden	1 Feb 1972	22 Jan 1974	1975
U 29	S 178	Howaldtswerke, Kiel	11 Jan 1972	5 Sep 1973	1975
U 30	S 179	Reinstahl Nordseewerke, Emden	29 Feb 1972	26 Mar 1974	1975

Displacement, tons: 400 surfaced; 600 dived
Length, feet (metres): 159·4 *(48·6)*
Beam, feet (metres): 15·4 *(4·7)*
Draught, feet (metres): 13·1 *(4·0)*
Torpedo tubes: 8—21 in *(533 mm)* (bow)
Main machinery: MTU diesel-electric; Diesels 1 500 hp; main motors 1 800 hp; 1 shaft
Speed, knots: 10 surfaced; 17 dived
Range, miles: 4 500 at 5 knots (surfaced)
Complement: 22

Authorised on 7 June 1969 from Howaldtswerke Deutsche Werft (8) and Rheinstahl Nordseewerke Emden, (10).
To be fitted with new minelaying equipment during refits from 1977.

Squadrons: First: U 25-30 U 1 and 2, 9-12. Third: U 13-24.

U 24   *2/1976, Reinhard Nerlich*

6 TYPE 205

Name	No.	Builders	Laid down	Launched	Commissioned
U 1	S 180	Howaldtswerke, Kiel	—	21 Oct 1961	—
U 2	S 181	Howaldtswerke, Kiel	—	25 Jan 1962	—
U 9	S 188	Howaldtswerke, Kiel	—	20 Oct 1966	—
U 10	S 189	Howaldtswerke, Kiel	—	20 July 1967	—
U 11	S 190	Howaldtswerke, Kiel	—	9 Feb 1968	21 June 1968
U 12	S 191	Howaldtswerke, Kiel	—	10 Sep 1968	14 Jan 1969

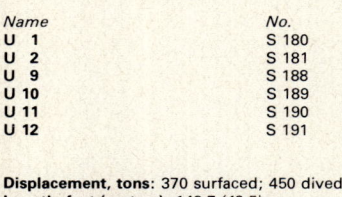

Displacement, tons: 370 surfaced; 450 dived
Length, feet (metres): 142·7 *(43·5)* oa
Beam, feet (metres): 15·1 *(4·6)*
Draught, feet (metres): 12·8 *(3·8)*
Torpedo tubes: 8—21 in *(533 mm)* (bow)
Main machinery: 2 Maybach (MTU) diesels; total 1 200 bhp; 2 Siemens electric motors, total 1 500 bhp; single screw
Speed, knots: 10 surfaced; 17 dived
Complement: 21

All built in floating docks. Fitted with snort mast. First submarines designed and built by Germany since the end of the Second World War. U 4-12 were built to a heavier and improved design. U 1 and U 2 were modified accordingly and refloated on 17 Feb 1967 and 15 July 1966 respectively. U 1 was reconstructed late 1963 to 4 Mar 1965. (See original appearance in the 1962-63 and 1963-64 editions). U 9-12 have hulls of different steel alloys of non-magnetic properties. U 3 of this class lent to Norway on 10 July 1962 and temporarily named *Kobben* (S 310), was returned to Germany in 1964 and decommissioned on 15 Sep 1967 for disposal.

Radar: French Thomson-CSF Calypso, nav/attack set.
Passive DF.

Torpedo equipment: The boats are trimmed by the stern to load through the bow caps. Also fitted for minelaying. Fire control by Hollandse. Mk 8.

U 9   *1975, Reinhard Nerlich*

1 CONVERTED TYPE XXI

Name	No.	Builders	Laid down	Launched	Commissioned
WILHELM BAUER (ex-*U 2540*)	Y 880	Blohm and Voss, Hamburg	1943	1944	1944

Displacement, tons: 1 620 surfaced; 1 820 dived
Length, feet (metres): 252·7 *(77·0)* pp
Beam, feet (metres): 21·7 *(6·6)*
Draught, feet (metres): 20·3 *(6·2)*
Torpedo tubes: 4—21 in *(533 mm)* (bow)
Main machinery: MTU diesel-electric drive; 2 diesels total 4 200 bhp; 2 electric motors total 5 000 hp
Speed, knots: 15·5 surfaced; 17·5 dived

Scuttled after air attack off Flensburg on 4 May 1945. Raised in 1957. Rebuilt in 1958-59 at Howaldtswerke, Kiel. Commissioned on 1 Sep 1960. Used for experiments on submarine equipment. Conning tower was modified.

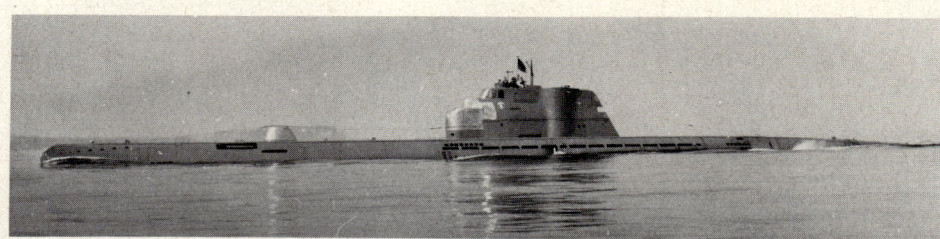

WILHELM BAUER   *1973, Howaldtswerke, Kiel*

DESTROYERS

GERMANY (FEDERAL) 189

3 US "CHARLES F. ADAMS" CLASS (DDGs)

Name	No.	Builders	Laid down	Launched	Commissioned
LÜTJENS (ex-US DDG 28)	D 185	Bath Iron Works Corp	1 Mar 1966	11 Aug 1967	12 Mar 1969
MÖLDERS (ex-US DDG 29)	D 186	Bath Iron Works Corp	12 April 1966	13 April 1968	12 Sep 1969
ROMMEL (ex-US DDG 30)	D 187	Bath Iron Works Corp	22 Aug 1967	1 Feb 1969	24 April 1970

Displacement, tons: 3 370 standard; 4 500 full load
Length, feet (metres): 431 *(131·4)* wl; 440 *(134·1)* oa
Beam, feet (metres): 47 *(14·3)*
Draught, feet (metres): 20 *(6·1)*
Missile launchers: 1 Tartar single (see notes)
Guns: 2—5 in *(127 mm)* single (see notes)
A/S weapons: Asroc; 2 triple torpedo; 1 DCT
Main engines: Geared steam turbines 70 000 shp; 2 shafts
Boilers: 4 Combustion Engineering; 1 200 psi *(84·4 kg/cm²)*
Speed, knots: 35
Oil fuel, tons: 900
Range, miles: 4 500 at 20 knots
Complement: 340 (21 officers, 319 men)

Modified to suit Federal German requirements and practice. 1965 contract.
Cost $43 754 000 each.

Appearance: Some differences from "Charles F Adams" in W/T aerials.

Electronics: SATIR I (similar to SENIT 2) automatic data system. TACAN beacon.

Modernisation: Work now in hand includes:
a. Replacement of after 5 in *(127 mm)* gun by 2 twin Harpoon launchers.
b. Improved Tartar and 5 in fire control with digital in place of analog computers.
c. Sundry minor modifications.

Radar: Three dimensional air search and target designator: one SPS 52 (after funnel)
Air surveillance: one SPS 40 (main-mast)
Tartar fire control: two SPG 51 (abaft after funnel)
Surface warning: one SPS 10.
Gun fire control: one GFCS 68.

Sonar: One SQS 23.

LÜTJENS
11/1976, Michael D. J. Lennon

LÜTJENS
4/1976, Reinhard Nerlich

LÜTJENS
1976, Michael D. J. Lennon

190 GERMANY (FEDERAL)

4 "HAMBURG" CLASS

Name	No.	Builders	Laid down	Launched	Commissioned
HAMBURG	D 181	H. C. Stülcken Sohn, Hamburg	1959	26 Mar 1960	23 May 1964
SCHLESWIG-HOLSTEIN	D 182	H. C. Stülcken Sohn, Hamburg	1959	20 Aug 1960	12 Oct 1964
BAYERN	D 183	H. C. Stülcken Sohn, Hamburg	1961	14 Aug 1962	6 July 1965
HESSEN	D 184	H. C. Stülcken Sohn, Hamburg	1962	4 May 1963	8 Oct 1968

Displacement, tons: 3 340 standard; 4 330 full load
Length, feet (metres): 420 *(128)* wl; 439·7 *(134·0)* oa
Beam, feet (metres): 44 *(13·4)*
Draught, feet (metres): 17 *(5·2)*
Missiles: 4 Exocet
Guns: 3—3·9 in *(100 mm)* (single); 8—40 mm (4 twin)
A/S weapons: 2 Bofors 4-barrel DC Mortars; 1 DCT
  4—12 in torpedo tubes for A/S torpedoes
Main engines: 2 Wahodag dr geared turbines; 68 000 shp; 2 shafts
Boilers: 4 Wahodag; 910 psi *(64 kg/cm²)*, 860°F *(460°C)*
Speed, knots: 35·8; 18 economical
Range, miles: 6 000 at 13 knots; 920 at 35 knots
Complement: 280 (17 officers, 263 men)

All named after countries of the German Federal Republic. Capable of minelaying. Carry one 20 barrelled SCLAR launcher.

Electronics: FCS for Bofors A/S launcher, torpedoes and DC from Hollandse Signaalapparaten. ECM fitted.

Modernisation: Replacement of 100 mm in X position by four MM 38 Exocet, replacement of 40 mm Bofors by Bredas and addition of two extra A/S torpedo tubes. Modernisation started in 1975 with *Claxton* to be followed by *Hamburg, Schleswig-Holstein* and *Bayern*, all completing by 1977. *Hessen* completed Nov 1975. *Hamburg* taken in hand by Blöhm and Voss 18 Aug 1975 completed mid-1976. *Schleswig-Holstein* taken in hand April 1976 completed Feb 1977. *Bayern* started early in 1977 to complete late 1977/early 1978.

Radar: All by Hollandse Signaalapparaten.
Navigation/surface warning: one set
Air warning: one LW.02/3
Target designator: one DAO 2

100 mm fire control: two M 45 series
40 mm fire control: two M 45 series

Sonar: One ELAC 1BV hull-mounted.

HAMBURG 10/1977, C. and S. Taylor

HAMBURG 6/1977, C. and S. Taylor

4 Ex-US "FLETCHER" CLASS

Name	No.	Builders	Laid down	Launched	Commissioned
Z 2 (ex-USS *Ringgold*, DD 500)	D 171	Federal SB & DD Co, Port Newark	25 June1942	11 Nov 1942	24 Dec 1942
Z 3 (ex-USS *Wadsworth*, DD 516)	D 172	Bath Iron Works Corporation, Maine	18 Aug 1942	10 Jan 1943	16 Mar 1943
Z 4 (ex-USS *Claxton*, DD 571)	D 178	Consolidated Steel Corporation, Orange	25 June1941	1 April1942	8 Dec 1942
Z 5 (ex-USS *Dyson*, DD 572)	D 179	Consolidated Steel Corporation, Orange	25 June1941	15 April1942	30 Dec 1942

Displacement, tons: 2 100 standard; 2 750 full load
Length, feet (metres): 368·4 *(112·3)* wl; 376·5 *(114·8)* oa
Beam, feet (metres): 39·5 *(12)*
Draught, feet (metres): 18 *(5·5)*
Guns: 4—5 in *(127 mm)* 38 cal;
  6—3 in *(76 mm)* 50 cal (twins) (Z 4; 4—3 in)
A/S weapons: 2 Hedgehogs; 1 DC rack
Torpedo tubes: 5—21 in *(533 mm)* (quintuple); 2 single 21 in tubes
Main engines: 2 sets GE geared turbines; 60 000 shp; 2 shafts
Boilers: 4 Babcock & Wilcox, 569 psi *(40 kg/cm²)*; 851°F *(455°C)*
Speed, knots: 32; 17 economical
Oil fuel, tons: 540
Range, miles: 3 450 at 15 knots (as modified)
Complement: 250

Former US "Fletcher" class destroyers. The original loan from the United States of a class of five for five years was extended. First ship arrived at Bremerhaven on 14 April 1958. Commissioned in FGN as follows: Z 2, 14 July 1959; Z 3, 6 Oct 1959; Z 4, 15 Dec 1959; Z 5, 23 Feb 1960. Purchased 7 Mar 1977.Capable of minelaying. Form 3rd Destroyer squadron.

Gunnery: Z 4 carried out trials of a containerised 3-in *(76 mm)* OTO Melara gun in 1975 in place of after 3-in mounting. On completion of trials OTO Melara mounting was removed but original twin 3-in was not replaced.

Radar: Air and surface search: one SPS 6
Surface surveillance: one SPS 10
Fire control: one GFCS 56 and 68.

Sonar: SQS 29.

Z 3 4/1976, Dr Giorgio Arra

GERMANY (FEDERAL) 191

FRIGATES

0 + 6 + 6 TYPE 122

Name	No	Builders	Commissioned
—	—	Bremer Vulkan	1981
—	—	AG Weser, Bremen	—
—	—	Howaldtswerke, Kiel	—
—	—	Nordseewerke, Emden	—
—	—	Blohm und Vess	—
—	—	Blohm und Voss	1984

Displacement, tons: 3 800 full load (approx)
Dimensions, feet (metres): 419·8 × 48·5 × 19·7 (128 oa × 14·8 × 6)
Aircraft: 2 helicopters
Missiles: 8 Harpoon; 1—8 cell Seasparrow; 2 multiple Stinger launchers
Guns: 1—76 mm 62 cal; Breda 105 mm 20 tube rocket launcher
A/S weapons: 6 Mk 32 torpedo tubes (triples)
Main engines: 2 GE-LM 2500 gas turbines; 53 200 hp; 2 MTU 20V-956-TB82 diesels; 9 000 hp; 2 shafts
Speed, knots: 30
Range, miles: 4 000 at 18 knots
Complement: 200

Approval given in early 1976 for six of this class, a modification of the Netherlands "Kortenaer" class. The first is expected in service in 1981 with six more planned. To replace "Fletcher", "Köln" and "Hamburg" classes. First six to be completed by 1984.

TYPE 122   *1976, Federal German Navy*

6 "KÖLN" CLASS

Name	No.	Builders	Laid down	Launched	Commissioned
KÖLN	F 220	H. C. Stülcken Sohn, Hamburg	—	6 Dec 1958	15 April 1961
EMDEN	F 221	H. C. Stülcken Sohn, Hamburg	—	21 Mar 1959	24 Oct 1961
AUGSBURG	F 222	H. C. Stülcken Sohn, Hamburg	—	15 Aug 1959	7 April 1962
KARLSRUHE	F 223	H. C. Stülcken Sohn, Hamburg	—	24 Oct 1959	15 Dec 1962
LÜBECK	F 224	H. C. Stülcken Sohn, Hamburg	—	23 July 1960	6 July 1963
BRAUNSCHWEIG	F 225	H. C. Stülcken Sohn, Hamburg	—	3 Feb 1962	16 June 1964

Displacement, tons: 2 100 standard; 2 550 full load
Length, feet (metres): 360·9 (110)
Beam, feet (metres): 36·1 (11·0)
Draught, feet (metres): 11·2 (3·4)
Guns: 2—3·9 in (100 mm)
    6—40 mm (2 twin and 2 single)
A/S weapons: 2 Bofors 4-barrel DC mortars (72 charges)
Torpedo tubes: 4—21 in (533 mm) (singles) for A/S torpedoes
Mines: Can carry 80
Main engines: Combined diesel and gas turbine plant; 4 MAN 16-cyl diesels; total 12 000 bhp; 2 Brown Boveri gas turbines, 24 000 bhp; total 36 000 bhp; 2 shafts
Speed, knots: 32; 23 economical
Oil fuel, tons: 333
Range, miles: 920 at 32 knots
Complement: 200

Ordered in Mar 1957. All ships of this class are named after towns of West Germany. Form 2nd Frigate Squadron.

Electronics: Hollandse Signaalapparaten FCS for Bofors A/S launchers. M9 torpedo fire control.

Engineering: Each of the two shafts is driven by two diesels coupled and geared to one BBC gas turbine. Controllable pitch propellers. A speed of 32 knots is reported to have been attained on full power trials.

Radar: All by Hollandse Signaalapparaten.
Navigation/surface search: one set.
Target designator: one DA 02.
Fire control (100 mm): two M 45 series.
Fire control (40 mm): two M 45 series.

Sonar: One PAE/CWE M/F set, hull-mounted.

EMDEN   *8/1977, Michael D. J. Lennon*

CORVETTES

5 "THETIS" CLASS

Name	No.	Builders	Commissioned
THETIS	P 6052	Rolandwerft, Bremen	1 July 1961
HERMES	P 6053	Rolandwerft, Bremen	16 Dec 1961
NAJADE	P 6054	Rolandwerft, Bremen	12 May 1962
TRITON	P 6055	Rolandwerft, Bremen	10 Nov 1962
THESEUS	P 6056	Rolandwerft, Bremen	15 Aug 1963

Displacement, tons: 564 standard; 650 full load
Dimensions, feet (metres): 229·7 × 27 × 14 (70 × 8·5 × 4·2)
Guns: 2—Breda 40 mm L 70 (twin mounting) (To be replaced by 1—3 in OTO Melara)
A/S weapons: Bofors DC mortar (4-barrelled)
Torpedo tubes: 4—21 in (533 mm)
Main engines: 2 MAN diesels; 2 shafts; 6 800 bhp = 24 knots
Complement: 48

Najade has computer house before bridge. Form Flotten Dienst Geschwäder with *Hans Bürckner*.

Electronics: HSA M9 series torpedo control.

Radar: Nav/surface warning: K-H14; TRS-N.

Sonar: ELAC 1BV.

THETIS   *8/1976, P. Crichton*

192 GERMANY (FEDERAL)

Name	No.	Builders	Commissioned
HANS BÜRKNER	A 1449	Atlaswerke, Bremen	18 May 1963

Displacement, tons: 950 standard; 1 000 full load
Dimensions, feet (metres): 265·2 oa × 30·8 × 10 (81 × 9·4 × 2·8)
A/S weapons: 1 DC mortar (four-barrelled) 2 DC racks
Torpedo tubes: 2—21 in (533 mm)
Main engines: 4 MAN diesels; 2 shafts; 13 600 shp = 24 knots
Complement: 50

Launched on 16 July 1961. Named after designer of German First World War battleships (1909-18). General purpose utility vessel.

Radar: TRS-N; KH14.

Sonar: Has small VDS aft.

HANS BÜRKNER   1975, Federal German Navy

LIGHT FORCES

TYPE 162 (FAST ATTACK HYDROFOIL—MISSILE)

On 19 Aug 1977 the cancellation of this order was announced. The "Zobel" class will be replaced by improved Type 143 boats.

10 TYPE 143 (FAST ATTACK CRAFT—MISSILE)

Name	No.	Builders	Commissioned
S 61	P 6111	Lürssen, Vegesack	1 Nov 1976
S 62	P 6112	Lürssen, Vegesack	14 April 1976
S 63	P 6113	Lürssen, Vegesack	2 June 1976
S 64	P 6114	Lürssen, Vegesack	14 Aug 1976
S 65	P 6115	Kröger, Rendsburg	27 Sep 1976
S 66	P 6116	Lürssen, Vegesack	25 Nov 1976
S 67	P 6117	Kröger, Rendsburg	17 Dec 1976
S 68	P 6118	Lürssen, Vegesack	28 Mar 1977
S 69	P 6119	Kroger, Rendsburg	May 1977
S 70	P 6120	Lürssen, Vegesack	18 July 1977

Displacement, tons: 295 nominal, 378 full load
Dimensions, feet (metres): 200·0 × 24·6 × 8·5 (57 × 7·8 × 2·4)
Missiles: 4 launchers for Exocet MM 38
Guns: 2—76 mm OTO Melara
Torpedoes: 2—21 in wire guided aft
Main engines: 4 MTU diesels; 16 000 hp; 4 shafts = 38 knots
Range, miles: 1 300 at 30 knots
Complement: 40

Ordered in 1972 as replacements for last ten boats of the "Jaguar" class from 1976 onwards. Final funds allocated 13 July 1972. First laid down late 1972. The first boat, S 61, started trials in Dec 1974. Wooden-hulled craft. Launch dates—S 61, 22 Oct 1973; S 62, 21 March 1974; S 63, 18 Sep 1974; S 64, 10 Dec 1974; S 65, 10 Dec 1974; S 66, 5 Sep 1975; S 67, 6 March 1975; S 68, 17 Nov 1975; S 69, 5 June 1975; S 70, 14 April 1976. Now form 2nd S Boat Squadron.

Electronics: Believed that data automation system AGIS is being fitted to permit use of Type 143 as control ship for concerted operation as Type 148 boats.

Radar: All by Hollandse Signaal. WM 27 in radome for Exocet, gun and torpedo control.

S 61   10/1975, Lürssen Werft

20 TYPE 148 (FAST ATTACK CRAFT—MISSILE)

Name	No.	Builders	Commissioned
		(see note re Lürssen)	
S 41	P 6141	C. M. de Normandie, Cherbourg	30 Oct 1972
S 42	P 6142	C. M. de Normandie, Cherbourg	8 Jan 1973
S 43	P 6143	C. M. de Normandie, Cherbourg	9 April 1973
S 44	P 6144	C. M. de Normandie, Cherbourg	14 June 1973
S 45	P 6145	C. M. de Normandie, Cherbourg	21 Aug 1973
S 46	P 6146	C. M. de Normandie, Cherbourg	17 Oct 1973
S 47	P 6147	C. M. de Normandie, Cherbourg	13 Nov 1973
S 48	P 6148	C. M. de Normandie, Cherbourg	9 Jan 1974
S 49	P 6149	C. M. de Normandie, Cherbourg	26 Feb 1974
S 50	P 6150	C. M. de Normandie, Cherbourg	27 Mar 1974
S 51	P 6151	C. M. de Normandie, Cherbourg	12 June 1974
S 52	P 6152	C. M. de Normandie, Cherbourg	17 July 1974
S 53	P 6153	C. M. de Normandie, Cherbourg	24 Sep 1974
S 54	P 6154	C. M. de Normandie, Cherbourg	27 Nov 1974
S 55	P 6155	C. M. de Normandie, Cherbourg	7 Jan 1975
S 56	P 6156	C. M. de Normandie, Cherbourg	12 Feb 1975
S 57	P 6157	C. M. de Normandie, Cherbourg	3 April 1975
S 58	P 6158	C. M. de Normandie, Cherbourg	22 May 1975
S 59	P 6159	C. M. de Normandie, Cherbourg	24 June 1975
S 60	P 6160	C. M. de Normandie, Cherbourg	6 Aug 1975

Displacement, tons: 234 standard; 265 full load
Dimensions, feet (metres): 154·2 × 23·0 × 5·9 (47 × 7 × 2)
Missiles: 4 launchers for Exocet MM 38
Guns: 1—76 mm OTO Melara; 1—40 mm (Bofors)
Main engines: 4 MTU diesels; 4 shafts; 12 000 bhp = 35·5 knots
Oil fuel, tons: 39
Range, miles: 600 at 30 knots
Complement: 30 (4 officers, 26 men)

S 60   6/1976, Reinhard Nerlich

Ordered in Oct 1970. For completion from 1973 onwards to replace the first 20 of the "Jaguar" class. Eight hulls contracted to Lürssen but all fitted out in France. Steel-hulled craft. Launch dates: S 41, 27 Sep 1972; S 42, 12 Dec 1972; S 43, 7 Mar 1973; S 44, 5 May 1973; S 45, 3 July 1973; S 46, 21 May 1973; S 47, 20 Sep 1973; S 48, 10 Sep 1973; S 49 11 Jan 1974; S 50, 10 Dec 1973; S 51, 11 June 1974; S 52, 25 May 1974; S 53, 4 July 1974; S 54, 8 July 1974; S 55, 15 Nov 1974; S 56, 30 Oct 1974; S 57, 18 Feb 1975; S 58, 26 Feb 1975; S 59, 15 May 1975; S 60, 26 May 1975.

Electronics: Thomson-CSF, Vega-Pollux PCET control system, controlling missiles, torpedoes and guns.

Radar: Navigation: three RM 20.
Air and surface search/target designator: Triton G-band
Tracking: Pollux I band.

Squadrons: Third: S 41-50. Fifth: S 51-60.

S 48   1977, Michael D, J. Lennon

GERMANY (FEDERAL) 193

10 "ZOBEL" CLASS (TYPE 142 FAST ATTACK CRAFT—TORPEDO)

Name	No.	Builders	Commissioned
ZOBEL	P 6092	Lürssen, Vegesack	1961
WIESEL	P 6093	Lürssen, Vegesack	1962
DACHS	P 6094	Lürssen, Vegesack	1962
HERMELIN	P 6095	Lürssen, Vegesack	1962
NERZ	P 6096	Lürssen, Vegesack	1963
PUMA	P 6097	Lürssen, Vegesack	1962
GEPARD	P 6098	Kröger, Rendsburg	1963
HYANE	P 6099	Kröger, Rendsburg	1963
FRETTCHEN	P 6100	Lürssen, Vegesack	1963
OZELOT	P 6101	Kröger, Rendsburg	1963

GEPARD *Lürssen Werft*

Displacement, tons: 225 full load
Dimensions, feet (metres): 139·4 × 23·4 × 7·9 *(42·5 × 7·2 × 2·4)*
Guns: 2—40 mm Bofors L 70 (single)
Torpedo tubes: 2—21 in for Seal wire-guided torpedoes
Main engines: 4 Mercedes-Benz (MTU) 20 cyl diesels; 4 shafts; 12 000 bhp = 40·5 knots
Complement: 39

Originally units of the "Jaguar" class, but, after conversion, known as the "Zobel" class. Form 7th Squadron.

Radar: Fire control: two M 20 series in radome

AMPHIBIOUS FORCES

22 TYPE 520 (LCUs)

FLUNDLER L 760	SCHLEI L 765	BUTT L 788	FORELLE L 794
KARPFEN L 761	STÖR L 766	BRASSE L 789	INGER L 795
LACHS L 762	TÜMMLER L 767	BARBE L 790	MAKRELE L 796
PLOTZE L 763	WELS L 768	DELPHIN L 791	MURÄNE L 797
ROCHEN L 764	ZANDER L 769	DORSCH L 792	RENKE L 798
		FELCHEN L 793	SALM L 799

Displacement, tons: 200 light; 403 full load
Dimensions, feet (metres): 136·5 × 28·9 × 6·9 *(41·6 × 8·8 × 2·1)*
Guns: 2—20 mm (see *Gunnery* notes)
Main engines: GM diesels; 2 shafts; 1 380 bhp = 12 knots
Complement: 17

Similar to the United States LCU (Landing Craft Utility) type. Provided with bow and stern ramp. Built by Howaldtswerke, Hamburg, 1964-67. To carry 160 tons load. *Inger* employed for seamanship training. *Renke* and *Salm* in reserve.

Gunnery: Have been rearmed with 2 modern 20 mm (twin).

DELPHIN *1976, J. A. Verhoog*

19 LCM TYPE 521

LCM 1-19

Displacement, tons: 116 standard; 140 full load
Dimensions, feet (metres): 67·6 wl × 21 × 4·3 *(20·6 × 6·4 × 1·3)*
Main engines: 2 diesels; 1 320 hp = 10 knots

Similar to US LCM 8 type. Built by Blöhm and Voss 1965-67. Can carry 50 tons.

MINE WARFARE FORCES

18 "LINDAU" CLASS (TYPE 320)
(MINESWEEPERS—COASTAL and MINEHUNTERS)

Name	No.	Builders	Commissioned
GÖTTINGEN	M 1070	Burmester, Bremen	1958
KOBLENZ	M 1071	Burmester, Bremen	1958
LINDAU	M 1072	Burmester, Bremen	1958
SCHLESWIG	M 1073	Burmester, Bremen	1958
TÜBINGEN	M 1074	Burmester, Bremen	1958
WETZLAR	M 1075	Burmester, Bremen	1958
PADERBORN	M 1076	Burmester, Bremen	1958
WEILHEIM	M 1077	Burmester, Bremen	1959
CUXHAVEN	M 1078	Burmester, Bremen	1959
DÜREN	M 1079	Burmester, Bremen	1959
MARBURG	M 1080	Burmester, Bremen	1959
KONSTANZ	M 1081	Burmester, Bremen	1959
WOLFSBURG	M 1082	Burmester, Bremen	1959
ULM	M 1083	Burmester, Bremen	1959
FLENSBURG	M 1084	Burmester, Bremen	1959
MINDEN	M 1085	Burmester, Bremen	1960
FULDA	M 1086	Burmester, Bremen	1960
VÖLKLINGEN	M 1087	Burmester, Bremen	1960

Displacement, tons: 370 standard; 420 full load
Dimensions, feet (metres): 137·8 pp; 147·7 oa × 27·2 × 8·5 *(49·7 × 8·3 × 2·5)*
Guns: 1—40 mm; 2—20 mm
Main engines: Maybach (MTU) diesels; 2 shafts; 4 000 bhp = 16·5 knots
Range, miles: 850 at 16·5 knots
Complement: 46

PADERBORN *8/1975, Michael D. J. Lennon*

Lindau, first German built vessel for the Federal German Navy since the Second World War, launched on 16 Feb 1957. Basically of NATO WU type but modified for German requirements. The hull is of wooden construction, laminated with plastic glue. The engines are of non-magnetic materials. The first six, *Göttingen, Koblenz, Lindau, Schleswig, Tubingen* and *Wetzlar*, were modified with lower bridges in 1958-59. *Schleswig* was lengthened by 6·8 feet *(2·07 metres)* in 1960—all others in 1960-64. *Fulda* and *Flensburg* were converted into minehunters in 1968-69 as part of a total of twelve ships to be so converted, with the second group started in 1975, *Lindau, Tübingen Minden, Koblenz, Wetzlar, Göttingen, Weilheim, Völkingen, Cuxhaven* and *Marburg* in that order. Owing to industrial problems delays caused all ten ships to be in the yards at the same time. *Lindau* eventually completed late 1975 and *Marburg* is hoped to complete in 1980.
These are being fitted with Plessey sonar and French PAP exploders.

Troika Conversion: The six ships *(Düren, Konstanz, Paderborn, Ulm, Schleswig* and *Wolfsburg)* not being converted to minehunters will, in 1980/81, be converted as guidance ships for Troika. Each will carry three of these unmanned minesweeping vehicles. The whole of this programme will replace the surviving "Schütze" class.

Squadrons: 4th MCM Squadron—*Fulda, Flensburg, Düren, Konstanz, Paderborn.* 6th MCM Squadron—*Ulm, Schleswig, Wolfsburg.*

FULDA (Hunter) *6/1975, Reinhard Nerlich*

194 GERMANY (FEDERAL)

22 "SCHÜTZE" CLASS (TYPE 340-341)
(MINESWEEPERS—COASTAL (FAST))

Name	No.	Builders	Commissioned
CASTOR	M 1051	Abeking and Rasmussen	1962
POLLUX	M 1054	Abeking and Rasmussen	1961
SIRIUS	M 1055	Abeking and Rasmussen	1961
RIGEL	M 1056	Abeking and Rasmussen	1962
REGULUS	M 1057	Abeking and Rasmussen	1962
MARS	M 1058	Abeking and Rasmussen	1960
SPICA	M 1059	Abeking and Rasmussen	1961
SKORPION	M 1060	Abeking and Rasmussen	1963
SCHÜTZE	M 1062	Abeking and Rasmussen	1959
WAAGE	M 1063	Abeking and Rasmussen	1962
DENEB	M 1064	Schürenstedt	1961
JUPITER	M 1065	Schürenstedt	1961
ATAIR	M 1067	Schlichting, Travemünde	1961
WEGA	M 1089	Abeking and Rasmussen	1963
PERSEUS	M 1090	Schlichting, Travemünde	1961
PLUTO	M 1092	Schürenstedt	1960
NEPTUN	M 1093	Schlichting, Travemünde	1960
WIDDER	M 1094	Schürenstedt	1960
HERKULES	M 1095	Schlichting, Travemünde	1960
FISCHE	M 1096	Abeking and Rasmussen	1960
GEMMA	M 1097	Abeking and Rasmussen	1960
STIER	Y 849	Abeking and Rasmussen	1961

Displacement, tons: 204 standard; 230 full load
Dimensions, feet (metres): 124·7 × 27·2 × 6·6 (43·8 × 8·2 × 2)
Gun: 1—40 mm (except Stier)
Main engines: MTU diesels = 14 knots
Range, miles: 2 000 at 13 knots
Complement: 24

30 originally built between 1959 and 1964. (Ex-*Uranus* is now German Navy League ship in Trier). The design is a development of the "R" boats of World War II. *Stier*, former number M 1061, carries no weapons, but has a recompression chamber, being a clearance diving vessel. Formerly classified as inshore minesweepers, but re-rated as fast minesweepers in 1966. Form the 1st and 5th MCM Squadrons. All to be replaced by Troika fitted "Lindau" class in early 1980s.

Radar: TRS-N.

Transfer: Five transferred to Greece, deleted in 1974.

HERKULES 1976, Reinhard Nerlich

STIER (with recompression chamber) 1975, Federal German Navy

10 "FRAUENLOB" CLASS (TYPE 394) (MINESWEEPERS—INSHORE)

Name	No.	Builders	Commissioned
FRAUENLOB	M 2658	Krögerwerft, Rendsburg	1966
NAUTILUS	M 2659	Krögerwerft, Rendsburg	1966
GEFION	M 2660	Krögerwerft, Rendsberg	1967
MEDUSA	M 2661	Krögerwerft, Rendsburg	1967
UNDINE	M 2662	Krögerwerft, Rendsburg	1967
MINERVA	M 2663	Krögerwerft, Rendsburg	1967
DIANA	M 2664	Krögerwerft, Rendsburg	1967
LORELEY	M 2665	Krögerwerft, Rendsburg	1968
ATLANTIS	M 2666	Krögerwerft, Rendsburg	1968
ACHERON	M 2667	Krögerwerft, Rendsburg	1969

Displacement, tons: 230 standard; 280 full load
Dimensions, feet (metres): 154·5 oa × 22·3 × 7·2 (47·2 × 7·2 × 2·2)
Gun: 1—40 mm
Mines: Laying capability
Main engines: Maybach (MTU) diesels; 2 shafts; Escher Wyss propellers; 3 600 bhp = 24·5 knots
Complement: 39

Launched in 1965-67. Originally designed coastguard boats with "W" numbers. Rated as inshore minesweepers in 1968 with the "M" numbers. All subsequently allocated Y numbers and later reallocated M numbers. 2nd MCM Squadron.

MINERVA 1977, J. A. Verhoog

8 "ARIADNE" CLASS (TYPE 393) (MINESWEEPERS—INSHORE)

Name	No.	Builders	Commissioned
ARIADNE	M 2650	Krögerwerft, Rendsburg	1961
FREYA	M 2651	Krögerwerft, Rendsburg	1962
VINETA	M 2652	Krögerwerft, Rendsburg	1962
HERTHA	M 2653	Krögerwerft, Rendsburg	1962
NYMPHE	M 2654	Krögerwerft, Rendsburg	1963
NIXE	M 2655	Krögerwerft, Rendsburg	1963
AMAZONE	M 2656	Krögerwerft, Rendsburg	1963
GAZELLE	M 2657	Krögerwerft, Rendsburg	1963

Displacement, tons: 184 standard; 210 full load
Dimensions, feet (metres): 124·3 × 27·2 × 6·6 (37·9 × 8·3 × 2)
Gun: 1—40 mm
Mines: Laying capability
Main engines: 2 Mercedes-Benz (MTU) diesels; 2 shafts; 2 000 bhp = 14 knots
Range, miles: 740 at 14 knots
Complement: 23

All launched between April 1960 (*Ariadne*) and June 1966 (*Freya*). All named after cruisers of 1897-1900. Formerly classified as patrol boats but re-rated as inshore minesweepers in 1966, and given new M numbers in Jan 1968, Y numbers in 1970, and M numbers once more in 1974. 3rd MCM Squadron.

VINETA 11/1976, Stefan Terzibaschitsch

GERMANY (FEDERAL) 195

1 TRIALS MINESWEEPER

Name	No.	Builders	Commissioned
HOLNIS	Y 836 (ex-M 2651)	Abeking and Rasmussen	1966

Displacement, tons: 180
Dimensions, feet (metres): 116·8 × 24·3 × 6·9 *(35·6 × 7·4 × 2·1)*
Gun: 1—20 mm
Main engines: 2 Mercedes-Benz (MTU) diesels; 2 shafts; 2 000 bhp = 14·5 knots
Complement: 21

Now serving for trials and evaluation. *Holnis* was launched on 22 May 1965 as the prototype of a new design projected as a class of 20 such vessels but she is the only unit of this type, the other 19 boats having been cancelled. Hull number changed from M 2651 to Y 836 in 1970.

HOLNIS *1975, Federal German Navy*

2 "NIOBE" CLASS (MINESWEEPERS—INSHORE)

Name	No.	Builders	Commissioned
HANSA	Y 806	Krögerwerft, Rendsburg	1958
NIOBE	Y 1643	Krögerwerft, Rendsburg	1958

Displacement, tons: 150 standard; 180 full load
Dimensions, feet (metres): 115·2 × 21·3 × 5·6 *(35·1 × 6·5 × 1·7)*
Gun: 1—40 mm
Mines: Laying capability
Main engines: *Hansa:* 1 Mercedes-Benz (MTU) diesel; 1 shaft; 950 bhp = 14 knots
  Niobe: 2 Mercedes-Benz (MTU) diesels; 2 shafts; 1 900 bhp = 16 knots
Range, miles: 1 100 at max speed
Complement: *Hansa* 19; *Niobe* 22

Hansa serves as support ship for clearance divers. *Niobe* is test and trials ship.

HANSA *1975, Federal German Navy*

SERVICE FORCES

11 "RHEIN" CLASS (DEPOT SHIPS)

Name	No.	Builders	Commissioned
ISAR	A 54	Blöhm and Voss	1964
LAHN	A 55	Flender, Lübeck	1964
LECH	A 56	Flender, Lübeck	1964
RHEIN	A 58	Schliekerwerft, Hamburg	1961
ELBE	A 61	Schliekerwerft, Hamburg	1962
MAIN	A 63	Lindenau, Kiel	1963
SAAR	A 65	Norderwerft, Hamburg	1963
NECKAR	A 66	Lürssen, Vegesack	1963
MOSEL	A 67	Schliekerwerft, Hamburg	1963
WERRA	A 68	Lindenau, Kiel	1964
DONAU	A 69	Schlichting, Travemünde	1964

Displacement, tons: 2 370 standard; 2 540 full load
  except *Lahn* and *Lech* 2 460 standard; 2 680 full load
Length, feet (metres): 304·5 *(92·8)* wl; 323·5 *(99)* oa
Beam, feet (metres): 38·8 *(11·8)*
Draught, feet (metres): 11·2 *(3·4)*; 12·2 *(3·7)* in *Lahn* and *Lech*
Guns: 2—3·9 in *(100 mm);* none in *Lahn, Lech;* 4—40 mm
Main engines: 6 Maybach or Daimler (MTU) diesels; diesel-electric drive in *Isar, Lahn, Lech, Mossel, Saar* 11 400 bhp; 2 shafts
Speed, knots: 20·5, 15 economical
Range, miles: 1 625 at 15 knots
Oil fuel, tons: 334
Complement: 110 (accommodation for 200); 198 *(Lahn* and *Lech)*

Originally a class of 13. Rated as depot ships for minesweepers *(Isar, Mosel, Saar),* submarines *(Lahn, Lech),* Type 206 submarines *(Rhein),* and motor torpedo boats (others) but these ships with their 3·9 in *(100 mm)* guns could obviously be used in lieu of frigates.

Conversion: *Lahn* major conversion in 1975.

Launch dates: *Donau* 26 Nov 1960, *Elbe* 5 May 1960, *Isar* 14 July 1962, *Lahn* 21 Nov 1961, *Lech* 4 May 1962, *Main* 23 July 1960, *Mosel* 15 Dec 1960, *Neckar* 26 June 1961, *Rhein* 10 Feb 1959, *Saar* 11 Mar 1961, *Werra* 26 Mar 1963.

Operation: *Saar,* 1st MCM Squadron; *Isar,* MCM Squadron; *Mosel,* 5th MCM Squadron; *Elbe,* 3rd FPB Squadron; *Main,* 5th FPB Squadron; *Lahn,* 1st Submarine Squadron; *Lech,* 3rd Submarine Squadron. Of the rest two are reported as civilian manned for SAR duties.

WERRA *5/1975, Reinhard Nerlich*

Radar: All by Hollandse. Search: HSA DA 02.
Fire control: Two HSA M 45 for 100 mm and 40 mm.

Status: Five of these comparatively new ships, namely *Donau, Isar, Lahn, Lech* and *Weser* (now deleted) were placed in reserve by July 1968. This was part of the economy programme announced by the Federal German Navy in Sep 1967 but all have subsequently been recommissioned or transferred.

Transfer: *Weser* to Greece 1975. *Rühr* to Turkey 1976.

2 Ex-US "ARISTAEUS" CLASS (REPAIR SHIPS)

ODIN (ex-USS *Diomedes,* ARB 11, ex-*LST 1119)* A 512
WOTAN (ex-USS *Ulysses,* ARB 9, ex-*LST 967)* A 513

Displacement, tons: 1 625 light; 3 455 full load
Dimensions, feet (metres): 328 oa × 50 × 9·2 *(100 × 15·2 × 2·8)*
Guns: 4—20 mm
Main engines: 2 GM diesels, 2 shafts; 1 800 bhp = 11·6 knots
Oil fuel, tons: 600
Range, miles: 2 000 at 9 knots
Complement: 187

Repair ships. Transferred under MAP in June 1961.
Odin commissioned in Jan 1966 and *Wotan* on 2 Dec 1965. *Wotan* now civilian-manned.

WOTAN *1975, Federal German Navy*

MEMMERT Y 805

The small repair ship *Memmert* Y 805 (ex-USN *106,* ex-*India,* ex-*BP 34),* 165 tons and 8 knots, rated as torpedo repair ship, salvage vessel with a derrick.

196 GERMANY (FEDERAL)

2 FLEET REPLENISHMENT SHIPS

Name	No.	Builder	Commissioned
SPESSART (ex-*Okapi*)	A 1442	Kröger, Rendsburg	1974
RHÖN (ex-*Okene*)	A 1443	Kröger, Rendsburg	1974

Measurement, tons: 6 103 brt; 10 800 d.wt.
Length, feet (metres): 426·7 *(130·1)*
Beam, feet (metres): 64·3 *(19·6)*
Main engines: 8 000 hp = 16 knots
Complement: 42

Completed for Terkol Group as Tankers. Acquired in 1976 for conversion which started in January 1977. (*Spessart* at Bremerhaven, *Rhön* at Kröger). The former commissioned 5 Sep 1977 and the latter on 23 Sep 1977. Unarmed and civilian manned.

1 "BODENSEE" CLASS (REPLENISHMENT TANKER)

Name	No.	Builders	Commissioned
WITTENSEE (ex-*Sioux*)	A 1407	Lindenau, Kiel	26 Mar 1959

Measurement, tons: 1 238 deadweight; 985 gross
Dimensions, feet (metres): 208·3 × 32·5 × 15 *(61·2 × 9·8 × 4·3)*
Main engines: Diesels; 1 050—1 250 bhp = 12 knots
Complement: 21

Launched on 23 Sep 1958.

WITTENSEE   11/1976, Stefan Terzibaschitsch

1 REPLENISHMENT TANKER

Name	No.	Builders	Commissioned
EIFEL (ex-*Friedrich Jung*)	A 1429	Norderwerft, Hamburg	27 May 1963

Displacement, tons: 4 720
Dimensions, feet (metres): 334 × 47·2 × 23·3 *(102 × 14·4 × 7·1)*
Main engines: 3 360 hp = 13 knots

Launched on 29 Mar 1958. Purchased in 1963 for service in the Federal German Navy.

EIFEL   1970, Federal German Navy

4 "WALCHENSEE" CLASS (TYPE 703) (SUPPORT TANKERS)

Name	No.	Builders	Commissioned
WALCHENSEE	A 1424	Lindenau, Kiel	29 June 1966
AMMERSEE	A 1425	Lindenau, Kiel	2 Mar 1967
TEGERNSEE	A 1426	Lindenau, Kiel	23 Mar 1967
WESTENSEE	A 1427	Lindenau, Kiel	6 Oct 1967

Displacement, tons: 2 174
Dimensions, feet (metres): 233 × 36·7 × 13·5 *(74·2 × 11·2 × 4·1)*
Main engines: Diesels; 2 shafts; 1 400 bhp = 12·6 knots

Launched on 22 Sep 1966, 22 Oct 1966, 10 July 1965 and 25 Feb 1966 respectively.

WALCHENSEE   1975, Reiner Nerlich

1 SUPPORT TANKER

Name	No.	Builders	Commissioned
HARZ (ex-*Claere Jung*)	A 1428	Norderwerft, Hamburg	27 May 1963 (see note)

Displacement, tons: 3 696 deadweight
Dimensions, feet (metres): 303·2 × 43·5 × 21·7 *(92·4 × 13·2 × 6·6)*
Main engines: 2 520 hp = 12 knots
Complement: 42

Built in 1953 and purchased in 1963 for service as a tanker.

HARZ   1970, Federal German Navy

GERMANY (FEDERAL) 197

8 "LÜNEBURG" CLASS (SUPPORT SHIPS)

Name	No.	Builders	Commissioned
LÜNEBURG*	A 1411	Flensburger, Schiffbau	9 July 1968
COBURG	A 1412	Flensburger Schiffbau	9 July 1968
FREIBURG	A 1413	Blöhm and Voss	27 May 1968
GLÜCKSBURG*	A 1414	Flensburger, Schiffbau	9 July 1968
SAARBURG*	A 1415	Blöhm and Voss	30 July 1968
NIENBURG	A 1416	Vulkan, Bremen	1 Aug 1968
OFFENBURG	A 1417	Blöhm and Voss	27 May 1968
MEERSBURG*	A 1418	Vulkan, Bremen	25 June 1968

*conversions

Displacement, tons: 3 254
Dimensions, feet (metres): 341·2 × 43·3 × 13·8 *(104 × 13·2 × 4·2)* (379 ft—115·5 m for lengthened ships)
Guns: 4—40 mm (cocooned)
Main engines: 2 Maybach (MTU) diesels; 2 shafts; 5 600 bhp = 17 knots
Complement: 103

Modernisation: Four of this class have been lengthened by 37·8 feet *(11·52 metres)* and modernised to serve the missile installations of the new classes of Fast Attack Craft and converted destroyers, including MM 38 Exocet maintenance. *Saarburg* completed 1975—*Lüneburg* 1976—*Meersburg* 1976—*Glücksburg* 1977.

MEERSBURG   1976, J. M. Verhoog

2 "WESTERWALD" CLASS (AMMUNITION TRANSPORTS)

Name	No.	Builders	Commissioned
WESTERWALD	A 1435	Lübecker, Masch	1 Feb 1967
ODENWALD	A 1436	Lübecker, Masch	23 Mar 1967

Displacement, tons: 3 460
Dimensions, feet (metres): 347·8 × 46 × 12·2 *(106 × 14 × 3·7)*
Guns: 4—40 mm
Main engines: MTU diesels; 5 600 bhp = 17 knots
Complement: 60

Odenwald was launched on 5 May 1966 and *Westerwald* was launched on 25 Feb 1966.

WESTERWALD   4/1976, Dr. Giorgio Arra

2 "SACHSENWALD" CLASS (MINE TRANSPORTS)

Name	No.	Builders	Commissioned
SACHSENWALD	A 1437	Blöhm and Voss, Hamburg	20 Aug 1969
STEIGERWALD	A 1438	Blöhm and Voss, Hamburg	20 Aug 1969

Displacement, tons: 3 850 full load
Dimensions, feet (metres): 363·5 × 45·6 × 11·2 *(111 × 13·9 × 3·4)*
Guns: 4—40 mm (two twin mountings)
Mines: Laying capacity
Main engines: 2 MTU diesels; 2 shafts; 5 600 hp = 17 knots
Range, miles: 3 500
Complement: 65

Built as mine transports. Laid down on 1 Aug 1966 and 9 May 1966. Launched on 10 Dec 1966 and 10 Mar 1967. Have mine ports in the stern and can be used as minelayers.

SACHSENWALD   1976, German Federal Navy

5 "FW" CLASS (WATER BOATS)

FW 1 Y 864   **FW 2** Y 865   **FW 3** Y 866   **FW 4** Y 867   **FW 5** Y 868

Measurement, tons: 350 deadweight
Dimensions, feet (metres): 144·4 × 25·6 × 8·2 *(44·1 × 7·8 × 2·5)*
Main engines: MWM diesel, 230 bhp = 9·5 knots

Built in pairs by Schiffbarges, Unterweser, Bremerhaven; H. Rancke, Hamburg and Jadewerft, Wilhelmshaven, in 1963-64. *FW 6* to Turkey 1975.

FW 5   8/1975, Stefan Terzibaschitsch

GERMANY (FEDERAL)

TRAINING SHIPS

1 "DEUTSCHLAND" CLASS

Name	No.	Builders	Commissioned
DEUTSCHLAND	A 59	Nobiskrug, Rendesburg	25 May 1963

Displacement, tons: 4 880 normal; 5 400 full load
Length, feet (metres): 452·8 *(138·0)* pp; 475·8 *(145·0)* oa
Beam, feet (metres): 59 *(18)*
Draught, feet (metres): 15·7 *(4·8)*
Guns: 4—3·9 in *(100 mm)* (single); 6—40 mm (2 twin and 2 single)
A/S weapons: 2 Bofors 4-barrel rocket launchers
Torpedo tubes: 2—21 in *(533 mm)* (surface targets); 4—21 in *(533 mm)* (A/S)
Mines: Laying capacity
Main engines: 6 800 bhp MTU diesels (2 Daimler-Benz and 2 Maybach); 2 shafts with vp propellers; 8 000 shp double reduction MAN geared turbines; 1 shaft
Boilers: 2 Wahodag; 768 psi *(54 km/cm²)*; 870°F *(465°C)*
Speed, knots: 22 (3 shafts); 17 (2 shafts) 14 economical (1 shaft)
Oil fuel, tons: 230 furnace; 410 diesel
Range, miles: 6 000 at 17 knots
Complement: 554 (33 officers, 271 men, 250 cadets)

DEUTSCHLAND — 6/1974, USN

Electronics: HSA fire control for Bofors A/S launchers and torpedoes.

Radar: All by Hollandse Signaalapparaten.
Navigation/surface warning: SGR 103, 105, 114.
Air warning: one LW-02/3
Target designator: one DA 02.
Fire control: two M 45 series (M2/2; M4).

Sonar: One ELAC 1BV hull-mounted set.

First West German naval ship to exceed the post-war limit of 3 000 tons. Designed with armament and machinery of different types for training purposes. The name originally planned for this ship was *Berlin*. Ordered in 1956. Laid down in 1959 and launched 5 Nov 1960. Carried out her first machinery sea trials on 15 Jan 1963.

SAIL TRAINING SHIPS

Name	No.	Builders	Commissioned
GORCH FOCK	A 60	Blöhm and Voss, Hamburg	17 Dec 1958

Displacement, tons: 1 760 standard; 1 870 full load
Dimensions, feet (metres): 257 oa × 39·2 × 15·8 *(81·3 × 12 × 4·8)*
Main engines: Auxiliary MAN diesel; 880 bhp = 11 knots
Sail area, sq ft: 21 141
Range, miles: 1 990 on auxiliary diesel
Complement: 206 (10 officers, 56 ratings, 140 cadets)

Sail training ship of the improved "Horst Wessel" type. Barque rig. Launched on 23 Aug 1958.

GORCH FOCK — 10/1975, Reinhard Nerlich

Name	No.	Builders	Commissioned
NORDWIND	Y 834	—	1944

Displacement, tons: 110
Dimensions, feet (metres): 78·8 × 22 × 9 *(24 × 6·4 × 2·5)*
Main engines: Diesel; 150 bhp = 8 knots (sail area 2 037·5 sq ft)

Ketch rigged.

There are over 70 other sailing vessels of various types serving for sail training and recreational purposes. *Achat, Alarich, Amsel, Argonaut, Borasco, Brigant, Dankwart, Diamont, Dietrich, Drossel, Dompfaff, Fafnir, Fink, Flibustier, Freibeuter, Gernot, Geiserich, Geuse, Giselher, Gödicke, Gunnar, Gunter, Hadubrand, Hagen, Hartnaut, Hilderbrand, Horand, Hunding, Jaspis, Kaper, Klipper, Korsar, Kuchkuch, Lerche, Likendeeler, Magellan, Michel, Mime, Meise, Mistral, Monsun, Nachtigall, Ortwin, Ostwind, Pampero, Pirol, Ruediger, Samum, Saphir, Schirocco, Seeteufel, Siegfried, Siegmund, Siegura, Smaragd, Star, Stieglitz, Storetbecker, Taifun, Teja, Topas, Tornadon, Totila, Vitalienbrüder, Volker, Walter, Wate, Westwind, Wiking, Wittigo, Zeisig.*

MISCELLANEOUS

7 COASTAL PATROL CRAFT

KW 15	Y 827	KW 19	Y 833
KW 16	Y 830	KW 17	Y 845
KW 18	Y 832	KW 20	Y 846

Displacement, tons: 45 standard; 60 full load
Dimensions, feet (metres): 93·5 oa × 15·5 × 4·0 *(28·9 × 4·9 × 1·5)*
Main engines: 2 Mercedes-Benz (MTU) diesels; 2 000 bhp = 25 knots
Complement: 14

Built in 1951-53.

13 TORPEDO RECOVERY VESSELS

TF 1-6 (Y 851-856)   **TF 101-104** (Y 883-886)   **TF 106-108** (Y 872-874)

All of approximately 30-40 tons. TF 1-6 and 106-108 built in 1966, the remainder a deal older.

TF 108 — 1974, Reiner Nerlich

KW 18 — 5/1975, Reiner Nerlich

KW 3 Y 829. Of 112 tons and 8 knots built in 1943.

GERMANY (FEDERAL) 199

TUGS

2 SALVAGE TUGS

Name	No.	Builders	Commissioned
HELGOLAND	A 1457	Unterweser, Bremerhaven	8 Mar 1966
FEHMARN	A 1458	Unterweser, Bremerhaven	1 Feb 1967

Displacement, tons: 1 310 standard; 1 643 full load
Dimensions, feet (metres): 223·1 × 41·7 × 14·4 *(68·0 × 12·7 × 4·4)*
Guns: 2—40 mm (removed in *Helgoland*)
Main engines: Diesel-electric; 4 MWM diesels; 2 shafts; 3 800 hp = 17 knots
Range, miles: 6 000 at 10 knots
Complement: 36-45

Launched on 25 Nov 1965 and 8 April 1965. Carry firefighting equipment.

FEHMARN   1974, Federal German Navy—Marineamt

6 SALVAGE TUGS

Name	No.	Builders	Commissioned
WANGEROOGE	A 1451	Schichau, Bremerhaven	9 April 1968
SPIEKEROOG	A 1452	Schichau, Bremerhaven	14 Aug 1968
LANGEOOG	A 1453	Schichau, Bremerhaven	14 Aug 1968
NORDERNEY	A 1455	Schichau, Bremerhaven	1968
JUIST	A 1456	Schichau, Bremerhaven	1968
BALTRUM	V 1661	Schichau, Bremerhaven	8 Oct 1968

Displacement, tons: 854 standard; 1 024 full load
Dimensions, feet (metres): 170·6 × 39·4 × 12·8 *(52·0 × 12·1 × 3·9)*
Gun: 1—40 mm (removed in *Wangerooge*)
Main engines: Diesel-electric; 2 shafts; 2 400 hp = 14 knots
Range, miles: 5 000 at 10 knots
Complement: 24-35

Wangerooge, prototype salvage tug, was launched on 4 July 1966, *Baltrum* on 8 Oct 1968. *Baltrum* diving training ship (1974). Pennant numbers of training ships changed in late 1976.

Duties: *Norderney*, *Juist* and *Langeoog* converted and employed as diving training ships 1976-77.

SPIEKEROOG   2/1976, Reiner Nerlich

1 COASTAL TUG

Name	No.	Builders	Commissioned
PELLWORM	Y 801	Schichau, Königsberg	1939

Displacement, tons: 437 standard; 500 full load
Dimensions, feet (metres): 138·7 × 27·9 × 3·6 *(38·7 × 8·5 × 1·2)*
Main engines: 1—MWM-DM Diesel; 1 shaft; 800 hp = 12 knots
Range, miles: 2 900 at 8 knots

4 HARBOUR TUGS

Name	No.	Builders	Commissioned
SYLT	Y 820	Schichau, Bremerhaven	1962
FÖHR	Y 821	Schichau, Bremerhaven	1962
AMRUM	Y 822	Schichau, Bremerhaven	1963
NEUWERK	Y 823	Schichau, Bremerhaven	1963

Displacement, tons: 266 standard
Dimensions, feet (metres): 100·7 oa × 25·2 *(30·6 × 7·5)*
Main engine: 1 Deutz diesel; 800 bhp = 12 knots
Complement: 10

Launched in 1961.

3 HARBOUR TUGS

Name	No.	Builders	Commissioned
NEUENDE	Y 1680	Schichau, Bremerhaven	1971
HEPPENS	Y 1681	Schichau, Bremerhaven	1971
ELLERBEK	Y 1682	Schichau, Bremerhaven	1971

Displacement, tons: 122
Dimensions, feet (metres): 87·2 × 24·3 × 8·5 *(26·6 × 7·4 × 2·6)*
Main engines: 1 MWM diesel; 1 shaft; 800 hp
Speed, knots: 12
Complement: 6

Harbour Type: There are also nine small harbour tugs all completed in 1958-60:—*Knechtsand* Y 814, *Langeness* Y 819, *Lütje Horn* Y 812, *Mellum* Y 813, *Nordstrand* Y 817, *Plon* Y 802, *Scharhörn* Y 815, *Trischen* Y 818 and *Vogelsand* Y 816.

ICEBREAKERS

Name	No.	Builders	Commissioned
HANSE	—	Wärtsilä, Helsinki	13 Dec 1966

Displacement, tons: 2 771
Dimensions, feet (metres): 226·6 × 57 × 28·9 *(69·1 × 17·4 × 8·8)*
Main engines: Diesel-electric; 4 shafts; 7 500 bhp = 16 knots

Laid down on 12 Jan 1965. Launched on 17 Oct 1966. Completed on 25 Nov 1966. Although owned by West Germany she sails under the Finnish flag, manned by a Finnish crew. Only when the winter is so severe that icebreakers are needed in the southern Baltic will she be transferred under the German flag and command. She is of improved "Karhu" class. She does not belong to the Bundesmarine.

Name	No.	Builders	Commissioned
EISVOGEL	A 1401	J. G. Hitzler, Lauenburg	11 Mar 1961
EISBAR	A 1402	J. G. Hitzler, Lauenburg	1 Nov 1961

Displacement, tons: 560 standard
Dimensions, feet (metres): 125·3 × 31·2 × 15·1 *(38·2 × 9·5 × 4·6)*
Gun: 1—40 mm
Main engines: 2 Maybach diesels; 2 shafts; 2 000 bhp = 14 knots

Launched on 28 April and 9 June 1960 respectively.

EISVOGEL   5/1975, Reiner Nerlich

AUXILIARY SHIPS

1 Ex-BRITISH "ISLES" CLASS (MC TRAINING SHIP)

Name	No.	Builders	Commissioned
EIDER	Y 1663	Davie & Sons	1942
(ex-*Catherine*, ex-*Dochet*)	(ex-A 50)	Lauzon, Canada	

Displacement, tons: 480 standard; 750 full load
Dimensions, feet (metres): 164·0 pp; 177·2 oa × 27·5 × 14·0 *(53·9 × 8·4 × 4)*
Guns: 1—40 mm; 1—20 mm
Main engines: Triple expansion; 1 shaft; 750 ihp = 12 knots
Range, miles: 3 700
Oil fuel, tons: 130
Complement: 45

Employed as a mine clearance training vessel. She has been civilian manned since 1 Jan 1968.

EIDER   5/1975, Reiner Nerlich

200 GERMANY (FEDERAL)

1 RADAR TRIALS SHIP

Name	No.	Builders	Commissioned
OSTE (ex-*Puddefjord*, ex-*USN 101*)	A 52	Akers Mekaniske V, Oslo	1943

Displacement, tons: 567 gross
Dimensions, feet (metres): 160 × 29.7 × 17 *(48.8 × 9 × 5.2)*
Main engines: 1 Akers diesel; 1 shaft; 1 600 bhp = 12 knots

Taken over from the US Navy. Converted in 1968.

OSTE 8/1976, P. Crichton

2 RADAR TRIALS SHIPS

Name	No.	Builders	Commissioned
ALSTE (ex-*Mellum*)	A 50	Unterweser, Bremen	1972
OKER (ex-*Hoheweg*)	A 53	Unterweser, Bremen	1972

Measurement, tons: 1 187
Dimensions, feet (metres): 237.8 × 34.4 × 16.1 *(72.5 × 10.5 × 4.9)*
Main engines: Diesel-electric; 1 screw = 15 knots
Complement: 30

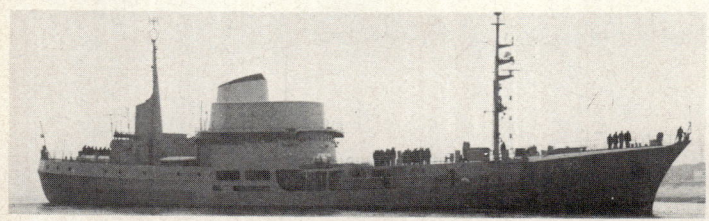

OKER 2/1977, Michael D. J. Lennon

1 TRIALS SHIP

Name	No.	Builders	Commissioned
WALTHER VON LEDEBUR	Y 841	Burmester, Bremen	1966

Displacement, tons: 725
Dimensions, feet (metres): 219.8 × 34.8 × 8.9 *(63 × 10.6 × 2.7)*
Main engines: Maybach (MTU) diesels; 2 shafts; 5 000 bhp = 19 knots
Complement: 11 + 10

Wooden hulled vessel. Trials ship. Launched on 30 June 1966.

WALTHER VON LEDEBUR 10/1975, Reinhard Nerlich

4 Ex-COASTAL MINESWEEPERS

OT 2 Y 847
H.C. OERSTED (ex-*Vinstra*, ex-*NYMS 247*) Y 877
ADOLF BESTELMEYER (ex-*BYMS 2213*) Y 881
RUDOLF DIESEL (ex-*BYMS 2279*) Y 889

Displacement, tons: 270 standard; 350 full load
Dimensions, feet (metres): 136 × 24.5 × 8 *(41.5 × 7.5 × 2.4)*
Main engines: 2 MTU diesels; 2 shafts; 1 000 bhp = 15 knots

Of US YMS type. Built in 1943. *Adolf Bestelmeyer* and *Rudolf Diesel* are used for gunnery trials. *H. C. Oersted* was acquired from the Royal Norwegian Navy and used as degaussing ship.

RUDOLF DIESEL 2/1976, Reinhard Nerlich

PLANET A 1450 of 1 943 tons and 13.5 knots. Built in 1965. Weapons research ship.

WILHELM PULLWER Y 838, **SP 1** Y 837 of 160 tons and 12.5 knots. Built in 1966. Trials ships.

HEINZ ROGGENKAMP Y 871. Of 785 tons and 12 knots. Built in 1952. Trials ship.

FRIEDRICH VOGE Y 888. Of 179 tons. Trials ship.

OTTO MEYCKE Diving Trials.

EF 3 Y 840 of 100 tons and 13.4 knots, ex-FPB built in 1943. Trials ship.

TB 1 Y 1678 of 70 tons and 14 knots. Diving boat built in 1972.

LP 1, 2 and **3**. Battery workshop craft of 180 tons built in 1963-73.

FÖRDE Y 1641   **JADE** Y 1642

Tank cleaning vessels. Of 600 tons, completed in 1967.

FÖRDE 8/1975, Stefan Terzibaschitsch

ARCONA (ex-*Royal Prince*) Y 809
KNURRHAHN Y 811 of 261 tons.

Both accommodation ships. *Arcona* ex-liner.

BARBARA Y 844, lifting ship of 3 500 tons.
HIEV Y 875, **GRIEP** Y 876, Floating cranes.

COASTGUARD VESSELS
(BUNDESGRENZSCHUTZ—SEE)

Note: This paramilitary force consists of about 1 000 men who operate the craft below as well as helicopters.

1 ICEBREAKING TUG

Name	No	Builders	Commissioned
RETTIN	BG 5	Mützelfeldwerft	3 Dec 1976

Measurement, tons: 120 brt
Dimensions, feet (metres): *(22.5 × 6.6 × 2.9)*
Main engines: 2 diesels; 590 hp = 9 knots
Complement: 4

Launched 29 Oct 1976.

8 LARGE PATROL CRAFT

NEUSTADT BG 11	**ESCHWEGE** BG 15
BAD BRAMSTEDT BG 12	**ALSFELD** BG 16
UELTZEN BG 13	**BAYREUTH** BG 17
DUDERSTADT BG 14	**ROSENHEIM** BG 18

Displacement, tons: 203
Length, feet (metres): 127·1 *(38·5)*
Guns: 2—40 mm
Main engines: 3 MTU diesels; 4 500 hp = 30 knots

All built between 1969 and late 1970—BG 13 by Schlichting, Travemünde, the remainder by Lürssen, Vegesack. Form two flotillas: BG 11-14 the 1st and BG 15-18 the 2nd. A third flotilla of smaller craft has been formed.

FISHERY PROTECTION SHIPS

Operated by Ministry of Agriculture and Fisheries.

ANTON DOHRN of 1 950 tons and 15 knots
FRITHJOF of 2 150 tons and 15 knots.
MEERKATZE of 2 250 tons and 14 knots. Completed 1977.
MINDEN of 973 tons and 16 knots.
ROTERSAND of 1 000 tons. Built in 1974.
SOLEA of 340 tons and 12 knots.
UTHÖRN of 110 tons and 9 knots.
WALTHER HERTWIG of 2 500 tons and 15 knots.

Previous *Meerkatze* sold in 1976 and *Nordenham* returned to her owners in 1977.

GERMANY (FEDERAL) / GHANA

SURVEY SHIPS

1 "VEGESACK" CLASS

PASSAU

Displacement, tons: 362 standard; 378 full load
Dimensions, feet (metres): 144·3 oa × 26·2 × 9 *(44·2 × 8 × 2·7)*
Main engines: 2 Mercedes-Benz (MTU) diesels; 1 500 hp; 2 shafts; cp propellers = 15 knots.

The last of 6 "Vegesack" class minesweepers built in Cherbourg 1959-60. Converted for oceanographic research. Other five transferred to Turkey.

The following ships operate for the Deutsches Hydrographisches Institut, under the Ministry of Transport.

METEOR (research ship) 3 085 tons, launched 1964, complement 55
KOMET (survey and research) 1 595 tons, launched 1969, complement 42
GAUSS (survey and research) 1 074 tons, launched 1949, complement 40
SÜDEROOG (survey ship) 211 tons, launched 1956, complement 16
ATAIR (survey and wrecks) 148 tons, launched 1962, complement 13
WEGA (survey and wrecks) 148 tons, launched 1962, complement 12
POSEIDON (survey) 1 266 tons, launched 1976, complement 28
VICTOR HENSEN (survey) 1 266 tons, launched 1976, complement 28
SENCKENBURG (research) 165 tons, launched 1976, complement 5

GAUSS
1974, Reiner Nerlich

GHANA

Administration

Commander of the Navy:
  Commodore C. K. Dzang

Personnel

(a) 1978: 2 000
(b) Voluntary service

General

The new orders with Lürssen may represent the four craft of the original order from Ruthof Werft. However, after a short fling with Soviet craft, it is notable that orders are now being directed to Western Europe. A programme for patrol craft to replace the aged British minesweepers would not be unreasonable as the new FACs seem an expensive way of patrolling off-shore limits.

Deletions

1973: 3 ex-Soviet "Poluchat I" Class Patrol Craft
1977 *Yogaga, Afadzato* ("Ham" class)

Mercantile Marine

Lloyd's Register of Shipping:
  79 vessels of 182 696 tons gross

Naval Bases

Secondi (Western Naval Command)
Tema, near Accra (Eastern Naval Command)

CORVETTES

2 "KROMANTSE" CLASS (VOSPER MARK I TYPE)

Name	No.	Builders	Commissioned
KROMANTSE	F 17	Vosper Ltd.	27 July 1964
KETA	F 18	Vickers Ltd (Tyne)	18 May 1965

Displacement, tons: 380 light; 440 standard; 500 full load
Dimensions, feet (metres): 162 wl; 177 oa × 28·5 × 13 *(49·4, 54 × 8·7 × 4)*
Guns: 1—4 in; 1—40 mm (see notes)
A/S weapons: 1 Squid triple-barrelled depth charge mortar
Main engines: 2 Bristol Siddeley Maybach (MTU) diesels; 2 shafts; 390 rpm; 7 100 bhp = 20 knots
Oil fuel, tons: 60
Range, miles: 2 000 at 16 knots; 2 900 at 14 knots
Complement: 54 (6 + 3 officers, 45 ratings)

Designed by Vosper Ltd, Portsmouth, a joint venture with Vickers-Armstrong's Ltd, one ship being built by each company. Vosper roll damping fins, and air conditioning throughout excepting machinery spaces. Generators 360 kW. The electrical power supply is 440 volts, 60 cycles ac. A very interesting patrol vessel design, an example of what can be achieved on a comparatively small platform to produce an inexpensive and quickly built anti-submarine vessel. *Kromantse* was launched at the Camber Shipyard, Portsmouth, on 5 Sep 1963. *Keta* was launched at Newcastle on 18 Jan 1965.

Radar: Search: Plessey AWS 1.

Refit: Both were fully refitted by Vosper Thornycroft Ltd (a £1·2 million contract) in 1974-75—*Keta* completed in April 1975 and *Kromantse* in Sep 1975.

Sonar: Both fitted with hull-mounted set.

KROMANTSE
9/1975, Vosper Thornycroft

GHANA

LIGHT FORCES

2 TYPE 45 (FAST ATTACK CRAFT—?MISSILE)

Displacement, tons: 255
Dimensions, feet (metres): 147·6 × 23 × 12·8 *(45 × 7 × 3·9)*
Missiles: 4—MM 38 Exocet (could be fitted)
Guns: 1—76 mm; 2—35 mm
Main engines: 4 MTU diesels; 14 000 hp; 4 shafts = 40 knots
Range, miles: 700 at 40 knots; 1 800 at 16 knots
Complement: 35

Ordered from Lürssen, Vegesack in 1976.

2 PB 57 TYPE (FAST ATTACK CRAFT—?MISSILE)

Displacement, tons: 410
Dimensions, feet (metres): 190·6 × 25 × 8·8 *(58·1 × 7·6 × 2·7)*
Missiles: ? MM 38 Exocet (could be fitted)
Guns: 1—76 mm; 2—35 mm
Main engines: 4 MTU diesels; 4 shafts; 12 000 hp = 42 knots
Range, miles: 700 at 35 knots.
Complement: ? 40

Ordered from Lürssen, Vegesack in 1977.

2 LARGE PATROL CRAFT

Name	No.	Builders	Commissioned
DIELA	P 24	Ruthof Werft, Mainz	1974
SAHENE	P 25	Ruthof Werft, Mainz	1974

Displacement, tons: 160
Dimensions, feet (metres): 115·5 × 21·3 × 5·9 *(35·2 × 6·5 × 1·8)*
Guns: 2—40 mm

Ordered from Ruthof Werft (Mainz) BRG in 1973 as part of a class of six. Only these two had been delivered when the builders went bankrupt in 1975—no further decisions known.

2 "FORD" CLASS (LARGE PATROL CRAFT)

Name	No.	Builders	Commissioned
ELMINA	P 13	—	—
ROMENDA	P 14	Yarrows, Scotstoun	Dec 1962

Displacement, tons: 120 standard; 142 full load
Dimensions, feet (metres): 110 wl; 117·5 oa × 20 × 7 *(33·6; 35·8 × 6·1 × 2·1)*
Gun: 1—40 mm, 60 cal Bofors
A/S weapons: Depth charge throwers
Main engines: 2 MTU (Maybach) diesels; type MD 16 V 53 87 B 90; 2 shafts = 3 000 hp at 1 790 rpm = 18 knots
Range, miles: 1 000 at 13 knots
Complement: 32 (3 officers, 29 ratings)

KOMENDA *1969, Ghana Navy*

MINEWARFARE FORCES

1 Ex-BRITISH "TON" CLASS (MINESWEEPER—COASTAL)

Name	No.	Builders	Commissioned
EJURA (ex-HMS *Aldington*)	M 16	Camper and Nicholson	1955

Displacement, tons: 360 standard; 425 full load
Dimensions, feet (metres): 140 pp; 153 oa × 28·8 × 8·2 *(42·7; 46·7 × 8·6 × 2·4)*
Guns: 1—40 mm forward; 2—20 mm aft
Main engines: Deltic diesels; 2 shafts; 3 000 bhp = 15 knots
Oil fuel, tons: 45
Range, miles: 2 300 at 13 knots
Complement: 27

Lent to Ghana by the United Kingdom in 1964. Acquired outright in 1974.

SERVICE CRAFT

ASUANTSI (ex-*MRC* 1122)

Displacement, tons: 657
Dimensions, feet (metres): 225 pp; 231·3 oa × 39 × 5 *(68·6; 70·5 × 11·9 × 1·5)*
Main engines: 4 Paxman; 1 840 bhp = 9 knots cruising

Acquired from the United Kingdom in 1965 and arrived in Ghana waters in July 1965. Used as a base workshop at Tema Naval Base. Is kept operational, and does a fair amount of seatime in general training and exercise tasks. Converted LCT.

GREECE

Ministerial

Minister of National Defence:
  Evangelos Averof

Headquarters Appointments

Chief Hellenic Navy:
  Vice-Admiral Konofaos
Deputy Chief:
  Rear-Admiral I. Deyiannis

Fleet Command

Commander of the Fleet:
  Vice-Admiral N. Andronopoulos

Diplomatic Representation

Naval Attaché in London:
  Captain Nikolaos Pappas
Naval Attaché in Washington:
  Captain O. Kapetos
Naval Attaché in Bonn:
  Captain T. Alicampiotis
Naval Attaché in Cairo:
  Captain P. Vossos
Naval Attaché in Ankara:
  Captain G. Tsakonas

Personnel

(a) 1977: 17 600 (1 900 officers and 15 700 ratings)
(b) 2 years national service

Naval Bases

Mitilini, Piraeus, Salamis, Salonika, Suda Bay and Volos (marines).

Naval Aviation

1 Squadron Alouette III helicopters with naval crews formed on 7 Aug 1975.
14 HU-16B Albatross are operated under naval command by mixed Air Force and Navy crews.
6 AB 212 ASW helicopters ordered 8 May 1977.

Harbour Corps

This force is equipped with coastal patrol craft and charged with harbour policing and coast-guard duties.

Prefix to Ships' Names

H.S. (Hellenic Ship)

Strength of the Fleet

Type	Active	Building
Destroyers	12	—
Frigates	4	—
Corvettes	5	—
Patrol Submarines	7	4
Fast Attack Craft—Missile	10	—
Fast Attack Craft—Torpedo	19	—
Large Patrol Craft	5	—
Fast Attack Craft—Patrol	—	10
Coastal Patrol Craft	5	—
Landing Ships	14	—
LCUs	6	—
Minor Landing Craft	47	—
Minelayers—Coastal	2	—
Minesweepers—Coastal	14	—
Survey Vessels	6	—
Depot Ship	1	—
Support Tankers	2	—
Harbour Tankers	5	—
Salvage Ship	2	—
Repair Ship	1	—
Lighthouse Tenders	4	—
Tugs	12	—
Netlayer	1	—
Water Boats	5	—
Auxiliary Transports	2	—

New Construction

It is reported that interest is being shown in the purchase of two A-69 Avisos from France.

Mercantile Marine

Lloyd's Register of Shipping:
  3 344 vessels of 29 517 059 tons gross

DELETIONS

Destroyers

1972 Doxa, Niki ("Gleaves" Class)

Submarines

1975 Poseidon

Light Forces

1971 Antiploiarkhos Laskos, Ploiarchos Meletopoulos
1972 Iniohos ("Nasty" Class)
1976 Plotarkhis Maridakis, Plotarkhis Vlachavas

Minesweepers—Coastal

1972 Paxi
1973 Afroessa, Kalymnos, Karteria, Kerkyra, Paralos, Zakynthos

Amphibious Forces

1971 Nafkratoussa (ex-Hyperion, ex-LSD 9)
1972 Ipopliarkhos Merlin (ex-US LSM 557) sunk in collision with a supertanker (15 Nov).
1975 Skopelos and Kea (ex-US LCT 6)

Survey Vessel

1973 Ariadne

Minesweeper Depot Ship

1973 Hermes (sunk as target)

Harbour Tanker

1976 Prometheus (target)

Tugs

1972 Aegeus, Adamastos

Water Boat

1972 Kaliroe

Light House Tenders

1976 St. Lykoudis, Skyros

PENNANT NUMBERS

Destroyers and Frigates

01 Aetos
06 Aspis
16 Velos
28 Thyella
31 Ierax
54 Leon
56 Lonchi
63 Navarinon
67 Panthir
85 Sfendoni
210 Themistocles
211 Miaoulis
212 Kanaris
213 Kontouriotis
214 Sachtouris

Submarines

S 86 Triaina
S 110 Glavkos
S 111 Nereus
S 112 Triton
S 113 Proteus
S 114 Papanikolis
S 115 Katsonis

Minelayers

N 04 Aktion
N 05 Amvrakia

Minesweepers

M 12 Armatolos
M 58 Mahitis
M 64 Navmachos
M 74 Polemistis
M 202 Atalanti
M 205 Antiopi
M 206 Faedra
M 210 Thalia
M 211 Alkyon
M 213 Argo
M 214 Avra
M 240 Pleias
M 241 Kichli
M 242 Kissa
M 245 Doris
M 246 Aigli
M 247 Dafni
M 248 Aedon
M 254 Niovi

Light Forces

P 14 Arslanoglou
P 15 Dolphin
P 16 Draken
P 17 Polikos
P 18 Polidefkis
P 19 Aiolos
P 20 Astrapi
P 21 Andromeda
P 22 N.I. Goulandris
P 23 Kastor
P 24 Kyknos
P 25 Pigassos
P 26 Toxotis
P 27 Foinix
P 28 Kelefstis Stamou
P 29 Diopos Antoniou
P 50 Antihliarpos Laskos
P 51 Plotarhis Blessas
P 52 Ipopliarhos Troupakis
P 53 Ipopliarhos Mikonios
P 54 Ipopliarhos Batsis
P 55 Ipopliarhos Arliotis
P 56 Anthipoploiarhos Anninos
P 57 Ipoploiarhos Konidis
P 70 A. Pezopoulos
P 96 P. Chadzikonstandis
P 196 Esperos
P 197 Kataigis
P 198 Kentauros
P 199 Kyklon
P 228 Lailaps
P 229 Scorpios
P 230 Tyfon

Amphibious Forces

L 144 Syros
L 145 Kassos
L 146 Karpathos
L 147 Kimolos
L 149 Kithos
L 150 Sifnos
L 152 Skiathos
L 153 Nafkratoussa
L 154 Ikaria
L 157 Rodos
L 158 Limnos
L 161 I. Grigoropoulos
L 162 I. Tournas
L 163 I. Daniolos
L 164 I. Roussen
L 165 I. Krystalidis
L 171 Kriti
L 172 Lesbos
L 179 Samos
L 195 Chios

Service Forces

A 215 Aegeon
A 307 Thetis
A 329 Sakipis
A 345 Sirios
A 372 Zeus
A 373 Kronos
A 374 Prometheus
A 376 Orion
A 377 Arethousa
A 384 Sotir
A 407 Antaios
A 408 Atlas
A 409 Achilleus
A 410 Atromitos
A 413 Hephestos
A 414 Ariadni
A 415 Pandora
A 416 Pandrosos
A 418 Romaleos
A 421 Minotauros
A 427 Patraikos
A 429 Perseus
A 430 Samson
A 431 Titan
A 432 Gigas
A 467 Volvi
A 469 Anemos
A 470 Kastoria
A 471 Vivies
A 472 Strimphalia
A 473 Trihonis
A 474 Iliki
A 476 Pyrpolitis
A 478 Naftilos
A 481 St. Lykoudis
A 485 I. Theophilopoulos Karavoyiannos
Evros
Kerkini
Kalliroe
Prespa

204 GREECE

"GEARING FRAM I" Class

"GEARING FRAM II" Class

"CANNON" Class

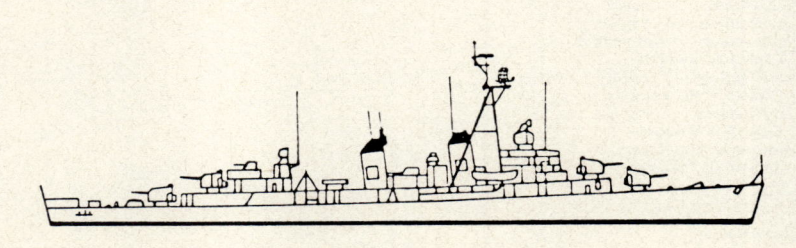

"FLETCHER" Class (4 Guns)

"ALGERINE" Class

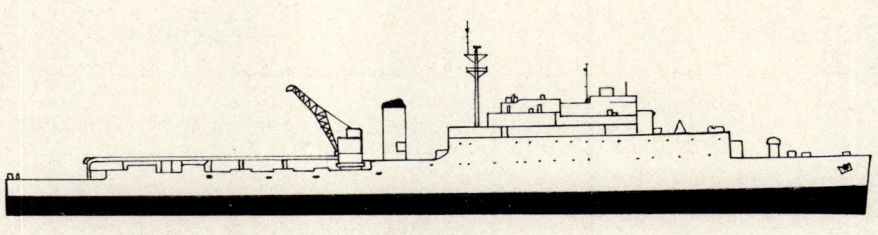

NAFKRATOUSSA

SUBMARINES

4 + 4 TYPE 209 "GLAVKOS" CLASS

Name	No.	Builders	Laid down	Launched	Commissioned
GLAVKOS	S 110	Howaldtswerke, Kiel	—	Sep 1971	5 Nov 1971
NEREUS	S 111	Howaldtswerke, Kiel	—	Sep 1971	10 Feb 1972
TRITON	S 112	Howaldtswerke, Kiel	—	1971	23 Nov 1972
PROTEUS	S 113	Howaldtswerke, Kiel	—	Dec 1971	8 Aug 1972
—	—	Howaldtswerke, Kiel	15 April 1976	1978	—
—	—	Howaldtswerke, Kiel	16 Sep 1978	—	—

Displacement, tons: 990 surfaced; 1 290 dived
Length, feet (metres): 177·1 (54·0)
Beam, feet (metres): 20·3 (6·2)
Draught, feet (metres): 17·9 (5·5)
Torpedo tubes: 8—21 in (with reloads) bow
Main machinery: Diesel-electric; 4 MTU; Siemens diesel-generators; 1 Siemens electric motor; 1 shaft
Speed, knots: 10 surfaced; 22 dived
Range: 50 days
Complement: 31

Designed by Ingenieurkontor, Lübeck for construction by Howaldtswerke, Kiel and sale by Ferrostaal Essen all acting as a consortium.
A single-hull design with two ballast tanks and forward and after trim tanks. Fitted with snort and remote machinery control. The single screw is slow revving. Very high capacity batteries with GRP lead-acid cells and battery cooling—by Wilh. Hagen and VARTA. Active and passive sonar, sonar detection equipment, sound ranging and underwater telephone. Fitted with two periscopes, radar and Omega receiver.

TRITON *1973, Hellenic Navy*

NEW CONSTRUCTION

A further three of this class were ordered from Howaldtswerke in a contract signed 1 Nov 1975 and a fourth in Sep 1976 all being launched in 1978.

GREECE 205

1 Ex-US "GUPPY III" CLASS

Name	No.	Builders	Laid down	Launched	Commissioned
KATSONIS (ex-USS *Remora*, SS 487)	S 115	Portsmouth Navy Yard	5 Mar 1945	12 July 1945	3 Jan 1946

Displacement, tons: 1 975 standard; 2 450 dived
Dimensions, feet (metres): 326 × 27 × 17 *(99·4 × 8·2 × 5·2)*
Torpedo tubes: 10—21 in; 6 bow, 4 stern
Main machinery: 4 diesels; 6 400 hp;
 2 electric motors; 5 400 shp; 2 shafts
Speed, knots: 20 surfaced; 15 dived
Range, miles: 12 000 at 10 knots (surfaced)
Complement: 85

Originally of the wartime "Tench" class, subsequently converted under the Guppy II programme and, in 1961-62 to Guppy III. Amongst other modifications this involved the fitting of BQG-4 Sonar (Puffs) for dived fire-control, in addition to the BQR-2 array sonar. Transferred 29 Oct 1973.

KATSONIS *1974, Commander Aldo Fraccaroli*

1 Ex-US "GUPPY IIA" CLASS

Name	No.	Builders	Laid down	Launched	Commissioned
PAPANIKOLIS (ex-USS *Hardhead*, SS 365)	S 114	Manitowoc SB Co	7 July 1943	12 Dec 1943	April 1944

Displacement, tons: 1 840 standard; 2 445 dived
Length, feet (metres): 306 *(93·2)*
Beam, feet (metres): 27 *(8·3)*
Draught, feet (metres): 17 *(5·2)*
Torpedo tubes: 10—21 inch; 6 bow, 4 stern
Main machinery: 3 diesels; 4 800 shp;
 2 motors, 5 400 shp; 2 shafts
Speed, knots: 17 surfaced; 15 dived
Range, miles: 12 000 at 10 knots (surfaced)
Complement: 84

Transferred 26 July 1972.

PAPANIKOLIS *1973, Hellenic Navy*

1 Ex-US "BALAO" CLASS

Name	No.	Builders	Laid down	Launched	Commissioned
TRIAINA (ex-USS *Scabbard Fish* SS 397)	S 86	Portsmouth Navy Yard	1943	27 Jan 1944	29 April 1944

Displacement, tons: 1 816 surfaced; 2 425 dived
Length, feet (metres): 311·5 *(94·9)* oa
Beam, feet (metres): 27·0 *(8·2)*
Draught, feet (metres): 17·0 *(5·2)*
Torpedo tubes: 10—21 in *(533 mm)*, 6 bow, 4 stern
Main machinery: 6 500 bhp diesels (surface), 4 610 hp motors (submerged)
Speed, knots: 20 on surface, 10 submerged
Range, miles: 12 000 at 10 knots (surfaced)
Complement: 85

Originally one of the wartime "Balao" class later having a streamlined fin fitted. Transferred 26 Feb 1965 and by sale in April 1976.

Spares: USS *Lapon* (SS 260) transferred by sale April 1976 for scrapping for spares.

TRIAINA *1974, Hellenic Navy*

DESTROYERS
1 Ex-US "ALLEN M. SUMNER" CLASS

Name	No.	Builders	Laid down	Launched	Commissioned
MIAOULIS (ex-USS *Ingraham*, DD 694)	211	Federal SB & DD Co	4 Aug 1943	16 Jan 1944	10 Mar 1944

Displacement, tons: 2 200 standard; 3 320 full load
Length, feet (metres): 376·5 *(114·8)* oa
Beam, feet (metres): 40·9 *(12·4)*
Draught, feet (metres): 19·0 *(5·8)*
Guns: 6—5 in *(127 mm)* 38 cal
A/S weapons: 2 triple torpedo launchers, Mk 32;
 2 ahead throwing Hedgehogs
Main engines: 2 geared turbines; 2 shafts; 60 000 shp
Boilers: 4
Speed, knots: 34
Range, miles: 4 600 at 15 knots
Complement: 269 (16 officers, 94 POs, 159 men)

Former fleet destroyer of the "Allen M. Sumner" class which had been modernised under the FRAM II programme. Transferred by USA July 1971.

MIAOULIS *1973, Hellenic Navy*

206 GREECE

1 Ex-US "GEARING FRAM II" CLASS
4 Ex-US "GEARING FRAM I" CLASS

Name	No.	Builders	Laid down	Launched	Commissioned
THEMISTOCLES (ex-USS *Frank Knox*, DD 742)	210	Bath Iron Works	8 May 1944	17 Sep 1944	11 Dec 1944
KANARIS (ex-USS *Stickell*, DD 888)	212	Consolidated Steel Corp	5 Jan 1945	16 June 1945	26 Sep 1945
KONTOURIOTIS (ex-USS *Rupertus*, DD 851)	213	Bethlehem (Quincy)	2 May 1945	21 Sep 1945	8 Mar 1946
SACHTOURIS (ex-USS *Arnold J. Isbell*, DD 869)	214	Bethlehem (Staten Island)	14 Mar 1945	6 Aug 1945	5 Jan 1946
TOMBASIZ (ex-USS *Gurke*, DD 783)	215	Todd Pacific Shipyards	Oct 1944	15 Feb 1945	12 May 1945

Displacement, tons: 2 425 standard; 3 500 full load
Length, feet (metres): 390·5 *(119·0)* oa
Beam, feet (metres): 40·9 *(12·4)*
Draught, feet (metres): 19·0 *(5·8)*
Aircraft: 1 helicopter
Missiles: See *Modernisation* note
Guns: 2—76 mm OTO Melara Compact *(Themistocles)* (See notes); 4—5 in (twin) (remainder) (See notes)
A/S weapons: 2 fixed Hedgehogs, *(Themistocles)*; 1 ASROC 8-barrelled launcher and facilities for small helicopter in remainder
Torpedo tubes: 2 triple (Mk 32)
Main engines: 2 Westinghouse geared turbines; 2 shafts; 60 000 shp
Boilers: 4 Babcock & Wilcox
Speed, knots: 34
Range, miles: 4 800 at 15 knots
Complement: 269 (16 officers, 253 men)

Themistocles was a FRAM II Radar Picket conversion, remainder are FRAM I DD conversions.

Gunnery: 1—76 mm OTO Melara and 1—40 mm added aft and forward respectively to *Sachtouris* and *Kanaris* early 1977.

Modernisation: Cantieri Navali Riuniti is carrying out a series of modernisations: the first, *Themistocles* in 1977. This major work consists of:
 a) Albatros 8-cell BPDM launcher
 b) Two 76 mm OTO Melara Compact guns
 c) Exocet launchers
 d) 2 NA-10 Argo fire control systems
 e) Helo deck extended to stern
 f) VDS fitted below helo deck
 g) Reduction in size of mast and bridge

Transfers: From USA: *Sachtouris*, 4 Dec 1973; *Kanaris*, 1 July 1972; *Kontouriotis*, 10 July 1973; *Themistocles* 30 Jan 1971; *Tombasiz* by sale 17 Mar 1977, commissioned 20 Mar 1977.

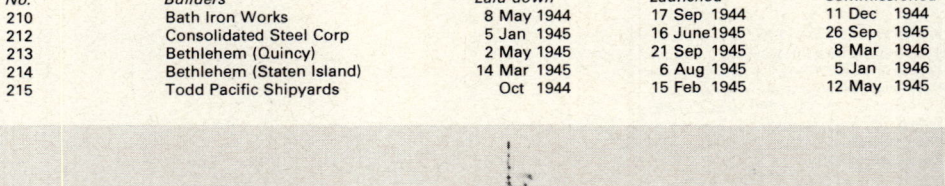

THEMISTOCLES (FRAM II) *1972, Hellenic Navy*

SACHTOURIS (FRAM I) *1977, D. Dervissis*

6 Ex-US "FLETCHER" CLASS

Name	No.
ASPIS (ex-USS *Conner*, DD 582)	06
VELOS (ex-USS *Charette*, DD 581)	16
THYELLA (ex-USS *Bradford*, DD 545)	28
LONCHI (ex-USS *Hall*, DD 583)	56
NAVARINON (ex-USS *Brown*, DD 546)	63
SFENDONI (ex-USS *Aulick*, DD 569)	85

Builders	Laid down	Launched	Commissioned
Boston Navy Yard	16 April 1942	18 July 1942	8 June 1943
Boston Navy Yard	20 Feb 1941	3 June 1942	18 May 1943
Bethlehem (S. Pedro)	28 April 1942	12 Dec 1942	12 June 1943
Boston Navy Yard	16 April 1942	18 July 1942	6 July 1943
Bethlehem (S. Pedro)	27 June 1942	22 Feb 1943	10 July 1943
Consolidated Steel Corp. Texas	14 May 1941	2 Mar 1942	27 Oct 1942

Displacement, tons: 2 100 standard; 3 050 full load
Length, feet (metres): 376·5 *(114·7)* oa
Beam, feet (metres): 39·5 *(12·0)*
Draught, feet (metres): 18 *(5·5)*
Guns: 4—5 in *(127 mm)* 38 cal. in *Aspis, Lonchi, Sfendoni* and *Velos*, 5 in *Navarinon* and *Thyella*
 6—3 in *(76 mm)*, 3 twin, in *Aspis, Lonchi, Sfendoni* and *Velos*.
 10—40 mm (2 quadruple, 1 twin) in *Navarinon* and *Thyella*
A/S weapons: Hedgehogs; DCs
Torpedo tubes: 5—21 in *(533 mm)*, quintuple bank, in *Aspis, Lonchi, Sfendoni* and *Velos*, none in *Navarinon* and *Thyella*
Torpedo racks: Side-launching for A/S torpedoes
Main engines: 2 sets GE geared turbines; 2 shafts; 60 000 shp
Boilers: 4 Babcock & Wilcox, 615 psi *(43·5 km/cm²)* 800°F *(427°C)*
Speed, knots: 32
Range, miles: 6 000 at 15 knots; 1 260 at full power
Oil fuel, tons: 506
Complement: 250

Transferred from USA, *Aspis, Lonchi* and *Velos* at Long Beach, Cal, on 15 Sep 1959, 9 Feb 1960 and 15 June 1959, respectively, *Sfendoni* at Philadelphia on 21 Aug 1959, *Navarinon* and *Thyella* at Seattle, Wash, on 27 Sep 1962. All purchased 25 April 1977.

Electronics: Reported that whole class has received extensive electronic modernisation.

Radar: Search: SPS 6, SPS 10.
Fire control: GFC 56 and 63 systems.

VELOS *1973, Dr. Giorgia Arra*

GREECE

FRIGATES

Note: Depot ship *Aegeon* currently employed on frigate duties.

4 Ex-US "CANNON" CLASS

Name	No.	Builders	Laid down	Launched	Commissioned
AETOS (ex-USS *Slater*, DE 766)	01	Tampa SB Co.	9 Mar 1943	13 Feb 1944	1 May 1944
IERAX (ex-USS *Elbert*, DE 768)	31	Tampa SB Co.	1 April 1943	23 May 1944	12 July 1944
LEON (ex-USS *Eldridge*, DE 173)	54	Federal SB & DD Co.	22 Feb 1943	25 June 1943	27 Aug 1943
PANTHIR (ex-USS *Garfield Thomas*, DE 193)	67	Federal SB & DD Co.	23 Sep 1943	12 Dec 1943	24 Jan 1944

Displacement, tons: 1 240 standard; 1 900 full load
Length, feet (metres): 306 *(93.3)* oa
Beam, feet (metres): 36.7 *(11.2)*
Draught, feet (metres): 14 *(4.3)*
Guns: 3—3 in *(76 mm)* 50 cal. 6—40 mm, (3 twin) 14—20 mm (7 twin)
A/S weapons: Hedgehog; 8 DCT; 1 DC rack
Torpedo racks: Side launching for A/S torpedoes
Main engines: 4 sets GM diesel-electric 6 000 bhp; 2 shafts
Speed, knots: 19.25
Oil fuel, tons: 316
Range, miles: 9 000 at 12 knots
Complement: 220

Aetos and *Ierax* were transferred on 15 Mar 1951 and *Leon* and *Panthir* on 15 Jan 1951. Their 3—21 in torpedo tubes in a triple mount were removed.

PANTHIR 1977, *Michael D. J. Lennon*

LIGHT FORCES

4 "LA COMBATTANTE III" CLASS (FAST ATTACK CRAFT—MISSILE)

Name	No.	Builders	Commissioned
ANTIPLOIARHOS LASKOS	P 50	Construction M. de Normandie	20 Apr 1977
PLOTARHIS BLESSAS	P 51	Construction M. de Normandie	19 July 1977
IPOPLOIARHOS TROUPAKIS	P 52	Construction M. de Normandie	8 Nov 1977
IPOPLOIARHOS MIKONIOS	P 53	Construction M. de Normandie	1977

Displacement, tons: 385 standard; 425 full load
Dimensions, feet (metres): 184 × 26 × 7 *(56.2 × 8 × 2.1)*
Missiles: 4 MM 38 Exocet
Guns: 2—76 mm OTO Melara; 4—30 mm Emerlec (twins)
Torpedo tubes: 2—21 in *(533 mm)*
Main engines: 4 MTU diesels; 18 000 bhp; 4 shafts (cp propellers) = 35.7 knots
Range, miles: 700 at 32.6 knots; 2 000 at 15 knots
Complement: 42

Ordered in Sept 1974, *A. Laskos* laid down 28 June 1975, launched 6 July 1976; *P. Blessas* laid down 5 Nov 1975, launched 10 Nov 1976; *I. Troupakis* laid down 27 Jan 1976, launched 25 Jan 1977, *I. Mikonios* laid down 7 April 1976, launched 5 May 1977.

Radar: Surveillance and navigation: one Triton
Fire control: 1 band

IPOPLOIARHOS TROUPAKIS 6/1977, *John Mortimer*

4 + 6 "LA COMBATTANTE II" CLASS
(FAST ATTACK CRAFT—MISSILE)

Name	No.	Builders	Commissioned
IPOPLOIARHOS BATSIS (ex-*Calypso*)	P 54	C. M. de Normandie, Cherbourg	Dec 1971
IPOPLOIARHOS ARLIOTIS (ex-*Evniki*)	P 55	C. M. de Normandie, Cherbourg	April 1972
ANTHIPLOIARHOS ANNINOS (ex-*Navsithoi*)	P 56	C. M. de Normandie, Cherbourg	June 1972
IPOPLOIARHOS KONIDIS (ex-*Kymothoi*)	P 57	C. M. de Normandie, Cherbourg	July 1972

Displacement, tons: 234 standard; 255 full load
Dimensions, feet (metres): 154.2 × 23.3 × 8.2 *(47 × 7.1 × 2.5)*
Missiles: 4 MM 38 Exocet surface-to-surface
Guns: 4—35 mm (2 twin)
Torpedo tubes: 2 aft for wire-guided torpedoes
Main engines: 4 MTU diesels; 4 shafts; 12 000 bhp = 36.5 knots
Oil fuel, tons: 39
Range, miles: 850 at 25 knots
Complement: 40 (4 officers, and 36 men)

Ordered in 1969. Fitted with Thomson CSF Triton radar and Plessey IFF Mk 10. *I. Arliotis* launched 26 April 1971. *I. Anninos* launched 8 Sep 1971. *I. Batsis* launched 26 Jan 1971. *I. Konidis* launched 20 Dec 1971. Six more ordered 23 Dec 1976, first pair to be built at Cherbourg (to complete Dec 1978 and Feb 1979), remainder in Greece. They will be fitted with Thomson CSF Vega II system and be armed with 6 Penguin II missiles, 1—76 mm OTO Melara and 2—40 mm guns.

IPOPLOIARHOS KONIDIS 1973, *Hellenic Navy*

208 GREECE

2 Ex-US "ASHEVILLE" CLASS (LARGE PATROL CRAFT)

Name	No.	Builders	Commissioned
— (ex-USS *Beacon*, PG 99)	—	Peterson Builders	21 Nov 1969
— (ex-USS *Green Bay*, PG 101)	—	Peterson Builders	5 Dec 1969

Displacement, tons: 225 standard; 245 full load
Dimensions, feet (metres): 164·5 × 23·5 × 9·5 *(50·2 × 7·2 × 2·9)*
Guns: 1—3 in *(76 mm)* 50 cal forward; 1—40 mm; 4—50 cal MG
Main engines: Codag; 2 Cummins diesels; 1 450 hp; 2 shafts = 16 knots.
  1 GE gas turbine; 13 300 hp; 2 shafts = 40+ knots
Complement: 27

Transferred Sep 1977. Not yet commissioned.

Ex-BEACON   9/1975, Dr. Giorgio Arra

5 "SILBERMÖWE" CLASS (FAST ATTACK CRAFT—TORPEDO)

Name	No.	Builders	Commissioned
DOLPHIN (ex-*Sturmmöwe*)	P 15	Lurrsen, Vegesack	1951-1956
DRAKON (ex-*Silbermöwe*)	P 16	Lurrsen, Vegesack	1951-1956
POLIKOS (ex-*Raubmöwe*)	P 17	Lurrsen, Vegesack	1951-1956
POLIDEFKIS (ex-*Wildschwan*)	P 18	Lurrsen, Vegesack	1951-1956
FOINIX (ex-*Eismöwe*)	P 27	Lurrsen, Vegesack	1951-1956

Displacement, tons: 119 standard; 155 full load
Dimensions, feet (metres): 116·1 × 16·7 × 5·9 *(35·5 × 5·1 × 1·8)*
Torpedo tubes: 2—21 in
Guns: 1—40 mm; 2—20 mm (1 twin)
Main engines: 3 diesels; 3 shafts; 9 000 bhp = 38 knots

Old S-Boote taken over from Germany 17 Dec 1968. Due for deletion.

2 FAST ATTACK CRAFT (MISSILE)

Name	No.	Builders	Commissioned
KELEFSTIS STAMOU	P 28	Ch. N. de l'Esterel	1975
DIOPOS ANTONIOU	P 29	Ch. N. de l'Esterel	1976

Displacement, tons: 80
Dimensions, feet (metres): 105 × 21 × 5·2 *(32 × 6·4 × 1·6)*
Missiles: 4—SS 12
Guns: 2—20 mm (twin); 1—0·50 MG
Main engines: 2 MTU 12V 331 TC81 diesels; 2 700 hp = 30 knots
Range, miles: 1 500 at 15 knots
Complement: 17

Wooden hulls. Originally ordered for Cyprus; later transferred to Greece.

5 "NASTY" CLASS (FAST ATTACK CRAFT—TORPEDO)

Name	No.	Builders	Commissioned
ANDROMEDA	P 21	Mandal, Norway	Feb 1967
KASTOR	P 23	Mandal, Norway	1967
KYKNOS	P 24	Mandal, Norway	1967
PIGASSOS	P 25	Mandal, Norway	1967
TOXOTIS	P 26	Mandal, Norway	1967

Displacement, tons: 69 standard; 76 full load
Dimensions, feet (metres): 75 pp; 80·4 oa × 24·6 × 6·9 *(22·9; 24·5 × 7·5 × 2·1)*
Torpedo tubes: 4—21 in
Guns: 2—40 mm
Main engines: 2 Napier Deltic T 18-37 K diesels; 3 100 bhp = 43 knots
Complement: 22

Andromeda and *Iniohos* (deleted 1972) were taken over in Feb 1967 from Mandal, Norway. *Kastor* and *Kyknos*, and the third pair, *Pigassos* and *Toxotis*, were delivered in succession in 1967.

ANDROMEDA   1974, Hellenic Navy

7 Ex-GERMAN "JAGUAR" CLASS
(FAST ATTACK CRAFT—TORPEDO)

Name	No.	Builders	Commissioned
HESPEROS (ex-*Seeadler* P 6068)	P 196	FDR	1958
KATAIGIS (ex-*Falke* P 6072)	P 197	FDR	1958
KENTAUROS (ex-*Habricht* P 6075)	P 198	FDR	1958
KYKLON (ex-*Grief* P 6071)	P 199	FDR	1958
LELAPS (ex-*Kondor* P 6070)	P 228	FDR	1958
SCORPIOS (ex-*Kormoran* P 6077)	P 229	FDR	1958
TYFON (ex-*Geier* P 6073)	P 230	FDR	1958

Displacement, tons: 160 standard; 190 full load
Dimensions, feet (metres): 139·4 × 23·4 × 7·9 *(42·5 × 7·2 × 2·4)*
Guns: 2—40 mm Bofors L70 (single)
Torpedo tubes: 4—21 in
Main engines: 4 diesels; 4 shafts; 12 000 bhp=42 knots
Complement: 39

Transferred 1976-77. *Kataigis, Kyklon, Tyfon* commissioned in Hellenic Navy 12 Dec 1976. *Hesperos* and *Lelaps* on 24 Mar 1977 and *Kentauros* and *Scorpios* on 22 May 1977. Three others (ex-*Albatros*, ex-*Bussard* and ex-*Sperber*) transferred at same time for spares. Built by Lürssen Vegesack or Kroger Rendsburg.

TYFON (before transfer)   1975, Reiner Nerlich

GREECE 209

1 VOSPER "BRAVE" CLASS (FAST ATTACK CRAFT—TORPEDO)

Name	No.	Builders	Commissioned
ASTRAPI (ex-*Strahl* P 6194)	P 20	Vosper, Portsmouth	21 Nov 1962

Displacement, tons: 95 standard; 110 full load
Dimensions, feet (metres): 99 oa × 25 × 7 *(30·2 × 7·6 × 2·1)*
Torpedo chutes: 4—21 in side launching
Guns: 2—40 mm
Main engines: 3 Bristol Siddeley Marine Proteus gas turbines; 3 shafts; 12 750 bhp = 55·5 knots

Launched on 10 Jan 1962. Commissioned in Federal German Navy on 21 Nov 1962. Transferred to Royal Hellenic Navy in April 1967. Refitted by Vosper in 1968. Of similar design to British "Brave" class.

ASTRAPI *1972, Hellenic Navy*

1 VOSPER "FEROCITY" CLASS (FAST ATTACK CRAFT—TORPEDO)

Name	No.	Builders	Commissioned
AIOLOS (ex-*Pfeil* P 6193)	P 19	Vosper, Portsmouth	27 June 1962

Displacement, tons: 75 standard; 80 full load
Dimensions, feet (metres): 92 wl; 95 oa × 23·9 × 6·5 *(28·1; 29 × 7·3 × 2)*
Torpedo chutes: 4—21 in side launching
Guns: 2—40 mm
Main engines: 2 Bristol Siddeley Marine Proteus gas turbines; 2 shafts; 8 500 bhp = 50 knots

Launched on 26 Oct 1961. Commissioned in German Navy on 27 June 1962. Transferred to Hellenic Navy in April 1967. Refitted by Vosper in 1968. Based on design of Vosper prototype *Ferocity*.

AIOLOS *1972, Hellenic Navy*

10 FAST ATTACK CRAFT—PATROL

Displacement, tons: 75
Dimensions, feet (metres): 95·1 × 16·2 × — *(29 × 5 × —)*
Speed, knots: 28
Complement: 20

Ordered from Skaramanga Shipyard in May 1976. The first was launched in November 1977.

2 Ex-US "PGM-9" CLASS (LARGE PATROL CRAFT)

PLOIARHOS ARSLANOGLOU (ex-*PGM 25*, ex-*PC 1565*) P 14
ANTHIPLOIARHOS PEZOPOULOS (ex-*PGM 21*, ex-*PC 1552*) P 70

Displacement, tons: 335 standard; 439 full load
Dimensions, feet (metres): 170 wl; 174·7 oa × 23 × 10·8 *(51·8; 53·3 × 7 × 3·3)*
Guns: 1—3 in; 6—20 mm
A/S weapons: Hedgehog; side launching torpedo racks; depth charges
Main engines: 2 GM diesels; 2 shafts; 3 600 bhp = 19 knots

All launched in 1943-44. Acquired from USA in Aug 1947. The two 40 mm guns were removed and a Hedgehog was installed in 1963.

ANTHIPLOIARHOS PEZOPOULOS *1973, Hellenic Navy*

3 + ? COASTAL PATROL CRAFT

Name	No.	Builders	Commissioned
N. I. GOULANDRIS I	P 22	Syros Shipyard	25 June 1975
E. PANAGOPOULOS	—	Syros Shipyard	23 June 1976
N. I. GOULANDRIS II	—	Syros Shipyard	6 June 1977

Displacement, tons: 38·5
Dimensions, feet (metres): 78·7 × 20·3 × 3·4 *(24 × 6·2 × 1·1)*
Main engines: 2 diesels; 2 700 hp = 30 knots
Range, miles: 1 600 at cruising speed

The first of these craft was donated to the Hellenic Navy by the wealthy shipowner after whom she is named. She is lead craft of a number of the same type, most of them donated by Greek shipowners.

2 Ex-FDR "KW" CLASS

ARHIKELEFSTIS STASSIS   ARHIKELEFSTIS MALIOPOULOS

Transferred 1976.

210 GREECE

AMPHIBIOUS FORCES

1 Ex-US "CABILDO" CLASS (LSD)

Name	No.	Builders	Commissioned
NAFKRATOUSSA (ex-USS *Fort Mandan*, LSD 21)	L 153	Boston Navy Yard	31 Oct 1945

Displacement, tons: 4 790 light; 9 357 full load
Dimensions, feet (metres): 457·8 oa × 72·2 × 18 *(139·6 × 22 × 5·5)*
Guns: 8—40 mm
Main engines: Geared turbines; 2 shafts; 7 000 shp = 15·4 knots
Boilers: 2

Laid down on 2 Jan 1945. Launched on 22 May 1945. Taken over from USA in 1971 replacing the previous *Nafkratoussa* (ex-*Hyperion,* ex-LSD 9) out of service in 1971 as Headquarters ship of Captain, Landing Forces.

NAFKRATOUSSA   1973, Hellenic Navy

2 Ex-US "TERREBONNE PARISH" CLASS (LSTs)

Name	No.	Builders	Commissioned
INOUSE (ex-USS *Terrell County*, LST 1157)	L 104	Bath Iron Works Corp	19 Mar 1953
KOS (ex-USS *Whitfield County*, LST 1169)	L 116	Christy Corp	14 Sep 1954

Displacement, tons: 2 590 light; 5 800 full load
Dimensions, feet (metres): 384 oa × 55 × 17 *(117·1 × 16·7 × 5·2)*
Guns: 6—3 in 50 cal
Main engines: 4 GM diesels; 6 000 bhp; 2 shafts (cp propellers) = 15 knots
Complement: 115
Troops: 395

Part of class of fifteen—Transferred 17 Mar 1977 by sale. Towed to Greece for reactivation and modernisation. Discussions on purchase of second pair.

8 Ex-US LSTs
(2 of 511—1152 series, 6 of 1—510 series)

511—1152 Series
IKARIA (ex-USS *Potter County,* LST 1086) L 154
KRITI (ex-USS *Page County,* LST 1076) L 171

1—510 Series
SYROS (ex-USS *LST 325*) L 144
RODOS (ex-USS *Bowman County,* LST 391) L 157
LIMNOS (ex-USS *LST 36*) L 158
LESBOS (ex-USS *Boone County,* LST 389) L 172
SAMOS (ex-USS *LST 33*) L 179
CHIOS (ex-USS *LST 35*) L 195

Displacement, tons: 1 653 standard; 2 366 beaching; 4 080 full load
Dimensions, feet (metres): 328 × 50 × 14 *(100 × 15·3 × 2·9)*
Guns: 8—40 mm; 6—20 mm (*Rodos* 10—40 mm)
Main engines: 2 GM diesels; 2 shafts; 1 700 bhp = 11·6 knots
Range, miles: 9 500 at 9 knots
Complement: 93 (8 officers, 85 men)

Former United States tank landing ships. Cargo capacity 2 100 tons. *Ikaria, Lesbos* and *Rodos* were transferred to the Hellenic Navy on 9 Aug 1960. *Syros* was transferred on 29 May 1964 at Portsmouth, Virginia, under MAP. *Kriti* was transferred in Mar 1971. Others under lease-lend in 1943.

RODOS   1976, Michael D. J. Lennon

5 Ex-US "LSM 1" CLASS

IPOPLOIARHOS GRIGOROPOULOS (ex-USS *LSM 45*) L 161
IPOPLOIARHOS TOURNAS (ex-USS *LSM 102*) L 162
IPOPLOIARHOS DANIOLOS (ex-USS *LSM 227*) L 163
IPOPLOIARHOS ROUSSEN (ex-USS *LSM 399*) L 164
IPOPLOIARHOS KRISTALIDIS (ex-USS *LSM 541*) L 165

Displacement, tons: 743 beaching; 1 095 full load
Dimensions, feet (metres): 196·5 wl; 203·5 oa × 34·2 × 8·3 *(59·9; 62·1 × 10·4 × 2·5)*
Guns: 2—40 mm; 8—20 mm
Main engines: Diesel direct drive; 2 shafts; 3 600 bhp = 13 knots

LSM 541 was handed over to Greece at Salamis on 30 Oct 1958 and *LSM 45, LSM 102, LSM 227* and *LSM 399* at Portsmouth, Virginia on 3 Nov 1958. All were renamed after naval heroes killed during World War 2.

IPOPLOIARHOS KRISTALIDIS   1974, Hellenic Navy

34 LCVPs

Transferred from USA.

14 LCPs

Ordered from Greek shipyards in 1977.

13 LCMs

Transferred from USA.

GREECE

6 Ex-US "LCU 501" CLASS (Ex-LCT 6)

Name	No.	Builders	Commissioned
KASSOS (ex-LCU 1382)	L 145	—	1944
KARPATHOS (ex-LCU 1379)	L 146	—	1944
KIMONOS (ex-LCU 971)	L 147	—	1944
KITHNOS (ex-LCU 763)	L 149	—	1944
SIFNOS (ex-LCU 677)	L 150	—	1944
SKIATHOS (ex-LCU 827)	L 152	—	1944

Displacement, tons: 143 standard; 309 full load
Dimensions, feet (metres): 105 wl; 119 oa × 32·7 × 5 *(32; 36·3 × 10 × 1·5)*
Guns: 2—20 mm
Main engines: Diesel; 3 shafts; 440 bhp = 8 knots
Complement: 13

Former US Utility Landing Craft of the *LCU* (ex-*LCT 6*) type. *Skiathos* acquired in 1959. *Kithnos* and *Sifnos* were transferred from USA in 1961, and *Karpathos*, *Kassos* and *Kimonos* in 1962.

KITHNOS *1971, Hellenic Navy*

MINE WARFARE FORCES

2 COASTAL MINELAYERS

Name	No.	Builders	Commissioned
AKTION (ex-LSM 301, ex-MMC 6)	N 04	Charleston Naval Shipyard	1 Jan 1945
AMVRAKIA (ex-LSM 303, ex-MMC 7)	N 05	Charleston Naval Shipyard	6 Jan 1945

Displacement, tons: 720 standard; 1 100 full load
Dimensions, feet (metres): 203·5 oa × 34·5 × 8·3 *(62·1 × 10·5 × 2·5)*
Guns: 8—40 mm (4 twin); 6—20 mm (single)
Mines: Capacity 100 to 130
Main engines: 2 diesels; 2 shafts; 3 600 bhp = 12·5 knots
Range, miles: 3 000 at 12 knots
Complement: 65

Former US "LSM 1" Class. *Aktion* was launched on 1 Jan 1945 and *Amvrakia* on 14 Nov 1944. Converted in the USA into minelayers for the Hellenic Navy. Underwent extensive rebuilding from the deck up. Twin rudders. Transferred on 1 Dec 1953.

AMVRAKIA *1974, Hellenic Navy*

10 US "MSC 294" CLASS (MINESWEEPERS—COASTAL)

Name	No.	Builders	Commissioned
ALKYON (ex-MSC 319)	M 211	Peterson Builders	3 Dec 1968
ARGO (ex-MSC 317)	M 213	Peterson Builders	7 Aug 1968
AVRA (ex-MSC 318)	M 214	Peterson Builders	3 Oct 1968
PLEIAS (ex-MSC 314)	M 240	Peterson Builders	22 June 1967
KICHLI (ex-MSC 308)	M 241	Peterson Builders	14 July 1964
KISSA (ex-MSC 309)	M 242	Peterson Builders	1 Sep 1964
DORIS (ex-MSC 298)	M 245	Tacoma, California	9 Nov 1964
AIGLI (ex-MSC 299)	M 246	Tacoma, California	4 Jan 1965
DAFNI (ex-MSC 307)	M 247	Peterson Builders	23 Sep 1964
AEDON (ex-MSC 310)	M 248	Peterson Builders	13 Oct 1964

Displacement, tons: 320 standard; 370 full load
Dimensions, feet (metres): 138 pp; 144 oa × 28 × 8·2 *(42·1; 43·3 × 8·5 × 2·5)*
Guns: 2—20 mm (twin)
Main engines: 2 GM diesels; 2 shafts; 880 bhp = 13 knots
Complement: 39

Built in USA for Greece. Wooden hulls.

AVRA *1974, Hellenic Navy*

5 Ex-US "ADJUTANT" CLASS (MINESWEEPERS—COASTAL)

ATALANTI (ex-Belgian *St. Truiden*, M 919, ex-USS *MSC 169*) M 202
ANTIOPI (ex-Belgian *Herve*, M 921, ex-USS *MSC 153*) M 205
FAEDRA (ex-Belgian *Malmedy*, M 922, ex-USS *MSC 154*) M 206
THALIA (ex-Belgian *Blankenberge*, M 923, ex-USS *MSC 170*) M 210
NIOVI (ex-Belgian *Laroche*, M 924, ex-USS *MSC 171*) M 254

Displacement, tons: 330 standard; 402 full load
Dimensions, feet (metres): 145·0 oa × 27·9 × 8·0 *(44·2 × 8·5 × 2·4)*
Guns: 2—20 mm Oerlikon (1 twin)
Main engines: 2 GM diesels; 2 shafts; 900 bhp = 14 knots
Complement: 38 officers and men

Originally supplied to Belgium under MDAP. Subsequently returned to USA and simultaneously transferred to Greece as follows: 29 July 1969 (*Herve* and *St. Truiden*) and 26 Sep 1969 (*Laroche*, *Malmedy* and *Blankenberge*). *Atalanti* employed on surveying duties.

ANTIOPI *1973, Dr. Giorgio Arra*

SURVEY AND RESEARCH VESSELS

Name	No.	Builders	Commissioned
NAFTILOS	A 478	Annastadiades Tsortanides (Perama)	3 April 1976

Displacement, tons: 1 400
Dimensions, feet (metres): 207 × 38 × 13·3 *(63·1 × 11·6 × 4·2)*
Main engines: 1 B & W diesel; 2 640 hp = 15 knots
Complement: 74 (8 officers, 66 men)

Launched 19 Nov 1975. Trials Feb 1976.

ATALANTI

Of "Adjutant" class MSCs. For details see Minewarfare Forces.

ANEMOS (ex-German *KFK KW7*) A 469

Displaces 112 tons, was launched in 1944 and has a complement of 16. Added to the Navy List in 1969.

212 GREECE

1 Ex-US "BARNEGAT" CLASS

Name	No.	Builders	Commissioned
HEPHESTOS (ex-USNS *Josiah Willard Gibbs*, T-AGOR 1, ex-USS *San Carlos*, AVP 51)	A 413	Lake Washington Shipyard, Houghton, Wash.	21 Mar 1944

Displacement, tons: 1 750 standard; 2 800 full load
Dimensions, feet (metres): 300·0 wl; 310·8 oa × 41·2 × 13·5 *(91·5; 94·8 × 12·6 × 4·1)*
Main engines: 2 Fairbanks-Morse diesels; 2 shafts; 6 080 bhp = 18 knots
Range, miles: 10 000 at 14 knots
Endurance: 30 days
Complement: 82 (8 officers and 74 men)

Former US seaplane tender converted for oceanographic research. Laid down on 7 Sep 1942, launched on 20 Dec 1942. Transferred to the Hellenic Navy on 7 Dec 1971. Purchased 15 Feb 1977. In reserve.

HEPHESTOS *1974, Hellenic Navy*

1 SURVEYING LAUNCH

Of 25 tons, launched in 1940. Complement 9.

SERVICE FORCES

1 NEW CONSTRUCTION TRAINING SHIP

Of 3 200 tons. Laid down in Oct 1976 at Salamis. Launched January 1978.

1 Ex-FDR DEPOT SHIP

Name	No.	Builders	Commissioned
AEGEON (ex-*Weser* A 62)	A 215	Elsflether Werft	1960

Displacement, tons: 2 370
Dimensions, feet (metres): 323·5 × 38·8 × 11·2 *(99 × 11·8 × 3·4)*
Guns: 2—3·9 in *(100 mm)*; 4—40 mm
Main engines: 6 diesels; 12 000 hp
Speed, knots: 20·5
Range, miles: 1 625 at 15 knots (economical)
Complement: 110

Transferred July 1975. Currently employed on frigate duties and as FAC support ship.

AEGEON *7/1976, Roland Wiegran*

2 Ex-US "PATAPSCO" CLASS (SUPPORT TANKERS)

Name	No.	Builders	Commissioned
ARETHOUSA (ex-USS *Natchaug*, AOG 54)	A 377	Cargill Inc, Savage, Minn.	1945
ARIADNI (ex-USS *Tombigbee*, AOG 11)	A 414	Cargill Inc, Savage, Minn.	12 July 1944

Displacement, tons: 1 850 light; 4 335 full load
Measurement, tons: 2 575 deadweight; cargo capacity 2 040
Dimensions, feet (metres): 292 wl; 310·8 oa × 48·5 × 15·7 *(89·1; 93·2 × 14·8 × 4·8)*
Guns: 4—3 in; 50 cal
Main engines: GM diesels; 2 shafts; 3 300 bhp = 14 knots
Complement: 43 (6 officers, 37 men)

Former US petrol carriers. *Arethousa* laid down on 15 Aug 1944. Launched on 16 Dec 1944. Transferred from the USA to Greece under the Mutual Defense Assistance Program in July 1959 and *Ariadni* transferred 7 July 1972, both at Pearl Harbor.

ARETHOUSA *1972, Hellenic Navy*

1 AMMUNITION SHIP

Name	No.	Builders	Commissioned
EVROS (ex-FDR *Schwarzwald* A1400, ex-*Amalthee*)	—	Ch. Dubigeon Nantes	1957

Measurement, tons: 1 667 gross
Dimensions, feet (metres): 263·1 × 39 × 15·1 *(80·2 × 11·9 × 4·6)*
Guns: 4—40 mm Bofors
Main engines: Sulzer diesel; 3 000 bhp = 15 knots

Bought by FDR from Societé Navale Caënnaise in Feb 1960. Transferred to Greece 6 June 1976.

EVROS (as *Schwarzwald*) *1971*

2 HARBOUR TANKERS

Name	No.	Builders	Commissioned
OURANOS	A 416	Greece	Feb 1977
HYPERION	—	Greece	Feb 1977

Displacement, tons: 1 200

Order announced 24 June 1976.

1 HARBOUR TANKER

SIRIOS (ex-*Poseidon*, ex-*Empire Faun*) A 345

Formerly on loan from the United Kingdom, but purchased outright in 1962. This ship was renamed *Sirios* when the name *Poseidon* was given to the submarine *Lapon* acquired from the USA in 1958. Capacity 850 tons.

GREECE 213

1 HARBOUR TANKER

VIVIES A 471

Originally a water carrier. Capacity 687 tons.

1 HARBOUR TANKER

KRONOS (ex-*Islay*, ex-*Dresden*) A 373

Displacement, tons: 311
Capacity: 110 tons

ORION (ex-US tanker Y 126) A 376

Formerly small United States yard tanker. Capacity 700 tons.

1 PETROL CARRIER

ZEUS (ex-YOG 98) A 372

Dimensions, feet (metres): 165 × 35 × 10 *(50·3 × 10·2 × 3·2)*

Former US yard petrol carrier. Launched in 1944. Capacity 900 tons.

1 HARBOUR TANKER

ORION   1969, Hellenic Navy

CORVETTES

2 Ex-BRITISH "ALGERINE" CLASS (TRAINING SHIPS)

Name	No.	Builders	Commissioned
PYRPOLITIS (ex-HMS *Arcturus*)	A 476	Redfern Construction Co	23 Oct 1943
POLEMISTIS (ex-HMS *Gozo*)	M 74	Redfern Construction Co	29 Sep 1943

Displacement, tons: 1 030 standard; 1 325 full load
Length, feet (metres): 225 *(68·6)* oa
Beam, feet (metres): 35·5 *(10·8)*
Draught, feet (metres): 11·5 *(3·5)*
Guns: 1—3 in *(76 mm)* (US Mark 21) (none in *Polemistis*);
4—20 mm (US), 2 MG
A/S weapons: 2 to 4 DCT
Main engines: 2 triple expansion, 2 shafts; 2 700 ihp
Speed, knots: 16
Boilers: 2 Yarrow, 250 psi *(17·6 kg cm²)*
Oil fuel, tons: 235
Range, miles: 5 000 at 10 knots; 2 270 at 14·5 knots
Complement: 85

Former British ocean minesweepers. Acquired from the Executive Committee of Surplus Allied Material.

Class: *Armatolos* sunk as target for Exocet on 25 May 1977. *Mahitis* and *Navmachos* deleted in 1976 one being sunk as a target.

Duties: Now employed variously as training ships and personnel transports.

MISCELLANEOUS

1 YACHT

THESSEUS

Ex-Royal Yacht used for VIP visits.

1 NETLAYER

Name	No.	Builders	Commissioned
THETIS (ex-USS *AN 103*)	A 307	Krüger, Rendsburg	April 1960

Displacement, tons: 680 standard; 805 full load
Dimensions, feet (metres): 146 wl; 169·5 oa × 33·5 × 11·8 *(44·5; 51·7 × 10·2 × 3·6)*
Guns: 1—40 mm; 4—20 mm
Main engines: MAN diesels; 1 shaft; 1 400 bhp = 12 knots
Complement: 48

US offshore order. Launched in 1959.

1 NEW CONSTRUCTION NETLAYER

Of 680 tons, building at Krögerwerft, Rendsburg.

5 SEA-AIR RESCUE LAUNCHES

| ADAMIDIS P 286 | KARNAVIAS | IOS |
| HERA P 289 | SAKELARIOU | |

Belong to the Air Force SAR Centre but are manned and maintained by the Navy.

2 AUXILIARY TRANSPORTS

Name	No.	Builders	Commissioned
PANDORA	A 415	Perama Shipyard	1973
PANDROSOS	A 420	Perama Shipyard	1974

Displacement, tons: 350
Length, feet (metres): 212·2 *(64·6)*
Speed, knots: 13

Launched 1972 and 1973. Transport capacity for 500 people.

3 NEW CONSTRUCTION OCEAN TUGS

Of 345 tons laid down 1977 at Perama Shipyard. 98·5 × 26 × 11·3 ft with one MWM diesel.

12 TUGS

AIAS (ex-USS *Ankachak*, YTM 767)
ANTAIOS (ex-USS *Busy*, YTM 2012) A 407
ATLAS (ex-*F 5*) A 408
ACCHILEUS (ex-USS *Confident*) A 409
ATROMITOS A 410
ROMALEOS A 418
MINOTAUROS (ex-*Theseus*, ex-*ST 539*) A 421
PATRAIKOS A 427
PERSEUS (ex-*ST 722*) A 429
SAMSON (ex-*F 16*) A 430
TITAN A 432
CIGAS A 432

Aias transferred on lease 1972. 3 more harbour tugs ordered 1977.

2 + 1 FLOATING CRANES

Two under construction in Greece with another ordered.

2 LIGHTHOUSE TENDERS

ST. LYKOUDIS A 481
I. THEOPHILOPOULOS KARAVOYIANNOS A 485 (?)

Displacement, tons: 1 350
Length, feet (metres): 207·3 *(63·2)*
Main engines: 1 diesel; 2 400 hp = 15 knots
Complement: 40

Built at Perama Shipyard 1976-77. Have facilities for small helicopter.

7 WATER BOATS

KERKINI (ex-FDR FW) A 433	KALLIROE A 468	TRIHONIS A 473
PRESPA A 434	KASTORIA A 470	ILIKI A 474
VOLVI A 467		

Capacity: *Iliki* and *Stymfalia* 120 tons, *Trichonis* 300 tons, *Volvi* 350 tons, *Kastoria* 520 tons. *Kerkini*, of 350 ton DWT transferred by FDR 1976. *Kalliroe* and *Prespa* completed at Perama Shipyard on 13 Dec 1976. (600 tons).

214 GRENADA / GUATEMALA

GRENADA

Grenada was granted self-government, in association with the United Kingdom (who was responsible for her defence) on 3 March 1967.
Full self-government was achieved in February 1973.

Mercantile Marine

Lloyd's Register of Shipping:
2 vessels of 226 tons gross

1 COASTAL PATROL CRAFT

Displacement, tons: 15
Dimensions, feet (metres): 40 × 12 × 2 *(12·2 × 3·7 × 0·6)*
Guns: 3 MG
Main engines: 2 diesels; 370 hp = 22 knots

Delivered by Brooke Marine, Lowestoft early in 1972.

GUATEMALA

On 5 January 1959 Guatemala announced the establishment of a navy for coastguard work. Subsequently the navy was assigned missions of search and rescue and the support of amphibious operations. The commissioning of a Marine Elevator (Synchrolift) at Santo Tomás on 23 June 1973 (230 ton lift) has greatly improved this navy's repair facilities.

Ministerial

Minister of National Defence:
General D. F. Rubio Coronado

Bases

Santo Tomás de Castillas (Atlantic); Sipacate (Pacific)

Personnel

(a) 1977: 400 (50 officers and 350 men, including 10 officers and 200 men of the Marines)
(b) 2 years national service

Mercantile Marine

Lloyd's Register of Shipping:
8 vessels of 11 854 tons gross

2 85 ft COASTAL PATROL CRAFT

Name	No.	Builders	Commissioned
UTATLAN	P 851	Sewart, Louisiana	May 1967
USORIO SARAVIA	P 852	Sewart, Louisiana	1972

Displacement, tons: 60
Dimensions, feet (metres): 85 × 18·7 × 3 *(25·9 × 5·7 × 0·9)*
Guns: 2 MG
Main engines: 2 GM diesels; 2 200 bhp = 23 knots
Range, miles: 400 at 12 knots
Complement: 12 (2 officers, 10 ratings)

Built to "Commercial Cruiser" design.

UTATLAN *1973, Guatemalan Navy*

3 "BROADSWORD" CLASS (COASTAL PATROL CRAFT)

Name	No.	Builder	Commissioned
—	P 1051	Halter Marine	4 Aug 1976
—	P 1052	Halter Marine	22 Oct 1976
—	P 1053	Halter Marine	1977

Displacement, tons: 90·5
Dimensions, feet (metres): 105 × 20·4 × 6·3 *(32 × 6·2 × 1·9)*
Guns: 1—75 mm recoilless; 1—81 mm mortar; 5—0·50 MG
Main engines: 2 GM diesels; 2 800 hp = 32 knots
Complement: 19

5 65 ft COASTAL PATROL CRAFT

Name	No.	Builders	Commissioned
TECUNUMAN	P 651	Halter Marine	1972
KAIBILBALAM	P 652	Halter Marine	1972
AZUMANCHE	P 653	Halter Marine	1972
—	P 654	Halter Marine	10 Mar 1976
—	P 655	Halter Marine	4 Aug 1976

Displacement, tons: 32
Dimensions, feet (metres): 64·5 × 17 × 3 *(19·7 × 5·2 × 0·9)*
Guns: 2 MG
Main engines: 2 GM diesels = 25 knots
Complement: 10 (2 officers, 8 ratings)

2 63 ft COASTAL CRAFT (ex-USCGS)

Name	No.	Builders	Commissioned
CABRAKAN	P 631	USA	—
HUNAHPU	P 632	USA	—

Displacement, tons: 32
Dimensions, feet (metres): 63·3 × 15·4 × 3 *(19·3 × 4·7 × 0·9)*
Guns: 2 MG
Main engines: 2 GM 8V71 diesels = 25 knots
Complement: 10 (2 officers, 8 men)

Transferred from USA—*Hunahpu*, 1964; *Cabrakan*, 1965.

2 "MACHETE" CLASS TROOP CARRIERS

Name	No.	Builder	Commissioned
—	D 361	Halter Marine	4 Aug 1976
—	D 362	Halter Marine	4 Aug 1976

Displacement, tons: 8·3
Dimensions, feet (metres): 36 × 12·5 × 2 *(11 × 3·8 × 0·6)*
Main engines: 2 diesels; 540 hp = 36 knots
Complement: 2 + 20 troops

Armoured open deck aluminium craft.

2 28 ft COASTAL PATROL CRAFT

XUCUXUY P 281   CAMALOTE P 282

Striker Utility Patrol Craft modified for one GM 6-53 diesel. 28 feet, 6·5 tons with 1 MG. Transferred in 1961.

2 Ex-USCG 40 ft UTILITY BOATS MK IV

TIKAL P 401   IXINCHE P 402

Transferred Aug 1963.

1 Ex-US LCM (6)

CHINALTENANGO 561

Transferred Dec 1965.

6 MOTOR LAUNCHES

Procured in late 1960s. Reported as inboard/outboard craft.

1 Ex-US REPAIR BARGE

Ex-US YR 40. Transferred in 1952.

1 TUG

Note: Three other names listed—*Escuintla, Mazatenango, Retalhuleu*—in addition to two yachts—*Mendieta* and one other.

GUINEA

Personnel
a) 1978: 350 officers and men
b) Conscript service—2 years

Bases
Conakry, Kakanda

Mercantile Marine
Lloyd's Register of Shipping:
11 vessels of 12 597 tons gross

LIGHT FORCES

6 Ex-CHINESE "SHANGHAI II" CLASS (FAST ATTACK CRAFT—GUN)

P 733   P 734   P 735   P 736   +2

Displacement, tons: 120 standard; 155 full load
Dimensions, feet (metres): 128 × 18 × 5·6 *(39 × 5·5 × 1·7)*
Guns: 4—37 mm (twin); 4—25 mm (twin)
A/S weapons: 8 DCs
Main engines: 4 diesels; 3 600 hp = 28 knots
Complement: 25

Transferred 1973-74 (first four) and 1976.

"SHANGHAI" Class

2 Ex-SOVIET "P 6" CLASS (FAST ATTACK CRAFT—TORPEDO)

Displacement, tons: 66 standard; 75 full load
Dimensions, feet (metres): 84·2 × 20·0 × 6·0 *(25·7 × 6·1 × 1·8)*
Guns: 4—25 mm
Torpedo tubes: 2—21 in (or mines or depth charges)
Main engines: 4 diesels; 4 shafts; 4 800 bhp = 43 knots
Range, miles: 450 at 30 knots
Complement: 25

It seems unlikely that the torpedo armament is operational.

3 Ex-SOVIET "POLUCHAT I" CLASS (COASTAL PATROL CRAFT)

Displacement, tons: 86 standard; 91 full load
Dimensions, feet (metres): 98·0 pp × 15·0 × 4·8 *(29·9 × 4·6 × 1·5)*
Guns: 2—14·5 mm (1 twin)
Main engines: 2 diesels; 2 shafts; 1 200 bhp = 18 knots
Oil fuel, tons: 9·25
Range, miles: 460 at 17 knots
Complement: 16 (2 officers, 14 ratings)

2 Ex-SOVIET "MO VI" CLASS (COASTAL PATROL CRAFT)

Displacement, tons: 64 standard; 73 full load
Dimensions, feet (metres): 83·6 × 19·7 × 4·0 *(25·5 × 6 × 1·2)*
Guns: 4—25 mm (twin)
A/S weapons: DC mortars and racks
Main engines: 4 diesels; 4 shafts; 4 800 hp = 40 knots

Transferred 1972-73.

Radar: Pot Head.

LANDING CRAFT

2 SMALL UTILITY TYPE

Recent visits by considerable numbers of Soviet ships may have increased these numbers.

GUINEA BISSAU

Personnel
a) 1978: 100 officers and men.
b) Voluntary service.

Base
Bissau.

Mercantile Marine
Lloyd's Register of Shipping:
1 vessel of 219 tons gross

1 Ex-SOVIET "P 6" CLASS (FAST ATTACK CRAFT—TORPEDO)

Details as in Guinea section. Reported 1977.

Several river craft and some small LCU type are reported in service.

216 GUYANA / HAITI

GUYANA

Ministerial
Premier and Minister of National Security:
L. F. S. Burnham

Mercantile Marine
Lloyd's Register of Shipping:
70 vessels of 16 274 tons gross

Bases
Georgetown, New Amsterdam

Prefix to Ships' Names
GDFS

1 VOSPER THORNYCROFT 103 ft TYPE (LARGE PATROL CRAFT)

Name	No.	Builders	Commissioned
PECCARI	—	Vosper Thornycroft	Mar 1977

Displacement, tons: 96 standard; 109 full load
Dimensions, feet (metres): 103 oa × 19·8 × 5·5 *(31·4 × 6·0 × 1·6)*
Guns: 2—40 mm
Main engines: 2 diesels, 3 500 hp = 27 knots
Range, miles: 1 400 at 14 knots
Complement: 22

Trials started 25 Nov 1976.

PECCARI 1977, Michael D. J. Lennon

3 VOSPER 12·2 METRE TYPE (COASTAL PATROL CRAFT)

Name	No.	Builders	Commissioned
JAGUAR	—	Vospers	28 April 1971
MARGAY	—	Vospers	21 May 1971
OCELOT	—	Vospers	22 June 1971

Displacement, tons: 10
Dimensions, feet (metres): 40 × 12 × 3·5 *(12·2 × 3·7 × 1·1)*
Guns: 1—7·62 mm MG
Main engines: 2 Cummins diesels; 370 hp = 19 knots
Range, miles: 150 at 12 knots
Complement: 6

They have glass fibre hulls with aluminium superstructures.

1 LIGHTER

YFN 960 transferred from US 1 Aug 1975. Under AIP.

JAGUAR 1971, C. and S. Taylor

HAITI

Ministerial:
Secretary for Interior and National Defence:
Pierre Biamby

Personnel
(a) 1978: Total 300 (40 officers and 260 men)
(b) Voluntary service

Base
Port Au Prince

New acquisitions:
Negotiations for the purchase of up to 26 Sewart 105 ft coastal patrol craft in the USA were unsuccessful.

DELETIONS

1977 *Jean Jacques Dessalines* ("Cohoes" class) returned to USA. *Admiral Killick, Seize Août 1946, Savannah, Artibonite, Sans Souci,* 6-83 ft cutters.

COAST GUARD VESSELS

2 Ex-USCG "CAPE" CLASS

Name	No.	Builders	Commissioned
LA CRETE A PIERROT (ex-USCG 95315)	MH 8	US Coast Guard Yard, Curtiss Bay, Maryland	—
VERTIERES	MH 9		—

Displacement, tons: 100
Dimensions, feet (metres): 95 × 19 × 5 *(29 × 5·8 × 1·5)*
Guns: 3—20 mm
Main engines: 4 diesels; 2 shafts; 2 200 bhp = 21 knots
Range, miles: 1 500
Complement: 15

Former US Coast Guard steel cutter. Acquired on 26 Feb 1956.

3 COASTAL PATROL CRAFT

MH 21, MH 22, MH 23.

65 foot *(19·8 metres)* built by Swiftships, USA

2 COASTAL PATROL CRAFT

MH 5, MH 6.

31 foot *(9·5 metres)* Bertram "Enforcer" Class.

Other craft listed—*Citadelle Henry, Haiti Cherie* and *22 Juin.*

HONDURAS / HONG KONG 217

HONDURAS

Ministerial

Minister of Defence:
Brigadier Gen. M. E. Chinchilla Carcamao

Personnel

(a) 1978: 50
(b) 8 months conscript service

Base

Puerto Cortes

Mercantile Marine

Lloyd's Register of Shipping:
63 vessels of 104 903 tons gross

4 "SWIFT 65 FT" CLASS (COASTAL PATROL CRAFT)

Name	No	Builder	Commissioned
GEN J. T. CABANAS	GC 6501	Swiftships	Dec 1973
—	GC 6502	Swiftships	Jan 1974
+2			

Displacement, tons: 36·3 full load
Dimensions, feet (metres): 65·3 × 18·4 × 5·2 *(19·9 × 5·6 × 1·6)*
Main engines: 2 GM diesels = 24 knots
Range, miles: 2 000 at 22 knots
Complement: 5

Originally built by Swiftships, Morgan City for Haiti. Contract cancelled and Honduras bought the two completed boats. No armament. Further two with MTU diesels (= 36 knots). Delivered in 1977.

1 "SWIFT 105 FT" CLASS (FAST PATROL CRAFT)

Dimensions, feet (metres): 105 × 24 × 5 *(32 × 7·3 × 1·5)*
Main engines: 3 MTU diesels; 4 290 hp = 38 knots

Delivered by Swiftships, Morgan City in 1977.

1 HYDROGRAPHIC LAUNCH

Of 56 ft, transferred from USA 1976.

HONG KONG

All the following craft are operated by the Marine District of the Royal Hong Kong Police Force.

Senior officers

District Police Commander:
Mr. Sze-to Che-yan CPM JP

Assistant Commissioner:
Mr. R. J. L. MacDonald

Personnel

(a) 1978: 71 officers, 330 NCOs, 891 constables
(b) Voluntary service

Deletion

1975: Logistic Craft No 24
45 ft Patrol Craft No 5 and 8

Mercantile Marine

Lloyd's Register of Shipping:
113 vessels of 609 679 tons gross

2 COMMAND VESSELS

No. 1   No. 2

Displacement, tons: 222·5
Dimensions, feet (metres): 111·3 × 24 × 10·5 *(33·9 × 7·3 × 3·2)*
Main engines: 2 diesels of 337 bhp = 11·8 knots
Range, miles: 5 200 at 11·8 knots
Complement: 25

Built at Taikoo 1965 (now Hong Kong United Dockyard). Can carry two platoons in addition to complement. Cost $HK 1 778 550.

POLICE LAUNCH No. 2   1974, RHKP

7 78 ft PATROL CRAFT

Nos. 50-56

Displacement, tons: 82
Dimensions, feet (metres): 78·5 oa × 17·2 × 5·6 *(23·9 × 5·2 × 1·7)*
Gun: 1—0·50 cal MG
Main engines: 2 Cummins diesels; 1 500 hp = 20·7 knots
Range, miles: 4 000 at 20 knots
Complement: 16

Steel hulled craft built by Thornycroft, Singapore. Delivered May 1972 to May 1973 to the Royal Hong Kong Police. Can carry an extra Platoon. Cost $HK 1 873 800.

POLICE LAUNCH No. 51   1974, RHKP

1 78 ft PATROL CRAFT

No. 4

Displacement, tons: 72
Dimensions, feet (metres): 78 × 15 × 4·5 *(22·8 × 4·6 × 1·4)*
Main engines: 3 diesels of 690 hp = 15·5 knots
Range, miles: 600 at 15·5 knots
Complement: 21

Built by Thornycroft, Singapore in 1958.

218 HONG KONG

9 70 ft PATROL CRAFT

Nos. 26-34

Displacement, tons: 52
Dimensions, feet (metres): 70 × 17 × 5·2 *(24·5 × 5·2 × 1·6)*
Main engines: 2 diesels of 215 bhp = 10 knots
Range, miles: 1 600 at 10 knots
Complement: 12

Built by Hong Kong SY (26-28) in 1954 and Cheoy Lee SY (29-34 in 1955).

POLICE LAUNCH No. 27   9/1977, Dr. Giorgio Arra

1 65 ft PATROL CRAFT

No. 6

Displacement, tons: 48
Dimensions, feet (metres): 65 × 14·5 × 5·5 *(19·8 × 4·4 × 1·8)*
Main engines: 1 diesel; 152 bhp = 10·5 knots
Range, miles: 1 400 at 9 knots
Complement: 11

8 45 ft PATROL CRAFT

Nos. 9-16

Displacement, tons: 27·7
Dimensions, feet (metres): 45 × 15 × 7 *(13·7 × 4·6 × 2·1)*
Main engines: 1 diesel; 144 bhp = 9 knots
Range, miles: 1 700 at 8 knots
Complement: 5

Built by Australian Ministry of Munitions in 1946.

POLICE LAUNCH No. 12   1976, RHKP

3 40 ft PATROL CRAFT

Nos. 20-22

Displacement, tons: 17
Dimensions, feet (metres): 40·3 × 11·6 × 2 *(12·3 × 3·5 × 0·6)*
Main engines: 2 diesels of 370 bhp = 24 knots
Range, miles: 380 at 24 knots
Complement: 5

Built in Choy Lee in 1971.

POLICE LAUNCH No. 22   1974, RHKP

1 58 ft LOGISTIC CRAFT

No. 3

Of 37 tons and 16 knots with a range of 240 miles at 15 knots. Complement 8. Built by Thornycroft Singapore in 1958.

POLICE LAUNCH No. 3   1976, RHKP

1 LOGISTIC CRAFT

No. 7

Displacement, tons: 18·5
Main engines: 2 diesels; 700 hp = 23·5 knots
Range, miles: 300+ at 20 knots
Complement: 6 plus 19 passengers

Built by Hip Hing Cheung shipyard in 1975.

POLICE LAUNCH No. 7 1977, Hip Hing Cheung Shipyard

11 22 ft LAUNCHES

Nos. 35-45

Of 4·8 tons and 20 knots with a range of 160 miles at full speed. Built by Choy Lee SY in 1970.

POLICE LAUNCH No. 38 9/1977, Dr. Giorgio Arra

HUNGARY

Ministerial

Minister of Defence:
 Lazos Czinege

Diplomatic Representation

Military and Air Attaché London:
 Colonel Imry Mózsik

Personnel

(a) 1978: 500 officers and men
(b) 2 years national service

Mercantile Marine

Lloyd's Register of Shipping:
 19 vessels of 63 016 tons gross

The Navy was dissolved by 1968 but a maritime wing of the Army is still very active on the Danube. The total number of craft operated is about 45.

LIGHT FORCES

10 100 ton PATROL CRAFT

Displacement, tons: 100
Gun: 1—14·7 mm
Main engines: 2 diesels

MINEWARFARE FORCES

Several riverine MCM vessels.

SERVICE FORCES

Several troop transports of up to 1 000 tons.
Five small LCUs.
A number of tugs.
Several river ice-breakers.
Transport barges which can double as landing craft or bridging element.

ICELAND

Ministerial

Minister of Justice:
 Olafur Johannesson

Senior Officer

Director of Coastguard:
 Pétur Sigurdsson

Personnel

1978: 170 officers and men

Duties

The Coast Guard Service (Landhelgisgaezlan) deals with fishery protection, salvage, rescue, hydrographic research, surveying and lighthouse duties.

Base

Reykjavik

Aircraft

2 Bell helicopter
1 Hughes helicopter
2 Fokker Friendship

Research Ships

A number of Government Research Ships bearing RE pennant numbers operate off Iceland.

Mercantile Marine

Lloyd's Register of Shipping:
 375 vessels of 166 702 tons gross

COAST GUARD PATROL VESSELS

Name	No.	Builders	Commissioned
AEGIR	—	Aalborg Vaerft, Denmark	1968
TYR	—	Aarhus Flyedock AS, Denmark	15 Mar 1975

Displacement, tons: 1 150 (Tyr 1500)
Dimensions, feet (metres): 204 × 33 × 14·8 (62·2 × 10 × 4·6) Aegir
229·6 × 32·8 × 19 (70 × 10 × 5·8) Tyr
Gun: 1—57 mm
Main engines: 2 MAN diesels; 2 shafts; 8 000 bhp = 19 knots (8 600 hp = 20 knots Tyr)
Complement: 22

Aegir was the first new construction patrol vessel for the Icelandic Coast Guard Service for about eight years. Projected in Feb 1965. Laid down in May 1967. Tyr, basically similar to Aegir, but a slightly improved design with higher speed was launched by Aarhus Flyedock AS, Denmark on 10 October 1974. Both have helicopter deck and hangar.

Radar: Three search sets.

Sonar: One hull mounted.

AEGIR 1969, Icelandic Coast Guard

Name	No.	Builders	Commissioned
ODINN	—	Aalborg Vaerft, Denmark	Jan 1960

Displacement, tons: 1 000
Dimensions, feet (metres): 187 pp × 33 × 13 (57 × 10 × 4)
Gun: 1—57 mm
Main engines: 2 B & W diesels; 2 shafts; 5 050 bhp = 18 knots
Complement: 22

Laid down in Jan 1959. Launched in Sept 1959. Refitted in Denmark by Aarhus Flydedock late 1975, with twin funnels and helicopter hangar.

Radar: Two search sets.

Sonar: One hull mounted.

ODINN 1976, Icelandic Coast Guard

Name	No.	Builders	Commissioned
THOR	—	Aalborg Vaerft, Denmark	Late 1951

Displacement, tons: 920
Dimensions, feet (metres): 183·3 pp; 206 oa × 31·2 × 13 (55·8; 62·8 × 9·5 × 4)
Gun: 1—57 mm
Main engines: 2—6-cyl MWM diesels; 3 200 bhp = 17 knots
Complement: 22

Launched in 1951. Fitted with helicopter platform during refit in 1972. Now has twin funnels and hangar.

Radar: Two search sets.

Sonar: One hull-mounted set.

THOR 1975, Icelandic Coast Guard

Name	No.	Builders	Commissioned
ARVAKUR	—	Bodewes, Netherlands	1962

Displacement, tons: 716
Dimensions, feet (metres): 106 × 33 × 13 *(32·3 × 10 × 4)*
Gun: 1 MG
Main engine: 1 diesel; 1 000 bhp = 12 knots
Complement: 12

Built as a lighthouse tender in the Netherlands. Acquired by Iceland for duty in the Coast Guard Service in 1969.

Radar: Two search sets.

Name	No.	Builders	Commissioned
ALBERT	—	Stalsmidjan, Reykjavik	April 1957

Displacement, tons: 200 gross
Dimensions, feet (metres): Length: 111·2 *(33·9)*
Gun: 1—47 mm
Main engine: 1 Nohab diesel; 650 bhp = 12·5 knots
Complement: 15

Launched in 1956. Refitted in 1972.

Radar: Two search sets.

ALBERT 1975, Icelandic Coast Guard

"21 SS SMUGGLER" CRAFT

A number of these craft fitted with Italian Castoldi jets (157 hp) and capable of 36 knots has recently been delivered by Smuggler Boats Trading AS Norway.

INDIA

Ministerial

Minister of Defence:
Bansi Lal

Headquarters Appointment

Chief of the Naval Staff:
Admiral J. Cursetji

Senior Appointments

Flag Officer C in C, Western Naval Command:
Vice-Admiral R. L. Pereira
Flag Officer Commanding Western Fleet:
Rear-Admiral M. R. Schunker
Flag Officer C in C Eastern Naval Command:
Vice-Admiral S. Parkash
Flag Officer Commanding Eastern Fleet:
Rear-Admiral D. S. Paintal
Flag Officer, Southern Naval Area:
Rear-Admiral V. E. C. Barboza

Diplomatic Representation

Naval Attaché in Bonn:
Commodore H. Johnson
Naval Adviser, Dacca:
Captain R. B. Mukherjee
Naval Attaché in Jakarta:
Captain R. V. Singh
Naval Adviser in London:
Commodore C. L. Sachdeva
Naval Attaché in Moscow:
Commodore I. J. S. Khurana
Defence Attaché in Washington:
Brigadier Srendra Singh MC

Personnel

(a) 1977: 46 000 officers and ratings (including Naval Air Arm)
(b) Voluntary service

Naval Bases and Establishments

Bombay (C in C Western Fleet, barracks and main Dockyard);
Vishakapatnam (C in C Eastern Command, submarine base, dockyard and barracks);
Cochin (FO Southern Area Naval Air Station, barracks and professional schools);
Lonavala and Jamnagar (professional schools);
Calcutta, Goa and Port Blair (small bases only);
New Delhi (HQ)

Naval Air Arm

Squadron No.	Aircraft	Role
300	Seahawk FGA6 (25)	Strike
310	Alize 1050 (10)	ASW
312	5 Super Constellations	MR
	3 Ilyushin IL38 May	
321	Alouette III (7)	SAR
330	Sea Kings (12)	ASW
331	Alouette III (7)	ASW
550	Alize, Alouette	Training
561	2 Devon	Training
	4 Hughes 300,	
	4 Vampire T-55,	
	7 HJT 16-Kiran	

Note: 5 Britten-Norman Defenders ordered in 1976

Prefix to Ships' Names

IS (Indian Ship)

Mercantile Marine

Lloyd's Register of Shipping:
566 vessels of 5 482 176 tons gross

Strength of the Fleet

Type	Active	Building
Attack Carrier (Medium)	1	—
Cruisers	2	—
Frigates	25	2
Corvettes	—	3
Patrol Submarines	8	—
Fast Attack Craft—Missile	16	—
Large Patrol Craft	1	—
Coastal Patrol Craft	7	—
Landing Ship	1	—
Landing Craft	6	—
Minesweepers—Coastal	4	—
Minesweepers—Inshore	4	—
Survey Ships	3	1
Submarine Tender	1	—
Submarine Rescue Ship	1	—
Replenishment Tankers	2	—
Support Tankers	3	—
Repair Ship	1	—
Ocean Tug	1	—
Harbour Craft	5	—

COAST GUARD

In March 1977 the Interim Coast Guard Force was formed with the transfer of the Type 14 frigates *Kirpan* and *Kuthar* from normal naval service. They remain armed and manned as before but carry the Coast Guard sign in place of pennant numbers. The Vice Chief of Naval Staff, Vice-Admiral V. A. Kamath took charge of this new organisation which will later be expanded to include additional ships and craft and aircraft. Five patrol craft previously belonging to the Home Department are being transferred.

DELETIONS

Destroyers

1976 *Rana, Rajput, Ranjit* (British "R" Class)

Frigates

1971 *Khukri* sunk in war with Pakistan (9 Dec)
1975 *Ganga* and *Gomati* ("Hunt" Class) paid off.

Survey Ship

1975 *Investigator* ("River" class) paid off.

Light Forces

1974 *Ajay* and *Akshay* to Bangladesh, *Amar* to Mauritius (April).
1975 *Savitri, Sharayu, Subhadra, Suvarna* paid off.

Minewarfare Forces

1973 *Konkan* (last of 6 "Bangor" class) paid off.

Harbour Tankers

1976 *Chilka, Sambhar*.

PENNANT LIST

Aircraft Carrier

R 11	Vikrant

Cruisers

C 60	Mysore
C 74	Delhi

Frigates

D 92	Godavari
F 11	Jamuna (Survey)
F 31	Brahmaputra
F 32	Nilgiri
F 33	Himgiri
F 34	Dunagiri
F 35	Udaygiri
F 36	Taragiri
F 37	Beas
F 38	Vindhyagiri
F 39	Betwa
F 40	Talwar
F 43	Trishul
F 46	Kistna
F 95	Sutlej (Survey)
F 110	Kaveri
F 256	Tir
CG	Kirpan
CG	Kuthar

Corvettes

K 71	Vijay Durg
K 72	Sinhu Durg
K 73	Nanuchka III
K 74	Nanuchka IV

Submarines

S 20	Kursura
S 21	Karanj
S 22	Kanderi
S 23	Kalvari
S 40	Vela
S 41	Vagir
S 42	Vagli
S 43	Vagsheer

Light Forces
(including "Petya" class with P numbers)

K 82	Veer
K 83	Vidyut
K 84	Vijeta
K 85	Vinash
K 86	Nipat
K 87	Nashat
K 88	Nirbhik
K 89	Nirghat
K 90	Prachand
K 91	Pralaya
K 92	Pralap
K 93	Prabal
K 94	Chapal
K 95	Chapmak
K 96	Osa II
K 97	Osa II
P 68	Arnala
P 69	Androth
P 73	Anjadip
P 74	Andaman
P 75	Amini
P 78	Kadmath
P 79	Kiltan
P 80	Kavaratti
P 81	Katchal
P 82	Kanjar
P 83	Amindivi
T 46	Panvel

Light Forces

T 47	Pamban
T 48	Puri
T 49	Panaji
T 50	Pulicat
SPB 3132	Sukanya
SPB 3133	Sharada
P 3135	Abhay

Minewarfare Forces

M 88	Bhaktal
M 89	Bulsar
M 90	Kuddalore
M 91	Cannanore
M 92	Karwar
M 93	Kakinada
M 2705	Bimlipitan
M 2707	Bassein

Amphibious Forces

L 11	Magar
L 12	Gharial
L 13	Guldar
L 14	Ghorpad
L 15	Kesari
L 16	Shardul
L 17	Sharab

Service Forces

A 14	Amba
A 15	Nistar
A 50	Deepak
A 57	Shakti
A 139	Darshak
A 306	Dharini
A 1750	Deepak

INDIA 223

VIKRANT

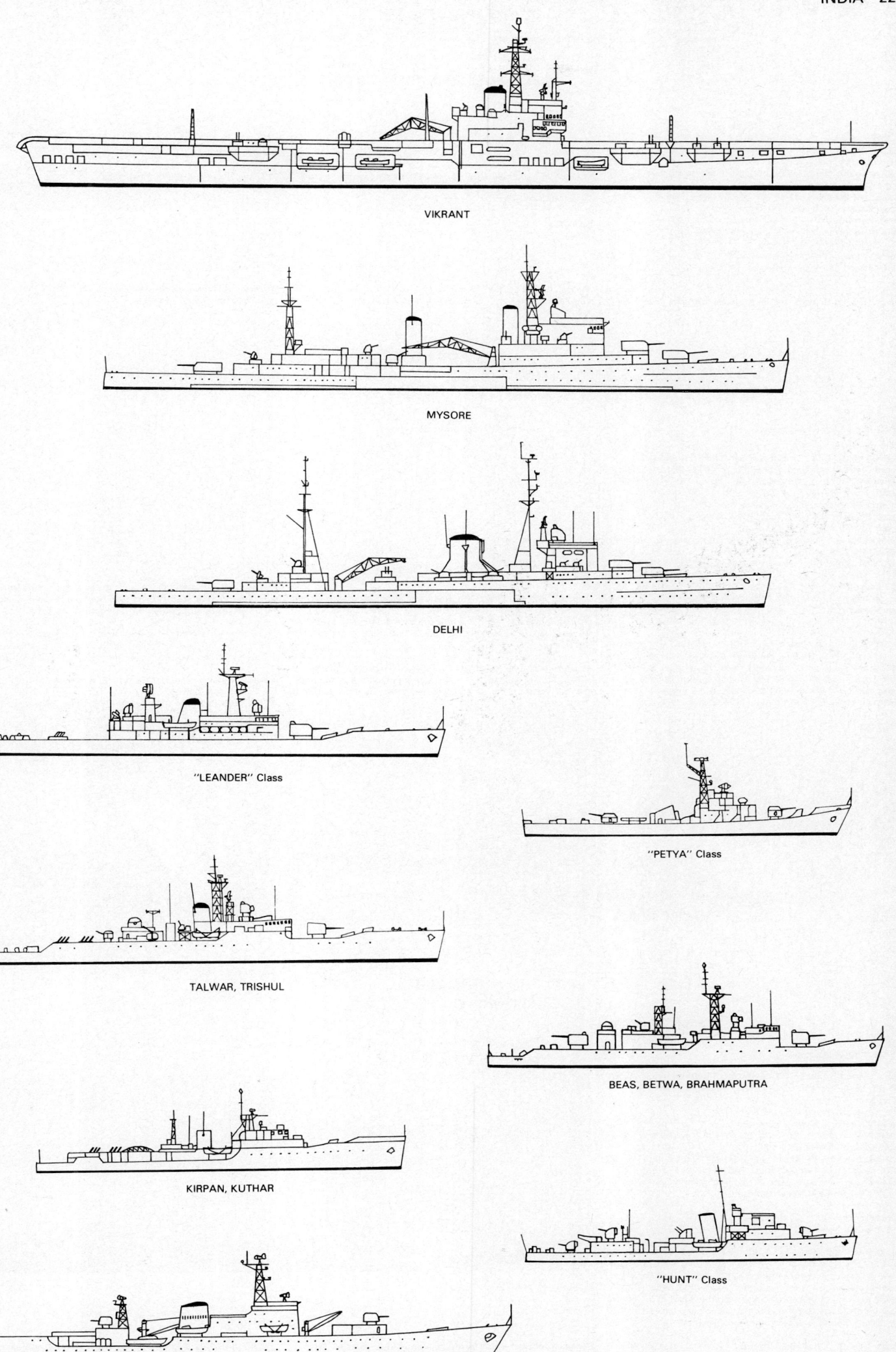

MYSORE

DELHI

"LEANDER" Class

"PETYA" Class

TALWAR, TRISHUL

BEAS, BETWA, BRAHMAPUTRA

KIRPAN, KUTHAR

"HUNT" Class

AMBA

224 INDIA

SUBMARINES

Note: India is still discussing plans to build her own submarines though no details have been released.

8 Ex-SOVIET "FOXTROT" CLASS

KURSURA S 20	**VELA** S 40
KARANJ S 21	**VAGIR** S 41
KANDERI S 22	**VAGLI** S 42
KALVARI S 23	**VAGSHEER** S 43

Displacement, tons: 2 000 surfaced; 2 300 dived
Length, feet (metres): 296·8 (90·5)
Beam, feet (metres): 42·1 (7·3)
Draught, feet (metres): 19·0 (5·8)
Torpedo tubes: 10—21 in (20 torpedoes carried)
Main machinery: 3 diesels; 3 shafts; 6 000 bhp; 3 electric motors; 6 000 hp
Speed, knots: 20 surfaced; 15 dived
Complement: 70

Kalvari arrived in India on 16 July 1968, *Kanderi* in Jan 1969.

KARANJ   1/1978

Karanj in Oct 1970 and *Kursura* in Dec 1970. *Vela* Nov 1973, *Vagir* Dec 1973, *Vagli* Sep 1974, *Vagsheer* May 1975.

Additions: There are reports, so far unconfirmed, that a further pair may be transferred later.

AIRCRAFT CARRIER

1 Ex-BRITISH "MAJESTIC" CLASS

Name	No.	Builders	Laid down	Launched	Commissioned
VIKRANT (ex-HMS *Hercules*)	R 11	Vickers-Armstrong Ltd, Tyne	14 Oct 1943	22 Sept 1945	4 Mar 1961

Displacement, tons: 16 000 standard; 19 500 full load
Length, feet (metres): 630 (192·0) pp; 700 (213·4) oa
Beam, feet (metres): 80 (24·4) hull
Width, feet (metres): 128 (39·0)
Draught, feet (metres): 24 (7·3)
Aircraft: 22 capacity (18 Seahawk, 4 Alize)
Guns: 15—40 mm (4 twin, 7 single)
Main engines: Parsons single reduction geared turbines; 40 000 shp; 2 shafts
Boilers: 4 Admiralty three-drum; 400 psi; 700°F
Speed, knots: 24·5
Oil fuel, tons: 3 200
Range, miles: 12 000 at 14 knots; 6 200 at 23 knots
Complement: 1 075 (peace); 1 345 (war)

Acquired from the United Kingdom in Jan 1957 after having been suspended in May 1946 when structurally almost complete and 75 per cent fitted out. Taken in hand by Harland & Wolff Ltd, Belfast, in April 1957 for completion in 1961. Commissioned on 4 March 1961 and renamed *Vikrant*. Completed extensive overhaul—1973 to Aug 1974.

Aircraft: Still equipped with Seahawks although re-equipment is planned. Harrier trials in mid-1972 showed promise, but subsequently the Indian Navy is understood to have preferred Soviet Yakovlev VTOL aircraft due to problems in purchasing the Harrier.

Engineering: One set of turbines and two boilers are installed side by side in each of the two propelling machinery spaces, on the unit system, so that the starboard propeller shaft is longer than the port.

Flight deck: The aircraft, including strike and anti-submarine aircraft, operate from an angled deck with steam catapult, landing sights and two electrically operated lifts.
Habitability: Partially air-conditioned and insulated for tropical service, the ship's sides being sprayed with asbestos cement instead of being lagged. Separate messes and dining halls.
Radar: Search: Type 960, Type 277.
Tactical: Type 293.
Miscellaneous: Type 963 Carrier Controlled Approach.

VIKRANT   1971, John G. Callis

CRUISERS

1 Ex-BRITISH "FIJI" CLASS

Name	No.	Builders	Laid down	Launched	Commissioned
MYSORE (ex-HMS *Nigeria*)	C 60	Vickers-Armstrong Ltd, Tyne	8 Feb 1938	18 July 1939	23 Sep 1940

Displacement, tons: 8 700 standard; 11 040 full load
Length, feet (metres): 538·0 (164·0) pp; 549·0 (176·3) wl 555·5 (169·3) oa
Beam, feet (metres): 62·0 (18·9)
Draught, feet (metres): 21·0 (6·4)
Guns: 9—6 in (152 mm), (3 triple); 8—4 in (102 mm), (4 twin); 12—40 mm (5 twin, 2 single)
Armour: Side 4½ in—3 in (114—76 mm); Deck 2 in (51 mm); Conning tower 4 in (102 mm); Turrets 2 in (51 mm)
Main engines: Parsons geared turbines; 4 shafts; 72 500 shp
Boilers: 4 Admiralty three-drum type
Speed, knots: 31·5
Complement: 800

Flagship at the Battle of Porsanger Fjord Sep 1941. Purchased from the United Kingdom on 8 April 1954 for £300 000. Extensively refitted and reconstructed by Cammell Laird & Co Ltd, Birkenhead, before commissioning. Formally handed over to the Indian Navy at Birkenhead and renamed *Mysore* on 29 Aug 1957. Involved in two serious collisions, the second in late 1972 with *Beas*, resulting in two months of repairs.

Radar: Search: Type 960, Type 277.
Tactical: Type 293.
Fire control: I Band.

MYSORE (*Vijadurg* alongside)   8/1977

Reconstruction: Ship formerly had tripod masts. During reconstruction the triple 6 inch turret in "X" position and the 6—21 inch torpedo tubes (tripled) were removed, the bridge was modified, two lattice masts were stepped, all electrical equipment was replaced and the engine room and other parts of the ship were refitted.

1 Ex-BRITISH "LEANDER" CLASS

Name	No.	Builders	Laid down	Launched	Commissioned
DELHI (ex-HMS Achilles)	C 74	Cammell Laird & Co Ltd, Birkenhead	11 June 1931	1 Sept 1932	5 Oct 1933

Displacement, tons: 7 114 standard; 9 740 full load
Length, feet (metres): 522·0 (159·1) pp; 544·5 (166·0) oa
Beam, feet (metres): 55·2 (16·8)
Draught, feet (metres): 20·0 (6·1)
Guns: 6—6 in (152 mm) (3 twins); 10—40 mm (2 twin, 6 single); 4—3 pdr saluting
Armour: 4 in-2 in side; 1 in gunhouses; 1 in bridge; 2 in deck
Main engines: Parsons geared turbines; 4 shafts 72 000 shp
Boilers: 4 Admiralty three-drum type
Oil fuel, tons: 1 800
Speed, knots: 32
Complement: 800

As HMS *Achilles*, then lent to the Royal New Zealand Navy, this ship, with HMS *Ajax* and HMS *Exeter*, defeated the German battleship *Admiral Graf Spee* in the Battle of the River Plate on 13 Dec 1939. Purchased from the United Kingdom and delivered on 5 July 1948. Refitted in 1955. Now used for training cadets. Reported as due for deletion.

Gunnery: Eight 4 in guns removed to provide space for deckhouses required for cadet accommodation. 40 mm armament reduced from fourteen to ten.

Radar: Search: Type 960, Type 277.
Tactical: Type 293.
Fire control: Early design.

Torpedo Tubes: In 1958 the original eight 21 in torpedo tubes, in two quadruple banks, were removed, and the forecastle deck plating was consequently extended aft to the twin 40 mm gun mounting abreast the boat stowage.

DELHI   1969, Graeme Andrews

FRIGATES

Note: It is reported that 2 "Kashin" class are to be transferred by the USSR in 1978

6 BRITISH "LEANDER" CLASS

Name	No.	Builders	Laid down	Launched	Commissioned
NILGIRI	F 32	Mazagon Docks Ltd, Bombay	Oct 1966	23 Oct 1968	3 June 1972
HIMGIRI	F 33	Mazagon Docks Ltd, Bombay	1967	6 May 1970	23 Nov 1974
DUNAGIRI	F 34	Mazagon Docks Ltd, Bombay	14 Sept 1970	24 Oct 1972	18 Feb 1976
UDAYGIRI	F 35	Mazagon Docks Ltd, Bombay	Jan 1973	9 Mar 1974	Feb 1977
TARAGIRI	F 36	Mazagon Docks Ltd, Bombay	1974	25 Oct 1976	?1979
VINDHYAGIRI	F 38	Mazagon Docks Ltd, Bombay	—	—	—

Displacement, tons: 2 450 standard; 2 800 full load
Length, feet (metres): 360 (109·7) wl; 372 (113·4) oa
Beam, feet (metres): 43 (13·1)
Draught, feet (metres): 18 (5·5)
Aircraft: 1 Alouette III helicopter
Missiles: 2 Seacat quadruple launchers (all but *Nilgiri*—one)
Guns: 2—4·5 in (115 mm) (1 twin); 2—20 mm
A/S weapons: 1 Limbo 3 barrelled DC mortar
Main engines: 2 geared turbines; 30 000 shp
Boilers: 2
Oil fuel, tons: 460
Speed, knots: 30
Range, miles: 4 500 at 12 knots
Complement: 263

First major warships built in Indian yards. Of similar design to later (broad beam) "Leander" class in the Royal Navy. Hangar has been enlarged to take Alouette III helicopter.

Missiles: *Nilgiri* has one Seacat launcher with UK GWS22 control. Remainder have two Seacat launchers with two Dutch M4 directors.

Radar: HSA radars in place of UK types.

UDAYGIRI   6/1977, C. and S. Taylor

HIMGIRI   6/1977

INDIA

ARNALA P 68
ANDROTH P 69
ANJADIP P 73
ANDAMAN P 74
AMINI P 75
KAMORTA P 77
KADMATH P 78
KILTAN P 79
KAVARATTI P 80
KATCHAL P 81
KANJAR P 82
AMINDIVI P 83

12 Ex-SOVIET "PETYA II" CLASS

Displacement, tons: 950 standard; 1 150 full load
Length, feet (metres): 250·0 (76·2) wl; 270 (82·3) oa
Beam, feet (metres): 29·9 (9·1)
Draught, feet (metres): 10·5 (3·2)
Guns: 4—3 in (76 mm) (2 twin)
A/S weapons: 4 MBU 2 500 (16-barrelled rocket launchers);
   2 internal DC racks
Torpedo tubes: 3—21 in (533 mm)
Mines: Have minerails
Main engines: 2 gas turbines; 30 000 hp;
   2 diesels; 2 shafts; 6 000 hp
Speed, knots: 30
Complement: 100

Transferred to the Indian Navy since 1969. *Andaman* delivered Mar 1974, *Amini* late 1974. All are of an export version of "Petya II" class with simplified communications.

Radar: Surface search: Slim Net.

ANDAMAN   6/1977

2 Ex-BRITISH "WHITBY" CLASS

Name	No.	Builders	Laid down	Launched	Commissioned
TALWAR	F 40	Cammell Laird & Co Ltd, Birkenhead	1957	18 July 1958	1960
TRISHUL	F 43	Harland & Wolff Ltd, Belfast	1957	18 June 1959	1960

Displacement, tons: 2 144 standard;
   2 545 full load (*Talwar*), 2 557 (*Trishul*)
Length, feet (metres): 360 (109·7) pp 369·8 (112·7) oa
Beam, feet (metres): 41 (12·5)
Draught, feet (metres): 17·8 (5·4)
Missiles: see note
Guns: 2—4·5 in (115 mm) (see missile note);
   4—40 mm (1 twin before Limbos, 2 singles abaft funnel)
A/S weapons: 2 Limbo 3-barrelled DC mortars
Main engines: 2 sets geared turbines; 30 000 shp; 2 shafts
Boilers: 2 Babcock & Wilcox
Oil fuel, tons: 400
Speed, knots: 30
Range, miles: 4 500 at 12 knots
Complement: 231 (11 officers, 220 men)

Generally similar to the British frigates of the "Whitby" class, but slightly modified to suit Indian conditions. *Trishul* acts as Squadron commander of 15th Frigate Squadron.

Missiles: In late 1975 *Talwar* was fitted with three SS-N-2 missile launchers from an "Osa" class in place of the 4·5 in turret.

Radar: Tactical: Type 293 and 277.
Fire control: I Band. (FPS 6 director).
Missile control (*Talwar*): Square Tie.

TALWAR (after SS-N-2 Mod)   1976

3 Ex-BRITISH "LEOPARD" CLASS

Name	No.	Builders	Laid down	Launched	Commissioned
BRAHMAPUTRA (ex-*Panther*)	F 31	John Brown & Co Ltd, Clydebank	1956	15 Mar 1957	28 Mar 1958
BEAS	F 37	Vickers-Armstrong Ltd, Tyne	1957	9 Oct 1958	24 May 1960
BETWA	F 39	Vickers-Armstrong Ltd, Tyne	1957	15 Sept 1959	8 Dec 1960

Displacement, tons: 2 251 standard; 2 515 full load
Length, feet (metres): 320·0 (97·5) pp; 330·0 (100·6) wl;
   339·8 (103·6) oa
Beam, feet (metres): 40·0 (12·2)
Draught, feet (metres): 16·0 (4·9)
Guns: 4—4·5 in (114 mm) (2 twin); 2—40 mm
A/S weapons: 1 Squid 3-barrelled DC motar
Main engines: Admiralty standard range diesels 2 shafts;
   12 380 bhp
Speed, knots: 25
Range, miles: 7 500 at 16 knots
Complement: 210

Brahmaputra, originally ordered as *Panther* for the Royal Navy on 28 June 1951, was the first major warship to be built in the United Kingdom for the Indian Navy since India became independent. All three ships are generally similar to the British frigates of the "Leopard" class, but modified to suit Indian conditions.
Form 16th Frigate Squadron.

Radar: Search: Type 960
Tactical: Type 293.
Fire control: I Band forward and aft.

BEAS   6/1977

INDIA 227

2 Ex-BRITISH "BLACKWOOD" CLASS (COAST GUARD)

Name	No.	Builders	Laid down	Launched	Commissioned
KIRPAN	Coast Guard	Alex Stephen & Sons Ltd, Govan, Glasgow	1957	19 Aug 1958	July 1959
KUTHAR	Coast Guard	J. Samuel White & Co Ltd, Cowes, Isle of Wight	1957	14 Oct 1958	1959

Displacement, tons: 1 180 standard; 1 456 full load
Length, feet (metres): 300 *(91·4)* pp; 310 *(94·5)* oa
Beam, feet (metres): 33 *(10·0)*
Draught, feet (metres): 15·5 *(4·7)*
Guns: 3—40 mm (single)
A/S weapons: 2 Limbo 3-barrelled DC mortars
Main engines: 1 set geared turbines; 15 000 shp; 1 shaft
Boilers: Babcock & Wilcox
Speed, knots: 27·8
Oil fuel, tons: 300
Range, miles: 4 000 at 12 knots
Complement: 150

Generally similar to the British frigates of the "Blackwood" class, but slightly modified to suit Indian requirements. *Khukri* of this class was sunk in the Pakistan war on 9 Dec 1971.

Radar: Fitted with E Band air and surface surveillance radar.

KHUKRI (*Kirpan* and *Kuthar* similar) *A. & J. Pavia*

1 Ex-BRITISH "HUNT" CLASS TYPE II

Name	No.	Builders	Laid down	Launched	Commissioned
GODAVARI (ex-HMS *Bedale*, ex-ORP *Slazak*, ex-HMS *Bedale*)	D 92	R. & W. Hawthorn, Leslie & Co Ltd, Hebburn	25 May 1940	23 July 1941	9 May 1942

Displacement, tons: 1 050 standard; 1 610 full load
Length, feet (metres): 264·2 *(80·5)* pp; 280·0 *(85·3)* oa
Beam, feet (metres): 31·5 *(9·6)*
Draught, feet (metres): 14·0 *(4·3)*
Guns: 6—4 in *(102 mm)* (twins); 4—20 mm; quad Pom-pom
Main engines: Parsons geared turbines; 2 shafts; 19 000 shp
Boilers: 2 Admiralty three-drum
Oil fuel, tons: 280
Speed, knots: 25
Range, miles: 3 700 at 14 knots
Complement: 150

Lent to Poland April 1942—Nov 1946. Transferred from the United Kingdom in May 1953. Lent to the Indian Navy for three years, subject to extension by agreement. Now used for training.
Ran aground in Maldives 1976—subsequently salvaged but may soon be deleted.

GANGA (Godavari similar) *A. & J. Pavia*

2 Ex-BRITISH "BLACK SWAN" CLASS

Name	No.	Builders	Laid down	Launched	Commissioned
KISTNA	F 46	Yarrow & Co Ltd, Scotstoun, Glasgow	14 July 1942	22 April 1943	23 Aug 1943
KAVERI	F 110	Yarrow & Co Ltd, Scotstoun, Glasgow	28 Oct 1942	15 June 1943	21 Oct 1943

Displacement, tons: 1 470 standard; 1 925 full load
Length, feet (metres): 283·0 *(86·3)* pp; 295·5 *(90·1)* wl; 299·5 *(91·3)* oa
Beam, feet (metres): 38·5 *(11·7)*
Draught, feet (metres): 11·2 *(3·4)*
Guns: 4—4 in *(102 mm)*; 4—40 mm
A/S weapons: 2 DCT
Main engines: Parsons geared turbines; 2 shafts; 4 300 shp
Boilers: 2 three-drum type
Speed, knots: 19
Oil fuel, tons: 370
Range, miles: 4 500 at 12 knots
Complement: 210

Former sloops of the British "Black Swan" class built for India and modified to suit Indian conditions.
Cauvery was renamed *Kaveri* in 1968.

Radar: Fitted with E band air and surface surveillance radar and ranging radar for the gunfire control systems.

KISTNA

1 Ex-BRITISH "RIVER" CLASS

Name	No.	Builders	Laid down	Launched	Commissioned
TIR (ex-HMS *Bann*)	F 256	Charles Hill & Sons Ltd, Bristol	18 June 1942	29 Dec 1942	7 May 1943

Displacement, tons: 1 463 standard; 1 934 full load
Length, feet (metres): 283·0 *(86·3)* pp; 303 *(92·4)* oa
Beam, feet (metres): 37·6 *(11·2)*
Draught, feet (metres): 14·5 *(4·4)*
Guns: 1—4 in *(102 mm)*; 1—40 mm; 2—20 mm
Main engines: Triple expansion; 2 shafts; 5 500 ihp
Boilers: 2 Admiralty three-drum type
Speed, knots: 18
Oil fuel, tons: 385
Range, miles: 4 200 at 12 knots
Complement: 120

Transferred on 3 Dec 1945. Converted to a Midshipman's Training Frigate by Bombay Dockyard in 1948.

TIR *1971, Indian Navy*

228 INDIA

CORVETTES

4 + (?2) Ex-SOVIET "NANUCHKA" CLASS

VIJAY DURG K 71   — K 73
SINHU DURG K 72   — K 74

Displacement, tons: 850 full load
Length, feet (metres): 196·8 *(60)*
Beam, feet (metres): 39·6 *(12)*
Draught, feet (metres): 9·9 *(3)*
Missiles: Probably SS-N-2 (mod)
Guns: 2—57 mm (twin)
Main engines: Diesels; 28 000 shp; 2 shafts
Speed, knots: 30
Complement: 70

A notable addition to Indian capabilities. *Vijay Durg* delivered March 1977.
Reported that a further two may be expected.

Radar: Search: Slim Net.
Navigation: Don.

VIJAY DURG   6/1977

LIGHT FORCES

16 Ex-SOVIET "OSA I and II" CLASS (FAST ATTACK CRAFT—MISSILE)

VEER K 82	NASHAT K 87	*PRATAP K 92
VIDYUT K 83	NIRBHIK K 88	*PRABAL K 93
VIJETA K 84	NIRGHAT K 89	*CHAPAL K 94
VINASH K 85	*PRACHAND K 90	*CHAMAK K 95
NIPAT K 86	*PRALAYA K 91	*+2 (K 96, K 97)

*Osa II

Displacement, tons: 165 standard; 200 full load
Dimensions, feet (metres): 128·7 × 25·1 × 5·9 *(37 × 7 × 1·8)*
Missiles: 4 in two pairs for SS-N-2
Guns: 4—30 mm (2 twin)
Main engines: 3 diesels; 3 shafts; 13 000 bhp = 36 knots
Complement: 25

Some of these craft took part in a night attack with Styx off Karachi on 4-5 Dec 1971. They sank the PNS *Khaibar*, damaged *Badr* and a CMS as well as one Panamanian m/s without damage to themselves.
Further eight delivered Feb-Oct 1976. ("Osa II" class). Three others reported sunk in Indo-Pakistani War 1971.

Missiles: *Vijeta* had three SS-N-2 launchers transferred to I. S. *Talwar* in late 1975.

Radar: Square Tie and Drum Tilt. IFF—Ski Pole.

INDIAN "OSA" Class   6/1977

4 + 4 "IMPROVED ABHAY" CLASS (FAST ATTACK CRAFT—PATROL)

Displacement, tons: 140
Dimensions, feet (metres): 123 × 24·6 × 5·9 *(37·5 × 7·5 × 1·8)*
Gun: 1—40 mm
Main engines: 2 Paxman diesels; 6 000 hp = 28 knots

First launched 16 July 1976, three more building at Garden Reach, Calcutta. Four more planned.
Indian Customs Service to purchase eight—"for but not with" armament.

1 "ABHAY" CLASS (LARGE PATROL CRAFT)

Name	No.	Builders	Commissioned
ABHAY	P 3135	Hoogly Docking & Engineering Co Ltd, Calcutta	13 Nov 1961

Displacement, tons: 120 standard; 151 full load
Dimensions, feet (metres): 110 pp; 117·2 oa × 20 × 5 *(33·6; 35·7 × 6·1 × 1·5)*
Gun: 1—40 mm
Main engines: 2 diesels; speed = 18 knots

Generally similar to the "Ford" class in the Royal Navy. Originally a class of six. *Ajay* and *Akshay* transferred to Bangladesh 1974, *Amar* to Mauritius April 1974.

5 Ex-SOVIET "POLUCHAT" CLASS (COASTAL PATROL CRAFT)

PANVEL T 46	PURI T 48	PULICAT T 50
PAMBAN T 47	PANAJI T 49	

Displacement, tons: 86 standard; 91 full load
Dimensions, feet (metres): 98 × 15 × 4·8 *(29·9 × 4·6 × 1·5)*
Guns: 2—14·5 mm (twin)
Main engines: 2 diesels; 2 shafts; 2 400 bhp = 18 knots
Range, miles: 460 at 17 knots
Complement: 16

One transferred to Bangladesh in 1973 but returned.

2 "SHARADA" CLASS (COASTAL PATROL CRAFT)

Name	No.	Builders	Commissioned
SUKANYA	SPB 3132	Yugoslavia	5 Dec 1959
SHARADA	SPB 3133	Yugoslavia	5 Dec 1959

Displacement, tons: 83 standard; 100 full load
Dimensions, feet (metres): 98·4 × 19·7 × 4·9 *(30 × 6 × 1·5)*
Guns: Small arms
Main engines: 2 Mercedes-Benz diesels; 1 900 hp = 18 knots
Complement: 16

Probably now laid up.

AMPHIBIOUS FORCES

Note: A new design of Landing Craft with a draught of no more than 4 feet is now available in India although no orders have yet been reported.

6 Ex-SOVIET "POLNOCNY" CLASS (LCT)

GHARIAL L 12	GHORPAD L 14	SHARDUL L 16
GULDAR L 13	KESARI L 15	SHARAB L 17

Displacement, tons: 780 standard; 1 000 full load (L 12 and L 13); 1 100 full load (remainder)
Dimensions, feet (metres): 239 × 29·5 × 9·8 *(72·9 × 9 × 3)* (L 12 and L 13); Remainder length 265 ft *(80·8)*, beam 31 ft *(9·5)*
Guns: 2—25 mm (twin) (L 12 and L 13); 4—30 mm (twins) (remainder)
Rocket launcher: Multi-barrelled 140 mm
Main engines: 2 diesels; 5 000 bhp = 18 knots

First pair transferred from USSR in 1966, *Ghorpad* in 1975, *Kesari* Sept 1975, *Shardul* Dec 1975 and *Sharab* March 1976. 350 ton cargo.

Radar: Drum Tilt not fitted.

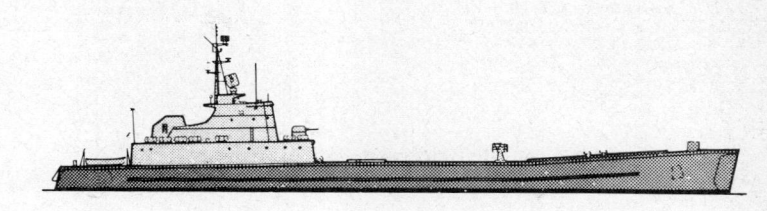

"POLNOCNY" Class

1 Ex-BRITISH LST (3)

MAGAR (ex-HMS *Avenger*) L 11

Displacement, tons: 2 256 light; 4 980 full load
Dimensions, feet (metres): 347·5 oa × 55·2 × 11·2 *(106 × 16·8 × 3·4)*
Guns: 2—40 mm; 6—20 mm; (2 twin, 2 single)
Main engines: Triple expansion; 2 shafts; 5 500 ihp = 13 knots

There is also LCT 4294 (ex-1294), yard craft of 200 tons, speed 9·5 knots.

MAGAR 1964, A. & J. Pavia

MINE WARFARE FORCES

4 Ex-BRITISH "TON" CLASS (MINESWEEPERS—COASTAL)

Name	No.	Builders	Commissioned
KUDDALORE (ex-HMS *Wennington*)	M 90	J. S. Doig Ltd, Grimsby	1955
CANNANORE (ex-HMS *Whitton*)	M 91	Fleetlands Shipyard Ltd, Gosport	1956
KARWAR (ex-HMS *Overton*)	M 92	Camper & Nicholson Ltd, Gosport	1956
KAKINADA (ex-HMS *Durweston*)	M 93	Dorset Yacht Co Ltd, Hamworthy	1955

Displacement, tons: 360 standard; 425 full load
Dimensions, feet (metres): 140·0 pp; 153·0 oa × 28·8 × 8·2 *(46·7 × 8·8 × 2·5)*
Guns: 2—20 mm
Main engines: Napier Deltic diesels; 2 shafts; 1 250 bhp = 15 knots
Oil fuel, tons: 45
Range, miles: 3 000 at 8 knots
Complement: 40

"Ton" class coastal minesweepers of wooden construction built for the Royal Navy, but transferred from the United Kingdom to the Indian Navy in 1956. *Cannanore* was launched 30 Jan 1956, *Karwar* was launched 30 Jan 1956. *Kuddalore* and *Kakinada* were taken over in Aug 1956, and sailed for India in Nov-Dec 1956. Named after minor ports in India. Constitute the 18th Mine Counter Measures Squadron, together with the inshore minesweepers.

KAKINADA 1977

4 "HAM" CLASS (MINESWEEPERS—INSHORE)

Name	No.	Builders	Commissioned
BHAKTAL	M 88	Magazon Dockyard, Bombay	1968
BULSAR	M 89	Magazon Dockyard, Bombay	1970
BIMLIPITAN (ex-HMS *Hildersham*)	M 2705	Vosper Ltd, Portsmouth	1954
BASSEIN (ex-HMS *Littleham*)	M 2707	Brooke Marine Ltd, Oulton Broad, Lowestoft	1954

Displacement, tons: 120 standard; 170 full load
Dimensions, feet (metres): 98·0 pp; 107·0 oa × 22·0 × 6·7 *(32·6 × 6·7 × 1·6)*
Gun: 1—20 mm
Main engines: 2 Paxman diesels; 550 bhp = 14 knots (9 knots sweeping)
Oil fuel, tons: 15
Complement: 16

Of wooden construction two of which were built for the Royal Navy but transferred from the United Kingdom to the Indian Navy in 1955. *Bassein* was launched on 4 May 1954; *Bimlipitan* was launched on 5 Feb 1954. *Bhaktal* was launched in April 1967, and *Bulsar* on 17 May 1969.

BASSEIN 1971, A & J Pavia

230 INDIA

SURVEY SHIPS

Name	No.	Builders	Commissioned
DARSHAK	A 139	Hindustan Shipyard, Vishakapatnam	28 Dec 1964

Displacement, tons: 2 790
Length, feet (metres): 319 *(97·2)* oa
Beam, feet (metres): 49 *(14·9)*
Draught, feet (metres): 28·8 *(8·8)*
Main engines: 2 diesel-electric units; 3 000 bhp
Speed, knots: 16
Complement: ~~150~~

First ship built by Hindustan Shipyard for the Navy. Launched on 2 Nov 1959. Provision was made to operate a helicopter. The ship is all welded.

DARSHAK 1967

Name	No.	Builders	Commissioned
SANDHAYAK	—	Garden Reach DY, Calcutta	1979

Displacement, tons: 1 200
Main engines: Diesel; 1 shaft

Launched 6 April 1977.

2 "SUTLEJ" CLASS

Name	No.	Builders	Laid down	Launched	Commissioned
JAMUNA (ex-*Jumna*)	F 11	Wm. Denny & Bros Ltd, Dumbarton	20 Feb 1940	16 Nov 1940	13 May 1941
SUTLEJ	F 95	Wm. Denny & Bros Ltd, Dumbarton	4 Jan 1940	10 Oct 1940	23 April 1941

Displacement, tons: 1 300 standard; 1 750 full load
Length, feet (metres): 276 *(84·1)* wl; 292·5 *(89·2)* oa
Beam, feet (metres): 37·5 *(11·4)*
Draught, feet (metres): 11·5 *(3·5)*
Main engines: Parsons geared turbines 3 600 shp; 2 shafts
Boilers: 2 Admiralty three-drum
Speed, knots: 18
Oil fuel, tons: 370
Range, miles: 5 600 at 12 knots
Complement: 150

Former frigates employed as survey ships since 1957 and 1955 respectively. Both ships are generally similar to the former British frigates of the "Egret" class.

JAMUNA 11/1975, P. Elliott

SERVICE FORCES

1 Ex-SOVIET "UGRA" CLASS (SUBMARINE TENDER)

AMBA A 14

Displacement, tons: 6 000 light; 9 000 full load
Length, feet (metres): 370 pp; 420 oa × 65 × 20 *(138 × 16·8 × 6·5)*
Guns: 4—3 in *(76 mm)* (twins)
Main engines: Diesels; 2 shafts; 7 000 bhp = 17 knots

Acquired from the USSR in 1968. Provision for helicopter. Can accommodate 750. Two cranes, one of 6 tons and one of 10 tons.

Radar: One Slim Net; two Hawk Screech.

AMBA 1977

1 Ex-SOVIET "T58" (Mod.) CLASS (SUBMARINE RESCUE SHIP)

NISTAR A 15

Displacement, tons: 790 standard; 900 full load
Dimensions, feet (metres): 220·0 × 29·5 × 7·9 *(67·7 × 9·1 × 2·3)*
Main engines: 2 diesels; 2 shafts; 5 000 bhp = 18 knots

Converted from a fleet minesweeper to a submarine rescue ship and transferred from USSR late-1971. Carries diving-bell and recompression chamber.

1 REPAIR SHIP

DHARINI (ex- *La Petite Hermine*) A 306

Displacement, tons: 6 000 (oil capacity 1 000)
Dimensions, feet (metres): 324·7 × 45·6 × 13·3 *(99 × 13·9 × 4)*
Main engines: Triple expansion; 809 ihp = 9 knots
Oil fuel, tons: 621

Cargo ship built by Foundation Maritime Ltd, Canada as *Ketowna Park*. Launched 25 July 1944. Sold to India for commercial use in 1953. Transferred to navy in 1957. Converted and commissioned in May 1960.

DHARINI 1964, Indian Navy

2 REPLENISHMENT TANKERS

Name	No.	Builders	Commissioned
DEEPAK	A 50	Bremer-Vulkan	1967
—	—	Bremer-Vulkan	31 Dec 1975

Displacement, tons: 15 800
Measurement, tons: 12 690·6 GRT
Dimensions, feet (metres): 552·6 oa × 75·5 × 30 *(168·4 × 23 × 9·2)*
Guns: 3—40 mm; 2—20 mm
Main engines: Steam turbines = 20 knots

On charter to Indian Navy from Mogul Lines. Fitted with a helicopter landing platform aft, but no hangar. Automatic tensioning fitted to replenishment gear. Also carries dry cargo. Second ship launched by Bremer-Vulkan Sept 1975.

1 SUPPORT TANKER

Name	No.	Builders	Commissioned
SHAKTI	A 57	Bremer-Vulkan	1975

Displacement, tons: 3 500
Dimensions, feet (metres): 318 × 44 × 18·4 *(97 × 13·5 × 5·6)*
Aircraft: 1 helicopter
Main engines: Diesel; speed = 13 knots

Fitted with helicopter deck and telescopic hangar.

SHAKTI   1/1978

1 SUPPORT TANKER

LOK ADHAR (ex-*Hooghly*)

Displacement, tons: 9 231

Formerly *Baqir* of Gulf Shipping Corp Ltd. Acquired in 1972.

1 TUG (OCEAN)

Name	No.	Builders	Commissioned
HATHI	—	Taikoo Dock & Engineering Company, Hong Kong	1933

Displacement, tons: 668
Dimensions, feet (metres): 147·5 × 23·7 × 15 *(45 × 7·2 × 4·6)*
Main engines: Triple expansion; speed = 13 knots

Launched in 1932.

1 SUPPORT TANKER

DESH DEEP

Measurement, tons: 11 000 DWT

Ex-Japanese merchant tanker taken over in 1972.

4 Ex-BRITISH HDML TYPE

SPC 3110 (ex-*HDML 1110*)   **SPC 3117** (ex-*HDML 1117*)
SPC 3112 (ex-*HDML 1112*)   **SPC 3118** (ex-*HDML 1118*)

Displacement, tons: 48 standard; 54 full load
Dimensions, feet (metres): 72 oa × 16 × 4·7 *(22 × 4·9 × 1·4)*
Guns: 2—20 mm
Main engines: Diesels; 2 shafts; 320 bhp = 12 knots
Complement: 14

Used as harbour craft.

A number of harbour tankers (approx 1 000 tons) have been built at Bombay.
A new class of fleet tug (approx 1 200 bhp) has been built recently at Garden Reach.

Barq (ex-*MMS 132*), *MMS 130* and *MMS 154*, former British motor minesweepers of the "105 ft" type of wooden construction, transferred from the United Kingdom, are employed as yard craft. *MMS 1632* and *MMS 1654* are yard craft in Bombay.

INDONESIA

Ministerial

Minister of Defence and Security:
  General Maraden Panggabean

Administration

Chief of the Naval Staff:
  Admiral R. Subiyakto
Deputy Chief of the Naval Staff Operations:
  Rear-Admiral Wulujo Sugito
Inspector General of the Navy:
  Commodore M. Wibowo
Chief for Naval Material:
  Commodore Urip Subiyanto
Chief for Naval Personnel:
  Commodore Imem Muharam
Commander of Navy Marine Corps:
  Major General Moch Anwar
Commander-in-Chief Indonesian Fleet:
  Rear-Admiral Rudy Purwana

Diplomatic Representation

Naval Attaché in Bangkok:
  Lieutenant Colonel Purnomo
Naval Attaché in Canberra:
  Colonel Eddy Tumengkol
Naval Attaché in Delhi:
  Lieutenant Colonel B. Sumitro
Naval Attaché and Naval Attaché for Air in London:
  Colonel Sumarjono
Naval Attaché in Moscow:
  Colonel Priyonggo
Naval Attaché in Tokyo:
  Colonel Agus Subroto
Naval Attaché and Naval Attaché for Air in Washington:
  Colonel Ariffin Roesady

Personnel

(a) 1978: 40 000 including 5 000 Marine Commando Corps and 1 000 Naval Air Arm
(b) Selective national service

Bases

Gorontalo, Kemajaran (Jakarta), Surabaja

Strength of the Fleet

Type	Active	Building
Frigates	11	3
Patrol Submarines	3	2
Fast Attack Craft—Missile	13	4
Fast Attack Craft—Torpedo	5	—
Large Patrol Craft	19	—
Coastal Patrol Craft	8	—
LSTs	9	—
LCUs	2	—
Minesweepers—Ocean	5	—
Minesweepers—Coastal	2	—
Survey Ships	4	—
Submarine Tenders	2	—
Destroyer Depot Ship	1	—
Repair Ship	1	—
Replenishment Tanker	1	—
Support Tankers	4	—
Harbour Tankers	3	—
Cable Ship	1	—
Tugs	3	—
Training Ship	1	—
Customs	19+	—
Army	23	—
Air Force	6	—

Ex-Soviet Ships

Indonesia obtained 104 ships from the USSR. Of these half have now been deleted and all will have gone in the near future.

Future Plans

It is planned, over the next 20 years, to provide a Navy of some 25 000 seamen and 5 000 marines to man a Fleet including 4 fast A/S Frigates, some Submarines, Light Forces of Fast Attack Craft—Missile and—Torpedo, Minelayers, Minesweepers, a fast HQ ship and a fast Supply Ship. 3 Corvettes/Frigates are being built by the Netherlands, 2 submarines in West Germany and 4 fast attack craft in South Korea.

Naval Air Arm

6—GAF Nomad (MR)
5—HU 16B Albatross (SAR)
6—C 47
3—Alouette II helicopters
3—Alouette III helicopters
4—Bell 47G helicopters
3—Commander

Prefix to Ships' Names

KRI (Kapal di Republik Indonesia)

Mercantile Marine

Lloyd's Register of Shipping:
  1 032 vessels of 1 163 173 tons gross

232 INDONESIA

DELETIONS

Cruiser

1972 *Irian*

Destroyers

1973 *Brawidjaja, Sandjaja, Sultan Babarudin*

Frigates

1973 *Kakiali, Slamet Rijadi*
1974 *Ngurah Rai* ("Riga" class)

Submarines

1974 *Alugoro, Hendradjala, Nagarangsang, Tjandrasa, Tjundmani, Trisula, Widjajadanu* (all "Whiskey" class)

Amphibious Forces

1974 3 ex-Yugoslav LCTs, *Tandjung Nusanive* (ex-US LST); 3 ex-US LCI Type

Minewarfare Forces

1974 4 ex-Dutch CMS, 5 "R" Class
1976 *Pulau Rondo* ("T 43" class), *Rau, Rindja, Rusa* ("R" class), *Pulau Alor, Pulau Anjer, Pulau Antang, Pulau Aru, Pulah Aruan, Pulau Impalasa* ("Falcon" class)

Light Forces

1970 *310, 314, 315, 316* (Kraljevica), *Dorang, Lajang, Rubara*
1974 2 "Jaguar" class, 25 HDMLs, 10 Motor Launches, *Palu, Tenggiri*

1975 14 "P 6" class, 18 "BK" class, *Landjuru, Lapai, Lumba Lumba, Madidihang, Tongkol, Tjutjut* ("Kronshtadt" class)
1976 *Katula, Momare* ("Kronshtadt" class), *Krapu* ("Kraljevica" class), *Katjabola, Tritusta* ("Komar" class)
1977 *Serigala* ("TNC 45" class)

Survey Ships

1972 *Hidral*
1973 *Dewa Kembar*

Auxiliaries

1974 2 Transports, 1 Salvage Vessel, 1 Tug, 37 Patrol Craft
1976 *Thamrin* ("Atrek" class), *Pangkalin Brandan, Wono Kromo* ("Uda" class)

PENNANT LIST

Frigates

341 Samadikun
342 Martadinata
343 Mongisidi
344 Ngurah Rai
351 Jos Sudarso
355 Iman Bondjol
356 Surapati
357 Lambung Makurat
360 Nuku
801 Pattimura
802 Sultan Hasanudin

Submarines

403 Nagga Banda
410 Pasopati
412 Bramastra

Light Forces

570 Bentang Kalakuang
571 Bentang Waitatire
572 Bentang Silunkang
601 Kelaplintah

Light Forces

602 Kalamisani
603 Sarpawasesa
604 Pulang Geni
605 Kalanada
608 Surotama
609 Sarpamina
611 Naga Pasa
612 Guawidjaja
652 Beruang
653 Matjan Kumbang
654 Harimau
655 Anoa
805 Hiu
806 Torani
807 Kakalang
808 Kelabang
809 Kompas
810 Kala Hitam
814 Pandorong
815 Sura
816 Kakap
817 Barakuda
818 Sembilang
819 Layang
820 Lemadang
821 Krapu

Light Forces

822 Dorang
823 Todak
846 Silinan
847 Sibarau

Minewarfare Forces

701 Pulau Rani
702 Pulau Ratewo
703 Pulau Roon
704 Pulau Rorbas
705 Pulau Raja
707 Pulau Rengat
708 Pulau Rapat

Amphibious Forces

501 Teluk Langsa
502 Teluk Bajur
503 Teluk Amboina
504 Teluk Kau
505 Teluk Manado
508 Teluk Tomini
509 Teluk Ratai

Amphibious Forces

510 Teluk Saleh
511 Teluk Bone

Support Ships

561 Multatuli
4101 Ratulangi

Service Forces

911 Sorong
921 Jaya Wijaya
923 Dumai
928 Rakata
934 Lampo Batang
935 Tambora
936 Bromo

Survey Ships

1002 Burdjamhal
1005 Jalanidhi
1006 Burudjulasad
1008 Aries

RATULANGI

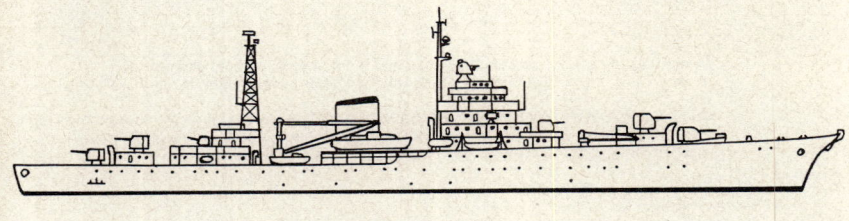

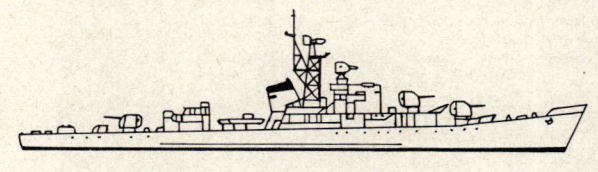

"RIGA" Class

"CLAUD JONES" Class

"SURAPATI" Class

SUBMARINES

2 TYPE 209

Standard class ordered from Howaldtswerke, Kiel on 2 April 1977.

3 Ex-SOVIET "WHISKEY" CLASS

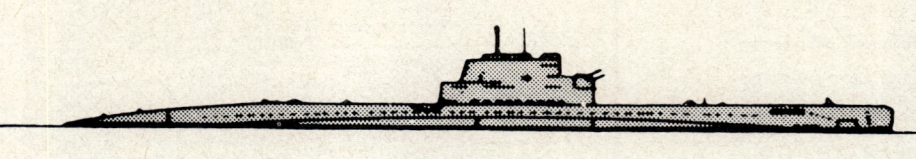

NAGGA BANDA 403	**BRAMASTRA** 412
PASOPATI 410	

Displacement, tons: 1 030 surfaced; 1 350 dived
Length, feet (metres): 249·3 *(76)*
Beam, feet (metres): 22 *(6·7)*
Draught, feet (metres): 15 *(4·6)*
Torpedo tubes: 6—21 in *(533 mm)* 4 forward, 2 aft; 18 torpedoes carried
Guns: 2—25 mm (403)
Mines: 40 in lieu of torpedoes
Main machinery: 4 000 bhp diesels; 2 500 hp electric motors, diesel-electric drive; 2 shafts
Speed, knots: 17 surfaced; 15 dived
Range, miles: 13 000 at 8 knots surfaced
Complement: 60

"WHISKEY" Class

The four Soviet submarines of the "Whiskey" class, which arrived in Indonesia on 28 June 1962, brought the total number of this class transferred to Indonesia to 14 units, but it was reported that only six would be maintained operational, while six would be kept in reserve and two used for spare parts. Now reduced to three operational boats of which two have been refitted and have received new batteries from UK. *Naga Banda* currently refitting.

INDONESIA

FRIGATES

3 NEW CONSTRUCTION

Displacement, tons: 1 200 standard
Dimensions, feet (metres): 276 × 36 × 10·7 *(84 × 11 × 3·3)*
Main engines: CODOG arrangement; 1 Olympus TM 3B turbine; 2 MTU diesels; 4 000 hp; 2 shafts = 30 knots
Guns: 1—76 mm; 2—40 mm
A/S weapons: Bofors 375 mm rocket projector

Ordered Aug 1975. Building by Wilton Fijenoord, Netherlands. First laid down 31 Jan 1977, and second on 28 July 1977. Officially rated as "Corvettes".

Radar: HSA—possibly WM 27.

NEW CONSTRUCTION FRIGATE   *1976, Wilton-Fijenoord*

4 Ex-US "CLAUD JONES" CLASS

Name	No.	Builders	Laid down	Launched	Commissioned
SAMADIKUN (ex-USS *John R. Perry* DE 1034)	341	Avondale Marine Ways	1 Oct 1957	29 July 1958	5 May 1959
MARTADINATA (ex-USS *Charles Berry* DE 1035)	342	American SB Co, Toledo, Ohio	29 Oct 1958	17 Mar 1959	25 Nov 1959
MONGISIDI (ex-USS *Claud Jones* DE 1033)	343	Avondale Marine Ways	1 June 1957	27 May 1958	10 Feb 1959
NGURAH RAI (ex-USS *McMorris* DE 1036)	344	American SB Co, Toledo, Ohio	5 Nov 1958	26 May 1959	4 Mar 1960

Displacement, tons: 1 450 standard; 1 750 full load
Length, feet (metres): 310 *(95)* oa
Beam, feet (metres): 37 *(11·3)*
Draught, feet (metres): 18 *(5·5)*
Guns: 1—3 in *(76 mm)* 50 cal; 2—37 mm (twin); 2—25 mm (twin) (341-342); 2—3 in *(76 mm)* (single); 2—25 mm (twin) (343-344)
A/S weapons: 2 triple torpedo tubes (Mk 32); 2 Hedgehogs
Main engines: 4 diesels; 9 200 hp; 1 shaft
Speed, knots: 22
Complement: 175

Samadikun served as fleet flagship.

Electronics: ECM/ESM gear removed

Gunnery: Fire control system Mk 70 for 3-in. Secondary armament is ex-Soviet artillery.

Radar: SPS 6 and 10.

Sonar: SQS 29-32 series.

Transfer: *Samadikun,* 20 Feb 1973; *Martadinata,* 31 Jan 1974; *Mongisidi* and *Ngurah Rai* 16 Dec 1974.

SAMADIKUN   *1975, Indonesian Navy*

3 Ex-SOVIET "RIGA" CLASS

JOS SUDARSO 351   **NUKU** 360
LAMBUNG MANGKURAT 357

Displacement, tons: 1 200 standard; 1 600 full load
Length, feet (metres): 298·8 *(91)*
Beam, feet (metres): 33·7 *(10·2)*
Draught, feet (metres): 11 *(3·4)*
Guns: 3—3·9 in *(100 mm)* (single); 4—37 mm
A/S weapons: 4 DC projectors
Torpedo tubes: 3—21 in *(533 mm)*
Mines: Fitted with mine rails
Main engines: Geared steam turbines; 2 shafts; 25 000 shp
Boilers: 2
Speed, knots: 28
Range, miles: 2 500 at 15 knots
Complement: 150

Built 1955-57.
Transferred in 1964.

Radar: Slim Net search and warning; Fire control Sun Visor A with Wasp Head director; Navigation Neptun; IFF, High Pole A.

JOS SUDARSO   *1974, John Mortimer*

234 INDONESIA

2 "SURAPATI" CLASS

Name	No.	Builders	Laid down	Launched	Commissioned
IMAN BONDJOL	355	Ansaldo, Genoa	8 Jan 1956	5 May 1956	19 May 1958
SURAPATI	356	Ansaldo, Genoa	8 Jan 1956	5 May 1956	28 May 1958

Displacement, tons: 1 150 standard; 1 500 full load
Dimensions, feet (metres): 325 × 36 × 8·5 (99 × 11 × 2·6)
Guns: 4—4 in (102 mm) (twins); 6—30 mm (twins); 6—20 mm (twins)
A/S weapons: 2 Hedgehogs; 4 DCT
Torpedo tubes: 3—21 in (533 mm)
Boilers: 2 Foster Wheeler
Main engines: 2 sets Parsons geared turbines, 2 shafts; 24 000 shp
Speed, knots: 32
Oil fuel, tons: 350
Range, miles: 2 800 at 22 knots
Complement: 200

Near sisters of the "Almirante Clemente" class of Venezuela. Both in reserve.

IMAN BONDJOL   Dr. Ing Luigi Accorsi

2 "PATTIMURA" CLASS

Name	No.	Builders	Laid down	Launched	Commissioned
PATTIMURA	801	Ansaldo, Leghorn	8 Jan 1956	1 July 1956	28 Jan 1958
SULTAN HASANUDIN	802	Ansaldo, Leghorn	8 Jan 1957	24 Mar 1957	8 Mar 1958

Displacement, tons: 950 standard; 1 200 full load
Length, feet (metres): 246 (75·0) pp; 270·2 (82·4) oa
Beam, feet (metres): 34 (10·4)
Draught, feet (metres): 9 (2·7)
Guns: 2—3 in (76 mm) 40 cal. 2—30 mm 70 cal (twin)
A/S weapons: 2 Hedgehogs; 4 DCT
Main engines: 3 Ansaldo-Fiat diesels; 3 shafts; 6 900 bhp
Speed, knots: 22
Range, miles: 2 400 at 18 knots
Oil fuel, tons: 100
Complement: 110

Similar to Italian "Albatros" class.
Sultan Hasanudin in reserve.

PATTIMURA   Dr.Ing Luigi Accorsi

LIGHT FORCES

6 Ex-SOVIET "KRONSHTADT" CLASS (LARGE PATROL CRAFT)

PANDORONG 814	KAKAP 816	SEMBILANG 818
SURA 815	BARAKUDA 817	TOHOK

Displacement, tons: 310 standard; 380 full load
Dimensions, feet (metres): 170·6 × 21·5 × 9 (52·0 × 6·5 × 2·7)
Guns: 1—3·5 in (85 mm); 2—37 mm; 6—12·7 mm
A/S weapons: 2 DCT; 2 RBU 1800; 2 dc racks
Mines: 2 mine rails for 10 mines
Main engines: 3 diesels; 3 shafts; 3 300 bhp = 19 knots
Oil fuel, tons: 20
Range, miles: 1 500 at 12 knots
Complement: 65

Built in 1951-54. Transferred to the Indonesian Navy on 30 Dec 1958. *Kakap* in reserve.

Radar: Ball Gun or Don 2; IFF, High Pole A

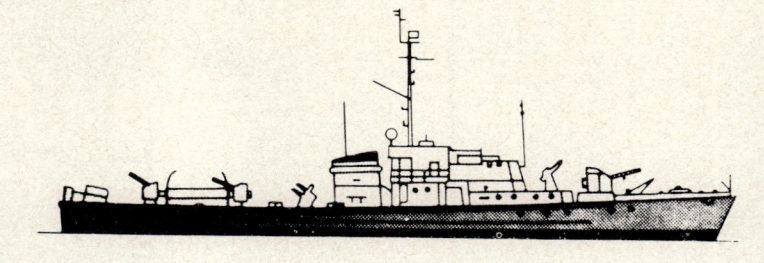

"KRONSHTADT" Class

3 Ex-US "PC-461" CLASS (LARGE PATROL CRAFT)

HIU (ex-USS *Malvern*, PC 580) 805
TORANI (ex-USS *Manville*, PC 581) 806
KAKALANG (ex-USS *Pierre*, PC 1141) 807

Displacement, tons: 280 standard; 450 full load
Dimensions, feet (metres): 170 wl; 173·7 oa × 23 × 10·8 (55·7; 53 × 7 × 3·3)
Guns: 1—37 mm; 4—25 mm (twin)
A/S weapons: 4 DCT
Main engines: 2 GM diesels; 2 shafts; 2 880 bhp = 20 knots
Oil fuel, tons: 60
Range, miles: 5 000 at 10 knots
Complement: 54 (4 officers, 50 men)

Gunnery: Original armament of 1—3 in (76 mm); 1—40 mm; 2—20 mm has been replaced in most ships by armament shown from deleted ex-Soviet ships.

Built in 1942-43. *Pierre* transferred from the US Navy at Pearl Harbor, Hawaii in Oct 1958 and *Malvern* and *Manville* in March 1960. *Kakalang* and *Torani* in reserve.

"PC-461" Class   1966, Indonesian Navy

INDONESIA 235

4 PSSM Mark 5 (FAST ATTACK CRAFT—MISSILE)

Displacement, tons: 290 full load
Dimensions, feet (metres): 165 × 24 × 9·5 (50·3 × 7·3 × 2·9)
Missiles: 4 launchers for Harpoon SSM
Guns: 1—3 in (76 mm) 50 cal; 2—20 mm
Main engines: 1 GE LM 2500 gas turbine; 2 MTU diesels; 2 shafts (cp propellers) = 45 knots (gas) 17 knots (diesels)
Complement: 32

Ordered from Korea-Tacoma Boatbuilding Co, Washington for delivery 1976-77. Building in South Korea.

BASIC PSSM Mk 5 DESIGN 1976

9 Ex-SOVIET "KOMAR" CLASS (FAST ATTACK CRAFT—MISSILE)

KELAPLINTAH 601	PULANG GENI 604	SARPAMINA 609
KALAMISANI 602	KALANADA 605	NAGA PASA 611
SARPAWASESA 603	SUROTAMA 608	GUAWIDJAJA 612

Displacement, tons: 70 standard; 80 full load
Dimensions, feet (metres): 83·7 × 19·8 × 5 (25·5 × 6·0 × 1·8)
Guns: 2—35 mm (1 twin)
Missiles: 2 launchers for SS-N-2
Main engines: 4 diesels; 4 800 hp = 40 knots
Range, miles: 400 at 30 knots
Complement: 20

Six were transferred to Indonesia in 1961-63, four more in Sept 1964 and two in 1965. Missiles probably of doubtful capability. *Guawidjaya* and *Naga Pasa* in reserve.

Hardadali of this class sank early 1976 after hitting an underwater obstacle.

SARPAMINA 1967

4 "LURSSEN TNC-45" CLASS (FAST ATTACK CRAFT—TORPEDO)

Name	No.	Builders	Commissioned
BERUANG	652	Lürssen Vegesack	1959
MATJAN KUMBANG	653	Lürssen Vegesack	1960
HARIMAU	654	Lürssen Vegesack	1960
ANOA	655	Lürssen Vegesack	1959

Displacement, tons: 160 standard; 190 full load
Dimensions, feet (metres): 131 pp; 138 oa × 22 × 7·5 (42·9; 42·1 × 6·7 × 2·3)
Guns: 2—40 mm (single)
Torpedo tubes: 4—21 in
Main engines: 4 Daimler-Benz (MTU) diesels; 4 shafts; 12 000 bhp = 42 knots
Complement: 39

Steel hulled—of the original eight, four had wooden hulls. Similar to German "Jaguar" class.

HARIMAU *Indonesia*

3 Ex-US "PGM 39" CLASS (LARGE PATROL CRAFT)

BENTANG KALUNGKANG (ex-*PGM 57*) 570
BENTANG WAITATIRE (ex-*PGM 56*) 571
BENTANG SILUNGKANG (ex-*PGM 55*) 572

Displacement, tons: 122 full load
Dimensions, feet (metres): 100 × 21 × 8·5 (30·5 × 6·4 × 2·6)
Guns: 2—20 mm; 2 MG
Main engines: 2 Mercedes-Benz MB 820 dB diesels; 2 shafts = 17 knots

Originally intended as Amphibious Control Craft. Now used for normal patrol duties. All transferred Jan 1962.

Gunnery: Original armament 4—12·7 mm MG (twin)

2 Ex-AUSTRALIAN "ATTACK" CLASS (LARGE PATROL CRAFT)

Name	No.	Builders	Commissioned
SILINAN (ex-HMAS *Archer*)	846	Australia	1968
SIBARAU (ex-HMAS *Bandolier*)	847	Australia	1968

Displacement, tons: 146 full load
Dimensions, feet (metres): 107·5 × 20 × 7·3 (32·8 × 6·1 × 2·2)
Guns: 1—40 mm; 2 medium MGs
Main engines: 2 Paxman diesels; 2 shafts = 21 knots
Complement: 19 (3 officers, 16 men)

Transferred from RAN after refit—*Bandolier* 16 Nov 1973, *Archer* in 1974. It is reported, though not confirmed, that another six may be transferred.

SIBARAU (old number) 1973, Graeme Andrews

236 INDONESIA

5 Ex-YUGOSLAV "KRALJEVICA" CLASS (LARGE PATROL CRAFT)

LAYANG (ex-*PBR 515*) 819　　**DORANG** (ex-*PBR 514*) 822
LEMADANG (ex-*PBR 517*) 820　　**TODAK** (ex-*PBR 518*) 823
KRAPU (ex-*PBR 513*) 821

Displacement, tons: 190 standard; 245 full load
Dimensions, feet (metres): 134·5 × 20·8 × 7 *(41 × 6·3 × 2·1)*
Guns: 1—3 in; 1—40 mm; 6—20 mm
A/S weapons: DC
Main engines: 2 MAN diesels; 2 shafts; 3 300 bhp = 20 knots
Oil fuel, tons: 15
Range, miles: 1 500 at 12 knots
Complement: 54

Purchased and transferred on 27th Dec 1958.

DORANG　　　　　　　　　　　　　　　　　　　　1968, *Indonesian Navy*

3 "KELABANG" CLASS (LARGE PATROL CRAFT)

KELABANG 808　　**KOMPAS** 809　　**KALA HITAM** 810

Displacement, tons: 147
Gun: 1—40/60 mm; 4—12·7 mm MG (twins)
Main engines: 2 MAN diesels = 21 knots

Built in Indonesia in 1966-70. *Kompas* in reserve.

KALAHITAM　　　　　　　　　　　　　　　　　　1968, *Indonesian Navy*

2 FAIREY MARINE "SPEAR" CLASS (COASTAL PATROL CRAFT)

Dimensions, feet (metres): 29·8 × 9·2 × 2·6 *(9·1 × 2·8 × 0·8)*
Main engines: Twin 180 hp diesels
Speed, knots: 30
Range, miles: 200 at 26 knots

Purchased in 1973-74.

6 AUSTRALIAN DE HAVILLAND TYPE (COASTAL PATROL CRAFT)

Name	No.	Builders	Commissioned
SAMADAR	—	Hawker-De Havilland Aust	Aug 1976
SASILA	—	Hawker-De Havilland Aust	Sept 1976
SABOLA	—	Hawker-De Havilland Aust	Oct 1976
SADARIN	—	Hawker-De Havilland Aust	Nov 1976
SAWANGI	—	Hawker-De Havilland Aust	—
SALMANETI	—	Hawker-De Havilland Aust	—

Displacement, tons: 27 full load
Dimensions, feet (metres): 52·5 × 16·4 × 3·9 *(16 × 5 × 1·2)*
Guns: 2 MGs
Main engines: 2 MTU diesels; 1 400 bhp = 30 knots
Range, miles: 950 at 18 knots
Endurance: 4/5 days
Complement: 10

First delivered June 1976.

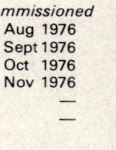

DE HAVILLAND SERIES 9311　　　　　　　　　　　10/1977, *Graeme Andrews*

AMPHIBIOUS FORCES

8 Ex-US "LST 1-511" and "512-1152" CLASSES

Name	No.	Builders	Commissioned
TELUK LANGSA (ex-USS *LST 1128*)	501	—	—
TELUK BAJUR (ex-USS *LST 616*)	502	—	—
TELUK KAU (ex-USS *LST 652*)	504	—	—
TELUK MANADO (ex-USS *LST 657*)	505	—	—
TELUK TOMINI (ex MV; ex-USS *Bledsoe County, LST 356*)	508	—	—
TELUK RATAI (ex-Liberian *Inagua Shipper*)	509	—	—
TELUK SALEH (ex-USS *Clark County, LST 601*)	510	—	—
TELUK BONE (ex-USS *Iredell County, LST 839*)	511	—	—

Displacement, tons: 1 653 standard; 4 080 full load
Dimensions, feet (metres): 316 × 50 × 14 *(103·6; 100 × 15·3 × 4·3)*
Guns: 7—40 mm; 2—20 mm (some); 6—37 mm (remainder)
Main engines: GM diesels; 2 shafts; 1 700 bhp = 11·6 knots
Oil fuel, tons: 600
Range, miles: 7 200 at 10 knots
Cargo capacity: 2 100 tons
Complement: 119 (accommodation for 266)

Gunnery: Older units and later unarmed ships fitted with ex-Soviet 37 mm.

Transfers: 505 in March 1960, 502, 510 and 511 in June 1961. 504 and 501 in July 1970.

3 LCU TYPE

AMURANG　　**BANTEN**　　**DORE**

Displacement, tons: 182 standard; 275 full load
Dimensions, feet (metres): 125·7 × 32·8 × 5·9 *(38·3 × 10 × 1·8)*
Main engines: Diesels; 210 hp = 8 knots
Complement: 17

Built in Austria.

3 + 10 INDONESIAN LCMs

First three completed in 1976.

25 + LCM TYPES

Possibly 25 ex-UK LCM 7.
Possibly 2 LCM 6.

1 JAPANESE TYPE LST

Name	No.	Builders	Commissioned
TELUK AMBOINA	503	Sasebo, Japan	1961

Displacement, tons: 2 200 standard; 4 200 full load
Dimensions, feet (metres): 327 × 50 × 15 *(99·7 × 15·3 × 4·6)*
Guns: 4—40 mm; 1—37 mm
Main engines: MAN diesels; 2 shafts; 3 000 bhp = 13·1 knots
Oil fuel, tons: 1 200
Range, miles: 4 000 at 13·1 knots
Complement: 88 (accommodation for 300)

Launched on 17 March 1961 and transferred in June 1961. A copy of US "LST 511" class.

20 + LCVP TYPE

Ex-US Craft, possibly with Indonesian Army Transportation Corps (See end of section).

INDONESIA 237

MINE WARFARE FORCES

5 Ex-SOVIET "T 43" CLASS (MINESWEEPERS—OCEAN)

| PULAU RANI | 701 | PULAU ROON | 703 | PULAU RAJA | 705 |
| PULAU RATEWO | 702 | PULAU RORBAS | 704 | | |

Displacement, tons: 500 standard; 610 full load
Dimensions, feet (metres): 190·2 × 28·2 × 6·9 (58 × 8·6 × 2·1)
Guns: 4—37 mm (twin); 8—12·7 mm (twin)
A/S weapons: 2 DCT

Main engines: 2 diesels; 2 shafts; 2 000 bhp = 17 knots
Range, miles: 1 600 at 10 knots
Complement: 40

Transferred to Indonesia by the USSR, four in 1962 and two in 1964.

2 "R" CLASS (MINESWEEPERS—COASTAL)

Name	No.	Builders	Commissioned
PULAU RENGAT	707	Abeking & Rasmussen Jacht-und Bootswerft, Lemwerder	—
PULAU RAPAT	708	Abeking & Rasmussen Jacht-und Bootswerft, Lemwerder	—

Displacement, tons: 139·4 standard
Dimensions, feet (metres): 129 × 18·7 × 5 (39·3 × 5·7 × 1·5)
Guns: 1—40 mm; 2—20 mm
Main engines: 2 MAN diesels; 12-cyl; 2 800 bhp = 24·6 knots
Complement: 26

"R" Class — Indonesian Navy

Originally a class of ten. These boats have a framework of light metal covered with wood. Both in reserve.

SURVEY SHIPS

Name	No.	Builders	Commissioned
BURUDJULASAD	1006	—	1967

Displacement, tons: 2 150 full load
Dimensions, feet (metres): 269·5 × 37·4 × 11·5 (82·2 × 11·4 × 3·5)
Main engines: 4 MAN diesels; 2 shafts; 6 850 bhp = 19·1 knots
Complement: 113

Burudjulasad was launched in 1966; her equipment includes laboratories for oceanic and meteorological research, a cartographic room, and a helicopter.

Name	No.	Builders	Commissioned
BURDJAMHAL	1002	Scheepswerf De Waal, Zaltbommel	6 July 1953

Displacement, tons: 1 500 full load
Dimensions, feet (metres): 211·7 oa; 192 pp × 33·2 × 10 (58·6 × 10·1 × 3·3)
Main engines: 2 Werkspoor diesels; 1 160 bhp = 10 knots
Complement: 90

Launched on 6 Sep 1952.

ARIES 1008

Displacement, tons: 35
Dimensions, feet (metres): 68·9 × 12·5 × 6·6 (21 × 3·8 × 2)
Main engines: Werkspoor diesel engines; 450 bhp
Complement: 13

Launched 1960. Ex-Soviet "PO 2" class.

JALANIDHI 1005

Displacement, tons: 985
Dimensions, feet (metres): 159·1 × 31·2 × 14·1 (48·5 × 9·5 × 4·3)
Speed, knots: 11·5
Complement: 58

Launched in 1962. Oceanographic Research ship.

COMMAND AND SUPPORT SHIPS

1 Ex-SOVIET "DON" CLASS (SUBMARINE TENDER)

RATULANGI (ex-*Kartasov*) 4101

Displacement, tons: 6 700 standard; 9 000 full load
Dimensions, feet (metres): 458·9 × 57·7 × 22·3 (140 × 17·6 × 6·8)
Guns: 4—3·9 in; 8—57 mm; 8—25 mm (twins)
Main engines: Diesels; 14 000 bhp = 21 knots
Complement: 300

A submarine support ship, escort vessel and maintenance tender transferred from the USSR to Indonesia in 1962, arriving in Indonesia in July. Fitted with Slim Net search and warning radar and with fire control radar.

RATULANGI — 1968, Indonesian Navy

1 SUBMARINE TENDER

Name	No.	Builders	Commissioned
MULTATULI	561	Ishikawajima-Harima Heavy Industries Co Ltd	Aug 1961

Displacement, tons: 3 220
Dimensions, feet (metres): 338 pp; 365·3 oa × 52·5 × 23 (103; 111·4 × 16 × 7)
Guns: 8—37 mm (2 twin, 4 single); 4—MG
Aircraft: 1 Alouette II helicopter
Main engines: B & W diesel; 5 500 bhp = 18·5 knots
Oil fuel, tons: 1 400
Range, miles: 6 000 at 16 knots cruising speed
Complement: 134

Built as a submarine tender. Launched on 15 May 1961. Delivered to Indonesia Aug 1961. Flush decker. Capacity for replenishment at sea (fuel oil, fresh water, provisions, ammunition, naval stores and personnel). Medical and hospital facilities. Equipment for supplying compressed air, electric power and distilled water to submarines. Air-conditioning and mechanical ventilation arrangements for all living and working quarters. Now used as fleet flagship.

Reconstruction: After 76 mm mounting replaced by helicopter deck.

1 Ex-SOVIET "ATREK" CLASS (SUBMARINE TENDER)

THAMRIN 4102

Displacement, tons: 3 500 standard
Dimensions, feet (metres): 336 × 49 × 20 (110 × 14·9 × 6·1)
Main engines: 2 turbines; 1 shaft; 2 450 hp = 13 knots
Range units: 3 500 at 13 knots

Converted from "Kolomna" class freighter. Built by Neptun, Rostock in 1955 and transferred in 1962.

238 INDONESIA

SERVICE FORCES

1 Ex-US "ACHELOUS" CLASS (REPAIR SHIP)

JAYA WIJAYA (ex-USS *Askari* 9109, ex-*ARL 30*, ex-*LST 1131*) 921

Displacement, tons: 1 625 light; 4 100 full load
Dimensions, feet (metres): 316·0 wl; 328·0 oa × 50·0 × 11·0 *(96·4; 100 × 15·3 × 3·4)*
Guns: 8—40 mm (2 quadruple)
Main engines: General Motors diesels; 2 shafts; 1 800 bhp = 11·6 knots
Complement: 280

Of wartime construction this ship was in reserve from 1956-66. She was recommissioned and reached Viet-Nam in 1967 to support River Assault Flotilla One. She was used by the USN and Vietnamese Navy working up the Mekong in support of the Cambodian operations in May 1970. Transferred on lease to Indonesia at Guam on 31 Aug 1971.

1 Ex-US "SHENANDOAH" CLASS (DESTROYER DEPOT SHIP)

DUMAI (ex-USS *Tidewater* AD31) 923

Displacement, tons: 8 165 standard; 16 635 full load
Dimensions, feet (metres): 465 wl; 492 oa × 69·5 × 27·2 *(141·8; 150·1 × 21·2 × 8·3)*
Gun: 1—5 in; 38 cal
Main engines: Geared turbines; 1 shaft; 8 500 shp = 18·4 knots
Boilers: 2 Babcock & Wilcox
Complement: 778

Transferred Feb 1971 as destroyer depot ship. No longer operational with most of equipment removed and used as accommodation ship for oil-field personnel.

1 REPLENISHMENT TANKER

SORONG 911

Measurement, tons: 5 100 dead weight
Dimensions, feet (metres): 367·4 × 50·5 × 21·6 *(112 × 15·4 × 6·6)*
Guns: 8—12·7 mm (twins)
Speed, knots: 15 (10 economical)

Built in Yugoslavia in 1965. Has underway replenishment facilities. Capacity 3 000 tons fuel and 300 tons water.

SORONG   1974, John Mortimer

1 Ex-SOVIET "UDA" CLASS (SUPPORT TANKER)

BALIKPAPAN

Displacement, tons: 5 500 standard; 7 200 full load
Dimensions, feet (metres): 400·3 × 51·8 × 20·3 *(122·1 × 15·8 × 6·2)*
Guns: 6—25 mm (twins)
Main engines: Diesels; 2 shafts; 8 000 bhp = 17 knots

1 Ex-SOVIET "KHOBI" CLASS (HARBOUR TANKER)

PAKAN BARU

Displacement, tons: 1 500 full load
Dimensions, feet (metres): 63 × 11·5 × 4·5 *(19·2 × 3·5 × 1·2)*
Main engines: Diesels; 2 shafts; 800 bhp = 11 knots

1 SUPPORT TANKER

SUNGAI JERONG

2 HARBOUR TANKERS

TARAKAN   BULA

Displacement, tons: 1 340 full load
Dimensions, feet (metres): 352·0 × 37·7 × 14·8 *(107·4 × 11·5 × 4·5)*
Main engines: Diesels; 1 shaft; 1 500 bhp = 13 knots

MISCELLANEOUS

5 "TISZA" CLASS (AKL)

KARIMATA, KARIMUDJAWA, MENTAWAI, NATUNA, TALAUD

Built in Hungary and transferred 1962 by USSR.

1 TRAINING SHIP

Name	No.	Builders	Commissioned
DEWARUTJI	—	H. C. Stülcken & Sohn, Hamburg	9 July 1953

Displacement, tons: 810 standard; 1 500 full load
Dimensions, feet (metres): 136·2 oa, 191·2 pp × 31·2 × 13·9 *(41·5; 58·3 × 9·5 × 4·2)*
Main engines: MAN diesels; 600 bhp = 10·5 knots
Complement: 110 (32 + 78 midshipmen)

Barquentine of steel construction. Sail area, 1 305 sq yards *(1 091 sq metres)*. Launched on 24 Jan 1953.

1 CABLE SHIP

Name	No.	Builders	Commissioned
BIDUK	—	J & K Smit, Kinderijk	30 July 1952

Displacement, tons: 1 250 standard
Dimensions, feet (metres): 213·2 oa × 39·5 × 11·5 *(65 × 12 × 3·5)*
Main engines: 1 triple expansion engine; 1 600 ihp = 12 knots
Complement: 66

Cable Layer, Lighthouse Tender, and multi-purpose naval auxiliary. Launched on 30 Oct 1951.

FLOATING DOCKS

There are three floating docks in Surabaya which are used for naval purposes.

TENDERS

2 SMALL TRANSPORTS

BANGGAI (ex-*Biscaya*) 925
NUSA TELU (ex-*Casablanca*) 952

Of 750 tons.

1 Ex-SOVIET "PODZHARNY" CLASS

Firefloat.

2 105 ft WATER BOATS

1 Ex-SOVIET "CHAYKA" CLASS

Patrol Launch.

4 35 ft PATROL LAUNCHES

TUGS

1 Ex-US "CHEROKEE" CLASS

RAKATA (ex-USS *Menominee*, ATF 73) 928

Displacement, tons: 1 235 standard; 1 675 full load
Dimensions, feet (metres): 195 wl; 205 oa × 38·5 × 15·5 *(59·5; 62·5 × 11·7 × 4·7)*
Guns: 1—3 in *(76 mm)*; 2—40 mm; 4—25 mm (twins)
Main engines: 4 diesels with electric drive; 3 000 bhp = 16·5 knots
Complement: 85

Launched on 14 Feb 1942. Transferred at San Diego in March 1961. Civilian manned.

INDONESIA 239

1 Ex-SOVIET "OKHTENSKY" CLASS

TAMRAU (ex-*Maraim*)

Displacement, tons: 835
Dimensions, feet (metres): 143 × 34 × 15 *(43·6 × 10·4 × 4·6)*
Guns: 1—3 in *(76 mm)*; 2—20 mm
Main engines: 2 BM diesels; 2 electric motors; 2 shafts; 1 875 bhp = 14 knots
Complement: 34

Ocean tug.

Name	No.	Builders	Commissioned
LAMPO BATANG	934	Japan	Nov 1961

Displacement, tons: 250
Dimensions, feet (metres): 86·7 pp; 92·3 oa × 23·2 × 11·3 *(26·4; 28·2 × 7·1 × 3·4)*
Main engines: 2 diesels; 1 200 bhp = 11 knots
Oil fuel, tons: 18
Range, miles: 1 000 at 11 knots
Complement: 43

Ocean tug. Launched in April 1961.

Name	No.	Builders	Commissioned
TAMBORA	935	Japan	June 1961
BROMO	936	Japan	Aug 1961

Displacement, tons: 150
Dimensions, feet (metres): 71·7 wl; 79 oa × 21·7 × 9·7 *(21·9; 24·1 × 6·6 × 3)*
Main engines: MAN diesel; 2 shafts; 600 bhp = 10·5 knots
Oil fuel, tons: 9
Range, miles: 690 at 10·5 knots
Complement: 15

Harbour tugs.

2 Ex-SOVIET "TUGUR" CLASS

DEMPO   MUTIS

Harbour tugs.

2 Ex-SOVIET "SITHOLE" CLASS

Harbour tugs.

ARMY CRAFT

A.D.R.I. operate fourteen 6-8000 GRT transports, two ex-US LSTs, five ex-Soviet "Keyla" class cargo ships *(Karmata, Karimundja, Mentawai, Natuna, Talaud)*, ex-Soviet "Okhtensky" class tug *(Tamrau)* and tug *Tambora* (sister to *Bromo* above).

AIR FORCE CRAFT

A.U.R.I. operates six cargo ships (all with bow doors).

CUSTOMS PATROL CRAFT

A very large force of which the following are examples.

6 "PAT" CLASS

PAT 01   PAT 02   PAT 03   PAT 04   PAT 05   PAT 06

Dimensions, feet (metres): 91·9 pp; 100 oa × 17 × 6 *(28; 30·5 × 5·2 × 1·8)*
Main engines: 2 Caterpillar diesels; 340 bhp

3 COASTAL PATROL CRAFT

Name	No.	Builders	Commissioned
—	BC 1001	Ch. Navals de l'Esterel	11 April 1975
—	BC 1002	Ch. Navals de l'Esterel	23 June 1975
—	BC 1003	Ch. Navals de l'Esterel	25 Sept 1975

Displacement, tons: 55
Dimensions, feet (metres): 91·8 × 17·1 × 5·2 *(28 × 5·2 × 1·6)*
Gun: 1—20 mm
Main engines: 2 MTU 12V 331 TC 81; 2 700 hp = 35 knots
Range, miles: 750 at 15 knots
Complement: 9

BC 1002   1976, Ch. N de l'Esterel

15 DKN TYPE

Name	No.	Builders	Commissioned
—	DKN 901	Lürssen, Vegesack	1958
—	DKN 902	Lürssen, Vegesack	1958
—	DKN 903	Abeking & Rasmussen Lemwerder	1958
—	DKN 904	Lürssen, Vegesack	1959
—	DKN 905	Abeking & Rasmussen Lemwerder	1959
—	DKN 907	Italy	1959
—	DKN 908	Italy	1960
—	DKN 909	Italy	1960
—	DKN 910	Italy	1960
—	DKN 911	Italy	1960
—	DKN 912	Italy	1960
—	DKN 913	Italy	1960
—	DKN 914	Italy	1960
—	DKN 915	Italy	1960
—	DKN 916	Italy	1960

Displacement, tons: 140
Dimensions, feet (metres): 128 × 19 × 5·2 *(39 × 5·8 × 1·6)*
Guns: 4—20 mm
Main engines: Maybach diesels; 2 shafts; 3 000 bhp = 24·5 knots

In addition are DKN 504-13.

IRAN

Ministerial

Minister of War:
General R. Azimi

Headquarters Appointments

Commander-in-Chief Imperial Iranian Navy:
Vice-Admiral Habibollahi
Deputy Commander-in-Chief:
Rear-Admiral Biglari

Fleet Command

Commander Fleet
Rear-Admiral Azadhi

Diplomatic Representation

Naval Attaché in London, Brussels and The Hague:
Captain M. Garachorlou
Naval Attaché in Rome and Paris:
Captain H. Keshvardoost
Naval Attaché in Washington and Ottawa:
Captain S. Bahrmast

Personnel

(a) 1978: 22 000 officers and men
(b) 2 years national service

Note: A Marine Battalion is being formed.

Bases

Persian Gulf
  Bandar Abbas (MHQ)
  Booshehr
  Kharg Island
  Khorramshar (Light Forces)
Indian Ocean
  Chah Bahar (under construction)
Caspian Sea
  Bandar—Pahlavi (Training)

Naval Air

7 Sikorsky SH-3D (Sea King) (11 on order)
7 Bell AB-212
2 Lockheed P-3C Orions (Maritime Patrol)
2 Fokker F-27 Mk 400 M (Transport)
6 Aero Commanders (Flag officers)
2 Mk 600 Friendship
5 Agusta—205A helicopters
14 Agusta—206A helicopters
3 RH.53D helicopters (3 on order)

Prefix to Ships' Names

IIS

Strength of the Fleet

Type	Active	Building (Planned)
Destroyers	3	4
Frigates	4	—
Corvettes	4	—
Submarines	—	(3)
Fast Attack Craft (Missile)	—	12
Large Patrol Craft	7	—
Hovercraft	14	—
Landing Ships (L)	2	1 (2 ?)
Landing Craft (U)	1	—
Minesweepers—Coastal	3	—
Minesweepers—Inshore	2	—
Replenishment Tanker	—	1
Supply Ships	2	1
Repair Ship	1	—
Harbour Tanker	1	—
Water Boat	1	—
Tugs	3	—
Yachts	2	—
Floating Dock	1	—
Survey Craft	3	—
Customs Craft	2	—
Coastguard (Coastal Patrol Craft)	30	—

Mercantile Marine

Lloyd's Register of Shipping:
193 vessels of 1 002 061 tons

DELETIONS

Mine Warfare Forces

1974 *Shahbaz* (ex-US *MSC*) after collision damage.

Service Forces

1974 *Sohrab* (ex-US *ARL 36*) sunk as A/S target.

Coastguard

1975 *Gohar, Shahpar, Shahram* (to Sudan)

PENNANT NUMBERS

Destroyers

51	Artemiz
61	Babr
62	Palang

Frigates

71	Saam
72	Zaal
73	Rostam
74	Faramarz

Corvettes

81	Bayandor
82	Naghdi
83	Milanian
84	Khanamuie

Submarines

101	Kusseh
102	Nahang
103	Dolfin

Light Forces

01-08	"Winchester" class hovercraft
101-106	"Wellington" class hovercraft
201	Kaivan
202	Tiran
203	Mehran
204	Mahan
211	Parvin
212	Bahram
213	Nahid
P 221	Kaman
P 222	Zoubin
P 223	Khadang
P 224	Peykan
P 225	Joshan
P 226	Falakhon
P 227	Shamshir
P 228	Gorz
P 229	Gardouneh
P 230	Khanjar
P 231	Neyzeh
P 232	Tabarzin

Mine Warfare Forces

301	Shahrokh
302	Simorgh
303	Karkas
311	Harischi
312	Riazi

Service and Auxiliary Forces

45	Bahmanshir
98	Kharg
401	Lengeh
402	Hormuz
421	Bandar Abbas
422	Booshehr
441	Chahbahar
501	Quesham
511	Hengam
512	Lerak

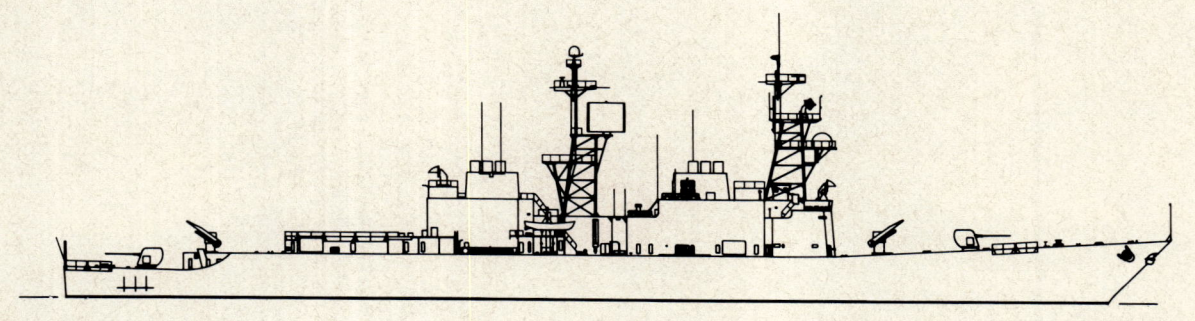

"DD 993" Class   1976, A. D. Baker III

IRAN 241

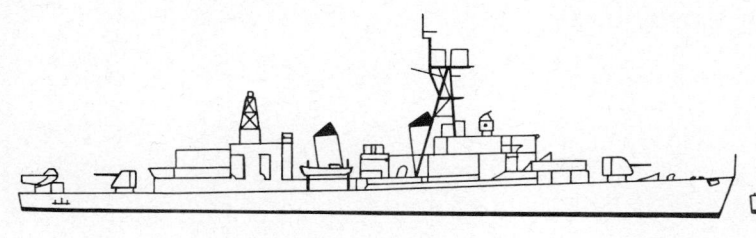

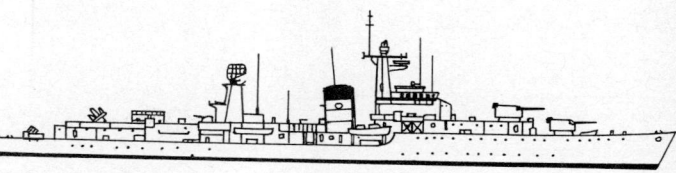

BABR and PALANG

ARTEMIZ

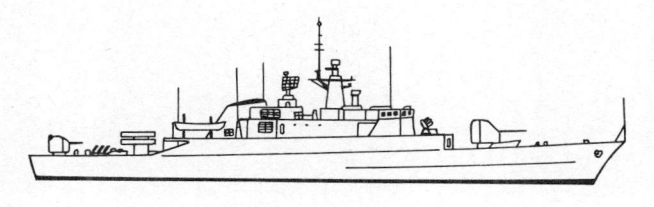

"SAAM" Class

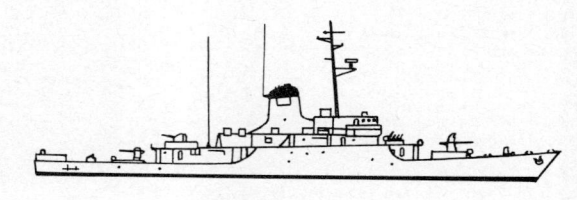

"BAYANDOR" Class

SUBMARINES

(3) Ex-US "TANG" CLASS (PATROL SUBMARINES)

Name	No.	Builders	Laid down	Launched	Commissioned
KUSSEH (ex-USS *Trout,* SS 566)	101	Electric Boat Co, Groton	1 Dec 1949	21 Aug 1951	27 June 1952
NAHANG (ex-USS *Wahoo,* SS 565)	102	Portsmouth Navy Yard	24 Oct 1949	16 Oct 1951	30 May 1952
DOLFIN (ex-USS *Tang,* SS 563)	103	Portsmouth Navy Yard	18 April 1949	April 1951	25 Oct 1951

Displacement, tons: 2 100 surfaced; 2 700 dived
Dimensions, feet (metres): 287 × 27·3 × 19 *(87·4 × 8·3 × 6·2)*
Torpedo tubes: 8—21 in *(533 mm)* (6 forward, 2 aft)
Main machinery: 3 diesels; 4 500 bhp;
 2 electric motors; 5 600 shp; 2 shafts
Speed, knots: 16 surfaced; 16 dived
Complement: 87 (8 officers, 79 men)

Agreement on transfer from USN reached in 1975 to provide training for the establishment of a larger submarine force.

Names: *Kusseh* (shark), *Nahang* (whale).

Transfer: *Kusseh* Aug 1978; *Nahang* 1979; *Dolfin* 1979-80.

"TANG" Class   1970, USN

DESTROYERS

4 US "DD 993 (MODIFIED SPRUANCE)" CLASS

Name	No.	Builders	Laid down	Launched	Commissioned
KOUROOSH (ex-US DD 993)	11	Litton Industries, USA	1978	—	—
DARYUSH (ex-US DD 994)	12	Litton Industries, USA	1978	—	—
ARDESHIR (ex-US DD 995)	13	Litton Industries, USA	1978	—	—
NADER (ex-US DD 996)	14	Litton Industries, USA	1978	—	—

Displacement, tons: approx 8 500 full load
Dimensions, feet (metres): 563·3 oa × 55 × 29
 (171·1 × 17·6 × 8·8)
Aircraft: 1 helicopter (Sea King)
Missiles: 2 twin Tartar-D launchers for Standard-MR SAM (Mk 26)
Guns: 2—5 in (127 mm) Mk 45, 54 cal
A/S weapons: 2 triple Mk 32 torpedo tubes
Main engines: 4 GE-LM 2500 gas turbines; 80 000 shp; 2 shafts
Speed, knots: 30+
Range, miles: 6 000 at 20 knots
Complement: approx 290

Ordered from Litton Industries, USA, in 1974, first to be delivered in 1980. Original order was for six ships, reduced 2 March 1976 with cancellation of *Shapour* and *Anoushirvan*. They are modifications of the "Spruance" design with improved AA capability, better radars, and more powerful air-conditioning.

Classification: Classed as CG by IIN.

Names: Called after ancient kings.

Radar: Radome; SPQ-9
Search; SPG-60
3-D; SPS-48
Fire control radars

Sonar: SQS 53 (mod) bow-mounted

"DD 993" Class   1975, Imperial Iranian Navy

242 IRAN

1 Ex-BRITISH "BATTLE" CLASS

Name	No.
ARTEMIZ (ex-HMS *Sluys*, D 60)	51

Builders	Laid down	Launched	Commissioned
Cammell Laird & Co Ltd, Birkenhead	24 Nov 1943	28 Feb 1945	30 Sept 1946

Displacement, tons: 2 325 standard; 3 360 full load
Length, feet (metres): 355·0 *(108·2)* pp; 379·0 *(115·5)* oa
Beam, feet (metres): 40·5 *(12·3)*
Draught, feet (metres): 17·5 *(5·2)*
Missiles: 4 Standard launchers with 8 missiles; 1 quadruple Seacat aft
Guns: 4—4·5 in *(115 mm)* (2 twin forward); 2—40 mm (single)
A/S weapons: 1 Squid 3-barrelled DC mortar
Main engines: Parsons geared turbines; 2 shafts; 50 000 shp
Boilers: 2 Admiralty three-drum type
Speed, knots: 35·5
Oil fuel, tons: 680
Range, miles: 3 000 at 20 knots
Complement: 270

Transferred to Iran at Southampton on 26 Jan 1967, and handed over to the Imperial Iranian Navy after a 3-year modernisation refit by the Vosper Thornycroft Group.

Radar: Search: Plessey AWS 1. Air surveillance with on-mounted IFF; Contraves Sea-Hunter fire control; Decca RDL 1 radar intercept; Racal DF equipment.

Refit: At Capetown 1975-76.

ARTEMIZ (old pennant number)   1975, Imperial Iranian Navy

2 Ex-US "ALLEN M. SUMNER" CLASS (FRAM II)

Name	No.
BABR (ex-USS *Zellers*, DD 777)	61
PALANG (ex-USS *Stormes*, DD 780)	62

Builders	Laid down	Launched	Commissioned
Todd Pacific Shipyards	24 Dec 1943	19 July 1944	25 Oct 1944
Todd Pacific Shipyards	15 Dec 1944	4 Nov 1944	27 Jan 1945

Displacement, tons: 2 200 standard; 3 320 full load
Length, feet (metres): 376·5 *(114·8)* oa
Beam, feet (metres): 40·9 *(12·4)*
Draught, feet (metres): 19 *(5·8)*
Aircraft: 1 A/S helicopter
Missiles: 4 Standard launchers with 8 missiles
Guns: 4—5 in *(127 mm)* 38 calibre (twin)
A/S weapons: 2 fixed Hedgehogs;
  2 triple torpedo launchers (Mk 32)
Main engines: 2 geared turbines; 60 000 shp; 2 shafts
Boilers: 4
Speed, knots: 34
Complement: 274 (14 officers, 260 ratings)

Two "FRAM II" conversion destroyers of the "Allen M. Sumner" class nominally transferred to Iran from the USN in March 1971 for delivery in 1972.

Conversion: Both ships received a full refit as well as conversion at Philadelphia NSY before sailing for Iran. This included a much-improved air-conditioning layout, the removal of B gun-mount with its magazine, altered accommodation, the fitting of a Canadian telescopic hangar, the siting of the four Standard missile launchers athwartships beside the new torpedo stowage between the funnels, the rigging of VDS and fitting of Hedgehogs in B position.

Electronics: Extensive intercept and jamming (ULQ/6) arrays fitted.

Names: *Babr* (Tiger), *Palang* (Leopard).

PALANG (old pennant number)   1975, Imperial Iranian Navy

Radar: SPS 10 search; SPS 37 air-surveillance with on-mounted IFF; Gun fire control system Mk 37 with radar Mk 25 on director. Navigational; one on bridge.

Sonar: SQS 29 series; VDS (*Babr*).

Spares: USS *Gainard* (DD 706) was to have been taken over in Mar 1971, but, being beyond repair, was replaced by USS *Stormes* (DD 780). Ex-USS *Kenneth D. Bailey* (DD 713) ("Gearing" class) purchased 13 Jan 1975 and ex-USS *Bordelon* (DD 881) on 1 Feb 1977 for spares.

FRIGATES

4 "SAAM" CLASS

Name	No.
SAAM	71
ZAAL	72
ROSTAM	73
FARAMARZ	74

Builders	Laid down	Launched	Commissioned
Vosper Thornycroft, Woolston	22 May 1967	25 July 1968	20 May 1971
Vickers, Barrow	3 Mar 1968	4 Mar 1969	1 Mar 1971
Vickers, Newcastle & Barrow	10 Dec 1967	4 Mar 1969	June 1972
Vosper Thornycroft, Woolston	25 July 1968	30 July 1969	28 Feb 1972

Displacement, tons: 1 110 standard; 1 290 full load
Length, feet (metres): 310·0 *(94·4)* oa
Beam, feet (metres): 34·0 *(10·4)*
Draught, feet (metres): 11·2 *(3·4)*
Missile launchers: 1 quintuple Seakiller; 1 triple Seacat
Guns: 1—4·5 in *(115 mm)* Mk 8
  2—35 mm Oerlikon (1 twin)
A/S weapons: 1 Limbo 3-barrelled DC mortar
Main engines: 2 Rolls-Royce "Olympus" gas turbines;
  46 000 shp; 2 Paxman diesels; 3 800 shp; 2 shafts
Speed, knots: 40
Complement: 125 (accommodation for 146)

It was announced on 25 Aug 1966 that Vosper Ltd, Portsmouth had received an order for four vessels for the Iranian Navy. Air-conditioned throughout. Fitted with Vosper stabilisers. *Rostam* was towed to Barrow for completion.

Names: All heroes of the Shah Nameh, the national epic.

Radar: Plessey AWS 1 air surveillance with on-mounted IFF. Two Contraves Seahunter systems for control of 35 mm, Seakillers and Seacats. Decca RDL 1 passive DF equipment.

Refit: *Saam* and *Zaal* taken in hand by HM Dockyard Devonport July/Aug 1975 for major refit including replacement of Mk 5 4·5 in gun by Mk 8. Completed 1977.

ZAAL   4/1977, C. and S. Taylor

IRAN

CORVETTES

4 Ex-US "PF 103" CLASS

Name	No.
BAYANDOR (ex-US PF 103)	81
NAGHDI (ex-US PF 104)	82
MILANIAN (ex-US PF 105)	83
KAHNAMUIE (ex-US PF 106)	84

Builders	Laid down	Launched	Commissioned
Levingstone Shipbuilding Co, Orange, Texas	20 Aug 1962	7 July 1963	18 May 1964
Levingstone Shipbuilding Co, Orange, Texas	12 Sept 1962	10 Oct 1963	22 July 1964
Levingstone Shipbuilding Co, Orange, Texas	1 May 1967	4 Jan 1968	13 Feb 1969
Levingstone Shipbuilding Co, Orange, Texas	12 June 1967	4 April 1968	13 Feb 1969

Displacement, tons: 900 standard; 1 135 full load
Length, feet (metres): 275·0 (83·8) oa
Beam, feet (metres): 33·0 (10·0)
Draught, feet (metres): 10·2 (3·1)
Guns: 2—3 in (76 mm); 2—40 mm (twin); 2—23 mm (twin)
A/S weapons: 4 DCT; 2 DC racks
Main engines: F-M diesels; 2 shafts; 6 000 bhp
Speed, knots: 20
Complement: 140

Built as two pairs, five years apart. Transferred from the USA to Iran under the Mutual Assistance programme in 1964 (Bayandor and Naghdi) and 1969 (Kahnamuie and Milanian).

Conversion: Mid-life conversion planned to include 76 mm OTO Melara guns.

Gunnery: The 23 mm guns were purchased from the Soviet army and replace the Hedgehog.

Names: Naval officers killed in the engagement with the British in 1941.

Radar: SPS 6 search.
Navigation: Raytheon.
Fire control: AN/SPG-34 on forward 76 mm (Mk 33) mount. Mk 63 for 76 mm. Mk 51 for 40 mm.

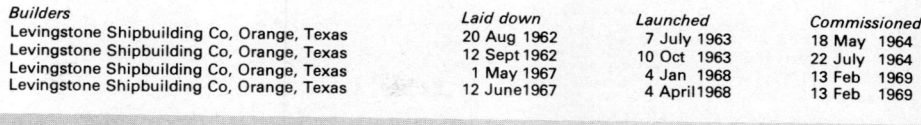

BAYANDOR (old pennant number)   1975, Imperial Iranian Navy

LIGHT FORCES

12 "KAMAN" CLASS (FAST ATTACK CRAFT—MISSILE)

Name	No.	Builders	Commissioned
KAMAN	P 221	Construction de Mécanique, Normandie	1977
ZOUBIN	P 222	Construction de Mécanique, Normandie	1977
KHADANG	P 223	Construction de Mécanique, Normandie	1977
PEYKAN	P 224	Construction de Mécanique, Normandie	1977
JOSHAN	P 225	Construction de Mécanique, Normandie	1978
FALAKHON	P 226	Construction de Mécanique, Normandie	1978
SHAMSHIR	P 227	Construction de Mécanique, Normandie	—
GORZ	P 228	Construction de Mécanique, Normandie	—
GARDOUNEH	P 229	Construction de Mécanique, Normandie	—
KHANJAR	P 230	Construction de Mécanique, Normandie	—
NEYZEH	P 231	Construction de Mécanique, Normandie	—
TABARZIN	P 232	Construction de Mécanique, Normandie	—

Displacement, tons: 249 standard; 275 full load
Dimensions, feet (metres): 154·2 × 23·3 × 6·4 (47 × 7·1 × 1·9)
Missiles: 2 twin Harpoon launchers
Guns: 1—76 mm OTO Melara; 1—40 mm Bofors
Main engines: 4 MTU diesels; 4 shafts; 14 400 bhp = 36 knots
Oil fuel, tons: 41
Range, miles: 700 at 30+ knots
Complement: 30

Of La Combattante II design. Ordered in Feb 1974. For completion by April 1979. Kaman laid down 5 Feb 1975, launched 8 Jan 1976; Zoubin laid down 4 April 1975, launched 31 March 1976; Khadang laid down 20 June 1975, launched 15 July 1976; Peykan laid down 15 Oct 1975, launched 12 Oct 1976. Joshan laid down 5 Jan 1976, launched 21 Feb 1977; Falakhon laid down 15 March 1976, launched 2 June 1977; Shamshir laid down 15 May 1976; Gorz laid down 5 Aug 1976; Gardouneh laid down 18 Oct 1976; Khanjar laid down 17 Jan 1977; Neyzeh laid down 12 April 1977; Tabarzin laid down 24 June 1977.

ZOUBIN   6/1977, Dr. Giorgio Arra

Names: Kaman (bow), Zoubin (javelin), Khadang (arrowhead), Peykan (arrow), Joshan (boiling oil), Falakhon (sling), Shamshir (scimitar), Gorz (mace), Gardouneh (roulette), Khanjar (dagger), Neyzeh (spear), Tabarzin (battleaxe).

Radar: Tactical and Fire control: WM 28 (Hollandse Signaalapparaten)

3 IMPROVED "PGM-71" CLASS (LARGE PATROL CRAFT)

Name	No.	Builders	Commissioned
PARVIN (ex-US PGM 103)	211	Peterson Builders Inc,	1967
BAHRAM (ex-US PGM 112)	212	Peterson Builders Inc,	1969
NAHID (ex-US PGM 122)	213	Peterson Builders Inc,	1970

Displacement, tons: 105 standard; 146 full load
Dimensions, feet (metres): 100 × 22 × 10 (30·5 × 6·7 × 3·1)
Guns: 1—40 mm; 2—20 mm; 2—50 cal MG
Main engines: 8 GM diesels; 2 000 bhp = 15 knots

Names: Parvin (Mercury), Bahram (Mars), Nahid (Venus).

PARVIN (original number)   1971

4 US COASTGUARD "CAPE" CLASS (LARGE PATROL CRAFT)

Name	No.	Builders	Commissioned
KAIVAN	201	USA	14 Jan 1956
TIRAN	202	US Coast Guard, Curtis Bay, Maryland	1957
MEHRAN	203	USA	1959
MAHAN	204	USA	1959

Displacement, tons: 85 standard; 107 full load
Dimensions, feet (metres): 90 pp; 95 oa × 20·2 × 6·8 (27·5; 28·9 × 6·2 × 2)
Gun: 1—40 mm
A/S weapons: 8-barrelled 7·2 in projector, 8—300 lb depth charges
Main engines: 4 Cummins diesels; 2 shafts; 2 200 bhp = 20 knots
Range, miles: 1 500 cruising
Complement: 15

Names: All Islands in the Gulf.

MAHAN (old pennant number)   1975, Imperial Iranian Navy

244 IRAN

6 "WELLINGTON" (BH.7) CLASS (HOVERCRAFT)

Name	No.	Builders	Commissioned
—	101	British Hovercraft Corporation	Nov 1970
—	102	British Hovercraft Corporation	Mar 1971
—	103	British Hovercraft Corporation	Mid 1974
—	104	British Hovercraft Corporation	Mid 1974
—	105	British Hovercraft Corporation	Late 1974
—	106	British Hovercraft Corporation	Early 1975

Displacement, tons: 50 max weight, 33 empty
Dimensions, feet (metres): 76 × 45 × 42 (23·2 × 13·7 × 12·8)
Missiles: SSMs in last four (see note)
Guns: 2 Browning MG
Main engines: 1 Proteus 15 M/541 gas turbine = 60 knots
Oil fuel, tons: 10

First pair are BH 7 Mk 4 and the next four are Mk 5 craft. Mk 5 craft fitted for, but not with, surface-to-surface missiles.

"Wellington" Hovercraft 101　　　　　　　　　　1975, Imperial Iranian Navy

8 "WINCHESTER" (SR.N6) CLASS (HOVERCRAFT)

Name	No.	Builders	Commissioned
—	01	British Hovercraft Corporation	1973
—	02	British Hovercraft Corporation	1973
—	03	British Hovercraft Corporation	1973
—	04	British Hovercraft Corporation	1974
—	05	British Hovercraft Corporation	1974
—	06	British Hovercraft Corporation	1975
—	07	British Hovercraft Corporation	1975
—	08	British Hovercraft Corporation	1975

Displacement, tons: 10 normal gross weight (basic weight 14 200 lbs; disposable load 8 200 lbs)
Dimensions, feet (metres): 48·4 × 25·3 × 15·9 (height) (14·8 × 7·7 × 4·8)
Guns: 1 or 2 50 cal .MGs
Main engines: 1 Gnome Model 1050 gas turbine = 58 knots
　1 Peters diesel as auxiliary power unit

Ordered 1970-72. The Imperial Iranian Navy has the world's largest fully operational hovercraft squadron, which is used for coastal defence and logistic duties.

"Winchester" Hovercraft 03　　　　　　　　　　1971

LANDING CRAFT

QESHM (ex-US *LCU 1431*) 501

Displacement, tons: 160 light; 320 full load
Dimensions, feet (metres): 119 × 32 × 5·7 (36·3 × 9·8 × 1·7)
Guns: 2—20 mm
Main engines: Diesels; 675 bhp = 10 knots
Complement: 14

LCU 1431 was transferred to Iran by US in Sept 1964 under the Military Aid Programme. Island in the Gulf.

QESHM　　　　　　　　　　1971

MINE WARFARE FORCES

3 Ex-US "MSC 292 and 268" CLASS (MINESWEEPERS—COASTAL)

Name	No.	Builders	Commissioned
SHAHROKH (ex-USS *MSC 276*)	301	Bellingham Shipyards Co	1960
SIMORGH (ex-USS *MSC 291*)	302	Tacoma Boatbuilding Co	1962
KARKAS (ex-USS *MSC 292*)	303	Petersen Builders Inc	1959

Displacement, tons: 320 light; 378 full load
Dimensions, feet (metres): 138 pp; 145·8 oa × 28 × 8·3 (42·1; 44·5 × 8·5 × 2·5)
Gun: 1—20 mm (double-barrelled)
Main engines: 2 GM diesels; 2 shafts; 890 bhp = 12·8 knots
Oil fuel, tons: 27
Range, miles: 2 400 at 11 knots
Complement: 40 (4 officers, 2 midshipmen, 34 men)

Originally class of four. Of wooden construction. Launched in 1958-61 and transferred from US to Iran under MAP in 1959-62. *Shahrokh* now in the Caspian Sea.

Names: *Shahrokh* (an ancient king), *Simorgh* (a fabled bird), *Karkas* (vulture).

SIMORGH (old pennant number)　　　　　　　　　　1975, Imperial Iranian Navy

IRAN 245

2 US "CAPE" CLASS (MINESWEEPERS—INSHORE)

Name	No.	Builders	Commissioned
HARISCHI (ex-*Kahnamuie*, ex-*MSI 14*)	311	Tacoma Boatbuilding Co	3 Sept 1964
RIAZI (ex-*MSI 13*)	312	Tacoma Boatbuilding Co	15 Oct 1964

Displacement, tons: 180 standard; 235 full load
Dimensions, feet (metres): 111 × 23 × 6 *(33·9 × 7·0 × 1·8)*
Gun: 1—50 cal MG
Main engines: Diesels; 650 bhp = 13 knots
Oil fuel, tons: 20
Range, miles: 1 000 at 9 knots
Complement: 23 (5 officers, 18 men)

Delivered to Iran under MAP. Laid down on 22 June 1962 and 1 Feb 1963, and transferred at Seattle, Washington, on 3 Sept 1964 and 15 Oct 1964, respectively. In Aug 1967 *Kahnamuie* was renamed *Harischi* as the name was required for one of the new US PFs (see Corvettes).

RIAZI (old pennant number)   *1975, Imperial Iranian Navy*

SERVICE FORCES

1 REPLENISHMENT SHIP

Name	No.	Builders	Commissioned
KHARG	431	Swan Hunter Ltd, Wallsend	1978

Displacement, tonnes: 10 890 light; 33 000 full load
Measurement, tons: 20 000 deadweight; 21 000 gross
Dimensions, feet (metres): 680 × 87 × 30 *(207·2 × 26·5 × 9·1)*
Aircraft: 3 helicopters
Guns: 1—76 mm OTO Melara; 2—40 mm (twin)
Main engines: Westinghouse geared turbine; 26 870 shp; 1 shaft
Boilers: 2 Babcock & Wilcox
Speed, knots: 21·5
Complement: 248

Ordered Oct 1974. Laid down Jan 1976. Launched 3 Feb 1977.
A design incorporating some of the features of the British "Ol" class but carrying ammunition and dry stores in addition to fuel.

4 LANDING SHIPS (LOGISTIC)

Name	No.	Builders	Commissioned
HENGAM	511	Yarrow, Clyde	12 Aug 1974
LARAK	512	Yarrow, Clyde	12 Nov 1974
LAVAN	513	Yarrow, Clyde	—
TONB	514	Yarrow, Clyde	—

Displacement, tons: 2 500
Dimensions, feet (metres): 305 × 49 × 7·3 *(93 × 15 × 2·4)*
Guns: 4—40 mm (single)
Main engines: 4 Paxman 12 YJCM diesels; 2 shafts; 5 600 bhp
Speed, knots: 14·5
Complement: 80 plus 227 embarked troops

Smaller than British *Sir Lancelot* design with no through tank deck. Carry up to nine tanks depending on size (one Chieftain abreast or two T54/55). Ordered 25 July 1972. *Hengam* laid down late 1972, launched 27 Sept 1973. *Larak* laid down 1973, launched 7 May 1974. Two under construction.

Names: Islands in the Gulf.

LARAK (old pennant number)   *5/1975, C. and S. Taylor*

2 FLEET SUPPLY SHIPS

Name	No.	Builders	Commissioned
BANDAR ABBAS	421	C. Lühring Yard, Brake, W. Germany	April 1974
BUSHEHR	422	C. Lühring Yard, Brake, W. Germany	Nov 1974

Measurement, tons: 3 250 deadweight
Dimensions, feet (metres): 354·2 × 54·4 × 14·8 *(108 × 16·6 × 4·5)*
Aircraft: 1 helicopter
Guns: 2—40 mm
Main engines: 2 MAN (MTU) diesels; 2 shafts; 6 000 bhp
Speed, knots: 16
Complement: 60

Combined tankers and store-ships carrying victualling, armament and general stores. *Bandar Abbas* launched 11 Aug 1973, *Bushehr* launched 23 March 1974.

BANDAR ABBAS (old pennant number)   *1975, Imperial Iranian Navy*

1 Ex-US "AMPHION" CLASS (REPAIR SHIP)

Name	No.	Builders	Commissioned
CHAHBAHAR (ex-USS *Amphion*, ex-*AR 13*)	441	Tampa Shipbuilding Co	30 Jan 1946

Displacement, tons: 7 826 standard; 14 490 full load
Dimensions, feet (metres): 456·0 wl; 492·0 oa × 70·0 × 27·5 *(139; 150·1 × 21·4 × 8·4)*
Guns: 2—3 in 50 cal
Main engines: Westinghouse turbines; 1 shaft; 8 500 shp = 16·5 knots
Boilers: 2 Foster-Wheeler
Complement: Accommodation for 921

Launched on 15 May 1945. Transferred to IIN on 1 Oct 1971. Based at Bandar Abbas as permanent repair facility, although she does go to sea occasionally.

CHAHBAHAR (old pennant number)   *1972, Imperial Iranian Navy*

246 IRAN

1 SUBMARINE RESCUE SHIP

— (ex-USS *Tringa* ASR 16)

1 HARBOUR TANKER

Name	No.	Builders	Commissioned
HORMUZ (ex-YO 247)	401	Cantiere Castellamàre di Stabia	1956

Displacement, tons: 1 250 standard; 1 700 full load
Dimensions, feet (metres): 171·2 wl; 178·3 oa × 32·2 × 14 *(52·2; 54·4 × 9·8 × 4·3)*
Guns: 2—20 mm
Main engines: 1 Ansaldo Q 370, 4 cycle diesel
Oil fuel, tons: 25

Cargo oil capacity: 5 000 to 6 000 barrels.

HORMUZ   *1970, Imperial Iranian Navy*

2 WATER TANKERS

Displacement, tons: 9 430
Dimensions, feet (metres): 460 pp × 70·5 × 16·5 *(139 × 21·2 × 5)*
Main engines: MAN diesel; 7 385 hp = 15 knots

First launched 24 March 1977.
Both building at Mazagon Docks, Bombay.

2 Ex-ITALIAN LINERS

RAFFELLO   MICHELANGELO

Purchased as barracks ships at Chahbahar and Bandar Abbas. Retain Italian names.

2 HARBOUR TUGS

No. 1 (ex-German *Karl*)   **No. 2** (ex-German *Ise*)

Sister ships of 134 tons taken over from W. Germany 17 June 1974. Both built 1962-63.

1 Ex-US "YW-83" CLASS (WATER TANKER)

LENGEH (ex-US YW 88) 402

Displacement, tons: 1 250 standard
Dimensions, feet (metres): 178·3 × 32·2 × 14 *(54·4 × 9·8 × 4·3)*
Main engines: Diesels; speed = 10 knots

Transferred to Iran by USA in 1964. Similar to tanker *Hormuz*.

1 TUG

BAHMANSHIR 451

Harbour tug (ex-US Army *ST 1002*), 150 tons, transferred in 1962.

26 BARGES

Built in Pakistan 1976-77 the largest being a 260 ft self-propelled lighter.

FLOATING DOCK

400 (ex-US *ARD 28*, ex- *FD 4*)

Lift: 3 000 tons

Transferred on loan Sept 1971. Of steel construction. Purchased 1 March 1977.

IMPERIAL YACHTS

Name	No.	Builders	Commissioned
KISH	—	Yacht und Bootswerft, Burmester, Germany	1970

Displacement, tons: 178
Dimensions, feet (metres): 122 × 25 × 7 *(37·2 × 7·6 × 2·1)*
Main engines: 2 MTU diesels; 2 920 hp

A smaller and more modern Imperial. In the Persian Gulf.

Name	No.	Builders	Commissioned
SHAHSAVAR	—	N.V. Boele's Scheepwerven, Bolnes, Netherlands	1936

Displacement, tons: 530
Dimensions, feet (metres): 176 × 25·3 × 10·5 *(53·7 × 7·7 × 3·2)*
Main engines: 2 sets diesels; 1 300 bhp

Launched in 1936. In the Caspian Sea.

COAST GUARD

20 65 ft TYPE (COASTAL PATROL CRAFT)

1201-1220

Built by Peterson Builders, Wisconsin 1975-76. Armed with 3—20 mm and 2—0·50 MG.

6 40 ft SEWART TYPE (COASTAL PATROL CRAFT)

| MAHNAVI-HAMRAZ | MAHNAVI-VAHEDI | MORVARID |
| MAHNAVI-TAHERI | MARDJAN | SADAF |

Displacement, tons: 10 standard
Dimensions, feet (metres): 40·0 × 11·0 × 3·7 *(12·2 × 3·4 × 1·1)*
Guns: Light MG
Main engines: 2 General Motors diesels = 30 knots

Small launches for port duties of Sewart (USA) standard 40 ft type. All transferred June 1953. Pennant numbers 5001 and above. Some serve in the Caspian Sea.

SURVEY VESSELS

(Operated by the Ministry of Finance except for *Abnegar*)

MEHR

Of 422 tons. Launched in 1964. Complement 22.

ABNEGAR

50 ton wooden oceanographic vessel built in Ireland. Operated by IIN.

HYDROGRAPH SHAHPOUR

Of 9 tons. Launched in 1965.

HYDROGRAPH PAHLAVI

Of 9 tons. Launched in 1966.

CUSTOMS VESSELS

TOUFAN   TOUSAN

Built by CN Inmar, La Spezia in 1954-55. Of 65 tons with twin diesels. 22 knots.

IRAQ

Ministerial

Minister of Defence:
Ahmad Hasan al-Bakr

Administration

Commander-in-Chief:
Rear-Admiral Abd Al Diri
Chief of Staff:
Commander Samad Sat Al Mufti

Personnel

(a) 1978: 3 000 officers and men
(b) 2 years national service

SOVIET-IRAQI TREATIES

Under the treaty, signed in April 1972, the Soviet fleet would have access to the Iraqi base of Umm Qasr, in return for Soviet assistance to strengthen Iraq's defences. This resulted in the acquisition by Iraq of 14 "Osa" class.
A further treaty signed in August 1976 has been kept secret but it is reported that, from the naval point of view, it includes provision for the Soviet occupation of Umm Qasr in return for the provision of "10 missile frigates" to Iraq. Whether these will be similar to the "Nanuchka" class sent to India remains to be seen.

Mercantile Marine

Lloyd's Register of Shipping:
110 vessels of 1 135 245 tons gross

Bases

Basra, Umm Qasr

AMPHIBIOUS FORCES

3 Ex-SOVIET "POLNOCNY" CLASS LCTs

ATIKA, GANDA +1

Displacement, tons: 870 standard: 1 000 full load
Dimensions, feet (metres): 239·4 × 29·5 × 9·8 (75 × 9 × 3)
Guns: 4—30 mm (twins); 2 rocket launchers
Main engines: 2 diesels; 5 000 bhp = 18 knots
Complement: 40

Built in Poland and transferred in 1977. Of original hull design but with a new type of deck-structure amidships. This would appear to be a form of helicopter platform were it not for the swimming-pool sized hole in the middle.

Iraqui "POLNOCNY" CLASS 5/1977, MOD

LIGHT FORCES

14 Ex-SOVIET "OSA" CLASS (FAST ATTACK CRAFT—MISSILE)

EL TAMI, HAZRAN NAUNI, NISAN, TAMUZ +10

Displacement, tons: 165 standard; 200 full load
Dimensions, feet (metres): 128·7 × 25·1 × 5·9 (39·3 × 7·7 × 1·8)
Missiles: 4 launchers for SS-N-2
Guns: 4—30 mm (twin)
Main engines: 3 diesels; 13 000 hp = 32 knots
Range, miles: 800 at 25 knots
Complement: 25

A combination of 6 "Osa I" delivered 1972-74 and 8 "Osa II" classes delivered in pairs in 1974, 75 and 1976.

Names: Some of those reported are very similar to Arabic names of the months and may, therefore, be suspect.

Radar: Drum Tilt.

"OSA I" Class

3 Ex-SOVIET "SO I" CLASS

210, 211, 212

Displacement, tons: 215 light; 250 full load
Dimensions, feet (metres): 138·6 × 20 × 9·2 (42·3 × 6·1 × 2·8)
Guns: 4—25 mm
A/S weapons: 4 5-barrelled MBU 1200
Main engines: 3 diesels; 7 500 bhp = 29 knots
Complement: 30

Delivered by the USSR to Iraq in 1962.

Radar: Pot Head.

Sonar: One Hull mounted.

"SO I" Class 1970, USN

248 IRAQ

10 Ex-SOVIET "P 6" CLASS (FAST ATTACK CRAFT—TORPEDO)

AL ADRISI, AL SHAAB, AL TAMI, ALEF, IBN SAID, LAMAKI, RAMADAN, SHULAB, TAMUR, TAREQ BEN ZAID

Displacement, tons: 66 standard; 75 full load
Dimensions, feet (metres): 84·2 × 20 × 6 *(25·7 × 6·1 × 1·8)*
Guns: 4—25 mm
Torpedo tubes: 2—21 in
Main engines: Diesels; 4 800 bhp = 45 knots
Complement: 25

Transferred from the USSR. Two were received in 1959, four in Nov 1960, and six in Jan 1961. Two deleted 1977.

"P 6" Class   1970, USN

2 Ex-SOVIET "POLUCHAT I" CLASS (LARGE PATROL CRAFT)

Displacement, tons: 100 standard
Dimensions, feet (metres): 98·4 × 19·0 × 5·9 *(30·0 × 5·8 × 1·8)*
Guns: 2—25 mm

Transferred by USSR in late 1960s. Also used for torpedo recovery.

"POLUCHAT I" Class   10/1975, MOD

4 COASTAL PATROL CRAFT

Name	No.	Builders	Commissioned
ABD AL RAHMAN	1	John I. Thornycroft & Co Ltd, Woolston, Southampton	1937
AL GHAZI	2	John I. Thornycroft & Co Ltd, Woolston, Southampton	1937
DAT AL DIYARI	3	John I. Thornycroft & Co Ltd, Woolston, Southampton	1937
JANNADA	4	John I. Thornycroft & Co Ltd, Woolston, Southampton	1937

Displacement, tons: 67
Dimensions, feet (metres): 100 × 17 × 3 *(30·5 × 5·2 × 0·9)*
Guns: 1—3·7 in howitzer; 2—3 in mortars; 4 MG
Main engines: 2 Thornycroft diesels; 2 shafts; 280 bhp = 12 knots

Protected by bullet-proof plating. All built by John I. Thornycroft & Co Ltd, Woolston, Southampton. All launched, completed and delivered in 1937.

2 Ex-SOVIET "PO 2" CLASS (COASTAL PATROL CRAFT)

Displacement, tons: 50 full load
Dimensions, feet (metres): 82 × 16·7 × 5·6 *(25 × 5·1 × 1·7)*
Guns: 2—25 mm or 2—12·7 mm
Main engines: 2 diesels = 30 knots

4 Ex-SOVIET "ZHUK" CLASS (COASTAL PATROL CRAFT)

Displacement, tons: 50
Dimensions, feet (metres): 75 × 16 × — *(22·9 × 4·9 × —)*
Guns: 2—14·5 mm MG; 1—12·7 mm MG
Main engines:
Speed, knots: 30

Transferred in 1975.

"ZHUK" Class

4 Ex-SOVIET "NYRYAT II" CLASS (COASTAL PATROL CRAFT)

Length, feet (metres): 70 *(21·3)*
Main engines: 150 bhp

Similar in appearance to "PO 2" class without bulwarks. Multi-purpose craft probably used as diving craft.

8 THORNYCROFT 36 ft TYPE

Length, feet (metres): 36 *(11·0)*
Main engines: 1 diesel; 125 bhp

Patrol boats built by John I. Thornycroft & Co for the Iraqi Ports Administration.

4 THORNYCROFT 21 ft TYPE

Length, feet (metres): 21 *(6·4)*
Main engines: 1 diesel; 40 bhp

Pilot despatch launches built by John I. Thornycroft & Co for the Iraqi Ports.

MINE WARFARE FORCES

2 Ex-SOVIET "T 43" CLASS (MINESWEEPERS—OCEAN)

AL YARMOUK 465   **AL KADISIA** 467

Transferred early 1970s. See USSR section for details.

3 Ex-SOVIET "YEVGENYA" CLASS (MINESWEEPERS—INSHORE)

Displacement, tons: 90 full load
Length, feet (metres): 88·6 *(27)*
Guns: 2—25 mm (twin)
Main engines: 2 diesels

GRP hulls. Delivered in 1975 under cover-name of "oceanographic craft".

HARBOUR AUTHORITY CRAFT

AL THAWRA (ex-*Malike Aliye*)

Displacement, tons: 746
Main engines: Diesels; 2 shafts; 1 800 shp = 14 knots

Royal Yacht before assassination of King Faisal II in 1958, after which she was renamed *Al Thawra* (The Revolution) instead of *Malike Aliye* (Queen Aliyah).

AL THAWRA   *1966, Aldo Fraccaroli*

MISCELLANEOUS

A number of customs craft and a large Dutch-built dredger of the Harbour Authority are also listed.

IRELAND (REPUBLIC)

Minister for Defence:
  Mr. R. Molloy
Commanding Officer and Director Naval Service:
  Captain P. Kavanagh, NS

The Irish Naval Service is administered from Naval Headquarters, Department of Defence, Dublin, by the Commanding Officer and Director Naval Service. The naval base and dockyard are on Haulbowline island in Cork Harbour.

Future Plans

At least two further patrol vessels may be added to the service and another five of similar 1 000 ton size may be acquired under an EEC plan to strengthen Ireland's fishery protection force. A sail training vessel, *Asgard II*, is to be built in 1978 although she may not come under naval control.

Personnel

(a) 1978: Approximately 700 officers and men (800 in 1979)
(b) Voluntary service

Mercantile Marine

Lloyd's Register of Shipping:
  98 vessels of 211 872 tons gross

DELETIONS

Cliona (ex-HMS *Bellwort*) and *Macha* (ex-HMS *Borage*), both built by George Brown, & Co (Marine) Ltd, Greenock, were sold for breaking up in 1970-71. *Maev* (ex-HMS *Oxlip*) deleted 1972. Tender *Wyndham* sold in 1968 and *General McHardy* in 1971.

250 IRELAND (REPUBLIC)

CORVETTES

Name	No.	Builders	Commissioned
DEIRDRE	P 20	Verolme, Cork	May 1972
EMER	P 21	Verolme, Cork	9 Jan 1978

Displacement, tons: 972 (Deirdre); 1 019·5 (Emer)
Dimensions, feet (metres): 184·3 pp × 34·1 × 14·4 (56·2 × 10·4 × 4·4) (Deirdre); 213·7 oa, 192 pp × 34·4 × 14·1 (65·2, 58·5 × 10·5 × 4·3) (Emer)
Gun: 1—40 mm Bofors
Main engines: 2 British Polar diesels (Deirdre), 2 Pielstick (Emer) coupled to 1 shaft; 4 200 bhp (Deirdre), 4 800 (Emer) = 18 knots
Oil fuel, tons: 170/155
Range, miles: 5 000 at 12 knots
Complement: 46 (5 officers, 41 men)

Controllable pitch propeller, stabilisers and sonar. Deirdre was the first vessel ever built for the Naval Service in the Republic of Ireland. Launched on 29 Dec 1971. The starboard life-boat and mainmast have been deleted in Emer. In Dec 1977 a contract for a third of this class was placed with Verolme, Cork for delivery in 1979 at a cost of £5 million.

Classification: Officially classified as "Patrol Vessels".

DEIRDRE 6/1977, Irish Naval Service

COASTAL MINESWEEPERS

3 Ex-BRITISH "TON" CLASS

Name	No.	Builders	Commissioned
GRÁINNE (ex-HMS Oulston, M 1129)	CM 10	Thornycroft	1955
BANBA (ex-HMS Alverton, M 1104)	CM 11	Camper and Nicholson	1953
FÓLA (ex-HMS Blaxton, M 1132)	CM 12	Thornycroft	1956

Displacement, tons: 360 standard; 425 full load
Dimensions, feet (metres): 140·0 pp; 153·0 oa × 28·8 × 8·2 (42·7; 46·7 × 8·8 × 2·5)
Guns: 1—40 mm; 2—20 mm
Main engines: 2 diesels; 2 shafts; 3 000 bhp = 15 knots
Oil fuel, tons: 45
Range, miles: 2 300 at 13 knots
Complement: 33

Former British "Ton" class coastal minesweepers. Double mahogany hulls and otherwise constructed of aluminium alloy and other materials with the lowest possible magnetic signature. Purchased from the United Kingdom in 1971 for fishery protection duties as replacements for previous corvettes.

GRÁINNE 5/1974, Irish Naval Service

TRAINING SHIP

Name	No.	Builders	Commissioned
SETANTA (ex-Isolde)	A 15	Liffey DY, Dublin	1953

Displacement, tons: 1 173
Dimensions, feet (metres): 208 pp × 38 × 13 (63·5 × 11·6 × 4)
Guns: 2—20 mm
Main engines: Steam recip: 1 500 ihp; 2 shafts = 11·5 knots
Oil fuel, tons: 276
Range, miles: 3 500 at 10 knots
Complement: 44

Acquired from the Commissioners of Irish Lights in 1976.

SETANTA 10/1977, Irish Naval Service

MISCELLANEOUS

Name	No.	Builders	Commissioned
FERDIA	A 16	Denmark	—

Originally used as a seismic survey vessel before being leased to Irish Naval Service. It is possible she may be converted for surveying duties instead of acting as a patrol vessel.

COLLEEN
Service launch of 35 ft, built in Wales in 1930. Single 30 hp diesel.

CHOWL
Oil barge of 100 tons with single 50 hp diesel.

Name	No.	Builders	Commissioned
JOHN ADAMS	—	Richard Dunston, Thorne, Yorks.	1934

Measurement, tons: 94 gross
Dimensions, feet (metres): 85 × 18·5 × 7 (25·9 × 5·6 × 2·1)
Main engines: Diesel; 216 bhp = 10 knots

Employed on harbour duties. New engine fitted in 1976. Civilian manned.

SIR CECIL ROMER, RAVEN, JACKDAW
Civilian manned passenger transports based at Cork. Taken over 1938.

ISRAEL

Headquarters Appointment

Commander in Chief of the Israeli Navy:
 Rear-Admiral Michael Barkai

Diplomatic Representation

Defence Attaché in London:
 Brigadier General R. Sivron
Naval Attaché in Rome:
 Captain P. Pinchasi
Naval Attaché in Washington:
 Captain M. Tabak

Personnel

(a) 1978: 3 300 (250 officers and 3 050 men, of whom 1 000 are conscripts. Includes a Naval Commando)
(b) 3 years national service for Jews and Druses.
Note (An additional 5 000 Reserves available on mobilisation).

Submarines

1975 *Leviathan* (ex-T class)
1977 *Dolphin* (ex-T class)

Bases

Haifa, Ashdod, Sharm-el-Sheikh
A repair base has been built at Eilat where a synchro-lift is installed.

Prefix to Ships' Names

INS (Israeli Naval Ship)

Mercantile Marine

Lloyd's Register of Shipping:
 58 vessels of 404 651 tons gross

DELETIONS

Light Forces

1975 12 Bertram Type; 14 Swift Type
1976 *Yarkon*

Strength of the Fleet

Type	Active	Building
Patrol Submarines	3	—
Corvettes	—	2 (?6)
Fast Attack Craft (Missile)	19	6
Coastal Patrol Craft	38	2
"Firefish"	3	—
LSMs	3	—
LCTs	6	—
LCMs	3	—
Transports	2	—
Support Ship	1	—
Training Ship	1	—

Deployment

At Sharm-el-Sheikh there are normally 4 "Reshef" class, 2 "Saar" class, some tugs, landing craft and a depot ship.

SUBMARINES

2 + 1 IKL/VICKERS TYPE 206

Name	No.	Builders	Laid down	Launched	Commissioned
GAL	—	Vickers Ltd, Barrow	1973	2 Dec 1975	Jan 1977
TANIN	—	Vickers Ltd, Barrow	1974	25 Oct 1976	1977
RAHAV	—	Vickers Ltd, Barrow	—	—	Dec 1977

Displacement, tons: 420 surfaced; 600 dived
Dimensions, feet (metres): 146·7 × 15·4 × 12 *(45·0 × 4·7 × 3·7)*
Torpedo tubes: 8—21 in bow
Main machinery: Diesels; 2 000 hp; electric motor; 1 800 hp; 1 shaft; diesel-electric
Speed, knots: 11 surfaced; 17 dived
Complement: 22

A contract was signed for the building of these boats by Vickers in April 1972.
Incorporated in the fin is the British SLAM missile launcher for Blowpipe missiles.

GAL

1977, Israeli Navy

CORVETTES

0 + 2 + ?6 NEW CONSTRUCTION

Displacement, tons: 850
Dimensions, feet (metres): 253·2 × 30·2 × 10·8 *(77·2 × 9·2 × 3·3)*
Aircraft: 1 helicopter
Missiles: 4 launchers for Gabriel II (see note)
Guns: 2—76 mm OTO Melara; 6—35 mm (Twins)
A/S Weapons: 1 twin Bofors 375 mm rocket launcher
Main engines: Codag; 1 GM LM2500 gas turbine; 24 000 bhp; 2 diesels; 2 shafts (cp propellers)
Speed, knots: 40-42
Range, miles: 4 500 on diesels
Complement: 45

A new design (QU-09-35) being built by Israel Shipyards Haifa. Will probably have a mix of Harpoon and Gabriel. Two building. These ships may well be intended for target acquisition for Harpoon fitted "Reshefs" with command and control facilities.

LIGHT FORCES

6 + 6 "RESHEF" CLASS (FAST ATTACK CRAFT—MISSILE)

Name	No.	Builders	Commissioned
RESHEF	—	Haifa Shipyard	April 1973
KESHET	—	Haifa Shipyard	Oct 1973
ROMAH	—	Haifa Shipyard	Mar 1974
KIDON	—	Haifa Shipyard	Sept 1974
TARSHISH	—	Haifa Shipyard	Mar 1975
YAFFO	—	Haifa Shipyard	April 1975

Displacement, tons: 415 standard
Dimensions, feet (metres): 190·6 × 25 × 8 *(58 × 7·8 × 2·4)*
Missile launchers: 6 Gabriel and 4 Harpoon
Guns: 2—76 mm OTO Melara; 2—20 mm Oerlikon (see Note)
Engines: 4 Maybach (MTU) diesels; 2 670 hp each; 2 shafts
Speed, knots: 32
Range, miles: 1 650 at 30 knots; 4 000 at 17·5 knots
Complement: 45

These steel-hulled boats carry Israeli-made missiles and electronics as well as chaff launchers.

Reshef was launched on 19 Feb 1973; *Keshet* 2 Aug 1973. This very interesting class has an extremely long range at cruising speed, two pairs having made the passage from Israel to the Red Sea via the Strait of Gibraltar and Cape of Good Hope, relying entirely on refuelling at sea. This is a great tribute not only to their endurance but also to their sea-keeping qualities. A further illustration of this was the appearance of two "Reshefs" in New York July 1976 (shown right).
The first pair was successfully engaged in the Arab-Israeli War, Oct 1973. The whole class will eventually be equipped with the new 22 mile range Gabriel missiles. At present carry a mix of Gabriel 1 and 2.

RESHEF

1974, Michael D. J. Lennon

An expansion of the building slips at Haifa Dockyard will allow the more rapid construction of the next six boats ordered in January 1975. These are slightly larger with an overall length of 202·6 ft *(61·7 m)* and may have increased speed of 36 knots. This batch has been delayed by the construction of South African "Reshefs". The last of these three due to sail from Haifa March 1978 so completion of the first of the new batch may be expected mid 1979. Numbers may be reduced with construction of new corvettes.
It is now reported, but not confirmed, that a further six ships have been ordered for a total of eighteen.

Sonar: Fitted in ships deployed in the Red Sea. (ELAC).

Deployment: *Tarshish* and *Yaffo* in Mediterranean. Other four of first six in Red Sea.

Missiles: Fitted with 4 Harpoon from Jan-Feb 1978 in addition to Gabriel 1 and 2.

Transfers: Six of this class building for South Africa in Haifa and Durban.

252 ISRAEL

12 "SAAR" CLASS (FAST ATTACK CRAFT—MISSILE)

Name	No.	Builders	Commissioned
Group A			
MIVTACH	311	Ch. de Normandie	1968
MIZNACH	312	Ch. de Normandie	1968
MISGAV	313	Ch. de Normandie	1968
EILAT	321	Ch. de Normandie	1968
HAIFA	322	Ch. de Normandie	1968
ACCO	323	Ch. de Normandie	1968
Group B			
SAAR	331	Ch. de Normandie	1969
SOUFA	332	Ch. de Normandie	1969
GAASH	333	Ch. de Normandie	1969
HEREV	341	Ch. de Normandie	1969
HANIT	342	Ch. de Normandie	1969
HETZ	343	Ch. de Normandie	1969

Displacement, tons: 220 standard; 250 full load
Dimensions, feet (metres): 147·6 oa × 23·0 × 8·2 *(45·0 × 7·0 × 2·5)*
Missile launchers: Gabriel surface to surface (see notes)
Guns: 40 mm or 76 mm (see notes)
Main engines: 4 Maybach (MTU) diesels; 13 500 bhp; 4 shafts = 40+ knots
Oil fuel, tons: 30
Range, miles: 2 500 at 15 knots; 1 600 at 20 knots; 1 000 at 30 knots
Complement: 35 to 40

"SAAR" Class with 76 mm and five Gabriel missiles   1973

Built from designs by Lürssen Werft of Bremen. Political problems caused their building in France instead of Germany—a political embargo kept the last five in France until their journey to Israel began on Christmas Eve 1969. Two batches were built, the first six (Group A) being fitted originally with three 40 mm AA guns and ordered in 1965. The second six (Group B) were ordered in 1966 and fitted with 76 mm OTO Melara guns. Five of these ships were delivered to Israel and two (*Acco* and *Saar*) made the journey on completion of local trials after the 1969 French arms embargo. The last five arrived off Haifa in January 1970 after a much-publicised passage which proved the remarkable endurance of this class.
The first batch was fitted for sonar but this was omitted from the 76 mm gun fitted group. Since their arrival in Israel provision of Gabriel surface to surface missiles has progressed. The first group can mount an armament varying from one 40 mm gun and eight Gabriel missiles (two single fixed mounts forward and two triple trainable mounts amidships) to three 40 mm guns. The second group can mount the two triple Gabriel launchers amidships as well as the 76 mm OTO Melara gun forward.
The Gabriel missile system is controlled by radar and optical sights and launches a low-altitude missile with a 150 lb HE head to a range of 12·5 miles in the first configuration and 22 miles in the later versions.

Sonar: ELAC sonar in Group A.

Torpedoes: Although Group A originally designed for four torpedo tubes for Mk 46 torpedoes these are no longer mounted.

"SAAR" Class with three 40 mm and torpedo tubes   1974

HANIT with one 40 mm and eight Gabriel missiles   1971, Israeli Navy

"SAAR" Class with 40 mm guns and torpedo tubes (see note)   1974

2 + ? US "FLAGSTAFF 2" CLASS (HYDROFOILS)

The first pair has been ordered in the USA with possibly 10 more to be built in Israel. Probably to replace the "Saar" class. To be fitted with Harpoon.

2 + ? "DVORA" CLASS (FAST ATTACK CRAFT—MISSILE)

Displacement, tons: 47
Dimensions, feet (metres): 75 × ? × ? *(23 × ? × ?)*
Missiles: 2 Gabriel launchers
Guns: 2—20 mm (singles)
Main engines: 2 MTU diesels = 36 knots
Range, miles: 700 at 27 knots

A private design of Israel Shipyards Ltd which is basically an improved "Dabur" class. The smallest missile craft so far built. First trials Dec 1977.

35 "DABUR" CLASS (COASTAL PATROL CRAFT)

Displacement, tons: 35 full load
Dimensions, feet (metres): 64·9 × 19 × 2·6 *(19·8 × 5·8 × 0·8)*
Guns: 2—20 mm; 2 twin 50 cal MGs (see note)
Main engines: 2 geared diesels; 960 shp; 2 shafts = 25 knots
Range, miles: 1 200 at 17 knots
Complement: 6/9 depending on armament

Twelve built in USA and remainder by Israel Aircraft Industry. Aluminium hull. There are several variations in their armament. Deployed in the Mediterranean and Red Seas, this being facilitated as these craft have been designed for overland transport. Good rough weather performance. A continuing programme in hand at the IAI plant at Ramta.

Missiles: There are reports that some may carry missiles of an unspecified type.

"DABUR" Class   1975, Israeli Navy

ISRAEL 253

3 Ex-US PBR TYPE (COASTAL PATROL CRAFT)

Dimensions, feet (metres): 32 × 11 × 2.6 (9.8 × 3.4 × 0.8)
Guns: 2—12.7 mm MG
Main engines: 2 geared diesels; waterjets = 25 knots
Complement: 5

Purchased 1974 and subsequently. GRP Hulls.

PBR Type — 1976, Israeli Navy

3 FIREFISH MODEL III

Displacement, tons: 6
Dimensions, feet (metres): 28 × 7.5 (8.5 × 2.3)
Main engines: 2 Mercruiser V-8; 430 hp
Speed, knots: 52
Range, miles: 250 cruising; 150 max speed

Built by Sandaire, San Diego. Glass fibre craft, can carry five men. Capable of being radio-controlled for attack missions or minesweeping under ship or aircraft control.

FIREFISH III — 1976, Israeli Navy

AMPHIBIOUS FORCES

3 Ex-US "LSM 1" CLASS

Displacement, tons: 1 095 full load
Dimensions, feet (metres): 203.5 oa × 34.5 × 7.3 (62.1 × 10.5 × 2.2)
Guns: 2—40 mm; 4—20 mm
Main engines: Diesels; 2 800 bhp; 2 shafts = 12.5 knots
Complement: 70

Purchased in 1972 from commercial sources.

"LSM 1" Class — 1976, Israeli Navy

3 "ASH" CLASS (LCT)

Name	No.	Builders	Commissioned
ASHDOD	61	Israel Shipyards, Haifa	1966
ASHKELON	63	Israel Shipyards, Haifa	1967
ACHZIV	65	Israel Shipyards, Haifa	1967

Displacement, tons: 400 standard; 730 full load
Dimensions, feet (metres): 180.5 pp; 205.5 oa × 32.8 × 5.8 (55.1; 62.7 × 10.0 × 1.8)
Guns: 2—20 mm
Main engines: 3 MWM diesels; 3 shafts; 1 900 bhp = 10.5 knots
Oil fuel, tons: 37
Complement: 20

"ASH" Class (being fitted with helicopter deck aft) — 1976, Israeli Navy

3 LC TYPE (LCT)

Name	No.	Builders	Commissioned
ETZION	51	Israel Shipyards, Haifa	1965
GUEBER	53	Israel Shipyards, Haifa	1965
SHIQMONA	55	Israel Shipyards, Haifa	1965

Displacement, tons: 182 standard; 230 full load
Dimensions, feet (metres): 120.0 × 23.2 × 4.7 (Etzion Geuber of only 90 ft length) (36.6 × 7.1 × 1.4 (27.5))
Guns: 2—20 mm
Main engines: 2 diesels; 2 shafts; 1 280 bhp = 10 knots
Complement: 12

LC Type — 1976, Israeli Navy

ISRAEL

3 Ex-US LCM TYPE

Displacement, tons: 22 tons standard; 60 full load
Dimensions, feet (metres): 50 × 14 × 3·2 *(15·3 × 4·3 × 1)*
Main engines: 2 diesels; 450 bhp = 11 knots

LCM Type 1976, Israeli Navy

MISCELLANEOUS

SUPPORT SHIPS

Note: Training ship *'Nogah'* converted from 500 ton coaster.

Name	No.	Builders	Commissioned
MA'OZ	—	Todd Marine, Washington	1976

Displacement, tons: 4 000?

Oil-rig tender for use as Light Forces Support ship.

1 "BAT SHEVA" CLASS (TRANSPORT)

Name	No.	Builders	Commissioned
BAT SHEVA	—	Netherlands	1967

Displacement, tons: 900
Dimensions, feet (metres): 311·7 × 36·7 × 26·9 *(95·1 × 11·2 × 8·2)*
Guns: 4—20 mm
Main engines: Diesels; speed = 10 knots
Complement: 26

Purchased from South Africa in 1968.

1 "BAT YAM" CLASS (TRANSPORT)

Name	No.	Builders	Commissioned
BAT YAM	T 82	Netherlands	—

A small armed merchant ship of 1 200 tons used as a transport. Bought from Netherlands in 1967.

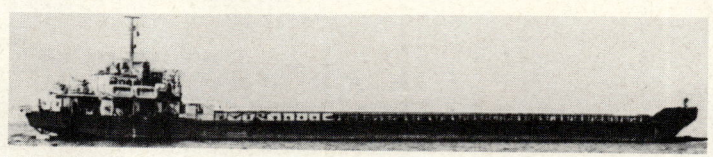

BAT SHEVA 1971, Israeli Navy

AUXILIARY

1 "YAR" CLASS (TRAINING CRAFT)

Name	No.	Builders	Commissioned
YARDEN	42	Yacht & Bootswerft, Burmester, Bremen	1958

Displacement, tons: 96 standard; 109 full load
Dimensions, feet (metres): 100 × 20 × 6 *(30·5 × 6·1 × 1·8)*
Guns: 2—20 mm
Main engines: MTU diesels; 2 shafts; speed 22 knots
Complement: 16

Has become non-naval training craft.

4 "KEDMA" CLASS (COASTAL PATROL CRAFT)

Name	No.	Builders	Commissioned
KEDMA	46	Japan	1968
YAMA	48	Japan	1968
NEGBA	52	Japan	1968
ZAFONA	60	Japan	1968

Displacement, tons: 32
Dimensions, feet (metres): 67·0 × 15·0 × 4·8 *(20·4 × 4·6 × 1·5)*
Guns: 2—20 mm
Main engines: 2 diesels; 2 shafts; 1 540 bhp = 25 knots
Complement: 10

Used for coastguard and police work in peace time.

YARDEN Israeli Navy

"KEDMA" Class 1976, Israeli Navy

ITALY

Headquarters Appointments

Chief of Naval Staff:
  Admiral Giovanni Torrisi
Vice Chief of Naval Staff:
  Vice-Admiral Giuliano Martinelli
Chief of Naval Personnel:
  Vice-Admiral Vittorio Gioncada

Principal Commands

Commander, Allied Naval Forces, Southern Europe (Naples) and Commander-in-Chief Dipartimento Basso Tirreno:
  Admiral Aldo Baldini
Commander-in-Chief of Fleet (and Comedcent):
  Admiral Girolamo Fantoni
Commander-in-Chief Dipartimento Alto Tirreno:
  Admiral Giuseppe Oriana
Commander-in-Chief Dipartimento Adriatico:
  Admiral Enzo Consolo
Commander-in-Chief Dipartimento dello Jonio e Canale d'Otranto:
  Admiral Mario Bini
Commander Sicilian Naval Area:
  Vice-Admiral Luigi de Ferrante
Commander Submarine Force:
  Rear-Admiral Renato Giovannetti

Diplomatic Representation

Naval Attaché in Bonn:
  Captain Pietro Scagliusi
Naval Attaché in London:
  Rear-Admiral Giulio Benini
Naval Attaché in Moscow:
  Captain Armando Vigliano
Naval Attaché in Paris:
  Commander Roberto Falciai
Naval Attaché in Washington:
  Commandant Antonio Conciarelli

Personnel

(a) 1978: 41 900 (including Naval Air Arm San Marco Battalion, Force of Marines)
(b) 1½ years national service

Bases

Main—La Spezia (Alto Tirreno), Taranto (Jonio e Canale d'Otranto), Ancona (Adriatico)
Secondary—Brindisi, Augusta, Messina, La Maddalena, Cagliari, Naples, Venice

Shipbuilding and Conversion Programme

In 1975 a law (Legge Navale) was approved which provided 1 000 000 million lire for the next ten years (1975-84), for the provision of new ships and helicopters over and above the normal annual expenditure.
The tentative new-construction programme is as follows:
```
 1      Light Anti-Submarine Cruiser
(2)     Guided Missile Destroyers
 6 (2)  Frigates "Maestrale" classes
 2      Submarines "Sauro" class
 6      "Sparviero" Hydrofoils
 4 (6)  Minehunters
(1)     LPD
 1      Salvage ship
 1      Replenishment Tanker; sister to Stromboli
27 (9)  AB212 Helicopters
```
Figures in brackets indicate ships not yet definitely decided upon or not ordered.

Ordinary budget:
```
 4   "Lupo" class frigates
 3   "Sparviero" class hydrofoils
 4   NATO hydrofoils
 2   "Sauro" class submarines
 4   Ocean Tugs
 8   Coastal Tugs
12   SH3D helicopters
```

All ships in service to be modernised.

Conversion programme (1977-1980)
10 MSCs to MSHs

Strength of the Fleet

Type	Active	Building (Ordered)
Cruisers	3	(1)
Destroyers	7	—
Frigates	11	3 (6)
Corvettes	9	—
Submarines	8	2 (2)
Hydrofoil—Missile	1	2 (4)
Fast Attack Craft	9	—
LSTs	2	—
Minehunters	1	(10)
Minesweepers—Ocean	4	—
Minesweepers—Coastal	30	—
Minesweepers—Inshore	10	—
Survey/Research Vessels	4	—
Replenishment Tankers	1	1
Transport	1	—
Fleet Support Ship	1	—
Coastal Transports	10	—
Transports (LCM)	20	—
Transports (LCVP)	39	—
Sail Training Ships	4	—
Netlayers	1	—
Lighthouse Tenders	3	—
Salvage Ships	1	(1)
Repair Craft	7	—
Water Carriers	13	—
Tugs—Large	8	—
Tugs—Small	31	—
Seaborne Helicopters	30	26

Naval Air Arm

2 LRMP Squadrons—18 Breguet Atlantics (BR 1150) (increasing to 32)
1 SRMP Squadron—Grumman Trackers (S2A/F)
2 Shore-based helicopter Squadrons (24 SH 3D)
3 ship-borne helicopter squadrons (27 AB 204, 28 AB 212) (26 more on order)

Note: Atlantics and Trackers operated by Navy with Air Force support and maintenance.

Mercantile Marine

Lloyd's Register of Shipping:
  1 690 vessels of 11 111 182 tons gross

DELETIONS

Destroyers

1977 Fanté

Frigates

1975 Aviere (target)
1976 Aldebaran (ex-US "Cannon" class)

Corvettes

1976-77 Sfinge, Bombarde, Chimera ("Ape" class)
1977 Vedetta (ex-US PC)

Submarines

1973 Leonardo da Vinci, Enrico Tazzoli
1975 Francesco Morosini ("Balao" Class) (15 Nov)
1976 Evangelista Torricelli
1977 Alfredo Cappellini ("Balao" Class)

Minesweepers (Coastal)

1974 Rovere, Acacia, Betulla, Ciliegio
1977 Abete

Minesweepers (Inshore)

1974 Arsella, Attinia, Calamaro, Conchiglia, Dromia, Ostrica, Paguro, Seppia, Tellina, Totano

Amphibious Forces

1974 Anteo, MTM 9903, 9904, 9906, 9921. MTP 9701, 9702, 9704-6, 9709, 9712, 9717, 9718, 9721, 9722, 9724, 9731
1976 MTP 9713, 9726. MTM 9908

Light Forces

1974 MS 472 (ex-813)
1975 MS 452 (ex-852) MS 473 (ex-813)
1977 Folgore

Miscellaneous

1974 Po, Flegetonte, Isonzo, Sesia, Metauro, Arno, Leno and Sprugola (water carriers). 24 tugs
1975 Aviere (experimental ship), Sterope (repl. tanker), Frigido (water carrier), MTM 9916-7, Porto Vecchio (tug)
1976 Volturno, Tevere (water carriers)
1977 Filicudi, Rampino

PENNANT NUMBERS

Cruisers

C 550	Vittorio Veneto
C 553	Andrea Dorea
C 554	Caio Duilio

Destroyers

D 550	Ardito
D 551	Audace
D 555	Geniere
D 558	Impetuoso
D 559	Indomito
D 562	San Giorgio
D 570	Impavido
D 571	Intrepido
F 565	Sagittario
F 566	Perseo
F 567	Orsa
F 570	Maestrale
F 571	Grecale
F 572	Libeccio
F 573	Scirocco
F 574	Aliseo
F 575	Euro

Frigates

D 564	Lupo
F 551	Canopo
F 553	Castore
F 554	Centauro
F 555	Cigno
F 580	Alpino
F 581	Carabiniere
F 593	Carlo Bergamini
F 594	Virginio Fasan
F 595	Carlo Margottini
F 596	Luigi Rizzo

Corvettes

F 540	Pietro De Cristofaro
F 541	Umberto Grosso
F 542	Aquila
F 543	Albatros
F 544	Alcione
F 545	Airone
F 546	Licio Visintini
F 550	Salvatore Todaro
F 597	Vedetta

Submarines

S 501	Primo Longobardo
S 502	Gianfranco Gazzana Priaroggia
S 505	Attilio Bagnolini
S 506	Enrico Toti
S 513	Enrico Dandolo
S 514	Lazzaro Mocenigo
S 515	Livio Piomarta
S 516	Romeo Romei

Light Forces

P 420	Sparviero
P 491	Lampo
P 492	Baleno
P 493	Freccia
P 494	Saetta
—	MS441
—	MS443
—	MS453
—	MS474
—	MS481

256 ITALY

Minesweepers

M 5430	Salmone
M 5431	Storione
M 5432	Sgombro
M 5433	Squalo
M 5450	Aragosta
M 5452	Astice
M 5457	Gambero
M 5458	Granchio
M 5459	Mitilo
M 5462	Pinna
M 5463	Polipo
M 5464	Porpora
M 5465	Riccio
M 5466	Scampo
M 5504	Castagno
M 5505	Cedro
M 5507	Faggio
M 5508	Frassino
M 5509	Gelso
M 5510	Larice
M 5511	Noce
M 5512	Olmo
M 5513	Ontano
M 5514	Pino
M 5516	Platano
M 5517	Quercia
M 5519	Mandorlo (hunter)
M 5521	Bambù
M 5522	Ebano
M 5523	Mango
M 5524	Mogano
M 5525	Palma
M 5527	Sandalo
M 5531	Agave
M 5532	Alloro

Minesweepers

M 5533	Edera
M 5534	Gaggia
M 5535	Gelsomino
M 5536	Giaggiolo
M 5537	Glicine
M 5538	Loto
M 5540	Timo
M 5541	Trifoglio
M 5542	Vischio

Amphibious Forces

L 9871	Andrea Bafile
L 9890	Grado
L 9891	Caorle

Service Forces

A 5301	Pietro Cavezzale
A 5302	Quarto
A 5303	Ammiraglio Magnaghi
A 5304	Alicudi
A 5305	Filicudi
A 5306	Mirto
A 5307	Pioppo
A 5309	Rampino
A 5310	Proteo
A 5311	Palinuro
A 5312	Amerigo Vespucci
A 5313	Stella Polare
A 5314	Quarto
A 5315	Barbara
A 5316	Corsaro II

Service Forces

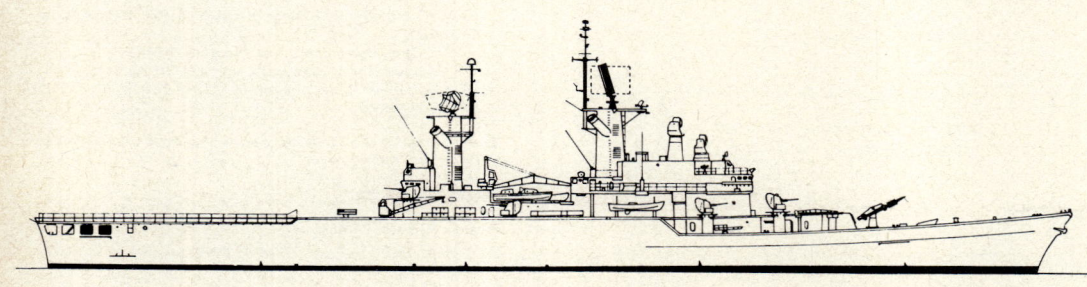

A 5317	Atlante
A 5318	Prometeo
A 5319	Ciclope
A 5320	Colosso
A 5321	Forte
A 5322	Gagliardo
A 5323	Robusto
A 5326	S. Giusto
A 5327	Stromboli
A 5328	Ape
A 5329	Vesuvio
A 5331-5338	MOC 1201-1208
A 5354	Piave
A 5356	Basento
A 5357	Bradano
A 5358	Brenta
A 5359	Bormida
A 5361-5363	MTF 1301-1303
A 5369	Adige
A 5374	Mincio
A 5376	Tanaro
A 5377	Ticino
Y 418	Caprera
Y 424	Favignana
Y 425	Levanzo
Y 432	Pantelleria
Y 434	Pianosa
Y 436	Porto d'Ischia
Y 438	Porta Pisano
Y 441	Porta Recanati
Y 443	Riva Trigoso
Y 445	Salvore
Y 447	Tino
Y 448	Ustica
Y 451	Vigoroso

VITTORIO VENETO

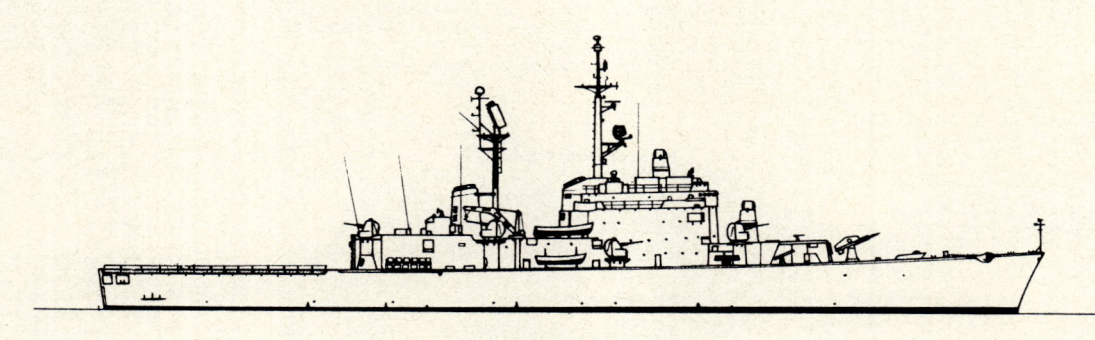

ANDREA DORIA

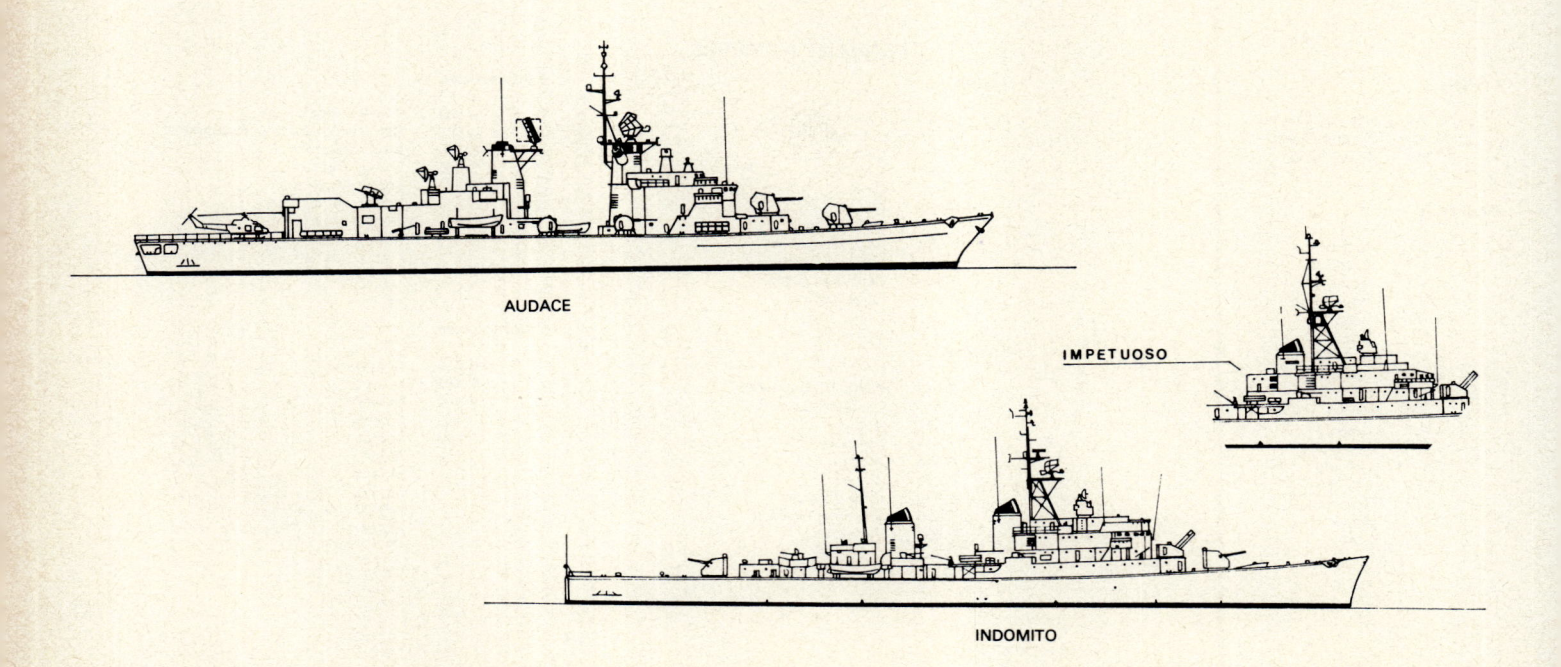

AUDACE

IMPETUOSO

INDOMITO

ITALY 257

FANTE

SAN GIORGIO

IMPAVIDO

LUPO

CENTAURO

ALPINO

PIETRO DE CRISTOFARO

ALBATROS

PIETRO CAVEZZALE

AMMIRAGLIO MAGNAGHI

STROMBOLI

Drawings, Lieutenant-Commander Erminio Bagnasco

258 ITALY

SUBMARINES

4 "SAURO" CLASS (1081 TYPE)

Name	No.	Builders	Laid down	Launched	Commissioned
NAZARIO SAURO	S 518	Italcantieri, Monfalcone	15 July 1974	9 Oct 1976	1978
FECIA DI COSSATO	S 519	Italcantieri, Monfalcone	15 Nov 1975	16 Nov 1977	Oct 1978
LEONARDO DA VINCI	S 520	Italcantieri, Monfalcone	1977	Nov 1974	Jan 1981
GUGLIELMO MARCONI	S 521	Italcantieri, Monfalcone	1977	May 1980	July 1981

Displacement, tons: 1 456 surfaced; 1 631 dived
Length, feet (metres): 210 *(63·9)*
Beam, feet (metres): 22·5 *(6·8)*
Draught, feet (metres): 18·9 *(5·7)*
Torpedo tubes: 6—21 in (bow) (6 reloads)
Main machinery: 3 diesel generators; 3 210 bhp; 1 electric motor; 3 650 hp; 1 shaft
Speed, knots: 11 surfaced; 20 dived; 12 (snorting)
Range, miles: 7 000 miles surfaced; 12 500 snorting at 4 knots; 400 miles dived at 4 knots; 20 miles dived at 20 knots
Endurance: 45 days
Complement: 42

Two of this class were originally ordered in 1967 but were cancelled in the following year. Reinstated in the building programme in 1972. Second pair provided for in Legge Navale and ordered 12 Feb 1976.

Diving depth: 800 feet + *(250 metres +)*.

Electronics: ECM; IFF, full communications fit.

Radar: One Search set (periscopic). 3 RM20/SMG

Sonar: Active and passive; Velox; Passive ranging; Acoustic ESM.

"SAURO" Class   *1976, Italcantieri*

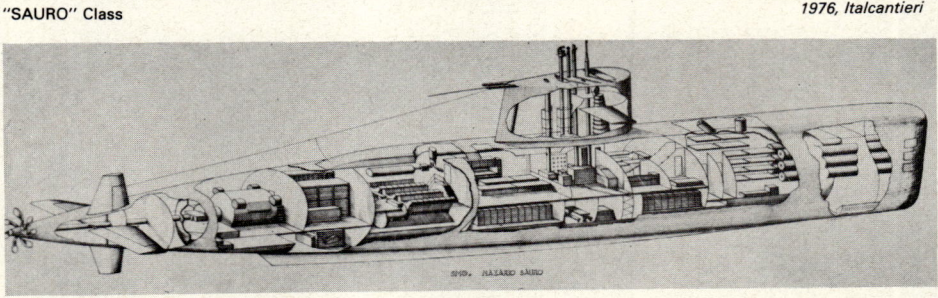

"SAURO" Class   *1976, CRDA*

4 "TOTI" CLASS (1075 TYPE)

Name	No.	Builders	Laid down	Launched	Commissioned
ATTILIO BAGNOLINI	S 505	Italcantieri, Monfalcone	15 April 1965	26 Aug 1967	16 June 1968
ENRICO TOTI	S 506	Italcantieri, Monfalcone	15 April 1965	12 Mar 1967	22 Jan 1968
ENRICO DANDOLO	S 513	Italcantieri, Monfalcone	10 Mar 1967	16 Dec 1967	25 Sept 1968
LAZZARO MOCENIGO	S 514	Italcantieri, Monfalcone	12 June 1967	20 April 1968	11 Jan 1969

Displacement, tons: 460 standard; 524 surfaced; 582 dived
Length, feet (metres): 151·5 *(46·2)*
Beam, feet (metres): 15·4 *(4·7)*
Draught, feet (metres): 13·1 *(4·0)*
Torpedo tubes: 4—21 in
Main machinery: 2 Fiat MB 820 N/I diesels, 1 electric motor, diesel-electric drive; 2 200 hp; 1 shaft
Speed, knots: 14 surfaced; 15 dived
Range, miles: 3 000 at 5 knots (surfaced)
Complement: 26 (4 officers, 22 men)

Italy's first indigenously-built submarines since the Second World War. The design was recast several times.

Diving depth: 600 feet *(180 metres)*.

Electronics: WT, HF, UHF and VLF equipment. Computer based fire control.

Radar: Search/nav set. 3 RM20/SMG. IFF, ECM.

Sonar: Passive set in stem. Active set in bow dome. Passive range finding. Ray path analyzer.

ENRICO DANDOLO   *9/1976, Commander Aldo Fraccaroli*

2 Ex-US "TANG" CLASS

Name	No.	Builders	Laid down	Launched	Commissioned
LIVIO PIOMARTA (ex-USS *Trigger*, SS 564)	S 515	General Dynamics (Electric Boat Div)	24 Feb 1949	3 Dec 1951	19 Aug 1952
ROMEO ROMEI (ex-USS *Harder*, SS 568)	S 516	General Dynamics (Electric Boat Div)	30 June 1950	14 June 1951	31 Mar 1952

Displacement, tons: 2 100 surfaced; 2 700 dived
Length, feet (metres): 287 *(87·4)*
Beam, feet (metres): 27·3 *(8·3)*
Draught, feet (metres): 19 *(6·2)*
Torpedo tubes: 8—21 in; 6 bow, 2 stern
Main machinery: 3 diesels 4 500 shp; 2 electric motors 5 600 hp
Speed, knots: 20 surfaced; 18 dived
Range, miles: 11 000 at 11 knots
Complement: 75 (7 officers, 68 men)

Transferred as follows: *Romeo Romei* 20 Feb 1974, *Livio Piomarta* 10 July 1973. Subsequently refitted at Philadelphia Navy Yard.

Radar: BPS-12.

ROMEO ROMEI   *11/1975, Dr. Giorgio Arra*

ITALY 259

2 Ex-US "GUPPY III" CLASS

Name	No.	Builders	Laid down	Launched	Commissioned
PRIMO LONGOBARDO(ex-USS *Volador*, SS 524)	S 501	Portsmouth Navy Yard	15 June 1945	17 Jan 1946	10 Jan 1948
GIANFRANCO GAZZANA PRIAROGGIA(ex-USS *Pickerel*, SS 524)	S 502	Boston Navy Yard	8 Feb 1944	15 Dec 1944	4 April 1949

Displacement, tons: 1 975 standard; 2 450 dived
Length, feet (metres): 326·5 *(99·4)* oa
Beam, feet (metres): 27 *(8·2)*
Draught, feet (metres): 17 *(5·2)*
Torpedo tubes: 10—21 in; 6 bow, 4 stern
Main machinery: 4 diesels; 6 400 bhp;
  2 electric motors; 5 400 shp; 2 shafts
Speed, knots: 20 surfaced; 15 dived
Oil fuel, tons: 300
Range, miles: 12 000 at 10 knots (surfaced)
Complement: 85 (10 officers, 75 men)

Both transferred 18 Aug 1972.

PRIMO LONGOBARDO *1975, Wright and Logan*

CRUISERS

1 NEW CONSTRUCTION AIRCRAFT CRUISER

Name	No.	Builders	Laid down	Launched	Commissioned
GIUSEPPE GARIBALDI	—	Italcantieri, Monfalcone	1980	—	1984?

Displacement, tons: 10 100 standard; 12 000 full load
Dimensions, feet (metres): 580 × 98 × 22 *(177 × 30 × 6·7)*
Aircraft: 16 Sea King or equivalent
Missiles: 3 "Tesco" launchers for 6 Otomat; 2 "Albatross"
  systems with Aspide missiles
Guns: 6—40/70 mm guns (3 twins) with Dardo control system
A/S weapons: 6 A/S torpedo tubes (2 triple)
Main engines: 4 Fiat/GE LM2 500 gas turbines; 80 000 hp
Speed, knots: 29·5
Range, miles: 7 000 at 20 knots
Complement: 550 (accommodation 825)

A new design ordered Dec 1977 to replace the "Andre Doria" class. A comparison with the British "Invincible" class shows that a longer flight deck and a similar complement of aircraft have been provided on two thirds of the British ships' displacement and with about the same proportion of power giving a similar if not higher speed and a somewhat increased range. However the design has already changed considerably and the final figures may be different.

Aircraft: VSTOL may also be included in the complement.

Electronics: System I PN 10 for data processing

Radar: Long range surveillance: RAN 3L
Air surveillance: RAN 10S
Combined search: SPQ 2D
Fire control: NA 10

Sonar: One, possibly SQS 23

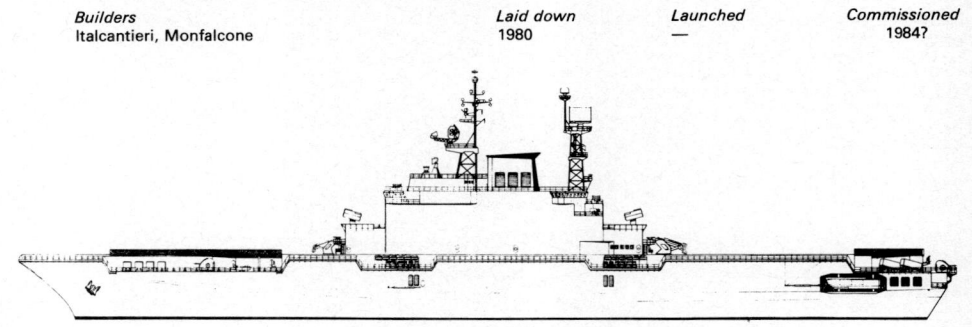

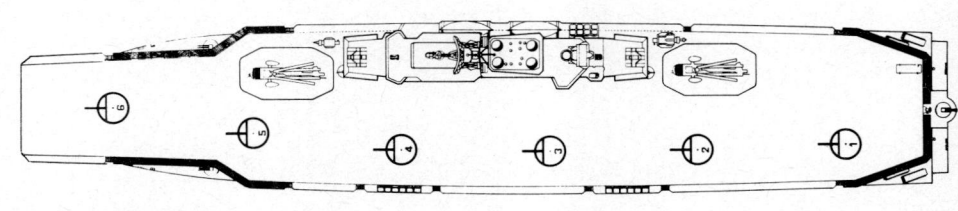

GIUSEPPE GARIBALDI *1977, Italian Navy*

1 HELICOPTER CRUISER

Name	No.	Builders	Laid down	Launched	Commissioned
VITTORIO VENETO	C 550	Italcantieri, Castellammare di Stabia	10 June 1965	5 Feb 1967	12 July 1969

Displacement, tons: 7 500 standard; 8 850 full load
Length, feet (metres): 589 *(179·6)* oa
Beam, feet (metres): 63·6 *(19·4)*
Draught, feet (metres): 19·7 *(6)*
Aircraft: 9 AB-204B or AB-212 helicopters
Missiles: 1 Terrier/Asroc twin launcher forward
Guns: 8—3 in *(76 mm)* 62 cal
A/S weapons: 2 triple US Mk 32 for A/S torpedoes; helicopter torpedoes
Main engines: 2 Tosi double reduction geared turbines; 73 000 shp; 2 shafts
Boilers: 4 Foster-Wheeler type (Ansaldo); 711 psi *(50 kg/cm²)*; 842°F *(450°C)*

Speed, knots: 32
Oil fuel, tons: 1 200
Range, miles: 6 000 at 20 knots
Complement: 550 (50 officers, 500 men)

Developed from the "Andrea Doria" class but with much larger helicopter squadron and improved facilities for anti-submarine operations. Projected under the 1959-60 New Construction Programme, but her design was recast several times. Started trials 30 April 1969. Flagship of C-in-C Fleet. Fitted with two sets of stabilisers.

Electronics: Tacan AN/URN-20 fitted.

Radar: Air search and target designator (3D on fore funnel): one SPS 52.
Long-range search (after funnel): one SPS 40.
Search: one SMA/SPQ-2.
Terrier fire control: two SPG 55B.
Gun fire control: four Orion radars in Argo/Elsag NA9 systems.
Navigation: Three RM7.

SCLAR: Fitted with control and launchers for SCLAR rockets—range 7 miles; fitted with HE heads, flares or chaff.

Sonar: One SQS 23.

VITTORIO VENETO *1973, Dr. Giorgio Arra*

King SH3Ds.

Radar: Air surveillance (3D on after funnel): one SPS 52
Tracking and missile guidance: two SPG 51
Air search: one SPS 12
Surface search: SPQ-2
Gun fire control: three Orion RTN 10X for Argo 10/Elsag NA 10 systems

Sonar: One CWE 610

SCLAR: fitted with SCLAR control and launch units for 105 mm rockets which can be fitted with chaff dispensers, flares or HE heads and have a range of 7 miles.

Torpedo tubes: The two triple Mk 32 launchers for Mk 44 torpedoes are on either beam amidships.

AUDACE *6/1976, Commander Aldo Fraccaroli*

ARDITO *6/1977, Michael D. J. Lennon*

260 ITALY

2 "ANDREA DORIA" CLASS

Name	No.	Builders	Laid down	Launched	Commissioned
ANDREA DORIA	C 553	Cantieri del Tirreno, Riva Trigoso	11 May 1958	27 Feb 1963	23 Feb 1964
CAIO DUILIO	C 554	Navalmeccanica di Stabia	16 May 1958	22 Dec 1962	30 Nov 1964

Displacement, tons: 5 000 standard; 6 500 full load
Length, feet (metres): 489·8 *(149·3)* oa
Beam, feet (metres): 56·4 *(17·2)*
Draught, feet (metres): 16·4 *(5·0)*
Aircraft: 4 AB-204B or AB-212 helicopters
Missiles: 1 Terrier twin launcher forward
Guns: 8—3 in *(76 mm)* 62 cal.
A/S weapons: 2 triple US Mk 32 torpedo tubes; helicopter torpedoes
Main engines: 2 double reduction geared turbines 60 000 shp *(Doria,* CNR; *Duilio,* Ansaldo); 2 shafts
Boilers: 4 Foster-Wheeler 711 psi *(50 kg/cm²)* (Ansaldo, *Duilio;* CNR, *Doria);* 842°F *(450°C)*
Speed, knots: 31
Range, miles: 6 000 at 20 knots
Oil fuel, tons: 1 100
Complement: 470 (45 officers, 425 men)

Escort cruisers of novel design with a good helicopter capacity in relation to their size. *Enrico Dandolo* was the name originally allocated to *Andrea Doria.* Both to be replaced in mid 1980s by *Giuseppi Garibaldi.*

Electronics: ECM and DF. Tacan beacon (AN/URN-20).

Gunnery: The anti-aircraft battery includes eight 3-in fully automatic guns, disposed in single turrets, four on each side amidships abreast the funnels and the bridge.

Helicopter platform: Helicopters operate from a platform aft measuring 98·5 feet by 52·5 feet *(30 by 16 metres).*

Roll damping: Both ships have Gyrofin-Salmoiraghi stabilisers.

Radar: Air surveillance and target designator (3D on mainmast): one SPS 52 *(Doria—*SPS 76B).
Long range search: one SPS 40
Navigation: one set.
Terrier fire-control: two SPG 55A *(Andrea Doria—*SPG 55C)
Gun fire control: four Orion radars in Argo/Elsag NA9 systems

SCLAR: Fitted with control and launchers for SCLAR rockets—range 7 miles; fitted with HE heads, flares or chaff.

Sonar: One SQS 23 *(Doria);* One SQS 39 *(Duilio)*

ANDREA DORIA   11/1975, Dr. Giorgio Arra

ANDREA DORIA   1973, Dr. Giorgio Arra

---

262 ITALY

2 "IMPAVIDO" CLASS (DDG)

Name	No.	Builders	Laid down	Launched	Commissioned
IMPAVIDO	D 570	Cantieri del Tirreno, Riva Trigoso	10 June 1957	25 May 1962	16 Nov 1963
INTREPIDO	D 571	Ansaldo, Leghorn	16 May 1959	21 Oct 1962	28 July 1964

Displacement, tons: 3 201 standard; 3 851 full load
Length, feet (metres): 429·5 *(131·3)*
Beam, feet (metres): 44·7 *(13·6)*
Draught, feet (metres): 14·8 *(4·5)*
Missiles: 1 Tartar/Standard launcher, aft
Guns: 2—5 in *(127 mm)* 38 cal forward; 4—3 in *(76 mm)* 62 cal
A/S weapons: 2 triple US Mk 32 torpedo tubes
Boilers: 4 Foster Wheeler; 711 psi *(50 kg/cm²);* 842°F *(450°C)*
Main engines: 2 double reduction geared turbines 70 000 shp; 2 shafts
Speed, knots: 34
Range, miles: 3 300 at 20 knots; 2 900 at 25 knots; 1 500 at 30 knots
Oil fuel, tons: 650
Complement: 340 (23 officers, 317 men)

Built under the 1956-57 and 1958-59 programmes respectively. Both ships have stabilisers.

Engineering: On first full power trials *Impavido,* at light displacement, reached 34·5 knots (33 knots at normal load).

Modernisation: In 1974-75 *Intrepido* underwent modernisation which included the improvement of the missile system and the replacement of the original gun fire-control system by Argo 10/Elsag NA 10 system. Same modifications carried out in *Impavido* 1976-77.

Radar: Search: SPS 12, SPS 39 (3-D) and SPQ-2.
Fire control: SPG 51 for Tartar (2); three Orion RTN 10X, Argo 10, Elsag NA 10 for guns.

SCLAR: Fitted with SCLAR control and launchers—for details see *Vittorio Veneto.*

Sonar: One SQS 23

IMPAVIDO   1975, Michael D. J. Lennon

INTREPIDO   6/1975, Dr. Giorgio Arra

1 "SAN GIORGIO" CLASS (DD)

Name	No.	Builders	Laid down	Launched	Commissioned
SAN GIORGIO (ex-*Pompeo Magno*)	D 562	Cantieri N. Riuniti Ancona	23 Sept 1939	28 Aug 1941	24 June 1943

Displacement, tons: 3 950 standard; 4 350 full load
Length, feet (metres): 455·2 *(138·8)* wl; 466·5 *(142·3)* oa
Beam, feet (metres): 47·2 *(14·4)*
Draught, feet (metres): 21·0 *(4·5)*
Guns: 4—5 in *(127 mm)* 38 cal; 3—3 in *(76 mm)* 62 cal
A/S weapons: 1 three-barrelled mortar (MENON); 2 triple torpedo tubes
Main engines: 2 Tosi Metrovick gas turbines; 15 000 bhp; 4 Fiat diesels; 16 600 hp; 2 shafts
Speed, knots: 20 (diesels), 28 (diesel and gas)

ITALY 263

2 "IMPETUOSO" CLASS

Name	No.	Builders	Laid down	Launched	Commissioned
IMPETUOSO	D 558	Cantieri del Tirreno, Riva Trigosa	7 May 1952	16 Sept 1956	25 Jan 1958
INDOMITO	D 559	Ansaldo, Leghorn (formerly OTO)	24 April 1952	7 Aug 1955	23 Feb 1958

Displacement, tons: 2 755 standard; 3 800 full load
Length, feet (metres): 405 *(123·4)* pp; 418·7 *(127·6)* oa
Beam, feet (metres): 43·5 *(13·3)*
Draught, feet (metres): 17·5 *(4·5)*
Guns: 4—5 in *(127 mm)* 38 cal. 16—40 mm 56 cal (twins)
A/S weapons: 2 triple US Mk 32 torpedo tubes; 1 three-barrelled mortar; 4 DCT; 1 DC rack 6 (2 triple)
Main engines: 2 double reduction geared turbines; 2 shafts; 65 000 shp
Boilers: 4 Foster-Wheeler; 711 psi *(50 kg/cm²)* working pressure; 842°F *(450°C)* superheat temperature
Speed, knots: 34 (see *Engineering* notes)
Oil fuel, tons: 650
Range, miles: 3 400 at 20 knots
Complement: 315 (15 officers, 300 men)

Italy's first destroyers built since Second World War. To be relieved in mid-1980s by "Improved Audace" class.

Engineering: On their initial sea trials these ships attained a speed of 35 knots at full load.

Gunnery: For 5 in—US Mk 37 director with Mk 25 radar. For 40 mm—four mounts have US Mk 34 radars. In addition six US Mk 51 directors.

Radar: Search: SPS-6 and SPQ-2.
Fire control: one US Mk 25 for Mk 37 FCS; four AN/SPG 34 for Mk 63 FCS.

Sonar: One SQS 11.

INDOMITO   1975, Commander Aldo Fraccaroli

IMPETUOSO   1975, Commander Aldo Fraccaroli

FRIGATES

0 + 6 "MAESTRALE" CLASS

Name	No.	Builders	Laid down	Launched	Commissioned
MAESTRALE	F 570	Cantiere Navali Riuniti	1978	Feb 1980	Aug 1980
GRECALE	F 571	Cantiere Navali Riuniti	—	Oct 1980	April 1981
LIBECCIO	F 572	Cantiere Navali Riuniti	—	April 1981	Oct 1981
SCIROCCO	F 573	Cantiere Navali Riuniti	—	Sept 1981	Mar 1982
ALISEO	F 574	Cantiere Navali Riuniti	—	Feb 1982	Aug 1982
EURO	F 575	Cantiere Navali Riuniti	—	July 1982	Jan 1983

Displacement, tons: 2 500 standard; 2 800 full load
Dimensions, feet (metres): 405 × 42·5 × 13·4 *(122·7 ×12·9 × 4·1)*
Aircraft: 2 AB 212 helicopters
Missiles: 4 OTO Melara Albatross PDMS
Guns: 1—5 in *(127 mm)* 54 OTO Melara Compact; 4—40 mm (twin) 70 cal Breda Compact
A/S weapons: 2 triple US Mk 32 torpedo tubes
Torpedo tubes: 2
Main engines: CODOG; 2 Fiat LM 2 500 gas turbines; 40 000 shp; 2 diesels GMT 2 320; 11 000 hp; 2 shafts (cp propellers)
Speed, knots: 30 (32·5 Trials)
Range, miles: 4 500 at 16 knots
Complement: 213 (23 officers, 190 ratings)

An improved "Lupo" class design provided for in Legge Navale. First six ordered Dec 1976. First ship due for trials Feb 1980. Fitted with stabilisers. Improved A/S capability and an integrated gun/missile control system.

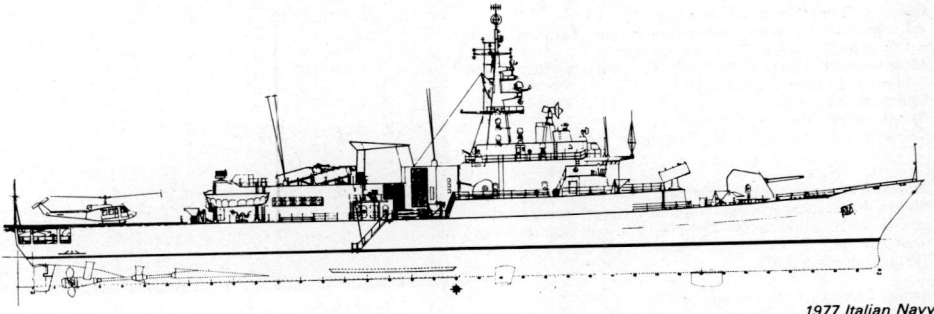

Radar: Air search: MM/SPS 774
Surface search: MM/SPS 702

"MAESTRALE" Class   1977 Italian Navy

Navigation: MM/SPS 703
Fire control: One Orion for Albatros; two Orion 20 for Dardo gun control system
Sonar: One Raytheon DE 1164 hull mounted: one VDS

Fire control: one Orion 3 for OG3 FCS.
Sonar: ELSAG DLB-1 fire control system. SQS 36 (hull-mounted and VDS)

LICIO VISINTINI   6/1975, Dr. Giorgio Arra

4 "ALBATROS" CLASS

Name	No.	Builders	Laid down	Launched	Commissioned
AQUILA	F 542	Breda Marghera, Mestre, Venice	25 July 1953	31 July 1954	2 Oct 1956
ALBATROS	F 543	Navalmeccanica, Castellammare di Stabia	1953	18 July 1954	1 June 1955
ALCIONE	F 544	Navalmeccanica, Castellammare di Stabia	1953	19 Sept 1954	23 Oct 1955
AIRONE	F 545	Navalmeccanica, Castellammare di Stabia	1953	21 Nov 1954	29 Dec 1955

Displacement, tons: 800 standard; 950 full load
Length, feet (metres): 250·3 *(76·3)* oa
Beam, feet (metres): 31·5 *(9·6)*
Draught, feet (metres): 9·2 *(2·8)*
Guns: 2—40 mm 70 cal Bofors (see *Gunnery*)
A/S weapons: 2 Hedgehogs Mk II; 2 DCT; 1 DC rack; 6 (2 triple) US Mk 32 A/S torpedo tubes
Main engines: 2 Fiat diesels; 2 shafts; 5 200 bhp
Speed, knots: 19
Oil fuel, tons: 100
Range, miles: 3 000 at 18 knots
Complement: 99

Eight ships of this class were built in Italy under US offshore MDAP orders. three for Italy, four for Denmark and one for the Netherlands. *Aquila*, laid down on 25 July 1953, was transferred to the Italian Navy on 18 Oct 1961 at Den Helder.

Gunnery: The two 3-in *(76 mm)* guns originally mounted, one forward and one aft, were temporarily replaced by two 40 mm guns in 1963. The ultimate armament was planned to include two 3-in *(76 mm)* OTO Melara guns.

Radar: Combined search and navigation: one SMA/SPQ-2.

Sonar: One QCU 2.

ALBATROS   1974, Dr. Giorgio Arra

264 ITALY

4 "LUPO" CLASS

Name	No.	Builders	Laid down	Launched	Commissioned
LUPO	F 564	Cantieri del Tirreno, Riva Trigoso	11 Oct 1974	29 July 1976	12 Sept 1977
SAGITTARIO	F 565	Cantieri del Tirreno, Riva Trigoso	4 Feb 1976	22 June1977	May 1978
PERSEO	F 566	Cantieri del Tirreno, Riva Trigoso	26 Feb 1977	April 1978	Feb 1979
ORSA	F 567	Cantieri del Tirreno, Riva Trigoso	Jan 1978	Nov 1978	Aug 1979

Displacement, tons: 2 208 standard; 2 500 full load
Length, feet (metres): 355·4 (108·4)
Beam, feet (metres): 37·1 (11·3)
Draught, feet (metres): 12·1 (3·7)
Aircraft: AB 204B or 212 helicopter
Missiles: 1—Otomat (OTO-Melara) surface-to-surface system with 8 launchers; 1—Octuple launcher for NATO Seasparrow
Guns: 1—5 in (127/54) OTO-Melara Compact; 4—40 mm 70 cal (Breda) (twin Dardo systems)
Rocket launcher: 1 SCLAR system with 2 multiple, trainable mountings
A/S weapons: 6 (2 triple) US Mk 32 torpedo tubes for Mk 46 torpedoes; helicopter torpedoes
Main engines: CODOG—2 Fiat LM 2 500 gas turbines; 50 000 hp; 2 GMT diesels; 7 800 hp; 2 shafts (cp propellers)
Speed, knots: 35 on turbines; 21 on diesels
Range, miles: 4 400 at 16 knots (diesels)
Complement: 185 (16 officers, 169 ratings)

First of class named after the most famous Italian torpedo-boat of Second World War. Fitted with stabilisers.

Aircraft: Although two helicopters can be carried there is hangar space for only one.

Construction: 14 watertight compartments; fixed-fin stabilisers; 90 days endurance.

Electronics: Automatic command and control system IPN 10 (Selenia); ECM System (Elettronica); Telecommunications System (Elmer).

Foreign sales: Similar ships being built for Peru and Venezuela.

Radar: Air search: one MM/SPS 774.
Combined search: one RAN 11L/X system (Selenia).

Gun fire control: Orion 20 for each Dardo system.

SCLAR: Fitted with control and launchers for SCLAR rockets; for details see *Vittorio Veneto*.

Sonar: One DE 1160B (Raytheon) hull-mounted set.

LUPO   1977, Italian Navy

---

266 ITALY

1 "APE" CLASS

Name	No.	Builders	Laid down	Launched	Commissioned
APE	A 5328	Navalmeccanica, Castellamare	1942	1942	1943

Displacement, tons: 670 standard; 771 full load
Length, feet (metres): 192·8 (58·8) wl; 212·6 (64·8) oa
Beam, feet (metres): 28·5 (8·7)
Draught, feet (metres): 8·9 (2·7)
Guns: 2—40 mm 56 cal
Main engines: 2 Fiat diesels; 2 shafts; 3 500 bhp
Speed, knots: 15
Oil fuel, tons: 64
Range, miles: 2 450 at 15 knots
Complement: 66 (6 officers, 60 men)

Originally fitted for minesweeping. Modified with navigating bridge. Now support ship for frogmen and commandos.

APE (Diving support ship)   6/1976, Dr. Giorgio Arra

LIGHT FORCES

1 + 6 "SPARVIERO" CLASS (HYDROFOIL—MISSILE)

Name	No.	Builders	Commissioned
SPARVIERO	P 420	Alinavi, La Spezia	15 July 1974
NIBBIO	—	Cantieri Navale Riuniti	April 1979
FALCONE	—	Cantieri Navale Riuniti	Aug 1979
ASTORE	—	Cantieri Navale Riuniti	Feb 1980
GRIFONE	—	Cantieri Navale Riuniti	June 1980
GHEPPIO	—	Cantieri Navale Riuniti	Oct 1980
CONDOR	—	Cantieri Navale Riuniti	Feb 1981

Displacement, tons: 62·5
Dimensions, feet (metres): 80·7 × 39·7 × 14·4 (24·6 × 12·1 × 4·4) (length and beam foils extended, draught hullborne)
Missile launchers: 2 fixed for Otomat ship-to-ship missiles
Gun: 1 OTO Melara 76 mm 62 cal
Main engines: Proteus gas turbine driving waterjet pump; 4 500 bhp; diesel and retractable propeller unit for hullborne propulsion
Range, miles: 400 at 45 knots; 1 200 at 8 knots
Speed, knots: 50 max, 42 cruising (sea state 4)
Complement: 10 (2 officers, 8 men)

Completed for trials 9 May 1973. Missiles made by OTO Melara/Matra. Fitted with Elsag NA-10 Mod 1 fire control system with Orion RTN-10X radar. Delivered to the Navy as class prototype on 15 July 1974. Eight more hydrofoils planned of this class although only six so far ordered. Four planned hydrofoils of US "Pegasus" design now cancelled. Alinavi, La Spezia transferred to CNR.

SPARVIERO   1974, Italian Navy

2 "FRECCIA" CLASS (FAST ATTACK CRAFT—CONVERTIBLE)

Name	No.	Builders	Commissioned
FRECCIA (ex-MC 590)	P 493	Cantiere del Tirreno, Riva Trigoso	6 July 1965
SAETTA (ex-MC 591)	P 494	CRDA, Monfalcone	25 April 1966

Displacement, tons: 188 standard; 205 full load
Dimensions, feet (metres): 150 × 23·8 × 5·5 (45·8 × 7·3 × 1·7)
Guns: *As Gunboat:* 3—40 mm, 70 cal or 2—40 mm, 70 cal. *As Fast Minelayer:* 1—40 mm with 8 mines. *As Torpedo Boat:* 2—40 mm, 70 cal
Torpedo tubes: *As Torpedo Boat:* 2—21 in
Main engines: 2 diesels; 7 600 bhp; 1 Bristol Siddeley Proteus gas turbine, 4 250 shp; cp propellers; total hp 11 850 = 40 knots
Complement: 37 (4 officers, 33 men)

Freccia was laid down on 30 April 1963 and launched on 9 Jan 1965. *Saetta* was laid down on 11 June 1963, launched on 11 April 1965. Can be converted in 24 hours to gunboat, torpedo boat, fast minelayer, or missile boat. Fitted with E band navigation and tactical radar. *Saetta* has been armed with Sea Killer Mk 1 system with 5 round trainable launcher.

Fire Control: *Freccia:* US Mk 51 optical FCS. *Saetta:* RTN 150 radar with TV camera on top for Contraves GFCS.

SAETTA experimentally armed with 5 Sea Killer I missiles   1970, Italian Navy

FRECCIA   1974, Italian Navy

2 "LAMPO" CLASS (FAST ATTACK CRAFT—CONVERTIBLE)

Name	No.	Builders	Commissioned
LAMPO (ex-MC 491)	P 491	Arsenale MM, Taranto	July 1963
BALENO (ex-MC 492)	P 492	Arsenale MM, Taranto	16 July 1965

Displacement, tons: 170 standard; 196 full load
Dimensions, feet (metres): 131·5 × 21 × 5 (40·1 × 6·4 × 1·5)
Guns: *As Gunboat:* 3—40 mm, 70 cal or 2—40 mm, 70 cal; *As Torpedo Boat:* 2—40 mm, 70 cal
Torpedo tubes: *As Torpedo Boat:* 2—21 in
Main engines: 2 MTU 518-D diesels; 1 Metrovick gas turbine; 3 shafts; total 11 700 hp = 39 knots
Complement: 33 (5 officers, 28 men)

Convertible gunboats, improved versions of the *Folgore* prototype. *Lampo* was laid down on 4 Jan 1958 and launched on 22 Nov 1960. *Baleno* was laid-down on the same slip on 22 Nov 1960, launched on 10 May 1964. She has been converted to an improved design. Both fitted with new diesels in 1976.

Fire control: US Mk 51 optical for 40/70 guns.

Radar: 3 ST 7-250.

LAMPO   6/1975, Dr. Giorgio Arra

ITALY 267

3 Ex-US "HIGGINS" CLASS (FAST PATROL CRAFT)

MS 441 (ex-GIS 841)   **MS 443** (ex-GIS 843)   **MS 453** (ex-GIS 853)

Displacement, tons: 64 full load
Dimensions, feet (metres): 78 × 20 × 6 *(23·8 × 6·1 × 1·8)*
Guns: 2—20 mm, 70 cal
Main engines: 3 CRM ASM 185 petrol motors; 3 shafts; 4 500 bhp = 34 knots
Range, miles: 1 000 at 20 knots
Complement: 11 (1 officer, 10 men)

Commissioned March 1948.
MS 441 and 453 converted for frogmen support with after weapons removed. Refitted in Italy in 1949-53.

Radar: One SPS-21.

M 453 (modified for frogmen support)   6/1975, Dr. Giorgio Arra

2 FAST ATTACK CRAFT—TORPEDO

Name	No.	Builders	Commissioned
—	MS 474 (ex-MS/MV 614, ex-MS 54)	CRDA, Monfalcone	1942
—	MS 481 (ex-MS/MV 615, ex-MS 55)	CRDA, Monfalcone	1942

Displacement, tons: 72 full load
Dimensions, feet (metres): 92 × 15 × 5 *(28·1 × 4·6 × 1·5)*
Guns: 1 or 2—40 mm, 56 cal
Torpedoes: 2—17·7 in (no tubes)
Main engines: Petrol motors; 3 shafts; 3 450 bhp = 27 knots
Range, miles: 600 at 16 knots
Complement: 19 (2 officers, 17 men)

Converted as MV (motovedette) with no tubes under the Peace Treaty. Reconverted in 1951-53. MS 481 refitted as convertible boat in 1960 and MS 474 in 1961. Originally class of four. Further refits 1965-69.

MS 481   1974, Italian Navy

14 COASTAL PATROL CRAFT

Twelve 5·25 ton craft of 23 knots built in 1976/77 and two 6·5 ton craft of 27 knots. May not have been built for the navy.

AMPHIBIOUS FORCES

Note: A new 6 000 ton LPD is to be built under Legge Navale to act as training ship in place of *San Giorgio* in addition to amphibious duties.

2 Ex-US "DE SOTO COUNTY" CLASS (LSTs)

Name	No.	Builders	Commissioned
GRADO (ex-USS *De Soto County*, LST 1171)	L 9890	Avondale, New Orleans	1957
CAORLE (ex-USS *York County*, LST 1175)	L 9891	Newport News SB & DD Co.	1957

Displacement, tons: 4 164 light; 8 000 full load
Dimensions, feet (metres): 444 × 62 × 16·5 *(133·4 × 18·9 × 5)*
Guns: 6—3 in *(76 mm)*
Main engines: 6 Fairbanks Morse diesels; 14 400 shp; 2 shafts; (cp propellers) = 17·5 knots
Range, miles: 16 500 at 13 knots
Complement: 165 (10 officers, 155 men)
Troops: Approx 575

Both completed 1957 and transferred 17 July 1972.

Radar: One 3 RM 20.

CAORLE   3/1977 J. A. Verhoog

1 Ex-US "KENNETH WHITING" CLASS (TRANSPORT)

Name	No.	Builders	Commissioned
ANDREA BAFILE (ex-USS *St. George*, AV 16, ex-A 5314)	L 9871	—	1944

Displacement, tons: 8 510 standard; 14 000 full load
Dimensions, feet (metres): 492 oa × 69·5 × 26 *(163 × 23 × 8·5)*
Aircraft: 1 or 2 helicopters
Guns: 2—5 in 38 cal
Main engines: Allis-Chalmers geared turbines; 1 shaft; 8 500 shp = 17 knots
Boilers: 2 Foster-Wheeler
Range, miles: 13 400 at 13 knots
Complement: 58 (10 officers, 48 men)

Former USN seaplane tender, launched on 14 Feb 1944. Purchased and commissioned in the Italian Navy on 11 Dec 1968 and modified. Depot ship for "Special Forces". In reserve at Taranto.

ANDREA BAFILE   1974, Italian Navy

268 ITALY

MINE WARFARE FORCES

10 NEW CONSTRUCTION (MINEHUNTERS/SWEEPERS)

Displacement, tons: 470
Dimensions, feet (metres): 163·7 × 30·8 × 8·2 *(49·9 × 9·4 × 2·5)*
Gun: 1—40 mm
Main engines: Passage—1 GMT 230 8 cyl diesel; 1 600 hp = 15 knots;
  Hunting—Hydraulic thrust jets = 0 to 7 knots
Range, miles: 2 500 at 12 knots
Endurance: 10 days
Complement: 39

To be ordered under Legge Navale from Intermarine, La Spezia.

Construction: Of GRP throughout hull, decks and bulkheads.

Electrics: 440 volt, 60 cycle 3 phase AC.

Engineering: All machinery is mounted on vibration dampers.

Minehunting: CGE-Fiart AN/SQQ 14 minehunting sonar; SMA navigation system with data processing; 2 underwater detection/destruction vehicles; diving equipment and recompression chamber.

Minesweeping: Oropesa wire sweep.

Radar: SMA.

NEW CONSTRUCTION   1976, Intermarine

Sonar: CGE-Fiart AN/SQQ-14 VDS (lowered from keel forward of bridge).

4 Ex-US "AGILE" CLASS (MINESWEEPERS—OCEAN)

Name	No.	Builders	Commissioned
SALMONE (ex-*MSO 507*)	M 5430	Martinolich SB Co	15 June 1956
STORIONE (ex-*MSO 506*)	M 5431	Martinolich SB Co	23 Feb 1956
SGOMBRO (ex-*MSO 517*)	M 5432	Tampa Marine Co	12 May 1957
SQUALO (ex-*MSO 518*)	M 5433	Tampa Marine Co	20 June 1957

Displacement, tons: 665 standard; 750 full load
Dimensions, feet (metres): 173 oa × 35 × 13·6 *(52·7 × 10·7 × 4)*
Gun: 1—40 mm, 56 cal
Main engines: 2 GM 8-278 ANW diesels; 2 shafts; 1 600 bhp = 14 knots
Oil fuel, tons: 46
Range, miles: 3 000 at 10 knots
Complement: 51 (7 officers, 44 men)

Wooden hulls and non-magnetic diesels of stainless steel alloy. Controllable pitch propellers. *Storione,* launched on 13 Nov 1954, *Salmone,* launched on 19 Feb 1955 transferred at San Diego, on 17 June 1956.

Radar: One 3 ST 7/DG.

STORIONE   6/1976, Dr. Giorgio Arra

13 Ex-US "ADJUTANT" CLASS (MINESWEEPERS/HUNTERS—COASTAL)

CASTAGNO M 5504	LARICE M 5510	PINO M 5514
CEDRO M 5505	NOCE M 5511	PLATANO M 5516
FAGGIO M 5507	OLMO M 5512	QUERCIA M 5517
FRASSINO M 5508	ONTANO M 5513	MANDORLO M 5519
GELSO M 5509		

Displacement, tons: 378 standard; 405 full load *(Mandorlo 360)*
Dimensions, feet (metres): 138 pp; 144 oa × 26·5 × 8·5 *(42·1; 43·9 × 8·1 × 2·6)*
Gun: 1—20 mm
Main engines: 2 diesels; 2 shafts; 1 200 bhp = 13·5 knots
Oil fuel, tons: 25
Range, miles: 2 500 at 10 knots
Complement: 31 (2 officers, 29 men)

Wooden hulled and constructed throughout of anti-magnetic materials. All commissioned Aug 1953-Dec 1954 and transferred by the US in 1953-54. Originally class of 18. *Pioppo* used for surveying. *Mandorlo* now converted for minehunting in 1975.

Builders: *Castagno* (Grebe, Chicago), *Cedro* (Berg SY), *Faggio* (Lake Union Co, Seattle), *Frassino* (Blaine), *Gelso* (Grebe, Chicago), *Larice* (Lake Union Co), *Noce* (Bellingham SY), *Olmo* (Bellingham SY), *Ontano* (Grebe, Chicago), *Pino, Platano* and *Quercia* (Bellingham SY).

ONTANO   6/1976, Dr. Giorgio Arra

17 "AGAVE" CLASS (MINESWEEPERS—COASTAL)

BAMBU M 5521	AGAVE M 5531	GLICINE M 5537
EBANO M 5522	ALLORO M 5532	LOTO M 5538
MANGO M 5523	EDERA M 5533	TIMO M 5540
MOGANO M 5524	GAGGIA M 5534	TRIFOGLIO M 5541
PALMA M 5525	GELSOMINO M 5535	VISCHIO M 5542
SANDALO M 5527	GIAGGIOLO M 5536	

Displacement, tons: 375 standard; 405 full load
Dimensions, feet (metres): 144 oa × 25·6 × 8·5 *(43 × 8 × 2·6)*
Guns: 2—20 mm 70 cal
Main engines: 2 diesels; 2 shafts; 1 200 bhp = 13·5 knots
Oil fuel, tons: 25
Range, miles: 2 500 at 10 knots
Complement: 38 (5 officers, 33 men)

Non-magnetic minesweepers of composite wooden and alloy construction similar to those transferred from the US but built in Italian yards; all completed Nov 1956-April 1957. Originally class of nineteen. *Mirto* now used for surveying.

Builders: CRDA Monfalcone: *Agave, Alloro, Edera, Bambu, Ebano, Mango, Mogano, Palma, Sandalo.* Baglietto, Varazze: *Gaggia, Gelsomino.* Picchiotti, Viareggio: *Giaggiolo, Glicine.* Celli, Venezia: *Loto.* Costaguta, Voltri: *Timo.* CN, Taranto: *Trifoglio.* Cant. Mediterraneo: *Vischio.*

Radar: 3 ST 7/DG.

AGAVE   6/1975, Dr. Giorgio Arra

ITALY 269

10 "ARAGOSTA" CLASS (MINESWEEPERS—INSHORE)

ARAGOSTA M 5450	**GRANCHIO** M 5458	**POLIPO** M 5463
ASTICE M 5452	**MITILO** M 5459	**PORPORA** M 5464
GAMBERO M 5457	**PINNA** M 5462	**RICCIO** M 5465
		SCAMPO M 5466

Displacement, tons: 188 full load
Dimensions, feet (metres): 106 × 21 × 6 *(32·5 × 6·4 × 1·8)*
Main engines: 2 diesels; 1 000 bhp = 14 knots
Oil fuel, tons: 15
Range, miles: 2 000 at 9 knots
Complement: 16 (4 officers, 12 men)

Similar to the British "Ham" class. All constructed to the order of NATO in 1955-57. All names of small sea creatures. Designed armament of one 20 mm gun not mounted. Originally class of twenty.

Builders: CRDA Monfalcone: *Aragosta, Astice.* Picchiotti, Viareggio: *Gambero, Granchio, Mitilo.* Costaguta, Voltri: *Pinna, Polipo, Porpora.* Apuano, Marina di Currara: *Riccio, Scampo.*

PORPORA   6/1976, Dr. Giorgio Arra

SURVEY VESSELS

Name	No.	Builders	Commissioned
AMMIRAGLIO MAGNAGHI	A 5303	Cantieri Navali di Tirreno é Riuniti	2 May 1975

Displacement, tons: 1 700
Dimensions, feet (metres): 271·3 × 44·9 × 11·5 *(82·7 × 13·7 × 3·5)*
Aircraft: 1—AB 204 helicopter
Gun: 1—40 mm
Main engines: 2 GM B 306 SS diesels = 3 000 hp; 1 shaft (cp propeller); Auxiliary electric motor—240 hp = 4 knots
Speed, knots: 16
Range, miles: 6 000 at 12 knots (1 diesel); 4 200 at 16 knots (2 diesels)
Complement: 140 (15 officers, 15 scientists, 110 men)

Ordered under 1972 programme. Laid down 13 June 1973. Launched 11 Oct 1974. Fitted with flight-deck and hangar, bow thruster, full air-conditioning, bridge engine controls, flume-type stabilisers and fully equipped for oceanographical studies.

Radar: Two RM 20.

AMMIRAGLIO MAGNAGHI   6/1976, Dr. Giorgio Arra

Name	No.	Builders	Commissioned
MIRTO	A 5306	Breda, Porta Marghera	4 Aug 1956
PIOPPO	A 5307	Bellingham SY, Seattle	31 July 1954

Mirto of the "Agave" class and *Pioppo* of the "Adjutant" class (see Minewarfare section for details) have been converted for surveying duties.

MIRTO   1973, Dr. Giorgio Arra

SERVICE FORCES

2 REPLENISHMENT TANKERS

Name	No.	Builders	Commissioned
STROMBOLI	A 5327	Cantiere Navali Riuniti, Riva Trigoso	1975
VESUVIO	A 5329	Cantiere del Muggiano	1978

Displacement, tons: 3 556 light; 8 706 full load
Dimensions, feet (metres): 403·4 oa × 59 × 21·3 *(123 oa × 18 × 6·5)*
Guns: 1—76 mm/62 cal OTO Melara; 2—40 mm
Main engines: 2 Fiat diesels C428 SS; 11 400 hp; 1 shaft; 4-bladed LIPS propeller
Speed, knots: 20
Complement: 115 (9 officers, 106 men)

Stromboli laid down on 1 Oct 1973. Launched 20 Feb 1975. *Vesuvio* ordered Aug 1976 and launched 4 June 1977. *Vesuvio* is the first large ship to be built at Muggiano (near La Spezia) since the war and the first with funds under Legge Navale 1975.

Aircraft: Helicopter flight deck but no hangar.

Capacity: 3 000 tons FFO; 1 000 tons dieso, 400 tons lub oil, 100 tons other stores.

Radar/Fire control: One Orion RTN 10X for Argo 10/Elsag NA 10 FCS.

STROMBOLI   10/1975, Commander Aldo Fraccaroli

270 ITALY

2 EXPERIMENTAL SHIPS

Name	No.	Builders	Commissioned
QUARTO	A 5314	Taranto Naval Shipyard	1967

Displacement, tons: 764 standard; 980 full load
Dimensions, feet (metres): 226·4 × 31·3 × 6 *(69·1 × 9·5 × 1·8)*
Guns: 4—40 mm (2 twin)
Main engines: 3 diesels; 2 300 bhp = 13 knots
Range, miles: 1 300 at 13 knots

Laid down on 19 March 1966 and launched on 18 March 1967. The design is intermediate between that of LSM and LCT. She is now being used as experimental ship for new weapon-systems trials and evaluation. Currently employed on Otomat trials with 2 launchers forward and requisite aerials on mast and bridge.

QUARTO (fitted for missile trials)   6/1975, Commander Aldo Fraccaroli

BARBARA

Displacement, tons: 195
Dimensions, feet (metres): 98·4 × 20·7 × 4·9 *(30 × 6·3 × 1·5)*
Main engines: 2 diesels; 600 hp = 12 knots

A fishing vessel purchased and converted for research work in 1975.
Built by Castracani, Ancona.

1 Ex-US "BARNEGAT" CLASS (SUPPORT SHIP)

Name	No.	Builders	Commissioned
PIETRO CAVEZZALE (ex-USS Oyster Bay, ex-AGP 6, AVP 28)	A 5301	Lake Washington Shipyard	1943

Displacement, tons: 1 766 standard; 2 800 full load
Dimensions, feet (metres): 311·8 oa × 41 × 13·5 *(95 × 12·5 × 3·7)*
Guns: 1—76 mm; 2—40 mm, 56 cal
Main engines: 2 sets Fairbanks Morse 38 D8 1/8 diesels; 2 shafts; 6 080 bhp = 16 knots
Oil fuel, tons: 300
Range, miles: 10 000 at 11 knots
Complement: 114 (7 officers, 107 men)

Former United States seaplane tender (previously motor torpedo boat tender). Launched on 7 Sept 1942. Transferred to the Italian Navy on 23 Oct 1957 and renamed.

Radar: SPS-60 and Jason.

PIETRO CAVEZZALE   6/1976, Dr. Giorgio Arra

9 Ex-GERMAN MFP TYPE (COASTAL TRANSPORTS)

MTC 1004	MTC 1006	MTC 1008	MTC 1010
MTC 1005	MTC 1007	MTC 1009	MTC 1101
			MTC 1102

Displacement, tons: 240 standard
Dimensions, feet (metres): 164 × 21·3 × 5·7 *(50 × 6·5 × 1·7)*
Guns: 2 or 3—20 or 37 mm
Main engines: 2 or 3 diesels; 500 bhp = 10 knots
Complement: 19 (1 officer, 18 men)

Moti-Trasporti Costieri, MTC 1004 to 1010 are Italian MZ *(Motozattere)*. MTC 1101 and 1102 ex-German built in Italy.

MTC 1006   1974, Italian Navy

19 Ex-US LCM TYPE

MTM 9901	MTM 9909	MTM 9914	MTM 9920	MTM 9925
MTM 9902	MTM 9911	MTM 9915	MTM 9922	MTM 9926
MTM 9905	MTM 9912	MTM 9918	MTM 9923	MTM 9927
	MTM 9913	MTM 9919	MTM 9924	MTM 9928

Displacement, tons: 20 standard
Dimensions, feet (metres): 49·5 × 14·8 × 4·2 *(15·1 × 4·5 × 1·3)*
Guns: 2—20 mm
Main engines: Diesels; speed 12 knots

Built in 1943-44. Transferred 1952-53.

37 US LCVP TYPE

MTP 9703	MTP 9715	MTP 9730	MTP 9739	MTP 9747
MTP 9707	MTP 9719	MTP 9732	MTP 9740	MTP 9748
MYP 9708	MTP 9720	MTP 9733	MTP 9741	MTP 9749
MTP 9710	MTP 9723	MTP 9734	MTP 9742	MTP 9750
MTP 9711	MTP 9727	MTP 9735	MTP 9743	MTP 9751
MTP 9714	MTP 9728	MTP 9736	MTP 9744	MTP 9752
	MTP 9729	MTP 9737	MTP 9745	MTP 9753
		MTP 9738	MTP 9746	MTP 9754

Displacement, tons: 8 standard
Dimensions, feet (metres): 36·5 × 10·8 × 3 *(11·1 × 3·3 × 0·9)*
Guns: 2 MG
Main engines: Diesels; speed 12 knots

MTP 9703 to 9723 are former US landing craft of the LCVP type. Transferred 1952, 1956, 1965, 1970, 1972. MTP 9727 and following craft of similar characteristics are of Italian construction.

1 HOVERCRAFT

HC 9801

SR N6 hovercraft from UK in service since 1968.

ITALY 271

MISCELLANEOUS

TRAINING SHIPS

Name	No.	Builders	Commissioned
AMERIGO VESPUCCI	A 5312	Castellammare	15 May 1931

Displacement, tons: 3 543 standard; 4 146 full load
Dimensions, feet (metres): 229·5 pp; 270 oa hull; 330 oa bowsprit × 51 × 22 *(70; 82·4; 100 × 15·5 × 7)*
Guns: 4—3 in, 50 cal; 1—20 mm
Main engines: 2 Fiat diesels with electric drive to 2 Marelli motors, 1 shaft; 2 000 hp = 10 knots
Sail area: 22 604 square feet
Endurance: 5 450 miles at 6·5 knots
Complement: 243 (13 officers, 230 men)

Launched on 22 March 1930. Hull, masts and yards are of steel. Extensively refitted at La Spezia Naval Dockyard in 1964.

AMERIGO VESPUCCI *1974, Wright and Logan*

Name	No.	Builders	Commissioned
PALINURO (ex-*Commandant Louis Richard*)	A 5311	Ch. Dubigeon, Nantes	1934

Displacement, tons: 1 042 standard; 1 450 full load
Measurement, tons: 858 gross
Dimensions, feet (metres): 204 pp; 226·3 oa × 32 × 18·7 *(59 × 10 × 4·8)*
Main engines: 1 diesel; 1 shaft; 450 bhp = 7·5 knots
Endurance, miles: 5 390 at 7·5 knots
Sail area: 1 152 square feet
Complement: 47

Barquentine launched in 1934. Purchased in 1951. Rebuilt in 1954-55 and commissioned in Italian Navy on 1 July 1955. She was one of the last two French Grand Bank cod-fishing Barquentines. Owned by the Armement Glâtre she was based at St Malo until bought by Italy.

PALINURO *1968, Italian Navy*

Name	No.	Builders	Commissioned
CORSARO II	A 5316	Costaguta Yard, Voltri	6 Jan 1961

Measurement, tons: 47
Dimensions, feet (metres): 69 × 15·4 × 9·8 *(21 × 4·7 × 3)*
Sail area: 2 200 square feet
Complement: 14 (12 officers, 2 men)

Special yacht for sail training and oceanic navigation. RORC class.

Name	No.	Builders	Commissioned
STELLA POLARE	A 5313	Sangermani, Chiavari	7 Oct 1965

Measurement, tons: 41
Dimensions, feet (metres): 68·6 × 15·4 × 9·5 *(20·9 × 4·7 × 2·9)*
Auxiliary engines: 1 Mercedes-Benz diesel, 96 bhp
Sail area: 2 117 square feet
Complement: 14 (8 officers, 6 men)

Yawl rigged built as a sail training vessel for the Italian Navy.

NETLAYERS

1 "ALICUDI" CLASS

Name	No.	Builders	Commissioned
ALICUDI (ex-USS *AN 99*)	A 5304	Ansaldo, Leghorn	1955

Displacement, tons: 680 standard; 834 full load
Dimensions, feet (metres): 151·8 pp; 165·3 oa × 33·5 × 10·5 *(46·3 × 10·2 × 3·2)*
Guns: 1—40 mm, 70 cal; 4—20 mm, 70 cal
Main engines: Diesel-electric; 1 200 shp = 12 knots
Complement: 51 (5 officers, 46 men)

Built to the order of NATO. Laid down on 22 April 1954 and launched on 11 July 1954.

ALICUDI *6/1975, Dr. Giorgio Arra*

LIGHTHOUSE TENDERS

3 Ex-BRITISH LCT (3) TYPE

MTF 1301 A 5361   MTF 1302 A 5362   MTF 1303 A 5363

Displacement, tons: 296 light; 700 full load
Dimensions, feet (metres): 192 × 31 × 7 *(58·6 × 9·5 × 2·1)*
Guns: 1—40 mm, 56 cal; 2—20 mm, 70 cal
Main engines: Diesel; 1 shaft = 8 knots
Complement: 23 (3 officers, 20 men)

Converted to lighthouse stores transports.

MTF 1301 *1968, Italian Navy*

SALVAGE SHIPS

1 NEW CONSTRUCTION

Name	No.	Builders	Commissioned
ANTEO	—	C.N. Breda-Mestre	April 1979

Displacement, tons: 3 200 full load
Dimensions, feet (metres): 324·7 × 47 × 31·7 *(98·4 × 15·8 × 9·6)*
Aircraft: 1 helicopter
Guns: 2—20 mm
Main engines: Diesel-electric; 3 Fiat GMT A-230 diesels; 8 100 hp; 1 electric motor; 4 000 hp
Speed, knots: 19
Range, miles: 4 000 at 14 knots

Comprehensively fitted with flight deck and hangar, extensive salvage gear, one DSRV to starboard, two LCVPs to port, two lifeboats under helicopter deck and one in chute aft. Three fire-fighting systems. Bow thruster. Full towing equipment.
Ordered mid 1977 for launch on Oct 1978.

Name	No.	Builders	Commissioned
PROTEO (ex-*Perseo*)	A 5310	Cantieri Navali Riuniti, Ancona	24 Aug 1951

Displacement, tons: 1 865 standard; 2 147 full load
Dimensions, feet (metres): 220·5 pp; 248 oa × 38 × 21 *(67·3; 75·6 × 11·6 × 6·4)*
Gun: 1—3·9 in
Main engines: 2 diesels; 4 800 bhp; single shaft = 16 knots
Range, miles: 7 500 at 13 knots
Complement: 130 (10 officers, 120 men)

Laid down at Cantieri Navali Riuniti, Ancona, in 1943. Suspended in 1944. Seized by Germans and transferred to Trieste. Construction re-started at Cantieri Navali Riuniti, Ancona, in 1949. Formerly mounted one 3·9 in gun and two 20 mm.

PROTEO (gun now removed) *Italian Navy*

272 ITALY

REPAIR CRAFT

7 Ex-BRITISH LCT 3s

| MOC 1201 A 5311 | MOC 1203 A 5313 | MOC 1205 A 5315 | MOC 1208 A 5318 |
| MOC 1202 A 5312 | MOC 1204 A 5314 | MOC 1207 A 5317 | |

Displacement, tons: 350 standard; 640 full load
Dimensions, feet (metres): 192 × 31 × 7 *(58·6 × 9·5 × 2·1)*
Guns: 2—40 mm; 2—20 mm (2 ships have 2—40 mm and 1 ship has 3—20 mm)
Main engines: Diesel = 8 knots
Complement: 24 (3 officers, 21 men)

Originally converted as repair craft. Other duties have been taken over—MOC 1207 and 1208 are ammunition transports and MOC 1201 is used for torpedo trials.

MOC 1201 (with torpedo tube)   6/1976, Dr. Giorgio Arra

WATER CARRIERS

PIAVE A 5354

4 973 tons full load—launched 1971 by Orlando (Livorno) and commissioned 23 May 1973. Complement 55 (7 officers, 48 men).

Guns: 4—40 mm (twins).

PIAVE   1/1977, J. A. Verhoog

Name	No.	Builders	Commissioned
BASENTO	A 5356	Inma di La Spezia	1970
BRADANO	A 5357	Inma di La Spezia	1971
BRENTA	A 5358	Inma di La Spezia	1972

1 914 tons. Laid down in 1969-70. Complement 24 (3 officers, 21 men)

Guns: 2—20 mm

BASENTO   6/1976, Dr. Giorgio Arra

ADIGE (ex-*YW 92*) A 5369   **TICINO** (ex-*YW 79*) A 5377
TANARO (ex-*YW 99*) A 5376

Ex-US Army YW type. 1 470 tons full load. Complement 35 (4 officers, 31 men).

Guns: 3—20 mm.

Builders: *Adige* and *Tanaro*, Rochester NY; *Ticino*, Bethlehem, New Orleans.

TANARO   6/1976, Dr. Giorgio Arra

MINCIO A 5374

645 tons. Launched in 1929. Complement 19 (1 officer, 18 men).

BORMIDA A 5359

Complement 11 (1 officer, 10 men)

TIMAVO

645 tons. Built by COMI, Venezia, 1926.

OFANTO

250 tons. Built 1913-14.

SIMETO   STURA

Small water carriers of 167 and 126 tons displacement, respectively.

TUGS

CICLOPE A 5319

Displacement, tons: 1 200
Dimensions, feet (metres): 157·5 × 32·5 × 13 *(48 × 9·8 × 4)*
Main engines: Triple expansion; 1 shaft; 1 000 ihp = 8 knots

Commissioned 1947.

Name	No.	Builders	Commissioned
ATLANTE	A 5317	Visentini-Donada	14 Aug 1975
PROMETEO	A 5318	Visentini-Donada	14 Aug 1975

Displacement, tons: 750 full load
Dimensions, feet (metres): 116·7 × 28·8 × 14·8 *(39 × 9·6 × 4·1)*
Main engines: Diesel; 1 shaft; cp propeller; 2 670 hp = 13·5 knots

Both launched 1974.

ATLANTE   1975, Dr. Luigi Accorsi

COLOSSO (ex-*LT 214*) A 5320   **FORTE** (ex-*LT 159*) A 5321

Displacement, tons: 525 standard; 835 full load
Dimensions, feet (metres): 142·8 × 32·8 × 11 *(43·6 × 10 × 3·4)*
Main engines: 2 diesel-electric; 690 hp = 11 knots

Ex-US Army. Built in 1943-44. Transferred 1948.

COLOSSO   6/1976, Dr. Giorgio Arra

SAN GIUSTO A 5326

Displacement, tons: 486 standard
Main engines: 900 hp = 12 knots

Built in 1952 by CNR, Palermo.

GAGLIARDO A 5322 (1938)   **ERCOLE** A 5388 (1971)
ROBUSTO A 5323 (1939)   **VIGOROSO** Y 451 (1971)

Displacement, tons: 389 standard; 506 full load
Main engines: 1 000 ihp = 8 knots

ITALY/IVORY COAST

PORTO D'ISCHIA Y 436   **RIVA TRIGOSO** Y 443

Displacement, tons: 296 full load
Dimensions, feet (metres): 83·7 × 23·3 × 10·8 (25·5 × 7·1 × 3·3)
Main engines: Diesel; 1 shaft; 850 bhp = 12·1 knots

Both launched in Sep 1969 by CNR Riva Trigoso. Controllable pitch propeller. *Porto d'Ischia* commissioned 1970, *Riva Trigosa*, 1969.

MISENO   **MONTE CRISTO**

Displacement, tons: 285
Main engines: 1 diesel GM 8/567, 700 shp.

Former United States Navy harbour tugs. Both commissioned 1 July 1948.

CAPRERA Y 418 (1972)   **PORTO PISANO** Y 438 (1937)
LEVANZO Y 426 (1973)   **PORTO RECANATI** Y 441 (1937)
PANTELLERIA Y 432 (1972)   **SALVORE** Y 445 (1927)
PIANOSA Y 434 (1914)   **TINO** Y 447 (1930)

Displacement, tons: 270
Dimensions, feet (metres): 88·8 × 22 × 10 (27·1 × 6·7 × 3·1)
Main engines: 600 ihp = 9 knots

Principally employed as harbour tugs.

FAVIGNANA Y 424 (1973)   **USTICA** Y 448 (1973)

Displacement, tons: 270 standard
Dimensions, feet (metres): 114·8 × 29·5 × 13 (35 × 9 × 4)
Main engines: Triple expansion; 1 shaft; 1 200 hp = 13 knots

AUSONIA   **PANARIA**

Displacement, tons: 240

Both launched in 1945. Coastal tugs for general duties.

VENTIMIGLIA

Displacement, tons: 230 standard
Dimensions, feet (metres): 108·2 × 23 × 7·2 (33 × 7 × 2·2)
Main engines: 627 hp = 11 knots

Commissioned Jan 1940.

PASSERO Y 439 (1934)   **RIZZUTO** Y 473 (1956)   **CIRCEO** Y 433 (1956)

Principally employed as ferry tugs.

ALBENGA Y 412 (1973)   **LINARO** Y 430 (1913)
ARZACHENA Y 414 (1931)   **MESCO** Y 435 (1933)
ASINARA Y 415 (1934)   **NISIDA** Y 437 (1943)
LAMPEDUSA Y 416 (1972)   **PIOMBINO** Y 440 (1969)
BOEO Y 417 (1943)   **SAN BENEDETTO** Y 446 (1941)
CARBONARA Y 419 (1936)   **SPERONE** Y 454 (1965)
CHIOGGIA Y 421 (1919)   **No 78** Y 469 (1965)
POZZI Y 422 (1912)   **No 96** Y 474 (1962)

Small tugs for harbour duties.

RP 101 Y 403 (1972)   **RP 105** Y 408 (1974)   **RP 109** Y 456 (1975)
RP 102 Y 404 (1972)   **RP 106** Y 410 (1974)   **RP 110** Y 458 (1975)
RP 103 Y 406 (1974)   **RP 107** Y 413 (1974)   **RP 111** Y 460 (1975)
RP 104 Y 407 (1974)   **RP 108** Y 452 (1975)   **RP 112** Y 462 (1975)

Displacement, tons: 36 standard
Dimensions, feet (metres): 61·6 × 14·6 × 5·9 (18·8 × 4·5 × 1·8)
Main engines: 1 diesel; 500 hp

Built by Cantiere Navale Visentini-Donado (Rovigo).

GOVERNMENT MARITIME FORCES

CAPTAINS OF THE PORTS
GUARDIA DI FINANZA DI MARE

Both organisations deploy considerable numbers of craft of differing sizes many of which are armed.

IVORY COAST

Ministerial

Minister of Defence and Civic Services:
Kouadio M'Bahia Ble

Bases

Use made of ports at Abidjan, Sassandra, Tabou and San Pedro

Personnel

1977: 240 officers and men

Mercantile Marine

Lloyd's Register of Shipping:
53 vessels of 114 191 tons gross

Future Plans

Eventually it is intended to organise the navy into two coastal patrol squadrons.

LIGHT FORCES

2 FRANCO-BELGE TYPE

Name	No.	Builders	Commissioned
VIGILANT	—	SFCN	1968
LE VALEUREUX	—	SFCN	25 Sept 1976

Displacement, tons: 235 standard (250 *Valeureux*)
Dimensions, feet (metres): 149·3 pp; 155·8 oa × 23·6 × 8·2 (45·5; 47·5 × 7 × 2·6)
 (*Valeureux* 157·5 feet oa *(48 metres)*)
Missiles: 8—SS12
Guns: 2—40 mm
Main engines: 2 AGO diesels; 2 shafts; 4 220 bhp = 18·5 knots (*Valeureux* 22 knots)
Range, miles: 2 000 at 15 knots
Complement: 25 (3 officers, and 22 men)

Vigilant laid down in Feb 1967. Launched on 23 May 1967. Sister ship to *Malaika* of Malagasy Navy and to *Saint Louis* and *Popenguine* of Senegal and similar craft in Tunisia and Cameroons. *Le Valeureux* ordered Oct 1974, laid down 20 Oct 1975, launched 8 March 1976.

1 "PATRA" TYPE (LARGE PATROL CRAFT)

Name	No.	Builders	Commissioned
—	—	A. et C. Auroux, Arcachon	1979

Displacement, tons: 115 standard; 130 full load
Dimensions, feet (metres): 187 × 18·0 × 5·2 (37 × 5·5 × 1·6)
Missiles: 6—SS-12
Gun: 1—40 mm
Main engines: 2 AGO V12 CZSHR diesels; 2 shafts (cp propellers); 4 000 shp = 26 knots
Range, miles: 750 at 20 knots
Complement: 19 (2 officers, 17 ratings)

Of similar design to French "Trident" class. Laid down 7 July 1977.

1 Ex-FRENCH VC TYPE

Name	No.	Builders	Commissioned
PERSEVERANCE (ex-*VC 9, P 759*)	—	Constructions Mécaniques de Normandie, Cherbourg	25 Feb 1958

Displacement, tons: 75 standard; 82 full load
Dimensions, feet (metres): 104·5 × 15·5 × 5·5 (31·8 × 4·7 × 1·7)
Guns: 2—20 mm
Main engines: 2 Mercedes-Benz (MTU) diesels; 2 shafts; 2 700 bhp = 28 knots
Oil fuel, tons: 10
Range, miles: 1 100 at 16·5 knots; 800 at 21 knots
Complement: 15

Former French seaward defence motor launch. Transferred from France to Ivory Coast 26 April 1963. Recently reported as unserviceable.

PERSEVERANCE   *1964, Ivory Coast Armed Forces*

5 RIVER PATROL CRAFT

Of varying sizes from 24—34 feet. Used for river and lake patrols.

274 IVORY COAST/JAMAICA

LANDING CRAFT

1 BATRAL TYPE (LIGHT TRANSPORT)

Name	No.	Builders	Commissioned
ELEPHANT	—	Dubigeon/Normandy Nantes	1976

Displacement, tons: 750 standard; 1 250 full load
Dimensions, feet (metres): 262·4 × 42·6 × 7·5 *(80 × 13 × 2·3)*
Guns: 2—40 mm; 2—81 mm mortars
Main engines: 2 diesels; 2 shafts; 1 800 hp = 16 knots
Range, miles: 3 500 at 13 knots
Complement: 39

Ordered 20 Aug 1974. Laid down 1975.

2 LCVP

Displacement, tons: 7
Guns: 2 MG
Main engines: Mercedes diesels
Speed, knots: 9

Built in Abidjan in 1970.

MISCELLANEOUS

LOKODJO

Displacement, tons: 450

Now used as a training and supply ship. Built in West Germany in 1953 and purchased in 1970. Trawler type.

1 SMALL TRANSPORT

Capable of carrying 25 men.

JAMAICA

Defence Force Coast Guard

Jamaica, which became independent within the Commonwealth on 6 Aug 1962, formed the Coast Guard as the Maritime Arm of the Defence Force. This is based at HMJS Cagway, Port Royal.

Administration

Commanding Officer Jamaica Defence Force Coast Guard:
  Commander L. E. Scott

Personnel

1978: 18 officers, 115 petty officers and ratings *(Coast Guard Reserve:* 16 officers, 30 men)

Training

a) Officers: BRNC Dartmouth and other RN Establishments, RCN and US Search and Rescue School.
b) Ratings: JMF Training depot, RN, RCN, US Search and Rescue School and MTU Engineering Germany.

Mercantile Marine

Lloyd's Register of Shipping: 5 vessels of 6 740 tons gross.

LIGHT FORCES

Name	No.	Builders	Commissioned
DISCOVERY BAY	P 4	Sewart Seacraft Inc, Berwick, La, USA	3 Nov 1966
HOLLAND BAY	P 5	Sewart Seacraft Inc, Berwick, La, USA	4 April 1967
MANATEE BAY	P 6	Sewart Seacraft Inc, Berwick, La, USA	9 Aug 1967

Displacement, tons: 60
Dimensions, feet (metres): 85 × 18 × 6·0 *(25·9 × 5·7 × 1·8)*
Guns: 3—0·50 cal Browning
Main engines: 3 MTU 8V 331 TC81 diesels, 3 shafts; 3 000 shp = 30 knots
Oil fuel, tons: 13
Range, miles: 800 at 20 knots
Complement: 11 (2 officers, 9 ratings)

All aluminium construction. *Discovery Bay,* the prototype was launched in Aug 1966. *Holland Bay* and *Manatee Bay* were supplied under the US Military Assistance programme. All three boats were extensively refitted and modified in 1972-73 by the builders with GM 12V 71 Turbo-injected engines to give greater range, speed and operational flexibility. They were again re-engined and refitted at Swift Ship Inc, Louisiana, USA—*Discovery Bay* in late 1975, *Holland Bay* in mid-1977 and *Manatee Bay* in late 1977.

DISCOVERY BAY   1973, Jamaica CG

Name	No.	Builders	Commissioned
FORT CHARLES	P 7	Sewart Seacraft Inc, Berwick, La, USA	1974

Displacement, tons: 103
Dimensions, feet (metres): 105 × 22 × 7 *(31·5 × 6·6 × 2·1)*
Guns: 1—20 mm; 2—0·50 cal MG
Main engines: 2 Maybach (MTU) MB 16V 538 TB90 diesels; 7 000 shp = 32 knots
Range, miles: 1 200 at 18 knots
Complement: 16 (3 officers, 13 ratings)

Of all aluminium construction launched July 1974. Navigation equipment includes Omega Navigator
Accommodation for 24 soldiers and may be used as 24 bed mobile hospital in an emergency.

FORT CHARLES   1975, Jamaican CG

1 40 ft INSHORE PATROL CRAFT

With 2 Caterpillar V-8 diesels and a crew of 3.

1 110 ft PATROL CRAFT

With 3 Cummings V-8 diesels and a crew of 5.

JAPAN

Naval Board

Chief of the Maritime Staff, Defence Agency:
  Admiral Teiji Nakamura
Commander-in-Chief, Self-Defence Fleet:
  Vice-Admiral Kiyonori Kunishima
Chief, Administration Division, Maritime Staff Office:
  Rear-Admiral Masayuki Akiyama

Diplomatic Representation

Defence (Naval) Attaché in London:
  Captain
Defence (Naval) Attaché in Washington:
  Captain Tameo Oki
Naval Attaché in Moscow:
  Captain Takao Endo
Defence Attaché in Paris:
  Colonel Yoshiaki Murata

Personnel

1976: 39 000 (including Naval Air)
1977: 42 199 (including Naval Air)

Bases

Naval—Yokosuka, Kure, Sasebo, Maizuru, Oominato
Naval Air—Atsugi, Hachinohe, Iwakuni, Kanoya, Komatsujima, Okinawa, Ozuki, Oominato, Oomura, Shimofusa, Tateyama, Tokushima.

Fleet Air Arm

14 Air ASW Sqns, P2-J, P2V-7, PS-1, S2F-1, HSS-2
4 Air Training Sqns, P2-J, P2V-7, YS-11, B-65, KM-2, Mentor, Bell-47, OH-6, HSS-2
1 Transport Sqn, YS-11
1 MCM Sqn

Present name	Incorporating	Building
1. Mitsubishi Heavy Industries	Mitsubishi Shipbuilders, Nagasaki; Shin-Mitsubishi Heavy Industries, Kobe; Mitsubishi-Nippon Heavy Industries, Yokohama	DDG and DD at Nagasaki. ASR at Yokohama. PT and ASH at Shimonoseki and Hiroshima. Submarines at Kobe.
2. Ishikawajima Harima Heavy Industries	Ishikawajima Heavy Industries, Tokyo; Kure Shipbuilders; Harima Shipbuilders	DDH, DD, DE and LST at Tokyo 1 and 2 (Yokohama) YF at Isogo.
3. Hitachi Shipbuilders	Hitachi Shipbuilders; Maizuru Heavy Industries (originally Iino Heavy Industries, Maizuru)	MSC and MSB at Maizuru and Kanagawa.
4. Sumitomo Heavy Industries	Uraga Heavy Industries (originally Uraga Dock Co); Sumitomo Machine Ltd.	DDK and DD.
5. Sasebo Heavy Industries	Originally Sasebo Senpak Kabushiki Kaishiya	LST, PC.
6. Mitsui Shipbuilders, Tamano	—	DD, DDE.
7. Kawasaki Heavy Industries, Kobe	—	Submarines.
Nippon Steel Tube Co.	—	Earlier MSC, MSB, AG at Tsurumi. Later MSC at Isogo.

Names

The practice of painting the ships' names on the broadsides of the hulls was discontinued in 1970. For submarines the painting of pennant numbers on the fins was stopped in Sept 1976.

Mercantile Marine

Lloyd's Register of Shipping:
  9 748 vessels of 41 663 188 tons gross

Defence Plan—New Construction

If programmes are agreed in period 1977-81 the fleet in 1982 will consist of: 60 DD, 16 SS, 40-45 MSC/MSB, 25-30 others, 15 supply ships, LST and special duty ships and 220 aircraft. (White Paper of 30 Oct 1976). Manpower 40 000.
In order to provide 2 DDH for each of four escort groups a further request for 4 DDH may be expected. Similarly 2 extra DDGs may be requested as well as a possible new frigate class of 6-8 ships. Further possible additions are 3 missile hydrofoils, 1 ARC, 1 AS, 1 ATS, 1 AGS and 4-5 500 ton LSMs.
The 1977 MSDF request for new construction as agreed by Dept. of Finance in Jan 1977 was for one 2 900 ton DD, one 1 500 ton frigate, one 2 200 ton submarine, two 440 ton MSC, one 4 500 ton ARC. This deleted one 3 900 ton DDG from the original request.

Naval Shipbuilders

Due to amalgamation the names of many Japanese shipyards have changed over the last twenty years and a number have been listed with their Japanese titles—Jyuko = Heavy Industries Co; Zoosen = Shipbuilders. The current situation is as follows.

Strength of the Fleet

Type	Active	Building (Projected)
Destroyers	31	3 (1)
Frigates	15	1
Corvettes	16	—
Submarines—Patrol	15	2
Fast Attack Craft—Torpedo	5	—
Patrol Craft—Coastal	10	—
LSTs	6	—
M/S Support Ships	2	—
Minesweepers—Coastal	29	3
MSBs	6	—
Training Ship	1	—
S/M Rescue Vessels	2	—
Support Tanker	1	(1)
Icebreaker	1	—
Auxiliaries	24	—
Survey Ships	6	(1)
Cable Layer	1	(1)
Training Support Ship	1	—

New Construction Programme

1973 1 DD, 1 DE, 1 SS, 2 MSC, 2 MSB, 1 PT, 1 LST
1974 1 DDK, 2 MSC, 1 LST
1975 1 DDH, 1 SS, 3 MSC, 1 LST
1976 1 DDH, 1 MSC, 1 AGS, 1 AOE
1977 MSDF request for 1 DDG, 1 DD, 1 PCE, 1 ARC, 1 SS, 2 MSC
1978 1—3 900 ton DDG, 1—2 900 ton DE, 1—1 200 ton DE, 2/3—440 ton MSC, 1—100 ton PHM, 1—2 700 ton AS

DELETIONS

Note: A number of ships on removal from the active list are classified as YAC (Harbour accommodation ship). As these have no operational value they are included as deletions marked *.

Destroyers

1974 *Ariake, Yugure* (Transferred to S. Korea for spares in 1976—scrapped).

Frigates

1972 *Kaya, Bura, Kashi, Moni, Tochi, Ume, Maki, Kusu, Matsu, Nata, Sakura,* (all ex-US PFs). *Wakaba*
1975 *Asahi* and *Hatsuhi* (ex-"Cannon" class) returned to US for disposal
1976 *Inazuma, Ikazuchi*, Akebono**
1977 *Nire** (sunk as target 19 Aug)

Corvettes

1977 *Kari, Kiji, Taka, Washi, Tsubame* (14 May), *Kamome* and *Misago* (1 Dec)

Submarine

1976 *Oyashio* (scrap list 30 Sept)

Light Forces

1972 PT 7, 9; PB 4, 11, 13-16, 18
1973 PB 1, 3, 12, 17; *Kosoku* 3
1974 PT 8; *Kosoku* 2, 4 and 5
1975 PT 10

LSTs

1972 *Hayatomo*
1974 *Oosumi*
1975 *Shimokita*
1976 *Shiretoko* (returned to US in Mar and passed to Philippines)

LSM

1974 3001

Minewarfare Forces

1972 MSB 01, 02
1974 MSB 03, 04, 05, 06 deleted, *Kusu**
1975 Five MSC converted
1976 One MSC converted

Tenders

1973 YAS 49 (ex-PT 2), YAS 52 (ex-PT 3), YAS 53 (ex-PT 4)
1974 YAS 48 (ex-PT 1), YAS 54 (ex-PT 5), YAS 55 (ex-PT 6), YAS 45 (*Suma*, ex-US YTL 749), YAS 59 (*Minho*, ex-US FS 524)
1976 YAS 51 (NAS *Ami* ex-US FS 409), YAS 3 (ex-US YTL 750), YAS 47 (ex-MSC 652)

PENNANT LIST

Submarines—Patrol

SS	521	Hayashio
	522	Wakashio
	523	Natsushio
	524	Fuyushio
	561	Ooshio
	562	Asashio
	563	Harushio
	564	Michishio
	565	Arashio
	566	Uzushio
	567	Makishio
	568	Isoshio
	569	Narushio
	570	Kuroshio
	571	Takashio
	572	New Construction
	573	New Construction

Destroyers

DD	101	Harukaze
	102	Yukikaze
	103	Ayanami
	104	Isonami
	105	Uranami
	106	Shikinami
	107	Murasame
	108	Yudachi
	109	Harusame
	110	Takanami
	111	Oonami
	112	Makinami
	113	Yamagumo
	114	Makigumo
	115	Asagumo
	116	Minegumo
	117	Natsugumo
	118	Murakumo
	119	Aokumo
	120	Akigumo
	121	New construction
	141	Haruna
	142	Hiei
	143	New Construction
	144	New Construction
	161	Akizuki
	162	Teruzuki
	163	Amatsukaze
	164	Takatsuki
	165	Kikuzuki
	166	Mochizuki
	167	Nagatsuki
	168	Tachikaze
	169	New Construction

Frigates

DE	211	Isuzu
	212	Mogami
	213	Kitakami
	214	Ooi
	215	Chikugo
	216	Ayase
	217	Mikuma
	218	Tokachi
	219	Iwase
	220	Chitose
	221	Niyodo
	222	Teshio
	223	Yoshino
	224	Kumano
	225	Noshiro

Light Forces

PC	305	Kamome
	306	Tsubame
	307	Misago
	309	Umitaka
	310	Otaka
	311	Mizutori
	312	Yamadori
	313	Otori
	314	Kasasagi
	315	Hatsukari
	316	Umidori
	317	Wakataka
	318	Kumataka
	319	Shiratori
	320	Hiyodori
811-815		PT 11-15
919-927		PB 19-27
06		Kosoku 6

Minesweepers—Coastal

MSC	617	Karato
	618	Hario
	619	Mutsure
	620	Chiburi
	621	Ootsu
	622	Kudako
	623	Rishiri
	624	Rebun
	625	Amami
	626	Urume
	627	Minase
	628	Ibuki
	629	Katsura
	630	Takami
	631	Iou
	632	Miyake
	633	Utone
	634	Awaji
	635	Toushi
	636	Teuri
	637	Murotsu
	638	Tashiro
	639	Miyato
	640	Takane
	641	Muzuki
	642	Yokose
	643	Sakate
	644	Oumi
	645	Fukue
	646	Okitsu
	647	Hashira
	648	Iwai

Minesweeping Boats

707	Nana-go
708	Hachi-go
709	Kyuu-go
710	Jyuu-go
711	Jyuu-Ichi-go
712	Jyuu-Ni-go

Minesweeper Tender

MST	473	Kouzu

MSC Support Ships

MMC	951	Souya
MST	462	Hayase

Amphibious Forces

LST	4101	Atsumi
	4102	Motobu
	4103	Nemuro
	4151	Miura
	4152	Ozika
	4153	Satsuma

Salvage Vessel

YE	41	Shobo

Submarine Rescue Ships

ASR	401	Chihaya
	402	Fusimir

Tanker

AO	411	Hamana

Fleet Support Ship

AOE	421	New Construction

Training Ship

TV	3501	Katori

Training Support Ship

ATS	4201	Azuma

Cable Layer

ARC	481	Tsugaru

Icebreaker

AGB	5001	Fuji

Surveying Ships

AGS	5101	Akashi
	5102	New Construction
	5111	Ichi-Go
	5112	Ni-Go
	5113	San-Go
	5114	Yon-Go
	5115	Go-Go

Tugs

YT	55
YT	56

Tenders

ASH	81-85	
ASY	91	Hayabusa
YAS	46	Yashima
	56	Atada
	57	Itsuki
	58	Yashiro
	60	Tsushima
	61	Toshima
	62	Shisaka
	63	Koshiki
	64	Sakito
	65	Kanawa
	66	Tsukumi
	67	Mikura
	68	Sikine
	69	Erimo
	70	Hotaka

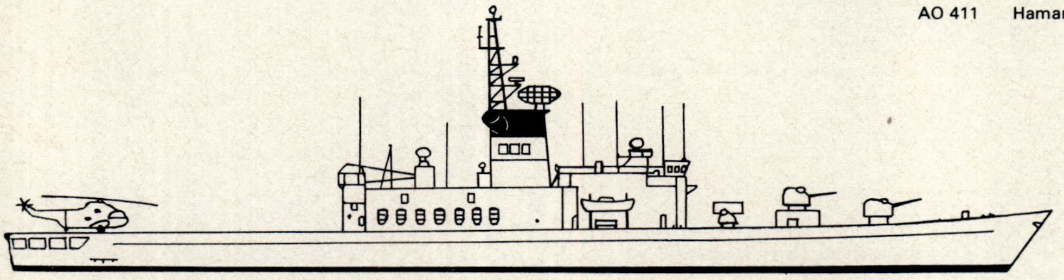

"HARUNA" Class

"TAKATSUKI" Class

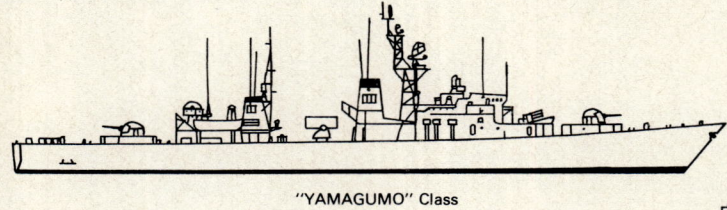

"YAMAGUMO" Class

"MINEGUMO" Class

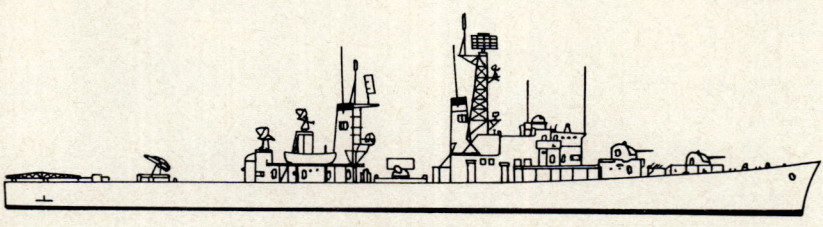

AMATSUKAZE

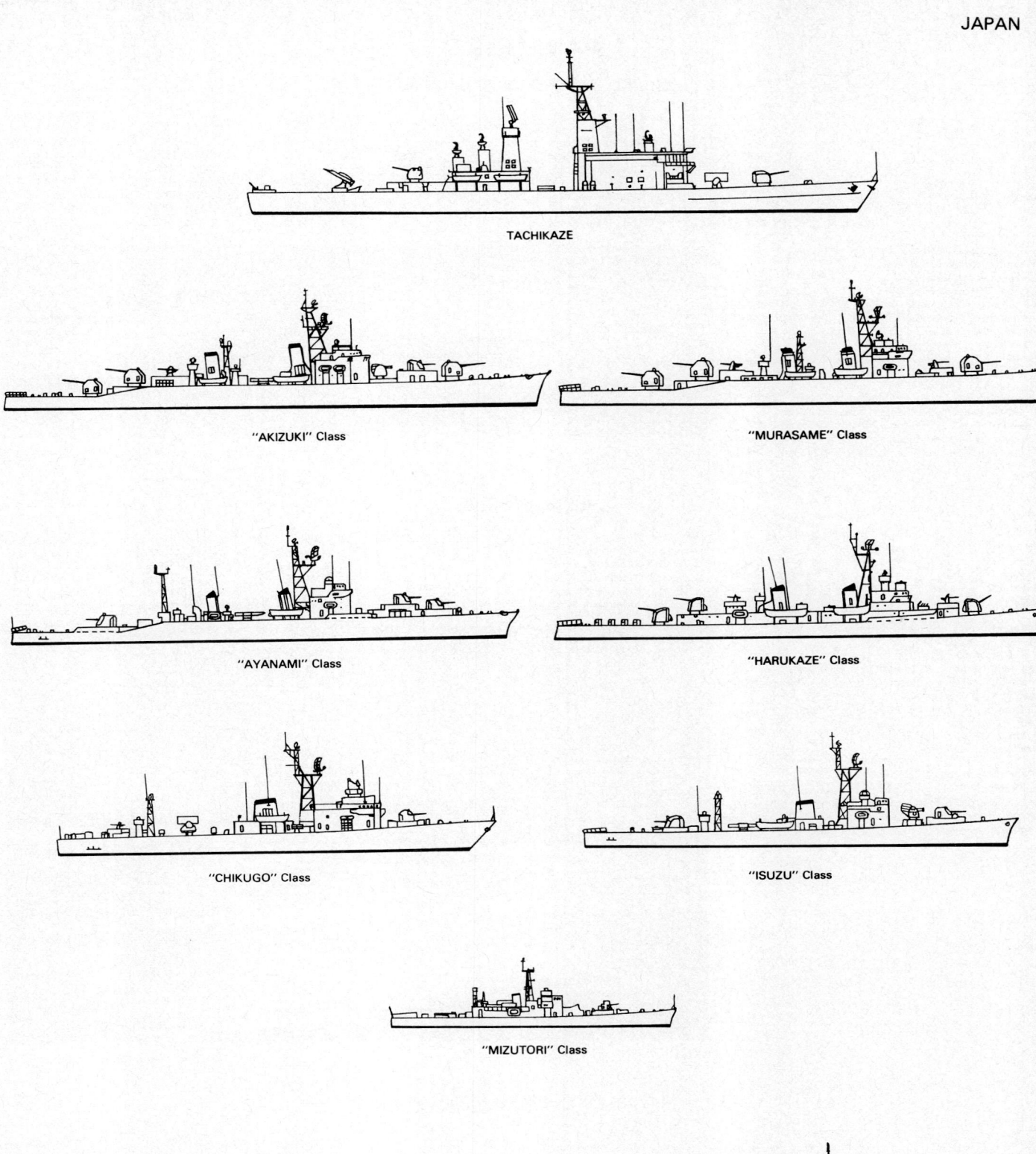

JAPAN 277

TACHIKAZE

"AKIZUKI" Class

"MURASAME" Class

"AYANAMI" Class

"HARUKAZE" Class

"CHIKUGO" Class

"ISUZU" Class

"MIZUTORI" Class

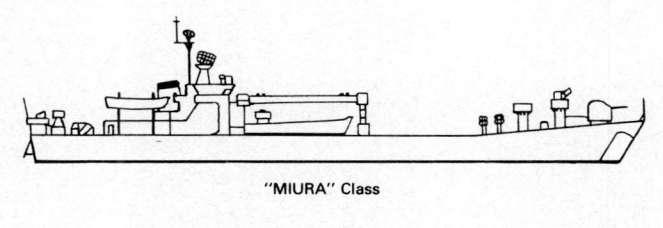

"MIURA" Class

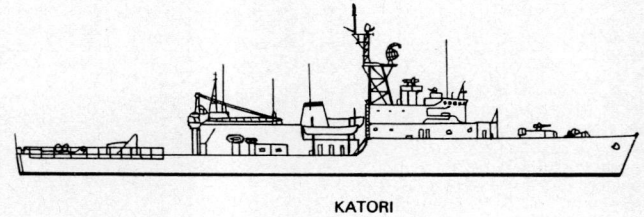

KATORI

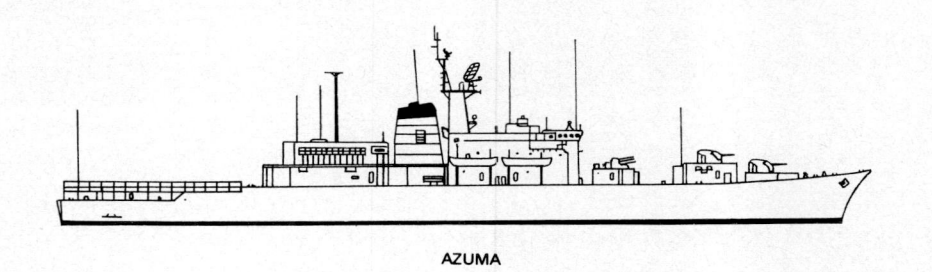

AZUMA

278 JAPAN

SUBMARINES

7 + 1 "UZUSHIO" and "IMPROVED UZUSHIO" CLASS

Name	No.	Builders	Laid down	Launched	Commissioned
UZUSHIO	SS 566	Kawasaki, Kobe	25 Sep 1968	11 Mar 1970	21 Jan 1971
MAKISHIO	SS 567	Mitsubishi, Kobe	21 June 1969	27 Jan 1971	2 Feb 1972
ISOSHIO	SS 568	Kawasaki, Kobe	9 July 1970	18 Mar 1972	25 Nov 1972
NARUSHIO	SS 569	Mitsubishi, Kobe	8 May 1971	22 Nov 1972	28 Sep 1973
KUROSHIO	SS 570	Kawasaki, Kobe	5 July 1972	22 Feb 1974	27 Nov 1974
TAKASHIO	SS 571	Mitsubishi, Kobe	6 July 1973	30 June 1975	30 Jan 1976
YAESHIO	SS 572	Kawasaki, Kobe	14 April 1975	19 May 1977	Mar 1978
—	SS 573	Mitsubishi, Kobe	3 Dec 1976	Mar 1978	1979

Displacement, tons: 1 850 standard
Length, feet (metres): 236·2 *(72·0)*
Beam, feet (metres): 29·5 *(9·0)*
Draught, feet (metres): 24·6 *(7·5)*
Torpedo tubes: 6—21 in *(533 mm);* amidships
Main machinery: 2 Kawasaki MAN diesels; 3 400 bhp; 1 shaft; 1 electric motor; 7 200 hp
Speed, knots: 12 surfaced; 20 dived
Complement: 80

Of double-hull construction and "tear-drop" form, built of HT steel to increase diving depth. New bow sonar fitted.
An enlarged version of 2 200 tons, 249·3 × 32·5 × 24·6 ft *(76 × 9·9 × 7·5 metres)* and with increased diving depth is building. First of "Improved" class is SS 573 to be equipped with Mascar.

MAKISHIO   1976, Japanese Maritime Self-Defence Force

5 "OOSHIO" CLASS

Name	No.	Builders	Laid down	Launched	Commissioned
OOSHIO	SS 561	Mitsubishi, Kobe	29 June 1963	30 April 1964	31 Mar 1965
ASASHIO	SS 562	Kawasaki, Kobe	5 Oct 1964	27 Nov 1965	13 Oct 1966
HARUSHIO	SS 563	Mitsubishi, Kobe	12 Oct 1965	25 Feb 1967	1 Dec 1967
MICHISHIO	SS 564	Kawasaki, Kobe	26 July 1966	5 Dec 1967	29 Aug 1968
ARASHIO	SS 565	Mitsubishi, Kobe	5 July 1967	24 Oct 1968	25 July 1969

Displacement, tons: 1 650 standard; *Ooshio* 1 600
Length, feet (metres): 288·7 *(88·0)*
Beam, feet (metres): 26·9 *(8·2)*
Draught, feet (metres): 16·2 *(4·9) Ooshio* 15·4 *(4·7)*
Torpedo tubes: 6—21 in *(533 mm)* (bow); 2—12·7 in A/S torpedoes in swim-out tubes
Main machinery: 2 diesels; 2 900 bhp; 2 shafts; 2 electric motors; 6 300 hp
Speed, knots: 14 surfaced; 18 dived
Complement: 80

Double-hulled boats. A bigger design to obtain improved seaworthiness, a larger torpedo capacity and more comprehensive sonar and electronic devices. *Ooshio* was built under the 1961 programme, *Asashio* 1963. Cost $5 600 000.

ASASHIO   1976, Japanese Maritime Self-Defence Force

4 "HAYASHIO" and "NATSUSHIO" CLASS

Name	No.	Builders	Laid down	Launched	Commissioned
HAYASHIO	SS 521	Shin Mitsubishi, Kobe	6 June 1960	31 July 1961	30 June 1962
WAKASHIO	SS 522	Kawasaki, Kobe	7 June 1960	28 Aug 1961	17 Aug 1962
NATSUSHIO	SS 523	Shin Mitsubishi, Kobe	5 Dec 1961	18 Sep 1962	29 June 1963
FUYUSHIO	SS 524	Kawasaki, Kobe	6 Dec 1961	14 Dec 1962	17 Sep 1963

Displacement, tons: 750 standard; (SS 521, 522); 790 standard (SS 523, 524)
Length, feet (metres): 193·6 *(59·0)* oa (SS 521, 522); 200·1 *(61·0)* oa (SS 523, 524)
Beam, feet (metres): 21·3 *(6·5)*
Draught, feet (metres): 13·5 *(4·1)*
Torpedo tubes: 3—21 in *(533 mm)* (bow)
Main machinery: 2 diesels; total 900 hp; 2 shafts; 2 electric motors, total 2 300 hp
Speed, knots: 11 surfaced; 15 dived (14 dived "Hayashio" class)
Complement: 40

Very handy and successful boats of their time, with a large safety factor, complete air-conditioning and good habitability.

"Hayashio" class SS 521-522
"Natsushio" class SS 523-524

NATSUSHIO   1976, Japanese Maritime Self-Defence Force

DESTROYERS

NEW CONSTRUCTION

Name	No.	Builders	Laid down	Launched	Commissioned
—	DD 122	Sumitomo, Uraga	—	—	—

Displacement, tons: 2 900
Aircraft: 1 HSS-2 A/S helicopter
Missiles: 2 Harpoon; 1 Seasparrow
Gun: 1—76 mm OTO Melara
A/S weapons: 1 Asroc; 2 triple US Mk 32 torpedo tubes
Main engines: COGOG; 2 Olympus TM3B; 56 000 shp; 2 Tyne RMIC; 2 shafts; 10 680 shp; (cp propellers)
Speed, knots: 30

DD 122 approved in 1977 estimates. Possible programme of 6-8 ships by 1981. Fitted with fin stabilisers.

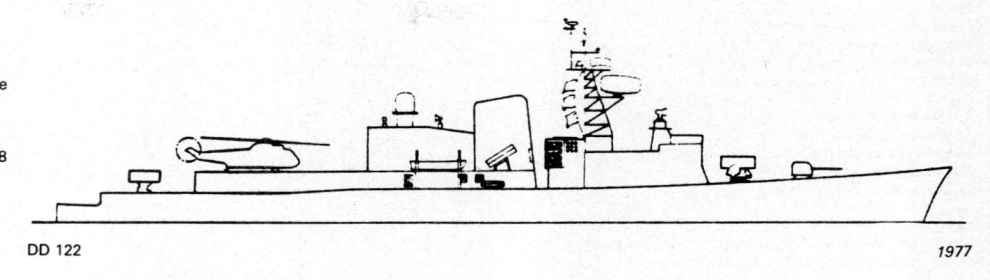

DD 122   1977

1 + 1 "TACHIKAZE" CLASS

Name	No.	Builders	Laid down	Launched	Commissioned
TACHIKAZE	DD 168	Mitsubishi, Nagasaki	19 June 1973	7 Dec 1974	26 Mar 1976
ASAKAZE	DD 169	Mitsubishi, Nagasaki	27 May 1976	Nov 1977	Mar 1979

Displacement, tons: 3 900
Dimensions, feet (metres): 443 × 47 × 15 (135 × 14·3 × 4·6)
Missiles: 1 Tartar D launcher Mk 13 Mod 3 for Standard RIM 60A SAM
Guns: 2—5 in (127 mm) 54 cal (singles)
A/S weapons: US Mk 16 Octuple Asroc launcher; 6 (2 triple) US Mk 32 torpedo tubes
Main engines: 2 turbines; 2 shafts; 60 000 hp
Speed, knots: 33
Complement: 260

DD 169 ordered 3 March 1975.

Gunnery: Mk 1 GFCS.

Radar: 3D search: AN/SPS 52.
Surface search: OPS 17.
Missile control: AN/SPG 51.

Sonar: VDS. SQS-35(J).

TACHIKAZE   1976, Japanese Maritime Self-Defence Force

2 "HARUNA" CLASS

Name	No.	Builders	Laid down	Launched	Commissioned
HARUNA	DD 141	Mitsubishi, Nagasaki	19 Mar 1970	1 Feb 1972	22 Feb 1973
HIEI	DD 142	Ishikawajima, Tokyo	8 Mar 1972	13 Aug 1973	27 Nov 1974

Displacement, tons: 4 700
Length, feet (metres): 502·0 (153·0)
Beam, feet (metres): 57·4 (17·5)
Draught, feet (metres): 16·7 (5·1)
Aircraft: 3 anti-submarine helicopters
Guns: 2—5 in (127 mm) (single)
A/S weapons: US Mk 16 Octuple Asroc launcher; 6 (2 triple) US Mk 32 torpedo tubes
Main engines: 2 turbines; 70 000 shp; 2 shafts
Speed, knots: 32
Complement: 364

Ordered under the third five-year defence programme (from 1967-71).

Gunnery: Mk 1 GFCS.

Radar: Air search: OPS-11.
Surface search: OPS-17.

Sonar: OQS-3.

HIEI   5/1976

280 JAPAN

0 + 2 "IMPROVED HARUNA" CLASS

Name	No.	Builders	Laid down	Launched	Commissioned
—	DD 143	Ishikawajima Harima, Tokyo	25 Feb 1977	Sept 1978	Mar 1980
—	DD 144	Ishikawajima Harima, Tokyo	—	1979	Mar 1981

Displacement, tons: 5 200
Length, feet (metres): 521 *(158·8)*
Beam, feet (metres): 57·5 *(17·5)*
Draught, feet (metres): 17·5 *(5·3)*
Aircraft: 3 anti-submarine helicopters
Missiles: 1 Sea Sparrow launcher
Guns: 2—5 in *(127 mm)* 54 cal (singles); 2—35 mm
A/S weapons: US Mk 16 Octuple Asroc launcher; 6 (2 triple) US Mk 32 torpedo tubes
Main engines: 2 turbines; 75 000 shp; 2 shafts
Speed, knots: 32
Complement: 370

One in 1975 programme and one in 1976 programme. To be twin funnelled. Contract for DD 144 signed 31 March 1977.

Gunnery: Mk 2 GFCS.

Radar: Air search: OPS-12 (not yet operational); OPS-28.

Sonar: OQS-101 (hull-mounted); SQS-35(J) (VDS).

4 "TAKATSUKI" CLASS

Name	No.	Builders	Laid down	Launched	Commissioned
TAKATSUKI	DD 164	Ishikawajima Harima, Tokyo	8 Oct 1964	7 Jan 1966	15 Mar 1967
KIKUZUKI	DD 165	Mitsubishi, Nagasaki	15 Mar 1966	25 Mar 1967	27 Mar 1968
MOCHIZUKI	DD 166	Ishikawajima Harima, Tokyo	25 Nov 1966	15 Mar 1968	25 Mar 1969
NAGATSUKI	DD 167	Mitsubishi, Nagasaki	2 Mar 1968	19 Mar 1969	12 Feb 1970

Displacement, tons: 3 100
Length, feet (metres): 446·2 *(136·0)* oa
Beam, feet (metres): 44·0 *(13·4)*
Draught, feet (metres): 14·5 *(4·4)*
Aircraft: 2 HSS-2 helicopters
Guns: 2—5 in *(127 mm)* 54 cal (single)
A/S weapons: 1 US Mk 16 Octuple Asroc launcher; 1 four-barrelled rocket launcher; 6 (2 triple) Mk 32 torpedo tubes
Main engines: 2 Mitsubishi WH geared turbines; 60 000 shp; 2 shafts
Boilers: 2 Mitsubishi CE
Speed, knots: 32
Range, miles: 7 000 at 20 knots
Complement: 270

Takatsuki was provided under the 1963 programme. Equipped with helicopter hangar.

Aircraft: 3 Dash helicopters exchanged for 2 HSS-2 helicopters during 1977.

Gunnery: US Mk 56 GFCS.

Radar: Air search: OPS-11.
Surface search: OPS-17.
Fire control: US Mk 35.

Sonars: VDS; SQS-35(J); *Takatsuki* (1970), *Kikuzuki* (1972). Remainder not so fitted though planned.
Hull: SQS-23 (164-165); OQS-3 (166-167).

NAGATSUKI   7/1976, USN

6 "YAMAGUMO" CLASS

Name	No.	Builders	Laid down	Launched	Commissioned
YAMAGUMO	DD 113	Mitsui, Tamano	23 Mar 1964	27 Feb 1965	29 Jan 1966
MAKIGUMO	DD 114	Uraga	10 June 1964	26 July 1965	19 Mar 1966
ASAGUMO	DD 115	Maizuru	24 June 1965	25 Nov 1966	29 Aug 1967
AOKUMO	DD 119	Sumitomo, Uraga	2 Oct 1970	30 Mar 1972	25 Nov 1972
AKIGUMO	DD 120	Sumitomo, Uraga	7 July 1972	23 Oct 1973	24 July 1974
YUUGUMO	DD 121	Sumitomo, Uraga	4 Feb 1976	31 May 1977	Mar 1978

Displacement, tons: 2 100
Length, feet (metres): 377 *(114·9)*
Beam, feet (metres): 38·7 *(11·8)*
Draught, feet (metres): 13·1 *(4)*
Guns: 4—3 in; 50 cal (2 twin)
A/S weapons: 1 US Mk 16 Octuple Asroc launcher; 1 four-barrelled rocket launcher; 6 (2 triple) Mk 32 torpedo tubes
Main engines: 6 diesels; 26 500 bhp; 2 shafts
Speed, knots: 27
Range, miles: 7 000 at 20 knots
Complement: 210

Class: DD 121 was to have been lead ship of an improved class—slightly larger with CODOG machinery giving possibly up to 32 knots. This plan has been replaced by the new DD 122 class of 2 900 tons.

Gunnery: 3 in guns to be replaced by OTO Melara 76 mm at refits.
US Mk 56 GFCS; US Mk 63 GFCS.

Radar: Air search: OPS-11.
Surface search: OPS-17.
Fire control: US Mk 35.

Sonar: Hull-mounted: SQS-23 (113-115); OQS-3 (119-121).
VDS: SQS-35(J) (113, 114, 120, 121).

AOKUMO   1976, Michael D. J. Lennon

JAPAN

3 "MINEGUMO" CLASS

Name	No.	Builders	Laid down	Launched	Commissioned
MINEGUMO	DD 116	Mitsui, Tamano	14 Mar 1967	16 Dec 1967	21 Aug 1968
NATSUGUMO	DD 117	Uraga	26 June 1967	25 July 1968	25 April 1969
MURAKUMO	DD 118	Maizuru	19 Oct 1968	15 Nov 1969	21 Aug 1970

All details as for "Yamagumo" class except:

Note difference in silhouettes between this and the "Yamagumo" class.

Aircraft: 2 Dash helicopter in place of Asroc although this will be reversed.

Gunnery: US Mk 56 GFCS; US Mk 63 GFCS.

Guns: In 1976 *Murakumo* had Y turret removed and replaced by an OTO Melara 76 mm Compact for trials. 3 in guns to be replaced by OTO Melara 76 mm at refits.

Radar: Air search: OPS-11.
Surface search: OPS-17.
Fire control: US Mk 35.

Refit: *Murakomo* refit to replace Dash with Asroc delayed until 1979.

Sonar: Hull-mounted: OQS 3.
VDS: SQS-35(J) (118).

NATSUGUMO 1972, Japanese Maritime Self-Defence Force

1 "AMATSUKAZE" CLASS

Name	No.	Builders	Laid down	Launched	Commissioned
AMATSUKAZE	DD 163	Mitsubishi, Nagasaki	29 Nov 1962	5 Oct 1963	15 Feb 1965

Displacement, tons: 3 050 standard; 4 000 full load
Length, feet (metres): 429·8 *(131·0)*
Beam, feet (metres): 44 *(13·4)*
Draught, feet (metres): 13·8 *(4·2)*
Aircraft: Helicopter
Missile launchers: 1 single Tartar
Guns: 4—3 in *(76 mm)* 50 cal, (2 twin)
A/S weapons: 1 US Mk 16 octuple Asroc launcher;
2 Hedgehogs Mk 15; 6 (2 triple) Mk 32 torpedo tubes
Main engines: 2 Ishikawajima GE geared turbines 2 shafts; 60 000 shp
Boilers: 2 Ishikawajima Foster Wheeler
Speed, knots: 33
Oil fuel, tons: 900
Range, miles: 7 000 at 18 knots
Complement: 290

Ordered under the 1960 programme. Refitted in 1967 when A/S Tubes and new Sonar were fitted.

Gunnery: US Mk 63 GFCS.

Guns: 3 in guns to be replaced by OTO Melara 76 mm at next refit.

Radar: 3D search: AN/SPS 52.
Air search: AN/SPS 29.
Surface search: OPS 16.
Missile control: AN.

Sonar: SQS 23.

AMATSUKAZE 1975, Japanese Maritime Self-Defence Force

2 "AKIZUKI" CLASS

Name	No.	Builders	Laid down	Launched	Commissioned
AKIZUKI	DD 161	Mitsubishi, Nagasaki	31 July 1958	26 June 1959	13 Feb 1960
TERUZUKI	DD 162	Shin Mitsubishi, Kobe	15 Aug 1958	24 June 1959	29 Feb 1960

Displacement, tons: 2 350 standard; 2 890 full load
Length, feet (metres): 387·2 *(118·0)* oa
Beam, feet (metres): 39·4 *(12·0)*
Draught, feet (metres): 13·1 *(4·0)*
Guns: 3—5 in *(127 mm)* 54 cal (single)
4—3 in *(76 mm)* 50 cal, (2 twin)
A/S weapons: 1—US Mk 108 Weapon Alfa rocket launcher; 2 US Mk 15 Hedgehogs; 2 US Mk 4 torpedo launchers (161); 6 (2 triple) Mk 32 torpedo tubes; 1 four-barrelled Bofors 375 mm rocket launcher (162) (see note)
Torpedo tubes: 4—21 in *(533 mm)* (quadruple)
Main engines: 2 geared turbines: *Akizuki*: Mitsubishi Escher-Weiss. *Teruzuki*: Westinghouse; 45 000 shp, 2 shafts
Boilers: 2 Mitsubishi CE type
Speed, knots: 32
Complement: 330

Built under the 1957 Military Aid Programme.

A/S weapons: *Teruzuki* rearmed Sept 1976-Jan 1977.

Gunnery: US Mk 57 GFCS; US Mk 63 GFCS.

Guns: 3 in guns to be replaced by OTO Melara 76 mm at next refit.

Radar: Air search: OPS 1.
Surface search: OPS 15.
Fire control: US Mk 34.

Refit: *Akikuzuki* expected to refit 1977 with similar change of A/S weapons to *Teruzuki*.

Sonar: Hull mounted: SQS-29.
VDS: OQA-1 (161 (1968)—162 (1967)).

TERUZUKI 1974, Japanese Maritime Self-Defence Force

282 JAPAN

3 "MURASAME" CLASS

Name	No.	Builders	Laid down	Launched	Commissioned
MURASAME	DD 107	Mitsubishi, Nagasaki	17 Dec 1957	31 July 1958	28 Feb 1959
YUDACHI	DD 108	Ishikawajima, Tokyo	16 Dec 1957	29 July 1958	25 Mar 1959
HARUSAME	DD 109	Uraga	17 June 1958	18 June 1959	15 Dec 1959

Displacement, tons: 1 800 standard; 2 500 full load
Length, feet (metres): 354·3 *(108·0)* oa
Beam, feet (metres): 36 *(11·0)*
Draught, feet (metres): 12·2 *(3·7)*
Guns: 3—5 in *(127 mm)* 54 cal
4—3 in *(76 mm)* 50 cal, (2 twin)
A/S weapons: 2 Mk 32 torpedo tubes; 1 Hedgehog;
1 DC rack; 1 Y-gun (see note)
Main engines: 2 sets geared turbines; 30 000 shp; 2 shafts
Boilers: 2 (see *Engineering* notes)
Speed, knots: 30
Range, miles: 6 000 at 18 knots
Complement: 250

Murasame and *Yudachi* were built under the 1956 Programme, *Harusame* 1957 Programme.

A/S weapons: *Murasame* fitted Sept 1975 with two triple tubes in place of those above. DC rack and Y-gun removed.

Engineering: *Murasame* has Mitsubishi Jyuko turbines and Mitsubishi CE boilers; and the other two have Ishikawajima Harima Jyuko turbines and Ishikawajima FW-D boilers.

Gunnery: US Mk 57 and 63 GFCS.

Radar: Air search: OPS 1.
Surface search: OPS 15.
Fire control: US Mk 34.

Sonar: Hull mounted: SQS 29.
VDS: OQA-1 (109 (1968)).

HARUSAME *1975, Japanese Maritime Self-Defence Force*

7 "AYANAMI" CLASS

Name	No.	Builders	Laid down	Launched	Commissioned
AYANAMI	DD 103	Mitsubishi, Nagasaki	20 Nov 1956	1 June 1957	12 Feb 1958
ISONAMI	DD 104	Shin Mitsubishi, Kobe	14 Dec 1956	30 Sept 1957	14 Mar 1958
URANAMI	DD 105	Kawasaki, Tokyo	1 Feb 1957	29 Aug 1957	27 Feb 1958
SHIKINAMI	DD 106	Mitsui, Tamano	24 Dec 1956	25 Sept 1957	15 Mar 1958
TAKANAMI	DD 110	Mitsui, Tamano	8 Nov 1958	8 Aug 1959	30 Jan 1960
OONAMI	DD 111	Ishikawajima, Tokyo	20 Mar 1959	13 Feb 1960	29 Aug 1960
MAKINAMI	DD 112	Iino, Maizuru	20 Mar 1959	25 April 1960	30 Oct 1960

Displacement, tons: 1 700 standard; 2 500 full load
Length, feet (metres): 357·6 *(109·0)* oa
Beam, feet (metres): 35·1 *(10·7)*
Draught, feet (metres): 12 *(3·7)*
Guns: 6—3 in *(76 mm)* 50 cal (3 twin)
A/S weapons: 6 (2 triple) Mk 32 torpedo tubes (103, 104, 105, 106, 112); 2 Mk 32 torpedo tubes (110, 111);
2 US Mk 15 Hedgehogs
Torpedo tubes: 4—21 in *(533 mm)* (quadruple) (see *Training Ship* note) (103, 105, 110, 111, 112)
Main engines: 2 Mitsubishi Escher-Weiss geared turbines;
2 shafts; 35 000 shp
Boilers: 2 (see *Engineering*)
Speed, knots: 32
Range, miles: 6 000 at 18 knots
Complement: 230

A/S weapons: Trainable Hedgehogs forward of the bridge.

Engineering: Types of boilers installed are as follows: Mitsubishi CE in *Ayanami, Isonami,* and *Uranami.* Hitachi, Babcock & Wilcox in *Oonami, Shikinami* and *Takanami.* Kawasaki Jyuko BD in *Makinami.*

Gunnery: US Mk 57 and 63 GFCS.

Radar: Air search: OPS 1 or 2.
Surface search: OPS 15 or 16.
Fire control: US Mk 34.

Training Ships: *Isonami* and *Shikinami* converted 1975-76 to training ships in place of *Asahi* and *Hatsuhi.* 21 in torpedo tubes removed and lecture hall built in the space.

Sonar: Hull mounted: OQS-12.
VDS: OQA-1 (103, 104, 110).

MAKINAMI *1975, Japanese Maritime Self-Defence Force*

JAPAN 283

2 "HARUKAZE" CLASS

Name	No.	Builders	Laid down	Launched	Commissioned
HARUKAZE	DD 101	Mitsubishi, Nagasaki	15 Dec 1954	20 Sept 1955	26 April 1956
YUKIKAZE	DD 102	Shin Mitsubishi, Kobe	17 Dec 1954	20 Aug 1955	31 July 1956

Displacement, tons: 1 700 standard; 2 340 full load
Length, feet (metres): 347·8 *(106·0)* wl; 358·5 *(190·3)* oa
Beam, feet (metres): 34·5 *(10·5)*
Draught, feet (metres): 12·0 *(3·7)*
Guns: 3—5 in *(127 mm)* 38 cal; 8—40 mm (2 quadruple)
A/S weapons: 2 Mk 32 torpedo tubes; 2 Hedgehogs;
 4 K-guns; 1 DC rack (see note)
Main engines: 2 sets geared turbines; *Harukaze;* 2 Mitsubishi
 Escher Weiss; *Yukikaze;* 2 Westinghouse; 2 shafts; 30 000
 shp
Boilers: *Harukaze:* 2 Hitachi-Babcock; *Yukikaze:* 2 Combustion
 Engineering
Speed, knots: 30
Range, miles: 6 000 at 18 knots
Oil fuel, tons: 557
Complement: 240

Authorised under the 1953 programme. First destroyer hulled vessels built in Japan after the Second World War. Electric welding was extensively used in hull construction; development of weldable high tension steel in main hull and light alloy in superstructure were also new.
Nearly all the armament was supplied from the USA under the MSA clause.

Gunnery: US Mk 57 and 63 GFCS.
Experimental Contraves GFCS in *Harukaze.*

Modifications: *Yukikaze* has been modified for experimental duties. 1—5 in (Y gun), 4 K-guns and 1 DC rack removed to make way for towed passive sonar array.

Radar: Air search: AN/SPS 6.
Surface search: OPS 37.
Fire control: US Mk 26 and 34.

Sonar: SQS-29.

HARUKAZE *1975, Japanese Maritime Self-Defence Force*

YUKIKAZE *1972, Toshio Tamura*

FRIGATES

6-8 NEW CONSTRUCTION

Builders	Laid down	Launched	Commissioned
Mitsui, Tamano	—	—	—

Displacement, tons: 1 200
Missiles: Quadruple Harpoon
Gun: 1—76 mm OTO Melara
A/S weapons: Quadruple Bofors launcher; 6 (2 triple) Mk 32
 torpedo tubes;
Main engines: CODOG; 1 Olympus TM3B; 28 000 shp; 1 DRV
 diesel; 5 000 shp; 2 shafts (cp propellers)

It is possible that this class will be built 1978-81 with the first requested in the 1977 programme. Aluminium bridge and superstructure.

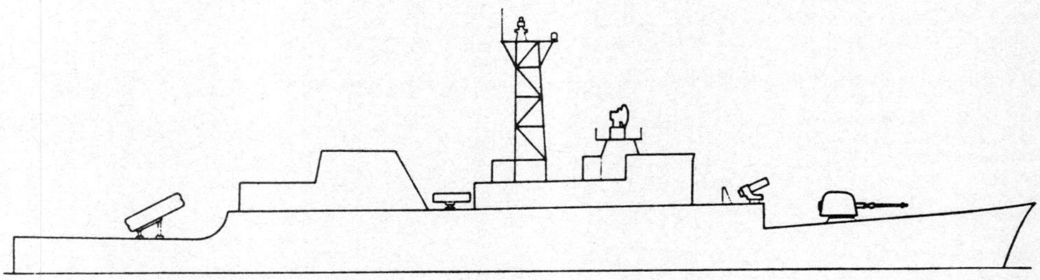

New Construction 1 200 ton Frigate 1977

11 "CHIKUGO" CLASS

Name	No.	Builders	Laid down	Launched	Commissioned
CHIKUGO	DE 215	Mitsui, Tamano	9 Dec 1968	13 Jan 1970	31 July 1970
AYASE	DE 216	Ishikawajima Harima	5 Dec 1969	16 Sept 1970	20 May 1971
MIKUMA	DE 217	Mitsui, Tamano	17 Mar 1970	16 Feb 1971	26 Aug 1971
TOKACHI	DE 218	Mitsui, Tamano	11 Dec 1970	25 Nov 1971	17 May 1972
IWASE	DE 219	Mitsui, Tamano	6 Aug 1971	29 June1972	12 Dec 1972
CHITOSE	DE 220	Hitachi, Maizuru	7 Oct 1971	25 Jan 1973	31 Aug 1973
NIYODO	DE 221	Mitsui, Tamano	20 Sept 1972	28 Aug 1973	8 Feb 1974
TESHIO	DE 222	Hitachi, Maizuru	11 July 1973	29 May 1974	10 Jan 1975
YOSHINO	DE 223	Mitsui, Tamano	28 Sept 1973	22 Aug 1974	6 Feb 1975
KUMANO	DE 224	Hitachi, Maizuru	29 May 1974	24 Feb 1975	19 Nov 1975
NOSHIRO	DE 225	Mitsui, Tamano	27 Jan 1976	23 Dec 1976	31 Aug 1977

Displacement, tons: 1 470 (216, 217-219,221); 1 480 (215, 220);
 1 500 (222 onwards)
Length, feet (metres): 305·5 *(93·1)* oa
Beam, feet (metres): 35·5 *(10·8)*
Draught, feet (metres): 11·5 *(3·5)*
Guns: 2—3 in *(76 mm)* 50 cal, (1 twin); 2—40 mm (1 twin)
A/S weapons: 1 US Mk 16 octuple Asroc launcher; 6 (2 triple)
 Mk 32 torpedo tubes
Main engines: 4 Mitsui B & W diesels (215, 217, 218, 219, 221,
 223, 225); 4 Mitsubishi UEV 30/40 N diesels (remainder); 2
 shafts; 16 000 shp
Speed, knots: 25
Complement: 165

These are the smallest warships in the world to mount Asroc.

Gunnery: Mk 1 GFCS.

Radar: Air search: OPS-14.
Surface search: OPS 17.
Fire control: —.

Sonar: Hull mounted: OQS-3.
VDS: SPS-35(J).

KUMANO *1976, Japanese Maritime Self-Defence Force*

284　JAPAN

4 "ISUZU" CLASS

Name	No.	Builders	Laid down	Launched	Commissioned
ISUZU	DE 211	Mitsui, Tamano	16 April 1960	17 Jan 1961	29 July 1961
MOGAMI	DE 212	Mitsubishi, Nagasaki	4 Aug 1960	7 Mar 1961	28 Oct 1961
KITAKAMI	DE 213	Ishikawajima Harima, Tokyo	7 June 1962	21 June 1963	27 Feb 1964
OOI	DE 214	Maizuru	10 June 1962	15 June 1963	22 Jan 1964

Displacement, tons: 1 490 standard; 1 700 full load
Length, feet (metres): 309·5 (94·3) oa
Beam, feet (metres): 34·2 (10·4)
Draught, feet (metres): 11·5 (3·5)
Guns: 4—3 in (76 mm) 50 cal, (2 twin)
A/S weapons: 4-barrelled Bofors rocket launcher; 6 (2 triple) Mk 32 torpedo tubes; 1 Y-gun; 1 DC rack (Ooi and Isuzu)
Torpedo tubes: 4—21 in (533 mm) (quadruple)
Main engines: 4 diesels, Mitsui in Ooi, Isuzu, Mitsubishi in Kitakami, Mogami, 16 000 hp; 2 shafts
Speed, knots: 25
Complement: 180

Modernisation: In 1966 (Mogami) and 1968 (Kitakami) 1 Y-gun and DC racks removed for VDS. Isuzu (1974-75) and Mogami (1974) modified for new Bofors rocket launcher.

Gunnery: US Mk 63 GFCS.

Radar: Air search: OPS 1.
Surface search: OPS 16.
Fire control: US Mk 34.

Sonar: Hull mounted: SQS-29.
VDS: OQA-1 (212-213).

OOI　1975

LIGHT FORCES

Note: Planned new construction of some 3 Missile hydrofoils of 100 tons, 45 knots armed with Harpoon and OTO Melara 76 mm gun. First in 1978 estimates.

8 "MIZUTORI" CLASS (LARGE PATROL CRAFT)

Name	No.	Builders	Laid down	Launched	Commissioned
MIZUTORI	311	Kawasaki, Kobe	13 Mar 1959	22 Sept 1959	27 Feb 1960
YAMADORI	312	Fujinagata, Osaka	14 Mar 1959	22 Oct 1959	15 Mar 1960
OTORI	313	Kure Shipyard	16 Dec 1959	27 May 1960	13 Oct 1960
KASASAGI	314	Fujinagata, Osaka	18 Dec 1959	31 May 1960	31 Oct 1960
HATSUKARI	315	Sasebo	25 Jan 1960	24 June 1960	15 Nov 1960
UMIDORI	316	Sasebo	15 Feb 1962	15 Oct 1962	30 Mar 1963
SHIRATORI	319	Sasebo	29 Feb 1964	8 Oct 1964	26 Feb 1965
HIYODORI	320	Sasebo	26 Feb 1965	25 Sept 1965	28 Feb 1966

Displacement, tons: 420 to 440 standard
Dimensions, feet (metres): 197·0 × 23·3 × 7·5 (60·0 × 7·1 × 2·3)
Guns: 2—40 mm (1 twin)
A/S weapons: 1 Hedgehog; 1 DC rack; 6 (2 triple) Mk 32 torpedo tubes (316, 319, 320); 2 Mk 32 torpedo tubes (remainder)
Main engines: 2 MAN diesels; 2 shafts; 3 800 bhp = 20 knots
Range, miles: 2 000 at 12 knots
Complement: 80

Gunnery: Mk 63 GFCS.

Radar: Surface search: OPS-35 (311-312); OPS-36 (313-316); OPS-16 (319-320).

Sonar: SQS-11A.

SHIRATORI　1975

4 "UMITAKA" CLASS (LARGE PATROL CRAFT)

Name	No.	Builders	Laid down	Launched	Commissioned
UMITAKA	309	Kawasaki, Kobe	13 Mar 1959	25 July 1959	30 Nov 1959
OTAKA	310	Kure Shipyard	18 Mar 1959	3 Sept 1959	14 Jan 1960
WAKATAKA	317	Kure Shipyard	5 Mar 1962	13 Nov 1962	30 Mar 1963
KUMATAKA	318	Fujinagata, Osaka	20 Mar 1963	21 Oct 1963	25 Mar 1964

Displacement, tons: 440 to 460 standard
Dimensions, feet (metres): 197·0 × 23·3 × 8·0 (60·0 × 7·1 × 2·4)
Guns: 2—40 mm (1 twin)
A/S weapons: 1 Hedgehog, 1 DC rack; 6 (2 triple) Mk 32 torpedo tubes (317, 318); 2 Mk 32 torpedo tubes (309, 310)
Main engines: 2 B & W diesels; 2 shafts; 4 000 bhp = 20 knots
Range, miles: 3 000 at 12 knots
Complement: 80

Gunnery: Mk 63 GFCS.

Radar: Surface search: OPS-35 (309-310); OPS-36 (317); OPS-16 (318)

Sonar: SQS-11A.

WAKATAKA　1976, Japanese Maritime Self-Defence Force

5 FAST ATTACK CRAFT—TORPEDO

Name	No.	Builders	Commissioned
PT 11	811	Mitsubishi, Shimonoseki	27 Mar 1971
PT 12	812	Mitsubishi, Shimonoseki	28 Mar 1972
PT 13	813	Mitsubishi, Shimonoseki	16 Dec 1972
PT 14	814	Mitsubishi, Shimonoseki	15 Feb 1974
PT 15	815	Mitsubishi, Shimonoseki	10 July 1975

Displacement, tons: 100
Dimensions, feet (metres): 116·4 × 30·2 × 3·9 (35·5 × 9·2 × 1·2)
Guns: 2—40 mm
Torpedo tubes: 4—21 in
Main engines: CODAG 2 Mitsubishi diesels; 2 IHI gas turbines; 3 shafts; 11 000 hp (PT 11; 10 500 hp) = 40 knots
Complement: 26-28

Laid down on 17 March 1970, 22 April 1971, 28 March 1972, 23 March 1973, and 23 April 1974 respectively.

Radar: OPS-13.

PT 14　1976, Japanese Maritime Self-Defence Force

9 COASTAL PATROL CRAFT

Name	No.	Builders	Commissioned
PB 19	919	Ishikawajima, Yokohama	31 Mar 1971
PB 20	920	Ishikawajima, Yokohama	31 Mar 1971
PB 21	921	Ishikawajima, Yokohama	31 Mar 1971
PB 22	922	Ishikawajima, Yokohama	31 Mar 1971
PB 23	923	Ishikawajima, Yokohama	31 Mar 1972
PB 24	924	Ishikawajima, Yokohama	31 Mar 1972
PB 25	925	Ishikawajima, Yokohama	29 Mar 1973
PB 26	926	Ishikawajima, Yokohama	29 Mar 1973
PB 27	927	Ishikawajima, Yokohama	29 Mar 1973

Displacement, tons: 18
Dimensions, feet (metres): 55·8 × 14·1 × 2·7 (17 × 4·3 × 0·8)
Gun: 1—20 mm
Main engines: 2 diesels; 760 hp = 20 knots
Complement: 6

GRP hulls.

Radar: OPS-29.

PB 22   11/1975, Toshio Tamura

Name	No.	Builders	Commissioned
KOSOKU 6	06	Mitsubishi, Shimonoseki	20 Mar 1967

Displacement, tons: 40
Dimensions, feet (metres): 75·9 × 18·2 × 3·3 (23·1 × 5·6 × 1)
Main engines: 3 diesels; 2 800 bhp = 30 knots

Of aluminium construction. Laid down on 28 June 1966 under the 1965 programme. Launched 22 Nov 1966.

Radar: OPS-4C.

KOSOKU 6   1974, Japanese Maritime Self-Defence Force

AMPHIBIOUS FORCES

Note: Possible new construction 1978-81 of 4/5 500 ton LSMs.

3 "MIURA" CLASS (LST)

Name	No.	Builders	Commissioned
MIURA	4151	Ishikawajima Harima, Tokyo	29 Jan 1975
OJIKA	4152	Ishikawajima Harima, Tokyo	22 Mar 1976
SATSUMA	4153	Ishikawajima Harima, Tokyo	17 Feb 1977

Displacement, tons: 2 000
Dimensions, feet (metres): 321·4 × 45·9 × 9·8 (98 × 14 × 3)
Guns: 2—3 in (76 mm) (twin); 2—40 mm (twin) (1—76 mm OTO Melara in Satsuma)
Main engines: 2 Kawasaki/MAN V8V 22/30 ATL diesels; 2 shafts; 4 400 hp = 14 knots
Complement: 115

Miura laid down 26 Nov 1973, launched 13 Aug 1974. Ojika laid down 10 June 1974, launched 2 Sept 1975. Satsuma laid down 26 May 1975, launched 12 May 1976. Carry 2 LCMs and 2 LCVPs, 10 type 74 tanks.

Radar: OPS-14; OPS-18.

MIURA   1976, Japanese Maritime Self-Defence Force

3 "ATSUMI" CLASS (LST)

Name	No.	Builders	Commissioned
ATSUMI	4101	Sasebo	27 Nov 1972
MOTOBU	4102	Sasebo	21 Dec 1973
NEMURO	4103	Sasebo	Oct 1977

Displacement, tons: 1 480 (Atsumi); 1 550 (Motobu); 1 500 (Nemuro)
Dimensions, feet (metres): 291·9 × 42·6 × 8·5 (89 × 13 × 2·6)
Guns: 4—40 mm (twins)
Main engines: 2 diesels; 4 400 hp = 13 knots (Motobu) = 14 knots (Atsumi)
Complement: 100 (Atsumi); 95 (Motobu)

Atsumi laid down 7 Dec 1971, launched 13 June 1972. Motobu laid down 23 April 1973, launched 3 Aug 1973. Nemuro laid down 18 Nov 1976; launched 16 June 1977.

Radar: OPS-9.

MOTOBU   1974, Japanese Maritime Self-Defence Force

286 JAPAN

MINE WARFARE FORCES

1 "SOUYA" CLASS (MINESWEEPER SUPPORT SHIP)

Name	No.	Builders	Laid down	Launched	Commissioned
SOUYA	951	Hitachi, Maizuru	9 July 1970	31 Mar 1971	30 Sept 1971

Displacement, tons: 2 150 standard; 3 050 full load
Length, feet (metres): 324·8 (99·0)
Beam, feet (metres): 49·5 (15·0)
Draught, feet (metres): 13·9 (4·2)
Guns: 2—3 in (76 mm) 50 cal (1 twin); 2—20 mm
A/S weapons: 6 (2 triple) Mk 32 A/S torpedo tubes
Main engines: 4 diesels; 4 000 bhp; 2 shafts
Speed, knots: 18
Complement: 185

With twin rails can carry 200 buoyant mines. Has helicopter platform aft and acts at times as command ship for MCM forces.

Fire control: GFCS Mk 1.

Radar: OPS-14; OPS 16 GFCS-Mk 1

Sonar: SQS-11A

SOUYA
1974, Japanese Maritime Self-Defence Force

1 "HAYASE" CLASS (MINESWEEPER SUPPORT SHIP)

Name	No.	Builders	Commissioned
HAYASE	462	Ishikawajima, Haruna	6 Nov 1971

Displacement, tons: 2 000 standard
Length, feet (metres): 324·8 (99·0)
Beam, feet (metres): 42·7 (13·0)
Draught, feet (metres): 12·5 (3·8)
Guns: 2—3 in (76 mm) 50 cal, (1 twin); 2—20 mm
A/S weapons: 6 (2 triple) Mk 32 A/S torpedo tubes
Main engines: 2 diesels; 4 000 bhp; 2 shafts
Speed, knots: 18
Complement: 185

Laid down 16 Sept 1970, launched 21 June 1971. Has helicopter platform aft.

Radar: OPS-14; OPS-16

Sonar: SQS-11A

HAYASE
1972, Japanese Maritime Self Defence Force

19 "TAKAMI" CLASS (MINESWEEPERS—COASTAL)

Name	No.	Builders	Commissioned
TAKAMI	MSC 630	Hitachi Kanagawa	15 Dec 1969
IOU	MSC 631	Nippon Steel Tube Co	22 Jan 1970
MIYAKE	MSC 632	Hitachi, Kanagawa	19 Nov 1970
UTONE	MSC 633	Nippon Steel Tube Co	3 Sept 1970
AWAJI	MSC 634	Hitachi, Kanagawa	29 Mar 1971
TOUSHI	MSC 635	Nippon Steel Tube Co	18 Mar 1971
TEURI	MSC 636	Hitachi, Kanagawa	10 Mar 1972
MUROTSU	MSC 637	Nippon Steel Tube Co	3 Mar 1972
TASHIRO	MSC 638	Hitachi, Kanagawa	30 July 1973
MIYATO	MSC 639	Nippon Steel Tube Co	24 Aug 1973
TAKANE	MSC 640	Hitachi, Kanagawa	28 Aug 1974
MUZUKI	MSC 641	Nippon Steel Tube Co	28 Aug 1974
YOKOSE	MSC 642	Hitachi, Kanagawa	15 Dec 1975
SAKATE	MSC 643	Nippon Steel Tube Co	17 Dec 1975
OUMI	MSC 644	Hitachi, Kanagawa	18 Nov 1976
FUKUE	MSC 645	Nippon Steel Tube Co	18 Nov 1976
OKITSU	MSC 646	Hitachi, Kanagawa	Sept 1977
HASHIRA	MSC 647	Nippon Steel Tube Co (Isogo)	31 Mar 1978
IWAI	MSC 648	Hitachi, Kanagawa	31 Mar 1978

Of similar dimensions to "Kasado" class below but of slightly different construction and with a displacement of 380 tons.
As minehunters fitted with mine-detecting sonar and carry four clearance divers.
Laid down—*Okitsu* 26 April 1976, *Hashira* 22 Feb 1977; *Iwai* 20 July 1976. Launch dates—*Okitsu* 4 March 1977, *Hashira* 8 Nov 1977, *Iwai* 24 Nov 1977.

Radar: OPS-9.

Sonar: ZQS-2.

SAKATE
1976, Japanese Maritime Self-Defence Force

JAPAN 287

1 +2 NEW CONSTRUCTION (MINESWEEPERS—COASTAL)

Name	No.	Builders	Commissioned
—	MSC 649	Nippon Steel Tube Co (Isogo)	Mar 1979
—	MSC 650	Hitachi, Kanagawa	—
—	MSC 651	Nippon Steel Tube Co (Isogo)	—

Displacement, tons: 440 standard
Dimensions, feet (metres): 180·4 × 30·8 × 13·8 *(55 × 9·4 × 4·2)*
Gun: 1—20 mm
Main engines: 2 diesels; 2 shafts; 1 440 bhp = 14 knots
Complement: 45

To be fitted with new S4 mine detonating equipment, a remote-controlled counter-mine charge. First of class ordered under 1976 programme. Contract for 649 signed 31 March 1977. Laid down 6 Dec 1977.

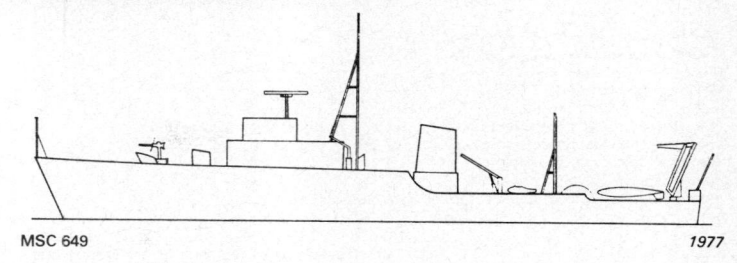

MSC 649   1977

13 "KASADO" CLASS (MINESWEEPERS—COASTAL)

Name	No.	Builders	Commissioned
KARATO	MSC 617	Nippon Steel Tube Co	23 Mar 1963
HARIO	MSC 618	Hitachi, Kanagawa	23 Mar 1963
MUTSURE	MSC 619	Nippon Steel Tube Co	24 Mar 1964
CHIBURI	MSC 620	Hitachi, Kanagawa	25 Mar 1964
OOTSU	MSC 621	Nippon Steel Tube Co	24 Feb 1965
KUDAKO	MSC 622	Hitachi, Kanagawa	24 Mar 1965
RISHIRI	MSC 623	Nippon Steel Tube Co	5 Mar 1966
REBUN	MSC 624	Hitachi, Kanagawa	24 Mar 1966
AMAMI	MSC 625	Nippon Steel Tube Co	6 Mar 1967
URUME	MSC 626	Hitachi, Kanagawa	30 Jan 1967
MINASE	MSC 627	Nippon Steel Tube Co	25 Mar 1967
IBUKI	MSC 628	Hitachi, Kanagawa	27 Feb 1968
KATSURA	MSC 629	Nippon Steel Tube Co	15 Feb 1968

Displacement, tons: 330 standard; (380 later ships); 448 full load (later ships)
Dimensions, feet (metres): 150·9 × 28 × 7·5 *(46 × 8·5 × 2·3)*; 171·6 × 28·9 × 7·9 *(52·3 × 8·8 × 2·4)* later ships
Gun: 1—20 mm
Main engines: 2 diesels; 2 shafts; 1 200 bhp (1 440 later ships) = 14 knots
Complement: 43

Originally a class of 29 ships. Hull is of wooden construction. Otherwise built of non-magnetic materials. Sixteen of this class converted as MCM support ship (1), survey craft (4), EOD (diving tenders) (3) and tenders (8).

Radar: OPS-9 or OPS-4.

IBUKI   1976, Japanese Maritime Self-Defence Force

1 "KOUZU" CLASS (MCM SUPPORT SHIP)

KOUZU MST 473 (ex-*MSC 609*)

Similar to "Kasado" class but has had minesweeping gear removed and was fitted as MCM command ship in June 1972.

6 "NANA-GO" CLASS (MSBs)

Name	No.	Builders	Commissioned
NANA-GO	707	Hitachi, Kanagawa	30 Mar 1973
HACHI-GO	708	Nippon Steel Tube Co	27 Mar 1973
KYUU-GO	709	Hitachi, Kanagawa	28 Mar 1974
JYUU-GO	710	Nippon Steel Tube Co	29 Mar 1974
JYUU-ICHI-GO	711	Hitachi, Kanagawa	10 May 1975
JYUU-NI-GO	712	Nippon Steel Tube Co	22 April 1975

Displacement, tons: 53
Dimensions, feet (metres): 73·8 × 17·7 × 3·3 *(22·5 × 5·4 × 1)*
Main engines: 2 Mitsubishi diesels; 2 shafts; 480 hp = 11 knots
Complement: 10

Laid down 26 May 1972, 3 Aug 1972, 5 July 1973, 7 June 1973, 2 July 1974, respectively. 712 launched 27 Jan 1975. No radar.

JYUU-GO   3/1974, Toshio Tamura

SERVICE FORCES

Note: One submarine tender to be included in future programmes.

Name	No.	Builders	Commissioned
AZUMA	ATS 4201	Maizuru	26 Nov 1969

Displacement, tons: 1 950 standard; 2 500 full load
Length, feet (metres): 323·4 *(98·6)*
Beam, feet (metres): 42·7 *(13·0)*
Draught, feet (metres): 12·5 *(3·8)*
Aircraft: 1 helicopter, 3 jetdrones, 7 propeller drones
Gun: 1—3 in *(76 mm)* 50 cal
A/S weapons: 2 A/S Short torpedo launchers
Main engines: 2 diesels; 2 shafts; 4 000 bhp
Speed, knots: 18
Complement: 185

Laid down on 15 July 1968, launched on 14 April 1969. Has drone hangar amidships and catapult on flight deck.
Training Support Ship.

Radar: OPS-16; SPS-40

Sonar: SQS-11A

AZUMA   1974, Japanese Maritime Self-Defence Force

288 JAPAN

Name	No.	Builders	Commissioned
KATORI	3501	Ishikawajima Harima, Tokyo	10 Sept 1969

Displacement, tons: 3 350 standard; 4 000 full load
Length, feet (metres): 422·4 *(128·7)*
Beam, feet (metres): 49·5 *(15·5)*
Draught, feet (metres): 14·6 *(4·5)*
Guns: 4—3 in *(76 mm)* 50 cal
A/S weapons: 1 four-barrelled rocket launcher; 6 (2 triple) for A/S torpedoes
Main engines: Geared turbines; 2 shafts; 20 000 shp
Range, miles: 7 000 at 18 knots
Speed, knots: 25
Complement: 460 (295 ship's company and 165 trainees)

Laid down 8 Dec 1967, launched on 19 Nov 1968. Training ship. Provided with a landing deck aft for a helicopter and large auditorium for trainees amidships.

Radar: Search: OPS-17 Tactical: SPS 12

Sonar: SQS-4

KATORI 8/1977, John Mortimer

1 E.O.D. TENDER

Name	No.	Builders	Commissioned
ERIMO	YAS 69 (ex-*AMC 491*)	Uraga	28 Dec 1955

Displacement, tons: 630 standard
Dimensions, feet (metres): 210 × 26 × 8 *(64·0 × 7·9 × 2·4)*
Guns: 2—40 mm; 2—20 mm
A/S weapons: 1 Hedgehog; 2 K-guns; 2 DC racks
Main engines: Diesel; 2 shafts; 2 500 bhp = 18 knots
Complement: 80

Conversion to tender for EOD (mine hunting diver) completed March 1976.

ERIMO (old pennant number) 1973, Japanese Maritime Self-Defence Force

4 E.O.D. TENDERS

YASHIMA (ex-US *AMS 144*) YAS 46
SAKITO (ex-*MSC 607*) YAS 64
TSUKUMI (e-*MSC 611*) YAS 66
HOTAKA (ex-*MSC 616*) YAS 70

YAS 46, former US AMS of 375 tons, and remainder of "Kasado" class (see Minewarfare Section for details) transferred after conversion to EOD (Mine Hunting diver) duties.

1 SUBMARINE RESCUE SHIP

Name	No.	Builders	Commissioned
FUSIMI	ASR 402	Sumitomo	10 Feb 1970

Displacement, tons: 1 430 standard
Dimensions, feet (metres): 249·5 × 41 × 12 *(76·0 × 12·5 × 3·7)*
Main engines: 2 diesels; 1 shaft; 3 000 bhp = 16 knots
Complement: 100

Laid down on 5 Nov 1968, launched 10 Sept 1969. Has a rescue chamber and two recompression chambers.

Radar: OPS-9.

Sonar: SQS-11A

FUSIMI 1976, Japanese Maritime Self-Defence Force

1 SUBMARINE RESCUE SHIP

Name	No.	Builders	Commissioned
CHIHAYA	ASR 401	Mitsubishi Nippon, Yokohama	15 Mar 1961

Displacement, tons: 1 340 standard
Dimensions, feet (metres): 239·5 × 39·3 × 12·7 *(73 × 12 × 3·9)*
Main engines: Diesels; 2 700 bhp = 15 knots
Complement: 90

Authorised under the 1959 programme. The first vessel of her kind to be built in Japan. Laid down on 15 March 1960. Launched on 4 Oct 1960. Has rescue chamber, two recompression chambers, four-point mooring equipment and a 12 ton derrick.

Radar: OPS-4.

Sonar: SQS-11A.

CHIHAYA 1976, Japanese Maritime Self-Defence Force

JAPAN 289

1 SALVAGE VESSEL

Note: One salvage and rescue ship to be included in future programmes.

Name	No.	Builders	Commissioned
SHOBO	YE 41	Azumo, Yokosuka	28 Feb 1964

Displacement, tons: 45
Dimensions, feet (metres): 75 × 18 × 3·3 *(22·9 × 5·5 × 1)*
Main engines: 4 diesels; 3 shafts; speed = 19 knots
Complement: 8

Four fixed fire hoses fitted. Now on auxiliary list.

1 NEW CONSTRUCTION CABLE LAYER

Name	No.	Builders	Commissioned
—	ARC 482	Mitsubishi, Shimonoseki	?

Displacement, tons: 4 500

To replace *Tsugaru*. Will have ocean survey capability.

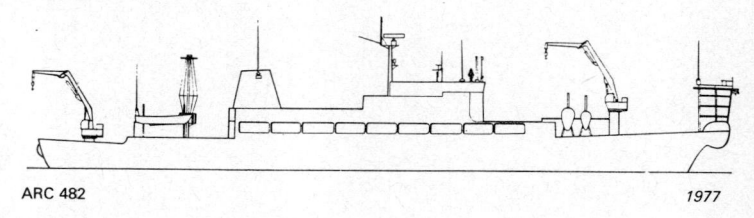

ARC 482   1977

1 CABLE LAYER

Name	No.	Builders	Commissioned
TSUGARU	ARC 481	Yokohama Shipyard	15 Dec 1955

Displacement, tons: 2 150 standard
Dimensions, feet (metres): 337·8 × 40·7 × 16 *(103 × 12·4 × 4·9)*
Guns: 2—20 mm
Main engines: 2 diesels; 2 shafts; 3 200 bhp = 13 knots
Complement: 103

Dual purpose cable layer and coastal minelayer. Built under the 1953 programme. Laid down on 18 Dec 1954. Launched on 19 July 1955. Converted to cable-layer 10 July 1969-30 April 1970 by Nippon Steel Tube Co.

TSUGARU   1972, Toshio Tamura

1 SUPPORT TANKER

Name	No.	Builders	Commissioned
HAMANA	AO 411	Uraga	10 Mar 1962

Displacement, tons: 2 900 light; 7 550 full load
Dimensions, feet (metres): 420 × 51·5 × 20·5 *(128·0 × 15·7 × 6·3)*
Guns: 2—40 mm
Main engines: 1 diesel; 5 000 bhp 1 shaft = 16 knots
Complement: 100

Built under the 1960 programme. Laid down on 17 April 1961, launched on 24 Oct 1961.

1 NEW CONSTRUCTION FLEET SUPPORT SHIP

Name	No.	Builders	Commissioned
—	AOE 421	Hitachi, Maizuru	Mar 1979

Displacement, tons: 4 500
Dimensions, feet (metres): 478·9 × 62·3 × 35·4 *(146 × 19 × 10·8)*
Main engines: 2 diesels; 2 shafts; 18 600 bhp
Speed, knots: 22
Range, miles: 9 500 at 20 knots
Complement: 131

Merchant type hull. Included in 1976 estimates. Ordered Dec 1976. Laid down Sept 1977, launched Aug 1978. Has six re-supply stations each side. No armament but can be fitted. Helicopter platform but no hangar.

AOE 421   1977

SURVEYING SHIPS
1 NEW CONSTRUCTION

Name	No.	Builders	Commissioned
—	AGS 5102	Mitsubishi, Shimonoseki	—

Displacement, tons: 2 000
Dimensions, feet (metres): 317·5 × 49·2 × 24·9 *(96·8 × 15·0 × 7·6)*
Main engines: 2 diesels; 2 shafts; 4 400 hp = 16 knots

Laid down Jan 1978. To be built to merchant marine design. Bow-thruster.

Radar: OPS-18.

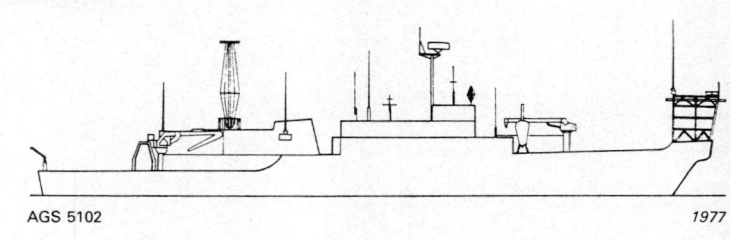

AGS 5102   1977

1 "AKASHI" CLASS (AGS)

Name	No.	Builders	Commissioned
AKASHI	5101	Nippon Steel Tube Co	25 Oct 1969

Displacement, tons: 1 420
Dimensions, feet (metres): 244·2 × 42·2 × 14·2 *(74·0 × 13·0 × 4·3)*
Main engines: 2 diesels; 2 shafts; 3 200 bhp
Speed, knots: 16
Range, miles: 16 500 at 14 knots
Complement: 65

Laid down 21 Sept 1968. Launched 30 May 1969.

Radar: OPS-9.

AKASHI   1974, Japanese Maritime Self-Defence Force

290　JAPAN

5 Ex-"KASADO" CLASS (AGS)

ICHI-GO (ex-*Kasado* MSC 604) 5111
NI-GO (ex-*Habushi* MSC 608) 5112
SAN-GO (ex-*Tatara* MSC 610) 5113
YON-GO (ex-*Hirado* MSC 614) 5114
GO-GO (ex-*AMS*) 5115

Displacement, tons: 340
Dimensions, feet (metres): 150·9 × 28 × 7·5 *(46 × 8·5 × 2·3)*
Main engines: 2 diesels; 2 shafts; 1 200 bhp = 14 knots

TENDERS
5 "500 TON" CLASS

Name	Laid down	Launched	Commissioned
ASH 81	10 Oct 1967	18 Jan 1968	30 Mar 1968
ASH 82	25 Sept 1968	20 Dec 1968	31 Mar 1969
ASH 83	2 April 1971	24 May 1971	30 Sept 1971
ASH 84	4 Feb 1972	15 June 1972	13 Sept 1972
ASH 85	20 Feb 1973	16 July 1973	19 Sept 1973

Displacement, tons: 500
Dimensions, feet (metres): 171·6 × 33·0 × 8·3 *(52·3 × 10·1 × 2·5)*
Main engines: 2 diesels; 2 shafts; 1 600 bhp = 14 knots

Training support and rescue.

Radar: OPS-19 (85);
OPS-29 (84);
OPS-10 (remainder).

ASH 81 (old pennant number)　　　1975, Japanese Maritime Self-Defence Force

1 "HAYABUSA" CLASS

Name	No.	Builders	Laid down	Launched	Commissioned
HAYABUSA	ASY 91	Mitsubishi, Nagasaki	23 May 1956	20 Nov 1956	10 June 1957

Displacement, tons: 380 standard
Dimensions, feet (metres): 190·2 × 25·7 × 7 *(58 × 7·8 × 2·1)*
Main engines: 2 diesels; 4 000 bhp; 2 shafts = 20 knots
Range, miles: 3 000 at 12 knots
Complement: 75

Built under the 1954 fiscal year programme.
A gas turbine was installed in March 1962 and removed in 1970. Now under reconstruction to ASY (Auxiliary Special Service Yacht) as from 1 Oct 1977.

Radar: Surface search: OPS-37.

Sonar: SQS-11A.

HAYABUSA (old pennant number)　　　1974, Japanese Maritime Self-Defence Force

8 Ex-"KASADO" CLASS

Name	No.	Builders	Commissioned
ATADA (ex-*MSC 601*)	YAS 56	Hitachi, Kanagawa	30 April 1956
ITSUKI (ex-*MSC 602*)	YAS 57	Hitachi, Kanagawa	20 June 1956
YASHIRO (ex-*MSC 603*)	YAS 58	Nippon Steel Tube Co	10 July 1956
SHISAKA (ex-*MSC 605*)	YAS 62	Nippon Steel Tube Co	16 Aug 1958
KOSHIKI (ex-*MSC 615*)	YAS 63	Nippon Steel Tube Co	29 Jan 1962
KANAWA (ex-*MSC 606*)	YAS 65	Hitachi, Kanagawa	24 July 1959
MIKURA (ex-*MSC 612*)	YAS 67	Nippon Steel Tube Co	27 May 1960
SHIKINE (ex-*MSC 613*)	YAS 68	Nippon Steel Tube Co	15 Nov 1960

Details as for "Kasado" class under Minewarfare Forces.

2 TENDERS

TOSHIMA (ex-USS *MSC*; ex-*AMS 258*) YAS 61
TSUSHIMA (ex-USS *MSC*; ex-*AMS 255*) YAS 60

Former US auxiliary minesweepers.

ICEBREAKER

Name	No.	Builders	Commissioned
FUJI	5001	Nippon Steel Tube Co	15 July 1965

Displacement, tons: 5 250 standard; 7 760 normal; 8 566 full load
Dimensions, feet (metres): 328 × 72·2 × 29 *(100 × 22 × 8·8)*
Aircraft: 3 helicopters
Main engines: 4 diesel-electric; 2 shafts; 12 000 bhp = 17 knots
Oil fuel, tons: 1 900
Range, miles: 15 000 at 15 knots
Complement: 200 plus 35 scientists and observers

Antarctic Support Ship. Laid down on 28 Aug 1964, launched on 18 March 1965. Hangar and flight deck aft. Can cope with ice up to 8·5 feet *(2·5 metres)*.

Radar: OPS-4; OPS-16.

Sonar: SQS-11A.

FUJI　　　1975, Japanese Maritime Self-Defence Force

---

2 TUGS

YT 55, YT 56

Displacement, tons: 195
Dimensions, feet (metres): 84·8 × 23 × 7·5 *(25·8 × 7 × 2·3)*
Main engines: 2 diesels; 500 hp = 11 knots
Complement: 15

YT 55 entered service 22 Aug 1975 and YT 56 on 13 July 1976.
Harbour tugs.

JAPAN 291

MARITIME SAFETY AGENCY

Establishment

Established in May 1948 as an external organisation of the Ministry of Transport to carry out patrol and rescue duties as well as hydrographic and navigation aids services.

Over the last 30 years a very considerable organisation with HQ in Tokyo has been built up. The Academy for the Agency is in Kure and the School in Maizuru.
The main operational branches are the Guard and Rescue Dept, the Hydrographic Dept and the Navigation Aids Dept. Regional Maritime Safety offices control the 11 Districts with their location as follows (air bases in brackets): RMS 1—Otaru (Chitose, Hakodate); 2—Shiogama (Sendai); 3—Yokohama (Haneda); 4—Nagoya (Ise); 5—Kobe (Yao); 6—Hiroshima (Hiroshima); 7—Kitakyushu (Fukuoka); 8—Maizuru (None); 9—Niigata (Niigata); 10—Kagoshima (Kagoshima); 11—Naha (Naha, Ishigaki). This organisation includes, as well as the RMS HQ, 65 MS officers, 51 MS Bases, 25 MS Detachments, 3 Control Communication Centres, 1 Traffic Advisory Centre, 4 Hydrographic Observatories and 144 Navigation Aids offices.

Commandant: Yasuhiko Sonomura

Personnel

1978: 11 188

Budget

FY 1977: 76 843 million yen.

New Construction

Under FY 1977 programme following are to be acquired:
1—3 800 ton PL, 4 "Bihoro" class, 1—350 ton PM, 1 "Hiryu" class FL, 2—30 m PC, 1 "AKizuki" class PC, 2 "Chiyokaze" class CL, 1 FM, 5 SS, 2 OR.

Strength of the Fleet

Guard and Rescue Service
Patrol Vessels:
Large (PL)	10
Medium (PM)	57
Small (PS)	24
Large Fire Fighting Boats (FL)	4

Patrol Craft:
Patrol Craft (PC)	44
Large (CL)	155
Small (CS)	10
Medium Fire Fighting Boats (FM)	7
Small Fire Fighting Boats (FS)	1

Special Service Craft:
Monitoring Boats (MS)	3
Surveillance Boats (SS)	21
Oil Recovery Boat (OR)	1
Oil Skimmers (OS)	3
Oil Boom Craft (OX)	19
Miscellaneous	5

Hydrographic Service
Surveying Vessels:
Large (HL)	3
Medium (HM)	3
Small (HS)	19

Strength of the Fleet

Navigation Aids Service
Lighthouse Supply Ship	1

Buoy Tenders:
Large (LL)	3
Medium (LM)	1

Navigation and Buoy Tenders:
Medium (LM)	11
Small (LS)	88

Aircraft Service
Fixed Wing:
NAMC YS-11A	2
Short Skyvan	1
Beechcraft E 18S, G 18S and H 18	11
Cessna 185C	1

Helicopters:
Mit-Sikorsky S 62A	1
Bell 212	6
Bell 206B	4
Kaw-Bell 47G3B	6
Kaw-Hughes 369HS	2

DELETIONS

1975: *Abukuma, Fuji, Ishikari, Isuzu, Kikuchi, Kuzuryu, Oyodo, Tenryu* ("Fuji", later "Sagami" class small patrol vessels)
Suzunami, Hayanami, Hatagumo, Makigumo, Tatsugumo (patrol craft)
CS 57, 58, 115 (harbour patrol craft)
FS 01, 02, 04, 05, 06 (salvage craft)

1976: *Sagami, Yoshino, Noshiro, Kiso, Nagara, Tone* (small patrol vessels)
Yaegumo (patrol craft)
CS 105, 117 (harbour patrol craft). FS 03 (salvage craft). M 601, 611, 616, 801, 802.

1977: *Mogami, Wakakusa, Shinano, Chikugo, Kumano* and *Kitakami*.
PC 34 and 35, CL 301 and 303, FS 07, M 618 and 902

GUARD AND RESCUE SERVICE
LARGE PATROL VESSELS

1 + 3 NEW CONSTRUCTION

Name	No.	Builders	Commissioned
—	PL —	Nippon Kokan, Tsurumi	Nov 1978

Displacement, tons: 3 750
Dimensions, feet (metres): 323·4 × 51·2 × 17·1 *(98·6 × 15·6 × 5·2)*
Aircraft: 1 Bell 212 helicopter with hangar
Guns: 1—40 mm; 1—20 mm
Main engines: 2 diesels; 15 600 shp; 2 shafts
Speed, knots: 20
Range, miles: 5 500 at 18 knots
Endurance: 25 days
Complement: 71

3 750 ton PL   1977

The first of class ordered under the FY 1977 programme and laid down 12 Sept 1977. Three further ships projected under the FY 1978 programme. The first and one subsequent ship are to have an ice-breaking capability. The first ship will be based at Kushiro for duty in the North in the 1st RMS District replacing *Soya*.

2 "IZU" CLASS

Name	No.	Builders	Commissioned
IZU	PL 31	Hitachi Mukai Shima	July 1967
MIURA	PL 32	Maizuru	Mar 1969

Displacement, tons: 2 080 normal
Dimensions, feet (metres): 313·3 oa × 38 × 12·8 *(95·6 × 11·6 × 3·9)*
Main engines: 2 diesels; 2 shafts; 10 400 bhp = 21·6 knots
Range, miles: 14 500 at 12·7 knots; 5 000 at 21 knots
Complement: 72

Izu was laid down in Aug 1966, launched in Jan 1967. *Miura* was laid down in May 1968, launched in Oct 1968. Employed in long range rescue and patrol and weather observation duties. Equipped with weather observation radar, various types of marine instruments. Ice strengthened hull.

Radar: One navigation set; one weather set.

Station: Yokohama.

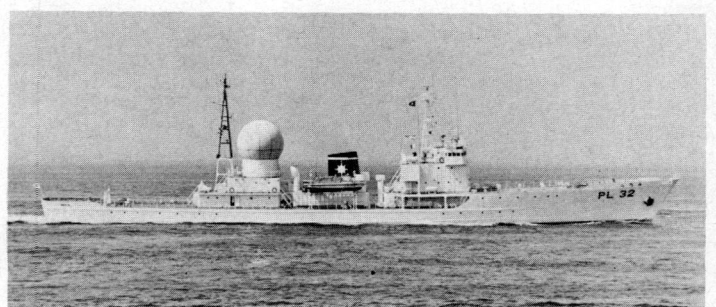

MIURA   5/1977, Yoshifumi Mayama

292 JAPAN

4 "ERIMO" AND "DAIO" CLASSES

Name	No.	Builders	Commissioned
ERIMO	PL 13	Hitachi	30 Nov 1965
SATSUMA	PL 14	Hitachi	30 July 1966
DAIO	PL 15	Hitachi Maizuru	28 Sept 1973
MUROTO	PL 16	Naikai	30 Nov 1974

Displacement, tons: 1 009 normal (1 194 *Daio*)
Dimensions, feet (metres): 251·3 oa × 30·2 × 9·9 (31·5 × 10·7 *Daio* and *Muroto*) (76·6 × 9·2 × 3) (9·6 × 3·3 *Daio* and *Muroto*)
Guns: 1—3 in 50 cal; 1—20 mm (1—40 mm; 1—20 mm *Daio* and *Muroto*)
Main engines: Diesels; 2 shafts; 4 800 bhp = 19·78 knots (7 000 bhp cp propellers = 20 knots, *Daio* and *Muroto*)
Range, miles: 5 000 at 17 knots
Complement: 72

Erimo was laid down on 29 March 1965 and launched on 14 Aug 1965. Her structure is strengthened against ice. Employed as a patrol vessel off northern Japan. *Satsuma*, is assigned to guard and rescue south of Japan. *Daio* was laid down 18 Oct 1972 and launched 19 June 1973. *Muroto* was laid down 15 Mar 1974 and launched 5 Aug 1974.

Stations: 13—Kushiro; 14—Kagoshima; 15—Kushiro; 16—Kagoshima.

Radar: One navigation set.

SATSUMA 5/1977, Yoshifumi Mayama

Name	No.	Builders	Commissioned
KOJIMA	PL 21	Kure	21 May 1964

Displacement, tons: 1 201
Dimensions, feet (metres): 228·3 oa × 33·8 × 10·5 (69·6 × 10·3 × 3·2)
Guns: 1—3 in; 1—40 mm; 1—20 mm
Main engines: Diesels; 2 600 hp = 17 knots
Range, miles: 6 000 at 13 knots
Complement: 17 officers, 42 men, 47 cadets

Maritime Safety Agency training ship at Kure Academy.

Radar: Two navigation sets.

KOJIMA 5/1977, Yoshifumi Mayama

2 "NOJIMA" CLASS

Name	No.	Builders	Commissioned
NOJIMA	PL 11	Uraga	30 April 1962
OJIKA	PL 12	Uraga	10 June 1963

Displacement, tons: 950 standard; 1 009 normal; 1 113 full load
Dimensions, feet (metres): 208·8 pp; 226·5 oa × 30·2 × 10·5 (63·7; 69·1 × 9·2 × 3·2)
Main engines: 2 diesels; 3 000 bhp = 17·5 knots
Range, miles: 9 270 at 17 knots
Complement: 51

Nojima laid down on 27 Oct 1961, launched on 12 Feb 1962. Both employed as patrol vessels and weather ships.

Radar: One navigation set.

Stations: 11—Yokohama; 12—Shiogama.

OJIKA 2/1977, Yoshifumi Mayama

Name	No.	Builders	Commissioned
SOYA	PL 107	Koyakijima	May 1938

Displacement, tons: 4 364 normal; 4 818 full load
Dimensions, feet (metres): 259·2 wl × 51·9 (including bulge) × 18·9 (79·1 × 15·8 × 5·8)
Main engines: 2 diesels; 4 800 bhp = 12·5 knots on trials
Range, miles: 10 000 at 12 knots
Complement: 96

Reconstructed IJN auxiliary. Commissioned in present form in 1955. Has icebreaking capability and will be replaced by new construction 3 750 ton class.

Radar: Two navigation sets.

Station: Hakodate.

SOYA 1975, Japanese Maritime Safety Agency

MEDIUM PATROL VESSELS

3 "MIYAKE" CLASS

Name	No.	Builders	Commissioned
MIYAKE	PM 70	Tohoku	25 Jan 1973
AWAJI	PM 71	Usuki	25 Jan 1973
YAEYAMA	PM 72	Usuki	20 Dec 1972

Displacement, tons: 530 standard; 574 full load
Dimensions, feet (metres): 190·4 oa × 24·2 × 8·2 (58·1 × 7·4 × 2·5)
Gun: 1—20 mm
Main engines: 2 diesels; 2 shafts; cp propellers; 3 200 hp = 17·8 knots
Range, miles: 3 580 at 16 knots
Complement: 36

Of similar hull design to "Kunashiri" class.

Radar: Two navigation sets.

MIYAKE 10/1974, Yoshifumi Mayama

16 "BIHORO" CLASS

Name	No.	Builders	Commissioned
BIHORO	PM 73	Tohoku	28 Feb 1974
KUMA	PM 74	Usuki	28 Feb 1974
FUJI	PM 75	Usuki	7 Feb 1975
KABASHIMA	PM 76	Usuki	25 Mar 1975
SADO	PM 77	Tohoku	1 Feb 1975
ISHIKARI	PM 78	Tohoku	13 Mar 1976
ABUKUMA	PM 79	Tohoku	30 Jan 1976
ISUZU	PM 80	Naikai	10 Mar 1976
KIKUCHI	PM 81	Usuki	6 Feb 1976
KUZURYU	PM 82	Usuki	18 Mar 1976
HOROBUTSU	PM 83	Tohoku	27 Jan 1977
SHIRAKAMI	PM 84	Tohoku	24 Mar 1977
SAGAMI	PM 85	Naikai	30 Nov 1976
TONE	PM 86	Usuki	30 Nov 1976
YOSHINO	PM 87	Usuki	28 Jan 1977
KUROBE	PM 88	Shikoku	15 Feb 1977

Displacement, tons: 636 standard; 657 full load
Dimensions, feet (metres): 208 × 25·6 × 8·3 *(63·4 × 7·8 × 2·5)*
Gun: 1—20 mm
Main engines: 2 diesels; 2 shafts; 3 000 hp = 18 knots
Range, miles: 3 200 at 18 knots
Complement: 34

New construction: In 1977 Estimates—*Takatori* PM 89, *Chikugo* PM 90, *Yamakuni* PM 91, *Katsura* PM 92, *Shinano* PM 93.

Radar: Two navigation sets.

KIKUCHI   5/1976, Yoshifumi Mayama

4 "KUNASHIRI" CLASS

Name	No.	Builders	Commissioned
KUNASHIRI	PM 65	Maizuru	28 Mar 1969
MINABE	PM 66	Maizuru	28 Mar 1970
SAROBETSU	PM 67	Maizuru	30 Mar 1971
KAMISHIMA	PM 68	Usuki	31 Jan 1972

Displacement, tons: 498 normal
Dimensions, feet (metres): 190·4 oa × 24·2 × 7·9 *(58·1 × 7·4 × 2·4)*
Gun: 1—20 mm
Main engines: 2 diesels; 2 600 bhp = 17·6 knots
Range, miles: 3 000 at 16·9 knots
Complement: 40

Kunashiri was laid down in Oct 1968 and launched in Dec 1968. *Minabe* was laid down in Oct 1969.

Radar: One navigation set.

KUNASHIRI   1970, Japanese Maritime Safety Agency

5 "MATSUURA" CLASS

Name	No.	Builders	Commissioned
MATSUURA	PM 60	Osaka	18 Mar 1961
SENDAI	PM 61	Osaka	14 April 1962
AMAMI	PM 62	Hitachi	29 Mar 1965
NATORI	PM 63	Hitachi	20 Jan 1966
KARATSU	PM 64	Hitachi	21 Mar 1967

Displacement, tons: 420 standard; 425 normal
Dimensions, feet (metres): 163·3 pp; 181·5 oa × 23 × 7·5 *(49·8; 55·4 × 7 × 2·3)*
Gun: 1—20 mm
Main engines: 2 diesels; 1 400 bhp = 16·5 knots *(Matsuura, Sendai)*;
1 800 bhp = 16·8 knots *(Amami, Natori)*; 2 600 bhp *(Karatsu)*
Range, miles: 3 500 at 12 knots
Complement: 37

Matsuura was laid down on 16 Oct 1960, launched on 24 Dec 1960. *Sendai* was laid down on 23 Aug 1961, launched on 18 Jan 1962.

Radar: One navigation set

NATORI   12/1974, Yoshifumi Mayama

7 "YAHAGI" CLASS

Name	No.	Builders	Commissioned
YAHAGI	PM 54	Niigata	31 July 1956
SUMIDA	PM 55	Niigata	30 June 1957
CHITOSE	PM 56	Niigata	30 April 1958
SORACHI	PM 57	Niigata	1 Mar 1959
YUBARI	PM 58	Niigata	15 Mar 1960
HORONAI	PM 59	Niigata	4 Feb 1961
OKINAWA	PM 69	Usuki	1 Oct 1970

Displacement, tons: 333·15 standard; 375·7 normal
Dimensions, feet (metres): 147·3 pp; 164·9 oa × 24 × 7·4 *(44·9; 50·3 × 7·3 × 2·3)*
Gun: 1—40 mm
Main engines: 2 diesels; 1 400 bhp = 15·5 knots
Range, miles: 3 500 at 12 knots
Complement: 37

Yahagi was laid down on 9 Dec 1955, launched on 19 May 1956. *Chitose* was laid down on 20 Sept 1957, launched on 24 Feb 1958.
Okinawa transferred to MSA in 1972.

Radar: One navigation set

OKINAWA   5/1976, Yoshifumi Mayama

294 JAPAN

Name	No.	Builders	Commissioned
TESHIO	PM 53	Uraga	19 Mar 1955

Displacement, tons: 421·5 normal
Dimensions, feet (metres): 149·4 pp; 165 oa × 23 × 8·2 (45·6; 50·3 × 7 × 2·5)
Gun: 1—40 mm
Main engines: 2 diesels; 1 400 bhp = 15·71 knots
Range, miles: 3 800 at 12 knots
Complement: 37

Laid down on 15 Sept 1954, launched on 12 Jan 1955.

Radar: One navigation set.

TESHIO   1975, Japanese Maritime Safety Agency

2 "TOKACHI" CLASS

Name	No.	Builders	Commissioned
TOKACHI	PM 51	Harima Dockyard, Kure	31 July 1954
TATSUTA	PM 52	Harima Dockyard, Kure	10 Sept 1954

Displacement, tons: 336 standard; 381 normal (Tokachi)
  324 standard; 369 normal (Tatsuta)
Dimensions, feet (metres): 157·5 pp; 164 wl; 170 oa × 21·9 × 11·2 (48; 50; 51·9 × 6·7 × 3·4)
Gun: 1—40 mm
Main engines: 2—4 cycle single acting diesels
  1 500 bhp = 16 knots (Tokachi)
  1 400 bhp = 15 knots (Tatsuta)
Range, miles: 3 800 at 12 knots
Complement: 37

Tokachi was laid down on 14 Nov 1953, launched on 8 May 1954.

Radar: One navigation set.

TOKACHI   1975, Japanese Maritime Safety Agency

5 "CHIFURI" CLASS

Name	No.	Builders	Commissioned
CHIFURI	PM 18	Nihonkai	30 April 1952
KUROKAMI	PM 19	Nihonkai	31 Mar 1952
KOZU	PM 20	Niigata	9 Dec 1951
SHIKINE	PM 21	Niigata	9 Jan 1952
DAITO	PM 22	Niigata	25 Feb 1952

Displacement, tons: 465 standard; 483 normal
Dimensions, feet (metres): 182·7 oa × 25·2 × 8·5 (55·9 × 7·7 × 2·6)
Guns: 1—3 in 50 cal; 1—20 mm
Main engines: 2 diesels; 1 300 bhp = 15·8 knots
Range, miles: 3 000 at 12 knots
Complement: 45

Radar: One navigation set.

DAITO   5/1977, Yoshifumi Mayama

14 "REBUN" CLASS

Name	No.	Builders	Commissioned
REBUN	PM 04	Hitachi	28 Feb 1951
IKI	PM 05	Hitachi	5 April 1951
OKI	PM 06	Mitsui Tamano	19 Feb 1951
GENKAI	PM 07	Mitsui Tamano	17 Mar 1951
HACHIJO	PM 08	Nakanihon	6 Mar 1951
AMAKUSA	PM 09	Nakanihon	8 Mar 1951
OKUSHIRI	PM 10	Hitachi	27 June 1951
KUSAKAKI	PM 11	Hitachi	30 July 1951
RISHIRI	PM 12	Fujinagata	30 June 1951
NOTO	PM 13	Fujinagata	25 Aug 1951
HEKURA	PM 14	Harima	30 June 1951
MIKURA	PM 15	Harima	19 July 1951
KOSHIKI	PM 16	Nishinihon	31 Aug 1951
HIRADO	PM 17	Nishinihon	4 Sept 1951

Displacement, tons: 450 standard; 495 normal
Dimensions, feet (metres): 155·2 pp; 164 wl; 171·9 oa × 26·5 × 8·5 (47·3; 50; 52·4 × 8·1 × 2·6)
Guns: 1—3 in 50 cal; 1—20 mm (2—20 mm only in some)
Main engines: 2 sets diesels; 1 300 bhp = 15 knots
Range, miles: 3 000 at 12 knots
Complement: 45

A development of the original "Awaji" class design all of which are now scrapped. *Kusakaki* due for disposal.

Radar: One navigation set.

REBUN   1975, Japanese Maritime Safety Agency

SMALL PATROL VESSELS
14 "HIDAKA" CLASS

Name	No.	Builders	Commissioned
HIDAKA	PS 32	Azuma	23 April 1962
HIYAMA	PS 33	Hitachi	13 Mar 1963
TSURUGI	PS 34	Mukaijima	13 Mar 1963
ROKKO	PS 35	Shikoku	31 Jan 1964
TAKANAWA	PS 36	Hayashikane	27 Jan 1964
AKIYOSHI	PS 37	Hashihama	29 Feb 1964
KUNIMI	PS 38	Hayashikane	15 Feb 1965
TAKATSUKI	PS 39	Kurashima	30 Mar 1965
KAMUI	PS 41	Hayashikane	15 Feb 1966
ASHITAKA	PS 43	Usuki	10 Feb 1967
KURAMA	PS 44	Usuki	28 Feb 1967
IBUKI	PS 45	Usuki	5 Mar 1968
TOUMI	PS 46	Usuki	20 Feb 1968
NOBARU	PS 49	Mukaijima	10 Dec 1963

Displacement, tons: 166·2 to 164·4 standard; 169·4 normal
Dimensions, feet (metres): 100 pp; 111 oa × 20·8 × 5·5 (30·5; 33·8 × 6·3 × 1·7)
Main engines: 1 set diesels; 1 shaft; 690 to 700 bhp = 13·5 knots
Range, miles: 1 200 at 12 knots
Complement: 17

Hidaka was laid down on 4 Oct 1961, launched on 2 March 1962. *Kunimi* was built under the 1964 programme, laid down on 15 Nov 1964, launched on 19 Dec 1964.

Radar: One navigation set.

ASHITAKA *1975, Japanese Maritime Safety Agency*

Name	No.	Builders	Commissioned
TSUKUBA	PS 31	Kanagawa	30 Mar 1962

Displacement, tons: 65
Dimensions, feet (metres): 80·5 × 21·5 × 3·7 (24·6 × 6·6 × 1·1)
Main engines: 2 Niigata diesels; 1 800 bhp = 18 knots
Range, miles: 230 at 15 knots
Complement: 19

Radar: One navigation set.

TSUKUBA *1974, Japanese Maritime Safety Agency*

Name	No.	Builders	Commissioned
BIZAN	PS 42	Shimonoseki	28 Mar 1966
ASAMA	PS 47	Shimonoseki	31 Jan 1969
SHIRAMINE	PS 48	Shimonoseki	15 Dec 1969

Displacement, tons: 40 normal; *Shiramine* 48 normal
Dimensions, feet (metres): 85·3 oa × 18·3 × 2·8 (26 × 5·6 × 0·9)
Gun: 1 MG aft
Main engines: 2 Mitsubishi diesels; 1 140 bhp = 21·6 knots. *Shiramine,* 2 Benz (MTU) diesels; 2 200 bhp = 25 knots
Range, miles: 400 at 18 knots; *Shiramine* 250 at 25 knots
Complement: 14

Of light metal construction.

Radar: One navigation set.

BIZAN *1974, Japanese Maritime Safety Agency*

Name	No.	Builders	Commissioned
AKAGI	PS 40	Kanagawa	24 Mar 1965

Displacement, tons: 42
Dimensions, feet (metres): 78·8 oa × 17·8 × 3·2 (24·0 × 5·4 × 1)
Main engines: 2 Mercedes-Benz diesels; 2 200 bhp = 28 knots
Range, miles: 350 at 21 knots
Complement: 19

Radar: One navigation set.

AKAGI *1974, Japanese Maritime Safety Agency*

JAPAN

COASTAL PATROL CRAFT

Note: Currently building at Mitsubishi is *Murakomo* with 2 diesels of 4 400 hp and capable of 30 knots. Probably first of new class.

9 "AKIZUKI" CLASS

Name	No.	Builders	Commissioned
AKIZUKI	PC 64	Mitsubishi	28 Feb 1974
SHINONOME	PC 65	Mitsubishi	25 Feb 1974
URAYUKI	PC 72	Mitsubishi	31 May 1975
ISEYUKI	PC 73	Mitsubishi	31 July 1975
MAKIGUMO	PC 75	Mitsubishi	19 Mar 1976
HATAGUMO	PC 76	Mitsubishi	21 Feb 1976
HAMAZUKI	PC 77	Mitsubishi	29 Nov 1976
ISOZUKI	PC 78	Mitsubishi	18 Mar 1977
SHIMANAMI	PC 79	Mitsubishi	—

Displacement, tons: 74
Dimensions, feet (metres): 83·5 oa × 20·7 × 9·8 *(26 × 6·3 × 3)*
Main engines: 3 Mitsubishi diesels; 3 000 bhp = 22·1 knots
Range, miles: 220 at 22 knots
Complement: 10

Shimanami laid down 29 June 1977.

Radar: One navigation set.

HATAGUMO 5/1977, Yoshifumi Mayama

17 "SHIKINAMI" CLASS

Name	No.	Builders	Commissioned
SHIKINAMI	PC 54	Mitsubishi, Shimonoseki	25 Feb 1971
TOMONAMI	PC 55	Mitsubishi, Shimonoseki	30 Mar 1971
WAKANAMI	PC 56	Mitsubishi, Shimonoseki	30 Oct 1971
ISENAMI	PC 57	Hitachi, Kanagawa	29 Feb 1972
TAKANAMI	PC 58	Mitsubishi, Shimonoseki	30 Nov 1971
MUTSUKI	PC 59	Hitachi, Kanagawa	18 Dec 1972
MOCHIZUKI	PC 60	Hitachi, Kanagawa	18 Dec 1972
HARUZUKI	PC 61	Mitsubishi, Shimonoseki	30 Nov 1972
KIYUZUKI	PC 62	Mitsubishi, Shimonoseki	18 Dec 1972
URAZUKI	PC 63	Hitachi, Kanagawa	30 Jan 1973
URANAMI	PC 66	Hitachi, Kanagawa	22 Dec 1973
TAMANAMI	PC 67	Mitsubishi, Shimonoseki	25 Dec 1973
MINEGUMO	PC 68	Mitsubishi, Shimonoseki	30 Nov 1973
KIYONAMI	PC 69	Mitsubishi, Shimonoseki	30 Oct 1973
OKINAMI	PC 70	Hitachi, Kanagawa	8 Feb 1974
WAKAGUMO	PC 71	Hitachi, Kanagawa	25 Mar 1974
ASOYUKI	PC 74	Hitachi, Kanagawa	16 June 1975

Displacement, tons: 44
Dimensions, feet (metres): 69 oa × 17·4 × 3·2 *(21 × 5·3 × 1)*
Main engines: 2 Mercedes-Benz (MTU) diesels; 2 200 bhp = 26·5 knots
Range, miles: 280 miles at near maximum speed
Complement: 10

Built completely of light alloy.

Radar: One navigation set.

KIYONAMI 1973, Japanese Maritime Safety Agency

14 "MATSUYUKI" CLASS

Name	No.	Builders	Commissioned
MATSUYUKI	PC 40	Hitachi, Kanagawa	28 Mar 1964
SHIMAYUKI	PC 41	Hitachi, Kanagawa	31 Jan 1966
TAMAYUKI	PC 42	Hitachi, Kanagawa	7 Feb 1966
HAMAYUKI	PC 43	Hitachi, Kanagawa	24 Mar 1966
YAMAYUKI	PC 44	Hitachi, Kanagawa	15 Mar 1967
KOMAYUKI	PC 45	Hitachi, Kanagawa	15 Mar 1967
UMIGIRI	PC 46	Hitachi, Kanagawa	15 Mar 1968
ASAGIRI	PC 47	Hitachi, Kanagawa	15 Mar 1968
HAMAGIRI	PC 48	Sumidagawa	19 Mar 1970
SAGIRI	PC 49	Hitachi, Kanagawa	31 Mar 1970
SETOGIRI	PC 50	Hitachi, Kanagawa	5 Mar 1970
HAYAGIRI	PC 51	Hitachi, Kanagawa	5 Mar 1970
HAYANAMI	PC 52	Sumidagawa	22 Mar 1971
MATSUNAMI	PC 53	Hitachi, Kanagawa	30 Mar 1971

Displacement, tons: 40-60 tons
Dimensions, feet (metres): 69 oa × 16·6 × 3·2 *(21 × 5·1 × 1)* (see note)
Gun: 1—13 mm
Main engines: 2 Mercedes-Benz (MTU) diesels; 2 200 bhp = 26·3 knots;
 PC 48 1 140 bhp = 14·6 knots; PC 52 = 21·8 knots; PC 53 = 20·8 knots
Range, miles: About 300 miles at near maximum speed
Complement: 10

Class: PCs 40-47 and 49-52 were built of light alloy frames with wooden hulls. PCs 48 and 52 were built of steel. PC 53 was built completely of light alloy and is sometimes classified as a separate class having larger dimensions (25 × 6 × 2·8 metres).

Radar: One navigation set.

MATSUYUKI 1975, Japanese Maritime Safety Agency

JAPAN 297

3 "HANAYUKI" CLASS

Name	No.	Builders	Commissioned
HANAYUKI	PC 37	Sumidagawa	Mar 1959
MINEYUKI	PC 38	Azuma	Mar 1959
ISOYUKI	PC 39	Sumidagawa	Feb 1960

Displacement, tons: 46
Dimensions, feet (metres): 72 oa × 17·6 × 3·2 (22 × 5·4 × 1)
Main engines: 3 diesels; 1 500 bhp = 20·7 knots (Hanayuki)
  2 diesels; 1 800 bhp = 21·3 knots (Isoyuki)
Complement: 13

Of light wooden hulls.

Radar: One navigation set.

2 "ASAGUMO" CLASS

Name	No.	Builders	Commissioned
ASAGUMO	PC 34	Sumidagawa	15 Mar 1955
MATSUGUMO	PC 35	Sumidagawa	31 Mar 1955

Displacement, tons: 42
Dimensions, feet (metres): 69 × 17·2 × 3·2 (21 × 5·2 × 1)
Main engines: 2 diesels; 1 400 bhp = 20·5 knots
Complement: 12

Completed in 1954-55. Wooden hulls.

Radar: One navigation set.

154 15 METRE TYPE

CL 21—156, 301—319

Displacement, tons: 20·2 full load
Dimensions, feet (metres): 49·2 × 13·5 × 3·1 (15 × 4·1 × 1)
Main engines: 2 diesels; 2 shafts; 520 bhp = 19 knots
Range, miles: 160 at 15 knots
Complement: 6

For coastal patrol and rescue duties. Built of high tensile steel, have been delivered each year.

Classes: This total includes six different classes of similar characteristics—"Yukikaze" (5), "Yakaze" (31), "Chiyokaze" (96), "Nogekaze" (4), "Hamakaze" (8), "Asashimo" (10).

Completions: 1962—2; 1963—2; 1964—3; 1965—3; 1966—6; 1967—6; 1968—6; 1969—9; 1970—13; 1971—26; 1972—22; 1973—21; 1974—4; 1975—7; 1976—5. Nineteen others of similar characteristics but built between 1948-53 were transferred to MSA by other ministries 1965-70.

Names: All but 24 of these craft have names ending in "-kaze". For convenience these have not been listed but are available.

CL 127   *1973, Japanese Maritime Safety Agency*

Radar: One navigation set.

10, 12 and 9 METRE TYPE

CS 100, 107, 108, 116, 119—120, 122—124, 126

Mainly of 7·7 tons displacement. All transferred to MSA by other ministries in 1966-69 having been built in 1948-52 with two later additions. Mostly of wooden construction. Classified as "Yaezakura" class plus *Hamayu* (100) and *Kogiku* (116).

FIRE FIGHTING CRAFT

5 "HIRYU" CLASS

Name	No.	Builders	Commissioned
HIRYU	FL 01	Asano Dockyard	4 Mar 1969
SHORYU	FL 02	Asano Dockyard	4 Mar 1970
NANRYU	FL 03	Asano Dockyard	4 Mar 1971
KAIRYU	FL 04	Asano Dockyard	18 Mar 1977
SUIRYU	FL 05	Asano Dockyard	1978

Displacement, tons: 251 normal
Dimensions, feet (metres): 90·2 oa × 34·1 × 7·2 (27·5 × 10·4 × 2·2)
Main engines: 2 sets diesels; 2 200 bhp = 13·5 knots
Range, miles: 395 at 13·4 knots
Complement: 14

Hiryu, a catamaran type fire boat, was laid down in Oct 1968, launched 21 Jan 1969. Designed and built for firefighting services to large tankers. *Shoryu* was launched on 18 Jan 1970, *Nanryu* on 16 Jan 1971, and *Kairyu* on 18 Jan 1977. *Suiryu* was ordered 7 June 1976.

Radar: One navigation set.

HIRYU   *5/1976, Yoshifumi Mayama*

7 "NUNOBIKI" CLASS

Name	No.	Builders	Commissioned
NUNOBIKI	FM 01	Yokohama Yacht Co Ltd	25 Feb 1974
YODO	FM 02	Yokohama Yacht Co Ltd	30 Mar 1975
OTOWA	FM 03	Sumidagawa	25 Dec 1974
SHIRAITO	FM 04	Yokohama Yacht Co Ltd	25 Feb 1975
KOTOBIKI	FM 05	Yokohama Yacht Co Ltd	31 Jan 1976
NACHI	FM 06	Sumidagawa	14 Feb 1976
KEGON	FM 07	Yokohama Yacht Co Ltd	29 Jan 1977

Displacement, tons: 87
Dimensions, feet (metres): 75·4 oa × 19·7 × 10·5 (23 × 6 × 3·2)
Main engines: 1 Mercedes-Benz (MTU) diesel plus 2 Nissan diesels;
  1 100 bhp + 500 bhp = 14 knots
Range, miles: 1 800 at 14 knots
Complement: 12

Radar: One navigation set.

OTOWA   *5/1976, Yoshifumi Mayama*

12 METRE FIREFIGHTING CRAFT

Name	No.	Builders	Commissioned
MINOO	FS 07	Kure (S)	28 Mar 1952

JAPAN

SURVEYING SERVICE

Note: *Shinkai*, ex-HU 06 now operates for the Academy at Kure.

Name	No.	Builders	Commissioned
SHOYO	HL 01	Hitachi, Maizuru	26 Feb 1972

Displacement, tons: 2 044 standard
Dimensions, feet (metres): 262·4 × 40·3 × 13·8 *(80 × 12·3 × 4·2)*
Main engines: 2 Fuji V-12 diesels; 4 800 hp; 1 shaft = 17·4 knots
Range, miles: 8 340 at 16 knots
Complement: 73

Launched 18 Sept 1971. Fully equipped for all types of hydrographic and oceanographic work. Based at Tokyo.

Radar: Two navigation sets.

SHOYO *1973, Japanese Maritime Safety Agency*

Name	No.	Builders	Commissioned
TAKUYO	HL 02	Niigata	12 Mar 1957

Displacement, tons: 880 standard
Dimensions, feet (metres): 204·7 oa × 31·2 × 10·7 *(62·4 × 9·5 × 3·3)*
Main engines: 2 diesels; 1 300 bhp = 14 knots
Range, miles: 8 000 at 12 knots
Complement: 50

Laid down on 19 May 1956, launched on 19 Dec 1956. Based at Tokyo.

Radar: One navigation set.

TAKUYO *1975, Japanese Maritime Safety Agency*

Name	No.	Builders	Commissioned
MEIYO	HL 03	Nagoya	15 Mar 1963

Displacement, tons: 486 normal
Measurement, tons: 360 gross
Dimensions, feet (metres): 133 wl; 146 oa × 26·5 × 9·5 *(40·6; 44·5 × 8·1 × 2·9)*
Main engine: 1 diesel; 700 bhp = 12 knots
Range, miles: 5 000 at 11 knots
Complement: 40

Laid down on 14 Sept 1962, launched 22 Dec 1962. Controllable pitch propeller. Based at Tokyo.

Radar: One navigation set.

MEIYO *1975, Japanese Maritime Safety Agency*

Name	No.	Builders	Commissioned
HEIYO	HM 04	Shimuzu Dockyard	22 Mar 1955

Displacement, tons: 69
Dimensions, feet (metres): 76·5 oa × 14·5 × 8 *(23·3 × 4·4 × 2·4)*
Main engine: 1 diesel; 150 bhp = 9 knots
Range, miles: 670 at 9 knots
Complement: 13

Radar: One navigation set.

HEIYO *1975, Japanese Maritime Safety Agency*

Name	No.	Builders	Commissioned
TENYO	HM 05	Yokohama Yacht Co	30 Mar 1961

Displacement, tons: 171
Dimensions, feet (metres): 99·1 oa × 19·2 × 9·2 *(30·2 × 5·9 × 2·8)*
Main engines: Diesels; 230 bhp = 10 knots
Range, miles: 3 160 at 10 knots
Complement: 25

Radar: One navigation set.

TENYO *1975, Japanese Maritime Safety Agency*

Name	No.	Builders	Commissioned
KAIYO	HM 06	Nagoya	14 Mar 1964

Displacement, tons: 378 normal
Dimensions, feet (metres): 132·5 wl; 146 oa × 26·5 × 7·8 *(40·4; 44·5 × 8·1 × 2·4)*
Main engines: 1 set diesels; 450 bhp = 12 knots
Range, miles: 6 100 at 11 knots
Complement: 34

Controllable pitch propeller.

Radar: One navigation set.

KAIYO
2/1976, Yoshifumi Mayama

SURVEYING CRAFT

11 "HAMASHIO" CLASS

HS 01-11

Completed 1969-72. 10 metre craft.

1 "HASHIMA" CLASS

HS 17

Completed 1951 by Yamanishi. Of 10 metres.

2 "FUKAE" CLASS

HS 20 and 21

Completed 1951. Of 12 metres.

5 "AKASHI" CLASS

HS 31-35

Completed 1973-75. Of 15 metres.

NAVIGATION AIDS SERVICE

Name	No.	Builders	Commissioned
TSUSHIMA	LL 01	Mitsui, Tamano	9 Sept 1977

Displacement, tons: 1 865 normal
Dimensions, feet (metres): 229·6 × 41 × 13·8 *(70 × 12·5 × 4·2)*
Main engines: 1 diesel; 4 000 shp; 1 shaft = 15·5 knots
Range, miles: 10 000 at 15 knots
Endurance: 30 days
Complement: 54

Built under FY 1975 programme. Laid down 10 June 1976, launched 7 April 1977. Replacement for *Wakakusa* as lighthouse Supply Ship, taking her pennant number. Fitted with bow thruster and tank stabilisers.

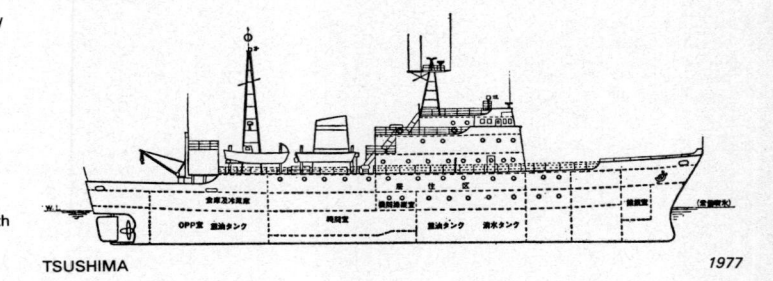

TSUSHIMA
1977

Name	No.	Builders	Commissioned
GINGA	LL 12	Osaka	30 June 1954

Displacement, tons: 500
Dimensions, feet (metres): 135·5 oa × 31·2 × 13·9 *(41·3 × 9·4 × 4·2)*
Main engines: 2 diesels; 420 bhp = 11·26 knots
Range, miles: 2 800 at 10 knots
Complement: 38

Ginga was laid down on 11 Nov 1953 and launched on 6 May 1954. Equipped with 15 ton derrick for laying buoys. Rated as Navigation Aid Vessel (Buoy Tender).

Radar: One navigation set

GINGA
1971, Japanese Maritime Safety Agency

Name	No.	Builders	Commissioned
HOKUTO	LL 11	Kawasaki	12 Mar 1952
KAIO	LL 13	Namura	24 Mar 1955

Displacement, tons: 616 standard
Dimensions, feet (metres): 153·8 × 33·8 × 8·9 *(46·9 × 10·3 × 2·7)*
Main engines: Recip; 400 ihp = 10·4 knots
Range, miles: 1 821
Complement: 38

HOKUTO
9/1975, Yoshifumi Mayama

300 JAPAN

Name	No.	Builders	Commissioned
MYOJO	LM 11	Asano	25 Mar 1974

Displacement, tons: 318 normal
Dimensions, feet (metres): 88·6 oa × 39·4 × 8·8 (27 × 12 × 2·7)
Main engines: 2 diesels; 600 bhp = 11·1 knots
Range, miles: 1 360 at 10 knots
Complement: 49

Completed in Mar 1974 to replace an identical ship of the same name, completed in 1967, which was lost in collision April 1972. Catamaran type buoy tender, propelled by controllable pitch propellers, this ship is employed in maintenance and position adjustment service to floating aids to navigation.

MYOJO   5/1976, Yoshifumi Mayama

NAVIGATION AND BUOY TENDERS

LM 101, 112 (30 metres); LM 102, 105-111, 113 (23 metres).
LS 204 (20 metres); LS 115, 124, 156, 184, 201-203, 206-208, 212-217 (17 metres); LS 122, 151-3, 171, 183, 205, 209-211, 218, 219 (12 metres); LS 154, 155, 181, 185, 186, 188-190, 192-5, 197, 198 ("Zuiko" and "Yuko" 10 metre classes); LS 104, 108, 111, 114, 132, 134, 138, 140, 147, 150, 159, 162, 167, 179, 180, 182, 199 ("Yoko", "Seiko" and "Yuko" 10 metre classes); LS 102, 103, 105, 106, 112, 113, 123, 125, 137, 163, 174, 177, 187, 191, 196 ("Eko", "Wako" and "Tenko" classes); LS 109, 110, 118, 130, 131, 142, 146, 148, 149, 172, 173, 175, 176 (Elderly craft of various types reaching retirement age).

UNDERWATER RESEARCH VESSEL

Name	No.	Builders	Commissioned
SHINKAI	HU 06	Kawasaki	Mar 1969

Displacement, tons: 91
Dimensions, feet (metres): 54·2 oa × 18·1 × 13 (16·5 × 5·5 × 4)
Main engines: 1 electric motor; 11 kW
Range, miles: 4·6 at 2·3 knots
Complement: 4

Laid down in Sept 1967, launched in Mar 1968. An underwater vehicle designed for carrying out research on biological and underground resources of the continental shelves. With a main propeller and two auxiliary ones installed on each side of the hull, this ship can dive to 2 000 feet and stay on the sea bed for sampling, observing and photographing.

SHINKAI   1970, Japanese Maritime Safety Agency

MISCELLANEOUS

MONITORING CRAFT

KINUGASA FS 01   SAIKAI FS 02   KATUREN FS 03

First two 10 metre catamaran craft, 03 of 16 metres.

SURVEILLANCE CRAFT

SS 01, 02, 04, 05-22

6 metre craft completed between 1972-1976.

OIL SKIMMERS

OS 01-03

Completed 1974-75 by Lockheed.

OIL BOOM CRAFT

M 101-119

20 metre dumb barges completed 1974-76.

UTILITY CRAFT

M 603, 615, 618, 804

Of varying sizes about 6 metres. M 803 renamed *Wakaba* operates for MSA Academy at Kure.

OIL RECOVERY CRAFT

SHIRASAGI OR 01

Completed 31 Jan 1977 by Sumidagawa.

SHIRASAGI   5/1977, Yoshifumi Mayama

# JORDAN

Ministerial

Minister of Defence:
 Mudar Badran (Premier)

Diplomatic Representation

Defence Attaché in London:
 Brigadier Mohammad Hussein

Coastal Guard

It was officially stated in 1969 that Jordan had no naval force known as such, but the Jordan Coastal Guard, sometimes called the Jordan Sea Force, took orders directly from the Director of Operations at General Headquarters. There is no longer a flotilla in the Dead Sea.

Base

Aqaba

Personnel

(a) 1978: 300 officers and men
(b) Voluntary service

Mercantile Marine

Lloyd's Register of Shipping:
 1 vessel of 200 tons gross

LIGHT FORCES

HUSSEIN ABDALLAH

Wooden hulled of 40 ft *(12 m)* acquired in Aug 1974.

1 BERTRAM TYPE (COASTAL PATROL CRAFT)

Displacement, tons: 7
Dimensions, feet (metres): 30·4 × 10·8 × 1·6 *(9·2 × 3·3 × 0·5)*
Guns: 1—12·7 mm; 1—7·2 mm
Main engines: Diesels = 24 knots
Complement: 8

Glass fibre hull.

4 25 ft TYPE (COASTAL PATROL CRAFT)

Aluminium hulls.

4 PATROL CRAFT

Wooden-hulled craft of about 18 ft—unarmed.

KAMPUCHEA (CAMBODIA)

The Marine Royale Khmer was established on 1 March 1954 and became Marine Nationale Khmer on 9 October 1970. With the imminent victory of the forces of Khmer Rouge in April-May 1975, several ships (listed in Deletions section) escaped from Khmer waters.
Originally Cambodia, became known as the Khmer Republic and is now officially called Democratic Kampuchea.

Note: The facts of this force are very uncertain. There is no postal link with Kampuchea now and what follows is probably "the worst possible case". It is probable that less than a third of the craft listed is operationsl.

Ministerial

Deputy Prime Minister for National Defence:
 Son Sen

Personnel

(a) 1975: 11 000 officers and men including Marine Corps (4 000 officers and men) (current situation not known)
(b) 18 months national service

Mercantile Marine

Lloyd's Register of Shipping:
 2 vessels of 1 208 tons gross

DELETIONS

Large Patrol Craft

1975 E 311 to Thailand (16 May), E 312 to Subic Bay, Philippines (2 May). P111 and P112 to Subic Bay (17 April) and to Philippine Navy.

Light Forces

1975 VR1 and VR2 (ex-Yugoslav "101" class) believed sunk by US aircraft during *Mayaguez* incident (13 May).

LIGHT FORCES

17 Ex-US "SWIFT" CLASS (COASTAL PATROL CRAFT)

Displacement, tons: 22·5
Dimensions, feet (metres): 50 × 13 × 3·5 *(15 × 4 × 1·1)*
Guns: 1—81 mm mortar; 3—50 cal MG
Main engines: 2 diesels; 960 hp; 2 shafts = 28 knots
Complement: 6

Transferred in 1972-73

2 Ex-US AVR TYPE (COASTAL PATROL CRAFT)

VR 3   VR 4

Displacement, tons: 30
Dimensions, feet (metres): 63 × 13 × 4·6 *(19·1 × 4 × 1·4)*
Guns: 4—12·7 mm MG
Main engines: GM diesel 500 bhp = 15 knots
Complement: 12

65 Ex-US PBR MARK 1 and II (RIVER PATROL CRAFT)

Displacement, tons: 8
Dimensions, feet (metres): 32 × 11 × 2·6 *(9·8 × 3·4 × 0·8)*
Guns: 3—50 cal MG; 1 grenade launcher
Main engines: 2 geared diesels; water jets = 25 knots
Complement: 5

Transferred 1973-74.

PBR Mk II Type   *United States Navy*

302 KAMPUCHEA

3 Ex-CHINESE "YU-LIN" CLASS (COASTAL PATROL CRAFT)

| VP 1 | VP 2 | VP 3 |

Displacement, tons: 7·7 standard; 9·7 full load
Dimensions, feet (metres): 40 × 9·5 × 3·5 *(13 × 2·9 × 1·1)*
Guns: 2—14·5 mm; 2—12·7 mm
Main engine: Diesel; 300 bhp = 24 knots
Complement: 10

Transferred from the People's Republic of China in Jan 1968. Built in Shanghai.

1 Ex-HDML TYPE (COASTAL PATROL CRAFT)

VP 212 (ex-*VP 748*, ex-*HDML 1223*)

Displacement, tons: 46 standard; 54 full load
Dimensions, feet (metres): 72 oa × 16 × 5·5 *(22 × 4·9 × 1·7)*
Guns: 2—20 mm; 4—7·5 mm MG
Main engines: 2 diesels; 2 shafts; 300 bhp = 10 knots
Complement: 8

Former British harbour defence motor launch of the HDML type. Transferred from the British Navy to the French Navy in 1950 and again transferred from the French Navy to the MNK in 1956.

AMPHIBIOUS VESSELS

2 Ex-US "LCU 1466" CLASS

T 917 (ex-US *YFU*, ex-*LCU 1577*)
SKILAK T 920 (ex-US *YFU 73*)

Displacement, tons: 320 full load
Dimensions, feet (metres): 119 oa × 32·7 × 5 *(36·3 × 10 × 1·5)*
Guns: 2—20 mm
Main engines: Diesels; 675 bhp; 3 shafts = 10 knots
Complement: 13

T 917 transferred Oct 1969. T 920 in Nov 1973.

US "LCU 1466" Class   *1970, Defoe Shipbuilding*

1 EDIC TYPE

T 916 (ex-*EDIC 606*)

Displacement, tons: 292 standard; 650 full load
Dimensions, feet (metres): 193·5 × 39·2 × 4·5 *(59 × 12 × 1·4)*
Guns: 1—81 mm mortar; 2—12·7 mm MG
Main engines: 2 MGO diesels; 2 shafts; 1 000 bhp = 10 knots
Complement: 16 (1 officer, 15 men)

Completed and transferred from the French Government in Aug 1969.

4 Ex-US "LCU 501" CLASS

T 914 (ex-US *LCU 783*)   T 918 (ex-US *LCU 646*)
T 915 (ex-US *LCU 1421*)   T 919 (ex-US *LCU 1385*)

Displacement, tons: 180 standard; 360 full load
Dimensions, feet (metres): 115 wl; 119 oa × 34 × 6 *(35·1; 36·3 × 10·4 × 1·8)*
Guns: 2—20 mm
Main engines: 3 diesels; 3 shafts; 675 bhp = 8 knots
Complement: 12

LCU 783 and LCU 1421 were transferred on 31 May 1962. T919 (ex-US *LCU 1577*) was sunk by a mine on 5 May 1970, her number being taken by new T919 transferred in Nov 1972 at same time as T918. Both these had operated as YFU—68 and 56 respectively.

US "LCU 501" Class   *1969, Marine Nat. Khmere*

MISCELLANEOUS

1 TUG

PINGOUIE R 911 (ex-US *YTL 556*)

2 FLOATING DOCKS

1 of 350 tons from France in 1955.
1 of 1 000 tons from USA in 1972.

KENYA

Ministerial

Minister of Defence:
James Samuel Gichuru

Establishment

The Kenya Navy was inaugurated on 12 Dec 1964, the first anniversary of Kenya's independence.

Administration

Commander, Kenya Navy:
Lieutenant Colonel J. C. J. Kimaro

General

With a coastline of only 350 miles the present force is probably adequate for coastal patrol duties. With a 200 mile limit to think about and with the three 31 metre craft probably well into the second half of their lives the possibility of some type of corvette replacement must be on the cards. Something of at least 500 tons would be necessary for offshore work, particularly in the NE Monsoon season.

Personnel

(a) 1978: 350 officers and men
(b) Voluntary service

Prefix to Ships' Names

KNS

Base

Mombasa

Mercantile Marine

Lloyd's Register of Shipping:
19 vessels of 15 469 tons gross

LIGHT FORCES

3 BROOKE MARINE 32·6 metre TYPE (LARGE PATROL CRAFT)

Name	No.	Builders	Commissioned
MADARAKA	P 3121	Brooke Marine, Lowestoft	16 June 1975
JAMHURI	P 3122	Brooke Marine, Lowestoft	16 June 1975
HARAMBEE	P 3123	Brooke Marine, Lowestoft	22 Aug 1975

Displacement, tons: 120 standard; 145 full load
Dimensions, feet (metres): 107 × 20 × 5·6 *(32·6 × 6·1 × 1·7)*
Guns: 2—40 mm
Main engines: 2 Ruston-Paxman Valenta diesels; 5 400 bhp; 2 shafts = 25·5 knots
Range, miles: 2 500 at 12 knots
Complement: 21 (3 officers, 18 men)

Ordered 10 May 1973. *Madaraka* launched 28 Jan 1975, *Jamhuri* 14 March 1975, *Harambe* 2 May 1975.

HARAMBEE *7/1976, Michael D. J. Lennon*

BROOKE MARINE 37·5 metre TYPE (LARGE PATROL CRAFT)

Name	No.	Builders	Commissioned
MAMBA	P 3100	Brooke Marine, Lowestoft	7 Feb 1974

Displacement, tons: 125 standard; 160 full load
Dimensions, feet (metres): 123 × 22·5 × 5·2 *(37·5 × 6·9 × 1·6)*
Guns: 2—40 mm Bofors
Main engines: 2—16-cyl Rustons diesels; 4 000 hp = 25 knots
Range, miles: 3 300 at 13 knots
Complement: 25 (3 officers, 22 men)

Laid down 17 Feb 1972.

MAMBA *1974*

3 VOSPER 31 metre TYPE (LARGE PATROL CRAFT)

Name	No.	Builders	Commissioned
SIMBA	P 3110	Vosper Ltd, Portsmouth	23 May 1966
CHUI	P 3112	Vosper Ltd, Portsmouth	7 July 1966
NDOVU	P 3117	Vosper Ltd, Portsmouth	27 July 1966

Displacement, tons: 96 standard; 109 full load
Dimensions, feet (metres): 95 wl; 103 oa × 19·8 × 5·8 *(28·8; 31·4 × 6 × 1·8)*
Guns: 2—40 mm Bofors
Main engines: 2 Paxman Ventura diesels; 2 800 bhp = 24 knots
Range, miles: 1 000 at economical speed; 1 500 at 16 knots
Complement: 23 (3 officers and 20 ratings)

The first ships specially built for the Kenya Navy. Ordered on 28 Oct 1964. *Simba* was launched on 9 Sept 1965. All three left Portsmouth on 22 Aug 1966 and arrived at their base in Mombasa on 4 Oct 1966. Air-conditioned. Fitted with roll damping fins.

SIMBA *1973, Kenyan Navy*

KOREA—North
(People's Democratic Republic)

Ministerial

Minister of Peoples Armed Forces:
O Chin-u

Administration

Commander of the Navy:
Rear-Admiral Yu Chang Kwon

Personnel

(a) 1978: 30 300 officers and men (40 000 reserves)
(b) National service; 5 years

Bases

Main: Wonsan (East), Nampo (West)
Minor: Ch'ongjin, Haeju, Najin (Naval Academy), Munchon, Pipa-got, Cha-ho, Mayang Do, Sagon-ni, Kimchaek, Kosong, Songjon Pando, Yoko Ri, Chodo, Kwangyang Ni.

Mercantile Marine

Lloyd's Register of Shipping:
19 vessels of 89 482 tons gross

Strength of the Fleet

Type	Active	Building
Submarines—Patrol	15	2
Frigates	3	1
Fast Attack Craft—Missile	18	—
Fast Attack Craft—Torpedo	165	2
Fast Attack Craft—Gun	134	4
Large Patrol Craft	26	—
Coastal Patrol Craft	30	—
LCAs (Large)	70	—
Trawlers etc.	105	—

SUBMARINES

Note: Up to five midget submarines reported as built in North Korea since 1974.

11 Ex-CHINESE "ROMEO" CLASS (PATROL TYPE)

Displacement, tons: 1 000 surfaced; 1 600 dived
Dimensions, feet (metres): 249·3 × 24 × 14·5 *(76 × 7·3 × 4·4)*
Torpedo tubes: 6—21 in (bow); 18 torpedoes
Main machinery: 2 diesels; 4 000 bhp; 2 electric motors; 4 000 hp; 2 shafts
Speed, knots: 17 surfaced; 14 dived
Range, miles: 16 000 at 10 knots (surfaced)
Complement: 65

Two transferred from China 1973, two in 1974 and two in 1975. Local building at Mayand Do provided two more in 1976. Continuing programme with slightly different dimensions etc. Stationed on West coast (Yellow Sea).

"ROMEO" Class   Bradley Hahn

4 Ex-SOVIET "WHISKEY" CLASS (PATROL TYPE)

Displacement, tons: 1 030 surfaced; 1 350 dived
Dimensions, feet (metres): 249·3 × 22 × 15 *(76 × 6·7 × 4·6)*
Torpedo tubes: 6—21 in (4 bow, 2 stern); 18 torpedoes carried normally (or up to 40 mines)
Main machinery: 2 diesels; 4 000 bhp; 2 electric motors; 2 500 hp; 2 shafts
Speed, knots: 17 surfaced; 15 dived
Range, miles: 13 000 at 8 knots (surfaced)
Complement: 60

Stationed on East Coast (Sea of Japan).

"WHISKEY" Class   Bradley Hahn

FRIGATES

3 + 1 "NAJIN" CLASS

3025	3026	3027

Displacement, tons: 1 500
Dimensions, feet (metres): 330 × 33 × 9 *(100 × 10 × 2·7)*
Guns: 2—3·9 in *(100 mm)*, 56 cal; 4—57 mm (twin); 4—25 mm (twin vertical); 8—14·5 mm
A/S weapons: 2—MBU 1800; 2 DC racks; 2 A/S mortars
Torpedo tubes: 3—21 in *(533 mm)*
Mines: 30 (estimated)
Main engines: 2 diesels; 15 000 bhp; 3 shafts
Speed, knots: 26
Range, miles: 4 000 at 14 knots
Complement: 180

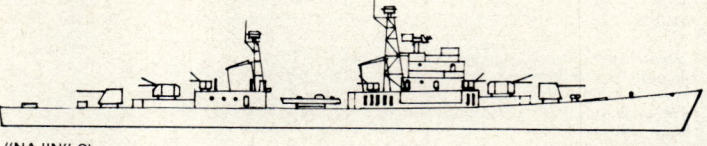

"NAJIN" Class   Bradley Hahn

Built in North Korea. First laid down 1971, completed 1973, second completed 1975, third completed 1976. Fourth laid down 1976.

Radar: Surface search: Skin Head, Pot Head.
IFF: Ski Pole.

KOREA (NORTH) 305

LIGHT FORCES

2 Ex-SOVIET "TRAL" CLASS (LARGE PATROL CRAFT)

Displacement, tons: 475
Dimensions, feet (metres): 203·5 pp × 23·8 × 7·8 *(62 × 7·2 × 2·4)*
Guns: 1—3·9 in *(100 mm)* 56 cal; 3—37 mm (singles); 4—12·7 mm MG
A/S weapons: 2 DC racks
Mines: 30
Main engines: 2 diesels; 2 800 hp; 2 shafts
Speed, knots: 18
Complement: 52

An elderly class of Fleet Minesweepers of which 8 were transferred by USSR in mid 1950s. Used for escort purposes.
All originally ex-commissioned in 1938. One (ex-*Strela,* ex-T 1) was transferred to Soviet Pacific Fleet via Panama Canal in 1939 and another (ex-*Paravan* ex-T 5) at the same time via Suez.

Radar: Surface search: Skin Head.
IFF: Yard Rake.

"TRAL" Class *Bradley Hahn*

3 "SARIWAN" CLASS (LARGE PATROL CRAFT)

725   726   727(?)

Displacement, tons: 475
Dimensions, feet (metres): 203·5 × 24 × 7·8 *(62·1 × 7·3 × 2·4)*
Guns: 1—85 mm; 2—57 mm (twin); 12/16—14·5 mm (quad—poss. ZPU-4 type)
Mines: 30
Main engines: 2 diesels; 3 000 bhp; 2 shafts
Speed, knots: 21 (estimated)
Complement: 65-70

Built in North Korea in the mid 1960s.

Radar: Surface search: Don 2. **IFF:** Ski Pole and Yard Rake.

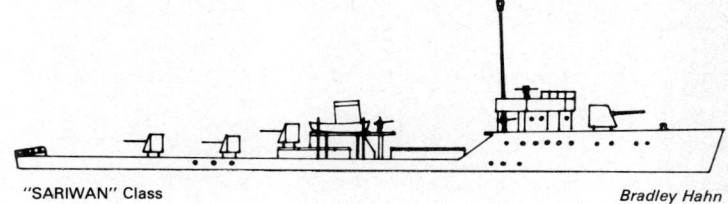

"SARIWAN" Class *Bradley Hahn*

4 Ex-CHINESE "HAI NAN" CLASS (LARGE PATROL CRAFT)

Displacement, tons: 360 standard; 400 full load
Dimensions, feet (metres): 197 × 24 × 6·1 *(60 × 7·4 × 2·1)*
Guns: 2—3 in *(76 mm);* 4—25 mm (twins)
A/S weapons: 4 MBU 1800; 2 DCT; 2 DC racks
Main engines: Diesels; 8 000 shp = 28 knots
Range, miles: 1 000 at 10 knots (est)
Complement: 60

Transferred in 1975 (2), 1976 (2).

"HAI NAN" Class   1976

6 + 9 SOVIET "SO 1" CLASS (LARGE PATROL CRAFT)

Displacement, tons: 215 light; 250 normal
Dimensions, feet (metres): 138·6 × 20·0 × 9·2 *(42·3 × 6·1 × 2·8)*
Guns: 1—85 mm; 2—37 mm (twin); 4—14·5 mm MG
Main engines: 3 diesels; 6 000 bhp = 29 knots
Range, miles: 1 100 at 13 knots
Complement: 30

Six transferred by USSR in 1957-61. Remainder built in North Korea—of modified form.

Radar: Fire control: Pot Head.
Navigation: Don 2.
IFF: Ski Pole.

Soviet "SO 1" Class (guns differ in Korean version)   1972

1 or 2 Ex-SOVIET "ARTILLERIST" CLASS (LARGE PATROL CRAFT)

Displacement, tons: 240
Dimensions, feet (metres): 160·8 × 19 × 6·5 *(49 × 5·8 × 2)*
Guns: 1—3·9 in *(100 mm);* 2—37 mm (singles); 4/6—25 mm (twin, vertical)
Main engines: 2 diesels; 3 300 bhp; 2 shafts
Speed, knots: 25
Complement: 30

Transferred in 1950s.

2 "TAECHONG" CLASS (LARGE PATROL CRAFT)

A North Korean class in series production.

306 KOREA (NORTH)

8 Ex-SOVIET "OSA 1" CLASS (FAST ATTACK CRAFT—MISSILE)

Displacement, tons: 165 standard; 200 full load
Dimensions, feet (metres): 128·7 × 25·1 × 5·9 *(39·3 × 7·7 × 1·8)*
Missile launchers: 4 in two pairs abreast for Styx missiles
Guns: 4—30 mm (1 twin forward, and aft)
Main engines: 3 diesels; 13 000 bhp = 32 knots
Range, miles: 800 at 25
Complement: 25

The combination of the "Osa" flotilla and the "Komar" units both armed with the very potent 23 mile range Styx missile, provides a powerful striking force on the South Korean border and within 250 miles of Japan.

Radar: Search: Square Tie.
Fire control: Pot Drum.
IFF: High Pole.

"OSA 1" Class   1970

10 Ex-SOVIET "KOMAR" CLASS (FAST ATTACK CRAFT—MISSILE)

Displacement, tons: 70 standard; 80 full load
Dimensions, feet (metres): 83·7 × 19·8 × 5·0 *(25·5 × 6·0 × 1·8)*
Missile launchers: 2 for Styx missiles
Guns: 2—25 mm (1 twin forward)
Main engines: 4 diesels; 4 shafts; 4 800 bhp = 40 knots
Range, miles: 400 at 30 knots

See note under "Osa" class above. Another class, "Sohung", may be a North Korean version of the "Komar".

"KOMAR" Class   Bradley Hahn

8 Ex-CHINESE "SHANGHAI" CLASS (FAST ATTACK CRAFT—GUN)

Displacement, tons: 120 standard; 155 full load
Dimensions, feet (metres): 128 × 18 × 5·6 *(39 × 5·5 × 1·7)*
Guns: 4—37 mm (twin); 4—25 mm (abaft bridge);
 2—3 in *(75 mm)* recoilless rifles (bow)
A/S weapons: 8 DC
Main engines: 4 diesels; 4 800 bhp = 30 knots
Mines: Rails can be fitted for 10 mines
Range, miles: 800 at 17 knots
Complement: 25

Acquired from China since 1967. Skin Head radar.

"SHANGHAI" Class   Bradley Hahn

8 Ex-CHINESE "SWATOW" CLASS (FAST ATTACK CRAFT—GUN)

Displacement, tons: 80
Dimensions, feet (metres): 83·5 × 19 × 6·5 *(25·5 × 5·8 × 2)*
Guns: 4—37 mm (twins); 4—12·7 mm (twins)
A/S weapons: 8 DC
Main engines: 4 diesels; 3 000 bhp = 28 knots
Range, miles: 500 at 28 knots
Complement: 17

Transferred from China in 1968.

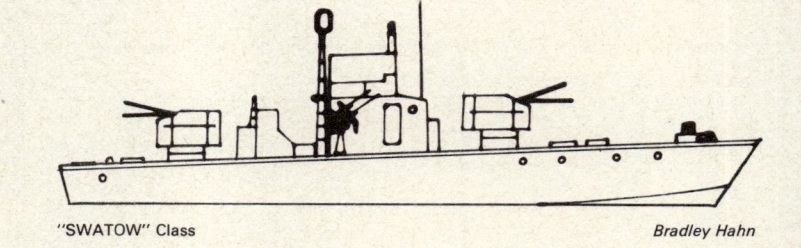

"SWATOW" Class   Bradley Hahn

4 "CHODO" CLASS (FAST ATTACK CRAFT—GUN)

Displacement, tons: 130 (estimated)
Dimensions, feet (metres): 140 × 19 × 8·5 *(42·7 × 5·8 × 2·6)*
Guns: 4—37 mm (single); 4—25 mm (twin, vertical)
Main engines: Diesels; 2 shafts; 6 000 bhp
Speed, knots: 25
Range, miles: 2 000 at 10 knots
Complement: 40

Built in North Korea in mid 1960s.

Radar. Skin Head.

"CHODO" Class   Bradley Hahn

KOREA (NORTH) 307

4 "K-48" CLASS (FAST ATTACK CRAFT—GUN)

Displacement, tons: 110 (estimated)
Dimensions, feet (metres): 125 × 18 × 5 *(38·1 × 5·5 × 1·5)*
Guns: 1—3 in *(76 mm)* 50 cal (forward); 3—37 mm (single); 4/6—14·5 mm MG (twin)
Main engines: Diesels; 4/5 000 bhp; 2 shafts
Speed, knots: 24 (estimated)

May have been built in North Korea in mid 1950s.

Radar: Skin Head.

"K-48" Class *Bradley Hahn*

20 Ex-SOVIET "MO IV" CLASS (FAST ATTACK CRAFT—GUN)

Displacement, tons: 56
Dimensions, feet (metres): 88·5 × 13·2 × 5 *(27 × 4 × 1·5)*
Guns: 1—37 mm; 1/2—14·5 mm MG
Main engines: 2 Skoda diesels; 2 600 hp = 25 knots
Complement: 20

Transferred in 1950s. Built in 1945-47. Wooden hulls.

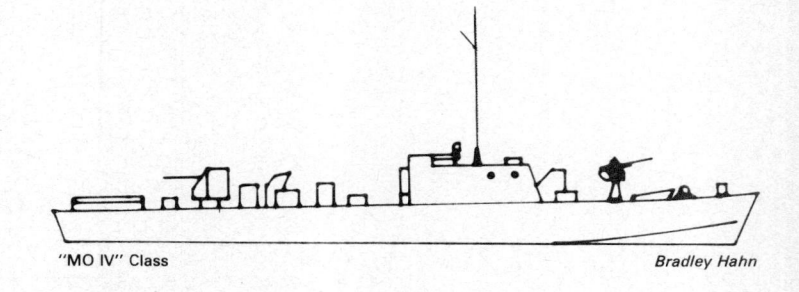

"MO IV" Class *Bradley Hahn*

60 "CHAHO" CLASS (FAST ATTACK CRAFT—GUN)

Displacement, tons: 80 full load
Dimensions, feet (metres): 84·2 × 20 × 6 *(27·7 × 6·1 × 1·8)*
Guns: 8—200 mm, 40 tube rocket launchers; 4—14·5 mm
Main engines: 4 diesels; 4 800 shp = 38-40 knots
Complement: 10-12 (est)

Reported as building in North Korea since 1974. Based on "P 6" hull.

"CHAHO" Class *Bradley Hahn*

30 "CHONG-JIN" CLASS (FAST ATTACK CRAFT—GUN)

Particulars similar to "Chaho" class of which this is an improved version. Building began about 1975.

4 Ex-SOVIET "SHERSHEN" CLASS
(FAST ATTACK CRAFT—TORPEDO)

Displacement, tons: 150 standard; 160 full load
Dimensions, feet (metres): 115·5 × 23 × 5 *(35·2 × 7·1 × 1·5)*
Guns: 4—30 mm (2 twin)
Torpedo tubes: 4—21 (single)
A/S weapons: 12 DC
Main engines: 3 diesels; 3 shafts; 13 000 bhp = 41 knots
Complement: 16

Transferred in 1973-74.

Radar: Search/Navigation: Pot Drum.
Fire control: Drum Tilt.
IFF: High Pole.

Soviet "SHERSHEN" Class *1970*

308 KOREA (NORTH)

62 Ex-SOVIET "P 6" CLASS (FAST ATTACK CRAFT—TORPEDO)

Displacement, tons: 66 standard; 75 full load
Dimensions, feet (metres): 84·2 × 20 × 6 *(25·7 × 6·1 × 1·8)*
Guns: 4—25 mm (original); 1—76 mm (modified); 2—37 mm (some)
Torpedo tubes: 2—21 in (or mines or DC)
Main engines: 4 diesels; 4 800 hp; 4 shafts = 43 knots
Range, miles: 450 at 30 knots
Complement: 19

There is a growing number of these craft in North Korea with local building programme in hand of a modified form. Some transferred originally by USSR and China. A further development, the six boats of the "Sinpo" class are reported to carry 6—14·5 mm MG.

Radar: Pot Head or Skin Head.

"P 6" Class   1972

"MODIFIED P 6" Class   Bradley Hahn

12 Ex-SOVIET "P 4" CLASS (FAST ATTACK CRAFT—TORPEDO)

Displacement, tons: 25
Dimensions, feet (metres): 62·7 × 11·6 × 5·6 *(19·1 × 3·5 × 1·7)*
Guns: 2—MG
Torpedo tubes: 2—18 in
Main engines: 2 diesels; 2 200 bhp = 50 knots.

Built in 1951-57. Aluminium hulls.

"P 4" Class   1971

15 "IWON" CLASS (FAST ATTACK CRAFT—TORPEDO)

Displacement, tons: 40
Dimensions, feet (metres): 63 × 12 × 5 *(19·2 × 3·7 × 1·5)*
Guns: 4—25 mm (twin, vertical)
Torpedo tubes: 2—21 in *(533 mm)*

Built in North Korea in late 1950s. Similar to older Soviet "P 2" class design.

Radar: Skin Head.

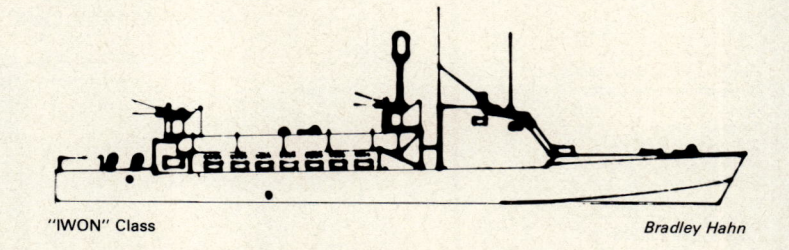

"IWON" Class   Bradley Hahn

6 "AN JU" CLASS (FAST ATTACK CRAFT—TORPEDO)

Displacement, tons: 35
Dimensions, feet (metres): 65 × 12 × 6 *(19·8 × 3·7 × 1·8)*
Guns: 2—25 mm (twin, vertical)
Torpedo tubes: 2—21 in *(533 mm)*
Main engines: Diesels; 4 screws
Range, miles: 1 300 at 20 knots
Complement: 20

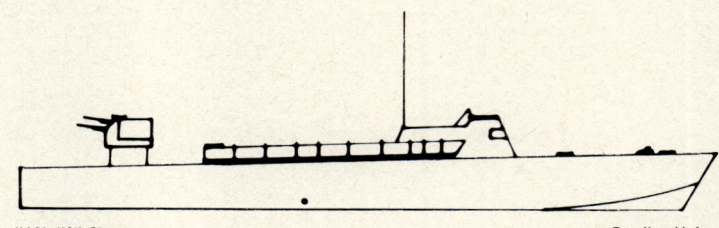

Built in North Korea in 1960s.

"AN JU" Class   Bradley Hahn

60 "SIN HUNG" and "KOSONG" CLASSES
(FAST ATTACK CRAFT—TORPEDO)

Displacement, tons: 35
Dimensions, feet (metres): 60 × 11 × 5·5 *(18·3 × 3·4 × 1·7)*
Guns: 2—14·5 mm (twin)
Torpedo tubes: 2—18 in or 2—21 in

Built in North Korea mid 1950s to 1970. Frequently operated on South Korean border. All resemble the Soviet "D-3" class of 25 years ago.

10 SOVIET "KM 4" CLASS (COASTAL PATROL CRAFT)

Displacement, tons: 10
Dimensions, feet (metres): 46 × 10·5 × 3 *(14 × 3·2 × 0·9)*
Guns: 1—36 mm; 1—14·5 mm MG
Main engines: Petrol; 146 shp; 2 shafts
Complement: 10

Built in North Korea to Soviet designs.

20 LIGHT GUNBOATS

Believed to be for inshore patrols. Locally built.

AMPHIBIOUS FORCES
70 "NAMPO" CLASS

Displacement, tons: 82
Dimensions, feet (metres): 84·2 × 20 × 6 *(27·7 × 6·1 × 1·8)*
Guns: 6—14·7 mm MG
Main engines: Diesels; 4 shafts; 4 800 bhp = 40 knots
Range, miles: 375 at 40 knots
Complement: 19

A class of assault landing craft based on a "P 6" hull. Building began about 1975. Have a retractable ramp in bows.

5-10 LCU and 15 LCM now in service with others building in North Korea. Used on South Korean border.

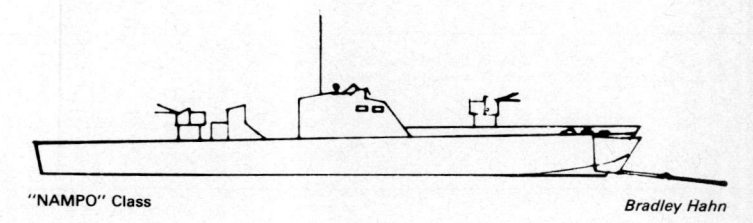

"NAMPO" Class *Bradley Hahn*

5 "HANCHON" CLASS (LCUs)

SERVICE FORCES

Five to ten Large Trawlers and small cargo vessels used as store ships. Some of the trawlers operate on the South Korean border where several have been sunk in the last few years. Some 100 craft in all of various types are employed as support craft with a secondary mission of coastal patrol.

KOREA, Republic (South)

Ministerial

Minister of National Defence:
  So Chong-Ch'ol

Senior Flag Officers

Chief of Naval Operations:

Vice Chief of Naval Operations:

Commander-in-Chief of Fleet:
  Rear-Admiral Chong-Yon Hwang

Diplomatic Representation

Naval Attaché in London:
  Commander Chang Hyon Paek
Naval Attaché in Paris:
  Colonel Ock-Sup Yoon (Army)
Naval Attaché in Washington:
  Captain Choong Hah Choi (Navy)

Personnel

(a) 1978: 20 000 (approx) Navy, 20 000 (approx) Marine Corps.
(b) 3 years (Navy), 33 months (Marines) national service.

Bases

Major: Chinhae, Inchon, Pusan.
Minor: Cheju, Mokpo, Mukho, Pohang.

Marine Corps

Over 20 000 organised into one division and one brigade plus smaller and support units. Since October 1973 the ROK Marine Force has been placed directly under the ROK Navy command with a Vice Chief of Naval Operations for Marine Affairs replacing the Commandant of Marine Corps.

Naval Aviation

The ROK Navy operates 23 S-2 A/F Tracker anti-submarine aircraft. Approximately ten utility aircraft and several helicopters are operated by the ROK Marine Corps. Additional Tracker aircraft are being acquired.
Base: Kimhae.

Strength of the Fleet

Type	Active	Building (Proposed)
Destroyers	9	—
Frigates	7	1 (3?)
Corvettes	6	—
Fast Attack Craft—Missile	8	(4)
Fast Attack Craft—Patrol	1	—
Large Patrol Craft	10	—
Coastal Patrol Craft	23	—
MSCs	8	—
MSB	1	—
LSTs	8	—
LSMs	12	—
LCU	1	—
Repair Ship	1	—
Supply Ships	6	—
Tankers	4	—
Tugs	2	—
Survey Ships and Craft	5	—

Mercantile Marine

Lloyd's Register of Shipping:
  1 042 vessels of 2 494 724 tons gross

DELETIONS

Frigates

1977 *Kang Won* (28 Oct), *Kyong Ki* (28 Dec) (ex-US "Cannon" class)

Corvettes

1977 *Han San, Ok Po* (15 Sept), *Ro Ryang, Myong Ryang* (28 Dec) (ex-US "PCE 827" class)

Minewarfare Forces

1977 *Kim Po, Ko Chang* (15 Sept) (ex-US "Albatross" class)

DESTROYERS

4 Ex-US "GEARING" CLASS (FRAM I and II)

Name	No.	Builders	Laid down	Launched	Commissioned
KWANG JU (ex-USS *Richard E. Kraus*, DD 849)	DD 90	Bath Iron Works Corp, Bath, Maine	31 July 1945	2 Mar 1946	23 May 1946
CHUNG BUK (ex-USS *Chevalier*, DD 805)	DD 95	Bath Iron Works Corp, Bath, Maine	12 June 1944	29 Oct 1944	9 Jan 1945
JEONG BUK (ex-USS *Everett F. Larson*, DD 830)	DD 96	Bath Iron Works Corp, Bath, Maine	4 Sept 1944	28 Jan 1945	6 April 1945
TAEJON (ex-USS *New*, DD 818)	DD 99	Consolidated Steel Corp	14 April 1945	18 Aug 1945	5 April 1946

Displacement, tons: 2 425 standard; approx 3 500 full load
Length, feet (metres): 383 *(116·7)* wl; 390·5 *(119·0)* oa
Beam, feet (metres): 40·9 *(12·4)*
Draught, feet (metres): 19 *(5·8)*
Guns: 6—5 in *(127 mm)* 38 cal (twin) (Mk 38); 1—20 mm Vulcan Gatling (DD 95 and 96); 2—30 mm (twin Emerlak) (DD 96 only)
A/S weapons: 6 (2 triple) Mk 32 A/S torpedo tubes; 2 fixed Hedgehogs (Mk 11)
Main engines: 2 geared turbines (General Electric); 60 000 shp; 2 shafts
Boilers: 4 (Babcock & Wilcox)
Speed, knots: 34
Complement: approx 275

DD 95 and 96 were converted to radar picket destroyers (DDR) in 1949; subsequently modernised under the US Navy's Fleet Rehabilitation and Modernisation programme—first pair to Fram II standards, second pair Fram I. Fitted with small helicopter hangar and flight deck. Anti-ship torpedo tubes have been removed.

A/S weapons: 15 in Mk 32 torpedo tubes are fitted with liners to reduce them to 12·75 in.

Guns: Vulcan Gatlings installed on after hangar deck in 1976.

Radar: SPS 10 and 40.

Sonar: SQS 29 series (hull mounted).

Transfers: First pair on loan on 5 July 1972 and 30 Oct 1972 respectively and by purchase by 31 Jan 1977. Second pair 23 Feb 1977.

JEONG BUK   1973

3 Ex-US "FLETCHER" CLASS

Name	No.	Builders	Laid down	Launched	Commissioned
CHUNG MU (ex-USS *Erben*, DD 631)	DD 91	Bath Iron Works, Bath, Maine	28 Oct 1942	21 Mar 1943	28 May 1943
SEOUL (ex-USS *Halsey Powell*, DD 686)	DD 92	Bethlehem Steel, Staten Island, New York	1943	30 June 1943	25 Oct 1943
PUSAN (ex-USS *Hickox*, DD 673)	DD 93	Federal SB & DD Co, Kearny, New Jersey	1943	4 July 1943	10 Sept 1943

Displacement, tons: 2 050 standard; 3 050 full load
Length, feet (metres): 360 *(110·3)* wl; 376·5 *(114·8)* oa
Beam, feet (metres): 39·6 *(12·0)*
Draught, feet (metres): 18 *(5·5)*
Guns: 5—5 in *(127 mm)* 38 cal (single) (Mk 30); 10—40 mm (2 quad, 1 twin) except *Seoul* (none)
A/S weapons: 6 (2 triple) Mk 32 A/S torpedo tubes; 2 Hedgehogs (Mk 10/11); depth charges
Main engines: Geared turbines (General Electric) 60 000 shp; 2 shafts
Boilers: 4 (Babcock & Wilcox)
Speed, knots: 35
Complement: approx 250

Radar: SPS-6 and -10.

Transfers: DD 91, 1 May 1963; DD 92, 27 April 1968; DD 93, 15 Nov 1968 on loan. All purchased 31 Jan 1977.

SEOUL   1968, United States Navy

KOREA (REPUBLIC) 311

2 Ex-US "ALLEN M. SUMNER" CLASS (FRAM II)

Name	No.	Builders	Laid down	Launched	Commissioned
DAE GU (ex-USS *Wallace L. Lind*, DD 703)	DD 97	Bath Iron Works Corp, Bath, Maine	April 1944	14 June 1944	8 Sept 1944
IN CHEON (ex-USS *De Haven*, DD 727)	DD 98	Federal SB & DD Co, Kearney, New Jersey	Oct 1943	9 Jan 1944	31 Mar 1944

Displacement, tons: 2 200 standard; 3 320 full load
Length, feet (metres): 376·5 *(114·8)* oa
Beam, feet (metres): 40·9 *(12·4)*
Draught, feet (metres): 19 *(5·8)* (Mk 38)
Guns: 6—5 in *(127 mm)* 38 calibre (twin) (Mk 38); 1—20 mm Vulcan Gatling
A/S weapons: 6 (2 triple) Mk 32 A/S torpedo tubes; 2 fixed Hedgehogs (Mk 11)
Main engines: 2 geared turbines (General Electric); 60 000 shp; 2 shafts
Boilers: 4 (Babcock & Wilcox)
Speed, knots: 34
Complement: approx 275

Both ships were modernised under the US Navy's Fleet Rehabilitation and Modernisation (FRAM II) programme. Fitted with small helicopter deck and hangar.

Radar: SPS 10 and 40 *(Dae Gu)*.
SPS 10 and 37 *(In Cheon)*.

Sonar: SQS-29 Series (hull-mounted).
SQA-10 (VDS).

Transfers: 3-4 Dec 1973.

DAE GU (as USS *Wallace L. Lind*)   1967, United States Navy

FRIGATES

1 + ?3 NEW CONSTRUCTION

A new frigate of approximately 1 600 tons with twin screws and CODAG driven is under construction at Hayunda. It is reported that three more may be ordered. Armament reported as one 5 in gun and SSM.

1 Ex-US "RUDDEROW" CLASS

Name	No.	Builders	Laid down	Launched	Commissioned
CHUNG NAM (ex-USS *Holt*, DE 706)	DE 73	Defoe Shipbuilding Co, Bay City, Michigan	Oct 1943	15 Dec 1943	9 June 1944

Displacement, tons: 1 450 standard; 1 890 full load
Length, feet (metres): 300 *(91·5)* wl; 306 *(83·2)* oa
Beam, feet (metres): 37 *(11·3)*
Draught, feet (metres): 14 *(4·3)*
Guns: 2—5 in *(127 mm)* 38 cal; 4—40 mm (twin)
A/S weapons: 6 (2 triple) Mk 32 A/S torpedo tubes; 1 Hedgehog; depth charges
Main engines: Turbo-electric drive (General Electric geared turbines); 12 000 shp; 2 shafts
Boilers: 2 (Combustion Engineering)
Speed, knots: 24
Complement: approx 210

Former US destroyer escort of the TEV design.

Radar: SPS-5 and 6.

Transfer: 19 June 1963 on loan and by purchase on 15 Nov 1974.

CHUNG NAM   1971, Korean Navy

6 Ex-US "CHARLES LAWRENCE" and "CROSSLEY" CLASSES

Name	No.	Builders	Launched	Commissioned	Transferred
KYONG NAM (ex-USS *Cavallaro*, APD 128)	APD 81	Defoe Shipbuilding Co, Bay City, Michigan	15 June 1944	13 Mar 1945	Oct 1959
AH SAN (ex-USS *Harry L. Corl*, APD 108)	APD 82	Bethlehem Shipbuilding Co, Higham, Mass	1 Mar 1944	5 June 1945	June 1966
UNG PO (ex-USS *Julius A. Raven*, APD 110)	APD 83	Bethlehem Shipbuilding Co, Higham, Mass	3 Mar 1944	28 June 1945	June 1966
KYONG PUK (ex-USS *Kephart*, APD 61)	APD 85	Charleston Navy Yard, South Carolina	6 Sept 1943	7 Jan 1944	Aug 1967
JONNAM (ex-USS *Hayter*, APD 80)	APD 86	Charleston Navy Yard, South Carolina	11 Nov 1943	16 Mar 1944	Aug 1967
CHR JU (ex-USS *William M. Hobby*, APD 95)	APD 87	Charleston Navy Yard, South Carolina	11 Feb 1944	4 April 1945	Aug 1967

Displacement, tons: 1 400 standard; 2 130 full load
Length, feet (metres): 300 *(91·4)* wl; 306 *(93·3)* oa
Beam, feet (metres): 37 *(11·3)*
Draught, feet (metres): 12·6 *(3·2)*
Guns: 1—5 in *(127 mm)* 38 cal; 6—40 mm (twin)
A/S weapons: depth charges
Main engines: Turbo-electric (General Electric turbines); 12 000 shp; 2 shafts
Boilers: 2 (Foster Wheeler "D" Express)
Speed, knots: 23·6
Complement: approx 200
Troop capacity: approx 160

All begun as destroyers escorts (DE), but converted during construction or after completion to high-speed transports (APD).
In Korean service four latter ships originally rated as gunboats (PG); changed in 1972 to APD. All are fitted to carry approximately 160 troops. Can carry four LCVPs.
Two different configurations; "Charles Lawrence (APD 37)" class with high bridge and lattice mast supporting 10-ton capacity boom; "Crossley (APD 87)" class with low bridge and tripod mast supporting 10-ton capacity boom.
All purchased by South Korea 15 Nov 1974.

KYONG NAM

312 KOREA (REPUBLIC)

CORVETTES
3 Ex-US "AUK" CLASS

Name	No.	Builders	Launched
SHIN SONG (ex-USS Ptarmigan, MSF 376)	PCE 1001	Savannah Machine & Foundry Co, Savannah, Georgia	15 Jan 1944
SUNCHON (ex-USS Speed, MSF 116)	PCE 1002	American SB Co, Lorain, Ohio	15 Oct 1942
KOJE (ex-USS Dextrous, MSF 341)	PCE 1003	Gulf SB Corp, Madisonville, Texas	8 Sept 1943

Displacement, tons: 890 standard; 1 250 full load
Dimensions, feet (metres): 215 (61·3) wl; 221·2 oa × 32·2 × 10·8 (63·2 × 9·2 × 3)
Guns: 2—3 in (76 mm) 50 cal (single); 4—40 mm (twin); 4—20 mm (twin)
A/S weapons: 3 (1 triple) Mk 32 A/S torpedo tubes; 1 Hedgehog; depth charges
Main engines: Diesel-electric (General Motors diesels); 3 532 bhp; 2 shafts = 18 knots
Complement: approx 110

Former US Navy minesweepers (originally designated AM). PCE 1001 transferred to ROK Navy in July 1963, PCE 1002 in Nov 1967, and PCE 1003 in Dec 1967.
The minesweeping gear was removed prior to transfer and a second 3 in gun fitted aft; additional anti-submarine weapons also fitted.

A/S weapons: Mk 32 tubes fitted with 12·75 in liners.

SHIN SONG

3 Ex-US "PCE 827" CLASS

Name	No.	Builders	Commissioned
PYOK PA (ex-USS Dania, PCE 870)	PCE 57	Albina Works, Portland Oreg.	5 Oct 1943
RYUL PO (ex-USS Somerset, PCE 892)	PCE 58	Willamette Corp, Portland, Oreg.	8 July 1943
SA CHON (ex-USS Batesburg, PCE 903)	PCE 59	Willamette Corp, Portland, Oreg.	16 May 1943

Displacement, tons: 640 standard; 950 full load
Dimensions, feet (metres): 180 (51·4) wl; 184·5 oa × 33 × 9·5 (52·7 × 9·4 × 2·7)
Guns: 1—3 in (76 mm) 50 cal (forward); 6—40 mm (twin); 4 or 8—20 mm (single or twin)
A/S weapons: 1 Hedgehog; depth charges
Main engines: Diesels (General Motors); 2 000 bhp; 2 shafts = 15 knots
Complement: approx 100

Original class of seven transferred on loan Dec 1961 and by sale 15 Nov 1974.

"PCE 827" Class   1969

LIGHT FORCES
7 TACOMA PSMM 5 TYPE (FAST ATTACK CRAFT—MISSILE)

Name	No.	Builders	Commissioned
PAEK KU 12	102	Tacoma Boatbuilding Co, Tacoma, Wash	14 Mar 1975
PAEK KU 13	103	Tacoma Boatbuilding Co, Tacoma, Wash	14 Mar 1975
PAEK KU 15	105	Tacoma Boatbuilding Co, Tacoma, Wash	1 Feb 1976
PAEK KU 16	106	Tacoma Boatbuilding Co, Tacoma, Wash	1 Feb 1976
PAEK KU 17	107	Korea—Tacoma International	1976-77
PAEK KU 18	108	Korea—Tacoma International	1976-77
PAEK KU 19	109	Korea—Tacoma International	1976-77

Displacement, tons: approx 250 full load
Dimensions, feet (metres): 165 oa × 24 × 9·5 (50·3 × 7·3 × 2·9)
Missile launchers: 4 launchers for Standard missiles (1 reload each)
Guns: 1—3 in (76 mm) 50 cal (forward)
  1—40 mm (aft; may have been removed with missile installation)
  2—50 cal MG
Main engines: 6 gas turbines (Avco Lycoming); 16 800 hp; 2 shafts (cp propellers) = 40+ knots
Complement: 32 (5 officers, 27 enlisted men)

Aluminium hulls. Based on the US Navy's *Asheville* (PG 84) design. Tacoma design designation was PSMM for multi-mission patrol ship. The Korean designation *Paek Ku* means seagull. *Paek Ku 12* launched 17 Feb 1975.

Engineering: The six TF 35 gas turbines turn two propeller shafts; the "Asheville" class ships have combination gas turbine-diesel power plants. In the Korean units one, two, or three turbines can be selected to provide each shaft with a variety of power settings.

PAEK KU 12 (old pennant number)   1975, Alfred W. Harris

1 + 4 Ex-US "ASHEVILLE" CLASS (FAST ATTACK CRAFT—MISSILE)

Name	No.	Builders	Commissioned
PAEK KU 11 (ex-USS Benicia, PG 96)	PGM 101 (ex-PGM 11)	Tacoma Boatbuilding Co, Tacoma, Washington	25 April 1970

Displacement, tons: 225 standard; 245 full load
Dimensions, feet (metres): 164·5 oa × 23·8 × 9·5 (50·1 × 7·3 × 2·9)
Missiles: Launchers for Standard SSM
Guns: 1—3 in (76 mm) (forward); 1—40 mm (aft); 4—50 cal MG (twin)
Main engines: CODAG; 2 diesels (Cummins); 1 450 bhp; 2 shafts = 16 knots; 1 gas turbine (General Electric); 13 300 shp; 2 shafts = 40+ knots
Complement: approx 25

Former US "Asheville" class patrol gunboat. Launched 20 Dec 1969; transferred to ROK Navy on 15 Oct 1971 and arrived in Korea in Jan 1972. No anti-submarine sensors or weapons are fitted. A further four to be purchased in near future.

Missiles: During 1971, while in US Navy service, this ship was fitted experimentally with one launcher for the Standard surface-to-surface missile. The box-like container/launcher held two missiles. Launchers fitted in South Korea 1975-76.

PAEK KU 11 (old pennant number)   1972

KOREA (REPUBLIC) 313

1 CPIC TYPE (FAST ATTACK CRAFT—PATROL)

Name	No.	Builders	Commissioned
GIREOGI	PKM 123	Tacoma Boatbuilding Co, Tacoma, Washington	1975

Displacement, tons: 71·25 full load
Dimensions, feet (metres): 100 oa × 18·5 × 6 *(30·5 × 5·6 × 1·8)*
Guns: 2—30 mm MG (twin) (Mk 74); 1—20 mm
Main engines: 3 gas turbines (Avco Lycoming); 6 750 shp; 3 shafts = 45 knots; 2 auxiliary diesels (Volvo); 500 bhp
Complement: approx 11 (varies with armament)

Transferred on 1 Aug 1975. A further seven were to be built in South Korea (PKM 125-131) but this order has been cancelled in favour of purchasing four more "Ashville" class PGMs from USA.

CPIC on trials   *1974, United States Navy*

8 Ex-US COAST GUARD "CAPE" CLASS (LARGE PATROL CRAFT)

PB 3 (ex-USCGC *Cape Rosier*, WPB 95333)
PB 5 (ex-USCGC *Cape Sable*, WPB 95334)
PB 6 (ex-USCGC *Cape Providence*, WPB 95335)
PB 8 (ex-USCGC *Cape Porpoise*, WPB 95327)
PB 9 (ex-USCGC *Cape Falcon*, WPB 95330)
PB 10 (ex-USCGC *Cape Trinity*, WPB 95331)
PB 11 (ex-USCGC *Cape Darby*, WPB 95323)
PB 12 (ex-USCGC *Cape Kiwanda*, WPB 95329)

Displacement, tons: 98 full load
Dimensions, feet (metres): 95 oa × 19 × 6 *(31·1 × 6·2 × 1·9)*
Guns: 1—·50 cal MG; 1—81 mm mortar; several 0·30 cal MG
Main engines: 4 diesels (Cummins); 2 200 bhp; 2 shafts = 20 knots
Complement: 13

Former US Coast Guard steel-hulled patrol craft. Built in 1958-1959. Nine units transferred to South Korea in Sept 1968.
Combination machinegun/mortar mount is forward; single light machineguns are mounted aft.
See US Coast Guard listings for additional details.

PB 11

2 100-ft PATROL TYPE (LARGE PATROL CRAFT)

PK 10   PK 11

Displacement, tons: 120
Dimensions, feet (metres): 100 oa *(32·7)*
Missiles: 2 Exocet
Guns: 1—40 mm; 1—20 mm
Main engines: Diesels (Mercedes-Benz-MTU); 10 200 bhp; 3 shafts = 35 knots

Two patrol craft reported built in Korea in 1971-72.

10+ "SCHOOLBOY" CLASS (COASTAL PATROL CRAFT)

Displacement, tons: 30
Dimensions, feet (metres): 72 oa × 11·5 × 3·6 *(23·6 × 3·8 × 1·2)*
Guns: 2—20 mm (single)
Main engines: 2 MTU diesels; 1 600 bhp; 2 shafts

At least 10 and possibly as many as 20 patrol craft of this type have been built in Korea, with the first units completed in 1973. Believed to be designated in the PB series.

9 US 65-ft SEWART TYPE (COASTAL PATROL CRAFT)

| FB 1 | FB 3 | FB 6 | FB 8 | FB 10 |
| FB 2 | FB 5 | FB 7 | FB 9 | |

Displacement, tons: 33 full load
Dimensions, feet (metres): 65 oa × 16 *(21·3 × 5·2)*
Guns: 2—20 mm (single)
Main engines: 3 diesels (General Motors); 1 590 bhp; 3 shafts = 25 knots
Complement: 5

These craft were built in the United States by Sewart. The design is adapted from a commercial 65-foot craft. Referred to as "Toksuuri" No. 1 etc. by the South Koreans. Transferred to South Korea in August 1967.

FB 10 on marine railway

4 US 40-ft SEWART TYPE (COASTAL PATROL CRAFT)

SB 1   SB 2   SB 3   SB 5

Displacement, tons: 9·25 full load
Dimensions, feet (metres): 40 oa × 12 × 3 *(13·1 × 3·9 × 0·9)*
Guns: 1—0·50 cal MG; 2—0·30 cal MG
Main engines: 2 diesels (General Motors); 500 bhp; 2 shafts = 31 knots
Complement: 7

These are aluminium-hulled craft built in the United States by Sewart. Transferred to South Korea in 1964.

314 KOREA (REPUBLIC)

MINE WARFARE FORCES

8 Ex-US "MSC 268" and "294" CLASSES

Name	No.	Builders	Commissioned
KUM SAN (ex-US *MSC 284*)	MSC 522	Peterson Builders, Wisconsin	1959
KO HUNG (ex-US *MSC 285*)	MSC 523	Peterson Builders, Wisconsin	1959
KUM KOK (ex-US *MSC 286*)	MSC 525	Peterson Builders, Wisconsin	1959
NAM YANG (ex-US *MSC 295*)	MSC 526	Peterson Builders, Wisconsin	1963
NA DONG (ex-US *MSC 296*)	MSC 527	Peterson Builders, Wisconsin	1963
SAM CHOK (ex-US *MSC 316*)	MSC 528	Peterson Builders, Wisconsin	1968
YONG DONG (ex-US *MSC 320*)	MSC 529	Peterson Builders, Wisconsin	1975
OK CHEON (ex-US *MSC 321*)	MSC 530	Peterson Builders, Wisconsin	1975

Displacement, tons: 320 light; 370 full load
Dimensions, feet (metres): 144 oa × 28 × 8·2 *(117·2 × 9·2 × 2·7)*
Guns: 2—20 mm
Main engines: Diesels; 1 200 bhp; 2 shafts = 14 knots
Complement: approx 40

Built by the United States specifically for transfer under the Military Aid Programme. Wood hulled with non-magnetic metal fittings.
Kum San transferred to South Korea in June 1959, *Ko Hung* in Sept 1959, *Kum Kok* in Nov 1959, *Nam Yang* in Sept 1963, *Na Dong* in Nov 1963, *Sam Chok* in July 1968, *Yong Dong* and *Ok Cheon* on 2 Oct 1975.

KUM KOK

1 Ex-US MSB

Name	No.
PI BONG (ex-US *MSB 2*)	MSB 1

Displacement, tons: 30 light; 39 full load
Dimensions, feet (metres): 57·2 oa × 15·3 × 4 *(18·7 × 5 × 1·3)*
Guns: Machine guns
Main engines: 2 geared diesels (Packard); 600 bhp; 2 shafts = 12 knots

Transferred on 1 Dec 1961 and by sale on 2 July 1975. Wood hulled.

PI BONG   1969, Korean Navy

AMPHIBIOUS FORCES

Note: Last year it was reported that USS *Fort Marion* LSD 22 had been transferred to South Korea. This transfer was cancelled and on 15 April 1977 the ship was transferred to Taiwan. On 10 Aug 1977 it was made known that South Korea would not be taking over an LSD.

8 Ex-US "1-510" and "511-1152" CLASSES (LST)

Name	No.	Commissioned
UN PONG (ex-USS *LST 1010*)	LST 807	25 April 1944
DUK BONG (ex-USS *LST 227*)	LST 808	14 Oct 1943
BI BONG (ex-USS *LST 218*)	LST 809	12 Aug 1943
KAE BONG (ex-USS *Berkshire County*, LST 288)	LST 810	20 Dec 1943
WEE BONG (ex-USS *Johnson County*, LST 849)	LST 812	16 Jan 1945
SU YONG (ex-USS *Kane County*, LST 853)	LST 813	11 Dec 1945
BUK HAN (ex-USS *Lynn County*, LST 900)	LST 815	28 Dec 1944
HWA SAN (ex-USS *Pender County*, LST 1080)	LST 816	29 May 1945

Displacement, tons: 1 653 standard; 2 366 beaching; 4 080 full load
Dimensions, feet (metres): 316 wl; 328 oa × 50 × 14 *(103·6; 107·5 × 16·4 × 4·6)*
Guns: 6 or 8—40 mm
Main engines: Diesels; 1 700 bhp; 2 shafts = 11·6 knots
Complement: approx 110

Former US Navy tank landing ships. Cargo capacity 2 100 tons. *Un Bong* transferred to South Korea in Feb 1955, *Duk Bong* in March 1955, *Bi Bong* in May 1955, *Kae Bong* in March 1956, *Wee Bong* in Jan 1959, *Su Yong* and *Buk Han* in Dec 1958, and *Hwa San* in Oct 1958. All purchased 15 Nov 1974.

DUK BONG

Launch dates: 807, 29 March 1944; 808, 21 Sept 1943; 809, 20 July 1943; 810, 7 Nov 1943; 812, 30 Dec 1944; 813, 17 Nov 1944; 815, 9 Dec 1944; 816, 2 May 1945.

1 Ex-US "ELK RIVER" CLASS (LSMR)

Name	No.	Builders
SI HUNG (ex-USS *St Joseph River* LSMR 527)	LSMR 311	Brown SB Co, Houston, Texas

Displacement, tons: 944 standard; 1 084 full load
Dimensions, feet (metres): 204·5 wl; 206·2 oa × 34·5 × 10 *(67·1; 67·6 × 11·3 × 3·3)*
Guns: 1—5 in *(127 mm)* 38 cal; 2—40 mm; 4—20 mm
Rocket launchers: 8 twin Mk 105 launchers for 5 in rockets
Main engines: 2 diesels (General Motors); 2 800 bhp; 2 shafts = 12·6 knots
Complement: approx 140

Former US Navy landing ship completed as a rocket-firing ship to support amphibious landing operations. Launched on 19 May 1945, transferred to South Korea on 15 Sept 1960 and purchased 15 Nov 1974. Configuration differs from conventional LSM type with "island" bridge structure and 5 in gun aft; no bow doors.

SI HUNG   1967, Korean Navy

KOREA (REPUBLIC) 315

11 Ex-US "LSM-1" CLASS

Name	No.
TAE CHO (ex-USS LSM 546)	LSM 601
TYO TO (ex-USS LSM 268)	LSM 602
KA TOK (ex-USS LSM 462)	LSM 605
KO MUN (ex-USS LSM 30)	LSM 606
PIAN (ex-USS LSM 96)	LSM 607
PUNG TO (ex-USS LSM 54)	LSM 608
WOL MI (ex-USS LSM 57)	LSM 609
KI RIN (ex-USS LSM 19)	LSM 610
NUNG RA (ex-USS LSM 84)	LSM 611
SIN MI (ex-USS LSM 316)	LSM 612
UL RUNG (ex-USS LSM 17)	LSM 613

Displacement, tons: 743 beaching; 1 095 full load
Dimensions, feet (metres): 196·5 wl; 203·5 oa × 34·6 × 8·5 *(64·4, 66·7 × 11·3 × 2·8)*
Guns: 2—40 mm (twin); several 20 mm
Main engines: 2 diesels (direct drive; Fairbanks Morse except *Tyo To* General Motors); 2 800 bhp; 2 shafts = 12·5 knots
Complement: approx 60

TYO TO   1969

Former US Navy medium landing ships. Built 1944-1945. LSM 601, 602, and 605 transferred to South Korea in 1955; others in 1956. *Sin Mi* served in Indochina as French L 9014 and *Ul Rung* as French L 9017 during 1954-1955; returned to United States in Oct 1955 and retransferred to South Korea in autumn 1956. All purchased 15 Nov 1974.

Pung To serves as mine force flagship fitted with mine-laying rails and designated LSML. Arrangement of 20 mm guns differs; some ships have two single mounts adjacent to forward 40 mm mount on forecastle; other 20 mm guns along sides of cargo well.

1 Ex-US "LCU 501" CLASS

LCU 1 (ex-USS *LCU 531*)

Displacement, tons: 309 full load
Dimensions, feet (metres): 105 wl; 119·1 oa × 32·66 × 5 *(34·4; 39 × 10·7 × 1·6)*
Main engines: Diesels (Gray Marine); 675 bhp; 3 shafts = 10 knots

Former US Navy utility landing craft. Built in 1943 as LCT(6) 531. Transferred to South Korea in Dec 1960. No name assigned.

SERVICE FORCES

1 Ex-US "ACHELOUS" CLASS (LIGHT REPAIR SHIP)

Name	No.	Builders	Commissioned
DUK SU (ex-USS *Minotaur*, ARL 15, ex-*LST 645*)	ARL 1	Chicago Bridge & Iron Co, Seneca, Illinois	30 Sept 1944

Displacement, tons: 2 366 standard; 4 100 full load
Dimensions, feet (metres): 316 wl; 328 oa × 50 × 11·2 *(103·6; 107·5 × 16·4 × 3·7)*
Guns: 8—40 mm; 12—20 mm
Main engines: Diesels (General Motors); 1 800 bhp; 2 shafts = 11·6 knots
Complement: approx 250

DUK SU

Former US Navy landing craft repair ship. Converted during construction from an LST. Launched on 20 Sept 1944, transferred to South Korea in Oct 1955 on loan and purchased 31 Jan 1977.

6 Ex-US ARMY FS TYPE (SUPPLY SHIPS)

Name	No.	Builders
IN CHON (ex-US Army *FS 198*)	AKL 902	Higgins Industries
CHI NAM PO (ex-US Army *FS 356*)	AKL 905	J. K. Welding
MOK PO (ex-USCGC *Trillium*, WAK 170, ex-US Army *FS 397*)	AKL 907	Ingalls, Decatur, Alabama
KU SAN (ex-USS *Sharps*, AKL 10, ex-*AG 139*, ex-US Army *FS 385*)	AKL 908	Ingalls, Decatur, Alabama
MA SAN (ex-USS *AKL 35*, ex-US Army *FS 383*)	AKL 909	Ingalls, Decatur, Alabama
UL SAN (ex-USS *Brule*, AKL 28, ex-US Army *FS 370*)	AKL 910	Sturgeon Bay

Displacement, tons: approx 700
Dimensions, feet (metres): 176·5 oa × 32·8 × 10 *(57·9 × 10·7 × 3·3)*
Guns: 2—20 mm (single) in most ships
Main engines: Diesel; 1 000 bhp; 1 shaft = 10 knots
Complement: approx 20

MA SAN   1957

Originally US Army freight and supply ships built in World War II for coastal operation.
In Chon and *Chin Nam Po* transferred to South Korea in 1951; *Mok Po, Kin San,* and *Ma San* in 1956; *Ul San* on 1 Nov 1971.
Many subsequently served in US Navy and Military Sea Transportation Service (later Military Sealift Command). Details and configurations differ.

1 Ex-NORWEGIAN TANKER

Name	No.	Builders	Launched
CHUN JI (ex-*Birk*)	AO 2	A/S Berken Mek Verks, Bergen	1951

Displacement, tons: 1 400 standard; 4 160 full load
Dimensions, feet (metres): 297·5 oa × 44·5 × 18·2 *(97·5 × 14·6 × 5·9)*
Guns: 1—40 mm; several 20 mm
Main engines: 2 diesels; 1 800 bhp; 1 shaft = 12 knots
Complement: approx 70

Transferred to South Korea in Sept 1953.

CHUN JI   1969

316 KOREA (REPUBLIC)

1 Ex-US 235-ft YO TYPE (HARBOUR TANKER)

Name	No.
HWA CHON (ex-*Paek Yeon* AO 5, ex-USS *Derrick* YO 59)	AO 5

Displacement, tons: 890 standard; 2 700 full load
Dimensions, feet (metres): 235 oa × 37 × 15 *(77 × 12·1 × 4·9)*
Guns: several 20 mm
Main engines: Diesel (Fairbanks Morse); 1 150 bhp; 1 shaft = 10·5 knots
Complement: approx 45

Former US Navy self-propelled fuel barge. Transferred to South Korea on 14 Oct 1955. Capacity 10 000 barrels petroleum. The ship has been laid up in reserve since 1974, although purchased on 2 July 1975.

HWA CHON   1969

2 Ex-US 174-ft YO TYPE (HARBOUR TANKERS)

KU YONG (ex-USS *YO 118*) AO 1 — (ex-USS *YO 179*) YO 6

Displacement, tons: 1 400 full load
Dimensions, feet (metres): 174 oa × 32 *(57 × 10·5)*
Guns: several 20 mm
Main engines: Diesel (Union); 500 bhp; 1 shaft = 7 knots
Complement: approx 35

Former US Navy self-propelled fuel barges. Transferred to South Korea on 3 Dec 1946 and 13 Sept 1971, respectively. Cargo capacity 6 570 barrels.

2 Ex-US "SOTOYOMO" CLASS (TUGS)

Name	No.	Builders	Launched
YONG MUN (ex-USS *Keosanqua*, ATA 198)	ATA 2	Levingston SB Co, Orange, Texas	17 Jan 1945
DO BONG (ex-USS *Pinola*, ATA 206)	ATA (S) 3	Gulfport Boiler & Welding Works, Port Arthur, Texas	14 Dec 1944

Displacement, tons: 538 standard; 835 full load
Dimensions, feet (metres): 133·66 wl × 143 oa × 33·8 *(43·8; 46·9 × 11·1)*
Guns: 1—3 in *(76 mm)* 50 cal; 4—20 mm
Main engines: Diesel (General Motors); 1 500 bhp; 1 shaft = 13 knots
Complement: approx 45

Former US Navy auxiliary ocean tugs. Both transferred to South Korea in Feb 1962. *Do Bong* modified for salvage work.

The South Korean Navy also operates nine small harbour tugs (designated YTL). These include one ex-US Navy craft (YTL 550) and five ex-US Army craft.

SERVICE CRAFT

The South Korean Navy operates approximately 35 small service craft in addition to the YO-type tankers listed above and the harbour tugs noted above. These craft include open lighters, floating cranes, diving tenders, dredgers, ferries, non-self-propelled fuel barges, pontoon barges, and sludge removal barges. Most are former US Navy craft.

HYDROGRAPHIC SERVICE

The following craft are operated by the Korean Hydrographic Service which is responsible to the Ministry of Transport.

2 Ex-BELGIAN MSI TYPE

SURO 5 (ex-Belgian *Temse*, ex-US MSI 470)
SURO 6 (ex-Belgian *Tournai*, ex-US MSI 481)

Displacement, tons: 160 light; 190 full load
Dimensions, feet (metres): 113·2 oa × 22·3 × 6 *(37·1 × 7·3 × 1·9)*
Main engines: Diesels; 1 260 bhp; 2 shafts = 15 knots
Complement: 16

Former Belgian inshore minesweepers. Built in Belgium, the *Tournai* being financed by United States. Launched on 6 Aug 1956 and 18 May 1957, respectively. Transferred to South Korea in March 1970.

1 Ex-US "YMS-1" CLASS

SURO 3 (ex-USC&GS *Hodgson*)

Displacement, tons: 289 full load
Dimensions, feet (metres): 136 oa × 24·5 × 9·25 *(44·6 × 8·1 × 3)*
Main engines: Diesels; 1 000 bhp; 2 shafts = 15 knots

YMS type transferred to South Korea from US Coast & Geodetic Survey in 1968.

SURO 2

Of 145 tons launched in 1942. Complement 12.

SURO 7   SURO 8

Of 30 tons with complement of 6.

COAST GUARD

The Korean Coast Guard operates about 25 small ships and craft including several tugs and rescue craft.

KUWAIT

Ministerial

Minister of Defence:
Sa'd al Abdallah al-Sabah

Personnel

(a) 1978: 500 (Coastguard) Administered by Ministry of the Interior
(b) Voluntary service

Future Plans

A contract was awarded to a Japanese firm in mid-1977 for the construction of a base. This will be necessary with the planned expansion of this force.

Mercantile Marine

Lloyd's Register of Shipping:
226 vessels of 1 831 194 tons gross

LIGHT FORCES

Note: There are reports, not substantiated by Vosper Thornycroft Ltd, of that firm receiving an order for 10 105 ft Fast Attack Craft with Breda gun armament.

10 THORNYCROFT 78 ft TYPE (COASTAL PATROL CRAFT)

AL SALEMI	AMAN	MASHHOOR	MURSHED
AL SHURTI	INTISAR	MAYMOON	WATHAH
AL MUBARAKI	MARZOOK		

Displacement, tons: 40
Dimensions, feet (metres): 78 oa × 15·5 × 4·5 (23·8 × 4·7 × 1·4)
Gun: 1 MG
Main engines: 2 Rolls-Royce V8 marine diesels; 1 340 shp at 1 800 rpm; 1 116 shp at 1 700 rpm = 20 knots
Range, miles: 700 at 15 knots
Complement: 12 (5 officers, 7 men)

Two were built by Thornycroft before the merger and eight by Vosper Thornycroft afterwards. *Al Salem* and *Al Mubaraki* were shipped to Kuwait on 8 Sept 1966 and the last pair *Al Shurti* and *Intisar* in 1972.
Hulls are of welded steel construction, with superstructures of aluminium alloy. Twin hydraulically operated rudders, Decca type D 202 radar. The later boats are slightly different in appearance with modified superstructure and no funnel, see photograph of *Intisar*.

INTISAR 1972, Vosper Thornycroft

2 VOSPER THORNYCROFT 56 ft TYPE (COASTAL PATROL CRAFT)

Name	No.	Builders	Commissioned
DASTOOR	—	Vosper Thornycroft Private Ltd, Singapore	June 1974
KASAR	—	Vosper Thornycroft Private Ltd, Singapore	June 1974

Displacement, tons: 25
Length, feet (metres): 56 (17·8)
Guns: 1—20 mm; 2 MG
Main engines: 2 MTU MB6 V.331 diesels; 1 350 hp = 26 knots
Range, miles: 320 at 20 knots
Complement: 8 (2 officers, 6 men)

Ordered Sept 1973. Both laid down 31 Oct 1973. Steel hulls and aluminium superstructure.

KASAR (guns not fitted) 1974, Vosper Thornycroft

7 THORNYCROFT 50 ft TYPE (COASTAL PATROL CRAFT)

Built by the Singapore Yard of Thornycroft (Malaysia) Limited, now the Tanjong Rhu, Singapore Yard of Vosper Thornycroft Private Ltd.

1 VOSPER THORNYCROFT 46 ft TYPE (COASTAL PATROL CRAFT)

Name	No.	Builders	Commissioned
MAHROOS	—	Vosper Thornycroft Private Ltd, Singapore	Jan 1976

Length, feet (metres): 46 (14)
Guns: Can mount 2—20 mm
Main engines: 2 Rolls-Royce C8M-410 diesels; 780 hp = 21+ knots
Complement: 5

Ordered in Oct 1974. Hull is of welded steel construction with aluminium superstructure.

MAHROOS (guns not fitted) 1975, Singapore Hilton

8 VOSPER THORNYCROFT 35 ft TYPE (COASTAL PATROL CRAFT)

Length, feet (metres): 35 (10·3)
Main engines: 2 turbocharged Perkins diesels = 25 knots

Ordered July 1972 from Vosper Thornycroft Private Ltd, Singapore. Built of double-skinned teak with Cascover sheathing. First four delivered late 1972, second four in May 1973.

318 KUWAIT / LEBANON

LANDING CRAFT
3 VOSPER THORNYCROFT 88 ft TYPE

Name	No.	Builders	Commissioned
WAHEED	—	Vosper Thornycroft Private Ltd, Singapore	May 1971
FAREED	—	Vosper Thornycroft Private Ltd, Singapore	May 1971
REGGA	—	Vosper Thornycroft Private Ltd, Singapore	Nov 1975

Dimensions, feet (metres): 88 × 22·6 × 4·3 *(27 × 6·9 × 1·3)*
Main engines: 2 Rolls-Royce C8M-410 diesels; 752 bhp = 10 knots
Complement: 9 (can carry 8 passengers)

First pair ordered in 1970 and third in Oct 1974 by Kuwait Ministry of the Interior. Can carry 6 400 gallons oil-fuel, 9 400 gallons water and 40 tons deck cargo, the last being handled by a 2·5 ton derrick. Used to support landing-parties working on Kuwait's off-shore islands.

WAHEED   1974, Vosper Thornycroft

LAOS

The situation in this force is uncertain.

Ministerial

Minister of National Defence:
Khamtai Siphandon

Personnel

(a) 1978:   550 officers and men
(b) 18 months national service

RIVER PATROL CRAFT

7	LCM (6) Type	28 tons	4 in commission, 3 in reserve
6	Cabin Type	21 tons	2 in commission, 4 in reserve
2	Chris Craft Type	15 tons	2 in commission
12	11 metre Type	10 tons	5 in commission, 7 in reserve
8	8 metre Type	6 tons	8 in reserve
7	Cargo Transport	50 tons	1 in commission, 6 in reserve

The above craft are formed into four squadrons, although at least half of them must be considered non-operational.

LEBANON

Diplomatic Representation

Naval Military and Air Attaché in London:
Colonel F. El Hussami

Personnel

1978:   250 officers and men

Mercantile Marine

Lloyd's Register of Shipping:
163 vessels of 227 009 tons gross

DELETION

1975   Djounieh (ex-*Fairmile B. ML*)

LIGHT FORCES

Note: (a) The 135 ton Large Patrol Craft ordered from Hamelin SY in Jan 1974 has not been delivered due to the internal Lebanese problems. Now transferred to Philippines.
(b) Reports that a number of Patrol Craft were transferred to the Christian forces by Israel during the recent Civil War are not confirmed.

1 LARGE PATROL CRAFT

Name	No.	Builders	Commissioned
TARABLOUS	31	Ch. Navals de l'Estérel	1959

Displacement, tons: 90
Dimensions, feet (metres): 124·7 × 18 × 5·8 *(38 × 5·6 × 1·6)*
Guns: 2—40 mm; 2—12·7 mm
Main engines: 2 MTU diesels; 2 shafts; 2 700 bhp = 27 knots
Range, miles: 1 500 at 15 knots
Complement: 19 (3 officers, 16 men)

Laid down in June 1958. Launched in June 1959. Completed in 1959.

TARABLOUS   1975, Chantiers Navals de l'Esterel

3 "BYBLOS" CLASS (COASTAL PATROL CRAFT)

Name	No.	Builders	Commissioned
BYBLOS	11	Ch. Navals de l'Estérel	1955
SIDON	12	Ch. Navals de l'Estérel	1955
BEYROUTH (ex-*Tir*)	13	Ch. Navals de l'Estérel	1955

Displacement, tons: 28 standard
Dimensions, feet (metres): 66 × 13·5 × 4 *(20·1 × 4·1 × 1·2)*
Guns: 1—20 mm; 2 MG
Main engines: General Motors diesels; 2 shafts; 530 bhp = 18·5 knots

French built ML type craft. Launched in 1954-55.

LANDING CRAFT
1 Ex-US "LCU 1466" CLASS

SOUR (ex-*LCU 1474*)

Displacement, tons: 180 standard; 360 full load
Dimensions, feet (metres): 115 × 34 × 6 *(35·1 × 10·4 × 1·8)*
Guns: 2—20 mm
Main engines: 3 diesels; 3 shafts; 675 bhp = 10 knots

Built in 1957, transferred in Nov 1958.

LIBERIA

Ministerial

Minister of National Defence:
 Hon E. Jonathan Goodridge
Assistant Minister of Defence:
 Hon W. R. Davis Jr

Command

This Coastguard force is controlled by a Coastguard Commandant who is responsible to the Minister of National Defence.

Commandant LNCG:
 Commander W. Kelly Garnett
Deputy Commandant LNCG:
 Lieutenant-Commander S. Weaka Peters

Personnel

(a) 1978: 225 officers and men
(b) Voluntary service

Base

Elijah Johnson CG Base, Monrovia.

DELETIONS

Presidential Yacht

1976 Liberian

Patrol Craft

1976 ML 4001, ML 4002 (40 ft USCG)

Mercantile Marine

Lloyd's Register of Shipping:
 2 617 vessels of 79 982 968 tons gross

LIGHT FORCES

1 US "PGM 71" CLASS

Name	No.	Builders	Commissioned
ALERT (ex-US PGM 102)	102	Peterson Ltd, Sturgeon Bay, USA	2 Dec 1966

Displacement, tons: 100
Dimensions, feet (metres): 100 × 19 × 5 (30·5 × 5·8 × 1·5)
Guns: 1—40 mm; 5—50 cal MGs
Main engines: 4—8-6-71 diesels; 2 shafts; 2 200 bhp = 21 knots
Complement: 15 (2 officers, 13 ratings)

PGM 102 (US number) was built in the United States for transfer under the Military Aid Programme. She was commissioned by the late President William V. S. Tubman. Similar to *Betelgeuse* in the Dominican Republic.

2 COASTAL PATROL CRAFT

Name	No.	Builders	Commissioned
CAVILLA	—	Swiftships Inc, Louisiana, USA	22 July 1976
MANO	—	Swiftships Inc, Louisiana, USA	22 July 1976

Displacement, tons: 38 full load
Dimensions, feet (metres): 65 × 19 × 2·6 (19·8 × 5·8 × 0·8)
Guns: 2—M-60 MGs (bridge); 1—81 mm mortar; 1—50 cal MG
Main engines: 2 V12-71 turbocharged diesels; 2 shafts; 1 920 shp = 24 knots
Range, miles: 600 at 21·5 knots
Complement: 20 (2 officers, 18 ratings)

Generally similar to US "Swift" class but with 16·7 ft more length and 4 ft more beam. Aluminium hulls.

MANO   1976

1 COASTAL PATROL CRAFT

Name	No.	Builders	Commissioned
ST. PAUL	—	Swiftships Inc, Louisiana, USA	22 July 1976

Displacement, tons: 11
Dimensions, feet (metres): 42 × 12 × 1·5 (12·8 × 3·7 × 0·6)
Guns: 2—M60 MGs (bridge)
Main engines: 2—V8-71 turbocharged diesels; 870 bhp = 20 knots
Complement: 4

LIBYA

Establishment

The Libyan Navy was established in Nov 1962 when a British Naval Mission was formed and first recruits were trained at HMS *St. Angelo*, Malta. Cadets were also trained at the Britannia Royal Naval College, Dartmouth, and technical ratings at HMS *Sultan*, Gosport, and HMS *Collingwood*, Fareham, England.

Headquarters Appointment

Senior Officer, Libyan Navy:
 Commander A. Shaksuki

Mining Capability

Although few of the listed Libyan ships are credited with a mining capability the fact that, in June 1973, two minefields were laid off Tripoli harbour, some eight miles out, suggests that a stock of mines is available.

Personnel

(a) 1978: Total 2 000 officers and ratings, including Coast Guard
(b) Voluntary service

Bases

Tripoli. Operating Ports at Benghazi, Darna, Tobruk, Burayqah. New bases are either under construction or on order in several localities. The main centre will probably be to the south of Benghazi.

Future programmes

In a manner reminiscent of some other countries, such as India, Libya is obtaining naval supplies from both West and East. The final result if all programmes are fulfilled (4 missile corvettes (Italian), 10 missile craft (French) and reportedly 24 (Soviet) plus up to 6 submarines (Soviet)) will be a large and up-to-date fleet at a crucial position in the Mediterranean. While the training task to man this fleet must be formidable the Libyans are also showing keen interest in the procurement of GRP minehunters/sweepers.
An expansion of this magnitude will clearly call for a large increase in the training programme which may well cause considerable problems.

Strength of the Fleet

Type	Active	Building (Planned)
Frigate	1	—
Submarines	2	?4
LSD	1	—
LSTs	2	—
Corvettes	2	3 (missiles)
Fast Attack Craft—Missile	10	15
Large Patrol Craft	10	—
Coastal Patrol Craft	1	—
MRC	1	—
Tugs	3	—

Mercantile Marine

Lloyd's Register of Shipping:
 53 vessels of 673 969 tons gross

DELETIONS

Inshore Minesweepers

1973 Brak and Zura ("Ham" Class)

320　LIBYA

SUBMARINES

Note: Because of a failure to reach agreement over training facilities the order for 4 "Daphne" class submarines reported last year has been cancelled.

2 + ?4 Ex-SOVIET "FOXTROT" CLASS

BABR + 1

Displacement, tons: 2 100 surfaced; 2 400 dived
Dimensions, feet (metres): 292 × 27·2 × 15·7 (89 × 8·3 × 4·8)
Torpedo tubes: 10—21 in (6 bow, 4 stern)
Main machinery: Diesel; 3 shafts; 6 000 bhp; electric motors; 5 000 hp
Speed, knots: 18 surfaced; 17 dived
Range, miles: 20 000 surfaced
Complement: 70

Coming from a re-activated building line in Leningrad. *Babr* arrived in Tripoli 27 Dec 1976; the second boat in mid-1977. Four more on order and building while Libyan crews continue training in USSR and Soviet officers (up to 12 in each boat) are attached to each submarine to ensure some measure of safety. In Egypt's case this surveillance continued for several years.

"FOXTROT" Class

FRIGATE
1 VOSPER THORNYCROFT MARK 7

Name	No.	Builders	Laid down	Launched	Commissioned
DAT ASSAWARI	F 01	Vosper Thornycroft	27 Sept 1968	Sept 1969	1 Feb 1973

Displacement, tons: 1 325 standard; 1 625 full load
Length, feet (metres): 310·0 (94·5) pp; 330·0 (100·6) oa
Beam, feet (metres): 36·0 (11·0)
Draught, feet (metres): 11·2 (3·4)
A/S weapons: 1 Mortar Mk 10
Missile launchers: 6 (2 triple) Seacat close range ship-to-air
Guns: 1—4·5 in; 2—40 mm (singles); 2—35 mm (twin)
Main engines: CODOG arrangement; 2 shafts; with Kamewa cp propellers; 2 Rolls-Royce Olympus gas turbines; 46 400 shp = 37·5 knots; 2 Paxman diesels; 3 500 bhp = 17 knots economical cruising speed
Range, miles: 5 700 at 17 knots

Mark 7 Frigate ordered from Vosper Thornycroft on 6 Feb 1968. Generally similar in design to the two Iranian Mark 5s built by this firm, but larger and with different armament. After trials she carried out work-up at Portland, England, reaching Tripoli autumn 1973.

Radar: AWS-1 air surveillance set; fire control radar and RDL-1 radar direction finder.

Refit: Reported that she is to return to United Kingdom for refit spring 1978.

DAT ASSAWARI　　　　　　　　　　　　　　　　　　　1973, John G. Callis

LOGISTIC SUPPORT SHIP
1 LSD TYPE

Name	No.	Builders	Laid down	Launched	Commissioned
ZELTIN	—	Vosper Thornycroft, Woolston	1967	29 Feb 1968	23 Jan 1969

Displacement, tons: 2 200 standard; 2 470 full load
Length, feet (metres): 300·0 (91·4) wl; 324·0 (98·8) oa
Beam, feet (metres): 48·0 (14·6)
Draught, feet (metres): 10·2 (3·1); 19·0 (5·8) aft when flooded
Dock:
Length, feet (metres): 135·0 (41·1)
Width, feet (metres): 40·0 (12·2)
Guns: 2—40 mm
Main engines: 2 Paxman 16-cyl diesels; 3 500 bhp; 2 shafts
Speed, knots: 15
Fuel, tons: 350
Range, miles: 3 000 at 14 knots
Complement: As Senior Officer Ship: 101 (15 officers and 86 ratings)

The ship provides full logistic support, including mobile docking maintenance and repair facilities for the Libyan fleet. Craft up to 120 feet can be docked. Used as tender for Light Forces. The Vosper Thornycroft Group received the order for this ship in Jan 1967 for delivery in late 1968.

Fitted with accommodation for a flag officer or a senior officer and staff. Operational and administrative base of the squadron. Workshops with a total area of approx 4 500 sq feet are situated amidships with ready access to the dock, and there is a 3-ton travelling gantry fitted with outriggers to cover ships berthed alongside up to 200 feet long.

Radar: Thomson-CSF Triton for Vega system.

ZELTIN　　　　　　　　　　　　　　　　　　　　　　　　1969

LIBYA 321

CORVETTES

1 + 3 550 TON MISSILE CORVETTES

Displacement, tons: 630 full load
Dimensions, feet (metres): 202·4 oa × 30·5 × 7·2 *(61·7 oa × 9·3 × 2·2)*
Missiles: 4 Otomat
Guns: 1—76/62 mm; 2—35 mm OTO-Oerlikon (twin)
A/S weapons: 6 (2 triple) Mk 32 A/S torpedo tubes
Mines: Can lay 16 mines
Main engines: 4 MTU MA 16 V956 TB91 diesels; 18 000 hp; 4 shafts = 33 knots
Range, miles: 4 400 at 14 knots
Complement: 56

Ordered from Cantieri Navali del Tirreno e Riuniti in 1974. Completion 1978 onwards. As this corvette can be provided with two, three or four diesels, the performance is very variable. The data given above is basic information for the missile variant (schedule 1).

Electronics: ECM equipment; ELMER telecommunications system.

Radar: Air and surface search: Selenia RAN 11 LX
Navigation: Decca TM 1226.
Fire control: Elsag NA 10.

Sonar: Diodon from Thomson CSF.

C 02 Corvette   11/1977, Commander Aldo Fraccaroli

Name	No.	Builders	Commissioned
TOBRUK	C 01	Vosper Ltd, Portsmouth and Vickers Ltd	20 April 1966

Displacement, tons: 440 standard; 500 full load
Dimensions, feet (metres): 162 wl; 177 oa × 28·5 × 13 *(49·4; 54 × 8·7 × 4)*
Guns: 1—4 in; 4—40 mm (single)
Main engines: 2 Paxman Ventura 16 YJCM diesels; 2 shafts; 3 800 bhp = 18 knots
Range, miles: 2 900 at 14 knots
Complement: 63 (5 officers and 58 ratings)

Launched on 29 July 1965, completed on 30 March 1966, commissioned for service at Portsmouth on 20 April 1966, and arrived in Tripoli on 15 June 1966. Fitted with surface warning radar, Vosper roll damping fins and air-conditioning. A suite of State apartments is included in the accommodation.

TOBRUK   1971, A. & J. Pavia

LIGHT FORCES

Note: There are reports, denied by some in France, that an order for six PR72 Large Patrol Craft has been placed for craft similar to those built for Morocco. Reports unsubstantiated.

2 + 8 "COMBATTANTE II G" CLASS (FAST ATTACK CRAFT—MISSILE)

Displacement, tons: 311
Dimensions, feet (metres): 160·7 × 24·9 × 7·9 *(49 × 7·6 × 2·4)*
Missiles: 4 Otomat
Guns: 1—76 mm OTO Melara (forward); 2—40 mm Bofors Breda (twin)
Main engines: 4 diesels; 20 000 bhp; 4 shafts = 40 knots
Range, miles: 1 600 at 15 knots
Complement: 31

Steel hull with alloy superstructure. Ordered from CMN Cherbourg in May 1977. Delivery expected 1978-80.

Radar: Thomson-CSF Triton and Castor radars for Vega system.

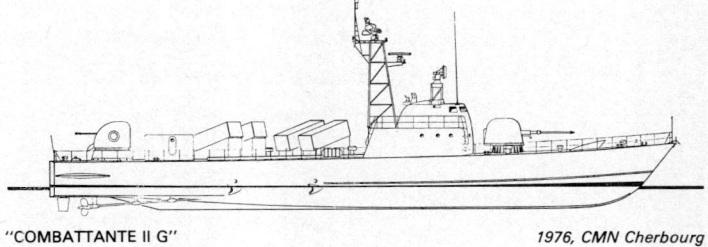

"COMBATTANTE II G"   1976, CMN Cherbourg

5 + ? 7 Ex-SOVIET "OSA II" CLASS
(FAST ATTACK CRAFT—MISSILE)

205 + 4

Displacement, tons: 165 standard; 210 full load
Dimensions, feet (metres): 128·7 × 25·1 × 5·9 *(39·3 × 7·7 × 1·8)*
Missile launchers: 4 for SS-N-2
Guns: 4—30 mm (two twins)
Main engines: 3 diesels; 12 000 bhp = 32 knots
Range, miles: 800 at 25 knots
Complement: 30

The first craft arrived in Oct 1976, two more in early 1977 and two more later in 1977. In Nov 1975 the Libyan government said that 24 of this class were to be acquired—subsequent reports suggest this may have been reduced to 12.

"OSA II" Class   1970

322 LIBYA

3 "SUSA" CLASS (FAST ATTACK CRAFT—MISSILE)

Name	No.	Builders	Commissioned
SUSA	P 01	Vosper Ltd, Portsmouth	23 Jan 1969
SIRTE	P 02	Vosper Ltd, Portsmouth	23 Jan 1969
SEBHA (ex-*Sokna*)	P 03	Vosper Ltd, Portsmouth	1969

Displacement, tons: 95 standard; 114 full load
Dimensions, feet (metres): 90·0 pp; 96·0 wl; 100·0 oa × 25·5 × 7·0 *(27·5; 29·3; 30·5 × 7·8 × 2·1)*
Missiles: 8—SS 12
Guns: 2—40 mm (single)
Main engines: 3 Bristol Siddeley "Proteus" gas turbines; 3 shafts; 12 750 bhp = 54 knots
Complement: 20

SEBHA (now carry pennant numbers)   1969, Wright and Logan

The order for these three fast patrol boats was announced on 12 Oct 1966. They are generally similar to the "Soloven" class designed and built by Vosper for the Royal Danish Navy. Fitted with air-conditioning and modern radar and radio equipment. *Suza* was launched on 31 Aug 1967, *Sirte* on 10 Jan 1968 and *Sokna* (renamed *Sebha*) on 29 Feb 1968. First operational vessels in the world to be armed with Nord-Aviation SS 12(M) guided weapons with sighting turret installation and other equipment developed jointly by Vosper and Nord. All three overhauled in Italy in 1977.

4 "GARIAN" CLASS (LARGE PATROL CRAFT)

Name	No.	Builders	Commissioned
KHAWLAN	—	Brooke Marine, Lowestoft	30 Aug 1969
MERAWA	—	Brooke Marine, Lowestoft	early 1970
SABRATHA	—	Brooke Marine, Lowestoft	early 1970
GARIAN	—	Brooke Marine, Lowestoft	30 Aug 1969

Displacement, tons: 120 standard; 159 full load
Dimensions, feet (metres): 100 pp; 106 oa × 21·2 × 5·5 *(30·5; 32·3 × 6·5 × 1·7)*
Guns: 1—40 mm; 1—20 mm
Main engines: 2 Paxman diesels; 2 200 bhp = 24 knots
Range, miles: 1 500 at 12 knots
Complement: 15 to 22

Launched on 21 April, 29 May, 25 Oct and 30 Sept 1969, respectively.

KHAWLAN   1970, Brooke Marine

6 THORNYCROFT TYPE (LARGE PATROL CRAFT)

Name	No.	Builders	Commissioned
AKRAMA	—	Vosper Thornycroft	early 1969
AR RAKIB	—	John I. Thornycroft, Woolston	4 May 1967
BENINA	—	Vosper Thornycroft	29 Aug 1968
FARWA	—	John I. Thornycroft, Woolston	4 May 1967
HOMS	—	Vosper Thornycroft	early 1969
MISURATA	—	Vosper Thornycroft	29 Aug 1968

Displacement, tons: 100
Dimensions, feet (metres): 100 × 21 × 5·5 *(30·5 × 6·4 × 1·7)*
Gun: 1—20 mm
Main engines: 3 Rolls-Royce DV8TLM diesels; 1 740 bhp = 18 knots
Range, miles: 1 800 at 14 knots

Welded steel construction. Slight difference in silhouette between first pair and the remainder.

FARWA   1969, Thornycroft

1 THORNYCROFT TYPE (COASTAL PATROL CRAFT)

Dimensions, feet (metres): 78 × 15 × 4·5 *(23·8 × 4·6 × 1·4)*
Gun: 1 MG
Main engines: 3 Rolls-Royce diesels; 3 shafts; 945 bhp = 22·5 knots
Range, miles: 400 at 15 knots

Built by John I. Thornycroft, Singapore in 1962. Two similar but smaller boats transferred to Malta in 1974.

AMPHIBIOUS FORCES

2 "PS 700" CLASS (LST)

Name	No.	Builders	Commissioned
IBN OUF	130	CNI de la Méditerranée	May 1977
IBN HARITHA	131	CNI de la Méditerranée	Mar 1978

Displacement, tons: 2 800 full load
Dimensions, feet (metres): 326·4 × 51·2 × 8·2 *(99·5 × 15·6 × 2·4)*
Aircraft: Deck for Alouette III
Guns: 6—40 mm (twin turrets) Breda Bofors
Main engines: 2 SEMT Pielstick diesels; 5 340 hp; 2 shafts (cp propellers) = 15·4 knots
Range, miles: 4 000 at 14 knots
Complement: 35

Can carry 240 troops under normal conditions. Have bow doors and ramp for the 11 tanks carried. Helicopter platform.
Ibn Ouf laid down 1 April 1976 and launched 22 Oct 1976; *Ibn Haritha* launched 18 April 1977.

IBN OUF   1977, Marius Bar, Toulon

1 Ex-SOVIET "POLNOCNY" CLASS (LCT)

IBN AL HADRAMI 112

Displacement, tons: 1 000 full load
Dimensions, feet (metres): 239·4 × 29·5 × 9·8 *(75 × 9 × 3)*
Guns: 4—30 mm; 2 rocket launchers
Main engines: 2 diesels; 5 000 hp = 18 knots
Complement: 40

Transferred Dec 1977.

IBN AL HADRAMI   12/1977

MAINTENANCE REPAIR CRAFT

ZLEITEN (ex-*MRC 1013*, ex-*LCT*)

Displacement, tons: 657 standard; 900 approx full load
Dimensions, feet (metres): 225·0 pp; 231·3 oa × 39·0 × 5·0 *(68·6; 70·5 × 11·9 × 1·5)*
Main engines: 4 Paxman diesels; 2 shafts; 1 840 bhp × 9 knots cruising

Built in 1944-45. Purchased from United Kingdom on 5 Sept 1966. Now a hulk.

TUGS

3 COASTAL TYPE

Name	No.	Builders	Commissioned
RAS EL-HELAL	—	Mondego, Portugal	22 Oct 1977
AL SHWEIRIF	—	Mondego, Portugal	17 Feb 1978
AL KERIAT	—	Mondego, Portugal	1978

Measurement, tons: 200 gross
Dimensions, feet (metres): 114 × 29·5 × 13 *(34·8 × 9 × 4)*
Main engines: 2 diesels, 2 300 hp = 14 knots

Laid down—*Ras El-Helal*, 5 Feb 1976; *Al Shweirif* 23 March 1976.

MADAGASCAR

Ministerial

Minister of Defence:
Lieutenant-Colonel Mampila Jaona

Personnel

(a) 1978: 600 officers and men (including Marine Company)
(b) 18 months national service

Mercantile Marine

Lloyd's Register of Shipping:
44 vessels of 39 850 tons gross

Bases and Ports

Diego Suarez, Tamatave, Majunga, Tulear, Nossi-Be, Fort Dauphin, Manakara.

DELETION
1976 *Jasmine* (Tender)

LIGHT FORCES

1 TYPE 48 (LARGE PATROL CRAFT)

Name	No.	Builders	Commissioned
MALAIKA	—	Chantiers Navals Franco-Belges (SFCN)	Dec 1967

Displacement, tons: 235 light
Dimensions, feet (metres): 149·3 pp; 155·8 oa × 23·6 × 8·2 *(45·5; 47·5 × 7·1 × 2·5)*
Guns: 2—40 mm
Main engines: 2 MGO diesels; 2 shafts; 2 400 bhp = 18·5 knots
Range, miles: 2 000 at 15 knots
Complement: 25

Ordered by the French Navy for delivery to Madagascar. Laid down in Nov 1966, launched on 22 March 1967.

5 PATROL BOATS

Displacement, tons: 46
Length, feet (metres): 78·7 *(24)*
Gun: 1—40 mm
Main engines: 2 diesels = 22 knots

Used by the Maritime Police. Built by Küstenwache in 1962.

AMPHIBIOUS FORCE

1 "BATRAM" CLASS

Name	No.	Builders	Commissioned
TOKY	—	Arsenal de Diego Suarez	Oct 1974

Displacement, tons: 810
Dimensions, feet (metres): 217·8 × 41 × 6·2 *(66·4 × 12·5 × 1·9)*
Missiles: 8—SS12
Guns: 2—40 mm
Main engines: 2 MGO diesels; 2 400 hp; 2 shafts = 13 knots
Complement: 27
Range, miles: 3 000 at 12 knots

Can carry 250 tons stores and 30 passengers or 120 troops over short distances. Paid for by the French Government as military assistance.
Fitted with a bow ramp and similar to, though larger, than the French EDIC.

324 MADAGASCAR / MALAYSIA

TRAINING SHIP

Name	No.	Builders	Commissioned
FANANTENANA (ex-*Richelieu*)	—	A. G. Weser, Bremen, Germany	1959

Displacement, tons: 1 040 standard; 1 200 full load
Dimensions, feet (metres): 183·7 pp; 206·4 oa × 30 × 14·8 *(56; 62·9 × 9·2 × 4·5)*
Guns: 2—40 mm
Main engines: 2 Deutz diesels; 1 shaft; 1 060 + 500 bhp = 12 knots

Trawler purchased and converted in 1966-67 to Coast Guard and training ship. 691 tons gross.

MALAWI

1 FAIREY MARINE "SPEAR" CLASS

Dimensions, feet (metres): 29·8 × 9·2 × 2·6 *(9·1 × 2·8 × ·8)*
Guns: 2—7·62 mm MG
Main engines: 2 Perkins diesels of 290 hp = 25 knots
Complement: 3

Acquired late 1976.

Three other small patrol-boats are deployed on Lake Nyasa (L. Malawi); the first was bought in 1968.

MALAYSIA
(see also Sabah)

Administration

Minister of Defence:
  Hon. Dato Hussein bin Onn

Headquarters Appointments

Chief of the Naval Staff:
  Rear-Admiral Dato Mohd. Zain bin Mohd. Salleh, DPMJ, KMN
Deputy Chief of the Naval Staff:
  Commodore Abdul Wahab bin Haji Nawi, KMN, SMJ

Senior Commands

Commander Naval Area 1:
  Commodore P. K. Nettur, KMN
Commander Naval Area 2:
  Commodore Aris Fadzillah bin Alang Ahmad

Diplomatic Representation

Services Adviser in London:
  Colonel M. Shah Bin Yahaya

Personnel

(a) 1978: 6 000 officers and ratings (Reserves about 1 000)
(b) Voluntary service

Bases

KD *Malaya*, Johore Straits; Labuan. (KD *Sri Labuan, Sri Tawau, Sri Rejang*).

Prefix to Ships' Names

The names of Malaysian warships are prefixed by KD, (Kapal Diraja).

Mercantile Marine

Lloyd's Register of Shipping:
  179 vessels of 563 666 tons gross

Strength of the Fleet

Type	Active	Building
Frigates	2	—
Fast Attack Craft—Missile	4	4
Fast Attack Craft—Gun	6	—
Large Patrol Craft	22	—
Minesweepers—Coastal	5	—
Diving Tender	1	—
Survey Vessels	2	—
LSTs	3	—
Police Launches	27	3

DELETIONS

Light Forces

1976 *Sri Kedah, Sri Pahang*
1977 *Gempita, Handalan, Penderkar, Perkase*

Frigate

1977 *Hang Tuah* ("Loch" Class)

Minewarfare Forces

1977 *Jerai* ("Ton" Class)

PENNANT LIST

Frigates

| F 24 | Rahmat |
| F 76 | Hang Tuah |

Light Forces

P 34	Kris
P 36	Sundang
P 37	Badek
P 38	Renchong
P 39	Tombak
P 40	Lembing
P 41	Serampang
P 42	Panah
P 43	Kerambit
P 44	Beledau
P 45	Kelewang
P 46	Rentaka
P 47	Sri Perlis

Light Forces

P 49	Sri Johor
P 3139	Sri Selangor
P 3140	Sri Perak
P 3142	Sri Kelantan
P 3143	Sri Trengganu
P 3144	Sri Sabah
P 3145	Sri Sarawak
P 3146	Sri Negri Sembilan
P 3147	Sri Melaka
P 3501	Perdana
P 3502	Serang
P 3503	Ganas
P 3504	Ganyang
P 3505	Jerong
P 3506	Todak
P 3507	Paus
P 3508	Yu
P 3509	Baung
P 3510	Pari

Minewarfare Forces

M 1127	Mahamiru
M 1134	Kinabalu
M 1143	Ledang
M 1163	Tahan
M 1172	Brinchang

Support Forces

A 151	Perantau
A 1109	Duyong
A 1500	Sri Langkawi
A 1501	Sri Banggi
A 1502	Rajah Jarom

Police Craft

| PX 1-30 | Coastal Patrol Craft |

MALAYSIA 325

FRIGATES
1 YARROW TYPE

Name	No.	Builders	Laid down	Launched	Commissioned
RAHMAT (ex-*Hang Jebat*)	F 24	Yarrow Shipbuilders & Co Ltd	Feb 1966	18 Dec 1967	Mar 1971

Displacement, tons: 1 250 standard; 1 600 full load
Length, feet (metres): 300·0 *(91·44)* pp; 308 *(93·9)* oa
Beam, feet (metres): 34·1 *(10·4)*
Draught, feet (metres): 14·8 *(4·5)*
Aircraft: Can land helo. on MacGregor hatch on Limbo well
Missile launchers: 1 quadruple Seacat surface-to-air
Guns: 1—4·5 in *(114 mm)*; 2—40 mm
A/S weapon: 1 Limbo three-barrelled mortar
Main engines: 1 Bristol Siddeley Olympus gas turbine; 19 500 shp; Crossley Pielstick diesel; 3 850 bhp; 2 shafts
Speed, knots: 26 boosted by gas turbine; 16 on diesel alone
Range, miles: 6 000 at 16 knots; 1 000 at 26 knots
Complement: 140

General purpose frigate of new design developed by Yarrow. Fully automatic with saving in complement. Ordered on 11 Feb 1966.

Radar: Air Surveillance: HSA LW 02. Fire control: M 20 with radar in spherical radome for guns; M 44 for Seacat.

RAHMAT   1972, Wright and Logan

1 YARROW TYPE

Name	No.	Builders	Laid down	Launched	Commissioned
HANG TUAH (ex-HMS *Mermaid*)	F 76	Yarrow Shipbuilders & Co Ltd	1965	29 Dec 1966	16 May 1973 (see notes)

Displacement, tons: 2 300 standard; 2 520 full load
Dimensions, feet (metres): 320 pp; 330 wl; 339·3 oa × 40 × 12 *(97·6; 100·7; 103·5 × 12·2 × 3·7)*
Guns: 2—4 in (twin); 2—40 mm
A/S weapons: 1—three-barrelled Limbo mortar
Main engines: 8 diesels; 14 400 shp; 2 shafts; 2 cp propellers = 24 knots
Oil fuel, tons: 230
Range, miles: 4 800 at 15 knots

Similar in hull and machinery to "Leopard" and "Salisbury" classes. Originally built for Ghana as a display ship for ex-President Nkrumah at a cost of £5m but put up for sale after his departure. She was launched without ceremony on 29 Dec 1966 and completed in 1968. She was transferred to Portsmouth Dockyard in April 1972 being acquired by the Royal Navy. Refit started Oct 1972 at Chatham. Commissioned in Royal Navy 16 May 1973. She was based at Singapore 1974-75 returning to UK early 1976.

Transfer: To Malaysia May 1977 as replacement for the previous *Hang Tuah*. She was refitted by Vosper Thornycroft and commissioned on 22 July 1977 sailing for Malaysia in August.

HANG TUAH   8/1977, Michael D. J. Lennon

LIGHT FORCES
0 + 4 "SPICA-M" CLASS (FAST ATTACK CRAFT—MISSILE)

Displacement, tons: 240
Dimensions, feet (metres): 142·6 × 23·3 × 7·4 *(43·6 × 7·1 × 2·4)*
Missiles: 4 Exocet aft; 1 Blowpipe
Guns: 1—57 mm; 1—40 mm
Main engines: 3 MTU diesels; 3 shafts; 10 800 hp = 34·5 knots
Range, miles: 1 850 at 14 knots

Bridge further forward than in Swedish class to accommodate Exocet. Ordered from Karlskrona Shipyard 15 Oct 1976 for delivery in 1979.

4 "PERDANA" CLASS (FAST ATTACK CRAFT—MISSILE)

Name	No.	Builders	Commissioned
PERDANA	P 3501	Constructions Mécaniques de Normandie	Dec 1972
SERANG	P 3502	Constructions Mécaniques de Normandie	31 Jan 1973
GANAS	P 3503	Constructions Mécaniques de Normandie	28 Feb 1973
GANYANG	P 3504	Constructions Mécaniques de Normandie	20 Mar 1973

Displacement, tons: 234 standard; 265 full load
Dimensions, feet (metres): 154·2 × 23·1 × 12·8 *(47·0 × 7·0 × 3·9)*
Missile launchers: 2 MM38 Exocet
Guns: 1—57 mm Bofors; 1—40 mm 70 cal Bofors
Main engines: 4 MTU diesels; 4 shafts; 14 000 bhp = 36·5 knots
Range, miles: 800 at 25 knots

Perdana launched 31 May 1972 and *Ganas* launched 26 Oct 1972, *Serang* launched 22 Dec 1971, and *Ganyang* launched 16 March 1972. All of basic "La Combattante II" design. Left Cherbourg for Malaysia 2 May 1973.

Radar: Thomson-CSF Triton and Pollux radars for Vega system.

PERDANA   1976, A. G. Burgoyne

326 MALAYSIA

6 "JERONG" CLASS (FAST ATTACK CRAFT—GUN)

Name	No.	Builders	Commissioned
JERONG	3505	Hong-Leong-Lürssen, Butterworth	27 Mar 1976
TODAK	3506	Hong-Leong-Lürssen, Butterworth	16 June 1976
PAUS	3507	Hong-Leong-Lürssen, Butterworth	16 Aug 1976
YU	3508	Hong-Leong-Lürssen, Butterworth	15 Nov 1976
BAUNG	3509	Hong-Leong-Lürssen, Butterworth	Jan 1977
PARI	3510	Hong-Leong-Lürssen, Butterworth	Mar 1977

Displacement, tons: 254 full load
Dimensions, feet (metres): 147·3 × 23 × 12·8 *(44·9 × 7 × 3·9)*
Guns: 1—57 mm; 1—40 mm
Main engines: 3 Maybach Mercedes-Benz diesels; 9 900 bhp = 32 knots
Range, miles: 2 000 at 15 knots

Launch dates: *Jerong*, 28 July 1975; *Todak*, 15 March 1976; *Paus*, 3 June 1976; *Yu*, 17 July 1976; *Baung*, 5 Oct 1976; *Pari*, Jan 1977.

JERONG 1976, Royal Malaysian Navy

4 "KEDAH" CLASS (LARGE PATROL CRAFT)

Name	No.	Builders	Commissioned
SRI SELANGOR	P 3139	Vosper Ltd, Portsmouth	25 Mar 1963
SRI PERAK	P 3140	Vosper Ltd, Portsmouth	June 1963
SRI KELANTAN	P 3142	Vosper Ltd, Portsmouth	12 Nov 1963
SRI TRENGGANU	P 3143	Vosper Ltd, Portsmouth	16 Dec 1963

4 "SABAH" CLASS (LARGE PATROL CRAFT)

Name	No.	Builders	Commissioned
SRI SABAH	P 3144	Vosper Ltd, Portsmouth	2 Sept 1964
SRI SARAWAK	P 3145	Vosper Ltd, Portsmouth	30 Sept 1964
SRI NEGRI SEMBILAN	P 3146	Vosper Ltd, Portsmouth	28 Sept 1964
SRI MELAKA	P 3147	Vosper Ltd, Portsmouth	2 Nov 1964

14 "KRIS" CLASS (LARGE PATROL CRAFT)

Name	No.	Builders	Commissioned
KRIS	P 34	Vosper Ltd, Portsmouth	1 Jan 1966
SUNDANG	P 36	Vosper Ltd, Portsmouth	29 Nov 1966
BADEK	P 37	Vosper Ltd, Portsmouth	15 Dec 1966
RENCHONG	P 38	Vosper Ltd, Portsmouth	17 Jan 1967
TOMBAK	P 39	Vosper Ltd, Portsmouth	2 Mar 1967
LEMBING	P 40	Vosper Ltd, Portsmouth	12 April 1967
SERAMPANG	P 41	Vosper Ltd, Portsmouth	19 May 1967
PANAH	P 42	Vosper Ltd, Portsmouth	27 July 1967
KERAMBIT	P 43	Vosper Ltd, Portsmouth	28 July 1967
BELEDAU	P 44	Vosper Ltd, Portsmouth	12 Sept 1967
KELEWANG	P 45	Vosper Ltd, Portsmouth	4 Oct 1967
RENTAKA	P 46	Vosper Ltd, Portsmouth	22 Sept 1967
SRI PERLIS	P 47	Vosper Ltd, Portsmouth	24 Jan 1968
SRI JOHOR	P 49	Vosper Ltd, Portsmouth	14 Feb 1968

Displacement, tons: 96 standard; 109 full load
Dimensions, feet (metres): 95 wl; 103 oa × 19·8 × 5·5 *(29; 31·4 × 6 × 1·7)*
Guns: 2—40 mm; 70 cal
Main engines: 2 Bristol Siddeley/Maybach (MTU) MD 655/18 diesels; 3 500 bhp = 27 knots
Range, miles: 1 400 (*Sabah* class 1 660) at 14 knots
Complement: 22 (3 officers, 19 ratings)

The first six boats, constituting the "Kedah" class were ordered in 1961 for delivery in 1963. The four boats of the "Sabah" class were ordered in 1963 for delivery in 1964. The remaining 14 boats of the "Kris" class were ordered in 1965 for delivery between 1966 and 1968. All are of prefabricated steel construction and are fitted with Decca radar, air-conditioning and Vosper roll damping equipment. The differences between the three classes are minor, the later ones having improved radar, communications, evaporators and engines of Maybach (MTU), as opposed to Bristol Siddeley construction. *Sri Johor*, the last of the 14 boats of the "Kris" class, was launched on 22 June 1967.

SRI SABAH ("Sabah" Class) 1976, A. G. Burgoyne

MINE WARFARE FORCES

5 Ex-BRITISH "TON" CLASS (MINESWEEPERS—COASTAL)

Name	No.	Builders	Commissioned
MAHAMIRU (ex-HMS *Darlaston*)	M 1127	Cook, Welton and Gemmell	1954
KINABALU (ex-HMS *Essington*)	M 1134	Camper and Nicholson	1955
LEDANG (ex-HMS *Hexton*)	M 1143	Cook, Welton and Gemmell	1954
TAHAN (ex-HMS *Lullington*)	M 1163	Harland and Wolff	1956
BRINCHANG (ex-HMS *Thankerton*)	M 1172	Camper and Nicholson	1957

Displacement, tons: 360 standard; 425 full load
Dimensions, feet (metres): 140 pp; 152 oa × 28·8 × 8·2 *(42·7; 46·4 × 8·8 × 2·5)*
Guns: 1—40 mm forward; 2—20 mm aft
Main engines: 2 Deltic diesels; 2 shafts; 2 500 bhp = 15 knots
Oil fuel, tons: 45
Range, miles: 2 300 at 13 knots
Complement: 39

Mahamiru transferred from the Royal Navy on May 1960. *Ledang*, refitted at Chatham Dockyard before transfer, commissioned for Malaysia in Oct 1963. *Jerai* and *Kinabalu*, refitted in Great Britain, arrived in Malaysia summer 1964. *Brinchang* and *Tahan*, refitted in Singapore, transferred to Malaysian Navy in May and April 1966, respectively. All six underwent a 9-month refit by Vosper Thornycroft, Singapore during 1972-73 which will extend their availability by some years.

KINABALU 1976, A. G. Burgoyne

MALAYSIA 327

AMPHIBIOUS FORCES

3 Ex-US "511-1152" CLASS (LSTs)

SRI LANGKAWI (ex-USS *Hunterdon County, AGP 838* ex-*LST 838*) A 1500
SRI BANGGI (ex-USS *Henry County LST 824*) A 1501
RAJAH JAROM (ex-USS *Sedgewick County LST 1123*) A 1502

Displacement, tons: 1 653 standard; 2 366 beaching; 4 080 full load
Dimensions, feet (metres): 316·0 wl; 328·0 oa × 50·0 × 14·0 *(96·4; 100 × 15·3 × 4·3)*
Guns: 8—40 mm (2 twin, 4 single)
Main engines: GM diesels; 2 shafts; 1 700 bhp = 11·6 knots
Complement: 138 (11 officers, 127 ratings)

Built in 1945. *Sri Langkawi* transferred on loan from the US Navy and commissioned in the Royal Malaysian Navy on 1 July 1971. Sold 1 Aug 1974. Other two transferred by sale 7 Oct 1976 and used as cargo support ships. Cargo capacity 2 100 tons.
Sri Langkawi operates as a tender to Light Forces.

SRI LANGKAWI   1976, A. G. Burgoyne

SURVEY VESSELS

Name	No.	Builders	Commissioned
MUTIARA	—	Hong-Leong-Lürssen, Butterworth	Dec 1977

Displacement, tons: 575
Complement: 154 (13 officers, 141 ratings)

Ordered in early 1975.

1 Ex-BRITISH "TON" CLASS

Name	No.	Builders	Commissioned
PERANTAU (ex-HMS *Myrmidon*, ex-HMS *Edderton*)	A 151	Doig	20 July 1964

Displacement, tons: 360 standard; 420 full load
Dimensions, feet (metres): 152 oa × 28·8 × 8·2 *(46·4 × 8·8 × 2·5)*
Main engines: 2 Mirrlees diesels; 2 shafts; 3 000 bhp = 15 knots
Range, miles: 2 300 at 13 knots
Complement: 35

A former coastal minesweeper of the "Ton" class, converted by the Royal Navy into a survey ship, renamed *Myrmidon* in April 1964, and commissioned for service on 20 July 1964. Paid off in 1968 and purchased by Malaysia in 1969. Service in Malaysian waters since 1970. To be replaced by *Mutiara*.

PERANTAU   1972, Royal Malaysian Navy

DIVING TENDER

Name	No.	Builders	Commissioned
DUYONG	A 1109	Kall Teck (Pte) Ltd, Singapore	5 Jan 1971

Displacement, tons: 120 standard; 140 full load
Dimensions, feet (metres): 99·5 wl; 110·0 oa × 21·0 × 5·8 *(30·3; 33·6 × 6·4 × 1·8)*
Gun: 1—20 mm
Main engines: 2 Cummins diesels; 1 900 rpm; 500 bhp = 10 knots
Complement: 23

Launched on 18 Aug 1970 as TRV.

DUYONG   1976, A. G. Burgoyne

ROYAL MALAYSIAN POLICE

18 PX CLASS

MAHKOTA PX 1	**BENTARA** PX 7	**PEKAN** PX 13	
TEMENGGONG PX 2	**PERWIRA** PX 8	**KELANG** PX 14	
HULUBALANG PX 3	**PERTANDA** PX 9	**KUALA KANGSAR** PX 15	
MAHARAJASETIA PX 4	**SHAHBANDAR** PX 10	**ARAU** PX 16	
MAHARAJALELA PX 5	**SANGSETIA** PX 11	**SRI GUMANTONG** PX 17	
PAHLAWAN PX 6	**LAKSAMANA** PX 12	**SRI LABUAN** PX 18	

Displacement, tons: 85
Dimensions, feet (metres): 87·5 oa × 19 × 4·8 *(26·7 × 5·8 × 1·5)*
Guns: 2—20 mm
Main engines: 2 Mercedes-Benz (MTU) diesels; 2 shafts; 2 700 hp = 25 knots
Range, miles: 700 at 15 knots
Complement: 15

328 MALAYSIA / MALTA

6 IMPROVED PX CLASS

ALOR STAR PX 19	KUALA TRENGGANU PX 21	SRI MENANTI PX 23
KOTA BAHRU PX 20	JOHORE BAHRU PX 22	KUCHING PX 24

Displacement, tons: 92
Dimensions, feet (metres): 91 oa (27·8)
Guns: 2—20 mm
Main engines: 2 (MTU) diesels; 2 460 hp = 25 knots
Range, miles: 750 at 15 knots
Complement: 18

All 24 boats built by Vosper Thornycroft Private, Singapore; PX class between 1963 and 1970, Improved PX class 1972-73. *Sri Gumantong* and *Sri Labuan* operated by Sabah Government, remainder by Royal Malaysian Police.

SRI MENANTI   1972, Yam Photos, Singapore

6 LÜRSSEN PATROL CRAFT

SRI — PX 25   SRI KUDAT PX 26   SRI TAWAU PX 27   + 3

Of 62·5 tons and 25 knots with 1—20 mm. First three completed mid-1973.

MALDIVES

A series of widely separated atolls where fishing has been interrupted by foreign craft and the small communities can be reached only by sea.

Mercantile Marine

Lloyd's Register of Shipping:
45 vessels of 110 681 tons gross.

1 Ex-BRITISH TARGET TOWING LAUNCH

Displacement, tons: 34·6
Dimensions, feet (metres): 68 × 19 × 6 (20·7 ×5·8 × 1·8)
Main engines: 2 Rolls-Royce Sea Griffon diesels; 11 000 bhp = 30 knots
Complement: 9

Transferred by RAF after their evacuation of Gan in 1976.

1 Ex-BRITISH PINNACE

Displacement, tons: 28·3
Dimensions, feet (metres): 63 × 15·5 × 5 (19·2 × 4·9 × 1·5)
Main engines: 2 Rolls-Royce C6 diesels; 190 bhp = 13 knots
Complement: 5

5 tons cargo capacity. Transferred by RAF in 1976.

4 Ex-BRITISH LANDING CRAFT

64 ft General Purpose craft transferred by RAF in 1976.

3 Ex-TAIWANESE TRAWLERS

Confiscated for illegal fishing. Fitted with one twin 25 mm (Soviet) gun on foc's'le.

1 FAIREY MARINE 45 ft TYPE

Provided for patrol and intercommunication duties in 1975.

MALI

Personnel

1978: 50 officers and men

Patrol Craft

A small river patrol service with 3 craft operating on headwaters of the Niger with bases at Bamako, Segou, Mopti and Timbuktu.

MALTA

A coastal patrol force of small craft was formed in 1973. It is manned by the Maltese Regiment and primarily employed as a coastguard.

Mercantile Marine

Lloyd's Register of Shipping:
44 vessels of 100 420 tons gross

1 CUSTOMS LAUNCH

C 21

Displacement, tons: 25
Dimensions, feet (metres): 54·1 × 12·8 × 4·9 (16·5 × 3·9 × 1·5)
Main engines: 2 Fiat 521 3M diesels
Complement: 6

Built by Malta Drydocks 1960 and purchased 1973.

MALTA 329

2 Ex-US "SWIFT" CLASS

C 23 (ex-US C 6823)   **C 24** (ex-US C 6824)

Displacement, tons: 22·5
Dimensions, feet (metres): 50 × 13 × 4·9 *(15·6 × 4 × 1·5)*
Guns: 3—0·50 cal Browning M2 MG; 81 mm mortars
Main engines: 2 GM 12V-71N diesels = 25 knots
Endurance: 24 hours
Complement: 6

Built by Sewart Seacraft Ltd in 1967. Bought in Feb 1971.

C 23   1977, Michael D. J. Lennon

2 Ex-LIBYAN CUSTOMS LAUNCHES

C 25   **C 26**

Displacement, tons: 86·2
Dimensions, feet (metres): 103 × 16·1 × 4·9 *(31·4 × 4·9 × 1·5)*
Gun: 1—0·50 cal Browning M2
Main engines: 2 Mercedes-Benz MB 820B diesels; 2 shafts; 630 bhp = 21 knots
Complement: 12

First transferred 16 Jan 1974.

C 26   1976, Michael D. J. Lennon

3 Ex-GERMAN CUSTOMS LAUNCHES

C 27 (ex-*Brunsbuttel*)

Displacement, tons: 105
Dimensions, feet (metres): 96·8 × 17·1 × 5·2 *(29·5 × 5·2 × 1·6)*
Gun: 1—0·50 cal Browning M2
Main engines: 2 Motoren Werke TRM 134S diesels
Complement: 9

Built in 1953 by Buschmann, Hamburg.

C 27   1976, Michael D. J. Lennon

C 28 (ex-*Geier*)

Displacement, tons: 125
Dimensions, feet (metres): 91·8 × 17·4 × 6·6 *(28 × 5 × 2)*
Main engines: 2 Mercedes-Benz diesel MB 846 AB—electric
Complement: 7

Built in 1955 by Bremen Burg. No guns.

C 28   1976, Michael D. J. Lennon

C 29 (ex-*Kondor*)

Displacement, tons: 100
Dimensions, feet (metres): 90·5 × 17·1 × 6·2 *(28 × 5·3 × 2)*
Gun: 1—0·50 cal Browning M2
Main engines: 1 Deutz R.T. 8M 233 diesel
Complement: 9

Built in 1953 by Lürssen, Bremen.

C 29   1975, D. Bateman

MAURITANIA

Ministerial

Minister of National Defence:
 Abdullahi Ould Bah

General

An interesting and rapid expansion from the four patrol craft of last year using the resources of both East and West.

Personnel

(a) 1978: 200 officers and men
(b) Voluntary service

Base

Port Etienne

Mercantile Marine

Lloyd's Register of Shipping:
 4 vessels of 1 113 tons gross

CORVETTES

2 Ex-SOVIET "MIRNY" CLASS

Name	No.	Builders	Commissioned
BOULANOUAR	—	Nikolaev	1956
IDINI	—	Nikolaev	1956

Displacement, tons: 850
Dimensions, feet (metres): 208 × 31·2 × 13·8 *(63·4 × 9·5 ×4·2)*
Guns: 2—30 mm; 1 MG
Main engines: Diesel-electric; 1 shaft = 17 knots

Ex-Whale-catchers converted for use as patrol craft and for support of Light Forces. Similar to Soviet AGIs.

"MIRNY" Class 1972

LIGHT FORCES

2 SPANISH "BARCELO" CLASS

Name	No.	Builders	Commissioned
—	—	Bazan-La Carraca	April 1978
—	—	Bazan-La Carraca	May 1978

Displacement, tons: 139
Dimensions, feet (metres): 118·7 × 18·9 × 8·2 *(36·2 × 5·8 × 2·5)*
Guns: 1—40 mm; 2—20 mm
Main engines: 2 MTU MD-16 TB-90 diesels; 6 000 shp = 40 knots
Range, miles: 1 200 at 17 knots
Complement: 19 (3 officers, 16 ratings)

The original Spanish *Barcelo* was built by Lürssen to their design, Bazan building the remainder. Ordered 21 July 1976.

BARCELO 3/1976, E. N. Bazán

2 Ex-SPANISH LARGE PATROL CRAFT

Name	No.	Builders	Commissioned
TICHITT	—	Chantiers Navals de l'Estérel	April 1969
DAR EL BARKA	—	Chantiers Navals de l'Estérel	June 1969

Displacement, tons: 75 standard; 80 full load
Dimensions, feet (metres): 105 × 18·9 × 5·2 *(31·4 × 5·8 × 1·6)*
Guns: 2—20 mm
Main engines: 2 Mercedes Maybach (MTU) 12V 331 TC81 diesels; 2 shafts; 2 700 bhp = 30 knots
Range, miles: 1 500 at 15 knots
Complement: 17

DAR EL BARKA *Chantiers Navals de l'Esterel*

Name	No.	Builders	Commissioned
— (ex-*Centinela* W 33)	—	Bazan, Ferrol	1953
— (ex-*Serviola* W 34)	—	Bazan, Ferrol	1953

Displacement, tons: 255 standard; 282 full load
Dimensions, feet (metres): 117·5 × 22·5 × 9·8 *(35·8 × 6·9 × 3)*
Guns: 2—37 mm
Main engine: 1 diesel; 430 bhp = 12 knots

Used as fishery protection ships in Spain. Transferred 5 March 1977.

SERVIOLA 1974, Spanish Navy

Name	No.	Builders	Commissioned
IM RAQ NI	—	Chantiers Navals de l'Estérel	Nov 1965
SLOUGHI	—	Chantiers Navals de l'Estérel	May 1968

Displacement, tons: 20
Dimensions, feet (metres): 59 × 13·5 × 3·8 (18 × 4·1 × 1·2)
Gun: 1—12·7 mm
Main engines: 2 GM 671M diesels; 512 bhp = 22·5 knots
Range, miles: 860 at 12 knots; 400 at 15 knots
Complement: 6

CHINGUETTI
Small patrol craft reaching the end of her life.

MAURITIUS

Ministerial

Minister of National Defence:
 Sir Seewoosagur Ramgoolam (Premier)

Mercantile Marine

Lloyd's Register of Shipping:
 17 vessels of 37 288 tons gross

1 Ex-INDIAN "ABHAY" CLASS (LARGE PATROL CRAFT)

AMAR

Displacement, tons: 120 standard; 151 full load
Dimensions, feet (metres): 110 pp; 117·2 oa × 20 × 5 (33·6 pp; 35·7 oa × 6·1 × 1·5)
Gun: 1—40 mm
Main engines: 2 diesels = 18 knots

Built by Hooghly D & E Co, Calcutta 1961. Transferred April 1974. Retained original name.

AMAR   1976

MEXICO

Ministerial

Secretary of National Defence:
 General Hermenegildo Cuenca Diaz

Headquarters Appointments

Secretary of the Navy:
 Admiral C. G. Demn. Luis M. Bravo Carrera
Under-Secretary of the Navy:
 Rear-Admiral Ing M. N. Ricardo Chazaro Lara
Commander-in-Chief of the Navy:
 Vice-Admiral C. G. Demn. Humberto Uribe Escandon
Chief of the Naval Staff:
 Rear-Admiral C. G. Demn. Miguel A. Gomez Ortega
Director Naval Air Services:
 Rear-Admiral Blanco Peyrefitte
Director of Services:
 Rear-Admiral C. G. Demn. Mario Artigas Fernandez

Diplomatic Representation

Naval Attaché in London:
 Rear-Admiral S. Gomez Bernard
Naval Attaché in Washington:
 Vice-Admiral Miguel Manzarraga

Personnel

(a) 1978: Total 11 000 officers and men (including Naval Air Force and 1 300 Marines)
(b) Voluntary service

Mercantile Marine

Lloyd's Register of Shipping:
 311 vessels of 673 964 tons gross

Naval Air Force

Naval air bases at Mexico City, Las Bajadas, Puerto Cortes, Isla Mujeres, Ensenada.

4 Hu-16 Albatros
2 Bell 47G helicopters
1 Bell 47J helicopter
4 Alouette III helicopters
5 Hughes 269A
4 DC 3 (Dakota)
1 Riley Turbo-Rocket
1 Cessna 402B
3 Beechcraft C45H
4 Cessna 150
1 Cessna 180-D
1 Cessna 337
1 Cessna 402B
1 Stearman
3 Mentor T-43B
1 Beech B-55 Baron
2 Beech F-33A Bonanza
1 Learjet 24D

General

One of the persistent problems facing the Mexican Navy is the incursion of foreign fishery poachers, frequently highly organised groups working from the USA. This explains the considerable emphasis which has been put on aircraft and medium sized patrol craft.

Naval Bases

The Naval Command is split between the Pacific and Gulf areas and each subdivided into Naval Zones and, subsequently, Naval Sectors.

Gulf Command: (odd numbered zones):
 Veracruz (HQ 3rd Naval Zone and Command HQ)
 Tampico (1st Naval Zone)
 Ciudad del Carmen (5th Naval Zone)
 Isla Mujeres (7th Naval Zone)
 Tuxpan, Coatzacoalcos, Progreso, Chetumal (Naval Sector HQs)

Pacific Command: (even numbered zones):
 Acapulco (HQ 8th Naval Zone and Command HQ)
 Puerto Cortes (2nd Naval Zone)
 Guaymas (4th Naval Zone)
 Manzanillo (6th Naval Zone)
 Ensenada, La Paz, Mazatlan, Salina Cruz (Naval Sector HQs)

Strength of the Fleet

Type	Active	Building
Destroyers	2	—
Frigates	6	—
Corvettes	34	—
Large Patrol Craft	22	9
Survey Vessels	2	—
Coastal and River Patrol Craft	14	—
Transport	1	—
LSTs (1 repair ship)	3	—
Tankers-Harbour	2	—
Tugs	6	—
Floating Docks	4	—
Floating Cranes	7	—

DELETIONS

Frigates

1972 *Potosi, Queretaro* ("Guanajato" class). *California* (APD type) standard (16 Jan)
1975 *Guanajato*
1976 *Papaloapan* (ex-US APD)

Survey Ships

1973 *Sotavento*
1975 *Virgilio Uribe*

Tug

1974 *R4*

332   MEXICO

DESTROYERS

2 Ex-US "FLETCHER" CLASS

Name
CUAUTHEMOC (ex-USS *Harrison,* DD 573)
CUITLAHUAC (ex-USS *John Rodgers,* DD 574)

No.	Builders	Laid down	Launched	Commissioned
IE 01 (ex-F 1)	Consolidated Steel Corp	25 July 1941	7 May 1942	25 Jan 1943
IE 02 (ex-F 2)	Consolidated Steel Corp	25 July 1941	7 May 1942	9 Feb 1943

Displacement, tons: 2 100 standard; 3 050 full load
Length, feet (metres): 376·5 *(114·7)* oa
Beam, feet (metres): 39·5 *(12·0)*
Draught, feet (metres): 18·0 *(5·5)*
Guns (original): 5—5 in *(127 mm);* 10—40 mm; (twin)
Torpedo tubes: 5—21 in *(533 mm)* (quintuple)
Main engines: 2 geared turbines; 2 shafts; 60 000 shp
Boilers: 4
Speed, knots: 36; 14 economical
Oil fuel, tons: 650
Range, miles: 5 000 at 14 knots
Complement: 197

Former US destroyers of the original "Fletcher" class. Transferred to the Mexican Navy in Aug 1970.

Radar and Fire control:
Mk 12 radar for Mk 37 director; SC and SG1 radars; 1 modern commercial radar; 5—Mk 51 GFCS for 40 mm.

CUAUTHEMOC (old pennant number)   *1972, Mexican Navy*

FRIGATES

1 Ex-US "EDSALL" CLASS

Name
COMO MANUEL AZUETA (ex-USS *Hurst,* DE 250)

No.	Builders	Laid down	Launched	Commissioned
A 06	Brown SB Co, Houston, Texas	27 Jan 1943	14 April 1943	30 Aug 1943

Displacement, tons: 1 200 standard; 1 850 full load
Dimensions, feet (metres): 302·7 × 36·6 × 13 *(92·3 × 11·3 × 4)*
Guns: 3—3 in *(76 mm),* 50 cal US Mk 22; 8—40 mm (1 quad, 2 twins)
Main engines: 4 Fairbanks-Morse 38D8 10-cyl diesels; 6 000 shp; 2 shafts
Speed, knots: 20; 12 economical
Range, miles: 13 000 at 12 knots
Complement: 216 (15 officers, 201 ratings)

Transferred to Mexico 1 Oct 1973. Employed as training ship with Gulf Fleet command. A/S weapons removed.

Radar: One Kelvin Hughes Type 14; One Kelvin Hughes Type 17.

Sonar: QCS-1.

COMO MANUEL AZUETA   *1975, Mexican Navy*

1 "DURANGO" CLASS

Name   **No.**
DURANGO   B-1 (ex-128)

Builders	Laid down	Launched	Commissioned
Union Naval de Levante, Valencia	1934	28 June 1935	1936

Displacement, tons: 1 600 standard; 2 000 full load
Length, feet (metres): 256·5 *(78·2)* oa
Beam, feet (metres): 36·6 *(11·2)*
Draught, feet (metres): 10·5 *(3·1)*
Guns: 2—4 in *(102 mm);* 2—2·24 in *(57 mm);* 4—20 mm
Main engines: 2 Enterprise DMR-38 diesels electric drive; 2 shafts; 5 000 bhp
Speed, knots: 18; 12 economical
Oil fuel, tons: 140
Range, miles: 3 000 at 12 knots
Complement: 149 (24 officers and 125 men)

Originally designed primarily as an armed transport with accommodation for 20 officers and 450 men. The two Yarrow boilers and Parsons geared turbines of 6 500 shp installed when first built were replaced with two 2 500 bhp diesels in 1967 when the ship was re-rigged with remodelled funnel.

DURANGO   *1972, Mexican Navy*

MEXICO 333

4 Ex-US "CHARLES LAWRENCE" and "CROSLEY" CLASSES

Name	No.	Builders	Laid down	Launched	Commissioned
COAHUILA (ex-USS *Rednour*, APD 102, ex-*DE 592*)	IB-02	Bethlehem SB Co, Hingham, Mass	9 Jan 1944	1 Mar 1944	15 Mar 1945
TEHUANTEPEC (ex-USS *Joseph M. Auman*, APD 117, ex-*DE 674*)	IB-05 (ex-H 5)	Consolidated Steel Corp	8 Nov 1943	5 Feb 1944	25 April 1945
USUMACINTA (ex-USS *Don O. Woods*, APD 118, ex-*DE 721*)	IB-06 (ex-H 6)	Consolidated Steel Corp	1 Dec 1943	19 Feb 1944	28 May 1945
CHIHUAHUA (ex-USS *Barber*, LPR, ex-*APD 57*, ex-*DE 161*)	IB-08	Norfolk Navy Yard, Norfolk, Va	27 April 1943	20 May 1943	10 Oct 1943

Displacement, tons: 1 400 standard; 2 130 full load
Length, feet (metres): 300·0 *(91·5)* wl; 306·0 *(93·3)* oa
Beam, feet (metres): 37·0 *(11·3)*
Draught, feet (metres): 11·3 *(3·4)*
Guns: 1—5 in *(127 mm)* 38 cal; 6—40 mm (3 twin); 6—20 mm (single)
Main engines: GE turbo-electric; 2 shafts; 12 000 shp
Speed, knots: 20; 13 economical
Boilers: 2 Foster Wheeler "D" with superheater
Range, miles: 5 000 at 15 knots
Oil fuel, tons: 350
Complement: 204 plus 162 troops

IB 5-6 were purchased by Mexico in December 1963 and IB 7 and 8 on 17 Feb 1969. *California* (ex-USS *Belet* APD 109) stranded and lost 16 Jan 1972 on Bahia Peninsula.

Fire control: 5 in: local control.
40 mm: 3—Mk 51 GFCS.

Radar: Combined search: SC.
Navigation: Commercial.

CHIHUAHUA 1976, Mexican Navy

CORVETTES

18 Ex-US "AUK" Class

Name	No.
LEANDRO VALLE (ex-USS *Pioneer*, MSF 105)	IG-01
GUILLERMO PRIETO (ex-USS *Symbol*, MSF 123)	IG-02
MARIANO ESCOBEDO (ex-USS *Champion*, MSF 314)	IG-03
PONCIANO ARRIAGA (ex-USS *Competent*, MSF 316)	IG-04
MANUAL DOBLADO (ex-USS *Defense*, MSF 317)	IG-05
SEBASTIAN L. DE TEJADA (ex-USS *Devastator*, MSF 318)	IG-06
SANTOS DEGOLLADO (ex-USS *Gladiator*, MSF 319)	IG-07
IGNACIO DE LA LLAVE (ex-USS *Spear*, MSF 322)	IG-08
JUAN N. ALVARES (ex-USS *Ardent*, MSF 340)	IG-09
MELCHOR OCAMPO (ex-USS *Roselle*, MSF 379)	IG-10
VALENTIN G. FARIAS (ex-USS *Starling*, MSF 64)	IG-11
IGNACIO ALTAMIRANO (ex-USS *Sway*, MSF 120)	IG-12
FRANCISCO ZARCO (ex-USS *Threat*, MSF 124)	IG-13
IGNACIO L. VALLARTA (ex-USS *Velocity*, MSF 128)	IG-14
JESUS G. ORTEGA (ex-USS *Chief*, MSF 315)	IG-15
GUTIERRIEZ ZAMORA (ex-USS *Scoter*, MSF 381)	IG-16
JUAN ALDAMA (ex-USS *Pilot*, MSF 104)	IG-18
HERMENEGILDO GALENA (ex-USS *Sage*, MSF 111)	IG-19

Displacement, tons: 890 standard; 1 250 full load
Dimensions, feet (metres): 215 wl; 221·2 oa × 32·2 × 10·8 *(65·6; 67·5 × 10 × 3·3)*
Guns: 1—3 in 50 cal; 4—40 mm (twins); 8—20 mm (twins)
Main engines: Diesel-electric; 2 shafts; 3 500 bhp
Speed, knots: 17; 10 economical
Complement: 9 officers and 96 ratings

Transferred—6 in Feb 1973, 4 in April 1973, 9 in Sept 1973. Employed on patrol duties—*Mariano Matamoros* of this class employed on surveying duties with after armament replaced by large deck-house. (see Survey section)

IGNACIO L. VALLARTA 2/1976

Appearance: Variations are visible in the mid-ships section where some have a bulwark running from the break of the fo'c'sle to the quarter-deck.

Radar: SO13 and commercial navigation set.

16 Ex-US "ADMIRABLE" CLASS

Name	No.
DM 01 (ex-USS *Jubilant* AM 255)	ID-01
DM 02 (ex-USS *Hilarity* AM 241)	ID-02
DM 03 (ex-USS *Execute* AM 232)	ID-03
DM 04 (ex-USS *Specter* AM 306)	ID-04
DM 05 (ex-USS *Scuffle* AM 298)	ID-05
DM 06 (ex-USS *Eager* AM 224)	ID-06
DM 10 (ex-USS *Instill* AM 252)	ID-10
DM 11 (ex-USS *Device* AM 220)	ID-11
DM 12 (ex-USS *Ransom* AM 283)	ID-12
DM 13 (ex-USS *Knave* AM 256)	ID-13
DM 14 (ex-USS *Rebel* AM 284)	ID-14
DM 15 (ex-USS *Crag* AM 214)	ID-15
DM 16 (ex-USS *Dour* AM 223)	ID-16
DM 17 (ex-USS *Diploma* AM 221)	ID-17
DM 18 (ex-USS *Invade* AM 254)	ID-18
DM 19 (ex-USS *Intrigue* AM 253)	ID-19

Displacement, tons: 650 standard; 945 full load
Dimensions, feet (metres): 184·5 oa × 33 × 9 *(56·3 × 10·1 × 3·1)*
Guns: 1—3 in, 50 cal; 4—40 mm; 6/8—20 mm (see note)
Main engines: 2 diesels; 2 shafts; 1 710 bhp = 15 knots
Range, miles: 4 300 at 10 knots
Complement: 104

DM 18 1976, Mexican Navy

Former US steel-hulled fleet minesweepers. All completed in 1943-44.

Gunnery: 20 mm armament varies from 6 (2 twin, 2 single) to 8 (4 twin).

334 MEXICO

LIGHT FORCES

22 + 9 "AZTECA" CLASS (LARGE PATROL CRAFT)

Name	No.	Builders	Commissioned
ANDRES QUINTANA ROOS	P 01	Ailsa Shipbuilding Co Ltd	1 Nov 1974
MATIAS DE CORDOVA	P 02	Scott & Sons, Bowling	22 Oct 1974
MIGUEL RAMOS ARIZPE	P 03	Ailsa Shipbuilding Co Ltd	23 Dec 1974
JOSE MARIA IZAZGU	P 04	Ailsa Shipbuilding Co Ltd	19 Dec 1974
JUAN BAUTISTA MORALES	P 05	Scott & Sons, Bowling	19 Dec 1974
IGNACIO LOPEZ RAYON	P 06	Ailsa Shipbuilding Co Ltd	19 Dec 1974
MANUEL CRECENCIO REJON	P 07	Ailsa Shipbuilding Co Ltd	4 July 1975
ANTONIO DE LA FUENTE	P 08	Ailsa Shipbuilding Co Ltd	4 July 1975
LEON GUZMAN	P 09	Scott & Sons, Bowling	7 April 1975
IGNACIO RAMIREZ	P 10	Ailsa Shipbuilding Co Ltd	17 July 1975
IGNACIO MARISCAL	P 11	Ailsa Shipbuilding Co Ltd	23 Sept 1975
HERIBERTO JARA CORONA	P 12	Ailsa Shipbuilding Co Ltd	7 Nov 1975
JOSE MARIA MAJA	P 13	J. Lamont & Co Ltd	13 Oct 1975
FELIX ROMERO	P 14	Scott & Sons, Bowling	23 June 1975
FERNANDO LIZARDI	P 15	Ailsa Shipbuilding Co Ltd	24 Dec 1975
FRANCISCO J. MUJICA	P 16	Ailsa Shipbuilding Co Ltd	21 Nov 1975
PASTOR ROUAIX	P 17	Scott & Sons, Bowling	7 Nov 1975
JOSE MARIA DEL CASTILLO VELASCO	P 18	Lamont & Co Ltd	14 Jan 1975
LUIS MANUEL ROJAS	P 19	Lamont & Co Ltd	3 April 1976
JOSE NATIVIDAD MACIAS	P 20	Lamont & Co Ltd	2 Sept 1976
ESTEBAN BACA CALDERON	P 21	Lamont & Co Ltd	18 June 1976
IGNACIO ZARAGOZA	P 22	Vera Cruz	1 June 1976

Displacement, tons: 130
Dimensions, feet (metres): 111·8 oa × 28·1 × 6·8 *(34·1 × 8·6 × 2·0)*
Guns: 1—40 mm; 1—20 mm
Main engines: 2—12-cyl Paxman Ventura diesels; 3 600 bhp = 24 knots
Range, miles: 2 500 at 12 knots
Complement: 24

Ordered by Mexico, for Fishery Protection duties, on 27 March 1973 from Associated British Machine Tool Makers Ltd.
HM Queen Elizabeth II went to sea in *Andres Quintana Roos* during her visit to Mexico in March 1975—an intention to place further orders for this class was announced shortly afterwards. Ten have been ordered for building in Mexican yards with ABMTM assistance (seven at Vera Cruz, three at Salina Cruz) and a final total of 80 is planned.

JOSE MARIA IZAZGU   1975, Mexican Navy

4 "POLIMAR" CLASS (COASTAL PATROL CRAFT)

Name	No.	Builders	Commissioned
POLIMAR 1	IF 01 (ex-G 1)	Astilleros de Tampico	1 Oct 1962
POLIMAR 2	IF 02 (ex-G 2)	Icacas Shipyard, Guerrero	1966
POLIMAR 3	IF 03 (ex-G 3)	Icacas Shipyard, Guerrero	1966
POLIMAR 4	IF 04 (ex-G 4)	Astilleros de Tampico	1968

Displacement, tons: 37 standard; 57 full load
Dimensions, feet (metres): 60·1 × 15·1 × 4·0 *(20·1 × 5·3 × 3·3)*
Gun: 1—20 mm
Main engines: 2 diesels; 456 bhp = 11 knots

Of steel construction.

POLIMAR 3   1972, Mexican Navy

2 "AZUETA" CLASS (COASTAL PATROL CRAFT)

Name	No.	Builders	Commissioned
AZUETA	IF 06 (ex-G 9)	Astilleros de Tampico	1959
VILLAPANDO	IF 07 (ex-G 6)	Astilleros de Tampico	1960

Displacement, tons: 80 standard; 85 full load
Dimensions, feet (metres): 85·3 × 16·4 × 7·0 *(26 × 5 × 2·1)*
Guns: 2—13·2 mm (1 twin)
Main engines: Superior diesels; 600 bhp = 12 knots

Of all steel construction.

8 RIVER TYPE (RIVER PATROL CRAFT)

Name	No.	Builders	Commissioned
AM 1	IF 11	Tampico	1960
AM 2	IF 12	Vera Cruz	1960
AM 3	IF 13	Tampico	1961
AM 4	IF 14	Vera Cruz	1961
AM 5	IF 15	Tampico	1961
AM 6	IF 16	Vera Cruz	1962
AM 7	IF 17	Tampico	1962
AM 8	IF 18	Vera Cruz	1962

Displacement, tons: 37
Dimensions, feet (metres): 56·1 × 16·4 × 8·2 *(17·1 × 5 × 2·5)*
Main engines: Diesel; speed = 6 knots

Of steel construction.

SURVEY VESSELS

1 Ex-US "ADMIRABLE" CLASS

OCEANOGRAFICO (ex-*DM 20*, ex-USS *Harlequin* AM 365) H 2 (ex-ID-20)

Details given in "Admirable" class under Corvettes. Now unarmed.

1 Ex-US "AUK" CLASS

MARIANO METAMOROS (ex-USS *Herald*, MSF 101) H 1 (ex-IG 17)

Details given in "Auk" class under Corvettes. Took over surveying duties from *Virgilio Uribe*. After guns replaced by large deck-house.

MARIANO METAMORUS   10/1977, Dr. Giorgio Arra

MEXICO 335

MISCELLANEOUS

SERVICE FORCES

TRANSPORT

Name	No.	Builders	Commissioned
ZACATECAS	B 2	Ulua Shipyard, Vera Cruz	1960

Displacement, tons: 785 standard
Dimensions, feet (metres): 158 × 27·2 × 10 *(48·2 × 8·3 × 2·7)*
Guns: 1—40 mm; 2—20 mm (single)
Main engines: 1 MAN diesel; 560 hp = 8 knots
Complement: 50 (13 officers and 37 men)

Launched in 1959. Cargo ship type. The hull is of welded steel construction. Cargo capacity 400 tons.

2 Ex-US "511-1152" CLASS (LSTs)

Name	No.	Builders	Commissioned
RIO PANUCO (ex-USS *Park County*, LST 1077)	IA 01	Bethlehem Steel Co, Hingham, Mass	8 May 1945
MANZANILLO (ex-USS *Clearwater County*, LST 602)	IA 02	Chicago Bridge and Iron Co Seneca, Illinois	31 Mar 1944

Displacement, tons: 1 653 standard; 2 366 beaching; 4 080 full load
Dimensions, feet (metres): 316 wl; 328 oa × 50 × 14 *(96·4; 100 × 15·3 × 4·3)*
Guns: 6—40 mm (1 twin; 4 singles)
Main engines: 2 GM diesels; 2 shafts; 1 700 bhp = 10·5 knots
Range, miles: 6 000 at 11 knots
Complement: 130
Troop capacity: 147

Transferred to Mexico on 20 Sept 1971 and 25 May 1972 respectively. Both employed as rescue ships.

RIO PANUCO   1976, Mexican Navy

1 Ex-US "FABIUS" CLASS (LIGHT FORCES TENDER)

Name	No.	Builders	Commissioned
GENERAL VINCENTE GUERRERO (ex-USS *Megara*, ARVA-6)	IA 05	American Bridge Co, Ambridge, Penn	27 June 1945

Displacement, tons: 1 625 light; 4 100 full load
Dimensions, feet (metres): 328 oa × 50 × 14 *(100 × 15·3 × 4·3)*
Guns: 8—40 mm
Main engines: 2 GM diesels; 2 shafts; 1 800 bhp = 14·6 knots
Range, miles: 10 000 at 10 knots
Complement: 250

Ex-aircraft repair ship sold to Mexico 1 Oct 1973.

GENERAL VINCENTE GUERRERO   1976, Mexican Navy

2 Ex-US YOG/YO TYPE (HARBOUR TANKERS)

Name	No.	Builders	Commissioned
AGUASCALIENTES (ex-*YOG 6*)	IA-03	Geo H. Mathis Co Ltd, Camden, N.J.	1943
TLAXCALA (ex-*YO 107*)	IA-04	Geo Lawley & Son, Neponset, Mass	1943

Displacement, tons: 440 light; 1 480 full load
Dimensions, feet (metres): 159·2 × 30 × 8·2 *(48·6 × 9·2 × 2·5)*
Gun: 1—20 mm
Main engine: Fairbanks-Morse diesel; 1 shaft; 500 bhp = 8 knots
Capacity: 6 570 barrels
Complement: 26 (5 officers and 21 ratings)

Former US self-propelled fuel oil barges. Purchased in Aug 1964. Entered service in Nov 1964.

AGUASCALIENTES   1975, Mexican Navy

AUXILIARY

4 Ex-US MARITIME ADMINISTRATION "V 4" CLASS (TUGS)

R-1 (ex-*Farallon*) A 11
R-2 (ex-*Montauk*) A 12
R-3 (ex-*Point Vicente*) A 13
R-5 (ex-*Burnt Island*) A 15

Measurement, tons: 786 deadweight; 1 117 gross
Dimensions, feet (metres): 185·6 × 37·7 × 18·7 *(56·6 × 11·5 × 5·7)*
Guns: 1—76 mm; 2—20 mm
Main engines: 2 Nat Supply 8-cyl diesels; 1 Kort nozzle = 14 knots
Range, miles: 19 000 at 14 knots

Part of a large class built 1943-45 by US Maritime Administration for civilian use. Not a successful design; most were laid up on completion. In 1968 six were taken from reserve and transferred by sale in Sept. Of the class R6 was paid off 1970 and R4 sank in 1973. All originally unarmed—guns fitted in Mexico. R1 and 5—Gulf Fleet; R2 and 3—Pacific Fleet.

Radar: Kelvin Hughes.

PRAGMAR   PATRON

Tugs acquired in 1973.

4 FLOATING DOCKS

Ex-US ARD 2   Ex-US ARD 11   Ex-US ARD 15

ARD 2 (150 × 24·7 m) transferred Aug 1963 and ARD 11 (same size) in June 1974. Lift 3 550 tonnes. Two 10 ton cranes and 1 100 kW generator. ARD 15 has the same capacity and facilities—transferred April 1971.

Ex-US AFDL 28

Lift capacity of 1 000 tons. Built of steel. (61 × 19·5 m).
Built in 1944 and transferred in Jan 1973.

7 FLOATING CRANES

Ex-US YDs 156, 157, 179, 180, 183, 194 and 203, transferred Sept 1964 to July 1971.

1 PILE DRIVER

Ex-US YPD 43 leased Aug 1968.

1 DREDGER

Ex-US YM. Date of transfer not known.

336 MONTSERRAT / MOROCCO

MONTSERRAT

Senior Officers

Commissioner of Police:
  Mr Galton B St John
CO Base:
  Cpl. Angus Prospere

Base

Plymouth

Marine Police

The following craft is employed on general patrol duties under control of Montserrat Police Force.

Mercantile Marine

Lloyd's Register of Shipping:
  3 vessels of 1 248 tons gross

1 BROOKE MARINE 12 metre TYPE

EMERALD STAR

Displacement, tons: 15
Length, feet (metres): 40 (12)
Guns: Can mount 3 MGs
Main engines: 2 diesels; 370 hp = 22 knots
Complement: 4

Purchased in 1971.

EMERALD STAR   1975, Montserrat Government

MOROCCO

Diplomatic Representation

Defence Attaché in London:
  Colonel Benomar Sbay

Personnel

(a) 1978: 1 800 officers and ratings (including 500 Marines)
(b) 18 months national service

General

At a time of tension in the Maghreb the increase in new construction is significant particularly with the increase from Soviet sources not only of the neighbouring Algerian force but also the long range capabilities, including submarines, of Libya. Frigates with an A/S capability are logical reinforcements and the choice of Spanish yards may also be a pointer.

Bases

Casablanca, Safi, Agadir, Kenitra, Tangier

New Construction Programme 1973-77

3—Frigates
4—"Lazaga" Class
2—PR 72 Large Patrol Craft
6—32 metre Coastal Patrol Craft

Strength of the Fleet

Type	Active	Building (Projected)
Frigates	—	1 (4)
Fast Attack Craft (Gun)	2	4 (2)
Large Patrol Craft	3	(2)
Coastal Patrol Craft	9	(6)
MSC	1	—
Landing Craft	4	—
Customs Craft	12	—

Mercantile Marine

Lloyd's Register of Shipping:
  91 vessels of 270 295 tons gross

DELETION

Frigate

1975 Al Maouna

FRIGATES

0 + 1 + (?4) MODIFIED "DESCUBIERTA" CLASS

Displacement, tons: 1 200 standard; 1 497 full load
Dimensions, feet (metres): 291·3 × 34 × 11·5 (88·8 × 10·5 × 3·5)
Missiles: Octuple Seasparrow fitted in Spanish ships
Guns: 1—76 mm OTO Melara; 2—40 mm
A/S weapons: 1—375 mm Bofors twin launcher; 6 (2 triple) Mk 32 torpedo tubes
Main engines: 4 MTU-Bazan 16V956 diesels; 16 000 bhp; 2 shafts; cp propellers
Speed, knots: 26
Range, miles: 4 000 cruising
Complement: 100

One ordered 14 June 1977 from Bazan, Spain with four more reportedly planned. Above data is for the Spanish ships of this class.

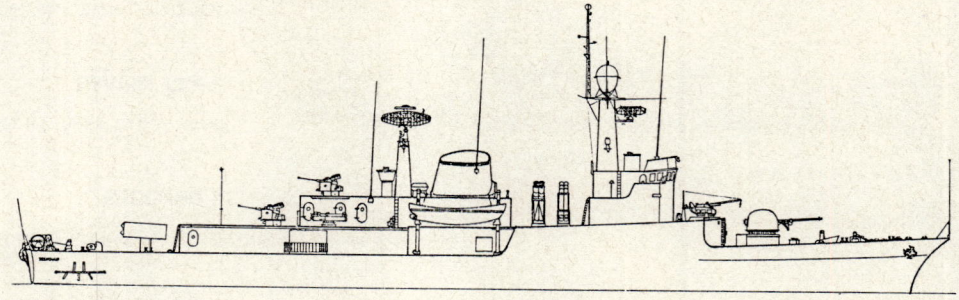

"DESCUBIERTA" Class

LIGHT FORCES

2 FRENCH PR 72 TYPE (FAST ATTACK CRAFT—GUN)

Name	No.	Builders	Commissioned
OKBA	—	Soc. Francaise de Construction Navale	16 Dec 1976
TRIKI	—	Soc. Francaise de Construction Navale	Feb 1977

Displacement, tons: 375 standard; 445 full load
Dimensions, feet (metres): 188·8 × 25 × 7·1 *(57·5 × 7·6 × 2·1)*
Guns: 1—76 mm OTO-Melara; 1—40 mm Breda Bofors; 2—20 mm
Main engines: 4 AGO V16 diesels; 4 shafts; 11 040 hp
Speed, knots: 28
Range, miles: 2 500 at 16 knots
Complement: 53 (5 officers; 48 ratings)

Ordered June 1973. This type can be fitted with Exocet—as the Vega control system will be installed this would be a simple operation. *Okba* launched 10 Oct 1975, *Triki* 1 Feb 1976. Two more in the New Construction Programme.

0 + 4 MODIFIED "LAZAGA" CLASS
(FAST ATTACK CRAFT—GUN)

Displacement, tons: 420 full load
Dimensions, feet (metres): 190·2 × 24·9 × 8·5 *(58 × 7·6 × 2·6)*
Guns: 1—76 mm OTO Melara; 1—40 mm; 2—20 mm
A/S weapons: 2 DC racks; possibly triple Mk 32 torpedo tubes
Main engines: 2 MTU-Bazan TB 91 diesels; 8 000 bhp
Speed, knots: 28
Range, miles: 6 100 at 17 knots
Complement: 30

Ordered from Bazan, Spain 14 June 1977.

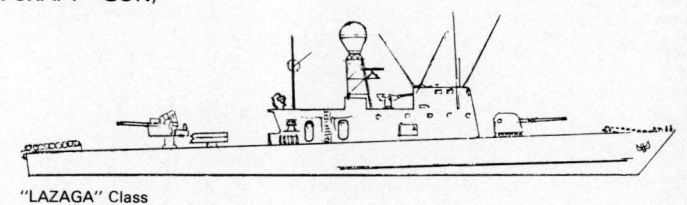

"LAZAGA" Class

1 LARGE PATROL CRAFT

Name	No.	Builders	Commissioned
LIEUTENANT RIFFI	32	Constructions Mécaniques de Normandie, Cherbourg	May 1964

Displacement, tons: 311 standard; 374 full load
Dimensions, feet (metres): 174 × 23 × 6·6 *(53 × 7 × 2)*
Guns: 1—76 mm; 2—40 mm
A/S weapons: 2—A/S mortars
Main engines: 2 SEMT Pielstick diesels; 2 cp propellers; 3 600 bhp = 19 knots
Range, miles: 3 000 at 12 knots
Complement: 49

Of modified "Fougeux" design. Laid down May 1963.

LIEUTENANT RIFFI   CMN

1 LARGE PATROL CRAFT

Name	No.	Builders	Commissioned
AL BACHIR	22 (ex-*12*)	Constructions Mécaniques de Normandie, Cherbourg	30 Mar 1967

Displacement, tons: 125 light; 154 full load
Dimensions, feet (metres): 124·7 pp; 133·2 oa × 20·8 × 4·7 *(38; 40·6 × 6·4 × 1·4)*
Guns: 2—40 mm; 2—MG
Main engines: 2 SEMT-Pielstick diesels; 2 shafts; 3 600 bhp = 25 knots
Oil fuel, tons: 21
Range, miles: 2 000 at 15 knots
Complement: 23

Ordered in 1964. Launched 25 Feb 1967.

AL BACHIR   CMN

1 Ex-FRENCH LARGE PATROL CRAFT

Name	No.	Builders	Commissioned
EL SABIQ (ex-*P 762*, VC 12)	11	Chantiers Navals de l'Estérel	1958

Displacement, tons: 60 standard; 82 full load
Dimensions, feet (metres): 104·5 × 18·9 × 5·5 *(31·8 × 5·8 × 1·7)*
Missiles: Can carry SS-12
Guns: 2—20 mm
Main engines: 2 MTU diesels; 2 shafts; 2 700 bhp = 30 knots
Range, miles: 1 400 at 15 knots
Complement: 17

Former French seaward defence motor launch of the VC type. Launched on 13 Aug 1957. Transferred from the French Navy to the Moroccan Navy on 15 Nov 1960 and renamed *El Sabiq*.

EL SABIQ (under French colours)   1960, C. N. de l'Esterel

338　MOROCCO

6 + (6) P 32 TYPE (COASTAL PATROL CRAFT)

Name	No.	Builders	Commissioned
EL WACIL	—	Constructions Mécaniques de Normandie, Cherbourg	9 Oct 1975
EL JAIL	—	Constructions Mécaniques de Normandie, Cherbourg	3 Dec 1975
EL MIKDAM	—	Constructions Mécaniques de Normandie, Cherbourg	30 Jan 1976
EL HARIS	—	Constructions Mécaniques de Normandie, Cherbourg	30 June 1976
EL KHAFIR	—	Constructions Mécaniques de Normandie, Cherbourg	16 April 1976
ESSAHIR	—	Constructions Mécaniques de Normandie, Cherbourg	16 July 1976

Displacement, tons: 90
Dimensions, feet (metres): 105 oa × 17·6 × 9·8 *(32 × 5·3 × 2·9)*
Guns: 2—20 mm
Main engines: 2 MGO-12V BZSHR diesels; 2 700 bhp; 2 shafts = 29 knots
Range, miles: 1 500 at 15 knots
Complement: 17

Wooden hull sheathed in plastic.
The first six of these patrol craft were ordered in Feb 1974. Launch dates—*El Wacil* 12 June 1975, *El Jail* 10 Oct 1975, *El Mikdam* 26 Nov 1975, *El Haris* 3 March 1976, *El Khafir* 1 Jan 1976, *El Sehir* 2 June 1976. Six more in the New Construction Programme.

Radar: One set Decca

EL WACIL　　　1976, CMN

3 COASTAL PATROL CRAFT

Arcor 31 type of 24 knots built by C. N. Arcor, Bordeaux.

MINE WARFARE SHIP

1 FRENCH "SIRIUS" CLASS (MINESWEEPER—COASTAL)

TAWFIC (ex-*Aries M 758*)

Displacement, tons: 365 standard; 424 full load
Dimensions, feet (metres): 152 oa × 28 × 8·2 *(46·3 × 8·5 × 2·1)*
Guns: 1—40 mm; 1—20 mm
Main engines: 2 diesels; 2 shafts; 2 000 bhp = 15 knots
Range, miles: 3 000 at 15 knots
Complement: 38

Launched 31 March 1956. Transferred on loan by France on 28 Nov 1974 for 4 years.

"SIRIUS" Class　　　1975, Dhr. J. van der Woude

AMPHIBIOUS FORCES

3 BATRAL TYPE

Name	No.	Builders	Commissioned
DAOUD BEN AICHA	—	Dubigeon, Normandie	28 May 1977
AHMED ES SAKALI	—	Dubigeon, Normandie	Sept 1977
ABOU ABDALLAH EL AYACHI	—	Dubigeon, Normandie	Mar 1978

Displacement, tons: 750 standard; 1 250 full load
Dimensions, feet (metres): 262·4 × 42·6 × 7·5 *(80× 13 × 2·3)*
Guns: 2—40 mm; 2—81 mm mortars
Main engines: 2 diesels; 2 shafts; 1 800 hp = 16 knots
Range, miles: 3 500 at 13 knots
Complement: 37

Fitted with helicopter landing platform and with vehicle-stowage above and below decks. Can carry an extra 140 men and twelve vehicles. Two ordered on 12 March 1975. Third ordered 19 Aug 1975. Of same class as the French *Champlain*.

BATRAL TYPE　　　1974, French Navy

Name	No.	Builders	Commissioned
LIEUTENANT MALGHAGH	21	Chantiers Navals Franco-Belges	1965

Displacement, tons: 292 standard; 642 full load
Dimensions, feet (metres): 193·6 × 39·2 × 4·3 *(59 × 12 × 1·3)*
Guns: 2—20 mm; 1—120 mm mortar
Main engines: 2 MGO diesels; 2 shafts; 1 000 bhp = 8 knots
Complement: 16 (1 officer, 15 men)

Ordered early in 1963. Similar to the French landing craft of the EDIC type built at the same yard.

LIEUTENANT MALGHAGH　　　1971, Royal Moroccan Navy

MISCELLANEOUS

There are also the yacht *Essaouira*, 60 tons, from Italy in 1967, used as a training vessel for watchkeepers; and twelve customs boats, four of 40 tons, 82 feet, diesels 940 bhp = 23 knots, and eight 42·7 feet; all built in 1963. The *Murene*, Coast Guard Cutter, has also been reported.

NETHERLANDS

Administration

Minister of Defence and State Secretary of Defence (Equipment):
 A. Stemerdink
State Secretary of Defence (Personnel):
 C. L. J. van Lent
Chief of the Defence Staff:
 Lieutenant General A. J. W. Wijting RNAF

Headquarters Appointments

Chief of the Naval Staff:
 Vice-Admiral B. Veldkamp
Vice Chief of the Naval Staff:
 Rear-Admiral H. L. van Beek
Flag Officer Naval Personnel:
 Rear-Admiral J. G. C. van de Linde
Flag Officer Naval Material:
 Rear-Admiral J. L. Langenberg

Commands

Admiral Netherlands Home Command:
 Rear-Admiral H. E. Rambonnet
Commander Netherlands Task Group:
 Rear-Admiral J. H. B. Hulshof
Commandant General Royal Netherlands Marine Corps:
 Major-General A. J. Romijn
Flag Officer Netherlands Antilles:
 Commodore W. Gonggrijp

Diplomatic Representation

Naval Attaché in Bonn:
 Captain R. H. Berts
Naval Attaché in London:
 Captain J. R. Roele
Naval Attaché in Paris:
 Captain C. J. van Westenbrugge
Naval Attaché in Washington and NLR SACLANT:
 Rear-Admiral J. J. Binnendijk

Personnel

(a) 1 January 1978: 17 200 officers and ratings (including the Navy Air Service, Royal Netherlands Marine Corps and about 360 officers and women of the W.R.NI.NS.)
(b) 14-17 months national service

Bases

Main Base: Den Helder
Minor Bases: Flushing and Curacao
Fleet Air Arm: NAS Valkenburgh (main),
 NAS De Kooy (helicopters)
R. Neth. Marines: Rotterdam
Training Bases: Amsterdam and Hilversum

Naval Air Force

Personnel: 1 700

3 MR Squadrons with 8 Atlantics, 15 Neptunes
12 Wasps and 6 Lynx helicopters
 (new MR aircraft and UH 14B helicopters by late 70s)

Prefix to Ships' Names

Hr Ms

Mercantile Marine

Lloyd's Register of Shipping:
 1 254 vessels of 5 290 360 tons gross

Strength of the Fleet

	Active	Building (Projected)
Destroyers	11	—
Frigates	6	12
Corvettes	6	—
Submarines (Patrol)	6	—
MCM Support Ships	4	—
Minehunters	4	15
Minesweepers—Coastal	11	—
Diving Ships	3	—
Minesweepers—Inshore	16	—
Large Patrol Craft	5	—
LCAs	11	—
Surveying Vessels	3	—
Combat Support Ships	2	—
Training Ships	2	—
Tugs	13	—
Tenders	6	—

Future New Construction Programme

1 Frigate (Command and Air Defence)
12 Frigates (ASW)
16 Lynx Helicopters

Planned Strength in 1980s

2 ASW Groups each of 6 ASW frigates, 1 DLG, 1 Support Ship (helicopters in all ships) to operate in Eastlant Area
1 ASW Group of 6 ASW frigates and 1 DLG to operate in Channel Approaches
1 ASW Group of 4 frigates to operate in Channel Command
6 Patrol Submarines
21 LRMP Aircraft in 3 squadrons (1 training)
2 MCM Groups of 12 ships each operating off Dutch ports
1 MCM Group of 7 ships for Channel command
2 R. Neth. Marine Commando Groups and 1 Cold Weather Reinforced Company

DELETIONS

Cruisers

Oct 1972 De Ruyter to Peru as Almirante Grau
Aug 1976 De Zeven Provincien to Peru as Aguirre

Destroyers

1973 Gelderland for harbour training
1974 Noord Brabant (after collision 9 Jan 1974)
1978 Holland (to Peru)

Submarines

Nov 1970 Zeeleeuw (ex-Hawkbill)
Nov 1971 Walrus (ex-Icefish)

MCM Support Ships

1976 Onversaagd (returned to US)

Minesweepers

1972 Onvermoeid, Bolsward, Breukelen, Bruinisse returned to USN
1973 Grijpskerk for harbour training
1974 Wildervank, Meppel, Goes, Brummen, Brouwershaven to disposal
 Axel, Aalsmeer to Oman
1975 Waalwijk, Leersum ("Wildervank" class)
 Beemster, Bedum, Beilen, Borculo, Borne, Blaricum, Brielle, Breskens, Boxtel ("Beemster" class MSC)

Survey Ships

1972 Luymes to disposal
1973 Snellius as accommodation ship and
1977 for disposal by sale

Amphibious Forces

1975 L 9515, 9521

Storeships

1972 Woendi
1973 Pelikaan

PENNANT NUMBERS

Destroyers

F801	Tromp
F806	De Ruyter
D809	Zeeland
D812	Friesland
D813	Groningen
D814	Limburg
D815	Overijssel
D816	Drenthe
D817	Utrecht
D818	Rotterdam
D819	Amsterdam

Frigates

F802	Van Speijk
F803	Van Galen
F804	Tjerk Hiddes
F805	Van Nes
F814	Isaac Sweers
F815	Evertsen

Submarines

S804	Potvis
S805	Tonijn
S806	Zwaardvis
S807	Tijgerhaai
S808	Dolfijn
S809	Zeehond

Corvettes

F817	Wolf
F818	Fret
F819	Hermelijn
F820	Vos
F821	Panter
F822	Jaguar

MCM Command/Support and Escort Ships

A855	Onbevreesd
A858	Onvervaard
A859	Onverdroten

Mine Hunters

M801	Dokkum
M818	Drunen
M828	Staphorst
M842	Veere

Coastal Minesweepers

M802	Hoogezand
M809	Naaldwijk
M810	Abcoude
M812	Drachten
M813	Ommen
M815	Giethoorn
M817	Venlo
M823	Naarden
M827	Hoogeveen
M830	Sittard
M841	Gemert

Inshore Minesweepers

M868	Alblas
M869	Bussemaker
M870	Lacomblé
M871	Van Hamel
M872	Van Straelen
M873	Van Moppes
M874	Chömpff
M875	Van Well-Groeneveld
M876	Schuiling
M877	Van Versendaal
M878	Van Der Wel
M879	Van 't Hoff
M880	Mahu
M881	Staverman
M882	Houtepen
M883	Zomer

340 NETHERLANDS

Diving Vessels

M806	Roermond
M820	Woerden
M844	Rhenen

Large Patrol Craft

P802	Balder
P803	Bulgia
P804	Freijer
P805	Hadda
P806	Hefring

Amphibious Forces

L9510-14
L9516-18
L9520
L9522
L9526

Auxiliary Ships

A832	Zuiderkruis
A835	Poolster
A847	Argus
A848	Triton
A849	Nautilus
A850	Hydra
A856	Mercuur
A870	Wamandai
A871	Wambrau
A872	Westgat
A873	Wielingen
A903	Zeefakkel
A904	Buyskes
A905	Blommendal
A906	Tydeman
A923	Van Bochove
Y8014	Harbour Tug
Y8016	Harbour Tug
Y8017	Harbour Tug
Y8020	Dreg IV
Y8022	Harbour Tug
Y8028	Harbour Tug
Y8037	Berkel
Y8038	Dintel
Y8039	Dommel
Y8040	Ijssel
Y8050	Urania

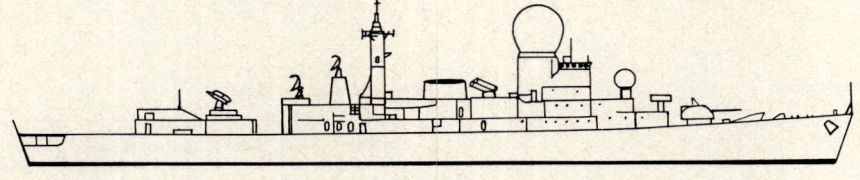

"TROMP" Class

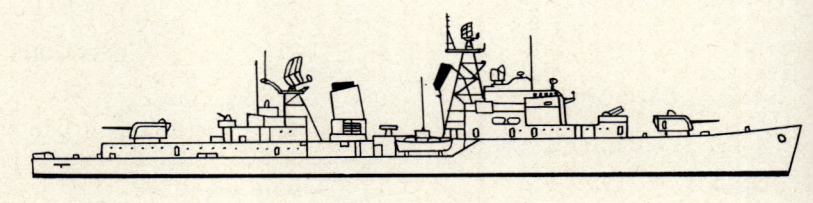

"FRIESLAND" Class

"HOLLAND" Class

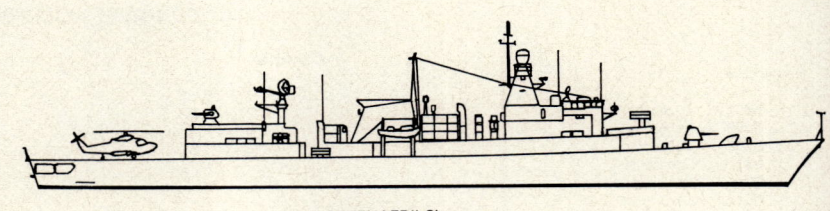

"KORTENAER" Class

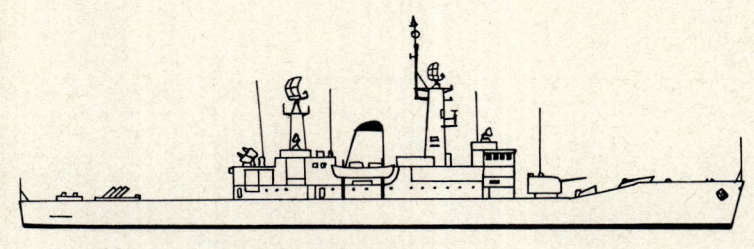

"VAN SPEIJK" Class

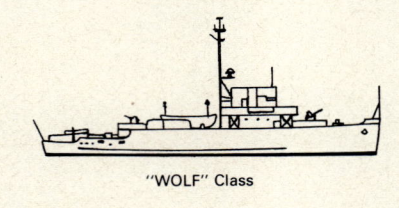

"WOLF" Class

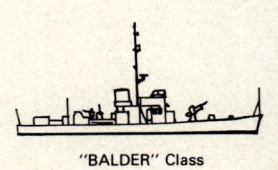

"BALDER" Class

NETHERLANDS 341

SUBMARINES

NEW CONSTRUCTION

In the 1975 estimates a sum was set aside for design work on a new class of submarine to be included in the 1979 order book. This design is ready and the price is set at 150 million guilders per boat. The order will probably be placed with Rotterdam Drydock Co in collaboration with Wilton-Fijenoord, the former being very much in need of orders to prevent unemployment. Main engines to be by SEMT-Pielstick.

2 "ZWAARDVIS" CLASS

Name	No.	Builders	Laid down	Launched	Commissioned
ZWAARDVIS	S 806	Rotterdamse Droogdok Mij, Rotterdam	14 July 1966	2 July 1970	18 Aug 1972
TIJGERHAAI	S 807	Rotterdamse Droogdok Mij, Rotterdam	14 July 1966	25 May 1971	20 Oct 1972

Displacement, tons: 2 350 surfaced; 2 640 dived
Length, feet (metres): 217·2 *(66·2)*
Beam, feet (metres): 33·8 *(10·3)*
Draught, feet (metres): 23·3 *(7·1)*
Torpedo tubes: 6—21 in *(533 mm)*
Main machinery: Diesel-electric; 3 diesel generators; 1 shaft
Speed, knots: 13 surfaced; 20 dived
Complement: 67

In the 1964 Navy Estimates a first instalment was approved for the construction of two conventionally powered submarines of tear-drop design. HSA M8 Fire control.

Radar: Type 1001.

TIGERHAAI 4/1977, Wright and Logan

2 "POTVIS" CLASS
2 "DOLFIJN" CLASS

Name	No.	Builders	Laid down	Launched	Commissioned
POTVIS	S 804	Wilton-Fijenoord, Schiedam	17 Sept 1962	12 Jan 1965	2 Nov 1965
TONIJN	S 805	Wilton-Fijenoord, Schiedam	27 Nov 1962	14 June 1965	24 Feb 1966
DOLFIJN	S 808	Rotterdamse Droogdok Mij, Rotterdam	30 Dec 1954	20 May 1959	16 Dec 1960
ZEEHOND	S 809	Rotterdamse Droogdok Mij, Rotterdam	30 Dec 1954	20 Feb 1960	16 Mar 1961

Displacement, tons: 1 140 standard; 1 494 surfaced; 1 826 dived
Length, feet (metres): 260·9 *(79·5)*
Beam, feet (metres): 25·8 *(7·8)*
Draught, feet (metres): 15·8 *(4·8)*
Torpedo tubes: 8—21 in *(533 mm)*
Main machinery: 2 MAN diesels; 3 100 bhp
  electric motors; 4 200 hp; 2 shafts
Speed, knots: 14·5 surfaced; 17 dived
Complement: 64

These submarines are of a triple-hull design, giving a diving depth 980 feet *(300 metres)*. *Potvis* and *Tonijn*, originally voted for in 1949 with the other pair, but suspended for some years, had several modifications compared with *Dolfijn* and *Zeehond* and were officially considered to be a separate class; but modernisation of both classes has been completed, and all four boats are now almost identical. HSA M8 Fire control.

Construction: The hull consists of three cylinders arranged in a triangular shape. The upper cylinder accommodates the crew, navigational equipment and armament. The lower two cylinders house the propulsion machinery comprising diesel engines, batteries and electric motors, as well as store-rooms.

Engineering: Main engines to be replaced by SEMPT-Pielstick diesels.

Radar: Type 1001.

POTVIS 8/1976, Wright and Logan

NETHERLANDS

DESTROYERS

2 "TROMP" CLASS (DLG)

Name	No.	Builders	Laid down	Launched	Commissioned
TROMP	F 801	Koninklijke Maatschappij De Schelde, Flushing	4 Sept 1971	4 June 1973	3 Oct 1975
DE RUYTER	F 806	Koninklijke Maatschappij De Schelde, Flushing	22 Dec 1971	9 Mar 1974	3 June 1976

Displacement, tons: 4 300 standard; 5 400 full load
Length, feet (metres): 429·5 *(130·9)* pp; 454·1 *(138·4)* oa
Beam, feet (metres): 48·6 *(14·8)*
Draught, feet (metres): 15·1 *(4·6)*
Aircraft: 1 Lynx helicopter
Missile launchers: 1 Tartar aft; Seasparrow Point defence missile system; Harpoon (2 quadruple) (8 missiles)
Guns: 2—4·7 in (twin turret)
A/S weapons: 6 (2 triple) Mk 32 ASW torpedo tubes
Main engines: 2 Olympus gas turbines; 50 000 hp; 2 Tyne cruising gas turbines, 8 000 hp
Speed, knots: 30
Complement: 306

First design allowance was voted for in 1967 estimates. Ordered (announced on 27 July 1970) for laying down in 1971. Hangar and helicopter spot landing platform aft. Fitted as flagships.

ECM: 2 Knebworth Corvus Chaff projectors (and illuminators).

Electronics: SEWACO I automated AIO.

Engineering: Each ship carries 4-1 000 kW diesel generators by Ruston Paxman, England.

Gunnery: Turrets from *Gelderland* with considerable modifications. Including full automation.

Radar: Search and designator; One HSA 3D in radome.
Search, tracker and fire control for Seasparrow and 4·7 in guns; one HSA WM 25.
Tartar control: Two SPG-51.
Navigation: Two Decca.

Sonar: One CWE 610.

TROMP 6/1977, Dr. Giorgio Arra

DE RUYTER 11/1976, Michael D. J. Lennon

TROMP 6/1977, C. and S. Taylor

NETHERLANDS 343

8 "FRIESLAND" CLASS

Name	No.	Builders	Laid down	Launched	Commissioned
FRIESLAND	D 812	Nederlandse Dok en Scheepsbouw Mij, Amsterdam	17 Dec 1951	21 Feb 1953	22 Mar 1956
GRONINGEN	D 813	Nederlandse Dok en Scheepsbouw Mij, Amsterdam	21 Feb 1952	9 Jan 1954	12 Sept 1956
LIMBURG	D 814	Koninklijke Maatschappij De Schelde, Flushing	28 Nov 1953	5 Sept 1955	31 Oct 1956
OVERIJSSEL	D 815	Dok-en-Werfmaatschappij Wilton-Fijenoord	15 Oct 1953	8 Aug 1955	4 Oct 1957
DRENTHE	D 816	Nederlandse Dok en Scheepsbouw Mij, Amsterdam	9 Jan 1954	26 Mar 1955	1 Aug 1957
UTRECHT	D 817	Koninklijke Maatschappij De Schelde, Flushing	15 Feb 1954	2 June 1956	1 Oct 1957
ROTTERDAM	D 818	Rotterdamse Droogdok Mij, Rotterdam	7 Jan 1954	26 Jan 1956	28 Feb 1957
AMSTERDAM	D 819	Nederlandse Dok en Schepsbouw Mij, Amsterdam	26 Mar 1955	25 Aug 1956	10 Aug 1958

Displacement, tons: 2 497 standard; 3 070 full load
Length, feet (metres): 370 *(112.8)* pp; 380.5 *(116.0)* oa
Beam, feet (metres): 38.5 *(11.7)*
Draught, feet (metres): 17 *(5.2)*
Guns: 4—4.7 in *(120 mm)* (twin turrets) 4—40 mm
A/S weapons: 2 four-barrelled 375 mm. Bofors rocket launchers; 2 DC racks
Main engines: 2 Werkspoor geared turbines, 60 000 shp; 2 shafts
Boilers: 4 Babcock
Speed, knots: 36
Complement: 284

These ships have side armour as well as deck protection. Twin rudders. Propellers 370 rpm. Named after provinces of the Netherlands, and the two principal cities. To be replaced by "Kortenaer" class of frigates.

Gunnery: The 4.7 in guns are fully automatic with a rate of fire of 42 rounds per minute. All guns are radar controlled. Originally six 40 mm guns were mounted.

Radar: Search: LW 03.
Tactical: DA 05.
Fire control: HSA M 45 for 4.7 in.
HSA fire control for 40 mm and A/S rockets.

Torpedo tubes: *Utrecht* was equipped with eight 21 in A/S torpedo tubes (single, four on each side) in 1960 and *Overijssel* in 1961, and the others were to have been, but the project was dropped and tubes already fitted were removed.

OVERIJSSEL   5/1977, Wright and Logan

OVERIJSSEL   6/1977, J. L. M. van der Burg

1 "HOLLAND" CLASS

Name	No.	Builders	Laid down	Launched	Commissioned
ZEELAND	D 809	Koninklijke Maatschappij De Schelde, Flushing	12 Jan 1951	27 June 1953	1 Mar 1955

Displacement, tons: 2 215 standard; 2 765 full load
Length, feet (metres): 360.5 *(109.9)* pp; 371.1 *(113.1)* oa
Beam, feet (metres): 37.5 *(11.4)*
Draught, feet (metres): 16.8 *(5.1)*
Guns: 4—4.7 in *(120 mm)*; 1—40 mm
A/S weapons: 2 four-barrelled 375 mm, Bofors rocket launchers; 2 DC racks
Main engines: Werkspoor Parsons geared turbines; 2 shafts; 45 000 shp
Boilers: 4 Babcock
Speed, knots: 32
Complement: 247

Two ships of this class were equipped with engines of the pre-war "Callenburgh" class design and the other two with engines of German construction. (The four "Callenburgh" class destroyers were being built in 1940. *Isaac Sweers* was towed to England and completed there, *Tjerk Hiddes* was completed by the Germans as ZH 1. The other two, *Callenburgh* and *Van Almonde*, were too severely damaged for further use and were scrapped, the engines being installed in the "Holland" class).

Gunnery: The 4.7 in guns are fully automatic with a rate of fire of 42 rounds per minute. All guns are radar controlled.

Radar: Search: LW 03.
Tactical: DA 02.
Fire control: HSA M 45 for 4.7 in.
HSA fire control for A/S rocket launcher.

Sisterships: *Gelderland* now a harbour-training hulk in Amsterdam. *Noord Brabant* too severely damaged in collision 9 Jan 1974 for repair. *Holland* paid off Dec 1977 and transferred to Peru. To be replaced by "Kortenaer" class.

ZEELAND   4/1976, J. L. M. van der Burg

344 NETHERLANDS

FRIGATES

1 + 11 "KORTENAER" CLASS

Name	No.	Builders	Laid down	Launched	Commissioned
KORTENAER	F 807	Koninklijke Maatschappij De Schelde, Flushing	8 April 1975	18 Dec 1976	Autumn 1978
CALLENBURGH	F 808	Koninklijke Maatschappij De Schelde, Flushing	30 June 1975	26 Mar 1977	Autumn 1979
VAN KINSBERGEN	F 809	Koninklijke Maatschappij De Schelde, Flushing	2 Sept 1975	16 April 1977	Summer 1980
BANCKERT	F 810	Koninklijke Maatschappij De Schelde, Flushing	25 Feb 1976	1979	Spring 1981
PIET HEYN	F 811	Koninklijke Maatschappij De Schelde, Flushing	28 April 1977	1978	Late 1981
PIETER FLORESZ	F 812	Koninklijke Maatschappij De Schelde, Flushing	1 July 1977	—	Spring 1982
WITTE DE WITH	F 813	Koninklijke Maatschappij De Schelde, Flushing	1978	—	Late Summer 1982
ABRAHAM CRIJNSSEN	F 816	Koninklijke Maatschappij De Schelde, Flushing	1978	—	Spring 1983
PHILIPS VAN ALMONDE	F 823	Dok en Werfmaatschappij Wilton, Fijenoord	3 Oct 1977	—	Summer 1982
BLOIS VAN TRESLONG	F 824	Dok en Werfmaatschappij Wilton, Fijenoord	1978	—	Summer 1983
JAN VAN BRAKEL	F 825	Koninklijke Maatschappij De Schelde, Flushing	1979	—	Autumn 1983
WILLEM VAN DER ZAAN	F 826	Koninklijke Maatschappij De Schelde, Flushing	1980	—	Spring 1984

Displacement, tons: 3 500
Dimensions, feet (metres): 419.8 × 47.2 × 14.3 *(128 × 14.4 × 4.4)*
Aircraft: 1 Lynx helicopter
Missiles: 8 Harpoon surface-to-surface; NATO Seasparrow PDMS
Guns: 2—76 mm OTO Melara (see notes)
A/S weapons: 4 (2 double) Mk 32 torpedo tubes for Mk 46 in after deckhouse
Main engines: 2 Rolls-Royce Olympus gas turbines = 50 000 shp; 2 Rolls-Royce Tyne gas turbines = 8 000 shp; 2 variable pitch propellers
Speed, knots: 30
Range, miles: 4 000 on Tyne cruising turbines
Complement: 176

First four of class ordered 31 Aug 1974, second four 28 Nov 1974. Third four 29 Dec 1976 (two to built by same constructors as rest of class, two by Wilton-Fijenoord). The thirteenth of class (SAM version) has been delayed. *Kortenaer* to be ready for trials 1 April 1978. *Callenburgh* to commission in Autumn 1979 and thereafter at 9 monthly intervals. These ships are to replace the "Holland" and "Friesland" classes. Cost at 1974 prices £37 m.

Building area: Covered area at No 6 repair dock at Wilton, Fijenoord now reaching completion.

"KORTENAER" Class   *1974, Royal Netherlands Navy*

Complement: Reduced to 176 by adoption of large amount of automation.

Gunnery: Twin 35 mm/90 is to be mounted on top of hangar when system becomes available. Until then second 76 mm will be mounted in lieu on first two ships and 40 mm on remainder.

Radar: Hollandse Signaal for radar and fire-control.

Sonar: SQS 505.

6 "VAN SPEIJK" CLASS

Name	No.	Builders	Laid down	Launched	Commissioned
VAN SPEIJK	F 802	Nederlandse Dok en Scheepsbouw Mij, Amsterdam	1 Oct 1963	5 Mar 1965	14 Feb 1967
VAN GALEN	F 803	Koninklijke Maatschappij De Schelde, Flushing	25 July 1963	19 June 1965	1 Mar 1967
TJERK HIDDES	F 804	Nederlandse Dok en Scheepsbouw Mij, Amsterdam	1 June 1964	17 Dec 1965	16 Aug 1967
VAN NES	F 805	Koninklijke Maatschappij De Schelde, Flushing	25 July 1963	26 Mar 1966	9 Aug 1967
ISAAC SWEERS	F 814	Nederlandse Dok en Scheepsbouw Mij, Amsterdam	5 May 1965	10 Mar 1967	15 May 1968
EVERTSEN	F 815	Koninklijke Maatschappij De Schelde, Flushing	6 July 1965	18 June 1966	21 Dec 1967

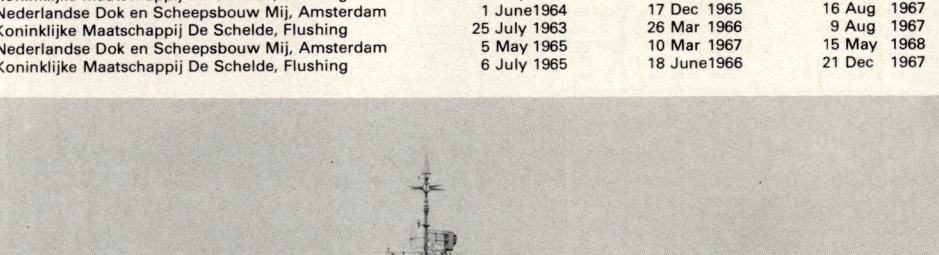

Displacement, tons: 2 200 standard; 2 850 full load
Dimensions, feet (metres): 360 wl, 372 oa × 41 × 18 *(109.8; 113.4 × 12.5 × 5.8)*
Aircraft: 1 Wasp helicopter
Missile: 2 quadruple Seacat anti-aircraft (see Modernisation note)
Guns: 2—4.5 in (twin turret) (see Modernisation note)
A/S weapons: 1 Limbo three-barrelled depth charge mortar (see Modernisation note)
Main engines: 2 double reduction geared turbines; 2 shafts; 30 000 shp (to be modernised)
Boilers: 2 Babcock & Wilcox (to be modernised)
Speed, knots: 30
Complement: 254 (after modernisation 231)

Four ships were ordered in Oct 1962 and two later.

Design: Although in general these ships are based on the design of the British Improved Type 12 ("Leander" class), there are a number of modifications to suit the requirements of the Royal Netherlands Navy. As far as possible equipment of Netherlands manufacture was installed. This resulted in a number of changes in the ship's superstructure compared with the British "Leander" class. To avoid delay these ships were in some cases fitted with equipment already available, instead of going through long development stages.

Electronics: SEWACO I integration system and Daisy data-processing to be fitted during modernisation.

Modernisation: This class is undergoing mid-life modernisation at Rykswerf Den Helder. This will take 18 months, one ship being accepted every 6 months from Jan 1977 when *Van Speijk* was taken in hand. This will consist of replacement of 4.5 in turret by one 76 mm OTO Melara, removal of Limbo, fitting of two quadruple Harpoon between the funnel and the main-mast, fitting of six (two triple) Mk 32 A/S torpedo tubes, conversion of hangar with telescopic door to take Lynx, new electronics and electrics, updating of Ops. Room, improved communications, extensive automation with reduction in complement and improved habitability. *Van Galen* is the second in hand and *Van Nes* the third

Electronics: ECM equipment.

Radar: (new radar systems to be fitted and integrated with Daisy during modernisation)
LW 02 air surveillance on mainmast
DA 05 target indicator on foremast
Kelvin-Hughes Surface-warning/nav set on foremast (to be replaced by new nav/helo control set)
1-M45 for 4.5 in guns
2-M44 for Seacat

Sonar: Hull-mounted and VDS.

EVERTSEN   *10/1977, C. and S. Taylor*

TJERK HIDDES   *10/1976, Wright and Logan*

NETHERLANDS 345

CORVETTES

6 "WOLF" CLASS

Name	No.	Builders	Commissioned
WOLF (ex-PCE 1607)	F 817	Avondale Marine Ways, Inc, New Orleans, La	26 Mar 1954
FRET (ex-PCE 1604)	F 818	General Shipbuilding and Engineering Works, Boston	4 May 1954
HERMELIJN (ex-PCE 1605)	F 819	General Shipbuilding and Engineering Works, Boston	5 Aug 1954
VOS (ex-PCE 1606)	F 820	General Shipbuilding and Engineering Works, Boston	2 Dec 1954
PANTER (ex-PCE 1608)	F 821	Avondale Marine Ways, Inc, New Orleans, La	11 June 1954
JAGUAR (ex-PCE 1609)	F 822	Avondale Marine Ways, Inc, New Orleans, La	11 June 1954

Displacement, tons: 870 standard; 975 full load
Dimensions, feet (metres): 180 pp; 184·5 oa × 33 × 14·5 (54·9; 56·2 × 10 × 4·4)
Guns: 1—3 in (76 mm); 6—40 mm (Jaguar, Panter: 4—40 mm); 8—20 mm (not mounted)
A/S weapons: 1 Hedgehog; 2 DCT (Jaguar, Panter: 4); 2 DC racks
Main engines: 2 GM diesels; 1 800 bhp; 2 shafts
Speed, knots: 15
Range, miles: 4 300 at 10 knots
Complement: 96

Built as part of the US "off-shore" agreement—all laid down 1952-53. 20 mm guns not fitted in peacetime.

Radar: Kelvin Hughes navigation set.

Sonar: One hull mounted set.

HERMELIJN   1976, Michael D. J. Lennon

LIGHT FORCES

5 "BALDER" CLASS (LARGE PATROL CRAFT)

Name	No.	Builders	Commissioned
BALDER	P 802	Rijkswerf Willemsoord	6 Aug 1954
BULGIA	P 803	Rijkswerf Willemsoord	9 Aug 1954
FREYR	P 804	Rijkswerf Willemsoord	1 Dec 1954
HADDA	P 805	Rijkswerf Willemsoord	3 Feb 1955
HEFRING	P 806	Rijkswerf Willemsoord	23 Mar 1955

Displacement, tons: 169 standard; 225 full load
Dimensions, feet (metres): 114·9 pp; 119·1 oa × 20·2 × 5·9 (35; 36·3 × 6·2 × 1·8)
Guns: 1—40 mm; 3—20 mm
A/S weapons: Mousetrap; depth charges
Main engines: Diesels; 2 shafts; 1 300 shp = 15·5 knots
Range, miles: 1 000 at 13 knots
Complement: 27

Built on US "off-shore" account.

Radar: Decca navigation set.

Sonar: One hull mounted.

HADDA   4/1976, J. L. M. van der Burg

MINE WARFARE FORCES

0 + 15 "ALKMAAR" CLASS (MINEHUNTERS)

Name	No.	Builders	Launched
ALKMAAR	850	Van der Giessen-de Noord-Albleasserdam	Jan 1981
DELFZIJL	851	Van der Giessen-de Noord-Albleasserdam	June 1981
DORDTRECHT	852	Van der Giessen-de Noord-Albleasserdam	Dec 1982
HAARLEM	853	Van der Giessen-de Noord-Albleasserdam	1982
HARLINGEN	854	Van der Giessen-de Noord-Albleasserdam	1982
HELLEVOETSLUIS	855	Van der Giessen-de Noord-Albleasserdam	1983
MAASSLUIS	856	Van der Giessen-de Noord-Albleasserdam	1983
MAKKUM	857	Van der Giessen-de Noord-Albleasserdam	1983
MIDDELBURG	858	Van der Giessen-de Noord-Albleasserdam	1984
SCHEVENINGEN	859	Van der Giessen-de Noord-Albleasserdam	1984
SCHIEDAM	860	Van der Giessen-de Noord-Albleasserdam	1985
URK	861	Van der Giessen-de Noord-Albleasserdam	1985
VEERE	862	Van der Giessen-de Noord-Albleasserdam	1985
VLAARDINGEN	863	Van der Giessen-de Noord-Albleasserdam	1986
WILLEMSTAD	864	Van der Giessen-de Noord-Albleasserdam	1986

Displacement, tons: 510
Dimensions, feet (metres): 154·5 pp × 29·2 × 8·2 (47·1 × 8·9 × 2·5)
Gun: 1—20 mm (an aditional short range missile system may be added for patrol duties)
Minehunting: 2 PAP systems
Minesweeping: Mechanical sweep gear
Main engine: 1 Werkspoor diesel; single axial propeller; 1 400 kW = 15 knots
Auxiliary propulsion: 2—88 kW motors = 7 knots
Range, miles: 3 000 at 12 knots
Endurance: 15 days
Complement: From 29-35 depending on task

This class is the Netherlands part of a cooperative plan with Belgium and France. The whole class will be built in a specially constructed "ship-factory" (472 × 141 ft) which was completed Dec 1977. First two ships ordered Nov 1977, to be laid down in Jan 1979 with GRP hulls. Subsequent keel laying—852-3, 1980; 854-6, 1981; 857-8, 1982; 859-61, 1983; 862-3, 1984; 864, 1985.

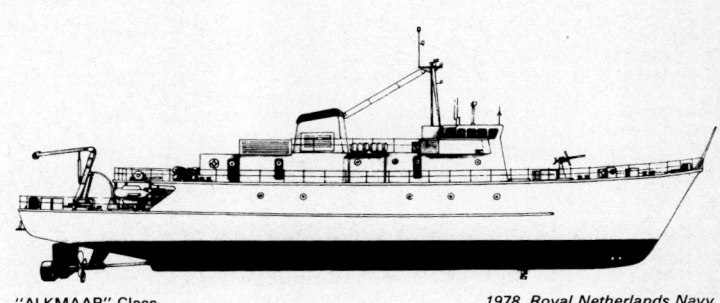

"ALKMAAR" Class   1978, Royal Netherlands Navy

Electronics: Automatic radar navigation system; automatic data processing and display; EVEC automatic pilot; automatic hovering.

Sonar: DUBM-21A.

Tasks: A 5 ton container can be shipped, stored for varying tasks—HQ-support; research; patrol; extended diving; drone control.

346 NETHERLANDS

4 "ONVERSAAGD" CLASS
(MCM SUPPORT SHIPS, ESCORTS and TORPEDO TENDER)

Name	No.	Builders	Commissioned
ONBEVREESD (ex-*AM 481*)	A 855 (ex-*M 885*)	Astoria Marine Construction Co	21 Sept 1954
MERCUUR (ex-*Onverschrokken*, ex-*AM 483*)	A 856 (ex-*M 886*)	Peterson Builders, Wisconsin	22 July 1954
ONVERVAARD (ex-*AM 482*)	A 858 (ex-*M 888*)	Astoria Marine Construction Co	31 Mar 1955
ONVERDROTEN (ex-*AM 485*)	A 859 (ex-*M 889*)	Peterson Builders, Wisconsin	22 Nov 1954

Displacement, tons: 735 standard; 790 full load
Dimensions, feet (metres): 165·0 pp; 172·0 oa × 36·0 × 10·6 *(50·3; 52·5 × 11 × 3·2)*
Gun: 1—40 mm
A/S weapons: 2 DC
Main engines: Diesels; 1 600 bhp = 15·5 knots
Oil fuel, tons: 46
Range, miles: 2 400 at 12 knots
Complement: 70

Built in USA for the Netherlands. Of wooden and non-magnetic construction. Originally designed as Minesweepers—Ocean—reclassified in 1966 and in 1972. Onbevreesd, Onverdroten and Onvervaard are MCM Command/Support Ships. Mercuur (ex-*Onverschrokken*) was converted into a Tender and Torpedo Trials Ship in 1972.

ONBEVREESD   1976, Michael D. J. Lennon

18 "DOKKUM" CLASS
(MINESWEEPERS, COASTAL and MINEHUNTERS)

DOKKUM M 801 (H)	OMMEN M 813	HOOGEVEEN M 827
HOOGEZAND M 802	GIETHOORN M 815	STAPHORST M 828 (H)
ROERMOND M 806 (D)	VENLO M 817	SITTARD M 830
NAALDWIJK M 809	DRUNEN M 818 (H)	GEMERT M 841
ABCOUDE M 810	WOERDEN M 820 (D)	VEERE M 842 (H)
DRACHTEN M 812	NAARDEN M 823	RHENEN M 844 (D)

Displacement, tons: 373 standard; 453 full load
Dimensions, feet (metres): 149·8 oa × 28 × 6·5 *(45·7 × 8·5 × 2)*
Guns: 2—40 mm
Main engines: 2 diesels; Fijenoord MAN; 2 500 bhp = 16 knots
Range, miles: 2 500 at 10 knots
Complement: 38

Of 32 Western Union type coastal minesweepers built in the Netherlands, 18 were under offshore procurement as the "Dokkum" class, with MAN engines, and 14 on Netherlands account as the "Wildervank" class, with Werkspoor diesels. All launched in 1954-56 and completed in 1955-56.
Of the "Dokkum" class four have been converted to minehunters (H), (1968-73) and three to diving vessels (D) (1962-68). The remaining eleven minesweepers of this class were subject to a fleet rehabilitation and modernisation programme completed by 1977. All "Wildervank" class deleted by 1976.

Sonar: Type 193 in hunters.

VEERE (Hunter)   7/1977, Dhr. J. van der Woude

HOOGEVEEN (Sweeper)   8/1977, Wright and Logan

16 "VAN STRAELEN" CLASS (MINESWEEPERS—INSHORE)

Name	No.	Builders	Commissioned
ALBLAS	M 868	Werf de Noord, Albasserdam	12 Mar 1960
BUSSEMAKER	M 869	G. de Vries Lentsch Jr, Amsterdam	1960
LACOMBLE	M 870	N.V. de Arnhemse Scheepsbouw Maatschappij	1960
VAN HAMEL	M 871	G. de Vries Lentsch Jr, Amsterdam	1960
VAN STRAELEN	M 872	N.V. de Arnhemse Scheepsbouw Maatschappij	1960
VAN MOPPES	M 873	Werf de Noord, Albasserdam	1960
CHOMPFF	M 874	Werf de Noord, Albasserdam	1961
VAN WELL GROENVELD	M 875	N.V. de Arnhemse Scheepsbouw Maatschappij	1961
SCHUILING	M 876	G. de Vries Lentsch Jr, Amsterdam	1961
VAN VERSENDAAL	M 877	Werf de Noord, Albasserdam	1961
VAN DER WEL	M 878	G. de Vries Lentsch Jr, Amsterdam	1961
VAN 'T HOFF	M 879	Werf de Noord, Albasserdam	1961
MAHU	M 880	Werf de Noord, Albasserdam	1962
STAVERMAN	M 881	G. de Vries Lentsch Jr, Amsterdam	1962
HOUTEPEN	M 882	N.V. de Arnhemse Scheepsbouw Maatschappij	1962
ZOMER	M 883	N.V. de Arnhemse Scheepsbouw Maatschappij	1962

Displacement, tons: 151 light; 169 full load
Dimensions, feet (metres): 90 pp; 99·3 oa × 18·2 × 5·2 *(27·5; 30·3 × 5·6 × 1·6)*
Gun: 1—20 mm
Main engines: Werkspoor diesels; 2 shafts; 1 100 bhp = 13 knots
Complement: 14

Eight were built under the offshore procurement programme, with MDAP funds, and the remaining eight were paid for by Netherlands. All ordered in mid-1957. Built of non-magnetic materials. Alblas, the first, was laid down on 26 Feb 1958, launched on 29 June 1959, started trials on 15 Jan 1960.

ALBLAS   7/1977, Dhr. J. van der Woude

AMPHIBIOUS FORCES

L 9526

Displacement, tons: 20
Dimensions, feet (metres): 50 × 11·8 × 5·8 (15·3 × 3·6 × 1·8)
Main engines: 2 Kromhout diesels; 75 bhp = 8 knots
Complement: 3

Now officially rated as LCA Type.
Built by Rijkswerf, Den Helder.

| L 9510 | L 9512 | L 9514 | L 9517 | L 9520 |
| L 9511 | L 9513 | L 9516 | L 9518 | L 9522 |

Displacement, tons: 13·6
Dimensions, feet (metres): 46·2 × 11·5 × 6 (14·1 × 3·5 × 1·8)
Main engines: Rolls-Royce diesel; Schottel propeller; 200 bhp = 12 knots
Complement: 3

Landing craft made of polyester, all commissioned in 1962-63, except L 9520 in 1964.
Built by Rijkswerf, Den Helder.

SURVEY SHIPS

1 "TYDEMAN" CLASS
(HYDROGRAPHIC/OCEANOGRAPHIC SHIP)

Name	No.	Builders	Commissioned
TYDEMAN	A 906	Scheepswerf En Machine Fabriek "de Merwede"	10 Nov 1976

Displacement, tons: 2 950
Dimensions, feet (metres): 295 × 47·2 × 15·7 (90 × 14·4 × 4·8)
Aircraft: 1 helicopter
Main engines: 3 diesels; 3 690 bhp; electric motor; 2 730 shp
Speed, knots: 15
Range, miles: 15 700 at 10·3 knots; 10 300 at 13·5 knots
Complement: 64 plus 15 scientists

Ordered in Oct 1974. Cost £6·7 m. Able to operate down to 7 000 metres. Fitted with eight laboratories. Supplied with two bow propellers. Laid down 29 April 1975, launched 18 Dec 1975. Built at Hardinxveld-Giessendam. The commissioning was delayed as the ship was rammed by a barge on 28 March 1976.

TYDEMAN 12/1976, Royal Netherlands Navy

2 "BUYSKES" CLASS

Name	No.	Builders	Commissioned
BUYSKES	A 904	Boele's Scheepswerven en Machinefabriek BV, Bolnes	9 Mar 1973
BLOMMENDAL	A 905	Boele's Scheepswerven en Machinefabriek BV, Bolnes	22 May 1973

Displacement, tons: 967 standard; 1 033 full load
Dimensions, feet (metres): 196·6 oa × 36·4 × 12 (60 × 11·1 × 3·7)
Main engines: Diesel-electric; 3 diesels; 2 100 hp = 13·5 knots
Complement: 43

Both designed primarily for hydrographic work but have also limited oceanographic and meteorological capability. They will operate mainly in the North Sea. A data logging system is installed as part of the automatic handling of hydrographic data. They carry two 22 feet survey launches capable of 15 knots and two work-boats normally used for sweeping. Both ships can operate two floats, each housing an echo-sounding transducer, one streaming on each beam. This will enable the running of three simultaneous sounding lines 100 metres apart.

BLOMMENDAL 1973, Royal Netherlands Navy

SERVICE FORCES

2 "POOLSTER" CLASS (FAST COMBAT SUPPORT SHIPS)

Name	No.	Builders	Commissioned
ZUIDERKRUIS	A 832	Verolme Shipyards, Albasserdam	27 June 1975
POOLSTER	A 835	Rotterdamse Droogdok Mij	10 Sept 1964

Displacement, tons: 16 800 full load; 16 900 (Zuiderkruis)
Measurement, tons: 10 000 deadweight
Dimensions, feet (metres): 515 pp; 556 oa × 66·7 × 27 (157·1 pp; 169·6 × 20·3 × 8·2) (Zuiderkruis 561 oa (171·1))
Aircraft: Capacity: 5 helicopters
Guns: 2—40 mm in *Poolster*; 2—20 mm in *Zuiderkruis*
Main engines: 2 turbines; 22 000 shp = 21 knots (*Poolster*)
2 Werkspoor diesels; 21 000 hp = 21 knots (*Zuiderkruis*)
Complement: 200

Poolster laid down on 18 Sept 1962. Launched on 16 Oct 1963. Trials mid-1964. Helicopter deck aft. Funnel heightened by 4·5 m. *Zuiderkruis* ordered Oct 1972. Laid down 16 July 1973, launched 15 Oct 1974.
Both carry A/S weapons for helicopters.

Radar: Kelvin Hughes navigation set.

Sonar: Hull mounted set.

POOLSTER 8/1975, Royal Netherlands Navy

ZUIDERKRUIS 4/1976, J. L. M. van der Burg

MISCELLANEOUS

TRAINING SHIPS

Name	No.	Builders	Commissioned
ZEEFAKKEL	A 903	J. & K. Smit, Kinderdijk	22 May 1951

Displacement, tons: 355 standard; 384 full load
Dimensions, feet (metres): 149 oa × 24·7 × 6·9 *(45·4 × 7·6 × 2·1)*
Guns: 1—3 in; 1—40 mm
Main engines: 2 Smit/MAN 8-cyl diesels; 2 shafts; 640 bhp = 12 knots
Complement: 29

Laid down Sept 1949, launched 21 July 1950. Former surveying vessel. Now used as local training ship at Den Helder.

Name	No.	Builders	Commissioned
URANIA (ex-*Tromp*)	Y 8050	—	23 April 1938

Displacement, tons: 38
Dimensions, feet (metres): 72 × 16·3 × 10 *(22 × 5 × 3·1)*
Main engines: Diesel; 65 hp
Complement: 15

Schooner used for training in seamanship.

Note: *Gelderland* (ex-destroyer) and *Grypskerk* (ex-minesweeper) are used at Amsterdam as harbour training and accommodation ships for the Technical Training establishment. *Soemba* (ex-sloop) used at Den Oever as harbour training and accommodation ship for divers and underwater-swimmers.

TUGS

Name	No.	Builders	Commissioned
WESTGAT	A 872	Rijkswerf, Willemsoord	10 Jan 1968
WIELINGEN	A 873	Rijkswerf, Willemsoord	4 April 1968

Displacement, tons: 185
Dimensions, feet (metres): 90·6 × 22·7 × 7·7 *(27·6 × 6·9 × 2·3)*
Guns: 2—20 mm
Main engines: Bolnes diesel; 750 bhp = 12 knots

Launched on 22 Aug 1967 and 6 Jan 1968, respectively. Equipped with salvage pumps and fire fighting equipment. Stationed at Den Helder.

Name	No.	Builders	Commissioned
WAMANDAI	A 870 (ex-Y 8035)	Rijkswerf, Willemsoord	1960

Displacement, tons: 159 standard; 201 full load
Dimensions, feet (metres): 89·2 × 21·3 × 7·5 *(27·2 × 6·5 × 2·3)*
Guns: 2—20 mm
Main engines: Diesel; 500 bhp = 11 knots

Launched on 28 May 1960. Equipped with salvage pumps and fire fighting equipment. In the Netherlands Antilles since 1964.

Name	No.	Builders	Commissioned
WAMBRAU	A 871	Rijkswerf, Willemsoord	8 Jan 1957

Displacement, tons: 154 standard; 179 full load
Dimensions, feet (metres): 86·5 oa × 20·7 × 7·5 *(26·4 × 6·3 × 2·3)*
Guns: 2—20 mm
Main engines: Werkspoor diesel and Kort nozzle; 500 bhp = 10·8 knots

Launched on 27 Aug 1956. Equipped with salvage pumps and fire fighting equipment. Stationed at Den Helder.

Name	No.	Builders	Commissioned
BERKEL	Y 8037	H. H. Bodewes, Millingen	1956
DINTEL	Y 8038	H. H. Bodewes, Millingen	1956
DOMMEL	Y 8039	H. H. Bodewes, Millingen	1957
IJSSEL	Y 8040	H. H. Bodewes, Millingen	1957

Displacement, tons: 139 standard; 163 full load
Dimensions, feet (metres): 82 oa × 20·5 × 7·3 *(25 × 6·3 × 2·2)*
Main engines: Werkspoor diesel and Kort nozzle; 500 bhp

Harbour tugs specially designed for use at Den Helder.

There are also five small harbour tugs—Y 8014, Y 8016, Y 8017, Y 8022, Y 8028.

ACCOMMODATION SHIPS

(See note under Training Ships)

Cornelis Drebbel is the name of the "Boatel"—775 tons, length 206·7 feet, beam 38·7 feet, draught 3·6 feet, complement 200, cost 3m guilders. Ordered in 1969 from Scheepswerf Voorwaarts at Hoogezand, launched on 19 Nov 1970 and completed in 1971. Serves as accommodation vessel for crews of ships refitting at private yards in the Rotterdam area. *Snellius* (ex-survey ship) was used for accommodation for R. Neth. N. personnel at the RN Submarine Base, Faslane and returned to Netherlands late 1976 and sold in 1977.

TENDERS

Name	No.	Builders	Commissioned
VAN BOCHOVE	A 923	Zaanlandse Scheepsbouw Mij, Zaandam	Aug 1962

Displacement, tons: 140
Dimensions, feet (metres): 97·2 × 18·2 × 6 *(29·6 × 5·6 × 1·8)*
Main engines: Kromhout diesel; Schottel propeller; 140 bhp = 8 knots
Complement: 8

Torpedo trials vessel. Ordered Oct 1961. Launched on 20 July 1962. Has two 21 in *(533 mm)* torpedo tubes.

4 DIVING TENDERS

Name	No.	Builders	Commissioned
ARGUS	A 847	Rijkswerf, Willemsoord	1939
TRITON	A 848	Rijkswerf, Willemsoord	4 April 1964
NAUTILUS	A 849	Rijkswerf, Willemsoord	20 April 1956
HYDRA	A 850	Rijkswerf, Willemsoord	20 April 1956

Displacement, tons: 44 *(Argus)*; 67 (remainder)
Dimensions, feet (metres): 75·4 × 15·4 × 3·3 *(23 × 4·7 × 1) (Argus)*; 76 × 16·4 × 4·6 *(23·2 × 5 × 1·4)* (remainder)
Main engines: Diesel; 144 hp = 8 knots *(Argus)*
diesel, 117 hp = 9 knots (remainder)
Complement: 8

DREG IV Y 8020

Displacement, tons: 46 standard; 48 full load
Dimensions, feet (metres): 65·7 × 15·1 × 4·9 *(20 × 4·6 × 1·5)*
Main engines: 120 hp = 9·5 knots
Complement: 10

Used for communication duties in Rotterdam area.

NEW ZEALAND

Ministerial

Minister of Defence:
Hon Allan McCready MP

Headquarters Appointments

Chief of Naval Staff:
Rear-Admiral N. D. Anderson, CBE
Deputy Chief of Naval Staff:
Commodore R. H. L. Humby

The three New Zealand Service Boards were formally abolished in 1971 as part of the Defence Headquarters reorganisation. The former three Service Headquarters and Defence Office have been reorganised into functional branches and offices.
On 1 June 1970 the command and control of the three New Zealand Services was vested in the Chief of Defence Staff who exercises this authority through the three Service Chiefs of Staff.

Diplomatic Representation

Head of New Zealand Defence Liaison Staff, London and Senior Naval Liaison Officer:
Commodore F. H. Bland, OBE
Deputy Head of New Zealand Defence Staff, Washington and Naval Attaché:
Captain E. R. Ellison, OBE

Personnel

(a) January 1974: 2 730 officers and ratings
January 1975: 2 690 officers and ratings
January 1976: 2 800 officers and ratings
January 1977: 2 648 officers and ratings
January 1978: 2 757 officers and ratings
(b) Voluntary service
Reserve; 326 RNZNVR

Base

Auckland (HMNZS Philomel)

Prefix to Ships' Names

HMNZS

Mercantile Marine

Lloyd's Register of Shipping:
102 vessels of 199 462 tons gross

Strength of the Fleet

Type	Active	Building
Frigates	4	—
Large Patrol Craft	4	—
Survey Ship	1 (converting)	—
Survey Craft	3	—
Research Vessel	1	—
Tender	1	—
Tug	1	—
Reserve Training HDMLs	4	—

Note: Construction of 10 000 ton Support Ship and offshore patrol craft as well as a new tug under discussion.

DELETIONS

Cruiser

Dec 1971 Black Prince

Frigate

April 1971 Blackpool returned to Royal Navy

Corvettes

Sept 1976 Inverell, Kiama

Patrol Craft

1972 Maroro (HDML)
1975 Kahawai, Mako, Parore, Tamure (HDMLs)
1977 Haku (HDML)

Survey Ships

June 1971 Endeavour (ex-US Namakagon) returned to USN for transfer to Taiwan (now Lung Chuan)
Dec 1974 Lachlan

PENNANT LIST

Frigates

F 55   Waikato
F 111   Otago
F 148   Taranaki
F 421   Canterbury

Light Forces

P 3552 Paea
P 3563 Kuparu
P 3564 Koura
P 3565 Haku
P 3567 Manga
P 3568 Pukaki
P 3569 Rotoiti
P 3570 Taupo
P 3571 Hawea

Surveying Vessels

A 06   Monowai
P 3556 Takapu
P 3566 Tarapunga

Research Vessel

A 2   Tui

FRIGATES

1 "LEANDER" and 1 "BROAD-BEAMED LEANDER" CLASSES

Name	No.	Builders	Laid down	Launched	Commissioned
WAIKATO	F 55	Harland & Wolff Ltd, Belfast	10 Jan 1964	18 Feb 1965	16 Sept 1966
CANTERBURY	F 421	Yarrow Ltd, Clyde	12 April 1969	6 May 1970	22 Oct 1971

Displacement, tons: 2 450 standard; 2 860 full load Waikato; 2 470 standard; 2 990 full load Canterbury
Length, feet (metres): 360·0 (109·7) pp; 372·0 (113·4) oa Waikato; 370·0 (112·8) pp Canterbury
Beam, feet (metres): 41·0 (12·5) Waikato; 43·0 (13·1) Canterbury
Draught, feet (metres): 18 (5·5)
Aircraft: 1 Wasp helicopter
Missiles: 1 quadruple Seacat
Guns: 2—4·5 in (155 mm) in twin turret; 2—20 mm
A/S weapons: 2—Mk 32 Mod 5 A/S torpedo tubes
Main engines: 2 sets dr geared turbines; 2 shafts; 30 000 shp
Boilers: 2 Babcock & Wilcox
Speed, knots: 30 Waikato; 28 Canterbury
Complement: 248 (14 officers, 234 ratings) Waikato; 243 (14 officers, 229 ratings) Canterbury

Waikato, ordered on 14 June 1963. Commissioned on 16 Sept 1966, trials in the United Kingdom until spring 1967, arrived in New Zealand waters in May 1967. Canterbury was ordered in Aug 1968, arrived in New Zealand in Aug 1972.
Canterbury has extensions fitted to her funnel uptakes.
Waikato completed long refit and modernisation mid-1977.

Radar: Search: Type 965.
Tactical: Type 993.
Fire control: MRS 3 System and I Band.

CANTERBURY

6/1977, C. and S. Taylor

350 NEW ZEALAND

2 "WHITBY" CLASS (TYPE 12)

Name	No.	Builders	Laid down	Launched	Commissioned
OTAGO (ex-HMS *Hastings*)	F 111	J. I. Thornycroft & Co Ltd, Woolston, Southampton	1957	11 Dec 1958	22 June 1960
TARANAKI	F 148	J. Samuel White & Co Ltd, Isle of Wight	1958	19 Aug 1959	28 Mar 1961

Displacement, tons: 2 144 standard; 2 557 full load
Length, feet (metres): 360·0 *(109·7)* pp; 370·0 *(112·8)* oa
Beam, feet (metres): 41·0 *(12·5)*
Draught, feet (metres): 17·3 *(5·3)*
Missiles: 1 quadruple Seacat
Guns: 2—4·5 in *(115 mm)* in twin turret; 2—20 mm *(Taranaki only)*
A/S weapons: 6 (2 triple) Mk 32 Mod 5 A/S torpedo tubes
Main engines: 2 sets dr geared turbines; 2 shafts; 30 000 shp
Boilers: 2 Babcock & Wilcox
Speed, knots: 30
Complement: 240 (13 officers, 227 ratings)

Taranaki was ordered direct (announced by J. Samuel White & Co on 22 Feb 1957). For *Otago* New Zealand took over the contract (officially stated on 26 Feb 1957) for *Hastings* originally ordered from John I. Thornycroft & Co in Feb 1956 for the Royal Navy. Both vessels are generally similar to the "Whitby" class in the Royal Navy, but were modified to suit New Zealand conditions and have had the most necessary "Rothesay" class alterations and additions. *Otago* has had enclosed foremast since 1967 refit; *Taranaki* was similarly fitted during 1969. *Taranaki* laid up at 48 hours notice in April 1977 owing to "a serious shortage of technical staff". To overcome this problem the loan of technical ratings from the RN and RAN is under consideration.

Radar: Search: Type 993 and Type 277.
Fire control: I Band.

Torpedo tubes: The original twelve 21 in *(533 mm)* A/S torpedo tubes (8 single and 2 twin) were removed.

OTAGO 1977, Royal New Zealand Navy

SURVEY VESSELS

Name	No.	Builders	Laid down	Launched	Commissioned
MONOWAI (ex-*Moana Roa*)	A 06		—	—	—

Measurement, tons: 2 893 gross; 1 318 net
Dimensions, feet (metres): 296·5 oa × 36 × 17 *(90·4 × 11 × 5·2)*
Aircraft: 1 helicopter
Main engines: 2 Sulzer 7-cyl diesels; 3 080 hp = 13·5 knots
Oil fuel, tons: 300
Complement: 120 approx

Previously employed on the Cook Islands service. Taken over 1974—put out to tender in early 1975 for conversion which included an up-rating of the engines, provision of a helicopter deck and hangar and fitting of cp propellers and a bow thruster. Conversion undertaken by Scott Lithgow Drydocks Ltd. Commissioned 4 Oct 1977.
May be used for training when available.

MONOWAI 1977, MOD

2 HDML TYPE

TAKAPU P 3556 (ex-*Q 1188*)
TARAPUNGA P 3566 (ex-*Q 1387*)

Of similar description as those listed under Light Forces.

2 NEW CONSTRUCTION

On 30 Nov 1977 the NZ Cabinet approved the construction of two 88·6 feet *(27 metres)* survey craft with hull and machinery similar to those of the new diving tender now building. Their equipment is being specifically designed to work with *Monowai*. They will replace *Takapu* and *Tarapunga*.

LIGHT FORCES

4 "LAKE" CLASS (LARGE PATROL CRAFT)

Name	No.	Builders	Commissioned
PUKAKI	P 3568	Brooke Marine, Lowestoft, England	24 Feb 1975
ROTOITI	P 3569	Brooke Marine, Lowestoft, England	24 Feb 1975
TAUPO	P 3570	Brooke Marine, Lowestoft, England	29 July 1975
HAWEA	P 3571	Brooke Marine, Lowestoft, England	29 July 1975

Displacement, tons: 105 standard; 134 full load
Dimensions, feet (metres): 107 oa × 20 × 11·8 *(32·8 × 6·1 × 3·6)*
Guns: 2—12·7 mm (0·50 cal) M2 MGs (forward); 1—81 mm mortar/0·50 cal MG combination (aft)
Main engines: 2 Paxman 12YJCM diesels; 3 000 bhp = 25 knots
Complement: 21 (3 officers, 18 ratings)

The first to complete, *Pukaki*, was finished on 20 July 1974. She and *Rotoiti* were shipped to New Zealand in Nov 1974. Launch dates—*Hawea*, 9 Sept 1974; *Pukaki*, 1 March 1974; *Rotoiti*, 8 March 1974; *Taupo*, 25 July 1974.

PUKAKI 1976, Royal New Zealand Navy

4 HDML TYPE

PAEA (ex-Q 1184) P 3552
KUPARU (ex-*Pegasus*, ex-Q 1349) P 3563
KOURA (ex-*Toroa*, ex-Q 1350) P 3564
MANGA (ex-Q 1185) P 3567

Displacement, tons: 46 standard; 54 full load
Dimensions, feet (metres): 72 × 16 × 5·5 *(22 × 4·9 × 1·7)*
Guns: Armament removed
Main engines: 2 diesels; 2 shafts; 320 bhp = 12 knots
Complement: 9

All built in various yards in the United States and Canada and shipped to New Zealand. All have been converted with lattice masts surmounted by a radar aerial.
Attached to RNZNVR divisions;
  Auckland: *Paea*.
  Canterbury: *Kuparu*.
  Otago: *Koura*.
  Wellington: *Manga*.

HAKU   1973, Royal New Zealand Navy

MISCELLANEOUS

TUGS

ARATAKI   MANAWANUI

Dimensions, feet (metres): Length: 75 *(22·9)*
Main engine: Diesel; 1 shaft; 320 hp

Steel tugs. *Arataki* is used as a dockyard tug and *Manawanui* as a diving tender. Built by Steel Ships Ltd, Auckland in 1947.

MANAWANUI   Royal New Zealand Navy

1 DIVING TENDER

A 88·6 feet *(27 metres)* diving tender is under construction by Whangarei Engineering Ltd.

RESEARCH VESSEL

Name	No.	Builders	Commissioned
TUI (ex-USS *Charles H. Davis*, T-AGOR 5)	A 2	Christy Corp, Sturgeon Bay, Wis.	25 Jan 1963

Displacement, tons: 1 200 standard; 1 380 full load
Dimensions, feet (metres): 208·9 × 37·4 × 15·3 *(63·7 × 11·3 × 4·7)*
Main engine: Diesel-electric; 1 shaft; 10 000 hp = 12 knots
Complement: 8 officers, 16 ratings, 15 scientists

Oceanographic research ship. Laid down on 15 June 1961, launched on 30 June 1962. On loan from US since 28 July 1970 for five years. Commissioned in the Royal New Zealand Navy on 11 Sept 1970. Announced that she will remain in RNZN until at least 1980. Operates for NZ Defence Research Establishment on acoustic research. Bow propeller 175 hp.

Appearance: Port after gallows removed—new gallows at stern—cable reels on quarterdeck and amidships—light cable-laying gear over bow.

TUI (now has gallows removed—see notes)   1971, Royal New Zealand Navy

---

NICARAGUA

Ministerial

Minister of Defence:
  Heberto Sanchez

Personnel

1978: 200 officers and men

All craft operated by Marine Section of the Guardia Naçional

Ports

Carinto, Puerto Cabezas, Puerto Somaza, San Juan del Sur.

Mercantile Marine

Lloyd's Register of Shipping:
  30 vessels of 34 588 tons gross

PATROL CRAFT

1 SEWART TYPE

Displacement, tons: 60
Dimensions, feet (metres): 85 × 18·8 × 5·9 *(25·9 × 5·6 × 1·8)*
Guns: 3—0·50 cal MG
Main engines: 3 GM diesels; 3 shafts; 2 000 shp = 26·5 knots
Range, miles: 1 000 at 20 knots
Complement: 10

Delivered July 1972.

RIO CRUTA

Dimensions, feet (metres): Length: 85 *(25·9)*
Gun: 1—20 mm (bow)
Main engines: Diesels; speed = 9 knots
Complement: 11

Wooden-hulled.

4 90 ft LARGE PATROL CRAFT

Wooden-hulled (27·5 metres).

2 80 ft LARGE PATROL CRAFT

Wooden hulled (24·4 metres)

1 75 ft LARGE PATROL CRAFT

Built in 1925 so present existence doubtful. Was used for training. (22·9 metres).

1 40 ft UTILITY CRAFT

Acquired in 1962.

1 26 ft COASTAL PATROL CRAFT

Armed with a 20 mm gun, capable of 25 knots and with a crew of 6. (7·9 metres).

1 Ex-US LCM 6

Acquired in 1970.

352 NIGERIA

NIGERIA

Headquarters Appointments

Chief of the Naval Staff:
  Rear-Admiral Michael Ayinde Adelanwa
Chief of Staff:
  Captain Hussaini Abdullahi

Commands

Western Naval Command:
  Captain Edwin Kentebe
Eastern Naval Command:
  Commander Raheem Adisa Adegbite

Diplomatic Representation

Naval Adviser in Delhi:
  Captain Akintunde Aduwo

Light Forces

1975 3 ex-Soviet "P6" class; *Kaduna, Ibadan II* ("Ford" class)

Personnel

(a) 1978: 260 officers and 2 700 ratings (2 000 reserves)
(b) Voluntary service

Bases

Apapa—Lagos:
  Western Naval Command
  Dockyard Training Schools
  New dockyard under construction
Calabar:
  Eastern Naval Command

Prefix to Ships' Names

NNS.

Strength of the Fleet

Type	Active	Building
Frigate	1	—
Corvettes	2	2
Fast Attack Craft (Missile)	0	6
Large Patrol Craft	12	—
Landing Craft	1	2
Survey Ships	2	—
Supply Ship	1	—
Training Ship	1	—
Tug	1	—
Police Craft	8	—

Mercantile Marine

Lloyd's Register of Shipping:
  94 vessels of 335 540 tons gross

DELETIONS

Survey Ship

1975 *Pathfinder*
1977 *Penelope*

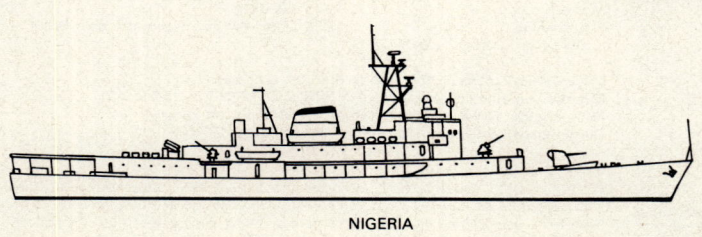

NIGERIA

LANA

FRIGATE

Note: Negotiations for purchase of a frigate from Blohm and Voss, Hamburg are reported.

Name	No.	Builders	Laid down	Launched	Commissioned
NIGERIA	F 87	Wilton-Fijenoord NV, Netherlands	9 April 1964	12 April 1965	16 Sept 1965

Displacement, tons: 1 724 standard; 2 000 full load
Length, feet (metres): 341·2 *(104·0)* pp; 360·2 *(109·8)* oa
Beam, feet (metres): 37·0 *(11·3)*
Draught, feet (metres): 11·5 *(3·5)*
Guns: 2—4 in *(102 mm)* (1 twin); 3—40 mm (single)
A/S weapons: 1—triple-barrelled Squid mortar
Main engines: 4 MAN diesels; 2 shafts; 16 000 bhp
Speed, knots: 26
Range, miles: 3 500 at 15 knots
Complement: 216

Cost £3·5 million. Helicopter platform aft.
Refitted at Birkenhead, 1973. Suffered a serious fire on return from refit. Further refit completed at Schiedam Oct 1977.

Radar: Type 293/AWS-4.

Sonar: Removed.

NIGERIA

10/1977, Michael D. J. Lennon

CORVETTES

2 Mk 9 VOSPER THORNYCROFT TYPE

Name	No.	Builders	Commissioned
ERIN'MI	—	Vosper Thornycroft Ltd	1978
ENYIMIRI	—	Vosper Thornycroft Ltd	1979

Displacement, tons: 820
Dimensions, feet (metres): 226·3 × 34·4 × 11·8 *(69 × 10·5 × 3·6)*
Missiles: 1 Seacat launcher
Guns: 1—76 mm OTO Melara; 1—40 mm; 2—20 mm
A/S weapons: 1 Bofors rocket launcher
Main engines: 4 MTU 20V 956 TB 92 diesels; 19 740 shp
Speed, knots: 29
Range, miles: 4 100 at 14 knots
Complement: 90 (including flag officer)

Ordered from Vosper Thornycroft 22 April 1975. *Erin'mi* laid down 14 Oct 1975 and launched 20 Jan 1977. *Enyimiri* laid down 11 Feb 1977 and launched 9 Feb 1978.

Radar: Search: Plessey AWS-2.

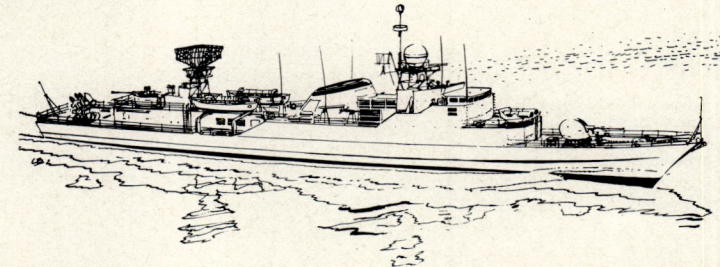

Vosper Thornycroft Mark 9 Corvette

1977, Vosper Thornycroft

NIGERIA 353

2 Mk 3 VOSPER THORNYCROFT TYPE

Name	No.	Builders	Commissioned
DORINA	F 81	Vosper Thornycroft	June 1972
OTOBO	F 82	Vosper Thornycroft	Nov 1972

Displacement, tons: 500 standard; 650 full load
Dimensions, feet (metres): 202 oa × 31 × 11·33 *(61·6 × 9·5 × 3·5)*
Guns: 2—4 in (1 twin) UK Mk 19; 2—40 mm Bofors (single) 2—20 mm
Main engines: 2 MAN diesels; = 23 knots
Range, miles: 3 500 at 14 knots
Complement: 66 (7 officers and 59 ratings)

Ordered on 28 March 1968. *Dorina* laid down 26 Jan 1970, launched 16 Sept 1970, *Otobo* laid down 28 Sept 1970, launched 25 May 1971. Both refitted by Vosper Thornycroft 1975.

Radar: Air search: Plessey AWS-1.
Fire control: HSA M20.
Navigation: Decca TM626.

DORINA   9/1976, Wright and Logan

LIGHT FORCES

0 + 3 LÜRSSEN S-143 CLASS (FAST ATTACK CRAFT—MISSILE)

Displacement, tons: 295 standard; 378 full load
Dimensions, feet (metres): 200 × 24·6 × 8·5 *(57 × 7·8 × 2·4)*
Missiles: 4 launchers for OTOmat
Guns: 2—76 mm
Torpedo tubes: 2—21 in *(533 mm)* aft
Main engines: 4 MTU diesels; 16 000 shp; 4 shafts = 38 knots
Range, miles: 1 300 at 30 knots
Complement: 40

Ordered from Lürssen, Vegesack late 1977. The above data is that of the West German S143 class with a change to OTOmat missiles. It is possible that, as in the following Combattante III class, the after 76 mm may be changed for a 40 mm and the torpedo tubes dispensed with. To carry HSA fire control.

Type 143   *Reinhard Nerlich*

0 + 3 COMBATTANTE IIIB CLASS (FAST ATTACK CRAFT—MISSILE)

Displacement, tons: 385 standard; 425 full load
Dimensions, feet (metres): 184 × 26 × 7 *(56·2 × 8 × 2·1)*
Missiles: 4 launchers for MM 38 Exocet
Guns: 1—76 mm OTO Melara Compact; 1—40 mm Breda; 4—30 mm (twins) Emerlec (bridge)
Main engines: 4 16-cyl MTU diesels; 20 000 shp; 4 shafts = 37 knots
Range, miles: 2 000 at 15 knots
Complement: 42

A 50 million franc order placed with CMN, Cherbourg in late 1977. Thomson CSF fire control. From previous building rates of this yard these craft could be in service in late 1979.

COMBATTANTE III Class (with 2—76 mm)   CMN

4 BROOKE MARINE TYPE (LARGE PATROL CRAFT)

Name	No.	Builders	Commissioned
MAKURDI	P 167	Brooke Marine, Lowestoft	14 Aug 1974
HADEJIA	P 168	Brooke Marine, Lowestoft	14 Aug 1974
JEBBA	P 171	Brooke Marine, Lowestoft	29 April 1977
OGUTA	P 172	Brooke Marine, Lowestoft	29 April 1977

Displacement, tons: 115 standard; 143 full load
Dimensions, feet (metres): 107 × 20 × 11·5 *(32·6 × 6·1 × 3·5)*
Guns: 2—40 mm; 2 Rocket flare launchers
Main engines: 2 Ruston Paxman YJCM diesels; 3 000 bhp; 2 shafts = 20·5 knots
Complement: 21

First pair ordered in 1971. Second pair ordered 30 Oct 1974, laid down 20 Jan 1975. Launch dates—*Hadejia*, 25 May 1974; *Makurdi*, 21 March 1974; *Jebba*, 1 Dec 1976; *Oguta* 17 Jan 1977. Completion dates for second pair 11 Feb 1977 and 18 March 1977 respectively.

HADEJIA   9/1974, C. and S. Taylor

4 Ex-BRITISH "FORD" CLASS (LARGE PATROL CRAFT)

Name	No.	Builders	Commissioned
BENIN (ex-HMS *Hinksford*)	P 03	Richards, Lowestoft	1955
BONNY (ex-HMS *Gifford*)	P 04	Scarr, Hessle	1954
ENUGU	P 05	Camper & Nicholson's, Gosport	14 Dec 1961
SAPELE (ex-HMS *Dubford*)	P 09	J. Samuel White, Cowes	1953

Displacement, tons: 120 standard; 160 full load
Dimensions, feet (metres): 110 pp; 117·2 oa × 20 × 5 *(33·6; 35·7 × 6·1 × 1·5)*
Guns: 1—40 mm Bofors; 2—20 mm Oerlikon
Main engines: Davey Paxman diesels; Foden engine on centre shaft; 1 100 bhp = 18 knots
Complement: 26

Enugu was the first warship built for the Nigerian Navy. Ordered in 1960. Sailed from Portsmouth for Nigeria on 10 April 1962. Fitted with Vosper roll damping fins. *Hinksford* purchased from the United Kingdom on 1 July 1966 and transferred at Devonport on 9 Sept 1966. *Dubford* and *Gifford* were purchased from the United Kingdom during 1967-68.

BENIN   1970, Nigerian Navy

354 NIGERIA

4 ABEKING AND RASMUSSEN TYPE (LARGE PATROL CRAFT)

Name	No.	Builders	Commissioned
ARGUNGU	P 165	Abeking & Rasmussen	Aug 1973
YOLA	P 166	Abeking & Rasmussen	Aug 1973
BRAS	P 169	Abeking & Rasmussen	Mar 1976
EPE	P 170	Abeking & Rasmussen	Mar 1976

Displacement, tons: 90
Dimensions, feet (metres): 95·1 × 18·0 × 5·2 *(29 × 5·5 × 1·6)*
Guns: 1—40 mm Bofors 60 cal in Mk 3 mtg; 1—20 mm
Main engines: 2 Paxman diesels; 2 200 hp; 2 shafts = 20 knots
Complement: 25

Launch dates—*Argungu,* 9 July 1973. *Yola,* 12 June 1973; *Bras,* 12 Jan 1976; *Epe,* 9 Feb 1976.

YOLA   10/1974, Michael D. J. Lennon

SURVEY SHIPS

Name	No.	Builders	Commissioned
LANA	—	Brooke Marine, Lowestoft	Sept 1976

Displacement, tons: 800 standard; 1 100 full load
Dimensions, feet (metres): 189 × 37·5 × 11·2 *(57·8 × 11·4 × 3·5)*
Main engines: 4 diesels; 2 shafts; 3 000 bhp = 16 knots
Range, miles: 4 500 at 12 knots
Complement: 38

Ordered in late 1973, laid down 5 April 1974, launched 4 March 1976. Sister to RN "Bulldog" Class.

LANA   10/1976, Wright and Logan

SERVICE FORCES

1 Ex-BRITISH LCT (4)

LOKOJA (ex-LCT (4) 1213)

Displacement, tons: 350 standard; 586 full load
Dimensions, feet (metres): 187·5 × 38·8 × 4·5 *(57·2 × 11·8 × 1·4)*
Guns: 2—20 mm
Main engines: 2 Paxman diesels; 920 bhp = 10 knots

Purchased from the United Kingdom in 1959. Allocated the name *Lokoja* in 1961. Underwent a major refit in 1966-67, including complete replating of the bottom, but currently in poor condition.

0 + 2 FRENCH LCT

Dimensions, feet (metres): 196·8 × 41·3 × 6 *(60 × 12·6 × 1·8)*
Main engines: 2 diesels; 800 hp = 9 knots

Ordered from La Manche, Dieppe June 1977.

1 TRAINING SHIP

Name	No.	Builders	Commissioned
RUWAN YARO (ex-*Ogina Brereton*)	A 497	Van Lent, Netherlands	1976

Displacement, tons: 400
Dimensions, feet (metres): 144·6 × 26·2 × 12·8 *(44·2 × 8 × 3·9)*
Main engines: 2 Deutz diesels; 3 000 hp = 17 knots
Range, miles: 3 000 at 15 knots
Complement: 42

Originally built in 1975 as a yacht. Used as navigational training vessel. Acquired 1976.

RUWAN YARO   12/1976, Michael D. J. Lennon

TUG

Name	No.	Builders	Commissioned
RIBADU	A 486	Oelkers, Hamburg	19 May 1973

Displacement, tons: 147
Dimensions, feet (metres): 93·5 × 23·6 × 12·1 *(28·5 × 7·2 × 3·7)*
Main engines: Diesel; 800 shp = 12 knots

Fitted for firefighting and salvage work.

POLICE CRAFT

8 VOSPER THORNYCROFT TYPE (COASTAL PATROL CRAFT)

Displacement, tons: 15
Dimensions, feet (metres): 34 oa × 10 × 2·8 *(10·4 × 3·1 × 0·9)*
Gun: 1 machine gun
Main engines: 2 diesels; 290 hp = 19 knots
Complement: 6

Ordered for Nigerian Police March 1971, completed 1971-72. GRP hulls.

NORWAY

Ministerial

Minister of Defence:
  Rolf Hansen

Headquarters Appointments

Inspector General:
  Rear-Admiral C. O. Herlofson
Commander Naval Logistics Services:
  Rear-Admiral N. A. Owren
Commodore Sea Training:
  Commodore Rolf Henningsen
Coast Guard Inspector:
  Commodore N. Tiltnes
Coast Artillery Inspector:
  Commodore R. Eichinger

Diplomatic Representation

Defence Attaché in Bonn:
  Lieutenant Colonel L. Tvilde
Defence Attaché in Helsinki:
  Lieutenant Colonel G. J. Jervaas
Defence Attaché in London:
  Commodore B. Eia
Defence Attaché in Moscow:
  Lieutenant Colonel T. Dypedal
Defence Attaché in Ottawa:
  Lieutenant Colonel O. Ravneberg
Defence Attaché in Stockholm:
  Lieutenant Colonel A. Riegels
Defence Attaché in Vienna:
  Colonel B. Gåsekjølen
Defence Attaché in Washington (for USA and Canada):
  Lieutenant General E. Tufte Johnsen

Training Ship

1974 Haakon VII

Personnel

(a) 1974: 8 400 officers and ratings
    1975: 8 400 officers and ratings
    1976: 8 000 officers and ratings
    1977: 8 400 officers and ratings
    1978: 8 400 officers and ratings
    (All above figures include 1 600 Coast Artillery)
    In 1977 a total of 265 was included in the Coast Guard which is to rise to 273 in 1978 and 364 in 1979.

(b) 15 months national service (5 000)
    12 months national service (Coast Artillery)

Naval Bases

Karl Johans Vern (Horten), Haakonsvern (Bergen), Ramsund (Harstad) and Olavsvern (Tromsø)

Prefix to Ships' Names

KNM; K/V (Coast Guard)

Mercantile Marine

Lloyd's Register of Shipping:
  2 738 vessels of 27 801 471 tons gross

DELETIONS

LCT

1975 Tjeldsund

Minelayers

1976 Gor, Tyr
1978 Brage, Uller

Depot Ship

1977 Valkyrien

Strength of the Fleet

Type	Active	Building
Frigates	5	—
Corvettes	2	—
Submarines—Coastal	15	—
Fast Attack Craft—Missile	27	13
Fast Attack Craft—Torpedo	20	—
Minelayers	3	—
Minesweepers—Coastal	10	—
Minesweepers—Inshore	—	1
LCUs	7	—
Depot Ships	1	1
Tenders	2	—
Royal Yacht	1	—
Research Ship	1	—
Coast Guard Vessels	14	5 (3)

Air Forces

5 Orion Maritime Patrol a/c (Air Force) 10 Seaking helicopters (Air Force SAR).
Note: The Coastguard will have 3 Maritime Patrol a/c and 6 helicopters.

PENNANT LIST

Frigates and Corvettes

F 300	Oslo
F 301	Bergen
F 302	Trondheim
F 303	Stavanger
F 304	Narvik
F 310	Sleipner
F 311	Aeger

Minesweepers

M 311	Sauda
M 312	Sira
M 313	Tana
M 314	Alta
M 315	Ogna
M 316	Vosso
M 317	Glomma
M 331	Tista
M 332	Kvina
M 334	Utla

Minelayers

N 51	Borgen
N 52	Vidar
N 53	Vale

Submarines

S 300	Ula
S 301	Utsira
S 302	Utstein
S 303	Utvaer
S 304	Uthaug
S 305	Sklinna
S 306	Skolpen
S 307	Stadt
S 308	Stord
S 309	Svenner
S 315	Kaura
S 316	Kinn
S 317	Kya
S 318	Kobben
S 319	Kunna

Light Forces

P 340	Vadsø
P 343	Tjeld
P 345	Teist
P 346	Jo
P 347	Lom
P 348	Stegg
P 349	—
P 350	Falk
P 357	Ravn
P 380	Skrei
P 381	Hai
P 382	Sel
P 383	Hval
P 384	Laks
P 385	Knurr
P 386	Delfin
P 387	Lyr
P 388	Gribb
P 389	Geir
P 390	Erle
P 960	Storm
P 961	Blink
P 962	Glimt
P 963	Skjold
P 964	Trygg
P 965	Kjekk
P 966	Djerv
P 967	Skudd
P 968	Arg
P 969	Steil
P 970	Brann
P 971	Tross
P 972	Hvass
P 973	Traust
P 974	Brott
P 975	Odd
P 976	Pil
P 977	Brask
P 978	Rokk
P 979	Gnist
P 980	Snøgg
P 981	Rapp
P 982	Snar

Light Forces

P 983	Rask
P 984	Kvikk
P 985	Kjapp
P 986	Hauk
P 987-999	New Construction

Amphibious Forces

A 4500	Kvalsund
A 4501	Raftsund
A 4502	Reinsöysund
A 4503	Söröysund
A 4504	Maursund
A 4505	Rotsund
A 4506	Borgsund

Service Force

A 533	Norge

Coast Guard

W 300	Nornen
W 301	Farm
W 302	Heimdal
W 303	Andenes
W 304	Senja
W 305	Nordkapp
W 311	Kr. Tønder
W 312	Sørfold
W 313	Møgsterfjord
W 314	Stålbas
W 315	Norviking
W 316	Voldstad Jr.
W 317	Rig Tugger

NORWAY

SUBMARINES

TYPE 210

A design contract for a new class of 750 ton patrol submarines has been placed with IKL (Lübeck). This is being carried out in conjunction with the navy of the Federal Republic of Germany.

15 TYPE 207

Name	No.	Builders	Laid down	Launched	Commissioned
ULA	S 300	Rheinstahl-Nordseewerke, Emden, West Germany	1962	19 Dec 1964	7 May 1965
UTSIRA	S 301	Rheinstahl-Nordseewerke, Emden, West Germany	1963	11 Mar 1965	1 July 1965
UTSTEIN	S 302	Rheinstahl-Nordseewerke, Emden, West Germany	1962	19 May 1965	9 Sept 1965
UTVAER	S 303	Rheinstahl-Nordseewerke, Emden, West Germany	1962	30 June 1965	1 Dec 1965
UTHAUG	S 304	Rheinstahl-Nordseewerke, Emden, West Germany	1962	8 Oct 1965	16 Feb 1966
SKLINNA	S 305	Rheinstahl-Nordseewerke, Emden, West Germany	1963	21 Jan 1966	27 May 1966
SKOLPEN	S 306	Rheinstahl-Nordseewerke, Emden, West Germany	1963	24 Mar 1966	17 Aug 1966
STADT	S 307	Rheinstahl-Nordseewerke, Emden, West Germany	1963	10 June 1966	15 Nov 1966
STORD	S 308	Rheinstahl-Nordseewerke, Emden, West Germany	1964	2 Sept 1966	9 Feb 1967
SVENNER	S 309	Rheinstahl-Nordseewerke, Emden, West Germany	1965	27 Jan 1967	1 July 1967
KAURA	S 315	Rheinstahl-Nordseewerke, Emden, West Germany	1961	16 Oct 1964	5 Feb 1965
KINN	S 316	Rheinstahl-Nordseewerke, Emden, West Germany	1960	30 Nov 1963	8 April 1964
KYA	S 317	Rheinstahl-Nordseewerke, Emden, West Germany	1961	20 Feb 1964	15 June 1964
KOBBEN	S 318	Rheinstahl-Nordseewerke, Emden, West Germany	1961	25 April 1964	17 Aug 1964
KUNNA	S 319	Rheinstahl-Nordseewerke, Emden, West Germany	1961	16 July 1964	1 Oct 1964

Displacement, tons: 370 standard; 435 dived
Length, feet (metres): 149 *(45.2)*
Beam, feet (metres): 15 *(4.6)*
Draught, feet (metres): 14 *(4.3)*
Torpedo tubes: 8—21 in *(533 mm)* (bow)
Main machinery: 2 MB 820 Maybach-Mercedes-Benz (MTU) diesels; 1 200 bhp; electric drive; 1 200 hp; 1 shaft
Speed, knots: 10 surfaced; 17 dived
Complement: 18 (5 officers, 13 men)

It was announced in July 1959 that the United States and Norway would share equally the cost of these submarines. These are a development of IKL Type 205 (West German U4-U8) with increased diving depth. *Svenner* has a second periscope for COs training operations—a metre longer.

Names: *Kobben* was the name of the first submarine in the Royal Norwegian Navy. Commissioned on 28 Nov 1909.

Sonar: Small dome fitted forward.

SVENNER (with second periscope) — 1972, Royal Norwegian Navy

KOBBEN — 1976, Michael D. J. Lennon

FRIGATES

5 "OSLO" CLASS

Name	No.	Builders	Laid down	Launched	Commissioned
OSLO	F 300	Marinens Hovedverft, Horten	1963	17 Jan 1964	29 Jan 1966
BERGEN	F 301	Marinens Hovedverft, Horten	1964	23 Aug 1965	15 June 1967
TRONDHEIM	F 302	Marinens Hovedverft, Horten	1963	4 Sept 1964	2 June 1966
STAVANGER	F 303	Marinens Hovedverft, Horten	1965	4 Feb 1966	1 Dec 1967
NARVIK	F 304	Marinens Hovedverft, Horten	1964	8 Jan 1965	30 Nov 1966

Displacement, tons: 1 450 standard; 1 745 full load
Length, feet (metres): 308 *(93.9)* pp; 317 *(96.6)* oa
Beam, feet (metres): 36.7 *(11.2)*
Draught, feet (metres): 17.4 *(5.3)*
Missiles: 6 Penguin, Octuple Seasparrow
Guns: 4—3 in *(76 mm)* (2 twin mounts US Mk 33)
A/S weapons: Terne system; 6 (2 triple) Mk 32 A/S torpedo tubes
Main engines: 1 set De Laval Ljungstrom double reduction geared turbines; 1 shaft; 20 000 shp
Boilers: 2 Babcock & Wilcox
Speed, knots: 25
Complement: 151 (11 officers, 140 ratings)

Built under the five-year naval construction programme approved by the Norwegian *Storting* (Parliament) late in 1960. Although all the ships of this class were constructed in the Norwegian Naval Dockyard, half the cost was borne by Norway and the other half by the United States. The design of these ships is based on that of the "Dealey" class destroyer escorts in the United States Navy, but considerably modified to suit Norwegian requirements.

Engineering: The main turbines and auxiliary machinery were all built by De Laval Ljungstrom, Sweden at the company's works in Stockholm-Nacka.

STAVANGER — 10/1977, C. and S. Taylor

Radar: Search: DRBV 22.
Tactical and fire control: HSA M 24 system.

Sonar: one Terne III Mk 3; one AN/SQS 36.

NORWAY 357

CORVETTES

2 "SLEIPNER" CLASS

Name	No.	Builders	Laid down	Launched	Commissioned
SLEIPNER	F 310	Nylands Verksted Shipyard	1963	9 Nov 1963	29 April 1965
AEGER	F 311	Akers, Oslo	1964	24 Sept 1965	31 Mar 1967

Displacement, tons: 600 standard; 780 full load
Dimensions, feet (metres): 227·8 oa × 26·2 × 8·2 *(69 × 8 × 2·4)*
Guns: 1—3 in *(76 mm)* (US Mk 34 mount); 1—40 mm
A/S weapons: Terne ASW system; 6 (2 triple) Mk 32 A/S torpedo tubes
Main engines: 4 Maybach (MTU) diesels; 2 shafts; 9 000 bhp = over 20 knots
Complement: 62

Under the five-year programme only two instead of the originally planned five new corvettes were built. Temporarily employed as training ships until new construction is available.

Radar and Fire Control: US Mk 63 GFCS with Mk 34 radar.

Sonar: one Terne III Mk 3; one AN/SQS 36.

AEGER *1977, J. L. M. van der Burg*

1 "VADSØ" CLASS

Name	No.	Builders	Laid down	Launched	Commissioned
VADSØ	P 340	A/S Stord Verft	1950	1951	1951

Displacement, tons: 631
Dimensions, feet (metres): 169·3 × 29·5 × 18 *(51 × 9 × 5·5)*
Gun: 1—40 mm
Main engine: 1 MAK 8M451 diesel
Complement: 20

Built as a whaler and rebuilt in 1976.

VADSØ *1977, Royal Norwegian Navy*

LIGHT FORCES

20 "STORM" CLASS (FAST ATTACK CRAFT—MISSILE)

Name	No.	Builders	Commissioned
STORM	P 960	Bergens MV	1968
BLINK	P 961	Bergens MV	18 Dec 1965
GLIMT	P 962	Bergens MV	1966
SKJOLD	P 963	Westermoen, Mandal	1966
TRYGG	P 964	Bergens MV	1966
KJEKK	P 965	Bergens MV	1966
DJERV	P 966	Westermoen, Mandal	1966
SKUDD	P 967	Bergens MV	1966
ARG	P 968	Bergens MV	1966
STEIL	P 969	Westermoen, Mandal	1967
BRANN	P 970	Bergens MV	1967
TROSS	P 971	Bergens MV	1967
HVASS	P 972	Westermoen, Mandal	1967
TRAUST	P 973	Bergens MV	1967
BROTT	P 974	Bergens MV	1967
ODD	P 975	Westermoen, Mandal	1967
PIL	P 976	Bergens MV	1967
BRASK	P 977	Bergens MV	1967
ROKK	P 978	Westermoen, Mandal	1968
GNIST	P 979	Bergens MV	1968

Displacement, tons: 100 standard; 125 full load
Dimensions, feet (metres): 120·0 oa × 20·5 × 5·0 *(36·5 × 6·2 × 1·5)*
Missile launchers: 6 Penguin
Guns: 1—3 in; 1—40 mm
Main engines: 2 Maybach (MTU) diesels; 2 shafts; 7 200 bhp = 32 knots

TRAUST with 6 Penguins fitted *1971, A/S Kongsbergvappenfabrikk*

The first of 20 (instead of the 23 originally planned) gunboats of a new design built under the five-year programme was *Storm*, launched on 8 Feb 1963, and completed on 31 May 1963, but this prototype was eventually scrapped and replaced by a new series construction boat as the last of the class. The first of the production boats was *Blink*, launched on 28 June 1965 and completed on 18 Dec 1965. The introduction of Penguin surface-to-surface guided missile launchers started in 1970, in addition to originally designed armament.

358 NORWAY

1 + 13 "HAUK" CLASS (FAST ATTACK CRAFT—MISSILE)

Name	No.	Builders	Commissioned
HAUK	P 986	Bergens Mek. Verksteder	17 Aug 1977
—	P 987-999	See notes	—

Displacement, tons: 120 standard; 150 full load
Dimensions, feet (metres): 119·7 oa × 20·3 × 5·5 (36·5 × 6·2 × 1·6)
Missiles: 6 Penguin
Guns: 1—40 mm; 1—20 mm
Torpedo tubes: 4—21 in (533 mm)
Main engines: 2 MTU diesels; 7 000 hp = 34 knots
Range, miles: 440 at 34 knots
Complement: 22

Ordered 12 June 1975—ten from Bergens Mek. Verksteder (Lakeseväg) and four from Westermöen (Alta). Very similar to "Snögg" class with improved fire control. *Hauk* laid down May 1976 and launched 21 Feb 1977.

Control system: Weapon control by MSI-80S developed by Kongsberg Vappenfabrikk.

Missiles: Of a longer-range version developed in collaboration with the Royal Swedish Navy.

HAUK (not fully armed) 1977, Royal Norwegian Navy

6 "SNÖGG" CLASS (FAST ATTACK CRAFT—MISSILE)

Name	No.	Builders	Commissioned
SNÖGG (ex-*Lyr*)	P 980	Batservice, Mandel	1970
RAPP	P 981	Batservice, Mandel	1970
SNAR	P 982	Batservice, Mandel	1970
RASK	P 983	Batservice, Mandel	1971
KVIKK	P 984	Batservice, Mandel	1971
KJAPP	P 985	Batservice, Mandel	1971

Displacement, tons: 100 standard; 125 full load
Dimensions, feet (metres): 120·0 × 20·5 × 5·0 (36·5 × 6·2 × 1·3)
Missile launchers: 4 Penguin
Gun: 1—40 mm
Torpedo tubes: 4—21 in (533 mm)
Main engines: 2 Maybach (MTU) diesels; 2 shafts; 7 200 bhp = 32 knots
Complement: 18

These steel hulled fast attack craft ordered from Batservice Werft, A/S, Mandal, Norway, started coming into service in 1970. Hulls are similar to those of the "Storm" class gunboats.

RAPP 1973, Royal Norwegian Navy

19 "TJELD" CLASS (FAST ATTACK CRAFT—TORPEDO)

Name	No.	Builders	Commissioned
TJELD	P 343	Båtservis, Mandal	June 1960
TEIST	P 345	Båtservis, Mandal	Dec 1960
JO	P 346	Båtservis, Mandal	Feb 1961
LOM	P 347	Båtservis, Mandal	April 1961
STEGG	P 348	Båtservis, Mandal	June 1961
—	P 349	Båtservis, Mandal	Aug 1961
FALK	P 350	Båtservis, Mandal	Sept 1961
RAVN	P 357	Båtservis, Mandal	Dec 1961
SKREI	P 380	Båtservis, Mandal	1962
HAI	P 381	Båtservis, Mandal	July 1964
SEL	P 382	Båtservis, Mandal	May 1963
HVAL	P 383	Båtservis, Mandal	Mar 1964
LAKS	P 384	Båtservis, Mandal	May 1964
KNURR	P 385	Båtservis, Mandal	1966
DELFIN	P 386	Båtservis, Mandal	20 May 1966
LYR	P 387	Båtservis, Mandal	1966
GRIBB	P 388	Båtservis, Mandal	Mar 1962
GEIR	P 389	Båtservis, Mandal	Aug 1962
ERLE	P 390	Båtservis, Mandal	June 1962

Displacement, tons: 70 standard; 82 full load
Dimensions, feet (metres): 80·3 oa × 24·5 × 6·8 (24·5 × 7·5 × 2·1)
Guns: 1—40 mm; 1—20 mm
Torpedo tubes: 4—21 in (533 mm)
Main engines: 2 Napier Deltic Turboblown diesels; 2 shafts; 6 200 bhp = 45 knots
Range, miles: 450 at 40 knots; 600 at 25 knots
Complement: 18

"TJELD" Class 1973, Royal Norwegian Navy

Built of mahogany to Båtservis design, known generally as "Nasty" class.

Transfers: Two to Turkey via West Germany, two to USA and six to Greece.

MINEWARFARE FORCES

2 COASTAL MINELAYERS

Name	No.	Builders	Commissioned
VIDAR	N 52	Mjellem and Karlsen, Bergen	21 Oct 1977
VALE	N 53	Mjellem and Karlsen, Bergen	Jan 1978

Displacement, tons: 1 500 standard; 1 673 full load
Dimensions, feet (metres): 212·6 × 39·4 × 13·1 (64·8 × 12 × 4)
Guns: 2—40 mm (twin)
Main engines: 2 Wichman 7AX diesels; 4 200 bhp; 2 shafts = 15 knots
Complement: 50

Ordered 11 June 1975. Laid down—*Vale*, 1 Feb 1976. *Vidar*, 1 March 1976. Launched—18 March 1977 and 5 Aug 1977 respectively. One to be used for training duties originally carried out by *Haakon VII* and then by *Sleipner* and *Aeger*.

Mines: To carry 320 on three decks with an automatic lift between. Loaded through hatches forward and aft each served by two cranes.

VIDAR 1977, Royal Norwegian Navy

NORWAY 359

1 CONTROLLED MINELAYER

Name	No.	Builders	Commissioned
BORGEN	N 51	Marinens Hovedverft, Horten	1961

Displacement, tons: 282 standard
Dimensions, feet (metres): 102·5 ao × 26·2 × 11 *(31·2 × 8 × 3·4)*
Main engines: 2 GM diesels; 2 Voith-Schneider propellers; 330 bhp = 9 knots

Launched 29 April 1960.

BORGEN 1977, Royal Norwegian Navy

10 Ex-US "FALCON" CLASS (MSC 60) (MINESWEEPERS—COASTAL)

Name	No.	Builders	Commissioned
SAUDA (ex-USS *MSC 102*)	M 311	Hodgeson Bros, Gowdy & Stevens, Maine	25 Aug 1953
SIRA (ex-USS *MSC 132*)	M 312	Hodgeson Bros, Gowdy & Stevens, Maine	28 Nov 1955
TANA (ex-*Roeselaere*, M 914, ex-*MSC 103*)	M 313	Hodgeson Bros, Gowdy & Stevens, Maine	1954
ALTA (ex-*Arlon* M 915, ex-*MSC 104*)	M 314	Hodgeson Bros, Gowdy & Stevens, Maine	1954
OGNA	M 315	Båtservis, Mandal	5 Mar 1955
VOSSO	M 316	Skaaluren Skibsbyggeri, Rosendal	16 Mar 1955
GLOMMA (ex-*Bastogne*, M 916, ex-*MSC 151*)	M 317	Hodgeson Bros, Gowdy & Stevens, Maine	1954
TISTA	M 331	Forende Batbyggeriex, Risör	27 April 1955
KVINA	M 332	Båtservis, Mandal	12 July 1955
UTLA	M 334	Båtservis, Mandal	15 Nov 1955

Displacement, tons: 333 standard; 384 full load
Dimensions, feet (metres): 144 × 28 × 8·5 *(44 × 8·1 × 2·6)*
Guns: 1—0·50 cal MG (2—20 mm in *Tana*)
Main engines: GM diesels; 880 bhp = 13·5 knots
Oil fuel, tons: 25
Complement: 38 (39 in *Tana*)

Hull of wooden construction. Five coastal minesweepers were built in Norway with US engines. *Alta, Glomma* and *Tana* were taken over from the Royal Belgian Navy in May, Sep and March 1966, respectively, having been exchanged for two Norwegian ocean minesweepers of the US MSO type, *Lagen* (ex-*MSO 498*) and *Nansen* (ex-*MSO 499*).

Minehunter: *Tana* converted as a minehunter in 1977.

TISTA 7/1975, J. L. M. van der Burg

TANA 1977, Royal Norwegian Navy

1 SWEDISH "GÄSSTEN" CLASS (MINESWEEPER—INSHORE)

M 70

Displacement, tons: 135 full load
Dimensions, feet (metres): 75·5 × 21·7 × 6·5 *(23 × 6·6 × 2)*
Gun: 1—40 mm
Main engines: Diesels = 11 knots

GRP hull. Ordered from Karlskrona, Sweden to be used in tests and evaluation.

AMPHIBIOUS FORCES

2 "KVALSUND" CLASS (LCT)

Name	No.	Builders	Commissioned
KVALSUND	L 4500	Mjellem & Karlsen, Bergen	1970
RAFTSUNDA	L 4501	Mjellem & Karlsen, Bergen	1970

KVALSUND (old pennant number) 1976, Royal Norwegian Navy

5 "REINØYSUND" CLASS (LCT)

Name	No.	Builders	Commissioned
REINØYSUND	L 4502	Mjellem & Karlsen, Bergen	Jan 1972
SØRØYSUND	L 4503	Mjellem & Karlsen, Bergen	June 1972
MAURSUND	L 4504	Mjellem & Karlsen, Bergen	Sept 1972
ROTSUND	L 4505	Mjellem & Karlsen, Bergen	1973
BORGSUND	L 4506	Mjellem & Karlsen, Bergen	1973

Displacement, tons: 590 ("Reinøysund" class 596)
Dimensions, feet (metres): 167·3 × 33·5 × 5·9 *(50 × 10·2 × 1·8)*
Guns: 2—20 mm (3 in "Reinøysund" class)
Speed, knots: 11

All capable of carrying 7 tanks. Both classes of same dimensions.

360 NORWAY

DEPOT SHIPS

1 NEW CONSTRUCTION

Name	No.	Builders	Commissioned
HORTEN	—	A/S Horten Verft	April 1978

Displacement, tons: 2 500
Dimensions, feet (metres): 285·5 × 42·6 × 23 *(87 × 13 × 7)*
Aircraft: 1 helicopter on deck
Guns: 2—40 mm
Main engines: 2 Wickmann diesels; 2 shafts = 16·5 knots
Complement: 85

Contract signed 30 March 1976. Laid down 28 Jan 1977; launched 12 Aug 1977. Cost approx £8 million. To serve both submarines and fast attack craft. Quarters for 60 extra and can cater for 190 extra.

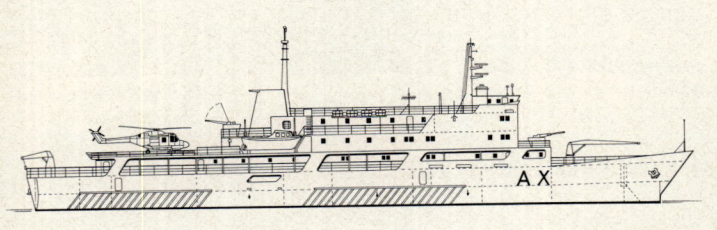

HORTEN   1976, Horten Verft

2 DIVING TENDERS

Name	No.	Builders	Commissioned
DRAUG	—	Nielsen, Harstad	1972
SARPEN	—	Nielsen, Harstad	1972

Small depot ships of 250 tons for frogmen and divers.

SARPEN   1977, Royal Norwegian Navy

ROYAL YACHT

Name	No.	Builders	Commissioned
NORGE (ex-*Philante*)	A 533	Camper & Nicholson's Ltd, Gosport, England	1937

Measurement, tons: 1 686 *(Thames yacht measurement)*
Dimensions, feet (metres): 263 oa × 28 × 15·2 *(80·2 × 8·5 × 4·6)*
Main engines: 8-cyl diesels; 2 shafts; 3 000 bhp = 17 knots

Built to the order of the late Mr. T. O. M. Sopwith as an escort and store vessel for the yachts *Endeavour I* and *Endeavour II*. Launched on 17 Feb 1937. Served in the Royal Navy as an anti-submarine escort during the Second World War, after which she was purchased by the Norwegian people for King Haakon at a cost of nearly £250 000 and reconditioned as a Royal Yacht at Southampton. Can accommodate about 50 people in addition to crew.

NORGE   1971, Royal Norwegian Navy

RESEARCH SHIP

Name	No.	Builders	Commissioned
H. U. SVERDRUP	—	Orens Mekaniske Verkstad, Trondheim	1960

Displacement, tons: 400
Measurement, tons: 295 gross
Dimensions, feet (metres): 127·7 × 25 × 13 *(38·9 × 7·6 × 4)*
Main engines: Wichmann diesel; 600 bhp = 11·5 knots
Oil fuel, tons: 65
Range, miles: 5 000 at 10 knots cruising speed
Complement: 10 crew; 9 scientists

Operates for Norwegian Defence Research Establishment. Trawler hull.

COASTGUARD

Set up in 1976 for combined duties of Fishery Protection and Oil Rig Patrol. The base for this force is still under discussion—Harstad, Sortland and Ramsund have all been mentioned.

Name	No.	Builders	Commissioned
O/S NORNEN	W 300	Mjellem & Karlsen, Bergen	1963

Measurement, tons: 930 gross
Dimensions, feet (metres): 201·8 × 32·8 × 15·8 *(61·5 × 10 × 4·8)*
Gun: 1—3 in *(76 mm)*
Main engines: 4 diesels; 3 500 bhp = 17 knots
Complement: 32

Launched 20 Aug 1962.

NORNEN   1970, Royal Norwegian Navy

Name	No.	Builders	Commissioned
O/S FARM	W 301	Ankerlokken Verft	1962
O/S HEIMDAL	W 302	Bolsones Verft, Molde	1962

Measurement, tons: 600 gross
Dimensions, feet (metres): 177 × 26·2 × 16·5 *(54·3 × 8·2 × 4·9)*
Gun: 1—3 in *(76 mm)*
Main engines: 2 diesels; 2 700 bhp = 16 knots
Complement: 29

Farm launched 22 Feb 1962 and *Heimdal* 7 March 1962.
Possibly not large enough for deepwater patrols to Spitsbergen.

Name	No.	Builders	Commissioned
O/S ANDENES	W 303	Netherlands	1957
O/S SENJA	W 304	Netherlands	1957
O/S NORDKAPP	W 305	Netherlands	1957

Measurement, tons: 500 gross
Dimensions, feet (metres): 186 × 31 × 16 *(56·7 × 9·5 × 4·9)*
Gun: 1—3 in *(76 mm)*
Main engines: MAN diesel; 2 300 bhp = 16 knots
Complement: 29

All three built in 1957 as whalers of varying appearance. Acquired by Norway in 1965 and converted into Fishery Protection Ships.
Possibly not large enough for deepwater patrols to Spitsbergen.

NORDKAPP   1974, Royal Norwegian Navy, Foto FRO

NORWAY / OMAN 361

7 TRAWLER TYPE

Name	No.	Tonnage	Completion
KR. TØNDER	W 311	984	1962
SØRFOLD	W 312	827	1951
MØGSTERFJORD	W 313	762	1975
STÅLBAS	W 314	498	1955
NORVIKING	W 315	1311	1965
VOLSTAD JR.	W 316	598	1950
RIG TUGGER	W 317	497	1973

Chartered in 1977 to fill the gap until completion of new construction patrol vessels.

RIG TUGGER *1977, Royal Norwegian Navy*

VOLDSTAD *1977, Royal Norwegian Navy*

NORVIKING *1977, Royal Norwegian Navy*

0 + 4 + (3) NEW CONSTRUCTION PATROL VESSELS

Displacement, tons: 1940
Dimensions, feet (metres): 231·2 pp × 37·7 × 16 *(70·5 pp × 11·5 × 4·9)*
Aircraft: 1 helicopter (? Sea King)
Guns: 1—76 mm; 4—20 mm (twin and singles)
A/S weapons: Possibly 2 Mk 32 mountings
Main engines: Diesels = 23 knots

Put to tender Nov 1976, the first to commission in 1980. Strengthened for ice, some A/S capacity, mention of (possibly) Penguin missiles. To be fitted for fire-fighting, anti-pollution work, diving (recompression chamber) with two motor cutters and a Gemini-type dinghy. In Nov 1977 the Coastguard Budget was cut from 2 000 million Kroner to 1 400 million resulting in a reduction of the immediate building programme from 7 to 4 ships.

Radar: Possibly DRBV 22.

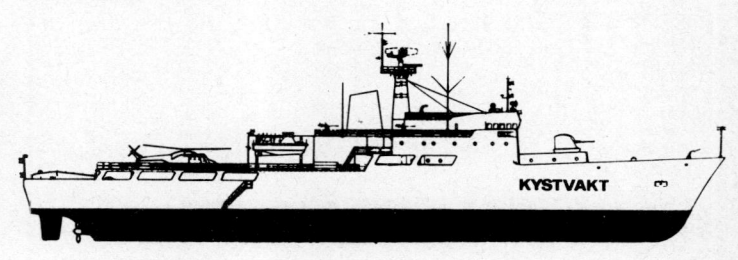

COASTGUARD PATROL VESSEL

1 NEW CONSTRUCTION SUPPORT SHIP

A new class designed to operate deep-diving vehicles capable of operations at 1 600 feet *(500 metres).*

OMAN

Personnel
(a) 1978: 600 officers and men
(b) Voluntary service

Senior Officers
Commander Sultan of Oman's Navy:
 Commodore H. Mucklow
Deputy Commander:
 Commander D. M. Connell

Bases
Qa'Adat Sultan Bin Ahmed Al Bahryya, Muscat (Main base and slipway). Raysut (advanced naval base).

Prefix to Ships' Names
SNV (Sultanate Naval Vessel)

Mercantile Marine
5 vessels of 3 149 tons gross

CORVETTES

Name	No.	Builders	Commissioned
AL SAID	—	Brooke Marine, Lowestoft	1971

Displacement, tons: 900
Dimensions, feet (metres): 203·4 × 35·1 × 9·8 *(62 × 10·7 × 3)*
Gun: 1—40 mm
Main engines: 2 Paxman Ventura 12-cyl diesels; 2 shafts; 2 470 bhp
Complement: 32 + 7 staff + 32 troops

Built by Brooke Marine, Lowestoft. Launched 7 April 1970 as a yacht for the Sultan of Muscat and Oman, she was converted for a dual purpose role with a gun on her forecastle as flagship of the Sultanate Navy. Carried on board is one Fairey Marine Spear patrol craft. Helicopter deck added in last refit.

Radar: Decca TM 626.

AL SAID *1971, Brooke Marine*

362 OMAN

2 Ex-NETHERLANDS "WILDERVANK" CLASS

Name	No.	Builders	Commissioned
AL NASIRI (ex-*Aalsmeer*, M 811)	P 1	Netherlands	1955
AL SALIHI (ex-*Axel*, M 808)	P 2	Netherlands	1955

Displacement, tons: 373 standard; 417 full load
Dimensions, feet (metres): 149·8 oa × 28 × 6·5 *(46·6 × 8·8 × 2)*
Guns: 3—40 mm
Main engines: 2 Werkspoor diesels; 2 500 bhp
Speed, knots: 16
Range, miles: 2 500 at 10 knots
Complement: 38

Acquired in March 1974 and converted for patrol duties at van der Giessen/de Noord in 1974-75.

Radar: Decca TM 916.

AL SALIHI 1976, Omani Dept. of Defence

LIGHT FORCES

7 BROOKE MARINE 37·5 metre TYPE (LARGE PATROL CRAFT)

Name	No.	Builders	Commissioned
AL BUSHRA	B 1	Brooke Marine, Lowestoft	22 Jan 1973
AL MANSUR	B 2	Brooke Marine, Lowestoft	26 Mar 1973
AL NEJAH	B 3	Brooke Marine, Lowestoft	13 May 1973
AL WAFI	B 4	Brooke Marine, Lowestoft	Mar 1977
AL FULK	B 5	Brooke Marine, Lowestoft	24 Mar 1977
AL AUL	B 6	Brooke Marine, Lowestoft	Aug 1977
AL JABBAR	B 7	Brooke Marine, Lowestoft	Aug 1977

Displacement, tons: 135 standard; 153 full load
Dimensions, feet (metres): 123 oa × 22·5 × 5·5 *(37·5 × 6·9 × 1·7)*
Missiles: 2—MM 38 Exocet (see note)
Guns: 2—40 mm (B 1-3); 1—76 mm/62 OTO Melara Compact; 1—20 mm (B 4-7)
Main engines: 2 Paxman Ventura diesels; 4 800 bhp = 29 knots
Range, miles: 3 300 at 15 knots
Complement: 25

First three ordered 5 Jan 1971.
4 more (B 4-7) ordered from Brooke Marine 26 April 1974.

Gunnery: Lawrence-Scott optical director in B 4-7.

Radar: Decca TM 916.

Refits: B 1-3 started refit Nov 1977 by Brooke Marine with addition of twin Exocet with Sea Archer fire control.

AL JABBAR 9/1977, John G. Callis

4 VOSPER THORNYCROFT 75 ft TYPE (COASTAL PATROL CRAFT)

HARAS 1-4

Displacement, tons: 45
Dimensions, feet (metres): 75 × 19·5 × 5 *(22·9 × 6 × 1·5)*
Guns: 2—20 mm
Main engines: 2 Caterpillar diesels; 1 840 hp = 24·5 knots
Range, miles: 600 at 20 knots; 1 000 at 11 knots
Complement: 11

Completed 22 Dec 1975 by Vosper Thornycroft. GRP hulls.

HARAS 4 9/1976, Dr. Giorgio Arra

3 27 ft CHEVERTON TYPE (COASTAL PATROL CRAFT)

W 1   W 2   W 3

Displacement, tons: 3·5
Dimensions, feet (metres): 27 × 9 × 2·8 *(8·2 × 2·7 × 0·8)*
Main engines: Twin diesels = 25 knots

Purchased April 1975.

OMAN 363

AMPHIBIOUS FORCES

1 LOGISTIC SHIP

Displacement, tons: 2 000
Dimensions, feet (metres): 276 × 49 × ? (84·1 × 14·9 × ?)
Gun: 1—76 mm
Main engines: 2 Mirrlees Blackstone diesels; 2 440 bhp

Ordered 1 March 1977 from Brooke Marine Ltd, Lowestoft. Helicopter deck, bow ramp. Full naval command facilities. Capable of carrying tanks, guns and troops. Helicopter deck suitable for large aircraft. Delivery mid-1979.

OMANI LOGISTIC SHIP   1977, Brooke Marine, Ltd

2 60 ft CHEVERTON "LOADMASTERS"

Name	No.	Builders	Commissioned
AL SANSOOR	—	Cheverton's, Cowes	Jan 1975
KINZEER AL BAHR	—	Cheverton's, Cowes	Jan 1975

Measurement, tons: 60 deadweight
Dimensions, feet (metres): 60 oa × 20 × 3·5 (18·3 × 6·1 × 1·1)
Main engines: 2 × 120 hp = 8·5 knots

Delivered Jan 1975.

AL SANSOOR   1975, Roger Smith

1 45 ft CHEVERTON "LOADMASTER"

Name	No.	Builders	Commissioned
SULHAFA AL BAHR	—	Cheverton's, Cowes	1975

Measurement, tons: 45
Dimensions, feet (metres): 45 × 15 × 3 (13·7 × 4·6 × 0·9)
Main engines: Twin Perkins 4 236 = 8·5 knots

MISCELLANEOUS

Name	No.	Builders	Commissioned
AL SULTANA	—	Conoship, Gröningen	4 June 1975

Measurement, tons: 1 380 deadweight
Dimensions, feet (metres): 214·3 oa × 35 × 13·5 (65·4 × 10·7 × 4·2)
Main engines: Mirrlees Blackstone diesel; 1 150 bhp = 11 knots
Complement: 12

Launched 18 May 1975.

1 TRAINING SHIP

DHOFAR

Displacement, tons: 1 500 full load
Dimensions, feet (metres): 219 oa × 34 × 13 (66·8 × 10·4 × 4)
Main engines: MAK diesel; 1 500 bhp = 10·5 knots
Complement: 22

Ex-Logistic ship now used for new entry training.

AL SULTANA   1975, Dick van der Heijde Jnr.

1 CHEVERTON LAUNCH

Of 9 tons, 39 feet and 10 knots—completed April 1975.

DHOFAR   1974, Omani Dept. of Defence

PAKISTAN

Ministerial

Minister of Defence:
General Mohammed Zia ul-Hak (Martial Law Administrator responsible for defence)

Headquarters Appointments

Chief of the Naval Staff:
Admiral M. Shariff HJ

Command Appointment

Commander Pakistan Fleet:
Rear-Admiral K. R. Niazi SJ

Diplomatic Representation

Naval Attaché in London:
Captain I. A. Sirohey
Naval Attaché in Paris:
Captain Y. H. Malik
Naval Attaché in Teheran:
Captain I. A. Sirohey
Naval Attaché in Washington:
Captain M. Saeed

Personnel

(a) 1978: 11 000 (950 officers; 10 050 ratings)
(b) Voluntary service

Naval Base and Dockyard

Karachi

Naval Air Arm

3 Breguet Atlantic BR 1150
6 Sea King helicopters
4 Alouette III helicopters
2 Cessna

Prefix to Ships' Names

PNS

Strength of the Fleet

(No building programme announced)

Type	Active
Cruiser	1
Destroyers	6
Frigate	1
Submarines—Patrol	4
Submarines—40 tons	6
Fast Attack Craft—Gun	12
Fast Attack Craft—Torpedo	4
Large Patrol Craft	3
Minesweepers—Coastal	7
Survey Ship	1
Tankers	2
Tugs—Ocean	2
Tugs—Harbour	2
Water-boat	1
Floating Docks	2

Mercantile Marine

Lloyd's Register of Shipping:
84 vessels of 475 600 tons gross

DELETIONS

Destroyer

1971 *Khaibar* (sunk in Indo-Pakistan War Dec 1971)

Submarine

1971 *Ghazi* (ex-US "Tench" class) (sunk in Indo-Pakistan War 4 Dec 1971)

Frigate

1977 *Tughril*

Large Patrol Craft

1971 *Comilla, Jessore* and *Sylhet* ("Town" class sunk in Indo-Pakistan War Dec 1971)

Minewarfare Forces

1971 *Muhafiz* (ex-US *MSC*) (sunk in Indo-Pakistan War Dec 1971)

PENNANT LIST

Cruiser

C 84	Babur

Destroyers

D 160	Alamgir
D 161	Badr
D 162	Jahangir
D 164	Shah Jahan
D 165	Tariq
D 166	Taimur

Frigate

F 260	Tippu Sultan

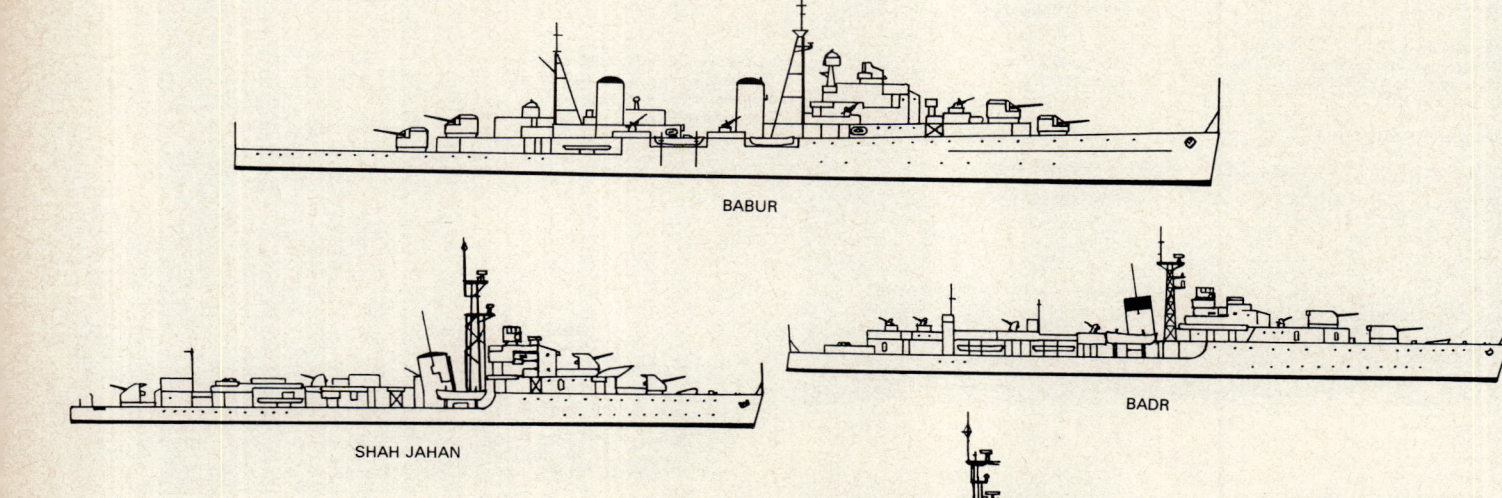

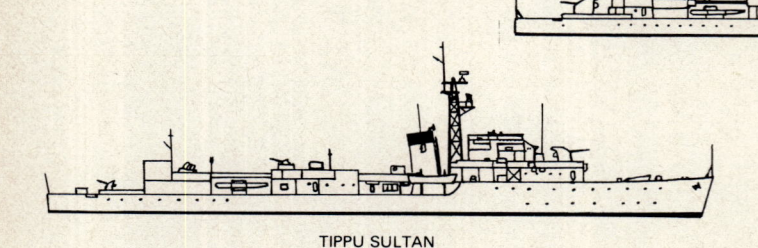

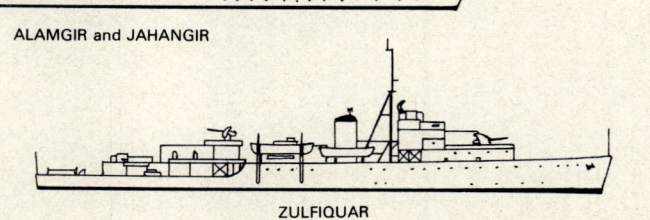

Submarines

S 131	Hangor
S 132	Shushuk
S 133	Mangro
S 134	Ghazi

Minesweepers

M 160	Mahmood
M 161	Momin
M 162	Murabak
M 164	Mujahid
M 165	Mukhtar
M 166	Munsif
M 167	Moshal

Light Forces

HDF 01-04	"Hu Chwan" Class
P 140	Rajshahi
P 141	Quetta
P 142	Lahore
P 143	Mardan
P 144	Gilgit
P 145	Pishin
P 147	Sukkur
P 148	Sehwan
P 149	Bahawalpur
P 154	Bannu
P 155	Baluchistan
P 156	Kalat
P 157	Larkana
P 159	Sind
P 160	Sahiwal

Service Forces

A 40	Attack
A 41	Dacca
A 42	Madadgar
YW 15	Zum Zum

Survey Ship

A 262	Zulfiquar

BABUR

SHAH JAHAN

BADR

ALAMGIR and JAHANGIR

TIPPU SULTAN

ZULFIQUAR

PAKISTAN 365

SUBMARINES

4 FRENCH "DAPHNE" CLASS

Name	No.	Builders	Laid down	Launched	Commissioned
HANGOR	S 131	Arsenal de Brest	1 Dec 1967	28 June 1969	12 Jan 1970
SHUSHUK	S 132	C. N. Ciotat (Le Trait)	1 Dec 1967	30 July 1969	12 Jan 1970
MANGRO	S 133	C. N. Ciotat (Le Trait)	8 July 1968	7 Feb 1970	8 Aug 1970
GHAZI (ex-*Cachalote*)	S 134	Dubigeon, Normandie	12 May 1967	23 Sept 1968	1 Oct 1969

Displacement, tons: 700 standard; 869 surfaced; 1 043 dived
Length, feet (metres): 189·6 *(57·8)*
Beam, feet (metres): 22·3 *(6·8)*
Draught, feet (metres): 15·1 *(4·6)*
Torpedo tubes: 12—21 in *(550 mm)* 8 bow, 4 stern (external)
Main machinery: Diesel-electric; 1 300 bhp (surfaced); electric motors 1 600 hp (dived); 2 shafts
Speed, knots: 13 surfaced; 15·5 dived
Complement: 45

The first three are the first submarines built for the Pakistan Navy. They are basically of the French "Daphne" class design, but slightly modified internally to suit Pakistan requirements and naval conditions. They are broadly similar to the submarines built in France for Portugal and South Africa and the submarines being constructed to the "Daphne" design in Spain.

Transfer: The Portuguese "Daphne" class *Cachalote* was bought by Pakistan in Dec 1975.

MANGRO   *1971, Contre Amiral M. J. Adam*

SHUSHUK   *1972*

6 "SX 404" CLASS

Displacement, tons: 40
Dimensions, feet (metres): 52·4 × 6·6 × — *(16 × 2 × —)*
Speed, knots: 11 surfaced; 6·5 dived
Range, miles: 1 200 surfaced; 60 dived
Complement: 4

Purchased 1972-73 from Cosmos, Livorno. With a diving depth of 330 feet *(100 metres)* and capable of carrying 12 passengers these submarines are valuable craft for clandestine raids, reconnaissance and a multitude of shallow-water tasks.

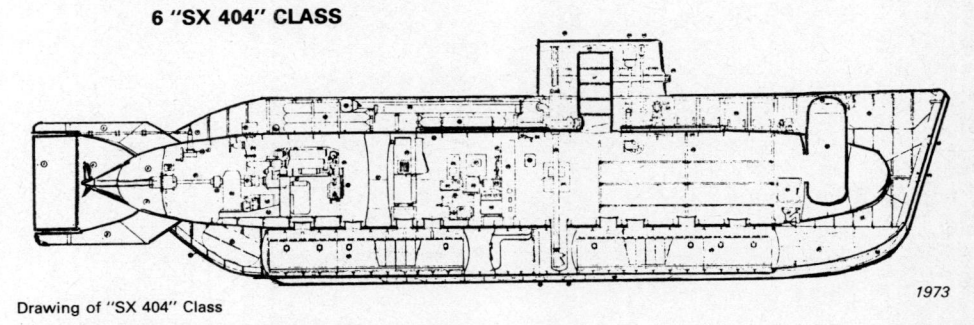

Drawing of "SX 404" Class   *1973*

CRUISER (CADET TRAINING SHIP)

1 Ex-BRITISH "MODIFIED DIDO" CLASS

Name	No.	Builders	Laid down	Launched	Commissioned
BABUR (ex-HMS *Diadem*)	C 84	R. & W. Hawthorn Leslie & Co Ltd, Hebburn-on-Tyne	15 Nov 1939	26 Aug 1942	6 Jan 1944

Displacement, tons: 5 900 standard; 7 560 full load
Length, feet (metres): 485 *(147·9)* pp; 512 *(156·1)* oa
Beam, feet (metres): 52·0 *(15·8)*
Draught, feet (metres): 18·5 *(5·6)*
Guns: 8—5·25 in *(133 mm)* (4 twin); 14—40 mm
Torpedo tubes: 6—21 in *(533 mm)* (2 triple)
Armour: 3 in *(76 mm)* sides; 2 in *(51 mm)* decks and turrets
Main engines: Parsons sr geared turbines; 4 shafts; 62 000 shp
Boilers: 4 Admiralty three-drum
Speed, knots: 20 (after training mods.)
Oil fuel, tons: 1 100
Range, miles: 4 000 at 18 knots
Complement: 588

Purchased on 29 Feb 1956. Refitted at HM Dockyard, Portsmouth and there transferred to Pakistan and renamed *Babur* on 5 July, 1957. Adapted as Cadet Training Ship in 1961.

Radar: Search: Type 960, Type 293.
Fire control: Type 284/285.

BABUR   *1976, Pakistan Navy*

DESTROYERS

2 Ex-US "GEARING" CLASS (FRAM 1)

Name	No.	Builders	Laid down	Launched	Commissioned
TARIQ (ex-USS *Wiltsie*, DD 716)	D 165	Federal SB & DD Co.	13 Mar 1945	31 Aug 1945	12 Jan 1946
TAIMUR (ex-USS *Epperson*, DD 719)	D 166	Todd Pacific Shipyards	20 June 1945	29 Dec 1945	19 Mar 1949

Displacement, tons: 2 425 standard; 3 500 full load
Length, feet (metres): 390·5 *(119)* oa
Beam, feet (metres): 40·9 *(12·4)*
Draught, feet (metres): 19 *(5·8)*
Guns: 4—5 in *(127 mm)* 38 cal (twins)
A/S weapons: 6 (2 triple) Mk 32 A/S torpedo tubes; facilities for small helicopter
Main engines: 2 geared turbines; 60 000 shp; 2 shafts
Boilers: 4 Babcock & Wilcox
Speed, knots: 30
Complement: 274

Transfer by purchase 29 April 1977. Reactivated and overhauled in USA during 1977. Arrival Pakistan mid 1978.

Radar: SPS 10 and 40.
Sonar: SQS 23.

TARIQ (as *Wiltsie*)   *1975, USN*

366 PAKISTAN

1 Ex-BRITISH "BATTLE" CLASS

Name	No.	Builders	Laid down	Launched	Commissioned
BADR (ex-HMS *Gabbard*, D 47)	D 161	Swan, Hunter & Wigham Richardson Ltd, Wallsend-on-Tyne	2 Feb 1944	16 Mar 1945	10 Dec 1946

Displacement, tons: 2 325 standard; 3 361 full load
Length, feet (metres): 355·0 *(108·2)* pp; 379·0 *(115·5)* oa
Beam, feet (metres): 40·2 *(12·3)*
Draught, feet (metres): 17·0 *(5·2)*
Guns: 4—4·5 in *(115 mm)*; 7—40 mm (2 twin; 3 single)
A/S weapons: Squid triple DC mortar
Torpedo tubes: 8—21 in *(533 mm)* (quadrupled)
Main engines: Parsons geared turbines; 2 shafts; 50 000 shp
Boilers: 2 Admiralty three-drum type
Speed, knots: 35·75
Oil fuel, tons: 680
Range, miles: 6 000 at 20 knots
Complement: 270

Purchased from Britain on 29 Feb 1956. Modernised with US funds under MDAP. Refitted at Palmers Hebburn, Yarrow, transferred to Pakistan on 24 Jan 1957 and sailed from Portsmouth for Karachi on 17 Feb 1957.

Radar: Search: Type 293. One Marconi set.
Fire Control: Type 275.

BADR
1977, Pakistan Navy

1 Ex-BRITISH "CH" CLASS

Name	No.	Builders	Laid down	Launched	Commissioned
SHAH JAHAN (ex-HMS *Charity*, D 29)	D 164	John I. Thornycroft Co Ltd, Woolston	9 July 1943	30 Nov 1944	19 Nov 1945

Displacement, tons: 1 710 standard; 2 545 full load
Length, feet (metres): 350·0 *(106·7)* wl; 362·7 *(110·5)* oa
Beam, feet (metres): 35·7 *(10·9)*
Draught, feet (metres): 17·0 *(5·2)*
Guns: 3—4·5 in *(115 mm)*; 6—40 mm
A/S weapons: 2 Squid triple DC mortars
Torpedo tubes: 4—21 in *(533 mm)* (quadrupled)
Main engines: Parsons geared turbines; 2 shafts; 40 000 shp
Boilers: 2 Admiralty three-drum type
Speed, knots: 36·75
Range, miles: 5 600 at 20 knots
Complement: 200

Purchased by USA and handed over to Pakistan on 16 Dec 1958, under MDAP, at yard of J. Samuel White & Co Ltd, Cowes, who refitted her. Sister ship *Taimur* (ex-HMS *Chivalrous*) was returned to the Royal Navy and scrapped in 1960-61.

Radar: Search: Type 293.
Fire control: Type 275.

SHAH JAHAN
1972, Pakistan Navy

2 Ex-BRITISH "CR" CLASS

Name	No.	Builders	Laid down	Launched	Commissioned
ALAMGIR (ex-HMS *Creole*, D 82)	D 160	J. Samuel White & Co Ltd, Cowes	3 Aug 1944	22 Nov 1945	14 Oct 1946
JAHANGIR (ex-HMS *Crispin*, ex-*Craccher*, D 168)	D 162	J. Samuel White & Co Ltd, Cowes	1 Feb 1944	23 June 1945	10 July 1946

Displacement, tons: 1 730 standard; 2 560 full load
Length, feet (metres): 350·0 *(106·7)* wl; 362·8 *(110·5)* oa
Beam, feet (metres): 35·7 *(10·9)*
Draught, feet (metres): 17·0 *(5·2)*
Guns: 3—4·5 in *(115 mm)*; 6—40 mm
A/S weapons: 2 Squid triple DC mortars
Torpedo tubes: 4—21 in *(533 mm)* (quadrupled)
Main engines: Parsons geared turbines; 2 shafts 40 000 shp
Boilers: 2 Admiralty three-drum type
Speed, knots: 36·75
Oil fuel, tons: 580
Range, miles: 5 600 at 20 knots
Complement: 200

Purchased by Pakistan in Feb 1956. Refitted and modernised in the United Kingdom by John I. Thornycroft & Co Ltd, Woolston, Southampton, in 1957-58 with US funds under MDAP. Turned over to the Pakistan Navy at Southampton in 1958 (*Crispin* on 18 March and *Creole* 20 June) and renamed.

Radar: Search: Type 293.
Fire control: Type 275.

Sonar: Types 170, 174.

JAHANGIR
1977, Pakistan Navy

FRIGATES

1 Ex-BRITISH TYPE 16

Name	No.	Builders	Laid down	Launched	Commissioned
TIPPU SULTAN (ex-HMS *Onslow*, ex-*Pakenham*, F 249)	F 260	John Brown & Co Ltd, Clydebank	1 July 1940	31 Mar 1941	8 Oct 1941

Displacement, tons: 1 800 standard; 2 300 full load
Length, feet (metres): 328·7 *(100·2)* pp; 345·0 *(107·2)* oa
Beam, feet (metres): 35·0 *(10·7)*
Draught, feet (metres): 15·7 *(4·8)*
Guns: 2—4 in *(102 mm)*; 5—40 mm
A/S weapons: 2 Squid triple DC mortars
Torpedo tubes: 4—21 in *(533 mm)*
Main engines: Parsons geared turbines; 2 shafts; 40 000 shp
Boilers: 2 Admiralty three-drum type
Speed, knots: 34
Complement: 170

Originally three "O" class destroyers were acquired from the United Kingdom, *Tippu Sultan* being handed over on 30 Sept 1949; *Tariq* on 3 Nov 1949; and *Tughril* on 6 March 1951. An agreement was signed in London between the United Kingdom and USA for refit and conversion in the United Kingdom of *Tippu Sultan* and *Tughril* (announced 29 April 1957) with US funds. All three ships were scheduled for conversion into fast anti-submarine frigates. *Tippu Sultan* and *Tughril* were converted at Liverpool by Grayson Rolls & Clover Docks Ltd, Birkenhead, and C. & H. Crighton Ltd, respectively. *Tariq* disposed of 1959 and *Tughril* in 1977.

Radar: Search: Type 293.

TIPPU SULTAN *1977, Pakistan Navy*

LIGHT FORCES

2 + 3 Ex-CHINESE "HAI NAN" CLASS (LARGE PATROL CRAFT)

BALUCHISTAN P 155   **SIND** P 159   + 3

Displacement, tons: 360 standard; 400 full load
Dimensions, feet (metres): 197 × 24 × 6·1 *(60 × 7·4 × 2·1)*
Guns: 2—3 in; 4—25 mm (twins)
A/S weapons: 4—MBU 1 800; 2 DCT; 2 DC Racks
Mines: Rails fitted
Main engines: Diesels; 8 000 shp
Speed, knots: 28
Range, miles: 1 000 at 10 knots
Complement: 60

First pair transferred mid 1976. Three more for delivery 1978.

Radar: Pot Head

BALUCHISTAN (old pennant number) *1976*

12 Ex-CHINESE "SHANGHAI II" CLASS (FAST ATTACK CRAFT—GUN)

QUETTA P 141	PISHIN P 145	BANNU P 154
LAHORE P 142	SUKKUR P 147	KALAT P 156
MARDAN P 143	SEHWAN P 148	LARKANA P 157
GILGIT P 144	BAHAWALPUR P 149	SAHIWAL P 160

Displacement, tons: 120 standard; 155 full load
Dimensions, feet (metres): 128 × 18 × 5·6 *(39·1 × 5·5 × 1·7)*
Guns: 4—37 mm (twin); 4—25 mm (twin)
Mines: Fitted with minerails for approx 10 mines
Main engines: 4 diesels; 3 000 bhp = 27 knots
Complement: 25

Transferred early 1972 (first eight) next four in 1974.

Radar: Pot Head.

"SHANGHAI" II Class *1977, Pakistan Navy*

4 Ex-CHINESE "HU CHWAN" CLASS
(FAST ATTACK HYDROFOIL—TORPEDO)

HDF 01, 02, 03, 04

Displacement, tons: 45
Dimensions, feet (metres): 70 × 16·5 × 3·1 *(21·4 × 5·0 × 0·9)*
Torpedo tubes: 2—21 in *(533 mm)*
Guns: 4—14·5 mm (twins)
Main engines: 2—12-cyl diesels; 2 shafts; 2 200 hp = 55 knots (calm)

Hydrofoil craft transferred by China in 1973.

PAKISTAN "HU CHWAN" Class *1973, Pakistan Navy*

368 PAKISTAN

1 "TOWN" CLASS (LARGE PATROL CRAFT)

Name	No.	Builders	Commissioned
RAJSHAHI	P 140	Brooke Marine	1965

Displacement, tons: 115 standard; 143 full load
Dimensions, feet (metres): 107 oa × 20 × 11 (32·6 × 6·1 × 3·4)
Guns: 2—40 mm; 70 cal Bofors
Main engines: 2 MTU 12V 538 diesels; 3 400 bhp = 24 knots
Complement: 19

The last survivor of a class of four built by Brooke Marine in 1965 (see "Deletions"). Steel hull and aluminium superstructure.

RAJSHAHI   1973, Pakistan Navy

78 ft COASTAL PATROL CRAFT

Several building by Halter Marine—New Orleans, USA.

MINE WARFARE FORCES

Note: Last year's report of two ex-US "Aggressive" class MSOs being transferred was wrong—the transfer was cancelled as the ships proved unfit for further service.

7 US MSC TYPE (MINESWEEPERS—COASTAL)

MAHMOOD (ex-*MSC 267*) M 160
MOMIN (ex-*MSC 293*) M 161
MURABAK (ex-*MSC 262*) M 162
MUJAHID (ex-*MSC 261*) M 164
MUKHTAR (ex-*MSC 274*) M 165
MUNSIF (ex-*MSC 273*) M 166
MOSHAL (ex-*MSC 294*) M 167

Displacement, tons: 335 light; 375 full load
Dimensions, feet (metres): 144 oa × 27 × 8·5 (43·9 × 8·2 × 2·6)
Guns: 2—20 mm
Main engines: GM diesels; 2 shafts; 880 bhp = 14 knots
Complement: 39

Transferred to Pakistan by the US under MAP. *Mukhtar* and *Munsif* on 25 June 1959, *Mujahid* in Nov 1956, *Mahmood* in May 1957, *Murabak* in 1957, *Momin* in Aug 1962 and *Moshal* on 13 July 1963.

MUNSIF   1972, Pakistan Navy

SURVEY SHIP

Name	No.	Builders	Commissioned
ZULFIQUAR (ex-*Dhanush*, ex-*Deveron* F 265)	A 262	Smith's Dock Co Ltd, South Bank-on-Tees	2 Mar 1943

Displacement, tons: 1 370 standard; 2 100 full load
Dimensions, feet (metres): 301·5 oa × 36·7 × 12·5 (91·9 × 11·2 × 3·8)
Guns: 1—4 in (102 mm); 2—40 mm
Main engines: Triple expansion; 5 500 ihp
Boilers: 2 Admiralty three-drum type
Speed, knots: 20
Range, miles: 6 000 at 12 knots
Complement: 150

Former British frigate of the "River" class converted into a survey ship, additional charthouse aft. She has strengthened davits and carries survey motor boats. The after 4-in gun was removed.

TANKERS

1 Ex-US "MISSION" CLASS

DACCA (ex-USNS *Mission Santa Cruz*, AO 132) A 41

Displacement, tons: 5 730 light; 22 380 full load
Dimensions, feet (metres): 523·5 oa × 68 × 30·9 (159·7 × 20·7 × 9·4)
Guns: 3—40 mm
Main engines: Turbo-electric; 6 000 shp = 15 knots
Boilers: 2 Babcock & Wilcox
Oil capacity: 20 000 tons
Complement: 160 (15 officers and 145 men)

Transferred on loan to Pakistan under MDAP. Handed over from the US on 17 Jan 1963. Purchased 31 May 1974.

DACCA

1 Ex-US YO TYPE

Name	No.	Builders	Commissioned
ATTOCK (ex-USS *YO 249*)	A 40	Trieste	1960

Displacement, tons: 600 standard; 1 255 full load
Dimensions, feet (metres): 177·2 oa × 32 × 15 (54 × 9·8 × 4·6)
Main engines: Direct coupled diesel; speed 8·5 knots
Complement: 26

A harbour oiler of 6 500 barrels capacity built for the Pakistan Navy. Transferred under the Mutual Defence Assistance Programme of USA.

MISCELLANEOUS

RESCUE SHIP

1 Ex-US "CHEROKEE" CLASS

Name	No.	Builders	Commissioned
MADADGAR (ex-USS Yuma, ATF 94)	A 42	Commercial Iron Works, Portland, Oregon	31 Aug 1943

Displacement, tons: 1 235 standard; 1 675 full load
Dimensions, feet (metres): 205 oa × 38·5 × 15·3 (62·5 × 11·7 × 4·7)
Main engines: 4 GM diesels; electric drive; 1 shaft; 3 000 bhp = 16·5 knots
Complement: 85

Ocean-going salvage tug. Laid down on 13 Feb 1943. Launched on 17 July 1943. Transferred from the US Navy to the Pakistan Navy on 25 March 1959 under MDAP. Fitted with powerful pumps and other salvage equipment.

MADADGAR 1976

TUGS

RUSTOM

Dimensions, feet (metres): 105 × 30 × 11 (32 × 9·1 × 3·3)
Main engines: Crossley diesel; 1 000 bhp = 9·5 knots
Range, miles: 3 000 at economic speed
Complement: 21

General purpose tug for the Pakistan Navy originally ordered from Werf-Zeeland at Hansweert, Netherlands, in Aug 1952, but after the liquidation of this yard the order was transferred to Worst & Dutmer at Meppel. Launched on 29 Nov 1955.

Name	No.	Builders	Commissioned
GAMA (ex-US YTL 754)	—	Costaguta-Voltz	Sept 1958
BHOLU (ex-US YTL 755)	—	Costaguta-Voltz	Sept 1958

Small harbour tugs built under an "off-shore" order.

AUXILIARIES

1 WATER CARRIER

ZUM ZUM YW 15

Built in Italy under MDA programme.

2 FLOATING DOCKS

PESHAWAR (ex-US ARD 6)

Transferred June 1961. 3 000 tons lift.

FD II

Built 1974. 1 200 tons lift.

PANAMA

Personnel

A Coastguard service split between both coasts.

(a) 1978: approx 300
(b) Voluntary service

Mercantile Marine

Lloyd's Register of Shipping:
3 267 ships of 19 458 419 tons gross

2 VOSPER TYPE (LARGE PATROL CRAFT)

Name	No.	Builders	Commissioned
PANQUIACO	GC 10	Vospers, Porchester, Portsmouth	Mar 1971
LIGIA ELENA	GC 11	Vospers, Porchester, Portsmouth	Mar 1971

Displacement, tons: 96 standard; 123 full load
Dimensions, feet (metres): 90·5 wl; 103·0 oa × 18·9 × 5·8 (30; 31·4 × 5·8 × 1·8)
Guns: 2—20 mm
Main engines: 2 Paxman Ventura 12-cyl diesels; 2 800 bhp = 24 knots
Complement: 23

Hull of welded mild steel and upperworks of welded or buck-bolted aluminium alloy. Vosper fin stabiliser equipment. *Panquiaco* was launched on 22 July 1970 and *Ligia Elena* on 25 Aug 1970.

2 Ex-US 63 ft AVR CLASS (COASTAL PATROL CRAFT)

Name	No.	Builders	Commissioned
AYANASI	GC 12	USA	1943
ZARTI	GC 13	USA	1943

Displacement, tons: 35
Dimensions, feet (metres): 63·3 × 15·3 × 3·3 (19·3 × 4·7 × 1)
Guns: 2—12·7 mm MGs
Main engines: 2 GM 8V-71 diesels; 2 shafts = 22·5 knots
Complement: 8

Transferred to Panama 1965 (*Ayanasi*) and 1966. Wooden hulls with glass-fibre sheathing.

Radar: Raytheon 1500B.

2 Ex-USCG 40 ft UTILITY TYPE (COASTAL PATROL CRAFT)

Name	No.	Builders	Commissioned
MARTI	GC 14	USA	1950
JUPITER	GC 15	USA	1950

Displacement, tons: 13
Dimensions, feet (metres): 40·3 × 11·2 × 3·3 (12·3 × 3·4 × 1)
Gun: 1—12·7 mm MG
Main engines: 2 GM 6-71 diesels = 18 knots
Range, miles: 160 at 18 knots
Complement: 4

Transferred under MAP in 1962. Steel hulled Mk 1 Type. No radar—magnetic compass only.

370 PANAMA / PAPUA NEW GUINEA

AMPHIBIOUS FORCES

1 Ex-US MODIFIED "ELK RIVER" CLASS

TIBURON (ex-USS *Smokey Hill River*) GN 9

Displacement, tons: 944 standard; 1 084 full load
Dimensions, feet (metres): 206·2 × 34·5 × 10 *(67·6 × 11·3 × 3·3)*
Guns: 1—5 in *(127 mm)*; 2—40 mm; 4—20 mm
Main engines: 2 GM diesels; 2 800 bhp = 12 knots
Complement: 140

Purchased 14 March 1975 from commercial sources. Armament may be removed. With a door cut in the bow she is used for logistic support. Originally a USN LSM Type completed as a rocket support ship with no bow doors—probably in 1945.

3 Ex-US "LCM 8" CLASS

GN 1, 2 and 3

Displacement, tons: 118 full load
Dimensions, feet (metres): 73·5 × 21 × 5·2 *(22·4 × 6·4 × 1·6)*
Main engines: 4 GM 6-71 diesels; 2 shafts = 10 knots
Complement: 6

Used for patrol and logistic duties with wheelhouse replaced by two deckhouses giving increased berthing thereby extending endurance. Unarmed. Transferred 1972.

MISCELLANEOUS

1 Ex-US YF-852 CLASS

— (ex-*YF 886*)

Displacement, tons: 590 full load
Dimensions, feet (metres): 132·9 × 29·9 × 8·9 *(40·5 × 9·1 × 2·7)*
Main engines: 2 GM diesels = 11 knots
Complement: 11

Built by Defoe SB Co in 1945. Acquired May 1975. Logistic support ship.

1 65 ft TRAWLER

— GN 8

Existence doubtful.

1 65 ft SHRIMP BOAT

Bought in 1976. Steel hulled. Single diesel = 11 knots. Can carry 150 troops on short hauls.

PAPUA NEW GUINEA

The Australian base at Manus in the Admiralty Islands, HMAS *Tarangau*, was de-commissioned on 14 Nov 1974 and handed over to the PNG Defence Force. It is now the PNGDF Patrol Boat Base Lombrun. The following ships were handed over to the PNGDF by the RAN.

Senior Officer
Brigadier E. R. Diro OBE (Commander PNGDF)

Bases
Port Moresby (HQ PNGDF); Lombrun.

Mercantile Marine
Lloyd's Register of Shipping:
64 ships of 16 217 tons gross

LIGHT FORCES

5 "ATTACK" CLASS (LARGE PATROL CRAFT)

Name	No.	Builders	Commissioned
AITAPE	84	Walkers Ltd, Maryborough	13 Nov 1967
SAMARAI	85	Evans Deakin & Co, Queensland	1 Mar 1968
LADAVA	92	Walkers Ltd, Maryborough	21 Oct 1968
LAE	93	Evans Deakin & Co, Queensland	3 April 1968
MADANG	94	Evans Deakin & Co, Queensland	28 Nov 1968

Displacement, tons: 146 full load
Dimensions, feet (metres): 107·5 × 20 × 7·3 *(32·8 × 6·1 × 2·2)*
Guns: 1—40 mm; 2 MG
Main engines: 2 Paxman 16 YJCM diesels; 2 shafts; 3 500 bhp = 24 knots
Complement: 18

Steel hulls with aluminium superstructure. Can lay mines.

LAE   1976, PNGDF

AMPHIBIOUS FORCES

2 LANDING CRAFT (LCH)

Name	No.	Builders	Commissioned
SALAMAUA	131	Walkers Ltd, Maryborough	1973
BUNA	132	Walkers Ltd, Maryborough	1973

Displacement, tons: 310 light; 503 full load
Dimensions, feet (metres): 146 × 33 × 6·5 *(44·5 × 10·1 × 1·9)*
Guns: 2—0·5 in MG
Main engines: 2 V12 GM diesels; twin screw = 10 knots
Complement: 13

BUNA   1974, John Mortimer

PARAGUAY

Ministerial

Minister of National Defence:
Major Gen. Marcial Samaniego

Personnel

1978: 1 900 officers and men including coastguard and 500 marines

Base

Asunciòn/Puerto Sajonia (main base, dockyard with one dry dock, one floating dock and one slipway)

Naval Air Arm (Escuadron de Caza de la Armada)

4 H-13 Sioux helicopters
2 North American T-6 (Trainers)
4 Cessna U-206
2 Cessna 150M

General

Accepting the fact that river water keeps circulating systems cleaner than does sea-water, thus extending machinery life, the age of some of these ships must be causing concern. On the whole their hulls have not had the wearing effect of wave-action but forty-seven years is a long time for any ship to be running. A replacement programme must be fairly close ahead.

Strength of the Fleet

2 River Defence Vessels
3 Corvettes
1 Large Patrol Craft
8 Coastal Patrol Craft
2 Tugs
1 Tender
1 Training Ship
2 LCUs
1 Floating Dock
7 Service Craft

Mercantile Marine

Lloyd's Register of Shipping:
26 vessels of 21 930 tons gross

RIVER DEFENCE VESSELS

2 "HUMAITA" CLASS

Name	No.	Builders	Commissioned
PARAGUAY (ex-Commodor Meza)	C 1	Odero, Genoa	May 1931
HUMAITA (ex-Capitan Cabral)	C 2	Odero, Genoa	May 1931

Displacement, tons: 636 standard; 865 full load
Dimensions, feet (metres): 231 × 35 × 5·3 (70 × 10·7 × 1·7)
Guns: 4—4·7 in; 3—3 in; 2—40 mm
Mines: 6
Armour: 0·5 in side amidships; 0·3 in deck; 0·8 in CT
Main engines: Parsons geared turbines; 2 shafts; 3 800 shp = 17 knots
Boilers: 2
Oil fuel, tons: 150
Range, miles: 1 700 at 16 knots
Complement: 86

PARAGUAY
1974, A. J. English

CORVETTES

3 "BOUCHARD" CLASS

Name	No.	Builders	Commissioned
NANAWA (ex-Bouchard M 7)	M 1	Rio Santiago Naval Yard	1937
CAPITAN MEZA (ex-Parker M 11)	M 2	Sanchez Shipyard, San Fernando	1938
TENIENTE FARINA (ex-Py M 10)	M 3	Rio Santiago Naval Yard	1939

Displacement, tons: 450 standard; 620 normal; 650 full load
Dimensions, feet (metres): 197 oa × 24 × 8·5 (60 × 7·3 × 2·6)
Guns: 4—40 mm Bofors; 2 MG
Main engines: 2 sets MAN 2-cycle diesels; 2 000 bhp = 16 knots
Oil fuel, tons: 50
Range, miles: 6 000 at 12 knots
Complement: 70

Former Argentinian minesweepers of the "Bouchard" class.
Launched on 20 March 1936, 2 May 1937, 30 March 1938. Can carry mines.
Transferred from the Argentinian Navy to the Paraguayan Navy; Capitan Meza, 1964; Teniente Farina, 1967; Nanawa, 1964.

Deletion: Hernandez (ex-Seaver M 12) was transferred in 1967 but is believed to have been deleted. She was launched 18 Aug 1938 by Hansen and Puccini, San Fernando.

NANAWA
11/1975, A. J. English

LIGHT FORCES

1 LARGE PATROL CRAFT

Name	No.	Builders	Commissioned
CAPITAN CABRAL (ex-Adolfo Riquelme)	A 1	Werf-Conrad, Haarlem	1908

Displacement, tons: 180 standard; 206 full load
Dimensions, feet (metres): 107·2 oa × 23·5 × 9·8 (32·7 × 7·2 × 3)
Guns: 1—3 in Vickers; 2—37 mm Vickers; 4 MG
Main engines: Triple expansion; 1 shaft; 300 ihp = 9 knots
Complement: 47

Former tug. Launched in 1907. Of wooden construction.

2 CG TYPE (COASTAL PATROL CRAFT)

P1 (ex-USCGC 20417)   P2 (ex-USCGC 20418)

Displacement, tons: 16
Dimensions, feet (metres): 45·5 oa × 13·5 × 3·5 (13·9 × 4·1 × 1·1)
Guns: 2—20 mm
Main engines: 2 petrol motors; 2 shafts; 190 hp = 20 knots
Complement: 10

Cf wooden construction. Built in the United States in 1944. Acquired from the United States Coast Guard in 1944. Existence now doubtful.

6 "701" CLASS (COASTAL PATROL CRAFT)

P 101   102   103   104   105   106

Patrol craft of 40 feet and 10 tons with 2—20 mm guns transferred by USA—two in Dec 1967, three in Sept 1970 and one in March 1971.

"701" Class
11/1975, A. J. English

372 PARAGUAY / PERU

TENDER
Ex-US LSM-1 CLASS (CONVERTED)

Name	No.	Builders	Commissioned
TENIENTE PRATTS GIL (ex-Argentine Corrientes, ex-US LSM 86)	PH 1	Brown SB Co, Houston	13 Oct 1944

Displacement, tons: 1 095
Guns: 4—40 mm
Speed, knots: 13

Transferred as a gift from Argentina 13 Jan 1972. Light Forces Tender with helicopter deck added aft. Officially classified as "helicopter-carrier" but whether she can carry one or two helicopters is not known—two might be a crowd.

TUGS
2 Ex-US YTL TYPE

Name	No.	Builders	Commissioned
— (ex-US YTL 211)	R 5	Everett Pacific SB & DD Co, Wash	1945
— (ex-US YTL 567)	R 11	Everett Pacific SB & DD Co, Wash	1945

Displacement, tons: 82 full load
Dimensions, feet (metres): 66·2 × 17 × 8·5 (20·2 × 5·2 × 2·6)
Main engine: 1 diesel; 300 bhp
Complement: 5

Small harbour tugs transferred to Paraguay by the USA under the Military Aid Programme in March 1967 (YTL 211) and April 1974 (YTL 567). By sale both on 11 Feb 1977.

AUXILIARIES
1 TRANSPORT/TRAINING SHIP

Name	No.	Builders	Commissioned
GUARANI	—	Tomas Ruiz de Valasco, Bilbao	Feb. 1968

Measurement, tons: 714 gross; 1 030 dw
Dimensions, feet (metres): 215 × 36 × 12 (65·6 × 11·9 × 3·7)
Main engines: Diesel; 1 300 hp = 13 knots

Repaired and refitted 1974 by Ast Olaveaja, Spain. Used occasionally for commercial purposes.

1 FLOATING DOCK

DF 1 (Ex-US AFDL 26)

Built 1944, leased June 1965. Purchased 11 Feb 1977. Lift 1 000 tons.

MISCELLANEOUS

1 FLOATING WORKSHOP
— (Ex-US YR 37)

Built in 1942. Transferred March 1963 and by sale 11 Feb 1977. No engines.

1 DREDGER
TENIENTE O CARRERAS SAGUIER

1 RIVER TRANSPORT
PTE. STROESNER T 1

4 STORE CARRIERS
No details available.

2 Ex-US LCU—501 CLASS

BT 1 (ex-US YFB 82)   BT 2 (ex-US YFB 86)

Built in 1945 and converted in 1960.
Leased by US in June 1970 and by sale 11 Feb 1977. Used as ferries.

PERU

Headquarters Appointments

Minister of Marine and Chief of Naval Operations:
Vice-Admiral Jorge Parodi Galliani
Chief of Naval Staff:
Vice-Admiral Guillermo Villa Pazos

Command

Commander-in-Chief of the Fleet:
Rear-Admiral Juan Egúsquiza Babilonia

Diplomatic Representation

Naval Attaché in London and Paris:
Rear-Admiral J. F. B. Egusquiza
Naval Attaché in Washington:
Vice-Admiral Rafael Durán Rey

Personnel

(a) 1978: 14 000 (1 200 officers, 12 800 men) (including Naval Air Arm and 1 000 marines)
(b) 2 years national service

Bases

Callao—Main naval base; dockyard with ship-building capacity, 1 dry dock, 2 floating docks, 1 floating crane; training schools.
Iquitos—River base for Amazon flotilla; small building yard, repair facilities, floating dock.
La Punta (naval academy), San Lorenzo (submarine base), Talara, Puno (Lake Titicaca)

Naval Air Arm

6 SH-3D Seakings (for *Aguirre*)
6 Bell AB 212 (on order for "Lupos")
2 Fokker 27 FPA MP aircraft (on order for mid/1977)
2 Alouette III helicopters
10 Bell 206 Jetrangers
2 Bell 47G
20 Bell UH-1D/H
9 Grumman S-2 (ASW)
6 Douglas C-47 (Transport)
1 Piper Aztec C (Liaison)
2 Beech T-34 Mentor (Training)

Following operated in maritime role by Peruvian Air Force.
4 Grumman HU-16B Albatros (ASW/SAR)

Marines

There is one battalion of 1 000 men, additionally armed with MOWAG amphibious vehicles (twin Oerlikon), 81 mm rocket launchers and armoured cars.

Coast Guard

A separate service set up in 1975 with a number of light forces transferred from the navy.

Prefix to Ships' Names

BAP (Baque Armada Peruana)

DELETIONS

Transports
Sept 1972 Callao
1973 Rimac (transferred to mercantile use on bare boat charter)

Strength of the Fleet

Type	Active	Building (Planned)
Aircraft Carriers	—	(4)
Cruisers	4	—
Destroyers	4	—
Frigates	3	3
Submarines—Patrol	8	4
Fast Attack Craft (Missile)	—	6
River Patrol Craft	3	—
Coastal Patrol Craft	4	—
Lake Patrol Craft	4	—
River Gunboats	5	—
Landing Ships	4	—
Transports	2	—
Tankers	7	1
Survey Vessels	4	1
Floating Docks	3	—
Tugs	5	—
Water Carriers	3	—
Floating Workshop	1	—
Hospital Craft	4	—

Coast Guard

Corvettes	2	—
Large Patrol Craft	14	—

Mercantile Marine

Lloyd's Register of Shipping:
681 vessels of 525 137 tons gross

Frigate
1974 Aguirre (target for Exocet tests)

Minewarfare Forces
1974 Bondy, San Martin (ex-YMS)

Amphibious Forces
1975 3 LCUs, 10 LCAs

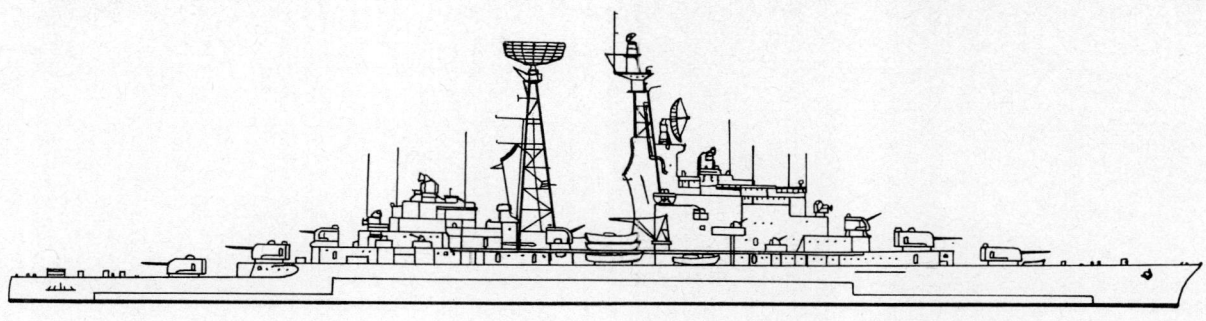

ALMIRANTE GRAU

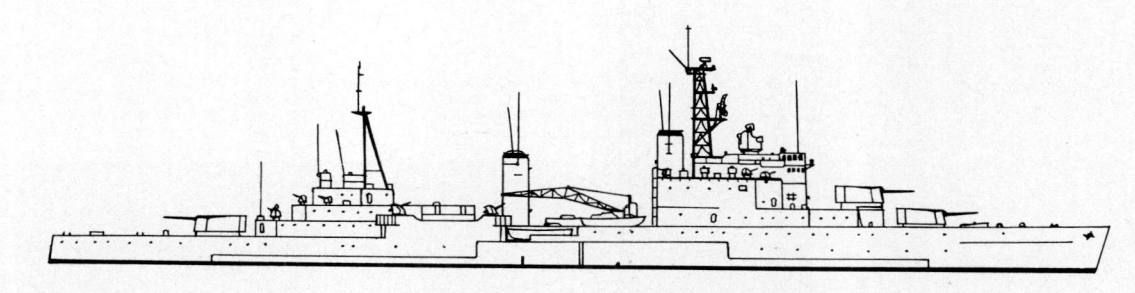

CORONEL BOLOGNESI *(Capitan Quiñones differs)*

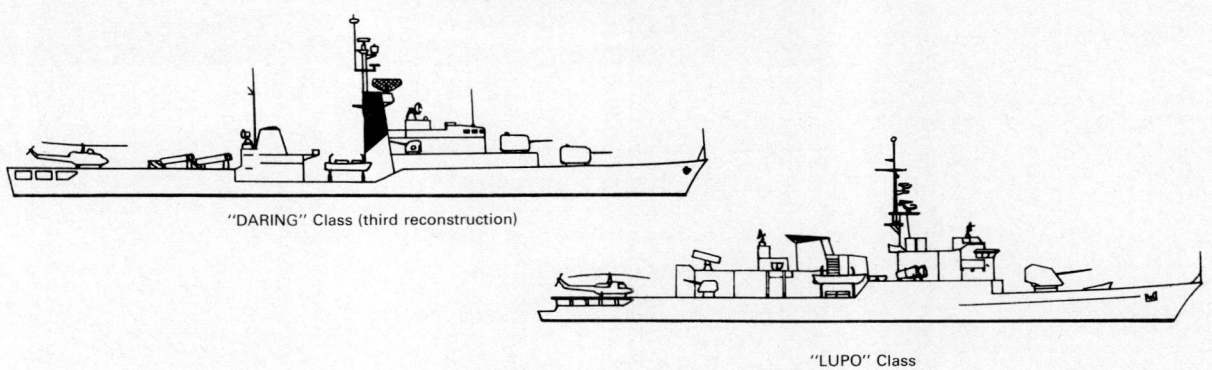

"DARING" Class (third reconstruction)

"LUPO" Class

SUBMARINES

2 + 2 + 2 TYPE 209

Name	No.	Builders	Laid down	Launched	Commissioned
ISLAY	S 45	Howaldtswerke, Kiel	1971	1973	28 Aug 1974
ARICA	S 46	Howaldtswerke, Kiel	1972	17 April 1974	21 Jan 1975
—	S 47	Howaldtswerke, Kiel	—	—	—
—	S 48	Howaldtswerke, Kiel	—	—	—

Displacement, tons: 990 surfaced; 1 290 dived
Length, feet (metres): 177·1 *(54·0)*
Beam, feet (metres): 20·3 *(6·2)*
Torpedo tubes: 8—21 in (with reloads)
Main machinery: Diesel-electric; 4 MTU Siemens diesel-generators; 1 Siemens electric motor; 1 shaft
Speed, knots: 10 surfaced; 22 dived
Range: 50 days
Complement: 31

Designed by Ingenieurkontor, Lübeck for construction by Howaldtswerke, Kiel and sale by Ferrostaal Essen all acting as a consortium.
A single-hull design with two ballast tanks and forward and after trim tanks. Fitted with snort and remote machinery control. The single screw is slow revving, very high capacity batteries with GRP lead-acid cells and battery cooling—by Wilh. Hagen and VARTTA. Active and passive sonar, sonar detection equipment, sound ranging gear and underwater telephone. Fitted with two periscopes, radar and Omega reciever. Fore-planes retract.
Islay ran trials in June 1974.
Two further boats ordered 12 Aug 1976 and two more ordered in March 1977.

ISLAY   1975, Peruvian Navy

374 PERU

2 Ex-US "GUPPY 1A" CLASS

Name	No.	Builders	Laid down	Launched	Commissioned
LA PEDRERA (ex-*Pabellon de Pica*, ex-USS *Sea Poacher* SS 406)	S 49	Portsmouth Navy Yard	23 Feb 1944	20 May 1944	31 July 1944
PACOCHA (ex-USS *Atule* SS 403)	S 50	Portsmouth Navy Yard	2 Dec 1943	6 Mar 1944	21 June 1944

Displacement, tons: 1 870 standard; 2 440 dived
Dimensions, feet (metres): 308 oa × 27 × 17 (93·8 × 8·2 × 5·2)
Torpedo tubes: 10—21 in; 6 forward 4 aft
Main machinery: 3 diesels; 4 800 hp; 2 electric motors; 5 400 shp; 2 shafts
Speed, knots: 18 surfaced; 15 dived
Complement: 85

Modernised under the 1951 Guppy programme. Purchased by Peru—*La Pedrera* on 1 July 1974, *Pacocha* on 31 July 1974. The name of *La Pedrera* was changed a fortnight after purchase. Both became operational in 1975 after refit. Ex-USS *Tench* (SS 417) purchased for spares 16 Sept 1976.

LA PEDRERA (as *Sea Poacher*)   1966, Dr. Giorgio Arra

4 "ABTAO" CLASS

Name	No.	Builders	Laid down	Launched	Commissioned
DOS DE MAYO (ex-*Lobo*)	S 41	General Dynamics (Electric Boat), Groton, Connecticut	12 May 1952	6 Feb 1954	14 June 1954
ABTAO (ex-*Tiburon*)	S 42	General Dynamics (Electric Boat), Groton, Connecticut	12 May 1952	27 Oct 1953	20 Feb 1954
ANGAMOS (ex-*Atun*)	S 43	General Dynamics (Electric Boat), Groton, Connecticut	27 Oct 1955	5 Feb 1957	1 July 1957
IQUIQUE (ex-*Merlin*)	S 44	General Dynamics (Electric Boat), Groton, Connecticut	27 Oct 1955	5 Feb 1957	1 Oct 1957

Displacement, tons: 825 standard; 1 400 dived
Length, feet (metres): 243 (74·1) oa
Beam, feet (metres): 22 (6·7)
Draught, feet (metres): 14 (4·3)
Guns: 1—5 in (127 mm) 25 cal (*Abtao* and *Dos de Mayo*)
Torpedo tubes: 6—21 in (533 mm); 4 bow, 2 stern
Main machinery: 2 GM 278A diesels; 2 400 bhp; electric motors; 2 shafts
Speed, knots: 16 surfaced, 10 dived
Oil fuel, tons: 45
Range, miles: 5 000 at 10 knots (surfaced)
Complement: 40

They are of modified US "Mackerel" class. Refitted at Groton as follows—*Dos de Mayo* and *Abtao* in 1965, other pair in 1968.

IQUIQUE   1975, Peruvian Navy

AIRCRAFT CARRIERS

Note: The following is from a highly respected source but unconfirmed from official sources.

4 NEW CONSTRUCTION

Displacement, tons: 12 500 full load
Dimensions, feet (metres): 574·2 × 98·5 × — (175 × 30 × —)
Missiles: Otomat; 3 eight-cell launchers for PDMS
Guns: 8 (twins) Breda/Bofors 40/70
A/S weapons: 6 (2 triple) torpedo tubes
Rocket launchers: 105 mm Breda-ELSAG 20 barrelled launchers

Two to be built by Cantieri Navali Riuniti and two by SIMA Callao.

Radar: Search: SMA RAN-3L and RAN-10S.
Tracking: Selenia RTN-10X.
Tactical: SMA SPQ-2D.

CRUISERS

2 Ex-NETHERLANDS "DE RUYTER" CLASS

Name	No.	Builders	Laid down	Launched	Commissioned
ALMIRANTE GRAU (ex-KMS *De Ruyter*)	CL 81 (ex-83)	Wilton-Fijenoord, Schiedam	5 Sept 1939	24 Dec 1944	18 Nov 1953
AGUIRRE (ex-KMS *De Zeven Provincien*)	CL 84	Rotterdamse Droogdok Maatschappij	19 May 1939	22 Aug 1950	17 Dec 1953

Displacement, tons: 9 529 standard; 12 165 full load (*Grau*); 9 850 and 12 250 (*Aguirre*)
Dimensions, feet (metres): 609 × 56·7 × 22 (185·6 × 17·3 × 6·7)
Aircraft: 3 helicopters (*Aguirre*)
Missiles: 4 MM 38 Exocet (*Aguirre*)
Guns: 8—6 in (twin turrets); 8—57 mm (twins); 8—40 mm (*Grau*); 4—6 in (twin turrets); 6—57 mm (twins); 4—40 mm (*Aguirre*)
Main engines: 2 De Schelde-Parsons geared turbines; 85 000 shp; 2 shafts
Boilers: 4 Werkspoor-Yarrow
Speed, knots: 32
Complement: 953 (49 officers, 904 ratings)

Almirante Grau transferred by purchase 7 March 1973 and *Aguirre* bought Aug 1976.
Almirante Grau commissioned in Peruvian Navy 23 May 1973 and sailed for Peru 18 June 1973.

Aircraft: 3 Seakings to be carried aboard *Aguirre* with 3 ashore. Hangar measures 67 × 54 ft and the flight deck 115 × 56 ft.

Reconstruction: After sale *Aguirre* was taken in hand by her original builders for conversion to a helicopter cruiser. The Terrier missile system has been returned to USA and a helicopter flight deck has been built from midships to the stern. Conversion completed 31 Oct 1977.

Radar: Search: LW-01 (*Grau*); LW-02 (*Aguirre*)
Heightfinder: SGR 104.
Tactical: DA 02.
Fire control: HSA M25 for 6 in guns and M45 for secondary battery.
Navigation: ZW-03.

AGUIRRE   10/1977, Dhr J. van der Woude

ALMIRANTE GRAU   1973, Peruvian Navy

2 Ex-BRITISH "CEYLON" CLASS

Name	No.
CORONEL BOLOGNESI (ex-HMS Ceylon)	CL 82
CAPITAN QUIÑONES	CL 83
(ex-Almirante Grau, ex-HMS Newfoundland)	

Builders	Laid down	Launched	Commissioned
Alexander Stephen & Sons Ltd, Govan, Glasgow	27 April 1939	30 July 1942	13 July 1943
Swan, Hunter & Wigham Richardson Ltd, Wallsend-on-Tyne	9 Nov 1939	19 Dec 1941	31 Dec 1942

Displacement, tons:
 Capitan Quiñones: 8 800 standard; 11 090 full load
 Col. Bolognesi: 8 781 standard; 11 110 full load
Length, feet (metres): 538 *(164.0)* pp; 549 *(167.4)* wl; 555.5 *(169.3)* oa
Beam, feet (metres): 63.6 *(19.4)*
Draught, feet (metres): 20.5 *(6.2)*
Guns: 9—6 in *(152 mm)* (triple turrets); 8—4 in (4 twin)
 12—40 mm *Capitan Quiñones*
 18—40 mm *Col. Bolognesi*
Armour: 4 in *(102 mm)* sides and CT; 2 in *(51 mm)* turrets and deck
Main engines: Parsons sr geared turbines; 72 500 shp; 4 shafts
Boilers: 4 Admiralty three-drum; 400 psi *(28 km/cm²)*; 720°F *(382°C)*
Speed, knots: 31.5
Oil fuel, tons: 1 620
Range, miles: 6 000 at 13 knots; 2 800 at full power
Complement: Capitan Quiñones: 743; Col. Bolognesi: 766

83 was transferred as *Almirante Grau* in Dec 1959, being renamed *Capitan Quiñones* on 15 May 1973. 82 was transferred as *Coronel Bolognesi* on 9 Feb 1960.

Radar: Search: Types 960, 277 and 293.
Fire control: E band surface, I band AA.

Reconstruction: 83 was reconstructed in 1951-53 at HM Dockyard, Devonport, with two lattice masts, new bridge and improved AA armaments, her torpedo tubes being removed. 82 was modified in 1955-56 with lattice foremast and covered bridge, her torpedo tubes being removed.

CORONEL BOLOGNESI   1975, Peruvian Navy

CAPITAN QUIÑONES   1975, Peruvian Navy

DESTROYERS

2 Ex-BRITISH "DARING" CLASS

Name	No.
PALACIOS (ex-HMS Diana)	DD 73
FERRÉ (ex-HMS Decoy)	DD 74

Builders	Laid down	Launched	Commissioned
Yarrow Co Ltd, Scotstoun	3 April 1947	8 May 1952	29 Mar 1954
Yarrow Co Ltd, Scotstoun	22 Sept 1946	29 Mar 1949	28 April 1953

Displacement, tons: 2 800 standard; 3 600 full load
Length, feet (metres): 366 *(111.7)* pp; 375 *(114.3)* wl; 390 *(118.9)* oa
Beam, feet (metres): 43 *(13.1)*
Draught, feet (metres): 18 *(5.5)*
Missiles: 8 MM 38 Exocet launchers abaft after funnel
Guns: 4—4.5 in *(115 mm);* (2 twin forward); 4—40 mm (twins)
Main engines: English Electric dr geared turbines; 2 shafts
Boilers: 2 Forster Wheeler; Pressure 650 psi *(45.7 kg/cm²)*; Superheat 850°F *(454°C)*
Oil fuel, tons: 580
Speed, knots: 34
Range, miles: 3 000 at 20 knots
Complement: 297

Purchased by Peru in 1969 and refitted by Cammel Laird (Ship Repairers) Ltd, Birkenhead, for further service.

Reconstruction: The first major reconstruction was carried out in 1970-73. The main points of this refit were the reconstructed and enclosed foremast carrying Plessey AWS-1 radar and the Exocet launcher positions in place of the Close Range Blind Fire Director forward of X Turret.
Commissioned after refit—*Palacios* Feb 1973. *Ferré* April 1973.

FERRÉ (after first reconstruction)   1975, Michael D. J. Lennon

The next major change took place 1975-76 when the Squid was removed to make way for a helicopter landing deck.
The third reconstruction was in 1977-78 when X-turret was removed to allow for a larger helicopter deck. The 2—40 mm guns were replaced by 2 twin 40 mm Breda-Bofors L70 Compact. The bridge was enclosed, the after funnel remodelled and new fire control system fitted. A drawing of this reconstruction is at the head of this section.
Radar: Fire control; TSF on fore-funnel.
Search; Plessey AWS-1.

PALACIOS (after second reconstruction)   1975, Dr. Robert L. Scheina

376 PERU

2 Ex-US "FLETCHER" CLASS

Name	No.	Builders	Laid down	Launched	Commissioned
VILLAR (ex-USS *Benham*, DD 796)	DD 71	Bethlehem Steel Co, Staten Island	Jan 1943	29 Aug 1943	20 Dec 1943
GUISE (ex-USS *Isherwood*, DD 520)	DD 72	Bethlehem Steel Co, Staten Island	12 May 1942	24 Nov 1942	10 April 1943

Displacement, tons: 2 120 standard; 2 715 normal; 3 050 full load
Length, feet (metres): 360·2 *(109·8)* pp; 370 *(112·8)* wl; 376·2 *(114·7)* oa
Beam, feet (metres): 39·7 *(12·1)*
Draught, feet (metres): 18 *(5·5)*
Guns: 4—5 in *(127 mm)* 38 cal; (5—5 in *Guise*); 6—3 in *(76 mm)* 50 cal (3 twin)
A/S weapons: 2 fixed Hedgehogs; 2 side-racks for A/S torpedoes
Torpedo tubes: 5—21 in *(533 mm)* (quintuple)
Main engines: 2 GE impulse reaction geared turbines; 60 000 shp; 2 shafts
Boilers: 4 Babcock & Wilcox; 600 psi *(42 kg/cm²)*; 850°F *(455°C)*
Speed, knots: 34
Oil fuel, tons: 650
Range, miles: 5 000 at 15 knots; 900 at full power
Complement: 245 (15 officers and 230 men)

Former United States destroyers of the later "Fletcher" class (*Villar*) and "Fletcher" class (*Guise*).
Two other "Fletcher" class, ex-USS *La Vallette* (DD 448) and *Terry* (DD 513) were transferred for spares in July 1974.

Helicopter: A helicopter deck without hangar or fuelling facilities was fitted on the quarter-deck in 1975-76.

Radar: Search: SPS 6, SPS 10.
Fire control: GFCS 68 system forward, GFCS 56 system aft.

Transfer: Transferred from the United States Navy to the Peruvian Navy at Boston, Massachusetts, on 8 Oct 1961, and at San Diego, California, on 15 Dec 1960 respectively.

VILLAR Note helo deck on fantail (GUISE same) *1975, USN*

FRIGATES

Note: It is reported that two "Maestrale" ("Improved Lupo") Class have been ordered from CNR.

1 + 3 ITALIAN "MODIFIED LUPO" CLASS

Name	No.	Builders	Laid down	Launched	Commissioned
MELITON CARVAJAL	51	CNR Riva Trigoso	8 Aug 1974	17 Nov 1976	1978
MANUEL VILLAVICENCIO	—	CNR Riva Trigoso	Nov 1975	—	1979
—	—	SIM Callao	Nov 1975	—	1979
—	—	SIM Callao			—

Displacement, tons: 2 208 standard; 2 500 full load
Dimensions, feet (metres): 347·7 × 39·5 × 12 *(106 × 12 × 3·7)*
Aircraft: 1 helicopter
Missiles: 2 Otomat twin-missile launchers; 1 Octuple Albatros (Aspide missiles) launcher for Point Defence
Guns: 1—127 mm OTO Melara; 4 (2 twin) Breda 40 mm L70 Compact
Rocket launchers: 2—105 mm Breda ELSAG multi-purpose 20-barrelled launchers
A/S weapons: 6 (2 triple) Mk 32 A/S torpedo tubes (port and starboard)
Main engines: CODOG with 2 GE Fiat LM 2500 gas turbines; 50 000 hp; 2 Fiat 20-cyl A 230 diesels; 7 800 hp
Speed, knots: 35

The second pair are being built at Servicio Industrial de la Marina at Callao with technical assistance from CNR. The design is similar to the "Lupo" class of Italy with a major modification in the inclusion of an A/S helicopter and fixed hangar at the expense of four surface-to-surface missiles and a reload capability for the Albatros PDMS.

"MODIFIED LUPO" Class *1975, Peruvian Navy*

2 Ex-US "CANNON" CLASS

Name	No.	Builders	Laid down	Launched	Commissioned
CASTILLA (ex-USS *Bangust*, DE 739)	DE 61	Western Pipe & Steel Co, San Pedro, California	Jan 1943	6 June 1943	30 Oct 1943
RODRIQUEZ (ex-USS *Weaver*, DE 741)	DE 63	Western Pipe & Steel Co, San Pedro, California	Jan 1943	20 June 1943	30 Nov 1943

Displacement, tons: 1 240 standard; 1 900 full load
Dimensions, feet (metres): 306 oa × 36·9 × 14·1 *(93·3 × 11·2 × 4·3)*
Guns: 3—3 in *(76 mm)* 50 cal; 6—40 mm (3 twin); 10—20 mm
A/S weapons: 1 Mk 10 Hedgehog; 8 K mortars; 2 DC racks aft
Main engines: 4 GM diesel-electric sets 6 000 hp; 2 shafts
Speed, knots: 21
Range, miles: 10 500 at 12 knots
Complement: 172 (12 officers and 160 men)

Transferred to Peru on 26 Oct 1951, under the Mutual Defence Assistance Programme. Reconditioned and modernised at Green Cove Springs and Jacksonville, Florida. Arrived in Peru on 24 May 1952.
Castilla now used as a training ship on the Amazon with home port Iquitos and *Rodriquez* as submarine accommodation ship.

RODRIQUEZ *1975, Peruvian Navy*

PERU 377

LIGHT FORCES

0 + 6 PR-72P CLASS (FAST ATTACK CRAFT—MISSILE)

Displacement, tons: 465 standard; 536 full load
Dimensions, feet (metres): 188·8 × 25 × 8·4 (57·5 × 7·6 × 2·5)
Missiles: 4—MM 38 Exocet
Guns: 1—76/62 mm OTO Melara; 2—40/70 Breda/Bofors; 2—20 mm Oerlikon
Main engines: 4 SACM AGO 240V16 diesels; 20 000 shp; 4 shafts = 37 knots
Range, miles: 700 at 30 knots; 2 000 at 16 knots
Complement: 45

Ordered late 1976 from SFCN, France.

Radar: Search: Thomson-CSF Triton.
Fire control: Thomson-CSF Vega/Pollux.
Navigation: Decca.

2 "MARAÑON" CLASS (RIVER GUNBOATS)

Name	No.	Builders	Commissioned
MARAÑON	CF 13	John I. Thornycroft & Co Ltd	July 1951
UCAYALI	CF 14	John I. Thornycroft & Co Ltd	June 1951

Displacement, tons: 365 full load
Dimensions, feet (metres): 154·8 wl × 32 × 4 (47·2 × 9·7 × 1·2)
Guns: 2—3 in 50 cal; 1—40 mm; 4—20 mm (twins)
Main engines: British Polar M 441 diesels; 800 bhp = 12 knots
Range, miles: 6 000 at 10 knots
Complement: 40

Ordered early in 1950 and both laid down in early 1951. Employed on police duties in Upper Amazon. Superstructure of aluminium alloy. Based at Iquitos.

UCAYALI   1975, Peruvian Navy

2 "LORETO" CLASS (RIVER GUNBOATS)

Name	No.	Builders	Commissioned
AMAZONAS	CF 11	Electric Boat Co, Groton	1935
LORETO	CF 12	Electric Boat Co, Groton	1935

Displacement, tons: 250 standard
Dimensions, feet (metres): 145 × 22 × 4 (44·2 × 6·7 × 1·2)
Guns: 2—3 in; 2—40 mm; 2—20 mm
Main engines: Diesel; 750 bhp = 15 knots
Range, miles: 4 000 at 10 knots
Complement: 35

Launched in 1934. In upper Amazon flotilla.

LORETO   1973, Peruvian Navy

1 RIVER GUNBOAT

Name	No.	Builders	Commissioned
AMERICA	CF 15	Tranmere Bay Development Co Ltd, Birkenhead	1904

Displacement, tons: 240
Dimensions, feet (metres): 133 × 19·5 × 4·5 (40·6 × 5·9 × 1·4)
Guns: 2—40 mm; 4—20 mm
Main engines: Triple expansion; 350 ihp = 14 knots
Complement: 26

Built of steel. Converted from coal to oil fuel burning. In the Upper Amazon Flotilla. The river gunboat *Iquitos* was discarded in 1967 and after 92 years service.

AMERICA   1975, Peruvian Navy

3 RIVER PATROL CRAFT

Name	No.	Builders	Commissioned
RIO ZARUMILLA	PL 250 (ex-*01*)	Viareggio, Italy	5 Sept 1960
RIO TUMBES	PL 251 (ex-*02*)	Viareggio, Italy	5 Sept 1960
RIO PIURA	PL 252 (ex-*04*)	Viareggio, Italy	5 Sept 1960

Displacement, tons: 37 full load
Dimensions, feet (metres): 65·7 × 17 × 3·2 (20 × 5·2 × 1)
Guns: 2—40 mm
Main engines: 2 GM diesels; 2 shafts; 1 200 bhp = 18 knots

Ordered in 1959 as a class of four laid down on 15 July 1959. Stationed at El Salto on Ecuadorian border.

RIO PIURA   1975, Peruvian Navy

378 PERU

4 COASTAL PATROL CRAFT

LA PUNTA PL 230 RÍO SANTA PL 232
RÍO CHILLÓN PL 231 RÍO MAJES PL 233

Of 16 tons with light MGs. Complement 4.

4 LAKE PATROL CRAFT

RÍO RAMIS PL 290 RÍO ILLAVE PL 291

Of 12 tons with light MGs. Complement 4.

RÍO COATA PL 292 RÍO HUANCANÉ PL 293

Of 10 tons with light MGs. Complement 4. All stationed on Lake Titicaca.

Patrol craft on Lake Titicaca *1973, Peruvian Navy*

AMPHIBIOUS FORCES

1 Ex-US "LST 1" CLASS

Name	No.	Builders	Commissioned
CHIMBOTE (ex-M/S *Rawhiti*, ex-US *LST 283*)	34	American Bridge Co, Ambridge, Penn	18 Nov 1943

Displacement, tons: 1 625 standard; 4 050 full load
Dimensions, feet (metres): 328 oa × 50 × 14·1 *(100 × 15·3 × 4·3)*
Gun: 1—3 in
Main engines: GM diesels; 2 shafts; 1 700 bhp = 10 knots
Oil fuel, tons: 600 oil tanks; 1 100 ballast tanks
Range, miles: 9 500 at 9 knots
Complement: Accommodation for 16 officers and 130 men

Laid down on 2 Aug 1943, launched on 10 Oct 1943. Sold to Peru by a British firm in March 1947. Served commercially until 1951 when she was transferred to the Peruvian Navy.

1 Ex-US "LST 511" CLASS

Name	No.	Builders	Commissioned
PAITA (ex-USS *Burnett County*, LST 512)	35 (ex-*AT 4*)	Chicago Bridge & Iron Co	8 Jan 1944

Displacement, tons: 1 653 standard; 4 080 full load
Dimensions, feet (metres): 328 oa × 50 × 14·5 *(100 × 15·3 × 4·4)*
Guns: 6—20 mm
Main engines: GM diesels; 2 shafts; 1 700 bhp = 10 knots
Range, miles: 9 500 at 9 knots
Complement: 13 officers, 106 men

Laid down on 29 July 1943. Launched on 10 Dec 1943. Purchased by Peru in Sep 1957. Unique deck-house forward of bridge. Helicopters are operated from upper deck amidships.

PAITA *1972, Peruvian Navy*

2 Ex-US "LSM-1" CLASS

Name	No.	Builders	Commissioned
LOMAS (ex-US *LSM 396*)	36	Charleston Navy Yard	23 Mar 1945
ATICO (ex-US *LSM 554*)	37	Charleston Navy Yard	14 Sept 1945

Displacement, tons: 513 standard; 913 full load
Dimensions, feet (metres): 203·5 oa × 34·5 × 7 *(62·1 × 10·5 × 2·1)*
Guns: 2—40 mm; 4—20 mm
Main engines: Diesels; 800 rpm; 2 shafts; 3 600 bhp = 12 knots
Range, miles: 5 000 at 7 knots
Complement: Accommodation for 116 (10 officers and 106 men)

Purchased in 1959.

LOMAS *1975, Peruvian Navy*

SURVEY VESSELS

1 NEW CONSTRUCTION OCEANOGRAPHIC SHIP

Displacement, tons: 1 200

Laid down 3 Jan 1977 for completion 1978 by SIMAC, Callao.

1 Ex-US "SOTOYOMO" CLASS

Name	No.	Builders	Commissioned
UNANUE (ex-USS *Wateree*, ATA 174)	136	Levingston SB Co, Orange, Texas	20 July 1944

Displacement, tons: 534 standard; 852 full load
Dimensions, feet (metres): 143 oa × 33·9 × 13·2 *(43·6 × 9 × 4)*
Main engines: GM diesel-electric; 1 500 bhp = 13 knots

Former United States auxiliary ocean tug. Laid down on 5 Oct 1943, launched on 18 Nov 1943. Purchased from the USA in Nov 1961 under MAP.

CARDENAS (ex-US *YP 99*) +2 (ex-US *YP 242* and *243*)

Of 19 tons, launched in 1950, with a complement of 4. Transferred Nov 1958. Last two operated by navy for Instituto del Mar.

1 RESEARCH CRAFT

Of 77 feet *(23·5 metres)* with accommodation for 16 operated on the Amazonas by El Instituto del Mar (Ministry of Marine). Commissioned May 1976.

PERU 379

SERVICE FORCES

1 Ex-US "BELLATRIX" CLASS (TRANSPORT)

Name	No.	Builders	Commissioned
INDEPENDENCIA (ex-USS Bellatrix, AKA 3, ex-Raven, AK 20)	TC 31 (ex-21)	Tampa Shipbuilding Co, Tampa, Florida	1941

Displacement, tons: 6 194 light
Dimensions, feet (metres): 459 oa × 63 × 26·5 *(140 × 19·2 × 8·1)*
Guns: 1—5 in 38 cal; 3—3 in 50 cal; 10—20 mm
Main engines: 1 Nordberg diesel; 1 shaft; 6 000 bhp = 16·5 knots

Former US attack cargo ship. Transferred to Peru at Bremerton, Washington on 20 July 1963 under the Military Aid Programme. Training ship for the Peruvian Naval Academy.

INDEPENDENCIA *1975, Peruvian Navy*

1 "ILO" CLASS (TRANSPORT)

Name	No.	Builders	Commissioned
ILO	131	Servicio Industrial de la Marina, Callao	Dec 1971

Displacement, tons: 18 400 full load
Measurement, tons: 13 000 deadweight
Dimensions, feet (metres): 507·7 × 67·3 × 27·2 *(154·8 × 20·5 × 8·3)*
Main engines: Diesels
Speed, knots: 15·6

The *Ilo* is used from time to time for commercial purposes. Her sister ship *Rimac* was launched at the same yard on 12 Dec 1971 and transferred from the navy for commercial use by State Shipping Company (CPV) on "bare-boat charter" in 1973.

ILO *1976, Michael D. J. Lennon*

2 "TALARA" CLASS (REPLENISHMENT TANKERS)

Name	No.	Builders	Commissioned
TALARA	AO 152	Servicio Industrial de la Marina, Callao	Mar 1977
BAYOVAR	—	Servicio Industrial de la Marina, Callao	1978

Measurement, tons: 25 000 dw
Dimensions, feet (metres): 561·5 × 82 × 31·2 *(171·2 × 25 × 9·5)*
Main engines: Diesels; 12 000 hp
Speed, knots: 15·5

Cargo space 35 662 cu metres. *Talara* laid down 1975, launched 9 July 1976. *Bayovar* laid down 9 July 1976, launched 18 July 1977 having been originally ordered by Petroperu and transferred to navy while building. A third, *Trompeteros*, of this class has been built for Petroperu.

2 "PARINAS" CLASS (REPLENISHMENT TANKERS)

Name	No.	Builders	Commissioned
PARINAS	155	Servicio Industrial de la Marina, Callao	13 June 1968
PIMENTEL	156	Servicio Industrial de la Marina, Callao	27 June 1969

Displacement, tons: 3 434 light; 13 600 full load
Measurement, tons: 10 000 deadweight
Dimensions, feet (metres): 410·9 × 63·1 × 26 *(125·3 × 19·2 × 7·9)*
Main engines: Burmeister & Wain Type 750 diesel; 5 400 bhp = 14·5 knots

All tankers may be used for commercial purposes if not required for naval use by Petroperu (State Oil Company).

PIMENTEL *1975, Peruvian Navy*

380 PERU

2 "SECHURA" CLASS (SUPPORT TANKERS)

Name	No.	Builders	Commissioned
ZORRITOS	158	Servicio Industrial de la Marina, Callao	1959
LOBITOS	159	Servicio Industrial de la Marina, Callao	1966

Displacement, tons: 8 700 full load
Measurement, tons: 4 300 gross; 6 000 deadweight
Dimensions, feet (metres): 385·0 oa × 52·0 × 21·2 *(117·4 × 15·9 × 6·4)*
Main engines: Burmeister & Wain diesels; 2 400 bhp = 12 knots
Boilers: 2 Scotch with Thornycroft oil burners for cargo tank cleaning

Zorritos launched 8 Oct 1958, *Lobitos* May 1965.

LOBITOS   1975, Peruvian Navy

1 SUPPORT TANKER

Name	No.	Builders	Commissioned
MOLLENDO (ex-*Amalienborg*)	ATP 151	Japan	Sept 1962

Displacement, tons: 6 084 standard; 25 670 full load
Dimensions, feet (metres): 534·8 oa × 72·2 × 30 *(164·3 × 22 × 9·2)*
Main engines: 674-VTFS-160 diesels; 7 500 bhp = 14·5 knots

This Japanese built tanker, completed Sept 1962, was acquired by Peru in April 1967. Used in commercial work when not required by navy.

— (Ex-US *YO 221*)

Transferred to Peru Feb 1975.

MOLLENDO   1975, Peruvian Navy

MISCELLANEOUS

TUGS

1 Ex-US "CHEROKEE" CLASS

Name	No.	Builders	Commissioned
GUARDIAN RIOS (ex-USS *Pinto*, ATF 90)	123	USA	1943

Displacement, tons: 1 235 standard; 1 675 full load
Dimensions, feet (metres): 205 oa × 38·5 × 15·5 *(62·5 × 11·7 × 4·7)*
Main engines: 4 GM diesel-electric; 3 000 bhp = 16·5 knots

Launched on 5 Jan 1943. Transferred to Peru in 1960 and delivered in Jan 1961. Fitted with powerful pumps and other salvage equipment.

CONTRAESTRE NAVARRO

50 ton tug for Amazon flotilla built in Peru in 1973.

Name	No.	Builders	Commissioned
OLAYA	—	Ruhrorter, SW. Duisburg	1967
SELENDON	—	Ruhrorter, SW. Duisburg	1967

Measurement, tons: 80 gross
Dimensions, feet (metres): 61·3 × 20·3 × 7·4 *(18·7 × 6·2 × 2·3)*
Main engines: 600 hp = 10 knots

Name	No.	Builders	Commissioned
FRANCO (ex-USS *Iwana*, YTM2)	ARA 124.	City Point Iron Works, Boston, USA	1892

Displacement, tons: 192
Dimensions, feet (metres): 92·6 pp × 20·1 × 8 *(28·2 × 6·4 × 2·4)*

Laid down April 1891. Transferred March 1946.

AUXILIARIES

1 CONVERTED RIVER GUNBOAT

Name	No.	Builders	Commissioned
NAPO	301	Yarrow Co Ltd, Scotstoun, Glasgow	1921

Displacement, tons: 98
Dimensions, feet (metres): 101·5 oa × 18 × 3 *(31 × 5·5 × 0·9)*
Main engines: Triple expansion; 250 ihp = 12 knots
Boilers: Yarrow
Complement: 22

Launched in 1920. Built of steel. Converted from wood to oil fuel burning. In the Upper Amazon Flotilla. Converted to a Dispensary Vessel in 1968.

NAPO   1975, Peruvian Navy

PERU 381

3 RIVER HOSPITAL CRAFT

Name	No.	Builders	Commissioned
MORONA	—	SIMAI, Iquitos	1976
—	—	SIMAI, Iquitos	1977
—	—	SIMAI, Iquitos	1977

Displacement, tons: 150
Dimensions, feet (metres): 98·4 × 19·6 × 1·5 *(30 × 6 × 0·6)*

For service on Rivers Amazonas, Putumayo and Yavari.

1 FLOATING DOCK

AFD 111 (ex-*WY 19*, ex-US *AFDL 33*)

Displacement, tons: 1 900
Dimensions, feet (metres): 288 × 64 × 8·2/31·5 *(92·2 × 19·5 × 2·5/9·6)*

Launched in Oct 1944. Transferred July 1959.

1 FLOATING DOCK

AFD 112 (ex-*WY 20*, ex-US *ARD 8*)

Displacement, tons: 5 200
Dimensions, feet (metres): 492 × 84 × 5·7/33·2 *(150·1 × 25·6 × 1·7/10·1)*

Transferred Feb 1961.

1 SMALL FLOATING DOCK

Dimensions, feet (metres): 194 × 61·3 × ? *(59·2 × 18·7 × ?)*
Lift: 600 tons

Built by John I. Thornycroft, Southampton in 1951. Based at Iquitos.

1 FLOATING WORKSHOP

PISCO (ex-US *YR 59*)

Transferred 8 Aug 1961.

1 FLOATING CRANE

At Callao; of 120 tons capacity.

Other names of unidentified types: *Duenas, Noguera, Neptuno, Corrillo*.

WATER CARRIERS

Name	No.	Builders	Commissioned
MANTILLA (ex-US *YW 22*)	141	Henry C. Grebe & Co Inc, Chicago, Illinois	1945

Displacement, tons: 1 235 full load
Dimensions, feet (metres): 174 × 32 × — *(52·3 × 9·8 × —)*
Gun: 1 MG forward
Speed, knots: 8
Capacity, gallons: 200 000

Former US water barge. Lent to Peru in July 1963. May now be 110 in place of 141.

ABA 091

Built in Peru 1972. Attached to Amazon Flotilla. Capacity 800 tons water.

ABA 113

Of 300 tons. Built in Peru 1972.

COASTGUARD
CORVETTES

2 Ex-US "AUK" CLASS

Name	No.	Builders	Commissioned
GALVEZ (ex-USS *Ruddy*, MSF 380)	68	Gulf Shipbuilding Corp	28 April 1945
DIEZ CANSECO (ex-USS *Shoveller*, MSF 382)	69	Gulf Shipbuilding Corp	28 June 1945

Displacement, tons: 890 standard; 1 250 full load
Dimensions, feet (metres): 221·2 oa × 32·2 × 11 *(67·5 oa × 9·8 × 3·4)*
Guns: 1—3 in 50 cal; 2—40 mm
A/S weapons: 1 Hedgehog
Main engines: Diesel-electric; 2 shafts; 3 532 bhp = 18 knots
Range, miles: 4 300 at 10 knots
Complement: 100

Recommissioned at San Diego, California, and transferred to the Peruvian Navy under the Mutual Defence Assistance Programme on 1 Nov 1960. Sonar equipment was fitted so that they could be used as patrol vessels. Both purchased by Peru in 1974. Transferred to the Coast Guard Service in 1975. Both still capable of minesweeping.

2 LARGE PATROL CRAFT

Name	No.	Builders	Commissioned
RIO CANETE	234	SIMA, Peru, Callao	1 April 1976
RIO CHIRA	235	SIMA, Peru, Callao	1976

Displacement, tons: 298 full load
Dimensions, feet (metres): 166·8 × 24·8 × 5·6 *(50·6 × 7·4 × 1·7)*
Gun: 1—40 mm
Main engines: 4—MTU diesels; 5 640 hp; 2 shafts = 22 knots
Complement: 39

Rio Canete launched 8 Aug 1974, *Rio Chira* on 8 Oct 1976.

6 VOSPER TYPE (LARGE PATROL CRAFT)

Name	No.	Builders	Commissioned
RIO CHICAWA (ex-*De Los Heros*)	224 (ex-*23*)	Vosper Ltd, Portsmouth	1965
RIO PATIVILCA (ex-*Herrera*)	225 (ex-*24*)	Vosper Ltd, Portsmouth	1965
RIO HUAORA (ex-*Larrea*)	226 (ex-*25*)	Vosper Ltd, Portsmouth	1965
RIO LOCUMBA (ex-*Sanchez Carrion*)	227 (ex-*26*)	Vosper Ltd, Portsmouth	1965
RIO ICA (ex-*Santillana*)	228 (ex-*27*)	Vosper Ltd, Portsmouth	1965
RIO VITOR (ex-*Velarde*)	229 (ex-*21*)	Vosper Ltd, Portsmouth	1965

Displacement, tons: 100 standard; 130 full load
Dimensions, feet (metres): 109·7 oa × 21 × 5·7 *(33·5 oa × 6·4 × 1·7)*
Guns: 2—20 mm
A/S weapons: DC racks
Main engines: 2 Napier Deltic 18-cyl, turbocharged diesels; 6 200 bhp = 30 knots
Range, miles: 1 100 at 15 knots
Complement: 25 (4 officers and 21 ratings)

Of all-welded steel construction with aluminium upperworks. Equipped with Vosper roll damping fins, Decca Type 707 true motion radar, comprehensive radio, up-to-date navigation aids, sonar, and air-conditioning. The first boat, 229, was launched on 10 July 1964, the last, 227, on 18 Feb 1965. Last arrived Callao 1 Dec 1965. Can be armed as gunboat, torpedo boat (four side-launched torpedoes) or minelayer. A twin rocket projector can be fitted forward instead of gun. All transferred to the Coast Guard Service in 1975 and renamed.

RIO LOCUMBA   1971, *Peruvian Navy*

2 US "PGM 71" CLASS (LARGE PATROL CRAFT)

Name	No.	Builders	Commissioned
RIO SAMA (ex-US *PGM 78*)	222 (ex-*PC 11*)	Peterson Builders, USA	Sept 1966
RIO CHIRA (ex-US *PGM 111*)	223 (ex-*PC 12*)	SIMA, Callao	1972

Displacement, tons: 130 standard; 147 full load
Dimensions, feet (metres): 101 × 21 × 6 *(30·8 × 6·4 × 1·8)*
Guns: 1—40 mm; 4—20 mm; 2—0·5 cal MG
Main engines: 2 diesels; 2 shafts; 1 800 hp = 18·5 knots
Range, miles: 1 500 at 10 knots
Complement: 15

Rio Sama completed under the US Military Aid Programme. *Rio Chira* transferred by US 30 June 1972. Transferred to the Coast Guard Service in 1975.

RIO SAMA   1971, *Peruvian Navy*

PHILIPPINES

Ministerial

Minister of National Defence:
  Juan Ponce Enrile

Senior Officers

Flag Officer in Command:
  Rear-Admiral Hilario M. Ruiz
Commander, Naval Operating Forces:
  Captain Simeon M. Alejandro

Diplomatic Representation

Armed Forces Attaché London:
  Captain Artemio A. Tadiar, Jr (Navy)
Naval Attaché Washington:
  Commander Ernesto M. Arzaga

Personnel

1978: approx 2 000 officers and 15 000 enlisted men

Prefix to Ships' Names

RPS for Republic of Philippines Ship.

Marine Corps

Commandant: Captain Rodolfo Punsalang
Personnel: 500 officers and 5 000 men (organised into a single brigade)

Coast Guard

Commandant: Commodore Ernesto R. Ogbinar
Personnel: 300 officers and 1 700 men

Naval Base

Sangley Point

Strength of the Fleet

	Active	Building
Frigates	8	—
Corvettes	11	—
Large Patrol Craft	10	—
Hydrofoils	4	—
Coastal Patrol Craft	61	?
Minesweepers (Coastal)	2	—
LSTs	27	—
LSMs	4	—
LSSLs	4	—
LSILs	4	—
Landing Craft	71	—
Repair Ships	3	—
Tankers	4	—
Miscellaneous	13	—
Tugs	8	—
Floating Docks	5	—
Survey Ships	4	—
Coast Guard Craft	33	—

Mercantile Marine

Lloyd's Register of Shipping:
  504 vessels of 1 146 529 tons gross

DELETIONS

Frigates

1976 ex-*Yukutat*, ex-*Cook Inlet* ("Casco" class USCG)

Corvettes

1976 2 MSO Type 4 (to US for disposal 1977). (*Davao del Norte, Davao del Sur*)
1977 *Datu Tupas* (ex-US "Admirable" Class)

Light Forces

1976 3 "Swift" Mk 1
1977 *Nueva Ecija* (ex-US "PC 461" class)

Coast and Geodetic Survey

1976 *Samar*

FRIGATES

1 Ex-US "SAVAGE" CLASS

Name	No.	Builders	Laid down	Launched	Commissioned
RAJAH LAKANDULA (ex-*Tran Hung Dao*, ex-USS *Camp*, DER 251)	PS 4	Brown SB & Co, Houston	27 Jan 1943	16 April 1943	16 Sept 1943

Displacement, tons: 1 590 standard; 1 850 full load
Length, feet (metres): 300 wl; 306 oa *(93.3)*
Beam, feet (metres): 36·6 *(11·2)*
Draught, feet (metres): 14 *(4·3)*
Guns: 2—3 in *(76 mm)* 50 cal (single)
A/S weapons: 6 (2 triple) Mk 32 torpedo tubes; 1 trainable Hedgehog (Mk 15); depth charge rack
Main engines: Diesel (Fairbanks Morse); 6 000 bhp; 2 shafts
Speed, knots: 19
Complement: approx 170

Former US Navy destroyer escort, of the FMR design group. After World War II this ship was extensively converted to radar picket configuration to serve as seaward extension of US aircraft attack warning system; redesignated DER with original DE hull number. Subsequently employed during 1960s in Indochina for coastal patrol and interdiction by US Navy (Operation MARKET TIME). Transferred to South Vietnamese Navy 6 Feb 1971. Acquired by the Philippines in 1975 and formally transferred on 5 April 1976.

Fire control: Mk 63 (forward) SPG 34 on gun mount. Mk 51 (aft).

Radar: SPS-28 and SPS-10 search radars on forward tripod mast. Apparently most electronic warfare equipment was removed prior to transfer. (See *Fire control*).

Sonar: SQS 31.

RAJAH LAKANDULA   6/1977, Dr. Giorgio Arra

PHILIPPINES

4 Ex-US "CASCO" CLASS COAST GUARD CUTTERS

Name	No.	Builders	Laid down	Launched	Commissioned
ANDRES BONIFACIO (ex-*Ly Thoung Kiet*, ex-USCGC *Chincoteague*, WHEC 375, ex-*AVP 24*)	PS 7	Lake Washington SY	1942	15 April 1942	12 April 1943
GREGORIO DE PILAR (ex-*Ngo Kuyen*, ex-USCGC *McCulloch*, WHEC 386, ex-USS *Wachapreague*, AGP 8, AVP 56)	PS 8	Lake Washington SY	1943	10 July 1943	17 May 1944
DIEGO SILANG (ex-*Tran Quang Khai*, ex-USCGC *Bering Strait*, WHEC 382, ex-*AVP 34*)	PS 9	Lake Washington SY	1943	15 Jan 1944	19 July 1944
FRANCISCO DAGAHOY (ex-*Tran Binh Trong*, ex-USCGC *Castle Rock*, WHEC 383, ex-*AVP 35*)	PS 10	Lake Washington SY	1943	11 Mar 1944	8 Oct 1944

Displacement, tons: 1 766 standard; 2 800 full load
Length, feet (metres): 300 wl; 310·75 oa *(94·7)*
Beam, feet (metres): 41·1 *(12·5)*
Draught, feet (metres): 13·5 *(4·1)*
Guns: 1—5 in *(127 mm)* 38 cal; 1 or 2—81 mm mortars in some ships; most have 2 or 3—40 mm aft; several MG
Main engines: Diesels (Fairbanks Morse); 6 080 bhp; 2 shafts
Speed, knots: approx 18
Complement: approx 200

Built as seaplane tenders of the "Barnegat" class for the US Navy.
All transferred to US Coast Guard in 1946-48, initially on loan designated WAVP and then on permanent transfer except ex-*McCulloch* transferred outright from US Navy to Coast Guard; subsequently redesignated as high endurance cutters (WHEC).

Appearance: These ships are distinguished from the former US Navy radar picket frigate of similar size by their pole masts forward, open side passages amidships, and radar antenna on second mast. Note combination 0·50 cal MG/81 mm mortar forward of bridge in "B" position.

Fire control: Mk 52 with Mk 26 radar for 5 in gun.

Radar: SPN 21 (foremast); SPS 29 (mainmast).

Transfers: Transferred from US Coast Guard to South Vietnamese Navy in 1971-72. Acquired by the Philippines in 1975 and formally transferred on 5 April 1976.
Ex-USCGC *Yukatat* and *Cook Inlet* transferred for spares 5 April 1976.

DIEGO SILANG   1971, Vietnamese Navy

3 Ex-US "CANNON" CLASS

Name	No.	Builders	Laid down	Launched	Commissioned
DATU KALANTIAW (ex-USS *Booth*, DE 170)	PS 76	Norfolk Navy Yard, Portsmouth Va.	30 Jan 1943	21 June 1943	19 Aug 1943
— (ex-*Asahi*, DE 262, ex-USS *Amick*, DE 168)	—	Federal Shipbuilding & Dry Dock Co, Newark, New Jersey	30 Nov 1942	27 May 1943	26 July 1943
— (ex-*Hatsuhi*, DE 263, ex-USS *Atherton*, DE 169)	—	Norfolk Navy Yard, Portsmouth Va.	14 Jan 1943	27 May 1943	29 Aug 1943

Displacement, tons: 1 220 standard; 1 620 full load
Length, feet (metres): 300 *(91·5)* wl; 306 *(93·2)* oa
Beam, feet (metres): 36·6 *(11·2)*
Draught, feet (metres): 14 *(4·3)*
Guns: 3—3 in *(76 mm)* 50 cal (single); 6—40 mm (twin); 2—20 mm (single) (6—20 mm in ex-Japanese)
A/S weapons: 1 Hedgehog; 6 (2 triple) Mk 32 torpedo tubes; depth charges (PS 76); 1 Hedgehog; 6 K-guns; 2 DC racks (ex-Japanese)
Main engines: Diesel-electric drive (General Motors diesels); 6 000 bhp; 2 shafts
Speed, knots: 21
Complement: approx 165

The USS *Booth* was completed by the Norfolk Navy Yard.

Appearance: Ex-Japanese ships have pole foremast.

Fire Control: Mk 52 GFCS with Mk 51 rangefinder and Mk 26 radar for 3 in gun; 3—Mk 51 Mod 2 GFCS for 40 mm.

Radar: The *Datu Kalantiaw* has been refitted with SPS-5 and SPS-6 radars with antennae mounted on tripod mast.

Transfers: PS 76 to Philippines 15 Dec 1967. Ex-Japanese ships *Asahi* and *Hatsuhi* originally transferred 14 June 1955 and were paid off June 1975. Transferred to Philippines 13 Sept 1976.

DATU KALANTIAW   Philippine Navy

CORVETTES

2 Ex-US "AUK" CLASS MSF TYPE

Name	No.	Builders	Commissioned
RIZAL (ex-USS *Murrelet*, MSF 372)	PS 69	Savannah Machine & Foundry Co, Georgia	21 Aug 1945
QUEZON (ex-USS *Vigilance*, MSF 324)	PS 70	Associated Shipbuilders, Seattle, Washington	28 Feb 1944

Displacement, tons: 890 standard; 1 250 full load
Dimensions, feet (metres): 215 wl; 221·2 oa × 32·2 × 10·8 *(70·5; 72·5 × 10·5 × 3·5)*
Guns: 2—3 in *(76 mm)* 50 cal (single); 4—40 mm (twin); 4—20 mm (twin)
A/S weapons: 3 (1 triple) Mk 32 torpedo tubes; 1 Hedgehog; depth charges
Main engines: Diesel-electric (General Motors diesels); 3 532 bhp; 2 shafts = 18 knots
Complement: approx 100

Upon transfer the minesweeping gear was removed and a second 3 in gun fitted aft; additional anti-submarine weapons also fitted. *Quezon* has bulwarks on iron-deck to end of superstructure which *Rizal* does not have.

Radar: SPS 5.

Transfers: PS 69 transferred to the Philippines on 18 June 1965 and PS 70 on 19 Aug 1967.

QUEZON   1976, Michael D. J. Lennon

384 PHILIPPINES

8 Ex-US "PCE 827" CLASS

Name	No.	Builders	Commissioned
MIGUEL MALVAR (ex-*Ngoc Hoi* ex-USS *Brattleboro*, EPCER 852)	PS 19	Pullman Standard Car Co, Chicago	1944
SULTAN KUDARAT (ex-*Dong Da II* ex-USS *Crestview*, PCE 895)	PS 22	Willamette Iron & Steel Corp, Portland	1943
DATU MARIKUDO (ex-*Van Kiep II* ex-USS *Amherst*, PCER 853)	PS 23	Pullman Standard Car Co, Chicago	1944
CEBU (ex-USS *PCE 881*)	PS 28	Albina E and M Works, Portland, Oregon	1944
NEGROS OCCIDENTAL (ex-USS *PCE 884*)	PS 29	Albina E and M Works, Portland, Oregon	1944
LEYTE (ex-USS *PCE 885*)	PS 30	Albina E and M Works, Portland, Oregon	1945
PANGASINAN (ex-USS *PCE 891*)	PS 31	Willamette Iron & Steel Corp, Portland	1944
ILOILO (ex-USS *PCE 897*)	PS 32	Willamette Iron & Steel Corp, Portland	1944

Displacement, tons: 640 standard; 850 full load
Dimensions, feet (metres): 180 wl; 184·5 oa × 33·1 × 9·5 *(59; 60·5 × 10·8 × 3·1)*
Guns: 1—3 in *(76 mm)* 50 cal; 3 or 6—40 mm (single or twin) (28-32); 2—40 mm (single) (remainder); 4—20 mm (single) (28-32); 8—20 mm (twin) (remainder)
Main engines: Diesels (General Motors); 2 000 bhp; 2 shafts = 15 knots
Complement: approx 90-100

Two originally were fitted as rescue ships (PCER).

Transfers: Five units transferred to the Philippines in July 1948; PS 22 to South Viet-Nam on 29 Nov 1961, PS 19 on 11 July 1966, and PS 23 in June 1970. PS 19 and 22 to Philippines Nov 1975 and PS 23 5 April 1976.

LEYTE   10/1977, Dr. Giorgio Arra

1 Ex-US "ADMIRABLE" CLASS

Name	No.	Builders	Commissioned
MAGAT SALAMAT (ex-*Chi Lang II*, ex-USS *Gayety*, MSF 239)	PS 20	Winslow Marine Railway & SB Co, Seattle, Wash	1944

Displacement, tons: 650 standard; 945 full load
Dimensions, feet (metres): 180 wl; 184·5 oa × 33 × 9·75 *(59; 60·5 × 10·8 × 3·2)*
Guns: 1—3 in *(76 mm)* 50 cal; 2—40 mm (single); up to 8—20 mm (twin)
Main engines: Diesel (Cooper Bessemer); 1 710 bhp; 2 shafts = 14 knots
Complement: approx 80

Launched 19 March 1944. Minesweeping equipment has been removed. Believed to have two 20 mm twin mounts at after end of bridge and one or two 20 mm twin mounts on quarterdeck.

Transfer: *Magat Salamat* transferred to South Viet-Nam in April 1962. To Philippines Nov 1975.

MAGAT SALAMAT (old name)   1962, Vietnamese Navy

LIGHT FORCES

6 LARGE PATROL CRAFT

Displacement, tons: 135
Dimensions, feet (metres): 118·1 × 20·3 × 5·6 *(36 × 6·2 × 1·7)*
Guns: 2—30 mm
Main engines: 2 MTU diesels; 5 000 hp; 2 shafts = 29 knots

Originally meant for Lebanon. Built by Hamelin SY FDR. Reported that another 14 are to be built locally.

4 Ex-US "PC 461" CLASS (LARGE PATROL CRAFT)

Name	No.	Builders	Commissioned
BATANGAS (ex-USS *PC 1134*)	PS 24	Defoe SB Corp	1943
CAPIZ (ex-USS *PC 1564*)	PS 27	Leathem D. Smith SB Co	1944
NEGROS ORIENTAL (ex-*E 312*, ex-*L'Inconstant, P 636*, ex-USS *PC 1171*)	PS 29	Leathem D. Smith SB Co	15 May 1943
NUEVA VISCAYA (ex-USAF *Altus*, ex-USS *PC 568*)	PS 80	Brown SB Co	1942

Displacement, tons: 280 standard; 450 full load
Dimensions, feet (metres): 170 wl; 173·66 oa × 23 × 10·8 *(55·7; 56·9 × 7·5 × 3·5)*
Guns: 1—3 in *(76 mm)* 50 cal; 1—40 mm; several—20 mm (single or twin)
A/S weapons: Depth charges (except *Negros Oriental*)
Main engines: Diesels (General Motors); 2 800 bhp; 2 shafts = 20 knots
Complement: approx 70

Deletion: *Nueva Ecija* deleted in 1977.

Transfers: PS 24 and 27 transferred July 1948 and PS 80 (which had served with USAF 1963-68) in March 1968. PS 29 to France in 1951, Khmer Republic 1956 and, after transferring to Philippines in 1975 acquired Dec 1976.

CAPIZ   Philippine Navy

PHILIPPINES 385

5 US PGM-39 and 71 CLASSES (LARGE PATROL CRAFT)

Name	No.	Builders	Commissioned
BASILAN (ex-*PGM 83*, ex-*Hon Troc*)	PG 60	Peterson Builders, Wisconsin	—
AGUSAN (ex-*PGM 39*)	PG 61	Tacoma Boatbuilding Co, Washington	Mar 1960
CATANDUANES (ex-*PGM 40*)	PG 62	Tacoma Boatbuilding Co, Washington	Mar 1960
ROMBLON (ex-*PGM 41*)	PG 63	Tacoma Boatbuilding Co, Washington	June 1960
PALAWAN (ex-*PGM 42*)	PG 64	Tacoma Boatbuilding Co, Washington	June 1960

Displacement, tons: 122 full load
Dimensions, feet (metres): 100·3 × 21·1 × 6·9 *(32·9 × 6·9 × 2·3)*
Guns: 1—40 mm; 4—20 mm (twins); 2—·50 cal MG *(Basilan)*; 4—·50 cal MGs remainder
Main engines: 2 Mercedes-Benz diesels; 1 900 bhp; 2 shafts = 17 knots
(*Basilan* 8 GM 6—71 diesels)
Complement: approx 15

Steel-hulled craft built under US military assistance programmes; PG 61-64 for the Philippines, PG 60 for South Viet-Nam. Assigned US PGM-series numbers while under construction. Transferred upon completion. *Basilan* transferred to South Viet-Nam in April 1967 and acquired by the Philippines Dec 1975.
These craft are lengthened versions of the US Coast Guard 95-foot "Cape" class patrol boat design. Heavier armament is provided in PG 60. No A/S weapons. PG 62 serves with the Coastguard.

CATANDUANES *10/1977, Dr. Giorgio Arra*

2 ITALIAN DESIGN (HYDROFOIL PATROL CRAFT)

Name	No.	Builders	Commissioned
SIQUIJOR	HB 76	Cantiere Navaltecnica, Messina	April 1965
CAMIGUIN	HB 77	Cantiere Navaltecnica, Messina	April 1965

Displacement, tons: 28
Dimensions, feet (metres): 15·3 (24·3 over foils) *(4·7 (7·4))* × 3·8 (8·9 foilborne) *(1·2 (2·7))*
Guns: MG
Main engines: Diesel (Mercedes-Benz-MTU); 1 250 bhp; 2 shafts = 38 knots
Complement: 9

Laid down on 26 May and 28 Oct 1964. For military and police patrol.

CAMIGUIN *Philippine Navy*

2 HITACHI PT 32 DESIGN (HYDROFOIL PATROL CRAFT)

Name	No.	Builders	Commissioned
BONTOC	HB 74	Hitachi, Kanagawa	Dec 1966
BALER	HB 75	Hitachi, Kanagawa	Dec 1966

Displacement, tons: 32 full load
Dimensions, feet (metres): 68·9 × 15·7 (24·6 over foils) *(21 × 4·8, 7·5)*
Guns: MG can be mounted fore and aft; normally unarmed
Main engines: Ikegai-Mercedes-Benz (MTU) diesel; 3 200 bhp = 37·8 knots (32 cruising). Also auxiliary engine
Complement: 14

For smuggling prevention. Also used as inter-island ferries. Based on Schertel-Sachsenburg foil system.

BALER on foils *Philippine Navy*

31 + ? De HAVILLAND SERIES 9209 (COASTAL PATROL CRAFT)

PC 326-331 + 25

Displacement, tons: 16·5 full load
Dimensions, feet (metres): 45·9 × 15·1 × 3·3 *(14 × 4·6 × 1)*
Guns: 2—0·5 in MGs
Main engines: 2 Cummins diesels; 740 hp = 25 knots
Range, miles: 500 at 12 knots
Complement: 8

GRP hulls. First six built by De Havilland Marine, Sydney NSW. Completed 20 Nov 1974-78 Feb 1975. In Aug 1975 80 further craft of this design were reported ordered from Marcelo Yard, Manila to be delivered 1976-78 at the rate of two per month. By the end of 1976, 25 more had been completed but a serious fire in the shipyard destroyed 14 new hulls and halted production temporarily.

DE HAVILLAND CPC *1977, De Havilland*

386 PHILIPPINES

15 SWIFT (Mk 1 and 2) TYPE (COASTAL PATROL CRAFT)

PCF 300	PCF 308	PCF 313
PCF 301	PCF 309	PCF 314
PCF 303	PCF 310	PCF 315
PCF 306	PCF 311	PCF 316
PCF 307	PCF 312	PCF 317

Displacement, tons: 22·5 full load
Dimensions, feet (metres): 50 × 13·6 × 4 (15·2 × 4·5 × 1·3) (Mk 1 300-303) 51·3 ft (15·6) (Mk 2 306-317)
Guns: 2—0·50 cal MG (twin)
Main engines: 2 geared diesels (General Motors); 860 bhp; 2 shafts = 28 knots

Most built in the United States. PCF 303 served in US Navy prior to transfer to the Philippines; others built for US military assistance programmes. PCF 300 and 301 transferred to Philippines in March 1966, PCF 303 in Aug 1966, PCF 306-313 in Feb 1968, PCF 314-316 in July 1970. PCF 317 built in 1970 in the Philippines (ferro concrete) with enlarged superstructure used as yacht for Señora Marcos.

PCF 308 10/1977, Dr. Giorgio Arra

13 IMPROVED SWIFT TYPE (COASTAL PATROL CRAFT)

PCF 318	PCF 323	PCF 337
PCF 319	PCF 333	PCF 338
PCF 320	PCF 334	PCF 339
PCF 321	PCF 336	PCF 340
PCF 322		

Displacement, tons: 33 full load
Dimensions, feet (metres): 65 oa × 16 × 3·4 (21·3 × 5·2 × 1·1)
Guns: 2—0·50 cal MG (twin); 2—·30 cal MG (single)
Main engines: 3 diesels (General Motors); 1 590 bhp; 3 shafts = 25 knots
Complement: 8

Improved Swift type inshore patrol boats built by Sewart for the Philippine Navy. First six delivered Jan-June 1972, 333 and 334 in April 1975, 337 and 338 in July 1975, 336 in Nov 1975 and 339 and 340 in Dec 1976.

2 COASTAL PATROL CRAFT

Name	No.
ABRA	FB 83
BUKINDON	FB 84

Displacement, tons: 40 standard
Dimensions, feet (metres): 87·5 oa × 19 × 4·75 (28·6 × 6·2 × 1·9)
Guns: 2—20 mm
Main engines: Diesels (Mercedes-Benz/MTU); 2 460 bhp; 2 shafts = approx 25 knots
Complement: 15 (3 officers, 12 men)

Abra built Singapore. Completed 8 Jan 1970. *Bukindon* completed Cavite 1970-71. Wood hulls and aluminium superstructure.

MINEWARFARE FORCES

2 Ex-US MSC 218 CLASS (MINESWEEPERS—COASTAL)

Name	No.	Builders	Commissioned
ZAMBALES (ex-USS *MSC 218*)	PM 55	Bellingham Shipyard, Washington	7 Mar 1956
ZAMBOANGA DEL NORTE (ex-USS *MSC 219*)	PM 56	Bellingham Shipyard, Washington	23 April 1956

Displacement, tons: 320 light; 385 full load
Dimensions, feet (metres): 144 oa × 28 × 8·2 (47·2 × 9·2 × 2·7)
Guns: 2—20 mm (twin)
Main engines: 2 diesels; 880 bhp; 2 shafts = 12 knots
Complement: approx 40

Built by the United States specifically for transfer under the military aid programme. Wood hull with non-magnetic metal fittings.

ZAMBALES

AMPHIBIOUS FORCES

27 Ex-US LST TYPE

Name	No.	Commissioned
BULACAN (ex-USS *LST 843*)	LT 38	1945
ALBAY (ex-USS *LST 865*)	LT 39	1945
MISAMIS ORIENTAL (ex-USS *LST 875*)	LT 40	1945
CAMBOANGA DEL SUR (ex-*Cam Ranh*, ex-USS *Marion County*, LST 975)	LT 86	1945
MINDORO OCCIDENTAL (ex-USNS *T-LST 222*)	LT 93	1944
SURIGAO DEL NORTE (ex-USNS *T-LST 488*)	LT 94	1944
SURIGAO DEL SUR (ex-USNS *T-LST 546*)	LT 95	1942
— (ex-*Thi Nai*, ex-USS *Cayuga County*, LST 529)	ex-HQ 502	1944
MAQUINDANAO (ex-USS *Caddo Parish*, LST 515)	LT 96	1944
CAGAYAN (ex-USS *Hickman County*, LST 825)	LT 97	1945
ILOCOS NORTE (ex-USS *Madera County*, LST 905)	LT 98	1945
— (ex-*Nha Trang*, ex-USS *Jerome County*, LST 848)	ex-HQ 505	1943
— (ex-USNS *T-LST 47*)		1943
— (ex-USNS *T-LST 230*)		1944
— (ex-USNS *T-LST 287*)		1944
— (ex-USNS *T-LST 491*)		1943
— (ex-USNS *T-LST 566*)		1944
— (ex-USNS *T-LST 607*)		Mar 1944
— (ex-USNS *Daggett County*, T-LST 689)		1944
— (ex-USNS *Davies County*, T-LST 692)		1944
— (ex-*Can Tho*, ex-USS *Garrett County*, AGP 786, ex-LST 786)		1944
— (ex-*My Tho*, ex-USS *Harnett County*, AGP 821, ex-LST 821)		1944
— (ex-USNS *Harris County*, T-LST 822)		1945
— (ex-USNS *Hillsdale County*, LST 835)		1944
— (ex-USNS *Nansemond County*, T-LST 1064)		1945
— (ex-USNS *Orleans Parish*, T-LST 1069, ex-*MSC 6*, LST 1069)		1945
— (ex-USNS *T-LST 1072*)		1945

Displacement, tons: 1 620 standard; 2 366 beaching; 4 080 full load
Dimensions, feet (metres): 316 wl; 328 oa × 50 × 14 (103·6; 107·5 × 19 × 4·9)
Guns: 7 or 8—40 mm (1 or 2 twin, 4 or 5 single); several 20 mm in former Vietnamese ships; former USNS ships are unarmed

Ex-NHA TRANG (tripod mast)

Main engines: Diesels (General Motors); 1 700 bhp; 2 shafts = 11·6 knots
Complement: varies; approx 60 to 110 (depending upon employment)

Cargo capacity 2 100 tons. Many of these ships served as cargo ships in the Western Pacific under the US Military Sealift Command (USNS/T-LST); they were civilian manned by Korean and Japanese crews.
The ex-HQ 505 and some of the later USNS ships have tripod masts; others have pole masts. The USNS ships lack troop accommodations and other amphibious warfare features. Many of these ships are used for general cargo work in Philippine service.

Transfers: LT 38-40 transferred to the Philippines in July 1948; LT 96-98 on 29 Nov 1969; LT 93-95 on 15 July 1972; 502, 505 transferred from US Navy to South Korean Navy in April 1962 and Dec 1963 and acquired by the Philippines in 1976. Ex-US 689, 835 and 1064 were transferred to Japan in April 1961 and thence to Philippines in 1975—remainder transferred from USN in 1976 with exception of ex-*My Tho* and ex-*Can Tho* which were used as light craft repair ships in South Viet-Nam and have retained amphibious capability (transferred to Viet-Nam 1970 and Philippines 1976 acquired by purchase 13 Sept 1977). Ex-US 529 and 975 transferred (grant aid) 17 Nov 1975. Ex-US 1064 acquired by purchase 24 Sept 1977. Several of these ships are undergoing major refit including replacement of frames and plating as well as engines and electrics.

PHILIPPINES 387

4 Ex-US "LSM-1" CLASS

Name	No.	Commissioned
ISABELA (ex-USS *LSM 463*)	LP 41	1945
BATANES (ex-*Huong Giang*, ex-USS *Oceanside*, LSM 175)	LP 65	1944
WESTERN SAMAR (ex-*Hat Giang*, ex-*LSM 9011*, ex-USS *LSM 335*)	LP 66	1945
ORIENTAL MINDORO (ex-USS *LSM 320*)	LP 68	1944

Displacement, tons: 743 beaching; 1 095 full load
Dimensions, feet (metres): 196·5 wl; 203·5 oa × 34·5 × 8·5 *(60·4; 66·7 × 11·3 × 2·7)*
Guns: 2—40 mm (twin); several 20 mm
Main engines: Diesels; 2 800 bhp; 2 shafts = 11·6 knots
Complement: approx 70

LP 41 transferred to the Philippines in March 1961 and LP 68 in April 1962; LP 66 originally transferred from US Navy to French Navy for use in Indochina in Jan 1954; subsequently transferred to South Viet-Nam in Dec 1955; LP 65 transferred from US Navy to South Viet-Nam on 1 Aug 1961. Acquired by the Philippines 17 Nov 1975.
LP 66 was fitted as hospital ship (LSM-H) for treating casualties retaining her armament. Has deck houses in and above well-deck.
LSM 110 (ex-Viet Nam (S)) transferred 17 Nov 1975 for spares and scrap.

WESTERN SAMAR (Old pennant number) *Vietnamese Navy*

4 Ex-US "LSSL-1" CLASS

Name	No.	Commissioned
CAMARINES SUR (ex-*Niguyen Duc Bong*, ex-US *LSSL 129*)	LS 48	1945
SULU (ex-*LSSL 96*)	LS 49	1944
— (ex-Japanese, ex-US *LSSL 68*)	—	1944
— (ex-Japanese, ex-US *LSSL 87*)	—	1944

Displacement, tons: 227 standard; 383 full load
Dimensions, feet (metres): 158 oa × 23·7 × 5·7 *(51·8 × 7·8 × 1·8)*
Guns: 1—3 in; 4—40 mm; 4—20 mm; 4 MG
Main engines: Diesel; 1 600 bhp; 2 shafts = 14 knots
Complement: 60

Former US Navy landing ships support; designed to provide close-in-fire support for amphibious assaults, but suitable for general gunfire missions.
Ex-*Doan Ngoc Tang* (ex-US *LSSL 9*) was transferred to France in 1951 *(Hallebarde* L. 9023) transferred to Japan 1956-1964; returned and transferred to South Viet-Nam in 1965 for spares. Acquired by Philippines for spares 1975 as was ex-*Lulu Phu Tho* (ex-US *LSSL 101*). LS 48 and 49 and ex-US *LSSL 68* transferred 17 Nov 1975. Ex-US *LSSL 87* transferred Sept 1976.

CAMARINES SUR (old pennant number) *Vietnamese Navy*

4 Ex-US LSIL TYPE

Name	No.	Commissioned
MARINDUQUE (ex-US *LSIL 875*)	LS 36	1944
SORSOGON (ex-*Thien Kich* ex-*L 9038*, ex-US *LSIL 872*)	LS 37	1944
CAMARINES NORTE (ex-*Loi Cong* ex-*L 9034*, ex-US *LSIL 699*)	LS 52	1944
MISAMIS OCCIDENTAL (ex-*Tam Set* ex-*L 9033*, ex-US *LSIL 871*)	LS 53	1944

Displacement, tons: 227 standard; 383 full load
Dimensions, feet (metres): 158 oa × 22·7 × 5·3 *(51·8 × 7·6 × 1·7)*
Guns: 1—3 in; 1—40 mm; 2—20 mm; 4 MG; and up to 4 army mortars (2—81 mm; 2—60 mm)
Main engines: Diesel; 1 600 bhp; 2 shafts = 14·4 knots
Complement: 55

Designed to carry 200 troops. LF 53 originally transferred to France in 1951 and others in 1953 for use in Indochina; subsequently retransferred in 1956 to South Viet-Nam. All acquired by the Philippines 17 Nov 1975. Ex-US *LSIL 476* transferred for spares at same time.

SORSOGON (old pennant number)

11 Ex-US "LCM-8" CLASS

TKM 90-1, TKM 90-2, LCM 257, 258, 260-266.

TKMs transferred March 1972, 257 and 258 June 1973, remainder June 1975.

50 Ex-US "LCM-6" CLASS

LCM 224-227, 229, 231-234, 237, 239, 240, 249, 255, 256, 259 + 34

One transferred in 1955, 13 in 1971-73, 24 in Nov 1975, remaining dozen 1973-75.

7 Ex-US "LCVP" CLASS

LCVP 175, 181 + 5

Five to be scrapped or sold in FY 1977. Two transferred in 1955-56, one in 1965, two in 1971 and 175 and 181 in June 1973.

3 Ex-US "LCU" CLASS

Ex US-LCU 1603, 1604, 1606

Transferred from Japan Nov 17 1975.

MISCELLANEOUS

SERVICE FORCES

3 Ex-US "ACHELOUS" CLASS (REPAIR SHIPS)

Name	No.	Commissioned
KAMAGONG (ex-*Aklan*, ex-USS *Romulus*, ARL 22, ex-*LST 926*)	AR 67	1944
NARRA (ex-USS *Krishna*, ARL 38, ex-*LST 1149*)	AR 88	1945
— (ex-USS *Satyr*, ARL 23, ex-*LST 852*)	—	1945

Displacement, tons: 4 100 full load
Dimensions, feet (metres): 316 wl; 328 oa × 50 × 14 *(103·6; 107·5 × 16·4 × 4·6)*
Guns: 8—40 mm (2 quad)
Main engines: Diesels (General Motors); 1 700 bhp; 2 shafts = 11·6 knots
Complement: approx 220

Converted during construction. Extensive machine shop, spare parts stowage, supplies, etc.

Transfers: AR 67 transferred to the Philippines in Nov 1961, AR 88 on 31 Oct 1971 and third on 24 Jan 1977.

KAMAGONG *1968, Philippine Navy*

388 PHILIPPINES

1 PRESIDENTIAL YACHT

Name	No.	Builders	Commissioned
ANG PANGULO (ex-*The President*, ex-*Roxas*, ex-*Lapu-Lapu*)	TP 777	Ishikawajima, Japan	1959

Dimensions, feet (metres): 275 oa × 42·6 × 21 *(90 × 13·9 × 6·9)*
Guns: 2—20 mm
Main engines: Diesels; 5 000 bhp; 2 shafts = 18 knots
Complement: approx 90

Built as war reparation; launched in 1958. Used as presidential yacht and command ship. Originally named *Lapu-Lapu* after the chief who killed Magellan; renamed *Roxas* on 9 Oct 1962 after the late Manuel Roxas, the first President of the Philippines Republic, renamed *The President* in 1967 and *Ang Pangulo* in 1975.

ANG PANGULO 11/1976, Dr. Giorgio Arra

1 Ex-US "ADMIRABLE" CLASS (PRESIDENTIAL YACHT)

Name	No.	Builders	Commissioned
MOUNT SAMAT (ex-*Pagasa*, ex-*Santa Maria*, ex-*Pagasa*, ex-*APO 21*, ex-USS *Quest*, AM 281)	TK 21	Gulf Shipbuilding Corp	25 Oct 1944

Displacement, tons: 650 standard; 945 full load
Dimensions, feet (metres): 190 oa × 33 × 9·8 *(57·9 × 10·8 × 3·2)*
Guns: 2—20 mm
Main engines: Diesels (Cooper Bessemer); 1 710 bhp; 2 shafts = 14·8 knots
Complement: approx 60

Former US Navy minesweeper (AM). Commissioned on 25 Oct 1944. Transferred to the Philippines in July 1948. Used as presidential yacht and command ship.

MOUNT SAMAT 10/1977, Dr. Giorgio Arra

1 YACHT

Name	No.	Builders	Commissioned
—	—	Vosper Thornycroft, Singapore	Dec 1975

Dimensions, feet (metres): 212·3 × 38 × 6 *(64·7 × 11·6 × 1·8)*
Main engines: 2 diesels; 7 500 hp = 28·5 knots

Used as a Command Ship.

1 Ex-US YON TYPE (FUEL BARGE)

— (Ex-US YON 279)

Transferred Dec 1975.

3 Ex-US YW TYPE (WATER CARRIERS)

LAKE LANAO (ex-US *YW 125*)	YW 42
LAKE BULUAN (ex-US *YW 111*)	YW 33
LAKE PAOAY (ex-US *YW 130*)	YW 34

Displacement, tons: 1 235 full load
Dimensions, feet (metres): 174 oa × 32 × 15 *(57 × 10·5 × 4·9)*
Guns: 2—20 mm
Main engines: Diesel, 560 bhp; 1 shaft = 8 knots

Basically similar to YOG type but adapted to carry fresh water. Cargo capacity 200 000 gallons. *Lake Lanao* transferred to the Philippines in July 1948; others on 16 July 1975—*YW 103* for spare parts and scrap.

3 Ex-US YO/YOG TYPE (TANKERS)

Name	No.	Commissioned
LAKE MAINIT (ex-US *YO 116*)	YO 35	1943
LAKE NAUJAN (ex-US *YO 173*)	YO 43	1943
LAKE BUHI (ex-US *YOG 73*)	YO 78	1944

Displacement, tons: 520 standard; approx 1 400 full load
Dimensions, feet (metres): 174 × 32 × 15 *(57 × 10·5 × 4·9)*
Guns: several 20 mm
Main engines: Diesels; 560 bhp; 1 shaft = 8 knots

Former US Navy harbour oiler (YO) and gasoline tankers (YOG). Cargo capacity 6 570 barrels. YO 43 carries fuel oil and the YO 78 gasoline and diesel oil.

Deletions: Two craft from South Viet-Nam ex-*YOG 33* and ex-*YOG 80* accepted for scrapping and spare parts 17 Nov 1975.

Transfers: YO 43 transferred to the Philippines in July 1948 YO 78 in July 1967 and YO 35 in July 1975. Ex-*YO 115* and *YOG 61* transferred from US Navy to the Philippines on 16 July 1975 for spare parts and scrap.

LAKE NAUJAN 10/1977, Dr. Giorgio Arra

1 Ex-US C1-M-AV1 TYPE (SUPPORT SHIP)

Name	No.	Builders	Commissioned
MACTAN (ex-USCGC *Kukui*, WAK 186, ex-USS *Colquitt*, AK 174)	TK 90	Froemming Brothers, Milwaukee	22 Sept 1945

Displacement, tons: 4 900 light; 5 636 full load
Dimensions, feet (metres): 320 wl; 338·5 oa × 50 × 18 *(104·9; 110·9 × 16·4 × 5·9)*
Guns: 2—20 mm
Main engines: Diesel (Nordberg); 1 750 bhp; 1 shaft = 11·5 knots

Commissioned in US Navy on 22 Sept 1945; transferred to the US Coast Guard two days later. Subsequently served as Coast Guard supply ship in Pacific until transferred to Philippines on 1 March 1972. Used to supply military posts and lighthouses in the Philippine archipelago.

1 LIGHTHOUSE TENDER

PEARL BANK (ex-US Army *LO 4*, ex-Australian *MSL*)

Displacement, tons: 160 standard; 300 full load
Dimensions, feet (metres): 120 oa × 24·5 × 8 *(39·3 × 8 × 2·6)*
Main engines: Diesels (Fairbanks Morse); 240 bhp; 2 shafts = 7 knots

Originally an Australian motor stores lighter; subsequently transferred to the US Army and then to the Philippines. Employed as a lighthouse tender.

4 Ex-US ARMY FS TYPE (BUOY TENDERS)

Name	No.
LAUIS LEDGE (ex-US Army *FS 185*)	TK 45
BOJEADOR (ex-US Army *FS 203*)	TK 46
LIMASAWA (ex-USCGC *Nettle* WAK 129, ex-US Army *FS 169*)	TK 79
— (ex-Japanese, ex-US Army *FS 408*)	—

Displacement, tons: 470 standard; 811 full load
Dimensions, feet (metres): 180 oa × 23 × 10 *(60 × 7 × 3)*
Main engines: Diesels; 1 000 shp; 1 shaft = 11 knots

Former US Army freight and supply ships. Employed as tenders for buoys and lighthouses. Ex-*FS 408* transferred Nov 1976.

LAUIS LEDGE 1969, Philippine Navy

1 TUG Ex-US ATR TYPE

Name	No.	Launched
IFUGAO (ex-HMS *Emphatic*, ex-US *ATR 96*)	AQ 44	27 Jan 1944

Displacement, tons: 783 full load
Dimensions, feet (metres): 134·6 wl; 143 oa × 33·8 × 13·5 *(44·1; 46·9 × 11 × 4·4)*
Guns: 1—3 in *(76 mm)* 50 cal; 2—20 mm
Main engines: Diesel; 1 500 bhp; 1 shaft = 13 knots

US-built rescue tug transferred to Royal Navy upon launching; subsequently returned to US Navy and retransferred to the Philippines in July 1948.

IFUGAO

1 TUG Ex-US ARMY

TIBOLI (ex-US Army *LT 1976*) YQ 58

Transferred March 1976.

6 TUGS Ex-US "YTL 422" CLASS

IGOROT (ex-*YTL 572*) YQ 222
TAGBANUA (ex-*YTL 429*) YQ 223
— (ex-*YTL 750*) —
ILONGOT (ex-*YTL 427*) YQ 225
TASADAY (ex-*YTL 425*) YG 226
— (ex-*YTL 748*) —

Former US Navy 66-foot harbour tugs.

Ex-748 and 750 transferred from Japan—17 Nov 1975 and 24 Sept 1976 by sale respectively.

5 FLOATING DOCKS

YD 200 (ex-*AFDL 24*)
YD 201 (ex-*AFDL 3681*)
YD 203 (ex-*AFDL 3682*)
YD 204 (ex-*AFDL 20*)
YD 205 (ex-*ADFL 44*)

Floating dry docks built in the United States; three are former US Navy units with YD 200 transferred in July 1948, YD 204 in Oct 1961, and YD 205 in Sept 1969; two other units built specifically for Philippine service were completed in May 1952 and Aug 1955, respectively.

2 FLOATING CRANES

YU 206 (ex-US *YD 163*) **YU 207** (ex-US *YD 191*)

SURVEY SHIPS

Operated by Coast and Geodetic Survey of Ministry of National Defence.

Name	No.	Builders	Commissioned
PATHFINDER	—	—	1909

Displacement, tons: 1 057
Guns: 2—20 mm
Complement: 69

Ex-US Coastguard vessel. Date of transfer unknown.

Name	No.	Builders	Commissioned
ALUNYA	—	Walkers, Maryborough, Australia	1964
ARINYA	—	Walkers, Maryborough, Australia	1962

Displacement, tons: 245 full load
Dimensions, feet (metres): 90 pp × 22 × 10·5 *(27·4 × 6·7 × 3·2)*
Main engines: 2 diesels; 336 bhp = 10 knots
Complement: 33 (6 officers, 27 ratings)

Coaster type with raised quarter deck.

PHILIPPINES 389

Name	No.	Builders	Commissioned
ATYIMBA	—	Walkers, Maryborough, Australia	1969

Displacement, tons: 611 standard; 686 full load
Dimensions, feet (metres): 161 × 33 × 12 *(49·1 × 10 × 3·7)*
Guns: 2—20 mm
Main engines: 2 Paxman diesels; 726 bhp = 11 knots
Range, miles: 5 000 at 8 knots
Complement: 54

Similar to HMAS *Flinders* with differences in displacement and use of davits aft instead of cranes.

ATYIMBA *1976, Dr. Giorgio Arra*

COASTGUARD

The Coast Guard operates a number of Coastal Patrol Craft numbered from 90 upwards. Of these the majority are of US construction although several come from foreign builders.

1 Ex-US COAST GUARD "BALSAM" CLASS (TENDER)

Name	No.	Builders	Commissioned
KALINGA (ex-USCGC *Redbud*, WAGL 398, ex-USNS *Redbud*, T-AKL 398)	TK 89	Marine Iron & Shipbuilding Co, Duluth	11 Sept 1943

Displacement, tons: 935 standard
Dimensions, feet (metres): 180 oa × 37 × 13 *(59 × 12·1 × 4·3)*
Guns: Unarmed
Main engines: Diesel-electric; 1 200 bhp; 1 shaft = 13 knots

Originally US Coast Guard buoy tender (WAGL 398). Transferred to US Navy on 25 March 1949 as AG 398; redesignated AKL 398 on 31 March 1949; transferred to Military Sea Transportation Service on 20 Feb 1952 (T-AKL 398); reacquired by Coast Guard on 20 Nov 1970; transferred to Philippines 17 May 1972.

KALINGA *10/1977, Dr. Giorgio Arra*

POLAND

Headquarters Appointments

Commander-in-Chief of the Polish Navy:
  Vice-Admiral Ludwik Janczyszyn

Chief of the Naval Staff:
  Rear-Admiral Henryk Pietraszkiewicz

Diplomatic Representation

Naval, Military and Air Attaché in London:
  Colonel A. Wasilewski
Naval, Military and Air Attaché in Washington:
  Colonel Henryk Nowaczyk
Naval, Military and Air Attaché in Moscow:
  Brigadier General Waclaw Jagas
Naval, Military and Air Attaché in Paris:
  Colonel Marian Bugaj

Personnel

(a) 1978: 25 000 (2 800 officers and 22 200 men)
(b) 3 years national service

Bases

Gdynia, Hel, Swinoujscie.

Naval Aviation

There is a Fleet Air Arm of about 50 fixed-wing aircraft (mainly MiG-17 and IL-28) and helicopters.

Prefix to Ships' Names

ORP, standing for *Okrety Polska Rzeczpospolita*

Mercantile Marine

Lloyd's Register of Shipping:
  733 vessels of 3 263 206 tons gross

Strength of the Fleet

Including WOP (Coastguard)

Type	Active
Destroyer	1
Submarines—Patrol	4
Fast Attack Craft—Missile	12
Fast Attack Craft—Torpedo	21
	(some as targets)
Large Patrol Craft	26
Coastal Patrol Craft	5
Minesweepers—Ocean	24
Minesweeping Boats	20
LCTs	23
LCPs	15+
Surveying Vessel	1
AGI	1
Training Ships	7
Salvage Ships	2
Tankers	6
TRVs	2+
Tugs	20
DGVs	3
Miscellaneous	40

DELETIONS

Destroyers

1974 *Blyskawica* (museum ship in Gdynia in place of *Burza*)
1975 *Grom* and *Wicher* (ex-"Skory" class) now immobile AA batteries at Gdynia.

Corvettes

1973 *Czuiny, Wytrwaly, Zawziety, Zrezczny, Zwinny, Zwrotny*
1974 *Grozny, Nieugiety* ("Kronshtadt" class)

Fast Attack Craft—Torpedo

1973 3 "P 6" class
1974 6 "P 6" class
1975 4 "P 6" class

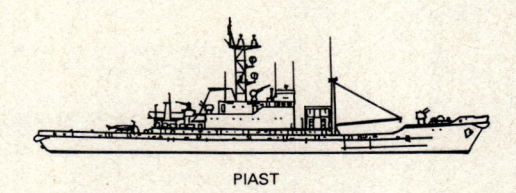

PIAST

SUBMARINES

4 Ex-SOVIET "WHISKEY" CLASS

ORZEL 292	KONDOR 294
SOKOL 293	BIELIK 295

Displacement, tons: 1 030 surfaced; 1 350 dived
Length, feet (metres): 249·3 *(76)*
Beam, feet (metres): 22 *(6·7)*
Draught, feet (metres): 15 *(4·6)*
Torpedo tubes: 6—21 in *(533 mm)*, (4 bow, 2 stern) 12 torpedoes carried
Mines: 40 mines in lieu of torpedoes
Main machinery: Diesel-electric; 2 diesels; 4 000 hp; 2 shafts; Electric motors; 2 500 hp
Speed, knots: 17 surfaced; 15 dived
Range, miles: 13 000 at 8 knots (surfaced)
Complement: 60

Built in the USSR and transferred to the Polish Navy.

Radar: Snoop Plate.

SOKOL *1971, Polish Navy*

KONDOR *1972*

DESTROYER

1 Ex-SOVIET "SAM KOTLIN" CLASS

WARSZAWA (ex-*Spravedlivy*) 275

Displacement, tons: 2 850 standard; 3 885 full load
Length, feet (metres): 415·0 *(126·5)* oa
Beam, feet (metres): 42·3 *(12·9)*
Draught, feet (metres): 16·1 *(4·9)*
Missile launchers: 1 twin SA-N-1 (Goa) aft
Guns: 2—5·1 in (1 twin); 4—45 mm (quad)
A/S weapons: 2—16 barrelled MBU
Torpedo tubes: 5—21 in *(533 mm)* (quin)
Main engines: Geared turbines; 2 shafts; 72 000 shp
Oil fuel, tons: 800
Range, miles: 5 500 at 16 knots
Speed, knots: 36
Complement: 285

Transferred from the USSR to the Polish Navy in 1970.

Radar: Air search: Head Net A.
Fire control: Peel Group (SA-N-1), Wasp Head/Sun Visor B (main armament), Hawk Screech.
IFF: High Pole B.

WARSZAWA *5/1975, C. and S. Taylor*

LIGHT FORCES

12 Ex-SOVIET "OSA" CLASS (FAST ATTACK CRAFT—MISSILE)

Displacement, tons: 165 standard; 200 full load
Dimensions, feet (metres): 128·7 × 25·1 × 5·9 *(39·3 × 7·7 × 1·8)*
Missiles: 4 launchers for SS-N-2
Guns: 4—30 mm (2 twin, 1 forward, 1 aft)
Main engines: 3 diesels; 13 000 bhp = 32 knots
Range, miles: 800 at 25 knots
Complement: 25

Most pennant numbers are in the 140-160 series as well as 084 and 136 and are carried on side-boards on the bridge.

Radar: Search: Square Tie.
Fire control: Drum Tilt.

"OSA" Class   1969

15 "WISLA" CLASS (FAST ATTACK CRAFT—TORPEDO)

Displacement, tons: 70 full load
Dimensions, feet (metres): 82·0 × 18·0 × 6·0 *(25 × 5·5 × 1·8)*
Guns: 2—30 mm (twin)
Torpedo tubes: 4—21 in *(533 mm)*
Main engines: Diesels; speed 30 knots

Polish built in a continuing programme since early 1970s. Most pennant numbers in 490 series but include 463.

"WISLA" Class   1975, S. Breyer

6 Ex-SOVIET "P 6" CLASS (FAST ATTACK CRAFT—TORPEDO)

Displacement, tons: 66 standard; 75 full load
Dimensions, feet (metres): 84·2 × 20 × 6 *(25·7 × 6·1 × 1·8)*
Guns: 4—25 mm; 8 DC
Torpedo tubes: 2—21 in *(533 mm)*
Main engines: 4 diesels; 4 800 bhp = 45 knots
Complement: 25

Acquired from the USSR in 1957-58. Torpedo tubes removed in some. At least two have been converted to target craft with reflectors similar to East German variant.

Radar: Surface search: Skin Head.

"P 6" Class   1971, Polish Navy

5 "OBLUZE" CLASS (LARGE PATROL CRAFT)

Note: All Polish-built Large Patrol Craft based on German R-boat design with modified bridge.

Name	No.	Builders	Commissioned
—	349	Oksywie Shipyard	1965
—	350	Oksywie Shipyard	1965
—	351	Oksywie Shipyard	1965
—	352	Oksywie Shipyard	1966
—	353	Oksywie Shipyard	1966

Displacement, tons: 170
Dimensions, feet (metres): 143·0 × 19·0 × 7·0 *(42 × 6 × 2·1)*
Guns: 4—30 mm (2 twins)
A/S weapons: 2 internal DC racks
Main engines: 2 diesels = 20 knots

Some belong to WOP (Coastguard).

Radar: Tamirio RN 231. Drum Tilt (not WOP craft).

"OBLUZE" Class (old number)   1969

8 "MODIFIED OBLUZE" CLASS (LARGE PATROL CRAFT)

301   302   303   304   305   306   307   308

Displacement, tons: 150
Dimensions, feet (metres): 137·8 × 19 × 6·6 *(41 × 6 × 2)*
Guns: 4—30 mm
A/S weapons: 2 internal DC racks
Main engines: 2 diesels = 20 knots

Slightly smaller than original "Obluze" class. Built late 1960s.

Radar: Tamirio RN 231 search. Drum Tilt.

Modified "OBLUZE" Class   1972, S. Breyer

POLAND

4 "OKSYWIE" CLASS (LARGE PATROL CRAFT)

336   337   338   339

Displacement, tons: 170 standard
Dimensions, feet (metres): 134·5 × 19·0 × 6·9 (41 × 6 × 2)
Guns: 2—37 mm; 4—12·7 mm
A/S weapons: 2 DC racks
Main engines: Diesels; speed = 20 knots

Some serve with WOP (coastguard). Built 1962-64.

Sonar: Tamirio.

"OKSYWIE" Class (old pennant number) 1972

9 "GDANSK" CLASS (LARGE PATROL CRAFT)

340-348

Displacement, tons: 120
Dimensions, feet (metres): 124·7 × 19·2 × 5·0 (35 × 5·8 × 1·5)
Guns: 2—37 mm; 2—12·7 mm (twin)
A/S weapons: DC rails
Main engines: Diesels = 20 knots

Built in Poland in 1960. Belong to WOP (Coastguard).

Sonar: Tamirio.

"GDANSK" Class (old pennant number) 1970

5 "PILICA" CLASS (COASTAL PATROL CRAFT)

701   702   703   704   705

Displacement, tons: 100 (approx)
Guns: 2—25 mm (twin)
Main engines: 2 diesels = 15 knots

Built in Poland since 1973. Belong to WOP (Coastguard).

MINE WARFARE FORCES

12 "KROGULEC" CLASS (MINESWEEPERS—OCEAN)

Name	No.	Builders	Commissioned
ORLIK	643	Stocznia, Gdynia	1964
KROGULEC	644	Stocznia, Gdynia	1963
JASTRAB	645	Stocznia, Gdynia	1964
KORMORAN	646	Stocznia, Gdynia	1963
CZAPLA	647	Stocznia, Gdynia	1964
ALBATROS	648	Stocznia, Gdynia	1965
PELIKAN	649	Stocznia, Gdynia	1965
TUKAN	650	Stocznia, Gdynia	1966
KANIA	651	Stocznia, Gdynia	1966
JASKOLKA	652	Stocznia, Gdynia	1966
ZURAW	653	Stocznia, Gdynia	1967
CZALPA	654	Stocznia, Gdynia	1967

Displacement, tons: 500
Dimensions, feet (metres): 190·3 × 24·6 × 8·2 (58 × 8·4 × 2·5)
Guns: 6—25 mm (twins)
Main engines: Diesels = 16 knots

PELIKAN (old pennant number) 5/1975, C. and S. Taylor

12 SOVIET "T 43" CLASS (MINESWEEPERS—OCEAN)

Name	No.	Builders	Commissioned
ZUBR*	631	Stocznia, Gdynia	1957
TUR*	632	Stocznia, Gdynia	1957
LOS*	633	Stocznia, Gdynia	1957
DZIK*	634	Stocznia, Gdynia	1958
BIZON	635	Stocznia, Gdynia	1958
BOBR	636	Stocznia, Gydnia	1959
ROSOMAK	637	Stocznia, Gdynia	1959
DELFIN	638	Stocznia, Gdynia	1960
FOKA	639	Stocznia, Gdynia	1960
MORS	640	Stocznia, Gdynia	1961
RYS	641	Stocznia, Gdynia	1961
ZBIK	642	Stocznia, Gdynia	1962

* 58 metre class.

Displacement, tons: 500 standard; 610 full load (*); 630 (remainder)
Dimensions, feet (metres): 190·2 × 28·2 × 6·9 (58 × 8·6 × 2·1) (*) 197 (60) (remainder)
Guns: 4—37 mm (twins), 4—25 mm (twins); 4—14·5 mm (twins)
A/S weapons: 2 DC throwers
Minelaying: Can lay mines
Main engines: 2 diesels; 2 shafts; 2 000 hp = 17 knots
Range, miles: 1 600 at 10 knots
Complement: 40

DELFIN (old pennant number) 1969, Polish Navy

20 "K 8" CLASS (MINESWEEPING BOATS)

Displacement, tons: 40 standard; 60 full load
Dimensions, feet (metres): 55·8 × 11·5 × 4 (17 × 3·5 × 1·2)
Guns: 2—25 mm (twin); 2 MG (twin)
Mines: Can lay mines
Main engines: 2 diesels; 2 shafts; 600 hp = 18 knots
Complement: 18

Now obsolescent and due for deletion.

POLAND 393

AMPHIBIOUS FORCES

23 "POLNOCNY" CLASS (LCT)

BALAS	JANOW	NARWIK
GRUNWALD 811	LENIN	WARTA	+ 17

Displacement, tons: 780 standard; 1 000 full load
Dimensions, feet (metres): 239·4 × 29·5 × 9·98 *(73 × 9 × 3)*
Guns: 4—30 mm (twin); 2—18 barrelled 140 mm rocket launchers
Main engines: 2 diesels; 5 000 bhp = 18 knots

Polish built in Gdansk, but same as the Soviet "Polnocny" class—can carry six tanks. Of various types including Polish variations. Pennant numbers—811/832 and 882.

Radar: Drum Tilt.

"POLNOCNY" Class (old pennant number) 1971

15 + LCPs

Length, feet (metres): 70 *(21·3)* approx
Gun: 1—30 mm

Pennant numbers in 500 series. Introduced 1975. Reported as "Marabut" and "Eichstaden" classes.

LCP 8/1975

MISCELLANEOUS

SURVEYING VESSEL

1 "MOMA" CLASS

KOPERNIK

Displacement, tons: 1 240 standard; 1 800 full load
Dimensions, feet (metres): 240 × 32·8 × 13·2 *(73·2 × 10 × 4)*
Main engines: Diesels = 16 knots

INTELLIGENCE VESSEL

1 B 10 TYPE

BALTYK

Displacement, tons: 1 200
Measurements, tons: 658 gross; 450 deadweight
Dimensions, feet (metres): 194·3 oa × 29·5 × 14 *(59·2 × 9·0 × 4·3)*
Main engines: Steam; 1 000 hp = 11 knots

Trawler of B-10 type. Built in 1954 in Gdansk. Converted and structure altered.

BALTYK 4/1976, S. Breyer

1 "MOMA" CLASS

NAWIGATOR

Details as for *Kopernik* above. Commissioned June 1975. Navigational training ship. Much altered in the upperworks and unrecognisable as a "Moma".

NAWIGATOR 1977, J. A. Verhoog

TRAINING SHIPS

1 SAIL TRAINING SHIP

Name	No.	Builders	Commissioned
ISKRA (ex-*Pigmy*, ex-*Iskra*, ex-*St. Blanc*, ex-*Vlissingen*)	—	Muller, Foxhol	1917

Displacement, tons: 560
Dimensions, feet (metres): 128 × 25 × 10 *(39 × 7·6 × 3·0)*
Main engines: Diesels; 250 bhp = 7·5 knots
Complement: 30, plus 40 cadets

A three masted schooner with auxiliary engines. Launched in 1917. Cadet training ship. Now used for harbour training.

— (ex-*Gryf*, ex-*Zetempowiec*, ex-*Opplem*, ex-*Omsk*, ex-*Empire Contees*, ex-*Irene Oldendorf*)

Apart from holding the record in this book for name changes this 1 959 ton ship launched in 1944, is now an alongside—accommodation ship for cadets. Due for deletion.

2 "WODNIK" CLASS

WODNIK	GRYF

Displacement, tons: 1 800
Dimensions, feet (metres): 239·4 × 39·4 × ?16·4 *(73 × 12 × ?5)*
Guns: 4—30 mm (twin); 2—25 mm (twin)
Main engines: Diesel = 17 knots

Built at Gdynia. *Wodnick* launched Nov 1975, *Gryf* March 1976.

"WODNIK" Class 9/1976, MOD

394 POLAND

3 "BRIZA" CLASS (TRAINING SHIPS)

BRIZA   KADET   PODCHORAZY

Displacement, tons: 150
Dimensions, feet (metres): 98·4 × 9·8 × 6·4 *(30 × 7 × 2)*
Main engines: Diesels = 10 knots
Complement: 11 plus 26 cadets

Podchorazy commissioned 30 Nov 1974, *Briza* 5 March 1975 and *Kadet* July 1975.

TANKERS

KRAB Z 1   MEDUSA Z 2   SLIMAK Z 3

Displacement, tons: approx 700
Guns: 2—30 mm (twin)

Z 5   Z 6   Z 7   Z 8   Z 9

Lighters of 300 tons gross with diesels, converted into tankers for coastal service.

TORPEDO RECOVERY VESSELS

2 + "PAJAK" CLASS

Some of this class, including K 11, have been reported.

TUGS

H 1-9, DP 51, HERCULES, NATEK, NEPTUNIA, POSEIDON, SMOK, SWAROZYC, SWIATOWID + 3

DEGAUSSING VESSELS

3 "MROWKA" CLASS

SD 11/13

A class of DGVs of which details are not yet available.

SALVAGE SHIPS

Name	No.	Builders	Commissioned
PIAST	—	Stocznia, Gdansk	26 Jan 1974
LECH	—	Stocznia, Gdansk	30 Nov 1974

Displacement, tons: 1 560 standard; 1 732 full load
Dimensions, feet (metres): 240 × 32·8 × 13·1 *(73·2 × 10 × 4)*
Guns: 8—25 mm (twins)
Main engines: 2 ZGODA diesels; 3 800 shp; 2 shafts
Speed, knots: 16·5
Range, miles: 3 000 at 12 knots

Carry a diving bell. Basically a "Moma" class hull.

"PIAST" Class   1977

AUXILIARIES

Ex-AGI *Kompas* now used as a barrack ship. Some 18 small diving craft, 4—180 ton salvage craft.
Hydrograf and *Kontroller,* of 30 and 80 tons are civilian-operated survey craft.
Icebreaker *Perkun* of 800 is civilian-operated but available for naval use.
Some fifteen other tenders.

PORTUGAL

Headquarters Appointment

Chief of Naval Staff:
  Admiral A. S. Silva Cruz

Diplomatic Representation

Naval Attaché in London:
  Captain I. M. Serpa Gouveia
Naval Attaché in Washington:
  Captain Jose L. Ferreira Lamas
Naval Attaché in Paris:
  Captain Pedro Azevedo Coutinho

Personnel

(a) 1978: 10 000 including marines (decreasing)
(b) 3 years national service

Naval Bases

Main Base: Lisbon
Dockyard: Arsenal do Alfeite

Maritime Reconnaissance Aircraft

Whilst there are no aircraft belonging to the Navy, P2V Neptunes of the Portuguese Air Force are placed under naval operational control for specific maritime operations.

Prefix to Ships' Names

NRP

Mercantile Marine

Lloyd's Register of Shipping:
  350 vessels of 1 281 439 tons gross

Strength of the Fleet

Type	Active	Building
Frigates	13	—
Submarines (Patrol)	3	—
Large Patrol Craft	10	—
Coastal Patrol Craft	8	—
Minesweepers (Coastal)	4	—
LCT	1	—
LCMs	12	1
LCA	1	—
Survey Ships and Craft	4	1
Replenishment Tanker	1	—
Sail Training Ship	1	—
Ocean Tug	1	—
Harbour Tugs	2	—
Harbour Tanker	1	—

DELETIONS
(see ANGOLA section)

Frigates

1970 *Francisco de Almeida, Pacheco Pereira*
1971 *Alvares Cabral, Vasco da Gama*
1975 *Pero Escobar*
1977 *Alfonso Cerqueira, Baptista de Andrade, Joao Roby, Oliveira E. Carmo* sold to Colombia.

Submarine

1975 *Cachalote* ("Daphne" class) (to Pakistan)

Amphibious Forces

1975 *Alfanage, Ariete, Cimitarra* ("Alfange" class LCTs)
  LDM 401-411, 413-417 ("400" class LCMs)
  LDM 304, 309 ("300" class LCMs)
  LDM 204 ("200" class LCM)
  LDM 101, 102, 105-118 ("100" class LCMs)
  LDP 301-303, 201, 203-217, 107, 108 (21 LCAs)
1976 *Bombarda* (LDG), *Montanee, Bacamarte* ("Alfange" class)

Large Patrol Craft

1971 *Cacheu*
1973 *Porto Sante, Fogo, Maio* ("Maio" class)
1975 *Boavista, Brava, Santa Luzia* ("Maio" class)
1976 *Sao Nicolau*

Light Forces

1975 *Cassiopeia, Escorpião, Lira, Orion, Pegaso* ("Argos" class)
  Sabre (River patrol craft)
  Albufeira, Aljezur, Alvor ("Alvor" class)
  Aldebaran, Altair, Arcturus, Bellatrix, Espiga, Fomalhaut, Pollux, Procion, Rigel, Sirius and *Vega* ("Bellatrix" class)
  Jupiter, Marte, Mercurio, Saturno, Urano and *Venus* ("Jupiter" class)
  Antares (Coastal patrol craft)
  Azevia, Corvina, Dourada ("Azevia" class)
1976 *Argos, Centauro, Dragao, Hidra, Sagitario* ("Argos" class) (some to Angola)
  Condor ("Albatroz" class), *Castor, Regulus, Bicuda* ("Azevia" class)

Survey Ships

1975 *Almirante Lacerda, Cavalho Araujo, Cruzeiro do Sul*
1976 *Pedro Nunes*

Service Forces

1975 *Sam Bras* (Fleet Supply Ship) (now used as accommodation ship), *Santo André*
1976 *São Rafael*

Minesweepers

1973 *Angra do Heroismo, Ponta Delgada, S. Pedro* (MSC), *Corvo, Pico, Graciosa, S. Jorge* (MSO)
1975 *Lajes, Santa Cruz* (MSC)
1976 *Horta, Velas, Vila do Porto*

PENNANT LIST

Frigates

F 471	Antonio Enes
F 472	Almirante Pereira Da Silva
F 473	Almirante Gago Coutinho
F 474	Almirante Magalhaes Correia
F 475	João Coutinho
F 476	Jacinto Candido
F 477	Gen. Pereira d'Eca
F 480	Comandante João Belo
F 481	Comandante Hermenegildo Capelo
F 482	Comandante Roberto Ivens
F 483	Comandante Sacadura Cabral
F 484	Augusto de Castilho
F 485	Honorio Barreto

Submarines

S 163	Albacora
S 164	Barracuda
S 166	Delfin

Minewarfare Forces

M 401	Sao Roque
M 402	Ribeira Grande
M 403	Lagoa
M 404	Rosario

Amphibious Forces

LDG 202 Alabarda
LDM 119-121
LDM 406
LDM 414
LDM 418-424
LDP 216

Light Forces and Corvettes

P 370	Rio Minho
P 1140	Cacine
P 1141	Cunene
P 1142	Mandovi
P 1143	Rovuma
P 1144	Cuanza
P 1145	Geba
P 1146	Zaire
P 1147	Zambese
P 1148	Dom Aleixo
P 1149	Dom Jeremias
P 1160	Limpopo
P 1161	Save
P 1162	Albatroz
P 1163	Acor
P 1164	Andorinha
P 1165	Aguia
P 1167	Cisne

Service Forces

A 520	Sagres
A 521	Schultz Xavier
A 526	Afonso de Albuquerque
A 527	Almeida Carvalho
A 5200	Mira
A 5206	São Gabriel

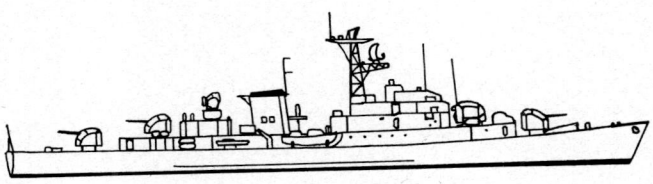

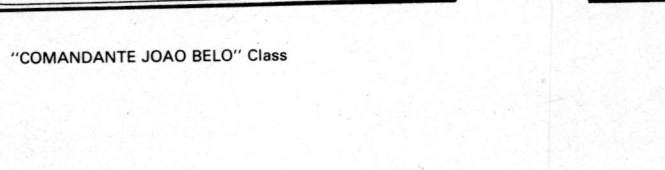

"COMANDANTE JOAO BELO" Class

"ALMIRANTE PEREIRA DA SILVA" Class

"JOAO COUTINHO" Class

ALFONSO DE ALBUQUERQUE

396 PORTUGAL

SUBMARINES

3 FRENCH "DAPHNE" CLASS

Name	No.
ALBACORA	S 163
BARRACUDA	S 164
DELFIN	S 166

Builders	Laid down	Launched	Commissioned
Dubigeon-Normandie	6 Sept 1965	13 Oct 1966	1 Oct 1967
Dubigeon-Normandie	19 Oct 1965	24 April 1967	4 May 1968
Dubigeon-Normandie	14 May 1967	23 Sept 1968	1 Oct 1969

Displacement, tons: 700 standard; 869 surfaced; 1 043 dived
Length, feet (metres): 189·6 *(57·8)*
Beam, feet (metres): 22·3 *(6·8)*
Draught, feet (metres): 15·1 *(4·6)*
Torpedo tubes: 12—21·7 in *(550 mm)*; (8 bow, 4 stern)
Main machinery: SEMT-Pielstick diesels, 1 300 bhp; electric motors; 450 kW, 1 600 hp; 2 shafts
Speed, knots: 13·2 surfaced; 16 dived
Oil fuel, tons: 90
Range, miles: 2 710 at 12·5 knots surfaced; 2 130 at 10 knots snorting
Complement: 50 (5 officers; 45 men)

The prefabricated construction of these submarines was begun between 1 Oct 1964 and 6 Sept 1965 at the Dubigeon-Normandie Shipyard. They are basically similar to the French "Daphne" type, but slightly modified to suit Portuguese requirements.

Transfer: *Cachalote* transferred to Pakistan as *Ghazi* 1975.

DELFIN   1972, Portuguese Navy

FRIGATES

4 "COMANDANTE JOÃO BELO" CLASS

Name
COMANDANTE JOÃO BELO
COMANDANTE HERMENEGILDO CAPELO
COMANDANTE ROBERTO IVENS
COMANDANTE SACADURA CABRAL

No.	Builders	Laid down	Launched	Commissioned
F 480	At et Ch de Nantes	6 Sept 1965	22 Mar 1966	1 July 1967
F 481	At et Ch de Nantes	13 May 1966	29 Nov 1966	26 April 1968
F 482	At et Ch de Nantes	13 Dec 1966	8 Aug 1967	23 Nov 1968
F 483	At et Ch de Nantes	18 Aug 1967	15 Mar 1968	25 July 1969

Displacement, tons: 1 990 standard; 2 230 full load
Length, feet (metres): 321·5 *(98)* pp; 338 *(103·0)* oa
Beam, feet (metres): 37·7 *(11·5)*
Draught, feet (metres): 14·5 *(4·42)*
Guns: 3—3·9 in *(100 mm)* single; 2—40 mm
A/S weapons: 1—12 in quadruple mortar
Torpedo tubes: 6—21·7 in *(550 mm)* A/S (triple)
Main engines: SEMT/Pielstick diesels; 2 shafts; 18 760 bhp
Speed, knots: 25
Range, miles: 4 500 at 15 knots; 2 300 at 25 knots
Complement: 200 (14 officers, 186 men)

Construction: The prefabricated construction of these frigates was begun on 1 Oct 1964.

Design: They are similar to the French "Commandant Rivière" class except for the 30 mm guns which were replaced by 40 mm guns.

Radar: Search: DRBV 22A
Tactical: DRBV 50
Fire control: DRBC 31D
Navigation: Decca RM 316

Sonar: Search: SQS 17A
Attack: DUBA-3A

COMANDANTE ROBERTO IVENS   1970, Portuguese Navy

3 "ALMIRANTE PEREIRA DA SILVA" CLASS

Name	No.
ALMIRANTE PEREIRA DA SILVA	F 472 (ex-US DE 1039)
ALMIRANTE GAGO COUTINHO	F 473 (ex-US DE 1042)
ALMIRANTE MAGALHÃES CORREA	F 474 (ex-US DE 1046)

Builders	Laid down	Launched	Commissioned
Estaleiros Navais (Lisnave), Lisbon	14 June 1962	2 Dec 1963	20 Dec 1966
Estaleiros Navais (Lisnave), Lisbon	2 Dec 1963	13 Aug 1965	29 Nov 1967
Estaleiros Navais de Viana do Castelo	30 Aug 1965	26 April 1966	4 Nov 1968

Displacement, tons: 1 450 standard; 1 914 full load
Length, feet (metres): 314·6 *(95·9)*
Beam, feet (metres): 36·68 *(11·18)*
Draught, feet (metres): 17·5 *(5·33)*
Guns: 4—3 in *(76 mm)* 50 cal
A/S weapons: 2 Bofors four-barrelled 375 mm rocket launchers;
 6 (2 triple) Mk 32 A/S torpedo tubes
Main engines: De Laval dr geared turbines; 1 shaft; 20 000 shp
Boilers: 2 Foster Wheeler, 300 psi, 850°F
Speed, knots: 27
Oil fuel, tons: 400
Range, miles: 3 220 at 15 knots
Complement: 166 (12 officers, 154 men)

Construction: The prefabrication of *Almirante Pereira da Silva* and *Almirante Gago Coutinho* was begun in 1961 at Lisnave (formerly Navais Shipyard, Lisbon) and of *Almirante Magalhães Correa* in 1962.

Design: Similar to the United States destroyer escorts of the "Dealey" class, but modified to suit Portuguese requirements.

Radar: Search: MLA-1b.
Fire control: AN/SPG 34 (on 3 in mounts)
Navigational: Decca RM 316P
Tactical: Type 978.
Extensive EW.

Sonar: Search: AN/SQS 30-32A. AN/SQA 10A (VDS).
Attack: DUBA-3A.

ALMIRANTE MAGALHAES CORREA   6/1977, C. and S. Taylor

PORTUGAL

6 "JOÃO COUTINHO" CLASS

Name	No.
ANTONIO ENES	F 471
JOÃO COUTINHO	F 475
JACINTO CANDIDO	F 476
GENERAL PEREIRA D'ECA	F 477
AUGUSTO DE CASTILHO	F 484
HONORIO BARRETO	F 485

Builders	Laid down	Launched	Commissioned
Empresa Nacional Bazan, Spain	Apr 1968	16 Aug 1969	18 June 1971
Blöhm and Voss AG, Hamburg, Germany	Sept 1968	2 May 1969	7 Mar 1970
Blöhm and Voss AG, Hamburg, Germany	April 1968	16 June 1969	16 June 1970
Blöhm and Voss AG, Hamburg, Germany	Oct 1968	26 July 1969	10 Oct 1970
Empresa Nacional Bazan, Spain	Aug 1968	4 July 1969	14 Nov 1970
Empresa Nacional Bazan, Spain	July 1968	11 April 1970	15 April 1971

Displacement, tons: 1 203 standard; 1 380 full load
Length, feet (metres): 227·5 *(84·6)*
Beam, feet (metres): 33·8 *(10·3)*
Draught, feet (metres): 11·8 *(3·6)*
Missiles: 2 MM 38 Exocet in 486-489
Guns: 2—3 in *(76 mm)* (twin); 2—40 mm (first six); 1—3·9 in *(100 mm)* 50 cal; 2 Bofors 40 mm (single) (486-489)
A/S weapons: 1 Hedgehog; 2 DC throwers (first six); 2 DC racks; (2 triple Mk 32 torpedo tubes in 486-489)
Main engines: 2 OEW 12-cyl Pielstick diesels; 10 560 bhp
Speed, knots: 24·4
Range, miles: 5 900 at 18 knots
Complement: 100 (9 officers, 91 men) plus marine detachment of 34

Fire control: 40 m Mk 51 GFCS (first six)

Radar: In first six:
Air search: MLA-1B.
Navigation: Decca TM 626.
Main guns: On-mounted radar SPG-34 (Mk 63 GFCS).
In 486-489:
Air search: Plessey AWS-2.
Navigation: Decca TM 626.
Gun fire control: Thomson CSF Pollux.

JOÃO COUTINHO   1971, Portuguese Navy

Transfer: Four of this class sold to Colombia in 1977.

LIGHT FORCES

10 "CACINE" CLASS (LARGE PATROL CRAFT)

Name	No.	Builders	Commissioned
CACINE	P 1140	Arsenal do Alfeite	1969
CUNENE	P 1141	Arsenal do Alfeite	1969
MANDOVI	P 1142	Arsenal do Alfeite	1969
ROVUMA	P 1143	Arsenal do Alfeite	1969
CUANZA	P 1144	Estaleiros Navais do Mendogo	May 1969
GEBA	P 1145	Estaleiros Navais do Mendogo	May 1969
ZAIRE	P 1146	Estaleiros Navais do Mendogo	Nov 1970
ZAMBEZE	P 1147	Estaleiros Navais do Mendogo	1971
LIMPOPO	P 1160	Arsenal do Alfeite	April 1973
SAVE	P 1161	Arsenal do Alfeite	May 1973

Displacement, tons: 292·5 standard; 310 full load
Dimensions, feet (metres): 144·0 oa × 25·2 × 7·1 *(44 × 7·7 × 2·2)*
Guns: 2—40 mm; 1—32 barrelled rocket launcher 37 mm
Main engines: 2 MTU 12V 538 Maybach (MTU) diesels; 4 000 bhp = 20 knots
Range, miles: 4 400 at 12 knots
Complement: 33 (3 officers, 30 men)

Radar: KH 975.

CACINE   1973, Portuguese Navy

2 "DOM ALEIXO" CLASS (COASTAL PATROL CRAFT)

Name	No.	Builders	Commissioned
DOM ALEIXO	P 1148	S. Jacintho Aveiro	7 Dec 1967
DOM JEREMIAS	P 1149	S. Jacintho Aveiro	22 Dec 1967

Displacement, tons: 62·6 standard; 67·7 full load
Dimensions, feet (metres): 82·1 oa × 17·0 × 5·2 *(25 × 5·2 × 1·6)*
Gun: 1—20 mm
Main engines: 2 Cummins diesels; 1 270 bhp = 16 knots
Complement: 10 (2 officers, 8 men)

Dom Aleixo in use as survey craft.

Radar: Decca 303.

DOM JEREMIAS   1973, Portuguese Navy

5 "ALBATROZ" CLASS (COASTAL PATROL CRAFT)

Name	No.	Builders	Commissioned
ALBATROZ	P 1162	Arsenal do Alfeite	1974
ACOR	P 1163	Arsenal do Alfeite	1974
ANDORINHA	P 1164	Arsenal do Alfeite	1975
AGUIA	P 1165	Arsenal do Alfeite	1975
CISNE	P 1167	Arsenal do Alfeite	1974

Displacement, tons: 45
Dimensions, feet (metres): 72 × 17 × 5 *(23·6 × 5·6 × 1·6)*
Guns: 1—20 mm; 2—50 cal MGs
Main engines: 2 Cummins diesels; 1 100 hp
Speed, knots: 20
Range, miles: 2 500 at 12 knots
Complement: 8 (1 officer, 7 men)

Radar: Decca RM 316P.

1 COASTAL PATROL CRAFT

Name	No.	Builders	Commissioned
RIO MINHO	P 370	Arsenal do Alfeite	1957

Displacement, tons: 14
Dimensions, feet (metres): 49·2 × 10·5 × 2·3 *(15 × 3·2 × 0·7)*
Guns: 2 light MG
Main engines: 2 Alfa Romeo diesels; 130 bhp = 9 knots
Complement: 7

Built for the River Minho on the Spanish border.

398   PORTUGAL

MINE WARFARE FORCES

4 "SAO ROQUE" CLASS (MINESWEEPERS—COASTAL)

Name	No.	Builders	Commissioned
SAO ROQUE	M 401	CUF Shipyard, Lisbon	6 June 1956
RIBEIRA GRANDE	M 402	CUF Shipyard, Lisbon	8 Feb 1957
LAGOA	M 403	CUF Shipyard, Lisbon	10 Aug 1956
ROSARIO	M 404	CUF Shipyard, Lisbon	8 Feb 1956

Displacement, tons: 394·4 standard; 451·9 full load
Dimensions, feet (metres): 140·0 (42·7) pp; 152·0 oa × 28·8 × 7·0 (46·3 × 8·8 × 2·3)
Guns: 2—20 mm (twin)
Main engines: 2 Mirrlees diesels; 2 shafts; 2 500 bhp = 15 knots
Complement: 47 (4 officers, 43 men)

Similar to British "Ton" class coastal minesweepers, laid down on 7 Sept 1954, under the OSP-MAP. *Lagoa* and *Sao Roque* were financed by USA and other two by Portugal. 40 mm gun removed 1972.

LAGOA (before change of armament)   1972, Portuguese Navy

AMPHIBIOUS FORCES

Note: One small landing craft under construction.

1 "BOMBARDA" CLASS LDG (LCT)

Name	No.	Builders	Commissioned
ALABARDA	LDG 202	Estaleiros Navais do Mondego	1970

Displacement, tons: 510 standard; 652 full load
Dimensions, feet (metres): 184·3 × 38·7 × 6·2 (56·2 × 11·8 × 1·9)
Main engines: 2 Maybach-Mercedes-Benz (MTU) diesels; 910 hp = 9·5 knots
Range, miles: 2 600 at 9·5 knots
Complement: 20 (2 officers, 18 men)

Radar: Decca RM 316.

BOMBARDA (ALABARDA similar)   1972, Portuguese Navy

9 "LDM 400" CLASS (LCM)

LDM 406   LDM 418   LDM 420   LDM 422   LDM 424
LDM 414   LDM 419   LDM 421   LDM 423

1 "LDP 200" (Ex-LD) CLASS (LCA)

Name	No.	Builders	Commissioned
—	LDP 216	Estaleiros Navais do Mondego	5 Feb 1969

Displacement, tons: 12 light; 18 full load
Dimensions, feet (metres): Length: 46 oa (14)
Main engines: 2 diesels; 187 bhp

3 "LDM 100" CLASS (LCM)

LDM 119   LDM 120   LDM 121

Displacement, tons: 50 full load
Dimensions, feet (metres): Length: 50 (15·25)
Main engines: 2 diesels; 450 bhp

All built at the Estaleiros Navais do Mondego in 1965.

SURVEY SHIPS

1 NEW CONSTRUCTION OCEANOGRAPHIC SHIP

Displacement, tons: 1 140
Dimensions, feet (metres): 196·8 × 39·4 × 15·1 (60 × 12 × 4·6)
Main engines: Diesel; 1 700 hp = 15 knots

Ordered 1976 from Arsenal do Alfeite.

1 Ex-US "KELLAR" CLASS

Name	No.	Builders	Commissioned
ALMEIDA CARVALHO (ex-USNS *Kellar*, T-AGS 25)	A 527	Marietta Shipbuilding Co.	31 Jan 1969

Displacement, tons: 1 200 standard; 1 400 full load
Dimensions, feet (metres): 190 oa × 39·0 × 15·0 (58 × 11·7 × 4·5)
Main engines: Diesel-electric; 1 shaft; 1 200 hp = 15 knots
Complement: 30 (5 officers, 25 men)

Laid down on 20 Nov 1962, launched on 30 July 1964. On loan from the US Navy since 21 Jan 1972.

Radar: One RCA CRM-N2A-30.
One Decca TM 829.

DOM ALEIXO

See Light Forces section for details.

MIRA (ex-*Fomalhaut*, ex-*Arrabida*) A 5200

Displacement, tons: 30 standard
Dimensions, feet (metres): 62·9 × 15·2 × 4 (19·2 × 4·6 × 1·2)
Main engines: 3 Perkins diesels; 300 bhp = 15 knots
Range, miles: 650 at 8 knots (economical speed)
Complement: 6 men

Launched 1961. No radar.

Name	No.	Builders	Commissioned
ALFONSO DE ALBUQUERQUE (ex-HMS *Dalrymple*, ex-HMS *Luce Bay*)	A 526	Wm. Pickersgill & Sons Ltd, Sunderland and HM Dockyard, Devonport	10 Feb 1949

Displacement, tons: 1 590 standard; 2 230 full load
Length, feet (metres): 286·0 (87·2) pp; 307·0 (93·6) oa
Beam, feet (metres): 38·5 (11·7)
Draught, feet (metres): 14·2 (4·3)
Main engines: 4-cyl triple expansion; 2 shafts; 5 500 ihp
Speed, knots: 19·5
Boilers: 2 Admiralty three-drum type
Range, miles: 7 055 at 9·1 knots
Complement: 109 (9 officers, 100 men)

Modified "Bay" class frigate. Built by Wm. Pickersgill & Sons Ltd, Sunderland, but completed at HM Dockyard, Devonport. Laid down on 29 April 1944. Launched on 12 April 1945. Purchased from the United Kingdom in April 1966.

PORTUGAL / QATAR 399

SERVICE FORCES

1 REPLENISHMENT TANKER

Name	No.	Builders	Commissioned
SÃO GABRIEL	A 5206	Estaleiros de Viana do Castelo	27 Mar 1963

Displacement, tons: 9 000 standard; 14 200 full load
Measurement, tons: 9 854 gross; 9 000 deadweight
Dimensions, feet (metres): 452·8 pp; 479·0 oa × 59·8 × 26·2 *(138; 146 × 18·2 × 8)*
Main engines: 1 Pametrada-geared turbine; 1 shaft; 9 500 shp = 17 knots
Boilers: 2
Range, miles: 6 000 at 15 knots
Complement: 98 (10 officers, 88 men)

Radar: Search: AN/SPS 6C.
Navigation: KH 975.

SÃO GABRIEL *1973, Portuguese Navy*

1 TRAINING SHIP

Name	No.	Builders	Commissioned
SAGRES (ex-*Guanabara*, ex-*Albert Leo Schlageter*)	A 520	Blöhm & Voss, Hamburg	1 Feb 1938

Displacement, tons: 1 725 standard; 1 869 full load
Dimensions, feet (metres): 293·5 oa × 39·3 × 17·0 *(89·5 × 12 × 4·6)*
Main engines: 2 MAN auxiliary diesels; 1 shaft; 750 bhp = 10 knots
Oil fuel, tons: 52
Range, miles: 3 500 at 6·5 knots
Complement: 153 (10 officers, 143 men)

Former German sail training ship. Built by Blöhm & Voss, Hamburg. Launched in June 1937 and completed on 1 Feb 1938. Sister of US Coast Guard training ship *Eagle* (ex-German *Horst Wessel*) and Soviet *Tovarisch*. Taken by USA as a reparation after the Second World War in 1945 and sold to Brazil in 1948. Purchased from Brazil and commissioned in the Portuguese Navy on 2 Feb 1972 at Rio de Janeiro and renamed *Sagres*.
Sail area 20 793 sq feet. Height of main-mast 142 feet.

SAGRES *1973, Portuguese Navy*

MISCELLANEOUS

1 HARBOUR TANKER

BC 3 (ex-US *YO 194*)

Transferred April 1962.

3 NEW CONSTRUCTION

SPARTACUS   ULISSES   + 1

Displacement, tons: 194
Dimensions, feet (metres): 94 × 28 × 7 *(28·7 × 8·5 × 2·1)*
Main engines: 2 400 hp; 2 shafts = 12·5 knots

First launched 18 Feb 1977, second on 9 March 1977.

TUGS

1 OCEAN TUG

Name	No.	Builders	Commissioned
SCHULTZ XAVIER	A 521	Alfeite Naval Yard	14 July 1972

Displacement, tons: 900
Main engines: 2 diesels; 2 shafts; 2 400 hp = 14·5 knots
Range, miles: 3 000 at 12·5 knots

A dual purpose ocean tug and buoy/lighthouse tender ordered late in 1968.

2 HARBOUR TUGS

RB 1 (ex-*ST 1994*)   RB 2 (ex-*ST 1996*)

Transferred from US Navy—RB 1 Dec 1961, RB 2 March 1962.

QATAR

Now possesses an expanding Marine Police Division of the Qatar Police Force. The geographical position of the state, dividing the Persian Gulf and covering Bahrain, gives this force added importance. The main oil-terminal is at Umm-Said.

Senior Officer
Commander Naval Force:
Colonel Salah Eddin Azab Saleem

Personnel
(a) 1978: 400 officers and men
(b) Voluntary service

Base
Doha

Mercantile Marine
Lloyd's Register of Shipping:
19 vessels of 84 710 tons gross

6 VOSPER THORNYCROFT 103 ft TYPE (LARGE PATROL CRAFT)

Name	No.	Builders	Commissioned
BARZAN	Q 11	Vosper Thornycroft Ltd	13 Jan 1975
HWAR	Q 12	Vosper Thornycroft Ltd	30 April 1975
THAT ASSUARI	Q 13	Vosper Thornycroft Ltd	3 Oct 1975
AL WUSAAIL	Q 14	Vosper Thornycroft Ltd	28 Oct 1975
FATEH-AL-KHAIR	Q 15	Vosper Thornycroft Ltd	22 Jan 1976
TARIQ	Q 16	Vosper Thornycroft Ltd	1 Mar 1976

Displacement, tons: 120
Dimensions, feet (metres): 103·7 pp; 110 oa × 21 × 5·5 *(31·1; 33·5 × 6·3 × 1·6)*
Guns: 2—20 mm
Main engines: 2 diesels; 4 000 hp = 27 knots
Complement: 25

Ordered in 1972-73. All laid down between Sept 1973 and Nov 1974.

AL WUSAAIL *12/1974, C. and S. Taylor*

QATAR / ROMANIA

2 75 ft COASTAL PATROL CRAFT

Length, feet (metres): 75 (22·5)
Guns: 2—20 mm
Main engines: 2 diesels; 1 420 hp

Built by Whittingham and Mitchell, Chertsey 1969.

25 FAIREY MARINE "SPEAR" CLASS
(COASTAL PATROL CRAFT)

Displacement, tons: 4·3
Dimensions, feet (metres): 29·8 × 9 × 2·8 (9·1 × 2·8 × 0·8)
Guns: 3—7·62 mm
Main engines: 2 diesels; 290 hp; 2 shafts = 26 knots
Complement: 4

First seven ordered early 1974. Delivered 19 June 1974, 16 Sept 1974, 18 Sept 1974, 2 Nov 1974, Dec 1974, Jan 1975, Feb 1975. Contract for further five signed December 1975. Third contract for three fulfilled with delivery of two on 30 June 1975 and one on 14 July 1975. Fourth order for ten (4 Mk 1—6 Mk 2) received Oct 1976 and delivery effected April 1977.

2 FAIREY MARINE "INTERCEPTOR" CLASS
(FAST ASSAULT/RESCUE CRAFT)

Displacement, tons: 1·25
Dimensions, feet (metres): 25 × 8 × 2·5 (7·9 × 2·4 × 0·8)
Main engines: 2 Johnson outboard motors; 270 bhp = 35 knots
Range, miles: 150 at 30 knots
Complement: 3

In assault role can carry 10 troops. In rescue role carry number of life rafts. GRP catamaran hull. Delivered 28 Nov 1975.

2 KEITH NELSON 45 ft TYPE (COASTAL PATROL CRAFT)

Displacement, tons: 13
Dimensions, feet (metres): 44 × 12·3 × 3·8 (13·5 × 3·8 × 1·1)
Guns: 1—12·7 mm; 2—7·62 mm (singles)
Main engines: 2 Caterpillar diesels; 800 hp = 26 knots
Complement: 6

The third vessel of this group has been converted into a pilot cutter.

FAIREY MARINE SPEARS   1974, Fairey Marine

RAS AL KHAIMAH
(see United Arab Emirates)

ROMANIA

Headquarters Appointment

Commander in Chief of the Navy:
 Rear-Admiral Sebastian Ulmeanu

Diplomatic Representation

Defence Attaché in London:
 Colonel C. Popa
Naval, Military and Air Attaché in Washington:
 Colonel Nicolae Gheorghe Plesa

Bases

Mangalia, Constanta, Dulcea (Danube base)

Personnel

(a) 1978: 10 000 officers and ratings
    (including 2 000 Coastal Defence)
(b) 2 years national service

Lloyd's Register of Shipping:
 207 vessels of 1 218 171 tons gross

Strength of the Fleet

(No details of building programme available)

Type	Active
Corvettes	3
Large Patrol Craft	3
Fast Attack Craft (Missile)	5
Fast Attack Craft (Gun and Patrol)	18
Fast Attack Craft (Torpedo)	23
River Patrol Craft	28
Minesweepers (Coastal)	4
Minesweepers (Inshore)	10
MSBs	8
Training Ships	1 + 1
Tugs	2

(Other unconfirmed vessels listed at end of section).

CORVETTES

3 Ex-SOVIET "POTI" CLASS

V 31   V 32   V 83

Displacement, tons: 550 standard; 600 full load
Dimensions, feet (metres): 193·5 × 26·2 × 9·2 (59 × 8 × 2·8)
Guns: 2—57 mm (twin)
Torpedo tubes: 2—21 in (533 mm)
A/S weapons: 2—16 barrelled MBU 2 500
Main engines: 2 gas turbines; 2 diesels; 2 shafts; total 20 000 hp = 28 knots
Complement: 50

Transferred from the USSR in 1970.

Radar: Don, Strut Curve, Muff Cob.

"POTI" Class   1971

LIGHT FORCES

3 Ex-SOVIET "KRONSHTADT" CLASS (LARGE PATROL CRAFT)

V-1   V-2   V-3

Displacement, tons: 310 standard; 380 full load
Dimensions, feet (metres): 170·6 × 21·5 × 9 (52 × 6·5 × 2·7)
Guns: 1—3·4 in; 2—37 mm (single); 6—12·7 mm (twins)
A/S weapons: 2 DC throwers; 2 depth charge racks
Main engines: 3 diesels; 3 shafts; 3 300 bhp = 24 knots
Range, miles: 1 500 at 12 knots
Complement: 65

Transferred by USSR in 1956.

Radar: Ball End.

"KRONSHTADT" Class

18 Ex-CHINESE "SHANGHAI" CLASS
(FAST ATTACK CRAFT—GUN and PATROL)

| VP 20-29 | VP 31 | VS 41-46 | VS 52 |

Displacement, tons: 120 standard; 155 full load
Dimensions, feet (metres): 128 × 18 × 5·6 *(39 × 5·5 × 1·7)*
Guns: VP type: 1—57 mm; 2—37 mm (twin). VS type: 1—37 mm; 4—14·5 mm MG
A/S weapons: VS type: 2—five-barrelled MBU 1200; 2 DC racks
Main engines: 4 diesels; 4 800 bhp = 30 knots
Complement: 25

Two variants of the "Shanghai" class of which the VS type (patrol A/S) is a new departure.
Built at Mangalia since 1973 in a continuing programme.

"SHANGHAI" Class—VS Type *8/1974*

5 Ex-SOVIET "OSA" CLASS (FAST ATTACK CRAFT—MISSILE)

194 to 198

Displacement, tons: 165 standard; 200 full load
Dimensions, feet (metres): 128·7 × 25·1 × 5·9 *(39·3 × 7·7 × 1·8)*
Missile launchers: 4 for SS-N-2
Guns: 4—30 mm (2 twin, 1 forward, 1 aft)
Main engines: 3 diesels; 13 000 bhp = 32 knots
Range, miles: 800 at 25 knots
Complement: 30

Transferred by USSR in 1964.

"OSA I" Class

10 CHINESE "HU CHWAN" CLASS
(FAST ATTACK CRAFT—TORPEDO)

VT 51-53 + 6

Displacement, tons: 45
Dimensions, feet (metres): 70 × 16·5 × 3·1 *(21·4 × 5 × 1)*
Guns: 4—14·5 mm (twins)
Torpedo tubes: 2—21 in *(533 mp)*
Main engines: 2 diesels; 2 200 hp = 55 knots (foilborne in calm conditions)
Range, miles: 500 cruising

Hydrofoils of the same class as the Chinese which were started in 1956.
Three with unknown pennant numbers imported from China. Further three (VT 51-53) locally
built in a continuing programme which started 1973-74.

"HU CHWAN" Class *8/1974*

13 Ex-SOVIET "P 4" CLASS (FAST ATTACK CRAFT—TORPEDO)

87 to 92 + 7

Displacement, tons: 25
Dimensions, feet (metres): 62·7 × 11·6 × 5·6 *(19·1 × 3·5 × 1·7)*
Guns: 2—14·5 mm (twin)
Torpedo tubes: 2—18 in
Main engines: 2 diesels; 2 200 bhp = 50 knots
Complement: 12

Built in 1955-56. Becoming obsolescent and ready for deletion. One has had guns removed.

"P 4" Class *1971*

402 ROMANIA

9 RIVER PATROL CRAFT

VB 76-82 + 2

Dimensions, feet (metres): 105 × 16 × 3 (32 × 4.8 × 0.9)
Guns: 1—85 mm; 4—25 mm (twins); 2—81 mm mortars
Complement: about 25

Built in Romania from 1973 in continuing programme. Belong to Danube Flotilla.

RIVER PATROL CRAFT 8/1974

10 "VG" CLASS (RIVER PATROL CRAFT)

Displacement, tons: 40
Dimensions, feet (metres): 52.5 × 14.4 × 4 (16 × 4.4 × 1.2)
Guns: 2 MG
Main engines: 2 diesels; 600 hp = 18 knots
Complement: 10

Steel-hulled craft built at Galata in 1954. Obsolescent. Belong to Danube Flotilla.

9 "SM 165" CLASS (RIVER PATROL CRAFT)

SM 161-169

Locally built from 1954-56. Belong to Danube Flotilla.

MINE WARFARE FORCES

4 Ex-GERMAN "M 40" CLASS (MINESWEEPERS—COASTAL)

| DESCATUSARIA DB 13 | DEMOCRATIA DB 15 |
| DESROBIREA DB 14 | DREPTATEA DB 16 |

Displacement, tons: 543 standard; 775 full load
Dimensions, feet (metres): 206.5 oa × 28 × 7.5 (62.3 × 8.5 × 2.6)
Guns: 6—37 mm (twin); 3—20 mm (singles)
A/S weapons: 2 DCT
Main engines: Triple expansion; 2 shafts; 2 400 ihp = 17 knots
Boilers: 2 three-drum water tube
Range, miles: 1 200 at 17 knots
Complement: 80

German "M Boote" design—designed as coal-burning minesweepers. Built at Galati. Converted to oil in 1951.

DEMOCRATIA and DREPTATEA 1968

10 Ex-SOVIET "T 301" CLASS (MINESWEEPERS—INSHORE)

DR 19, 21-29

Displacement, tons: 150 standard; 180 full load
Dimensions, feet (metres): 128 × 18 × 4.9 (39 × 5.5 × 1.5)
Guns: 2—37 mm; 4—12.7 mm MG (twins)
Main engines: 2 diesels; 1 440 bhp; 2 shafts = 17 knots
Complement: 30

Transferred to Romania by the USSR in 1956-60. Probably half of these are non-operational. Two deleted 1975.

8 Ex-POLISH "TR-40" CLASS (MSBs)

VD-241 VD-242 VD-243 VD-244 VD-245 VD-246 VD-247 VD-248

Displacement, tons: 50 standard; 70 full load
Dimensions, feet (metres): 92 × 13.6 × 2.5 (28 × 4.1 × 0.7)
Guns: 2 MG (twin)
Main engines: 2 diesels; 2 shafts = 14 knots
Complement: 18

Employed on shallow water and river duties. These were originally a Polish class begun in 1955 but completed in Romania in late 1950s.

MISCELLANEOUS

TRAINING SHIPS

Name	No.	Builders	Commissioned
MIRCEA	—	Blohm & Voss, Hamburg	29 Mar 1939

Displacement, tons: 1 604
Dimensions, feet (metres): 239.5 oa; 267.3 (with bowsprit) × 39.3 × 16.5 (73; 81.5 × 12 × 5)
Sail area: 18 830 sq ft
Main engines: Auxiliary MAN 6-cyl diesel; 500 bhp = 9.5 knots
Complement: 83 + 140 midshipmen for training

Laid down on 30 April 1938. Launched on 22 Sept 1938. Refitted at Hamburg in 1966.

1 NEW CONSTRUCTION TRAINING SHIP

Name	No.	Builders	Commissioned
NEPTUN	—	Stettin	1976

Of 5 600 tons and launched 29 April 1976.

TUGS

4 "ROSLAVL" CLASS

VITEAZUL RM 101   VOINICUL —   + 2

Displacement, tons: 450
Dimensions, feet (metres): 135 × 29.3 × 11.8 (41.2 × 8.9 × 3.6)
Main engines: Diesels; 1 250 hp = 12.5 knots
Complement: 28

Built in Galata shipyard 1953-54.

AUXILIARIES

Although details are not available the following have been reported—two survey craft, three tankers, ten transports and twelve "Braila" class LCUs.

MIRCEA 1970, Michael D. J. Lennon

SABAH
(see also Malaysia)

Base

Labuan

2 91 ft PATROL BOATS

Name	No.	Builders	Commissioned
SRI GUMANTONG	—	Vosper Thornycroft Ltd, Singapore	8 April 1970
SRI LABUAN	—	Vosper Thornycroft Ltd, Singapore	6 April 1970

Sri Gumantong launched 18 Aug 1969. On detachment from Royal Malaysian Police (see Malaysian section for details).

1 YACHT

Name	No.	Builders	Commissioned
PUTRI SABAH	—	Vosper Thornycroft Ltd, Singapore	11 July 1971

Displacement, tons: 117
Dimensions, feet (metres): 91 × 19 × 5·5 *(27·8 × 5·8 × 1·7)*
Main engines: 1 diesel = 12 knots
Complement: 22

2 55 ft PATROL BOATS

Name	No.	Builders	Commissioned
SRI SEMPORNA	—	Chevertons, Isle of Wight	Feb 1975
SRI BANGJI	—	Chevertons, Isle of Wight	Feb 1975

Displacement, tons: 50
Dimensions, feet (metres): 55 × 15 × 3 *(16·8 × 4·6 × 0·9)*
Gun: 1—MG
Main engines: Diesels; 1 200 hp = 20 knots
Range, miles: 300 at 15 knots
Complement: 11

ST. KITTS

Senior Appointment

Chief of Police:
O. A. Hector

Mercantile Marine

Lloyd's Register of Shipping:
1 vessel of 256 tons

Base

Basseterre.

1 FAIREY MARINE "SPEAR" CLASS

Displacement, tons: 4·3
Dimensions, feet (metres): 29·8 × 9 × 2·8 *(9·1 × 2·8 × 0·8)*
Guns: Mountings for 2—7·62 mm
Main engines: 2 diesels; 360 hp = 30 knots
Complement: 2

Ordered for the Police in June 1974—delivered 10 Sept 1974.

ST. LUCIA

Mercantile Marine

Lloyd's Register of Shipping:
3 vessels of 928 tons gross

1 BROOKE MARINE PATROL CRAFT

HELEN

Displacement, tons: 14
Dimensions, feet (metres): 40 × 11·7 × 4 *(12·2 × 3·4 × 1·3)*
Main engines: 2 Cummins V8 diesels; 2 shafts = 21 knots (12 at present)

Completed 20 July 1970.

ST. VINCENT

Senior Appointment

Commissioner of Police:
R. J. O'Garro

Base

Kingstown

Mercantile Marine

Lloyd's Register of Shipping:
25 vessels of 8 428 tons gross

1 BROOKE MARINE PATROL CRAFT

CHATOYER

Displacement, tons: 15
Dimensions, feet (metres): 45 × 13 × 3·8 *(13·7 × 4 × 1·2)*
Guns: 3 MG
Main engines: 2 Cummins diesels; 370 hp; 2 shafts = 21 knots

CHATOYER   1976, St. Vincent Police

404 SAUDI ARABIA

SAUDI ARABIA

Ministerial

Minister of Defence:
Amir Sultan ibn 'Abd al-'Aziz

Diplomatic Representation

Defence Attaché in London:
Major-General Mohammed Sabri

Personnel

(a) 1978: 2 200 officers and men
(b) Voluntary service

Bases

Jiddah, Al Qatif/Jubail, Ras Tanura, Damman, Yanbo, Ras al-Mishab (under construction).

Coastguard Bases

Haqi, Ash Sharmah, Qizan.

Strength of the Fleet

	Active	Building
Corvettes—Missile	—	9
Fast Attack Craft—Missile	—	4
Fast Attack Craft—Torpedo	3	—
Large Patrol Craft	1	—
Coastal Patrol Craft and Patrol Boats	115	—
Hovercraft	8	—
MSCs	2	2
LCUs	4	—
Tugs	2	—
Royal Yacht	1	—

New Construction

In January 1972 an agreement was signed with the USA for a ten-year programme to provide 6 corvettes, 4 MSC, 2 coastal patrol craft, 4 LCTs, 3 training ships and 2 tugs. In addition orders have been placed in France, Germany and the United Kingdom.
To man a proportion of these a considerable training programme is under way in the USA.

Mercantile Marine

Lloyd's Register of Shipping:
119 vessels of 1 018 713 tons gross

CORVETTES

9 NEW CONSTRUCTION

Name	No.	Builders	Commissioned
AS SADDIQ	511	Peterson Builders, Wisconsin	April 1980
AL FAROUQ	513	Peterson Builders, Wisconsin	Aug 1980
ABDUL AZIZ	515	Peterson Builders, Wisconsin	Nov 1980
FAISAL	517	Peterson Builders, Wisconsin	April 1981
KAHLID	519	Peterson Builders, Wisconsin	May 1981
AMYR	521	Peterson Builders, Wisconsin	July 1981
TARIQ	523	Peterson Builders, Wisconsin	Oct 1981
OQBAH	525	Peterson Builders, Wisconsin	Jan 1982
ABU OBAIDAH	527	Peterson Builders, Wisconsin	April 1982

Displacement, tons: 720
Dimensions, feet (metres): 234·5 × 27·6 × 8·8 *(71·4 × 8·4 × 2·7)*
Missiles: 8 Harpoon SSM
Guns: 1—76 mm OTO Melara; 1—81 mm mortar; 2—40 mm mortars; 2—20 mm
A/S weapons: 6 (2 triple) Mk 32 A/S torpedo tubes
Main engines: CODOG; 1 GE gas turbine; 16 500 hp; 2 diesels; 3 000 hp
Speed, knots: 30 on gas turbines; 20 on diesels
Complement: 53 (5 officers, 48 ratings)

Ordered 16 Feb 1977. First craft (511) laid down Nov 1977. Last (527) to be laid down May 1980. First launch June 1979—last, Aug 1981.

Radar: Surface warning: AN/SPS 60.
Air warning: AN/SPS 40B.
Fire control system: Mk 92.

Sonar: AN/SQS 56.

MINEWARFARE FORCES

4 "MSC 322" CLASS (MINESWEEPERS—COASTAL)

Name	No.	Builders	Commissioned
ADDRIYAH	MSC 412	Peterson Builders, Wisconsin	1978
AL-QUYSUMAH	MSC 414	Peterson Builders, Wisconsin	1978
AL-WADEEAH	MSC 416	Peterson Builders, Wisconsin	1979
SAFWA	MSC 418	Peterson Builders, Wisconsin	1979

Ordered on 30 Sept 1975 under the international Logistics Programme.
Laid down—412, 12 May 1976; 414, 24 Aug 1976; 416, 28 Dec 1976; 418, March 1977.
412 launched 20 Dec 1976.

LIGHT FORCES

Note: Reports of transfer of three "Osa" class, probably from Egypt, are unconfirmed.

4 FAST ATTACK CRAFT (MISSILE)

Name	No.	Builders	Commissioned
BADR	612	Tacoma Boatbuilding Co, Washington, USA	Aug 1980
AL YARMOOK	614	Tacoma Boatbuilding Co, Washington, USA	Jan 1981
HITTEEN	616	Tacoma Boatbuilding Co, Washington, USA	April 1981
TABUK	618	Tacoma Boatbuilding Co, Washington, USA	July 1981

Displacement, tons: 320
Dimensions, feet (metres): 184·4 × 25 × 5·8 *(56·2 × 7·6 × 1·8)*
Missiles: 2 twin Harpoon launchers
Guns: 1—76 mm OTO Melara; 1—81 mm mortar; 2—40 mm mortars; 2—20 mm
Main engines: CODOG; 1 GE gas turbine; 16 500 hp; 2 diesels; 1 500 hp
Speed, knots: 38 (gas turbine); 18 (diesel)
Complement: 35

Ordered 30 Aug 1977. To be laid down Dec 1978, July 1979, Oct 1979, Jan 1980.

Radar: Surface warning: AN/SPS 60
Air warning: AN/SPS 40 B
Fire control: Mk 92 system

3 GERMAN "JAGUAR" CLASS (FAST ATTACK CRAFT—TORPEDO)

Name	No.	Builders	Commissioned
DAMMAM	—	Lürssen Vegesack	1969
KHAY BAR	—	Lürssen Vegesack	1969
MACCAH	—	Lürssen Vegesack	1969

Displacement, tons: 160 standard; 190 full load
Dimensions, feet (metres): 139·4 × 23·4 × 7·9 *(42·5 × 7 × 2·4)*
Guns: 2—40 mm
Torpedo tubes: 4—21 in *(533 mm)*
Main engines: 4 MTU diesels; 12 000 bhp = 42 knots
Complement: 33 (3 officers, 30 men)

Refitted in Germany 1976.

"JAGUAR" Class   1974, Reiner Nerlich

SAUDI ARABIA 405

1 USCG TYPE (LARGE PATROL CRAFT)

RYADH

Displacement, tons: 100 standard
Dimensions, feet (metres): 95·0 × 19·0 × 6·0 *(29 × 5·8 × 1·9)*
Gun: 1—40 mm
Main engines: 4 diesels; 2 shafts; 2 200 bhp = 21 knots
Complement: 15

Steel-hulled patrol boat transferred to Saudi Arabia in 1960.

8 P 32 TYPE (COASTAL PATROL CRAFT)

Displacement, tons: 90
Dimensions, feet (metres): 105 × 17·6 × 9·8 *(32 × 5·3 × 2·9)*
Guns: 2—20 mm
Main engines: 2 MGO 12V diesels; 2 700 bhp; 2 shafts = 29 knots
Range, miles: 1 500 at 15 knots
Complement: 17

Wooden hulls sheathed with GRP. Sisters to Moroccan "El Wacil" class. Ordered from CMN (Cherbourg) Jan 1976.

P 32 Type 1976, CMN

12 "RAPIER" CLASS (COASTAL PATROL CRAFT)

Length, feet (metres): 50 *(15·2)*
Guns: 2 MG
Main engines: 2 diesels; 1 300 bhp = 28 knots
Complement: 9

Three completed 1976, remainder in 1977 by Halter Marine, New Orleans.

20 45 ft COASTAL PATROL CRAFT

Built by Whittingham and Mitchell, Chertsey, England. Armed with one 0·5 cal MG and powered with two 362 hp diesels.

2 Ex-US 40 ft UTILITY BOATS

Transferred late 1960s.

43 30 ft "C-80" CLASS (COASTAL PATROL CRAFT)

Displacement, tons: 2·8
Dimensions, feet (metres): 29·3 oa × 9·3 × 1·5 *(8·9 × 2·9 × 0·6)*
Main engines: 1 Caterpillar diesel; 210 bhp; Castoldi pump jet unit = 20 knots
Gun: 1 MG

All delivered 1975 to Saudi Coastguard. Built by Northshore Yacht Yards under sub-contract to Planning Associates Ltd (London). Contract 1974.

"C-80" Class 1975, Northshore

10 23 ft "HUNTRESS" PATROL BOATS

Built by Fairey Marine, Hamble, England. Capable of 20 knots with a cruising range of 150 miles and a complement of four.

20 20 ft PATROL BOATS

Smaller editions of the 45 feet craft above, built by Whittingham and Mitchell.

8 SRN-6 HOVERCRAFT

Displacement, tons: 10 normal (load 8 200 lbs)
Dimensions, feet (metres): 48·4 × 25·3 × 15·9 (height) *(14·8 × 7·7 × 4·8)*
Main machinery: 1 Gnome model 1050 gas turbine.
Speed, knots: 58

Acquired from British Hovercraft Corporation Ltd, between Feb and Dec 1970.

SRN-6 hovercraft 1971

406 SAUDI ARABIA / SENEGAL

2 AIR SEA-RESCUE LAUNCHES

ASR 1   ASR 2

With two diesels of 1 230 hp and capable of 25 knots. Belong to Ministry of Transportation.

MISCELLANEOUS

SERVICE FORCES

1 TRAINING SHIP

Name	No.	Builders	Commissioned
TEBUK	—	Bayerischen Schiffbau, Erlenbach, FDR	Dec 1977

Displacement, tons: 350
Dimensions, feet (metres): 196·8 × 32·8 × 5·8 *(60 × 10 × 1·8)*
Main engines: 2 MTU diesels; 5 260 bhp = 20 knots
Complement: 60

Ordered 1976.

2 Ex-US YTB TYPE (HARBOUR TUGS)

EN 111 (ex-*YTB 837*)   EN 112 (ex-*YTB 838*)

Displacement, tons: 350 full load
Dimensions, feet (metres): 109 oa × 30 × 13·8 *(31·1 × 9·8 × 4·5)*
Main engines: 2 diesels; 2 000 bhp; 2 shafts
Complement: 12

Transferred by USN 15 Oct 1975.

4 Ex-US LCUs

SA 310   SA 311   SA 312   SA 313

Transferred June/July 1976.

1 ROYAL YACHT

Name	No.	Builders	Commissioned
AL RIYADH	—	Van Lent (de Kaag), Netherlands	1978

Displacement, tons: 650
Dimensions, feet (metres): 212 oa × 32 × 10 *(69·5 × 10·5 × 3·3)*
Main engines: 2 diesels; 6 300 hp = 26 knots
Complement: 26 (accommodation for 24 passengers)

Ordered 12 Dec 1975. Laid down 6 May 1976. Launched 17 Dec 1977. Cost £7 million.

Fittings: Helicopter pad, sauna, swimming pool, hospital with intensive care unit.

SENEGAL

Ministerial
Minister of Armed Forces:
  Amadu Sall

Personnel
(a) 1978: approx 350 officers and men
(b) 2 years conscript service

Base
Dakar

Mercantile Marine
Lloyd's Register of Shipping:
  65 vessels of 26 621 tons gross

DELETION
Light Forces
1974 Sénégal

LIGHT FORCES

3 "P 48" CLASS (LARGE PATROL CRAFT)

Name	No.	Builders	Commissioned
SAINT LOUIS	—	Ch. Navales Franco-Belges	1 Mar 1971
POPENGUINE	—	Soc. Francais de Constructions Navales	10 Aug 1974
PODOR	—	Soc. Francais de Constructions Navales	13 July 1977

Displacement, tons: 250 full load
Dimensions, feet (metres): 149·3 pp; 156 oa × 23·3 × 8·1 *(45·5; 47·5 × 7·1 × 2·5)*
Guns: 2—40 mm
Main engines: 2 MGO diesels; 1 shaft; 2 400 bhp = 23 knots
Range, miles: 2 000 at 18 knots
Complement: 33

Saint Louis laid down on 20 April 1970, launched on 5 Aug 1970. *Popenguine* laid down in Dec 1973, launched 22 March 1974. Sisters to *Malaika* of Malagasy, *Vigilant* of Ivory Coast and "Bizerte" Class of Tunisian Navy. *Podor* ordered Aug 1975, laid down Dec 1975, launched 20 July 1976.

SAINT LOUIS   1972

2 Ex-FRENCH VC TYPE

Name	No.	Builders	Commissioned
CASAMANCE (ex-*VC 5*, ex-*P 755*)	—	Constructions Mécaniques de Normandie, Cherbourg	1958
SINE-SALOUM (ex-*Reine N'Galifourou*, ex-*VC 4*, ex-*P 754*)	—	Constructions Mécaniques de Normandie, Cherbourg	1958

Displacement, tons: 75 standard; 82 full load
Dimensions, feet (metres): 104·5 × 15·5 × 5·5 *(31·8 × 4·7 × 1·7)*
Guns: 2—20 mm
Main engines: 2 Mercedes-Benz (MTU) diesels; 2 shafts; 2 700 bhp = 28 knots
Complement: 15

Former French patrol craft (Vedettes de Surveillance Côtière). *Casamance* was transferred from France to Senegal in 1963. *Sine-Saloum* was given to Senegal on 24 Aug 1965 after having been returned to France by the Congo in Feb 1965.

SINE-SALOUM   1967, Senegalese Navy

1 TRAWLER TYPE

LES ALMADIES

Used previously on fishery protection.

12 VOSPER 45 ft TYPE

Dimensions, feet (metres): 45 × 13·2 × 3·5 *(13·7 × 4 × 1·1)*
Guns: 1—12·7 mm; 2—7·62 mm
Main engines: 2 diesels; 920 hp = 25 knots
Complement: 6

1 FAIREY MARINE "LANCE" CLASS (COASTAL PATROL CRAFT)

Displacement, tons: 15·7 light
Dimensions, feet (metres): 48·7 × 15·3 × 4·3 (14·8 × 4·7 × 1·3)
Guns: 2—7·62 mm
Main engines: 2 GM 8 V 71 T1; 850 hp = 24 knots
Complement: 7

Completed June 1977. Has capacity for boarding party of 12. Air conditioned.

"LANCE" Class
1977, Fairey Marine

1 FAIREY MARINE "SPEAR" CLASS
(COASTAL PATROL CRAFT)

Displacement, tons: 4·3
Dimensions, feet (metres): 29·8 × 9 × 2·8 (9·1 × 2·8 × 0·8)
Guns: 1—12·7 mm; 2—7·62 mm
Main engines: 2 diesels; 360 hp = 30 knots
Complement: 4

Completed 28 Feb 1974 for Senegal Customs.

2 FAIREY MARINE "HUNTRESS" CLASS
(COASTAL PATROL CRAFT)

Dimensions, feet (metres): 23·2 × 8·8 × 2·8 (7·1 × 2·7 × 0·8)
Main engines: 1 diesel; 180 hp; 29 knots
Complement: 2

Completed March 1974 for Senegal Customs.

AMPHIBIOUS FORCES

1 Ex-FRENCH EDIC

LA FALENCE (ex-9095) (LCT)

Displacement, tons: 250 standard; 670 full load
Dimensions, feet (metres): 193·5 × 39·2 × 4·5 (59 × 12 × 1·3)
Guns: 2—20 mm
Main engines: 2 MGO diesels; 2 shafts; 1 000 bhp = 8 knots
Complement: 6

Launched 7 April 1958. Transferred 1 July 1974.

2 Ex-US "LCM 6" CLASS

DIOU LOULOU (ex-6723)   DIOMBOS (ex-6733)

Transferred July 1968. Of 26 tons.

1 TENDER

CRAME JEAN

18 ton fishing boat used as training craft.

SHARJAH
(see United Arab Emirates)

SIERRA LEONE

Personnel

(a) 1978: 150 officers and men
(b) Voluntary service

Base

Freetown

Mercantile Marine

Lloyd's Register of Shipping:
13 vessels of 17 209 tons gross

3 Ex-CHINESE "SHANGHAI II" CLASS
(FAST ATTACK CRAFT—GUN)

Displacement, tons: 120 standard; 155 full load
Dimensions, feet (metres): 128 × 18 × 5·6 (39 × 5·5 × 1·7)
Guns: 4—37 mm; 4—25 mm
A/S weapons: 8 DCs
Mines: Mine rails can be fitted
Main engines: 4 diesels; 4 800 hp = 30 knots
Complement: 25

Transferred by China June 1973.

Radar: Skin Head.

"SHANGHAI II" Class

SINGAPORE

Headquarters Appointments

Commander of the Republic of Singapore Navy:
Colonel Khoo Eng An

Personnel

(a) 1978: 3 000 officers and men
(b) 2-3 years national service and regular volunteers

Prefix to Ships' Names

RSS

Mercantile Marine

Lloyd's Register of Shipping:
872 vessels of 6 791 398 tons gross

LIGHT FORCES

6 LÜRSSEN VEGESACK "TNC 48" CLASS
(FAST ATTACK CRAFT—MISSILE)

Name	No.	Builders	Commissioned
SEA WOLF	P 76	Lürssen Werft, Vegesack	1972
SEA LION	P 77	Lürssen Werft, Vegesack	1972
SEA DRAGON	P 78	Singapore Shipbuilding & Engineering Co	1974
SEA TIGER	P 79	Singapore Shipbuilding & Engineering Co	1974
SEA HAWK	P 80	Singapore Shipbuilding & Engineering Co	1975
SEA SCORPION	P 81	Singapore Shipbuilding & Engineering Co	1975

Displacement, tons: 230
Dimensions, feet (metres): 158 × 23 × 7·5 *(48 × 7 × 2·3)*
Missiles: 5 Gabriel
Guns: 1—57 mm; 1—40 mm
Main engines: 4 MTU diesels; 4 shafts; 14 400 hp = 34 knots
Complement: 40

Designed by Lürssen Werft who built the first pair, *Sea Wolf* and *Sea Lion*, which arrived autumn 1972.

SEA TIGER 4/1977, Dr. Giorgio Arra

6 VOSPER THORNYCROFT DESIGN
3 "TYPE A" (FAST ATTACK CRAFT—GUN)

Name	No.	Builders	Commissioned
INDEPENDENCE	P 69	Vosper Thornycroft Ltd, UK	8 July 1970
FREEDOM	P 70	Vosper Thornycroft Private Ltd, Singapore	11 Jan 1971
JUSTICE	P 72	Vosper Thornycroft Private Ltd, Singapore	23 April 1971

Displacement, tons: 100 standard
Dimensions, feet (metres): 103·6 wl; 109·6 × 21·0 × 5·6 *(31·6; 33·5 × 6·4 × 1·8)*
Guns: 1—40 mm (forward); 1—20 mm (aft)
Main engines: 2 Maybach (MTU 16 V538) diesels; 7 200 bhp = 32 knots
Range, miles: 1 100 at 15 knots
Complement: 19 to 22

On 21 May 1968 the Vosper Thornycroft Group announced the receipt of an order for six of their 110-foot fast patrol boats for the Republic of Singapore. Two sub-types, the first of each (*Independence* and *Sovereignty*) built in UK, the remainder in Singapore. *Independence* was launched 15 July 1969. *Freedom* 18 Nov 1969 and *Justice* 20 June 1970.

INDEPENDENCE 1971, Vosper Thornycroft

3 "TYPE B" (FAST ATTACK CRAFT—GUN)

Name	No.	Builders	Commissioned
SOVEREIGNTY	P 71	Vosper Thornycroft Ltd, Portsmouth, England	Feb 1971
DARING	P 73	Vosper Thornycroft Private Ltd, Singapore	18 Sept 1971
DAUNTLESS	P 74	Vosper Thornycroft Private Ltd, Singapore	1971

Displacement, tons: 100 standard; 130 full load
Dimensions, feet (metres): 103·6 wl; 109·6 × 21·0 × 5·6 *(31·6; 33·5 × 6·4 × 1·8)*
Guns: 1—76 mm Bofors; 1—20 mm Oerlikon
Main engines: 2 Maybach (MTU 16 V538) diesels; 7 200 bhp = 32 knots
Range, miles: 1 100 at 15 knots
Complement: 19 (3 officers, 16 ratings)

Sovereignty was launched 25 Nov 1969. *Dauntless* launched 6 May 1971. Steel hulls of round bilge form. Aluminium alloy superstructure.

SOVEREIGNTY 1976, A. G. Burgoyne

MINEWARFARE FORCES

2 Ex-US "REDWING" CLASS (MINESWEEPERS—COASTAL)

JUPITER (ex-USS *Thrasher* MSC 203)	M 101
MERCURY (ex-USS *Whippoorwill* MSC 207)	M 102

Displacement, tons: 370 full load
Dimensions, feet (metres): 144 × 28 × 8·2 *(43·9 × 8·5 × 2·5)*
Gun: 1—20 mm
Main engines: 2 GM diesels; 1 760 bhp; 2 shafts = 12 knots
Range, miles: 2 500 at 10 knots
Complement: 39

Transferred by sale 5 Dec 1975.

MERCURY 1976, Singapore Navy

SINGAPORE 409

TRAINING SHIPS

1 "FORD" CLASS (LARGE PATROL CRAFT)

Name	No.	Builders	Commissioned
PANGLIMA	P 68	United Engineers, Singapore	May 1956

Displacement, tons: 119 standard; 134 full load
Dimensions, feet (metres): 117·0 × 20·0 × 6·0 (35·7 × 6·1 × 1·8)
Guns: 1—40 mm 60 cal; 1—20 mm
Main engines: Paxman YHAXM supercharged B 12 diesels = 14 knots
Oil fuel, tons: 15
Complement: 15 officers and men

Laid down in 1954. Launched on 14 Jan 1956. Similar to the British seaward defence boats of the "Ford" class. Transferred to the Royal Malaysian Navy on the formation of Malaysia. Transferred to the Republic of Singapore in 1967.

PANGLIMA   1975, Singapore Navy

Name	No.	Builders	Commissioned
ENDEAVOUR	P 75	Shiffswarft Oberwinter, Germany	30 Sept 1970

Displacement, tons: 250
Dimensions, feet (metres): 135 × 25 × 8 (40·9 × 7·6 × 2·4)
Guns: 2—20 mm
Main engines: 2 Maybach diesels; 2 600 bhp
Range, miles: 800 at 8 knots
Complement: 24

ENDEAVOUR   1976, Singapore Navy

AMPHIBIOUS FORCES

6 Ex-US "511-1152" CLASS (LSTs)

Name	No.	Builders	Commissioned
ENDURANCE (ex-USS *Holmes County*, LST 836)	A 81	American Bridge Co	1944
EXCELLENCE (ex-US *LST 629*)	A 82	Chicago Bridge & Iron Co.	1944
INTREPID (ex-US *LST 579*)	A 83	Chicago Bridge & Iron Co	1944
RESOLUTION (ex-US *LST 649*)	A 84	Chicago Bridge & Iron Co	1944
PERSISTENCE (ex-US *LST 613*)	A 85	Chicago Bridge & Iron Co	1944
PERSEVERANCE (ex-US *LST 623*)	A 86	Chicago Bridge & Iron Co	1944

Displacement, tons: 1 653 light; 4 080 full load
Dimensions, feet (metres): 316·0 wl; 328·0 oa × 50·0 × 14·0 (96·3; 100 × 15·2 × 4·3)
Guns: 8—40 mm (4 twin)
Main engines: GM diesels; 2 shafts; 1 700 bhp = 11·6 knots
Complement: 120

Endurance loaned from the United States Navy on 1 July 1971 and sold on 5 Dec 1975. Remainder transferred 4 June 1976. *Endurance* leased commercially in 1976; *Excellence* and *Intrepid* active; *Persistence* and *Perseverance* in reserve.

EXCELLENCE   1976, A. G. Burgoyne

6 LANDING CRAFT (RPL)

BRANI, BERLAYER + 4

Of 30-50 tons—all ex-Australian.

RPL 56   5/1977, Dr. Giorgio Arra

POLICE PATROL CRAFT

4 VOSPER THORNYCROFT TYPE

Name	No.	Builders	Commissioned
—	PX 10	Vosper Thornycroft Ltd, Portsmouth, England	1969
—	PX 11	Vosper Thornycroft Ltd, Portsmouth, England	1969
—	PX 12	Vosper Thornycroft Ltd, Portsmouth, England	1969
—	PX 13	Vosper Thornycroft Ltd, Portsmouth, England	1969

Displacement, tons: 40 standard
Length, feet (metres): 87·0 (26·5)
Guns: 2—20 mm

Built for marine police duties.

SOMALIA

Personnel
(a) 1978: 350 officers and men
(b) Voluntary service

Bases
Berbera, Mogadishu and Kismayu

Mercantile Marine
Lloyd's Register of Shipping:
31 vessels of 158 166 tons gross

General

With the withdrawal of the Soviet element from Somalia and the cessation of imports of equipment and spares the state of this navy will deteriorate unless replacements and refits are arranged outside the Soviet bloc.

LIGHT FORCES

3 Ex-SOVIET "OSA II" CLASS (FAST ATTACK CRAFT—MISSILE)

Displacement, tons: 165 standard; 200 full load
Dimensions, feet (metres): 128·7 × 25·1 × 5·9 *(39·3 × 7·7 × 1·8)*
Missiles: 4—SS-N-2
Guns: 4—30 mm (twins)
Main engines: 3 diesels; 1 300 bhp = 32 knots
Range, miles: 800 at 25 knots
Complement: 30

Transferred in Dec 1975.

"OSA II" Class

4 Ex-SOVIET "MOL" CLASS
(FAST ATTACK CRAFT—TORPEDO/PATROL)

Displacement, tons: 240 full load
Dimensions, feet (metres): 126·6 × 25·6 × 9·5 *(38·6 × 7·8 × 2·9)*
Guns: 4—30 mm (twins)
Torpedo tubes: 4—21 in *(533 mm)* can be mounted on sponsons
Main engines: 3 M504 diesels; 15 500 bhp; 2 shafts = 40 knots
Complement: 25

Transferred 1976. Some do not carry torpedo tubes.

"MOL" Class 1976

4 Ex-SOVIET "P6" CLASS (FAST ATTACK CRAFT—TORPEDO)

Displacement, tons: 66 standard; 75 full load
Dimensions, feet (metres): 84·2 × 20·0 × 6·0 *(27·6 × 6·5 × 2)*
Guns: 4—25 mm
Torpedo tubes: 2—21 in *(533 mm)*
Main engines: 4 diesels; 4 shafts; 4 800 hp = 43 knots
Range, miles: 450 at 30 knots
Complement: 25

Transferred in 1968.

6 Ex-SOVIET "POLUCHAT I" CLASS (LARGE PATROL CRAFT)

Displacement, tons: 100 standard; 120 full load
Dimensions, feet (metres): 98·4 × 20·0 × 5·9 *(32·3 × 6·5 × 1·9)*
Guns: 2—25 mm
Main engines: Diesels = 15 knots

Transferred two in 1965, four in 1966.

AMPHIBIOUS FORCES

1 Ex-SOVIET "POLNOCNY" CLASS (LCT)

Displacement, tons: 800 full load
Dimensions, feet (metres): 239·4 × 29·5 × 9·8 *(73 × 9 × 3)*
Guns: 2—25 mm (twin)
Rocket launchers: 2—18 barrelled 140 mm launchers
Main engines: 2 diesels; 5 000 bhp = 18 knots

Can carry 6 tanks. Transferred Dec 1976.

Soviet "POLNOCNY" Class

4 Ex-SOVIET "T4" CLASS (LCM)

Displacement, tons: 70
Dimensions, feet (metres): 62·3 × 14·1 × 3·3 *(19 × 4·3 × 1)*
Main engines: 2 diesels; 2 shafts = 10 knots

Transferred 1968-69.

SOUTH AFRICA

Ministerial

Minister of Defence:
 Mr. P. W. Botha

Headquarters Appointments

Chief of South African Defence Force:
 General M. A. de M. Malan, SSA, SM
Chief of the Navy:
 Vice-Admiral J. C. Walters, SM
Chief of Naval Staff (Operations):
 Rear-Admiral P. A. H. Tomlinson, SM

Diplomatic Representation

Naval Attaché in London:
 Captain P. R. Le Roux
Defence Attaché in Bonn:
 Captain P. E. Blitzker
Defence Attaché in Washington:
 Commodore W. N. Du Plessis
Naval Attaché in Paris:
 Captain J. A. de Kock
Armed Forces Attaché in Buenos Aires:
 Captain W. H. Kelly, SM

Personnel

(a) 1974: Total 4 204 (475 officers, 2 329 ratings and 1 400 national service ratings)
 1975: Total 4 250 (475 officers, 2 375 ratings and 1 400 national service ratings)
 1976: Total 4 700 (500 officers, 2 800 ratings and 1 400 national service ratings)
 1977: Total 4 800 (500 officers, 2 900 ratings and 1 400 national service ratings)
(b) Voluntary service plus 18 months national service

Naval Bases

HM Dockyard at Simonstown was transferred to the Republic of South Africa on 2 April 1957. The new submarine base at Simonstown, SAS *Drommedaris*, incorporating offices, accommodation and operations centre alongside a Synchrolift marine elevator, capable of docking all South African ships except the *Tafelberg*, was opened in July 1972.
A new Maritime Headquarters was opened in March 1973 at Silvermine on the Cape Peninsula.

Air Sea Rescue Base

The SAAF Maritime Group base at Langebaan was transferred to the South African Navy on 1 Nov 1969, becoming SAN Sea Rescue Base (SAS *Flamingo*). The ASR launches were given Naval Coastal Forces numbers to replace SAAF "R" numbers.

Maritime Air

The SAAF operates an MP group consisting of 18 Piaggio P166s and 7 Shackleton MR 3. In addition 11 Wasp helicopters are available for embarkation in the frigates.

Prefix to Ships' Names

SAS (Suid Afrikaanse Skip)

Mercantile Marine

Lloyd's Register of Shipping:
 297 vessels of 476 324 tons gross

Strength of the Fleet

Type	Active	Building
Destroyer	1	—
Frigates	3	—
Submarines Patrol	3	—
Fast Attack Craft—Missile	2	4
Large Patrol Craft	4	—
Minesweepers (Coastal)	10	—
Survey Ships	2	—
Fleet Replenishment Ship	1	—
BDV	1	—
TRV	1	—
Training Ship	1	—
Tugs	2	—
SAR Launches	4	—

General

The delivery of the two French A69 frigates and the two "Agosta" class submarines has been stayed by a UN resolution banning the sale of weapons to South Africa. Of the two frigates *Good Hope* had started trials and *Transvaal* was completing. The first submarine was launched 14 Dec 1977 without name or ceremony.
As the South Africans are unlikely to see themselves operating in alliance in the near future and coast defence therefore becomes a top priority the non-arrival of the frigates may be a blessing in some ways allowing them to concentrate on larger numbers of home-built craft of the "Reshef" type.

DELETIONS

Destroyer

1976 *Simon van der Stel*

Frigates

1976 *Vrystaat* (sunk as target in April)
 Good Hope, Transvaal,
 Pietermaritzburg (shore accommodation ship)

Survey Ship

1972 *Natal* (sunk as target Sept)

Training Ship

1975 HDML 1204

PENNANT LIST

Destroyer

D 278	Jan Van Riebeeck

Frigates

F 145	President Pretorius
F 147	President Steyn
F 150	President Krüger

Submarines

S 97	Maria Van Riebeeck
S 98	Emily Hobhouse
S 99	Johanna Van der Merwe

Minewarfare Forces

M 291	Pietermaritzburg
M 1207	Johannesburg
M 1210	Kimberley
M 1212	Port Elizabeth
M 1213	Mosselbaai
M 1214	Walvisbaai
M 1215	East London
M 1498	Windhoek
M 1499	Durban

Light Forces

P 285	Somerset (BDV)
P 1556	Pretoria
P 1557	Kaapstad
P 3105	Gelderland
P 3120	Nautilus
P 3125	Reijger
P 3126	Haerlem
P 3127	Oosterland
P 3148	Fleur (TRV)

Service Force

A 243	Tafelberg
A 324	Protea

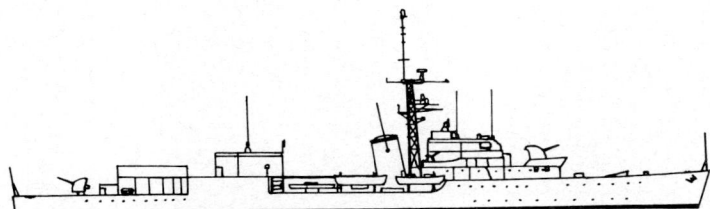

Ex-British "W", Class

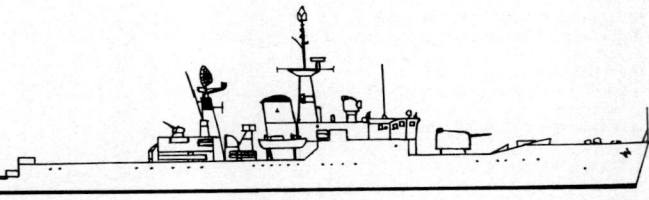

"PRESIDENT" Class

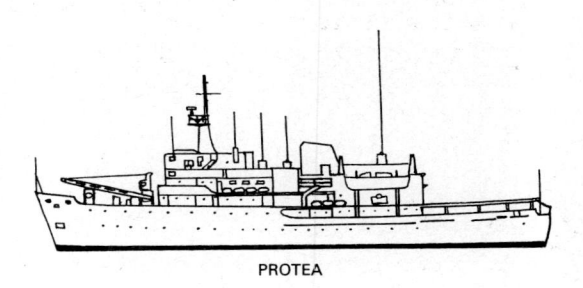

PROTEA

412 SOUTH AFRICA

SUBMARINES
2 FRENCH "AGOSTA" CLASS

Name	No.
—	—
—	—

Builders	Laid down	Launched	Commissioned
Dubigeon—Normandie (Nantes)	15 Sept 1976	14 Dec 1977	?
Dubigeon—Normandie (Nantes)	—	—	?

Delivery of these two submarines was stayed by the UN resolution banning arms sales to South Africa. The first was launched without name or ceremony.

3 FRENCH "DAPHNE" CLASS

Name	No.
MARIA VAN RIEBEECK	S 97
EMILY HOBHOUSE	S 98
JOHANNA VAN DER MERWE	S 99

Builders	Laid down	Launched	Commissioned
Dubigeon—Normandie, Nantes-Chantenay	14 Mar 1968	18 Mar 1969	22 June 1970
Dubigeon—Normandie, Nantes-Chantenay	18 Nov 1968	24 Oct 1969	25 Jan 1971
Dubigeon—Normandie, Nantes-Chantenay	24 April 1969	21 July 1970	21 July 1971

Displacement, tons: 850 surfaced; 1 040 dived
Length, feet (metres): 190·3 *(58)*
Beam, feet (metres): 22·3 *(6·8)*
Draught, feet (metres): 15·4 *(4·7)*
Torpedo tubes: 12—21·7 in *(550 mm)* (8 bow, 4 stern)
Main machinery: SEMT-Pielstick diesel electric; 1 300 bhp surfaced; 1 600 hp dived; 2 shafts
Speed, knots: 16 surfaced and dived
Range, miles: 4 500 at 5 knots (snorting)
Complement: 47 (6 officers, 41 men)

First submarines ordered for the South African Navy. They are of the French "Daphne" design, similar to those built in France for that country, Pakistan and Portugal and also built in Spain.

EMILY HOBHOUSE   1973, South African Navy

DESTROYER
1 Ex-BRITISH "W" CLASS

Name
JAN VAN RIEBEECK (ex-HMS *Wessex*, ex-*Zenith*)

No.	Builders	Laid down	Launched	Commissioned
D 278	Fairfield SB & Eng Co Ltd, Govan, Glasgow	20 Oct 1942	2 Sept 1943	11 May 1944

Displacement, tons: 2 205 standard; 2 850 full load
Length, feet (metres): 339·5 *(103·6)* pp; 362·8 *(110·6)* oa
Beam, feet (metres): 35·7 *(10·9)*
Draught, feet (metres): 17·1 *(5·2)*
Aircraft: 2 Westland Wasp helicopters
Guns: 4—4 in *(102 mm)* (twin); 2—40 mm (single); 4—3 pdr (saluting)
A/S weapons: 6 (2 triple) Mk 32 torpedo tubes; 2 DCT; 2 DC racks
Boilers: 2 Admiralty three-drum type; 300 psi; 670°F
Main engines: 2 Parsons sr geared turbines; 2 shafts; 40 000 shp
Speed, knots: 36
Range, miles: 3 260 at 14 knots; 1 000 at 30 knots
Oil fuel, tons: 579 (95%)
Complement: 192 (11 officers, 181 men)

Purchased from the United Kingdom. Transferred to South Africa on 29 March 1950.

JAN VAN RIEBEECK   1973, South African Navy

Aircraft: Landing patch on fo'c'sle. Helo deck aft.

Gunnery: The main armament formerly comprised four 4·7 in guns.

Modernisation: Modernised in 1964-66.

Radar: Search: Type 293.
Fire control: I Band (NSG NA 9 system).

FRIGATES
3 "PRESIDENT" CLASS

Name	No.
PRESIDENT PRETORIUS	F 145
PRESIDENT STEYN	F 147
PRESIDENT KRUGER	F 150

Builders	Laid down	Launched	Commissioned
Yarrow & Co, Scotstoun	21 Nov 1960	28 Sept 1962	4 Mar 1964
Alex Stephen & Sons, Govan	20 May 1960	23 Nov 1961	25 April 1963
Yarrow & Co, Scotstoun	6 April 1959	20 Oct 1960	1 Oct 1962

Displacement, tons: 2 250 standard; 2 800 full load
Dimensions, feet (metres): 370 oa × 41·1 × 17·1 *(112·8 × 12·5 × 5·2)*
Aircraft: 1 Wasp helicopter
Guns: 2—4·5 in *(115 mm)* (1 twin); 2—40 mm Bofors; 4—3 pdr (saluting)
A/S weapons: 6 (2 triple) Mk 32 torpedo tubes; 1 Limbo three-barrel DC mortar
Main engines: 2 sets dr geared turbines; 2 shafts; 30 000 shp
Boilers: 2 Babcock & Wilcox 550 psi; 850°F
Speed, knots: 30
Oil fuel, tons: 430
Range, miles: 4 500 at 12 knots
Complement: 203 (13 officers, 190 men)

Originally "Rothesay" Type 12 frigates, *President Kruger* arrived in South Africa on 27 March 1963.

Modernisation: Refitted to carry a Wasp A/S helicopter, with hangar and landing deck. To accommodate this, one Limbo A/S mortar was removed and the two single 40 mm remounted on the hangar roof. *President Kruger* completed refit and recommissioned on 5 Aug 1969, *President Steyn* completed refit in 1971, when *President Pretorius* was taken in hand although delayed to take advantage gained from the previous conversions. Refit completed 12 July 1977. The refits were carried out at S.A. Naval Dockyard, Simonstown and included replacement of the lattice foremast by a truncated pyramid tower. *Kruger* retained her original GDS5 director but will later be brought into line with the other pair. Small differences exist between all three ships.

PRESIDENT STEYN (*President Pretorius* similar)   12/1976, South African Navy

PRESIDENT KRUGER   7/1976, USN

Radar: Surveillance: Thomson CSF Jupiter.
Air/Surface search: Type 293.
Fire control: Elsag NA9C.

SOUTH AFRICA

2 Ex-FRENCH "A69" CLASS

Name	No.	Builders	Laid down	Launched	Commissioned
GOOD HOPE (ex-*Lieutenant de Vaisseau Le Hénaff*)	—	Lorient Naval DY	12 Mar 1976	Mar 1977	?
TRANSVAAL (ex-*Commandant l'Herminier*)	—	Lorient Naval DY	1 Oct 1976	Sept 1977	?

Delivery of these two ships has been stayed by the UN resolution banning the sale of arms to South Africa. Trials of *Good Hope* were stopped in Nov 1977 and she was berthed in the Inner Harbour.

LIGHT FORCES

2 + 4 "RESHEF" CLASS (FAST ATTACK CRAFT—MISSILE)

Displacement, tons: 430 full load
Dimensions, feet (metres): 204 × 25 × 8 *(62·2 × 7·8 × 2·4)*
Missiles: 6—Gabriel (Selenia control)
Guns: 2—76 mm
Main engines: 4 Maybach diesels; 2 shafts; 5 340 hp = 32 knots
Range, miles: ? 1 500 at 30 knots; 4 000+ at economical speed
Complement: 45

Contract signed with Israel in late 1974; first three under construction at Haifa and three in Durban. Completion of order expected 1978. Two launched 1976.

"RESHEF" Class   1974, Michael D. J. Lennon

5 BRITISH "FORD" CLASS (LARGE PATROL CRAFT)

Name	No.	Builders	Commissioned
GELDERLAND (ex-*Brayford*)	P 3105	A. & J. Inglis Ltd, Glasgow	30 Aug 1954
NAUTILUS (ex-*Glassford*)	P 3120	Dunston, Thorne	23 Aug 1955
REIJGER	P 3125	Vosper Ltd, Portsmouth	1958
HAERLEM	P 3126	Vosper Ltd, Portsmouth	1959
OOSTERLAND	P 3127	Vosper Ltd, Portsmouth	1959

Displacement, tons: 120 standard; 160 full load
Dimensions, feet (metres): 110·0 wl; 117·2 oa × 20·0 × 4·5 *(35; 38·4 × 6·5 × 1·3)*
Gun: 1—40 mm
A/S weapons: 2 DCT in *Oosterland* and *Reijger*
Main engines: 2 Davey Paxman diesels; Foden engine on centre shaft; 1 100 bhp = 18 knots

Gelderland was purchased from Britain, and handed over to South Africa at Portsmouth on 30 Aug 1954. Second ship, *Nautilus* was handed over 23 Aug 1955, *Reijger* was launched on 6 Feb 1958, *Haerlem* on 18 June 1958, *Oosterland* on 27 Jan 1959. All three of these later ships are fitted with Vosper roll damping fins. *Haerlem* had a charthouse added aft as an inshore survey craft.

REIJGER   12/1976, South African Navy

MINE WARFARE FORCES

10 BRITISH "TON" CLASS (MINESWEEPERS—COASTAL)

Name	No.	Builders	Commissioned
JOHANNESBURG (ex-HMS *Castleton*)	M 1207	White, Southampton	1958
KIMBERLEY (ex-HMS *Stratton*)	M 1210	Dorset Yacht Co	1958
PORT ELIZABETH (ex-HMS *Dumbleton*)	M 1212	Harland & Wolff, Belfast	1958
MOSSELBAAI (ex-HMS *Oakington*)	M 1213	Harland & Wolff, Belfast	1959
WALVISBAAI (ex-HMS *Packington*)	M 1214	Harland & Wolff, Belfast	1959
EAST LONDON (ex-HMS *Chilton*)	M 1215	Cook Welton and Gemmell	1958
WINDHOEK	M 1498	Thornycroft, Southampton	1959
DURBAN	M 1499	Camper & Nicholson, Gosport	1957
PRETORIA (ex-HMS *Dunkerton*)	P 1556	Goole Shipbuilding Co	1954
KAAPSTAD (ex-HMS *Hazleton*)	P 1557	Cook Welton and Gemmell	1954

Displacement, tons: 360 standard; 425 full load
Dimensions, feet (metres): 140·0 pp; 152·0 oa × 28·8 × 8·2 *(45·9; 49·8 × 9·4 × 2·7)*
Guns: 1—40 mm Bofors; 2—20 mm
Main engines: Mirrlees diesels in *Kaapstad* and *Pretoria*, 2 500 bhp; Deltic diesels in remainder; 3 000 bhp = 15 knots
Range, miles: 2 300 at 13 knots

Kaapstad and *Pretoria*, open bridge and lattice mast, were purchased in 1955 and converted with enclosed bridge and lattice mast in 1973. *Windhoek*, enclosed bridge and tripod mast, was launched by Thornycroft, Southampton, on 27 June 1957. *Durban*, enclosed bridge and tripod mast, was launched at Camper & Nicholson, Gosport, on 12 June 1957. *East London* and *Port Elizabeth*, transferred from the Royal Navy at Hythe on 27 Oct 1958, sailed for South Africa in Nov 1958. *Johannesburg*, *Kimberley* and *Mosselbaai* were delivered in 1959. *Walvisbaai* was launched by Harland & Wolff, Belfast on 3 July 1958 and delivered in 1959. Some now used on patrol duties. (Note change of pennant numbers for *Kaapstad* and *Pretoria*).

EAST LONDON   1977, Michael D. J. Lennon

KAAPSTAD (as Patrol Craft)   1977, Michael D. J. Lennon

SURVEY SHIPS

Name	No.	Builders	Commissioned
PROTEA	A 324	Yarrow (Shipbuilders) Ltd.	23 May 1972

Displacement, tons: 1 930 standard; 2 750 full load
Length, feet (metres): 235 *(71·6)* pp; 260·1 *(79·3)* oa
Beam, feet (metres): 49·1 *(15·0)*
Draught, feet (metres): 15·1 *(4·6)*
Aircraft: 1 helicopter
Main engines: 4 Paxman/Ventura diesels geared to 1 shaft and cp propeller; 4 880 bhp
Speed, knots: 16
Range, miles: 12 000 at 11 knots
Oil fuel, tons: 560
Complement: Total 121 (10 officers, 104 ratings plus 7 scientists)

An order was placed with Yarrow (Shipbuilders) Ltd, for a "Hecla" class survey ship on 7 Nov 1969. Equipped for hydrographic survey with limited facilities for the collection of oceanographical data and for this purpose fitted with special communications equipment, naval surveying gear, survey launches and facilities for helicopter operations. Hull strengthened for navigation in ice and fitted with a transverse bow thrust unit and passive roll stabilisation system. Laid down 20 July 1970. Launched 14 July 1971.

PROTEA 1973, South African Navy

HAERLEM P 3126

Converted July 1963 from "Ford" class for survey duties. Complement 23. See Light Forces section for details.

FLEET REPLENISHMENT SHIP

Name	No.	Builders	Commissioned
TAFELBERG (ex-*Annam*)	A 243	Nakskovs Skibsvaert, Denmark	1959

Measurement, tons: 12 500 gross; 18 980 deadweight
Dimensions, feet (metres): 559·8 × 72·1 × — *(170·6 × 21·9 × —)*
Main engines: B & W diesels; 8 420 bhp = 15·5 knots
Complement: 100

Built as Danish East Asiatic Co tanker. Launched on 20 June 1958. Purchased by the Navy in 1965. Accommodation rehabilitated by Barens Shipbuilding & Engineering Co, Durban with extra accommodation, air conditioning, re-wiring for additional equipment, new upper RAS (replenishment at sea) deck to contain gantries, re-fuelling pipes. Remainder of conversion by Jowies, Brown & Hamer, Durban. A helicopter flight-deck was added aft during refit in 1975.

TAFELBERG 1973, South African Navy

TORPEDO RECOVERY VESSEL

Name	No.	Builders	Commissioned
FLEUR	P 3148	Dorman Long (Africa) Ltd.	3 Dec 1969

Displacement, tons: 220 standard; 257 full load
Dimensions, feet (metres): 115·0 wl; 121·5 oa × 27·5 × 11·1 *(37·7; 39·8 × 9·0 × 3·6)*
Main engines: 2 Paxman Ventura diesels; 1 400 bhp
Complement: 22 (4 officers, 18 ratings)

Combined Torpedo Recovery Vessel and Diving Tender.

FLEUR 1973, South African Navy

BOOM DEFENCE VESSEL

Name	No.	Builders	Commissioned
SOMERSET (ex-HMS *Barcross*)	P 285	Blyth Dry Dock & SB Co Ltd	14 April 1942

Displacement, tons: 750 standard; 960 full load
Dimensions, feet (metres): 150·0 pp; 182·0 oa × 32·2 × 11·5 *(49·2; 59 × 10·5 × 3·8)*
Main engines: Triple expansion; 850 hp = 11 knots
Boilers: 2 single ended
Oil fuel, tons: 186

Originally two in the class. Laid down on 15 April 1941, launched on 21 Oct 1941. Engined by Swan, Hunter & Wigham Richardson Ltd, Tyne.

SOMERSET 12/1976, South African Navy

TRAINING VESSEL

Name	No.	Builders	Commissioned
NAVIGATOR	—	Fred Nicholls (Pty) Ltd, Durban	1964

Navigational Training Vessel. 75 tons displacement; 63 × 20 feet; 2 Foden diesels, 200 bhp = 9·5 knots. Based at Naval College, Gordon's Bay. Round bilge fishing boat wooden hull.

MISCELLANEOUS

TUGS

Name	No.	Builders	Commissioned
DE NEYS	—	Globe Engineering Works Ltd, Cape Town	23 July 1969
DE NOORDE	—	Globe Engineering Works Ltd, Cape Town	Dec 1961

Displacement, tons: 180 and 170 respectively
Dimensions, feet (metres): 94·0 × 26·5 × 15·75 and 104·5 × 25·0 × 15·0 *(30·8 × 8·7 × 5·2, 34·2 × 8·2 × 4·9)*
Main engines: 2 Lister Blackstone diesels; 2 shafts; 608 bhp = 9 knots
Complement: 10

De Neys fitted with Voith-Schneider screws.

DE NOORDE   12/1976, South African Navy

AIR SEA RESCUE LAUNCHES

2 FAIREY MARINE "TRACKER" CLASS

Name	No.	Builders	Commissioned
—	P 1554	Groves and Gutteridge, Cowes	1973
—	P 1555	Groves and Gutteridge, Cowes	1973

Displacement, tons: 26
Dimensions, feet (metres): 64 × 16 × 5 *(19·5 × 4·9 × 1·5)*
Main engines: 2 diesels; 1 120 bhp = 28 knots

Built by subsidiary of Fairey Marine.

P 1554   1973, South African Navy

2 KROGERWERFT TYPE

Name	No.	Builders	Commissioned
—	P 1551 (ex-*R 31*)	Krogerwerft, Rendsburg	1962
—	P 1552 (ex-*R 30*)	Krogerwerft, Rendsburg	1961

Displacement, tons: 87
Dimensions, feet (metres): 96 × 19 × 4 *(29·3 × 5·8 × 1·2)*
Main engines: 2 diesels; 4 480 bhp = 30 knots

There are also two 24 foot tenders.

P 1552   1977, Michael D. J. Lennon

DEPARTMENT OF TRANSPORT

1 NEW CONSTRUCTION (ANTARCTIC SURVEY AND SUPPLY VESSEL)

Measurement, tons: 3 050 dw
Dimensions, feet (metres): 358·3 × 59 × 19 *(109·2 × 18 × 5·8)*
Aircraft: 2 helicopters
Main engines: 2 Mirrlees-Blackstone diesels; 6 000 shp; 1 shaft = 14 knots
Complement: 40 (92 spare berths)

Ordered 11 Aug 1976 from Mitsubishi, Shimonoseki. Laid down April 1977.

SPAIN

Headquarters Appointments

Minister of the Navy:
  Admiral Excmo Sr Don Gabriel Pita da Veiga
Chief of the Naval Staff:
  Admiral Excmo Sr Don Carlos Buhigas
Chief of Fleet Support:
  Admiral Excmo Sr Don Pedro Durán
Vice Chief of the Naval Staff:
  Vice-Admiral Excmo Sr Don Guillermo Mateu

Commands

Commander-in-Chief of the Fleet:
  Vice-Admiral Excmo Sr Don Juan C. Muñoz-Delgado
Captain General, Cantabrian Zone:
  Admiral Excmo Sr Don Pedro Español Iglesias
Captain General, Straits Zone:
  Admiral Excmo Sr Don Vicente Alberto y Lloveres
Captain General, Mediterranean Zone:
  Admiral Excmo Sr Don Francisco J de Elizalde
Commandant General, Marines:
  Lieutenant-General Excmo Sr Don Carlos Arriaga

Diplomatic Representation

Naval Attaché in London:
  Captain Don Gabino Aranda de Carranza
Naval Attaché in Washington:
  Captain Sr Don Adolfo Gregorio Alvarez

Personnel

(a) 1978: Total 44 799 (4 085 officers, 32 668 ratings, 8 046 civil branch).
  Infanteria Marina 10 614 (614 officers, 10 000 marines)
(b) 18 months national service

Bases

Main:
  El Ferrol del Caudillo (Cantabrian Zone)
  San Fernando, Cádiz (Straits Zone)
  Cartagena (Mediterranean Zone)
Secondary:
  La Graña (Ferrol area), Rota (Cadiz), Tarifa (Straits of Gibraltar), Marin (Pontevedra—Naval School), Vigo (Electronics School), Las Palmas de Gran Canaria (arsenal), Palma de Majorca and Sóller (Majorca), Port Mahón (Minorca), La Algameca (near Cartagena).
New base to be built at Gando (Canary Is).

Naval Air Service

- 5 Harrier AV-8A (Matador) (5 on order)
- 2 Harrier TAV-8A
- 12 Bell 47G helicopters
- 3 AB 212
- 4 AB 204B
- 10 Sikorsky SH-3D Sea King
- 12 Hughes 500 ASW
- 6 Bell AH-1G "Hueycobra"
- 3 Sikorsky S-55 (phasing out)
- 2 Piper Comanche
- 2 Twin Comanche
- (6 helicopters, probably Sea Kings, on order)

Notes:
First Harrier AV-8 aircraft ordered from US Marine Corps in 1973. Initial order of 8.

US Agreement

Under 1976 Agreement US is to provide four minesweepers—Ocean and one Repair Ship (the latter now cancelled).

Strength of the Fleet

Type	Active	Building	Proposed
Aircraft Carriers	1	1	—
Destroyers	13	—	—
Frigates	14	9	2
Submarines—Patrol	8	4	—
Fast Attack Craft (Patrol)	12	—	—
Coastal Patrol Craft	22	—	—
LSD	1	—	—
Attack Transports	2	—	—
LSTs	3	—	—
LCTs	8	—	—
Minor Landing Craft	26	—	—
Minesweepers—Ocean	8 + 4	—	—
Minesweepers—Coastal	12	—	—
Survey Ships	6	—	—
Replenishment Tanker	1	—	—
Harbour Tankers	13	—	—
Training Ship	1	—	—
Auxiliary Patrol Craft	7	—	—
Tugs (Ocean, Coastal and Harbour)	28	—	—
Miscellaneous	64	—	—

New Construction

Because of financial considerations the current programme has been cut to the following; three FFG-7 class frigates; eight corvettes, two or four "Agosta" class submarines, six 400 ton Large Patrol Craft, six 140 ton Large Patrol Craft.
Of the above, eight corvettes and two submarines are building whilst two oceanographic vessels and two survey vessels have been completed. Most patrol craft are completed.
Proposed but not yet approved—one Sea Control Ship, two additional "Agosta" class submarines and two additional corvettes.

Mercantile Marine

Lloyd's Register of Shipping:
2 792 vessels of 6 027 763 tons gross

DELETIONS

Submarines

1971 *D 2* (S 21), *D 3* (S 22), *G 7* (ex-U573 VII C)
  Midget submarines *SA 41* (F 1), *SA 42* (F 2)
1977 *SA 51, SA 52* ("Tiburon" Class)
  Narciso Menturiol

Minewarfare Forces

1971 *Lerez* ("Bidasoa" Class)
1972 *Bidasoa, Nervion, Segura, Tambre, Ter* ("Bidasoa" Class)
1976 *Tinto* ("Guardioro" Class) (31 Jan)
1977 *Eume* (1 Sept); *Guardiaro* (15 May) ("Guardiaro" Class)

Amphibious Forces

1974 *LSM 3*
1976 *LSM 1, LSM 2*

Light Forces

1971 *Javier Quiroga* (ex-US PC)
1973 *Ciés* (Fishery Protection)
1974 *V 2, V 12, V 13, V 18, Candido Pérez, AR 10* (Coastal Launches)
1977 *LT 30, LT 31* (Lürssen Type). RR 19, 20 (20 April)
  Centinela and *Serviola* (Fishery Protection—to Mauritania 5 March 1977)

Survey Ships

1971 *Malaspina*
1975 *Tofiño, Juan de la Cosa* (30 April)

Service Forces

1974 *PP 1, 3, 4, PB 5, 6, 17* (tankers)
1977 *Almirante Lobo* (30 April), *A 1* (14 March), *A 8* (30 April), *AB 10* (19 May), *BL 11* (20 April)

Cruiser

1975 *Canarias* (17 Dec)

Frigates

1971 *Magallanes, Vasco Nunez de Balboa, Hernan Cortes* ("Pizarro" Class) *Marte* ("Jupiter" Class)
1972 *Eolo, Triton* ("Eolo" Class), *Neptuno* ("Jupiter" Class)
1973 *Osado* ("Audaz" Class)
1974 *Audaz, Furor, Rayo* ("Audaz" Class), *Jupiter* ("Jupiter" Class), *Sarmiento de Gamboa* ("Pizarro" Class)
1975 *Meteoro, Relampago, Temerario,* ("Audaz" Class)
1977 *Vulcano* ("Jupiter" Class)

Corvettes

1971 *Descubierta* ("Atrevida" Class)
1973 *Diana* ("Atrevida" Class)

LIST OF PENNANT NUMBERS

Aircraft Carrier

PA 01	Dédalo

Destroyers

D 21	Lepanto
D 22	Almirante Ferrandiz
D 23	Almirante Valdes
D 24	Alcala Galiano
D 25	Jorge Juan
D 41	Oquendo
D 42	Roger de Lauria
D 43	Marques de la Ensenada
D 61	Churruca
D 62	Gravina
D 63	Mendez Nuñez
D 64	Langara
D 65	Blas de Lezo

Frigates

D 38	Intrépido
D 51	Liniers
D 52	Alava
F 31	Descubierta
F 32	Diana
F 33	Infanta Elena
F 34	Infanta Cristina
F 35	New Construction
F 36	New Construction
F 37	New Construction
F 38	New Construction
F 41	Vicente Yáñez Pinzon
F 42	Legazpi
F 61	Atrevida
F 62	Princesa
F 64	Nautilus
F 65	Villa de Bilbao
F 71	Baleares
F 72	Andalucia
F 73	Cataluña
F 74	Asturias
F 75	Extremadura
F 91-3	Proposed New Construction

Submarines

S 31	Almirante Garcia de los Reyes
S 32	Isaac Peral
S 34	Cosme Garcia
S 35	(no name)
S 61	Delfin
S 62	Tonina
S 63	Marsopa
S 64	Narval
S 71-72	New Construction
S 73-74	Proposed New Construction

Light Forces

P 01	Lazaga
P 02	Alsedo
P 03	Cadarso
P 04	Villaamil
P 05	Bonifaz
P 06	Recalde
P 11	Barceló
P 12	Laya
P 13	Javier Quiroga
P 14	Ordóñez
P 15	Acevedo
P 16	Candido Pérez
LPI 1-5	
LAS 10, 20, 30	
RR 29	
V-1	
V-4	
V-5	
V-6	
V-9	
V-10	
V-11	
V-21	
V-31	
V-32	
V-33	
V-34	
W 01	Gaviota
W 32	Salvora
—	Cabo Fradera

Amphibious Forces

TA 11	Aragon
TA 21	Castilla
TA 31	Galicia
L 11	Velasco
L 12	Martin Alvarez
L 13	C. de Venadito
K 1-8	BDK 1-8

Minewarfare Forces

M 14	Almanzora
M 15	Navia
M 16	Guadalhorce
M 17	Eo
M 21	Nalón
M 22	Llobregat
M 23	Jucar
M 24	Ulla
M 25	Miño

SPAIN 417

M 26	Ebro		Survey Ships			Service Forces	
M 27	Turia						
M 28	Duero		A 21	Castor		BP 11	Teide
M 29	Sil		A 22	Pollux			
M 30	Tajo		A 23	Antares			
M 31	Genil		A 24	Rigel			
M 32	Odiel		A 31	Malaspina			
M 41	Guadalete		A 32	Tofiño			
M 42	Guadalmedina						
M 43	Guadalquivir						
M 44	Guadiana						

DEDALO

"DESCUBIERTA" ("F 30") Class

"MOD OQUENDO" Class

ALM. FERRANDIZ, LEPANTO

OQUENDO

ALCALA GALIANO, JORGE JUAN and VALDES

"Ex-US" GEARING" ("D 60") Class

"BALEARES" ("F70") Class

INTREPIDO

"LAZAGA" ("P 00") Class

"BARCELO" ("P 10") Class

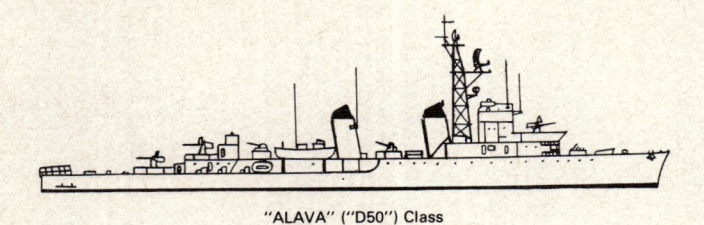

418 SPAIN

"ALAVA" ("D50") Class

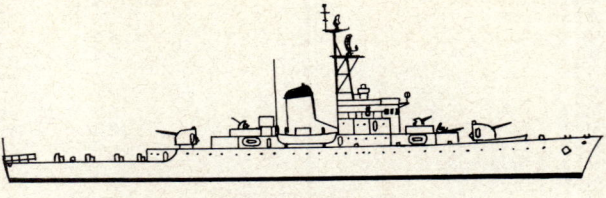

Mod. "PIZARRO" ("F 40") Class

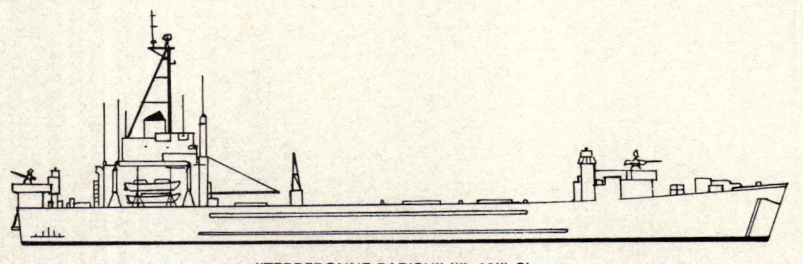

"TERREBONNE PARISH" ("L 10") Class

SUBMARINES

0 + 4 "S 70" CLASS (FRENCH "AGOSTA" CLASS)

Name	No.	Builders	Laid down	Launched	Commissioned
—	S 71	Bazán, Cartagena	late 1975	1977	1981
—	S 72	Bazán, Cartagena	early 1976	1977	1981
—	S 73	Bazán, Cartagena	—	—	—
—	S 74	Bazán, Cartagena	—	—	—

Displacement, tons: 1 450 surfaced; 1 725 dived
Dimensions, feet (metres): 221·7 × 22·3 × 17·7 (67·6 × 6·8 × 5·4)
Torpedo tubes: 4—21·7 in (550 mm) (16 reloads)
Main machinery: Diesel-electric; 2 diesels; 3 600 hp; 1 Main motor; 6 400 hp; 1 cruising motor; 1 shaft
Speed, knots: 12 surfaced; 20 dived
Range, miles: 9 000 at 9 knots (snorting); 350 at 3·5 knots (dived)
Endurance: 45 days
Complement: 50

Two ordered 9 May 1975. Building by Bazán Cartagena with some French advice. Two more orders placed 25 May 1976.

Missiles: Submarine Exocet may be carried.

Radar: Calypso I Band.

Sonar: Two DUUA active; one DSUV passive.

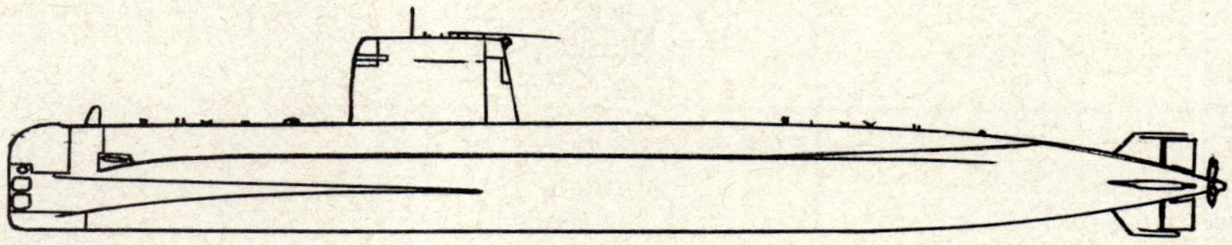

"S 70" Class 1974

4 "S 60" CLASS (FRENCH "DAPHNE" CLASS)

Name	No.	Builders	Laid down	Launched	Commissioned
DELFIN	S 61	Bazán, Cartagena	13 Aug 1968	25 Mar 1972	3 May 1973
TONINA	S 62	Bazán, Cartagena	1969	3 Oct 1972	10 July 1973
MARSOPA	S 63	Bazán, Cartagena	19 Mar 1971	15 Mar 1974	12 April 1975
NARVAL	S 64	Bazán, Cartagena	1971	14 Dec 1974	22 Nov 1975

Displacement, tons: 870 surfaced; 1 040 dived
Length, feet (metres): 189·6 (57·8)
Beam, feet (metres): 22·3 (6·8)
Draught, feet (metres): 15·1 (4·6)
Torpedo tubes: 12—21·7 in (550 mm) (8 bow, 4 stern) (no reloads — mining capability)
Main machinery: SEMT-Pielstick diesel-electric; 2 600 bhp surfaced; 2 700 hp dived; 2 shafts
Speed, knots: 13·2 surfaced; 15·5 dived
Range, miles: 4 500 at 5 knots (snorting); 2 710 at 12·5 knots (surfaced)
Complement: 47 (6 officers, 41 men)

Identical to the French "Daphne" class and built with extensive French assistance in the Cartagena Yard. First pair ordered 26 Dec 1966 and second pair in March 1970. S 63 cost 1 040 million pesetas.

Radar: Thompson CSF DRUA-31 plus ECM.

Sonar: Active, DUUA 1; Passive with rangefinding, DSUV. Goniometer; DUUG-1.

TONINA 6/1975, Dr. Giorgia Arra

SPAIN 419

3 "S 30" CLASS (Ex-US GUPPY IIA TYPE)

No.	Builders	Laid down	Launched	Commissioned
S 32	Portsmouth Navy Yard	9 Sept 1943	27 Jan 1944	22 April 1944
S 34	Portsmouth Navy Yard	30 April 1943	30 Aug 1943	4 Dec 1943
S 35	Manitowoc SB Corp	29 Sept 1943	12 Mar 1944	8 July 1944

Name
ISAAC PERAL (ex-USS *Ronquil*, SS 396)
COSME GARCIA (ex-USS *Bang*, SS 385)
— (ex-USS *Jallao*, SS 385)

Displacement, tons: 1 840 surfaced; 2 445 dived
Length, feet (metres): 306·0 *(93·3)* oa
Beam, feet (metres): 27·0 *(8·2)*
Draught, feet (metres): 17·0 *(5·2)*
Torpedo tubes: 10—21 in *(533 mm)* 6 bow, 4 stern
Main machinery: 3 Fairbanks-Morse diesels; total 4 800 bhp; 2 shafts; 2 Elliot electric motors; 5 400 shp
Speed, knots: 18 surfaced; 14 dived
Oil fuel, tons: 464 (472 in SS 35)
Range, miles: 12 000 at 10 knots
Complement: 74

Transferred to Spain on 1 July 1971 *(Peral)* 1 Oct 1972 *(Garcia)* and (ex-*Jallao*) 26 June 1974. *Monturiol* and *Garcia* purchased 18 Nov 1974 the other pair being transferred by sale. *Narciso Monturiol* deleted, as expected after her mechanical problems of 1975, on 30 April 1977.

Diving Depth: 450 feet *(140 metres)*.

Electronics: Mk 106 TDC.

Radar: SS 2.

Sonar: BQS, BQR.

COSME GARCIA   1973, X. I. Taibo

S-35   1977, X. I. Taibo

1 Ex-US "BALAO" CLASS

No.	Builders	Laid down	Launched	Commissioned
S 31	Manitowoc SB Co	1943	30 April 1944	8 Sept 1944

Name
ALMIRANTE GARCIA DE LOS REYES (ex-USS *Kraken*, SS 370)

Displacement, tons: 1 816 surfaced; 2 400 dived
Dimensions, feet (metres): 311·5 × 27·2 × 17·2 *(95 × 8·3 × 5·2)*
Torpedo tubes: 10—(6—21 in *(533 mm)* and 4 for A/S torpedoes)
Main machinery: 4 diesels; 6 400 bhp; 2 main motors; 4 600 shp; 2 shafts
Speed, knots: 18·5 surfaced; 10 dived
Oil fuel, tons: 472
Range, miles: 12 000 at 10 knots (surfaced)
Complement: 80

Transferred 24 Oct 1959 after modernisation at Pearl Harbor. Although due to be paid off in 1975 retained in service (see note under "S 30" class).

ALMIRANTE GARCIA DE LOS REYES   1977, X. I. Taibo

HELICOPTER CARRIERS

ALMIRANTE CARRERA

She will be built by Bazán Ferrol to the Sea Control ship design obtained from the USA. Bazán is working with Gibbs and Cox of USA with a plan to lay down this ship in late 1978 for completion 1982-84.

Name: *Almirante Carrera* was originally chosen. *Canarias* has been mentioned.

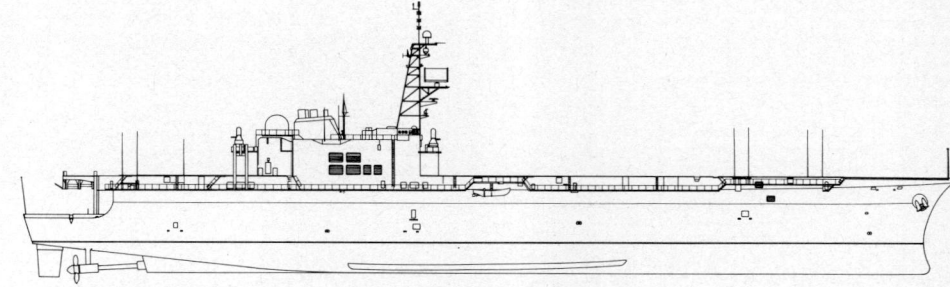

Possible New Helicopter Carrier   1977

420 SPAIN

1 Ex-US "INDEPENDENCE" CLASS (CVL)

Name	No.	Builders	Laid down	Launched	Commissioned
DÉDALO (ex-USS *Cabot*, AVT 3, ex-*CVL 28*, ex-*Wilmington*, CL 79)	PA 01	New York Shipbuilding Corp	16 Aug 1942	4 April 1943	24 July 1943

Displacement, tons: 13 000 standard; 16 416 full load
Length, feet (metres): 600·0 *(182·8)* wl; 623·0 *(189·9)* oa
Beam, feet (metres): 71·5 *(21·8)* hull
Width, feet (metres): 109·0 *(33·2)*
Draught, feet (metres): 26·0 *(7·9)*
Aircraft: 7 Harriers (5 AV-8A, 2 TAV-8A) (Matador) 20 helicopters (ASW/Sea Kings—Combat/Huey Cobras—Landings/specially embarked Bell 212s or 204s)
Guns: 26—40 mm (2 quadruple, 9 twin)
Armour: 2 to 5 in sides; 2 to 3 in deck
Main engines: GE geared turbines; 4 shafts; 100 000 shp
Boilers: 4 Babcock & Wilcox
Speed, knots: 32
Range, miles: 7 200 at 15 knots
Oil fuel, tons: 1 800
Complement: 1 112 (without Air Groups)

Completed as an aircraft carrier from the hull of a "Cleveland" class cruiser. Originally carried over 40 aircraft. Converted with strengthened flight and hangar decks, large port side catapult, revised magazine arrangements, new electronic gear, with stability corrected to offset the added top-weight. Hangar capacity altered to take 20 aircraft. Flight deck: 545 × 108 feet *(166·1 × 32·9 metres)*.
Reactivated and modernised at Philadelphia Naval Shipyard, where she was transferred to Spain on 30 Aug 1967, on loan for five years. Purchased Dec 1973. Fleet flagship.
Rerated "Portaaronaves" on 28 Sept 1976 with change of flag superior from PH to PA.

Aircraft: Hangar capacity—18 Sea Kings. Six more can be spotted on flight deck.

Electronics: AN/WLR1 ECM; Tacan.

Gunnery: Reported that Meroka 20 mm system is to be shipped.

Radar: Three dimensional: SPS 52B.
Air search: SPS 6 and SPS 40.
Tactical: SPS 10
Fire control: Four sets

DÉDALO *1974, Michael D. J. Lennon*

DÉDALO *1974, Michael D. J. Lennon*

DESTROYERS

2 "ROGER DE LAURIA" CLASS

Name	No.	Builders	Laid down	Launched (see note)	Commissioned
ROGER DE LAURIA	D 42	Bazán, Ferrol/Cartagena	4 Sept 1951	12 Nov 1958	30 May 1969
MARQUÉS DE LA ENSENADA	D 43	Bazán, Ferrol/Cartagena	4 Sept 1951	15 July 1959	10 Sept 1970

Displacement, tons: 3 012 standard; 3 785 full load
Length, feet (metres): 391·5 *(119·3)*
Beam, feet (metres): 42·7 *(13·0)*
Draught, feet (metres): 18·4 *(5·6)*
Aircraft: 1 Hughes 369 HM ASW helicopter
Guns: 6—5 in *(127 mm)* 38 cal (3 twin)
A/S weapons: 2 triple Mk 32 tubes for Mk 44 A/S torpedoes
Torpedo tubes: 2—21 in *(533 mm)* fixed single Mk 25 tubes for Mk 37 torpedoes
Main engines: 2 Rateau-Bretagne geared turbines; 2 shafts; 60 000 shp
Boilers: 3 three-drum type
Speed, knots: 28
Oil fuel, tons: 700
Range, miles: 4 500 at 15 knots
Complement: 318 (20 officers, 298 men)

Ordered in 1948. Originally of the same design as *Oquendo*. Towed to Cartegena for reconstruction to a new design. *Roger de Lauria* was re-launched after being lengthened and widened on 29 Aug 1967 and *Marqués de la Ensenada* on 2 March 1968. Weapons and electronics identical to Gearing Fram II.

Electronics: ESM; AL/WLRI. Torpedo control; ? Mk 114.

Fire control: One Mk 37 director with Mk 25 radar.
One Mk 56 director with Mk 35 radar.

MARQUÉS DE LA ENSENADA *1976, Royal Spanish Navy*

Gunnery: To be fitted with Meroka 20 mm system.

Radar: Search: SPS 40.
Tactical: SPS 10.

Sonar: One hull mounted, SQS 32C; one VDS, SQA 10.

SPAIN 421

5 "D 60" CLASS (Ex-US "GEARING" FRAM I CLASS)

Name	No.	Builders	Laid down	Launched	Commissioned
CHURRUCA (ex-USS *Eugene A. Greene*, DD 711)	D 61	Federal SB & DD Co.	1944	18 Mar 1945	8 June 1945
GRAVINA (ex-USS *Furse*, DD 882)	D 62	Consolidated Steel Corp	1944	9 Mar 1945	10 July 1945
MENDEZ NUÑEZ (ex-USS *O'Hare*, DD 889)	D 63	Consolidated Steel Corpn	1945	22 June 1945	29 Nov 1945
LANGARA (ex-USS *Leary*, DD 879)	D 64	Consolidated Steel Corpn	1944	20 Jan 1945	7 May 1945
BLAS DE LEZO (ex-USS *Noa*, DD 841)	D 65	Bath Iron Works	1945	30 July 1945	2 Nov 1945

Displacement, tons: 2 425 standard; 3 480 full load
Length, feet (metres): 390·5 *(119·0)* oa
Beam, feet (metres): 40·9 *(12·4)*
Draught, feet (metres): 19 *(5·8)*
Aircraft: 1 Hughes 500 helicopter
Guns: 4—5 in *(127 mm)* 38 cal (twin)
A/S weapons: 1 Asroc launcher; 2 triple Mk 32 tubes
Main engines: 2 geared turbines (GE or Westinghouse) 60 000 shp; 2 shafts
Boilers: 4 Babcock & Wilcox
Speed, knots: 34
Fuel, tons: 650
Range, miles: 4 800 at 15 knots (economical)
Complement: 274 (17 officers, 257 ratings)

Appearance: *Blas de Lezo* has two forward gun mounts and torpedo tubes by after funnel.

Electronics: ESM; AL/WLRI.

Fire control: Radar directed Mk 37 Director.

Radar: Air search: D61 and 62, SPS 40—remainder, SPS 37; Surface search: SPS 10.

Refits: The first pair were refitted at El Ferrol on transfer. The remainder arrived at El Ferrol on 23 July 1974 after refit in the USA.

Sonar: SQS 23 (hull mounted).

Torpedo control: ? Mk 114.

Transfers: D61 and 62—31 Aug 1972; D63-65—31 Oct 1973. (All finally purchased 1975).

LANGARA   1975, Spanish Navy

5 "D 20" CLASS (Ex-US "FLETCHER" CLASS)

Name	No.	Builders	Laid down	Launched	Commissioned
LEPANTO (ex-USS *Capps*, DD 550)	D 21	Gulf SB Corp, Chickasaw, Ala	12 June 1941	31 May 1942	23 June 1943
ALMIRANTE FERRANDIZ (ex-USS *David W. Taylor*, DD 551)	D 22	Gulf SB Corp, Chickasaw, Ala	12 June 1941	4 July 1942	18 Sept 1943
ALMIRANTE VALDES (ex-USS *Converse*, DD 509)	D 23	Bath Iron Works	23 Feb 1942	30 Aug 1942	8 June 1943
ALCALA GALIANO (ex-USS *Jarvis*, DD 799)	D 24	Todd Pacific Shipyards	7 June 1943	14 Feb 1944	3 June 1944
JORGE JUAN (ex-USS *McGowan*, DD 678)	D 25	Federal SB & DD Co	May 1943	14 Nov 1943	20 Dec 1943

Displacement, tons: 2 080 standard; 2 750 normal; 3 050 full load
Length, feet (metres): 376·5 *(114·8)* oa
Beam, feet (metres): 39·5 *(12·0)*
Draught, feet (metres): 18·0 *(5·5)*
Guns: D21, D22: 5—5 in *(127 mm)* 38 cal; Others: 4—5 in *(127 mm)* single
D21, D22: 6—40 mm, 60 cal Mk 1, (3 twin); 6—20 mm, 70 cal Mk 4, (single); Others: 6—3 in *(76 mm)* 50 cal Mk 33, (3 twin)
A/S weapons: 2 Mk 11 Hedgehogs; 6 DCT in D21 and D22, 4 in D23; 2 DC racks in D21, D22, 1 in others
Torpedo tubes: 3—21 in *(533 mm)* in D23, 24 and 25 only
Torpedo racks: 2 side launching Mk 4 each with 3 Mk 32 A/S torpedoes (to be replaced by torpedo tubes)
Main engines: Geared turbines; Westinghouse in D21, D22, GE in others; 2 shafts; 60 000 shp
Boilers: 4 Babcock & Wilcox
Speed, knots: 35
Oil fuel, tons: 506
Range, miles: 5 000 at 15 knots
Complement: 290 (17 officers, 273 men)

Lepanto and *Almirante Ferrandiz* were reconditioned at San Francisco, Cal, and there turned over to the Spanish Navy on 15 May 1957, sailing for Spain on 1 July 1957. *Valdes* was transferred at Philadelphia on 1 July 1959, *Jorge Juan* was transferred at Barcelona on 1 Dec 1960 and *Alcala Galiano* at Philadelphia on 3 Nov 1960, both being of the later "Fletcher" class. Modernisation of A/S equipment is planned. All purchased from US on 1 Oct 1972. *Lepanto* damaged on grounding 16 April 1977.

Electronics: Torpedo director Mk 5. A/S director Mk 105.

Fire control: Radar controlled Mk 37 directors; Mk 56 director with Mk 35 radar (D 23, 24 and 25); Mk 63 director with SPG 34 radar for 3 in *(76 mm)* guns (D 23, 24 and 25).

Radar: Search: SPS 6C.
Tactical: SPS 10.

Sonar: One hull mounted set. SQS-29 or SQS-4.

ALMIRANTE VALDES   1974, Wright and Logan

ALCALA GALIANO   1977, X. I. Taibo

422 SPAIN

1 "OQUENDO" CLASS

Name	No.	Builders	Laid down	Launched	Commissioned
OQUENDO	D 41	Bazán, Ferrol	15 June 1951	5 Sept 1956	13 Sept 1960

Displacement, tons: 2 342 standard; 3 005 full load
Length, feet (metres): 382 *(116·4)*
Beam, feet (metres): 36·5 *(11·1)*
Draught, feet (metres): 12·5 *(3·8)*
Guns: 4—4·7 *(120 mm)* 50 cal (2 twin NG 53); 6—40 mm, 70 cal (single SP 48)
A/S weapons: 2 Mk 11 Mod 0 Hedgehogs; 2 Mk 4 side-launchers with 3 Mk 32 torpedoes each
Main engines: 2 Rateau-Bretagne geared turbines; 2 shafts; 60 000 shp
Boilers: 3 three-drum type
Speed, knots: 32·4
Oil fuel, tons: 659
Range, miles: 5 000 at 15 knots
Complement: 250 (17 officers, 233 men)

Ordered in 1947. Initially completed on 13 Sept 1960. Completed modernisation on 22 April 1963.

Construction: Designed as a conventional destroyer but modified during construction. Seven 21-in torpedo tubes and two depth charge throwers were replaced by different anti-submarine weapons.

OQUENDO   1974, Spanish Navy

Gunnery: This is the only ship with Spanish-built NG 53 120 mm twin mountings.

Radar: Search: British 293 type.
Air search: Marconi SNW 10 (960).

Navigation: one set.
Fire control: British type 275 on Mark 6 DCT and British Type 262 on CRBFD (or MRS 8).

Sonar: QHBa.

FRIGATES

0 + 1 + 2 US "FFG 7" CLASS (NEW CONSTRUCTION)

Name	No.	Builders	Laid down	Launched	Commissioned
—	—	Bazán-Ferrol	1978	—	?1981
—	—	Bazán-Ferrol	—	—	—
—	—	Bazán-Ferrol	—	—	—

Displacement, tons: 3 605 full load
Length, feet (metres): 445 *(135·6)* oa
Beam, feet (metres): 45 *(13·7)*
Draught, feet (metres): 24·5 *(7·5)*
Aircraft: 2 helicopters
Missile launchers: 1 single launcher for Standard/Harpoon missiles (Mk 13 Mod 4)
Guns: 1—76 mm 62 calibre (Mk 75); 1—Meroka system
A/S weapons: 2 triple torpedo tubes (Mk 32)
Main engines: 2—LM 2500 gas turbines (General Electric); 41 000 shp; 1 shaft (cp propeller)
Speed, knots: 30
Range, miles: 4 500 at 20 knots
Complement: 163 (11 officers, 152 ratings)

Three ordered in Sept 1977. Pennant numbers not yet known.

Sonar: DE 1160B or SQS 56 with TACTAS.

"FFG 7" Class   Drawing, A. D. Baker III

3 + 5 "F 30" CLASS (NEW CONSTRUCTION)

Name	No.	Builders	Laid down	Launched	Commissioned
DESCUBIERTA	F 31	Bazán, Cartagena	16 Nov 1974	8 July 1975	mid-1978
DIANA	F 32	Bazán, Cartagena	8 July 1975	26 Jan 1976	1978
INFANTA ELENA	F 33	Bazán, Cartagena	26 Jan 1976	14 Sept 1976	1978
INFANTA CRISTINA	F 34	Bazán, Cartagena	14 Sept 1976	25 April 1977	1979
—	F 35	Bazán, Ferrol	14 Dec 1977	—	1980
—	F 36	Bazán, Ferrol	—	—	—
—	F 37	Bazán, Ferrol	—	—	—
—	F 38	Bazán, Ferrol	—	—	—

Displacement, tons: 1 200 standard; 1 497 full load
Dimensions, feet (metres): 291·3 × 34 × 11·5 *(88·8 × 10·4 × 3·4)*
Missiles: 1 Octuple Seasparrow mounting (16 reloads) (see note)
Guns: 1—3 in *(76 mm)* 62 cal Oto Melara; 2—40 mm 70 cal Breda-Bofors (singles); 1 or 2 Meroka 20 mm 120 cal (12 barrels non-rotating) (possible)
A/S weapons: 1—375 mm Bofors twin-barrelled rocket launcher; 6 (2 triple) Mk 32 for Mk 46 torpedoes
Main engines: 4 MTU-Bazan 16V956 "TB 91" diesels; 16 000 bhp (18 000 bhp supercharged for 2 hours); 2 shafts; cp propellers
Speed, knots: 26
Range, miles: 4 000 at 18 knots
Complement: approx 100

Similar to the Portuguese "improved João Coutinho" class built by Bazán with modifications to the armament and main engines. Officially rated as corvettes. Reported as designed to carry 30 marines. *Diana* (tenth of the name) originates with the Armada of 1588. Infanta Elena and Cristina are the daughters of King Juan Carlos. Approval for second four ships given on 21 May 1976. First four ordered 7 Dec 1973 (83 per cent Spanish components) and four more from Bazán, Ferrol on 25 May 1976.

Appearance: Altered from original design by use of Y-shaped funnel.

Design: Original Portuguese "improved João Coutinho" design by Comodoro de Oliveira PN developed by Captain Remigio Diez Davó of Spain.

Electrical: 1 700 kVA—4 diesel alternators with Bazán-MAN RBV 16 TLS of 520 hp and emergency gas turbine alternator of 450 kVA.

"F 30" Class   1976, X. I. Taibo

Electronics: ECM Elettronica SpA "Beta".

Engineering: Bridge control as well as control centre.

Gunnery: 144 ready rounds for 40 mm. Secondary optical director, DME ("CSEE").

Missiles: Selenia system (Albatros) for Seasparrow. This is built partly in Spain. SSMs will be MM 39 or Harpoon with two 4-cell launchers between bridge and funnel.

Radar: Air/surface search: HSA DA 05/2.
Navigation and helo control: HSA ZW-06.
Fire control: HSA WM 22/41 system.

Sonar: Raytheon 1160B (combined hull mounted and VDS).

SPAIN 423

5 "BALEARES (F 70)" CLASS

Name	No.	Builders	Laid down	Launched	Commissioned
BALEARES	F 71	Bazán, Ferrol	31 Oct 1968	20 Aug 1970	24 Sept 1973
ANDALUCIA	F 72	Bazán, Ferrol	2 July 1969	30 Mar 1971	23 May 1974
CATALUÑA	F 73	Bazán, Ferrol	20 Aug 1970	3 Nov 1971	16 Jan 1975
ASTURIAS	F 74	Bazán, Ferrol	30 Mar 1971	13 May 1972	2 Dec 1975
EXTREMADURA	F 75	Bazán, Ferrol	3 Nov 1971	21 Nov 1972	10 Nov 1976

Displacement, tons: 3 015 standard; 4 177 full load
Length, feet (metres): 415·0 *(126·5)* pp; 438·0 *(133·6)* oa
Beam, feet (metres): 46·9 *(14·3)*
Draught, feet (metres): 15·4 *(4·7)*
Missile launchers: 1 single for Tartar/Standard missiles (lightweight Mk 22)
Gun: 1—5 in *(127 mm)* 54 cal Mk 42 Mod 9
A/S weapons: 1 8-tube ASROC launcher (8 reloads);
4 Mk 32 for Mk 46 torpedoes;
2 Mk 25 for Mk 37 torpedoes (stern)
Main engines: 1 set Westinghouse geared turbines; 1 shaft; 35 000 shp
Boilers: 2 high pressure V2M type; 1 200 psi *(84·4 kg/cm²)*
Speed, knots: 28
Range: 4 500 miles at 20 knots
Complement: 256 (15 officers, 241 men)

This class resulted from a very close co-operation between Spain and the USA. Programme approved 17 Nov 1964, technical support agreement with USA being signed 31 March 1966. USN supplied weapons, sensors, major hull sections—turbines and gearboxes made at El Ferrol, superstructures at Alicante, boilers, distilling plants and propellers at Cadiz.

Design: This class replaced the "Leander" class from the United Kingdom which order was cancelled in 1962 as the result of political insults in that country. Generally similar to USN "Knox" class although they differ in the missile system, hull sonar, Mk 25 torpedo tubes and lack of helicopter facilities. The last is a cause of criticism along with similar criticisms in USN of low speed, lack of manoeuvrability (1 screw) and inadequate missile stowage.
The anchor arrangement provides for a 2-ton anchor on the port bow and a 4-ton anchor in the keel aft of the sonar dome.

Fire control: Mk 68 GFCS with SPG-53B radar for guns and missiles; Mk 74 missile control system integrating Mk 73 missile control director and SPG-51C radar. Mk 111 replaced by digital control Mk 152 calculator. Mk 114 torpedo control system.

Gunnery: 600—5 in rounds carried.
Meroka system due to be shipped in 1978.

Missile system: Mk 22 launcher with stowage for 16 missiles. Single director with two lines of fire against different targets with Mk 68 GFCS. To receive SSMs.

Radar: Search: SPS 52A (3D).
Tactical: SPS 10.
Fire control: SPG-51C continuous wave for missiles; Mk 68 with SPG 53B for guns with continuous wave injection for limited use with missiles.

Torpedoes and tubes: All are fitted fixed internally the Mk 32 being angled at 45°. Total of 41 torpedoes carried.

Sonar: SQS 23 bow mounted; SQS 35V VDS below quarterdeck.

ASTURIAS   7/1976, Arthur D. Baker III

CATALUÑA   9/1975, Dr. Giorgio Arra

1 "AUDAZ" CLASS

Name	No.	Builders	Laid down	Launched	Commissioned
INTRÉPIDO	D 38	Bazán, Ferrol	14 July 1945	15 Feb 1961	25 Mar 1965

Displacement, tons: 1 227 standard; 1 550 full load
Length, feet (metres): 295·2 *(90·0)* pp; 308·2 *(94·0)* oa
Beam, feet (metres): 30·5 *(9·3)*
Draught, feet (metres): 17·1 *(5·2)*
Guns: 2—3 in *(76 mm)* 50 cal US Mk 34; 2—40 mm 70 cal (SP 48)
A/S weapons: 2 Mk 11 Hedgehogs; 8 mortars; 2 DC racks;
2 side launching racks for Mk 32 A/S torpedoes (6 torpedoes)
Main engines: 2 Rateau-Bretagne geared turbines; 2 shafts; 28 000 shp (32 500 max)
Boilers: 3 La Seine three-drum type
Speed, knots: 28
Oil fuel, tons: 290
Range, miles: 3 800 at 14 knots
Complement: 199 (13 officers, 186 men)

Based on the French "Le Fier" design. Allocated D Pennant number in 1961.

Engineering: The boilers are in two compartments separated by the engine rooms.

Radar: Surface search, SPS 5B.
Air search: MLA-1B.
Fire control: one Mk 63.

Sonar: One QHBa hull mounted-set.

INTRÉPIDO   1969, Spanish Navy

424　SPAIN

2 "ALAVA" CLASS

Name	No.	Builders	Laid down	Launched	Commissioned
LINIERS	D 51 (ex-*21*)	Bazán, Cartagena	1 Jan 1945	1 May 1946	27 Jan 1951
ALAVA	D 52 (ex-*23*)	Bazán, Cartagena	21 Dec 1944	19 May 1947	21 Dec 1950

Displacement, tons: 1 842 standard; 2 287 full load
Length, feet (metres): 336·3 *(102·5)*
Beam, feet (metres): 31·5 *(9·6)*
Draught, feet (metres): 19·7 *(6·0)*
Guns: 3—3 in *(76 mm)* 50 cal, Mk 34; 3—40 mm, 70 cal (SP 48)
A/S weapons: 2 Hedgehogs; 8 DC mortars; 2 DC racks;
　2 side launching racks for Mk 32 A/S torpedoes (6 torpedoes)
Main engines: Parsons geared turbines; 2 shafts; 31 500 shp
Boilers: 4 Yarrow three-drum type
Speed, knots: 29
Oil fuel, tons: 370
Range, miles: 4 100 at 15 knots
Complement: 222 (15 officers, 207 men)

Ordered in 1936, but construction was held up by the Civil War. After being resumed, was again suspended in 1940, but restarted at Empresa Nacional Bazán in 1944. These are the last of the old "Churruca" class of which 18 were built.

Fire control: Mk 63 FCS with Mk 34 radar.

Radar: Air search: MLA 1B.
Surface search: SG-6B.
Navigation: Decca TM 626.

Sonar: One SQS 30A hull-mounted set.

ALAVA　　　　　　　　　　　　　　　　　　　　　1974, Spanish Navy

2 MODERNISED "PIZARRO" CLASS

Name	No.	Builders	Laid down	Launched	Commissioned
VICENTE YAÑEZ PINZON	F 41	Bazán, Ferrol	Sept 1943	8 Aug 1945	5 Aug 1949
LEGAZPI	F 42	Bazán, Ferrol	Sept 1943	8 Aug 1945	8 Aug 1951

Displacement, tons: 1 924 standard; 2 228 full load
Length, feet (metres): 279·0 *(85·0)* pp; 312·5 *(95·3)* oa
Beam, feet (metres): 39·5 *(12·0)*
Draught, feet (metres): 17·7 *(5·4)*
Guns: 2—5 in *(127 mm)* 38 cal; 4—40 mm, 70 cal (SP 48)
A/S weapons: 2 Hedgehogs; 8 mortars; 2 DC racks;
　2 side launching racks for Mk 32 torpedoes (3 torpedoes each)
Main engines: 2 sets Parsons geared turbines; 2 shafts; 6 000 shp
Boilers: 2 Yarrow type
Speed, knots: 18·5
Range, miles: 3 000 at 15 knots
Oil fuel, tons: 390
Complement: 255 (16 officers, 239 men)

Originally designed to carry 30 mines.

Fire control: GFCS Mk 52 with Mk 29 radar on one director.

Modernisation: *Legazpi* completed 14 Jan 1960 and *Pinzon* 25 March 1960.

Radar: Surface search: SPS 5B.
Air search: MLA-1B.
Navigation: Decca TM 626.

VICENTE YAÑEZ PINZON　　　　　　　　　　　　　1974, Spanish Navy

4 "ATREVIDA - F 60" CLASS

Name	No.	Builders	Laid down	Launched	Commissioned
ATREVIDA	F 61	Bazán, Cartagena	26 June 1950	2 Dec 1952	19 Aug 1954
PRINCESA	F 62	Bazán, Cartagena	18 Mar 1953	31 Mar 1956	2 Oct 1957
NAUTILUS	F 64	Bazán, Cadiz	27 July 1953	23 Aug 1956	10 Dec 1959
VILLA DE BILBAO	F 65	Bazán, Cadiz	18 Mar 1953	19 Feb 1958	2 Sept 1960

Displacement, tons: 1 031 standard; 1 135 full load
Length, feet (metres): 247·8 *(75·5)* oa
Beam, feet (metres): 33·5 *(10·2)*
Draught, feet (metres): 9·8 *(3·0)*
Guns: 1—3 in *(76 mm)* 50 cal Mk 22; 3—40 mm, 70 cal (SP 48)
A/S weapons: 2 Hedgehogs; 8 mortars; 2 DC racks
Mines: 20 can be carried
Main engines: Sulzer diesels; 2 shafts; 3 000 bhp
Speed, knots: 18·5
Oil fuel, tons: 105
Range, miles: 8 000 at 10 knots
Complement: 132 (9 officers, 123 men)

All have been modernised, F 61 in 1959-60, remainder while building. No funnel, the diesel exhaust being on the starboard side waterline. Allocated F pennant numbers in 1961 although still officially classed as corvettes.

Aircraft: Although no deck is fitted helicopters can be refuelled in flight.

Radar: Modified SPS-5B combined air/surface search.

Sonar: One QHBa.

PRINCESA　　　　　　　　　　　　　　　　　　　　X. I. Taibo

SPAIN 425

LIGHT FORCES

Note: The following programme, worth 780 million pesetas, was agreed 13 May 1977, to be funded jointly by the Ministry of Marine and Ministry of Commerce (similarly to the "Lazaga" class). Contracts offered 16 Nov 1977. All to be manned by the Navy:

30 3-ton inshore launches at 3 million pesetas each.
20 20-ton Coastal launches at 22 million pesetas each (from Aresa, Barcelona).
4 80-ton Coastal launches at 62·5 million pesetas each.

This supersedes the 36-ton launch programme listed in last year's Addendum.
Two fishery protection vessels at 500 million pesetas each are to be built but it is uncertain whether these will be Naval-manned.

6 "LAZAGA (P-00)" CLASS (FAST ATTACK CRAFT—PATROL)

Name	No.	Builders	Commissioned
LAZAGA	P 01	Lürssen Vegesack	16 July 1975
ALSEDO	P 02	Bazán, La Carraca	28 Feb 1977
CADARSO	P 03	Bazán, La Carraca	10 July 1976
VILLAAMIL	P 04	Bazán, La Carraca	26 April 1977
BONIFAZ	P 05	Bazán, La Carraca	11 July 1977
RECALDE	P 06	Bazán, La Carraca	17 Dec 1977

Displacement, tons: 275 standard; 399 full load
Dimensions, feet (metres): 190·6 × 24·9 × 8·5 (58·1 × 7·6 × 2·6)
Guns: 1—3 in 62 cal OTO Melara; 1—40 mm 70 cal Breda-Bofors 350P; 2—20 mm Oerlikon GK 204
A/S weapons: 2 DC racks; provision for 2 triple Mk 32 torpedo tube mountings
Main engines: 2 MTU-Bazan MA15 TB91 diesels; 8 000 bhp
Speed, knots: 30
Range, miles: 6 100 at 17 knots
Complement: 34 (4 officers, 30 ratings)

Ordered in 1972, primarily for Fishery Protection duties. Although all will be operated by the Navy half the cost is being borne by the Ministry of Commerce. Of similar hull form to Israeli "Reshef" class and to S-143 class of FDR and of basic Lürssen Type 57 design but with only two engines.
Lazaga launched on 10 Oct.1974. She was steamed to Spain in April 1975 for equipping and arming. Laid down dates—01-03 May, 1974; 04-05, 8 Jan 1975; 06, 1975. Launch dates—01, 30 Sept 1974; 02 and 03, 8 Jan 1975; 04 and 05 24 May 1975; 06, 9 Nov 1975.

Design: A modified version of this class, "Cormoran" of 169·2 feet *(51·6 metres)*, 355 tons full load, 36 knots, 2 500 miles at 15 knots with 4 Exocet, 1—76/62 OTO Melara, 1—40/70 mm gun, M-20 series radar and CSEE secondary director is under discussion with foreign purchasers and may have been bought by Morocco (see Moroccan section where information is given for "Lazaga" class).

Electronics: ECM and IFF.

Fire control: Optical director CSEE (HSM Mk 22).

LAZAGA   1975, Lürssen

Gunnery: All guns assembled under licence by Bazán.

Missiles: Provision has been made for fitting surface-to-surface missiles (four Exocet or eight Harpoon or MM 39), without change of gun armament.

Radar: Surface search and target indication: HSA-M 20 series.
Navigation: Decca TM626.

Sonar: One hull-mounted set (?ELAC).

6 "BARCELO (P 10)" CLASS (FAST ATTACK CRAFT—PATROL)

Name	No.	Builders	Commissioned
BARCELÓ	P 11	Lürssen Vegesack	20 Mar 1976
LAYA	P 12	Bazán, La Carraca	23 Dec 1976
JAVIER QUIROGA	P 13	Bazán, La Carraca	4 April 1977
ORDÓÑEZ	P 14	Bazán, La Carraca	7 June 1977
ACEVEDO	P 15	Bazán, La Carraca	14 July 1977
CÁNDIDO PÉREZ	P 16	Bazán, La Carraca	25 Nov 1977

Displacement, tons: 134 full load
Dimensions, feet (metres): 118·7 × 19 × 6·2 *(36·2 × 5·8 × 1·9)*
Guns: 1—40 mm Breda Bofors 350; 2—20 mm Oerlikon GAM 204; 2—12·7 mm
Torpedo tubes: Provision for 2—21 in *(533 mm)*
Main engines: 2 MTU-Bazán MD-16V TB 90 diesels; 5 760 bhp; 2 shafts
Speed, knots: 36; 20 cruising
Range, miles: 1 200 at 17 knots
Complement: 19

Of Lürssen TNC 36 design.
Ordered 5 Dec 1973, the prototype, *Barcelo*, being built by Lürssen, Vegesack with MTU engines. Laid down 3 March 1975 for launch in Nov 1975. All to be manned by the Navy although the cost is being borne by the Ministry of Commerce.
Launch dates—P 11, Nov 1975, P 12-13, 18 Dec 1975, P 14-15, 10 Sept 1976, P 16, 3 March 1977.

Fire control: CSEE optical director for 40 mm.

Missiles: Reported as able to take two or four Surface-to-Surface missiles.

BARCELO   3/1976, E. N. Bazán

5 "LP 1" CLASS (COASTAL PATROL CRAFT)

Name	No.	Builders	Commissioned
—	LP 1	Bazán, La Carraca	Feb 1965
—	LP 2	Bazán, La Carraca	Feb 1965
—	LP 3	Bazán, La Carraca	Mar 1965
—	LP 4	Bazán, La Carraca	Mar 1965
—	LP 5	Bazán, La Carraca	Mar 1965

Displacement, tons: 17·2 standard; 25 full load
Dimensions, feet (metres): 46 × 15·4 × 3·3 *(14 × 4·7 × 1)*
Guns: 2—7·62 mm (twin)
Main engines: 2 Gray Marine diesels; 450 hp = 13 knots
Complement: 8

Laid down 1964 by Bazán, La Carraca. Wooden-hulled.

LP 3   1965, Spanish Navy

426 SPAIN

3 USCG 83 ft TYPE (COASTAL PATROL CRAFT)

Name	No.	Builders	Commissioned
—	LAS 10 (ex-LAS 1)	Bazán, Cartagena	26 April 1965
—	LAS 20 (ex-LAS 2)	Bazán, Cartagena	4 May 1965
—	LAS 30 (ex-LAS 3)	Bazán, Cartagena	3 Sept 1965

Displacement, tons: 49 standard; 63 full load
Dimensions, feet (metres): 78·0 pp; 83·3 oa × 16·1 × 6·6 (23·8; 25·4 × 4·9 × 2)
Guns: 1—20 mm; 2—7 mm (single)
A/S weapons: 2 Mousetrap Mk 20 (4 rockets each)
Main engines: 800 bhp; 2 shafts = 15 knots
Complement: 15

Of wooden hull construction. All launched 1964.

Radar: Decca 978.

Sonar: QCU 2.

LAS 30   1974, Spanish Navy

1 FISHERY PROTECTION VESSEL

SALVORA (ex-*Virgen de la Almudena*, ex-*Mendi Eder*) W 32

Displacement, tons: 180 standard; 275 full load
Dimensions, feet (metres): 107·0 × 20·5 × 9·0 (31 × 6·1 × 2·5)
Gun: 1—20 mm Mk 4 70 cal
Main engines: 1 Sulzer diesel; 1 shaft; 400 bhp = 12 knots
Oil fuel, tons: 25
Complement: 31

Trawler. Built in 1948 by SA Juliana, Gijon. Commissioned 25 Sept 1954. Based in Coruña.

Radar: Decca RM 914.

1 PATROL VESSEL

RR 29

Displacement, tons: 364 standard; 498 full load
Dimensions, feet (metres): 124·0 × 29·0 × 10·0 (38 × 8·4 × 3)
Guns: 1—1·5 in, 85 cal; 1—20 mm
Main engines: Triple expansion; 1 shaft; 800 ihp = 10 knots
Boilers: 1 cylindrical, (13 kg/cm)
Fuel, tons: 100 coal
Range, miles: 620 at 10 knots

Former tug launched in 1941. To be retired soon in wake of sisters RR 19-20.

Radar: DK 12.

13 COASTAL/RIVER PATROL LAUNCHES

Name	No.	Builders	Commissioned
—	V 1	Kiel, Germany	1926
—	V 4	Egaña, Motrico	10 April 1947
—	V 5	Arsenal, Cartagena	13 June 1969
—	V 6 (ex-V 22)	—	—
—	V 9 (ex-V 19)	—	—
—	V 10	—	—
—	V 11	—	—
—	V 21	UK	—
—	V 31	Barcelona	23 Mar 1974
—	V 32	Barcelona	23 Mar 1974
—	V 33	Barcelona	14 July 1977
—	V 34	Barcelona	14 July 1977
GAVIOTA	W 01	Germany	1944

Gaviota W 01, 104·2 tons standard, 27·5 × 5·2 × 2 *metres*, 2 MG, complement 14, ex-smuggler, commissioned in Spanish Navy 26 Nov 1970; V 1 (ex-*Azor*) 112 tons, 31·1 × 5·7 × 2·1 *metres*, complement 16, yacht employed by Naval School, Marin; V 4, 65 tons, 19 × 4·6 × 2·1 *metres*, speed 8 knots, complement 13; V 5, 5 tons, 8·2 × 2·9 × 1 *metres*, 5 knots, complement 7; V 6 (ex-V 22), 42 tons standard, 22 × 4·8 × 1·6 *metres*, 19 knots, complement 7; V 9 (ex-V 19), 30 tons standard, 14·4 × 4·7 × 1·5 *metres*, 9 knots, complement 7; V 10 and 11, 11·7 tons standard, 14·8 × 3 × 1 *metres*, 8 knots, complement 7; V 21 (ex-British ML, smuggler taken over April 1961), commissioned 23 July 1962, complement 12; V 31, 32, 33, 34, 5 tons, 27 knots, first pair purchased 1974, second pair 1977; *Cabro Fradera* (doubtful pennant number) 28 tons, 1—7·62 mm MG, based at Tuyon River Miño for border patrol with Portugal—built by Bazán, La Carraca, Commissioned 25 Feb 1963.

CABO FRADERA   1976, Royal Spanish Navy

AMPHIBIOUS FORCES

1 Ex-US "HASKELL" CLASS (ATTACK TRANSPORT)

Name	No.	Builders	Commissioned
ARAGÓN (ex-USS *Noble*, APA 218)	TA 11	USA	1945

Displacement, tons: 6 720 light; 12 450 full load
Dimensions, feet (metres): 455 oa × 63·5 × 24 (138·8 × 19·3 × 7·2)
Guns: 12—40 mm 60 cal (1 quad, 4 twin)
Main engines: 1 geared turbine; 8 500 shp = 17 knots
Boilers: 2 Babcock & Wilcox
Oil fuel, tons: 1 150
Range, miles: 14 700 at 16 knots
Complement: 357

Former US Attack Transport, transferred at San Francisco on 19 Dec 1964. Can carry 1 190 men and 680 tons cargo (or 11—2½ ton trucks and 49—¾ ton trucks). 24 landing craft. Amphibious forces flagship.

Radar: Air search: SPS 6.
Surface search: SPS 4.

ARAGÓN   1975, Spanish Navy

1 Ex-US "ANDROMEDA" CLASS (ATTACK CARGO SHIP)

Name	No.	Builders	Commissioned
CASTILLA (ex-USS *Achernar*, AKA 53)	TA 21	USA	1944

Displacement, tons: 7 430 light; 11 416 full load
Dimensions, feet (metres): 457·8 oa × 63 × 24 (140 × 19·2 × 7·4)
Guns: 1—5 in 38 cal; 8—40 mm 60 cal (twins) (Mk 1)
Main engines: 1 GE geared turbine; 6 000 shp = 16 knots
Boilers: 2 Foster-Wheeler
Oil fuel, tons: 1 400
Range, miles: 18 500 at 12 knots
Complement: 324

Former US Attack Cargo Ship transferred at New York on 2 Feb 1965. Can carry 98 men, 6—M 48 tanks, 36—2½ ton trucks and 267 Jeeps. 24 landing craft.

Radar: Surface search: SPS 10

CASTILLA   1975, Spanish Navy

SPAIN 427

1 Ex-US "CABILDO" CLASS (LSD)

Name	No.	Builders	Commissioned
GALICIA (ex-USS *San Marcos*, LSD 25)	TA 31	Philadelphia Navy Yard	15 April 1945

Displacement, tons: 4 790 standard; 9 375 full load
Dimensions, feet (metres): 475·4 oa × 72·6 × 18·0 *(139 × 21·9 × 4·9)*
Guns: 12—40 mm, 60 cal (2 quadruple, 2 twin)
Main engines: Geared turbines; 2 shafts; 7 000 shp = 15·4 knots
Boilers: 2—three-drum cylindrical
Oil fuel, tons: 1 727
Range, miles: 8 000 at 15 knots
Complement: 301 (18 officers, 283 men)

Transferred to Spain on 1 July 1971 and by sale Aug 1974. Fitted with helicopter platform. Can carry 3 LCUs or 18 LCMs. 1 347 tons of cargo or 100—2½ ton trucks or 27—M 48 tanks or 11 heavy helicopters. Accommodation for 137 troops (overnight) or 500 for short haul.

Fire control: GFCS with Mk 51 radar.

Radar: SPS 10.

GALICIA 1975, Spanish Navy

3 Ex-US "TERREBONNE PARISH" CLASS (LST)

Name	No.	Builders	Commissioned
VELASCO (ex-USS *Terrebonne Parish*, LST 1156)	L 11	Bath Iron Works	21 Nov 1952
MARTIN ALVAREZ (ex-USS *Wexford County*, LST 1168)	L 12	Christy Corp	15 June 1954
CONDE DE VENADITO (ex-USS *Tom Green County*, LST 1159)	L 13	Bath Iron Works	12 Sept 1953

Displacement, tons: 2 590 standard; 5 800 full load
Dimensions, feet (metres): 384·0 oa × 55·0 × 17·0 *(117·4 × 16·7 × 3·7)*
Guns: 6—3 in, 50 cal (3 twin, 2 forward, 1 aft)
Main engines: 4 GM diesels; 2 shafts; 6 000 bhp = 15 knots
Range, miles: 15 000 at 9 knots
Complement: 116 (troops 395)

LST 1156 and 1168 transferred on 29 Oct 1971, LST 1159 on 5 Jan 1972. Can carry 395 men, 10 M-48 tanks or 17 LVTP. 4 landing craft. Purchase approved 5 Aug 1976 and carried out 1 Nov 1976.

Fire control: 2 Mk 63 GFCS with SPG 34 radar.

Radar: SPS 10 surface search.

MARTIN ALVAREZ 5/1976, P. Crichton

2 Ex-BRITISH LCT (4)

BDK 1	K 1	BDK 2	K2

Displacement, tons: 440 standard; 868 full load
Dimensions, feet (metres): 185·3 × 38·7 × 6·2 *(56·5 × 11·8 × 1·9)*
Guns: 2—20 mm (single)
Main engines: 2 Paxman diesels; 2 shafts; 920 bhp = 9 knots
Range, miles: 1 100 at 8 knots

Can carry 350 tons or 500 men. Both laid down 1945 and commissioned 11 Nov 1948.

BDK 1 1975, Spanish Navy

3 EDIC TYPE (LCT)

Name	No.	Builders	Commissioned
BDK 6	K 6	Bazán, La Carraca	6 Dec 1966
BDK 7	K 7	Bazán, La Carraca	30 Dec 1966
BDK 8	K 8	Bazán, La Carraca	30 Dec 1966

Displacement, tons: 279 standard; 665 full load
Dimensions, feet (metres): 193·5 oa × 39·0 × 5·0 *(59 × 11·9 × 1·3)*
Guns: 2—12·7 mm MG; 1—81 mm mortar
Main engines: 2 diesels; 2 shafts; 1 040 bhp = 9·5 knots
Range, miles: 1 500 at 9 knots
Complement: 17

Landing craft of the French EDIC type.

Radar: One navigation set.

BDK 6 1976, Royal Spanish Navy

428 SPAIN

3 SPANISH BUILT LCTs

Name	No.	Builders	Commissioned
BDK 3	K 3	Bazán, Ferrol	15 June 1959
BDK 4	K 4	Bazán, Ferrol	15 June 1959
BDK 5	K 5	Bazán, Ferrol	15 June 1959

Displacement, tons: 902 full load
Dimensions, feet (metres): 186 × 38·4 × 6 (56·6 × 11·6 × 1·7)
Guns: 2—20 mm (singles)
Main engines: 2 M60 V8 AS diesels; 2 shafts; 1 000 hp = 8·5 knots
Range, miles: 1 000 at 7 knots
Complement: Complement 20 (1 officer, 19 men)

All laid down 1958. Can carry 300 tons or 400 men.

BDK 5 — 1971, Spanish Navy

2 Ex-US LCUs

LCU 1 (ex-*LCU 1471*)
LCU 2 (ex-*LCU 1491*)

Displacement, tons: 360
Dimensions, feet (metres): 119·7 × 31·5 × 5·2 (36·5 × 9·6 × 1·6)
Speed, knots: 7·6
Complement: 13

Transferred June 1972. Sold Aug 1976.

6 US LCM (8)

E 81 E 82 E 83 E 84 E 85 E 86

Displacement, tons: 115 full load
Dimensions, feet (metres): 74·5 × 21·7 × 5·9 (22·7 × 6·6 × 1·8)
Speed, knots: 9
Complement: 5

This new class was ordered from Oxnard, California in 1974. Assembled in Spain. All commissioned in July-Sept 1975.

Note: Total of landing craft (including those attached to *Aragón, Castilla,* and LSTs):
2 LCU; 12 LCM (3) and (6); 6 LCM (8); 16 LCP (L); 1 LCP (R); 49 LCVP.
All of US origin except 8 LCP (L), built at Cartagena.

MINE WARFARE FORCES

4 + 4 Ex-US "AGGRESSIVE" CLASS (MINESWEEPERS—OCEAN)

Name	No.	Builders	Commissioned
GUADALETE (ex-USS *Dynamic,* MSO 432)	M 41	Colbert BW, Stockton, Calif	15 Dec 1953
GUADALMEDINA (ex-USS *Pivot,* MSO 463)	M 42	Wilmington BW, Calif	12 July 1954
GUADALQUIVIR (ex-USS *Persistant,* MSO 491)	M 43	Tacoma, Washington	3 Feb 1956
GUADIANA (ex-USS *Vigor,* MSO 473)	M 44	Burgess Boat Co, Manitowoc	8 Nov 1954

Displacement, tons: 665 standard; 750 full load
Dimensions, feet (metres): 165·0 wl; 172·0 oa × 36·0 × 13·6 (52·3 × 10·4 × 4·2)
Guns: 2—20 mm (twin)
Main engines: 4 Packard diesels; 2 shafts; cp propellers; 2 280 bhp = 15·5 knots
Oil fuel, tons: 46
Range, miles: 3 000 at 10 knots
Complement: 74 (6 officers, 68 men)

The first three were transferred and commissioned on 1 July 1971. The fourth unit was delivered 4 April 1972. All purchased Aug 1974. A further four to be provided under the 1976 US Agreement.

Radar: Surface search: SPS 5C.

Sonar: SQQ 14 (VDS) with mine classification capability.

GUADALETE — 1973, X. I. Taibo

12 "NALON" (M 20) CLASS (Ex-US MSC TYPE)
(MINESWEEPERS—COASTAL)

Name	No.	Builders	Commissioned
NALÓN (ex-*MSC 139*)	M 21	S. Coast SY, Calif	Feb 1954
LLOBREGAT (ex-*MSC 143*)	M 22	S. Coast SY, Calif	Nov 1954
JUCAR (ex-*MSC 220*)	M 23	Bellingham SY	June 1956
ULLA (ex-*MSC 265*)	M 24	Adams YY, Mass	July 1958
MIÑO (ex-*MSC 266*)	M 25	Adams YY, Mass	Oct 1956
EBRO (ex-*MSC 269*)	M 26	Bellingham SY	Dec 1958
TURIA (ex-*MSC 130*)	M 27	Hildebrand DD, NY	Jan 1955
DUERO (ex-*Spoonbill,* MSC 202)	M 28	Tampa Marine Corp	Jan 1959
SIL (ex-*Redwing,* MSC 200)	M 29	Tampa Marine Corp	Jan 1959
TAJO (ex-*MSC 287*)	M 30	Tampa Marine Corp	July 1959
GENIL (ex-*MSC 279*)	M 31	Tacoma, Seattle	Sept 1959
ODIEL (ex-*MSC 288*)	M 32	Tampa Marine Corp	Oct 1959

Displacement, tons: 355 standard; 384 full load
Dimensions, feet (metres): 138·0 pp; 144·0 oa × 27·2 × 8·0 (41·5; 43 × 8 × 2·6)
Guns: 2—20 mm (1 twin)
Main engines: 2 diesels; 2 shafts; 900 bhp = 14 knots
Oil fuel, tons: 30
Range, miles: 2 700 at 10 knots
Complement: 39

Wooden-hulled.
Two sub-types: (a) with derrick on mainmast: M 21, 22, 23, 24, 25, 27, 28, 29, (b) with no mainmast but crane abreast the funnel: M 26, 30, 31, 32.

Radar: Decca TM 626 or RM 914.

Sonar: AN/UQS-1.

EBRO, Class B, small crane — 1974, Dr. Giorgio Arra

DUERO, Class A, with mainmast — 1975, Wright and Logan

4 "GUADIARO" CLASS
(MINESWEEPERS—OCEAN AS PATROL VESSELS)

Name	No.	Builders	Commissioned
ALMANZORA	M 14	Cadiz	Nov 1954
NAVIA	M 15	Cadiz	Mar 1955
GUADALHORCE	M 16	Cadiz	Dec 1953
EO	M 17	Cadiz	Mar 1955

Displacement, tons: 671 standard; 770 full load
Dimensions, feet (metres): 203·4 × 27·4 × 8·5 *(62 × 8·5 × 2·6)*
Guns: 2—20 mm
A/S weapons: 2 Mk 20 Mousetrap
Main engines: Triple expansion and exhaust turbines; 2 shafts; 2 400 hp = 13 knots after modernisation
Boilers: 2 Yarrow
Oil fuel, tons: 90
Range, miles: 1 000 at 6 knots
Complement: 68 (as patrol ships)

Modernised in 1959-61. Currently employed on patrol duties. Will be paid off when replaced by "Lazaga" class.

Radar: Decca TM 626 or RM 914.

Sonar: AN/UQS-1.

GUADALHORCE *1971, Commander Aldo Fraccaroli*

SURVEY SHIPS

4 "CASTOR" (A 20) CLASS

Name	No.	Builders	Commissioned
CASTOR	A 21 (ex-H 4)	Bazán, La Carraca	10 Nov 1966
POLLUX	A 22 (ex-H 5)	Bazán, La Carraca	6 Dec 1966
ANTARES	A 23	Bazán, La Carraca	21 Nov 1974
RIGEL	A 24	Bazán, La Carraca	21 Nov 1974

Displacement, tons: 327 standard; 383 full load
Dimensions, feet (metres): 111 pp; 125·9 oa × 24·9 × 8·9 *(33·8; 38·4 × 7·6 × 2·8)*
Main engines: 1 Sulzer 4TD-36 diesel; 720 hp = 11·7 knots
Range, miles: 3 620 at 8 knots
Complement: 39 (A 23 and 24) 37 (A 21 and 22)

Antares and *Rigel* ordered summer 1972, launched 1973. Fitted with Raydist, Omega and digital presentation of data. Cost of later ships 105 million pesetas.

Appearance: A 21 and 22 have gaps in the gunwhale aft for Oropesa sweep. In A 23 and 24 this is a full run to the stern.

Radar: Raytheon.

CASTOR *1974, Spanish Navy*

---

2 "MALASPINA" (A 30) CLASS (OCEANOGRAPHIC SHIPS)

Name	No.	Builders	Commissioned
MALASPINA	A 31	Bazán, La Carraca	21 Feb 1975
TOFIÑO	A 32	Bazán, La Carraca	23 April 1975

Displacement, tons: 820 standard; 1 090 full load
Dimensions, feet (metres): 188·9 × 38·4 × 11·8 *(57·6 × 11·7 × 3·6)*
Guns: 2—20 mm (single)
Main engines: 2 San Carlos MWM TbRHS-345-61 diesels; 3 600 bhp; 2 vp propellers = 15·3 knots
Range, miles: 4 000 at 12 knots; 3 140 at 14·5 knots
Complement: 63 (9 officers, 54 men)

Ordered mid-1972.
Malaspina laid down early 1973, launched 15 Aug 1973. *Tofiño* laid down 15 Aug 1973, launched 22 Dec 1973. Both named after their immediate predecessors. Of similar design to British "Bulldog" class costing 380 million pesetas each.

Electrical: Three—250 kVA alternators and one emergency 30 kVA.

Equipment: Fitted with Atlas Echograph *(4 500 metres)*, Raydist and Transit, Hewlett Packard 2100A computer inserted into Magnavox Transit satellite navigation system, active rudder with fixed pitch auxiliary propeller.

TOFIÑO *1976, Royal Spanish Navy*

SERVICE FORCES

1 REPLENISHMENT TANKER

Name	No.	Builders	Commissioned
TEIDE	BP 11	Bazán, Cartagena	20 Oct 1956

Displacement, tons: 2 747 light; 8 030 full load
Oil capacity: 5 350 cu m
Dimensions, feet (metres): 385·5 × 48·5 × 20·3 *(117·5 × 14·8 × 6·2)*
Gun: 1—4·1 in (not mounted)
Main engines: 2 diesels; 3 360 bhp = 12 knots
Complement: 98

Ordered in December 1952. Laid down on 11 Nov 1954. Launched on 20 June 1955. Modernised in 1962 with refuelling at sea equipment (300 tons/hr).

Radar: Navigation: Decca TM 707.

TEIDE *1976, Royal Spanish Navy*

430 SPAIN

1 HARBOUR TANKER

PP 1

Displacement, tons: 470
Dimensions, feet (metres): 147·5 oa × 25 × 9·5 (45 × 7·6 × 2·9)
Main engines: Deutz diesel; 220 bhp = 10 knots
Complement: 12

Built at Santander and launched in 1939.

3 HARBOUR TANKERS

PP 3   PP 4   PP 5

Displacement, tons: 510
Dimensions, feet (metres): 121·4 × 22·3 × 9·8 (37 × 6·8 × 3)

9 HARBOUR TANKERS

PB 1, 2, 3, 4, 5, 6, 20, 21, 22

Displacement, tons: 200
Dimensions, feet (metres): 111·5 × 19·7 × 8·9 (34 × 6 × 2·7)

Small harbour tankers with capacity; 1-3, 100 tons capacity; 4-6, 300 tons capacity; 20-22, 193 tons capacity (of similar construction to water carriers AB 1-3). All built by Bazán between 1960 and 1965.

1 SAIL TRAINING SHIP

Name	No.	Builders	Commissioned
JUAN SEBASTIAN DE ELCANO	—	Echevarrieta, Cadiz	28 Feb 1928

Displacement, tons: 3 420 standard; 3 754 full load
Dimensions, feet (metres): 269·2 pp; 308·5 oa × 43 × 23 (94·1 × 13·6 × 7)
Guns: 2—37 mm
Main engines: 1 Sulzer diesel; 1 shaft; 1 500 bhp = 9·5 knots
Oil fuel, tons: 230
Range, miles: 10 000 at 9·5 knots
Complement: 292 + 80 cadets

Four masted top-sail schooner—near sister of Chilean *Esmeralda*. Named after the first circumnavigator of the world (1519-26) who succeeded to the command of the expedition led by Magellanes after the latter's death. Laid down 24 Nov 1925. Launched on 5 March 1927.

Radar: Two Decca TM 626.

JUAN SEBASTIAN DE ELCANO and friends   7/1976, US Navy

1 ROYAL YACHT

Name	No.	Builders	Commissioned
AZOR	W0	Bazán, Ferrol	20 July 1949

Displacement, tons: 442 standard; 486 full load
Dimensions, feet (metres): 153·0 × 25·2 × 10·9 (47 × 7·7 × 3·3)
Main engines: 2 diesels; 1 200 bhp = 13·3 knots
Range, miles: 4 000
Complement: 47

Built as the Caudillo's yacht. Launched on 9 June 1949. Underwent an extensive refit in 1960, her hull being cut to admit an extension in length. Now painted royal blue with a buff funnel.

Radar: Decca TM 626.

AZOR   1970, X. I. Taibo

PBP 1, 2 and 3

Dimensions, feet (metres): 73·1 × 28·5 × 2·6 (22·3 × 8·7 × 0·8)

Gate Vessels.
Delivered 1959-60.

PR 1-5

Dimensions, feet (metres): 72·2 × 28·5 × 4·3 (22 × 8·7 × 4·3)

Net laying barges.
Delivered 1959-60.

MISCELLANEOUS

PRA 1-8

Dimensions, feet (metres): 91·8 × 27·9 × 2·3 (28 × 8·5 × 0·7)

Tugs for PBPs and PRs.
Delivered 1959-60.

1 BOOM DEFENCE VESSEL

Name	No.	Builders	Commissioned
—	CR 1 (ex-G 6)	Penhoët, France	29 July 1955

Displacement, tons: 630 standard; 831 full load
Dimensions, feet (metres): 165·5 × 34 × 10·5 (50·5 × 10·2 × 3·2)
Guns: 1—40 mm; 4—20 mm (single) 70 cal
Main engines: 2 diesels; electric drive; 1 shaft; 1 500 bhp = 12 knots
Oil fuel, tons: 126
Range, miles: 5 200 at 12 knots
Complement: 40

US off-shore order. Launched on 28 Sept 1954. Transferred from the US in 1955 under MDAP. Sister ship of French "Cigale" class. Based at Cartagena.

Radar: One navigation set.

CR 1   1976, Royal Spanish Navy

SPAIN

2 OCEAN TUGS

Name	No.	Builders	Commissioned
—	RA 1	Bazán, Cartagena	9 July 1955
—	RA 2	Bazán, Cartagena	12 Sept 1955

Displacement, tons: 757 standard; 1 039 full load
Dimensions, feet (metres): 184 × 33·5 × 12 *(56·1 × 10·1 × 3·9)*
Guns: 2—20 mm (singles)
Mines: Can lay 24
Main engines: 2 Sulzer diesels; 3 200 bhp; 1 shaft; cp propeller = 15 knots
Oil fuel, tons: 142
Range, miles: 5 500 at 15 knots
Complement: 49

Originally known as "Valen" class.

Radar: Decca 12.

RA 2 *1974, Reiner Nerlich*

1 OCEAN TUG

Name	No.	Builders	Commissioned
— (ex-*Metinda III*)	RA 3	Wellington, England	1945

Displacement, tons: 762 standard; 1 080 full load
Dimensions, feet (metres): 137 × 33·1 × 15·5 *(41·8 × 10·1 × 4·5)*
Main engines: Triple expansion; 3 200 ihp = 10 knots
Fuel: Coal
Complement: 44

Purchased by Spain 26 May 1961.

RA 3 *1976, Royal Spanish Navy*

3 OCEAN TUGS

Name	No.	Builders	Commissioned
POSEIDÓN	BS 1 (ex-*RA 6*)	Bazán, La Carraca	8 Aug 1964
—	RA 4	Bazán, La Carraca	25 Mar 1964
—	RA 5	Bazán, La Carraca	11 April 1964

Displacement, tons: 951 standard; 1 069 full load
Dimensions, feet (metres): 183·5 × 32·8 × 13·1 *(55·9 × 10 × 4)*
Main engines: 2 Sulzer diesels; 3 200 bhp = 15 knots
Range, miles: 4 640
Complement: 49 (*Poseidón* 60)

RA 6 was renumbered BS 1 when she became a frogman support ship, known as *Poseidón*. She carries a 300 metre/6 hour bathyscope.

Radar: Decca TM 626.

POSEIDÓN *1973, Dr. Giorgio Arra*

7 COASTAL TUGS

Name	No.	Builders	Commissioned
—	RR 50	Bazán, Cartagena	1963
—	RR 51	Bazán, Cartagena	1963
—	RR 52	Bazán, Cartagena	1963
—	RR 53	Bazán, Cartagena	1967
—	RR 54	Bazán, Cartagena	1967
—	RR 55	Bazán, Cartagena	1967

Displacement, tons: 205 (RR 50-52); 227 (RR 53-55) standard; 320 full load
Dimensions, feet (metres): 91·2 × 23 × 8·2 *(27·8 × 7 × 2·6)*
Main engines: Diesels; 1 shaft; 1 400 bhp (53 to 55), 800 bhp (50 to 52)
Complement: 13

Radar: Pilot 7D 20 in RR 50, 51 and 52.

RR 16

81 feet *(27 metres)* long with complement of 10.
Built by Bazán, La Carraca. Commissioned 26 April 1962.

14 HARBOUR TUGS

RP 1-12

Dimensions, feet (metres): 60·7 × 15·5 × — *(18·5 × 4·7 × —)*

Of 65 tons and 200 bhp (diesel). Commissioned 1965-67.

RP 40

Dimensions, feet (metres): 69·7 × 19·4 × — *(21·3 × 5·9 × —)*
Complement: 8

Of 150 tons and 600 bhp (diesel). Commissioned 27 Dec 1961.

RP 18

Displacement, tons: 160 standard
Dimensions, feet (metres): 81·0 × 17·7 × 7·9 *(24·7 × 5·4 × 2·4)*
Main engines: Triple expansion; 1 shaft (Kort nozzle)
Fuel: Coal

Laid down 1946 at Cartagena. Commissioned 1952.

Note: Five tug-launches of less than 50 tons—LR 47, 51, 67, 68, 69.

12 WATER CARRIERS

A 2

Built in 1936. Of 1 785 tons full load with 1 000 tons capacity. Ocean going.

A 6

Displacement, tons: 1 785
Dimensions, feet (metres): 200 × 31·5 × 14·1 *(61 × 9·6 × 4·3)*
Main engines: Triple expansion; 1 shaft; 800 ihp = 9 knots
Complement: 27

Commissioned 30 Jan 1952.

A 7   A 9   A 10   A 11

Displacement, tons: 610 full load (A 7-8; 706 full load)
Dimensions, feet (metres): 146·9 × 24·9 × 9·8 *(44·8 × 7·6 × 3)*
Main engines: 1 shaft = 9 knots
Range, miles: 1 000
Complement: 16

All built at Bazán, La Carraca. A 7-8 commissioned 1952. A 9-11 24 Jan 1963. All oceangoing.

Radar: Pilot 7 D20 (A 9-11).

A 11 *1973, Spanish Navy*

AB 1, 2, 3, 10, 17, 18

All of less than 400 tons. Harbour water boats with 200 tons (AB 1-3) capacity.

432 SPAIN / SRI LANKA

9 TORPEDO RECOVERY CRAFT

BTM 1-6

Built by Bazán 1961-63 of 60-190 tons. To carry torpedoes and mines and, in emergency, can act as minelayers. Complement 8.

ST 5

Torpedo tracking craft on range at Alcudia, Majorca. 36 feet *(11 metres)* long.

LRT 3 and 4

TRVs built in 1956. 58·2 tons—58·1 × 6·6 × —*(17·7 × 2·2 ×–)*. Can carry six torpedoes. Have stern ramp and crane. Based at submarine base, Cartagena.

RESEARCH CRAFT

An unpropelled underwater research base under construction 1976 by Bazán Cartagena. Can accommodate 4: 40·7 × 20·7 *(12·4 × 6·3)*; hull diameter 11·8 *(3·6)*.

8 SPANISH LCP (L)

LCP 4, 5, 6, 7, 10, 11, 12, 13

All operate as diving tenders.

4 DIVING CRAFT

BZL 1, 3, 9   **NEREIDA** (BZL 10)

Small self-propelled craft of less than 50 tons.

BL 13

Dumb barge for diving.

8 FLOATING CRANES

SANSÓN GRI (100 tons lift)
GR 3, 4 and 5 (30 tons lift)
GR 6, 7, 8, 9 (15 tons lift)

Based at Cartagena, Ferrol, La Carraca and Mahon.

CUSTOMS SERVICE

3 "AGUILUCHO" CLASS (COASTAL PATROL CRAFT)

Name	No.	Builders	Commissioned
AGUILUCHO	—	J. Roberto Rodriguez e Hijos, Vigo	1973
GAVILAN I	—	J. Roberto Rodriguez e Hijos, Vigo	1975
GAVILAN II	—	J. Roberto Rodriguez e Hijos, Vigo	1976

Displacement, tons: 45
Dimensions, feet (metres): 85·5 oa × 16·7 × 4·3 *(26·1 × 5·1 × 1·3)*
Main engines: Diesels; 2 shafts; 2 750 bhp = 30 knots
Range, miles: 750 at 30 knots

Aguilucho launched 19 Feb 1973 for Customs duties. *Gavilan I* launched 22 July 1975.

3 Ex-FRENCH "VC" CLASS

Name	No.	Builders	Commissioned
ALBATROS	—	CMN Cherbourg	1958
ALBATROS II	—	CMN Cherbourg	1958
ALBATROS III	—	CMN Cherbourg	1958

Displacement, tons: 82 full load
Dimensions, feet (metres): 104·5 × 15·5 × 5·5 *(31·8 × 4·7 × 1·7)*
Gun: 1—20 mm
Main engines: 2 diesels; 2 shafts; 2 700 bhp = 28 knots
Complement: 15

In addition a number of other craft, some of modern French construction, some of wartime British and German classes, operate for the Finance ministry. Some named *Milano, Sacre, Nebli, Basanta Silva, Sanqual*.

ALBATROS   *CMN*

SRI LANKA

Formation

The Royal Ceylon Navy was formed on 9 Dec 1950 when the Navy Act was proclaimed. Called the Sri Lanka Navy since Republic Day 22 May 1972.

Headquarters Appointment

Commander of the Navy:
Rear-Admiral D. B. Goonesekera

Diplomatic Representation

Services Attaché in London:
Withdrawn from 1 November 1970

General

Emphasis now being placed on local building of Coastal Patrol craft although a 200 mile EEZ will call for larger craft than the Shanghais, more suitable craft than the "MOL" and, therefore, some ship or ships to replace *Gajabahu*, probably foreign built.

Personnel

(a) 1978: 2 573 (203 officers and 2 370 sailors)
(b) Voluntary service
(c) SLNR; 550 (50 officers, 500 sailors)

Strength of the Fleet

Type	Active	Building
Frigate	1	—
Fast Attack Craft—Gun	6	—
Coastal Patrol Craft	28	1
Survey Craft	4	—

Naval Bases

A Naval Base established at Trincomalee, which was a British base from 1795 until 1957.
Minor bases at Karainagar, Colombo, Welisara, Tangale, Kalpitiya and Talaimannar.

Prefix to Ships' Names

SLNS

Mercantile Marine

Lloyd's Register of Shipping:
37 vessels of 92 581 tons gross

DELETIONS

1974   Short hydrofoil and 1 Thornycroft Patrol Craft (101)
1975   Tug *Aliya*

FRIGATE
1 Ex-CANADIAN "RIVER" CLASS

Name	No.	Builders	Laid down	Launched	Commissioned
GAJABAHU (ex-*Misnak*, ex-HMCS *Hallowell*)	F 232	Canadian Vickers Ltd, Montreal	144	8 Aug 1944	Jan 1945

Displacement, tons: 1 445 standard; 2 360 full load
Length, feet (metres): 282 *(86·3)* pp; 295·5 *(90·1)* wl; 310·5 *(91·9)* oa
Beam, feet (metres): 36·5 *(11·1)*
Draught, feet (metres): 13·8 *(4·2)*
Guns: 1—4 in *(102 mm)*; 3—40 mm
Main engines: Triple expansion; 5 500 ihp; 2 shafts
Boilers: 2 three-drum type
Speed, knots: 20
Range, miles: 4 200 at 12 knots
Oil fuel, tons: 585
Complement: 160

Acquired from Canada by Israel in 1950 and sold by Israel to Ceylon in 1959. Guns above replaced 3—4·7 in, 8—20 mm in 1965.

GAJABAHU   *1971, Royal Ceylon Navy*

LIGHT FORCES

Note: Tenders called for mid-1977 for five Coastal Patrol Boats.

5 "SOORAYA" CLASS (Ex-CHINESE "SHANGHAI II") (FAST ATTACK CRAFT—GUN)

BALAWATHA SOORAYA
DAKSAYA WEERAYA
RAMAKAMI

Displacement, tons: 120 full load
Dimensions, feet (metres): 130 × 18 × 5·6 *(42·6 × 5·9 × 1·8)*
Guns: 4—37 mm (2 twin); 4—25 mm (2 twin abaft the bridge)
Main engines: 4 diesels; 5 000 bhp = 30 knots
Complement: 25

All of the "Shanghai" class.
The first pair was transferred by China in Feb 1972, the second pair in July 1972 and the last in Dec 1972. In monsoonal conditions off the coast of Sri Lanka these boats are lively and uncomfortable.

Radar: Pot Head.

SOORAYA *1974, Sri Lanka Navy*

1 Ex-SOVIET "MOL" CLASS (FAST ATTACK CRAFT—GUN)

Name	No.	Builders	Commissioned
SAMUDRA DEVI	—	USSR	31 Dec 1975

Displacement, tons: 205 standard; 245 full load
Dimensions, feet (metres): 126·6 × 25·6 × 9·5 *(38·6 × 7·8 × 2·9)*
Guns: 4—30 mm (twin)
Main engines: 3 M 504 diesels; 13 500 bhp; 2 shafts
Speed, knots: 40
Complement: 25

Built 1975. Has certain variations from standard Soviet craft although the hull is a basic "Osa" type. The after radar pedestal mounts only a Kolonka optical sight and the torpedo tubes have been unshipped although the sponsons remain. An additional section of superstructure has been added abaft the after pedestal.

Radar: Don and High Pole IFF.

SAMUDRA DEVI *12/1975, Sri Lanka Navy*

2 + 1 COASTAL PATROL CRAFT

Name	No.	Builders	Commissioned
PRADEEPA	—	Colombo DY Ltd	1976
—	—	Colombo DY Ltd	1977

Displacement, tons: 57
Dimensions, feet (metres): 62 × 18 × 7 *(18·9 × 5·5 × 2·1)*
Guns: 2—20 mm
Main engines: 2 Berquins-Kelvin Co UK diesels
Range, miles: 1 200 at 14 knots
Complement: 12

Ordered June 1976 (first pair) and Nov 1976.

2 COASTAL PATROL CRAFT

Name	No.	Builders	Commissioned
HANSAYA	—	Korody Marine Corp, Venice	1956
LIHINIYA	—	Korody Marine Corp, Venice	1956

Displacement, tons: 36
Dimensions, feet (metres): 63·5 pp; 66 oa × 14 × 4 *(20·8; 21·6 × 4·6 × 1·3)*
Main engines: 3 General Motors diesels; 450 bhp = 16 knots

5 COASTAL PATROL CRAFT

Name	No.	Builders	Commissioned
BELIKAWA	421	Cheverton Workboats (UK)	1977
DIYAKAWA	422	Cheverton Workboats (UK)	1977
KORAWAKKA	423	Cheverton Workboats (UK)	1977
SERUWA	424	Cheverton Workboats (UK)	1977
TARAWA	425	Cheverton Workboats (UK)	1977

Displacement, tons: 22
Dimensions, feet (metres): 55·9 × 14·8 × 3·9 *(17 × 4·5 × 1·2)*
Guns: 3 MG
Main engines: Twin diesels; 640 hp = 23 knots
Range, miles: 1 000 at 12 knots
Complement: 7

Decca Navigation radar.

BELIKAWA *1977, Cheverton Workboats*

1 COASTAL PATROL CRAFT

Name	No.	Builders	Commissioned
—	—	Colombo DY Ltd	1976

Displacement, tons: 15
Dimensions, feet (metres): 45 × 12 × 3 *(13·7 × 3·6 × 0·9)*
Main engines: 2 diesels; 1 240 hp = ?19 knots
Range, miles: 250 at 16 knots
Complement: 8

18 (+ 2 SURVEY CRAFT) THORNYCROFT TYPE
(COASTAL PATROL CRAFT)

Name	No.	Builders	Commissioned
—	102	Thornycroft (Malaysia) Ltd, Singapore	1966
—	103	Thornycroft (Malaysia) Ltd, Singapore	1966
—	104	Thornycroft (Malaysia) Ltd, Singapore	1967
—	105	Thornycroft (Malaysia) Ltd, Singapore	1967
—	106	Thornycroft (Malaysia) Ltd, Singapore	1967
—	107	Thornycroft (Malaysia) Ltd, Singapore	1967
—	108	Thornycroft (Malaysia) Ltd, Singapore	1967
—	109	Thornycroft (Malaysia) Ltd, Singapore	1967
—	110	Thornycroft (Malaysia) Ltd, Singapore	1967
—	201	Thornycroft (Malaysia) Ltd, Singapore	1967
—	202	Thornycroft (Malaysia) Ltd, Singapore	1967
—	203	Thornycroft (Malaysia) Ltd, Singapore	1968
—	204	Thornycroft (Malaysia) Ltd, Singapore	1968
—	205	Thornycroft (Malaysia) Ltd, Singapore	1968
—	206	Thornycroft (Malaysia) Ltd, Singapore	1968
—	207	Thornycroft (Malaysia) Ltd, Singapore	1968
—	208	Thornycroft (Malaysia) Ltd, Singapore	1968
—	209	Thornycroft (Malaysia) Ltd, Singapore	1968
—	210	Thornycroft (Malaysia) Ltd, Singapore	1968
—	211	Thornycroft (Malaysia) Ltd, Singapore	1968

Displacement, tons: 13
Dimensions, feet (metres): 45·5 × 12 × 3 *(14·9 × 3·9 × 0·9)*
Main engines: 102: Thornycroft K6SMI engines; 500 bhp; 2 shafts = 25 knots.
  Remainder: General Motors 6 71-Series; 500 bhp; 2 shafts = 25 knots

The hulls are of hard chine type with double skin teak planking. Equipped with radar, radio, searchlight etc. Two ordered in 1965. Seven ordered in 1966. Assembled in Sri Lanka and completed by Sept 1968. Originally 21 boats.
They are based, as two squadrons, at Kalpitiya and Karainagar. 2 (Pennant numbers not known) employed as surveying craft HV 11 and 12 (see below).

SURVEY CRAFT

Name	No.	Builders	Commissioned
SERUWA	—	Italy	1955
TARAWA	—	Italy	1955

HV 11   HV 12
Thornycroft type of coastal patrol craft converted to survey craft, 1977

Of 13 tons and 15 knots with two Foden diesels.

SUDAN

Establishment

The navy was established in 1962 to operate on the Red Sea coast and on the River Nile. The original training staff was from Yugoslav Navy, but this staff left in 1972.

Personnel

(a) 1978: 600 officers and men
(b) Voluntary service

Diplomatic Representation

Naval, Military and Air Attaché in London:
  Colonel A. El-Tayeb El-Mihaina

Mercantile Marine

Lloyd's Register of Shipping:
  13 vessels of 43 375 tons gross

Bases

Port Sudan for Red Sea operations with a separate riverine unit on the Nile based at Khartoum.

LIGHT FORCES

2 Ex-YUGOSLAV "KRALJEVICA" CLASS (LARGE PATROL CRAFT)

Name	No.	Builders	Commissioned
EL FASHER	522	Yugoslavia	1954
EL KHARTOUM	523	Yugoslavia	1955

Displacement, tons: 190 standard; 245 full load
Dimensions, feet (metres): 134·5 × 20·7 × 7·2 *(41 × 6·3 × 2·2)*
Guns: 2—40 mm; 2—20 mm
Main engines: Diesel; 2 shafts; 3 300 bhp = 20 knots
Range, miles: 1 500 at 12 knots

Transferred from the Yugoslav Navy during 1969.

"KRALJEVICA" Class

6 Ex-YUGOSLAV "101" CLASS (FAST ATTACK CRAFT—GUN)

Displacement, tons: 55 standard; 60 full load
Dimensions, feet (metres): 78 × 21·3 × 7·8 *(23·8 × 6·5 × 2·4)*
Guns: 2—40 mm; 2—20 mm (single)
Main engines: 3 Packard petrol motors; 3 shafts; 5 000 bhp = 36 knots
Complement: 14

Transferred in this "Gun" version of the class in 1970. Same characteristics as US "Higgins" class.

"101" Class

3 Ex-IRANIAN COASTAL PATROL CRAFT

Name	No.	Builders	Commissioned
— (ex-*Gohar*)	—	Abeking and Rasmussen	1970
— (ex-*Shahpar*)	—	Abeking and Rasmussen	1970
— (ex-*Shahram*)	—	Abeking and Rasmussen	1970

Displacement, tons: 70
Dimensions, feet (metres): 75·2 × 16·5 × 6 *(22·9 × 5 × 1·8)*
Main engines: 2 diesels; 2 shafts; 2 200 hp = 27 knots
Complement: 19

Built for Iran. Transferred to Iranian Coastguard 1975 and to Sudan later that year.

4 Ex-YUGOSLAV PBR TYPE (LARGE PATROL CRAFT)

Name	No.	Builders	Commissioned
GIHAD	PB 1	Mosor Shipyard, Trogir, Yugoslavia	1961
HORRIYA	PB 2	Mosor Shipyard, Trogir, Yugoslavia	1961
ISTIQLAL	PB 3	Mosor Shipyard, Trogir, Yugoslavia	1962
SHAAB	PB 4	Mosor Shipyard, Trogir, Yugoslavia	1962

Displacement, tons: 100
Dimensions, feet (metres): 115 × 16·5 × 5·2 *(35 × 5 × 1·7)*
Guns: 1—40 mm; 1—20 mm; 2—7·6 mm MG
Main engines: Mercedes-Benz (MTU 12V 493) diesels; 2 shafts; 1 800 bhp = 20 knots
Range, miles: 1 400 at 12 knots
Complement: 20

Of steel construction. First craft acquired by the newly established Sudanese Navy.

GIHAD

AMPHIBIOUS FORCES

2 Ex-YUGOSLAV "DTK 221" CLASS (LCTs)

SOBAT   DINDER

Displacement, tons: 410
Dimensions, feet (metres): 144·3 × 19·7 × 7 *(44 × 6 × 2·1)*
Guns: 1—20 mm; 2—12·7 mm
Speed, knots: 10
Complement: 15

Transferred during 1969.

"DTK 221" Class

1 Ex-YUGOSLAV "DTM 231" CLASS (LCU)

Transferred by Yugoslavia 1970—of 40 tons.

"DTM 231" Class

SERVICE FORCES

1 SUPPORT TANKER

FASHODA (ex-PN 17)

Displacement, tons: 420 standard; 650 full load
Dimensions, feet (metres): 141·5 × 22·8 × 13·6 *(43·2 × 7 × 4·2)*
Main engines: 300 bhp = 7 knots

Former Yugoslav Tanker rehabilitated and transferred to the Sudanese Navy in 1969.

1 SURVEY SHIP

TIENGA

A small vessel, converted into a hydrographic ship, acquired from Yugoslavia in 1969.

1 WATER BOAT

BARAKA (ex-PV 6)

A small water carrier, transferred from Yugoslavia to the Sudanese Navy in 1969.

SURINAM

Formerly Dutch Guiana—granted independence in 1975.

3 LARGE PATROL CRAFT

Name	No.	Builders	Commissioned
—	S 401	De Vries, Aalsmeer, Netherlands	Nov 1976
—	S 402	De Vries, Aalsmeer, Netherlands	May 1977
—	S 403	De Vries, Aalsmeer, Netherlands	Nov 1977

Displacement, tons: 127
Dimensions, feet (metres): 105 × 21·3 × 5·5 *(32 × 6·5 × 1·7)*
Guns: 2—40 mm
Main engines: 2 Paxman 12 YHCM diesels; 2 110 hp = 17·5 knots
Range, miles: 1 200 at 13·5 knots
Complement: 15

This design has far greater speed and armament potential but Surinam apparently opted for the scaled-down version.

1 COASTAL PATROL CRAFT

Length, feet (metres): 32·8 *(10)*
Main engine: 1 Dorman 8 JT; 280 hp

Ordered Dec 1974 from Schottel, Netherlands. Delivered Aug 1975.

3 COASTAL PATROL CRAFT

Length, feet (metres): 72·2 *(22)*
Gun: 1—40 mm Bofors
Main engines: 2 Paxman 12 YHCM diesels; 2 110 hp; 2 shafts

Ordered April 1975 from Schottel, Netherlands. Delivered 1976.

3 COASTAL PATROL CRAFT

Length, feet (metres): 41·4 *(12·6)*
Main engine: 1 Dorman 8 JT; 280 hp

Ordered Dec 1974 from Schottel, Netherlands. Delivered Aug 1975.

SWEDEN

Headquarters Appointments

Commander-in-Chief:
  Vice-Admiral Per Rudberg
Chief of Naval Material Department:
  Rear-Admiral Gunnar Grandin
Chief of Naval Staff:
  Major-General Bo Varenius (Coastal Artillery)

Senior Command

Commander-in-Chief of Coastal Fleet:
  Rear-Admiral Bengt Rasin

Diplomatic Representation

Naval Attaché in London:
  Captain L. Jedeur-Palmgren
Naval Attaché in Washington:
  Captain L. Forsman

Personnel

(a) 1978: 15 100 officers and men of Navy and Coast Artillery made up of 4 500 regulars, 2 900 Reservists and 7 700 National Servicemen. In addition 7 000 conscripts receive annual training.
(b) 9-18 months

Bases

Stockholm, Karlskrona, Göteborg.
Minor base at Härnösand

Composition of the Navy

In addition to seagoing personnel the Navy includes the Coastal Artillery, manning 20 mobile and 45 coastal batteries of both major guns and SSMs. A number of amphibious and patrol craft are also controlled by the Coastal Artillery.

Naval Air Arm

  5 Alouette II helicopters (training)
 10 Jet Ranger helicopters
 10 Vertol 107 (Hkp-4B)

Mercantile Marine

Lloyd's Register of Shipping:
  764 vessels of 7 971 246 tons gross

Strength of the Fleet

Type	Active	Building (Planned)
Destroyers	6	—
Frigates	6	—
Submarines—Patrol	17	3
Fast Attack Craft—Missile	2	14
Fast Attack Craft—Torpedo	32	—
Large Patrol Craft	1	—
Coastal Patrol Craft	31	—
Minelayers	3	1
Minelayers—Coastal	9	—
Minelayers—Small	37	—
Minesweepers—Coastal	18	—
Minesweepers—Inshore	18	—
LCMs	9	—
LCUs	84	—
LCAs	54	—
Mine Transports	2	—
Survey Ships	5	1
Tanker—Support	1	—
Supply Ship	1	—
Tugs	20	—
Salvage Ship	1	—
Sail Training Ships	2	—
Ice Breakers	8	—
TRVs	5	—
Tenders	5	—
Water Boats	2	—

DELETIONS

Cruiser

1971 Göta Lejon to Chile *(Latorre)*

Frigates

1974 Karlskrona

Submarines

1975 Gäddan, Siken ("Abborren" Class)
1976 Abborren, Laxen, Makrillen ("Abborren" Class)

Light Forces

1973 TV 101
1975 T 38, 39, 40
1976 T 102-106
1977 T 108-109, T 111, Orust, Tjörn

Depot Ship

1972 Patricia
1976 Marieholm

Surveying Vessels

1972 Johen Nordenankar, Petter Gedda
1973 Anden
1975 Lederen

Miscellaneous

1973 Gälnan (water carrier)
1974 Ymer (Icebreaker)
1975 Urd (experimental ship)

PENNANT LIST

Destroyers

J 18	Halland
J 19	Smaaland
J 20	Ostergotland
J 21	Södermanland
J 22	Gästrikland
J 23	Hälsingland

Frigates

F 11	Visby
F 12	Sundsvall
F 13	Halsingborg
F 14	Kalmar
F 16	Öland
F 17	Uppland

Submarines

Bäv	Bävern
Del	Delfinen
Dra	Draken
Gri	Gripen
Haj	Hajen
Iln	Illern
Näc	Näcken
Naj	Najad } building
Nep	Neptun
Nor	Nordkaparen
Säl	Sälen
Sbj	Sjöbjörnen
Shu	Sjöhunden
Shä	Sjöhästen
Sle	Sjölejonet
Sor	Sjöormen
Spr	Springaren
Utn	Uttern
Val	Valen
Vgn	Vargen

Light Forces

P 150	Jägaren
P 151	Hugin
P 152	Munin
P 153	Magne
P 154	Mode
P 155	Vale
P 156	Vidar
P 157	Mjölner
P 158	Nysing
P 159	Kaparen
P 160	Väktaren
P 161	Snapphanen
P 162	Spejaren
P 163	Styrbjörn
P 164	Starkodder
P 165	Tordón
P 166	Tirfing
T 45-56	"T 42" class
T 107	Aldebaran
T 110	Arcturus
T 112	Astrea
T 121	Spica
T 122	Sirius
T 123	Capella
T 124	Castor
T 125	Vega
T 126	Virgo
T 131	Norrköping
T 132	Nynäshamn
T 133	Norrtälje
T 134	Varberg
T 135	Västeräs
T 136	Västervik
T 137	Umea
T 138	Pitea
T 139	Lulea
T 140	Halmstad
T 141	Strömstad
T 142	Ystad
V 01	Skanór
V 02	Smyge
V 03	Arild
V 04	Viken

Amphibious Forces

A 333	Skagul
A 335	Sleipner
L 51-56	LCUs
201-276	LCUs
280-284	LCUs
301-354	LCAs

Minewarfare Forces

M 01	Alvsnabben
M 02	Alvsborg
M 03	Visborg
M 04	New Construction
MUL 11-19	Coastal Minelayers
M 15-16, 21-26	MSI
M 31	Gässten
M 32	Norsten
M 33	Viksten
M 42	Tjörn
M 43	Hisingen
M 44	Blackan
M 45	Dämman
M 46	Galten
M 47	Gillöga
M 48	Rödlöga
M 49	Svartlöga
M 51	Hanö
M 52	Tärnö
M 53	Tjurkö
M 54	Sturkö
M 55	Ornö
M 56	Utö
M 57	Arkö
M 58	Spärö
M 59	Karlsö
M 60	Iggö
M 61	Styrsö
M 62	Skaftö
M 63	Aspö
M 64	Hasslö
M 65	Vinö
M 66	Vällö
M 67	Nämdö
M 68	Blidö
501-536	Small Minelayers

Service Forces

S 01	Gladen
S 02	Falken
A 201	Marieholm
A 211	Belos
A 216	Unden
A 217	Fryken
A 221	Freja
A 228	Brännaren
A 231	Lommen
A 232	Spoven
A 236	Fällaren
A 237	Minören
A 242	Skuld
A 246	Hagern
A 247	Pelikanen
A 248	Pingvinen
A 251	Achilles
A 252	Ajax
A 253	Hermes
A 256	Sigrun
A 321	Hector
A 322	Heros
A 323	Hercules
A 324	Hera
A 326	Hebe
A 327	Passop
A 328	Ran
A 329	Henrik
A 330	Atlas
A 332	Mársgarn
A 336	Vitsgarn
A 341	ATB 1
A 342	ATB 2
A 343	ATB 3
A 345	Granaten
A 347	Edda
A 349	Gerda

SWEDEN 437

"ÖSTERGÖTLAND" Class

"ÖLAND" Class

NACKEN

"ÄLVSBORG" Class

"HALLAND" Class

"VISBY" Class

M 04

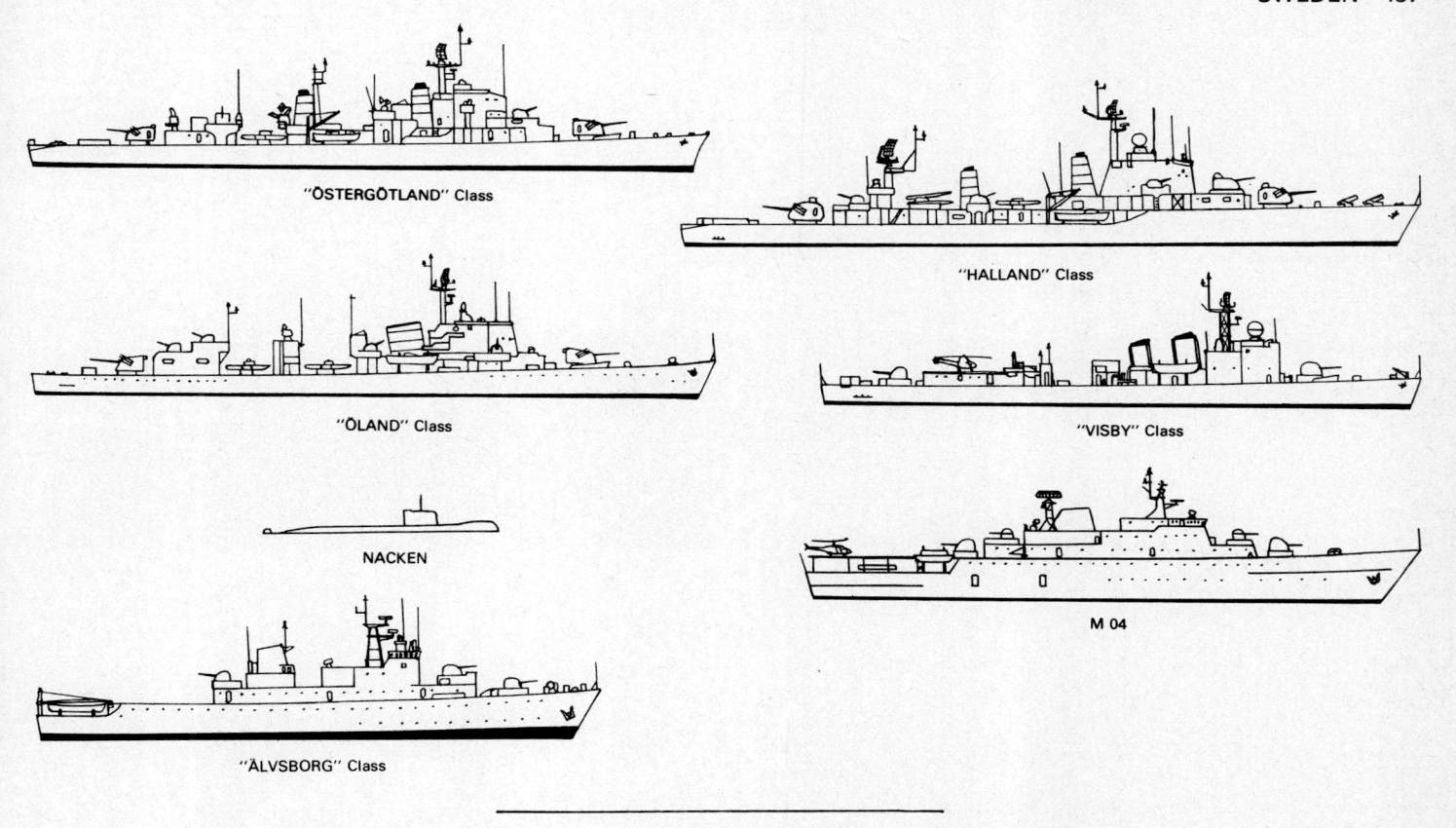

SUBMARINES

Note: Submarines do not have pennant numbers on fin but carry distinctive letters in their place.

NEW CONSTRUCTION "A 17" CLASS

In design stage for completion mid 1980s.

3 "NÄCKEN" CLASS (A14)

Name	No.	Builders	Laid down	Launched	Commissioned
NÄCKEN	NÄC	Kockums, Malmö	Nov 1972	Jan 1975	1977
NAJAD	NAJ	Karlskronavervarver	Sept 1973	Oct 1975	1978
NEPTUN	NEP	Kockums, Malmö	Mar 1974	April 1976	1978

Displacement, tons: 980 surfaced; 1 125 dived
Length, feet (metres): 135 *(41)*
Beam, feet (metres): 20·0 *(6·1)*
Draught, feet (metres): 16·7 *(5·1)*
Torpedo tubes: 4—21 in *(533 mm)* (8 reloads)
Main machinery: Diesels; electric motors; 1 shaft with large five-bladed propeller
Speed, knots: 20 surfaced and dived
Complement: 25

The very high beam to length ratio is notable in this Albacore hull design. Have large bow mounted sonar. Main accommodation space is abaft the control room with machinery spaces right aft.

5 "SJÖORMEN" CLASS (A11B)

Name	No.	Builders	Laid down	Launched	Commissioned
SJÖORMEN	SOR	Kockums, Malmö	1965	25 Jan 1967	31 July 1967
SJÖLEJONET	SLE	Kockums, Malmö	1966	29 June 1967	16 Dec 1968
SJÖHUNDEN	SHU	Kockums, Malmö	1966	21 Mar 1968	25 June 1969
SJÖBJÖRNEN	SBJ	Karlskronavervarver	1967	6 Aug 1968	28 Feb 1969
SJÖHÄSTEN	SHÄ	Karlskronavervarver	1966	9 Jan 1968	15 Sept 1969

Displacement, tons: 1 125 standard; 1 400 dived
Length, feet (metres): 167·3 *(50·5)*
Beam, feet (metres): 20·0 *(6·1)*
Draught, feet (metres): 16·7 *(5·1)*
Torpedo tubes: 4—21 in *(533 mm)* 2 A/S tubes
Main machinery: 2 Pielstick diesels; 1 large five-bladed propeller; 2 200 bhp; 1 electric motor
Speed, knots: 15 surfaced; 20 dived
Endurance: 3 weeks
Complement: 23

Albacore hull. Twin-decked. Diving depth 500 feet.

SJÖHÄSTEN   5/1976, Reinhard Nerlich

438 SWEDEN

6 "DRAKEN" CLASS (A 11)

Name	No.	Builders	Laid down	Launched	Commissioned
DELFINEN	DEL	Karlskronavervarver	1959	7 Mar 1961	7 June 1962
DRAKEN	DRA	Kockums, Malmö	1958	1 April 1960	4 April 1962
GRIPEN	GRI	Karlskronavervarver	1959	31 May 1960	28 April 1962
NORDKAPAREN	NOR	Kockums, Malmö	1959	8 Mar 1961	4 April 1962
SPRINGAREN	SPR	Kockums, Malmö	1960	31 Aug 1961	7 Nov 1962
VARGEN	VGN	Kockums, Malmö	1958	20 May 1960	15 Nov 1961

Displacement, tons: 770 standard; 835 surfaced; 1 110 dived
Length, feet (metres): 226·4 *(69·0)*
Beam, feet (metres): 16·7 *(5·1)*
Draught, feet (metres): 16·4 *(5·0)*
Torpedo tubes: 4—21 in *(533 mm)* bow
Main machinery: 2 Pielstick diesels; 1 660 bhp; 1 large five-bladed propeller; 1 electric motor
Speed, knots: 17 surfaced; 20 dived
Complement: 36

DELFINEN   5/1976, Reinhard Nerlich

6 "HAJEN" CLASS

Name	No.	Builders	Laid down	Launched	Commissioned
BÄVERN	BAV	Kockums, Malmö	1956	3 Feb 1958	29 May 1959
HAJEN	HAJ	Kockums, Malmö	1953	11 Dec 1954	28 Feb 1957
ILLERN	ILN	Kockums, Malmö	1956	15 Nov 1957	31 Aug 1959
SÄLEN	SAL	Kockums, Malmö	1954	3 Oct 1955	8 April 1957
UTTERN	UTN	Kockums, Malmö	1957	14 Nov 1958	15 Mar 1960
VALEN	VAL	Karlskronavervarver	1953	24 April 1955	4 Mar 1957

Displacement, tons: 720 standard; 785 surfaced; 1 000 dived
Length, feet (metres): 216·5 *(66·0)*
Beam, feet (metres): 16·7 *(5·1)*
Draught, feet (metres): 16·4 *(5·0)*
Torpedo tubes: 4—21 in *(533 mm)* bow (8 torpedoes)
Main machinery: 2 SEMT-Pielstick diesels; 1 660 bhp; 2 electric motors; 2 shafts
Speed, knots: 16 surfaced; 17 dived
Complement: 44

ILLERN (old lettering)   1972, Royal Swedish Navy

DESTROYERS

4 "SÖDERMANLAND" CLASS

Name	No.	Builders	Laid down	Launched	Commissioned
ÖSTERGÖTLAND	J 20	Götaverken, Göteborg	1 Sept 1955	8 May 1956	3 Mar 1958
SÖDERMANLAND	J 21	Eriksberg Mek Verkstads	1 June 1955	28 May 1956	27 June 1958
GÄSTRIKLAND	J 22	Götaverken, Göteborg	1 Oct 1955	6 June 1956	14 Jan 1959
HÄLSINGLAND	J 23	Kockums Mek Verkstads A/B	1 Oct 1955	14 Jan 1957	17 June 1959

Displacement, tons: 2 150 standard; 2 600 full load
Length, feet (metres): 367·5 *(112·0)* oa
Beam, feet (metres): 36·8 *(11·2)*
Draught, feet (metres): 12·0 *(3·7)*
Missile launchers: 1 quadruple Seacat (RB 07) surface-to-air; 1—RB 08A (Mk 20) surface-to-surface
Guns: 4—4·7 in *(120 mm)*, (2 twin); 4—40 mm (single)
A/S weapons: 1 Squid (triple-barrelled)
Torpedo tubes: 6—21 in *(533 mm)* (1 mount)
Mines: 60 can be carried
Main engines: De Laval turbines; 2 shafts; 47 000 bhp
Boilers: 2 Babcock & Wilcox
Speed, knots: 35
Oil fuel, tons: 330
Range, miles: 2 200 at 20 knots
Complement: 244 (18 officers, 226 men)

Modernisation: *Gästrikland* in 1965, *Södermanland* in 1967, *Hälsingland* in 1968, *Östergötland* in 1969.

Radar: Search and target designator: Thomson CSF Saturn.
Fire control: HSA M 44 for Seacat—M 45 series for guns.

SÖDERMANLAND   1977, Royal Swedish Navy

SWEDEN 439

2 "HALLAND" CLASS

Name	No.
HALLAND	J 18
SMÅLAND	J 19

Builders	Laid down	Launched	Commissioned
Götaverken, Göteborg	1951	16 July 1952	8 June 1955
Eriksberg Mek Verkstads	1951	23 Oct 1952	12 Jan 1956

Displacement, tons: 2 800 standard; 3 400 full load
Length, feet (metres): 380·5 *(116·0)* wl; 397·2 *(121·0)* oa
Beam, feet (metres): 41·3 *(12·6)*
Draught, feet (metres): 14·8 *(4·5)*
Missiles: 1 RB 08A (Mk 20) launcher (see note)
Guns: 4—4·7 in *(120 mm)* (2 twin); 2—57 mm (twin); 6—40 mm
A/S weapons: 2 four-barrelled rocket-launcher (Bofors)
Torpedo tubes: 8—21 in *(533 mm)* (1 quin, 1 triple)
Mines: Can be fitted for minelaying
Main engines: De Laval double reduction geared turbines; 2 shafts; 58 000 bhp
Boilers: 2 Penhöet
Speed, knots: 35
Oil fuel, tons: 500
Range, miles: 3 000 at 20 knots
Complement: 290 (18 officers, 272 men)

Both ordered in 1948. The first Swedish destroyers of post-war design. Fully automatic gun turrets forward and aft. Both modernised in 1962.

Missiles: Being re-equipped with missiles 1977-78.

Radar: Search and target designator: Thomson CSF Saturn (foremast).
Air warning: LW 02/03 (mainmast).
Fire control, search and tracking: M 22 and associated sets (radome).
ECM.

SMÅLAND 1977, Royal Swedish Navy

FRIGATES

2 "ÖLAND" CLASS

Name	No.
ÖLAND	F 16
UPPLAND	F 17

Builders	Laid down	Launched	Commissioned
Kockums Mek Verkstads A/B, Malmö	1943	15 Dec 1945	5 Dec 1947
Karlskrona Dockard	1943	5 Nov 1946	31 Jan 1949

Displacement, tons: 2 000 standard; 2 400 full load
Length, feet (metres): 351 *(107·0)* pp; 367·5 *(112·0)* oa
Beam, feet (metres): 36·8 *(11·2)*
Draught, feet (metres): 11·2 *(3·4)*
Guns: 4—4·7 in *(120 mm)* (2 twin); 6—40 mm (single)
A/S weapon: 1 triple-barrelled Squid mortar
Torpedo tubes: 6—21 in *(533 mm)* (2 triple)
Mines: 60 capacity
Main engines: De Laval geared turbines; 2 shafts; 44 000 bhp
Boilers: 2 Penhöet
Speed, knots: 35
Oil fuel, tons: 300
Range, miles: 2 500 at 20 knots
Complement: 210

Superstructure and machinery spaces lightly armoured. Pennant numbers changed to F superior 1975.

Gunnery: 4·7 in guns semi-automatic with 80° elevation. 40 mm gun near jackstaff was removed in 1962, and eight 20 mm guns in 1964.

Radar: Search and target designator: Thomson CSF Saturn.
Fire control: two M 45 series.
Navigation: one set.

ÖLAND (Old pennant number) 1975, Royal Swedish Navy

Reconstruction: *Öland* was modernised with new bridge in 1960 and again modernised in 1969; and *Uppland* with new bridge and helicopter platform in 1963.

4 "VISBY" CLASS

Name	No.
VISBY	F 11
SUNDSVALL	F 12
HÄLSINGBORG	F 13
KALMAR	F 14

Builders	Laid down	Launched	Commissioned
Götaverken, Göteborg	1941	16 Oct 1942	10 Aug 1943
Eriksberg Mek Verkstads	1941	20 Oct 1942	17 Sept 1943
Karlskronavarvet	1942	23 Mar 1943	30 Nov 1943
Eriksberg Mek Verkstads	1942	20 July 1943	3 Feb 1944

Displacement, tons: 1 150 standard; 1 320 full load
Length, feet (metres): 310·0 *(94·5)* wl; 321·5 *(98·0)* oa
Beam, feet (metres): 30 *(9·1)*
Draught, feet (metres): 12·5 *(3·8)*
Aircraft: 1 helicopter platform
Guns: 3—4·7 in *(120 mm)*; 2—57 mm; 3—40 mm
A/S weapons: 1—375 mm Bofors 4-tube rocket launcher
09 De Laval geared turbines; 2 shafts; 36 000 shp
Boilers: 3 three-drum type
Speed, knots: 39
Range, miles: 1 600 at 20 knots
Oil fuel, tons: 150
Complement: 140

All of the class of four were originally fitted for minelaying. Will be paid off for disposal in the near future.

Radar: Thompson CSF Saturn S-band long-range search and target designator
M 24 fire control systems with co-mounted radars for search and tracking for guns.

SUNDSVALL 1972, Royal Swedish Navy

440 SWEDEN

LIGHT FORCES

2 + 15 "HUGIN" (Ex-"JÄGAREN") CLASS
(FAST ATTACK CRAFT—MISSILE)

Name	No.	Builders	Commissioned
JÄGAREN	P 150	Norway	8 June 1972
HUGIN	P 151	Norway	3 June 1977
MUNIN	P 152	Norway	1978
MAGNE	P 153	Norway	—
MODE	P 154	Norway	—
VALE	P 155	Norway	—
VIDAR	P 156	Norway	—
MJÖLNER	P 157	Norway	—
NYSING	P 158	Norway	—
KAPAREN	P 159	Norway	—
VÄKTAREN	P 160	Norway	—
SNAPPHANEN	P 161	Norway	—
SPEJAREN	P 162	Norway	—
STYRBJÖRN	P 163	Norway	—
STARKODDER	P 164	Norway	—
TORDÖN	P 165	Norway	—
TIRFING	P 166	Norway	—

Displacement, tons: 140
Dimensions, feet (metres): 118 × 20·3 × 4·9 (36 × 6·2 × 1·5)
Missile launchers: 6 Penguin Mark 2
Gun: 1—57 mm Bofors L 70
Torpedo tubes: Fitted for 4—21 in (533 mm) (except with missiles)
Main engines: 2 MTU MB20V 672 TY90 diesels; 2 shafts; 7 000 bhp = 35 knots
Complement: 19

JÄGAREN (old pennant number) 1976, Royal Swedish Navy

Instead of the motor gunboats projected for several years a choice was made of fast attack craft similar to the Norwegian "Hauk" class armed with Penguin missiles. They can be fitted for minelaying at the expense of missiles or torpedoes.

Jägaren underwent extensive trials and, on 15 May 1975, an order for a further 11 was placed with Bergens Mekaniske Verksted, Norway and 5 from Westermoen. Guns and electronics are being provided from Sweden. Fitted for alternative minelaying capability aft.
An extra deck-mounting ring is fitted amidships though now blanked by Penguin mounts.

12 "SPICA T 131" CLASS (FAST ATTACK CRAFT—TORPEDO)

Name	No.	Builders	Commissioned
NORRKÖPING	T 131	Karlskronavarvet	11 Mar 1973
NYNÄSHAMN	T 132	Karlskronavarvet	28 Sept 1973
NORRTÄLJE	T 133	Karlskronavarvet	1 Feb 1974
VARBERG	T 134	Karlskronavarvet	13 June 1974
VÄSTERÅS	T 135	Karlskronavarvet	25 Oct 1974
VÄSTERVIK	T 136	Karlskronavarvet	15 Jan 1975
UMEÅ	T 137	Karlskronavarvet	15 May 1975
PITEA	T 138	Karlskronavarvet	13 Sept 1975
LULEA	T 139	Karlskronavarvet	28 Nov 1975
HALMSTAD	T 140	Karlskronavarvet	9 April 1976
STRÖMSTAD	T 141	Karlskronavarvet	13 Sept 1976
YSTAD	T 142	Karlskronavarvet	10 Jan 1976

Displacement, tons: 230 standard
Dimensions, feet (metres): 134·5 × 23·3 × 5·2 (41 × 7·1 × 1·6)
Gun: 1—57 mm Bofors L 70
Rocket launchers: 8 for 57 mm flare rockets
Torpedo tubes: 6—21 in (533 mm) for wire-guided torpedoes
Main engines: 3 Rolls-Royce Proteus gas turbines; 3 shafts; 12 900 bhp = 40·5 knots
Complement: 27

Similar to the original "Spica" class from which they were developed. Launched—*Norrköping* 16 Nov 1972, *Nynäshamn* 24 April 1973, *Norrtälje* 18 Sept 1973, *Varberg* 2 Feb 1974, *Västerås* 15 May 1974, *Västervik* 2 Sept 1974, *Umea* 13 Jan 1975, *Pitea* 12 May 1975. Laid down—*Lulea* 6 Sept 1974, *Halmstad* 7 Feb 1975.

Missiles: Plans exist for the fitting of 2 twin missile launchers aft post-1978 in place of after pair of torpedo tubes.

Radar: Philips Teleindustrie 9 LV 200-simultaneous air and surface search in I band with tracking in separate band.

VÄSTERVIK 1975, Kapten Goran Frisk

6 "SPICA T 121" CLASS (FAST ATTACK CRAFT—TORPEDO)

Name	No.	Builders	Commissioned
SPICA	T 121	Götaverken, Göteborg	1966
SIRIUS	T 122	Götaverken, Göteborg	1966
CAPELLA	T 123	Götaverken, Göteborg	1966
CASTOR	T 124	Karlskronavervarvet	1967
VEGA	T 125	Karlskronavervarvet	1967
VIRGO	T 126	Karlskronavervarvet	1967

Displacement, tons: 200 standard; 230 full load
Dimensions, feet (metres): 134·5 × 23·3 × 5·2 (41 × 7·1 × 1·6)
Gun: 1—57 mm Bofors
Torpedo tubes: 6—21 in (533 mm) (single, fixed)
Rocket launchers: 6—57 mm flare rockets; 4—103 mm flare rockets
Main engines: 3 Bristol Siddeley Proteus 1 274 hp gas turbines; 3 shafts; 12 720 shp = 40 knots
Complement: 28 (7 officers, 21 ratings)

The 57 mm gun is in a power operated turret controlled by a radar equipped director.

Missiles: Plans exist for the fitting of two twin missile launchers aft in place of after pair of torpedo tubes (post 1978).

Radar: M 22 fire control system with co-mounted radars in radome for guns and torpedoes.

SPICA 1977, Royal Swedish Navy

SWEDEN 441

3 "PLEJAD" CLASS (FAST ATTACK CRAFT—TORPEDO)

Name	No.	Builders	Commissioned
ALDEBARAN	T 107	Lürssen, Vegesack	1956
ARCTURUS	T 110	Lürssen, Vegesack	1957
ASTREA	T 112	Lürssen, Vegesack	1956

Displacement, tons: 155 standard; 170 full load
Dimensions, feet (metres): 147.6 × 19 × 5.2 *(45 × 5.8 × 1.6)*
Guns: 2—40 mm Bofors
Rocket launchers: 4—103 mm flare rockets; 1—12 rail 57 mm flare launcher
Torpedo tubes: 6—21 in *(533 mm)*
Main engines: 3 Mercedes-Benz (MTU 20 V 672) diesels; 3 shafts; 9 000 bhp = 37.5 knots
Range, miles: 600 at 30 knots
Complement: 33

Launched between 1954 and 1957.

"PLEJAD" Class   1975, Royal Swedish Navy

11 "T 42" CLASS (FAST ATTACK CRAFT—TORPEDO)

Name	No.	Builders	Commissioned
—	T 46	Kockums, Malmö	1957
—	T 47	Kockums, Malmö	1957
—	T 48	Kockums, Malmö	1957
—	T 49	Kockums, Malmö	1957
—	T 50	Kockums, Malmö	1958
—	T 51	Kockums, Malmö	1958
—	T 52	Kockums, Malmö	1958
—	T 53	Naval Dockyard, Stockholm	1958
—	T 54	Naval Dockyard, Stockholm	1959
—	T 55	Naval Dockyard, Stockholm	1959
—	T 56	Naval Dockyard, Stockholm	1959

Displacement, tons: 40 standard
Dimensions, feet (metres): 75.5 × 19.4 × 4.6 *(23 × 5.9 × 1.4)*
Gun: 1—40 mm Bofors
Rocket launchers: 1—12 rail 57 mm flare launcher
Torpedo tubes: 2—21 in *(533 mm)*
Main engines: 3 Isotta Fraschini petrol engines; 4 500 bhp = 45 knots

T42-45 converted to "V 01" class (see below).

T 56   1975, Royal Swedish Navy

1 LARGE PATROL CRAFT

V 57

Displacement, tons: 115 standard
Dimensions, feet (metres): 98 × 17.3 × 7.5 *(30 × 5.3 × 2.3)*
Gun: 1—20 mm
Main engines: Diesel; 500 bhp = 13.5 knots
Complement: 12

Built at Stockholm. Launched in 1953. Fitted for minelaying. Attached to Coastal Artillery.

5 COASTAL PATROL CRAFT

SVK 1   SVK 2   SVK 3   SVK 4   SVK 5

Displacement, tons: 19 standard
Dimensions, feet (metres): 52.5 × 12.1 × 3.9 *(16 × 3.7 × 1.2)*
Gun: 1—20 mm
Main engines: Diesel; 100 to 135 bhp = 10 knots
Complement: 12

Patrol craft of the Sjövarnskarens (RNVR). All launched in 1944.

17 COASTAL PATROL CRAFT

61-77

Displacement, tons: 28 standard
Dimensions, feet (metres): 69 × 15 × 5 *(21 × 4.6 × 1.5)*
Gun: 1—20 mm
Main engines: Diesel; speed = 18 knots

These are attached to the Coastal Artillery. "60" series launched in 1960-61 and "70" series in 1966-67.

Radar: One navigation set.

PATROL CRAFT 66   1975, Royal Swedish Navy

4 "V 01" CLASS (COASTAL PATROL CRAFT)

Name	No.	Builders	Commissioned (after reconstruction)
SKANÖR	V 01	Kockums, Malmö	Dec 1976
SMYGE	V 02	Kockums, Malmö	1977
ARILD	V 03	Kockums, Malmö	1977
VIKEN	V 04	Kockums, Malmö	1977

Displacement, tons: 40 standard
Dimensions, feet (metres): 75.5 × 19.4 × 4.6 *(23 × 5.9 × 1.4)*
Gun: 1—40 mm Bofors
Rocket launcher: 1—12 rail 57 mm
Main engines: 3 diesels

These four craft were originally of the "T-42" class (T42-45) which commissioned in 1957. They were reconstructed at Karlskrona having their torpedo tubes removed and their petrol engines replaced by diesels.

SKÄNOR   1976, Royal Swedish Navy

442 SWEDEN

5 COASTGUARD PATROL CRAFT

TV 103-107

Displacement, tons: 50
Dimensions, feet (metres): 87·6 × 16·5 × 3·6 *(26·7 × 5·2 × 1·1)*
Main engines: 2 diesels; 1 800 hp; 2 shafts = 25 knots
Range, miles: 1 000
Complement: 8 (accommodation for 16)

All welded aluminium hull and upperworks. Twin rudders. Equipped for salvage divers. Built since 1969 at Karlskrona.

Radar: One Navigational radar.

Sonar: One hull mounted.

MINE WARFARE FORCES

1 NEW CONSTRUCTION

Name	No.	Builders	Commissioned
—	M 04	Karlskrona Naval DY	1980

Displacement, tons: 3 000
Length, feet (metres): 328 *(100)*
Guns: 2—57 mm (single); 2—40 mm (single)
Complement: 95 plus 185 trainees

Laid down 1977. When completed is planned to relieve *Alvsnabben* as Cadet Training Ship as well as serving as a minelayer. Fitted with helicopter deck.

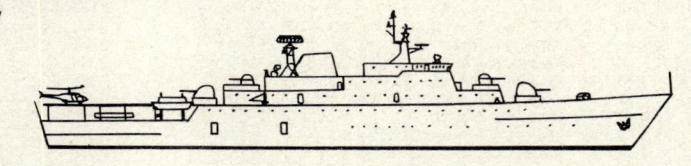

M 04

2 "ALVSBORG" CLASS (MINELAYERS)

Name	No.	Builders	Commissioned
ÄLVSBORG	M 02	Karlskrona Naval DY	10 April 1971
VISBORG	M 03	Karlskrona Naval DY	6 Feb 1976

Displacement, tons: 2 660 (M 02); 2 540 (M 03)
Length, feet (metres): 301·8 *(92)*
Beam, feet (metres): 48·2 *(14·7)*
Draught, feet (metres): 13·2 *(4·0)*
Aircraft: 1 helicopter
Guns: 3—40 mm Bofors
Main engines: 2 Nohab-Polar 12-cyl diesels; 1 shaft; 4 200 bhp
Speed, knots: 16
Complement: 95 (accommodation for 205 submariners in M 02—158 admiral's staff in M 03)

Älvsborg was ordered in 1968 and launched on 11 Nov 1969. She replaced the submarine depot ship *Patricia* which was sold in 1972.
Visborg, laid down on 16 Oct 1973 and launched 22 Jan 1975 has succeeded *Marieholm* as Command Ship for C-in-C Coastal Fleet.

Fire control: M 20 Series.

ÄLVSBORG
1975, Royal Swedish Navy

1 MINELAYER/TRAINING SHIP

Name	No.	Builders	Commissioned
ÄLVSNABBEN	M 01	Eriksberg Mek Verkstads	8 May 1943

Displacement, tons: 4 250 standard
Length, feet (metres): 317·6 *(96·8)* wl; 334·7 *(102·0)* oa
Beam, feet (metres): 44·6 *(13·6)*
Draught, feet (metres): 16·4 *(5·0)*
Guns: 2—6 in *(152 mm)*; 2—57 mm Bofors; 2—40 mm; 4—37 mm saluting
Main engines: Diesels; 1 shaft; 3 000 bhp
Speed, knots: 14
Complement: 255 (63 cadets)

Built on a mercantile hull. Laid down on 31 Oct 1942, launched on 19 Jan 1943. Employed as a training ship during 1953-58. Relieved the anti-aircraft cruiser *Gotland* as Cadets' Seagoing Training Ship in 1959. Re-armed in 1961. Formerly carried 4—6 in, 8—40 mm, 6—20 mm.

Radar: Search and target designator: Thomson CSF Saturn.
Fire control: M45 series.

ÄLVSNABBEN
7/1976, US Navy

Note: A new construction coastal minelayer MUL 20 projected for Coast Artillery.

1 COASTAL MINELAYER

MUL 11

Displacement, tons: 200 full load
Dimensions, feet (metres): 98·8 × 23·7 × 11·8 *(32·4 × 7·8 × 3·9)*
Guns: 2—20 mm
Main engines: 2 Atlas diesels; 300 bhp = 10 knots

Launched in 1946. Operated by Coast Artillery.

Radar: One navigation set.

MUL 11
1976, Royal Swedish Navy

SWEDEN 443

8 COASTAL MINELAYERS

| MUL 12 (1952) | MUL 14 (1953) | MUL 16 (1956) | MUL 18 (1956) |
| MUL 13 (1952) | MUL 15 (1953) | MUL 17 (1956) | MUL 19 (1956) |

Displacement, tons: 245 full load
Dimensions, feet (metres): 95·1 × 24·3 × 10·2 *(29 × 7·4 × 3·1)*
Gun: 1—40 mm
Main engines: 2 Nohab diesel-electric; 460 bhp = 10·5 knots

Launch dates in brackets. All completed by 1957. Operated by Coast Artillery.

Radar: One navigation set.

MUL 12   *1975, Royal Swedish Navy*

36 SMALL MINELAYERS

501-536

Ordered in 1969. Of 15 tons and 14 knots with diesel engines. Mines are laid from single traps on either beam. Nine more projected.

Radar: One navigation set.

SMALL MINELAYER 502   *1975, Royal Swedish Navy*

6 "HANÖ" CLASS (MINESWEEPERS—COASTAL)

Name	No.	Builders	Commissioned
HANÖ	M 51	Karlskrona	1954
TÄRNÖ	M 52	Karlskrona	1954
TJURKÖ	M 53	Karlskrona	1954
STURKÖ	M 54	Karlskrona	1954
ORNÖ	M 55	Karlskrona	1954
UTÖ	M 56	Karlskrona	1954

Displacement, tons: 275 standard
Dimensions, feet (metres): 131·2 × 23 × 8 *(40 × 7 × 2·4)*
Guns: 2—40 mm (except *Utö;* 1—40mm)
Main engines: 2 Nohab diesels; 2 shafts; 910 bhp = 14·5 knots

Steel hulls.

TJURKÖ   *1975, Royal Swedish Navy*

12 "ARKÖ" CLASS (MINESWEEPERS—COASTAL)

Name	No.	Builders	Commissioned
ARKÖ	M 57	Karlskrona	1958
SPÄRÖ	M 58	Hälsingborg	1958
KARLSÖ	M 59	Karlskrona	1958
IGGÖ	M 60	Hälsingborg	1961
STYRSÖ	M 61	Karlskrona	1962
SKAFTÖ	M 62	Hälsingborg	1962
ASPÖ	M 63	Karlskrona	1962
HASSLÖ	M 64	Hälsingborg	1962
VINÖ	M 65	Karlskrona	1962
VÅLLÖ	M 66	Hälsingborg	1963
NÄMDÖ	M 67	Karlskrona	1964
BLIDÖ	M 68	Hälsingborg	1964

Displacement, tons: 285 standard; 300 full load
Dimensions, feet (metres): 131 pp; 144·5 oa × 23 × 8 *(42 × 7 × 2·4)*
Gun: 1—40 mm
Main engines: 2 Mercedes-Benz (MTU 12V 493) diesels; 2 shafts; 1 600 bhp = 14·5 knots

Of wooden construction. There is a small difference in the deck-line between M 57-59 and M 60-68. *Arkö* was launched on 21 Jan 1957.

ASPÖ   *1975, Royal Swedish Navy*

444 SWEDEN

3 "M 47" CLASS (MINESWEEPERS—INSHORE)

GILLÖGA M 47   RÖDLÖGA M 48   SVARTLÖGA M 49

Details same as "M 44" class. Built in 1964. Trawler type.

RÖDLÖGA   1976, Royal Swedish Navy

4 "M 44" CLASS (MINESWEEPERS—INSHORE)

HISINGEN M 43   DÄMMAN M 45
BLACKAN M 44   GALTEN M 46

Displacement, tons: 140
Dimensions, feet (metres): 72·2 × 21 × 11·2 (22 × 6·4 × 3·4)
Gun: 1—40 mm
Main engines: 1 diesel; 380 bhp = 9 knots

Built in 1960. Trawler type.

3 "M 31" CLASS (MINESWEEPERS—INSHORE)

Name	No.	Builders	Commissioned
GÄSSTEN	M 31	Knippla Skeppsvarv	16 Nov 1973
NORSTEN	M 32	Hellevikstrands Skeppsvarv	12 Oct 1973
VIKSTEN	M·33	Karlskrona	1 July 1974

Displacement, tons: 120 standard; 135 full load
Dimensions, feet (metres): 79 oa × 21·7 × 12·2 (24 × 6·6 × 3·7)
Gun: 1—40 mm
Main engines: 1 diesel; 460 bhp = 11 knots

Ordered 1972. *Viksten* built of glass reinforced plastic as a forerunner to new minehunters to be built at Karlskrona. Others have wooden hulls. *Gässten* launched Nov 1972. *Norsten* April 1973, *Viksten* April 1974.

VIKSTEN   1975, Royal Swedish Navy

8 "M 15" CLASS (MINESWEEPERS—INSHORE)

M 15   M 16   M 21   M 22   M 23   M 24   M 25   M 26

Displacement, tons: 70 standard
Dimensions, feet (metres): 85·3 × 16·5 × 4·5 (26 × 5 × 1·4)
Gun: 1—20 mm
Main engines: 2 diesels; 320-430 bhp = 12-13 knots

All launched in 1941. M 17, M 18 and M 20 of this class were re-rated as tenders and renamed *Lommen*, *Spoven* and *Skuld* respectively: see later page.

M 25   1975, Royal Swedish Navy

2 MINE TRANSPORTS

FÄLLAREN A 236   MINÖRENA 237

Displacement, tons: 165 standard
Dimensions, feet (metres): 97 × 19 × 6·7 (31·8 × 6·2 × 2·2)
Main engines: 2 diesels; 1 shaft; 240 bhp = 9 knots

Launched in 1941 and 1940 respectively.

SWEDEN 445

AMPHIBIOUS FORCES

3 LCM

Name	No.	Builders	Commissioned
BORE	—	Åsigeverken	1967
GRIM	—	Åsigeverken	1962
HEIMDAL	—	Åsigeverken	1967

Displacement, tons: 340 full load
Dimensions, feet (metres): 118·1 × 27·9 × 8·5 *(36 × 8·5 × 2·6)*
Guns: 2—20 mm
Main engines: Diesels; 800 bhp = 12 knots

Launched in 1961 *(Grim)* and other two in 1966. Attached to Coastal Artillery.

BORE *1969, Royal Swedish Navy*

2 LCM

Name	No.	Builders	Commissioned
SKAGUL	A 333	—	1960
SLEIPNER	A 335	—	1960

Displacement, tons: 335 standard
Dimensions, feet (metres): 114·8 × 27·9 × 9·5 *(35 × 8·5 × 2·9)*
Main engines: Diesels; 640 bhp = 10 knots

Sleipner was launched in 1959 and *Skagul* in 1960. Attached to Coastal Artillery.

4 "ANE" CLASS (LCM)

ANE 324   BALDER 325   LOKE 326   RING 327

Displacement, tons: 135 standard
Dimensions, feet (metres): 91·9 × 26·2 × 6·0 *(28 × 8 × 1·2)*
Guns: 1—20 mm; 1 or 2 MG
Main engines: Speed = 8·5 knots

Built in 1943-45. Attached to Coastal Artillery.

81 LCUs

Nos. 201-276 and 280-284

Displacement, tons: 31
Dimensions, feet (metres): 69 × 13·8 × 4·2 *(20 × 4·2 × 1·3)*
Guns: 2—6·5 mm MG
Main engines: Diesels; 600 hp = 17 knots

"201" Class (201-241) launched 1957-1960. "242" class (242-255) built in 1971-73; "256" class (256-276); 256-263 completed 1975, 264-269 and 274-276 completed 1976, 270-273 completed 1977; 280 class (280-284) completed 1976-77.

LCU 227 ("201" Class) *1975, Royal Swedish Navy*

5 "L 51" CLASS (LCU)

L 51   L 52   L 53   L 54   L 55

Displacement, tons: 32 standard
Dimensions, feet (metres): 50·8 × 16 × 3·2 *(14 × 4·8 × 1)*
Main engines: Diesel; 140 bhp = 7 knots

Launched in 1947-48.

54 LCAs

337-354 of 6 tons and 21 knots. Built 1970-73.
332-336 of 5·4 tons and 25 knots. Built in 1967.
331 of 6 tons and 20 knots. Built in 1965.
301-330 of 4 tons and 9·5 knots. Built in 1956-59.

ICEBREAKERS

2 + 1 FINNISH "URHO" CLASS

Name	No.	Builders	Commissioned
ATLE	—	Wärtsilä, Helsinki	21 Oct 1974
FREJ	—	Wärtsilä, Helsinki	30 Sept 1975
YMER	—	Wärtsilä, Helsinki	1977

Displacement, tons: 7 900
Dimensions, feet (metres): 337·8 × 77·1 × 24·6 *(104·6 × 23·8 × 7·3)*
Aircraft: 1 helicopter
Main engines: 5 Wärtsilä-Pielstick diesels of 25 000 bhp; 4 Stromberg electric motors; 4 shafts (2 forward, 2 aft); 22 000 shp = 18 knots
Complement: 54 (16 officers, 38 men)

Atle laid down 10 May 1973, launched 27 Nov 1973. *Frej* launched 3 June 1974. *Ymer* ordered 24 March 1975, laid down 12 Feb 1976 and launched 3 Sept 1976. Sister ships of Finnish "Urho" class.

YMER

446 SWEDEN

Name	No.	Builders	Commissioned
NJORD	—	Wärtsilä, Helsinki	Dec 1969

Displacement, tons: 5 150 standard; 5 686 full load
Dimensions, feet (metres): 283·8 oa × 69·6 × 20·3 *(86·5 × 20·5 × 6·2)*
Main engines: Wärtsilä diesel-electric; 4 shafts, (2 forward, 2 aft); 12 000 hp = 18 knots

Launched on 20 Oct 1968. Near sister ship of *Tor.*
Has deck-rings for 4—40 mm guns.

NJORD 1971, Royal Swedish Navy

Name	No.	Builders	Commissioned
TOR	—	Wärtsilä, Crichton-Vulcan Yard, Turku	31 Jan 1964

Displacement, tons: 4 980 standard; 5 290 full load
Dimensions, feet (metres): 277·2 oa × 69·6 × 20·3 *(84·5 × 20·5 × 6·2)*
Main engines: Wärtsilä-Sulzer diesel-electric; 4 shafts; (2 forward; 2 aft); 12 000 hp = 18 knots

Launched on 25 May 1963. Towed to Sandvikens Skeppsdocka, Helsingfors, for completion. Larger but generally similar to *Oden,* and a near-sister to *Tarmo* built for Finland.
Has deck-rings for 4—40 mm guns

TOR 1972, Royal Swedish Navy

Name	No.	Builders	Commissioned
ALE	—	Wärtsilä, Helsinki	19 Dec 1973

Displacement, tons: 1 488
Dimensions, feet (metres): 150·9 × 42·6 × 16·4 *(46 × 13 × 5)*
Main engines: Diesels; 4 750 hp; 2 shafts = 14 knots
Complement: 21

Built for operations on Lake Vänern. Launched 1 June 1973.

Name	No.	Builders	Commissioned
THULE	—	Naval Dockyard, Karlskrona	1953

Displacement, tons: 2 200 standard; 2 280 full load
Dimensions, feet (metres): 204·2 oa × 52·8 × 19·4 *(57 × 16·1 × 5·9)*
Main engines: Diesel-electric; 3 shafts (1 forward); 4 800 bhp = 14 knots
Complement: 43

Launched in Oct 1951.

Name	No.	Builders	Commissioned
ODEN	—	Sandviken, Helsingfors	1958

Displacement, tons: 4 950 standard; 5 220 full load
Dimensions, feet (metres): 273·5 oa × 63·7 × 22·7 *(78 × 19·4 × 6·9)*
Main engines: Diesel-electric; 4 shafts (2 forward); 10 500 shp = 16 knots
Fuel, tons: 740
Complement: 75

...the Finnish *Voima* and three Soviet icebreakers. Launched on 16 Oct 1956.

ODEN 1972, Royal Swedish Navy

MISCELLANEOUS

ANDERS BURE (ex-*Rali*)

Displacement, tons: 54
Dimensions, feet (metres): 82·0 × 19·4 × 6·9 *(25 × 5·9 × 2·1)*
Main engines: Diesels = 15 knots
Complement: 11

Built in 1968 as *Rali.* She was purchased in 1971 and renamed.

SURVEY SHIPS

...sport but manned and operated by the navy).

...2·6 × 11·5 *(64·5 × 13 × 3·5)*
...shaft = 14 knots

...on 1 Jan 1979.

...7 × 2·6)

...in 1946.

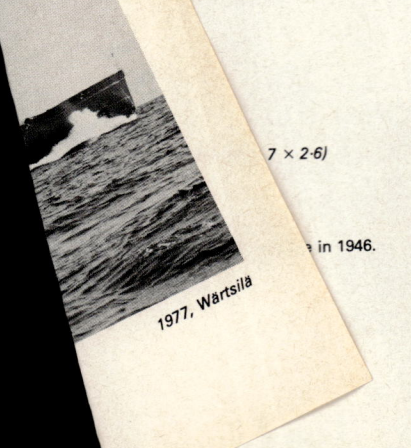

1977, Wärtsilä

ANDERS BURE 1976, Royal Swedish Navy

SWEDEN 447

JOHAN MÅNSSON

Displacement, tons: 977 standard; 1 030 full load
Dimensions, feet (metres): 183·7 × 36·1 × 11·5 (56 × 11 × 3·5)
Main engines: Diesels; 3 300 bhp = 15 knots
Complement: 85

Launched on 14 Jan 1966. Her surveying launches are lowered and recovered over a stern ramp.

JOHAN MÅNSSON 1975, Royal Swedish Navy

GUSTAF AF KLINT

Displacement, tons: 750 standard
Dimensions, feet (metres): 170·6 × 36·2 × 15·4 (52 × 11 × 4·7)
Main engines: Diesels; 640 bhp = 10 knots
Complement: 66

Launched in 1941. Reconstructed in 1963. She formerly displaced 650 tons with a length of 154 feet (47 metres).

GUSTAV AF KLINT 1976, Royal Swedish Navy

NILS STRÖMCRONA

Displacement, tons: 140 standard
Dimensions, feet (metres): 88·6 × 17·0 × 8·2 (27 × 5·2 × 2·5)
Guns: None in peacetime
Main engines: Diesels; 300 bhp = 9 knots
Complement: 14

Launched in 1894, and reconstructed in 1952.

NILS STRÖMCRONA 1976, Royal Swedish Navy

SERVICE FORCES

1 SUPPLY SHIP

Name	No.	Builders	Commissioned
FREJA	A 221	Kroger, Rendsburg	1954

Displacement, tons: 415 standard; 465 full load
Dimensions, feet (metres): 160·8 × 27·9 × 12·1 (49 × 8·5 × 3·7)
Main engines: Diesels; 600 bhp = 11 knots

Launched in 1953. Employed as a provision ship.

1 SUPPORT TANKER

BRÄNNAREN A 228

Displacement, tons: 857
Dimensions, feet (metres): 203·4 × 28·2 × 12·1 (62 × 8·6 × 3·7)
Speed, knots: 11

Ex-German merchant tanker *Indio* purchased early 1972. Built 1965.

1 SALVAGE SHIP

Name	No.	Builders	Commissioned
BELOS	A 211	—	29 May 1963

Displacement, tons: 1 000 standard
Dimensions, feet (metres): 204·4 × 37·0 × 12·0 (58 × 11·2 × 3·8)
Aircraft: 1 helicopter
Main engines: Diesels; 2 shafts; 1 200 bhp = 13 knots

Launched on 15 Nov 1961. Equipped with decompression chamber.

BELOS 1970, Royal Swedish Navy

2 SAIL TRAINING SHIPS

Name	No.	Builders	Commissioned
GLADAN	S 01	—	1947
FALKEN	S 02	—	1948

Displacement, tons: 220 standard
Dimensions, feet (metres): 93 wl; 129·5 oa × 23·5 × 13·5 (30·5; 42·5 × 7·7 × 4·4)
Main engines: Auxiliary diesel; 120 bhp

Sail training ships. Two masted schooners. Launched 1947 and 1946 respectively. Sail area 5 511 square feet (512 square metres).

GLADAN 1977, Royal Swedish Navy

TENDERS

3 TRVs

Name	No.	Builders	Commissioned
PELIKANEN	A 247	—	26 Sept 1963

Displacement, tons: 130 standard
Dimensions, feet (metres): 108·2 × 19·0 × 6·0 (33 × 5·8 × 1·8)
Main engines: 2 Mercedes-Benz diesels; 1 040 bhp = 15 knots

Torpedo recovery and rocket trials vessel.

HÄGERN A 246

Displacement, tons: 50 standard
Dimensions, feet (metres): 88·6 × 16·4 × 4·9 (29 × 5·4 × 1·6)
Main engines: 2 diesels; 240 bhp = 10 knots

Launched in 1951.

448 SWEDEN

Name	No.	Builders	Commissioned
PINGVINEN	A 248	Lundevarv-Ooverkstads AB, Kramfors	Mar 1975

Displacement, tons: 191
Dimensions, feet (metres): 108·2 × 20 × 6 *(33 × 6·1 × 1·8)*
Main engines: 2 diesels; 1 100 hp = 13 knots

Ordered 1972. Torpedo recovery and rocket trials ship. Launched 26 Sept 1973.

PINGVINEN   *1976, Royal Swedish Navy*

5 TENDERS

SIGRUN A 256

Displacement, tons: 250 standard
Dimensions, feet (metres): 105·0 × 22·3 × 11·8 *(32 × 6·8 × 3·6)*
Main engines: Diesels: 320 bhp = 11 knots

Launched in 1961. Laundry ship.

URD (ex-*Capella*) A 241

Displacement, tons: 63 standard; 90 full load
Dimensions, feet (metres): 73·8 × 18·3 × 9·2 *(22 × 5·6 × 2·8)*
Main engines: Diesels; 200 bhp = 8 knots

Experimental vessel added to the official list in 1970. Launched in 1969.

LOMMEN (ex-*M 17*) A 231   **SKULD** (ex-*M 20*) A 242
SPOVEN (ex-*M 18*) A 232

Displacement, tons: 70 standard
Dimensions, feet (metres): 85·3 × 16·5 × 4·5 *(26 × 5 × 1·4)*
Main engines: 2 diesels; 410 bhp = 13 knots

Former inshore minesweepers of the "M 15" Class. All launched in 1941.

TUGS

HERMES A 253   **HECTOR** A 321   **HEROS** A 322

Displacement, tons: 185 standard
Dimensions, feet (metres): 75·5 × 22·6 × 11·1 *(24·5 × 7·4 × 3·6)*
Main engines: Diesels; 600 bhp = 11 knots

Launched in 1953-57. Icebreaking tugs.

HERCULES A 323   **HERA** A 324

Displacement, tons: 127 tons
Dimensions, feet (metres): 65·3 × 21·3 × 12·5 *(21·4 × 6·9 × 4·1)*
Main engines: Diesels; 615 bhp = 11·5 knots

Launched 1969 and 1971. Icebreaking tugs.

ACHILLES A 251   **AJAX** A 252

Displacement, tons: 450
Dimensions, feet (metres): 108·2 × 28·9 × 12 *(35·5 × 9·5 × 3·9)*
Main engines: Diesel; 1 650 bhp = 12 knots

Achilles was launched in 1962 and *Ajax* in 1963. Both are icebreaking tugs.

AJAX   *5/1976, Reinhard Nerlich*

Also listed:
HEBE A326; **PASSOP** A327; **RAN** A328; **HENRIK** A329; **ATLAS** A330; **MÄRSGARN** A332; **VITS-GARN** A336.

ATB 1 A341; **ATB 2** A342; **ATB 3** A343.

GRANATEN A345; **EDDA** A347; **GERDA** A349.

WATER CARRIERS

UNDEN A 216

Displacement, tons: 540 standard
Dimensions, feet (metres): 121·4 × 23·3 × 9·8 *(39·8 × 7·6 × 3·2)*
Main engines: Steam reciprocating; 225 ihp = 9 knots

Launched in 1946.

FRYKEN A 217

Displacement, tons: 307 standard
Dimensions, feet (metres): 105·0 × 18·7 × 8·9 *(34·4 × 6·1 × 2·9)*
Main engines: Diesels; 370 bhp = 10 knots

A naval construction water carrier. Launched in 1959 and completed in 1960.

FRYKEN   *1976, Royal Swedish Navy*

SWITZERLAND

Diplomatic Representation

Defence Attaché in London:
 Colonel W. Dudli

Mercantile Marine

Lloyd's Register of Shipping:
 28 vessels of 252 746 tons gross

The Swiss Army operates ten Coastal Patrol Craft on the lakes. These were originally built in 1942 against possible German operations and have been modernised. Fitted with machine guns and radar. New construction would seem imminent. There are also water-transport detachments and other detachments with smaller patrol craft.

SWISS PATROL CRAFT 2/1976, Commander Aldo Fraccaroli

SWISS PATROL CRAFT 1966, Swiss Army

SYRIA

Ministerial

Minister of Defence:
 Major General Mustafa Tlass

Headquarters Appointments

Commander-in-Chief Navy:
 Commodore Fadl Husayn
Chief of Staff:
 Commodore Mustafa Tayyare
Director of Naval Operations:
 Commodore Muhammad Hamud

Personnel

(a) 1978: 2 500 officers and men
(b) 18 months national service

Naval Aviation

6-10 Ka25 Hormone helicopters.

Bases

Latakia, Baniyas, Tartus, Al-Mina-al-Bayda

New Acquisition

There are varying reports, none confirmed, of a Syrian order for 24 Patrol Craft in UK and of Syrian interest in French built patrol craft.

Mercantile Marine

Lloyd's Register of Shipping:
 32 vessels of 20 679 tons gross

FRIGATES

2 Ex-SOVIET "PETYA I" CLASS

Displacement, tons: 950 standard; 1 150 full load
Dimensions, feet (metres): 270 × 29·9 × 10·5 *(82·3 × 9·1 × 3·2)*
Guns: 4—3 in *(76 mm)* (twin)
A/S weapons: 4—16 barrelled MBU 2500
Torpedo tubes: 3—21 in *(533 mm)*
Main engines: 1 diesel; 6 000 hp; 2 gas-turbines; 30 000 hp; 3 shafts
Speed, knots: 30
Complement: 100

Transferred by USSR in 1975-76.

"PETYA I" Class 3/1975, MOD

450 SYRIA

LIGHT FORCES

6 Ex-SOVIET "OSA I" CLASS (FAST ATTACK CRAFT—MISSILE)

Displacement, tons: 165 standard; 200 full load
Dimensions, feet (metres): 128·7 × 25·1 × 5·9 (42·2 × 8·2 × 1·9)
Missile launchers: 4, two pairs abreast, for SS-N-2 (Styx)
Guns: 4—30 mm (twins) (1 forward, 1 aft)
Main engines: 3 diesels; 13 000 bhp = 32 knots
Range, miles: 800 at 25 knots
Complement: 25

Original pair sunk in Oct 1973 war. Up to six replacements reported.

Syrian "OSA" Class   12/1972

6 Ex-SOVIET "KOMAR" CLASS (FAST ATTACK CRAFT—MISSILE)

Displacement, tons: 70 standard; 80 full load
Dimensions, feet (metres): 83·7 × 19·8 × 5 (27·4 × 6·5 × 1·6)
Missile launchers: 2 for SS-N-2 (Styx)
Guns: 2—25 mm
Main engines: 4 diesels; 4 shafts; 4 800 bhp = 40 knots
Range, miles: 400 at 30 knots

Transferred between 1963 and 1966. Three reported lost in Israeli War October 1973, but were replaced.

"KOMAR" Class

8 Ex-SOVIET "P 4" CLASS (FAST ATTACK CRAFT—TORPEDO)

Displacement, tons: 25 standard
Dimensions, feet (metres): 62·7 × 11·6 × 5·6 (20·5 × 3·8 × 1·8)
Torpedo tubes: 2—18 in
Guns: 2—MG (twin)
Main engines: 2 diesels; 2 200 bhp; 2 shafts = 50 knots

Five torpedo boats were transferred from the USSR at Latakia on 7 Feb 1957, and at least 12 subsequently. One reported lost in Israeli War October 1973. Four transferred to Egypt in 1970. Only eight of the remainder considered operational.

3 Ex-FRENCH CH TYPE (LARGE PATROL CRAFT)

ABABEH IBN NEFEH   ABDULLAH IBN ARISSI   TAREK IBN ZAYED

Displacement, tons: 107 standard; 131 full load
Dimensions, feet (metres): 116·5 pp; 121·8 oa × 17·5 × 6·5 (38·2; 39·9 × 5·7 × 2·1)
Guns: 2—20 mm
A/S weapons: Depth charges
Main engines: MAN diesels; 2 shafts; 1 130 bhp = 16 knots
Oil fuel, tons: 50
Range, miles: 1 200 at 8 knots; 680 at 13 knots
Complement: 28

All built in France and completed in 1940. Rebuilt in 1955-56 when the funnels were removed. These were transferred in 1962 to form the nucleus of the Syrian Navy. Two of these ships are probably non-operational.

"Ch" Type   M Henri Le Masson

MINE WARFARE FORCES

1 Ex-SOVIET "T 43" CLASS (MINESWEEPER—OCEAN)

YARMOUK

Displacement, tons: 500 standard; 610 full load
Dimensions, feet (metres): 190·2 × 28·1 × 6·9 (58 × 9·2 × 2·3)
Guns: 4—37 mm (twins); 8—12·7 mm (twins)
Main engines: 2 diesels motors; 2 shafts; 2 000 hp = 17 knots
Range, miles: 1 600 at 10 knots
Complement: 40

Reported in 1962 to have been transferred from the Soviet Navy. The second of this class was sunk in the Israeli War October 1973.

2 Ex-SOVIET "VANYA" CLASS (MINESWEEPERS—COASTAL)

Displacement, tons: 225 standard; 250 full load
Dimensions, feet (metres): 130·7 × 24 × 6·9 (39·9 × 7·3 × 2·1)
Guns: 2—30 mm (twin)
Main engines: 2 diesels; 2 200 bhp = 18 knots
Complement: 30

Transferred Dec 1972.

MISCELLANEOUS

1 Ex-SOVIET "NYRYAT" CLASS

Displacement, tons: 145
Main engines: Diesel = 12·5 knots
Complement: 15

Used as divers' base-ship.

TAIWAN

Ministerial

Minister of National Defence:
  Kao K'uei-yuan

Senior Flag Officers

Commander-in-Chief:
  Admiral Soong Chang-chih
Deputy Commanders-in-Chief:
  Vice-Admiral Chih Meng-ping
  Vice-Admiral Tsou Chien
Chief of Staff:
  Vice-Admiral Chen Tung-hai
Commander, Fleet Command:
  Vice-Admiral Li Pei-chou
Commandant of Marine Corps:
  Lieutenant-General Kung Lin-cheng

Diplomatic Representation

Naval Attaché in Washington:
  Rear-Admiral Chiu Hua-ku

Bases

Tsoying, Makung (Pescadores), Keelung.

Personnel

(a) 1978, 7 100 officers and 28 000 men in Navy, 3 000 officers and 26 000 men in Marine Corps. (2 divisions with armour, APCs and heavy artillery).
(b) 2 years conscript service.

Naval Aviation

One squadron of Air Force S-2A tracker ASW aircraft is under Navy operational control.
The Marine Corps operates several observation aircraft and helicopters.

Pennant Numbers

A major revision of warship pennant numbers was reported to have taken place early in 1976.

Strength of the Fleet

Type	Active	Building
Destroyers	22	—
Frigates	11	—
Corvettes	3	—
Submarines (Patrol)	2	—
Fast Attack Craft (Missile)	1	1
Fast Attack Craft (Torpedo)	9	—
Coastal Patrol Craft	14	—
Coastal Minesweepers	14	—
Minesweeping Boats	8	—
LSDs	2	—
Landing Ships	27	—
Utility Landing Craft	22	—
Repair Ship	1	—
Transports	2	—
Survey Ships	4	—
Support Tankers	7	—
Cargo Ship	1	—
Tugs	9	—
Floating Docks	5	—
Service Craft	25	—
Customs	7+	—

Mercantile Marine

Lloyd's Register of Shipping:
  443 vessels of 1 558 713 tons gross

DELETIONS

Destroyers

1975 Lo Yang, Han Yang, Nan Yang (ex-US "Benson" class) (all names transferred to later ships)
1976 Hsien Yang (sunk for film unit)

Frigates

1972 Tai Kang
1972-73 Tai Cho, Tai Chong, Tai (ex-US "Cannon" class)
1975 Tai Hu (ex-US "Cannon" class)
1976 Heng Shan, Lung Shan (APDs)

Submarines

1974-75 3 SX404 small submarines

Repair Ship

1974 Tien Tai

Survey Ship

1976 Yang Ming

Tankers

1972 Tai Yun
1975 Kuichi

Tugs

1975-76 YTLs 3, 8 and 10

Customs

1974 PC122

SUBMARINES

2 Ex-US GUPPY II TYPE

Name	No.	Builders	Launched	Commissioned
HAI SHIH (ex-USS Cutlass, SS 478)	SS 91	Portsmouth Navy Yard	5 Nov 1944	17 Mar 1945
HAI PAO (ex-USS Tusk, SS 426)	SS 92	Federal SB & DD Co, Kearney, New Jersey	8 July 1945	11 April 1946

Displacement, tons: 1 870 standard; 2 420 dived
Length, feet (metres): 307·5 (93·6) oa
Beam, feet (metres): 27·2 (8·3)
Draught, feet (metres): 18 (5·5)
Torpedo tubes: 10—21 in (533 mm); (6 fwd; 4 aft)
Main machinery: 3 diesels (Fairbanks Morse); 4 800 bhp; 2 electric motors (Elliott); 5 400 shp; 2 shafts
Speed, knots: 18 surfaced; 15 dived
Complement: 81 (11 officers, 70 ratings)

Originally fleet-type submarines of the US Navy "Tench" class; extensively modernised under the GUPPY II programme. These submarines each have four 126-cell electric batteries; fitted with snorkel.
Taiwan is the only nation in the Western Pacific currently to operate former US Navy submarines.

Torpedoes: A number of Italian torpedoes suitable for submarine operations were sold to Taiwan in 1976. The submarine torpedo-tubes, "sealed" by the US Navy, must, therefore, have been "unsealed" in Taiwan and these submarines must be considered operational.

Transfers: 91, 12 April 1973; 92, 18 Oct 1973.

HAI SHIH   1972, US Navy

452 TAIWAN

DESTROYERS

9 Ex-US "GEARING" CLASS (FRAM I and II)

Name	No.	Builders	Laid down	Launched	Commissioned
DANG YANG (ex-USS *Lloyd Thomas*, DD 764) (FRAM II)	DD 11	Bethlehem Steel, San Francisco	1945	5 Oct 1945	21 Mar 1947
CHIEN YANG (ex-USS *James E. Kyes*, DD 787)	DD 12	Todd Pacific SY, Seattle, Wash	1945	4 Aug 1945	8 Feb 1946
HAN YANG (ex-USS *Herbert J. Thomas*, DD 833)	DD 15	Bath Iron Works Corp	1944	25 Mar 1945	29 May 1945
LAO YANG (ex-USS *Shelton*, DD 790)	DD 20	Todd Pacific SY, Seattle, Wash	1945	8 Mar 1945	21 June 1946
LIAO YANG (ex-USS *Hanson*, DD 832)	DD 21	Bath Iron Works Corp	1944	11 Mar 1945	11 May 1945
KAI YANG (ex-USS *Richard B. Anderson*, DD 786)	—	Todd Pacific SY, Seattle, Wash	1945	7 July 1945	26 Oct 1945
TE YANG (ex-USS *Sarsfield*, DD 837)	—	Bath Iron Works Corp	1945	27 May 1945	31 July 1945
SHEN YANG (ex-USS *Power*, DD 839)	—	Bath Iron Works Corp	1945	30 June 1945	13 Sept 1945
— (ex-USS *Leonard F. Mason*, DD 852)	—	Bethlehem (Quincy)	1945	4 Jan 1946	28 June 1946

Displacement, tons: 2 425 standard; approx 3 500 full load
Length, feet (metres): 390·5 *(119·0)* oa
Beam, feet (metres): 40·9 *(12·4)*
Draught, feet (metres): 19 *(5·8)*
Aircraft: 1 helicopter and hangar
Missiles: 3 Gabriel *(Dang Yang)*
Guns: 4—5 in *(127 mm)* 38 cal (twin) (Mk 38); 4—40 mm (twins) (*Han Yang* only); several 0·50 cal MG fitted in some ships
A/S weapons: ASROC 8-tube launcher except in DD 11, ex-DD 786 and ex-DD 782; DD 11 has trainable Hedgehog (Mk 15); 6—(2 triple) Mk 32 A/S torpedo tubes
Main engines: 2 geared turbines (General Electric); 60 000 shp; 2 shafts
Boilers: 4
Speed, knots: 34
Complement: approx 275

Dang Yang was modified to a special anti-submarine configuration and reclassified as an escort destroyer (DDE) in 1950; changed again to "straight" DD upon modernisation in 1962. Armament listed above was at time of transfer. *Lao Yang* has twin 5 in gun mounts in "A" and "B" positions with A/S torpedo tubes alongside second funnel; other ships have the "A" and "Y" gun mounts with torpedo tubes in "B" position except *Dang Yang* has torpedo tubes between funnels.
In 1963-64 *Herbert J. Thomas* was modified for protection against biological, chemical, and atomic attack; the ship could be fully sealed with enclosed lookout and control positions, special air-conditioning. Upon transfer to Taiwan *Herbert J. Thomas,* originally transferred for spares but re-activated, assumed name and pennant number of an ex-US "Benson" class destroyer in Taiwan service.
Three of the FRAM I ships were initially scheduled for transfer to Spain; however, they were declined by Spain and allocated to Taiwan.

Deletions: *Chao Yang* (ex-USS *Rowan* DD 782) ran aground 22 Aug 1977 while in tow to Taiwan. Beyond salvage—being stripped for spares.

Electronics: Most have ULQ-6 ECM and WLR-1 and WLR-3 passive warning receivers.

Radar: At time of transfer three of these ships had SPS-37 and SPS-10 search radar antennae on their tripod mast; *Dang Yang* had older SPS-6 and SPS-10 antennae; *Chien Yang* had SPS-40 and SPS-10. *Lao Yang* now has SPS-10 and SPS-29.
Navigation: Mk 5 (TDS).

Sonar: SQS 23 except *Dang Yang* with SQS 29 series.

Transfers: 11, 12 Oct 1972; 12, 18 April 1973; 15, 6 May 1974; 20, 18 April 1973; 21, 18 April 1973; ex-DD 786 and 782, 10 June 1977 by sale; ex-DD 837 and 839, 1 Oct 1977 by sale; ex-DD 852, Jan 1978.

DANG YANG (as USS *Lloyd Thomas*)   1970, US Navy   LIAO YANG (as USS *Hanson*)   1971, US Navy

1 Ex-US "GEARING" CLASS RADAR PICKET (FRAM II)

Name	No.	Builders	Laid down	Launched	Commissioned
FU YANG (ex-USS *Ernest G. Small*, DD 838)	DD 7	Bath Iron Works Corp	1945	14 June 1945	21 Aug 1945

Displacement, tons: 2 425 standard; approx 3 500 full load
Length, feet (metres): 390·5 *(119·0)* oa
Beam, feet (metres): 40·8 *(12·4)*
Draught, feet (metres): 19 *(5·8)*
Missiles: 3 Gabriels
Guns: 6—5 in *(127 mm)* 38 calibre (twin) (Mk 38); 8—40 mm (twin); 4—0·50 cal MG (single)
A/S weapons: 6 (2 triple) torpedo tubes (Mk 32); 2 fixed Hedgehogs
Main engines: 2 geared turbines; (General Electric); 60 000 shp; 2 shafts
Boilers: 4 Babcock & Wilcox
Speed, knots: 34
Complement: approx 275

Converted to a radar picket destroyer (DDR) during 1952 and subsequently modernised under the FRAM II programme; redesignated as a "straight" destroyer (DD), but retained specialised electronic equipment. Not fitted with helicopter flight deck or hangar. The 40 mm guns were installed after transfer to Taiwan.

Fire control: US Mk 25 and Mk 37; Taiwan built Mk 51 (adapted from F86 aircraft).

Radar: At time of transfer *Fu Yang* had SPS-37 and SPS-10 search radars on forward tripod mast, and large TACAN antenna on second tripod mast.
Navigation: Mk 5 (TDS).

Sonar: SQS-29 (hull-mounted); SQS-10 (VDS)

Transfer: Feb 1971.

FU YANG

8 Ex-US "ALLEN M. SUMNER" CLASS

Name	No.	Builders	Laid down	Launched	Commissioned
HSIANG YANG (ex-USS *Brush*, DD 745)	DD 1	Bethlehem Steel, Staten Island	1943	28 Dec 1943	17 April 1944
HENG YANG (ex-USS *Samuel N. Moore*, DD 747)	DD 2	Bethlehem Steel, Staten Island	1943	23 Feb 1944	24 June 1944
HUA YANG (ex-USS *Bristol*, DD 857)	DD 3	Bethlehem Steel, San Pedro	1944	29 Oct 1944	17 Mar 1945
YUEN YANG (ex-USS *Haynsworth*, DD 700)	DD 5	Federal SB & DD Co	1943	15 April 1944	22 June 1944
HUEI YANG (ex-USS *English*, DD 696)	DD 6	Federal SB & DD Co	1943	27 Feb 1944	4 May 1944
PO YANG (ex-USS *Maddox*, DD 731)	DD 10	Bath Iron Works Corp	1943	19 Mar 1944	2 June 1944
LO YANG (ex-USS *Taussig*, DD 746)	DD 14	Bethlehem Steel, Staten Island	1943	25 Jan 1944	20 May 1944
NAN YANG (ex-USS *John W. Thomason*, DD 760)	DD 17	Bethlehem Steel, San Francisco	1944	30 Sept 1944	11 Oct 1945

Displacement, tons: 2 200 standard; 3 320 full load
Length, feet (metres): 376·5 *(114·8)* oa
Beam, feet (metres): 40·9 *(12·4)*
Draught, feet (metres): 19 *(5·8)*
Missiles: 7 Gabriels (1 triple, 2 twin) in DD 1, 3 and 5
Guns: 6—5 in *(127 mm)* 38 calibre (twin) (Mk 38); 4—3 in *(76 mm)* 50 calibre (2 twin); some including *Heng Yang* and *Yuen Yang*, have 8—40 mm (1 quad, 2 twin); several ·50 cal MG (single) in most ships
A/S weapons: 6 (2 triple) A/S torpedo tubes (Mk 32); 2 fixed Hedgehogs; depth charges in some ships
Main engines: 2 geared turbines (General Electric or Westinghouse); 60 000 shp; 2 shafts
Boilers: 4 Babcock & Wilcox
Speed, knots: 34
Complement: approx 275

These ships have not been modernised under the FRAM programmes, but retain their original configurations with removal of original torpedo tubes, and 40 mm and 20 mm guns, and installation of improved electronic equipment. Secondary gun battery now varies; during the 1950s most of these ships were rearmed with six 3 in guns (two single alongside forward funnel and two twin amidships); number retained apparently varies from ship to ship, with some ships retaining original 40 mm guns. Tripod mast fitted.
Lo Yang and *Nan Yang* have names and numbers previously assigned to older ex-US destroyers.

Fire control: US Mk 25, 37 and 51.

Radar: Surface search: SPS-6 and SPS-10 (*Po Yang* has SPS-40 and SPS-10, *Nan Yang* has SPS-37 and SPS-10 and *Lo Yang* has SPS-10 and SPS-29.
Navigation: Mk 5 (TDS).

Transfers: 1, 9 Dec 1969; 2, Feb 1970; 3, 9 Dec 1969; 5, 12 May 1970; 6, Sept 1970; 10, 6 July 1972; 14, 6 May 1974; 17, 6 May 1974.

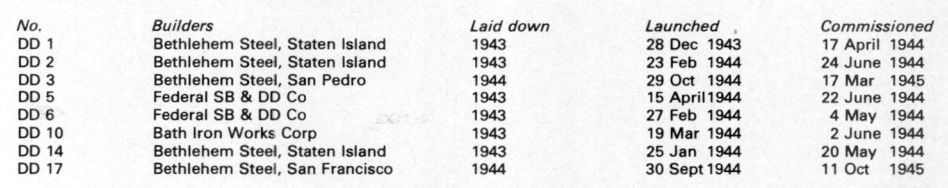

HSIANG YANG   *1971, US Navy*

HENG YANG   *"Ships of the World"*

4 Ex-US "FLETCHER" CLASS

Name	No.	Builders	Laid down	Launched	Commissioned
KWEI YANG (ex-USS *Twining*, DD 540)	DD 8	Bethlehem Steel, San Francisco	1943	11 July 1943	1 Dec 1943
CHIANG YANG (ex-USS *Mullany*, DD 528)	DD 9	Bethlehem Steel, San Francisco	1942	12 Oct 1942	23 April 1943
AN YANG (ex-USS *Kimberly*, DD 521)	DD 18	Bethlehem Steel, Staten Island	1942	4 Feb 1943	22 May 1943
KUEN YANG (ex-USS *Yarnall*, DD 541)	DD 19	Bethlehem Steel, San Francisco	1943	25 July 1943	30 Dec 1943

Displacement, tons: 2 100 standard; 3 050 full load
Length, feet (metres): 376·5 *(114·7)* oa
Beam, feet (metres): 35·9 *(11·9)*
Draught, feet (metres): 18 *(5·5)*
Missiles: Sea Chaparral launcher (SAM) above "X" 5 in mount
Guns: 5—5 in *(127 mm)* 38 calibre (single) except 4 guns in *Chiang Yang* (Mk 30); 5—3 in *(76 mm)* 50 calibre in *Kwei Yang* and *Chiang Yang*; 6—40 mm (twin) in *An Yang* and *Kuen Yang*
A/S weapons: 6 (2 triple) A/S torpedo tubes (Mk 32) in *Kwei Yang* and *Chiang Yang*; 2 fixed Hedgehogs and depth charges in some ships
Torpedo tubes: 5—21 in *(533mm)* (quintuple) in *Kuen Yang*
Main engines: 2 geared turbines (General Electric in *An Yang*, Allis Chalmers in *Kuen Yang*, Westinghouse in others); 60 000 shp; 2 shafts
Boilers: 4 Babcock & Wilcox
Speed, knots: 36
Complement: approx 250

All now have tripod mast. Only *Kuen Yang* retains anti-ship torpedo tubes installed between second funnel and third 5 in gun mount. Reportedly, the ship has been fitted for minelaying.

Electronics: BLR-1 or SLR-2 passive detection.

Fire control: US Mk 25 and 37.

Radar: SPS 6 and 10 (DD 8, 9, 19); SPS 10 and 12 (DD 18). Navigation: Mk 5 (TDS).

Transfers: 8, 6 Oct 1971 (sale); 9, 6 Oct 1971 (sale); 18, 2 June 1967; 19, 10 June 1968. Last pair purchased Jan 1974.

KEUN YANG (5 main guns)   *C. B. Mulholland*

454 TAIWAN

FRIGATES

10 Ex-US "APD 37" and "APD 87" CLASSES

Name	No.	Builders	Laid down	Launched	Commissioned
YU SHAN (ex-USS *Kinzer*, APD 91/DE 232)	PF 32	Charleston Navy Yard, South Carolina	1943	9 Dec 1943	1 Nov 1944
HUA SHAN (ex-USS *Donald W. Wolf*, APD 129/DE 713)	PF 33	Defoe SB Co, Bay City, Michigan	1944	22 July 1944	13 April 1945
WEN SHAN (ex-USS *Gantner*, APD 42/DE 60)	PF 34	Bethlehem SB Co, Higham, Mass	1942	17 April 1943	23 July 1943
FU SHAN (ex-USS *Truxton*, APD 98/DE 282)	PF 35	Charleston Navy Yard, South Carolina	1943	9 Mar 1943	9 July 1943
LU SHAN (ex-USS *Bull*, APD 78/DE 693)	PF 36	Defoe SB Co, Bay City, Michigan	1942	25 Mar 1943	12 Aug 1943
SHOA SHAN (ex-USS *Kline*, APD 120/DE 687)	PF 37	Bethlehem, Quincy, Mass	1944	27 June 1944	18 Oct 1944
TAI SHAN (ex-USS *Register*, APD 92/DE 233)	PF 38	Charleston Navy Yard, South Carolina	1943	20 Jan 1944	11 Jan 1945
KANG SHAN (ex-USS *G. W. Ingram*, APD 43/DE 62)	PF 42	Bethlehem SB Co, Higham, Mass	1942	8 May 1943	11 Aug 1943
CHUNG SHAN (ex-USS *Blessman*, APD 48/DE 69)	PF 43	Bethlehem SB Co, Higham, Mass	1943	19 June 1943	19 Sept 1943
TIEN SHAN (ex-USS *Kleinsmith*, APD 134/DE 718)	APD 215	Defoe SB Co, Bay City, Michigan	1944	27 Jan 1945	12 June 1945

Displacement, tons: 1 400 standard; 2 130 full load
Length, feet (metres): 300 *(91·4)* wl; 306 *(93·3)* oa
Beam, feet (metres): 37 *(11·3)*
Draught, feet (metres): 12·6 *(3·2)*
Guns: 2—5 in *(127 mm)* 38 cal; 6—40 mm (twin); 4—20 mm (single) except *Hua Shan* and possibly others have 8 guns (twin mounts)
A/S weapons: 6—12·75 in *(324 mm)* torpedo tubes (Mk 32 triple) except some have two Hedgehogs; depth charges
Main engines: Geared turbines (General Electric) with electric drive; 12 000 shp; 2 shafts
Boilers: 2 Foster Wheeler
Speed, knots: 23·6
Complement: approx 200

All begun as destroyer escorts (DE), but converted during construction or after completion to high speed transports carrying 160 troops, commandoes, or frogmen.
The ex-USS *Walter B Cobb* (APD 106/DE 596) transferred to Taiwan in 1966 was lost at sea while under tow to Taiwan; replaced by ex-USS *Bull*.

Appearance: APD 37 class has high bridge; APD 87 class has low bridge. Radars and fire control equipment vary. Davits amidships can hold four LCVP-type landing craft but usually carry only one each.

Fire control: Most have US Mk 26 Mod 4.

Gunnery: All ships are now believed to have been refitted with a second 5 in gun aft. One twin 40 mm gun mount is forward of bridge and two twin mounts are amidships.

Radar: Most have SPS-5. Some have Decca 707 in addition.

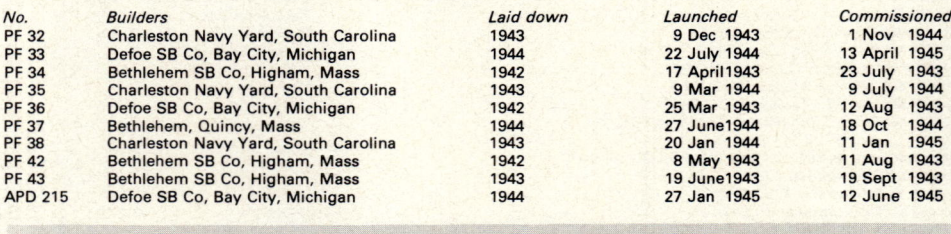

Transfers: PF 32, April 1962; 33, May 1965; 34, May 1966; 35, March 1966; 36, Aug 1966; 37, March 1966; 38, Oct 1966; 42, July 1967; 43, July 1967; APD 215, June 1967.

HUA SHAN *C. B. Mulholland*

1 Ex-US "RUDDEROW" CLASS

Name	No.	Builders	Laid down	Launched	Commissioned
TAI YUAN (ex-USS *Riley*, DE 579)	PF 27	Bethlehem Steel Co, Higham, Mass	1943	29 Dec 1943	13 Mar 1944

Displacement, tons: 1 450 standard; approx 2 000 full load
Length, feet (metres): 300 *(91·4)* wl; 306 *(93·3)* oa
Beam, feet (metres): 37 *(11·3)*
Draught, feet (metres): 14 *(4·3)*
Guns: 2—5 in *(127 mm)* 38 calibre (single); 4—40 mm (twin); 4—20 mm (single)
A/S weapons: 6—(2 triple) A/S torpedo tubes (Mk 32); 1 Hedgehog; depth charges
Main engines: Geared turbines (General Electric) with electric drive; 12 000 shp; 2 shafts
Boilers: 2 Foster Wheeler
Speed, knots: 24
Complement: approx 200

Refitted with tripod mast and platforms before bridge for 20 mm guns. (Hedgehog is on main deck, behind forward 5 in mount). Fitted for minelaying.
Designation changed from DE to PF in 1975.

Radar: SPS 6 and 10.

Transfer: 10 July 1968; sale March 1974.

TAI YUAN *C. B. Mulholland*

CORVETTES

3 Ex-US "AUK" CLASS

Name	No.	Builders	Commissioned
WU SHENG (ex-USS *Redstart*, MSF 378)	PCE 66	Savannah Machine & Foundry Co, Georgia	4 April 1945
CHU YUNG (ex-USS *Waxwing*, MSF 389)	PCE 67	American SB Co, Cleveland, Ohio	6 Aug 1945
MO LING (ex-USS *Steady*, MSF 118)	PCE 70	American SB Co, Cleveland, Ohio	16 Nov 1942

Displacement, tons: 890 standard; 1 250 full load
Dimensions, feet (metres): 215 wl; 221·1 oa × 32·1 × 10·8 *(70·4; 61·4 × 10·5 × 3·5)*
Guns: 2—3 in *(76 mm)* 50 cal (single); 4—40 mm (twin); 4—20 mm (twin)
A/S weapons: 1 Hedgehog; 3—12·75 in *(324 mm)* torpedo tubes (Mk32 triple); depth charges
Mines: Minerails fitted in *Chu Yung* (1975).
Main engines: Diesel-electric (General Motors diesels); 3 530 bhp; 2 shafts = 18 knots
Complement: approx 80

Minesweeping equipment removed and second 3 in gun fitted aft in Taiwan service. One fitted for minelaying.

Transfers: 66, July 1965; 67, Nov 1965; 70, March 1968.

WU SHENG

TAIWAN 455

LIGHT FORCES

1 + 1 FAST ATTACK CRAFT (MISSILE)

LUNG CHIANG PGG 582 + 1

Displacement, tons: 240 standard; 270 full load
Dimensions, feet (metres): 164.5 × 23.9 × 7.5 *(50.2 × 7.3 × 2.3)*
Missiles: 4 Otomat launchers
Guns: 1—76 mm OTO Melara; 2—30 mm (Emerson) (twin); 2—0.50 cal MG
Main engines: CODAG; 3 Avco Lycoming gas turbines; 13 800 shp (15 000 max); 3 diesels; 2 880 shp; 3 shafts (cp propellers)
Speed, knots: 20 knots (diesels); 40 knots (gas turbines)
Range, miles: 2 700 at 12 knots (1 diesel); 1 900 at 20 knots (3 diesels); 700 at 40 knots (3 gas turbines)
Complement: 34 (5 officers, 29 ratings)

Ordered from Tacoma Boatbuilding Co Inc, Washington, USA. The first built at Tacoma, the second in Taiwan. Designated Patrol Ship Multi-Mission Mk 5 (PSMM Mk 5). Originally to be a class of 15 but 13 cancelled for financial reasons and to be replaced by Taiwan—designed Patrol Craft.

Fire control: NA 10 Mod 0 GFCS with Selenia RAN 11 L/X and IPN 10. Otomat MFCS.

PSMM Mk 5

2 79 ft TYPE (FAST ATTACK CRAFT—TORPEDO)

Name	No.	Builders	Commissioned
FU KWO	—	Hutchins Yacht Corp, Jacksonville, Florida	—
TIAN KWO	—	Hutchins Yacht Corp, Jacksonville, Florida	—

Displacement, tons: 46 light; 53 full load
Dimensions, feet (metres): 79 oa × 23.25 × 5.5 *(25.9 × 7.6 × 1.8)*
Guns: 1—40 mm; 2—0.50 cal MG (single)
Torpedo launchers: 2
Main engines: 3 petrol engines; 3 shafts = 39 knots max; 32 knots cruising
Complement: 12

Transferred to Taiwan on 1 Sept 1957.

2 71 ft TYPE (FAST ATTACK CRAFT—TORPEDO)

Name	No.	Builders	Commissioned
FAAN KONG	—	Annapolis Yacht Yard, Annapolis, Maryland	—
SAO TANG	—	Annapolis Yacht Yard, Annapolis, Maryland	—

Displacement, tons: 39 light; 46 full load
Dimensions, feet (metres): 71 oa × 19 × 5 *(23.3 × 6.3 × 1.6)*
Guns: 1—20 mm; 4—50 cal MG (twin)
Torpedo launchers: 2 (?)
Main engines: 3 petrol engines; 3 shafts = 42 knots max; 32 knots cruising
Complement: 12

Transferred to Taiwan on 19 Aug 1957 and 1 Nov 1957, respectively.

2 JAPANESE TYPE (FAST ATTACK CRAFT—TORPEDO)

Name	No.	Builders	Commissioned
FUH CHOW	—	Mitsubishi SB Co	—
HSUEH CHIH	—	Mitsubishi SB Co	—

Displacement, tons: 33 light; 40 full load
Dimensions, feet (metres): 69 oa × 19.9 *(22.6 × 6.5)*
Guns: 1—40 mm; 2—20 mm (twin)
Torpedo launchers: 2—18 in *(457 mm)*
Main engines: 3 petrol engines; 3 shafts = 40 knots max; 27 knots cruising
Complement: 12

Transferred to Taiwan on 1 June 1957 and 6 Nov 1957, respectively.

Note: At least three additional fast attack craft (torpedo) are known to be in service; details are not available.

FUH CHOW (forward 40 mm unshipped)

14 COASTAL PATROL CRAFT

Displacement, tons: approx 30 tons
Gun: 1—40 mm

Small patrol boats designated PB. Constructed in Taiwan with the first of a reported 14 units completed about 1971. These are believed the first warships of indigenous Taiwan construction.

PB 1

456 TAIWAN

MINEWARFARE FORCES

Note: Previously reported transfer of ex-USS *Bold* and *Bulwark* ("Agile" class MSOs) did not take place.

14 US "ADJUTANT" CLASS (MINESWEEPERS—COASTAL)

Name	No.	Builders	Commissioned
YUNG PING (ex-US *MSC 140*)	MSC 155	USA	June 1955
YUNG AN (ex-US *MSC 123*)	MSC 156	USA	June 1955
YUNG NIEN (ex-US *MSC 277*)	MSC 157	USA	Dec 1958
YUNG CHOU (ex-US *MSC 278*)	MSC 158	USA	July 1959
YUNG HSIN (ex-US *MSC 302*)	MSC 159	USA	Mar 1965
YUNG JU (ex-US *MSC 300*)	MSC 160	USA	April 1965
YUNG LO (ex-US *MSC 306*)	MSC 161	USA	June 1960
YUNG FU (ex-*Diest*, ex-USS *Macaw* MSC 77)	MSC 162	USA	1953
YUNG CHING (ex-*Eekloo*, ex-US *MSC 101*)	MSC 163	USA	1955
YUNG SHAN (ex-*Lier*, ex-US *MSC 63*)	MSC 164	USA	1954
YUNG CHENG (ex-*Maaseick*, ex-US *MSC 78*)	MSC 165	USA	1955
YUNG CHI (ex-*Charleroi*, ex-US *MSC 152*)	MSC 166	USA	1955
YUNG JEN (ex-*St Nicholas*, ex-US *MSC 64*)	MSC 167	USA	1953
YUNG SUI (ex-*Diksmude*, ex-US *MSC 65*)	MSC 168	USA	1954

Displacement, tons: approx 380 full load
Dimensions, feet (metres): 144 oa × 28 × 8·5 *(47·2 × 9·2 × 2·8)*
Guns: 2—20 mm (twin)
Main engines: Diesels (General Motors); 2 shafts = 13·5 knots
Complement: 40 to 50

YUNG SHAN (pole mast aft)

Non-magnetic, wood-hulled minesweepers built in the United States specifically for transfer to allied navies. First seven units listed above transferred to Taiwan upon completion: MSC 160 in April 1965, and MSC 161 in June 1966.
All are of similar design; the ex-Belgian ships have a small boom aft on a pole mast. They carried a single 40 mm gun forward in Belgian service.

Transfers: Last seven originally built for Belgium and transferred to Taiwan Nov 1969. *De Panne* (ex-US *MSC 131*) was also transferred but has been stripped for spares.

YUNG CHOU (no pole mast aft)

1 MINESWEEPING BOAT

MSB 12 (ex-US *MSB 4*)

Former US Army minesweeping boat; assigned hull number MSB 4 in US Navy and transferred to Taiwan in Dec 1961.

7 MINESWEEPING LAUNCHES

MSML 1	MSML 5	MSML 7	MSML 11
MSML 3	MSML 6	MSML 8	

Fifty-foot minesweeping launches built in the United States and transferred to Taiwan in March 1961.

AMPHIBIOUS FORCES

1 Ex-US "ASHLAND" CLASS (LSD)

Name	No.	Builders	Commissioned
CHUNG CHENG (ex-USS *White Marsh*, LSD 8, ex-*Tung Hai*)	LSD 639 (ex-LSD 191)	Moore Dry Dock Co, Oakland, California	2 July 1945

Displacement, tons: 4 790 standard; 8 700 full load
Dimensions, feet (metres): 454 wl; 457·8 oa × 72 × 18 *(148·8; 150 × 23·6 × 5·9)*
Guns: 12—40 mm (2 quad and 2 twin)
Main engines: Skinner Unaflow; 7 400 ihp; 2 shafts = 15 knots
Boilers: 2

Launched on 19 July 1943. Designed to serve as parent ship for landing craft and coastal craft. Transferred from the US Navy to Taiwan on 17 Nov 1960. Purchased May 1976.
Renamed to honour the late President Chiang Kai-Shek on 18 Feb 1976; pennant number also changed.

CHUNG CHENG (as LSD 191)

1 Ex-US "CASA GRANDE" CLASS (LSD)

Name	No.	Builders	Commissioned
CHEN HAI (Ex-USS *Fort Marion*, LSD 22)	—	Gulf SB Co, Chickasaw, Alabama	29 Jan 1946

Displacement, tons: 4 790 standard; 9 375 full load
Dimensions, feet (metres): 475·4 oa × 76·2 × 18 *(155·8 × 24·9 × 5·9)*
Guns: 12—40 mm (2 quad and 2 twin)
Main engines: Geared turbines; 7 000 shp; 2 shafts = 15·4 knots
Boilers: 2

Launched on 22 May 1945 and transferred to Taiwan on 15 April 1977.
Docking well is 392 × 44 feet; can accommodate 3 LCUs or 18 LCMs or 32 LVTs (amphibious tractors) in docking well. Fitted with helicopter platform over well (which also can be used for truck parking; see photograph).

Electronics: UPX-12 IFF.

Fire control: US Mk 26 Mod 4.

Radar: SPS-5.

"CASA GRANDE" Class   1965, US Navy

22 Ex-US "LST 1-510" and "511-1152" CLASSES

Name	No.
CHUNG HAI (ex-USS LST 755)	201
CHUNG TING (ex-USS LST 537)	203
CHUNG HSING (ex-USS LST 557)	204
CHUNG CHIEN (ex-USS LST 716)	205
CHUNG CHI (ex-USS LST 1017)	206
CHUNG SHUN (ex-USS LST 732)	208
CHUNG LIEN (ex-USS LST 1050)	209
CHUNG YUNG (ex-USS LST 574)	210
CHUNG KUANG (ex-USS LST 503)	216
CHUNG SUO (ex-USS *Bradley County*, LST 400)	217
CHUNG CHIE (ex-USS *Berkley County*, LST 279)	218
CHUNG CHUAN (ex-LST 1030)	221
CHUNG SHENG (ex-LST 211, ex-USS LSTH 1033)	222
CHUNG FU (ex-USS *Iron County*, LST 840)	223
CHUNG CHENG (ex-USS *Lafayette County*, LST 859)	224
CHUNG CHIANG (ex-USS *San Bernardino County*, LST 1110)	225
CHUNG CHIH (ex-USS *Sagadahoc County*, LST 1091)	226
CHUNG MING (ex-USS *Sweetwater County*, LST 1152)	227
CHUNG SHU (ex-USS LST 520)	228
CHUNG WAN (ex-USS LST 535)	229
CHUNG PANG (ex-USS LST 578)	230
CHUNG YEH (ex-USS *Sublette County*, LST 1144)	231

Displacement, tons: 1 653 standard; 4 080 full load
Dimensions, feet (metres): 316 wl; 328 oa × 50 × 14 *(103·6; 107·5 × 16·4 × 4·6)*
Guns: Varies; up to 10—40 mm (2 twin, 6 single) with some modernised ships rearmed with 2—3 in (single) and 6—40 mm (twin)
 Several 20 mm (twin or single)
Main engines: Diesel (General Motors); 1 700 bhp; 2 shafts = 11·6 knots
Complement: Varies: 100 to 125 in most ships

Constructed during World War II. These ships have been rebuilt in Taiwan. Hull numbers of LSTs are being changed to 600 series.

Appearance: Some have davits forward and aft.

Electronics: Some have UPX-5 or 12 IFF.

Radar: US SO-1, 2 or 8.

Transfers: 201-208, 1946; 209 and 222, 1947; 228, 1948; 217, 223-230, 1958; 210, 1959; 216 and 218, 1960; 231, 1961.

CHUNG CHIE (*Ho Shan* alongside) 1974

CHUNG SHUN

1 Ex-US "LST 511-1152" CLASS (FLAGSHIP)

Name	No.	Builders	Commissioned
KAO HSIUNG (ex-*Chung Hai*, LST 219, ex-USS *Dukes County*, LST 735)	AGC 1	Dravo Corp, Neville Island, Penn	26 April 1944

Displacement, tons: 1 653 standard; 4 080 full load
Dimensions, feet (metres): 316 wl; 328 oa × 50 × 14 *(103·6; 107·5 × 16·4 × 4·6)*
Guns: Several 40 mm (twin)
Main engines: Diesel (General Motors); 1 700 bhp; 2 shafts = 11·6 knots

Launched on 11 March 1944. Transferred to Taiwan in May 1957 for service as an LST. Converted to a flagship for amphibious operations and renamed and redesignated (AGC) in 1964. Purchased Nov 1974.
Note lattice mast atop bridge structure, modified bridge levels, and antenna mountings on main deck.

KAO HSIUNG

4 Ex-US "LSM-1" CLASS

Name	No.
MEI CHIN (ex-USS LSM 155)	LSM 341
MEI SUNG (ex-USS LSM 457)	LSM 347
MEI PING (ex-USS LSM 471)	LSM 353
MEI LO (ex-USS LSM 362)	LSM 356

Displacement, tons: 1 095 full load
Dimensions, feet (metres): 196·5 wl; 203·5 oa × 34·5 × 7·3 *(66·4; 66·7 × 11·3 × 2·4)*
Guns: 2—40 mm (twin); 4 or 8—20 mm (4 single or 4 twin)
Main engines: Diesels; 2 800 bhp; 2 shafts = 12·5 knots
Complement: 65 to 75

Constructed during World War II. Originally numbered in the 200-series in Taiwan service. These ships are being rebuilt in Taiwan.

Radar: Surface search: SO-8.

Transfers: 341 and 347 1946; 353, 1956; 356, 1962.

MEI PING

22 Ex-US "LCU 501" and "LCU 1466" CLASSES

Name	No.	Name	No.
HO CHUN (ex-LCU 892)	481	HO SHUN (ex-LCU 1225)	494
HO TSUNG (ex-LCU 1213)	482	HO YUNG (ex-LCU 1271)	495
HO CHUNG (ex-LCU 849)	484	HO CHIEN (ex-LCU 1278)	496
HO CHANG (ex-LCU 512)	485	HO CHI (ex-LCU 1212)	401
HO CHENG (ex-LCU 1145)	486	HO HOEI (ex-LCU 1218)	402
HO SHAN (ex-LCU 1596)	488	HO YAO (ex-LCU 1244)	403
HO CHUAN (ex-LCU 1597)	489	HO DENG (ex-LCU 1367)	404
HO SENG (ex-LCU 1598)	490	HO FENG (ex-LCU 1397)	405
HO MENG (ex-LCU 1599)	491	HO CHAO (ex-LCU 1429)	406
HO MOU (ex-LCU 1600)	492	HO TENG (ex-LCU 1452)	407
HO SHOU (ex-LCU 1601)	493	HO CHIE (ex-LCU 700)	SB1

"LCU 501" Class

Displacement, tons: 158 light; 268 full load
Dimensions, feet (metres): 115·1 oa × 32 × 4·2 *(37·7 × 10·5 × 1·4)*
Guns: 2—20 mm (single); some units also may have 2—0·50 cal MG
Main engines: 3 diesels; 675 bhp; 3 shafts = 10 knots
Complement: 10 to 25

"LCU 1466" Class

Displacement, tons: 130 light; 280 full load
Dimensions, feet (metres): 115·1 oa × 34 × 4·1 *(37·7 × 10·5 × 1·4)*
Guns: 3—20 mm (single); some units may also have 2—0·50 cal MG
Main engines: 3 diesels; 675 bhp; 3 shafts = 10 knots
Complement: 15 to 25

The LCU 501 series were built in the United States during World War II; initially designated LCT(6) series. The six of LCU 1466 series built by Ishikawajima Heavy Industries Co, Tokyo, Japan, for transfer to Taiwan; completed in March 1955. All originally numbered in 200-series; subsequently changed to 400 series.

Transfers: 401-407; Nov/Dec 1959. SB1, 494-496; Jan/Feb 1958. Remainder: 1946-48.

458 TAIWAN

SURVEY SHIPS

1 Ex-US C1-M-AV1 TYPE

Name	No.	Builders	Commissioned
CHIU HUA (ex-USNS *Sgt. George D. Keathley*, T-AGS 35, ex-T-APC 117)	AGS 564	—	—

Displacement, tons: 6 090 tons
Dimensions, feet (metres): 338·8 oa × 50·3 × 17·5 *(111·1 × 16·5 × 5·7)*
Guns: 1—40 mm; 2—20 mm
Main engine: Diesel; 1 750 bhp; 1 shaft = 11·5 knots
Complement: 72

Built in 1945 as merchant ship; subsequently acquired by US Army for use as transport, but assigned to Navy's Military Sea Transportation Service in 1950 and designated as coastal transport (T-APC 117). Refitted for oceanographic survey work in 1966-67 and redesignated T-AGS 35. Transferred to Taiwan on 29 March 1972 and by sale 19 May 1976.

1 Ex-US "SOTOYOMO" CLASS

Name	No.	Builders	Commissioned
CHIU LIEN (ex-USS *Geronimo*, ATA 207)	AGS 563	Gulfport Boiler & Welding Works, Port Arthur, Texas	1 Mar 1945

Displacement, tons: 835
Dimensions, feet (metres): 143 oa × 33·9 × 13·2 *(46·9 × 11·1 × 4·3)*
Main engine: Diesel-electric (General Motors); 1 500 bhp; 1 shaft = 13 knots

Former US Navy auxiliary tug. Launched 4 Jan 1945. Transferred to Taiwan in Feb 1969 and converted to surveying ship. Currently employed as research ship for the Institute of Oceanology. Civilian manned. Painted white.

1 Ex-US "LSIL 351" CLASS

Name	No.	Builders	Commissioned
LIEN CHANG (ex-USS *LSIL 1017*)	AGSC 466	Albina Engineering & Machinery Works, Portland, Oregon	12 April 1944

Dimensions, feet (metres): 153 wl; 159 oa × 23·6 × 5·6 *(50·2; 52·1 × 7·7 × 1·8)*
Guns: 2—40 mm (twin); several 20 mm
Main engines: 2 diesels (General Motors); 2 320 bhp; 2 shafts = 14 knots

Launched on 14 March 1944. Transferred to Taiwan in Mar 1958. Employed as surveying ship; retains basic LSIL appearance.

1 SURVEY SHIP

WU KANG

Of 907 tons, launched 1943 with complement of 59.

CHIU LIEN

MISCELLANEOUS

SERVICE FORCES

Notes: (a) Reported that USS *Tappahannock*, AO 43 is to be transferred.
(b) ex-USS *Grapple* ARS 7 transferred 1 Dec 1977 as *Ta Hu*

1 Ex-US "AMPHION" CLASS (REPAIR SHIP)

Name	No.	Builders	Commissioned
YU TAI (ex-USS *Cadmus*, AR 14)	ARG 521	Tampa Shipbuilding Co, Tampa, Florida	23 April 1946

Displacement, tons: 7 826 standard; 14 490 full load
Dimensions, feet (metres): 456 wl; 492 oa × 70 × 27·5 *(149·5; 161·3 × 22·9 × 9)*
Gun: 1—5 in *(127 mm)* 38 calibre
Main engines: Turbines (Westinghouse); 8 500 shp; 1 shaft = 16·5 knots
Boilers: 2 (Foster Wheeler)

Launched on 5 Aug 1945. Transferred to Taiwan on 15 Jan 1974. Replaced *Tien Tai* (ex-USS *Tutuila*, ARG-4).

1 Ex-US "ACHELOUS" CLASS (TRANSPORT)

Name	No.	Builders	Commissioned
WU TAI (ex-*Sung Shan*, ARL 336, ex-USS *Agenor*, ARL 3, ex-*LST 490*)	AP 520	Kaiser Co, Vancouver, Wash	20 Aug 1943

Displacement, tons: 1 625 light; 4 100 full load
Dimensions, feet (metres): 316 wl; 328 oa × 50 × 11 *(103·6; 107·5 × 16·4 × 3·6)*
Guns: 8—40 mm (quad)
Main engines: Diesels (General Motors); 1 800 bhp; 2 shafts = 11·6 knots
Troops: 600

Begun for the US Navy as an LST completed as a repair ship for landing craft (ARL). Launched on 3 April 1943. Transferred to France in 1951 for service in Indochina; subsequently returned to United States and retransferred to Taiwan on 15 Sept 1957
Employed as a repair ship (ARL 336, subsequently ARL 236) until converted in 1973-1974 to troop transport.

WU TAI (as repair ship)

1 TAIWAN TYPE (TRANSPORT)

Name	No.	Builders	Commissioned
LING YUEN	522	Taiwan Shipbuilding Co, Keelung	15 Aug 1975

Measurement, tons: 2 510 DWT; 3 040 gross
Dimensions, feet (metres): 328·7 × 47·9 × 16·4 *(100·2 × 14·6 × 5)*
Guns: 2—20 mm (single); 2—0·5 in MG (single)
Main engines: Diesel 6 cyl
Complement: 55
Accommodation for troops: 500

Designed by Chinese First Naval Shipyard at Tsoying.
Launched 27 Jan 1975.

LING YUEN 1975

1 JAPANESE TYPE (SUPPORT TANKER)

Name	No.	Builders	Commissioned
WAN SHOU	AOG 512	Ujina Shipbuilding Co, Hiroshima, Japan	1 Nov 1969

Displacement, tons: 1 049 light; 4 150 full load
Dimensions, feet (metres): 283·8 oa × 54 × 18 *(93·1 × 17·7 × 5·9)*
Guns: 2—40 mm (single); 2—20 mm
Main engine: Diesel; 2 100 bhp; 1 shaft = 13 knots
Complement: 70
Cargo: 73 600 gallons fuel; 62 000 gallons water

Employed in resupply of offshore islands.

TAIWAN 459

3 Ex-US "PATAPSCO" CLASS (SUPPORT TANKERS)

Name	No.	Builders	Commissioned
CHANG PEI (ex-USS *Pecatonica* AOG 57)	AOG 507	Cargill, Inc, Savage Minnesota	28 Nov 1945
LUNG CHUAN (ex-HMNZS *Endeavour*, ex-USS *Namakagon*, AOG 53)	AOG 515	Cargill, Inc, Savage, Minnesota	1945
HSIN LUNG (ex-USS *Elkhorn* AOG 7)	AOG 517	Cargill, Inc, Savage, Minnesota	12 Feb 1944

Displacement, tons: 1 850 light; 4 335 full load
Dimensions, feet (metres): 292 wl; 310·75 oa × 48·5 × 15·7 *(95·7; 101·9 × 15·9 × 5·1)*
Main engines: Diesels (General Motors); 3 300 bhp; 2 shafts = 14 knots

Chang Pei was launched on 17 March 1945 and transferred to Taiwan on 24 April 1961. The ex-USS *Namakagon* was launched on 4 Nov 1944 and transferred to New Zealand on 5 Oct 1962 for use as an Antarctic resupply ship; stengthened for polar operations and renamed *Endeavour*; returned to the US Navy on 29 June 1971 and retransfered to Taiwan the same date. *Hsin Lung* was launched on 15 May 1943 and was transferred to Taiwan on 1 July 1972. All three transferred by sale 19 May 1976.

Radar: *Chang Pei* has SPS-21.

CHANG PEI

1 Ex-US YO TYPE (SUPPORT TANKER)

Name	No.	Builders	Commissioned
SZU MING (ex-US *YO 198*)	AOG 504 (ex-*AOG 304*)	Manitowoc SB Co, Manitowoc, Wisconsin	1945

Displacement, tons: 650 light; 1 595 full load
Dimensions, feet (metres): 174 oa × 32 *(57·1 × 10·5)*
Guns: 1—40 mm; 5—20 mm (single)
Main engine: Diesel (Union); 560 bhp; 1 shaft = 10·5 knots
Complement: approx 65

Transferred to Taiwan in Dec 1949. Reportedly placed in reserve in 1976.

Radar: SO-8.

2 JAPANESE TYPE (SUPPORT TANKERS)

Also reported to be in service.

1 Ex-US "MARK" CLASS (CARGO SHIP)

Name	No.	Builders	Commissioned
YUNG KANG (ex-USS *Mark*, AKL 12, ex-*AG 143* ex-US Army *FS 214*)	AKL 514	Higgins	1944

Displacement, tons: approx 700
Dimensions, feet (metres): 176·5 oa × 32·8 × 10 *(57·8 × 10·7 × 3·3)*
Guns: 2—20 mm
Main engine: Diesel; 1 000 bhp; 1 shaft = 10 knots

Built as a small cargo ship (freight and supply) for the US Army. Transferred to US Navy on 30 Sept 1947; operated in South East Asia from 1963 until transferred to Taiwan on 1 June 1971 and by sale 19 May 1976.

TUGS

2 Ex-US "CHEROKEE" CLASS

Name	No.	Builders	Commissioned
TA TUNG (ex-USS *Chickasaw*, ATF 83)	ATF 548	United Engineering Co, Alameda, California	4 Feb 1943
TA WAN (ex-USS *Apache*, ATF 67)	ATF 550	Charleston SB & DD Co, South Carolina	12 Dec 1942

Displacement, tons: 1 235 standard; 1 675 full load
Dimensions, feet (metres): 195 wl; 205 oa × 38·5 × 15·5 *(63·9; 67·2 × 12·6 × 5·1)*
Guns: 1—3 in *(76 mm)* 50 cal AA; several light AA
Main engines: Diesels (electric drive); 3 000 bhp; 1 shaft = 15 knots

Launched on 23 July 1942 and 8 May 1942 respectively. *Ta Tung* transferred to Taiwan in Jan 1966 and by sale 19 May 1976 and *Ta Wan* on 30 June 1974.

3 Ex-US "SOTOYOMO" CLASS

Name	No.	Builders	Commissioned
TA SUEH (ex-USS *Tonkawa*, ATA 176)	ATA 547	Levingston SB Co, Orange, Texas	19 Aug 1944
TA PENG (ex-USS *Mohopac*, ATA 196)	ATA 549	Levingston SB Co, Orange, Texas	21 Dec 1944
TA TENG (ex-USS *Cahokia*, ATA 186)	ATA 550	Levingston SB Co, Orange, Texas	24 Nov 1944

Displacement, tons: 435 standard; 835 full load
Dimensions, feet (metres): 134·5 wl; 143 oa × 33·9 × 13 *(44·1; 46·9 × 11·1 × 4·3)*
Guns: 1—3 in *(76 mm)* 50 cal; several light MG
Main engine: Diesel-electric (General Motors diesel); 1 500 bhp; 1 shaft = 13 knots

Ta Sueh launched on 1 March 1944 and transferred to Taiwan in April 1962. *Ta Teng* launched on 18 Sept 1944; assigned briefly to US Air Force in 1971 until transferred to Taiwan on 29 March 1972. *Ta Peng* transferred on 1 July 1971. Latter two by sale 19 May 1976. A fourth tug of this class serves as a surveying ship.

TA YU (ex-US *LT 310*) ATA 545

Transferred April 1949. Also reported.

1 Ex-US ARMY ST TYPE

YTL 9 (ex-US Army *ST 2004*)

Former US Army 76-foot harbour tug.

3 Ex-US "YLT 422" CLASS

YTL 11 (ex-USN *YTL 454*)   **YTL 14** (ex-USN *YTL 585*)
YTL 12 (ex-USN *YTL 584*)

Former US Navy 66-foot harbour tugs.

5 Ex-US FLOATING DRY DOCKS

Name	No.	Builders	Commissioned
HAY TAN (ex-USN *AFDL 36*)	AFDL 1	—	—
KIM MEN (ex-USN *AFDL 5*)	AFDL 2	—	—
HAN JIH (ex-USN *AFDL 34*)	AFDL 3	—	—
FO WU 5 (ex-USN *ARD 9*)	ARD 5	—	—
FO WU 6 (ex-USS *Windsor*, ARD 22)	ARD 6	—	—

Former US Navy floating dry docks; see United States section for characteristics.

Transfers: AFDL 1 in March 1947, 2 in Jan 1948, 3 in July 1959, 5 in Oct 1967, 6 in June 1971. ARD 6 by sale 19 May 1976 and ARD 5 on 12 Jan 1977.

SERVICE CRAFT

Approximately 25 non-self-propelled service craft are in use; most are former US Navy service craft.

CUSTOMS SERVICE

Several small ships and small craft are in service with the Customs Service of Taiwan, an agenc of the Ministry of Finance as well as the ships listed below.

2 Ex-US "ADMIRABLE" CLASS

Name	No.	Builders	Commiss
HUNG HSING (ex-USS *Embattle*, AM 226)	A 7	American Shipbuilding Co, Lorain, Ohio	25 April
— (ex-USS *Improve*, AM 247)	—	Savannah Machine & Foundry Co, Georgia	29 Feb

Dimensions, feet (metres): 180 wl; 184·5 oa × 33 × 9·75 *(59; 60·5 × 10·8 × 3·2)*
Guns: 2—20 mm
Main engines: Diesel (Cooper Bessemer); 1 710 bhp; 2 shafts = 14 knots

Former US Navy minesweepers (AM). Launched on 17 Sept 1944 and 26 Sept 1943 re

3 Ex-US "PC-461" CLASS

Name	No.	Builders
Ex-*Tung Kiang* (ex-USS *Placerville*, PC 1087)	PC 119	USA
Ex-*Hsi Kiang* (ex-USS *Susanville*, PC 1149)	PC 120	USA
Ex-*Pei Kiang* (ex-USS *Hanford* PC 1142)	PC 122	USA

Displacement, tons: 450 full load
Dimensions, feet (metres): 173·66 oa × 23 × 10·8 *(56·9 × 7·5 × 3·5)*
Guns: 2—20 mm
Main engines: Diesels (General Motors); 2 880 bhp; 2 shafts = 20 knots
Range, miles: 5 000 at 10 knots
Complement: 65

Former US Navy steel-hulled submarine chasers. Originally transferred tc subsequently allocated to the Customs Service. Transferred in July 19 All sold in May 1976.

2 HALTER 78 ft PATROL CRAFT

Purchased in 1977.

460 TANZANIA

TANZANIA
(see also Zanzibar)

Ministerial

Minister of Defence:
 Mr. Rashidi Kawawa

Personnel

(a) 1978: 700 (approx)
(b) Voluntary service

Base

Dar Es Salaam. A new base area built under Chinese supervision.

New acquisitions

Reported that the "Riga" class frigate *Friedrich Engels* from East Germany, paid off in 1969, has been refitted in USSR for transfer to Tanzania.

Mercantile Marine

Lloyd's Register of Shipping:
 22 vessels of 35 613 tons gross

LIGHT FORCES

7 Ex-CHINESE "SHANGHAI" CLASS (FAST ATTACK CRAFT—GUN)

JW 9861-7

Displacement, tons: 120 full load
Dimensions, feet (metres): 130 × 18·0 × 5·6 *(42·6 × 5·9 × 1·8)*
Guns: 4—37 mm (twin) 4—25 mm (twins)
Main engines: 4 diesels; 5 000 bhp = 30 knots
Complement: 25

Transferred by the Chinese People's Republic in 1970-71.

"SHANGHAI" Class

4 Ex-CHINESE "HU CHWAN" CLASS
(FAST ATTACK CRAFT—HYDROFOIL (TORPEDO))

Displacement, tons: 45
Dimensions, feet (metres): 70 × 16·5 × 3·1 *(22·9 × 5·4 × 1)*
Guns: 4—12·7 mm (twins)
Torpedo tubes: 2—21 in (533 mm)
Main engines: 2 diesels; 2 200 bhp = 55 knots (calm)
Range, miles: 500 at cruising speed

...ferred 1975.

1 Ex-SOVIET "POLUCHAT" CLASS (LARGE PATROL CRAFT)

Displacement, tons: 120 full load
Dimensions, feet (metres): 98·4 × 20 × 5·9 *(32·3 × 6·5 × 1·9)*
Guns: 2—25 mm
Main engines: Diesels = 15 knots

2 Ex-EAST GERMAN "SCHWALBE" CLASS
(COASTAL PATROL CRAFT)

ARAKA   SALAAM

Displacement, tons: 70 full load
Dimensions, feet (metres): 85·2 × 14·8 × 4·6 *(26 × 4·5 × 1·4)*
Guns: 2—25 mm (twin); 2 MG
Main engines: Diesel; 300 hp = 17 knots

Launched 1955-56. Transferred 1966-67.

"SCHWALBE" Class

2 Ex-EAST GERMAN COASTAL PATROL CRAFT

RAFIKI   UHURU

Displacement, tons: 50
Dimensions, feet (metres): 78·7 × 16·4 × 4·3 *(24 × 5 × 1·3)*
Guns: 1—40 mm; 4 MG

Purchased 1967, via Portugal.

4 Ex-CHINESE "YU LIN" CLASS (COASTAL PATROL CRAFT)

Displacement, tons: 27
Dimensions, feet (metres): 42·6 × 13 × 4·2 *(13 × 4 × 1·2)*
Gun: 1—12·7 mm MG
Speed, knots: 20
Complement: 10

Transferred late 1966.

1 SURVEY LAUNCH

Dimensions, feet (metres): 91·8 × 15·7 × 3·3 *(28 × 4·8 × 1)*
Main engine: 1 Caterpillar diesel; 480 hp = 14 knots

Ordered from Bayerische Schiffbau West Germany for completion end 1978.

2 Ex-CHINESE LCMs

THAILAND

Ministerial

Minister of Defence:
  Admiral Sa-Ngad Chaloryu

Administration

Commander-in-Chief of the Navy:
  Admiral Amorn Sirigaya
Deputy Commander-in-Chief:
  Admiral Ching Chullasukhum
Chief of Staff (RTN):
  Admiral M. R. Pandhum Davivongs
Commander-in-Chief, Fleet:
  Admiral Satap Keyanon

Diplomatic Representation

Naval Attaché in London:
  Captain Amnuay Iamsuro
Naval Attaché in Washington:
  Captain Vinit Tapasanan

Personnel

(a) 1978: Navy, 20 000 (2 000 officers and 18 000 ratings) including Marine Corps: 7 000 (500 officers and 6 500 men)
(b) 2 years national service

Bases

Bangkok, Sattahip, Songkhla, Paknam. A new base on the West coast has been reported.

Prefix to Ships' Names

HTMS.

General

With three Frigates, three Fast Attack Craft (with three building) and a few coastal patrol craft as the only ships of under ten years of age this is an aged fleet. Replacement will presumably take account of the problems of extended off-shore limits and the continued upheavals in the Kampuchea—Viet-Nam area. The navies of the latter pair present no great threat at the moment with lack of fuel and training but intrusions into the offshore areas and the Malaysian border areas suggest a need for fast patrol craft with fairly light armament but considerable range and sea-keeping qualities.

Strength of the Fleet

Type	Active	Building
Frigates	6	—
Fast Attack Craft (Missile)	3	3
Large Patrol Craft	27	1
Coastal Patrol Craft	20	—
Coastal Minelayers	2	—
Coastal Minesweepers	4	—
MCM Support Ship	1	—
MSBs	10	—
LSTs	5	—
LSMs	3	—
LCG	1	—
LSILs	2	—
LCUs	6	—
LCMs	26	—
LCVPs	6	—
Survey Vessels	4	—
Support Tankers	2	—
Harbour Tankers	2	—
Water Boats	2	—
Tugs	4	—
Transports	2	—
Training Ships	3	—

Mercantile Marine

Lloyd's Register of Shipping:
  100 vessels of 260 664 tons gross

DELETIONS

Note: Frigates *Bangpakong*, *Maeklong* and *Phosamton* transferred to training duties.

Large Patrol Craft

1973 SC 7
1976 *Chumporn*, *Phuket* and *Trad*; *Kantang* and *Klongyai*

Coastal Patrol Craft

1973 CGC1 and 11, T 31, 33, 34 and 35
1976 T 93

Harbour Tankers

1975 *Prong* and *Samui*

FRIGATES

1 YARROW TYPE

Name	No.	Builders	Laid down	Launched	Commissioned
MAKUT RAJAKUMARN	7	Yarrow & Co Ltd, Scotstoun	11 Jan 1970	18 Nov 1971	7 May 1973

Displacement, tons: 1 650 standard; 1 900 full load
Length, feet (metres): 305 *(93)* wl; 320·0 *(97·6)* oa
Beam, feet (metres): 36·0 *(11·0)*
Draught, feet (metres): 18·1 *(5·5)*
Missile launchers: 1 quadruple Seacat
Guns: 2—4·5 in Mk 8 *(114 mm)* (single)
  2—40 mm 60 cal Bofors (single)
A/S weapons: 1 triple barrelled Limbo mortar; 1 DC rack; 2 depth charge throwers
Main engines: 1 Rolls-Royce Olympus gas turbine; 23 125 shp; 1 Crossley-Pielstick 12 PC2V diesel; 2 shafts; 6 000 bhp
Speed, knots: 26, 18 on diesel
Range, miles: 5 000 at 18 knots (diesel); 1 200 at 26 knots
Complement: 140 (16 officers, 124 ratings)

An order was placed on 21 Aug 1969 for a general purpose frigate. The ship is largely automated with a consequent saving in complement, and has been most successful in service. Fitted as flagship.

Electronics: HSA CIC system. Racal DF.

Radar: Surveillance: one LW 04 (amidships)
Fire control: one M 20 series (radome)
Seacat control: one M 44 Series (aft)
Navigation: one Decca Type 626
IFF: UK Mk 10.

Sonar: UK Type 170 and Plessey Type MS 27.

MAKUT RAJAKUMARN 9/1973, Wright and Logan

2 US "PF-103" CLASS

Name	No.	Builders	Laid down	Launched	Commissioned
TAPI	5	American SB Co, Toledo, Ohio	1 April 1970	17 Oct 1970	1 Nov 1971
KHIRIRAT	6	Norfolk SB & DD Co	18 Feb 1972	2 June 1973	10 Aug 1974

Displacement, tons: 900 standard; 1 135 full load
Length, feet (metres): 275 *(83·8)* oa
Beam, feet (metres): 33 *(10·0)*
Draught, feet (metres): 10 *(3·0)*
Guns: 2—3 in *(76 mm)*; 2—40 mm (twin)
A/S weapons: Hedgehogs; 6 (2 triple) Mk 32 A/S torpedo tubes
Main engines: 2 FM Diesels; 6 000 bhp
Speed, knots: 20
Complement: 150

Of similar design to the Iranian ships of the "Bayandor" class. *Tapi* was ordered on June 27 1969. *Khirirat* was ordered on 25 June 1971.

Fire control: Mk 63 GFCS (SPG 34). Mk 51 GFCS (40 mm).

Radar: Air search: SPS 6.
Fire control: SPG 34.

TAPI 1975, Royal Thai Navy

462 THAILAND

1 Ex-US "CANNON" CLASS

Name	No.	Builders	Laid down	Launched	Commissioned
PIN KLAO (ex-USS *Hemminger*, DE 746)	3 (ex-1)	Western Pipe & Steel Co.	1943	12 Sept 1943	30 May 1944

Displacement, tons: 1 240 standard; 1 900 full load
Length, feet (metres): 306·0 (93·3) oa
Beam, feet (metres): 37·0 (11·3)
Draught, feet (metres): 14·1 (4·3)
Guns: 3—3 in (76 mm) 50 cal; 6—40 mm
A/S weapons: 8 DCT
Torpedo tubes: 6 (2 triple) Mk 32 for A/S torpedoes
Main engines: GM diesels with electric drive; 2 shafts; 6 000 bhp
Speed, knots: 20
Oil fuel, tons: 300
Range, miles: 11 500 at 11 knots
Complement: 220

Transferred from US Navy to Royal Thai Navy at New York Navy Shipyard in July 1959 under MDAP and by sale 6 June 1975. The 3—21 in torpedo tubes were removed and the 4—20 mm guns were replaced by 4—40 mm. The six A/S torpedo tubes were fitted in 1966. Finally purchased 6 June 1975.

Radar: SPS-5 and SC.

PIN KLAO   1977, Royal Thai Navy

2 Ex-US "TACOMA" CLASS

Name	No.
TAHCHIN (ex-USS *Glendale*, PF 36)	1
PRASAE (ex-USS *Gallup*, PF 47)	2

Builders	Laid down	Launched	Commissioned
Consolidated Steel Corp, Los Angeles	6 April 1943	28 May 1943	1 Oct 1943
Consolidated Steel Corp, Los Angeles	18 Aug 1943	17 Sept 1943	29 Feb 1944

Displacement, tons: 1 430 standard; 2 100 full load
Length, feet (metres): 304·0 (92·7) oa
Beam, feet (metres): 37·5 (11·4)
Draught, feet (metres): 13·7 (4·2)
Guns: 3—3 in (76 mm) 50 cal; 2—40 mm; 9—20 mm
A/S weapons: 6 (2 triple) Mk 32 A/S torpedo tubes; 8 DCT
Main engines: Triple expansion; 2 shafts; 5 500 ihp
Boilers: 2 small water tube three-drum type
Speed, knots: 19
Oil fuel, tons: 685
Range, miles: 7 800 at 12 knots
Complement: 180

Delivered to the Royal Thai Navy on 29 Oct 1951. *Prasae* partially non-operational after collision in Jan 1972 and *Tahchin* may also be non-operational.

PRASAE   8/1977, Royal Thai Navy

LIGHT FORCES

3 FAST ATTACK CRAFT—MISSILE

Name	No.	Builders	Commissioned
RATCHARIT	4	C. N. Breda (Venezia)	1979
WITTHAYAKHOM	5	C. N. Breda (Venezia)	1979
UDOMDET	6	C. N. Breda (Venezia)	1979

Displacement, tons: 235 standard; 270 full load
Dimensions, feet (metres): 163·4 × 24·6 × 5·6 (49·8 × 7·5 × 1·7)
Missiles: 4—MM 38 Exocet
Guns: 1—76 mm OTO Melara; 1—40 mm Bofors
Main engines: 3 MTU diesels; 13 500 hp = 36 knots
Range: 2 000 at 15 knots
Complement: 45

Ordered June 1976. Standard Breda BMB 30 design.

3 45 METRE TYPE (FAST ATTACK CRAFT—MISSILE)

Name	No.	Builders	Commissioned
PRABPARAPAK	1	Singapore Shipbuilding and Engineering Ltd	28 July 1976
HANHAK SATTRU	2	Singapore Shipbuilding and Engineering Ltd	6 Nov 1976
SUPHAIRIN	3	Singapore Shipbuilding and Engineering Ltd	1 Feb 1977

Displacement, tons: 224 standard; 260 full load
Dimensions, feet (metres): 147·3 × 22·9 × 6·9 (44·9 × 7·0 × 2·1)
Missiles: 5 Gabriel launchers (1 triple, 2 single)
Guns: 1—57 mm 70 Bofors (forward); 1—40 mm 70 Bofors (aft)
Main engines: 4 Maybach (MTU) diesels; 14 400 shp = 34 knots
Range: 2 000 cruising
Complement: 41

Ordered June 1973. Launch dates—*Prabparapak* 29 July 1975, *Hanhak Sattru* 28 Oct 1975, *Suphairin* 20 Feb 1976.

SUPHAIRIN   1977, Royal Thai Navy

THAILAND 463

4 "TRAD" CLASS (LARGE PATROL CRAFT)

Name	No.	Builders	Commissioned
PATTANI	13	Cantieri Riunti dell' Adriatico, Monfalcone	1937
SURASDRA	21	Cantieri Riunti dell' Adriatico, Monfalcone	1937
CHANDHABURI	22	Cantieri Riunti dell' Adriatico, Monfalcone	1937
RAYONG	23	Cantieri Riunti dell' Adriatico, Monfalcone	1938

Displacement, tons: 318 standard; 470 full load
Dimensions, feet (metres): 223 oa × 21 × 7 (68 × 6·4 × 2·1)
Guns: 2—3 in; 1—40 mm; 2—20 mm
Torpedo tubes: 4—18 in (2 twin)
Main engines: Parsons geared turbines; 2 shafts; 9 000 hp = 31 knots
Boilers: 2 Yarrow
Oil fuel, tons: 102
Range, miles: 1 700 at 15 knots
Complement: 70

Survivors of class of seven. Armament was supplied by Vickers-Armstrong Ltd. First boat reached 32·34 knots on trials with 10 000 hp. 2 single 18 in torpedo tubes and the 4—8 mm guns were removed.

"TRAD" Class

7 "LIULOM" CLASS (LARGE PATROL CRAFT)

SARASIN (ex-PC *495*) PC 1
THAYANCHON (ex-PC *575*) PC 2
PHALI (ex-PC *1185*) PC 4
SUKRIP (ex-PC *1218*) PC 5
TONGPLIU (ex-PC *616*) PC 6
LIULOM (ex-PC *1253*) PC 7
LONGLOM (ex-PC *570*) PC 8

Displacement, tons: 280 standard; 400 full load
Dimensions, feet (metres): 174 oa × 23·2 × 6·5 (53 × 7 × 2)
Guns: 1—3 in; 1—40 mm; 5—20 mm
A/S weapons: 2 (single) Mk 32 ASW torpedo tubes (except *Sarasin*)
Main engines: Diesel; 2 shafts; 3 600 bhp = 19 knots
Oil fuel, tons: 60
Range, miles: 6 000 at 10 knots
Complement: 62 to 71

Launched in 1941-43 as US PCs. All transferred between March 1947 and Dec 1952.

Radar: SPS 25.

PHALI   8/1976, Dr. Giorgio Arra

1 "KLONGYAI" CLASS (LARGE PATROL CRAFT)

Name	No.	Builders	Commissioned
SATTAHIP	8	Royal Thai Naval Dockyard, Bangkok	1958

Displacement, tons: 110 standard; 135 full load
Dimensions, feet (metres): 131·5 × 15·5 × 4 (42 × 4·6 × 1·5)
Guns: 1—3 in; 1—20 mm
Torpedo tubes: 2—18 in
Main engines: Geared turbines; 2 shafts; 2 000 shp = 19 knots
Boilers: 2 water-tube
Range, miles: 480 at 15 knots
Oil fuel, tons: 18
Complement: 31

Sattahip was laid down on 21 Nov 1956, launched on 28 Oct 1957.

10 Ex-US "PGM 71" CLASS (LARGE PATROL CRAFT)

Name	No.	Builders	Commissioned
—	T 11 (ex-US *PGM 71*)	Peterson Builders Inc	1 Feb 1966
—	T 12 (ex-US *PGM 79*)	Peterson Builders Inc	1967
—	T 13 (ex-US *PGM 107*)	Peterson Builders Inc	28 Aug 1967
—	T 14 (ex-US *PGM 116*)	Peterson Builders Inc	18 Aug 1969
—	T 15 (ex-US *PGM 117*)	Peterson Builders Inc	18 Aug 1969
—	T 16 (ex-US *PGM 115*)	Peterson Builders Inc	12 Feb 1970
—	T 17 (ex-US *PGM 113*)	Peterson Builders Inc	12 Feb 1970
—	T 18 (ex-US *PGM 114*)	Peterson Builders Inc	12 Feb 1970
—	T 19 (ex-US *PGM 123*)	Peterson Builders Inc	25 Dec 1970
—	T 110 (ex-US *PGM 124*)	Peterson Builders Inc	Oct 1970

Displacement, tons: 130 standard; 147 full load
Dimensions, feet (metres): 101·0 oa × 21·0 × 6·0 (30·8 × 6·4 × 1·9)
Guns: 1—40 mm; 4—20 mm; 2—50 cal MG
Main engines: Diesels; 2 shafts; 1 800 bhp = 18·5 knots
Range, miles: 1 500 at 10 knots
Complement: 30

T 11 was launched on 5 May 1965.

T 11   8/1976, Dr. Giorgio Arra

1 Ex-US SC TYPE (LARGE PATROL CRAFT)

T 85 (ex-*SC 32*, ex-US *SC 162*)

Displacement, tons: 110 light; 125 full load
Dimensions, feet (metres): 111 × 17 × 6 (36·4 × 5·5 × 1·9)
Guns: 1—40 mm; 3—20 mm
A/S weapons: Depth charges, Mousetrap
Main engines: High-speed diesel = 18 knots
Range, miles: 2 000 at 10 knots

Wooden hulled. Non-operational.

464   THAILAND

4 Ex-US CG "CAPE" CLASS (LARGE PATROL CRAFT)

T 81 (ex-CG 13)   **T 83** (ex-CG 15)
T 82 (ex-CG 14)   **T 84** (ex-CG 16)

Displacement, tons: 95 standard; 105 full load
Dimensions, feet (metres): 95 × 20·2 × 5 (29 × 5·8 × 1·6)
Gun: 1—20 mm
A/S weapons: 2 DC racks; 2 Mousetraps
Range, miles: 1 500 at 14 knots
Complement: 15

US coastguard cutters transferred in 1954. Similar to those built for USCG by US Coast Guard Yard, Curtis Bay in 1953. Cost £475 000 each.

T 82 (as CG 14)   Royal Thai Navy

2 + 1 THAI BUILT (COASTAL PATROL CRAFT)

Name	No.	Builders	Commissioned
—	T 91	Royal Thai Naval Dockyard, Bangkok	1971
—	T 92	Royal Thai Naval Dockyard, Bangkok	1971

Displacement, tons: 87·5 standard
Dimensions, feet (metres): 104·3 × 17·5 × 5·5 (30·8 × 6·4 × 1·9)
Guns: 1—40 mm; 1—20 mm
Main engines: Diesels; 2 shafts; 1 600 bhp = 25 knots
Complement: 21

One more laid down 1977.

T 91   1970, Royal Thai Navy

12 Ex-US "SWIFT" CLASS (COASTAL PATROL CRAFT)

T 27   T 29   T 31   T 33   T 35   T 211
T 28   T 30   T 32   T 34   T 210 T 212

Displacement, tons: 20 standard; 22 full load
Dimensions, feet (metres): 50 × 13 × 3·5 (15·2 × 4 × 1·1)
Guns: 2—81 mm mortars; 2—0·50 cal (1 twin)
Main engines: Diesels; 2 shafts; 480 bhp = 25 knots
Complement: 5

"Swift" class patrol craft transferred from USN; T 28 in Aug 1968, T 29-31 in Feb 1970. T 27 in May 1970, T 32 in March 1970, T 33 in April 1970, T 34, 35, 210-212 in 1975.

6 Ex-US RPC TYPE (COASTAL PATROL CRAFT)

T 21   T 22   T 23   T 24   T 25   T 26

Displacement, tons: 10·4 standard; 13·05 full load
Dimensions, feet (metres): 35 × 10 (11·5 × 3·2)
Guns: 2—0·50 cal (1 twin); 2—0·30 cal
Main engines: Diesels; 2 shafts; 225 bhp = 14 knots
Complement: 7

Transferred March 1967.

T 21   8/1976, Dr. Giorgio Arra

1 COASTAL PATROL CRAFT

Dimensions, feet (metres): 16·4 × 6·6 × — (5 × 2 × —)
Main engine: 1 Castoldi marine jet engine Mod 3000/05 = 38 knots

Fibreglass tri-maran built in Thailand.

There are reports that a patrol of Riverine Craft is maintained on the Upper Mekong although details are not available.

MINE WARFARE FORCES

Note: Transfer of ex-USS *Prime* and *Reaper* ("Agile" class MSOs) was cancelled.

2 "BANGRACHAN" CLASS (COASTAL MINELAYERS)

Name	No.	Builders	Commissioned
BANGRACHAN	MMC 1	Cantiere dell'Adriatico, Monfalcone	1937
NHONG SARHAI	MMC 2	Cantiere dell'Adriatico, Monfalcone	1936

Displacement, tons: 368 standard; 408 full load
Dimensions, feet (metres): 160·8 × 25·9 × 7·2 (52·7 × 8·5 × 2·4)
Guns: 2—3 in; 2—20 mm
Mines: 142
Main engines: Burmeister & Wain diesels; 2 shafts; 540 bhp = 12 knots
Oil fuel, tons: 180
Range, miles: 2 700 at 10 knots
Complement: 55

Launched in 1936.

BANGRACHAN

THAILAND 465

4 US "BLUEBIRD" CLASS (MINESWEEPERS—COASTAL)

Name	No.	Builders	Commissioned
LADYA (ex-US MSC 297)	5	Peterson Builders Inc, Sturgeon Bay, Wisc	14 Dec 1963
BANGEKO (ex-US MSC 303)	6	Dorchester SB Corp, Camden	9 July 1965
TADINDENG (ex-US MSC 301)	7	Tacoma Boatbuilding Co, Tacoma, Wash	26 Aug 1965
DONCHEDI (ex-US MSC 313)	8	Peterson Builders Inc, Sturgeon Bay, Wisc	17 Sept 1965

Displacement, tons: 330 standard; 362 full load
Dimensions, feet (metres): 145·3 oa × 27 × 8·5 *(43 × 8 × 2·6)*
Guns: 2—20 mm
Main engines: 4 GM diesels; 2 shafts; 1 000 bhp = 13 knots
Range, miles: 2 500 at 10 knots
Complement: 43 (7 officers, and 36 men)

Constructed for Thailand.

BANGEKO 8/1976, Dr. Giorgio Arra

1 MCM SUPPORT SHIP

Name	No.	Builders	Commissioned
RANG KWIEN (ex-*Umihari Maru*)	MSC 11	Mitsubishi Co	1944

Displacement, tons: 586 standard
Dimensions, feet (metres): 162·3 × 31·2 × 13·0 *(49 × 9·5 × 4)*
Guns: 2—20 mm
Main engines: Triple expansion steam; speed = 10 knots

Originally built as a tug. Acquired by Royal Thai Navy on 6 Sept 1967.

RANG KWIEN 1969, Royal Thai Navy

5 MSB

MSML 6-10

Thai built. 50 feet, 30 tons with 2—20 mm guns.

5 MSB

MSML 1-5

Thai built. 40 feet, 25 tons with 2—20 mm guns.

AMPHIBIOUS FORCES

5 Ex-US "1-510" and "511-1152 CLASSES (LST)

Name	No.	Builders	Commissioned
ANGTHONG (ex-USS LST 294)	LST 1	American Bridge Co, Pa.	Jan 1944
CHANG (ex-USS *Lincoln County*, LST 898)	LST 2	Dravo Corp	29 Dec 1944
PANGAN (ex-USS *Stark County*, LST 1134)	LST 3	Chicago Bridge and Iron Co, Ill.	7 April 1945
LANTA (ex-USS *Stone County*, LST 1141)	LST 4	Chicago Bridge and Iron Co, Ill.	7 April 1945
PRATHONG (ex-USS *Dodge County*, LST 722)	LST 5	Jefferson B & M Co, Ind.	13 Sept 1944

Displacement, tons: 1 625 standard; 4 080 full load
Dimensions, feet (metres): 328 oa × 50 × 14 *(100 × 15·2 × 4·4)*
Guns: 6—40 mm; 4—20 mm
Main engines: GM diesels; 2 shafts; 1 700 bhp = 11 knots
Range, miles: 9 500 at 9 knots
Complement: 80
Cargo capacity: 2 100 tons

CHANG 1967, Royal Thai Navy

Angthong is employed as training ship. *Chang*, transferred to Thailand in 1962, was laid down on 15 Oct 1944. *Pangan* was transferred on 16 May 1966, *Lanta* on 12 March 1970 and *Prathong* on 17 Dec 1975.

3 Ex-US "LSM-1" CLASS

Name	No.	Builders	Commissioned
KUT (ex-USS *LSM 338*)	LSM 1	Pullman Std Car Co, Chicago	16 Jan 1945
PHAI (ex-USS *LSM 333*)	LSM 2	Pullman Std Car Co, Chicago	25 Nov 1945
KRAM (ex-USS *LSM 469*)	LSM 3	Brown SB Co, Houston, Tex	17 Mar 1945

Displacement, tons: 743 standard; 1 095 full load
Dimensions, feet (metres): 203·5 oa × 34·5 × 8·3 *(62 × 10·5 × 2·4)*
Guns: 2—40 mm
Main engines: Diesel direct drive; 2 shafts; 2 800 bhp = 12·5 knots
Range, miles: 2 500 at 12 knots
Complement: 55

Former United States landing ships of the LCM, later LSM (Medium Landing Ship) type. *Kram* was transferred to Thailand under MAP at Seattle, Wash, on 25 May 1962.

1 Ex-US "LSIL 351" CLASS

PRAB (ex-*LSIL 670*) LSIL 1   SATAKUT (ex-*LSIL 739*) LSIL 2

Displacement, tons: 230 standard; 387 full load
Dimensions, feet (metres): 157 × 23 × 6 *(47 × 7 × 1·7)*
Guns: 2—20 mm
Main engines: Diesel; 2 shafts; 1 320 bhp = 14 knots
Complement: 54

Prab non-operational.

466 THAILAND

1 Ex-US LCG TYPE

NAKHA (ex-USS *LSSL* 102) LSSL 3

Displacement, tons: 233 standard; 287 full load
Dimensions, feet (metres): 158 oa × 23 × 4·25 *(47·5 × 7 × 1·4)*
Guns: 1—3 in; 4—40 mm; 4—20 mm; 4—81 mm mortars
Main engines: Diesels; 2 shafts; 1 320 bhp = 15 knots
Range, miles: 4 700 at 10 knots

Transferred in 1966. Acquired when Japan returned her to USA.

26 Ex-US LCM 6

14-16, 61-68, 71-78, 81-82, 85-87

First 21 delivered 1969.

8 Ex-US LCVP

6 Ex-US "LCU" CLASS

| MATAPHON LCU 1 | ARDANG LCU 3 | KOLUM LCU 5 |
| RAWI LCU 2 | PHETRA LCU 4 | TALIBONG LCU 6 |

Displacement, tons: 134 standard; 279 full load
Dimensions, feet (metres): 112 × 32 × 4 *(37 × 9·7 × 1·2)*
Guns: 2—20 mm
Main engines: Diesel; 3 shafts; 675 bhp = 10 knots
Complement: 37

Employed as transport ferries. Originally LCT-6 class.

1 LCA

Dimensions, feet (metres): 39·4 × 9·8 × — *(12 × 3 × —)*
Main engines: 2 Chrysler diesels; 2 Castoldi Mod 06 jet units = 25 Knots
Capacity: 35 troops

Built in Thailand. Fibreglass hull with bow ramp.

LCAs

There is also a large but unknown number of Thai-built LCAs.

MISCELLANEOUS

TRAINING SHIPS

1 Ex-BRITISH "ALGERINE" CLASS

Name	No.	Builders	Commissioned
PHOSAMTON (ex-HMS *Minstrel*)	MSF 1	Redfern Construction Co	1945

Displacement, tons: 1 040 standard; 1 335 full load
Length, feet (metres): 225·0 *(68·6)* oa
Beam, feet (metres): 35·5 *(10·8)*
Draught, feet (metres): 10·5 *(3·2)*
Guns: 1—4 in *(102 mm)* ; 6—20 mm
A/S weapons: 4 DCT
Main engines: Triple expansion; 2 shafts; 2 000 ihp
Boilers: 2 three-drum type
Speed, knots: 16
Oil fuel, tons: 270
Range, miles: 5 000 at 10 knots
Complement: 103

Transferred in April 1947. The 20 mm guns were increased from three to six, and the DCTs from two to four in 1966. Marginally operational—now used for training.

Name	No.	Builders	Commissioned
MAEKLONG	4	Uraga Dock Co, Japan	June 1937

Displacement, tons: 1 400 standard; 2 000 full load
Length, feet (metres): 269·0 *(82·0)*
Beam, feet (metres): 34·0 *(10·4)*
Draught, feet (metres): 10·5 *(3·2)*
Guns: 4—3 in *(76 mm)* 50 cal (singles); 3—40 mm; 3—20 mm
Main engines: Triple expansion; 2 shafts; 2 500 ihp
Boilers: 2 water tube
Speed, knots: 14
Oil fuel, tons: 487
Range, miles: 8 000 at 12 knots
Complement: 155 as training ship

Employed as training ship. The 4—18 in torpedo tubes were removed.

Armament: 4—4·7 in guns replaced by 3 in guns in 1974.

1 Ex-BRITISH "FLOWER" CLASS

Name	No.	Builders	Commissioned
BANGPAKONG (ex-*Gondwana*, ex- HMS *Burnet*)	P4	Ferguson Bros, Port Glasgow	23 Sept 1943

Displacement, tons: 1 060 standard; 1 350 full load
Dimensions, feet (metres): 203·2 × 33 × 14·5 *(61·9 × 10 × 4·4)*
Guns: 1—3 in *(76 mm)* 50 cal; 1—40 mm; 6—20 mm
A/S weapons: 4 DCT
Main engines: Triple expansion; 2 880 ihp = 16 knots
Boilers: 2 three-drum type
Range, miles: 4 800 at 12 knots
Complement: 100

Served in Indian Navy before transfer to Thailand 15 May 1947. Now used for training.

SURVEY SHIPS

Name	No.	Builders	Commissioned
CHANDHARA	AGS 11	C. Melchers & Co, Bremen, Germany	1961

Displacement, tons: 870 standard; 996 full load
Dimensions, feet (metres): 229·2 oa × 34·5 × 10 *(71 × 10·5 × 3)*
Gun: 1—20 mm
Main engines: 2 diesels; 2 shafts; 1 000 bhp = 13·25 knots
Range, miles: 10 000 (cruising)
Complement: 72

Laid down on 27 Sept 1960. Launched on 17 Dec 1960.

3 OCEANOGRAPHIC CRAFT

Of 90 tons, with a crew of eight launched in 1955.

SERVICE FORCES

2 SUPPORT TANKERS

CHULA AO 2   MATRA AO 3

Displacement, tons: 2 395 standard; 4 744 full load
Dimensions, feet (metres): 328 × 45·2 × 20 *(100 × 14 × 6·1)*
Main engines: Steam turbines

Built in Japan during World War II. Exact sisters *Chula* employed as floating storage, *Matra* as freighting and fleet replenishment tanker and naval stores ship.

1 HARBOUR TANKER

Name	No.	Builders	Commissioned
SAMED	YO 11	Royal Thai Naval Dockyard, Bangkok	15 Dec 1970

Displacement, tons: 360 standard; 485 full load
Dimensions, feet (metres): 120 × 20 × 10 *(39 × 6·1 × 3·1)*
Main engine: Diesel; 500 bhp = 9 knots

Launched on 8 July 1966.

1 HARBOUR TANKER

Name	No.	Builders	Commissioned
PROET	YO 9	Royal Thai Naval Dockyard, Bangkok	16 Jan 1970

Displacement, tons: 360
Dimensions, feet (metres): 122·7 × 19·7 × 8·7 *(37·4 × 6 × 2·7)*
Main engines: Diesels; 500 bhp = 9 knots

1 TRANSPORT

Name	No.	Builders	Commissioned
SICHANG	AKL 1	Harima Co, Japan	Jan 1938

Displacement, tons: 815 standard
Dimensions, feet (metres): 160 × 28 × 16 *(48·8 × 8·5 × 4·9)*
Main engine: Diesel; 2 shafts; 550 bhp = 16 knots
Complement: 30

Sichang was launched on 10 Nov 1937. Completed in Jan 1938.

1 TRANSPORT

KLED KEO AF 7

Displacement, tons: 382 standard; 450 full load
Dimensions, feet (metres): 154·9 × 25·4 × 14 *(46 × 7·6 × 4·3)*
Guns: 3—20 mm
Main engine: 1 diesel; 600 hp = 12 knots
Complement: 54

Operates with patrol boat squadron.

2 WATER CARRIERS

Name	No.	Builders	Commissioned
CHUANG	YW 8	Royal Thai Naval Dockyard, Bangkok	1965
CHARN	YW 6	Royal Thai Naval Dockyard, Bangkok	1965

Displacement, tons: 305 standard; 485 full load
Dimensions, feet (metres): 136 × 25 × 10 *(42 × 7·5 × 3·1)*
Main engine: GM diesel; 500 bhp = 11 knots
Complement: 29

Chuang launched on 14 Jan 1965.

TUGS

Name	No.	Builders	Commissioned
SAMAE SAN (ex-*Empire Vincent*)	YTM 1	Cochrane & Sons Ltd, Selby, Yorks, England	—

Displacement, tons: 503 full load
Dimensions, feet (metres): 105·0 × 26·5 × 13·0 *(32 × 8·1 × 4)*
Main engine: Triple expansion; 850 ihp = 10·5 knots
Complement: 27

3 Ex-US "YTL 422" CLASS

KLUENG BADEN YTL 2
MARN VICHAI YTL 3
RAD (ex-USN *YTL 340*) YTL 4

Displacement, tons: 63 standard (*Rad* 52 standard)
Dimensions, feet (metres): 64·7 × 16·5 × 6·0 *(18·6 × 4·5 × 1·8)*
  Rad 60·7 × 17·5 × 5·0 *(18·3 × 5·3 × 1·5)*
Main engines: Diesels; speed = 8 knots (*Rad* 6 knots)

Rad transferred May 1955 from US, the other pair bought from Canada 1953.

RAD   8/1976, Dr. Giorgio Arra

TOGO

Ministerial

Minister of National Defence:
General Gnassingbe Eyadema (President)

Personnel

(a) 1978: 200
(b) Voluntary service

Base

Lome

Mercantile Marine

Lloyd's Register of Shipping:
1 vessel of 134 tons gross

2 COASTAL PATROL CRAFT

Name	No.	Builders	Commissioned
MONO	—	Chantiers Navals de l'Esterel	1976
KARA	—	Chantiers Navals de l'Esterel	1976

Displacement, tons: 80
Dimensions, feet (metres): 105 × 19·6 × 5·8 *(32 × 5·8 × 1·6)*
Missiles: Can carry SS-12
Guns: 2—20 mm
Main engines: 2 MTU diesels; 2 700 bhp = 30 knots
Range, miles: 1 400 at 15 knots
Complement: 17

Radar: One navigation set

Note: Reports of three other patrol craft and a river gunboat are unsubstantiated.

MONO and KARA   1976, Ch. Navals de l'Esterel

TONGA

On 10 March 1973 King Taufa'ahau Tupou IV commissioned the first craft of Tonga's Maritime Force, a necessary service in a Kingdom of seven main groups of islands spread over 270 square miles.

Mercantile Marine

Lloyd's Register of Shipping:
12 vessels of 14 180 tons gross

2 COASTAL PATROL CRAFT

Name	No.	Builders	Commissioned
NGAHAU KOULA	P 101	Brooke Marine, Lowestoft	10 Mar 1973
NGAHAU SILIVA	P 102	Brooke Marine, Lowestoft	10 May 1976

Displacement, tons: 15
Dimensions, feet (metres): 45 × 13 × 3·8 *(13·7 × 4 × 1·2)*
Guns: 2—0·50 Browning MG
Main engines: 2 Cummins V8 diesels; 2 shafts = 21 knots
Range, miles: 800 (101), 1 000 (102)
Complement: 7

DF and echo-sounder (Ferrograph). Manned by volunteers from the Maritime Defence Division Tongan Defence Service. *Ngahau Siliva* was completed 2 Feb 1976 and commissioned by HM Queen Halaevalu Mata'aho in May. Names mean Golden and Silver Arrow respectively.

Radar: Decca 101.

NGAHAU SILIVA   1977, Royal Tongan Defence Service

468 TRINIDAD AND TOBAGO

TRINIDAD AND TOBAGO
COAST GUARD

Ministerial

Minister of National Security:
Senator John Donaldson

Headquarters Appointment

Commanding Officer:
Commander M. O. Williams, MOM

Personnel

(a) 1978: 286 (30 officers, 256 ratings)
(b) Voluntary service

Base

Staubles Bay

Mercantile Marine

Lloyd's Register of Shipping:
42 vessels of 17 192 tons gross

DELETIONS
1975-76 Sea Hawk and Sea Scout

2 LATER VOSPER TYPE (LARGE PATROL CRAFT)

Name	No.	Builders	Commissioned
CHAGUARAMUS	CG 3	Vosper Ltd, Portsmouth	18 Mar 1972
BUCCOO REEF	CG 4	Vosper Ltd, Portsmouth	18 Mar 1972

Displacement, tons: 100 standard; 125 full load
Dimensions, feet (metres): 103·0 × 19·8 × 5·8 (31·5 × 5·9 × 1·6)
Gun: 1—20 mm Hispano Suiza
Main engines: 2 Paxman Ventura diesels; 2 900 bhp = 24 knots
Oil fuel, tons: 20
Range, miles: 2 000 at 13 knots
Complement: 19 (3 officers, 16 ratings)

Chaguaramus was laid down on 1 Feb 1971 and launched on 29 March 1971. Fitted with air-conditioning and roll-damping. Both commissioned at Portsmouth, England.

CHAGUARAMUS   1975, Trinidad and Tobago Coast Guard

2 VOSPER TYPE (LARGE PATROL CRAFT)

Name	No.	Builders	Commissioned
TRINITY	CG 1	Vosper Ltd, Portsmouth	20 Feb 1965
COURLAND BAY	CG 2	Vosper Ltd, Portsmouth	20 Feb 1965

Displacement, tons: 96 standard; 123 full load
Dimensions, feet (metres): 102·6 oa × 19·7 × 5·5 (31·4 × 5·9 × 1·7)
Gun: 1—40 mm Bofors
Main engines: 2 12-cyl Paxman Ventura YJCM turbo-charged diesels; 2 910 bhp = 24·5 knots
Oil fuel, tons: 18
Range, miles: 1 800 at 13·5 knots
Complement: 17 (3 officers, 14 ratings)

Designed by Vosper Limited, Portsmouth. Of steel construction with aluminium alloy superstructure. The boats are air-conditioned throughout except the engine room. Vosper roll-damping equipment is fitted. Laid down Oct 1963. *Trinity* was launched on 14 April 1964. *Trinity* is named after Trinity Hills, so named by Columbus on making his landfall in 1498, and *Courland Bay* after a bay in Tobago where a settlement was founded by the Duke of Courland in the 17th century. Both commissioned at Portsmouth, England.

TRINITY   1975, Trinidad and Tobago Coast Guard

MISCELLANEOUS

1 NEW CONSTRUCTION COASTAL PATROL CRAFT

Length, feet (metres): 55 (16·7)
Main engines: 2 GM diesels
Complement: 6

Under construction by Tugs and Lighters Ltd.

1 COASTAL PATROL CRAFT

CG 9

Locally built of glass fibre, 23 ft long with one Caterpillar diesel. Capable of 27 knots. Used for inshore patrol work, mainly in the Gulf of Paria.

1 SAIL TRAINING SHIP

HUMMING BIRD II

40 foot cutter-rigged ketch with three-cylinder Lister auxiliary diesel. Built in Trinidad 1966.

1 COASTAL PATROL CRAFT

Name	No.	Builders	Commissioned
NAPARIMA	—	Tugs and Lighters, Port of Spain	13 Aug 1976

Dimensions, feet (metres): 50 × 16 × 8 (16·4 × 52·5 × 26·2)
Main engines: 2 GM 8V 71 diesels; 460 bhp
Complement: 5

NAPARIMA   1976 Trinidad and Tobago Coast Guard

TUNISIA

Headquarters Appointment

Chief of Naval Staff:
 Capitaine de Fregate Jedidi Bechir

Diplomatic Representation

Defence Ataché in Paris (and for London):
 Colonel A. El-Fehri

Personnel

(a) 1978: 2 600 officers and men
(b) 1 year national service

Mercantile Marine

Lloyd's Register of Shipping:
 39 vessels of 100 128 tons gross

Strength of the Fleet

Type	Active	Building
Frigate	1	—
MSC	2	—
Large Patrol Craft	5	1
Coastal Patrol Craft	10	—
Tugs	3	—

FRIGATES

1 Ex-US "SAVAGE" CLASS

Name	No.	Builders	Commissioned
PRÉSIDENT BOURGUIBA	E 7	Consolidated Steel Corp	27 Nov 1943
(ex-USS *Thomas J. Gary* DER 326, ex-DE 326)			

Displacement, tons: 1 590 standard; 2 100 full load
Dimensions, feet (metres): 306 oa × 36·6 × 14 *(93·3 × 11·1 × 4·3)*
Guns: 2—3 in *(76 mm)* 50 cal; 2—20 mm
A/S weapon: 6 (2 triple) Mk 32 A/S torpedo tubes
Main engines: 4 diesels; 6 000 bhp; 2 shafts = 19 knots
Range, miles: 11 500 at 11 knots
Complement: 169

Completed as "Edsall" class DE. Converted to Radar Picket "Savage" class in 1958. Transferred 27 Oct 1973.

Radar: SPS 29 and SPS 10.

PRESIDENT BOURGUIBA   1977, Tunisian Navy

COASTAL MINESWEEPERS

2 Ex-US "ADJUTANT" CLASS

Name	No.	Builders	Commissioned
HANNIBAL (ex-*Coquelicot*, ex-USN *MSC 84*)	—	Stephen Bros, Calif	May 1953
SOUSSE (ex-*Marjolaine*, ex-USN *MSC 66*)	—	Harbor BB Co, Calif	Mar 1953

Displacement, tons: 320 standard; 372 full load
Dimensions, feet (metres): 141 oa × 26 × 8·3 *(43 × 8 × 2·6)*
Guns: 2—20 mm
Main engines: 2 GM diesels; 2 shafts; 1 200 bhp = 13 knots
Oil fuel, tons: 40
Range, miles: 2 500 at 10 knots
Complement: 38

Built for France under MDAP *Hannibal* delivered in 1953—to Tunisia in 1973. *Sousse* transferred mid-1977. Of French "Acacia" class. Currently in use for patrol duties.

HANNIBAL   1974, Tunisian Navy

LIGHT FORCES

1 Ex-FRENCH "LE FOUGEUX" CLASS (LARGE PATROL CRAFT)

Name	No.	Builders	Commissioned
SAKIET SIDI YOUSSEF	P 303	Dubigeon, Nantes	1956
(ex-*UW 12*)			

Displacement, tons: 325 standard; 440 full load
Dimensions, feet (metres): 170 pp × 23 × 6·5 *(53 × 7·3 × 2)*
Guns: 1—40 mm; 2—20 mm
A/S weapons: Mousetrap; 4 DCT; 2 DC racks
Main engines: 4 SEMT-Pielstick diesels; 3 240 bhp = 18·7 knots
Range, miles: 2 000 at 15 knots
Complement: 4 officers, 59 men

Built in France, under US off-shore order. Purchased by West Germany in 1957 and served as A/S trials vessel. Transferred to Tunisia in Dec 1969.

SAKIET SIDI YOUSSEF   1977, Tunisian Navy

2 VOSPER THORNYCROFT 103 ft TYPE
(FAST ATTACK CRAFT—PATROL)

Name	No.	Builders	Commissioned
TAZARKA	P205	Vosper Thornycroft	27 Oct 1977
MENZEL BOURGUIBA	P206	Vosper Thornycroft	27 Oct 1977

Displacement, tons: 120
Dimensions, feet (metres): 103 × 19·5 × 5·5 *(31·4 × 5·9 × 1·7)*
Guns: 2—20 mm
Main engines: 2 diesels; 4 000 hp = 27 knots
Range, miles: 1 500 cruising
Complement: 24

Ordered 9 Sept 1975. P205 laid down 23 March 1976 and launched 19 July 1976.

TAZARKA   10/1977 Michael D. J. Lennon

470 TUNISIA

3 "P 48" CLASS (LARGE PATROL CRAFT)

Name	No.	Builders	Commissioned
BIZERTE	P 301	Ch. Franco-Belges (Villeneuve, la Garenne)	10 July 1970
HORRIA (ex-*Liberté*)	P 302	Ch. Franco-Belges (Villeneuve, la Garenne)	Oct 1970
MONASTIR	P 304	Soc. Francaise Constructions Navale	25 Mar 1975

Displacement, tons: 250
Dimensions, feet (metres): 157·5 × 23·3 × 7 *(48 × 7·1 × 2·3)*
Missiles: 8—SS 12
Guns: 2—40 mm
Main engines: 2 MTU diesels; 4 800 bhp = 20 knots
Range, miles: 2 000 at 16 knots

First pair ordered in 1968. *Bizerte* was launched on 20 Nov 1969. *Horria* launched 12 Feb 1970. *Monastir* ordered in Aug 1973, laid down Jan 1974, launched 25 June 1974, completed 20 Feb 1975 but commissioned on 25 March.

HORRIA   1974, *Tunisian Navy*

4 32-metre COASTAL PATROL CRAFT

Name	No.	Builders	Commissioned
ISTIKLAL (ex-*VC 11, P 761*)	P 201	Ch. Navals de l'Esterel	1957
JQUMHOURIA	P 202	Ch. Navals de l'Esterel	Jan 1969
AL JALA	P 203	Ch. Navals de l'Esterel	Nov 1963
REMADA	P 204	Ch. Navals de l'Esterel	July 1967

Displacement, tons: 60 standard; 82 full load
Dimensions, feet (metres): 104·5 × 15·5 × 5·6 *(31·5 × 5·8 × 1·7)*
Gun: 1—20 mm
Main engines: 2 MTU 12V 493 (Mercedes-Benz) diesels; 2 shafts; 2 700 bhp = 28 knots
Range, miles: 1 400 at 15 knots
Complement: 17

Istiklal transferred from France March 1959.

ISTIKLAL   1971, *Tunisian Navy*

6 25-metre COASTAL PATROL CRAFT

Name	No.	Builders	Commissioned
—	V 101	Ch. Navals de l'Esterel	1961
—	V 102	Ch. Navals de l'Esterel	1961
—	V 103	Ch. Navals de l'Esterel	1962
—	V 104	Ch. Navals de l'Esterel	1962
—	V 105	Ch. Navals de l'Esterel	1963
—	V 106	Ch. Navals de l'Esterel	1963

Displacement, tons: 38
Dimensions, feet (metres): 83 × 15·6 × 4·1 *(25 × 4·8 × 1·3)*
Gun: 1—20 mm
Main engines: 2 twin GM diesels; 2 400 hp = 23 knots
Range, miles: 900 at 16 knots
Complement: 11

V 104   1970, *Tunisian Navy*

Two further craft of the same design (V 107 and V 108) but unarmed were supplied to the Fisheries Administration in 1971.

V 105   1974, *Tunisian Navy*

TUGS

Name	No.	Builders	Commissioned
RAS ADAR (ex-*Zeeland*, ex-*Pan American*, ex-*Ocean Pride*, ex-HMS *Oriana*, BAT 1)	—	Gulfport Boilerworks & Eng Co.	1942

Name	No.	Builders	Commissioned
JAOUEL EL BAHR	T 1	Ch. Navals de l'Esterel	—
SABBACK EL BAHR	T 2	Ch. Navals de l'Esterel	—

Displacement, tons: 540 standard
Dimensions, feet (metres): 144·4 × 33 × 13·5 *(43 × 10 × 4)*

Built in 1942 and lend leased to the Royal Navy in that year as BAT 1 HMS *Oriana*, returned and sold in 1946 as *Ocean Pride*, then *Pan America* in 1947, then *Zeeland* in 1956.

TURKEY

Headquarters Appointment

Commander in Chief, Turkish Naval Forces:
   Admiral Bulend Ulusu

Senior Command

Fleet Commander:
   Vice-Admiral Nejat Tumer

Diplomatic Representation

Naval Attaché in Athens:
   Captain Y. Günçer
Naval Attaché in Bonn:
   Captain T. Özkan
Naval Attaché in Cairo:
   Commander Y. Erel
Naval Attaché in London:
   Lieutenant-Commander B. Alpkaya
Naval Attaché in Moscow:
   Captain R. Maldemir
Naval Attaché in Oslo:
   Captain T. Erdinç
Naval Attaché in Rome:
   Captain E. Akman
Naval Attaché in Tokyo:
   Commander E. Erdilek
Naval Attaché in Washington:
   Captain Aydan Erol

Personnel

(a) 1978: 45 000 officers and ratings
(b) 20 months national service

Naval Bases

Headquarters: Ankara
Main Naval Base: Gölçük
Senior Flag Officers: Istanbul, Izmir
Other Flag Officers: Eregli, Bosphorus,
   Heybeliada (Training), Dardanelles, Iskenderun
Dockyards: Gölçük, Taşkizak (Istanbul)

Naval Air Arm

3 AB-204B Helicopters
16 S2E ASW Aircraft

Mercantile Marine

Lloyd's Register of Shipping:
   448 vessels of 1 288 282 tons gross

Strength of the Fleet

Type	Active	Building
Destroyers	13	—
Frigates	2	—
Submarines—Patrol	12	2
Fast Attack Craft—Missile	7	1
Fast Attack Craft—Torpedo	13	—
Large Patrol Craft	43	(13)
Coastal Patrol Craft	4	—
Minelayer—Large	1	—
Minelayers—Coastal	6	—
Minesweepers—Coastal	21	—
Minesweepers—Inshore	4	—
Minehunting Boats	9	—
LSTs	4	—
LCTs	17	—
LCUs	16	—
LCMs	20	—
Support Tankers	5	—
Harbour Tanker	1	—
Water Tankers	3	—
Repair Ships	3	—
Transports	8	—
Submarine Rescue Ships	3	—
BDVs	4	—
Gate Vessels	3	—
Tug—Ocean	5	—
Tugs—Harbour	3	—
Floating Docks	7	—
Training Ship	1	—
Survey Vessels	4	—
Depot Ships	2	—

DELETIONS

Destroyers

1973 Gaziantep, Giresun
1974 Kocatepe (ex-USS Harwood) sunk on 22 July. Gemlik.
1976 Gelibolu

Corvettes

1973 Edremit, Eregli (ex-MSF)
1974 Çardak, Çesme, Edincik (ex-MSF)
1975 Alanya, Ayvalik

Submarines

(Most replaced by submarines of same name).

1973 Birinci Inönü, Çanakkale, Çerbe, Ikinci Inönü, Piri Reis
1974 Gür (ex-Chub), Sakarya (ex-Boarfish)
1977 Dumlupinar, Hizir Reis, Turgut Reis

Fast Attack Craft

1973 Dogan, Marti ("Nasty" class), AB 1-4, 6-7

Support Tanker

1975 Akar

Boom Defence Vessels

1975 AG 2, AG 3, Kaldaray

Training Ship

1977 Savarona

Survey Craft

1975 Mesaha 3 and 4

Tug

1975 Önder

PENNANT LIST

Destroyers

D 340	Istanbul
D 341	Izmir
D 342	Izmit
D 343	Iskenderun
D 344	Içel
D 351	M. Fevzi Çakmak
D 352	Gayret
D 353	Adatepe
D 354	Kocatepe
D 355	Tinaztepe
D 356	Zafer
D 357	Muavenet

Frigates

| D 358 | Berk |
| D 359 | Peyk |

Submarines

S 333	Ikinci Inönü
S 335	Burak Reis
S 336	Murat Reis
S 337	Oruc Reis
S 338	Uluçali Reis
S 339	Dumlupinar
S 340	Çerbe
S 341	Çanakkale
S 342	Turgut Reis
S 344	Hizir Reis
S 345	Preveze
S 346	Birinci Inönü
S 347	Atilay
S 348	Saldiray
S 349	Yildiray
S 350	Batiray

Amphibious Forces

L 401	Ertugrul
L 402	Serdar
L 403	Bayraktar
L 404	Sancaktar
C 101 and 103-106	LCTs
C 107-118	LCTs
C 201-204	LCUs
C 205-216	LCUs
C 301-320	LCMs

Minewarfare Forces (Sweepers)

M 500	Foça
M 501	Fethiye
M 502	Fatsa
M 503	Finike
M 507	Seymen
M 508	Selcuk
M 509	Seyhan
M 510	Samsun
M 511	Sinop
M 512	Sumene
M 513	Seddulbahir
M 514	Silifke
M 515	Saros
M 516	Sigacik
M 517	Sapanca
M 518	Sariyer
M 520	Karamürsel
M 521	Kerempe
M 522	Kilimli
M 523	Kozlu
M 524	Kuşadasi
M 530	Trabzon
M 531	Terme
M 532	Tirebolu
M 533	Tekirdag

Minewarfare Forces (Layers)

N 101	Mordogan
N 102	Meriç
N 103	Marmaris
N 104	Mersin
N 105	Mürefte
N 110	Nusret
N 115	Mehemedcik

Service Forces

A 403	Bayraktar
A 404	Sancaktar
A 571	Yuzbaşi Tolunay
A 572	Albay Hakki Burak
A 573	Binbaşi Saadettin Gürçan
A 574	Akpina
A 575	Inebolu
A 579	Gazi Hasan Paşa
A 581	Onaran
A 582	Başaran
A 583	Donatan
A 584	Kurtaran
A 585	Akin
A 586	Ülkü
A 587	Gazal
A 588	Umur Bey
A 591	Erkin
A 593	Çandarli (survey)
A 594	Çarşamba (survey)
Y 1081-1087	Floating Docks
Y 1117	Sonduren
Y 1118	Akbas
Y 1119	Kepez
Y 1121	Yedekci
Y 1122	Kuvvet
Y 1123	Öncu
Y 1129	Kudret
Y 1155	Kanaria
Y 1156	Sarköy
Y 1163	Lapseki
Y 1164	Erdek
Y 1166	Kilya
Y 1168	Tuzla
Y 1207	Gölçük
Y 1208	Van
Y 1209	Ulabat
Y 1217	Sogut

Light Forces

P 111	Sultanhisar
P 112	Demirhisar
P 113	Yarhisar
P 114	Akhisar
P 115	Sivrihisar
P 116	Koçhisar
P 301	AG 1 (BDV)
P 304	AG 4 (BDV)
P 305	AG 5 (BDV)
P 306	AG 6 (BDV)
P 311-4	MTB 1-4
P 316-20	MTB 6-10
P 321	Denizkuzu
P 322	Atmaca
P 323	Sahin
P 324	Kartal
P 325	Melten
P 326	Pelikan
P 327	Albatros
P 328	Şimşek
P 329	Kasirga
P 330	Firtina
P 331	Tufan
P 332	Kiliç
P 333	Mizrak
P 334	Yildiz
P 335	Kalkan
P 336	Karayel
P 338	Yildirim
P 339	Bora
P 340	Dogan
P 341	Marti
P 342	Tayfun
P 343	Volkan
P 1209-12	LS 9-12
P 1221-34	AB 21-34
J 12-30	Large Patrol Craft

472 TURKEY

Ex-US "GEARING" Class

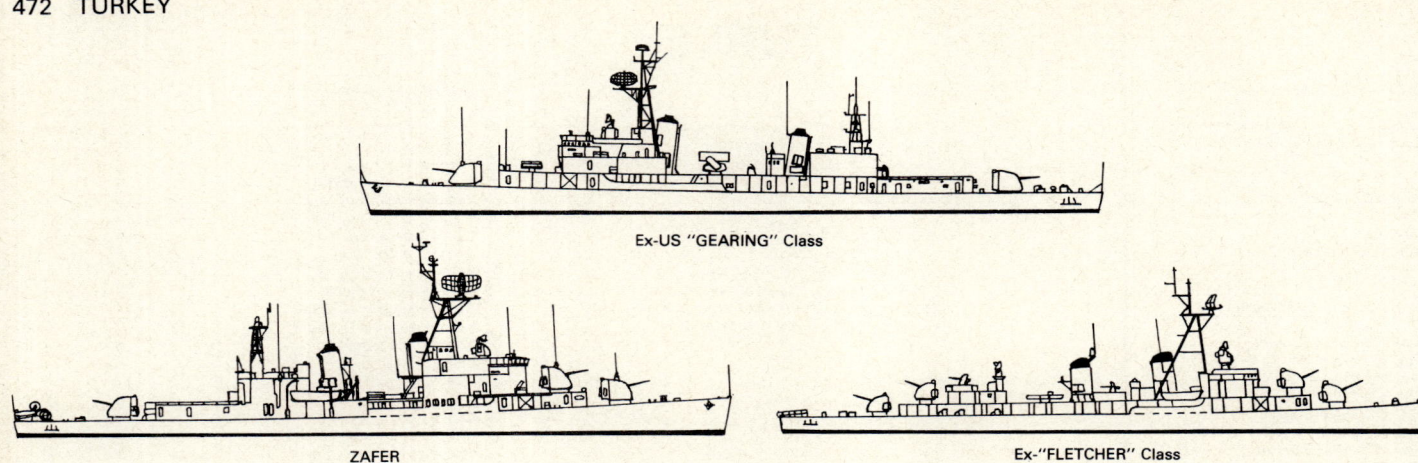

ZAFER

Ex-"FLETCHER" Class

SUBMARINES

3 + 1 TYPE 209 (HOWALDTSWERKE)

Name	No.	Builders	Laid down	Launched	Commissioned
ATILAY	S 347	Howaldtswerke, Kiel	2 Aug 1972	23 Oct 1974	23 July 1975
SALDIRAY	S 348	Howaldtswerke, Kiel	1973	14 Feb 1975	16 Jan 1977
BATIRAY	S 349	Gölcük	11 June 1975	1977	1979
YILDIRAY	S 350	Gölcük	—	—	1980

Displacement, tons: 990 surfaced; 1 290 dived
Length, feet (metres): 183·7 (56·0)
Beam, feet (metres): 20·3 (6·2)
Torpedo tubes: 8—21 in (with reloads)
Main machinery: Diesel-electric; 4 MTU Siemens diesel-generators; 1 Siemens electric motor; 1 shaft
Speed, knots: 10 surfaced; 22 dived
Range: 50 days
Complement: 31

Designed by Ingenieurkontor, Lübeck for construction by Howaldtswerke, Kiel and sale by Ferrostaal, Essen all acting as a consortium.
A single-hull design with two ballast tanks and forward and after trim tanks. Fitted with snort and remote machinery control. The single screw is slow revving. Very high capacity batteries with GRP lead-acid cells and battery cooling—by Wilh. Hagen and VARTA. Active and passive sonar, sonar detection equipment, sound ranging gear and underwater telephone. Fitted with two periscopes, radar and Omega receiver. Foreplanes retract. Saldiray completed 21 Oct 1975 but was not taken over until Jan 1977.

ATILAY 2/1975, Reinhard Nerlich

Future Construction: Two of this class are the first submarines ever built in Turkey. If this class is to replace the ex-USN boats a considerable programme must be planned.

2 Ex-US "GUPPY III" CLASS

Name	No.	Builders	Laid down	Launched	Commissioned
ÇANAKKALE (ex-USS Cobbler SS 344)	S 341	Electric Boat Co	3 April 1944	1 April 1945	8 Aug 1945
IKINCI INONÜ (ex-USS Corporal SS 346)	S 333	Electric Boat Co	27 April 1944	10 June 1945	9 Nov 1945

Displacement, tons: 1 975 standard; 2 540 dived
Dimensions, feet (metres): 326·5 × 27 × 17 (99·4 × 8·2 × 5·2)
Torpedo tubes: 10—21 in (533 mm) 6 bow, 4 stern
Main machinery: 4 diesels; 6 400 shp; 2 electric motors 5 400 bhp; 2 shafts
Speed: 20 surfaced; 15 dived
Complement: 86

Transferred 21 Nov 1973.

Future Additions: When the US Congress imposed an arms embargo on exports to Turkey in 1975 arrangements were well-advanced for the transfer of the two "Guppy III" class, Clamagore and Tiru. It is reported that these will possibly be transferred in 1978-79.

IKINCI INONÜ (ex-US number) Turkish Navy

7 Ex-US "GUPPY II A" CLASS

Name	No.	Builders	Laid down	Launched	Commissioned
BURAK REIS (ex-USS Seafox, SS 402)	S 335	Portsmouth Navy Yard	2 Nov 1943	28 Mar 1944	13 June 1944
MURAT REIS (ex-USS Razorback, SS 394)	S 336	Portsmouth Navy Yard	9 Sept 1943	27 Jan 1944	3 April 1944
ORUC REIS (ex-USS Pomfret, SS 391)	S 337	Portsmouth Navy Yard	14 July 1943	27 Oct 1943	19 Feb 1944
ULUÇ ALI REIS (ex-USS Thornback, SS 418)	S 338	Portsmouth Navy Yard	5 April 1944	7 July 1944	13 Oct 1944
ÇERBE (ex-USS Trutta, SS 421)	S 340	Portsmouth Navy Yard	22 Dec 1943	22 May 1944	16 Nov 1944
PREVEZE (ex-USS Entemedor, SS 340)	S 345	Electric Boat Co	3 Feb 1944	17 Dec 1944	6 April 1945
BIRINCI INÖNÜ (ex-USS Threadfin, SS 410)	S 346	Portsmouth Navy Yard	18 Mar 1944	26 June 1944	30 Aug 1944

Displacement, tons: 1 840 standard; 2 445 dived
Dimensions, feet (metres): 306 × 27 × 17 (93·2 × 8·2 × 5·2)
Torpedo tubes: 10—21 in (533 mm) (6 bow, 4 stern); 24 torpedoes carried
Main machinery: 3 GM diesels; 4 800 hp; 2 electric motors; 5 400 hp
Speed, knots: 17 surfaced; 15 dived
Range, miles: 12 000 at 10 knots surfaced
Complement: 85

The fact that the same names are used for replacement submarines as for their predecessors can be confusing. eg "Cerbe" was used for both ex-USS Hammerhead and now for ex-USS Trutta.

Transfers: Burak Reis Dec 1970, Murat Reis 17 Nov 1970, Oruç Reis 3 May 1972, Çerbe, June 1972, Preveze, Uluç Ali Reis 24 Aug 1973, Birinci Inönü 15 Aug 1973.

ULUÇ ALI REIS 1975, Turkish Navy

TURKEY 473

DESTROYERS

5 Ex-US "GEARING" CLASS (FRAM I and II)

Name	No.	Builders	Laid down	Launched	Commissioned
M. FEVZI ÇAKMAK (ex-USS *Charles H. Roan*, DD 853)	D 351	Bethlehem Steel Corp, Quincy	1944	15 May 1945	12 Sept 1946
GAYRET (ex-USS *Eversole*, DD 789)	D 352	Todd Pacific Shipyard	1945	8 Jan 1946	10 July 1946
ADATEPE (ex-USS *Forrest Royal*, DD 872)	D 353	Bethlehem, Staten Is.	1945	17 Jan 1946	28 June 1946
KOCATEPE (ex-USS *Norris*, DD 859)	D 354	Bethlehem Steel Corp, San Pedro	1944	25 Feb 1945	9 June 1945
TINAZTEPE (ex-USS *Keppler*, DD 765)	D 355	Bethlehem Steel Corp, San Francisco	1944	24 June 1945	23 May 1947

Displacement, tons: 2 425 standard; 3 500 full load
Length, feet (metres): 390·5 *(119·0)* oa
Beam, feet (metres): 40·9 *(12·5)*
Draught, feet (metres): 19·0 *(5·8)*
Aircraft: Helicopter deck and hangar
Guns: 4—5 in *(127 mm)* 38 cal (2 twin)
A/S weapons: FRAM I; 1 Asroc 8-tube launcher; 2 triple torpedo tubes (Mk 32); FRAM II; 1 trainable Hedgehog; 2 triple torpedo tubes (Mk 32)
Main engines: 2 geared turbines; 2 shafts; 60 000 shp
Boilers: 4 Babcock & Wilcox
Speed, knots: 34
Oil fuel, tons: 650
Range, miles: 4 800 at 15 knots; 2 400 at 25 knots
Complement: 275 (15 officers, 260 ratings)

Adatepe, Gayret and *Çakmak* FRAM I conversions and *Kocatepe* and *Tinaztepe* FRAM II. They were transferred to Turkey on 27 March 1971 *(Adatepe)* 30 June 1972 *(Tinaztepe)* 11 July 1973 *(Gayret)* and 21 Sept 1973 *(Çakmak)*, *Adatepe* purchased 15 Feb 1973 and *Kocatepe* 7 July 1974, commissioned 24 July 1975.

Fire control: GFCS Mk 37 with Mk 25 radar.

Radar: Long range air search: SPS 40 (FRAM I) SPS 6 (FRAM II). Surface search: SPS 10.

Replacement: The previous *Kocatepe* D 354 was sunk 22 July 1974. USS *Norris* had been purchased for spares on 7 July 1974 and has been re-activated to replace *Kocatepe*.

Sonar: FRAM I, SQS 23. FRAM II, SQS 29 series.

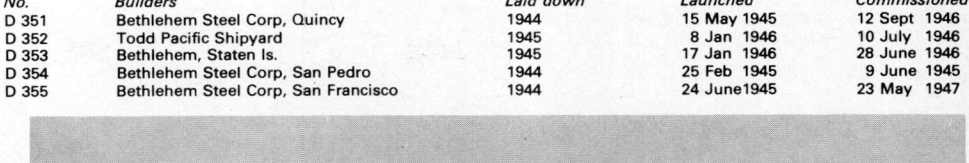

ADATEPE 1973, Dr. Giorgio Arra

TINAZTEPE 6/1975, Dr. Giorgio Arra

1 Ex-US "ROBERT H. SMITH" CLASS

Name	No.	Builders	Laid down	Launched	Commissioned
MUAVENET (ex-USS *Gwin*, ex-*MMD 33*, ex-*DD 772*)	D 357	Bethlehem Steel Corp, San Pedro	1943	9 April 1944	30 Sept 1944

Displacement, tons: 2 250 standard; 3 375 full load
Dimensions, feet (metres): 376·5 × 41 × 19 *(114·8 × 12·5 × 5·8)*
Guns: 6—5 in *(127 mm)* 38 cal (twins); 12—40 mm (2 quad, 2 twin); 11—20 mm
Mines: 80
Main engines: Geared turbines; 60 000 shp; 2 shafts
Boilers: 4 Babcock & Wilcox
Speed, knots: 34
Range, miles: 4 600 at 15 knots
Complement: 274

Modified "Allen M. Sumner" class converted for minelaying. After modernisation at Philadelphia she was transferred on 22 Oct 1971.

Fire control: GFCS director Mk 37 with Mk 28 radar. Mk 34 director for Mk 51 GFCS for a quad 40 mm.

Radar: Air search: SPS 6.
Surface search: SPS 10

Sonar: QCU or QHB.

MUAVENET (old pennant number) Godfrey H. Walker

1 Ex-US "ALLEN M. SUMNER (FRAM II)" CLASS

Name	No.	Builders	Laid down	Launched	Commissioned
ZAFER (ex-USS *Hugh Purvis* DD 709)	D 356	Federal SB and DD Co	1944	17 Dec 1944	1 Mar 1945

Displacement, tons: 2 200 standard; 3 320 full load
Length, feet (metres): 376·5 *(114·8)*
Beam, feet (metres): 40·9 *(12·5)*
Draught, feet (metres): 19·0 *(5·8)*
Guns: 6—5 in 38 cal (twins)
A/S weapons: 6 (2 triple) Mk 32 A/S torpedo tubes; 2 Hedgehogs
Main engines: 2 geared turbines; 2 shafts; 60 000 shp
Boilers: 4 Babcock & Wilcox
Speed, knots: 34
Oil fuel, tons: 650
Range, miles: 4 600 at 15 knots
Complement: 275 (15 officers, 260 ratings)

Zafer is of "Allen M. Sumner" class of modified FRAM II having been used as a USN trials ship for planar passive sonar. There is an extra deck-house on the hangar. Purchased 15 Feb 1972.

Radar: Air search: SPS 40.
Surface search: SPS 10.

Sonar: SQS 29 series.

474 TURKEY

5 Ex-US "FLETCHER" CLASS

Name	No.	Builders	Laid down	Launched	Commissioned
ISTANBUL (ex-USS *Clarence K. Bronson*, DD 668)	D 340	Federal SB & DD Co, Newark	1942	18 April 1943	11 June 1943
IZMIR (ex-USS *Van Valkenburgh*, DD 656)	D 341	Gulf Shipbuilding Corp	1943	19 Dec 1943	2 Aug 1944
IZMIT (ex-USS *Cogswell*, DD 651)	D 342	Bath Iron Works, Corpn	1942	5 June 1943	17 Aug 1943
ISKENDERUN (ex-USS *Boyd*, DD 544)	D 343	Bethlehem Co, San Pedro	1942	29 Oct 1942	8 May 1943
IÇEL (ex-USS *Preston*, DD 795)	D 344	Bethlehem Co, San Pedro	1943	12 Dec 1943	20 Mar 1944

Displacement, tons: 2 050 standard; 3 000 full load
Length, feet (metres): 376·5 *(114·8)* oa
Beam, feet (metres): 39·5 *(12·1)*
Draught, feet (metres): 18·0 *(5·5)*
Guns: 4—5 in *(127 mm)* 38 cal; 6—3 in *(76 mm)*
A/S weapons: 2 Hedgehogs
Torpedo tubes: 5—21 in *(533 mm)* (quintuple)
Main engines: GE geared turbines; 2 shafts; 60 000 shp
Boilers: 4 Babcock & Wilcox
Speed, knots: 34
Oil fuel, tons: 650
Range, miles: 5 000 at 15 knots
Complement: 250

Fire control: Mk 37 GFCS forward with Mk 25 radar. Mk 56 GFCS aft with Mk 35 radar. Two Mk 51 GFCS amidships.

Radar: Search: SPS 6.
Tactical: SPS 10.

Transfers: Transferred as follows: *Istanbul* 14 Jan 1967, *Izmir* 28 Feb 1967, *Iskenderun* and *Izmit* on 1 Oct 1969, and *Içel* on 15 Nov 1969.

ISTANBUL 1975, Turkish Navy

FRIGATES

2 "BERK" CLASS

Name	No.	Builders	Laid down	Launched	Commissioned
BERK	D 358	Gölcük Naval Yard	9 Mar 1967	25 June 1971	12 July 1972
PEYK	D 359	Gölcük Naval Yard	18 Jan 1968	7 June 1972	24 July 1975

Displacement, tons: 1 450 standard; 1 950 full load
Length, feet (metres): 311·7 *(95·0)*
Beam, feet (metres): 38·7 *(11·8)*
Draught, feet (metres): 18·1 *(5·5)*
Aircraft: 1 helicopter
Guns: 4—3 in *(76 mm)* 50 cal (2 twin Mk 33)
A/S weapons: 6 (2 triple) Mk 32 A/S torpedo tubes; 1 DC rack
Main engines: 4 Fiat diesels; 2 shafts; 24 000 bhp
Speed, knots: 25

First major warships built in Turkey, the start of a most important era in the Eastern Mediterranean. Both are named after famous ships of the Ottoman Navy. Of modified US "Claud Jones" design.

Fire control: Each mounting has GFCS Mk 63.

Radar: SPG 34;
Air search: SPS 40
Surface search: SPS 10

BERK 6/1977, Dr. Giorgio Arra

LIGHT FORCES

4 LÜRSSEN TYPE (FAST ATTACK CRAFT—MISSILE)

Name	No.	Builders	Commissioned
DOĞAN	P 340	Lürssen, Vegesack	Late 1976
MARTI	P 341	Taşkizak Yard, Istanbul	1978
TAYFUN	P 342	Taşkizak Yard, Istanbul	1978
VOLKAN	P 343	Taşkizak Yard, Istanbul	—

Displacement, tons: 410
Dimensions, feet (metres): 190·6 × 25 × 8·8 *(58·1 × 7·6 × 2·7)*
Missiles: 8—Harpoon
Guns: 2—76 mm OTO Melara
Main engines: 4—16-cyl MTU diesels; 18 000 hp = 38 knots
Range, miles: 700 at 35 knots

Ordered 3 Aug 1973. *Dogan* laid down 2 June 1975 (launched 16 June 1976), *Marti* 1 July 1975, *Tayfun* 1 Dec 1975.

Radar: HSA WM 27 system for missile control.

DOGAN 1976, Lürssen

TURKEY 475

9 "KARTAL" CLASS (FAST ATTACK CRAFT—MISSILE/TORPEDO)

Name	No.	Builders	Commissioned
DENIZKUSU	P 321 (ex-P 336)	Lürssen, Vegesack	1967
ATMACA	P 322 (ex-P 335)	Lürssen, Vegesack	1967
SAHIN	P 323 (ex-P 334)	Lürssen, Vegesack	1967
KARTAL	P 324 (ex-P 333)	Lürssen, Vegesack	1967
MELTEM	P 325 (ex-P 330)	Lürssen, Vegesack	1968
PELIKAN	P 326	Lürssen, Vegesack	1968
ALBATROS	P 327 (ex-P 325)	Lürssen, Vegesack	1968
ŞIMŞEK	P 328 (ex-P 332)	Lürssen, Vegesack	1968
KASIRGA	P 329 (ex-P 338)	Lürssen, Vegesack	1967

Displacement, tons: 160 standard; 180 full load
Dimensions, feet (metres): 140·5 × 23·5 × 7·2 (42·8 × 7·1 × 2·2)
Missiles: (see note)
Guns: 2—40 mm
Torpedo tubes: 4—21 in
Main engines: 4 MTU 16V 538 (Maybach) diesels; 4 shafts; 12 000 bhp = 42 knots
Complement: 39

Of the German Jaguar type. Launch dates—*Atmaca* 6 May 1966, *Kartal* 4 Nov 1965, *Meltem* 28 Dec 1966.

Missiles: Harpoon surface-to-surface missiles embarked in *Albatros, Meltem, Pelikan* and *Şimşek* during 1975.

DENIZKUSU   1975, Turkish Navy

7 Ex-FDR "JAGUAR" CLASS (FAST ATTACK CRAFT—TORPEDO)

Name	No.	Builders	Commissioned
FIRTINA (ex-FDR *Pelikan*, P 6086)	P 330	Lürssen, Vegesack	1962
TUFAN (ex-FDR *Storch*, P 6085)	P 331	Lürssen, Vegesack	1962
KILIÇ (ex-FDR *Löwe*, P 6065)	P 332	Lürssen, Vegesack	1960
MIZRAK (ex-FDR *Hähner*, P 6087)	P 333	Lürssen, Vegesack	1962
YILDIZ (ex-FDR *Tiger*, P 6063)	P 334	Lürssen, Vegesack	1959
KALKAN (ex-FDR *Wolf*, P 6062)	P 335	Lürssen, Vegesack	1959
KARAYEL (ex-FDR *Pinguin*, P 6090)	P 336	Lürssen, Vegesack	1962

Displacement, tons: 160 standard; 190 full load
Dimensions, feet (metres): 139·4 × 23·4 × 7·9 (42·5 × 7·2 × 2·4)
Guns: 2—40 mm L 70 Bofors (single)
Torpedo tubes: 4—21 in (2 tubes can be removed to embark 4 mines)
Main engines: 4 Maybach (MTU) diesels; 4 shafts; 12 000 bhp = 42 knots
Complement: 39

In late 1975-early 1976 seven "Jaguar" class were transferred by the FDR to Turkey. In addition three more were transferred for spare parts—*Alk* P 6084, *Fuchs* P 6066 and *Reiher* P 6089.

FIRTINA   1976, Reinhard Nerlich

1 + ? "NASTY" CLASS (FAST ATTACK CRAFT—TORPEDO)

Name	No.	Builders	Commissioned
GIRNE	P—	Taskizak Naval Yard	1976

Displacement, tons: 63·5 standard; 74·5 full load
Dimensions, feet (metres): 80·4 × 21 × 6·9 (24·5 × 6·4 × 2·1)
Guns: 2—40 mm
Torpedo tubes: 4—21 in (533 mm)
Main engines: 2 Deltic diesels; 6 200 hp; 2 shafts = 44 knots
Range, miles: 450 at 38 knots
Complement: 20

First of a series currently under construction.

2 Ex-US "ASHEVILLE" CLASS (LARGE PATROL CRAFT)

Name	No.	Builders	Commissioned
YILDIRIM (ex-USS *Defiance*, PG 95)	P 338	Petersons, Wisconsin	24 Sept 1969
BORA (ex-USS *Surprise*, PG 97)	P 339	Petersons, Wisconsin	17 Oct 1969

Displacement, tons: 225 standard; 245 full load
Dimensions, feet (metres): 164·5 oa × 23·8 × 9·5 (50·1 × 7·3 × 2·9)
Guns: 1—3 in 50 cal; 1—40 mm; 4—50 cal MG
Main engines: CODAG; 2 Cummins diesels; 1 450 hp = 16 knots; 1 GE gas turbine; 13 300 shp = 40 knots
Complement: 25

These vessels belong to the largest Patrol Type built by the USN since World War II and the first of that Navy to have gas turbines. Transferred to Turkey on 11 June 1973 and 28 Feb 1973 respectively.

BORA (as *Surprise*)   1975, Turkish Navy

10 LARGE PATROL CRAFT

Name	No.	Builders	Commissioned
AB 25	P 1225	Taskizak Naval Yard	1967
AB 26	P 1226	Taskizak Naval Yard	1967
AB 27	P 1227	Taskizak Naval Yard	1967
AB 28	P 1228	Taskizak Naval Yard	1968
AB 29	P 1229	Taskizak Naval Yard	1968
AB 30	P 1230	Taskizak Naval Yard	1969
AB 31	P 1231	Taskizak Naval Yard	1969
AB 32	P 1232	Taskizak Naval Yard	1970
AB 33	P 1233	Taskizak Naval Yard	1970
AB 34	P 1234	Taskizak Naval Yard	1970

Displacement, tons: 170
Dimensions, feet (metres): 132 × 21 × 5·5 (40·2 × 6·4 × 1·7)
Guns: 2—40 mm
Speed, knots: 22

AB 28 (Old pennant number)   1970, Turkish Navy

First was launched on 9 March 1967. Six similar launches are operated by the Gendarmerie.

476 TURKEY

6 Ex-US "PC 1638" CLASS (LARGE PATROL CRAFT)

Name	No.	Builders	Commissioned
SULTANHISAR (ex-*PC 1638*)	P 111	Gunderson Bros Engineering Co, Portland, Oregon	1943
DEMIRHISAR (ex-*PC 1639*)	P 112	Gunderson Bros Engineering Co, Portland, Oregon	1943
YARHISAR (ex-*PC 1640*)	P 113	Gunderson Bros Engineering Co, Portland, Oregon	1943
AKHISAR (ex-*PC 1641*)	P 114	Gunderson Bros Engineering Co, Portland, Oregon	1943
SIVRIHISAR (ex-*PC 1642*)	P 115	Gunderson Bros Engineering Co, Portland, Oregon	1943
KOÇHISAR (ex-*PC 1643*)	P 116	Gölcük Dockyard, Turkey	1965

Displacement, tons: 280 standard; 412 full load
Dimensions, feet (metres): 173·7 oa × 23 × 10·2 *(54 × 7 × 3·1)*
Guns: 1—3 in; 1—40 mm
A/S weapons: 4 DCT; 1 Hedgehog
Main engines: 2 FM diesels; 2 shafts; 2 800 bhp = 19 knots
Range, miles: 6 000 at 10 knots
Complement: 65 (5 officers, and 60 men)

Transferred in May 1964, 22 April 1965, Sept 1964, 3 Dec 1964, June 1965 and July 1965 respectively.

DEMIRHISAR   1975, Turkish Navy

4 US "PGM 71" CLASS (LARGE PATROL CRAFT)

Name	No.	Builders	Commissioned
AB 21 (ex-*PGM 104*)	P 1221	Peterson, Sturgeon Bay, USA	Dec 1967
AB 22 (ex-*PGM 105*)	P 1222	Peterson, Sturgeon Bay, USA	Dec 1967
AB 23 (ex-*PGM 106*)	P 1223	Peterson, Sturgeon Bay, USA	Dec 1967
AB 24 (ex-*PGM 108*)	P 1224	Peterson, Sturgeon Bay, USA	April 1968

Displacement, tons: 130 standard; 147 full load
Dimensions, feet (metres): 101 × 21 × 7 *(30·8 × 6·4 × 1·9)*
Guns: 1—40 mm; 4—20 mm
Main engines: 2 diesels; 2 shafts; 1 850 hp = 18·5 knots
Range, miles: 1 500 at 10 knots
Complement: 15

AB 23 (Old pennant number)   1970, Turkish Navy

19 LARGE PATROL CRAFT

Name	No.	Builders	Commissioned
—	J 12	Schweers, Bardenfleth	1961
—	J 13	Schweers, Bardenfleth	1961
—	J 14	Schweers, Bardenfleth	1961
—	J 15	Schweers, Bardenfleth	1961
—	J 16	Schweers, Bardenfleth	1962
—	J 17	Schweers, Bardenfleth	1962
—	J 18	Schweers, Bardenfleth	1962
—	J 19	Schweers, Bardenfleth	1962
—	J 20	Schweers, Bardenfleth	1962
—	J 21	Gölcük Navy Yard	1968
—	J 22	Gölcük Navy Yard	1968
—	J 23	Taskizak Naval Yard	1969
—	J 24	Taskizak Naval Yard	1969
—	J 25	Taskizak Naval Yard	1969
—	J 26	Taskizak Naval Yard	1969
—	J 27	Taskizak Naval Yard	1969
—	J 28	Taskizak Naval Yard	1970
—	J 29	Taskizak Naval Yard	1971
—	J 30	Taskizak Naval Yard	1971

Displacement, tons: 150
Dimensions, feet (metres): 129·3 × 20·6 × 4·9¯-4 × 6·3 × 1·5*)*
Guns: 2—40 mm
Main engines: 4 MTU 12V 493 diesels; 2 shafts; 3 200 bhp = 22 knots

Some operated by Gendarmerie.

J TYPE   1976, Michael D. J. Lennon

1 + 13 SAR 33 TYPE (LARGE PATROL CRAFT)

Displacement, tons: 190
Dimensions, feet (metres): 108·3 × 28·3 × 9·7 *(33 × 8·6 × 3)*
Guns: 1—40 mm; 2 MG
Main engines: 3 SCAM diesels; 12 000 hp = 40 knots
Range, miles: 450 at 35 knots

Prototype ordered from Abeking and Rasmussen, Lemwerder in May 1976. Laid down Oct 1976 for trials late 1977. As these trials were very successful it is now most probable that the remaining 13 are being built in Turkey. Ordered for Gendarmerie.

Armament: Could carry 2 SSM, 1—76 mm and 2—35 mm (twin) but guns shown to be fitted for Gendamerie.

4 Ex-US COASTGUARD "83 ft" CLASS (COASTAL PATROL CRAFT)

LS 9 P 1209 (ex-US *A 001*)   LS 11 P 1211 (ex-US *C 001*)
LS 10 P 1210 (ex-US *B 001*)   LS 12 P 1212 (ex-US *D 001*)

Displacement, tons: 63 standard
Dimensions, feet (metres): 83·0 × 14·0 × 5·0 *(25·3 × 4·3 × 1·6)*
Gun: 1—20 mm
A/S weapons: 2 Mousetrap
Main engines: 2 Cummins diesels; 1 100 bhp = 20 knots

Transferred on 25 June 1953.

TURKEY 477

MINE WARFARE FORCES

1 MINELAYER

Name	No.	Builders	Commissioned
NUSRET	N 110 (ex-*N 108*)	Frederikshaven Dockyard, Denmark	16 Sept 1964

Displacement, tons: 1 880 standard
Length, feet (metres): 246 *(75·0)* pp; 252·7 *(77·0)* oa
Beam, feet (metres): 41 *(12·6)*
Draught, feet (metres): 11 *(3·4)*
Guns: 4—3 in *(76 mm)* (2 twin)
Mines: 400
Main engines: GM diesels; 4 800 hp; 2 shafts
Speed, knots: 18
Complement: 146

Laid down in 1962, launched in 1964. Similar to Danish "Falster" class.

Radar: Search: RAN 7S.
Fire control: one Band.
Navigation Radar.

NUSRET 1975, Turkish Navy

5 Ex-US MODIFIED "LSM 1" CLASS (COASTAL MINELAYERS)

Name	No.	Builders	Commissioned
MORDOĞAN (ex-US *LSM 484* ex-*MMC 11*)	N 101	Brown SB Co, Texas	15 April 1945
MERIÇ (ex-US *LSM 490*, ex-*MMC 12*)	N 102	Brown SB Co, Texas	28 April 1945
MARMARIS (ex-US *LSM 481*, ex-*MMC 10*)	N 103	Brown SB Co, Texas	8 April 1945
MERSIN (ex-US *LSM 494*, ex-*MMC 13*)	N 104	Brown SB Co, Texas	8 May 1945
MÜREFTE (ex-US *LSM 492*, ex-*MMC 14*)	N 105	Brown SB Co, Texas	1 May 1945

Displacement, tons: 743 standard; 1 100 full load
Dimensions, feet (metres): 203·2 oa × 34·5 × 8·5 *(61·9 × 10·5 × 2·4)*
Guns: 2—40 mm; 2—20 mm
Main engines: Diesels; 2 shafts; 2 880 bhp = 12 knots
Oil fuel, tons: 60
Range, miles: 2 500 at 12 knots
Complement: 89

Ex-US Landing Ships Medium. All launched in 1945, converted into coastal minelayers by the US Navy in 1952 and taken over by the Turkish Navy (LSM 481, 484 and 490) and the Norwegian Navy (LSM 492 and 494) in Oct 1952 under MAP. LSM 492 *(Vale)* and LSM 494 *(Vidar)* were retransferred to the Turkish Navy on 1 Nov 1960 at Bergen, Norway.

MERIÇ 1975, Turkish Navy

1 Ex-US YMP TYPE (COASTAL MINELAYEER)

Name	No.	Builders	Commissioned
MEHMETCIK (ex-US *YMP 3*)	N 115	Higgins Inc, New Orleans	1958

Displacement, tons: 540 full load
Dimensions, feet (metres): 130 × 35 × 6 *(39·6 × 10·7 × 1·9)*
Main engines: Diesels; 2 shafts; 600 bhp = 10 knots
Complement: 22

Former US motor mine planter. Steel hulled. Transferred under MAP in 1958. For harbour defence.

MEHMETCIK (old pennant number)

12 Ex-US "ADJUTANT" "MSC 268" and "MSC 294" CLASSES
(MINESWEEPERS—COASTAL)

SEYMEN (ex-*MSC 131*) M 507
SELCUK (ex-*MSC 124*) M 508
SEYHAN (ex-*MSC 142*) M 509
SAMSUN (ex-USS *MSC 268*) M 510
SINOP (ex-USS *MSC 270*) M 511
SURMENE (ex-USS *MSC 271*) M 512
SEDDULBAHIR (ex-*MSC 272*) M 513
SILIFKE (ex-USS *MSC 304*) M 514
SAROS (ex-USS *MSC 305*) M 515
SIGACIK (ex-USS *MSC 311*) M 516
SAPANCA (ex-USS *MSC 312*) M 517
SARIYER (ex-USS *MSC 315*) M 518

Displacement, tons: 320 standard; 370 full load
Dimensions, feet (metres): 138·0 pp; 144·0 oa × 28·0 × 9·0 *(41·5; 43 × 8 × 2·6)*
Guns: 2—20 mm
Main engines: 2 diesels; 2 shafts; 1 200 bhp = 14 knots
Oil fuel, tons: 25
Range, miles: 2 500 at 10 knots
Complement: 38 (4 officers, 34 men)

Transferred on 19 Nov, 1970, 24 March 1970, 24 March 1970, 30 Sept 1958, Feb 1959, 27 March 1959, May 1959, Sept 1965, Feb 1966, June 1965, 26 July 1965, 8 Sept 1967, respectively. *Selcuk* and *Seyhan* were transferred from France (via USA) and *Seymen* from Belgium (via USA).

SURMENE 1975, Turkish Navy

4 Ex-CANADIAN MCB TYPE (MINESWEEPERS—COASTAL)

TRABZON (ex-HMCS *Gaspe*) M 530
TERME (ex-HMCS *Trinity*) M 531
TIREBOLU (ex-HMCS *Comax*) M 532
TEKIRDAG (ex-HMCS *Ungava*) M 533

Displacement, tons: 390 standard; 412 full load
Dimensions, feet (metres): 152·0 oa × 20·8 × 7·0 *(50 × 9·2 × 2·8)*
Gun: 1—40 mm
Main engines: Diesels; 2 shafts; 2 400 bhp = 16 knots
Oil fuel, tons: 52
Range, miles: 4 500 at 11 knots
Complement: 44

Sailed from Sydney, Nova Scotia, to Turkey on 19 May 1958. Built by Davie SB Co. 1951-53. Of similar type to British "Ton" class.

478 TURKEY

5 Ex-FDR "VEGESACK" CLASS (MINESWEEPERS—COASTAL)

Name	No.	Builders	Commissioned
KARAMÜRSEL (ex-*Worms* M 1253)	M 520	Amiot, Cherbourg	1960
KEREMPE (ex-*Detmold* M 1252)	M 521	Amiot, Cherbourg	1960
KILIMLI (ex-*Siegen* M 1254)	M 522	Amiot, Cherbourg	1960
KOZLU (ex-*Hameln* M 1251)	M 523	Amiot, Cherbourg	1960
KUŞADASI (ex-*Vegesack* M 1250)	M 524	Amiot, Cherbourg	1960

Displacement, tons: 362 standard; 378 full load
Dimensions, feet (metres): 144·3 × 26·2 × 9 *(47·3 × 8·6 × 2·9)*
Guns: 2—20 mm
Main engines: 2 Mercedes-Benz (MTU) diesels; 2 shafts; 1 500 bhp = 15 knots (cp propellers)

Of similar class to French *Mercure*. Transferred by FDR to Turkey late 1975-early 1976.

KARAMÜRSEL (*Kerempe* behind) 8/1975, Reinhard Nerlich

4 Ex-US "CAPE" CLASS (MINESWEEPERS—INSHORE)

Name	No.	Builders	Commissioned
FOÇA (ex-*MSI 15*)	M 500	USA	Aug 1967
FETHIYE (ex-*MSI 16*)	M 501	USA	Aug 1967
FATSA (ex-*MSI 17*)	M 502	USA	Sept 1967
FINIKE (ex-*MSI 18*)	M 503	Peterson Builders Inc	8 Nov 1967

Displacement, tons: 180 standard; 235 full load
Dimensions, feet (metres): 111·9 × 23·5 × 7·9 *(34 × 7·1 × 2·4)*
Gun: 1—0·50 cal
Main engines: 4 diesels; 2 shafts; 960 bhp = 13 knots
Complement: 30

Built in USA and transferred under MAP at Boston, Mass, Aug-Dec 1967.

FOÇA 1970, Turkish Navy

9 MINEHUNTING BOATS

MTB 1 P 311	MTB 3 P 313	MTB 6 P 316	MTB 8 P 318
MTB 2 P 312	MTB 4 P 314	MTB 7 P 317	MTB 9 P 319
			MTB 10 P 320

Displacement, tons: 70 standard
Dimensions, feet (metres): 71·5 × 13·8 × 8·5 *(21·8 × 4·2 × 2·6)*
Main engines: Diesel; 2 000 bhp = 20 knots

All launched in 1942. Now employed as minehunting base ships.

MTB 10 1972, Turkish Navy

AMPHIBIOUS FORCES

Note: Unidentified amphibious vessel *Çake Bey* launched at Taşkizak on 30 June 1977.

2 Ex-US "TERREBONNE PARISH" CLASS (LSTs)

Name	No.	Builders	Commissioned
ERTUĞRUL (ex-USS *Windham County*, LST 1170)	L 401	Christy Corp	1954
SERDAR (ex-USS *Westchester County*, LST 1167)	L 402	Christy Corp	1954

Displacement, tons: 2 590 light; 5 800 full load
Dimensions, feet (metres): 384 oa × 55 × 17 *(117·4 × 16·8 × 3·7)*
Guns: 6—3 in 50 cal (twins)
Main engines: 4 GM diesels; 2 shafts (cp propellers); 6 000 bhp = 15 knots
Complement: 116
Troops: 395

Transferred by US June 1973. (L 401) and 27 Aug 1974 (L 402).

ERTUĞRUL 1975, Turkish Navy

2 Ex-US LST 511-1152 SERIES (COASTAL MINELAYERS)

BAYRAKTAR (ex-FDR *Bottrop*, ex-USS *Saline County* L 1101) L 403 (ex-N-111, ex-A 579)
SANCAKTAR (ex-FDR *Bochum*, ex-USS *Rice County* L 1089) L 404 (ex-N-112, ex-A 580)

Displacement, tons: 1 653 standard; 4 080 full load
Dimensions, feet (metres): 328 oa × 50 × 14 *(100 × 15·2 × 4·3)*
Guns: 6—40 mm (2 twin, 2 single)
Main engines: 2 GM diesels; 2 shafts; 1 700 bhp = 11 knots
Range, miles: 15 000 at 9 knots
Complement: 125

Transferred to West Germany in 1961 and thence to Turkey on 13 Dec 1972. Converted into minelayers in West Germany 1962-64. Minelaying gear removed 1974-75.

BAYRAKTAR (old pennant number) 1973, Reinhard Nerlich

TURKEY 479

5 Ex-BRITISH LCTs

C 101 and 103-106

Displacement, tons: 500 light; 700 full load
Dimensions, feet (metres): 180·9 × 27·7 × 5·4 (55·2 × 8·4 × 1·6)
Guns: 2—20 mm
Complement: 15

Built in UK in 1942. Transferred 25 Sept 1967.

C 104 1975, Turkish Navy

MISCELLANEOUS

12 TURKISH-BUILT LCTs

C 107-118

Displacement, tons: 400 light; 600 full load
Dimensions, feet (metres): 180·9 × 36·8 × 4·8 (55·2 × 11·2 × 1·4)
Guns: 2—20 mm
Speed, knots: 10·5
Complement: 15

Built in Turkey 1966-1973. Of French EDIC type.

12 TURKISH-BUILT LCUs

C 205-216

Displacement, tons: 320 light; 405 full load
Dimensions, feet (metres): 142 × 28 × 5·7 (43·3 × 8·5 × 1·7)
Guns: 2—20 mm
Main engines: GM diesels; 2 shafts; 600 bhp = 10 knots

Built in Turkey 1965-66. Of US LCU type.

C 207 1975, Turkish Navy

4 Ex-US LCU 501 SERIES

C201-204 (ex-US *LCU 588, 608, 666* and *667*)

Displacement, tons: 160 light; 320 full load
Dimensions, feet (metres): 119 oa × 32·7 × 5 (36·3 × 10 × 1·5)
Guns: 2—20 mm
Main engines: 3 diesels; 675 bhp = 10 knots
Complement: 13

Transferred from USA July 1967.

C 204 1975, Turkish Navy

20 TURKISH-BUILT LCM 8 TYPE

C 301-320

Displacement, tons: 58 light; 113 full load
Dimensions, feet (metres): 72 × 20·5 × 4·8 (22 × 6·3 × 1·4)
Guns: 2—12·7 mm
Main engines: GM diesels; 2 shafts; 660 bhp = 9·5 knots
Complement: 9

Built in Turkey in 1965.

SURVEY SHIPS

2 Ex-US "AUK" CLASS

ÇANDARLI (ex-US *BAM 28*) A 593   ÇARSAMBA (ex-US *BAM 32*) A 594

Displacement, tons: 1 125 full load
Dimensions, feet (metres): 221 oa × 32 × 10·8 (67·4 × 9·8 × 3·3)
Main engines: Diesel-electric; 2 shafts; 3 500 bhp
Speed, knots: 18
Complement: 98 (8 officers, 90 ratings)

Ex-US "Auk" class minesweepers. Both launched in 1942, they are the survivors of a class of seven transferred via the United Kingdom in 1947.

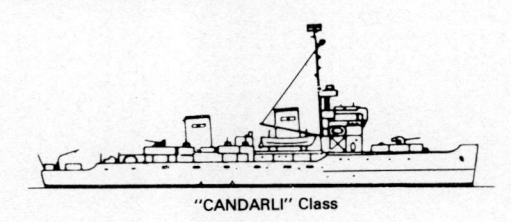

"CANDARLI" Class

MESAHA 1 and 2

Of 45 tons with a complement of eight—built in 1966.

SERVICE FORCES

1 Ex-FDR DEPOT SHIP (TRAINING SHIP)

Name	No.	Builders	Commissioned
CEZAYIRLI GAZI HASAN PAŞA (ex-FDR *Ruhr*)	A 579	Schiekerwerft, Hamburg	1963

Displacement, tons: 2 370 standard; 2 540 full load
Dimensions, feet (metres): 323·5 oa × 38·8 × 11·2 (99 × 11·8 × 3·4)
Guns: 2—3·9 in (100 mm)
Main engines: 6 diesels; 11 400 bhp; 2 shafts
Speed, knots: 20·5
Range, miles: 1 625 at 15 knots
Complement: 110 (accommodation for 200)

Used as Training Ship. Commissioned in Turkish Navy 16 Jan 1977.

Radar: Search: HSA DA 02.
Fire control: Two HSA M 45.

Transfer: 12 July 1975 followed by major refit.

CEZAYIRLI GAZI HASAN PAŞA 12/1976, Roland Wiegran

1 SUPPORT TANKER

Name	No.	Builders	Commissioned
BINBASI SAADETTIN GÜRÇAN	A 573	Taskizak Naval DY, Istanbul	1970

Displacement, tons: 1 505 standard; 4 460 full load
Dimensions, feet (metres): 299 × 39·4 × 18 (89·7 × 11·8 × 5·4)
Main engines: Diesels; 4 400 bhp

Launched 1 July 1969.

480 TURKEY

1 SUPPORT TANKER

ALBAY HAKKI BURAK A 572

Displacement, tons: 3 800 full load
Dimensions, feet (metres): 274·7 oa × 40·2 × 18 (83·7 × 12·3 × 5·5)
Main engines: 2 GM diesels; electric drive; 4 400 bhp = 16 knots
Complement: 88

Built in 1964.

ALBAY HAKKI BURAK 1975, Turkish Navy

1 SUPPORT TANKER

Name	No.	Builders	Commissioned
YUZBASI TOLUNAY	A 571	Taşkizak, Naval DY, Istanbul	1951

Displacement, tons: 2 500 standard; 3 500 full load
Dimensions, feet (metres): 260 × 41 × 19·5 (79 × 12·4 × 5·9)
Main engines: Atlas-Polar diesels; 2 shafts; 1 920 bhp = 14 knots

Launched on 22 Aug 1950.

YUZBASI TOLUNAY 1975, Turkish Navy

1 Ex-US SUPPORT TANKER

Name	No.	Builders	Commissioned
AKPINAR (ex-USS Chiwankum, AOG 26)	A 574	East Coast SY Inc, Bayonne	22 July 1944

Displacement, tons: 700 light; 2 700 full load
Measurement, feet (metres): 1 453 deadweight
Dimensions, feet (metres): 212·5 wl; 220·5 oa × 37 × 12·8 (64·8; 67·3 × 11·3 × 3·9)
Main engines: Diesel; 800 bhp = 10 knots

Laid down on 2 April 1944. Launched on 5 May 1944. Transferred to Turkey in May 1948.

AKPINAR 1975, Turkish Navy

1 Ex-FDR SUPPORT TANKER

Name	No.	Builders	Commissioned
INEBOLU (ex-Bodensee, A 1406, ex-Unkas)	A 575	Lindanau, Kiel	26 Mar 1959

Measurement, tons: 985 gross; 1 238 dw
Dimensions, feet (metres): 219·8 × 32·5 × 15 (67 × 9·8 × 4·3)
Main engines: Diesels; 1 050 bhp = 12 knots
Complement: 26

Launched 19 Nov 1955. Transferred Sept 1977 at Wilhelmshavn, under West German military aid programme. Has replenishment capability.

"BODENSEE" Class 5/1975, Reinhard Nerlich

1 Ex-US REPAIR SHIP

DONATAN (ex-USS *Anthedon*, AS 24) A 583

Displacement, tons: 8 100 standard
Dimensions, feet (metres): 492 × 69·5 × 26·5 (150 × 21·8 × 8·1)
Main engines: Geared turbines; 1 shaft; 8 500 shp = 14·4 knots
Boilers: 2

Former US submarine tender of the "Aegir" class transferred to Turkey on 7 Feb 1969.

DONATAN 1972, Turkish Navy

2 Ex-US REPAIR SHIPS

Name	No.	Builders	Commissioned
ONARAN (ex-*Alecto*, AGP 14, ex-*LST 558*)	A 581	Missouri Valley Bridge & Iron Co.	1945
BAŞARAN (ex-*Patroclus*, ARL 19, ex-*LST 955*)	A 582	Bethlehem Hingham Shipyard	1945

Displacement, tons: 1 625 standard; 4 080 full load
Dimensions, feet (metres): 328 oa × 50 × 14 (100 × 15·2 × 4·4)
Guns: 2—40 mm; 8—20 mm
Main engines: Diesel; 2 shafts; 1 700 bhp = 11 knots
Oil fuel, tons: 1 000
Range, miles: 9 000 at 9 knots
Complement: 80

Former US repair ship and MTB tender, respectively, of the LST type. *Başaran* was launched on 22 Oct 1944, *Onaran* on 14 April 1944. Acquired from the USA in Nov 1952 and May 1948, respectively.

ONARAN 1973, Dr. Giorgio Arra

1 HARBOUR TANKER

Name	No.	Builders	Commissioned
GÖLCÜK (ex-*A 573*)	Y 1207	Gölcük Dockyard	1954

Displacement, tons: 1 255
Measurement, feet: 750 deadweight
Dimensions, feet (metres): 185 × 31·1 × 10 (56·4 × 9·5 × 3·1)
Main engines: B & W diesel; 700 bhp = 12·5 knots

Launched on 4 Nov 1953.

1 SUBMARINE DEPOT SHIP

ERKIN (ex-*Trabzon*, ex-*Imperial*) A 591

Dimensions, feet (metres): 441 × 58·5 × 23 (133 × 17·5 × 7)
Guns: 2—40 mm
Speed, knots: 16
Complement: 128

Built in 1938. Purchased in 1968 and placed on the Navy list in 1970.

2 Ex-US "CHANTICLEER" CLASS (SUBMARINE RESCUE SHIPS)

Name	No.	Builders	Commissioned
AKIN (ex-USS *Greenlet*, ASR 10)	A 585	Moore SB & DD Co.	29 May 1943
— (ex-USS *Tringa*, ASR 16)	—	Savannah M & F Co	1947

Displacement, tons: 1 770 standard; 2 321 full load
Dimensions, feet (metres): 251·3 × 42·2 × 14·7 (75·5 × 12·7 × 4·3)
Guns: 1—40 mm; 2—20 mm (twin)
Main engines: Diesel-electric; 1 shaft; 3 000 bhp = 15 knots
Complement: 85

Akin transferred 12 June 1970 and purchased 15 Feb 1973. USS *Tringa* transferred 1977.

TURKEY 481

1 SUBMARINE RESCUE SHIP

KURTARAN (ex-USS *Bluebird*, ASR 19, ex-*Yurak* AT 165) A 584

Displacement, tons: 1 294 standard; 1 675 full load
Dimensions, feet (metres): 205·0 oa × 38·5 × 11·0 *(62·5 × 12·2 × 3·5)*
Guns: 1—3 in; 2—40 mm
Main engines: Diesel-electric; 3 000 bhp = 16 knots

Former salvage tug adapted as a submarine rescue vessel in 1947. Transferred from the US Navy on 15 Aug 1950.

KURTARAN   9/1976, Michael D. J. Lennon

2 Ex-FDR "ANGELN" CLASS (DEPOT SHIPS)

Name	No.	Builders	Commissioned
ULKU (ex-*FDR Angeln*)	A 586	A. C. de Bretagne	1955
UMUR BEY (ex-*FDR Dithmarschen*)	A 588	A. C. de Bretagne	1956

Displacement, tons: 2 600 full load
Dimensions, feet (metres): 296·9 × 43·6 × 20·3 *(90·5 × 13·3 × 6·2)*
Main engines: Pielstick diesel; 1 shaft; 3 000 bhp = 17 knots
Complement: 57

Ex-cargo ships bought by FDR in 1959. Transferred 22 March 1972 and Dec 1975. *Umur Bey* employed as submarine depot ship and *Ulku* as Light Forces depot ship.

UMUR BEY   12/1976, Roland Wiegran

4 TRANSPORTS

LAPSEKI Y 1163 **ERDEK** Y 1164 **KILYA** Y 1166 **TUZLA** Y 1168

Measurement, tons: 700
Dimensions, feet (metres): 183·7 × 37·2 × 8·9 *(56 × 12·2 × 2·7)*
Main engines: Steam; 700 hp = 9·5 knots

Have a minelaying capability. Survivors of a class of 11 car-ferries built in UK. 1940-1942.

2 Ex-US TRANSPORTS

Y 1204 (ex-US *APL 47*)
Y 1205 (ex-US *APL 53*)

Transferred: Y 1204 on Oct 1972 and Y 1205 on 6 Dec 1974.

1 WATER TANKER

SOGUT (ex-FDR *FW 6*) Y 1217

Measurement, tons: 350 dw
Dimensions, feet (metres): 144·4 × 25·6 × 8·2 *(44·1 × 7·8 × 2·5)*
Main engines: MWM diesels; 230 bhp = 9·5 knots

Transferred by West Germany 18 July 1975.

SOGUT   9/1976, Michael D. J. Lennon

2 WATER TANKERS

Name	No.	Builders	Commissioned
VAN	Y 1208	Gölcük Dockyard	1970
ULABAT	Y 1209	Gölcük Dockyard	1969

Displacement, tons: 1 200
Main engines: Designed for a speed of 14·5 knots

Two small tankers for the Turkish Navy built in 1968-70.

BOOM DEFENCE VESSELS

Name	No.	Builders	Commissioned
AG 6 (ex-USS *AN 93*, ex-Netherlands *Cerberus*, A 895)	P 306	Bethlehem Steel Corp, Staten Island	10 Nov 1952

Displacement, tons: 780 standard; 902 full load
Dimensions, feet (metres): 165·0 × 33·0 × 10·0 *(50·8 × 10·4 × 3·1)*
Guns: 1—3 in; 4—20 mm
Main engines: Diesel-electric; 1 shaft; 1 500 bhp = 12·8 knots

Netlayer. Launched in May 1952. Transferred from USA to Netherlands in Dec 1952. Used first as a boom defence vessel and latterly as salvage and diving tender since 1961 but retained her netlaying capacity. Handed back to USN on 17 Sept 1970 but immediately turned over to the Turkish Navy.

AG 6   1975, Turkish Navy

Name	No.	Builders	Commissioned
AG 5 (ex-*AN 104*)	P 305	Kröger, Rendsburg	5 Feb 1961

Displacement, tons: 680 standard; 860 full load
Dimensions, feet (metres): 148·7 pp; 173·8 oa × 35·0 × 13·5 *(52·5 × 10·5 × 4·1)*
Guns: 1—40 mm; 3—20 mm
Main engines: 4 MAN diesels; 2 shafts; 1 450 bhp = 12 knots

Netlayer AN 104 built in US off-shore programme for Turkey. Launched on 20 Oct 1960.

Name	No.	Builders	Commissioned
AG 4 (ex-USS *Larch*, ex-*AN 21*)	P 304	American SB Co, Cleveland	1941

Displacement, tons: 560 standard; 805 full load
Dimensions, feet (metres): 163·0 oa × 30·5 × 10·5 *(50 × 9·3 × 3·2)*
Gun: 1—3 in
Main engines: Diesel-electric; 800 bhp = 12 knots

Former US netlayer of the "Aloe" class. Laid down in 1940. Launched on 2 July 1941. Acquired in May 1946.

AG 4   1969

1 "BAR" CLASS

Name	No.	Builders	Commissioned
AG 1 (ex-HMS *Barbarian*)	P 301	Blyth SB Co	1938

Displacement, tons: 750 standard; 1 000 full load
Dimensions, feet (metres): 150·0 pp; 173·8 oa × 32·2 × 9·5 *(52·9 × 9·4 × 2·7)*
Gun: 1—3 in
Main engines: Triple expansion; 850 ihp = 11·5 knots
Boilers: 2 SE

Former British boom defence vessel.

482 TURKEY

3 GATE VESSELS

KAPI, I, II, III (Y 1201, 1202, 1203)

Displacement, tons: 360
Dimensions, feet (metres): 102·7 × 34 × 4·7 *(30·8 × 10·2 × 1·3)*

These gate vessels were built by US for Turkey under MAP. Transferred March 1961.

TUGS

1 Ex-US OCEAN TUG

GAZAL (ex-USS *Sioux* ATF 75) A 587

Displacement, tons: 1 235 standard; 1 675 full load
Dimensions, feet (metres): 205 oa × 38·5 × 16 *(60·7 × 11·6 × 4·7)*
Gun: 1—3 in
Main engines: Diesel-electric; 3 000 bhp = 16 knots
Complement: 85

Transferred 30 Oct 1972. Purchased 15 Aug 1973. Can be used for salvage.

AKBAS Y 1118   **KEPEZ** Y 1119

Displacement, tons: 971
Dimensions, feet (metres): 149 × 33·9 × 14 *(44·7 × 10·2 × 4·3)*
Speed, knots: 12

1 Ex-US OCEAN TUG

KUVVET (ex-US *ATA*) Y 1122

Displacement, tons: 390
Dimensions, feet (metres): 107 × 26·5 × 12 *(32·1 × 8 × 3·6)*

Transferred Feb 1962.

2 Ex-US "YTL" TYPE (HARBOUR TUGS)

SONDUREN (ex-US *YTL 751*) Y 1117   **YEDEKCI** (ex-US *YTL 155*) Y 1121

Transferred July 1957 and Nov. 1954.

1 HARBOUR TUG

ÖNCU Y 1123

Displacement, tons: 500
Speed, knots: 12

Transferred under MAP.

1 HARBOUR TUG

KUDRET Y 1129

Displacement, tons: 128
Dimensions, feet (metres): 65 × 19·6 × 9 *(21·3 × 6·4 × 2·9)*

FLOATING DOCKS

Y 1081

16 000 tons lift.

Y 1082

12 000 tons lift.

Y 1083 (ex-US *AFDL*)

2 500 tons lift.

Y 1084

4 500 tons lift.

Y 1085

400 tons lift.

Y 1086

3 000 tons lift.

Y 1087 (ex-US *ARD 12*)

3 500 tons lift. Transferred Nov 1971.

AUXILIARIES

Note: Others listed but not identified; *Ersen Bayrak* Y 1134, L-1 *Samandira* Y 1148, L-2 *Samandira* Y 1149, *Odev* Y 1228.

2 SMALL TRANSPORTS

SARKÖY Y 1156   **KANARYA**

1 HARBOUR PATROL CRAFT

Y 1223

1 NAVAL DREDGER

TARAK Y 1209

Of 200 tons.

1 FLOATING CRANE

ALGARNA III Y 1023 (ex-US *YD 185*)

Transferred Sept 1963.

UNION OF SOVIET SOCIALIST REPUBLICS

Flag Officers Soviet Navy

Commander-in-Chief of the Soviet Navy and Deputy Minister of Defence:
  Admiral of the Fleet of the Soviet Union Sergei Georgiyevich Gorshkov
First Deputy Commander-in-Chief of the Soviet Navy:
  Admiral of the Fleet N. I. Smirnov
Deputy Commander-in-Chief:
  Admiral N. N. Amelko
Deputy Commander-in-Chief:
  Admiral G. A. Bondarenko
Deputy Commander-in-Chief:
  Admiral V. V. Mikhaylin
Deputy Commander-in-Chief:
  Engineer Admiral P. G. Kotov
Deputy Commander-in-Chief:
  Engineer Admiral V. G. Novikov
Deputy Commander-in-Chief (Rear Services):
  Admiral L. Y. Mizin
Commander of Naval Aviation:
  Colonel-General A. A. Mironenko
Chief of the Political Directorate:
  Admiral V. M. Grishanov
Chief of Naval Training Establishments:
  Vice-Admiral I. M. Kuznetsov
Chief of Main Naval Staff:
  Admiral of the Fleet G. M. Yegorov
1st Deputy Chief of the Main Naval Staff:
  Vice-Admiral P. M. Navoytsev
Chief of the Hydrographic Service:
  Admiral A. I. Rassokho

Northern Fleet

Commander-in-Chief:
  Vice-Admiral V. N. Chernavin
1st Deputy Commander-in-Chief:
  Vice-Admiral V. S. Kruglyakov
Chief of Staff:
  —
In Command of the Political Department:
  Rear-Admiral Y. Padorin

Pacific

Commander-in-Chief:
  Admiral V. P. Maslov
1st Deputy Commander-in-Chief:
  Vice-Admiral E. N. Spiridonov
Chief of Staff:
  Vice-Admiral Ya. M. Kudelkin
In Command of the Political Department:
  Rear-Admiral V. D. Sabaneyev

Black Sea

Commander-in-Chief:
  Admiral N. I. Khovrin
1st Deputy Commander-in-Chief:
  Vice-Admiral V. Samoylov
Chief of Staff:
  Vice-Admiral V. I. Akimov
In Command of the Political Department:
  Vice-Admiral P. N. Medvedev

Baltic

Commander-in-Chief:
  Vice-Admiral A. M. Kosov
1st Deputy Commander-in-Chief:
  Vice-Admiral V. V. Sidorov
Chief of Staff:
  Vice-Admiral A. M. Kalinin
In Command of the Political Department:
  Vice-Admiral N. I. Shablikov

Caspian Flotilla

Commander-in-Chief:
  Vice-Admiral G. G. Kasumbekov
Chief of Staff:
  Rear-Admiral V. M. Buynov
In Command of the Political Department:
  Captain I. R. Likhvonin

Leningrad Naval Base

Commanding Officer:
  Admiral V. M. Leonenkov
In Command of the Political Department:
  Vice-Admiral A. A. Plekhanov
Head of the Order of Lenin Naval Academy:
  Admiral V. S. Sysoyev
Head of Frunze Naval College:
  Rear-Admiral V. V. Platonov

Diplomatic Representation

Naval Attaché London:
  Captain I. Ivanov

Personnel

(a) 1978: Approximately 425 000 officers and ratings (including Naval Infantry) (approximately 50 000 officers, 25 000 senior ratings and 350 000 junior ratings. Of these 40 per cent are seagoing, 45 per cent are ashore (including 12 000 Naval Infantry) and 15 per cent are Naval Air Force)
(b) Approximately 18 per cent volunteers (officers and senior ratings)—remainder 3 years national service at sea and 2 if ashore

Mercantile Marine

Lloyd's Register of Shipping:
  8 167 vessels of 21 438 291 tons gross

Main Naval Bases

North: Severomorsk (HQ), Archangelsk, Polyarny, Severodvinsk (building).
Baltic: Leningrad (Kronshtadt), Tallinn, Lepaia, Baltiisk (HQ)
Black Sea: Sevastopol (HQ), Tuapse, Poti, Nikolayev (building)
Pacific: Vladivostock (HQ), Nakhodka, Sovetskaia Gavan, Magadan, Petropavlovsk.

Pennant Numbers

The Soviet Navy has frequent changes of pennant numbers and so these are of little use in identifying individual ships. For that reason such a list has been omitted in this section. It will be noticed that, in some cases, the same ship has different numbers in different photographs.

Deletions and Conversions

Whilst it is not possible to provide an accurate estimate of total deletions and conversions during the last year the following is a guide to those estimates used in this section.

Cruiser
Conversion of *Oktyabrskaya Revolutsiya*

Destroyers
"Kashin" class conversions with SSM appear to be postponed, at least.
"Krupny" class conversion to "Kanin" class completed.
"Kildin" class conversions appear to be completed—one outstanding.

Frigates
Conversion of "Petya 1A" class continues slowly.

Fast Attack Craft
Deletion of 10 "P6" class.

Service Forces
Conversion of several more tankers for underway replenishment.

River Patrol Craft
Deletion of "BK 2-4" classes.

Building Programme

The following is an abstract of the programme used in estimating force levels.

Aircraft Carriers
1 "Kiev" class building—continuing programme.

Submarines
Continuing programme for "Delta II", "Delta III", "Charlie II", "Victor II" and "Tango" classes.

Cruisers
Continuing programme for "Kara" and "Kresta II" classes.

Destroyers
"Krivak" class continues now "Krivak II"

Frigates
New "Koni" class.
"Petya" class may be continuing—no current evidence.

Corvettes
"Grisha III" and "Nanuchka" classes continue.

Light Forces
"Sarancha" class hydrofoils continue.
"Turya" class hydrofoils continue.
"Zhuk" class coastal patrol craft continues. "Stenka" class continues.

Mine Warfare Forces
"Sonya" class (MSC) and "Natya" class continue.
New "Olya" class building.

Amphibious Forces
"Ropucha" class LST continues.

Air Cushion Vehicles
A large programme of unknown size.

Support and Depot Ships
"Amur" class continuing.

Service Forces
"Boris Chilikin" class continues.
"Ingul", "Sorum" and "Pamir" class tugs continue.

Several types and classes have been revised from new information, not necessarily as new construction.

484 USSR

Strength of the Fleet

Aircraft Carriers	2 + 1 building	Fast Attack Craft (Hydrofoil)	50	Training Ships	2	
Helicopter Cruisers	2	Fast Attack Craft (Torpedo)	80	Fleet Replenishment Ships	7	
Submarines (SSBN)	68 + 6 building	Large Patrol Craft	60	Replenishment Tankers	23	
Submarines (SSB)	22	River Patrol Craft	80	Coastal Tankers	22	
Submarines (SSGN)	46 + 2 building	Coastal Patrol Craft	25	Salvage Vessels	21	
Submarines (SSG)	26	Minesweepers—Ocean	175 + 3 building	Rescue Ships	24	
Submarines (SSN)	41 + ?2 building	Minesweepers—Coastal	109 + 3 building	Lifting Ships	15	
Submarines (SS)	*154 + 2 building	Minesweepers—Inshore	125	Tenders	135 +	
Cruisers (CG)	25 + 3 building	LSTs	24 + 1 building	Icebreakers (Nuclear)	3 + 1 building	
Cruisers (Gun)	12	LCTs	60	Icebreakers	44 + 4 building	
Destroyers (DDG)	58 + 4 building	LCUs	105	Cable Ships	10	
Destroyers (Gun)	54	LCMs	100 +	Large Tugs	75 +	
Frigates	108 + ? building (a number in reserve)	Depot and Repair Ships	65 + 1 building	Transports	76	
		Intelligence Collectors (AGI)	53			
Corvettes (Missile)	17 + 3 building	Survey Ships	104 + 33 (civilian) + 1 building			
Corvettes	94 + 2 building					
Fast Attack Craft (Missile)	120	Research Ships	15 + 1 building 27 (civilian)			
Hydrofoil (Missile)	3 + ? building					
Fast Attack Craft (Patrol)	62 + 2 building	Space Associated Ships	15 + 9 (civilian)	* plus 100 or more in reserve.		

Approximate Deployments

The following figures do not attempt to give an exact deployment of the Soviet Navy but offer an approximate apportionment of the totals given above. It must be remembered that at any normal time at least some ten per cent of submarines, cruisers, destroyers, frigates, amphibious forces, depot ships and service forces are deployed "out of area" ie in the Mediterranean, Indian Ocean, West Africa etc or on passage. This figure is normally higher for ballistic missile submarines.

Fleets

Type	Northern	Baltic	Black Sea	Pacific	Type	Northern	Baltic	Black Sea	Pacific
SSBN	48	—	—	20	CL	1	2	6	3
SSB	10	6	—	6	DD**	5	24	16	13
SSGN	27	—	—	19	FF and Corvettes	43	60	65	36
SSG	14	3	3	6	FAC(M) and Missile Corvettes	35	44	29	35
SSN	25	—	—	16	Light Forces	55	145	72	85
SS*	65	29	27	33	MSO/MSC	60	84	70	70
CV	1	—	1	—	LST	5	6	5	4
CHG	—	—	2	—	LCT and LCU	20	48	50	47
CG	10	2	7	6	Depot Ships	25	2	17	21
DDG	14	11	18	15	Service Forces (large)	21	3	14	16

* In addition about 100 believed in reserve.
** A considerable number of the older destroyers in reserve.

SOVIET NAVAL AVIATION

The Soviet Navy operates some 1 300 fixed-wing aircraft and helicopters in *Voyenno Morskaya Aviatsiya*, the world's second largest naval air arm. The primary combat components are
(1) Long range and medium bombers employed in the maritime reconnaissance role.
(2) Medium bombers mostly equipped with air-to-surface missiles in the anti-ship strike role.
(3) Land based patrol aircraft, amphibians and helicopters in the anti-submarine role.
(4) The "Forger" V/STOL aircraft operating from the "Kiev" class aircraft carriers.

Bombers: The Soviet naval air arm has about 80 heavy and 530 medium bombers in the anti-shipping, strike, tanker and reconnaissance roles. The main strike force comprises over 300 "Badger" equipped with "Kipper" and "Kelt" air-to-surface missiles as well as an increasing number (now about 30) "Backfire" supersonic bombers first introduced in 1974 and the earlier "Blinder" conventional bombers. The reconnaissance aircraft are about 50 "Bear D" (long range recce); 60 "Badger" and a similar number of "Blinders". About 100 "Badgers" are equipped as tankers.

ASW Helicopters: Over 250 anti-submarine helicopters are believed to be in the naval air arm, mostly Ka-25 "Hormone" (a twin-turbine craft) and some of the older Mi-4 "Hound" helicopters which are now being replaced for shore-based ASW by the "Haze" helicopters. The "Hormone" anti-submarine helicopters, armed with torpedoes or other ASW weapons operate from the "Kiev" class and *Moskva* and *Leningrad* which can each operate some 15 to 20 helicopters, servicing them in a hangar below the flight deck. They have also been seen in the "Kara", "Kresta I" and "Kresta II" class cruisers which are the first Soviet ships of this type to be fitted with a helicopter hangar. In some of these ships the radar fitted helicopter ("Hormone B") may also have a reconnaissance role associated with the surface-to-surface missile system. Other types of helicopter are also used in the transport role ashore. The presence of *Kiev* and, later, her sisters notably increases the seaborne helicopter capability.

ASW Patrol Aircraft: The Soviet Union is the only nation other than Japan maintaining modern military flying boats, about 100 Be-12 "Mail" (turboprop) aircraft of this type being operational. The latter aircraft, an amphibian often-photographed on runways, has an advanced anti-submarine capability evidenced by a radome extending forward, a Magnetic Anomaly Detector (MAD) boom extending aft and a weapons bay in the rear fuselage.
The "May", of which some 60 are in service, is a militarised version of the four-turboprop commercial air freighter (code name "Coot") in wide commercial service. The patrol/anti-submarine version has been lengthened and fitted with a MAD boom as well as other electronic equipment and a weapons capability. Some of these are being transferred to India. There is also another variant of the "Bear" bomber, the "Bear F" engaged in ASW operations in increasing numbers.

Transports/Training Aircraft: There are also about 300 transports, utility, and training fixed-wing aircraft and helicopters under Navy control.

Aircraft names are NATO code names; "B" names indicate bombers, "H" names for helicopters, and "M" names for miscellaneous aircraft. Single syllable names are propeller driven and two syllable names are jet-propelled.

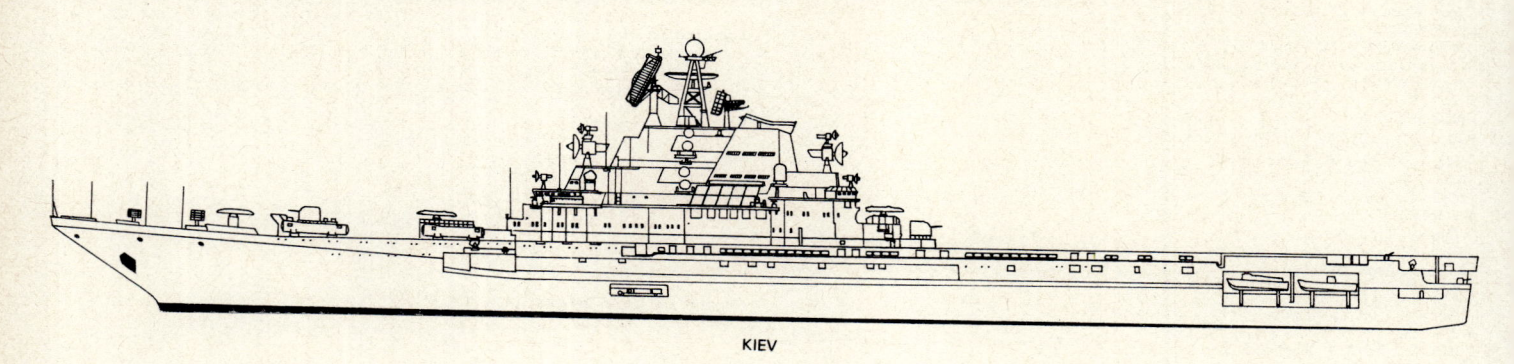

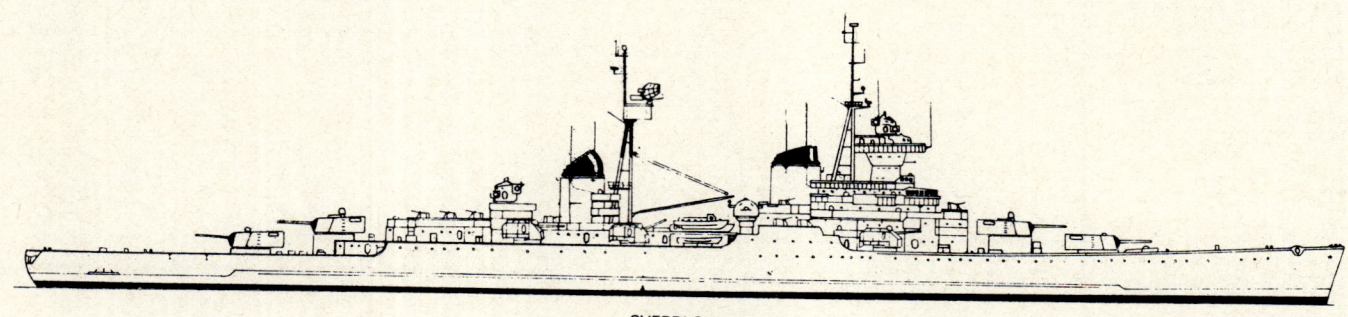

KIEV

SVERDLOV

USSR 485

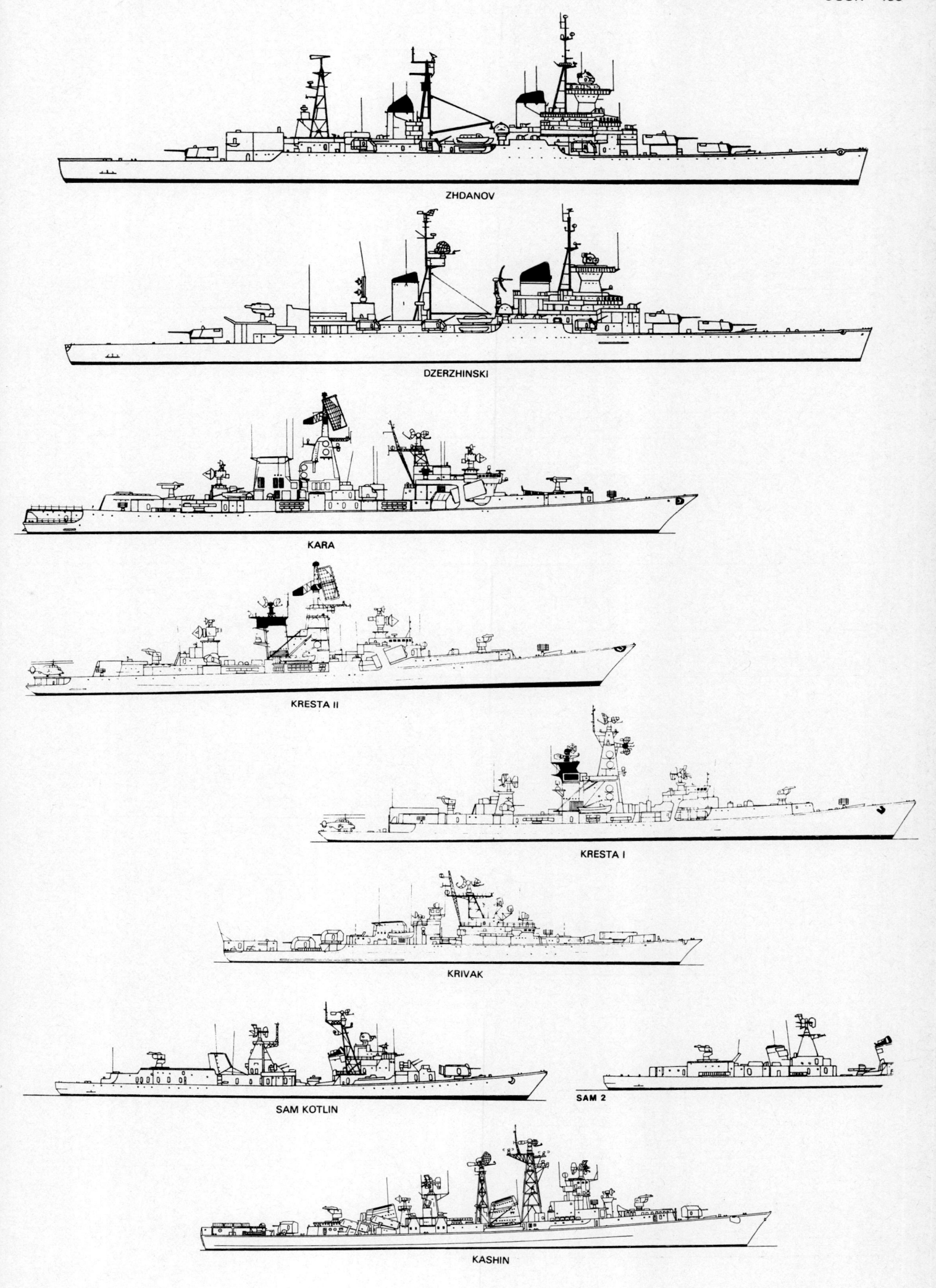

ZHDANOV

DZERZHINSKI

KARA

KRESTA II

KRESTA I

KRIVAK

SAM KOTLIN

SAM 2

KASHIN

486 USSR

KOTLIN

SKORY I

OSKOL

SKORY II

YANKEE

VICTOR

NATYA

NANUCHKA

PETYA

MIRKA II

MIRKA I

ROPUCHA

POLNOCHNY I and II

OSA I

AMUR

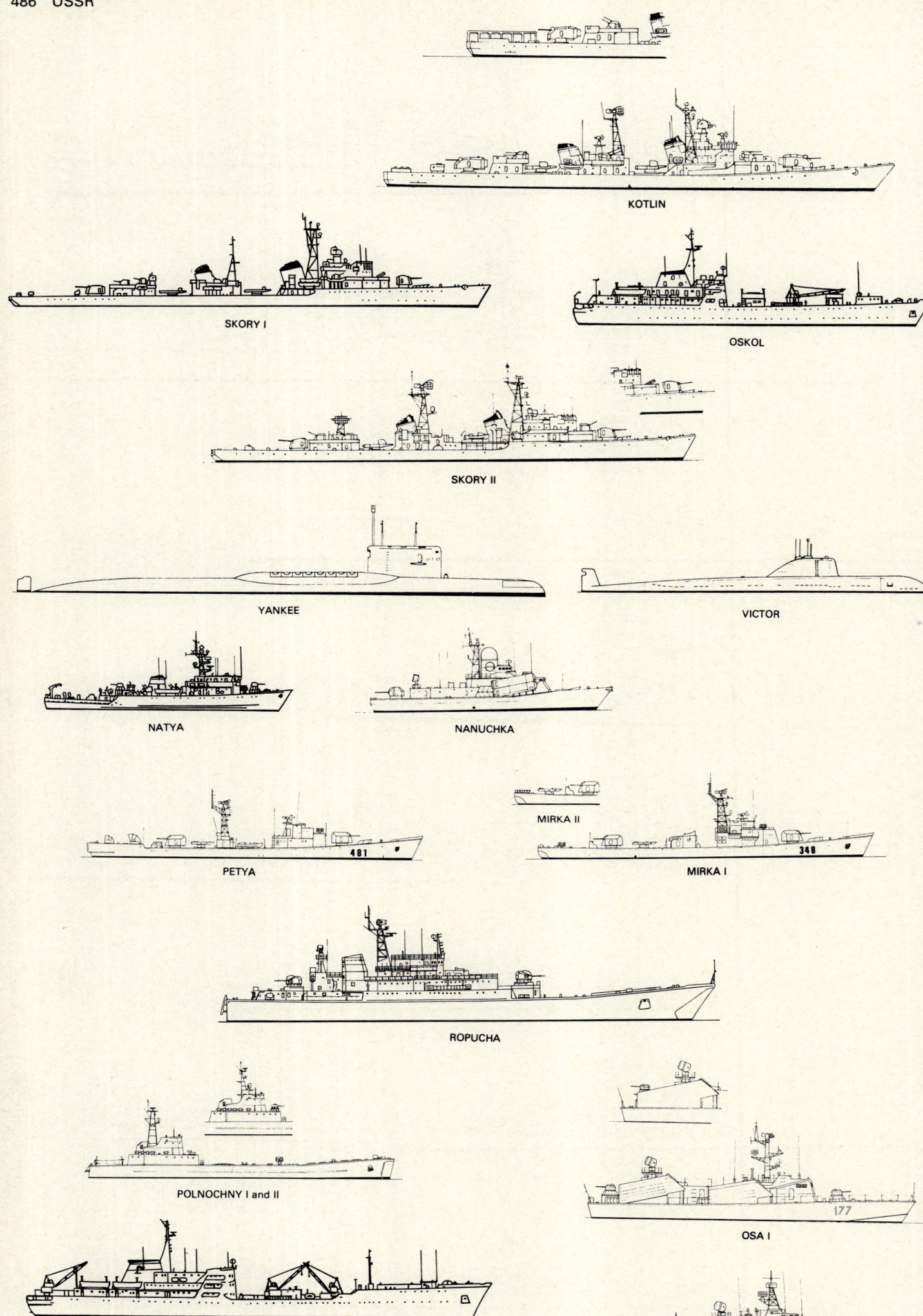

SHERSHEN

Note: Line drawings by courtesy of Erminio Bagnasco and Siegfried Breyer. Scale is 1 : 1200 except for Osa I, Osa II and Shershen classes, which are 600.

SUBMARINES
Ballistic Missile Classes

Note: The development of Soviet submarine launched ballistic missiles dates from early trials with German V2 (A4) missiles. The Lafferentz Project of 1944 was for the launching of V-2 from capsules towed by U-boats. The Soviets probably attempted such operations with the Golem series of missiles without success and then turned to tube launchers.

The deployment of operational missiles dates from the development of the 300 mile surface launched SS-N-4 missile which was first launched in September 1955. The "Zulu V" class was converted to carry this missile in two tubes in the fin. All this class now deleted. In 1958 the diesel-propelled "Golf" class appeared and in 1959 the nuclear "Hotel" class. Both originally carried the SS-N-4 but from 1962 all the "Hotels" and thirteen of the "Golfs" were converted for the 700 mile SS-N-5 which had the added advantage of dived-launch capability. Both the 4 and 5 missiles carried a megaton head and were 42·5 feet long but the apparent lack of an inertial navigation system in the submarines may have presented targetting problems. In 1969 the first evidence of a new missile, later to be known as SS-N-X-13, appeared, apparently a two stage weapon with some form of guidance head and a range of about 300 miles. This may have been intended for the "Yankee" class, of which the first was delivered in 1967 and may have had an anti-shipping role but it has never become operational although expected in 1974. The less sophisticated SS-N-6 was installed in the "Yankees", of similar size (31·6 feet long) to the SS-N-X-13 but with a 1 300 mile range. In 1971 Mk II and III of SS-N-6 with 1 600 mile range and MRV warheads were tested and are now operational. Recently the SS-N-17, with a range of some 1 800 miles and with solid propellant has become operational and is now in at least some of the "Yankees".

In the late 1960s the SS-N-8 was first tested and this was fitted in the "Delta I" class and subsequently the "Delta II". This is a much larger missile (42·5 feet long) than its predecessors and required the increased size of the "Deltas" to house it. The SS-N-18, its longer range follow-up (5 200 miles and 46 feet long), is now being fitted in the "Delta III" class.

The Soviet navy is now inching over the SALT I agreed limits—if the level is to be maintained some deletions are required or building must cease. The latter appears unlikely in view of reports of a new class, "Typhoon", which will presumably be larger and more heavily armed than "Delta III".

6 + 3 "DELTA III" CLASS
(BALLISTIC MISSILE SUBMARINES SSBN)

Similar in dimensions and other data to "Delta II" class (below). Carry 16 tubes for SS-N-18 missiles (5 200 mile range with MIRV capability). Building at Severodvinsk and Komsomolsk.

5 + 3 "DELTA II" CLASS
(BALLISTIC MISSILE SUBMARINES SSBN)

Displacement, tons: 9 000 surfaced; 11 000 dived
Dimensions, feet (metres): 500 × 39·4 × 29·5 (152·5 × 12 × 9)
Missiles: 16—SS-N-8 tubes
Torpedo tubes: 6—21 in (533 mm)
Main machinery: Nuclear reactors; steam turbines; 2 shafts
Speed, knots: 20 surfaced; 25 dived
Complement: 110

First reported Nov 1973. Building yards—Severodvinsk and Komsomolsk.
Of the total of twelve submarines per year completing in Soviet yards at least half are probably of the "Delta II and III" classes. With the limitations of the SALT agreement this programme could result in the deletion of other earlier classes.

15 "DELTA I" CLASS
(BALLISTIC MISSILE SUBMARINES SSBN)

Displacement, tons: 8 500 surfaced; 10 500 dived
Dimensions, feet (metres): 442·8 × 39·4 × 29·5 (135 × 12 × 9)
Missiles: 12—SS-N-8 tubes
Torpedo tubes: 6—21 in (533 mm)
Main machinery: Nuclear reactors; 2 steam turbines; 2 shafts; 40 000 shp
Speed, knots: 20 surfaced; 26 dived
Complement: 100

This advance on the "Yankee" class SSBNs was announced at the end of 1972. The missile armament is twelve SS-N-8s with a range of 4 200 n. miles, at present believed to carry single heads, rather than MRVs. As the SS-N-6 has already been tested with MRV warheads, however, it is not unlikely that these missiles will in due course be similarly armed. The longer-range SS-N-8 missiles are of greater length than the SS-N-6s and, as this length cannot be accommodated below the keel, they stand several feet proud of the after-casing. At the same time their presumed greater diameter and the need to compensate for the additional top-weight would seem to be the reasons for the reduction to twelve missiles in this class. The total "Delta" class building programme depends on the final outcome of the various Strategic Arms Limitation Talks (SALT). Programme probably completed 1973-77.

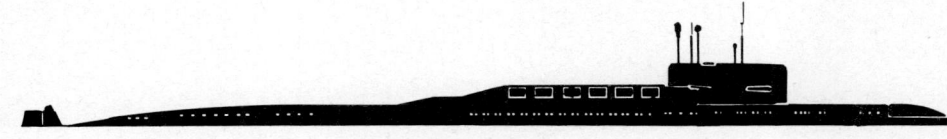

"DELTA I" Class

"DELTA" Class
1973

488   USSR

34 "YANKEE" CLASS
(BALLISTIC MISSILE SUBMARINES SSBN)

Displacement, tons: 8 000 surfaced; 10 000 dived
Dimensions, feet (metres): 426·5 × 36·1 × 27·9 *(130·0 × 11 × 8·5)*
Missile launchers: 16 tubes for SS-N-6 missiles (see note)
Torpedo tubes: 8—21 in
Main machinery: Nuclear reactors; 2 steam turbines; 2 shafts; 40 000 shp
Speed, knots: 20 surfaced; 25 dived
Complement: 100

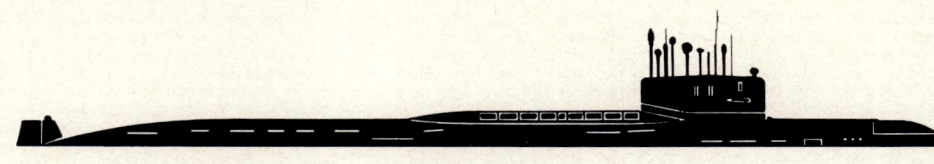

"YANKEE" Class

The vertical launching tubes are arranged in two rows of eight, and the SS-N-6 missiles have a range of 1 300/1 600 n. miles. These missiles have been tested with MRV warheads and these are now operational. At about the time that the USS *George Washington* was laid down (1 Nov 1957) as the world's first SSBN it is likely that the Soviet Navy embarked on its own major SSBN programme. With experience gained from the diesel-propelled "Golf" class and the nuclear-propelled "Hotel" class, the "Yankee" design was completed. The first of the class was delivered late-1967 and the programme then accelerated from four boats in 1968 to eight in 1971, the last of the class being completed in 1976. Construction took place at Severodvinsk and Komsomolsk. The original deployment of this class was to the Eastern seaboard of the US giving a coverage at least as far as the Mississippi. Increase in numbers allowed a Pacific patrol to be established off California extending coverage at least as far as the Rockies.

Appearance: More like the USN "Ethan Allen" class than any other submarines. Fin mounted fore-planes.

Engineering: The twin screws and great horsepower give this class a speed advantage over some western counterparts.

Missiles: Some of this class are now being fitted to launch the 1 800 mile SS-N-17 missiles.

"YANKEE" Class

"YANKEE" Class

"YANKEE" Class

1 "HOTEL III" CLASS
7 "HOTEL II" CLASS
(BALLISTIC MISSILE SUBMARINES SSBN)

Displacement, tons: 5 000 surfaced; 6 000 dived
Dimensions, feet (metres): 377·2 × 29·1 × 25 *(115·2 × 9 × 7·6)*
Missile launchers: 3—SS-N-5 tubes
Torpedo tubes: 6—21 in (bow); 4—16 in (stern)
Main machinery: 2 nuclear reactors; steam turbines; 2 shafts; 30 000 shp
Speed, knots: 20 surfaced; 22 dived
Complement: 90

"HOTEL II" Class

Three vertical ballistic missile tubes in the large fin. All this class was completed between 1958 and 1962. Originally fitted with SS-N-4 system with Sark missiles (300 miles). Between 1962 and 1967 this system was replaced by the dived launch SS-N-5 system with Serb missiles capable of over 700 mile range. A number of these boats was deployed off both coasts of the USA and Canada. As the limitations of SALT are felt the "Hotel IIs" will probably be phased-out to allow the maximum number of "Delta" class to be built. The "Hotel III" was a single unit converted for the test firings of the SS-N-8. The earlier boats of this class, which was of a similar hull and reactor design to the "Echo" class, will, by the late 1970s, be reaching their twentieth year in service.

Appearance: Of similar hull form to the "November" and "Echo I" class although the huge fin is distinctive.

Navigation: There has been no evidence that these submarines are fitted with an inertial navigation system.

"HOTEL II" Class damaged in North Atlantic   2/1972, USN

"HOTEL II" Class   1972

490 USSR

9 "GOLF I" and 13 "GOLF II" CLASS
(BALLISTIC MISSILE SUBMARINES SSB)

Displacement, tons: 2 350 surfaced; 2 800 dived
Dimensions, feet (metres): 321·4 × 27·9 × 19·6 (98 × 8·5 × 6·0)
Missile launchers: 3—SS-N-4 (G I); 3—SS-N-5 (G II)
Torpedo tubes: 10—21 in (6 bow; 4 stern)
Main machinery: 3 diesels; 3 shafts; 6 000 hp; electric motors; 6 000 hp
Speed, knots: 17·6 surfaced; 13 dived
Range, miles: 22 700 surfaced cruising
Complement: 86 (12 officers, 74 men)

This class has a very large fin fitted with three vertically mounted tubes and hatches for launching ballistic missiles. Built at Komsomolsk and Severodvinsk. Building started in 1958 and finished in 1961-62. After the missile conversion of the "Hotel" class was completed in 1967 thirteen of this class ("Golf II") were converted to carry the SS-N-5 system with 700 miles Serb missiles in place of the shorter range (300 mile) Sarks. One sank in the Pacific in 1968 and was partially raised by the USA in 1974.
Some of the "Golf I" class have probably been modified as missile test platforms.
One of this class has been built by China, although apparently lacking missiles.

Deployment: Six deployed in the Baltic since 1976, the first SSBs to enter that sea.

SALT I: The "Golf" class hulls are not included in the SALT I totals. However if new missiles are embarked these are to be counted in the overall missile total.

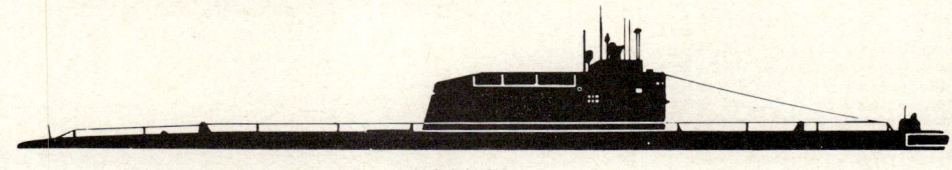

"GOLF I" Class

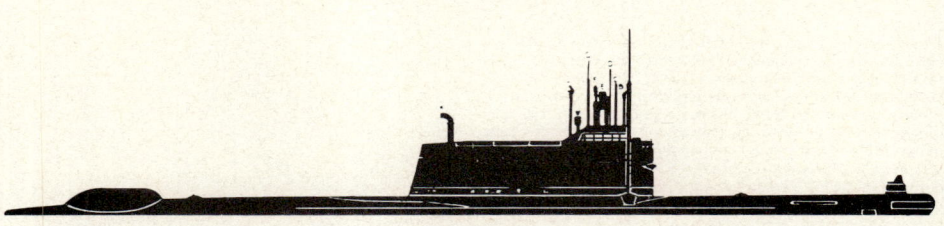

"GOLF II" Class

"GOLF II" Class   7/1973

"GOLF I" Class

"GOLF II" Class (in the Caribbean)   5/1974, USN

Cruise Missile Classes

Note: The first appearance of cruise-missiles at sea in Soviet submarines was in the Twin-cylinder variant of the "Whiskey" class in 1958-60. These carried two SS-N-3 missiles with a maximum range of 400 miles, optimum range 150 and requiring external (aircraft or ship) targetting and guidance. The fact that the USN had carried out trials with Loon missiles in the submarines *Cusk* and *Carbonero* in 1948-49 and soon afterwards converted several submarines, some to fire and some to guide the 80 foot Regulus cruise-missile, shows that at this stage the Soviet navy had lagged far behind. In fact in the FY 1956 programme the US Navy included the first nuclear-propelled cruise missile submarine *Halibut*, designed to carry five 560 mile Regulus I missiles. By 1965 the cruise-missile programme had been abandoned by the US Navy. Meanwhile the Soviet Navy had gone ahead faster than the US Navy in the production of the first ballistic-missile submarines, diverting effort from that programme to submarine cruise-missiles to face the threat of US Navy carriers with nuclear-armed aircraft. The first "Echo I" nuclear-propelled cruise missile submarines appeared in 1961 followed very closely by the "Echo II" nuclears and the conventional "Juliett" class which were building over the same period. By 1968 both production lines had stopped when the first "Charlie" class appeared with underwater launch capability for its 25 mile SS-N-7 missiles. The problem which had faced all the earlier boats, that of having to surface to launch, had been overcome and improvements of the "Charlies", "Charlie II" and "Papa", have been in service for five years.

2 "PAPA" CLASS
(CRUISE MISSILE SUBMARINES SSGN)

Displacement, tons (approx): 5 500 surfaced; 6 500 dived
Dimensions, feet (metres): 328 × 33·3 × 26·3 *(100 × 12 × 8)*
Missile launchers: 10 for SS-N-7
Torpedo tubes: 8—21 in *(533 mm)*
Main machinery: Nuclear reactor; 2 steam turbines; 2 shafts; 24 000 shp
Speed, knots: 20 surfaced; 28 dived
Complement: 85

A single member of an SSGN class apparently a development of the "Charlie" class first reported in 1973. The fin is of a much more angular shape than the "Charlies" with a higher casing, a more rounded bow and with the missile tubes having square covers. Second reported 1976.

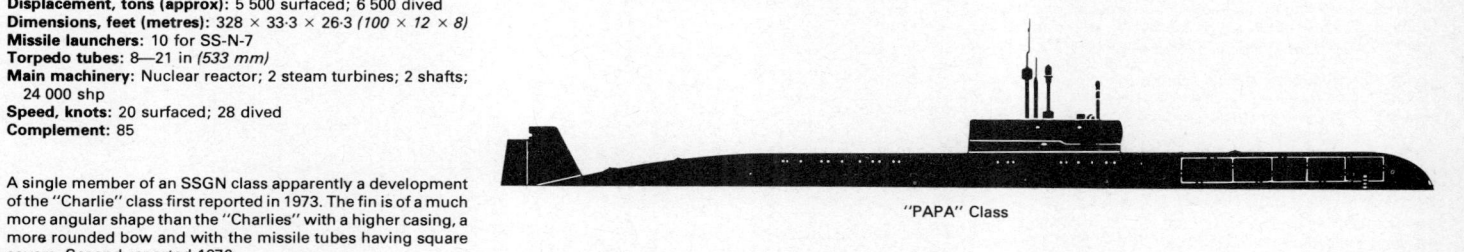

"PAPA" Class

3 "CHARLIE II" CLASS
(CRUISE MISSILE SUBMARINES SSGN)

Displacement, tons: 4 500 surfaced; 5 600 dived
Dimensions, feet (metres): 324·7 × 32·8 × 24·6 *(99 × 10 × 7·5)*
Missile launchers: 8 tubes for SS-N-7
Torpedo tubes: 6—21 in *(533 mm)* (see note)
Main machinery: Nuclear reactor; 2 steam turbines; 1 shaft
Speed, knots: 20 surfaced; 28 dived
Complement: 80

Enlarged "Charlie" class, first reported in 1973 and now in production at Gorky in place of the earlier version.
The increase in size may be due to the fitting of equipment for firing the SS-N-15, a Subroc-type weapon, from her torpedo tubes.

"CHARLIE II" Class

12 "CHARLIE" CLASS
(CRUISE MISSILE SUBMARINES SSGN)

Displacement, tons: 4 000 surfaced; 5 100 dived
Dimensions, feet (metres): 295·2 × 32·8 × 24·6 *(90 × 10 × 7·5)*
Missile launchers: 8 tubes for SS-N-7 missiles
Torpedo tubes: 6—21 in *(533 mm)*
Main machinery: 1 nuclear reactor; steam turbines; 25 000-30 000 shp; 1 shaft
Speed, knots: 20 surfaced; 30 dived
Complement: 80

A class of cruise-missile submarines built at Gorky. The first of class was delivered in 1968, representing a very significant advance in the cruise-missile submarine field. With a speed of at least 30 knots and mounting eight missile tubes for the SS-N-7 system (25 n. miles range) which has a dived launch capability, this is a great advance on the "Echo" class. These boats have an improved hull and reactor design and must be assumed to have an organic control for their missile system therefore posing a notable threat to any surface force. Their deployment to the Mediterranean, the area of the US 6th Fleet, is only a part of their general and world-wide operations.

Appearance: Although similar to the "Victor" class the bulge at the bow, the almost vertical drop of the forward end of the fin, a slightly lower after casing and a different arrangement of free-flood holes in the casing give a clear differentiation.

Sonar: Fin sonar fitted. This may be of value when tracking for missile firing data, although bound to be speed-limited.

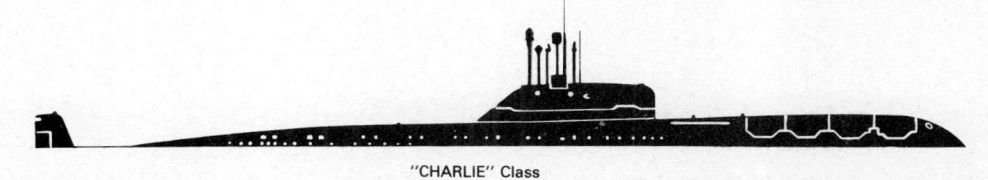

"CHARLIE" Class

"CHARLIE" Class — 1974, MOD(N)

"CHARLIE II" Class (all masts up) — 4/1974

492 USSR

29 "ECHO II" CLASS
(CRUISE MISSILE SUBMARINES SSGN)

Displacement, tons: 4 800 surfaced; 6 000 dived
Length, feet (metres): 390·7 *(119)*
Beam, feet (metres): 31·3 *(9·5)*
Draught, feet (metres): 25·9 *(7·9)*
Missile launchers: 8—SS-N-3 tubes (see note)
Torpedo tubes: 6—21 in (bow); 4—16 in (stern)
Main machinery: 1 nuclear reactor; 2 steam turbines; 2 shafts; 22 500 shp
Speed, knots: 20 surfaced; 22 dived
Complement: 92

"ECHO II" Class

The decision to produce this class may have been due to the failure of the "Echo I", the availability of slips and hull components probably intended for another type of submarine and the production of SS-N-3 launchers for the "Juliett" class which probably started construction about a year earlier than "Echo II".
With a slightly lengthened hull, a fourth pair of launchers was installed and between 1963 and 1967 at least 29 of this class were built. They are now deployed evenly between the Pacific and Northern fleets and still provide a useful group of boats some being deployed to the Mediterranean. Some may be fitted with SS-N-12 missiles.
Built at Severodvinsk and Komsomolsk.

Design: This was a new design from the "Echo I", longer and carrying eight launchers instead of six. The "Echo I" was probably a stop-gap and a not very successful one at that as all were stripped of their missile equipment in 1971-74. "Echo II" class carry a mid-course guidance radar for SS-N-3.

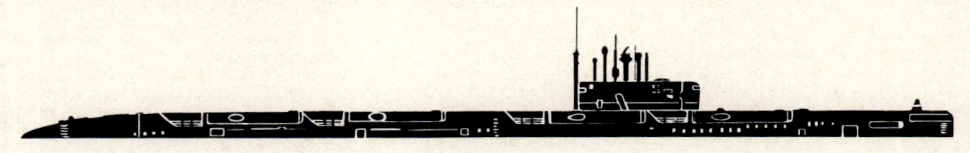

"ECHO II" Class 1973

"ECHO II" Class 1973, MOD(N)

"ECHO II" Class 6/1973

USSR 493

16 "JULIETT" CLASS
(CRUISE MISSILE SUBMARINES SSG)

Displacement, tons: 3 200 surfaced; 3 600 dived
Dimensions, feet (metres): 285·4 × 32·8 × 19·6 *(87 × 10 × 6)*
Missile launchers: 4—SS-N-3 tubes; 2 before and 2 abaft the fin
Torpedo tubes: 6—21 in (bow)
Main machinery: Diesels; 7 000 bhp; electric motors; 5 000 hp; 2 shafts
Speed, knots: 16 surfaced; 16 dived
Range, miles: 15 000 surfaced cruising
Complement: 90

Completed at Leningrad between 1962 and 1967. Four SS-N-3 launchers, one pair either end of the fin which appears to be comparatively low. This class was the logical continuation of the "Whiskey" class conversions. A number of this class has in the past been deployed to the Mediterranean. Some may be fitted with SS-N-12 missiles.

Appearance: The massive casing and fairly low fin make this an unmistakable class.

Engineering: The unusually broad beam for a diesel submarine has prompted speculation that some form of unconventional propulsion requiring more space or shielding has been used in this class. Although this view is not generally supported it has certainly not been disproved.

Radar: Mid-course guidance radar for SS-N-3.

"JULIETT" Class

"JULIETT" Class 7/1973

"JULIETT" Class 1973, MOD(N)

"JULIETT" Class 5/1972, US Navy

494   USSR

7 "WHISKEY LONG-BIN" CLASS
(CRUISE MISSILE SUBMARINES SSG)

Displacement, tons: 1 200 surfaced; 1 600 dived
Dimensions, feet (metres): 275·5 × 23·9 × 16·3 *(84 × 7·3 × 5)*
Missile launchers: 4—SS-N-3 tubes
Torpedo tubes: 6—21 in *(533 mm)*
Main machinery: Diesels; 4 000 bhp; electric motors; 2 500 hp
Speed, knots: 16 surfaced; 14 dived
Range, miles: 13 000 surfaced, cruising
Complement: 75

A more efficient modification of the "Whiskey" class than the "Twin-Cylinder" with four SS-N-3 launchers built into a remodelled fin on a hull lengthened by 33 feet. Converted between 1960-63—no organic guidance and therefore reliance must be made on aircraft or surface-ship cooperation. Must be a very noisy boat when dived.
Two or three probably in reserve.

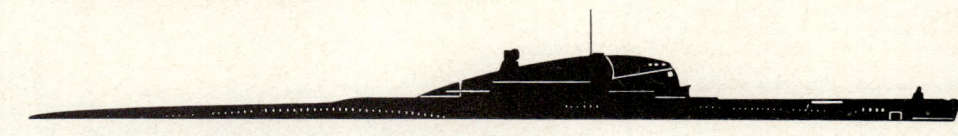

"WHISKEY LONG-BIN" Class

"WHISKEY LONG BIN" Class   1975

3 "WHISKEY TWIN CYLINDER" CLASS
(CRUISE MISSILE SUBMARINES SSG)

Displacement, tons: 1 100 surfaced; 1 400 dived
Dimensions, feet (metres): 246 × 22 × 16·4 *(75 × 7·3 × 5)*
Missile launchers: 2—SS-N-3 tubes
Torpedo tubes: 4—21 in *(533 mm)*
Main machinery: Diesels; 4 000 bhp; electric motors; 2 500 hp
Speed, knots: 17 surfaced; 15 dived
Range, miles: 13 000, surfaced, cruising
Complement: 70

A 1958-60 modification of the conventional "Whiskey" class designed to test out the SS-N-3 system at sea. Probably never truly operational being a thoroughly messy conversion which must make a noise like a train if proceeding at any speed above dead slow when dived. The modification consisted of fitting a pair of launchers abaft the fin. Probably now in reserve before deletion. Six originally modified.

"WHISKEY TWIN CYLINDER" Class

"WHISKEY TWIN CYLINDER" Class   7/1973

Fleet Submarine Classes

Note: The use of nuclear power for marine propulsion was developed from 1950 onwards, the first submarine reactor being put in hand in 1953 probably about the same time as a larger reactor for the icebreaker *Lenin* was under construction. The latter commissioned in September 1959, a year after the first of the "November" class entered service. These submarines, of which 14 were built in five years had a very long hull, and this long form was also used in the "Hotel" and "Echo I" designs. It was a new concept designed to take full advantage of the available horse-power and, in the "Novembers", was fitted with a small streamlined fin.

Apparently no prototype was produced before series production of the "Novembers" began and this was also true for the "Victors" which followed after a five year pause. Since the early "Novembers" provided sea-experience of this new form of submarine some seven years of redesign was therefore available before the first "Victor" was laid down. The ability to produce hydrodynamically advanced hull forms was further proved by the efficiency of the "Victor" and her near sister the "Charlie". Five years after the first "Victor" came the "Victor II", an enlarged edition whose increase in size may be due to the fitting of the new tube-launched weapon system, SS-N-15, probably similar to the Subroc of the USN.

The "Alfa" class remains an enigma but may be a prototype particularly as it is built at Sudomekh.

2 + ? "ALFA" CLASS
(FLEET SUBMARINES SSN)

Displacement, tons: 2 500 surfaced; 3 000 dived
Dimensions, feet (metres): 255·8 × 32·8 × 26·2 *(78 × 10 × 8)*
Torpedo tubes: 6—21 in *(533 mm)*
Main machinery: 1 nuclear reactor; steam turbine; 25 000 shp; 1 shaft
Speed, knots: 16 surfaced; 28 dived

One unit of this class was completed in 1970 at Sudomekh, Leningrad. The building time was very long and it seems most likely that this is a prototype of a new class, with some advanced design or propulsion aspects. If so additional units of this class or its successor can be expected over the next few years.

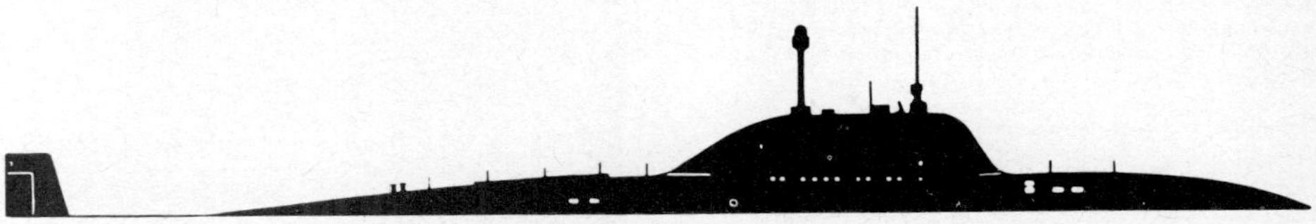

"ALFA" Class

5 + ? "VICTOR II" CLASS
(FLEET SUBMARINES SSN)

Displacement, tons: 4 700 surfaced; 6 000 dived
Dimensions, feet (metres): 308·3 × 32·8 × 26·2 *(94 × 10 × 8)*
Torpedo tubes: 8—21 in *(533 mm)* see note
Main machinery: 1 nuclear reactor; 2 steam turbines; 1 shaft; 30 000 shp
Speed, knots: 26 surfaced; 33 dived
Complement: 90

An enlarged "Victor" design, 7 metres longer. This additional length may be needed to house the equipment needed for firing the tube-launched SS-N-15, a Subroc type weapon.

Radar: Snoop Tray.

Sonar: Apparently none in the fin.

"VICTOR II" Class

16 "VICTOR" CLASS
(FLEET SUBMARINES SSN)

Displacement, tons: 4 000 surfaced; 5 200 dived
Dimensions, feet (metres): 285·4 × 32·8 × 26·2 *(87 × 10 × 8)*
Torpedo tubes: 8—21 in *(533 mm)*
Main machinery: 1 nuclear reactor; 2 steam turbines; 25 000-30 000 shp; 1 shaft
Speed, knots: 20 surfaced; 30 plus dived
Complement: 85

Designed purely as a torpedo carrying submarine its much increased speed makes it a menace to all but the fastest ships. The first of class entered service in 1967-68 with a subsequent building rate of about two per year, which may now have been superseded by the "Victor II" programme. Built at Admiralty Yard, Leningrad.

The majority is deployed with the Northern Fleet, although some have joined the Pacific Fleet.

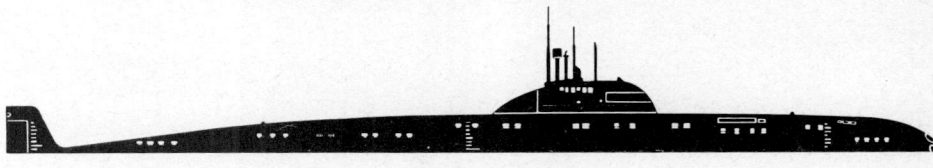

"VICTOR" Class

"VICTOR" Class (in S. China Sea) 4/1974

"VICTOR" Class 4/1974, MOD

496 USSR

13 "NOVEMBER" CLASS
(FLEET SUBMARINES SSN)

Displacement, tons: 4 200 surfaced; 5 000 dived
Dimensions, feet (metres): 357·5 × 32·1 × 24·3 *(109 × 9·8 × 7·4)*
Torpedo tubes: 10; 6—21 in *(533 mm)* (bow);
 4—16 in *(406 mm)* (stern)
Main machinery: 2 nuclear reactors; steam turbines;
 32 500 shp
Speed, knots: 20 surfaced; 25 dived
Complement: 88

"NOVEMBER" Class

The first class of Soviet nuclear submarines which entered service between 1958 and 1963. Built at Severodvinsk. The hull form with the great number of free-flood holes in the casing suggests a noisy boat and it is surprising that greater efforts have not been made to supersede this class with the "Victors". In April 1970 one of this class sank south-west of the United Kingdom.

Diving Depth: Reported as 1 650 feet *(500 metres)*.

"NOVEMBER" Class

"NOVEMBER" Class (in Gulf of Mexico) 7/1969, USN

5 "ECHO I" CLASS
(FLEET SUBMARINES SSN)

Displacement, tons: 4 300 surfaced; 5 500 dived
Dimensions, feet (metres): 367·4 × 31·2 × 25·9 *(112 × 9·5 × 7·9)*
Torpedo tubes: 6—21 in (bow)
Main machinery: 1 nuclear reactor; 2 steam turbines;
 25 000-30 000 shp; 1 shaft
Speed, knots: 20 surfaced; 25 dived
Complement: 92 (12 officers, 80 men)

"ECHO I" Class

This class was completed in 1960-62. Originally mounted six SS-N-3 launchers raised from the after casing.
The hull of this class is very similar to the "Hotel"/"November" type and it is probably powered by similar nuclear plant. Only five "Echo Is" were built, being followed immediately by the "Echo IIs". In 1971-74 the "Echo I" class was converted into fleet submarines with the removal of the missile system, a decision which may have been due to a basic inefficiency of this hull form for the planned task. It has been reported that in their original configuration this class carried only two torpedo tubes.

"ECHO I" Class (as SSN) 8/1975 MOD

USSR 497

Patrol Submarine Classes

Note: When the time came to rebuild the Soviet navy after the Revolution the first major new construction programme was that for submarines. By 1939 this force numbered 185 and by the start of the Great Patriotic War in June 1941, 218 were listed. At the end of the war new German ideas became available to the USSR—new designs, new concepts. This new knowledge was incorporated in a 1948 plan to build 1 200 submarines between 1950 and 1965 at an initial rate of 78 a year, increasing to 100. This programme was probably split into three sections, representing the three zones of defence—200 long-range boats ("Zulu" and, later, "Foxtrot" classes), 900 medium-range boats, ("Whiskey" and, later, "Romeo" classes) and 100 coastal boats of the "Quebec" class, the last being fitted with either Walther turbines or closed-cycle diesels. These last were German designs as were the hull-forms of the submarines, being similar to the German Type XXI.

This plan was largely amended with the post-Stalin readjustments and the successful experiments with nuclear power plants. Of the projected boats only 28 out of 40 "Zulus" were built, 60 out of 160 "Foxtrots", 240 out of 340 "Whiskeys" (albeit in seven years), 20 out of 560 "Romeos" and 40 out of 100 "Quebecs". After the arrival of the nuclears the "Golfs" and "Julietts" were the only other diesel submarines completed until 1968. Then the "Bravos" appeared and set a problem for Western analysts until they were classified as "padded targets". Finally, the "Tangos" joined the fleet in 1973. These last, apparently possessing excellent underwater performance and a considerable fire-power, may be the logical product of the twin facts that the USSR has large areas of shallow water around her coasts in which nuclear submarines cannot develop their full potential and that the diesel-boat is still the quietest listening platform.

7 + ? "TANGO" CLASS
(PATROL SUBMARINES SS)

Displacement, tons: 3 000 surfaced; 3 500 dived
Dimensions, feet (metres): 296·3 × 30 × 19·6 *(91 × 9·1 × 6)*
Torpedo tubes: ? 6—21 in *(533 mm)* see note
Main machinery: 3 diesels; 6 000 shp; 3 electric motors; 6 000 shp; 3 shafts
Speed, knots: 16 surfaced; 20 dived
Complement: 62

This class was first seen at the Sevastopol Review in July 1973. Notable features are the rise in the forecasing and a new shape for the snort exhaust. This class, following five years after the "Bravo", shows a continuing commitment to diesel-propelled boats which is of interest in view of the comparatively slow building programme of nuclear attack submarines. As this is clearly an advanced design it may be intended to cover the large shallow-water areas around the USSR where nuclear submarines would be less efficiently deployed. Continuing programme of two a year at Gorky and Sudomekh.

Torpedoes: The increase in the bow section suggests that these submarines can launch the SS-N-15 (Subroc type) weapon.

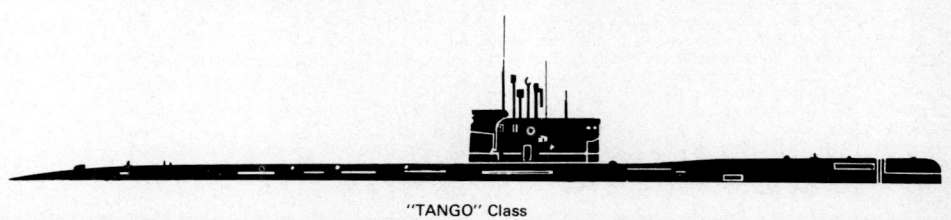

"TANGO" Class

"TANGO" Class 1975, MOD

"TANGO" Class 1973, Tass

4 "BRAVO" CLASS
(PATROL SUBMARINES SS)

Displacement, tons: 2 300 surfaced; 2 800 dived
Dimensions, feet (metres): 219·8 × 30 × 23·2 *(67 × 9·1 × 7)*
Torpedo tubes: 6—21 in *(533 mm)*
Main machinery: Diesel-electric
Speed, knots: 16 dived

The beam-to-length ratio is larger than normal in a diesel submarine which would account in part for the large displacement for a comparatively short hull.
First completed in 1968. One attached to each of the main fleets, reinforcing the view that these are "padded targets" for torpedo and A/S firings.

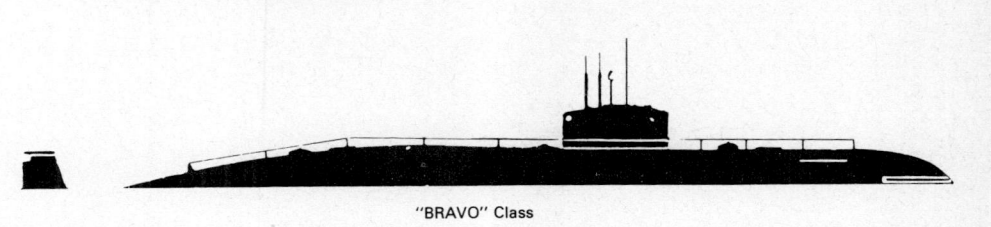

"BRAVO" Class

USSR

60 "FOXTROT" CLASS
(PATROL SUBMARINES SS)

Displacement, tons: 2 100 surfaced; 2 400 dived
Dimensions, feet (metres): 298·5 × 26·2 × 16·4 (91 × 8 × 5)
Torpedo tubes: 10—21 in (6 bow, 4 stern) (20 torpedoes carried)
Main machinery: Diesels; 6 000 bhp; 3 electric motors; 5 000 hp; 3 shafts
Speed, knots: 18 surfaced; 17 dived
Range: 20 000 miles surfaced, cruising
Complement: 70

Built since 1958 at Sudomekh although the Soviet naval programme finished in late 1960s. A follow-on of the "Zulu" class with similar propulsion to the "Golf" class. Only 60 out of a total programme of 160 were completed as the change over to nuclear boats took effect. A most successful class which has been deployed world-wide, forming the bulk of the Soviet submarine force in the Mediterranean. Four transferred to India in 1968-69 with a further four new construction following. This is a continuing programme for export, now including Libya—one delivered to that country in 1976 with five more reportedly on order.

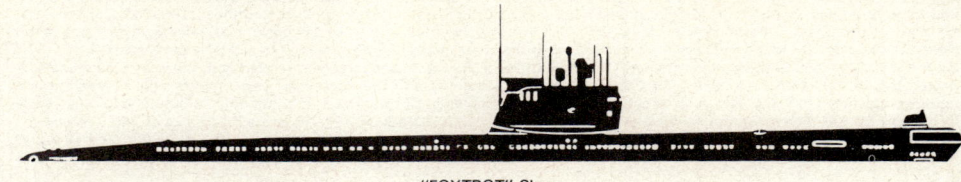

"FOXTROT" Class

"FOXTROT" Class (Indian Ocean)   5/1974, USN

Frozen "FOXTROT" with bow guard   7/1973

"FOXTROT" Class (Mediterranean—USS *Jonas Ingram* behind)   12/1973, USN

USSR 499

19 "ZULU IV" CLASS
(PATROL SUBMARINES SS)

Displacement, tons: 2 000 surfaced; 2 400 dived
Length, feet (metres): 295 (89·6)
Beam, feet (metres): 24 (7·4)
Draught, feet (metres): 15·7 (4·8)
Torpedo tubes: 10—21 in (6 bow, 4 stern); (24 torpedoes carried or 40 mines)
Main machinery: Diesel-electric; 3 shafts; 3 diesels; 8 000 bhp; 3 electric motors; 3 500 hp
Speed, knots: 18 surfaced; 15 dived
Range, miles: 20 000 surfaced, cruising
Complement: 70

The first large post-war patrol submarines built by USSR. 28 completed from late 1951 to 1955 out of an original programme of 40. General appearance is streamlined with a complete row of free-flood holes along the casing. Eighteen were built by Sudomekh Shipyard, Leningrad, in 1952-55 and others at Severodvinsk. The general external similarity to the later German U-boats of World War II is notable. All now appear to be of the "Zulu IV" type. This class, although the majority are probably still operational, is obsolescent and will soon be disposed of.
The six "Zulu V" conversions of this class provided the first Soviet ballistic missile submarines with SS-N-4 systems, the first becoming operational in 1955.

"ZULU IV" Class

"ZULU IV" Class   1969, USN

"ZULU IV" Class   1974

10 "ROMEO" CLASS
(PATROL SUBMARINES SS)

Displacement, tons: 1 400 surfaced; 1 800 dived
Dimensions, feet (metres): 249·3 × 23 × 16·4 (76 × 7 × 5)
Torpedo tubes: 6—21 in (533 mm) 18 torpedoes or 36 mines in place of torpedoes
Main machinery: Diesels; 4 000 bhp; electric motors; 3 000 hp; 2 shafts
Speed, knots: 17 surfaced; 14 dived
Range, miles: 13 000 at 10 knots (surfaced)
Complement: 60

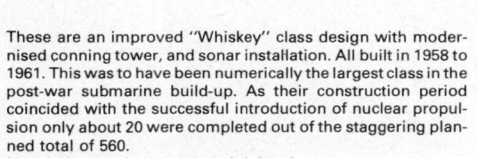

"ROMEO" Class

These are an improved "Whiskey" class design with modernised conning tower, and sonar installation. All built in 1958 to 1961. This was to have been numerically the largest class in the post-war submarine build-up. As their construction period coincided with the successful introduction of nuclear propulsion only about 20 were completed out of the staggering planned total of 560.
Now being put in reserve and deleted.

Transfers: Six to Egypt in 1966. China and North Korea building submarines of similar design.

"ROMEO" Class   1974

"ROMEO" Class   1970

500 USSR

50 "WHISKEY" CLASS (see note)
(PATROL SUBMARINES SS)

Displacement, tons: 1 030 surfaced; 1 350 dived
Dimensions, feet (metres): 249·3 × 22 × 16·5 *(76 × 6·7 × 5)*
Torpedo tubes: 6—21 in (4 bow, 2 stern); 18 torpedoes carried (or 40 mines)
Main machinery: Diesel-electric; 2 shafts
  2 diesels; 4 000 bhp
  2 electric motors; 2 500 hp
Speed, knots: 17 surfaced; 15 dived
Range, miles: 13 000 at 8 knots (surfaced)
Complement: 60

"WHISKEY V" Class

This was the first post-war Soviet design for a medium-range submarine. Like its larger contemporary the "Zulu", this class shows considerable German influence. About 240 of the "Whiskeys" were built between 1951 and 1957 at yards throughout the USSR. Like its successor, the "Romeo", this class was cut back from the original planned total of 340 as nuclear propulsion became established. Built in six types—I and IV had guns forward of the conning tower. II had guns both ends, whilst III and V have no guns. V is the most common variant whilst VA has a diver's exit hatch forward of the conning tower. The inclusion of 100 mm guns on the original "Whiskey II" type must have resulted in considerable noise and turbulence on what was basically a very smooth design although the mounting of smaller guns forward of the fin had already broken up the streamline. It is difficult to understand the purpose of such heavy artillery on a class designed, presumably, as a medium range protective force against the most advanced navies in the world.

Class Total: There may be about 50 operational although decreasing numbers are seen out of area. Some 100 are probably in reserve, a sizeable proportion probably unmaintained.

Conversions: Two of this class, named *Severyanka* and *Slavyanka*, were converted for oceanographic and fishery research.

Foreign Transfers: Has been the most popular export model; currently in service in Albania (4), Bulgaria (4), China (21), Egypt (6), Indonesia (3), North Korea (4) and Poland (4).

"WHISKEY V" Class   1974, J. D. R. Rawlings

"WHISKEY V" Class   1977, Selçuk Emre

"WHISKEY V" Class   1973

4 "WHISKEY CANVAS BAG" CLASS
(RADAR PICKET SUBMARINES SSR)

Displacement, tons: 1 030 surfaced; 1 350 dived
Dimensions, feet (metres): 249·3 × 22 × 16·5 *(76 × 6·7 × 5)*
Torpedo tubes: 6—21 in *(533 in)* (4 bow, 2 stern)
Main machinery: Diesel-electric; 2 shafts; 2 diesels; 4 000 bhp; electric motors; 2 500 hp
Speed, knots: 17 surfaced; 15 dived
Range, miles: 13 000 at 8 knots surfaced
Complement: 65

Basically of same design as the "Whiskey" class but with long-range Boat-Sail radar aerial mounted on the fin. The coy way in which this was covered prompted the title "Canvas Bag". Converted in 1959 to 1963 as surveillance pickets. The introduction of "Bear" aircraft around 1963 probably rendered this plan redundant and thus very few were converted. They have, however, remained in service so presumably a task has been found for them.

"WHISKEY CANVAS BAG" Class

"WHISKEY CANVAS BAG" Class (with radar aerial abeam) 1975

20 "QUEBEC" CLASS
(PATROL SUBMARINES SS)

Displacement, tons: 470 surfaced; 550 dived
Dimensions, feet (metres): 185·0 × 18 × 13·2 *(56·4 × 5·5 × 4·0)*
Torpedo tubes: 4—21 in *(533 mm)* bow
Main machinery: Diesel-electric; 3 shafts; 2 diesels; 2 000 bhp; 3 electric motors; 2 000 hp
Speed, knots: 18 surfaced; 16 dived
Oil fuel, tons: 50
Range, miles: 7 000 surfaced cruising
Complement: 42

Short range, coastal submarines. Built from 1954 to 1957. Thirteen were constructed in 1955 by Sudomekh Shipyard, Leningrad. The original planned total was cut from 100 to at least 22, overtaken by nuclear propulsion and with the failure of the unconventional propulsion in the earlier boats.

Class Total: Five may be still running but most are in reserve and may be deleted in the near future.

Propulsion system: In the late 1930s both closed cycle diesels and a closed cycle turbine were under development in Germany. After initial sea trials both were tried out in the Type XVII and later submarines. Thus when the Soviet Union occupied a large part of Germany at the war's end they had a great deal of knowledge available and experiments continued at Leningrad. The Walther/Kreislof Turbine was certainly put to sea and possibly also closed cycle diesels. The fuels required, high test peroxide for the turbines and liquid oxygen for the diesels, was dangerous to handle, frequently causing fires and explosions. Consequently this class reverted to normal diesel and electric propulsion, losing their title of "Cigarette Lighters".

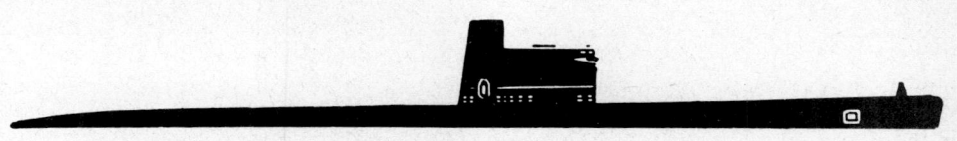

"QUEBEC" Class

"QUEBEC" Class 1970

"QUEBEC" Class 1970

502 USSR

Name	No.
KIEV	—
MINSK	—
KOMSOMOLEC	—

Displacement, tons: 43 000 full load
Length, feet (metres): 898·7 *(274)* oa
Beam, feet (metres): 135 *(41·2)* (hull); 157·4 *(48)* (overall, including flight deck and sponsons)
Aircraft (estimated): 30-35—normal mix, 12 Forger, 20 Hormones
Missile launchers: 8 (4 twin) SS-N-12 SSM launchers; 2 twin SA-N-3; 1 SUW-N A/S launcher; 2 SA-N-4 launchers
Guns: 4—76 mm; 8 Air Defence Gatling mounts
A/S weapons: 2—12 barrelled MBU 2500A launchers forward
Torpedo tubes: 10—21 in *(533 mm)* recessed below waterline
Main engines: Steam turbines; 4 shafts
Speed, knots: At least 30
Range, miles: 13 000 at 18 knots (?)

After years of argument and indecision the first sign of Soviet acceptance of the need for organic air was the appearance of *Moskva* and *Leningrad* in 1968-69, the first ships built with a flat deck in the post-war years. They carried the embarked helicopter concept a long stage further than the cruisers and destroyers with a single embarked helicopter. It is most probable that a much larger number was projected and the reason for the cancellation of the remainder might be because of any or all of a number of factors. Two appear to be of considerable importance—the growing Soviet realisation of the important part their navy could play in overseas affairs and the appearance of the prototype of the first Soviet V/STOL aircraft, the Yakovlev *Freehand.* This first appeared in public in 1967 and its capabilities were known at least a year before that. This was ten years before *Kiev* became operational, a reasonable lead time for Soviet designers and constructors.

The task of this class is probably twofold—an advanced ASW role in wartime and an intervention capability in so-called peacetime with excellent command, control and communication capabilities. The inclusion of the very considerable SSM capability, A/S weapons as well as sonar equipment, and a gun armament as well as both missile and gun Point Defence Systems shows a continuation of the Soviet plan for multi-purpose ships.

Aircraft: The complement appears to be a mix of *Hormone* helicopters and *Forger* (Yak 36) V/STOL aircraft. The *Forger* comes in two versions—A, a single seater of which about a dozen were embarked in July-August 1976 and B, a twin-seat trainer of which only one was seen. Some 20 *Hormones,* mostly A but with one or two B, were also carried on the same trip.

The functions of the *Forger* have not been fully revealed and may not yet, in fact, be fully evaluated. It appears to have the potential to carry both air-to-air and air-to-surface missiles as well as A/S weapons. All this, combined with a reconnaissance role, means that a new dimension in Soviet capability has been achieved.

ECM: A full fit is carried including Side Globe housings.

Flight Deck: 620 feet *(189 metres)* long with a 4 degree angle, 68 feet *(20·7 metres)* wide with two lifts, one larger one abaft the island for V/STOL and a smaller one amidships abreast the bridge. Six spots are provided with a seventh at the forward tip of the flight deck. A larger spot amidships aft is apparently for V/STOL.

Missiles: The four twin SSM launchers carry SS-N-12 missiles, an advance on the SS-N-3 with a range of over 250 miles at a speed of Mach 2/3.
The SAM armament is standard.
The A/S missile launcher can presumably launch either SS-N-14 or FRAS-1.

Operations: With a relative wind of up to 15 knots fine on the port bow (sometimes requiring a very slow ship's speed) a maximum of two aircraft is normally launched. Take off and landing is normally very cautious, possibly a combination of inexperience and doubt. The inexperience has been reflected on the flight-deck where the customary accessories (bulldozer etc) have not been visible.

Radar: 3D search: Top Sail.
Search: Head Net.
Fire control: Head Light (SA-N-3); Pop Group (SA-N-4); Owl Screech *(76 mm).*
In addition two other types of radar, the radome and twin sets aft are fitted.

Sonar: Hull-mounted and VDS.

Soviet Type Name: Protivo Lodochny Kreyser meaning anti-submarine cruiser. This is an interesting designation for a ship of this size, continuing the Soviet practice of calling nearly all major surface units by an ASW title.

AIRCRAFT CARRIERS

2 + 1 "KIEV" CLASS (AIRCRAFT CARRIERS)

Builders	Laid down	Launched	Commissioned
Nikolayev South	1971	31 Dec 1972	1976
Nikolayev South	1972	1974	1977
Nikolayev South	1973	1976	1979

KIEV

KIEV (with "Forgers" on deck) 8/1976, MOD

KIEV 8/1976, MOD

USSR 503

KIEV ("Forgers" and "Hormones" on deck)   12/1977, MOD

KIEV   7/1976, USN

KIEV   7/1976, Selçuk Emre

KIEV   10/1976, USN

504 USSR

HELICOPTER CRUISERS

2 "MOSKVA" CLASS

Name	No.	Builders	Laid down	Launched	Commissioned
MOSKVA	—	Nikolayev South	1962	—	1968
LENINGRAD	—	Nikolayev South	1963	—	1969

Displacement, tons: 14 500 standard; 19 200 full load
Length, feet (metres): 624·8 (190·5); 644·8 oa (196·6)
Flight deck, feet (metres): 295·3 (90·0) aft of superstructure
Width, feet (metres): 115·0 (35·0)
Beam, feet (metres): 111·5 (34)
Draught, feet (metres): 24·9 (7·6)
Aircraft: 18 Hormone A ASW helicopters
Missile launchers: 4 (2 twin) SA-N-3 systems (180 reloads)
Guns: 4—57 mm (2 twin mountings)
A/S weapons: 1 twin SUWN-1 A/S missile launcher; 2—12 tube MBU 2500A on forecastle
Torpedo tubes: 2 quintuple 21 in (533 mm)
Main engines: Geared turbines; 2 shafts; 100 000 shp
Boilers: 4 watertube
Speed, knots: 30
Complement: 800

This class represented a radical change of thought in the Soviet fleet. The design must have been completed while the "November" class submarines were building and the heavy A/S armament and efficient sensors (helicopters and VDS) suggest an awareness of the problem of dealing with nuclear submarines. Alongside what is apparently a primary A/S role these ships have a capability for A/A warning and self-defence as well as a command function. With a full fit of radar and ECM equipment they clearly represent good value for money. Both ships handle well in heavy weather and are capable of helicopter-operations under adverse conditions. Why only two were built is discussed earlier in the notes on the "Kiev" class aircraft carriers.

Modification: In early 1973 Moskva was seen with a landing pad on the after end of the flight deck, probably for flight tests of VTOL aircraft. Since removed.

Radar: Search: Top Sail 3-D and Head Net C 3-D.
Fire control: Head Light (2). Muff Cob.
Miscellaneous: Electronic warfare equipment.

Sonar: VDS and, probably, hull mounted set. In addition all helicopters have dunking-sonar.

Soviet Type Name: Protivo Lodochny Kreyser meaning Anti-Submarine Cruiser.

"MOSKVA" Class

MOSKVA 5/1974, USN

LENINGRAD 11/1974, MOD

MOSKVA 1975, MOD

CRUISERS

6 + 2 "KARA" CLASS (CG)

NIKOLAYEV	OCHAKOV	
KERCH	AZOV	
PETROPAVLOVSK	+1	+2 building

Displacement, tons: 8 200 standard; 10 000 full load
Length, feet (metres): 570 *(173·8)*
Beam, feet (metres): 60 *(18·3)*
Draught, feet (metres): 20 *(6·2)*
Aircraft: 1 Hormone A or B helicopter (Hangar aft)
Missile Systems: 8—SS-N-14 (two quad launchers abreast bridge)
4—SA-N-4 (twins either side of mast)
4—SA-N-3 (twins)
Guns: 4—76 mm (2 twins abaft bridge)
4—Gatling type close range weapons (abreast funnel) (see *Gunnery* note)
A/S weapons: 2—12 barrelled MBU launchers (forward)
2—6 barrelled DC throwers
Torpedo tubes: 10—21 in *(533 mm)* (2 quintuple mountings abaft funnel)
Main engines: Gas-turbine; 120 000 hp
Speed, knots: Approximately 34

Apart from the specialised "Moskva" class this is the first class of large cruisers to join the Soviet navy since the "Sverdlovs". *Nikolayev* was first seen in public when she entered the Mediterranean from the Black Sea on 2 March 1973. Clearly capable of prolonged operations overseas.
All built or building at Nikolayev. *Azov* is of a modified design but has not yet emerged from the Black Sea. Continuing programme of about one a year.

ECM: A full outfit appears to be housed on the bridge and mast.

Gunnery: The siting of both main and secondary armament on either beams in the waist follows the precedent of both "Kresta" classes, although the weight of the main armament is increased. The single mountings are Gatling.

Missiles: In addition to the "Kresta II" armament of eight tubes for the SS-N-14 A/S system (possibly with a surface-to-surface capability) and the pair of twin launchers for SA-N-3 system with Goblet missiles, "Kara" mounts the SA-N-4 system in two silos, either side of the mast. The combination of such a number of systems presents a formidable capability, matched by no ship other than *Kiev*.

Radar: Surveillance: Top Sail and Head Net C.
SA-N-3 control: Head Light
SA-N-4 control: Pop Group (2).
76 mm gun control: Owl Screech.
Gatling gun control: Bass Tilt.

Sonar and A/S: VDS is mounted below the helicopter pad and is presumably complementary to a hull-mounted set or sets. The presence of the helicopter with dipping-sonar and an A/S weapon load adds to her long-range capability.

Soviet Type Name: Bolshoy Protivolodochny Korabl, meaning Large Anti-Submarine Ship.

"KARA" Class

KERCH (Hull 3) (same pennant number as *Ochakov* a year earlier) — 2/1976, MOD

OCHAKOV (Hull 2) (same pennant number as *Nikolayev* a year earlier) — 3/1975, MOD

NIKOLAYEV (Hull 1) — 1974, MOD

USSR

10 "KRESTA II" CLASS (CG)

ADMIRAL ISACHENKOV
ADMIRAL ISAKOV
ADMIRAL MAKAROV
ADMIRAL NAKHIMOV
ADMIRAL OKTYABRSKY
ADMIRAL YUMASCHEV
KRONSHTADT
MARSHAL TIMOSHENKO
MARSHAL VOROSHILOV
VASILIY CHAPAEV
+ 1

Displacement, tons: 6 000 standard; 8 000 full load
Length, feet (metres): 519·9 *(158·5)*
Beam, feet (metres): 55·1 *(16·8)*
Draught, feet (metres): 19·7 *(6·0)*
Aircraft: 1 Hormone A or B helicopter (hangar aft)
Missile launchers: 2 quadruple for SS-N-14; 2 twin for SA-N-3
Guns: 4—57 mm (2 twin); 4—Gatling Close Range Weapons
A/S weapons: 2—12 barrelled MBU (forward);
  2—6 barrelled DC throwers (aft)
Torpedo tubes: 10—21 in *(533 mm)* (two quintuple)
Main engines: 2 steam turbines; 2 shafts; 100 000 shp
Boilers: 4 watertube
Speed, knots: 35
Range, miles: 5 500 at 18 knots
Complement: 500

The design was developed from that of the "Kresta I" class, but the layout is more up-to-date. The missile armament shows an advance on the "Kresta I" SAM armament and a complete change of practice in the fitting of the SS-N-14 A/S missile system. The fact that it has subsequently been fitted in the "Kara" and "Krivak" classes and that it must have a very limited anti-surface-ship capability indicates a possible change in tactical thought. Built at Zhdanov, Leningrad 1968 onwards. There are indications that these slipways may now be in use for a new class.

New construction: Two building at Zhdanov Yard Leningrad (1977).

Radar: 3D search: Top Sail.
Search: Head Net C.
SA-N-3 control: Head Light (2).
SA-N-4 control: Pop Group.
57 mm control: Muff Cob (2).
Gatling control: Bass Tilt.

Soviet Type Name: Bolshoy Protivolodochny Korabl, meaning Large Anti-Submarine Ship.

"KRESTA II" Class

ADMIRAL MAKAROV   7/1974, USN

ADMIRAL MAKAROV   5/1975, MOD

ADMIRAL OKTYABRSKY   1975, MOD

USSR 507

4 "KRESTA I" CLASS (CG)

VICE-ADMIRAL DROZD **SEVASTOPOL**
ADMIRAL ZOZULYA **VLADIVOSTOK**

Displacement, tons: 6 140 standard; 8 000 full load
Length, feet (metres): 510 *(155·5)*
Beam, feet (metres): 55·7 *(17)*
Draught, feet (metres): 19·7 *(6)*
Aircraft: 1 Hormone A and B helicopter with hangar aft
Missile launchers: 2 twin for SS-N-3 for Shaddock (no reloads);
 2 twin SA-N-1 for Goa
Guns: 4—57 mm (2 twin); 4 Gatling Close Range Weapons
 (*Drozd* only)
A/S weapons: 2—12 barrelled MBU (60 reloads) (forward);
 2—6 barrelled DC throwers (aft)
Torpedo tubes: 10 (two quintuple) 21 in
Main engines: Steam turbines; 2 shafts; 100 000 shp
Boilers: 4 watertube
Speed, knots: 35
Range, miles: 5 500 at 18 knots
Complement: 400

"KRESTA I" Class

Provided with a helicopter landing deck and hangar aft for the first time in a Soviet ship. This gives an enhanced A/S capability and could certainly provide carried-on-board target-location facilities for the 250 mile SS-N-3 system at a lower, possibly optimum, range. The "Kresta I" was therefore the first Soviet missile cruiser free to operate alone and distant from own shore-based aircraft.
Built at the Zhdanov Shipyard, Leningrad. The prototype ship was laid down in Sept 1964, launched in 1965 and carried out sea trials in the Baltic in Feb 1967. The second ship was launched in 1966 and the others in 1967-68.

ECM: Full kit.

Radar: Search: Head Net C, Big Net and Plinth Net.
Fire control: Scoop Pair for Shaddock system;
Peel Group (2) for Goa system.
57 mm control: Muff Cob.
Gatling control: Bass Tilt (*Drozd* only).

Refit: The first ship undergoing a major refit, *Vice-Admiral Drozd,* was completed in 1975 with new Bass Tilt radar and Gatling guns on a new superstructure between the bridge and the tower mast.

Soviet Type Name: Bolshoy Protivolodochny Korabl, meaning Large Anti-Submarine Ship.

VICE-ADMIRAL DROZD (after 1975 refit with new Bass Tilt radar and Gatling guns)   *2/1976, MOD(N)*

VLADIVOSTOK   *1974, USN*

VICE-ADMIRAL DROZD (after 1975 refit—see top picture)   *2/1976, MOD(N)*

508   USSR

4 "KYNDA" CLASS (CG)

ADMIRAL FOKIN	GROZNY
ADMIRAL GOLOVKO	VARYAG

Displacement, tons: 4 800 standard; 5 700 full load
Length, feet (metres): 465·8 *(142·0)*
Beam, feet (metres): 51·8 *(15·8)*
Draught, feet (metres): 17·4 *(5·3)*
Aircraft: Pad for helicopter on stern
Missile launchers: 2 quadruple mounts, 1 forward, 1 aft, for SS-N-3 system (1 reload per tube)
  1 twin mount on forecastle for SA-N-1 system (30 reloads)
Guns: 4—3 in *(76 mm)* (2 twin)
A/S weapons: 2—12 barrelled MBUs on forecastle
Torpedo tubes: 6—21 in *(533 mm)* (2 triple amidships)
Main engines: 2 sets geared turbines; 2 shafts; 100 000 shp
Boilers: 4 high pressure
Speed, knots: 35
Range, miles: 7 000 at 15 knots
Complement: 390

The first ship of this class was laid down in June 1960, launched in April 1961 at Zhdanov Shipyard, Leningrad, and completed in June 1962. The second ship was launched in Nov 1961 and fitted out in Aug 1962. The others were completed by 1965. Two enclosed towers, instead of masts, are stepped forward of each raked funnel. In this class there is no helicopter embarked, so guidance, for the SS-N-3 system would be more difficult than in later ships. She will therefore be constrained in her operations compared with the later ships with their own helicopters.

Radar: This class showed at an early stage the Soviet ability to match radar availability to weapon capability. The duplicated aerials provide not only a capability for separate target engagement but also provide a reserve in the event of damage.
Search: Head Net A.
Fire control: Scoop Pair (2) for Shaddock systems, Peel Group for Goa systems and Owl Screech for guns.
Navigation: Don.

Soviet Type Name: Raketny Kreyser meaning Large Rocket Cruiser.

"KYNDA" Class

ADMIRAL GOLOVKO   7/1973, MOD

"KYNDA" Class   1975

ADMIRAL GOLOVKO   7/1974, USN

"KYNDA" Class   4/1975, MOD (N)

USSR 509

1 "SVERDLOV" CLASS ((CG)
2 "SVERDLOV" CLASS (CC)
9 "SVERDLOV" CLASS (CL)

ADMIRAL LAZAREV	ALEKSANDR NEVSKI	DZERZHINSKI	OKTYABRSKAYA REVOLUTSIYA
ADMIRAL SENYAVIN	ALEKSANDR SUVOROV	MIKHAIL KUTUZOV	SVERDLOV
ADMIRAL USHAKOV	DMITRI POZHARSKI	MURMANSK	ZHDANOV

Displacement, tons: 16 000 standard; 17 500 full load
Length, feet (metres): 656·2 *(200·0)* pp; 689·0 *(210·0)* oa
Beam, feet (metres): 72·2 *(22·0)*
Draught, feet (metres): 24·5 *(7·5)*
Aircraft: Helicopter pad in *Zhdanov*. Pad and hangar in *Senyavin*
Armour: Belts 3·9—4·9 in *(100–125 mm)*; forward and aft 1·6—2 in *(40–50 mm)*; turrets 4·9 in *(125 mm)*; C.T. 5·9 in *(150 mm)*; decks 1—2 in *(25–50 mm)* and 2—3 in *(50–75 mm)*
Missile launchers: Twin SA-N-2 aft in *Dzerzhinski*; 2 SA-N-4 in *Zhdanov* and *Senyavin* (twin) (see *Conversions*)
Guns: 12—6 in *(152 mm)*, (4 triple) (9—6 in in *Dzerzhinski* and *Zhdanov*); 6—6 in in *Senyavin*); 12—3·9 in *(100 mm)*, (6 twin), 16—37 mm (twin), 8—30 mm (twin) *(Zhdanov)*; 16—30 mm (twins) *(Senyavin)*; 8 Gatlings *(O. Revolutsiya)*
Mines: 150 capacity—(except *Zhdanov* and *Senyavin*)
Main engines: Geared turbines; 2 shafts; 110 000 shp
Boilers: 6 watertube
Speed, knots: 30
Oil fuel, tons: 3 800
Range, miles: 8 700 at 18 knots
Complement: 1 000 average

Of the 24 cruisers of this class originally projected, 20 keels were laid and 17 hulls were launched from 1951 onwards, but only 14 ships were completed by 1956. There were two slightly different types. *Sverdlov* and sisters had the 37 mm guns near the fore-funnel one deck higher than in later cruisers. All ships except *Zhdanov* and *Senyavin* are fitted for minelaying. Mine stowage is on the second deck. Two in reserve.

Conversions: *Dzerzhinski* has been fitted with an SA-N-2 launcher aft replacing X-Turret the only ship so fitted—presumably the experiment was not sufficiently successful to extend this item. In 1972 *Admiral Senyavin* returned to service with both X and Y turrets removed and replaced by a helicopter pad and a hangar surmounted by four 30 mm mountings and an SA-N-4 mounting. At about the same time *Zhdanov* had only X-turret removed and replaced by a high deckhouse mounting an SA-N-4.
Oktyabrskaya Revolutsiya completed refit in early 1977 which included the extension of her bridge work aft and the fitting of 8 Gatling mounts with associated 4 Bass Tilt radars.

Flagships: *Admiral Senyavin* is a flagship in the Pacific Fleet and *Zhdanov* is a flagship in the Black Sea Fleet.

Gunnery: The refit of *O. Revolutsiya* with the fitting of Gatlings around the bridge shows an intention to keep this big-gun class in commission.

Names: The ship first named *Molotovsk* was renamed *Oktyabrskaya Revolutsiya* in 1957.

Torpedoes: All torpedo tubes removed by 1960.

Radar: Unmodified ships—
Air search: Big Net or Knife Rest or Top Trough or Hair/Slim Net.
Surface search: Low or High Sieve.
Target indication: Half Bow.
Fire control: Top Bow (152 mm); Egg Cup (152 mm turrets); Sun Visor (100 mm); Bass Tilt (Gatlings in *O. Revolutsiya*).
Navigation: Don.
Dzerzhinski—
Air search: Big Net; Slim Net.
Surface search: Low Sieve.
Missile control: Fan Song E.
Fire control: As in unmod.
Navigation: Neptun.
Senyavin and *Zhdanov*—
Air search: Top Trough.
Surface search, navigation and fire control: As in *Dzerzhinski*.
30 mm control: Drum Tilt.
SA-N-4 control: Pop Group.

Soviet Type Name: Kreyser meaning Cruiser.

OKTYABRSKAYA REVOLUTSIYA

ADMIRAL SENYAVIN

OKTYABRSKAYA REVOLUTSIYA   4/1977, MOD

SVERDLOV   7/1976, MOD(N)

510 USSR

ZHDANOV 9/1976, Arrigo Barilli

ADMIRAL SENYAVIN 1973

1 "CHAPAEV" CLASS (CA)

KOMSOMOLETS (ex-*Chkalov*)

Displacement, tons: 11 300 standard; 15 000 full load
Length, feet (metres): 659·5 *(201·0)* wl; 665 *(202·8)*
Beam, feet (metres): 62 *(18·9)*
Draught, feet (metres): 24 *(7·3)*
Armour: Side 3 in *(75 mm)*; deck 2 in *(50 mm)*; gunhouses 3·9 in *(100 mm)* CT 3 in *(75 mm)*
Guns: 12—6 in *(152 mm)* 57 cal, (4 triple); 8—3·9 in *(100 mm)* 70 cal, (4 twin); 24—37 mm (12 twin)
Mines: 200 capacity; 425 ft rails
Main engines: Geared turbines, with diesels for cruising speeds; 4 shafts; 110 000 shp
Boilers: 6 watertube
Speed, knots: 30
Range, miles: 7 000 at 20 knots
Oil fuel, tons: 2 500
Complement: 900

Originally a class of six ships of which one was never completed—shows signs of both Italian and German influence. Laid down in 1939-40. Launched during 1941-47. All work on these ships was stopped during the war, but was resumed in 1946-47. Completed in 1950 in Leningrad. Catapults were removed from all ships of this type. Remaining ship serves as training cruiser.

Gunnery: Turret guns fitting allows independent elevation to 45 degrees.

Radar: Air search: Slim Net.
Surface search: Low Sieve.
Fire control: Top Bow (152 mm), Egg Cup (152 mm turrets), Sun Visor (100 mm).
Navigation: Neptun.

Soviet Type Name: Kreyser meaning Cruiser.

KOMSOMOLETS 11/1970

DESTROYERS

15 "KRIVAK I" CLASS, 4 "KRIVAK II" CLASS (DDG)

BDITELNY	DRUZHNY	REZKY*	SVIREPY
BODRY	RAZUMNY	REZVY*	ZHARKI
DEIATELNY	RAZYASCHY	SILNY	+2 "Krivak I" Class
DOBLESTNY	RAZYTELNY*	STOROZHEVOY	+1 "Krivak II" Class
DOSTOYNY	RETIVY		

* "Krivak II" class

Displacement, tons: 3 300 standard; 3 600 full load (3 700, "Krivak II")
Length, feet (metres): 404·8 *(123·4)* 418 *(127·4)* ("Krivak II")
Beam, feet (metres): 45·9 *(14·0)*
Draught, feet (metres): 16·4 *(5·0)*
Missile launchers: 4 for SS-N-14 system, in A position (quad); 4 for SA-N-4 system (twins)
Guns: 4—3 in *(76 mm)* (2 twin) X and Y positions in "Krivak I"; 2—100 mm (singles, aft) in "Krivak II"
A/S weapons: 2 12-barrelled MBU (forward)
Torpedo tubes: 8—21 in *(533 mm)* (2 quads)
Main engines: 4 sets gas turbines; 2 shafts; 80 000 shp
Speed, knots: 32
Complement: 250

"KRIVAK" CLASS

This handsome class, the first ship of which appeared in 1971, appears to be a most successful design incorporating A/S and anti-air capability, a VDS with associated MBUs, two banks of tubes, all in a hull designed for both speed and sea-keeping. The use of gas-turbines gives the "Krivak" class a rapid acceleration and availability. Building continues at about four per year at Kaliningrad, Kerch and Leningrad.

Class: "Krivak II" Class has X-gun mounted higher and a larger VDS apart from other variations noted.

Missiles: The missiles of the SS-N-14 system continue the A/S trend of the "Kresta II" class and the "Kara" class. The SA-N-4 SAMs are of the same design which is now mounted also in the "Kiev", "Kara", "Nanuchka", "Grisha" and other classes. The launcher retracts into the mounting for stowage and protection, rising to fire and retracting to reload. The two mountings are forward of the bridge and abaft the funnel.

Problems: The widely reported mutiny in *Storozhevoy* in late 1975 was followed soon after by her transfer to the Pacific. Numerous suggestions that this event indicated a deep-seated lack of discipline in the Soviet Navy have little foundation in fact.

"KRIVAK" CLASS   7/1976, MOD(N)

Radar: Search: Head Net C.
Missile control: Eye Bowl (SS-N-14), Pop Group (SA-N-4) (2).
Gunnery control: Kite Screech (Owl Screech—"Krivak II")
Navigation: Don 2 (Low Trough—"Krivak II")

Sonar: One hull mounted set in bow; 1 VDS.

Soviet Type Name: Bolshoy Protivolodochny Korabl, meaning Large Anti-Submarine Ship.

REZKY ("KRIVAK II")   6/1977, MOD

STOROZHEVOY   1975, J. A. Verhoog

BODRY   10/1975, USN

512　USSR

19 "KASHIN" and "MODIFIED KASHIN" CLASS (DDG)

KOMSOMOLETS UKRAINY
KRASNY-KAVKAZ
KRASNY-KRIM
OBRAZTSOVY
ODARENNY
(* modified)

OGNEVOY*
PROVORNY
SKORY
RESHITELNY
SDERZHANNY*

SLAVNY*
SMELY*
SMETLIVY
SMYSHLENY*
SOOBRAZITELNY

SPOSOBNY
STEREGUSHCHY
STROGIY
STROYNY

Displacement, tons: 3 750 standard; 4 500 full load (4 700 (mod))
Length, feet (metres): 470·9 *(143·3)* or 481 *(146·5)* (mod)
Beam, feet (metres): 52·5 *(15·9)*
Draught, feet (metres): 15·4 *(4·7)*
Missile launchers: 4 (2 twin) SA-N-1 in B and X positions; 4 SS-N-2 (mod) in mod-class
Guns: 4—3 in *(76 mm)* (2 twin) in A and Y positions; 4—23 mm Gatlings in mod-class
A/S weapons: 2—12 barrelled MBU forward; 2—6 barrelled DC throwers aft (unmodified)
Torpedo tubes: 5—21 in *(533 mm)* quintuple, amidships
Main engines: 4 sets gas turbines; 96 000 hp; 2 shafts
Speed, knots: 35
Complement: 300

The first class of warships in the world to rely entirely on gas-turbine propulsion giving them the quick getaway and acceleration necessary for modern tactics. These ships were delivered from 1962 onwards from the Zhdanov Yard, Leningrad and the Nosenko Yard, Nikolayev.
As they were built at the same time as "Kynda" class they may originally have been intended as AA support for the latter.

Conversion: In order to bring this class up-to-date with SSM, new SAM system and VDS a conversion programme was started in 1974. This conversion consists of lengthening the hull by 10 feet, shipping 4—SS-N-2 (mod) launchers (SSM), 4 Gatling close range weapons, a VDS under a new stern helicopter platform and removing the DC throwers. By 1977 five had been so converted. One of this class may have a separate and distinctive conversion from the remainder.

Loss: *Otvazhny* of this class (on trials after conversion) foundered in the Black Sea in Sept 1974, apparently as the result of an internal explosion followed by a fire which lasted for five hours. Nearly 300 of the ship's company were lost, making this the worst peacetime naval loss for many years.

Radar: Unmodified ships—
Search: Head Net C and Big Net in some ships; Head Net A (2) in others.
Fire control: Peel Group (2) for Goa system and Owl Screech (2) for guns.
Modified ships—
Search: Head Net C and Big Net or 2 Head Net A.
Fire control: As in unmod plus Bass Tilt for Gatlings.

Sonar: Hull mounted plus VDS in modernised ships.

Soviet Type Name: Bolshoy Protivolodochny Korabl, meaning Large Anti-Submarine Ship.

"KASHIN" Class

Modified "KASHIN" Class

SMELY　　　　　　　　　　　　　　　　　　　　　　　9/1976, Arrigo Barilli

OBRAZTSOVY at Portsmouth　　　　　　　　　　　　5/1976, C. and S. Taylor

SDERZHANNY (modified)　　　　　　　　　　　　　　6/1975, MOD(N)

4 "KILDIN" CLASS (DDG)

BEDOVY* NYEULOVIMY*
NEUDERSIMY PROZORLIVY*

* modified

Displacement, tons: 3 000 standard; 3 600 full load
Length, feet (metres): 414·9 *(126·5)*
Beam, feet (metres): 42·6 *(13·0)*
Draught, feet (metres): 16·1 *(4·9)*
Missile launchers: 1—SS-N-1 (before conversion);
4 for SS-N—2 (mod) system (conversions)
A/S weapons: 2—16 barrelled MBU on forecastle
Guns: 4—76 mm (twins aft) (after conversion);
16—57 mm (quads—2 forward, 2 between funnels)
Torpedo tubes: 4—21 in (2 twin)
Main engines: Geared turbines: 2 shafts; 72 000 shp
Boilers: 4 high pressure
Speed, knots: 35
Range, miles: 4 000 at 16 knots
Complement: 300 officers and men

Converted "KILDIN" Class

These were the last four "Kotlin" hulls with an SS-N-1 launcher replacing the after turret and the forward turret removed. *Bedovy* built at Nikolaev, *Neudersimy* at Komsomolsk, *Neulovimy* at Leningrad and *Prozorlivy* at Nikolaev. All completed in 1958.

Conversion: In 1972 *Neulovimy* was taken in hand for modification. This was completed in mid-1973 and consisted of the replacement of the SS-N-1 on the quarterdeck by two superimposed twin 76 mm turrets, the fitting of four SS-N-2 (Mod) launchers abreast the after funnel and the fitting of new radar. The Substitution of the 40 n. mile SS-N-2 (Mod) system (a modified Styx) for the obsolescent SS-N-1 system and the notable increase in gun armament illustrate two trends in Soviet thought. *Bedovy* and *Prozorlivy* have now completed this conversion. All modified ships serve in the Black Sea.

Radar: Original ships—
Air search: Slim Net.
Fire control: Top Bow; Hawk Screech.
Conversions—
Air search: Head Net C (2 Strut Curve in *Bedovy*)
Fire control: Owl Screech (76 mm); Hawk Screech (57 mm).

Sonar: Hull mounted.

Soviet Type Name: Bolshoy Protivolodochny Korabl meaning Large Anti-Submarine Ship.

"KILDIN" Class (before conversion) 3/1975, USN

NEULOVIMY after conversion 1974

BEDOVY after conversion 4/1975, MOD(N)

514　USSR

8 "KANIN" CLASS (DDG)

BOYKY	**GNEVNY**	**GREMYASHCHYI**	**ZHGUCHY**
DERZKY	**GORDY**	**UPORNY**	**ZORKY**

Displacement, tons: 3 700 standard; 4 700 full load
Length, feet (metres): 455·9 *(139)*
Beam, feet (metres): 48·2 *(14·7)*
Draught, feet (metres): 16·4 *(5·0)*
Aircraft: Helicopter platform
Missile launchers: 1 twin SA-N-1 mounted aft
Guns: 8—57 mm (2 quadruple forward); 8—30 mm (twin) (by after funnel)
A/S weapons: 3—12 barrelled MBU
Torpedo tubes: 10—21 in *(533 mm)* A/S (2 quintuple)
Main engines: 2 sets geared steam turbines; 2 shafts; 84 000 shp
Boilers: 4 watertube
Speed, knots: 34
Oil fuel, tons: 900
Range, miles: 4 500 at 16 knots
Complement: 350

All ships of this class have been converted from "Krupnys" at Zhdanov Yard, Leningrad from 1967 onwards, being given a SAM capability instead of the latter's SSM armament.

Appearance: As compared with the "Krupny" class these ships have enlarged bridge, converted bow (probably for a new sonar) and larger helicopter platforms.

Gunnery: The 4 twin 30 mm around the after funnel were a late addition to the armament.

Radar: Search: Head Net C
Fire control: Peel Group for SA-N-1,
Hawk Screech for guns.
Drum Tilt for additional 30 mm guns.
Navigation: Don

Sonar: Hull mounted.

Soviet Type Name: Bolshoy Protivolodochny Korabl, meaning Large Anti-Submarine Ship.

"KANIN" Class

BOYKY with additional 30 mm guns　　　10/1973, MOD(N)

ZHGUCHY　　　1976, Michael D. J. Lennon

"KANIN" Class (in Caribbean)　　　8/1970, USN

USSR 515

8 "SAM KOTLIN I and II" CLASS (DDG)

| BRAVY ("Sam Kotlin I") | NASTOYCHIVY | SKROMNY | SOZNATELNY* |
| NAKHODCHIVY | NESOKRUSHIMY* | SKRYTNY* | VOZBUZHDENNY |

* Modified

Displacement, tons: 2 850 standard; 3 600 full load
Length, feet (metres): 414·9 *(126·5)*
Beam, feet (metres): 42·6 *(13·0)*
Draught, feet (metres): 16·1 *(4·9)*
Missile launchers: 1 twin SA-N-1 mounted aft
Guns: 2—5·1 in *(130 mm)* (1 twin); 4—45 mm (1 quadruple or twins); (12—45 mm in *Bravy)*; 8—30 mm (twins) in (mods)
Torpedo tubes: 1 quintuple 21 in mounting (not in *Bravy)*
A/S weapons: 2—12 barrelled MBU (2—16 barrelled in *Bravy* and modified ships))
Main engines: Geared turbines; 2 shafts; 72 000 shp
Boilers: 4 high pressure
Speed, knots: 36
Range, miles: 4 000 at 16 knots
Complement: 360

"SAM KOTLIN" Class

Converted "Kotlin" class destroyers with a surface-to-air missile launcher in place of the main twin turret aft and anti-aircraft guns reduced to one quadruple mounting.
The prototype conversion was completed about 1962 and the others since 1966. One ship transferred to Poland. Three subsequently modified with 30 mm armament and Drum Tilt radar.

Appearance: The prototype "Kotlin" SAM class has a different after funnel and different radar pedestal from those in the standard "Kotlin" SAM class.

Radar: Search: Head Net C or Head Net A.
Fire control: Peel Group for Goa system;
Sun Visor for 130 mm guns;
Egg Cup in turret;
Hawk Screech for 45 mm guns;
Drum Tilt for 30 mm in modified ships.

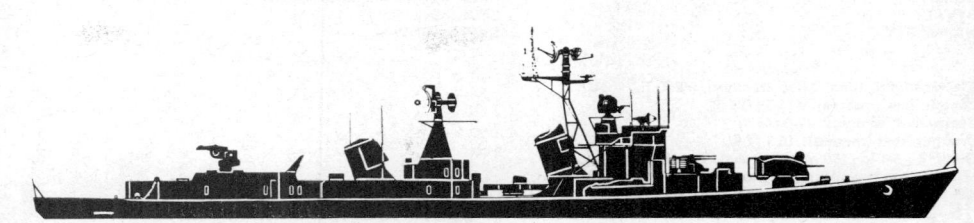

"BRAVY" ("SAM KOTLIN I") 4/1975, USN

Later "SAM KOTLIN" (with 2 extra Drum Tilt and 8—30 mm by after funnel) 1973

"SAM KOTLIN" Class (off Hawaii) 9/1971, USN

518 USSR

FRIGATES

1 + ? "KONI" CLASS

Displacement, tons: 2 000-2 500 approx
Length, feet (metres): 330 *(100)* approx
Guns: 4—3 in *(76 mm)* (twins); 2 Gatlings; ? 30 mm

---

520 USSR

37 "RIGA" CLASS

BARSUK	KOBCHIK	SHAKAL
BUYVOL	LISA	TURMAN
BYK	MEDVED	VOLK
GEPARD	PANTERA	+25
GIENA		

Displacement, tons: 1 200 standard; 1 300 full load
Length, feet (metres): 298·8 *(91·0)*
Beam, feet (metres): 31·2 *(9·5)*
Draught, feet (metres): 11 *(3·4)*
Guns: 3—3·9 in *(100 mm)* (single); 4—37 mm (2 twin); 4—25 mm (twin) in some
A/S weapons: 2—MBU (in some)
Torpedo tubes: 2 or 3—21 in *(533 mm)* in some
Mines: 50
Main engines: Geared turbines; 2 shafts; 20 000 shp
Boilers: 2
Speed, knots: 28
Range, miles: 2 000 at 10 knots
Complement: 150

Built from 1952 to 1959. Successors to the "Kola" class escorts, of which they are lighter and less heavily armed but improved versions. Fitted with mine rails. At least one third in reserve.

Anti-submarine: The two 12 barrelled MBU rocket launchers are mounted just before the bridge abreast B gun.

Conversion: A small number of this class has been converted. Some have had the triple torpedo-tube mountings replaced by more modern twin mountings and have a twin 25 mm gun mounting on either side of the funnel.
One or more now fitted with main mast carrying extensive electronic arrays.

Radar: Search: Slim Net.
Fire control: Sun Visor
Navigation: Don

Sonar: One hull-mounted.

Soviet Type Name: Storozhevoy Korabl meaning Escort Ship.

Transfers: Bulgaria (2), East Germany (4), Finland (2), Indonesia (6).

"RIGA" Class

"RIGA" Class   6/1974, MOD

"RIGA" Class   6/1974, MOD

3 "KOLA" CLASS

SOVIETSKY AZERBAIDJAN
SOVIETSKY DAGESTAN
SOVIETSKY TURKMENISTAN

Displacement, tons: 1 200 standard; 1 600 full load
Length, feet (metres): 321·4 *(98)*
Beam, feet (metres): 31·2 *(9·5)*
Draught, feet (metres): 10·6 *(3·2)*
Guns: 4—3·9 in *(100 mm)* (single); 4—37 mm; 4—25 mm (twin) (some)
A/S weapons: 4 DC rails
Torpedo tubes: 3—21 in *(533 mm)*
Mines: 30
Main engines: Geared turbines; 2 shafts; 25 000 shp
Boilers: 2
Speed, knots: 30
Range, miles: 3 500 at 12 knots
Complement: 190

Built in 1950-52. In design this class of flushdecked frigates appears to be a combination of the former German "Elbing" class destroyers, with a similar hull form, and of the earlier Soviet "Birds" class escorts. All now serving in the Caspian Sea.

Radar: Surface search: Ball Gun
Air search: Cross Bird
Fire control: Sun Visor (100 mm)
IFF: High Pole

Soviet Type Name: Storozhevoy Korabl meaning Escort Ship.

"KOLA" Class

USSR 521

CORVETTES

18 "GRISHA I", 4 "GRISHA II" and 8 "GRISHA III" CLASSES

AMETYST, BRILLANT, BURYA, JEMCHUG, METEL, RUBIN, URAGAN +23

Displacement, tons: 900 standard; 1 000 full load
Dimensions, feet (metres): 236·2 × 32·8 × 11 *(72 × 10 × 3·6)*
Missile launchers: SA-N-4 surface-to-air (1 twin) ("Grisha I" class)
Guns: 2—57 mm (1 twin) (4 in "Grisha II" class); Gatling mount aft ("Grisha III")
Torpedo tubes: 4 (2 twin)—21 in *(533 mm)*
A/S weapons: 2 MBU; internal DC racks
Mines: Fitted for minelaying
Main engines: 1 gas turbine; 12 000 shp; 2 diesels; 18 000 shp; 3 shafts = 30 knots

"GRISHA I" Class

Reported to have started series production in the late 1969-70 period. Five built by end of 1972, with a continuing programme of 4 a year. SA-N-4 launcher mounted on the forecastle in "Grisha I" class. This is replaced by a second twin 57 mm in "Grisha II" class some of which may be operated by KGB. "Grisha III" class has Muff Cob radar removed, Bass Tilt and Gatling (fitted aft), and Rad-haz-screen removed from abaft funnel.

Radar: Air search: Strut Curve.
Fire control: Pop Group (SA-N-4 Grisha I only);
Muff Cob (57 mm) (except in "Grisha III");
Bass Tilt (Gatlings) ("Grisha III")
Navigation: Don.

"GRISHA III" Class

Sonar: One hull mounted. Some have a similar VDS to that used in Hormone helicopters.

Soviet Type Name: Maly Protivolodochny Korabl meaning Small Anti-Submarine Ship.

"GRISHA II" Class 7/1974, MOD

"GRISHA II" Class 7/1974, MOD

"GRISHA I" Class 7/1974

IFF: High Pole.
Soviet Type Name: Maly Protivo Lodochny Korabl meaning Small Anti-Submarine Ship.

Transfers: Algeria (6), Bulgaria (6), Cuba (12), Egypt (12), East Germany (12), Iraq (3), North Korea (12), Viet-Nam (2 or 3), South Yemen (2).

"SO I" Class 1970, USN

522 USSR

17 "NANUCHKA" CLASS (MISSILE CORVETTES)

Displacement, tons: 800 standard; 950 full load
Length, feet (metres): 193·5 *(59)*
Beam, feet (metres): 39·6 *(12·0)*
Draught, feet (metres): 9·9 *(3·0)*
Missile launchers: 6 (2 triple) for SS-N-9; 1—SA-N-4 system forward (twin)
Guns: 2—57 mm (1 twin)
Main engines: 6 diesels; 28 000 shp; 3 shafts
Speed, knots: 32
Complement: 70

Probably mainly intended for deployment in coastal waters although several have been deployed in the Mediterranean and North Sea. Built from 1969 onwards. Has received many type designations including "Missile Cutter". Building continues at rate of about 3 a year at

---

524 USSR

62 "STENKA" CLASS (FAST ATTACK CRAFT—PATROL)

Displacement, tons: 170 standard; 210 full load
Dimensions, feet (metres): 128·7 × 25·1 × 5·9 *(39·3 × 7·7 × 1·8)*
Guns: 4—30 mm (2 twin)
Torpedo tubes: 4—16 in *(406 mm)* anti-submarine
A/S weapons: 2 depth charge racks
Main engines: 3 diesels; 12 000 bhp = 33 knots
Complement: 25

Based on the hull design of the "Osa" class. Built from 1967-68 onwards. Continuing programme of about two a year. A variant of this class, the "Mol", is in production apparently for export. (See Sri Lanka and Somalia.)

Radar: Search: Square Tie or Pot Drum.
Fire control: Drum Tilt.
IFF: High Pole; Square Head (2).

Sonar: Some have Hormone type dipping sonar.

"STENKA" Class   11/1970

30 "TURYA" CLASS (FAST ATTACK CRAFT—TORPEDO HYDROFOIL)

Displacement, tons: 200 standard; 230 full load
Dimensions, feet (metres): 128·7 × 25·1 × 5·9 *(39·3 × 7·7 × 1·8)*
Guns: 2—57 mm (twin, aft); 2—25 mm (twin, forward)
Torpedo tubes: 4—21 in *(533 mm)*
Main engines: 3 diesels; 14 000 shp
Speed, knots: 40
Complement: 30

A new class of hydrofoil with a naval orientation rather than the earlier "Pchela" class. Entered service from 1973—in series production, possibly 4-5 per year. Basically "Osa" hull.

Radar: Search: Pot Drum.
Fire control: Drum Tilt.
IFF: High Pole and Square Head.

Sonar: A form of VDS is fitted on the transom (similar to Hormone sonar). In view of this the apparent lack of A/S weapons is surprising. Could operate with shore-based helicopters.

"TURYA" Class   1977

20 "PCHELA" CLASS (FAST ATTACK CRAFT—PATROL HYDROFOIL)

Displacement, tons: 70 standard; 80 full load
Dimensions, feet (metres): 88·4 × 18 × 5·2 *(27 × 5·5 × 1·6)*
Guns: 4 MG (2 twin)
A/S weapons: DCs
Main engines: 2 diesels; 6 000 bhp = 50 knots
Complement: 12

This class of hydrofoil is reported to have been built since 1964-65. Also carry depth charges. Used for frontier guard duties by KGB in Baltic and Black Seas.

Radar: Search: Pot Drum.
IFF: High Pole.

Sonar: One type of VDS.

"PCHELA" Class   1970

50 "SHERSHEN" CLASS (FAST ATTACK CRAFT—TORPEDO)

Displacement, tons: 150 standard; 160 full load
Dimensions, feet (metres): 115·5 × 23·1 × 5·0 *(35·2 × 7 × 1·5)*
Guns: 4—30 mm (2 twin)
Torpedo tubes: 4—21 in (single)
A/S weapons: 12 DC
Main engines: 3 diesels; 3 shafts; 12 000 bhp = 38 knots
Complement: 35

First of class produced in 1963. Programme apparently completed.

Radar: Search: Pot Drum.
Fire control: Drum Tilt.
IFF: High Pole and Square Head.

Transfers: Bulgaria (4), East Germany (15), Egypt (6), North Korea (4), Viet-Nam (2), Yugoslavia (13).

"SHERSHEN" Class   1977

USSR 525

30 "P 6" CLASS (FAST ATTACK CRAFT—TORPEDO)

Displacement, tons: 66 standard; 75 full load
Dimensions, feet (metres): 84·2 × 20·0 × 6·0 (25·7 × 6·1 × 1·8)
Guns: 4—25 mm (twins)
A/S weapons: DCs (or mines)
Torpedo tubes: 2—21 in (533 mm)
Main engines: 4 diesels; 4 shafts; 4 800 bhp = 43 knots
Range, miles: 450 at 30 knots
Complement: 20

The "P 6" class (Soviet Type 184 originally) was of a standard medium sized type running into series production. Launched during 1951 to 1960. Known as "MO VI" class in the patrol craft version. The later versions, known as the "P 8" and "P 10" classes, were powered with gas-turbines, and had different bridge and funnel; "P 8" boats with hydrofoils. The "P 6" class is now being deleted because of old age; some have been converted to radio-controlled target craft. "P 8" and "P 10" classes are reported to have been completely deleted. Originally 250-300 boats of these classes were built.

Radar: Search: Skin Head or Pot Head.
IFF: High Pole.

Transfers: Algeria (12), China (80, indigenous construction), Cuba (12), Egypt (24), East Germany (18), Guinea (4), Indonesia (14), Iraq (12), Nigeria (3), Poland (20), North Viet-Nam (6), Somalia (4).

"P 6" Class   1970

15 "MO VI" CLASS (FAST ATTACK CRAFT—PATROL)

Displacement, tons: 64 standard; 73 full load
Dimensions, feet (metres): 84·2 × 20 × 6 (25·7 × 6·1 × 1·8)
Guns: 4—25 mm (twin)
A/S weapons: 2 depth charge mortars; 2 depth charge racks
Main engines: 4 diesels; 4 shafts; 4 800 bhp = 40 knots

Built in 1956 to 1960. Based on the hull design of the "P 6".

"MO VI" Class   1972

25 "ZHUK" CLASS (COASTAL PATROL—CRAFT)

Displacement, tons: 60
Dimensions, feet (metres): 75 × 16 × 6 (24·6 × 5·2 × 1·9)
Guns: 2—14·5 mm (twin forward); 1—12·7 mm (aft)
Main engines: 2 diesels; 4 000 hp = 34 knots
Complement: 17 (?)

A new class of patrol craft mainly manned by the KGB. Export versions have twin (over/under) 14·5 mm aft.

Transfers: Cuba (5 in 1975), Iraq (4 in 1975).

"ZHUK" Class (on transport)

RIVER PATROL CRAFT

Attached to Black Sea and Pacific Fleets for operations on the Danube, Amur and Usuri Rivers, and to the Caspian Flotilla.

80 "SHMEL" CLASS

Displacement, tons: 70
Dimensions, feet (metres): 92 × 16·4 × 3·3 (28·1 × 5·0 × 1)
Guns: 1—76 mm; 2—25 mm (twin)
Main engines: 2 diesels; 2 400 hp; 2 shafts
Speed, knots: 24
Complement: 15

Forward gun mounted in a tank-type turret. Some also mount a 10-barrelled rocket launcher amidships. Built since 1958.

"SHMEL" Class   1977

1 COMMAND SHIP

PS 10

Displacement, tons: 300
Guns: 2—20 mm
Speed, knots: 12

PS 10   4/1975 Heinz Stockinger

526   USSR

MINE WARFARE FORCES

Note: The "Alësha" class (under Support and Depot Ships) probably has a primary minelaying role.

24 "NATYA" CLASS (MINESWEEPERS—OCEAN)

MINER, NAVODVHIK, RULEVOY, SIGNALCHIK +20

Displacement, tons: 650 full load
Dimensions, feet (metres): 190·2 × 29·5 × 7·2 (60 × 9 × 2·2)
Guns: 4—30 mm (2 twin); 4—25 mm (2 twin)
A/S weapons: 2—MBU 1 800
Main engines: 2 diesels; 4 800 bhp; 2 shafts = 18 knots
Complement: 50

First reported in 1971, evidently intended as successors to the "Yurka" class. Steel hulls. Building rate of 3 a year. Usually operate in home waters but have been deployed to the Mediterranean.

Radar: Drum Tilt and Don.

"NATYA" Class

"NATYA" Class   1974, MOD

47 "YURKA" CLASS (MINESWEEPERS—OCEAN)

SAKHALINSKY KOMSOMOLETS, PRIMORSKY KOMSOMOLETS +45

Displacement, tons: 450 full load
Dimensions, feet (metres): 164 × 26·3 × 6·5 (52 × 8 × 2)
Guns: 4—30 mm (2 twin)
Main engines: 2 diesels; 4 000 bhp; 2 shafts = 18 knots
Range, miles: 1 100 at 18 knots
Complement: 50

A class of medium fleet minesweepers with steel hull. Built from 1963 to the late 1960s.

Radar: Drum Tilt and Don.

Transfer: Four to Egypt.

"YURKA" Class

"YURKA" Class   1975

20 "T 58" CLASS (MINESWEEPERS—OCEAN)

Displacement, tons: 790 standard; 900 full load
Dimensions, feet (metres): 229·9 × 29·5 × 7·9 (70·1 × 9 × 2·4)
Guns: 4—57 mm (2 twin)
A/S weapons: 2—MBU 1800; 2 DCT
Main engines: 2 diesels; 2 shafts; 4 000 bhp = 18 knots

Built from 1957 to 1964. Steel hulls. Of this class 14 were converted to submarine rescue ships with armament and sweeping gear removed, see later page ("Valdai" class). Frequently deployed to the Indian Ocean.

Radar: Muff Cob, Ball End and Neptun.

"T 58" Class

"T 58" Class   1/1975, MOD

84 "T 43" CLASS (MINESWEEPERS—OCEAN)

Displacement, tons: 500 standard; 570 full load
Dimensions, feet (metres): 190·2 × 28·2 × 6·9 *(58 × 8·6 × 2·1)* (older units)
 (198 *(60 m)* in later ships)
Guns: 2—45 mm (singles); 4—25 mm or 37 mm (2 twin) (not in older units)
Main engines: 2 diesels; 2 shafts; 2 000 bhp = 17 knots
Range, miles: 1 600 at 10 knots
Complement: 40

Built in 1948-57 in shipyards throughout the Soviet Union. Steel hulls. A number of this class were converted into radar pickets. The remainder are gradually being replaced by newer types of fleet minesweepers and at least half are probably in reserve.

Radar: Don.

Transfers: Algeria (2), Albania (2), Bulgaria (3), China (20); Egypt (6), Indonesia (6), Poland (12), Syria (2).

"T 43" Class

"T 43" Class   4/1973

5 "T 43/AGR" CLASS

Displacement, tons: 500 standard; 570 full load
Dimensions, feet (metres): 190·2 × 28·2 × 6·9 *(58 × 8·6 × 2·1)*
Guns: 4—37 mm; 2—25 mm
Main engines: 2 diesels; 2 shafts; 2 000 bhp = 17 knots
Range, miles: 1 600 at 10 knots
Complement: 60

Former fleet minesweepers of the "T 43" class converted into radar pickets with comprehensive electronic equipment. It is reported that there may be a dozen vessels of this type. A large Big Net-like radar is mounted on the mainmast.

"T43-AGR" Class   1973, USN

15 "SONYA" CLASS (MINESWEEPERS—COASTAL)

Displacement, tons: 400
Dimensions, feet (metres): 154·1 × 21·3 × 6·2 *(47 × 6·5 × 1·9)*
Guns: 2—30 mm (twin); 2—25 mm (twin)
Main engines: 2 diesels; 2 400 shp; 2 shafts = 18 knots

GRP hull. Now in series production at about 3/4 a year. First reported 1973.

Radar: Search/navigation: Don 2.
IFF: Square Head and High Pole B.

"SONYA" Class   7/1976

528 USSR

4 "ZHENYA" CLASS (MINESWEEPERS—COASTAL)

Displacement, tons: 320
Dimensions, feet (metres): 141 × 25 × 7 *(43 × 7·6 × 2·1)*
Guns: 2—30 mm (twin)
Main engines: 2 diesels; 2 400 shp; 2 shafts = 18 knots

Reported to be a trial class for GRP hulls. First reported 1972.

"ZHENYA" Class　　　　　1974, S. Breyer

70 "VANYA" CLASS (MINESWEEPERS—COASTAL)

Displacement, tons: 250 full load
Dimensions, feet (metres): 141 × 24 × 6 *(40 × 7·3 × 1·8)*
Guns: 2—30 mm (1 twin)
Main engines: 2 diesels; 2 200 bhp = 18 knots
Range, miles: 1 100 at 18 knots
Complement: 30

A coastal class with wooden hulls of a type suitable for series production built from 1961 onwards. Class now believed completed.

Conversion: One or more have been converted with superstructure extended forward, with 25 mm mounting on foc's'le in place of 30 mm, lattice mast at break amidships and two boats stowed on quarterdeck. Probably guidance ships for "Olya" class (following).

Transfers: Four to Bulgaria.

"VANYA" Class　　　　　1975

20 "SASHA" CLASS (MINESWEEPERS—COASTAL)

Displacement, tons: 250 standard; 280 full load
Dimensions, feet (metres): 150·9 × 20·5 × 6·6 *(46 × 6·3 × 2)*
Guns: 1—57 mm; 4—25 mm (2 twin)
Main engines: 2 diesels; 2 200 bhp; 2 shafts = 18 knots
Complement: 25

Of steel construction. Built between 1956-60. Now phasing out.

"SASHA" Class　　　　　1968, S. Breyer

25 "EVGENYA" CLASS (MINESWEEPERS—INSHORE)

Displacement, tons: 80
Dimensions, feet (metres): 85 × 18 × 4·1 *(26 × 5·5 × 1·2)*
Guns: 2—14·7 mm (twin)
Main engines: 2 diesels; 1 200 hp = 16 knots
Range, miles: 1 000 at 9 knots
Complement: 12

GRP hulls. Production started 1972. Can also lay mines.

Transfers: Three to Iraq.

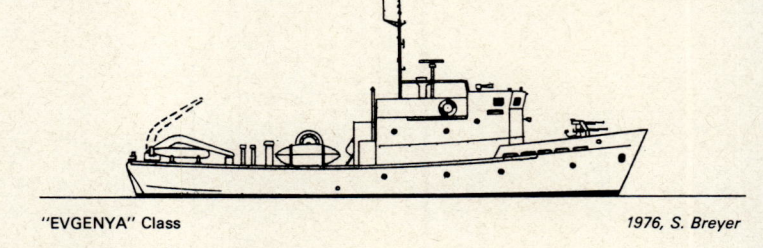

"EVGENYA" Class　　　　　1976, S. Breyer

8 "ILYUSHA" CLASS (MINESWEEPERS—INSHORE)

Displacement, tons: 70
Dimensions, feet (metres): 78·7 × 16·4 × 4·3 *(24 × 5 × 1·3)*
Guns: 2—14·7 mm (twin)
Main engine: 1 diesel; 450 shp = 12 knots
Radar: One Spin Trough.

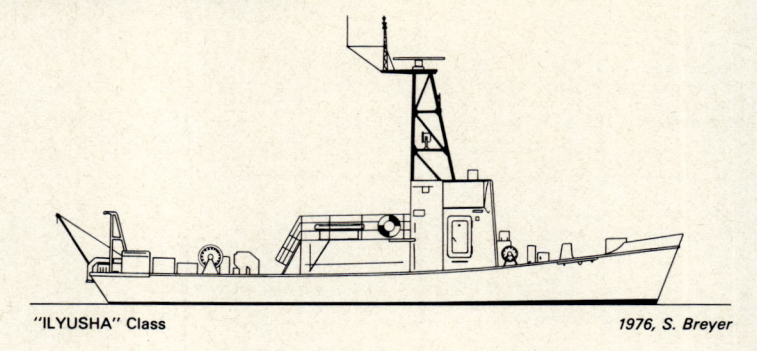

"ILYUSHA" Class　　　　　1976, S. Breyer

2 "OLYA" CLASS (MINESWEEPERS—INSHORE)

Displacement, tons: 70
Dimensions, feet (metres): 83·6 × 14·8 × 4·6 *(25·5 × 4·5 × 1·4)*
Guns: 2—25 mm
Main engines: 2 diesels; 2 200 shp = 15 knots
Complement: 15

An improvement of "Ilyusha" class with large foremast carrying electronic arrays. Probably capable of operating unmanned and radio controlled. (see "Vanya" Class—preceding).

Radar: One Spin Trough.

20 "TR 40" CLASS (MINESWEEPING BOATS)

Displacement, tons: 70 full load
Dimensions, feet (metres): 92·0 × 13·5 × 2·3 *(28 × 4·1 × 0·7)*
Guns: 2 MG (twin)
Main engines: Diesels; 600 bhp = 14 knots

USSR 529

70 "K 8" CLASS (MINESWEEPING BOATS)

Displacement, tons: 26 full load
Dimensions, feet (metres): 55·8 × 11·5 × 4·0 *(17 × 3·5 × 1·2)*
Guns: 2 MG (twin)
Main engines: 2 diesels; 700 shp = 18 knots
Complement: 6

"K 8" Class 1975

AMPHIBIOUS FORCES

Note: The fitting out in the Baltic of a large LSD type is reported.

14 "ALLIGATOR" CLASS (LST)

ALEKSANDR TORTSEV
DONETSKY SHAKHTĖR
KRASNAYA PRESNYA
KRYMSKY KOMSOMOLETS
NIKOLAI FILCHENKOV

NIKOLAI VILKOV
PĖTR ILICHEV
SERGEJ LAZO
TOMSKY KOMSOMOLETS
VORONEZHSKY KOMSOMOLETS
50 LET SHEFTSVA VLKSM
+3

Displacement, tons: 4 100 standard; 4 600 full load
Dimensions, feet (metres): 370·7 × 50·9 × 12·1 *(113 × 16 × 4·4)*
Guns: 2—57 mm (twin); 2 rocket launchers; 2 or 4—25 mm (some); mortars (Type III)
Main engines: 4 diesels; 8 000 bhp; 2 shafts = 18 knots

Largest type of landing ship in operation in the Soviet navy to date. First ship built in 1965-66 and commissioned in 1966. These ships have ramps on the bow and stern. Carrying capacity 1 700 tons. There are three variations of rig. In earlier type two or three cranes are carried—later types have only one crane. In the third type the bridge structure has been raised and the forward deck house has been considerably lengthened to accommodate 25 mm guns and mortars. These ships operate regularly off West Africa and in the Mediterranean and the Indian Ocean, usually with Naval Infantry units embarked.

Radar: Don and Muff Cob (in some).

KRYMSKY KOMSOMOLETS (Type I) 10/1974, MOD

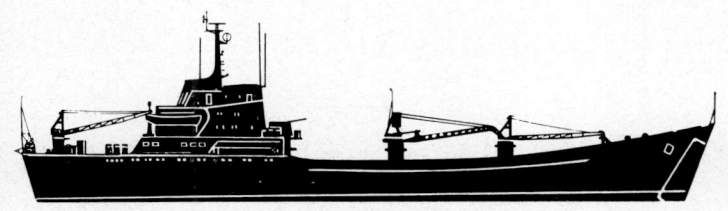

"ALLIGATOR I" Class

"ALLIGATOR III" Class

"ALLIGATOR" Class 1972

NIKOLAI VILKOV (Type III) (Hull 14) 4/1976, MOD

"ALLIGATOR" Class (Type II) 4/1973, USN

530　USSR

10 + 1 "ROPUCHA" CLASS (LST)

Displacement, tons: 2 500 standard; 4 200 full load
Dimensions, feet (metres): 360 × 49·2 × 11·5 (113 × 15 × 3·5)
Guns: 4—57 mm (twins)
Main engines: 2 diesels; 8 000 shp; 2 shafts
Speed, knots: 18

Building at Gdansk, Poland at a rate of about two a year. Appears to be a "roll-on-roll-off" design.
These ships have a higher troop-to-vehicle ratio than the "Alligator" class and thus the two provide a distant-ocean assault capability hitherto unavailable in the Soviet navy.

Radar: Muff Cob, Strut Curve, Don.

"ROPUCHA" Class

"ROPUCHA" Class　　　　　　　　　　　　　　　　　7/1976, MOD(N)

"ROPUCHA" Class　　　　　　　　　　　　　　　　　10/1975, MOD

60 "POLNOCHNIY" CLASS (LCT)

Displacement, tons: 800 standard; 1 000 full load (Type IX 1 300)
Dimensions, feet (metres): 239·4 × 29·5 × 9·8 (73 × 9 × 3) (246 (77) in Type VI to VIII) (Type IX 285 × 27·7 × 9·8 (81 × 8·4 × 3))
Guns: 2 or 4—30 mm (twin) in all but earliest ships (see note); 2 rocket launchers
Main engines: 2 diesels; 5 000 bhp = 18 knots
Complement: 40 (original)

Carrying capacity 350 tons. Can carry 6 tanks. Up to 9 types of this class have been built. In I to IV the mast and funnel are combined—in V onwards the mast is stepped on the bridge—in VI to VIII there is a redesign of the bow-form—IX is a completely new design of greater length with corresponding increase in tonnage and with 4—30 mm (2 twins).

Missiles: Some reported with SA-7 Grail.

Radar: Don and Drum Tilt (in those with 30 mm); Muff Cob (Type IX)

Transfers: One to Algeria, six to Egypt, three to India, two to Iraq, one to Libya, one to Somalia, two to South Yemen.

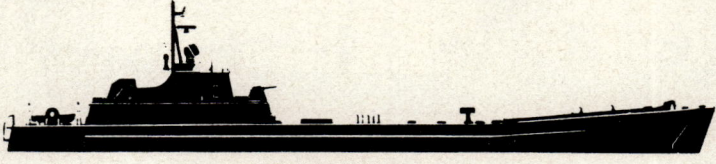

"POLNCHNIY V" Class

"POLNOCHNIY" Class—latest variant with higher funnel　　　1974, S. Breyer

"POLNOCHNIY" Class with 2—30 mm before bridge and fire control radar on bridge

"POLNOCHNIY" (Type IX) Class　　　　　　　　　　　　1973, USN

USSR 531

35 "VYDRA" CLASS (LCU)

Displacement, tons: 300 standard; 475 full load
Dimensions, feet (metres): 157·4 × 24·6 × 7·2 *(48 × 7·5 × 2·2)*
Main engines: 2 diesels; 2 shafts; 400 hp = 10 knots

Built from 1967-69. No armament. Carrying capacity 250 tons. Fifteen active, fifteen in reserve—rest in auxiliary roles.

Transfers: Ten to Bulgaria, ten to Egypt.

"VYDRA" Class   1971

20 "MP 4" CLASS (LCU)

Displacement, tons: 800 full load
Dimensions, feet (metres): 183·7 × 26·2 × 8·9 *(56 × 8 × 2·7)*
Guns: 4—25 mm (2 twin)
Main engines: Diesels; 2 shafts; 1 100 bhp = 10 knots

Built in 1956-58. Of the small freighter type in appearance. Two masts, one abaft the bridge and one in the waist. Gun mountings on poop and forecastle. Can carry six to eight tanks. Several ships now serve as transports—remainder in reserve.

"MP 4" Class   1973, J. Rowe

10 "MP 10" CLASS (LCU)

Displacement, tons: 200 standard; 420 full load
Dimensions, feet (metres): 157·5 × 21·3 × 6·5 *(48 × 6·5 × 2)*
Main engines: 2 diesels; 2 shafts; 400 hp = 11 knots

A type of landing craft basically similar to the German wartime type in silhouette and layout. Can carry four tanks. Loading capacity about 150 tons. Built 1959-66. Probably all in reserve.

"MP 10" Class   1971

40 "SMB 1" CLASS (LCU)

Displacement, tons: 400
Dimensions, feet (metres): 157·4 × 19·6 × 3·2 *(48 × 6 × 2)*
Main engines: 2 diesels; 4 000 hp = 10 knots

Built in 1960-65. Capacity 180 tons. In reserve.

100+ "T 4" CLASS (LCM)

Displacement, tons: 70
Dimensions, feet (metres): 62·3 × 14·1 × 3·3 *(19 × 4·3 × 1)*
Main engines: 2 diesels; 2 shafts = 10 knots

More than a hundred reported in service (1975).

AIR CUSHION VEHICLES

(Numbers in service are not accurately known. The following gives an indication of Soviet capability. Fuller details appear in the latest *Jane's Surface Skimmers*).

3 "LEBED" CLASS

Operating weight: 15 tons
Dimensions, feet (metres): 70 × 30 *(21·4 × 9·2)*
Propulsion: 2—350 hp aircraft radial engines
Lift: 1—350 hp aircraft radial with centrifugal fan
Speed, knots: 50

In use in the Soviet Navy since 1967 for tests and evaluation.

"LEBED" Class   Jane's Surface Skimmers

532 USSR

30 "GUS" CLASS

Operating weight: 27 tons
Dimensions, feet (metres): 70 × 24 (21·4 × 7·3)
Propulsion: 2—780 hp marine gas turbines (vp and reversible propellers)
Lift: 1—780 hp marine gas turbine
Speed, knots: 58
Range, miles: 230 cruising

This is a naval version of a 50-seat passenger carrying design (Skate). In production for Naval Infantry. Deployed to all four fleets.

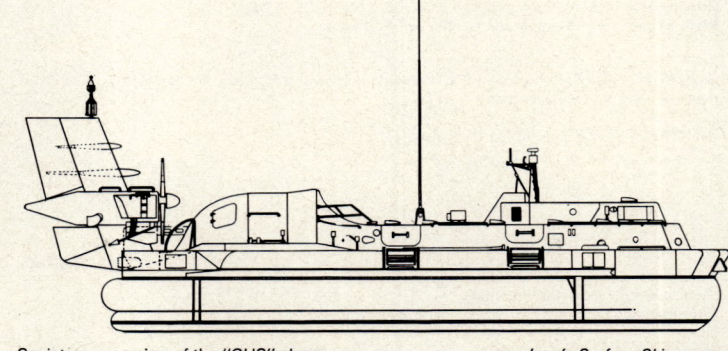

Soviet navy version of the "GUS" class   Jane's Surface Skimmers

5 "AIST" CLASS

Operating weight: 220 tons
Dimensions, feet (metres): 150 × 60 (45·7 × 18·3)
Guns: 2—30 mm (twin)
Main engines: 6 gas turbines (2 for lift, 4 for propulsion)
Speed, knots: 70 approx

Currently in production at Leningrad for Naval Infantry. Is the first large Soviet hovercraft for naval use. Similar to British SR.N4.

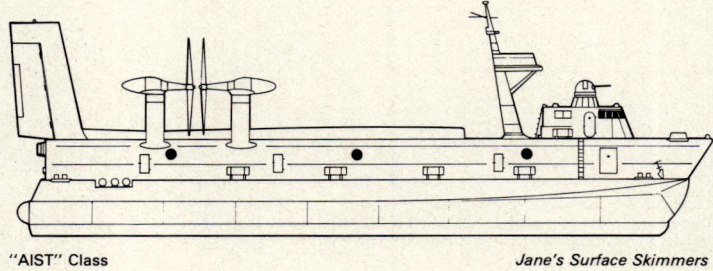

"AIST" Class   Jane's Surface Skimmers

EKRANOPLAN CRAFT (WIG)

Dimensions, feet (metres): 400 × 125 (approx wing span) (122 × 38)
Propulsion: 10 gas turbines (2 to assist take-off then 8 for cruising)
Speed, knots: 300 approx

An experimental craft, a wing-in-ground-effect machine, with a carrying capacity of about 900 troops and with potential for a number of naval applications such as ASW, minesweeping or patrol. Claimed to be capable of operations in heavy weather as well as crossing marshes, ice and low obstacles. Several other prototypes of unknown characteristics exist.

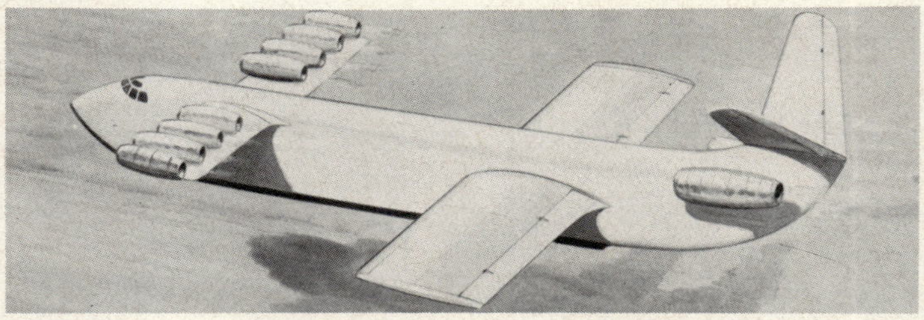

EKRANOPLAN   Jane's Surface Skimmers

SUPPORT AND DEPOT SHIPS

9 "UGRA" CLASS (SUBMARINE DEPOT SHIPS)

BORODINO*
GANGUT*
IVAN KOLYSHKIN
IVAN KUCHERENKO
IVAN VADREMEEV
TOBOL
VOLGA
+2
*Training

Displacement, tons: 6 750 standard; 9 000 full load
Length, feet (metres): 452·6 (141)
Beam, feet (metres): 57·6 (17·6)
Draught, feet (metres): 19·8 (6·0)
Aircraft: 1 helicopter
Guns: 8—57 mm (twin)
Main engines: 4 diesels; 2 shafts; 14 000 bhp = 20 knots
Range, miles: 10 000 at 12 knots
Complement: 300

Improved versions of the "Don" class. Built from 1961 onwards, all in Nikolayev. Equipped with workshops. Provided with a helicopter platform and, in later versions, a hangar. Carries a large derrick to handle torpedoes. Has mooring points in hull about 100 feet apart, and has baggage ports possibly for coastal craft and submarines. The last pair of this class (Borodino and Gangut) mount a large superstructure from the mainmast to quarter-deck and are used for training.

Aerials: Volga and some others have lattice mainmast with Vee-cone HF aerial.

Radar: Search: Strut Curve.
Fire control: Muff Cob.
Navigation: Don

Transfer: A tenth ship, Amba, which had four 76 mm guns, was transferred to India.

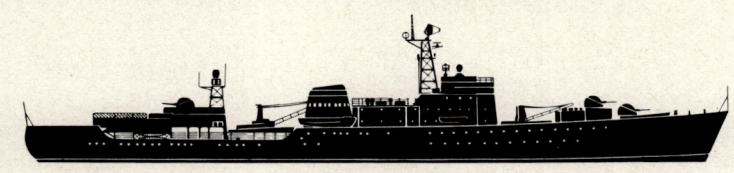

"UGRA" Class

"UGRA" Class   5/1974, MOD

USSR 533

6 "DON" CLASS (SUBMARINE SUPPORT)

DMITRI GALKIN
FEDOR VIDYAEV
KAMCHATSKY KOMSOMOLETS (ex-*Mikhail Tukhachevsky*)
MAGOMED GADZHIEV
NIKOLAY STOLBOV
VIKTOR KOTELNIKOV

Displacement, tons: 6 800 standard; 9 000 full load
Length, feet (metres): 458·9 *(139·9)*
Beam, feet (metres): 54·1 *(16·5)*
Draught, feet (metres): 22·3 *(6·8)*
Aircraft: Provision for helicopter in two ships
Guns: 4—3·9 in *(100 mm)*; 8—57 mm (4 twin) (see notes)
Main engines: 4 diesels; 14 000 bhp; 2 shafts
Speed, knots: 21
Range, miles: 10 000 at 12 knots
Complement: 300

Support ships, all named after officers lost in WW II. Built in 1957 to 1962. Originally seven ships were built, all in Nikolayev. Quarters for about 450 submariners.

Aerials: Some have lattice mainmast with Vee-Cone HF aerials.

Gunnery: In hull number III only 2—3·9 in. In IV no 3·9 in mounted. In some of class 8—25 mm (twin) are mounted.

Radar: Search: Slim Net and probably Strut Curve in some.
Fire control: Sun Visor.

Transfers: One to Indonesia in 1962.

"DON" Class

DMITRI GALKIN with Vee-Cone HF aerial on mainmast   8/1974, MOD

6 "LAMA" CLASS (MISSILE SUPPORT)

Displacement, tons: 4 600 full load
Length, feet (metres): 370·0 *(112·8)* oa
Beam, feet (metres): 60·7 *(18·3)*
Draught, feet (metres): 19·0 *(5·8)*
Guns: 8—57 mm, (2 quadruple, 1 on the forecastle; 1 on the break of the quarter deck) (in 2 units);
4—57 mm (quad) (in one unit); 2—57 mm;
4—25 mm (in two units); 2—57 mm (in one unit)
Main engines: Diesels; 2 shafts; 5 000 shp
Speed, knots: 15

The engines are sited aft to allow for a very large and high hangar or hold amidships for carrying missiles or weapons' spares. This is about 12 feet high above the main deck. There are doors at the forward end with rails leading in and a raised turntable gantry or travelling cranes for transferring armaments to combatant ships.
There are mooring points along the hull for ships of low freeboard such as submarines to come alongside. The well deck is about 40 feet long, enough for a missile to fit horizontally before being lifted vertically for loading.

Radar: Search: Slim Net or Strut Curve.
Fire control: Hawk Screech, (2) or Muff Cob. Various combinations in different ships.
Navigation: Don

"LAMA" Class

"LAMA" Class   1972, USN

2 "AMGA" CLASS (MISSILE SUPPORT)

Displacement, tons: 6 350
Dimensions, feet (metres): 361 × 56 × 19 *(102 × 17 × 5·8)*
Guns: 4—25 mm (twins)
Main engines: Diesels; 10 000 hp = 18 knots

Ships of similar size and duties to the "Lama" class. May be distinguished from those ships by the break at the bridge, giving a lower freeboard than that of the "Lamas". Fitted with a large 50 ton crane forward and thus capable of handling much larger missiles than their predecessors. Probably, therefore, designed for servicing submarines, particularly those armed with SS-N-8 missiles and others of equal size.

Radar: Search; Strut Curve.
Fire control; Hawk Screech.
Navigation; Don.

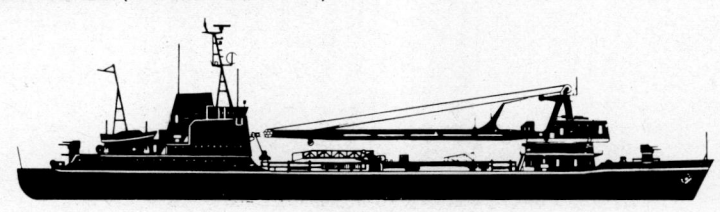

"AMGA" Class

"AMGA" Class   1976

534 USSR

14 + 1 "AMUR" CLASS (REPAIR SHIPS)

Displacement, tons: 6 400 full load
Dimensions, feet (metres): 377·3 × 57·4 × 18·0 (115 × 17·5 × 5·5)
Main engines: Diesels; 2 shafts = 18 knots

General purpose depot ships built since 1969. Successors to the "Oskol" class. In series production.

"AMUR" Class

"AMUR" Class 1976

1 "URAL" CLASS (? NUCLEAR SUPPORT SHIP)

URAL

Displacement, tons: 4 000 (approx)
Dimensions, feet (metres): 340 × 45 × 20 (103 × 14 × 6) (approx)
Main engines: Diesel

Radar: Don.

URAL 7/1973

1 "WILHELM BAUER" CLASS (SUBMARINE TENDER)

PECHORA (ex-*Otto Wünche*)

Displacement, tons: 4 726 standard; 5 600 full load
Dimensions, feet (metres): 446·0 × 52·5 × 14·5 (136 × 16 × 4·4)
Main engines: 4 MAN diesels; 2 shafts; 12 400 bhp = 20 knots

Former German ship. Launched in 1939.

3 "ALËSHA" CLASS (MINELAYERS)

075   083   +1

Displacement, tons: 3 400 standard; 3 900 full load
Dimensions, feet (metres): 337·9 × 47·6 × 15·7 (96 × 14·5 × 4·8)
Guns: 4—57 mm (1 quadruple forward)
Mines: 400
Main engines: 4 diesels; 2 shafts; 8 000 bhp = 20 knots
Range, miles: 8 000 at 14 knots
Complement: 150

In service since 1965. Fitted with four mine tracks to provide stern launchings. Also have a capability in general support role.

"ALESHA" Class 1969, MOD

3 "TOMBA" CLASS (REPAIR SHIPS)

Displacement, tons: 5 200
Dimensions, feet (metres): 351 × 50 × 20 (107 × 15 × 6) (approx)
Main engines: 1 diesel; 1 shaft

A new type of medium repair ship, first completed 1975. One in Northern Fleet, one in Pacific After funnel serves propulsion diesel, forefunnel serves the auxiliaries.

"TOMBA" Class

"TOMBA" Class 5/1976, MOD

USSR 535

10 "OSKOL" CLASS (REPAIR SHIPS)

Displacement, tons: 2 500 full load
Dimensions, feet (metres): 295·2 × 39·4 × 14·8 (90 × 12 × 4·5)
Guns: See notes
Main engines: 2 diesels; 2 shafts; speed = 16 knots

Three series: "Oskol I" class, well-decked hull, no armament; "Oskol II" class, well-decked hull, armed with 2—57 mm guns (1 twin) and 4—25 mm guns (2 twin); "Oskol III" class, flush-decked hull. General purpose tenders and repair ships. Built from 1963 to 1970 in Poland.

Radar: Fire control: Muff Cob (In "II").
Navigation: Don.

"OSKOL" Class

"OSKOL" Class 1971, MOD

6 "ATREK" CLASS (SUBMARINE SUPPORT)

ATREK AYAT BAKHMUT DVINA MURMATS OSIPOV

Displacement, tons: 3 500 standard
Measurement, tons: 3 258 gross
Dimensions, feet (metres): 336 × 49 × 20 (110 × 14·9 × 6·1)
Main engines: Expansion and exhaust turbines; 1 shaft; 2 450 hp = 13 knots
Boilers: 2 water tube
Range, miles: 3 500 at 13 knots

Built in 1956-58, and converted to naval use from "Kolomna" class freighters. There are six of these vessels employed as submarine tenders and replenishment ships. Some may have up to 6—37 mm (twins).

BAKHMUT 1974

4 "DNEPR" CLASS (SUBMARINE TENDERS)

Displacement, tons: 4 500 standard; 5 250 full load
Dimensions, feet (metres): 370·7 × 54·1 × 14·4 (113 × 16·5 × 4·4)
Main engines: Diesels; 2 000 bhp = 12 knots

Bow lift repair ships for S/M support and maintenance. Built in 1957-66 and equipped with workshops and servicing facilities. The last two ships of this class form the "Dnepr II" Class.

"DNEPR II" Class 1974

INTELLIGENCE COLLECTORS (AGIs)

6 "PRIMORYE" CLASS

PRIMORYE   KRYM   ZAPOROZHIYE
KAVKAZ   ZABAIKALYE   ZAKARPATYE

Displacement, tons: 5 000
Dimensions, feet (metres): 274 × 45 × 26·2 (83·6 × 13·7 × 8)
Main engines: Diesels

The most modern intelligence collectors in the world, apparently with built-in processing and possibly, analysis capability. The aerials carried would seem to dispose of the contention that these are fishery research ships.

"PRIMORYE" Class 1972

2 "NIKOLAI ZUBOV" CLASS

GAVRIL SARYCHEV   KHARITON LAPTEV

Displacement, tons: 3 021 full load
Dimensions, feet (metres): 295·2 × 42·7 × 15 (90 × 13 × 4·6)
Main engines: Diesels; 2 shafts = 16·5 knots

Built in Poland.

GAVRIL SARYCHEV 1973, Michael D. J. Lennon

536 USSR

GIDROGRAF PELENG

Measurement, tons: 2 000 gross
Dimensions, feet (metres): 256 oa × 42 × 13·5 *(78 × 12·8 × 4·1)*
Main engines: 2—4 stroke diesels; 2 shafts; 4 200 bhp = 17 knots

Built in Sweden 1959-60. Originally salvage tugs and have higher deckhouse abaft bridge than other ships of class.

2 "PAMIR" CLASS

PELENG 4/1970, USN

6 "MOMA" CLASS

ARKHIPELAG	NAKHODKA
ILMEN	PELORUS
YUPITER	SELIGER

Displacement, tons: 1 240 standard; 1 400 full load
Dimensions, feet (metres): 240 × 32·8 × 13·2 *(75 × 10 × 4)*
Main engines: Diesels = 16 knots

The modernised version has a new foremast in the fore well-deck. Similar class operate as Survey Ships.

YUPITER 10/1975, MOD

4 "MIRNY" CLASS

BAKAN	VAL
LOTSMAN	VERTIKAL

Displacement, tons: 850
Dimensions, feet (metres): 208 × 31·2 × 13·8 *(63·4 × 9·5 × 4·2)*
Main engines: Diesel; 1 shaft = 15 knots

Converted from whale-catchers in 1965.

"MIRNY" Class 8/1972, USN

8 "MAYAK" CLASS

ANEROID	KURSOGRAF
GIRORULEVOY	LADOGA
KHERSONES	GS 239
KURS	GS 242

Measurement, tons: 680 gross, 252 net
Dimensions, feet (metres): 178 × 30·6 × 15·9 *(54·3 × 9·3 × 4·8)*
Main engines: Diesel; 1 shaft; 800 hp = 12 knots

Built in USSR from 1967. Advance on "Okean" class.

GIRORULEVOY (new aerial arrays) 9/1975, MOD(N)

15 "OKEAN" CLASS

ALIDADA	EKHOLOT	REDUKTOR
AMPERMETR	GIDROFON	REPITER
BAROGRAF	KRENOMETR	TEODOLIT
BAROMETR	LINZA	TRAVERZ
DEFLEKTOR	LOTLIN	ZOND

Displacement, tons: 720
Dimensions, feet (metres): 178 × 30·6 × 15·9 *(51 × 9·3 × 4·8)*
Main engines: Diesel; 1 shaft; 800 hp = 12 knots

Built in USSR 1965. Have the same variations in the superstructure with the port side closed in and the starboard side open as in the "Mayak" class.

Modified "OKEAN" Class (open starboard side)   9/1974, MOD

8 "LENTRA" CLASS

GS 34	GS 43	GS 55
GS 36	GS 46	GS 59
GS 41	GS 47	

Displacement, tons: 250
Measurement, tons: 334 gross; 186 deadweight
Dimensions, feet (metres): 143 × 25 × 12·5 *(43·6 × 7·6 × 3·8)*
Main engines: Diesel; 400 hp = 10·5 knots

All built in USSR and East Germany 1957-63. Now have names in addition to numbers. Two known as *Neringa* and *Izvalta*. Mainly employed in-area.

GS 43   MOD

2 "DNEPR" CLASS

IZMERITEL   PROTRAKTOR

Measurement, tons: 500 gross
Dimensions, feet (metres): 150 × 30 × 8 *(45·8 × 9·2 × 2·4)*
Main engines: Diesel = 11 knots

NAVAL SURVEY SHIPS

Note: Two converted "Zulu V" class submarines *Lira* and *Vega* are employed on oceanographical research.

9 "NIKOLAI ZUBOV" CLASS

A. CHIRIKOV	F. LITKE	SEMYEN DEZHNEV
A. VILKITSKY	NIKOLAI ZUBOV	T. BELLINSGAUSEN
BORIS DAVIDOV	S. CHELYUSKIN	V. GOLOVNIN

Displacement, tons: 2 674 standard; 3 021 full load
Dimensions, feet (metres): 295·2 × 42·7 × 15 *(90 × 13 × 4·6)*
Main engines: 2 diesels; speed = 16·5 knots
Complement: 108 to 120, including scientists

Oceanographic research ships built at Szczecin Shipyard, Poland in 1964. Also employed on navigational, sonar and radar trials.

"NIKOLAI ZUBOV" Class

ANDREY VILKITSKY 1973, Michael D. J. Lennon

23 "MOMA" CLASS (+6 AGIs)

ALTAIR	ASKOLD	KRILON	
ANADIR	BEREZAN	KOLGUEV	RYBACHI
ANDROMEDA	CHELEKEN	LIMAN	SEVER
ANTARES	EKVATOR	MARS	TAYMYR
ANTARKTYDA	ELTON	MORSOVIETS	VEGA
ARTIKA	KILDIN	OKEAN	ZAPOYLARA

Displacement, tons: 1 240 standard; 1 400 full load
Dimensions, feet (metres): 240 × 32·8 × 13·2 *(75 × 10 × 4)*
Main engines: Diesels; 16 knots

Eight ships of this class were reported to have been built from 1967 to 1970 and the remainder since. Naval manned.

"MOMA" Class

LIMAN 10/1975, MOD

5 "TELNOVSK" CLASS

| AYTODOR | ULYANA GROMOVA | SIRENA | STVOR | SVIYAGA |

Displacement, tons: 1 200 standard
Measurement, tons: 1 217 gross, 448 net
Dimensions, feet (metres): 229·6 × 32·8 × 13·1 *(70 × 10 × 4)*
Main engines: 4 diesels; 1 600 shp = 10 knots

Formerly coastal freighters. Built in Hungary in 1950s. Refitted and modernised for naval supply and surveying duties. Naval manned. *Stvor* has additional accommodation forward of the bridge and a gantry foremast.

AYTODOR 1974, Michael D. J. Lennon

15 "SAMARA" CLASS

AZIMUT	GRADUS	SOTNIKOV
DEVIATOR	KOLESNIKOV	TROPIK
GIGROMETR	KOMPAS	VAGACH
GLUBOMER	PAMYAT MERKURYIA	VOSTOK
GORIZONT	RUMB	ZENIT

Displacement, tons: 800 standard; 1 200 full load
Measurement, tons: 1 276 gross; 1 000 net
Dimensions, feet (metres): 198 × 36·3 × 10·8 *(60·4 × 11·1 × 3·3)*
Main engines: Diesels; 3 000 hp; 2 shafts = 16 knots

Built at Gdansk, Poland since 1962 for hydrographic surveying and research. Naval manned.

GIGROMETR 1975, J. A. Verhoog

USSR 539

12 "BIYA" CLASS

Displacement, tons: 1 000
Dimensions, feet (metres): 229·6 × 32·8 × 11·5 (70 × 10 × 3·5)
Main engines: 2 diesels = 16 knots

10 "KAMENKA" CLASS

BELBEK, SIMA, WIERNIER +7

Displacement, tons: 1 000 full load
Dimensions, feet (metres): 180·5 × 31·2 × 11·5 (55·1 × 9·5 × 3·5)
Main engines: 2 diesels; 3 000 shp = 16 knots

The ships of these classes are not named but have a number with the prefix letters "GS". All reported to have been built since 1967-68. Naval manned.

"KAMENKA" Class   1974, MOD

20 "Ex-T 43" CLASS

Of 570 tons full load. Details under Minewarfare Forces. Now about to be phased out.

10 "LENTRA" CLASS (+8 AGIs)

POLYARNIK, TAIFUN +8

Displacement, tons: 250
Dimensions, feet (metres): 143 × 25 × 12·5 (43·6 × 7·6 × 3·8)
Main engines: Diesel; 400 hp = 10·5 knots

"LENTRA" Class   MOD

CIVILIAN MANNED SURVEY SHIPS

2 "ONEGA" CLASS (NEW CONSTRUCTION)

Main engines: Gas turbines = 20 knots

Built 1977. Have helicopter deck but no hangar.

17 + 1 "DMITRI OVSTYN" CLASS

A. SMIRNOV
DMITRI LAPTEV
DMITRI OVSTYN
DMITRI STERLEGOV
E. TOLL
FEDOR MATISEN
N. KOLOMEYTSEV
N. YEVGENOV*
PAVEL BASHMAKOV
PROFESSOR BOGOROV
PROFESSOR KURENTSOV
PROFESSOR VODNANITSKY
S. KRAKOV*
STEFAN MALYGIN
VALERIAN ALBANOV
V. SUKHOTSKY*
YAKOV SMIRNITSKY

Displacement, tons: 1 800 full load
Dimensions, feet (metres): 220 × 39 × 15 (67·1 × 11·9 × 4·6)
Main engine: 1—6-cyl Deutz diesel; 2 200 bhp = 13·5 knots

Built by Abo at Laivateollisuus, Finland except P. Bogorov at Turku, Finland. Civilian manned. Fitted with bow thruster. Employed largely on geological research oceanographic work and survey in the Arctic. Those marked *, completed Jan-Aug 1974. P. Bogorov launched 11 Oct 1975, P. Kurentsov 17 Dec 1975, Professor Vodnanitsky 3 March 1976, Fedor Matisen 6 May 1976, Paval Bashmakov 10 Dec 1976, Yakov Smirnitsky 14 Feb 1977. Average time from launch to completion, seven months. Continuing programme.
Owned by Ministry of Merchant Marine.

DMITRI OVSTYN

3 + ? "VALERIAN URYVAEV" CLASS

VALERIAN URYVAEV   VSEVOLOD BERYOZKIN   YAKOV GAKKEL

Measurement, tons: 350 dwt; 697 gross; 85 net
Dimensions, feet (metres): 180·1 × 31·2 × 13·1 (54·9 × 9·5 × 4)
Main engine: 1 Deutz diesel; 850 bhp = 12 knots

Built at Khabarovsk—1974, V. Uryvaev; 1975, other two.
Hydromet ships based at Sakhalin (V. Uryvaev), Murmansk (V. Beryozkin), Odessa (Y. Gakkel). Reports of another and similar ship ordered from Abo, Laivatteollisuus, Finland on 26 Jan 1977 could refer to a fourth of this class.

YAKOV GAKKEL   9/1977, Giorgio Ghiglione

540 USSR

1 "KOLOMNA" CLASS

MIKHAIL LOMONOSOV

Displacement, tons: 5 960 normal
Measurement, tons: 3 897 gross; 1 195 net
Dimensions, feet (metres): 336·0 × 47·2 × 14·0 (102·5 × 14·4 × 4·3)
Main engines: 1—4-cyl Liebknecht triple-expansion; 2 450 ihp = 13 knots

Built by Neptun, Rostock, in 1957 from the hull of a freighter of the "Kolomna" class. Operated for the Academy of Sciences by Ukraine Institute of Oceanology, Black Sea. Equipped with 16 laboratories. Carries a helicopter for survey. Civilian manned.

MIKHAIL LOMONOSOV   1970, Michael D. J. Lennon

5 "AKADEMIK L. ORBELI" CLASS

AKADEMIK KOVALEVSKY	AKADEMIK VAVILOV	
AKADEMIK L. ORBELI	PERVENETS	+1

Measurement, tons: 284 gross (Vavilov 255)
Dimensions, feet (metres): 126·8 × 23·7 × 11·5 (38·1 × 7·2 × 3·5); (Vavilov 119·7 × 24·1 × 11·5 (36·5 × 7·4 × 3·5)
Main engine: 1 diesel = 10 knots

Built in East Germany in 1949. Civilian manned oceanographic ships run by Acadamy of Sciences.

AKADEMIK KOVALEVSKY   1974, Michael D. J. Lennon

3 "MELITOPOL" CLASS

MAYAK, NIVELIR, PRIZMA

Displacement, tons: 775
Dimensions, feet (metres): 189 × 29·5 × 14·1 (57·6 × 9 × 4·3)
Main engines: 2 diesels; 2 000 hp = 10 knots
Complement: 21

AKADEMIK ARKHANGELSKY	YURIJ GODIN

Measurement, tons: 416 tons gross
Dimensions, feet (metres): 132·9 × 25 × 13 (40·5 × 7·6 × 4)
Main engine: 1 diesel = 10 knots

Built in USSR in 1963.

AKADEMIK ARKHANGELSKY   1974, Michael D. J. Lennon

MGLA

Measurement, tons: 299 gross
Dimensions, feet (metres): 129·5 × 24·3 × 11·8 (39·5 × 7·4 × 3·6)
Main engine: 1 diesel = 8·5 knots

Hydromet research ship. Civilian manned.

MGLA   1974, Michael D. J. Lennon

ZARYA

Measurement, tons: 333 gross; 71 net

Built in 1952 for geomagnetic survey work. Civilian manned. Run by Academy of Sciences.

ZARYA   1972, Michael D. J. Lennon

USSR 541

NEREY   NOVATOR

Measurement, tons: 369 gross
Dimensions, feet (metres): 118·1 × 24·7 × 11·5 *(36 × 7·5 × 3·5)*
Main engines: 2 diesels = 11 knots

Built in USSR in 1956 and 1955. Originally fleet tugs. Converted for seismic research. Civilian manned.
Run by Academy of Sciences.

NEREY   1972, Michael D. J. Lennon

PETRODVORETS (ex-*Bore II*)

Measurement, tons: 1 965 gross; 985 net
Dimensions, feet (metres): 254·2 × 39·4 × 24·9 *(77·5 × 12 × 7·6)*
Main engines: Diesel = 13·5 knots

Built at Abo, Finland for Finnish owners in 1938. Sold to USSR in 1950 and renamed.

ZVEZDA

Measurement, tons: 348 gross
Dimensions, feet (metres): 129 × 24·2 × 11·4 *(39·3 × 7·4 × 3·5)*
Main engines: Diesel = 10 knots

Built in East Germany in 1957. Carries winches in the chains on the quarters. Sister ships *Zarnitsa* and *Yug* are used for transporting crews to ships building outside the USSR.

ZVEZDA   1974, Ian Brooke

NAVAL RESEARCH SHIPS

4 + 1 "AKADEMIK KRILOV" CLASS

ADMIRAL VLADIMIRSKY   IVAN KRUZENSTERN
AKADEMIK KRILOV   LEONID SOBOLEV   +1

Displacement, tons: 9 100
Dimensions, feet (metres): 469·1 × 60·7 × 20·3 *(143 × 18·5 × 6·2)*
Main engines: Diesels = 15 knots

A new class of research ships, the fifth is building in Stettin. Naval manned.

Radar: Two Don 2.

"AKADEMIK KRILOV" Class

"AKADEMIK KRILOV   7/1976, MOD

4 "ABKHASIA" CLASS

ABKHASIA   ADZHARIYA   BASHKIRIYA   MOLDAVYA

Displacement, tons: 7 000 full load
Dimensions, feet (metres): 409·2 × 56 × 21·1 *(124·8 × 17·1 × 6·4)*
Aircraft: 1 helicopter
Main engines: 2 MAN diesels; 8 000 bhp = 18·2 knots
Range, miles: 20 000 at 15 knots
Endurance: 60 days

Built by Mathias Thesen Werft at Wismar. Fitted with helicopter platform and hangar aft. Naval manned. Completed; 1971, *Abkhasia*, 1972, *Adzhariya*, 1973, other two. Some are hydromet reporting ships. Fitted with two bow thrusters.

"ABKHASIA" Class

BASHKIRIYA   1/1974

542 USSR

3 "ANDIZHAN" CLASS ("KOVEL" TYPE)

BAIKAL   BALKHASH   POLYUS

Displacement, tons: 6 900 standard
Measurement, tons: 3 897 gross; 1 195 net
Dimensions, feet (metres): 365·8 × 46·2 × 20·7 *(111·6 × 14·1 × 6·3)*
Main engines: Diesel-electric; 1 shaft; 4 000 bhp = 13·5 knots

These ships are a part of the "Andizhan" class of some 45 ships. They were converted whilst building by Schiffswerft Neptun of Rostock. *Polyus* in 1962 and the other two in 1964. Oceanographic research ships. Naval manned.

POLYUS   MOD

1 "NEVELSKOY" CLASS

NEVELSKOY

Displacement, tons: 2 350
Dimensions, feet (metres): 272·3 × 49·2 × 11·5 *(83 × 15 × 3·5)*
Main engines: 1 diesel; 2 000 hp = 18 knots
Complement: 45

Was predecessor to "Zubov" class. Naval manned. Serves in the Pacific.

NEVELSKOY   1969, MOD

3 "MODIFIED VASILY PRONCHISHTCHEV" CLASS

GEORGY SEDOV   PETR PAKHTUSOV   VLADIMIR KAVRASKY

Displacement, tons: 2 800 full load
Dimensions, feet (metres): 223·1 × 59·1 × 18·1 *(68 × 18 × 5·5)*
Main engines: 3 shafts = 13·8 knots

Part of a numerous class of icebreakers built at Leningrad in the early 1960s—converted for polar research in 1972 under Ministry of Shipping.

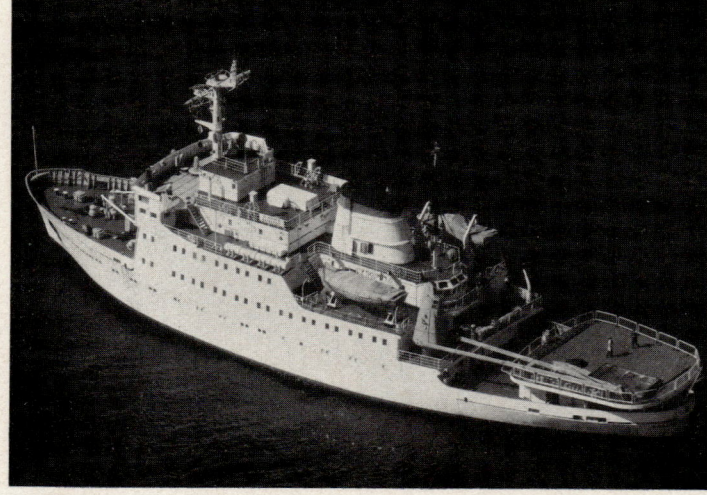

VLADIMIR KAVRASKY   5/1975, MOD

CIVILIAN RESEARCH SHIPS

Note: There are some 180 ships ranging downwards from 3 200 tons engaged on Fishery Research worldwide. The larger ships are of the "Mayakovsky", "Tropik", "Atlantik", "Leskov" and "Luchecorsk" classes of 3 200-2 400 tons. Two of the "Mayakovsky" class carry submersibles and one "Whiskey" class submarine *Severyanka* is also operated.

MIKHAIL SOMOV

Displacement, tons: 7 000

Operates under Arctic and Antarctic Research Institute for research duties and Antarctic support.

7 "AKADEMIK KURCHATOV" CLASS

AKADEMIK KOROLEV	DMITRI MENDELEYEV
AKADEMIK KURCHATOV	PROFESSOR ZUBOV
AKADEMIK SHIRSHOV	PROFESSOR VIZE
AKADEMIK VERNADSKY	

Displacement, tons: 6 681 full load
Measurement, tons: 1 986 deadweight; 5 460 gross; 1 387 net
Dimensions, feet (metres): 400·3 to 406·8 × 56·1 × 15·0 *(122·1 to 124·1 × 17·1 × 4·6)*
Main engines: 2 Halberstadt 6-cyl diesels; 2 shafts; 8 000 bhp = 18 to 20 knots

All built by Mathias Thesen Werft at Wismar, East Germany between 1966 and 1968. All have a hull of the same design as the "Mikhail Kalinin" class of merchant vessels. There are variations in mast and aerial rig. *Professor Vize* is similar to *A. Shirshov* whilst *A. Kurchatov, A. Vernadsky* and *D. Mendeleyev* are the same. Civilian manned. Two bow thrusters.

Duties: Hydromet (Vladivostock): *A. Korolev, A. Shirshov.*
Inst. Oceanology (Baltic): *A. Kurchatov.*
Inst. Oceanology (Vladivostock): *D. Mendeleyev.*
Ukraine Inst. Oceanology: *A. Vernadsky.*
Hydromet (Baltic): *P. Vize, P. Zubov.*

AKADEMIK KURCHATOV   1973, Michael D. J. Lennon

VITYAZ (ex-*Mars*, ex-*Empire Forth*, ex-*Equator*)

Displacement, tons: 5 700 standard
Dimensions, feet (metres): 357·5 × 48·9 × 15·5 *(109 × 14·9 × 4·7)*
Main engines: Diesels; 3 000 bhp = 14·5 knots
Range, miles: 18 400 at 14 knots
Complement: 137 officers and men including 73 scientists

The first post-war Soviet oceanographic research ship. Formerly a German freighter built at Wismar in 1939 which was taken over by the British in 1949, transferred to the USSR in 1949. Renamed on conversion in 1957. Equipped with 13 laboratories. Has now steamed over 2 million miles.
Run for Academy of Sciences by Institute of Oceanology, Vladivostock.

VITYAZ   1972, Michael D. J. Lennon

IZUMRUD

Measurement, tons: 3 862 gross, 465 net
Dimensions, feet (metres): 326 × 46 × 15·5 *(99·4 × 14 × 4·7)*
Main engines: Diesel-electric; 4 generators; one shaft = 13·8 knots

A research ship built in 1970 at Nikolaev. Civilian manned for structural and material tests Owned by Ministry of Shipping. Operated by Naval Institute of Shipbuilding, Black Sea.

IZUMRUD   1972, Michael D. J. Lennon

9 "PASSAT" CLASS (B 88 TYPE)

ERNST KRENKEL (ex-*Vikhr*)	OKEAN	PRILIV
GEORGI USHAKOV (ex-*Schkval*)	PASSAT	VIKTOR BUGAEV (ex-*Poriv*)
MUSSON	PRIBOI	VOLNA

Measurement, tons: 3 280 gross; 3 311 (*E. Krenkel, V. Bugaev*)
Dimensions, feet (metres): 319 × 45 × 15·5 *(97·1 × 13·9 × 4·7)*;
328 × 48·5 × 15·5 *(100 × 14·8 × 4·7)* (*E. Krenkel, V. Bugaev*)
Main engines: 2 Sulzer 8-cyl Cegielski diesels; 2 shafts; 4 800 bhp = 16 knots

Hydromet ships built at Szczecin, Poland—1968, *Musson, Passat, Volna;* 1969, *Okean, Priboi;* 1970, *Priliv;* 1971, *G. Ushakov, V. Krenkel, V, Bugaev.*

Duties: Based at:
Vladivostock: *Okean, Priboi, Priliv, Volna, Passat.*
Black Sea: Remainder.

GEORGI USHAKOV   1975, Michael D. J. Lennon

2 "LEBEDEV" CLASS

PETR LEBEDEV   **SERGEI VAVILOV**

Measurement, tons: 3 642 gross; 1 164 net
Dimensions, feet (metres): 308·3 × 45·9 × 19·7 *(94 × 14 × 5·6)*
Main engine: 1—6-cyl Sulzer diesel; 2 400 hp = 14 knots

Research vessels with comprehensive equipment and accommodation. Both built by Crichton-Vulcan, Finland in 1954.
Run by Hydroacoustic Institute, Baltic. Civilian manned. Freighter conversions.

Radar: One Neptun.

PETR LEBEDEV   1975, J. A. Verhoog

544   USSR

2 "MODIFIED MAYAKOVSKY" CLASS

AKADEMIK VOEYKOV, YURI M. SHOKALSKY

Displacement, tons: 3 000

Operated by Hydromet Service, Vladivostock.

2 "TROPIK" CLASS

KALLISTO   PEGAS

Measurement, tons: 1 200 deadweight; 2 345 gross; 1 100 net
Dimensions, feet (metres): 262 × 43 × ? *(79.8 × 13.2 × ?)*
Main engines: 2—8-cyl Liebknecht diesels; 2 shafts; 1 660 bhp = 12.5 knots

Operated by Scientific Research Institute, Sakhalin. Modified for geological and biological research. Originally stern-trawler factory ships of the 70 strong class built by Volkswerft, Stralsund, East Germany between 1962 and 1966. Nine others converted for fishery research.

VLADIMIR OBRUCHEV

Measurement, tons: 534 gross
Dimensions, feet (metres): 156.5 × 32.2 × 16.4 *(47.7 × 9.8 × 5)*
Main engines: 2 diesels; = 11 knots

One of the "Gromovoy" class tugs built in Romania in 1959 and subsequently converted for seismic research duties. Civilian manned.

VLADIMIR OBRUCHEV   1972, Michael D. J. Lennon

NAVAL SPACE ASSOCIATED SHIPS

3 "DESNA" CLASS

CHAZHMA (ex-*Dangara*)   **DSHANKOY**   **CHUMIKAN** (ex-*Dolgeschtschelje*)

Displacement, tons: 5 300 light; 12 700 full load
Dimensions, feet (metres): 457.7 × 59.0 × 25.9 *(139.6 × 18 × 7.9)*
Aircraft: 1 helicopter
Main engines: 2—7-cyl diesels = 18 knots

Formerly bulk ore-carriers of the "Dshankoy" class (7 265 tons gross). Soviet Range Instrumentation Ships (SRIS). Active since 1963. Naval manned.

"DESNA" Class

8 "VYTEGRALES" CLASS

APSHERON (ex-*Tosnoles*)   **DONBASS** (ex-*Kirishi*)
BASKUNCHAK (ex-*Vostok 4*)   **SEVAN** (ex-*Vyborgles*)
DAURIYA (ex-*Suzdal*)   **TAMAN** (ex-*Vostok 3*)
DIKSON (ex-*Vagales*)   **YAMAL** (ex-*Svirles*)

Measurement, tons: 6 450 deadweight; 4 896 gross; 2 215 net
Dimensions, feet (metres): 400.3 × 55.1 × 14.0 *(122.1 × 16.8 × 4.3)*
Main engines: B & W 9-cyl diesels = 15 knots

Standard timber carriers of a class of 27 modified with helicopter flight deck. Built at Zhdanov Yard, Leningrad between 1963 and 1966. Entirely manned by naval personnel.

Class name: The first of class, completed in 1962, was originally *Vytegrales*, but this was later changed to *Kosmonaut Pavel Belyayev*. Since these and the four others of the same class (but civilian manned) have been taken over for scientific work they have been variously, but incorrectly, called "Vostok", "Baskunchak" etc.

TAMAN   1972, Michael D. J. Lennon

4 "SIBIR" CLASS

SAKHALIN   SIBIR   SPASSK (ex-*Chukotka*)   **SUCHAN**

Displacement, tons: 7 100 full load
Measurement, tons: 3 767 gross (*Spassk* 3 800, *Suchan* 3 710)
Dimensions, feet (metres): 354 × 49.2 × 20 *(108 × 15 × 6.1)*
Main engines: Triple expansion; 2 shafts; 3 300 ihp = 15 knots
Range, miles: 3 300 at 12 knots

Converted bulk ore carriers employed as Missile Range Ships in the Pacific. *Sakhalin* and *Sibir* have three radomes forward and aft, and carry helicopters. *Suchan* is also equipped with a helicopter flight deck. Launched in 1957-59. Formerly freighters of the Polish B 31 type. Rebuilt in 1958-59 as missile range ships in Leningrad. Naval manned.

Names: Reported that *Suchan* has become *Spassk* although no information on latter's new name.

Refit: One ship (believed to be *Spassk* and possibly renamed) refitted and now has new funnel, mast and electronics.

"SIBIR" Class

CIVILIAN SPACE ASSOCIATED SHIPS

Note: See "Kazbek" class tankers under Service Forces.

1 "GAGARIN" CLASS

KOSMONAVT YURI GAGARIN

Displacement, tons: 45 000
Measurement, tons: 32 291 gross; 5 247 net
Dimensions, feet (metres): 773·3 oa × 101·7 × 30·0 (235·9 oa × 31 × 9·2)
Main engine: 2 geared steam turbines; 1 shaft; 19 000 shp = 17 knots

Design based on the "Sofia" or "Akhtuba" (ex-"Hanoi") class steam tanker. Built at Leningrad by Baltic SB & Eng Works in 1970, completed in 1971. Used for investigation into conditions in the upper atmosphere, and the control of space vehicles. She is the largest Soviet research vessel. Has bow and stern thrust units for ease of berthing. With all four aerials vertical and facing forward she experiences a loss in speed of 2 knots. Based in Black Sea.

KOSMONAVT YURI GAGARIN   2/1977
KOSMONAVT YURI GAGARIN   2/1977 

1 "KOMAROV" CLASS

KOSMONAVT VLADIMIR KOMAROV (ex-*Genichesk*)

Displacement, tons: 17 500 full load
Measurement, tons: 6 650 deadweight; 13 935 gross; 5 304 net
Dimensions, feet (metres): 510·8 × 75·5 × 29·5 (155·8 × 23 × 9)
Main engine: 1—6-cyl Bryansk diesel; 9 000 bhp
Speed, knots: 17·5

She was launched in 1966 at Kherson as *Genichesk* and operated as a "Poltava" class dry cargo ship in the Black Sea for about six months. Converted to her present role at Leningrad in 1967. The ship is named in honour of the Soviet astronaut who died when his space craft crashed in 1967. Based in Black Sea.

KOSMONAVT VLADIMIR KOMAROV   1977, Seiçuk Emre
KOSMONAVT VLADIMIR KOMAROV   2/1977 

1 "KOROLEV" CLASS

AKADEMIK SERGEI KOROLEV

Displacement, tons: 21 250
Measurement, tons: 17 114 gross; 2 158 net
Dimensions, feet (metres): 597·1 × 82·0 × 30·0 (182·1 × 25 × 9·2)
Main engine: 1—8-cyl Bryansk diesel; 12 000 shp
Speed, knots: 17

Built at Chernomorsky Shipyard, Nikolayev in 1970, completing in 1971. Equipped with the smaller type radome and two "saucers". Based in Black Sea.

AKADEMIK SERGEI KOROLEV   1972, Michael D. J. Lennon
AKADEMIK SERGEI KOROLEV   1977, MOD

546 USSR

1 "BEZHITSA" CLASS

BEZHITSA

Measurement, tons: 13 935 gross; 6 650 deadweight
Dimensions, feet (metres): 510·4 × 75·5 × 29·5 (155·7 × 20·6 × 9)
Main engine: 1—6-cyl Bryansk diesel; 8 750 bhp = 17·5 knots

Former freighter of "Poltava" class launched at Kherson in 1963, and subsequently converted as a research ship. The Vee-cone horns were fitted in 1971. Directional aerials similar to those in *Dolinsk* and *Ristna* fitted on crane stowage forward of the bridge. Based in Baltic.

BEZHITSA 1972, Michael D. J. Lennon

4 NEW CONSTRUCTION

KOSMONAVT VOLKOV   KOSMONAVT BELYAYEV
KOSMONAVT DOBROVOLSKY   KOSMONAVT SAYEV

Displacement, tons: 9 000

New space associated research ships under construction, 1978.

1 "POVENETS" (Conversion) CLASS

RISTNA

Measurement, tons: 4 200 deadweight; 3 724 gross; 1 819 net
Dimensions, feet (metres): 347·8 × 47·9 × 14·0 (106·1 × 14·6 × 4·3)
Main engine: 1—MAN 6-cyl diesel; 3 250 bhp = 15 knots

Converted from a "Povnets" class merchant ship. Built in East Germany at Rostok by Schiffswerft—Neptun in 1963. Painted white. Fitted with directional aerials on top of bridge wings.
Space monitoring ship. Based in Baltic.

RISTNA 1970, Michael D. J. lennon

4 "VYTEGRALES" CLASS

BOROVICHI (ex-*Svirles*)   KEGOSTROV (ex-*Taimyr*)   MORZHOVETS   NEVEL

Former timber carriers built at Zhdanov Yard, Leningrad in 1965-66 and completely modified with a comprehensive array of tracking, direction finding and directional aerials in 1967. Additional laboratories built above the forward holds. Sister ships to the naval-manned "Vytegrales" class. Based in the Baltic.

NEVEL 1972, Michael D. J. Lennon

TRAINING SHIPS

In addition to the naval training ships listed here a considerable fleet of other training ships, mainly mercantile marine, may be encountered. These are mainly in the 300-400 feet bracket. Names: *Equator, Gorizont, Meridian, Professor Anichkov, P. Khlyustin, P. Kudrevich, P. Minyayev, P. Pavlenko, P. Rybaltovsky, P. Shchyogolev, P. Ukhov, P. Yushenko, Zenit.*

2 "SMOLNY" CLASS

SMOLNY   PEREKOP

Displacement, tons: 6 500
Dimensions, feet (metres): 452·6 × 59 × 20·3 (138 × 18 × 6·2)
Guns: 4—76 mm (twins); 4—30 mm (twin)
A/S weapons: 2—MBU 2500A
Main engines: 2 diesels; 2 shafts; 12 000 shp = 20 knots
Range, miles: 20 000 at 15 knots

Built at Stettin, Poland, 1976.

Radar: Search: one Head Net C.
Fire control: one Owl Screech.
Navigation/Training: four Don 2.

SMOLNY 5/1977, MOD

CABLE SHIPS

6 "KLASMA" CLASS

DONETZ   INGUL*   TSNA   YANA*   ZEYA   + 1
*Type I

Displacement, tons: 6 000 standard; 6 900 full load
Measurement, tons: 3 400 deadweight; 5 786 gross
Dimensions, feet (metres): 427·8 × 52·5 × 19 *(130·5 × 16 × 5·8)*
Main engines: 5 Wärtsila Sulzer diesels; 5 000 shp = 14 knots
Complement: 110

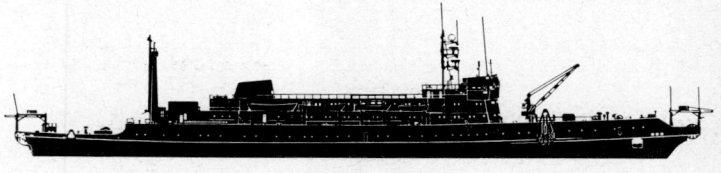

Ingul and *Yana* were built by Wärtsilä, Helsingforsvarvet, Finland, laid down on 10 Oct 1961 and 4 May 1962 and launched on 14 April 1962 and 1 Nov 1962 respectively. *Donetz* and *Tsna* were built at the Wärtsilä, Abovarvet, Abo. *Donetz* was launched on 17 Dec 1968 and completed 3 July 1969. *Tsna* was completed in summer 1968. *Zeya* was delivered on 20 Nov 1970. *Donetz*, *Tsna* and *Zeya* are of slightly modified design.

"KLASMA" Class

YANA (Type I—no gantry aft)   3/1976, MOD

TSNA (Type II—with gantry aft)   Wärtsila

4 "KALAR" CLASS

KALAR   KATUNJ   + 2

First pair ordered in 1972/73 the first being launched 20 March 1974. Two more ordered 16 July 1974. First laid down 14 April 1976 and launched 21 Oct 1976 and second laid down 21 Oct 1976.

COMMUNICATIONS RELAY SHIPS

20 "LIBAU" CLASS

Displacement, tons: 310 standard; 380 full load
Dimensions, feet (metres): 170·6 × 21·5 × 9·0 *(52 × 6·6 × 2·7)*
Main engines: 3 diesels; 2 shafts; 3 300 bhp = 24 knots
Range, miles: 1 500 at 12 knots

Converted "Kronshtadt" class.

SERVICE FORCES

Note: With the Soviet merchant fleet under State control any ships of the merchant service, including tankers, may be diverted to a fleet support role at any time. Over half the Soviet navy's support out-of-area is from merchant tankers.

1 NEW CONSTRUCTION (FLEET REPLENISHMENT SHIP)

Displacement, tons: 30 000 approx

Working up in Black Sea 1978. Possibly as aircraft carrier support ship.

5 "BORIS CHILIKIN" CLASS (FLEET REPLENISHMENT SHIPS)

BORIS CHILIKIN   IVAN BUBNOV
DNESTR   VLADIMIR KOLECHITSKY
GENRIK GASANOV

Displacement, tons: 23 400 full load
Dimensions, feet (metres): 531·5 × 70·2 × 28·1 *(162·1 × 21·4 × 8·6)*
Guns: 4—57 mm (2 twin) (guns removed in all ships)
Main engines: Diesel; 9 900 hp; 1 shaft = 16·5 knots

Based on the "Veliky Oktyabr" merchant ship tanker design *Boris Chilikin* was built at Leningrad completing in 1971. This is the first Soviet Navy class of purpose built underway fleet replenishment ships for the supply of both liquids and solids, indicating a growing awareness of the need for afloat support for a widely dispersed fleet.
Carry 13 000 tons fuel oil, 400 tons ammunition, 400 tons spares and 400 tons victualling stores.
A continuing programme.

"BORIS CHILIKIN" Class

DNESTR   9/1974, MOD

548   USSR

2 "MANYCH" CLASS (FLEET REPLENISHMENT SHIPS)

MANYCH   TAGIL

Displacement, tons: 7 500
Dimensions, feet (metres): 377·2 × 52·5 × 19·7 *(115 × 16 × 6)*

Completed 1972, probably in Finland. A smaller edition of the *Boris Chilikin* but showing the new interest in custom-built replenishment ships. The high point on the single gantry is very similar to that on *Boris Chilikin's* third gantry. Reported in use as water-carrier.

MANYCH   2/1973

2 "DUBNA" CLASS (REPLENISHMENT TANKERS)

Note: 4 "Improved Dubna" class to be built in Finland.

DUBNA   IRKUT

Displacement, tons: 12 000
Measurement, tons: 6 800 deadweight; 6 022 gross; 2 990 net
Dimensions, feet (metres): 426·8 × 65·8 × 23·8 *(130 × 21·6 × 7·8)*
Main engine: Diesel; 6 000 hp = 16 knots

Dubna completed 1974, *Irkut* launched Jan 1975, completed Dec 1975 both at Rauma-Repola, Finland.

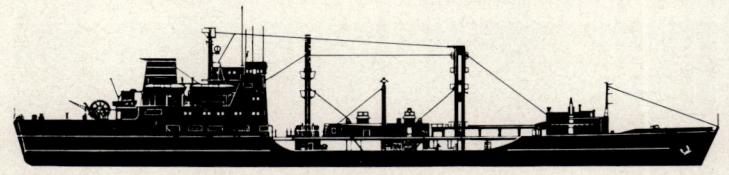

"DUBNA" Class

DUBNA   1976, MOD

1 "SOFIA" CLASS (REPLENISHMENT TANKER)

AKHTUBA (ex-*Hanoi*)

Displacement, tons: 45 000 full load
Measurement, tons: 62 000 deadweight; 32 840 gross, 16 383 net
Dimensions, feet (metres): 757·9 × 101·7 × 32·8 *(231·2 × 31 × 10)*

Built as the merchant tanker *Hanoi* in 1963 at Leningrad, she was taken over by the Navy in 1969 and renamed *Akhtuba*. The hull type was used in the construction of the space associated ship *Kosmonaut Yuri Gagarin*.

AKHTUBA (as *Hanoi*)   1971, MOD

3 "KAZBEK" CLASS (REPLENISHMENT TANKERS)

ALATYR   DESNA   VOLKHOV

Displacement, tons: 16 250 full load
Measurement, tons: 12 000 deadweight; 8 230 gross; 3 942 net
Dimensions, feet (metres): 447·4 × 63·0 × 23·0 *(136·5 × 19·2 × 7)*
Main engines: 2 diesels; single shaft

Former "Leningrad" class merchant fleet tankers taken over by the Navy. Built at Leningrad and Nikolaev from 1951 to 1961. Seven others—*Karl Marx, Kazbek, Dzerzhinsk, Grodno, Cheboksary, Liepaya* and *Buguzuslan* have acted in support of naval operations. The original class numbered 64. All now modified for alongside replenishment.

Radar: Don 2.

DESNA   1976, MOD

7 "ALTAY" (IMPROVED "OLEKMA") CLASS (SUPPORT TANKERS)

ALTAY   IZHORA   KOLA   PRUT   TARKHANKUT   YEGORLIK   YELNYA

Displacement, tons: 5 500 standard
Dimensions, feet (metres): 348 × 51 × 19·7 *(106·2 × 15·5 × 6)*
Main engines: Diesels; speed = 14 knots

Building from 1967 onwards. Most now modified for alongside replenishment. This class is part of 38 ships, being the third group of Rouma types built in Finland in 1967. Of similar hull to "Olekma" class (following) though with bridge aft.

PRUT   4/1977, MOD

USSR 549

3 "OLEKMA" CLASS (SUPPORT TANKERS)

IMAN   OLEKMA   ZOLOTOY ROG

Displacement, tons: 4 000 standard
Measurement, tons: 4 400 deadweight; 3 300 gross; 1 550 net
Dimensions, feet (metres): 344·5 × 47·9 × 20·0 *(105·1 × 14·6 × 6·1)*
Main engines: Diesels; 2 900 bhp = 14 knots

Part of the second group of 34 tankers built by Rauma-Repola, Finland between 1960 and 1966. Similar hull to "Altay" class (preceding) though with bridge amidships.

"OLEKMA" Class   *1973, Michael D. J. Lennon*

1 REPLENISHMENT TANKER

POLYARNIK (ex-*Kärnten*, ex-*Netherlands*)

Measurement, tons: 4 320 dwt
Dimensions, feet (metres): 344 × 48 × ? *(105 × 14·7 × ?)*
Main engine: Diesel = 13·5 knots

Thought to have been deleted. Sighted in 1977 in Pacific.

POLYARNIK   *USN*

6 "UDA" CLASS (SUPPORT TANKERS)

DUNAY   KOIDA   LENA   SHEKSNA   TEREK   VISHERA

Displacement, tons: 5 500 standard; 7 200 full load
Dimensions, feet (metres): 400·3 × 51·8 × 20·3 *(122·1 × 15·8 × 6·2)*
Main engines: Diesels; 2 shafts; 8 000 bhp = 17 knots

All have a beam replenishment capability.
Built since 1961.

"UDA" Class

LENA   *1/1975, MOD*

1 "USEDOM" CLASS (SUPPORT TANKER)

USEDOM (ex-*Jeverland*)

Displacement, tons: 5 250
Dimensions, feet (metres): 297·8 × 45·2 × 18·3 *(90·8 × 13·8 × 5·6)*
Main engines: 2 Schichau diesels; 2 shafts; 3 500 shp = 15 knots
Cargo, tons: 2 600
Complement: 65

Built by Howaldtswerke, Hamburg in 1938. Rebuilt for naval service May 1942. Taken from Germany 1946.

5 "KONDA" CLASS (SUPPORT TANKERS)

KONDA   ORSK   ROSSOSH   SOYANNA   YAKHROMA

Displacement, tons: 1 178 standard; 1 300 full load
Dimensions, feet (metres): 210 × 14 × 6·6 *(64 × 4·5 × 2)*
Main engines: 1 100 bhp = 10·5 knots

Originally of the "Iskra" class of merchant tankers built in 1955.

3 "NERCHA" CLASS (SUPPORT TANKERS)

DORA   IRTYSH   IRBIT

Measurement, tons: 1 303 deadweight; 1 081 gross; 524 net
Dimensions, feet (metres): 208 × 33 × 9·9 *(69 × 10 × 3)*
Main engines: 6-cyl diesels

Built in Finland 1952-55 as part of class of 12. Renamed in naval service.

15 "KHOBI" CLASS (SUPPORT TANKERS)

CHEREMSHAN	METAN	SHACHA	TARTU
INDIGA	MOKSHA	SHELON	TITAN
KHOBI	ORSHA	SOSVA	TUNGUSKA
LOVAT	SEIMA	SYSOLA	

Displacement, tons: 800 light; 2 000 approx full load
Dimensions, feet (metres): 207 × 12 × 6·6 *(63 × 3·8 × 2)*
Speed, knots: 12·5

Built from 1957 to 1959. Part of a class of 25.

LOVAT   *3/1974, MOD*

550 USSR

SALVAGE VESSELS

10 "PRUT" CLASS

| ALTAI | BRESHTAU | VLADIMIR TREFOLEV | ZHIGUILI | + 6 |

Displacement, tons: 2 120 standard; 2 800 full load
Dimensions, feet (metres): 296·0 × 36·1 × 13·1 *(90·3 × 11 × 4)*
Guns: 2—25 mm
Main engines: Diesels; 4 200 bhp = 18 knots

Large rescue vessels. Built since 1960.

"PRUT" Class

"PRUT" Class *1970, S. Breyer*

10 "SURA" CLASS

Displacement, tons: 3 150 full load
Dimensions, feet (metres): 285·4 × 48·6 × 16·4 *(87 × 14·8 × 5)*
Main engines: Diesels; 1 770 bhp = 13·2 knots

Heavy lift ships built as mooring and buoy tenders since 1965 in East Germany. Six built by 1972. Continuing programme.

"SURA" Class

"SURA" Class *6/1974*

15 "NEPTUN" CLASS

Displacement, tons: 700 light; 1 230 standard
Dimensions, feet (metres): 170·6 × 36·1 × 12·5 *(52 × 11 × 3·8)*
Main engines: Oil fuelled, speed = 12 knots

Mooring tenders similar to Western boom defence vessels. Built in 1957-60 by Neptun Rostock. Have a crane of 75 tons lifting capacity on the bow. One of this class is now based at Murmansk for the Maritime Fleet. She is acting as a diving vessel for hydrogeologists and construction personnel.

"NEPTUN" Class

SUBMARINE RESCUE SHIPS

1 "NEPA" CLASS

KARPATY

Displacement, tons: 3 500 light; 6 100 standard
Dimensions, feet (metres): 410·1 × 52·5 × 16·4 *(130 × 16 × 5)*
Main engines: Diesels; 2 shafts

Submarine rescue and salvage ship of improved design with a special high stern which extends out over the water for rescue manoeuvres. *Karpaty* completed 1969.

"NEPA" Class

KARPATY *1972, A. Nubert*

15 "VALDAY" CLASS (Ex-"T 58" CLASS)

Displacement, tons: 725 standard; 850 full load
Dimensions, feet (metres): 229·9 × 29·5 × 7·9 *(70·1 × 9 × 2·4)*
Main engines: 2 diesels; 2 shafts; 4 000 bhp = 18 knots

Basically of similar design to that of the "T 58" class fleet minesweepers, but they were completed as emergency salvage vessels and submarine rescue ships at Leningrad. Equipped with diving bell, recompression chamber and emergency medical ward. It has been reported that there may be an extra six smaller rescue ships based on the "T 43" hull. One transferred to India *(Nistar)*.

"VALDAY" Class *1970, S. Breyer*

9 Ex-"T 43" CLASS

Details under Mine Warfare Forces. Carry recompression chambers and diving bells.

TRANSPORTS

1 "YAVZA" CLASS

YAVZA

Displacement, tons: 13 200
Dimensions, feet (metres): 436 × 62 × 29 *(133 × 19 × 8·6)*
Main engines: Diesel-electric; 9 000 hp = 15 knots

3 "CHULYM" CLASS

CHULYM	INSAR	KUZNETSKY

Displacement, tons: 5 050 full load
Dimensions, feet (metres): 311 × 44·5 × 18·3 *(101·9 × 14·6 × 6)*
Main engines: Compound 4-cyl; 1 650 hp = 14 knots
Range, miles: 5 500 at 11 knots
Complement: 40

Built by Stocznia Szczecinska, Poland from 1953-57. Nineteen others of this B 32 type operate with the merchant navy. *Chulym* original name—others appear to have been renamed.

2 "KAMCHATKA" CLASS

KAMCHATKA	SHILKA

Measurement, tons: 4 300 deadweight; 3 745 gross; 1 800 net
Dimensions, feet (metres): 347 × 48 × ? *(105·8 × 14·6 × ?)*
Main engine: MAN 6-cyl diesel; 3 250 bhp = 13·5 knots

Part of a class of 40 ships built at Rostock 1964-66 by Schiffswerft Neptun. Sister ship *Ristna* converted to space-events ship.

2 "ISHIM" CLASS

ISHIM	MONGOL

Measurement, tons: 2 638 deadweight; 3 560 gross; 1 560 net
Dimensions, feet (metres): 326 × 46 × ? *(99·4 × 14 × ?)*
Main engine: Diesel-electric; 1 shaft = 13·5 knots

Built at Nosenko, Nikolaiev 1964-66 as fish carriers. Funnel and bridge aft, twin-legged foremast. *Ishim* is Coast Guard transport.

1 "BAIKAL" CLASS

OB

Displacement, tons: 12 400 full load
Dimensions, feet (metres): 427 oa × 61·8 × 27 *(140 × 20·3 × 8·9)*
Main engines: Diesel-electric; 4 generators; 7 000 shp = 15·5 knots
Range, miles: 13 500 at 15 knots
Complement: 60

Built by Konmij de Scheldt, Flushing. Ice-strengthened. *Ob* is operated by Academy of Sciences as Antarctic Transport/Support ship. Five others of the same class come under the Ministry of Merchant Marine.

OB *1973, Michael D. J. Lennon*

552   USSR

1 "MIKHAIL KALININ" CLASS

KUBAN (ex-*Nadeshda-Krupskaya*)

Measurement, tons: 5 261 gross; 2 323 net
Dimensions, feet (metres): 401 × 52 × ? *(122·2 × 16 × ?)*
Main engines: 2 MAN 6-cyl diesels; 2 shafts; 8 000 bhp = 18 knots

Built in 1963 by Mathias Thesen Werft, Wismar, East Germany. Part of "Mikhail Kalinin" class originally to have been 24 ships of which only 19 were completed 1958-64. Name changed on transfer to naval service.
Employed under naval command as personnel support ship for the Soviet Mediterranean Squadron.

KUBAN   9/1976, Michael D. J. Lennon

9 "KEILA" CLASS

BEREZINA, ERUSLAN, MEZEN, ONEGA, PONOI, RITSA, TERIBERKA, TULOMA, UNJA

Displacement, tons: 1 400
Dimensions, feet (metres): 258·4 × 34·4 × 15·1 *(78·8 × 10·5 × 4·6)*
Main engine: Diesel = 12 knots

15 "LENTRA" CLASS

Details under AGIs.

10 "MAYAK" CLASS

Details under AGIs.

9 "MUNA" CLASS

Torpedo transports.

8 "MP 6" CLASS

2 000 ton ex-amphibious craft.

16 "TELNOVSK" CLASS

Of 1 650 tons. Light freighters.

TORPEDO RECOVERY/PATROL CRAFT

Note: A number of "Kronshtadt" class has been converted for torpedo recovery.

90 "POLUCHAT I" CLASS

Displacement, tons: 100 standard
Dimensions, feet (metres): 98·4 × 19·7 × 5·9 *(30 × 6 × 1·8)*
Guns: 2 MG (1 twin) (in some)

Employed as specialised or dual purpose torpedo recovery vessels and/or patrol boats. They have a stern slipway. Several exported as patrol craft.

"POLUCHAT I" Class   10/1975, MOD

DIVING TENDERS/PATROL CRAFT

"NYRYAT I" CLASS

Displacement, tons: 145
Dimensions, feet (metres): 93 × 18 × 5·5 *(28·4 × 5·5 × 1·7)*
Gun: 1—12·5 MG (in some)
Main engine: Diesel; 1 shaft; 450 hp = 12·5 knots
Range, miles: 1 500 at 10 knots
Complement: 15

Built from 1955. Can operate as patrol craft.

Transfers: Cuba, Iraq (2), North Yemen.

FIRE/PATROL CRAFT

"POZHARNY I" CLASS

Displacement, tons: 180
Dimensions, feet (metres): 114·5 × 20 × 6 *(34·9 × 6·1 × 1·8)*
Guns: 4—12·7 mm or 14·5 mm (in some)
Main engines: 2 diesels; 1 shaft; 1 800 hp = 12·5 knots

Built in USSR in mid 1950s. Harbour fire boats but can be used for patrol duties.

Transfers: Iraq (2), North Yemen.

WATER CARRIERS

14 "VODA" CLASS

Displacement, tons: 2 100 standard
Dimensions, feet (metres): 267·3 × 37·7 × 14 *(81·5 × 11·5 × 4·3)*
Main engines: Diesels; speed = 12 knots

Built in 1956 onwards. No armament.

9 "LUZA" CLASS

ALAMBAI, ARAGVI, BARGUZIN, DON, ENISSEL, KANA, OKA, SASIMA, SALENGA

Of 3 000 tons and 12 knots.

DEGAUSSING SHIPS

1 "KHABAROV" CLASS

KHABAROV

Displacement, tons: 500 full load
Dimensions, feet (metres): 150·3 × 26·5 × 8 *(45·8 × 8·1 × 2·4)*
Main engines: Diesel; 1 shaft; 400 bhp = 10·5 knots
Range, miles: 1 130 at 10 knots
Complement: 30

Steel-hulled. Prominent deckhouse and stern anchors. One of class, *Kilat*, transferred to Indonesia 1961—subsequently disposed of.
Several others known to exist.

USSR 553

ICEBREAKERS

Note: The majority of these ships is operated by Ministry of Merchant Marine—only a small number being naval manned. No excuse is offered for including them here as they are an indispensible part of many operations not only in the Baltic, Northern and Pacific Fleet areas but also on rivers, lakes and canals.

1 PROJECTED LARGE NUCLEAR POWERED

Main engines: Nuclear reactors; steam turbines; 80 000 hp

Reported as in the design stage in Oct 1974.

2 "ARKTIKA" CLASS

ARKTIKA   SIBIR

Displacement, tons: 19 300 standard; 24 460 full load
Dimensions, feet (metres): 446·1 × 91·8 × 36·1 *(148 × 28 × 11)*
Aircraft: Helicopter with hangar
Main engines: 2 nuclear reactors; steam turbines; 66 000 shp; 3 shafts aft
Speed, knots: 21

Building yard—Leningrad. *Arktika* launched summer 1973, started trials on 30 Nov 1974 and was operational late 1975. Fitted with new type of reactor, the development of which may have retarded these ships' completion. *Sibir* on trials June 1977. Civilian manned.

"ARKTIKA" Class

ARKTIKA

1 NUCLEAR POWERED

LENIN

Displacement, tons: 15 300 standard; 19 240 full load
Dimensions, feet (metres): 406·7 × 87·9 × 34·4 *(124 × 26·8 × 10·5)*
Aircraft: 2 helicopters
Main engines: 3 pressurised water-cooled nuclear reactors, 4 steam turbines; 3 shafts; 39 200 shp = 19·7 knots
Complement: 230

The world's first nuclear powered surface ship to put to sea. Reported to have accommodation for 1 000 personnel. Civilian manned.

Construction: Built at the Admiralty Yard, Leningrad. Launched on 5 Dec 1957. Commissioned on 15 Sept 1959.

Engineering: The original reactors, prototype submarine variety, were replaced during refit at Murmansk 1966-72. The new reactors presumably have a longer core-life than the 18 months of their predecessors. The turbines were manufactured by the Kirov plant in Leningrad. Three propellers aft, but no forward screw.

Operation: Can maintain a speed of 3-4 knots in 8 feet ice, giving a path of some 100 feet.

LENIN   1972

3 "YERMAK" CLASS

Name	No.	Builders	Commissioned
ADMIRAL MAKAROV	—	Wärtsilä, Helsinki	2 June 1975
YERMAK	—	Wärtsilä, Helsinki	30 June 1974
KRASIN	—	Wärtsilä, Helsinki	Jan 1976

Displacement, tons: 20 241 full load
Dimensions, feet (metres): 442·8 × 85·3 × 36·1 *(135 × 26 × 11)*
Aircraft: 2 helicopters
Main engines: 9 Wärtsilä-Sulzer 12-cyl 12 ZH 40/48 diesels of 4 600 bhp each (total 41 400 hp) with Stromberg Ab generators feeding three Stromberg electric motors of total 36 000 shp; 3 shafts
Speed, knots: 19·5
Range, miles: 40 000 at 15 knots
Complement: 118 plus 28 spare berths

The Soviet Union ordered three large and powerful Icebreakers on 29 April 1970 from Wärtsilä Shipyard, Helsinki, for delivery in 1974, 1975 and 1976. Six Wärtsilä auxiliary diesels, 7 200 bhp. Propelling and auxiliary nachinery controlled electronically. These are the first vessels to be fitted with Wärtsilä mixed-flow air-bubbling system to decrease friction between hull and ice. *Yermak* launched 7 Sept 1973. A *Makarov* laid down 10 Sept 1973 and launched 26 April 1974. *Krasin* laid down 9 July 1974, launched 18 April 1975. Civilian manned.

ADMIRAL MAKAROV   1976, Wärtsilä

554 USSR

5 "MOSKVA" CLASS

VLADIVOSTOCK KIEV LENINGRAD MOSKVA MURMANSK

Displacement, tons: 13 290 standard; 15 360 full load
Dimensions, feet (metres): 368·8 wl; 400·7 oa × 80·3 × 34·5 (112·5 wl; 122·2 oa × 24·5 × 10·5)
Aircraft: 2 helicopters
Main engines: 8 Sulzer diesel-electric; 3 shafts; 22 000 shp = 18 knots
Oil fuel, tons: 3 000
Range, miles: 20 000
Complement: 145

Civilian manned.

Construction: Built by Wärtsilä Shipyard, Helsinki. *Moskva* was launched on 10 Jan 1959 and completed in June 1960. *Leningrad* was laid down in Jan 1959. Launched on 24 Oct 1959, and completed in 1962. *Kiev* was completed in 1966. *Murmansk* was launched on 14 July 1967, and *Vladivostock* on 28 May 1968.

Design: Designed to stay at sea for a year without returning to base. The concave embrasure in the ship's stern is a housing for the bow of a following vessel when additional power is required. There is a landing deck for helicopters and hangar space for two machines.

Engineering: Eight generating units of 3 250 bhp each comprising eight main diesels of the Wärtsilä-Sulzer 9 MH 51 type which together have an output of 26 000 hp. Four separate machinery compartments. Two engine rooms, four propulsion units in each. Three propellers aft. No forward propeller. Centre propeller driven by electric motors of 11 000 hp and each of the side propellers by motors of 5 500 hp. Two Wärtsilä-Babcock & Wilcox boilers for heating and donkey work.

Operation: *Moskva* has four pumps which can move 480 tonnes of water from one side to the other in two minutes to rock the icebreaker and wrench her free of thick ice.

MOSKVA   1960, Wärtsilä

2 "KAPITAN SOROKIN" CLASS

Name	No.	Builders	Commissioned
KAPITAN SOROKIN	—	Wärtsilä, Helsinki	14 July 1977
KAPITAN NIKOLAEV	—	Wärtsilä, Helsinki	1978

Displacement, tons: 14 900
Dimensions, feet (metres): 432·6 × 86·9 × 27·9 (131·9 × 26·5 × 8·5)
Aircraft: 2 helicopters
Main engines: 6 Wärtsilä-Sulzer 9 ZL 40/48 diesels; 24 800 shp; 6 AC generators; 22 000 shp; 3 shafts with DC motors
Speed, knots: 19
Complement: 76 (16 spare berths)

Shallow draught polar icebreakers fitted with Wärtsilä bubbling system. Fitted with single cabins (except spare berths), sauna, swimming pool, gymnasium, library, cinema and hospital.

KAPITAN SOROKIN   1977, Wärtsilä

1 NEW CONSTRUCTION

OTTO SCHMIDT

Displacement, tons: 3 650
Main engines: Diesel-electric; 5 400 shp
Range, miles: 11 000

Building at Admiralty Yard, Leningrad. Icebreaker/polar research ship.

1 "PURGA" CLASS

Displacement, tons: 2 250 standard; 3 000 full load
Length, feet (metres): 295·2 (90)
Beam, feet (metres): 44·3 (13·5)
Draught, feet (metres): 17·1 (5·2)
Guns: 4—3·9 in (100 mm) (singles)
Mines: 50 capacity
Main engines: Diesels
Speed, knots: 18
Complement: 250

Laid down in 1939 in Leningrad and completed in 1948. Equipped as icebreaker. Fitted with director similar to those in the "Riga" class frigates. Modernised in 1958-60.

"PURGA" Class

3 "KAPITAN BELOUSOV" CLASS

Name	No.	Builders	Commissioned
KAPITAN BELOUSOV	—	Wärtsilä, Helsinki	1955
KAPITAN MELEKHOV	—	Wärtsilä, Helsinki	1957
KAPITAN VORONIN	—	Wärtsilä, Helsinki	1956

Displacement, tons: 4 375 to 4 415 standard; 5 350 full load
Dimensions, feet (metres): 265 wl; 273 oa × 63·7 × 23 (80·8 wl; 83·3 oa × 19·4 × 7)
Main engines: Diesel-electric; 6 Polar 8-cyl; 10 500 bhp = 14·9 knots
Oil fuel, tons: 740
Complement: 120

The ships have four screws, two forward under the forefoot and two aft. Civilian manned *K. Belousov* launched 1954, *K. Voronin* 1955 and *K. Melechov* 19 Oct 1956.

KAPITAN BELOUSOV   1970, Michael D. J. Lennon

USSR 555

20 "VASILY PRONCHISHTCHEV" CLASS

AFANASY NIKITIN (ex-Ledokol 2)	SADKO
BURAN	SEMYEN CHELYUSKIN
DOBRINYA NIKITCH	SEMYEN DEZHNEV
FËDOR LITKE	VASILY POIARKOV (ex-Ledokol 4)
ILIA MUROMETS	VASILY PRONCHISHTCHEV (ex-Ledokol 1)
IVAN MOSKVITIN	VLADIMIR RUSANOV (ex-Ledokol 7)
IVAN KRUZENSTERN (ex-Ledokol 6)	VYUGA
KHARITON LAPTEV (ex-Ledokol 3)	YEMELYAN PUGATCHEV
PERESVET	YEROFEI KHABAROV (ex-Ledokol 5)
PLUG	YURI LISYANSKIY (ex-Ledokol 8)

Displacement, tons: 2 500 standard (average)
Measurements, tons: 2 305 gross (ships vary)
Dimensions, feet (metres): 223·1 × 26·2 × 19·9 *(68 × 8 × 6·1)*
Guns: 2—57 mm; 2—25 mm *(Peresvet and Plug)*
Main engines: 3 shafts (1 bow, 2 stern); 5 400 hp = 13·8 knots

All built at Leningrad between 1961 (first, ship *Vasily Pronchishtchev*) and 1965 (last ship, *Ivan Moskvitin*). Divided between the Baltic, Black Sea and Far East. All civilian manned except *Buran*, *Peresvet* and *Plug*. Last two are armed.

YURIK LISANSKIY   1972, Michael D. J. Lennon

AFANASY NIKITIN   Michael D. J. Lennon

2 + 4 "KAPITAN CHECHKIN" CLASS

Name	No.	Builders	Commissioned
KAPITAN CHECHKIN	—	Wärtsilä	6 Nov 1977
KAPITAN PLAHIN	—	Wärtsilä	30 Dec 1977

Displacement, tons: 2 240
Dimensions, feet (metres): 254·5 × 53·5 × 10·7 *(77·6 × 16·3 × 3·3)*
Main engines: Diesel-electric; 3 shafts; 4 490 hp = 14 knots
Complement: 28

Ordered 16 May 1975. *K. Chechkin* laid down 22 Oct 1976 and launched 29 April 1977. *K. Plahin* launched 30 June 1977. Designed for service on Volga-Baltic waterways and Siberian rivers. Fitted with three rudders, air-bubbling system and an automatic lowering system for masts, radar and aerials. Four more ordered.

KAPITAN PLAHIN   1978, Wärtsilä

3 "KAPITAN IZMAYLOV" CLASS

Name	No.	Builders	Commissioned
KAPITAN M. IZMAYLOV	—	Wärtsilä, Helsinki	15 June 1976
KAPITAN KOSOLAPOV	—	Wärtsilä, Helsinki	14 July 1976
KAPITAN A. RADZABOV	—	Wärtsilä, Helsinki	5 Oct 1976

Displacement, tons: 2 045
Dimensions, feet (metres): 185·3 × 51·5 × 13·8 *(56·5 × 15·7 × 4·2)*
Main engines: Diesel-electric; 3 400 shp; 2 shafts; 2 rudders
Speed, knots: 13

Contract signed with Wärtsilä, Helsinki on 22 March 1974 for the building of these three icebreakers for delivery in 1976. All fitted with Wärtsilä air-bubbler system. Machinery by Wärtsilä Vasa. Electrical machinery by Oy Strömberg Ab.
Laid down: *K. Izmaylov* 12 June 1975 (launched 11 Dec 1975), *K. Kosolapov* 19 Aug 1975 (launched 13 Feb 1976), *K. Radzabov* 17 June 1975 (launched 9 March 1976). Civilian manned.

KAPITAN IZMAYLOV   10/1976, Wärtsilä

ARMED ICEBREAKERS

4 MODIFIED "VASILY PRONCHISHTCHEV" CLASS

AISBERG   IMENI XXV SYEZDA KPSS   IVAN SUSANIN   RUSLAN

Of similar major characteristics to Icebreakers of same class but lengthened by 80 feet and modified with new bridge structure, twin 76 mm forward, 2—30 mm Gatling guns aft (in all but *Aisberg*) and a helicopter platform. May be operated by KGB.

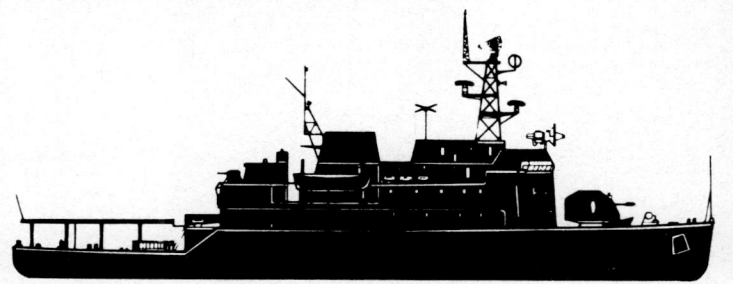

"MOD VASILY PRONCHISHTCHEV" Class

IVAN SUSANIN   7/1974

556 USSR

TUGS

2 "INGUL" CLASS

PAMIR   MASHUK

Displacement, tons: 4 050
Dimensions, feet (metres): 295 × 52 × 18 *(92·8 × 15·4 × 5·8)*
Main engines: 2—16-cyl 58D-4R diesels; 9 000 hp = 18·7 knots
Complement: 35 (plus salvage party of 18)

NATO class-name the same as one of the "Klasma" class cable-ships.
Naval manned Arctic salvage and rescue tugs.
Two more civilian manned—one named *Jaguar*. This class has an interesting underwater shape with a large protruding bulb at the forefoot.

Name: Reported that *Pamir* has been renamed *Ingul*.

PAMIR   4/1975, MOD(N)

2 "PAMIR" CLASS

AGATAN   ALDAN

Measurement, tons: 2 032 gross
Dimensions, feet (metres): 256 oa × 42 × 13·5 *(78 × 12·8 × 4·1)*
Main engines: 2 10-cyl 4 stroke diesels; 2 shaft; 4 200 bhp = 17 knots

Salvage tugs built at AB Gävie, Varv, Sweden, in 1959-60. Equipped with strong derricks, powerful pumps, air compressors, diving gear, fire fighting apparatus and electric generators.

ALDAN   4/1975, MOD(N)

9 "SORUM" CLASS

AMUR   KAMCHATKA   SAKHALIN   + 6

Displacement, tons: 1 630
Dimensions, feet (metres): 190·2 × 41·3 × 15·1 *(58 × 12·6 × 4·6)*
Guns: 4—30 mm (twins) (3 twins—*Amur, Kamchatka, Sakhalin*)
Main engines: Diesels; 2 100 hp

A new class of ocean tugs first seen in 1973. All are naval manned and *Amur*, *Kamchatka* and *Sakhalin*, are KGB operated. Last four building at Uusikaupunki, Finland. Two launched 8 Dec 1976 and 27 May 1977.

KAMCHATKA   5/1976, MOD

50 "OKHTENSKY" CLASS

Displacement, tons: 835
Dimensions, feet (metres): 134·5 wl; 143 oa × 34 × 15 *(41 wl; 43·6 × 10·4 × 4·6)*
Guns: 1—3 in; 2—20 mm
Main engines: 2 BM diesels; 2 electric motors; 2 shafts; 1 875 bhp = 14 knots
Oil fuel, tons: 187
Complement: 34

Oceangoing salvage and rescue tugs. Fitted with powerful pumps and other apparatus for salvage. Pennant numbers preceded by MB.

"OKHTENSKY" Class

5 "OREL" CLASS SALVAGE TUGS

Measurement, tons: 1 070 gross
Dimensions, feet (metres): 201·2 × 39·2 × 18·1 *(61·4 × 12 × 5·5)*
Main engines: 2 diesels = 14 knots

Class of salvage and rescue tugs normally operated by Ministry of Fisheries with the fishing fleets although at least two are naval manned. Built in Finland in late 1950s and early 1960s.

STREMITELNY—"Orel" Class   1972, Michael D. J. Lennon

7 "KATUN" CLASS

Displacement, tons: 950
Length, feet (metres): 210 *(64)*

Built in 1970-71.

FINNISH "530 TON" CLASS

Measurement, tons: 533 gross
Dimensions, feet (metres): 157·1 × 31·3 × 15·5 *(47·9 × 9·5 × 4·7)*
Main engines: Steam = 9·5 knots

Numerous class built in Finland in 1950s.

EAST GERMAN BERTHING TUGS

Measurement, tons: 233 gross
Main engines: Diesels

Numerous class built in 1970 in East Germany.

EAST GERMAN HARBOUR TUGS

Measurement, tons: 132 gross
Dimensions, feet (metres): 94·5 × 21·3 × 9·8 *(28·8 × 6·5 × 3)*
Main engine: 1 diesel = 10 knots

Very numerous class built in East Germany in 1964.

There are a large number of other tugs available in commercial service which could be directed to naval use.

UAE 557

UNITED ARAB EMIRATES

Headquarters Staff

Commander, Naval Forces:
 To be named

Deputy Commander, Naval Forces:
 Colonel Madwar

General

This federation of the former Trucial States (Abu Dhabi, Ajman, Dubai, Fujairah, Ras al Khaimah, Sharjah, Umm al Qaiwan) was formed under a provisional constitution in 1971 with a new constitution coming into effect on 2 Dec 1976.
Following a decision of the UAE Supreme Defence Council on 6 May 1976 the armed forces of the member states were unified and the organisation of the UAE Armed Forces was furthered by decisions taken on 1 Feb 1978. Overall control will be exercised by GHQ (UAE) in Abu Dhabi with a newly appointed Commander, Naval Forces coming under the general direction of that GHQ.

Personnel

(a) 1978: 986 (120 officers, 866 ratings)
(b) Voluntary service

Ports

Mina Zayed (Abu Dhabi).

LIGHT FORCES

6 VOSPER THORNYCROFT TYPE (LARGE PATROL CRAFT)

Name	No.	Builders	Commissioned
ARDHANA	P 1101	Vosper Thornycroft	24 June 1975
ZURARA	P 1102	Vosper Thornycroft	14 Aug 1975
MURBAN	P 1103	Vosper Thornycroft	16 Sept 1975
AL GHULLAN	P 1104	Vosper Thornycroft	16 Sept 1975
RADOOM	P 1105	Vosper Thornycroft	1 July 1976
GHANADHAH	P 1106	Vosper Thornycroft	1 July 1976

Displacement, tons: 110 standard; 175 full load
Dimensions, feet (metres): 110 oa × 21 × 6·6 *(33·5 × 6·4 × 2·0)*
Guns: 2—30 mm A32 (twin); 1—20 mm A41A (carry 2—2 in flare projectors)
Main engines: 2 Paxman Valenta diesels; 5 400 hp = 30 knots
Range, miles: 1 800 at 14 knots
Complement: 26

A class of round bilge steel hull craft. 1101-2 and 1105-6 transported to Abu Dhabi by heavy-lift ships. 1103 and 1104 were sailed out.

Radar: Decca TM 1626.

MURBAN 9/1975, John G. Callis

3 KEITH NELSON TYPE (COASTAL PATROL CRAFT)

Name	No.	Builders	Commissioned
KAWKAB	P 561	Keith Nelson, Bembridge	7 Mar 1969
THOABAN	P 562	Keith Nelson, Bembridge	7 Mar 1969
BANI YAS	P 563	Keith Nelson, Bembridge	27 Dec 1969

Displacement, tons: 32 standard; 38 full load
Dimensions, feet (metres): 57 × 16·5 × 4·5 *(17·4 × 5·0 × 1·4)*
Guns: 2—20 mm (single)
Main engines: 2 Caterpillar diesels. 750 bhp = 19 knots
Range, miles: 445 at 15 knots
Complement: 11 (2 officers, 9 men)

Of glass fibre hull construction.

Radar: Decca TM 1626.

BANI YAS 11/1976, UAE Armed Forces

POLICE CRAFT

(under control of Ministry of Interior)

6 "DHAFEER" CLASS (COASTAL PATROL CRAFT)

Name	No.	Builders	Commissioned
DHAFEER	P 401	Keith Nelson, Bembridge	1 July 1968
GHADUNFAR	P 402	Keith Nelson, Bembridge	1 July 1968
HAZZA	P 403	Keith Nelson, Bembridge	1 July 1968
DURGHAM	P 404	Keith Nelson, Bembridge	7 June 1969
TIMSAH	P 405	Keith Nelson, Bembridge	1 June 1969
MURAYJIB	P 406	Keith Nelson, Bembridge	7 June 1970

Displacement, tons: 10
Dimensions, feet (metres): 40·3 × 11 × 3·5 *(12·3 × 3·4 × 1·1)*
Guns: 2—7·62 mm MG
Main engines: 2 Cummins diesels; 370 bhp = 19 knots
Range, miles: 350 at 15 knots
Complement: 6 (1 officer, 5 men)

Of glass fibre hull construction. Transferred to Ministry of Interior (Marine Police) in July 1977.

TIMSAH 11/1976, UAE Armed Forces

558　UAE

2 50 ft CHEVERTON TYPE

Name	No.	Builders	Commissioned
AL SHAHEEN	—	Chevertons, Cowes	Feb 1975
AL AQAB	—	Chevertons, Cowes	Feb 1975

Displacement, tons: 20
Dimensions, feet (metres): 50 × 14 × 4·5 *(15·2 × 4·3 × 1·4)*
Gun: 1 MG
Main engines: 2 GM diesels; 2 shafts; 850 bhp = 23 knots
Range, miles: 1 000 at 20 knots
Complement: 8

GRP hull.

AL SHAHEEN　　　　　　　　　　　　　　　1975, Roger M. Smith

6 FAIREY MARINE "SPEAR" CLASS (COASTAL PATROL CRAFT)

Dimensions, feet (metres): 29·8 × 9·2 × 2·6 *(9·1 × 2·8 × 0·8)*
Guns: 2—7·62 mm MGs
Main engines: 2 Perkins diesels of 290 hp = 25 knots
Complement: 3

Order placed in Feb 1974. Craft delivered between July 1974 and Jan 1975.

"SPEAR" Class　　　　　　　　　　　　　　　1974, Faireys

2 27 FT CHEVERTON TYPE (TENDERS)

A 271　　　A 272

Displacement, tons: 3·3
Dimensions, feet (metres): 27 × 9 × 2·7 *(8·2 × 2·7 × 0·8)*
Main engine: 1 Lister RMW3 diesel; 150 hp = 15 knots

Built of GRP. Acquired from Chevertons, Cowes, Isle of Wight in 1975.
A 272 has a 2 ton hoist.

4 20 ft Coastal PATROL CRAFT

Ordered 1976.

1 FAIREY MARINE "INTERCEPTOR" CLASS

25 feet *(7·6 metres)* craft with catamaran hull. Powered by twin 135 hp outboard motors—speed 30 knots. Can carry a platoon of soldiers or eight life-rafts.

UNITED KINGDOM

Admiralty Board

Secretary of State for Defence (Chairman):
  The Right Hon F. W. Mulley, MP
Minister of State: Ministry of Defence (Vice-Chairman) and Minister of State for Defence Procurement:
  Dr J. W. Gilbert, MP
Parliamentary Under-Secretary of State for Defence for the Royal Navy:
  Dr Patrick Duffy, MP
Chief of the Naval Staff and First Sea Lord:
  Admiral Sir Terence Lewin, GCB, MVO, DSC, ADC
Chief of Naval Personnel and Second Sea Lord:
  Admiral Sir Gordon Tait, KCB, DSC
Controller of the Navy:
  Admiral Sir Richard Clayton, KCB
Chief of Fleet Support:
  Vice-Admiral J. H. F. Eberle
Vice-Chief of the Naval Staff:
  Vice-Admiral Sir Anthony Morton, KCB

Commanders-in-Chief

Commander-in-Chief, Naval Home Command:
  Admiral Sir David Williams, GCB, ADC
Commander-in-Chief, Fleet:
  Admiral Sir Henry Leach, KCB

Flag Officers

Flag Officer, Naval Air Command:
  Vice-Admiral D. A. Cassidi
Flag Officer, Carriers and Amphibious Ships:
  Rear-Admiral W. D. M. Staveley
Flag Officer, Sea Training:
  Rear-Admiral G. I. Pritchard
Flag Officer, Gibraltar:
  Rear-Admiral M. L. Stacey
Flag Officer, Malta:
  Rear-Admiral O. N. A. Cecil
Flag Officer, Medway:
  Rear-Admiral C. B. Williams, OBE
Flag Officer, Plymouth:
  Vice-Admiral J. M. Forbes
Flag Officer, Portsmouth:
  Rear-Admiral: W. J. Graham
Flag Officer, Scotland and Northern Ireland:
  Vice-Admiral C. Rusby, MVO

General Officers, Royal Marines

Commandant-General, Royal Marines:
  Lieutenant-General J. C. C. Richards
Chief of Staff to Commandant-General, Royal Marines:
  Major-General R. P. W. Wall, CB
Major-General Training Group, Royal Marines:
  Major-General P. L. Spurgeon
Major-General Commando Forces, Royal Marines:
  Major-General Sir Steuart Pringle

Diplomatic Representation

British Naval Attaché in Bonn:
  Captain B. R. Outhwaite
British Naval Adviser in Canberra:
  Captain P. A. Pinkster
British Naval Attaché in Moscow:
  Captain P. H. Coward
British Naval Adviser in Ottawa:
  Captain A. A. Hensher, MBE
British Naval Attaché in Paris:
  Captain W. S. Gueterbock
British Naval Attaché in Rome:
  Captain G. J. Byers
British Naval Attaché in Washington:
  Rear-Admiral R. M. Burgoyne

Personnel (including Royal Marines)

(a) 1973: 77 600 (10 200 officers, 67 400 ratings and ORs) plus 3 600 servicewomen
    1974: 74 700 (10 200 officers, 64 500 ratings and ORs) plus 3 600 servicewomen
    1975: 72 500 (10 000 officers, 62 500 ratings and ORs) plus 3 700 servicewomen
    1976: 72 300 (9 900 officers, 62 300 ratings and ORs) plus 3 900 servicewomen
    1977: 72 200 (9 800 officers, 62 400 ratings and ORs) plus 3 900 servicewomen
    1978: 71 500 (9 600 officers, 61 900 ratings and ORs) plus 4 000 servicewomen
(b) Voluntary service
(c) RNR (1978): 2 234 officers, 3 208 ratings
(d) RMR (1978): 64 officers, 913 men

Mercantile Marine

Lloyd's Register of Shipping:
  3 549 vessels of 32 923 308 tons gross

Strength of the Fleet

Type	Active	Building (Projected)	Reserve
Aircraft Carriers	1+1 (A/S)	—	—
A/S Carriers (Cruisers)	—	2 (1)	—
Helicopter Cruisers	2	—	—
Light Cruisers	8 (1 refit)	—	—
Destroyers	5	5	—
Frigates	53 (9 refit)	4	6
SSBNs	4 (1 refit)	—	—
Submarines—Fleet	10 (1 refit)	3	—
Submarines—Patrol	17 (5 refit)	—	2
Commando Ship	1	—	—
Assault Ships (LPD)	1	—	1
LSLs	6 (1 refit)	—	—
LCLs	2	—	—
LST	1	—	—
LCTs	3	2	—
LCMs	27	—	—
LCVPs	26	—	—
LCPLs	3	—	—
Offshore Patrol Craft	5	2	—
Fast Attack Craft—Patrol	1	—	—
Large Patrol Craft	11	—	—
Fast Training Boats	3	—	—
MCM Support Ship	1	—	—
Minehunters	16 (1 refit)	2	—
Minesweepers—Coastal	18 (2 refit)	—	—
Minesweepers—Inshore	5	—	—
Maintenance Ships	3	—	—
Target Ship	1	—	—
Survey Ships	4 (1 refit)	—	—
Coastal Survey Ships	4	—	—
Inshore Survey Craft	5	—	—
Ice Patrol Ship	1	—	—
Royal Yacht	1	—	—
Hovercraft	5	—	—
Diving Trials Ship	1	—	—
Large Fleet Tankers	5	—	—
Support Tankers	4	—	—
Coastal Tanker	1	—	—
Small Fleet Tankers	6	—	—
Helicopter Support Ship	1	—	—
Stores Support Ships	3	—	—
Fleet Replenishment Ships	5	1	—
Store Carriers	2	—	—
MSBVs	12	—	—
Trials Ships	5	—	—
TRVs	10	—	—
Cable Ship	1	—	—
Armament Carriers	1	—	5
Water Carriers	7	1	3
Ocean Tugs	15	—	1
Harbour Tugs	52	—	—
Tenders	47	—	—
RNXS Craft	11	4	—
DG Vessels	3	—	—
TCVs	6	—	—
Diving Tenders	6	—	—

Fleet Disposition

First Flotilla (Rear-Admiral R. R. Squires)
Blake (Flag), 4 "County" class, 4 Frigate Squadrons: 1st (*Galatea* + 5 frigates), 2nd (*Apollo* + 5 frigates), 5th (*Hermione* + 1 destroyer and 4 frigates), 6th (*Sirius* + 1 destroyer and 5 frigates)

Second Flotilla (Rear-Admiral M. La T. Wemyss)
Tiger (Flag), 3 "County" class, 4 Frigate Squadrons: 3rd (*Diomede* + 1 destroyer and 4 frigates), 4th (*Cleopatra* + 4 frigates), 7th (*Jupiter* + 4 frigates), 8th (*Ajax* + 5 frigates).

Submarine Command (Rear-Admiral J. D. E. Fieldhouse) HQ at Northwood:
1st Squadron (*Dolphin*, Portsmouth) 8 Patrol Submarines; 2nd Squadron (Devonport) 5 Fleet Submarines, 2 Patrol Submarines; 3rd Squadron (*Neptune,* Faslane) 3 Fleet Submarines, 2 Patrol Submarines; 10th Squadron (*Neptune*, Faslane) 3 SSBN

MCM Commands:
1st Squadron (Rosyth), 2nd Squadron (Portsmouth), 3rd Squadron (Portland), FPS (Rosyth), 10th Squadron (RNR).

Fleet Air Arm

Aircraft	Role	Deployment	No. of sqdns or flights
Buccaneer 2	Strike	Carrier	1 Sqdn
Gannet 3	AEW	Carrier	1 Flight
Gannet 3	AEW	Lossiemouth	1 Sqdn
Phantom FG1	FGA	Carrier	1 Sqdn

Helicopters

Lynx	Aircrew Training	Yeovilton	1 Sqdn
Lynx	ASW	Destroyers and Frigates	4 Flights
Sea King	ASW	Carrier	1 Sqdn
Sea King	ASW	ASW Carrier	1 Sqdn
Sea King	ASW	Cruisers	2 Sqdns
Sea King	ASW	Prestwick	1 Sqdn
Sea King	Aircrew Training	Culdrose	1 Sqdn
Sea King	ASW	RFAs	2 Flights
Wasp	ASW	"Leander" Class	}
Wasp	ASW	"Rothesay" Class	}
Wasp	ASW	"Tribal" Class	} 35 Flights
Wasp	ASW	Type 21	}
Wasp	ASW	Type 42	}
Wasp	Aircrew Training	Portland	1 Sqdn
Wessex 3	ASW	"County" Class	7 Flights
Wessex 3	Aircrew Training	Portland	1 Sqdn
Wessex 5	Commando Assault	Yeovilton/HMS *Hermes*	2 Sqdns
Wessex 5	Aircrew Training	Yeovilton	1 Sqdn
Wessex 5	Fleet Requirements	Portland	1 Sqdn

560 UK

DELETIONS
(**Note:** Disposal List following)

Carriers (of all kinds)

1972 *Centaur* and *Albion*

Cruiser

1975 *Lion* (b.u. Inverkeithing 24 April)

Light Cruiser

1976 *Hampshire*

Destroyers

1970 *Aisne, Trafalgar, Camperdown*
1971 *Daring, Delight, Scorpion, Cambrian*
1972 *Crossbow, Defender, Saintes*
1974 *Agincourt* (b.u. Sunderland 27 Oct)
1975 *Corunna* (b.u. Blyth 11 Sept)

Frigates

1070 *Loch Killisport, Loch Fada, Ulysses, Zest, Murray*
1971 *Urania, Relentless, Pellew, Wakeful, Alert, Grafton*
1972 *Verulam, Venus*
1974 *Tenby, Scarborough. Whirlwind* (target 28 Oct)
1976 *Blackwood, Puma. Llandaff* (to Bangladesh), *Volage*
1977 *Mermaid* (to Malaysia), *Scarborough* (b.u.)
1978 *Jaguar* (to Bangladesh). *Leopard*

Submarines

1970 *Talent, Thermopylae, Anchorite, Astute*
1971 *Ambush, Alaric, Trump, Taciturn, Auriga*
1972 *Artemis, Acheron, Alderney, Aeneas, Alcide, Alliance*
1976 *Rorqual*
1977 *Andrew* (b.u.—4 May)

Depot Ship

1977 *Maidstone* to Rosyth for b.u. (Jan)

MCM Vessels

1970 *Dalswinton, Invermoriston, Puncheston, Quainton, Wilkieston*
1974 *Woolaston*
1975 *Boulston, Maddiston* (scrapped). *Birdham, Odiham*
1976 *Highburton, Woolaston, Arlingham. Fittleton* (sunk in collision Sept b.u. after salvage)
1977 *Ashton* (Aug). *Dufton* (b.u.—10 June), *Chawton* (b.u.—6 Aug)

Fast Attack Craft

1976 *Dark Gladiator* (sunk as target—Portland)

Service Forces

1970 *Girdleness* (scrapped)
1973 *Moorsman, Foulness*
1974 *Wave Chief, Derwentdale* (returned to owners), *Brown Ranger* (Tankers). *Barmond* (MSBV), *Miner III*
1975 *Dispenser*, (MSBV), *Robert Middleton* (Stores Carrier), *Icewhale* (Trials Ship), *Freshmere* (Water boat), *Bowstring* (Armament Carrier). *Ironbridge, Nordenfeld*
1976 *Tideflow* (to b.u. Bilbao 4 May). *Spalake, Spaburn, Freshpool, Freshpond*
1977 *Tidesurge* (Tanker, b.u.—April). *Barfoot* (MSBV, b.u.—23 Aug). *Reliant* (Airstores Ship, b.u.—23 Aug). *Throsk* (Stores Ship, b.u.—12 June)

Survey Ship

1976 *Vidal* (b.u. Bruges—June)

Tugs

1975 *Diver, Driver, Eminent, Empire Ace, Empire Demon, Empire Fred, Empire Rosa, Fidget, Foremost, Freedom, Frisky, Handmaid, Impetus, Integrity,* (*Lilian* and *May*—existence doubted), *Prompt, Security, Tampeon, Trunnion, Vagrant, Weasel.*
1976 *Reward* (to disposal after salvage 29 Aug)

DISPOSAL LIST

The following ships not on the Active or Reserve list are held in the ports shown pending disposal by sale or scrap.

Aircraft Carrier

Eagle R 05 (Plymouth)

Light Cruiser

Hampshire D 06 (Chatham)

Destroyers

Caprice D 01 (Plymouth)
Barrosa D 68 (Portsmouth)

Submarines

1977 *Narwhal* S 03, *Cachalot* S 06

Frigates

Blackpool F 77 (Rosyth Target Ship)
Grenville F 197 (Portsmouth)
Keppel F 85 (Portsmouth)
Palliser F 94 (Portsmouth)
Rapid F 138 (Milford Haven—Target)
Undaunted F 53 (Gibraltar—Target)
Whitby F 36 (Portsmouth)
1978 *Chichester, Eastbourne, Dundas*

Minesweepers—Coastal

Belton M 1199 (Rosyth)

Fast Attack Craft

Brave Borderer (Pembroke Dock)
Brave Swordsman (Pembroke Dock)
Dark Hero (Pembroke Dock)

Submarine Depot Ship

1978 *Forth* (Mar)

Service Forces

1978 *Tidereach*

LSTs

Lofoten (Rosyth)
Messina (Plymouth)
Stalker (Rosyth)
Zeebrugge (Plymouth)

Immobile Tenders

Diamond D 35. Attached to *Sultan* for engineering training at Portsmouth
Ulster F 83. Accommodation ship at Plymouth
Russell F 97. Attached to *Sultan Collingwood*—Portsmouth
Grampus S 04. Harbour Training—*Dolphin*—Portsmouth
Duncan F 80. Attached to *Caledonia*—Rosyth
Cavalier D 73 (Museum Ship, Southampton)
Eastbourne F 73. Attached to *Caledonia*—Rosyth (approved for disposal 1978)

LIST OF PENNANT NUMBERS

Note: Not displayed on Submarines or RMAS craft.

*Disposal List

		Aircraft Carriers
R	05	Eagle*
R	08	Bulwark
R	09	Ark Royal
R	12	Hermes

		Submarines
S	01	Porpoise
S	03	Narwhal*
S	04	Grampus*
S	05	Finwhale
S	06	Cachalot*
S	07	Sealion
S	08	Walrus
S	09	Oberon
S	10	Odin
S	11	Orpheus
S	12	Olympus
S	13	Osiris
S	14	Onslaught
S	15	Otter
S	16	Oracle
S	17	Ocelot
S	18	Otus
S	19	Opossum
S	20	Opportune
S	21	Onyx
S	22	Resolution
S	23	Repulse
S	26	Renown
S	27	Revenge
S	46	Churchill
S	48	Conqueror
S	50	Courageous
S	101	Dreadnought
S	102	Valiant
S	103	Warspite
S	104	Sceptre
S	108	Sovereign
S	109	Superb
S	111	Spartan
S	112	Severn
S	113	Trafalgar
S	126	Swiftsure

		Cruisers
C	20	Tiger
C	99	Blake

		Light Cruisers and Destroyers
D	01	Caprice*
D	02	Devonshire
D	06	Hampshire*
D	12	Kent
D	16	London
D	18	Antrim
D	19	Glamorgan
D	20	Fife
D	21	Norfolk
D	23	Bristol
D	35	Diamond
D	68	Barrosa*
D	80	Sheffield
D	86	Birmingham
D	87	Newcastle
D	88	Glasgow
D	108	Cardiff
D	118	Coventry
D	—	Exeter
D	—	Southampton
D	—	Nottingham
D	—	New Construction

		Frigates
F	10	Aurora
F	12	Achilles
F	15	Euryalus
F	16	Diomede
F	18	Galatea
F	27	Lynx
F	28	Cleopatra
F	32	Salisbury
F	38	Arethusa

UK 561

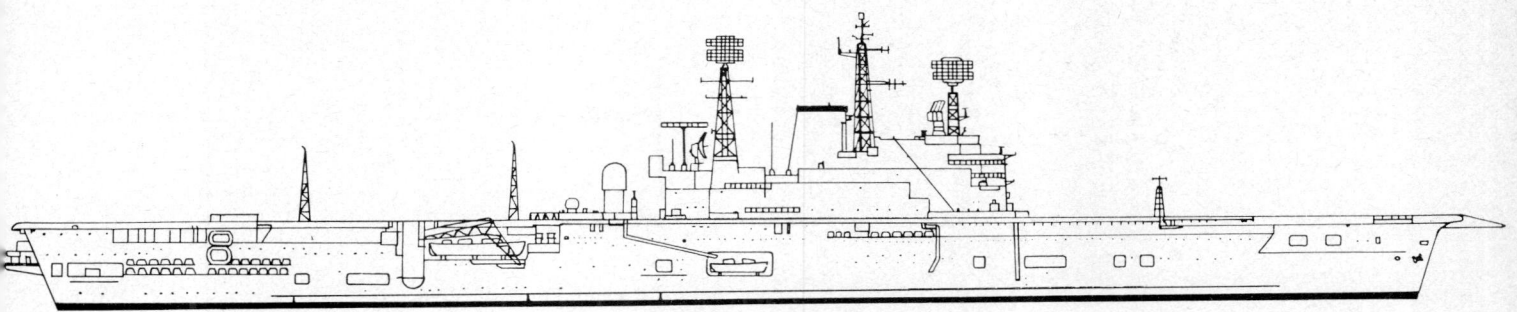

Frigates

F	39	Naiad
F	40	Sirius
F	42	Phoebe
F	43	Torquay
F	45	Minerva
F	47	Danae
F	52	Juno
F	53	Undaunted*
F	54	Hardy
F	56	Argonaut
F	57	Andromeda
F	58	Hermione
F	59	Chichester
F	60	Jupiter
F	69	Bacchante
F	70	Apollo
F	71	Scylla
F	72	Ariadne
F	75	Charybdis
F	77	Blackpool*
F	80	Duncan*
F	83	Ulster*
F	85	Keppel*
F	88	Broadsword
F	—	Battleaxe
F	—	Brilliant
F	—	Boxer
F	94	Palliser*
F	97	Russell*
F	99	Lincoln
F	101	Yarmouth
F	103	Lowestoft
F	104	Dido
F	106	Brighton
F	107	Rothesay
F	108	Londonderry
F	109	Leander
F	113	Falmouth
F	114	Ajax
F	115	Berwick
F	117	Ashanti
F	119	Eskimo
F	122	Gurkha
F	124	Zulu
F	125	Mohawk
F	126	Plymouth
F	127	Penelope
F	129	Rhyl
F	131	Nubian
F	133	Tartar
F	138	Rapid*
F	169	Amazon
F	170	Antelope
F	171	Active
F	172	Ambuscade
F	173	Arrow
F	174	Alacrity
F	184	Ardent
F	185	Avenger
F	197	Grenville*

Assault Ships

L	10	Fearless
L	11	Interpid

Logistic Landing Ships and LCTs

L	700-711	LCM 9
L	3004	Sir Bedivere
L	3005	Sir Galahad
L	3027	Sir Geraint
L	3029	Sir Lancelot
L	3036	Sir Percivale
L	3505	Sir Tristram
L	3507-8	LCM 9
L	3513	Empire Gull
L	4001	Ardennes
L	4002	Agheila
L	4041	Abbeville
L	4061	Audemer
L	—	Arakan

LCMs (RCT)

RPL	01	Avon
RPL	02	Bude
RPL	03	Clyde
RPL	04	Dart
RPL	05	Eden
RPL	06	Forth
RPL	07	Glen
RPL	08	Hamble
RPL	10	Kennet
RPL	11	Loddon
RPL	12	Medway

Helicopter Support Ship

K	08	Engadine

Minelayer

N	21	Abdiel

Support Ships and Auxiliaries

A	00	Britannia
A	70	Echo
A	71	Enterprise
A	72	Egeria
A	75	Tidespring
A	76	Tidepool
A	77	Pearleaf
A	78	Plumleaf
A	80	Orangeleaf
A	82	Cherryleaf
A	85	Faithful
A	86	Forceful
A	87	Favourite
A	88	Agile
A	89	Advice
A	90	Accord
A	93	Dexterous
A	94	Director
A	95	Typhoon
A	99	Beaulieu
A	100	Beddgelert
A	101	Bembridge
A	102	Airedale
A	103	Bibury
A	104	Blakeney
A	105	Brodick
A	106	Alsatian
A	108	Triumph
A	111	Cyclone
A	113	Alice
A	116	Agatha
A	117	Audrey
A	121	Agnes
A	122	Olwen
A	123	Olna
A	124	Olmeda
A	126	Cairn
A	127	Torrent
A	128	Torrid
A	129	Dalmatian
A	133	Hecla
A	134	Rame Head
A	137	Hecate
A	138	Herald
A	144	Hydra
A	145	Daisy
A	155	Deerhound
A	162	Elkhound
A	168	Labrador
A	169	Husky
A	171	Endurance
A	176	Bullfinch
A	177	Edith
A	179	Whimbrel
A	180	Mastiff
A	182	Saluki
A	187	Sealyham
A	188	Pointer
A	189	Setter
A	191	Berry Head
A	201	Spaniel
A	210	Charlotte
A	217	Christine
A	218	Clare
A	220	Loyal Moderator
A	222	Spapool
A	231	Reclaim
A	232	Kingarth
A	236	Wakeful
A	250	Sheepdog
A	252	Doris
A	259	St. Margarets
A	261	Eddyfirth
A	268	Green Rover
A	269	Grey Rover
A	270	Blue Rover
A	271	Gold Rover
A	273	Black Rover
A	274	Ettrick
A	277	Elsing
A	280	Resurgent
A	281	Kinbrace
A	288	Sea Giant
A	289	Confiance
A	290	Confident
A	310	Invergordon
A	317	Bulldog
A	318	Ixworth
A	319	Beagle
A	320	Fox
A	322	Bridget
A	323	Betty
A	324	Barbara
A	325	Fawn
A	327	Basset
A	328	Collie
A	329	Retainer
A	330	Corgi
A	332	Caldy
A	334	Bern
A	335	Fawn
A	336	Lundy
A	338	Skomer
A	339	Lyness
A	340	Graemsay
A	344	Stromness
A	345	Tarbatness
A	346	Switha
A	352	Epworth
A	353	Elkstone
A	354	Froxfield
A	361	Roysterer
A	364	Whitehead
A	367	Newton
A	377	Maxim
A	378	Kinterbury
A	382	Vigilant (ex-Loyal Factor)
A	384	Felsted
A	385	Fort Grange
A	386	Fort Austin
A	389	Clovelly
A	393	Dunster
A	394	Foxhound
A	404	Bacchus
A	406	Hebe
A	480	Resource
A	482	Kinloss
A	486	Regent
A	502	Rollicker
A	507	Uplifter
A	510	Alert (ex-Loyal Governor)
A	1771	Loyal Proctor
A	1772	Holmwood
A	1773	Horning

Auxiliaries

Y	15	Watercourse
Y	16	Waterfowl
Y	17	Waterfall
Y	18	Watershed
Y	19	Waterspout
Y	20	Waterside
Y	21	Oilpress
Y	22	Oilstone
Y	23	Oilwell
Y	24	Oilfield
Y	25	Oilbird
Y	26	Oilman

Boom Defence Vessels

P	190	Laymoor
P	191	Layburn
P	192	Mandarin
P	193	Pintail
P	194	Garganey
P	195	Goldeneye
P	196	Goosander
P	197	Pochard

Light Forces

P	260	Kingfisher
P	261	Cygnet
P	262	Peterel
P	263	Sandpiper
P	271	Scimitar
P	274	Cutlass
P	275	Sabre
P	276	Tenacity
P	295	Jersey
P	297	Guernsey
P	298	Shetland
P	299	Orkney
P	300	Lindisfarne
P	301	—
P	302	—
P	1007	Beachampton
P	1055	Monkton
P	1089	Wasperton
P	1093	Wolverton
P	1096	Yarnton
P	3104	Dee (ex-Beckford)
P	3113	Droxford

Coastal Minesweepers

M	29	Brecon
M	1103	Alfriston
M	1109	Bickington
M	1110	Bildeston
M	1113	Brereton
M	1114	Brinton
M	1115	Bronington
M	1116	Wilton
M	1124	Crichton
M	1125	Cuxton
M	1133	Bossington
M	1140	Gavinton
M	1141	Glasserton
M	1146	Hodgeston
M	1147	Hubberston
M	1151	Iveston
M	1153	Kedleston
M	1154	Kellington
M	1157	Kirkliston
M	1158	Laleston
M	1165	Maxton
M	1166	Nurton
M	1167	Repton
M	1173	Pollington
M	1180	Shavington
M	1181	Sheraton
M	1182	Shoulton
M	1187	Upton
M	1188	Walkerton
M	1195	Wotton
M	1199	Belton*
M	1200	Soberton
M	1204	Stubbington
M	1208	Lewiston
M	1216	Crofton

Inshore Minesweepers

M	2002	Aveley
M	2010	Isis (ex-Cradley)
M	2611	Bottisham (RAF 5001) R
M	2614	Bucklesham TRV
M	2616	Chelsham (RAF 5000) R
M	2621	Dittisham
M	2622	Downham TRV
M	2626	Everingham TRV
M	2628	Flintham
M	2630	Fritham TRV
M	2635	Haversham TRV
M	2636	Lasham TRV
M	2716	Pagham RNXS
M	2717	Fordham DGV
M	2720	Waterwitch (ex-Powderham)
M	2726	Shipham RNXS
M	2733	Thakeham RNXS
M	2735	Tongham RNXS
M	2737	Warmingham DGV
M	2780	Woodlark (ex-Yaxham)
M	2781	Portisham RNXS
M	2783	Odiham RNXS
M	2784	Puttenham RNXS
M	2785	Birdham RNXS
M	2790	Thatcham DGV
M	2793	Thornham

DGV	=	Degaussing Vessels
RNXS	=	Royal Naval Auxiliary Service
TRV	=	Torpedo Recovery Vessels
R	=	Reserve (ex-RAF)

ARK ROYAL (scale = 1:1300)

562 UK

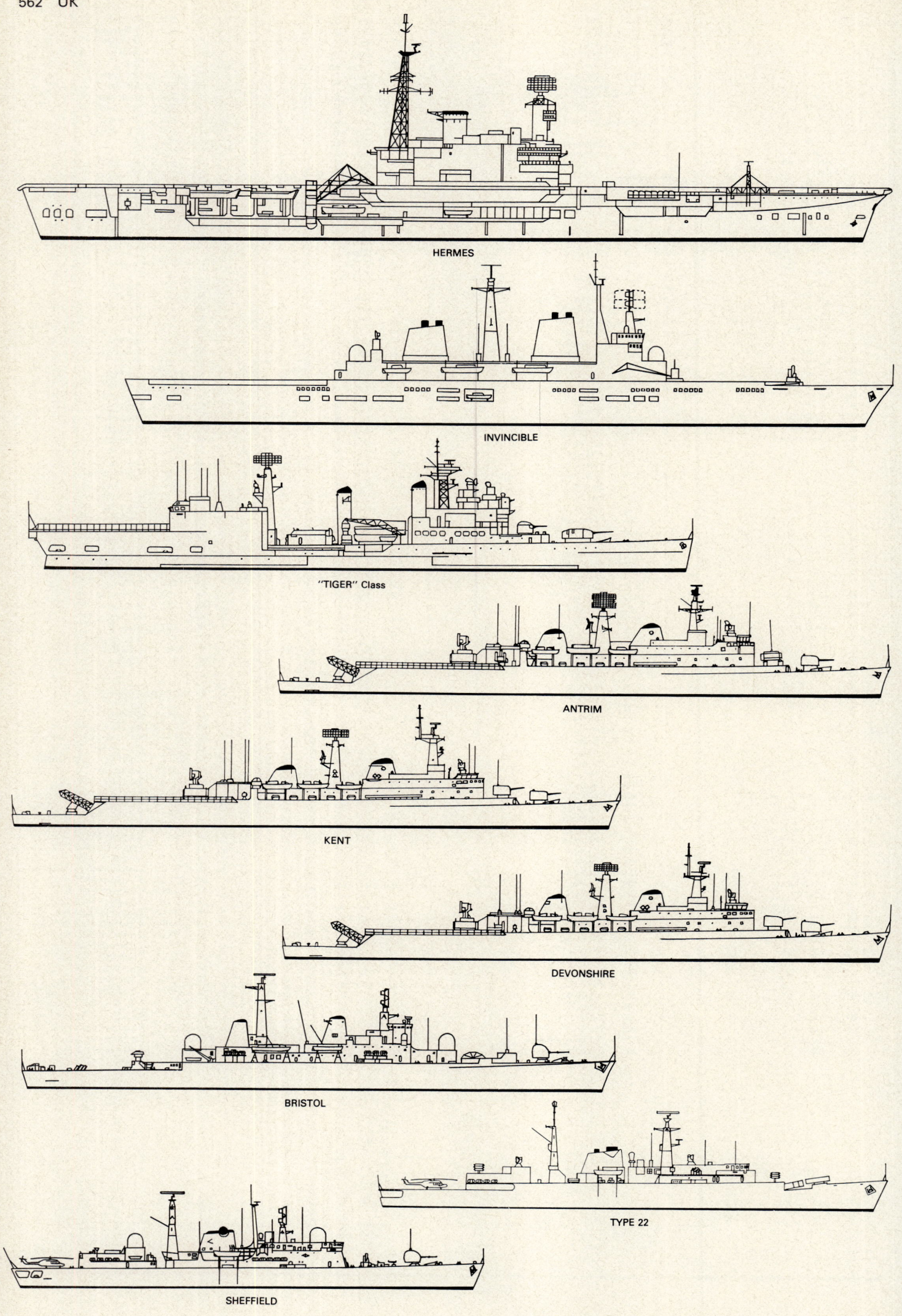

HERMES

INVINCIBLE

"TIGER" Class

ANTRIM

KENT

DEVONSHIRE

BRISTOL

TYPE 22

SHEFFIELD

UK 563

"LEANDER" Class (Ikara)

"LEANDER" Class (Exocet)

"LEANDER" Class (4-5")

"ROTHESAY" Class

TORQUAY

"AMAZON" Class

"TRIBAL" Class

LYNX

"SALISBURY" Class (except *Chichester*)

"BLACKWOOD" Class

564 UK

SUBMARINES
Nuclear Powered Ballistic Missile Submarines (SSBN)
4 "RESOLUTION" CLASS

Name	No.	Builders	Laid down	Launched	Commissioned
RESOLUTION	S 22	Vickers (Shipbuilding) Ltd, Barrow-in-Furness	26 Feb 1964	15 Sept 1966	2 Oct 1967
REPULSE	S 23	Vickers (Shipbuilding) Ltd, Barrow-in-Furness	12 Mar 1965	4 Nov 1967	28 Sept 1968
RENOWN*	S 26	Cammell Laird & Co Ltd, Birkenhead	25 June 1964	25 Feb 1967	15 Nov 1968
REVENGE	S 27	Cammell Laird & Co Ltd, Birkenhead	19 May 1965	15 Mar 1968	4 Dec 1969

* Refit

Displacement, tons: 7 500 surfaced; 8 400 dived
Length, feet (metres): 360 *(109.7)* pp; 425 *(129.5)* oa
Beam, feet (metres): 33 *(10.1)*
Draught, feet (metres): 30 *(9.1)*
Missiles, surface: 16 tubes amidships for Polaris A—3 SLBMs
Torpedo tubes: 6—21 in *(533 mm)* (bow)
Nuclear reactors: 1 pressurised water cooled
Main machinery: Geared steam turbines; 1 shaft
Speed, knots: 20 surfaced; 25 dived
Complement: 143 (13 officers, 130 ratings); 2 crews (see *Personnel*)

In Feb 1963 it was officially stated that it was intended to order four or five 7 000 ton nuclear powered submarines, each to carry 16 Polaris missiles, and it was planned that the first would be on patrol in 1968. Their hulls and machinery would be of British design. As well as building two submarines Vickers (Shipbuilding) would give lead yard service to the builder of the other two. Four Polaris submarines were in fact ordered in May 1963. The plan to build a fifth Polaris submarine was cancelled on 15 Feb 1965. Britain's first SSBN, *Resolution,* put to sea on 22 June 1967 and completed six weeks trial in the Firth of Clyde and Atlantic on 17 Aug 1967.

Cost: *Resolution,* £40·24 million; *Renown,* £39·95 million; *Repulse,* £37·5 million; *Revenge,* £38·6 million; completed ships excluding missiles.

Personnel: Each submarine, which has accommodation for 19 officers and 135 ratings, is manned on a two-crew basis, in order to get maximum operational time at sea.

Radar: Search: I-band
Periscope radar.

Sonar: Types 2001 and 2007.

REVENGE at Faslane   3/1976, Wren Veronica Evans (MOD(N))

RENOWN   10/1976, Wright and Logan

REPULSE   11/1976, MOD(N)

Fleet Submarines

0 + 1 NEW CONSTRUCTION "TRAFALGAR" CLASS

Name	No.	Builders	Laid down	Launched	Commissioned
TRAFALGAR	S 113	Vickers (Shipbuilding) Ltd, Barrow-in-Furness	1978	—	—

The first of an improved class of Fleet Submarines was ordered in Sept 1977. The second is planned for ordering in 1978. Improvements include equipment, endurance and speed.

4 + 2 "SWIFTSURE" CLASS

Name	No.	Builders	Laid down	Launched	Commissioned
SCEPTRE	S 104	Vickers (Shipbuilding) Ltd, Barrow-in-Furness	25 Oct 1973	20 Nov 1976	Mid 1978
SOVEREIGN	S 108	Vickers (Shipbuilding) Ltd, Barrow-in-Furness	17 Sept 1970	17 Feb 1973	11 July 1974
SUPERB	S 109	Vickers (Shipbuilding) Ltd, Barrow-in-Furness	16 Mar 1972	30 Nov 1974	13 Nov 1976
SPARTAN	S 111	Vickers (Shipbuilding) Ltd, Barrow-in-Furness	24 April 1976	? Dec 1978	? 1980
SPLENDID	S 112	Vickers (Shipbuilding) Ltd, Barrow-in-Furness	1 Nov 1977	? April 1980	? 1981
SWIFTSURE	S 126	Vickers (Shipbuilding) Ltd, Barrow-in-Furness	15 April 1969	7 Sept 1971	17 April 1973

Displacement, tons: 4 000 light; 4 200 standard; 4 500 dived
Length, feet (metres): 272·0 *(82·9)*
Beam, feet (metres): 32·3 *(9·8)*
Draught, feet (metres): 27 *(8·2)*
Torpedo tubes: 5—21 in *(533 mm)* (20 reloads)
Nuclear reactor: 1 pressurised water-cooled
Main machinery: English Electric geared steam turbines; 15 000 shp; 1 Paxman auxiliary diesel; 4 000 hp; 1 shaft
Speed, knots: 30 dived
Complement: 97 (12 officers, 85 men)

Compared with the "Valiant" class submarines these are slightly shorter with a fuller form with the fore-planes set further forward with one less torpedo tube and with a deeper diving depth.
Sovereign visited the North Pole 1976.

Armament: It is planned to provide Sub-Harpoon in all Fleet Submarines from the early 1980s.

Costs: Building—*Swiftsure* £37·1 million, *Superb* £41·3 million. Running cost £3·8 million per submarine per year.

Design: The pressure hull in the "Swiftsures" maintains its diameter for much greater length than previously.

Electrical: 112 cell emergency battery.

Engineering: Whilst the basic reactor design remains similar to previous types core-life has probably increased.

Orders: *Swiftsure*, 3 Nov 1967; *Sovereign*, 16 May 1969; *Superb*, 20 May 1970; *Sceptre*, 1 Nov 1971; *Spartan*, 17 Feb 1973; *Severn*, 26 May 1976.

Radar: Search: Type 1003.

Sonar: Type 2001 in "chin" position, Types 2007, 197 and 183.

Torpedoes: Individual reloading in 15 seconds.

SUPERB   6/1977, John G. Callis

SOVEREIGN   9/1975, John G. Callis

SUPERB   6/1977, Michael D. J. Lennon

566 UK

5 "VALIANT" CLASS

Name	No.	Builders	Laid down	Launched	Commissioned
CHURCHILL	S 46	Vickers (Shipbuilding) Ltd, Barrow-in Furness	30 June 1967	20 Dec 1968	15 July 1970
CONQUEROR	S 48	Cammell Laird & Co Ltd, Birkenhead	5 Dec 1967	28 Aug 1969	9 Nov 1971
COURAGEOUS	S 50	Vickers (Shipbuilding) Ltd, Barrow-in-Furness	15 May 1968	7 Mar 1970	16 Oct 1971
VALIANT*	S 102	Vickers (Shipbuilding) Ltd, Barrow-in-Furness	22 Jan 1962	3 Dec 1963	18 July 1966
WARSPITE	S 103	Vickers (Shipbuilding) Ltd, Barrow-in-Furness	10 Dec 1963	25 Sept 1965	18 April 1967

* Refit

Displacement, tons: 4 000 light; 4 400 standard; 4 900 dived
Length, feet (metres): 285 *(86·9)*
Beam, feet (metres): 33·2 *(10·1)*
Draught, feet (metres): 27 *(8·2)*
Torpedo tubes: 6—21 in *(533 mm)* (26 reloads)
Nuclear reactor: 1 pressurised water cooled
Main machinery: English Electric geared steam turbines; 1 shaft
Speed, knots: 28 dived
Complement: 103 (13 officers, 90 men)

It was announced on 31 Aug 1960 that the contract for a second nuclear powered submarine *(Valiant)* had been awarded to Vickers Ltd, the principal sub-contractors being Vickers-Armstrong (Engineers) Ltd, for the machinery and its installation, and Rolls-Royce and Associates for the nuclear steam raising plant. The class, of which she is the first, is broadly of the same design as that of *Dreadnought*, but slightly larger. She was originally scheduled to be completed in Sept 1965, but work was held up by the Polaris programme.

Armament: It is planned to provide Sub-Harpoon in all Fleet Submarines from the early 1980s.

Cost: Vary from £24 million *(Warspite)* to £30 million *(Conqueror)*.

Electrical: 112 cell emergency battery.

Endurance: On 25 April 1967 *Valiant* completed the 12 000-mile homeward voyage from Singapore, the record submerged passage by a British submarine, after 28 days non-stop.

Engineering: *Valiant's* reactor core was made in the United Kingdom, with machinery of British design and manufacture similar to the shore prototype installed in the Admiralty Reactor Test Establishment at Dounreay. The main steam turbines and condensers were designed and manufactured by the English Electric Company, Rugby, and the electrical propulsion machinery and control gear by Laurence, Scott & Electromotors Ltd.

Orders: *Valiant,* 31 Aug 1960—*Warspite*, 12 Dec 1962—*Churchill*, 21 Oct 1965—*Conqueror*, 9 Aug 1966—*Courageous*, 1 March 1967.

Radar: Search: Type 1003.

Sonar: Type 2001 in "chin" position; Types 2007, 197 and 183.

Torpedoes: Individual reloading in 15 seconds.

CHURCHILL   6/1977, Michael D. J. Lennon

CHURCHILL   6/1977, Dr. Giorgio Arra

1 "DREADNOUGHT" CLASS

Name	No.	Builders	Laid down	Launched	Commissioned
DREADNOUGHT	S 101	Vickers-Armstrong, Barrow-in-Furness	12 June 1959	21 Oct 1960	17 April 1963

Displacement, tons: 3 000 standard; 3 500 surfaced; 4 000 dived
Length, feet (metres): 265·8 *(81·0)*
Beam, feet (metres): 32·2 *(9·8)*
Draught, feet (metres): 26 *(7·9)*
Torpedo tubes: 6—21 in *(533 mm)* (bow)
Nuclear reactor: 1 S5W pressurised water-cooled
Main machinery: Geared steam turbines; 1 shaft
Speed, knots: 28 dived
Complement: 88 (11 officers, 77 men)

As originally planned *Dreadnought* was to have been fitted with a British designed and built nuclear reactor, but in 1958 an agreement was concluded with the United States Government for the purchase of a complete set of propulsion machinery of the type fitted in USS *Skipjack*. This agreement enabled the submarine to be launched far earlier. The supply of this machinery was made under a contract between the Westinghouse Electric Corporation and Rolls-Royce. The latter were also supplied with design and manufacturing details of the reactor and with safety information and set up a factory in this country to manufacture similar cores. *Dreadnought* has a hull of British design both as regards structural strength and hydrodynamic features, although the latter are based on the pioneering work of the US Navy in *Skipjack* and *Albacore*. From about amidships aft, the hull lines closely resemble *Skipjack* to accommodate the propulsion machinery. The forward end is wholly British in concept. In the Control Room and Attack Centre the instruments are fitted into consoles.

The improved water distilling plant for the first time provides unlimited fresh water for shower baths and for washing machines in the fully equipped laundry.

She is fitted with an inertial navigation system and with means of measuring her depth below ice and was the first British submarine to surface at the North Pole, in 1970.

Radar: Search: I-band.

Sonar: Type 2001 in "chin" position; Type 2007.

DREADNOUGHT   6/1977, Wright and Logan

Patrol Submarines

13 "OBERON" CLASS   4 "PORPOISE" CLASS

"OBERON" CLASS

Name	No.	Builders	Laid down	Launched	Commissioned
OBERON	S 09	HM Dockyard, Chatham	28 Nov 1957	18 July 1959	24 Feb 1961
ODIN	S 10	Cammell Laird & Co Ltd, Birkenhead	27 April 1959	4 Nov 1960	3 May 1962
ORPHEUS	S 11	Vickers (Shipbuilding) Ltd, Barrow-in Furness	16 April 1959	17 Nov 1959	25 Nov 1960
OLYMPUS	S 12	Vickers (Shipbuilding) Ltd, Barrow-in Furness	4 Mar 1960	14 June 1961	7 July 1962
OSIRIS*	S 13	Vickers (Shipbuilding) Ltd, Barrow-in-Furness	26 Jan 1962	29 Nov 1962	11 Jan 1964
ONSLAUGHT	S 14	HM Dockyard, Chatham	8 April 1959	24 Sept 1960	14 Aug 1962
OTTER*	S 15	Scotts (Shipbuilding) Co Ltd, Greenock	14 Jan 1960	15 May 1961	20 Aug 1962
ORACLE*	S 16	Cammell Laird & Co Ltd, Birkenhead	26 April 1960	26 Sept 1961	14 Feb 1963
OCELOT*	S 17	HM Dockyard, Chatham	17 Nov 1960	5 May 1962	31 Jan 1964
OTUS*	S 18	Scotts (Shipbuilding) Co Ltd, Greenock	31 May 1961	17 Oct 1962	5 Oct 1963
OPOSSUM	S 19	Cammell Laird & Co Ltd, Birkenhead	21 Dec 1961	23 May 1963	5 June 1964
OPPORTUNE	S 20	Scotts (Shipbuilding) Co Ltd, Greenock	26 Oct 1962	14 Feb 1964	29 Dec 1964
ONYX	S 21	Cammell Laird & Co Ltd, Birkenhead	16 Nov 1964	18 Aug 1966	20 Nov 1967

* Refit

"PORPOISE" CLASS

Name	No.	Builders	Laid down	Launched	Commissioned
PORPOISE	S 01	Vickers (Shipbuilding) Ltd, Barrow-in-Furness	15 June 1954	25 April 1956	17 April 1958
FINWHALE	S 05	Cammell Laird & Co Ltd, Birkenhead	18 Sept 1956	21 July 1959	19 Aug 1960
SEALION	S 07	Cammell Laird & Co Ltd, Birkenhead	5 June 1958	31 Dec 1959	25 July 1961
WALRUS	S 08	Scotts (Shipbuilding) Co Ltd, Greenock	12 Feb 1958	22 Sept 1959	10 Feb 1961

Displacement, tons: 1 610 standard; 2 030 surfaced; 2 410 dived
Length, feet (metres): 241 *(73·5)* pp; 295·2 *(90·0)* oa
Beam, feet (metres): 26·5 *(8·1)*
Draught, feet (metres): 18 *(5·5)*
Torpedo tubes: 8—21 in *(533 mm)* (6 bow, 2 stern); 24 torpedoes carried
Main machinery: 2 Admiralty Standard Range 1, 16 VMS diesels; 3 680 bhp; 2 electric motors; 6 000 shp; 2 shafts
Speed, knots: 12 surfaced; 17 dived
Complement: 68 (6 officers, 62 men) in "Oberon" class 71 (6 officers, 65 men) in "Porpoise" class

As a result of the 1975 Defence Review the following have been retired some years before the end of hull life:—
Rorqual to disposal 1976
Grampus to reserve 1976
Narwhal to reserve 1977.

Cost: Running cost, at 1976 prices, £1·1 million per boat per year.

Construction: For the first time in British submarines plastic was used in the superstructure construction of the "Oberon" class. Before and abaft the bridge the superstructure is mainly of glass fibre laminate in most units of this class. The superstructure of *Orpheus* is of light alloy aluminium.

Engineering: Three bladed, 7 foot diameter propellers; 400 rpm.

Gunnery: "O" class submarines serving in the Far East carried a 20 mm Oerlikon gun during Indonesian Confrontation.

Modification: *Oberon* has been modified with deeper casing to house equipment for the initial training of personnel for nuclear powered submarines. Others of this class are currently undergoing modification.

Radar: Search: I-band.

Sonar: Types 186 and 187.

Transfer: The submarine of the "Oberon" class laid down on 27 Sept 1962 at HM Dockyard, Chatham as *Onyx* for the Royal Navy was launched on 29 Feb 1964 as *Ojibwa* for the Royal Canadian Navy. She was replaced by another "Oberon" class submarine named *Onyx* for the Royal Navy built by Cammell Laird, Birkenhead.
Cachalot paid off for disposal 2 Sept 1977 is to be transferred to Egypt after refit.

ORPHEUS   6/1977, Michael D. J. Lennon

SEALION   5/1977, John G. Callis

OBERON   4/1977, Wright and Logan

568 UK

AIRCRAFT CARRIERS

Note: *Eagle*, see Disposal List.

1 "ARK ROYAL" CLASS

Name	No.	Builders	Laid down	Launched	Commissioned
ARK ROYAL	R 09	Cammell Laird and Co Ltd, Birkenhead	3 May 1943	3 May 1950	25 Feb 1955

Displacement, tons: 43 060 standard; 50 786 full load
Length, feet (metres): 720·0 *(219·5)* pp; 845·0 *(257·6)* oa
Beam, feet (metres): 112·8 *(34·4)* hull
Draught, feet (metres): 36·0 *(11·0)*
Width, feet (metres): 168 *(51·2)*
Catapults: 2 improved steam
Aircraft: 30 fixed wing + 9 helicopters
Armour: 4·5 in belt; 4 in flight deck; 2·5 in hangar deck; 1·5 in hangar side
Main engines: Parsons single reduction geared turbines; 4 shafts; 152 000 shp
Boilers: 8 Admiralty three-drum type; pressure 400 psi *(28·1 kg/cm²)*; superheat 600°F *(316°C)*
Speed, knots: 31·5
Oil fuel, tons: 5 500 capacity
Complement: 260 officers (as Flagship); 2 380 ratings (with Air Staff)

First British aircraft carrier with steam catapults. Had first side lift in a British aircraft carrier, situated amidships on the port side and serving the upper hangar, but in 1959 this was removed, the deck park provided by the angled deck having obviated its necessity, leaving her with two centre lifts. In 1961, the deck landing projector sight, "Hilo" long range guidance system, and more powerful steam catapults were installed. Ship originally cost £21·428 million.
To be replaced by *Bulwark* when *Ark Royal* goes into reserve in Dec 1978.

Aircraft: Phantom FG1, 892 Squadron (12).
Buccaneer 2, 809 Squadron (14).
Gannet AEW, 849 B Squadron (4).
Sea King ASW, 824 Squadron (7).
Wessex 3, SAR (2).

Costs: Running costs (at 1976 prices) including aircraft costs £17·1 million per year.

Corvus: Four six-tubed Knebworth Corvus launchers for Chaff; single RFL Mk 5 51 mm rocket flare-launcher co-mounted.

Electrical: Ten generators—total output 9 000 kW.

Electronics: Fitted with Skynet and Tacan.

Engineering: Five bladed propellers of 15 feet diameter. 230 rpm.

Fuel: Capacity: 5 450 tons FFO, 560 tons diesel, 1 600 tons Avcat.
Consumption (average flying): 500 tons FFO, 20 tons diesel, 300 tons Avcat.

Modernisation: A three-years "special refit" and modernisation costing £32·5 million, from March 1967 to Feb 1970, enables her to operate both Phantom and Buccaneer Mk 2 aircraft. A fully angled deck 8·5 degrees off the centre line was fitted, involving two large extensions to the flight deck and the size of the island was increased. A new waist catapult with an increased launching speed allows her to operate aircraft at almost "nil" wind conditions. A new direct acting gear was installed to enable bigger aircraft to be landed at greater speeds.

Radar: Search: two Type 965.
Aircraft direction: one Type 982.
Heightfinder: two Type 983.
CCA: one set.
Navigation: one Type 975.

ARK ROYAL 6/1977, John G. Callis

ARK ROYAL 6/1977, Dr. Giorgio Arra

ARK ROYAL 6/1977, Wright and Logan

UK 569

1 HELICOPTER/VSTOL CARRIER

Name	No.	Builders	Laid down	Launched	Commissioned
HERMES	R 12	Vickers (Shipbuilding) Ltd, Barrow-in-Furness	21 June 1944	16 Feb 1953	18 Nov 1959

Displacement, tons: 23 900 standard; 28 700 full load
Length, feet (metres): 650·0 *(198·1)* pp; 744·3 *(226·9)* oa
Beam, feet (metres): 90·0 *(27·4)* hull
Draught, feet (metres): 28·5 *(8·7)*
Width, feet (metres): 160·0 *(48·8)* overall
Aircraft: A squadron of Sea King, and Wessex 5 helicopters
Armour: Reinforced flight deck (0·75 in); 1—2 in over magazines and machinery spares
Missiles: 2 quadruple Seacat launchers either side abaft the after lift
Main engines: Parsons geared turbines; 2 shafts; 76 000 shp
Boilers: 4 Admiralty three-drum type
Speed, knots: 28
Oil fuel, tons: 4 200 furnace; 320 diesel
Complement: 1 350 (143 officers, 1 207 ratings). In emergency a Commando can be embarked

Originally name ship of a class including *Albion, Bulwark* and *Centaur*, but design was modified to a more advanced type, incorporating new equipment and improved arrangements, including five post-war developments— angled deck, steam catapult, landing sight, 3D radar, and deck edge-lift. Air-conditioned. Embarked air squadrons and joined the Fleet summer 1960. Long refit 1964 to 1966, costing £10 million.

Aircraft: Current complement (1978): nine Sea Kings and four Wessex 5. From 1980: five Sea Harriers and nine Sea Kings. The armament for the Sea Harriers (the first squadron to form) will be the P3T ASM and Sidewinder AIM9L AAM both controlled by Blue Fox radar. By 1980 all Sea Kings are expected to be modified to the standard of the Mk 2 helicopters now in production. They will all have improved radar and communications, an acoustic processor and sono-buoys to supplement the dunking sonar.

Conversion: *Hermes* was taken in hand for conversion to a Commando Carrier on 1 March 1971, commissioning for this role on 17 Aug 1973. Fixed wing facilities such as catapults and arrester gear were removed. The whole performance cost over £25 million.
In 1976, as a result of the Defence Review and pressure from other NATO countries, *Hermes*' role was altered to that of A/S carrier with the retention of a capability for commando support. As a result she underwent yet another conversion at Devonport which was completed Jan 1977. How long she continues in this role depends on how much extra delay is experienced on the "Invincible" class but it seems likely that she will continue to run until at least 1984-85. When the Harriers are eventually in naval service they will fly from this ship amongst others. The first operational squadron is due for embarkation in *Hermes* in 1980.

Electrical: Five turbo and four diesel alternators = 9 000 kW.

Engineering: 15 ft 6 in diameter propellers; 230 rpm.

Flight deck: Angled 6·5 degree off centre line of ship, the biggest angle that could be contrived in an aircraft carrier of this size. Strengthened to take Harrier aircraft.

Radar: Surveillance: one Type 965 with single AKE-1 array.
Search: one Type 993.
Navigation: one Type 975.
Fire control: two GWS 22.
Tacan beacon.

Sonar: Type 184.

Turning circle: 800 yards.

HERMES *10/1977, C. and S. Taylor*

HERMES *6/1977, John G. Callis*

1 HELICOPTER/VSTOL CARRIER

Name	No.	Builders	Laid down	Launched	Commissioned
BULWARK	R 08	Harland & Wolff Ltd, Belfast	10 May 1945	22 June 1948	4 Nov 1954

Displacement, tons: 23 300 standard; 27 705 full load
Length, feet (metres): 650 *(198·1)* pp; 737·8 *(224·9)* oa
Beam, feet (metres): 90 *(27·4)* hull
Draught, feet (metres): 28 *(8·5)*
Width, feet (metres): 123·5 *(37·7)* overall
Aircraft: 20 Wessex and Sioux helicopters
Landing craft: 4 LCVP
Guns: 8—40 mm (twins) Bofors on UK Mk V mountings
Main engines: Parsons geared turbines; 76 000 shp; 2 shafts
Boilers: 4 Admiralty three-drum
Speed, knots: 28
Oil fuel, tons: 3 880 furnace; 320 diesel
Complement: 980 plus 750 Royal Marine Commando and troops

Former fixed-wing aircraft carrier. Converted into commando ship in Portsmouth Dockyard, Jan 1959 to Jan 1960. Her arrester gear and catapults have been removed but, with a helicopter and VSTOL capability she was placed in reserve in April 1976 as a result of the 1975 Defence Review. In late 1977 it was decided to reactivate *Bulwark* to cover the period after *Ark Royal* pays off in Dec 1978 and before *Invincible* enters service. Due to manpower shortages her commissioning will have to await the availability of *Ark Royal*'s complement.

BULWARK *7/1973, C. and S. Taylor*

570 UK

0 + 2 ANTI-SUBMARINE CRUISERS

Name	No.	Builders	Laid down	Launched	Commissioned
INVINCIBLE	CAH 1	Vickers (Shipbuilding) Ltd, Barrow-in-Furness	20 July 1973	3 May 1977	?1979
ILLUSTRIOUS	CAH 2	Swan Hunter Ltd, Wallsend	7 Oct 1976	—	?1980

Displacement, tons: 16 000 standard; 19 500 full load
Length, feet (metres): 632 pp *(192·9)*; 677 oa *(206·6)*
Beam, feet (metres): 90 wl *(27·5)*; 104·6 deck *(31·9)*
Draught, feet (metres): ?24 *(7·3)*
Flight deck length, feet (metres): 550 *(167·8)*
Aircraft: Total of 15: 10 Sea King helicopters (also to carry 5 Sea Harriers)
Missile launchers: Twin Sea Dart (see notes)
Main engines: 4 Olympus gas turbines; 112 000 shp; 2 shafts (reversible gear box)
Speed, knots: 28
Range, miles: 5 000 at 18 knots
Complement: 900 (31 officers, 265 senior ratings, 604 junior ratings) (excluding aircrew)

The history of this class is a long and complex one starting almost sixteen years ago. The first of class, the result of many compromises, was ordered from Vickers on 17 April 1973. At that time completion might have been expected in 1977-78 but changes in design and labour problems have delayed this by probably two years. The results of this must be the running-on of the "Tiger" class and *Hermes* to provide the necessary aircraft platforms at sea. The order for the second ship, to be named *Illustrious*, was placed on 14 May 1976, whilst a third is now planned. Present indications are that *Invincible* will replace *Bulwark* and *Illustrious* the two "Tiger" class.
The primary task of this class, apart from providing a command centre for maritime air forces, is the operation of both helicopters and VTOL/STOL aircraft. Provision has been made for sufficiently large lifts and hangars to accommodate the next generation of both these aircraft.
The design allows for an open foc'sle head and a slightly angled deck which will allow the Sea Dart launcher to be set almost amidships.

Aircraft: The second squadron of Sea Harriers will be embarked in *Invincible* and subsequently all such squadrons will be deployed in ships of this class. (See *Aircraft* note under *Hermes* for further details.)

INVINCIBLE at launch   5/1977, Vickers Ltd.

Cost: Although originally estimated at approximately £60 million the estimated cost of *Invincible* at 1976 prices = £167 million.

Design: In 1976/77 an amendment was incorporated to allow for the transport and landing of a Commando.

Flight deck: Various angles of lift are being tested for the forward end of the flight-deck (ski-jump) to allow V/STOL aircraft of greater all-up weight to operate more efficiently. It is not known whether this will be incorporated in *Invincible*.

Missiles: Original drawing below shows four Exocet launchers subsequently apparently deleted.

Radar: Surveillance: one Type 965 with double AKE 1 array.
Search: one Type 992 R.
Fire control: two Type 909 for Sea Dart.
Navigation: one Type 1006.

Sonar: Type 184.

INVINCIBLE   1977, Vickers Ltd.

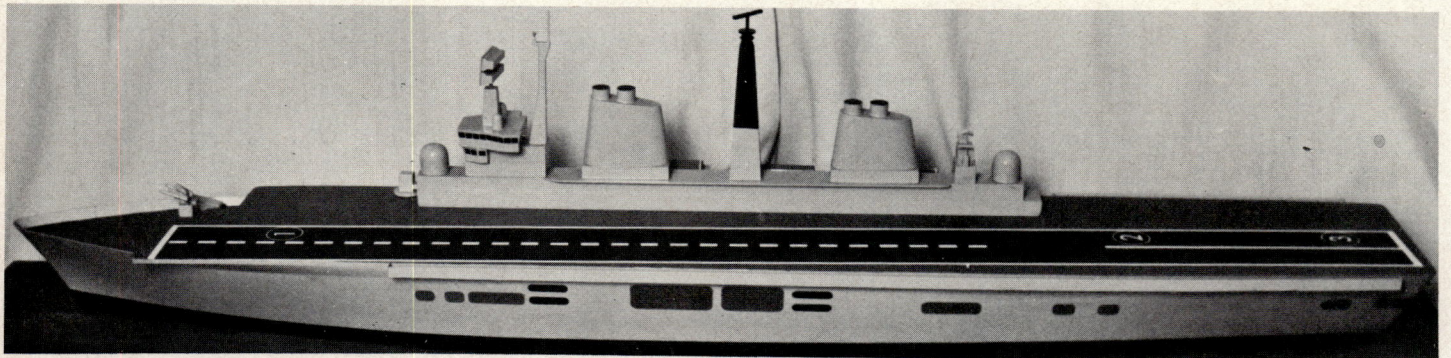

INVINCIBLE model   1973, MOD

UK 571

CRUISERS

2 "TIGER" CLASS (HELICOPTER CRUISERS)

Name	No.	Builders	Laid down	Launched	Commissioned
TIGER (ex-*Bellerophon*)	C 20	John Brown Ltd, Clydebank	1 Oct 1941	25 Oct 1945	18 Mar 1959
BLAKE (ex-*Tiger*, ex-*Blake*)	C 99	Fairfield SB & Eng, Govan	17 Aug 1942	20 Dec 1945	8 Mar 1961

Displacement, tons: 9 500 standard; 12 080 full load
Length, feet (metres): 538·0 *(164·0)* pp; 550·0 *(167·6)* wl; 566·5 *(172·8)* oa
Beam, feet (metres): 64·0 *(19·5)*
Draught, feet (metres): 23·0 *(7·0)*
Aircraft: 4 Sea King helicopters
Missile launchers: 2 quadruple Seacat
Guns: 2—6 in *(152 mm)* (1 twin); 2—3 in *(76 mm)* (twin)
Armour: Belt 3·5 in—3·2 in *(89–83 mm)*; deck 2 in *(51 mm)*; turret 3 in—1 in *(76–25 mm)*
Main engines: 4 Parsons geared turbines; 4 shafts; 80 000 shp
Boilers: 4 Admiralty three-drum type
Speed, knots: 30
Oil fuel, tons: 1 850
Range, miles: 2 000 at 30 knots; 4 000 at 20 knots; 6 500 at 13 knots
Complement: 85 officers, 800 ratings

This design was originally an improvement on that of *Superb/Swiftsure. Bellerophon* and *Hawke* of a similar design were cancelled in 1945-46 as were the projected ships *Centurion, Edgar, Mars* and *Neptune.* There was much juggling of names between ships; *Blake* was renamed *Tiger* in Dec 1944 and back to *Blake* in Feb 1945.
Defence was renamed *Lion* in Oct 1957. *Bellerophon* was renamed *Tiger* in Feb 1945. Work on all three of the surviving ships was suspended in July 1946, the decision to complete them being announced on 15 Oct 1954. Subsequent redesign delayed work even further and it was not completed until 1959-61. By this time *Tiger* had cost £13·113 million and *Blake* £14·940 million. The next stage was conversion to command helicopter cruisers (official title). *Lion* was not converted and was eventually sent for scrap in April 1975. *Blake* was transformed by Portsmouth Dockyard at a cost of £5·5 million from early 1965 until recommissioning on 23 April 1969. *Tiger* was in hand from 1968 to 1972 at Devonport Dockyard, her cost reaching the staggering sum of £13·25 million. (As a considerable amount of equipment from *Lion* was used in *Tiger's* conversion the latter was unofficially known for a time as "Liger").

Electrical: Four turbo-generators provide 4 000 kW AC, the first time this type of power had been used in British cruisers although it was already in use in the "Daring" class destroyers.

Engineering: Main machinery is largely automatic and can be remotely controlled. Steam conditions 400 psi pressure and 640°F. Propellers 11 feet diameter, 285 rpm.

Radar: Search: one Type 965 and one Type 993.
Height finder: one Type 277 or 278.
Fire control: four MRS 3 fire control directors.
Navigation: one Type 975.

Turning circle: 800 yards.

BLAKE 6/1977, C. and S. Taylor

TIGER 6/1977, John G. Callis

TIGER 6/1977, C. and S. Taylor

572 UK

LIGHT CRUISERS

1 TYPE 82

Name	No.	Builders	Laid down	Launched	Commissioned
BRISTOL	D 23	Swan Hunter Ltd.	15 Nov 1967	30 June 1969	31 Mar 1973

Displacement, tons: 6 100 standard; 7 100 full load
Length, feet (metres): 490·0 (149·4) wl; 507·0 (154·5) oa
Beam, feet (metres): 55·0 (16·8)
Draught, feet (metres): 16·8 (5·2); 23 (7) (sonar dome)
Aircraft: Landing platform for 1 Wasp helicopter
Missile launchers: 1 twin Sea Dart GWS 30 launcher aft
A/S weapons: 1 Ikara single launcher forward; 1 Limbo three-barrelled depth charge mortar (Mark 10) aft
Guns: 1—4·5 in (115 mm) Mark 8 forward; 2—20 mm
Main engines: COSAG arrangement (combined steam and gas turbines) 2 sets Standard Range geared steam turbines, 30 000 shp; 2 Bristol-Siddeley marine Olympus TMIA gas turbines, 30 000 shp; 2 shafts
Boilers: 2
Speed, knots: 30
Fuel, tons: 900
Range, miles: 5 000 at 18 knots
Complement: 407 (29 officers, 378 ratings)

Designed around Sea Dart GWS 30 weapons system. Fully stabilised to present a steady weapon platform. The gas turbines provide emergency power and high speed boost. The machinery is remotely-controlled from a ship control centre. Automatic steering, obviating the need for a quartermaster. Many labour-saving items of equipment fitted to make the most efficient and economical use of manpower resulting in a smaller ship's company for tonnage than any previous warship. Fitted with Action Data Automation Weapon System. Started trials 10 April 1972. Remainder of class cancelled owing to high cost and cancellation of aircraft-carrier building programme for which they were intended as A/A escorts. Officially listed as "destroyer" which is in some measure borne out by her limited fire-power, lack of embarked helicopter, limited ESM, as well as lack of jammers and Knebworth Corvus launchers.

Appearance: Three funnels, one amidships and two aft abreast the mainmast.

A/S weapons: Ikara is GWS 40.

Communications: By GEC-Marconi to include SCOT satellite system compatible with both SKYNET and the US Defence satellites.

Cost: £22·5 million (£27 million overall). GEC-Marconi equipment for radar, weapons and communications cost over £3 million.

Missiles: The Sea Dart ship missile system has a reasonable anti-ship capability.

Radar: Surveillance: one Type 965 with double AKE array and IFF.
Search: one Type 992.
Fire control: two Type 909 (Sea Dart)
Navigation: one Type 1006; One Type 978.

Sonar: Types 162, 170, 182, 184, 185, 189.

BRISTOL   2/1978, Michael D. J. Lennon

BRISTOL   2/1978, Michael D. J. Lennon

BRISTOL   9/1975, John G. Callis

7 "COUNTY" CLASS

Name	No.	Builders	Laid down	Launched	Commissioned
DEVONSHIRE	D 02	Cammell Laird & Co Ltd, Birkenhead	9 Mar 1959	10 June 1960	15 Nov 1962
KENT	D 12	Harland & Wolff Ltd, Belfast	1 Mar 1960	27 Sept 1961	15 Aug 1963
LONDON	D 16	Swan, Hunter & Wigham Richardson, Wallsend	26 Feb 1960	7 Dec 1961	4 Nov 1963
ANTRIM	D 18	Fairfield SB & Eng Co Ltd, Govan	20 Jan 1966	19 Oct 1967	14 July 1970
GLAMORGAN*	D 19	Vickers (Shipbuilding) Ltd, Newcastle upon Tyne	13 Sept 1962	9 July 1964	11 Oct 1966
FIFE	D 20	Fairfield SB & Eng Co Ltd, Govan	1 June 1962	9 July 1964	21 June 1966
NORFOLK	D 21	Swan, Hunter & Wigham Richardson, Wallsend	15 Mar 1966	16 Nov 1967	7 Mar 1970

* Refit

Displacement, tons: 5 440 standard; 6 200 full load
Length, feet (metres): 505·0 *(153·9)* wl; 520·5 *(158·7)* oa
Beam, feet (metres): 54·0 *(16·5)*
Draught, feet (metres): 20·5 *(6·3)*
Aircraft: 1 Wessex helicopter
Missile launchers: 4 Exocet in four ships (see *Missiles* note): 1 twin Seaslug aft; 2 quadruple Seacat either side abreast hangar
Guns: 4—4·5 in *(115 mm)*, 2 twin turrets forward; 2—20 mm, (single) (2—4·5 only in ships with Exocet)
Main engines: Combined steam and gas turbines; 2 sets geared steam turbines, 30 000 shp; 4 gas turbines, 30 000 shp; 2 shafts
Boilers: 2 Babcock & Wilcox
Speed, knots: 30
Complement: 471 (33 officers and 438 men)

Fife, Glamorgan, Antrim and *Norfolk,* have the more powerful Seaslug II systems. All fitted with stablisers and are fully air-conditioned. Original cost varied from £13·8 million *(Hampshire)* to £16·8 million *(Antrim)*. Officially rated as "destroyers".

Appearance: *Kent* and *London* have mainmast stepped further aft than remainder. The last four of the class have distinctive tubular foremast and twin AKE radar aerial.

Costs: Running costs (at 1976 prices, excluding helicopter) £4·9 million per ship).

Disposal: As a result of the Defence Review *Hampshire* was paid off in April 1976—at least seven years before she might have been expected on the disposal list.

Electrical: Two 1 000 kW turbo-alternators and three gas turbines alternators total 3 750 kW, at 440 V a/c SCOT fitted in *London*.

Engineering: These are the first ships of their size to have COSAG (combined steam and gas turbine machinery). Boilers work at a pressure of 700 psi and a temperature of 950°F. The steam and gas turbines are geared to the same shaft. Each shaft set consists of a high pressure and low pressure steam turbine of 15 000 shp combined output plus two G.6 gas turbines each of 7 500 shp. The gas turbines are able to develop their full power from cold within a few minutes, enabling ships lying in harbour without steam to get under way instantly in emergency.

Gunnery: The 4·5 in guns are radar controlled fully automatic dual-purpose. The 20 mm guns were added for picket duties in S. E. Asia, but have been retained for general close range duties.

Missiles: Four Exocet fitted in *Norfolk, Antrim, Glamorgan* and *Fife*. No reloads carried. *Norfolk* Exocet trials on French missile range (Mediterranean) in April 1974.
Approx 36 Seaslug missiles carried.

Radar: Air search: one type 965 (double AKE-2 array in *Norfolk, Glamorgan, Antrim* and *Fife*—remainder single AKE-1).
Surveillance: one Type 992.
Height finder: one Type 277.
Seaslug fire control: one Type 901.
Gunnery fire control: MRS 3 (forward) with Type 903.
Seacat fire control: GWS 23 in *London;* GWS 22 with Type 904 in *Kent, Norfolk, Antrim, Fife* and *Glamorgan;* GWS 21 in *Devonshire*.
Navigation: one Type 975.

Sonar: Type 184.

KENT 5/1977, Wright and Logan

ANTRIM 6/1977, Wright and Logan

GLAMORGAN 6/1977, Dr. Giorgio Arra

DEVONSHIRE 6/1977, Michael D. J. Lennon

LONDON 6/1977, C. and S. Taylor

574 UK

DESTROYERS

5 + 5 "SHEFFIELD" (TYPE 42) CLASS

Name	No.	Builders	Laid down	Launched	Commissioned
SHEFFIELD	D 80	Vickers (Shipbuilding) Ltd, Barrow-in-Furness	15 Jan 1970	10 June 1971	16 Feb 1975
BIRMINGHAM	D 86	Cammell Laird & Co Ltd, Birkenhead	28 Mar 1972	30 July 1973	3 Dec 1976
NEWCASTLE	D 87	Swan Hunter Ltd, Wallsend on Tyne	21 Feb 1973	24 April 1975	23 Mar 1978
GLASGOW	D 88	Swan Hunter Ltd, Wallsend on Tyne	7 Mar 1974	14 April 1976	1978
CARDIFF	D 108	Vickers (Shipbuilding) Ltd Barrow-in-Furness (see note)	3 Nov 1972	22 Feb 1974	1978
COVENTRY	D 118	Cammell Laird & Co Ltd, Birkenhead	22 Mar 1973	21 June 1974	1978
EXETER	—	Swan Hunter Ltd, Wallsend on Tyne	1976	—	—
SOUTHAMPTON	—	Vosper Thornycroft Ltd	21 Oct 1976	—	—
NOTTINGHAM	—	Vosper Thornycroft Ltd	—	—	—
	—	Cammell Laird & Co Ltd, Birkenhead	—	—	—

Displacement, tons: 3 150 standard; 4 100 full load
Length, feet (metres): 392·0 *(119·5)* wl; 410·0 *(125·0)* oa
Beam, feet (metres): 46 *(14)*
Draught, feet (metres): 19 *(5·8)*
Aircraft: 1 Lynx Mk 2 helicopter
Missile launchers: 1 twin Sea Dart medium range surface-to-air (surface-to-surface capability) GWS 30 system
Guns: 1—4·5 in automatic, Mark 8, 2—20 mm Oerlikon; 2 saluting
A/S weapons: Helicopter-launched Mk 44 torpedoes; 6 A/S torpedo tubes (triples) for Mk 46 (except in *Sheffield*)
Main engines: COGOG arrangement of Rolls-Royce Olympus gas turbines for full power 50 000 shp; 2 Rolls-Royce Tyne gas turbines for cruising 8 000 shp; cp propellers; 2 shafts
Speed, knots: 30
Range: 4 500 miles at 18 knots
Complement: 299 (26 officers, 80 senior rates, 193 junior rates) (accommodation for 312)

This is a class of all gas-turbine ships fitted with four sets of stabilisers and twin rudders. The helicopter will carry the Skua (CK 834) air-to-surface weapon for use against lightly defended surface ship targets such as fast patrol boats. Advantages include ability to reach maximum speed with great rapidity, reduction in space and weight and 25 per cent reduction in technical manpower. Originally to cost approximately £23 million per ship, although this may well be increased by delays and rising costs of raw materials and labour.
Exeter ordered 22 Jan 1976. *Southampton* ordered 18 March 1976. *Nottingham* ordered 1 March 1977 and tenth on 27 May 1977.
Glasgow damaged by fire whilst fitting out 23 Sept 1976.
Newcastle started trials June 1977, handed over 27 Feb 1978. Further orders are planned for ships of this class which may possibly be of slightly increased length.

Completion: *Cardiff*, whose completion was delayed by lack of man-power at Vickers Ltd, Barrow, was towed to Swan Hunters, Ltd, Wallsend in Feb 1976 for completion in 1978.

Costs: Building costs—*Sheffield* £23·2 million; *Birmingham* £30·9 million. Running costs (1976 prices, excluding helicopter) £5·2 million per year per ship.

Electronics: Twin SCOT Skynet satellite communication aerials; ADAWS 4 for coordination of action information. ECM D/F.

Engineering: Considerable automation has allowed a number of machinery spaces to be operated unmanned. Propellers by Stone Manganese (Type XX).

Radar: Search: one Type 965 with double AKE-2 array and IFF. Surveillance and target indication: one Type 992Q.
Sea Dart fire control and target: two Type 909
Navigation, HDWS and helicopter control: one Type 1006

Sonar: Type 184 hull mounted. Type 162 classification.

BIRMINGHAM 6/1977, Dr. Giorgio Arra

NEWCASTLE 2/1978, Michael D. J. Lennon

BIRMINGHAM 6/1977, John G. Callis

SHEFFIELD 6/1977, C. and S. Taylor

UK 575

FRIGATES

8 "AMAZON" (TYPE 21) CLASS

Name	No.	Builders	Laid down	Launched	Commissioned
AMAZON	F 169	Vosper Thornycroft Ltd, Woolston	6 Nov 1969	26 April 1971	11 May 1974
ANTELOPE	F 170	Vosper Thornycroft Ltd, Woolston	23 Mar 1971	16 Mar 1972	19 July 1975
ACTIVE	F 171	Vosper Thornycroft Ltd, Woolston	23 July 1971	23 Nov 1972	17 June 1977
AMBUSCADE	F 172	Yarrow (Shipbuilders) Ltd, Glasgow	1 Sept 1971	18 Jan 1973	5 Sept 1975
ARROW	F 173	Yarrow (Shipbuilders) Ltd, Glasgow	28 Sept 1972	5 Feb 1974	29 July 1976
ALACRITY	F 174	Yarrow (Shipbuilders) Ltd, Glasgow	5 Mar 1973	18 Sept 1974	2 July 1977
ARDENT	F 184	Yarrow (Shipbuilders) Ltd, Glasgow	26 Feb 1974	9 May 1975	13 Oct 1977
AVENGER	F 185	Yarrow (Shipbuilders) Ltd, Glasgow	30 Oct 1974	20 Nov 1975	April 1978

Displacement, tons: 2 750 standard; 3 250 full load
Length, feet (metres): 360·0 *(109·7)* wl; 384·0 *(117·0)* oa
Beam, feet (metres): 41·8 *(12·7)*
Draught, feet (metres): 19 *(5·8)*
Aircraft: 1 Lynx Mk 2 helicopter (see note)
Missile launchers: 1 quadruple Seacat surface-to-air; 4 Exocet MM 38
Guns: 1—4·5 in Mk 8; 2—20 mm Oerlikon (singles)
A/S weapons: Helicopter launched torpedoes; 6 (2 triple) torpedo tubes for Mk 46 (from F 171 onwards)
Main engines: COGOG arrangement of 2 Rolls-Royce Olympus gas turbines 56 000 bhp; 2 Rolls-Royce Tyne gas turbines for cruising 8 500 shp; 2 shafts; cp, five-bladed propellers
Speed, knots: 32; 18 on Tyne GTs
Range, miles: 3 500 at 18 knots; 1 200 at 30 knots
Complement: 177 (13 officers, and 164 ratings) (accommodation for 192)

A contract was awarded to Vosper Thornycroft, on 27 Feb 1968 for the design of a patrol frigate to be prepared in full collaboration with Yarrow Ltd. This is the first custom built gas turbine frigate (designed and constructed as such from the keel up, as opposed to conversion) and the first warship designed by commercial firms for many years.

A/S weapons: Torpedo tubes to be fitted in all ships.

Costs: Building costs between £14·4 million *(Antelope)* and £20·2 million *(Arrow)*. Running costs (at 1976 prices, excluding helicopter) £3·3 million per ship per year.

Electronics: SCOT satellite communication to be fitted in last four ships, CAAIS fitted.

Helicopter: Provided with Wasp until Lynx is available.

Missiles: Although Seawolf was planned for the last four, it was not ready in time so all will mount Seacat. Presumably retro-fitting may take place at subsequent major refits. All fitted with Exocet.

Radar: Surveillance and target Indicator: one Type 992Q.
Navigation: one Type 978.
Seacat control: two GWS 24.
Gun fire control: Orion RTN-10X WSA 4 system.
IFF Interrogator: Cossor Type 1010.
IFF Transponder: Plessey PTR 461.

Sonar: Type 184M hull mounted.
Type 162M classification.

ACTIVE *9/1977, Michael D. J. Lennon*

ARDENT *11/1977, Michael D. J. Lennon*

AMAZON *6/1977, C. and S. Taylor*

1 + 3 "BROADSWORD" CLASS (TYPE 22)

Name	No.	Builders	Laid down	Launched	Commissioned
BROADSWORD	F 88	Yarrow (Shipbuilders) Ltd, Glasgow	7 Feb 1975	12 May 1976	Late 1978?
BATTLEAXE	—	Yarrow (Shipbuilders) Ltd, Glasgow	1976	18 May 1977	—
BRILLIANT	—	Yarrow (Shipbuilders) Ltd, Glasgow	1977	—	—
BOXER	—	Yarrow (Shipbuilders) Ltd, Glasgow	1978	—	—

Displacement, tons: 3 500 standard; 4 000 full load
Dimensions, feet (metres): 430 oa × 48·5 × 14 *(131·2 × 14·8 × 4·3)*
Aircraft: 2 Lynx Mk 2 helicopters with ASM and A/S torpedoes
Missile launchers: 2 Sea Wolf surface-to-air systems; 4 Exocet launchers forward
Guns: 2—40 mm
A/S weapons: 6 (2 triple) Mk 32 torpedo tubes for Mk 46; helicopter-carried A/S torpedoes
Main engines: COGOG arrangement of 2 Rolls-Royce Olympus gas turbines; 56 000 bhp and 2 Rolls-Royce Tyne gas turbines; 8 500 bhp; 2 shafts
Speed, knots: 30+ (18 on Tynes)
Range, miles: 4 500 at 18 knots (on Tynes)
Complement: 250 (approx)

Designed as successors to the "Leander" class, the construction of which ceased with the completion of the scheduled programme of 26 ships. Order for the first of class, Broadsword, was placed on 26 Feb 1974, Battleaxe ordered 5 Sept 1975. Order for Brilliant 7 Sept 1976 and Boxer on 21 Oct 1977. This class is primarily designed for A/S operations and is capable of acting as OTC and helicopter control ship. These are the first major ships for the RN which have no main gun armament (apart from the "Blackwood" class.)
It is reported that fourteen of this class are planned and the fifth ship is to be ordered in 1978.

Radar: Surveillance: two Type 967/8.
Navigation: one Type 1006.

Sonar: Type 2016.

BROADSWORD model *1974, MOD*

576 UK

26 "LEANDER" CLASS

IKARA GROUP

Name	No.	Builders	Laid down	Launched	Commissioned
AURORA	F 10	John Brown & Co (Clydebank) Ltd	1 June 1961	28 Nov 1962	9 April 1964
EURYALUS	F 15	Scotts Shipbuilding & Eng Co, Greenock	2 Nov 1961	6 June 1963	16 Sept 1964
GALATEA	F 18	Swan Hunter & Wigham Richardson, Tyne	29 Dec 1961	23 May 1963	25 April 1964
ARETHUSA	F 38	J. Samuel White & Co Ltd, Cowes	7 Sept 1962	5 Nov 1963	24 Nov 1965
NAIAD	F 39	Yarrow & Co Ltd, Scotstoun, Glasgow	30 Oct 1962	4 Nov 1963	15 Mar 1965
LEANDER	F 109	Harland & Wolff Ltd, Belfast	10 April 1959	28 June 1961	27 Mar 1963
AJAX	F 114	Cammell Laird & Co Ltd, Birkenhead	12 Oct 1959	16 Aug 1962	10 Dec 1963
PENELOPE (see "Trials" note)*	F 127	Vickers-Armstrong Ltd, Tyne	14 Mar 1961	17 Aug 1962	31 Oct 1963

EXOCET GROUP

Name	No.	Builders	Laid down	Launched	Commissioned
CLEOPATRA	F 28	HM Dockyard, Devonport	19 June 1963	25 Mar 1964	4 Jan 1966
SIRIUS	F 40	HM Dockyard, Portsmouth	9 Aug 1963	22 Sept 1964	15 June 1966
PHOEBE	F 42	Alex Stephen & Sons Ltd, Glasgow	3 June 1963	8 July 1964	15 April 1966
MINERVA*	F 45	Vickers-Armstrong Ltd, Tyne	25 July 1963	19 Dec 1964	14 May 1966
DANAE*	F 47	HM Dockyard, Devonport	16 Dec 1964	31 Oct 1965	7 Sept 1967
JUNO	F 52	John I. Thornycroft Ltd, Woolston	16 July 1964	24 Nov 1965	18 July 1967
ARGONAUT*	F 56	Hawthorn Leslie Ltd, Hebburn-on-Tyne	27 Nov 1964	8 Feb 1966	17 Aug 1967
DIDO*	F 104	Yarrow & Co Ltd, Scotstoun, Glasgow	2 Dec 1959	22 Dec 1961	18 Sept 1963

BROAD-BEAMED GROUP

Name	No.	Builders	Laid down	Launched	Commissioned
ACHILLES	F 12	Yarrow & Co Ltd, Scotstoun, Glasgow	1 Dec 1967	21 Nov 1968	9 July 1970
DIOMEDE	F 16	Yarrow & Co Ltd, Scotstoun, Glasgow	30 Jan 1968	15 April 1969	2 April 1971
ANDROMEDA*	F 57	HM Dockyard, Portsmouth	25 May 1966	24 May 1967	2 Dec 1968
HERMIONE	F 58	Alex Stephen & Sons Ltd, Glasgow	6 Dec 1965	26 April 1967	11 July 1969
JUPITER	F 60	Yarrow & Co Ltd, Scotstoun, Glasgow	3 Oct 1966	4 Sept 1967	9 Aug 1969
BACCHANTE	F 69	Vickers-Armstrong Ltd, Tyne	27 Oct 1966	29 Feb 1968	17 Oct 1969
APOLLO	F 70	Yarrow & Co Ltd, Scotstoun, Glasgow	1 May 1969	15 Oct 1970	28 May 1972
SCYLLA	F 71	HM Dockyard, Devonport	17 May 1967	8 Aug 1968	12 Feb 1970
ARIADNE	F 72	Yarrow & Co Ltd, Scotstoun, Glasgow	1 Nov 1969	10 Sept 1971	10 Feb 1973
CHARYBDIS	F 75	Harland & Wolff Ltd, Belfast	27 Jan 1967	28 Feb 1968	2 June 1969

* Refit

Displacement, tons: 2 450 standard; 2 860 full load (Ikara); 3 200 full load (Exocet group); 2 500 standard; 2 962 full load (Broad-beamed)
Length, feet (metres): 360 (109·7) wl; 372 (113·4) oa
Beam, feet (metres): 41 (12·5) (Leanders) 43 (13·1) (Broad-beamed)
Draught, feet (metres): 18 (5·5); 18·5 (5·6) (Exocet group)
Aircraft: 1 Lynx Mk 2 or Wasp helicopter
Missiles: Ikara Group: 2 quad Seacat
 Exocet Group: 4 MM 38 Exocet (forward); 3 quad Seacat (2 aft, 1 forward)
 Broad-Beamed Group: 1 quad Seacat
Guns: Ikara Group: 2—40 mm
 Exocet Group: 2—40 mm
 Broad-Beamed Group: 2—4·5 in (115 mm) (twin); 2—20 mm
A/S weapons: Ikara Group: Ikara (forward); 1 Limbo (aft)
 Exocet Group: 2 triple Mk 32 torpedo tubes
 Broad-Beamed Group: 1 Limbo
Main engines: 2 double reduction geared turbines; 2 shafts; 30 000 shp (see Notes)
Boilers: 2
Speed, knots: 29
Oil fuel, tons: 460
Range, miles: 4 000 at 15 knots
Complement: 251 (Leanders); 260 (Broad-beamed) (19 officers, 241 ratings)

This class, whose construction extended over ten years, was an improvement on the Type 12. As originally designed there were several significant improvements—a helicopter, VDS and long-range air warning radar being the most important. Recently a number of conversions have been put in hand (see Notes below).

Conversions:
(a) Ikara Group
Leander (Devonport) completed Dec 1972;
Ajax (Devonport) completed Sept 1973;
Galatea (Devonport) completed Sept 1974;
Naiad (Devonport) completed July 1975;
Euryalus (Devonport) completed March 1976;
Aurora (Chatham) completed March 1976;
Arethusa (Portsmouth) completed Nov 1976;
Penelope on completion of Seawolf trials.
(b) Exocet Group
Cleopatra (Devonport) completed 28 Nov 1975;
Phoebe (Devonport) completed April 1977;
Sirius (Devonport) completed Oct 1977.
Dido (Devonport) completed Oct 1978;
Argonaut (Devonport) completed Oct 1978;
Minerva (Chatham) completed Oct 1978;
Juno (Portsmouth) completed Oct 1978;
Danae (Devonport) completed Oct 1978;
(c) The conversion of the Broad-beamed Group started with Andromeda (late 1977) and will include the provision of four MM 38 Exocet launchers, the Seawolf SAM system, improved sonar and modern EW equipment.

Costs: Building costs—earlier ships averaged £4·7 million, later ones £7·0 million. Running costs (at 1976 prices, excluding helicopter) £2·9 million per ship per year.

Electrical: 440 volts, 60 cycle AC. 1 900 kW in earlier ships, 2 500 KW in later ones.

Electronics: SCOT satellite communications being fitted at later conversions.

Engineering: The first ten have Y-100 machinery, the remainder of the "Leanders" Y-136. "Broad-beamed Leanders" have Y-160 machinery.

Gunnery: 4·5 in turret removed in Exocet and Ikara conversions and in Penelope. 40 mm are not fitted in unconverted ships mounting Seacat. Conversions mount 2 single 40 mm abaft the bridge.

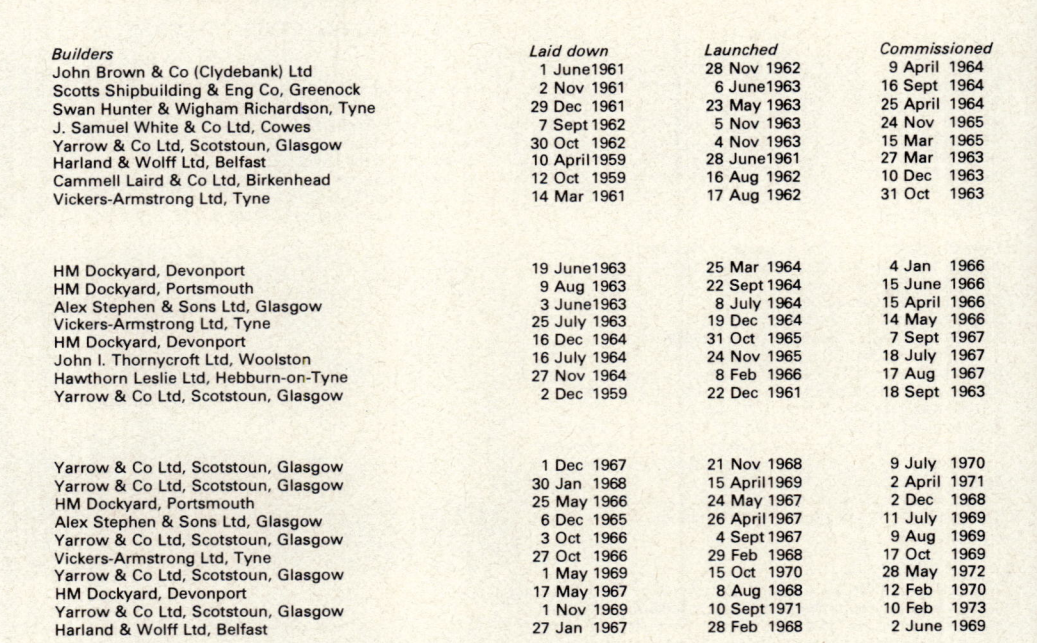

ARETHUSA (Ikara Group)   6/1977, C. and S. Taylor

PHOEBE (Exocet Group)   6/1977, Wright and Logan

CHARYBDIS (Broad-Beamed Group)   6/1977 C. and S. Taylor

Radar: Air surveillance: one Type 965 with single AKE array (except in Ikara ships)
Combined air/surface warning: one Type 993.
Fire control: MRS 3/GWS 22.
Navigation: one Type 975. Type 1006 (conversions)

Sonar: VDS was originally fitted in all but Diomede. In some the VDS has been removed leaving the well—in others the well has been plated over to provide extra accommodation for RMs. Can be replaced. Currently all Ikara conversions have VDS.

Trials: Seawolf trials are continuing in Penelope who has had her armament removed and will undergo Ikara conversion on completion of trials.

UK 577

7 "TRIBAL" CLASS (TYPE 81)

Name	No.	Builders	Laid down	Launched	Commissioned
ASHANTI	F 117	Yarrow & Co Ltd, Scotstoun	15 Jan 1958	9 Mar 1959	23 Nov 1961
ESKIMO	F 119	J. Samuel White & Co Ltd, Cowes	22 Oct 1958	20 Mar 1960	21 Feb 1963
GURKHA	F 122	J. I. Thornycroft & Co Ltd, Woolston	3 Nov 1958	11 July 1960	13 Feb 1963
ZULU	F 124	Alex Stephen & Sons Ltd, Govan	13 Dec 1960	3 July 1962	17 April 1964
MOHAWK	F 125	Vickers-Armstrong Ltd, Barrow	23 Dec 1960	5 April 1962	29 Nov 1963
NUBIAN	F 131	HM Dockyard, Portsmouth	7 Sept 1959	6 Sept 1960	9 Oct 1962
TARTAR*	F 133	HM Dockyard, Devonport	22 Oct 1959	19 Sept 1960	26 Feb 1962

* Refit

Displacement, tons: 2 300 standard; 2 700 full load
Length, feet (metres): 350·0 *(106·7)* wl; 360·0 *(109·7)* oa
Beam, feet (metres): 42·3 *(12·9)*
Draught, feet (metres): 18 *(5·5)*
Aircraft: 1 Wasp helicopter
Missile launchers: 2 quadruple Seacats
Guns: 2—4·5 in (singles); 2—20 mm
A/S weapons: 1 Limbo three-barrelled mortar
Main engines: Combined steam and gas turbine; Metrovick steam turbine; 12 500 shp; Metrovick gas turbine; 7 500 shp; 1 shaft
Boilers: 1 Babcock & Wilcox (plus 1 auxiliary boiler)
Speed, knots: 25
Oil fuel, tons: 400
Complement: 253 (13 officers and 240 ratings)

Ashanti, Eskimo and *Gurkha* were ordered under the 1955-56 estimates, *Nubian* and *Tartar* 1956-57, and *Mohawk* and *Zulu* 1957-58. Designed as self-contained units for service in such areas as the Persian Gulf. *Ashanti* cost £5·22 million. Some still have 4 in flare rocket launchers. *Ashanti* in Stand-by Squadron.

Construction: All-welded prefabrication. Denny Brown stabilisers fitted. Enclosed bridge and twin rudders.

Corvus: Knebworth Corvus Chaff launchers fitted.

Electrical: Generator capacity of 1 500 kW.

Engineering: The gas turbine is used to boost the steam turbines for sustained bursts of high speed and also enables the ship lying in harbour without steam up to get under way instantly in emergency. The machinery is remotely controlled. The main boiler works at a pressure of 550 psi and a temperature of 850°F. Five-bladed propeller, 11·75 feet diameter, 280 rpm. The forward funnel serves the boilers, the after one the gas turbine.

Radar: Search: one Type 965 with single AKE 1 array and IFF.
Air and surface warning: one Type 993.
Navigation: one Type 978.
Fire control: MRS 3 system.
Seacat: GWS 21.

Sonar: Types 177, 170 and 162. Type 199. VDS fitted in *Ashanti* and *Gurkha* in 1970.

ESKIMO   5/1977, Wright and Logan

TARTAR   6/1977, Dr. Giorgio Arra

GURKHA   3/1977, Wright and Logan

NUBIAN   6/1977, C. and S. Taylor

578 UK

9 "ROTHESAY" CLASS (MODIFIED TYPE 12)

Name	No.	Builders	Laid down	Launched	Commissioned
YARMOUTH	F 101	John Brown & Co Ltd, Clydebank	29 Nov 1957	23 Mar 1959	26 Mar 1960
LOWESTOFT	F 103	Alex Stephen & Sons Ltd, Govan	9 June 1958	23 June 1960	18 Oct 1961
BRIGHTON	F 106	Yarrow & Co Ltd, Scotstoun	23 July 1957	30 Oct 1959	28 Sept 1961
ROTHESAY*	F 107	Yarrow & Co Ltd, Scotstoun	6 Nov 1956	9 Dec 1957	23 April 1960
LONDONDERRY*	F 108	J. Samuel White & Co Ltd, Cowes	15 Nov 1956	20 May 1958	22 July 1960
FALMOUTH	F 113	Swan Hunter, Wigham Richardson	23 Nov 1957	15 Dec 1959	25 July 1961
BERWICK	F 115	Harland & Wolff Ltd, Belfast	16 June 1958	15 Dec 1959	1 June 1961
PLYMOUTH	F 126	HM Dockyard, Devonport	1 July 1958	20 July 1959	11 May 1961
RHYL	F 129	HM Dockyard, Portsmouth	29 Jan 1958	23 April 1959	31 Oct 1960

* Refit

Displacement, tons: 2 380 standard; 2 800 full load
Length, feet (metres): 360·0 (109·7) wl; 370·0 (112·8) oa
Beam, feet (metres): 41·0 (12·5)
Draught, feet (metres): 17·3 (5·3)
Aircraft: 1 Wasp helicopter
Missile launchers: 1 quadruple Seacat
Guns: 2—4·5 in (115 mm) (1 twin); 2—20 mm (single)
A/S weapons: 1 Limbo three-barrelled DC mortar
Main engines: 2 double reduction geared turbines; 2 shafts; 30 000 shp
Boilers: 2 Babcock & Wilcox
Speed, knots: 30
Oil fuel, tons: 400
Complement: 235 (15 officers and 220 ratings)

Provided under the 1954-55 programme. Originally basically similar to the "Whitby" class but with modifications in layout.

Cost: £3·6 million average building cost.

Electrical: Two turbo generators and two diesel generators in all ships. Total 1 140 kW. Alternating current, 440 volts, three phase, 60 cycles per second.

Engineering: Two Admiralty Standard Range turbines each rated at 15 000 shp. Propeller revolutions 220 rpm. Boilers 550 psi (38·7 kg/cm²) pressure and 850°F (450°C) temperature.

Modernisation: The "Rothesay" class was reconstructed and modernised from 1966-72 during which time they were equipped to operate a Wessex Wasp helicopter armed with homing torpedoes. A flight deck and hangar were built on aft, necessitating the removal of one of their anti-submarine mortars. A Seacat replaced the 40 mm gun. A new operations room, new GFCS and full air-conditioning were provided.

Radar: Search: one Type 993
Fire control: MRS 3
Navigation: one Type 978

Refits: *Londonderry* started refit at Rosyth in Nov 1975 to become trials ship for Admiralty Surface Weapons Establishment. *Rothesay* to have similar refit in 1978.

Seacat: Optical Director—GWS 20

Sonar: New sonar fitted aft in *Lowestoft*.

ROTHESAY 8/1977, Wright and Logan

BRIGHTON 6/1977, Dr. Giorgio Arra

BERWICK 6/1977, Wright and Logan

PLYMOUTH 4/1976, C. and S. Taylor

UK 579

2 "SALISBURY" CLASS (TYPE 61)

Name	No.
SALISBURY	F 32
LINCOLN	F 99

Builders	Laid down	Launched	Commissioned
HM Dockyard, Devonport	23 Jan 1952	25 June 1953	27 Feb 1957
Fairfield SB & Eng Co Ltd, Govan	20 May 1955	6 April 1959	7 July 1960

Displacement, tons: 2 170 standard; 2 408 full load
Length, feet (metres): 320·0 (97·5) pp; 330·0 (100·6) wl; 339·8 (103·6) oa
Beam, feet (metres): 40·0 (12·2)
Draught, feet (metres): 15·5 (4·7)
Missile launchers: 1 quadruple Seacat in *Lincoln* and *Salisbury*
Guns: 2—4·5 in (115 mm); 1—40 mm (Chichester); 2—20 mm (remainder)
A/S weapons: 1 Squid triple-barrelled DC mortar (only *Lincoln*)
Main engines: 8 ASR 1 diesels in three engine rooms; 2 shafts; 14 400 bhp; 4 engines geared to each shaft
Speed, knots: 24
Oil fuel, tons: 230
Range, miles: 2 300 at full power; 7 500 at 16 knots
Complement: 237 (14 officers and 223 ratings)

Class of three designed primarily for the direction of carrier-borne and shore-based aircraft. Ordered on 28 June 1951 except *Salisbury*, the prototype ship. Construction was all welded and largely prefabricated. The construction of three other ships *Exeter*, *Gloucester* and *Coventry* cancelled in 1957 being replaced by first three "Leander" class. *Salisbury* fitted with stabilisers. Original lattice masts replaced by tower masts during 1960s. *Lincoln* was fitted with wooden bow sheathing for Cod War 1976 but has subsequently been returned to reserve.

Corvus: Knebworth Corvus Chaff launchers fitted.

Cost: Average £3·3 million building cost.

Engineering: Powered by Admiralty Standard Range 1 diesel engines coupled to the propeller shafts through hydraulic couplings and oil operated reverse and reduction gear boxes. *Lincoln* is fitted with controllable pitch propellers, rotating at 200 rpm, which are 12 feet in diameter, manufactured by Stone Marine & Engineering Co Ltd. The fuel tanks are fitted with compensating system.

Fire control: Seacat control. GWS 20 (optical).

Hong Kong Guardship: In 1973 *Chichester* was re-equipped for service as permanent HK Guardship. This involved removal of Type 965. *Chichester* returned to UK early 1976 to reserve and to Disposal List 1978.

Radar: Long range surveillance: one Type 965 with double AKE 2 array with IFF.
Combined warning: one Type 993.
Height-finder: one Type 277Q.
Target indication: one Type 982.
Fire control: Mk 6M director with Type 275.
Navigation: one Type 975.

Sonar: Types 174 and 170B.

Transfer: *Llandaff* to Bangladesh as *Oomar Farooq* (F 16) on 1 Dec 1976.

LINCOLN (with wooden sheath on bow for Cod War) 5/1976, MOD(N)

SALISBURY 6/1977, Michael D. J. Lennon

1 "LEOPARD" CLASS (TYPE 41)

Name	No.
LYNX	F 27

Builders	Laid down	Launched	Commissioned
John Brown & Co Ltd, Clydebank	13 Aug 1953	12 Jan 1955	14 Mar 1957

Displacement, tons: 2 300 standard; 2 520 full load
Length, feet (metres): 320 (97·5) pp; 330 (100·6) wl; 339·8 (103·6) oa
Beam, feet (metres): 40 (12·2)
Draught, feet (metres): 16 (4·9)
Guns: 4—4·5 in (115 mm) (twin turrets); 1—40 mm
A/S weapons: 1 Squid three-barrelled DC mortar
Main engines: 8 ASR 1 diesels in three engine rooms; 14 400 bhp; 2 shafts; 4 engines geared to each shaft
Speed, knots: 24
Oil fuel, tons: 220
Range, miles: 2 300 at full power; 7 500 at 16 knots
Complement: 235 (15 officers, 220 ratings)

Originally a class of four, a fifth ship having been cancelled for a "Leander" class. Designed primarily for anti-aircraft protection. All welded. Fitted with stabilisers. *Lynx* to Stand-by Squadron June 1977 at Chatham.

Cost: Average £3·2 million building cost.

Radar: Air search: one Type 965 with single AKE 1 array and IFF.
Combined warning: Type 993 (AKD aerial).
Fire control: Mk 6 M I-band. Type 275.
Navigation: one Type 978.

Reconstruction: *Lynx* was extensively refitted in 1963 with new mainmast.

Sonar: Types 174 and 170.

Transfers: Another ship of this class, *Panther*, was transferred to India while building and renamed *Brahmaputra*. *Jaguar* to Bangladesh July 1978.

LYNX 6/1977, Dr. Giorgio Ar

580 UK

1 "WHITBY" CLASS (TYPE 12)

Builders	Laid down	Launched	Commissioned
Harland & Wolff Ltd, Belfast	11 Mar 1953	1 July 1954	10 May 1956

Name: TORQUAY
No.: F 43

Displacement, tons: 2 150 standard; 2 560 full load
Length, feet (metres): 360·0 (109·7) wl; 369·8 (112·7) oa
Beam, feet (metres): 41·0 (12·5)
Draught, feet (metres): 17 (5·2)
Guns: 2—4·5 in (115 mm) (twin)
A/S weapons: 1 Limbo three-barrelled DC mortar
Main engines: 2 sets dr geared turbines; 2 shafts; 30 430 shp
Boilers: 2 Babcock & Wilcox; pressure 550 psi (38·7 kg/cm²); temperature 850°F (454°C)
Speed, knots: 31
Oil fuel, tons: 370
Complement: 225 (12 officers, and 213 ratings)

Ordered in 1951. Twin-rudders.

Class: Originally class of six. *Torquay* used as Navigation/Direction training and trials ship at Portsmouth, having a large deck-house aft and carrying the first CAAIS (Computer Assisted Action Information System) to go to sea. *Eastbourne*, alongside at Rosyth for engine-room trainees from HMS *Caledonia* and approved for disposal, 1978. *Blackpool* now in use as target ship—laid up. *Scarborough* scrapped.

Radar: Search: one Type 993.
Navigation: Type 1006.
Fire control: Type 275 (Mk 6 MDCT)

Sonar: Types 177, 170 and 162.

TORQUAY   6/1977, Michael D. J. Lennon

1 "BLACKWOOD" CLASS (TYPE 14)

Builders	Laid down	Launched	Commissioned
Yarrow & Co Ltd	4 Feb 1953	25 Nov 1953	12 Dec 1955

Name: HARDY
No.: F 54

Displacement, tons: 1 180 standard; 1 456 full load
Length, feet (metres): 300 (91·4) wl; 310 (94·5) oa
Beam, feet (metres): 33·0 (10·1)
Draught, feet (metres): 11·2 (3·4) (mean)
Guns: 2—40 mm Bofors
A/S weapons: 2 Limbo three-barrelled DC mortars
Main engines: 1 set geared turbines; 1 shaft; 15 000 shp
Boilers: 2 Babcock & Wilcox; pressure 550 psi (38·7 kg/cm²); temperature 850°F (454°C)
Speed, knots: 26
Oil fuel, tons: 275
Range, miles: 4 000 at 12 knots
Complement: 140 (8 officers, and 132 ratings)

Originally a class of twelve. Of comparatively simple construction. Built in prefabricated sections. In 1958-59 their hulls were strengthened to withstand severe and prolonged sea and weather conditions on fishery protection in Icelandic waters.

Class: *Hardy* currently operational. *Duncan* is at Rosyth for harbour training and *Russell* at Portsmouth for similar duties with HMS *Sultan*. *Dundas* approved for disposal 1978.

Cost: Average £1·6 million building cost.

Radar: General search: one Type 978.

Sonar: Types 174, 170 and 162.

Turning circle: 350 yards.

HARDY   6/1977, Michael D. J. Lennon

TYPE 15

For *Grenville, Rapid, Undaunted* and *Volage* see Disposal List. With *Ulster*, acting as accommodation ship at Plymouth, these are the sole survivors of the wartime "R", "T", "U", "V", "W", and "Z" classes of destroyers, launched in 1942-43. Of the 48 ships of these classes 33 were converted into Type 15 frigates and 7 ("T" Class) into Type 16 (limited conversion) frigates. A number have been transferred to other navies.

UK 581

AMPHIBIOUS WARFARE FORCES

2 ASSAULT SHIPS (LPD)

Name	No.	Builders	Laid down	Launched	Commissioned
FEARLESS	L 10 (ex-L 3004)	Harland & Wolff Ltd, Belfast	25 July 1962	19 Dec 1963	25 Nov 1965
INTREPID	L 11 (ex-L 3005)	John Brown & Co (Clydebank) Ltd	19 Dec 1962	25 June 1964	11 Mar 1967

Displacement, tons: 11 060 standard; 12 120 full load; 16 950 ballasted
Length, feet (metres): 500 *(152·4)* wl; 520 *(158·5)* oa
Beam, feet (metres): 80 *(24·4)*
Draught, feet (metres): 20·5 *(6·2)*
Draught, ballasted: 32 *(9·8)* aft; 23 *(7·0)* forward
Landing craft: 4 LCM(9) in dock; 4 LCVP at davits
Vehicles: Specimen load: 15 tanks, 7 three-ton and 20 quarter-ton trucks
Aircraft: Flight deck facilities for 5 Wessex helicopters
Missiles: 4 Seacat systems
Guns: 2—40 mm Bofors
Main engines: 2 EE turbines; 22 000 shp; 2 shafts
Boilers: 2 Babcock & Wilcox
Speed, knots: 21
Range, miles: 5 000 at 20 knots
Complement: 580 (see *Troops* note)

They carry landing craft which are floated through the open stern by flooding compartments of the ship and lowering her in the water; are able to deploy tanks, vehicles and men; have seakeeping qualities much superior to those of tank landing ships, and greater speed and range. Capable of operating independently. Another valuable feature is a helicopter platform which is also the deckhead of the dock from which the landing craft are floated out. Officially estimated building cost: *Fearless* £11·25 million; *Intrepid* £10·5 million.
Intrepid to reserve in 1976 for refit in 1977-1978 and to relieve *Fearless* (to reserve) 1979.

Countermeasures: Mount 2 Knebworth Corvus launchers.

Electrical: Power at 440V 60c/s 3-phase a/c is supplied by four 1 000 kW AE1 turbo-alternators.

Electronics: Fitted with CAAIS.

Engineering: The two funnels are staggered across the beam of the ship, indicating that the engines and boilers are arranged *en echelon,* two machinery spaces having one turbine and one boiler installed in each space. The turbines were manufactured by the English Electric Co, Rugby, the gearing by David Brown & Co, Huddersfield. Boilers work at a pressure of 550 psi and a temperature of 850°F. Two five-bladed propellers, 12·5 feet diameter, 200 rpm in *Fearless*.

Operational: Each ship is fitted out as a Naval Assault Group/Brigade Headquarters with an Assault Operations Room from which naval and military personnel can mount and control the progress of an assault operation.

Radar: Air and surface search: one Type 993.
Navigation: one Type 975.

Satellite system: The Royal Navy fitted its first operational satellite communications system in *Intrepid* in 1969, the contract having been awarded to Plessey Radar—now removed.

Training: *Fearless* used for the sea training of officers from the Britannia Royal Naval College, Dartmouth, retaining full amphibious capabilities.

Troops: Each ship can carry 380 to 400 troops at ship's company standards, and an overload of 700 marines and military personnel can be accommodated for short periods.

INTREPID 4/1975, John G. Callis

FEARLESS 6/1977. C. and S. Taylor

FEARLESS 6/1977, Michael D. J. Lennon

582 UK

6 LOGISTIC LANDING SHIPS
(RFA MANNED)

Name	No.	Builders	Laid down	Launched	Commissioned
SIR BEDIVERE	L 3004	Hawthorn Leslie	Oct 1965	20 July 1966	18 May 1967
SIR GALAHAD	L 3005	Alex Stephen	Feb 1965	19 April 1966	17 Dec 1966
SIR GERAINT	L 3027	Alex Stephen	June 1965	26 Jan 1967	12 July 1967
SIR LANCELOT	L 3029	Fairfield	Mar 1962	25 June 1963	16 Jan 1964
SIR PERCIVALE	L 3036	Hawthorn Leslie	April 1966	4 Oct 1967	23 Mar 1968
SIR TRISTRAM	L 3505	Hawthorn Leslie	Feb 1966	12 Dec 1966	14 Sept 1967

Displacement, tons: 3 270 light; 5 674 full load (3 370 and 5 550 in *Sir Lancelot*)
Dimensions, feet (metres): 366·3 pp; 412·1 oa × 59·8 × 13·0 (120; 135·1 × 19·6 × 4·3)
Guns: Fitted for 2—40 mm—not normally carried
Main engines: 2 Mirrlees diesels; 9 400 bhp; 2 shafts; (2 Denny/Sulzer diesels; 9 520 bhp in *Sir Lancelot*)
Speed, knots: 17
Oil fuel, tons: 815
Range, miles: 8 000 at 15 knots
Complement: 68 (18 officers, 50 ratings)
Military lift: 340

Sir Lancelot was the prototype of this class which was originally built for the Army but transferred to RFA in Jan and March 1970. Fitted for bow and stern loading with drive-through facilities and deck-to-deck ramps. Facilities provided for on-board maintenance of vehicles and for laying out pontoon equipment.

Aircraft: Helicopters can be operated from the well-deck and the after platform by day or night in the later ships. In *Sir Lancelot* well-deck operations are limited to fair weather-day conditions. If required to carry helicopters 11 can be stowed on the Tank Deck and nine on the Vehicle Deck.

SIR LANCELOT 6/1977, Michael D. J. Lennon

2 LOGISTIC LANDING CRAFT (RCT)

Name	No.	Builders	Laid down	Launched	Commissioned
ARDENNES	L 4001	Brooke Marine, Lowestoft	27 Aug 1975	29 July 1976	1977
ARAKAN	L —	Brooke Marine, Lowestoft	16 Feb 1976	23 May 1977	1978

Displacement, tons: 870 standard; 1 413 full load
Dimensions, feet (metres): 240 oa × 47·5 × 5·8 (73·1 × 14·4 × 1·8)
Main engines: 2 diesels; 2 000 bhp = 10·3 knots
Fuel, tons: 150 dieso
Range, miles: 4 000 at 10 knots
Complement: 36 (plus 34 troops)

Both ordered in Oct 1974. Can carry 350 tonnes of Stores or five Chieftain tanks.

ARDENNES 8/1977, Michael D. J. Lennon

1 LST (3) (RFA)

EMPIRE GULL (ex-*Trouncer*) L 3513

Displacement, tons: 2 260 light; 4 960 full load
Dimensions, feet (metres): 347 × 54·1 × 12 (105·8 × 16·5 × 3·7)
Main engines: 2 triple expansion; 2 shafts; 5 500 shp = 10 knots
Boilers: 2 Water Tube
Oil fuel, tons: 950
Complement: 63 officers and men
Troop accommodation: 8 officers, 72 ORs

Built by Davie Shipbuilding, Quebec. Launched 9 July 1945. To be paid off in 1978. The last survivor in the Navy List of a huge number of British LSTs. Chinese crew.

EMPIRE GULL 7/1977, Wright and Logan

3 LCT (8) TYPE (RCT)

AGHEILA L 4002   **AUDEMER** L 4061
ABBEVILLE L 4041

Displacement, tons: 657 light; 895 to 1 017 loaded
Dimensions, feet (metres): 231·2 oa × 39 × 3·2 forward; 5 aft (70·5 × 11·9 × 1 forward; 1·8 aft) Beaching draughts
Main engines: 4 Paxman engines; 1 840 bhp = 12·6 knots
Complement: 33 to 37

All transferred to the Army's Royal Corps of Transport from the Royal Navy. Originally nine of these ships were operated by the RCT. *Agheila* has low bridge with radar central and platform forward of bridge with life-rafts disposed differently from other pair.

AUDEMER 6/1977, John Mortimer

UK 583

14 LCM (9) TYPE

Name	No.	Builders	Commissioned
—	L 700	Brooke Marine Ltd	1964
—	L 701	Brooke Marine Ltd	1964
—	L 702	Brooke Marine Ltd	1965
—	L 703	brooke Marine Ltd	1965
—	L 704	R. Dunston (Thorne)	1964
—	L 705	R. Dunston (Thorne)	1965
—	L 706	R. Dunston (Thorne)	1965
—	L 707	R. Dunston (Thorne)	1965
—	L 708	R. Dunston (Thorne)	1966
—	L 709	R. Dunston (Thorne)	1966
—	L 710	J. Bolson (Poole)	1965
—	L 711	J. Bolson (Poole)	1965
—	L 3507	Vosper Ltd	1963
—	L 3508	Vosper Ltd	1963

Displacement, tons: 75 light; 176 loaded
Dimensions, feet (metres): 85 oa × 21·5 × 5·5 *(25·7 × 6·5 × 1·7)*
Capacity: 2 tanks or 100 tons of vehicles
Main engines: 2 Paxman 6-cyl YHXAM diesels; 2 shafts; 624 bhp = 10 knots. Screws enclosed in Kort nozzles to improve manoeuvrability

LCM (9) 3507 and LCM (9) 3508 were the first operational minor landing craft to be built since the Second World War. Ramped in the traditional manner forward, a completely enclosed radar-fitted wheelhouse is positioned aft. Upon completion they carried out familiarisation trials to perfect the new techniques required in launching and recovering LCMs from the flooded sterns of the parent assault ships. Now operated by RCT. Four each of the 700 Series allocated to assault ships.

LCM 707 (from HMS *Intrepid*)   5/1975, Wright and Logan

LCM 3507 (RCT)   4/1975, John G. Callis

2 LCM (7)

7037   7100

Displacement, tons: 28 light; 63 loaded
Dimensions, feet (metres): 60·2 × 16 × 3·7 *(18·4 × 4·9 × 1·2)*
Main engines: 290 bhp = 9·8 knots

Employed as naval servicing boats and store carriers. Re-engined with Gray Marine diesels.

11 "AVON" CLASS LCM (RCT)

AVON RPL 01   **GLEN** RPL 07
BUDE RPL 02   **HAMBLE** RPL 08
CLYDE RPL 03   **KENNET** RPL 10
DART RPL 04   **LODDON** RPL 11
EDEN RPL 05   **MEDWAY** RPL 12
FORTH RPL 06

Diesel-driven LCMs manned by RCT and available for short coastal hauls.

LODDON   1976, Michael D. J. Lennon

26 LCVP (1) (2) and (3)

LCVP (1) 102, 112, 118, 120, 123, 127, 128, 134, 136
LCVP (2) 142-149
LCVP (3) 150-158

Displacement, tons: 8·5 light; 13·5 full load
Dimensions, feet (metres): 41·5 (LCVP (2)); 43 (LCVP (3)) × 10 × 2·5 *(12·7; 13·1 × 3·1 × 0·8)*
Main engines: 130 bhp = 8 knots; 2 Foden diesels; 200 bhp = 10 knots (LCVP (2))

LCVP (2)s carried by *Intrepid* and *Fearless* can carry 35 troops or two Land Rovers. Crew four. LCA (2)s were redesignated LCVPs (Landing Craft Vehicle and Personnel) in 1966. There were also a number of variations and prototypes of about the same length (43 feet).

Note: Raiding Landing Craft, including LCR 5507 and 5508, and Navigational Landing Craft, including LCN 604 (ex-LCR 5505).

LCVP   8/1976, C. and S. Taylor

3 LCP (L) (3)

LCP (L) (3) 501, 503, 556

Displacement, tons: 6·5 light; 10 loaded
Dimensions, feet (metres): 37 × 11 × 3·2 *(11·3 × 3·4 × 1)*
Main engines: 225 bhp = 12 knots

HELICOPTER SUPPORT SHIP

Name	No.	Builders	Commissioned
ENGADINE	K 08	Henry Robb Ltd, Leith	15 Dec 1967

Displacement, tons: 8 000 full load
Measurement, tons: 6 384 gross; 2 848 net
Dimensions, feet (metres): 424·0 oa × 58·4 × 22·1 *(129·3 × 17·8 × 6·7)*
Aircraft: 4 Wessex and 2 Wasp or 2 Sea King helicopters
Main engines: 1 Sulzer two stroke, 5-cyl turbocharged 5RD68 diesel; 5 500 bhp = 14·5 knots
Complement: RFA: 63 (15 officers, 48 men); RN: 14 (2 officers, 12 ratings)
  Accommodation for a further RN 113 (29 officers and 84 ratings)

Projected under the 1964-65 Navy Estimates. Ordered on 18 Aug 1964. Laid down on 9 Aug 1965. Officially named on 15 Sept 1966. Largest ship then built by the company. Intended for the training of helicopter crews in deep water operations. She does not carry her own flight but embarks aircraft as necessary. Fitted with Denny Brown stabilisers, the only RFA vessel so equipped. Also fitted with PTA hangar immediately abaft the funnel.

ENGADINE   5/1977, Michael D. J. Lennon

584 UK

MINE WARFARE FORCES

Name	No.	Builders	Commissioned
ABDIEL	N 21	John I. Thornycroft Ltd, Woolston, Southampton	17 Oct 1967

Displacement, tons: 1 375 standard; 1 500 full load
Dimensions, feet (metres): 244·5 pp; 265 oa × 38·5 × 10 *(80·2; 86·8 × 12·6 × 3·3)*
Mines: 44 carried
Main engines: 2 Paxman Ventura 16-cyl pressure charged diesels; 1 250 rpm; 2 690 bhp = 16 knots
Complement: 77

Exercise minelayer ordered in June 1965. Laid down on 23 May 1966. Launched on 27 Jan 1967. Main machinery manufactured by Davey Paxman, Colchester. Main gearing supplied by Messrs Wisemans. Her function is to support mine countermeasure forces, maintain these forces when they are operating away from their shore bases and minelaying. Cost £1·5 million.

ABDIEL   1/1977, C. and S. Taylor

0 + 2 "HUNT" CLASS
(MINESWEEPERS/MINEHUNTERS—COASTAL)

Name	No.	Builders	Commissioned
BRECON	M 29	Vosper Thornycroft Ltd.	1978
LEDBURY	—	Vosper Thornycroft Ltd.	—

Displacement, tons: 615 standard; 725 full load
Dimensions, feet (metres): 197 × 32·3 × 7·3 *(60 × 9·9 × 2·2)*
Gun: 1—40 mm
Main engines: 2 Ruston-Paxman Deltic diesels; 3 540 bhp = 17 knots
Complement: 45

A new class of MCM Vessels combining both hunting and sweeping capabilities. Hulls of GRP. Will be equipped with two French PAP 104 mine destructor outfits. *Ledbury* ordered 31 March 1977. *Brecon* laid down 15 Sept 1975 for launch 1977. It is reported that twelve of this class are planned. Agreement of March 1976 provided for Yarrow Ltd equipping their yard to build ships of this class. Further orders are planned for 1978.

Artist's Impression of "BRECON" Class   1974, MOD (N)

1 MINESWEEPER/MINEHUNTER (COASTAL)

Name	No.	Builders	Commissioned
WILTON	M 1116	Vosper Thornycroft, Woolston	14 July 1973

Displacement, tons: 450 standard
Dimensions, feet (metres): 153·0 oa × 28·8 × 8·5 *(46·3 × 8·8 × 2·5)*
Gun: 1—40 mm Mark VII
Main engines: 2 English Electric Deltic 18 diesels; 2 shafts; 3 000 bhp = 16 knots
Complement: 37 (5 officers and 32 ratings)

The world's first GRP warship. Contract signed on 11 Feb 1970. Laid down 16 Nov 1970 and launched on 18 Jan 1972. Prototype built of glass reinforced plastic to the existing minehunter design by Vosper Thornycroft at Woolston. Similar to the "Ton" class and fitted with reconditioned machinery and equipment from the scrapped *Derriton*.

Cost: Building cost £2·3 million.

Radar: Type 975.

Sonar: Type 193M.

WILTON   6/1977, John Mortimer

UK 585

33 "TON" CLASS

15 MINEHUNTERS

(* = RNR Training Ship)

Name	No.	Builders	Commissioned
BILDESTON†	M 1110	J. S. Doig (Grimsby) Ltd	28 April 1953
BRERETON	M 1113	Richards Ironworks	9 July 1954
BRINTON	M 1114	Cook Welton and Gemmell	4 Mar 1954
BRONINGTON	M 1115	Cook Welton and Gemmell	4 June 1954
BOSSINGTON	M 1133	J. I. Thornycroft & Co, Southampton	11 Dec 1956
GAVINTON	M 1140	J. S. Doig (Grimsby) Ltd	14 July 1954
HUBBERSTON	M 1147	Fleetlands Shipyards Ltd, London	14 Oct 1955
IVESTON	M 1151	Philip & Sons Ltd, Dartmouth	29 June 1955
*KEDLESTON	M 1153	William Pickersgill & Son	2 July 1955
*KELLINGTON	M 1154	William Pickersgill & Son	4 Nov 1955
KIRKLISTON	M 1157	Harland & Wolff Ltd, Belfast	21 Aug 1954
MAXTON	M 1165	Harland & Wolff Ltd, Belfast	19 Feb 1957
NURTON	M 1166	Harland & Wolff Ltd, Belfast	21 Aug 1957
SHERATON	M 1181	White's Shipyard Ltd, Southampton	24 Aug 1956
SHOULTON	M 1182	Montrose Shipyard Ltd	16 Nov 1955

† Refit

SHOULTON 6/1977, Wright and Logan

18 MINESWEEPERS—COASTAL

(* = RNR Training Ship)

Name	No.	Builders	Commissioned
ALFRISTON†	M 1103	J. I. Thornycroft & Co., Southampton	16 Mar 1954
BICKINGTON	M 1109	White's Shipyard Ltd, Southampton	27 May 1954
CRICHTON	M 1124	J. S. Doig (Grimsby) Ltd	23 April 1954
CUXTON	M 1125	Camper and Nicholson Ltd, Gosport	1953
GLASSERTON	M 1141	J. S. Doig (Grimsby) Ltd	31 Dec 1954
*HODGESTON	M 1146	Fleetlands Shipyards Ltd, London	17 Dec 1954
LALESTON	M 1158	Harland and Wolff	1954
*REPTON	M 1167	Harland & Wolff Ltd, Belfast	12 Dec 1957
POLLINGTON	M 1173	Camper & Nicholson Ltd, Gosport	5 Sept 1958
SHAVINGTON	M 1180	White's Shipyard Ltd, Southampton	1 Mar 1956
*UPTON	M 1187	J. I. Thornycroft & Co, Southampton	24 July 1956
WALKERTON	M 1188	J. I. Thornycroft & Co, Southampton	10 Jan 1958
WOTTON†	M 1195	Philip & Sons Ltd, Dartmouth	13 June 1957
SOBERTON	M 1200	Fleetlands Shipyards Ltd, Gosport	17 Sept 1957
STUBBINGTON	M 1204	Camper & Nicholson Ltd, Gosport	30 July 1957
WISTON	M 1205	Wivenhoc Shipyard Ltd	17 Feb 1960
LEWISTON	M 1208	Herd & Mackenzie, Buckie, Banff	16 June 1960
*CROFTON	M 1216	J. I. Thornycroft & Co, Southampton	26 Aug 1958

† Refit

Displacement, tons: 360 standard; 425 full load
Dimensions, feet (metres): 140·0 pp; 153·0 oa × 28·8 × 8·2 (42·7; 46·3 × 8·8 × 2·5)
Guns: Vary in different ships, some sweepers having no 40 mm, some 1—40 mm and 2—20 mm whilst hunters have 1—40 mm
Main engines: 2 diesels; 2 shafts; 2 500 bhp (JVSS 12 Mirrlees), 3 000 bhp (18A-7A Deltic)
Speed, knots: 15
Oil fuel, tons: 45
Range, miles: 2 300 at 13 knots
Complement: 29 (38 in minehunters, 5 officers and 33 ratings)

The survivors of a class of 118 built between 1953 and 1960, largely as a result of lessons from the Korean War. John I. Thornycroft & Co Ltd, Southampton were the lead yard for these ships which have double mahogany hull and incorporate a considerable amount of non-magnetic material. Fitted with Vospers stabilisers. The majority has now been fitted with nylon in place of copper sheathing. *Cuxton* commissioned finally in Oct 1975 after 22 years in "moth-balls".

Appearance: Frigate bridges in *Bildeston, Brereton, Brinton, Crofton, Cuxton, Iveston, Kellington, Kirkliston, Lewiston, Bossington, Bronington, Gavinton, Hubberston, Kedleston, Maxton, Repton, Pollington, Nurton, Sheraton, Shoulton, Soberton, Stubbington, Walkerton, Wiston.* Enclosed bridges being fitted in remainder.

Conversions: *Beachampton, Monkton, Wasperton, Wolverton* and *Yarnton* were converted into coastal patrol vessels late in 1971, (see Light Forces). *Laleston* was converted into diving trials ship in 1966-67. *Walkerton* used by Dartmouth RN College as Navigation Training Ship, to be relieved by *Alfriston* in 1978. *Shoulton* was the original minehunter conversion, fitted with pump-jet and bow thruster.

Cost: Average running cost at 1976 prices £0·3 million per ship.

Diving: *Laleston* is diving training ship.

Engineering: Earlier vessels had Mirrlees diesels, but later units had Napier Deltic lightweight diesels. *Highburton*, the first with Deltic diesels, was accepted on 21 April 1955. All minehunters have Deltics and active rudders. Generators for electrical power are in a separate engine room in Mirrlees, Deltic-conversions and minehunters. Deltic built minesweepers have a generator in the main engine-room and two generators in the generator-room. Mirrlees still fitted in *Glasserton, Laleston, Cuxton* and *Repton*. Three-bladed propellers, 6 feet diameter, 400 rpm. *Shoulton*, refitted 1965-67, has pump-jet propulsion.

Fishery protection: Carried out by *Bickington, Brereton, Brinton, Cuxton, Crichton, Pollington, Shavington, Sheraton, Soberton* and *Stubbington*. All FPS ships carry a large Signal Projector (searchlight).

Osbourne sweep: *Glasserton* is fitted with derricks for Osbourne sweep. *Highburton* used in initial trials.

Radar: Type 975 (*Kirkliston*, Type 1006).

Royal Naval Reserve: The practice of temporarily renaming ships attached to RNR divisions has been abandoned as the six vessels now operate for various groupings. *Kedleston*—Forth; *Repton* and *Wiston*—Tyne; *Kellington*—Sussex; *Crofton*—Solent; *Upton*—Severn; *Hodgeston*—Mersey. Other RNR training ships are provided from the "Kingfisher" class (see Light Forces).

Sonar: Type 193 in minehunters (Type 193M in *Iveston*).

Transfers: Argentine (six in 1968), Australia (six in 1962), Ghana (one in 1964), India (four in 1956), Ireland (three in 1971), Malaysia (seven in 1960-68), South Africa (ten in 1958-59).

MAXTON 6/1977, Michael D. J. Lennon

KEDLESTON 6/1976, Dr. Giorgio Arra

CUXTON 6/1977, Michael D. J. Lennon

UPTON 6/1977, C. and S. Taylor

LALESTON 6/1977, C. and S. Taylor

586 UK

3 "HAM" CLASS (MINESWEEPERS—INSHORE)

Name	No.	Builders	Commissioned
DITTISHAM	M 2621	Fairlie Yacht Slip	1954
FLINTHAM	M 2628	Bolson & Co	1955
THORNHAM (Aberdeen)	M 2793	Taylor, Shoreham	1957

Displacement, tons: 120 standard; 159 full load
Dimensions, feet (metres): 2601 Series: 100 pp; 106·5 oa × 21·2 × 5·5 (30·5; 32·4 × 6·5 × 1·7).
  Thornham: 100 pp; 107·5 oa × 22 × 5·8 (30·5; 32·1 × 6·6 × 1·8)
Gun: 1—20 mm Oerlikon forward
Main engines: 2 Paxman diesels; 1 100 bhp = 14 knots
Oil fuel, tons: 15
Complement: 15 (2 officers, 13 ratings)

The first inshore minesweeper, *Inglesham*, was launched by J. Samuel White & Co Ltd, Cowes, on 23 April 1952. The 2601 series were of composite construction. In all 95 of this class were built.
Thornham attached to Aberdeen University RNU, other two at Plymouth.

Transfers: Australia (three in 1966-68), France (15 in 1954-55), Ghana (two in 1959), India (two in 1955), Libya (two in 1963), Malaysia (four in 1958-59), South Yemen (three in 1967). Ships subsequently returned are not listed.

DITTISHAM 6/1977, Dr. Giorgio Arra

2 "LEY" CLASS M 2001 SERIES (MINEHUNTERS—INSHORE)

Name	No.	Builders	Commissioned
AVELEY	M 2002	J. S. White & Co Ltd, Cowes	1953
ISIS (ex-*Cradley*)	M 2010	Saunders Roe Ltd	1955

Displacement, tons: 123 standard; 164 full load
Dimensions, feet (metres): 100 pp; 107 oa × 21·8 × 5·5 (30·5; 32·3 × 6·5 × 1·7)
Gun: 1—40 mm (*Isis*); 1—20 mm (*Aveley*)
Main engines: 2 Paxman diesels; 700 bhp = 13 knots
Complement: 15 (2 officers, 13 ratings)

The "Ley" class, originally of ten ships, differed from the "Ham" class. They were of composite (non-magnetic metal and wooden) construction, instead of all wooden construction. Their superstructure and other features also differed. They had no winch or sweeping gear, as they were minehunters, not sweepers. *Aveley* is attached to Plymouth. *Isis*, renamed in 1963, was affiliated with Southampton University RNU on 1 April 1974. RN Crew.

ISIS 6/1977, Dr. Giorgio Arra

MAINTENANCE SHIPS

Name	No.	Builders	Laid down	Launched	Commissioned
TRIUMPH	A 108 (ex-R 16)	R & W Hawthorn Leslie, Hebburn	27 Jan 1943	2 Oct 1944	9 April 1946

Displacement, tons: 13 500 standard; 17 500 full load
Length, feet (metres): 630·0 (192·0) pp; 650·0 (198·1) wl; 699·0 (213·1) oa
Beam, feet (metres): 80·0 (24·4)
Draught, feet (metres): 23·7 (7·2)
Width, feet (metres): 112·5 (34·3) overall
Aircraft: 3 helicopters in flight deck hangar
Guns: 4—40 mm; 3 saluting (now removed)
Main engines: Parsons geared turbines; 2 shafts; 40 000 shp
Boilers: 4 Admiralty three-drum type; pressure 400 psi (28·1 kg/cm²); temperature 700°F (371°C)
Speed, knots: 24·25
Oil fuel, tons: 3 000
Range, miles: 10 000 at 14 knots; 5 500 at full speed
Complement: 500 (27 officers, 473 men) plus 285 (15 officers, 270 men) on maintenance staff

Originally an aircraft carrier of the "Colossus" class. Converted for present role at a cost of £10·2 million. at Portsmouth between 1958 and 1965. Now in reserve at Chatham in preservation.

TRIUMPH 9/1974, Dr Giorgio Arra

2 "HEAD" CLASS

Name	No.	Builders	Laid down	Launched	Commissioned
RAME HEAD	A 134	Burrard DD Co, Vancouver	12 July 1944	22 Nov 1944	18 Aug 1945
BERRY HEAD	A 191	North Vancouver Ship Repairers	15 June 1944	21 Oct 1944	30 May 1945

Displacement, tons: 9 000 standard; 11 270 full load
Length, feet (metres): 416·0 (126·8) pp; 441·5 (134·6) oa
Beam, feet (metres): 57·5 (17·5)
Draught, feet (metres): 22·5 (6·9)
Guns: 11—40 mm
Main engines: Triple expansion; 2 500 ihp
Boilers: 2 Foster Wheeler
Speed, knots: 10 approx
Oil fuel, tons: 1 600 capacity
Complement: 425

Escort Maintenance Ships. To reserve in 1972.
Rame Head accommodation ship at Portsmouth since June 1976. *Berry Head*, at Devonport.

RAME HEAD 6/1976, Dr. Giorgio Arra

UK 587

ROYAL YACHT

Name	No.	Builders	Laid down	Launched	Commissioned
BRITANNIA	A 00	John Brown & Co Ltd, Clydebank	July 1952	16 April 1953	14 Jan 1954

Displacement, tons: 3 990 light; 4 961 full load
Measurement, tons: 5 769 gross
Dimensions, feet (metres): 380·0 wl; 412·2 oa × 55·0 × 17·0 *(115·9; 125·7 × 16·8 × 5·2)*
Main engines: Single reduction geared turbines; 2 shafts; 12 000 shp = 21 knots
Boilers: 2
Oil fuel, tons: 330 (490 with auxiliary fuel tanks)
Range, miles: 2 100 at 20 knots; 2 400 at 18 knots; 3 000 at 15 knots
Complement: 270

Designed as a medium sized naval hospital ship for use by Her Majesty The Queen in peacetime as the Royal Yacht. Construction conformed to mercantile practice. Fitted with Denny-Brown single fin stabilisers to reduce roll in bad weather from 20 to 6 degrees. Cost £2·098 million. To pass under the bridges of the St. Lawrence Seaway when she visited Canada, the top 20 feet of her mainmast and the radio aerial on her foremast were hinged in Nov 1958 so that they could be lowered as required.

BRITANNIA 6/1977, John Mortimer

ICE PATROL SHIP

Name	No.	Builders	Laid down	Launched	Commissioned
ENDURANCE (ex-*Anita Dan*)	A 171	Krögerwerft, Rendsburg	1955	May 1956	Dec 1956

Displacement, tons: 3 600
Measurement, tons: 2 641 gross
Length, feet (metres): 273·5 *(89·7)* pp; 300 *(91·44)* oa; 305 *(92·96);* including helicopter deck extension
Beam, feet (metres): 46 *(14·02)*
Draught, feet (metres): 18 *(5·5)*
Aircraft: 2 Whirlwind Mk IX helicopters
Guns: 2—20 mm
Main engine: 1 B & W 550 VTBF diesel; 3 220 ihp; 1 shaft
Speed, knots: 14·5
Range, miles: 12 000 at 14·5 knots
Complement: 119 (13 officers, 106 men, including a small Royal Marine detachment) plus 12 spare berths for scientists

Purchased from J. Lauritzen Lines, Copenhagen (announced on 20 Feb 1967). Strengthened for operation in ice. Converted by Harland & Wolff, Belfast 1967-68 into an ice patrol ship for southern waters, undertaking hydrographic and oceanographic surveys and acting as support ship for the British Antarctic Survey and guard vessel. Original cost £1·8 million.
An unusual feature for one of HM ships is her hull painted a vivid red for easy identification in the ice.

ENDURANCE 6/1977, Wright and Logan

HOVERCRAFT

Note: The RN Hovercraft Trials Unit was established at Lee-on-the-Solent in 1974.

2 WINCHESTER (SR.N6) TYPE

Displacement, tons: 10 normal gross weight
Dimensions, feet (metres): 48·4 × 23·0 × 15·0 oa (height); 4·0 (skirt) *(14·8 × 7 × 4·6; 1·3)*
Main engine: 1 Rolls-Royce Gnome gas turbine; 900 shp = 50 knots
Range, miles: 200

Modified with radar and military communications equipment for its primary role of a fast amphibious communication craft to support Royal Marine units.

SR.N6 1975, BHC

588 UK

1 WELLINGTON (BH.N7) TYPE

Displacement, tons: 50 max weight; 33 light
Dimensions, feet (metres): 78·3 × 45·5 × 34·0 oa (height); 5·5 (skirt) (23·9 × 13 × 10·4; 1·7)
Main engine: 1 Rolls-Royce Proteus gas turbine; 4 250 shp = 60 knots
Complement: 14 plus trials crew

Costing about £700 000, delivered to the inter-Service Hovercraft Trials Unit at the Royal Naval Air Station, Lee-on-Solent, in April 1970. She could be used as a missile armed fast patrol craft or amphibious assault craft. Winter trials in Swedish waters in Feb 1972. Records established: longest open sea voyage, furthest north, and sustained speeds of over 55 knots in the Baltic.

BH.N7   6/1977, Dr. Giorgio Arra

1 SR.N5 TYPE

This small hovercraft is used for crew training.

SR.N5   4/1976, C. and S. Taylor

CHARTER

The Vosper Thornycroft VT2 hovercraft was chartered for trials in 1976 by MOD.
An SR.N4 hovercraft was chartered for a short period of trials in 1976.

DIVING TRIALS SHIP

Name	No.	Builders	Commissioned
RECLAIM (ex-*Salverdant*)	A 231	Wm Simons & Co Ltd, Renfrew	Oct 1948

Displacement, tons: 1 200 standard; 1 800 full load
Dimensions, feet (metres): 200 pp; 217·8 oa × 38 × 15·5 (61; 66·4 × 11·6 × 4·7)
Main engines: Triple expansion; 2 shafts; 1 500 ihp = 12 knots
Oil fuel, tons: 310
Range, miles: 3 000
Complement: 100

Engined by Aitchison Blair Ltd. Laid down on 9 April 1946. Launched on 12 March 1948. Construction based on the design of a "King Salvor" class naval ocean salvage vessel. First deep diving and submarine rescue vessel built as such for the Royal Navy. Fitted with sonar, radar, echo-sounding apparatus for detection of sunken wrecks, and equipped for submarine rescue work. Due for replacement, a design contract for a "sea-bed operations vessel" having been awarded to Scotts, Greenock in June 1977. An order could be forthcoming in 1978.

RECLAIM   6/1977, Dr. Giorgio Arra

LIGHT FORCES

(See Deletion List for "Dark" and "Brave" Classes).
(See Tenders section for "Alert" patrol craft).

5 +2 "ISLAND" CLASS (OFFSHORE PATROL CRAFT)

Name	No.	Builders	Commissioned
JERSEY	P 295	Hall Russell & Co Ltd	15 Oct 1976
GUERNSEY	P 297	Hall Russell & Co Ltd	28 Oct 1977
SHETLAND	P 298	Hall Russell & Co Ltd	14 July 1977
ORKNEY	P 299	Hall Russell & Co Ltd	25 Feb 1977
LINDISFARNE	P 300	Hall Russell & Co Ltd	1978

Displacement, tons: 925 standard; 1 250 full load
Dimensions, feet (metres): 195·3 oa × 35·8 × 14 (59·6 × 10·9 × 4·3)
Gun: 1—40 mm
Main engines: 2 diesels; 1 shaft; 4 380 hp = 16 knots
Range, miles: 7 000 at 12 knots
Complement: 34 (accommodation for 40)

Order announced 11 Feb 1975. Order placed 2 July 1975. *Jersey* launched 18 March 1976, *Orkney* 29 June 1976, *Shetland* 22 Oct 1976 *Guernsey* 17 Feb 1977 and *Lindisfarne* 1 June 1977. Can carry small RM detachment.
Two more of class ordered from Hall Russell 21 Oct 1977.

Cost: For *Jersey* and *Orkney* building cost £3·3 million. Running cost £0·5 million per ship per year at 1976 prices.

JERSEY   6/1977, Michael D. J. Lennon

UK 589

4 "BIRD" CLASS (LARGE PATROL CRAFT)

Name	No.	Builders	Commissioned
KINGFISHER	P 260	R. Dunston Ltd, Hessle	8 Oct 1975
CYGNET	P 261	R. Dunston Ltd, Hessle	8 July 1976
*PETEREL	P 262	R. Dunston Ltd, Hessle	7 Feb 1977
*SANDPIPER	P 263	R. Dunston Ltd, Hessle	16 Sept 1977

*RNR

Displacement, tons: 190
Dimensions, feet (metres): 120 oa × 23 × 6·5 (36·6 × 7·0 × 2)
Guns: 1—40 mm; 2 MG
Main engines: 2 Paxman 16YJCM diesels; 4 200 bhp = 21 knots
Oil fuel, tons: 35
Range, miles: 2 000 at 14 knots
Complement: 24 (4 officers, 20 ratings)

Based on the smaller "Seal" class RAF rescue launches with some improvement to sea-keeping qualities and fitted with stabilisers. *Kingfisher* launched 20 Sept 1974. *Cygnet* 6 Oct 1975. *Peterel* 14 May 1976. *Sandpiper* 20 Jan 1977.

Cost: Average cost for building £1 million each.

Design: Comparison of later craft with *Kingfisher* shows an expected attempt to cut down topweight eg radar cross-trees, deletion of scuttles.

Duties: *Kingfisher* and *Cygnet* attached to MCM Rosyth having been found unsuitable for Fishery Protection; *Peterel* RNR North Western group (Clyde); *Sandpiper* RNR Channel group (London).

PETEREL 6/1977, Michael D. J. Lennon

3 FAST TRAINING BOATS

Name	No.	Builders	Commissioned
SCIMITAR	P 271	Vosper Thornycroft Group, Porchester Shipyard	19 July 1970
CUTLASS	P 274	Vosper Thornycroft Group, Porchester Shipyard	12 Nov 1970
SABRE	P 275	Vosper Thornycroft Group, Porchester Shipyard	5 Mar 1971

Displacement, tons: 102 full load
Dimensions, feet (metres): 90·0 wl; 100·0 oa × 26·6 × 6·4 (27·4; 30·5 × 8·1 × 1·9)
Main engines: 2 Rolls-Royce Proteus gas turbines; 9 000 hp = 40 knots (2 Foden diesels for cruising in CODAG arrangement)
Range, miles: 425 at 35 knots; 1 500 at 11·5 knots
Complement: 12 (2 officers, 10 ratings)

Hull of glued laminated wood construction. Design developed from that of "Brave" class fast patrol boats. Design permits fitting of third gas-turbine and a gun armament if required. Launch dates:— *Cutlass* 19 Feb 1970, *Sabre* 21 April 1970, *Scimitar* 4 Dec 1969.

SCIMITAR 6/1977, Michael D. J. Lennon

1 VOSPER THORNYCROFT (FAST ATTACK CRAFT—PATROL)

Name	No.	Builders	Commissioned
TENACITY	P 276	Vosper Thornycroft Ltd	17 Feb 1973

Displacement, tons: 165 standard; 220 full load
Dimensions, feet (metres): 144·5 oa × 26·6 × 7·8 (44·1 × 8·1 × 2·4)
Guns: 2 MGs
Main engines: 3 Rolls-Royce Proteus gas turbines; 3 shafts; 12 750 bhp = 40 knots; 2 Paxman Ventura 6-cyl diesels on wing shafts for cruising = 16 knots
Range, miles: 2 500 at 15 knots
Complement: 32 (4 officers, 28 ratings)

Built as a private venture and launched on 18 Feb 1969 at Camber Shipyard, Portsmouth. Steel hull and aluminium alloy superstructure. Purchased by the Ministry of Defence (Navy) on 25 Jan 1972 for approximately £750 000 "as lying" and refitted with minor alterations and additions to meet naval requirements. To be used for exercises and fishery protection. Decca nav, radar.

Cost: After conversion £1·26 million.

TENACITY 1974, Michael D. J. Lennon

5 MODIFIED "TON" CLASS

Name	No.	Builders	Commissioned
BEACHAMPTON	P 1007 (ex-M 1107)	Goole SB Co	1953
MONKTON	P 1055 (ex-M 1155)	Herd & Mackenzie, Buckie	1956
WASPERTON	P 1089 (ex-M 1189)	J. Samuel White & Co Ltd	1956
WOLVERTON	P 1093 (ex-M 1193)	Montrose SY Co	1957
YARNTON	P 1096 (ex-M 1196)	Pickersgill	1956

Displacement, tons: 360 standard; 425 full load
Dimensions, feet (metres): 140·0 pp; 153·0 oa × 28·8 × 8·2 (42·7; 46·3 × 8·8 × 2·5)
Guns: 2—40 mm Bofors (single, 1 forward, 1 aft)
Main engines: 2 diesels; 2 shafts; 3 000 bhp = 15 knots
Oil fuel, tons: 45
Range, miles: 2 300 at 13 knots
Complement: 30 (5 officers and 25 ratings, but varies)

Former coastal minesweepers of the "Ton" class, refitted at the end of 1971, re-designated as coastal patrol vessels with limited wire-sweeping capability. Fitted with limited armour in bridge area. Form 6th Patrol Squadron Hong Kong.

MONKTON 6/1977, Dr. Giorgio Arra

2 "FORD" CLASS (SDBs)

Name	No.	Builders	Commissioned
DEE (ex-*Beckford*)	P 3104	Wm. Simons, Renfrew	1953
DROXFORD	P 3113	Pimblott, Northwich	1954

Displacement, tons: 120 standard; 142 full load
Dimensions, feet (metres): 110·0 wl; 117·2 oa × 20·0 × 7·0 (33·6; 35·7 × 6·1 × 2·1)
A/S weapons: DC rails; large and small DC
Main engines: Davey Paxman diesels. Foden engine on centre shaft. 1 100 bhp = 18 knots
Oil fuel, tons: 23
Complement: 19

Built in 1953-57. Last survivors of a class of 20. *Dee* attached to Liverpool University RNU (administered by RNR Mersey) and *Droxford* to Glasgow University RNU (administered by RNR Clyde). *Dee* renamed 1965, this name having been used for *Droxford* 1955-65.

DEE 8/1977, Michael D. J. Lennon

590 UK

SURVEY SHIPS

1 IMPROVED "HECLA" CLASS

Name	No.	Builders	Commissioned
HERALD	A 138	Robb Caledon, Leith	31 Oct 1974

Displacement, tons: 2 000 standard; 2 945 full load
Dimensions, feet (metres): 260·1 oa × 49·1 × 15·6 *(79·3 × 15 × 4·7)*
Aircraft: 1 Wasp helicopter
Main engines: Diesel-electric drive; 1 shaft
Speed, knots: 14
Range, miles: 12 000 at 11 knots
Complement: 128

A later version of the "Hecla" class design. Fitted with Hydroplot Satellite navigation system, computerised data logging, gravimeter, magnetometer, sonars, echo-sounders, coring and oceanographic winches, passive stabilisation tank, bow thruster and two 35 foot surveying motor-boats.
Laid down 9 Nov 1972. Launched by Mrs Mary Hall, wife of the Hydrographer, on 4 Oct 1973.

Cost: £5·2 million building cost.

HERALD 4/1977, Wright and Logan

3 "HECLA" CLASS

Name	No.	Builders	Commissioned
HECLA	A 133	Yarrow & Co, Blythswood	9 Sept 1965
HECATE	A 137	Yarrow & Co Ltd, Scotstoun	20 Dec 1965
HYDRA	A 144	Yarrow & Co, Blythswood	5 May 1966

Displacement, tons: 1 915 light; 2 733 full load
Measurement, tons: 2 898 gross
Length, feet (metres): 235 *(71·6)* pp; 260·1 *(79·3)* oa
Beam, feet (metres): 49·1 *(15·0)*
Draught, feet (metres): 15·6 *(4·7)*
Aircraft: 1 Wasp helicopter
Main engines: Diesel-electric drive; 1 shaft; 3 Paxman Ventura 12-cyl Vee turbocharged diesels; 3 840 bhp; 1 electric motor; 2 000 shp
Speed, knots: 14
Oil fuel, tons: 450
Range, miles: 12 000 at 11 knots
Complement: 118 (14 officers, 104 ratings)

The first RN ships to be designed with a combined oceanographical and hydrographic role. Of merchant ship design and similar in many respects to the Royal Research ship *Discovery*. The hull is strengthened for navigation in ice, and a bow thruster is fitted. The fore end of the superstructure incorporates a Landrover garage and the after end a helicopter hangar with adjacent flight deck. Equipped with chartroom, drawing office and photographic studio; two laboratories, dry and wet; electrical, engineering and shipwright workshops, large storerooms and two surveying motor-boats. Air-conditioned throughout.
Average cost £1·25 million. *Hecate* laid down 26 Oct 1964, launched 31 March 1965. *Hecla*; 6 May 1964, 21 Dec 1964; *Hydra* 14 May 1964, 14 July 1965.

HECATE 6/1977, C. and S. Taylor

COASTAL SURVEY SHIPS

4 "BULLDOG" CLASS

Name	No.	Builders	Commissioned
BULLDOG	A 317	Brooke Marine Ltd, Lowestoft	21 Mar 1968
BEAGLE	A 319	Brooke Marine Ltd, Lowestoft	9 May 1968
FOX	A 320	Brooke Marine Ltd, Lowestoft	11 July 1968
FAWN	A 325	Brooke Marine Ltd, Lowestoft	10 Sept 1968

Displacement, tons: 800 standard; 1 088 full load
Dimensions, feet (metres): 189 oa × 37·5 × 12 *(60·1 × 11·4 × 3·6)*
Guns: Fitted for 2—20 mm
Main engines: 4 Lister Blackstone ERS8M, 8-cyl, 4 stroke diesels, coupled to 2 shafts; cp propellers; 2 000 bhp = 15 knots
Range, miles: 4 000 at 12 knots
Complement: 41 (5 officers, 36 ratings)

Originally designed for duty overseas, working in pairs. Launch dates: *Bulldog* on 12 July 1967, *Beagle* on 7 Sept 1967, *Fox* on 6 Nov 1967 and *Fawn* on 29 Feb 1968. Built to commercial standards. Fitted with passive tank stabilizer, precision ranging radar, Decca "Hifix" system, automatic steering. Air-conditioned throughout. Carry 28·5 ft surveying motor-boat.

FOX 6/1977, Michael D. J. Lennon

INSHORE SURVEY CRAFT

Note: Orders expected for two inshore survey craft to replace *Waterwitch* and *Woodlark* with three to follow to replace the "E" class.

3 "E" CLASS

Name	No.	Builders	Commissioned
ECHO	A 70	J. Samuel White & Co Ltd, Cowes	12 Sept 1958
ENTERPRISE	A 71	M. W. Blackmore & Sons Ltd, Bideford	1959
EGERIA	A 72	Wm. Weatherhead & Sons Ltd, Cockenzie	1959

Displacement, tons: 120 standard; 160 full load
Dimensions, feet (metres): 106·8 oa × 22·0 × 6·8 *(32·6 × 7 × 2·1)*
Gun: Fitted for 1—40 mm
Main engines: 2 Paxman diesels; 2 shafts; cp propellers; 1 400 bhp = 14 knots
Oil fuel, tons: 15
Range, miles: 1 600 at 10 knots
Complement: 18 (2 officers, 16 ratings); accommodation for 22 (4 officers, 18 ratings)

Echo, the first Inshore Survey Craft, was launched on 1 May 1957. Equipped with two echo sounding machines, sonar, radar, wire sweep gear and surveying motor boat.

EGERIA 6/1977, Michael D. J. Lennon

2 "HAM" CLASS

Name	No.	Builders	Commissioned
WATERWITCH (ex-*Powderham*)	M 2720	J. Samuel White & Co Ltd, Cowes	1959
WOODLARK (ex-*Yaxham*)	M 2780	J. Samuel White & Co Ltd, Cowes	1958

Displacement, tons: 120 standard; 160 full load
Dimensions, feet (metres): 107·5 oa × 22 × 5·5 *(32·4 × 6·5 × 1·7)*
Main engines: Diesels; 2 shafts; 1 100 bhp = 14 knots
Endurance, miles: 1 500 at 12 knots
Complement: 18 (2 officers, 16 ratings)

Former inshore minesweepers of the "Ham" class converted to replace the old survey motor launches *Meda* and *Medusa* for operation in inshore waters at home. *Waterwitch*, operated by RMAS.

WOODLARK — 6/1977, Michael D. J. Lennon

ROYAL FLEET AUXILIARY SERVICE

Note: Many of large RFAs carry two boxed 40 mm guns

Commodore, RFA: Commodore S. C. Dunlop, MBE

LARGE FLEET TANKERS (AOF(L))

3 "OL" CLASS

Name	No.	Builders	Commissioned
OLWEN (ex-*Olynthus*)*	A 122	Hawthorn Leslie, Hebburn	21 June 1965
OLNA	A 123	Hawthorn Leslie, Hebburn	1 April 1966
OLMEDA (ex-*Oleander*)	A 124	Swan Hunter, Wallsend	18 Oct 1965

* Refit

Displacement, tons: 10 890 light; 36 000 full load
Measurement, tons: 25 100 deadweight; 18 600 gross
Dimensions, feet (metres): 611·1 pp; 648·0 oa × 84·0 × 34·0 *(185·9; 197·5 × 25·6 × 10·5)*
Aircraft: 2 Wessex helicopters (can carry 3)
Main engines: Pametrada double reduction geared turbines; 26 500 shp = 19 knots
Boilers: 2 Babcock & Wilcox, (750 psi; 950°F)
Complement: 87 (25 officers and 62 ratings)

Largest and fastest ships when they joined the Royal Fleet Auxiliary Service. *Olmeda* was launched on 19 Nov 1964, while *Olna* and *Olwen* were launched on 28 July 1965 and 10 July 1964, respectively.
Designed for underway replenishment of the Fleet both alongside or by helicopter. Specially strengthened for operations in ice, fully air-conditioned. *Olna* has a transverse bow thrust unit for improved manoeuvrability in confined waters and a new design of replenishment-at-sea systems.

Capacity: Original figures as follows; 18 400 tons FFO; 1 720 tons diesel; 130 tons lub oil; 3 730 tons Avcat; 280 tons Mogas. The proportions of FFO and diesel may now be changed.

Hangar: On port side of funnel can house three helicopters. On starboard side acts as garage for vehicles.

OLWEN — 6/1977, Dr. Giorgio Arra

2 LATER "TIDE" CLASS

Name	No.	Builders	Commissioned
TIDESPRING	A 75	Hawthorn Leslie, Hebburn	18 Jan 1963
TIDEPOOL	A 76	Hawthorn Leslie, Hebburn	28 June 1963

Displacement, tons: 8 531 light; 27 400 full load
Measurement, tons: 18 900 deadweight; 14 130 gross
Dimensions, feet (metres): 550·0 pp; 583·0 oa × 71·0 × 32·0 *(167·7; 177·6 × 21·6 × 9·8)*
Aircraft: 2 Wessex helicopters (can carry 3)
Main engines: Double reduction geared turbines; 15 000 shp = 18·3 knots
Boilers: 2 Babcock & Wilcox
Complement: 110 (30 officers and 80 ratings)

Highly specialised ships for fuelling (13 000 tons cargo fuel) and storing naval vessels at sea. *Tidespring* was laid down on 24 July 1961, launched on 3 May 1962. *Tidepool* was laid down on 4 Dec 1961, launched on 11 Dec 1962.

Hangar: On port side of funnel can house three helicopters. On starboard side acts as garage for vehicles.

TIDESPRING — 6/1977, Dr. Giorgio Arra

592　UK

SMALL FLEET TANKERS (AOF(S))

5 "ROVER" CLASS

Name	No.	Builders	Commissioned
GREEN ROVER	A 268	Swan Hunter, Hebburn-on-Tyne	15 Aug 1969
GREY ROVER	A 269	Swan Hunter, Hebburn-on-Tyne	10 April 1970
BLUE ROVER	A 270	Swan Hunter, Hebburn-on-Tyne	15 July 1970
GOLD ROVER	A 271	Swan Hunter, Wallsend-on-Tyne	22 Mar 1974
BLACK ROVER	A 273	Swan Hunter, Wallsend-on-Tyne	23 Aug 1974

Displacement, tons: 4,700 light; 11 522 full load
Measurement, tons: 6 692 (A 271 and 273), 6 822 (remainder) deadweight; 7 510 gross; 3 185 net
Dimensions, feet (metres): 461·0 oa × 63·0 × 24·0 (140·6 × 19·2 × 7·3)
Main engines: 2 Pielstick 16-cyl diesels; 1 shaft; cp propeller; 15 300 bhp = 18 knots
Range, miles: 15 000 at 15 knots
Complement: 47 (16 officers and 31 men)

Small fleet tankers designed to replenish HM ships at sea with fuel, fresh water, limited dry cargo and refrigerated stores under all conditions while underway. A helicopter landing platform is provided served by a stores lift, to enable stores to be transferred at sea by "vertical lift". *Green Rover* was launched on 19 Dec 1968, *Grey Rover* on 17 April 1969, *Blue Rover* on 11 Nov 1969. *Gold Rover* on 7 March 1973 and *Black Rover* on 30 Oct 1973. Cargo capacity 6 600 tons fuel.

Cost: *Gold Rover* cost £7·7 million, an increase of £4·7 million over *Green Rover*. Running costs at 1976 prices £1·0 million per ship per year.

Training: *Gold Rover* employed on training duties at Portland.

BLACK ROVER (variation in stern)　　9/1975, C. and S. Taylor

GREEN ROVER (variation in stern)　　8/1975, Wright and Logan

SUPPORT TANKERS (AOS)

Note: Majority under long-term charter; *Dewdale* returned to owners September 1977.

Name	No.	Builders	Commissioned
PEARLEAF	A 77	Blythswood Shipbuilding Co Ltd, Scotstoun	Jan 1960

Displacement, tons: 25 790 full load
Measurement, tons: 18 711 deadweight; 12 353 gross; 7 215 net
Dimensions, feet (metres): 535 pp; 568 oa × 71·7 × 30 (162·7; 173·2 × 21·9 × 9·2)
Main engines: Rowan Doxford 6-cyl diesels; 8 800 bhp = 16 knots
Complement: 55

Chartered from Jacobs and Partners Ltd, London on completion. Launched on 15 Oct 1959. Can carry three different grades of cargo. Astern and abeam fuelling.

PEARLEAF　　6/1977, Dr. Giorgio Arra

Name	No.	Builders	Commissioned
PLUMLEAF	A 78	Blyth DD & Eng Co Ltd	July 1960

Displacement, tons: 26 480 full load
Measurement, tons: 19 430 deadweight; 12 459 gross
Dimensions, feet (metres): 534 pp; 560 oa × 72 × 30 (162·9; 170·8 × 22 × 9·2)
Main engines: N.E. Doxford 6-cyl diesels; 9 500 bhp = 15·5 knots
Complement: 55

Launched 29 March 1960. Astern and abeam fuelling.

PLUMLEAF　　4/1976, Dr. Giorgio Arra

Name	No.	Builders	Commissioned
ORANGELEAF (ex-MV *Southern Satellite*)	A 80	Furness Shipbuilding Co Ltd, Haverton Hill on Tees	June 1955

Measurement, tons: 18 222 deadweight; 12 146 gross; 6 800 net
Dimensions, feet (metres): 525 pp; 556·5 oa × 71·7 × 30·5 (160·1; 169·7 × 21·9 × 9·3)
Main engines: Doxford 6-cyl diesel; 6 800 bhp = 14 knots
Oil fuel, tons: 1 610
Complement: 55

Launched on 8 Feb 1955. Chartered from South Georgia Co Ltd, 25 May 1959. Astern and abeam fuelling. Under refit. To be returned to owners 1978.

ORANGELEAF　　4/1976

UK 593

Name	No.	Builders	Commissioned
CHERRYLEAF (ex-*Overseas Adventurer*)	A 82	Rheinstahl Nordseewerke	1963

Measurement, tons: 19 700 deadweight; 13 700 gross; 7 648 net
Dimensions, feet (metres): 559 × 72 × 30 *(170·5 × 22 × 9·2)*
Machinery: 7-cyl MAN diesel; 8 400 bhp = 16 knots
Complement: 55

Ordered and completed in 1963. Transferred to RFA March 1973. No RAS capability. Under refit.

CHERRYLEAF　　　　　　　　　　　　　　　　　　　8/1975, C. and S. Taylor

COASTAL TANKER (AO(H))

1 "EDDY" CLASS

Name	No.	Builders	Commissioned
EDDYFIRTH	A 261	Lobnitz & Co Ltd, Renfrew	10 Feb 1954

Displacement, tons: 1 960 light; 4 160 full load
Measurement, tons: 2 200 deadweight; 2 222 gross
Dimensions, feet (metres): 270 pp; 286 oa × 44 × 17·2 *(82·4; 87·2 × 13·4 × 5·2)*
Main engines: 1 set triple expansion; 1 shaft; 1 750 ihp = 12 knots
Boilers: 2 oil burning cylindrical

The last of a class of eight, all completed 1952-54. Cargo capacity: 1 650 tons oil.

EDDYFIRTH　　　　　　　　　　　　　　　　　　　10/1976, Wright and Logan

FLEET REPLENISHMENT SHIPS (AEFS)

Name	No.	Builders	Commissioned
FORT GRANGE	A 385	Scott-Lithgow	1978
FORT AUSTIN	A 386	Scott-Lithgow	1979

Displacement, tonnes: 20 000+
Measurement, tons: 9 843 dw
Dimensions, feet (metres): 603 × 79 × 29·5 *(183·9 × 24·1 × 9)*
Aircraft: 1 Wessex helicopter
Main engines: 1—8-cyl Sulzer diesel; 23 300 hp; 1 shaft = 20 knots
Complement: 201

Ordered in Nov 1971. To be fitted with a helicopter flight-deck and hangar, thus allowing not only for vertical replenishment but also a fuelling point for Force A/S helicopters. *Fort Grange* laid down 9 Nov 1973, launched 9 Dec 1976. *Fort Austin* laid down 9 Dec 1975. A/S stores for helicopters carried on board. To replace *Resurgent* and *Retainer*.

FORT GRANGE　　　　　　　　　　　　　　　　　　1972, MOD (N) Drawing

Name	No.	Builders	Commissioned
RESOURCE	A 480	Scotts Shipbuilding & Eng Co, Greenock	16 May 1967
REGENT	A 486	Harland & Wolff, Belfast	6 June 1967

Displacement, tons: 22 890 full load
Measurements, tons: 18 029 gross
Dimensions, feet (metres): 600·0 pp; 640·0 oa × 77·2 × 26·1 *(182·8; 195·1 × 23·5 × 8)*
Aircraft: 1 Wessex helicopter
Guns: Fitted for 2—40 mm Bofors (single) which are not carried in peacetime
Main engines: AEI steam turbines; 20 000 shp = 21 knots
Complement: 119 RFA officers and ratings; 52 Naval Dept industrial and non-industrial civil servants; 11 Royal Navy (1 officer and 10 ratings) for helicopter flying and maintenance

Ordered on 24 Jan 1963. They have lifts for armaments and stores, and helicopter platforms for transferring loads at sea. Designed from the outset as Fleet Replenishment Ships (previous ships had been converted merchant vessels). Air-conditioned. *Resource* was launched at Greenock on 11 Feb 1966, *Regent* at Belfast on 9 March 1966. Official title is Ammunition, Explosives, Food, Stores Ship (AEFS).

RESOURCE　　　　　　　　　　　　　　　　　　　1976, Michael D. J. Lennon

ARMAMENT SUPPORT SHIPS (AE)

Name	No.	Builders	Commissioned
RESURGENT (ex-*Changchow*)	A 280	Scotts Shipbuilding & Engineering Co Ltd, Greenock	1951
RETAINER (ex-*Chungking*)	A 329	Scotts Shipbuilding & Engineering Co Ltd, Greenock	1950

Displacement, tons: 14 400
Measurement, tons: *Resurgent* 9 357 gross; *Retainer* 9 498 gross
Dimensions, feet (metres): 477·2 oa × 62 × 29 *(145·8 × 18·9 × 8·8)*
Main engines: Doxford diesel; 1 shaft; 6 500 bhp = 16 knots
Oil fuel, tons: 925
Complement: 107

Retainer was purchased in 1952 and converted into a naval storeship during autumn 1954-April 1955 by Palmers Hebburn Co Ltd, where further conversion was carried out March-Aug 1957 to extend her facilities as a stores ship, including the fitting out of holds to carry naval stores, the installation of lifts for stores, the provision of extra cargo handling gear and new bridge wings. *Resurgent* was taken over on completion. To be replaced by "Fort" class.

RETAINER　　　　　　　　　　　　　　　　　　　9/1977, Michael D. J. Lennon

594 UK

STORES SUPPORT SHIPS (AVS/AFS)

Name	No.	Builders	Commissioned
LYNESS	A 339	Swan Hunter & Wigham Richardson Ltd, Wallsend-on-Tyne	22 Dec 1966
STROMNESS	A 344	Swan Hunter & Wigham Richardson Ltd, Wallsend-on-Tyne	21 Mar 1967
TARBATNESS	A 345	Swan Hunter & Wigham Richardson Ltd, Wallsend-on-Tyne	10 Aug 1967

Displacement, tons: 9,010 light; 16 792 full load (14 000 normal operating)
Measurement, tons: 7 782 deadweight; 12 359 gross; 4 744 net
Dimensions, feet (metres): 490 pp; 524 oa × 72 × 22 (149·4; 159·7 × 22 × 6·7)
Aircraft: Helicopter deck
Main engines: Wallsend-Sulzer 8-cyl RD.76 diesel; 11 520 bhp = 18 knots
Range, miles: 12 000 at 16 knots
Complement: 151 (25 officers, 82 ratings, 44 stores personnel)

Lifts and mobile appliances provided for handling stores internally, and a new replenishment at sea system and a helicopter landing platform for transferring loads at sea. A novel feature of the ships is the use of closed-circuit television to monitor the movement of stores. All air-conditioned. *Lyness* was launched on 7 April 1966, *Stromness* on 16 Sept 1966, and *Tarbatness* 22 Feb 1967. *Lyness* is an Air-Stores Support Ship and cost £3·5 million.

Cost: Running cost, at 1976 prices, £1·6 million per ship per year.

LYNESS 4/1977, Dr. Giorgio Arra

STORE CARRIERS (AK)

Name	No.	Builders	Commissioned
BACCHUS	A 404	Henry Robb Ltd, Leith	Sept 1962
HEBE	A 406	Henry Robb Ltd, Leith	May 1962

Displacement, tons: 2 740 light; 8 173 full load
Measurement, tons: 5 312 deadweight; 4 823 gross; 2 441 net
Dimensions, feet (metres): 379 oa × 55 × 22 (115·6 × 16·8 × 6·4)
Main engines: Swan Hunter Sulzer diesel; 1 shaft; 5 500 bhp = 15 knots
Oil fuel, tons: 720
Complement: 57

Built for the British India Steam Navigation Co for charter to the Royal Navy on completion. Crew accommodation and engines aft as in tankers. In 1973 both purchased by P and O SN Co, remaining on charter to MOD (N). Boxed 40 mm guns carried on board.

HEBE 6/1977, Dr. Giorgio Arra

ROYAL MARITIME AUXILIARY SERVICE

Notes: (a) The Royal Maritime Auxiliary Service and Port Auxiliary Service were combined as RMAS on 1 October 1976.
(b) To avoid over complication the ships and vessels of the Royal Naval Auxiliary Service and some of the Royal Corps of Transport are included here.

MOORING, SALVAGE AND BOOM VESSELS

Note: *Scarab* ("Insect" Class tender) acts as mooring vessel.

2 "WILD DUCK" CLASS (A)

2 "IMPROVED WILD DUCK" CLASS (B)

2 "LATER WILD DUCK" CLASS (C)

Name		No.	Builders	Commissioned
MANDARIN	} A	P 192	Cammell Laird & Co Ltd, Birkenhead	5 Mar 1964
PINTAIL		P 193	Cammell Laird & Co Ltd, Birkenhead	Mar 1964
GARGANEY	} B	P 194	Brooke Marine Ltd, Lowestoft	20 Sept 1966
GOLDENEYE		P 195	Brooke Marine Ltd, Lowestoft	21 Dec 1966
GOOSANDER	} C	P 196	Robb Caledon Ltd	10 Sept 1973
POCHARD		P 197	Robb Caledon Ltd	11 Dec 1973

Displacement, tons: (A) 750 light; 1 200 full load. (B) 850 light; 1 300 full load.
(C) 941 light; 1 622 full load
Dimensions, feet (metres): (A) 181·8 × 36·6 × 13 (55·4 × 11·2 × 4).
(B) 189·8 × 36·6 × 13 (57·9 × 11·2 × 4). (C) 197·6 × 40·1 × 13·8 (60·2 × 12·2 × 4·2)
Main engine: 1 Davey Paxman 16-cyl diesel; 1 shaft; cp propeller; 550 bhp (A and B); 750 bhp (C)
Speed, knots: 10 (A and B); 10·8 (C)
Range, miles: 3 260 at 9·5 knots (C); 3 000 at 10 knots (A and B)
Complement: 26

Mandarin was the first of a new class of marine service vessels. Launched on 17 Sept 1963. *Pintail* was launched on 3 Dec 1963. *Garganey* and *Goldeneye* were built in 1965-67. *Goosander* and *Pochard* of the later "Later Wild Duck" class were launched 12 April 1973 and 21 June 1973 respectively. Previously their three tasks were separately undertaken by specialist vessels. Capable of laying out and servicing the heaviest moorings used by the Fleet and also maintaining booms for harbour defence. Heavy lifting equipment enables a wide range of salvage operations to be performed, especially in harbour clearance work. The special heavy winches have an ability for tidal lifts over the apron of 200 tons. Boxed 40 mm guns carried on board.

4 "KIN" CLASS

Name	No.	Builders	Commissioned
KINGARTH	A 232	A. Hall, Aberdeen	1944
KINBRACE	A 281	A. Hall, Aberdeen	1945
KINLOSS	A 482	A. Hall, Aberdeen	1945
UPLIFTER	A 507	Smith's Dock Co Ltd	1944

Displacement, tons: 950 standard; 1 050 full load
Measurement, tons: 262 deadweight; 775 gross
Dimensions, feet (metres): 179·2 oa × 35·2 × 12·0 (54 × 10·6 × 3·6)
Main engines: 1 British Polar Atlas M44M diesel; 630 bhp = 9 knots
Complement: 34

Originally a class of eight classified as Coastal Salvage Vessels, but re-rated Mooring, Salvage and Boom Vessels in 1971. Equipped with horns and heavy rollers. Can lift 200 tons deadweight over the bow. *Kinbrace*, *Kingarth* and *Uplifter* were refitted with diesel engines in 1966-67, and *Kinloss* in 1963-64.

KINLOSS 5/1977, Michael D. J. Lennon

2 "LAY" CLASS

Name	No.	Builders	Commissioned
LAYMOOR (RN)	P 190	Wm. Simons & Co Ltd (Simons-Lobnitz Ltd)	9 Dec 1959
LAYBURN	P 191	Wm. Simons & Co Ltd (Simons-Lobnitz Ltd)	7 June 1960

Displacement, tons: 800 standard; 1 050 full load
Dimensions, feet (metres): 192·7 oa × 34·5 × 11·5 (59 × 10·3 × 3·4)
Main engines: Triple expansion; 1 shaft; 1 300 ihp = 10 knots
Boilers: 2 Foster-Wheeler "D" type; 200 psi
Complement: 26 (4 officers; 22 ratings)

Layburn, cost £565 000. Designed for naval or civilian manning. Good accommodation enables them to be operated in any climate. Oil-fuelled.

LAYBURN   1973, John G. Callis

COASTAL TANKERS

6 "OILPRESS" CLASS

Name	No.	Builders	Commissioned
OILPRESS	Y 21	Appledore Shipbuilders Ltd	1969
OILSTONE	Y 22	Appledore Shipbuilders Ltd	1969
OILWELL	Y 23	Appledore Shipbuilders Ltd	1969
OILFIELD	Y 24	Appledore Shipbuilders Ltd	1969
OILBIRD	Y 25	Appledore Shipbuilders Ltd	1969
OILMAN	Y 26	Appledore Shipbuilders Ltd	1969

Displacement, tons: 280 standard; 530 full load
Dimensions, feet (metres): 130·0 wl; 139·5 oa × 30·0 × 8·3 (39·6; 41·5 × 9 × 2·5)
Main engines: 1 Lister Blackstone ES6 diesel; 1 shaft; 405 shp at 900 rpm
Complement: 11 (4 officers and 7 ratings)

Ordered on 10 May 1967. Three are diesel oil carriers and three FFO carriers. Launched:— *Oilbird* 21 Nov 1968, *Oilfield* 5 Sept 1968, *Oilman* 18 Feb 1969, *Oilpress* 10 June 1968, *Oilstone* 11 July 1968, *Oilwell* 20 Jan 1969. Near sisters to "Water" class.

OILFIELD   6/1977, Dr. Giorgio Arra

TRIALS SHIPS

Name	No.	Builders	Commissioned
NEWTON	A 367	Scott Lithgow Ltd	17 June 1976

Displacement, tons: 3 940
Dimensions, feet (metres): 323·5 × 53 × 18·5 (98·6 × 16 × 5·7)
Main engines: Diesel-electric; 3 Mirrlees Blackstone diesels; 1 shaft; 4 350 bhp = 15 knots
Range, miles: 5 000 at 13 knots
Complement: 61 (including 12 scientists)

Ordered Nov 1971. Laid down 19 Dec 1973. Launched 25 June 1975. Fitted with bow thruster and Kort nozzle. Propulsion system is very quiet. Passive tank stabilisation. Prime duty sonar propagation trials. Can serve as cable-layer with large cable tanks. Special winch system. Based at Plymouth.

NEWTON   6/1977, John G. Callis

UK 595

Name	No.	Builders	Commissioned
WHITEHEAD	A 364	Scotts Shipbuilding Co Ltd, Greenock	1971

Displacement, tons: 3 040 full load
Dimensions, feet (metres): 291·0 wl; 319·0 oa × 48·0 × 17·0 (88·8; 97·3 × 14·6 × 5·2)
Torpedo tubes: 1—21 in (bow, submerged); 3 (1 triple) Mk 32 A/S mounting
Main engines: 2 Paxman 12 YLCM diesels; 1 shaft; 3 400 bhp = 15·5 knots
Range, miles: 4 000 at 12 knots
Complement: 10 officers, 32 ratings, 15 trials and scientific staff

Designed to provide mobile preparation, firing and control facilities for weapons and research vehicles. Launched on 5 May 1970. Named after Robert Whitehead, the torpedo development pioneer and engineer. Fitted with equipment for tracking weapons and target and for analysing the results of trials. Based at Plymouth.

WHITEHEAD   9/1977, Michael D. J. Lennon

Name	No.	Builders	Commissioned
CRYSTAL	RDV 01	HM Dockyard, Devonport	30 Nov 1971

Displacement, tons: 3 040
Dimensions, feet (metres): 413·5 × 56·0 × 5·5 (126·1 × 17·1 × 1·7)
Complement: 60, including scientists

Unpowered floating platform for Sonar Research and Development. Ordered in Dec 1969. Launched 22 March 1971. A harbour-based laboratory without propulsion machinery or steering which provides the Admiralty Underwater Weapons Establishment at Portland with a stable platform on which to carry out acoustic tests and other research projects. Under Dockyard Control.

CRYSTAL   10/1975, C. and S. Taylor

2 "MINER" CLASS

Name	No.	Builders	Commissioned
BRITANNIC (ex-*Miner V*)	—	Philip & Son Ltd, Dartmouth	26 June 1941
STEADY (ex-*Miner VII*)	—	Philip & Son Ltd, Dartmouth	31 Mar 1944

Displacement, tons: 300 standard; 355 full load
Dimensions, feet (metres): 110·2 × 26·5 × 8·0 (33·6 × 8·1 × 2·4)
Main engines: Ruston & Hornsby diesels; 2 shafts; 360 bhp = 10 knots

Last of a class of eight small controlled-minelayers. *Miner V* was converted into a harbour cable-layer and renamed *Britannic* in 1960. *Miner VII* was adapted as a stabilisation trials ship at Portsmouth and renamed *Steady* in 1960. *Britannic* laid-up at Portland as spare ship for *Steady* who normally operates off the Channel Islands.

BRITANNIC   8/1976, Wright and Logan

596 UK

TORPEDO RECOVERY VESSELS

Note: Four new TRVs ordered 1977 from Hall Russell, Aberdeen.

Name	No.	Builders	Commissioned
TORRENT	A 127	Cleland SB Co, Wallsend	10 Sept 1971
TORRID	A 128	Cleland SB Co, Wallsend	Jan 1972

Measurement, tons: 550 gross
Dimensions, feet (metres): 151·0 × 31·5 × 11 (46·1 × 9·6 × 3·4)
Main engines: Paxman diesels; 700 bhp = 12 knots
Complement: 19

Torrent was launched on 29 March 1971 and *Torrid* on 7 Sept 1971. These ships have a stern ramp for torpedo recovery—can carry 22 torpedoes in hold and 10 on deck.
Torrent—Clyde. *Torrid*—Portsmouth.

TORRID   6/1977, Michael D. J. Lennon

Name	No.	Builders	Commissioned
THOMAS GRANT	—	Charles Hill & Sons Ltd, Bristol	July 1953

Displacement, tons: 209 light; 461 full load
Measurement, tons: 252 deadweight; 218 gross
Dimensions, feet (metres): 113·5 × 25·5 × 8·8 (34·6 × 7·8 × 2·7)
Main engines: 2 Mirrlees diesels; 500 hp = 9 knots

Built as a local store carrier. Launched on 11 May 1953. Converted into torpedo recovery vessel in 1968. Based in Clyde area.

THOMAS GRANT   1969

6 "HAM" CLASS

BUCKLESHAM M 2614	**EVERINGHAM** M 2626	**HAVERSHAM** M 2635
DOWNHAM M 2622	**FRITHAM** M 2630	**LASHAM** M 2636

Details similar to other "Ham" class in Mine Warfare section but converted for TRV in 1964 onwards. Now fitted with stern ramp.

TRV 72 TYPE

A number of this SAR type are still in use. Ex-RAF SAR craft.
L 72 in Clyde area.

ENDEAVOUR

Displacement, tons: 88
Dimensions, feet (metres): 76 × 14·5 × 9·8 (23·2 × 4·4 × 3)
Main engine: 1 Lister-Blackstone diesel; 337 hp; 1 shaft = 10·5 knots

Built for Liverpool Customs by R. Dunston & Co in 1966. Subsequently bought by M.O.D. Operates as TRV and range safety craft at Bincleaves Torpedo Range, Portland.

ENDEAVOUR   8/1977, Michael D. J. Lennon

EXPERIMENTAL SHIP

1 Ex-LCT (3)

WHIMBREL (ex-NSC (E) 1012) A 179

Displacement, tons: 300
Dimensions, feet (metres): 187 × 29·5 × 5 (57 × 9 × 1·5)
Main engines: Diesels; 2 shafts

Employed for weapon research by Underwater Weapons Establishment, Portland.

WHIMBREL   1974, Michael D. J. Lennon

CABLE SHIP

Name	No.	Builders	Commissioned
ST. MARGARETS	A 259	Swan Hunter & Wigham Richardson Ltd.	1944

Displacement, tons: 1 300 light; 2 500 full load
Measurement, tons: 1 524 gross; 1 200 deadweight
Dimensions, feet (metres): 228·8 pp; 252 oa × 36·5 × 16·3 (76 × 10·9 × 4·8)
Main engines: Triple expansion; 2 shafts; 1 250 ihp = 12 knots

Provision was made for mounting one 4 inch gun and four 20 mm guns but no armament is fitted. Sister ship *Bullfinch* paid off at Plymouth.

ST. MARGARETS   4/1976, John G. Callis

TARGET SHIP

WAKEFUL (ex-*Dan*, ex-*Heracles*) A 236

Displacement, tons: 900 approx
Measurement, tons: 492 gross
Dimensions, feet (metres): 127·5 oa × 35 × 15·5 (38·9 × 10·7 × 4·7)
Main engines: 2—9-cyl Ruston diesels; 4 750 bhp
Complement: 18

Purchased from Sweden in 1974 at cost of £600 000. Built as a tug by Cochranes, Selby, Yorks and now operated as Submarine Target Ship in the Clyde after undergoing a £1·6 million refit.

WAKEFUL   12/1976, Michael D. J. Lennon

ARMAMENT STORE CARRIERS (AKF)

Name	No.	Builders	Commissioned
THROSK	A 379	Cleland SB Co, Wallsend	Sept 1977

Displacement, tons: 1 968 full load
Measurement, tons: 1 150 dw
Dimensions, feet (metres): 210·9 × 39 × 15 *(64·3 × 11·9 × 4·6)*
Main engines: 2 Mirrlees-Blackstone diesels; 3 000 bhp; 1 shaft = 14 knots
Range, miles: 5 000 at 10 knots
Complement: 22 (plus 10 spare bunks)

Ordered 9 Dec 1975. Laid down 25 Aug 1976, launched 31 March 1977. To carry armament stores in two holds. Two 5 tonne derricks.

THROSK   8/1977, Michael D. J. Lennon

Name	No.	Builders	Commissioned
KINTERBURY	A 378	Philip & Son Ltd	4 Mar 1943

Displacement, tons: 1 490 standard; 1 770 full load
Measurement, tons: 600 deadweight
Dimensions, feet (metres): 199·8 × 34·3 × 13 *(60·9 × 10·2 × 4)*
Main engines: Triple expansion; 1 shaft; 900 ihp = 11 knots
Coal, tons: 154

Launched on 14 Nov 1942. Rated as naval armament carrier. Converted in 1959 with hold stowage and a derrick for handling guided missiles.
In reserve. Sister *Throsk* deleted 1977.

CATAPULT   FLINTLOCK   HOWITZER

Of differing displacements and data.

Name	No.	Builders	Commissioned
MAXIM	A 377	Lobnitz & Co Ltd, Renfrew	1945

Displacement, tons: 604
Measurement, tons: 340 deadweight
Dimensions, feet (metres): 144·5 × 25 × 8 *(44·1 × 7·6 × 2·3)*
Main engines: Reciprocating; 500 ihp = 9 knots
Complement: 13

Launched 6 Aug 1945. Laid up at Pembroke Dock.

WATER CARRIERS

1 "SPA" CLASS

Name	No.	Builders	Commissioned
SPAPOOL	A 222	Charles Hill & Sons Ltd, Bristol	1947

Displacement, tons: 1 219 full load
Measurement, tons: 630 deadweight; 672 to 719 gross
Dimensions, feet (metres): 172 oa × 30 × 12 *(52·5 × 9·2 × 3·6)*
Main engines: Triple expansion; 675 ihp = 9 knots
Coal, tons: 90

Reported as based in Mombasa. Originally class of six with 1—3 in and 2—20 in guns. *Spabeck* carried HTP for submarines *Explorer* and *Excalibur*. Deleted May 1977. *Spa* deleted 1970. *Spalake* and *Spaburn* deleted 1976, *Spabrook* 1977.

UK 597

6 +1 "WATER" CLASS

Name	No.	Builders	Commissioned
WATERCOURSE	Y 15	Drypool Engineering & Drydock Co, Hull	1974
WATERFOWL	Y 16	Drypool Engineering & Drydock Co, Hull	25 May 1974
WATERFALL	Y 17	Drypool Engineering & Drydock Co, Hull	1967
WATERSHED	Y 18	Drypool Engineering & Drydock Co, Hull	1967
WATERSPOUT	Y 19	Drypool Engineering & Drydock Co, Hull	1967
WATERSIDE	Y 20	Drypool Engineering & Drydock Co, Hull	1968
WATERMAN	—	R. Dunston (Hessle) Ltd	1979

Measurement, tons: 285 gross
Dimensions, feet (metres): 131·5 oa × 24·8 × 8 *(40·1 × 7·5 × 2·3)*
Main engine: 1 diesel; 1 shaft; 600 bhp = 11 knots
Complement: 11

Latest pair have after deck-house extended forward. *Waterman* ordered in June 1977 and launched 24 Nov 1977.

WATERSHED   6/1977, John Mortimer

3 "FRESH" CLASS

FRESHBURN   FRESHLAKE   FRESHSPRING

Displacement, tons: 594
Dimensions, feet (metres): 126·2 × 25·5 × 10·8 *(38·5 × 7·8 × 3·3)*
Main engines: Triple expansion; 450 ihp = 9 knots

Freshspring was converted from coal to oil fuel, in 1961. In reserve. Last of a wartime class of 14.

"FRESH" Class   1966, Dr. Giorgio Arra

TUGS

Note: Appearance of RMAS tugs—black hull with white line, buff upperworks, buff funnel with black top. The blue on the funnel now removed.

3 OCEAN TUGS

Name	No.	Builders	Commissioned
ROYSTERER	A 361	Charles D. Holmes, Beverley Shipyard, Hull	26 April 1972
ROLLICKER	A 502	Charles D. Holmes, Beverley Shipyard, Hull	Feb 1973
ROBUST	—	Charles D. Holmes, Beverley Shipyard, Hull	6 April 1974

Displacement, tons: 1 630 full load
Dimensions, feet (metres): 162·0 pp; 179·7 oa × 38·5 × 18·0 *(54 × 11·6 × 5·5)*
Main engines: 2 Mirrlees KMR 6 diesels (by Lister Blackstone Mirrlees Marine Ltd); 2 shafts; 4 500 bhp at 525 rpm = 15 knots
Range, miles: 13 000 at 12 knots
Complement: 31 (10 officers and 21 ratings) (and able to carry salvage party of 10 RN officers and ratings)

Bollard pull—50 tons. Designed principally for salvage and long range towage but can be used for general harbour duties, which *Robust* now undertakes. Cost well over £2 million apiece. Ordered Nov 1968 *(Rollicker, Roysterer)* and May 1970 *(Robust)*. Launch dates: *Robust* 7 Oct 1971, *Rollicker* 29 Jan 1971, *Roysterer* 20 April 1970.

ROYSTERER   7/1977, Michael D. J. Lennon

598 UK

Name	No.	Builders	Commissioned
TYPHOON	A 95	Henry Robb & Co Ltd, Leith	1960

Displacement, tons: 800 standard; 1 380 full load
Dimensions, feet (metres): 200·0 oa × 40·0 × 13·0 (60·5 × 12 × 4)
Main engines: 2 turbocharged Vee type 12-cyl diesels; 1 shaft; 2 750 bhp = over 16 knots

Launched on 14 Oct 1958. The machinery arrangement of two diesels geared to a single shaft was an innovation for naval ocean tugs in the RN. Controllable pitch propeller, 150 rpm. Fitted for fire fighting, salvage and ocean rescue, with a heavy mainmast and derrick attached. Bollard pull 32 tons.

TYPHOON 1976, Michael D. J. Lennon

5 "CONFIANCE" CLASS

Name	No.	Builders	Commissioned
AGILE	A 88	Goole SB Co.	July 1959
ADVICE	A 89	A. & J. Inglis Ltd, Glasgow	Oct 1959
ACCORD	A 90	A. & J. Inglis Ltd, Glasgow	Sept 1958
CONFIANCE	A 289	A. & J. Inglis Ltd, Glasgow	27 Mar 1956
CONFIDENT	A 290	A. & J. Inglis Ltd, Glasgow	Jan 1956

Displacement, tons: 760 full load
Dimensions, feet (metres): 140·0 pp; 154·8 oa × 35·0 × 11·0 (42·7; 47·2 × 10·7 × 3·4)
Main engines: 4 Paxman HAXM diesels; 2 shafts; 1 800 bhp = 13 knots
Complement: 29 plus 13 salvage party

Fitted with 2·5 m diameter Stone Kamewa controllable pitch propellers. *Accord, Advice* and *Agile*, formerly rated as dockyard tugs were officially added to the "Confiance" class in 1971 as part of the Royal Maritime Auxiliary Service ocean towing force although there are minor differences between these three and the "Confiance" pair. Fitted for 1—40 mm gun.

CONFIANCE 6/1977, John G. Callis

2 "SAMSON" CLASS

Name	No.	Builders	Commissioned
SEA GIANT	A 288	Alexander Hall & Co Ltd, Aberdeen	1955
SUPERMAN	—	Alexander Hall & Co Ltd, Aberdeen	1954

Displacement, tons: 1 200 full load
Measurement, tons: 850 gross
Dimensions, feet (metres): 180 oa × 37 × 14 (54 × 11·2 × 4·3)
Main engines: Triple expansion; 2 shafts; 3 000 ihp = 15 knots
Complement: 30

Superman laid up in reserve at Devonport. *Samson* sold commercially 1977.

SEA GIANT 6/1977, Dr. Giorgio Arra

1 "BUSTLER" CLASS

Name	No.	Builders	Commissioned
CYCLONE (ex-*Growler*)	A 111	Henry Robb Ltd, Leith	Sept 1943

Displacement, tons: 1 118 light; 1 630 full load
Dimensions, feet (metres): 190·0 pp; 205·0 oa × 40·2 × 16·8 (58; 62·5 × 12·3 × 5·1)
Main engines: 2 Atlas Polar 8-cyl diesels; 1 shaft; 4 000 bhp = 16 knots
Oil fuel, tons: 405
Range, miles: 17 000 (economical)
Complement: 42

Last of class of eight. In Gibraltar. Launch date: 10 Sept 1942.

CYCLONE 1975, Michael D. J. Lennon

5 "DIRECTOR" CLASS (PAS)

Name	No.	Builders	Commissioned
FAITHFUL	A 85	Yarrow & Sons Ltd	1958
FORCEFUL	A 86	Yarrow & Sons Ltd	1958
FAVOURITE	A 87	Ferguson & Co Ltd	1959
DEXTEROUS	A 93	Yarrow & Sons Ltd	1957
DIRECTOR	A 94	Yarrow & Sons Ltd	1957

Displacement, tons: 710 full load
Dimensions, feet (metres): 157·2 oa × 30 (60 over paddle boxes) × 10 (47·9 × 9·2 (18·4) × 3·1)
Main engines: Paxman diesels and BTH motors; diesel-electric; 2 shafts; 2 paddle wheels; 2 000 bhp = 13 knots
Complement: 21

Dexterous at Gibraltar. The only class of paddlers run by any navy in the world, this being considered the best arrangement for working with aircraft carriers.

FORCEFUL 6/1977, Michael D. J. Lennon

19 "DOG" CLASS

AIREDALE A 102	HUSKY A 169	SPANIEL A 201
ALSATIAN A 106	MASTIFF A 180	SHEEPDOG A 250
CAIRN A 126	SALUKI A 182	BASSET (ex-*Beagle*) A 327
DALMATIAN A 129	SEALYHAM A 187	COLLIE A 328
DEERHOUND A 155	POINTER A 188	CORGI A 330
ELKHOUND A 162	SETTER A 189	FOXHOUND (ex-*Boxer*) A 394
LABRADOR A 168		

Displacement, tons: 170 full load
Dimensions, feet (metres): 94 × 24·5 × 12 (28·7 × 7·5 × 3·7)
Main engines: Lister-Blackstone diesels; 1 320 bhp = 12 knots
Complement: 8

Harbour berthing tugs. *Airedale* and *Sealyham* at Gibraltar. Bollard pull 16 tons. Completed 1962-72. *Foxhound* renamed 22 Oct 1977 to free the name *Boxer* for new Type 22 frigate.

SHEEPDOG 6/1977, Wright and Logan

UK 599

8 "GIRL" CLASS

| ALICE A 113 | AUDREY A 117 | BRIDGET A 322 | BARBARA A 324 |
| AGATHA A 116 | AGNES A 121 | BETTY A 323 | BRENDA A 335 |

Of 40 tons. 495 bhp = 10 knots. "A" names built by P. K. Harris, "B" names by Dunstons. Completed 1962-72. *Barbara* in Chatham.

BARBARA 6/1977, Michael D. J. Lennon

8 "MODIFIED GIRL" CLASS

| DAISY A 145 | CHARLOTTE A 210 | CLARE A 218 | DAPHNE |
| EDITH A 177 | CHRISTINE A 217 | DORIS A 252 | DOROTHY |

Of 38 tons. 495 bhp = 10 knots. *Dorothy* and *Clare* in Hong Kong. *Edith* at Gibraltar. "C" names built by Pimblott and "D" and "E" names by Dunstons. Completed 1971-1972. *Celia* sold to Sembawang Dockyard, Singapore in 1971.

CHRISTINE 8/1977, Michael D. J. Lennon

12 "TRITON" CLASS

IRENE	JOYCE	LESLEY	MYRTLE
ISABEL	KATHLEEN	LILAH	NANCY
JOAN	KITTY	MARY	NORAH

All completed by Aug 1974 by Dunstons. "Water-tractors" with small wheelhouse and adjoining funnel. 58 feet *(17·7 metres)* and of 107·5 tons. 330 bhp = 8 knots.

ISABEL 6/1977, Wright and Logan

5 "FELICITY" CLASS

| FELICITY | GEORGINA | HELEN |
| FIONA | GWENDOLINE | |

"Water tractors". Of 80 tons. 600 bhp = 10 knots. *Felicity* built by Dunstons and remainder by Hancocks. Completed 1973.

HELEN 6/1976, Michael D. J. Lennon

FLEET TENDERS

DOLWEN (ex-*Hector Gull*)

Displacement, tons: 602 full load
Measurement, tons: 354·6 gross; 115·9 net
Dimensions, feet (metres): 135 × 29·5 × 14·5 *(41·1 × 9·0 × 4·4)*
Main engine: 1 National FSSM6 diesel; 1 shaft (cp propeller)

Built at Appledore by P. K. Harris in 1962 as stern trawler. Converted to buoy tender and now operates as range safety ship for RAE, Aberporth.

DOLWEN 1/1978, Michael D. J. Lennon

7 "INSECT" CLASS

Name	No.	Builders	Commissioned
BEE	—	C. D. Holmes Ltd, Beverley, Yorks	1970
CICALA	—	C. D. Holmes Ltd, Beverley, Yorks	1971
COCKCHAFER	—	C. D. Holmes Ltd, Beverley, Yorks	1971
CRICKET	—	C. D. Holmes Ltd, Beverley, Yorks	1972
GNAT	—	C. D. Holmes Ltd, Beverley, Yorks	1972
LADYBIRD	—	C. D. Holmes Ltd, Beverley, Yorks	1973
SCARAB	—	C. D. Holmes Ltd, Beverley, Yorks	1973

Displacement, tons: 450 full load
Dimensions, feet (metres): 111·8 oa × 28 × 11 *(34·1 × 8·5 × 3·4)*
Main engines: Lister-Blackstone diesels; 1 shaft; 660 bhp = 10·5 knots
Complement: 10

First three built as stores carriers, three as armament carriers and *Scarab*, as mooring vessel capable of lifting 10 tons over the bows.

BEE 6/1977, Dr. Giorgio Arra

600 UK

1 DIVING TENDER

Name	No.	Builders	Commissioned
DATCHET	—	Vospers Ltd (Singapore)	1972

Main engines: 2 Gray diesels, 2 shafts, 450 bhp = 12 knots

DATCHET   1976, Michael D. J. Lennon

5 DIVING TENDERS

Name	No.	Builders	Commissioned
IRONBRIDGE (ex-*Invergordon*)	A 310	Gregson Ltd, Blyth	1974
IXWORTH	A 318	Gregson Ltd, Blyth	1974
CLOVELLY	A 389	I. Pimblott & Sons, Northwich	1972
ILCHESTER	—	Gregson Ltd, Blyth	1974
INSTOW	—	Gregson Ltd, Blyth	1974

Of similar characteristics to "Cartmel" class. RN manned.

28 "CARTMEL" CLASS

Name	No.	Builders	Commissioned
ETTRICK	A 274	J. Cook, Wivenhoe	1972
ELSING	A 277	J. Cook, Wivenhoe	1971
EPWORTH	A 352	J. Cook, Wivenhoe	1972
ELKSTONE	A 353	J. Cook, Wivenhoe	1971
FROXFIELD	A 354	R. Dunston, Thorne	1972
FELSTED	A 384	R. Dunston, Thorne	1972
DUNSTER	A 393	R. Dunston, Thorne	1972
HOLMWOOD	A 1772	R. Dunston, Thorne	1973
HORNING	A 1773	R. Dunston, Thorne	1973
CARTMEL	—	I. Pimblott & Sons, Northwich	1971
CAWSAND	—	I. Pimblott & Sons, Northwich	1971
CRICCIETH	—	I. Pimblott & Sons, Northwich	1972
CRICKLADE	—	C. D. Holmes, Beverley	1971
CROMARTY	—	J. Lewis, Aberdeen	1972
DENMEAD	—	C. D. Holmes, Beverley	1972
DORNOCH	—	J. Lewis, Aberdeen	1972
FINTRY	—	J. Lewis, Aberdeen	1972
FOTHERBY	—	R. Dunston, Thorne	1972
FULBECK	—	C. D. Holmes, Beverley	1972
GLENCOVE	—	I. Pimblott & Sons, Northwich	1972
GRASMERE	—	J. Lewis, Aberdeen	1972
HAMBLEDON	—	R. Dunston, Thorne	1973
HARLECH	—	R. Dunston, Thorne	1973
HEADCORN	—	R. Dunston, Thorne	1973
HEVER	—	R. Dunston, Thorne	1973
LAMLASH	—	R. Dunston, Thorne	1974
LECHLADE	—	R. Dunston, Thorne	1974
LLANDOVERY	—	R. Dunston, Thorne	1974

Displacement, tons: 143 full load
Dimensions, feet (metres): 80 oa × 21 × 6·6 *(24·1 × 6·4 × 3)*
Main engines: 1 Lister-Blackstone diesel; 1 shaft; 320 bhp = 10·5 knots
Complement: 6

All fleet tenders of an improved "Aberdovey" class. *Elsing* and *Ettrick* at Gibraltar (RN manned). Of three types—A. Cargo only; B. Passengers or cargo; C. Training tenders (complement 12).

HEVER   6/1977, Wright and Logan

6 + 4 "LOYAL" CLASS (RNXS)

LOYAL MODERATOR A 220
VIGILANT (ex-*Loyal Factor*) A 382
ALERT (ex-*Loyal Governor*) A 510
LOYAL PROCTOR A 1771
LOYAL CHANCELLOR
LOYAL HELPER

Details as for "Cartmel" class. *Alert* and *Vigilant* classified as "Patrol Craft" as they have, from time to time, carried out patrols off Ulster. (RN manned). *Loyal Helper* launched 23 Sept 1977 with four more ordered. *Loyal Proctor* at Rosyth (RNXS). *Loyal Moderator,* Portland/Plymouth.

LOYAL MODERATOR   6/1977, Dr. Giorgio Arra

12 "ABERDOVEY" CLASS

Name	No.	Builders	Commissioned
ABERDOVEY	—	Isaac Pimblott & Sons, Northwich	1963
ABINGER	—	Isaac Pimblott & Sons, Northwich	1964
ALNESS	—	Isaac Pimblott & Sons, Northwich	1965
ALNMOUTH	—	Isaac Pimblott & Sons, Northwich	1966
APPLEBY	—	Isaac Pimblott & Sons, Northwich	1967
ASHCOTT	—	Isaac Pimblott & Sons, Northwich	1968
BEAULIEU	A 99	J. S. Doig, Grimsby	1966
BEDDGELERT	A 100	J. S. Doig, Grimsby	1967
BEMBRIDGE	A 101	J. S. Doig, Grimsby	1968
BIBURY	A 103	J. S. Doig, Grimsby	1969
BLAKENEY	A 104	J. S. Doig, Grimsby	1970
BRODICK	A 105	J. S. Doig, Grimsby	1971

Displacement, tons: 117·5 full load
Dimensions, feet (metres): 79·8 oa × 18 × 5·5 *(24 × 5·4 × 2·4)*
Main engines: 1 Lister-Blackstone diesel; 1 shaft; 225 bhp = 10·5 knots
Complement: 6

Multi-purpose for stores (25 tons), passengers (200 standing) plus a couple of torpedoes. *Ashcott* at Gibraltar (RN manned). *Alnmouth* operates from Devonport for Sea Cadet Corps training. *Aberdovey* with RMs, Poole. *Bembridge* at Portsmouth.

ALNMOUTH   5/1976, Michael D. J. Lennon

6 "HAM" CLASS (RNXS)

PAGHAM M 2716
SHIPHAM M 2726
THAKEHAM M 2733
TONGHAM M 2735
PORTISHAM M 2781
PUTTENHAM M 2784

Details in Mine Warfare Section. Due for replacement by new construction "Loyal" class.

PORTISHAM   10/1976, Wright and Logan

30 MFV TYPES

A number of MFV types are used in dockyard ports, not necessarily under naval control.

TANK CLEANING VESSELS

6 "ISLES" CLASS

Name	No.	Builders	Commissioned
CALDY	A 332	John Lewis and Sons	1943
BERN	A 334	Cook Welton and Gemmell	1942
LUNDY	A 336	Cook Welton and Gemmell	1943
SKOMER	A 338	John Lewis and Sons	1943
GRAEMSAY	A 340	Ardrossan Dockyard Co	1943
SWITHA	A 346	A. and J. Inglis Ltd	1942

Displacement, tons: 770 full load
Dimensions, feet (metres): 164 oa × 27·5 × 14 *(49 × 8·4 × 4·2)*
Main engines: Triple expansion; 1 shaft; 850 ihp = 12 knots
Boiler: 1 cylindrical
Coal, tons: 183

Last survivors, in UK service of a class of 145 built for minesweeping and escort duties during the war, most of them were employed on wreck dispersal after the war until conversion to their present role in 1951-57.

GRAEMSAY *5/1977, Michael D. J. Lennon*

DEGAUSSING VESSELS

3 "HAM" CLASS

FORDHAM M 2717   **WARMINGHAM** M 2737   **THATCHAM** M 2790

Of the "Ham" class of Inshore Minesweepers. For details see Mine Warfare Section.

WARMINGHAM *10/1974, C. and S. Taylor*

SCOTTISH FISHERY PROTECTION VESSELS

2 "JURA" CLASS

Name	No.	Builders	Commissioned
JURA	—	Hall, Russell & Co, Aberdeen	1973
WESTRA	—	Hall, Russell & Co, Aberdeen	1975

Displacement, tons: 778 light; 1 285 full load
Measurement, tons: 942 gross
Dimensions, feet (metres): 195·3 oa × 35 × 14·4 *(59·6 × 10·7 × 4·4)*
Main engines: 2 British Polar SP112VS-F diesels; 4 200 bhp; 1 shaft = 17 knots
Complement: 28

Jura was leased by the Ministry of Defence for oil-rig patrol and armed with 1—40 mm. Returned from RN service Jan 1977 and disarmed. *Westra* was launched on 6 Aug 1974. Three other craft are operated by Department of Agriculture and Fisheries for Scotland.

JURA (fitted for North Sea Patrol) *1975, MOD (N)*

UK 601

ROYAL CORPS OF TRANSPORT

As well as "Ardennes", "Abbeville" and "Avon" classes listed in the Amphibious Warfare Section the following craft are operated by the RCT.

1 "HAM" CLASS

R. G. MASTERS (ex-RAF 5012, ex-HMS *Halsham*)

Details in Mine Warfare section.

R. G. MASTERS *1976, Michael D. J. Lennon*

1 90 ft MFV

YARMOUTH NAVIGATOR

Of 90 ft. *Yarmouth Seaman* sold 1976.

YARMOUTH NAVIGATOR *1976, Michael D. J. Lennon*

1 GENERAL SERVICE LAUNCH

TREVOSE

Of 72 ft.

7 GENERAL SERVICE LAUNCHES

JACKSON	RADDLE
MARTIN	SMIKE
NEWMAN NOGGS	URIAH HEEP
OLIVER TWIST	

Of 50 ft.

7 GENERAL DUTIES LAUNCHES

CARP WB 01	ROACH WB 05
CHUB WB 02	PERCH WB 06
BREAM WB 03	PIKE WB 07
BARBEL WB 04	

47 ft work-boats.

6 COMMAND and CONTROL CRAFT

PETREL L 01	SKUA L 04
TERN L 02	SHEARWATER L 05
FULMAR L 03	SHELDUCK L 06

41 ft craft.

PETREL *2/1977, Michael D. J. Lennon*

602 UK

2 Ex-SAR CRAFT

HYPERION
MINORU

ROYAL AIR FORCE MARINE CRAFT

Officer-in-Charge: Group Captain J. F. Burgess

New Construction: All wooden craft to be replaced by "Seal" class, "Spitfire" class and 27 ft workboats by end 1981.

3 "SEAL" CLASS (LRRSC)

Name	No.	Builders	Commissioned
SEAL	5000	Brooke Marine, Lowestoft	Aug 1967
SEAGULL	5001	Fairmile Construction, Berwick on Tweed	1970
SEA OTTER	5002	Fairmile Construction, Berwick on Tweed	1970

Displacement, tons: 159 full load
Dimensions, feet (metres): 120·3 × 23·5 × 6·5 (36·6 × 7·2 × 2)
Main engines: 2 Paxman diesels; 2 200 hp = 21 knots
Complement: 18

All welded steel hulls. Aluminium alloy superstructure.

SEAGULL 1973, RAF

4 "SPITFIRE" CLASS (RTTL Mk 3)

Name	No.	Builders	Commissioned
SPITFIRE	4000	James and Stone, Brightlingsea	1972
SUNDERLAND	4001	James and Stone, Brightlingsea	1976
STIRLING	4002	James and Stone, Brightlingsea	1976
HALIFAX	4003	James and Stone, Brightlingsea	1977

Displacement, tons: 70
Dimensions, feet (metres): 77·7 × 18 × 4·9 (23·7 × 5·5 × 1·5)
Main engines: 2 Paxman diesels; 2 100 hp = 22 knots
Complement: 9

All welded steel hulls; aluminium alloy superstructure. *Spitfire* has twin funnels, remainder none.

SUNDERLAND 1976, RAF

4 RESCUE TARGET TOWING LAUNCHES Mk 2 (RTTL Mk 2)

2752, 2757, 2768, 2771

Displacement, tons: 34·6
Dimensions, feet (metres): 68 × 19 × 6 (20·7 × 5·8 × 1·8)
Main engines: 2 Rolls-Royce Sea Griffon; 11 000 bhp = 30 knots
Complement: 9

Hard chine, wooden hulls. Built by Vospers, Saunders Roe and Groves and Gutteridge. To be replaced by RTTL Mk 3.

10 PINNACES 1300 SERIES

Displacement, tons: 28·3
Dimensions, feet (metres): 63 × 15·5 × 5 (19·2 × 4·9 × 1·5)
Main engines: 2 Rolls-Royce C6 diesels; 190 bhp = 13 knots
Complement: 5

Hard chine, wooden hulls. Built by Groves and Gutteridge, Robertsons (Dunoon) and Dorset Yacht Co (Poole). 5 tons cargo capacity.

1300 Series Pinnace 1975, RAF

7 RANGE SAFETY LAUNCHES 1600 SERIES

Displacement, tons: 12 full load
Dimensions, feet (metres): 43 × 13 × 4 (13·1 × 4 × 1·2)
Main engines: 2 Rolls-Royce C6 diesels; 190 bhp = 16 knots
Complement: 4

Hard chine, wooden double diagonal hulls.

HARBOUR CRAFT

24 ft tenders and Gemini craft in current use. To be replaced by 27 ft Cheverton workboats by 1980-81.

HM CUSTOMS

The Customs and Excise (Waterguard) of HM Treasury operate a considerable number of craft around the United Kingdom, including Fairey Marine Trackers. The following photograph of *Active* shows the general appearance and fittings.

ACTIVE C. and S. Taylor

POLICE SERVICE

Police craft of many sizes operate in all the major ports, although rarely met with beyond the port limits.

TRINITY HOUSE

A number of vessels of varying types—buoy-layers, pilot craft, lighthouse tenders—may be met throughout the waters of the United Kingdom.

UNITED STATES OF AMERICA

Administration

Secretary of the Navy:
Hon. W. Graham Claytor Jr

There are one Under Secretary and four Assistant Secretaries.

Principal Commands by Flag Officers' Seniority

Chief of Naval Operations:
Admiral James L. Holloway III
Commander-in-Chief, Atlantic, Commander-in-Chief, US Atlantic Fleet and Supreme Allied Commander, Atlantic (NATO):
Admiral Isaac C. Kidd, Jr
Commander-in-Chief, Pacific:
*Admiral Maurice F. Weisner
Commander-in-Chief, Allied Forces, Southern Europe:
Admiral Harold E. Shear
Chief of Naval Material:
Admiral Frederick H. Michaelis
Commander-in-Chief, US Pacific Fleet:
Admiral Thomas B. Hayward
Vice-Chief of Naval Operations:
Admiral Robert L. J. Long
Commander Seventh Fleet:
Vice-Admiral Robert B. Baldwin
Commander-in-Chief, US Naval Forces, Europe:
Vice-Admiral Joseph P. Moorer
Commander Naval Surface Force, US Pacific Fleet:
Vice-Admiral William R. St George
Commander Sixth Fleet and Commander Strike Force South (NATO):
Vice-Admiral Harry D. Train II
Commander Naval Air Force, US Atlantic Fleet:
Vice-Admiral Howard E. Greer
Commander Naval Air Force, US Pacific Fleet:
Vice-Admiral Robert P. Coogan
Commander Naval Air Systems Command:
Vice-Admiral Forrest S. Petersen
Commander Naval Sea Systems Command:
Vice-Admiral Clarence R. Bryan
Commander Third Fleet:
Vice-Admiral Samuel L. Gravely, Jr
Commander Submarine Force, US Atlantic Fleet:
Vice-Admiral Kenneth M. Carr
Commander Naval Surface Force, US Atlantic Fleet:
Vice-Admiral William L. Read
Commander, Second Fleet:
Vice-Admiral Wesley L. McDonald
Commander US Naval Forces, Caribbean:
Rear-Admiral William R. Flanagan
Commander, Naval Forces, Japan:
Rear-Admiral Thomas B. Russell, Jr
Commander Military Sealift Command:
Rear-Admiral John D. Johnson, Jr
Commander Submarine Force, US Pacific Fleet:
Rear-Admiral William J. Cowhill
Commander Naval Electronics Systems Command:
Rear-Admiral Earl B. Fowler, Jr
Commander Mine Warfare Command:
Rear-Admiral Albert J. Monger
Commander Middle East Force:
Rear-Admiral Samuel H. Packer II
Commander South Atlantic Force:
Rear-Admiral James A. Sagerholm

Note: *Unified Command with the Commander-in-Chief directing all US Army, Navy, and Air Force activities in the area.

Marine Corps

Commandant:
General Louis H. Wilson, Jr
Assistant Commandant:
General Samuel Jaskilka

Diplomatic Representation

Defense Attaché and Naval Attaché in London:
Rear-Admiral Francis T. Brown
Naval Attaché and Naval Attaché for Air in Moscow:
Captain Leonard A. Braken
Naval Attaché and Naval Attaché for Air in Paris:
Captain Neil L. Harvey

Personnel

	30 Sept 1976 (Actual)	30 Sept 1977 (Actual)	30 Sept 1978 (Planned)
Navy			
Officers	63 176	63 312	62 973
Enlisted	460 231	461 571	464 502
Marine Corps			
Officers	18 581	18 584	} 191 500
Enlisted	171 204	173 057	

Mercantile Marine

Lloyd's Register of Shipping:
4 740 vessels of 15 299 681 tons gross

US Commerce Department (Vessels over 1 000 tons) (1 Oct 1977):
Active: 589 vessels of 11 023 100 tons gross
Reserve: 158 vessels of 1 239 362 tons gross

Strength of the Fleet

Number of ships listed in the table are actual as of 1 Feb 1978, based on official tabulations and include ships and craft attached to the Naval Reserve Force (NRF).

Type		Active	Building	Reserve	Conversion
Strategic Missile Submarines					
SSBN	Ballistic Missile Submarines	40	7	—	1
Submarines					
SSN	Submarines (nuclear)	68	28	2	—
SS	Attack Submarines (diesel)	8	—	—	—
SSG	Guided Missile Submarines (diesel)	—	—	1	—
Aircraft Carriers					
CVN	Aircraft Carriers (nuclear)	3	1	—	—
CV	Aircraft Carriers	10	—	1	—
CVS	Anti-Submarine Carriers	—	—	4	—
CVA	Attack Carrier	—	—	1	—
Battleships					
BB	Battleships	—	—	4	—
Cruisers					
CGN	Guided Missile Cruisers (nuclear)	7	2	—	—
CG	Guided Missile Cruisers	20	—	2	1
CA	Heavy Cruisers	—	—	5	—
Destroyers					
DDG	Guided Missile Destroyers	39	1	—	—
DD	Destroyers	54	20	—	—
DDH	Helicopter Destroyer (ASW)	—	1	—	—
Frigates					
FFG	Guided Missile Frigates	7	25	—	—
FF	Frigates	58	—	—	—
Light Forces					
PHM	Patrol Combatants—Missile (hydrofoil)	1	5	—	—
PCH	Patrol Craft (hydrofoil)	1	—	—	—
PG	Patrol Combatants	2	—	—	—
PTF	Fast Patrol Craft	4	—	—	—
Command Ships					
CC	Command Ships	—	2	—	—
Amphibious Warfare Forces					
LCC	Amphibious Command Ships	2	—	—	—
LHA	Amphibious Assault Ships (GP)	2	3	—	—
LKA	Amphibious Cargo Ships	6	—	—	—
LPA	Amphibious Transports	2	—	—	—
LPD	Amphibious Transport Docks	14	—	—	—
LPH	Amphibious Assault Ships	7	—	—	—
LSD	Landing Ships Dock	13	—	—	—
LST	Landing Ships Tank	20	—	—	—
Mine Warfare Forces					
MSO	Minesweepers—Ocean	25	—	—	—
Auxiliary Ships					
AD	Destroyer Tenders	9	3	1	—
AE	Ammunition Ships	13	—	—	—
AFS	Combat Stores Ships	7	—	1	—
AG	Miscellaneous	1	—	1	—
AGDS	Auxiliary Deep Submergence Support Ship	1	—	—	—
AGEH	Hydrofoil Research Ship	1	—	—	—
AGF	Miscellaneous Command Ship	1	—	—	—
AGFF	Frigate Research Ship	1	—	—	—
AGSS	Auxiliary Submarines	1	—	1	—
AH	Hospital Ship	—	—	1	—
AO	Oilers	8	5	—	—
AOE	Fast Combat Support Ships	4	—	—	—
AOR	Replenishment Fleet Oilers	7	—	—	—
AR	Repair Ships	5	—	2	—
ARL	Landing Craft Repair Ships	—	—	2	—
ARS	Salvage Ships	10	—	1	—
AS	Submarine Tenders	11	3	2	—
ASR	Submarine Rescue Ships	6	—	—	—
ATA	Auxiliary Ocean Tugs	—	4	—	—
ATF	Fleet Ocean Tugs	14	—	1	—
ATS	Salvage and Rescue Ships	3	—	—	—
AVM	Guided Missile Ship	1	—	—	—
CVT	Training Aircraft Carrier	1	—	—	—
Service Craft					
All Types		1 093*	—	1 093*	3
Military Sealift Command (Nucleus)		63	—	4	1

Note: *Total Number of service craft in US Navy. Breakdown for each category not available.

604 USA

Special Notes

To provide similar information to that included in other major Navies' Deployment Tables the fleet assignment (abbreviated "F/S") status of each ship in the US Navy has been included. The assignment appears in a column immediately to the right of the commissioning date. In the case of the Floating Drydock section this system is not used. In the case of harbour tugs (YTB, YTM), the "F/S" column appears immediately to the right of the hull number. The following abbreviations are used to indicate fleet assignments:

AA	Active, Atlantic Fleet
AR	In Reserve, Out of Commission, Atlantic Fleet
ASA	Active, In Service, Atlantic Fleet
ASR	In Reserve, Out of Service, Atlantic Fleet
Bldg	Building
LOAN	Ship or craft loaned to another government, or non-government agency, but US Navy retains title and the ship or craft is on the NVR
MAR	In Reserve, Out of Commission, Atlantic Fleet and laid up in the temporary custody of the Maritime Administration
MPR	Same as "MAR", but applies to the Pacific Fleet
NRF	Assigned to the Naval Reserve Force (ships so assigned are listed in a special table, at the end of each major category, that indicates NRF homeport, date assigned to NRF and which ship, if any, it replaced)
PA	Active, Pacific Fleet
PR	In Reserve, Out of Commission, Pacific Fleet
PSA	Active, In Service, Pacific Fleet
PSR	In Reserve, Out of Service, Pacific Fleet
TAA	Active, Military Sealift Command, Atlantic Fleet
TAR	In Ready Reserve, Military Sealift Command, Atlantic Fleet
TPA	Active, Military Sealift Command, Pacific Fleet
TPR	In Ready Reserve, Military Sealift Command, Pacific Fleet
TWWR	Active, Military Sealift Command, World-wide Routes

Ship Status Definitions

In Commission: As a rule any ship, except a Service Craft, that is active, is in commission. The ship has a Commanding Officer and flies a commissioning pennant.

In Service: All Service Craft (Drydocks and with classifications that start with "Y"), with the exception of *Constitution*, that are active, are "in service". The ship has an Officer-in-Charge and does not fly a commissioning pennant.

Ships "in reserve, out of commission" or "in reserve, out of service" are put in a state of preservation for future service. Depending on the size of the ship or craft, a ship in "mothballs" usually takes from 30 days to nearly a year to restore to full operational service.

The above statuses do not apply to the Military Sealift Command.

Shipbuilding/Conversion Programmes

Note: During the final review of the Defense Dept requests, in December 1977, for the Fiscal Year 1979 budget, the Carter Administration deleted one SSN-688, one CGN, one FFG and one Auxiliary from the Navy's Shipbuilding request. Since the approved version of a Fiscal Year Shipbuilding Programme often differs from the requested version, the four deleted ships have been retained in the Fiscal Year 1979 table below.

Planned Five Year Shipbuilding/Conversion Programme (Fiscal Year 1979/1983)

Shipbuilding*
- 7 "Ohio" Class SSBNs
- 10 "Los Angeles" Class SSNs
- 2 Aircraft Carriers (Medium) (CVV)
- 6 Improved "Virginia" Class Guided Missile Cruisers (nuclear propulsion) (CGN)
- 8 Guided Missile Destroyers (AEGIS) (DDG 47 Class)
- 42 Guided Missile Frigates (FFG 7 Class)
- 1 Guided Missile Frigates (FFGX Class)
- 2 Dock Landing Ships (LSD 41 Class)
- 5 Mine Countermeasures Vehicles (MCM)
- 2 Destroyer Tenders (AD)
- 4 Oilers (AO 177 Class)
- 12 Ocean Surveillance Ships (AGOS)
- 1 Cable Repair Ship (ARC)

Conversions*
- 2 Aircraft Carrier Service Life Extension Programme (SLEP)
- 23 Anti-Air Warfare Modernisation "Charles F. Adams" Class (DDG)
- 1 Cargo Ship Conversion (AK)

Proposed Fiscal Year 1979 Programme

Shipbuilding
- 1 "Ohio" Class SSBN (SSBN-733)
- 2 "Los Angeles" Class SSNs (SSN-720/721)
- 1 Improved "Virginia" Class Guided Missile Cruiser (nuclear propulsion) (CGN-42)
- 9 "Oliver Hazard Perry" Class FFG (FFG-35/43)
- 2 Destroyer Tenders (AD-44/45)
- 3 Ocean Surveillance Ships (AGOS)
- 1 Cable Repair Ship (ARC-7)

Long Term Lead Items
- 1 Aircraft Carrier (Medium) (CVV) ($75 million)
- 1 Aircraft Carrier Service Life Extension Programme (SLEP) ($32 million)
- 4 Anti-Air Warfare Modernisation "Charles F. Adams" Class DDGs ($167 million)

Miscellaneous
$35 million requested for construction of service craft
$12 million requested for construction of landing craft

Approved Fiscal Year 1978 Programme

Shipbuilding
- 2 "Ohio" Class SSBNs (SSBN-731/732)
- 1 "Los Angeles" Class SSN (SSN-719)
- 8 "Oliver Hazard Perry" Class FFGs (FFG-27/34)
- 1 Guided Missile Destroyer (AEGIS) (DDG-47)
- 2 Oilers (AO-180, 186)
- 3 "Powhatan" Class ATFs (ATF-170/172)
- 1 Improved "Spruance" Class ASW Helicopter Destroyer DDH (DDH-997)**

Long Term Lead Items
- 1 Improved "Virginia" Class CGN (CGN-42)
- 6 "Charles F. Adams" Class AAW Modernisation (DDG)
- 1 Aircraft Carrier Service Life Extension Programme (SLEP)

Notes: *As of 20 Sept 1977. Subject to revision.
**This unit was added to the Shipbuilding Programme by Congress and is not a Navy initiated programme.

Source: Data based on Hearing Report on 'Department of Defense Appropriations for 1978, Part 4', material from the Naval Sea Systems Command Public Affairs Office and other official sources.

Naval Aviation

US Naval Aviation currently consists of approx 7 000 aircraft flown by the Navy and Marine Corps. The principal naval aviation organisations are 13 carrier air wings, 24 maritime reconnaissance/patrol squadrons, and three Marine Aircraft Wings. In addition, the Naval Reserve and Marine Corps Reserve operate 7 fighter squadrons, 11 attack squadrons, and 12 patrol squadrons, plus various reconnaissance, electrical warfare, tanker, helicopter and transport units.

Fighter: 26 Navy squadrons with F-4 Phantom and F-14 Tomcat aircraft; 12 Marine squadrons with F-4 Phantoms.
Attack: 39 Navy squadrons with A-6 Intruder and A-7 Corsair aircraft; 13 Marine squadrons with A-4 Skyhawk, A-6 Intruder, AV-8 Harrier aircraft.
Reconnaissance: 10 Navy RA-5C Vigilante and RF-8G Crusader aircraft; 3 Marine squadrons with RF-4B Phantoms.
Airborne Early Warning: 12 Navy squadrons with E-2 Hawkeye aircraft.
Electronic Warfare: 8 Navy squadrons with EA-6B Prowler aircraft (Marines operate EA-6A Intruder aircraft in composite reconnaissance squadrons).
Anti-Submarine: 9 Navy squadrons with S-3 Viking aircraft replacing S-2 Trackers.
Maritime Patrol: 24 Navy squadrons with P-3 Orion aircraft.
Helicopter Anti-Submarine: 16 Navy squadrons with SH-3 Sea King and SH-2 LAMPS helicopters.
Helicopter Mine Countermeasures: 1 Navy squadron with RH-53 Sea Stallion.
Helicopter Support: 4 Navy squadrons with UH-46 Sea Knight helicopters.
Electronic Reconnaissance: 2 Navy squadrons with EP-3E Orion and EC-121 Warning Star aircraft.
Communications Relay: 2 Navy squadrons with EC-130 Hercules aircraft.
Observation: 3 Marine squadrons with OV-10 Bronco aircraft.
Helicopter Gunship: 3 Marine squadrons with AH-1 Sea Cobra helicopters.
Helicopter Transport: 21 Marine squadrons with UH-1 Iroquois (Huey), CH-46 Sea Knight, and CH-53 Sea Stallion helicopters.

BASES

Naval Air Stations and Air Facilities (44)

NAS Alameda, Calif; NAF China Lake, Calif; NAF El Centro, Calif; NAS Los Alamitos, Calif; NAS Mirimar, Calif; NAS Moffett Field (San Jose), Calif; NAS Point Mugu, Calif; NAS North Island (San Diego), Calif; NAF Andrews, Washington DC; NAS Cecil Field (Pensacola), Fla; NAS Jacksonville, Fla; NAS Key West, Fla; NAS Mayport, Fla; NAS Roosevelt Roads, Puerto Rico; NAS Whiting Field (Milton), Fla; NAS Saufley Field (Pensacola), Fla; NAS Pansacola, Fla; NAS Atlanta (Marietta), Ga; NAS Glenview, Ill; NAS Barbers Point (Oahu), Hawaii; NAS New Orleans, La; NAS Brunswick, Me; NAS Paxtuxent River, Md; NAS South Weymouth, Mass; NAF Detroit, Mich; NAS Meridan, Miss; NAS Fallon, Nev; NAS Lakehurst, NJ; NAF Warminster, Penna; NAS Willow Grove, Penna; NAS Memphis (Millington), Tenn; NAS Chase Field (Beeville), Texas; NAS Corpus Christi, Texas; NAS Dallas, Texas; NAS Kingsville, Texas; NAS Norfolk, Va; NAS Whidbey Island (Oak Harbor), Wash; NAF Lajes, Azores; NAS Bermuda; NAS Guantanamo Bay, Cuba; NAF Naples, Italy; NAF Atsugi, Japan; NAS Agana, Guam; NAF Okinawa; NAS Subic Bay, Philippines; NAF Mildenhall (Suffolk), England.

Naval Stations and Naval Bases (25)

Yokosuka, Japan; Subic Bay, Philippines; Apra Harbour, Guam; Midway Is; Adak, (Alaska); Pearl Harbor, (Hawaii); Treasure Is (San Francisco) Calif; San Diego, Calif; Coronado (San Diego) Calif (Amphibs); Long Beach (Calif); Mayport, Fla; Roosevelt Roads, Puerto Rico; Guantanamo Bay, Cuba; Charleston, SC; Norfolk, Va; Little Creek (Norfolk) Va (Amphibs); Philadelphia, Pa; Brooklyn, NY; New London (Conn) (Submarines); Newport, RI; Boston, Mass; Argentia, Newfoundland; Keflavik, Iceland; Rota, Spain; Naples, Italy.

Strategic Missile Submarine Bases (6)

Holy Loch, Scotland; Apra Harbour, Guam; Rota, Spain (being phased out by 1980); Charleston, SC; Bangor, Wash (under construction as Trident base); Kings Bay, Ga (projected).

Navy Yards (1)

Washington, DC (administration and historical activities only).

Naval Shipyards (8)

Pearl Harbor, Hawaii; Puget Sound, Bremerton, Wash; Long Beach, Calif; Mare Is, Vallejo, Calif; Charleston, SC; Norfolk, Va; Philadelphia, Pa; Portsmouth, NH (located in Kittery, Me).

Note: None engaged in new construction. All refitting and repair yards.

Naval Ship Repair Facilities (2)

Subic Bay, Philippines; Yokosuka, Japan.

Marine Air Stations and Air Facilities (7)

El Toro (Santa Ana), Calif; Kaneohe Bay (Oahu), Hawaii; Cherry Point, NC; New River (Jacksonville), Fla; Quantico, Va; Iwakuni, Japan; Futema, Okinawa.

Marine Corps Bases (5)

Camp Pendleton, Calif; Twentynine Palms, Calif; Camp H.M. Smith (Oahu), Hawaii; Camp Lejeune, NC; Camp Smedley D. Butler (Kawasaki), Okinawa.

MAJOR COMMERCIAL SHIPYARDS

Avondale Shipyards, Inc, New Orleans, Louisiana
Bath Iron Works Corp, Bath, Maine
Bethlehem Steel Corp, Sparrows Point, Maryland
General Dynamics Corp, Electric Boat Division, Groton, Connecticut (formerly Electric Boat Company)
General Dynamics Corp, Quincy Shipbuilding Division, Quincy, Massachusetts (formerly Bethlehem Steel Corp Yard)
Ingalls Shipbuilding Division (Litton Industries), Pascagoula, Mississippi
Lockheed Shipbuilding & Construction Co, Seattle, Washington
National Steel & Shipbuilding Co, San Diego, California
Newport News Shipbuilding & Dry Dock Co, Newport News, Virginia
Todd Shipyards Corp, San Pedro, California
Todd Shipyards Corp, Seattle, Washington

Note: All of the above yards have engaged in naval shipbuilding, overhaul, or modernisation except for the General Dynamics/Electric Boat yard which is engaged only in submarine work.

CLASSIFICATION OF NAVAL SHIPS AND SERVICE CRAFT

The following is the official US Navy list of classifications of naval ships and service craft as promulgated by the Secretary of the Navy on 6 Jan 1975 and amended 11 Jan 1978.
The following data should be noted: the use of an "E" before a classification indicates that the ship or craft is experimental in nature; the use of a "T" indicates that the ship or craft is assigned to the Military Sealift Command and is civilian manned. In either case the letters "E" and "T" are not an official part of the ship classification.
From time to time classifications, such as AGOS, appear which are not on the official classification list. These classifications indicate new ship types which were developed after the last official list was published. They are usually added to the list by change or revision. Some classifications listed below are no longer employed in the US Navy, but are retained because ships of this type are still on the Naval Vessel Register (NVR) in some other capacity than as a US Naval Ship. In some cases, there are no more ships of the type in any capacity. Examples are MSC, MCS, CPIC, ATA, FFR. The letter "X" is often added to existing classifications, such as FFGX, ARX, to indicate a new class whose characteristics have not been defined.

COMBATANT SHIPS

Warships

Aircraft Carriers:
Aircraft Carrier	CV
Aircraft Carrier (nuclear propulsion)	CVN
ASW Aircraft Carrier	CVS

Surface Combatants:
Battleships
Battleship	BB

Cruisers
Gun Cruiser	CA
Guided Missile Cruiser	CG
Guided Missile Cruiser (nuclear propulsion)	CGN

Destroyers
Destroyer	DD
Guided Missile Destroyer	DDG
Helicopter Destroyer	DDH

Frigates
Frigate	FF
Guided Missile Frigate	FFG
Radar Picket Frigate	FFR

Patrol Combatants
Patrol Combatant	PG
Guided Missile Patrol Combatant (hydrofoil)	PHM
Patrol Escort	PCE

Command Ships
Command Ship	CC

Submarines
Submarine (conventional propulsion)	SS
Guided Missile Submarine (conventional propulsion)	SSG
Submarine (nuclear propulsion)	SSN
Ballistic Missile Submarine (nuclear propulsion)	SSBN
Auxiliary Submarine	AGSS

Amphibious Warfare Ships

Amphibious Command Ship	LCC
Inshore Fire Support Ship	LFR
Amphibious Assault Ship (general purpose)	LHA
Amphibious Cargo Ship	LKA
Amphibious Transport	LPA
Amphibious Transport Dock	LPD
Amphibious Assault Ship (helicopter)	LPH
Amphibious Transport (small)	LPR
Amphibious Transport Submarine	LPSS
Dock Landing Ship	LSD
Tank Landing Ship	LST

Mine Warfare Ships

Mine Countermeasures Ship	MCS
Minesweeper, Coastal	MSC
Minesweeper, Ocean	MSO

COMBATANT CRAFT

Patrol Craft

Coastal Patrol Boat	CPC
Coastal Patrol and Interdiction Craft	CPIC
Patrol Boat	PB
Patrol Craft (fast)	PCF
Patrol Craft (hydrofoil)	PCH
Patrol Gunboat (hydrofoil)	PGH
Fast Patrol Craft	PTF

Landing Craft

Amphibious Assault Landing Craft	AALC
Landing Craft, Air Cushion	LCAC
Landing Craft, Mechanised	LCM
Landing Craft, Personnel, Large	LCPL
Landing Craft, Personnel, Ramped	LCPR
Landing Craft, Utility	LCU
Landing Craft, Vehicle, Personnel	LCVP
Amphibious Warping Tug	LWT

Mine Countermeasures Craft

Minesweeping Boat	MSB
Minesweeping, Drone	MSD
Minesweeper, Inshore	MSI
Minesweeper, River (converted LCM-6)	MSM
Minesweeper, Patrol	MSR

Riverine Warfare Craft

Assault Support Patrol Boat	ASPB
Mini-Armoured Troop Carrier	ATC
River Patrol Boat	PBR
Shallow Water Attack Craft, Medium	SWAM
Shallow Water Attack Craft, Light	SWAL

Special Warfare Craft

Landing Craft Swimmer Reconnaissance	LCSR
Light SEAL Support Craft	LSSC
Medium SEAL Support Craft	MSSC
Swimmer Delivery Vehicle	SDV
Special Warfare Craft, Light	SWCL
Special Warfare Craft, Medium	SWCM

Mobile Inshore Undersea Warfare (MIUW) Craft

MIUW Attack Craft	MAC

AUXILIARY SHIPS

Destroyer Tender	AD
Degaussing Ship	ADG
Ammunition Ship	AE
Store Ship	AF
Combat Store Ship	AFS
Miscellaneous	AG
Deep Submergence Support Ship	AGDS
Hydrofoil Research Ship	AGEH
Environmental Research Ship	AGER
Miscellaneous Command Ship	AGF
Frigate Research Ship	AGFF
Patrol Combatant Support Ship	AGHS
Missile Range Instrumentation Ship	AGM
Major Communications Relay Ship	AGMR
Oceanographic Research Ship	AGOR
Patrol Craft Tender	AGP
Surveying Ship	AGS
Auxiliary Submarine	AGSS
Hospital Ship	AH
Cargo Ship	AK
Light Cargo Ship	AKL
Vehicle Cargo Ship	AKR
Net Layer	ANL
Oiler	AO
Fast Combat Support Ship	AOE
Gasoline Tanker	AOG
Replenishment Oiler	AOR
Transport	AP
Self-propelled Barracks Ship	APB
Repair Ship	AR
Battle Damage Repair Ship	ARB
Cable Repairing Ship	ARC
Internal Combustion Engine Repair Ship	ARG
Repair Ship, Small	ARL
Salvage Ship	ARS
Submarine Tender	AS
Submarine Rescue Ship	ASR
Auxiliary Ocean Tug	ATA
Fleet Ocean Tug	ATF
Salvage and Rescue Ship	ATS
Guided Missile Ship	AVM
Training Aircraft Carrier	CVT
Surface Effects Ship	SES

SUPPORT CRAFT (including Service Craft, Lighters and Miscellaneous)*

Large Auxiliary Floating Dry Dock	AFDB
Small Auxiliary Floating Dry Dock	AFDL
Medium Auxiliary Floating Dry Dock	AFDM
Barracks Craft (non-self-propelled)	APL
Auxiliary Repair Dry Dock	ARD
Medium Auxiliary Repair Dry Dock	ARDM
Deep Submergence Rescue Vehicle	DSRV
Deep Submergence Vehicle	DSV
Unclassified Miscellaneous	IX
Submersible Research Vehicle (nuclear propulsion)	NR
Miscellaneous Auxiliary (self-propelled)	YAG
Bowdock	YBD
Open Lighter	YC
Car Float	YCF
Aircraft Transportation Lighter	YCV
Floating Crane	YD
Diving Tender	YDT
Covered Lighter (self-propelled)	YF
Ferryboat or Launch (self-propelled)	YFB
Yard Floating Dry Dock	YFD
Covered Lighter	YFN
Large Covered Lighter	YFNB
Dry Dock Companion Craft	YFND
Lighter (special purpose)	YFNX
Floating Power Barge	YFP
Refrigerated Covered Lighter (self-propelled)	YFR
Refrigerated Covered Lighter	YFRN
Covered Lighter (Range Tender) (self-propelled)	YFRT
Harbour Utility Craft (self-propelled)	YFU
Garbage Lighter (self-propelled)	YG
Garbage Lighter (non-self-propelled)	YGN
Salvage Lift Craft, Heavy	YHLC
Dredge (self-propelled)	YM
Salvage Lift Craft, Medium	YMLC
Gate Craft	YNG
Fuel Oil Barge (self-propelled)	YO
Gasoline Barge (self-propelled)	YOG
Gasoline Barge	YOGN
Fuel Oil Barge	YON
Oil Storage Barge	YOS
Patrol Craft (self-propelled)	YP
Floating Pile Driver	YPD
Floating Workshop	YR
Repair and Berthing Barge	YRB
Repair, Berthing and Messing Barge	YRBM
Floating Dry Dock Workshop (hull)	YRDH
Floating Dry Dock Workshop (machine)	YRDM
Radiological Repair Barge	YRR
Salvage Craft Tender	YRST
Seaplane Wrecking Derrick (self-propelled)	YSD
Sludge Removal Barge	YSR
Large Harbour Tug (self-propelled)	YTB
Small Harbour Tug (self-propelled)	YTL
Medium Harbour Tug (self-propelled)	YTM
Water Barge (self-propelled)	YW
Water Barge	YWN

*Self-propelled barges are indicated in parenthesis. The final letter "N" generally indicates non-self-propelled.

606 USA

ELECTRONIC EQUIPMENT CLASSIFICATION

The "AN" nomenclature was designed so that a common designation could be used for Army, Navy and Air Force equipment. The system indicator "AN" does not mean that the Army, Navy and Air Force use the equipment, but means that the type number was assigned in the "AN" system.

"AN" nomenclature is assigned to complete sets of equipment and major components of military design; groups of articles of either commercial or military design which are grouped for military purposes; major articles of military design which are not part of or used with a set; and commercial articles when nomenclature will not facilitate military identification and/or procedures.

"AN" nomenclature is not assigned to articles catalogued commercially except as stated above; minor components of military design which other adequate means of identification are available; small parts such as capacitors and resistors; and articles having other adequate identification in joint military specifications. Nomenclature assignments remain unchanged regardless of later installation and/or application.

Installation

A	Airborne (installed and operated in aircraft).
B	Underwater mobile, submarine.
C	Air transportable (inactivated, do not use).
D	Pilotless carrier.
F	Fixed.
G	Ground, general ground use (includes two or more ground-type installations).
K	Amphibious.
M	Ground, mobile (installed as operating unit in a vehicle which has no function other than transporting the equipment).
P	Pack or portable (animal or man).
S	Water surface craft.
T	Ground, transportable.
U	General utility (includes two or more general installation classes, airborne, shipboard, and ground).
V	Ground, vehicular (installed in vehicle designed for functions other than carrying electronic equipment, etc, such as tanks).
W	Water surface and underwater.

Type of Equipment

A	Invisible light, heat radiation.
B	Pigeon.
C	Carrier.
D	Radiac.
E	Nupac.
F	Photographic.[1]
G	Telegraph or teletype.
I	Interphone and public address.
J	Electromechanical or inertial wire covered.
K	Telemetering.
L	Countermeasures.
M	Meteorological.
N	Sound in air.
P	Radar.
Q	Sonar and underwater sound.
R	Radio.
S	Special types, magnetic, etc, or combinations of types.
T	Telephone (wire).
V	Visual and visible light.
W	Armament (peculiar to armament, not otherwise covered).
X	Facsimile or television.
Y	Data processing.

Purpose

A	Auxiliary assemblies (not complete operating sets used with or part of two or more sets or sets series).
B	Bombing.
C	Communications (receiving and transmitting).
D	Direction finder, reconnaissance and/or surveillance.
E	Ejection and/or release.
G	Fire-control or searchlight directing.
H	Recording and/or reproducing (graphic meteorological and sound).
K	Computing.
L	Searchlight control (inactivated, use G).
M	Maintenance and test assemblies (including tools).
N	Navigational aids (including altimeters, beacons, compasses, racons, depth sounding, approach, and landing).
P	Reproducing (inactivated, do not use).
Q	Special, or combination of purposes.
R	Receiving, passive detecting.
S	Detecting and/or range and bearing, search.
T	Transmitting.
W	Automatic flight or remote control.
X	Identification and recognition.

1. Not for US use except for assigning suffix letters to previously nomenclatured items.

Example: AN/URD-4A. AN: "AN" System; U: General Utility; R: Radio; D: Direction Finder, Reconnaissance, and/or Surveillance; 4: Model Number; A: Modification Letter.

CLASSIFICATION OF MARITIME ADMINISTRATION SHIP DESIGNS

The US Maritime Administration is a Division of the US Department of Commerce. All US flag merchant vessels are built under the jurisdiction of the US Maritime Administration and are assigned Maritime Administration design classifications. These classifications consist of three groups of letters and numbers.

A number of US Naval Auxiliaries were originally built to Maritime Administration specifications and were acquired during construction or after the ship was completed. It should be noted that the Maritime Administration acts as a "ship broker" for the US government and does not build ships for itself. The Maritime Administration generally oversees the operation and administration of the US Merchant Marine.

Merchant Ship Design Classifications

Type and Length of Vessel

		Length in Feet at Load Water Line			
Type		1	2	3	4
C	Cargo	Under 400	400-450	450-500	500-550
P	Passenger	Under 500	500-600	600-700	700-800
N	Coastal Cargo	Under 200	200-250	250-300	300-350
R	Refrigerated Cargo	Under 400	400-450	450-500	500-550
S	Special (Navy)	Under 200	200-300	300-400	400-500
T	Tanker	Under 450	450-500	500-550	550-600

Type of Propulsion; Number of Propellers and Passengers

	Single Screw		Twin Screw	
Power	1/12 Passengers	13+ Passengers	1/12 Passengers	13+ Passengers
Steam	S	S1	ST	S2
Motor (Diesel)	M	M1	MT	M2
Turbo-Electric	SE	SE1	SET	SE2

Example: C4-S-B1. C4: Cargo Ship between 500 and 550 ft long; S: steam powered; B1: 1st variation ("1") of the original design ("B"). If the third group of letters and numbers read BV1 instead of B1, the translation of the code would be, the 1st variation ("1") of the 22nd modification ("V") of the original design ("B").

UNITED STATES COAST GUARD

Icebreakers

1976	*Edisto* (WAGB 284), *Staten Island* (WAGB 278) (both sold)

High Endurance Cutters

1976	*Chautauqua* (WHEC 41), *Mendota* (WHEC 69), *Minnetonka* (WHEC 67), *Pontchatrain* (WHEC 70), *Winona* (WHEC 65), (all scrapped)

DELETIONS

Patrol Craft

1976	*Cape Higgon* (WPB 95302), *Cape Gull* (WPB 95304), *Cape Upright* (WPB 95303), *Cape Hatteras* (WPB 95305) (all scrapped)

Buoy Tenders

1976	*Clematis* (WLI 74286), *Shadbush* (WLI 74287), *Blueberry* (WLI 65302) (all sold)
1977	*Verbena* (WLI 317) (scrapped)

DELETIONS

Note: Disposals listed in parentheses after each entry. For those ships whose disposal is indicated as "transfer", see succeeding pages for further details on the transfer.

Submarines

1975	12 June	*Clamagore* (SS 343) (transfer)
	27 June	*Tigrone* (AGSS 419) (sunk as target 25 Oct 1976)
	1 July	*Tiru* (SS 416) (transfer)
1977	1 Oct	*Salmon* (SS 573) (transfer)

Aircraft Carriers

1976	31 Jan	*Hancock* (CV 19) (scrapped)
1977	30 Sept	*Franklin D. Roosevelt* (CV 42) (scrapped)

Cruisers

1976	9 Aug	*Columbus* (CG 12) (scrapped)
	22 Nov	*Little Rock* (CG 4) (memorial at Buffalo, NY as of 21 June 1977)

Destroyers

1975	1 March	*Porterfield* (DD 682), *Picking* (DD 685) (targets)
	29 March	*Laffey* (DD 724) (target)
	1 April	*Theodore E. Chandler* (DD 717) (scrapped)
	1 June	*Ozbourn* (DD 846) (scrapped), *Stoddard* (DD 566) (target)
	2 June	*Noa* (DD 841), *Leary* (DD 879), *Furse* (DD 882), *O'Hare* (DD 889), *Chevalier* (DD 805), *Everett F. Larson* (DD 830), *Eugene A. Greene* (DD 711), *Erben* (DD 630), *Hickox* (DD 673), *Halsey Powell* (DD 686), *Hale* (DD 642) (all transfers)
	1 Sept	*Heermann* (DD 532), *Dortch* (DD 670), *Stembel* (DD 644), *Bradford* (DD 545), *Brown* (DD 546), *Aulick* (DD 569), *Charrette* (DD 581), *Conner* (DD 582), *Hall* (DD 583), *Wadleigh* (DD 689), *Rooks* (DD 804) (all transfers)
	1 Dec	*Epperson* (DD 719) (transfer)
	18 Dec	*Rowan* (DD 782) (transfer)
	20 Dec	*Richard B. Anderson* (DD 786) (transfer)
1976	23 Jan	*Wiltsie* (DD 716) (transfer)
	30 Jan	*Gurke* (DD 783) (transfer)
	1 July	*Stribling* (DD 867) (target), *New* (DD 818), *Richard E. Kraus* (DD 849) (both transfers)
	30 Sept	*Brownson* (DD 868) (scrapped)
	1 Oct	*Glennon* (DD 840), *Holder* (DD 819) (both scrapped), *George K. MacKenzie* (DD 836) (sunk as target 17 Oct 1976)
	2 Nov	*Leonard F. Mason* (DD 852) (transfer)
	1 Dec	*Vesole* (DD 878), *William M. Wood* (DD 715) (transfers)
1977	1 Feb	*Bordelon* (DD 881) (transfer)
	1 Oct	*Power* (DD 839), *Sarsfield* (DD 837) (both transfers)
	1 Nov	*Basilone* (DD 824) (scrapped)
	15 Dec	*Rich* (DD 820) (scrapped)

Frigates

1975	15 June	*Amick* (FF 168), *Atherton* (FF 169) (both transfers)

Radar Picket Frigates (FFR) (ex-Radar Picket Escort Ships—DER)

1975	1 March	*Chambers* (DER 391) (scrapped)
	1 June	*Falgout* (DER 324), *Savage* (DER 386), *Vance* (DER 387), *Hissem* (DER 400) (all targets)
	30 Dec	*Camp* (FFR 251) (transfer)

Command Ships

1977	1 Dec	*Northampton* (CC 1), *Wright* (CC 2) (scrapped)

Light Forces

1975	21 Aug	*Chehalis* (PG 94) (reclassified as "boat" and assigned to Naval Ship Research and Development Centre as M/V *Athena* this date)
1976	July	PTF 17/22 ("Trumpy" Class taken out of service this date. Sold); PTF 3, 5/7, 10/12 "Nasty" Class taken out of service this date. Sold)
1977	31 Jan	*Ashville* (PG 84), *Marathon* (PG 89) (to Mass Maritime Academy as training ships 11 and 18 April 1977 respectively); *Gallup* (PG 85), *Canon* (PG 90) (pending); *Crockett* (PG 88) (to Environmental Protection Agency 18 April 1977. Based Lake Michigan)
	1 Oct	*Antelope* (PG 86) (pending); *Ready* (PG 87) (to Mass Maritime Academy in late 1977); *Grand Rapids* (PG 98) (Same as *Chehalis* (PG 94) on 1 Oct 1977: new name not available); *Douglas* (PG 100)
1978	17 Jan	*Antelope* (PG 86) to US Environmental Protection Agency
	Feb	*Douglas* (PG 100) to NSRDC as M/V *Athena II*

Amphibious Command Ships

1976	30 July	*Mount McKinley* (LCC 7), *Estes* (LCC 12) (scrapped)
	1 Dec	*Pocono* (LCC 16), *Taconic* (LCC 17) (scrapped)

Amphibious Cargo Ships

1976	1 Sept	*Seminole* (LKA 104), *Union* (LKA 106), *Washburn* (LKA 108), *Merrick* (LKA 97), *Winston* (LKA 94) (scrapped)
1977	1 Jan	*Thuban* (LKA 19), *Algol* (LKA 54), *Capricornus* (LKA 57), *Muliphen* (LKA 61), *Yancey* (LKA 93), *Rankin* (LKA 103), *Vermillion* (LKA 107) (scrapped)

Amphibious Transports

1976	1 Sept	*Magoffin* (LPA 199), *Talladega* (LPA 208), *Navarro* (LPA 215), *Pickaway* (LPA 222), *Bexar* (LPA 237) (scrapped)
	1 Dec	*Sandoval* (LPA 194), *Mountrail* (LPA 213) (scrapped)

Amphibious Transports (small)

1975	1 March	*Laning* (LPR 55) (scrapped)
	15 May	*Begor* (LPR 127) (scrapped)
	15 July	*Balduck* (LPR 132) (scrapped)
1977	31 Oct	*Ruchamkin* (LPR 89) (transfer)

Amphibious Transport Submarine

1977	15 March	*Sealion* (LPSS 315) (target)

Dock Landing Ships

1976	15 April	*Whitemarsh* (LSD 8) (transfer)
	30 April	*Whetstone* (LSD 27) (laid up Maritime Administration, Suisun Bay, Calif)
	30 June	*Comstock* (LSD 19) (pending)
	15 Oct	*Cabildo* (LSD 16), *Colonial* (LSD 18), *Tortuga* (LSD 26) (same as *Whetstone*, LSD 27 for all)
	1 Nov	*Rushmore* (LSD 14) (laid up Maritime Administration, James River, Va)
	11 Nov	*Donner* (LSD 20) (transfer to Energy Resources Development Administration along with *Shadwell*, LSD 15)

Tank Landing Ships

1975	1 April	*Floyd County* (LST 762), *Hampshire County* (LST 819), *Litchfield County* (LST 901), *Meeker County* (LST 980), *Pitkin County* (LST 1082), *St Clair County* (LST 1096) (all sold), *Kemper County* (LST 854), *Henry County* (LST 824) (both transfers)
	15 May	*Sedgewick County* (LST 1123) (transfer)
	30 June	USNS LST 47 (T-LST 47), USNS LST 230 (T-LST 230), USNS LST 287 (T-LST 287), USNS LST 491 (T-LST 491), USNS LST 566 (T-LST 566), USNS LST 579 (T-LST 579), USNS LST 607 (T-LST 607), USNS *Davies County* (T-LST 692), USNS LST 613 (T-LST 613), USNS LST 623 (T-LST 623), USNS LST 629 (T-LST 629), USNS LST 649 (T-LST 649), USNS *Harris County* (T-LST 822), USNS *Orleans Parish* (T-LST 1069), USNS LST 1072 (T-LST 1072) (all transfers)
1976	15 Aug	*Whitfield County* (LST 1169), *Terrell County* (LST 1157) (both transfers)
	1 Nov	*Terrebonne Parish* (LST 1156), *Tom Green County* (LST 1159), *Wexford County* (LST 1168), *Summitt County* (LST 1146), *Duval County* (LST 578) (all transfers)

Mine Warfare Forces

1975	28 Feb	*Aggressive* (MSO 422), *Bold* (MSO 424), *Bulwark* (MSO 425), *Embattle* (MSO 434), *Prime* (MSO 466), *Reaper* (MSO 467) (all scrapped)
	1 July	*Peacock* (MSC 198), *Phoebe* (MSC 199), *Shrike* (MSC 201) (scrapped), *Thrasher* (MSC 203), *Vireo* (MSC 205), *Warbler* (MSC 206), *Whippoorwill* (MSC 207), *Woodpecker* (MSC 209) (all transfers)
1976	1 May	*Falcon* (MSC 190), *Frigate Bird* (MSC 191), *Hummingbird* (MSC 192), *Jacana* (MSC 193), *Limpkin* (MSC 195), *Meadowlark* (MSC 196) (returned from loan to Indonesia and struck this date)
	15 May	*Lucid* (MSO 458), *Acme* (MSO 508), *Advance* (MSO 510) (scrap)
	1 Nov	*Nimble* (MSO 459) (scrap)
1977	1 July	*Energy* (MSO 436), *Firm* (MSO 444) (returned from loan to Philippines and struck this date. Scrap)
	1 Aug	*Thrush* (MSC 204) (returned from lease to Virginia Institute of Marine Science where employed as research ship and struck this date. Scrap)
	1 Sept	*Agile* (MSO 421), *Observer* (MSO 461), *Pinnacle* (MSO 462), *Skill* (MSO 471), *Vital* (MSO 474), *Sturdy* (MSO 494), *Swerve* (MSO 495), *Venture* (MSO 496) (all scrap)

AUXILIARY SHIPS

Destroyer Tenders

1976	15 Sept	*Isle Royal* (AD 29) (sold)

Degaussing Ships

1975	21 Feb	*Surfbird* (ADG 383) (ex-MSF), *Lodestone* (ADG 8) (both scrap); *Magnet* (9), *Deperm* (ADG 10) (both sunk as targets)

Ammunition Ships

1976	15 July	*Firedrake* (AE 14) (sold)
	1 Oct	*Mauna Loa* (AE 8), *Wrangell* (AE 12) (both sold)

Store Ships

1976	30 April	*Denebola* (AF 56) (sold)
	1 June	*Zelima* (AF 49), *Pictor* (AF 54), *Aludra* (AF 55), *Procyon* (AF
	1 Oct	*Arcturus* (AF 52), *Hyades* (AF 28) (both sold)
1977	29 April	*Vega* (AF 59) (pending)

Miscellaneous

1975	17 July	USNS *Flyer* (T-AG 169) (sold)
1976	15 Aug	USNS *Pvt Jose E. Valdes* (T-AG 169) (sold)
1977	30 Sept	*Alacrity* (AG 520), *Assurance* (AG 521) (both ex-MSO

Major Communications Relay Ships

1975	15 Aug	*Arlington* (AGMR 2) (ex-CVL: scrapped)
1976	15 Oct	*Annapolis* (AGMR 1) (ex-CVE: scrapped)

Oceanographic Research Ships

1977	15 Feb	USNS *Joshiah Willard Gibbs* (T-AGOR 1) (tr
	30 Dec	*Chain* (AGOR 17) (scrapped)

Patrol Craft Tender

1977	1 March	*Graham County* (AGP 1176) (scrapped

Survey Ships

1975	15 April	USNS *Michelson* (T-AGS 23) (per
1976	15 April	USNS *Sgt George D. Keathley* (T
	30 April	USNS *Coastal Crusader* (T-AGS

Cargo Ships

1975	1 April	USNS *Sgt Morris E. Crain*

608 USA

Light Cargo Ship

1976 15 April   *Mark* (AKL 12) (transfer)

Oilers

1975	15 April	*Tolovana* (AO 64) (sold)
	15 May	*Guadalupe* (AO 32) (sold)
1976	15 July	*Kennebec* (AO 36) (sold); *Tappahannock* (AO 43) (transfer)
	1 Dec	*Sabine* (AO 25), *Chikaskia* (AO 54), *Aucilla* (AO 56) (all sold)

Gasoline Tankers

1975	1 July	*Chewaucan* (AOG 50) (transfer); *Nespelen* (AOG 55), *Noxubee* (AOG 56) (both sold)
1976	15 April	*Elkhorn* (AOG 7), *Namakagon* (AOG 53), *Pecatonica* (AOG 57) (transfer)

Repair Ships

1976	1 Sept	*Markab* (AR 23) (scrapped)
	1 Nov	*Amphion* (AR 13) (transfer)
1977	1 Jan	*Briareus* (AR 12) (scrap)
	1 Oct	*Delta* (AR 9) (scrap)

Battle Damage Repair Ships

1976	15 April	*Midas* (ARB 5) (transfer); *Sarpedon* (ARB 7) (scrap)
	10 Dec	*Helios* (ARB 12) (transfer)

Cable Repair Ship

1977 20 Dec   *Thor* (ARC 4)

Landing Craft Repair Ships

1975	15 June	*Satyr* (ARL 23) (transfer)
1976	1 Nov	*Minotaur* (ARL 15) (transfer)
1977	1 Oct	*Egeria* (ARL 8), *Bellerophon* (ARL 31) (scrapped)
	31 Dec	*Indra* (ARL 37) (transferred to Maritime Administration)

Salvage Ships

1977	15 April	*Cable* (ARS 19) (sold)
	1 Dec	*Grapple* (ARS 7) (transfer)
1978	31 March	*Grasp* (ARS 24) (pending)

Submarine Rescue Ships

	15 Sept	*Coucal* (ASR 8) (target)
	30 Sept	*Tringa* (ASR 16) (transfer)

Ocean Tugs

Salish (ATA 187), *Catawba* (ATA 210) (transfer)
Penobscot (ATA 188) (sold)
Umpqua (ATA 209) (paid off by Colombia)
Cahokia (ATA 186), *Mahopac* (ATA 196) (both transfer)
Tatnuck (ATA 195) (sold)
Kalmia (ATA 184) (transfer)

(ATF 92) (sold)
(ATF 156) (transfer)
(ATF 100) (transfer); *Mataco* (ATF 86) (sold)
(ATF 70) (transfer)
(ATF 81) (transfer)

Refrigerated Covered Lighter (self-propelled)

1977 31 Oct   YFR 443 (transfer)

Covered Lighter (Range Tender)

1975 1 May   YFRT 411, 519 (both sold)

Harbor Utility Craft

1975	1 June	YFU 53 (scrapped)
1976	1 April	YFU 67 (sunk as target)
	15 Nov	YFU 99 (scrapped)
1977	1 April	YFU 80 (scrapped)
	1 July	YFU 55 (sold)
	15 Sept	YFU 44 (sold)

Dredge

1975 1 May   YM 22 (sold)

Salvage Lift Craft, Medium

1975 15 Feb   YMLC 5 and 6 (both sold)

Fuel Oil Barges

1975	1 Feb	YO 211, YO 60 (both sunk as targets); YO 248 (sold)
	1 April	YO 179 (transfer); YO 59 (sunk as target)
	1 July	YO 154 (sold)
1976	1 June	YO 227 (sunk as target 19 March 1977)
	1 July	YO 199 (sunk as target Aug 1976)
1977	1 March	*Crownblock* (YO 48) (sunk as target)
	15 June	YO 205 (sunk as target 25 Oct 1977)
	1 July	YO 219 (sunk as target)

Gasoline Barge (self-propelled)

1975	1 May	*Lt Thomas W. Fowler* (YOG 107), YOG 89 (both sunk as targets)
	1 July	YOG 65 (sold)
	16 July	YOG 61 (transfer)
1976	5 April	YOG 80 (transfer)

Oil Storage Barge

1976 1 Aug   YOS 22 (sold)

Patrol Craft

1976	1 July	YP 589, 590 (sold)
1977	1 Sept	YP 587 (sold)

Floating Workshops

1975	1 April	YR 66 (transfer)
1976	1 Sept	YR 32 (transfer)

Repair and Berthing Barge

1976 1 March   YRB 28 (sold)

Small Harbour Tugboat

1976 1 Sept   YTL 211, 567 (transfer)

Medium Harbour Tugboats

1975	1 March	*Shahaska* (YTM 533) (sold)
	15 March	*Orono* (YTM 190) (transfer)
	1 May	*Abinago* (YTM 493), *Barboncito* (YTM 495), *Olathe* (YTM 273), *Washakie* (YTM 386), *Connewango* (YTM 388), *Chiquito* (YTM 765), *Chohonaga* (YTM 766) (all sold)
	1 Sept	*Mantee* (YTM 751), *Kewaunee* (YTM 752), *Woonsocket* (YTM 754), *Waukegan* (YTM 755) (all sold)
	15 Sept	*Satanta* (YTM 270), *Smohalla* (YTM 371), *Minniska* (YTM 408), *Topawa* (YTM 419), *Cholocco* (YTM 764), *Hastwiana* (YTM 775) (all sold); *Wallacut* (YTM 420), *Windigo* (YTM 421) (both sunk as targets)
	1 Nov	*Black Fox* (YTM 177) (to University of Georgia 9 Nov 1975); *Mazapeta* (YTM 181) (sold)
1976	1 March	*Wabanaquet* (YTM 525) (sold)
	1 April	YTM 510 (sunk as target)
	15 May	*Satago* (YTM 414) (sunk as target 21 Jan 1977)
	1 July	*Tensaw* (YTM 418) (sold)
1977	15 April	*Panameta* (YTM 402) (sunk as target)
	1 May	*Chilkat* (YTM 773) (to Maritime Administration 17 March 1976 for service); *Oomulgee* (YTM 532) (sold)
	1 Oct	*Mahoa* (YTM 519) (sunk as target)

Water Barges (self-propelled)

1975	1 Feb	YW 115, 129 (both sunk as targets)
	1 July	YW 84 (sold)
	16 July	YW 103, 111, 130 (transfer)
	1 Aug	YW 89, 157 (both sunk as targets)

Water Barge (non-self-propelled)

1975 1 July   YWN 67 (to NOAA on 26 April 1977)

US NAVAL SHIPS AND CRAFT TRANSFERRED TO FOREIGN COUNTRIES

This section comprises a list of ships and craft, arranged by date transferred, to a foreign country, since 1 January 1975. All transfers, except where noted took place under the International Logistics Programme (formerly the Military Defense Assistance Pact). The six methods of transfer are as follows:

Sale: The recipient buys the vessel(s) and receives the title(s). Most ship sales usually fall in this category.
Loan: Vessel(s) is loaned to recipient. US Navy retains title; recipient pays operating and maintenance costs.
Grant Aid: The recipient receives the vessel(s) in lieu of a grant of money. The United States does not retain title, but pays for activation (if needed), modernisation, and all other costs to make the vessel(s) suitable for transfer. After the transfer, the recipient country assumes all costs.
Lease: Similar to a loan, only the navy of the recipient country, rather than its government, makes the request to lease a vessel(s) directly to the US Navy rather than to the US government.
Off-Shore Procurement (OSP): Vessel(s) built in a foreign yard (usually in a yard in country of the recipient) and the United States pays half the costs of construction and/or provides equipment and technical assistance. US Navy hull numbers are assigned for accounting purposes.
Special: Vessel(s) transferred under methods other than the five listed above will be listed in the "Mode" column as Special.

Notes:
(a) A single asterisk before a date in the "Date of Transfer" column indicates that the ship in question had previously been loaned or leased to the indicated country at an earlier date.
(b) In the "USN Name/Hull Number" column asterisks appearing after the former USN name hull number indicate the following: * formerly with the Republic of South Viet-Nam Navy; ** formerly with the Khmer Republic (ex-Cambodia) Navy; *** formerly with the Japanese Maritime Self-Defense Force.
(c) Those ships indicated as transferred by "Special*" in the "Mode" column were transferred to the indicated country via the Agency for International Development (AID).
(d) A "—" in the "Recipient Name/Hull Number" column indicates that as of writing the foreign name and pennant number were unknown.
(e) Those ships whose disposal is indicated as "transfer" in the deletion list, but are not listed below are pending. In some cases, some of the transfers pending are already on loan/lease to their prospective purchasers.

Date of Transfer	Recipient	USN Name/Hull Number	Recipient Name/Hull Number	Mode
1975				
13 Jan	Iran	Kenneth D. Bailey (DD 713)	(for cannibalisation and scrapping)	Sale
16 Jan	Spain	Unnamed (DEG 9)	Cataluna (F 73)	OSP
*19 Feb	Guatemala	YR 40	YR 44	Sale
24 Feb	Peru	YO 221	—	Sale
20 May	Guyana	Orono (YTM 190)	—	Sale
* 6 June	Thailand	Hemminger (DE 746)	Pin Klao (DE 3)	Special*
1 July	Columbia	Chewaucan (AOG 50)	Tumaco (BT 65)	Grant Aid
1 July	Argentina	Luiseno (ATF 156)	Francisco De Gurruchaga (A 3)	Sale
* 2 July	South Korea	Derrick (YO 59)	Hwa Chon (AO 5)	Sale
* 2 July	South Korea	YO 179	YO 6	Sale
* 2 July	South Korea	MSB 2	Pi Bong (MSB 1)	Sale
16 July	Philippines	YOG 61	(for cannibalisation and scrapping)	Sale
16 July	Philippines	YW 130	Lake Paoay (YW 34)	Loan
16 July	Philippines	YO 115	(for cannibalisation)	Loan
16 July	Philippines	YO 116	Lake Mainit (YO 35)	Loan
16 July	Philippines	YW 103	(for cannibalisation)	Loan
16 July	Philippines	YW 111	Lake Bulan (YW 33)	Loan
1 Aug	South Korea	CPIC-X	Gireogi (PKM 123)	Grant Aid
1 Aug	Guyana	YFN 960	—	Special*
2 Oct	South Korea	Unnamed (MSC 320)	Yong Dong (MSC 529)	Grant Aid
2 Oct	South Korea	Unnamed (MSC 321)	Ok Cheon (MSC 530)	Grant Aid
13 Oct	Saudi Arabia	YTB 837	Tuwaig (YTB 111)	Grant Aid
13 Oct	Saudi Arabia	YTB 838	Dareen (YTB 113)	Grant Aid
14 Oct	Fiji	Vireo (MSC 205)	Kula (205)	Sale
14 Oct	Fiji	Warbler (MSC 206)	Kiro (206)	Sale
17 Nov	Philippines	Gayety (MSF 239)*	Magat Salamat (PS 20)	Grant Aid
17 Nov	Philippines	Shelter (MSF 301)*	(for cannibalisation and scrapping)	Grant Aid
17 Nov	Philippines	Crestview (PCE 895)*	Sultan Kudarat (PS 22)	Grant Aid
17 Nov	Philippines	Brattleboro (PCER 852)*	Miguel Malvar (PS 19)	Grant Aid
17 Nov	Philippines	Marion County (LST 975)*	Zamboanga Del Sur (LT 86)	Grant Aid
17 Nov	Philippines	Cayuga County (LST 529)*	—	Grant Aid
17 Nov	Philippines	LSM 110*	(for cannibalisation)	Grant Aid
17 Nov	Philippines	Oceanside (LSM 175)*	Batanes (LP 65)	Grant Aid
17 Nov	Philippines	LSM 355*	Western Samar (LP 66)	Grant Aid
17 Nov	Philippines	LSIL 699*	Camarines Norte (LS 52)	Grant Aid
17 Nov	Philippines	LSIL 871*	Misamis Occidental (LS 53)	Grant Aid
17 Nov	Philippines	LSIL 872*	Sorsogon (LS 37)	Grant Aid
17 Nov	Philippines	LSIL 875**	Marinduque (LS 36)	Grant Aid
17 Nov	Philippines	LSIL 476**	(for cannibalisation and scrapping)	Grant Aid
17 Nov	Philippines	LSSL 9*	(for cannibalisation and scrapping)	Grant Aid
17 Nov	Philippines	LSSL 96*	Sulu (LS 49)	Grant Aid
17 Nov	Philippines	LSSL 101*	(for cannibalisation and scrapping)	Grant Aid
17 Nov	Philippines	LSSL 129*	Camarines Sur (LS 48)	Grant Aid
17 Nov	Philippines	YOG 33*	(for cannibalisation and scrapping)	Grant Aid
17 Nov	Philippines	YOG 80*	(for cannibalisation and scrapping)	Grant Aid
17 Nov	Philippines	Daggett County (LST 689)***	—	Grant Aid
17 Nov	Philippines	LSSL 68***	—	Grant Aid
17 Nov	Philippines	LCU 1603***	—	Grant Aid
17 Nov	Philippines	LCU 1604***	—	Grant Aid
17 Nov	Philippines	LCU 1606***	—	Grant Aid
17 Nov	Philippines	YTL 748***	—	Grant Aid
2 Dec	Spain	Unnamed (DEG 10)	Asturias (F 74)	Grant Aid
3 Dec	Philippines	PC 1171*	Negros Oriental (PS 29)	OSP
3 Dec	Philippines	PGM 83*	Basilan (PG 60)	Grant A
5 Dec	Singapore	Thrasher (MSC 203)	Mercury (M 84)	Grant
5 Dec	Singapore	Whippoorwill (MSC 207)	Jupiter (M 85)	Sale
17 Dec	Thailand	Dodge County (LST 722)	Prathong (LST 5)	Sale
Dec	Philippines	YON 279	—	Sal Sp
1976				
6 Jan	Barbados	Kemper County (LST 854)	—	
*14 Feb	Argentina	Salish (ATA 187)	Comodoro Somellera (A 10)	
*14 Feb	Argentina	Catawba (ATA 210)	Alfrez Sobral (A-9)	
*14 Feb	Argentina	M/V Dry Tortugas (ATF)	Goyena (Q 17)	
March	Philippines	M/V Sombrero Key (ATF)	Thompson (A 14)	
* March	Ethiopia	LT 1976 (ex-US Army)	Tiboli (YQ 58)	
5 April	Philippines	Orca (AVP 49)	Ethiopia (A 01)	
5 April	Philippines	Camp (FFR 251)*	Rajah Lakandula (PS 4)	
5 April	Philippines	Chincoteague (WHEC 375)*	Andres Bonifacio (PS 7)	
5 April	Philippines	Yakutat (WHEC 380)*	(for cannibalisation and scrapping)	
5 April	Philippines	Bering Strait (WHEC 382)*	Diego Silang (PS 9)	
5 April	Philippines	Castle Rock (WHEC 383)*	Francisco Dagahoy (PS 10)	
5 April	Philippines	Cook Inlet (WHEC 384)*	(for cannibalisation and scrapping)	
5 April	Philippines	McCulloch (WHEC 386)*	Gregorio de Pilar (PS 8)	
5 April	Philippines	Amherst (PCER 853)*	Datu Marikudo (PS 23)	
5 April	Philippines	Jerome County (LST 848)*	—	
5 April	Philippines	Garrett County (AGP 786)*	—	
5 April	Philippines	Harnett County (AGP 821)*	—	
* April	Greece	YOG 80*	—	
* April	Greece	Lapon (SS 260)	(for cannibalisation and scrapping	
*19 May	Taiwan	Scabbardfish (SS 397)	(for cannibalisation and scrapping	
*19 May	Taiwan	White Marsh (LSD 8)	Triaina (S 86)	
*19 May	Taiwan	Chickasaw (ATF 83)	Chung Cheng (LSD 191)	
		Pecatonica (AOG 57)	Ta Tung (ATF 548)	
			Chang Pei (AOG 507)	

610 USA

Date of Transfer	Recipient	USN Name/Hull Number	Recipient Name/Hull Number	Mode
*19 May	Taiwan	Namakagon (AOG 53) (ex-HMNZS)	Lung Chuan (AOG 515)	Sale
*19 May	Taiwan	Mahopac (ATA 196)	Ta Peng (ATA 549)	Sale
*19 May	Taiwan	Mark (AKL 12)	Yung Kang (AKL 514)	Sale
*19 May	Taiwan	Cahokia (ATA 186)	Ta Teng (ATA 550)	Sale
*19 May	Taiwan	Elkhorn (AOG 7)	Hsing Lung (AOG 517)	Sale
*19 May	Taiwan	Windsor (ARD 22)	Fo Wu No 6	Sale
*19 May	Taiwan	Sgt George D. Keathley (AGS 35)	Chu Hwa (AGS 564)	Sale
*19 May	Taiwan	Placerville (PC 1087)	—	Sale
*19 May	Taiwan	Hanford (PC 1142)	—	Sale
*19 May	Taiwan	Susanville (PC 1149)	—	Sale
4 June	Singapore	USNS LST 579 (T-LST 579)	Intrepid (L 203)	Sale
4 June	Singapore	USNS LST 613 (T-LST 613)	Persistance (L 205)	Sale
4 June	Singapore	USNS LST 623 (T-LST 623)	Perseverence (L 206)	Sale
4 June	Singapore	USNS LST 629 (T-LST 629)	Excellence (L 202)	Sale
4 June	Singapore	USNS LST 649 (T-LST 649)	Resolution (L 204)	Sale
17 June	Fiji	Woodpecker (MSC 209)	Kikau (204)	Sale
*23 June	Uruguay	Chickadee (MSF 59)	Cdmt Pedro Campbell (MSF 1)	Sale
8 July	Saudi Arabia	Unnamed (LCU type)	Al-Uqair (LCU 311)	Grant Aid
Aug	Spain	LCU 1471	—	Sale
Aug	Spain	LCU 1491	—	Sale
13 Sept	Philippines	Amick (DE 168)***	—	Sale
13 Sept	Philippines	Atherton (DE 169)***	—	Sale
13 Sept	Philippines	USNS LST 47 (T-LST 47)	—	Sale
13 Sept	Philippines	USNS LST 230 (T-LST 230)	—	Sale
13 Sept	Philippines	USNS LST 287 (T-LST 287)	—	Sale
13 Sept	Philippines	USNS LST 491 (T-LST 491)	—	Sale
13 Sept	Philippines	USNS LST 566 (T-LST 566)	—	Sale
13 Sept	Philippines	USNS LST 607 (T-LST 607)	—	Sale
13 Sept	Philippines	USNS Davies County (T-LST 692)	—	Sale
13 Sept	Philippines	USNS Harris County (T-LST 822)	—	Sale
13 Sept	Philippines	USNS Orleans Parish (T-LST 1069)	—	Sale
13 Sept	Philippines	USNS LST 1072 (T-LST 1072)	—	Sale
16 Sept	Peru	Tench (SS 417)	(for cannibalisation and scrapping)	Sale
24 Sept	Philippines	Nansemond County (LST 1064)***	—	Sale
24 Sept	Philippines	LSSL 87***	—	Sale
24 Sept	Philippines	YTL 750***	—	Sale
24 Sept	Philippines	FS 408***	—	Sale
29 Sept	Dominican Republic	Etlah (AN 79)	Cambiaso (P 207)	Sale
29 Sept	Dominican Republic	Passaconaway (AN 86)	Separacion (P 208)	Sale
29 Sept	Dominican Republic	Passaic (AN 87)	Caleras (P 209)	Sale
7 Oct	Malaysia	Henry County (LST 824)	Sri Banggi (A 1501)	Sale
7 Oct	Malaysia	Sedgewick County (LST 1123)	Rajah Jarom (A 1502)	Sale

1977

Date of Transfer	Recipient	USN Name/Hull Number	Recipient Name/Hull Number	Mode
*12 Jan	Taiwan	ARD 9	Fo Wu No 5	Sale
*14 Jan	Argentina	Heermann (DD 532)	Brown (D 20)	Sale
*14 Jan	Argentina	Dortch (DD 670)	(for cannibalisation and scrapping)	Sale
*14 Jan	Argentina	Stembel (DD 644)	Rosales (D 22)	Sale
24 Jan	Philippines	Satyr (ARL 23)	—	Sale
*31 Jan	South Korea	Minotaur (ARL 15)	Duk Su (ARL 1)	Sale
*31 Jan	South Korea	Erben (DD 631)	Chung Mu (DD 91)	Sale
31 Jan	South Korea	Hickox (DD 673)	Pusan (DD 93)	Sale
1 Jan	South Korea	Halsey Powell (DD 686)	Seoul (DD 92)	Sale
Jan	South Korea	Chevalier (DD 805)	Chung Buk (DD 95)	Sale
Jan	South Korea	Everett F. Larson (DD 830)	Jeong Buk (DD 96)	Sale
eb	Paraguay	YFB 82	—	Sale
b	Paraguay	YFB 86	YTL 559	Sale
	Paraguay	YTL 211	—	Sale
	Paraguay	YTL 567	—	Sale
	Paraguay	YR 37	—	Sale
	Paraguay	AFDL 26	Hualcopo (T 55)	Sale
	Ecuador	Summit County (LST 1148)	Taejon (DD 99)	Sale
	South Korea	New (DD 818)	Kwang Ju (DD 90)	Sale
	South Korea	Richard E. Kraus (DD 849)	Chahbahar (A 41)	Sale
	Iran	Amphion (AR 13)	FD 4	Sale
	Iran	Arco (ARD 29)	Z 2 (D 171)	Sale
	West Germany	Ringgold (DD 500)	Z 3 (D 172)	Sale
	West Germany	Wadsworth (DD 516)	Z 4 (D 178)	Sale
	West Germany	Claxton (DD 571)	Z 5 (D 179)	Sale
	West Germany	Dyson (DD 572)	Tombazis (D 215)	Sale
	Greece	Gurke (DD 783)	Oinoussa (L 104)	Sale
	Greece	Terrell County (LST 1157)	Kos (L 116)	Sale
		Whitfield County (LST 1169)	— (LSD 618)	Sale
		Fort Marion (LSD 22)	Sfendoni (D 85)	Sale
		Aulick (DD 569)	Velos (D 16)	Sale
		Charette (DD 581)	Aspis (D 06)	Sale
		Conner (DD 582)	Lonchi (D 56)	Sale
		Hall (DD 583)	Thyella (D 28)	Sale
		Bradford (DD 545)	Navarinon (D 63)	Sale
		Brown (DD 546)	Tariq (D 165)	Sale
		Wiltsie (DD 716)	Taimur (D 166)	Sale
		Epperson (DD 719)	Chao Yang	Sale
		Rowan (DD 782)	Kai Yang	Sale
		Richard B. Anderson (DD 786)	Chulupi (R 10)	Sale
		YTL 426	Mocovi (R 5)	Sale
		YTL 441	Capayan (R 16)	Sale
		YTL 443	Chiquiyon (R 18)	Sale
		YTL 444	Calchaqui (R 6)	Sale
		YTL 445	Morcoyan (R 19)	Sale
		YTL 448	Te Yang	Sale
		Sarsfield (DD 837)	Shen Yang	Sale
		Powers (DD 839)	Chimborazo (106)	Sale
		Chowanoc (ATF 100)	Ta Hu	Sale
		Grapple (ARS 7)	Alfredo Cappellini (S 507)	Sale
		Capitaine (SS 336)	Gianfranco Gazzana Friaroggia (S 501)	Sale
		Volador (SS 490)	Primo Longobardo (S 502)	Sale
		Pickerel (SS 524)		

USA 611

STRATEGIC MISSILE SUBMARINES

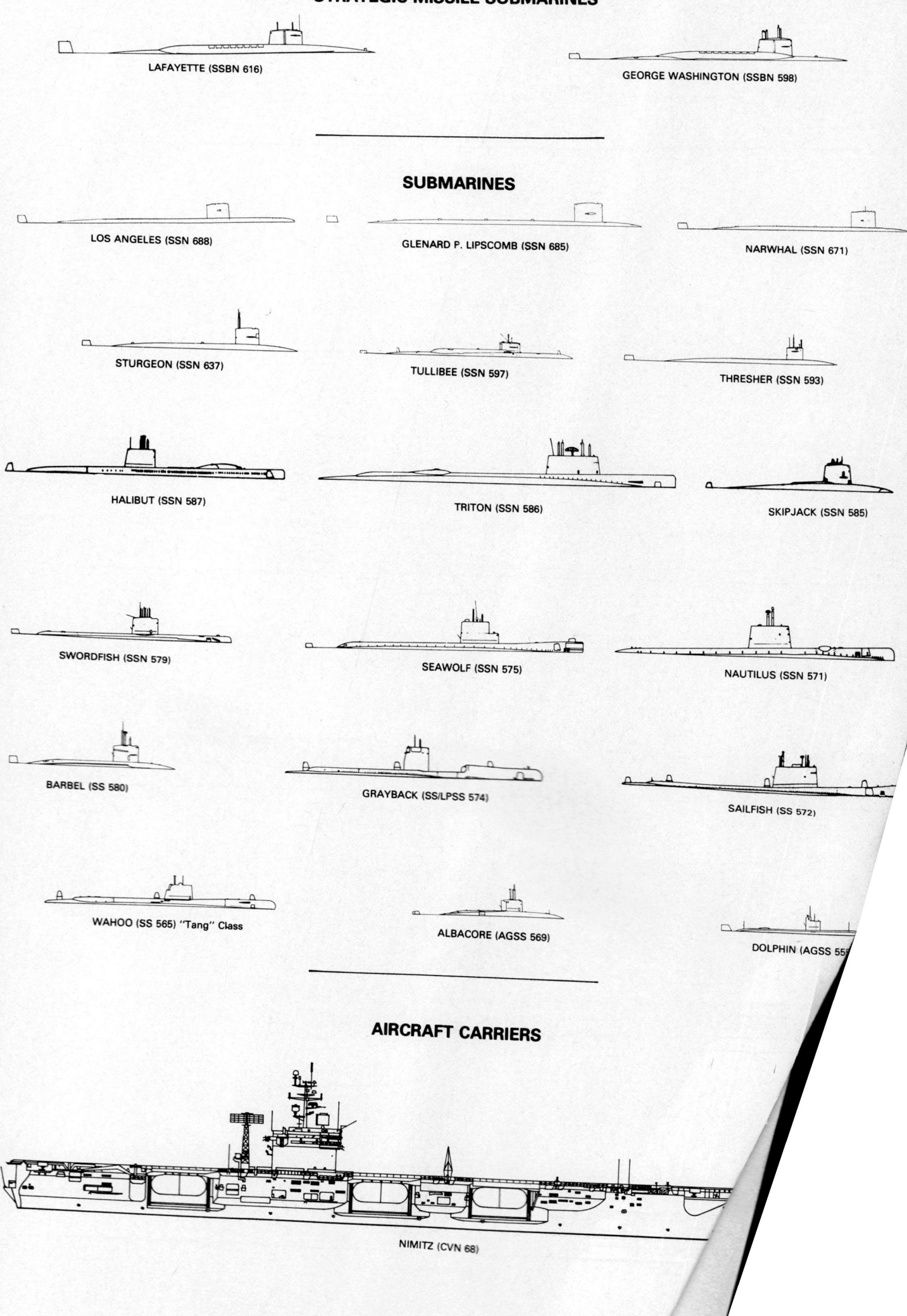

LAFAYETTE (SSBN 616)

GEORGE WASHINGTON (SSBN 598)

SUBMARINES

LOS ANGELES (SSN 688)

GLENARD P. LIPSCOMB (SSN 685)

NARWHAL (SSN 671)

STURGEON (SSN 637)

TULLIBEE (SSN 597)

THRESHER (SSN 593)

HALIBUT (SSN 587)

TRITON (SSN 586)

SKIPJACK (SSN 585)

SWORDFISH (SSN 579)

SEAWOLF (SSN 575)

NAUTILUS (SSN 571)

BARBEL (SS 580)

GRAYBACK (SS/LPSS 574)

SAILFISH (SS 572)

WAHOO (SS 565) "Tang" Class

ALBACORE (AGSS 569)

DOLPHIN (AGSS 555)

AIRCRAFT CARRIERS

NIMITZ (CVN 68)

612 USA

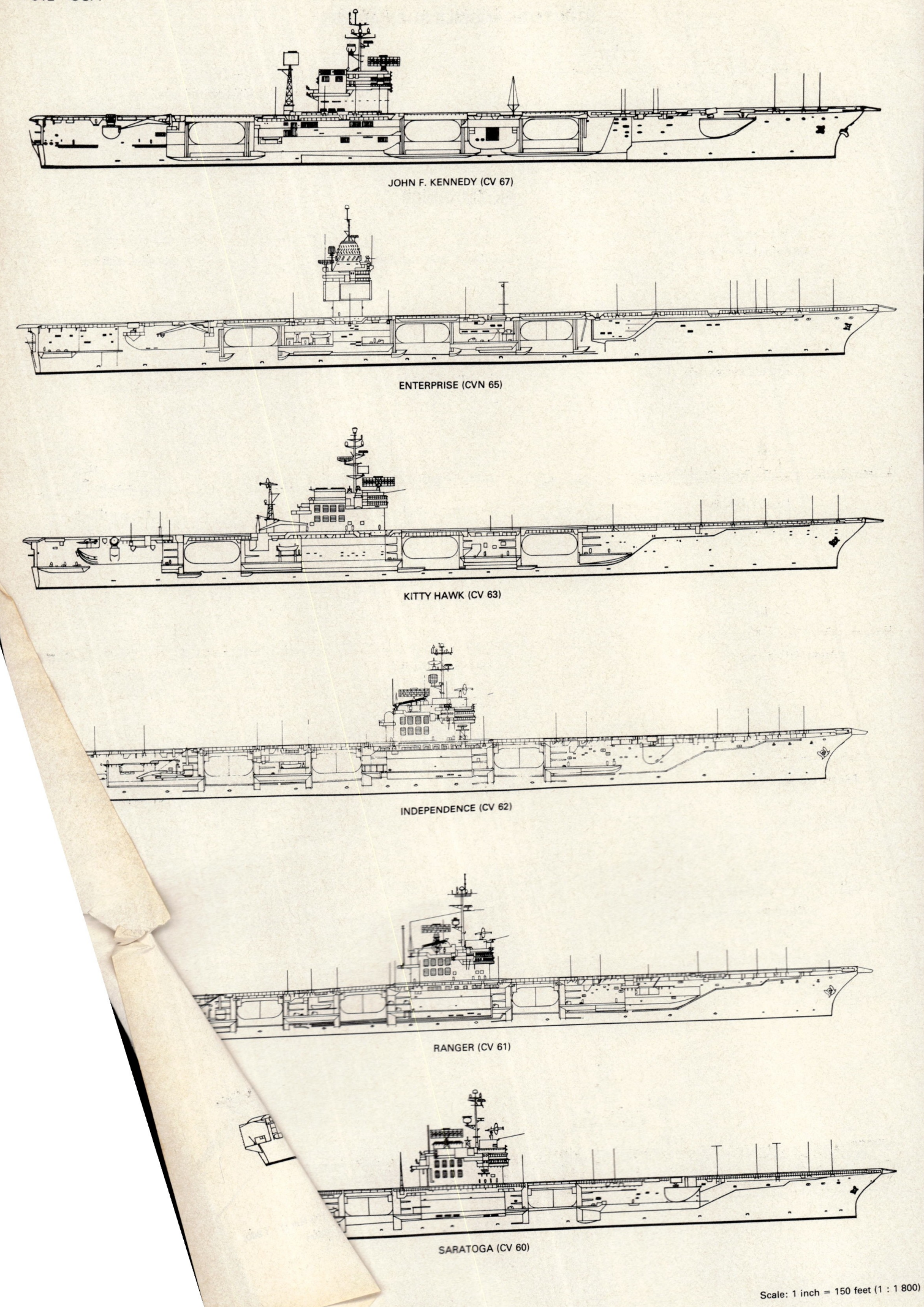

JOHN F. KENNEDY (CV 67)

ENTERPRISE (CVN 65)

KITTY HAWK (CV 63)

INDEPENDENCE (CV 62)

RANGER (CV 61)

SARATOGA (CV 60)

Scale: 1 inch = 150 feet (1 : 1 800)

USA 613

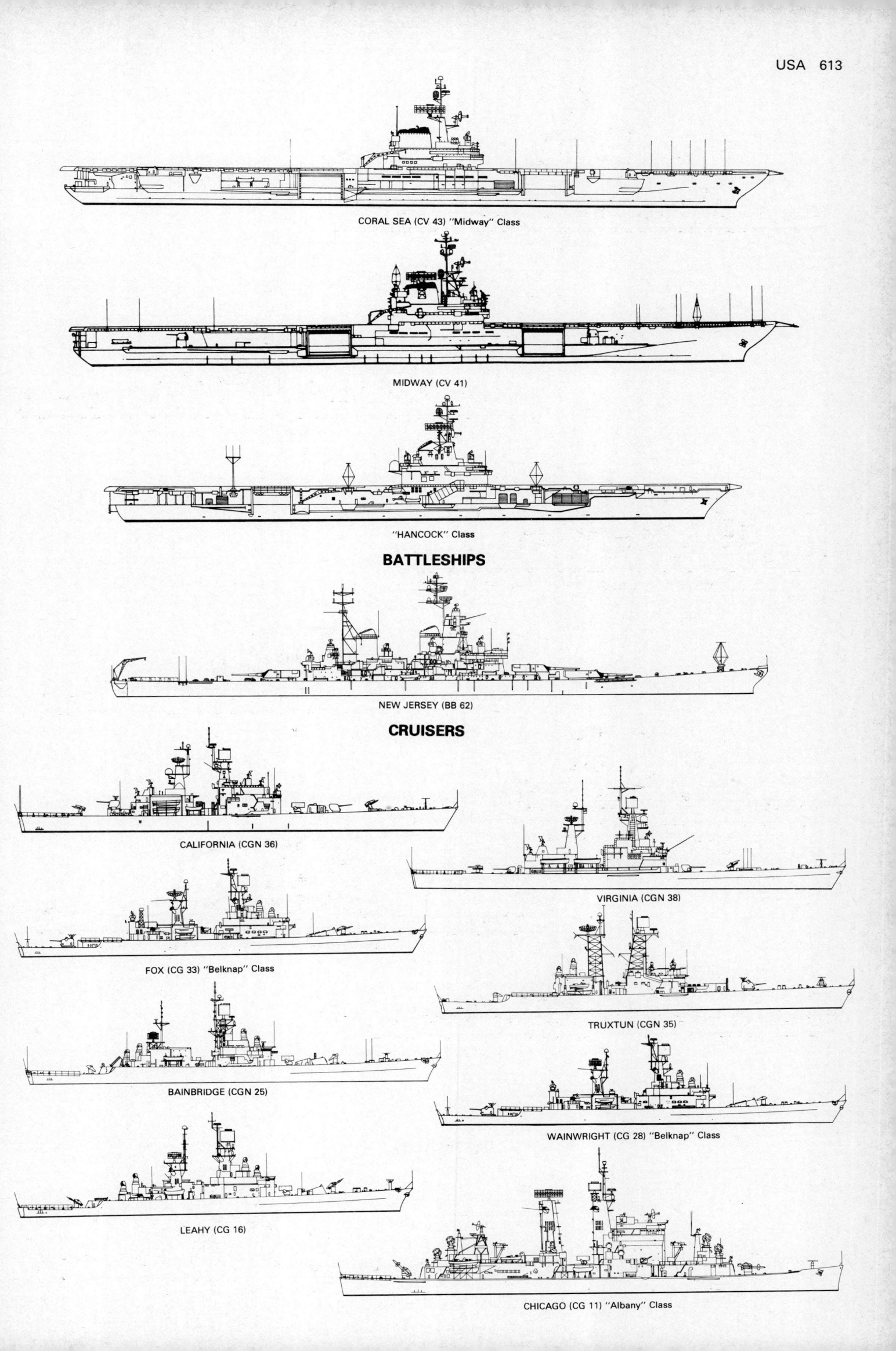

CORAL SEA (CV 43) "Midway" Class

MIDWAY (CV 41)

"HANCOCK" Class

BATTLESHIPS

NEW JERSEY (BB 62)

CRUISERS

CALIFORNIA (CGN 36)

VIRGINIA (CGN 38)

FOX (CG 33) "Belknap" Class

TRUXTUN (CGN 35)

BAINBRIDGE (CGN 25)

WAINWRIGHT (CG 28) "Belknap" Class

LEAHY (CG 16)

CHICAGO (CG 11) "Albany" Class

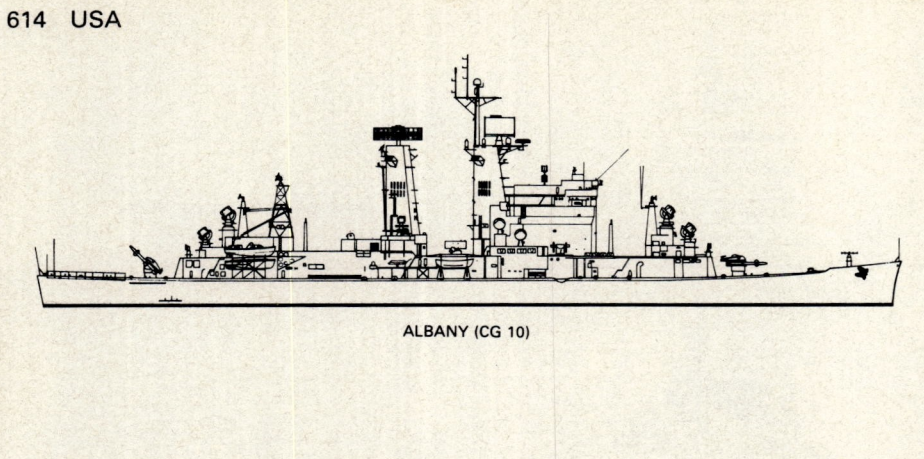

614 USA

ALBANY (CG 10)

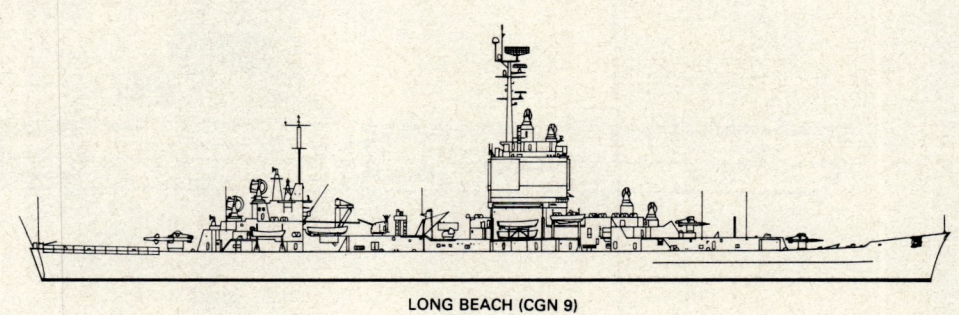

LONG BEACH (CGN 9)

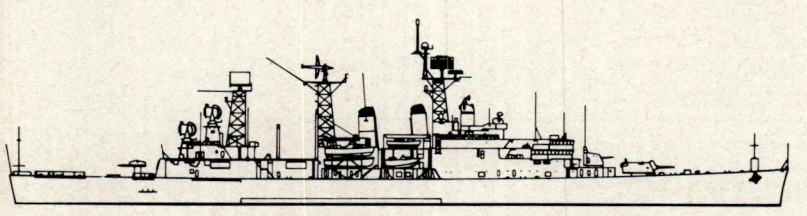

PROVIDENCE (CG 6) Converted "Cleveland" Class (Terrier)

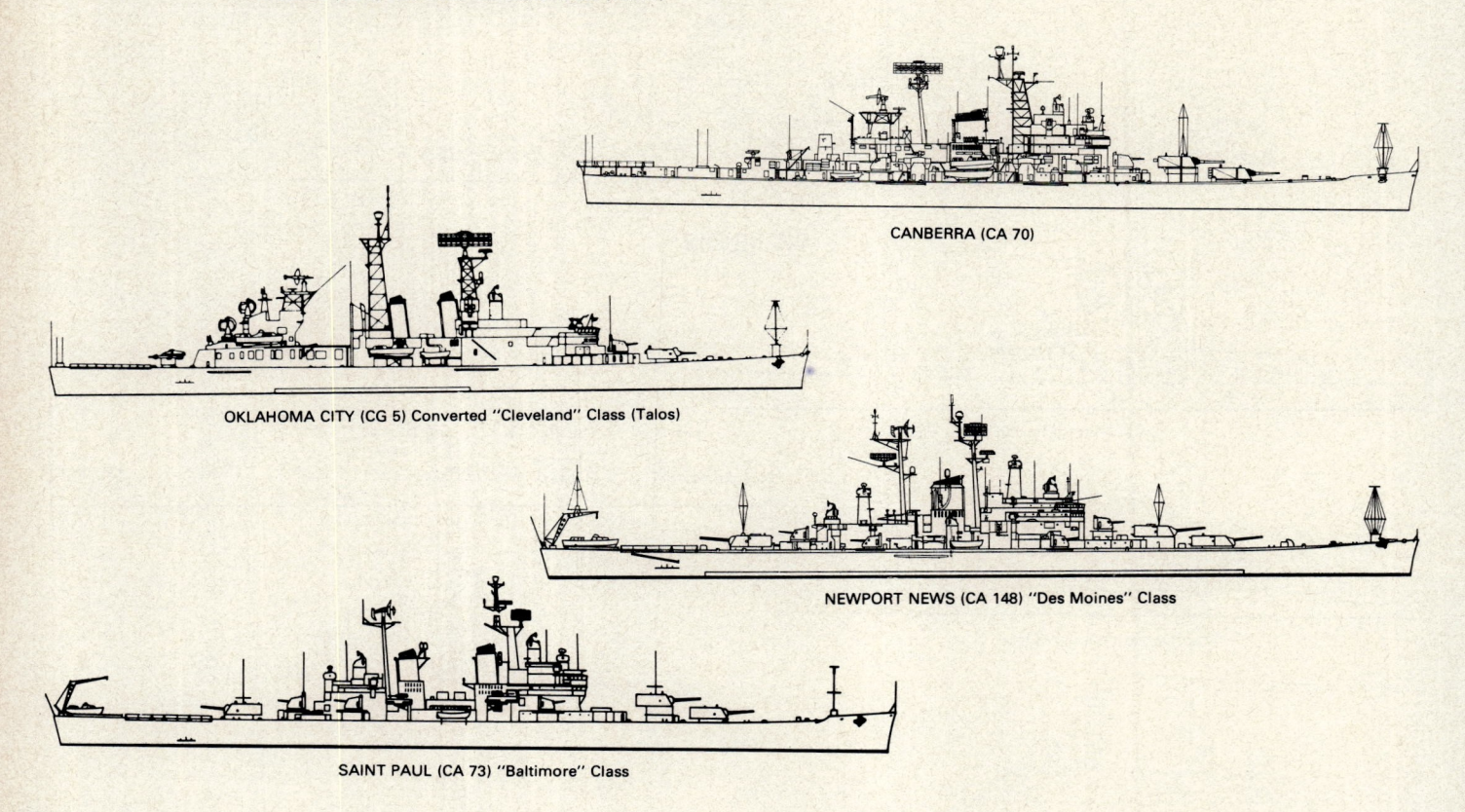

CANBERRA (CA 70)

OKLAHOMA CITY (CG 5) Converted "Cleveland" Class (Talos)

NEWPORT NEWS (CA 148) "Des Moines" Class

SAINT PAUL (CA 73) "Baltimore" Class

DESTROYERS

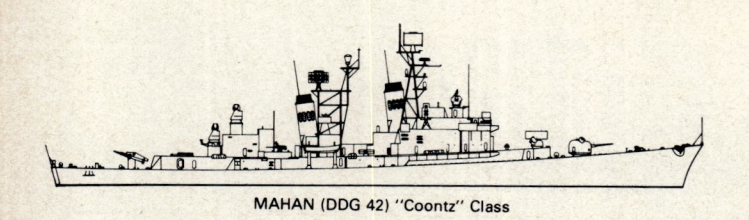

MAHAN (DDG 42) "Coontz" Class

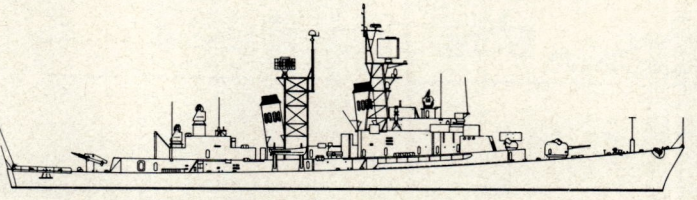

FARRAGUT (DDG 37) "Coontz" Class

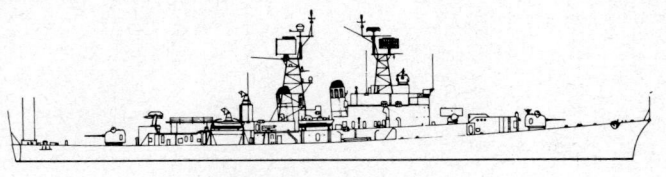

USA 615

MITSCHER (DDG 35)

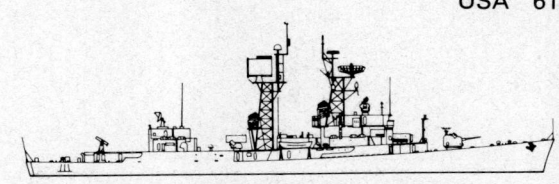

SOMERS (DDG 34) Converted "Forrest Sherman" Class

WADDELL (DDG 24) "Charles F. Adams" Class

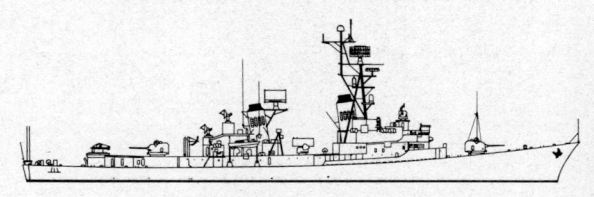

BARNEY (DDG 6) "Charles F. Adams" Class

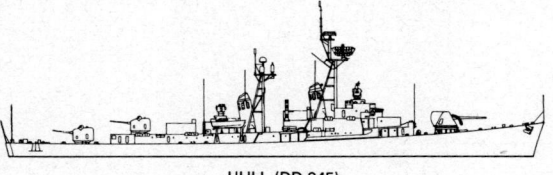

HULL (DD 945)

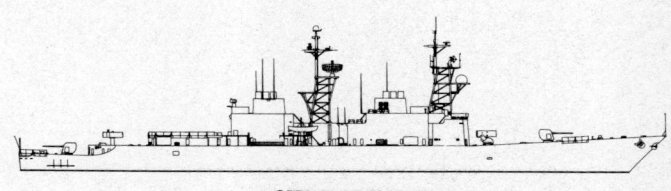

SPRUANCE (DD 963)

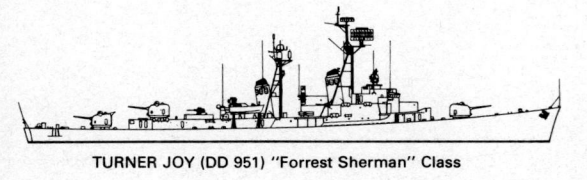

TURNER JOY (DD 951) "Forrest Sherman" Class

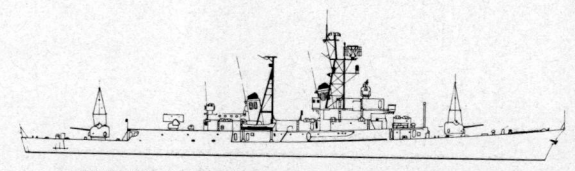

JONAS INGRAM (DD 938) "Forrest Sherman" Class (ASW)

BARRY (DD 933) "Forrest Sherman" Class (ASW)

"GEARING" Class FRAM I (guns forward and aft)

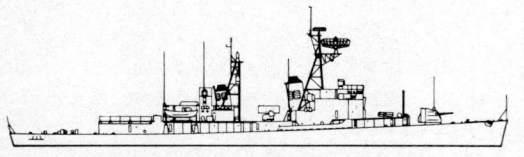

ROBERT A. OWENS (DD 827) "Carpenter" Class FRAM I

"GEARING" Class FRAM I (all guns forward)
(Agerholm DD 824 and Meredith, DD 890)

FRIGATES

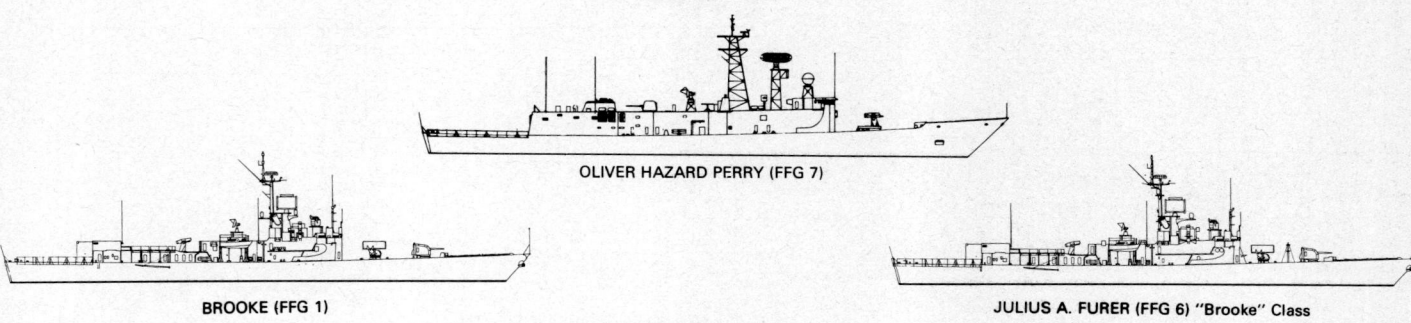

OLIVER HAZARD PERRY (FFG 7)

BROOKE (FFG 1)

JULIUS A. FURER (FFG 6) "Brooke" Class

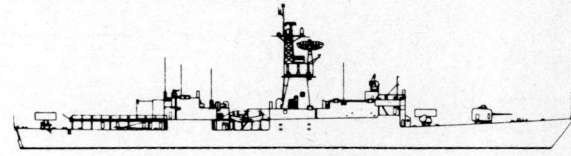

"KNOX" Class (improved)

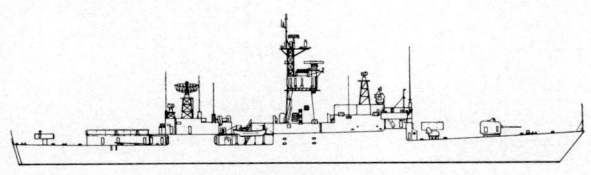

DOWNES (FF 1070) NATO Sea Sparrow

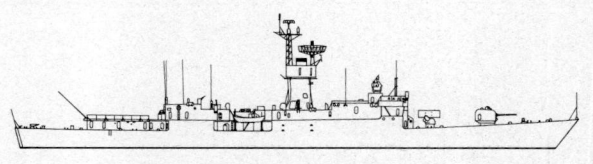

"KNOX" Class

Scale: 1 inch = 150 feet (1 : 1 800)

616 USA

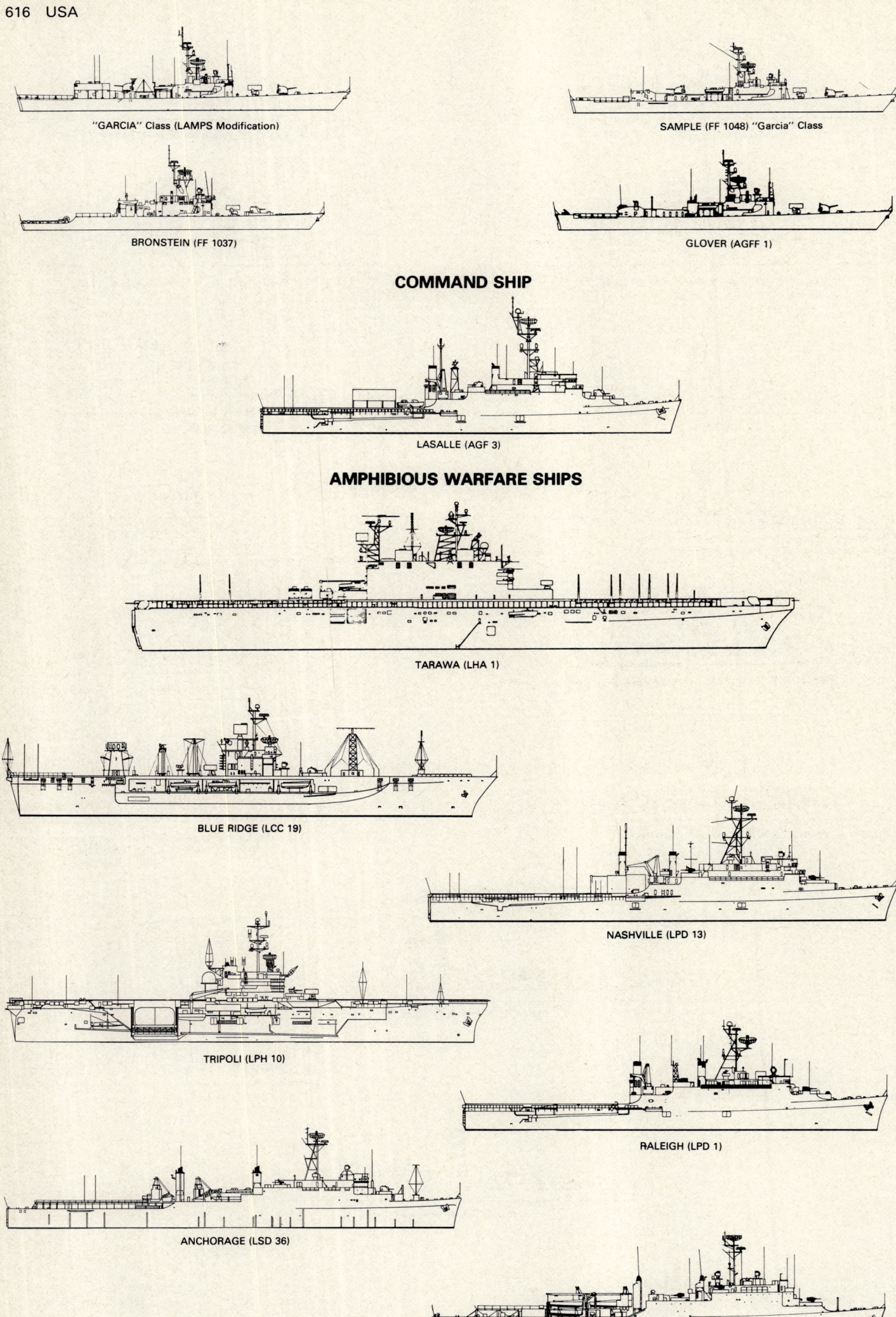

"GARCIA" Class (LAMPS Modification)

SAMPLE (FF 1048) "Garcia" Class

BRONSTEIN (FF 1037)

GLOVER (AGFF 1)

COMMAND SHIP

LASALLE (AGF 3)

AMPHIBIOUS WARFARE SHIPS

TARAWA (LHA 1)

BLUE RIDGE (LCC 19)

NASHVILLE (LPD 13)

TRIPOLI (LPH 10)

RALEIGH (LPD 1)

ANCHORAGE (LSD 36)

HERMITAGE (LSD 34) "Thomaston" Class

USA 617

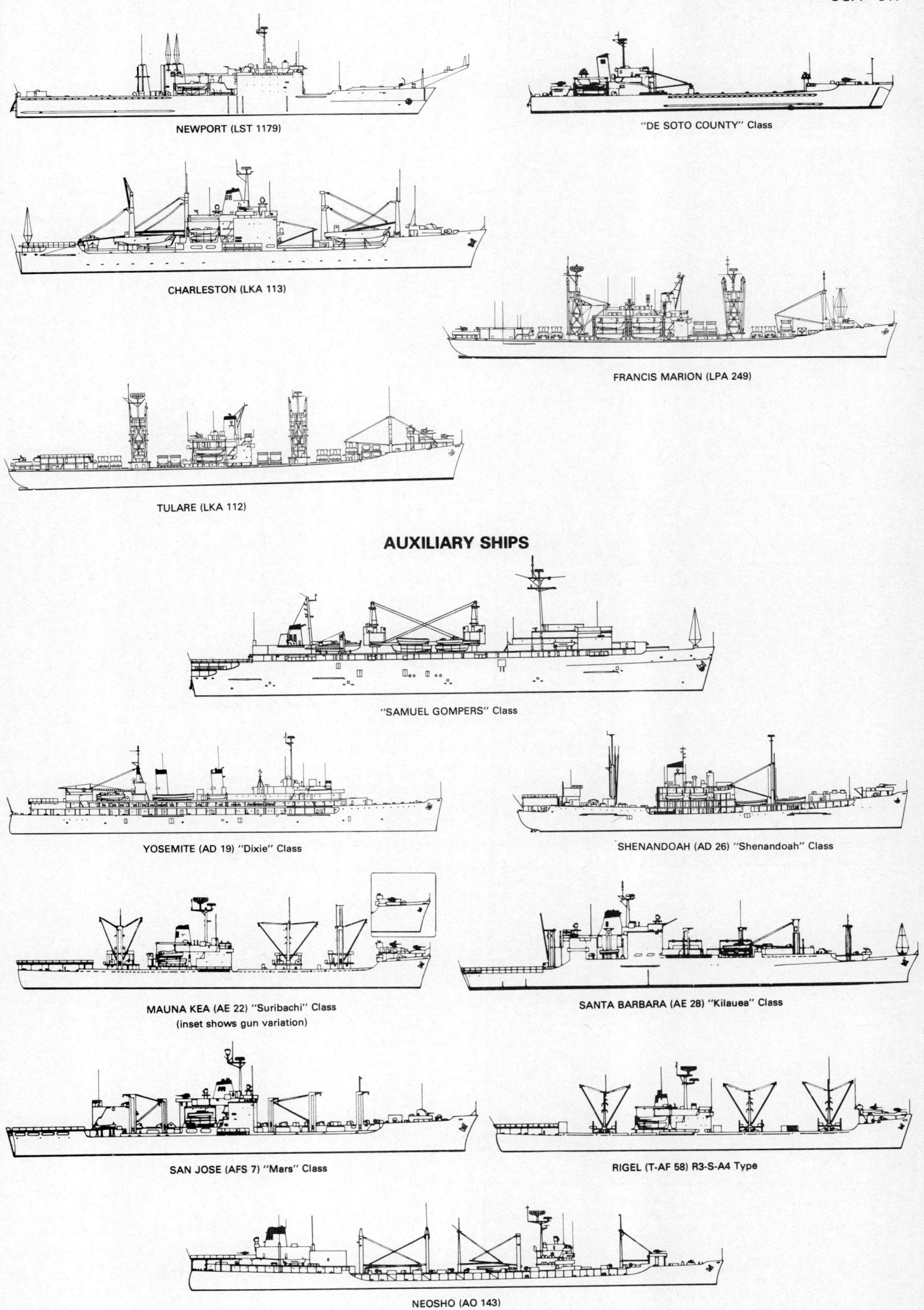

NEWPORT (LST 1179)

"DE SOTO COUNTY" Class

CHARLESTON (LKA 113)

FRANCIS MARION (LPA 249)

TULARE (LKA 112)

AUXILIARY SHIPS

"SAMUEL GOMPERS" Class

YOSEMITE (AD 19) "Dixie" Class

SHENANDOAH (AD 26) "Shenandoah" Class

MAUNA KEA (AE 22) "Suribachi" Class
(inset shows gun variation)

SANTA BARBARA (AE 28) "Kilauea" Class

SAN JOSE (AFS 7) "Mars" Class

RIGEL (T-AF 58) R3-S-A4 Type

NEOSHO (AO 143)

618 USA

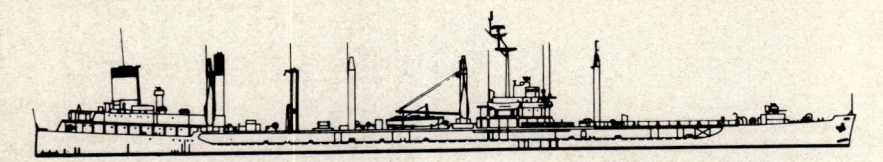

MISPILLION (T-AO 105) Jumboised T3-S2-A3

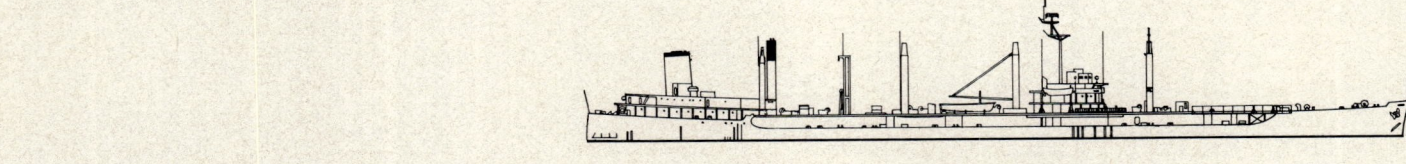

"MISPILLION" Class T-AO

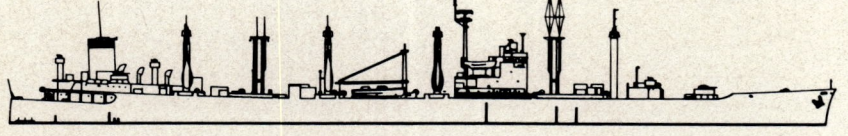

CANISTEO (AO 99) Jumboised T3-S2-A1

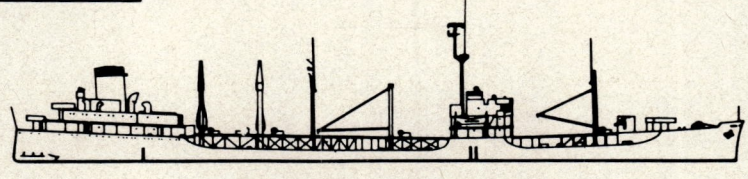

"CIMARRON" Class T-AO T3-S2-A1 Type

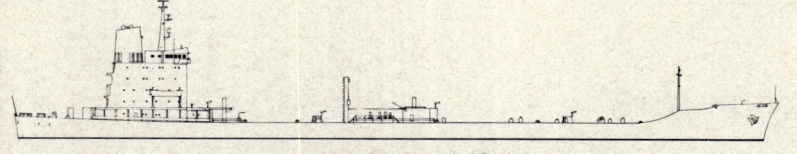

"SEALIFT" Class (T-AO 168)

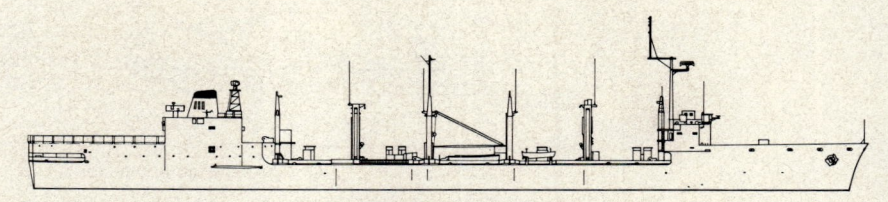

ROANOKE (AOR 7) "Wichita" Class

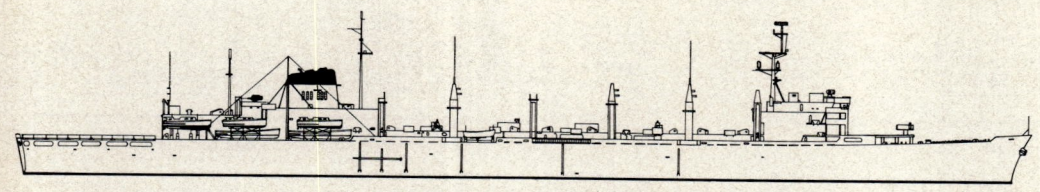

CAMDEN (AOE 2) "Sacramento" Class

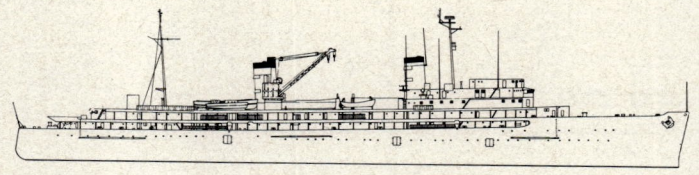

VULCAN (AR 5)

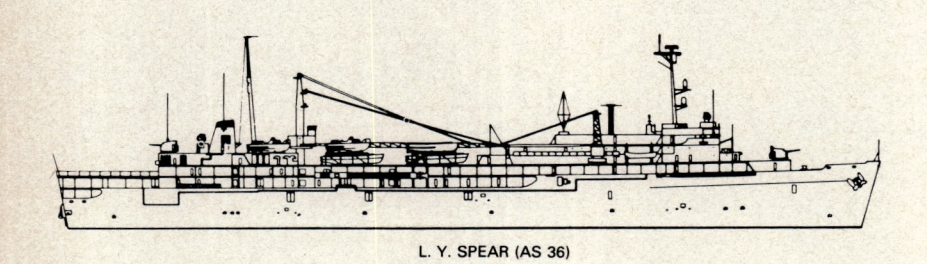

L. Y. SPEAR (AS 36)

Scale: 1 inch = 150 feet (1 : 1 800)

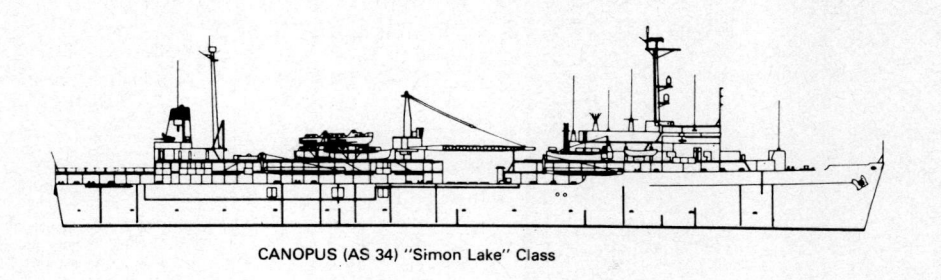

CANOPUS (AS 34) "Simon Lake" Class

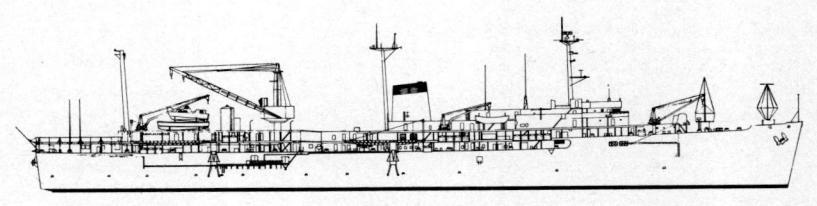

HUNLEY (AS 31)

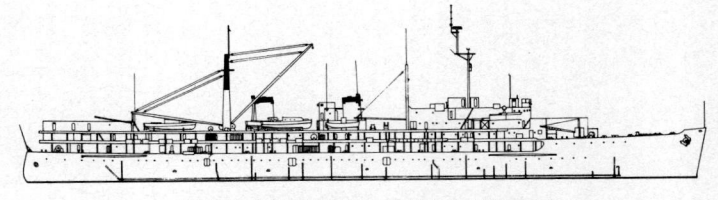

HOWARD W. GILMORE (AS 16) "Fulton" Class

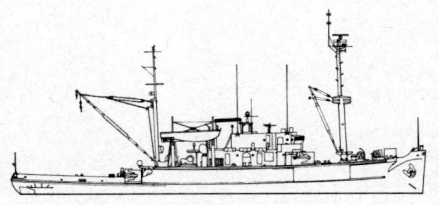

CONSERVER (ARS 39)

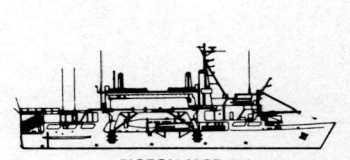

PIGEON (ASR 21)

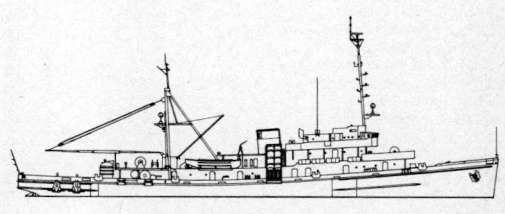

SUNBIRD (ASR 15)

"ABNAKI" Class ATF
(Please note Scale: 1 inch = 100 feet 1 : 1 200))

"AGGRESSIVE" Class MSO
(Please note Scale: 1 inch = 100 feet (1 : 1 200))

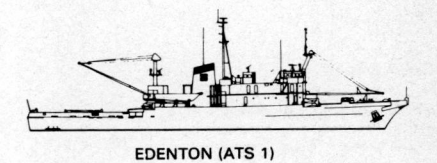

EDENTON (ATS 1)

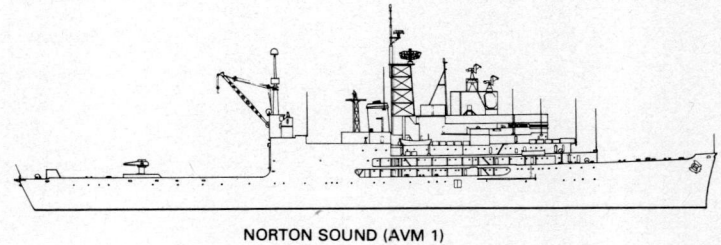

NORTON SOUND (AVM 1)

PATROL SHIPS AND CRAFT

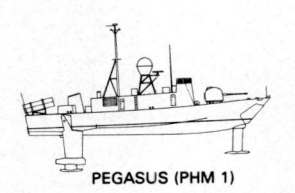

PEGASUS (PHM 1)

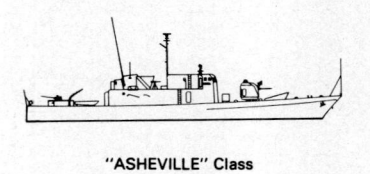

"ASHEVILLE" Class

Scale: 1 inch = 100 feet (1 : 1 200)

620 USA

UNITED STATES SHIP HULL NUMBERS

(Type designations in order of arrangement within this volume; ships are in numerical sequence)

Strategic Missile Submarines

SSBN—Fleet Ballistic Missile Submarines

"Geo. Washington" Class
- 598 George Washington
- 599 Patrick Henry
- 600 Theodore Roosevelt
- 601 Robert E. Lee
- 602 Abraham Lincoln

"Ethan Allen" Class
- 608 Ethan Allen
- 609 Sam Houston
- 610 Thomas A. Edison
- 611 John Marshall

"Lafayette" Class
- 616 Lafayette
- 617 Alexander Hamilton

"Ethan Allen" Class (Cont'd)
- 618 Thomas Jefferson

"Lafayette" Class (Cont'd)
- 619 Andrew Jackson
- 620 John Adams
- 622 James Monroe
- 623 Nathan Hale
- 624 Woodrow Wilson
- 625 Henry Clay
- 626 Daniel Webster
- 627 James Madison
- 628 Tecumseh
- 629 Daniel Boone
- 630 John C. Calhoun
- 631 Ulysses S. Grant
- 632 Von Steuben
- 633 Casimir Pulaski
- 634 Stonewall Jackson
- 635 Sam Rayburn
- 636 Nathanael Greene
- 640 Benjamin Franklin
- 641 Simon Bolivar
- 642 Kamehameha
- 643 George Bancroft
- 644 Lewis and Clark
- 645 James K. Polk
- 654 George C. Marshall
- 655 Henry L. Stimson
- 656 George Washington Carver
- 657 Francis Scott Key
- 658 Mariano G. Vallejo
- 659 Will Rogers

"Ohio" Class
- 726 Ohio
- 727 Michigan

Submarines

SS/SSN—Attack Submarines
AGSS—Auxiliary Submarines
SSG—Guided Missile Submarines

"Dolphin" Class (AGSS)
- 555 Dolphin

"Tang" Class (SS)
- 563 Tang (AGSS)
- 565 Wahoo
- 566 Trout
- 567 Gudgeon

"Albacore" Class (AGSS)
- 569 Albacore

"Nautilus" Class (SSN)
- 571 Nautilus

"Sailfish" Class (SS)
- 572 Sailfish

"Grayback" Class (LPSS)
- 574 Grayback SS

"Seawolf" Class (SSN)
- 575 Seawolf

"Darter" Class (SS)
- 576 Darter

"Grayback" Class (SSG)
- 577 Growler

"Skate" Class (SSN)
- 578 Skate
- 579 Swordfish

"Barbel" Class (SS)
- 580 Barbel
- 581 Blueback
- 582 Bonefish

"Skate" Class (SSN) (Cont'd)
- 583 Sargo
- 584 Seadragon

"Skipjack" Class (SSN)
- 585 Skipjack

"Triton" Class (SSN)
- 586 Triton

"Halibut" Class (SSN)
- 587 Halibut

"Skipjack" Class (SSN) (Cont'd)
- 588 Scamp
- 590 Sculpin
- 591 Shark
- 592 Snook

"Thresher" Class (SSN)
- 594 Permit
- 595 Plunger
- 596 Barb

"Tullibee" Class (SSN)
- 597 Tullibee

"Thresher" Class (SSN) (Cont'd)
- 603 Pollack
- 604 Haddo
- 605 Jack
- 606 Tinosa
- 607 Dace
- 612 Guardfish
- 613 Flasher
- 614 Greenling
- 615 Gato
- 621 Haddock

"Sturgeon" Class (SSN)
- 637 Sturgeon
- 638 Whale
- 639 Tautog
- 646 Grayling
- 647 Pogy
- 648 Aspro
- 649 Sunfish
- 650 Pargo
- 651 Queenfish
- 652 Puffer
- 653 Ray
- 660 Sand Lance
- 661 Lapon
- 662 Gurnard
- 663 Hammerhead
- 664 Sea Devil
- 665 Guitarro
- 666 Hawkbill
- 667 Bergall
- 668 Spadefish
- 669 Seahorse
- 670 Finback

"Narwhal" Class (SSN)
- 671 Narwhal

"Sturgeon" Class (SSN) (Cont'd)
- 672 Pintado
- 673 Flying Fish
- 674 Trepang
- 675 Bluefish
- 676 Billfish
- 677 Drum
- 678 Archerfish
- 679 Silversides
- 680 William H. Bates
- 681 Batfish
- 682 Tunny
- 683 Parche
- 684 Cavalla

"Glenard P. Lipscomb" Class (SSN)
- 685 Glenard P. Lipscomb

"Sturgeon" Class (SSN) (Cont'd)
- 686 L. Mendel Rivers
- 687 Richard B. Russell

"Los Angeles" Class (SSN)
- 688 Los Angeles
- 689 Baton Rouge
- 690 Philadelphia
- 691 Memphis
- 692 Omaha
- 693 Cincinnati
- 694 Groton
- 695 Birmingham
- 696 New York City
- 697 Indianapolis
- 698 Bremerton
- 699 Jacksonville
- 700 Dallas
- 701 La Jolla
- 702 Phoenix
- 703 Boston
- 704 Baltimore
- 711 San Francisco

Aircraft Carriers

CV CVA CVN—Attack Aircraft Carriers
CVS—ASW Aircraft Carriers
CVT—Training Aircraft Carriers

"Intrepid" Class
- 11 Intrepid (CVS)

"Essex" Class
- 12 Hornet (CVS)

"Intrepid" Class (Cont'd)
- 16 Lexington (CVT)

"Essex" Class (Cont'd)
- 20 Bennington (CVS)

"Hancock" Class
- 31 Bon Homme Richard (CVA)
- 34 Oriskany (CV)

"Intrepid" Class (Cont'd)
- 38 Shangri-La (CVS)

"Midway" Class (CV)
- 41 Midway
- 43 Coral Sea

"Forrestal" Class (CV)
- 59 Forrestal
- 60 Saratoga
- 61 Ranger
- 62 Independence

"Kitty Hawk" Class (CV)
- 63 Kitty Hawk
- 64 Constellation

"Enterprise" Class (CVN)
- 65 Enterprise

"Kitty Hawk" Class (CV) (Cont'd)
- 66 America

"John F. Kennedy" Class (CV)
- 67 John F. Kennedy

"Nimitz" Class (CVN)
- 68 Nimitz
- 69 Dwight D. Eisenhower
- 70 Carl Vinson

Battleships

BB—Battleships

"Iowa" Class
- 61 Iowa
- 62 New Jersey
- 63 Missouri
- 64 Wisconsin

Cruisers

CG/CGN—Guided Missile Cruisers

Converted "Cleveland" Class (CG)
- 5 Oklahoma City
- 6 Province
- 7 Springfield

"Long Beach" Class (CGN)
- 9 Long Beach

"Albany" Class (CG)
- 10 Albany
- 11 Chicago

"Leahy" Class
- 16 Leahy
- 17 Harry E. Yarnell
- 18 Worden
- 19 Dale
- 20 Richmond K. Turner
- 21 Gridley
- 22 England
- 23 Halsey
- 24 Reeves

"Bainbridge" Class (CGN)
- 25 Bainbridge

"Belknap" Class (CG)
- 26 Belknap
- 27 Josephus Daniels
- 28 Wainwright
- 29 Jouett
- 30 Horne
- 31 Sterett
- 32 William H. Standley
- 33 Fox
- 34 Biddle

"Truxtun" Class (CGN)
35 Truxtun

"California" Class (CGN)
36 California
37 South Carolina

"Virginia" Class (CGN)
38 Virginia
39 Texas
40 Mississippi
41 Arkansas

CA—Heavy Cruisers

"Boston" Class
70 Canberra

"Baltimore" Class
73 St. Paul

"Des Moines" Class
134 Des Moines
139 Salem
148 Newport News

Destroyers

DDG—Guided Missile Destroyers

"Charles F. Adams" Class
2 Charles F. Adams
3 John King
4 Lawrence
5 Claude V. Ricketts
6 Barney
7 Henry B. Wilson
8 Lynde McCormack
9 Towers
10 Sampson
11 Sellers
12 Robison
13 Hoel
14 Buchanan
15 Berkeley
16 Joseph Strauss
17 Conyngham
18 Semmes
19 Tattnall
20 Goldsborough
21 Cochrane
22 Benjamin Stoddert
23 Richard E. Byrd
24 Waddell

Converted "Forrest Sherman" Class
31 Decatur
32 John Paul Jones
33 Parsons
34 Somers

Converted "Mitscher" Class
35 Mitscher
36 John S. McCain

"Coontz" Class
37 Farragut
38 Luce
39 MacDonough
40 Coontz
41 King
42 Mahan
43 Dahlgren
44 William V. Pratt
45 Dewey
46 Preble

DD—Destroyers

"Gearing" Class
714 William R. Rush
718 Hamner
743 Southerland
763 William C. Lawe
784 McKean
785 Henderson
788 Hollister
806 Higbee
817 Corry
821 Johnston
822 Robert H. McCard

"Carpenter" Class
825 Carpenter

"Gearing" Class (Cont'd)
826 Agerholm

"Carpenter" Class (Cont'd)
827 Robert A. Owens

"Gearing" Class (Cont'd)
829 Myles C. Fox
835 Charles P. Cecil
842 Fiske
845 Bausell
862 Vogelgesang
863 Steinaker
864 Harold J. Ellison
866 Cone
871 Damato
873 Hawkins

876 Rogers
880 Dyess
883 Newman K. Perry
885 John R. Craig
886 Orleck
890 Meredith

"Forrest Sherman" Class
931 Forrest Sherman
933 Barry
937 George F. Davis
938 Jonas Ingram
940 Manley
941 Dupont
942 Bigelow
943 Blandy
944 Mullinnix

"Hull" Class
945 Hull
946 Edson
948 Morton
950 Richard S. Edwards
951 Turner Joy

"Spruance" Class
963 Spruance
964 Paul F. Foster
965 Kinkaid
966 Hewitt
967 Elliot
968 Arthur W. Radford
969 Peterson
970 Caron
971 David R. Ray
972 Oldendorf
973 John Young
974 Comte de Grasse
975 O'Brien
976 Merrill
977 Briscoe
978 Stump
979 Conolly
980 Moosburgger
981 John Hancock
982 Nicholson
983 John Rodgers
984 Leftwich
985 Cushing
986 Harry W. Hill
987 O'Bannon
988 Thorn
989 Deyo
990 Ingersoll
991 Fife
992 Fletcher

Frigates

FFG—Guided Missile Frigates

"Brooke" Class
1 Brooke
2 Ramsey
3 Schofield
4 Talbot
5 Richard L. Page
6 Julius A. Furer

"Oliver Hazard Perry" Class
7 Oliver Hazard Perry
8 McInerney
9 Wadsworth
10 Duncan

FF—Frigates

"Bronstein" Class
1037 Bronstein
1038 McCloy

"Garcia" Class
1040 Garcia
1041 Bradley
1043 Edward McDonnell
1044 Brumby
1045 Davidson
1047 Voge
1048 Sample
1049 Koelsch
1050 Albert David
1051 O'Callahan

"Knox" Class
1052 Knox
1053 Roark
1054 Gray
1055 Hepburn
1056 Connole
1057 Rathburne
1058 Mayerkord
1059 W. S. Sims
1060 Lang
1061 Patterson
1062 Whipple
1063 Reasoner
1064 Lockwood
1065 Stein
1066 Marvin Shields
1067 Francis Hammond
1068 Vreeland
1069 Bagley
1070 Downes
1071 Badger

1072 Blakely
1073 Robert E. Peary
1074 Harold E. Holt
1075 Trippe
1076 Fanning
1077 Ouellet
1078 Joseph Hewes
1079 Bowen
1080 Paul
1081 Aylwin
1082 Elmer Montgomery
1083 Cook
1084 McCandless
1085 Donald B. Beary
1086 Brewton
1087 Kirk
1088 Barbey
1089 Jesse L. Brown
1090 Ainsworth
1091 Miller
1092 Thomas C. Hart
1093 Capodanno
1094 Pharris
1095 Truett
1096 Valdez
1097 Moinester

Patrol Ships and Craft

PHM—Guided Missile Patrol Combatants (Hydrofoil)

"Pegasus" Class
1 Pegasus
2 Hercules

PCH—Hydrofoil Patrol Craft

"High Point" Class
1 High Point

PG—Patrol Combatants

"Asheville" Class
92 Tacoma
93 Welch

Amphibious Warships

LCC—Amphibious Command Ships (ex-AGC)

"Blue Ridge" Class
19 Blue Ridge
20 Mount Whitney

LHA—Amphibious Assault Ships (General Purpose)

"Tarawa" Class
1 Tarawa
2 Saipan
3 Belleau Wood
4 Nassau
5 Da Nang

LKA—Amphibious Cargo Ships

"Tulare" Class
112 Tulare

"Charleston" Class
113 Charleston
114 Durham
115 Mobile
116 St. Louis
117 El Paso

LPH—Amphibious Assault Ships (Helicopter)

"Iwo Jima" Class
2 Iwo Jima
3 Okinawa
7 Guadalcanal
9 Guam
10 Tripoli
11 New Orleans
12 Inchon

LPA—Amphibious Transports

"Paul Revere" Class
248 Paul Revere
249 Francis Marion

LPD—Amphibious Transport Docks

"Raleigh" Class
1 Raleigh
2 Vancouver

"Austin" Class
4 Austin
5 Ogden
6 Duluth
7 Cleveland
8 Dubuque
9 Denver
10 Juneau

622 USA

11 Coronado
12 Shreveport
13 Nashville
14 Trenton
15 Ponce

LSD—Dock Landing Ships

"Thomaston" Class
28 Thomaston
29 Plymouth Rock
30 Fort Snelling
31 Point Defiance
32 Speigel Grove
33 Alamo
34 Hermitage
35 Monticello

"Anchorage" Class
36 Anchorage
37 Portland
38 Pensacola
39 Mt Vernon
40 Fort Fisher

LST—Tank Landing Ships

"De Soto County" Class
1173 Suffolk County
1177 Lorain County
1178 Wood County

"Newport" Class
1179 Newport
1180 Manitowac
1181 Sumter
1182 Fresno
1183 Peroria
1184 Frederick
1185 Schenectady
1186 Cayuga
1187 Tuscaloosa
1188 Saginaw
1189 San Bernardino
1190 Boulder
1191 Racine
1192 Spartanburg County
1193 Fairfax County
1194 La Moure County
1195 Barbour County
1196 Harlan County
1197 Barnstable County
1198 Bristol County

Mine Warfare Ships

MSO—Ocean Minesweepers

"Agile" Class
421 Agile

"Aggressive" and "Dash" Classes
427 Constant
428 Dash
429 Detector
430 Direct
431 Dominant
433 Engage
437 Enhance
438 Esteem
439 Excel
440 Exploit
441 Exultant
442 Fearless
443 Fidelity
446 Fortify
448 Illusive
449 Impervious
455 Implicit
456 Inflict
464 Pluck
488 Conquest
489 Gallant
490 Leader
492 Pledge

"Acme" Class
509 Adroit
511 Affray

Auxiliary Ships

AD—Destroyer Tenders

"Dixie" Class
14 Dixie
15 Prairie
17 Piedmont
18 Sierra
19 Yosemite

"Klondike" and "Shenandoah" Classes
24 Everglades
26 Shenandoah
36 Bryce Canyon

"Samuel Gompers" Class
37 Samuel Gompers
38 Puget Sound

AE—Ammunition Ships

"Suribachi" Class
21 Suribachi
22 Mauna Kea
23 Nitro
24 Pyro
25 Haleakala

"Kilauea" Class
26 Kilauea
27 Butte
28 Santa Barbara
29 Mount Hood
32 Flint
33 Shasta
34 Mount Baker
35 Kiska

AF—Store Ship

"Rigel" Class
58 Rigel

AFS—Combat Store Ships

"Mars" Class
1 Mars
2 Sylvania
3 Niagara Falls
4 White Plains
5 Concord
6 San Diego
7 San Jose

AGF—Miscellaneous Flagship

3 La Salle

AGFF—Frigate Research Ship

"Glover" Class
1 Glover

AH—Hospital Ship

17 Sanctuary

AO—Oilers

"Jumboised" "Cimarron" Class
51 Ashtabula
98 Caloosahatchee
99 Canisteo

"Neosho" Class
143 Neosho
144 Mississinewa (MSC)
145 Hassayampa
146 Kawishiwi
147 Truckee
148 Ponchatoula

AOE—Fast Combat Support Ships

"Sacramento" Class
1 Sacramento
2 Camden
3 Seattle
4 Detroit

AOR—Replenishment Oilers

"Wichita" Class
1 Wichita
2 Milwaukee
3 Kansas City
4 Savannah
5 Wabash
6 Kalamazoo
7 Roanoke

APB/IX—Self-Propelled Barracks Ships

504 Echols/IX
502 Mercer/IX
503 Nueces/IX

AR—Repair Ships

"Vulcan" Class
5 Vulcan
6 Ajax
7 Hector
8 Jason

"Grand Canyon" Class
28 Grand Canyon

ARL—Landing Craft Repair Ships

"Achelous" Class
24 Sphinx

ARS—Salvage Ships

"Diver" and "Bolster" Classes
6 Escape
8 Preserver
23 Deliver
24 Grasp
25 Safeguard
33 Clamp
34 Gear
38 Bolster
39 Conserver
40 Hoist
41 Opportune
42 Reclaimer
43 Recovery

AS—Submarine Tenders

"Fulton" Class
11 Fulton
12 Sperry
15 Bushnell
16 Howard W. Gilmore
17 Nereus
18 Orion

"Proteus" Class
19 Proteus

"Hunley" Class
31 Hunley
32 Holland

"Simon Lake" Class
33 Simon Lake
34 Canopus

"L.Y. Spear" Class
36 L.Y. Spear
37 Dixon
39 Emory S. Land
40 Frank Cable

ASR—Submarine Rescue Ships

"Chanticleer" Class
9 Florikan
13 Kittiwake
14 Petrel
15 Sunbird

"Pigeon" Class
21 Pigeon
22 Ortolan

ATA—Auxiliary Tugs

"Sotoyomo' Class
181 Accokeek
190 Samoset
193 Stallion
213 Keywadin

ATF—Fleet Tugs

"Cherokee" and "Abnaki" Classes
76 Ute
84 Cree
85 Lipan
91 Seneca
96 Abnaki
101 Cocopa
103 Hitchiti
105 Moctobi
106 Molala
110 Quapaw
113 Takelma
114 Tawakoni
149 Atakapa
157 Nipmuc
158 Mosospelea
159 Paiute
160 Papago
161 Salinan
162 Shakori

ATS—Salvage and Rescue Ships

"Edenton" Class
1 Edenton
2 Beaufort
3 Brunswick

Military Sealift Command

Note: All ships of MSC have T prefix.

AG—Hydrographic Research Ship

164 Kingsport

AGM—Range Instrumentation Ships

- 8 Wheeling
- 9 General H. H. Arnold
- 10 General Hoyt S. Vandenberg
- 19 Vanguard
- 20 Redstone
- 22 Range Sentinel

AGOR—Oceanographic Research Ships

- 4 James M. Gilliss
- 7 Lynch
- 11 Mizar
- 12 De Steiguer
- 13 Bartlett
- 16 Hayes

AGS—Surveying Ships

- 21 Bowditch
- 22 Dutton
- 26 Silas Bent
- 27 Kane
- 29 Chauvenet
- 32 Harkness
- 33 Wilkes
- 34 Wyman
- 38 H. H. Hess

AK—Cargo Ships

"Greenville Victory" Class
- 237 Greenville Victory
- 240 Pvt. John R. Towle
- 242 Sgt. Andrew Miller
- 254 Sgt. Truman Kimbro

"Private Leonard C. Brostrom" Class
- 255 Pvt. Leonard C. Brostrom

"Marine Fiddler" Class
- 267 Marine Fiddler

"Eltanin" Class
- 271 Mirfak

"Greenville Victory" Class (Cont'd)
- 274 Lieut. James E. Robinson

"Schuyler Otis Bland" Class
- 277 Schuyler Otis Bland

"Norwalk" Class
- 279 Norwalk
- 280 Furman
- 281 Victoria
- 282 Marshfield

"Wyandot" Class
- 283 Wyandot

AKR—Vehicle Cargo Ships

"Comet" Class
- 7 Comet

"Meteor" Class
- 9 Meteor

AO—Tankers

"Suamico" Class
- 50 Tallulah

"Cimarron" Class
- 57 Marias
- 62 Taluga

"Suamico" Class (Cont'd)
- 73 Millicoma
- 75 Saugatuck
- 76 Schuylkill

"Jumboised Mispillion" Class
- 105 Mispillion
- 106 Navasota
- 107 Pasumpsic
- 108 Pawcatuck
- 109 Waccamaw

"Maumee" Class
- 149 Maumee
- 151 Shoshone
- 152 Yukon

"American Explorer" Class
- 165 American Explorer

"Sealift" Class
- 168 Sealift Pacific
- 169 Sealift Arabian Sea
- 170 Sealift China Sea
- 171 Sealift Indian Ocean
- 172 Sealift Atlantic
- 173 Sealift Mediterranean
- 174 Sealift Caribbean
- 175 Sealift Arctic
- 176 Sealift Antarctic

"Potomac" Class
- 181 Potomac

"Falcon" Class
- 182 Columbia
- 183 Neches
- 184 Hudson
- 185 Susquehanna

AOG—Gasoline Tankers

"Peconic" Class
- 77 Rincon
- 78 Nodaway
- 79 Petaluma

ARC—Cable Ships

- 2 Neptune
- 3 Aeolus
- 4 Thor
- 6 Albert J. Myer

6th Fleet at Sea

SHIPBOARD SYSTEMS

AEGIS (formerly Advanced Surface Missile System) Advanced surface-to-air missile system intended for use in guided missile destroyer (DDG 47 class) and cruisers (CGN 42 class) scheduled for delivery during the 1980s. To have a capability against high-performance aircraft and air, surface and sub-surface launched, anti-ship missiles. Launcher is Mk 26. AEGIS will have an electronic scanning radar with fixed antenna which will be capable of controlling friendly aircraft as well as surveillance, detection and tracking. Elements will include the AN/UYK-7 computer and illuminators for missile guidance for use with Standard surface-to-air missile.
Status: Development.

ASROC (Anti-Submarine Rocket) Anti-Submarine missile launched from surface ships with homing torpedo or nuclear depth charge as warhead. Launcher is Mk 10 or Mk 26 combination ASROC/surface-to-air missile launcher or Mk 16 eight-cell "pepper box". Installed in US Navy cruisers, destroyers, and frigates; Japanese, Italian, West German, and Canadian destroyer-type ships.
Weight of missile approximately 1 000 lb; length 15 ft; diameter 1 ft; span of fins 2·5 ft. Payload: Mk 44 or Mk 46 acoustic-homing torpedo or nuclear depth charge; range one to six miles.
Designation: RUR-5.
Status: Operational.

BPDMS (Basic Point Defence Missile System) Close-in-air-defence system employing the Sparrow AIM-7E or 7F series missile designated Sea Sparrow and a modified ASROC-type "pepper box" launcher. Installed in aircraft carriers, ocean escorts, and amphibious ships.
Status: Operational.

CAPTOR (Encapsulated Torpedo). Mk 46 torpedo inserted in mine casing. Can be launched by aircraft or submarine.
Status: Operational.

CIWS (Close-in Weapon System) "Family" of advanced gun and missile systems to provide close-in or "point" defence for ships against anti-ship missiles and aircraft. Specific weapons being developed or evaluated under this programme include the Chaparral, Hybrid launcher, Pintle, Vulcan Air Defence, Phalanx, and OTO Melara 35 mm twin gun mount.

LAMPS (Light Airborne Multi-Purpose System) Ship-launched helicopter intended for anti-submarine and missile-defence missions, with secondary roles of search-and-rescue and utility (eg, parts and personnel transfer). For use aboard destroyer-type ships with hangars. Sensors include Magnetic Airborne Detection (MAD), and sonobuoys with digital relays to permit control and attack direction by launching ship. Radar provided to extend detection range.
Weapons: 2 Mk 46 ASW torpedoes. Crew: pilot, co-pilot, one operator.
Status: 105 Kaman Seasprite helicopters being modified to SH-2 configuration as interim LAMPS. Deployed in cruisers, destroyers, and frigates.
LAMPS III Improved Light Airborne Multi-Purpose System based on Army Utility Tactical Transport Aircraft System (UTTAS) helicopter.
Status: Development.

MCLWG (Major Calibre Light-Weight Gun). Light-weight 8-in gun (Mk 71) planned for advanced surface combatants.
Status: Evaluation in destroyer *Hull* (DD 945).

(Naval Tactical Data System) Combination of digital computers, displays, and transmission links to increase an individual ship commander's capability to assess tactical data and take action by integrating input from various sensors (eg, radars) and providing display of tactical situation and the defence or offence options available. Data can be transmitted among NTDS-equipped ships. An automatic mode initiates action to respond to greatest threats in a tactical situation. Also can be linked to airborne Tactical Data System (ATDS) in E-2 Hawkeye aircraft. Fitted in US Navy aircraft carriers, missile-armed cruisers, destroyers ("Coontz" class), amphibious command ships, and two frigates (*Voge* [FF 1047] and *Koelsch* [FF 1049]).
Status: Operational.

NATO SEA SPARROW Follow-on to BPDMS with a Target Acquisition System (TAS), powered director, smaller launcher, and control console combined with the Sea Sparrow missile. Planned for US amphibious and auxiliary ships.
Status: Under development; also a NATO co-operative programme with Belgium, Denmark, Italy, Netherlands and Norway. Being evaluated in *Downes* (FF 1070).

PHALANX Rapid-fire, close-in gun system being developed to provide close range defence against anti-ship missiles. Fires 20 mm ammunition from six-barrel "gatling" gun with "dynamic gun aiming" with fire control radar tracking projectiles and target(s). Theoretical rate of fire 3 000 rounds-per-minute. Initially planned for "Spruance" class destroyers, frigates, and some auxiliary ships; tentative programme calls for approx 359 units in 192 ships and three trainers.
Status: Development.
Average cost for installation: $100 000 (new construction), $150 000 (retrofitting).

QUICKSTRIKE Advanced mine system; details classified.
Status: Development.

SINS (Ships' Inertial Navigation System) Navigation system providing exact navigation information without active input from terrestrial sources. Prime components are gyroscopes and accelerometers that relate movement of the ship in all directions, ship speed through water and over the ground, and true north to give a continuous report of the ship's position.
Status: Operational.

SIRCS (Shipboard Intermediate Range Combat System). Programme to integrate shipboard self-defence systems (existing and planned).
Status: Development.

SUBROC (Submarine Rocket) Anti-submarine missile launched from submarines with nuclear warhead. Launched from 21-in torpedo tube. Carried in US Navy submarines of "Thresher" and later classes with amidships torpedo tubes, BQQ-2 or BQQ-5 sonar and Mk 113 or later torpedo fire control systems. The missile is fired from the submerged submarine, rises up through the surface, travels through air towards the hostile submarine, and then re-enters the water to detonate.
Weight of missile approximately 4 000 lb, length 21 ft; diameter 1·75 ft (maximum); estimated range 25 to 30 miles.
Designation: UUM-44.
Status: Operational.

TACTAS (Tactical Towed Array Sonar). Ship-towed long-range acoustic detection system.

TOMAHAWK A cruise missile whose details are listed below. Both submarines and surface ships will be able to launch the SLCM version. Mentioned here as one of the most significant advances in missile design of the last ten years.

NAVAL MISSILES

Name	Launch Platform (tubes/launchers)	Range miles (km)	Length feet (metres)	Weight lb (kg)	Notes(b)
Polaris A-3	"Ethan Allen", "George Washington" submarines (16)	2 500 (4 023·4)	32 (9·8)	30 000 (13 608)	Thermo-nuclear; MRV warhead
Poseidon C-3	"Lafayette" submarines (16)	approx 2 500 (4 023·4)	34 (10·4)	65 000 (29 484)	Thermo-nuclear; MIRV warhead
...dent (I) C-4	"Ohio" submarines (24)	approx 4 000 (6 432)	34·1 (10·4)	70 000 (31 752)	Thermo-nuclear; MIRV and MARV warhead
...(II) D-5	Trident submarines (24)	approx 6 000 (9 656)	45·75 (13·9)	126 000 (57 153)	Proposed
...wk	Attack submarines (torpedo tubes) Surface ships (box launchers)	approx 1 500 (2 414)	20·5 (6·3)	2 400-2 700 (1 088-1 224)	Nuclear land attack and 300 mile (HE) anti-ship; under development
...-ARM	some surface ships (ASROC launcher)	15 (24·14)	15 (4·6)	1 400 (635)	HE
	Surface ships	50 (80·5)	15 (4·6)	1 470 (666·1)	Operational; HE
Harpoon	Attack submarines (torpedo tubes)	60 (96·6)	21 (6·4)	2 355 (1 068)	Development; HE; operational 1978-79
	Cruisers (1 or 2 twin); "Coontz" destroyers (1 twin); "Kitty Hawk", "America" carriers (2 twin)	20+ (32·2+)	26·1 (8)	3 000 (1 361)	Nuclear or HE
	Surface ships	8 (12·9)	12 (3·7)	500 (226·8)	HE; Mk 25 or Mk 29 (NATO) multiple launcher; Basic Point Defence Missile System
	"Albany", "Long Beach" cruisers (2 twin)	65+ (104·6+)	31·2 (9·5)	7 000 (3 175)	Nuclear or HE
	"Albany" cruisers (2 twin); "Chas. ...dams" destroyers (1 twin or single); "...rooke" frigates (1 single); later cruisers	10+ (16·1+)	15 (4·6)	1 425 (646·4)	HE
	S... replacement	20+ (32·2+)	14·4 (4·4)	1 200-1 400 (546·3-635)	HE
	SA...	60+ (96·6+)			Long range with mid-course guidance; development
	SAM ...placement	20+ (32·2+)			Medium range—development
	AAM	35+ (56·3+)	26·2 (8)	2 900 (1 315·4)	HE
	AAM ...cement	60+ (96·6+)			Long range—development
	AAM ...ent	9-16 (14·5-25·8)	12 (3·7)	500 (226·8)	
	ASM ...ters	8 (12·9)	9·5 (2·9)	185 (83·9)	
	...ghters	60+ (96·6+)	13 (4)	985 (446·8)	
		7 (11·3)	10 (3·1)	571 (259)	

NAVAL MISSILES

ASM	AGM-12D	Bullpup-B	Attack/patrol aircraft	10 (16·1)	13·5 (4·1)	1 785 (809·7)	Nuclear or HE
ASM	AGM-45	Shrike	Attack/patrol aircraft	8–10 (12·9–16·1)	10 (3·1)	390 (176·9)	Anti-radiation
ASM	AGM-53	Condor	Attack/patrol aircraft	40–60 (64·4–96·6)	13·8 (4·2)	2 130 (966·2)	Nuclear or HE; production planned
ASM	AGM-62	Walleye I	Attack/patrol aircraft	16 (25·7)	11·2 (3·5)	1 100 (499)	Nuclear or HE
ASM	AGM-62	Walleye II	Attack/patrol aircraft	35 (56·3)	13·2 (4·0)	2 400 (1 089)	Nuclear or HE
ASM	AGM-78	Standard-ARM	Attack/patrol aircraft	35 (56·3)	15 (4·6)	1 356 (615·1)	Anti-radiation
ASM	AGM-83	Bulldog	Attack/patrol aircraft	35 (56·3)	9·8 (3·0)	600 (272·1)	Modified Bullpup
ASM	AGM-84	Harpoon	Attack/patrol aircraft	120 (193·1)	12·6 (3·8)	1 168 (529·8)	Operational; HE
ASM	AGM-88	Harm	Attack/patrol aircraft		13·7 (4·2)	780 (353·8)	Development; High-speed Anti-Radiation Missile; larger than Shrike
ASW	RUR-5	ASROC	Cruisers, destroyers, frigates	1–6 (1·6–9·7)	15 (4·6)	1 000 (453·6)	Nuclear depth charge, Mk 44, or Mk 46 torpedo; multiple launcher in most ships; Mk 26 launcher in later ships; 570 lb (256·5 kg) with Mk 46
ASW	UUM-44	SUBROC	"Thresher" and later attack submarines (torpedo tubes)	25–30 (40·2–48·3)	21 (6·4)	4 000 (1 814·4)	Nuclear

(a) FBM = Fleet Ballistic Missile; SLCM = Sea-Launched Cruise Missile; SSM = Surface-to-Surface Missile; SAM = Surface-to-Air Missile; AAM = Air-to-Air Missile; ASM = Air-to-Surface Missile; ASW = Anti-Submarine Warfare.
(b) MRV = Multiple re-entry Vehicle; MIRV = Multiple Independently targeted re-entry Vehicle; MaRV = Maneouvring re-entry Vehicle; HE = High Explosive.

TORPEDOES

Designation	Launch Platform	Weight lb (kg)	Length feet (metres)	Diameter, in (mm)	Propulsion	Guidance	Notes
Mk 37 Mod 2	Submarines	1 690 (766·6)	13·4 (4·1)	19 (482·6)	Electric	Wire; active-passive acoustic homing	Anti-submarine
Mk 37 Mod 3	Submarines	1 430 (648·6)	11·25 (3·4)	19 (482·6)	Electric	Active-passive acoustic homing	Anti-submarine
Mk 37C	Submarines				Liquid mono-propellant	Active-passive acoustic homing	Anti-submarine; modified Mk 37-2/3 for allied navies; in production
Mk 44 Mod 1	Surface ships (Mk 32 tubes and ASROC); aircraft	433 (196·4)	8·4 (2·6)	12·75 (323·9)	Electric	Active acoustic homing	Anti-submarine
Mk 45 Mod 1 & Mod 2 (ASTOR)	Submarines	2 213 (1 003·8)	18·9 (5·8)	19 (482·6)	Electric	Wire	Anti-submarine; nuclear warhead; 10+ mile range; being replaced by Mk 48
Mk 46 Mod 0	Surface ships (Mk 32 tubes and ASROC); aircraft	568 (257·6)	8·5 (2·6)	12·75 (323·9)	Solid-propellant	Active-passive acoustic homing	Anti-submarine; successor to Mk 44
Mk 46 Mod 1 & Mod 2	Surface ships (Mk 32 tubes and ASROC); aircraft	508 (230·4)	8·5 (2·6)	12·75 (323·9)	Liquid mono-propellant	Active-passive acoustic homing	Anti-submarine; successor to Mk 44; Mod 4 used in CAPTOR (Encapsulated Torpedo) mine
Mk 48 Mod 1 & Mod 3	Submarines	3 480 (1 578·5)	19·1 (5·8)	21 (533·6)	Liquid mono-propellant	Wire/terminal acoustic homing	Anti-submarine and anti-shipping; in production; range approx 20 miles
ALWT	Aircraft; submarines						Advanced Light-Weight Torpedo; to replace Mk 46; in development

626 USA

SUBMARINES

STRATEGIC MISSILE SUBMARINES (SSBN)

The current SSBN force, with the completion of the last Poseidon conversion in 1977, provides over 5 000 separate warheads or "re-entry" vehicles, or about 55 per cent of US strategic warheads. (Each Poseidon missile is believed normally to carry ten separately targetable RVs, while the Polaris A-3 missile delivers three RVs on the same target, thus the latter weapon is considered to deliver only one warhead). The Trident strategic missile submarine programme has been initiated to replace the older Polaris/Poseidon submarines from about 1980 onwards. All 41 existing submarines will reach their 20th year of active service between 1981 and 1987. The urgency of the original SSBN programme will thus result in block obsolescence at this time causing a substantial decrease in overall SLBM capability in the late 1980s and early 1990s.

Trident Programme: The Trident programme provides for an improved nuclear-propelled submarine and longer-range missiles. The Trident submarine is described below; the Trident I missile now under development will have a nominal range of approximately 4 000 n. miles. This missile will be installed in the new construction submarines and retrofitted in ten of the Poseidon-armed submarines. The longer range (approx 6 000-mile) Trident II missile is under study. This weapon, which could be available in the mid-1980s, would also have a greater throw weight and accuracy than the Trident I.
When the Trident programme was initiated, the Navy planned to construct the first submarine with the Fiscal Year 1974 funding and three submarines each year thereafter for the initial ten-SSBN class. However, in 1974 the Department of Defense slowed the rate to 1-2-2-2-2-1; in 1975 this was again revised to 1-2-1-2-1-2-1.
In early 1976, Secretary of Defense Donald H. Rumsfeld announced that for planning purposes additional submarines beyond the ten-submarine force would be procured at the 1-2-1-2 rate continuously consistent with Strategic Arms Limitation Talks (SALT) agreements.

Narwhal Programme: Proposals to develop a type of smaller Trident-carrying submarines from the "Los Angeles" or "Narwhal" class designs have been dropped because of the increased costs which would result.

Strategic Cruise Missiles: The US Navy is in advanced development of a strategic Sea-Launched Cruise Missile (SLCM) (Tomahawk). This is an underwater-launched weapon with ram-jet propulsion which could deliver nuclear warheads to a range of approximately 1 500 n. miles. A shorter-range (300-mile) version of the weapon with a conventional warhead is planned for use as an over-the-horizon anti-ship weapon. The strategic cruise missile would have a low-level, terrain following flight path over land, much like that of a manned bomber in contrast to the ballistic trajectory of a Polaris/Poseidon/Trident missile.

Names: US ballistic missile submarines (SSBN) have been named for "distinguished Americans who were known for their devotion to freedom" since 1958 when the Polaris submarine programme was initiated. Included as "Americans" were Latin American and Hawaiian leaders, and several Europeans who supported the American fight for independence. In 1976 the SSBN name source was changed to States of the Union with the first Trident submarine (SSBN 726) being named *Ohio*. This move thoroughly confuses the US ship nomenclature scheme because since 1971 guided missile cruisers have been assigned state names and four state-named battleships of the "Iowa" class remain on the Navy List (in reserve).

WILL ROGERS in Holy Loch, Scotland

0 + 13 + ? "OHIO" CLASS (FLEET BALLISTIC MISSILE SUBMARINES (SSBN))

Name	No.	Builders	Laid down	Launch	Commission	F/S
OHIO	SSBN 726	General Dynamics (Electric Boat)	10 April 1976	Late 1977	Late 1979	Building
MICHIGAN	SSBN 727	General Dynamics (Electric Boat)	4 April 1977	Late 1978	Late 1980	Building
	SSBN 728	General Dynamics (Electric Boat)	—	Mid 1979	Mid 1981	
	SSBN 729	General Dynamics (Electric Boat)	—	Early 1980	Late 1981	
	SSBN 730	General Dynamics (Electric Boat)	—	—	Mid 1982	
	SSBN 731	Proposed FY 1978 programme				
	SSBN 732	Proposed FY 1978 programme				
	SSBN 733	Planned FY 1979 programme				
	SSBN 734	Planned FY 1980 programme				
	SSBN 735	Planned FY 1980 programme				
	SSBN 736	Planned FY 1981 programme				
	SSBN 737	Planned FY 1982 programme				
	SSBN 738	Planned FY 1982 programme				

Displacement, tons: 16 600 surfaced; 18 700 dived
Length, feet (metres): 560 *(170·7)* oa
Beam, feet (metres): 42 *(12·8)*
Draught, feet (metres): 35·5 *(10·8)*
Missiles: 24 tubes for Trident I Submarine-Launched Ballistic Missile (SLBM)
Torpedo tubes: 4—21 in *(533 mm)* Mk 68 (bow)
Main machinery: 1 pressurised-water cooled S8G (General Electric) reactor; geared turbines; 1 shaft
Complement: 133 (16 officers, 117 enlisted men)

These submarines will be the largest undersea craft yet constructed, being significantly larger than the Soviet "Delta" class missile submarines which are now the largest afloat. The lead submarine was contracted to the Electric Boat Division of the General Dynamics Corp (Groton, Connecticut) on 25 July 1974. The only other US shipyard currently capable of building submarines of this class is the Newport News SB & DD Co in Virginia.
A series of problems both in Washington and in the shipbuilding yards has resulted in progressive delays to this class.

Design: The size of the Trident submarine is dictated primarily by the larger size missile required for 4 or 6 000-mile range and the larger reactor plant to drive the ship. The submarine will have 24 tubes in a vertical position.
The principle characteristics of the Trident concept as proposed were: (1) long-range missile (eventually of 6 000 miles (Trident II)) to permit targeting the Soviet Union while the submarine cruises in remote areas, making effective ASW virtually impossible for the foreseeable future, (2) extremely quiet submarines, (3) a high at-sea to in-port ratio.

Designation: Initially the hull number SSBN 711 was planned for the first Trident submarine. However, on 21 Feb 1974 the designation SSBN 1 was assigned, confusing the Navy's submarine designation system which goes back to USS *Holland* (SS 1), commissioned in 1900. Subsequently, the designation was again changed on 10 April 1974, with the "block" SSBN 726-735 being reserved for the Trident programme. Three more 736-738 now added.

Electronics: UYK-7 computer is provided to support electronic and weapon systems. Mk 118 digital torpedo fire control system is installed.

Engineering: These submarines will have a nuclear core life of about nine years between refuellings. A prototype of the S8G reactor plant has been constructed at West Milton, New York.

Fiscal: Costs of the first four SSBNs have increased over the initial appropriations. See 1975-76 edition for initial costs. SSBNs 731 and 732 in the Fiscal Year 1978 are funded at $1 703 million for the pair.

Missiles: The Trident submarines will be armed initially with the Trident I missile, scheduled to become operational late in 1978. This missile is expected to have a range of 4 000 n. miles, a range already exceeded by the SS-N-8 missile in the Soviet "Delta" class submarines. However, the US missile will have a MIRV warhead, which at present is not fitted to SS-N-8, although SS-N-6 (Mod III) has an MRV head.
The Trident missile is expected to carry more than the 10 to 14 re-entry vehicles that the Poseidon can lift. In addition, the Mk 500 MaRV (Manoeuvring re-entry Vehicle) is under development for the purpose of demonstrating its compatability with the Trident I missile. This re-entry vehicle intended to evade ABM interceptor missiles and is not terminally guided to increase its accuracy.

Navigation: Each submarine will have two Mk 2 Ships Inertial Navigation Systems; to be fitted with satellite navigation receivers.

Sonar: BQQ-5 (passive only).

USA 627

31 "BENJAMIN FRANKLIN" and "LAFAYETTE" CLASSES (FLEET BALLISTIC MISSILE SUBMARINES (SSBN))

Name	No.	Builders	Laid down	Launched	Commissioned	F/S
LAFAYETTE	SSBN 616	General Dynamics (Electric Boat Div)	17 Jan 1961	8 May 1962	23 April 1963	AA
ALEXANDER HAMILTON	SSBN 617	General Dynamics (Electric Boat Div)	26 June 1961	18 Aug 1962	27 June 1963	AA
ANDREW JACKSON	SSBN 619	Mare Island Naval Shipyard	26 April 1961	15 Sept 1962	3 July 1963	AA
JOHN ADAMS	SSBN 620	Portsmouth Naval Shipyard	19 May 1961	12 Jan 1963	12 May 1964	AA
JAMES MONROE	SSBN 622	Newport News Shipbuilding & DD Co	31 July 1961	4 Aug 1962	7 Dec 1963	AA
NATHAN HALE	SSBN 623	General Dynamics (Electric Boat Div)	2 Oct 1961	12 Jan 1963	23 Nov 1963	AA
WOODROW WILSON	SSBN 624	Mare Island Naval Shipyard	13 Sept 1961	22 Feb 1963	27 Dec 1963	AA
HENRY CLAY	SSBN 625	Newport News Shipbuilding & DD Co.	23 Oct 1961	30 Nov 1962	20 Feb 1964	AA
DANIEL WEBSTER	SSBN 626	General Dynamics (Electric Boat Div)	28 Dec 1961	27 April 1963	9 April 1964	AA
JAMES MADISON	SSBN 627	Newport News Shipbuilding & DD Co	5 Mar 1962	15 Mar 1963	28 July 1964	AA
TECUMSEH	SSBN 628	General Dynamics (Electric Boat Div)	1 June 1962	22 June 1963	29 May 1964	AA
DANIEL BOONE	SSBN 629	Mare Island Naval Shipyard	6 Feb 1962	22 June 1963	23 April 1964	AA
JOHN C. CALHOUN	SSBN 630	Newport News Shipbuilding & DD Co	4 June 1962	22 June 1963	15 Sept 1964	AA
ULYSSES S. GRANT	SSBN 631	General Dynamics (Electric Boat Div)	18 Aug 1962	2 Nov 1963	17 July 1964	AA
VON STEUBEN	SSBN 632	Newport News Shipbuilding & DD Co	4 Sept 1962	18 Oct 1963	30 Sept 1964	AA
CASIMIR PULASKI	SSBN 633	General Dynamics (Electric Boat Div)	12 Jan 1963	1 Feb 1964	14 Aug 1964	AA
STONEWALL JACKSON	SSBN 634	Mare Island Naval Shipyard	4 July 1962	30 Nov 1963	26 Aug 1964	AA
SAM RAYBURN	SSBN 635	Newport News Shipbuilding & DD Co	3 Dec 1962	20 Dec 1963	2 Dec 1964	AA
NATHANAEL GREENE	SSBN 636	Portsmouth Naval Shipyard	21 May 1962	12 May 1964	19 Dec 1964	AA
BENJAMIN FRANKLIN	SSBN 640	General Dynamics (Electric Boat Div)	25 May 1963	5 Dec 1964	22 Oct 1965	AA
SIMON BOLIVAR	SSBN 641	Newport News Shipbuilding & DD Co	17 April 1963	22 Aug 1964	29 Oct 1965	AA
KAMEHAMEHA	SSBN 642	Mare Island Naval Shipyard	2 May 1963	16 Jan 1965	10 Dec 1965	AA
GEORGE BANCROFT	SSBN 643	General Dynamics (Electric Boat Div)	24 Aug 1963	20 Mar 1965	22 Jan 1966	AA
LEWIS AND CLARK	SSBN 644	Newport News Shipbuilding & DD Co	29 July 1963	21 Nov 1964	22 Dec 1965	AA
JAMES K. POLK	SSBN 645	General Dynamics (Electric Boat Div)	23 Nov 1963	22 May 1965	16 April 1966	AA
GEORGE C. MARSHALL	SSBN 654	Newport News Shipbuilding & DD Co	2 Mar 1964	21 May 1965	29 April 1966	AA
HENRY L. STIMSON	SSBN 655	General Dynamics (Electric Boat Div)	4 April 1964	13 Nov 1965	20 Aug 1966	AA
GEORGE WASHINGTON CARVER	SSBN 656	Newport News Shipbuilding & DD Co	24 Aug 1964	14 Aug 1965	15 June 1966	AA
FRANCIS SCOTT KEY	SSBN 657	General Dynamics (Electric Boat Div)	5 Dec 1964	23 April 1966	3 Dec 1966	AA
MARIANO G. VALLEJO	SSBN 658	Mare Island Naval Shipyard	7 July 1964	23 Oct 1965	16 Dec 1966	AA
WILL ROGERS	SSBN 659	General Dynamics (Electric Boat Div)	20 Mar 1965	21 July 1966	1 April 1967	AA

Displacement, tons: 6 650 light surfaced; 7 250 standard surfaced; 8 250 dived
Length, feet (metres): 425 *(129·5)* oa
Beam, feet (metres): 33 *(10·1)*
Draught, feet (metres): 31·5 *(9·6)*
Missile launchers: 16 tubes for Poseidon C-3 SLBM (see *Missile* notes)
Torpedo tubes: 4—21 in *(533 mm)* Mk 65 (bow)
Main machinery: 1 pressurised-water cooled S5W (Westinghouse) reactor; 2 geared turbines; 15 000 shp; 1 shaft
Speed, knots: 20 surfaced; approx 30 dived
Complement: 168 (20 officers, 148 enlisted men) (SSBN 640 onward); 140 (14 officers, 126 enlisted men) (remainder)

These submarines are the largest undersea craft to be completed in the West. The first four submarines (SSBN 616, 617, 619, 620) were authorised in the Fiscal Year 1961 shipbuilding programme with five additional submarines (SSBN 622-626) authorised in a supplemental the FY 1961 programme; SSBN 627-636 (ten) in the FY 1962, SSBN 640-645 (six) in the FY 1963, and SSBN 654-659 (six) in the FY 1964. Cost for the earlier ships of this class was approximately $109·5 million per submarine.

Design: *Benjamin Franklin* and later submarines are officially considered a separate class; however, differences are minimal (eg, quieter machinery).

Electronics: Fitted with Mk 113 Mod 9 torpedo fire control system.

Engineering: *Benjamin Franklin* and subsequent submarines of this class have been fitted with quieter machinery. All SSBNs have diesel-electric stand-by machinery, snorts, and "outboard" auxiliary propeller for emergency use.
The nuclear cores inserted in refuelling these submarines during the late 1960s and early 1970s cost approximately $3·5 million and provide energy for approximately 400 000 miles.

Missiles: The first eight ships of this class were fitted with the Polaris A-2 missile (1 500 n. mile range) and the 23 later ships with the Polaris A-3 missile (2 500 n. mile range).
The SSBN 620 and SSBN 622-625 (five ships) were rearmed with the Polaris A-3 missile during overhaul-refuellings from 1968 to 1970. Subsequently, all converted to carry the Poseidon C-3 missile.
Andrew Jackson launched the first Polaris A-3 missile to be fired from a submarine on 26 Oct 1963. *Daniel Webster* was the first submarine to deploy with the A-3 missile, beginning her first patrol on 28 Sept 1964. *Daniel Boone* was the first Polaris submarine to deploy to the Pacific, beginning her first patrol with the A-3 missile on 25 Dec 1964. *James Madison* launched the first Poseidon C-3 missile from a submarine on 3 Aug 1970; the submarine began the first Poseidon deployment on 31 March 1971.
James Madison was the first submarine to undergo conversion to carry the Poseidon missile. She began conversion in Feb 1969 and was completed in June 1970. (See conversion table on following page).
Poseidon conversion, overhaul, and reactor refuelling are conducted simultaneously. In addition to changes in missile tubes to accommodate larger Poseidon, the conversion provides replacement of Mk 84 fire control system with Mk 88 system. The Poseidon conversion programme completed in 1977. This conversion makes no change to the submarines' external appearance.
Current planning provides for the first of ten of these classes of SSBNs to be refitted with the Trident I missile.
During the FY 1979, *Francis Scott Key* (SSBN 657) will be converted to fire the Trident I missile. The conversion will be done during a tender availability alongside an AS(FBM) and the conversion will entail minor modifications to the launcher and to the ballasting of the submarine to accommodate the greater weight of the Trident missile. More extensive modifications will be required to the installed fire control, instrumentation and missile checkout subsystems to support the increased sophistication of the longer range missile. *Francis Scott Key* will serve as a sea going test bed for the at sea testing phase of the Trident I missile. During this time *Francis Scott Key* will not be employed on deterrent patrols.

SIMON BOLIVAR   9/1976, Dr. Giorgio Arra

SIMON BOLIVAR   9/1976, Dr. Giorgio Arra

Navigation: These submarines are equipped with an elaborate Ship's Inertial Navigation System (SINS), a system of gyroscopes and accelerometers which relates movement of the ship in all directions, true speed through the water and over the ocean floor, and true north to give a continuous report of the submarine's position. Navigation data produced by SINS can be provided to each missile's guidance package until the instant the missile is fired.

As converted, all Poseidon submarines have three Mk 2 Mod 4 SINS; all fitted with navigational satellite receivers.

Personnel: Each submarine is assigned two alternating crews designated "Blue" and "Gold". Each crew mans the submarine during a 60-day patrol and partially assists during the intermediate 28-day refit alongside a Polaris tender.

628 USA

MARIANO C. VALLEJO   1974, USN

POSEIDON CONVERSION SCHEDULE

No.	Programme	Conversion Yard	Start	Complete
SSBN 616	FY 1973	General Dynamics Corp (Electric Boat)	15 Oct 1972	7 Nov 1974
SSBN 617	FY 1973	Newport News SB & DD Co	15 Jan 1973	11 April 1975
SSBN 619	FY 1973	General Dynamics Corp (Electric Boat)	19 Mar 1973	15 Aug 1975
SSBN 620	FY 1974	Portsmouth Naval Shipyard	1 Feb 1974	15 April 1976
SSBN 622	FY 1975	Newport News SB & DD Co	15 Jan 1975	14 May 1977
SSBN 623	FY 1973	Puget Sound Naval Shipyard	15 June 1973	27 June 1975
SSBN 624	FY 1974	Newport News SB & DD Co	1 Oct 1973	23 Oct 1975
SSBN 625	FY 1975	Portsmouth Naval Shipyard	29 April 1975	29 July 1977
SSBN 626	FY 1975	General Dynamics Corp (Electric Boat)	1 Dec 1975	? 1978
SSBN 627	FY 1968	General Dynamics Corp (Electric Boat)	3 Feb 1969	28 June 1970
SSBN 628	FY 1970	Newport News SB & DD Co	10 Nov 1969	18 Feb 1971
SSBN 629	FY 1968	Newport News SB & DD Co	11 May 1969	11 Aug 1970
SSBN 630	FY 1969	Mare Island Naval Shipyard	4 Aug 1969	22 Feb 1971
SSBN 631	FY 1970	Puget Sound Naval Shipyard	3 Oct 1969	16 Dec 1970
SSBN 632	FY 1969	General Dynamics Corp (Electric Boat)	11 July 1969	19 Nov 1970
SSBN 633	FY 1970	General Dynamics Corp (Electric Boat)	10 Jan 1970	30 April 1971
SSBN 634	FY 1971	General Dynamics Corp (Electric Boat)	15 July 1970	29 Oct 1971
SSBN 635	FY 1970	Portsmouth Naval Shipyard	19 Jan 1970	2 Sept 1971
SSBN 636	FY 1971	Newport News SB & DD Co	22 July 1970	21 Sept 1971
SSBN 640	FY 1971	General Dynamics Corp (Electric Boat)	25 Feb 1971	15 May 1972
SSBN 641	FY 1971	Newport News SB & DD Co	15 Feb 1971	12 May 1972
SSBN 642	FY 1972	General Dynamics Corp (Electric Boat)	15 July 1971	27 Oct 1972
SSBN 643	FY 1971	Portsmouth Naval Shipyard	28 April 1971	31 July 1972
SSBN 644	FY 1971	Puget Sound Naval Shipyard	30 April 1971	21 July 1972
SSBN 645	FY 1972	Newport News SB & DD Co	15 July 1971	17 Nov 1972
SSBN 654	FY 1972	Puget Sound Naval Shipyard	14 Sept 1971	8 Feb 1973
SSBN 655	FY 1972	Newport News SB & DD Co	15 Nov 1971	22 Mar 1973
SSBN 656	FY 1972	General Dynamics Corp (Electric Boat)	12 Nov 1971	7 April 1973
SSBN 657	FY 1972	Puget Sound Naval Shipyard	20 Feb 1972	17 May 1973
SSBN 658	FY 1973	Newport News SB & DD Co	21 Aug 1972	19 Dec 1973
SSBN 659	FY 1973	Portsmouth Naval Shipyard	16 Oct 1972	8 Feb 1974

THOMAS A. EDISON in rear, passing FRANCIS SCOTT KEY in Panama Canal   1973, USN

TECUMSEH approaching PROTEUS   USN

USA 629

5 "ETHAN ALLEN" CLASS (FLEET BALLISTIC MISSILE SUBMARINES (SSBN))

Name	No.	Builders	Laid down	Launched	Commissioned	F/S
ETHAN ALLEN	SSBN 608	General Dynamics (Electric Boat Div, Groton)	14 Sept 1959	22 Nov 1960	8 Aug 1961	PA
SAM HOUSTON	SSBN 609	Newport News Shipbuilding & DD Co	28 Dec 1959	2 Feb 1961	6 Mar 1962	PA
THOMAS A. EDISON	SSBN 610	General Dynamics (Electric Boat Div, Groton)	15 Mar 1960	15 June 1961	10 Mar 1962	PA
JOHN MARSHALL	SSBN 611	Newport News Shipbuilding & DD Co	4 April 1960	15 July 1961	21 May 1962	PA
THOMAS JEFFERSON	SSBN 618	Newport News Shipbuilding & DD Co	3 Feb 1961	24 Feb 1962	4 Jan 1963	PA

Displacement, tons: 6 955 surfaced; 7 880 dived
Length, feet (metres): 410 *(125)* oa
Beam, feet (metres): 33 *(10·1)*
Draught, feet (metres): 32 *(9·8)*
Missile launchers: 16 tubes for Polaris A-3 SLBM
Torpedo tubes: 4—21 in *(533 mm)* bow
Main machinery: 1 pressurised-water cooled S5W (Westinghouse) reactor; 2 geared turbines (General Electric); 15 000 shp; 1 shaft
Speed, knots: 20 surfaced; 30 dived
Complement: 142 (15 officers, 127 enlisted men)

These submarines were designed specifically for the ballistic missile role and are larger and better arranged than the earlier "George Washington" class submarines. The first four ships of this class were authorised in the Fiscal Year 1959 programme; *Thomas Jefferson* was in the FY 1961 programme. These submarines and the previous "George Washington" class will not be converted to carry the Poseidon missile because of materiel limitations and the age they would be after conversion. This class is depth limited compared with the later SSBN classes.

Design: These submarines and the subsequent "Lafayette" class are deep-diving submarines with a depth capability similar to the "Thresher" class attack submarines; pressure hulls of HY-80 steel.

Missiles: These ships were initially armed with the Polaris A-2 missile (1 500 n. mile range). *Ethan Allen* launched the first A-2 missile fired from a submarine on 23 Oct 1961. She was the first submarine to deploy with the A-2 missile, beginning her first patrol on 26 June 1962. *Ethan Allen* fired a Polaris A-2 missile in the Christmas Island Pacific Test Area on 6 May 1962 in what was the first complete US test of a ballistic missile including detonation of the nuclear warhead. All five of these submarines have been modified to fire the A-3 missile (2 500 n. mile range).

Navigation: Fitted with two Mk 2 Mod 3 Ship's Inertial Navigation Systems (SINS) and navigational satellite receiver.

THOMAS JEFFERSON 6/1976, USN

ETHAN ALLEN 1971, USN

THOMAS JEFFERSON 6/1976, USN

USA

5 "GEORGE WASHINGTON" CLASS (FLEET BALLISTIC MISSILE SUBMARINES (SSBN))

Name	No.	Builders	Laid down	Launched	Commissioned	F/S
GEORGE WASHINGTON	SSBN 598	General Dynamics (Electric Boat Div, Groton)	1 Nov 1957	9 June 1959	30 Dec 1959	PA
PATRICK HENRY	SSBN 599	General Dynamics (Electric Boat Div, Groton)	27 May 1958	22 Sept 1959	9 April 1960	PA
THEODORE ROOSEVELT	SSBN 600	Mare Island Naval Shipyard	20 May 1958	3 Oct 1959	13 Feb 1961	PA
ROBERT E. LEE	SSBN 601	Newport News Shipbuilding & DD Co	25 Aug 1958	18 Dec 1959	16 Sept 1960	PA
ABRAHAM LINCOLN	SSBN 602	Portsmouth Naval Shipyard	1 Nov 1958	14 May 1960	11 Mar 1961	PA

Displacement, tons: 6 019 standard surfaced; 6 888 dived
Length, feet (metres): 381·7 *(116·3)* oa
Beam, feet (metres): 33 *(10·1)*
Draught, feet (metres): 29 *(8·8)*
Missile launchers: 16 tubes for Polaris A-3 SLBM
Torpedo tubes: 6—21 in *(533 mm)* Mk 59 (bow)
Main machinery: 1 pressurised-water cooled S5W (Westinghouse) reactor; 2 geared turbines (General Electric); 15 000 shp; 1 shaft
Speed, knots: 20 surfaced; 31 dived
Complement: 112 (12 officers, 100 enlisted men)

George Washington was the West's first ship to be armed with ballistic missiles. A supplement to the Fiscal Year 1958 new construction programme signed on 11 Feb 1958 provided for the construction of the first three SSBNs. The Navy ordered the just-begun attack submarine *Scorpion* (SSN 589) to be completed as a missile submarine on 31 Dec 1957. The hull was redesignated SSBN 598 and completed as *George Washington*. *Patrick Henry* similarly was re-ordered on the last day of 1957, her materials having originally been intended for the not-yet started SSN 590. These submarines and three sister ships (two authorised in the FY 1959) were built to a modified "Skipjack" class design with almost 130 feet being added to the original design to accommodate two rows of eight missile tubes, fore control and navigation equipment, and auxiliary machinery. All are depth limited compared with later designs.

Appearance: Note that "hump" of hull extension for housing missile tubes is more pronounced in these submarines than later classes.

Engineering: *George Washington* was the first FBM submarine to be overhauled and "refuelled". During her 4½ years of operation on her initial reactor core she carried out 15 submerged missile patrols and steamed more than 100 000 miles.

Missiles: These ships were initially armed with the Polaris A-1 missile (1 200 n. mile range). *George Washington* successfully fired two Polaris A-1 missiles while submerged off Cape Canaveral on 20 July 1960 in the first underwater launching of a ballistic missile from a US submarine. She departed on her initial patrol on 15 Nov 1960 and remained submerged for 66 days, 10 hours. All five submarines of this class have been refitted to fire the improved Polaris A-3 missile (2 500 n. mile range). Missile refit and first reactor refuelling were accomplished simultaneously during overhaul. *George Washington* from 20 June 1964 to 2 Feb 1966, *Patrick Henry* from 4 Jan 1965 to 21 July 1966, *Theodore Roosevelt* from 28 July 1965 to 14 Jan 1967, *Robert E. Lee* from 23 Feb 1965 to 2 July 1966, and *Abraham Lincoln* from 25 Oct 1965 to 3 June 1967, four at Electric Boat yard in Groton, Connecticut, and *Robert E. Lee* at Mare Island Naval Shipyard (California). These submarines all have Mk 84 fire control systems and gas-steam missile ejectors (originally fitted with Mk 80 fire control systems and compressed air missile ejectors, changed during A-3 missile refit). These submarines will not be modified to carry and launch the advanced Poseidon ballistic missile.

Navigation: Fitted with three Mk 2 Mod 4 Ship's Inertial Navigation System (SINS) and navigational satellite receiver.

ABRAHAM LINCOLN — USN

GEORGE WASHINGTON — USN

ROBERT E. LEE — USN

SUBMARINES (SSN and SS)

The US Navy's submarine forces consist of two principal categories: strategic missile submarines (SSBN), listed in the previous section, and attack submarines (SS and SSN).
The Navy's attack submarine force is almost entirely nuclear. The few remaining diesel-electric submarines are all of post-World War II construction; their age and the demand of foreign transfers to US allies will result in an all-nuclear submarine force by the mid-1980s, if not earlier. At that time the Navy will have some 85 to 90 SSNs ("Skipjack" class and later).
A construction rate of two SSNs per year from the FY 1979 for the foreseeable future has been proposed by the Department of Defense.
Construction of the submarines recently has been slowed by the late delivery of component equipment and problems in the hiring of shipyard workers. Further complicating the situation has been the start of the Trident missile submarine programme and the loss to the SSN construction programme of the Litton/Ingalls yard at Pascagoula, Mississippi, which delivered its last nuclear submarine in 1974. This leaves only two shipyards in the United States building nuclear submarines. (No diesel-propelled submarines have been built in the United States since 1959).
In Jan 1977 Secretary of Defence D. H. Rumsfeld reported "It has been decided to continue the production of the SSN 688 *(Los Angeles)* class until at least the mid-1980s rather than to introduce a new generation submarine. We plan to procure eight SSN-688s in the five year programme. A faster building rate will be necessary in the 1980s." The initial sea trials of *Los Angeles* gave an increase over the designed speed and showed improved sound quieting.

Ancillary Programmes: These include development of a wide-aperture array sonar for rapid localisation of targets and attack, the retrofitting of BQQ-5 sonar in all submarines of the "Sturgeon" class and deployment of submarine-launched Harpoon.

Anti-ship Missiles: An encapsulated version of the Harpoon anti-ship missile has been developed for launching from submarines. The Harpoon, also capable of surface ship and aircraft launch, is a 15-foot weapon carrying a conventional high-explosive warhead. In the encapsulated version (length 21 feet), the Harpoon is launched from a torpedo tube and travels to the surface where the protective capsule is discarded, the missile's fins extend, and the rocket engine ignites. The Harpoon has a range of about 60 n. miles and will be operational in the FY 1978/9.

Deep Submergence Vehicles: The US Navy's Deep Submergence Vehicles (DSV), including the nuclear-propelled *NR-1*, are rated as Service Craft and are listed at the end of this section.

Force Levels: As of 1 Jan 1978 there were 76 SS/SSNs in commission. In addition 28 SSN were under construction and 2 SSN and 1 SSG in reserve.

Names: US submarines generally have been named for fish and other marine life except that fleet ballistic missile submarines have been named for famous Americans. The tradition of naming "fleet" and "attack" submarines for fish was broken in 1971 when three submarines of the "Sturgeon" class and the one-of-a-kind SSN 685 were named after deceased members of Congress. Previously US destroyer-type ships have been named after members of Congress.
Later in 1971 the SSN 688, lead ship for a new class of attack submarines, was named *Los Angeles*, introducing "city" names to US submarines. This was the third name source applied to US submarines within a year.
(Of late, several types of auxiliary ships also have been named for cities, a name source traditionally applied to cruisers in the US Navy.)

Transfers: Three of the four remaining "Tang" class submarines *(Tang, Wahoo* and *Trout)* are scheduled for transfer to the Imperial Iranian Navy in 1978-79.

6 + 26 (+8) NUCLEAR POWERED SUBMARINES (SSN) "LOS ANGELES" CLASS

Name	No.	Builders	Laid down	Launched	Commissioned	F/S
*LOS ANGELES	SSN 688	Newport News SB & DD Co	8 Jan 1972	6 April 1974	13 Nov 1976	AA
BATON ROUGE	SSN 689	Newport News SB & DD Co	18 Nov 1972	26 April 1975	25 June 1977	AA
PHILADELPHIA	SSN 690	General Dynamics (Electric Boat)	12 Aug 1972	19 Oct 1974	25 June 1977	AA
MEMPHIS	SSN 691	Newport News SB & DD Co	23 June 1973	3 April 1976	17 Dec 1977	AA
OMAHA	SSN 692	General Dynamics (Electric Boat)	27 Jan 1973	21 Feb 1976	31 Dec 1977	AA
CINCINNATI	SSN 693	Newport News SB & DD Co	6 April 1974	19 Feb 1977	1978	AA
GROTON	SSN 694	General Dynamics (Electric Boat)	3 Aug 1973	9 Oct 1976	1978	Bldg
BIRMINGHAM	SSN 695	Newport News SB & DD Co	26 April 1975	29 Oct 1977	1978	Bldg
NEW YORK CITY	SSN 696	General Dynamics (Electric Boat)	15 Dec 1973	18 June 1977	1978	Bldg
INDIANAPOLIS	SSN 697	General Dynamics (Electric Boat)	19 Oct 1974	30 July 1977	1979	Bldg
BREMERTON	SSN 698	General Dynamics (Electric Boat)	8 May 1976	1978	1979	Bldg
JACKSONVILLE	SSN 699	General Dynamics (Electric Boat)	21 Feb 1976	1978	1979	Bldg
DALLAS	SSN 700	General Dynamics (Electric Boat)	9 Oct 1976	1978	1979	Bldg
LA JOLLA	SSN 701	General Dynamics (Electric Boat)	16 Oct 1976	1979	1980	Bldg
PHOENIX	SSN 702	General Dynamics (Electric Boat)	30 July 1977	1979	1980	Bldg
BOSTON	SSN 703	General Dynamics (Electric Boat)	1977	1979	1980	Bldg
BALTIMORE	SSN 704	General Dynamics (Electric Boat)	1978	1980	1981	Bldg
—	SSN 705	General Dynamics (Electric Boat)	1978	1980	1981	Ord
—	SSN 706	General Dynamics (Electric Boat)	1979	1980	1981	Ord
—	SSN 707	General Dynamics (Electric Boat)	1979	1980	1982	Ord
—	SSN 708	General Dynamics (Electric Boat)	1979	1981	1982	Ord
—	SSN 709	General Dynamics (Electric Boat)	1980	1981	1982	Ord
—	SSN 710	General Dynamics (Electric Boat)	1980	1981	1982	Ord
SAN FRANCISCO	SSN 711	Newport News SB and DD Co	26 May 1977	1979	1980	Bldg
—	SSN 712	Newport News SB and DD Co	1978	1980	1981	Ord
—	SSN 713	Newport News SB and DD Co	1979	1980	1982	Ord
—	SSN 714	Newport News SB and DD Co	1979	1981	1982	Ord
—	SSN 715	Newport News SB and DD Co	1980	1981	1983	Ord
Three submarines	SSN 716-718	Newport News SB and DD Co	1980-81	1981-82	1983-84	
One submarine	SSN 719	Approved FY 1978 programme				
Two submarines	SSN 720-721	Proposed FY 1979 programme				
Two submarines	SSN 722-723	Proposed FY 1980 programme				
Two submarines	SSN 724-725	Proposed FY 1981 programme				
Two submarines	SSN —	Proposed FY 1982 programme				

Displacement, tons: 6 000 standard; 6 900 dived
Length, feet (metres): 360 *(109·7)* oa
Beam, feet (metres): 33 *(10·1)*
Draught, feet (metres): 32·3 *(9·85)*
Missiles: Tube launched Harpoon
Torpedo tubes: 4—21 in *(533 mm)* amidships
A/S weapons: SUBROC and Mk 48 A/S torpedoes
Main machinery: 1 pressurised-water cooled S6G (GE) reactor; 2 geared turbines; 1 shaft
Speed, knots: 30+ dived
Complement: 127 (12 officers, 115 enlisted men)

The SSN 688-690 were authorised in the Fiscal Year 1970 new construction programme, SSN 691-694 in the FY 1971, SSN 695-699 in the FY 1972, SSN 700-705 in the FY 1973, SSN 706-710 in the FY 1974, SSN 711-713 in the FY 1975, SSN 714-715 in the FY 1976 and SSN 716-718 in the FY 1977 programme. Additional submarines are planned at the rate of two units per year into the mid-1980s and then at a faster rate.
Detailed design of the SSN 688 class as well as construction of the lead submarine was contracted to the Newport News Shipbuilding & Dry Dock Company, Newport News, Virginia.
Due to controversy in Washington, strikes and other shipyard problems these submarines are considerably behind schedule with the lead ship being completed over two years behind the original date. Thus, *Los Angeles* was nearly five years from keel laying to commissioning.

Design: Every effort has been made to improve sound quieting and the trials of *Los Angeles* have shown success in this area.

Electronics: UYK-7 computer is installed to assist command and control functions: Mk 113 Mod 10 torpedo fire control system fitted in SSN 688-699 (to be replaced by Mk 117 in near future); Mk 117 in later submarines.

Engineering: The S6G reactor is reportedly a modified version of the D2G type fitted in *Bainbridge* and *Truxtun*. The D2G reactors each produce approximately 30 000 shp. Reactor core life between refuellings is estimated at ten years.

Fiscal: The costs of these submarines have increased in every fiscal year programme. In the FY 1976 an average cost of $221·25 million per unit was estimated for a 38-submarine class. However, the FY 1977 units are estimated to cost approximately $330 million each.

Radar: BPS-15.

Sonar: BQQ-5 long range acquisition; BQS-15 close range; Towed array fitted.

PHILADELPHIA

5/1977, USN

632   USA

1 NUCLEAR/POWERED SUBMARINE (SSN) "GLENARD P. LIPSCOMB" CLASS

Name	No.	Builders	Laid down	Launched	Commissioned	F/S
GLENARD P. LIPSCOMB	SSN 685	General Dynamics (Electric Boat)	5 June 1971	4 Aug 1973	21 Dec 1974	AA

Displacement, tons: 5 813 standard; 6 480 dived
Length, feet (metres): 365 oa *(111·3)*
Beam, feet (metres): 31·7 *(9·7)*
Missiles: To be fitted for Harpoon
Torpedo tubes: 4—21 in *(533 mm)* amidships
A/S weapons: SUBROC and A/S torpedoes
Main machinery: 1 pressurised-water cooled S5Wa (Westinghouse) reactor. Turbine-electric drive (General Electric); 1 shaft
Speed, knots: approx 25+ dived
Complement: 120 (12 officers, 108 enlisted men)

Studies of a specifically "quiet" submarine were begun in Oct 1964. After certain setbacks approval for the construction of this submarine was announced on 25 Oct 1968 and the contract awarded to General Dynamics on 14 Oct 1970.
The Turbine-Electric Drive Submarine (TEDS) was constructed to test "a combination of advanced silencing techniques" involving "a new kind of propulsion system, and new and quieter machinery of various kinds", according to the Department of Defense. The TEDS project will permit an at-sea evaluation of improvements in ASW effectiveness due to noise reduction.
No further class of turbine-electric nuclear submarines has been proposed. Rather, quieting features developed in *Glenard P. Lipscomb* which do not detract from speed have been incorporated in the "Los Angeles" design.
Authorised in the Fiscal Year 1968 new construction programme, estimated construction cost was approximately $200 million.

Electronics: Mk 113 Mod 8 TFCS. To be replaced by Mk 117 Mod 3.

Engineering: Turbine-electric drive eliminates the noisy reduction gears of standard steam turbine power plants. The turbine-electric power plant is larger and heavier than comparable steam turbine submarine machinery.
Tullibee (SSN 597) was an earlier effort at noise reduction through a turbine-electric nuclear plant.

GLENARD P. LIPSCOMB   *1974, General Dynamics, Electric Boat Division*

1 NUCLEAR POWERED SUBMARINE (SSN) "NARWHAL" CLASS

Name	No.	Builders	Laid down	Launched	Commissioned	F/S
NARWHAL	SSN 671	General Dynamics (Electric Boat)	17 Jan 1966	9 Sept 1967	12 July 1969	PA

Displacement, tons: 4 450 standard; 5 350 dived
Length, feet (metres): 314·6 *(95·9)* oa
Beam, feet (metres): 43 *(13·1)*
Draught, feet (metres): 27 *(8·2)*
Missiles: To be fitted for Harpoon
Torpedo tubes: 4—21 in *(533 mm)* amidships
A/S weapons: SUBROC and A/S torpedoes
Main machinery: 1 pressurised water-cooled S5G (General Electric) reactor. 2 steam turbines; 17 000 shp; 1 shaft
Speed, knots: 20+ surfaced; 30+ dived
Complement: 107 (12 officers, 95 enlisted men)

Authorised in the Fiscal Year 1964 new construction programme.

Design: *Narwhal* is similar to the "Sturgeon" class submarines in hull design.

Electronics: Mk 113 Mod 6 torpedo fire control system. To be replaced by Mk 117 system.

Engineering: *Narwhal* is fitted with the prototype sea-going S5G natural circulation reactor plant. According to Admiral H. G. Rickover the natural circulation reactor "offers promise of increased reactor plant reliability, simplicity, and noise reduction due to the elimination of the need for large reactor coolant pumps and associated electrical and control equipment by taking maximum advantage of natural convection to circulate the reactor coolant".
The Atomic Energy Commission's Knolls Atomic Power Laboratory was given prime responsibility for development of the power plant. Construction of a land-based prototype plant began in May 1961 at the National Reactor Testing Station in Idaho. The reactor achieved initial criticality on 12 Sept 1965.

Sonar: BQS-8 upward-looking sonar for under-ice work (photo). BQQ-2 system (BQS-6 active and BQR-7 passive). BQS-6 is fitted in a 15 foot sphere and BQR-7 with conformal hydrophone array forward.

NARWHAL   *2/1974, USN*

37 NUCLEAR POWERED SUBMARINES (SSN) "STURGEON" CLASS

Name	No.	Builders	Laid down	Launched	Commissioned	F/S
STURGEON	SSN 637	General Dynamics (Electric Boat)	10 Aug 1963	26 Feb 1966	3 Mar 1967	AA
WHALE	SSN 638	General Dynamics (Quincy)	27 May 1964	14 Oct 1966	12 Oct 1968	AA
TAUTOG	SSN 639	Ingalls Shipbuilding Corp	27 Jan 1964	15 April 1967	17 Aug 1968	PA
GRAYLING	SSN 646	Portsmouth Naval Shipyard	12 May 1964	22 June 1967	11 Oct 1969	AA
POGY	SSN 647	Ingalls Shipbuilding Corp	4 May 1964	3 June 1967	15 May 1971	PA
ASPRO	SSN 648	Ingalls Shipbuilding Corp	23 Nov 1964	29 Nov 1967	20 Feb 1969	PA
SUNFISH	SSN 649	General Dynamics (Quincy)	15 Jan 1965	14 Oct 1966	15 Mar 1969	AA
PARGO	SSN 650	General Dynamics (Electric Boat)	3 June 1964	17 Sept 1966	5 Jan 1968	AA
QUEENFISH	SSN 651	Newport News SB & DD Co	11 May 1965	25 Feb 1966	6 Dec 1966	PA
PUFFER	SSN 652	Ingalls Shipbuilding Corp	8 Feb 1965	30 Mar 1968	9 Aug 1969	PA
RAY	SSN 653	Newport News SB & DD Co	1 April 1965	21 June 1966	12 April 1967	AA
SAND LANCE	SSN 660	Portsmouth Naval Shipyard	15 Jan 1965	11 Nov 1969	25 Sept 1971	AA
LAPON	SSN 661	Newport News SB & DD Co	26 July 1965	16 Dec 1966	14 Dec 1967	AA
GURNARD	SSN 662	San Francisco NSY (Mare Island)	22 Dec 1964	20 May 1967	6 Dec 1968	PA
HAMMERHEAD	SSN 663	Newport News SB & DD Co	29 Nov 1966	14 April 1967	28 June 1968	AA
SEA DEVIL	SSN 664	Newport News SB & DD Co	12 April 1966	5 Oct 1967	30 Jan 1969	AA
GUITARRO	SSN 665	San Francisco NSY (Mare Island)	9 Dec 1965	27 July 1968	9 Sept 1972	PA
HAWKBILL	SSN 666	San Francisco NSY (Mare Island)	12 Sept 1966	12 April 1969	4 Feb 1971	PA
BERGALL	SSN 667	General Dynamics (Electric Boat)	16 April 1966	17 Feb 1968	13 June 1969	AA
SPADEFISH	SSN 668	Newport News SB & DD Co	21 Dec 1966	15 May 1968	14 Aug 1969	AA
SEAHORSE	SSN 669	General Dynamics (Electric Boat)	13 Aug 1966	15 June 1968	19 Sept 1969	AA
FINBACK	SSN 670	Newport News SB & DD Co	26 June 1967	7 Dec 1968	4 Feb 1970	AA
PINTADO	SSN 672	San Francisco NSY (Mare Island)	27 Oct 1967	16 Aug 1969	11 Sept 1971	PA
FLYING FISH	SSN 673	General Dynamics (Electric Boat)	30 June 1967	17 May 1969	29 April 1970	AA
TREPANG	SSN 674	General Dynamics (Electric Boat)	28 Oct 1967	27 Sept 1969	14 Aug 1970	AA
BLUEFISH	SSN 675	General Dynamics (Electric Boat)	13 Mar 1968	10 Jan 1970	8 Jan 1971	AA
BILLFISH	SSN 676	General Dynamics (Electric Boat)	20 Sept 1968	1 May 1970	12 Mar 1971	PA
DRUM	SSN 677	San Francisco NSY (Mare Island)	20 Aug 1968	23 May 1970	15 April 1972	AA
ARCHERFISH	SSN 678	General Dynamics (Electric Boat)	19 June 1969	16 Jan 1971	17 Dec 1971	AA
SILVERSIDES	SSN 679	General Dynamics (Electric Boat)	13 Oct 1969	4 June 1971	5 May 1972	AA
WILLIAM H. BATES (ex-Redfish)	SSN 680	Ingalls Shipbuilding (Litton)	4 Aug 1969	11 Dec 1971	5 May 1973	AA
BATFISH	SSN 681	General Dynamics (Electric Boat)	9 Feb 1970	9 Oct 1971	1 Sept 1972	AA
TUNNY	SSN 682	Ingalls Shipbuilding (Litton)	22 May 1970	10 June 1972	26 Jan 1974	AA
PARCHE	SSN 683	Ingalls Shipbuilding (Litton)	10 Dec 1970	13 Jan 1973	17 Aug 1974	AA
CAVALLA	SSN 684	General Dynamics (Electric Boat)	4 June 1970	19 Feb 1972	9 Feb 1973	AA
L. MENDEL RIVERS	SSN 686	Newport News SB & DD Co	26 June 1971	2 June 1973	1 Feb 1975	AA
RICHARD B. RUSSELL	SSN 687	Newport News SB & DD Co	19 Oct 1971	12 Jan 1974	16 Aug 1975	AA

Displacement, tons: 3 640 standard; 4 640 dived
Length, feet (metres): 292·2 *(89·0)* oa (see *Design* notes)
Beam, feet (metres): 31·7 *(9·5)*
Draught, feet (metres): 26 *(7·9)*
Missiles: To be fitted for Harpoon
Torpedo tubes: 4—21 in *(533 mm)* Mk 63 amidships
A/S weapons: SUBROC and A/S torpedoes
Main machinery: 1 pressurised-water cooled S5W (Westinghouse) reactor; 2 steam turbines; 15 000 shp; 1 shaft
Speed, knots: 20+ surfaced; 30+ dived
Complement: 107 (12 officers, 95 enlisted men)

The 37 "Sturgeon" class attack submarines comprise the largest US Navy group of nuclear-powered ships built to the same design to date.
They are similar in design to the previous "Thresher" class but are slightly larger. SSN 637-639 were authorised in the Fiscal Year 1962 new construction programme. SSN 646-653 in the FY 1963, SSN 660-664 in the FY 1964, SSN 665-670 in the FY 1965, SSN 672-677 in the FY 1966, SSN 678-682 in the FY 1967, SSN 683-684 in the FY 1968, and SSN 686-687 in the FY 1969.

Construction: *Pogy* was begun by the New York Shipbuilding Corp (Camden, New Jersey), contract with whom was terminated on 5 June 1967; contract for completion awarded to Ingalls Shipbuilding Corp on 7 Dec 1967.
Guitarro sank in 35 feet of water on 15 May 1969 while being fitted out at the San Francisco Bay Naval Shipyard. According to a congressional report, the sinking, caused by Shipyard workers, was "wholly avoidable". Subsequently raised; damage estimated at $25 million. Completion delayed more than two years.

Design: These submarines are slightly larger than the previous "Thresher" class and can be identified by their taller sail structure and the lower position of their diving planes on the sail (to improve control at periscope depth). Sail height is 20 feet, 6 inches above deck. Sail-mounted diving planes rotate to vertical for breaking through ice when surfacing in arctic regions. These submarines probably are slightly slower than the previous "Thresher" and "Skipjack" classes because of their increased size with the same propulsion system as in the earlier classes.
SSN 678/684, 686 and 687 are ten feet longer than remainder of class to accommodate extra sonar and electronic gear.

Electronics: Mk 113 torpedo fire control system. To be replaced by Mk 117 Mod 2.

Name: *William H. Bates* (SSN 680) previously *Redfish* renamed 25 June 1971.

Operational: *Whale, Pargo,* and older nuclear submarine *Sargo* conducted exercises in the Arctic ice pack during March-April 1969. *Whale* surfaced at the geographic North Pole on 6 April, the 60th anniversary of Rear-Admiral Robert E. Peary's reaching the North Pole. This was the first instance of single-screw US nuclear submarines surfacing in the Arctic ice.

Radar: BPS 14 Search.

Sonar: BQQ-2 sonar system. Principal components of the BQQ-2 include the BQS-6 active sonar, with transducers mounted in a 15-foot diameter sonar sphere, and BQR-7 passive sonar, with hydrophones in a conformal array on sides of forward hull. The active sonar sphere is fitted in the optimum bow position, requiring placement of torpedo tubes amidships. These submarines also have BQS-8 under-ice sonar and BQS-12 (first 16 units) or BQS-13 active/passive sonars. Transducers for the BQS-8, intended primarily for under-ice navigation, are in two small domes aft of the sail structure.
Sonar suites of the *Guitarro* and *Cavalla* have been modified. All "Sturgeon" class submarines are to be refitted with replacement of the BQQ-2 by BQQ-5 during regular overhauls.

HAWKBILL — 2/1977, Dr. Giorgio Arra

BILLFISH — 6/1977, John G. Callis

PINTADO (with DSRV 1 embarked and fluorescent markings to aid homing) — 3/1977, USN

Submersibles: *Hawkbill* and *Pintado* have been modified to carry and support the Navy's Deep Submergence Rescue Vehicles (DSRV). See section on Deep Submergence Vehicles for additional DSRV details.

634 USA

13 NUCLEAR POWERED SUBMARINES (SSN) "THRESHER" CLASS

Name	No.	Builders	Laid down	Launched	Commissioned	F/S
PERMIT	SSN 594	Mare Island Naval Shipyard	16 July 1959	1 July 1961	29 May 1962	PA
PLUNGER	SSN 595	Mare Island Naval Shipyard	2 Mar 1960	9 Dec 1961	21 Nov 1962	PA
BARB	SSN 596	Ingalls Shipbuilding Corp	9 Nov 1959	12 Feb 1962	24 Aug 1963	AA
POLLACK	SSN 603	New York Shipbuilding Corp	14 Mar 1960	17 Mar 1962	26 May 1964	AA
HADDO	SSN 604	New York Shipbuilding Corp	9 Sept 1960	18 Aug 1962	16 Dec 1964	PA
JACK	SSN 605	Portsmouth Naval Shipyard	16 Sept 1960	24 April 1963	31 Mar 1967	AA
TINOSA	SSN 606	Portsmouth Naval Shipyard	24 Nov 1959	9 Dec 1961	17 Oct 1964	AA
DACE	SSN 607	Ingalls Shipbuilding Corp	6 June 1960	18 Aug 1962	4 April 1964	AA
GUARDFISH	SSN 612	New York Shipbuilding Corp	28 Feb 1961	15 May 1965	20 Dec 1966	AA
FLASHER	SSN 613	General Dynamics (Electric Boat)	14 April 1961	22 June 1963	22 July 1966	PA
GREENLING	SSN 614	General Dynamics (Electric Boat)	15 Aug 1961	4 April 1964	3 Nov 1967	PA
GATO	SSN 615	General Dynamics (Electric Boat)	15 Dec 1961	14 May 1964	25 Jan 1968	AA
HADDOCK	SSN 621	Ingalls Shipbuilding Corp	24 April 1961	21 May 1966	22 Dec 1967	AA

Displacement, tons: 3 750 standard; *Flasher, Greenling* and *Gato* 3 800; 4 300 dived except *Jack* 4 470 dived, *Flasher, Greenling* and *Gato* 4 242 dived
Length, feet (metres): 278·5 *(84·9)* oa except *Jack* 297·4 *(90·7)* oa, *Flasher, Greenling* and *Gato* 292·2 *(89·1)*
Beam, feet (metres): 31·7 *(9·6)*
Draught, feet (metres): 28·4 *(8·7)*
Missiles: To be fitted for Harpoon
Torpedo tubes: 4—21 in *(533 mm)* Mk 63 amidships
A/S weapons: SUBROC and A/S torpedoes
Main machinery: 1 pressurised-water cooled S5W (Westinghouse) reactor; 2 steam turbines, 15 000 shp; 1 shaft
Speed, knots: 20+ surfaced; 30+ dived
Complement: 103 (12 officers, 91 enlisted men)

PLUNGER   4/1976, USN

They have a greater depth capability than previous nuclear-powered submarines and are the first to combine the SUBROC anti-submarine missile capability with the advanced BQQ-2 sonar system. The lead ship of the class, *Thresher* (SSN 593), was authorised in the Fiscal Year 1957 new construction programme, the SSN 594-596 in the FY 1958. SSN 603-607 in the FY 1959, SSN 612-615 in the FY 1960, and SSN 621 in the FY 1961. *Thresher* (SSN 593) was lost off the coast of New England on 10 April 1963 while on post-overhaul trials. She went down with 129 men on board (108 crewmen plus four naval officers and 17 civilians on board for trials).

Construction: *Greenling* and *Gato* were launched by the Electric Boat Division of the General Dynamics Corp (Groton, Connecticut); towed to Quincy Division (Massachusetts) for lengthening and completion.

Design: *Jack* was built to a modified design to test a modified power plant (see *Engineering* notes).
Flasher, Gato and *Greenling* were modified during construction; fitted with SUBSAFE features, heavier machinery, and larger sail structures.
These submarines have a modified "tear-drop" hull design. Their bows are devoted to sonar and their four torpedo tubes are amidships, angled out, two to port and two to starboard.
The sail structure height of these submarines is 13 feet 9 inches to 15 feet above the deck, with later submarines of this class having a sail height of 20 feet.

Electronics: These submarines have the Mk 113 Mod 6 torpedo fire control system. To be replaced by Mk 117 Mod 1.

Engineering: *Jack* is fitted with two propellers on essentially one shaft (actually a single shaft within a sleeve-like shaft) and a counter-rotating turbine without a reduction gear. Both innovations are designed to reduce operating noises. To accommodate the larger turbine, the engine spaces were lengthened 10 feet and the shaft structure was lengthened seven feet to mount the two propellers. The propellers are of different size and are smaller than in the other submarines of this class. Also eliminated in *Jack* was a clutch and secondary-propulsion electric motor.
Jack's propulsion arrangement provides a 10 per cent increase in power efficiency, but no increase in speed.

PLUNGER   12/1976, Dr. Giorgio Arra

Names: Names changed during construction: *Plunger* ex-*Pollack; Barb* ex-*Pollack* ex-*Plunger; Pollack* ex-*Barb.*

Sonar: BQQ-2 (BQS-6 active and BQR-7 passive). The positioning of the conformal array for BQR-7 in the bow dictates the use of midships tubes.

1 NUCLEAR POWERED SUBMARINE (SSN) "TULLIBEE" CLASS

Name	No.	Builders	Laid down	Launched	Commissioned	F/S
TULLIBEE	SSN 597	General Dynamics (Electric Boat)	26 May 1958	27 April 1960	9 Nov 1960	AA

Displacement, tons: 2 317 standard; 2 640 dived
Length, feet (metres): 273 *(83·2)* oa
Beam, feet (metres): 23·3 *(7·1)*
Draught, feet (metres): 21 *(6·4)*
Torpedo tubes: 4—21 in *(533 mm)* Mk 64 amidships
A/S weapons: A/S torpedoes
Main machinery: 1 pressurised-water cooled S2C (Combustion Engineering) reactor; turbo-electric drive with steam turbine (Westinghouse); 2 500 shp; 1 shaft
Speed, knots: 15+ surfaced; 20+ dived
Complement: 56 (6 officers, 50 enlisted men)

Tullibee was designed specifically for anti-submarine operations and was the first US submarine with the optimum bow position devoted entirely to sonar. No additional submarine of this type was constructed because of the success of the larger, more-versatile "Thresher" class. *Tullibee* was authorised in the Fiscal Year 1958 new construction programme. She is no longer considered a "first line" submarine.

Design: She has a modified, elongated "tear-drop" hull design. Originally she was planned as a 1 000-ton craft, but reactor requirements and other considerations increased her size during design and construction.
Her four amidships torpedo tubes are angled out from the centreline two to port and two to starboard. Not fitted to fire SUBROC.

Electronics: Mk 112 Mod 3 torpedo fire control system.

Engineering: She has a small nuclear power plant designed and developed by the Combustion Engineering Company. The propulsion system features turbo-electric drive rather than conventional steam turbines with reduction gears in an effort to reduce operating noises.

Navigation: Fitted with Ships Inertial Navigation System (SINS).

Sonar: BQQ-2 system (BQS-6 active and BQR-7 passive) the first submarine so fitted.
BQG-4 passive (PUFFS—Passive Underwater Fire Control Feasibility System) with three (originally two) domes on top of hull.

TULLIBEE   1968, USN

USA 635

5 NUCLEAR POWERED SUBMARINES (SSN) "SKIPJACK" CLASS

Name	No.	Builders	Laid down	Launched	Commissioned	F/S
SKIPJACK	SSN 585	General Dynamics (Electric Boat)	29 May 1956	26 May 1958	15 April 1959	AA
SCAMP	SSN 588	Mare Island Naval Shipyard	23 Jan 1959	8 Oct 1960	5 June 1961	PA
SCULPIN	SSN 590	Ingalls Shipbuilding Corp	3 Feb 1958	31 Mar 1960	1 June 1961	PA
SHARK	SSN 591	Newport News SB & DD Co	24 Feb 1958	16 Mar 1960	9 Feb 1961	AA
SNOOK	SSN 592	Ingalls Shipbuilding Corp	7 April 1958	31 Oct 1960	24 Oct 1961	PA

Displacement, tons: 3 075 surfaced; 3 513 dived
Length, feet (metres): 251·7 *(76·7)* oa
Beam, feet (metres): 31·5 *(9·6)*
Draught, feet (metres): 29·4 *(8·9)*
Torpedo tubes: 6—21 in *(533 mm)* bow (Mk 59)
A/S weapons: A/S torpedoes
Main machinery: 1 pressurised-water cooled S5W (Westinghouse) reactor; 2 steam turbines (Westinghouse in *Skipjack;* General Electric in others); 15 000 shp; 1 shaft
Speed, knots: 16+ surfaced; 30+ dived
Complement: 93 (8 officers, 85 enlisted men)

Combine the high-speed endurance of nuclear propulsion with the high-speed "tear-drop" "Albacore" hull design. *Skipjack* was authorised in the Fiscal Year 1956 new construction programme and the five other submarines of this class were authorised in the FY 1957.
These submarines are still considered suitable for "first line" service. Officially described as fastest US nuclear submarines in service.
Each cost approximately $40 million.
Scorpion (SSN 589) of this class was lost some 400 miles southwest of the Azores while *en route* from the Mediterranean to Norfolk, Virginia, in May 1968. She went down with 99 men on board.

Construction: *Scorpion's* keel was laid down twice; the original keel, laid down on 1 Nov 1957, was renumbered SSBN 598 and became the Polaris submarine *George Washington;* the second SSN 589 keel became *Scorpion*. *Scamp's* keel laying was delayed when materiel for her was diverted to SSBN 599. This class introduced the Newport News Shipbuilding and Dry Dock Company and the Ingalls Shipbuilding Corporation to nuclear submarine construction. Newport News had not previously built submarines since before World War I.

Design: *Skipjack* was the first US nuclear submarine built to the "tear-drop" design. These submarines have a single propeller shaft (vice two in earlier nuclear submarines) and their diving planes are mounted on sail structures to improve underwater manoeuvrability. No after torpedo tubes are fitted because of their tapering sterns.

Electronics: Fitted with Mk 101 Mod 17 TFCS.

Engineering: The "Skipjack" class introduced the S5W fast attack submarine propulsion plant which has been employed in all subsequent US attack and ballistic missile submarines except the "Los Angeles" class (SSN 688) *Narwhal* (SSN 671) and *Glenard P. Lipscomb* (SSN 685). The plant was developed by the Bettis Atomic Power Laboratory.

Sonar: Modified BQS-4.

SCAMP *12/1976, Dr. Giorgio Arra*

SCAMP *12/1976, Dr. Giorgio Arra*

SCAMP *12/1976, Dr. Giorgio Arra*

636　USA

1 NUCLEAR POWERED SUBMARINE (SSN) "HALIBUT" CLASS

Name	No.	Builders	Laid down	Launched	Commissioned	F/S
HALIBUT	SSN 587 (ex-SSGN 587)	Mare Island Naval Shipyard, Vallejo, Calif.	11 April 1957	9 Jan 1959	4 Jan 1960	PR

Displacement, tons: 3 850 standard; 5 000 dived
Length, feet (metres): 350 *(106·6)* oa
Beam, feet (metres): 29·5 *(8·9)*
Draught, feet (metres): 21·5 *(6·5)*
Torpedo tubes: 6—21 in *(533 mm)* 4 bow (Mk 61); 2 stern (Mk 62)
Main machinery: 1 pressurised-water cooled S3W (Westinghouse) reactor; 2 steam turbines (Westinghouse); 6 600 shp; 2 shafts
Speed, knots: 15+ surfaced; 20+ dived
Complement: 98 (10 officers, 88 enlisted men)

Halibut is believed to have been the first submarine designed and constructed specifically to fire guided missiles.
She was originally intended to have diesel-electric propulsion but on 27 Feb 1956 the Navy announced she would have nuclear propulsion. She was the US Navy's only nuclear-powered guided missile submarine (SSGN) to be completed. Authorised in the Fiscal Year 1956 new construction programme and built for an estimated cost of $45 million.
She was reclassified as an attack submarine on 25 July 1965 after the Navy discarded the Regulus submarine-launched missile force. Her missile equipment was removed. Reportedly she has been fitted with a ducted bow thruster to permit precise control and manoeuvring. When active employed on research duties.
She can carry the 50-foot Deep Submergence Rescue Vehicle (DSRV) and other submersibles on her after deck and operate these while dived.
Decommissioned on 30 June 1976 and laid up at Bremerton.

Design: Built with a large missile hangar faired into her bow (see *picture*). Her hull was intended primarily to provide a stable surface launching platform rather than for speed or manoeuvrabilty.

Electronics: Mk 101 Mod 11 torpedo fire control system (removed 1977).

Missiles: Designed to carry two Regulus II surface-to-surface missiles. The Regulus II was a transonic missile which could carry a nuclear warhead and had a range of 1 000 miles. The Regulus II was cancelled before becoming operational and *Halibut* operated from 1960 to 1964 carrying five Regulus I missiles, subsonic cruise missiles which could deliver a nuclear warhead on targets 575 n miles from launch.
During this period the US Navy operated a maximum of five Regulus guided (cruise) missile submarines, *Halibut*, the post-war constructed *Grayback* (SSG 574 now SS 574) and *Growler* (SSG 577), and the World War II-built *Tunny* (SSG 282 subsequently LPSS 282) and *Barbero* (SSG 317).
As SSGN *Halibut* carried a complement of 11 officers and 108 enlisted men.

Navigation: Fitted with Ship's Inertial Navigation System (SINS).

Sonar: BQS-4.

HALIBUT　　　1970, USN

1 NUCLEAR POWERED SUBMARINE (SSN) "TRITON" CLASS

Name	No.	Builders	Laid down	Launched	Commissioned	F/S
TRITON	SSN 586 (ex-SSRN 586)	General Dynamics (Electric Boat)	29 May 1956	19 Aug 1958	10 Nov 1959	AR

Displacement, tons: 5 940 surfaced; 6 670 dived
Length, feet (metres): 447 *(136·2)* oa
Beam, feet (metres): 37 *(11·3)*
Draught, feet (metres): 24 *(7·3)*
Torpedo tubes: 6—21 in *(533 mm)* 4 bow; 2 stern (Mk 60)
Main machinery: 2 pressurised-water cooled S4G (General Electric) reactors; 2 steam turbines (General Electric); 34 000 shp; 2 shafts
Speed, knots: 27+ surfaced; 20+ dived
Complement as SSRN: 170 (14 officers, 156 enlisted men)

Triton was designed and constructed to serve as a radar picket submarine to operate in conjunction with surface carrier task forces.
Authorised in the Fiscal Year 1956 new construction programme and built for an estimated cost of $109 million.
Triton circumnavigated the globe in 1960, remaining submerged except when her sail structure broke the surface to enable an ill sailor to be taken off near the Falkland Islands. The 41 500-mile cruise took 83 days and was made at an average speed of 18 knots.
Reclassified as an attack submarine (SSN) on 1 March 1961 as the Navy dropped the radar picket submarine programme. She is no longer considered a "first line" submarine and was decommissioned on 3 May 1969 to become the first US nuclear submarine placed in preservation. Laid up at Norfolk.
There had been proposals to operate the *Triton* as an underwater national command post afloat, but no funds were provided.

Design: *Triton* was fitted with an elaborate combat information centre and large radar antenna which retracted into the sail structure. Until the Trident SSBN programme *Triton* was the longest US submarine ever constructed.

Electronics: Mk 101 Mod 11 torpedo fire control system.

Engineering: *Triton* is the only US submarine with two nuclear reactors. The Atomic Energy Commission's Knolls Atomic Power Laboratory was given prime responsibility for development of the power plant. After 2½ years of operation, during which she steamed more than 110 000 miles, *Triton* was overhauled and refuelled from July 1962 to March 1964.

Sonar: BQS-4.

TRITON　　　1959, USN

USA 637

4 NUCLEAR POWERED SUBMARINES (SSN) "SKATE" CLASS

Name	No.	Builders	Laid down	Launched	Commissioned	F/S
SKATE	SSN 578	General Dynamics (Electric Boat)	21 July 1955	16 May 1957	23 Dec 1957	AA
SWORDFISH	SSN 579	Portsmouth Naval Shipyard	25 Jan 1956	27 Aug 1957	15 Sept 1958	PA
SARGO	SSN 583	Mare Island Naval Shipyard	21 Feb 1956	10 Oct 1957	1 Oct 1958	PA
SEADRAGON	SSN 584	Portsmouth Naval Shipyard	20 June 1956	16 Aug 1958	5 Dec 1959	PA

Displacement, tons: 2 310 light; 2 360 full load (578-9); 2 384 light; 2 547 full load (583-4)
Length, feet (metres): 267·7 *(81·5)* oa
Beam, feet (metres): 25 *(7·6)*
Draught, feet (metres): 22 *(6·7)*
Torpedo tubes: 8—21 in *(533 mm)* 6 bow; 2 stern (short)
Main machinery: 1 pressurised-water cooled S3W (Westinghouse) reactor in *Skate* and *Sargo*, 1 pressurised-water cooled S4W (Westinghouse) in *Swordfish* and *Seadragon*; 2 steam turbines (Westinghouse); 6 600 shp; 2 shafts
Speed, knots: 20+ surfaced; 25+ dived
Complement: 87 (11 officers, 76 enlisted men)

The first production model nuclear-powered submarines, similar in design to *Nautilus* but smaller. *Skate* and *Swordfish* were authorised in the Fiscal Year 1955 new construction programme and *Sargo* and *Seadragon* in the FY 1956.
Skate was the first submarine to make a completely submerged transatlantic crossing. In 1958 she established a (then) record of 31 days submerged with a sealed atmosphere, on 11 Aug 1958 she passed under the North Pole during a polar cruise, and on 17 March 1959 she became the first submarine to surface at the North Pole. *Sargo* undertook a polar cruise during Jan-Feb 1960 and surfaced at the North Pole on 9 Feb 1960. *Seadragon* sailed from the Atlantic to the Pacific via the Northwest Passage (Lancaster Sound, Barrow and McClure Straits) in Aug 1960. *Skate*, operating from New London, Connecticut and *Seadragon*, based at Pearl Harbour, rendezvoused under the North Pole on 2 Aug 1962 and then conducted antisubmarine exercises under the polar ice pack and surfaced together at the North Pole.
Skate also operated in the Arctic Ocean during April-May 1969, conducting exercises under the Arctic ice pack with the later nuclear-powered attack submarines *Pargo* and *Whale*; and again during the spring of 1971 with the nuclear attack submarine *Trepang*.

Electronics: Fitted with Mk 101 Mod 19 torpedo fire control system.

Engineering: The reactors for this class were developed by the Atomic Energy Commission's Bettis Atomic Power Laboratory, the new propulsion system was similar to that of *Nautilus* but considerably simplified with improved operation and maintenance. The propulsion plant developed under this programme had two arrangements, the S3W configuration in *Skate*, *Sargo* and *Halibut* and the S4W configuration in *Swordfish* and *Seadragon*. Both arrangements proved satisfactory. *Skate* began her first overhaul and refuelling in January 1961 after steaming 120 862 miles on her initial reactor core during three years of operation. *Swordfish* began her first overhaul and refuelling in early 1962 after more than three years of operation in which time she steamed 112 000 miles.

Sonar: BQS-4.

SWORDFISH   *1970, USN*

1 NUCLEAR POWERED SUBMARINE (SSN) "SEAWOLF" CLASS

Name	No.	Builders	Laid down	Launched	Commissioned	F/S
SEAWOLF	SSN 575	General Dynamics (Electric Boat)	15 Sept 1953	21 July 1955	30 Mar 1957	PA

Displacement, tons: 3 765 surfaced; 4 200 dived
Length, feet (metres): 337·5 *(102·9)* oa
Beam, feet (metres): 27·7 *(8·4)*
Draught, feet (metres): 23 *(7)*
Torpedo tubes: 6—21 in *(533 mm)* bow
Main machinery: 1 pressurised-water cooled S2Wa (Westinghouse) reactor; 2 steam turbines (General Electric), 15 000 shp; 2 shafts
Speed, knots: 20+ surfaced; 20+ dived
Complement: 101 (11 officers, 90 enlisted men)

Seawolf was the world's second nuclear-propelled vehicle; she was constructed almost simultaneously with *Nautilus* to test a competitive reactor design. Funds for *Seawolf* were authorised in the Fiscal Year 1952 new construction programme.
She is no longer considered a "first line" submarine and has been engaged primarily in research work since 1969.

Design: GUPPY-type hull with stepped sail.

Electronics: Mk 101 Mod 8 torpedo fire control system.

Engineering: Initial work in the development of naval nuclear propulsion plants investigated a number of concepts, two of which were of sufficient interest to warrant full development: the pressurised water and liquid metal (sodium). *Nautilus* was provided with a pressurised-water reactor plant and *Seawolf* was fitted initially with a liquid-metal reactor. Originally known as the Submarine Intermediate Reactor (SIR), the liquid-metal plant was developed by the Atomic Energy Commission's Knolls Atomic Power Laboratory.
The SIR Mark II/S2G reactor in *Seawolf* achieved initial criticality on 25 June 1956. Steam leaks developed during the dockside testing. The plant was shut down and it was determined that the leaks were caused by sodium-potassium alloy which had entered the super-heater steam piping. After repairs and testing *Seawolf* began sea trials on 21 Jan 1957. The trials were run at reduced power and after two years of operation *Seawolf* entered the Electric Boat yard for removal of her sodium-cooled plant and installation of a pressurised-water plant similar to that installed in *Nautilus* (designated S2Wa). When the original *Seawolf* plant was shut down in Dec 1958 the submarine had steamed a total of 71 611 miles. She was recommissioned on 30 Sept 1960. The pressurised-water reactor was refuelled for the first time between May 1965 and Aug 1967, having propelled *Seawolf* for more than 161 000 miles on its initial fuel core.

Sonar: BQS-4.

SEAWOLF   *1974, William Whalen, Jr.*

638 USA

1 NUCLEAR POWERED SUBMARINE (SSN) "NAUTILUS" CLASS

Name	No.	Builders	Laid down	Launched	Commissioned	F/S
NAUTILUS	SSN 571	General Dynamics (Electric Boat)	14 June 1952	21 Jan 1954	30 Sept 1954	AA

Displacement, tons: 3 764 surfaced; 4 040 dived
Length, feet (metres): 319·4 *(97·4)*
Beam, feet (metres): 27·6 *(8·4)*
Draught, feet (metres): 22 *(6·7)*
Torpedo tubes: 6—21 in *(533 mm)* bow (Mk 50)
Main machinery: 1 pressurised-water cooled S2W (Westinghouse) reactor; 2 steam turbines (Westinghouse), approx 15 000 shp; 2 shafts
Speed, knots: 20+ surfaced; 20+ dived
Complement: 105 (13 officers, 92 enlisted men)

Nautilus was the world's first nuclear-propelled vehicle. She predated the first Soviet nuclear-powered submarine by an estimated five years.
The funds for her construction were authorised in the Fiscal Year 1952 budget. She put to sea for the first time on 17 Jan 1955 and signalled the historic message: "Underway on nuclear power".
On her shakedown cruise in May 1955 she steamed submerged from London, Connecticut, to San Juan, Puerto Rico, travelling more than 1 300 miles in 84 hours at an average speed of almost 16 knots; she later steamed submerged from Key West, Florida, to New London, a distance of 1 397 miles, at an average speed of more than 20 knots.
During 1958 she undertook extensive operations under the Arctic ice pack and in August she made history's first polar transit from the Pacific to the Atlantic, steaming from Pearl Harbour to Portland, England. She passed under the geographic North Pole on 3 Aug 1958.
During 1972-74 she underwent a 30-month overhaul and modification at the Electric Boat yard in Groton, Connecticut, where the submarine was built. Modified for submarine communications research. Due to decommission in the FY 1979.

Electronics: Mk 101 Mod 6 torpedo fire control system.

Engineering: In Jan 1948 the Department of Defense requested the Atomic Energy Commission to undertake the design, development, and construction of a nuclear reactor for submarine propulsion. Initial research and conceptual design of the Submarine Thermal Reactor (STR) was undertaken by the Argonne National Laboratory. Subsequently the Atomic Energy Commission's Bettis Atomic Power Laboratory, operated by the Westinghouse Electric Corporation, undertook development of the first nuclear propulsion plant.
Nautilus STR Mark II nuclear plant (redesignated S2W) was first operated on 20 Dec 1954 and first developed full power on 3 Jan 1955.
After more than two years of operation, during which she steamed 62 562 miles, she began an overhaul which included refuelling in April 1957. She was again refuelled in 1959 after steaming 91 324 miles on her second fuel core, and again in 1964 after steaming approximately 150 000 miles on her third fuel core.

Sonar: BQS-4.

NAUTILUS 1975, General Dynamics, Electric Boat Division

NAUTILUS 1975, General Dynamics, Electric Boat Division

3 SUBMARINES (SS) "BARBEL" CLASS

Name	No.	Builders	Laid down	Launched	Commissioned	F/S
BARBEL	SS 580	Portsmouth Naval Shipyard	18 May 1956	19 July 1958	17 Jan 1959	PA
BLUEBACK	SS 581	Ingalls Shipbuilding Corp	15 April 1957	16 May 1959	15 Oct 1959	PA
BONEFISH	SS 582	New York Shipbuilding Corp	3 June 1957	22 Nov 1958	9 July 1959	PA

Displacement, tons: 2 145 surfaced; 2 894 dived
Length, feet (metres): 219·1 *(66·8)* oa
Beam, feet (metres): 29 *(8·8)*
Draught, feet (metres): 28 *(8·5)*
Torpedo tubes: 6—21 in *(533 mm)* bow (Mk 58)
Main machinery: 3 diesels; 4 800 bhp (Fairbanks-Morse); 2 electric motors (General Electric); 3 150 shp; 1 shaft
Speed, knots: 15 surfaced; 21 dived
Complement: 77 (8 officers, 69 men)

These submarines were the last non-nuclear combatant submarines built by the US Navy. All three were authorised in the Fiscal Year 1956 new construction programme.

Construction: *Blueback* was the first submarine built by the Ingalls Shipbuilding Corp at Pascagoula, Mississippi, and *Bonefish* was the first constructed at the New York Shipbuilding Corp yard in Camden, New Jersey. None of the three shipyards that built this class is now employed in submarine construction.

Design: These submarines have the "tear drop" hull design which was tested in the experimental submarine *Albacore*. As built, their fore planes were bow-mounted; subsequently moved to the sail.
They introduced a new concept in centralised arrangement of controls in an "attack centre" to increase efficiency; which has been adapted for all later US combat submarines.

Electronics: Mk 101 Mod 20 torpedo fire control system.

Sonar: BQS-4.

BLUEBACK 1967, USN

1 GUIDED MISSILE SUBMARINE (SSG) "GRAYBACK" CLASS

Name	No.	Builders	Laid down	Launched	Commissioned	F/S
GROWLER	SSG 577	Portsmouth Naval Shipyard	15 Feb 1955	5 April 1958	30 Aug 1958	PR

Displacement, tons: 2 540 standard; 3 515 dived
Length, feet (metres): 317·6 *(96·8)* oa
Beam, feet (metres): 27·2 *(8·2)*
Draught, feet (metres): 19 *(5·8)*
Torpedo tubes: 6—21 in *(533 mm)* 4 bow; 2 stern
Main machinery: 3 diesels (Fairbanks-Morse); 4 600 bhp; 2 electric motors (Elliott); 5 500 shp; 2 shafts
Speed, knots: 20 surfaced; 17 dived
Complement: 87 (9 officers, 78 enlisted men)

Growler was authorised in the Fiscal Year 1955 new construction programme; completed as a guided missile submarine to fire the Regulus surface-to-surface cruise missile (see *Halibut*, SSN 587, for *Missile* notes).

When the Regulus submarine missile programme ended in 1964, *Growler* and her near-sister *Grayback* were withdrawn from service, *Growler* being decommissioned on 25 May 1964. *Grayback* was subsequently converted to an amphibious transport submarine (LPSS). *Growler* was scheduled to undergo a similar conversion when *Grayback* was completed, but the second conversion was deferred late in 1968 because of rising ship conversion costs.

Growler is in reserve at Bremerton.

Design: *Grayback* and *Growler* were initially designed as attack submarines of the "Darter" class. Upon redesign as missile submarines they were cut in half on the building ways and were lengthened approximately 50 feet, two cylindrical hangars, each 11 feet high and 70 feet long, were superimposed on their bows, a missile launcher was installed between the hangars and sail structure, and elaborate navigation and fire control systems were fitted. The height of the sail structure on *Growler* is approximately 30 feet above the deck; *Grayback's* lower sail structure was increased during LPSS conversion.

Electronics: Mk 106 Mod 13 torpedo fire control system.

Sonar: BQS-4.

GROWLER   1958, USN

1 SUBMARINE (SS, ex-LPSS) "GRAYBACK" CLASS

Name	No.	Builders	Laid down	Launched	Commissioned	F/S
GRAYBACK	SS 574 (ex-LPSS 574, ex-SSG 574)	Mare Island Naval Shipyard	1 July 1954	2 July 1957	7 Mar 1958	PA

Displacement, tons: 2 670 standard; 3 650 dived
Length, feet (metres): 334 *(101·8)* oa
Beam, feet (metres): 27 *(8·2)*
Draught, feet (metres): 19 *(5·8)*
Torpedo tubes: 8—21 in *(533 mm)* 6 bow (Mk 52); 2 stern (Mk 53)
Main machinery: 3 diesels (Fairbanks-Morse); 4 500 bhp; 2 electric motors (Elliott); 5 500 shp; 2 shafts
Speed, knots: 20 surfaced; 16·7 dived
Complement: 89 (12 officers, 77 enlisted men)
Troops: 67 (7 officers, 60 enlisted men)

Grayback has been fully converted to a transport submarine of the "Darter" Class. She was originally intended to be an attack submarine, being authorised in the Fiscal Year 1953 new construction programme, but redesigned in 1956 to provide a Regulus missile launching capability; completed as SSG 574 in 1958, similar in design to *Growler* (SSG 577). See *Growler* listing above for basic design notes.

Classification: *Grayback* was reclassified as an attack submarine (SS) on 30 June 1975 although she retains her transport configuration and capabilities. The reclassification was an administrative change associated with funding support.

Conversion: She began conversion to a transport submarine at Mare Island in Nov 1967. The conversion was originally estimated at $15·2 million but was actually about $30 million. She was reclassified from SSG to LPSS on 30 Aug 1968 (never officially designated APSS).

During conversion she was fitted to berth and mess 67 troops and carry their equipment including landing craft or swimmer delivery vehicles (SDV). Her torpedo tubes and hence attack capability are retained. As completed (SSG) she had an overall length of 322 feet 4 inches; lengthened 12 feet during LPSS conversion. Conversion was authorised in the Fiscal Year 1965 programme and completed with her new commissioning on 9 May 1969; delayed because of higher priorities being allocated to other submarine projects.

Electronics: Mk 106 Mod 12 torpedo fire control system.

Sonar: BQS-2; BQS-4 (PUFFS).

GRAYBACK   1975, USN

640 USA

1 SUBMARINE (SS) "DARTER" CLASS

Name	No.	Builders	Laid down	Launched	Commissioned	F/S
DARTER	SS 576	General Dynamics (Electric Boat)	10 Nov 1954	28 May 1956	26 Oct 1956	PA

Displacement, tons: 1 720 surfaced; 2 388 dived
Length, feet (metres): 284·5 *(86·7)*
Beam, feet (metres): 27·2 *(8·3)*
Draught, feet (metres): 19 *(5·8)*
Torpedo tubes: 8—21 in *(533 mm)* 6 bow; 2 stern
Main machinery: 3 diesels (Fairbanks-Morse); 4 500 bhp; electric motors (Elliott); 5 500 shp; 2 shafts
Speed, knots: 19·5 surfaced; 14 dived
Complement: 83 (8 officers, 75 men)

Designed for high submerged speed with quiet machinery. Planned sister submarines *Growler* and *Grayback* were completed to missile-launching configuration.
Basic design of *Darter* is similar to the "Tang" class described later.
Authorised in the Fiscal Year 1954 shipbuilding programme. No additional submarines of this type were built because of shift to high-speed hull design and nuclear propulsion.

Electronics: Mk 106 Mod 11 torpedo fire control system.

Sonar: BQG-4 (PUFFS).

DARTER   1967, Dr. Giorgio Arra

1 SUBMARINE (SS) "SAILFISH" CLASS

Name	No.	Builders	Laid down	Launched	Commissioned
SAILFISH	SS 572 (ex-SSR 572)	Portsmouth Naval Shipyard	8 Dec 1953	7 Sept 1955	14 April 1956

Displacement, tons: 2 625 standard; 3 168 dived
Length, feet (metres): 350·4 *(106·8)* oa
Beam, feet (metres): 28·4 *(8·8)*
Draught, feet (metres): 18 *(5·5)*
Torpedo tubes: 6—21 in *(533 mm)* Mk 49 bow
Main machinery: 4 diesels (Fairbanks-Morse); 6 000 bhp; 2 electric motors (Elliott); 8 200 shp; 2 shafts
Speed, knots: 19·5 surfaced; 14 submerged
Complement: 108 (12 officers, 96 enlisted men)

Sailfish (with *Salmon*) was built as radar picket submarine (SSR) with air search radars on and elaborate aircraft control centre. Subsequently modified for "straight" attack operations. The largest non-nuclear submarines built by the US Navy since 1930 and believed to be the largest conventional submarine now operated by any navy.
Authorised in the Fiscal Year 1952 programme; modernised under the FRAM II programme.
Salmon deleted in late 1977. *Sailfish* for deletion 30 Sept 1978.

Classification: Reclassified from radar picket submarine (SSR) to SS on 1 March 1961.

Electronics: Mk 106 Mod 21 torpedo fire control system.

Sonar: BQG-4 (PUFFS).

SAILFISH   6/1974, USN

3 SUBMARINES (SS) / 1 AUXILIARY SUBMARINE (AGSS) "TANG" CLASS

Name	No.	Builders	Laid down	Launched	Commissioned	F/S
TANG	AGSS 563	Portsmouth Naval Shipyard	18 April 1949	19 June 1951	25 Oct 1951	PA
WAHOO	SS 565	Portsmouth Naval Shipyard	24 Oct 1949	16 Oct 1951	30 May 1952	PA
TROUT	SS 566	Electric Boat Co, Groton	1 Dec 1949	21 Aug 1951	27 June 1952	PA
GUDGEON	SS 567	Portsmouth Naval Shipyard	20 May 1950	11 June 1952	21 Nov 1952	PA

Displacement, tons: 2 050 standard; 2 700 dived
Length, feet (metres): 287 *(87·4)* oa
Beam, feet (metres): 27·3 *(8·3)*
Draught, feet (metres): 19 *(6·2)*
Torpedo tubes: 8—21 in *(533 mm)* 6 bow; 2 stern
Main machinery: 3 diesels (Fairbanks-Morse); 4 500 bhp; 2 electric motors; 5 600 shp; 2 shafts
Speed, knots: 15·5 surfaced; 16 dived
Complement: 83 (8 officers, 75 men)

Six submarines of this class were constructed, incorporating improvements based on German World War II submarine developments. *Tang* was authorised in the Fiscal Year 1947 new construction programme, *Wahoo* and *Trout* in the FY 1948, and *Gudgeon* in the FY 1949. *Gudgeon* was the first US submarine to circumnavigate the world during Sept 1957-Feb 1958. All modernised under FRAM II programme.

Classification: *Tang* was reclassified as a research submarine (AGSS) on 30 June 1975 for use in acoustic research.

Electronics: Mk 106 Mod 18 torpedo fire control system.

Sonar: BQG-4 (PUFFS).

Transfers: *Trigger* (SS 564) transferred to Italy on 10 July 1973; *Harder* (SS 568) transferred to Italy on 15 March 1974.
(These were the first US submarines of past-World War II construction to be transferred to foreign navies).
Tang, *Wahoo* and *Trout* to be transferred to Iran. When this takes place *Gudgeon* will replace *Tang* as AGSS.

GUDGEON   1970, USN

1 AUXILIARY SUBMARINE (AGSS) "ALBACORE" CLASS

Name	No.	Builders	Laid down	Launched	Commissioned	F/S
ALBACORE	AGSS 569	Portsmouth Naval Shipyard	15 Mar 1952	1 Aug 1953	5 Dec 1953	AR

Displacement, tons: 1 500 standard; 1 850 dived
Length, feet (metres): 204 *(62·2)*
Beam, feet (metres): 22 *(6·7)*
Draught, feet (metres): 18·5 *(5·6)*
Torpedo tubes: None
Main machinery: 2 diesels; radial pancake type (General Motors) electric motor (Westinghouse) 15 000 shp; 1 shaft
Speed, knots: 25 surfaced; 33 dived
Complement: 54 (5 officers, 49 men)

Built as a high-speed experimental submarine to test an advanced hull form. Officially described as a hydrodynamic test vehicle. Streamlined, whale shaped hull without casing.

Decommissioned and placed in reserve on 1 Sept 1972 at Philadelphia.

Experimental: She has been extensively modified to test advanced submarine design and engineering concepts.
Phase I modifications were made from July 1954 to Feb 1955 to eliminate the many bugs inherent with completely new construction and equipment.
Phase II modifications from Dec 1955 to March 1956 during which conventional propeller-rudder-stern diving plane arrangement was modified; the new design provided for the propeller to be installed aft of the control surfaces. (At this time a small auxiliary rudder on the sail was removed).

A concave bow sonar dome was fitted for tests in 1960. Phase III modifications from Nov 1960 to Aug 1961 during which an entirely new stern was installed featuring the stern planes in an "X" configuration, a system of ten hydraulic operated dive brakes around the hull amidships, a dorsal rudder, and a new bow sonar dome. Phase IV modifications from Dec 1962 to Mar 1965 during which a silver-zinc battery was installed and counter-rotating stern propellers rotating around the same axis were fitted.
Albacore conducted trials with towed sonar arrays from May to July 1966.
All modifications were made at the Portsmouth Naval Shipyard.

ALBACORE USN

1 AUXILIARY SUBMARINE (AGSS) "DOLPHIN" CLASS

Name	No.	Builders	Laid down	Launched	Commissioned	F/S
DOLPHIN	AGSS 555	Portsmouth Naval Shipyard	9 Nov 1962	8 June 1968	17 Aug 1968	PA

Displacement, tons: 800 standard; 930 full load
Length, feet (metres): 152 *(46·3)*
Beam, feet (metres): 19·3 *(5·9)*
Draught, feet (metres): 18 *(5·5)* (maximum)
Torpedo tubes: Removed
Main machinery: Diesel-electric (2 Detroit 12 V71 diesels), 1 650 hp; 1 shaft
Speed, knots: 15+ dived
Complement: 22 (7 officers, 15 enlisted men) plus 4 to 7 scientists

Specifically designed for deep-diving operations. Authorised in the Fiscal Year 1961 new construction programme but delayed because of changes in mission and equipment coupled with higher priorities being given to other submarine projects. Fitted for deep-ocean sonar and oceanographic research. She is highly automated and has three computer-operated systems, a safety system, hovering system, and one that is classified. The digital-computer submarine safety system monitors equipment and provides data on closed-circuit television screens; malfunctions in equipment set off an alarm and if they are not corrected within the prescribed time the system, unless overridden by an operator, automatically brings the submarine to the surface. There are several research stations for scientists and she is fitted to take water samples down to her operating depth.
Underwater endurance is limited (endurance and habitability were considered of secondary importance in design).

Assigned to Submarine Development Group 1 at San Diego.

Design: Has a constant diameter cylindrical pressure hull approximately 15 feet in outer diameter closed at both ends with hemispherical heads. Pressure hull fabricated of HY-80 steel with aluminium and fibre-glass used in secondary structures to reduce weight. No conventional hydroplanes are mounted, improved rudder design and other features provide manoeuvring control and hovering capability.

Engineering: Fitted with 330 cell silver-zinc battery. Submerged endurance is approximately 24 hours with an at-sea endurance of 14 days.

DOLPHIN USN

GUPPY SUBMARINES

All 52 submarines modernised to the GUPPY (Greater Underwater Propulsion Project) configurations have been deleted or transferred to other navies. The last GUPPY submarines to serve with the US Navy were *Clamagore* (SS 343) deleted on 27 June 1975 and *Tiru* (SS 416) deleted on 1 July 1975. They were not transferred to Turkey, as planned, but are still awaiting transfer in 1978.
Corrections to the comprehensive list of GUPPY submarine disposals and transfers provided in the 1974-75 edition include: *Blenny* (SS 324) deleted on 15 Aug 1973 (sunk as target); *Sea Poacher* (SS 406) transferred to Peru on 1 July 1974; *Atule* (SS 403) transferred to Peru on 31 July 1974. *Tench* (SS 417) to Peru 16 Sept 1976 for spares.

DEEP SUBMERGENCE VEHICLES

The US Navy operates several deep submergence vehicles for scientific, military research, and operational military missions. The US Navy acquired its first deep submergence vehicle with the purchase of the bathyscaph *Trieste* in 1958. *Trieste* was designed and constructed by Professor Auguste Piccard. The US Navy sponsored research dives in the Mediterranean Sea with *Trieste* in 1957 after which the bathyscaph was purchased outright and brought to the United States.

Trieste reached a record depth of 35 800 feet *(10 910 metres)* in the Challenger Deep off the Marianas on 23 Jan 1960, being piloted by Lieutenant Don Walsh, USN, and Jacques Piccard (son of Auguste). Rebuilt and designated *Trieste II*, the craft was subsequently used in the search for wreckage of the nuclear-powered submarine *Thresher* (SSN 593) which was lost in 1963 and *Scorpion* (SSN 589) lost in 1968.

After the loss of *Thresher* the US Navy initiated an extensive deep submergence programme that led to construction of two Deep Submergence Rescue Vehicles (DSRV); however, other vehicles proposed in the recommended programme were not built because of a lack of interest, changing operational concepts, and funding limitations.

Several of these deep submergence vehicles and other craft and support ships are operated by Submarine Development Group One at San Diego, California. The Group is a major operational command that includes advanced diving equipment; divers trained in "saturation" techniques; the DSVs *Trieste II*, *Turtle*, *Sea Cliff*, DSRV-1, DSRV-2; the submarine *Dolphin* (AGSS 555); several submarine rescue ships.

The hull of the original *Trieste* and Krupp sphere are in the Navy Yard in Washington, DC.

NUCLEAR POWERED RESEARCH VEHICLE: PROPOSED ("NR-2" Class)

A second nuclear-powered submersible research vehicle has been proposed by Admiral H. G. Rickover, Deputy Commander for Nuclear Propulsion, Naval Sea Systems Command. The craft would have a greater depth capability than the NR-1 (described below) and would employ a nuclear plant similar to that of the earlier craft. The vehicle would have a pressure hull of HY-130 steel.

Reportedly, Admiral Rickover began development of the so-called "NR-2" in 1971. The term HTV for Hull Test Vehicle also has been used for this vehicle, reportedly to avoid critical association with the NR-1 programme.

Estimated construction time would be 2½ years; however, construction has not yet been approved. To be built of HY 130 steel reportedly at General Electric, Electric Boat Division. Unofficial estimates of construction costs ranged to more than $300 million in the Fiscal Year 1975 funding. At the beginning of 1978 construction had been stalled owing to financial problems.

1 NUCLEAR POWERED OCEAN ENGINEERING AND RESEARCH VEHICLE

Name	Builders	F/S
NR 1	General Dynamics (Electric Boat), Groton	AA

Displacement, tons: 400 submerged
Length, feet (metres): 136·4 oa × 12·4 × 14·6 *(41·6 × 3·8 × 4·5)*
Diameter, feet (metre): 12 *(3·7)*
Machinery: Electric motors; 2 propellers; four ducted thrusters
Reactor: 1 pressurised-water cooled
Complement: 7 (2 officers, 3 enlisted men, 2 scientists)

NR 1 was built primarily to serve as a test platform for a small nuclear propulsion plant; however, the craft additionally provides an advanced deep submergence ocean engineering and research capability. Vice-Admiral Rickover conceived and initiated NR 1 in 1964-65 (the craft was not proposed in a Navy research or shipbuilding budget).

Laid down on 10 June 1967; launched on 25 Jan 1969; placed in service 27 Oct 1969. Commanded by an officer-in-charge vice commanding officer. First nuclear-propelled service craft. Describing the craft Admiral Rickover has stated: "The (NR 1) will be able to perform detailed studies and mapping of the ocean bottom, temperature, currents, and other oceanographic parameters for military, commercial, and scientific use. The submarine (NR 1) will have viewing ports for visual observation of its surroundings and the ocean bottom. In addition, a remote grapple will be installed to permit collection of marine samples and other items. With its depth capability, the NR 1 is expected to be capable of exploring areas of the Continental Shelf.

Construction: Originally costed at $30 million in March 1965. During detailed design of NR 1 the Navy determined that improved equipment had to be developed and a larger hull than originally planned would be required. Consequently, in July 1967 the Navy obtained Congressional approval to proceed with construction of NR 1 at an estimated cost of $58·03 million. The final estimated ship construction cost at time of launching was $67 million plus $19·9 million for oceanographic equipment and sensors, and $11·8 million for research and development (mainly related to the nuclear propulsion plant), for a total estimated cost of $99·2 million.

Design: The NR 1 is fitted with wheels beneath the hull to permit "bottom crawling". This will obviate the necessity of hovering while exploring the ocean floor. Submarine wheels, a concept proposed as early as the first decade of this century by submarine inventor Simon Lake, were tested in the small submarine *Mackerel* (SST 1).

The NR 1 is fitted with external lights, external television cameras, a remote-controlled manipulator, and various recovery devices. No periscopes, but fixed television mast. Credited with a 30 day endurance, but limited habitability makes missions of only a few days feasible. Reportedly, a surface "mother" ship is required to support the NR 1.

Engineering: The NR-1 reactor plant was designed by the Atomic Energy Commission's Knolls Atomic Power Laboratory. She is propelled by two propellers driven by electric motors outside the pressure hull with power provided by a turbine generator within the pressure hull. Four ducted thrusters, two horizontal and two vertical, are provided for precise manoeuvring.

NR 1 — *1969, General Dynamics, Electric Boat*

NR 1 — *1969, General Dynamics, Electric Boat*

2 DEEP SUBMERGENCE RESCUE VEHICLES

No.	Builders	F/S
DSRV 1	Lockheed Missiles and Space Co	PSA
DSRV 2	(Sunnyvale, Calif)	ASA

Weight in air, tons: 32
Length, feet (metres): 49·2 oa *(15·0)*
Diameter, feet (metres): 8 *(2·4)*
Propulsion: Electric motors, propeller mounted in control shroud and four ducted thrusters
Speed, knots: 5 (maximum)
Endurance: 12 hours at 3 knots
Operating depth, feet (metres): 5 000 *(1 525)*
Complement: 3 (pilot, co-pilot, rescue sphere operator) +24 rescued men

The Deep Submergence Rescue Vehicle is intended to provided a quick-reaction world-wide, all-weather capability for the rescue of survivors in a disabled submarine. The DSRV is transportable by road, aircraft (in C 141 and C 5 jet cargo aircraft), surface ship (on "Pigeon" ASR 21 class submarine rescue ships), and specially modified submarines (SSN type).

The operational effectiveness of the craft is limited severely by the lack of large numbers of ships and submarines that air transport and support the craft. They will be used for the forseeable future for evaluation and research.

The carrying submarine will launch and recover the DSRV while submerged and, if necessary, while under ice. A total of six DSRVs were planned, but only two were funded. DSRV-1 was placed in service 7 Aug 1971 and DSRV-2 on 7 Aug 1972. DSRV-1 activated for rescue duty on 4 Nov 1977 and DSRV-2 on 1 Jan 1978. They will alternate their duties every two months.

Cost: The construction cost for the DSRV-1 was $41 million and for the DSRV-2 $23 million. The development, construction, test, and support of both vehicles through the Fiscal Year 1975 was $220 million. This expenditure includes the design and construction, research, spares and training.

Design: The DSRV outer hull is constructed of formed fibreglass. Within this outer hull are three interconnected spheres which form the main pressure capsule. Each sphere is 7·5 feet in diameter and is constructed of HY-140 steel. The forward sphere contains the vehicle's control equipment and is manned by the pilot and co-pilot, the centre and after spheres accommodate 24 passengers and a third crewman. Under the DSRVs centre sphere is a hemispherical protrusion or "skirt" which seals over the disabled submarine's hatch. During the mating operation the skirt is pumped dry to enable personnel to transfer.

Electronics: Elaborate search and navigational sonar, and closed-circuit television (supplemented by optical devices) are installed in the DSRV to determine the exact location of a disabled submarine within a given area and for pinpointing the submarine's escape hatches. Side-looking sonar can be fitted for search missions.

USA 643

Engineering: Propulsion and control of the DSRV are achieved by a stern propeller in a movable control shroud and four ducted thrusters, two forward and two aft. These, plus a mercury trim system, permit the DSRV to manoeuvre and hover with great precision and to mate with submarines lying at angles up to 45 degrees from the horizontal. An elaborate Integrated Control and Display (ICAD) system employs computers to present sensor data to the pilots and transmit their commands to the vehicle's control and propulsion system.

Names: Unofficially named *Avalon* (DSRV 1) and *Mystic* (DSRV 2).

DSRV 1 on HAWKBILL (SSN 666)   1971, USN

2 DEEP SUBMERGENCE VEHICLES: MODIFIED "ALVIN" TYPE

Name	No.	Builders	F/S
TURTLE (ex-*Autec II*)	DSV 3	General Dynamics (Electric Boat), Groton, Conn	PA
SEA CLIFF (ex-*Autec I*)	DSV 4	General Dynamics (Electric Boat), Groton, Conn	PSA

Weight, tons: 21
Length, feet (metres): 25 oa *(7·6)*
Beam, feet (metres): 8 *(2·4)*
Propulsion: Electric motors, trainable stern propeller; 2 rotating propeller pods
Speed, knots: 2·5
Endurance: 8 hours at 2 knots
Operating depth, feet (metres): 6 500 *(1 980)*
Complement: 2 (pilot, observer)

Intended for deep submergence research and work tasks. Designated *Autec I* and *Autec II* during construction, but assigned above names in dual launching on 11 Dec 1968.
Designated DSV 4 and DSV 3, respectively, on 1 June 1971 when they were placed in service. DSV 3 placed in commission (miscellaneous) in Jan 1973 and DSV 4 placed in service (miscellaneous) in the same month.

Construction: Three pressure spheres were fabricated for the *Alvin* submersible programme, one for installation in *Alvin*, a spare, and one for testing. The second and third spheres subsequently were allocated to these later submersibles.

Design: Twin-arm manipulator fitted to each submersible. Propulsion by stern propeller and two smaller, manoeuvring propeller "pods" on sides of vehicles; no thrusters.

SEA CLIFF   USN

1 DEEP SUBMERGENCE VEHICLE: "ALVIN" TYPE

Name	No.	Builders	F/S
ALVIN	DSV 2	General Mills Inc, Minneapolis, Minn	PSA

Weight, tons: 16
Length, feet (metres): 22·5 oa *(6·9)*
Beam, feet (metres): 8·5 *(2·6)*
Propulsion: Electric motors; trainable stern propeller; 2 rotating propeller pods
Speed, knots: 2
Endurance: 8 hours at 1 knot
Operating depth, feet (metres): 12 000 *(3 658)*
Complement: 3 (1 pilot, 2 observers)

Alvin was built for operation by the Woods Hole Oceanographic Institution for the Office of Naval Research. Original configuration had an operating depth of 6 000 feet. Named for Allyn C. Vine of Woods Hole Oceanographic Institution.
Alvin accidentally sank in 5 051 feet of water on 16 Oct 1968; subsequently raised in Aug 1969; refurbished 1970-71 in essentially original configuration. Placed in service on Navy List 1 June 1971. Subsequently refitted with titanium pressure sphere to provide increased depth capability and again operational in Nov 1973.

ALVIN   1974

1 DEEP SUBMERGENCE VEHICLE: "TRIESTE" TYPE

Name	No.	F/S
TRIESTE II	DSV 1 (ex-X-2)	PSA

Weight, tons: 84
Displacement, tons: 303 submerged
Length, feet (metres): 78·6 *(24·0)*
Beam, feet (metres): 15·3 *(4·7)*
Propulsion: Electric motors, 3 propellers aft, ducted thruster forward (see *Design* notes)
Speed, knots: 2
Endurance: 10-12 hours at 2 knots
Operating depth, feet (metres): 12 000 *(3 658)* (see *Design* notes)
Complement: 3 (2 operators, 1 observer)

Trieste II is the successor to *Trieste I* which the US Navy purchased in 1958 from Professor Auguste Piccard. The original *Trieste* was built at Castellammare, Italy; launched on 1 Aug 1953. The vehicle is operated by Submarine Development Group One at San Diego, California, and is used primarily as a test bed for underwater equipment and to train deep submergence vehicle operators (hydronauts).
Designated as a "submersible craft" and assigned the designation X-2 on 1 Sept 1969; subsequently changed to DSV 1 on 1 June 1971. Placed in service, (miscellaneous) Jan 1973.
Used in location of wreckage of *Scorpion* and *Thresher*.

Design: *Trieste II* is essentially a large float with a small pressure sphere attached to the underside. The float, which is filled with aviation petrol, provides buoyancy. Designed operating depth is 20 000 feet but dives have been limited to approximately 12 000 feet. (The record-setting Challenger Deep dive was made with a Krupp sphere which has a virtually unlimited depth capability).
Trieste II was built at the Mare Island Naval Shipyard in Sept 1965-Aug 1966 with a modified float, pressure sphere, propulsion system, and mission equipment being fitted. In the broadside view the sphere is now largely hidden by protective supports to keep the sphere clear of the welldeck when the craft rests in a floating dry dock.
Fitted with external television cameras and mechanical manipulator; computerised digital navigation system installed.

TRIESTE II   1970, USN

Transfers: The 600-foot capability *Nemo* DSV 5 is on loan to the Southwest Research Institute, San Antonio, Texas, since 1974.

644 USA

AIRCRAFT CARRIERS

The US Navy currently operates 13 aircraft carriers: ten ships of post-World War II construction (including three nuclear powered) and two "Midway" class ships completed shortly after the war. In addition, an obsolescent "Intrepid" class ship serves as a training carrier.

One additional nuclear carrier is under construction, *Carl Vinson* (CVN 70), to commission in 1981.

With the ever increasing size and costs of aircraft carriers, alternative designs to the "Nimitz" class have been sought to maintain a planned force level of 12 carriers beyond the mid-1980s when the first of the "Forrestal" class nears the end of its service life. Among the alternatives discussed was a concept known as "CVNX". A Navy study group, at the request of the then Secretary of Defense, James R. Schlesinger, was formed and directed to examine the feasibility of constructing "medium" size aircraft carriers of approx 50 000 tons standard displacement as an alternative to the "Nimitz" class. The group submitted its report in Jan 1976. Known collectively as the "CVNX" concept, it proposed three designs for further development (see 1976-77 edition of Jane's, page 560, bottom for further details). This concept was later discarded. The current planned procurement of a fourth "Nimitz" class (CVN 71), for which long term lead items were requested under FY 1977, has been held in abeyance while alternatives to this class are investigated. As of 1978 the choice has narrowed to the new Medium-sized Aircraft Carrier (CVV) or at least two more "Nimitz" class (CVN).

Air Wings: Each large aircraft carrier (CV/CVN) normally operates an air wing of some 85 to 95 aircraft: two fighter squadrons of 24 F-4 Phantom or F-14 Tomcats; two light attack squadrons of 24 A-7 Corsairs; one medium attack squadron of 12 A-6 Intruders; one anti-submarine squadron of 10 S-3 Viking aircraft; one A/S squadron of 8 SH-3 Sea King helicopters; and smaller squadrons or detachments of 3 RA-5C Vigilante reconnaissance aircraft, 4 EA-6B Prowler electronic warfare aircraft, 4 KA-6 Intruder tankers, and 4 E-2 Hawkeye early-warning/control aircraft.

The "Midway" class carriers cannot accommodate the full wing described above, and normally would not operate the Vigilante and Viking aircraft.

The carriers generally also embark a Carrier On-board Delivery (COD) aircraft in addition to the air wing.

Classification: From 1972 onward attack aircraft carriers (CVA) were reclassified as aircraft carriers (CV) upon being fitted with anti-submarine control centres and facilities to support A/S aircraft and helicopters (in addition to fighter/attack aircraft). The muti-purpose configuration was dictated by the phasing out of dedicated anti-submarine aircraft carriers (CVS), the last being decommissioned in 1974.

All active ships still classified as attack aircraft carriers (CVA/CVAN) on 30 June 1975 were changed to CV/CVN regardless of their ability to support anti-submarine aircraft.

Service Life Extension Programme (SLEP): While the new CVVs are being designed and constructed, beginning with the FY 1980 programme, the Carrier Service Life Extension Programme (SLEP) will be initiated. Each carrier, beginning with *Saratoga* (CV 60), will undergo a two year modernisation and overhaul which is designed to extend each ship's life by 10-15 years. The chart below shows the long term implications of the SLEP programme. Also shown are the projected retirement dates of the ships after they have been through the SLEP programme as well as the two remaining "Midway" class ships.

The US Navy's long-range plan provides for 14 or 15 CV/CVN aircraft carriers plus 8 VSTOL support ships. It is considered unlikely that the former force level can be achieved.

Training Carrier: The "Intrepid" class carrier *Lexington* (CVT 16) operates as a training ship and is based at Pensacola, Florida. The ship has no aircraft maintenance or arming capabilities, and is not considered as a combat ship. In an emergency, aircraft could be embarked on a very restricted operational basis.

It is anticipated that *Coral Sea* (CV 43) will replace *Lexington* in the training role about 1980 or earlier.

Names: US aircraft carriers traditionally have been named for American battles and earlier Navy ships. However, during the past few years they have increasingly been named for statesmen and naval leaders.

CARRIER SERVICE LIFE EXTENSION PROGRAMME
(From Annual Defense Department Report FY 1978)

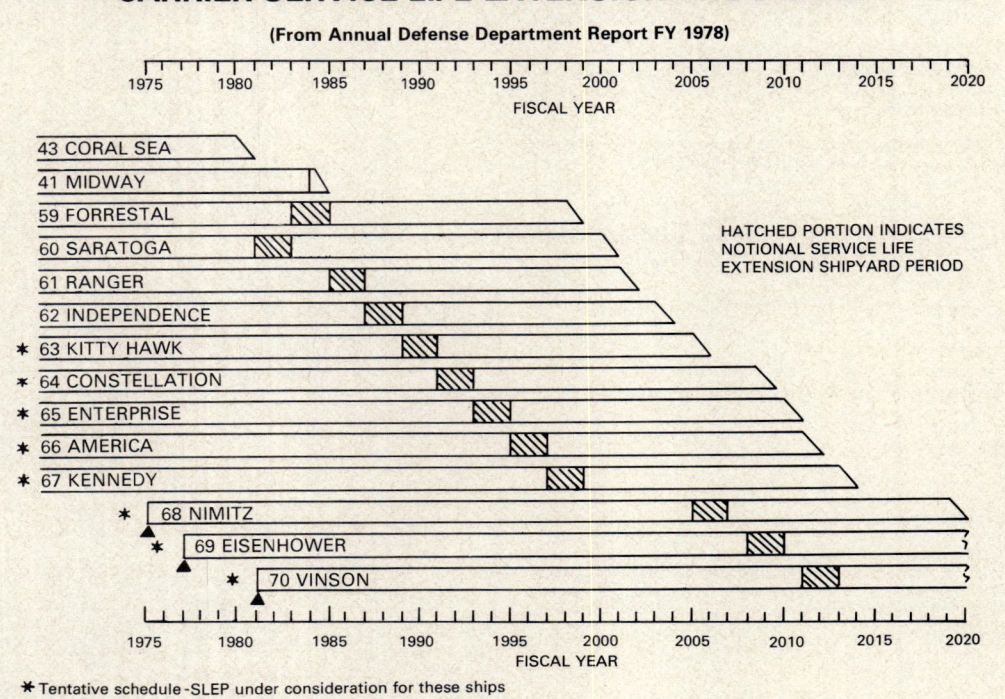

[Chart showing FY 1975 to 2020 service life timelines for carriers:
43 CORAL SEA
41 MIDWAY
59 FORRESTAL
60 SARATOGA
61 RANGER
62 INDEPENDENCE
* 63 KITTY HAWK
* 64 CONSTELLATION
* 65 ENTERPRISE
* 66 AMERICA
* 67 KENNEDY
* 68 NIMITZ
* 69 EISENHOWER
* 70 VINSON

HATCHED PORTION INDICATES NOTIONAL SERVICE LIFE EXTENSION SHIPYARD PERIOD]

* Tentative schedule - SLEP under consideration for these ships

(2) AIRCRAFT CARRIERS (MEDIUM) (CVV): PROPOSED

Displacement, tons: 59 000 full load
Length, feet (metres): approx 780 oa *(237·7)*
Beam, feet (metres): approx 100 *(30·5)* (extreme)
Draught, feet (metres): approx 25 *(7·6)* (max)
Aircraft: approx 55 (see notes)
Catapults: 2 or 3 steam (C-13)
Elevators: 2
Main engines: Steam turbines; 100 000 shp; 2 shafts
Speed, knots: approx 30

The Navy is investigating the possibility of replacing the "Nimitz" class in future building programmes with a new class of Medium Aircraft carriers (CVV). These ships would operate Vertical and Short Take off and Landing (V/STOL) aircraft and helicopters. If it is decided to go ahead with this class current plans are for two initial ships, one to be authorised in the FY 1979 and one in the FY 1981. The first ship would be operational in the mid-1980s. Cost of the first ship in the FY 1979 would be $1·31 billion. The two CVVs would replace CVN 71 in the current programme.

Congress refused to fund a V/STOL carrier known as the Sea Control Ship (SCS) that the Navy had planned for the FY 1975 shipbuilding programme. This ship was opposed on the basis of limited size, capability, and speed. Accordingly, the Navy has examined a number of designs that would provide a more flexible employment of sea-based tactical aircraft in a wide range of "low threat" situations as well as being able to conduct anti-submarine operations.

The CVV design will be suitable for sea control, amphibious assault, close air support, mine countermeasures, and low-intensity Anti-Air Warfare (AAW) operations. This multi-mission concept overcomes many of the objections which led to Congressional refusal to fund the smaller Sea Control Ship previously proposed by the Navy. In addition, the CVV would have sufficient speed to accompany carrier task forces or fast merchant ships.

The feasibility of the Sea Control Ship/CVV concept was demonstrated from 1972 to 1974 by the amphibious assault ship *Guam* (LPH 9) which operated as an interim SCS. *Guam* carried AV-8 Harrier VSTOL fighter-attack aircraft, SH-3 Sea King helicopters, and SH-2 LAMPS helicopters during several exercises. She subsequently reverted to the amphibious role, keeping her AV-8A Harrier aircraft.

Aircraft: The V/STOL strike aircraft is the AV-8 Harrier or its successor; the large anti-submarine helicopter is the SH-3 Sea King or SH-53 Sea Stallion (in an A/S configuration); the LAMPS (Light Airborne Multi-Purpose System) is actually a medium-size helicopter primarily configured for A/S search and attack. The current LAMPS helicopter is the SH-2, while a later aircraft based on the Army's Utility Tactical Transport Aircraft System (UTTAS) programme will be developed as the LAMPS III.

Several advanced V/STOL aircraft are under development in the United States for ship-based use, with the more promising candidates being the Hawker Siddeley-McDonnell Douglas AV-16 Advanced Harrier, the Rockwell XFV-12 Thrust-Augmented Wing (TAW) aircraft, and the Grumman "Nutcracker" design.

Gunnery: All the CVV designs provide for the installation of at least two Close-In Weapon Systems (CIWS), probably the rapid-fire, multi-barrel 20 mm Phalanx gun system.

Missiles: Harpoon anti-ship missiles in storage/launcher canisters could be fitted in all of these ships.

Propulsion: Despite the Title VIII legislation passed by Congress which encourages nuclear propulsion for surface combatants, all CVV designs provide for fossil-fuel propulsion because of the high development and procurement costs of nuclear power plants.

USA 645

3 "NIMITZ" CLASS (NUCLEAR POWERED AIRCRAFT CARRIERS (CVN))

Name	No.	Builders	Laid down	Launched	Commissioned	F/S
NIMITZ	CVN 68	Newport News Shipbuilding & Dry Dock Co	22 June 1968	13 May 1972	3 May 1975	AA
DWIGHT D. EISENHOWER	CVN 69	Newport News Shipbuilding & Dry Dock Co	15 Aug 1970	11 Oct 1975	18 Oct 1977	AA
CARL VINSON	CVN 70	Newport News Shipbuilding & Dry Dock Co	11 Oct 1975	Mar 1979	1981	Bldg

Displacement, tons: 72 700 light (condition A); 81 600 standard; 91 487 full load
Length, feet (metres): 1 040 *(317·0)* wl; 1 092 *(332·0)* oa
Beam, feet (metres): 134 *(40·8)*
Draught, feet (metres): 37 *(11·3)*
Flight deck width, feet (metres): 252 *(76·8)*
Catapults: 4 steam (C13-1)
Aircraft: 90+
Missiles: 3 Basic Point Defence Missile System (BPDMS) launchers with Sea Sparrow missiles (Mk 25 in *Nimitz*; Mk 29 in remainder); see notes
Guns: See notes
Main engines: Geared steam turbines; 280 000 shp; 4 shafts
Nuclear reactors: 2 pressurised-water cooled (A4W/A1G)
Speed, knots: 30+
Complement: 3 300 plus 3 000 assigned to air wing for a total of 6 300 per ship

The lead ship for this class and the world's second nuclear-powered aircraft carrier was ordered 9½ years after the first such ship, *Enterprise* (CVN 65). *Nimitz* was authorised in the Fiscal Year 1967 new construction programme; *Dwight D. Eisenhower* in the FY 1970 programme; and *Carl Vinson* in the FY 1974 programme. The builders are the only US shipyard now capable of constructing large, nuclear-propelled warships.
The completion of the first two ships has been delayed almost two years because of delays in the delivery and testing of nuclear plant components. *Eisenhower* was contracted for delivery to the Navy 21 months after *Nimitz*. However, the official Navy construction schedule notes that past undermanning by the shipbuilder has resulted in slippage beyond contract delivery date.

Originally it was planned to procure two more ships of this class (CVN 71 and 72). Long lead items for CVN 71 were requested under the FY 1977 and $350 million were authorised. President Ford's request to cancel CVN 71 was backed by President Carter but Congress allowed $268·4 million of the original authorisation to stand, a sum already contractually agreed. The stipulation was made that this sum should be used for spare components for CVN 68/70 or for long lead items for CVN 71 should the Administration decide to go ahead with her. This all came about at a time when Congress and the Pentagon were debating the future Carrier programme in the light of increasing cost, size and building time of the CVNs and studies being undertaken as to the advisability of changing to a new class (The "fossil-fuelled" Medium Carrier—CVV) or continuing with the "Nimitz" class CVN 71. A decision on this option has to be reached by the submission of the FY 1979 budget.

Classification: *Nimitz* and *Eisenhower* were ordered as attack aircraft carriers (CVAN): reclassified CVN on 30 June 1975. First two ships will be refitted with A/S control centre and facilities for A/S aircraft and helicopters for their new multi-mission role (attack/ASW). *Vinson* will be completed with these facilities.

Electronics: These ships have the Naval Tactical Data System (NTDS).

Endurance: 13 years for reactors, 16 days for aviation fuel (steady flying).

Engineering: These carriers have only two nuclear reactors compared with the eight reactors required for *Enterprise*. The nuclear cores for the reactors in these ships are expected to provide sufficient energy for the ships each to steam for at least 13 years, an estimated 800 000 to 1 million miles between refuelling.

Fiscal: A number of cost growth factors have had an impact on these ships, including delays in schedule. The cost of *Nimitz* in the Fiscal Year 1976 dollars was equivalent to $1 881 million; the two later ships will cost in excess of $2 000 million each in equivalent dollars.

Gunnery: It is planned to add three 20 mm Mk 15 CIWS to each ship, which at present have only two 40 mm saluting guns.

Missiles: *Nimitz* will shortly receive Mk 29 Sea Sparrow in place of Mk 25.

Names: *Dwight D. Eisenhower* is believed to be the first major US surface warship to be named after an Army officer.
Carl Vinson is believed to be the first US naval ship to be named after a living person since the American Revolution. Carl Vinson was a member of the House of Representatives from Georgia from 1914 to 1965; he served as Chairman of the House Naval Affairs Committee and later the House Armed Services Committee.

Protection: Sides with system of full and empty compartments. 2·5 in plating over certain areas of side shell.

Radar: 3D air search: SPS 48.
Air search: SPS 43A.
Surface search: SPS 10.
Navigational: SPN 42, 43 and 44.

Sonar: None.

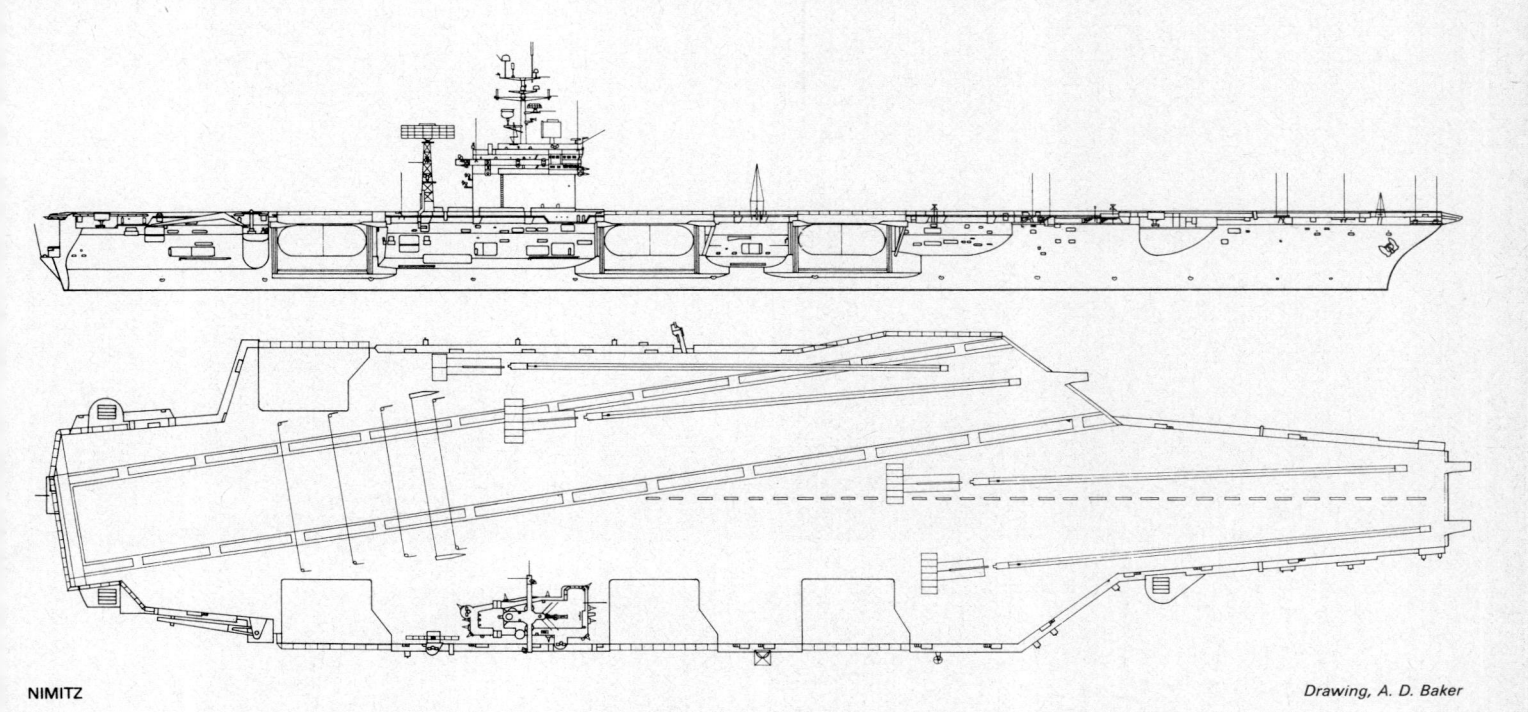

NIMITZ   *Drawing, A. D. Baker*

NIMITZ   *1976, J. L. M. van der Burg*

646 USA

DWIGHT D. EISENHOWER   8/1977, USN

NIMITZ   4/1975, USN

DWIGHT D. EISENHOWER   8/1977, USN

1 NUCLEAR-PROPELLED AIRCRAFT CARRIER (CVN) "ENTERPRISE" CLASS

Name	No.	Builders	Laid down	Launched	Commissioned	F/S
ENTERPRISE	CVN 65	Newport News Shipbuilding & Dry Dock Co.	4 Feb 1958	24 Sept 1960	25 Nov 1961	PA

Displacement, tons: 75 700 standard; 89 600 full load
Length, feet (metres): 1 040 *(317·0)* wl; 1 102 *(335·9)* oa
Beam, feet (metres): 133 *(40·5)*
Draught, feet (metres): 35·8 *(10·8)*
Flight deck width, feet (metres): 252 *(76·8)* maximum
Aircraft: approx 84
Catapults: 4 steam (C 13)
Missile launchers: 2 Basic Point Defence Missile Systems (BPDMS) launchers (Mk 25) with Sea Sparrow missiles
Main engines: 4 geared steam turbines (Westinghouse); approx 280 000 shp; 4 shafts
Nuclear reactors: 8 pressurised-water cooled A2W (Westinghouse)
Speed, knots: approx 35
Complement: 3 100 (162 officers, approx 2 940 enlisted men) plus 2 400 assigned to attack air wing for a total of 5 500)

At the time of her construction, *Enterprise* was the largest warship ever built and is rivalled in size only by the nuclear-powered "Nimitz" class ships. *Enterprise* was authorised in the Fiscal Year 1958 new construction programme. She was launched only 19 months after her keel was laid down.
The cost of *Enterprise* was $451·3 million.
The Fiscal Year 1960 budget provided $35 million to prepare plans and place orders for components of a second nuclear-powered carrier, but the project was cancelled.

Armament: *Enterprise* was completed without any armament in an effort to hold down construction costs. Space for Terrier missile system was provided. Mk 25 Sea Sparrow BPDMS subsequently was installed in late 1967 and this is planned to be replaced by Mk 29 and to be supplemented with three 20 mm Mk 15 CIWS in the near future.

Classification: Originally classified as CVAN; reclassified as CVN on 30 June 1975.

Design: Built to a modified "Forrestal" class design. The most distinctive feature is the island structure. Nuclear propulsion eliminated requirement for smoke stack and boiler air intakes. Rectangular fixed-array radar antennae ("billboards") are mounted on sides of island; electronic countermeasure (ECM) antennae ring dome-shaped upper levels of island structure. Fixed antennae have increased range and performance (see listing for cruiser *Long Beach*). *Enterprise* has four deck-edge lifts, two forward of island and one aft on starboard side and one aft on port side.
A re-shaping of the island will take place in the next refit in 1979. This will include the removal of the mast and dome (which carries obsolete ECM gear) which will be replaced with a mast similar to that of the "Nimitz" class. The "billboards" of the SPS 32 and 33 radars will also be removed to be replaced by the antennas of AN/SPS 48 and 49 radars on the new mast.

Electronics: Fitted with the Naval Tactical Data System (NTDS); Tacan.

Engineering: *Enterprise* was the world's second nuclear-powered warship (the cruiser *Long Beach* was completed a few months earlier). Design of the first nuclear-powered aircraft carrier began in 1950 and work continued until 1953 when the programme was deferred pending further work on the submarine reactor programme. The large ship reactor project was reinstated in 1954 on the basis of technological advancements made in the previous 14 months. The Atomic Energy Commission's Bettis Atomic Power Laboratory was given prime responsibility for developing the nuclear power plant.
The first of the eight reactors installed in *Enterprise* achieved initial criticality on 2 Dec 1960, shortly after the carrier was launched. After three years of operation during which she steamed more than 207 000 miles, *Enterprise* was overhauled and refuelled from Nov 1964 to July 1965. Her second set of cores provided about 300 000 miles steaming. The eight cores initially installed in *Enterprise* cost $64 million; the second set cost about $20 million.
Enterprise underwent an extensive overhaul from October 1969 to January 1971, which included installation of a new set of uranium cores in the ship's eight nuclear reactors. The overhaul and refuelling took place at the Newport News shipyard. Estimated cost of the overhaul was approximately $30 million, with $13 million being for non-nuclear repairs and alterations, and $17 million being associated with installation of the new nuclear cores (the latter amount being in addition to the $80 million cost of the eight cores). This third set of cores is expected to fuel the ship for 10 to 13 years.
There are two reactors for each of the ship's four shafts. The eight reactors feed 32 heat exchangers. *Enterprise* developed more horsepower during her propulsion trials than any other ship in history (officially "in excess of 200 000 shaft horsepower"; subsequently. Navy officials stated that she can generate 280 000 shp).

Radar: Search: SPS 32 and 33 ("billboards").
Low level search: SPS 58.
Search: SPS 10 and 12.
Navigational radars: SPN 10.

ENTERPRISE *12/1976, Dr. Giorgio Arra*

ENTERPRISE *12/1976, Dr. Giorgio Arra*

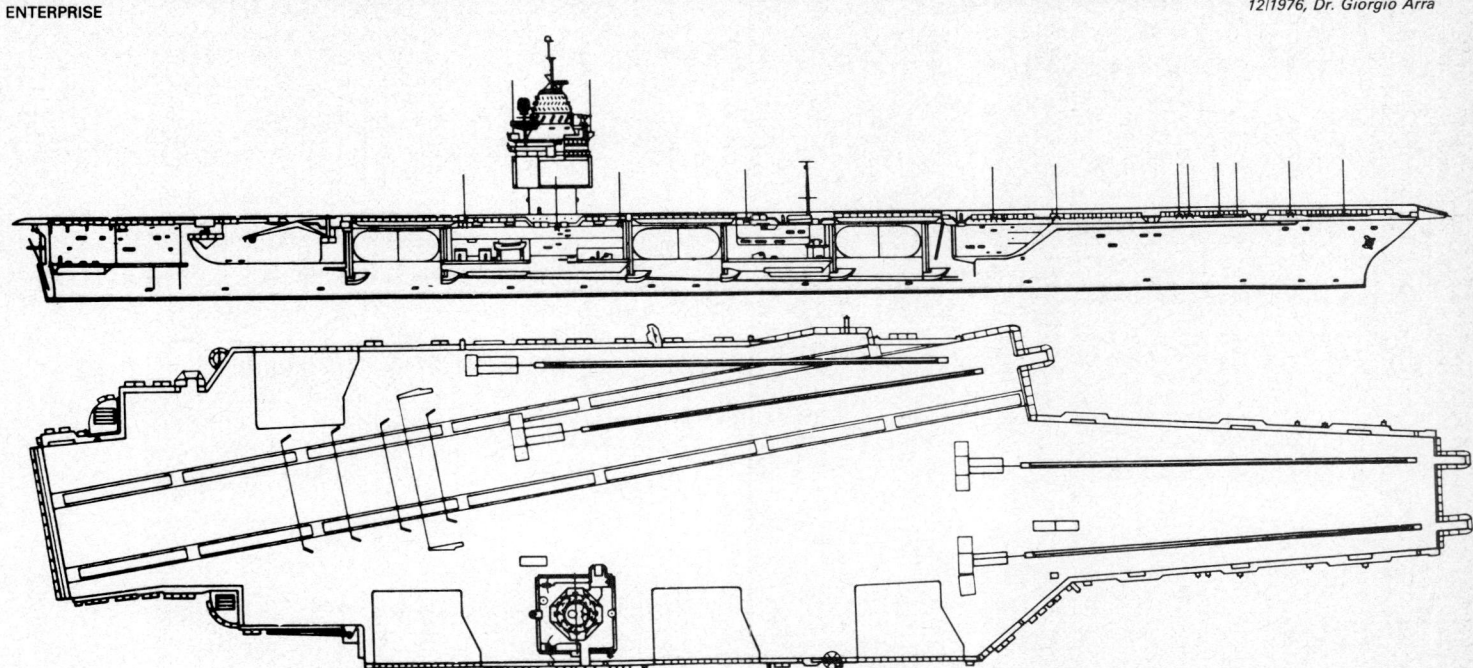

ENTERPRISE *Drawing, A. D. Baker III*

648 USA

4 AIRCRAFT CARRIERS (CV): "KITTY HAWK" and "JOHN F. KENNEDY" CLASSES

Name	No.	Builders	Laid down	Launched	Commissioned	F/S
KITTY HAWK	CV 63	New York Shipbuilding Corp, Camden, NJ	27 Dec 1956	21 May 1960	29 April 1961	PA
CONSTELLATION	CV 64	New York Naval Shipyard	14 Sept 1957	8 Oct 1960	27 Oct 1961	PA
AMERICA	CV 66	Newport News Shipbuilding & Dry Dock Co	9 Jan 1961	1 Feb 1964	23 Jan 1965	AA
JOHN F. KENNEDY	CV 67	Newport News Shipbuilding & Dry Dock Co	22 Oct 1964	27 May 1967	7 Sept 1968	AA

Displacement, tons:
  Kitty Hawk: 60 100 standard; 80 800 full load
  Constellation: 60 100 standard; 80 800 full load
  America: 60 300 standard; 78 500 full load
  John F. Kennedy: 61 000 standard; 82 000 full load
Length, feet (metres): 990 *(301·8)* wl
  Kitty Hawk and *Constellation:* 1 046 *(318·8)* oa
  America: 1 047·5 *(319·3)* oa
  J. F. Kennedy: 1 052 *(320·7)* oa
Beam, feet (metres): 130 *(39·6)*
Draught, feet (metres):
  J. F. Kennedy: 35·9 *(10·9)*
  Remainder: 37 *(11·3)*
Flight deck width, feet (metres): 252 *(76·9)*
Catapults: 4 steam
Aircraft: approx 85
Missile launchers: 2 twin Terrier surface-to-air launchers (Mk 10) in *Constellation, America* (40 missiles per twin launcher)
  3 Basic Point Defence Missile System (BPDMS) launchers (Mk 25) with Sea Sparrow missiles in *John F. Kennedy*;
  3 Mk 29 BPDMS launchers in *Kitty Hawk*
Guns: See note
Main engines: 4 geared turbines (Westinghouse) 280 000 shp; 4 shafts
Boilers: 8 (Foster-Wheeler)
Speed, knots: 30+
Complement: 2 800 (150 officers, approx 2 645 enlisted men) plus approx 2 150 assigned to attack air wing for a total of 4 950 officers and enlisted men per ship

These ships were built to an improved "Forrestal" design and are easily recognised by their smaller island structure which is set farther aft than the superstructure in the four "Forrestal" class ships. Lift arrangements also differ (see *Design* notes). *Kitty Hawk* was authorised in the Fiscal Year 1956 new construction programme, *Constellation* in the FY 1957, *America* in the FY 1961, and *John F. Kennedy* in the FY 1963. Completion of *Constellation* was delayed because of a fire which ravaged her in the New York Naval Shipyard in Dec 1960. Construction of *John F. Kennedy* was delayed because of debate over whether to provide her with conventional or nuclear propulsion.

Classification: As completed, all four ships were classified as attack aircraft carriers (CVA); first two changed to multi-mission aircraft carriers (attack and anti-submarine) when modified with A/S command centres and facilities for S-3 Viking fixed-wing aircraft and SH-3 Sea King helicopters. *Kitty Hawk* to CV vice CVA on 29 April 1973; *John F. Kennedy* to CV vice CVA on 1 Dec 1974; *Constellation* and *America* from CVA to CV on 30 June 1975, prior to A/S modifications.

Design: They have two deck-edge lifts forward of the superstructure, a third lift aft of the structure, and the port-side lift on the after quarter. This arrangement considerably improves flight deck operations. Four C13 catapults (with one C13-1 in each of later ships). *John F. Kennedy* and *America* have stern anchors because of their bow sonar domes (see *Sonar* notes). All have a small radar mast abaft the island.

Electronics: All four ships of this class have highly sophisticated electronic equipment including the Naval Tactical Data System (NTDS). Tacan in all ships.

Fire Control: *Kitty Hawk:* 2—Mk 91 MFCS for Mk 29 BPDMS.
Constellation: 4—Mk 76 MFCS for Terrier.
America: 3—Mk 76 MFCS for Terrier.
John F. Kennedy: 3—Mk 115 MFCS for Mk 25 BPDMS.
It is planned to replace Mk 76 and Mk 115 systems with Mk 91 in *Constellation* and *John F. Kennedy.*

Fiscal: Construction costs were $265·2 million for *Kitty Hawk*, $264·5 million for *Constellation*, $248·8 million for *America*, and $277 million for *John F. Kennedy.*

Gunnery: Planned to mount 3—20 mm Mk 15 CIWS in each ship. All currently have only 40 mm saluting guns (2 in 63 and 64, 4 in 66 and 1 in 67).

Missiles: The two Terrier-armed ships have a Mk 10 Mod 3 launcher on the starboard quarter and a Mod 4 launcher on the port quarter.
America has updated Terrier launchers and guidance system that can accommodate Standard missiles; *Constellation* retains older Terrier HT systems which will be replaced by three NATO Sea Sparrow launchers (Mk 29).
Three Sea Sparrow BPDMS launchers were fitted in *John F. Kennedy* early in 1969. It is planned to replace *Constellation's* Terrier system with Mk 29 BPDMS and *John F. Kennedy's* Mk 25 with Mk 29 BPDMS. *America* is to retain her Terrier until 1978-79.

Names: *Kitty Hawk* honours the site where the Wright brothers made their historic flights.

Radar: 3D search: SPS 52 (3 ships).
Search: SPS 43.
Search: SPS 30 (3 ships).
Search: SPS 48 and 58 (*John F. Kennedy*).

Rockets: Mk 28 Mod 5 rocket launching systems fitted in *America* and *John F. Kennedy.*

Sonar: SQS 23 (*America* only).
This is the only US attack carrier so fitted, although it was planned also for *John F. Kennedy* but not fitted.

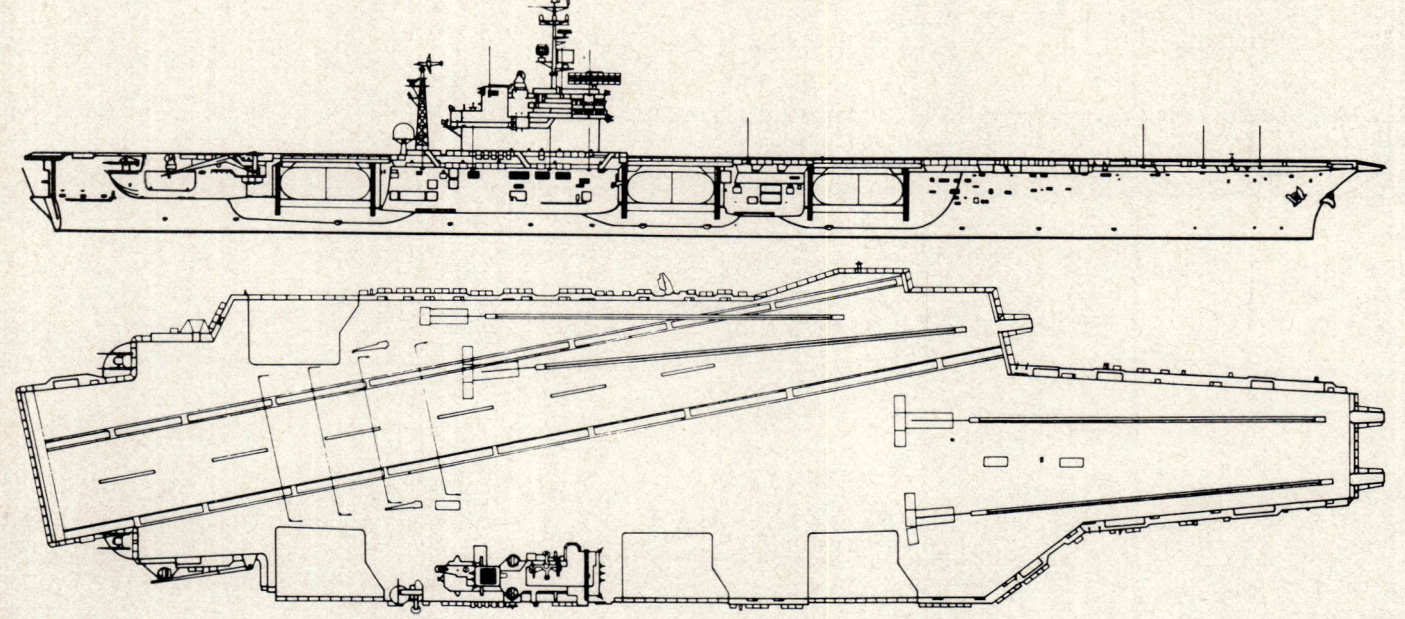

CONSTELLATION 10/1975, USN

CONSTELLATION 8/1977, Dr. Giorgio Arra

AMERICA

Drawing by A. D. Baker

JOHN F. KENNEDY   10/1976, Michael D. J. Lennon

AMERICA   10/1974, USN

JOHN F. KENNEDY   1974, USN

650 USA

4 AIRCRAFT CARRIERS (CV): "FORRESTAL" CLASS

Name	No.	Builders	Laid down	Launched	Commissioned	F/S
FORRESTAL	CV 59	Newport News SB & DD Co	14 July 1952	11 Dec 1954	1 Oct 1955	AA
SARATOGA	CV 60	New York Naval Shipyard	16 Dec 1952	8 Oct 1955	14 April 1956	AA
RANGER	CV 61	Newport News SB & DD Co	2 Aug 1954	29 Sept 1956	10 Aug 1957	PA
INDEPENDENCE	CV 62	New York Naval Shipyard	1 July 1955	6 June 1958	10 Jan 1959	AA

Displacement, tons:
Forrestal and *Saratoga*: 59 060 standard; 75 900 full load
Others: 60 000 standard; 79 300 full load
Length, feet (metres):
Forrestal: 1 086 *(331)* oa
Ranger: 1 071 *(326·4)* oa
Saratoga: 1 063 *(324)* oa
Independence: 1 070 *(326·1)* oa
Beam, feet (metres): 129·5 *(39·5)*
Draught, feet (metres): 37 *(11·3)*
Flight deck width, feet (metres): 252 *(76·8)* maximum
Catapults: 4 steam
Aircraft: approx 70
Guns: 2—5 in *(127 mm)* 54 cal (Mk 42) (single) in *Ranger*
Missile launchers: 2 Basic Point Defence Missile Systems (BPDMS) launchers (Mk 25) with Sea Sparrow missiles in all except *Ranger*
Main engines: 4 geared turbines (Westinghouse) 4 shafts; 260 000 shp *(Forrestal)*; 280 000 shp (remainder)
Boilers: (Babcock & Wilcox)
Speed, knots:
Forrestal: 33
Others: 34
Complement: 2 790 (145 officers, approx 2 645 enlisted men) plus approx 2 150 assigned to attack air wing for a total of 4 940+ per ship

Forrestal was the world's first aircraft carrier built after World War II. The *Forrestal* design drew heavily from the aircraft carrier *United States* (CVA 58) which was cancelled immediately after being laid down in April 1949. *Forrestal* was authorised in the Fiscal Year 1952 new construction programme; *Saratoga* followed in the FY 1953 programme, *Ranger* in the FY 1954 programme, and *Independence* in the FY 1955 programme.

Classification: *Forrestal* and *Saratoga* were initially classified as Large Aircraft Carriers (CVB); reclassified as Attack Aircraft Carriers (CVA) on 1 October 1952 to reflect their purpose rather than size.
Saratoga redesignated CV on 30 June 1972; *Independence* on 28 Feb 1973; *Forrestal* and *Ranger* on 30 June 1975.

Design: The "Forrestal" class ships were the first aircraft carriers designed and built specifically to operate jet-propelled aircraft. *Forrestal* was redesigned early in construction to incorporate British-developed angled flight deck and steam catapults. These were the first US aircraft carriers built with an enclosed bow area to improve seaworthiness. Four large deck-edge lifts are fitted, one forward of island structure to starboard, two aft of island structure to starboard and one at forward edge of angled flight deck to port. Other features include armoured flight deck and advanced underwater protection and internal compartmentation to reduce effects of conventional and nuclear attack. Mast configurations differ; *Forrestal* originally had two masts, one of which was removed in 1967.
The first two ships have two C7 and two C11 catapults; the others have four C7.

Electronics: Naval Tactical Data System (NTDS) and Tacan

Engineering: *Saratoga* and later ships have an improved steam plant; increased machinery weight of the improved plant is more than compensated for by increased performance and decreased fuel consumption. *Forrestal* boilers are 615 psi *(42·7 kg/cm²)*; 1 200 psi *(83·4 kg/cm²)* in other ships.

Fiscal: Construction costs were $188·9 million for *Forrestal*, $213·9 million for *Saratoga*, $173·3 million for *Ranger*, and $225·3 million for *Independence*.

Gunnery: All four ships initially mounted 8—5 in guns (Mk 42) in single mounts, two on each quarter and two on each bow. The forward sponsons carrying the guns interfered with ship operations in rough weather, tending to slow the ships down. The forward sponsons and guns were subsequently removed (except in *Ranger*), reducing armament to four guns per ship. The after guns were removed with installation of BPDMS launchers (see below). *Ranger's* two 5 in guns removed in 1976. Each ship carries four 40 mm saluting guns. It is planned to fit all these ships with three 20 mm Mk 15 CIWS in the immediate future.

Missiles: The four after 5 in guns were removed from *Forrestal* late in 1967 and a single BPDMS launcher for Sea Sparrow missiles was installed forward on the starboard side. An additional launcher was provided aft on the port side in 1972. Two BPDMS launchers fitted in *Independence* in 1973, *Saratoga* in 1974; *Forrestal* in 1976. These are soon to be replaced by three Mk 29 BPDMS—the same fitting is to be carried out in *Ranger*.

Names: *Forrestal* is named after James V. Forrestal, Secretary of the Navy from 1944 until he was appointed the first US Secretary of Defense in 1947.

Radar: Low angle air search: SPS 58
Search: SPS 30 and 43 (*Saratoga* —to be replaced by SPS 48 and 49 during SLEP); SPS 48 and 49 in remainder.
Navigation: SPN 10.

Rockets: One Mk 28 rocket launching system fitted in all but *Ranger*.

Service Life Extension Programme (SLEP): Owing to current building costs this programme is intended to extend carriers' lives from 30 to 45 years. The "Forrestal" class will be the first to undergo this modernisation—*Saratoga* first, *Forrestal* in the FY 1982, *Independence* in the FY 1984 and *Ranger* in the FY 1986. Cost per ship approx $426 million.

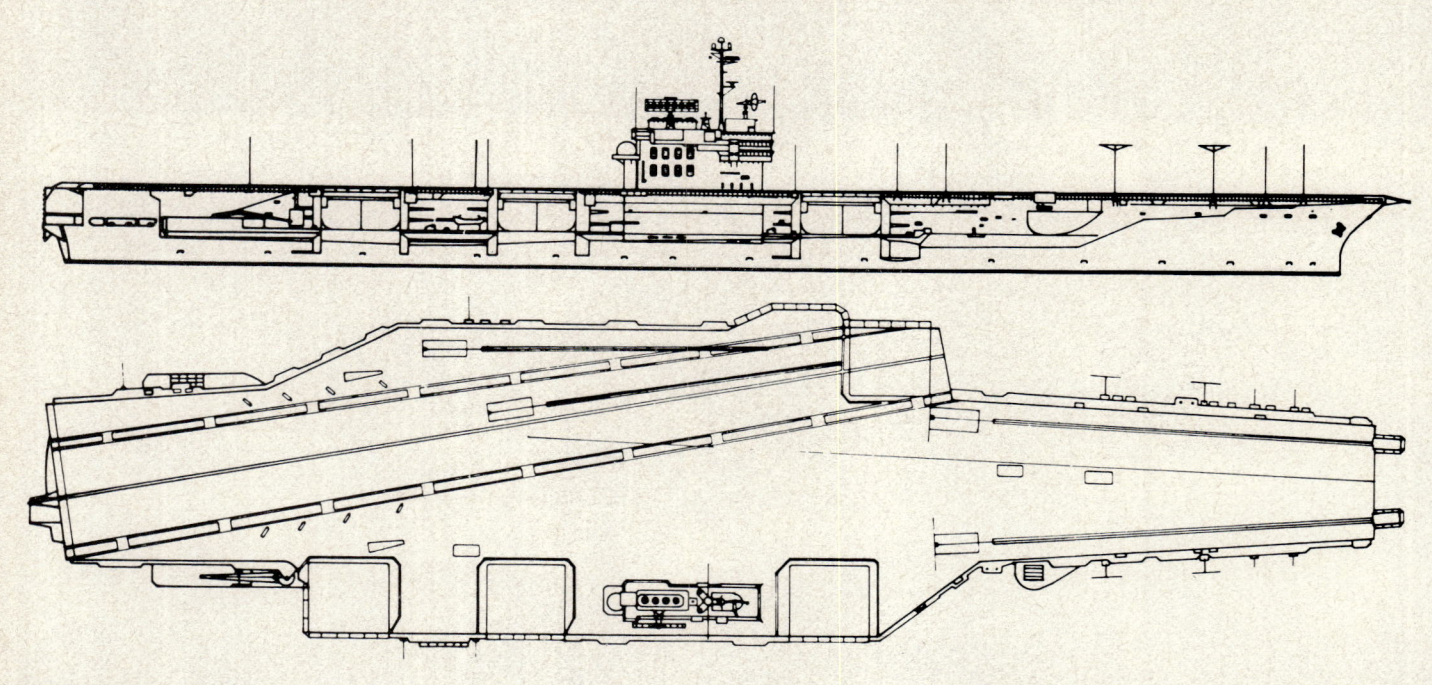

FORRESTAL 7/1976, A. D. Baker III

FORRESTAL Drawing, A. D. Baker III

USA 651

SARATOGA
1975, USN

INDEPENDENCE
9/1976, Dr. Giorgio Arra

RANGER
2/1976, USN

652 USA

2 AIRCRAFT CARRIERS (CV) "MIDWAY" CLASS

Name	No.	Builders	Laid down	Launched	Commissioned	F/S
MIDWAY	CV 41	Newport News SB & DD Co	27 Oct 1943	20 Mar 1945	10 Sept 1945	PA
CORAL SEA	CV 43	Newport News SB & DD Co	10 July 1944	2 April 1946	1 Oct 1947	PA

Displacement, tons: *Midway:* 51 000 standard; *Coral Sea:* 52 500 standard; 62 200 full load
Length, feet (metres): 900 *(274·3)* wl; 979 *(298·4)* oa
Beam, feet (metres): 121 *(36·9)*
Draught, feet (metres): 35·3 *(10·8)*
Flight deck width, feet (metres): 238 *(72·5)* maximum
Catapults: 2 steam in *Midway* (C 13); 3 in *Coral Sea* (C 11)
Aircraft: approx 75
Guns: 3—5 in *(127 mm)* 54 cal (Mk 39) (single) (see *Gunnery* notes)
Main engines: 4 geared turbines (Westinghouse); 212 000 shp; 4 shafts
Boilers: 12 (Babcock & Wilcox)
Speed, knots: 30+
Complement: 2 615 (140 officers, approx 2 475 enlisted men) except *Coral Sea* 2 710 (165 officers, approx 2 545 enlisted men) plus approx 1 800 assigned to attack air wing for a total of 4 400 to 4 500 per ship

The original three carriers of this class were the largest US warships constructed during World War II. Completed too late for service in that conflict, they were the backbone of US naval strength for the first decade of the Cold War. The entire class has been in active service (except for overhaul and modernisation) since the ships were completed. *F. D. Roosevelt* deleted in 1977.
Midway was homeported at Yokosuka, Japan, in October 1973; she is the only US aircraft carrier to be based overseas.
Coral Sea is due to transfer to the Atlantic Fleet in 1978.
Midway will probably be retained in service until 1985 to provide a 13 carrier force level.
The unnamed CVB 44, 56 and 57 of this class were cancelled prior to the start of construction.

Classification: These ships were initially classified as large Aircraft Carriers (CVB); reclassified as Attack Aircraft Carriers (CVA) in October 1952. Both ships reclassified as Aircraft Carriers (CV) on 30 June 1975.

Design: These ships were built to the same design with a standard displacement of 45 000 tons, full load displacement of 60 100 tons, and an overall length of 968 feet. They have been extensively modified since completion (see notes below). These ships were the first US aircraft carriers with an armoured flight deck and the first US warships with a designed width too large to enable them to pass through the Panama Canal.

Electronics: Naval Tactical Data System (NTDS); Tacan.

Fire control: One Mk 37 and one Mk 56 GFCS.

Fiscal: Construction cost of *Midway* was $85·6 million and *Coral Sea* $87·6 million.

Gunnery: As built, these ships mounted 18—5 in guns (14 in *Coral Sea*), 84—40 mm guns, and 28—20 mm guns. Armament reduced periodically with 3 in guns replacing lighter weapons. Minimal 5 in armament remains. The 5 in guns are 54 calibre Mk 39, essentially modified 5 in/38 calibre with a longer barrel for greater range; not to be confused with rapid-fire 5 in/54s of newer US warships.
Midway is to be fitted with three 20 mm Mk 15 CIWS in near future.
Both ships carry two 40 mm saluting guns.

MIDWAY *2/1977, Dr. Giorgio Arra*

MIDWAY *2/1977, Dr. Giorgio Arra*

Missiles: *Midway* is to be fitted with two Mk 25 Sea Sparrow launchers (BPDMS) in near future.

Modernisation: All were extensively modernised. Their main conversion gave them angled flight decks, steam catapults, enclosed bows, new electronics, and new lift arrangement *(Franklin D. Roosevelt* from 1954 to 1956, *Midway* from 1955 to 1957, and *Coral Sea* from 1958 to 1960; all at Puget Sound Naval Shipyard). Lift arrangement was changed in *Franklin D. Roosevelt* and *Midway* to one centreline lift forward, one deck-edge lift aft of island on starboard side, and one deck-edge lift at forward end of angled deck on port side. *Coral Sea* has one lift forward and one aft of island on starboard side and third lift outboard on port side aft. *Midway* began another extensive modernisation at the San Francisco Bay Naval Shipyard in Feb 1966; she was recommissioned on 31 Jan 1970 and went to sea in March 1970.
Her modernisation included provisions for handling newer aircraft, new catapults, new lifts (arranged as in *Coral Sea*), and new electronics.
Midway is now the more capable of the two ships.

Radar: Low angle air search: SPS 58
Search: SPS 10, 30 and 43
Navigation: SPN 6 and 10

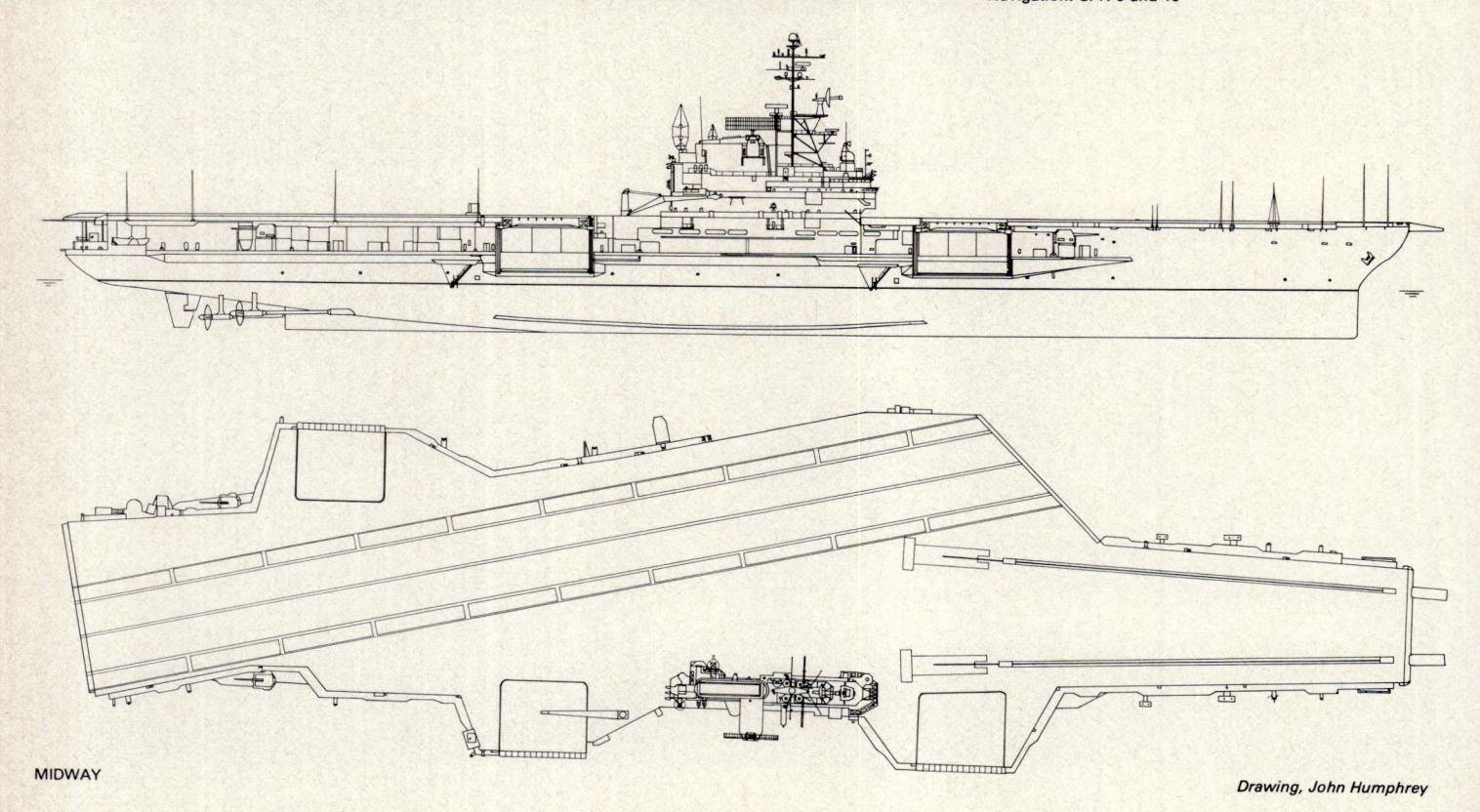

MIDWAY *Drawing, John Humphrey*

5 AIRCRAFT CARRIERS (2 CVA/CV, 2 CVS, 1 CVT) "HANCOCK" and "INTREPID" CLASSES

Name	No.	Builders	Laid down	Launched	Commissioned	F/S
INTREPID	CVS 11	Newport News Shipbuilding & Dry Dock Co	1 Dec 1941	26 April 1943	16 Aug 1943	AR
LEXINGTON	CVT 16	Bethlehem Steel Co, Quincy, Mass	15 July 1941	26 Sept 1942	17 Feb 1943	AA
BON HOMME RICHARD	CVA 31	New York Navy Yard	1 Feb 1943	29 April 1944	26 Nov 1944	PR
ORISKANY	CV 34	New York Navy Yard	1 May 1944	13 Oct 1945	25 Sept 1950	PR
SHANGRI-LA	CVS 38	Norfolk Navy Yard	15 Jan 1943	24 Feb 1944	15 Sept 1944	AR

Displacement, tons: 29 600 light; 41 900 full load. (*Oriskany* 28 200 light; 40 600 full load)
Length, feet (metres): 820 *(249·9)* wl; 899 *(274)* oa (889 *(270·9) Shangri-La, Lexington)*
Beam, feet (metres): 103 *(30·8)* except *Oriskany* 106·5 *(32·5)*
Draught, feet (metres): 31 *(9·4)*
Flight deck width, feet (metres): 172 *(52·4)* except *Lexington* 192 *(58·5)* and *Oriskany* 195 *(59·5)*
Catapults: 2 steam
Aircraft: 70 to 80 for CVA/CV type; approx 45 for CVS type; none assigned to *Lexington*
Guns: 2—5 in *(127 mm)* 38 cal (Mk 24) (single) in *Oriskany;* 4 guns in other ships except all removed from *Lexington*
Main engines: 4 geared turbines (Westinghouse) 150 000 shp; 4 shafts
Boilers: 8 (Babcock & Wilcox)
Speed, knots: 30+
Complement: CVA/CV type: 2 090 (110 officers, 1 980 enlisted men); plus approx 1 185 (135 officers, 1 050 enlisted men) in air wing for a total of approx 3 200 per ship
CVS type: 1 615 (115 officers, approx 1 500 enlisted men) plus approx 800 assigned to ASW air group for a total of 2 400 per ship
Lexington: 1 440 (75 officers, 1 365 enlisted men); no air unit assigned

These ships (formerly six including *Hancock*) originally were "Essex" class aircraft carriers; extensively modernised during 1950s, being provided with enclosed bow, angled flight deck, improved elevators, increased aviation fuel storage, and steam catapults. Construction of *Oriskany* suspended after World War II and she was completed in 1950 to a modified "Essex" design.
Bon Homme Richard decommissioned on 2 July 1971, *Shangri-La* on 30 July 1971, *Intrepid* on 15 March 1974, *Oriskany* on 30 Sept 1976; *Lexington* remains in commission as a training carrier (with no aircraft support capability) but is reported to be in poor material condition and will probably be deleted in the near future. It is also reported that *Shangri-La* will be deleted in 1978.

Classification: All "Essex" class ships originally were designated as Aircraft Carriers (CV); reclassified as Attack Aircraft Carriers (CVA) on 1 Oct 1952. *Intrepid* reclassified as ASW Support Aircraft Carrier (CVS) on 31 March 1962, *Lexington* on 1 Oct 1962, *Shangri-La* on 30 June 1969. *Lexington* became the Navy's training aircraft carrier in the Gulf of Mexico on 29 Dec 1962; reclassified CVT on 1 Jan 1969.
Oriskany redesignated as CV on 30 June 1975 (as was now-stricken *Hancock*).

Electronics: *Oriskany* conducted the initial sea trials of the Naval Tactical Data System (NTDS) in 1961-62; Tacan.

Fire control: Fitted with one Mk 37 gunfire control system and two Mk 56 GFCS except *Oriskany* with two Mk 37 GFCS.

LEXINGTON 5/1975, USN

ORISKANY 8/1970, USN

Modernisation: These ships have been modernised under several programmes to increase their ability to operate more-advanced aircraft. *Oriskany* was completed with some post-war features incorporated. The most prominent difference from their original configuration is angled flight deck and removal of twin 5-in gun mounts from flight deck forward and aft of island structure. Three elevators fitted; "Pointed" centreline lift forward between catapults, deckedge lift on port side at leading edge of angled deck, and deckedge lift on starboard side aft of island structure. Minimal gun battery retained (see description of original armament under "Essex" class listings). Remaining guns removed from *Lexington* in 1969; by 1975 *Oriskany* had only 2—5 in guns fitted.

Radar: Search: SPS 10, 30 and 43.
Navigation: SPN 10.
Lexington:
Search: SPS 10, 12 and 43.
Navigation: SPN 10.

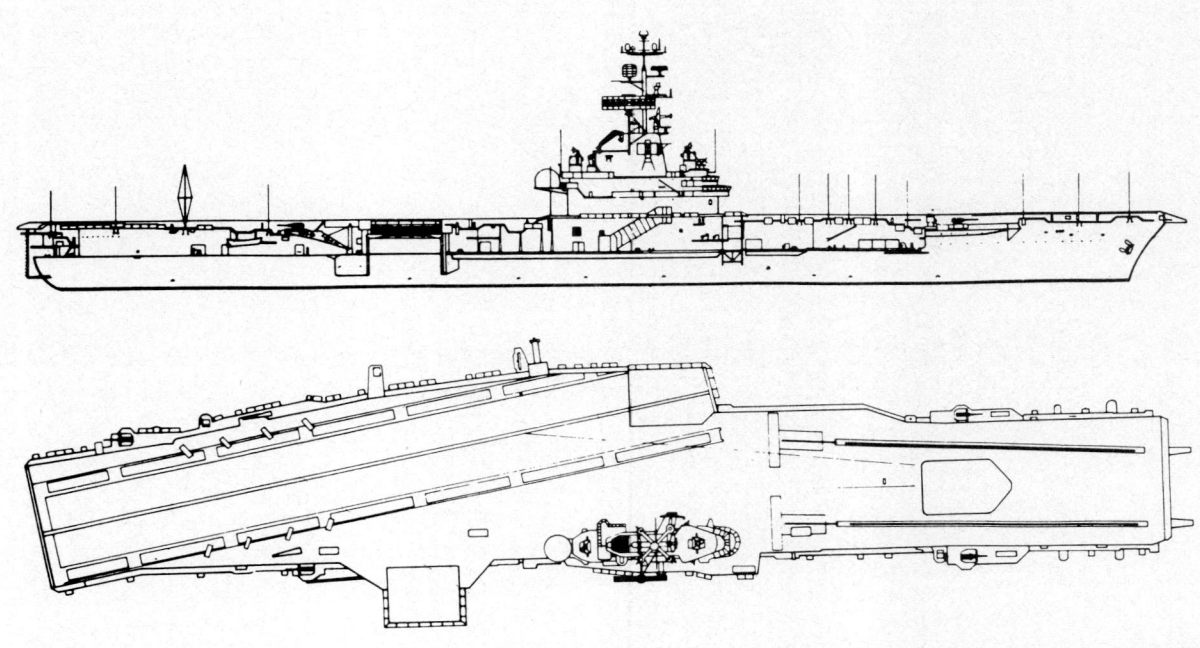

ORISKANY Drawing, A. D. Baker III

654 USA

2 ASW AIRCRAFT CARRIERS (CVS): MODERNISED "ESSEX" CLASS

Name	No.	Builders	Laid down	Launched	Commissioned	F/S
HORNET	CVS 12	Newport News Shipbuilding & Dry Dock Co	3 Aug 1942	29 Aug 1943	29 Nov 1943	PR
BENNINGTON	CVS 20	New York Navy Yard	15 Dec 1942	26 Feb 1944	6 Aug 1944	PR

Displacement, tons: approx 33 000 standard; approx 40 600 full load
Length, feet (metres): 820 *(249·9)* wl; 899 *(274)* oa
Beam, feet (metres): 101 *(30·7)*
Draught, feet (metres): 31 *(9·4)*
Flight deck width, feet (metres): 172 *(52·4)* maximum
Catapults: 2 hydraulic (H-8)
Aircraft: 45 (including 16 to 18 helicopters)
Guns: 4—5 in *(127 mm)* 38 cal (Mk 24) (single)
Main engines: 4 geared turbines (Westinghouse); 150 000 shp; 4 shafts
Boilers: 8 (Babcock & Wilcox)
Speed, knots: 30+
Complement: 1 615 (115 officers, approx 1 500 enlisted men) plus approx 800 assigned to ASW air group for a total of 2 400 per ship

The two above ships and the previously listed "Hancock" and "Intrepid" classes are the survivors of the 24 "Essex" class fleet carriers built during World War II (with one ship, *Oriskany*, not completed until 1950). Both of the above ships were extensively modernised during the 1950s; however, they lack the steam catapults and other features of the "Hancock" and "Intrepid" classes.
Bennington was decommissioned on 15 Jan 1970 and *Hornet* on 26 June 1970.

Classification: These ships originally were designated as Aircraft Carriers (CV); reclassified as Attack Carriers (CVA) on 1 Oct 1952. Subsequently they became ASW Support Aircraft Carriers (CVS): *Hornet* on 27 June 1958, and *Bennington* on 30 June 1959.

Design: All 24 "Essex" class ships were built to the same basic design except for the delayed *Oriskany*. Standard displacement as built was 27 100 tons, full load displacement was 36 380 tons, and overall length 888 or 872 feet.

Fire control: One Mk 37 and three Mk 56 GFCS.

Modernisation: These ships have been modernised under several programmes to increase their ability to operate advanced aircraft and to improve sea keeping. Also modernised to improve anti-submarine capabilities under the Fleet Rehabilitation and Modernisation (FRAM II) programme.

Radar: Search: SPS 10, 30 and 43; Tacan.

Sonar: SQS 23 (bow-mounted).

BENNINGTON (starboard lift raised during replenishment)   1968, USN

HORNET   1968, USN

BATTLESHIPS

4 "IOWA" CLASS

Name	No.	Builders	Laid down	Launched	Commissioned	F/S
IOWA	BB 61	New York Navy Yard	27 June 1940	27 Aug 1942	22 Feb 1943	AR
NEW JERSEY	BB 62	Philadelphia Navy Yard	16 Sept 1940	7 Dec 1942	23 May 1943	PR
MISSOURI	BB 63	New York Navy Yard	6 Jan 1941	29 Jan 1944	11 June 1944	PR
WISCONSIN	BB 64	Philadelphia Navy Yard	25 Jan 1941	7 Dec 1943	16 April 1944	AR

Displacement, tons: 45 000 standard; 58 000 full load
Length, feet (metres): 860 *(262·1)* wl; 887·2 *(270·4)* oa except *New Jersey* 887·6 *(270·5)*
Beam, feet (metres): 108·2 *(33·0)*
Draught, feet (metres): 38 *(11·6)*
Guns: 9—16 in *(406 mm)* 50 cal (triple); 20—5 in *(127 mm)* 38 cal (twin); 20—40 mm guns in *Missouri* only
Main engines: 4 geared turbines (General Electric in BB 61 and BB 63; Westinghouse in BB 62 and BB 64); 212 000 shp; 4 shafts
Boilers: 8 (Babcock & Wilcox)
Speed, knots: 33 (all may have reached 35 knots in service)
Oil fuel, tons: 9 000
Range, miles: 5 000 at 30 knots; 15 000 at 17 knots
Complement: designed complement varied, averaging 95 officers and 2 270 enlisted men in wartime; *New Jersey* was manned by 70 officers and 1 556 enlisted men (requirements reduced with removal of all light anti-aircraft weapons, floatplanes, and reduced operational requirements) in 1968-69.

These ships were the largest battleships ever built except for the Japanese *Yamato* and *Musashi* (64 170 tons standard, 863 feet overall, 9—18·1 in guns). All four "Iowa" class ships were in action in the Pacific during World War II, primarily screening fast carriers and bombarding amphibious invasion objectives. Three were mothballed after the war with *Missouri* being retained in service as a training ship. All four ships again were in service during the Korean War (1950-53) as shore-bombardment ships; all mothballed 1954-58.
New Jersey began reactivation in mid-1967 at a cost of approximately $21 million; recommissioned on 6 April 1968. *Iowa* and *Wisconsin* remained in reserve at the Philadelphia Naval Shipyard where *New Jersey* had been berthed and reactivated; and the mothballed *Missouri* at the Puget Sound Naval Shipyard, Bremerton, Washington.
New Jersey was again decommissioned on 17 Dec 1969 and mothballed at Bremerton with *Missouri*. Two additional ships of this class were laid down, but never completed: *Illinois* (BB 65), laid down 15 Jan 1945, and *Kentucky* (BB 66), laid down 6 Dec 1944. *Illinois* was 22 per cent complete when cancelled on 11 Aug 1945. *Kentucky* was 69·2 per cent complete when construction was suspended late in the war; floated from its building dock on 20 Jan 1950. Conversion to a missile ship (BBG) was proposed but no work was undertaken and she was stricken on 9 June 1958 and broken up for scrap.
Approximate construction cost was $114·485 million for *Missouri*; other ships cost slightly less.

Aircraft: As built, each ship carried three floatplanes for scouting and gunfire spotting and had two quarterdeck catapults. Catapults removed and helicopters carried during the Korean War.

Armour: These battleships are the most heavily armoured US warships ever constructed, being designed to survive ship-to-ship combat with enemy ships armed with 16 in guns. The main armour belt consists of Class A steel armour 12·1 in thick tapering vertically to 1·62 in; a lower armour belt aft of Turret No. 3 to protect propeller shafts is 13·5 in; turret faces are 17 in; turret tops are 7·25 in; turret backs are 12 in; barbettes have a maximum of 11·6 in of armour; second deck armour is 6 in; and the three-level conning tower sides are 17·3 in with an armoured roof 7·25 in (the conning tower levels are pilot house navigation bridge and flag-signal bridge).

Design: These ships carried heavier armament than previous US battleships and had increased protection and larger engines accounting for additional displacement and increased speed.
All fitted as fleet flagships with additional accommodations and bridge level for admiral and staff. When *New Jersey* was reactivated in 1967-8 this accommodation remained mothballed.

Gunnery: The Mk VII 16 in guns in these ships fire projectiles weighing up to 2 700 lb *(1 225 kg)* (armour piercing) a maximum range of 23 miles *(39 km)*. As built, these ships had 80—40 mm and 49 to 60—20 mm anti-aircraft guns (except *Iowa*, only 19 quad 40 mm mounts); all 20 mm guns now removed.
When recommissioned in 1968 *New Jersey* was fitted with two Mk 38 fire control directors in addition to the Mk 40 and four Mk 51 previously installed. Mk 48 shore bombardment computer installed when reactivated. Also fitted with four Mk 37 and six Mk 56 GFCS.

Operational: *New Jersey* made one deployment to the Western Pacific during her third commission (1968-69).
During the deployment she was on the "gun line" off South Viet-Nam for a total of 120 days with 47 days being the longest sustained period at sea.
While in action *New Jersey* fired 5 688 rounds of ammunition from her 16 in main battery guns and a total of 6 200 rounds during the commission, the additional firings being for tests and training. While off Viet-Nam she also fired some 15 000 rounds from her 5 in secondary battery guns.
(In comparison, during World War II *New Jersey* fired 771 main battery rounds and during two deployments in the Korean War and midshipmen training cruises she fired 6 671 main battery rounds.)

Radar: SPS 6 and 10 (fitted in *New Jersey* 1968-69).

NEW JERSEY (off Viet-Nam)   4/1969, USN

WISCONSIN   USN

CRUISERS

The US Navy's active cruiser force consists of 27 guided missile ships. Twenty-four of these ships (including seven nuclear powered) have been completed during the past 15 years with the three older ships being modernised World War II-built cruisers. All of these ships are oriented primarily toward Anti-Air Warfare (AAW) with the three older ships additionally configured to serve as flagships for the US Navy's numbered fleets. In addition, the collision-damaged *Belknap* (CG 26) is undergoing a two-year repair/modernisation programme (1978-80).

Three additional nuclear-propelled missile cruisers are under construction. With nine nuclear cruisers available by 1980 the Navy could operate two all-nuclear carrier task forces.

Future cruiser construction consists of four "Modified Virginia" class Aegis-equipped CGNs. On Feb 22 1977 Secretary of Defense Harold Brown announced the cancellation of the nuclear strike cruiser (CSGN) programme preferring the option of two DDG-47 Aegis-equipped destroyers for the price of one CSGN. He promised "study in depth" before "changing the five-year shipbuilding plan" (Details of the proposed CSGN are in *Jane's Fighting Ships* 1976-77).

4 GUIDED MISSILE CRUISERS (nuclear propulsion) (CGN): "MODIFIED VIRGINIA" CLASS

No.	Programme	Commission
CGN 42	Planned FY 1979	est 1984
CGN 43	Planned FY 1981	est 1986
CGN 44	Planned FY 1983	est 1987
CGN 45	Planned FY 1985	est 1989

Displacement, tons: 12 000 full load
Length, feet (metres): 560 *(172·2)* waterline
Beam, feet (metres): 63 *(19·2)*
Draught, feet (metres): 24 *(7·3)*
Helicopters: approx 2
Missile launchers: approx 2 combination twin Tartar D/ASROC launchers (Mk 26) firing Standard MR surface-to-air missiles
Guns: 2—5 in *(127 mm)* 54 calibre (Mk 45) single; 2—20 mm Mk 15 CIWS; 2—40 mm (saluting)
A/S weapons: (approx) ASROC *(see above)*; 2 triple Mk 32 torpedo tubes firing Mk 46 torpedoes
Main engines: 2 geared turbines; 2 shafts
Reactors: 2 pressurised-water cooled D2W (Westinghouse)
Speed, knots: 30+
Complement: 634 (52 officers, 582 enlisted men)

The "Modified Virginia" Class is to be built in place of the eight Nuclear Strike Cruisers (CSGN) proposed by the Ford Administration in late 1976. CGN 42 was originally to be the fifth unit of the "Virginia" Class, but was cancelled in the FY 1976.

It is more than likely that all four ships of this class will be built by Newport News SB & DD Co. Contract for long term lead items awarded to Newport News in Nov 1977.

Design: To save on design and research and development costs this class is using the same basic design as the "Virginia" Class (CGN 38/41). The major difference is that the existing design has been modified to accommodate the AEGIS system. Another difference between this class and the "Virginia" class is that this class employs the latest electronic, fire control and weapons systems.

Electronics: Fitted with Naval Tactical Data System (NTDS).

Fire control: Estimated to be Mk 74 missile control directors and digital Mk 116 ASW FCS. Will carry the AEGIS AN/SPY 1 system with UYK 7 computers to control radar.

Fiscal: In the FY 1979 the initial ship will cost $1 082 million dollars with costs decreasing to between $840 million and $1 000 million dollars for the follow on ships.

Gunnery: Mk 86 gunfire control directors.

Missiles: Magazines will carry a mixed Standard MR/ASROC load for each launcher. Harpoon SSM will be fitted during construction.

Radar: Data not available.

Sonar: Probably SQS 53 series (bow mounted).

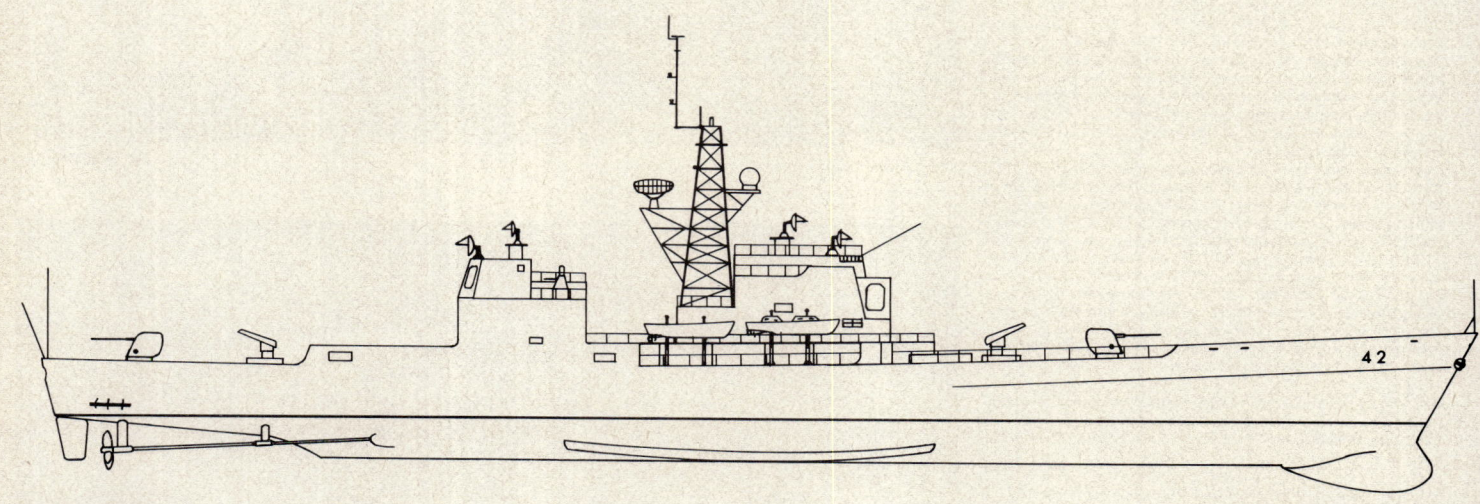

CGN 42 (Provisional)

Drawing, John Humphrey

USA 657

3 + 1 NUCLEAR-POWERED GUIDED MISSILE CRUISERS (CGN): "VIRGINIA" CLASS

Name	No.	Builders	Laid down	Launched	Commissioned	F/S
VIRGINIA	CGN 38 (ex-*DLGN 38*)	Newport News Shipbuilding Co	19 Aug 1972	14 Dec 1974	11 Sept 1976	AA
TEXAS	CGN 39 (ex-*DLGN 39*)	Newport News Shipbuilding Co	18 Aug 1973	9 Aug 1975	10 Sept 1977	AA
MISSISSIPPI	CGN 40 (ex-*DLGN 40*)	Newport News Shipbuilding Co	22 Feb 1975	31 July 1976	July 1978	Bldg
ARKANSAS	CGN 41	Newport News Shipbuilding Co	17 Jan 1977	—	May 1980	Bldg

Displacement, tons: 10 000 full load
Length, feet (metres): 585 *(177·3)* oa
Beam, feet (metres): 63 *(18·9)*
Draught, feet (metres): 29·5 *(9·0)*
Aircraft: 2 (see *Helicopter* notes)
Missile launchers: 2 combination twin Tartar-D/ASROC launchers firing Standard MR surface-to-air missile (Mk 26)
Guns: 2—5 in *(127 mm)* 54 calibre (Mk 45) (single)
A/S weapons: ASROC (see above);
2 triple torpedo tubes (Mk 32)
Main engines: 2 geared turbines; 60 000 shp; 2 shafts
Reactors: 2 pressurised-water cooled D2G (General Electric)
Speed, knots: 30+
Complement: 442 (27 officers, 415 enlisted men)

Virginia was authorised in the Fiscal Year 1970 new construction programme, *Texas* in the FY 1971, *Mississippi* in the FY 1972, and *Arkansas* in the FY 1975.
CGN 42 was proposed in the FY 1976 new construction programme but was not funded by the Congress.
Construction of this class has been delayed because of a shortage of skilled labour in the shipyard. Newport News SB & DD Co (Virginia) is the only shipyard in the United States now engaged in the construction of nuclear surface ships. The first three ships of the class are more than one year behind their original construction schedules. Additional delays are anticipated.

Classification: These ships were originally classified as guided missile frigates (DLGN); subsequently reclassified as guided missile cruisers (CGN) on 30 June 1975.

Design: The principal differences between the "Virginia" and "California" classes are the improved anti-air warfare capability, electronic warfare equipment, and anti-submarine fire control system. The deletion of the separate ASROC Mk 16 launcher permitted the "Virginia" class to be 10 feet shorter.

Electronics: Naval Tactical Data System (NTDS).

Fiscal: These ships have incurred major cost growth/escalation during their construction. Fiscal data on the earlier ships were in the 1974-75 and earlier editions.

Fire control: Mk 74 missile control directors.
Digital Mk 116 ASW FCS.

Gunnery: Mk 86 gunfire control directors. Two 20 mm Mk 15 CIWS will be fitted in each ship.

Each ship has two 40 mm saluting guns.

Helicopters: A hangar for helicopters is installed beneath the fantail flight-deck with a telescoping hatch cover and an electro-mechanical elevator provided to transport helicopters between the main deck and hangar. These are the first US post-World War II destroyer/cruiser ships with a hull hangar.

Missiles: The initial design for this class provided for a single surface-to-air missile launcher; revised in 1969 to provide two Mk 26 launchers that will fire the Standard-Medium Range (MR) surface-to-air missile and the ASROC anti-submarine missile. "Mixed" Standard/ASROC magazines are planned for each launcher.
Harpoon SSM will be fitted in the immediate future or as new ships complete.

Radar: 3D search: SPS 48A.
Search: SPS 40B and 55.

Rockets: Mk 36 "Chaffroc" RBOC (Rapid Bloom Overhead Chaff) to be fitted.

Sonar: SQS 53A (bow-mounted).

VIRGINIA
9/1976, Dr. Giorgio Arra

TEXAS
7/1977, USN

2 NUCLEAR-POWERED GUIDED MISSILE CRUISERS (CGN) "CALIFORNIA" CLASS

Name	No.	Builders	Laid down	Launched	Commissioned	F/S
CALIFORNIA	CGN 36	Newport News Shipbuilding Co	23 Jan 1970	22 Sept 1971	16 Feb 1974	AA
SOUTH CAROLINA	CGN 37	Newport News Shipbuilding Co	1 Dec 1970	1 July 1972	25 Jan 1975	AA

Displacement, tons: 9 561 full load
Length, feet (metres): 596 (181·7) oa
Beam, feet (metres): 61 (18·6)
Draught, feet (metres): 31·5 (9·6)
Missile launchers: 2 single Tartar-D surface-to-air launchers firing Standard MR (Mk 13) to be fitted with Harpoon in near future
Guns: 2—5 in (127 mm) 54 calibre (Mk 45) (single)
A/S weapons: 4 torpedo tubes (Mk 32); 1 ASROC 8-tube launcher (Mk 16)
Main engines: 2 geared turbines; 60 000 shp; 2 shafts
Nuclear reactors: 2 pressurised-water cooled D2G (General Electric)
Speed, knots: 30+
Complement: 540 (28 officers, 512 enlisted men)

California was authorised in the Fiscal Year 1967 new construction programme and *South Carolina* in the FY 1968 programme. The construction of a third ship of this class (DLGN 38) was also authorised in FY 1968, but the rising costs of these ships and development of the DXGN/DLGN 38 design (now "Virginia" class) caused the third ship to be cancelled.

Classification: These ships were originally classified as guided missile frigates (DLGN); subsequently reclassified as guided missile cruisers (CGN) on 30 June 1975.

Design: These ships have tall, enclosed towers supporting radar antennae in contrast to the open lattice masts of the previous nuclear frigates *Truxtun* and *Bainbridge*.
No helicopter support facilities provided.

Electronics: Fitted with the Naval Tactical Data System (NTDS).

Engineering: Estimated nuclear core life for these ships provides 700 000 miles range; estimated cost is $11·5 million for the two initial nuclear cores in each ship.

Fire control: Two Mk 74 MFCS; one Mk 86 GFCS; one Mk 11 Weapons direction system (to be replaced by Mk 13)

Fiscal: Estimated cost is $200 million for *California* and $180 million for *South Carolina*.

Gunnery: Two Phalanx 20 mm CIWS (Mk 15) to be fitted. Each ship carries two 40 mm saluting guns.

Missiles: Reportedly, these ships carry some 80 surface-to-air missiles divided equally between a magazine beneath each launcher.

Radar: 3D air search: SPS 48
Search: SPS 10 and 40.
Fire control: SPG 51D, SPG 60 and SPQ 9A.

Rockets: Mk 36 Chaffroc RBOC to be fitted in place of Mk 28 system.

Sonar: SQS 26CX (bow mounted).

CALIFORNIA   6/1977, C. and S. Taylor

SOUTH CAROLINA   9/1976, USN

CALIFORNIA   6/1977, C. and S. Taylor

USA 659

1 NUCLEAR-PROPELLED GUIDED MISSILE CRUISER (CGN): "TRUXTUN" CLASS

Name	No.	Builders	Laid down	Launched	Commissioned	F/S
TRUXTUN	CGN 35	New York SB Corp (Camden, New Jersey)	17 June 1963	19 Dec 1964	27 May 1967	PA

Displacement, tons: 8 200 standard; 9 127 full load
Length, feet (metres): 564 (117.9) oa
Beam, feet (metres): 58 (17.7)
Draught, feet (metres): 31 (9.4)
Aircraft: Facilities for helicopter
Missile launchers: 1 twin Standard ER/ASROC launcher (Mk 10) Harpoon to be fitted
Guns: 1—5 in (127 mm) 54 calibre (Mk 42)
2—3 in (76 mm) 50 calibre (Mk 34) (single)
A/S weapons: ASROC (see above);
4 fixed torpedo tubes (Mk 32)
Main engines: 2 geared turbines; 60 000 shp; 2 shafts
Nuclear reactors: 2 pressurised-water cooled D2G (General Electric)
Speed, knots: 29
Complement: 528 (36 officers, 492 enlisted men)
Flag accommodations: 18 (6 officers, 12 enlisted men)

Truxtun was the US Navy's fourth nuclear-powered surface warship. The Navy had requested seven oil-burning frigates in the Fiscal Year 1962 shipbuilding programme; Congress authorised seven ships, but stipulated that one ship must be nuclear-powered.
Although the *Truxtun* design is adapted from the "Belknap" class design, the nuclear ship's gun-missile launcher arrangement is reversed from the non-nuclear ships.
Construction cost was $138.667 million.

Ammunition: 60 rounds for the missile launcher of which no more than 20 can be ASROC.

Classification: *Truxtun* was originally classified as a guided missile frigate (DLGN); subsequently reclassified as a guided missile cruiser (CGN) on 30 June 1975.

Electronics: Naval Tactical Data System (NTDS); Tacan.

Engineering: Power plant is identical to that of the cruiser *Bainbridge*.

Fire control: Two Mk 76 missile control systems, one Mk 68 gunfire control system, one Mk 11 weapon direction system, one SPG 53A and two SPG 55B weapon control radars (Mk 11 WDS to be replaced by Mk 14).

Gunnery: 2 Phalanx 20 mm systems (Mk 15) to be fitted.
Two 40 mm saluting guns fitted.

Missiles: The twin missile launcher aft can fire Standard ER anti-aircraft missiles and ASROC anti-submarine rockets.

Name: *Truxtun* is the fifth ship to be named after Commodore Thomas Truxton *(sic)* who commanded the frigate *Constellation* (38 guns) in her successful encounter with the French frigate *L'Insurgente* (44) in 1799.

Radar: 3D search: SPS 48.
Search: SPS 10 and 40.

Rockets: Mk 36 Chaffroc RBOC will be fitted soon replacing the Mk 28 system.

Sonar: SQS 26 (bow-mounted).

Torpedoes: Fixed Mk 32 tubes are below 3-in gun mounts, built into superstructure.

TRUXTUN   1/1977, Dr. Giorgio Arra

TRUXTUN   1/1977, Dr. Giorgio Arra

TRUXTUN   1/1977, Dr. Giorgio Arra

660 USA

9 GUIDED MISSILE CRUISERS (CG): "BELKNAP" CLASS

Name	No.	Builders	Laid down	Launched	Commissioned	F/S
BELKNAP	CG 26	Bath Iron Works Corp	5 Feb 1962	20 July 1963	7 Nov 1964	AR
JOSEPHUS DANIELS	CG 27	Bath Iron Works Corp	23 April 1962	2 Dec 1963	8 May 1965	AA
WAINWRIGHT	CG 28	Bath Iron Works Corp	2 July 1962	25 April 1964	8 Jan 1966	AA
JOUETT	CG 29	Puget Sound Naval Shipyard	25 Sept 1962	30 June 1964	3 Dec 1966	PA
HORNE	CG 30	San Francisco Naval Shipyard	12 Dec 1962	30 Oct 1964	15 April 1967	PA
STERETT	CG 31	Puget Sound Naval Shipyard	25 Sept 1962	30 June 1964	8 April 1967	PA
WILLIAM H. STANDLEY	CG 32	Bath Iron Works Corp	29 July 1963	19 Dec 1964	9 July 1966	PA
FOX	CG 33	Todd Shipyard Corp	15 Jan 1963	21 Nov 1964	8 May 1966	PA
BIDDLE	CG 34	Bath Iron Works Corp	9 Dec 1963	2 July 1965	21 Jan 1967	AA

Displacement, tons: 6 570 standard; 7 900 full load
Length, feet (metres): 547 (166·7) oa
Beam, feet (metres): 54·8 (16·7)
Draught, feet (metres): 28·8 (8·7)
Aircraft: 1 SH-2D LAMPS helicopter
Missile launchers: 1 twin Standard ER/ASROC launcher (Mk 10); Harpoon to be fitted
Guns: 1—5 in (127 mm) 54 cal (Mk 42)
2—3 in (76 mm) 50 cal (Mk 34) (single)
A/S weapons: ASROC (see above); 2 triple torpedo tubes (Mk 32)
Main engines: 2 geared turbines (General Electric except De Laval in CG 33): 85 000 shp; 2 shafts
Boilers: 4 (Babcock & Wilcox in CG 26-28, 32-34; Combustion Engineering in CG 29-31)
Speed, knots: 32·5
Complement: 418 (31 officers, 387 enlisted men) including squadron staff
Flag accommodations: 18 (6 officers; 12 enlisted men)

These ships were authorised as guided missile frigates; DLG 26-28 in the FY 1961 shipbuilding programme; DLG 29-34 in the FY 1962 programme.
All ships of this class are active except *Belknap*, which was severely damaged in a collision with the carrier *John F. Kennedy* (CV 67) on 22 Nov 1975 near Sicily; the cruiser was towed back to the United States for rebuilding at Philadelphia Naval Shipyard. Placed "Out of Commission—Special" 20 Dec 1975. Rebuilding began 9 Jan 1978. Estimated completion 8 Jan 1980.

Ammunition: 60 missiles for Mk 10 launcher of which only 20 can be ASROC.

Classification: These ships were originally classified as guided missile frigates (DLG); reclassified as guided missile cruisers (CG) on 30 June 1975.

Design: These ships are distinctive by having their single missile launcher forward and 5 in gun mount aft. This arrangement allowed missile stowage in the larger bow section and provided space aft of the superstructure for a helicopter hangar and platform. The reverse gun-missile arrangement, preferred by some commanding officers, is found in *Truxtun*.

Electronics: Naval Tactical Data System (NTDS); Tacan.

Fire control: Two Mk 76 missile control systems, one Mk 68 gunfire control system, two Mk 51 gun directors (removed from *Sterett* in 1976 and *Josephus Daniels*, *Belknap* and *Fox* in 1977), one Mk 11 weapon direction system (Mk 7 in *Josephus Daniels* and *Belknap*), one SPG 53A and two SPG 55B weapon control radars. (Mk 14 WDS to be fitted in place of present system in all ships soon).

Gunnery: All of this class will be fitted with two Phalanx 20 mm Mk 15 CIWS as will *Belknap* during rebuilding. Two 76 mm 50 cal removed from *Sterett* in 1976.

Helicopters: These ships are the only conventionally powered US cruisers with a full helicopter support capability. All fitted with the Light Airborne Multi-Purpose System, now the SH-2D helicopter. *Belknap* embarked the first operational SH-2D/LAMPS in Dec 1971.

Missiles: *Truxtun* and "Belknap" class ships have a twin Terrier/ASROC Mk 10 missile launcher. A "triple-ring" rotating magazine stocks both Terrier anti-craft missiles and ASROC anti-submarine rockets, feeding either weapon to the launcher's two firing arms. The rate of fire and reliability of the launcher provide a potent AAW/ASW capability to these ships. The class will be fitted in the near future with Harpoon. *Fox* was fitted with an experimental Tomahawk cruise-missile system in 1977.

Radar: 3D search: SPS 48.
Search: SPS 10 and 37 (26-28) or 40 (remainder).

Rockets: Mk 36 "Chaffroc" RBOC to be fitted in place of Mk 28.

Sonar: SQS 26 (bow mounted).

Torpedoes: As built, these ships each had two 21 in tubes for anti-submarine torpedoes installed in the structure immediately forward of the 5 in mount, one tube angled out to port and one to starboard; subsequently removed.

JOUETT 3/1976, USN

JOUETT 3/1976, USN

STERETT 8/1976, USN

USA 661

9 GUIDED MISSILE CRUISERS (CG) "LEAHY" CLASS

Name	No.	Builders	Laid down	Launched	Commissioned	F/S
LEAHY	CG 16	Bath Iron Works Corp	3 Dec 1959	1 July 1961	4 Aug 1962	PA
HARRY E. YARNELL	CG 17	Bath Iron Works Corp	31 May 1960	9 Dec 1961	2 Feb 1963	AA
WORDEN	CG 18	Bath Iron Works Corp	19 Sept 1960	2 June 1962	3 Aug 1963	PA
DALE	CG 19	New York SB Corp	6 Sept 1960	28 July 1962	23 Nov 1963	AA
RICHMOND K. TURNER	CG 20	New York SB Corp	9 Jan 1961	6 April 1963	13 June 1964	AA
GRIDLEY	CG 21	Puget Sound Bridge & Dry Dock Co	15 July 1960	31 July 1961	25 May 1963	PA
ENGLAND	CG 22	Todd Shipyards Corp	4 Oct 1960	6 Mar 1962	7 Dec 1963	PA
HALSEY	CG 23	San Francisco Naval Shipyard	26 Aug 1960	15 Jan 1962	20 July 1963	PA
REEVES	CG 24	Puget Sound Naval Shipyard	1 July 1960	12 May 1962	15 May 1964	PA

Displacement, tons: 5 670 standard; 7 800 full load
Length, feet (metres): 510 pp (155·5); 533 (162·5) oa
Beam, feet (metres): 54·9 (16·6)
Draught, feet (metres): 24·8 (7·6)
Missile launchers: 2 twin Standard ER launchers (Mk 10)
Guns: 4—3 in (76 mm) 50 cal (Mk 33) (twin)
A/S weapons: 1 ASROC 8-tube launcher; 2 triple torpedo tubes (Mk 32)
Main engines: 2 geared turbines (see Engineering notes); 85 000 shp; 2 shafts
Boilers: 4 (Babcock & Wilcox in CG 16-20, Foster-Wheeler in 21-24)
Speed, knots: 32·7
Fuel, tons: 1 800
Range, miles: 8 000 at 20 knots
Complement: 377 (18 officers, 359 enlisted men) (16, 17, 21, 23); 413 (32 officers, 381 men) (18-20, 22, 24)
Flag accommodations: 18 (6 officers, 12 enlisted men)

These ships are "double-end" missile cruisers especially designed to screen fast carrier task forces. They are limited in only having 3 in guns. Authorised as DLG 16-18 in the Fiscal Year 1958 new construction programme and DLG 19-24 in the FY 1959 programme.

Classification: These ships were originally classified as guided missile frigates (DLG); reclassified as guided missile cruisers (CG) on 30 June 1975.

Design: These ships are distinctive in having twin missile launchers forward and aft with ASROC launcher between the forward missile launcher and bridge on main deck level.
There is a helicopter landing area aft but only limited support facilities are provided; no hangar.

Electronics: Naval Tactical Data System (NTDS) fitted during AAW modernisation.

Engineering: General Electric turbines in CG 16-18, De Laval turbines in CG 19-22, and Allis-Chalmers turbines in CG 23 and CG 24.

Fire control: Four Mk 76 missile control systems, two Mk 63 gunfire control systems (Reeves only), one Mk 11 weapon direction system, (to be replaced by Mk 14 WDS) and four SPG 55 radars. Mk 114 ASW fire control system.

Gunnery: Two Phalanx 20 mm CIWS Mk 15 to be fitted.
Two 40 mm saluting guns fitted.

Missiles: Reportedly, each ship carries 80 missiles divided between the two magazines. Harpoon to be fitted.

Modernisation: These ships were modernised between 1967 and 1972 to improve their Anti-Air Warfare (AAW) capabilities. Superstructure enlarged to provide space for additional electronic equipment, including NTDS; improved Tacan fitted and improved guidance system for Terrier/Standard missiles installed, and larger ship's service turbo generators provided.
All ships modernised at Bath Iron Works except Leahy at Philadelphia Naval Shipyard.
Cost of Leahy modernisation was $36·1 million.

Radar: 3D search: SPS 48 (replacing SPS 39 or 52 in some ships)
Search: SPS 10, 37

Rockets: Mk 36 Chaffroc RBOC to be fitted

Sonar: SQS 23 bow-mounted.

HALSEY 9/1975, USN

HARRY E. YARNELL 10/1977, C. and S. Taylor

LEAHY 1976, Michael D. J. Lennon

662 USA

1 NUCLEAR-PROPELLED GUIDED MISSILE CRUISER (CGN) "BAINBRIDGE" CLASS

Name	No.	Builders	Laid down	Launched	Commissioned	F/S
BAINBRIDGE	CGN 25	Bethlehem Steel, Co Quincy, Mass	15 May 1959	15 April 1961	6 Oct 1962	PA

Displacement, tons: 7 600 standard; 8 580 full load
Length, feet (metres): 550 *(167·6)* wl; 565 *(172·5)* oa
Beam, feet (metres): 57·9 *(17·6)*
Draught, feet (metres): 25·4 *(7·7)*
Missile launchers: 2 twin Terrier/Standard ER surface-to-air Mk 10 launchers
Guns: 4—3 in *(76 mm)* 50 calibre (Mk 33) (twins)
A/S weapons: 1 ASROC 8-tube launcher; 2 triple torpedo tubes (Mk 32)
Main engines: 2 geared turbines, approx 60 000 shp; 2 shafts
Nuclear reactors: 2 pressurised-water cooled D2G (General Electric)
Speed, knots: 30+
Complement: 470 (34 officers, 436 enlisted men)
Flag accommodations: 18 (6 officers, 12 enlisted men)

(All data prior to modernisation).

Bainbridge was the US Navy's third nuclear powered surface warship (after the cruiser *Long Beach* and the aircraft carrier *Enterprise*). Authorised in the FY 1956 shipbuilding programme. Construction cost was $163·61 million.

Classification: *Bainbridge* was originally classified as a guided missile frigate (DLGN); reclassified as a guided missile cruiser (CGN) on 30 June 1975.

Design: The ship is similar in basic arrangements to the "Leahy" class cruisers.

Engineering: Development of a nuclear power plant suitable for use in a large "destroyer type" warship began in 1957. The Atomic Energy Commission's Knolls Atomic Power Laboratory undertook development of the destroyer power plant (designated D1G/D2G).

Fire control: Four Mk 76 missile control systems, one Mk 11 weapons direction system, four SPG 55A weapon control radars (Mk 14 WDS to replace Mk 11).

Gunnery: Two 20 mm Mk 15 CIWS to be fitted. Two 40 mm saluting guns carried.

Missiles: *Bainbridge* has a Terrier Mk 10 Mod 5 launcher forward and a Mk 10 Mod 6 launcher aft. Reportedly, the ship carries 80 missiles divided between the forward and aft rotating magazines. Terrier system to be replaced by Standard 1 (ER) in near future. To be fitted with Harpoon.

Modernisation: *Bainbridge* underwent an Anti-Air Warfare (AAW) modernisation at the Puget Sound Naval Shipyard from 30 June 1974 to 24 Sept 1976. The ship was fitted with the Naval Tactical Data System (NTDS) and improved guidance capability for missiles. Estimated cost of modernisation $103 million.

Radar: 3D search: SPS 52
Search: SPS 10 and 37

Rockets: Mk 36 Chaffroc RBOC to be fitted.

Sonar: SQS 23 (bow-mounted)

BAINBRIDGE 4/1977, USN

1 NUCLEAR-PROPELLED GUIDED MISSILE CRUISER (CGN) "LONG BEACH" CLASS

Name	No.	Builders	Laid down	Launched	Commissioned	F/S
LONG BEACH	CGN 9 (ex-CGN 160, CLGN 160)	Bethlehem Steel Co, Quincy, Mass	2 Dec 1957	14 July 1959	9 Sept 1961	PA

Displacement, tons: 14 200 standard; 15 540 light; 17 100 full load
Length, feet (metres): 721·2 *(219·8)* oa
Beam, feet (metres): 73·2 *(22·3)*
Draught, feet (metres): 29·7 *(9·1)*
Aircraft: Deck for utility helicopter
Missile launchers: 1 twin Talos surface-to-air launcher (Mk 12); 2 twin Terrier/Standard-ER surface-to-air launchers (Mk 10)
Guns: 2—5 in *(127 mm)* 38 calibre (Mk 30) (single)
A/S weapons: 1 ASROC 8-tube launcher; 2 triple torpedo tubes (Mk 32)
Main engines: 2 geared turbines (General Electric); 80 000 shp; 2 shafts
Nuclear reactors: 2 pressurised-water cooled C1W (Westinghouse)
Speed, knots: 30
Complement: 1 160 (79 officers, 1 081 enlisted men)
Flag accommodations: 68 (10 officers, 58 enlisted men)

Long Beach was the first ship to be designed as a cruiser for the United States since the end of World War II. She is the world's first nuclear-powered surface warship and the first warship to have a guided missile main battery. She was authorised in the FY 1957 new construction programme. Estimated construction cost was $332·85 million.

Aegis: Long-lead funding for the installation of an Aegis system was provided in the FY 1977 programme.
The conversion was due to start in Oct 1978 for completion in Oct 1981. It was cancelled in Dec 1976 and the authorised funds rescinded (see *Conversion* note below).

Conversion: As a result of the Aegis cancellation (above) *Long Beach* is to undergo a mid-life conversion in FY 1980. This is planned to include updating of missile systems, restoration of the missile radars, the present SPS 32 and 33 air search to be replaced by SPS 48 and 49 systems, replacement of the ship's computer and modernisation of the communications system. Estimated cost of conversion—$267 million. Estimated length of conversion—three years.

Classification: Ordered as a guided missile light cruiser (CLGN 160) on 15 Oct 1956; reclassified as a guided missile cruiser (CGN 160) early in 1957 and renumbered (CGN 9) on 1 July 1957.

Design: Initially planned at about 7 800 tons (standard) to test the feasibility of a nuclear-powered surface warship. Early in 1956 her displacement was increased to 11 000 tons and a second Terrier missile launcher was added. A Talos missile launcher was also added which, with other features, increased displacement to 14 200 tons.

Electronics: Naval Tactical Data System (NTDS).

Fire control: Four Mk 76 missile fire control systems, one Mk 77 Mod 4 missile fire control system, two Mk 56 gunfire control systems, one Mk 6 weapon direction system, two SPG 49B and four SPG 55A weapon-control radars.

Engineering: The reactors are similar to those of *Enterprise* (CVN 65). *Long Beach* first got underway on nuclear power on 5 July 1961. After four years of operation and having steamed more than 167 700 miles she underwent her first overhaul and refuelling at the Newport News Shipbuilding and Dry Dock Company from Aug 1965 to Feb 1966.

Gunnery: Completed with an all-missile armament. Two single 5 in mounts were fitted during 1962-63. two Phalanx 20 mm CIWS Mk 15 to be fitted. Two 40 mm saluting guns carried.

Missiles: *Long Beach* has two Terrier twin missile launchers stepped forward and one Talos twin missile launcher aft. Reportedly, her magazines hold 120 Terrier missiles and approx 46 Talos missiles. Harpoon to be fitted.
In the FY 1978 Talos is reportedly to be replaced. Terrier system to be replaced by Standard 1 (ER) system in near future.

Radar: Long range fixed air search: SPS 32
Long range target tracking: SPS 33
(Fixed arrays "billboards" on bridge, SPS 32 horizontal and 33 vertical—both modified in 1970).
Search: SPS 10 and 12

Rockets: Mk 36 Chaffroc RBOC to be fitted in place of Mk 28.

Sonar: SQS 23.

LONG BEACH 1968, USN

2 GUIDED MISSILE CRUISERS (CG) "ALBANY" CLASS

Name	No.	Builders	Laid down	Launched	Commissioned	F/S
ALBANY	CG 10 (ex-CA 123)	Bethlehem Steel Co, Fore River	6 Mar 1944	30 June 1945	15 June 1946	AA
CHICAGO	CG 11 (ex-CA 136)	Philadelphia Navy Yard	28 July 1943	20 Aug 1944	10 Jan 1945	PA

Displacement, tons: 13 700 standard; 17 700 full load *(Chicago)* 18 240 *(Albany)*
Length, feet (metres): 664 *(202·4)* wl; 674 *(205·4)* oa
Beam, feet (metres): 71 *(21·6)*
Draught, feet (metres): 33·5 *(10·2)*
Missile launchers: 2 twin Talos surface-to-air launchers (Mk 12); 2 twin Tartar surface-to-air launchers (Mk 11)
Guns: 2—5 in *(127 mm)* 38 calibre (Mk 24) (single)
A/S weapons: 1 ASROC 8-tube launcher; 2 triple torpedo tubes (Mk 32)
Helicopters: Deck for utility helicopters
Main engines: 4 geared turbines (General Electric); 120 000 shp; 4 shafts
Boilers: 4 (Babcock & Wilcox)
Speed, knots: 32
Complement: 1 222 (72 officers, 1 150 enlisted men)
Flag accommodations: 68 (10 officers, 58 enlisted men)

These ships were fully converted from heavy cruisers, *Albany* having been a unit of the "Oregon City" class and *Chicago* of the "Baltimore" class. Although the two heavy cruiser classes differed in appearance they had the same hull dimensions and machinery. These ships form a new, homogeneous class.
The cruiser *Fall River* (CA 131) was originally scheduled for missile conversion, but was replaced by *Columbus* (now deleted). Proposals to convert two additional heavy cruisers (CA 124 and CA 130) to missile ships (CG 13 and CG 14) were dropped, primarily because of high conversion costs and improved capabilities of newer missile-armed frigates.

Conversion: During conversion these ships were stripped down to their main hulls with all cruiser armament and superstructure being removed. New superstructures make extensive use of aluminium to reduce weight and improve stability. *Albany* was converted at the Boston Naval Shipyard between Jan 1959 and new commissioning on 3 Nov 1962; *Chicago* at San Francisco Naval Shipyard from July 1959 to new commissioning on 2 May 1964.

Electronics: Naval Tactical Data System (NTDS) is fitted in *Albany*.

Fire control: Two Mk 77 missile fire control systems, four Mk 74 missile fire control systems, two Mk 56 gunfire control systems, one Mk 6 weapon direction system, four SPG 49B and four SPG 51C weapon control radars.

Gunnery: No guns were fitted when these ships were converted to missile cruisers. Two single open-mount 5 in guns were fitted subsequently to provide low-level defence.
Two Phalanx 20 mm Mk 15 CIWS to be fitted. Two 40 mm saluting guns fitted.

Missiles: One twin Talos launcher is forward and one aft, a twin Tartar launcher is on each side of the main bridge structure. During conversion, space was allocated amidships for installation of eight Polaris missile tubes, but the plan to install ballistic missiles in cruisers was cancelled in mid-1959. Reportedly 92 Talos and 80 Tartar missiles are carried.
It is reported that the Talos system and associated fire control systems will be removed in the FY 1978 and not replaced. Harpoon to be fitted.

Modernisation: *Albany* underwent an extensive anti-air warfare modernisation at the Boston Naval Shipyard, including installation of NTDS, a digital Talos fire-control system and improved radars. This began in Feb 1967 and was completed in August 1969. She was formally recommissioned on 9 Nov 1968.
Both are due for major overhauls—*Albany* July 1978-June 1979, *Chicago* March 1979. Costs for *Albany* $20·1 million for repairs and $1·6 million for alterations. Costs for *Chicago* $20·6 million for repairs and $4·1 million in alterations. The higher expenditure on *Chicago* is designed to bring her closer to the capabilities of *Albany*.

Radar: *Albany*:
3D search: SPS 48
Search: SPS 10, 30 and 43

ALBANY 8/1975, USN

ALBANY 1976, Michael D. J. Lennon

Chicago:
Search: SPS 10, 30, 43 and 52

Rockets: Mk 28 Chaffroc RBOC to be replaced by Mk 36.

Sonar: SQS 23 (bow mounted)

ALBANY 9/1975, Reinhard Nerlich

664 USA

3 GUIDED MISSILE CRUISERS (CG) CONVERTED "CLEVELAND" CLASS

Name	No.	Builders	Laid down	Launched	Commissioned	F/S
OKLAHOMA CITY	CG 5 (ex-CLG 5, ex-CL 91)	Cramp Shipbuilding, Philadelphia	8 Mar 1942	20 Feb 1944	22 Dec 1944	PA
PROVIDENCE	CG 6 (ex-CLG 6, ex-CL 82)	Bethlehem Steel Co, Quincy, Mass	27 July 1943	28 Dec 1944	15 May 1945	PR
SPRINGFIELD	CG 7 (ex-CLG 7, ex-CL 66)	Bethlehem Steel Co, Quincy, Mass	13 Feb 1943	9 Mar 1944	9 Sept 1944	AR

Displacement, tons: 10 670 standard; 15 200 full load
Length, feet (metres): 600 *(182·9)* wl; 610 *(185·9)* oa
Beam, feet (metres): 66·3 *(20·1)*
Draught, feet (metres): 25 *(7·6)*
Aircraft: Utility helicopter carried
Missile launchers:
 CG 5: 1 twin Talos surface-to-air launcher (Mk 7)
 CG 6, 7: 1 twin Terrier surface-to-air launcher (Mk 9)
Guns: 3—6 in *(152 mm)* 47 cal (triple);
 2—5 in *(127 mm)* 38 cal (Mk 32) (twin)
Main engines: 4 geared turbines (General Electric);
 100 000 shp; 4 shafts
Boilers: 4 (Babcock & Wilcox)
Speed, knots: 30·6 knots (CG 5); 32 (others)
Complement: approx 1 350 (89/92 officers; 1 245/1 288 enlisted men)
Flag accommodations: 216 (50 officers; 166 enlisted men)

Originally a series of six ships were converted from light cruisers of the "Cleveland" class; three ships converted to Terrier missile configuration aft and three ships to Talos missile aft, with two ships of each missile type configured to serve as fleet flagships.
The surviving ships are all fitted as fleet flagships.
Providence was decommissioned on 31 Aug 1973 and *Springfield* on 15 June 1974; *Oklahoma City* is flagship of the US Seventh Fleet in the Western Pacific (homeported in Yokosuka, Japan).

Classification: Upon conversion to missile configuration these ships were reclassified as guided missile light cruisers (CLG). On 30 June 1975 the surviving three ships were reclassified as guided missile cruisers (CG).

Conversion: All six of these ships had their two after 6 in gun turrets replaced by a twin surface-to-air missile launcher, superstructure enlarged to support missile fire control equipment, lattice masts fitted to carry antennae, 5 in battery reduced from original 12 guns and all 40 mm and 20 mm light anti-aircraft guns removed. The four ships fitted as fleet flagships additionally had their No 2 turret of 6 in guns removed and their forward superstructure enlarged to provide command and communications spaces. *Oklahoma City* began conversion at the Bethlehem Steel shipyard in San Francisco in May 1957 and was commissioned on 7 Sept 1960; *Providence* began conversion at the Boston Naval Shipyard in June 1957 and was commissioned on 17 Sept 1959; *Springfield* began conversion at the Bethlehem Steel shipyard in Quincy, Massachusetts, in Aug 1957, but was moved to the Boston Naval Shipyard in March 1960 for completion and commissioning on 2 July 1960. There is a helicopter landing area on the fantail, but only limited support facilities are provided; no hangar.

Fire control: CG 5 has one Mk 77 missile fire control system and the Terrier ships one Mk 73; CG 5 has one Mk 2 weapon direction system and two SPG 49A weapon control radars; Terrier ships one Mk 3 weapon direction system and two SPQ 5A radars.

Gunnery: Two Phalanx 20 mm Mk 15 CIWS to be fitted in *Oklahoma City*. Two 40 mm saluting guns fitted in each ship.

Missiles: Reportedly, the cruisers armed with Terrier each carry 120 missiles and the ship armed with Talos carries 46 missiles. As of FY 1978 *Oklahoma City* is the only USN ship fitted with Talos.

Radar: 3D search: SPS 52 (6 and 7)
Search: SPS 10, 30 and 43 (5 and 7)
SPS 10, 30 and 37 (6)

Rockets: One Mk 36 Chaffroc RBOC to be fitted in *Oklahoma City*.

Sonar: None.

PROVIDENCE   USN

SPRINGFIELD   1973, USN

OKLAHOMA CITY

9/1977, Dr. Giorgio Arra

USA 665

3 HEAVY CRUISERS (CA) "DES MOINES" CLASS

Name	No.	Builders	Laid down	Launched	Commissioned	F/S
DES MOINES	CA 134	Bethlehem Steel Co, Fore River	28 May 1945	27 Sept 1946	16 Nov 1948	AR
SALEM	CA 139	Bethlehem Steel Co, Fore River	4 July 1945	25 Mar 1947	14 May 1949	AR
NEWPORT NEWS	CA 148	Newport News SB & DD Co	1 Oct 1945	6 Mar 1947	29 Jan 1949	AR

Displacement, tons: 17 000 standard; 20 950 full load
Length, feet (metres): 700 *(213·4)* wl; 716·5 *(218·4)* oa
Beam, feet (metres): 76·3 *(23·3)*
Draught, feet (metres): 25·4 *(7·7)*
Guns: 9—8 in *(203 mm)* 55 cal (triple) except 6—8 in guns in *Newport News* (see *Gunnery* notes); 12—5 in *(127 mm)* 38 cal (Mk 32) twin; 20—3 in *(76 mm)* 50 cal *(Des Moines)* (twin); 22—3 in *(Salem)*; 4—3 in *(Newport News)*
Main engines: 4 geared turbines (General Electric); 120 000 shp; 4 shafts
Boilers: 4 (Babcock & Wilcox)
Speed, knots: 31·5
Complement: 1 803 (116 officers, 1 687 enlisted men) *(Des Moines)*
1 738 (115 officers, 1 623 enlisted men (remainder)
Flag accommodations: 267 (65 officers, 206 enlisted men) in *Newport News*

These ships were the largest and most powerful 8 in gun cruisers ever built. Completed too late for World War II, they were employed primarily as flagships for the Sixth Fleet in the Mediterranean and the Second Fleet in the Atlantic. *Salem* was decommissioned on 30 Jan 1959 and *Des Moines* on 14 July 1961. *Newport News* served as flagship of the US Second Fleet in the Atlantic. Her decommissioning was delayed several times to enable her to provide gunfire support in Viet-Nam. Decommissioned on 27 June 1975, the last active all-gun cruiser of the US Navy.

Aircraft: As completed *Des Moines* had two stern catapults and carried four floatplanes; catapults later removed.

Design: These ships are an improved version of the previous "Oregon City" class. The newer cruisers have automatic main batteries, larger main turrets, taller fire control towers, and larger bridges. *Des Moines* and *Newport News* are fully air-conditioned.
Additional ships of this class were cancelled: *Dallas* (CA 140) and the unnamed CA 141-142, CA 149-153.

Electronics: Tacan.

Fire control: Two Mk 56 gunfire control systems, two Mk 54 gunfire control directors and four Mk 37 GFCS *(Newport News)*.

Gunnery: These cruisers were the first ships to be armed with fully automatic 8 in guns firing cased ammunition. The guns can be loaded at any elevation from −5 to +41 degrees; rate of fire is four times faster than earlier 8 in guns. Mk XVI 8-in guns in these ships; other heavy cruisers remaining on Navy List have Mk XV guns.
As built, these ships mounted 12—5 in guns, 24—3 in guns (in twin mounts), and 12—20 mm guns (single mounts). The 20 mm guns were removed almost immediately and the 3 in battery was reduced gradually as ships were overhauled. With full armament the designed wartime complement was 1 860. The No. 2 main gun turret of *Newport News* was severely damaged by a turret explosion in Oct 1972; not repaired and centre gun subsequently removed. The turret is not operable. Two saluting guns in each ship.

Modernisation: *Newport News* was extensively modified to provide improved flagship facilities.

Radar: SPS 6, 8, 10 and 37 *(Newport News)*.

NEWPORT NEWS   10/1974, USN

NEWPORT NEWS   10/1974, USN

666　USA

1 HEAVY CRUISER (CA) "BALTIMORE" CLASS

Name	No.	Builders	Laid down	Launched	Commissioned	F/S
SAINT PAUL	CA 73	Bethlehem Steel Co, Fore River	3 Feb 1943	16 Sept 1944	17 Feb 1945	PR

Displacement, tons: 13 600 standard; 17 350 full load
Length, feet (metres): 664 *(204·4)* wl; 674·7 *(205·6)* oa
Beam, feet (metres): 70·6 *(21·5)*
Draught, feet (metres): 24·3 *(7·4)*
Guns: 9—8 in *(203 mm)* 55 cal (triple); 10—5 in *(127 mm)* 38 cal (Mk 32) (twin); 12—3 in *(76 mm)* 50 cal (Mk 33) (twin)
Main engines: 4 geared turbines (General Electric); 120 000 shp; 4 shafts
Boilers: 4 (Babcock & Wilcox)
Speed, knots: 31
Complement: 1 777 (106 officers, 1 671 enlisted men)
Flag accommodations: 217 (37 officers, 180 enlisted men)

Saint Paul is the last all-gun cruiser of the "Baltimore" class. Fourteen of these ships were completed 1943-45. This was the largest class of heavy (8-in gun) cruisers built by any navy. Two missile ship conversions remain on the Navy List (see *Conversion* notes). *Saint Paul* was decommissioned 30 April 1971 and placed in reserve.

Aircraft: As completed the "Baltimore" class ships had two stern catapults and carried four floatplanes; catapults removed after World War II. Hangar under fantail.

Conversions: Two ships of this class were converted to partial missile configurations, *Boston* (CA 69/CAG 1) (since deleted) and *Canberra* (CA 70/CAG 2); and two ships were converted to all-missile configurations, *Columbus* (CA 74/CG 12) (since deleted) and *Chicago* (CA 136 now CG 11).

Fire control: Two Mk 37 GFCS, four Mk 56 GFCS, two Mk 34 gun directors, one Mk 5 target designation system.

Gunnery: As built the "Baltimore" class cruisers were armed with nine 8 in guns, 12—5 in guns, 48—40 mm guns, and 23—20 mm guns. After World War II all 20 mm weapons were removed and the 40 mm guns were replaced by 20—3 in guns. Subsequently the 5 in twin mount forward of the bridge was removed from *Saint Paul* and the number of 3 in twin gun mounts was reduced.
Two 40 mm saluting guns fitted.

Modernisation: *Saint Paul* was extensively modified to serve as flagship for the Seventh Fleet in the western Pacific; advanced communications equipment installed and amidships structure built up to provide more office space.

Name: *Saint Paul* was renamed during construction; ex-*Rochester*.

Radar: (On decommissioning): SPS 8 and 37.

SAINT PAUL　　　　　　　　　　　　　　　　　　　　　　　　　　　　　　　　　　USN

1 HEAVY CRUISER (CA-ex-CAG) "CANBERRA" CLASS

Name	No.	Builders	Laid down	Launched	Commissioned	F/S
CANBERRA	CA 70 (ex-CAG 2)	Bethlehem Steel Co, Fore River	3 Sept 1941	19 April 1943	14 Oct 1943	PR

Displacement, tons: 13 300 standard; 17 800 full load
Length, feet (metres): 664 *(222·3)* wl; 674 *(205·4)* oa
Beam, feet (metres): 70·9 *(21·6)*
Draught, feet (metres): 29 *(8·8)*
Guns: 6—8 in *(203 mm)* 55 cal (triple); 10—5 in *(127 mm)* 38 cal (Mk 32) (twin); 4—3 in *(76 mm)* 50 cal (Mk 33) (twin); 2—40 mm saluting guns
Main engines: 4 geared turbines (General Electric); 120 000 shp; 4 shafts
Boilers: 4 (Babcock & Wilcox)
Speed, knots: 33
Complement: 1 730 (110 officers, 1 620 enlisted men)
Flag accommodations: 72 (10 officers, 62 enlisted men)

Canberra and her sister ship *Boston* (CA 69 ex-CAG 1) (since deleted) were the US Navy's first guided missile surface ships. They originally were heavy cruisers (CA) of the "Baltimore" class. *Canberra* was converted 1952-1956 to a combination gun-missile configuration and reclassified CAG 2 on 4 Jan 1952. Subsequently reverted to original classification of CA 70 on 1 May 1968; as a CA *Canberra* retained the Terrier missile systems until late 1969.
Retention of 8 in guns forward made *Boston* and *Canberra* valuable in the fire support role during the Viet-Nam War. *Canberra* was decommissioned on 16 Feb 1970 and placed in reserve.

Conversion: *Canberra* was converted to a missile configuration at the New York Shipbuilding Corp, Camden, New Jersey. Conversion included removal of after 8-in gun turret (143 tons) and after twin 5-in gun mount; all 40 mm and 20 mm guns replaced by six 3-in twin mounts (subsequently reduced to two mounts). Original superstructure modified and twin funnels replaced by single large funnel as in "Oregon City" class. Forward pole mast replaced by lattice radar mast and radar platform fitted aft of pole mast. Missile systems included rotating magazine below decks, loading and check-out equipment, two large directors, and two launchers.

Electronics: Tacan.

Fire control: One Mk 37 and four Mk 56 gunfire control systems, one Mk 34 gun director, and one Mk 1 target designation system.

Missiles: Reportedly, *Canberra* could carry 144 Terrier missiles in two rotating magazines. Each launcher could load and fire two missiles every 30 seconds; loading was completely automatic with the missiles sliding up onto the launchers when in the vertical position. Both missile launchers removed prior to decommissioning—late 1969.

Name: *Canberra* was originally named *Pittsburgh*; renamed while under construction in commemoration of the Australian cruiser of that name which was sunk at the Battle of Savo Island with several US Navy ships in August 1942. She is the only US warship named after a foreign capital city.

Radar: Search: SPS 30 and 43 (on decommissioning).

CANBERRA　　　　　　　　　　　　　　　　　　　　　　　　　　　　　　　　　　1968, USN

DESTROYERS

The rapid drop in destroyer numbers began to slow in Sept 1975 when the first of 30 "Spruance" class destroyers was commissioned. These ships will be completed at regular intervals through 1979. At this time the Navy plans to follow the "Spruance" class with a guided missile destroyer based on the same hull and machinery, but employing the Aegis missile system.
The US Navy destroyer force in early-1977 consisted of 61 ships (including 10 former "frigates") plus 29 ships assigned to the Naval Reserve Force (NRF) and manned partially by reservists.
Increasingly the Navy is using frigates for operations that previously required destroyers. Although the frigates have modern anti-submarine weapons and sensors similar to destroyers, and in some classes superior, the frigates lack the guns, electronics, 30-knot speeds, and in most cases the surface-to-air missiles considered necessary for modern anti-air warfare and surface warfare operations.
Soon after the last of the "Spruance" class ships are completed in 1979, the destroyer force is expected to consist of 69 ships: the 39 missile-armed DDG type and the 30 "Spruance" class non-missile DD type. Most or all of the "Forrest Sherman" class destroyers and the few surviving "Gearing" class ships will probably be assigned to the Naval Reserve Force by that time.

CLASSIFICATION

All guided missile frigates (DLG/DLGN) on the Navy List as of 30 June 1975 were reclassified as guided missile cruisers (CG/CGN) except for the ten ships of the "Coontz" class which were reclassified as guided missile destroyers (DDG). Previously two all-gun frigates had been reclassified as guided missile destroyers upon conversion to a missile configuration: *Mitscher* DDG 35 (ex-DL 2, ex-DD 927) and *John S. McCain* DDG 36 (ex-DL 3, ex-DD 928).

1 + (15) GUIDED MISSILE DESTROYERS (DDG): AEGIS TYPE

	No.	Programme	Commission	F/S
One Ship	DDG 47	Approved FY 1978	1982 (est)	Bldg
One Ship	DDG 48	Proposed FY 1980	—	Proj
Two Ships	DDG 49-50	Proposed FY 1981	—	Proj
Two Ships	DDG 51-52	Proposed FY 1982	—	Proj
Three Ships	DDG 53-55	Proposed FY 1983	—	Proj
Three Ships	DDG 56-58	Proposed FY 1984	—	Proj
Three Ships	DDG 59-61	Proposed FY 1985	—	Proj
One Ship	DDG 62	Proposed FY 1986	1990 (est)	Proj

Displacement, tons: 9 055 full load
Length, feet (metres): approx 563·3 *(171·1)* oa
Beam, feet (metres): 55 *(17·6)*
Draught, feet (metres): 31 app *(9·5)*
Aircraft: 2 LAMPS helicopters
Missile launchers: 2 twin Standard-MR/ASROC launchers (Mk 26); Harpoon surface-to-surface cannisters
Guns: 2—5 in *(127 mm)* 54 cal; 2—20 mm Phalanx Close-In Weapon Systems (CIWS)
A/S weapons: ASROC; torpedo tubes (Mk 32)
Main engines: 4 LM 2500 gas turbines; 80 000 shp; 2 shafts
Speed, knots: 30+
Complement: 316 (27 officers, 289 enlisted men)

The DDG 47 class fulfils the proposal for a non-nuclear Aegis-armed ship as proposed in the early 1970s with the designation DG, but subsequently dropped to avoid conflict with the Navy's nuclear-propelled cruiser programme.
The DDG 47 budget request is for $938 million for the lead ship; follow-on ships will cost between $700-750 million each, still many times that of the late DG proposal. The high cost of these ships and the view that all high-capability Aegis ships should have nuclear propulsion have made the class the target of intensive Congressional criticism. The Navy-Department of Defense five-year plan provides for ten of these ships.

Builder: Ingall SB Divn Litton Industries is suggested as a likely builder for the first ships along with Bath Iron Works.

Design: The DDG 47 design is a modification of the "Spruance" class (DD 963). The same basic hull will be used, with the same gas turbine propulsion system. The design calls for 1 in steel armour plate to protect the magazines.

Electronics: Aegis is described under "Shipboard Systems". DDG 47 will have the full Aegis electronics suite.

Fire control: Aegis Weapons Control System Mk 1 with UYK-7 computers to control radar phasing, Mk 86 gunfire control system, four Mk 99 missile guidance illuminators. Mark 116 Underwater FCS.

Missiles: Two launchers will be provided for the Standard-MR surface-to-air missile. Standard Missile—2 (now under trial). The Harpoon surface-to-surface missiles would be carried in two eight-tube deck canisters.

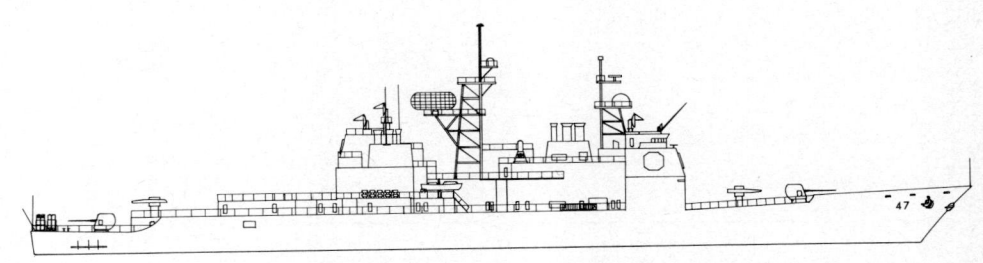

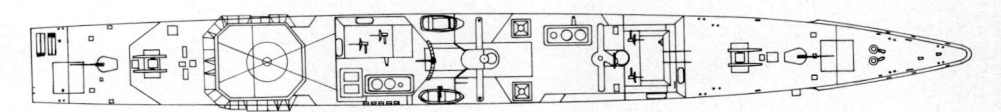

Radar: SPY 1A paired arrays (one forward, one aft)
Search: SPS 49
Weapons: SPQ 9

Sonar: SQS 53 and TACTAS towed array.

DDG 47 Class — 1978, John Humphrey

DDG 47 Class — 1976, USN Drawing

668　USA

1 ASW HELICOPTER DESTROYER (DDH) IMPROVED "SPRUANCE" CLASS

Name	No.	Programme	Commission
—	DDH 997	Approved FY 1978	est 1982

Displacement, tons: est 9 000
Length, feet (metres): 529 *(161·2)* wl; 563·3 *(171·1)* oa
Beam, feet (metres): 55 *(16·8)*
Draught, feet (metres): est 29 *(8·8)*
Aircraft: Up to 4 SH-2F LAMPS III helicopters
Missile launchers: 1—8-tubed NATO Sea Sparrow (Mk 29)
Guns: 2—5 in *(127 mm)* 54 cal (Mk 45) (single)
A/S weapons: 1 ASROC 8-tube launcher
　2 triple torpedo tubes (Mk 32)
Main engines: 4 gas turbines (General Electric); 80 000 shp;
　2 shafts
Speed, knots: 30+
Complement: 369 (36 officers, 333 enlisted men)

This single ship class was added to the Navy's 1978 programme by Congress and is not Navy initiated. Originally two of this class were added by the US Senate. The House of Representatives failed to approve funds for any of this class. During the House-Senate Conference about the FY 1978 Military Budget, agreement was reached to provide $310 million for one ship. This sum was authorised with the proviso that no more than this should be spent on this ship. When bids are solicited from shipbuilders should they be over the $310 million, weapons, electronics and other equipment will have to be deleted to bring the cost under the limit. It is conceivable that the Navy will have 31 "Spruance" Class. Since this ship is to be the only one of the class and was added to the shipbuilding programme due to a heavy lobbying effort by interested parties it is considered probable that she will be the "white elephant" of the fleet.

Design: The design duplicates that of the "Spruance" Class Destroyer with the exception that the hangar and landing area have been enlarged.

Electronics: All radars, sonar and fire control will be fairly similar to that of the "Spruance" Class. Naval Tactical Data System will be fitted.

Engineering: Propulsion system will duplicate that of the "Spruances".

Missiles: Space and weight are reserved for the installation of two quadruple Harpoon SSM missile launchers.

Gunnery: Weight and space are reserved for installation of two Phalanx 20 mm (Mk 15) CIWS systems.

Rockets: Two Mk 36 Chaffroc (RBOC) launchers are to be fitted.

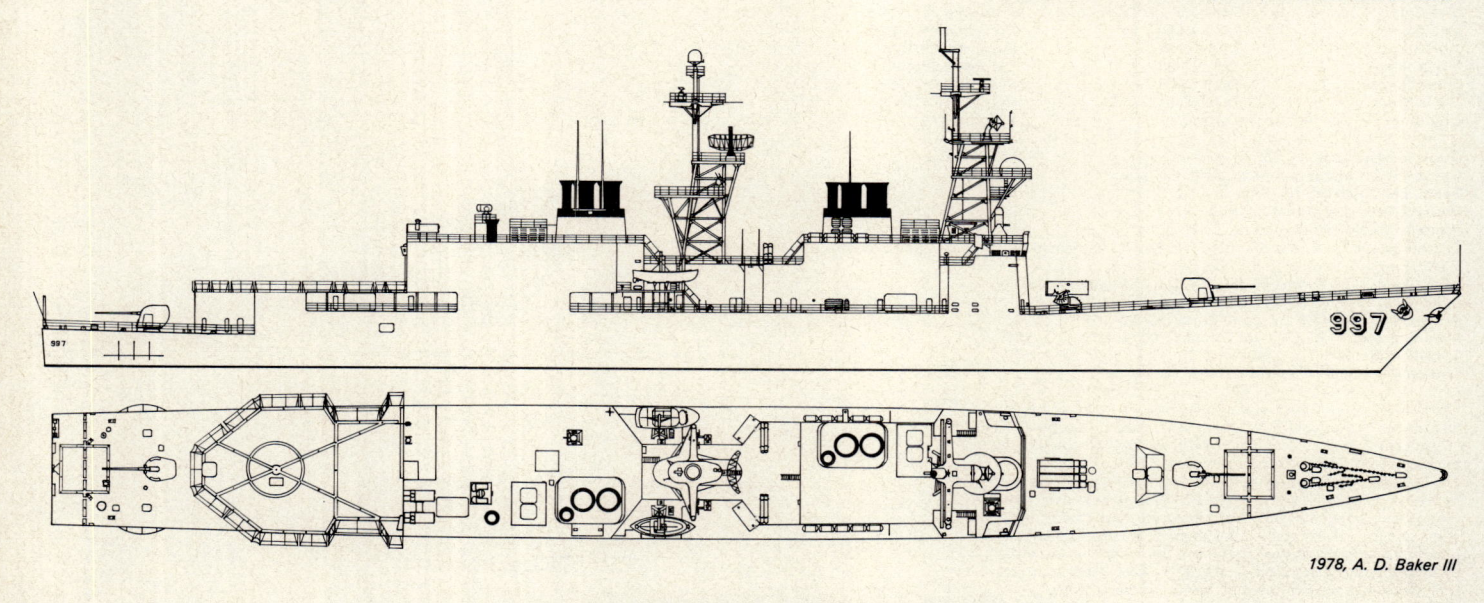

1978, A. D. Baker III

18 + 12 DESTROYERS (DD) "SPRUANCE" CLASS

Name	No.	Builders	Laid down	Launched	Commissioned	F/S
SPRUANCE	DD 963	Ingalls Shipbuilding Corp	17 Nov 1972	10 Nov 1973	20 Sept 1975	AA
PAUL F. FOSTER	DD 964	Ingalls Shipbuilding Corp	6 Feb 1973	23 Feb 1974	21 Feb 1976	PA
KINKAID	DD 965	Ingalls Shipbuilding Corp	19 April 1973	25 May 1974	10 July 1976	PA
HEWITT	DD 966	Ingalls Shipbuilding Corp	23 July 1973	24 Aug 1974	25 Sept 1976	PA
ELLIOTT	DD 967	Ingalls Shipbuilding Corp	15 Oct 1973	19 Dec 1974	22 Jan 1976	PA
ARTHUR W. RADFORD	DD 968	Ingalls Shipbuilding Corp	14 Jan 1974	1 Mar 1975	16 April 1977	AA
PETERSON	DD 969	Ingalls Shipbuilding Corp	29 April 1974	21 June 1975	9 July 1977	AA
CARON	DD 970	Ingalls Shipbuilding Corp	1 July 1974	24 June 1975	1 Oct 1977	AA
DAVID R. RAY	DD 971	Ingalls Shipbuilding Corp	23 Sept 1974	23 Aug 1975	19 Nov 1977	PA
OLDENDORF	DD 972	Ingalls Shipbuilding Corp	27 Dec 1974	21 Oct 1975	1978	Bldg
JOHN YOUNG	DD 973	Ingalls Shipbuilding Corp	17 Feb 1975	7 Feb 1976	1978	Bldg
COMTE DE GRASSE	DD 974	Ingalls Shipbuilding Corp	4 April 1975	26 Mar 1976	1978	Bldg
O'BRIEN	DD 975	Ingalls Shipbuilding Corp	9 May 1975	8 July 1976	17 Dec 1977	PA
MERRILL	DD 976	Ingalls Shipbuilding Corp	16 June 1975	1 Sept 1976	1978	Bldg
BRISCOE	DD 977	Ingalls Shipbuilding Corp	21 July 1975	15 Dec 1976	1978	Bldg
STUMP	DD 978	Ingalls Shipbuilding Corp	25 Aug 1975	29 Jan 1977	1978	Bldg
CONOLLY	DD 979	Ingalls Shipbuilding Corp	29 Sept 1975	19 Feb 1977	1978	Bldg
MOOSBURGGER	DD 980	Ingalls Shipbuilding Corp	3 Nov 1975	23 July 1977	1978	Bldg
JOHN HANCOCK	DD 981	Ingalls Shipbuilding Corp	16 Jan 1976	29 Oct 1977	1979	Bldg
NICHOLSON	DD 982	Ingalls Shipbuilding Corp	20 Feb 1976	11 Nov 1977	1979	Bldg
JOHN RODGERS	DD 983	Ingalls Shipbuilding Corp	12 Aug 1976	1977	1979	Bldg
LEFTWICH	DD 984	Ingalls Shipbuilding Corp	12 Nov 1976	1978	1979	Bldg
CUSHING	DD 985	Ingalls Shipbuilding Corp	27 Dec 1976	1978	1979	Bldg
HARRY W. HILL	DD 986	Ingalls Shipbuilding Corp	3 Jan 1977	1978	1979	Bldg
O'BANNON	DD 987	Ingalls Shipbuilding Corp	21 Feb 1977	1978	1979	Bldg
THORN	DD 988	Ingalls Shipbuilding Corp	29 Aug 1977	1978	1979	Bldg
DEYO	DD 989	Ingalls Shipbuilding Corp	14 Oct 1977	1978	1979	Bldg
INGERSOLL	DD 990	Ingalls Shipbuilding Corp		1978	1980	Bldg
FIFE	DD 991	Ingalls Shipbuilding Corp	1977	1978	1980	Bldg
FLETCHER	DD 992	Ingalls Shipbuilding Corp	1978	1979	1980	Bldg

Displacement, tons: 7 810 full load
Length, feet (metres): 529 *(161·2)* wl; 563·3 *(171·1)* oa
Beam, feet (metres): 55 *(17·6)*
Draught, feet (metres): 29 *(8·8)*
Aircraft: 1 SH-3 Sea King or 2 SH-2D LAMPS helicopters
Guns: 2—5 in *(127 mm)* 54 calibre (Mk 45) (single)
A/S weapons: 1 ASROC 8-tube launcher
　2 triple torpedo tubes (Mk 32)
Main engines: 4 gas turbines (General Electric); 80 000 shp;
　2 shafts
Speed, knots: 33
Range, miles: 6 000 at 20 knots
Complement: 296 (24 officers, 272 enlisted men)

According to official statements, "the primary mission of these ships is anti-submarine warfare including operations as an integral part of attack carrier task forces."

The Fiscal Year 1969 new construction programme requested funding for the first five ships of this class, although, funds were denied by Congress. In the FY 1970 programme Congress approved funds for five ships, but increasing costs forced the Department of Defense to construct only three ships under the FY 1970 programme (DD 963-965); six ships were authorised in the FY 1971 programme (DD 966-971); seven ships (DD 972-978) in the FY 1972 programme; seven ships (DD 979-985) in the FY 1974 programme, and seven ships (DD 986-992) in the FY 1975 programme.

A/S weapons: The ASROC reload magazine is located under the launcher with the twin-cell launcher nacelles depressing to a vertical position. Capacity 24 rounds. 14 torpedoes carried for Mk 32 tubes.

Design: Extensive use of the modular concept is used to facilitate initial construction and block modernisation of the ships. The ships are highly automated, resulting in about 20 per cent reduction in personnel over a similar ship with conventional systems.

Engineering: These ships are the first large US warships to employ gas turbine propulsion. Each ship has four General Electric LM2500 marine gas turbine engines, a shaft-power version of the TF39 turbofan aircraft engine, and controllable-pitch propellers, because gas turbine engines cannot use a reversible shaft. Fitted with advanced self-noise reduction features.

Fire control: Mk 116 digital underwater fire control system and one Mk 86 gunfire control system, one Mk 91 missile FCS, one SPG 60 and one SPG 9 radars.

Helicopters. Full helicopter facilities are provided to accommodate the Light Airborne Multi-Purpose System (LAMPS), now the SH-2D helicopter. However, the ship can handle the larger SH-3 Sea King series.

Gunnery: An improved 5 in 54 calibre Mk 65 gun is being considered for use in later ships of the class. The "Spruance" design can accommodate the 8-in Major Calibre Light-Weight Gun (MCLWG) (Mk 71). There are now plans to install that weapon in DD 963-968 during each overhaul beginning 1980. The 5 in mount will be retained aft.
Two 20 mm Phalanx Mk 15 CIWS are planned for installation. 600 rounds per gun carried (5 in).

Missiles: The NATO Sea Sparrow multiple missile launcher (Mk 29) is planned for installation in these ships (between helicopter deck and after 5 in gun mount).

Radar: Search: SPS 40

Rockets: Mk 36 Chaffroc system is to be retrofitted in 1978-79 in DD 963-972 (in place of Mk 33) and in remainder during construction.

Sonar: SQS 53 (bow mounted) (SQS 35 VDS not fitted due to success with SQS 53).

Torpedoes: The triple Mk 32 torpedo tubes are inside the superstructure to facilitate maintenance and reloading; they are fired through side ports.

PETERSON

7/1977, Litton Industries

CARON

7/1977, Litton Industries

10 GUIDED MISSILE DESTROYERS (DDG) "COONTZ" CLASS

Name	No.	Builders	Laid down	Launched	Commissioned	F/S
FARRAGUT	DDG 37 (ex-DLG 6)	Bethlehem Co, Quincy, Mass	3 June 1957	18 July 1958	10 Dec 1960	AA
LUCE	DDG 38 (ex-DLG 7)	Bethlehem Co, Quincy, Mass	1 Oct 1957	11 Dec 1958	20 May 1961	AA
MACDONOUGH	DDG 39 (ex-DLG 8)	Bethlehem Co, Quincy, Mass	15 April 1958	9 July 1959	4 Nov 1961	AA
COONTZ	DDG 40 (ex-DLG 9)	Puget Sound Naval Shipyard	1 Mar 1957	6 Dec 1958	15 July 1960	AA
KING	DDG 41 (ex-DLG 10)	Puget Sound Naval Shipyard	1 Mar 1957	6 Dec 1958	17 Nov 1960	AA
MAHAN	DDG 42 (ex-DLG 11)	San Francisco Naval Shipyard	31 July 1957	7 Oct 1959	25 Aug 1960	AA
DAHLGREN	DDG 43 (ex-DLG 12)	Philadelphia Naval Shipyard	1 Mar 1958	16 Mar 1960	8 April 1961	AA
WILLIAM V. PRATT	DDG 44 (ex-DLG 13)	Philadelphia Naval Shipyard	1 Mar 1958	16 Mar 1960	4 Nov 1961	AA
DEWEY	DDG 45 (ex-DLG 14)	Bath Iron Works, Maine	10 Aug 1957	30 Nov 1958	7 Dec 1959	AA
PREBLE	DDG 46 (ex-DLG 15)	Bath Iron Works, Maine	16 Dec 1957	23 May 1959	9 May 1960	PA

Displacement, tons: 4 150/4 580 standard; 5 709/5 907 full load
Length, feet (metres): 512·5 *(156·2)* oa
Beam, feet (metres): 52·5 *(15·9)*
Draught, feet (metres): 23·4 *(7·1)*
Missile launchers: 1 twin Terrier/Standard-ER surface-to-air launcher (Mk 10) (see Missile note)
Gun: 1—5 in *(127 mm)* 54 cal (Mk 42) (see *Gunnery* note)
A/S weapons: 1 ASROC 8-tube launcher; 2 triple torpedo tubes (Mk 32)
Main engines: 2 geared turbines; 85 000 shp; 2 shafts
Boilers: 4 (Foster-Wheeler in DDG 37-39; Babcock & Wilcox in DDG 40-46)
Speed, knots: 33
Fuel, tons: 900
Range, miles: 5 000 at 20 knots
Flag accommodations: 19 (7 officers, 12 enlisted men)
Complement: 377 (21 officers, 356 enlisted men)

These ships are an improvement of the "Mitscher" class (DL/DDG). DDG 37-42 were authorised in the FY 1956 programme; DDG 43-46 in the FY 1957 programme. Average cost per ship was $52 million.
Although now classified as "destroyers", these ships have many of the capabilities of the larger US cruiser classes, including the Terrier/Standard-ER missile system and Naval Tactical Data System (NTDS).

Classification: *Farragut, Luce* and *MacDonough* were initially classified as frigates (DL 6-8, respectively); changed to guided missile frigate (DLG) 6-8 on 14 Nov 1956. The first ship ordered as a missile frigate was *Coontz* which became the name ship for the class. All ten ships were classified as guided missile frigates (DLG 6-15) from completion until 30 June 1975 when reclassified as guided missile destroyers (DDG 37-46).

Design: These ships were the only US guided missile "frigates" with separate masts and funnels. They have aluminium superstructures to reduce weight and improve stability. Early designs for this class had a second 5 in gun mount in the "B" position; design revised when ASROC launcher was developed.
Helicopter landing area on stern, but no hangar and limited support capability.

Electronics: *King* and *Mahan* along with the aircraft carrier *Oriskany* (CV 34) were the first ships fitted with the Naval Tactical Data System (NTDS), conducting operational evaluation of the equipment in 1961-62. NTDS now in all ships.

Engineering: De Laval turbines in DDG 37-39 and DDG 46; Allis-Chalmers turbines in DDG 40-45.

Fire control: Two Mk 76 missile fire control systems, one Mk 68 gunfire control system, one SPG 53A and two SPG-55B weapon control radars (plus two SPG 50—*Macdonough* only). One Mk 11 WDS and one Mk 111 ASW FCS.

Gunnery: These ships have a Mk 42 single 5 inch gun forward. The original 4—3 in 50 cal guns were removed during modernisation.
King was fitted with the 20 mm Phalanx Mk 15 CIWS for at-sea evaluation from Aug 1973 to March 1974. All ships to be fitted with Phalanx in near future.
Two 40 mm saluting guns fitted.

Missiles: The first five ships of this class originally fitted with Terrier BW-1 beam-riding missile systems; five later ships built with Terrier BT-3 homing missile systems. Reportedly, each ship carries 40 missiles (BT-3). Harpoon to be fitted in all ships in near future.

Modernisation: These ships have been modernised to improve their Anti-Air Warfare (AAW) capabilities. Superstructure enlarged to provide space for additional electronic equipment, including NTDS (previously fitted in *King* and *Mahan*); improved Tacan installed, improved guidance system for Terrier/Standard missiles (SPG 55 fire control radar), and larger ship's service turbo generators fitted. *Farragut* also had improved ASROC reload capability provided (with additional structure forward of bridge) and second mast increased in height. (Other ships are not believed to carry ASROC reloads).
All ships modernised at Philadelphia Naval Shipyard, except *Mahan* at Bath Iron Works, Bath, Maine, and *King* at Boland Machine & Manufacturing Co, New Orleans, Louisiana between 1969 and 1977.
Cost of modernisation was $39 million per ship in the FY 1970 conversion programme.

Names: DDG 38 was to have been named *Dewey;* renamed *Luce* in 1957.

Radar: (After modernisation)
3D search: SPS 48 (SPS 52 in *King* and *Pratt*)
Search: SPS 10 and 37

Rockets: Mark 36 Chaffroc (RBOC) system to be fitted.

Sonar: SQS 23.

WILLIAM V. PRATT 7/1976, A. D. Barker

MACDONOUGH 10/1977, C. and S. Taylor

FARRAGUT 9/1976, Dr. Giorgio Arra

PREBLE 10/1977. Dr. Giorgio Arra

USA 671

2 GUIDED MISSILE DESTROYERS (DDG) "MITSCHER" CLASS

Name	No.	Builders	Laid down	Launched	Commissioned	F/S
MITSCHER	DDG 35 (ex-DL 2, ex-DD 927)	Bath Iron Works	3 Oct 1949	26 Jan 1952	15 May 1953	AA
JOHN S. McCAIN	DDG 36 (ex-DL 3, ex-DD 928)	Bath Iron Works	24 Oct 1949	12 July 1952	12 Oct 1953	PA

Displacement, tons: 5 200 full load
Length, feet (metres): 493 *(150·3)* oa
Beam, feet (metres): 50 *(15·2)*
Draught, feet (metres): 21 *(6·7)*
Missile launchers: 1 single Tartar surface-to-air launcher (Mk 13)
Guns: 2—5 in *(127 mm)* 54 calibre (Mk 42) (single)
A/S weapons: 1 ASROC 8-tube launcher;
2 triple torpedo tubes (Mk 32)
Main engines: 2 geared turbines (General Electric); 80 000 shp; 2 shafts
Boilers: 4 (Foster-Wheeler)
Speed, knots: 32
Complement: 377 (28 officers, 349 enlisted men)

These ships are former "Mitscher" class all-gun frigates which have been converted to a guided missile and improved ASW configuration.

Appearance: Both ships now have the smaller Tacan (Tactical Air Navigation) antenna on the main mast.

Classification: These ships were originally classified as destroyers (DD); reclassified as destroyer leaders (DL) on 9 Feb 1951 while under construction. The DL symbol was changed to "frigate" on 1 Jan 1955. Both ships were changed to DDG on 15 March 1967 during Tartar missile conversion.

Conversion: Both ships were converted to DDG at the Philadelphia Naval Shipyard. *Mitscher* began conversion in March 1966, commissioning on 29 June 1968 and *John S. McCain* in June 1966, commissioning on 6 Sept 1969. Superstructure was modified with ASROC launcher installed forward of the bridge in "B" position; two heavy lattice masts fitted; triple Mk 32 torpedo tubes retained amidships; and single Tartar launcher installed aft (system weighs approximately 135 000 lb).

Fire control: Two Mk 74 gun/missile fire control systems, one Mk 67 gunfire control system, two SPG 51C missile control radars and one Mk 4 WDS and one Mk 114 ASW FCS.

Missiles: Tartar magazine capacity is reported to be 40 missiles.

Radar: 3D search: SPS 48
Search: SPS 10 and 37

Rockets: Mk 36 Chaffroc (RBOC) to be fitted.

Sonar: SQS 23 (hull mounted)

JOHN S. McCAIN — 1975, USN

MITSCHER — 1971, USN

MITSCHER — 1973, Dr. Giorgio Arra

672 USA

4 GUIDED MISSILE DESTROYERS (DDG) CONVERTED "FORREST SHERMAN" CLASS

Name	No.	Builders	Laid down	Launched	Commissioned	F/S
DECATUR	DDG 31 (ex-DD 936)	Bethlehem Steel Co, Quincy, Mass	13 Sept 1954	15 Dec 1955	7 Dec 1956	PA
JOHN PAUL JONES	DDG 32 (ex-DD 932)	Bath Iron Works	18 Jan 1954	7 May 1955	5 April 1956	PA
PARSONS	DDG 33 (ex-DD 949)	Ingalls Shipbuilding Corp	17 June 1957	19 Aug 1958	29 Oct 1959	PA
SOMERS	DDG 34 (ex-DD 947)	Bath Iron Works	4 Mar 1957	30 May 1958	3 April 1959	PA

Displacement, tons: 4 150 full load
Length, feet (metres): 418·4 *(127·5)* oa
Beam, feet (metres): 44 *(13·4)*
Draught, feet (metres): 20 *(6·1)*
Missile launcher: 1 single Tartar surface-to-air launcher (Mk 13)
Gun: 1—5 in *(127 mm)* 54 calibre (Mk 42)
A/S weapons: 1 ASROC 8-tube launcher; 2 triple torpedo tubes (Mk 32)
Main engines: 2 geared turbines (Westinghouse in *John Paul Jones* and *Decatur*; General Electric in others); 70 000 shp; 2 shafts
Boilers: 4 (Foster-Wheeler in *Decatur*; Babcock & Wilcox in *John Paul Jones, Somers* and *Parsons*)
Speed, knots: 31 knots
Fuel, tons: 500
Range, miles: 4 500 at 20 knots
Complement: 337 (22 officers, 315 enlisted men) *(Decatur* and *John Paul Jones)*
364 (25 officers and 339 enlisted men) *(Parsons* and *Somers)*

"Forrest Sherman" class destroyers that have been converted to a guided missile and improved ASW configuration. Plans for additional DDG conversions of this class were dropped. *Decatur* was reclassified as DDG 31 on 15 Sept 1966; *John Paul Jones, Somers* and *Parsons* became DDG on 15 March 1967. See "Forrest Sherman" class DDs for additional notes.

Conversion: *Decatur* began conversion to a DDG at the Boston Naval Shipyard on 15 June 1965, *John Paul Jones* at the Philadelphia Naval Shipyard on 2 Dec 1965, *Parsons* at the Long Beach (California) Naval Shipyard on 30 June 1965, and *Somers* at the San Francisco Bay Naval Shipyard on 30 March 1966.
Commissioned as DDGs on 29 April 1967, 23 April 1967, 3 Nov 1967 and 10 Feb 1968 respectively.
During conversion all existing armament was removed except the forward 5 in gun; two triple ASW torpedo tubes were installed forward of the bridge; two heavy lattice masts fitted; ASROC launcher mounted aft of second stack; single Tartar Mk 13 launcher installed aft (on 01 level; system weighs approximately 135 000 lb).
Original DDG conversion plans provided for Drone Anti-Submarine Helicopter (DASH) facilities; however, ASROC was substituted in all four ships as DASH lost favour in the Navy.

Fire control: One Mk 74 missile fire control system, one Mk 68 gunfire control system, one SPG 51C and one SPG 53B weapon control radars.
One Mk 4 WDS and one Mk 114 ASW FCS.

Gunnery: These ships and the "Coontz" class are the only US destroyers with one 5 in gun.

Missiles: Reportedly Tartar magazine capacity is 40 missiles.

Radar: 3D search: SPS 48.
Search: SPS 10 and 37 (40 in *Somers)*

Rockets: Mk 36 Chaffroc (RBOC) to be fitted.

Sonar: SQS 23 (hull mounted)

PARSONS 12/1976, Dr. Giorgio Arra

DECATUR 1/1977, Dr. Giorgio Arra

DECATUR 1/1977, Dr. Giorgio Arra

23 GUIDED MISSILE DESTROYERS (DDG) "CHARLES F. ADAMS" CLASS

USA 673

Name	No.	Builders	Laid down	Launched	Commissioned	F/S
CHARLES F. ADAMS	DDG 2	Bath Iron Works	16 June 1958	8 Sept 1959	10 Sept 1960	AA
JOHN KING	DDG 3	Bath Iron Works	25 Aug 1958	30 Jan 1960	4 Feb 1961	AA
LAWRENCE	DDG 4	New York Shipbuilding Corp	27 Oct 1958	27 Feb 1960	6 Jan 1962	AA
CLAUDE V. RICKETTS	DDG 5	New York Shipbuilding Corp	18 May 1959	4 June 1960	5 May 1962	AA
BARNEY	DDG 6	New York Shipbuilding Corp	18 May 1959	10 Dec 1960	11 Aug 1962	AA
HENRY B. WILSON	DDG 7	Defoe Shipbuilding Co	28 Feb 1958	23 April 1959	17 Dec 1960	PA
LYNDE McCORMICK	DDG 8	Defoe Shipbuilding Co	4 April 1958	9 Sept 1960	3 June 1961	PA
TOWERS	DDG 9	Todd Shipyards Inc, Seattle	1 April 1958	23 April 1959	6 June 1961	PA
SAMPSON	DDG 10	Bath Iron Works	2 Mar 1959	9 Sept 1960	24 June 1961	AA
SELLERS	DDG 11	Bath Iron Works	3 Aug 1959	9 Sept 1960	28 Oct 1961	AA
ROBISON	DDG 12	Defoe Shipbuilding Co	23 April 1959	27 April 1960	9 Dec 1961	PA
HOEL	DDG 13	Defoe Shipbuilding Co	1 June 1960	4 Aug 1960	16 June 1962	PA
BUCHANAN	DDG 14	Todd Shipyards Inc, Seattle	23 April 1959	11 May 1960	7 Feb 1962	PA
BERKELEY	DDG 15	New York Shipbuilding Corp	1 June 1960	29 July 1961	15 Dec 1962	PA
JOSEPH STRAUSS	DDG 16	New York Shipbuilding Corp	27 Dec 1960	9 Dec 1961	20 April 1963	PA
CONYNGHAM	DDG 17	New York Shipbuilding Corp	1 May 1961	19 May 1962	13 July 1963	AA
SEMMES	DDG 18	Avondale Marine Ways Inc	18 Aug 1960	20 May 1961	10 Dec 1962	AA
TATTNALL	DDG 19	Avondale Marine Ways Inc.	14 Nov 1960	26 Aug 1961	13 April 1963	AA
GOLDSBOROUGH	DDG 20	Puget Sound Bridge & Dry Dock Co	3 Jan 1961	15 Dec 1961	9 Nov 1963	PA
COCHRANE	DDG 21	Puget Sound Bridge & Dry Dock Co	31 July 1961	18 July 1962	21 Mar 1964	PA
BENJAMIN STODDERT	DDG 22	Puget Sound Bridge & Dry Dock Co	11 June 1962	8 Jan 1963	12 Sept 1964	PA
RICHARD E. BYRD	DDG 23	Todd Shipyards Inc, Seattle	12 April 1961	6 Feb 1962	7 Mar 1964	AA
WADDELL	DDG 24	Todd Shipyards Inc, Seattle	6 Feb 1962	26 Feb 1963	28 Aug 1964	PA

Displacement, tons: 3 370 standard; 4 500 full load
Length, feet (metres): 437 *(133.2)* oa
Beam, feet (metres): 47 *(14.3)*
Draught, feet (metres): 27.2 *(8.3)*
Missile launchers: DDG 2-14: 1 twin Tartar surface-to-air launcher (Mk 11)
  DDG 15-24: 1 single Tartar surface-to-air launcher (Mk 13)
  (see *Missile* note)
Guns: 2—5 in *(127 mm)* 54 calibre (Mk 42) (single)
A/S weapons: 1 ASROC 8-tube launcher;
  2 triple torpedo tubes (Mk 32)
Main engines: 2 geared steam turbines (General Electric in DDG 2, 3, 7, 8, 10-13, 15-22; Westinghouse in DDG 4-6, 9, 14, 23, 24); 70,000 shp; 2 shafts
Boilers: 4 (Babcock & Wilcox in DDG 2, 3, 7, 8, 10-13, 20-22; Foster-Wheeler in DDG 4-6, 9, 14, 23, 24; Combustion Engineering in DDG 15-19)
Speed, knots: 31+
Complement: 354 (24 officers, 330 enlisted men)

DDG 2-9 were authorised in the Fiscal Year 1957 new construction programme, DDG 10-14 in the FY 1958, DDG 15-19 in the FY 1959, DDG 20-22 in the FY 1960, DDG 23-24 in the FY 1961. Excellent general-purpose ships.

Classification: The first eight ships were to be a continuation of "Hull" class DDs and carried hull numbers DD 952-959. Redesigned as Guided Missile Destroyers and assigned DDG numbers. DDG 1 was *Gyatt* (ex-DD 712), which operated as a missile destroyer from 1956 to 1962 armed with a twin Terrier launcher.

Design: These ships were built to an improved "Forrest Sherman" class design with aluminium superstructures and a high level of habitability including air conditioning in all living spaces. DDG 20-24 have stem anchors because of sonar arrangement.
Several ships have been modified with an extension of the bridge structure on the starboard side on the 02 level.

Fire control: Two Mk 74 MFCS, one Mk 68 GFCS (to be replaced by Mk 86), one Mk 4 weapon system (to be replaced by Mk 13 which is already fitted in DDG 9, 12, 15 and 21), one SPG 51C, one SPG 53A weapon control radars and one Mk 114 ASW FCS.

Missiles: DDG 2-14 have a twin Mk 11 Tartar missile launcher while DDG 15-24 have a single Mk 13 Tartar launcher. Reportedly, their magazine capacities are 42 and 40 missiles, respectively, and ships equipped with either launcher can load, direct, and fire about six missiles per minute. *Lawrence* and *Hoel* fitted in 1972-1973 with multiple launcher for Chaparral (MIM-72A) for operational testing, in addition to their Tartar launcher. Harpoon to be fitted.

Modernisation: Beginning in the FY 1980 it is planned to give this class a mid-life modernisation to improve their capabilities, ease the maintenance and extend their service lives by 15 years over the current estimate of 20. This modernisation will provide Harpoon and Standard-ARM armament, with Mk 11 or 13 launchers, up-date the weapons systems and provide major improvements to the radar, sonar and fire-control systems. Work will take 15-18 months and cost $125.7 to 178.5 million (1979$) per ship. $167 million for long lead items is in the FY 1979 programme. The planned schedule is the FY 1980: DDG 3, 8, 10, 19, 22 and 23; the FY 1981: DDG 4, 7, 12, 15, 18 and 21; the FY 1982: DDG 5, 6, 9, 11, 16 and 20; the FY 1983: DDG 2, 13, 14, 17 and 24.

Names: DDG 5 was originally named *Biddle*; renamed *Claude V. Ricketts* on 28 July 1964.

Radar: 3D search: SPS 39 (52 being fitted)
Search: SPS 10 and 37 (2-14)
SPS 10 and 40 (15-24); SPS 39

Rockets: Mk 36 Chaffroc (RBOC) will be fitted.

Sonar: SQS 23 (bow-mounted) (20-24)
SQS 23 (hull-mounted) (remainder)

WADDELL *1/1977, Dr. Giorgio Arra*

CHARLES F. ADAMS *1976, Michael D. J. Lennon*

RICHARD E. BYRD *10/1977, C. and S. Taylor*

674 USA

14 DESTROYERS (DD) "FORREST SHERMAN" and "HULL" CLASSES

Name	No.	Builders	Laid down	Launched	Commissioned	F/S
FORREST SHERMAN	DD 931	Bath Iron Works	27 Oct 1953	5 Feb 1955	9 Nov 1955	AA
BIGELOW	DD 942	Bath Iron Works	6 July 1955	2 Feb 1957	8 Nov 1957	AA
MULLINNIX	DD 944	Bethlehem Steel Co, Quincy, Mass	5 April 1956	18 Mar 1957	7 Mar 1958	AA
HULL	DD 945	Bath Iron Works	12 Sept 1956	10 Aug 1957	3 July 1958	PA
EDSON	DD 946	Bath Iron Works	3 Dec 1956	1 Jan 1958	7 Nov 1958	NRF
TURNER JOY	DD 951	Puget Sound Bridge & Dry Dock Co	30 Sept 1957	5 May 1958	3 Aug 1959	PA

ANTI-SUBMARINE MODERNISATION

Name	No.	Builders	Laid down	Launched	Commissioned	F/S
BARRY	DD 933	Bath Iron Works	15 Mar 1954	1 Oct 1955	31 Aug 1956	AA
DAVIS	DD 937	Bethlehem Steel Co, Quincy, Mass	1 Feb 1955	28 Mar 1956	28 Feb 1957	AA
JONAS INGRAM	DD 938	Bethlehem Steel Co, Quincy, Mass	15 June 1955	8 July 1956	19 July 1957	AA
MANLEY	DD 940	Bath Iron Works	10 Feb 1955	12 April 1956	1 Feb 1957	AA
DU PONT	DD 941	Bath Iron Works	11 May 1955	8 Sept 1956	1 July 1957	AA
BLANDY	DD 943	Bethlehem Steel Co, Quincy, Mass	29 Dec 1955	19 Dec 1956	26 Nov 1957	AA
MORTON	DD 948	Ingalls Shipbuilding Corp	4 Mar 1957	23 May 1958	26 May 1959	PA
RICHARD S. EDWARDS	DD 950	Puget Sound Bridge & Dry Dock Co	20 Dec 1956	24 Sept 1957	5 Feb 1959	PA

Displacement, tons: 2 800/3 000 standard; 3 960/4 200 full load
Length, feet (metres): 418 *(127·4)* oa
Beam, feet (metres): 45 *(13·7)*
Draught, feet (metres): 20 *(6·1)*
Guns: A/S Mod: 2—5 in *(127 mm)* 54 cal (Mk 42) (single)
  Others: 3—5 in *(127 mm)* 54 cal Mk 42 (except DD 945 which has 1—8 in *(203 mm)* (Mk 71)); 1—3 in *(76 mm)* 50 cal Mk 33 (in DD 931, 946 and 951 only)
A/S weapons: 2 triple torpedo tubes (Mk 32);
  1 ASROC 8-tube launcher in A/S modified ships
Main engines: 2 geared turbines (Westinghouse in DD 931, 933, 937 and 938; General Electric in others); 70 000 shp; 2 shafts
Boilers: 4 Babcock & Wilcox (Foster-Wheeler in DD 937, 938, 940-942)
Speed, knots: 33 knots
Oil fuel, tons: 750
Range, miles: 4 500 at 20 knots
Complement: 292 (17 officers, 275 enlisted men) in unmodified ships; 304 in A/S Mod ships (17 officers, 287 enlisted men)

These ships were the first US destroyers of post-World War II design and construction to be completed with the DD designation. Four have been converted to a guided missile configuration (DDGs) and are listed separately. They were authorised in the Fiscal Year 1952-56 new construction programmes. These ships each cost approximately $26 million.
Edson was assigned to the NRF on 1 April 1977 for employment as school ship for engine-room training and for reservist training at Newport, Rhode Island.

Armament: As built all 18 ships of this class had three single 5 in guns, two twin 3 in mounts, four fixed 21 in ASW torpedo tubes (amidships); two ASW Hedgehogs (forward of bridge), and depth charge racks.

Design: The entire superstructure of these ships is of aluminium to obtain maximum stability with minimum displacement. All living spaces are air conditioned. *Davis* and later ships have higher bows; *Hull* and later ships have slightly different bow designs. *Barry* had her sonar dome moved forward in 1959 and a stem anchor fitted.

Electronics: Several of the unmodified ships have elaborate electronic warfare antennas on the main mast.

Fire control: One Mk 56 and one Mk 68 GFCS, one Mk 105 ASW FCS, one Mk 5 target designation system, one SPG 53A radar (SPG 50 in *Hull*).

Gunnery: With original armament of one 5 in mount forward and two 5 in mounts aft, these were the first US warships with more firepower aft than forward. Note that *Barry* and later ships have their Mk 68 gunfire control director forward and Mk 56 director aft; positions reversed in earlier ships.
During 1974-75 *Hull* was fitted with an 8 in gun forward to determine feasibility of installing a Major Calibre Light Weight Gun (MCLWG) in destroyer-type ships for shore bombardment. Forward 5 in gun removed. There are no plans to remove the 8 in gun.
Single Phalanx 20 mm Mk 15 CIWS to be installed in *Bigelow*.

Modernisation: Eight ships of this class were extensively modified in 1967-71 to improve their anti-submarine capabilities: *Barry, Davis, Du Pont* at the Boston Naval Shipyard; *Jonas Ingram, Manley, Blandy* at the Philadelphia Naval Shipyard; and *Morton, Richard S. Edwards* at the Long Beach (California) Naval Shipyard. During modernisation the anti-submarine torpedo tubes installed forward of bridge (on 01 level), deckhouse aft of second funnel extended to full width of ship, ASROC launcher installed in place of after gun mounts on 01 level, and variable depth sonar fitted at stern. Six ships of this class were not modernised because of increased costs.

Radar: Search: SPS 10, 37 or 40.

Sonar: SQS 23 (bow mounted in *Barry*, the first US ship so fitted).
VDS in ASW ships.

HULL with 8 in gun forward   4/1975, USN

DU PONT (ASW modernisation)   1976, Wright and Logan

MULLINNIX   1976, Michael D. J. Lennon

USA 675

28 DESTROYERS (DD) "GEARING" CLASS (FRAM I)

Name	No.	Builders	Laid down	Launched	Commissioned	F/S
WILLIAM R. RUSH	DD 714	Federal SB & DD Co	19 Oct 1944	8 July 1945	21 Sept 1945	NRF
HAMNER	DD 718	Federal SB & DD Co	23 April 1945	24 Nov 1945	11 July 1946	NRF
SOUTHERLAND	DD 743	Bath Iron Works Corp	27 May 1944	5 Oct 1944	22 Dec 1944	NRF
WILLIAM C. LAWE	DD 763	Bethlehem, San Francisco	12 Mar 1944	21 May 1945	18 Dec 1946	NRF
McKEAN	DD 784	Todd Pacific Shipyards	15 Sept 1944	31 Mar 1945	9 June 1945	NRF
HENDERSON	DD 785	Todd Pacific Shipyards	27 Oct 1944	28 May 1945	4 Aug 1945	NRF
HOLLISTER	DD 788	Todd Pacific Shipyards	27 Dec 1944	9 Oct 1945	26 Mar 1946	NRF
HIGBEE	DD 806	Bath Iron Works Corp	26 June 1944	12 Nov 1944	27 Jan 1945	NRF
CORRY	DD 817	Consolidated Steel Corp	5 April 1945	28 July 1945	26 Feb 1946	NRF
JOHNSTON	DD 821	Consolidated Steel Corp	6 May 1945	19 Oct 1945	10 Oct 1945	NRF
ROBERT H. McCARD	DD 822	Consolidated Steel Corp	20 June 1945	9 Nov 1945	26 Oct 1946	NRF
AGERHOLM	DD 826	Bath Iron Works Corp	10 Sept 1945	30 Mar 1946	20 June 1946	PA
MYLES C. FOX	DD 829	Bath Iron Works Corp	14 Aug 1944	13 Jan 1945	20 Mar 1945	NRF
CHARLES P. CECIL	DD 835	Bath Iron Works Corp	2 Dec 1944	22 April 1945	29 June 1945	NRF
FISKE	DD 842	Bath Iron Works Corp	9 April 1945	8 Sept 1945	28 Nov 1945	NRF
BAUSELL	DD 845	Bath Iron Works Corp	28 May 1945	19 Nov 1945	7 Feb 1947	PA
VOGELGESANG	DD 862	Bethlehem, Staten Island	3 Aug 1944	15 Jan 1945	28 April 1945	NRF
STEINAKER	DD 863	Bethlehem, Staten Island	1 Sept 1944	13 Feb 1945	26 May 1945	NRF
HAROLD J. ELLISON	DD 864	Bethlehem, Staten Island	3 Oct 1944	14 Mar 1945	23 June 1945	NRF
CONE	DD 866	Bethlehem, Staten Island	30 Nov 1944	10 May 1945	18 Aug 1945	NRF
DAMATO	DD 871	Bethlehem, Staten Island	10 May 1945	21 Nov 1945	27 April 1946	NRF
HAWKINS	DD 873	Consolidated Steel Corp	14 May 1944	7 Oct 1944	10 Feb 1945	NRF
ROGERS	DD 876	Consolidated Steel Corp	3 June 1944	20 Nov 1944	26 Mar 1945	NRF
DYESS	DD 880	Consolidated Steel Corp	17 Aug 1944	26 Jan 1945	21 May 1945	NRF
NEWMAN K. PERRY	DD 883	Consolidated Steel Corp	10 Oct 1944	17 Mar 1945	26 July 1945	NRF
JOHN R. CRAIG	DD 885	Consolidated Steel Corp	17 Nov 1944	14 April 1945	20 Aug 1945	NRF
ORLECK	DD 886	Consolidated Steel Corp	28 Nov 1944	12 May 1945	15 Sept 1945	NRF
MEREDITH	DD 890	Consolidated Steel Corp	27 Jan 1945	28 June 1945	31 Dec 1945	NRF

Displacement, tons: 2 425 standard; 3 480 to 3 520 full load
Length, feet (metres): 390·5 (119·0) oa
Beam, feet (metres): 41·2 (12·6)
Draught, feet (metres): 19 (5·8)
Guns: 4—5 in (127 mm) 38 calibre (Mk 38) (twin)
A/S weapons: 1 ASROC 8-tube launcher;
2 triple torpedo tubes (Mk 32)
Main engines: 2 geared turbines (General Electric; Westinghouse in DD 743, 822, 871, 880 and Allis-Chalmers in DD 788); 60 000 shp; 2 shafts
Boilers: 4 Babcock & Wilcox
Speed, knots: 32·5
Range, miles: 5 800 at 15 knots
Complement: 274 (14 officers, 260 enlisted men); 307 in Naval Reserve training ships (12 officers, 176 enlisted active duty; 7 officers, 112 enlisted reserve)

The US Navy survivors of the several hundred destroyers constructed in the United States during World War II.
The "Gearing" class initially covered hull numbers DD 710-721, 742, 743, 763-769, 782-791, 805-926. Forty-nine of these ships were cancelled in 1945 (DD 768, 796, 809-816, 854-856, and 891-926); four ships were never completed and were scrapped in the 1950s; Castle (DD 720), Woodrow R. Thompson (DD 721), Lansdale (DD 766), and Seymour D. Owens (DD 767).
Two similar ships completed to a modified design after World War II are listed separately as the "Carpenter" class.
Twenty-six ships are assigned to Naval Reserve training and are manned by composite active duty-reserve crews.

Armament-Design: As built, these ships had a pole mast and carried an armament of six 5 in guns (twin mounts), 12—40 mm guns (2 quad, 2 twin), 11—20 mm guns (single), and 10—21 in torpedo tubes (quin). After World War II, the after bank of tubes was replaced by an additional quad 40 mm mount. All 40 mm and 20 mm guns were replaced subsequently by six 3 in guns (2 twin, 2 single) and a tripod mast was installed to support heavier radar antennae. The 3 in guns and remaining anti-ship torpedo tubes were removed during FRAM modernisation.

Electronics: Electronic warfare equipment fitted to most ships.

Engineering: During Nov 1974 Johnston conducted experiments using liquefied coal as fuel in one boiler (Project Seacoal).

Fire control: Single Mk 37 gunfire control system, Mk 114 ASW FCS (Mk 111 in DD 763, 785, 788, 826, 845 and 890) and Mk 5 target designation system.

Helicopters: Fitted to operate the Drone Anti-Submarine Helicopter (DASH) during FRAM modernisation—never carried.

Modernisation: All of these ships underwent extensive modernisation under the Fleet Rehabilitation and Modernisation (FRAM I) programme between 1961 and 1965.
There are two basic FRAM I configurations: Agerholm, Bausell and Meredith have twin 5 in mounts in "A" and "B" positions and Mk 32 torpedo launchers abaft second funnel; others have twin 5 in mounts in "A" and "Y" positions and Mk 32 launchers on 01 level in "B" position.

Radar: SPS 10, 37 or 40.

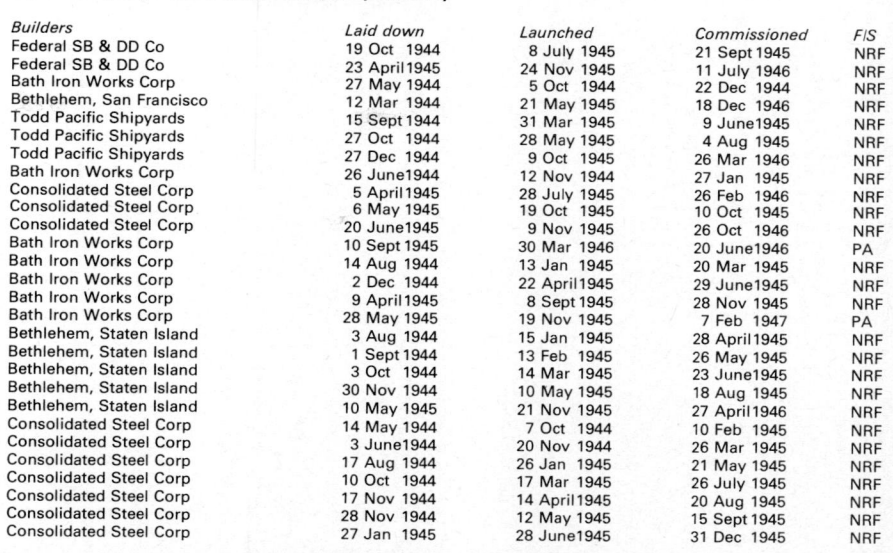

Sonar: SQS 23.

HAWKINS 9/1976, Dr. Giorgio Arra

BAUSELL (both 5 in mounts forward) 2/1977, Dr. Giorgio Arra

HAMNER 3/1976, USN

676 USA

2 DESTROYERS (DD) "CARPENTER" CLASS (FRAM I)

Name	No.	Builders	Laid down	Launched	Commissioned	F/S
CARPENTER	DD 825	Consolidated Steel Corp, Orange, Texas	30 July 1945	30 Dec 1945	15 Dec 1949	NRF
ROBERT A. OWENS	DD 827	Bath Iron Works Corp	29 Oct 1945	15 July 1946	5 Nov 1949	NRF

Displacement, tons: 2 425 standard; 3 540 full load
Length, feet (metres): 390·5 *(119·0)* oa
Beam, feet (metres): 41 *(12·5)*
Draught, feet (metres): 20·9 *(6·4)*
Guns: 2—5 in *(127 mm)* 38 calibre (Mk 38) (twin)
A/S weapons: 1 ASROC 8-tube launcher;
  2 triple torpedo tubes (Mk 32)
Main engines: 2 geared turbines (General Electric) 60 000 shp; 2 shafts
Boilers: 4 (Babcock & Wilcox)
Speed, knots: 33
Complement: 282 (12 officers, 176 enlisted active duty; 8 officers, 86 enlisted reserve)

These ships were laid down as units of the "Gearing" class. Their construction was suspended after World War II until 1947 when they were towed to the Newport News Shipbuilding and Dry Dock Co for completion as DDK. As specialised ASW ships they mounted 3 in *(76 mm)* guns in place of 5 in mounts and were armed with improved ahead-firing anti-submarine weapons (Hedgehogs and Weapon Able/Alfa); special sonar equipment installed. The DDK and DDE classifications were merged in 1950 with both of these ships being designated DDE on 4 March 1950. Upon being modernised to the FRAM I configuration they were reclassified DD on 30 June 1962.

Both of these ships are assigned to Naval Reserve training; they are manned by composite active duty and reserve crews.

Electronics: These ships have electronic warfare antennas on a smaller tripod mast forward of their second funnel.

Fire control: One Mk 56 gunfire control system, one Mk 114 ASW FCS, Mk 1 target designation system and one SPG 35 fire control radar.

Radar: Search: SPS 10 and 40.

Sonar: SQS 23.

CARPENTER

"ALLEN M. SUMNER" (FRAM II) CLASS

All surviving ships of the 70-destroyer "Allen M. Sumner" class have been stricken or transferred to other navies. Between 1943 and 1945, 58 destroyers and 12 minelayers were completed to this design. See 1974-75 and earlier editions for characteristics.

Ships of this class serve in the navies of Argentina, Brazil, Chile, Colombia, Greece, Iran, South Korea, Taiwan, Turkey and Venezuela.

"FLETCHER" CLASS

The survivors of 175 "Fletcher" class destroyers have been stricken or transferred to other navies. See 1975-76 and previous editions for characteristics.

Ships of this class serve in the navies of Argentina, Brazil, Chile, Colombia, West Germany, Greece, Italy, South Korea, Mexico, Peru, Spain, Taiwan and Turkey.

NAVAL RESERVE FORCE TRAINING DESTROYERS

Name/Hull No.	NRF Homeport	Date of Assignment	Remarks
WILLIAM R. RUSH (DD 714)	New York City	2 July 1973	Replaced *Moale* (DD 693)
HAMNER (DD 718)	Portland, Oreg	1 June 1975	Replaced *Ozbourn* (DD 846)
SOUTHERLAND (DD 743)	San Diego, Calif	2 July 1973	Replaced *Bridget* (DE 1024)
WILLIAM C. LAWE (DD 763)	New Orleans, La	31 Aug 1973	Replaced *Putnam* (DD 757)
McKEAN (DD 784)	Seattle, Wash	1 Oct 1975	Replaced *Epperson* (DD 719)
HENDERSON (DD 785)	Long Beach, Calif	1 Oct 1973	Replaced *Arnold J. Isbell* (DD 869)
HOLLISTER (DD 788)	Long Beach, Calif	2 July 1973	Replaced *Hooper* (DE 1026)
HIGBEE (DD 806)	Seattle, Wash	1 July 1975	Replaced *Theodore E. Chandler* (DD 717)
CORRY (DD 817)	Philadelphia, Pa	31 Aug 1973	Replaced *Lowry* (DD 770)
JOHNSTON (DD 821)	Philadelphia, Pa	1 July 1972	Replaced *Hank* (DD 702)
ROBERT H. McCARD (DD 822)	Tampa, Fla	18 Dec 1972	Replaced *Beatty* (DD 756)
CARPENTER (DD 825)	San Francisco, Calif	15 Jan 1973	Replaced *Perkins* (DD 877)
ROBERT A. OWENS (DD 827)	Pensacola, Fla	15 June 1977	
MYLES C. FOX (DD 829)	New York City	2 July 1973	Replaced *John R. Pierce* (DD 753)
CHARLES P. CECIL (DD 835)	New London, Conn	2 July 1973	Replaced *Gearing* (DD 710)
FISKE (DD 842)	Bayonne, NJ	31 Aug 1973	Replaced *Robert K. Huntington* (DD 781)
VOGELGESANG (DD 862)	Newport, RI	1 Mar 1974	
STEINAKER (DD 863)	Baltimore, Md	2 July 1973	Replaced *Allan M. Sumner* (DD 692)
HAROLD J. ELLISON (DD 864)	Philadelphia, Pa	30 Nov 1974	Replaced *Robert L. Wilson* (DD 847)
CONE (DD 866)	Charleston, SC	31 Aug 1973	Replaced *Strong* (DD 758)
DAMATO (DD 871)	Newport, RI	1 Feb 1974	
HAWKINS (DD 873)	Philadelphia, Pa	15 Dec 1977	Replaced *Rich* (DD 820)
ROGERS (DD 876)	Portland, Oreg	1 Oct 1973	Replaced *Wallace L. Lind* (DD 703)
DYESS (DD 880)	Brooklyn, NY	16 Feb 1971	Replaced *Zellars* (DD 777)
NEWMAN K. PERRY (DD 883)	Newport, RI	1 July 1975	
JOHN R. CRAIG (DD 885)	San Diego, Calif	26 Aug 1973	Replaced *Bauer* (DE 1025)
ORLECK (DD 886)	Tacoma, Wash	1 Oct 1973	Replaced *Brinkley Bass* (DD 887)
MEREDITH (DD 890)	Mayport, Fla	31 Aug 1973	Replaced *Waldron* (DD 699)
EDSON (DD 946)	Newport, RI	1 April 1977	Replaced *Holder* (DD 819)

USA 677

FRIGATES

There are 65 frigates (FF/FFG) in commission with another 73 ships planned for construction during the next few years. All ships now in commission have the large SQS 26 sonar, ASROC anti-submarine rockets, and a helicopter capability. However, only seven have a surface-to-air missile capability for limited area defence. The 74 ships of the "Oliver Hazard Perry" class (FFG 7) will have the smaller SQS 56 sonar. The ASROC will be deleted but the ships will be able to operate two LAMPS (Light Airborne Multi-Purpose System) helicopters and will have a surface-to-air/surface-to-surface missile capability. The "Perry" class ships will be more versatile than the previous "Knox" class frigates and several other navies have expressed interest in the newer design. The Royal Australian Navy has ordered two of the ships.

The US Navy's frigates could be supplemented in the ocean escort role by the 12 "Hamilton" class high-endurance cutters operated by the Coast Guard. The Coast Guard ships are fitted with sonar and are armed with Mk 32 torpedo tubes (as well as a single 5-in gun). They also have facilities for operating a large helicopter.

Future Programmes: Preliminary studies for a successor class to the "Oliver Hazard Perry" class, currently known as the "FFGX" programme are in hand. At present construction of the first ship is to be requested under the FY 1983 programme.

1 + 17 + (56) GUIDED MISSILE FRIGATES (FFG) "OLIVER HAZARD PERRY" CLASS

Name	No.	Builders	Laid down	Launched	Commission	F/S
OLIVER HAZARD PERRY	FFG 7 (ex-PF 109)	Bath Iron Works, Bath, Maine	12 June 1975	25 Sept 1976	17 Dec 1977	AA
McINERNEY	FFG 8	Bath Iron Works, Bath, Maine	7 Nov 1977	1978	1980	Bldg
WADSWORTH	FFG 9	Todd Shipyards Corp, San Pedro, Calif	13 July 1977	1978	1980	Bldg
DUNCAN	FFG 10	Todd Shipyards Corp, Seattle, Wash	29 April 1977	1978	1980	Bldg
CLARK	FFG 11	Bath Iron Works, Bath, Maine	1978	1979	1980	Bldg
GEORGE PHILIP	FFG 12	Todd Shipyards Corp, San Pedro, Calif	1978	1979	1980	Bldg
	FFG 13	Bath Iron Works, Bath, Maine	1979	1979	1980	Bldg
	FFG 14	Todd Shipyards Corp, San Pedro, Calif	1979	1979	1980	Bldg
	FFG 15	Bath Iron Works, Bath, Maine	1979	1980	1981	Bldg
	FFG 16	Bath Iron Works, Bath, Maine	1979	1980	1981	Bldg
	FFG 19	Todd Shipyards Corp, San Pedro, Calif	1979	1980	1981	Bldg
	FFG 20	Todd Shipyards Corp, Seattle, Wash	1978	1979	1981	Bldg
	FFG 21	Bath Iron Works, Bath, Maine	1979	1980	1981	Bldg
	FFG 22	Todd Shipyards Corp, Seattle, Wash	1979	1979	1981	Bldg
	FFG 23	Todd Shipyards Corp, San Pedro, Calif	1979	1980	1981	Bldg
	FFG 24	Bath Iron Works, Bath, Maine	1980	1980	1981	Bldg
	FFG 25	Todd Shipyards Corp, San Pedro, Calif	1980	1980	1982	Bldg
	FFG 26	Bath Iron Works, Bath, Maine	1980	1981	1982	Bldg
Eight ships	FFG 27/34	Approved Fiscal Year 1978 programme				
Nine ships	FFG 35/43	Requested FY 1979 programme				
Eight ships	FFG 44/51	Planned FY 1980 programme				
Eight ships	FFG 52/59	Planned FY 1981 programme				
Eight ships	FFG 60/67	Planned FY 1982 programme				
Nine ships	FFG 68/76	Planned FY 1983 programme				
Six ships	FFG 77/82	Planned FY 1984 programme				

Displacement, tons: 3 605 full load
Length, feet (metres): 445 *(135·6)* oa
Beam, feet (metres): 45 *(13·7)*
Draught, feet (metres): 24·5 *(7·5)*
Aircraft: 2 SH-2 LAMPS helicopters
Missile launchers: 1 single launcher Mk 13 for Standard/Harpoon missiles
Guns: 1—76 mm 62 calibre (Mk 75)
A/S weapons: 2 triple torpedo tubes (Mk 32)
Main engines: 2—LM 2500 gas turbines (General Electric); 41 000 shp; 1 shaft (cp propeller)
Speed, knots: 30
Range, miles: 4 500 at 20 knots
Complement: 164 (11 officers, 153 enlisted men)

They are follow-on ships to the large number of frigates (formerly DE) built in the 1960s and early 1970s, with the later ships emphasising anti-ship/aircraft/missile capabilities while the previous classes were oriented primarily against submarines (eg, larger SQS 26 sonar and ASROC).
The lead ship (FFG 7) was authorised in the Fiscal Year 1973 shipbuilding programme; three ships (FFG 8-10) in the FY 1975 programme; and six ships (FFG 11-16) in the FY 1976 programme. Congress authorised nine ships in the FY 1976, but cost escalation permitted the construction of only six ships, eight ships in the FY 1977 (FFG 19-26) and eight ships in the FY 1978 (FFG 27-34).
The Navy proposes to build 48 additional ships of this class under the FY 1979-84 programmes.
The two additional ships of this class under construction at the Todd-Seattle shipyard for the Royal Australian Navy are assigned US Navy hull numbers FFG 17 and FFG 18 for accounting purposes.

Classification: These ships were originally classified as "patrol frigates" (PF) at a time when the term "frigate" was used in the US Navy for the DL/DLG/DLGN. *Oliver Hazard Perry* was designated PF 109 at time of keel laying and designated FFG 7 on 30 June 1975.

Design: These ships are slightly longer but lighter than the earlier "Knox" class. The original single hangar has been changed to two adjacent hangars, each to house an SH-2 or follow-on LAMPS helicopters.
Several weapon and sensor systems for this class were evaluated at sea in the guided missile frigate *Talbot* (FFG 4). Fin stabilisers may be fitted at a later date (space and weight reserved).

Engineering: Two auxiliary retractable propeller pods are provided aft of the sonar dome to provide "get home" power in the event of a casualty to the main engines or propeller shaft. Each pod has a 325 hp engine to provide a ship speed of 3 to 5 knots.

Fire control: The Mk 92 weapons control system is installed with a dome-shaped antenna atop the bridge. (The Mk 92 is the Americanised version of the WM-28 system developed by NV Hollandse Signaalapparaten). Mk 13 weapon direction system.

Fiscal: The design-to-cost estimate of $45·7 million in the Fiscal Year 1973 dollars based on a 49-ship programme has increased to $55·3 million in the same dollars due to design and cost estimating changes. However, adding the estimated inflation and contract escalation factors brings the estimated cost per ship in the FY 1977 programme to $191 111 000. This is approximately $53 836 500 more per ship than estimated one year earlier.

Gunnery: The principal gun on this ship is the single 76 mm OTO Melara with a 90-round-per-minute firing rate (designated Mk 75 in US service). Space and weight are reserved for one 20 mm Phalanx Mk 15 CIWS.

Missiles: The single-arm Tartar-type missile launcher will be capable of firing both Standard-MR surface-to-air and Harpoon surface-to-surface missiles: "mixed" missile magazines will be provided. Harpoon to be fitted in near future.

Radar: Long-range search: SPS 49.
Search and navigation: SPS 55.
Weapons control: STIR (modified SPG 60).

Rockets: Mk 36 Chaffroc RBOC launcher fitted.

Sonar: SQS 56 (hull mounted).
TACTAS (towed passive sonar).

OLIVER HAZARD PERRY 12/1977, USN

USA

6 GUIDED MISSILE FRIGATES (FFG) "BROOKE" CLASS

Name	No.	Builders	Laid down	Launched	Commissioned	F/S
BROOKE	FFG 1	Lockheed SB & Construction Co	10 Dec 1962	19 July 1963	12 Mar 1966	PA
RAMSEY	FFG 2	Lockheed SB & Construction Co	4 Feb 1963	15 Oct 1963	3 June 1967	PA
SCHOFIELD	FFG 3	Lockheed SB & Construction Co	15 April 1963	7 Dec 1963	11 May 1968	PA
TALBOT	FFG 4	Bath Iron Works	4 May 1964	6 Jan 1966	22 April 1967	AA
RICHARD L. PAGE	FFG 5	Bath Iron Works	4 Jan 1965	4 April 1966	5 Aug 1967	AA
JULIUS A. FURER	FFG 6	Bath Iron Works	12 July 1965	22 July 1966	11 Nov 1967	AA

Displacement, tons: 2 640 standard; 3 426 full load
Length, feet (metres): 414·5 *(126·3)* oa
Beam, feet (metres): 44·2 *(13·5)*
Draught, feet (metres): 24·2 *(7·4)*
Aircraft: 1 SH-2D LAMPS helicopter
Missile launcher: 1 single Tartar/Standard-MR surface-to-air launcher (Mk 22)
Gun: 1—5 in *(127 mm)* 38 calibre (Mk 30)
A/S weapons: 1 ASROC 8-tube launcher; 2 triple torpedo tubes (Mk 32)
Main engines: 1 geared turbine (Westinghouse in FFG 1-3, General Electric in others); 35 000 shp; 1 shaft
Boilers: 2 Foster-Wheeler
Speed, knots: 27·2
Complement: 248 (17 officers, 231 enlisted men)

These ships are identical to the "Garcia" class escorts except for the Tartar missile system in lieu of a second 5 in gun mount and different electronic equipment. Authorised as DEG 1-3 in the Fiscal Year 1962 new construction programme and DEG 4-6 in the FY 1963 programme. Plans for ten additional DEGs in the FY 1964 and possibly three more DEGs in a later programme were dropped because of the $11 million additional cost of a DEG over FF. In 1974-75 *Talbot* was reconfigured as test and evaluation ship for systems being developed for the "Oliver Hazard Perry" class (FFG 7) frigates and "Pegasus" class (PHM 7) hydrofoil missile combatants.

Classification: Reclassified as FFG 1-6 on 30 June 1975.

Fire control: One Mk 74 MFCS, one Mk 56 GFCS, one Mk 114 ASW FCS, one Mk 4 weapon direction system, one SPG 51 and one SPG 35 fire control radars.

Helicopters: These ships were designed to operate Drone Anti-Submarine Helicopters (DASH), but the programme was cut back before helicopters were provided. They were fitted to operate the Light Airborne Multi-Purpose System (LAMPS), currently the SH-2D helicopter during 1972-75 refits.

Missiles: These ships have a single Tartar Mk 22 launching system which weighs 92 395 lb. Reportedly, the system has a rate of fire similar to the larger Mk 11 and Mk 13 systems installed in guided missile destroyers, but the FFG system has a considerably smaller magazine capacity (16 missiles according to unofficial sources).
The FFG 4-6 have automatic ASROC loading system (note angled base of bridge structure aft of ASROC in these ships).

Radar: 3D search: SPS 52.
Search: SPS 10.
Missile control: SPG 51C.

Rockets: Mk 33 Chaffroc RBOC. Mk 36 to replace Mk 33 in FFG 1 and 3.

Sonar: SQS 26 AX (bow-mounted). (SQS 56 evaluated in *Talbot*).

JULIUS A. FURER (with LAMPS helicopter) 7/1976, A. D. Baker III

RICHARD L. PAGE 2/1976, USN

RAMSEY 1/1977, Dr. Giorgio Arra

USA 679

46 FRIGATES (FF) "KNOX" CLASS

Name	No.	Builders	Laid down	Launched	Commissioned	F/S
KNOX	FF 1052	Todd Shipyards, Seattle	5 Oct 1965	19 Nov 1966	12 April 1969	PA
ROARK	FF 1053	Todd Shipyards, Seattle	2 Feb 1966	24 April 1967	22 Nov 1969	PA
GRAY	FF 1054	Todd Shipyards, Seattle	19 Nov 1966	3 Nov 1967	4 April 1970	PA
HEPBURN	FF 1055	Todd Shipyards, San Pedro	1 June 1966	25 Mar 1967	3 July 1969	PA
CONNOLE	FF 1056	Avondale Shipyards	23 Mar 1967	20 July 1968	30 Aug 1969	AA
RATHBURNE	FF 1057	Lockheed SB & Constn Co	8 Jan 1968	2 May 1969	16 May 1970	PA
MEYERKORD	FF 1058	Todd Shipyards, San Pedro	1 Sept 1966	15 July 1967	28 Nov 1969	PA
W. S. SIMS	FF 1059	Avondale Shipyards	10 April 1967	4 Jan 1969	3 Jan 1970	AA
LANG	FF 1060	Todd Shipyards, San Pedro	25 Mar 1967	17 Feb 1968	28 Mar 1970	PA
PATTERSON	FF 1061	Avondale Shipyards	12 Oct 1967	3 May 1969	14 Mar 1970	AA
WHIPPLE	FF 1062	Todd Shipyards, Seattle	24 April 1967	12 April 1968	22 Aug 1970	PA
REASONER	FF 1063	Lockheed SB & Constn Co	6 Jan 1969	1 Aug 1970	31 July 1971	PA
LOCKWOOD	FF 1064	Todd Shipyards, Seattle	3 Nov 1967	5 Sept 1964	5 Dec 1970	PA
STEIN	FF 1065	Lockheed SB & Constn Co	1 June 1970	19 Dec 1970	8 Jan 1972	PA
MARVIN SHIELDS	FF 1066	Todd Shipyards, Seattle	12 April 1968	23 Oct 1969	10 April 1971	PA
FRANCIS HAMMOND	FF 1067	Todd Shipyards, San Pedro	15 July 1967	11 May 1968	25 July 1970	PA
VREELAND	FF 1068	Avondale Shipyards	20 Mar 1968	14 June 1969	13 June 1970	AA
BAGLEY	FF 1069	Lockheed SB & Constn Co	22 Sept 1970	24 April 1971	6 May 1972	PA
DOWNES	FF 1070	Todd Shipyards, Seattle	5 Sept 1968	13 Dec 1969	28 Aug 1971	PA
BADGER	FF 1071	Todd Shipyards, Seattle	17 Feb 1968	7 Dec 1968	1 Dec 1970	PA
BLAKELY	FF 1072	Avondale Shipyards	3 June 1968	23 Aug 1969	18 July 1970	AA
ROBERT E. PEARY	FF 1073	Lockheed SB & Constn Co	20 Dec 1970	23 June 1971	23 Sept 1972	PA
HAROLD E. HOLT	FF 1074	Todd Shipyards, San Pedro	11 May 1968	3 May 1969	26 Mar 1971	PA
TRIPPE	FF 1075	Avondale Shipyards	29 July 1968	1 Nov 1969	19 Sept 1970	AA
FANNING	FF 1076	Todd Shipyards, San Pedro	7 Dec 1968	24 Jan 1970	23 July 1971	PA
OUELLET	FF 1077	Avondale Shipyards	15 Jan 1969	17 Jan 1970	12 Dec 1970	PA
JOSEPH HEWES	FF 1078	Avondale Shipyards	15 May 1969	7 Mar 1970	24 April 1971	AA
BOWEN	FF 1079	Avondale Shipyards	11 July 1969	2 May 1970	22 May 1971	AA
PAUL	FF 1080	Avondale Shipyards	12 Sept 1969	20 June 1970	14 Aug 1971	AA
AYLWIN	FF 1081	Avondale Shipyards	13 Nov 1969	29 Aug 1970	18 Sept 1971	AA
ELMER MONTGOMERY	FF 1082	Avondale Shipyards	23 Jan 1970	21 Nov 1970	30 Oct 1971	AA
COOK	FF 1083	Avondale Shipyards	20 Mar 1970	23 Jan 1971	18 Dec 1971	PA
McCANDLESS	FF 1084	Avondale Shipyards	4 June 1970	20 Mar 1971	18 Mar 1972	AA
DONALD B. BEARY	FF 1085	Avondale Shipyards	24 July 1970	22 May 1971	22 July 1972	AA
BREWTON	FF 1086	Avondale Shipyards	2 Oct 1970	24 July 1971	8 July 1972	PA
KIRK	FF 1087	Avondale Shipyards	4 Dec 1970	25 Sept 1971	9 Sept 1972	PA
BARBEY	FF 1088	Avondale Shipyards	5 Feb 1971	4 Dec 1971	11 Nov 1972	PA
JESSE L. BROWN	FF 1089	Avondale Shipyards	8 April 1971	18 Mar 1972	17 Feb 1973	AA
AINSWORTH	FF 1090	Avondale Shipyards	11 June 1971	15 April 1972	31 Mar 1973	AA
MILLER	FF 1091	Avondale Shipyards	6 Aug 1971	3 June 1972	30 June 1973	AA
THOMAS C. HART	FF 1092	Avondale Shipyards	8 Oct 1971	12 Aug 1972	28 July 1973	AA
CAPODANNO	FF 1093	Avondale Shipyards	12 Oct 1971	21 Oct 1972	17 Nov 1973	AA
PHARRIS	FF 1094	Avondale Shipyards	11 Feb 1972	16 Dec 1972	26 Jan 1974	AA
TRUETT	FF 1095	Avondale Shipyards	27 April 1972	3 Feb 1973	1 June 1974	AA
VALDEZ	FF 1096	Avondale Shipyards	30 June 1972	24 Mar 1973	27 July 1974	AA
MOINESTER	FF 1097	Avondale Shipyards	25 Aug 1972	12 May 1973	2 Nov 1974	AA

Displacement, tons: 3 011 standard; 3 877 (1052-1077) 3 963 (remainder) full load
Length, feet (metres): 438 *(133·5)* oa
Beam, feet (metres): 46·75 *(14·25)*
Draught, feet (metres): 24·75 *(7·55)*
Aircraft: 1 SH-2 LAMPS helicopter (except 1061 and 1070)
Missile launchers: 1 Sea Sparrow BPDMS multiple launcher (Mk 25) in 1052-1069 and 1071-1083; 1 NATO Sea Sparrow multiple launcher (Mk 29) in *Downes*; Harpoon in *Thomas C. Hart* and *Ainsworth* (see *Missile* note)
Gun: 1—5 in *(127 mm)* 54 calibre (Mk 42)
A/S weapons: 1 ASROC 8-tube launcher; 4 fixed torpedo tubes (Mk 32)
Main engines: 1 geared turbine (Westinghouse) 35 000 shp; 1 shaft
Boilers: 2 Combustion Engineering (except FF 1056, 1057, 1061, 1063, 1065, 1072, 1073, 1075, 1077 which have Babcock & Wilcox)
Speed, knots: 27
Complement: 245 (17 officers, 228 enlisted men); increased to 283 (22 officers, 261 enlisted men) with BPDMS and LAMPS installation; (as built 12 ships had accommodation for 2 staff officers)

The 46 frigates of the "Knox" class comprise the largest group of destroyer or frigate type warships built to the same design in the West since World War II. These ships are similar to the previous "Garcia" and "Brooke" classes, but slightly larger because of the use of non-pressure-fired boilers.
Although now classified as frigates they were authorised as DE 1052-1061 (10 ships) in the Fiscal Year 1964 new construction programme, DE 1062-1077 (16 ships) in the FY 1965, DE 1078-1087 (10 ships) in the FY 1966, DE 1088-1097 (10 ships) in the FY 1967, and DE 1098-1107 (10 ships) in the FY 1968. However, construction of six ships (DE 1102-1107) was deferred in 1968 as US Navy emphasis shifted to the more versatile and faster DX/DXG ships; three additional ships (DE 1098-1100) were cancelled on 24 Feb 1969 to finance cost overruns of the FY 1968 nuclear-powered attack submarines and to comply with a Congressional mandate to reduce expenditures; the last ship of the FY 1968 programme (DE 1101) was cancelled on 9 April 1969.
The DEG 7-11 guided missile "frigates" constructed in Spain are similar to this design.

Classification: Originally classified as ocean escorts (DE); reclassified as frigates (FF) on 30 June 1975.

Construction: The ships built at Avondale Shipyards in Westwego, Louisiana, were assembled with mass production techniques. The hulls were built keel-up to permit downhead welding. Prefabricated, inverted hull modules were first assembled on a permanent platen, then lifted by hydraulic units and moved laterally into giant turning rings which rotated the hull into an upright position. Avondale, which also built the "Hamilton" class cutters for the Coast Guard, side launched these ships.

Design: A 4 000-lb lightweight anchor is fitted on the port side and an 8 000-lb anchor fits into the after section of the sonar dome.

JESSE L. BROWN   1976, Michael D. J. Lennon

LOCKWOOD   2/1977, Dr. Giorgio Arra

Engineering: DE 1101 was to have had gas turbine propulsion; construction of the ship was cancelled when decision was made to provide gas turbine propulsion in the "Spruance" class (DD 963) destroyers.
These ships can steam at 22 knots on one boiler. They have a single 5-blade, 15-foot diameter propeller.

Fire control: One Mk 68 gunfire control with SPG 53A radar, one Mk 115 MFCS, one Mk 114 ASW FCS and one Mk 1 target designation system.

Fiscal: These ships have cost considerably more than originally estimated. Official programme cost for the 46 ships as of Jan 1974 was $1 424 million an average of $30·959 million per ship not including the LAMPS, Standard missile, VDS, or BPDMS installation.

Helicopters: These ships were designed to operate the now-discarded DASH unmanned helicopter. From the FY 1972 to the FY 1976 they were modified to accommodate the Light Airborne Multi-Purpose System, the SH-2D anti-submarine

680 USA

helicopter; hangar and flight deck are enlarged. Cost approximately $1 million per ship for LAMPS modification. Modification of FF 1061 and 1070 cancelled.

Missiles: Sea Sparrow Basic Point Defence Missile System (BPDMS) launcher installed in 31 ships from 1971-75 (FF 1052-1069, 1071-1083).
Modified NATO Sea Sparrow installed in *Downes* for evaluation.
In addition, some ships are being fitted with the Standard interim surface-to-surface missile which is fired from the ASROC launcher forward of the bridge. Two of the eight "cells" in the launcher are modified to fire a single Standard.
Cost was approximately $400 000 per ship for BPDMS and $750 000 for Standard missile modification.
Downes and *Lockwood* have been used in at-sea firing tests and shipboard compatability for the Harpoon ship-to-ship missiles.
Harpoon fitted in *Ainsworth* in Aug 1976 (first production model in USN) followed by *Thomas C. Hart*. To be fitted in all other ships in immediate future.

Names: DE 1073 originally was named *Conolly;* changed on 12 May 1971.

Radar: Search: SPS 10 and 40.
(Note: *Downes* has SPS 58 threat detection radar, and Improved Point Defence/Target Acquisition System (IPD/TAS) radar).

Rockets: Mk 36 Chaffroc RBOC to be fitted in near future replacing Mk 33 system in FF 1052, 1055, 1061, 1065, 1068, 1072, 1074-76, 1078-1085 and 1087.

Sonar: SQS 26 CX (bow-mounted).
SQS 35 (Independent VDS) (except FF 1053-55, 1057-62, 1072 and 1077).

Torpedoes: Improved ASROC-torpedo reloading capability as in some ships of previous "Garcia" class (note slanting face of bridge structure immediately behind ASROC). Four Mk 32 torpedo tubes are fixed in the amidships structure, two to a side, angled out at 45 degrees. The arrangement provides improved loading capability over exposed triple Mk 32 torpedo tubes.

LANG — 1976, Michael D. J. Lennon

MEYERKORD — 10/1976, Dr. Giorgio Arra

RATHBURNE (with LAMPS helicopter) — 1/1977, Dr. Giorgio Arra

VALDEZ — 11/1977, C. and S. Taylor

USA 681

10 FRIGATES (FF) "GARCIA" CLASS

Name	No.	Builders	Laid down	Launched	Commissioned	F/S
GARCIA	FF 1040	Bethlehem Steel, San Francisco	16 Oct 1962	31 Oct 1963	21 Dec 1964	AA
BRADLEY	FF 1041	Bethlehem Steel, San Francisco	17 Jan 1963	26 Mar 1964	15 May 1965	PA
EDWARD McDONNELL	FF 1043	Avondale Shipyards	1 April 1963	15 Feb 1964	15 Feb 1965	AA
BRUMBY	FF 1044	Avondale Shipyards	1 Aug 1963	6 June 1964	5 Aug 1965	AA
DAVIDSON	FF 1045	Avondale Shipyards	20 Sept 1963	2 Oct 1964	7 Dec 1965	PA
VOGE	FF 1047	Defoe Shipbuilding Co	21 Nov 1963	4 Feb 1965	25 Nov 1966	AA
SAMPLE	FF 1048	Lockheed SB & Construction Co	19 July 1963	28 April 1964	23 Mar 1968	PA
KOELSCH	FF 1049	Defoe Shipbuilding Co	19 Feb 1964	8 June 1965	10 June 1967	AA
ALBERT DAVID	FF 1050	Lockheed SB & Construction Co	29 April 1964	19 Dec 1964	19 Oct 1968	PA
O'CALLAHAN	FF 1051	Defoe Shipbuilding Co	19 Feb 1964	20 Oct 1965	13 July 1968	PA

Displacement, tons: 2 620 standard; 3 403 full load
Length, feet (metres): 414·5 *(126·3)* oa
Beam, feet (metres): 44·2 *(13·5)*
Draught, feet (metres): 24 *(7·3)*
Aircraft: 1 SH-2D LAMPS helicopter (except *Sample* and *Albert David*)
Guns: 2—5 in *(127 mm)* 38 calibre (Mk 30) (single)
A/S weapons: 1 ASROC 8-tube launcher;
2 triple torpedo tubes (Mk 32)
Main engines: 1 geared turbine (Westinghouse, 1040, 1041, 1043-1045; remainder, GE); 35 000 shp; 1 shaft
Boilers: 2 (Foster-Wheeler)
Speed, knots: 27·5
Complement: 239 (13 officers, 226 enlisted men (1040, 1041, 1043, 1044)
247 (16 officers, 231 enlisted men) (remainder)

These ships exceed some of the world's destroyers in size and ASW capability, but are designated as frigates by virtue of their single propeller shaft and limited speed. The FF 1040 and FF 1041 were authorised in the Fiscal Year 1961 new construction programme, FF 1043-1045 in the FY 1962, and FF 1047-1051 in the FY 1963.

Classification: Originally classified as ocean escorts (DE); reclassified as frigates (FF) on 30 June 1975. The hull numbers DE 1039, 1042, and 1046 were assigned to frigates built overseas for Portugal to US "Dealey" design.

Design: Anchors are mounted at stem and on portside, just forward of 5 in gun. Hangar structure of this class modified during the early 1970s to handle LAMPS except in *Sample* and *Albert David.*

Electronics: *Voge* and *Koelsch* are fitted with a specialised ASW Naval Tactical Data System (NTDS).

Fire control: One Mk 56 gunfire control system, one Mk 114 ASW FCS and one Mk 1 target designation system, one SPG 35 fire control radar.

Helicopters: The Drone Anti-Submarine Helicopter (DASH) programme was cut back before these ships were provided with helicopters. Reportedly only *Bradley* actually operated with DASH.
All but two of these ships were fitted to operate the Light Airborne Multi-Purpose System (LAMPS), now the SH-2D helicopter between FY 1972-75.

Missiles: *Bradley* was fitted with a Sea Sparrow Basic Point Defense Missile System (BPDMS) in 1967-68; removed for installation in the carrier *Forrestal* (CV 59).

Radar: Search: SPS 10 and 40.

Sonar: SQS 26 AXR (bow mounted) in FF 1040-1041, 1043-1045.
SQS 26 BR (bow mounted) in FF 1047-1051.

Torpedoes: Most of these ships were built with two Mk 25 torpedo tubes built into their transom for launching wire-guided ASW torpedoes. However, they have been removed from the earlier ships and deleted in the later ships. *Voge* and later ships have automatic ASROC reload system (note angled base of bridge structure behind ASROC in these ships).

O'CALLAHAN about to refuel from *Kitty Hawk* — 1975 USN

GARCIA — 1975

EDWARD McDONNELL — 3/1975, Wright and Logan

682 USA

2 FRIGATES (FF) "BRONSTEIN" CLASS

Name	No.	Builders	Laid down	Launched	Commissioned	F/S
BRONSTEIN	FF 1037	Avondale Shipyards, Westwego, Lousiana	16 May 1961	31 Mar 1962	16 June 1963	PA
McCLOY	FF 1038	Avondale Shipyards, Westwego, Lousiana	15 Sept 1961	9 June 1962	21 Oct 1963	AA

Displacement, tons: 2 360 standard; 2 650 full load
Length, feet (metres): 371·5 *(113·2)* oa
Beam, feet (metres): 40·5 *(12·3)*
Draught, feet (metres): 23 *(7·0)*
Guns: 2—3 in *(76 mm)* 50 calibre (Mk 33) (twin)
A/S weapons: 1 ASROC 8-tube launcher;
  2 triple torpedo tubes (Mk 32);
  facilities for small helicopter
Main engines: 1 geared turbine (De Laval); 20 000 shp; 1 shaft
Boilers: 2 (Foster-Wheeler)
Speed, knots: 26
Complement: 196 (16 officers, 180 enlisted men)

These two ships may be considered the first of the "second generation" of post-World War II frigates which are comparable in size and ASW capabilities to conventional destroyers. *Bronstein* and *McCloy* have several features such as hull design, large sonar and ASW weapons that subsequently were incorporated into the mass-produced "Garcia", "Brooke", and "Knox"classes.
Both ships were built under the Fiscal Year 1960 new construction programme.

Classification: These ships were originally classified as ocean escorts (DE); reclassified as frigates (FF) on 30 June 1975.

Design: Position of stem anchor and portside anchor (just forward of gun mount) necessitated by large bow sonar dome. As built, a single 3 in (Mk 34) open mount was aft of the helicopter deck; removed for installation of towed sonar.

Fire control: One Mk 56 gunfire control system, one Mk 114 ASW FCS, Mk 1 target designation system and SPG 35 fire control radar.

Radar: Search: SPS 10 and 40.

Sonar: SQS 26 (bow-mounted).
TASS (Towed Array Surveillance System) installed mid-1970s. Cable reel on quarterdeck.

BRONSTEIN 7/1975, USN

RADAR PICKET FRIGATES

All surviving radar picket frigates (FFR) (ex-DER) of the converted "Edsall" class DEs have been deleted except for *Forster* (FFR-334). She had been transferred to the South Viet-Nam Navy in Sept 1971. When South Viet-Nam fell to the Communists in late April 1975, she was in a shipyard undergoing overhaul. With her engines disassembled, she was unable to escape as did her sistership the ex-USS *Camp* (FFR 251) (now in the Philippine Navy). Her current status is unknown. See the 1975-76 and previous editions for characteristics.

LIGHT FORCES

The US Navy's programme to construct a series of 30 hydrofoil missile ships has been sharply curtailed, with only six units now planned probably as a result of a 130 per cent increase in estimated unit costs. Designated "patrol combatant missile (hydrofoil)".
Initial problems in the pump, gearbox, and electrical system of the prototype PHM have been overcome.
The six PHMs will be operated as a tactical squadron to develop tactics and gain technical experience with this type of craft. An earlier hydrofoil craft, *High Point* (PCH 1) is operated in a test and evaluation status. During 1974-75 *High Point* was evaluated by the US Coast Guard (subsequently returned to Navy control). Finally, several patrol and riverine warfare craft are operated by the Naval Reserve Force, and one new design (PB) is being developed for US and foreign use. US use of these craft will be minimal; rather they are intended to compete with contemporary small craft built overseas in the foreign sales market.

1 + 5 PATROL COMBATANTS MISSILE (HYDROFOILS)

Name	No.	Builders	Commissioned	F/S
PEGASUS	PHM 1	Boeing Co, Seattle	9 July 1977	PA
HERCULES	PHM 2	Boeing Co, Seattle	1982	Bldg
	PHM 3	Boeing Co, Seattle	1981	Bldg
	PHM 4	Boeing Co, Seattle	1981	Bldg
	PHM 5	Boeing Co, Seattle	1981	Bldg
	PHM 6	Boeing Co, Seattle	1982	Bldg

Displacement, tons: 239 full load
Dimensions, feet (metres):
  foils extended: 131·2 *(40·0)* oa × 28·2 *(8·6)* hull × 23·2 *(7·1)*
  foils retracted: 147·5 *(45·0)* oa × 28·2 *(8·6)* hull × 6·2 *(1·9)*
Missile launchers: 8 canisters (quad) for Harpoon surface-to-surface missile
Gun: 1—76 mm 62 calibre (Mk 75) OTO Melara
Main engines: Foil borne; 1 gas turbine (General Electric LM 2500); 18 000 shp;
  waterjet propulsion units = 48 knots
  Hull borne; 2 diesels (Mercedes-Benz); 1 600 bhp; 2 waterjet propulsion units = 12 knots
Complement: 21 (4 officers, 17 enlisted men)

The PHM design was developed in conjunction with the Italian and West German navies in an effort to produce a small combatant that would be universally acceptable to NATO navies with minor modifications.
The US Navy plans to construct six ships of this class. *Pegasus* and *Hercules* were authorised in the Fiscal Year 1973 R and D programme, and four additional ships in the FY 1975 shipbuilding programme. Planning for 24 additional units was cancelled in 1975. *Pegasus* was laid down on 10 May 1973 and launched on 9 Nov 1974 and made her first foil-borne trip on 25 Feb 1975. *Hercules* was laid down on 30 May 1974 and was originally named *Delphinus*. Renamed 26 April 1974. Due to cost increases and inflation, construction of PHM-2 was suspended in August 1975 when 40·9 per cent complete. PHM 2 was to be completed with funds from the FY 1976 shipbuilding programme, but a further re-examination of this programme led to the cancellation of PHM 2/6 on 6 April 1977. The Carter Administration then requested rescindment of the funds to complete PHM 2 and construct PHM 3/6. PHM 1 was to serve as a High Speed Test Vehicle. In August 1977, the Secretary of Defense released the $272·7 million appropriated to complete the six ship programme. Subsequently, a contract to complete PHM 2 and construct PHM 3/6 was awarded to Boeing Co on 20 Oct 1977. Four of the five uncompleted PHMs will be completed as such. The fifth will be completed for use as test ship (believed to be *Hercules*) and will be unarmed.

Classification: The designation PHM originally was for Patrol Hydrofoil-Missile; reclassified Patrol Combatant Missile (Hydrofoil) on 30 June 1975.

Fire control: Fitted with the Mk 92 fire control system (Americanised version of the WM-28 radar and weapons control system developed by NV Hollandse Signaalapparaten).

PEGASUS 10/1975, USN

Missiles: Each PHM will have two lightweight four-tube cannister launchers. This is double the Harpoon armament originally planned.

Rockets: Mk 34 Chaffroc being fitted.

USA 683

2 PATROL COMBATANTS (PG) "ASHEVILLE" CLASS

Name	No.	Builders	Commissioned	F/S
TACOMA	PG 92	Tacoma Boatbuilding	14 July 1969	AA
WELCH	PG 93	Peterson Builders	8 Sept 1969	AA

Displacement, tons: 225 standard; 235 full load
Dimensions, feet (metres): 164·5 oa × 23·8 × 9·5 (50·1 × 7·3 × 2·9)
Guns: 1—3 in (76 mm) 50 cal (forward); 1—40 mm (aft); 4—·50 cal MG (twin)
Main engines: CODAG: 2 diesels (Cummins); 1 450 shp; 2 shafts = 16 knots
   1 gas turbine (General Electric LM 2500); 13 300 shp; 2 shafts = 40+ knots
Range, miles: 1 700 at 16 knots; 325 at 37 knots
Complement: 24 (3 officers, 21 enlisted men)

Originally a class of 17 patrol gunboats (PG ex-PGM) designed to perform patrol, blockade, surveillance, and support missions. No anti-submarine capability. Requirement for these craft was based on the volatile Cuban situation in the early 1960s.
PG 92 and 93, authorised in the FY 1966. Ships took approximately 18 months from keel laying to completion. Cost per ship approximately $5 million.
Tacoma and *Welch* are at Little Creek, Virginia, involved in training Saudi Arabian naval personnel.
Chehalis (PG 94) was stripped of armament and assigned as a research craft to the Naval Scientific Research & Development Center in Annapolis, Maryland, on 21 Aug 1975; renamed *Athena* (no hull number assigned) and civilian manned. *Grand Rapids* followed her on 1 Oct 1977 and *Douglas* (PG 100) (as *Athena II*) in Feb 1978. *Antelope* (PG 86) transferred to US Environmental Protection Agency 17 Jan 1978. All 17 of this class still exist, some with other Government agencies or foreign navies (see *Deletion* list).

Classification: These ships were originally classified as motor gunboats (PGM); reclassified as patrol boats (PG) with same hull numbers on 1 April 1967 and as Patrol Combatants (PG) on 30 June 1975.

Design: All-aluminium hull and aluminium-fibreglass superstructure. Because of the heat-transmitting qualities of the aluminium hull and the amount of waste heat produced by a gas turbine engine the ships are completely air conditioned.

Engineering: The transfer from diesel to gas turbine propulsion (or vice versa) can be accomplished while under way with no loss of speed. From full stop these ships can attain 40 knots in one minute; manoeuvrability is excellent due in part to controllable pitch-propellers.

Fire control: Mk 63 Gunfire Control System with SPG 50 fire control radar.

Gunnery: 3 in (Mk 34) gun forward in closed mount with 40 mm (Mk 3) gun in open mount aft.

"ASHEVILLE" Class   7/1976, Dr. Giorgio Arra

"ASHEVILLE" Class   6/1973, USN

Missiles: *Benicia* (PG 96) was experimentally fitted with a single launcher aft for the Standard interim anti-ship missile in 1971; removed prior to transfer to South Korea later that year.

1 PATROL CRAFT—HYDROFOIL (PCH) "HIGH POINT" CLASS

Name	No.	Builders	In Service	F/S
HIGH POINT	PCH 1	Boeing Co, Seattle	15 Aug 1963	PSA

Displacement, tons: 110 full load
Dimensions, feet (metres): 115 (35) oa × 31 (9·4) × 6 (1·8) (foils retracted) or 17 (5·2) (foils extended)
Guns: removed
A/S weapons: removed
Main engines: Foil borne; 2 gas turbines (Bristol Siddeley Marine Proteus); 6 200 shp; 2 paired counter-rotating propellers = 48 knots
   Hull borne; diesel (Packard); 600 bhp; retractable outdrive with 1 propeller = 12 knots
Complement: 13 (1 officer, 12 enlisted men)

Experimental craft authorised under the Fiscal Year 1960 programme. Built at Martinac Boatyard, Tacoma. Laid down 27 Feb 1961, launched 17 Aug 1962. During March 1975 *High Point* was evaluated by the Coast Guard.

Design: *High Point's* forward foil is supported by a single strut and the after foil by twin struts. Twin underwater nacelles at the junction of the vertical struts and main foil housed contra-rotating, super-cavitating propellers for foil-borne propulsion. After foils modified in 1973 and nacelles repositioned to improve performance in heavy sea states. Also, forward foil strut made steerable to improve manoeuvrability

Gunnery: A single 40 mm gun was mounted forward in 1968; subsequently removed.

Missiles: During 1973-74 *High Point* was employed as a test ship for the lightweight cannister launchers for the Harpoon surface-to-surface missile intended for the PHM.

HIGH POINT   1975, US Coast Guard

4 FAST PATROL CRAFT (PTF) "OSPREY" CLASS

PTF 23   **PTF 24**   **PTF 25**   **PTF 26**

Displacement, tons: 105 full load
Dimensions, feet (metres): 94·7 oa × 23·2 × 7 (28·8 × 7·1 × 2·1)
Guns: 1—81 mm mortar; 1—·50 cal MG (mounted over mortar);
   1—40 mm (aft); 2—20 mm (single)
Main engines: 2 diesels (Napier-Deltic); 6 200 bhp; 2 shafts = approx 40 knots
Complement: approx 20

PTF 23-26 built by Sewart Seacraft Division of Teledyne Inc of Berwick, Louisiana. First unit completed in 1967, others in 1968. Aluminium hulls. Commercial name is "Osprey".
Two units based at Little Creek (Va) and two at Coronado Amphibious base. All except *PTF 25* assigned to NRF. *PTF 25* fitted with gas turbines on an experimental basis in early 1978. To be removed in 1980.

PTF 23   1976, Dr. Giorgio Arra

684 USA

COASTAL PATROL AND INTERDICTION CRAFT (CPIC)

The US Navy's prototype CPIC was transferred to South Korea on 1 Aug 1975. No additional craft of this type is planned for the US Navy.

15 PATROL BOATS (PB) Mk I and III Series

2 **PB** Mark I series
13 **PB** Mark III series

Displacement, tons:
 Mk I: 26·9 light; 36·3 full load
 Mk III: 31·5 light; 41·25 full load
Dimensions, feet (metres):
 Mk I: 65 oa × 16 × 4·9 *(19·8 × 4·9 × 1·5)*
 Mk III: 65 oa × 18 × 5·9 *(19·8 × 5·5 × 1·8)*
Guns: 6—20 mm or 0·50 cal MG (1 twin, 4 single)
Main engines: Diesel (Detroit); 1 635 bhp; 3 shafts = 26 knots

The PB series is being developed as replacements for the "Swift" type inshore patrol craft (PCF). Mk I built by Sewart Seacraft, Berwick, Louisiana; Mk III by Peterson Builders Sturgeon Bay, Wisconsin. Two Mark I prototypes completed in 1972 and delivered to the Navy in 1973 for evaluation; assigned to Naval Reserve Force. Procurement of the PB Mk III for the US Navy is under consideration. (The PB Mark II design was not built).

The Mk III design has the pilot house offset to starboard to provide space on port side for installation of additional weapons.

PB Mk III 9/1976, Dr. Giorgio Arra

5 INSHORE PATROL CRAFT (PCF) Mk I and II Series

Displacement, tons: 22·5 full load
Dimensions, feet (metres): 50·1 oa × 13 × 3·5 *(15·3 × 4·0 × 1·1)*
Guns: 1—81 mm mortar, 3—0·50 cal MG (twin MG mount atop pilot house and single MG mounted over mortar)
Main engines: 2 geared diesels (General Motors); 960 shp; 2 shafts = 28 knots
Complement: 6 (1 officer, 5 enlisted men)

The PCF design is adapted from the all-metal crew boat which is used to support off-shore drilling rigs in the Gulf of Mexico. Approximately 125 built since 1965.
Designation changed from Fast Patrol Craft (PCF) to Inshore Patrol Craft (PCF) on 14 Aug 1968.

Transfers: PCF 33, 34, and 83-86 transferred to the Philippines in 1966. Additional PCFs of this type constructed specifically for transfer to Thailand, the Philippines, and South Korea; not assigned US hull numbers in the PCF series; 104 PCFs formerly manned by US Navy personnel transferred to South Viet-Nam in 1968-70.

PCF Mk I Type 1969, USN

38 RIVER PATROL BOATS (PBR) Mk I and II Series

Displacement, tons: 8
Dimensions, feet (metres): 32 oa × 11 × 2·6 *(9·8 × 3·4 × 0·8)*
Guns: 3—0·50 cal MG (twin mount forward; single aft); 1—40 mm grenade launcher; 1—60 mm mortar in some boats
Main engines: 2 geared diesels (General Motors); water jets = 25+ knots
Complement: 4 or 5 (enlisted men)

Fibreglass hull river patrol boats. Approximately 500 built 1967-73; most transferred to South Viet-Nam.

PBR Mk II Type USN

1 COMMAND AND CONTROL BOAT (CCB)

Displacement, tons: 80 full load
Dimensions, feet (metres): 61 oa × 17·5 × 3·4 *(18·6 × 5·3 × 1·0)*
Guns: 3—20 mm; 2—0·30 cal MG; 2—40 mm high velocity-grenade launchers
Main engines: 2 diesels (Detroit); 2 shafts = 8·5 knots max (6 knots sustained)
Complement: 11

This craft serves as afloat command post providing command and communications facilities for ground force and boat group commanders. Heavily armoured. Armament changed to above configuration in 1968. Converted from LCM-6 landing craft.

Note: All other small craft, ie Assault Support Patrol Boats (ASPB), "Mini" Armoured Troop Carriers (ATC) and Swimmer Support Craft were disposed of 1976-77.

COMMAND AND CONTROL BOAT USN

AMPHIBIOUS WARFARE FORCES

The relatively large and modern US amphibious warfare force is being improved with deliveries now under way of the five large, "Tarawa" class amphibious assault ships (LHA). These ships are the size (and configuration) of aircraft carriers, and each can embark a reinforced Marine battalion complete with equipment, trucks, landing craft, and helicopters.
The current force of 65 large amphibious ships can simultaneously lift the assault elements of slightly more than one Marine Amphibious Force (MAF) even when one includes a ship non-availability factor of 15 percent for overhauls. An MAF is a division/aircraft wing team and their supporting elements with a total of approximately 30 000 troops.
Upon completion of all five "Tarawa" class assault ships, the amphibious lift will be sufficient for one and one-third division/wing teams (excluding ships in overhaul). When the last LHA is delivered, the amphibious force will have 66 active ships and three Naval Reserve Force (NRF) ships. All are capable of 20-knot or higher sustained speeds and have helicopter facilities.
Although the MAF lift capability is used as measurement criteria for US Navy amphibious ships by defence officials, a more realistic consideration is the number of reinforced battalions which can be maintained afloat in forward areas, primarily the Mediterranean and the Western Pacific. The US Navy is now able to keep two reinforced battalions continuously afloat in "WesPac" and one in the "Med", albeit one of the former without helicopters because of a shortage of LPH/LHA-type ships. In addition, a reinforced battalion is intermittently deployed in the Atlantic, generally without helicopters. The availability of the five "Tarawa" class LHAs will alleviate the lack of helicopter ships in the deployed forces. NRF assignments are listed at end of section.

Landing ship (LX): The Navy plans to begin replacement of the "Thomaston" class dock landing ships (LSD) in the mid-1980s as they reach the end of their 30-year service life. Conceptual design work is under way for a new landing ship, originally designated LX, now designated "LSD 41" class. First ship scheduled for construction under the FY 1980 programme; at least six ships were being planned but this was cut to two by the Secretary of Defense who considered the technology being used was outmoded. The two ships will be of improved "Anchorage" class design.

V/STOL operations: *Guam* (LPH 9) operated as an interim sea control ship from 1972 to 1974, during which period she operated AV-8A Harrier V/STOL (Vertical/Short Take-Off and Landing) aircraft in the light attack and intercept role, and SH-3 Sea King helicopters in the anti-submarine role. See 1974-75 edition for additional data.
Guam has continued to carry 12 Marine-flown Harriers upon return to the LPH role. Increasing V/STOL aircraft operations from the LPH/LHA ships have been undertaken.

Minesweeping Operations: Several LPHs were used to operate RH-53D Sea Stallion helicopters in the mine countermeasures role during the 1973 sweeping of North Vietnamese ports and the 1974 sweeping of the Suez Canal.

Transport submarines: The transport submarine *Grayback* (SS 574, ex-*LPSS 574*) is in active commission and is listed in the Submarine section of this edition.

2 AMPHIBIOUS COMMAND SHIPS (LCC) "BLUE RIDGE" CLASS

Name	No.	Builders	Laid down	Launched	Commissioned	F/S
BLUE RIDGE	LCC 19	Philadelphia Naval Shipyard	27 Feb 1967	4 Jan 1969	14 Nov 1970	PA
MOUNT WHITNEY	LCC 20	Newport News Shipbuilding & Dry Dock Co.	8 Jan 1959	8 Jan 1970	16 Jan 1971	AA

Displacement, tons: 17 100 full load
Length, feet (metres): 620 *(188·5)* oa
Beam, feet (metres): 82 *(25·3)*
Main deck width, feet (metres): 102 *(31·1)*
Draught, feet (metres): 29 *(8·8)*
Aircraft: Utility helicopter can be carried
Missile launchers: 2 Basic Point Defence Missile System (BPDMS) launchers for Sea Sparrow missile (Mk 25)
Guns: 4—3 in *(76 mm)* 50 cal (Mk 33) (twin)
Main engine: 1 geared turbine (General Electric); 22 000 shp; 1 shaft
Boilers: 2 (Foster-Wheeler)
Speed, knots: 20
Complement: 720 (40 officers, 680 enlisted men)
Flag accommodations: 700 (200 officers, 500 enlisted men)

These are large amphibious force command ships of post-World War II design. They can provide integrated command and control facilities for sea, air and land commanders in amphibious operations. *Blue Ridge* was authorised in the Fiscal Year 1965 new construction programme, *Mount Whitney* in the FY 1966. One more was planned but cancelled late in 1969. It was proposed that the last ship combine fleet as well as amphibious force command-control facilities. The phasing out of the converted "Cleveland" class (CG) fleet flagships has fostered discussion of the potential use of these ships in that role. Their capabilities are greater than would be required by a fleet commander while they are considered too slow for striking fleet operations.

Classification: Originally designated Amphibious Force Flagships (AGC); redesignated Amphibious Command Ships (LCC) on 1 Jan 1969.

Design: General hull design and machinery arrangement are similar to the "Iwo Jima" class assault ships.

Electronics: Tactical Aircraft Navigation (Tacan).
These ships have three computer systems to support their Naval Tactical Data System (NTDS), Amphibious Command Information System (ACIS), and Naval Intelligence Processing System (NIPS).

Fire control: Each ship has two Mk 56 gunfire control systems, two Mk 115 missile fire control systems and one Mk 1 target designation system. SPG 35 radar also carried.

Gunnery: At one stage of design two additional twin 3 in mounts were provided on forecastle; subsequently deleted from final designs. Antennae and their supports severely restrict firing arcs of guns. Two 20 mm Mk 15 CIWS to be fitted. Two 40 mm saluting guns carried.

Missiles: Two BPDMS launchers installed on each ship during 1974 (on antenna deck, aft of superstructure).

Personnel: The ships' complements includes one Marine officer and 12 enlisted men to maintain communications equipment for use by Marine Corps command and staff.

Radar: 3D search: SPS 48.
Search: SPS 10 and 40.

Rockets: One Mk 36 Chaffroc (RBOC) launcher to be fitted.

MOUNT WHITNEY   10/1977, Leo van Ginderen

BLUE RIDGE   1/1977, Dr. Giorgio Arra

686 USA

3 + 2 AMPHIBIOUS ASSAULT SHIPS G.P. (LHA) "TARAWA" CLASS

Name	No.	Builders	Erection of First Module	Launched	Commissioned	F/S
TARAWA	LHA 1	Ingalls Shipbuilding Corp	15 Nov 1971	1 Dec 1973	29 May 1976	PA
SAIPAN	LHA 2	Ingalls Shipbuilding Corp	21 July 1972	18 July 1974	15 Oct 1977	AA
BELLEAU WOOD	LHA 3	Ingalls Shipbuilding Corp	5 Mar 1973	11 April 1977	Late 1978	Bldg
NASSAU	LHA 4	Ingalls Shipbuilding Corp	13 Aug 1973	Early 1978	Late 1979	Bldg
DA NANG	LHA 5	Ingalls Shipbuilding Corp	12 Nov 1976	Mid 1978	Early 1980	Bldg

Displacement, tons: 39 300 full load
Length, feet (metres): 778 *(237·8)* wl; 820 *(250)* oa
Beam, feet (metres): 106 *(32·3)*
Draught, feet (metres): 26 *(7·9)*
Aircraft: 16 CH-46, 6 CH-53, 4 UH-IE helicopters or Harrier AV-8 V/STOL aircraft in place of some helicopters
Missile launchers: 2 Basic Point Defence Missile Systems (BPDMS) launchers firing Sea Sparrow missiles (Mk 25)
Guns: 3—5 in *(127 mm)* 54 cal (Mk 45) (single)
6—20 mm (Mk 67) (single)
Main engines: 2 geared turbines (Westinghouse); 140 000 shp; 2 shafts
Boilers: 2 (Combustion Engineering)
Speed, knots: 24
Complement: 902 (90 officers, 812 enlisted men)
Troops: 1 903 (172 officers, 1 731 enlisted men)

LHA 1 was authorised in the Fiscal Year 1969 new construction programme, the LHA 2 and LHA 3 in the FY 1970 and LHA 4 and LHA 5 in the FY 1971. The Navy announced on 20 Jan 1971 that four additional ships of this type previously planned would not be constructed. All ships of this class are under construction at a new ship production facility known as "Ingalls West". The new yard was developed specifically for multi-ship construction of the same design.
Late in 1971, the Navy announced that the LHA design work was behind schedule. Subsequently the Secretary of Defense announced that the ships will be delivered 24-38 months beyond original completion date.

Aircraft: The flight deck can operate a maximum of 9 CH-53 Sea Stallion or 12 CH-46 Sea Knight helicopters; the hangar deck can accommodate 19 CH-53 Sea Stallion or 30 CH-46 Sea Knight helicopters. A mix of these and other helicopters and at times AV-8 Harriers could be embarked.

Contract: These ships were procured by the US Navy with the acquisition processes known as Concept Formulation, Contract Definition, and Total Package Procurement. The proposals of Litton Systems Inc, and two other shipbuilding firms were submitted in response to specific performance criteria. The firms submitted detailed designs and cost estimates for series production of not less than five ships of this type. This procurement process has subsequently been abandoned.

Design: Beneath the full-length flight deck are two half-length hangar decks, the two being connected by an elevator amidships on the port side and a stern lift; beneath the after elevator is a floodable docking well measuring 268 feet in length and 78 feet in width which is capable of accommodating four LCU 1610 type landing craft. Also included is a large garage for trucks and AFVs and troop berthing for a reinforced battalion. Storage for 10 000 gallons (US) of vehicle petrol and 400 000 gallons (US) of JP-5 helicopter petrol.

TARAWA

7/1976, USN

Electronics: Helicopter navigation equipment provided. Each ship also will have an Integrated Tactical Amphibious Warfare Data System (ITAWDS) to provide computerised support in control of helicopters and aircraft, shipboard weapons and sensors, navigation, landing craft control, and electronic warfare.

Engineering: A 900 hp fixed bow thruster is provided for holding position while unloading landing craft.

Fire control: One Mk 86 gunfire control system and two Mk 15 Missile fire control systems; also one SPG 60 and one SPG 9A weapon control radars.

Gunnery: To be fitted with two 20 mm Mk 15 CIWS. Two 40 mm saluting guns fitted.

Fiscal: In early 1974 the estimated total cost to the government of the five LHAs was $1 145 million or an average of $229 million per ship. A cancellation fee of $109·7 million was due to the shipyard for cancellation of LHA 6-9.

Medical: These ships are fitted with extensive medical facilities including operating rooms, X-ray room, hospital ward, isolation ward, laboratories, pharmacy, dental operating room and medical store rooms.

Radar: 3D search: SPS 52.
Search: SPS 10 and 40.
Air/navigation: SPN 35.

Rockets: One Mk 36 Chaffroc (RBOC) to be fitted.

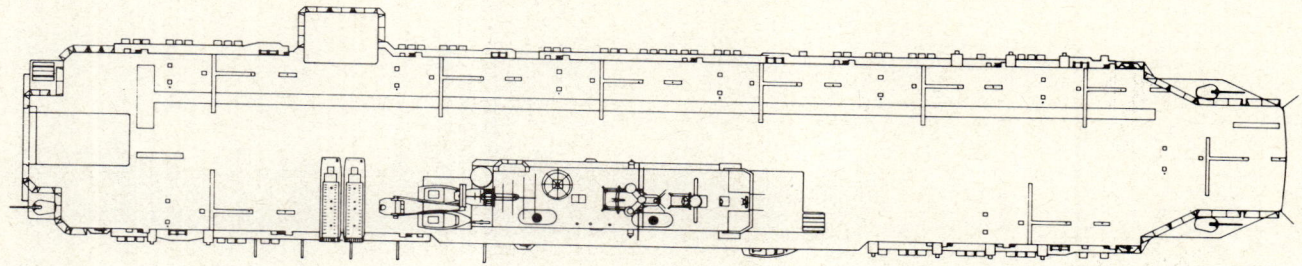

"TARAWA" Class

Drawing, A. D. Baker III

TARAWA

1975, Litton Industries

USA 687

7 AMPHIBIOUS ASSAULT SHIPS (LPH) "IWO JIMA" CLASS

Name	No.	Builders	Laid down	Launched	Commissioned	F/S
IWO JIMA	LPH 2	Puget Sound Naval Shipyard	2 April 1959	17 Sept 1960	26 Aug 1961	AA
OKINAWA	LPH 3	Philadelphia Naval Shipyard	1 April 1960	14 Aug 1961	14 April 1962	PA
GUADALCANAL	LPH 7	Philadelphia Naval Shipyard	1 Sept 1961	16 Mar 1963	20 July 1963	AA
GUAM	LPH 9	Philadelphia Naval Shipyard	15 Nov 1962	22 Aug 1964	16 Jan 1965	AA
TRIPOLI	LPH 10	Ingalls Shipbuilding Corp	15 June 1964	31 July 1965	6 Aug 1966	PA
NEW ORLEANS	LPH 11	Philadelphia Naval Shipyard	1 Mar 1966	3 Feb 1968	16 Nov 1968	PA
INCHON	LPH 12	Ingalls Shipbuilding Corp	8 April 1968	24 May 1969	20 June 1970	AA

Displacement, tons: 17 000 light; 18 000 (2, 3 and 7), 18 300 (9 and 10), 17 706 (11), 17 515 (12) full load
Length, feet (metres): 592 *(180·0)* oa
Beam, feet (metres): 84 *(25·6)*
Draught, feet (metres): 26 *(7·9)*
Flight deck width, feet (metres): 104 *(31·9)* maximum
Aircraft: 20-24 medium (CH-46) helicopters;
 4 heavy (CH-53) helicopters;
 4 observation (HU-1) helicopters;
 4 AV-8 Harriers in place of some troop helicopters
Guns: 4—3 in *(76 mm)* 50 cal (Mk 33) (twin)
Missile launchers: 2 Basic Point Defence Missile System (BPDMS) launchers firing Sea Sparrow missiles (Mk 25)
Main engines: 1 geared turbine (De Laval—10, GE—12, Westinghouse in others); 22 000 shp; 1 shaft
Boilers: 2 (Combustion Engineering; Babcock & Wilcox in *Guam*)
Speed, knots: 23
Complement: 652 (47 officers, 605 enlisted men)
Troops: 1 724 (143 officers, 1 581 enlisted men)

IWO JIMA *1976, Dr. Giorgio Arra*

Iwo Jima was the world's first ship designed and constructed specifically to operate helicopters. Each LPH can carry a Marine battalion landing team, its guns, vehicles, and equipment, plus a reinforced squadron of transport helicopters and various support personnel.

Iwo Jima was authorised in the Fiscal Year 1958 new construction programme, *Okinawa* in the FY 1959, *Guadalcanal* in the FY 1960, *Guam* in the FY 1962, *Tripoli* in the FY 1963, *New Orleans* in the FY 1965, and *Inchon* in the FY 1966. Estimated cost of *Iwo Jima* was $40 million.

Guam was modified late in 1971 and began operations in January 1972 as an interim sea control ship. She operated Harrier AV-8 V/STOL aircraft and SH-3 Sea King A/S helicopters in convoy escort exercises; she reverted to the amphibious role in 1974 but kept 12 AV-8As on board. Several of these ships operated RH-53 minesweeping helicopters to clear North Vietnamese ports in 1973 and the Suez Canal in 1974.

Aircraft: The flight decks of these ships provide for simultaneous take off or landing of seven CH-46 Sea Knight or four CH-53 Sea Stallion helicopters during normal operations. The hangar decks can accommodate 19 CH-46 Sea Knight or 11 CH-53 Sea Stallion helicopters, or various combinations of helicopters.

Design: Each ship has two deck-edge lifts, one to port opposite the bridge and one to starboard aft of island. Full hangars are provided; no arresting wires or catapults. Two small elevators carry cargo from holds to flight deck. Storage provided for 6 500 gallons (US) of vehicle petrol and 405 000 gallons (US) of JP-5 helicopter petrol.

Electronics: Tacan; advanced electronic warfare equipment fitted.

Fire control: As rearmed with BPDMS these ships have two Mk 63 gunfire control systems and two SPG 50 weapon control radars (removed from LPH 10 and 12). Two Mk 115 missile fire control systems. One Mk 1 Target Designation System.

Gunnery: As built, each ship had eight 3 in guns in twin mounts, two forward of the island structure and two at stern. Gun battery reduced by half with substitution of BPDMS launchers (see *Missile* notes). Two 20 mm Mk 15 CIWS to be fitted. Two 40 mm saluting guns fitted.

Medical: These ships are fitted with extensive medical facilities including operating room, X-ray room, hospital ward, isolation ward, laboratory, pharmacy, dental operating room, and medical store rooms.

GUAM (with AV-8A Harriers) *7/1976, USN*

Missiles. One Sea Sparrow launcher forward of island structure and one on the port quarter. *Okinawa* had one BPDMS launcher fitted in 1970 and the second in 1973; *Tripoli* and *Inchon* rearmed in 1972, *Iwo Jima* and *New Orleans* in 1973, *Guam* and *Guadalcanal* in 1974.

Radar: Search: SPS 10 and 40.
Navigation: SPN 10.

Rockets: One Mk 36 Chaffroc (RBOC) to be fitted.

OKINAWA *1/1977, Dr. Giorgio Arra*

688 USA

12 AMPHIBIOUS TRANSPORT DOCKS (LPD) "AUSTIN" CLASS

Name	No.	Builders	Commissioned	F/S
AUSTIN	LPD 4	New York Naval Shipyard	6 Feb 1965	AA
OGDEN	LPD 5	New York Naval Shipyard	19 June 1965	PA
DULUTH	LPD 6	New York Naval Shipyard	18 Dec 1965	PA
CLEVELAND	LPD 7	Ingalls Shipbuilding Corp	21 April 1967	PA
DUBUQUE	LPD 8	Ingalls Shipbuilding Corp	1 Sept 1967	PA
DENVER	LPD 9	Lockheed Shipbuilding & Const Co	26 Oct 1968	PA
JUNEAU	LPD 10	Lockheed Shipbuilding & Const Co	12 July 1969	PA
CORONADO	LPD 11	Lockheed Shipbuilding & Const Co	23 May 1970	PA
SHREVEPORT	LPD 12	Lockheed Shipbuilding & Const Co	12 Dec 1970	AA
NASHVILLE	LPD 13	Lockheed Shipbuilding & Const Co	14 Feb 1970	AA
TRENTON	LPD 14	Lockheed Shipbuilding & Const Co	6 Mar 1971	AA
PONCE	LPD 15	Lockheed Shipbuilding & Const Co	10 July 1971	AA

Displacement, tons: 10 000 light; 13 900 (4-6), 16 550 (7-10), 16 900 (11-13), 17 000 (14 and 15) full load
Length, feet (metres): 570 (173·3) oa
Beam, feet (metres): 100 (30·5)
Draught, feet (metres): 23 (7·0)
Aircraft: up to 6 UH-34 or CH-46
Guns: 8—3 in (76 mm) 50 cal (Mk 33) (twin) (only 4 (twins) in LPD 5 and 12)
Main engines: 2 steam turbines (De Laval); 24 000 shp; 2 shafts
Boilers: 2 Foster-Wheeler (Babcock & Wilcox in LPD 5 and 12)
Speed, knots: 21
Complement: 473 (27 officers, 446 enlisted men)
Troops: 930 in LPD 4-6 and LPD 14-15; 840 in LPD 7-13
Flag accommodations: Approx 90 in LPD 7-13

These ships are enlarged versions of the earlier "Raleigh" class; most notes for the "Raleigh" class apply to these ships.
The dates of laying down and launching are: *Austin* and *Ogden* 4 Feb 1963 and 27 June 1964; *Duluth* 18 Dec 1963 and 14 Aug 1965; *Cleveland* 30 Nov 1964 and 7 May 1966; *Dubuque* 25 Jan 1965 and 6 Aug 1966; *Denver* 7 Feb 1964 and 23 Jan 1965; *Juneau* 23 Jan 1965 and 12 Feb 1966; *Coronado* 3 May 1965 and 30 July 1966; *Shreveport* 27 Dec 1965 and 25 Oct 1966; *Nashville* 14 March 1966 and 7 Oct 1967; *Trenton* 8 Aug 1966 and 3 Aug 1968; *Ponce* 31 Oct 1966 and 20 May 1970. *Duluth* completed at Philadelphia Naval Shipyard.
LPD 4-6 were authorised in the Fiscal Year 1962 new construction programme, LPD 7-10 in the FY 1963, LPD 11-13 in the FY 1964, LPD 14 and LPD 15 in the FY 1965, and LPD 16 in the FY 1966. LPD 16 was deferred in favour of LHA programme; officially cancelled in Feb 1969.

Fire control: One Mk 56 GFCS, two Mk 63 GFCS with two SPG 50 and one SPG 35 radars. One Mk 1 target designation system. (None of the foregoing in LPD 6, 7 and 9).

Gunnery: Two 20 mm Mk 15 CIWS to be fitted.

Rockets: Each ship will be fitted with Mk 36 Chaffroc.

NASHVILLE 7/1976, A. D. Barker III

SHREVEPORT 7/1977, USN

DUBUQUE 1/1977, Dr. Giorgio Arra

2 AMPHIBIOUS TRANSPORT DOCKS (LPD) "RALEIGH" CLASS

Name	No.	Builders	Commissioned	F/S
RALEIGH	LPD 1	New York Naval Shipyard	8 Sept 1962	AA
VANCOUVER	LPD 2	New York Naval Shipyard	11 May 1963	PA

Displacement, tons: 8 040 light; 13 600 full load
Length, feet (metres): 500 (152·0) wl; 521·8 (158·4) oa
Beam, feet (metres): 100 (30·5)
Draught, feet (metres): 22 (6·7)
Guns: 8—3 in (76 mm) 50 cal (Mk 33) (twin)
Helicopters: up to 6 UH-34 or CH-46
Main engines: 2 steam turbines; (De Laval); 24 000 shp; 2 shafts
Boilers: 2 (Babcock & Wilcox)
Speed, knots: 21
Complement: 490 (30 officers, 460 enlisted men)
Troops: 1 039 (143 officers, 996 enlisted men)

The amphibious transport dock was developed from the dock landing ship (LSD) concept but provides more versatility. The LPD replaces the amphibious transport (LPA) and, in part, the amphibious cargo ship (LKA) and dock landing ship. The LPD can carry a "balanced load" of assault troops and their equipment, has a docking well for landing craft, a helicopter deck, cargo holds and vehicle garages. *Raleigh* was authorised in the Fiscal Year 1959 new construction programme, *Vancouver* in the FY 1960. *Raleigh* was laid down on 23 June 1960 and launched on 17 March 1962; *Vancouver* on 19 Nov 1960 and 15 Sept 1962. Approximate construction cost was $29 million per ship.
A third ship of this class, *La Salle* (LPD 3), was reclassified as a miscellaneous command ship (AGF 3) on 1 July 1972.

Design: These ships resemble dock landing ships (LSD) but have fully enclosed docking well with the roof forming a permanent helicopter platform. The docking well is 168 feet long and 50 feet wide, less than half the length of wells in newer LSDs; the LPD design provides more space for vehicles, cargo and troops. Ramps allow vehicles to be driven between helicopter deck, parking area and docking well, side ports provide roll-on/roll-off capability when docks are available. An overhead monorail in the docking well with six cranes facilitates loading landing craft. The docking well in these ships can hold one LCU and three LCM-6s or four LCM-8s or 20 LVTs (amphibious tractors). In addition, two LCM-6s or four LCPLs are carried on the boat deck which are lowered by crane.

Fire control: One Mk 56 GFCS, two Mk 51 gun directors, one SPG 35 radar (LPD 2 only), and one Mk 1 Target Designation System.

Gunnery: Two 20 mm Mk 15 CIWS to be fitted.

Helicopters: These ships are not normally assigned helicopters because they lack integral hangars and maintenance facilities. It is intended that a nearby amphibious assault ship (LHA or LPH) would provide helicopters during an amphibious operation. Telescoping hangars have been fitted.

Rockets: Mk 36 Chaffroc system to be fitted.

RALEIGH 1/1976, USN

VANCOUVER 1/1977, Dr. Giorgio Arra

USA 689

5 DOCK LANDING SHIPS (LSD) "ANCHORAGE" CLASS

Name	No.	Builders	Commissioned	F/S
ANCHORAGE	LSD 36	Ingalls Shipbuilding Corp	15 Mar 1969	PA
PORTLAND	LSD 37	General Dynamics, Quincy, Mass	3 Oct 1970	AA
PENSACOLA	LSD 38	General Dynamics, Quincy, Mass	27 Mar 1971	AA
MOUNT VERNON	LSD 39	General Dynamics, Quincy, Mass	13 May 1972	PA
FORT FISHER	LSD 40	General Dynamics, Quincy, Mass	9 Dec 1972	PA

Displacement, tons: 8 600 light; 13 600 full load
Dimensions, feet (metres): 553·3 oa × 84 × 20 (168·6 × 25·6 × 6)
Guns: 8—3 in (76 mm) 50 cal (Mk 33) (twin) (12 twins) in LPD 37 and 40)
Main engines: Steam turbines (De Laval); 24 000 shp; 2 shafts = 20 knots sustained
Boilers: 2 (Foster-Wheeler except Combustion Engineering in *Anchorage*)
Complement: 397 (21 officers, 376 enlisted men)
Troops: 376 (28 officers, 348 enlisted men)

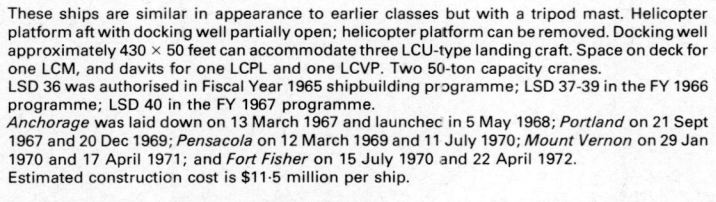

These ships are similar in appearance to earlier classes but with a tripod mast. Helicopter platform aft with docking well partially open; helicopter platform can be removed. Docking well approximately 430 × 50 feet can accommodate three LCU-type landing craft. Space on deck for one LCM, and davits for one LCPL and one LCVP. Two 50-ton capacity cranes.
LSD 36 was authorised in Fiscal Year 1965 shipbuilding programme; LSD 37-39 in the FY 1966 programme; LSD 40 in the FY 1967 programme.
Anchorage was laid down on 13 March 1967 and launched in 5 May 1968; *Portland* on 21 Sept 1967 and 20 Dec 1969; *Pensacola* on 12 March 1969 and 11 July 1970; *Mount Vernon* on 29 Jan 1970 and 17 April 1971; and *Fort Fisher* on 15 July 1970 and 22 April 1972.
Estimated construction cost is $11·5 million per ship.

Fire control: One Mk 56 and two Mk 63 GFCS, two SPG 50 radars (none in LSD 37 and 40) and one Mk 1 Target Designation System.

Gunnery: Two 20 mm Mk 15 CIWS to be fitted.

Rockets: One Mk 36 Chaffroc (RBOC) to be fitted.

PENSACOLA 6/1975, Dr. Giorgio Arra

PENSACOLA 6/1975, Dr. Giorgio Arra

8 DOCK LANDING SHIPS (LSD) "THOMASTON" CLASS

Name	No.	Builders	Commissioned	F/S
THOMASTON	LSD 28	Ingalls Shipbuilding Corp	17 Sept 1954	PA
PLYMOUTH ROCK	LSD 29	Ingalls Shipbuilding Corp	29 Nov 1954	AA
FORT SNELLING	LSD 30	Ingalls Shipbuilding Corp	24 Jan 1955	AA
POINT DEFIANCE	LSD 31	Ingalls Shipbuilding Corp	31 Mar 1955	PA
SPIEGEL GROVE	LSD 32	Ingalls Shipbuilding Corp	8 June 1956	AA
ALAMO	LSD 33	Ingalls Shipbuilding Corp	24 Aug 1956	PA
HERMITAGE	LSD 34	Ingalls Shipbuilding Corp	14 Dec 1956	AA
MONTICELLO	LSD 35	Ingalls Shipbuilding Corp	29 Mar 1957	PA

Displacement, tons: 6 880 light; 11 270 full load
Dimensions, feet (metres): 510 oa × 84 × 19 (155·5 × 25·6 × 5·8)
Guns: 8—3 in (76 mm) 50 cal (Mk 33) (twin) (12 twins) in LSD 28 and 31)
Main engines: Steam turbines (General Electric); 24 000 shp; 2 shafts = 22·5 knots
Boilers: 2 (Babcock & Wilcox)
Complement: 400
Troops: 340

LSD 28-31 launched in 1954 on 9 Feb, 7 May, 16 July and 28 Sept respectively; LSD 32 launched on 10 Nov 1955; LSD 33-35 launched in 1956 on 20 Jan, 12 June and 10 Aug. Fitted with helicopter platform over docking well; two 5-ton capacity cranes; can carry 21 LCM-6 or 3 LCU and 6 LCM landing craft or approximately 50 LVTs (amphibious tractors) in docking well plus 30 LVTs on mezzanine and super decks (with helicopter landing area clear). Welldeck measures 391 × 48 feet.
Note pole mast compared to tripod mast of "Anchorage" class which have enclosed 3 in gun mounts forward of bridge.

Fire control: Two Mk 56 and two Mk 63 GFCS and one Mk 5 Target Designation System. Two SPG 34 and two SPG 35 radars (in LSD 29, 32, 34, 35—none in remainder).

Gunnery: As built, each ship had 16—3 in guns; twin mount on each side wall (abaft boats davits) has been removed and subsequently, two more twin mounts removed except in LSD 28 and 31. Two 20 mm Mk 15 CIWS to be fitted.

Rockets: One Mk 36 Chaffroc (RBOC) to be fitted.

MONTICELLO 1/1977, Dr. Giorgio Arra

POINT DEFIANCE 7/1976, Dr. Giorgio Arra

690   USA

20 TANK LANDING SHIPS (LST) "NEWPORT" CLASS

Name	No.	Laid down	Launched	Commissioned	F/S
NEWPORT	LST 1179	1 Nov 1966	3 Feb 1968	7 June 1969	AA
MANITOWOC	LST 1180	1 Feb 1967	4 June 1969	24 Jan 1970	AA
SUMTER	LST 1181	14 Nov 1967	13 Dec 1969	20 June 1970	AA
FRESNO	LST 1182	16 Dec 1967	28 Sept 1968	22 Nov 1969	PA
PEORIA	LST 1183	22 Feb 1968	23 Nov 1968	21 Feb 1970	PA
FREDERICK	LST 1184	13 April 1968	8 Mar 1969	11 April 1970	PA
SCHENECTADY	LST 1185	2 Aug 1968	24 May 1969	13 June 1970	PA
CAYUGA	LST 1186	28 Sept 1968	12 July 1969	8 Aug 1970	PA
TUSCALOOSA	LST 1187	23 Nov 1968	6 Sept 1969	24 Oct 1970	PA
SAGINAW	LST 1188	24 May 1969	7 Feb 1970	23 Jan 1971	AA
SAN BERNARDINO	LST 1189	12 July 1969	28 Mar 1970	27 Mar 1971	PA
BOULDER	LST 1190	6 Sept 1969	22 May 1970	4 June 1971	AA
RACINE	LST 1191	13 Dec 1969	15 Aug 1970	9 July 1971	PA
SPARTANBURG COUNTY	LST 1192	7 Feb 1970	11 Nov 1970	1 Sept 1971	AA
FAIRFAX COUNTY	LST 1193	28 Mar 1970	19 Dec 1970	16 Oct 1971	AA
LA MOURE COUNTY	LST 1194	22 May 1970	13 Feb 1971	18 Dec 1971	AA
BARBOUR COUNTY	LST 1195	15 Aug 1970	15 May 1971	12 Feb 1972	PA
HARLAN COUNTY	LST 1196	7 Nov 1970	24 July 1971	8 April 1972	AA
BARNSTABLE COUNTY	LST 1197	19 Dec 1970	2 Oct 1971	27 May 1972	AA
BRISTOL COUNTY	LST 1198	13 Feb 1971	4 Dec 1971	5 Aug 1972	PA

Displacement, tons: 8 450 full load
Dimensions, feet (metres): 522·3 hull oa × 69·5 × 15 (aft) *(159·2 × 21·2 × 4·6)*
Guns: 4—3 in *(76 mm)* 50 cal (Mk 33) (twin)
Main engines: 6 diesels (Alco) (GM in 1179-1181); 16 000 bhp, 2 shafts = 20 knots
Complement: 196 (12 officers, 174 enlisted men)
Troops: 431 (20 officers, 411 enlisted men)

These ships are of an entirely new design; larger and faster than previous tank landing ships. They operate with 20-knot amphibious squadrons to transport tanks, other heavy vehicles, engineer equipment, and supplies which cannot be readily landed by helicopters or landing craft. These are the only recent construction amphibious ships with a pole mast *vice* tripod-lattice mast.

Newport was authorised in the Fiscal Year 1965 new construction programme and laid down on 1 Nov 1966. LST 1180-1187 (8 ships) in the FY 1966, and LST 1188-1198 (11 ships) in the FY 1967. LST 1179-1181 built by Philadelphia Naval Shipyard, LST 1182-1198 built by National Steel & SB Co, San Diego, California. Seven additional ships of this type that were planned for the Fiscal Year 1971 new construction programme were cancelled.

Design: These ships are the first LSTs to depart from the bow-door design developed by the British early in World War II. The hull form required to achieve 20 knots would not permit bow doors, thus these ships unload by a 112-foot ramp over their bow. The ramp is supported by twin derrick arms. A ramp just forward of the superstructure connects the lower tank deck with the main deck and a vehicle passage through the superstructure provides access to the parking area amidships. A stern gate to the tank deck permits unloading of amphibious tractors into the water, or unloading of other vehicles into an LCU or onto a pier. Vehicle stowage is rated at 500 tons and 19 000 square feet (5 000 square feet more than previous LSTs). Length over derrick arms is 562 feet; full load draught is 11·5 feet forward and 17·5 feet aft. Bow thruster fitted to hold position offshore while unloading amphibious tractors.

Fire control: Two Mk 63 GFCS and one Mk 1 Target Designation System. Two SPG 50 radars (none in LST 1183, 1186, 1188 and 1195).

Gunnery: Two 20 mm Mk 15 CIWS to be fitted.

Rockets: One Mk 36 Chaffroc RBOC to be fitted.

RACINE   1/1977, Dr. Giorgio Arra

BARNSTABLE COUNTY   10/1976, Michael D. J. Lennon

RACINE   1/1977, Dr. Giorgio Arra

3 TANK LANDING SHIPS (LST) "DE SOTO COUNTY" CLASS

Name	No.	Builders	Commissioned	F/S
SUFFOLK COUNTY	LST 1173	Boston Navy Yard	15 Aug 1957	AR
LORAIN COUNTY	LST 1177	American SB Co, Lorrain, Ohio	3 Oct 1959	MAR
WOOD COUNTY	LST 1178	American SB Co, Lorrain, Ohio	5 Aug 1969	MAR

Displacement, tons: 4 164 light; 7 100 full load
Dimensions, feet (metres): 445 oa × 62 × 17·5 *(138·7 × 18·9 × 5·3)*
Guns: 6—3 in *(76 mm)* 50 cal (Mk 33) (twin)
Main engines: 6 diesels (Fairbanks-Morse—1173) (Cooper Bessemer—others); 13 700 bhp; 2 shafts; (cp propellers) = 16·5 knots
Complement: 188 (15 officers, 173 men)
Troops: 634 (30 officers, 604 enlisted men)

Originally a class of seven tank landing ships (LST 1171, 1173-1178 with LST 1172 not built). They were faster and had a greater troop capacity than earlier LSTs; considered the "ultimate" design attainable with the traditional LST bow-door configuration.
Suffolk County launched on 5 Sept 1956, *Lorain County* on 22 June 1957, and *Wood County* on 14 Dec 1957.
Suffolk County decommissioned 25 Aug 1972, *Lorain County* on 1 Sept 1972 and *Wood County* on 1 May 1972. All in reserve.
Graham County (LST 1176) was converted to a gunboat support ship (AGP); now stricken.

Conversion: *Wood County* was to have been converted to Patrol Combatant Support Ship (AGHS) under the original FY 1978 programme but this was deleted by the new administration.

Design: High degree of habitability with all crew and troop living spaces air conditioned. Can carry 23 medium tanks or vehicles up to 75 tons on 288-foot-long (lower) tank deck. Davits for four LCVP-type landing craft. Liquid cargo capacity of 170 000 gallons (US) diesel or jet fuel plus 7 000 gallons (US) of petrol for embarked vehicles; some ships had reduced troop spaces to carry additional 250 000 gallons (US) of aviation petrol for pumping ashore or to other ships.

SUFFOLK COUNTY   1971, USN

USA 691

5 AMPHIBIOUS CARGO SHIPS (LKA) "CHARLESTON" CLASS

Name	No.	Builders	Commissioned	F/S
CHARLESTON	LKA 113	Newport News SB & DD Co.	14 Dec 1968	AA
DURHAM	LKA 114	Newport News SB & DD Co.	24 May 1969	PA
MOBILE	LKA 115	Newport News SB & DD Co.	29 Sept 1969	PA
ST. LOUIS	LKA 116	Newport News SB & DD Co.	22 Nov 1969	PA
EL PASO	LKA 117	Newport News SB & DD Co.	17 Jan 1970	AA

Displacement, tons: 10 000 light; 18 600 full load
Dimensions, feet (metres): 575·5 oa × 62 × 25·5 (175·4 × 18·9 × 7·7)
Guns: 8—3 in (76 mm) 50 cal (Mk 33) (twin)
Main engines: 1 steam turbine (Westinghouse); 19 250 shp; 1 shaft = 20 knots
Boilers: 2 (Combustion Engineering)
Complement: 334 (24 officers, 310 enlisted men)
Troops: 226 (15 officers, 211 enlisted men)

Charleston laid down 5 Dec 1966, launched 2 Dec 1967; *Durham* laid down 10 July 1967, launched 29 March 1968; *Mobile* laid down 15 Jan 1968, launched 19 Oct 1968; *St. Louis* 3 April 1968 and 4 Jan 1969 and *El Paso* 22 Oct 1968 and 17 May 1969.
These ships are designed specifically for the attack cargo ship role; can carry nine landing craft (LCM) and supplies for amphibious operations. Design includes two heavy-lift cranes with a 78·4 ton capacity, two 40-ton capacity booms, and eight 15-ton capacity booms; helicopter deck aft.
The LKA 113-116 were authorised in the FY 1965 shipbuilding programme; LKA 117 in the FY 1966 programme.
Cost of building was approximately $21 million per ship.

Classification: Originally designated Attack Cargo Ship (AKA), *Charleston* redesignated Amphibious Cargo Ship (LKA) on 14 Dec 1968; others to LKA on 1 Jan 1969.

Engineering: These are among the first US Navy ships with a fully automated main propulsion plant; control of plant is from bridge or central machinery space console. This automation permitted a 45-man reduction in complement.

Fire control: Two Mk 56 GFCS, one Mk 1 Target Designation System. Two SPG 35 radars. (No fire control in LKA 116).

Gunnery: Two 20 mm Mk 15 CIWS to be fitted.

Rockets: One Mk 36 Chaffroc RBOC to be installed.

CHARLESTON 10/1976, Michael D. J. Lennon

DURHAM 1/1977, Dr. Giorgio Arra

1 AMPHIBIOUS CARGO SHIP (LKA) "TULARE" CLASS

Name	No.	Builders	Commissioned	F/S
TULARE (ex-*Evergreen Mariner*)	LKA 112	Bethlehem, San Francisco	13 Jan 1956	NRF

Displacement, tons: 9 050 light; 17 500 full load
Dimensions, feet (metres): 564 oa × 80 × 28 (171·9 × 24·4 × 8·5)
Guns: 12—3 in (76 mm) 50 cal (Mk 33) (twin)
Main engines: Steam turbine (De Laval); 22 000 shp; 1 shaft = 23 knots
Boilers: 2 (Combustion Engineering)
Complement: 393 (10 officers, 154 enlisted active duty; 21 officers, 208 enlisted reserve)
Troops: 319 (18 officers, 301 enlisted men)

Laid down on 16 Feb 1953; launched on 22 Dec 1953; acquired by Navy during construction; C4-S-1A type. Has helicopter landing platform and booms capable of lifting 60-ton landing craft. Carries 9 LCM-6 and 11 LCVP landing craft as deck cargo. Fitted with five Mk 63 gunfire control systems. Designation changed from AKA 112 to LKA 112 on 1 Jan 1969.
Tulare was assigned to the Naval Reserve Force on 1 July 1975 and is partially manned by reserve personnel.

Class: Thirty-five "Mariner" design C4-S-1A merchant ships built during the early 1950s; five acquired by Navy, three for conversion to amphibious ships (AKA-APA) and two for support of Polaris-Poseidon programme (designated AG). Acquisition of sixth ship cancelled.

Fire control: Five Mk 63 GFCS and five SPG 35 radars.

TULARE 1969, USN

2 AMPHIBIOUS TRANSPORTS (LPA) "PAUL REVERE" CLASS

Name	No.	Builders	Commissioned	F/S
PAUL REVERE (ex-*Diamond Mariner*)	LPA 248	New York SB Corp	3 Sept 1958	NRF
FRANCIS MARION (ex-*Prairie Mariner*)	LPA 249	New York SB Corp	6 July 1961	NRF

Displacement, tons: 10 709 light; 16 838 full load
Dimensions, feet (metres): 563·5 oa × 76 × 27 (171·8 × 23·2 × 8·2)
Guns: 8—3 in (76 mm) 50 cal (Mk 33) (twin)
Main engines: Steam turbine (General Electric); 19 250 shp; 1 shaft = 22 knots
Boilers: 2 (Foster-Wheeler)
Complement: 307 (13 officers, 187 enlisted active duty; 15 officers, 237 enlisted reserve)
Troops: 1 657 (96 officers, 1 561 enlisted men)

Paul Revere launched 13 Feb 1954, *Francis Marion* launched 11 April 1953. "Mariner" C4-S-1A merchant ships acquired for conversion to attack transports; *Paul Revere* converted by Todd Shipyard Corp, San Pedro, California, under the Fiscal Year 1957 conversion programme; *Francis Marion* converted by Bethlehem Steel Corp, Key Highway Yard, Baltimore, Maryland, under the FY 1959 programme. Helicopter platform fitted aft; 7 LCM-6 and 16 LCVP landing craft carried as deck cargo; each ship has four Mk 63 gunfire control systems. Fitted to serve as force flagships.
Designation of both ships changed from APA to LPA on 1 Jan 1969.
Paul Revere and *Francis Marion* assigned to the Naval Reserve Force are partially manned by reserve personnel.

Fire control: Four Mk 63 GFCS, one Mk 5 Target Designation System and four SPG 50 radars (LPA 249 only).

FRANCIS MARION 6/1977, Wright and Logan

692 USA

LANDING CRAFT

1 AMPHIBIOUS ASSAULT LANDING CRAFT (AALC)
AEROJET-GENERAL DESIGN (JEFF-A)

Weight, tons: 90 empty; 167 gross
Dimensions, feet (metres): 96·2 oa × 48 × (height) 23·2 *(29·3 × 14·6 × 7·1)*
Main engines: 4 gas turbines (Avco-Lycoming T40); 15 000 hp; 4 aircraft type propellers in rotating shrouds for propulsive thrust = approx 50 knots cruising
Lift engines: 2 gas turbines (Avco-Lycoming T40); 7 500 hp; 8 horizontal fans (2 sets) for cushion lift
Range, miles: 200
Complement: 6

This is an Air Cushion Vehicle (ACV) landing craft being developed by the Aerojet-General Corp and being built by Todd Shipyards, Seattle, Washington, under Navy contract. Construction completed in February 1975 with one year of contractor testing before delivery to Navy in February 1976. (Construction shifted from Tacoma Boatbuilding Co.)
Above dimensions are for craft on air cushion; when at rest dimensions will be 97 × 44 × 19 feet. Designed to carry 120 000 lb payload at a design speed of 50 knots (same as Jeff-B). Design features include aluminium construction, bow and stern ramps, cargo deck area of 2 100 square feet; two sound-insulated compartments each hold four persons; three engines housed in each side structure; two propellers in rotating shrouds provide horizontal propulsion and steering. Performance parameters include four-hour endurance (200 n. mile range), 4 foot obstacle clearance, and capability to maintain cruise speed in Sea State 2 with 25-knot headwind. Delivered 1976.

Project: Aerojet-General and Bell Aerosystems were awarded contracts in 1971 to design competitive assault landing craft employing ACV technology and to build and test one craft per company.

AEROJET-GENERAL DESIGN (Model)

These are air cushion or bubble craft, supported above the land or water surface by a continuously generated cushion or bubble of air held by flexible "skirts" that surround the base of the vehicle. According to US Navy usage, they differ from surface effect ships (SES) which have rigid sidewalls that penetrate the water surface to help hold the cushion or bubble. Official designation of these craft is Amphibious Assault Landing Craft (AALC), with the Aerojet-General design being referred to as AALC—Jeff(A) and the Bell Aerosystems craft as AALC—Jeff(B).

1 AMPHIBIOUS ASSAULT LANDING CRAFT (AALC)
BELL DESIGN (JEFF-B)

Weight, tons: 165 gross
Dimensions, feet (metres): 86·75 oa × 47 × (height) 23·5 *(26·4 × 14·3 × 7·2)*
Main/lift engines: 6 gas turbines (Avco-Lycoming T40); 16 800 hp; interconnected with 2 aircraft-type propellers in rotating shrouds for propulsive thrust and 4 horizontal fans for cushion lift = approx 50 knots cruising
Range, miles: 200
Complement: 6

ACV landing craft built by Bell Aerosystems. Completed 1976. Above dimensions are for craft on air cushion; when at rest dimensions are 80 × 43 × 19 feet. Aluminium construction; bow and stern ramps; cargo area of 1 738 square feet; three engines housed in each side structure with raised pilot house on starboard side. Performance parameters similar to Jeff (A).
Distinguished from Aerojet-General craft by having only two shrouded propellers for thrust and steering. Delivered 1976. Currently running extensive trials.

BELL AEROSYSTEMS DESIGN (Model)

60 UTILITY LANDING CRAFT: LCU 1610 SERIES

LCU 1613	LCU 1627	LCU 1641	LCU 1651	LCU 1661	LCU 1671
LCU 1614	LCU 1628	LCU 1642	LCU 1652	LCU 1662	LCU 1672
LCU 1616	LCU 1629	LCU 1643	LCU 1653	LCU 1663	LCU 1673
LCU 1617	LCU 1630	LCU 1644	LCU 1654	LCU 1664	LCU 1674
LCU 1618	LCU 1631	LCU 1645	LCU 1655	LCU 1665	LCU 1675
LCU 1619	LCU 1632	LCU 1646	LCU 1656	LCU 1666	LCU 1676
LCU 1621	LCU 1633	LCU 1647	LCU 1657	LCU 1667	LCU 1677
LCU 1623	LCU 1634	LCU 1648	LCU 1658	LCU 1668	LCU 1678
LCU 1624	LCU 1635	LCU 1649	LCU 1659	LCU 1669	LCU 1679
LCU 1626	LCU 1637	LCU 1650	LCU 1660	LCU 1670	LCU 1680

Displacement, tons: 200 light; 375 full load
Dimensions, feet (metres): 134·9 oa × 29 × 6·1 *(44·2 × 9·5 × 2)*
Guns: 2—50 cal machine guns
Main engines: 4 diesels (Detroit); 1 000 bhp; 2 shafts (Kort nozzles) = 11 knots
Range, miles: 1 200 at 8 knots
Complement: 12 to 14 (enlisted men)

Improved landing craft, larger than previous series; can carry three M-103 or M-48 tanks (approx 64 tons and 48 tons respectively). Cargo capacity 170 tons.
LCU 1610-1612 built by Christy Corp, Sturgeon Bay, Wisconsin; LCU 1613-1619, 1623, 1624 built by Gunderson Bros Engineering Corp, Portland, Oregon; LCU 1620, 1621, 1625, 1626, 1629, 1630 built by Southern Shipbuilding Corp, Slidell, Louisiana; LCU 1622 built by Weaver Shipyards, Texas; LCU 1627, 1628, 1631-1636 built by General Ship and Engine Works (last six units completed in 1968); LCU 1638-1645 built by Marinette Marine Corp, Marinette, Wisconsin (completed 1969-1970); LCU 1646-1666 built by Defoe Shipbuilding Co, Bay City, Michigan

LCU 1661 1976, Dr. Giorgio Arra

(completed 1970-1971). The one-of-a-kind aluminium hull, 133·8 foot LCU 1637 built by Pacific Coast Engineering Co, Alameda, California; LCU 1667-1670 built by General Ship & Engine Works, East Boston, in 1973-1974; LCU 1671-1680 built by Marinette Marine Corp, 1974-1976. LCU 1636, 1638, 1639, 1640 reclassified as YFB 88-91 in Oct 1969 LCU 1620 and 1625 to YFU 92 and 93 respectively, in April 1971; LCU 1611, 1615, 1622 to YFU 97-99 in Feb 1972; LCU 1610, 1612 to YFU 100 and 101 respectively, in Aug 1972.

Engineering: Only two diesels fitted with vertical cycloidal propellers shipped in LCU 1621 and ex-LCUs 1620 and 1625.

24 UTILITY LANDING CRAFT: LCU 1466 SERIES

LCU 1466	LCU 1470	LCU 1485	LCU 1490	LCU 1537
LCU 1467	LCU 1472	LCU 1486	LCU 1492	LCU 1539
LCU 1468	LCU 1477	LCU 1487	LCU 1525	LCU 1547
LCU 1469	LCU 1482	LCU 1488	LCU 1535	LCU 1548
	LCU 1484	LCU 1489	LCU 1536	LCU 1559

Displacement, tons: 180 light; 360 full load
Dimensions, feet (metres): 115 wl; 119 oa × 34 × 6 *(37·7; 39 × 11·1 × 1·9)*
Guns: 2—20 mm
Main engines: 3 diesels (Gray Marine); 675 bhp; 3 shafts = 18 knots
Complement: 14

These are enlarged versions of the World War II-built LCTs; constructed during the early 1950s. LCU 1608 and 1609 have modified propulsion systems; LCU 1582 and later craft have Kort nozzle propellers. LCU 1496 reclassified as YFU 70 on 1 March 1966; LCU 1471 to YFU 88 in May 1968; LCU 1576, 1582 and 1608 to YFU 89-91, respectively, in June 1970; LCU 1488, 1491, and 1609 to YFU 94-96 on 1 June 1971; YFU 94 reverted to LCU 1488 on 1 Feb 1972.

Classification: The earlier craft of this series were initially designated as Utility Landing Ships (LSU); redesignated Utility Landing Craft (LCU) on 15 April 1952 and classified as service craft.

LCU 1488 1965, USN

USA 693

21 UTILITY LANDING CRAFT: LCU 501 SERIES

LCU 539	LCU 660	LCU 768	LCU 1124	LCU 1430
LCU 588	LCU 666	LCU 803	LCU 1241	LCU 1451
LCU 599	LCU 667	LCU 871	LCU 1348	LCU 1462
LCU 608	LCU 674	LCU 893	LCU 1348	
LCU 654	LCU 742	LCU 1045	LCU 1387	

Displacement, tons: 143-160 light; 309 to 320 full load
Dimensions, feet (metres): 105 wl × 119 oa × 32·7 × 5 *(34·6; 39 × 10·7 × 1·6)*
Guns: 2—20 mm
Main engines: Diesels (Gray Marine); 675 bhp; 3 shafts = 10 knots
Complement: 13 (enlisted men)

Formerly LCT(6) 501-1465 series; built in 1943-44. Can carry four tanks or 200 tons of cargo.

LCU 524, 529, 550, 562, 592, 600, 629, 664, 666, 668, 677, 686, 742, 764, 776, 788, 840, 869, 877, 960, 973, 974, 979, 980, 1056, 1082, 1086, 1124, 1136, 1156, 1159, 1162, 1195, 1224, 1236, 1250, 1283, 1286, 1363, 1376, 1378, 1384, 1386, 1398, 1411, and 1430 reclassified as YFU 1 through 46, respectively, on 18 May 1958; LCU 1040 reclassified YFB 82 on 18 May 1958; LCU 1446 reclassified YFU 53 in 1964; LCU 509, 637, 646, 709, 716, 776, 851, 916, 973, 989, 1126, 1165, 1203, 1232, 1385, and 1388 reclassified as YFU 54 through 69, respectively, on 1 March 1966; LCU 780 reclassified as YFU 87. YFU 9 reverted to LCU 666 on 1 Jan 1962; LCU 1459 converted to YLLC 4; LCU 1462 to YFU 102 on 1 Aug 1973. Changes reflect employment as general cargo craft assigned to shore commands (see section on Service Craft).

Classification: All LCUs were originally rated as Landing Craft, Tank (LCT(6)); redesignated Utility Landing Ships (LSU) in 1949 to reflect varied employment; designation changed to Utility Landing Craft (LCU) on 15 April 1952 and classified as service craft.

MECHANISED LANDING CRAFT: LCM 8 TYPE

Displacement, tons: 115 full load (steel) or 105 full load (aluminium)
Dimensions, feet (metres): 75·6 × 73·7 oa or 21 × 5·2 *(24·8 × 24·2 or 6·9 × 1·7)*
Main engines: 2 diesels (Detroit or General Motors); 650 bhp; 2 shafts = 9 knots
Complement: 5 (enlisted men)

Constructed of welded-steel or (later units) aluminium. Can carry one M-48 or M-60 tank (both approx 48 tons) or 60 tons cargo; range is 150 nautical miles at full load. Also operated in large numbers by the US Army.

LCM 8   *1976, Dr. Giorgio Arra*

MECHANISED LANDING CRAFT: LCM 6 TYPE

Displacement, tons: 60 to 62 full load
Dimensions, feet (metres): 56·2 oa × 14 × 3·9 *(18·4 × 4·6 × 1·3)*
Main engines: Diesels; 2 shafts; 450 bhp = 9 knots

Welded-steel construction. Cargo capacity is 34 tons or 80 trops.

LCM 6   *9/1976, Dr. Giorgio Arra*

LANDING CRAFT VEHICLE AND PERSONNEL (LCVP)

Displacement, tons: 13·5 full load
Dimensions, feet (metres): 35·8 oa × 10·5 × 3·5 *(11·7 × 3·4 × 1·1)*
Main engines: Diesel; 325 bhp; 1 shaft = 9 knots

Constructed of wood or fibreglass-reinforced plastic. Fitted with 30-calibre machine guns when in combat areas. Cargo capacity, 8 000 lb; range, 110 n. miles at full load.

2 WARPING TUGS (LWT)

LWT 1   LWT 2

Displacement, tons: 61 (hoisting weight)
Dimensions, feet (metres): 85 oa × 22 × 6·75 *(27·9 × 7·2 × 2·2)*
Main engines: 2 diesels (Harbormaster); 420 bhp; 2 steerable shafts = 9 knots
Complement: 6 (enlisted men)

These craft are employed in amphibious landings to handle pontoon causeways. The LWT 1 and 2 are prototypes of an all-aluminium design completed in 1970. A collapsible A-frame is fitted forward to facilitate handling causeway anchors and ship-to-shore fuel lines. They can be "side loaded" on the main deck of an LST 1179 class ship or carried in an LPD/LSD type ship. The propulsion motors are similar to outboard motors, providing both steering and thrust, alleviating the need for rudders.
Built by Campbell Machine, San Diego, California.

LWT 2   *USN*

WARPING TUGS (LWT)

Displacement, tons: approx 120
Dimensions, feet (metres): 92·9 oa × 23 × 6·5 *(30·4 × 7·5 × 2·1)*
Main engines: 2 outboard propulsion units = 6·5 knots

These craft are fabricated from pontoon sections and are assembled by the major amphibious commands as required.

LWT 85   *USN*

NAVAL RESERVE FORCE TRAINING AMPHIBIOUS WARFARE SHIPS

Name/Hull No.	NRF Homeport	Date of Assignment	Remarks
TULARE (LKA 112)	San Francisco, Calif	1 July 1975	Replaced *Hamner* (DD 718)
PAUL REVERE (LPA 248)	Long Beach, Calif	1 July 1975	Replaced *Higbee* (DD 806) and *McKean* (DD 784)
FRANCIS MARION (LPA 249)	Norfolk, Va	14 Nov 1975	

694 USA

MINE WARFARE FORCES

The US Navy has initiated a programme to construct a new class of mine countermeasures ships especially for deep water operations.
Currently the Navy operates three active and 22 Naval Reserve Force (NRF) minesweepers. The active ships provide support to mine research and development activities at the Naval Coastal Systems Laboratory in Panama City, Florida; the NRF ships are manned by composite active-reserve crews. In addition, the Navy flies 21 specially equipped RH-53D Sea Stallion helicopters. These helicopters, which tow mine countermeasure devices, are readily deployable to aircraft carriers or amphibious ships in overseas areas. They can counter mines laid in shallow waters but have no capability against deep-water mines.
The US Navy maintains no surface ships with a minelaying capability. Rather, the Navy can plant mines by carrier-based aircraft, land-based maritime patrol aircraft, and attack submarines. The large B-52 Stratofortress bombers of the Strategic Air Command can also plant sea mines.

(5) MINE COUNTERMEASURE SHIPS (MCM)

One ship	MCM 1	Planned under FY1980
Two ships	MCM 2-3	Planned under FY 1982
Two ships	MCM 4-5	Planned under FY 1983

Dimensions, feet (metres): 239·5 × 44·3 × 11·8 (app.) *(73 × 13·5 × 3·6)*
Main engines: 4 diesels
Accommodation: About 100

Cost approx $100-110 million per ship.

2 "ACME" CLASS (OCEAN MINESWEEPERS (MSO))

Name	No.	Launched	Commissioned	F/S
ADROIT	MSO 509	20 Aug 1955	4 Mar 1957	NRF
AFFRAY	MSO 511	18 Dec 1956	8 Dec 1958	NRF

Displacement, tons: 633 light; 750 full load
Dimensions, feet (metres): 173 oa × 35 × 14 *(52·7 × 10·7 × 4·3)*
Guns: 2—20 mm (twin)
Main engines: 2 diesels (Packard), 2 280 bhp; 2 shafts (cp propellers) = 15 knots
Complement: 81 (7 officers, 37 enlisted active duty; 4 officers, 33 enlisted reserve)

This class is different from the "Aggressive" class but has similar basic particulars. Built by Frank L. Sample, Jr, Inc, Boothbay Harbor, Maine. Plans to modernise these ships were cancelled (see notes under "Aggressive" class).
Adroit and *Affray* are assigned to Naval Reserve training, manned partially by active and partially by reserve personnel (see notes under "Aggressive" class).

AFFRAY   1969, USN

23 OCEAN MINESWEEPERS (MSO)
"AGGRESSIVE" and "DASH" CLASSES

Name	No.	Launched	Commissioned	F/S
CONSTANT	MSO 427	14 Feb 1952	8 Sept 1954	NRF
DASH	MSO 428	20 Sept 1952	14 Aug 1953	NRF
DETECTOR	MSO 429	5 Dec 1952	26 Jan 1954	NRF
DIRECT	MSO 430	27 May 1953	9 July 1954	NRF
DOMINANT	MSO 431	5 Nov 1953	8 Nov 1954	NRF
ENGAGE	MSO 433	18 June 1953	29 June 1954	NRF
ENHANCE	MSO 437	11 Oct 1952	16 April 1955	NRF
ESTEEM	MSO 438	20 Dec 1952	10 Sept 1955	NRF
EXCEL	MSO 439	25 Sept 1953	24 Feb 1955	NRF
EXPLOIT	MSO 440	10 April 1953	31 Mar 1954	NRF
EXULTANT	MSO 441	6 June 1953	22 June 1954	NRF
FEARLESS	MSO 442	17 July 1953	22 Sept 1954	NRF
FIDELITY	MSO 443	21 Aug 1953	19 Jan 1955	AA
FORTIFY	MSO 446	14 Feb 1953	16 July 1954	NRF
ILLUSIVE	MSO 448	12 July 1952	14 Nov 1953	AA
IMPERVIOUS	MSO 449	29 Aug 1952	15 July 1954	NRF
IMPLICIT	MSO 455	1 Aug 1953	10 Mar 1954	NRF
INFLICT	MSO 456	6 Oct 1953	11 May 1954	NRF
PLUCK	MSO 464	6 Feb 1954	11 Aug 1954	NRF
CONQUEST	MSO 488	20 May 1954	20 July 1955	NRF
GALLANT	MSO 489	4 June 1954	14 Sept 1955	NRF
LEADER	MSO 490	15 Sept 1954	16 Nov 1955	AA
PLEDGE	MSO 492	20 July 1955	20 April 1956	NRF

Displacement, tons: 620 light; 735 full load (428-431); 720 (remainder)
Dimensions, feet (metres): 165 wl; 172 oa × 36 × 13·6 *(52·4 × 11·0 × 4·2)*
Gun: 1—20 mm Mk 68 (single); (all modernised ships are unarmed)
Main engines: 4 diesels (Packard) (Waukesha in modernised ships); 2 280 bhp; 2 shafts; cp propellers = 14 knots; *Dash, Detector, Direct* and *Dominant,* have 2 diesels (General Motors); 1 520 bhp (see *Modernisation* notes)
Range, miles: 2 400 at 10 knots
Complement: 76 (6 officers, 70 enlisted men); 86 in NRF ships (3 officers, 36 enlisted active duty; 3 officers, 44 enlisted reserve) (see *Modernisation* note)

These ships were built on the basis of mine warfare experience in the Korean War (1950-53); 58 built for US service and 35 transferred upon completion to NATO navies. (One ship cancelled, MSO 497). They have wooden hulls and non-magnetic engines and other equipment. All surviving ships were built in private shipyards.
Initially designated as minesweepers (AM); reclassified as ocean minesweepers (MSO) in Feb 1955. Originally fitted with UQS 1 mine detecting sonar. Active MSOs serve as tenders.

Engineering: Diesel engines are fabricated of non-magnetic stainless steel alloy.

Modernisation: The 62 ocean minesweepers in commission during the mid-1960s were all to have been modernised; estimated cost and schedule per ship were $5 million and ten months in shipyard. However, some of the early modernisations took as long as 26 months which, coupled with changes in mine countermeasures techniques, led to cancellation of programme after 13 ships were modernised: MSO 433, 437, 438, 441-443, 445, 446, 448, 449, 456, 488, and 490.
The modernisation provided improvements in mine detection, engines, communications, and habitability: four Waukesha Motor Co diesel engines installed (plus two or three diesel generators for sweep gear), SQQ 14 sonar with mine classification as well as detection capability provided, twin 20 mm in some ships (replacing single 40 mm because of space requirements for sonar hoist mechanism), habitability improved, and advanced communications equipment fitted; bridge structure in modernised ships extended around mast and aft to funnel. Complement in active modernised ships is 6 officers and 70 enlisted men.
Some MSOs have received SQQ 14 sonar but not full modernisation.

DOMINANT   11/1975, USN

EXPLOIT   9/1976, Dr. Giorgio Arra

Transfers: Ships of this class serve in the navies of Belgium, France, Italy, Netherlands, Norway, Portugal, Spain, and Uruguay.

USA 695

COASTAL MINESWEEPERS (MSC): NEW CONSTRUCTION

Four coastal minesweepers are under construction for transfer to Saudi Arabia; designated MSC 322-325 for accounting purposes. Contract awarded 30 Sept 1975 to Peterson Builders, Sturgeon Bay, Wisconsin; scheduled to complete June through October 1978. Hull numbers MSC 320 and MSC 321 assigned to units built in the United States for South Korea. See Saudi Arabia and South Korea sections for details.

2 Ex-MINESWEEPERS (RESEARCH SHIPS (MSI))

Name	No.	Builders	In service
COVE	MSI 1	Bethlehem Shipyards Co, Bellingham	20 Nov 1958
CAPE	MSI 2	Bethlehem Shipyards Co, Bellingham	27 Feb 1959

Displacement, tons: 120 light; 240 full load
Dimensions, feet (metres): 105 × 22 × 10 *(32·0 × 6·7 × 3·0)*
Guns: Removed
Main engines: Diesel (General Motors); 650 bhp; 1 shaft = 12 knots
Complement: 21 (3 officers, 18 men)

These ships were prototype inshore minesweepers (MSI) authorised under the Fiscal Year 1956 new construction programme. *Cape* laid down on 1 May 1957 and launched on 5 April 1968; *Cove* laid down 1 Feb 1957 and launched 8 Feb 1958.
Cape is operated by the Naval Undersea Research Development Center, San Diego, California; neither in service nor in commission. *Cove* transferred to Johns Hopkins Applied Physics Laboratory on 31 July 1970; she remains on the Navy List. Both conduct Navy research. Both active.

CAPE
1968, USN

8 MINESWEEPING BOATS (MSB)

| MSB 15 | MSB 25 | MSB 29 | MSB 51 |
| MSB 16 | MSB 28 | MSB 41 | MSB 52 |

Displacement, tons: 30 light; 39 full load except MSB 29, 80 full load
Dimensions, feet (metres): 57·2 × 15·5 × 4 except MSB 29, 82 × 19 × 5·5 *(17·4 × 4·7 × 1·2—25 × 5·8 × 1·7)*
Guns: several MG
Main engines: 2 geared diesels (Packard); 600 bhp; 2 shafts = 12 knots
Complement: 6 (enlisted)

Wooden-hull minesweepers intended to be carried to theatre of operations by large assault ships; however, they are too large to be easily handled by cranes and are assigned to sweeping harbours. From 1966 to 1972 they were used extensively in Viet-Nam for river minesweeping operations.
Of 49 minesweeping boats of this type built only eight remain in active service, all based at Charleston, South Carolina.
MSB 1-4 were ex-Army minesweepers built in 1946 (since discarded), MSB 5-54 (less MSB 24) were completed in 1952-1956. MSB 24 was not built. MSB 29 built to enlarged design by John Trumpy & Sons, Annapolis, Maryland, in an effort to improve seakeeping ability.
Normally commanded by chief petty officer or petty officer first class.

Gunnery: MSBs serving in South Viet-Nam were fitted with several machineguns and removable fibreglass armour.

NAVAL RESERVE FORCE TRAINING MINE WARFARE SHIPS

Name/Hull No.	NRF Homeport	Date of Assignment	Remarks
CONSTANT (MSO 427)	Long Beach, Calif	1 July 1972	Replaced *Embattle* (MSO 434)
DASH (MSO 428)	Newport, RI	1 Mar 1976	Replaced *Jacana* (MSC 193)
DETECTOR (MSO 429)	Newport, RI	15 Aug 1977	Replaced *Adroit* (MSO 509)
DIRECT (MSO 430)	Perth Amboy, NJ	1 Sept 1971	Replaced *Limpkin* (MSC 195) and *Meadowlark* (MSC 196)
DOMINANT (MSO 431)	St. Petersburg, Fla	1 Sept 1971	
ENGAGE (MSO 433)	St. Petersburg, Fla	1 Aug 1974	
ENHANCE (MSO 437)	San Diego, Calif	1 July 1974	
ESTEEM (MSO 438)	Seattle, Wash	1 Sept 1975	Replaced *Vireo* (MSC 205), *Warbler* (MSC 206) and *Woodpecker* (MSC 209)
EXCEL (MSO 439)	San Francisco, Calif	1 July 1972	
EXPLOIT (MSO 440)	Little Creek, Va	30 Sept 1973	
EXULTANT (MSO 441)	St. Petersburg, Fla	1 July 1972	
FEARLESS (MSO 442)	Charleston, SC	1 July 1974	
FORTIFY (MSO 446)	Little Creek, Va	1 Aug 1974	
IMPERVIOUS (MSO 449)	Mayport, Fla	1 Aug 1974	
IMPLICIT (MSO 455)	Tacoma, Wash	1 July 1972	
INFLICT (MSO 456)	Little Creek, Va	1 Aug 1974	
PLUCK (MSO 464)	San Diego, Calif	1 July 1972	
CONQUEST (MSO 488)	Seattle, Wash	1 Sept 1975	See *Esteem* (MSO 438)
GALLANT (MSO 489)	San Francisco, Calif	1 July 1972	Replaced *Reaper* (MSO 467)
PLEDGE (MSO 492)	Long Beach, Calif	1 July 1972	
ADROIT (MSO 509)	Portsmouth, NH	15 Aug 1977	Replaced *Detector* (MSO 429)
AFFRAY (MSO 511)	Portland, Maine	30 June 1973	

696   USA

AUXILIARY SHIPS

The Auxiliary Ships of the US Navy are usually divided into two broad categories, Underway Replenishment Ships and Fleet Support Ships. Underway Replenishment Ships are distinguished by their primary role, the direct support of deployed forces in the forward area of operations.

Most US Navy replenishment ships are fitted with helicopter platforms to allow the transfer of supplies by vertical replenishment (VERTREP). Helicopters are carried specifically for this purpose by the newer ammunition ships (AE), the combat store ships (AFS), the fast combat support ships (AOE), and some replenishment oilers (AOR). Carrier-based helicopters are sometimes employed in this role.

Planned Underway Replenishment (UNREP) ship force levels provide a wartime capability to support deployed carrier and amphibious task groups in up to four or five locations simultaneously. This plan is based on the availability of some storage depots on foreign territory, and the use of Military Sealift Ships to carry fuels, munitions, and the stores from the United States or overseas sources for transfer to UNREP ships in overseas areas.

During peacetime some 16 to 18 UNREP ships normally are forward deployed in the Mediterranean and western Pacific areas in support of the 6th and 7th Fleets, respectively.

The Navy's plan for modernisation of the UNREP forces provides for 14 fleet oilers (AO) in the new construction programme.

Fleet support ships provide primarily maintenance and related towing and salvage services at advanced bases and at ports in the United States. These ships normally do not provide fuel, munitions, or other supplies except when ships are alongside for maintenance.

Most fleet support ships operate from bases in the United States. The five Polaris/Poseidon submarine tenders (AS) are based at Holy Loch, Scotland; Rota, Spain; Charleston, South Carolina; and Apra harbour, Guam, with one ship generally in transit or overhaul. The Rota facility will be disestablished in about 1980. In addition, two support ships (AD/AR/AS type) generally are forward deployed in the Mediterranean and two in the western Pacific.

Underway replenishment ships and fleet support ships are mainly Navy manned and armed; however, an increasing number are being operated by the Military Sealift Command (MSC) with civilian crews. The latter ships are not armed and have T- prefix before their designations.

2 + 3 + (2) DESTROYER TENDERS (AD)
"AD 41" and "SAMUEL GOMPERS" CLASSES

Name	No.	Builders	Laid down	Commissioned	F/S
SAMUEL GOMPERS	AD 37	Puget Sound Naval SY, Bremerton	9 July 1964	1 July 1967	PA
PUGET SOUND	AD 38	Puget Sound Naval SY, Bremerton	15 Feb 1965	27 April 1968	AA
YELLOWSTONE	AD 41	National Steel BB Co, San Diego	27 June 1977	Early 1980	Bldg
ACADIA	AD 42	National Steel BB Co, San Diego	—	Mid 1980	Bldg
	AD 43	Approved FY 1977 programme		Late 1980	Bldg
	AD 44	Proposed FY 1979 programme		1981	
	AD 45	Proposed FY 1979 programme		1982	

Displacement, tons: 20 500 full load
Dimensions, feet (metres): 644 oa × 85 × 22·5 (196·3 × 25·9 × 6·9)
Guns: 1—5 in (127 mm) 38 cal (Mk 30) (Puget Sound only); 4—20 mm Mk 67
Missile launchers: 1 NATO Sea Sparrow system planned for AD 41 and later ships
Main engines: Steam turbines (De Laval); 20 000 shp; 1 shaft = 18 knots
Boilers: 2 (Combustion Engineering)
Complement: 1 803 (135 officers, 1 668 enlisted men)

These are the first US destroyer tenders of post-World War II design; capable of providing repair and supply services to new destroyer classes. The tenders also have facilities for servicing nuclear power plants. Services can be provided simultaneously to six guided-missile destroyers moored alongside. Basic hull design similar to "L. Y. Spear" and "Simon Lake" submarine tenders. Provided with helicopter platform and hangar; two 7 000-lb capacity cranes.
Samuel Gompers authorised in the Fiscal Year 1964 new construction programme and *Puget Sound* in the FY 1965 programme.
Two sisters of *Samuel Gompers* AD 39 of the FY 1969 programme, cancelled—AD 39 on 11 Dec 1965 prior to start of construction to provide funds for overruns in other new ship programmes and AD 40, authorised in the FY 1973 new construction programme, cancelled in April 1974. AD 41 in the FY 1975 programme and AD 42 in the FY 1976 programme with three additional ships planned (AD 41 and later ships of a slightly modified design.)
Estimated cost of AD 43 is $260·4 million and estimated cost of AD 44 is $289·1 million.

Gunnery: Proposed armament of AD 41-43 is 2—20 mm Phalanx CIWS, 2—40 mm Mk 64 (singles), 2—20 mm Mk 67 (singles). Two 40 mm saluting guns (AD 37 and 38).

Particulars: Apply only to "Samuel Gompers" class.

SAMUEL GOMPERS   1/1977, Dr. Giorgio Arra

SAMUEL GOMPERS   1/1977, Dr. Giorgio Arra

3 DESTROYER TENDERS (AD)
"KLONDIKE" and "SHENANDOAH" CLASSES

Name	No.	Builders	Commissioned	F/S
EVERGLADES	AD 24	Los Angeles SB & DD Co	25 May 1951	AR
SHENANDOAH	AD 26	Todd Shipyards, Los Angeles	13 Aug 1945	AA
BRYCE CANYON	AD 36	Charleston NY	15 Sept 1950	PA

Displacement, tons: 8 165 standard; 14 700 full load (15,460 AD 24)
Dimensions, feet (metres): 465 wl; 492 oa × 69·5 × 27·2 (150·0 × 21·2 × 8·3)
Guns: 1—5 in (127 mm) 38 cal Mk 37 (AD 36)
  2—3 in (76 mm) 50 cal Mk 26 (AD 24)
  4—20 mm Mk 68 (AD 26)
Main engines: Steam turbines (Westinghouse); 8 500 shp 1 shaft = 18·4 knots
Boilers: 2 (Foster-Wheeler)
Complement: 778 to 918

These ships are of modified C-3 design completed as destroyer tenders. Originally class of four. *Everglades* launched 28 Jan 1945, *Shenandoah* 29 March 1945; *Bryce Canyon* 7 March 1946. Originally 13 ships of two similar designs, the "Klondike" class of AD 22-25 and "Shenandoah" class of AD 26, 27, 28, 29, 30, 31, 33, 35, 36. *Great Lakes* (AD 30), *Canopus* (AD 33, ex-AS 27), *Arrow Head* (AD 35) cancelled before completion; *Klondike* (AD 22) reclassified AR 22 (since deleted); *Grand Canyon* (AD 28) reclassified AR 28 (see under ARs).
Two ships remain in active service with *Everglades* in reserve as accommodation and depot ship at Philadelphia Navy Yard. *Yellowstone* (AD 27) paid off 12 Sept 1974.

Gunnery: Original armament for "Klondike" class was 1—5 in gun, 4—3 in guns, and 4—40 mm guns; for "Shenandoah" class was 2—5 in guns and 8—40 mm guns.
Two 40 mm saluting guns in AD 24 and 26.

Modernisation: These ships have been modernised under the FRAM II programme to service modernised destroyers fitted with ASROC, improved electronics, helicopters etc.

SHENANDOAH   9/1976, Dr. Giorgio Arra

USA 697

5 DESTROYER TENDERS (AD) "DIXIE" CLASS

Name	No.	Builders	Commissioned	F/S
DIXIE	AD 14	NY Shipbuilding Corp, NJ	25 April 1940	PA
PRAIRIE	AD 15	NY Shipbuilding Corp, NJ	5 Aug 1940	PA
PIEDMONT	AD 17	Tampa Shipbuilding Co, Florida	5 Jan 1944	AA
SIERRA	AD 18	Tampa Shipbuilding Co, Florida	20 Mar 1944	AA
YOSEMITE	AD 19	Tampa Shipbuilding Co, Florida	25 Mar 1944	AA

Displacement, tons: 9 450 standard; 17 190 to 18 000 full load
Dimensions, feet (metres): 520 wl; 530·5 oa × 73·3 × 25·5 *(161·7 × 22·3 × 7·8)*
Guns: 4—20 mm Mk 67 (singles)
Main engines: Steam turbines (New York SB Corp in AD 14 and 15; Allis Chalmers in remainder); 12 000 shp; 2 shafts = 18·2 knots
Boilers: 4 (Babcock & Wilcox)
Complement: 1 131 to 1 271

Launched on 27 May 1939, 9 Dec 1939, 7 Dec 1942, 23 Feb 1943 and 16 May 1943 respectively. All five ships are active with *Dixie* the oldest ship currently in service with the US Navy except for the sail frigate *Constitution*. Two 40 mm saluting guns carried.

Modernisation: All of these ships have been modernised under the FRAM II programme to service destroyers fitted with ASROC, improved electronics, helicopters, etc. Two or three 5 in guns and eight 40 mm guns removed during modernisation.

DIXIE   4/1976, USN

8 AMMUNITION SHIPS (AE) "KILAUEA" CLASS

Name	No.	Builders	Commissioned	F/S
KILAUEA	AE 26	General Dynamics Corp, Quincy, Mass	10 Aug 1968	PA
BUTTE	AE 27	General Dynamics Corp, Quincy, Mass	14 Dec 1968	AA
SANTA BARBARA	AE 28	Bethlehem Steel Corp, Sparrows Pt, Md	11 July 1970	AA
MOUNT HOOD	AE 29	Bethlehem Steel Corp, Sparrows Pt, Md	1 May 1971	PA
FLINT	AE 32	Ingalls SB Corp, Pascagoula, Miss	20 Nov 1971	PA
SHASTA	AE 33	Ingalls SB Corp, Pascagoula, Miss	26 Feb 1972	PA
MOUNT BAKER	AE 34	Ingalls SB Corp, Pascagoula, Miss	22 July 1972	AA
KISKA	AE 35	Ingalls SB Corp, Pascagoula, Miss	16 Dec 1972	PA

Displacement, tons: 18 088 full load (17 931, AE 26 and 27)
Dimensions, feet (metres): 564 oa × 81 × 28 *(171·9 × 24·7 × 8·5)*
Helicopters: 2 UH-46 Sea Knight cargo helicopters normally embarked
Guns: 8—3 in *(76 mm)* 50 cal (twin) (Mk 33) (AE 28-33); 4—3 in (twin) (remainder)
Main engines: Geared turbines (General Electric); 22 000 shp; 1 shaft = 20 knots
Boilers: 3 (Foster-Wheeler)
Complement: 411 (38 officers, 373 enlisted men)

Fitted for rapid transfer of missiles and other munitions to ships alongside or with helicopters in vertical replenishment operations (VERTREP). Helicopter platform and hangar aft. AE 26 and 27 authorised in the Fiscal Year 1965 new construction programme, AE 28 and 29 in the FY 1966, AE 32 and 33 in the FY 1967, and AE 34 and 35 in the FY 1968. AE 26 laid down 10 March 1966; AE 27, 21 July 1966; AE 28, 20 Dec 1966; AE 29, 8 May 1967; AE 32, 4 Aug 1969; AE 33, 10 Nov 1969; AE 34, 10 May 1970; AE 35, 4 Aug 1971.

FLINT   10/1976, Dr. Giorgio Arra

Fire control: One Mk 56 GFCS, one Mk 1 Target Designation System and one SPG 35 radar (AE 27, 29, 34 and 35 only).

Gunnery: The 3 in guns are arranged in twin closed mounts forward and twin open mounts aft, between funnel and after booms. Two 20 mm Mk 15 CIWS to be fitted.

Missiles: Plans to instal NATO Seasparrow cancelled.

Rockets: Mk 36 Chaffroc (RBOC) to be fitted.

5 AMMUNITION SHIPS (AE) "SURIBACHI" and "NITRO" CLASSES

Name	No.	Builders	Commissioned	F/S
SURIBACHI	AE 21	Bethlehem Steel Corp, Sparrows Point, Md	17 Nov 1956	AA
MAUNA KEA	AE 22	Bethlehem Steel Corp, Sparrows Point, Md	30 Mar 1957	PA
NITRO	AE 23	Bethlehem Steel Corp, Sparrows Point, Md	1 May 1959	AA
PYRO	AE 24	Bethlehem Steel Corp, Sparrows Point, Md	24 July 1959	PA
HALEAKALA	AE 25	Bethlehem Steel Corp, Sparrows Point, Md	3 Nov 1959	PA

Displacement, tons: 7 470 light; 10 000 standard; 15 500 full load (21 and 22), 15 900-16 083 (rest)
Dimensions, feet (metres): 512 oa × 72 × 29 *(156·1 × 21·9 × 8·8)* (21 and 22; 502 oa *(153)*)
Guns: 4—3 in *(76 mm)* 50 cal (twin) (Mk 33)
Main engines: Geared turbines (Bethlehem); 16 000 shp; 1 shaft = 18 knots (AE 21 and 22); 20·6 (rest)
Boilers: 2 (Combustion Engineering)
Complement: 386 (16 officers, 370 enlisted men) (AE 21 and 22); 350 (20 officers, 330 enlisted men) (rest)

Designed specifically for underway replenishment. A sixth ship of this class to have been built under the FY 1959 programme was cancelled.
All five ships were modernised in 1960s, being fitted with high-speed transfer equipment, three holds configured for stowage of missiles up to and including the 33-foot Talos, and helicopter platform fitted aft (two after twin 3 in gun mounts removed).

NITRO   9/1975, Dr. Giorgio Arra

Arrangements of twin 3 in gun mounts differ, some ships have them in tandem and others side-by-side.

Fire control: One Mk 63 director with one Mk 1 Target Designation System and one SPG 34 radar (21 and 22); two Mk 51 directors; one Mk 1 target designation system (24 and 25); two SPG 52 radars (24 only).

Rockets: Mk 36 Chaffroc (RBOC) to be fitted.

7 COMBAT STORE SHIPS (AFS) "MARS" CLASS

Name	No.	Builders	Commissioned	F/S
MARS	AFS 1	National Steel and SB Co, San Diego	21 Dec 1963	PA
SYLVANIA	AFS 2	National Steel and SB Co, San Diego	11 July 1964	AA
NIAGARA FALLS	AFS 3	National Steel and SB Co, San Diego	29 April 1967	PA
WHITE PLAINS	AFS 4	National Steel and SB Co, San Diego	23 Nov 1968	PA
CONCORD	AFS 5	National Steel and SB Co, San Diego	27 Nov 1968	AA
SAN DIEGO	AFS 6	National Steel and SB Co, San Diego	24 May 1969	AA
SAN JOSE	AFS 7	National Steel and SB Co, San Diego	23 Oct 1970	AA

Displacement, tons: 16 500 full load (1-3) 15 900 (remainder)
Dimensions, feet (metres): 581 oa × 79 × 24 *(177·1 × 24·1 × 7·3)*
Guns: 8—3 in *(76 mm)* 50 cal (twin) Mk 33
Helicopters: 2 UH-46 Sea Knight helicopters normally assigned
Main engines: Steam turbines (De Laval except AFS 6—Westinghouse); 22 000 shp; 1 shaft = 20 knots
Boilers: 3 (Babcock & Wilcox)
Complement: 486 (45 officers, 441 enlisted men)

WHITE PLAINS   12/1976, Dr. Giorgio Arra

On building represented a new design with a completely new replenishment at sea system. "M" frames replace conventional king posts and booms, which are equipped with automatic tensioning devices to maintain transfer lines taut. Computers provide data on stock status with data displayed by closed-circuit television. Five holds (one refrigerated). Cargo capacity 2 625 tons dry stores and 1 300 tons refrigerated stores (varies with specific loadings).
Automatic propulsion system with full controls on bridge. The large SPS 40 radar fitted in *Mars* and *Sylvania* have been removed; some ships have Tacan (tactical aircraft navigation) radar. *Mars* authorised in the Fiscal Year 1961 shipbuilding programme, *Sylvania* in the FY 1962,

Niagara Falls in the FY 1964, *White Plains* and *Concord* in the FY 1965, *San Diego* in the FY 1966, *San Jose* in the FY 1967.
Plans to construct three additional ships of this type in the FY 1977-1978 programmes have been dropped.

Fire control: Two Mk 56 GFCS, two SPG 35 radars, Mark 1 Target Designation System (only fitting in AFS 7).

Rockets: Mk 36 Chaffroc (RBOC) to be fitted.

698 USA

2 SONAR RESEARCH SHIPS (AG) CONVERTED "ABILITY" CLASS

Name	No.	Builders	Commissioned
ALACRITY	AG 520 (ex-MSO 520)	Peterson Builders Inc, Wisconsin	1 Oct 1958
ASSURANCE	AG 521 (ex-MSO 521)	Peterson Builders Inc, Wisconsin	21 Nov 1958

Displacement, tons: 810 light; 960 full load
Dimensions, feet (metres): 190 oa × 36 × 12 (58·0 × 11·0 × 3·7)
Guns: Removed
Main engines: 2 diesels (General Motors); 2 700 bhp; 2 shafts (cp propellers) = 15 knots

Former ocean minesweepers. Launched on 8 June 1957 and 31 Aug 1957. Wood-hulled with non-magnetic engines and fittings. Both ships modified for sonar test activities and redesignated as miscellaneous auxiliaries (AG) on 1 June 1973 and 1 March 1973, respectively. Fitted with Towed Acoustic Surveillance System (TASS).

ASSURANCE   USN

1 MISCELLANEOUS (AG) Ex-MERCHANT DEEP SALVAGE SHIP

Name	No.	Builders	Completed	F/S
(ex-M/V Hughes Glomar Explorer)	AG 193	Sun SB and Drydock Co, Chester, Pa	July 1973	MPR

Displacement, tons: 63 300 full load
Tonnage: 27 445 gross; 18 511 net; 39 705 deadweight
Dimensions, feet (metres): 618·8 × 115·7 × 50·8 (188·6 × 35·3 × 15·5)
Aircraft: Landing area for 1 medium helicopter; no support facilities
Main engines: 5 Nordberg diesels, 6 electric motors (diesel-electric drive); 13 200 shp; 2 shafts = approx 15 + knots
Boilers: 4
Complement: not available

Built for the Summa Corp 1972-73, this vessel was officially classified by the American Bureau of Shipping as a "Survey Ship". After her actual mission and career had been widely disclosed 1975-76, the US Navy took her over on 30 Sept 1976 and classified her as AG 193. She was then inactivated and given to the Maritime Administration on 17 Jan 1977 for layup at the reserve fleet in Suisun Bay, Calif. The plan is to keep her there at least five years.

1 MISCELLANEOUS (AG) "COMPASS ISLAND" CLASS

Name	No.	Builders	Commissioned	F/S
COMPASS ISLAND (ex-Garden Mariner)	AG 153 (ex-YAG 56)	New York SB Corp, NJ	3 Dec 1956	AA

Displacement, tons: 17 600 full load
Dimensions, feet (metres): 564 oa × 78 × 31 (171·6 × 23·8 × 9·5)
Main engines: Geared turbines (General Electric); 19 250 shp; 1 shaft = 20 knots
Boilers: 2 (Foster-Wheeler)
Complement: 250 (18 officers, 232 enlisted men)

Originally a "Mariner" class merchant ship (C4-S-1a type). Acquired by the Navy on 29 March 1956.
Converted by New York Naval Shipyard for the development of the Fleet Ballistic Missile guidance and ship navigation systems. Her mission is to assist in the development and valuation of a navigation system independent of shore-based aids. Navy manned.
Observation Island (AG 154), a sister ship, serves with the Military Sealift Command.

COMPASS ISLAND   USN

1 AUXILIARY DEEP SUBMERGENCE SUPPORT SHIP (AGDS) Ex-DOCK CARGO SHIP

Name	No.	Builders	Commissioned	F/S
POINT LOMA (ex-Point Barrow)	AGDS 2 (ex-AKD 1)	Maryland SB & DD Co	28 Feb 1958	PA

Displacement, tons: 9 415 standard; 14 000 full load
Dimensions, feet (metres): 475 wl; 492 oa × 78 × 22 (150·0 × 23·8 × 6·7)
Guns: None
Main engines: Steam turbines (Westinghouse); 6 000 shp; 2 shafts = 15 knots
Boilers: 2 (Foster-Wheeler)
Complement: 160 (Including scientific personnel and submersible operators)

A docking ship designed to carry cargo, vehicles, and landing craft (originally designated AKD). Built for the Military Sea Transportation Service (now Military Sealift Command); launched on 25 May 1957 decommissioned and delivered to MSTS on 29 May 1958. Maritime Administration S2-ST-23A design; winterised for arctic service. Fitted with internal ramp and garage system. Subsequently refitted with hangar over docking well and employed in transport of large booster rockets to Cape Kennedy Space Center. Primarily used to carry the second stage of the Saturn V moon rocket and Lunar Modules. Placed out of service in reserve on 28 Sept 1972.
Reactivated in mid-1972 for cargo work; transferred from Military Sealift Command to Navy on 28 Feb 1974 for modification to support deep submergence vehicles, especially the bathyscaph Trieste II. Placed in commission "special" on 28 Feb 1974 as the AGDS 2; renamed Point Loma for the location of the San Diego submarine base where Submarine Development Group 1 operates most of the Navy's submersibles. Point Loma was placed in commission on 30 April 1975. Aviation gas capacity increased to approximately 100 000 gallons (US) to support Trieste II which uses lighter-than-water avgas for flotation.

Classification: The designation AGDS was established on 3 Jan 1974; originally it was a service craft designation rather than a ship designation. AGDS 1 was assigned briefly to the floating dry dock White Sands (ARD 20), the previous Trieste II support ship. Point Loma renamed and reclassified AGDS 2 on 28 Feb 1974.

POINT LOMA   6/1976, J. L. M. van der Burg

USA 699

1 HYDROFOIL RESEARCH SHIP (AGEH) "PLAINVIEW" CLASS

Name	No.	Builders	In service	F/S
PLAINVIEW	AGEH 1	Lockheed SB & Cons Co, Seattle	1 Mar 1969	PSA

Displacement, tons: 309 full load
Dimensions, feet (metres): 220 oa × 40·5 × 10 (hull borne) or 25 (with foils down) (67·1 × 12·3 × 3·0 or 7·6)
A/S weapons: 2 triple torpedo tubes (Mk 32)
Main engines: 2 gas turbines (General Electric Mod J-79); 28 000 hp; 2 diesels (Detroit); 1 200 shp = 50 knots
Complement: 20 (4 officers, 16 men)

Aluminium hull experimental hydrofoil. Three retractable foils, 25 feet in height, each weighing 7 tons, fitted port and starboard and on stern, and used in waves up to 15 feet. Initial maximum speed of about 50 knots, with later modifications designed to raise the speed to 80 knots. Fitted with the largest titanium propellers made. Power plant and transmission designed to permit future investigation of various types of foils. Laid down on 8 May 1964, launched on 28 June 1965. Delayed because of engineering difficulties. In service vice being in commission.

PLAINVIEW 1972, USN

1 COMMAND SHIP (AGF) CONVERTED "RALEIGH" CLASS

Name	No.	Builders	Laid down	Launched	Commissioned	F/S
LA SALLE	AGF 3 (ex-LPD 3)	New York Naval Shipyards	2 April 1962	3 Aug 1963	22 Feb 1964	AA

Displacement, tons: 8 040 light; 13 900 full load
Length, feet (metres): 500 (152·0) wl; 521·8 (158·4) oa
Beam, feet (metres): 104 (31·7)
Draught, feet (metres): 21 (6·4)
Guns: 8—3 in (76 mm) 50 cal (Mk 33) (twin)
Main engines: Steam turbines (De Laval); 24 000 shp; 2 shafts
Boilers: 2 (Babcock & Wilcox)
Speed, knots: 20
Complement: 387 (18 officers, 369 enlisted men)
Flag accommodations: 59 (12 officers, 47 enlisted men)

La Salle is a former amphibious transport dock (LPD) of the "Raleigh" class. Authorised in the Fiscal Year 1961 new construction programme. La Salle served as an amphibious ship from completion until 1972; the ship retains an amphibious assault capability.
La Salle serves as flagship for the US commander Middle East Force, operating in the Persian Gulf, Arabian Sea, and Indian Ocean; the ship is based at Bahrain. She replaced Valcour (AGF 1) in 1972.

Conversion: Converted in 1972 at Philadelphia Navy Yard. Elaborate command and communications facilities installed; accommodations provided for admiral and staff; additional air-conditioning fitted; painted white to help retard heat of Persian Gulf area. Reclassified as a flagship and designated AGF 3 on 1 July 1972 (the designation AGF 2 not used because of ship's previous "3" hull number).

Fire control: One Mk 56 and one Mk 70 gunfire control system.

Gunnery: To be fitted with 20 mm Mk 15 CIWS.
Two 40 mm saluting guns.

Radar: Search; SPS 10 and 40.

Rockets: One Mk 36 Chaffroc (RBOC) to be fitted.

LA SALLE 8/1975, USN

1 FRIGATE RESEARCH SHIP (AGFF) "GLOVER" CLASS

Name	No.	Builders	Laid down	Launched	Commissioned	F/S
GLOVER	AGFF 1 (ex-AGDE 1, ex-AG 163)	Bath Iron Works	29 July 1963	17 April 1965	13 Nov 1965	AA

Displacement, tons: 2 643 standard; 3 426 full load
Length, feet (metres): 414·5 (126·3) oa
Beam, feet (metres): 44·2 (13·5)
Draught, feet (metres): 24 (7·3)
Gun: 1—5 in (127 mm) 38 calibre (Mk 30)
A/S weapons: 1 ASROC 8-tube launcher; 2 triple torpedo tubes (Mk 32); facilities for small helicopter
Main engines: 1 geared turbine (Westinghouse); 35 000 shp; 1 shaft
Boilers: 2 (Foster-Wheeler)
Speed, knots: 27
Complement: 248 plus 38 civilian technicians

Glover was built to test an advanced hull design and propulsion system, and has a full combat capability.
The ship was originally authorised in the Fiscal Year 1960 new construction programme, but was postponed and re-introduced in the FY 1961 programme. Estimated construction cost was $29·33 million.

Classification: Glover was originally classified as a miscellaneous auxiliary (AG 163); completed as an escort research ship (AGDE 1). Subsequently changed to frigate research ship on 30 June 1975.

Design: Glover has a massive bow sonar dome integral with her hull and extending well forward underwater.
No reload capability for ASROC because of space requirements for equipment and technical personnel.

Electronics: The ship has a prototype tactical assignment console that integrates signals from the three sonars and radars to present combined and coordinated tactical situation presentations in the Combat Information Centre (CIC). Reportedly, this increases the combat effectiveness of the ship to a considerable extent.

Fire control: Mk 56 GFCS with SPG 35; one Mk 114 ASW FCS and one Mk 1 target designation system.

Radar: Search: SPS 10 and 40.

Sonar: Bow-mounted SQS 26 AXR active sonar, hull-mounted SQR 13 Passive/Active Detection and Location (PADLOC) sonar, and SQS 35 Independent Variable Depth Sonar (IVDS) lowered from the stern.

GLOVER

700 USA

1 HOSPITAL SHIP (AH) "HAVEN" CLASS

Name	No.	Builders	Commissioned	F/S
SANCTUARY (ex-*Marine Owl*)	AH 17	Sun SB & DD Co, Chester	20 June 1945	AR

Displacement, tons: 11 141 standard; 15 100 full load
Dimensions, feet (metres): 496 wl; 520 oa × 71·5 × 24 *(158·5 × 21·8 × 7·3)*
Main engines: Steam turbines (General Electric); 9 000 shp; 1 shaft = 18·33 knots
Boilers: 2 (Babcock & Wilcox)
Complement: 675 (87 officers, 588 enlisted)

Sanctuary is the survivor of six hospital ships (AH) of the "Haven" class. Built on C4-S-B2 merchant hull and launched on 15 Aug 1944. *Sanctuary* recommissioned from reserve in 1966 for service off Viet-Nam; decommissioned on 15 Dec 1971 for modification to "dependent support ship" at Hunter's Point Naval Shipyard, San Francisco, California. Subsequently recommissioned on 18 Nov 1972.
As a dependent support ship *Sanctuary* had special facilities for obstetrics, gynaecology, maternity, and nursery services; fitted as a 74-bed hospital which can be expanded to 300 beds in 72 hours. She was the first US Navy ship with mixed male-female crew (although previously female nurses have been assigned to hospital ships and transports). The medical personnel consisted of 50 officers and approx 120 enlisted including several female nurse officers; the ship's company consisted of 20 officers (including two women) and approx 330 enlisted (including 60 women). The ship was modified to support US dependents of ships homeported in Piraeus, Greece. However, she was not deployed to Greece, but was decommissioned on 28 March 1974 and laid up at Philadelphia.

SANCTUARY   1974, USN

0 + 3 + 15 OILERS (AO) "AO 177" CLASS

	No.		Commissioned	F/S
	AO 177	Approved FY 1976 programme	Early 1980	Bldg
	AO 178	Approved FY 1976 programme	Mid 1980	Bldg
	AO 179	Approved FY 1977 programme	Late 1980	Bldg
	AO 180	Proposed FY 1978 programme		
	AO 186	Proposed FY 1978 programme		
	AO 187	Planned FY 1980 programme		
	AO 188	Planned FY 1981 programme		
Two ships	AO 189-190	Planned FY 1981 programme		
Nine ships	AO 191-199	Planned Post FY 1983 programme		

Displacement, tons: 27 500 full load
Dimensions, feet (metres): 588·5 oa × 88 × 35 *(179·4 × 26·8 × 10·7)*
Guns: 2—20 mm Phalanx CIWS
Rockets: 1—Mk 36 Chaffroc
Main engine: 1 geared turbine; 24 000 shp; 1 shaft = 20 knots
Boilers: 2
Complement: 135

This class of fleet oilers is significantly smaller than the previous built-for-the-purpose AOs of the "Neosho" class; the newer ships are "sized" to provide two complete refuellings of a fossil-fuelled aircraft carrier and six to eight accompanying destroyers. The lead ship was requested in the Fiscal Year 1975 new construction programme but was not approved by Congress. Subsequently, two ships (AO 177 and AO 178) approved in the FY 1976.
A contract for the construction of AO 177 and 178 was awarded to Avondale Shipyards Inc. Westwego, La on 9 Aug 1976 and for AO 179 of the FY 1977 programme on 25 Jan 1977. Fifteen more of this class planned or proposed.
Each ship has a capacity of 120 000 barrels, will have two Phalanx 20 mm CIWS (forward and aft) and a helicopter platform aft.

Classification: The hull numbers AO 168-176 are assigned to the "Sealift" class tankers; AO 181 is USNS *Potomac*; AO 182-185 assigned to "Columbia" class. All listed under Military Sealift Command section.

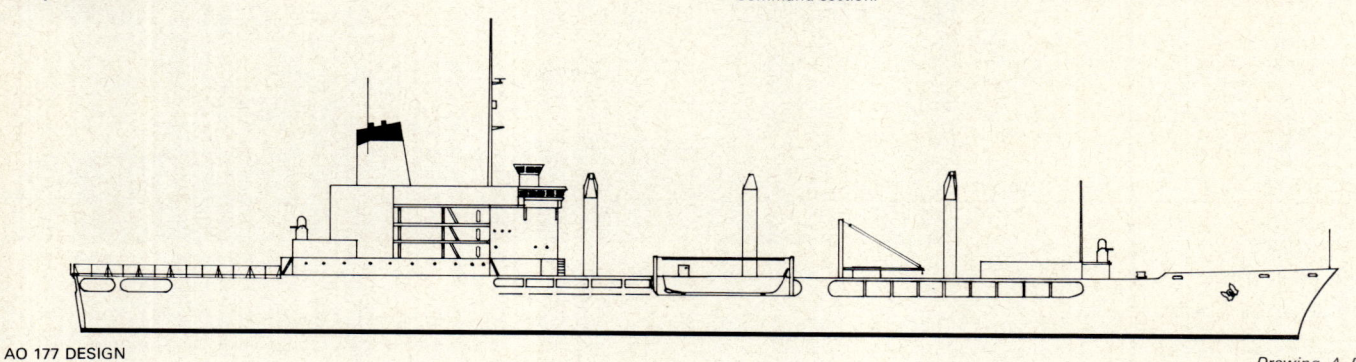

AO 177 DESIGN   Drawing, A. D. Baker III

6 OILERS (AO) "NEOSHO" CLASS

Name	No.	Launched	Commissioned	F/S
NEOSHO	AO 143	10 Nov 1953	24 Sept 1954	AA
MISSISSINEWA	T-AO 144	12 June 1954	18 Jan 1955	TAA
HASSAYAMPA	AO 145	12 Sept 1954	19 April 1955	PA
KAWISHIWI	AO 146	11 Dec 1954	6 July 1955	PA
TRUCKEE	AO 147	10 Mar 1955	23 Nov 1955	AA
PONCHATOULA	AO 148	9 July 1955	12 Jan 1956	PA

Displacement, tons: 11 600 light; 38 000 full load
Dimensions, feet (metres): 640 wl; 655 oa × 86 × 35 *(199·6 × 26·2 × 10·7)*
Guns: 8—3 in *(76 mm)* 50 cal (twin) (Mk 33) (4—3 in in AO 145; none in T-AO 144)
Main engines: Geared turbines (General Electric); 28 000 shp; 2 shafts = 20 knots
Boilers: 2 (Babcock & Wilcox)
Complement: 324 (21 officers and 303 enlisted men including staff) when navy manned

Neosho built by Bethlehem Steel Co, Quincy, Massachusetts; others by New York Shipbuilding Corp, Camden, New Jersey. These are the largest "straight" fleet oilers (AO) constructed specifically for the Navy. Cargo capacity is approximately 180 000 barrels of liquid fuels. Original armament was two 5 in guns and twelve 3 in guns; former removed in 1969. Two twin 3 in gun mounts removed from *Neosho*, *Mississinewa*, and *Truckee* and helicopter platform installed. Those ships also have additional superstructure installed forward of after superstruc-

TRUCKEE   8/1975, USN

ture. All fitted to carry a service force commander and staff (12 officers).
Mississinewa assigned to Military Sealift Command on 15 Nov 1976 (guns removed; civilian manned); others will follow into MSC operation.

Fire control: Armed ships except AO 145 have two Mk 56 GFCS.

3 OILERS (AO) "JUMBOISED CIMARRON" CLASS

Name	No.	Launched	Commissioned	F/S
ASHTABULA	AO 51	22 May 1943	7 Aug 1943	PA
CALOOSAHATCHEE	AO 98	2 June 1945	10 Oct 1945	AA
CANISTEO	AO 99	6 July 1945	3 Dec 1945	AA

Displacement, tons: 34 040 full load
Dimensions, feet (metres): 644 oa × 75 × 35 *(196·3 × 22·9 × 10·7)*
Guns: 4—3 in *(76 mm)* 50 cal (single) (Mk 26)
Main engines: Geared turbines (Bethlehem); 13 500 shp; 2 shafts = 18 knots
Boilers: 4 (Foster-Wheeler)
Complement: 317 (19 officers and 298 enlisted men)

ASHTABULA   10/1976, Dr. Giorgio Arra

All built by Bethlehem Steel Co, Sparrows Point, Maryland. Originally T3-S2-A1 oilers; converted mid-1960s under "jumbo" programme. Enlarged midsections added to increase cargo capacity to approximately 143 000 barrels plus 175 tons of munitions and 100 tons refrigerated stores. Provided with one Mk 52 gunfire control system. No helicopter platform fitted.
All three ships naval manned.

USA 701

4 FAST COMBAT SUPPORT SHIPS (AOE) "SACRAMENTO" CLASS

Name	No.	Laid down	Launched	Commissioned	F/S
SACRAMENTO	AOE 1	30 June 1961	14 Sept 1963	14 Mar 1964	PA
CAMDEN	AOE 2	17 Feb 1964	29 May 1965	1 April 1967	PA
SEATTLE	AOE 3	1 Oct 1965	2 Mar 1968	5 April 1969	AA
DETROIT	AOE 4	29 Nov 1966	21 June 1969	28 Mar 1970	AA

Displacement, tons: 19 200 light; 51 400-53 600 full load
Dimensions, feet (metres): 793 oa × 107 × 39·3 (241·7 × 32·6 × 12·0)
Aircraft: 2 UH-46 Sea Knight normally assigned
Missiles: One Mk 29 Nato Sea Sparrow System (AOE 1 and 4)
Guns: 8—3 in (76 mm) 50 cal (twin) (Mk 33) (6 twins in AOE 1 and 4)
Main engines: Geared turbines (General Electric); 100 000 shp; 2 shafts = 26 knots
Boilers: 4 (Combustion Engineering)
Complement: 600 (33 officers, 567 enlisted men) (AOE 1 and 2);
680 (33 officers, 647 enlisted men) (AOE 3 and 4)

These ships provide rapid replenishment at sea of petroleum, munitions, provisions, and fleet freight. Fitted with helicopter platform, internal arrangements, and large hangar for vertical replenishment operations (VERTREP). Cargo capacity 177 000 barrels plus 2 150 tons munitions, 500 tons dry stores, 250 tons refrigerated stores (varies with specific loadings). Built by Puget Sound Naval Shipyard except *Camden* by New York Shipbuilding Corp, Camden, New Jersey. *Sacramento* authorised in the Fiscal Year 1961 new construction programme; *Camden* in the FY 1963, *Seattle* in the FY 1965, and *Detroit* in the FY 1966. Construction of AOE 5 in the FY 1968 was deferred and then cancelled in Nov 1969. No additional ships of this type were planned because of high cost, the availability of new-construction ammunition ships, and the great success of the smaller "Wichita" class replenishment oilers; however, in 1976 the Department of Defense announced plans to construct another AOE in the Fiscal Year 1980 shipbuilding programme. Approximate cost of *Camden* was $70 million.

Appearance: These ships can be distinguished from the smaller "Wichita" class replenishment oilers by their larger superstructures and funnel, helicopter deck at higher level, and hangar structure aft of funnel.

SEATTLE 9/1976, Dr. Giorgio Arra

Engineering: *Sacramento* and *Camden* have machinery taken from the cancelled battleship *Kentucky* (BB 66).

Fire control: Two Mk 56 GFCS (AOE 3); one Mk 91 MFCS (AOE 1 and 4)

Gunnery: Two Phalanx 20 mm CIWS to be fitted.

Missiles: NATO Sea Sparrow system with Mark 91 director to be fitted in AOE 2 and 3.

Rockets: One Mk 36 Chaffroc (RBOC) to be fitted.

7 REPLENISHMENT OILERS (AOR) "WICHITA" CLASS

Name	No.	Laid down	Launched	Commissioned	F/S
WICHITA	AOR 1	18 June 1966	18 Mar 1968	7 June 1969	PA
MILWAUKEE	AOR 2	29 Nov 1966	17 Jan 1969	1 Nov 1969	AA
KANSAS CITY	AOR 3	20 April 1968	28 June 1969	6 June 1970	PA
SAVANNAH	AOR 4	22 Jan 1969	25 April 1970	5 Dec 1970	AA
WABASH	AOR 5	21 Jan 1970	6 Feb 1971	20 Nov 1971	PA
KALAMAZOO	AOR 6	28 Oct 1970	11 Nov 1972	11 Aug 1973	AA
ROANOKE	AOR 7	19 Jan 1974	7 Dec 1974	30 Oct 1976	PA

Displacement, tons: 37 360 full load
Dimensions, feet (metres): 659 oa × 96 × 33·3 (206·9 × 29·3 × 10·2)
Aircraft: 2 UH-46 Sea Knight can be embarked
Missils: 1 NATO Sea Sparrow system (Mk 29) in *Roanoke* and *Kansas City*
Guns: 4—3 in (76 mm) 50 cal (twin) (Mk33) (in AOR 1, 5-6); 4—20 mm Mk 67 single (AOR 2 and 7)
Main engines: Geared turbines (General Electric); 32 000 shp; 2 shafts = 20 knots (18 knots on 2 boilers)
Boilers: 3 (Foster-Wheeler)
Complement: 390 (27 officers, 363 enlisted men); 457 (30 and 427 in AOR 7)

These ships provide rapid replenishment at sea of petroleum and munitions with a limited capacity for provision and fleet freight. Fitted with helicopter platform and internal arrangement for vertical replenishment operations (VERTREP), but no hangar originally provided; some subsequently fitted with hangar. Cargo capacity 175 000 barrels of liquid fuels plus 600 tons munitions, 425 tons dry stores, 150 tons refrigerated stores.
All built by General Dynamics Corp, Quincy Massachusetts except AOR 7 by National Steel and Shipbuilding Co, San Diego, California. *Wichita* and *Milwaukee* authorised in the Fiscal Year 1965 new construction programme, *Kansas City* and *Savannah* in the FY 1966, *Wabash* and *Kalamazoo* in the FY 1967, and *Roanoke* in the FY 1972. Approximate cost of *Milwaukee* was $27·7 million.

Fire control: One Mk 91 MFCS (AOR 3 and 7); two Mk 56 GFCS (remainder)

Gunnery: Two 20 mm Mk 15 CIWS to be fitted; four 20 mm Mk 67 (single) to be fitted in AOR 1 and 3-6.

Rockets: One Mk 36 Chaffroc (RBOC) to be fitted.

ROANOKE 7/1976, National Steel and SB Co San Diego

WICHITA 6/1976, J. L. M. van der Burg

REPAIR SHIPS (AR) NEW CONSTRUCTION

Navy plans to build a new class of repair ships have been deferred indefinitely. The first unit of the class was to have been requested in the FY 1979 programme.

1 REPAIR SHIP (AR) CONVERTED "SHENANDOAH" CLASS

Name	No.	Builders	Commissioned	F/S
GRAND CANYON	AR 28 (ex-AD 28)	Todd Shipyards Corp, Los Angeles	5 April 1946	AA

Displacement, tons: 8 165 standard; 17 430 full load
Dimensions, feet (metres): 492 oa × 69·5 × 27·2 (150·0 × 21·2 × 8·3)
Guns: 4—20 mm Mk 67 (singles)
Main engines: Steam turbines (Allis-Chalmers); 12 000 shp; 1 shaft = 18·4 knots
Boilers: 2 (Babcock & Wilcox)
Complement: 1 271 (80 officers, 1 191 enlisted men)

Grand Canyon is a modified C-3 cargo ship completed as a destroyer tender and subsequently reclassified as a repair ship; AR 28 on 12 March 1971. Designed armament was 2—5 in guns and 8—40 mm guns.
Launched on 27 April 1945. Modernised; fitted with helicopter platform and hangar aft. Due for deletion 1 Sept 1978.

GRAND CANYON 1971, USN

702   USA

1 REPAIR SHIP (AR) "DELTA" CLASS

Name	No.	Builders	Commissioned	F/S
DELTA (ex-*Hawaiian Packer*)	AR 9 (ex-AK 29)	Newport News SB & DD Co, Virginia	15 June 1941	None

Displacement, tons: 8 975 standard; 13 009 full load
Dimensions, feet (metres): 465·5 wl; 490·5 oa × 69·5 × 24·3 (*149·5 × 21·2 × 7·4*)
Guns: 4—3 in (*76 mm*) 50 cal Mk 26 (single)
Main engines: Steam turbines (Newport News); 8 500 shp; 1 shaft = 16 knots
Boilers: 2 (Babcock & Wilcox)
Complement: 1 003 (46 officers, 957 enlisted men)

C-3 type. Launched in 1941. The 5 in and 4—40 mm guns originally fitted now removed. *Delta*, decommissioned on 20 June 1970. Stricken 1 Oct 1977 but retained indefinitely for use as station ship at Bremerton, Washington.

DELTA   1969, USN

4 REPAIR SHIPS (AR) "AJAX" CLASS

Name	No.	Builders	Commissioned	F/S
VULCAN	AR 5	New York SB Corp	16 June 1941	AA
AJAX	AR 6	Los Angeles SB & DD Corp	30 Oct 1942	PA
HECTOR	AR 7	Los Angeles SB & DD Corp	7 Feb 1944	PA
JASON	AR 8 (ex-ARH 1)	Los Angeles SB & DD Corp	19 June 1944	PA

Displacement, tons: 9 140 standard; 16 160-16 380 full load
Dimensions, feet (metres): 520 wl; 529·3 oa × 73·3 × 23·3 (*161·3 × 22·3 × 7·1*)
Guns: 4—20 mm (singles) (Mk 67)
Main engines: Steam turbines (Allis-Chalmers except AR 5—New York SB Corp); 11 000 shp; 2 shafts = 19·2 knots
Boilers: 4 (Babcock & Wilcox)
Complement: 1 336 (63 officers, 1 273 enlisted men)

Vulcan was built under the 1939 programme and the other three under the 1940 programme. Launched on 14 Dec 1940, 22 Aug 1942, 11 Nov 1942 and 3 April 1943 respectively. All carry a most elaborate equipment of machine tools to undertake repairs of every description. *Jason*, originally designated ARH 1 and rated as heavy hull repair ship, was reclassified AR 8 on 9 Sept 1957. Eight 40 mm guns (twin) have been removed; the four 5 in guns previously fitted were the standard main battery of large fleet support ships and oilers during World War II.

VULCAN   9/1975, Dr. Giorgio Arra

2 LANDING CRAFT REPAIR SHIPS (ARL) "ACHELOUS" CLASS

Name	No.	Builders	Commissioned
SPHINX	ARL 24 (ex-*LST 963*)	Bethlehem Steel Co, Higham, Mass	12 Dec 1944
INDRA	ARL 37 (ex-*LST 1147*)	Chicago Bridge & Iron Co, Seneca, Illinois	28 May 1945

Displacement, tons: 1 625 light; 4 325 full load
Dimensions, feet (metres): 316 wl; 328 oa × 50 × 11 (*100·0 × 15·2 × 3·4*)
Guns: 8—40 mm (quad)
Main engines: Diesels (General Motors); 1 800 bhp; 2 shafts = 12 knots
Complement: 266 (18 officers, 248 enlisted men)

Tank landing ships converted during construction to landing craft repair ships (ARL). Launched 21 May 1945 and 18 Nov 1944 respectively. Fitted with machine shops, parts storage, lifting gear, etc and 60-ton capacity booms. The ARLs cater for small amphibious, minesweeping, and riverine craft. Tripod mast in 37. Both reactivated during Viet-Nam War.
Indra has been "in service, in reserve" as a station ship at Norfolk Va, since July 1975.

SPHINX   1968, USN

Fire control: Two Mark 51 directors.

Transfers: Former US Navy LSTs modified to fleet support ships (AGP-ARB-ARL-ARVE) are operated by the navies of Greece, Indonesia, South Korea, Malaysia, Philippines, Taiwan, Turkey and Venezuela.

12 SALVAGE SHIPS (ARS) "DIVER" and "BOLSTER" CLASSES

Note: Plans for new Salvage Ships indefinitely postponed.

Name	No.	Builders	Commissioned	F/S
ESCAPE	ARS 6	Basalt Rock Co, Napa, Calif	20 Nov 1943	AA
PRESERVER	ARS 8	Basalt Rock Co, Napa, Calif	11 Jan 1944	AA
DELIVER	ARS 23	Basalt Rock Co, Napa, Calif	18 July 1944	PA
SAFEGUARD	ARS 25	Basalt Rock Co, Napa, Calif	31 Oct 1944	PA
CLAMP	ARS 33	Basalt Rock Co, Napa, Calif	23 Aug 1943	MPR
GEAR	ARS 34	Basalt Rock Co, Napa, Calif	24 Sept 1943	Loan
BOLSTER	ARS 38	Basalt Rock Co, Napa, Calif	1 May 1945	PA
CONSERVER	ARS 39	Basalt Rock Co, Napa, Calif	9 June 1945	PA
HOIST	ARS 40	Basalt Rock Co, Napa, Calif	21 July 1945	AA
OPPORTUNE	ARS 41	Basalt Rock Co, Napa, Calif	5 Oct 1945	AA
RECLAIMER	ARS 42	Basalt Rock Co, Napa, Calif	20 Dec 1945	PA
RECOVERY	ARS 43	Basalt Rock Co, Napa, Calif	15 May 1946	AA

Displacement, tons: 1 530 standard; 1 970 full load (ARS 38-43 2 040)
Dimensions, feet (metres): 207 wl; 213·5 oa × 41 except later ships 44 × 13 (*65·1 × 12·5 or 13·4 × 4·0*)
Guns: 1—40 mm (ARS 39, 41 and 42); 2—20 mm (remainder)
Main engines: Diesel-electric (Cooper Bessemer); (Caterpillar in ARS 23, 25, 38, 39, 42); 2 440 shp; 2 shafts = 14·8 knots
Complement: 96-157

These ships are fitted for salvage and towing; equipped with compressed air diving equipment. Launched on 22 Nov 1942, 1 April 1943, 25 Sept 1943, 20 Nov 1943, 24 Oct 1942, 24 Oct 1942, 23 Dec 1944, 27 Jan 1945, 31 March 1945, 31 March 1945, 25 June 1945 and 4 Aug 1945 respectively. Early ships have 8-ton and 10-ton capacity booms; later ships have 10-ton and 20-ton booms. ARS 38 and later ships are of a slightly different design, known as the "Bolster" class.
Gear is operated by a commercial firm in support of Navy activities; *Curb* ARS 21 on loan to private salvage firm, supports naval requirements as needed. *Clamp* was stricken from the Navy List in 1963 but reacquired in 1973 and is still laid up in Maritime Administration Reserve Fleet.

RECLAIMER   12/1976, Dr. Giorgio Arra

Conversions: *Chain* ARS 20 and *Snatch* ARS 27 converted to oceanographic research ships, designated AGOR 17 and AGOR 18, respectively. Both since deleted.

Disposals: *Grapple* and *Grasp* deleted 1977.

USA 703

2 + 3 SUBMARINE TENDERS (AS)
"EMORY S. LAND" and "L. Y. SPEAR" CLASSES

Name	No.	Builders	Commissioned	F/S
L. Y. SPEAR	AS 36	General Dynamics Corp, Quincy	28 Feb 1970	AA
DIXON	AS 37	General Dynamics Corp, Quincy	7 Aug 1971	PA
EMORY S. LAND	AS 39	Lockheed SB & Cons Co, Seattle	1979	Bldg
FRANK CABLE	AS 40	Lockheed SB & Cons Co, Seattle	1979	Bldg
McKEE	AS 41	Lockheed SB & Cons Co, Seattle	1981	Bldg

Displacement, tons: 13 000 standard; 22 640 full load (AS 36 and AS 37); 24 000 (AS 39-41)
Dimensions, feet (metres): 643·8 oa × 85 × 28·5 (196·2 × 25·9 × 8·7)
Guns: 4—20 mm Mk 67 (single) (AS 37); 2—40 mm Mk 64 (single) (AS 39-41)
Main engines: Steam turbines (General Electric); 20 000 shp; 1 shaft = 20 knots
Boilers: 2 (Foster-Wheeler)
Complement: 1 348 (96 officers, 1 252 enlisted men) (AS 36 and 37); 1 158 (50 officers, 1 108 enlisted men) (AS 39-41)
Flag accommodations: 69 (25 officers, 44 enlisted men)

These ships are the first US submarine tenders designed specifically for servicing nuclear-propelled attack submarines with later ships built to a modified design to support SSN 688 class submarines. Basic hull design similar to "Samuel Gompers" class destroyer tenders. Provided with helicopter deck but no hangar. Each ship can simultaneously provide services to four submarines moored alongside. AS 39 and later ships ("Emory S. Land" class) are especially configured to support SSN 688 class submarines.
L. Y. Spear authorised in the Fiscal Year 1965 shipbuilding programme, laid down 5 May 1966 and launched 7 Sept 1967; Dixon authorised in the FY 1966, laid down 7 Sept 1967 and launched 20 June 1970; AS 38 of the FY 1969 not built to provide funds for cost increases in other ship programmes. Cancelled 27 March 1969. Emory S. Land authorised in the FY 1972, and Frank Cable in the FY 1973 both laid down on 2 March 1976 and launched in 1977. No additional submarine tenders planned through the FY 1983.
Estimated cost of AS 41 is $260·9 million.

L. Y. SPEAR 9/1976, Dr. Giorgio Arra

2 SUBMARINE TENDERS (AS) "SIMON LAKE" CLASS

Name	No.	Builders	Commissioned	F/S
SIMON LAKE	AS 33	Puget Sound Naval Shipyard	7 Nov 1964	AA
CANOPUS	AS 34	Ingalls SB Co, Pascagoula	4 Nov 1965	AA

Displacement, tons: 19 934 full load (AS 33); 21 089 (AS 34)
Dimensions, feet (metres): 643·7 × 85 × 30 (196·2 × 25·9 × 9·1)
Guns: 4—3 in (76 mm) 50 cal (twin) (Mk 33)
Main engines: Steam turbines (De Laval); 20 000 shp; 1 shaft = 20 knots
Boilers: 2 (Combustion Engineering)
Complement: 1 428 (90 officers, 1 338 men) (AS 33); 1 421 (95 officers, 1 326 enlisted men) (AS 34)

These ships are designed specifically to service fleet ballistic missile submarines (SSBN), with three submarines alongside being supported simultaneously.
Simon Lake was authorised in the Fiscal Year 1963 new construction programe, laid down on 7 Jan 1963 and launched 8 Feb 1964. Canopus was authorised in the FY 1964, laid down on 2 March 1964 and launched on 12 Feb 1965. AS 35 was authorised in the FY 1965 programme, but her construction was cancelled 3 Dec 1964.

Conversions: Conversions to permit of Poseidon C-3 missile handling and repairing and support of related systems carried out at Puget Sound Navy yard as follows: Canopus, completed 3 Feb 1970; Simon Lake, completed 9 March 1971.

Fire control: Two Mk 63 GFCS with two SPG 50 radars.

CANOPUS 1966, USN

2 SUBMARINE TENDERS (AS) "HUNLEY" CLASS

Name	No.	Builders	Commissioned	F/S
HUNLEY	AS 31	Newport News SB & DD Co	16 June 1962	PA
HOLLAND	AS 32	Ingalls SB Co, Pascagoula	7 Sept 1963	AA

Displacement, tons: 10 500 standard; 19 000 full load
Dimensions, feet (metres): 599 × 83 × 27 (182·6 × 25·3 × 8·2)
Guns: 4—20 mm (singles)
Main engines: Diesel-electric (6 Fairbanks-Morse diesels); 15 000 bhp; 1 shaft = 19 knots
Complement: 2 568 (144 officers, 2 424 enlisted men)

These are the first US submarine tenders of post-World War II construction; they are designed specifically to provide repair and supply services to fleet ballistic missile submarines (SSBN). Have 52 separate workshops to provide complete support. Helicopter platform fitted aft but no hangar. Both ships originally fitted with a 32-ton-capacity hammerhead crane; subsequently refitted with two amidships cranes as in "Simon Lake" class.
Hunley authorised in the Fiscal Year 1960 shipbuilding programme, laid down on 28 Nov 1960 and launched on 28 Sept 1961; Holland authorised in the FY 1962 programme, laid down on 5 March 1962 and launched on 19 Jan 1963. Former ship cost $24 359 800.

Conversions: Conversions to provide for Poseidon C-3 missile handling and repairing and support of related systems carried out at Puget Sound Navy Yard as follows: Hunley, completed 22 Jan 1974; Holland, completed 20 June 1975.

HOLLAND USN

704 USA

7 SUBMARINE TENDERS (AS)
"FULTON" and "PROTEUS" CLASSES

Name	No.	Builders	Commissioned	F/S
FULTON	AS 11	Mare Island Navy Yard	12 Sept 1941	AA
SPERRY	AS 12	Moore SB & DD Co, Oakland	1 May 1942	PA
BUSHNELL	AS 15	Mare Island Navy Yard	10 April 1943	AR
HOWARD W. GILMORE (ex-Neptune)	AS 16	Mare Island Navy Yard	24 May 1944	AA
NEREUS	AS 17	Mare Island Navy Yard	27 Oct 1945	PR
ORION	AS 18	Moore SB & DD Co, Oakland	30 Sept 1943	AA
PROTEUS	AS 19	Moore SB & DD Co, Oakland	31 Jan 1944	PA

Displacement, tons: 9 734 standard; 16 230-17 020 full load (19 200, AS 19)
Dimensions, feet (metres): 530·5 oa except *Proteus* 574·5 oa × 73·3 × 25·5 *(161·7 Proteus 175·1 × 22·3 × 7·8)*
Guns: 2—5 in *(127 mm)* 38 cal in AS 15 and 17; 4—20 mm (Mk 67) (single) in active ships; 2—20 mm (Mk 24) (twin) in AS 17 only
Main engines: Diesel-electric (General Motors) (Allis Chalmers in AS 19); 11 200 bhp; 2 shafts = 15·4 knots
Complement: 1 286-1 937 except *Proteus* 1 300 (86 officers, 1 214 enlisted men)

These venerable ships are contemporaries of the similar-design "Dixie" class destroyer tenders. Launched on 27 Dec 1940, 17 Dec 1941, 14 Sept 1942, 16 Sept 1943, 12 Feb 1945, 14 Oct 1942 and 12 Nov 1942 respectively. As built, they carried the then-standard large auxiliary armament of four 5 in guns plus 8—40 mm guns (twin). The original 20-ton capacity cylinder cranes have been replaced in *Howard W. Gilmore*.

Conversion: *Proteus* AS 19 was converted at the Charleston Naval Shipyard, under the Fiscal Year 1959 conversion programme, at a cost of $23 million to service nuclear-powered fleet ballistic missile submarines (SSBN). Conversion was begun on 19 Jan 1959 and she was recommissioned on 8 July 1960. She was lengthened by adding a 44 feet section amidships, and the bare hull weight of this six-deck high insertion was approximately 500 tons. Three 5 in guns were removed and her upper decks extended aft to provide additional workshops. Storage tubes for Polaris missiles installed; bridge crane amidships loads and unloads missiles for alongside submarines.

Modernisation: All except *Proteus* have undergone FRAM II modernisation to service nuclear-powered attack submarines. Additional maintenance shops provided to service nuclear plant components and advanced electronic equipment and weapons. After two 5 in guns and eight 40 mm guns (twin) removed.

HOWARD W. GILMORE 6/1976, Dr. Giorgio Arra

SPERRY 3/1973, USN

2 SUBMARINE RESCUE SHIPS (ASR) "PIGEON" CLASS

Name	No.	Builders	Commissioned	F/S
PIGEON	ASR 21	Alabama DD & SB Co, Mobile	28 April 1973	PA
ORTOLAN	ASR 22	Alabama DD & SB Co, Mobile	14 July 1973	AA

Displacement, tons: 3 411 full load
Dimensions, feet (metres): 251 oa × 86 (see *Design* notes) × 21·25 *(76·5 × 26·2 × 6·5)*
Guns: 2—20 mm (single)
Main engines: 4 diesels (Alco); 6 000 bhp; 2 shafts = 15 knots
Range, miles: 8 500 at 13 knots
Complement: 115 (6 officers, 109 enlisted men)
Staff accommodation: 14 (4 officers, 10 enlisted men)
Submersible operators: 24 (4 officers, 20 enlisted men)

These are the world's first ships designed specifically for this role, all other ASR designs being adaptations of tug types. The "Pigeon" class ships serve as (1) surface support ships for the Deep Submergence Rescue Vehicles (DSRV), (2) rescue ships employing the existing McCann rescue chamber, (3) major deep-sea diving support ships and (4) operational control ships for salvage operations. Each ASR is capable of transporting, servicing, lowering, and raising two Deep Submergence Rescue Vehicles (DSRV) (see section on Deep Submergence Vehicles). The Navy had planned in the 1960s to replace the 10-ship ASR force with new construction ASRs. However, only two ships were funded, with procurement of others deferred.
Pigeon authorised in the Fiscal Year 1967 new construction programme and *Ortolan* in the FY 1968 programme. *Pigeon* was laid down on 17 July 1968 and launched on 13 Aug 1969; *Ortolan* was laid down on 22 Aug 1968 and launched on 10 Sept 1969; they were delayed more than two years by a shipyard strike and technical difficulties; additional delays encountered in special equipment installation.

Design: These ships have twin, catamaran hulls, the first ocean-going catamaran ships to be built for the US Navy since Robert Fulton's steam gunboat *Demologus* of 1812. The design provides a large deck working area, facilities for raising and lowering submersibles and underwater equipment, and improved stability when operating equipment at great depths. Each of the twin hulls is 251 feet long and 26 feet wide. The well between the hulls is 34 feet across, giving the ASR a maximum beam of 86 feet. Fitted with helicopter platform and with precision three-dimensional sonar system for tracking submersibles.

Diving: These ships have been fitted with the Mk II Deep Diving System to support conventional or saturation divers operating at depths to 850 feet. The system consists of two decompression chambers, two personnel transfer capsules to transport divers between the ship and ocean floor, and the associated controls, winches, cables, gas supplies etc. Submarine rescue ships are the US Navy's primary diving ships and the only ones fitted for helium-oxygen diving.

Engineering: Space and weight are reserved for future installation of a ducted thruster in each bow to enable the ship to maintain precise position while stopped or at slow speeds.

ORTOLAN 9/1976, Dr. Giorgio Arra

ORTOLAN 9/1976, Dr. Giorgio Arra

USA 705

4 SUBMARINE RESCUE SHIPS (ASR) "CHANTICLEER" CLASS

Name	No.	Builders	Commissioned	F/S
FLORIKAN	ASR 9	Moore SB & DD Co, Oakland	5 April 1943	PA
KITTIWAKE	ASR 13	Savannah Machine & Foundry Co	18 July 1946	AA
PETREL	ASR 14	Savannah Machine & Foundry Co	24 Sept 1946	AA
SUNBIRD	ASR 15	Savannah Machine & Foundry Co	28 Jan 1947	AA

Displacement, tons: 1 653 standard; 2 320 full load
Dimensions, feet (metres): 240 wl; 251·5 oa × 44 × 16 (76·7 × 13·4 × 4·9)
Guns: 2—20 mm (single) (Mk 68)
Main engines: Diesel-electric (Alco ARS 9 and 15; General Motors remainder); 3 000 bhp; 1 shaft = 15 knots
Complement: 116-221

Large tug-type ships equipped with powerful pumps, heavy air compressors, and rescue chambers for submarine salvage and rescue operations. Launched on 29 May 1942, 14 June 1942, 10 July 1945, 29 Sept 1945, 3 April 1945 and 25 June 1945 respectively.
Fitted for Helium-oxygen diving.
As built, each ship was armed with 2—3 in guns; removed 1957-58. Some ships subsequently fitted with two 20 mm guns.

Transfers: Former US Navy submarine rescue ships serve in the navies of Brazil and Turkey—*Tringa* to Turkey late 1978.

SUNBIRD 9/1975, Dr. Giorgio Arra

5 AUXILIARY TUGS (ATA) "SOTOYOMO" CLASS

Name	No.	Builders	Commissioned	F/S
ACCOKEEK	ATA 181	Levingston SB Co, Orange, Texas	7 Oct 1944	MAR
SAMOSET	ATA 190	Levingston SB Co, Orange, Texas	1 Jan 1945	MAR
STALLION	ATA 193	Levingston SB Co, Orange, Texas	26 Feb 1945	MAR
TATNUCK	ATA 195	Levingston SB Co, Orange, Texas	1 Feb 1945	MAR
KEYWADIN	ATA 213	Gulfport Boiler & Welding Works, Port Arthur, Texas	1 June 1945	MAR

Displacement, tons: 534 standard; 860 full load
Dimensions, feet (metres): 134·5 wl; 143 oa × 33·9 × 13 (43·6 × 10·3 × 4·0)
Main engines: Diesel-electric (General Motors diesels); 1 500 bhp; 1 shaft = 13 knots
Complement: 49 (7 officers, 42 enlisted men)

Steel-hulled tugs formerly designated as rescue tugs (ATR); designation changed to ATA in 1944. Launched on 27 July 1944, 26 Oct 1944, 14 Dec 1944, 24 Nov 1944 and 9 April 1945 respectively. During 1948 they were assigned names that had been carried by discarded fleet and yard tugs.
All of the surviving ships were decommissioned in 1969-71 and placed in reserve. Two ships of this class serve in the Coast Guard.

Transfers: Ships of this class serve with Argentina, Colombia, Dominican Republic and Taiwan.

ACCOKEEK 1970, USN

19 FLEET TUGS (ATF) "CHEROKEE" and "ABNAKI" CLASSES

Note: For characteristics of "Powhatan" (ATF 166) Class see Military Sealift Command Section.

Name	No.	Builders	Commissioned	F/S
UTE	T-ATF 76	United Engineering Co, Alameda, Calif	31 Dec 1942	TPA
CREE	ATF 84	United Engineering Co, Alameda, Calif	28 Mar 1943	PA
LIPAN	T-ATF 85	United Engineering Co, Alameda, Calif	29 April 1943	TPA
SENECA	ATF 91	Cramp SB Co, Philadelphia	30 April 1943	MAR
ABNAKI	ATF 96	Charleston SB & DD Co, SC	15 Nov 1943	PA
COCOPA	ATF 101	Charleston SB & DD Co, SC	25 Mar 1944	PA
HITCHITI	ATF 103	Charleston SB & DD Co, SC	27 May 1944	PA
MOCTABI	ATF 105	Charleston SB & DD Co, SC	25 July 1944	NRF
MOLALA	ATF 106	United Engineering Co, Alameda, Calif	29 Sept 1943	PA
QUAPAW	ATF 110	United Engineering Co, Alameda, Calif	6 May 1944	NRF
TAKELMA	ATF 113	United Engineering Co, Alameda, Calif	3 Aug 1944	PA
TAWAKONI	ATF 114	United Engineering Co, Alameda, Calif	15 Sept 1944	PA
ATAKAPA	T-ATF 149	Charleston SB & DD Co, SC	8 Dec 1944	TAA
NIPMUC	ATF 157	Charleston SB & DD Co, SC	8 July 1945	AA
MOSOPELEA	T-ATF 158	Charleston SB & DD Co, SC	28 July 1945	TAA
PAIUTE	ATF 159	Charleston SB & DD Co, SC	27 Aug 1945	NRF
PAPAGO	ATF 160	Charleston SB & DD Co, SC	3 Oct 1945	NRF
SALINAN	ATF 161	Charleston SB & DD Co, SC	9 Nov 1945	AA
SHAKORI	ATF 162	Charleston SB & DD Co, SC	20 Dec 1945	AA

Displacement, tons: 1 235 standard; 1 640 full load
Dimensions, feet (metres): 195 wl; 205 oa × 38·5 × 17 (62·5 × 11·7 × 5·2)
Gun: 1—3 in (76 mm) 50 cal (Mk 22) gun removed from MSC ships and ATF 84, 103, 105, 114 and 159)
Main engines: Diesel-electric drive (GM or Alco); 3 000 bhp; 1 shaft = 15 knots
Complement: 75 (5 officers, 70 enlisted men) navy; 24 civilians plus 6 navy communications personnel in MSC ships.

PAIUTE 1976, Michael D. J. Lennon

Large ocean tugs fitted with powerful pumps and other salvage equipment. ATF 96 and later ships ("Abnaki" class) have smaller funnel. As built these ships mounted 2—40 mm guns in addition to 3 in gun. Launched on 24 June 1942, 17 Aug 1942, 17 Sept 1942, 22 April 1943, 20 Aug 1943, 5 Oct 1943, 29 Jan 1944, 25 March 1944, 23 Dec 1942, 15 May 1943, 18 Sept 1943, 28 Oct 1943, 11 July 1944, 12 April 1945, 7 March 1945, 4 June 1945, 21 June 1945, 20 July 1945 and 9 Aug 1945 respectively.
Beginning in 1973 several fleet tugs have been assigned to the Military Sealift Command and provided with civilian crews; these ships are designated T-ATF and are unarmed. ATF 85 and ATF 158 assigned to MSC in July 1973; ATF 76, and ATF 149 to MSC in July-Aug 1974.
Three ships of this class serve with the US Coast Guard.

Deletions: Following planned in the FY 1977/78: *Abnaki, Cocopa, Cree, Hitchiti, Molala, Nipmuc, Salinan* and *Tawakoni*.

Naval Reserve: Following transferred to Naval Reserve Force: *Moctabi*, 1 Jan 1977; *Paiute*, 1 Feb 1977; *Papago*, 1 Aug 1977; *Quapaw*, 30 Sept 1977.

Transfers: Ships of this class serve with Argentina, Chile, Dominican Republic, Peru, Turkey, Taiwan and Venezuela.

706 USA

3 SALVAGE AND RESCUE SHIPS (ATS) "EDENTON" CLASS

Name	No.	Builders	Commissioned
EDENTON	ATS 1	Brooke Marine, Lowestoft, England	23 Jan 1971
BEAUFORT	ATS 2	Brooke Marine, Lowestoft, England	22 Jan 1972
BRUNSWICK	ATS 3	Brooke Marine, Lowestoft, England	19 Dec 1972

Displacement, tons: 2 929 full load
Dimensions, feet (metres): 282·6 oa × 50 × 15·1 *(86·1 × 15·2 × 4·6)*
Guns: 2—20 mm Mk 68 (single) (ATS 2 and 3); 2—20 mm (twin) Mk 24 (ATS 1)
Main engines: 4 diesels (Paxman); 6 000 bhp; 2 shafts (cp propellers) = 16 knots
Complement: 100 (9 officers and 91 enlisted men)

These ships are designed specifically for salvage operations and are capable of (1) ocean towing, (2) supporting diver operations to depths of 850 feet, (3) lifting submerged objects weighing as much as 600 000 lb from a depth of 120 feet by static tidal lift or 30 000 lb by dynamic lift, (4) fighting ship fires, and (5) performing general salvage operations. Fitted with 10-ton capacity crane forward and 20-ton capacity crane aft.
ATS 1 was authorised in the Fiscal Year 1966 shipbuilding programme; ATS 2 and ATS 3 in the FY 1967 programme. Laid down on 1 April 1967, 19 Feb 1968 and 5 June 1968 respectively; launched on 15 May 1968, 20 Dec 1968 and 14 Oct 1969. In service the British-made components have created certain supply problems.
ATS 4 was authorised in the FY 1972 new construction programme and ATS 5 in the FY 1973 programme, with several additional ships being planned. However, construction of these ships was deferred in 1973 with the smaller modification of a commercial design ATF being substituted in their place.
Classification changed from salvage tug (ATS) to salvage and rescue ship (ATS) on 16 Feb 1971.

Diving: These ships can carry the air-transportable Mk 1 Deep Diving System which can support four divers working in two-man shifts at depths to 850 feet. The system consists of a double-chamber recompression chamber and a personnel transfer capsule to transport divers between the ship and ocean floor. The ships' organic diving capability is compressed air only.

Engineering: Fitted with tunnel bow thruster for precise manoeuvring.

BEAUFORT   8/1974, USN

1 GUIDED MISSILE SHIP (AVM) CONVERTED "CURRITUCK" CLASS

Name	No.	Builders	Commissioned
NORTON SOUND	AVM 1 (ex-AV 11)	Los Angeles SB & DD Co, San Pedro	8 Jan 1945

Displacement, tons: 9 106 standard; 15 170 full load
Dimensions, feet (metres): 540·6 oa × 71·6 × 23·5 *(164·8 × 21·8 × 7·2)*
Missile launchers: 1 twin Standard surface-to-air launcher (Mk 26)
Machinery: Geared turbines (Allis-Chalmers); 12 000 shp; 2 shafts = 19 knots
Boilers: 4 (Babcock & Wilcox)
Complement: 750 (86 officers, 664 enlisted men)

Norton Sound is a seagoing laboratory and test centre for advanced weapon systems. Constructed as a seaplane tender (AV 7); laid down 7 Sept 1942, launched 28 Nov 1943. After operating briefly in the Pacific War and afterward as a seaplane tender; in 1948 she was converted to a guided missile test ship.
Subsequently served as test ship for a number of research and weapon programmes, and is currently employed as a test platform for the Aegis advanced fleet defence system.

Classification: Changed from AV 11 to AVM 1 on 8 Aug 1951.

Conversion: *Norton Sound* was initially fitted as a guided missile (test) ship in 1948 during a seven-month conversion at the Philadelphia Naval Shipyard; 30-ton capacity boom removed from fantail (similar boom retained on hangar structure); helicopter deck provided forward; provision for fuelling, checking out, monitoring, and firing rockets and missiles.
Converted from Nov 1962 to June 1964 at Maryland SB & DD Co, Baltimore, Maryland, to test ship for the Typhon advanced weapons control system (intended for a new class of nuclear-powered guided missile cruisers); Typhon system removed in July 1966.
Modified in 1974 to serve as test ship for the Aegis advanced fleet defence system. SPY-1 paired radar arrays to provide 180° coverage (12 × 12 foot, six-sided "faces") installed atop forward superstructure; Mk 110 radar control system installed (including five UYK-7 computers to control phase steering of radars). Twin Standard surface-to-air missile launcher fitted on stern. SPS 52 radar also fitted.

Gunnery: Fitted in 1968 with light-weight 5 in 54 calibre gun and associated Mk 86 gunfire control system for operational test and evaluation.

Missiles: Missiles and rockets test fired from *Norton Sound* include the Aerobee, Loon (US version of the German V-1), Lark, Regulus, Terrier, Tartar, and Sea Sparrow. During Project Argus in 1958 from a position south of the Falkland Islands she launched three multi-stage missiles carrying low-yield nuclear warheads which were detonated approximately 300 miles above the earth. (The ship was also used to launch high-altitude balloons in Project Skyhook during 1949).

NORTON SOUND   11/1974, USN

NAVAL RESERVE FORCE TRAINING AUXILIARY SHIPS

Name/Hull Number	NRF Homeport	Date of Assignment
MOCTABI (ATF 105)	Everett, Wash	1 Jan 1977
QUAPAW (ATF 110)	Port Hueneme, Calif	30 Sept 1977
PAIUTE (ATF 159)	Mayport, Fla	1 Feb 1977
PAPAGO (ATF 160)	Little Creek, Va	1 Aug 1977

USA 707

EXPERIMENTAL SHIPS

1 EXPERIMENTAL SURFACE EFFECT SHIP (SES) AEROJET-GENERAL DESIGN

SES-100A

Weight, tons: 100 gross
Dimensions, feet (metres): 81·9 oa × 41·9 *(25·0 × 12·8)*
Main/lift engines: 4 gas turbines (Avco-Lycoming) 12 000 hp; three fans for lift and two water-jet propulsion systems = 80+ knots (designed)

Surface effect ship developed by Aerojet-General Corp, and built by Tacoma Boatbuilding Co, Tacoma, Washington, to test feasibility of large SES for naval missions. Christened in July 1971; underway in mid-1972 in competition with the Bell design described below. Aluminium construction with rigid sidewalls to hold cushion or bubble of air. Cargo capacity ten tons (instrumentation during evaluation); provision for crew of four and six observers. Fitted with four TF-35 gas turbine engines, marine version of the T55-L-11A developed for the CH-47C helicopter. The SES-100A is reported to have reached 76 knots on trials.

SES-100A   *1972, Aerojet General*

1 EXPERIMENTAL SURFACE EFFECT SHIP (SES) BELL AEROSYSTEMS DESIGN

SES-100B

Weight, tons: 100 gross
Dimensions, feet (metres): 78 oa × 35 *(23·8 × 10·7)*
Main engines: 3 gas turbines (Pratt & Whitney); 13 500 hp; 2 semi submerged, super cavitating propellers = 80+ knots
Lift engines: 3 gas turbines (United Aircraft of Canada); 1 500 hp; eight lift fans

Surface effect ship developed by Bell Aerospace Division of the Textron Corp; built at Bell facility in Michoud, Louisiana. Christened on 6 March 1971; underway in Feb 1972 as competitive development platform for Navy.
Aluminium hull with rigid sidewalls to hold cushion or bubble of air. Cargo capacity ten tons (instrumentation during evaluation); provision for crew of four and six observers.
Fitted with three Pratt & Whitney FT-12 gas turbine engines and three United Aircraft of Canada ST-6J-70 gas turbine engines.
The SES-100B is credited with having set an SES speed record of 82·3 knots during trials in 1975.

SES-100B   *1974, Bell Aerosystems*

SPECIAL VESSELS

ADVANCED NAVAL VEHICLES
(Not included in US Naval Vessels Register)

The US Navy has applied the term Advanced Naval Vehicles (ANV) to a number of platforms being considered for future construction programmes. These include airships, Small Waterplane Area Twin Hull (SWATH) ships, hydrofoils, Surface Effect Ships (SES), Air Cushion Vehicles (ACV), and Wing-In-Ground (WIG) effect machines, among others.
Some of these concepts are relatively old, such as the airship (which the US Navy discarded in 1962) and hydrofoils; the latter now being in production for the US Navy after several years of experimentation. After successful tests of two 100-ton SES designs the US Navy had planned to construct prototypes of a 2 000-ton ocean-going SES combatant. Preliminary characteristics of such an Advanced Naval Vehicle are provided below and the artist concept is shown on this page.
Navy plans for the 2 000-ton SES were slowed in 1975 by a Department of Defense decision that the Navy should undertake a comprehensive analysis of all advanced platform concepts, determine their potential roles, and relate estimated costs. Accordingly, in that year the Navy established the Advanced Naval Vehicles Concept Evaluation effort which was expected to complete the analysis in 1977.
The Navy's overall SES programme continues to be the largest ANV effort in terms of current funding, with $48 000 000 million requested for the Fiscal Year 1977. Still, this is a paltry sum when compared to research and development efforts in a number of other areas.

2 000-ton SURFACE EFFECT SHIP (SES)

Weight, tons: 2 000 gross
Length, feet (metres): approx 240 *(73·2)*
Beam, feet (metres): approx 100 *(30·5)*
Helicopters: 2 large (SH-3 Sea King type)
Missile launchers: Harpoon surface-to-surface launchers; Sea Sparrow surface-to-air launchers
Main/lift engines: gas turbines
Speed, knots: 80-100

The above characteristics are those of a 2 000-ton national combat-capable surface effect ship. Contracts were awarded to the Bell Aerospace Division of Textron and to Rohr Industries to undertake the development and design of such a ship. Although the nominal weight of 2 000 tons is in general use, it has become obvious that the SES will in reality be close to 3 000 tons.
After evaluation of the designs submitted by Rohr and Bell a contract for design with option to construct was awarded to Rohr Marine Inc, San Diego.
Money to build a prototype was to be requested under the FY 1979 budget, cost was to be about $90 million. However, the Carter Administration deleted all building funds from the FY 1979 request in Dec 1977. Research work is to continue.
In A/S operations the large SES would employ the sprint-and-drift technique, whereby it would travel at high speeds—between 60 and 100 knots—to an area, slow to use its sensors to search the area, and then speed on to another area.

Classification: During the early 1970s the Navy used the classification DSX for planning purposes to indicate a large SES employed in destroyer/frigate roles.

Design: The SES concept differs from the Air Cushion Vehicle (ACV) by having rigid "sidewalls" that pentrate into the water to provide stability for high-speed operation. Flexible "skirts" forward and aft trap the air bubble under the hull.

2 000-ton Advanced Naval Vehicle /Surface Effect Ship design   *Bell Aerospace*

708 USA

SERVICE CRAFT

As of 1 Jan 1978, the US Navy has 1 093 service craft, primarily small craft, on the US Naval Vessel Register. A majority of them provide services to the fleet in various harbors and ports. Others are ocean going ships such as *Elk River* that provide services to the fleet in the research area. Only the self propelled craft and relics are listed here. The non-self propelled craft, such as floating cranes, dredges are not included. Most of the service craft are rated as "Active, in Service", but a few are rated as "in commission".

FLOATING DRY DOCKS

The US Navy operates a number of floating dry docks to supplement dry dock facilities at major naval activities, to support fleet ballistic missile submarines (SSBN) at advanced bases, and to provide repair capabilities in forward combat areas.

The larger floating dry docks are made sectional to facilitate movement overseas and to render them self docking. The ARD-type docks have the forward end of their docking well closed by a structure resembling the bow of a ship to facilitate towing. Berthing facilities, repair shops, and machinery are housed in sides of larger docks. None is self-propelled.

Eighteen floating dry docks are in Navy service (including one partial dock), seven are out of service in reserve (including two partial docks), and 32 are on lease to commercial firms for private use. Several are on loan to other US services and foreign navies (including one partial dock). Asterisks indicate docks in active US service.

ARDM 4 is under construction at the Bethlehem Steel Co, Sparrows Point, Maryland. Designed specifically to service "Los Angeles" class (SSN 688) submarines and to be based at New London, Conn.

Figures in parenthesis indicate the number of sections for sectional docks. Each section of the AFDB docks has a lifting capacity of about 10 000 tons. Four sections of the AFDB 7 form the floating dry dock *Los Alamos* at Holy Loch, Scotland and two sections are in reserve. (The AFDB sections each are 256 feet long, 80 feet in width, with wing walls 83 feet high; the wing walls, which contain compartments, fold down when the sections are towed).

White Sands (ARD 20) was reclassified as auxiliary deep submergence support vehicle (AGDS 1) on 1 Aug 1973; subsequently stricken. ARD 5 named *Waterford* 16 Nov 1976 and ARD 7 *West Milton* on 18 May 1976.

Transfers: The following floating dry docks are in foreign service: ARD 23 to Argentina; AFDL 39, ARD 14 to Brazil; ARD 32 to Chile; ARD 28 to Columbia; ARD 13 to Ecuador; AFDL 11 to Kampuchea (Cambodia); ARD 15, AFDL 28 to Mexico; ARD 6 to Pakistan; AFDL 26 to Paraguay; AFDL 33, ARD 8 to Peru; AFDL 20, AFDL 44 to Philippines; ARD 9, *Windsor* (ARD 22) to Taiwan; ARD 13 to Venezuela; AFDL 22 to South Viet-Nam; ARD 12 to Turkey; *Arco* (ARD 29) to Iran; ARD 25 to Chile; AFDL 24 to Philippines; ARD 11 to Mexico.

LARGE AUXILIARY FLOATING DRY DOCKS (AFDB)

AFDB 1	1943	90 000 tons	Steel (5)	Reserve (B/F only)
AFDB 2	1944	90 000 tons	Steel (10)	Reserve
AFDB 3	1944	81 000 tons	Steel (9)	Reserve
AFDB 4	1944	55 000 tons	Steel (7)	Reserve
AFDB 5	1944	55 000 tons	Steel (7)	Reserve
AFDB 7 (partial)	1944	20 000 tons	Steel (2)	Reserve (C and D)
LOS ALAMOS AFDB 7 (partial)	—	40 000 tons	Steel (4)	Holy Loch, Scotland (A, E, F and G only)

MEDIUM AUXILIARY FLOATING DRY DOCKS (AFDM)

AFDM 1 (ex-YFD 3)	1942	15 000 tons	Steel (3)	Commercial lease
AFDM 2 (ex-YFD 4)	1942	15 000 tons	Steel (3)	Commercial lease
AFDM 3 (ex-YFD 6)	1943	18 000 tons	Steel (3)	Commercial lease
AFDM 5 (ex-YFD 21)	1943	18 000 tons	Steel (3)	Reserve
AFDM 6 (ex-YFD 62)	1944	18 000 tons	Steel (3)	Subic Bay, Philippines
AFDM 7 (ex-YFD 63)	1945	18 000 tons	Steel (3)	Norfolk, Va
RICHLAND AFDM 8 (ex-YFD 64)	1944	18 000 tons	Steel (3)	Guam, Marianas
AFDM 9 (ex-YFD 65)	1945	18 000 tons	Steel (3)	Commercial lease
AFDM 10	1945	18 000 tons	Steel (3)	Commercial lease

AFDM 6 1/1977, Dr. Giorgio Arra

SMALL AUXILIARY FLOATING DRY DOCKS (AFDL)

Name-No.	Completed	Capacity	Construction	Notes
AFDL 1	1943	1 000 tons	Steel	Guantanamo Bay, Cuba
AFDL 2	1943	1 000 tons	Steel	Commercial lease
AFDL 6	1944	1 000 tons	Steel	Little Creek, Virginia
AFDL 7	1944	1 900 tons	Steel	Subic Bay, Philippines
AFDL 8	1943	1 000 tons	Steel	Commercial lease
AFDL 9	1943	1 000 tons	Steel	Commercial lease
AFDL 10	1943	1 000 tons	Steel	Reserve
AFDL 12	1943	1 000 tons	Steel	Commercial lease
AFDL 15	1943	1 000 tons	Steel	Commercial lease
AFDL 16	1943	1 000 tons	Steel	Commercial lease
AFDL 19	1944	1 000 tons	Steel	Commercial lease
AFDL 21	1944	1 000 tons	Steel	Commercial lease
AFDL 23	1944	1 900 tons	Steel	Subic Bay, Philippines
AFDL 25	1944	1 000 tons	Steel	Commercial lease
AFDL 29	1943	1 000 tons	Steel	Commercial lease
AFDL 30	1944	1 000 tons	Steel	Commercial lease
AFDL 35	1944	2 800 tons	Concrete	Commercial lease
AFDL 37	1944	2 800 tons	Concrete	Commercial lease
AFDL 38	1944	2 800 tons	Concrete	Commercial lease
AFDL 40	1944	2 800 tons	Concrete	Commercial lease
AFDL 41	1944	2 800 tons	Concrete	Commercial lease
AFDL 43	1944	2 800 tons	Concrete	Commercial lease
AFDL 45	1944	2 800 tons	Concrete	Commercial lease
AFDL 47	1946	6 500 tons	Steel	Commercial lease
AFDL 48	1956	4 000 tons	Concrete	Long Beach Naval Shipyard

AFDL 6 9/1976, Dr. Giorgio Arra

AUXILIARY REPAIR DRY DOCKS and MEDIUM AUXILIARY REPAIR DRY DOCKS

WATERFORD (ARD 5)	1942	3 000 tons	Steel	New London, Connecticut
WEST MILTON (ARD 7)	1943	3 000 tons	Steel	New London, Connecticut
ARDM 3 (ex-ARD 18)	1944	3 000 tons	Steel	Charleston, South Carolina
ARDM 4	1978		Steel	Under construction
OAK RIDGE ARDM 1 (ex-ARD 19)	1944	3 000 tons	Steel	Rota, Spain
ARD 24	1944	3 000 tons	Steel	San Francisco, Calif
ALAMAGORDO ARDM 2 (ex-ARD 26)	1944	3 000 tons	Steel	Charleston, South Carolina
SAN ONOFRE (ARD 30)	1944	3 000 tons	Steel	Pearl Harbor Naval Shipyard

SAN ONOFRE (ARD 30) 6/1970, USN

USA 709

YARD FLOATING DRY DOCKS

YFD 7	1943	18 000 tons	Steel (3)	Commercial lease
YFD 8	1942	20 000 tons	Wood	Commercial lease
YFD 9	1942	16 000 tons	Wood	Commercial lease
YFD 23	1943	10 500 tons	Wood	Commercial lease
YFD 54	1943	5 000 tons	Wood	Commercial lease
YFD 68	1945	14 000 tons	Steel (3)	Commercial lease
YFD 69	1945	14 000 tons	Steel (3)	Commercial lease
YFD 70	1945	14 000 tons	Steel (3)	Commercial lease
YFD 71	1945	14 000 tons	Steel (3)	San Diego Naval Base
YFD 83 (ex-AFDL 31)	1943	1 000 tons	Steel	US Coast Guard

3 UNCLASSIFIED MISCELLANEOUS (IX)
"BENEWAH" CLASS (ex-APB)

Name	No.	Builders	Commissioned	F/S
MERCER	IX 502 (ex-APB 39, ex-APL 39)	Boston Navy Yard	19 Sept 1945	PSA
NUECES	IX 503 (ex-APB 40, ex-APL 40)	Boston Navy Yard	30 Nov 1945	PSA
ECHOLS	IX 504 (ex-APB 37, ex-APL 37)	Boston Navy Yard	1 Jan 1947	ASA

Displacement, tons: 2 189 light; 4 080 full load
Dimensions, feet (metres): 136 wl; 328 oa × 50 × 11 *(100·0 × 15·2 × 3·4)*
Guns: Vary
Main engines: Diesels (General Motors); 1 600 to 1 800 bhp; 2 shafts = 10 knots
Complement: 193 (13 officers, 180 enlisted men) as APB
Troops: 1 226 (26 officers, 1 200 enlisted men) as APB

Originally built as self-propelled barracks ships (APB) built to provide support and accommodation for small craft and riverine forces. Launched on 30 July 1945, 17 Nov 1944, 6 May 1945, respectively. *Echols* placed in reserve Jan 1947. All ex-LST type ships of the same basic characteristics. *Mercer* and *Nueces* recommissioned in 1968 for service in Viet-Nam; decommissioned in 1969-71 as US riverine forces in South Viet-Nam were reduced.
Each APB has troop berthing and messing facilities, evaporators which produce up to 40 000 gallons of fresh water per day, a 16-bed hospital, X-ray room, dental room, bacteriological laboratory, pharmacy, laundry, library, and tailor shop; living and most working spaces are air-conditioned.
Mercer and *Nueces* again reactivated in 1974 to serve as barrack ships for ships in overhaul at Puget Sound Naval Shipyard, Bremerton, Washington. *Echols* (in reserve since 1947) reactivated in 1976 to provide berthing for crews of Trident missile submarines being built by General Dynamics Electric Boat Division in Groton, Connecticut. *Kingman* remains in reserve.

Classification: *Mercer* and *Nueces* reclassified as "unclassified miscellaneous" (IX) on 1 Nov 1975; *Echols* changed to IX on 1 Feb 1976.

MERCER (as APB 39)   1968, USN

1 UNCLASSIFIED MISCELLANEOUS (IX)
CONVERTED "ELK RIVER" CLASS (Ex-LSMR)

Name	No.	Builders	Commissioned	F/S
ELK RIVER	IX 501 (ex-LSMR 501)	Brown SB Co, Houston	27 May 1945	PSA

Displacement, tons: 1 785 full load
Dimensions, feet (metres): 229·7 oa × 50 × 9·2 *(70 × 15·2 × 2·8)*
Main engines: Diesels; 1 400 bhp; 2 shafts = 11 knots
Complement: 25 + 20 technical personnel

Elk River is a former rocket landing ship specifically converted to support Navy deep submergence activities on the San Clemente Island Range off the coast of southern California. Launched 21 April 1945.
The ship is capable of supporting (1) deep diving for man-in-the-sea programmes, (2) deep diving for salvage programmes, (3) submersible test and evaluation, (4) underwater equipment testing, and (5) deep mooring operations. Operated by combined Navy-civilian crew.

Conversion: She was withdrawn from the Reserve Fleet and converted to a range support ship in 1967-68 at Avondale Shipyards Inc, Westwego, Louisiana, and the San Francisco Bay Naval Shipyard.
The basic LSMR hull was lengthened and eight-foot sponsons were added to either side to increase deck working space and stability; superstructure added forward. An open centre well was provided to facilitate lowering and raising equipment; also fitted with 65-ton-capacity gantry crane (on tracks) to handle submersibles and active positioning mooring system to hold ship in precise location without elaborate mooring and permit shifting within the moor. Five anchors including bow anchor. Fitted with prototype Mk 2 Deep Diving System.

ELK RIVER   6/1976, J. L. M. van der Burg

1 UNCLASSIFIED MISCELLANEOUS (IX)
CONVERTED 'MARK" CLASS (Ex-AKL)

Name	No.	F/S
NEW BEDFORD	IX 308 (ex-AKL 17, ex-FS 289)	PSA

Displacement, tons: approx 700
Dimensions, feet (metres): 176·5 oa × 32·8 × 10 *(53·8 × 10·0 × 3·1)*
Main engines: Diesel; 1 000 bhp; 1 shaft = 10 knots

Former Army cargo ship (freight and supply) acquired by Navy on 1 March 1950 for cargo work and subsequently converted to support torpedo testing. Operated since 1963 by Naval Torpedo Station, Keyport, Washington. Employed as Torpedo Test ship.

NEW BEDFORD   1973, USN

710   USA

1 UNCLASSIFIED MISCELLANEOUS (IX)
Ex-US COAST GUARD BUOY TENDER (Ex-WLI)

Name	No.	F/S
BRIER	IX 307 (ex-WLI 299)	ASA

Displacement, tons: 178
Dimensions, feet (metres): 100 × 24 × 5 *(30·1 × 7·3 × 1·5)*
Machinery: Diesel with electric drive; 600 bhp; 2 shafts = 12 knots

Former Coast Guard buoy tender built in 1943; acquired by the Navy on 10 March 1969 for use as instrument platform for explosive testing; redesignated IX 307 on 29 Aug 1970.

BRIER (Old pennant number)   *USCG*

1 UNCLASSIFIED MISCELLANEOUS (IX)
CONVERTED ARMY SUPPLY SHIP

IX 306 (ex-FS 221)

Displacement, tons: 906 full load
Dimensions, feet (metres): 179 oa × 33 × 10 *(54·6 × 10·1 × 3·1)*
Main engine: Diesel; 1 shaft = 12 knots

Former Army cargo ship (freight and supply) acquired by the Navy in Jan 1969 and subsequently converted to a weapon test ship, being placed in service late in 1969. Conducts research for the Naval Underwater Weapons Research and Engineering Station, Newport, Rhode Island; operates in Atlantic Underwater Test and Evaluation Centre (AUTEC) range in Caribbean. Manned by Navy and civilian RCA personnel. Note white hull with blue bow and torpedo tube opening on starboard side just aft of hull number.

IX 306   *1969, USN*

1 UNCLASSIFIED MISCELLANEOUS (IX) BARGE GROUP

IX 310

A group of barges used by Naval Underwater Sound Laboratory, Newport, Rhode Island. Placed "in service" 1 April 1971. Consists of two barges joined by a deckhouse. Based on Lake Seneca, NY.

1 UNCLASSIFIED MISCELLANEOUS (IX) SAIL FRIGATE

Name	No.	Under Way	F/S
CONSTITUTION	None	23 July 1798	AA

The oldest ship remaining on the Navy List. *Constitution* is one of the six frigates authorised by act of Congress on 27 March 1794. Has been in full commission since Oct 1971, having been "in commission, special" prior to that date. Served as Flagship of the First Naval District until 1 Oct 1977 when she was transferred to the control of the Director of Naval History, Department of the Navy. Every year she is taken out into Boston Harbor and "turned around" so she will wear evenly on both sides of her masts. Overhauled at the former Boston Naval Shipyard from April 1973 to early 1975 at the cost of $4·2 million to "spruce her up" for the American Bicentennial. The "Unclassified Miscellaneous" classification of IX-21, assigned to her on 8 Jan 1941 was dropped on 1 Sept 1975 for some unfathomable reason. With her classification dropped, she is the only US Navy ship carried on the Naval Vessel Register without a classification. Since a ship in commission can not be on the Naval Register without a classification, her legal status as a naval ship is hazy.

The sailing ship *Constellation,* which survives under private ownership at Baltimore, Maryland, is apparently the last sailing man-of-war built for the US Navy; she was constructed at the Norfolk (Virginia) Navy Yard in 1853-1854, built in part with material from the earlier frigate *Constellation* (launched 1797).

1 MISCELLANEOUS AUXILIARY (YAG)
CONVERTED "YW 83" CLASS

Name		F/S
MONOB I	YAG 61 (ex-IX 309, ex-YW 87)	ASA

Displacement, tons: 440 light; 1 390 full load
Dimensions, feet (metres): 174 oa × 33 *(57 × 10·8)*
Main engine: 1 diesel = 7 knots

Monob I is a mobile listening barge converted from a self-propelled water barge. Built in 1943 and completed conversion for acoustic research in May 1969, being placed in service in May 1969. Conducts research for the Naval Mine Defence Laboratory, Panama City, Fla. Designation changed from IX 309 to YAG 61 on 1 July 1970.

MONOB I   *1969, USN*

2 DIVING TENDERS (YDT)

Tenders used to support shallow-water diving operations. Two self-propelled diving tenders are on the Navy List: *Phoebus* YDT 14 (ex-YF 294), and *Suitland* YDT 15 (ex-YF 336). (Two non-self-propelled YDTs are in service).

3 COVERED LIGHTERS (YF)

Lighters used to transport material in harbours; self-propelled; three are on the Navy List: *YF 862, YF 856* and *Keyport* (YF 885). Only *Keyport* is in service.

USA 711

6 FERRYBOATS (YFB)

Ferryboats used to transport personnel and vehicles in large harbours; self-propelled; YFB 83 and 87-91; all are active, in service. YFB 88-91 are the former LCU 1636, 1638-1640, all reclassified on 1 Sept 1969. *Aquidneck* (YFB 14) transferred to State of Washington on 23 Dec 1975.

YFB 88 (ex-LCU 1636)   USN

1 REFRIGERATED COVERED LIGHTER (YFR)

Used to store and transport food and other materials which require refrigeration. YFR 888 remains on the Navy List in reserve.

5 COVERED LIGHTERS (RANGE TENDER (YFRT))

Lighters used for miscellaneous purposes; YFRT 287, 451, 520, and 523 active; YFRT 418 is in reserve. Note Mk 32 torpedo tubes on YFRT 520.

YFRT 520   1969, USN

11 HARBOUR UTILITY CRAFT (YFU)

YFU 71	YFU 74	YFU 76	YFU 79	YFU 81
YFU 72	YFU 75	YFU 77	YFU 80	YFU 82
				YFU 83

Dimensions, feet (metres): 125 oa × 36 × 7·5 *(40·9 × 11·8 × 2·4)*
Main engines: Diesels = 8 knots
Guns: 2—0·50 cal MG

Militarised versions of a commercial lighter design and a single craft *(YFU 83)* built to LCU 1646 design and of similar characteristics. Used for off-loading large ships in harbours and ferrying cargo from one coastal port to another. Built by Pacific Coast Engineering Co, Alameda, California; completed 1967-68. Can carry more than 300 tons cargo; considerable cruising range.
YFU 71-77 and YFU 80-82 loaned to US Army in 1970 for use in South Viet-Nam; returned to Navy control in 1973. Only YFU 80 and 83 are active—rest in reserve.

Transfer: YFU 73 transferred to Khmer Republic (Cambodia) on 15 Nov 1973.

YFU 75   1968, USN

10 HARBOUR UTILITY CRAFT (YFU) LCU TYPE

YFU 44 (ex-LCU 1398)	YFU 91 (ex-LCU 1608)	YFU 100 (ex-LCU 1610)
YFU 50 (ex-LCU 1486)	YFU 93 (ex-LCU 1625)	YFU 101 (ex-LCU 1612)
YFU 55 (ex-LCU 637)	YFU 97 (ex-LCU 1611)	YFU 102 (ex-LCU 1462)
	YFU 98 (ex-LCU 1615)	

Former utility landing craft employed primarily as harbour and coastal cargo craft (see section on Landing Craft for basic characteristics). YFU 44 has an open centre well for lowering research equipment into the water; assigned to the Naval Undersea Research and Development Centre in Long Beach, California.
Several YFUs were loaned to the US Army in 1970 for use in Viet-Nam after withdrawal of US Navy riverine and coastal forces. YFU 44, 55, 91, 98, 100-102 active; rest in reserve.

21 FUEL OIL BARGES (YO)

Small liquid fuel carriers intended to fuel ships where no pierside fuelling facilities are available; self-propelled. One named unit, *Crownlock* (YO 48), is in reserve.

10 GASOLINE BARGES (YOG)

Similar to the fuel barges (YO), but carry gasoline and aviation fuels; self-propelled; ten are on the Navy List.

23 SEAMANSHIP TRAINING CRAFT (YP)

YP 591	YP 657	YP 661	YP 665	YP 669	YP 673
YP 654	YP 658	YP 662	YP 666	YP 670	YP 674
YP 655	YP 659	YP 663	YP 667	YP 671	YP 675
YP 656	YP 660	YP 664	YP 668	YP 672	

YP 591:

Displacement, tons: 50
Dimensions, feet (metres): 75 oa × 16 × 4·5 *(24·6 × 5·2 × 1·5)*
Main engines: 2 diesels (Superior); 400 bhp; 2 shafts = 12 knots

YP 654 series:

Displacement, tons: 69·5 full load
Dimensions, feet (metres): 80·4 oa × 18·75 × 5·3 *(26·4 × 6·1 × 1·7)*
Main engines: 4 diesels (General Motors); 660 bhp; 2 shafts = 13·5 knots

These craft are used for instruction in seamanship and navigation at the Naval Academy, Annapolis, Maryland; Naval Officer Candidate School, Newport, Rhode Island; and Surface Warfare Officers School at Newport. Fitted with surface search radar, Fathometer, gyro compass, and UHF and MF radio; YP 655 additionally fitted for instruction in oceanographic research at the Naval Academy.
YP 591 is an older craft of a once-numerous type employed for training and utility work. YP 654-663 built by Stephens Bros, Inc, Stockton, California; completed in 1958; YP 664 and 665 built by Elizabeth City Shipbuilders, Inc, Elizabeth City, North Carolina; YP 666 and 667 built by Stephens Bros; YP 668 built by Peterson Boatbuilding Co, Tacoma, Washington, completed in 1968; YP 669-672 built by Peterson completed in 1971-72.
These craft are of wooden construction with aluminium deck houses.

YP 669   1971, Peterson Builders

New Construction: YP 673-675 authorised in the FY 1977. Builders, Peterson Builders Inc, Sturgeon Bay, Wisconsin completing Jan-May 1979. New class—no details available.

712   USA

81 LARGE HARBOUR TUGS (YTB)

Name	Number	Name	Number
EDENSHAW	YTB 752	TAMAQUA	YTB 797
MARIN	YTB 753	OPELIKA	YTB 789
PONTIAC	YTB 756	NATCHITOCHES	YTB 799
OSHKOSH	YTB 757	EUFAULA	YTB 800
PADUCAH	YTB 758	PALATKA	YTB 801
BOGALUSA	YTB 759	CHERAW	YTB 802
NATICK	YTB 760	NANTICOKE	YTB 803
OTTUMWA	YTB 761	AHOSKIE	YTB 804
TUSCUMBIA	YTB 762	OCALA	YTB 805
MUSKEGON	YTB 763	TUSKEGEE	YTB 806
MISHAWAKA	YTB 764	MASSAPEQUA	YTB 807
OKMULGEE	YTB 765	WENATCHEE	YTB 808
WAPAKONETA	YTB 766	AGAWAN	YTB 809
APALACHICOLA	YTB 767	ANOKA	YTB 810
ARCATA	YTB 768	HOUMA	YTB 811
CHESANING	YTB 769	ACCONAC	YTB 812
DAHLONEGA	YTB 770	POUGHKEEPSIE	YTB 813
KEOKUK	YTB 771	WAXAHATCHIE	YTB 814
NASHUA	YTB 774	NEODESHA	YTB 815
WAUWATOSA	YTB 775	CAMPTI	YTB 816
WEEHAWKEN	YTB 776	HAYANNIS	YTB 817
NOGALES	YTB 777	MECOSTA	YTB 818
APOPKA	YTB 778	IUKA	YTB 819
MANHATTAN	YTB 779	WANAMASSA	YTB 820
SAUGUS	YTB 780	TONTOGANY	YTB 821
NIANTIC	YTB 781	PAWHUSKA	YTB 822
MANISTEE	YTB 782	CANONCHET	YTB 823
REDWING	YTB 783	SANTAQUIN	YTB 824
KALISPELL	YTB 784	WATHENA	YTB 825
WINNEMUCCA	YTB 785	WASHTUCNA	YTB 826
TONKAWA	YTB 786	CHETEK	YTB 827
KITTANNING	YTB 787	CATAHECASSA	YTB 828
WAPATO	YTB 788	METACOM	YTB 829
TOMAHAWK	YTB 789	PUSHMATHA	YTB 830
MENOMINEE	YTB 790	DEKANAWIDA	YTB 831
MARINETTE	YTB 791	PETALESHARO	YTB 832
ANTIGO	YTB 792	SHABONEE	YTB 833
PIQUA	YTB 793	NEWGAGON	YTB 834
MANDAN	YTB 794	SKENANDOA	YTB 835
KETCHIKAN	YTB 795	POKAGON	YTB 836
SACO	YTB 796		

WATHENA

Displacement, tons: 350 full load
Dimensions, feet (metres): 109 oa × 30 × 13·8 (35·7 × 9·8 × 4·5)
Machinery: 2 diesels; 2 000 bhp; 2 shafts
Complement: 10 to 12 (enlisted)

Large harbour tugs; 81 are in active service. YTB 752 completed in 1959, YTB 753 in 1960, YTB 756-762 in 1961, YTB 763-766 in 1963, YTB 770 and YTB 771 in 1964, YTB 767-769, 776 in 1965, YTB 774, 775, 777-789 in 1966, YTB 790-793 in 1967, YTB 794 and 795 in 1968, YTB 796-803 in 1969, and YTB 804-815 completed in 1970-72, YTB 816-827 completed 1972-73, YTB 828-836 completed 1974-75. YTB 837 and YTB 838 transferred upon completion in late 1975 to Saudi Arabia.

9 SMALL HARBOUR TUGS (YTL)

Unnamed. Six are active and three in reserve.

67 MEDIUM HARBOUR TUGS (YTM)

HOGA (YTM 146)	WINGINA (YTM 395)	NAHOKE (YTM 536)
TOKA (YTM 149)	YANEGUA (YTM 397)	CHEGODEGA (YTM 542)
KONOKA (YTM 151)	NATAHKI (YTM 398)	ETAWINA (YTM 543)
JUNALUSKA (YTM 176)	NUMA (YTM 399)	YATANOCAS (YTM 544)
DEKAURY (YTM 178)	OTOKOMI (YTM 400)	ACCOHANOC (YTM 545)
MADOKAWANDO (YTM 180)	PITAMAKAN (YTM 403)	TAKOS (YTM 546)
NEPANET (YTM 189)	COSHECTON (YTM 404)	YANABA (YTM 547)
SASSACUS (YTM 193)	CUSSETA (YTM 405)	MATUNAK (YTM 548)
DEKANISORA (YTM 252)	KITTATON (YTM 406)	MIGADAN (YTM 549)
HIAWATHA (YTM 265)	ANAMOSA (YTM 409)	ACOMA (YTM 701)
RED CLOUD (YTM 268)	POROBAGO (YTM 413)	ARAWAK (YTM 702)
PAWTUCKET (YTM 359)	SECOTA (YTM 415)	MORATOC (YTM 704)
SASSABA (YTM 364)	TACONNET (YTM 417)	MANKTAO (YTM 734)
WAUBANSEE (YTM 366)	— (YTM 496)	YUMA (YTM 748)
CHEPANOC (YTM 381)	MAHOA (YTM 519)	HACKENSACK (YTM 750)
COATOPA (YTM 382)	NABIGWON (YTM 521)	MASCOUTAH (YTM 760)
COCHALI (YTM 383)	SAGAWAMICK (YTM 522)	MENASHA (YTM 761)
WANNALANCET (YTM 385)	SENASQUA (YTM 523)	APOHOLA (YTM 768)
GANADOGA (YTM 390)	TUTAHACO (YTM 524)	MIMAC (YTM 770)
ITARA (YTM 391)	WAHAKA (YTM 526)	HIAMONEE (YTM 776)
MECOSTA (YTM 392)	WAHPETON (YTM 527)	LELAKA (YTM 777)
NAKARNA (YTM 393)	NADLI (YTM 534)	POCASSET (YTM 779)
WINAMAC (YTM 394)		

ETAWINA (YTM 543)   1975, Dr. Giorgio Arra

Former YTBs renumbered YTMs in the mid-1960s. Some are former Army Tugboats. About half are in reserve and half active. One unit, YTM-759 was reclassified IX-505 on 1 Nov 1976.

11 WATER BARGES (YW)

Barges modified to carry water to ships in harbour; self-propelled. Three active, eight in reserve.

TORPEDO WEAPONS RETRIEVERS (TWR)

Displacement, tons: 97·4 light; 152 full load
Dimensions, feet (metres): 102 oa × 21 × 7·75 (33·4 × 6·9 × 2·5)
Main engines: 4 diesels; 2 shafts = 18 knots
Range, miles: 1 900 at 10 knots
Complement: 15 (enlisted)

These are the largest of several types of torpedo recovery craft operated by the Navy. They are fitted to recover torpedoes and perform limited torpedo maintenance during exercises. An internal stern ramp facilitates recovery and up to 17 tons of torpedoes can be carried. These large TWRs also perform harbour utility duties. Range is 1 900 miles at 10 knots. Some are numbered—one is given the distinguished Royal Naval name of "Diamond". None carried on Naval Vessel Register.

TWR   9/1975, Dr. Giorgio Arra

USA 713

MILITARY SEALIFT COMMAND
(See also under Auxiliaries Section)

Sealift ships provide ocean transportation for all components of the Department of Defense. These ships are operated by the Navy's Military Sealift Command (MSC), renamed on 1 Aug 1970 from Military Sea Transportation Service (MSTS). Sealift cargo ships and tankers are not configured to provide underway replenishment (UNREP) of other ships, or land stores over the beach in amphibious landings. Four MSC-operated cargo ships are fitted to carry Submarine-Launched Ballistic Missiles (SLBM) and other supplies for US Polaris/Poseidon submarines. On 30 Dec 1977 there was a total of 69 ships active in the MSC nucleus fleet of which 64 were fully active and five in reduced operating status.

Most US defence cargo is carried in commercial merchant ships under charter to the government (through the Military Sealift Command).
The Commander, Deputy Commander, and Area Commanders of the MSC (Atlantic, Pacific, and Far East) are flag officers of the Navy on active duty. All ships are civilian manned with most of their crews being Civil Service employees of the Navy. However, the tankers are operated under contract to commercial tanker lines and are manned by merchant seamen.
The Military Sealift Command also operates a number of underway replenishment (UNREP) ships, fleet support ships, and special projects ships that support other defence-related activities, mostly research, surveying and missile-range support ships.
This section also includes research ships on loan to various civilian research institutions.

Armament: No ship of the Military Sealift Command is armed.

Classification: Military Sealift Command ships are assigned standard US Navy hull designations with the added designation prefix "T". Ships in this category are referred to as "USNS" (United States Naval Ship) *vice* "USS" (United States Ship) which is used for Navy-manned ships.

1 STORE SHIP (AF) "RIGEL" CLASS

Name	No.	Launched	Commissioned	F/S
RIGEL	T-AF 58	15 Mar 1955	2 Sept 1955	TAA

Displacement, tons: 7 950 light; 15 540 full load
Dimensions, feet (metres): 475 wl; 502 oa × 72 × 29 *(153·0 × 22·0 × 8·8)*
Guns: none
Main engines: Geared turbine (General Electric); 16 000 shp; 1 shaft = 20 knots
Boilers: 2 (Combustion Engineering)
Complement: approx 350

Built by Ingalls Shipbuilding Co, Pascagoula. R3-S-A4 type. Helicopter platform fitted aft. *Rigel* was assigned to Military Sealift Command on 23 June 1975 (guns removed; civilian manned).

"RIGEL" Class
1974, USN

1 MISCELLANEOUS (AG) CONVERTED "VICTORY" TYPE

Name	No.	Builders	F/S
KINGSPORT (ex-*Kingsport Victory*)	T-AG 164	California SB Corp	TAA

Displacement, tons: 7 190 light; 10 680 full load
Dimensions, feet (metres): 455 oa × 62 × 22 *(138·7 × 18·9 × 6·7)*
Main engines: Geared turbines; 8 500 shp; 1 shaft = 15·2 knots
Boilers: 2
Complement: 73 (13 officers, 42 men, 15 technicians)

Maritime Administration type VC2-S-AP3. Employed as cargo ship by Military Sea Transportation Service prior to conversion. Name shortened, ship reclassified and converted in 1961-62 by Willamette Iron & Steel Co, Portland, Oregon, into the world's first satellite communications ship, for Project Advent, involving the promotion of a terminal to meet the required military capability for high capacity, world-wide radio communications using high altitude hovering satellites, and the installation of ship-to-shore communications facilities, additional electric power generating equipment, a helicopter landing platform, aerological facilities, and a 30-foot parabolic communication antenna housed in a 53-foot diameter plastic radome abaft the superstructure. Painted white for operations in the tropics. Protect Advent Syncom satellite relay operations were completed in 1966, and *Kingsport* was reassigned to hydrographic research. Antenna sphere now removed.
Note antenna mast on helicopter platform in photograph; exhaust ducts fitted to funnel.
Operated by Military Sealift Command for Naval Electronic Systems Command; civilian manned.

KINGSPORT
1/1976, Michael D. J. Lennon

1 MISCELLANEOUS (AG) "OBSERVATION ISLAND" CLASS

Name	No.	Builders	Commissioned
OBSERVATION ISLAND (ex-*Empire State Mariner*)	AG 154 (ex-YAG 57)	New York SB Corp, NJ	5 Dec 1958

Displacement, tons: 16 076 full load
Dimensions, feet (metres): 529·5 wl; 563 oa × 76 × 29 *(171·6 × 23·2 × 8·8)*
Main engines: Geared turbines (General Electric); 19 250 shp; 1 shaft = 20 knots
Boilers: 2 (Foster-Wheeler)
Complement: 428 (35 officers, 393 enlisted men)

Built as a "Mariner" class merchant ship (C4-S-1A type); launched on 15 Aug 1953; acquired by the Navy on 10 Sept 1956 for use as a Fleet Ballistic Missile (FBM) test ship. Converted at Norfolk Naval Shipyard.
Was fitted to test fire Polaris and later Poseidon missiles. Navy manned. Decommissioned on 29 Sept 1972 and placed in Maritime Administration reserve; remains in Navy List.
On 18 Aug 1977, *Observation Island* was reacquired by the US Navy from the Maritime Administration and was transferred to the Military Sealift Command for administrative control. She will undergo a two to three year conversion for operation as a Missile Range Instrumentation Ship (AGM). Her name and AG classification will be retained and she will be under the operational control of the US Air Force. Manned by a civil service crew, US Navy will retain title.

Missile Testing: The ship was fitted with complete missile testing, servicing and firing systems. She fired the first ship-launched Polaris missile at sea on 27 Aug 1959. Refitted to fire the improved Poseidon missile in 1969 and launched the first Poseidon test missile fired afloat on 16 Dec 1969.

OBSERVATION ISLAND
1971, USN

714 USA

1 MISSILE RANGE INSTRUMENTATION SHIP (AGM)
CONVERTED "HASKELL" CLASS

Name	No.	Builders	Commissioned	F/S
RANGE SENTINEL (ex-Sherburne)	T-AGM 22 (ex-APA 205)	Permanente Metals Corp, Richmond, Calif	20 Sept 1944	TAA

Displacement, tons: 11 800 full load
Dimensions, feet (metres): 455 oa × 62 × 23 *(138·7 × 18·9 × 7·0)*
Main engines: Turbine (Westinghouse); 8 500 hp; 1 shaft = 17·7 knots
Boilers: 2 (Combustion Engineering)
Complement: 95 (14 officers, 54 men, 27 technical personnel)

Former attack transport (APA) converted specifically to serve as a range instrumentation ship in support of the Poseidon Fleet Ballistic Missile (FBM) programme. Maritime Administration VC2-S-AP5 type. Renamed *Range Sentinel* on 26 April 1971.
Stricken from the Navy List on 1 Oct 1958 and transferred to Maritime Administration reserve fleet; reacquired by the Navy on 22 Oct 1969 for AGM conversion.
Converted from Oct 1969 to Oct 1971; placed in service as T-AGM 22 on 14 Oct 1971. Operated by Military Sealift Command and civilian manned.

RANGE SENTINEL   1973, USN

2 RANGE INSTRUMENTATION SHIPS (AGM)
"CONVERTED" MISSION CLASS

Name	No.	Builders	Delivered	F/S
VANGUARD (ex-Muscel Shoals, ex-Mission San Fernando)	T-AGM 19 (ex-T-AO 122)	Marine Ship Corp, Sausalito, Calif	29 Feb 1944	TAA
REDSTONE (ex-Johnstown, ex-Mission de Pala)	T-AGM 20 (ex-T-AO 114)	Marine Ship Corp, Sausalito, Calif	22 April 1944	TAA

Displacement, tons: 22 310 full load
Dimensions, feet (metres): 595 oa × 75 × 25 *(181·4 × 22·9 × 7·6)*
Main engines: Turbo-electric (Westinghouse); 10 000 shp; 1 shaft = 14 knots
Boilers: 2 (Babcock & Wilcox)
Complement: *Vanguard* 19 officers, 71 enlisted men, 108 technical personnel; *Redstone* 20 officers, 71 enlisted men, 120 technical personnel

Former "Mission" class tankers converted in 1964-66 to serve as mid-ocean communications and tracking ships in support of the Apollo manned lunar flights. Maritime Administration T2-SE-A2 type.
Converted to range instrumentation ships by General Dynamics Corp, Quincy Division, Massachusetts; each ship was cut in half and a 72-foot mid-section was inserted, increasing length, beam, and displacement; approximately 450 tons of electronic equipment installed for support of lunar flight operations, including communications and tracking systems; balloon hangar and platform fitted aft. Cost of converting the three ships was $90 million. Operated by Military Sealift Command for Air Force Eastern Test Range in Atlantic (*Vanguard*) and for NASA Goddard Space Flight Center (*Redstone*). Civilian crews.
Note different bow structure configurations and deck houses.

REDSTONE   1970, United States Air Force

VANGUARD   1967, USN

2 MISSILE RANGE INSTRUMENTATION SHIPS (AGM) CONVERTED C4-S-A1 TYPE

Name	No.	Builders	Commissioned	F/S
GENERAL H. H. ARNOLD (ex-USNS *General R. E. Callan*)	T-AGM 9 (ex-T-AP 139)	Kaiser Co, Richmond Calif	17 Aug 1944	TPA
GENERAL HOYT S. VANDENBERG (ex-USNS *General Harry Taylor*)	T-AGM 10 (ex-T-AP 145)	Kaiser Co, Richmond Calif	1 April 1944	TAA

Displacement, tons: 16 600 full load
Dimensions, feet (metres): 552·9 oa × 71·5 × 26·3 *(168·5 × 21·8 × 8·0)*
Main engines: Geared turbines (Westinghouse); 9 000 shp; 1 shaft = 14 knots
Boilers: 2 (Babcock & Wilcox)
Complement: 205 (21 officers, 71 men, 113 technical personnel)

Former troop transports converted in 1962-63 for monitoring Air Force missiles firing and satellite launches. Maritime Administration C4-S-A1 type. Upon conversion to range instrumentation ships they were placed in service in 1963 under Air Force operation, however assigned to MSTS for operation on 1 July 1964 (*Arnold*) and 13 July 1964 (*Vandenberg*).
Both ships are operated by Military Sealift Command for Air Force Eastern Test Range in Atlantic. Civilian manned.

GEN. HOYT S. VANDENBERG   USN

1 MISSILE RANGE INSTRUMENTATION SHIP (AGM) "VICTORY" CLASS

Name	No.	Builders	Commissioned	F/S
WHEELING (ex-*Seton Hall Victory*)	T-AGM 8	Oregon SB Corp, Portland	1944	TPA

Displacement, tons: 11 500 full load
Dimensions, feet (metres): 455·3 oa × 62·2 × 22 *(138·8 × 19·0 × 6·7)*
Main engines: Geared turbines (Westinghouse); 8 500 shp; 1 shaft = 17 knots
Boilers: 2 (Combustion Engineering)
Complement: 107 (13 officers, 46 men, 48 technical personnel)

Wheeling is the only survivor of six "Victory" type military cargo and merchant ships converted to missile range instrumentation ships during the massive US space and military missile programmes of the 1960s. Maritime Administration VC2-S-AP3 type. Assigned to Military Sea Transportation Service on 28 May 1964; operated in support of Pacific Missile Range. Fitted with helicopter hangar and platform aft. Employed to test AWG-9 fire control system for use in the F-14 Tomcat fighter aircraft. Civilian manned.

WHEELING   USN

USA 715

2 OCEANOGRAPHIC RESEARCH SHIPS (AGOR) "GYRE" CLASS

Name	No.	Builders	Completed
GYRE	AGOR 21	Halter Marine Service, New Orleans	14 Nov 1973
MOANA WAVE	AGOR 22	Halter Marine Service, New Orleans	16 Jan 1974

Displacement, tons: 950 full load
Dimensions, feet (metres): 165 oa × 36 × 14·5 (50·3 × 11·0 × 4·4)
Main engines: Turbo-charged diesels (Caterpillar); 1 700 bhp; 2 shafts (cp propellers) = 12 knots
Complement: 21 (10 crew, 11 scientists)

Laid down on 9 Oct 1972 and 10 Oct 1972 respectively; launched on 25 May 1973 and 18 June 1973. They are based on a commercial ship design. Fitted with a 150 hp retractable propeller pod for low-speed or station keeping with main machinery shut down. Open deck aft provides space for equipment vans to permit rapid change of mission capabilities. Each ship cost approximately $1·9 million.
The Navy plans to construct several of these small, utility oceanographic research ships to replace older and obsolescent ships now operated by civilian research and educational institutions in support of Navy programmes. The above ships are assigned for operation to Texas A & M University and the University of Hawaii, respectively.

GYRE   1973, Halter Marine Services

1 OCEANOGRAPHIC RESEARCH SHIP (AGOR) "HAYES" CLASS

Name	No.	Builders	Commissioned	F/S
HAYES	T-AGOR 16	Todd Shipyards, Seattle	21 July 1971	TAA

Displacement, tons: 2 876 full load
Dimensions, feet (metres): 220 wl; 246·5 oa × 75 (see *Design* notes) × 22 (75·1 × 22·9 × 6·7)
Main engines: Geared diesels (GM); 5 400 bhp; 2 shafts (cp propeller) = 15 knots
Range, miles: 6 000 at 13·5 knots
Complement: 74 (11 officers, 33 men, 30 scientists)

Hayes is one of two classes of modern US naval ships to have a catamaran hull, the other being the ASR 21 class submarine rescue ships. Laid down 12 Nov 1969; launched 2 July 1970. Estimated cost was $15·9 million.
Operated by the Military Sealift Command for the Office of Naval Research under the Technical control of the Oceanographer of the Navy; civilian crew.

Design: Catamaran hull design provides large deck working area, centre well for operating equipment at great depths, and removes laboratory areas from main propulsion machinery. Each hull is 246·5 feet long and 24 feet wide (maximum). There are three 36-in diameter instrument wells in addition to the main centre well.

Engineering: An auxiliary 165-bhp diesel is fitted in each hull to provide "creeping" speed of 2 to 4 knots. Separation of controllable pitch propellers by catamaran hull separation provides high degree of manoeuvrability eliminating the need for bow thrusters.

HAYES   1971, Todd Shipyards Corp

7 OCEANOGRAPHIC RESEARCH SHIPS (AGOR) "ROBERT D. CONRAD" CLASS

Name	No.	Builders	Completed
ROBERT D. CONRAD	AGOR 3	Gibbs Corp, Jacksonville	29 Nov 1962
JAMES M. GILLISS	AGOR 4	Christy Corp, Sturgeon Bay	5 Nov 1962
LYNCH	T-AGOR 7	Marinette Mfg Co, Point Pleasant	27 Mar 1965
THOMAS G. THOMPSON	AGOR 9	Marinette Marine Corp, Wisc	24 Aug 1965
THOMAS WASHINGTON	AGOR 10	Marinette Marine Corp, Wisc	27 Sept 1965
DE STEIGUER	T-AGOR 12	Northwest Marine Iron Works, Portland, Oregon	28 Feb 1969
BARTLETT	T-AGOR 13	Northwest Marine Iron Works, Portland, Oregon	31 Mar 1969

Displacement, tons: 950-1 200 light; 1 362-1 370 full load
Dimensions, feet (metres): 191·5 wl; 208·9 oa × 40 × 15·3 (63·7 × 12·2 × 4·7)
Main engines: Diesel-electric (Caterpillar Tractor Co diesels (3 and 4); Cummins in rest); 1 000 bhp; 1 shaft = 13·5 knots
Range, miles: 12 000 at 12 knots
Complement: 41 (9 officers, 17 men, 15 scientists except *De Steigeur* and *Bartlett*, 8 officers, 18 men)

This is the first class of ships designed and built by the US Navy for oceanographic research. Fitted with instrumentation and laboratories to measure gravity and magnetism, water temperature, sound transmission in water, and the profile of the ocean floor. Special features include 10 ton capacity boom and winches for handling over-the-side equipment; bow thruster; 620 hp gas turbine (housed in funnel structure) for providing "quiet" power when conducting experiments; can propel the ship at 6·5 knots.
Robert D. Conrad laid down on 19 Jan 1961 and launched on 26 May 1962. Operated by Lamont Geological Observatory of Columbia University under technical control of the Oceanographer of the Navy; civilian crew.
James H. Gilliss laid down on 31 May 1961 and launched on 19 May 1962. Operated by the University of Miami (Florida) since 1970 in support of Navy programmes
Lynch laid down on 7 Sept 1962 and launched on 17 March 1964. Operated by Military Sealift Command under the technical control of the Oceanographer of the Navy; civilian crew.
Thomas G. Thompson laid down on 12 Sept 1963 and launched on 18 July 1964. Operated by University of Washington (State) under technical control of the Oceanographer of the Navy; civilian crew.
Thomas Washington laid down on 12 Sept 1963 and launched on 1 Aug 1964. Operated by Scripps Institution of Oceanography (University of California) under technical control of the Oceanographer on the Navy; civilian crew.
De Steiguer and *Bartlett* laid down on 12 Nov 1965 and 18 Nov 1965 and launched on 21 March 1966 and 24 May 1966. Operated by Military Sealift Command under the technical control of the Oceanographer of the Navy; civilian crew. Active in Pacific and Atlantic Fleets respectively.

Transfers: Ships of this class are in service with Brazil *(Sands)* and New Zealand *(Charles H. Davies)*.

JAMES M. GILLISS   USN

LYNCH   1974, Dr. Giorgio Arra

716   USA

2 OCEANOGRAPHIC RESEARCH SHIPS (AGOR) "MELVILLE" CLASS

Name	No.	Builders	Completed
MELVILLE	AGOR 14	Defoe SB Co, Bay City, Mich	27 Aug 1969
KNORR	AGOR 15	Defoe SB Co, Bay City, Mich	14 Jan 1970

Displacement, tons: 1 915 full load
Dimensions, feet (metres): 244·9 × 46·3 × 15 *(74·7 × 14·1 × 4·6)*
Main engines: 2 De Laval diesels; 2 500 bhp; 2 cycloidal propellers = 12·5 knots
Range, miles: 10 000 at 12 knots
Complement: 50 (9 officers, 16 men, 25 scientists)

Oceanographic research ships of an advanced design. AGOR 19 and AGOR 20 of this type in the FY 1968 programme, but construction of the latter ships was cancelled. These ships are fitted with internal wells for lowering equipment; underwater lights and observation ports. Facilities for handling small research submersibles.
Melville and *Knorr* laid down on 12 July 1967 and 9 Aug 1967 respectively; launched 10 July 1968 and 21 Aug 1968. *Melville* operated by Scripps Institution of Oceanography and *Knorr* by Woods Hole Oceanography Institution for the Office of Naval Research; under technical control of the Oceanographer of the Navy.

Engineering: First US Navy ocean-going ships with cycloidal propellers permitting the ships to turn 360 degrees in their own length. One propeller is fitted at each end of the ship, providing movement in any direction and optimum station keeping without use of thrusters. They have experienced engineering difficulties.

MELVILLE   1969, Defoe Shipbuilding

1 OCEANOGRAPHIC RESEARCH SHIP (AGOR) "ELTANIN" CLASS

Name	No.	Builders	In Service	F/S
MIZAR	T-AGOR 11 (ex-T-AK 272)	Avondale Marine Ways, New Orleans	7 Mar 1958	TPA

Displacement, tons: 2 036 light; 3 481 full load
Dimensions, feet (metres): 256·8 wl; 262·2 oa × 51·5 × 18·7 *(79·9 × 15·7 × 5·7)*
Main engines: Diesel-electric (ALCO diesels, Westinghouse electric motors) 2 700 bhp; 2 shafts = 12 knots
Complement: 56 (11 officers, 30 enlisted men, 15 scientists)

Built for Military Sea Transportation Service. Designed for Arctic operation with hull strengthened against ice. C1-ME2-13a type. Delivered as cargo ship to MSTS and subsequently converted to oceanographic research ship.
As a research ship *Mizar* was operated by the Military Sealift Command for Naval Research Laboratory, under technical control of the Oceanographer of the Navy; civilian crew. Transferred to technical control of Naval Electronics Command on 1 July 1975.

Conversion: *Mizar* converted in 1962 into deep sea research ship. Equipped with centre well for lowering oceanographic equipment including towed sensor platforms, fitted with laboratories and elaborate photographic facilities, hydrophone system and computer for seafloor navigation and tracking towed vehicles. *Mizar* had key roles in the searches for the US nuclear submarines *Thresher* and *Scorpion*; the French submarine *Eurydice*; and recovery of the H-bomb lost at sea off Palomares, Spain.

MIZAR   1973, Wright and Logan

OCEANOGRAPHIC RESEARCH CRAFT

The Navy also owns a number of smaller oceanographic research craft that are operated by various educational and research institutions in support of Navy programmes; under technical control of the Oceanographer of the Navy; no Navy hull numbers are assigned; all are 100 feet in length or smaller except for *Lamb*, a converted 136-foot minesweeper (YMS/AMS type) operated by the Lamont Geophysical Laboratory.

0 + 12 OCEAN SURVEILLANCE SHIPS (AGOS)

Three ships	T-AGOS	Requested FY 1979 programme
Five ships	T-AGOS	Planned FY 1980 programme
Four ships	T-AGOS	Planned FY 1981 programme

The Navy plans to construct 12 ocean surveillance ships to operate the new SURTASS (Surface Towed Array Surveillance System). These ships will have a hull design similar to the fleet tugs (T-ATF) now under construction, but will be specially configured for the ocean surveillance mission. They will be operated by the Military Sealift Command, apparently with civilian crews and Navy personnel to operate the classified SURTASS equipment.

1 SURVEYING SHIP (AGS) CONVERTED MERCHANT TYPE

Name	No.	Builders	In Service	F/S
H. H. HESS (ex-*Canada Mail*)	T-AGS 38	National Steel & SB Co.	16 Jan 1978	TPA

Displacement, tons: 22 625 full load
Measurement, tons: 14 747 dwt
Dimensions, feet (metres): 535·7 × 76 × 41 *(163·3 × 23·2 × 12·5)*
Main engines: Geared turbines (GE); 19 250 shp; 1 shaft = 20 knots
Boilers: 2 (Foster-Wheeler)
Complement: 57

Merchant ship completed in 1965 and acquired by the Navy 9 July 1976 for conversion to replace the "Victory" class surveying ship *Michelson* (T-AGS 23). Above data as merchant ship. As a hydrographic survey ship she is operated by the Military Sealift Command (Pacific Fleet) for the Oceanographer of the Navy with a civilian crew. Converted at National Steel and SB Co San Diego between March 1977 and Jan 1978.

H. H. HESS (as *Canada Mail*)

USA 717

2 SURVEYING SHIPS (AGS) "CHAUVENET" CLASS

Name	No.	Builders	Completed	F/S
CHAUVENET	T-AGS 29	Upper Clyde Shipbuilders, Glasgow	13 Nov 1970	TPA
HARKNESS	T-AGS 32	Upper Clyde Shipbuilders, Glasgow	29 Jan 1971	TAA

Displacement, tons: 3 670 full load
Dimensions, feet (metres): 393·2 oa × 54 × 16 *(119·8 × 16·5 × 4·9)*
Main engine: 1 Alco diesel; 3 600 bhp; 1 shaft = 15 knots
Complement: 175 (13 officers, approx 150 men and technical personnel, 12 scientists)

Capable of extensive military hydrographic and oceanographic surveys, supporting coastal surveying craft, amphibious survey teams and helicopters. Fitted with two helicopter hangars and platform.
Chauvenet authorised in the Fiscal Year 1965 new construction programme; *Harkness* in the FY 1966 programme. Laid down on 24 May 1967 and 30 June 1967 respectively; launched on 13 May 1968 and 12 June 1968
These ships are operated by the Military Sealift Command for the Oceanographer of the Navy with Navy detachments on board. Civilian crews.

CHAUVENET   1971, USN

4 SURVEYING SHIPS (AGS) "SILAS BENT" and "WILKES" CLASSES

Name	No.	Builders	Delivered	F/S
SILAS BENT	T-AGS 26	American SB Co, Lorain	23 July 1965	TPA
KANE	T-AGS 27	Christy Corp, Sturgeon Bay	19 May 1967	TAA
WILKES	T-AGS 33	Defoe SB Co, Bay City, Mich	28 June 1971	TAA
WYMAN	T-AGS 34	Defoe SB Co, Bay City, Mich	3 Nov 1971	TAA

Displacement, tons: 1 935 standard; 2 420-2 580 full load
Dimensions, feet (metres): 285·3 oa × 48 × 15·1 *(87·0 × 14·6 × 4·6)*
Main engines: Diesel-electric (diesels; Westinghouse, 26; Alco, 27; GE, rest); 3 000 bhp; 1 shaft = 15 knots
Complement: 77/78 (12 officers, 35 or 36 men, 30 scientists)

These ships were designed specifically for surveying operations. Bow propulsion unit for precise manoeuvrability and station keeping. All four ships operated by Military Sealift Command for the Oceanographer of the Navy; civilian crews.
Laid down on 2 March 1964, 19 Dec 1964, 18 July 1968 and 18 July 1968 respectively; launched on 16 May 1964, 20 Nov 1965, 31 July 1969 and 30 Oct 1969.
Wilkes laid up in ready reserve.

WILKES   6/1971, USN

2 SURVEYING SHIPS (AGS) "BOWDITCH" CLASS

Name	No.	Builders	F/S
BOWDITCH (ex-SS *South Bend Victory*)	T-AGS 21	Oregon SB Co.	TAA
DUTTON (ex-SS *Tuskegee Victory*)	T-AGS 22	South Coast Co, Newport Beach	TPA

Displacement, tons: 13 050 full load
Dimensions, feet (metres): 455·2 oa × 62·2 × 25 *(138·7 × 19·0 × 7·6)*
Main engine: Geared turbine (GE, 21; Westinghouse, 22); 8 500 shp; 1 shaft = 15 knots
Boilers: 2
Complement: 100 (13 officers, 47 men, approx 40 technical personnel)

VC2-S-AP3 type ships. Converted to support the Fleet Ballistic Missile Programme, *Dutton* at Philadelphia Naval Shipyard 8 Nov 1957 to 16 Nov 1958 and *Bowditch* at Charleston Naval Shipyard 10 Oct 1957 to 30 Sept 1958.
Designed for general surveying and to record magnetic fields and gravity.
Operated by Military Sealift Command for the Oceanographer of the Navy; civilian crews.

BOWDITCH   1976, Michael D. J. Lennon

1 CARGO SHIP (AK) PROPOSED CONVERSION

Under the Fiscal Year 1981 programme it is proposed to convert a merchant freighter to a Cargo Ship (AK 284). Estimated cost of conversion $50 million. Details and planned task not available.

1 CARGO SHIP (AK) CONVERTED "ANDROMEDA" CLASS

Name	No.	Builders	Commissioned
WYANDOT	T-AK 283 (ex-T-AKA 92)	Moore DD Co, Oakland	30 Sep 1944

Displacement, tons: 7 430 light; 11 000 full load
Dimensions, feet (metres): 435 wl; 459·2 oa × 63 × 28 *(140·0 × 19·2 × 8·5)*
Main engines: Geared turbines (General Electric); 6 000 shp; 1 shaft = 16·5 knots
Boilers: 2 (Combustion Engineering)
Complement: 423 (38 officers, 385 enlisted men)

Former attack cargo ship (AKA) of the "Andromeda" class; C2-S-B1 type. Launched on 28 June 1944; commissioned as AKA 92. Designation changed to T-AK 283 on 1 Jan 1969. Winterised for arctic service.
On 5 March 1976 was transferred to Maritime Administration for lay-up in the fleet at Suisun Bay. Remains on Navy List.

718　USA

4 CARGO SHIPS (AK) "NORWALK" CLASS

Name	No.	F/S
NORWALK (ex-*Norwalk Victory*)	T-AK 279	TAA
FURMAN (ex-*Furman Victory*)	T-AK 280	TPA
VICTORIA (ex-*Ethiopia Victory*)	T-AK 281	TAA
MARSHFIELD (ex-*Marshfield Victory*)	T-AK 282	TAA

Displacement, tons: 6 700 light; 11 000/11 300 full load
Dimensions, feet (metres): 455·25 oa × 62 × 22 *(138·8 × 18·9 × 7·2)*
Main engine: Geared turbine; 8 500 shp; 1 shaft = 17 knots
Boilers: 2 (Babcock & Wilcox, 279-280; Combustion Engineering, 281-282)
Complement: 80 to 90 plus Navy detachment

Former merchant ships of the VC2-S-AP3 "Victory" type built during World War II. Extensively converted to supply tenders for Fleet Ballistic Missile (FBM) submarines. Fitted to carry torpedoes, spare parts, packaged petroleum products, bottled gas, black oil and diesel fuel, frozen and dry provisions, and general cargo as well as missiles. No 3 hold converted to carry 16 Polaris missiles in vertical position; tankage provided for 355 000 gallons (US) of diesel oil and 430 000 gallons (US) of fuel oil (for submarine tenders). All subsequently modified to carry Poseidon missiles. All four ships are operated by the Military Sealift Command with civilian operating crews; a small Navy detachment in each ship provides security and technical services.

Conversion: *Norwalk* converted to FBM cargo ship by Boland Machine & Manufacturing Co, and accepted for service on 30 Dec 1963; *Furman* converted by American Shipbuilding Co, and accepted on 7 Oct 1964; *Victoria* converted by Philadelphia Naval Shipyard, and accepted on 15 Oct 1965; and *Marshfield* converted by Boland Machine & Manufacturing Co, and accepted on 28 May 1970.

MARSHFIELD　1970, USN

1 VEHICLE CARGO SHIP (AKR) "CALLAGHAN" CLASS

Name	No.	Builders
ADMIRAL WM. M. CALLAGHAN	—	Sun SB & DD Co, Chester, Pennsylvania

Displacement, tons: 24 500 full load
Dimensions, feet (metres): 694 oa × 92 × 29 *(211·5 × 28·0 × 8·8)*
Main engines: 2 LM2500 gas turbines (General Electric); 50 000 shp; 2 shafts = 26 knots
Complement: 33

Roll-on/roll-off vehicle cargo ship built specifically for long-term charter to the Military Sealift Command. Launched on 17 Oct 1967. Internal parking decks and ramps for carrying some 750 vehicles on 167 537 square feet of parking area; unloading via four side ramps and stern ramp, she can off load and reload full vehicle capacity in 27 hours.
Active with MSC in Atlantic Fleet. This ship is not on the Naval Vessels Register but is included here for information.

Engineering: She was the first Navy-sponsored all gas-turbine ship; has similar turbines to those of the "Spruance" class destroyers (DD 963) and "Oliver Hazard Perry" class frigates (FFG 7).

ADM. WM. M. CALLAGHAN　USN

1 CARGO SHIP (AK) "SCHUYLER OTIS BLAND" CLASS

Name	No.	F/S
SCHUYLER OTIS BLAND	T-AK 277	TPA

Displacement, tons: 15 910 full load
Dimensions, feet (metres): 454 oa × 66 × 27 *(138·4 × 20·1 × 8·2)*
Main engine: Geared turbine (GE); 13 750 shp; 1 shaft = 18·5 knots
Boilers: 2 (Foster-Wheeler)
Complement: 51 (14 officers, 37 enlisted men)

Acquired from the Maritime Administration by the Military Sea Transportation Service in July 1961. The only ship of the type (C3-S-DX1), built in 1961; prototype of the "Mariner" cargo ship design.

SCHUYLER OTIS BLAND　USN

1 CARGO SHIP (AK) "ELTANIN" CLASS

Name	No.	Builders	In Service	F/S
MIRFAK	T-AK 271	Avondale Marine Ways, New Orleans	30 Dec 1957	TAA

Displacement, tons: 2 022 light; 3 886 full load
Dimensions, feet (metres): 256·8 wl; 262·2 oa × 51·5 × 18·7 *(79·9 × 15·7 × 5·7)*
Main engines: Diesel-electric (ALCO diesels with Westinghouse electric motors); 2 700 bhp; 2 shafts = 13 knots
Complement: 48

Built for Military Sea Transportation Service, Louisiana. Designed for Arctic operation with hull strengthened against ice. C1-M E2-13a type. Launched on 5 Aug 1957. Note icebreaking prow in photo.

Conversion: Two other ships of this class converted for oceanographic research: *Eltanin*, reclassified from T-AK 270 to T-AGOR 8 on 15 Nov 1962 loaned to Argentina as *Islas Orcadas*; *Mizar* T-AK 272 was reclassified T-AGOR 11 on 15 April 1964 (see AGORs "Eltanin" Class).

MIRFAK　USN

USA 719

1 CARGO SHIP (AK) "PRIVATE LEONARD C. BROSTROM" CLASS

Name	No.	Acquired	F/S
PVT. LEONARD C. BROSTROM (ex-*Marine Eagle*)	T-AK 255	9 Aug 1950	TPA

Displacement, tons: 8 590 light; 12 056 full load
Dimensions, feet (metres): 520 oa × 71·5 × 33 *(158·5 × 21·8 × 10·1)*
Main engine: Geared turbine (GE); 9 000 shp; 1 shaft = 15·8 knots
Boilers: 2 (Babcock & Wilcox)
Complement: 57 (14 officers, 43 men)

She is fitted with 150-ton capacity booms, providing the most powerful lift capability of any US ship. C4-S-B1 type built in 1943.

PVT. LEONARD C. BROSTROM   USN

5 CARGO SHIPS (AK) "GREENVILLE VICTORY" CLASS

Name	No.	F/S
GREENVILLE VICTORY	T-AK 237	MAR
PVT. JOHN R. TOWLE (ex-*Appleton Victory*)	T-AK 240	TAA
SGT. ANDREW MILLER (ex-*Radcliffe Victory*)	T-AK 242	MAR
SGT. TRUMAN KIMBRO	T-AK 254	MPR
LT. JAMES E. ROBINSON (ex-T-AG 170, ex-T-AK 274, ex-AKV 3, ex-*Czechoslovakia Victory*)	T-AK 274	MAR

Displacement, tons: 6 700 light; 15 199 full load
Dimensions, feet (metres): 455·5 oa × 62 × 28·5 *(138·9 × 18·9 × 8·9)*
Main engine: Geared turbine (GE; 242: Westinghouse; rest); 8 500 shp; 1 shaft = 17 knots except T-AK 254 15 knots
Boilers: 2

Former merchant ships of the "Victory" type built during World War II. All near sisters. VC2-S-AP3 type capable of 17 knots except T-AK 254 is VC2-S-AP2 type capable of 15 knots. "Victory" type cargo ships configured as Fleet Ballistic Missile (FBM) cargo ships are listed separately.

Classification: The former Military Sea Transportation Service aircraft cargo and ferry ships *Lt. James E. Robinson* AKV 3 reclassified as cargo ship on 7 May 1959. *Kingsport Victory* T-AK 239, was renamed and reclassified *Kingsport* T-AG 164 in 1962.
Lt. James E. Robinson T-AK 274, was to have been transferred to the Maritime Administration, but was modified for special project work and reclassified as T-AG 170 in 1963, and reverted to the original classification T-AK 274 on 1 July 1964. Transferred to Maritime Administration for lay-up at James River. Ship remains on Navy List.
Sgt. Truman Kimbro, Sgt. Andrew Miller and *Greenville Victory* transferred to Maritime Administration on 6 March and 22 and 23 March 1976 for lay-up at Suisun Bay and James River (last two). Remain on Navy List.

GREENVILLE VICTORY   USN

PVT. JOHN R. TOWLE in Antarctic   1961, USN

1 VEHICLE CARGO SHIP (AKR) "METEOR" CLASS

Name	No.	Builders	Delivered	F/S
METEOR (ex-*Sea Lift*)	T-AKR 9 (ex-LSV 9)	Puget Sound Bridge & DD Co	25 April 1967	TPA

Displacement, tons: 11 130 light; 16 940 standard; 21 700 full load
Dimensions, feet (metres): 540 oa × 83 × 27 *(164·7 × 25·5 × 8·2)*
Main engines: Geared turbines; 19 400 shp; 2 shafts = 20 knots
Boilers: 2
Complement: 54
Passengers: 12

Maritime Administration C4-ST-67a type. Roll-on/roll-off vehicle cargo ship. Cost of $15 895 500. Authorised under the Fiscal Year 1963 programme. Laid down on 19 May 1964 and launched on 18 April 1965. Delivered to Military Sea Transportation Service on 25 April 1967. Designed for point-to-point sea transportation of Department of Defense self-propelled, fully loaded, wheeled, tracked and amphibious vehicles and general cargo. Internal ramps, stern ramp and side openings provide for quick loading and unloading. Designation changed from T-LSV to T-AKR on 1 Jan 1969. Originally authorised as AK-278.

METEOR   1966, Lockheed Shipbuilding

Name: Originally named *Sea Lift*. Renamed *Meteor* on 12 Sept 1975 to avoid confusion with "Sealift" class tankers.

1 VEHICLE CARGO SHIP (AKR) "COMET" CLASS

Name	No.	Builders	Commissioned	F/S
COMET	T-AKR 7 (ex-*T-LSV 7*, ex-*T-AK 260*)	Sun SB & DD Co	27 Jan 1958	TAA

Displacement, tons: 7 605 light; 18 286 full load
Dimensions, feet (metres): 465 oa; 499 oa × 78 × 28·8 *(152·1 × 23·8 × 8·8)*
Main engines: Geared turbines (General Electric); 13 200 shp; 2 shafts = 18 knots
Boilers: 2 (Babcock & Wilcox)
Complement: 73

Roll-on/roll-off vehicle carrier built for Military Sea Transportation Service C3-ST-14A type. Laid down on 15 May 1956. Launched on 31 July 1957. Maritime Administration Design includes ramp system for loading and discharging. The hull is strengthened against ice. Can accommodate 700 vehicles in two after holds; the forward holds are for general cargo. Equipped with Denny-Brown stabilisers. Reclassified from T-AK to T-LSV on 1 June 1963, and changed to T-AKR on 1 Jan 1969.

COMET   USN

720   USA

4 TANKERS (AO) "COLUMBIA" CLASS

Name	No.	Builders	Delivered	F/S
COLUMBIA (ex-*Falcon Lady*)	T-AO 182	Ingalls SB Co, Pascagoula	11 Mar 1971	TWWR
NECHES (ex-*Falcon Duchess*)	T-AO 183	Ingalls SB Co, Pascagoula	4 Aug 1971	TWWR
HUDSON (ex-*Falcon Princess*)	T-AO 184	Ingalls SB Co, Pascagoula	4 May 1972	TWWR
SUSQUEHANNA (ex-*Falcon Countess*)	T-AO 185	Ingalls SB Co, Pascagoula	13 Jan 1972	TWWR

Displacement, tons: 37 276 deadweight
Dimensions, feet (metres): 672 oa × 89 × 36 *(204·8 × 27·1 × 11·0)*
Main engines: Geared turbine; 1 shaft = 16·5 knots
Boilers: 2

Former merchant tankers originally chartered to the Military Sealift Command. All four acquired on bareboat charter on 3 May 1974 (182 and 183), 10 April 1974 (184) and 17 April 1974 (185). Acquired by USN for MSC service on 15 Jan 1976 (182), 11 Feb 1976 (183), 23 April 1976 (184) and 11 May 1976 (185). Operated under contract by Cove Shipping Inc. Cargo capacity 310 000 barrels. Civilian manned.

HUDSON (as *Falcon Princess*)

1 TANKER (AO) "POTOMAC" CLASS

Name	No.	Acquired	F/S
POTOMAC (ex-*Shenandoah*)	T-AO 181	12 Jan 1976	TWWR

Displacement, tons: 27 467 deadweight
Dimensions, feet (metres): 620 oa × 83·5 × 34 *(189·0 × 25·5 × 10·4)*
Main engine: Geared turbine; 20 460 shp; 1 shaft = 18 knots
Boilers: 2

The merchant tanker *Shenandoah* was built from the stern of the naval tanker *Potomac* (T-AO 150) destroyed by fire on 26 Sept 1961, and new bow and mid-body sections. After being chartered by the Military Sealift Command since 14 Dec 1964 the ship was formally acquired on 12 Jan 1976, assigned the name *Potomac* and placed in MSC service. Cargo capacity 200 000 barrels. Operated under charter by Hudson Waterways Corp.

9 TANKERS (AO) "SEALIFT" CLASS

Name	No.	Builders	Delivered	F/S
SEALIFT PACIFIC	T-AO 168	Todd Shipyards	14 Aug 1974	TWWR
SEALIFT ARABIAN SEA	T-AO 169	Todd Shipyards	6 May 1975	TWWR
SEALIFT CHINA SEA	T-AO 170	Todd Shipyards	9 May 1975	TWWR
SEALIFT INDIAN OCEAN	T-AO 171	Todd Shipyards	29 Aug 1975	TWWR
SEALIFT ATLANTIC	T-AO 172	Bath Iron Works	26 Aug 1974	TWWR
SEALIFT MEDITERRANEAN	T-AO 173	Bath Iron Works	6 Nov 1974	TWWR
SEALIFT CARIBBEAN	T-AO 174	Bath Iron Works	10 Feb 1975	TWWR
SEALIFT ARCTIC	T-AO 175	Bath Iron Works	22 May 1975	TWWR
SEALIFT ANTARCTIC	T-AO 176	Bath Iron Works	1 Aug 1975	TWWR

Displacement, tons: 34 100 full load
Dimensions, feet (metres): 587 oa × 84 × 34·6 *(178·9 × 25·6 × 10·6)*
Main engines: 2 turbo-charged diesels; 19 200 bhp; 1 shaft (cp propeller) = 16 knots
Range, miles: 12 000 at 16 knots
Complement: 30 + 2 Maritime Academy cadets

Built specially for long term-charter by the Military Sealift Command. T-AO 168 launched on 13 Oct 1973; others launched in 1974 on 26 Jan, 20 April, 27 July, 26 Jan, 9 March, 8 June, 31 Aug and 26 Oct respectively. Operated for MSC under charter by Marine Transport Lines Inc. Fitted with bow thruster to assist docking; automated engine room. Approximately 25 000 tons deadweight; cargo capacity 225 154 barrels. Estimated cost $146·5 million for the nine-ship class.

SEALIFT ANTARCTIC   1975, USN

1 TANKER (AO) "AMERICAN EXPLORER" CLASS

Name	No.	Builders	Commissioned	F/S
AMERICAN EXPLORER	T-AO 165	Ingalls SB Co, Pascagoula	27 Oct 1959	TWWR

Displacement, tons: 8 400 light; 31 300 full load
Measurement, tons: 22 525 deadweight
Dimensions, feet (metres): 615 oa × 80 × 32 *(187·5 × 24·4 × 9·8)*
Main engines: Steam turbines (De Laval); 22 000 shp; 1 shaft = 20 knots
Boilers: 2 (Babcock & Wilcox)
Complement: 53

T5-S-RM2A type. Laid down on 9 July 1957; launched on 11 April 1958. Built for the Maritime Administration, but acquired by Military Sea Transportation Service. Cargo capacity 190 300 barrels.
Operated for Military Sealift Command under charter by Hudson Waterways Corp.

AMERICAN EXPLORER   USN

USA 721

3 TANKERS (AO) "MAUMEE" CLASS

Name	No.	Builders	Delivered	F/S
MAUMEE	T-AO 149	Ingalls SB Co, Pascagoula	12 Dec 1956	TWWR
SHOSHONE	T-AO 151	Sun SB & DD Co, Chester	15 April 1957	TWWR
YUKON	T-AO 152	Ingalls SB Co, Pascagoula	17 May 1957	TWWR

Displacement, tons: 7 761 light; 32 953 full load
Measurement, tons: 25 000 deadweight
Dimensions, feet (metres): 591 wl; 620 oa × 83·5 × 32 (189·0 × 25·5 × 9·8)
Main engine: Geared turbine (Westinghouse); 18 600 shp; 1 shaft = 18 knots
Boilers: 2 (Combustion Engineering)
Complement: 53

Yukon laid down 16 May 1955, launched 16 March 1956; *Maumee* laid down 8 March 1955, launched 16 Feb 1956; *Shoshone* laid down 15 Aug 1955, launched 17 Jan 1957, T5-S-12A type. *Potomac* T-AO 150 sank after explosion in 1961, but was rebuilt in 1963-64; see previous listing fot *Potomac* (T-AO 181). Cargo capacity 203 216 barrels.
Maumee provided with ice-strengthened bow during 1969-70 modification at Norfolk SB & DD Co; employed in transporting petroleum products to Antarctica in support of US scientific endeavours.
These ships are operated for the Military Sealift Command under charter by Hudson Waterways Corp.

YUKON   1/1976, Michael D. J. Lennon

5 TANKERS (AO) "JUMBOISED MISPILLION" CLASS

Name	No.	Launched	Commissioned	F/S
MISPILLION	T-AO 105	10 Aug 1945	29 Dec 1945	TPA
NAVASOTA	T-AO 106	30 Aug 1945	27 Feb 1946	TPA
PASSUMPSIC	T-AO 107	31 Oct 1945	1 April 1946	TPA
PAWCATUCK	T-AO 108	19 Feb 1945	10 May 1946	TAA
WACCAMAW	T-AO 109	30 Mar 1946	25 June 1946	TAA

Displacement, tons: 11 600 light; 34 179 full load (33 750 in T-AO 106 and 109)
Dimensions, feet (metres): 644 oa × 75 × 35·5 (196·3 × 22·9 × 10·8)
Guns: Removed
Main engines: Geared turbines (Westinghouse); 13 500 shp; 2 shafts = 16 knots
Boilers: 4 (Babcock & Wilcox)
Complement: 290 (16 officers, 274 men) when Navy manned

All built by Sun Shipbuilding & Dry Dock Co, Chester, Pennsylvania. Originally T3-S2-A3 oilers; converted during mid-1960s under "jumbo" programme. Enlarged midsections added to increase cargo capacity to approximately 150 000 barrels. Helicopter platform fitted forward. As "jumboised" these ships had four 3 in single gun mounts; removed in MSC service. *Passumpsic* was assigned to the Military Sealift Command on 24 July 1973. *Mispillion* on 26 July 1974, *Waccamaw* on 24 Feb 1975, *Pawcatuck* on 15 July 1975 and *Navasota* on 13 Aug 1975. All operate in fleet support with civilian crews and naval detachments.

Appearance: Two funnels in the *Passumpsic*.

NAVASOTA   2/1977, Dr. Giorgio Arra

4 TANKERS (AO) "SUAMICO" CLASS

Name	No.	Builders	Commissioned	F/S
TALLULAH (ex-*Valley Forge*)	T-AO 50	Sun SB & DD Co, Chester	5 Sept 1942	MAR
MILLICOMA (ex-*Conastoga*, ex-*King's Mountain*)	T-AO 73	Sun SB & DD Co, Chester	5 Mar 1943	MAR
SAUGATUCK (ex-*Newton*)	T-AO 75	Sun SB & DD Co, Chester	19 Feb 1943	MAR
SCHUYLKILL (ex-*Louisburg*)	T-AO 76	Sun SB & DD Co, Chester	9 April 1943	MAR

Displacement, tons: 5 252 light; 21 880 full load
Dimensions, feet (metres): 503 wl; 523·5 oa × 68 × 33 (159·6 × 20·7 × 10·1)
Main engines: Turbo-electric drive (GE except Westinghouse in 75); 6 000 shp; 1 shaft = 15 knots
Boilers: 2 (Babcock & Wilcox)
Complement: 52

T2-SE-A1 tankers begun as merchant ships but acquired by Navy and completed as fleet oilers. During the post World War II period, all of these ships were employed in the tanker role, carrying petroleum point-to-point. Launched on 25 June 1942, 21 Jan 1943, 7 Dec 1942, 16 Feb 1943 respectively.
Cargo capacity approximately 134 000 barrels.
Transferred to Maritime Administration for lay-up at James River—T-AO 50, 29 May 1975; T-AO 73, 16 July 1975; T-AO 75, 5 Nov 1974; T-AO 76, 8 Sept 1975. All remain on Navy List—replaced by "Sealift" class AOs.

SCHUYLKILL   USN

2 OILERS (AO) "JUMBOISED CIMARRON" CLASS

Name	No.	Launched	Commissioned	F/S
MARIAS	T-AO 57	21 Dec 1943	12 Feb 1944	TAA
TALUGA	T-AO 62	10 July 1944	25 Aug 1944	TPA

Displacement, tons: 25 450 full load
Dimensions, feet (metres): 553 oa × 75 × 33 (168·6 × 22·9 × 10·1)
Guns: Unarmed
Main engines: Geared turbines (Bethlehem); 13 500 shp; 2 shafts = 18 knots
Boilers: 4 (Foster-Wheeler)
Complement: 274 (14 officers, 260 enlisted men)

These ships are survivors of a class of 26 of twin-screw (S2) fleet oilers built during World War II; some converted to escort carriers. These ships have been enlarged through the "jumbo" process. Both ships were built by Bethlehem Steel Co, Sparrows Point, Maryland. Original armament consisted of one 5 in gun, four 3 in guns and up to eight 40 mm guns. Cargo capacity 145 000 barrels of liquid fuels.
Marias and *Taluga* were assigned to the Military Sealift Command (MSC) on 2 Oct 1973 and 4 May 1972 respectively; manned by civilian crews and guns removed. Operate in fleet support.

MARIAS   10/1976, Michael D. J. Lennon

722 USA

2 GASOLINE TANKERS (AOG) "ALATNA" CLASS

Name	No.	Completed	F/S
ALATNA	T-AOG 81	July 1957	MPR
CHATTAHOOCHEE	T-AOG 82	Oct 1957	MPR

Displacement, tons: 7 300 (81); 5 720 (82) full load
Measurement, tons: 3 659 gross
Dimensions, feet (metres): 302 oa × 61 × 19 (92·1 × 18·6 × 5·8)
Main engines: Turbo-electric (Alco built diesels); 4 000 bhp; 2 shafts = 13 knots
Complement: 51

Built as T1-MET-24a type gasoline tankers by Bethlehem Steel Co, Staten Island. Bows strengthened for navigation in ice. Equipped with small helicopter deck. *Chattahoochee* transferred to the temporary custody of the Maritime Administration on 8 Aug 1972 for lay-up at Suisun Bay. *Alatna* followed on 8 Aug 1972. Both scheduled to be reacquired by the US Navy in December 1978 for reactivation and operation by MSC. Scheduled to be in service by mid-1979. Cargo capacity 30 000 barrels.

3 GASOLINE TANKERS (AOG) "PECONIC" CLASS

Name	No.	Builders	Completed	F/S
RINCON (ex-*Tarland*)	T-AOG 77	Todd Shipyards, Houston	Oct 1945	TPA
NODAWAY (ex-*Belridge*)	T-AOG 78	Todd Shipyards, Houston	Sept 1945	TPA
PETALUMA (ex-*Raccoon Bend*)	T-AOG 79	Todd Shipyards, Houston	Nov 1945	TPA

Displacement, tons: 2 100 light; 6 047 full load
Dimensions, feet (metres): 325·2 oa × 48·2 × 19·1 (99·1 × 14·7 × 5·8)
Main engine: 1 Nordberg diesel; 1 400 bhp; 1 shaft = 10 knots
Complement: 41

RINCON   USN

T1-M-BT2 gasoline tankers. Launched as merchant tankers on 5 Jan 1945, 15 May 1945 and 9 Aug 1945 respectively. All acquired by Navy 1 July 1950 (77) and 7 Sept 1950 (78 and 79) and assigned to Military Sea Transportation Service and employed in point-to-point carrying of petroleum. Cargo capacity approximately 30 000 barrels.
These are the only survivors in US service of a once large number of small gasoline tankers. Several survive in foreign navies.

2 CABLE REPAIR SHIPS (ARC) PROJECTED

Two Cable Repair Ships are programmed to be built in the five year programme (1979-83). One is to be requested under the FY 1979 programme and will replace *Thor* (ARC 4). Estimated cost $175 million. The second unit is to be requested under the FY 1981 programme as a replacement for *Aeolus* (ARC 3). Estimated cost $198 million. Characteristics not available.

1 CABLE REPAIR SHIP (ARC) "AEOLUS" CLASS

Name	No.	Builders	Commissioned
AEOLUS (ex-*Turandot*)	T-ARC 3 (ex-AKA 47)	Walsh-Kaiser Co, Providence, RI	18 June 1945

Displacement, tons: 7 810 full load
Dimensions, feet (metres): 400 wl; 438 oa × 58·2 × 19·25 (133·5 × 17·7 × 5·9)
Main engines: Turbo-electric (Westinghouse); 6 000 shp; 2 shafts = 14 knots
Boilers: 2 (Wickes)
Complement: 221 (23 officers, 198 enlisted men)

AEOLUS   USN

Built as S4-SE2-BE1 attack cargo ship. Transferred to Maritime Administration and laid up in reserve from 1946 until reacquired by Navy for conversion to cable repair ship in 1955-56 at the Key Highway Plant of Bethlehem Steel Corp, Baltimore, Maryland, being recommissioned on 14 May 1955. Fitted with cable-laying bow sheaves, cable stowage tanks, cable repair facilities, and helicopter platform aft.
Employed in hydrographic and cable operations. Naval manned until 1973 when transferred to Military Sealift Command and provided with civilian crew.

2 CABLE REPAIR SHIPS (ARC) "NEPTUNE" CLASS

Name	No.	Builders	Commissioned
NEPTUNE (ex-*William H. G. Bullard*)	T-ARC 2	Pusey & Jones Corp, Wilmington, Del	1 June 1953
ALBERT J. MEYER	T-ARC 6	Pusey & Jones Corp, Wilmington, Del	13 May 1963

Displacement, tons: 7 810 full load
Dimensions, feet (metres): 322 wl; 370 oa × 47 × 25 (112·8 × 14·3 × 7·6)
Main engines: Reciprocating (Skinner); 4 800 ihp; 2 shafts = 14 knots
Boilers: 2 (Combustion Engineering)
Complement: 173

Built as S3-S2-BP1 type cable ships for the Maritime Administration.
Neptune acquired by the Navy from the Maritime Administration in 1953 and sister ship *Albert J. Meyer* from US Army in 1966. They have been fitted with electric cable handling machinery (in place of steam equipment) and precision navigation equipment; helicopter platform in *Neptune*.
Both ships are operated by the Military Sealift Command with civilian crews; *Neptune* was Naval-manned until 8 Nov 1973 when transferred to MSC.
The USNS *Neptune* (T-ARC 2) should not be confused with the commercial cable ship *Neptun* of the United States Undersea Cable Corp.

NEPTUNE   1975, Dr. Giorgio Arra

1 + 3 + 3 FLEET TUGS (ATF) "POWHATAN" CLASS

Name	No	Builders	Commissioned	F/S
POWHATAN	T-ATF 166	Marinette Marine Corp, Wisconsin	Mid 1978	Bldg
NARRAGANSETT	T-ATF 167	Marinette Marine Corp, Wisconsin	Mid 1979	Bldg
CATAWBA	T-ATF 168	Marinette Marine Corp, Wisconsin	Mid 1979	Bldg
NAVAJO	T-ATF 169	Marinette Marine Corp, Wisconsin	Mid 1979	Bldg
Three ships	T-ATF 170 172	Approved Fiscal Year 1978 programme		

Displacement, tons: 2 400 full load
Dimensions, feet (metres): 240 × 48 × 17 (73·2 × 14·6 × 5·2)
Guns: See notes
Main engines: 2 diesels (General Motors); 4 500 bhp; 2 shafts (cp propellers) = 15 knots
Complement: 47 (43 civilians, 4 Navy communications ratings)

This is a new class of fleet tugs built to commercial standards intended as successors to "Cherokee" class. The ships will be operated by the Military Sealift Command and manned by civilian crews. Space provided to fit 2—20 mm (single) and 2—0·50 cal MG if required. A 300 hp bow thruster will be provided; 10 ton capacity crane.
Estimated cost of the lead ship is $11·5 million; an average of $15 million for the FY 1976 ships and $16 million for the FY 1978 ships. No further construction planned.

COAST GUARD

Senior Officers

Commandant:
  Admiral Owen W. Siler (to be relieved 1 July 1978)
Vice Commandant:
  Vice-Admiral Ellis L. Perry
Chief of Staff:
  Rear-Admiral James S. Gracey
Commander, Atlantic Area:
  Vice-Admiral William F. Rea, III
Commander, Pacific Area:
  Vice-Admiral Austin C. Wagner

Establishment

The United States Coast Guard was established by an Act of Congress approved 28 Jan 1915, which consolidated the Revenue Cutter Service (founded in 1790) and the Life Saving Service (founded in 1848). The act of establishment stated the Coast Guard "shall be a military service and a branch of the armed forces of the United States at all times. The Coast Guard shall be a service in the Treasury Department except when operating as a service in the Navy". Congress further legislated that in time of national emergency or when the President so directs, the Coast Guard operates as a part of the Navy. The Coast Guard did operate as a part of the Navy during the First and Second World Wars.
The Lighthouse Service (founded in 1789) was transferred to the Coast Guard on 1 July 1939. The Coast Guard was transferred to the newly established Department of Transportation on 1 April 1967.

Missions

The current missions of the Coast Guard are to (1) enforce or assist in the enforcement of applicable Federal laws upon the high seas and waters subject to the jurisdiction of the United States including environmental protection; (2) administer all Federal laws regarding safety of life and property on the high seas and on waters subject to the jurisdiction of the United States, except those laws specifically entrusted to other Federal agencies; (3) develop, establish, maintain, operate, and conduct aids to maritime navigation, ocean stations, icebreaking activities, oceanographic research, and rescue facilities; and (4) maintain a state of readiness to function as a specialised service in the Navy when so directed by the President.

Personnel

Oct 1978: 4 874 officers, 31 575 enlisted men.

Aviation

Only the larger "Hamilton" class cutters and certain classes of icebreakers can support helicopters at sea.
As of 13 Jan 1978 the Coast Guard's aviation strength consisted of 65 fixed-wing aircraft and 118 helicopters:

29	HC-130	Hercules
17	HC-131	Convair
17	HU-16	Albatross
1	VC-4A	Gulfstream I
1	VC-11A	Gulfstream II
38	HH-3F	Pelican
80	HH-52A	Sea Guard

The Coast Guard plans to acquire approximately 40 land-based patrol and rescue aircraft in the period 1979-83 to replace the long-serving HU-16 Albatross amphibians.

Cutter Strength

All Coast Guard vessels are referred to as "cutters". Cutter names are preceded by USCGC. Cutter serial numbers are prefixed with letter designations similar to the US Navy classification system with the prefix letter "W". The first two digits of serial numbers for cutters less than 100 feet in length indicate their approximate length overall. All Coast Guard cutters are active unless otherwise indicated.
Approximately 600 small rescue and utility craft also are in service.

The following table provides a tabulation of the ship strength of the United States Coast Guard. Ship arrangement is based on function and employment. Numbers of ships listed are actual as of 1 Jan 1978. Some projections of changes are also included.

Category/Classification		Active*	Reserve	New Construction
Cutters				
WHEC	High Endurance Cutters	17	1	—
WMEC	Medium Endurance Cutters	23	—	4
Icebreakers				
WAGB	Icebreaker	7		
Patrol Craft				
WPGH	Patrol Gunboat (Hydrofoil)	1	—	—
WPB	Patrol Craft, Large	75	—	—
Training Cutters				
WIX	Training Cutters	2	—	—
WTR	Reserve Training Cutter	1	—	—
Oceanographic Cutters				
WAGO	Oceanographic Cutters	2	—	—
Buoy Tenders				
WLB	Buoy Tender, Seagoing	29	4	—
WLM	Buoy Tender, Coastal	15	—	—
WLI	Buoy Tender, Inland	13	—	—
WLR	Buoy Tender, River	22	—	—
Construction Tenders				
WLIC	Construction Tender, Inland	14	—	—
Lightships				
WLV	Lightships	2	1	—
Harbour Tugs				
WYTM	Harbor Tugs, Medium	14	—	4
WYTL	Harbor Tugs, Small	15	—	—

Shipbuilding Programmes

Approved FY 1978 Programme

4 WMEC (270 ft Class)

Proposed FY 1979 Programme

2 WMEC (270 ft Class)
2 WYTM (140 ft Class)

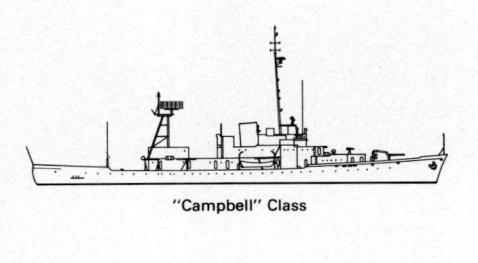

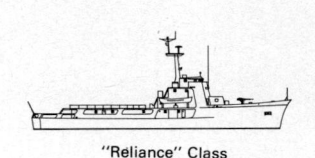

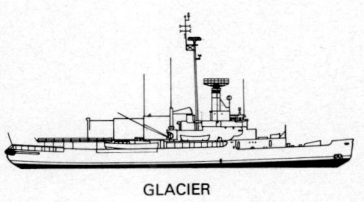

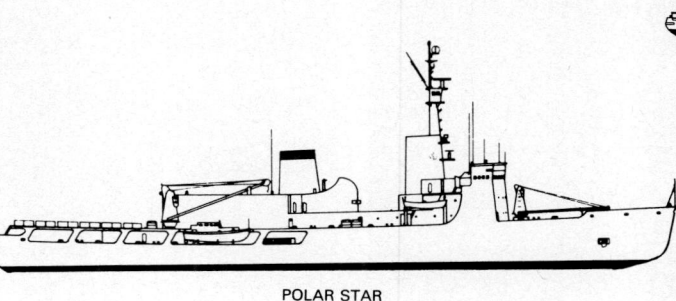

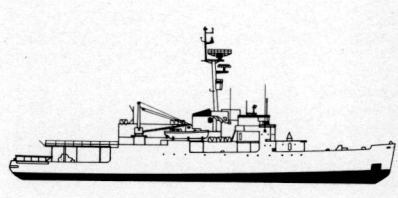

"Campbell" Class

"Reliance" Class

"Hamilton" Class

GLACIER

"Wind" Class

POLAR STAR

Scale: 1 inch = 150 feet (1 : 1 800)

Drawings, A. D. Baker III

724 USA

ICEBREAKERS

2 ICEBREAKERS (WAGB) "POLAR STAR" CLASS

Name	No.	Builders	Commissioned	F/S
POLAR STAR	WAGB 10	Lockheed Shipbuilding Co, Seattle, Wash	17 Jan 1976	PA
POLAR SEA	WAGB 11	Lockheed Shipbuilding Co, Seattle, Wash	23 Feb 1978	PA

Displacement, tons: 12 087 full load
Dimensions, feet (metres): 399 oa × 86 × 31 (121·6 × 26·2 × 9·5)
Helicopters: 2 HH-52A
Guns: None
Main engines: Diesel-electric; 6 ALCO diesels; 18 000 shp; 3 gas turbines (Pratt & Whitney FT4A-12); 60 000 shp; 3 shafts (cp propellers) = 18 knots
Range, miles: 28 000 at 13 knots
Complement: 148 (13 officers, 125 enlisted men) plus 10 scientists

These ships are the first icebreakers built for US service since *Glacier* was constructed two decades earlier. The programme is intended to replace the World War II-built "Wind" class icebreakers. *Polar Star* authorised in the Fiscal Year 1971 budget of the Department of Transportation; *Polar Sea* in the FY 1973 budget. *Polar Star* was laid down on 15 May 1972 and launched on 17 Nov 1973; *Polar Sea* was laid down on 27 Nov 1973 and launched on 24 June 1975. No additional ships are planned for the near future. *Polar Star* based at Seattle.

Design: The "Polar Star" class icebreakers are the largest ships operated by the US Coast Guard. At a continuous speed of 3 knots these ships can break ice 6 feet thick and by riding on the ice they can break 21 feet pack.
These ships have a conventional icebreaker hull form with cutaway bow configuration and well rounded body sections to prevent being trapped in ice. Two 15-ton capacity cranes fitted aft; hangar and flight deck aft; extensive research laboratories provided for arctic and oceanographic research.

Engineering: This CODOG design provides for conventional diesel engines for normal cruising in field ice and gas turbines for heavy icebreaking. The diesel engines drive generators producing AC power; the main propulsion DC motors draw power through rectifiers permitting absolute flexibility in the delivery of power from alternate sources. The use of controllable-pitch propellers on three shafts will permit manoeuvring in heavy ice without the risk to the propeller blades caused by stopping the shaft while going from ahead to astern. The Coast Guard had given consideration to the use of nuclear power for an icebreaker; however, at this time the gas turbine-diesel combination can achieve the desirable power requirements without the added cost and operating restrictions of a nuclear powerplant. From Jan 1976 until Nov 1977 (her first deployment) *Polar Star* had serious engineering problems which resulted in her being alongside for most of that period.

Gunnery: Two single 40 mm and four 20 mm guns to be fitted.

POLAR STAR   6/1976, United States Coast Guard

POLAR STAR   6/1976, United States Coast Guard

1 ICEBREAKER (WAGB) "GLACIER" CLASS

Name	No.	Builders	USN Commissioned	F/S
GLACIER	WAGB 4 (ex-AGB 4)	Ingalls Shipbuilding Corp, Pascagoula, Mississippi	27 May 1955	PA

Displacement, tons: 8 449 full load
Dimensions, feet (metres): 309·6 oa × 74 × 29 (94·4 × 6·9 × 8·8)
Helicopters: 2 helicopters normally embarked
Main engines: Diesel-electric (10 Fairbanks-Morse diesels and 2 Westinghouse electric motors); 21 000 hp; 2 shafts = 17·6 knots
Range, miles: 29 200 at 12 knots; 12 000 at 17·6 knots
Complement: 241 (15 officers, 226 enlisted men)

The largest icebreaker in US service prior to the "Polar Star" class; laid down on 3 Aug 1953 and launched on 27 Aug 1954. Transferred from Navy (AGB 4) to Coast Guard on 30 June 1966. During 1972 *Glacier* and assigned helicopters were painted red to improve visibility in Arctic regions. All other icebreakers painted red during 1973.

Engineering: When built *Glacier* had the largest capacity single-armature DC motors ever built and installed in a ship.

Gunnery: As built *Glacier* was armed with two 5 in guns (twin), six 3 in guns (twin), and four 20 mm guns; lighter weapons removed prior to transfer to Coast Guard; 5 in guns removed in 1969. Two single 40 mm guns to be fitted.

GLACIER   1976, John A. Jedrlinic

USA 725

3 ICEBREAKERS (WAGB) "WIND" CLASS

Name	No.	Builders	Launched	F/S
WESTWIND	WAGB 281 (ex-AGB 6)	Western Pipe & Steel Co, San Pedro, California	31 Mar 1943	GLA
NORTHWIND	WAGB 282	Western Pipe & Steel Co, San Pedro, California	25 Feb 1945	AA
BURTON ISLAND	WAGB 283 (ex-AGB 1, ex-AG 88)	Western Pipe & Steel Co, San Pedro, California	30 April 1946	PA

Displacement, tons: 3 500 standard; 6 515 full load
Dimensions, feet (metres): 250 wl; 269 oa × 63·5 × 29 *(82·0 × 19·4 × 8·8)*
Helicopters: 2 helicopters normally embarked (HH 52 A)
Main engines: Diesel-electric; 4 diesels (Fairbanks-Morse 38D81/8—283, Enterprise—281, 282); 10 000 bhp; 2 shafts = 16 knots
Range, miles: 38 000 at 10·5 knots; 16 000 at 16 knots
Complement: 135

Originally seven ships in this class built. Five ships were delivered to the US Coast Guard during World War II and two to the US Navy in 1946. *Westwind* served in the Soviet Navy from 1945 to 1951 (named *Severni Polus* in Soviet service). *Burton Island* was transferred from the US Navy to the Coast Guard on 15 Dec 1966.
Westwind operates on the Great Lakes. *Burton Island* was scheduled to be assigned to Office of Naval Research on Oct 31 1977 for use in Arctic trials. This plan was cancelled due to the recurrent problems in *Polar Star*. She is now due to decommission in April 1978 although this may be delayed indefinitely until the difficulties with the "Polar Star" class are resolved. Crews of *Northwind* and *Westwind* reduced from 181 to approx 135 during 1975.

Engineering: These ships were built with a bow propeller shaft in addition to the two stern shafts; bow shaft removed from all units because it would continually break in heavy ice. *Westwind* re-engined in 1973-74, and *Northwind* in 1974-75.

Gunnery: As built the five Coast Guard ships each mounted four 5 in guns (one twin mount forward and one twin mount aft on 01 level) and twelve 40 mm guns (quad); the two Navy Ships were completed with only forward twin 5 in mount (as built a catapult and cranes were fitted immediately abaft the funnel and one floatplane was carried). Armament reduced after war and helicopter platform eventually installed in all ships.
During the 1960s *Northwind* carried two 5 in guns (twin), and the other ships each mounted one 5 in gun; all primary gun batteries removed in 1969-70. Two single 40 mm guns to be shipped in *Westwind* and *Northwind*.

WESTWIND   *2/1976, United States Coast Guard*

1 ICEBREAKER (WAGB) "MACKINAW" CLASS

Name	No.	Builders	Commissioned	F/S
MACKINAW (ex-*Manitowac*)	WAGB 83	Toledo Shipbuilding Co, Ohio	20 Dec 1944	GLA

Displacement, tons: 5 252
Dimensions, feet (metres): 290 oa × 74 × 19 *(88·4 × 22·6 × 5·8)*
Helicopters: 1 helicopter
Main engines: 2 diesels (Fairbanks-Morse); with electric drive (Elliot); 3 shafts (1 forward, 2 aft); 10 000 bhp = 18·7 knots
Range, miles: 60 000 at 12 knots; 10 000 at 18·7 knots
Complement: 127 (10 officers, 117 enlisted men)

Laid down on 20 March 1943; launched 6 March 1944 and completed in Jan 1945. Specially designed and constructed for service as icebreaker on the Great Lakes. Equipped with two 12-ton capacity cranes. Clear area for helicopter is provided on the quarterdeck.

MACKINAW   *United States Coast Guard*

1 MEDIUM ENDURANCE CUTTER (WMEC) "STORIS" CLASS

Name	No.	Builders	Commissioned	F/S
STORIS (ex-*Eskimo*)	WMEC 38 (ex-WAGB 38)	Toledo Shipbuilding Co, Ohio	30 Sept 1942	PA

Displacement, tons: 1 715 standard; 1 925 full load
Dimensions, feet (metres): 230 oa × 43 × 15 *(70·1 × 13·1 × 4·6)*
Guns: 2—40 mm single MR64
Main engines: Diesel-electric; 1 shaft; 1 800 bhp = 14 knots
Range, miles: 22 000 at 8 knots; 12 000 at 14 knots
Complement: 106 (10 officers, 96 enlisted men)

Laid down on 14 July 1941; launched on 4 April 1942. Ice patrol tender. Strengthened for ice navigation and sometimes employed as icebreaker. Employed in Alaskan service for search, rescue and law enforcement.
Designation changed from WAG to WAGB on 1 May 1966; redesignated as medium endurance cutter (WMEC) on 1 July 1972.

STORIS   *1975, United States Coast Guard*

726 USA

HIGH ENDURANCE CUTTERS

12 HIGH ENDURANCE CUTTERS (WHEC) "HAMILTON" and "HERO" CLASSES

Name	No.	Builders	Laid down	Launched	Commissioned	F/S
HAMILTON	WHEC 715	Avondale Shipyards Inc, New Orleans, Louisiana	Jan 1965	18 Dec 1965	20 Feb 1967	AA
DALLAS	WHEC 716	Avondale Shipyards Inc, New Orleans, Louisiana	7 Feb 1966	1 Oct 1966	1 Oct 1967	AA
MELLON	WHEC 717	Avondale Shipyards Inc, New Orleans, Louisiana	25 July 1966	11 Feb 1967	22 Dec 1967	PA
CHASE	WHEC 718	Avondale Shipyards Inc, New Orleans, Louisiana	15 Oct 1966	20 May 1967	1 Mar 1968	AA
BOUTWELL	WHEC 719	Avondale Shipyards Inc, New Orleans, Louisiana	12 Dec 1966	17 June 1967	14 June 1968	PA
SHERMAN	WHEC 720	Avondale Shipyards Inc, New Orleans, Louisiana	13 Feb 1967	23 Sept 1967	23 Aug 1968	AA
GALLANTIN	WHEC 721	Avondale Shipyards Inc, New Orleans, Louisiana	17 April 1967	18 Nov 1967	20 Dec 1968	AA
MORGENTHAU	WHEC 722	Avondale Shipyards Inc, New Orleans, Louisiana	17 July 1967	10 Feb 1968	14 Feb 1969	AA
RUSH	WHEC 723	Avondale Shipyards Inc, New Orleans, Louisiana	23 Oct 1967	16 Nov 1968	3 July 1969	AA
MUNRO	WHEC 724	Avondale Shipyards Inc, New Orleans, Louisiana	18 Feb 1970	5 Dec 1970	10 Sept 1971	PA
JARVIS	WHEC 725	Avondale Shipyards Inc, New Orleans, Louisiana	9 Sept 1970	24 April 1971	30 Dec 1971	PA
MIDGETT	WHEC 726	Avondale Shipyards Inc, New Orleans, Louisiana	5 April 1971	4 Sept 1971	17 Mar 1972	PA

Displacement, tons: 2 716 standard; 3 050 full load
Length, feet (metres): 350 wl; 378 oa *(115·2)*
Beam, feet (metres): 42·8 *(13·1)*
Draught, feet (metres): 20 *(6·1)*
Guns: 1—5 in *(127 mm)* 38 cal (Mk 30); 2—20 mm in 715, 716, 718, 720-722; 2—81 mm mortars in remainder; 2—0·50 MGs
A/S weapons: 2 triple topedo tubes (Mk 32)
Helicopters: 1 HH-52A or HH-3 helicopter
Main engines: Combined diesel and gas turbine (CODAG): 2 diesels (Fairbanks-Morse) 7 000 bhp; 2 gas turbines (Pratt & Whitney FT-4A), 28 000 shp; aggregate 36 000 hp; 2 shafts (cp propellers)
Speed, knots: 29
Range, miles: 14 000 at 11 knots (diesels); 2 400 at 29 knots (gas)
Complement: 164 (15 officers, 149 enlisted men)

All active.

Anti-submarine armament: Hedgehog anti-submarine weapons have been removed from earlier ships during overhaul and Mk 309 fire control system for Mk 32 torpedo tubes are installed. Hedgehogs deleted in later ships. *Hamilton* was first to drop hedgehogs and receive Mk 309 during 1970 overhaul.

Design: These ships have clipper bows, twin funnels enclosing a helicopter hangar, helicopter platform aft. All are fitted with oceanographic laboratories, elaborate communications equipment, and meteorological data gathering facilities. Superstructure is largely of aluminium construction. Bridge control of manoeuvring is by aircraft-type joy-stick rather than wheel.

Engineering: The "Hamiltons" were the largest US "military" ships with gas turbine propulsion prior to the Navy's "Spruance" class destroyers. The Fairbanks-Morse diesels are 12 cylinder.
Engine and propeller pitch consoles are located in wheelhouse and at bridge wing stations as well as engine room control booth.
A retractable bow propulsion unit is provided for station keeping and precise manoeuvring (unit is located directly forward of bridge, immediately aft of sonar dome).

Gunnery: Planned to ship 2—40 mm guns in all vessels and to replace 2—81 mm mortars with 2—20 mm in ships still carrying them. Mk 56 GFCS and SPG 35 fire control radar.

Radar: Search: SPS 29 and 51.

Sonar: SQS 38.

SHERMAN 5/1975, USN

MORGENTHAU 7/1976, A. D. Baker III

CHASE 1976, Michael D. J. Lennon

USA 727

6 HIGH ENDURANCE CUTTERS (WHEC) "CAMPBELL" (327 ft) CLASS

Name	No.	Builders	Laid down	Launched	Commissioned	F/S
BIBB (ex-*George M. Bibb*)	WHEC 31	Charleston Navy Yard	10 May 1935	14 Jan 1937	10 Mar 1937	AA
CAMPBELL (ex-*George W. Campbell*)	WHEC 32	Philadelphia Navy Yard	1 May 1935	3 June 1936	16 June 1936	PA
DUANE (ex-*William J. Duane*)	WHEC 33	Philadelphia Navy Yard	1 May 1935	3 June 1936	16 Aug 1936	AA
INGHAM (ex-*Samuel D. Ingham*)	WHEC 35	Philadelphia Navy Yard	1 May 1935	3 June 1936	12 Sept 1936	AA
SPENCER (ex-*John C. Spencer*)	WHEC 36	New York Navy Yard	11 Sept 1935	3 Jan 1936	1 Mar 1937	AR
TANEY (ex-*Roger B. Taney*)	WHEC 37	Philadelphia Navy Yard	1 May 1935	3 June 1936	20 Nov 1936	AA

Displacement, tons: 2 216 standard; 2 656 full load
Length, feet (metres): 308 wl; 327 oa *(99·7)*
Beam, feet (metres): 41 *(12·5)*
Draught, feet (metres): 15 *(4·6)*
Guns: 1—5 in *(127 mm)* 38 cal (Mk 30); 2—81 mm mortars (except 35) see notes
A/S weapons: Removed
Main engines: Geared turbines (Westinghouse); 6 200 shp; 2 shafts
Boilers: 2 (Babcock & Wilcox)
Speed, knots: 19·8
Range, miles: 4 000 at 20 knots; 8 000 at 10·5 knots
Complement: 144 (13 officers, 131 enlisted men)

These were the Coast Guard's largest cutters until *Hamilton* was completed in 1967.
Duane served as an amphibious force flagship during the invasion of Southern France in August 1944 and was designated AGC 6 (Coast Guard manned); the other ships of this class, except the lost *Alexander Hamilton* (PG 34), were similarly employed but retained Coast Guard number with WAGC prefix (amidships structure built up and one or two additional masts installed); all reverted to gunboat configuration after war (WPG designation). Redesignated WHEC on 1 May 1966.
All of these cutters remain in active service except *Spencer*, decommissioned on 1 Feb 1974 and placed in reserve at the Coast Guard Yard, Curtis Bay, Maryland. *Spencer* is employed as a non-operable engineering school ship.
Taney mans weather station "Hotel" off Norfolk, Va. WSR-S1 storm tracking radar in dome.

Anti-submarine armament: During the 1960s these ships each had an ASW armament of one ahead-firing fixed hedgehog and two Mk 32 triple torpedo tube mounts; subsequently removed from all ships.

Gunnery: As built these ships had two 5 in 51 cal guns (single mounts forward) and two 6 pdr guns; rearmed during World War II with an additional single 5 in 51 cal gun installed aft plus two or three 3 in 50 cal anti-aircraft guns, and several 20 mm anti-aircraft guns (depth charge racks installed); *Taney* was experimentally armed with four 5 in 38 cal guns in single mounts. Present armament fitted after World War II.
Planned to fit all of class with 2—40 mm Mk 64 (single) and 2—20 mm Mk 67 (single) the latter replacing the 2—81 mm mortars. 20 mm shift already done in *Ingham, Bibb* and *Duane*.

TANEY   1975, United States Coast Guard

INGHAM   6/1976, C. and S. Taylor

1 HIGH ENDURANCE CUTTER (WHEC) "CASCO" (311 ft) CLASS

Name	No.	Builders	Laid down	Launched	Commissioned	F/S
UNIMAK	WHEC 379 (ex-WTR 379, ex-WHEC 379, ex-AVP 31)	Associated Shipbuilders, Seattle, Wash	15 Feb 1942	27 May 1942	31 Dec 1943	AA

Displacement, tons: 1 766 standard; 2 800 full load
Length, feet (metres): 300 wl; 310·75 oa *(94·7)*
Beam, feet (metres): 41 *(12·5)*
Draught, feet (metres): 13·5 *(4·1)*
Guns: 1—5 in *(127 mm)* 38 cal; 2—81 mm mortars
A/S weapons: Removed
Main engines: Diesels (Fairbanks-Morse); 6 080 bhp; 2 shafts
Speed, knots: 18
Range, miles: 8 000 at 18 knots
Complement: 150 (13 officers; 137 enlisted men)

Unimak is the sole survivor of 18 former Navy seaplane tenders (AVP) transferred to the Coast Guard in 1946-48 (WAVP/WHEC 370-387). *Unimak* operated as a training cutter (WTR) from 1969 until decommissioned on 30 May 1975 at Baltimore. Replaced by *Reliance* WTR 615. Towed to Boston in Jan 1977 for reactivation which was delayed by a serious engine-room fire. Recommissioned 15 Aug 1977 to assist in patrolling the 200 mile EEZ. Due to her age and engineering problems in wake of the fire her active career may be short.

Classification: The former Navy AVPs were designated WAVP by the Coast Guard until changed to high endurance cutters (WHEC) on 1 May 1966. *Unimak* subsequently became a training cutter (WTR) on 28 Nov 1969. Reclassified WHEC on 15 Aug 1977.

Transfers: Ships of this class (originally "Barnegat" class) serve in the navies of Ethiopia, Italy, Philippines and Viet-Nam.

UNIMAK   1970, United States Coast Guard

728 USA

MEDIUM ENDURANCE CUTTERS

0 + 4 + 9 MEDIUM ENDURANCE CUTTERS (WMEC) "270-foot" CLASS

Name	No.	Builders	Commissioned	F/S
BEAR	WMEC 901	Tacoma Boatbuilding Co Inc, Wash	Early 1981	Bldg
TAMPA	WMEC 902	Tacoma Boatbuilding Co Inc, Wash	Mid 1981	Bldg
HARRIET LANE	WMEC 903	Tacoma Boatbuilding Co Inc, Wash	Late 1981	Bldg
NORTHLAND	WMEC 904	Tacoma Boatbuilding Co Inc, Wash	Early 1982	Bldg
2 ships	905-6	Requested FY 1979		
7 ships (minimum)	—	Planned FY 1980-84		

Displacement, tons: 1 780 full load
Dimensions, feet (metres): 270 oa × 38 × 13·5 (82·3 × 11·6 × 4·1)
Helicopters: 1 HH-52A or 1 LAMPS III
Gun: 1—76 mm 62 calibre (Mk 75) OTO-Melara (single)
A/S weapons: See notes
Main engines: Diesels; 7 000 bhp; 2 shafts = 19·5 knots
Complement: 95 (13 officers, 82 enlisted men)

The Coast Guard plans to construct up to 25 medium endurance cutters of this class over a seven-year period. They will replace the "Campbell" class and other older medium and high endurance cutters when they become operational from about 1981 onwards.

A/S weapons: These ships will have no shipboard A/S weapons, but will rely on helicopters to deliver torpedoes against submarines detected by the ships' towed sonar array.

Design: They will be the only medium endurance cutters with helicopter hangars, and the first cutters with automated command and control centre. Fin stabilisers to be fitted.

Electronics: Fitted with Mk 92 weapons control system, easily identified by radome atop pilot house. These ships will not have hull-mounted sonar, but instead the tactical Towed Array Sonar System (TTASS), capable of providing long-range targeting data for A/S helicopter attack.

Engineering: Diesels were selected over gas turbine propulsion because of the Coast Guard requirement for long on-station time at slow speeds vice high-speed naval operations.

Fiscal: The Coast Guard Fiscal Year 1977 programme provides $49 million for the first two ships of this class.

Gunnery: Weight and space for CIWS.

Helicopters: The design is sized to accommodate the HH-52 Sea Guard helicopter or its Coast Guard successor, or the Navy's planned LAMPS III (Light Airborne Multi-Purpose System) helicopter. The helicopter hangar is extendable. Weight and space reserved for helicopter landing and traversing system.

Missiles: Weight and space reserved for Harpoon.

Names: Others approved: *Seneca, Pickering, Escanaba, Legare* and *Argus*.

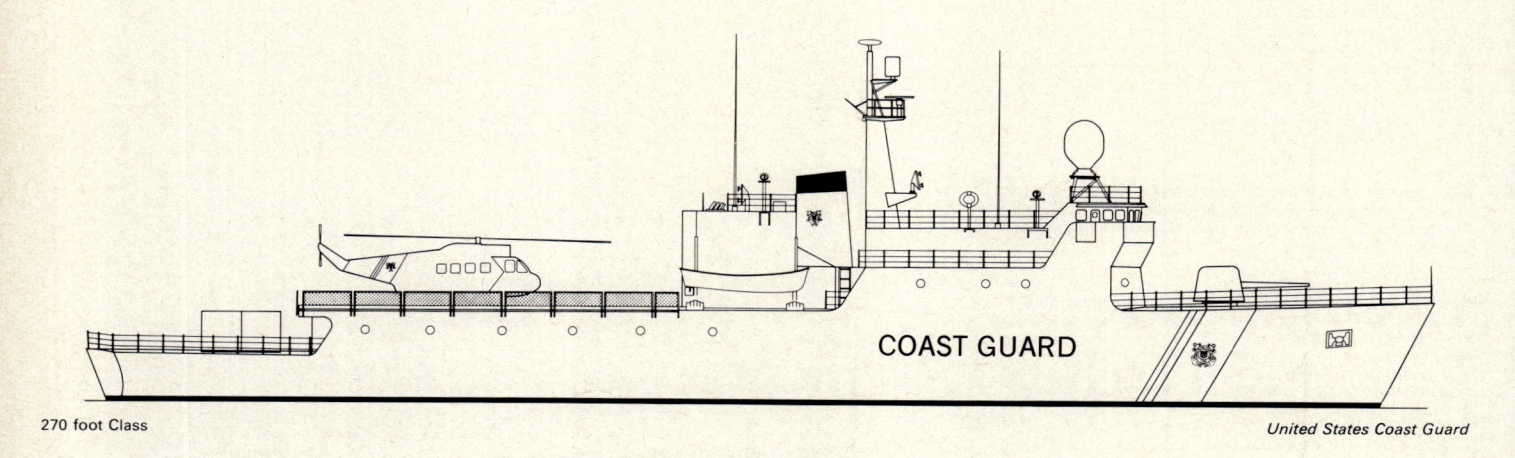

270 foot Class United States Coast Guard

15 MEDIUM ENDURANCE CUTTERS (WMEC) } "RELIANCE" (210 ft) CLASS
1 TRAINING CUTTER (WTR)

Name	No.	Builders	Commissioned	F/S
RELIANCE	WTR 615	Todd Shipyards	20 June 1964	AA
DILIGENCE	WMEC 616	Todd Shipyards	26 Aug 1964	AA
VIGILANT	WMEC 617	Todd Shipyards	3 Oct 1964	AA
ACTIVE	WMEC 618	Christy Corp	17 Sept 1966	AA
CONFIDENCE	WMEC 619	Coast Guard Yard, Curtis Bay, Baltimore	19 Feb 1966	PA
RESOLUTE	WMEC 620	American Shipbuilding Co	8 Dec 1966	PA
VALIANT	WMEC 621	American Shipbuilding Co	28 Oct 1967	AA
COURAGEOUS	WMEC 622	American Shipbuilding Co	10 April 1968	AA
STEADFAST	WMEC 623	American Shipbuilding Co	25 Sept 1968	AA
DAUNTLESS	WMEC 624	American Shipbuilding Co	10 June 1968	AA
VENTUROUS	WMEC 625	Coast Guard Yard, Curtis Bay, Baltimore	16 Aug 1968	PA
DEPENDABLE	WMEC 626	American Shipbuilding Co	22 Nov 1968	AA
VIGOROUS	WMEC 627	American Shipbuilding Co	2 May 1969	AA
DURABLE	WMEC 628	Coast Guard Yard, Curtis Bay, Baltimore	8 Dec 1967	AA
DECISIVE	WMEC 629	Coast Guard Yard, Curtis Bay, Baltimore	23 Aug 1968	AA
ALERT	WMEC 630	American Shipbuilding Co	4 Aug 1969	AA

Displacement, tons: 950 standard; 1 007 full load (except WTR and WMEC 616-619, 970 full load)
Dimensions, feet (metres): 210·5 oa × 34 × 10·5 (64·2 × 10·4 × 3·2)
Guns: 1—3 in (76 mm) 50 calibre; 2—40 mm singles (Mk 64) (see *Gunnery* note)
Helicopters: 1 HH-52A helicopter embarked for missions
Main engines: 2 turbo-charged diesels (ALCO 251B); 2 shafts; 5 000 bhp = 18 knots (WTR 615 and WMEC 616-619 have 2 Solar gas turbines in addition (4 000 shp))
Range, miles: 6 100 at 13 knots (615-619); 6 100 at 14 knots; 2 700 at 18 knots (remainder)
Complement: 61 (7 officers, 54 enlisted men)

Designed for search and rescue duties. Design features include 360 degree visibility from wheelhouse; helicopter flight deck (no hangar); and engine exhaust vent at stern in place of conventional funnel. Capable of towing ships up to 10 000 tons. Air-conditioned throughout except engine room; high degree of habitability.
Launched, respectively, on the following dates: 25 May 1963, 20 July 1963, 24 Dec 1963, 21 July 1965, 8 May 1965, 30 April 1966, 14 Jan 1967, 18 March 1967, 24 June 1967, 21 Oct 1967, 11 Nov 1967, 16 March 1968, 4 May 1968, 29 April 1967, 14 Dec 1967, 19 Oct 1968.
All these cutters are active. *Reliance* is the Coast Guard's reserve training cutter based at Yorktown, Virginia, and retains full search, rescue, and patrol capabilities.

Designation: These ships were originally designated as patrol craft (WPC); changed to WMEC on 1 May 1966.

Gunnery: Two 20 mm single (Mk 67) to be fitted in all ships.

Helicopters: *Alert* was the first US ship fitted with the Canadian-developed "Beartrap" helicopter hauldown system. No further procurement of this system has been funded.

VIGILANT

9/1976, Dr. Giorgio Arra

USA 729

1 PATROL GUNBOAT (HYDROFOIL) (WPGH) "FLAGSTAFF" CLASS

Name	No.	Builders	USN In Service	F/S
FLAGSTAFF	WPGH 1	Grumman Aircraft Corp, Stuart, Fla.	14 Sept 1968	AA

Displacement, tons: 56·8 full load
Dimensions, feet (metres): 74·4 oa *(22·7)* × 21·4 *(6·2)* × 4·5 *(1·4)* (foils retracted) or 13·5 *(4·1)* (foils extended)
Guns: 1—81 mm mortar; 2—0·50 cal machine guns
Main engines: foil borne: 1 gas turbine (Rolls-Royce Tyne Mk 621); 3 620 hp;
  cp propeller = 40+ knots
  hull borne: 2 diesels (Packard); 300 bhp; water-jet propulsion = 8 knots
Complement: 13 (1 officer, 12 enlisted men)

Flagstaff was a competitive prototype evaluated with *Tucumcari* (PGH 2). Laid down 15 July 1966 and launched 9 Jan 1968. Construction cost was $3·6 million. She has conducted sea trials with a 152 mm howitzer (see *Gunnery* notes), foil-mounted sonars, and towed shapes representing Variable Depth Sonar (VDS). From 1 Nov 1974 to 20 Dec 1974, She was evaluated by the Coast Guard to determine possible roles for this type of craft and was transferred to the Coast Guard permanently on 29 Sept 1976. After running evaluation tests out of Wood's Hole, Mass, she was commissioned on 2 March 1977 for duty in patrolling the new 200 mile fishing and conservation zone with *Unimak* (WHEC-379).

Design: *Flagstaff* has a conventional foil arrangement with 70 per cent of the craft's weight supported by the forward set of foils and 30 per cent of the weight supported by the stern foils. Steering is accomplished by movement of the stern strut about its vertical axis. Foil-borne operation is automatically controlled by a wave-height sensing system. The foils are fully retractable for hull-borne operations. Aluminium construction.

Engineering: During foil-borne operation the propeller is driven by a geared transmission system contained in the tail strut, and in the pod located at the strut-foil connection. During hull borne operation two diesel engines drive a water-jet propulsion system. Water enters the pump inlets through openings in the hull and the thrust is exerted by water flow through nozzles in the transome. Steering in the hull-borne mode is by deflection vanes in the water stream.

Gunnery: Originally armed with one 40 mm gun forward, four 0·50 cal MG amidships, and an 81 mm mortar aft. Rearmed in 1971 with a 152 mm gun forward. After firing trials in 1971 the gun was removed. As a Coast Guard craft she carries the same armament as a WPB of the "Point" or "Cape" Class.

FLAGSTAFF 1974, United States Coast Guard

22 PATROL CRAFT—LARGE (WPB) "CAPE" CLASS

Name	No.	Builders	F/S
"A" Series			
CAPE SMALL	95300	Coast Guard Yard, Curtis Bay, Maryland	PA
CAPE CORAL	95301	Coast Guard Yard, Curtis Bay, Maryland	PA
CAPE GEORGE	95306	Coast Guard Yard, Curtis Bay, Maryland	AA
CAPE CURRENT	95307	Coast Guard Yard, Curtis Bay, Maryland	AA
CAPE STRAIT	95308	Coast Guard Yard, Curtis Bay, Maryland	AA
CAPE CARTER	95309	Coast Guard Yard, Curtis Bay, Maryland	PA
CAPE WASH	95310	Coast Guard Yard, Curtis Bay, Maryland	PA
CAPE HEDGE	95311	Coast Guard Yard, Curtis Bay, Maryland	PA
"B" Series			
CAPE KNOX	95312	Coast Guard Yard, Curtis Bay, Maryland	AA
CAPE MORGAN	95313	Coast Guard Yard, Curtis Bay, Maryland	AA
CAPE FAIRWEATHER	95314	Coast Guard Yard, Curtis Bay, Maryland	AA
CAPE FOX	95316	Coast Guard Yard, Curtis Bay, Maryland	AA
CAPE JELLISON	95317	Coast Guard Yard, Curtis Bay, Maryland	AA
CAPE NEWAGEN	95318	Coast Guard Yard, Curtis Bay, Maryland	PA
CAPE ROMAIN	95319	Coast Guard Yard, Curtis Bay, Maryland	PA
CAPE STARR	95320	Coast Guard Yard, Curtis Bay, Maryland	AA
"C" Series			
CAPE CROSS	95321	Coast Guard Yard, Curtis Bay, Maryland	AA
CAPE HORN	95322	Coast Guard Yard, Curtis Bay, Maryland	AA
CAPE SHOALWATER	95324	Coast Guard Yard, Curtis Bay, Maryland	AA
CAPE CORWIN	95326	Coast Guard Yard, Curtis Bay, Maryland	PA
CAPE HENLOPEN	95328	Coast Guard Yard, Curtis Bay, Maryland	AA
CAPE YORK	95332	Coast Guard Yard, Curtis Bay, Maryland	AA

Displacement, tons: 105
Dimensions, feet (metres): 95 oa × 20 × 6 *(29·0 × 6·1 × 1·8)*
Guns: 1—81 mm mortar and 2—0·50 cal MG or 2—0·50 cal MG
Main engines: 4 diesels (Cummings); 2 324 bhp; 2 shafts = 20 knots
Range, miles: 2 600 (A series); 3 000 (B series); 2 800 (C series); all at 9 knots (economical); 460 at 20 knots (C Series 500 at 21 knots)
Complement: 14 (1 officer, 13 enlisted men)

Designed for port security, search, and rescue. Steel hulled. A series built in 1953; B series in 1955-56, and C series in 1958-59.
Plans to dispose of this class from 1974-75 onward in favour of new WPB construction have been cancelled; instead all 22 remaining units will be modernised (see below). Eight "Cape" class cutters serve in the South Korean Navy.

Modernisation: All 22 units will be modernised to extend their service life for an estimated ten years. Cost in 1976 was estimated at $500 000 per cutter. They will receive new engines, electronics, and deck equipment; superstructure will be modified or replaced; and habitability will be improved. The programme will begin in July 1977 and complete by 1981. Each unit will take five months to modernise. This modernisation replaces the planned construction of a new class of Patrol Craft.

CAPE FAIRWEATHER 7/1976, A. D. Baker III

730 USA

53 PATROL CRAFT—LARGE (WPB) "POINT" CLASS

Name	No.	Builders	F/S
"A" Series			
POINT HOPE	82302	Coast Guard Yard, Curtis Bay, Maryland	AA
POINT VERDE	82311	Coast Guard Yard, Curtis Bay, Maryland	AA
POINT SWIFT	82312	Coast Guard Yard, Curtis Bay, Maryland	AA
POINT THATCHER	82314	Coast Guard Yard, Curtis Bay, Maryland	AA
"C" Series			
POINT HERRON	82318	Coast Guard Yard, Curtis Bay, Maryland	AA
POINT ROBERTS	82332	Coast Guard Yard, Curtis Bay, Maryland	AA
POINT HIGHLAND	82333	Coast Guard Yard, Curtis Bay, Maryland	AA
POINT LEDGE	82334	Coast Guard Yard, Curtis Bay, Maryland	PA
POINT COUNTESS	82335	Coast Guard Yard, Curtis Bay, Maryland	PA
POINT GLASS	82336	Coast Guard Yard, Curtis Bay, Maryland	PA
POINT DIVIDE	82337	Coast Guard Yard, Curtis Bay, Maryland	PA
POINT BRIDGE	82338	Coast Guard Yard, Curtis Bay, Maryland	PA
POINT CHICO	82339	Coast Guard Yard, Curtis Bay, Maryland	PA
POINT BATAN	82340	Coast Guard Yard, Curtis Bay, Maryland	AA
POINT LOOKOUT	82341	Coast Guard Yard, Curtis Bay, Maryland	AA
POINT BAKER	82342	Coast Guard Yard, Curtis Bay, Maryland	AA
POINT WELLS	82343	Coast Guard Yard, Curtis Bay, Maryland	AA
POINT ESTERO	82344	Coast Guard Yard, Curtis Bay, Maryland	AA
POINT JUDITH	82345	Martinac SB, Tacoma, Washington	PA
POINT ARENA	82346	Martinac SB, Tacoma, Washington	AA
POINT BONITA	82347	Martinac SB, Tacoma, Washington	AA
POINT BARROW	82348	Martinac SB, Tacoma, Washington	PA
POINT SPENCER	82349	Martinac SB, Tacoma, Washington	AA
POINT FRANKLIN	82350	Coast Guard Yard, Curtis Bay, Maryland	AA
POINT BENNETT	82351	Coast Guard Yard, Curtis Bay, Maryland	PA
POINT SAL	82352	Coast Guard Yard, Curtis Bay, Maryland	AA
POINT MONROE	82353	Coast Guard Yard, Curtis Bay, Maryland	AA
POINT EVANS	82354	Coast Guard Yard, Curtis Bay, Maryland	PA
POINT HANNON	82355	Coast Guard Yard, Curtis Bay, Maryland	AA
POINT FRANCIS	82356	Coast Guard Yard, Curtis Bay, Maryland	AA
POINT HURON	82357	Coast Guard Yard, Curtis Bay, Maryland	AA
POINT STUART	82358	Coast Guard Yard, Curtis Bay, Maryland	PA
POINT STEELE	82359	Coast Guard Yard, Curtis Bay, Maryland	AA
POINT WINSLOW	82360	Coast Guard Yard, Curtis Bay, Maryland	PA
POINT CHARLES	82361	Coast Guard Yard, Curtis Bay, Maryland	AA
POINT BROWN	82362	Coast Guard Yard, Curtis Bay, Maryland	AA
POINT NOWELL	82363	Coast Guard Yard, Curtis Bay, Maryland	AA
POINT WHITEHORN	82364	Coast Guard Yard, Curtis Bay, Maryland	AA
POINT TURNER	82365	Coast Guard Yard, Curtis Bay, Maryland	AA
POINT LOBOS	82366	Coast Guard Yard, Curtis Bay, Maryland	AA
POINT KNOLL	82367	Coast Guard Yard, Curtis Bay, Maryland	AA
POINT WARDE	82368	Coast Guard Yard, Curtis Bay, Maryland	AA
POINT HEYER	82369	Coast Guard Yard, Curtis Bay, Maryland	PA
POINT RICHMOND	82370	Coast Guard Yard, Curtis Bay, Maryland	AA
"D" Series			
POINT BARNES	82371	Coast Guard Yard, Curtis Bay, Maryland	AA
POINT BROWER	82372	Coast Guard Yard, Curtis Bay, Maryland	PA
POINT CAMDEN	82373	Coast Guard Yard, Curtis Bay, Maryland	AA
POINT CARREW	82374	Coast Guard Yard, Curtis Bay, Maryland	PA
POINT DORAN	82375	Coast Guard Yard, Curtis Bay, Maryland	PA
POINT HARRIS	82376	Coast Guard Yard, Curtis Bay, Maryland	PA
POINT HOBART	82377	Coast Guard Yard, Curtis Bay, Maryland	PA
POINT JACKSON	82378	Coast Guard Yard, Curtis Bay, Maryland	AA
POINT MARTIN	82379	Coast Guard Yard, Curtis Bay, Maryland	AA

POINT HURON 9/1976, Dr. Giorgio Arra

POINT BRIDGE 1/1977, United States Coast Guard

Displacement, tons: A series 67; C series 66; D series 69
Dimensions, feet (metres): 78·1 wl; 83 oa × 17·2 × 5·8 (25·3 × 5·2 × 1·8)
Guns: 1—81 mm mortar and 1—0·50 cal MG or 2—0·50 cal MG; some boats unarmed
Main engines: 2 diesels; 1 600 bhp; 2 shafts = 23·5 knots except D series 22·6 knots
Range, miles: 1 500 at 8 knots (1 200 D series)
Complement: 8 (1 officer, 7 enlisted men; see notes)

Designed for search, rescue, and patrol. Of survivors, A series built 1960-61; C series in 1961-67; and D series in 1970.
Twenty-six cutters of the "A" and "B" series were transferred to South Viet-Nam in 1969-70.

Names: WPB 82301-82314 were assigned "Point" names in Jan 1964.

Personnel: Most of these units now have an officer assigned; a few still operate with an all-enlisted crew.

TRAINING CUTTERS

1 TRAINING CUTTER (WIX) "ACTIVE" CLASS

		F/S
CUYAHOGA WIX 157 (ex-WMEC 157, ex-WPC 157, ex-WAG 26)		AA

Displacement, tons: 290 full load
Dimensions, feet (metres): 125 oa × 24 × 8 (38·1 × 7·3 × 2·4)
Guns: Removed
Main engines: Diesel; 2 shafts; 800 bhp = 13·2 knots
Range, miles: 2 800 at 6 knots
Complement: 11 (1 officer, 10 enlisted men)

Built in 1926 as one of the 33 "Active" class steel patrol boats. *Cuyahoga* is the only cutter of this type remaining on the Coast Guard list. *Cuyahoga* is based at Yorktown, Virginia, for the training of officer candidates.

CUYAHOGA 1974, United States Coast Guard

1 SAIL TRAINING CUTTER (WIX) "EAGLE" CLASS

Name	No.	Builders	F/S
EAGLE (ex-*Horst Wessel*)	WIX 327	Blohm & Voss, Hamburg	AA

Displacement, tons: 1 784 full load
Dimensions, feet (metres): 231 wl; 295·2 oa × 39·1 × 17 (90·0 × 11·9 × 5·2)
Sail area, square feet: 25 351
Height of masts, feet (metres): fore and main 150·3 (45·8); mizzen 132 (40·2)
Main engines: Auxiliary diesel (MAN); 700 bhp; 1 shaft = 10·5 knots (as high as 18 knots under full sail alone)
Range, miles: 5 450 at 7·5 knots (diesel only)
Complement: 245 (19 officers, 46 enlisted men, 180 cadets)

Former German training ship. Launched on 13 June 1936. Taken by the United States as part of reparations after the Second World War for employment in US Coast Guard Practice Squadron. Taken over at Bremerhaven in Jan 1946; arrived at home port of New London, Connecticut, in July 1946.
(Sister ship *Albert Leo Schlageter* was also taken by the United States in 1945 but was sold to Brazil in 1948 and re-sold to Portugal in 1962. Another ship of similar design, *Gorch Foch*, transferred to the Soviet Union in 1946 and survives as *Tovarisch*).

Appearance: When the Coast Guard added the orange-and-blue marking stripes to cutters in the 1960s *Eagle* was exempted because of their affect on her graceful lines; however, in early 1976 the stripes and words "Coast Guard" were added in time for the July 1976 Operation Sail in New York harbour.

EAGLE 7/1976, USN

USA 731

SEAGOING TENDERS

Note: *Acushnet* WAGO 167 serves as Oceanographic cutter with *Evergreen* WAGO 295 from class below. 167 operates from Gulfport, Miss and *Evergreen* from New London, Conn.

33 BUOY TENDERS (SEAGOING) (WLB)/OCEANOGRAPHIC CUTTER (WAGO) "BALSAM" CLASS

Name	No.	Launched	F/S	Name	No.	Launched	F/S
BALSAM*	WLB 62	1942	PR	BITTERSWEET	WLB 389	1944	AA
LAUREL	WLB 291	1942	PA	BLACTHAW*	WLB 390	1944	AA
CLOVER	WLB 292	1942	PA	BLACKTHORN	WLB 391	1944	AA
EVERGREEN	WAGO 295	1943	AA	BRAMBLE*	WLB 392	1944	GLA
SORREL*	WLB 296	1943	AA	FIREBUSH	WLB 393	1944	AA
IRONWOOD	WLB 297	1944	PA	HORNBEAM	WLB 394	1944	AA
CITRUS*	WLB 300	1943	PA	IRIS	WLB 395	1944	PA
CONIFER	WLB 301	1943	AA	MALLOW	WLB 396	1944	PA
MADRONA	WLB 302	1943	AA	MARIPOSA	WLB 397	1944	GLA
TUPELO	WLB 303	1943	PR	SAGEBRUSH	WLB 399	1944	AA
MESQUITE	WLB 305	1943	GLA	SALVIA	WLB 400	1944	AA
BUTTONWOOD	WLB 306	1943	PA	SASSAFRAS	WLB 401	1944	AA
PLANETREE	WLB 307	1943	PA	SEDGE*	WLB 402	1944	PA
PAPAW	WLB 308	1943	A	SPAR*	WLB 403	1944	AA
SWEETGUM	WLB 309	1943	AA	SUNDEW*	WLB 404	1944	AA
BASSWOOD	WLB 388	1944	PA	SWEETBRIER	WLB 405	1944	AA
				WOODRUSH	WLB 407	1944	GLA

Displacement, tons: 935 standard; 1 025 full load
Dimensions, feet (metres): 180 oa × 37 × 13 *(59 × 12·1 × 4·2)*
Guns: 1—3 in *(76 mm)* 50 calibre in *Citrus*, (original armament); 2—20 mm guns in *Ironwood, Bittersweet, Firebush, Sedge* and *Sweetbrier* rest unarmed
Main engines: Diesel-electric; 1 000 bhp in tenders numbered WLB 62-303 series, except *Ironwood*; 1 shaft = 12·8 knots; others 1 200 bhp; 1 shaft = 15 knots
Complement: 53 (6 officers, 47 enlisted men)

Seagoing buoy tenders. *Ironwood* built by Coast Guard Yard at Curtis Bay, Maryland; others by Marine Iron & Shipbuilding Co, Duluth, Minnesota, or Zeneth Dredge Co, Duluth, Minnesota. Completed 1943-45. Eight ships indicated by asterisks are strengthened for icebreaking. Three ships, *Cowslip, Bittersweet,* and *Hornbeam,* have controllable-pitch, bow-thrust propellers to assist in manoeuvring. All WLBs have 20-capacity booms. *Evergreen* has been refitted as an oceanographic cutter (WAGO) and is painted white; *Balsam* and *Tupelo* are laid up in reserve.

Modernisation: All of this class, except WLB 62, 277, 290-292, 296 and 300-303 are undergoing or have completed modernisation. This has involved a rebuilding of the main engines and overhaul of the propulsion motors, improvement of habitability, installation of hydraulic cargo-handling equipment and the addition of a bow thruster. *Sorrel* completed in mid-1977 under the FY 1977 programme, *Sundew* is to be completed under the FY 1978 and *Firebush* under the FY 1979 programme. This last will complete the plan.

MARIPOSA   1975, United States Coast Guard

COASTAL TENDERS

5 BUOY-TENDERS COASTAL (WLM) "RED" CLASS

Name	No.	Launched	F/S	Name	No.	Launched	F/S
RED WOOD	WLM 685	1965	AA	RED CEDAR	WLM 688	1971	AA
RED BEECH	WLM 686	1965	AA	RED OAK	WLM 689	1972	AA
RED BIRCH	WLM 687	1966	AA				

Displacement, tons: 471 standard; 512 full load
Dimensions, feet (metres): 157 oa × 33 × 6 *(51·5 × 10·8 × 1·9)*
Main engines: 2 diesels; 2 shafts; 1 800 hp = 12·8 knots
Range, miles: 3 000 at 11·6 knots
Complement: 31 (4 officers, 27 enlisted men)

All built by Coast Guard Yard, Curtis Bay, Maryland. WLM 685-7 completed 1965-66 and other pair 1971-72. Fitted with controllable-pitch propellers and bow thrusters; steel hulls strengthened for light icebreaking. Steering and engine controls on each bridge wing as well as in pilot house. Living spaces are air conditioned. Fitted with 10-ton capacity boom.

RED BEECH   1976, Dr. Giorgio Arra

3 BUOY-TENDERS COASTAL (WLM) "HOLLYHOCK" CLASS

		F/S
FIR	WLM 212	PA
HOLLYHOCK	WLM 220	AA
WALNUT	WLM 252	PA

Displacement, tons: 989
Dimensions, feet (metres): 175 × 34 × 12 *(57·4 × 10·9 × 3·9)*
Main engines: Diesel reduction; 2 shafts; 1 350 bhp = 12 knots
Complement: 40 (5 officers, 35 enlisted men)

Launched in 1937 *(Hollyhock)* and 1939 *(Fir* and *Walnut). Walnut* was re-engined by Williamette Iron & Steel Co, Portland, Oregon, in 1958. Redesignated coastal tenders, (WLM), instead of buoy tenders, (WAGL) on 1 Jan 1965. Fitted with 20-ton capacity boom.

WALNUT   1976, John A. Jedrlinic

732 USA

7 BUOY-TENDERS COASTAL (WLM) "WHITE SUMAC" CLASS

		F/S			F/S
WHITE SUMAC	WLM 540	AA	WHITE HEATH	WLM 545	AA
WHITE BUSH	WLM 542	PA	WHITE LUPINE	WLM 546	AA
WHITE HOLLY	WLM 543	AA	WHITE PINE	WLM 547	AA
WHITE SAGE	WLM 544	AA			

Displacement, tons: 435 standard; 600 full load
Dimensions, feet (metres): 133 oa × 31 × 9 (43.6 × 10.1 × 2.9)
Main engines: Diesel; 2 shafts; 600 bhp = 9.8 knots
Complement: 21 (1 officer, 20 enlisted men)

All launched in 1943. All seven ships are former US Navy YFs, adapted for the Coast Guard. The *White Alder* (WLM 541) was sunk in a collision on 7 Dec 1968. Fitted with 10-ton capacity boom.

WHITE BUSH   1969, United States Coast Guard

BUOY-TENDERS (INLAND) (WLI)

		F/S
TERN	WLI 80801	AA

Displacement, tons: 168 full load
Dimensions, feet (metres): 80 oa × 25 × 5 (26.2 × 8.2 × 1.6)
Main engines: Diesels; 2 shafts; 450 hp = 10 knots
Complement: 7 (enlisted men)

Tern is prototype for a new design. A cutaway stern and gantry crane (the first installed in a Coast Guard tender) permit lifting buoys aboard from the stern. The crane moves on rails that extend forward to the deck house. Fitted with 125 hp bow thruster to improve manoeuvrability. Air conditioned.
Built by Coast Guard Yard at Curtis Bay, Baltimore, Maryland. Launched on 15 June 1968 and placed in service on 7 Feb 1969.

TERN   1969, United States Coast Guard

		F/S
AZALEA	WLI 641	AA

Displacement, tons: 200 full load
Dimensions, feet (metres): 100 oa × 24 × 5 (32.8 × 7.8 × 1.6)
Main engines: Diesels; 2 shafts; 440 bhp = 9 knots
Complement: 14 (1 officer, 13 enlisted men)

Built in 1958. Fitted with pile driver.

		F/S
COSMOS	WLI 293	AA
RAMBLER	WLI 298	AA
BLUEBELL	WLI 313	AA
SMILAX	WLI 315	AA
PRIMROSE	WLI 316	AA

Displacement, tons: 178 full load
Dimensions, feet (metres): 100 oa × 24 × 5 (32.8 × 7.8 × 1.6)
Main engines: Diesels; 2 shafts 600 bhp = 10.5 knots
Complement: 15 (1 officer, 14 enlisted men)

Cosmos completed in 1942, *Bluebell* in 1945, others in 1944. *Primrose* fitted with pile drivers.

PRIMROSE (with pile driver)   1976, John A. Jedrlinic

		F/S
BUCKTHORN	WLI 642	GLA

Displacement, tons: 200 full load
Dimensions, feet (metres): 100 oa × 24 × 4 (32.8 × 7.8 × 1.3)
Main engines: Diesels; 2 shafts; 600 bhp = 7.3 knots
Complement: 14 (1 officer, 13 enlisted men)

Completed in 1963.

BUCKTHORN   1975, United States Coast Guard

		F/S
BLACKBERRY	WLI 65303	AA
CHOKEBERRY	WLI 65304	AA
LOGANBERRY	WLI 65305	AA

Displacement, tons: 68 full load
Dimensions, feet (metres): 65 oa × 17 × 4 (21.3 × 5.6 × 4.6)
Main engines: Diesels; 1 shaft; 220 hp = 9 knots
Complement: 5 enlisted men)

Completed in 1946.

		F/S
BAYBERRY	WLI 65400	PA
ELDERBERRY	WLI 65401	AA

Displacement, tons: 68 full load
Dimensions, feet (metres): 65 oa × 17 × 4 (21.3 × 5.6 × 4.6)
Main engines: Diesels; 2 shafts; 400 hp = 11.3 knots
Complement: 5 (enlisted men)

Completed in 1954.

USA 733

BUOY TENDERS (RIVER) (WLR)

Note: All are based on rivers of USA especially the Mississippi and the Missouri and its tributaries.

SUMAC WLR 311

Displacement, tons: 404 full load
Dimensions, feet (metres): 115 oa × 30 × 6 *(37.7 × 9.8 × 1.9)*
Main engines: Diesels; 3 shafts; 960 hp = 10.6 knots
Complement: 23 (1 officer, 22 enlisted men)

Built in 1943.

FOXGLOVE WLR 285

Displacement, tons: 350 full load
Dimensions, feet (metres): 114 oa × 30 × 6 *(37.4 × 9.8 × 1.9)*
Main engines: Diesels; 3 shafts; 8 500 hp = 13.5 knots
Complement: 21 (1 officer, 20 enlisted men)

Built in 1945.

GASCONADE	WLR 75401	**CHEYENNE**	WLR 75405
MUSKINGUM	WLR 75402	**KICKAPOO**	WLR 75406
WYACONDA	WLR 75403	**KANAWHA**	WLR 75407
CHIPPEWA	WLR 75404	**PATOKA**	WLR 75408
		CHENA	WLR 75409

Displacement, tons: 145 full load
Dimensions, feet (metres): 75 oa × 22 × 4 *(24.5 × 7.2 × 1.3)*
Main engines: Diesel; 2 shafts; 600 hp = 10.8 knots
Complement: 12 (enlisted men)

Built 1964-71.

OUACHITA	WLR 65501	**SCIOTO**	WLR 65504
CIMARRON	WLR 65502	**OSAGE**	WLR 65505
OBION	WLR 65503	**SANGAMON**	WLR 65506

Displacement, tons: 139 full load
Dimensions, feet (metres): 65.6 oa × 21 × 5 *(21.5 × 6.9 × 1.6)*
Main engines: Diesel; 2 shafts; 600 hp = 12.5 knots
Complement: 10 (enlisted men)

Built in 1960-62.

DOGWOOD WLR 259   **FORSYTHIA** WLR 263   **SYCAMORE** WLR 268

Displacement, tons: 230 full load, except *Forsythia* 280
Dimensions, feet (metres): 114 oa × 26 × 4 *(37.4 × 8.5 × 1.3)*
Main engines: Diesels; 2 shafts; 2 800 hp = 11 knots
Complement: 21 (1 officer, 20 enlisted men)

Dogwood and *Sycamore* built in 1940; *Forsythia* in 1943.

LANTANA WLR 80310

Displacement, tons: 235 full load
Dimensions, feet (metres): 80 oa × 30 × 6 *(26.2 × 9.8 × 1.9)*
Main engines: Diesels; 3 shafts; 10 000 hp = 10 knots
Complement: 20 (1 officer, 19 enlisted men)

Built in 1943.

OLEANDER WLR 73264

Displacement, tons: 90 full load
Dimensions, feet (metres): 73 oa × 18 × 5 *(23.9 × 5.9 × 1.6)*
Main engines: Diesel; 2 shafts; 300 hp = 12 knots
Complement: 10 (enlisted men)

Built in 1940.

OSAGE pushing barge — *United States Coast Guard*

CONSTRUCTION TENDERS, INLAND (WLIC)

		F/S			F/S
PAMLICO	WLIC 800	AA	**KENNEBEC**	WLIC 803	AA
HUDSON	WLIC 801	AA	**SAGINAW**	WLIC 804	AA

Displacement, tons: 413 light
Dimensions, feet (metres): 160.9 × 30 × 4 *(49.1 × 9.1 × 1.2)*
Main engines: 2 diesels = 11.5 knots
Complement: 15

Built in 1975-77 at the Coast Guard Yard, Curtis Bay, Maryland.

	F/S			F/S			F/S
ANVIL WLIC 75301	AA	**MALLET** WLIC 75304	AA	**WEDGE** WLIC 75307	AA
HAMMER WLIC 75302	AA	**VISE** WLIC 75305	AA	**SPIKE** WLIC 75308	AA
SLEDGE WLIC 75303	AA	**CLAMP** WLIC 75306	AA	**HATCHET** WLIC 75309	AA
				AXE WLIC 75310	

Displacement, tons: 145 full load
Dimensions, feet (metres): 75 oa (WLIC 75306-75310 are 76 oa) × 22 × 4 *(24.6 × 7.2 × 1.3)*
Main engines: Diesels; 2 shafts; 600 hp = 10 knots
Complement: 9 or 10 (1 officer in *Mallet, Sledge* and *Vise;* 9 enlisted men in all)

Completed 1962-65.

SPIKE pushing barge — *1971, United States Coast Guard*

734 USA

OCEANGOING TUGS

1 MEDIUM ENDURANCE CUTTER (WMEC)/1 OCEANOGRAPHIC CUTTER (WAGO) "DIVER" CLASS

Name	No.	Builders	USN Comm.	F/S
ACUSHNET (ex-USS *Shackle*)	WAGO 167 (ex-WAT 167, ARS 9)	Basalt Rock Co, Napa, California	5 Feb 1944	AA
YOCONA (ex-USS *Seize*)	WMEC 168 (ex-WAT 168, ARS 26)	Basalt Rock Co, Napa, California	3 Nov 1944	PA

Displacement, tons: 1 557 standard; 1 745 full load
Dimensions, feet (metres): 213·5 oa × 39 × 15 *(70 × 12·8 × 4·9)*
Guns: Removed
Main engines: Diesels (Cooper Bessemer); 3 000 bhp; 2 shafts = 15·5 knots
Complement: *Acushnet* 64 (7 officers, 57 enlisted men); *Yocona* 72 (7 officers, 65 enlisted men)

Large, steel-hulled salvage ships transferred from the Navy to the Coast Guard after World War II and employed in tug and oceanographic duties. Launched 1 April 1943 and 8 April 1944 respectively. *Acushnet* modified for handling environmental data buoys and reclassified WAGO in 1968; *Yocona* reclassified as WMEC in 1968.

ACUSHNET   8/1975, United States Coast Guard

3 MEDIUM ENDURANCE CUTTERS (WMEC) "CHEROKEE" CLASS

Name	No.	Builders	USN Comm.	F/S
CHILULA	WMEC 153 (ex-WAT 153, ATF 153)	Charleston Shipbuilding & Drydock Co, Charleston, South Carolina	5 April 1945	AA
CHEROKEE	WMEC 165 (ex-WAT 165, ATF 66)	Bethlehem Steel Co, Staten Island, New York	26 April 1940	AA
TAMAROA (ex-*Zuni*)	WMEC 166 (ex-WAT 166, ATF 95)	Commercial Iron Works, Portland, Oregon	9 Oct 1943	AA

Displacement, tons: 1 731 full load
Dimensions, feet (metres): 205 oa × 38·5 × 17 *(62·5 × 11·7 × 5·2)*
Guns: 1—3 in 50 calibre; 2—0·50 cal MG
Main engines: Diesel-electric (General Motors diesel); 3 000 bhp; 1 shaft = 16·2 knots
Complement: 72 (7 officers, 65 enlisted men)

Steel-hulled tugs transferred from the Navy to the Coast Guard on loan in 1946; transferred permanently 1 June 1969. Classification of all three ships changed to WMEC in 1968. Launched on 1 Dec 1944, 10 Nov 1939, and 13 July 1943, respectively.

CHEROKEE   1975, Dr. Giorgio Arra

2 MEDIUM ENDURANCE CUTTERS (WMEC) "SOTOYOMO" CLASS

Name	No.	Builders	USN Comm.	F/S
MODOC (ex-USS *Bagaduce*)	WMEC 194 (ex-WATA 194, ATA 194)	Levingston Shipbuilding Co, Orange, Texas	14 Feb 1945	PA
COMANCHE (ex-USS *Wampanoag*)	WMEC 202 (ex-WATA 202, ATA 202)	Gulfport Boiler & Welding Works, Port Arthur, Texas	8 Dec 1944	AA

Displacement, tons: 534 standard; 860 full load
Dimensions, feet (metres): 143 oa × 33·8 × 14 *(46·8 × 11 × 4·9)*
Armament: 2—0·50 cal MG
Main engines: Diesel-electric (General Motors diesel); 1 shaft; 1 500 hp = 13·5 knots
Complement: 47 (5 officers, 42 enlisted men)

Steel-hulled tugs. Launched on 4 Dec 1944 and 10 Oct 1944, respectively. *Modoc* was stricken from the Navy List after World War II and transferred to Maritime Administration; transferred to Coast Guard on 15 April 1959. *Comanche* transferred on loan from Navy to Coast Guard from 25 Feb 1959 until stricken from Navy List on 1 June 1969 and transferred permanently. Both ships reclassified as WMEC in 1968.

MODOC   1977, United States Coast Guard

HARBOUR TUGS

10 MEDIUM HARBOUR TUGS (WYTM) "140-FOOT" CLASS

Name	No.	Builders	Commissioned	F/S
KATMAI BAY	WYTM 101	Tacoma Boatbuilding Co Inc, Tacoma	Late 1978	Bldg
BRISTOL BAY	WYTM 102	Tacoma Boatbuilding Co Inc, Tacoma	Early 1979	Bldg
MOBILE BAY	WYTM 103	Tacoma Boatbuilding Co Inc, Tacoma	Mid 1979	Bldg
BISCAYNE BAY	WYTM 104	Tacoma Boatbuilding Co Inc, Tacoma	Late 1979	Bldg
NEAH BAY	WYTM 105	Approved under FY 1979 programme		
MORRO BAY	WYTM 106	Requested under FY 1979 programme		
PENOBSCOT BAY	WYTM 107	Planned FY 1980-84 programme		
THUNDER BAY	WYTM 108	Planned FY 1980-84 programme		
STURGEON BAY	WYTM 109	Planned FY 1980-84 programme		
	WYTM 110	Planned FY 1980-84 programme		

Displacement, tons: 662 full load
Dimensions, feet (metres): 140 oa × 37·6 × 12·5 *(42·7 × 11·4 × 3·8)*
Main engines: Diesel-electric; 2 500 bhp; 1 shaft = 14·7 knots
Range, miles: 14 days
Complement: 17 (3 officers, 14 enlisted men)

This class is designed to replace the 110 foot class. The size, manoeuvrability and other operational characteristics of these new vessels will be tailored for operations in harbours and other restricted waters and for fulfilling present and anticipated multi-mission requirements. All units will be ice strengthened for operation on the Great Lakes, coastal waters and in rivers.

USA 735

13 HARBOUR TUGS MEDIUM (WYTM) 110 ft CLASS

MANITOU	WYTM 60	MOHICAN	WYTM 73	CHINOOK	WYTM 96
KAW	WYTM 61	ARUNDEL	WYTM 90	OBJIBWA	WYTM 97
APALACHEE	WYTM 71	MAHONING	WYTM 91	SNOHOMISH	WYTM 98
YANKTON	WYTM 72	NAUGATUCK	WYTM 92	SAUK	WYTM 99
		RARITAN	WYTM 93		

Displacement, tons: 370 full load
Dimensions, feet (metres): 110 oa × 27 × 11 *(36 × 8·8 × 3·6)*
Main engines: Diesel-electric; 1 shaft; 1 000 hp = 11·2 knots
Complement: 20 (1 officer, 19 enlisted men)

Built in 1943 except WYTM 90-93 built in 1939. WYTM 60, 71-73, 91, 96, 98, 99 active in the Atlantic Fleet. Remainder active on inland waterways.

CHINOOK   1/1977, United States Coast Guard

1 HARBOUR TUG MEDIUM (WYTM) 85 ft CLASS

MESSENGER   WYTM 85009   F/S AA

Displacement, tons: 230 full load
Dimensions, feet (metres): 85 oa × 23 × 9 *(27·8 × 7·5 × 2·9)*
Main engine: Diesel; 1 shaft; 700 hp = 9·5 knots
Complement: 10 (enlisted)

Built in 1944.

15 HARBOUR TUGS SMALL (WYTL) 65 ft CLASS

CAPSTAN	WYTL 65601	CATENARY	WYTL 65606	LINE	WYTL 65611
CHOCK	WYTL 65602	BRIDLE	WYTL 65607	WIRE	WYTL 65612
SWIVEL	WYTL 65603	PENDANT	WYTL 65608	BITT	WYTL 65613
TACKLE	WYTL 65604	SHACKLE	WYTL 65609	BOLLARD	WYTL 65614
TOWLINE	WYTL 65605	HAWSER	WYTL 65610	CLEAT	WYTL 65615

Displacement, tons: 72 full load
Dimensions, feet (metres): 65 oa × 19 × 7 *(21·3 × 6·2 × 2·3)*
Main engines: Diesel; 1 shaft; 400 hp = 9·8 knots except WYTL 65601-65606 10·5 knots
Complement: 10 (enlisted men)

Built from 1961 to 1967. All active in the Atlantic fleet.

LINE   7/1976, A. D. Baker III

LIGHTSHIPS (WLV)

LIGHTSHIP COLUMBIA WLV 604   LIGHTSHIP RELIEF WLV 613
LIGHTSHIP NANTUCKET WLV 612

Displacement, tons: 617 full load, except WLV 612 and 613 are 607 full load
Dimensions, feet (metres): 128 oa × 30 × 11 *(41·9 × 9·8 × 3·8)*
Main engines: Diesel; 550 bhp; 1 shaft = 10·7 knots, except WLV 612 and 613 = 11 knots

All launched 1950. *Lightship Columbia* assigned to Astoria, Oregon; *Lightship Nantucket* (612) and *Lightship Relief* (605) to Boston, Massachusetts.
Coast Guard lightships exchange names according to assignment; hull numbers remain constant.

NATIONAL OCEANIC AND ATMOSPHERIC ADMINISTRATION

Command

Director, National Ocean Survey:
  Rear-Admiral Allen L. Powell
Associate Director, Office of Fleet Operations:
  Rear-Admiral Herbert R. Lippold, Jnr.
Director, Atlantic Marine Center:
  Rear-Admiral Robert C. Munson
Director, Pacific Marine Center:
  Rear-Admiral Eugene A. Taylor

Establishment

The "Survey of the Coast" was established by an act of Congress on 10 Feb, 1807. Renamed US Coast Survey in 1834 and again renamed Coast and Geodetic Survey in 1878. The commissioned officer corps was established in 1917. The Coast and Geodetic Survey was made a component of the Environmental Science Services Administration on 13 July, 1965, when that agency was established within the Department of Commerce. The Environmental Science Services Administration subsequently became the National Oceanic and Atmospheric Administration in October 1970 with the Coast and Geodetic Survey being renamed National Ocean Survey and its jurisdiction expanded to include the US Lake Survey, formerly a part of the US Army Corps of Engineers; the Coast Guard's national data buoy development project; and the Navy's National Oceanographic Instrumentation Centre.

Missions

The National Ocean Survey operates the ships of the National Oceanic and Atmospheric Administration (NOAA), a federal agency created in 1970. During 1972-73 the National Marine Fisheries Service (formerly the Bureau of Commercial Fisheries of the Department of Interior) was consolidated into the NOAA fleet which is operated by the National Ocean Survey. Approximately 15 small ships and craft 65 feet or longer are counted in the National Marine Fisheries Service. The former National Marine Fisheries vessels are not described because of the specialised, non-military nature of their work. The National Ocean Survey prepares nautical and aeronautical charts; conducts geodetic, geophysical, oceanographic, and marine surveys; predicts tides and currents; tests, evaluates, and calibrates sensing systems for ocean use; and conducts the development of and eventually will operate a national system of automated ocean buoys for obtaining environmental information.

The National Ocean Survey is a civilian agency that supports national civilian and military requirements. During time of war the ships and officers of NOAA can be expected to operate with the Navy, either as a separate service or integrated into the Navy.

Ships

The following ships may be met with at sea.
Oceanographic Survey Ships: *Researcher, Oceanographer, Discoverer, Surveyor.*
Hydrographic Survey Ships: *Fairweather, Rainier, Mt. Mitchell.*
Coastal Survey Ships: *McArthur, Davidson, Peirce, Whiting.*
Coastal Vessels: *Rude, Heck, Ferrel.*

Personnel

The National Ocean Survey has approximately 225 commissioned officers and 250 officers and 2 250 civil service personnel. In addition, another 125 commissioned officers serve elsewhere in NOAA and several US Navy officers are assigned to NOAA.

URUGUAY

Headquarters Appointment

Commander-in-Chief of the Navy:
 Vice-Admiral Victor González Ibargoyen

Diplomatic Representation

Naval Attaché in Washington:
 Captain Jorge Laborde

Personnel

(a) 1978: Total: 3 500 officers and men
 (including Naval Infantry)
(b) Voluntary service

Base

Montevideo: Main naval base with a drydock and a slipway

Coast Guard

The Prefectura Maritima operates six coastal patrol craft.

Naval Air Arm

2 SH-34C helicopters
1 Bell 47G
2 Bell CH-13H
3 Grumman S-2A Tracker (ASW)
4 Beech SNB-5 (Training-Transport)
3 North American SNJ (Training)
1 Beech T-34 B Mentor (Training)

Prefix to Ships' Names

R.O.U.

Mercantile Marine

Lloyd's Register of Shipping:
 45 vessels of 192 792 tons gross

Strength of the Fleet

	Active	Building
Frigates	3	—
Corvettes	2	—
Large Patrol Craft	1	—
Coastal Patrol Craft	6	—
Survey Ships	2	—
Salvage Vessel	1	—
Tankers	3	—
Tenders	3	—

Deletion

Frigate

1975 *Montevideo*

SUBMARINES

There is no confirmation of the previous report of a possible order for two Type 209.

FRIGATES

1 Ex-US "DEALEY" CLASS

Name	No.	Builders	Laid down	Launched	Commissioned
18 DE JULIO (ex-USS *Dealey*, DE 1006)	DE 3	Bath Iron Works Corpn	15 Oct 1952	8 Nov 1953	3 June 1954

Displacement, tons: 1 450 standard; 1 900 full load
Length, feet (metres): 314·5 *(95·9)* oa
Beam, feet (metres): 36·8 *(11·2)*
Draught, feet (metres): 13·6 *(4·2)*
Guns: 4—3 in *(76 mm)* (twins)
A/S weapons: 2 triple torpedo tubes (Mk 32)
Main engine: 1 De Laval geared turbine; 20 000 shp; 1 shaft
Boilers: 2 Foster-Wheeler
Speed, knots: 25
Complement: 165

Purchased 28 July 1972. *Dealey* was the first US escort ship built after the war.

Fire control: Mk 63 forward and aft with SPG 34 radar.

Radar: SPS 6, SPS 10.

18 DE JULIO *1975, Uruguayan Navy*

2 Ex-US "CANNON" CLASS

Name	No.	Builders	Laid down	Launched	Commissioned
URUGUAY (ex-USS *Baron*, DE 166)	DE 1	Federal SB & DD Co, Pt Newark	Dec 1942	9 May 1943	5 July 1943
ARTIGAS (ex-USS *Bronstein*, DE 189)	DE 2	Federal SB & DD Co, Pt Newark	Aug 1943	14 Nov 1943	13 Dec 1943

Displacement, tons: 1 240 standard; 1 900 full load
Length, feet (metres): 306·0 *(93·3)* oa
Beam, feet (metres): 37·0 *(11·3)*
Draught, feet (metres): 17·1 *(5·2)*
Guns: 3—3 in *(76 mm)* (single); 2—40 mm (see *Gunnery* notes)
A/S weapons: Hedgehog; 8 DCT; 1 DCR (see *Torpedo Tubes* note)
Main engines: Diesel-electric; 2 shafts; 6 000 bhp
Speed, knots: 19
Oil fuel, tons: 315 (95 per cent)
Range, miles: 8 300 at 14 knots
Complement: 160

Appearance: Practically identical, but *Uruguay* can be distinguished by the absence of a mainmast, whereas *Artigas* has a small pole mast aft.

Gunnery: Formerly also mounted ten 20 mm anti-aircraft guns, but these have been removed.

Radar: Search: SPS 6.
Tactical: SPS 10.

Torpedo tubes: The three 21-in torpedo tubes in a triple mounting, originally carried, were removed.

Transfers: *Uruguay,* May 1952; *Artigas,* March 1952.

URUGUAY *1975, Uruguayan Navy*

URUGUAY 737

CORVETTES

1 Ex-US "AUK" CLASS

Name	No.	Builders	Commissioned
COMANDANTE PEDRO CAMPBELL	MS 31	Defoe B & M	9 Nov 1942
(ex-USS *Chickadee* MSF 59)	(ex-MSF 1)	Works	

Displacement, tons: 890 standard; 1 250 full load
Dimensions, feet (metres): 221·2 oa × 32·2 × 10·8 *(67·5 × 9·8 × 3·5)*
Guns: 1—3 in, 50 cal; 4—40 mm (twin); 4—20 mm (twin)
Main engines: Diesel-electric; 2 shafts; 3 118 bhp = 18 knots
Complement: 105

Former United States fleet minesweeper. Launched on 20 July 1942. Transferred on loan and commissioned at San Diego on 18 Aug 1966. Purchased 15 Aug 1976.

COMANDANTE PEDRO CAMPBELL   1971

1 Ex-US "AGGRESSIVE" CLASS

Name	No.	Builders	Commissioned
MALDONADO	MS 33	USA	24 Feb 1954
(ex-*Bir Hakeim* M 614, ex-USS *MSO 451*)			

Displacement, tons: 700 standard; 795 full load
Dimensions, feet (metres): 171·0 oa × 35·0 × 10·3 *(50·3 × 10·7 × 3·2)*
Gun: 1—40 mm
Main engines: 2 GM diesels; 2 shafts; 1 600 bhp = 13·5 knots
Range, miles: 3 000 at 10 knots
Complement: 54

Former US ocean minesweeper launched 1 Oct 1953 and transferred to France in Feb 1954. Returned to the US Navy and transferred to Uruguay in Sept 1970. All sweeping gear removed.

MALDONADO   1975, Uruguayan Navy

LIGHT FORCES

1 US "ADJUTANT" CLASS (LARGE PATROL CRAFT)

Name	No.	Builders	Commissioned
RIO NEGRO	MS 32	USA	1954
(ex-*Marguerite*, ex-USS *MSC 94*)			

Displacement, tons: 370 standard; 405 full load
Dimensions, feet (metres): 141·0 oa × 26·0 × 8·3 *(43 × 8 × 2·6)*
Guns: 2—20 mm
Main engines: 2 GM diesels; 2 shafts; 1 200 bhp = 13 knots
Oil fuel, tons: 40
Range, miles: 2 500 at 10 knots
Complement: 38

Built for France under MDAP. Returned to US in 1969. She was transferred to Uruguay at Toulon on 10 Nov 1969. All sweeping gear removed.

RIO NEGRO   1975, Uruguayan Navy

1 Ex-US 63 ft AVR (COASTAL PATROL CRAFT)

COLONIA PR 10 (ex-*AR 1*)

Displacement, tons: 25 standard; 34 full load
Dimensions, feet (metres): 63 × 15 × 3·8 *(20·6 × 4·9 × 1·2)*
Guns: 4 MGs
Main engines: 2 Hall Scott Defender; 1 260 bhp = 33·5 knots
Range, miles: 600 at 15 knots
Complement: 8

Launched 4 July 1944.

COLONIA   1975, Uruguayan Navy

738 URUGUAY

1 COASTAL PATROL CRAFT

Name	No.	Builders	Commissioned
CARMELO	PR 11	Lürssen, Vegesack	1957

Displacement, tons: 70
Dimensions, feet (metres): 93·0 × 19·0 × 7·0 (28·7 × 5·9 × 2·1)
Gun: 1—20 mm
Speed, knots: 25

CARMELO 1975, Uruguayan Navy

1 COASTAL PATROL CRAFT

Name	No.	Builders	Commissioned
PAYSANDU	PR 12	Sewart, USA	1968

Displacement, tons: 60
Dimensions, feet (metres): 83·0 × 18·0 × 6·0 (26 × 5·6 × 1·6)
Guns: 3—0·50 cal MG
Main engines: 2 GM diesels; 2 shafts = 22 knots

PAYSANDU 1975, Uruguayan Navy

3 COASTAL PATROL CRAFT

701   702   703

43 ft craft transferred by US Navy in Feb 1970.

SURVEY SHIPS

Name	No.	Builders	Commissioned
CAPITAN MIRANDA	GS 20 (ex-GS 10)	Sociedad Espanola de Construccion Naval, Matagorda, Cadiz	1930

Displacement, tons: 516 standard; 527 full load
Dimensions, feet (metres): 148 pp; 179 oa × 26 × 10·5 (45; 53 × 8·4 × 3·2)
Main engine: 1 MAN diesel; 500 bhp = 11 knots
Oil fuel, tons: 37
Complement: 49

Originally a three-masted schooner with pronounced clipper bow used as a cadet training ship.

CAPITAN MIRANDA (old pennant number) 1971

Name	No.	Builders	Commissioned
SALTO	GS 24 (ex-PR 2)	Cantieri Navali Riuniti, Ancona	1936

Displacement, tons: 150 standard; 180 full load
Dimensions, feet (metres): 137 × 18 × 10 (42·1 × 5·8 × 3)
Gun: 1—40 mm
Main engines: 2 Germania-Krupp diesels; 2 shafts; 1 000 bhp = 17 knots
Range, miles: 4 000 at 10 knots
Complement: 26

Now used also as a buoy-tender.

SALTO (old pennant number) 1971

URUGUAY 739

SALVAGE VESSEL
1 Ex-US "COHOES" CLASS

Name	No.	Builders	Commissioned
HURACAN (ex-USS *Nahant AN 83*)	AM 25 (ex-*BT 30*)	Commercial Ironworks, Portland, Oregon	1945

Displacement, tons: 650 standard; 855 full load
Dimensions, feet (metres): 168·5 × 33·8 × 11·7 *(51·4 × 10·2 × 3·3)*
Guns: 3—20 mm (single)
Main engines: Diesel-electric; 1 shaft; 1 200 bhp = 11·5 knots
Complement: 48

Former US netlayer, transferred Dec 1968 for salvage services carrying divers and underwater swimmers. In 1954 diving equipment and a recompression chamber were installed.

HURACAN   *1975, Uruguayan Navy*

AMPHIBIOUS CRAFT
2 Ex-US "LCM 6" CLASS

LD 40   LD 41

Transferred on lease Oct 1972.

TANKERS

Note: All operate under commercial charter to ANCAP (State Oil Company) when not required for naval purposes.

Name	No.	Builders	Commissioned
JUAN A. LAVALLEJA (ex-MV *Solfonn*)	AO 27	Kawasaki, Kobe	1975

Measurement, tons: 68 931 gross; 131 663 deadweight
Dimensions, feet (metres): 895·8 × 144·6 × 51·6 *(273 × 44·1 × 15·7)*
Main engines: 2 steam turbines; 24 500 shp = 15·5 knots

Former Norwegian tanker laid-up on 13 Oct 1975. Bought by Uruguyan Navy 13 Jan 1977.

JUAN A. LAVALLEJA   *1977, J. van der Woude*

Name	No.	Builders	Commissioned
PRESIDENTE RIVERA	AO 28	EN Bazán, Spain	1971

Measurement, tons: 19 686 gross; 31 885 deadweight
Dimensions, feet (metres): 636·3 × 84 × 32 *(194 × 25·6 × 9·8)*
Main engines: 15 300 bhp = 15 knots
Complement: 58

PRESIDENTE RIVERA   *1975, Uruguayan Navy*

Name	No.	Builders	Commissioned
PRESIDENTE ORIBE	AO 29 (ex- *AO 9*)	Ishikawajima-Harima Ltd, Japan	22 Mar 1962

Measurement, tons: 18 584 gross; 28 474 deadweight
Dimensions, feet (metres): 620 oa × 84·3 × 33 *(189 × 25·7 × 10·1)*
Main engines: 1 Ishikawajima turbine; 12 500 shp = 16·75 knots
Boilers: 2 Ishikawajima-Harima Foster-Wheeler type
Range, miles: 16 100 at 16 knots
Complement: 76

Can carry out alongside replenishment. Refitted in Durban, RSA in May 1977.

PRESIDENTE ORIBE (old pennant number)   *1971*

TENDERS

VANGUARDIA AM 26 (ex-US YTL 589)

Transferred Sept 1965.

Following also reported: UA 12 (ex-US) repair ship, *Anapal* No 1, ex-US 20 LH, ex-US 26 MW, *Banco Ingles*, LV 21 (ex-US WLV *Portland*) (no longer a light-ship).

740 VENEZUELA

VENEZUELA

Administration

Commander General of the Navy (Chief of Naval Operations):
 Vice-Admiral Magin Lagrave Fry
Deputy Chief of Naval Operations:
 Rear-Admiral Ernesto Reyes Leal
Chief of Naval Staff:
 Rear-Admiral Alfredo Bello Borges

Diplomatic Representation

Naval Attaché in London:
 Captain Ramon Sanoja Medina
Naval Attaché in Washington:
 Rear-Admiral Rafael Silveira
Assistant Naval Attache in Washington:
 Commander Carlos A. Colmenares

Personnel

(a) 1978: 7 500 officers and men including 4 000 of the Marine Corps (3 battalions)
(b) 2 years national service

National Guard

The Fuerzas Armadas de Cooperacion, generally known as the National Guard, is a paramilitary organisation, 10 000 strong. It is concerned, amongst other things, with customs and internal security—the Maritime Wing operates the Coastal Patrol Craft listed under Light Forces, though these nominally belong to the Navy.

Bases

Caracas: Main HQ.
Puerto Cabello: Main Naval Base (Dockyard, 1 Drydock, 1 synchrolift, 1 floating crane).
La Guaira: Small Naval Base (Naval Academy).
Puerto de Hierro: Naval Supply Base.

Naval Air Arm

2 Bell 47J helicopters
6 Grumman S-2E Trackers (ASW)
4 Grumman Hu-16A Albatros (SAR)
3 Douglas C-47 (Transports)

Strength of the Fleet

Type	Active	Building
Destroyers	4	—
Frigates	5	5
Submarines, Patrol	4	2
Fast Attack Craft—Missile/Gun	6	—
Coastal Patrol Craft	21	—
LST	1	—
LSMs	4	—
Transport Landing Ship	1	—
Transports	4	—
Survey Ships and Craft	3	—
Ocean Tug	1	—
Harbour Tugs	13	—
Floating Dock	1	—
National Guard CPC	16	—

Mercantile Marine

Lloyd's Register of Shipping:
 179 vessels of 639 396 tons gross

DELETIONS

Submarine

1977 *Carite* (ex-USS *Tilefish*) (28 Jan)

Destroyer

1975 *Aragua* (D 31)

Light Forces

1976-77 *Albatros, Alcatraz, Calamar, Camaron, Caracol, Gaviota, Mejillon, Petrel, Pulpo, Togogo* (US "PC-461" class)

Frigates

1976 *General José de Austria*
1977 *General José Garcia*

Survey Ships

1975 *Puerto Miranda* (H 03), *Puerto de Nutrius* (H 02)

PENNANT LIST

Submarines

S 21	Tiburon
S 22	Picuda
S 31	Sabalo
S 32	Caribe

Destroyers

D 11	Nueva Esparta
D 12	Zulia
D 21	Carabobo
D 22	Falcon

Frigates

—	Sucre
—	Urdaneto
—	New "Lupo" class
F 11	Almirante Clemente
F 12	General José Trinidad Moran
F 13	General Juan José Flores
F 14	Almirante Brion

Light Forces

C 87	Rio Orinoco
C 88	Rio Ventuari
C 89	Rio Caparo
C 90	Rio Venamo
C 91	Rio Torres
C 92	Rio Escalante
C 93	Rio Limon
C 94	Rio San Juan
C 95	Rio Tucuyo
C 96	Rio Turbio
C 128-138	"Rio Orinoco" class
P 11	
P 12	
P 13	
P 14	
P 15	
P 16	
P 119	Gabriela (Survey)
P 121	Lely (Survey)

Amphibious Forces

T 21	Los Monjes
T 22	Los Roques
T 23	Los Frailes
T 24	Los Testigos
T 31	Guyana
T 51	Amazonas

Transports

T 12	Las Aves
T ?	Punta Cabana
T 41	Maracaibo
T ?	New ship

Survey Ships

H 01	Puerto Santo
P 119	Gabriela
IP 121	Lely

Tugs

C 139-142	Harbour Tugs
R 11	Fernando Gomes
R 13	General José Felix Ribas
R 14	Fabrio Gallipoli
R 21	Felipe Larrazabal
R ?	Diana III

Floating Dock

| DF 11 | Golfo de Carriaco |

NUEVA ESPARTA

CARABOBO

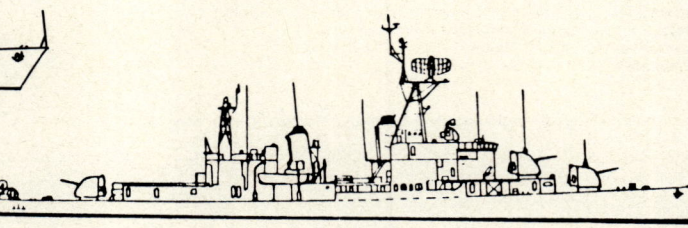

FALCON

"ALMIRANTE CLEMENTE" Class

VENEZUELA

SUBMARINES

2 + 2 HOWALDTSWERKE TYPE 209

Name	No.	Builders	Laid down	Launched	Commissioned
SABALO	S 31 (ex-S 21)	Howaldtswerke, Kiel	1973	21 Aug 1975	6 Aug 1976
CARIBE	S 32	Howaldtswerke, Kiel	1973	16 Dec 1975	11 Mar 1977

Displacement, tons: 990 surfaced; 1 350 dived
Dimensions, feet (metres): 177·1 × 20·3 × 18 *(54·0 × 6·2 × 5)*
Torpedo tubes: 8—21 in (with reloads) bow
Main machinery: Diesel-electric; 4 MTU-Siemens diesel generators; 1 Siemens electric motor 5 000 hp; 1 shaft
Speed, knots: 10 surfaced; 22 dived
Range, miles: 50 days
Complement: 31

Type 209, IK81 designed by Ingenieurkontor Lübeck for construction by Howaldtswerke, Kiel and sale by Ferrostaal, Essen, all acting as a consortium.
A single-hull design with two main ballast tanks and forward and after trim tanks. Fitted with snort and remote machinery control. Slow revving single screw. Very high capacity batteries with GRP lead-acid cells and battery-cooling—by W. Hagen and VARTA. Active and passive sonar, sonar detection set, sound-ranging equipment and underwater telephone. Have two periscopes, radar and Omega receiver. Fore-planes retract. Ordered in 1971.
Second pair ordered 10 March 1977.

SABALO   *1976, Howaldtswerke*

2 Ex-US "GUPPY II" CLASS

Name	No.	Builders	Laid down	Launched	Commissioned
TIBURON (ex-USS *Cubera*, SS 347)	S 21 (ex-S 12)	Electric Boat Co, Groton	11 May 1944	17 June 1945	19 Dec 1945
PICUDA (ex-USS *Grenadier*, SS 525)	S 22 (ex-S 13)	Boston Navy Yard	8 Feb 1944	15 Dec 1944	10 Feb 1951

Displacement, tons: 1 870 surfaced; 2 420 dived
Length, feet (metres): 307·5 *(93·8)*
Beam, feet (metres): 27·0 *(8·2)*
Draught, feet (metres): 18·0 *(5·5)*
Torpedo tubes: 10—21 in *(533 mm)* (6 bow, 4 stern)
Main machinery: 3 diesels; 4 800 shp; 2 electric motors; 5 400 shp; 2 shafts
Speed, knots: 18 surfaced; 15 dived
Range, miles: 12 000 at 10 knots
Oil fuel, tons: 300
Complement: 80

Transferred as follows—*Tiburon* 5 Jan 1972, *Picuda* 15 May 1973.

PICUDA (as GRENADIER)   *USN*

DESTROYERS

2 "ARAGUA" CLASS

Name	No.	Builders	Laid down	Launched	Commissioned
NUEVA ESPARTA	D 11	Vickers Ltd, Barrow	24 July 1951	19 Nov 1952	8 Dec 1953
ZULIA	D 12 (ex-D 21)	Vickers Ltd, Barrow	24 July 1951	29 June 1953	15 Sept 1954

Displacement, tons: 2 600 standard; 3 670 full load
Length, feet (metres): 384·0 *(117·0)* wl; 402·0 *(122·5)* oa
Beam, feet (metres): 43·0 *(13·1)*
Draught, feet (metres): 19·0 *(5·8)*
Missiles: 2 quadruple Seacat in D 11
Guns: 6—4·5 *(114 mm)* (twins); 16—40 mm (twins) in D 12; 4—40 mm (twins) in D 11
A/S weapons: 2 Hedgehogs; 2 DCT; 2 DC racks
Main engines: Parsons geared turbines; 2 shafts; 50 000 shp
Boilers: 2 Yarrow
Speed, knots: 34
Range, miles: 5 000 at 10 knots
Complement: 256 (20 officers, 236 men)

Ordered in 1950 as class of three. Air conditioned. Two engine rooms and two boiler rooms served by a single uptake. The 4·5 in guns are fully automatic.

Fire control: Two UK type 276 on DCT for 4·5 in.
Two optical GWS 20 directors for Seacat in D 11.

Radar: Search: AWS 2 *(Nueva Esparta)* SPS 6 *(Zulia)*.
SPS 12 (both).
Fire control: I Band.

ZULIA (Old pennant number)   *7/1976, A. D. Baker III*

Refits: Both refitted at Palmers Hebburn Works, and Vickers in 1959, and at New York Navy Yard in 1960 to improve anti-submarine and anti-aircraft capabilities. *Nueva Esparta* at Cammell Laird in 1968-69 when Seacat launchers were fitted and some 40 mm and the torpedo tubes removed.

742 VENEZUELA

1 Ex-US "ALLEN M. SUMNER (FRAM II)" CLASS

Name	No.	Builders	Laid down	Launched	Commissioned
FALCON (ex-USS *Robert K. Huntington* DD 781)	D 22 (ex-D 51)	Todd Pacific Shipyards	1944	5 Dec 1944	3 Mar 1945

Displacement, tons: 2 200 standard; 3 320 full load
Dimensions, feet (metres): 376·5 × 40·9 × 19 (114·8 × 12·4 × 5·8)
Guns: 6—5 in 38 cal (twins)
A/S weapons: 2 Hedgehogs; 2 triple torpedo tubes (Mk 32); facilities for small helicopter
Main engines: 2 geared turbines; 60 000 shp; 2 shafts
Boilers: 4
Speed, knots: 34
Range, miles: 4 600 at 15 knots
Complement: 274

Purchase from US Navy 31 Oct 1973. Modernised under the FRAM II programme.

Radar: SPS 40 and SPS 10.

Sonar: Hull mounted; SQS 29 series. VDS.

"ALLEN M. SUMNER (FRAM II)" Class *USN*

1 Ex-US "ALLEN M. SUMNER" CLASS

Name	No.	Builders	Laid down	Launched	Commissioned
CARABOBO (ex-USS *Beatty*, DD 756)	D 21 (ex-D 41)	Bethlehem, Staten Is.	1944	30 Nov 1944	31 Mar 1945

Displacement, tons: 2 200 standard; 3 320 full load
Dimensions, feet (metres): 376·5 × 40·9 × 19·0 (114·8 × 12·4 × 5·8)
Guns: 6—5 in (twins)
A/S weapons: 2 fixed Hedgehogs; DCs; 2 triple torpedo tubes (Mk 32)
Main engines: 2 geared turbines; 60 000 shp; 2 shafts
Boilers: 4
Speed, knots: 34
Range, miles: 4 600 at 15 knots
Complement: 274

Transferred from US Navy 14 July 1972.

Fire control: Mk 37 GFCS forward with Mk 25 radar; Mk 51 GFCS aft (no radar).

Radar: SPS 6, SPS 10.

Sonar: SQS 29 series.

CARABOBO (as *Beatty*) *1965, Dr. Giorgio Arra*

FRIGATES

1 + 5 "LUPO" CLASS

Name	No.	Builders	Laid down	Launched	Commissioned
SUCRE	—	CNR, Riva Trigoso	19 Nov 1976	1977	Oct 1978
URDANETO	—	CNR, Riva Trigoso			
—	—	CNR, Riva Trigoso			
—	—	CNR, Riva Trigoso			
—	—	CNR, Riva Trigoso			
—	—	CNR, Riva Trigoso			

Displacement, tons: 2 208 standard; 2 500 full load
Dimensions, feet (metres): 366 × 39·4 × 11·8 (111·6 × 12 × 3·6)
Aircraft: 1 AB212 helicopter (fixed hangar)
Missiles: 4 Otomat 2 (singles); 8 cell Albatros SAM system
Guns: 1—5 in (127 mm) 54 cal OTO Melara; 4—40 mm 70 cal (singles)
Rocket launchers: 2 SCLAR 4·1 in multi-tube mountings
A/S weapons: 6 tubes for A/S torpedoes (triples)
Main engines: CODAG. 2 Fiat-GELM 2 500 gas turbines; 34 400 bhp; 2 GMT A230/20M diesels; 7 800 hp; 2 shafts
Speed, knots: 35; 21 on diesels
Complement: 185

Letter of intent signed 24 Oct 1975.

Missiles: With fixed hangar only 4 Otomat carried with no reloads for Albatros system.

Radar: Search: Selenia MM/SPS 74.
Navigation: SMA SPQ/2F.
Fire control (guns): Elsag Mark 10 Mod O Argo.
Fire control (missiles): EX 77 Mod O.

Sonar: SQS 29.

"LUPO" Class *1976, Italian Navy*

VENEZUELA 743

4 "ALMIRANTE CLEMENTE" CLASS

Name	No.	Builders	Laid down	Launched	Commissioned
ALMIRANTE CLEMENTE	F 11 (ex-D 12)	Ansaldo, Leghorn	5 May 1954	12 Dec 1954	1956
GENERAL JOSÉ TRINIDAD MORAN	F 12 (ex-D 22)	Ansaldo, Leghorn	5 May 1954	12 Dec 1954	1956
GENERAL JUAN JOSÉ FLORES	F 13 (ex-D 13)	Ansaldo, Leghorn	5 May 1954	7 Feb 1955	1956
ALMIRANTE BRION	F 14 (ex-D 23)	Ansaldo, Leghorn	12 Dec 1954	4 Sept 1955	1957

Displacement, tons: 1 300 standard; 1 500 full load
Length, feet (metres): 325·11 *(99·1)* oa
Length, feet (metres): 35·5 *(10·8)*
Draught, feet (metres): 12·2 *(3·7)*
Guns: 4—4 in *(102 mm)* (2 twin) or 2—76 mm OTO Melara Compact; 4—40 mm; 8—20 mm (modified group 40 mm only) (see note)
A/S weapons: 2 Hedgehogs, 4 DCT and 2 DC racks in original group; 1 A/S Mortar, 4 DCT and 2 DC racks in modified group
Torpedo tubes: 3—21 in *(533 mm)* triple (only F 13)
Main engines: 2 sets geared turbines; 2 shafts; 24 000 shp
Boilers: 2 Foster-Wheeler
Speed, knots: 32
Oil fuel, tons: 350
Range, miles: 3 500 at 15 knots
Complement: 162 (12 officers, 150 men)

The first three of this class of six were ordered in 1953. Three more were ordered in 1954. Aluminium alloys were widely employed in the building of all superstructure. All ships fitted with Denny-Brown fin stabilisers and air conditioned throughout the living and command spaces.

Gunnery: The 4 in anti-aircraft guns are fully automatic and radar controlled—replaced by two OTO Melara 76 mm in F 11 and 12.

ALMIRANTE BRION (Old pennant number) — 1975, Dhr. J. Van der Woude

Modernisation: *Almirante José Garcia, Almirante Brion* and *General José de Austria* were refitted by Ansaldo, Leghorn, in 1962 to improve their anti-submarine and anti-aircraft capabilities: the survivor of this group is known as "Modified Almirante Clemente" type. *Almirante Clemente* and *General José Trinidad Moran* were taken in hand for refit by Cammell Laird/Plessey group in April 1968. 4 in guns replaced by 76 mm OTO Melara Compact. *Almirante Clemente* started her post-refit trials in Feb 1975 and *General Jose Moran* after trials sailed mid-Jan 1976 for Venezuela.

Radar: Search: MLA 1—some, Plessey AWS-1.
Fire control: I Band

LIGHT FORCES

Note: Also reported three ex-US 43 ft PBs transferred Feb 1970

6 VOSPER-THORNYCROFT 121 FT CLASS (FAST ATTACK CRAFT—MISSILE AND GUN)

Name	No.	Builders	Laid down	Launched	Commissioned
CONSITUCION	P 11	Vosper-Thornycroft Ltd	Jan 1973	1 June 1973	16 Aug 1974
*FEDERACION	P 12	Vosper-Thornycroft Ltd	Aug 1973	26 Feb 1974	25 Mar 1975
INDEPENDENCIA	P 13	Vosper-Thornycroft Ltd	Feb 1973	24 July 1973	20 Sept 1974
*LIBERTAD	P 14	Vosper-Thornycroft Ltd	Sept 1973	5 Mar 1974	12 June 1975
PATRIA	P 15	Vosper-Thornycroft Ltd	Mar 1973	27 Sept 1973	9 Jan 1975
*VICTORIA	P 16	Vosper-Thornycroft Ltd	Mar 1974	3 Sept 1974	22 Sept 1975

* Missile craft

Displacement, tons: 150
Dimensions, feet (metres): 121 oa × 23·3 × 5·6 *(36·9 × 7·6 × 1·7)*
Missiles: 2 Otomat (P 12, 14 and 16)
Gun: 1—76 mm OTO Melara (P 11, 13 and 15); 1—40 mm gun (P 12, 14 and 16)
Main engines: 2 MTU diesels; 7 200 hp; 2 shafts
Speed, knots: 27
Range, miles: 1 350 at 16 knots
Complement: 18

A £6 million order the first laid down in Jan 1973. A new design, fitted with Elsag fire-control system NA 10 mod 1 and Selenia radar in 76 mm gun craft. Ten more fast attack craft (missile) projected.

Radar: SPQ 2D.

FEDERACION — 4/1975, Vosper Thornycroft

21 "RIO ORINOCO" CLASS (COASTAL PATROL CRAFT)

Name	No.	Builders	Commissioned
RIO ORINOCO	C 87	Inma, La Spezia	1974
RIO VENTUARI	C 88	Inma, La Spezia	1974
RIO CAPARO	C 89	Inma, La Spezia	1974
RIO VENAMO	C 90	Inma, La Spezia	1974
RIO TORRES	C 91	Inma, La Spezia	1974
RIO ESCALANTE	C 92	Inma, La Spezia	1975
RIO LIMON	C 93	Inma, La Spezia	1975
RIO SAN JUAN	C 94	Inma, La Spezia	1975
RIO TUCUYO	C 95	Inma, La Spezia	1975
RIO TURBIO	C 96	Inma, La Spezia	1975
—	C 128-138	Dianca, Puerto Cabello	—

Displacement, tons: 65
Dimensions, feet (metres): 92·8 × 15·7 × 4·9 *(28·3 × 4·8 × 1·5)*
Main engines: 2 MTU diesels; 2 200 bhp = 25 knots

Ordered in May 1973. Assistance given in overseeing at Puerto Cabello by Inma. First Cabello built craft launched March 1974 and six were completed by end 1975.

744 VENEZUELA

AMPHIBIOUS FORCES

1 Ex-US "TERREBONNE PARISH" CLASS (LST)

Name	No.	Builders	Commissioned
AMAZONAS (ex-USS *Vernon County* LST 1161)	T 51 (ex-T 21)	Ingalls Shipbuilding Corpn	1953

Displacement, tons: 2 590 light; 5 800 full load
Dimensions, feet (metres): 384 oa × 55 × 17 *(117.4 × 16.8 × 3.7)*
Guns: 6—3 in 50 cal (twins)
Main engines: 4 GM diesels; 2 shafts; cp propeller; 6 000 bhp = 15 knots
Complement: 116
Troops: 395

Built 1952-53. Carries four LCVP landing craft. Transferred on loan 29 June 1973. Purchased 1977.

4 Ex-US "LSM I" CLASS

Name	No.	Builders	Commissioned
LOS MONJES (ex-USS *LSM 548*)	T 21 (ex-T 13)	Brown Shipbuilding Co, Houston, Texas	1945
LOS ROQUES (ex-USS *LSM 543*)	T 22 (ex-T 14)	Brown Shipbuilding Co, Houston, Texas	1945
LOS FRAILES (ex-USS *LSM 544*)	T 23 (ex-T 15)	Brown Shipbuilding Co, Houston, Texas	1945
LOS TESTIGOS (ex-USS *LSM 545*)	T 24 (ex-T 16)	Brown Shipbuilding Co, Houston, Texas	1945

Displacement, tons: 743 beaching; 1 095 full load
Dimensions, feet (metres): 196.5 wl; 203.5 oa × 34.5 × 8.3 *(59.9; 62.1 × 10.5 × 2.5)*
Guns: 1—40 mm; 4—20 mm
Main engines: Direct drive diesels; 2 shafts; 2 800 bhp = 12 knots
Range, miles: 9 000 at 11 knots
Complement: 59

LOS MONJES (old pennant number)   *1970, Venezuelan Navy*

Transferred to Venezuela under MAP—Feb 1959 (T 21), Sept 1959 (T 22), Dec 1959 (T 23), Jan 1960 (T 24).

1 Ex-US "ACHELOUS" CLASS

Name	No.	Builders	Commissioned
GUYANA (ex-USS *Quirinus*, ARL 39, ex-*LST 1151*)	T 31 (ex-T 18)	Chicago Bridge & Iron Co, Seneca, Illinois	1945

Displacement, tons: 1 625 light; 4 100 full load
Dimensions, feet (metres): 316 wl; 328 oa × 50 × 11.2 *(103.6; 107.7 × 15.3 × 3.7)*
Guns: 8—40 mm (two quadruple mountings)
Main engines: GM diesels; 2 shafts; 1 800 bhp = 11.6 knots
Complement: 81 (11 officers, 70 men)

Former US Navy landing craft repair ship. Laid down on 3 March 1945. Loaned to Venezuela in June 1962 and now used as a transport.

GUYANA (old pennant number)   *1970, Venezuelan Navy*

12 LCVPS

Built by Dianca, Puerto Cabello 1972-73.

MISCELLANEOUS

TRANSPORTS

Name	No.	Builders	Commissioned
— (ex-M/V *Ciudad de Valencia*)	—	Vickers, Canada	1953

Measurement, tons: 4 297 gross; 5 885 dwt
Dimensions, feet (metres): 420.5 × 55 × 22.3 *(128.15 × 16.76 × 6.78)*
Main engine: 1 Nordberg diesel; 4 275 hp = 15 knots

Acquired from state shipping company in 1977.

MARACAIBO   T 41 (ex-T 19)

Displacement, tons: 7 450 full load
Dimensions, feet (metres): 338.8 × 50.3 × 21 *(103.3 × 15.3 × 6.4)*
Main engine: Diesel; 1 shaft; 1 750 bhp = 11.5 knots

Built in Canada in 1949.

1 JAPANESE TYPE

Name	No.	Builders	Commissioned
PUNTA CABANA	T ? (ex-T 17)	Uraga Dockyard, Japan	—

Displacement, tons: 3 200
Dimensions, feet (metres): 373.9 × 52.5 × 22.9 *(114 × 16 × 7)*
Main engine: Diesel; 5 500 hp = 17 knots
Range, miles: 6 000 at 15 knots

Name	No.	Builders	Commissioned
LAS AVES (ex-*Dos de Diciembre*)	T ? (ex-T 12)	Chantiers Dubigeon, Nantes-Chantenay	1955

Displacement, tons: 944
Dimensions, feet (metres): 234.2 × 33.5 × 10 *(71 × 10.2 × 3.1)*
Guns: 4—20 mm (2 twin)
Main engines: 2 diesels; 2 shafts; 1 600 bhp = 15 knots
Radius, miles: 2 600 at 11 knots

Launched in Sept 1954. Light transport for naval personnel. Renamed *Las Aves* in 1961. Can be used as Presidential Yacht.

LAS AVES   *1970, Venezuelan Navy*

VENEZUELA 745

SURVEY SHIPS

Note: One Oceanographic ship projected.

1 Ex-US "COHOES" CLASS

Name	No.	Builders	Commissioned
PUERTO SANTO (ex-USS *Marietta*, AN 82)	H 01	Commercial Iron Works, Portland, Oregon	1945

Displacement, tons: 650 standard; 855 full load
Dimensions, feet (metres): 168·5 oa × 33·8 × 11·7 *(51·4 × 10·2 × 3·3)*
Guns: 3—20 mm
Main engines: Bush-Sulzer diesel-electric; 1 shaft; 1 500 bhp = 12 knots
Complement: 46

Puerto Santo loaned from USA in Jan 1961 under MAP and converted into Hydrographic survey vessel and buoy tender by US Coast Guard Yard, Curtis Bay, Maryland, in Feb 1962. Originally carried one 3-in 50 cal gun. Since 1977 used full-time as a buoy tender.

PUERTO SANTO   1970, Venezuelan Navy

2 SURVEY LAUNCHES

Name	No.	Builders	Commissioned
GABRIELA	P 119	Abeking and Rasmussen, Lemwerder	5 Feb 1974
LELY	P 121	Abeking and Rasmussen, Lemwerder	7 Feb 1974

Displacement, tons: 90
Dimensions, feet (metres): 88·6 × 18·4 × 4·9 *(27 × 5·6 × 1·5)*
Main engines: 2 diesels; 2 300 hp = 20 knots
Complement: 16

Lely laid down 28 May 1973, launched 12 Dec 1973 and *Gabriela* laid down 10 March 1973, launched 29 Nov 1973. Non-naval—civilian manned by Instituto de Canalizaciones.

TUGS

1 Ex-US OCEAN TUG

Name	No.	Builders	Commissioned
FELIPE LARRAZABAL (ex-USS *Utina*, ATF 163)	R 21	—	—

Displacement, tons: 1 235 standard; 1 675 full load
Dimensions, feet (metres): 205 oa × 38·5 × 15·5 *(61·7 × 11·6 × 4·7)*
Gun: 1—3 in 50 cal
Main engines: Diesel-electric; 3 000 bhp; 1 shaft
Speed, knots: 15
Complement: 85

Transferred 3 Sept 1971. This is the third tug of this name. The first (ex-USS *Discoverer*) was deleted in 1962. The second (ex-USS *Tolowa*, ATF 116) was deleted in 1972 after damage when grounded.

4 HARBOUR TUGS

C 139   C 140   C 141   C 142

Built by Dianca, Puerto Cabello. Two Werkspoor diesels; two shafts; 1 600 bhp. Ordered in 1973—C 139 launched in 1974 for completion 1975, other three completed 1976.

1 Ex-US HARBOUR TUG

FERNANDO GOMEZ (ex-YTM 744) R 11 (ex-R 12)

Displacement, tons: 161
Dimensions, feet (metres): 80 × 19 × 8 *(24·5 × 5·8 × 2·5)*
Main engines: Clark diesel; 6-cyl, 315 rpm; 380 bhp = 15 knots
Complement: 10

1 Ex-US HARBOUR TUG

GENERAL JOSE FELIX RIBAS (ex-USS *Oswegatchie*, YTM 778, ex-YTB 515) R 13

Displacement, tons: 345
Dimensions, feet (metres): 100 × 26 × 9·7 *(30·5 × 7·3 × 2·9)*
Speed, knots: 12
Complement: 10

Transferred in March 1965 at San Diego, Calif.

2 Ex-US MEDIUM HARBOUR TUGS

FABRIO GALLIPOLI (ex-USS *Wannalancet* YTM 385) R 14
DIANA III (ex-USS *Sassacus* YTM 193)

Leased to Venezuela in Aug 1965.

5 Ex-US SMALL HARBOUR TUGS

Ex-US YTL 446, 451, 455, 590, 592

80 feet long, leased in Jan 1963.

REPAIR CRAFT

GOLFO DE CARIACO DF 11 (ex-USS *ARD 13*, ex-DF 1)

Floating dock of 3 000 tons and built of steel. Transferred on loan to Venezuela in Feb 1962. Purchased 1977.

Ex-US YR 48 (Floating Workshop) transferred 1965. Purchased 1977.
One Floating Crane with 40 ton lift.

NATIONAL GUARD

6 COASTAL PATROL CRAFT

RIO META   RIO URIBANTE
RIO PORTUGUESA   + 3

Displacement, tons: 45
Dimensions, feet (metres): 88·6 × 16 × 4·9 *(27 × 4·9 × 1·5)*
Guns: 1—20 mm; 1 MG
Main engines: 2 diesels; 3 300 hp = 30 knots
Range, miles: 1 500 at 15 knots
Complement: 12

Built at Chantiers Navals de l'Esterel in 1971-76. Manned by National Guard.

8 "RIO" CLASS (COASTAL PATROL CRAFT)

Name	No.	Builders	Commissioned
RIO APURE	—	Chantiers Navals de l'Esterel, Cannes	1954
RIO ARAUCA	—	Chantiers Navals de l'Esterel, Cannes	1954
RIO CABRIALES	—	Chantiers Navals de l'Esterel, Cannes	1954
RIO CARONI	—	Chantiers Navals de l'Esterel, Cannes	1954
RIO GUARICO	—	Chantiers Navals de l'Esterel, Cannes	1954
RIO NEGRO	—	Chantiers Navals de l'Esterel, Cannes	1954
RIO NEVERI	—	Chantiers Navals de l'Esterel, Cannes	1954
RIO TUX	—	Chantiers Navals de l'Esterel, Cannes	1954

Displacement, tons: 38
Dimensions, feet (metres): 82 oa × 15 × 4 *(28 × 4·7 × 1·3)*
Main engines: 2 MTU 12 V 493 diesels; 1 400 rpm; 1 350 bhp = 27 knots

Manned by National Guard.

RIO NEGRO   1972, Venezuelan Navy

1 COASTAL PATROL CRAFT

GOLFO DE CARIACO

Displacement, tons: 37
Dimensions, feet (metres): 65 × 18 × 9 *(20 × 5·5 × 2·8)*
Main engines: Diesels; speed = 19 knots
Complement: 10

Manned by National Guard.

1 COASTAL PATROL CRAFT

RIO SANTO DOMINGO

Displacement, tons: 40
Dimensions, feet (metres): 70 × 15 × 6 *(22 × 4·6 × 1·9)*
Main engines: 2 GM diesels; 1 250 bhp = 24 knots
Complement: 10

Manned by National Guard.

746 VIET-NAM

VIET-NAM

Administration

Commander in Chief of the Navy:
Rear-Admiral Ta Xuan Thu

Strength of the Fleet

It is impossible to give an accurate estimate of this fleet—the details following refer to the known classes in 1975 including their names and pennant numbers at that time. There is no evidence as to which ships have been made operational. All that can be said is that those listed did not get away.
So far as operational availability is concerned only a very small proportion of this considerable force can be considered fit for sea. Of those that are seaworthy very few can steam any distance due to a chronic lack of fuel oil.

Personnel

1978: ?

Mercantile Marine

Lloyd's Register of Shipping:
69 vessels of 128 525 tons gross

FRIGATES

1 Ex-US "BARNEGAT" CLASS

Name	No.	Builders	Launched	Commissioned
THAM NGU LAO (ex-USCGC *Absecon*, WHEC 374, ex-AVP 23)	HQ 15	Lake Washington SY	8 Mar 1942	28 Jan 1943

Displacement, tons: 1 766 standard; 2 800 full load
Length, feet (metres): 310·75 *(94·7)*
Beam, feet (metres): 41·1 *(12·5)*
Draught, feet (metres): 13·5 *(4·1)*
Guns: 1—5 in *(127 mm)* 0·38 cal; 2—81 mm mortars; several MG
Main engines: Diesels (Fairbanks-Morse); 6 080 bhp; 2 shafts
Speed, knots: approx 18
Complement: approx 200

Last of a group built as seaplane tenders for the US Navy. Transferred to US Coast Guard in 1948, initially on loan designated WAVP and then on permanent transfer subsequently redesignated as high endurance cutter (WHEC). Transferred from US Coast Guard to South Vietnamese Navy in 1971.

Ex-US "BARNEGAT" Class   *1971, Vietnamese Navy*

1 Ex-US "SAVAGE" CLASS

Name	No.	Builders	Launched	Commissioned
TRAN KHANH DU (ex-USS *Forster*, DER 334)	HQ 04	Consolidated Steel Corp, Orange, Texas	13 Nov 1943	25 Jan 1944

Displacement, tons: 1 590 standard; 1 850 full load
Length, feet (metres): 306 *(93·3)*
Beam, feet (metres): 36·6 *(11·2)*
Draught, feet (metres): 14 *(4·3)*
Guns: 2—3 in *(76 mm)* 50 cal (single)
A/S weapons: 6 (Mk 32 triple) torpedo tubes; 1 trainable Hedgehog (Mk 15); depth charge rack
Main engines: Diesel (Fairbank-Morse); 6 000 bhp; 2 shafts
Speed, knots: 21
Complement: approx 170

Former US Navy destroyer escort of the FMR design group. Employed during 1960s in Indochina for coastal patrol and interdiction by US Navy (Operation MARKET TIME). Transferred to South Vietnamese Navy on 25 Sept 1971. Was in overhaul at time of occupation of South Viet-Nam.

Radar: Search: SPS 10 and 28.

TRAN KHANH DU   *1971, Vietnamese Navy*

CORVETTES

2 Ex-US "ADMIRABLE" CLASS

Name	No.	Launched
KY HOA (ex-USS *Sentry*, MSF 299)	HQ 09	15 Aug 1943
HA HOI (ex-USS *Prowess*, IX 305, ex-MSF 280)	HQ 13	17 Feb 1944

Displacement, tons: 650 standard; 945 full load
Dimensions, feet (metres): 184·5 × 33 × 9·75 *(56·3 × 10 × 3)*
Guns: 1—3 in *(76 mm)* 50 cal; 2—40 mm (single); up to 8—20 mm (twin)
A/S weapons: 1 fixed Hedgehog; depth charges
Main engines: Diesel (Cooper Bessemer); 1 710 bhp; 2 shafts = 14 knots
Complement: approx 80

Former US Navy minesweepers of the "Admirable" class (originally designated AM). *Ky Hoa* built by Winslow Marine Railway & SB Co, Winslow, Washington, and *Ha Hoi* by Gulf SB Corp, Chicasaw, Alabama.
Ky Hoa transferred in Aug 1962, *Ha Hoi* transferred on 4 June 1970. Minesweeping equipment has been removed and two depth charge racks fitted on fantail; employed in patrol and escort roles.

VIET-NAM

LIGHT FORCES

3 Ex-SOVIET "SO 1" CLASS

Displacement, tons: 215 light; 250 normal
Dimensions, feet (metres): 138·6 × 20 × 9·2 *(45·4 × 6·5 × 3)*
Guns: 4—25 mm (2 twin mountings)
A/S weapons: 4—5-barrelled MBU; 2 DCT
Range, miles: 1 100 at 13 knots
Main engines: 3 diesels; 6 000 hp = 29 knots
Complement: 30

Four of Soviet "SO 1" class were originally transferred to North Viet-Nam, two in 1960-61 and two in 1964-65, but one was sunk by US Navy aircraft on 1 Feb 1966.

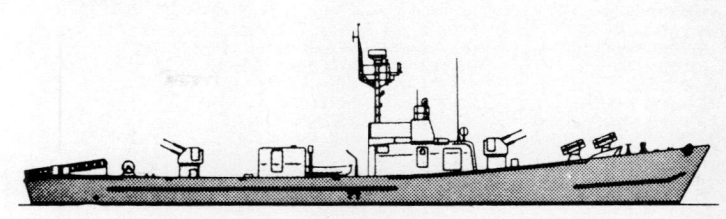

"SO 1" Class

19 Ex-US "PGM 59" and "71" CLASSES (LARGE PATROL CRAFT)

Name	No.	Transferred
PHU DU	HQ 600 (PGM 64)	Feb 1963
TIEN MOI	HQ 601 (PGM 65)	Feb 1963
MINH HOA	HQ 602 (PGM 66)	Feb 1963
KIEN VANG	HQ 603 (PGM 67)	Feb 1963
KEO NGUA	HQ 604 (PGM 68)	Feb 1963
KIM QUI	HQ 605 (PGM 60)	May 1963
MAY RUT	HQ 606 (PGM 59)	May 1963
NAM DU	HQ 607 (PGM 61)	May 1963
HOA LU	HQ 608 (PGM 62)	July 1963
TO YEN	HQ 609 (PGM 63)	July 1963
DINH HAI	HQ 610 (PGM 69)	Feb 1964
TRUONG SA	HQ 611 (PGM 70)	April 1964
THAI BINH	HQ 612 (PGM 72)	Jan 1966
THI TU	HQ 613 (PGM 73)	Jan 1966
SONG TU	HQ 614 (PGM 74)	Jan 1966
TAT SA	HQ 615 (PGM 80)	Oct 1966
HOANG SA	HQ 616 (PGM 82)	April 1967
PHU QUI	HQ 617 (PGM 81)	April 1967
THO CHAU	HQ 619 (PGM 91)	April 1967

KIM QUI *1970, Vietnamese Navy*

Displacement, tons: 117 full load
Dimensions, feet (metres): 100·3 oa × 21·1 × 6·9 *(30·6 × 6·4 × 2·1)*
Guns: 1—40 mm; 2 or 4—20 mm (twin); 2—MG
Main engines: Diesel; 1 900 bhp; 2 shafts = 17 knots
Complement: approx 15

Welded-steel patrol gunboats built in the United States specifically for foreign transfer; assigned PGM numbers for contract purposes. Enlarged version of US Coast Guard 95-foot patrol boats with commercial-type machinery and electronic equipment. HQ 600-605 built by J. M. Martinac SB Corp, Tacoma, Washington; HQ 606-610 built by Marinette Marine Corp. Wisconsin.

2 Ex-SOVIET "KOMAR" CLASS
(FAST ATTACK CRAFT—MISSILE)

Displacement, tons: 70 standard; 80 full load
Dimensions, feet (metres): 83·7 × 19·8 × 5·0 *(27·4 × 6·5 × 1·6)*
Missiles: 2—SS-N-2 launchers
Guns: 2—25 mm (twin forward)
Main engines: 4 diesels; 4 shafts; 4 800 hp = 40 knots
Range, miles: 400 at 30 knots

A sister ship was reported sunk on 19 Dec 1972.

6 Ex-SOVIET "P 4" CLASS (FAST ATTACK CRAFT—TORPEDO)

Displacement, tons: 25 standard
Dimensions, feet (metres): 62·7 × 11·6 × 5·6 *(20·5 × 3·8 × 1·8)*
Guns: 2 MG (1 twin)
Torpedo tubes: 2—18 in
Main engines: 2 diesels; 2 200 bhp = 50 knots

Approximately a dozen aluminium hulled motor torpedo boats were transferred from the Soviet Union in 1961 and 1964 and some from China. A number have been lost in action.

6 Ex-CHINESE "P 6" CLASS (FAST ATTACK CRAFT—TORPEDO)

Displacement, tons: 66 standard; 75 full load
Dimensions, feet (metres): 84·1 × 20 × 6 *(27·7 × 6·5 × 1·9)*
Guns: 4—25 mm (2 twin)
Torpedo tubes: 2—21 in (single)
Mines: 4
Main engines: 4 diesels; 4 800 bhp; 4 shafts = 43 knots
Range, miles: 450 at 30 knots
Complement: 25

Built in China and transferred in 1967. Some may have been lost in action.

"P 6" Class

8 Ex-CHINESE "SHANGHAI" CLASS
(FAST ATTACK CRAFT—GUN)

Displacement, tons: 120 full load
Dimensions, feet (metres): 128 × 18 × 5·5 *(39 × 5·5 × 1·7)*
Guns: 4—37 mm (2 twin mountings); 4—25 mm (twins)
Main engines: 4 diesels; 4 800 bhp = 30 knots
Complement: 25

Four were received from the People's Republic of China in May 1966.

"SHANGHAI II" Class *1972, Aviation Fan*

14 Ex-CHINESE "SWATOW" CLASS
(FAST ATTACK CRAFT—GUN)

Displacement, tons: 80 full load
Dimensions, feet (metres): 83·5 × 19 × 6·5 *(27·4 × 6·2 × 2·1)*
Guns: 4—37 mm; 2—20 mm
A/S weapons: 8 depth charges
Main engines: 4 diesels; 4 800 bhp = 40 knots
Range, miles: 750 at 15 knots
Complement: 17

Approximately 30 "Swatow" class built in China were transferred in 1958, and 20 were delivered in 1964 to replace those lost in action. Pennant numbers run in a 600 series.

748 VIET-NAM

26 Ex-USCG 82-ft "POINT" CLASS
(COASTAL PATROL CRAFT)

Name	No.
LE PHUOC DUI	HQ 700 (ex-*Point Garnet* 82310)
LE VAN NGA	HQ 701 (ex-*Point League* 82304)
HUYNH VAN CU	HQ 702 (ex-*Point Clear* 82315)
NGUYEN DAO	HQ 703 (ex-*Point Gammon* 82328)
DAO THUC	HQ 704 (ex-*Point Comfort* 82317)
LE NGOC THANH	HQ 705 (ex-*Point Ellis* 82330)
NGUYEN NGOC THACH	HQ 706 (ex-*Point Slocum* 82313)
DANG VAN HOANH	HQ 707 (ex-*Point Hudson* 82322)
LE DINH HUNG	HQ 708 (ex-*Point White* 82308)
THUONG TIEN	HQ 709 (ex-*Point Dume* 82325)
PHAM NGOC CHAU	HQ 710 (ex-*Point Arden* 82309)
DAO VAN DANG	HQ 711 (ex-*Point Glover* 82307)
LE DGOC AN	HQ 712 (ex-*Point Jefferson* 82306)
HUYNH VAN NGAN	HQ 713 (ex-*Point Kennedy* 82320)
TRAN LO	HQ 714 (ex-*Point Young* 82303)
BUI VIET THANH	HQ 715 (ex-*Point Patrige* 82305)
NGUYEN AN	HQ 716 (ex-*Point Caution* 82301)
NGUYEN HAN	HQ 717 (ex-*Point Welcome* 82329)
NGO VAN QUYEN	HQ 718 (ex-*Point Banks* 82327)
VAN DIEN	HQ 719 (ex-*Point Lomas* 82321)
HO DANG LA	HQ 720 (ex-*Point Grace* 82323)
DAM THOAI	HQ 721 (ex-*Point Mast* 82316)
HUYNH BO	HQ 722 (ex-*Point Grey* 82324)
NGUYEN KIM HUNG	HQ 723 (ex-*Point Orient* 82319)
HO DUY	HQ 724 (ex-*Point Cypress* 82326)
TROUNG BA	HQ 725 (ex-*Point Maromc* 82331)

Displacement, tons: 64 standard; 67 full load
Dimensions, feet (metres): 83 × 17·2 × 5·8 *(25·3 × 5·2 × 1·8)*

"POINT" Class   1970, Vietnamese Navy

Guns: 1—81 mm/50 cal MG (combination) plus 2 to 4—50 cal MG (single) or 1—20 mm
Main engines: 2 diesels; 1 200 bhp; 2 shafts = 16·8 knots
Complement: 8 to 10

Former US Coast Guard 82-foot patrol boats (designated WPB). All served in Vietnamese waters, manned by US personnel, comprising Coast Guard Squadron One. HQ 700-707 transferred to South Vietnamese Navy in 1969, HQ 708-HQ 725 in 1970.

30 MOTOR LAUNCH TYPES (COASTAL PATROL CRAFT)

Some 30 motor launches were reported to have been incorporated into the North Viet-Nam Navy before May 1966, but not all are still in service.

AMPHIBIOUS FORCES

3 Ex-US "501-1152" CLASS (LSTs)

Name	No.	Launched
DA NANG (ex-USS *Maricopa County*, LST 938)	HQ 501	15 Aug 1944
VUNG TAU (ex-USS *Cochino County*, LST 603)	HQ 503	14 Mar 1944
QUI NHON (ex-USS *Bullock County*, LST 509)	HQ 504	23 Nov 1943

Displacement, tons: 2 366 beaching; 4 080 full load
Dimensions, feet (metres): 328 oa × 50 × 14 *(100 × 15·2 × 4·6)*
Guns: 7 or 8—40 mm (1 or 2 twin; 4 or 5 single); several 20 mm
Main engines: Diesel (General Motors); 1 700 bhp; 2 shafts = 11 knots
Complement: 110

Former US Navy tank landing ships HQ 501 built by Bethlehem Steel Co, Hingham, Massachusetts; HQ 504 by Jeffersonville B & M Co, Jeffersonville, Indiana; HQ 503 by Chicago Bridge & Iron Co. Illinois. Lattice tripod masts.

QUI NHON   1971, Vietnamese Navy

5 Ex-US "LSM-1" CLASS

Name	No.	Launched
HAN GIANG (ex-LSM 9012, ex-USS LSM 110)	HQ 401	28 Oct 1944
LAM GIANG (ex-USS LSM 226)	HQ 402	4 Sept 1944
NINH GIANG (ex-USS LSM 85)	HQ 403	15 Sept 1944
TIEN GIANG (ex-USS LSM 313)	HQ 405	24 May 1944
HAU GIANG (ex-USS LSM 276)	HQ 406	20 Sept 1944

Displacement, tons: 743 beaching; 1 095 full load
Dimensions, feet (metres): 203·5 × 34·5 × 8·3 *(62 × 10·5 × 2·5)*
Guns: 2—40 mm; 4—20 mm
Main engines: Diesel; 2 shafts; 2 800 bhp = 12 knots
Complement: 73

First three transferred to French Navy for use in Indo-China, Jan 1954. *Han Giang* transferred to Viet-Nam Navy, Dec 1955. *Tien Giang* transferred in 1962, *Hau Giang* on 10 June 1965.

LAM GIANG   Vietnamese Navy

1 Ex-US "LSSL-1" CLASS

Name	No.	Launched
NGUYEN NGOC LONG (ex-USS LSSL 96)	HQ 230	6 Jan 1945

Displacement, tons: 227 standard; 383 full load
Dimensions, feet (metres): 158 × 23·7 × 5·7 *(48·3 × 7·6 × 1·8)*
Guns: 1—3 in; 4—40 mm; 4—20 mm; 4 MG
Main engines: Diesel; 2 shafts; 1 600 bhp = 14 knots
Complement: 60

Served in Japanese Navy in 1953 to 1964; retransferred to South Viet-Nam in 1965.

LSSL Type   Vietnamese Navy

VIET-NAM

18 Ex-US LCU TYPE

HQ 533 (ex-US LCU 1479)	HQ 543 (ex-US LCU 1493)
HQ 534 (ex-US LCU 1480)	HQ 544 (ex-US LCU 1485)
HQ 535 (ex-US LCU 1221)	HQ 545 (ex-US LCU 1484)
HQ 536 (ex-US LCU 1595)	HQ 546 (ex-US YFU 90, ex-LCU 1582)
HQ 537 (ex-US LCU 1501)	HQ 547 (ex-US LCU 1481)
HQ 538 (ex-US LCU 1594)	HQ 548 (ex-US LCU 1498)
HQ 539 (ex-US LCU 1502)	HQ 560 (ex-US YLLC 1, LCU 1348)
HQ 540 (ex-US LCU 1475)	HQ 561 (ex-US YLLC5, YFU 2, LCU 529)
HQ 542 (ex-US LCU 1494)	HQ 562 (ex-US YLLC 3, YFU 33, LCU 1195)

LCU 501 series

Displacement, tons: 309 to 320 full load
Dimensions, feet (metres): 119 × 32·7 × 5 *(36·3 × 10 × 1·5)*
Main engines: Diesels (Gray Marine); 675 bhp; 3 shafts = 10 knots

LCU 1466 series

Displacement, tons: 360 full load
Dimensions, feet (metres): 119 × 34 × 5·25 *(36·3 × 10·6 × 1·7)*
Main engines: Diesels (Gray Marine); 675 bhp; 3 shafts = 8 knots

501 series built during World War II with LCT (6) designation; 1466 series built during the early 1950s. Transferred to South Viet-Nam from 1954 to 1971, with some of the earlier craft serving briefly in French Navy in Indo-China waters.

Most units armed with two 20 mm guns.

HQ 538   *1971, Vietnamese Navy*

MISCELLANEOUS

RIVERINE CRAFT

The US Navy transferred approximately 700 armed small craft to South Viet-Nam since 1965. A few former French riverine craft also survive. The exact number of these craft now in service is not known.

In addition to the armed craft grouped here under the category of Riverine (Warfare) Craft, there are numerous small landing craft which are armed.

107 Ex-US "SWIFT" CLASS

Displacement, tons: 22·5 full load
Dimensions, feet (metres): 50 × 13 × 3·5 *(15·2 × 3·8 × 1·1)*
Guns: 1—81 mm mortar/1—50 cal MG combination mount: 2—0·50 cal MG (twin)
Main engines: 2 geared diesels (General Motors); 960 bhp; 2 shafts = 28 knots
Complement: 6

All-metal inshore patrol craft (PCF). Transferred to South Viet-Nam from 1968 to 1970. Numbered in HQ 3800-3887 and later series.

HQ 3825   *1970, Vietnamese Navy*

293 Ex-US PBR TYPE

Displacement, tons: PBR I series: 7·5; PBR II series: 8
Dimensions, feet (metres): PBR I series: 31 × 10·5 × 2·5 *(9·1 × 3·1 × 0·8)*
PBR II series: 32 × 11 × 2·6 *(9·3 × 3·2 × 0·8)*
Guns: 3—0·50 cal MG (twin mount forward; single gun aft)
Main engines: 2 geared diesels; 440 bhp; water-jet propulsion = 25+ knots
Complement: 4 or 5

River patrol boats (PBR) with fibreglass (plastic) hulls. Transferred to South Viet-Nam from 1968 to 1970. Numbered in HQ 7500-7749 and 7800 series.

PBR Type   *1970, Vietnamese Navy*

27 Ex-US RCP TYPE

Displacement, tons: 15·6
Dimensions, feet (metres): 35·75 × 10·3 × 3·6 *(10·9 × 3·1 × 1·2)*
Guns: varies: 2—0·50 cal MG (twin); 3—0·30 cal MG (twin mount aft and single gun at conning station); some units have additional twin 0·30 cal mount in place of 0·50 cal MH
Main engines: 2 geared diesels; 2 shafts = 14 knots

River patrol craft (RPC); predecessor to PBR type. Welded-steel hulls. Few used by US Navy as minesweepers, but most of the 34 units built were transferred to South Viet-Nam upon completion in 1965; others in 1968-69. Numbered HQ 7000-7028.

RCP Type   *1970, Vietnamese Navy*

84 Ex-US ASPB TYPE

Displacement, tons: 36·25 full load
Dimensions, feet (metres): 50 × 15·6 × 3·75 *(15·2 × 4·8 × 1·1)*
Guns: varies: 1 or 2—20 mm (with 2—0·50 cal MG in boats with one 20 mm); 2—0·30 cal MG; 2—40 mm grenade launchers
Main engines: 2 geared diesels; 2 shafts = 14 knots sustained
Complement: 6

Assault support patrol boats (ASPB) with welded-steel hulls. Transferred to South Viet-Nam from 1969 to 1970. Numbered in HQ 5100 series.

ASPB Type   *1970, Vietnamese Navy*

42 Ex-US MONITORS

Displacement, tons: 80 to 90 full load
Dimensions, feet (metres): 60·5 × 17·5 × 3·5 *(18·3 × 5·3 × 1·1)*
Guns: 1—105 mm howitzer; 2—20 mm; 3—0·30 cal MG; 2—40 mm grenade launchers
Main engines: 2 geared diesels; 2 shafts = 9 knots
Complement: 11

River monitors (MON). Transferred to South Viet-Nam in 1969-70. Numbered in HQ 6500 series.

VIET-NAM / VIRGIN ISLANDS

22 Ex-US LCM MONITORS

Displacement, tons: 75 full load
Dimensions, feet (metres): 60 × 17 × 3·5 (18·3 × 5·2 × 1·1)
Guns: varies: 1—81 mm mortar or 2 M10-8 flame throwers; 1—40 mm; 1—20 mm; 2—0·50 cal MG; possibly 2 to 4—0·30 cal MG
Main engines: 2 geared diesels; 2 shafts = 8 knots
Complement: approx 10

Twenty-four LCM-6 landing craft converted to this configuration from 1964 to 1967. Predecessor to the Monitor listed above. Transferred to South Viet-Nam from 1965 to 1970. Numbered in HQ 1800 series.

LCM MONITOR 1970, Vietnamese Navy

100 Ex-US ATC TYPE

Displacement, tons: 66 full load
Dimensions, feet (metres): 65·5 × 17·5 × 3·25 (20 × 5·4 × 1)
Guns: varies: 1 or 2—20 mm; 2—0·50 cal MG; several 0·30 cal MG; 2—40 mm grenade launchers
Main engines: 2 geared diesels; 2 shafts = 8·5 knots (6 knots sustained)

Armoured troop carriers (ATC). Some fitted with steel helicopter platforms for evacuation of wounded. Transferred to South Viet-Nam in 1969. Numbered in HQ 1200 series.

9 Ex-US CCB TYPE

Displacement, tons: 80 full load
Dimensions, feet (metres): 61 × 17·5 × 3·4 (18·6 × 5·4 × 1·1)
Guns: 3—20 mm; 2—0·30 cal MG; 2—40 mm grenade launchers
Main engines: 2 geared diesels; 2 shafts = 8·5 knots maximum (6 knots sustained)
Complement: 11

Transferred to South Viet-Nam in 1969-1970. Numbered HQ 6100-6108.

4 Ex-US CSB TYPE

Dimensions, feet (metres): 56 × 18·75 × 6 (17·1 × 5·7 × 1·7)
Guns: 4—0·50 cal MG (twin)
Main engines: 2 geared diesels; 2 shafts = 6 knots
Complement: 6

Combat salvage boats (CSB) converted from LCM-6 landing craft; configured for river salvage and to support diving operations. Ten-ton capacity "A" frame forward.

Ex-FRENCH CRAFT

The Vietnamese Navy listed 43 ex-French STCAN/FOM and 14 LCM Commandement as being in service. The latter are converted LCM-3 landing craft.

MINESWEEPING LAUNCHES

Before cessation of hostilities 24 minesweeping launches were listed in the South Vietnamese Navy; ten MLMS 50-foot type transferred in 1963 from US Navy (numbered HQ 150-155, 157-160; HQ 156 and 161 stricken in 1971); eight MSM 56-foot type transferred in 1970 (numbered HQ 1700-1707); six MSR 50-foot type transferred in 1970 (numbered HQ 1900-1905). Other riverine craft had a minesweeping capability.

MLMS 1971, Vietnamese Navy

TANKERS

4 Ex-US YOG TYPE

HQ 472 (ex-US YOG 67)   HQ 474 (ex-YOG 131)
HQ 473 (ex-US YOG 71)   HQ 475 (ex-YOG 56)

Displacement, tons: 450 light; 1 253 full load
Dimensions, feet (metres): 174·0 × 32·0 × 10·9 (53 × 9·8 × 3·1)
Main engines: Diesels; 1 shaft = 10 knots
Cargo Capacity: 6 570 barrels

Former US Navy small gasoline tankers.
Transfers: HQ 472 in July 1967, HQ 473 in Mar 1970; HQ 474 in April 1971, and HQ 475 in June 1972.

WATER CARRIERS

2 Ex-US YW TYPE

HQ 9118 (ex-US YW 152)   HQ 9113 (ex-US YW 153)

Former US Navy self-propelled water carriers. Transferred to South Viet-Nam in 1956.

HARBOUR TUGS

9 Ex-US YTL TYPE

HQ 9500 (ex-US YTL 152)   HQ 9508 (ex-US YTL 452)
HQ 9501 (ex-US YTL 245)   HQ 9509 (ex-US YTL 456)
HQ 9502 (ex-US YTL)   HQ 9510 (ex-US YTL 586)
HQ 9503 (ex-US YTL 200)   HQ 9511 (ex-US YTL 457)
HQ 9504 (ex-US YTL 206)

Former US Navy harbour tugs. HQ 9500 transferred to South Viet-Nam in 1955; HQ 9501, 9503, 9504 in 1956; others from 1968 to 1970.

VIRGIN ISLANDS

An area of some 40 islands, large and small.

Chief of Police:
Mr. Rex K. Jones, MVO, QPM

Base
Road Town

1 BROOKE MARINE PATROL CRAFT

VIRGIN CLIPPER

Displacement, tons: 15
Dimensions, feet (metres): 40 × 12 × 2 (13·1 × 3·9 × 0·6)
Gun: 1 MG
Main engines: 2 diesels; 370 hp = 22 knots
Complement: 4

Standard Brooke Marine patrol craft attached to the Royal Virgin Islands Police Force.

VIRGIN CLIPPER 1975, Virgin Islands Police Force

YEMEN—NORTH
(Arab Republic)

Personnel
(a) 1978: 300 officers and men
(b) 3 years national service

Base
Hodeida

Mercantile Marine
Lloyd's Register of Shipping:
4 vessels of 1 436 tons gross

4 Ex-SOVIET "P 4" CLASS (FAST ATTACK CRAFT—TORPEDO)

Displacement, tons: 25
Dimensions, feet (metres): 62·7 × 11·6 × 5·6 (20·5 × 3·7 × 1·8)
Guns: 2 MG
Torpedo tubes: 2—18 in
Main engines: 2 diesels; 2 shafts; 2 200 hp = 50 knots

Transferred by USSR in late 1960s.

4 Ex-SOVIET "POLUCHAT" CLASS (LARGE PATROL CRAFT)

Displacement, tons: 70 standard; 90 full load
Dimensions, feet (metres): 98·4 × 19 × 5·9 (30 × 5·8 × 1·8)
Guns: 2—14·5 mm (twin)
Main engines: 2 diesels; 2 shafts; 2 400 shp = 20 knots
Complement: 20

Transferred 1970.

Note: In addition a dozen smaller Patrol Craft and two small landing craft have been reported.

YEMEN—SOUTH
(People's Democratic Republic)

Personnel
(a) 1978: 450 officers and men
(b) 2 years national service

Bases
Aden, Mukalla

Mercantile Marine
Lloyd's Register of Shipping:
16 vessels of 6 390 tons gross

LIGHT FORCES

Note: Also reported, but unconfirmed, that the USSR has transferred three "Osa" class fast attack craft (missile).

2 Ex-SOVIET "SO I" CLASS (LARGE PATROL CRAFT)

Displacement, tons: 215 standard; 250 full load
Dimensions, feet (metres): 138·6 × 20·0 × 9·2 (42·3 × 6·1 × 2·8)
Guns: 4—25 mm (twins)
A/S weapons: 2—5-barrelled RBUs; 2 DC racks
Main engines: 3 diesels; 6 000 shp = 29 knots
Range, miles: 1 100 at 13 knots
Complement: 30

Transferred in April 1972.

Soviet "SO I" Class   USN

2 Ex-SOVIET "P 6" CLASS (FAST ATTACK CRAFT—TORPEDO)

111   112

Displacement, tons: 66 standard; 75 full load
Dimensions, feet (metres): 84·2 × 20 × 6·0 (25·7 × 6·1 × 1·8)
Guns: 4—25 mm (twins)
Torpedo tubes: 2—21 in
Main engines: 4 diesels; 4 shafts; 4 800 bhp = 43 knots
Range, miles: 450 at 30 knots
Complement: 25

Transferred 1971

2 "ZHUK" CLASS (FAST ATTACK CRAFT—PATROL)

Displacement, tons: 60
Dimensions, feet (metres): 75 × 16 × 5 (22·9 × 4·9 × 1·5)
Guns: 4—14·5 mm (twin)
Main engines: 2 diesels = 34 knots

Transferred Feb 1975.

1 Ex-SOVIET "POLUCHAT" CLASS (LARGE PATROL CRAFT)

Displacement, tons: 70 standard; 90 full load
Dimensions, feet (metres): 98·4 × 19 × 5·9 (30 × 5·8 × 1·8)
Guns: 2—14·5 mm (twin)
Main engines: 2 diesels; 2 shafts; 2 400 shp = 20 knots
Complement: 20

3 FAIREY MARINE "SPEAR" CLASS
(COASTAL PATROL CRAFT)

Dimensions, feet (metres): 29·8 × 9·2 × 2·6 (9·1 × 2·8 × 0·8)
Guns: 3—7·62 mm MG
Main engines: 2 diesels; 290 hp = 25 knots

Delivered 30 Sept 1975.

1 FAIREY MARINE "INTERCEPTOR" CLASS

Of 25 feet (7·6 metres) with a catamaran hull. Can carry eight 25-man liferafts or a platoon of troops. Twin 135 outboard motors = 30 knots. Delivered 27 July 1975.

AMPHIBIOUS FORCES

2 Ex-SOVIET "POLNOCNY" CLASS (LCT)

Displacement, tons: 780 standard; 1 000 full load
Dimensions, feet (metres): 246 × 29·5 × 9·8 (73 × 9 × 3)
Guns: 4—25 mm (twin); 2—18-barrelled 140 mm rocket launchers
Main engines: 2 diesels; 5 000 bhp = 18 knots

Can carry six tanks. Transferred in Aug 1973.

1 "Z" LIGHTER

3 Ex-SOVIET T4 (LCVPs)

Main engines: 3 diesels; 3 shafts; 3 300 bhp = 24 knots
Range, miles: 1 500 at 12 knots

Transferred Nov 1970.

INSHORE MINESWEEPERS

3 Ex-BRITISH "HAM" CLASS

JIBLA (ex-HMS *Bodenham*, ex-*Al Saqr*)
SOCOTRA (ex-HMS *Blunham*, ex-*Al Dairak*)
ZINGAHAR (ex-HMS *Elsenham*, ex-*Al Ghazala*)

Displacement, tons: 120 standard; 160 full load
Dimensions, feet (metres): 106·5 oa × 21·2 × 5·5 (32·4 × 6·5 × 1·7)
Gun: 1—20 mm
Main engines: 2 Paxman diesels; 1 100 bhp = 14 knots
Oil fuel, tons: 15
Complement: 15 officers and men

Transferred to the South Arabian Navy established by the Federal Government in 1967. All three were renamed after local islands in 1975.

752 YUGOSLAVIA

YUGOSLAVIA

Ministerial

Federal Secretary for Peoples' Defence:
  General Nikola Ljubicic
Assistant Secretary for Peoples' Defence (Navy):
  Admiral Branko Mamula

Headquarters Appointments

Chief of General Staff:
  Colonel General Stane Potocar
Commander of Split Naval Region:
  Admiral Branko Mamula
Commander of the Fleet:
  Rear-Admiral Sveto Letica

Diplomatic Representation

Defence Attaché in London:
  Colonel M. Surlan
Naval, Military and Air Attaché in Moscow:
  Colonel S. Krivokapic
Naval, Military and Air Attaché in Washington:
  Colonel Milan Mavric

Personnel

(a) 1978: 20 000 (2 000 officers and 18 000 men)
(b) 18 months national service

Bases and Organisation

Split Naval Region: Major commands are the Fleet, Pula Naval District (HQ at Pula), Sibenik Naval District (HQ at Sibenik), Boka Naval Sector (HQ at Kumbor).
River Flotilla (Novi Sad) under operational command of Belgrade Army Region.
Main bases: Lora/Split: Minor bases: Pula, Sibenik, Ploce, Gulf of Cattaro.

Naval Air Arm

ASW helicopter squadron (Divulje) was formed in 1974-75 and has a number of Ka-25 Hormones.
There is also an air-liaison detachment (Divulje) composed of a few Mi-8 and S-55 helicopters and DHC-2 Beavers.

New Construction

As well as the new submarines, fast attack craft and LSTs it is reported that the first of a new class of surface ship, possibly of some 1 000 tons with two diesels and one Olympus Gas Turbine, is now in hand.

Strength of the Fleet

Type	Active	Building
Destroyer	1	—
Corvettes	3	—
Submarines—Patrol	5	2 + ?
Fast Attack Craft—Missile	14	6
Fast Attack Craft—Gun	6	—
Fast Attack Craft—Torpedo	14	—
Large Patrol Craft	24	—
Minesweepers—Coastal	4	—
Minesweepers—Inshore	10	—
River Minesweepers	17	?
LSTs	—	1
LCTs/Minelayers	24	—
LCAs	2	?
Training Ships	2	—
Survey Ship	1	—
HQ Ships	2	—
Salvage Vessel	1	—
Tankers	6	—
Transports	10	—
Ammunition Transports	4	—
Tugs	12	—
Water Carriers	3	—
Presidential Yacht	1	—

Mercantile Marine

Lloyd's Register of Shipping:
  459 vessels of 2 284 526 tons gross

DELETIONS

Destroyers

1971 *Kotor* (ex-*Kempenfelt*, ex-*Valentine*)
       Pula (ex-*Wager*)

Frigates

1971 *Biokovo* (ex-*Aliseo*), *Triglav* (ex-*Indomito*)

Submarines

1971 *Sava* (ex-*Nautilo*)

Large Patrol Craft

1975 Two "Kraljevica" class to Bangladesh, one to Ethiopia

SUBMARINES

0 + 2 "IMPROVED HEROJ" CLASS

Displacement, tons: 964 dived
Length, feet (metres): 215·8 *(65·8)*
Torpedo tubes: 6—21 in *(533 mm)* (10 reloads or 20 mines)
Main machinery: Diesel-electric
Speed, knots: 16·1 dived
Complement: 35

A new class of diesel propelled submarine now under construction in Yugoslavia. Diving depth 1 000 feet. Have Soviet electronic equipment and armament.

3 "HEROJ" CLASS (PATROL SUBMARINES)

Name	No.	Builders	Laid down	Launched	Commissioned
HEROJ	821	Uljanik Shipyard, Pula	1964	1967	1968
JUNAK	822	Uljanik Shipyard, Pula	1965	1968	1969
USKOK	823	Uljanik Shipyard, Pula	1966	1969	1970

Displacement, tons: 1 068 dived
Length, feet (metres): 210·0 *(64)*
Beam, feet (metres): 23·6 *(7·2)*
Draught, feet (metres): 16·4 *(5·0)*
Torpedo tubes: 6—21 in *(533 mm)* (bow)
Main machinery: Diesels; electric motors; 2 400 hp
Speed, knots: 16 surfaced; 10 dived
Complement: 55

Have Soviet electronic equipment and armament.

JUNAK   1972, S. and DE. Factory, Split

2 "SUTJESKA" CLASS (PATROL SUBMARINES)

Name	No.	Builders	Laid down	Launched	Commissioned
SUTJESKA	811	Uljanik Shipyard, Pula	1957	28 Sept 1958	16 Sept 1960
NERETVA	812	Uljanik Shipyard, Pula	1957	1959	1962

Displacement, tons: 820 surfaced; 945 dived
Length, feet (metres): 196·8 *(60·0)*
Beam, feet (metres): 22·3 *(6·8)*
Draught, feet (metres): 16·1 *(4·9)*
Torpedo tubes: 6—21 in *(533 mm)* (bow)
Main machinery: Diesels; electric motors; 1 800 hp
Speed, knots: 14 surfaced; 9 dived
Range, miles: 4 800 at 8 knots
Complement: 38

The first class of submarines to be built in a Yugoslav yard. Were later modernised and received Soviet electronic equipment and armament.

NERETVA   1969, Dr. Giorgio Arra

YUGOSLAVIA 753

"MALA" CLASS (2 MAN SUBMARINES)

Dimensions, feet (metres): 25 × 6 approx *(8·2 × 1·9 approx)*
Main motors: 1 electric motor; single screw
Complement: 2

This is a free-flood craft with the main motor, battery, navigation-pod and electronic equipment housed in separate watertight cylinders. Constructed of light aluminium it is fitted with fore- and after-hydroplanes, the tail being a conventional cruciform with a single rudder abaft the screw. Large perspex windows give a good all-round view.

Class name: This is not certain.

"MALA" Class *1973, S. and DE. Factory, Split*

DESTROYER

1 "SPLIT" CLASS

Name	No.	Builders	Laid down	Launched	Commissioned
SPLIT (ex-*Spalato*)	R 11	Brodogradiliste, Rijeka (see note)	July 1939	1940	1959 (see note)

Displacement, tons: 2 400 standard; 3 000 full load
Length, feet (metres): 376·3 *(114·7)* pp; 393·7 *(120·0)* oa
Beam, feet (metres): 36·5 *(11·1)*
Draught, feet (metres): 12·3 *(3·8)*
Guns: 4—5 in *(127 mm)*; 12—40 mm
A/S weapons: 2 Hedgehogs; 6 DCT; 2 DC racks
Torpedo tubes: 5—21 in *(533 mm)*
Mines: Capacity 40
Main engines: Geared turbines; 2 shafts; 50 000 shp
Boilers: 2 watertube type (1 operational)
Speed, knots: 24
Oil fuel, tons: 590
Complement: 240

Built by Brodogradiliste "3 Maj", Rijeka. The original ship was laid down in July 1939 by Chantieres de Loire, Nantes, in 1939 at Split Shipyard. Completed on 4 July 1958. Ready for operational service in 1959. The original design provided for an armament of 5—5·5 in guns, 10—40 m guns and 6—21·7 in torpedo tubes (tripled), but the plans were subsequently modified.
Only one boiler now operational. Serves as flagship of the Torpedo Boat Brigade.

Fire control: Mk 37 GFCS forward with Mk 12 and 22 radars; Mk 51 GFCS for 40 mm.

Radar: SC and SG1.

SPLIT *Commander Aldo Fraccaroli*

CORVETTES

2 "MORNAR" CLASS

Name	No.	Builders	Laid down	Launched	Commissioned
MORNAR	PBR 551	Tito SY, Kraljevica	1957	1958	10 Sept 1959
BORAC	PBR 552	Tito SY, Kraljevica	1964	1965	1965

Displacement, tons: 330 standard; 430 full load
Dimensions, feet (metres): 170 pp; 174·8 × 23 × 6·6 *(51·8; 53·3 × 7 × 2)*
Guns: 1—76 mm; 2—40 mm (single); 4—20 mm (quad, aft)
A/S weapons: 4 MBU-1200; 2 DCT; 2 DC racks
Main engines: 4 SEMT-Pielstick diesels; 2 shafts; 3 240 bhp
Speed, knots: 20
Range, miles: 3 000 at 12 knots; 2 000 at 15 knots
Complement: 60

The design is an improved version of that of *Udarnik*. Modernised in 1970-73 at Naval repair yard, "Sava Kovacevic", Tivat, Gulf of Cattaro. Probably now fitted with Soviet sonar equipment.

Type name: Patrolni Brod.

BORAC *Commander Aldo Fraccaroli*

754 YUGOSLAVIA

1 "LE FOUGUEUX" CLASS

Name	No.	Builders	Laid down	Launched	Commissioned
UDARNIK (ex-P 6)	PBR 581	F.C. Mediterranee (Le Havre)	1954	1 June 1954	1955

Displacement, tons: 325 standard; 400 full load
Dimensions, feet (metres): 170 pp; 174·8 oa × 23 × 6·6 *(51·8; 53·3 × 7 × 2)*
Guns: 2—40 mm; 2—20 mm
A/S weapons: 1 Hedgehog; 4 DCT; 2 DC racks
Main engines: 4 SEMT Pielstick diesels; 3 240 bhp = 18·7 knots
Range, miles: 3 000 at 12 knots; 2 000 at 15 knots
Complement: 62

USA offshore procurement.

UDARNIK *1972, Yugoslav Navy*

LIGHT FORCES

4 +6 "RADE KONCAR" CLASS (Type 211)
(FAST ATTACK CRAFT—MISSILE/GUN)

Name	No.	Builders	Commissioned
RADE KONCAR	401	Tito SY, Kraljevica	April 1977
VLADO CETKOVIC	402	Tito SY, Kraljevica	?
—	403	Tito SY, Kraljevica	?
—	404	Tito SY, Kraljevica	?

Displacement, tons: 240 full load
Dimensions, feet (metres): 147·6 × 27·6 × 7·5 *(45 × 8·4 × 2·5)*
Missiles: 2 launchers for SS-N-2
Guns: 2 Bofors 57 mm/L 70
Main engines: 2 Rolls-Royce Proteus gas turbines; 11 600 shp; 2 MTU diesels; 7 200 shp
Speed, knots: 40
Range, miles: 500 at 35 knots
Complement: 30

Designed by the Naval Shipping Institute in Zagreb. *Rade Koncar* was completed for trials Autumn 1976.

Radar: Philips TAB in radome.

Type name: Raketna Topovnjaca.

10 Ex-SOVIET "OSA" CLASS (FAST ATTACK CRAFT—MISSILE)

M. ACEV	Z. JOVANOVIC-SPANAC RC 310	K. ROJC
V. BAGAT RC 302	N. MARTINOVIC RC 306	F. ROZMAN-STANE RC 309
P. DRAPSIN	J. MAZAR	V. SKORPIK
S. FILIPOVIC		

Displacement, tons: 165 standard; 205 full load
Dimensions, feet (metres): 128·7 × 25·1 × 5·9 *(39·3 × 7·7 × 1·8)*
Missile launchers: 4 for SS-N-2 system
Guns: 4—30 mm (2 twin, 1 forward, 1 aft)
Main engines: 3 diesels; 12 000 bhp = 40 knots
Fuel, tons: 40
Range, miles: 800 at 30 knots
Complement: 29 (4 officers, 25 men)

Acquired between 1965 and 1969. Pennant numbers from 301-310.

Names: Named after war heroes.

Radar: Search: Square Tie.
Fire control: Drum Tilt.
IFF: High Pole.

Type name: Raketni Camac.

"OSA" Class *1972, Yugoslav Navy*

"OSA" Class *1972*

14 Ex-SOVIET "SHERSHEN" CLASS (201 TYPE)
(FAST ATTACK CRAFT—TORPEDO)

CRVENA ZVIJEZDA TC 220	KORNAT
PARTIZAN II TC 222	PROLETER
BIKOVAC	STRELJKO
IVAN	+ 7

Displacement, tons: 140 standard; 170 full load
Dimensions, feet (metres): 115·5 × 23·1 × 5·0 *(35·2 × 7 × 1·5)*
Guns: 4—30 mm (2 twin)
Torpedo tubes: 4—21 in (single)
Mines: 4-6
Main engines: 3 diesels; 3 shafts; 12 000 bhp = 45 knots
Fuel, tons: 30
Complement: 23 (3 officers, 20 men)

Four craft (TC 211, 212, 215, 216) acquired from USSR, 1965. Remainder built under licence by Tito Shipyard, Kraljevica between 1966 and 1971.

Names: Named after partisan craft of World War II.

Pennant numbers: TC 211-224.

CRVENA ZVIJEZDA *1972*

Radar: Search: Pot Head.
Fire control: Drum Tilt.
IFF: High Pole.

Type name: Torpedni Camac.

YUGOSLAVIA 755

6 "158" CLASS (Ex-108) (FAST ATTACK CRAFT—GUN)

TOP 146, 154, 162, 168, 169, 174

Displacement, tons: 50 standard; 60 full load
Dimensions, feet (metres): 69 pp; 78 oa × 21·3 × 4·5 *(21; 23·8 × 6·5 × 1·3)*
Guns: 2—40 mm Bofors L 60; 4—12·7 mm Browning MGs (twins)
Mines: 2-4
Main engines: 3 Packard motors; 3 shafts; 4 500 bhp = 26 knots
Range, miles: 320 at 21 knots
Complement: 14

Of the same class as US "Higgins". Built in Yugoslavia 1951-60 as "108" class. About 25 were reconstructed from 1963 on as gunboats classified as "158" class. Now considered obsolete and mainly used for auxiliary duties.

Transfers: Six to Sudan in April 1970. Two to Ethiopia in 1960 (deleted 1969).

Type name: Topovnjaca.

"158" Class — *Yugoslav Navy*

14 "KRALJEVICA" CLASS ("501" and "509" TYPES)
(LARGE PATROL CRAFT)

501, 503-4, 506-8 ("501" Type)

510-12, 519-21, 523, 524 ("509" Type)

Displacement, tons: 180 standard; 202 (full load) ("501" Type); 195; 245 ("509" Type)
Dimensions, feet (metres): 134·5 × 20·7 × 5·5 *(41 × 6·3 × 1·7)* ("501" Type);
  141·4 × 20·7 × 5·7 *(43·1 × 6·3 × 1·8)* ("509" Type)
Guns: 1—40 mm; 4—20 mm ("501" Type);
  1—3 in *(76 mm)* US Mk 22; 1—40 mm; 4—20 mm ("509" Type)
A/S weapons: 2 Mousetraps (or 1 Hedgehog); 2 DCT; 2 DC Racks
Main engines: 2 diesels; 2 shafts; 3 000 bhp = 17 knots ("501" Type);
  3 300 bhp = 19 knots ("509" Type)
Complement: 45 ("501" Type); 49 ("509" Type)

Built at Tito SY, Kraljevica—"501" Type 1953-56 and "509" Type 1957-59

Modernisation: Two MBU 1200 being fitted as elderly 3 in guns are replaced by extra 40 mm. All export models have this 40 mm shipped.

Radar: Search: Decca 45.

"KRALJEVICA" Class — *Yugoslav Navy*

Sonar: QCU-2.

Transfers: Six to Indonesia in 1959 (built as separate order); two to Sudan in 1969; one to Ethiopia in 1975; two to Bangladesh in 1975.

10 TYPE 131 (LARGE PATROL CRAFT)

KALNIK PC 132	COPAONIK
LOVCEN PC 136	KOZUF
DURMITOR PC 139	ROMANIJA
CER	+ 3

Displacement, tons: 85 standard; 120 full load
Dimensions, feet (metres): 91·9 × 14·8 × 8·3 *(28 × 4·5 × 2·5)*
Guns: 6—20 mm (triple Hispano-Suiza HS 831 mounts)
Main engines: 2 diesels; 900 bhp = 15 knots

Built at Trogir SY between 1965 and 1968. Serve in Maritime Border Brigade.

Type name: Patrolni Camac.

Pennant numbers: 131-140.

Type 131 — *1968, Yugoslavian Navy*

MINE WARFARE FORCES

4 "VUKOVKLANAC" CLASS (MINESWEEPERS—COASTAL)

Name	No.	Builders	Commissioned
VUKOVKLANAC (ex-*Hrabri*)	M 151 (ex-*D 25*)	A. Normand, France	Sept 1957
PODGORA (ex-*Smeli*)	M 152 (ex-*D 26*)	A. Normand, France	Sept 1957
BLITVENICA (ex-*Slobodni*)	M 153 (ex-*D 27*)	A. Normand, France	Sept 1957
GRADAC (ex-*Snazni*)	M 161	Mali Losinj SY, Yugoslavia	1960

Displacement, tons: 365 standard; 424 full load
Dimensions, feet (metres): 140 pp; 152 oa × 28 × 8·2 *(42·7; 46·4 × 8·6 × 2·5)*
Guns: 2—20 mm
Main engines: SIGMA free piston generators; (gas turbines in *Gradac*);
  2 shafts; 2 000 bhp = 15 knots
Oil fuel, tons: 48
Range, miles: 3 000 at 10 knots
Complement: 40

BLITVENIC (ex-*Slobodni*) — *1966, Yugoslav Navy*

The first three were built as US "off-shore" orders. *Gradac* (ex-*Snazni*) was built in Yugoslavia in 1960 with French assistance.

6 "M 117" CLASS (MINESWEEPERS—INSHORE)

M 117 M 118 M 119 M 121 M 122 M 123

Displacement, tons: 120 standard; 131 full load
Dimensions, feet (metres): 98·4 × 18 × 4·9 *(30 × 5·5 × 1·5)*
Guns: 1—40 mm; 2—12·7 mm MG
Main engines: 2 GM diesels; 1 000 bhp = 12 knots

Built in Yugoslav shipyards between 1966 and 1968.

M 121 — *1968, Yugoslav Navy*

756 YUGOSLAVIA

4 BRITISH "HAM" CLASS (MINESWEEPERS—INSHORE)

M 141   M 142   M 143   M 144

Displacement, tons: 123 standard; 164 full load
Dimensions, feet (metres): 100 × 21·8 × 5·5 (32·4 × 6·3 × 1·7)
Guns: 2—20 mm
Main engines: 2 Paxman diesels; 1 100 bhp = 14 knots
Range, miles: 2 000 at 9 knots
Complement: 22

Built in Yugoslavia 1964-66 under the US Military Aid Programme. Of same design as British "Ham" class.

"158" Class 1968, Yugoslav Navy

3 + ? "NESTIN" CLASS (RIVER MINESWEEPERS)

Name	No.	Builders	Commissioned
NESTIN	M 331	Brodotehnika, Belgrade	20 Dec 1975
MOTAJICA	M 332	Brodotehnika, Belgrade	18 Dec 1976
BELEGIS	M 333	Brodotehnika, Belgrade	Jan 1977

Displacement, tons: 65
Dimensions, feet (metres): 88·6 × 20·7 × 5·2 (27 × 6·3 × 1·6)
Guns: 3—20 mm Hispano (triple, aft)
Main engines: 2 diesels; 260 bhp = 15 knots

Continuing programme.

14 "M 301" CLASS (RIVER MINESWEEPERS)

| M 301 | M 303 | M 305 | M 307 | M 309 | M 311 | M 313 |
| M 302 | M 304 | M 306 | M 308 | M 310 | M 312 | M 314 |

Displacement, tons: 38
Gun: 1—20 mm
Main engines: Speed = 12 knots

All launched in 1951-53. Serve on the Danube.

AMPHIBIOUS FORCES

NEW CONSTRUCTION LST

Displacement, tons: 2 980
Dimensions, feet (metres): 334·6 × 46·6 × 10·2 (102 × 14·2 × 3·1)
Guns: 2—40 mm
Main engines: 2 diesels; 6 800 shp

A new class capable of carrying six tanks, a number of LCAs and fitted with a helicopter deck now being built in Yugoslavia.

24 DTM 211 TYPE (LCT/MINELAYERS)

DTM 215, 217-223, 229-31 +13

Displacement, tons: 410
Dimensions, feet (metres): 144·3 × 19·7 × 7 (47·3 × 6·4 × 2·3)
Guns: 1—20 mm; 2—12·7 mm
Speed, knots: 9
Complement: 15

Capable of carrying at least two, possibly three of the heaviest tanks. Unlike other tank landing craft in that the centre part of the bow drops to form a ramp down which the tanks go ashore, the vertical section of the bow being articulated to form outer end of ramp. Built in Yugoslavia. Can also act as minelayers.

Transfers: Two to Sudan in 1969.

DTM 230 B. Hinchcliffe

2 601 TYPE (LCAs)

DJC 601 and 602

Displacement, tons: 32
Dimensions, feet (metres): 70·2 × 15·1 × 2 (21·4 × 4·6 × 0·6)
Gun: 1—20 mm
Main engines: Diesels; 1 125 shp = 22 knots

A programme is under way for the construction of a considerable number of LCAs built of polyester and glass fibre. Probably to be carried in the new class of LSTs. First in service Sept 1976, second 1977.

MISCELLANEOUS

TRAINING SHIPS

1 "GALEB" CLASS

Name	No.	Builders	Commissioned
GALEB (ex-Kuchuk, ex-Ramb III)	M 11	Ansaldo, Genoa	1939

Displacement, tons: 5 182 standard
Measurement, tons: 3 667 gross
Length, feet (metres): 384·8 (117·3)
Beam, feet (metres): 51·2 (15·6)
Draught, feet (metres): 18·4 (5·6)
Main engines: 2 diesels; 2 shafts; 7 200 bhp
Speed, knots: 17

Ex-Italian. Launched in 1938. Sunk as an auxiliary cruiser in 1944, refloated and reconstructed in 1952. Serves as fleet flagship, Presidential Yacht and training ship. Former armament was four 3·5 in, four 40 mm and 24—20 mm (six quadruple) guns. The guns were landed. Can act as minelayer.

GALEB 1976, Dhr J. van der Woude

YUGOSLAVIA

JADRAN (ex-*Marco Polo*)

Displacement, tons: 720
Dimensions, feet (metres): 190 × 29·2 × 13·8 *(58 × 8·8 × 4·2)*
Sail area: 8 600 sq feet *(800 sq metres)*
Main engine: 1 Linke-Hofman Diesel; 375 hp = 8 knots

Topsail schooner. Built by Blöhm and Voss, Hamburg. Served in Italian navy during World War II *(Marco Polo)*. Launched in 1932. Accommodation for 150 Cadets.

PRESIDENTIAL YACHT

Name	No.	Builders	Commissioned
JADRANKA (ex-*Bjeli Orao*)	—	C. R. dell Adriatico, San Marco, Trieste	Oct 1939

Displacement, tons: 567 standard; 660 full load
Dimensions, feet (metres): 213·2 oa × 26·5 × 9·3 *(60·5 × 7·9 × 2·8)*
Main engines: 2 Sulzer diesels; 1 900 bhp = 18 knots

Launched on 3 June 1939. While in Italian hands was named *Alba*, for some days only, then *Zagaria*.

JADRANKA   1970, Yugoslav Navy

HQ SHIPS

KOZARA

Former Presidential Yacht on Danube. Now acts as flagship of the river flotilla.

VIS

Built in 1956. Serves as flagship of missile boat brigade.

SURVEY SHIP

Name	No.	Builders	Commissioned
ANDRIJA MOHOROVICIC	PH 33	Gdansk Shipyard, Poland	1972

Displacement, tons: 1 240 standard; 1 800 full load
Dimensions, feet (metres): 240 × 32·8 × 13·2 *(73·2 × 10 × 4)*
Main engines: 2 diesels = 16 knots
Complement: 37

Built in 1971 at the shipyard in Gdansk, Poland, and added to the Yugoslav Navy List in 1972. Of Soviet "Moma" class.

A. MOHOROVICIC   1972, Yugoslav Navy

SALVAGE VESSEL

SPASILAC PS 12

New construction to replace ship of same name which was built in Italy in 1929-30 and is now deleted. Built at Tito SY, Belgrade. In service, Sept 1976.

TANKERS

2 PN 24 TYPE (HARBOUR TANKERS)

PN 24   PN 25

Built at Split in mid-1950s.

4 PN 13 TYPE (HARBOUR TANKERS)

PN 13 (ex-*Lovcen*)   PN 14   PN 15   PN 16

Displacement, tons: 695 standard
Speed, knots: 8·5

PN 13 (ex-*Lovcen*) was launched in 1932. PN 17 was transferred to the Sudanese Navy in 1969.

TRANSPORTS

4 PT 71 TYPE

PT 71—PT 74

Displacement, tons: 310 standard; 428 full load
Dimensions, feet (metres): 141·5 × 22·2 × 16 *(46·4 × 7·2 × 5·2)*
Main engines: 300 bhp = 7 knots

Built in 1953

6 PT 61 TYPE

PT 61—66

Built at Pula and Sibenik 1951-54.

4 PO TYPE (AMMUNITION TRANSPORTS)

PO 52—55

TUGS

4 COASTAL TUGS

PR 37—40

Speed, knots: 11
Type name: PR = Pomorski Remorker.

8 HARBOUR TUGS

LR 67—74

Displacement, tons: 130
Type name: LR = Lucki Remorker.

WATER CARRIERS

PV 11   PV 12   PV 13

Of various types and of modern construction.

ZAIRE

Ministerial

State Commissioner for Defence:
Lieutenant-General Mobuto Sese Seko (President)

Personnel

(a) 1978: 200 officers and men
(b) Voluntary service

Bases

Matadi; Lake Tanganyika

Mercantile Marine

Lloyd's Register of Shipping:
34 vessels of 109 785 tons gross

LIGHT FORCES

Note: Also reported, but not confirmed, that three ex-Chinese "Hu Chwan" class hydrofoils have been transferred.

1 COASTAL PATROL CRAFT

ZAIRE (ex-*President Mobuto*, ex-*General Olsen*, ex-*Congo*)

A 70 ton craft, the first in this naval force.

6 SEWART TYPE (COASTAL PATROL CRAFT)

Displacement, tons: 33
Length, feet (metres): 65 *(19·8)*
Guns: 6 MG
Main engines: 2 GM diesels = 26 knots
Range, miles: 1 000 at 18 knots

Purchased in USA in 1971.

3 Ex-KOREAN (N) "P 4" CLASS

Displacement, tons: 22
Dimensions, feet (metres): 62·7 × 11·6 × 5·6 *(19·1 × 3·5 × 1·7)*
Guns: 2—14·7 mm MG
Torpedo tubes: 2—18 in
Main engines: 2 diesels; 2 shafts; 2 200 hp = 50 knots
Complement: 12

Transferred 1974.

12 COASTAL PATROL CRAFT

Ordered in 1974 in France. No further information.

1 COASTAL PATROL CRAFT

Of 18 tons, 25 knots and mounting three MG. Purchased in USA in 1968.

3 Ex-US COASTAL PATROL CRAFT

Purchased in 1974. Of same type as Swiftboats.

4 COASTAL PATROL CRAFT

Reported as transferred by China in late 1960s.

ZANZIBAR

(see also Tanzania)

Although part of the United Republic of Tanzania, Zanzibar retains a separate Executive and Legislature, the President of Zanzibar being First Vice-President of Tanzania.

4 VOSPER THORNYCROFT 75 ft TYPE

Displacement, tons: 70
Dimensions, feet (metres): 75 × 19·5 × 8 *(22·9 × 6·0 × 1·5)*
Guns: 2—20 mm
Main engines: 2 diesels; 1 840 hp
Speed, knots: 24·5
Range, miles: 800 at 20 knots
Complement: 11

This was one of the first orders for the new Keith Nelson 75 foot craft. First pair delivered 6 July 1973, second pair 1974.

75 ft Type   *1974, Vosper Thornycroft*

NAVAL STRENGTHS

760 NAVAL STRENGTHS

Figures in brackets indicate ships under construction or planned.

	Aircraft Carriers (L=light)	Cruisers and Light Cruisers	Destroyers	Frigates	Corvettes	Ballistic Missile Submarines (N = Nuclear D = Diesel)	Cruise Missile Submarines (N = Nuclear D = Diesel)	Fleet Submarines	Patrol Submarines	FAC Missile	FAC Torpedo	FAC Gun	Patrol Craft	Mine-layers
ARGENTINA	1 (L)	2	9 (1)	(?8)	9				4 (2)	(2)	2	2	6	
AUSTRALIA	1 (L)		5	6 (2)					6				12 (15)	
BELGIUM				2 (2)									6	
BRAZIL	1 (L)		14 (2)		10 (?6)				9 (1)				22	
BULGARIA				2	3				2	4	10			
BURMA				2	4								71	
CANADA			4	16					3				13	
CHILE		2	6	5	3				3		4		5	
CHINA, PEOPLE'S REPUBLIC			9 (2)	14 (2)		1 (D)		1 (?)	72 (6)	162 (20)	200 (10)	404 (10)	140+	
COLOMBIA			3	5					2+4 (small)				23	
CUBA				1 Res						26	24		17	
DENMARK				7 (3)	3				6	10	6		46	7
DOMINICAN REP				1 (2 Res)	3 (2 Res)								17	
ECUADOR				3	2				2	3	3		7	
EGYPT			5	3 (2)					12 (2)	16	26	4 (6)	35	
FINLAND				2 (2)	2					4+1 (5)		14	5	1 (1)
FRANCE	2 (1)	2	22 (1)	24 (7)		4 (1) (N) 1 (D)		(1) (4)	23	5			29	
GERMANY (Democratic)				1						15	65		22	
GERMANY (Federal)			11	6 (12)	6				24	30	10			
GREECE			12	4	5				7 (4)	10	19		10 (10)	2
INDIA	1 (L)	2		25 (2)	4 (2)				8	16			8	
INDONESIA				11 (3)					3 (2)	13 (4)	5		27	
IRAN			3 (4)	4	4				(3)	3 (9)			7	
IRAQ										14	10	4	31	
ISRAEL					(2)				3	20 (5)			41	
ITALY		3 (1)	7	11 (3+6)	9				8 (2+2)		9			
JAPAN			31 (3+1)	15 (1)	16				15 (2)		5		10	
KOREA (N)				3 (1)					15 (2)	18	165 (2)	134 (4)	56	
KOREA (S)			9	7 (1)	6					8 (4)			34	
MALAYSIA				3						8		6 (4)	22	
MEXICO			2	6	35								36 (9)	
NETHERLANDS			12	6 (8+4)	6				6				5	
NEW ZEALAND				4									4	
NORWAY				5	2				15	27 (13)	20			3
PAKISTAN		1	6	1					4+6 small		4	12	3	
PERU		4	4	3					8 (2)				16	
PHILIPPINES				8	11							9	46	
POLAND			1						4	12	21		29	
PORTUGAL				13					3				18	
ROMANIA					3					5	23	18	31	
SOUTH AFRICA			1	3					3	2 (4)			4	
SPAIN	1 (L) (1)		13	14 (9)					8 (4)				34	
SWEDEN			6	6					17 (3)	2 (14)	32		32	49 (1)
TAIWAN			22	11	3				2	1 (1)	9		14	
THAILAND				6						3 (3)			47 (1)	2
TURKEY			12	2					12 (2)	7 (1)	13		47 (13)	7
UNION OF SOVIET SOCIALIST REPUBLICS	2 (1)	37 (3)	112 (4)	108 (1)	111 (5)	68 (6) (N) 22 (D)	46 (2) (N) 28 (D)	41 (2)	154 (2) (+100 res)	123 (?2)	80	50	202 (2)	2
UNITED KINGDOM	1+2 (L)	10 (2)	5 (5)	53 (4) 6 Res	4			10 (3)	17				21 (2)	1
UNITED STATES OF AMERICA	13 (3N) +(1N) +6 res	27 (2) (+8 res)	93 (22)	65 (25)		40 (N) (7N) (1N)	1 res (D)	69 (27+2 res)	8	1 (5)			7	
VENEZUELA			4	4 (6)					4 (2)	3		3	21	
YUGOSLAVIA				1	3				5 (2)	12 (4)	14	20	23	

NAVAL STRENGTHS

Ocean Mine-sweepers	Coastal Mine-sweepers/ Mine-hunters	Inshore Mine-sweepers	Mine-sweeping Boats	Assault Ships	Landing Ships	Landing Craft	Depot Repair Main-tenance Ships	Survey Research Ships (Large and Small)	Supply Ships	Large Tankers	Hydrofoils Small Tankers	and ACVs	Misc-ellaneous	
	4/2				4 (1)	28		8 (2)		1	2		20 (1)	ARGENTINA
	3				(1)	6	1	4 (1 + 2)		1			18	AUSTRALIA
7	4/2 (15)	14						2	2				14	BELGIUM
	6				2	20	1	14	1	1	2		28	BRAZIL
2	4		12			20		3			3		22	BULGARIA
								2					10	BURMA
							2	5	3		2	1	71	CANADA
					4	7	2	1		1 (2)	2		17	CHILE
23					44	467	1	20	24 (?12)		18	70	375+	CHINA, PEOPLE'S REPUBLIC
								3			1		14	COLOMBIA
						7		6					8	CUBA
	8										2		4	DENMARK
2					1	2		2			2		9	DOMINICAN REP
						2		2	1				9 (1)	ECUADOR
10		4				19						3	9	EGYPT
		6 (10)				13							74	FINLAND
6	22/12 (15)			2	7	49	9	8	6	4 (1)	5		158 (10)	FRANCE
	52				8	12		4	4		4		50	GERMANY (Democratic)
	40	18				41	14	1	12		11		80	GERMANY (Federal)
	14			1	14	53	1	6			7		27	GREECE
	4	4			1	6	1	3 (1)		2	3		14	INDIA
5	2				9	2	4	4		1	7		5	INDONESIA
	3	2			2 (1)	1	1	3	2	(1)	1	14	7	IRAN
						3							3	IRAQ
					3	9						(2)	9	ISRAEL
4	34/1 (10)	10			2	59	7	4	1	2		1 (2+4)	137	ITALY
	29 (3)		6		6		4	6 (1)	(1)	(1)	1 (1)		50 (2)	JAPAN
						70							105	KOREA (N)
	8		1		20	1	1	5	6		4		2	KOREA (S)
	6					3		1	1				28 (3)*	MALAYSIA
17					3			1			2		8	MEXICO
	11/4 (15)	16				11	4	3	2				24	NETHERLANDS
								4					6	NEW ZEALAND
	10	(1)				7	1 (1)	1					3	NORWAY
	7							1			2		7	PAKISTAN
					4			4 (1)			7 (1)		14	PERU
	2				39	71	3				4	4	30	PHILIPPINES
24			20			38		1			6		78+1 AGI	POLAND
	4					14		4		1	1		4	PORTUGAL
	4	10	8										?	ROMANIA
	8							2	1				8	SOUTH AFRICA
8/4	12			1	5	87	1 (2)	6		1	13		100	SPAIN
	18	18				147		5 (1)	1		1		43	SWEDEN
	14		8		29	22	1	4			7		42	TAIWAN
	4		10		10	39		4			4		11	THAILAND
	21	4	9 (Hunters)		4	53	5	4	2		6		36	TURKEY
175 (3)	109 (3)	125			24 (1)	165 +100 small	65 (1)	179 (2)	7	23	22	50	400+ 53 AGIs	UNION OF SOVIET SOCIALIST REPUBLICS
	17/16 (2)	5		2	7	61	3	4+9	8 (1)	15	6	5	192	UNITED KINGDOM
25			11 (3)		55	100	20 (6) (25 res)	40	24	15 (5) (2)	MSC		1 093 plus MSC	UNITED STATES OF AMERICA
						6		3					18	VENEZUELA
	4	10	17 (river)		(1)	25		1			10		30	YUGOSLAVIA

* Police

NAVAL EQUIPMENT

AIRCRAFT

Notes: (a) For technical details see under country of origin; (b) Class: A Carrier based B Helicopters C Land based

Country/Manufacturer	Strength	Role	Class (See note)	Country of Origin	Max Speed	Service Ceiling	Range	Max Endurance	T/O Weight
ARGENTINA									
McDonnell Douglas Skyhawk (A-4Q)	15	Attack Bomber F/W	A	USA	(a)				
Grumman Tracker (S-2A/E)	12	Attack A/S, F/W	A	USA					
Grumman Albatross (HU-16B)	3	Amphibian, Search and Rescue, F/W	C	USA					
Aerospatiale Alouette III	4	Helicopter	B	France					
Sikorsky Sea King (S-61D-4)	4	Helicopter	B	USA					
Westland Lynx Mk 23	3	A/S Helicopter	B	UK					
Aermacchi MB 326GB	12	Trainer and F/W Light Attack	C	Italy					
Lockheed Neptune (P-2H)	8	Maritime F/W Patrol Bomber	C	USA					
AUSTRALIA									
McDonnell Douglas Skyhawk (A-4G)	13	Attack F/W	A	USA	Plus 3 TA-4G trainers				
Lockheed Orion (P-3B/C)	19	A/S Recce F/W	C	USA	Operated by Air Force				
Grumman Tracker (S-2E/G)	19	A/S F/W and Maritime Patrol	A, C	USA					
Government Aircraft Factories (GAF) Search Master		F/W Maritime Patrol	C	Australia	168 knots (cruising)	22 500 ft (6 860 m)	730 n. miles at 10 000 ft (3 050 m)		8 500 lb (3 855 kg)
Bell Iroquois (UH-1D)	7	Helicopter	B	USA					
Westland Wessex (HAS 31B)	10	Helicopter	B	UK					
Westland Sea King (HAS 50)	7	Helicopter	B	UK					
BELGIUM									
Aerospatiale Alouette III	3	Coast Guard Helicopter	B	France					
Westland Sea King Mk 48	5	Helicopter	B	UK	Operated by Air Force				
BRAZIL									
Embraer EMB-111	16	F/W Maritime Reconnaissance	C	Brazil	Operated by Air Force 218 knots (cruising)	22 500 ft (6 860 m)	1 550 n. miles		15 432 lb (7 000 kg)
Grumman Tracker (S-2E)	8	A/S F/W	A	USA	Operated by Air Force				
Bell 47G-2 & 47J	2	Helicopter	B	USA					
Bell JetRanger II	18	Helicopter	B	USA					
Hughes 269/300	6	Helicopter	B	USA					
Sikorsky Sea King (SH-3D)	5	Helicopter	B	USA					
Westland Wasp	5	A/S Helicopter	B	UK					
Westland Whirlwind	3	Helicopter	B	UK					
Westland Lynx	9	A/S Helicopter	A	UK/France	Carried on new destroyers				
CANADA									
Sikorsky CHSS-2 Sea King (CH-124)	32	Helicopter	B	USA					
Canadair Argus (CP-107)	26	F/W Maritime Reconnaissance	C	Canada	20,000 ft 274 knots	20,000 ft plus (6 100 m plus)	5 124 n. miles at 194 knots		148 000 lb (67 130 kg)
Canadair CL-215		F/W Amphibian	C	Canada	157 knots (cruising)		1 220 n. miles		Land 43 500 lb (19 731 kg) Sea 37 700 lb (17 100 kg)
Grumman CS2F-3 Tracker (CP-121)	30	F/W A/S	C	USA					
CHILE									
Embraer EMB-111N	6	F/W Maritime Reconnaissance	C	Brazil					
Bell JetRanger	4	Helicopter	B	USA					
Grumman Albatross (HU-16B)	5	Maritime F/W Amphibian	C	USA					
Lockheed Neptune (SP-2E)	4	Maritime Recce F/W	C	USA					

AIRCRAFT / NAVAL EQUIPMENT

Wing span Rotor diameter	Length	Height	Power Plant	Armament Capacity	Remarks
54 ft 0 in (16·46 m)	41 ft 2·4 in (12·56 m)	18 ft 1·5 in (5·52 m)	2 × 400 shp Allison 250-B17B turboprop engines	Provision for underwing stores	Used by Indonesian Navy (Not by Australia)
52 ft 4·5 in (15·96 m)	48 ft 7·75 in (14·83 m)	15 ft 6·5 in (4·74 m)	2 × 750 shp Pratt & Whitney (Canada) PT6A-34 turboprop engines		
142 ft 3·5 in (43·38 m)	128 ft 9·5 in (39·25 m)	36 ft 8·5 in (11·19 m)	4 × Wright R-3350 EA-1 turbo-compound radial piston engines 3 700 hp each	15 600 lb of weapons (7 075 kg)	In service with 4 Sqdns. (Nos. 404, 405, 407 and 415)
93 ft 10 in (28·6 m)	65 ft (19·82 m)	29 ft 3 in (8·92 m)	2 × 2 100 hp Pratt & Whitney R-2800 radial piston engines		Used by Greek and Spanish Air Forces for search and rescue (Not by Canada)

766 NAVAL EQUIPMENT / AIRCRAFT

Country/ Manufacturer	Strength	Role	Class (See note)	Country of Origin	Max Speed	Service Ceiling	Range	Max Endurance	T/O Weight
CHINA, PEOPLE'S REPUBLIC									
Ilyushin Il-28T	100	Torpedo Bomber	C	USSR (built in China)	14 765 ft (4 000 m) 485 knots	40 350 ft (12 300 m)	at 415 knots (770 km/h) 1 175 n. miles		46 300 lb (21 000 kg)
Shenyang F-6 (MiG-19SF) ("Farmer")	250	F/W Fighter	C	USSR (built in China)	32 800 ft (10 000 m) 783 knots	58 725 ft (17 900 m)	with ext tanks 1 187 n. miles	2 hrs 38 min	19 180 lb (8 700 kg)
Shenyang F-9 ("Fantan")	50	F/W Fighter	C	China	nearly Mach 2		combat radius 430 n. miles		22 050 lb (10 000 kg)
DENMARK									
Aerospatiale Alouette III	8	Helicopter	B	France	Flown from frigates				
Westland Lynx	7	Helicopter	B	UK	Delivery in 1979, for fishery patrol				
FRANCE									
Breguet Br 1050 Alizé	40	A/S F/W	A	France	10 000 ft (3 050 m) 254 knots	26 250 ft (8 000 m)	normal 1 350 n. miles	7 hrs 40 min	18 100 lb (8 200 kg)
Vought Crusader F-8E(FN)	35	F/W Interceptor	A	USA					
Dassault Etendard IV-M, IV-P	42	F/W Attack Recce	A	France	36 000 ft (11 000 m) Mach 1·02	49 000 ft (15 000 m)	at 442 knots (820 km/h) with ext tanks 1 520 n. miles		22 650 lb (10 275 kg)
Dassault Super Etendard	71 ordered	F/W Fighter	A	France	36 000 ft (11 000 m) approx Mach 1	45 000 ft (13 700 m)	with anti-ship missile 350 n. miles		25 350 lb (11 500 kg)
Aerospatiale Super Frelon SA321G	21	A/S and Minesweeping Helicopter	B	France	at S/L 148 knots	10 325 ft (3 150 m)	at S/L 442 n. miles		28 660 lb (13 000 kg)
Aerospatiale Alouette III	20	General-Purpose Helicopter	B	France	at S/L 113 knots	10 500 ft (3 200 m)	290 n. miles		4 840 lb (2 200 kg)
Westland/Aérospatiale Lynx	26 ordered	A/S Helicopter	B	UK/ France					
Breguet Br 1150 Atlantic	35	Long-Range F/W Maritime Patrol	C	France	High Altitude 355 knots	32 800 ft (10 000 m)	4 854 n. miles	at 169 knots 18 hours	95 900 lb (43 500 kg)
Aerospatiale N262/Frégate	20	F/W Transport	C	France	208 knots	23 500 ft (7 160 m)	with max payload 525 n. miles		23 370 lb (10 600 kg)
Lockheed Neptune (P-2H)	20	F/W Maritime Patrol	C	USA					
GERMANY (Federal Republic)									
Westland Sea King (HAS Mk 41)	22	Helicopter	B	UK					
Breguet Br 1150 Atlantic	20	F/W Maritime Recce	C	France					
Dornier Do 28D-2 Skyservant	20	F/W General Duty	C	Germany	10 000 ft (3 050 m) 175 knots	25 200 ft (7 680 m)	1 090 n. miles		8 470 lb (3 842 kg)
Lockheed Starfighter (F-104G)	120	F/W Fighter	C	USA (built in Germany)	To be replaced by Panavia Tornado Includes RF-104G				
Panavia Tornado	113	Swing-wing Strike and Reconnaissance	C	Germany/ Italy/UK	36 000 ft (11 000 m) 1 146 knots				38 000- 40 000 lb (17 240- 18 145 kg)
INDIA									
Ilyushin Il-38 ("May")	4	F/W Maritime Recce	C	USSR					
Breguet Br 1050 Alizé	18	F/W A/S	A	France					
Armstrong Whitworth Sea Hawk	25	F/W Fighter-Bomber	A	UK	Max cruise speed at S/L 512 knots				16 200 lb (7 355 kg)
Aerospatiale Alouette III	18	Helicopter	B	France					
Westland Sea King Mk 42	17	A/S Helicopter	B	UK					
INDONESIA									
Aerospatiale Alouette III	3	Helicopter	B	France					
Grumman Albatross (HU-16A)	5	F/W Maritime Patrol Amphibian	C	USA					
GAF Search Master	12	F/W Maritime Patrol	C	Australia					
IRAN									
Lockheed Orion (P-3F)	9	F/W Maritime Patrol	C	USA	Operated by Air Force				
Sikorsky Sea King (SH-3D)	20	A/S Helicopter	B	USA (built in Italy)					
Sikorsky RH-53D	6	Mine Countermeasures	B	USA					
Agusta-Bell 212ASW	6	Anti-ship Helicopter	B	Italy					

Wing span Rotor diameter	Length	Height	Power Plant	Armament Capacity	Remarks
70 ft 4·75 in (21·45 m)	57 ft 10·75 in (17·65 m)		2 × Klimov VK-1 turbojets	2 torpedoes	
29 ft 6·5 in (9·00 m)	48 ft 10·5 (14·90 m)	13 ft 2·25 in (4·02 m)	2 × Klimov R-9B turbojets (Chinese-built)	3 × 30 mm cannon, rockets, bombs	Limited all-weather version also operational
33 ft 5 in (10·20)	50 ft 0 in (15·25 m)		2 × unidentified turbojets		Evolved from F-6
51 ft 2 in (15·6 m)	45 ft 6 in (13·86 m)	16 ft 5 in (5·00 m)	1 × 2 100 eshp Rolls-Royce Dart R.Da 21 turboprop	Depth charges, torpedo, rockets, AS.12 missiles	
31 ft 6 in (9·60 m)	47 ft 3 in (14·40 m)	14 ft 1 in (4·30 m)	1 × SNECMA Atar 8B turbojet	2 × 30 mm cannon, 3 000 lb (1,360 kg) rockets, bombs, Sidewinder missiles	Those embarked on *Clemenceau* and *Foch* are fitted to carry 2 Matra R530 missiles each
31 ft 6 in (9·60 m)	46 ft 11·5 in (14·31 m)	12 ft 8 in (3·85 m)	1 × SNECMA Atar 8K-50 turbojet	2 × 30 mm cannon, rockets, bombs, missiles	Deliveries started in 1978
62 ft 0 in (18·90 m)	Inc tail rotor 65 ft 10·75 in (20·08 m)	21 ft 10·25 in (6·66 m)	3 × 1 550 shp Turbomeca Turmo III C6 turboshaft engines	Four homing torpedoes, search radar, sonar. Provision for 27 passengers	
36 ft 1·75 in (11·02 m)	42 ft 1·5 in (12·84 m)	9 ft 10 in (3·00 m)	1 × 570 shp Turbomeca Artouste IIIB turboshaft engine	Provision for gun, missiles, torpedoes, MAD equipment	
119 ft 1 in (36·3 m)	104 ft 2 in (31·75 m)	37 ft 2 in (11·33 m)	2 × 6 106 ehp Rolls-Royce Tyne R.Ty.20 Mk 21 turboprop engines	Bombs, depth charges, homing torpedoes, rockets or ASMs	
71 ft 10 in (21·90 m)	63 ft 3 in (19·28 m)	20 ft 4 in (6·21 m)	2 × 1 080 hp Turbomeca Bastan VIC turboprop engines	Seating for 29	Used by French Navy as light transports and aircrew trainers
51 ft 0·25 in (15·55 m)	37 ft 5·25 in (11·41 m)	12 ft 9·5 in (3·90 m)	2 × 380 hp Lycoming IGSO-540-A1E piston engines	Seating for 12 or 13	
Swept: 28 ft 2·5 in (8·60 m)	54 ft 9·5 in (16·70 m)	18 ft 8·5 in (5·70 m)	2 × Turbo-Union RB.199-34R-4 turbojets	2 × 27 mm cannon, bombs, missiles	To equip MFG1 and 2
39 ft (11·89 m)	39 ft 8 in (12·09 m)	8 ft 8 in (2·64 m)	1 × Rolls-Royce Nene 103 turbojet	Cannon, bombs or rockets	Operational in carrier *Vikrant*

768 NAVAL EQUIPMENT / AIRCRAFT

Country/ Manufacturer	Strength	Role	Class (See note)	Country of Origin	Max Speed	Service Ceiling	Range	Max Endurance	T/O Weight
ITALY									
Agusta-Sikorsky SH-3D	24	Helicopter	B	USA (built in Italy)					
Agusta-Bell 204AS	24	A/S Helicopter	B	Italy	at S/L 104 knots	4 500 ft (1 370 m)	340 n. miles		9 500 lb (4 310 kg)
Agusta-Bell 212ASW	48	A/S Helicopter	B	Italy	at S/L 106 knots		360 n. miles	5 hrs	11 196 lb (5 079 kg)
Breguet Br 1150 Atlantic	18	F/W Long-Range Maritime	C	France	Operated by Air Force				
Grumman Tracker (S-2F)	10	F/W ASW	C	USA	To be retired in 1978-79				
Piaggio P.166S Albatross		F/W Coastal Patrol	C	Italy	9 500 ft (2 900 m) 193 knots	25 500 ft (7 770 m)			8 115 lb (3 680 kg)
JAPAN									
Sikorsky Sea King (SH-3A)	80	A/S Helicopter	B	USA (built in Japan)					
Kawasaki-Boeing KV 107/II-3	9	Mine Countermeasures Helicopter	B	Japan USA					
Grumman Tracker (S-2A)	24	F/W A/S	C	USA					
Kawasaki-Lockheed P-2J	82	F/W A/S and Maritime Patrol Bomber	C	Japan	Max cruising 217 knots	30 000 ft (9 150 m)	with max fuel 2 400 n. miles		75 000 lb (34 019 kg)
Lockheed Neptune (P-2H)	40	F/W A/S and Maritime Patrol Bomber	C	USA					
Shin Meiwa PS-1	22	A/S F/W Flying-Boat	C	Japan	Max level at 5 000 ft (1 525 m) 295 knots	29 500 ft (9 000 m)	1 169 n. miles	15 hrs	94 800 lb (43 000 kg)
MEXICO									
Grumman Albatross (HU-16A)	12	F/W Search and Rescue Amphibian	C	USA					
Aerospatiale Alouette III	2	Helicopter	B	France					
NETHERLANDS									
Westland Wasp (HAS Mk 1)	11	Helicopter	B	UK					
Westland Lynx	24	A/S Helicopter	B	UK/France					
Breguet Br 1150 Atlantic	8	F/W A/S	C	France					
Lockheed Neptune (SP-2H)	11	Maritime Patrol F/W	C	USA					
Fokker-VFW F.27MPA		Maritime Patrol F/W	C	Netherlands	230 knots (cruising)	23 200 ft (7 070 m)	2 215 n. miles		45 000 lb (20 410 kg)
NEW ZEALAND									
Westland Wasp (HAS Mk 1)	2	A/S Helicopter	B	UK					
Lockheed Orion (P-3B)	5	Maritime Patrol F/W	C	USA	Operated by RNZAF				
NORWAY									
Westland Sea King (Mk 43)	10	ASR. Helicopter	B	UK	Operated by Norwegian Air Force				
Lockheed Orion (P-3B)	5	Maritime Patrol F/W	C	USA	Operated by Norwegian Air Force				
PAKISTAN									
Breguet Br 1150 Atlantic	3	F/W A/S	C	France	Operated by Pakistan Air Force				
Westland Sea King (Mk 45)	6	A/S Helicopter	B	UK					
PERU									
Grumman Tracker (S-2E)	9	F/W A/S	C	USA					
Agusta-Bell 212ASW	6	A/S Helicopter	B	Italy					
Bell UH-1D/H	6	Helicopter	B	USA					
Bell JetRanger	10	Helicopter	B	USA					
Aerospatiale Alouette III	2	Helicopter	B	France					
Grumman Albatross (HU-16B)	4	Maritime Patrol F/W	C	USA	Operated by Peruvian Air Force				
Fokker-VFW F.27MPA	2	Maritime Patrol F/W	C	Netherlands					
POLAND									
Ilyushin Il-28 ("Beagle")	8	F/W Recce and ECM	C	USSR					
PORTUGAL									
Lockheed Neptune (SP-2E)	6	LRMP F/W	C	USA	Operated by Portuguese Air Force				

Wing span Rotor diameter	Length	Height	Power Plant	Armament Capacity	Remarks
48 ft (14·63 m)	57 ft (17·37 m)		1 × 1 290 shp General Electric T58-GE-3 turboshaft	2 × Mk 44 torpedoes, dipping sonar	
48 ft (14·63 m)	57 ft 1 in (17·40 m)	14 ft 5 in (4·40 m)	1 × 1 290 shp Pratt & Whitney (Canada) PT6T-3 Turbo Twin Pac twin turboshaft	2 × Mk 44 or Mk 46 torpedoes, depth charges, missiles, dipping sonar	
46 ft 9 in (14·25 m)	38 ft 1 in (11·60 m)	16 ft 5 in (5·00 m)	Two 340 hp Lycoming GSO-480-B1C6 piston engines		Used by South African Air Force (not by Italy)
97 ft 8·5 in (29·78 m)	95 ft 10·75 in (29·23 m)	29 ft 3·5 in (8·93 m)	Two General Electric T64-IHI-10 turboprop engines and two pod-mounted J3-IHI-7C turbojets	Classified; equipment includes radar, smoke detector and MAD	
108 ft 9 in (33·15 m)	109 ft 9·25 in (33·46 m)	32 ft 2·75 in (9·82 m)	Four Ishikawajima-built General Electric T64-IHI-10 turboprop engines each 3 060 ehp	Torpedoes, air-to-surface rockets, bombs, radar, MAD, sonobuoys	Also 3 US-1 search and rescue amphibians
95 ft 2 in (29·00 m)	77 ft 3·5 in (23·56 m)	27 ft 11 in (8·50 m)	Two 2 140 shp Rolls-Royce Dart 532-7R turboprop engines	Normally unarmed. Equipment includes underfuselage radome	Used by Peruvian Navy, Spanish Navy (not by Netherlands)

NAVAL EQUIPMENT / AIRCRAFT

Country/ Manufacturer	Strength	Role	Class (See note)	Country of Origin	Max Speed	Service Ceiling	Range	Max Endurance	T/O Weight
SOUTH AFRICA									
Westland Wasp (HAS Mk 1)	11	A/S Helicopter	B	UK	Embarked in Destroyers: *Jan Van Riebeeck; Simon van der Stel* Embarked in Frigates: *President Kruger; President Pretorius; President Steyn*				
Avro Shackleton MR.3	7	LRMP F/W	C	UK	Operated by SAAF				
Piaggio P.166S Albatross	20	F/W Coastal Patrol	C	Italy					
SPAIN									
Hawker Siddeley Matador (Harrier)	10	V/STOL F/W Strike/Recce	A	UK	Supplied via USA for operation from carrier *Dedalo* (+2 Harrier TAV-8A)				
Agusta-Bell 212ASW	4	A/S Helicopter	B	Italy					
Agusta-Bell 204AS	4	Search and Rescue Helicopter	B	Italy					
Bell AH-1G HueyCobra	6	Armed Helicopter	B	USA					
Sikorsky Sea King (SH-3D)	11	A/S Helicopter	B	USA					
Lockheed Orion (P-3A)	3	Maritime Patrol F/W	C	USA	Operated by Spanish Air Force				
Fokker-VFW F.27MPA	3	F/W Search and Rescue	C	Netherlands	Operated by Spanish Air Force				
Grumman Albatross (HU-16B)	11	F/W Maritime Patrol Amphibian	C	USA	Operated by Spanish Air Force				
Hughes 500 M	12	A/S Helicopter	B	USA					
SWEDEN									
Agusta-Bell 206A JetRanger	10	Search and Rescue Helicopter	B	USA					
Boeing Vertol-Kawasaki 107-II	20	A/S and General Duty Helicopter	B	USA Japan					
Saab-Scania SH-37 Viggen	15	Maritime Recce F/W	C	Sweden	Mach 2				
SYRIA									
Kamov Ka-25 ("Hormone")	9	A/S Helicopter	B	USSR					
THAILAND									
Grumman Tracker (S-2F)	10	A/S, Maritime Patrol F/W	C	USA					
Grumman Albatross (HU-16B)	2	Search and Rescue F/W	C	USA					
TURKEY									
Agusta-Bell 205AS	3	A/S Helicopter	B	Italy					
Agusta-Bell 212ASW	12	A/S Helicopter	B	Italy					
Grumman Tracker (S-2A/E)	20	F/W A/S Attack	C	USA					
UNION OF SOVIET SOCIALIST REPUBLICS									
Yakovlev Yak-36 ("Forger-A")	25	VTOL Attack and Reconnaissance	A	USSR	Mach 1·3				22 050 lb (10 000 kg)
Mil ("Haze")		A/S Helicopter	C	USSR					26 455 lb (12 000 kg)
Mil Mi-8 ("Hip")		General Purpose Helicopter	C	USSR	140 knots	14 760 ft (4 500 m)	248 n. miles		26 455 lb (12 000 kg)
Kamov Ka-25 ("Hormone")	200 approx	A/S and Strike Helicopter	B	USSR	119 knots	11 500 ft (3 500 m)	350 n. miles		16 100 lb (7 300 kg)
Tupolev ("Backfire")	50	V/G Recce Bomber F/W	C	USSR	approx Mach 2·5		approx 4 775- 5 200 n. miles		270 000 lb (122 500 kg)
Tupolev Tu-16 ("Badger")	425	L. Range Bomber Maritime Recce F/W	C	USSR	at 35 000 ft 510 knots	42 650 ft (13 000 m)	with max bomb load 2 605 n. miles		150 000 lb (68 000 kg)
Tupolev Tu-95 ("Bear")	75	L. Range Bomber Maritime Recce F/W	C	USSR	Cruising at 32 000 ft 410 knots		with max load 6 775 n. miles		340 000 lb (154 220 kg)
Tupolev Tu-22 ("Blinder")	60	Recce Bomber F/W	C	USSR	at 40 000 ft Mach 1·4	60 000 ft (18 300 m)	1 215 n. miles		185 000 lb (83 900 kg)
Sukhoi Su-17 ("Fitter-C/D")		V/G A/S and close support Fighter	C	USSR	Mach 2·17	59 050 ft (18 000 m)	Combat radius 195-340 n. miles		41 887 lb (19 000 kg)
Beriev M-12 ("Mail")	100	A/S Recce Amphibian F/W	C	USSR	329 knots	39 977 ft (12 185 m)	2 160 n. miles		65 035 lb (29 500 kg)
Ilyushin Il-38 ("May")	60	A/S Recce F/W	C	USSR	365 knots	32 800 ft (10,000 m)	3 900 n. miles		

Wing span Rotor diameter	Length	Height	Power Plant	Armament Capacity	Remarks
34 ft 9·25 in (10·60 m)	53 ft 5·75 in (16·30 m)	19 ft 0·25 in (5·80 m)	One Volvo Flygmotor RM8A turbojet	Two air-to-air missiles. Provision for attack weapons	
23 ft 0 in (7·00 m)	49 ft 3 in (15·00 m)		One conventional turbojet and two lift-jets	Gun pods and rocket pods	Also a two-seat training version ("Forger-B")
69 ft 10·25 in (21·29 m)			Two 1 500 shp Isotov turboshaft		Similar to Mi-8 transport, but with retractable landing gear, undernose radome, towed MAD, boat hull, etc.
69 ft 10·25 in (21·29 m)	82 ft 9·75 in (25·24 m)	18 ft 6·5 in (5·65 m)	Two 1 500 shp Isotov TV2-117A turboshaft	Normally unarmed but can carry external stores on outriggers	
51 ft 8 in (15·75 m)	32 ft 0 in (9·75 m)	17 ft 7·5 in (5·37 m)	Two 900 shp Glushenkov GTD-3 turboshaft	A/S torpedoes, flares, small stores	
*113 ft (34·45 m)	132 ft (40·23 m)	33 ft (10·06 m)	Possibly two Kuznetsov turbofans	Air-to-surface missiles	
110 ft (33·5 m)	120 ft (36·5 m)	35 ft 6 in (10·8 m)	Two Mikulin AM-3M turbojets	Up to 7 × 23 mm cannon in dorsal, ventral and tail turrets and nose. 19 800 lb (9 000 kg) of bombs or missiles	Total includes 90 flight refuelling tankers
159 ft (48·5 m)	155 ft 10 in (47·5 m)	39 ft 9 in (12·12 m)	Four 14 795 ehp Kuznetsov NK-12MV turboprops	Bombs, missiles, 2 to 6 × 23 mm cannon	
90 ft 10·5 in (27·70 m)	132 ft 11·5 in (40·53 m)	17 ft 0 in (5·18 m)	Two turbojets with afterburners	Cameras. Provision for bombs and missiles	Data for "Blinder-C"
*45 ft 11·25 in (14·00 m)	61 ft 6·25 in (18·75 m)	15 ft 7 in (4·75 m)	One Lyulka AL-21F-3 afterburning turbojet	Two 30 mm cannon. 11 023 lb (5 000 kg) of bombs, rockets, missiles	Data for "Fitter-C". "Fitter-D" has undernose radar
97 ft 6 in (29·70 m)	99 ft (30·20 m)	22 ft 11·5 in (7·00 m)	Two 4 000 shp Ivchenko AI-20D turboprops	Torpedoes, depth charges, sonobuoys, MAD gear, nose radome	
122 ft 8·5 in (37·4 m)	129 ft 10 in (39·6 m)	33 ft 4 in (10·15 m)	Four 4 250 ehp Ivchenko AI-20 turboprops	A/S weapons, MAD gear, undernose radar	

*wings spread

NAVAL EQUIPMENT / AIRCRAFT

Country/Manufacturer	Strength	Role	Class (See note)	Country of Origin	Max Speed	Service Ceiling	Range	Max Endurance	T/O Weight
UNITED KINGDOM									
Hawker Siddeley Buccaneer S Mk 2	17	All Weather Strike and Recce F/W	A	UK	at 200 ft (60 m) Mach 0·85 approx		Tactical radius 1 000 n. miles	9 hours with two flight refuellings	62 000 lb (28 123 kg)
Westland (Fairey) Gannet AEW Mk 3	5	AEW F/W	A	UK	220 knots approx		Approx 695 nm	5-6 hours at 120 knots	
Hawker Siddeley Harrier (AV-8A)		V/STOL F/W Strike and Recce	A	UK	over 640 knots	over 50 000 ft (15 240 m)	over 3 000 n. miles with one flight refuelling		over 25 000 lb (11 339 kg)
Hawker Siddeley Sea Harrier FRS.1	24 ordered	V/STOL F/W Recce Strike Fighter	A	UK					
McDonnell Douglas Phantom F.G.1 (F-4K)	16	Interceptor and Ground Attack F/W	A	USA	Mach 2+		Ferry Range 2 000 n. miles		
Westland/Aerospatiale Gazelle HT.2	29	Helicopter Trainer	B	UK France	at S/L 167 knots	16 400 ft (5 000 m)	at S/L with full fuel 361 n. miles		3 970 lb (1 800 kg)
Westland Lynx HAS.2	60 ordered	Helicopter Search and Strike	B	UK	145 knots (cruising)		Mission radius 154 n. miles	2 hrs 24 min	9 500 lb (4 309 kg)
Westland Sea King (HAS.1 and HAS.2)	69	A/S Helicopter	B	UK	Normal operating 112 knots	10 000 ft (3 050 m)	664 n. miles with normal fuel		21 000 lb (9 525 kg)
Westland Wasp HAS.1	80	G/P and A/S Helicopter	B	UK	at S/L 104 knots		approx 234 n. miles		5 600 lb (2 495 kg)
Westland Wessex (HAS.1/3 & HU.5)	150	A/S, Assault and GP Helicopter	B	UK	at S/L 115 knots	(HAS.1) 14 000 ft (4 300 m)	Max fuel 10% reserve 415 n. miles		13 500 lb (6 120 kg)
Hawker Siddeley Nimrod MR.1	35	Long Range Maritime Recce F/W	C	UK	500 knots		Ferry 4 500-5 000 n. miles	12 hrs (typical)	177 500-192 000 lb (80 510-87 090 kg)
Avro Shackleton MR.3		L R M Recce AEW F/W	C	UK	at S/L 152 knots		2 515 n. miles		
Hawker Siddeley (Avro) Shackleton AEW.2	11	Airborne Early Warning F/W	C	UK	226 knots			10 hrs	98 000 lb (44 452 kg)
UNITED STATES OF AMERICA									
Rockwell International Bronco OV-10A	114 built	Multi-purpose Counter Insurgency F/W	C	USA	at S/L W/O Weapons 244 knots		Ferry with aux. fuel 1 240 n. miles	Combat radius with max weapon load 198 n. miles	14 466 lb (6 563 kg)
Vought A-7E Corsair II	950 built	Single-seat Attack Aircraft F/W	A	USA	at S/L 600 knots		Ferry 2 800 n. miles		42 000 lb (19 050 kg)
F-8H Crusader	Total all versions 200	Single-seat Fighter F/W	A	USA	F-8A, B, C 868 knots + F-8D, E, H & J nearly Mach 2		F-8A 520 n. miles		34 000 lb (15 420 kg)
Grumman C-2A Greyhound	25	COD Transport F/W	A	USA	at 11 000 ft (3 450 m) 306 knots		at cruising speed and height 1 432 n. miles		54 830 lb (24 870 kg)
Grumman Hawkeye E-2B/C	94	AEW F/W	A	USA	314 knots	30 800 ft (9 390 m)	Ferry 1 394 n. miles		51 569 lb (23 391 kg)
Grumman A-6E Intruder	Total built 546	Strike and Recce F/W	A	USA	at S/L 558 knots	46 800 ft (14 265 m)	2 365 n. miles		60 400 lb (27 400 kg)
McDonnell Douglas F-4B Phantom II	Total built 1 189	All Weather Fighter F/W	A	USA	Mach 2·5	Combat 71 000 ft (21 640 m)	Ferry 1 997 n. miles		54 600 lb (24 765 kg)
McDonnell Douglas A-4M Skyhawk	500	Attack Bomber F/W	A	USA	with 4 000 lb of bombs 561 knots		Ferry 1 740 n. miles		24 500 lb (11 113 kg)
McDonnell Douglas EA-3B Skywarrior	60	Electronic Countermeasures F/W	A	USA	at 10 000 ft (3 050 m) 530 knots	45 000 ft (13 780 m)	Normal 2 520 n. miles		73 000 lb (33 112 kg)
Grumman F-14A Tomcat	390 ordered	All Weather Fighter F/W	A	USA	Mach 2·40	over 56 000 ft (17 070 m)			74 348 lb (33 724 kg)
Grumman S-2E Tracker	180	A/S Attack F/W	A	USA	at S/L 230 knots	21 000 ft (6 400 m)	Ferry 1 128 n. miles	Max endurance 9 hrs	29 150 lb (13 222 kg)
Lockheed S-3A Viking	187 built	A/S F/W	A	USA	450 knots	over 35 000 ft (10 670 m)	Ferry 3 000 n. miles+		42 500 lb (19 277 kg)
Rockwell International RA-5C Vigilante	100	Tactical Recce F/W	A	USA	Mach 2·1	64 000 ft (19 500 m)	2 600 n. miles		66 800 lb (30 300 kg)
Sikorsky SH-34 Seabat/Seahorse (S-58)		A/S and GP Helicopter	B	USA	at S/L 107 knots	9 000 ft (2 740 m)	214 n. miles +10% reserve		14 000 lb (6 350 kg)
Bell AH-1J SeaCobra	Total 101	Close Support Helicopter	B	USA	180 knots	10 550 ft (3 215 m)	310 n. miles		10 000 lb (4 535 kg)
Sikorsky SH-3A/D/G Sea King	325	ASW and Transport Helicopter	B	USA	144 knots	14 700 ft (4 480 m)	542 n. miles 10% reserve		18 626 lb (8 450 kg)
Boeing Vertol UH-46D Sea Knight	450 built	Transport and Utility Helicopter	B	USA	144 knots	14 000 ft (4 265 m)	approx 198 n. miles		Max 23 000 lb (10 433 kg)
Kaman SH-2F Seasprite	100	ASW Helicopter	B	USA	at S/L 143 knots	22 500 ft (6 860 m)	367 n. miles		12 500 lb (5 670 kg)

AIRCRAFT / NAVAL EQUIPMENT

Wing span Rotor diameter	Length	Height	Power Plant	Armament Capacity	Remarks
44 ft (13·41 m)	63 ft 5 in (19·33 m)	16 ft 3 in (4·95 m)	Two Rolls-Royce RB 168-1A Spey Mk 101 turbofan engines	Bombs, rockets, air-to-surface missiles—camera. Max load 16 000 lb (7 257 kg)	Expected to be transferred to the RAF, 1979
54 ft 6 in (16·61 m)	44 ft (13·41 m)	16 ft 10 in (5·13 m)	One Bristol Siddeley Double Mamba 102 turboprop 3 875 ehp	Electronics, early warning for long range ship and aircraft detection	Expected to be scrapped, 1979
25 ft 3 in (7·70 m)	45 ft 6 in (13·87 m)	Approx 11 ft 3 in (3·43 m)	One Rolls-Royce Pegasus 103 vectored-thrust turbofan engine	Aden gun pods, bombs, rockets, Sidewinder missiles, flares, camera	In service with USMC and Spain. Total includes 8 TAV-8As
25 ft 3·25 in (7·70 m)	47 ft 7 in (14·50 m)	12 ft 2 in (3·71 m)	One Rolls-Royce Pegasus 104 vectored-thrust turbofan engine	Aden gun pods, bombs, rockets, Sidewinder missiles, air-to-surface missiles, etc	For service from 1979
38 ft 5 in (11·71 m)	62 ft 11·75 in (19·20 m)		Two Rolls-Royce Spey Mk 201 turbofan engines with afterburners	Sparrow III air-to-air missiles, bombs, rockets, etc.	Expected to be transferred to the RAF, 1979
34 ft 5·75 in (10·50 m)	39 ft 3·25 in (11·97 m)	10 ft 2·25 in (3·15 m)	One 590 shp Turbomeca Astazou IIIA turboshaft engine		
42 ft (12·80 m)	49 ft 9 in (15·16 m)	11 ft 9·75 in (3·60 m)	Two 900 shp Rolls-Royce BS 360.07.26 Gem turboshaft engines	Two Mk 44 or Mk 46 homing torpedoes, depth charges or missiles	
62 ft 0 in (18·90 m)	72 ft 8 in (22·15 m)	16 ft 10 in (5·13 m)	Two 1 660 shp Rolls-Royce Gnome H 1400-1 turboshaft engines	Dipping sonar type 195 system, radar, smoke floats, AD580 doppler navigation, torpedoes, depth charges, machine gun	Data for current Mk 2 version. Eight Sea King HAR.3s ordered for RAF search and rescue
32 ft 3 in (9·83 m)	40 ft 4 in (12·29 m)	11 ft 8 in (3·56 m)	One Rolls-Royce Bristol Nimbus 503 turboshaft engine, derated to 710 shp	Two Mk 44 homing torpedoes or other stores	
56 ft 0 in (17·07 m)	65 ft 9 in (20·03 m)	16 ft 2 in (4·93 m)	One Rolls-Royce Bristol Gnome 112 and one Gnome 113 turboshaft engines, each 1 350 shp	Up to 13 troops or 7 stretchers A/S version (HAS.1) can carry weapons	
114 ft 10 in (35·3 m)	126 ft 9 in (38·63 m)	29 ft 8·5 in (9·08 m)	Four Rolls-Royce RB168 Spey Mk 250 turbofan engines	Bombs, mines, depth charges, MAD, full range ASW detection equipment	Operated by RAF. Being uprated to MR.2
119 ft 10 in (36·52 m)	87 ft 4 in (26·52 m)	23 ft 4 in (7·11 m)	Four Rolls-Royce Griffon 57A piston engines 2 455 hp each		Operated by SAAF
119 ft 10 in (36·52 m)	92 ft 6 in (28·19 m)	23 ft 4 in (7·11 m)	Four Rolls-Royce/Griffon 67 piston engines, 2 450 hp each	Early warning electronics	Operated by RAF
40 ft 0 in (12·19 m)	41 ft 7 in (12·67 m)	15 ft 2 in (4·62 m)	Two 715 ehp Garrett AiResearch T76-G-416/417 turboprops	4 × 0·30 in machine guns, air-to-air missiles, bombs, rockets, etc. Max weapon load 3,600 lb (1,633 kg)	
38 ft 9 in (11·80 m)	46 ft 1·5 in (14·06 m)	16 ft 0·75 in (4·90 m)	One Allison TF41-A-2 turbofan	Air-to-air, air-to-surface missiles, guns, rockets, bombs, drop tanks	Total includes A-7A/B/C
35 ft 8 in (10·87 m)	54 ft 6 in (16·61 m)	15 ft 9 in (4·80 m)	One Pratt & Whitney J57-P-20 turbojet	Cannon, rockets, bombs, missiles	Also F-8J/K and RF-8G
80 ft 7 in (24·56 m)	56 ft 8 in (17·27 m)	15 ft 11 in (4·85 m)	Two 4 050 ehp Allison T56-A-8A turboprops	10 000 lb freight	
80 ft 7 in (24·56 m)	57 ft 7 in (17·55 m)	18 ft 4 in (5·59 m)	Two 4 910 ehp Allison T56-A-425 turboprops	Early warning and command electronics	Data for E-2C
53 ft 0 in (16·15 m)	54 ft 7 in (16·64 m)	16 ft 2 in (4·93 m)	Two Pratt & Whitney J52-P-8A turbojets	Bombs, missiles and other stores	Total includes A-6A/B/C
38 ft 5 in (11·70 m)	58 ft 0 in (17·76 m)	16 ft 0 in (4·88 m)	Two General Electric J79-GE-8 turbojets with afterburners	Missiles, bombs, rockets	Also F-4J/N and 50 RF-4Bs
27 ft 6 in (8·38 m)	40 ft 4 in (12·27 m)	15 ft 0 in (4·57 m)	One Pratt & Whitney J52-P-408A turbojet	Cannon, bombs, rockets, missiles	Total includes A-4C/E/F/L
72 ft 6 in (22·07 m)	76 ft 4 in (23·27 m)	22 ft 8 in (6·91 m)	Two Pratt & Whitney J57-P-10 turbojets	Provision for bombs, torpedoes, cannon	Total includes tankers
Unswept 64 ft 1·5 in (19·54 m)	61 ft 11·9 in (18·89 m)	16 ft 0 in (4·88 m)	Two Pratt & Whitney TF30-P-412A turbofans with afterburners	Guns, missiles, bombs	
72 ft 7 in (22·13 m)	43 ft 6 in (13·26 m)	16 ft 7 in (5·06 m)	Two 1 525 hp Wright R-1820-82WA piston engines	Depth charges, torpedoes, rockets, sonobuoys	Total includes S-2D/G
68 ft 8 in (20·93 m)	53 ft 4 in (16·26 m)	22 ft 9 in (6·93 m)	Two General Electric TF34-GE-2 turbofan engines	Bombs, depth bombs, rockets, missiles, mines, torpedoes, flares	
53 ft 0 in (16·15 m)	76 ft 7·25 in (23·35 m)	19 ft 5 in (5·92 m)	Two General Electric J79-GE-10 turbojets	Variety of weapons inc. thermo-nuclear bombs	
56 ft 0 in (17·07 m)	56 ft 8·25 in (17·27 m)	15 ft 11 in (4·85 m)	One 1 525 hp Wright R-1820-84B/D piston engine	12 passengers	
44 ft 0 in (13·41 m)	53 ft 4 in (16·26 m)	13 ft 8 in (4·15 m)	One 1 800 shp Pratt & Whitney T400-CP-400 turboshaft	Cannon and rockets	Total includes improved AH-1T
62 ft 0 in (18·90 m)	72 ft 8 in (22·15 m)	16 ft 10 in (5·13 m)	Two 1 400 shp General Electric T58-GE-10 turboshaft	Torpedoes, missiles 840 lb (381 kg) of weapons	Data for SH-3D
60 ft 0 in (18·29 m)	Fuselage 51 ft 0 in (15·54 m)	16 ft 8·5 in (5·09 m)	Two 1 400 shp General Electric T58-GE-10 turboshaft	Up to 10 000 lb load	Total includes CH-46s
44 ft 0 in (13·41 m)	52 ft 7 in (16·03 m)	15 ft 6 in (4·72 m)	Two 1 350 shp GE T58-GE-8F turboshaft	LAMPS equipment. Details in JAWA	

NAVAL EQUIPMENT / AIRCRAFT—GUNS

Country/Manufacturer	Strength	Role	Class (See note)	Country of Origin	Max Speed	Service Ceiling	Range	Max Endurance	T/O Weight
Sikorsky CH-53A/D Sea Stallion	275	Assault Transport Helicopter	B	USA	170 knots	21 000 ft (6 400 m)	223 n. miles		42 000 lb (19 050 kg)
Sikorsky RH-53D	30	Mine Countermeasures Helicopter	B	USA				over 4 hr	50 000 lb (22 680 kg)
Bell UH-1E	190	Assault Support Helicopter	B	USA	140 knots	21 000 ft (6 400 m)	248 n. miles		9 500 lb (4 309 kg)
Hawker Siddeley AV-8A Harrier	80	V/STOL Strike/Recce F/W	A	UK					
Grumman EA-6A/B Prowler	104	ECM/ELINT F/W	A	USA	570 knots at S/L	46 300 ft (14 110 m)	2 182 n. miles with max load		65 000 lb (26 535 kg)
Lockheed C-130 Hercules	117	LR Transport and Recce and Tanker F/W	C	USA	335 knots	33 000 ft (10 060 m)	4 460 n. miles		155 000 lb (70 310 kg)
Lockheed SP-2H Neptune	50	LRMP F/W	C	USA	at 10 000 ft (3 050 m) 350 knots	22 000 ft (6 700 m)	3 200 n. miles		79 895 lb (36 240 kg)
Lockheed P-3A/B/C and EP-3E Orion	400	A/S Recce F/W	C	USA	at 15 000 ft (4 570 m) 411 knots	28 300 ft (8 625 m)	Mission radius 2 070 n. miles		142 000 lb (64 410 kg)
URUGUAY									
Bell 47G-2	2	Helicopter	B	USA					
Sikorsky SH-34J	2	A/S and Search and Rescue Helicopter	B	USA					
Grumman Tracker (S-2A)	3	A/S Patrol F/W	C	USA					
VENEZUELA									
Bell 47G	4	Helicopter	B	USA					
Grumman Tracker (S-2E)	3	A/S Patrol F/W	C	USA					
YUGOSLAVIA									
Kamov Ka-25 ("Hormone")		A/S Helicopter	B	USSR					
Mil Mi-8 ("Hip")		Coastal Patrol	B	USSR					

GUNS

Calibre mm	Length in Calibres	Country and Year Introduced	Number of Barrels	Elevation Degrees	Rate of Fire per Barrel (Rounds per Minute)	Weight of Shell kg (Explosive)	Range km (Surface/Height)	AA Slant	Associated Radar/Director
HEAVY									
406	50	US Navy 1936	Single		2	1 235	42 km		Mk 34 Fire Control Director
203	55	US Navy 1971	Single	−5°, +65°, 20°/sec	10-12 rpm	118 kg max	Estimated over 55 km		Mk 68 fire control system on destroyer Hull
203	55	US Navy 1927, 1944	3 Mk XV Mk XVI	30 41	5 10 cased	125	23 km 28		Mk 34 fire control director with Mk 13 radar
152	53	Bofors, Sweden 1942	Triple and twin	70° 60°	10-15	46	18/10 km 26 max		
152	50	Vickers, UK 1951	Twin Mk 26	80	20		15 km		MRS-3 F.C.S.
152	50	Vickers, UK, 1934	Triple	45	8	50	23 km max		
152	50	Vickers, UK, 1923	Twin	60	8	45	23 km		
152	47	US Navy 1933	Triple Mk 16		10	47	23 km max		Mk 33 F.C.S. Mk 34 Director
150	50	USSR 1938	Triple Semi-auto	50	4/10	50	27 km max		26 foot range finder (built-in)
MEDIUM									
133		UK	Twin	70	12	36	21	13 km ceiling	
130	60	USSR 1953	Twin Auto	70	15	27	17/8 28/13 max		
130	50	USSR 1936	Twin semi- auto single	40	10	27	24 max 15 opt		
130	58	USSR	Twin semi-auto Dual purpose	50	15	27	28 000 metres max 18 000 opt	13 000 max	Sun Visor, Egg Cup and Wasp Head
127	54	US Navy 1969	Single Mk 45	65	20	32			Mk 86 F.C.3 with AN/SPG-60 radar
127	54	OTO Melara, 1968	Single	85	45	32	15/7		
127	54	US Navy 1953	Single Mk 42	85	45	46 (32)	24/14 max		Mk 68 Director with AN/SPG-53 radar
127	54	France 1948	Twin semi-auto	80	18	— (32)	18/9 22/13 max		
127	54	US Navy 1944	Single Mk 39	80	15	— (32)	12/8 22/13 max		

GUNS—AIRCRAFT / NAVAL EQUIPMENT

Wing span Rotor diameter	Length	Height	Power Plant	Armament Capacity	Remarks
72 ft 3 in (22·02 m)	88 ft 3 in (26·90 m)	24 ft 11 in (7·60 m)	Two 2 850 shp GE T64-GE-6 turboshaft	37 passengers or 24 stretchers with 4 attendants	Data for CH-53D
72 ft 3 in (22·02 m)			Two 4 380 shp GE T64-GE-415 turboshaft	Two machine-guns	
44 ft 0 in (13·41 m)	53 ft 0 in (16·15 m)	12 ft 7·25 in (3·84 m)	One Lycoming T53-L-11 turboshaft	Machine guns, rockets, 8 passengers or 4 000 lb cargo	Total includes UH-1D/H/L
53 ft 0 in (16·15 m)	59 ft 5 in (18·11 m)		Two Pratt & Whitney J52-P-8A turbojets	Normally unarmed ECM equipment	Data for EA-6B
132 ft 7 in (40·41 m) inc. tip tanks	97 ft 9 in (29·78 m)	38 ft 3 in (11·66 m)	Four 4 508 ehp Allison T56-A-15 turboprop	Cargo up to 26 640 lb (12 080 kg) 92 troops, 64 paras or 74 stretchers	Data for late-model transport
103 ft 10 in (31·65 m)	91 ft 8 in (27·94 m)	29 ft 4 in (8·94 m)	Two 3 500 hp Wright R-3350-32W radial piston + 2 Westinghouse J34 turbojets	8 000 lb (3 630 kg) bombs, torpedoes, depth charges and rockets	
99 ft 8 in (30·37 m)	116 ft 10 in (35·61 m)	33 ft 8·5 in (10·29 m)	Four 4 910 ehp Allison T56-A-14 turboprops	Mines, depth bombs, torpedoes	Data for P-3C

Remarks

US Navy Reserve Battleships of "Iowa" class.

MCLWG (Major Calibre Lightweight Gun) at present only in destroyer *Hull* for trials. Destined for "Spruance" class if accepted. Intended for surface fire. Digital Mk 86 GECS in new constructions.

Mk XV manually operated fitted to *Saint Paul* and *Canberra*. Mk XVI automatically operated on US cruisers of "Salem" class.

Fitted in cruisers *A. Grau* (Peru) and *A. Latorre* (Chile). *A. Latorre* has the only existing triple mount. Single Bofors 152 mm open shielded mountings in Swedish minelayer *Alvsnabben* are believed to belong to the same general type.

Only on board cruisers HMS *Blake* and *Tiger*. One mounting per ship.

Now only found in British-built cruisers—Indian *Mysore* and Peruvian "Bolognesi" class. Mk 23 gun on Mk 23 mounting.

Only aboard Indian Navy cruiser *Delhi*.

Only aboard US cruiser "Brooklyn" class owned by Argentina (2) and Chile (1).

Independent-elevating barrels often referred as L.57 long. On "Chapaiev" and "Sverdlov" classes of Soviet cruisers.

Dual purpose mounting exists only aboard British built cruiser *Babur* (Pakistan).

"Kotlin" class and variants (USSR and Polish "Warszawa"). Sometimes referred to as 58 calibres long × 50.

"Skory" class destroyers (USSR). "Luta" class Chinese Navy. Single only on Ex-Soviet "Gordy" class of Chinese Navy.

"Skory" (Mod) and "Kotlin" classes.

Ordered by US Navy ("Virginia", "California", "Spruance" and "Tarawa" classes) also Iran "Spruances", Mk 65 improvement, proposed for late "Spruance" class.

In use by Canada (four "Iroquois" class destroyers) and Italy (two "Audace" class) ordered for "Lupo" class frigates of Italy, Peru and Venezuela. Probably for Italian "Maestrale" class.

Aboard US carriers, cruisers, destroyers and frigates of post war design. Also in Australia, West Germany, Japan and Spain.

Twin gun using American ammunition only remaining aboard four T53 destroyers ("La Bourdonnais" class).

Aboard US carriers of the original "Midway" class and in Japanese "Akizuki" and "Murasame" classes (five destroyers). Semi-automatic.

776 NAVAL EQUIPMENT / GUNS

Calibre mm	Length in Calibres	Country and Year Introduced	Number of Barrels	Elevation Degrees	Rate of Fire per Barrel (Rounds per Minute)	Weight of Shell kg (Explosive)	Range km (Surface/Height)	AA Slant	Associated Radar/Director
127	38	US Navy 1935	Single Mk 30 Twin Mk 38	80	15	37	13/8 17/11		
127	50	US Navy 1923	Single		8	27			
120	50	Bofors, Sweden, 1950	Twin	85	42	24	13/7 20/12 max		Dutch fire control Director L.A.-01. See note
120	50	San Carlos, Spain, 1950	Twin NG-53	80	15	25	18/11		
120	50	Bofors, Sweden, 1934	Single	70	12	24	20 max		
120	45	Vickers, UK, 1931	Single	40	12	23	18		
120	50	Ansaldo, Italy, 1926	Twin			23			
120	46	Bofors, Sweden, 1967	Single	80	80	35 (21)	12/8 19/12		
120	45	Bofors, Sweden, 1945	Twin	80	20	24	19/13		
114	55	Vickers, UK, 1971	Single Mk 8	53-55	20-25		13/6		
114	50	Vickers, UK, 1946	Twin Mk 6	80	11-25	25	13/6 19		
114	45	Vickers, UK, 1937	Twin Mk 3 Single Mk 4	80 55	15	25 25	18 "Battle" Class 17 "Tribal" Class		
105	50	Bofors, Sweden, 1932	Single						
102	60	Vickers, UK, 1955	Single	75	40	16	12/8 18/12		
102	—	Vickers, UK, 1935	Various	80	up to 16	16	19/13		
100	60	USSR, 1942	Twin	80 or 90	15-20	16	11/8 18/12 max		Sun Visor
100	56	China							
100	55	France 1959	Single, various versions	80	60	23·2 (13·4)	13/7 17/11 max		
100	50	USSR	Twin	80	15	16	20 12	15 000 max 9,000 Slan	Sun Visor
100	50	USSR 1947	Single	40 or 80	15	13·5	18/11 16/6	6,000	Sun Visor
85	55	USSR 1943	Single, Twin	70 or 75	10-20	9·5	9/6 14/9	6,000	
76	70	Vickers, UK, 1951	Twin Mk 6	80 or 90	60	7 approx	5 max 17 surface		
76	62	OTO Melara, Italy, 1964	Single	85	85	6	8/5 16/12 max		
76	62	OTO Melara, Italy, 1961	Single	85	60	6	8/5 16/12 max		
76	60	USSR 1961	Twin	85	60	16	15/10	14,000	
76	50	Bofors, Sweden, 1965	Single	30	30	11	7·5/— 13/— max		
76	50	US Navy 1944	See Note	7·5 or 85	45 or 50	6	7/5·5 13/8		
76	50	US Navy 1936	Single Mks 21-22 & 26		20 or 33		12/—		Mk 52

LIGHT

57	80	USSR, about 1965	Twin	85	120	2·7	5/1 12/5 max		Muff Cobb
57	70	USSR 1959	Single, Twin, Quad	85	120	2·8	—/4 9/6 max	6 000	Hawk Screech
57	70	Bofors, Sweden, 1971	Single	75	200	5·9	14/—		Dutch M-20 series
57	60	Bofors, Sweden, 1950	Twin	90	120-130	2·6	—/5 14/9		

Remarks

Twin Mk-38 aboard US-built destroyers "Gearing" and "Sumner" classes in many navies; Danish, Italian and Spanish built escorts. Single Mk 30 on other wartime escorts; US built in many foreign navies. Cruisers, "Long Beach", "Brooke" and "Garcia" classes of frigates, auxiliaries, and a few Spanish and Yugoslav built frigates. Both models employ Mk 12 barrel and usually Mk 37 fire control director, sometimes complemented for Mk 56. In austere installations Mk 52 fire control system, including Mk 51 manual director. Other variants of this widely used wartime gun are Mk 32 in several old US cruisers. Single Mk 24 in "Albany" class cruisers also "Hancock"/"Essex" classes of carriers. Open mountings without shield are used in auxiliaries and known as either Mk-37 or Mk-30 Mod 24, both singles.

Single open mountings used (eight per ship) in US built "Brooklyn" class cruisers remaining in Argentine Navy (2) and Chilean Navy (1)

Dutch fire control director LA-01 aboard destroyers of the "Halland" class. (Sweden 2, Columbia 2) and of the Dutch "Tromp", "Holland" and "Friesland" classes.

Data is estimated. Derived from NG-50. NG-53 is semi-automatic. Only in service in Spanish destroyer *Oquendo*.

Only aboard *Halsingborg* and *Kalmar* frigates of the Royal Swedish Navy.

Manually operated. Surface fire only in "R" class destroyers of the Indian Navy (3). Mk 9 gun on Mk CP-18 mounting.

Believed to be used in the two "Paraguay" class gunboats of Paraguayan Navy.

Turret has a 4 mm shield 51 rounds per minute. Private venture only mounted in the two Finnish "Turunma" class escorts. One mounting per ship.

Swedish destroyers of "Öland" and "Östergotland" classes. Semi-automatic light shield. Originally employing Mk-45 fire control.

Developed from the "Abbot" field gun. Aboard British "Amazon", "Bristol" and "Sheffield" classes.

Data is estimated: semi-automatic aboard escorts of Australia (where it is locally built under licence) Chile, India, Netherlands, New Zealand, Peru, South Africa and UK navies. Sometimes referred to as 46 calibres long with automatic version used in "County" class destroyers with rate of fire of 50 rpm per barrel. Dates from 1960.

Fitted to British "Tribal" class, Pakistan "C" class and Malaysian frigate *Rahmat* open turret hand loaded. It is assumed that closed twin turrets in "Battle" class destroyers of Iran and Pakistan navies and Venezuelan "Aragua" class use the same gun but are semi-automatic.

Two Argentinan "King" class frigates. Three guns per ship. Hand loaded. Open shield.

Used exclusively aboard two "Almirante Williams" class destroyers of Chilean Navy. Closed turrets. Four mountings per ship.

These performance figures belong to the pre-war 3·4 ton 4 in barrel made by Vickers. This is most widely used in British-built ships in different mountings. All believed to use the above barrel. The single and twin Mk 19 can be found in the navies of Burma, Dominican Republic, Ecuador, Egypt, India, Malaysia, Nigeria, Pakistan, South Africa, Sri Lanka, Thailand. A twin lightweight anti-aircraft British 4 in gun is used on Peruvian and Indian cruisers. A modern short barrelled-enclosed mounting, also from Vickers, serves in "Vosper Mk 1" class corvettes owned by Libya and Ghana. Sometimes referred to as the 102 or 100 mm are the twin guns of the Italian-made frigates owned by Venezuela ("A. Clemente" class) and Indonesia ("Surapati" type).

Only in Russian cruisers ("Sverdlov" and "Chapaev" class) and "Kotlin" class destroyers. The gunnery of the Chinese "Kiangtung" class could be considered as a local development. Each turret uses its own Egg Cup radar. Fire control is managed with Sun Visor radars.

Known to exist in Chinese "Kiang-Nan" class. Probably the same as those aboard North Korean frigates of "Najin" class and corvettes of the "Sariwan" and "Tral" classes. The last being Russian built. The guns are thought to be a Chinese refit of a Soviet weapon, possibly the 100/50 1947 model.

Two versions: *Modèle 1953* with analogic fire control and *Modèle 68* associated with digital fire control. Integrating DRBC 32 radar. Aboard two ("Clémenceau") carriers, one "Colbert" cruiser, two "Suffren" frigates, *Jeanne d'Arc* and escorts of the "C 65", "C 70", "A 69", "F 67", "T 47", "ASW", "T 53 ASW", "T 56" and "Commandant Rivière" classes. Total of 36 ships including those under construction in French Navy. Also fitted in Belgian "E 71" class (4); Federal Germany ("Hamburg", "Köln" and "Rhein") classes and *Deutschland*, Portugal ("C. João Belo" and "João Countinho" classes); Tunisia; South Africa (A69 class new Avisos); and Turkish ("Rhein") class. The newest 1976 turret, which is lighter than its predecessors is claimed to reach 90 rounds per minute.

"Sverdlov" and "Chapaev" classes.

"Riga", "Kola", "Don" and "Purga" class ships of Soviet Navy. Semi-automatic.

Twin mounts in "Skory" class. Single mounts in "Kronshtadt" class. New enclosed mounting, single, on "Krivak" class ships built since 1976.

Fully automatic aboard Canadian frigates and HMS *Blake* and *Tiger* cruisers.

Ordered by Argentina, Denmark, Fed. Germany, Iran, Israel, Italy, Libya, Morocco, Netherlands, Nigeria, Oman, Spain, Turkey, Venezuela and USA. The USA has standardised the weapon as the Mk 75 to start its employment in "Pegasus" and "WMEC-630" classes; a variety of fire control systems is used, notably the Dutch M.20 series.

Aboard Italian Navy ships "V Veneto," "A. Doria," "Impavido," "Alpino," "Bergamini," "Centauro" and "De Cristofaro" classes. Sometimes referred to as Brescia model. Also in use on ships of Greek and Ecuadorian Navies.

"Kiev", "Kara", "Kynda", "Krivak", "Kashin", converted "Kildin", "Mirka", and "Petya" classes.

Surface fire only. Used aboard fast attack craft of Norwegian "Storm" class (20) and Singapore "Type B" Vosper class (3).

Most usual versions are single Mk 34 single mount (weight 7·7 tons). Mk 27 and Mk 33 twin mounts (weight 14·5 tons). In both open and semi-protected versions, the last using a fibre-glass shield. Aboard US-built cruisers, destroyers, frigates and auxiliaries. Extensively used in foreign navies and foreign-built ships; notably Japan. Built under licence (Mk 34) in Spain. Mk 56 and Mk 63 gunfire control systems usually employed.

Semi-automatic; intended for surface fire only; widely used in many obsolete ships of US Navy (auxiliary, amphibious) and abroad including wartime-built escort destroyers. Also Greek "Algerine" class. Many other 76 mm of obsolete types remain in service in small quantities. A single 76/40, probably OTO Melara-built, is used aboard Italian built corvettes ("Albatross" class) owned by Denmark (4) and Indonesia (2). Also a 76/40, probably Vickers' 1914 model is used by the Paraguayan Navy on its "Humaita" and "C. Cabral" classes. These have single mounts. Another 76 mm tank turret 76/41·2 is used by Soviet river patrol launches of "Shmel" and "PB" classes. "Trad" and "Bangrachan" classes of Thai Navy probably use Japanese wartime guns of 76 or 75 mm by 40 or 50 calibres long.

Soviet Navy "Moskva", "Kresta I" and "Kresta II", "Grisha I" and "II", "Nanuchka", "Poti", "Turya" and "T.58" classes. Amphibious and auxiliary ships sometimes referred to as 73 calibres long. Water cooled.

Only twin mod. has muzzle brake. This and quadruple are aboard Soviet "Kildin", "Kanin" and "Kotlin" classes. Singles are aboard Soviet "Skory" (modified) destroyers and various classes of minesweepers. Also East Germany's amphibious ships. A single Chinese 57 mm gun is used in "Shanghai II" class fast attack craft (including some transferred to Albania) and the new "Luta" class.

Plastic-enclosed turret used by navies of Denmark *(Willemoes)* Malaysia *(Perdana)*; Singapore ("Sea" class); Sweden ("Visby", class frigates and 38 fast attack craft); Thailand's "Prabarapak" class. Single 57 mm guns in Sweden's "Alvsnabben" class are of unidentified model—they have very long barrels.

Current Swedish original turret for this gun weighs 20-24 tons and is aboard Peruvian "A Grau" class and Chilean *A Latorre* Sweden's "Halland" class destroyers use French turret weighing 15 tons with only 80° elevation. Also fitted to French cruiser *Colbert* and escorts of the T47, T53, E50 and E52 classes. Open, unprotected, small and obsolete single 57 mm mountings are operated in five patrol vessels of Icelandic Navy. A similar weapon of 47 mm calibre is aboard its sixth fishery protection vessel. Peruvian "Loreto" class (2 ships) also use a similar 47 mm gun but might be of the American 30 calibre long model.

778 NAVAL EQUIPMENT / GUNS—MISSILES

Calibre mm	Length in Calibres	Country and Year Introduced	Number of Barrels	Elevation Degrees	Rate of Fire per Barrel (Rounds per Minute)	Weight of Shell kg (Explosive)	Range km (Surface/Height)	AA Slant	Associated Radar/Director
45	85	USSR 1953	Quad	90	160-220	1·5	—/4 9/6 max	7 000	Hawk Screech
40	70	Bofors, Sweden, 1946	Single 2·4-3·3 Also Twin	80-90	240-300	2·4	4/— 13/9		
40	60	Bofors, Sweden, 1942	Various	80	120-160	0·89	—12·7 10/4·5 max		
37	80	Krupp, Germany, 1932	Single	85	80	0·745	4/3		
37	63	USSR, 1944	Twin	80	130	0·7	8/5 max	3 000	Eye Shooting
37	63	USSR, 1044	Single	80	130	0·7	8/5 max	3 000	Eye Shooting
35	90	Oerlikon, Switzerland, 1972	Twin	85	550	1·55	6/5 max		
30	75	Oerlikon, Switzerland, 1974	Twin	80-85	650	1 0·36	3 10·2 max		
30	70	Hispano Suiza, France, 1962	Single	83	600	0·42	2·8 8·5 max		
30	65	USSR 1960	Twin	80 or 85	500		2·5 4 max		Drum Tilt

MISSILES

Further details can be found in the current edition of JANE'S WEAPON SYSTEMS
Note: Maximum range given can be up to twice the optimum range.

Country/ Manufacturer	Classification	Name	No.	Length ft	Launch weight lb	Power plant	Guidance	Max Range n. miles	Mach speed	Warhead	Remarks
AUSTRALIA Dept of Productivity	A/S	Ikara	—	11·3		Solid fuel rocket	Command link	13	—	Torpedo-HE	Acoustic homing torpedo. Digital control system in RAN. In RN version computer service from ADAS. Branik system in Brazilian "Niteroi" class linked to ships WCS with two Ferranti FM1600B computers
FRANCE Aerospatiale	SLBM	MSBS	M1	34·1	39 683	Solid fuel rocket 2 stage	Inertial	1 350	—	Nuclear 500 KT	In "Le Redoubtable" class SSBN
	SLBM	MSBS	M2	34·1	44 000	as above	Inertial	1 860	—	Nuclear 500 KT	In production to replace M1
	SLBM	MSBS	M20	34·1	44 000	as above	Inertial	1 860	—	Thermonuclear 1 MT	First embarked mid-1976
	SLBM	MSBS	M4	34·1	73 300	as above with 3 stages	Inertial	2 500+	—	Thermonuclear with seven MRV each of 150 KT	Production by late 1970s
CNIM	SSM	—	RP14	6·5	118	Solid fuel rocket	Nil	9	—	HE	22 rocket multiple launcher
Matra (with Oto Melara)	SSM	Otomat	—	14·6	1 694	Turbojet	Inertial cruise Active homer	112	0·9	132 lb HE	Sea-skimmer for last 2 miles; can be ASM
Aerospatiale	SSM	Exocet	MM38	17·1	1 617	2 stage solid fuel rocket	Inertial cruise Active radar homer	26	0·9	363 lb HE	Sea-skimmer throughout flight Variants — AM 39, air-launched; MM 39, ship-launched version of AM 39; MM 40, improved MM 38 with 40 n. mile range; SM 39, projected submarine launched MM 39
	SSM	—	SS11	3·9	66	2 stage solid fuel rocket	Wire-guided	2·0	330 knots	HE or torpedo	Same characteristics as AS-11. Harpon is very similar with improved guidance
	SSM	—	SS12	6·2	165	2 stage solid fuel rocket	Wire-guided	4·4	—	66 lb HE	Same characteristics as AS-12
Ecan Ruelle	SAM	Masurca	Mk 2	28·2 (with booster)	4 070	2 stage solid fuel rocket	Mod 2 Beam rider. Mod 3. semi active homer	25 (slant)	2·5	105 lb HE	Mounted in *Colbert*, *Suffren* and *Duquesne*
	SAM	Hirondelle Super 530	—	—	—	—	—	—	—	—	Project for PDMS for small ships and craft
	SAM	Catulle	—	—	—	—	—	—	—	—	Development. Multi-barrelled rocket system firing salvoes of 40 mm shells
Matra	SAM	Crotale Navale	R440	9·5	176	Solid fuel rocket	Infra-red/ command	10 (slant)	0·9 to 1·2	33 lb HE	Being installed in French Navy
Matra-Hawker Siddeley	ASM	Martel	AS37/ AJ168	13·8 12·8	—	Solid fuel rocket	TV on AJ168; passive radar homing on AS37	?30	—	HE	Air-to-surface weapon also in service with RAF
Aerospatiale	ASM	—	AS20	8·5	315	2 stage solid fuel rocket	Radio command	4	—	66 lb HE	In service
	ASM	—	AS30	12·4	1 100	2 stage solid fuel rocket	Radio command	6	1·5	506 lb HE	In service
Matra	AAM	Magic	R550	9·2	200	Solid fuel rocket	Infra-red	4	—	HE	In service 1975
	AAM	—	R530	10·8 11·6 (Super)	430	Solid fuel rocket	Infra-red or semi-active radar. EMD electro-magnetic, semi-active in Super 530	9·5	2·7	HE	Proximity fused head. Being replaced by Super 530
Latecoere	A/S	Malafon Mk 2	—	20·1	3 300	2 stage solid fuel rocket and booster	Radio/acoustic homing	8·1	450 knots	Torpedo	Torpedo dropped by parachute 300 yards from target

MISSILES—GUNS / NAVAL EQUIPMENT

Remarks

"Kildin" and "Kotlin" classes. Semi-automatic.

The original 1946 model has appeared in a very wide range of variations built in many western countries. Usually 1958 versions: SP-48 type built in Spain, British Mk 7 and Italian Breda improvements. (106 twin and 107 single) with 32 ready use rounds per barrel; Twin type 64 (200 ready use rounds/barrel) and type 350P/564 single (144 ready use rounds). Latest improvement is Breda Compatto twin 40/70 using either 736 ready use rounds or 444 ru rounds. Ordered for Italy, Peru and Venezuela ("Lupo" class) and Libya. This weapon uses "Dardo" system. Non-Italian models use 20 ready use rounds.

Many local versions have been manufactured from the original system. Most common are the American (twin Mk 1 and quad Mk 2 water-cooled mountings, single Mk 3 aircooled.) Other variants are the British twin Mk 5 weighing 3 tons and a French single.

Single mounting built in Spain around 1950. Derived from standard German twin mounting. Remaining examples aboard seven Spanish patrol and auxiliary ships. Semi-automatic.

"Sverdlov", "Chapaev", "Skory (modified)" and "Riga" classes. Twin Chinese mountings in "Whampoa", "Shantung" and "Shanghai", "Swatow" classes.

"Kronshtadt", "T301" class. Minesweepers use new enclosed version turret called 70-K.

The original weapon (GDM-A) is only found in Greek "Navsithoi" class fast attack craft, Iranian "Saam" class Libyan *Dat Assawari*, Turkish "Dogan" class and Ecuadorean Lurssen craft. Also possibly in two Japanese "Improved Haruna" class. An Italian mounting variant (Oerlikon OTO) was proposed for Peruvian "Lupo" and Libyan 550 ton corvettes. Probably abandoned in favour of twin Breda 40/70 KDC barrel weighing 120 kg. Has 112 ready use rounds per barrel.

GMC-A muzzle braked barrel KCB, HEX, HS 8, 31SLH. Manufactured in UK and in service. In Abu Dhabi patrol craft and Indonesian "Surapati" class frigates. American Emerlec Mk 74 twin mounting (950 ready use rounds) was first embarked in South Korean "Gireogi" coastal patrol craft. Now also used on Greek FPBs.

Mounting (215 ready use rounds) in French "Commandant Rivière" class. "Ouragan" class and single "La Combattante" Fast attack craft. Hispano Suiza system is now owned by Oerlikon.

Water cooled. Small enclosed turret used in Soviet ships of "Kanin" some "Kotlin" and "Sverdlov" (CC version) classes. Also some "Rigas", fast attack craft, minesweepers and amphibious craft. In the German "Hai" class and patrol ships is a 30 mm single mounting which was introduced in the new Polish (series 500) landing craft. This might belong to the same system.

Country/Manufacturer	Classification	Name	No.	Length ft	Launch weight lb	Power plant	Guidance	Max Range n. miles	Mach speed	Warhead	Remarks
GERMANY (Federal Republic)											
Messerschmitt-Bölkow-Blöhm	ASW	Kormoran	—	14·4	1 323	3 stage solid fuel rocket	Active or passive radar	20	0·95	350 lb HE	Suitable for all fixed and rotary-wing aircraft
ISRAEL											
Israel Aircraft Industries	SSM	Gabriel I and II	—	11·0	882 (I) 1 100 (II)	Two stage solid fuel rocket	Active radar or optical	14 (I) 26 (II)	0·7	400 lb HE	Mounted in "Saar" and "Saar IV" classes. Now being exported, eg Singapore, South Africa
ITALY											
Sistel	SSM	Sea Killer I (Nettuno)	—	12·3	375	1 stage solid fuel rocket	Beam rider/ radio-command or optical	6+	1·9	77 lb HE	Operational for use in ships or helicopters (Marte). Five round launcher in ships
	SSM	Sea Killer II (Vulcano)	—	15·4	660	2 stage solid rocket motor	as above	13	1·9	155 lb HE	
	SSM	Sea Killer III	—	17·4	1 200	1 booster 2 sustainers	Active homer	24	1·9	330 lb HE	Under development
Otomat (with Matra)	SSM	Otomat (see "France")									
Sistel	SAM	Sea Indigo	—	11	266	1 stage solid fuel rocket	Radio command/ beam rider	5·5 (slant)	2·5	46 lb HE	Automatic reloading in ships over 500 tons
	ASM	Airtos	—	12·8	421	1 stage solid fuel rocket	Active radar homing	6	1·5	77 lb HE	All-weather system under development
NORWAY											
Kongsberg Vaapenfabrikk	SSM	Penguin I and II	—	9·8	726	2 stage solid fuel rocket	Inertial/infra-red homing	14·5 20 (II)	0·7	264 lb HE	Fitted in frigates and fast attack craft
	A/S	Terne III	—	6·6	298	2 stage solid fuel rocket	Nil	1·5	—	110 lb HE depth charge	Full salvo of six can be fired in 5 seconds. Reload time 40 seconds
SWEDEN											
Saab-Scania	SSM	—	RB 08A	18·8	1 984	Marboré turbo-jet	Radar homing	?100	0·85	HE	For ship and coast artillery use. Entered service 1967
Bofors	A/S	—	Type 375	—	550	Rocket	Nil	0·5/1·0/ 2·2	—	HE	Have three different rocket motors M50 (0·5 m), Erika (1·0 m), Nelli (2·2 m)
UNION OF SOVIET SOCIALIST REPUBLICS											
(NATO designations used—further details at head of USSR section)	SLBM	Sark	SS-N-4	42·5	41 000 app.	2 stage solid fuel rocket	Inertial	370	—	Nuclear megaton	Tested 1955. Operational 1958 Obsolete. Surface launched
	SLBM	Serb	SS-N-5	42·5	41 000 app.	2 stage solid fuel rocket	Inertial	700	—	Nuclear megaton	Operational 1963. Dived launched
	SLBM	Sawfly	SS-N-6	31·6	?	2 stage liquid fuel rocket	Inertial	1 300 (1 600 Mks II and III)	—	Nuclear Megaton (3 MRV in Mk III)	Operational 1967. "Yankee" class. (Mks II and III in 1974-75)
	SLBM	—	SS-N-8	42·5	?	2 stage liquid fuel rocket	Stellar-Inertial	4 200	—	Nuclear	Operational 1972, "Delta". Now in "Delta II" class

NAVAL EQUIPMENT / MISSILES

Country/ Manufacturer	Classification	Name	No.	Length ft	Launch Weight, lb	Powerplant	Guidance	Max Range n. mile	Mach Speed	Warhead	Remarks
USSR	SLBM	—	SS-N-X-13	?32	?	2 stage	Inertial	370	—	Nuclear	Appears to have been unsuccessful. Never operational. Possibly anti-task force
	SLBM	—	SS-N-17	36.3	?	2 stage solid fuel rocket with Post Boost Vehicle (PBV)	Inertial	2 400	—	Nuclear megaton	Probably being deployed in "Yankee" class from 1977 and in new class
	SLBM	—	SS-N-18	46.3	?	2 stage liquid fuel rocket with Post Boost Vehicle (PBV)	Inertial	5 200	—	Nuclear	Sea trials Nov 1976—deployed in "Delta III" class
	SSM	Scrubber	SS-N-1	22.5	—	—	Radar Infra-red homing	130	0.9	—	Operational 1958. Soon obsolete
	SSM	Styx	SS-N-2	15	—	2 stage solid fuel rocket	Active radar homing	23	0.9	HE	Operational 1960 SS-N-2 mod (once designated SS-N-11) now in service
	SSM	Shaddock	SS-N-3	36	—	2 boosters Turbojet sustainer	Radar head, mid-course guidance Radar or IR homing	150-250	1.5	HE or Nuclear	Operational 1961-62 Surface launch in submarines
	SLCM	—	SS-N-7	22	—	—	Autopilot radar homing	30	1.5	—	Operational 1969-70 Submarine launched from dived
	SSM	—	SS-N-9	30 (est)	—	—	Radar head with mid-course guidance	150	1.0+	HE or Nuclear	Operational 1968-69. In "Nanuchka" class
	SSM	—	SS-N-12	—	—	—	? Radar—mid course guidance	? 250	—	—	Replacement for Shaddock in both s/ms and surface ships including "Kiev" class
	SAM	Goa	SA-N-1	22 (booster)	—	2 stage solid fuel rocket	Beam-rider semi-active radar	17 (slant)	2	HE	Operational 1961
	SAM	Guideline	SA-N-2	34.7	5 000	Solid booster liquid sustainer	Radar	25	3.5	HE (290 lb)	Only in *Dzerzhinsky*
	SAM	Goblet	SA-N-3	20	1 200	2 stage solid fuel rocket	Rocket/ramjet	20-30	1.5/2.8	HE (90 lb)	Probably similar to SA-6 (Gainful). Operational 1967
	SAM	—	SA-N-4	10.5?	—	—	Radar-command	8?	2?	HE	Probably PDMS. Operational 1969
	SAM	—	SA-N-5	4.9	32	Rocket	Optical with IR homing	5-6	?1.5	HE	Seaborne form of SA-7 (Grail) in Light and Amphibious forces
	ASM	Kennel	AS-1	29	6 000?	1 Turbojet	Beam-rider with radar homing	55	0.9	HE	Obsolete. Used by Badger aircraft
	ASM	Kipper	AS-2	33	—	1 Turbojet	Autopilot. Radar homing	115	1.0+	—	Operational 1960. Used by Badger C aircraft
	ASM	Kangaroo	AS-3	49.2	—	1 Turbojet	—	? 350	1.5+	Nuclear	Operational 1961. Used by Bear aircraft
	ASM	Kitchen	AS-4	37	—	1 stage liquid fuel rocket	? Inertial guidance	145	2+	Nuclear	Operational 1965. Used by Bear, Blinder and, probably, Backfire aircraft
	ASM	Kelt	AS-5	28	—	1 stage liquid fuel rocket	Active radar homing	85	0.9	—	Operational 1968. Used by Badger aircraft
	ASM	—	AS-6	—	—	1 stage	Inertial mid-course active radar homing	120	3	—	Operational 1970-71. Used by Badger and Backfire aircraft
	A/S	—	FRAS I	—	—	—	?Pre-programme	15	—	?Nuclear	Operational 1968 in "Moskva" and "Kiev" classes on SUWN-1 mounting. Similar to USN ASROC
	A/S	—	SSN-14	—	—	—	—	30	—	—	Operational 1968 in "Kresta II", "Kara" and "Krivak" classes and also in place of FRASI (above)
	A/S	—	SSN-15	—	—	—	—	20	—	?Nuclear	Operational 1974 for use from "Victor II", "Charlie II" and "Tango" class submarines in A/S operations. When fitted with a torpedo in place of war head known as SS-N-16

Note: Also reported are two types of Air to Surface Missiles. These are:
(a) Unnamed AS-7 with a range of 5 miles and a 200 lb HE head carried by the Forger aircraft of the "Kiev" class.
(b) AS-9, also unnamed with a 50 mile range and a 300 lb HE head carried by Badger and Backfire aircraft.

Country/ Manufacturer	Classification	Name	No.	Length ft	Launch Weight, lb	Powerplant	Guidance	Max Range n. mile	Mach Speed	Warhead	Remarks
UNITED KINGDOM	SLBM	Polaris A3 (see USA)	—	—	—	—	—	—	—	UK made 3×200 KT Thermo-nuclear MRV	Carried in "Resolution" class
Hawker Siddeley	SAM/ SSM	Sea Dart	CF 299	14.3	1 212	Solid fuel booster Liquid ramjet sustainer	Radar guidance (Type 909) semi-active radar homing	25	—	HE	Fitted in *Bristol* and Type 42 destroyers with GWS 30 system

MISSILES / NAVAL EQUIPMENT

Country/ Manufacturer	Classification	Name	No.	Length ft	Launch Weight, lb	Powerplant	Guidance	Max Range n. mile	Mach speed	Warhead	Remarks
UK Hawker Siddeley	SAM	Sea Slug Mk 1 and 2	—	19·7	—	4 solid fuel boosters, solid fuel sustainer	Beam-riding (Type 901)	24(Mk 1) approx	—	HE Proximity fuse	Surface-to-surface capability. Mk 2 has a longer range and better low-level capability
British Aircraft Corp	SAM	Sea Wolf	PX 430	6·5	About 200	Solid fuel rocket	Radio command with TV or radar tracking (Type 910)	—	—	HE	Entire system GWS 25. (Normally to be used from 6-barrelled launcher). Lightweight version for ships smaller than frigates Seawolf VM 40 — under study
Short Bros and Harland	SAM	Sea Cat	—	4·9	140	2 stage solid fuel rocket	Optical, Radar or TV	2·9	—	HE	Fitted in many systems GWS 20 (visual) GWS 22 and 24 (Radar). M4/1 (Radar), Signaal M40. Normally 4-barrelled launcher. 3-barrelled launcher (less than half the weight) in service
	ASM	Sea Skua	CL 834	9·2	462	Solid fuel rocket	Radar/radio control radar homing	?5	—	45 lb HE	Developed for use from helicopters with Sea Spray radar
Hawker-Siddeley	AAM	Firestreak	—	10·5	320	Solid fuel rocket	Infra-red homing	4·3	2+	50 lb HE	Being replaced by Red Top (below)
	AAM	Red Top	—	10·8	330	Solid fuel rocket	Infra-red homing	6	3	68 lb HE	A much improved version of Firestreak
Short Bros and Harland	SAM	Slam (Blow pipe)	—	4·6	40	2 stage solid fuel rocket	Optical with radio guidance	—	—	4·8 lb HE	Privately developed system. Suitable for submarines or surface ships.
UNITED STATES OF AMERICA											
Lockheed	SLBM	Polaris A3	UGM 27C	32	30 000(3)	2 stage solid fuel rocket	Inertial	2 500	10 at burn-out	Thermonuclear MRV head	See USA and UK sections for fitting policy.
	SLBM	Poseidon (C-3)	UGM 73A	34	65 000	2 stage solid fuel rocket	Inertial	2 500		Thermonuclear MIRV head	As above. Double A3 payload
	SLBM	Trident I (C-4)	UGM 96A	34·1	70 000	3 stage solid fuel rocket	Inertial	4 000 approx		Thermonuclear MIRV and MARV head	To replace Poseidon using same tubes
	SLBM	Trident II (D-5)	UGM	45·8	126 000	3 stage solid fuel rocket	Inertial	6 000 approx		Thermonuclear	For fitting in "Trident" class SSBNs
McDonnell Douglas	SSM/ USM	Harpoon	RGM 84	15 21 (s/m)	1 470 2 355 (s/m)	Solid fuel booster Turbojet sustainer	Pre-programmed Active radar homing	50 60 (s/m)	0·9	HE	For general surface-ship fitting. Submarine version under trial
GDC-Convair	SLCM	Tomahawk	BGM 109	20·5	2 400-2 700	Solid boost-turbofan cruise	TAINS (Strat) Inertial with radar homing (Tact)	1 750 (Strat) 275 (Tact)	475 knots	HE (Tact) Nuclear (Strat)	Under development in both strategic and tactical forms in parallel with ALCM
	ASM	Harpoon	AGM 84	12·6	1 168	As RGM 84	As RGM 84	120	0·9	HE	
	ASM	Condor	AGM 53	5·5	2 130	1 solid fuel rocket	Radio control TV homing	40-60	1·1	HE or nuclear	For carrier-borne A/C particularly A6. Production planned.
Maxson	ASM	Bullpup A and B	AGM 12B and C	10(A) 13·5(B)	571(A) 1 785(B)	1 liquid fuel rocket	Command	7(A) 10(B)	2	HE 250 lb(A) 1 000 lb(B) or nuclear	Operational 1959
Texas Instruments Inc	ASM	Harm	AGM 88	13·7	780	1 liquid fuel rocket	—	—	—	—	High-speed anti-radiation missile Development
	ASM	Bulldog	AGM 83	9·8	600	1 liquid fuel rocket	Command	35	—	—	Modified Bullpup
NASC/NWC	ASM	Shrike	AGM 45	10	390	1 solid fuel rocket	Passive radar homing	8-10	2	HE	Production 1963. Anti-radiation
Martin, Marietta	ASM	Walleye I and II	AGM 62	11·2 (I) 13·2 (II)	1 100 (I) 2 400 (II)	Nil	TV guided	16 (I) 35 (II)		HE or nuclear	Glide bombs
GDC-Pomona	ASM	Standard ARM	AGM 78	15	1 356	Dual-thrust solid fuel rocket	Passive Radar homing	35	2	HE	Production 1968
GDC-Pomona	SAM	Standard-MR (SM-1)	RIM 66	14·4	1 300	Dual thrust solid fuel rocket	Semi-active radar homing	20+	—	HE	Tartar replacement
GDC-Pomona	SAM	Standard (SM-2)	RIM 66C					60+			Mid-course guidance for long-range. Talos replacement. Standard-MR (SM-2) with 20+range for Aegis. Standard-ER (SM-2) (RIM 67B) under development
GDC-Pomona	SAM	Standard-ER (SM-1)	RIM 67	26·2	2 900	2 stage solid fuel rocket	Semi-active radar homing	35+	—	HE	SSM capability. Terrier replacement (ER)
Raytheon	SAM	Seasparrow	RIM 7H	12	500	1 solid fuel rocket	Semi-active radar homing	12(E) 24+(F)	—	HE	Can also be used as UK version XJ 521. Mk 25 or 29 (NATO) launcher. BPDMS
Bendix	SAM	Talos	RIM 8F, G and H	31·3	7 000 (booster)	Solid fuel booster ram-jet sustainer	Beam rider semi-active radar homing	65+	2·5	HE/ nuclear	SSM capability. RIM H has anti-radiation housing. Replacement by RIM 66C
GDC-Pomona	SAM	Tartar	RIM 24B	15	1 425	Dual-thrust solid fuel rocket	Semi-active radar homing	14	2	HE	Ceiling 40 000 ft Replacement by RIM 66
GDC-Pomona	SAM	Terrier	RIM 2F	26·1	3 000 (booster)	2 stage solid-fuel rocket	Semi-active radar homing	20+	2·5	HE	Ceiling 65 000 ft Operational 1963 Replacement by RIM 67
NWC-Hughes	AAM	Agile	AIM 95	8	250	Solid fuel	Infra-red	2	—	HE	Planned replacement for Sidewinder
Hughes	AAM	Phoenix	AIM 54	13	985	1 solid-fuel rocket	Radar homing	60+	2+	HE	In use in F14 Operational 1973
Raytheon/NWC/ Philco Ford	AAM	Sidewinder-1B	AIM 9G, J H and L	9·5	185	1 solid fuel rocket	Infra-red	8	2	HE	Ceiling 50 000 ft+ First AIM9B entered service 1962
Raytheon	AAM	Sparrow III	AIM 7E and F	12	450(E) 500(F)	1 solid fuel rocket	Semi-active radar homing	9(E) 16(F)	3·5	HE	For carrier-borne aircraft
Honeywell	A/S	ASROC	RUR 5	15·4	1 000(Mk 44) 570(Mk 46)	1 solid fuel rocket	Pre-programme	1—6	—	Mk 44 or 46 torpedo or Nuclear D/C	Fired from multi-barrelled launcher. Mk 26 in later ships. 10 mile version under development
Goodyear	A/S or anti-surface-ship	SUBROC	UUM 44	21	4 000	2 stage solid fuel rocket	Pre-programme inertial	25-30	1+	Nuclear	Fired from 21 in torpedo tubes

RADAR

Country/Number	Type	Transmitter frequency	Transmitter peak power	Range
DENMARK				
Scanter	I Band Navigation Radar	9 375±30 MHz	20 KW± 1dB Measured at output flange	—
FRANCE				
ELI 4	Naval IFF Interrogator	1 030± 0·5 Mcs	Selectable 0·5 or 2 kW	—
ELR 3	IFF Transponder	—	—	—
Triton	C band surface search radar	C Band	250 kW	—
Castor TRS	3200 Band target tracking radar	I/J Band Tunable	36 kW	—
Pollux	I Band fire control radar	I Band	200 kW	20 m
Pollux II	Improved version of above fire control	Probably I Band	—	—
Calypso II	TH D 1030 I Band S/M Radar	X Band	70 kW	30 km for 10 m² air target
Calypso III	TRS 3100 X Band S/M Radar	X Band	—	35 km for 10 m² air target
Jupiter I	TH D 1077 long range surveillance Radar C Band 2 MW	C/D Band 23 cm	2 MW	180 km for 2 m² air target
Jupiter II	TRS 3010 air search radar	L Band	—	—
Ramses	TH D 1022 short range nav & surveillance radar	I Band	36 kW	60 n. miles
Lynx	TH D 1051	—	—	—
Saturne II	TH D 1041. TRS.3043	S Band	1 MW	—
Sea Tiger	Surveillance radar. TRS 3001	S Band	Average 1 kW	60 n. miles on 2 m² fluctuation target—with P.D 50%
DRBC 32	Gun fire control radar	I Band	—	—
DRBI 10	Height finder	E/F Band	Between 1 and 2 MW	Between 100 and 140 n. miles
DRBV 13	Air search radar	E/F Band	—	—
DRBV 20	Long range search radar	Metric	—	—
DRBV 22	Air search radar	C Band	—	—
DRBV 23	Air search and surveillance	C Band	—	—
DRBR 51	Tracking and missile guidance	I Band	—	—
DRBI 23	Surveillance and target designator	C/D Band (23 cm)	—	—
GERMANY (Federal Republic)				
Atlas 1555	Navigation radar	—	—	—
INTERNATIONAL				
EX 77 Mod O	Director for NATO Sea Sparrow	Probably I Band	—	—
ITALY				
Argus 5000	Early warning radar	—	5 MW	—
Orion 250	Fire control radar	I Band	200 kW	—
Orion RTN 10X	Fire control radar	I Band	—	40 n. miles
Orion RTN 16X	Monopulse fire control radar	I Band	—	—
Orion RTN 20 X	Fire control radar	I Band	—	—
Orion RTN 30X	Fire control radar	I Band	—	—
RAN 2C	Surveillance radar	G Band	—	—
RAN 3L	Early warning radar	C/D Band	—	Approx 200 n. miles
RAN 7S	10 cm air and surface search radar	10 cm	—	—
RAN 10S	Air and sea search on small ships	E/F Band	—	40 n. miles
RAN 11L/X	Air warning and weapons control	C and I Bands	28 kW C Band, 80 kW I Band	35 n. miles
RAN 13X	Search radar	I Band	—	—
RAN 14X	Low altitude and surface search	I Band	—	—
RAN 57	Surface search radar	—	—	—
Sea Hunter	Search radar	I/J Band	180 kW	—
Sea Hunter	Tracker radar	I/J Band	—	—
SPQ 2D	Search radar	I Band	—	—
3 RM	Navigation radar	—	7 or 20 kW	—
JAPAN				
OPS 1	Air search	—	—	—
OPS 2	Air search	—	—	—
OPS 11	Air search	—	—	—
OPS 12	Air search	—	—	—
OPS 14	Air search	—	—	—
OPS 15	Surface search	—	—	—
OPS 16	Surface search	—	—	—
OPS 17	Surface search	—	—	—
OPS 28	Not available	—	—	—
OPS 35	Surface search	—	—	—
OPS 37	Surface search	—	—	—
ZPS 2	Surface search	—	—	—
ZPS 3	Surface search	—	—	—
—	Fire control	—	—	—
—	Fire control	—	—	—
—	Fire control	—	—	—
—	Fire control	—	—	—
NETHERLANDS				
DA 01	Surface search	—	—	—
DA 02	Surface search	—	—	—
DA 04	Surface search	—	—	—
DA 05	Surface search	S Band	—	—
DA 08	Air search	S Band	—	—
LW 01	Air search	Probably L Band	—	—
LW 02	Air search	L Band	500 kW	100 n. miles
LW 04	Air search	L Band	—	—
LW 06	Air search	L Band	—	—
LW 08	Air search	L Band	—	145 n. miles
SD-X	Surface search	X Band	—	—
SGR 101	Fire control	X Band	—	—
SGR 107	Fire control	X Band	—	—
SGR 108	Fire control	X Band	—	—
SGR 120	Fire control	X Band	—	—
V 1	Height finder	S Band	400 kW	150 n. miles
WM 4/42	Fire control	—	—	—
ZW 01	Surface search	Probably X Band	—	—
ZW 06	Surface search	X Band	—	—
ZW 07	Surface search	X Band	—	—
ZW 08	Surface search	X Band	—	—
3D MTTR	Multi target tracking radar	—	—	—
SWEDEN				
9 GR 600	Transmitter/receiver	I Band	200 kW	—
9 LV 200	Mk 2 Tracking radar	J Band	65 kW	—
SUBFAR	S/M radar	I Band	—	—

P.R.F.	Manufacturer	Remarks
Short NOM 4000 Hz±200 Hz Long NOM 2000 Hz±200 Hz	TERMA	
—	LMT	Receiver frequency: 1 090 Mc/s
—	LMT	Includes selective identification feature and side lobe suppression
—	Thompson CSF	Associated with Thompson fire control systems
Variable	Thompson CSF	Used in some versions of Vega series fire control system; 20 kW
—	Thompson CSF	Used in some versions of Vega series fire control system; 200 kW
Variable	Thompson CSF	Used for surface search. Used on board submarines
Variable	Thompson CSF	Improvement of above
—	—	
450 per sec	Thompson CSF	Naval air surveillance radar (long range)
—	Thompson CSF	
—	Thompson CSF	
—	Thompson CSF	Dual radar. Coastal mine watching system
—	Thompson CSF	Medium range air and surface surveillance radar
—	Thompson CSF	Can be used in Thompson CSF series ship fire control systems
—	Thompson CSF	A, C and D, versions fitted in various classes of French ships
—	Thompson CSF	Robinson scanner mounted on French carriers and *Jeanne d'Arc*
—	Thompson CSF	Pulse doppler air search radar. Multi mode operation
—	Thompson CSF	Operates in metric wave band A, B and C versions C model on aircraft carriers
—	Thompson CSF	Search radar A, C and D versions in service on French and other vessels
—	Thompson CSF	Long range naval air search and surveillance radar
—	Thompson CSF	Part of Masurca surface-to-air missile system
—	Thompson CSF	3D surveillance-target designator radar. Stacked beam system mounted on board "Sufren" class
—	Krupp Atlas Elektronic	
—	NATO Consortium	Provides search, target designation tracking and illumination for Sea Sparrow point defence missile system
—	Selenia	High power. Ship's early warning radar
—	Selenia	Used in NA 9. System conical scan; 200 kW
—	Selenia	Fire control radar used by RN
—	Selenia	
—	Selenia	Used in Dardo system
—	Selenia	Used in Albatros system
—	Selenia	Dual purpose air and surface surveillance radar
—	Selenia	Digital. Signal processing
—	Selenia	Air and surface target warning
—	Selenia	Air and surface surveillance
—	Selenia	D Band air detection, I/J Band surface detection
—	Selenia	Surface and low flying search
—	Selenia	Low altitude and surface search radar
—	Selenia	
Variable	Contraves	
—	Contraves	
—	SMA	Surface search and short range air search
750-6 000 Hz range	SMA	Series of I Band nav and surface warning radars
—	—	Similar in appearance to US AN/SPS 6; parameters are probably also similar
—	—	
—	—	Not yet operational
—	—	
—	—	Similar in appearance to US AN/SPS 5; parameters are probably also similar
—	—	
—	—	Not yet operational
—	—	
—	—	Found on board old patrol craft
—	—	Employed by submarines
—	—	
—	—	Associated with fire control director Contraves
—	—	Associated with fire control director Type 0
—	—	Associated with fire control director Type 1
—	—	Associated with fire control director Type 2
—	Hollandse Signaalapparaten	On board Colombian Halland class plus numerous Dutch and West German units
—	Hollandse Signaalapparaten	
—	Hollandse Signaalapparaten	
—	—	Land version designated DA 05/M
—	Hollandse Signaalapparaten	
—	Hollandse Signaalapparaten	Only on board Argentine *25 de Mayo* and Peruvian *Almirante Grau*
—	Hollandse Signaalapparaten	Designed for destroyer size ships. Employed by numerous navies
—	Hollandse Signaalapparaten	
—	Hollandse Signaalapparaten	
—	Hollandse Signaalapparaten	
—	Hollandse Signaalapparaten	
—	Hollandse Signaalapparaten	Associated with fire control directors M1, M2, M3
—	Hollandse Signaalapparaten	Associated with fire control director M3
—	Hollandse Signaalapparaten	Associated with fire control director M4
—	Hollandse Signaalapparaten	Associated with fire control director M2
1 000	Hollandse Signaalapparaten	Only on board Argentine *25 de Mayo* and Peruvian *Almirante Grau*
—	Hollandse Signaalapparaten	Radar for most M20 series and WM series fire control
—	Hollandse Signaalapparaten	Alternative designation SGR 103
—	Hollandse Signaalapparaten	
—	Hollandse Signaalapparaten	
—	Hollandse Signaalapparaten	Anti submarine radar
—	Hollandse Signaalapparaten	3D air search
2-3 000 Hz	Philips	
Approx 2 000 Hz	Philips	Frequency agility naval fire control
Variable 250-3 000/sec	Philips	Air and surface search

NAVAL EQUIPMENT / RADAR

Country/Number	Type	Transmitter frequency	Transmitter peak power	Range

UNION OF SOVIET SOCIALIST REPUBLICS

Country/Number	Type	Transmitter frequency	Transmitter peak power	Range
Square Tie	Lightweight search radar	I Band	—	—
Square Head	Naval radar	—	—	—
Pop Group	Fire control radar	Probably I Band	—	—
Head Net B	Air surveillance radar	Probably D or E/F Band	—	—
Drum Tilt	Fire control radar	Probably I Band	—	—
Sun Visor	Fire control radar	Probably I or G Band	—	—
Cylinder Head	Fire control radar	—	—	—
Big Net	Air search radar	D or E Band	—	—
Fan Song E	Fire control radar	G/H Band	—	—
Hair Net	Naval radar	—	—	—
Plinth Net	Air search radar	—	—	—
Pot Drum	Naval radar	Probably I Band	—	—
Pot Head	Naval radar	Probably I Band	—	—
Scoop Pair	Missile control radar	—	—	—
Hawk Screech	Gun fire control	Probably I Band. Possibly G Band	—	—
Owl Screech	Gun fire control	Probably I Band. Possibly G Band	—	—
High Lune	Naval height finder	Probably E/F Band	—	—
Muff Cob	Fire control radar	G/H or I Band	—	—
Slim Net	Air warning radar	Probably E/F Band	—	—
Flat Spin	Surveillance radar	D or E/F Band	—	—
Head Net C	Air surveillance radar	—	—	—
Top Sail	3D radar	Probably C Band	—	—
Head Light	Fire control	Probably I and G/H Band	—	—
Strut Curve	Air search radar	Probably E/F Band	—	—
Peel Group	Fire control radar	Probably G Band or I Band	—	—
Head Net A	Air surveillance radar	D or E Band	—	—
Boat Sail	Submarine radar air search	D or E Band	—	—
Skin Head	Naval radar	Probably I/J Band	—	—
Top Trough	Air surveillance radar	—	—	—
Knife Rest B	Early warning radar	—	—	—
High Sieve	Surface search radar	—	—	—
Top Bow	Gun fire control radar	—	—	—
Seagull	Air search	—	—	—

UNITED KINGDOM

Country/Number	Type	Transmitter frequency	Transmitter peak power	Range
AWS/2	Surface search	E/F Bands	—	60 nm
Decca 45	Navigation	—	—	—
Decca 202	Navigation	—	—	—
Decca 212	Navigation	—	—	—
Decca 303	Navigation	—	—	—
Decca 416	Navigation	—	—	—
Decca 909	Navigation	—	—	—
Decca 1226	Navigation	—	—	—
Decca 2400	Navigation	—	—	—
MRS 3/GWS 22	Fire control	—	—	—
RN Type 268	Surface search	—	—	—
RN Type 285	Fire control	—	—	—
RN Type 291	Air search	—	—	—
RN Type 765	Air search	—	—	—
RN Type 901	Fire control	Possibly G Band	—	—
RN Type 904	Fire control	—	—	—
RN Type 909	Fire control	Possibly G Band	—	—
RN Type 910	Fire control	I Band	—	—
RN Type 912	Fire control	I Band	—	—
RN Type 965	Air search	Metric	—	—
RN Type 967	Air search	E/F Bands	—	—
RN Type 968	Surface search	C/D Bands	—	—
RN Type 974	Navigation	—	—	—
RN Type 975	Surface search	I Band	50 kW	48 nm
RN Type 978	Surface search	I Band	—	—
RN Type 992Q	Surface search	E/F Bands	—	—
RN Type 993	Air search	—	—	—
RN Type 1006	Navigation	—	—	—
S 604 HN	Surface search	I Band	2/3 MW	—
S 810	Surface search	I Band	200 kW	—
SNW 12	Air search	—	—	—
14/9	Navigation	—	—	—

UNITED STATES OF AMERICA

Country/Number	Type	Transmitter frequency	Transmitter peak power	Range
RTN 10	Fire control for Sea Sparrow III	I Band	—	—
SPG 49	Guidance for Talos and Terrier. Surface-to-air	Used with SPW 2	—	120 km
SPG 51	Tartar missile guidance	I Band	—	—
SPG 53	Fire control radar	—	—	—
SPG 55	Terrier guidance radar	G/H Band	Approx 50 kW	50 km
SPG 60	Doppler search and tracking	I Band	—	50 km
SPQ 9	Lockheed MK 86 fire control system	I/J Band	—	20 nm
SPQ 5	Missile guidance	G/H Band	—	—
SPS 6	Air surveillance	D Band	Approx 500 kW	100-200 km
SPS 10	Surface search	G/H Band	—	—
SPS 12	Long range air search	D Band	0·1 and 1·0 MW	—
SPS 30	Long range 3D radar	—	—	—
SPS 32	Air and surface surveillance	—	—	—
SPS 33	Fire control radar	—	—	—
SPS 37	Long range air surveillance	—	—	—
SPS 39	3D radar air surveillance	—	—	200-300 km
SPS 40	Search and surveillance for air targets	? E/F Band	? 1 MW	—
SPS 43	High power very long range search radar	? Metric	1-2 MW	—
SPS 48	Air surveillance radar	? E/F Band	—	—
SPS 49	Air search radar	—	—	—
SPS 52	3D air surveillance	? E/F Band	—	—
SPS 55	Surface search and navigation	—	130 kW	—
SPS 58	Pulse Doppler air search and target acquisition radar	D Band	—	—
SPY 1	Multi function array radar	E/F Band	Several MW	—

RADAR / NAVAL EQUIPMENT

P.R.F.	Manufacturer	Remarks
—	—	Probably include target detection and tracking for anti-ship missile direction.
—	—	Possible IFF interrogator or directional array for transmission of guidance signals to surface-to-surface missiles
—	—	Associated with Soviet Navy's SAN-4 surface-to-air missile system
—	—	Air search and surveillance and in connection with fire control radars carried for direction of surface-to-air missiles and guns
—	—	
—	—	Believed now obsolete
—	—	Very large long range air surveillance radar
—	—	Shipboard version of Guideline surface-to-air missile control and guidance radar
—	—	Medium range general purpose search and surveillance radar
—	—	Medium range general purpose search radar
—	—	Small surface search radar
—	—	Surface target detection; short range
—	—	Twin radar group for Shaddock SSM
—	—	
—	—	
—	—	Gun fire control
—	—	High definition surface target radar
—	—	Long range air search radar
—	—	Dual V beam 3D installation of Head Net A
—	—	Long range 3D air surveillance radar
—	—	Missile fire control group
—	—	Lightweight search radar
—	—	Missile control group for Goa
—	—	Long range air surveillance radar
—	—	Air search for submarine pickets
—	—	Surface target detection radar for light forces
—	—	High definition surface target radar
—	—	Long wavelength early warning radar
—	—	Target acquisition radar for naval guns
—	—	Long range air search radar
400-1 000 pps	Plessey	
—	Decca	
—	Decca	
—	Decca	
—	Decca	
—	Decca	On board some modern French ships
—	Decca	
—	Decca	On board some modern French ships
—	Decca	
—	Sperry	Control for MRS 3 guns and missiles GWS/22
—	Marconi	Introduced during WW II now obsolete
—	—	Mainly obsolete still found on Egyptian and South American units
—	—	Introduced during WW II now obsolete
—	—	On board *Hermes*
—	Marconi	Guidance for Seaslug missile
—	—	Guidance for Sea Dart
—	Marconi	Guidance for Sea Wolf
—	—	
—	Marconi	Long Range air search also target designation for guided weapons and IFF Mk 10 facilities. Can be combined with Type 968 for medium to short range defence radar
—	Kelvin Hughes	
—	Decca	
—	Kelvin Hughes	
—	Decca	
—	Marconi	
—	Kelvin Hughes	
—	Marconi	Long range surveillance
1 500 or 4 400 Hz	Marconi	Lightweight surveillance
—	Marconi	
—	Kelvin Hughes	
—	Raytheon	
—	Sperry	
—	Raytheon	Part of Mk 73 FCS
—	—	Associated with Mk 68 fire control system
—	Sperry	
—	Lockheed	
—	Lockheed	
—	Sperry	Now obsolescent
—	Westinghouse	Now obsolescent. Found in a number of Latin American navies
—	Sylvania	First produced in late 1940s extensively modified through Model F
—	RCA Moorestown	Used on older units of Japanese MSDF
—	GEC	
—	Hughes	Companion in use with SPS 33
—	Hughes	
—	Westinghouse	
—	Hughes	Now obsolete
—	Lockheed	
—	Westinghouse	Generally carries IFF antenna
—	ITT-Gilfillan	3D long range air surveillance
—	—	Narrow beam very long range for air search
—	Hughes	In use in NATO navies
750-2 250 pps	Cordion Electronics	Replacement for SPS 10.
—	Westinghouse	Designed to operate with USN point defence Surface Missile System
—	—	Under development for US Navy Aegis fleet air defence missile system

SONAR EQUIPMENT

Country/Designation	Description	Manufacturer	Mounting
AUSTRALIA			
Mulloka	Sonar project for Royal Australian Navy	—	—
Barra	Project Barra is RAAF/RAN project to develop advanced sonobuoy and airborne detection system	Amalgamated Wireless	—
CANADA			
HS 1000	Lightweight search and attack sonar either hull mounted or towed	Canadian Westinghouse	—
SQS 505	Medium search/attack sonar	Canadian Westinghouse	—
SQS 507 (Helen)	Lightweight variable depth towed sonar	Canadian Westinghouse	—
FRANCE			
DUBV/23D	Active surface vessel search/attack sonar	CIT/ALCATEL	Bow mounted
DUBV/43B	Variable depth sonar	CIT/ALCATEL	Towed
DUUX 2A/B/C	Passive sonar. Submarine detection system	CIT/ALCATEL	—
DUBV 24/C	Low frequency panoramic search/attack sonar	CIT/ALCATEL	—
PASCAL Sonar	Surveillance and tracking sonar for small and medium ships	CIT/ALCATEL	—
DUUA 2A	Simultaneous search and attack sonar for modernised Daphne class S/M	CIT/ALCATEL	—
HS-71/DUAV-4	Helicopter Sonar	CIT/ALCATEL	—
TSM 2 400/DUBA 25	Surface vessel sonar (TARPON). Attack sonar	Thomson CSF	Hull or towed
Diodon (TSM 2314)	Submarine detection, target tracking and attack operations	Thomson CSF	Hull or towed
Piranha (TSM 2140)	Attack sonar	Thomson CSF	Hull
DUBM 41A	Side looking sonar	Thomson CSF	Towed
DUBM 21A IBIS	Mine counter measure sonar	Thomson CSF	Hull mounted
DUBM 40B	Active mine hunting sonar	Thomson CSF	Towed
ITALY			
IP 64 MD 64	Submarine sonars	USEA	—
NETHERLANDS			
LWS 30	Passive sonar/intercept system. Omni-directional surveillance against surface or sub-surface targets	Hollandse Signaalapparaten BV	—
PSH 32	High performance search and attack sonar	Hollandse Signaalapparaten BV	Hull
UNITED KINGDOM			
PMS.26.27	Lightweight search/attack sonar	Plessey	Hull
Type 195	Helicopter sonar	Plessey	Dunking type
PMS 32	Active/passive panoramic sonar	Plessey	Hull
Type 162M	Sideways looking sonar	Kelvin Hughes	Hull
Type 186	Submarine sonar	EMI	Hull
Type 187	Submarine sonar	EMI	Hull
Type 193	RN mine hunting system (Acoustic)	Plessey	Hull
Type 193M	Solid state improved version of type 193 mine hunting sonar	Plessey	Hull
Type 199	Variable depth towed sonar	EMI	Towed
Type 719	Submarine sonar	EMI	Hull
SADE	Sensitive Acoustic Detection Equipment. Intruder detection system	Plessey	—
Project 35	Advanced fleet escort sonar in development	Plessey	
UNITED STATES OF AMERICA			
AQS 13	Helicopter sonar	Bendix	Dunking type
BQG 1/4	Submarine passive fire control sonars	Sperry/Raytheon	Hull
BQQ 1	Search and fire control sonars	Raytheon	Hull
BQQ 2	Sonar for Subroc system	Raytheon	Hull
BQQ 5	Nuclear attack submarine sonar	Hughes/GE/IBM	Hull
BQR 2B	Submarine passive sonar	EDO	Hull
BQR 3	Submarine passive sonar	Raytheon	Hull
BQR 7	Passive sonar. Part of BQQ 2 system	EDO	Hull
BQR 15	Towed submarine sonar	Western Electric	Towed
BQR 19	Submarine sonar	Raytheon	Hull
BQR 21	Submarine passive detection and tracking set (DIMUS)	Honeywell	Hull
BQS 6	Active submarine sonar. Part of BQQ-2 system	Raytheon	Hull
BQS 8	Under ice navigation sonar	EDO/Hazeltine	Hull
BQS 13	Submarine search sonar. Passive/active	IBM	Hull
SQA 10	Variable depth sonar	Litton	Towed
SQA 13	Variable depth sonar Hoist	EDO/Litton	Hull
SQA 14	"Searchlight" sonar	Raytheon	Towed
SQA 16	"Searchlight" sonar	Raytheon	Hull
SQA 19	Variable depth sonar	Litton	Towed
SQG 1	A/S attack sonar	Raytheon	Hull
SQQ 14	Mine hunting and classification sonar	GE	Hull
SQQ 23	Sonar for A/S patrol ships	—	Hull
SQR 14	Surface sonar	—	Hull
SQR 18	Passive towed array	EDO	VDS
SQS 4	Short range active sonar	Sangamo/GE	Hull
SQS 23	Long range active sonar	Sangamo	Hull
SQS 26	Bow mounted "Bottom Bounce" mode sonar to replace SQS 23	EDO/GE	Hull
SQS 29/32	Surface vessel active sonars. Nos relate to differing frequencies	—	—
SQS 35	Variable depth towed sonar		Towed
SQS 36	Medium range hull sonar	EDO	Hull
SQS 38	Medium range hull sonar	EDO	Hull
SQS 56	Lightweight sonar under development for USN PF ships	Raytheon	Hull
UQS 2	Mine hunting sonar	GE	Hull
610	Long range hull sonar	EDO	Hull
700 series	Medium range hull and variable depth versions	EDO	Hull and Towed
Model 900	Submarine mine avoidance	EDO	Hull
Model 910	Surface ship mine avoidance	EDO	Hull
1102/1105	Submarine active/passive	EDO	Hull

Frequency	Power	Ship Type	Remarks
—	—	—	
—	—	—	
—	—	—	
—	—	—	
4 operating frequencies around 5 kHz, 2 of which are operational	96 kW (2 × 48 kW)	A/S escorts Types T47/T56 "Suffren" class frigates and type C67 and corvettes type C70 of French Navy	
—	—	A/S escorts T47 and T56 also C67 series and C70 series	
4 operating frequencies around 5 kHz, 2 of which are operational	48 kW (2 × 24 kW)	—	
10 and 11·5 kHz	5 kW	—	
8·4 kHz	30 kW	Daphne class S/M	
—	—	Helicopter	
—	—	"Aviso" type	
Selectable: 11·12 or 13 kHz	—	ASW small or medium tonnage	
11, 12 or 13 kHz	10 kVa	Small ship	
8, 9 or 10 kHz	5 kVa	Small ship	
100 kHz mod ±10 kHz	—	Mine hunters	
730 kHz	1 kW	Mine hunters	
—	—	Small or medium size S/M	
—	—	Corvette to frigate size ships	
—	—	Ships and patrol craft over 150 tons	
—	—	Westland Sea King ASW	
—	—	A/S escort ships	
—	—	Vosper glassfibre 45 metre minehunter	
—	—	Minehunters	
—	—	Submarines	
—	—	Submarines	
—	—	—	
—	—	—	
—	—	Shore based	
—	—	Helicopter	
—	—	S/M	
—	—	—	
—	—	S/M	
—	—	S/M	
—	—	S/M	
—	—	S/M	
—	—	—	
—	—	SSBNs	
—	—	S/M	
—	—	SSBNs and SSNs	
—	—	S/M	
—	—	S/M	
—	—	S/M	
—	—	—	
—	—	—	
—	—	—	
—	—	MCM	
—	—	—	
—	—	—	
—	—	—	Re-designated AN/SQS 53. Specified for 30 "Spruance" Class DD 963 destroyers
—	—	—	
—	—	—	
—	—	—	
—	—	—	
—	—	—	
—	—	—	
—	—	—	
—	—	—	

TORPEDOES

No.	Name/Note	Length	Diameter	Weight	Speed knots	Range	Explosive charge	Guidance	Target/Role	Carrier
FRANCE										
Z 16	Now probably obsolete	720 cm	550 mm	1 700 kg	30	10 km	300 kg	Preset plus Pattern	A/S	S/M
E 14	Acoustic Torpedo	429·1 cm	550 mm	900 kg	25	5·5 km	200 kg	Acoustic	A/Surface (up to 20 knots) +S/M at shallow depth	S/M
E 15	Acoustic Torpedo	600 cm	550 mm	1 350 kg	25	12 km	300 kg	Acoustic	A/Surface 0-20 knots +S/M at shallow depth	S/M
L 3	Acoustic Torpedo	430 cm	550 mm	910 kg	25	5·5 km	200 kg	Acoustic	A/S 0-20 knots up to 300 m depth	S/M only
L 4	Acoustic Torpedo	313 cm inc parachute stabiliser	533 mm	540 kg	30			Acoustic	A/S up to 20 knots	Airborne
L 5 Mod 1	Multi purpose		533 mm	1 000 kg	35			Direct Attack or Programmed Search		Ship
L 5 Mod 3			533 mm	1 300 kg	35					S/M
GERMANY (Federal Republic)										
SST 4	Wire Guided Torpedo	639 cm inc 46 cm wire casket	533 mm				260 kg	Wire Guided Active Passive Sonar Homing	A/Surface	Ship or S/M
	Sea Eel	639 cm	533 mm	1 370 kg	35/23	13/28 km		Wire guided, active/ Passive Sonar Homing	A/S	S/M or FPBs
	Sut	613 and 670 cm inc wire casket	533 mm							S/M or ship
	Seal	639 cm inc wire casket	533 mm	1 370 kg			260 kg	Wire		Ships
	Seeschlange	400 cm inc wire casket	533 mm				100 kg	Wire	A/S	
ITALY										
G 6E	Kangaroo	620 cm	533 mm					Wire Guided	Obsolescent	
A 184		600 cm	533 mm					Wire Guided Active/Passive Sonar	A/S or A/Surface	Ship or S/M
A 244		270 cm	324 mm					Homing Course and Depth		Ship or aircraft
SWEDEN										
Type 41		244 cm	400 mm	250 kg				Passive Homing Sonar	Limited A/Surface or A/S	S/M
Type 42		244 cm + 18 cm wire section	400 mm	270 kg				Passive Homing Sonar or Wire Guidance	A/S	Ship S/M and helicopter
Type 61		70·25 cm	533 mm	1 765 kg			250 kg	Wire Guided	A/Ship	Ship or S/M

TORPEDOES / NAVAL EQUIPMENT

No.	Name/Note	Length	Diameter	Weight	Speed knots	Range	Explosive charge	Guidance	Target/Role	Carrier
UNION OF SOVIET SOCIALIST REPUBLICS										
—	—	—	533 mm	—	—	—	—	—	—	Surface ships, submarines and aircraft
—	—	?500 cm	406 mm	—	—	—	—	—	—	
UNITED KINGDOM										
Mark 8		670 cm	533 mm	1 535 kg	45	45 km		Preset Course Angle & Depth	A/Surface	S/M
	Tigerfish	646·4 cm	533 mm	1 550 kg	Dual high or low			Wire Guided Acoustic Homing	Primarily A/S	S/M
MW 30 Mark 44	Drill and Practice	256 cm	324 mm	233 kg				Active/Acoustic Homing	A/Surface	Aircraft, ship, helicopter
UNITED STATES OF AMERICA										
Mark 14	Mod 5	525 cm	533 mm	1 780 kg	32-46	46·9 km	230 kg	Preset depth & Course Angles	A/Surface	S/M
Mark 37	Mod 3	340 cm	484·5 mm	649 kg	24	—	150 kg HE	Free running then Sonar Auto Homing	A/S	S/M
Mark 37	Mod 2	409 cm	484·5 mm	766 kg	24	—	150 kg HE	Wire Guidance Active/Passive Sonar Homing	A/S	S/M
NT 37 2C Dimensions and warheads as for Mk 37 Mod 2/3 but speed increased by 40%, range by over 100% and wire guided capability in excess of 13 000 yds. Improvements to sonar and homing logic plus additional A/Ship attack modes									A/Surface, A/S	Ship or S/M
Mark 44	Mod 1	260 cm	324 mm	196·4 kg	—	—		Active Acoustic	A/S	Ships (Mk 32 or Asroc), aircraft
Mark 45	Mod 1 Astor (Mod 2)	580 cm	484·5 mm	1 003·8 kg	approx 11 km		Nuclear Warhead	Wire Guided	A/S	S/M being replaced by Mk 48
Mark 46	Mod 0, 1 and 2	260 cm	324 mm	257 kg 230 kg (1 and 2)	—	—		Active/Passive Acoustic Homing	A/S	Ships, (Mk 32 or Asroc), aircraft, helicopter Mod 1 and 2 have liquid propellant
Mark 46	Captor Mod 4	Mk 46 inserted in mine casing and sown in narrow seas. See Jane's Weapon System 2541.441.								
Mark 48	Mod 1 and 2	580 cm	533 mm	1 579 kg	93 km/h	46 km	—	Wire Guided and Active/Passive Acoustic Homing	A/Surface, A/S	S/M
—	Freedom Torpedo	572 cm	484·5 mm	1 237 kg	40	18·5 km	minimum of 295 kg	Wire Guided to hit or free run to intercept followed by pattern run if target missed	A/Surface, A/S	Ship or S/M

DEXTOR (Deep EXperimental TORpedo) Mk 48 replacement
ALWT (Advanced LightWeight Torpedo) Mk 46 replacement

ADDENDA

792 ADDENDA

ALGERIA

There is a considerable Coast Guard force made up of French and Italian built craft as well as the ex-Soviet "P6" class which have been disarmed.
GC 100 of 85 tons and GC 114 of 44 tons were delivered by Baglietto of Italy in Aug 1976 GC 112, 113, 221 and 222 were built in France. Other Italian built craft include *Ombrine* (GC 223), *Dorade* (GC 224), GC 235, GC 236, GC 237, *Requin* (GC 331), *Espadon* (GC 332), *Marsouin* (GC 333), *Murène* (GC 334), all of which are reportedly built by Baglietto. This information replaces that in the main text.

ARGENTINA

Puerto Deseada (survey ship) laid down 17 March 1976 and launched Dec 1977. Range 12 000 miles at 12 knots; complement 83.
Transports *Canal Beagle* and *Bahia san Blas* laid down 10 Jan 1977 and 11 April 1977 respectively.
PNA is considering orders for 30-40 new ships and craft including six patrol craft.
A contract is to be signed with Nordseewerke, Emden for the construction of one 1 700 ton submarine in Emden, three more to be built in Argentina. Financial guarantees have been provided by West German government.

Brown (D 20) (ex-USS *Heermann*, DD 532) and *Espora* (D 21) (ex-USS *Dortch*, DD 670) decommissioned 13 Dec 1977 for disposal. Will be stripped of parts first. Ex-USS *Mansfield* (DD 728), may be reactivated as replacement for *Brown*.
The icebreaker *Almirante Irizar* was launched on 3 Feb 1978. She is scheduled for delivery in Oct 1978.

Displacement, tons: 10 000

Cost, approx: US $61·5 million

Page 25: correct commissioning date for *Nueve de Julio* (ex-USS *Boise*) 12 Aug 1938.
Page 27: dates of laying down of *Bouchard* 29 Feb 1944 and *Segui* 17 Jan 1944.
Page 33: tugs *Querandi* and *Tehuelche* ordered 10 March 1977 and laid down 1 May 1977. Of 270 tons; range 1 100 miles at 12 knots; complement 30.

AUSTRALIA

Third US "Oliver Hazard Perry" (FFG 7) class unit ordered in Nov 1977. To cost $186 million.

BAHAMAS

Page 47: new Vosper Thornycroft 60 ft patrol craft are *Exuma* P 25, *Abaco* P 26, *Iragua* P 27.
Photograph in section is of *Inagua*, not *Marlin*.

BELGIUM

Page 50: "E-71" class frigates carry rocket launchers by Le Creusot-Loire with Bofors rockets. Tonnage now reported as 1 880 light, 2 283 deep load.
Page 51: type 498 MSOs (M/H) have range of 300 miles at 10 knots.
Page 50: *Wielingen* (F 910) and *Westdiep* (F 911) both commissioned 20 Jan 1978.

BRAZIL

Pennant numbers for "Niteroi" class—*Constituição* F42, *Liberal* F43. Numbers F 44 and 45 being used for Brazilian-built pair.
Planned new construction programme of 49 ships includes a new carrier, submarines, missile cruisers and frigates as well as continuing programme of amphibious vessels.
Tonelero sailed from Clyde 12 Feb 1978.

CAMEROON

Three small patrol craft delivered in Aug 1977 by Chantiers Plascoa, Cannes. Three more building.

CANADA

3 in guns in "Annapolis" class are US Mk 33. "Restigouche" and "Mackenzie" classes have same arrangement of 3 in guns.
Tenders called for by Canadian government for six frigates of 3 500-4 200 tons armed with Harpoon missiles, Seasparrow, one 76 mm gun and one Sea King helicopter.

CHILE

6 in guns in *Latorre* originally ordered in 1940 for Netherlands "De Zeven Provincien" class.

COLOMBIA

Reported that transfer of Portuguese frigates is now doubtful. Ex-USS *Duval County* (LST 758) transferred in early 1978. To be overhauled in the USA prior to sailing for Colombia.

ESPADON *11/1977, Carlo Martinelli, Genova*

GC 237 *11/1977, Carlo Martinelli, Genova*

CUBA

Now reported to carry 8 "Zhuk" class.

DENMARK

Lindormen launched 9 Sept. 1977. Capacity 50/60 mines.

ECUADOR

Ex-USS *Chowanoc* ATF 100 renamed *Chimborazo*.

EGYPT

Tariq carries DC racks in addition to throwers.

ETHIOPIA

Two landing craft L 1035 and 1036 completed in France, 4 May 1977.

FINLAND

New Wärtsila minelayer/training ship (No 421) ordered late 1977.

FRANCE

Aconit undergoing modernisation 1977-78 including removal of radome, fitting of Exocet and, possibly, helicopter facilities.
Meuse laid down 2 June 1977.
Eridan, first and name ship of new minehunter class laid down 20 Dec 1977.
Gazelle delivered 26 Oct 1977; fifth of class (*Isard*) ordered 1977.
S 616 to be launched in 1979

GERMANY (FDR)

4th and 6th M/S Squadrons combined in 1977 to form MCM Squadron, North Sea.

Page 193: six "Lindau" class minesweepers being converted for Troika operation will also have a minehunting capability and will be the "Type 351". Eighteen "Hohlstab" boats for Troika operation (three to each ship) to be built by Blohm & Voss, the whole programme to be completed by 1982.
Length of "Lindau" class 156.5 feet *(47.7 metres)*. The last pair of "Lindau" minehunter conversions *Lindau* and *Tubingen* completed in October and December 1977.

GREECE

The ten Skaramanga built craft in Light Forces are to carry Torpedo tubes. Two ex-US "Asheville" class *Beacon* and *Green Bay* renamed *Arsanoglou* and *Pegopoulos*.

GUYANA

Peccari launched on 26 March 1976.

INDIA

Three Sea King helicopters ordered. The British Government has given permission for negotiations to buy 6 single seat and 2 Training Sea Harriers.
Taragiri launched Oct 1977.
Report of future transfer of two Soviet modified—"Kashin" class.
Tankers *Deepak* and *Shakti* of same class with details as listed for *Deepak*.
Page 222: *Ranjit* (D 141) was not deleted in 1976 and remained active in late 1977.

ADDENDA

INDONESIA

Two more "Attack" class transferred by RAN: names *Sawangi* 854 and *Sandarin* 855. Two more to follow in 1978.
Five more GAF Nomad aircraft ordered from Australia in 1978.

Page 233: The names and pennant numbers of the three new frigates under construction are *Kri Fatahilla* (361) (launched 12/77), *Kri Malahayati* (362) and *Kri Nala* (363). All to be delivered 1978-79.
Page 232: the names and pennant numbers of the two new West German *Type* 209s are *Cakra* (401) and *Candrasa* (402).

IRAN

Reported that the three MSCs are to be converted to minehunting with Sperry equipment.
Reported that Iran is planning to build an extra 18 destroyers, 8-12 frigates, 16 submarines, 18 MCMV and several patrol craft, the bulk of the order to be placed in the Netherlands and West Germany.
Page 241: US hull numbers of "Spruance" class should read 993, 994, 996, 998 allowing for two deletions to date.

ITALY

Modernisation of *Andrea Doria* which started late 1977 to include provision of eight Otomat missiles, one Albatross system, alteration of Terrier system to take Standard missiles and new electronics and AIO systems.

JAPAN

Launch dates: Page 279: *Asakaze* DD 169, 15 Oct 1977; page 293: *Chikugo* PM90, 28 Sept 1977; page 296: *Shimanami* PC 79, 14 Sept 1977.
Commissioning dates: page 285: *Nemuro* L 4103, 27 Oct 1977; page 286: *Okitso* MSC 646, 20 Sept 1977.

KENYA

Reported to have bought surplus Israeli patrol craft.

KOREA, SOUTH

Grasp (ARS 24) transferred, by sale, on 31 March 1978 and renamed *Chang Won*.

KUWAIT

It may now be unlikely that the order for ten Fast Attack Craft will be placed with Vosper Thornycroft.

LIBYA

Page 321: first 550 ton corvette named *Wadi Mrach*—launched 29 Sept 1977.

MALAYSIA

Survey ship KD *Mutiara* of 1 905 tons, 71 × 13 × 4 metres, with 2 Deutz diesels = 16 knots and with range of 4 500 n. miles. Complement 156.

MOROCCO

Page 337: *Triki* commissioned 12 July 1977.

NETHERLANDS

Eight more Lynx (Type SH 14C with towed MAD) ordered Dec 1977 to add to previous ten (Type SH 14B with dipping sonar) ordered earlier. Twelve more to be ordered in future to bring total to 36.
Funds released Feb 1978 for construction of one submarine at Rotterdam Drydock.

Page 341: "Zeehond" class with draught of 16.4 feet *(5 metres)* have four tubes at each end.
Page 342: "Tromp" class missile load reported as 40 Tartar, 60 Sea Sparrow and 16 Harpoon when fitted. Speed believed to be nearer 28 than 30 knots.

NIGERIA

120 metre frigate ordered from Blohm & Voss late 1977.

OMAN

New Brooke Logistic Ship named *Munassir* A1. Training schooner *Youth of Oman* bought from Dulverton Trust.

PERU

Netherlands destroyer *Holland* transferred 20 Jan 1978; named *Garcia y Garcia*.
Page 374: pennant number of *Pacocha* (ex-USS *Atule*, SS 403) is "48" not "50".
Page 379: the new oiler *Talara* commissioned in Feb 1978.

SWEDEN

"Spica" (T121 and T131) classes to start fitting of Penguin 2 missiles in 1978.
Minelayer M04 to be laid down in 1978.

MUTIARA *1978, Royal Malaysian Navy*

UNITED ARAB EMIRATES

Four fast attack craft ordered from Lürssen in late 1977.

UNITED KINGDOM

Rear-Admiral W. D. M. Staveley relieved as Flag Officer, Carriers and Amphibious Ships in July 1978 by Rear-Admiral P. G. M. Herbert OBE.
RFA *Fort Austin* launched 9 March 1978.
RFA *Fort Grange* commissioned March 1978.

TAIWAN

Grapple (ARS 7) transferred, by sale, on 1 Dec 1977 as *TA HU*.
Page 452: *Leonard F. Mason* (DD 852) transferred, by sale, on 10 March 1978.

UNITED STATES OF AMERICA

Admiral James L. Holloway III relieved as Chief of Naval Operations in July 1978 by Admiral Thomas B. Hayward.
Vice-Admiral Donald C. Davis will relieve Vice-Admiral Robert B. Baldwin as Commander, Seventh Fleet.
Vice-Admiral George E. R. Kinnear II will relieve Vice-Admiral Howard E. Greer as Commander, Naval Air Force, US Atlantic Fleet.
General Samuel Jasklika, USMC, will retire as Assistant Commandant of the Marine Corps on 1 July 1978. His relief will be General Robert H. Barrow, USMC.

Mahoa (YTM 519) deleted 1 October 1977. To be sunk as target.
Nautilus (SSN 571) is scheduled to decommission in Feb 1980 at Mare Island Naval Shipyard. In the spring of 1980 she will be towed back to Annapolis, Md for permanent berthing at the United States Naval Academy as a memorial.
Corrected and additional characteristics of the new Mine Countermeasures Ships (MCM) to begin construction under the FY 1980 programme.

Displacements, tons: 1 640 standard, 2 200 full load
Length, feet (metres): 239·5 *(73·0)*
Beam, feet (metres): 44·3 *(13·5)*
Draught, feet (metres): 11·2 *(3·4)*
Main engines: 2 diesels, 2 shafts = 18 knots, 6 800 bhp
Screws: Controllable pitch
Sonar: Probably AN/SQQ-14
Armament: Probably one 20 mm
Complement: About 100 total
Known characteristics of the new T-ARC are as follows:

Length, feet (metres): 450 *(137·2)*
Beam, feet (metres): 60 *(18·3)*
Engines: Diesel-electric, 2 screws, 16 knot max
Complement: 112

Known characteristics of the new Ocean Surveillance Ships (AGOS):

Length, feet (metres): approx 217 *(66·1)*
Beam, feet (metres): 42 *(12·8)*
Main engines: Diesel-electric, 2 shafts, 11 knots max.
The mission of this class is "to support SURTASS system as unit of the Military Sealift Command."

The design characteristics of the Aircraft Carrier (Medium) (CVV) are as follows:

Displacement, tons: 62 427 full load, 52 220 standard
Length, feet (metres): 912 oa *(278·0)*
Beam, feet (metres): 126 hull *(38·4)*
Beam, feet (metres): 256·5 flight deck *(78·2)*
Draught, feet (metres): 34 max *(10·4)*

Catapults: 2 steam (C 13)
Aircraft: 50 to 64 planes
Elevators: 2
Main engines: Steam turbines, 100 000 shp, 2 shafts
Speed, knots: 27-29
Endurance: 8 000 n. miles at 20 knots
Complement: 3 400-3 900 including air wing

If it is decided to build this design the first ship is due to be authorised under FY 1980 not 1979.
ARD 12 and YFN 903 were sold to Brazil on 28 Dec 1977, for service, having previously been on loan.
Vernon County (LST 1161), *Quirinus* (ARL 39), ARD 13, YR 48, *Wannalancet* (YTM 385), *Sassacus* (YTM 193), *Oswegatchie* (YTM 778), *Utina* (ATF 163), *Marietta* (AN 82), *Tunxis* (AN 90) and *Waxsaw* (AN 91) were sold to Venezuela on 30 Dec 1977, for service, having previously been on loan.
Grant County (LST 1174) deleted 30 Dec 1977 for sale to Brazil. Currently on loan.
Frank Cable (AS 40) launched 14 Jan 1978. *Emory S. Land* (AS 39), the lead ship of the class, was launched on 4 May, 1977.
Construction contracts for the approved FY 1978 "Oliver Hazard Perry" Class (FFG 7) have been awarded to Todd Pacific Shipyards Corp, Seattle, Todd Pacific Shipyards Corp, San Pedro and Bath Iron Works, Bath, Maine. Breakdown as to which hull numbers were awarded to which shipbuilder is not available.
Naval Submarine Support Base Kings Bay, Georgia to be activated on 1 May 1979 as a replacement for the Rota, Spain FBM Base. The Kings Bay base will provide a facility for the refit of FBM submarines and eventually refitting some of existing FBM submarines with TRIDENT I missiles. The base is currently an inactivated military ocean terminal owned by the Army.
Thrush (MSC 204) was originally leased to the Virginia Institute of Marine Science, Gloucester Point, Va in July 1975. She was returned to the US Navy on 1 July 1977 and retransferred to the same organisation, permanently, on the same date. Struck from the Naval Vessel Register on 1 Aug 1977.
Unnamed (AG 193) (ex-M/V *Huges Glomar Explorer*) to be reactivated and leased to Global Marine Development Inc, Newport Beach, Calif on or about 1 June 1978 for a period of 13 months. Global Marine will pay for all reactivation and operating costs as well as mothballing costs once the lease expires. The ship is to be used for "scientific and mineral exploration and mining in the deep ocean".
Nassau (LHA 4) and *Nicholson* (DD 982) both launched on 28 Jan 1978.
On 18 Jan 1978, after dropping an old YO hulk off at the bombing range near San Diego, *Cree* (ATF 84) was accidentally bombed by a US A-6 Intruder aircraft. After the incident has been investigated, *Cree* will be deleted and sold for scrapping.
Estimated repair and modernisation of *Belknap* (CG 26) to cost $213 million. Modernisation to include new improved 5 in gun (probably lightweight 5 in), updated missile armament, sonar, communications and radar suits as well as improvement in hability.
In January 1978 the Defense Department approved the Navy's request to start production of the 8 in major caliber lightweight gun (MCLWG). Present plans call for the outfitting of all "Spruance" Class DD's with the new gun.
Mitscher (DDG 35) and *John S. McCain* (DDG 36) deleted from the US Naval Vessel Register on 1 June 1978 and 29 April 1978 respectively. To be scrapped.
A total of five of the "AO-177" Class have been authorised for construction (AO 177, 180, 186). The number of units projected for this class has temporarily been reduced to nine, leaving AO 187, 190 to be authorised in the FY 1980 (187) FY 1981 (188) and the FY 1983 (189, 190) programmes.
AFDL 43 deleted from the Naval Vessel Register on 1 Feb 1978. The drydock had been on lease to Campbell Industries.
The reported removal of the TALOS systems from CGN 9, CG 10, 11 has been confirmed. The systems will be replaced by the Standard (MR) system. In the meantime, the Talos system on CG-5 will be retained and the systems from CGN 9, CG 10, 11 cannibalised to keep hers going until the ship is retired.

794 ADDENDA

The following is the projected ship changes in the US Navy from 4 March 1978 to 30 Sept 1978.

Date	Name/Hull Number	From Status	To Status
4 March 1978	**OLDENDORF** (DD 972)	Building	Active
4 March 1978	**OMAHA** (SSN 692)	Building	Active
11 March 1978	**MERRILL** (DD 976)	Building	Active
31 March 1978	**GRASP** (ARS 24)	Active	Stricken
1 April 1978	**NEOSHO** (AO 143)	Active	Military Sealift Command
15 April 1978	**GROTON** (SSN 694)	Building	Active
30 April 1978	**JOHN S. McCAIN** (DDG 36)	Active	Stricken
27 May 1978	**JOHN YOUNG** (DD 973)	Building	Active
30 May 1978	**BAUSELL** (DD 845)	Active	Stricken
31 May 1978	**CINCINNATI** (SSN 693)	Building	Active
1 June 1978	**TAWAKONI** (ATF 114)	Active	Stricken
1 June 1978	**MITSCHER** (DDG 35)	Active	Stricken
1 July 1978	**WILLIAM R. RUSH** (DD 714)	Active	Stricken
1 July 1978	**MOLALA** (ATF 106)	Active	Stricken
8 July 1978	**BRISCOE** (DD 977)	Building	Active
1 Aug 1978	**CREE** (ATF 84)	Active	Stricken
1 Sept 1978	**GRAND CANYON** (AR 28)	Active	Stricken
1 Sept 1978	**ESCAPE** (ARS 6)	Active	Stricken
1 Sept 1978	**NIPMUC** (ATF 157)	Active	Stricken
1 Sept 1978	**SALINAN** (ATF 161)	Active	Stricken
19 Sept 1978	**COMTE DE GRASSE** (DD 974)	Building	Active
28 Sept 1978	**BELLEAU WOOD** (LHA 3)	Building	Active
30 Sept 1978	**PLAINVIEW** (AGEH 1)	Active	Stricken
30 Sept 1978	**ABNAKI** (ATF 96)	Active	Stricken
30 Sept 1978	**COCOPA** (ATF 101)	Active	Stricken
30 Sept 1978	**HITCHITI** (ATF 103)	Active	Stricken
30 Sept 1978	**MISSISSIPPI** (CGN 40)	Building	Active
30 Sept 1978	**STUMP** (DD 978)	Building	Active
30 Sept 1978	**SAILFISH** (SS 572)	Active	Stricken
30 Sept 1978	**DARTER** (SS 576)	Active	Stricken

The above list is subject to revision.

Actual FY 1979 proposal submitted to Congress on 20 Jan 1978.

(Supersedes that given on page 604).

Shipbuilding

1	"Ohio" Class SSBN (SSBN 733)	$1 186·7 million total
1	"Los Angeles" Class (SSN 720)	$433 million total
8	"Oliver Hazard Perry" Class FFG's (FFG 35/42)	$1 533·1 million total
1	Destroyer Tender (AD 44)	$318 million total
3	Ocean Surveillance Ships (AGOS)	$98 million total
1	Cable Repair Ship (T ARC 7)	$1 186·7 million total

Long Term Lead Items

1	Aircraft Carrier Service Life Extension Program (SLEP)	$32·2 million total
4	Anti-Air Warfare Modernisation "Charles F. Adams" Class DDG's	$151 million total

Notes: The new Guided Missile Cruiser (AEGIS) Class (CGN-42) was deleted by the Carter Administration, but it is more than probable that Congress will re-instate it.

Planned Five Year Shipbuilding/Conversion Programme (FY 1979/1983) (Supersedes that on page 604).
(Deletions from previous programme marked in brackets).

Shipbuilding

- 6 "Ohio" Class SSBN's (minus one)
- 5 "Los Angeles" Class SSN's (minus five)
- 2 Aircraft Carriers (Medium) (CVV)
- 1 Improved "Virginia" Class Guided Missile Cruisers (nuclear propulsion) (CGN) (minus three)
- 7 Guided Missile Destroyers (AEGIS) (DDG-47 Class) (minus one)
- 26 Guided Missile Frigates (FFG 7 Class) (minus sixteen)
- 2 Dock Landing Ships (LSD 41 Class)
- 5 Mine Countermeasures Vehicles (MCM)
- 1 Destroyer Tender (AD) (minus one)
- 1 Oiler (AO 177 Class) (minus three)
- 1 New design Ocean Tug (minus one)
- 12 Ocean Surveillance Ships (AGOS)
- 1 Cable Repair Ship (ARC)

Conversions

- 2 Aircraft Carrier Service Life Extension Programme (SLEP)
- 10 Anti-Air Warfare Modernisation "Charles F. Adams" Class (DDG) (minus thirteen)
- 1 Cargo Ship Conversion (AK)

Following is quoted from covering report:

This plan proposes to build six Trident strategic missile submarines over the five year period. Since each Trident submarine has launch tubes for 24 missiles, the plan would add 144 Trident missiles to the strategic force.

For general purpose forces, we would continue to build ships for a balanced Navy than can maintain forward presence for deterrence in peacetime, keep the sea lines of communications open in a war between the Warsaw Pact and NATO, and protect the US interests in non-NATO contingencies. It would have a growing anti-submarine warfare capability and a greatly enhanced anti-air warfare capability.

In order to maintain our forward presence for deterrence, the shipbuilding plan includes money to start major service life extensions for the Forrestal-class conventional carriers. This programme will allow us to keep these conventional carriers in the force structure until at least the year 2000. We also have proposed a new carrier approximately the same size as the Midway. These carriers, along with our four nuclear carriers, will provide at least 12 deployable carriers. If we continue to homeport one in Japan, we will be able to maintain our current posture of four forward deployed and have another four to six that could respond to a surge demand.

We are tentatively planning to begin construction of a new class of amphibious ships in this period. This would help ensure enough lift to keep the same level of forward deployments that we have had for the past few years.

Forces particularly important for the defense of the vital sea lanes include the continuation of the SSN-688 at the rate of one per year, the FFG 7 class Frigate, and 12 Mobile undersea surveillance ships (T AGOS) for anti-submarine warfare. To enhance our anti-air warfare capability, we plan to build seven DDG-47 AEGIS ships and modernise ten of the DDG 2 guided missile destroyers.

Our carriers, the DDG 47, the CGN 42, and the amphibious ships will sustain our ability to project sea power into any ocean of the world where US vital interests are threatened. This shipbuilding plan—when added to the current fleet and ships previously authorised but not delivered—will increase the fleet size from about 466 ships at the end of this fiscal year to over 525 ships by end of Fiscal Year 1984. Although projections beyond that time are more uncertain, the logical extension of this plan should allow the fleet to remain at or above 500 ships through the turn of the century.

Oldendorf (DD 972) was commissioned on 4 March 1978. She is assigned to the Pacific Fleet.

Merrill (DD 976) was commissioned on 11 March 1978. She is assigned to the Pacific Fleet.

Ex-*Rowe* (DD 564) sunk as a target on 23 Feb 1978, in a fleet exercise, by missiles, gunfire and aircraft.

It is the Navy plan to rely on a force of 12 CV/CVN's through the 1990's. A thirteenth carrier, *Coral Sea* (CV 43), is presently active, but has no air wing and is used as a contingency CV. She will be replaced in the active fleet by *Carl Vinson* (CVN 70).

Saratoga (CV 60) will begin a 28 month SLEP modernisation/overhaul in the autumn of 1980. Each modernisation/overhaul is to cost approx. $496 million. After *Saratoga* is completed *Forrestal* (CV 59) will receive her SLEP.

The contract for construction of SSBN 731/732 was awarded to Electric Boat on 27 Feb 1978. The number of TRIDENT units to be constructed has been set at 14.

Duncan (FFG 10) launched on 1 March 1978).

Omaha (SSN 692) commissioned on 4 March 1978. Assigned to the Atlantic Fleet.

Memphis (SSN 691) commissioned on 17 Dec 1977. Assigned to the Atlantic Fleet.

Capitaine (SS 336), on loan to Italy since 5 March 1966, was striken from the Naval Vessel Register on 5 Dec 1977.

Leonard F. Mason (DD 852) transferred to Tailwan by sale on 10 March 1978.

Grasp (ARS 24) transferred to South Korea by sale on 31 March 1978.

The name of *LHA 5* was changed from *Da Nang* to *Peleliu* on 15 Feb 1978.

UNITED STATES COAST GUARD

Rear-Admiral John B. Hayes will be promoted to Admiral and relieve Admiral Owen W. Siler as Commandant of the Coast Guard on 1 June 1978. Rear-Admiral R. H. Scarborough, Jr will be promoted to Vice-Admiral and relieve Vice-Admiral Ellis L. Perry as Vice-Commandant of the Coast Guard on 1 July 1978.

The following ships decommissioned for disposal on the indicated dates: *Oleander* (WLR 73264) on 1 June 1977, *Forsythia* (WLR 63) on 12 Aug 1977, *Sycamore* (WLR 268) on 30 June 1977, *Foxglove* (WLR 285) on 8 July 1977, *Loganberry* (WLI 65305) on 30 Sept 1976, *Tern* (WLI 80801) on 1 July 1977, *Verbena* (WLI 317) on 1 Sept 1977 and *Clematis* (WIL 74286) on 12 Nov 1976. All to be scrapped.

INDEXES

Albania	Alb	Guinea	Gn	Peru	Per
Algeria	Alg	Guinea Bissau	GB	Philippines	Plp
Angola	Ang	Guyana	Guy	Poland	Pol
Anguilla	Ana	Haiti	Hai	Portugal	Por
Argentina	Arg	Honduras	Hon	Qatar	Qat
Australia	Aust	Hong Kong	HK	Romania	Rom
Austria	Aus	Hungary	Hun	St Kitts	StK
Bahamas	Bhm	Iceland	Ice	St Lucia	StL
Bahrain	Bhr	India	Ind	St Vincent	StV
Bangladesh	Ban	Indonesia	Indo	Sabah	Sab
Barbados	Bar	Iran	Iran	Saudi Arabia	SAr
Belgium	Bel	Iraq	Iraq	Senegal	Sen
Belize	Blz	Ireland	Ire	Sierra Leone	SL
Bolivia	Bol	Israel	Isr	Singapore	Sin
Brazil	Brz	Italy	Ita	Somalia	Som
Brunei	Bru	Ivory Coast	IC	South Africa	SA
Bulgaria	Bul	Jamaica	Jam	Spain	Spn
Burma	Bur	Japan	Jap	Sri Lanka	Sri
Cameroon	Cam	Jordan	Jor	Sudan	Sud
Canada	Can	Kampuchea	Kam	Surinam	Sur
Chile	Chi	Kenya	Ken	Sweden	Swe
China, People's Republic	CPR	Korea, Democratic		Syria	Syr
Colombia	Col	People's Republic (North)	DPRK	Taiwan	RoC
Comoro Islands	Com	Korea, Republic (South)	RoK	Tanzania	Tan
Congo	Con	Kuwait	Kwt	Thailand	Tld
Costa Rica	CR	Laos	Lao	Togo	Tog
Cuba	Cub	Lebanon	Leb	Tonga	Ton
Cyprus	Cyp	Liberia	Lbr	Trinidad and Tobago	TT
Czechoslovakia	Cz	Libya	Lby	Tunisia	Tun
Denmark	Den	Madagascar	Mad	Turkey	Tur
Dominican Republic	DR	Malawi	Mlw	Uganda	Uga
Ecuador	Ecu	Malaysia	Mly	Union of Soviet	
Egypt	Egy	Malta	Mlt	Socialist Republics	USSR
El Salvador	ElS	Mauritania	Mtn	United Arab Emirates	UAE
Equatorial Guinea	EqG	Mauritius	Mrt	United Kingdom	UK
Ethiopia	Eth	Mexico	Mex	United States of America	USA
Fiji	Fij	Montserrat	Mnt	Uruguay	Uru
Finland	Fin	Morocco	Mor	Venezuela	Ven
France	Fra	Netherlands	Nld	Viet-Nam	Vtn
Gabon	Gab	New Zealand	NZ	Virgin Isles	VI
Gambia	Gam	Nicaragua	Nic	Yemen Arab Republic (North)	YAR
Germany, Democratic		Nigeria	Nig	Yemen, People's	
Republic	GDR	Norway	Nor	Democratic Republic (South)	YPDR
Germany, Federal Republic	GFR	Oman	Omn	Yugoslavia	Yug
Ghana	Gha	Pakistan	Pak	Zaire	Zai
Greece	Gre	Panama	Pan	Zambia	Zam
Grenada	Gra	Papua New Guinea	PNG	Zanzibar	Zan
Guatemala	Gua	Paraguay	Par		

NAMED SHIPS

A

A. Barbosa (Brz) 63
A. Chirikov (USSR) 538
A. F. Dufour (Bel) 51
A. Smirnov (USSR) 539
A. Vilkitsky (USSR) 538
Aarøsund (Den) 121
AB 21-24 (Tur) 476
AB 25-34 (Tur) 475
Ababeh Ibn Nefeh (Syr) 450
Abbeville (UK) 582
Abcoude (Nld) 346
Abd Al Rahman (Iraq) 248
Abdiel (UK) 584
Abdul Aziz (SAr) 404
Abdullah Ibn Arissi (Syr) 450
Aber wrach (Fra) 171
Aberdovey (UK) 600
Abhay (Ind) 228
Abinger (UK) 600
Abkhasia (USSR) 541
Abnaki (USA) 705
Abnegar (Iran) 246
Abon Abdallah El Ayachi (Mor) 338
Abra (Plp) 386
Abraham Crijnssen (Nld) 344
Abraham Lincoln (USA) 630
Abrolhos (Brz) 60
Abtao (Per) 374
Abu Obaidah (SAr) 404
Abukuma (Jap) 293
Acacia (Fra) 168
Acadia (USA) 696
Acadian (Can) 77
Acajou (Fra) 178
Acanthe (Fra) 168
Acara (Brz) 60
Acchileus (Gre) 213
Acco (Isr) 252
Accohanoc (USA) 712
Accokeek (USA) 705
Acconac (USA) 712
Accord (UK) 598
Acevedo (Spn) 425
Acharné (Fra) 178
Achat (GFR) 198
Acheron (GFR) 194
Achilles (Swe) 448
Achilles (UK) 576
Achziv (Isr) 253
Acklins (Bhm) 47
Acoma (USA) 712
Aconit (Fra) 161
Acor (Por) 397
Actif (Fra) 178
Active (UK) 575
Active (USA) 728
Acushnet (USA) 734
Acute (Aust) 41
Adam Kuckhoff (GDR) 181
Adamidis (Gre) 213
Adatepe (Tur) 473
Addriyah (SAr) 404
Adelaide (Aust) 40
Adige (Ita) 272
Admiral Fokin (USSR) 508
Admiral Golovko (USSR) 508
Admiral Isachenkov (USSR) 506
Admiral Isakov (USSR) 506
Admiral Lazarev (USSR) 509
Admiral Makarov (USSR) 506, 553
Admiral Nakhimov (USSR) 506
Admiral Oktyabrsky (USSR) 506
Admiral Senyavin (USSR) 509
Admiral Ushakov (USSR) 509
Admiral Vladimirsky (USSR) 541
Admiral Wm. M. Callaghan (USA) 718
Admiral Yumaschev (USSR) 506
Admiral Zozulya (USSR) 507
Adolf Bestelmeyer (GFR) 200
Adroit (Aust) 41
Adroit (USA) 694
Advance (Aust) 41
Advance (Can) 79
Adversus (Can) 77
Advice (UK) 598
Adzhariya (USSR) 541
Aedon (Gre) 211
Aegeon (Gre) 212
Aeger (Nor) 357
Aegir (Ice) 220
Aeolus (USA) 722
Aetos (Gre) 207
Afanasy Nitikin (USSR) 555
Affray (USA) 694
Afonso Pena (Brz) 63
AG 1.4.5.6. (Tur) 481
Agatan (USSR) 556
Agatha (UK) 599
Agave (Ita) 268
Agawan (USA) 712
Agdleq (Den) 118
Agerholm (USA) 675
Agheila (UK) 582
Agile (UK) 598
Agnes (UK) 599
Agosta (Fra) 150
Agpa (Den) 118
Aguascalientes (Mex) 335
Aguia (Por) 397
Aguila (Chi) 92
Aguilucho (Spn) 432
Aguirre (Per) 374
Agulha (Brz) 60
Agusan (Plp) 385
Ah San (RoK) 311
Ahmed Es Sakali (Mor) 338
Ahoskie (USA) 712
Ahrenshoop (GDR) 183
Aias (Gre) 213
Aigli (Gre) 211
Aigrette (Fra) 178
Aiguiere (Fra) 178
Ainsworth (USA) 680
Aiolos (Gre) 209
Air Sprite (Aust) 45
Airedale (UK) 598
Airone (Ita) 265
Aisberg (USSR) 555
Aitape (PNG) 370
Aiyar Lulin (Bur) 68
Ajax (Swe) 448
Ajax (UK) 576
Ajax (USA) 702
Ajonc (Fra) 176
Akademik Arkhangelsky (USSR) 540
Akademik Korolev (USSR) 543
Akademik Kovalevsky (USSR) 540
Akademik Krilov (USSR) 541
Akademik Kurchatov (USSR) 543
Akademik L. Orbeli (USSR) 540
Akademik Sergei Korolev (USSR) 545
Akademik Shirshov (USSR) 543
Akademik Vavilov (USSR) 540
Akademik Vernadsky (USSR) 543
Akademik Voeykov (USSR) 544
Akagi (Jap) 295
Akashi (Jap) 289
Akbas (Tur) 482
Akhisar (Tur) 476
Akhtuba (USSR) 548
Akigumo (Jap) 280
Akin (Tur) 480
Akiyoshi (Jap) 295
Akizuki (Jap) 281, 296
Akpinar (Tur) 480
Akrama (Lby) 322
Aktion (Gre) 211
Al Adrisi (Iraq) 248
Al Aqab (UAE) 558
Al Aul (Omn) 362
Al Bachir (Mor) 337
Al Bushra (Omn) 362
Al Farouq (SAr) 404
Al Fulk (Omn) 362
Al Ghazi (Iraq) 248
Al Ghullan (UAE) 557
Al Jabbar (Omn) 362
Al Jala (Tun) 470
Al Kadisia (Iraq) 249
Al Keriat (Lby) 323
Al Makas (Egy) 135
Al Mansur (Omn) 362
Al Mubaraki (Kwt) 317
Al Nasiri (Omn) 362
Al Nejah (Omn) 362
Al Quysumah (SAr) 404
Al Riyadh (SAr) 406
Al Said (Omn) 361
Al Salemi (Kwt) 317
Al Salihi (Omn) 362
Al Sansoor (Omn) 363
Al Shaab (Iraq) 248
Al Shurti (Kwt) 317
Al Shaheen (UAE) 558
Al Shweirif (Lby) 323
Al Sultana (Omn) 363
Al Tami (Iraq) 248
Al Thawra (Iraq) 249
Al Wadeach (SAr) 404
Al Wafi (Omn) 362
Al Wusaail (Qat) 399
Al Yarmook (SAr) 404
Al Yarmouk (Iraq) 249
Al Zaffer (Egy) 131
Alabarda (Por) 398
Alacrity (UK) 575
Alacrity (USA) 698
Alagoas (Brz) 58
Alakush (Arg) 30
Alamagordo (USA) 708
Alambai (USSR) 552
Alamgir (Pak) 366
Alamo (USA) 689
Alarich (GFR) 198
Alatna (USA) 722
Alatyr (USSR) 548
Alava (Spn) 424
Albacora (Por) 396
Albacore (USA) 641
Albany (USA) 663
Albardão (Brz) 60
Albatros (Ita) 265
Albatros (Pol) 392
Albatros (Spn) 432
Albatros II (Spn) 432
Albatros III (Spn) 432
Albatros (Tur) 475
Albatroz (Por) 397
Albay (Plp) 386
Albay Hakki Burak (Tur) 480
Albenga (Ita) 273
Albert (Ice) 221
Albert David (USA) 679
Albert J. Meyer (USA) 722
Alblas (Nld) 346
Alcalá Galiano (Spn) 421
Alcione (Ita) 265
Aldan (USSR) 556
Aldebarán (DR) 124
Aldebaran (Swe) 441
Ale (Swe) 446
Alef (Iraq) 248
Aleksandr Nevski (USSR) 509
Aleksandr Suvorov (USSR) 509
Aleksandr Tortsev (USSR) 529
Alençon (Fra) 167
Alert (Can) 85
Alert (Lbr) 319
Alert (UK) 600
Alert (USA) 728
Alexander Hamilton (USA) 627
Alexander Henry (Can) 83
Alexander Mackenzie (Can) 85
Alferez Sobral (Arg) 28
Alfonso de Albuquerque (Por) 398
Alfonso Vargas (Col) 108
Alfriston (UK) 585
Algarna III (Tur) 482
Algonquin (Can) 73
Ali Hyder (Ban) 48
Alice (UK) 599
Alicudi (Ita) 271
Alidada (USSR) 537
Aliseo (Ita) 263
Alkmaar (Nld) 345
Alkyon (Gre) 211
Alloro (Ita) 268
Almanzora (Spn) 429
Almirante Brásil (Brz) 63
Almeida Carvalho (Por) 398
Almirante Brion (Ven) 743
Almirante Brown (Arg) 27
Almirante Camara (Brz) 61
Almirante Clemente (Ven) 743
Almirante Domecq Garcia (Arg) 27
Almirante Ferrandiz (Spn) 421
Almirante Gago Coutinho (Por) 396
Almirante Garcia de los Reyes (Spn) 419
Almirante Grau (Bol) 53
Almirante Grau (Per) 374
Almirante Irizar (Arg) 32
Almirante Jeronimo Goncalves (Brz) 63
Almirante Lynch (Chi) 91
Almirante Magalhaes Correa (Por) 396
Almirante Pereira Da Silva (Por) 396
Almirante Riveros (Chi) 90
Almirante Saldanha (Brz) 61
Almirante Storni (Arg) 27
Almirante Valdes (Spn) 421
Almirante Williams (Chi) 90
Alness (UK) 600
Alnmouth (UK) 600
Alor Star (Mly) 328
Alouette (Fra) 178
Alphée (Fra) 176
Alpino (Ita) 264
Alsatian (UK) 598
Alsedo (Spn) 425
Alsfeld (GFR) 201
Alssund (Den) 121
Alste (GFR) 200
Alta (Nor) 359
Altai (USSR) 550
Altair (Fra) 166
Altair (USSR) 538
Altay (USSR) 548
Altentreptow (GDR) 183
Alunya (Plp) 389
Alvaro Alberto (Brz) 60
Alvin (USA) 643
Alvsborg (Swe) 442
Alvsnabben (Swe) 442
Amakusa (Jap) 294
Amami (Jap) 287, 293
Aman (Kwt) 317
Amapa (Brz) 60
Amar (Mrt) 331
Amatsukaze (Jap) 281
Amazon (UK) 575
Amazonas (Brz) 55
Amazonas (Ecu) 129
Amazonas (Per) 377
Amazonas (Ven) 744
Amazone (Fra) 151
Amazone (GFR) 194
Amba (Ind) 230
Ambuscade (UK) 575
America (Per) 377
America (USA) 648
American Explorer (USA) 720
Amerigo Vespucci (Ita) 271
Ametyst (USSR) 521
AMI-8 (Mex) 334
Amindin (Ind) 226
Amini (Ind) 226
Amiral Charner (Fra) 161
Ammersee (GFR) 196
Ammiraglio Managhi (Ita) 269
Ampermetr (USSR) 537
Amrum (GFR) 199
Amsel (GFR) 198
Amsterdam (Nld) 343
Amur (USSR) 556
Amurang (Indo) 236
Amvrakia (Gre) 211
Amyot D'Inville (Fra) 163
Amyr (SAr) 404
An Yang (RoC) 453
Anadir (USSR) 538
Anamosa (USA) 712
Anapal (Uru) 739
Anchorage (USA) 689
Anchova (Brz) 60
Ancud (Chi) 94
Andagoya (Col) 110
Andalucia (Spn) 423
Andaman (Ind) 226
Andenes, O/S (Nor) 360
Andenne (Bel) 51
Anders Bure (Swe) 446
Andorinha (Por) 397
Andrea Bafile (Ita) 267
Andrea Doria (Ita) 260
Andres Bonifacio (Plp) 383
Andres Quintana Roos (Mex) 334
Andrew Jackson (USA) 627
Andrija Mohorovicic (Yug) 757
Andromeda (Gre) 208
Andromeda (USSR) 538
Andromeda (UK) 576
Andros (Bhm) 47
Androth (Ind) 226
Ane (Swe) 445
Anemos (Gre) 211
Aneriod (USSR) 536
Ang Pangulo (Plp) 388
Angamos (Chi) 93
Angamos (Per) 374
Angostura (Brz) 59
Angthong (Tld) 465
Anhatomirim (Brz) 60
Anita Garibaldi (Brz) 65
Anjadip (Ind) 226
Anklam (GDR) 183
Annapolis (Can) 74
Anoa (Indo) 235
Anoka (USA) 712
Anshan (CPR) 97
Antaios (Gre) 213
Antar (Egy) 135
Antares (Fra) 166
Antares (Spn) 429
Antares (USSR) 538
Antarktyda (USSR) 538
Antelope (UK) 575
Anteo (Ita) 271
Anthiploiarthos Anninos (Gre) 207
Anthiploiarthos Pezopoulos (Gre) 209
Antigo (USA) 712
Antiopi (Gre) 211
Antiploiarhos Laskos (Gre) 207
Antizana (Ecu) 129
Anton Dohrn (GFR) 201
Anton Saefkow (GDR) 181
Antonio Enes (Por) 397
Antonio de la Fuente (Mex) 334
Antonio Joa (Brz) 63
Antrim (UK) 573
Anvil (USA) 733
Aokumo (Jap) 280
Apalachee (USA) 735
Apalachicola (USA) 712
Ape (Ita) 266
Apohola (U.S.A.) 712
Apollo (UK) 576
Apopka (USA) 712
Appleby (UK) 600
Aprendiz Ledio Conceiçao (Brz) 63
Apsheron (USSR) 544
Apu (Fin) 141
Aquila (Ita) 265
Aquiles (Chi) 93
Ar Rakib (Lby) 322
Ara (Fra) 178
Aracatuba (Brz) 60
Aragon (Spn) 426
Aragosta (Ita) 269
Aragir (USSR) 552
Araka (Tan) 460
Arakan (UK) 582
Arkansas (USA) 657
Arashio (Jap) 278
Arataki (NZ) 351
Aratu (Brz) 60
Arau (Mly) 327
Arauca (Col) 108
Araucano (Chi) 94
Arawak (USA) 712
Arcata (USA) 712
Archerfish (USA) 633
Archimède (Fra) 174
Arcona (GFR) 200
Arcturus (Fra) 166
Arcturus (Swe) 441
Ardang (Tld) 466
Ardennes (UK) 582
Ardent (Aust) 41
Ardent (UK) 575
Ardeshir (Iran) 241
Ardhana (UAE) 557
Ardito (Ita) 261
Arenque (Brz) 60
Arethusa (Gre) 212
Arethusa (UK) 576
Aréthuse (Fra) 151
Arg (Nor) 357
Argens (Fra) 164
Argo (Gre) 211
Argonaut (GFR) 198
Argonaut (UK) 576
Argonaute (Fra) 151
Argungu (Nig) 354
Argus (Brz) 61
Argus (Nld) 348
Arhikelefstis Maliopoulos (Gre) 209
Arhikelefstis Stassis (Gre) 209
Ariadne (UK) 576
Ariadne (GFR) 194
Ariadni (Gre) 212
Ariane (Fra) 151
Arica (Per) 373
Ariel (Fra) 176
Aries (Indo) 237
Arild (Swe) 441
Arinya (Plp) 389
Ark Royal (UK) 568
Arkhipelag (USSR) 536
Arkö (Swe) 443
Arkona (GDR) 184
Arktika (USSR) 553
Armoise (Fra) 177
Arnala (Ind) 226
Arrow (UK) 575
Artemiz (Iran) 242
Artevelde (Bel) 51
Arthur Becker (GDR) 181
Arthur W. Radford (USA) 668
Artigas (Uru) 736
Artika (USSR) 538
Aruana (Brz) 60
Arundel (USA) 735
Arvakur (Ice) 221
Arvid Harnack (GDR) 181
Ary Parreiras (Brz) 62
Arzachena (Ita) 273
As Saddiq (SAr) 404
Asagiri (Jap) 296
Asagumo (Jap) 280, 297
Asakaze (Jap) 279
Asama (Jap) 295
Asashio (Jap) 278
Ash 81-85 (Jap) 290
Ashanti (UK) 577
Ashcott (UK) 600
Ashdod (Isr) 253
Ashitaka (Jap) 295
Ashkelon (Isr) 253
Ashtabula (USA) 700
Asinara (Ita) 273
Askar (Bhr) 47
Askø (Den) 120
Askold (USSR) 538
Asoyuki (Jap) 296
Aspis (Gre) 206
Aspö (Swe) 443
Aspro (USA) 633
Assail (Aust) 41
Assiniboine (Can) 75
Assiut (Egy) 134
Assurance (USA) 698
Astice (Ita) 269
Astove (Ita) 266

798 INDEX / NAMED SHIPS

Astrapi (Gre) 209
Astrea (Swe) 441
Asturias (Spn) 423
Asuantsi (Gha) 202
Aswan (Egy) 134
Atada (Jap) 290
Atahualpa (Ecu) 129
Atair (GFR) 194, 201
Atakapa (USA) 705
Atalaia (Brz) 60
Atalanti (Gre) 211
ATB 1, 2, 3 (Swe) 448
Athabaskan (Can) 73
Atico (Per) 378
Atika (Iraq) 247
Atilay (Tur) 472
Atlante (Ita) 272
Atlantida (DR) 124
Atlantis (GFR) 194
Atlas (Gre) 213
Atlas (Swe) 448
Atle (Swe) 445
Atmaca (Tur) 475
Atrek (USSR) 535
Atrevida (Spn) 424
Atromitos (Gre) 213
Atsumi (Jap) 285
Attack (Aust) 41
Attilio Bagnolini (Ita) 258
Attock (Pak) 368
Atum (Brz) 60
Atún (DR) 124
Atyimba (Plp) 389
Audace (Ita) 260
Audaz (Brz) 63
Audemer (UK) 582
Audrey (UK) 599
Augsburg (GFR) 191
August Lüttgens (GDR) 181
Augusto de Castilho (Por) 397
Aunis (Fra) 173
Aurora (UK) 576
Ausonia (Ita) 273
Austin (USA) 688
Autun (Fra) 167
Aveley (UK) 586
Avenger (UK) 575
Avon (UK) 583
Avra (Gre) 211
Awaji (Jap) 286, 292
Aware (Aust) 41
Awl (Aust) 45
Axe (USA) 733
Ayanami (Jap) 282
Ayanasi (Pan) 369
Ayase (Jap) 283
Ayat (USSR) 535
Aylwin (USA) 680
Aytador (USSR) 538
Azalea (USA) 732
Azalée (Fra) 168
Azimut (USSR) 538
Azov (USSR) 505
Azor (Spn) 430
Azueta (Mex) 334
Azuma (Jap) 287
Azumanche (Gua) 214

B

Baagø (Den) 120
Babr (Iran) 242
Babr (Lby) 320
Babur (Pak) 365
Baccarat (Fra) 167
Bacchante (UK) 576
Bacchus (UK) 594
Bad Bramstedt (GFR) 201
Bad Doberan (GDR) 181
Badek (Mly) 326
Badger (USA) 680
Badr (Pak) 366
Badr (SAr) 404
Bagley (USA) 680
Bahaira (Egy) 134
Bahawalpur (Pak) 367
Bahia (Brz) 55
Bahia Aguirre (Arg) 31
Bahia Buen Suceso (Arg) 31
Bahia Camarones 31
Bahia San Blas (Arg) 31
Bahia Utria (Col) 110
Bahmanshir (Iran) 246
Bahaira (Egy) 134
Bahram (Iran) 243
Bahrain I (Bhr) 47
Baiana (Brz) 59
Baikal (USSR) 542
Bainbridge (USA) 662
Bakan (USSR) 536
Bakasi (Cmn) 69
Bakhmut (USSR) 535
Balas (Pol) 393
Balawatha (Sri) 433
Balder (Nld) 345
Balder (Swe) 445
Baleares (Spn) 423
Baleno (Ita) 266
Baler (Plp) 385
Balikpapan (Aust) 44
Balikpapan (Indo) 238
Balkhash (USSR) 542
Balny (Fra) 161
Balsa (Fra) 178
Balsam (USA) 731
Baltimore (USA) 631
Baltrum (GFR) 199
Baltyk (Pol) 393
Baluchistan (Pak) 367
Bambu (Ita) 268
Banba (Ire) 250
Banckert (Nld) 344
Banco Ingles (Uru) 739
Bandar Abbas (Iran) 245
Bangeko (Tld) 465
Banggai (Indo) 238
Bangrachan (Tld) 464
Bangpakong (Tld) 466
Bani Yas (UAE) 557
Banks (Aust) 45
Bannu (Pak) 367
Bansin (GDR) 183
Baraka (Sud) 435
Barakuda (Indo) 234
Barb (USA) 634
Barbara (GFR) 200
Barbara (Ita) 270
Barbara (UK) 599
Barbe (GFR) 193
Barbel (UK) 601
Barbel (USA) 638
Barbette (Aust) 41
Barbey (USA) 680
Barbour County (USA) 690
Barcelo (Spn) 425
Barguzin (USSR) 552
Barney (USA) 673
Barnstable County (USA) 690
Barograf (USSR) 537
Barometr (USSR) 537
Barq (Ind) 231
Barracuda (Por) 396
Barricade (Aust) 41
Barroso Pereira (Brz) 62
Barry (USA) 674
Barsø (Den) 119
Barsuk (USSR) 520
Bartlett (Can) 84
Bartlett (USA) 715
Barzan (Qat) 399
Basanta (Spn) 432
Basaran (Tur) 480
Basento (Ita) 272
Bashkiriya (USSR) 541
Basilan (Plp) 385
Baskunchak (USSR) 544
Bass (Aust) 45
Bassein (Ind) 229
Basset (UK) 598
Basswood (USA) 731
Bat Sheva (Isr) 254
Bat Yam (Isr) 254
Batanes (Plp) 387
Batangas (Plp) 384
Batiray (Tur) 472
Batfish (USA) 633
Baton Rouge (USA) 631
Battleaxe (UK) 575
Baung (Mly) 326
Baurú (Brz) 62
Bausell (USA) 675
Bauten (Indo) 236
Bävern (Swe) 438
Bayandor (Iran) 243
Bayberry (USA) 732
Bayern (GFR) 190
Bayonet (Aust) 41
Bayovar (Peru) 379
Bayraktar (Tur) 478
Bayreuth (GFR) 201
Bdi (Arg) 29
Bditelny (USSR) 511
BDK 1 & 2, 3, 4, 5.
BDK 6, 7, & 8 (Spn) 427
Beachampton (UK) 589
Beagle (Chi) 94
Beagle (UK) 590
Beamsville (Can) 79
Bear (USA) 728
Beas (Ind) 226
Beaufort (USA) 706
Beauport (Can) 86
Beaulieu (UK) 600
Beddgelert (UK) 600
Bedovy (USSR) 513
Bee (UK) 599
Belbek (USSR) 539
Beledau (Mly) 326
Belegis (Yug) 756
Belikawa (Sri) 433
Belize (Blz) 53
Belknap (USA) 660
Bellatrix (DR) 124
Belleau Wood (USA) 686
Bellona (Den) 117
Belmonte (Brz) 62
Belmopan (Blz) 53
Belos (Swe) 447
Bembridge (UK) 600
Bendahara (Bru) 64
Bengali (Fra) 178
Benin (Nig) 353
Benin (Lby) 322
Benjamin Franklin (USA) 627
Benjamin Stoddert (USA) 673
Bennington (USA) 654
Bentang Kalakuang (Indo) 235
Bentang Silungkang (Indo) 235
Bentang Waitatire (Indo) 235
Bentara (Mly) 327
Berezan (USSR) 538
Berezina (USSR) 552
Bergall (USA) 633
Bergen (GDR) 183
Bergen (Nor) 356
Berk (Tur) 474
Berkel (Nld) 348
Berkeley (USA) 673
Berlaimont (Fra) 167
Berlayer (Sin) 409
Berlin (GDR) 185
Bern (UK) 601
Bernau (GDR) 183
Berneval (Fra) 167
Bernhard Bästlein (GDR) 181
Berry (Fra) 173
Berry Head (UK) 586
Bertha (Cub) 114
Bervang (Indo) 235
Berwick (UK) 578
Beskytteren (Den) 116
Besnervny (USSR) 517
Bessledny (USSR) 516
Bessmenny (USSR) 517
Bessmertny (USSR) 517
Betano (Aust) 44
Betelgeuse (DR) 124
Bételgeuse (Fra) 168
Betty (UK) 599
Betwa (Ind) 226
Bévéziers (Fra) 150
Beyrouth (Leb) 318
Bezhitsa (USSR) 546
Bezukoriznenny (USSR) 517
Bezuprechniy (USSR) 517
Bhaktal (Ind) 229
Bholu (Pak) 369
Bi Bong (RoK) 314
Bibb (USA) 727
Bibury (UK) 600
Bickington (UK) 585
Bidassoa (Fra) 164
Biddle (USA) 660
Biduk (Indo) 238
Bielik (Pol) 590
Bigelow (USA) 674
Bihoro (Jap) 293
Bij (Bel) 52
Bikovac (Yug) 754
Bildeston (UK) 585
Bille (Den) 117
Billfish (USA) 633
Bimbia (Cmn) 69
Bimlipitan (Ind) 229
Binbasi Saadettin Gurcan (Tur) 479
Birinci Inönü (Tur) 472
Birmingham (UK) 574
Birmingham (USA) 631
Biscayne Bay (USA) 734
Bitt (USA) 735
Bitterfeld (GDR) 183
Bittersweet (USA) 731
Bizan (Jap) 295
Bizerte (Tun) 470
Bizon (Pol) 392
Black Rover (UK) 592
Blackan (Swe) 444
Blackberry (USA) 732
Blacthaw (USA) 731
Blackthorn (USA) 731
Blagorodny (USSR) 516
Blake (UK) 571
Blakely (USA) 680
Blakeney (UK) 600
Blanco Encalada (Chi) 89
Blandy (USA) 674
Blas de Lezo (Spn) 421
Blavet (Fra) 164
Blestyashchy (USSR) 516
Blidö (Swe) 443
Blink (Nor) 357
Blitvenica (Yug) 755
Blois van Treslong (Nld) 344
Blommendal (Nld) 347
Blue Ridge (USA) 685
Blue Rover (UK) 592
Blueback (USA) 638
Bluebell (USA) 732
Bluefish (USA) 633
Bluethroat (Can) 77
Bobr (Pol) 392
Bodry (USSR) 511
Boeo (Ita) 273
Bogalusa (USA) 712
Bogra (Ban) 48
Bohechio (DR) 125
Bojeador (Plp) 379
Bollard (USA) 735
Bolster (USA) 702
Boltenhagen (GDR) 183
Bombard (Aust) 41
Bon Homme Richard (USA) 653
Bonefish (USA) 638
Bonifaz (Spn) 425
Bonite (Fra) 178
Bonny (Nig) 353
Bontoc (Plp) 385
Bora (Tur) 475
Borac (Yug) 753
Borasco (GFR) 198
Bore (Swe) 445
Borgen (Nor) 359
Borgsund (Nor) 359
Boris Chilikin (USSR) 547
Boris Davidov (USSR) 538
Bormida (Ita) 272
Borodino (USSR) 532
Borovichi (USSR) 546
Bossington (UK) 585
Boston (USA) 631
Bouchard (Arg) 27
Boulanouar (Mrt) 330
Boulder (USA) 690
Bouleau (Fra) 178
Boussole (Fra) 169
Boutwell (USA) 726
Bouvet (Fra) 160
Bowditch (USA) 717
Bowen (USA) 680
Boxer (UK) 575
Boyaca (Col) 107
Boyyo (USSR) 514
Bradano (Ita) 272
Bradley (USA) 679
Brahmaputra (Ind) 226
Bramastra (Indo) 232
Bramble (USA) 731
Brani (Sin) 409
Brann (Nor) 357
Brännaren (Swe) 447
Bras (Nig) 354
Bras D'Or (Can) 77
Brask (Nor) 357
Brasse (GFR) 193
Braunschweig (GFR) 191
Bravy (USSR) 515
Bream (UK) 601
Brecon (UK) 584
Bredal (Den) 118
Breitling (GDR) 184
Bremerton (USA) 631
Brenda (UK) 599
Brenta (Ita) 272
Brereton (UK) 585
Breshtau (USSR) 550
Brewton (USA) 680
Breydel (Bel) 51
Bridget (UK) 599
Bridle (USA) 735
Brier (USA) 710
Brigadier M'Bonga Tounda (Cmn) 69
Brigant (GFR) 198
Brighton (UK) 578
Brillant (USSR) 521
Brilliant (UK) 575
Brinchang (Mly) 326
Brinton (UK) 585
Brisbane (Aust) 38
Briscoe (USA) 668
Bristol (UK) 572
Bristol Bay (USA) 734
Bristol County (USA) 690
Britannia (UK) 587
Brittanic (UK) 595
Briza (Pol) 594
Broadsword (UK) 575
Brodick (UK) 600
Bromo (Indo) 239
Bronington (UK) 585
Bronstein (USA) 682
Brooke (USA) 678
Brott (Nor) 357
Brule (Can) 79
Brumby (USA) 679
Brunei (Aust) 44
Bruno Kühn (GDR) 181
Bruno Racua (Bol) 53
Brunswick (USA) 706
Bryce Canyon (USA) 696
Buccaneer (Aust) 41
Buccoo Reef (TT) 468
Buchanan (USA) 673
Bucklesham (UK) 596
Buckthorn (USA) 732
Bude (UK) 583
Buena Piedra (Arg) 27
Bui Viet Thanh (Vtn) 748
Buk (GDR) 184
Buk Han (RoK) 314
Bukindon (Plp) 386
Bula (Indo) 238
Bulacan (Plp) 386
Bulgia (Nld) 345
Bulldog (UK) 590
Bulsar (Indo) 229
Bulwark (UK) 569
Buna (PNG) 370
Burak Reis (Tur) 472
Buran (USSR) 555
Burdjamhal (Ind) 237
Burlivy (USSR) 516
Burrard (Can) 79
Burton Island (USA) 725
Burudjulasad (Indo) 237
Burya (USSR) 521
Bushehr (Iran) 245
Bushnell (USA) 704
Bussemaker (Nld) 346
Butt (GFR) 193
Butte (USA) 697
Buttonwood (USA) 731
Bützow (GDR) 181
Buyskes (Nld) 347
Buyvol (USSR) 520
Byblos (Leb) 318
Byk (USSR) 520
Byvaly (USSR) 516

C

Cabacla (Brz) 59
Cabo Fradera (Spn) 426
Cabo Odger (Chi) 92
Cabo San Antonio (Arg) 29
Cabo San Gonzalo (Arg) 29
Cabo San Isidro (Arg) 29
Cabo San Pio (Arg) 29
Cabrakan (Gua) 214
Cacine (Por) 397
Cadarso (Spn) 425
Cagayan (Plp) 386
Caio Duilio (Ita) 260
Cairn (UK) 598
Calchaqui (Arg) 33
Calderas (DR) 123, 125
Caldy (UK) 601
Calibio (Col) 108
Calicuchima (Ecu) 129
California (USA) 658
Callenburgh (Nld) 344
Calliope (Fra) 167
Calmar (Fra) 175
Caloosahatchee (USA) 700
Camalote (Gua) 214
Camarines Norte (Plp) 387
Camarines Sur (Plp) 387
Cambiaso (DR) 123
Camboanga del Sur (Plp) 386
Cambaroa (Brz) 59
Camden (USA) 701
Camélia (Fra) 168
Camiguin (Plp) 385
Camilo (Cub) 114
Camocim (Brz) 61
Campbell (USA) 727
Campti (USA) 712
Camsell (Can) 82
Canakkale (Tur) 472
Canal Beagle (Arg) 31
Canberra (Aust) 40
Canberra (USA) 666
Candarli (Tur) 479
Candido De Lasala (Arg) 29
Candido Leguizamo (Col) 110
Candido Pérez (Spn) 425
Canisteo (USA) 700
Cannanore (Ind) 229
Canonchet (USA) 712
Canopo (Ita) 265
Canopus (Brz) 61
Canopus (Fra) 166
Canopus (USA) 703
Canterbury (NZ) 349
Cantho (Fra) 167
Caonabo (DR) 125
Caorle (Ita) 267
Capayan (Arg) 33
Cape (USA) 695
Cape Breton (Can) 76
Cape Carter (USA) 729
Cape Coral (USA) 729
Cape Corwin (USA) 729
Cape Cross (USA) 729
Cape Current (USA) 729
Cape Fairweather (USA) 729
Cape Fox (USA) 729
Cape George (USA) 729
Cape Harrison (Can) 85
Cape Hedge (USA) 729

NAMED SHIPS / INDEX 799

Cape Henlopen (USA) 729
Cape Horn (USA) 729
Cape Jellison (USA) 729
Cape Knox (USA) 729
Cape Morgan (USA) 729
Cape Newagen (USA) 729
Cape Rogers (Can) 85
Cape Romain (USA) 729
Cape Shoalwater (USA) 729
Cape Small (USA) 729
Cape Starr (USA) 729
Cape Strait (USA) 729
Cape Wash (USA) 729
Cape York (USA) 729
Capella (DR) 124
Capella (Fra) 168
Capella (Swe) 440
Capitan Alsina (DR) 124
Capitan Alvaro Ruiz (Col) 110
Capitan Beotegui (DR) 125
Capitan Cabral (Par) 371
Capitan Castro (Col) 110
Capitan Meza (Par) 371
Capitan Miranda (Uru) 738
Capitan Quiñones (Per) 375
Capitan R. D. Binney (Col) 108
Capitan Rigoberto Giraldo (Col) 110
Capitan W. Arvelo (DR) 125
Capiz (Plp) 384
Capodanno (USA) 680
Capotillo (DR) 125
Caprera (Ita) 273
Capricorne (Fra) 168
Capstan (USA) 735
Captor (Can) 77
Capucine (Fra) 177
Carabiniere (Ita) 264
Carabobo (Ven) 742
Caravelas (Brz) 61
Carbonara (Ita) 273
Cardenas (Per) 378
Cardiff (UK) 574
Caribe (Cub) 114
Caribe (Ven) 741
Carite (DR) 124
Carl Vinson (USA) 645
Carlo Bergamini (Ita) 264
Carlo Margottini (Ita) 264
Carlos Alban (Col) 108
Carlos E. Restrepo (Col) 108
Carlos Galindo (Col) 108
Carmelo (Uru) 738
Caron (USA) 668
Carp (UK) 601
Carpenter (USA) 676
Carsamba (Tur) 479
Cartagena (Col) 108
Cartmel (UK) 600
Casabianca (Fra) 160
Casamance (Sen) 406
Cascade (Fra) 178
Casimir Pulaski (USA) 627
Castagno (Ita) 268
Castelhanos (Brz) 61
Castilla (Per) 376
Castilla (Spn) 426
Castor (Chi) 94
Castor (GFR) 194
Castor (Spn) 429
Castor (Swe) 440
Castore (Ita) 265
Catahecassa (USA) 712
Cataluña (Spn) 423
Catanduanes (Plp) 385
Catapult (UK) 597
Catawba (USA) 722
Catenary (USA) 735
Caupolican (Chi) 94
Cavalla (USA) 633
Cavilla (Lbr) 319
Cawsand (UK) 600
Cayambe (Ecu) 129
Cayuga (USA) 690
Ceara (Brz) 55
Cebu (Plp) 384
Cedro (Ita) 268
Centaure (Fra) 177
Centauro (Brz) 63
Centauro (Ita) 265
Centennial (Can) 79
Céphée (Fra) 168
Cer (Yug) 755
Cerbe (Tur) 472
Ceres (Fra) 167
Cezayirli Gazi Hasan Paşa (Tur) 479
Chaco (Arg) 30
Chaguaramus (TT) 468
Chahbahar (Iran) 245
Chaleur (Can) 78
Chamak (Ind) 228
Chamois (Fra) 172
Champlain (Fra) 164
Chandhaburi (Tld) 463
Chandhara (Tld) 466
Chang (Tld) 465
Chang Chiang (CPR) 99
Chang Chun (CPR) 97
Chang Pai Shan (CPR) 103
Chang Pei (RoC) 459
Chang Pi (CPR) 99
Chapare (Bol) 53
Chapal (Ind) 228
Charkieh (Egy) 134
Charles F. Adams (USA) 673
Charles P. Cecil (USA) 675
Charleston (USA) 691
Charlotte (UK) 595
Charme (Fra) 178
Charn (Tld) 467
Charybdis (UK) 576
Chase (USA) 726
Chataigner (Fra) 178
Chatoyer (St V) 403
Chattahoochee (USA) 722
Chaudiere (Can) 74
Chauvenet (USA) 717
Chazhma (USSR) 544
Chegodega (USA) 712
Cheleken (USSR) 538
Chen Hai (RoC) 456
Chena (USA) 733
Chène (Fra) 178
Ch'eng Tu (CPR) 98
Chepanoc (USA) 712
Cheraw (USA) 712
Cheremshan (USSR) 549
Cherokee (USA) 734
Cherryleaf (UK) 593
Chesaning (USA) 712
Chetek (USA) 712
Chevreul (Fra) 172
Cheyenne (USA) 733
Chi Lin (CPR) 97
Chi Nam Po (Rok) 315
Chi Nan (CPR) 99
Chiang Sha (CPR) 99
Chiang Yang (RoC) 453
Chiburi (Jap) 287
Chicago (USA) 663
Chien Yang (Roc) 452
Chifuri (Jap) 294
Chignecto (Can) 78
Chihaya (Jap) 288
Chihuahua (Mex) 333
Chikugo (Jap) 283
Chilula (USA) 734
Chimbote (Per) 378
Chimère (Fra) 177
Chinaltenango (Gua) 214
Ch'ing Kang Shan (CPR) 103
Chinguetti (Mtn) 331
Chinook (USA) 735
Chioggia (Ita) 273
Chios (Gre) 210
Chippewa (USA) 733
Chiquillan (Arg) 33
Chiriguano (Arg) 33
Chitose (Jap) 283, 293
Chiu Hua (RoC) 458
Chiu Lien (RoC) 458
Chock (USA) 735
Chokeberry (USA) 732
Chömpff (Nld) 346
Chowl (Ire) 250
Chr Ju (RoK) 311
Christine (UK) 599
Chu Yung (RoC) 454
Chuang (Tld) 467
Chub (UK) 601
Chubut (Arg) 30
Chui (Ken) 303
Chula (Tld) 466
Chulupi (Arg) 33
Chulym (USSR) 551
Chumikan (USSR) 544
Chun Ji (RoK) 315
Chung Buk (RoK) 310
Chung Cheng (RoC) 457
Chung Chiang (RoC) 457
Chung Chie (RoC) 457
Chung Chien (RoC) 457
Chung Chih (RoC) 457
Chung Chuan (RoC) 457
Chung Fu (RoC) 457
Chung Hai (RoC) 457
Chung Hsing (RoC) 457
Chung Kuang (RoC) 457
Chung Lien (RoC) 457
Chung Ming (RoC) 457
Chung Mu (RoK) 310
Chung Nam (RoK) 311
Chung Pang (RoC) 457
Chung Shan (RoC) 454
Chung Sheng (RoC) 457
Chung Shu (RoC) 457
Chung Shun (RoC) 457
Chung Suo (RoC) 457
Chung Ting (RoC) 457
Chung Tung (CPR) 98
Chung Wan (RoC) 457
Chung Yeh (RoC) 457
Chung Yung (RoC) 457
Churchill (UK) 566
Churruca (Spn) 421
Cicala (UK) 599
Ciclope (Ita) 272
Cidade de Natal (Brz) 63
Cienfuegos (Cub) 114
Cigale (Fra) 175
Cigas (Gre) 213
Cigno (Ita) 265
Cigogne (Fra) 178
Cimarron (USA) 733
Cincinnati (USA) 631
Circe (Fra) 167
Circeo (Ita) 273
Cirujano Videla (Chi) 94
Cisne (Por) 397
Citrus (USA) 731
Ciudad de Quibdo (Col) 110
Clamp (USA) 702, 733
Clare (UK) 599
Clark (USA) 677
Claude V. Ricketts (USA) 673
Cleat (USA) 735
Clemenceau (Fra) 152
Cleopatra (UK) 576
Cleveland (USA) 688
Clio (Fra) 167
Clovelly (UK) 600
Clover (USA) 731
Clyde (UK) 583
Coahuila (Mex) 333
Coatopa (USA) 712
Coburg (GFR) 197
Cochali (USA) 712
Cochrane (Chi) 89
Cochrane (USA) 673
Cockhafer (UK) 599
Cocopa (USA) 705
Colac (Aust) 45
Colbert (Fra) 155
Colibri (Fra) 178
Colleen (Ire) 250
Collie (UK) 598
Colmar (Fra) 167
Colocolo (Chi) 94
Colonia (Uru) 737
Colosso (Ita) 272
Columbia (Can) 74
Columbia (USA) 720
Comanche (USA) 734
Comandante Arandia (Bol) 53
Comandante Hemmerdinger (Chi) 92
Comandante Hermenegildo Capelo (Por) 396
Comandante João Belo (Por) 396
Comandante Pedro Campbell (Uru) 737
Comandante Roberto Ivens (Por) 396
Comandante Sacadura Cabral (Por) 396
Comet (USA) 719
Commandant Blaison (Fra) 163
Commandant Bory (Fra) 161
Commandant Bourdais (Fra) 161
Commandant de Pimodan (Fra) 163
Commandant l'Herminier (Fra) 163
Commandant Rivière (Fra) 161
Commandante General Irigoyen (Arg) 28
Commander Marshall (Bar) 49
Como Manuel Azueta (Mex) 332
Comodoro Rivadavia (Arg) 31
Comodoro Somellera (Arg) 28
Compass Island (USA) 698
Comte de Grasse (USA) 668
Concord (USA) 697
Conde de Venadito (Spn) 427
Condell (Chi) 91
Condor (Ita) 266
Cone (USA) 675
Confiance (UK) 598
Confidence (USA) 728
Confident (UK) 598
Conifer (USA) 731
Connole (USA) 680
Conolly (USA) 668
Conqueror (UK) 566
Conquest (USA) 694
Conserver (USA) 702
Constant (USA) 694
Constellation (USA) 648
Constitucion (Ven) 743
Constituição (Brz) 57
Constitution (USA) 710
Contraestre Navarro (Per) 380
Conyngham (USA) 673
Cook (Aust) 42
Cook (USA) 680
Coolie (Fra) 178
Coontz (USA) 670
Copaonik (Yug) 755
Corail (Fra) 170
Coral Sea (USA) 652
Cordoba (Col) 107
Corgi (UK) 598
Cormier (Fra) 178
Cormoran (Arg) 31
Cormorant (Can) 78
Cornelis Drebbel (Nld) 348
Coronado (USA) 688
Coronel Bolognesi (Per) 375
Coronel Edvardo Avaroa (Bol) 53
Corrillo (Per) 381
Corry (USA) 675
Corsaro II (Ita) 271
Cortez (Chi) 94
Coshecton (USA) 712
Cosme Garcia (Spn) 419
Cosmos (USA) 732
Cotopaxi (Ecu) 129
Courageous (UK) 566
Courageous (USA) 728
Courageux (Fra) 178
Courland Bay (TT) 468
Cove (USA) 695
Coventry (UK) 574
Cowichan (Can) 78
Cree (Can) 79
Cree (USA) 705
Crame Jean (Sen) 407
Criccieth (UK) 600
Crichton (UK) 585
Cricket (UK) 599
Cricklade (UK) 600
Criquet (Fra) 175
Cristobal Colon (DR) 123
Crofton (UK) 585
Croix du Sud (Fra) 166
Cromarty (UK) 600
Crvena Zvijezda (Yug) 754
Crystal (UK) 595
Cuanza (Por) 397
Cuartel (Cub) 114
Cuauthemoc (Mex) 332
Cuenca (Ecu) 128
Cuitlahuac (Mex) 332
Cunene (Por) 397
Curlew (Aust) 41
Cushing (USA) 668
Cusseta (USA) 712
Custódio de Mello (Brz) 62
Cutlass (UK) 589
Cuxhaven (GFR) 193
Cuxton (UK) 585
Cuyahoga (USA) 730
Cybèle (Fra) 167
Cyclamen (Fra) 168
Cyclone (UK) 598
Cygne (Fra) 178
Cygnet (UK) 589
Czapla (Pol) 392

D

10 De Agosto (Ecu) 128
D'Entrecasteaux (Fra) 168
D'Estienne D'Orves (Fra) 163
D'Estrées (Fra) 160
D'Iberbille (Can) 82
Da Nang (USA) 686
Da Nang (Vtn) 748
Dacca (Pak) 368
Dace (USA) 634
Dachs (GFR) 193
Dae Gu (RoK) 311
Dafni (Gre) 211
Dahlgren (USA) 670
Dahlia (Fra) 177
Dahlonega (USA) 712
Daio (Jap) 292
Daisy (UK) 599
Daito (Jap) 294
Dakhla (Egy) 134
Daksaya (Sri) 433
Dale (USA) 661
Dallas (USA) 631, 726
Dalmatian (UK) 598
Dalnevostochny Komsomolets (USSR) 516
Dam Thoai (Vtn) 748
Damato (USA) 675
Dammam (SAr) 404
Damman (Swe) 444
Damuan (Bru) 64
Danae (UK) 576
Danbjørn (Den) 121
Dang Van Hoanh (Vtn) 748
Dang Yang (RoC) 452
Daniel Boone (USA) 627
Daniel Webster (USA) 627
Dankwart (GFR) 198
Dannebrog (Den) 122
Dao Thuc (Vtn) 748
Dao Van Dang (Vtn) 748
Daoud Ben Aicha (Mor) 338
Daphne (Den) 118
Daphné (Fra) 151
Daphne (UK) 599
Dar El Barka (Mtn) 330
Daring (Can) 85
Daring (Sin) 408
Darshak (Ind) 230
Dart (UK) 583
Darter (USA) 640
Daryush (Iran) 241
Dash (USA) 694
Dasser Ort (GDR) 184
Dastoor (Kwt) 317
Dat Al Diyari (Iraq) 248
Dat Assawari (Lby) 320
Datchet (UK) 600
Datu Kalantiaw (Plp) 383
Datu Marikudo (Plp) 383
Dauntless (Sin) 408
Dauntless (USA) 728
Dauphin (Fra) 151
Dauriya (USSR) 544
David R. Ray (USA) 668
Davidson (USA) 679, 735
Davis (USA) 674
De Brouwer (Bel) 51
De Grasse (Fra) 158
De Julio, 18 (Uru) 754
De Neys (SA) 415
De Noorde (SA) 415
De Ruyter (Nld) 342
De Steiguer (USA) 715
Decatur (USA) 672
Decisive (USA) 728
Dédalo (Spn) 420
Dee (UK) 589
Deepak (Ind) 231
Deerhound (UK) 598
Defensora (Brz) 57
Deflektor (USSR) 537
Deiatelny (USSR) 511
Deirdre (Ire) 250
Dekanawida (USA) 712
Dekaury (USA) 712
Dekanisora (USA) 712
Delfin (Arg) 30
Delfin (Nor) 358
Delfin (Pol) 392
Delfin (Por) 396
Delfin (Spn) 418
Delfinen (Den) 115
Delfinen (Swe) 438
Delfzijl (Nld) 345
Delhi (Ind) 225
Deliver (USA) 702
Delphin (GFR) 193
Delta (USA) 702
Demirhisar (Tur) 476
Demmin (GDR) 183
Democratia (Rom) 402
Dempo (Indo) 239
Deneb (GFR) 194
Denizkusu (Tur) 475
Denmead (UK) 600
Denver (USA) 688
Dependable (USA) 728
Derwent (Aust) 40
Derzky (USSR) 514
Des Moines (USA) 665
Descatusaria (Rom) 402
Descubierta (Spn) 422
Desh Deep (Ind) 231
Desna (USSR) 548
Desrobirea (Rom) 402
Dessau (GDR) 183
Detector (Can) 77, 86
Detector (USA) 694
Detroit (USA) 701
Détroyat (Fra) 163
Deutschland (GFR) 198
Deviator (USSR) 538
Devonshire (UK) 573
Dewarutji (Indo) 238
Dewey (USA) 670
Dexterous (UK) 598
Deyo (USA) 668
Dhafeer (UAE) 557
Dharini (Ind) 230
Dhofar (Omn) 363
Diaguita (Arg) 28
Diamantina (Aust) 42
Diamiette (Egy) 131
Diamont (GFR) 198
Diana (GFR) 194
Diana (Spn) 422
Diana III (Ven) 745
Diane (Fra) 151
Dido (UK) 576
Diego Silang (Plp) 383
Diela (Gha) 202
Dietrich (GFR) 198
Diez Canseco (Per) 381
Dikson (USSR) 544
Diligence (USA) 728
Diligente (Col) 108
Dinant (Bel) 51
Dinder (Sud) 435
Dinh Hai (Vtn) 747
Dintel (Nld) 348
Diombos (Sen) 407
Diomede (UK) 576

800 INDEX / NAMED SHIPS

Diopos Antoniou (Gre) 208
Diou Loulou (Sen) 407
Direct (USA) 694
Director (UK) 598
Discoverer (USA) 735
Discovery Bay (Jam) 274
Dittisham (UK) 586
Dives (Fra) 164
Dixie (USA) 697
Dixon (USA) 703
Diyakawa (Sri) 433
Djerv (Nor) 357
DM01-06 (Mex) 333
DM10-19 (Mex) 333
Dmitri Galkin (USSR) 533
Dmitri Laptev (USSR) 539
Dmitri Mendeleyev (USSR) 543
Dmitri Ovstyn (USSR) 539
Dmitri Pozharski (USSR) 509
Dmitri Sterlegov (USSR) 539
Dnestr (USSR) 547
Dnog (Brz) 63
Do Bong (RoK) 316
Doblestny (USSR) 511
Dobrinya Nikitch (USSR) 555
Dogan (Tur) 474
Dogwood (USA) 733
Dokkum (Nld) 346
Dolfijn (Nld) 341
Dolfin (Iran) 241
Dolphin (Gre) 208
Dolphin (USA) 641
Dolwen (UK) 599
Dom Aleixo (Por) 397, 398
Dom Jeremias (Por) 397
Dominant (USA) 694
Dommel (Nld) 348
Dompaire (Fra) 167
Dompfaff (GFR) 198
Don (USSR) 552
Donald B. Beary (USA) 680
Donatan (Tur) 480
Donau (GFR) 195
Donbass (USSR) 544
Donchedi (Tld) 465
Donetsky Shakhter (USSR) 529
Donetz (USSR) 547
Dora (USSR) 549
Dorang (Indo) 236
Dordrecht (Nld) 345
Dore (Indo) 236
Dorina (Nig) 353
Doris (Fra) 151
Doris (Gre) 211
Doris (UK) 599
Dornbusch (GDR) 184
Dornoch (UK) 600
Dorothy (UK) 599
Dorsch (GFR) 193
Dos de Mayo (Per) 374
Dostoyny (USSR) 511
Doudart de LaGrée (Fra) 161
Downes (USA) 680
Downham (UK) 596
Dr. Gondim (Brz) 63
Dr. Jamot (Cmn) 69
Drachten (Nld) 346
Draken (Swe) 438
Drakon (Gre) 208
Draug (Nor) 360
Dreadnought (UK) 566
Dreg IV (Nld) 348
Drejø (Den) 119
Drenthe (Nld) 343
Dreptatea (Rom) 402
Drogou (Fra) 163
Drossel (GFR) 198
Droxford (UK) 589
Drozny (USSR) 696
Drum (USA) 633
Drunen (Nld) 346
Druzhny (USSR) 511
Druzki (Bul) 65
Dryade (Fra) 176
Dryaden (Den) 118
Dshankoy (USSR) 544
DSRV 1 & 2 (USA) 642
Du Chayla (Fra) 160
Du Pont (USA) 674
Duana (USA) 727
Duarte (DR) 125
Dubna (USSR) 548
Dubuque (USA) 688
Duderstadt (GFR) 201
Duenas (Per) 381
Duero (Spn) 428
Dufferin (Can) 79
Duguay-Trouin (Fra) 158
Duk Bong (RoK) 314
Duk Su (RoK) 315
Duluth (USA) 688
Dumai (Indo) 238
Dumit (Can) 86
Dunagiri (Ind) 225
Dunay (USSR) 549
Duncan (Can) 79
Duncan (USA) 677
Dundalk (Can) 76
Dundurn (Can) 76
Dunster (UK) 600
Duperré (Fra) 159
Dupetit Thouars (Fra) 160
Dupleix (Fra) 156
Duque de Caxais (Brz) 59
Duquesne (Fra) 157
Durable (USA) 728
Durance (Fra) 170
Durango (Mex) 332
Durban (SA) 413
Düren (GFR) 193
Durgham (UAE) 557
Durham (USA) 691
Durmitov (Yug) 755
Dutton (USA) 717
Duyong (Mly) 327
Dvina (USSR) 535
Dwight D. Eisenhower (USA) 645
Dyess (USA) 675
Dzerzhinski (USSR) 509
Dzik (Pol) 392

E

E. Toll (USSR) 539
E. Panagopoulos (Gre) 209
Eagle (USA) 730
East London (SA) 413
Eastwood (Can) 79
Ebano (Ita) 268
Ebène (Fra) 178
Eberswalde (GDR) 182
Ebro (Spn) 428
Echo (UK) 590
Echols (USA) 709
Eckaloo (Can) 86
Edda (Swe) 448
Eddyfirth (UK) 593
Eden (UK) 583
Edenshaw (USA) 712
Edenton (USA) 706
Edera (Ita) 268
Edgar André (GDR) 181
Edith (UK) 599
Edson (USA) 674
Edward Cornwallis (Can) 84
Edward McDonnell (USA) 679
EF 3 (GFR) 200
Efficace (Fra) 178
Egeria (UK) 590
Egernsund (Den) 121
Eglantine (Fra) 168
Eider (Can) 86
Eider (Fra) 178
Eider (GFR) 199
Eifel (GFR) 196
Eilat (Isr) 252
Eilenburg (GDR) 183
Eisbar (GDR) 184
Eisbar (GFR) 199
Eisleben (GDR) 183
Eisvogel (GDR) 183
Eisvogel (GFR) 199
Ejura (Gha) 202
Ekholot (USSR) 537
Ekvator (USSR) 538
El Austral (Arg) 31
El Fasher (Sud) 434
El Fateh (Egy) 131
El Fayoud (Egy) 134
El Harris (Mor) 338
El Horriya (Egy) 135
El Jail (Mor) 338
El Khafir (Mor) 338
El Khartoum (Sud) 434
El Manufieh (Egy) 134
El Mikdam (Mor) 338
El Paso (USA) 691
El Sabiq (Mor) 337
El Tami (Iraq) 247
El Wacil (Mor) 338
Elan (Fra) 172
Elbe (GFR) 195
Elbjørn (Den) 121
Elderberry (USA) 732
Eléphant (Fra) 178
Eléphant (IC) 274
Elevthera (Bhm) 47
Elfe (Fra) 176
Elicura (Chi) 93
Elk River (USA) 709
Elkhound (UK) 598
Elkstone (UK) 600
Ellerbek (GFR) 199
Elliott (USA) 668
Elmer Montgomery (USA) 680
Elmina (Gha) 202
Elsenhüttenstadt (GDR) 182
Elsing (UK) 600
Elton (USSR) 538
Embrun (Fra) 178
Emden (GFR) 191
Emer (Ire) 250
Emerald Star (Mnt) 336
Emily Hobhouse (SA) 412
Emory S. Land (USA) 703
Empire Gull (UK) 582
Endeavour (Can) 77
Endeavour (Sin) 409
Endeavour (UK) 596
Endurance (Sin) 409
Endurance (UK) 587
Engadine (UK) 583
Engage (USA) 694
Engageante (Fra) 177
England (USA) 661
Engoulevent (Fra) 178
Enhance (USA) 694
Enissel (USSR) 552
Enø (Den) 120
Enrico Dandolo (Ita) 258
Enrico Toti (Ita) 258
Enrique Collazo (Cub) 113
Enseigne de Vaisseau Henry (F) 161
Enseigne de Vaisseau Jacoubet (Fra) 163
Enterprise (UK) 590
Enterprise (USA) 647
Enugu (Nig) 353
Enyimiri (Nig) 352
Eo (Spn) 429
Epe (Nig) 354
Epée (Fra) 165
Epworth (UK) 600
Equator (USSR) 546
Equeurdiville (Fra) 178
Erable (Fra) 178
Ercole (Ita) 272
Erdek (Tur) 481
Erezcano (Arg) 30
Eridan (Fra) 166
Erimo (Jap) 288, 292
Erin'mi (Nig) 352
Erkin (Tur) 480
Erle (Nor) 358
Ernest Lapointe (Can) 83
Ernest Thälmann (GDR) 180, 185
Ernest Grube (GDR) 181
Ernst Krenkel (USSR) 543
Ernst Schneller (GDR) 181, 185
Ersen Bayrak (Tur) 482
Ertugrul (Tur) 478
Eruslan (USSR) 552
Escambray (Cub) 114
Escape (USA) 702
Eschwege (GFR) 201
Eskimo (UK) 577
Esmeralda (Chi) 93
Esmeraldas (Ecu) 127
Espadon (Fra) 151
Espartana (Col) 108
Espérance (Fra) 169
Esper Ort (GDR) 184
Espirito Santo (Brz) 58
Essahir (Mor) 338
Essaouira (Mor) 338
Estafette (Fra) 169
Esteban Baca Calderon (Mex) 334
Esteban Jaramillo (Col) 108
Esteem (USA) 694
Etawina (USA) 712
Etchbarne (Brz) 63
Ethan Allen (USA) 629
Ethiopia (Eth) 136
Etoile Polaire (Fra) 166
Ettrick (UK) 600
Etzion (Isr) 253
Eufaula (USA) 712
Euro (Ita) 263
Euryalus (UK) 576
Everglades (USA) 696
Evergreen (USA) 731
Everingham (UK) 596
Evertsen (Nld) 344
Evros (Gre) 212
Excel (USA) 694
Excellence (Sin) 409
Exeter (UK) 574
Exploit (USA) 694
Extremadura (Spn) 423
Exultant (USA) 694

F

F. Bovesse (Bel) 51
F. Litke (USSR) 538
F. Rozman-Stane (Yug) 754
Faan Kong (RoC) 455
Fabrio Gallipoli (Ven) 745
Faedra (Gre) 211
Fafnir (GFR) 198
Faggio (Ita) 268
Fairfax County (USA) 690
Fairweather (USA) 735
Faisal (SAr) 404
Faithful (UK) 598
Falakhon (Iran) 243
Falcon (Ven) 742
Falcone (Ita) 266
Falk (Nor) 358
Falken (Swe) 447
Fällaren (Swe) 444
Falmouth (UK) 578
Falster (Den) 120
Fanantenana (Mad) 324
Fanning (USA) 680
Faramarz (Iran) 242
Fareed (Kwt) 318
Farfadet (Fra) 177
Farm, O/S (Nor) 360
Farø (Den) 119
Farol N. Santos (Brz) 63
Faroleiro Areas (Brz) 61
Faroleiro Nascimento (Brz) 61
Faroleiro Santana (Brz) 61
Faroleiro Wanderley (Brz) 63
Farragut (USA) 670
Farwa (Lby) 322
Fashoda (Sud) 435
Fateh-Al-Khair (Qat) 399
Fatsa (Tur) 478
Faune (Fra) 176
Fauvette (Fra) 178
Favignana (Ita) 273
Favourite (UK) 598
Fawn (UK) 590
Fearless (UK) 581
Fearless (USA) 694
Fecia di Cossato (Ita) 258
Federacion (Ven) 743
Fedor Litke (USSR) 555
Fedor Matisen (USSR) 539
Fedor Vidyaev (USSR) 533
Fehmarn (GFR) 199
Felchen (GFR) 193
Felicity (UK) 599
Felipé Larrazabal (Ven) 745
Felix Romero (Mex) 334
Felsted (UK) 600
Ferdia (Ire) 250
Fernando Gomez (Ven) 745
Fernando Lizardi (Mex) 334
Ferré (Per) 375
Ferrel (USA) 735
Fethiye (Tur) 478
Fidelity (USA) 694
Fiete Schulze (GDR) 181
Fife (UK) 573
Fife (USA) 668
Finback (USA) 633
Finike (Tur) 478
Fink (GFR) 198
Finlay (Cub) 114
Fintry (UK) 600
Finwhale (UK) 567
Fiona (UK) 599
Fir (USA) 731
Firebush (USA) 731
Firtina (Tur) 475
Fische (GFR) 194
Fiske (USA) 675
F. L. Jahn (GDR) 185
Flaggtief (GDR) 183
Flagstaff (USA) 729
Flamingo (?) (Bhm) 47
Flasher (USA) 634
Flensburg (GFR) 193
Fletcher (USA) 668
Fleur (SA) 414
Flibustier (GFR) 198
Flinders (Aust) 42
Flint (USA) 697
Flintham (UK) 586
Flintlock (UK) 597
Flora (Den) 117
Flore (Fra) 151
Florikan (USA) 705
Flundler (GFR) 193
Flying Fish (USA) 633
Fo Wu 5-6 (RoC) 459
Foça (Tur) 478
Foch (Fra) 152
Föhr (GFR) 199
Foinix (Gre) 208
Foka (Pol) 392
Fóla (Ire) 250
Forbin (Fra) 159
Forceful (UK) 598
Förde (GFR) 200
Fordham (UK) 601
Forelle (GFR) 193
Formosa (Arg) 30
Forrest Sherman (USA) 674
Forrestal (USA) 650
Forsythia (USA) 733
Fort Austin (UK) 593
Fort Charles (Jam) 274
Fort Fisher (USA) 689
Fort Grange (UK) 593
Fort McLeod (Can) 79
Fort Snelling (USA) 689
Fort Steele (Can) 78
Forte (Ita) 272
Forte de Coimbra (Brz) 59
Forth (UK) 583
Fortify (USA) 694
Fortuana (Arg) 33
Fotherby (UK) 600
Fou Chou (CPR) 104
Fourmi (Fra) 175
Fox (UK) 590
Fox (USA) 660
Foxglove (USA) 733
Foxhound (UK) 598
Francis Garnier (Fra) 164
Francis Hammond (USA) 680
Francis Marion (USA) 691
Francis Scott Key (USA) 627
Francisco Dagahoy (Plp) 383
Francisco de Gurruchaga (Arg) 28
Francisco J. Mujica (Mex) 334
Francisco Zarco (Mex) 333
Franco (Per) 380
Frank Cable (USA) 703
Frankenland (Ger) 182
Fraser (Can) 75
Frassino (Ita) 268
Frauenlob (GFR) 194
Freccia (Ita) 266
Frederick (USA) 690
Freedom (Sin) 408
Freesendorf (GDR) 184
Freibeuter (GFR) 198
Freiburg (GFR) 197
Frej (Swe) 445
Freja (Swe) 447
Fréne (Fra) 178
Freshburn (UK) 597
Freshlake (UK) 597
Freshspring (UK) 597
Fresia (Chi) 92
Fresno (USA) 690
Fret (Nld) 345
Frettchen (GFR) 193
Freundschaft (GDR) 185
Freya (GFR) 194
Freyr (Nld) 345
Friedrich Voge (GFR) 200
Friesland (Nld) 343
Fritham (UK) 596
Frithjof (GFR) 201
Fritz Behn (GDR) 181
Fritz Gast (GDR) 181
Fritz Hagale (Col) 108
Fritz Heckert (GDR) 181
Froxfield (UK) 600
Fryken (Swe) 448
Fu Chun (CDR) 97
Fu Kwo (RoC) 455
Fu Shan (RoC) 454
Fu Yang (RoC) 452
Fuh Chow (RoC) 455
Fuji (Jap) 290, 293
Fukue (Jap) 286
Fulbeck (UK) 600
Fulda (GFR) 193
Fulmar (UK) 601
Fulton (USA) 704
Fundy (Can) 78
Furman (USA) 718
Fusimi (Jap) 288
Fuyushio (Jap) 278
FW1-FW5 (GFR) 197
Fyen (Den) 120
Fylla (Den) 117

G

G. Truffaut (Bel) 51
Gaash (Isr) 252
Gabriela (Ven) 745
Gadebusch (GDR) 181
Gaggia (Ita) 268
Gagliardo (Ita) 272
Gajabahu (Sri) 432
Gal (Isr) 251
Galatea (UK) 576
Galatée (Fra) 151
Galeb (Yug) 756
Galicia (Spn) 427
Gallant (USA) 694
Gallantin (USA) 726
Galten (Swe) 444
Galvez (Chi) 94
Galvez (Per) 381
Gama (Pak) 369
Gambero (Ita) 269
Ganadoga (USA) 712
Ganda (Iraq) 247

Gangut (USSR) 532
Ganas (Mly) 325
Ganges (Can) 79
Gangut (USSR) 532
Ganyang (Mly) 325
Garcia (USA) 679
Garcia D'Avila (Brz) 59
Gardénia (Fra) 176
Gardouneh (Iran) 243
Garganey (UK) 594
Garian (Lby) 322
Garigliano (Fra) 167
Garonne (Fra) 171
Gasconade (USA) 733
Gässten (Swe) 444
Gastao Moutinho (Brz) 62
Gästrikland (Swe) 438
Gatineau (Can) 75
Gato (USA) 634
Gauss (GFR) 201
Gave (Fra) 178
Gavilan I, II (Spn) 432
Gavinton (UK) 585
Gaviota (Spn) 426
Gavril Sarychev (USSR) 535
Gayret (Tur) 473
Gayundah (Aust) 45
Gazal (Tur) 482
Gazelle (Fra) 172
Gazelle (GFR) 194
GB 21, GB 22, GB 23, GB 24 (Eth) 137
Gear (USA) 702
Geba (Por) 397
Gefion (GFR) 194
Geir (Nor) 358
Geiserich (GFR) 198
Gelderland (Nld) 348
Gelderland (SA) 413
Gelinotte (Fra) 178
Gelso (Ita) 268
Gelsomino (Ita) 268
Gemert (Nld) 346
Gemma (GFR) 194
Gen J. T. Cabanas (Hon) 217
General Belgrano (Arg) 26
General H. H. Arnold (USA) 714
General Hoyt S. Vandenberg (USA) 714
General José Felix Ribas (Ven) 745
General José Trinidad Moran (Ven) 743
General Juan José Flores (Ven) 743
General Pereira D'Eca (Por) 397
General San Martin (Arg) 32
General Vasques Cobo (Col) 108
General Vincente Guerro (Mex) 335
Genil (Spn) 428
Genkai (Jap) 294
Genrik Gasanov (USSR) 547
Genthin (GDR) 183
George Bancroft (USA) 627
George C. Marshall (USA) 627
George Ferguson (Bar) 49
George Philip (USA) 677
George Washington (USA) 630
George Washington Carver (USA) 627
George Leygues (Fra) 156
Georgi Ushakov (USSR) 543
Georgina (UK) 599
Georgy Sedov (USSR) 542
Gepard (GFR) 193
Gepard (USSR) 520
Géranium (Fra) 166
Gerda (Swe) 448
Gerhard Prenzier (GDR) 183
Gernot (GFR) 198
Getulio Lima (Brz) 63
Geuse (GFR) 198
Geyser (Fra) 178
Ghadunfar (UAE) 557
Ghanadhah (UAE) 557
Gharbia (Egy) 134
Gharial (Ind) 229
Ghazi (Pak) 365
Gheppio (Ita) 266
Ghorpad (Ind) 229
Giaggiolo (Ita) 268
Gianfranco Gazzana Priariggia (Ita) 259
Gidrofon (USSR) 537
Gidrograf (USSR) 536
Giena (USSR) 520
Giethoorn (Nld) 346
Gigrometr (USSR) 538
Gihad (Sud) 435
Gilgit (Pak) 367
Gillöga (Swe) 444
Ginga (Jap) 299
Girelle (Fra) 177
Gireogi (RoK) 313
Girne (Tur) 475
Girorulevoy (USSR) 536
Giselher (GFR) 198
Giuseppe Garibaldi (Ita) 259
Giza (Egy) 134
Glacier (USA) 724
Gladan (Swe) 447
Glaive (Fra) 165
Glamorgan (UK) 573
Glasgow (UK) 574
Glasserton (UK) 585
Glavkos (Gre) 204
Glen (UK) 583
Glenard P. Lipscombe (USA) 632
Glenbrook (Can) 79
Glencove (UK) 600
Glendale (Can) 79
Glendyne (Can) 79
Glenevis (Can) 79
Glenside (Can) 79
Glicine (Ita) 268
Glimt (Nor) 357
Glomma (Nor) 359
Gloria (Col) 110
Glover (USA) 699
Glubomer (USSR) 538
Glücksburg (GFR) 197
Glycine (Fra) 168
Gnat (UK) 599
Gnevny (USSR) 514
Gnist (Nor) 357
Godavari (Ind) 227
Godetia (Bel) 52
Gödicke (GFR) 198
Goeland (Fra) 178
Go-Go (Jap) 290
Goiza (Brz) 55
Gölcük (Tur) 480
Gold Rover (UK) 592
Goldeneye (UK) 594
Goldsborough (USA) 673
Golfo de Cariaco (Ven) 745
Goliath (Fra) 178
Golwitz (GDR) 184
Good Hope (SA) 413
Goosander (UK) 594
Gorch Fock (GFR) 198
Gordy (USSR) 514
Gorgona (Col) 109
Gorizont (USSR) 538, 546
Gorz (Iran) 243
Göttingen (GFR) 193
Goyena (Arg) 31
Graal-Müritz (GDR) 183
Graça Aranha (Brz) 61
Gradac (Yug) 755
Grado (Ita) 267
Gradus (USSR) 538
Graemsay (UK) 601
Gráinne (Ire) 250
Granaten (Swe) 448
Granchio (Ita) 269
Grand Canyon (USA) 701
Grand Duc (Fra) 178
Granma (Cub) 114
Grasmere (UK) 600
Grass Ort (GDR) 184
Gravina (Spn) 421
Gray (USA) 680
Grayback (USA) 639
Grayling (USA) 633
Grecale (Ita) 263
Green Rover (UK) 592
Greenling (USA) 634
Greenville Victory (USA) 719
Gregorio de Pilar (Plp) 383
Gregorio Luperon (DR) 122
Greifswald (GDR) 183
Gremyashchyi (USSR) 514
Grevesmühlen (GDR) 181
Grey Rover (UK) 592
Gribb (Nor) 358
Gridley (USA) 661
Griep (GFR) 200
Griffon (Can) 82
Griffon (Fra) 174
Grifone (Ita) 266
Grillon (Fra) 175
Grim (Swe) 445
Grimma (GDR) 182
Grimmen (GDR) 182
Gripen (Swe) 438
Gromova (USSR) 736
Groningen (Nld) 343
Grønsund (Den) 121
Groton (USA) 631
Growler (USA) 639
Grozny (USSR) 508
Grumete (Brz) 63
Grunwald (Pol) 393
Gryf (Pol) 393
Grypskerk (Nld) 348
Guacanagarix (DR) 125
Guacolda (Chi) 92
Guairia (Brz) 63
Guadalcanal (USA) 687
Guadalete (Spn) 428
Guadalhorce (Spn) 429
Guadalmedina (Spn) 428
Guadalquivir (Spn) 428
Guadiana (Spn) 428
Guam (USA) 687
Guanabacoa (Cub) 114
Guanabara (Brz) 55
Guarani (Brz) 63
Guarani (Par) 372
Guarapari (Brz) 59
Guardfish (USA) 634
Guardian Rios (Per) 380
Guawidjaja (Indo) 235
Guayaquil (Ecu) 128
Guayas (Ecu) 129
Guaycuru (Arg) 33
Guben (GDR) 183
Gudgeon (USA) 640
Gueber (Isr) 253
Guépratte (Fra) 160
Guernsey (UK) 588
Guglielmo Marconi (Ita) 258
Guillermo Prieto (Mex) 333
Guise (Per) 376
Guitarro (USA) 633
Guldar (Ind) 229
Guldborgsund (Den) 121
Gunnar (GFR) 198
Gunter (GFR) 198
Gurkha (UK) 577
Gurnard (USA) 633
Gustaf af Klint (Swe) 447
Gustave Zedé (Fra) 174
Gutierriez Zamora (Mex) 333
Guyana (Ven) 744
Gwendoline (UK) 599
Gymnote (Fra) 150
Gyre (USA) 715

H

H. C. Oersted (GFR) 200
H. H. Hess (USA) 716
H. U. Sverdrup (Nor) 360
Ha Hoi (Vtn) 746
Haarlem (Nld) 345
Hachi-Go (Jap) 287
Hachijo (Jap) 294
Hackensack (USA) 712
Hadda (Nld) 345
Haddo (USA) 634
Haddock (USA) 634
Hadejia (Nig) 353
Hadubrand (GFR) 198
Haerlem (SA) 413
Hagen (GFR) 198
Hägern (Swe) 447
Hai (Nor) 358
Hai Chiu (CPR) 104
Hai Pao (RoC) 451
Hai Sheng (CPR) 103
Hai Shih (RoC) 451
Hai Yu (CPR) 104
Hai Yun (CPR) 104
Haifa (Isr) 252
Hait'se (CPR) 104
Häjen (Swe) 438
Haleakala (USA) 697
Halibut (USA) 636
Halifax (UK) 602
Halland (Swe) 439
Halmstad (Swe) 446
Halsey (USA) 661
Hälsingborg (Swe) 439
Hälsingland (Swe) 438
Hamagiri (Jap) 296
Hamana (Jap) 289
Hamayu (Jap) 297
Hamayuki (Jap) 296
Hamazuki (Jap) 296
Hamble (UK) 583
Hambledon (UK) 600
Hamburg (GFR) 190
Hameenma (Fin) 138
Hamilton (USA) 726
Hammer (Den) 117
Hammer (USA) 733
Hammerhead (USA) 633
Hamner (USA) 675
Han Giang (Vtn) 748
Han Jih (RoC) 459
Han Yang (RoC) 452
Hanayuki (Jap) 297
Hang Tuah (Mly) 325
Hangor (Pak) 365
Hanhak Sattru (Tld) 462
Hanit (Isr) 252
Hannibal (Tun) 469
Hanö (Swe) 443
Hans Bürkner (GFR) 192
Hans Coppi (GDR) 181
Hansa (GFR) 195
Hansaya (Sri) 433
Hanse (GFR) 199
Harambee (Ken) 303
Haras 1-4 (Omn) 362
Hardy (UK) 580
Harimau (Indo) 235
Hario (Jap) 287
Harischi (Iran) 245
Harkness (USA) 717
Harlan County (USA) 690
Harlech (UK) 600
Harlingen (Nld) 345
Harold E. Holt (USA) 680
Harold J. Ellison (USA) 675
Harriet Lane (USA) 728
Harry E. Yarnell (USA) 661
Harry W. Hill (USA) 668
Hartnaut (GFR) 198
Harukaze (Jap) 283
Haruna (Jap) 279
Harusame (Jap) 282
Harushio (Jap) 278
Haruzuki (Jap) 296
Harvison (Can) 79
Harz (GFR) 196
Hashira (Jap) 286
Hassayampa (USA) 700
Hasselt (Bel) 51
Hasslö (Swe) 443
Hatagumo (Jap) 296
Hatchet (USA) 733
Hathi (Ind) 231
Hatsukari (Jap) 284
Hau Giang (Vtn) 748
Hauk (Nor) 358
Haversham (UK) 596
Havfruen (Den) 118
Havmanden (Den) 118
Hawea (NZ) 350
Hawkbill (USA) 633
Hawkins (USA) 675
Hawser (USA) 735
Hay Tan (RoC) 459
Hayabusa (Jap) 290
Hayagiri (Jap) 296
Hayanami (Jap) 296
Hayannis (USA) 712
Hayase (Jap) 286
Hayashio (Jap) 278
Hayes (USA) 715
Hazran Nauni (Iraq) 247
Hazza (UAE) 557
Headcorn (UK) 600
Hebe (Swe) 448
Hebe (UK) 594
Hecate (UK) 590
Heck (USA) 735
Hecla (UK) 590
Hector (Swe) 448
Hector (USA) 702
Hefring (Nld) 345
Heimdal, O/S (Nor) 360
Heimdal (Swe) 445
Heinrich Dorrenbach (GDR) 181
Heinz Kapelle (GDR) 181
Heinz Roggenkamp (GFR) 200
Heinz Wilkowski (GDR) 183
Heist (Bel) 52
Heiyo (Jap) 298
Hekura (Jap) 294
Helen (StL) 403
Helen (UK) 599
Helgoland (GFR) 199
Hellevotsluis (Nld) 345
Henderson (USA) 675
Hengam (Iran) 245
Heng Yang (RoC) 453
Henri Poincaré (Fra) 173
Henrik (Swe) 448
Henry B. Wilson (USA) 673
Henry Clay (USA) 627
Henry L. Stimson (USA) 627
Hepburn (USA) 680
Hephestos (Gre) 212
Heppens (GFR) 199
Hera (Gre) 213
Hera (Swe) 448
Herald (UK) 590
Hercule (Fra) 178
Hercules (Arg) 26
Hercules (DR) 125
Hercules (Pol) 394
Hercules (Swe) 448
Hercules (USA) 682
Herev (Isr) 252
Heriberto Jara Corona (Mex) 334
Herkules (GFR) 194
Herluf Trolle (Den) 116
Hermelijn (Nld) 345
Hermelin (GFR) 193
Hermenegildo Galena (Mex) 333
Hermes (GFR) 191
Hermes (Swe) 448
Hermes (UK) 569
Hermione (UK) 576
Hermitage (USA) 689
Hernando Gutierrez (Col) 110
Heroj (Yug) 752
Héron (Fra) 178
Heros (Swe) 448
Herstal (Bel) 51
Hertha (GFR) 194
Hesperos (Gre) 208
Hessen (GFR) 190
Hétre (Fra) 178
Hetz (Isr) 252
Hévéa (Fra) 178
Hever (UK) 600
Hewitt (USA) 668
Hiamonee (USA) 712
Hiawatha (USA) 712
Hibiscus (Fra) 177
Hidaka (Jap) 295
Hiei (Jap) 279
Hiev (GFR) 200
Higbee (USA) 675
High Point (USA) 683
Hilderbrand (GFR) 198
Himgiri (Ind) 225
Hippopotame (Fra) 178
Hirado (Jap) 294
Hiryu (Jap) 297
Hisingen (Swe) 444
Hitchiti (USA) 705
Hitteen (SAr) 404
Hiu (Indo) 234
Hiyama (Jap) 295
Hiyodori (Jap) 284
Hjortø (Den) 120
Ho Chang (RoC) 457
Ho Chao (RoC) 457
Ho Cheng (RoC) 457
Ho Chi (RoC) 457
Ho Chie (RoC) 457
Ho Chien (RoC) 457
Ho Chuan (RoC) 457
Ho Chun (RoC) 457
Ho Chung (RoC) 457
Ho Dang (Vtn) 748
Ho Deng (RoC) 457
Ho Duy (Vtn) 748
Ho Feng (RoC) 457
Ho Hoei (RoC) 457
Ho Meng (RoC) 457
Ho Mou (RoC) 457
Ho Seng (RoC) 457
Ho Shan (RoC) 457
Ho Shou (RoC) 457
Ho Shun (RoC) 457
Ho Teng (RoC) 457
Ho Tsung (RoC) 457
Ho Yao (RoC) 457
Ho Yung (RoC) 457
Hoa Lu (Vtn) 747
Hoang Sa (Vtn) 747
Hobart (Aust) 38
Hodgeston (UK) 585
Hoel (USA) 673
Hoga (USA) 712
Hoist (USA) 702
Hokuto (Jap) 299
Holland (USA) 703
Holland Bay (Jam) 274
Hollister (USA) 675
Hollyhock (USA) 731
Holmwood (UK) 600
Holnis (GFR) 195
Hommel (Bel) 52
Homs (Lby) 322
Honorio Barreto (Por) 397
Hoogeveen (Nld) 346
Hoogezand (Nld) 346
Horand (GFR) 198
Hormuz (Iran) 246
Hornbeam (USA) 731
Horne (USA) 660
Hornet (USA) 654
Horning (UK) 600
Horobutsu (Jap) 293
Horonai (Jap) 293
Horria (Tun) 470
Horriya (Sud) 435
Horten (Nor) 360
Hortensia (Fra) 177
Hotaka (Jap) 288
Houma (USA) 712
Houtepen (Nld) 346
Howard W. Gilmore (USA) 704
Howar (Bhr) 47
Howitzer (UK) 597
Hoyerswerda (GDR) 182
Hsi An (CPR) 99
Hsiang Yang (RoC) 453
Hsiang Yang Hung San (CPR) 103
Hsiang Yang Hung Wu (CPR) 103
Hsin Lung (RoC) 459
Hsueh Chih (RoC) 455
Hua Shan (RoC) 454
Hua Yang (RoC) 453
Huancavilca (Ecu) 126
Huarpe (Arg) 33
Huascar (Chi) 94
Hubberston (UK) 585
Hudson (USA) 720, 733
Huei Yang (RoC) 453
Hugin (Swe) 440
Hui An (CPR) 99
Huitfelde (Den) 117
Hull (USA) 674
Hulubalang (Mly) 327
Humaita (Brz) 55

802 INDEX / NAMED SHIPS

Humaita (Par) 371
Humberto Cortes (Col) 108
Humming Bird II (TT) 468
Hunahpu (Gua) 214
Hunding (GFR) 198
Hung Hsing (RoC) 459
Hunley (USA) 703
Huracan (Uru) 739
Huron (Can) 73
Husky (UK) 598
Hussein Abdallah (Jor) 301
Huy (Bel) 51
Huynh Bo (Vtn) 748
Huynh Van Cu (Vtn) 748
Huynh Van Ngan (Vtn) 748
Hval (Nor) 358
Hvass (Nor) 357
Hvidbjørnen (Den) 117
Hwa Chon (RoK) 316
Hwa San (RoK) 314
Hwar (Qat) 399
Hyäne (GFR) 193
Hyatt (Chi) 88
Hydra (Nld) 348
Hydra (UK) 590
Hydrograf (Pol) 394
Hydrograph (GDR) 183
Hydrograph Pahlavi (Iran) 246
Hydrograph Shahpour (Iran) 246
Hyperion (Gre) 212
Hyperion (UK) 602

I

I. Meng Shan (CPR) 103
I. Theophilopoulos
Karavoyiannos (Gre) 213
Ibare (Bol) 53
Ibis (Aust) 41
Ibn Al Hadrami (Lby) 323
Ibn Haritha (Lby) 322
Ibn Ouf (Lby) 322
Ibn Said (Iraq) 248
Ibuki (Jap) 287, 295
Icel (Tur) 474
Ichi-Go (Jap) 290
Ichilo (Bol) 53
Idini (Mrt) 330
Ierax (Gre) 207
Ifugao (Plp) 389
Iggö (Swe) 443
Ignacio Altamirano (Mex) 333
Ignacio de la Llave (Mex) 333
Ignacio L. Vallarta (Mex) 333
Ignacio Lopez Rayon (Mex) 334
Ignacio Mariscal (Mex) 334
Ignacio Ramirez (Mex) 334
Ignacio Zaragoza (Mex) 334
Igorot (Plp) 389
Iguassu (Brz) 63
Iguatemi (Brz) 59
Ijssel (Nld) 348
Ikaria (Gre) 210
Iki (Jap) 294
Ikinci Inönü (Tur) 472
Ilchester (UK) 600
Ile d'Oléron (Fra) 173
Ilia Muromets (USSR) 555
Iliki (Gre) 213
Illern (Swe) 438
Illusive (USA) 674
Illustrious (UK) 569
Ilmen (USSR) 536
Ilo (Per) 379
Ilocos Norte (Plp) 386
Iloilo (Plp) 384
Ilongot (Plp) 389
Im Raq Ni (Mtn) 331
Iman (USSR) 549
Iman Bondjol (Indo) 234
Imeni XXV Syezda KPSS
(USSR) 555
Impavido (Ita) 262
Imperial Marinheiro (Brz) 59
Impervious (USA) 694
Impetuoso (Ita) 263
Implicit (USA) 694
In Cheon (RoK) 311
In Chon (RoK) 315
Inchon (USA) 687
Indépendance (Cmn) 69
Independence (Sin) 408
Independence (USA) 650
Independencia (Bol) 53
Independencia (Brz) 57
Indépendencia (DR) 123
Independencia (Per) 379
Independencia (Ven) 743
Indianapolis (USA) 631
Indiga (USSR) 549
Indomable (Col) 106
Indomita (Arg) 30
Indomito (Ita) 263
Indra (USA) 702
Inebolu (Tur) 480
Infanta Cristina (Spn) 422
Infanta Elena (Spn) 422
Inflict (USA) 694
Ingeniero Mery (Chi) 94
Inger (GFR) 193
Ingersoll (USA) 668
Ingham (USA) 727
Ingolf (Den) 117
Ingul (USSR) 547
Inlay (Bur) 68
Inma (Bur) 68
Inouse (Gre) 210
Insar (USSR) 551
Instow (UK) 600
Intisar (Kwt) 317
Intishat (Egy) 135
Intrepid (Sin) 409
Intrepid (UK) 581
Intrepid (USA) 653
Intrepida (Arg) 30
Intrepido (Col) 106
Intrepido (Ita) 262
Intrépido (Spn) 423
Invincible (UK) 570
Inya (Bur) 68
Ios (Gre) 213
Iou (Jap) 286
Iowa (USA) 655
Ipiranga (Brz) 59
Ipoploiarhos Arliotis (Gre) 207
Ipoploiarhos Batsis (Gre) 207
Ipopliarkhos Daniolos (Gre) 210
Ipopliarkhos Grigoropoulos
(Gre) 210
Ipoploiarhos Konidis (Gre) 207
Ipopliarhos Kristalidis (Gre) 210
Ipopliarkhos Mikonios (Gre) 207
Ipopliarkhos Roussen (Gre) 210
Ipopliarkhos Tournas (Gre) 210
Ipoploiarhos Troupakis (Gre) 207
Iquique (Per) 374
Irbit (USSR) 549
Irene (UK) 599
Iris (USA) 731
Irkut (USSR) 548
Ironbridge (UK) 600
Ironwood (USA) 731
Iroquis (Can) 73
Irtysh (USSR) 549
Isaac Peral (Spn) 419
Isaac Sweers (Nld) 344
Isabel (UK) 599
Isabela (DR) 125
Isabela (Plp) 387
Isar (GFR) 195
Isbjørn (Den) 121
Isenami (Jap) 296
Isère (Fra) 170
Iseyuki (Jap) 296
Ishikari (Jap) 293
Ishim (USSR) 551
Isis (UK) 586
Iskara (Pol) 393
Iskenderun (Tur) 474
Isku (Fin) 139
Isla de la Plata (Ecu) 129
Isla Puna (Ecu) 129
Islas de Noronha (Brz) 63
Islas Orcadas (Arg) 31
Islay (Per) 373
Isonami (Jap) 282
Isoshio (Jap) 278
Isoyuki (Jap) 297
Isozuki (Jap) 296
Issole (Fra) 165
Istanbul (Tur) 474
Istiklal (Tur) 470
Istiqlal (Sud) 435
Isuzu (Jap) 284, 293
Itacurussa (Brz) 61
Itapura (Brz) 63
Itara (USA) 712
Itati (Arg) 33
Itenez (Bol) 53
Itsuki (Jap) 290
Iuka (USA) 712
Ivan (Yug) 754
Ivan Bubnov (USSR) 547
Ivan Koyshkin (USSR) 532
Ivan Kruzenstern (USSR) 541, 555
Ivan Kucherenko (USSR) 532
Ivan Moskvitin (USSR) 555
Ivan Susanin (USSR) 555
Ivan Vadremeev (USSR) 532
Iveston (UK) 585
Iwai (Jap) 286
Iwase (Jap) 283
Iwo Jima (USA) 687
Ixinche (Gua) 214
Ixworth (UK) 600
Izhora (USSR) 548
Izmeritel (USSR) 537
Izmir (Tur) 474
Izmit (Tur) 474
Izu (Jap) 291
Izumrud (USSR) 543
Izvalta (USSR) 537

J

J. E. Bernier (Can) 82
J. E. Van Haverbeke (Bel) 51
J. Mazar (Yug) 754
J. T. C. Ramsay (Bar) 49
Jacinthe (Fra) 168
Jacinto Candido (Por) 397
Jack (USA) 634
Jackdaw (Ire) 250
Jackson (UK) 601
Jacksonville (USA) 631
Jade (GFR) 200
Jadran (Yug) 757
Jadranka (Yug) 757
Jägaren (Swe) 440
Jaguar (Guy) 216
Jaguar (Nld) 345
Jahangir (Pak) 366
Jalanidhi (Indo) 237
Jambeli (Ecu) 128
James K. Polk (USA) 627
James M. Gilliss (USA) 715
James Madison (USA) 627
James Monroe (USA) 627
Jamhuri (Ken) 303
Jamuna (Ind) 230
Jan Van Brakel (Nld) 344
Jan Van Riebeeck (SA) 412
Jannada (Iraq) 248
Janow (Pol) 393
Jaquel El Bahr (Tun) 470
Jarvis (USA) 726
Jaskolka (Pol) 392
Jasmin (Fra) 166
Jason (USA) 702
Jaspis (GFR) 198
Jastrab (Pol) 392
Javier Quiroga (Spn) 425
Jaya Wijaya (Indo) 238
Jebba (Nig) 353
Jean de Vienne (Fra) 156
Jeanne d'Arc (Fra) 154
Jebel Antar (Alg) 22
Jebel Honda (Alg) 22
Jemchug (USSR) 521
Jeong Buk (RoK) 310
Jerong (Mly) 326
Jersey (UK) 588
Jervis Bay (Aust) 44
Jesse L. Brown (USA) 680
Jesus G. Ortega (Mex) 333
Jibla (YPDR) 751
Jida (Bhr) 47
Jo (Nor) 358
Joan (UK) 599
Joao Coutinho (Por) 397
Joe Mann (Aust) 45
Johan Mansson (Swe) 447
Johanna Van Der Merwe (SA) 412
Johannesburg (SA) 413
John A. MacDonald (Can) 81
John Adams (Ire) 250
John Adams (USA) 627
John Cabot (Can) 81
John C. Calhoun (USA) 627
John F. Kennedy (USA) 648
John Hancock (USA) 668
John King (USA) 673
John Marshall (USA) 629
John Paul Jones (USA) 672
John R. Craig (USA) 675
John Rodgers (USA) 668
John S. McCain (USA) 671
John Young (USA) 668
Johnston (USA) 675
Johore Bahru (Mly) 328
Jonas Ingram (USA) 674
Jonnam (RoK) 311
Jonny Scheer (GDR) 185
Jonquille (Fra) 166
Jordan (GDR) 183
Jorge Juan (Spn) 421
Jorge Soto del Corval (Col) 108
Jos Sudarso (Indo) 233
Jose Maria del Castillo
Velasco (Mex) 334
Jose Maria Izazagu (Mex) 334
Jose Maria Maja (Mex) 334
Jose Natividad Macias (Mex) 334
Josef Schares (GDR) 181
Joseph Hewes (USA) 680
Joseph Strauss (USA) 673
Josephus Daniels (USA) 660
Joshan (Iran) 243
Jouett (USA) 660
Joumhouria (Tun) 470
Joves Fiallo (Col) 110
Joyce (UK) 599
Juan A. Lavalleja (Uru) 739
Juan Aldama (Mex) 333
Juan Alejandro Acosta (DR) 123
Juan Bautista Morales (Mex) 334
Juan Lucio (Col) 108
Juan N. Alvarez (Mex) 333
Juan Sebastian de Elcano (Spn) 430
Juana (Arg) 33
Jucar (Spn) 428
Juist (GFR) 199
Jules Verne (Fra) 172
Julius A. Furer (USA) 678
Junak (Yug) 752
Junaluska (USA) 712
Juneau (USA) 688
Juno (UK) 576
Junon (Fra) 151
Jupiter (Bul) 66
Jupiter (Pan) 369
Jupiter (UK) 576
Jupiter (GFR) 194
Jupiter (Sin) 408
Jura (UK) 601
Jurel (DR) 124
Justice (Sin) 408
Jyuu-Go (Jap) 287
Jyuu-Ichi-Go (Jap) 287
Jyuu-Ni-Go (Jap) 287

K

K. Rojc (Yug) 754
KR Tønder (Nor) 361
Ka Tok (RoK) 315
Kaakkuri (Fin) 143
Kaapstad (SA) 413
Kabashima (Jap) 293
Kadet (Pol) 394
Kadmath (Ind) 226
Kae Bong (RoK) 314
Kahlid (SAr) 404
Kahnamuie (Iran) 243
Kai Feng (CPR) 104
Kai Yang (RoC) 452
Kaibilbalam (Gua) 214
Kaibokan (CPR) 104
Kaio (Jap) 299
Kairyu (Jap) 297
Kaivan (Iran) 243
Kaiyo (Jap) 299
Kakalang (Indo) 234
Kakap (Indo) 234
Kakinada (Ind) 229
Kala 1-6 (Fin) 142
Kala Hitam (Indo) 236
Kalamazoo (USA) 701
Kalamisani (Indo) 235
Kalanada (Indo) 235
Kalar (USSR) 547
Kalat (Pak) 367
Kalinga (Plp) 389
Kalispell (USA) 712
Kalkan (Tur) 475
Kalliroe (Gre) 213
Kallisto (USSR) 544
Kalmar (Swe) 439
Kalnik (Yug) 755
Kalvari (Ind) 224
Kamagong (Plp) 387
Kaman (Iran) 243
Kamchatka (USSR) 551, 556
Kamchatsky Komsomolets
(USSR) 533
Kamehameha (USA) 627
Kamenz (GDR) 183
Kamishima (Jap) 293
Kamorta (Ind) 226
Kampela 1 (Fin) 142
Kampela 2 (Fin) 142
Kamui (Jap) 295
Kana (USSR) 552
Kanaris (Gre) 206
Kanawa (Jap) 290
Kanawha (USA) 733
Kanderi (Ind) 224
Kane (USA) 717
Kang Shan (RoC) 454
Kania (Pol) 392
Kanjar (Ind) 226
Kansas City (USA) 701
Kao Hsiung (RoC) 457
Kaparen (Swe) 440
Kaper (GFR) 198
Kapi I, II, III (Tur) 482
Kapitan A. Radzabov (USSR) 555
Kapitan Belousov (USSR) 554
Kapitan Chechkin (USSR) 555
Kapitan Izmaylov (USSR) 555
Kapitan Kosolapov (USSR) 555
Kapitan Melekhov (USSR) 554
Kapitan Nikolaev (USSR) 554
Kapitan Plahin (USSR) 555
Kapitan Sorokin (USSR) 554
Kapitan Voronin (USSR) 554
Kara (Tog) 467
Karamürsel (Tur) 478
Karanj (Ind) 224
Karato (Jap) 287
Karatsu (Jap) 293
Karayel (Tur) 475
Karhu (Fin) 141
Karimata (Indo) 238
Karimudjawa (Indo) 238
Karjala (Fin) 138
Karkas (Iran) 244
Karl F. Gaus (GDR) 183
Karl Meseberg (GDR) 181
Karlsö (Swe) 443
Karlsruhe (GFR) 191
Karnaphuli (Ban) 49
Karnavias (Gre) 213
Karpathos (Gre) 211
Karpaty (USSR) 551
Karpfen (GFR) 193
Kartal (Tur) 475
Karwar (Ind) 229
Kasar (Kwt) 317
Kasasagi (Jap) 284
Kasirga (Tur) 475
Kassos (Gre) 211
Kastor (Gre) 208
Kastoria (Gre) 213
Kataigis (Gre) 208
Katchal (Ind) 226
Kathleen (UK) 599
Katmai Bay (USA) 734
Katori (Jap) 288
Katsonis (Gre) 205
Katsura (Jap) 287
Katunj (USSR) 547
Katuren (Jap) 300
Kaura (Nor) 356
Kavaratti (Ind) 226
Kave 1-4 and 6 (Fin) 142
Kaveri (Ind) 227
Kavkaz (USSR) 535
Kaw (USA) 735
Kawishiwi (USA) 700
Kawkab (UAE) 557
Kedleston (UK) 585
Kedma (Isr) 254
Kegon (Jap) 297
Kegostrov (USSR) 546
Keihässalmi (Fin) 140
Kelabang (Indo) 236
Kelang (Mly) 327
Kelaplintah (Indo) 235
Kelefstis Stamou (Gre) 208
Kelewang (Mly) 326
Kellington (UK) 585
Kemaindera (Bru) 64
Kemper County (Bar) 49
Kennebec (USA) 733
Kennet (UK) 583
Kenoki (Can) 85
Kent (UK) 573
Kentauros (Gre) 208
Keo Ngua (Vtn) 747
Keokuk (USA) 712
Kepez (Tur) 482
Kerambit (Mly) 326
Kerch (USSR) 505
Kerempe (Tur) 478
Kerkini (Gre) 213
Kersaint (Fra) 160
Kesari (Ind) 229
Keshet (Isr) 251
Keta (Gha) 201
Ketchikan (USA) 712
Keywadin (USA) 705
Khabarov (USSR) 552
Khadang (Iran) 243
Khanjar (Iran) 243
Kharg (Iran) 245
Khariton Laptev (USSR) 535, 555
Khataf (Bhr) 47
Khawlan (Lby) 322
Khay Bat (SAr) 404
Khersones (USSR) 536
Khirirat (Tld) 461
Khobi (USSR) 549
Ki Rin (RoK) 315
Kichli (Gre) 211
Kickapoo (USA) 733
Kidon (Isr) 251
Kien Vang (Vtn) 747
Kiev (USSR) 502, 554
Kiisla (Fin) 143
Kikau (Fij) 137
Kikuchi (Jap) 293
Kikuzuki (Jap) 280
Kilauea (USA) 697
Kildin (USSR) 538
Kiliç (Tur) 475
Kilimli (Tur) 478
Kiltan (Ind) 226
Kilya (Tur) 481
Kim Men (RoC) 459
Kim Qui (Vtn) 747
Kimberley (SA) 413
Kimbla (Aust) 43
Kimonos (Gre) 211
Kinabalu (Mly) 326
Kinbrace (UK) 594
King (Arg) 28
King (USA) 670
Kingarth (UK) 594
Kingfisher (UK) 589

Kingsport (USA) 713
Kinkaid (USA) 668
Kinloss (UK) 594
Kinn (Nor) 356
Kinterbury (UK) 597
Kinugasa (Jap) 300
Kinzeer Al Bahr (Omn) 363
Kirk (USA) 680
Kirkliston (UK) 585
Kiro (Fij) 137
Kirpan (Ind) 227
Kish (Iran) 246
Kiska (USA) 697
Kissa (Gre) 211
Kistna (Ind) 227
Kitakami (Jap) 284
Kithnos (Gre) 211
Kittanning (USA) 712
Kittaton (USA) 712
Kittiwake (USA) 705
Kitty (UK) 599
Kitty Hawk (USA) 648
Kiyonami (Jap) 296
Kiyuzuki (Jap) 296
Kjapp (Nor) 358
Kjekk (Nor) 357
Kled Keo (Tld) 466
Klipper (GFR) 198
Klueng Baden (Tld) 467
Klütz (GDR) 183
Knechtsand (GFR) 199
Knechtsand II (GDR) 185
Knorr (USA) 716
Knox (USA) 680
Knurr (Nor) 358
Knurrhahn (GFR) 200
Ko Hung (RoK) 314
Ko Mun (RoK) 315
Kobben (Nor) 356
Kobchik (USSR) 520
Koblenz (GFR) 193
Kocatepe (Tur) 473
Kochisar (Tur) 476
Koelsch (USA) 679
Kogiku (Jap) 297
Koida (USSR) 549
Koje (RoK) 312
Kojima (Jap) 292
Koksijde (Bel) 51
Kola (USSR) 548
Kolesnikov (USSR) 538
Kolguev (USSR) 538
Köln (GFR) 191
Kolum (Tld) 466
Komayuki (Jap) 296
Komet (GDR) 183
Komet (GFR) 201
Kompas (Indo) 236
Kompas (Pol) 394
Kompas (USSR) 538
Komsomolec (USSR) 502
Komsomolets (USSR) 510
Komsomolets Ukrainy (USSR) 512
Konda (USSR) 549
Kondor (Pol) 390
Konoka (USA) 712
Konstanz (GFR) 193
Kontouriotis (Gre) 206
Kontroller (Pol) 394
Kootenay (Can) 75
Kopernick (Pol) 393
Korawakka (Sri) 433
Kormoran (Pol) 392
Kornat (Yug) 754
Korrigan (Fra) 176
Korsar (GFR) 198
Korsholm (Fin) 142
Kortenaer (Nld) 344
Kortryk (Bel) 51
Kos (Gre) 210
Koshiki (Jap) 290, 294
Koskelo (Fin) 143
Kosmonavt Belyayev (USSR) 546
Kosmonavl Dobrovolsky (USSR) 546
Kosmonavt Sayev (USSR) 546
Kosmonavt Vladimir Komarov (USSR) 545
Kosmonavt Volkov (USSR) 546
Kosmonavt Yuri Gagarin (USSR) 545
Kosoku 6 (Jap) 285
Kota Bahru (Mly) 328
Kotobiki (Jap) 297
Kouroosh (Iran) 241
Koura (NZ) 351
Kouzu (Jap) 287
Kozara (Yug) 757
Kozlu (Tur) 478
Kozu (Jap) 294
Kozuf (Yug) 755
Krab (Pol) 394
Kram (Tld) 465
Krapu (Indo) 236
Krasin (USSR) 553
Krasnaya Presnya (USSR) 529
Krasny-Kavkaz (USSR) 512
Krasny-Krim (USSR) 512
Krekel (Bel) 52
Krenometr (USSR) 537
Krieger (Den) 117
Krilon (USSR) 538
Kris (Mly) 326
Kriti (Gre) 210
Krogulec (Pol) 392
Kromantse (Gha) 201
Kronos (Gre) 213
Kronshtadt (USSR) 506
Krym (USSR) 535
Krymsky Komsomolets (USSR) 529
Ku San (RoK) 315
Ku Yong (RoK) 316
Kuala Kangsar (Mly) 327
Kuala Trengganu (Mly) 328
Kuang Chou (CPR) 99
Kuban (USSR) 552
Kuching (Mly) 328
Kuchkuch (GFR) 198
Kudako (Jap) 287
Kuddalore (Ind) 229
Kudret (Tur) 482
Kuei Lin (CPR) 98
Kuei Yang (CPR) 98
Kuen Yang (RoC) 453
Kuha 21-26 (Fin) 140
Kuhlungsborn (GDR) 183
Kuikka (Fin) 143
Kula (Fij) 137
Kum Kok (RoK) 314
Kum San (RoK) 314
Kuma (Jap) 293
Kumano (Jap) 283
Kumataka (Jap) 284
K'un Ming (CPR) 98
Kunashiri (Jap) 293
Kunimi (Jap) 295
Kunna (Nor) 356
Kuovi (Fin) 143
Kuparu (NZ) 351
Kurama (Jap) 295
Kurki (Fin) 143
Kurobe (Jap) 293
Kurokami (Jap) 294
Kuroshio (Jap) 278
Kurs (USSR) 536
Kursograf (USSR) 536
Kursura (Ind) 224
Kurtaran (Tur) 481
Kusadasi (Tur) 478
Kusakaki (Jap) 294
Kusseh (Iran) 241
Kut (Tld) 465
Kuthar (Ind) 227
Kuznetsky (USSR) 551
Kuzuryu (Jap) 293
Kuvvet (Tur) 482
Kvalsund (Nor) 359
Kvikk (Nor) 358
Kvina (Nor) 359
KW3 (GFR) 198
KW15-KW20 (GFR) 198
Kwang Ju (RoK) 310
Kwei Yang (RoC) 453
Ky Hoa (Vtn) 746
Kya (Nor) 356
Kyklon (Gre) 208
Kyknos (Gre) 208
Kyong Nam (RoK) 311
Kyong Puk (RoK) 311
Kyritz (GDR) 183
Kyuu-Go (Jap) 287

L

L. Mendel Rivers (USA) 633
L. Y. Spear (USA) 703
L'Adroit (Fra) 166
L'Agenais (Fra) 162
L'Alsacien (Fra) 162
L'Archéonaute (Fra) 174
L'Ardent (Fra) 166
L'Astrolabe (Fra) 169
L'Audacieux (Cam) 69
L'Etoile (Fra) 177
L'Indomptable (Fra) 149
L'Inflexible (Fra) 149
La Bayonnaise (Fra) 166
La Belle Poule (Fra) 177
La Charente (Fra) 170
La Combattante (Fra) 165
La Crete a Pierrot (Hai) 216
La Dieppoise (Fra) 166
La Douane (Fra) 178
La Dunkerquoise (Fra) 166
La Falence (Sen) 407
La Fidèle (Fra) 175
La Galissonière (Fra) 158
La Grande Hermine (Fra) 177
La Jolla (USA) 631
La Lorientaise (Fra) 166
La Malouine (Fra) 166
La Moure County (USA) 690
La Paimpolaise (Fra) 166
La Pedrera (Per) 374
La Persévérante (Fra) 175
La Praya (Fra) 150
La Prudente (Fra) 175
La Punta (Per) 378
La Recherche (Fra) 169
La Salle (USA) 699
La Saône (Fra) 170
Laborieux (Fra) 178
Labrador (Can) 82
Labrador (UK) 598
Labuan (Aust) 44
Lac Tonlé Sap (Fra) 171
Lachs (GFR) 193
Lacomblé (Nld) 346
Ladava (PNG) 370
Ladislaoo Cabrea (Bol) 53
Ladoga (USSR) 536
Ladya (Tld) 465
Ladybird (UK) 599
Lae (PNG) 370
Laesø (Den) 119
Lafayette (USA) 627
Lagoa (Por) 398
Lahmeyer (Brz) 63
Lahn (GFR) 195
Lahore (Pak) 367
Lake Buhi (Plp) 388
Lake Buluan (Plp) 388
Lake Lanao (Plp) 388
Lake Mainit (Plp) 388
Lake Naujan (Plp) 388
Lake Paoay (Plp) 388
Laks (Nor) 358
Laksamana (Mly) 327
Laleston (UK) 585
Lamego (Brz) 63
Lam Giang (Vtn) 748
Lamaki (Iraq) 248
Lambung Mangkurat (Indo) 233
Lamlash (UK) 600
Lampedusa (Ita) 273
Lampo (Ita) 266
Lampo Batang (Indo) 239
Lana (Nig) 354
Landtieff (GDR) 184
Lang (USA) 680
Langara (Spn) 421
Langeland (Den) 121
Langeness (GFR) 199
Langeoog (GFR) 199
Lanta (Tld) 465
Lantana (USA) 733
Lao Yung (RoC) 452
Lapon (USA) 633
Lapseki (Tur) 481
Larak (Iran) 245
Larice (Ita) 268
Larkana (Pak) 367
Las Aves (Ven) 744
Lasham (UK) 596
Latanier (Fra) 178
Latorre (Chi) 89
Lauis Ledge (Plp) 388
Laurel (USA) 731
Laurier (Fra) 168
Laurindo Pitta (Brz) 63
Lautaro (Chi) 91
Lavan (Iran) 245
Lawrence (USA) 673
Lawrenceville (Can) 79
Laya (Spn) 425
Layang (Indo) 236
Layburn (UK) 595
Laymoor (UK) 595
Lazaga (Spn) 425
Lazzaro Mocenigo (Ita) 258
Le Basque (Fra) 162
Le Béarnais (Fra) 162
Le Boulonnais (Fra) 162
Le Dgoc An (Vtn) 748
Le Dinh Hung (Vtn) 748
Le Fort (Fra) 178
Le Foudroyant (Fra) 149
Le Fringant (Fra) 166
Le Gascon (Fra) 162
Le Ngoc Thanh (Vtn) 748
Le Normand (Fra) 162
Le Picard (Fra) 162
Le Phuoc Dui (Vtn) 748
Le Provençal (Fra) 162
Le Redoubtable (Fra) 149
Le Savoyard (Fra) 162
Le Terrible (Fra) 149
Le Tonnant (Fra) 149
Le Valeureux (Cmn) 69
Le Valeureux (IC) 273
Le Van Nga (Vtn) 748
Le Vendéen (Fra) 162
Leader (USA) 694
Leahy (USA) 661
Leander (UK) 576
Leandro Valle (Mex) 333
Lech (GFR) 195
Lech (Pol) 394
Lechlade (UK) 600
Ledang (Mly) 326
Ledbury (UK) 584
Leftwich (USA) 668
Legazpi (Spn) 424
Lei Chou (CPR) 104
Leie (Bel) 52
Lelaka (USA) 712
Lelaps (Gre) 208
Lely (Ven) 745
Lemadang (Indo) 236
Lembing (Mly) 326
Lena (USSR) 549
Lengeh (Iran) 246
Lenin (Pol) 393
Lenin (USSR) 553
Leningrad (USSR) 504, 554
Leon (Gre) 207
Leon Guzman (Mex) 334
Leonardo Da Vinci (Ita) 258
Leonid Sobolev (USSR) 541
Lepanto (Spn) 421
Lerche (GFR) 198
Lerido (Aust) 46
Les Almadies (Sen) 406
Lesbos (Gre) 210
Lesley (UK) 599
Leticia (Col) 108
Levanzo (Ita) 273
Lewis and Clark (USA) 627
Lewiston (UK) 585
Lexington (USA) 653
Leyte (Plp) 384
Liao Yang (RoC) 452
Libeccio (Ita) 263
Liberal (Brz) 57
Liberation (Bel) 52
Libertad (Arg) 32
Libertad (DR) 123
Libertad (Ven) 743
Licio Visintini (Ita) 265
Lien Chang (RoC) 458
Lientur (Chi) 91
Lieut. James E. Robinson (USA) 719
Lieutenant de Vaisseau Lavallée (Ita) 163
Lieutenant De Vaisseau Le Henaff (Fra) 163
Lieutenant Malghagh (Mor) 338
Lieutenant Riffi (Mor) 337
Lightship Columbia (USA) 735
Lightship Nantucket (USA) 735
Lightship Relief (USA) 735
Ligia Elena (Pan) 369
Lihiniya (Sri) 433
Likendeeler (GFR) 198
Lilah (UK) 599
Lilas (Fra) 168
Liman (USSR) 538
Limasawa (Plp) 388
Limburg (Nld) 343
Limnos (Gre) 210
Limpopo (Por) 397
Lin I (CPR) 99
Linaro (Ita) 273
Lincoln (UK) 579
Lindau (GFR) 193
Lindisfarne (UK) 588
Lindormen (Den) 120
Line (USA) 735
Ling Yuen (RoC) 458
Liniers (Spn) 424
Linza (USSR) 537
Lipan (USA) 705
Lisa (USSR) 520
Liseron (Fra) 176
Listerville (Can) 79
Litoral (Bol) 53
Liulom (Tld) 463
Livio Piomarta (Ita) 258
Llandovery (UK) 600
Llobregat (Spn) 428
Lo Yang (RoC) 453
Lobélia (Fra) 168
Lobitos (Per) 380
Lockwood (USA) 680
Loddon (UK) 583
Loganberry (USA) 732
Loganville (Can) 79
Loire (Fra) 171
Lok Adhar (Ind) 231
Loke (Swe) 445
Lokeren (Bel) 51
Lokodjo (IC) 274
Lokoja (Nig) 354
Lom (Nor) 358
Lomas (Per) 378
Lommen (Swe) 448
Lonchi (Gre) 206
London (UK) 573
Londonderry (UK) 578
Long Beach (USA) 662
Longlom (Tld) 463
Lorain County (USA) 690
Loreley (GFR) 194
Loreto (Per) 377
Loriot (Fra) 178
Los (Pol) 392
Los Alamos (USA) 708
Los Angeles (USA) 631
Los Frailes (Ven) 744
Los Monjes (Ven) 744
Los Roques (Ven) 744
Los Testigos (Ven) 744
Lossen (Den) 120
Lotlin (USSR) 537
Loto (Ita) 268
Lotsman (USSR) 536
Louhi (Fin) 141
Louis St. Laurent (Can) 81
Lovat (USSR) 549
Lovcen (Yug) 755
Lowestoft (UK) 578
Loyal Chancellor (UK) 600
Loyal Helper (UK) 600
Loyal Moderator (UK) 600
Loyal Proctor (UK) 600
Loyang (CPR) 99
LP 1, 2 & 3 (GFR) 200
LS 9-12 (Tur) 476
Lu Shan (RoC) 454
Lübben (GDR) 182
Lübeck (GFR) 191
Lübz (GDR) 181
Luce (USA) 670
Ludwigslust (GDR) 181
Luigi Rizzo (Ita) 264
Luis Manuel Rojas (Mex) 334
Lulea (Swe) 440
Lumme (GDR) 184
Lundy (UK) 601
Lüneburg (GFR) 197
Lung Chiang (RoC) 455
Lung Chuan (RoC) 459
Lupo (Ita) 264
Lutin (Fra) 176
Lütje Horn (GFR) 199
Lütjens (GFR) 189
Lutteur (Fra) 178
Lynch (Arg) 30
Lynch (USA) 715
Lynde McCormick (USA) 673
Lyness (UK) 594
Lynx (UK) 579
Lyø (Den) 120
Lyr (Nor) 358
Lyre (Fra) 166

M

M. Acev (Yug) 754
M. Fevzi Cakmak (Tur) 473
Ma San (RoK) 315
Ma'oz (Ist) 254
Maagen (Den) 118
Maassluis (Nld) 345
Maccah (SAr) 404
Macdonough (USA) 670
Maceo (Cub) 114
Mackenzie (Can) 74
Mackinaw (USA) 725
Machtigal (Cmn) 69
Macorix (DR) 125
Macreuse (Fra) 178
Mactan (Plp) 388
Madadgar (Pak) 369
Madang (PNG) 370
Madaraka (Ken) 303
Madera (Bol) 53
Madokawando (USA) 712
Madrona (USA) 731
Maeklong (Tld) 466
Maestrale (Ita) 263
Magar (Ind) 229
Magat Salamat (Plp) 384
Magellan (GFR) 198
Magne (Swe) 440
Magnolia (Fra) 176
Magomed Gadzhiev (USSR) 533
Maguana (DR) 125
Mahamiru (Mly) 326
Mahan (Iran) 243
Mahan (USA) 670
Maharajalela (Bru) 64
Maharajalela (Mly) 327
Maharajasetia (Mly) 327
Mahkota (Mly) 327
Mahmood (Pak) 368
Mahnavi-Hamraz (Iran) 246
Mahnavi-Taheri (Iran) 246
Mahnavi-Vahedi (Iran) 246
Mahoa (USA) 712
Mahoning (USA) 735
Mahroos (Kwt) 317
Mahu (Nld) 346
Maille-Brézé (Fra) 160
Main (GFR) 195
Makigumo (Jap) 280, 296
Makinami (Jap) 282

804 INDEX / NAMED SHIPS

Makishio (Jap) 278
Makkum (Nld) 345
Makrele (GFR) 193
Makurdi (Nig) 353
Makut Rajakumarn (Tld) 461
Malabar (Fra) 177
Malaika (Mad) 323
Malaspina (Spn) 429
Maldonado (Uru) 737
Mallard (Can) 86
Mallemukken (Den) 118
Mallet (USA) 733
Mallow (USA) 731
Mamba (Ken) 303
Manabi (Ecu) 127
Manatee Bay (Jam) 274
Manawanui (NZ) 351
Mandan (USA) 712
Mandarin (USA) 594
Mandorio (Ita) 268
Mandovi (Por) 397
Manga (NZ) 351
Mango (Ita) 268
Mangro (Pak) 365
Manhattan (USA) 712
Manistee (USA) 712
Manitou (USA) 735
Manitowoc (USA) 690
Manktao (USA) 712
Manley (USA) 674
Manø (Den) 120
Mano (Lbr) 319
Manoka (Cmn) 69
Manquier (Fra) 178
Mansa Kila IV (Gam) 179
Manta (Ecu) 128
Mantilla (Col) 110
Mantilla (Per) 381
Manuel Crecencio Rejon (Mex) 334
Manuel Doblado (Mex) 333
Manuel Lara (Col) 110
Manuel Villavicencio (Per) 376
Manych (USSR) 548
Manzanillo (Mex) 335
Mapiri (Bol) 53
Maquindanao (Plp) 386
Marabout (Fra) 178
Maracaibo (Ven) 744
Marajo (Brz) 62
Maranhao (Brz) 58
Marañón (Per) 377
Marburg (GFR) 193
Marcilio Dias (Brz) 58
Mardan (Pak) 367
Mardjan (Iran) 246
Margaree (Can) 75
Margay (Guy) 216
Maria Quiteria (Brz) 63
Maria Van Riebeeck (SA) 412
Mariano Escobedo (Mex) 333
Mariano G. Vallejo (USA) 627
Mariano Metamoros (Mex) 334
Marias (USA) 721
Marin (USA) 712
Marinduque (Plp) 387
Marinero Fuentealba (Chi) 92
Marinette (USA) 712
Mario Serpa (Col) 110
Mariposa (USA) 731
Mariscal Santa Cruz (Bol) 53
Marisco (Brz) 63
Mariz E. Barros (Brz) 58
Markab (USA) 629
Marlin (Bhm) 47
Marmaris (Tur) 477
Marn Vichai (Tld) 467
Marionier (Fra) 178
Marqués De La Ensenada (Spn) 420
Mars (GFR) 194
Mars (USA) 697
Mars (USSR) 538
Märsgarn (Swe) 448
Marshal Timoshenko (USSR) 506
Marshal Voroshilov (USSR) 506
Marshfield (USA) 718
Marsopa (Spn) 418
Marsouin (Fra) 151
Martadinata (Indo) 233
Marti (Cub) 114
Marti (Pan) 369
Marti (Tur) 474
Martin (UK) 601
Martin Alvarez (Spn) 467
Martin Pécheur (Fra) 178
Martinet (Fra) 178
Martins de Oliveira (Brz) 62
Marvin Shields (USA) 680
Mary (UK) 599
Marysville (Can) 79
Marzook (Kwt) 317
Mascoutah (USA) 712
Mashhoor (Kwt) 317
Mashuk (USSR) 556
Masna (Bru) 64
Massapequa (USA) 712
Mastiff (UK) 598
Mataphon (Tld) 466
Matias de Cordova (Mex) 334
Matjan Kumbang (Indo) 235
Mato Grosso (Brz) 58
Matra (Tld) 466
Matsugumo (Jap) 297
Matsunami (Jap) 296
Matsuura (Jap) 293
Matsuyuki (Jap) 296
Matunak (USA) 712
Maumee (USA) 721
Mauna Kea (USA) 697
Maursund (Nor) 359
Max Reichpietsch (GDR) 181
Max Reichpietsch II (GDR) 185
Maxim (UK) 597
Maxton (UK) 585
May Rut (Vtn) 747
Mayak (USSR) 540
Mayberries (Can) 79
Maymoon (Kwt) 317
Mayor Arias (Col) 110
Mayta Kapac (Bol) 53
Mayu (Bur) 67
McArthur (USA) 735
McCandless (USA) 680
McCloy (USA) 682
McInerney (USA) 677
McKean (USA) 675
McKee (USA) 703
McLennan (Can) 79
Mearim (Brz) 59
Mechelen (Bel) 52
Mecosta (USA) 712
Medusa (GFR) 194
Medusa (Pol) 394
Medved (USSR) 520
Medway (UK) 583
Meerkatze (GFR) 201
Meersburg (GFR) 197
Mehmetcik (Tur) 477
Mehr (Iran) 246
Mehran (Iran) 243
Mei Chin (RoC) 457
Mei Lo (RoC) 457
Mei Ping (RoC) 457
Mei Sung (RoC) 457
Meise (GFR) 198
Meiyo (Jap) 298
Melbourne (Aust) 37
Melchor Ocampo (Mex) 333
Méléze (Fra) 178
Meliton Carvajal (Per) 376
Mella (DR) 122
Mellon (USA) 726
Mellum (GFR) 199
Meltem (Tur) 475
Mélusine (Fra) 176
Melville (USA) 716
Memmert (GFR) 195
Memphis (USA) 631
Menasha (USA) 712
Mendez Nuñez (Spn) 421
Menominee (USA) 712
Mentawai (Indo) 238
Menzel Bourguiba (Tun) 469
Merawa (Lby) 322
Mercer (USA) 709
Mercure (Fra) 168
Mercury (Sin) 408
Mercuur (Nld) 346
Meredith (USA) 675
Meric (Tur) 477
Meridian (USSR) 546
Merisier (Fra) 178
Merksem (Bel) 51
Merle (Fra) 178
Merlin (Fra) 176
Merrickville (Can) 79
Merrill (U.S.A.) 668
Mersin (Tur) 477
Mesaha 1-2 (Tur) 479
Mésange (Fra) 178
Mesco (Ita) 273
Mesquite (USA) 731
Messenger (USA) 735
Mestre Joao Dos Santos (Brz) 61
Metacom (USA) 712
Metan (USSR) 549
Metel (USSR) 521
Meteor (GDR) 183
Meteor (GFR) 201
Meteor (USA) 719
Meteoro (Chi) 94
Meuse (Bel) 52
Meuse (Fra) 170
Meyerkord (USA) 680
Mezen (USSR) 552
Mgla (USSR) 540
Miaoulis (Gre) 205
Michel (GFR) 198
Michelangelo (Iran) 246
Michigan (USA) 626
Michishio (Jap) 278
Middelburg (Nld) 345
Midgett (USA) 726
Midway (USA) 652
Mier (Bel) 52
Migadan (USA) 712
Miguel dos Santos (Brz) 63
Miguel Malvar (Plp) 384
Miguel Ramos Arizpe (Mex) 334
Mikhail Kutusov (USSR) 509
Mikhail Lomonosov (USSR) 540
Mikhail Somov (USSR) 543
Mikula (Can) 86
Mikuma (Jap) 283
Mikura (Jap) 290, 294
Milanian (Iran) 243
Milano (Spn) 432
Miller (USA) 680
Millicoma (USA) 721
Milwaukee (USA) 701
Mimac (USA) 712
Mime (GFR) 198
Mimosa (Fra) 168
Minabe (Jap) 293
Minas Gerais (Brz) 56
Minase (Jap) 287
Mincio (Ita) 272
Minden (GFR) 193, 201
Mindoro Occidental (Plp) 386
Minegumo (Jap) 281, 296
Minerva (GFR) 194
Minerva (UK) 576
Mineyuki (Jap) 297
Minh Hoa (Vtn) 747
Ministro Portales (Chi) 90
Ministro Zenteno (Chi) 90
Mink (Can) 86
Miño (Spn) 428
Minoo (Jap) 297
Minorena (Swe) 444
Minoru (UK) 602
Minotauros (Gre) 213
Minsk (USSR) 502
Mira (Por) 398
Miramichi (Can) 78
Mircea (Rom) 402
Mirfak (USA) 718
Mirto (Ita) 269
Misamis Occidental (Plp) 387
Misamis Oriental (Plp) 386
Miseno (Ita) 273
Misgav (Isr) 252
Mishawaka (USA) 712
Miskanaw (Can) 86
Mispillion (USA) 721
Mississinewa (USA) 700
Mississippi (USA) 657
Missouri (USA) 655
Mistral (GFR) 198
Misurata (Lby) 322
Mitilo (Ita) 269
Mitscher (USA) 671
Miura (Jap) 285, 291
Mivtach (Isr) 252
Miyake (Jap) 286, 292
Miyato (Jap) 286
Mizar (USA) 716
Miznach (Isr) 252
Mizrak (Tur) 475
Mizutori (Jap) 284
Mjölner (Swe) 440
Mo Ling (RoC) 454
Moana Wave (USA) 715
Mobile (USA) 691
Mobile Bay (USA) 734
Mochizuki (Jap) 280, 296
Mocovi (Arg) 33
Moctabi (USA) 705
Mode (Swe) 440
Modoc (USA) 734
Møen (Den) 120
Mogami (Jap) 284
Mogano (Ita) 268
Møgsterfjord (Nor) 361
Mohawk (UK) 577
Mohican (USA) 735
Moineau (Fra) 178
Moinester (USA) 680
Mok Po (RoK) 315
Moksha (USSR) 549
Molala (USA) 705
Moldavya (USSR) 541
Mölders (GFR) 189
Mollendo (Per) 380
Momin (Pak) 368
Monastir (Tun) 470
Moncada (Cub) 114
Mongisidi (Indo) 233
Mongol (USSR) 551
Monkton (UK) 589
Mono (Tog) 467
Monob I (USA) 710
Monowai (NZ) 350
Monreal (Chi) 94
Monsun (GFR) 198
Montcalm (Can) 83
Montcalm (Fra) 156
Monte Cristo (Ita) 273
Monticello (USA) 689
Montmagny (Can) 85
Montmorency (Can) 84
Moorhen (Can) 86
Moosburgger (U.S.A.) 668
Moosomin II (Can) 79
Moran Valverde (Ecu) 127
Moratoc (USA) 712
Morcoyan (Arg) 33
Mordogan (Tur) 477
Moresby (Aust) 42
Morgane (Fra) 176
Morgenthau (USA) 726
Mornar (Yug) 753
Morona (Per) 381
Morro Bay (USA) 734
Mors (Pol) 392
Morse (Fra) 151
Morsoviets (USSR) 538
Morton (USA) 674
Morvarid (Iran) 246
Morzhovets (USSR) 546
Mosel (GFR) 195
Moselle (Fra) 172
Moshal (Pak) 368
Moskovsky Komsomolets (USSR) 516
Moskva (USSR) 504, 554
Mosospelea (USA) 705
Mosselbaai (SA) 413
Motajica (Yug) 756
Motobu (Jap) 285
Mouette (Fra) 178
Mount Baker (USA) 697
Mount Hood (USA) 697
Mount Mitchell (USA) 735
Mount Samat (Plp) 388
Mount Vernon (USA) 689
Mount Whitney (USA) 685
Muavenet (Tur) 473
Muchula (Bol) 53
Muguet (Fra) 168
Mujahid (Pak) 368
Mukhtar (Pak) 368
Mul 11 (Swe) 442
Mul 12-19 (Swe) 443
Mullinnix (USA) 674
Multatuli (Indo) 237
Mungo (Cmn) 69
Munin (Swe) 440
Munro (USA) 726
Munsif (Pak) 368
Murabak (Pak) 368
Murakumo (Jap) 281
Muräne (GFR) 193
Murasame (Jap) 282
Murat Reis (Tur) 472
Murature (Arg) 28
Murayjib (UAE) 557
Murban (UAE) 557
Mürefte (Tur) 477
Murene (Fra) 178
Murene (Mor) 338
Murmansk (USSR) 509, 554
Murmats (USSR) 535
Muroto (Jap) 292
Murotsu (Jap) 286
Murshed (Kwt) 317
Murtaja (Fin) 141
Muskegon (USA) 712
Muskingum (USA) 733
Musson (USSR) 543
Mutiara (Mly) 327
Mutilla (Chi) 94
Mutin (Fra) 177
Mutis (Indo) 239
Mutsuki (Jap) 296
Mutsure (Jap) 286
Muzuki (Jap) 286
Myles C. Fox (USA) 675
Myojo (Jap) 300
Myosotis (Fra) 177
Myrtle (UK) 599
Mysore (Ind) 224
Mytho (Fra) 167

N

9 De Octubre (Ecu) 128
N.B. McLean (Can) 83
N. I. Goulandrias I (Gre) 209
N. I. Goulandrias II (Gre) 209
N. Kolomeytsev (USSR) 539
N. Martinovic (Yug) 754
N. Yevgenov (USSR) 539
N'Golo (Gab) 179
N'Guene (Gab) 179
Na Dong (RoK) 314
Naaldwijk (Nld) 346
Naarden (Nld) 346
Nabigwon (USA) 712
Nachi (Jap) 297
Nachtigall (GFR) 198
Näcken (Swe) 437
Nader (Iran) 241
Nadli (USA) 712
Nafkratoussa (Gre) 210
Naftilos (Gre) 211
Nagakyay (Bur) 68
Naga Pasa (Indo) 235
Nagatsuki (Jap) 280
Nagga Banda (Indo) 232
Naghdi (Iran) 243
Nahang (Iran) 241
Nahid (Iran) 243
Nahidik (Can) 86
Nahoke (USA) 712
Naiad (UK) 576
Najad (Swe) 437
Najade (GFR) 191
Najaden (Den) 118
Nakarna (USA) 712
Nakha (Tld) 466
Nakhodchivy (USSR) 515
Nakhodka (USSR) 536
Nalón (Spn) 428
Nam Du (Vtn) 747
Nam Yang (RoK) 314
Namao (Can) 85
Namdö (Swe) 443
Nan Chang (CPR) 99
Nan Yang (RoC) 453
Nana-Go (Jap) 287
Nanawa (Par) 371
Nancy (UK) 599
Nanryu (Jap) 297
Nanticoke (USA) 712
Naparima (TT) 468
Napo (Per) 380
Naporisty (USSR) 516
Narhvalen (Den) 115
Narra (Plp) 387
Narragansett (USA) 722
Narushio (Jap) 278
Narval (Fra) 151
Narval (Spn) 418
Narvik (Fra) 167
Narvik (Nor) 356
Narwhal (Can) 83
Narwhal (USA) 632
Narwik (Pol) 393
Nashat (Ind) 228
Nashua (USA) 712
Nashville (USA) 688
Nassau (USA) 686
Nastoychivy (USSR) 515
Natahki (USA) 712
Natchitoches (USA) 712
Natek (Pol) 394
Nathan Hale (USA) 627
Nathanael Greene (USA) 627
Natick (USA) 712
Natori (Jap) 293
Natsugumo (Jap) 281
Natsushio (Jap) 278
Natuna (Indo) 238
Naugatuck (USA) 735
Nautilus (GFR) 194
Nautilus (Nld) 348
Nautilus (SA) 413
Nautilus (Spn) 424
Nautilus (USA) 638
Navajo (USA) 722
Navarinon (Gre) 206
Navasota (USA) 721
Navia (Spn) 429
Navigator (SA) 414
Nawarat (Bur) 68
Nawigator (Pol) 393
Nazario Sauro (Ita) 258
Ndovu (Ken) 303
Neah Bay (USA) 734
Nebil (Spn) 432
Neches (USA) 720
Neckar (GFR) 195
Negba (Isr) 254
Negros Occidental (Plp) 384
Negros Oriental (Plp) 384
Nemuro (Jap) 285
Neodesha (USA) 712
Neosho (USA) 700
Nepanet (USA) 712
Neptun (Den) 118
Neptun (GFR) 194
Neptun (Rom) 402
Neptun (Swe) 437
Neptune (USA) 722
Neptunia (Pol) 394
Neptuno (DR) 125
Neptuno (Per) 381
Nereida (Spn) 432
Nereide (Fra) 176
Neretva (Yug) 752
Nereus (Gre) 204
Nereus (USA) 704
Nerey (USSR) 541
Nereida (Spn) 432
Neringa (USSR) 537
Nerz (GFR) 193
Nesokrushimy (USSR) 515
Nestin (Yug) 756
Neudersimy (USSR) 513
Neuende (GFR) 199

NAMED SHIPS / INDEX 805

Neuquen (Arg) 30
Neuruppin (GDR) 183
Neustadt (GFR) 201
Neustrelitz (GDR) 183
Neuwerk (GFR) 199
Nevel (USSR) 546
Nevelskoy (USSR) 542
New Bedford (USA) 709
New Jersey (USA) 655
New Orleans (USA) 687
New York City (USA) 631
Newcastle (UK) 574
Newgagon (USA) 712
Newman K. Perry (USA) 675
Newman Noggs (UK) 601
Newport (USA) 690
Newport News (USA) 665
Newton (UK) 595
Neyzeh (Iran) 243
Ngahau Koula (Ton) 467
Ngahan Siliva (Ton) 467
Ngo Van Quyen (Vtn) 748
Ngurah Rai (Indo) 233
Nguyen An (Vtn) 748
Nguyen Dao (Vtn) 748
Nguyen Han (Vtn) 748
Nguyen Kim Hung (Vtn) 748
Nguyen Ngoc Long (Vtn) 748
Nguyen Ngoc Thach (Vtn) 748
Nhong Sarhai (Tld) 464
Ni-Go (Jap) 290
Niagara Falls (USA) 697
Niantic (USA) 712
Nibbio (Italy) 266
Nicholson (Can) 77
Nicholson (USA) 668
Nicolas Suarez (Bol) 53
Nicolet (Can) 86
Niederösterreich (Aus) 46
Niels Juel (Den) 116
Nienburg (GFR) 197
Nieuwpoort (Bel) 51
Nigeria (Nig) 352
Nikolai Filchenkov (USSR) 529
Nikolai Vilkov (USSR) 529
Nikolai Zubov (USSR) 538
Nikolay Stolbov (USSR) 533
Nikolayev (USSR) 505
Nilgiri (Ind) 225
Nils Strömcrona (Swe) 447
Nimitz (USA) 645
Nimpkish (Can) 79
Ninh Giang (Vtn) 748
Niobe (GFR) 195
Niovi (Gre) 211
Nipat (Ind) 228
Nipigon (Can) 74
Nipmuc (USA) 705
Nirbhik (Ind) 228
Nirghat (Ind) 228
Nisan (Iraq) 247
Nisida (Ita) 273
Nisr 1, 2, 3 (Egy) 133
Nistar (Ind) 230
Niteroi (Brz) 57
Nito Restrepo (Col) 108
Nitro (USA) 697
Nivelir (USSR) 540
Nixe (GFR) 194
Niyodo (Jap) 283
Njord (Swe) 446
Noakhali (Ban) 48
Nobaru (Jap) 295
Noce (Ita) 268
Nodaway (USA) 722
Nogah (Isr) 254
Nogales (USA) 712
Nogueira Da Gama (Brz) 61
Noguera (Per) 381
Nojima (Jap) 292
Nokomis (Can) 85
Noon (Bhr) 47
Norah (UK) 599
Norain (Bru) 64
Norby (Den) 117
Norderney (GFR) 199
Nordkaperen (Den) 115
Nordkaperen (Swe) 438
Nordkapp, O/S (Nor) 360
Nordstrand (GFR) 199
Nordwind (GFR) 198
Norfolk (UK) 573
Norge (Nor) 360
Norman McLeod Rogers (Can) 81
Nornen, O/S (Nor) 360
Norrköping (Swe) 440
Norrtälje (Swe) 440
Norsten (Swe) 444
Northwind (USA) 725, 728
Norton Sound (USA) 706
Norviking (Nor) 361
Norwalk (USA) 718
Noshiro (Jap) 283
Noto (Jap) 294
Nottingham (UK) 574
Novator (USSR) 541
Noyer (Fra) 178
NR 1 (USA) 642
Nubian (UK) 577
Nueces (USA) 709
Nueva Esparta (Ven) 741
Nueve de Julio (Arg) 26
Nueva Viscaya (Plp) 384
Nuevo Rocafuerte (Ecu) 128
Nuku (Indo) 233
Numa (USA) 712
Nung Ra (RoK) 315
Nunobiki (Jap) 297
Nuoli 1-13 (Fin) 139
Nurton (UK) 585
Nusa Telu (Indo) 238
Nusret (Tur) 477
Nymfen (Den) 118
Nymphe (GFR) 194
Nynäshamn (Swe) 440
Nyenlouimy (USSR) 513
Nysing (Swe) 440

O

18 de Julio (Uru) 736
O/Lt Valcke (Bel) 52
Oak Ridge (USA) 708
Ob (USSR) 551
O'Bannon (USA) 668
Oberon (UK) 567
Oberst Brecht (Aus) 33
Obion (USA) 733
Objibwa (USA) 735
Obraztsovy (USSR) 512
O'Brien (Chi) 88
O'Brien (USA) 668
Observation Island (USA) 713
Ocala (USA) 712
O'Callahan (USA) 679
Oceanografico (Mex) 334
Oceanographer (USA) 735
Ocelot (Guy) 216
Ocelot (UK) 567
Ochakov (USSR) 505
Ockero (Fin) 143
Ocoa (DR) 124
Octant (Fra) 169
October, 6 (Egy) 131
Odarenny (USSR) 512
Odd (Nor) 357
Oden (Swe) 446
Odenwald (GFR) 197
Odev (Tur) 482
Odiel (Spn) 428
Odin (GFR) 195
Odin (UK) 567
Odinn (Ice) 220
Oeillet (Fra) 177
Ofanto (Ita) 272
Offenburg (GFR) 197
Ogden (USA) 688
Ogna (Nor) 359
Ognenny (USSR) 517
Ognevoy (USSR) 512
Oguta (Nig) 353
O'Higgins (Chi) 89
Ohio (USA) 626
Oilbird (UK) 595
Oilfield (UK) 595
Oilman (UK) 595
Oilpress (UK) 595
Oilstone (UK) 595
Oilwell (UK) 595
Oiseau Des Iles (Fra) 166
Ojibwa (Can) 72
Ojika (Jap) 285, 292
Ok Cheon (RoK) 314
Oka (USSR) 552
Okanagan (Can) 72
Okba (Mor) 337
Okean (USSR) 538, 543
Oker (GFR) 200
Oki (Jap) 294
Okinami (Jap) 296
Okinawa (Jap) 293
Okinawa (USA) 687
Okitsu (Jap) 286
Oklahoma City (USA) 664
Okmulgee (USA) 712
Okoume (Fra) 178
Oktyabrskaya Revolutsiya (USSR) 509
Okushiri (Jap) 294
Öland (Swe) 439
Olaya (Per) 380
Olaya Herrera (Col) 108
Oldendorf (USA) 668
Oleander (USA) 733
Olekma (USSR) 549
Olfert Fischer (Den) 116
Olivier (Fra) 178
Oliver Hazard Perry (USA) 677
Oliver Twist (UK) 601
Olmeda (UK) 591
Olmo (Ita) 268
Olna (UK) 519
Olwen (UK) 519
Olympus (UK) 567
Omaha (USA) 631
Ommen (Nld) 346
Omøsund (Den) 121
Onaran (Tur) 480
Onbevreesd (Nld) 346
Öncu (Tur) 482
Ondire (Fra) 176
Onega (USSR) 552
Onondaga (Can) 72
Onslaught (UK) 567
Onslow (Aust) 36
Ontano (Ita) 268
Onverdroten (Nld) 346
Onvervaard (Nld) 346
Onyx (UK) 567
Ooi (Jap) 284
Oonami (Jap) 282
Ooshio (Jap) 278
Oosterland (SA) 413
Ootsu (Jap) 287
Opelika (USA) 712
Operario Luis Leal (Brz) 63
Opossum (UK) 567
Opportune (UK) 567
Opportune (USA) 702
Oqbah (SAr) 404
Oquendo (Spn) 422
Oracle (UK) 567
Orage (Fra) 164
Orangeleaf (UK) 592
Oranienburg (GDR) 183
Ordóñez (Spn) 425
Orella (Chi) 91
Oriental Mindoro (Plp) 387
Origny (Fra) 169
Oriole (Can) 78
Orion (Aust) 36
Orion (Brz) 61
Orion (Ecu) 129
Orion (Gre) 213
Orion (USA) 704
Oriskany (USA) 653
Orkney (UK) 588
Orleck (USA) 675
Orlik (Pol) 392
Ornö (Swe) 443
Orompello (Chi) 93
Orpheus (UK) 567
Orsa (Ita) 264
Orsha (USSR) 549
Orsk (USSR) 549
Ortolan (USA) 704
Ortwin (GFR) 198
Oruc Reis (Tur) 472
Orzel (Pol) 390
Osage (USA) 733
Oshkosh (USA) 712
Osipov (USSR) 535
Osiris (UK) 567
Oslo (Nor) 356
Oste (GFR) 200
Östergötland (Swe) 438
Ostervenely (USSR) 517
Ostorozny (USSR) 517
Ostroglazy (USSR) 517
Ostwind (GFR) 198
OT 2 (GFR) 200
Otago (NZ) 350
Otaka (Jap) 284
Otama (Aust) 36
Otchayanny (USSR) 517
Otobo (Nig) 353
Otokomi (USA) 712
Otori (Jap) 284
Otowa (Jap) 297
Otretovenny (USSR) 517
Ottawa (Can) 75
Otter (UK) 567
Otto Meycke (GFR) 200
Otto Schmidt (USSR) 554
Otto Tost (GDR) 181
Otto von Guericke (GDR) 184
Ottumwa (USA) 712
Otus (UK) 567
Otvetstvenny (USSR) 517
Otway (Aust) 36
Ouachita (USA) 733
Oudenaarde (Bel) 51
Oued (Fra) 178
Ouellet (USA) 680
Ouessant (Fra) 150
Ougree (Bel) 51
Ouistreham (Fra) 167
Oumi (Jap) 286
Ouragan (Cmn) 69
Ouragan (Fra) 164
Ouranos (Gre) 212
Outlook (Can) 79
Ovens (Aust) 36
Overijssel (Nld) 343
Oxley (Aust) 36
Ozelot (GFR) 193
Ozhestochenny (USSR) 517
Ozhivlenniy (USSR) 517

P

P. Drapsin (Yug) 754
Pabna (Ban) 48
Pacocha (Per) 374
Paderborn (GFR) 193
Padma (Ban) 49
Paducah (USA) 712
Paea (NZ) 351
Paek Ku II (RoK) 312
Paek Ku II, 12, 13, 15, 16, 17, 18, 19 (RoK) 312
Pagham (UK) 600
Pahlawan (Mly) 327
Paita (Per) 378
Paiute (USA) 705
Pakan Baru (Indo) 238
Palacios (Per) 375
Palang (Iran) 242
Palangrin (Fra) 174
Palatka (USA) 712
Palawan (Plp) 385
Palétuvier (Fra) 178
Palinuro (Ita) 271
Palma (Ita) 268
Palmer Ort (GDR) 184
Pamban (Ind) 228
Pamir (USSR) 556
Pamlico (USA) 733
Pampeiro (Brz) 60
Pampero (GFR) 198
Pamyat Merkuryia (USSR) 538
Panah (Mly) 326
Panaji (Ind) 228
Panaria (Ita) 273
Pandora (Gre) 213
Pandrong (Indo) 234
Pandrosos (Gre) 213
Pangan (Tld) 465
Pangasinan (Plp) 384
Pangkalan Brandan (Ind) 239
Panglima (Sin) 409
Panquiaco (Pan) 369
Pansio (Fin) 142
Pantelleria (Ita) 273
Panter (Nld) 345
Pantera (USSR) 520
Panthir (Gre) 207
Panvel (Ind) 228
Papago (USA) 705
Papanikolis (Gre) 205
Papaw (USA) 731
Papenoo (Fra) 171
Papayer (Fra) 178
Papudo (Chi) 92
Paquerette (Fra) 166
Para (Brz) 58
Paraguassu (Brz) 63
Paraguay (Par) 371
Paraiba (Brz) 58
Paraibano (Brz) 61
Parana (Brz) 58
Parati (Brz) 60
Parche (USA) 633
Parchim (GDR) 181
Pargo (USA) 633
Pari (Mly) 326
Parinas (Per) 379
Parksville (Can) 79
Parnaiba (Brz) 59
Parramatta (Aust) 40
Parsons (USA) 672
Partisan (GDR) 185
Partizan II (Yug) 754
Parvin (Iran) 243
Pasewalk (GDR) 183
Pasopati (Indo) 232
Passat (USSR) 543
Passau (GFR) 201
Passereau (Fra) 178
Passero (Ita) 273
Passo da Patria (Brz) 63
Passop (Swe) 448
Passumpsic (USA) 721
Pastor Rouaix (Mex) 334
Pathfinder (Plp) 389
Patoka (USA) 733
Patos (Alb) 20
Patraikos (Gre) 213
Patria (Ven) 743
Patrick Henry (USA) 630
Patron (Mex) 335
Pattani (Tld) 463
Patterson (USA) 680
Pattimura (Indo) 234
Patuakhali (Ban) 48
Paul (USA) 680
Paul Eisenschneider (GDR) 181
Paul F. Foster (USA) 668
Paul Revere (USA) 691
Paul Wieczorek (GDR) 181
Paulo Afonso (Brz) 63
Paus (Mly) 326
Pavel Bashmakov (USSR) 539
Pawcatuck (USA) 721
Pawhuska (USA) 712
Pawtucket (USA) 712
Paysandu (Uru) 738
PB 19-27 (Jap) 285
PC 11 (Eth) 137
PC 13 (Eth) 137
PC 14 (Eth) 137
PC 15 (Eth) 137
Pearkes (Can) 79
Pearl Bank (Plp) 388
Pearleaf (UK) 592
Peccari (Guy) 216
Pechora (USSR) 534
Peder Skram (Den) 116
Pedro de Heredia (Col) 110
Pedro Gual (Col) 108
Pedro Santana (DR) 122
Pedro Teixeira (Brz) 59
Pegas (USSR) 544
Pegase (Fra) 176
Pegasus (USA) 682
Pehuenche (Arg) 33
Peieplier (Fra) 178
Peirce (USA) 735
Pekan (Mly) 327
Peleng (USSR) 536
Pélican (Fra) 175
Pelikan (Pol) 392
Pelikan (Tur) 475
Pelikanen (Swe) 447
Pellworm (GFR) 199
Pelorus (USSR) 536
Pemburu (Bru) 64
Pendant (USA) 735
Penedo (Brz) 60
Penelope (Nig) 345
Penelope (UK) 576
Penobscot Bay (USA) 734
Pensacola (USA) 689
Penyarang (Bru) 60
Peoria (USA) 690
Perantau (Mly) 327
Perch (UK) 601
Perdana (Mly) 325
Perekop (USSR) 546
Peresvet (USSR) 555
Perkun (Pol) 394
Perleberg (GDR) 181
Permit (USA) 634
Pernambuco (Brz) 58
Perseo (Ita) 264
Perseus (GFR) 194
Perseus (Gre) 213
Perseverance (Sin) 409
Perseverence (IC) 273
Persistence (Sin) 409
Pertanda (Mly) 327
Perth (Aust) 38
Pertuisane (Fra) 165
Pervenche (Fra) 168
Pervenets (USSR) 540
Perwira (Bru) 64
Perwira (Mly) 327
Peshawar (Pak) 369
Petalesharo (USA) 712
Petaluma (USA) 722
Peter Tordenskjold (Den) 116
Peterel (UK) 589
Peterson (USA) 668
Petr Ilichev (USSR) 529
Petr Lebedev (USSR) 543
Petr Pakhtusov (USSR) 542
Petrel (Arg) 31
Pétrel (Fra) 176
Petrel (UK) 601
Petrel (USA) 705
Petrodvorets (USSR) 541
Petropavlovsk (USSR) 505
Pétunia (Fra) 166
Peyk (Tur) 474
Peykan (Iran) 243
Phai (Tld) 465
Phali (Tld) 463
Pham Ngoc Chau (Vtn) 748
Pharris (USA) 680
Phénix (Fra) 168
Phetra (Tld) 466
Philadelphia (USA) 631
Philips van Almonde (Nld) 344
Phoebe (UK) 576
Phoenix (USA) 631
Phosamton (Tld) 466
Phu Du (Vtn) 747
Phu Qui (Vtn) 747
Pi Bong (RoK) 314
Pian (RoK) 315
Pianosa (Ita) 273
Piast (Pol) 394
Piaui (Brz) 58
Piave (Ita) 272
Picúa (DR) 124
Picuda (Ven) 741
Piedmont (USA) 697
Pierre Radisson (Can) 81
Piet Heyn (Nld) 344

806 INDEX / NAMED SHIPS

Pieter Floresz (Nld) 344
Pietro Cavezzale (Ita) 270
Pietro de Christofaro (Ita) 265
Pigassos (Gre) 208
Pigeon (USA) 704
Pijao (Col) 105
Pike (UK) 601
Pil (Nor) 357
Piloto Pardo (Chi) 94
Pimentel (Per) 379
Pin (Fra) 178
Pin Klao (Tld) 462
Pingouie (Kam) 302
Pingouin (Fra) 178
Pingvinen (Swe) 448
Pinna (Ita) 269
Pino (Ita) 268
Pinson (Fra) 178
Pintado (USA) 633
Pintail (UK) 594
Piombino (Ita) 273
Pionier (GDR) 185
Pioppo (Ita) 269
Piqua (USA) 712
Piraja (Brz) 60
Piratini (Brz) 60
Pirol (GFR) 198
Pirttisaari (Fin) 142
Pisco (Per) 381
Pishin (Pak) 367
Pitamakan (USA) 712
Piteä (Swe) 440
Pivert (Fra) 178
Pivoine (Fra) 168
Plainsville (Can) 79
Plainview (USA) 699
Plamenny (USSR) 516
Planet (GFR) 200
Planetree (USA) 731
Platane (Fra) 178
Platano (Ita) 268
Pledge (USA) 694
Pleias (Gre) 211
Ploiarhos Arslanoglou (Gre) 209
Plon (GFR) 199
Plotarhis Blessas (Gre) 207
Plotze (GFR) 193
Pluck (USA) 694
Plug (USSR) 555
Plumleaf (UK) 592
Plunger (USA) 634
Pluto (GFR) 194
Plymouth (UK) 578
Plymouth Rock (USA) 689
Po Yang (RoC) 453
Pobeda (Bul) 65
Pocasset (USA) 712
Pochard (UK) 594
Podchorazy (Pol) 394
Podgora (Yug) 755
Podor (Sen) 406
Pogy (USA) 633
Point Arena (USA) 730
Point Baker (USA) 730
Point Barnes (USA) 730
Point Barrow (USA) 730
Point Batan (USA) 730
Point Bennet (USA) 730
Point Bonita (USA) 730
Point Bridge (USA) 730
Point Brower (USA) 730
Point Brown (USA) 730
Point Camden (USA) 730
Point Carrew (USA) 730
Point Charles (USA) 730
Point Chico (USA) 730
Point Countess (USA) 730
Point Defiance (USA) 689
Point Divide (USA) 730
Point Doran (USA) 730
Point Estero (USA) 730
Point Evans (USA) 730
Point Francis (USA) 730
Point Franklin (USA) 730
Point Glass (USA) 730
Point Hannon (USA) 730
Point Harris (USA) 730
Point Herron (USA) 730
Point Heyer (USA) 730
Point Highland (USA) 730
Point Hobart (USA) 730
Point Hope (USA) 730
Point Huron (USA) 730
Point Jackson (USA) 730
Point Judith (USA) 730
Point Knoll (USA) 730
Point Ledge (USA) 730
Point Lobos (USA) 730
Point Loma (USA) 698
Point Lookout (USA) 730
Point Martin (USA) 730
Point Monroe (USA) 730
Point Nowell (USA) 730
Point Richmond (USA) 730
Point Roberts (USA) 730
Point Sal (USA) 730
Point Spencer (USA) 730
Point Steele (USA) 730
Point Stuart (USA) 730
Point Swift (USA) 730
Point Thatcher (USA) 730
Point Turner (USA) 730
Point Verde (USA) 730
Point Warde (USA) 730
Point Wells (USA) 730
Point Whitehorn (USA) 730
Point Winslow (USA) 730
Pointer (UK) 598
Pokagon (USA) 712
Polar Sea (USA) 724
Polar Star (USA) 724
Polemistis (Gre) 213
Polidefkis (Gre) 208
Polikos (Gre) 208
Polimar 1-4 (Mex) 334
Polipo (Ita) 269
Pollack (USA) 634
Pollington (UK) 585
Pollux (GFR) 194
Pollux (Spn) 429
Polyarnik (USSR) 539, 549
Polyus (USSR) 542
Ponce (USA) 688
Ponchatoula (USA) 700
Ponciano Arriaga (Mex) 333
Ponoi (USSR) 552
Pontiac (USA) 712
Poolster (Nld) 347
Popenguine (Sen) 406
Porkkala (Fin) 142
Porobago (USA) 712
Porpoise (Aust) 45
Porpoise (UK) 567
Porpora (Ita) 269
Port Elizabeth (SA) 413
Port Said (Egy) 132
Porte Dauphine (Can) 78
Porte de la Reine (Can) 78
Porte Quebec (Can) 78
Porte St. Jean (Can) 78
Porte St. Louis (Can) 78
Portisham (UK) 600
Portland (USA) 689
Porto D'Ischia (Ita) 273
Porto Pisano (Ita) 273
Porto Recanati (Ita) 273
Poseidon (Fra) 177
Poseidon (GFR) 201
Poseidon (Pol) 394
Poseidón (Spn) 431
Potengi (Brz) 62
Poti (Brz) 60
Potomac (USA) 720
Potsdam (GDR) 185
Potvis (Nld) 341
Poughkeepsie (USA) 712
Powhatan (USA) 722
Pozzi (Ita) 273
Prab (Tld) 465
Prabal (Ind) 228
Prabparapak (Tld) 462
Prachand (Ind) 228
Pradupa (Sri) 433
Pragmar (Mex) 335
Prairie (USA) 697
Pralaya (Ind) 228
Prasae (Tld) 462
Prat (Chi) 89
Pratap (Ind) 228
Prathong (Tld) 465
Pratico Juvencio (Brz) 63
Preble (USA) 670
Premier-Maitre l'Her (Fra) 163
Prerow (GDR) 183
Preserver (Can) 76
Preserver (USA) 702
President Albert Bernard Bongo (Gab) 179
President Bourguiba (Tun) 469
President Kruger (SA) 412
President Leon M'ba (Gab) 179
President Pretorius (SA) 412
President Steyn (SA) 412
Presidente Alfaro (Ecu) 127
Presidente Busch (Bol) 53
Presidente Kennedy (Bol) 53
Presidente Oribe (Uru) 739
Presidente Rivera (Uru) 739
Presidente Sarmiento (Arg) 33
Presidente Velasco Ibarra (Ecu) 127
Prespa (Gre) 213
Prestol Botello (DR) 123
Pretoria (SA) 413
Preveze (Tur) 472
Priboi (USSR) 543
Priliv (USSR) 543
Primo Longobardo (Ita) 259
Primorye (USSR) 535
Primrose (USA) 732
Princesa (Spn) 424
Pritzwalk (GDR) 183
Private John R. Towle (USA) 719
Private Leonard C. Brostrom (USA) 719
Prizma (USSR) 540
Procion (DR) 124
Proet (Tld) 466
Professor Anichkov (USSR) 546
Professor Bogorov (USSR) 539
Professor Khlyustin (USSR) 546
Professor Krümmel (GDR) 183
Professor Kudrevich (USSR) 546
Professor Kurentsov (USSR) 539
Professor Minyayev (USSR) 546
Professor Pavlenko (USSR) 546
Professor Rybaltovsky (USSR) 546
Professor Schyogolev (USSR) 546
Professor Ukhov (USSR) 546
Professor Vodnanitsky (USSR) 539
Professor Vize (USSR) 543
Professor Yushchenko (USSR) 546
Professor Zubov (USSR) 543
Prometeo (Ita) 272
Protea (SA) 414
Proctecteur (Can) 76
Proleter (Yug) 754
Proteo (Ita) 271
Protet (Fra) 161
Proteus (Gre) 204
Proteus (USA) 704
Protraktor (USSR) 537
Providence (USA) 664
Provider (Can) 76
Provo Wallis (Can) 84
Provorny (USSR) 512
Prozorlivy (USSR) 513
Prut (USSR) 548
Psyché (Fra) 151
PT 11-15 (Jap) 284
Pte. Stroesner (Par) 372
Puerto Deseado (Arg) 31
Puerto Santo (Ven) 745
Puffer (USA) 633
Puget Sound (USA) 696
Pukaki (NZ) 350
Pukkio (Fin) 142
Pulang Geni (Indo) 235
Pulau Raja (Indo) 237
Pulau Rani (Indo) 237
Pulau Rapat (Indo) 237
Pulau Ratewo (Indo) 237
Pulau Rengat (Indo) 237
Pulau Roon (Indo) 237
Pulau Rorbas (Indo) 237
Pulicat (Ind) 228
Puma (GFR) 193
Punaruu (Fra) 171
Pung To (RoK) 315
Puni (Bru) 64
Punta Alta (Arg) 32
Punta Cabana (Ven) 744
Punta Delgada (Arg) 32
Punta Medanos (Arg) 32
Purha (Fin) 142
Puri (Ind) 228
Purus (Brz) 59
Pusan (RoK) 310
Pushmatha (USA) 712
Putri Sabah (Sab) 403
Putsaari (Fin) 142
Puttenham (UK) 600
Putumayo (Ecu) 129
Py (Arg) 27
Pyhtää (Fin) 142
Pyok Pa (RoK) 312
Pyro (USA) 697
Pyrpolitis (Gre) 213

Q

Qena (Egy) 134
Qeshm (Iran) 244
Quadra (Can) 80
Quapaw (USA) 705
Qu'Appelle (Can) 74
Quartier-Matre Alfred Motto (Cmn) 69
Quartier-Matre Anquetil (Fra) 163
Quarto (Ita) 270
Queenfish (USA) 633
Queensville (Can) 79
Querandi (Arg) 33
Quercia (Ita) 268
Quest (Can) 77
Quetta (Pak) 367
Quezon (Plp) 383
Qui Nhon (Vtn) 748
Quidora (Chi) 92
Quilmes (Arg) 33
Quindio (Col) 109
Quita Sueno (Col) 106
Quito (Ecu) 128

R

R1, 2, 3, 5 (Mex) 335
R. G. Masters (UK) 601
Racer (Can) 85
Racine (USA) 690
Rad (Tld) 467
Raddle (UK) 601
Radoom (UAE) 557
Rade Koncar (Yug) 754
Rafiki (Tan) 460
Raftsunda (Nor) 359
Raffello (Iran) 246
Rahav (Isr) 251
Rahmat (Mly) 325
Raimundo Nonato (Brz) 63
Rainier (USA) 735
Raisio (Fin) 140
Rajah Jarom (Mly) 327
Rajah Lakandula (Plp) 382
Rajshahi (Pak) 368
Rakata (Indo) 238
Raleigh (USA) 688
Rally (Can) 85
Ramadan (Iraq) 248
Ramakami (Sri) 433
Rambler (USA) 732
Rame Head (UK) 586
Ramsey (USA) 678
Ramzow (GDR) 184
Ran (Den) 118
Ran (Swe) 446, 448
Rance (Fra) 171
Rang Kwien (Tld) 465
Rangamati (Ban) 48
Range Sentinel (USA) 714
Ranger (USA) 650
Rapid (Can) 85
Raposo Taveres (Brz) 59
Rapp (Nor) 358
Raritan (USA) 735
Ras Adar (Tun) 470
Ras El-Helal (Lby) 323
Rashid (Egy) 132
Rask (Nor) 358
Ratcharit (Tld) 462
Rathburne (USA) 680
Rathenow (GDR) 183
Ratulangi (Indo) 237
Raven (Ire) 250
Ravn (Nor) 358
Rawi (Tld) 466
Ray (USA) 633
Rayong (Tld) 463
Razumny (USSR) 511
Razyashchy (USSR) 511
Razytelny (USSR) 511
Ready (Can) 85
Reasoner (USA) 680
Rebun (Jap) 287, 294
Recalde (Spn) 425
Reclaim (UK) 588
Reclaimer (USA) 702
Recovery (USA) 702
Red Beech (USA) 731
Red Birch (USA) 731
Red Cedar (USA) 731
Red Cloud (USA) 712
Red Oak (USA) 731
Red Wood (USA) 731
Redstone (USA) 714
Reduktor (USSR) 537
Redwing (USA) 712
Reeves (USA) 661
Regent (UK) 593
Regga (Kwt) 318
Regina (Can) 79
Regulus (GFR) 194
Reijger (SA) 413
Reinøysund (Nor) 359
Relay (Can) 85
Reliance (USA) 728
Remada (Tun) 470
Renchong (Mly) 326
Renke (GFR) 193
Renown (UK) 564
Rentaka (Mly) 326
Repiter (USSR) 537
Repton (UK) 585
Repulse (UK) 564
Requin (Fra) 151
Researcher (USA) 735
Réséda (Fra) 168
Reshef (Isr) 251
Reshitelny (USSR) 512
Resolute (USA) 728
Resolution (Sin) 409
Resolution (UK) 564
Resource (UK) 593
Restauracion (DR) 123
Restigouche (Can) 75
Resurgent (UK) 593
Retainer 593
Retivy (USSR) 511
Rettin (GFR) 200
Reunification (Cmn) 69
Revenge (UK) 564
Reyes (Chi) 94
Rezky (USSR) 511
Rezvy (USSR) 511
Rhein (GFR) 195
Rhenen (Nld) 346
Rhin (Fra) 171
Rhinocéros (Fra) 178
Rhon (GFR) 196
Rhône (Fra) 171
Rhyl (UK) 578
Riachuelo (Brz) 55
Riazi (Iran) 245
Ribadu (Nig) 354
Ribeira Grande (Por) 398
Ribnitz-Damgarten (GDR) 181
Riccio (Ita) 269
Richard B. Russell (USA) 633
Richard E. Byrd (USA) 673
Richard L. Page (USA) 678
Richard S. Edwards (USA) 674
Richard Sorge (GDR) 181
Richland (USA) 708
Richmond K. Turner (USA) 661
Rider (Can) 85
Riesa (GDR) 183
Rig Tugger (Nor) 361
Rigel (DR) 124
Rigel (Ecu) 129
Rigel (GFR) 194
Rigel (Spn) 429
Rigel (USA) 713
Rihtniemi (Fin) 140
Rimfaxe (Den) 121
Rincon (USA) 722
Ring (Swe) 445
Rio Apure (Ven) 745
Rio Arauca (Ven) 745
Rio Branco (Brz) 61
Rio Cabriales (Ven) 745
Rio Canete (Per) 381
Rio Caparo (Ven) 743
Rio Caroni (Ven) 745
Rio Chicawa (Per) 381
Rio Chillón (Per) 378
Rio Chira (Per) 381
Rio Chui (Brz) 63
Rio Coata (Per) 378
Rio Cruta (Nic) 351
Rio Das Contas (Brz) 62
Rio De Janeiro (Brz) 55
Rio Doce (Brz) 62
Rio Escalante (Ven) 743
Rio Formoso (Brz) 62
Rio Grande Do Norte (Brz) 58
Rio Grande Do Sul (Brz) 55
Rio Guarico (Ven) 745
Rio Huancané (Per) 378
Rio Huaora (Per) 381
Rio Ica (Per) 381
Rio Illave (Per) 378
Rio Limon (Ven) 743
Rio Locumba (Per) 381
Rio Majes (Per) 378
Rio Meta (Ven) 745
Rio Minho (Por) 397
Rio Negro (Arg) 30
Rio Negro (Brz) 63
Rio Negro (Uru) 737
Rio Negro (Ven) 745
Rio Neveri (Ven) 745
Rio Oiapoque (Brz) 63
Rio Orinoco (Ven) 743
Rio Panuco (Mex) 335
Rio Pardo (Brz) 63
Rio Pativilca (Per) 381
Rio Piura (Per) 377
Rio Portuguesa (Ven) 745
Rio Ramis (Per) 378
Rio Real (Brz) 62
Rio Sama (Per) 381
Rio San Juan (Ven) 743
Rio Santa (Per) 378
Rio Santo Domingo (Ven) 745
Rio Torres (Ven) 743
Rio Tucuyo (Ven) 743
Rio Tumbes (Per) 377
Rio Turbio (Ven) 743
Rio Turvo (Brz) 62
Rio Tux (Ven) 745
Rio Uribante (Ven) 745
Rio Venamo (Ven) 743
Rio Ventuari (Ven) 743
Rio Verde (Brz) 62
Rio Vitor (Per) 381
Rio Zarumilla (Per) 377
Riohacha (Col) 108
Rishiri (Jap) 287, 294
Ristna (USSR) 546
Ritsa (USSR) 552
Riva Trigoso (Ita) 273
Riverton (Can) 79
Rivett-Carnac (Can) 79
Rizal (Plp) 383
Rizzuto (Ita) 273
Roach (UK) 601
Roanoke (USA) 701
Roark (USA) 680
Robel (GDR) 183

NAMED SHIPS / INDEX 807

Robert A. Owens (USA) 676
Robert D. Conrad (USA) 715
Robert E. Lee (USA) 630
Robert E. Peary (USA) 680
Robert Foulis (Can) 85
Robert H. McCard (USA) 675
Robison (USA) 673
Robust (UK) 597
Robuste (Fra) 178
Robusto (Ita) 272
Rochefort (Bel) 51
Rochen (GFR) 193
Rödlöga (Swe) 444
Rodos (Gre) 210
Rodriguez (Col) 108
Rodriguez Zamora (Col) 110
Rodriquez (Per) 376
Rodsteen (Den) 118
Roermond (Nld) 346
Roger De Lauria (Spn) 420
Rogers (USA) 675
Rokk (Nor) 357
Rokko (Jap) 295
Rolf Peters (GDR) 183
Rollicker (UK) 597
Romah (Isr) 251
Romaleos (Gre) 213
Romanija (Yug) 755
Romblon (Plp) 385
Romenda (Gha) 202
Romeo Romei (Ita) 258
Rommel (GFR) 189
Romø (Den) 119
Romsø (Den) 119
Roncador (Col) 106
Rondonia (Brz) 60
Roraima (Brz) 60
Rosales (Arg) 27
Rosario (Por) 398
Rosenheim (GFR) 201
Rosen Ort (GDR) 184
Rosomak (Pol) 392
Rosslau (GDR) 183
Rossosh (USSR) 549
Rostam (Iran) 242
Rostock (GDR) 185
Rota (Den) 118
Rotersand (GFR) 201
Rothesay (UK) 578
Rotoiti (NZ) 350
Rotsund (Nor) 359
Rotterdam (Nld) 343
Rouget (Fra) 178
Rovuma (Por) 397
Roysterer (UK) 597
Röyttä (Fin) 140
Rubin (USSR) 521
Rude (USA) 735
Ruden (GDR) 184
Rudolf Breitscheid (GDR) 181
Rudolf Diesel (GFR) 200
Rudolf Egelhofer (GDR) 181
Ruediger (GFR) 198
Rugen (GDR) 184
Ruissalo (Fin) 140
Rumb (USSR) 538
Rush (USA) 726
Ruslan (USSR) 555
Rustom (Pak) 369
Ruve (Fij) 137
Ruwan Yaro (Nig) 354
Ryadh (SAr) 405
Rybachi (USSR) 538
Rymättylä (Fin) 140
Rys (Pol) 392
Ryul Po (RoK) 312

S

6 October (Egy) 131
S. Chelyuskin (USSR) 538
S. Filipovic (Yug) 754
S. Krakov (USSR) 539
S41-S60 (GFR) 192
S61-S70 (GFR) 192
Sa Chon (RoK) 312
Saam (Iran) 242
Saar (GFR) 195
Saar (Isr) 252
Saarburg (GFR) 197
Sabalo (Ven) 741
Saban (Bur) 68
Sabback El Bahr (Tun) 470
Sabola (Indo) 236
Sabratha (Lby) 322
Sabre (UK) 589
Sachsenwald (GFR) 197
Sachtouris (Gre) 206
Sackville (Can) 77
Saco (USA) 712
Sacramento (USA) 701
Sacre (Spn) 432
Sadaf (Iran) 246
Sadarin (Indo) 236
Sadko (USSR) 555
Sado (Jap) 293
Saetta (Ita) 266
Safeguard (USA) 702
Safra (Bhr) 47
Sagami (Jap) 293
Sagawamick (USA) 712
Sagebrush (USA) 731
Saginaw (USA) 690, 733
Sagiri (Jap) 296
Sagittaire (Fra) 166
Sagittario (Ita) 264
Sagres (Por) 399
Sagu (Bur) 68
Saguenay (Can) 75
Saham (Bhr) 47
Sahel (Fra) 171
Sahene (Gha) 202
Sahin (Tur) 475
Sahiwal (Pak) 367
Saikai (Jap) 300
Sailfish (USA) 640
St. Anthony (Can) 79
St. Charles (Can) 79
St. Croix (Can) 74
St. Louis (Sen) 406
St. Louis (USA) 691
St. Lykoudis (Gre) 213
St. Margarets (UK) 596
St. Paul (Lbr) 319
St. Paul (USA) 666
St. Sylvestre (Cam) 69
Saintonge (Fra) 172
Saipan (USA) 686
Sakate (Jap) 286
Sakelariou (Gre) 213
Sakhalin (USSR) 544, 556
Sakiet Sidi Youssef (Tun) 469
Sakito (Jap) 288
Salaam (Tan) 460
Salamaua (PNG) 370
Saldiray (Tur) 472
Saleha (Bru) 64
Salem (USA) 665
Sälen (Swe) 438
Salenga (USSR) 552
Salinan (USA) 705
Salisbury (UK) 579
Salm (GFR) 193
Salmaneti (Indo) 236
Salmone (Ita) 268
Salta (Arg) 25
Salto (Uru) 738
Saluki (UK) 598
Salvatore Todaro (Ita) 265
Salvia (USA) 731
Salvora (Spn) 426
Salvore (Ita) 273
Sam Chok (RoK) 314
Sam Houston (USA) 629
Sam Rayburn (USA) 627
Samadar (Indo) 236
Samadikun (Indo) 233
Samae San (Tld) 467
Samana (DR) 124
Samandira (Tur) 482
Samarai (PNG) 370
Sambre (Bel) 52
Samed (Tld) 466
Samos (Gre) 210
Samoset (USA) 705
Sample (USA) 679
Sampo (Fin) 141
Sampson (USA) 673
Samsø (Den) 119
Samson (Chi) 94
Samson (Gre) 213
Samsun (Tur) 477
Samudra Devi (Sri) 433
Samuel Gompers (USA) 696
Samum (GFR) 198
San Andres (Col) 109
San Benedetto (Ita) 273
San Bernardino (USA) 690
San Diego (USA) 697
San Francisco (USA) 631
San Francisco dos Santos (Brz) 63
San Giorgio (Ita) 262
San Giusto (Ita) 272
San-Go (Jap) 290
San Jose (USA) 697
San Luis (Arg) 25
San Onofre (USA) 708
San Salvador (Bhm) 47
Sanaga (Cmn) 69
Sanaviron (Arg) 33
Sancaktar (Tur) 478
Sanctuary (USA) 700
Sandalo (Ita) 268
Sand Lance (USA) 633
Sandhayak (Ind) 230
Sandpiper (UK) 589
Sangamon (USA) 733
Sangay (Ecu) 129
Sangsetia (Mly) 327
Sanson Gri (Spn) 432
Santa Barbara (USA) 697
Santa Catarina (Brz) 58
Santal (Fra) 178
Santander (Col) 106
Santaquin (USA) 712
Sanqual (Spn) 432
Santa Fe (Arg) 25
Santiago del Estero (Arg) 25
Santissima Trinidad (Arg) 26
Santos Degollado (Mex) 333
Sao Gabriel (Por) 399
Sao Roque (Por) 398
Sao Tang (RoC) 455
Sapanca (Tur) 477
Sapele (Nig) 353
Saphir (GFR) 198
Sarasin (Tld) 463
Saratoga (USA) 650
Sarcelle (Fra) 178
Sardius (Aust) 45
Sargo (USA) 637
Sariyer (Tur) 477
Sarköy (Tur) 482
Sarobetso (Jap) 293
Saros (Tur) 477
Sarpamina (Indo) 235
Sarpawasesa (Indo) 235
Sarpen (Nor) 360
Sasila (Indo) 236
Sasima (USSR) 552
Saskatchewan (Can) 74
Sassaba (USA) 712
Sassacus (USA) 712
Sassafras (USA) 731
Satakut (Tld) 465
Satsuma (Jap) 285, 292
Sattahip (Tld) 463
Satzhaff (GDR) 184
Sauda (Nor) 359
Saugatuck (USA) 721
Saugus (USA) 712
Sauk (USA) 735
Saule (Fra) 178
Savannah (USA) 701
Save (Por) 397
Sawangi (Indo) 236
Scamp (USA) 635
Scampo (Ita) 269
Scarab (UK) 599
Scarabée (Fra) 175
Sceptre (UK) 565
Scharhörn (GFR) 199
Schelde (Bel) 52
Schenectady (USA) 690
Scheveningen (Nld) 345
Schiedam (Nld) 345
Schirocco (GFR) 198
Schlei (GFR) 193
Schleswig (GFR) 193
Schleswig-Holstein (GFR) 190
Schofield (USA) 678
Schönebeck (GDR) 183
Schuiling (Nld) 346
Schultz Xavier (Por) 399
Schütze (GFR) 194
Schuyler Otis Bland (USA) 718
Schuylkill (USA) 721
Schwedt (GDR) 182
Scimitar (UK) 589
Scioto (USA) 733
Scirocco (Ita) 263
Scorpios (Gre) 208
Sculpin (USA) 635
Scylla (UK) 576
Sderzhanny (USSR) 512
Sea Cliff (USA) 643
Sea Devil (USA) 633
Sea Dog (Gam) 179
Sea Dragon (Sin) 408
Sea Giant (UK) 598
Sea Hawk (Sin) 408
Sea Lion (Sin) 408
Sea Otter (UK) 602
Sea Scorpion (Sin) 408
Sea Tiger (Sin) 408
Sea Wolf (Sin) 408
Seadragon (USA) 637
Seagull (UK) 602
Seahorse (USA) 633
Seal (Aust) 45
Seal (UK) 602
Sealift Antarctic (USA) 720
Sealift Arabian Sea (USA) 720
Sealift Arctic (USA) 720
Sealift Atlantic (USA) 720
Sealift Caribbean (USA) 720
Sealift China Sea 720
Sealift Indian Ocean (USA) 720
Sealift Mediterranean (USA) 720
Sealift Pacific (USA) 720
Sealion (UK) 567
Sealyham (UK) 598
Seattle (USA) 701
Seawolf (USA) 637
Sebastian L. de Tejada (Mex) 333
Sebha (Lby) 322
Second Maitre le Bihan (Fra) 163
Secota (USA) 712
Seddulbahir (Tur) 477
Sedge (USA) 731
Seeteufel (GFR) 198
Segui (Arg) 27
Sehested (Den) 117
Sehwan (Pak) 367
Seid Bereil (GDR) 185
Seima (USSR) 549
Seinda (Bur) 68
Sel (Nor) 358
Selcuk (Tur) 477
Selendon (Per) 380
Seliger (USSR) 536
Sellers (USA) 673
Semani (Alb) 20
Sembilang (Indo) 234
Semen Chelyuskin (USSR) 555
Semmes (USA) 673
Semois (Bel) 52
Semyen Dezhnev (USSR) 538, 555
Senasqua (USA) 712
Senckenburg (GFR) 201
Sendai (Jap) 293
Seneca (USA) 705
Senja, O/S (Nor) 360
Seoul (RoK) 310
Separacion (DM) 123
Seraing (Bel) 51
Serampang (Mly) 325
Serang (Mly) 325
Serdar (Tur) 478
Sergei Vavilov (USSR) 543
Sergej Lazo (USSR) 529
Serdity (USSR) 517
Sergento Aldea (Chi) 91
Sergipe (Brz) 58
Seriozny (USSR) 517
Serrano (Chi) 91
Seruwa (Sri) 433, 434
Setanta (Ire) 250
Setkaya (Bur) 68
Setogiri (Jap) 296
Setter (UK) 598
Setyahat (Bur) 68
Sevan (USSR) 544
Sevastopol (USSR) 507
Sever (USSR) 538
Seyhan (Tur) 477
Seymen (Tur) 477
Sfendoni (Gre) 206
Sgombro (Ita) 268
Sgt. Andrew Miller (USA) 719
Sgt. Truman Kimbro (USA) 719
Shaab (Sud) 435
Shabonee (USA) 712
Shacha (USSR) 549
Shackle (USA) 735
Shah Jahan (Pak) 366
Shahbandar (Mly) 327
Shaheed Ruhul Amin (Ban) 49
Shahrokh (Iran) 244
Shahsavar (Iran) 246
Shakal (USSR) 520
Shakori (USA) 705
Shakti (Ind) 231
Shamshir (Iran) 243
Shangri-La (USA) 653
Sharab (Ind) 229
Sharada (Ind) 228
Shardul (Ind) 229
Shark (USA) 635
Shasta (USA) 697
Shavington (UK) 585
Shearwater (UK) 601
Sheepdog (UK) 598
Sheffield (UK) 574
Sheksna (USSR) 549
Shelduck (UK) 601
Shelon (USSR) 549
Shen Yang (RoC) 452
Shenandoah (USA) 696
Sheraton (UK) 585
Sherman (USA) 726
Shetland (UK) 588
Shih Jian (CPR) 103
Shikinami (Jap) 282, 296
Shikine (Jap) 290, 294
Shilka (USSR) 551
Shimanami (Jap) 296
Shimayuki (Jap) 296
Shin Song (RoK) 312
Shinkai (Jap) 299
Shinonome (Jap) 296
Shipham (UK) 600
Shiqmona (Isr) 253
Shiraito (Jap) 297
Shirakami (Jap) 293
Shiramine (Jap) 295
Shirasagi (Jap) 300
Shiratori (Jap) 284
Shisaka (Jap) 290
Shoa Shan (RoC) 454
Shobo (Jap) 289
Shoryu (Jap) 297
Shoshone (USA) 721
Shoulton (UK) 585
Shoyo (Jap) 298
Shreveport (USA) 688
Shu Kuang (CPR) 104
Shulab (Iraq) 248
Shushuk (Pak) 365
Shwepazun (Bur) 68
Shwethida (Bur) 68
Shyri (Ecu) 126
Si Hung (RoK) 314
Sibarau (Indo) 235
Sibir (USSR) 544, 553
Sichang (Tld) 466
Sidney (Can) 77
Sidon (Leb) 318
Siegfried (GFR) 198
Siegmund (GFR) 198
Siegura (GFR) 198
Sierra (USA) 697
Siete de Agosto (Col) 106
Sifnos (Gre) 211
Sigacik (Tur) 477
Sigrun (Swe) 448
Sil (Spn) 428
Silas Bent (USA) 717
Silifke (Tur) 477
Silinan (Indo) 235
Silmä (Fin) 143
Silny (USSR) 511
Silva (Spn) 432
Silversides (USA) 633
Sima (USSR) 539
Simba (Ken) 303
Simcoe (Can) 84
Simeto (Ita) 272
Simon Bolivar (USA) 627
Simon Fraser (Can) 84
Simon Lake (USA) 703
Simorgh (Iran) 244
Simpson (Chi) 88
Simsek (Tur) 475
Sin Mi (RoK) 315
Sinai (Egy) 134
Sind (Pak) 367
Sine-Saloum (Sen) 406
Sinhu Durg (Ind) 228
Sinmin (Bur) 68
Sinop (Tur) 477
Siquijor (Plp) 385
Sir Bedivere (UK) 582
Sir Cecil Romer (Ire) 250
Sir Galahad (UK) 582
Sir Geraint (UK) 582
Sir Humphrey Gilbert (Can) 83
Sir James Douglas (Can) 85
Sir Lancelot (UK) 582
Sir Percivale (UK) 582
Sir Tristram (UK) 582
Sir William Alexander (Can) 83
Sira (Nor) 359
Sirena (USSR) 538
Siréne (Fra) 151
Sirio (DR) 125
Sirios (Gre) 212
Sirius (Brz) 61
Sirius (GFR) 194
Sirius (Swe) 440
Sirius (UK) 576
Sirte (Lby) 322
Sisu (Fin) 141
Sittard (Nld) 346
Sivrihisar (Tur) 476
Sjaelland (Den) 120
Sjöbjörnen (Swe) 437
Sjöhästen (Swe) 437
Sjöhunden (Swe) 437
Sjölejonet (Swe) 437
Sjöormen (Swe) 437
Skaftö (Swe) 443
Skagul (Swe) 445
Skanör (Swe) 441
Skate (USA) 637
Skeena (Can) 75
Skenandoa (USA) 712
Skenderbeu (Alb) 20
Skiathos (Gre) 211
Skidegate (Can) 86
Skilak (Kam) 302
Skinfaxe (Den) 121
Skipjack (USA) 635
Skjold (Nor) 357
Sklinna (Nor) 356
Skolpen (Nor) 356
Skomer (UK) 601
Skorpion (GFR) 194
Skory (USSR) 512
Skrei (Nor) 358
Skromny (USSR) 515
Skrytny (USSR) 515
Skua (Can) 86
Skua (UK) 601
Skudd (Nor) 357
Skuld (Swe) 448
Slava (Bul) 65
Slavny (USSR) 512
Sledge (USA) 733
Sleipner (Den) 121

808 INDEX / NAMED SHIPS

Sleipner (Nor) 357
Sleipner (Swe) 445
Slimak (Pol) 394
Sloughi (Mtn) 331
Småland (Swe) 439
Smaragd (GFR) 198
Smeli (Bul) 65
Smely (USSR) 512
Smetilvy (USSR) 512
Smike (UK) 601
Smilax (USA) 732
Smok (Pol) 394
Smolny (USSR) 546
Smotryashchy (USSR) 517
Smyge (Swe) 441
Smyshleny (USSR) 512
Snar (Nor) 358
Snappharen (Swe) 440
Snellius (Nld) 348
Snipe (Aust) 41
Snögg (Nor) 358
Snohomish (USA) 735
Snook (USA) 635
Soares Dutra (Brz) 62
Sobat (Sud) 435
Sobenes (Chi) 94
Soberton (UK) 585
Søbjoren (Den) 118
Socorro (Col) 110
Socotra (YPDR) 751
Södermanland (Swe) 438
Soemba (Nld) 348
Sogut (Tur) 481
Sohag (Egy) 134
Søhesten (Den) 118
Søhunden (Den) 118
Sokol (Pol) 390
Sokrushitelny (USSR) 517
Solea (GFR) 201
Solidny (USSR) 517
Solimoes (Brz) 59
Søløven (Den) 118
Somers (USA) 672
Somerset (SA) 414
Sömmera (GDR) 183
Song Tu (Vtn) 747
Sonduren (Tur) 482
Songhee (Can) 79
Soobrazitelny (USSR) 512
Sooraya (Sri) 433
Sorachi (Jap) 293
Sørfold (Nor) 361
Søridderen (Den) 118
Sorong (Indo) 238
Sørøysund (Nor) 359
Sorrell (USA) 731
Sorsogon (Plp) 387
Sosva (USSR) 549
Sotnikov (USSR) 538
Souellaba (Cam) 69
Soufa (Isr) 252
Søulven (Den) 118
Sour (Leb) 318
Sousse (Tun) 469
South Carolina (USA) 658
Southampton (UK) 574
Southerland (USA) 675
Souya (Jap) 286
Sovereign (UK) 565
Sovereignty (Sin) 408
Sovershenny (USSR) 517
Sovietsky Azerbaidjan (USSR) .. 520
Sovietsky Dagestan (USSR) 520
Sovietsky Turkmenistan (USSR) 520
Soya (Jap) 292
Soyanna (USSR) 549
Soznatelny (USSR) 515
Spa (Bel) 52
Spadefish (USA) 633
Spaekhuggeren (Den) 115
Spaniel (UK) 598
Spapool (UK) 597
Spar (USA) 731
Sparö (Swe) 443
Spartacus (Por) 399
Spartan (UK) 565
Spartanburg County (USA) 690
Sparviero (Ita) 266
Spasilac (Yug) 757
Spassk (USSR) 544
Spejaren (Swe) 440
Spencer (USA) 727
Sperone (Ita) 273
Sperry (USA) 704
Speshny (USSR) 516
Spessart (GFR) 196
Sphinx (USA) 702
Spica (GFR) 194
Spica (Swe) 440
Spiegel Grove (USA) 689
Spiekeroog (GFR) 199
Spike (USA) 733
Spindrift (Can) 86
Spiro (Arg) 28
Spitfire (UK) 602
Splendid (UK) 565
Split (Yug) 753
Spokojny (USSR) 516
Sposobny (USSR) 512
Spoven (Swe) 448
Spray (Can) 86
Springaren (Swe) 438
Springeren (Den) 115
Springfield (USA) 664
Spruance (USA) 668
Spume (Can) 86
Squalo (Ita) 268
Sri — (Mly) 328
Sri Banggi (Mly) 327
Sri Bangji (Sab) 403
Sri Gumantong (Mly) 327
Sri Gumantong (Sab) 403
Sri Johor (Mly) 326
Sri Kelantan (Mly) 326
Sri Kudat (Mly) 328
Sri Labuan (Mly) 327
Sri Labuan (Sab) 403
Sri Langkawi (Mly) 327
Sri Melaka (Mly) 326
Sri Menanti (Mly) 328
Sri Negri Sembilan (Mly) 326
Sri Perak (Mly) 326
Sri Perilis (Mly) 326
Sri Sabah (Mly) 326
Sri Sarawak (Mly) 326
Sri Selangor (Mly) 326
Sri Semporna (Sab) 403
Sri Tawau (Mly) 328
Sri Trengganu (Mly) 326
Stadt (Nor) 356
Stalbas (Nor) 361
Stallion (USA) 705
Stalwart (Aust) 43
Stand Off (Can) 79
Staphorst (Nld) 346
Star (GFR) 198
Starkodder (Swe) 440
Statny (USSR) 517
Stavanger (Nor) 356
Stavelot (Bel) 51
Staverman (Nld) 346
Steadfast (USA) 728
Steady (UK) 595
Stefan Malygin (USSR) 539
Stegg (Nor) 358
Steigerwald (GFR) 197
Steil (Nor) 357
Stein (USA) 680
Steinaker (USA) 675
Stella Polare (Ita) 271
Stepenny (USSR) 517
Stephan Jantzen (GDR) 185
Steregushchy (USSR) 512
Sterett (USA) 660
Sternberg (GDR) 181
Stieglitz (GFR) 198
Stier (GFR) 194
Stirling (UK) 602
Stonewall Jackson (USA) 627
Stör (GFR) 193
Stord (Nor) 356
Storetbecker (GFR) 198
Storione (Ita) 268
Storis (USA) 725
Storm (Nor) 357
Storozhevoy (USSR) 511
Stoyky (USSR) 517
Stralsund (GDR) 183
Strasburg (GDR) 183
Streljko (Yug) 754
Stremitelny (USSR) 517, 556
Strogiy (USSR) 512
Stromboli (Ita) 269
Stromness (UK) 594
Strömstad (Swe) 440
Stroyny (USSR) 512
Stuart (Aust) 40
StubbenKammer (GDR) 184
Stubbington (UK) 585
Stump (USA) 668
Stura (Ita) 272
Sturgeon (USA) 633
Sturgeon Bay (USA) 734
Sturkö (Swe) 443
Stvor (USSR) 538
Styrbjörn (Swe) 440
Styrsö (Swe) 443
Su Yong (RoK) 314
Suchan (USSR) 544
Sucre (Ven) 742
Süderoog (GFR) 201
Suenson (Den) 117
Suez (Egy) 131
Suffolk County (USA) 690
Suffren (Fra) 157
Suiryu (Jap) 297
Sukanya (Ind) 228
Sukkur (Pak) 367
Sukrip (Tld) 463
Sulhafa Al Bahr (Omn) 363
Sultan Hasanudin (Indo) 234
SultanHisar (Tur) 476
Sultan Kudarat (Plp) 384
Sulu (Plp) 387
Sumac (USA) 733
Sumida (Jap) 293
Sumter (USA) 690
Sunbird (USA) 705
Sunchon (RoK) 312
Sundang (Mly) 326
Sunderland (UK) 602
Sundew (USA) 731
Sundsvall (Swe) 439
Sunfish (USA) 633
Sungai Jerong (Indo) 238
Superb (UK) 565
Superman (UK) 598
Suphairin (Tld) 462
Supply (Aust) 43
Sura (Indo) 234
Surapati (Indo) 234
Surasdra (Tld) 463
Suribachi (USA) 697
Surigao Del Norte (Plp) 386
Surigao Del Sur (Plp) 386
Surma (Ban) 49
Surma (Ban) 49
Surmene (Tur) 477
Suro 2, 3, 5-8 (RoK) 316
Surotama (Indo) 235
Surovy (USSR) 517
Surubi (Arg) 30
Surveyor (USA) 735
Susa (Lby) 322
Susquehanna (USA) 720
Sutjeska (Yug) 752
Sutlej (Ind) 230
Suwad (Bhr) 47
Svartlöga (Swe) 444
Svedujschy (USSR) 516
Svenner (Nor) 356
Sverdlov (USSR) 509
Svetly (USSR) 516
Svirepy (USSR) 511
Sviyaga (USSR) 538
Svobodny (USSR) 517
Swan (Aust) 40
Swarozye (Pol) 394
Sweetbrier (USA) 731
Sweetgum (USA) 731
Swiatowid (Pol) 394
Swiftsure (UK) 565
Switha (UK) 601
Swivel (USA) 735
Swordfish (USA) 637
Sycamore (USA) 733
Sycomore (Fra) 178
Sydney (Aust) 29
Sylphe (Fra) 176
Sylt (GFR) 199
Sylvania (USA) 697
Syros (Gre) 210
Sysola (USSR) 549
Szu Ch'ing Shan (CPR) 103
Szu Ming (RoC) 459

T

3 De Noviembre (Ecu) 128
T. Bellingsgausen (USSR) 538
T.T. Lewis (Bar) 49
Ta Chih (CPR) 103
Ta Hu (RoC) 458
Ta Pieh Shan (CPR) 103
Ta Peng (RoC) 459
Ta Sueh (RoC) 459
Ta Teng (RoC) 459
Ta Tung (RoC) 459
Ta Wan (RoC) 459
Ta Yu (RoC) 459
Tabarzin (Iran) 243
Tabuk (SAr) 404
Tachikaze (Jap) 279
Tackle (USA) 735
Tacoma (USA) 683
Taconnet (USA) 712
Tadindeng (Tld) 465
Tae Cho (RoK) 315
Taejon (RoK) 310
Tafelberg (SA) 414
Tagbanua (Plp) 389
Tagil (USSR) 548
Tahan (Mly) 326
Tahchin (Tld) 462
Tahuamanu (Bol) 53
Tai Hsing Shan (CPR) 103
Tai Shan (RoC) 454
Tai Yuan (RoC) 454
Taifun (GFR) 198
Taifun (USSR) 539
Taimur (Pak) 365
Tajo (Spn) 428
Takami (Jap) 286
Takanami (Jap) 282, 296
Takanawa (Jap) 295
Takane (Jap) 286
Takapu (NZ) 350
Takashio (Jap) 278
Takatsuki (Jap) 280, 295
Takelma (USA) 705
Takos (USA) 712
Taku Shan (CPR) 103, 105
Takuyo (Jap) 298
Talara (Per) 379
Talaud (Indo) 238
Talbot (USA) 678
Talibong (Tld) 466
Tallulah (USA) 721
Taluga (USA) 721
Talwar (Ind) 226
Taman (USSR) 544
Tamanami (Jap) 296
Tamaqua (USA) 712
Tamaroa (USA) 734
Tamayuki (Jap) 296
Tambora (Indo) 239
Tampa (USA) 728
Tamrau (Indo) 239
Tamur (Iraq) 248
Tamuz (Iraq) 247
Tana (Nor) 359
Tanaro (Ita) 272
Taney (USA) 727
Tang (USA) 640
Tangerhütte (GDR) 183
Tanin (Isr) 251
Tapi (Tld) 461
Tarablous (Leb) 318
Taragiri (Ind) 225
Tarak (Tur) 482
Tarakan (Aust) 44
Tarakan (Indo) 238
Taranaki (NZ) 350
Tarapunga (NZ) 350
Tarawa (Sri) 433, 434
Tarawa (USA) 686
Tarbatness (UK) 594
Tarek Ibn Zayed (Syr) 450
Tareq Ben Zaid (Iraq) 248
Tariq (Egy) 131
Tariq (Pak) 365
Tariq (Qat) 399
Tariq (SAr) 404
Tarkhankut (USSR) 548
Tarmo (Fin) 141
Tärnö (Swe) 443
Tarqui (Ecu) 128
Tarshish (Isr) 251
Tartar (UK) 577
Tartu (Fra) 159
Tartu (USSR) 549
Tasaday (Plp) 389
Tashiro (Jap) 286
Tatnuck (USA) 705
Tat Sa (Vtn) 747
Tatsuta (Jap) 294
Tattnall (USA) 673
Taupo (NZ) 350
Taurus (Brz) 61
Tazarka (Tun) 469
Tutog (USA) 633
Tavi (Fin) 143
Tawakoni (USA) 705
Tawfic (Mor) 338
Tayfun (Tur) 474
Taymyr (USSR) 538
Tayrona (Col) 105
TB 1 (GFR) 200
Te Yang (RoC) 452
Tebuk (SAr) 406
Tecumseh (USA) 627
Tecunuman (Gua) 214
Tegernsee (GFR) 196
Tegualda (Chi) 92
Tehuantepec (Mex) 333
Tehuelche (Arg) 33
Teide (Spn) 429
Teist (Nor) 358
Teja (GFR) 198
Tejsten (Den) 119
Tekirdag (Tur) 477
Telkkä (Fin) 143
Teluk Amboina (Indo) 236
Teluk Bajur (Indo) 236
Teluk Bone (Indo) 236
Teluk Kau (Indo) 236
Teluk Langsa (Indo) 236
Teluk Manado (Indo) 236
Teluk Ratai (Indo) 236
Teluk Saleh (Indo) 236
Teluk Tomini (Indo) 236
Tembah (Can) 86
Temenggong (Mly) 327
Templin (GDR) 183
Tenace (Fra) 177
Tenacity (UK) 589
Tenente Claudio (Brz) 63
Tenente Fabio (Brz) 63
Tenente Raul (Brz) 63
Teniente Farina (Par) 371
Teniente Luis Bernal (Col) 110
Teniente Pratts Gil (Par) 372
Tenente O. Carreras Saguier (Par) 372
Teniente Sorzano (Col) 110
Tenyo (Jap) 298
Teodolit (USSR) 537
Terek (USSR) 549
Teriberka (USSR) 552
Terme (Tur) 477
Tern (UK) 601
Tern (USA) 732
Terra Nova (Can) 75
Teruzuki (Jap) 281
Teshio (Jap) 283, 294
Teterow (GDR) 181
Teuri (Jap) 286
Texas (USA) 657
TF 1-6 (GFR) 198
TF 101-104 (GFR) 198
TF 106-108 (GFR) 198
Thai Binh (Vtn) 747
Thakeham (UK) 600
Thalia (Gre) 211
Tham Ngu Lao (Vtn) 746
Thamrin (Indo) 237
That Assuari (Qat) 399
Thatcham (UK) 601
Thayanchon (Tld) 463
The Luke (Aust) 46
Themistocles (Gre) 206
Theodore Roosevelt (USA) 630
Theseus (GFR) 191
Thesseus (Gre) 213
Thetis (GFR) 191
Thetis (Gre) 213
Thi Tu (Vtn) 747
Thoaban (UAE) 557
Tho Chau (Vtn) 747
Thomas A. Edison (USA) 629
Thomas C. Hart (USA) 680
Thomas Carleton (Can) 84
Thomas G. Thompson (USA) 715
Thomas Grant (UK) 596
Thomas Jefferson (USA) 629
Thomas Washington (USA) 715
Thomaston (USA) 689
Thompson (Arg) 31
Thor (Ice) 220
Thorn (USA) 668
Thornham (UK) 586
Throsk (UK) 597
Thu Tay Thi (Bur) 68
Thule (Swe) 446
Thuong Tien (Vtn) 748
Thunder (Can) 78
Thunder Bau (USA) 734
Thurø (Den) 119
Thyella (Gre) 206
Tian Kwo (RoC) 455
Tianée (Fra) 175
Tiboli (Plp) 389
Tiburon (Pan) 370
Tiburon (Ven) 741
Tichitt (Mtn) 330
Ticino (Ita) 272
Tidepool (UK) 591
Tidespring (UK) 591
Tien Giang (Vtn) 748
Tien Moi (Vtn) 747
Tien Shan (RoC) 454
Tienga (Sud) 435
Tierra Del Fuego (Arg) 30
Tiger (UK) 571
Tijerhaai (Nld) 341
Tikal (Gua) 214
Timavo (Ita) 272
Timban (Brz) 59
Timo (Ita) 268
Timsah (UAE) 557
Tinaztepe (Tur) 473
Tino (Ita) 273
Tinosa (USA) 634
Tippu Sultan (Pak) 367
Tir (Ind) 227
Tiran (Iran) 243
Tirebolu (Tur) 477
Tirfing (Swe) 440
Tista (Ban) 49
Tista (Nor) 359
Titan (Gre) 213
Titan (USSR) 549
Tjeld (Nor) 358
Tjerk Hiddes (Nld) 344
Tjurkö (Swe) 443
Tlaxcala (Mex) 335
To Yen (Vtn) 747
Toba (Arg) 33
Tobol (USSR) 532
Tobruk (Aust) 44
Tobruk (Lby) 321
Todak (Indo) 236
Todak (Mly) 326
Tofino (Can) 79
Tofino (Spn) 429
Tohok (Indo) 234

NAMED SHIPS / INDEX 809

Toka (USA) 712
Tokachi (Jap) 283, 294
Toky (Mad) 323
Toll (Arg) 30
Tomahawk (USA) 712
Tombak (Mly) 326
Tombasiz (Gre) 206
Tomonami (Jap) 296
Tomsky Komsomolets (USSR) 529
Tonb (Iran) 245
Tone (Jap) 293
Tonelero (Brz) 55
Toneleros (Brz) 63
Tongeren (Bel) 51
Tongham (UK) 600
Tongpliu (Tld) 463
Tonijn (Nld) 341
Tonina (Spn) 418
Tonkawa (USA) 712
Tonocote (Arg) 33
Tontogany (USA) 712
Topas (GFR) 198
Topater (Bol) 53
Tor (Swe) 446
Torani (Indo) 234
Tordön (Swe) 440
Toribio (Bol) 53
Tornade (Cmn) 69
Tornadon (GFR) 189
Torquay (UK) 580
Torrens (Aust) 40
Torrent (UK) 596
Torrid (UK) 596
Tortuguero (DR) 123
Toshima (Jap) 290
Totila (GFR) 198
Toucan (Fra) 178
Toufan (Iran) 246
Toumi (Jap) 295
Tourmaline (Fra) 167
Tourterelle (Fra) 178
Tourville (Fra) 158
Tousan (Iran) 246
Toushi (Jap) 286
Tovda (USSR) 719
Towers (USA) 673
Towline (USA) 735
Towwora (Arg) 30
Toxotis (Gre) 208
Trabzon (Tur) 477
Tracy (Can) 83
Trafalgar (UK) 565
Tramandai (Brz) 59
Tran Khanh Du (Vtn) 746
Tran Lo (Vtn) 748
Transvaal (SA) 413
Traust (Nor) 357
Travailleur (Fra) 178
Traverz (USSR) 537
Trenton (USA) 688
Trepang (USA) 633
Trevose (UK) 601
Triaina (Gre) 205
Trident (Fra) 165
Tridente (Brz) 63
Trieste II (USA) 643
Trieux (Fra) 164
Trifoglio (Ita) 268
Trihonis (Gre) 213
Triki (Mor) 337
Trinity (TT) 468
Tripoli (USA) 687
Trippe (USA) 680
Trischen (GFR) 199
Trishul (Ind) 226
Tritao (Brz) 63
Triton (Den) 117
Triton (Fra) 174
Triton (GFR) 191
Triton (Gre) 204
Triton (Nld) 348
Triton (USA) 636
Triumph (UK) 586
Triunfo (Brz) 63
Tromp (Nld) 342
Trondheim (Nor) 356
Tropik (USSR) 538
Tross (Nor) 357
Troung Ba (Vtn) 748
Trout (USA) 640
Truckee (USA) 700
Truett (USA) 680
Truong Sa (Vtn) 747
Truxtun (USA) 659
Trygg (Nor) 357
Tsna (USSR) 547
Tsugaru (Jap) 289
Tsukuba (Jap) 295
Tsukumi (Jap) 288
Tsurugi (Jap) 295
Tsushima (Jap) 290, 299
Tübingen (GFR) 193
Tufan (Tur) 475
Tui (NZ) 351
Tuima (Fin) 139
Tuiska (Fin) 139
Tukan (Pol) 392
Tulare (USA) 691
Tulcan (Ecu) 128
Tulipe (Fra) 177
Tullibee (USA) 634
Tuloma (USSR) 552
Tumaco (Col) 109
Tumleren (Den) 115
Tümmler (GFR) 193
Tung An (CPR) 99
Tung Fan Hung (CPR) 103
Tunguska (USSR) 549
Tunny (USA) 633
Tupa (Fra) 175
Tupelo (USA) 731
Tupper (Can) 84
Tur (Pol) 392
Turja (Spn) 428
Turja (Fin) 143
Turman (USSR) 520
Turner Joy (USA) 674
Turnhout (Bel) 51
Tursas (Fin) 143
Turtle (USA) 643
Turunmaa (Fin) 138
Tuscaloosa (USA) 690
Tuscumbia (USA) 712
Tuskegee (USA) 712
Tutahaco (USA) 712
Tuuli (Fin) 139
Tuzla (Tur) 481
Tydeman (Nld) 347
Tyfon (Gre) 208
Tyo To (RoK) 315
Typhoon (UK) 598
Tyr (Ice) 220
Tyrsky (Fin) 139

U

U1-U2 (GFR) 188
U9-U12 (GFR) 188
U13-U30 (GFR) 188
Ubirajara dos Santos (Brz) 63
Ucayali (Per) 377
Uckermünde (GDR) 183
Udarnik (Yug) 754
Udaygiri (Ind) 225
Ueltzen (GFR) 201
Uhuru (Tan) 460
Uisko (Fin) 143
Ul Rung (RoK) 315
Ul San (RoK) 315
Ula (Nor) 356
Ulabat (Tur) 481
Ulisses (Por) 399
Ulku (Tur) 481
Ulla (Spn) 428
Ulm (GFR) 193
Uluç Ali Reis (Tur) 472
Ulvsund (Den) 121
Ulyana Gromova (USSR) 538
Ulysses S. Grant (USA) 627
Umar Farooq (Ban) 48
Umberto Grosso (Ita) 265
Umeå (Swe) 440
Umidori (Jap) 284
Umigiri (Jap) 296
Umitaka (Jap) 284
Umur Bey (Tur) 481
Un Pong (RoK) 314
Unanue (Per) 378
Unden (Swe) 448
Undine (GFR) 194
Ung Po (RoK) 311
Uniao (Brz) 57
Unimak (USA) 727
Unja (USSR) 552
Uplifter (UK) 594
Uporny (USSR) 514
Uppland (Swe) 439
Upton (UK) 585
Uragan (USSR) 521
Ural (USSR) 534
Uranami (Jap) 282, 296
Urania (Nld) 348
Urayuki (Jap) 296
Urazuki (Jap) 296
Urd (Swe) 448
Urdaneto (Ven) 742
Urho (Fin) 141
Uriah Heep (UK) 601
Uribe (Chi) 91
Urk (Nld) 345
Uruguay (Arg) 33
Uruguay (Uru) 736
Urume (Jap) 287
Usedom (GDR) 184
Usedom (USSR) 549
Uskok (Yug) 752
Usorio Saravia (Gua) 214
Ustica (Ita) 273
Usumacinta (Mex) 333
Utatlan (Gua) 214
Ute (USA) 705
Uthaug (Nor) 356
Uthörn (GFR) 201
Utile (Fra) 178
Utla (Nor) 359
Utö (Swe) 443
Utone (Jap) 286
Utrecht (Nld) 343
Utsira (Nor) 356
Utstein (Nor) 356
Uttern (Swe) 438
Utvaer (Nor) 356
Uusimaa (Fin) 138
Uzushio (Jap) 278

V

24 De Mayo (Ecu) 127
25 De Julio (Ecu) 127
V. Bagat (Yug) 754
V. Golovnin (USSR) 538
V. Skorpik (Yug) 754
V. Sukhotsky (USSR) 539
Vadso (Nor) 357
Vaedderen (Den) 117
Vagach (USSR) 538
Vagir (Ind) 224
Vagli (Ind) 224
Vagsheer (Ind) 224
Väktaren (Swe) 440
Val (USSR) 536
Valdez (USA) 680
Valdivia (Chi) 93
Vale (Nor) 358
Vale (Swe) 440
Valen (Swe) 438
Valentin G. Farias (Mex) 333
Valerian Albanov (USSR) 539
Valerian Uryvaev (USSR) 539
Valeureux (Fra) 178
Valiant (UK) 566
Valiant (USA) 728
Valleyfield II (Can) 79
Vällö (Swe) 443
Valpas (Fin) 142
Vampire (Aust) 39
Van (Tur) 481
Van Bochove (Nld) 348
Van der Wel (Nld) 346
Van Dien (Vtn) 748
Van Galen (Nld) 344
Van Hamel (Nld) 346
Van Kinsbergen (Nld) 344
Van Moppes (Nld) 346
Van Nes (Nld) 344
Van Speijk (Nld) 344
Van Straelen (Nld) 346
Van 'T Hoff (Nld) 346
Van Versendaal (Nld) 346
Van Well Groenveld (Nld) 346
Vancouver (Can) 80
Vancouver (USA) 688
Vanguard (USA) 714
Vanguardia (Uru) 739
Vanneau (Fra) 178
Varberg (Swe) 440
Vargen (Swe) 438
Varma (Fin) 141
Varyag (USSR) 508
Vasama 2 (Fin) 139
Vasiliy Chapaev (USSR) 506
Vasily Poiarkov (USSR) 555
Vasily Pronchishtchev (USSR) 555
Vasouya (Alg) 22
Västerås (Swe) 440
Västervik (Swe) 440
Vauquelin (Fra) 160
Vazhny (USSR) 517
Vdokhnovenny (USSR) 516
Vdumchivy (USSR) 517
Vedushchy (USSR) 517
Veer (Ind) 228
Veere (Nld) 346, 345
Vega (Fra) 166
Vega (Swe) 440
Vega (USSR) 538
Veinte de Julio (Col) 106
Veinticinco de Mayo (Arg) 25
Vejrø (Den) 119
Vela (Ind) 224
Velasco (Spn) 427
Velos (Gre) 206
Vendetta (Aust) 39
Vengadora (Col) 108
Venlo (Nld) 346
Ventimiglia (Ita) 273
Venturous (USA) 728
Venus (Fra) 151
Verendrye (Can) 85
Verny (USSR) 517
Verseau (Fra) 168
Vertieres (Hai) 216
Vertikal (USSR) 536
Verviers (Bel) 51
Vesky (USSR) 516
Vesuvio (Ita) 269
Veurne (Bel) 51
Vice-Admiral Drozd (USSR) 507
Vicente Yañez Pinzon (Spn) 424
Victor Cubillos (Col) 110
Victor Hensen (GFR) 201
Victor Schoelcher (Fra) 161
Victoria (USA) 718
Victoria (Ven) 743
Vidar (Nor) 358
Vidar (Swe) 440
Vidny (USSR) 517
Vidyut (Ind) 228
Vigilant (IC) 273
Vigilant (UK) 600
Vigilant (USA) 728
Vigilante (Fra) 177
Vigoroso (Ita) 272
Vigorous (USA) 728
Vii (Fin) 143
Vijay Durg (Ind) 228
Vijeta (Ind) 228
Viken (Swe) 441
Vikhrevoy (USSR) 517
Vikrant (Ind) 224
Viksten (Swe) 444
Viktor Bugaev (USSR) 543
Viktor Kotelnikov (USSR) 533
Villa de Bilbao (Spn) 424
Villaamil (Spn) 425
Villapando (Mex) 334
Villar (Per) 376
Ville Marie (Can) 86
Vilm (GDR) 184
Vilsund (Den) 121
Vinash (Ind) 228
Vindhyagiri (Ind) 225
Vineta (GFR) 194
Vinh Long (Fra) 167
Vinö (Swe) 443
Violette (Fra) 177
Virgin Clipper (VI) 750
Virginia (USA) 657
Virginio Fasan (Ita) 264
Virgo (Swe) 440
Vis (Yug) 757
Visborg (Swe) 442
Visby (Swe) 439
Vischio (Ita) 268
Vise (Bel) 51
Vise (USA) 733
Vishera (USSR) 549
Vitalienbrüder (GFR) 198
Viteazul (Rom) 402
Vitsgarn (Swe) 448
Vitte (GDR) 183
Vittorio Veneto (Ita) 259
Vityaz (USSR) 543
Vivies (Gre) 213
Vlaardingen (Nld) 345
Vladimir Kavrasky (USSR) 542
Vladimir Kolechitsky (USSR) 547
Vladimir Obruchev (USSR) 544
Vladimir Rusanov (USSR) 555
Vladimir Trefolev (USSR) 550
Vladimir Zaimov (Bul) 66
Vladivostock (USSR) 507, 554
Vlado Cetkovic (Yug) 754
Vlijatelny (USSR) 516
Vnezapny (USSR) 517
Vnimatelny (USSR) 517
Voge (USA) 679
Vogelgesang (USA) 675
Vogelsand (GFR) 199
Voima (Fin) 141
Voinicul (Rom) 402
Volkan (Tur) 474
Volevoy (USSR) 517
Volga (USSR) 532
Volk (USSR) 520
Volker (GFR) 198
Volkhov (USSR) 548
Völklingen (GFR) 193
Volna (USSR) 543
Volstad Jr (Nor) 361
Voluntario (Brz) 63
Volvi (Gre) 213
Von Steuben (USA) 627
Voronezhsky Komsomolets (USSR) 529
Vos (Nld) 345
Vosso (Nor) 359
Vostok (USSR) 538
Vozbuzhdenny (USSR) 515
Vozmuschenny (USSR) 516
Vrazumitelny (USSR) 517
Vreeland (USA) 680
Vsevolod Beryozkin (USSR) 539
Vukovklanac (Yug) 755
Vulcan (USA) 702
Vung Tau (Vtn) 748
Vyderzhanny (USSR) 516
Vyuga (USSR) 555
Vyzvyajuschy (USSR) 516

W

W. S. Sims (USA) 680
Waage (GFR) 194
Wabash (USA) 701
Waccamaw (USA) 721
Waddell (USA) 673
Wadsworth (USA) 677
Wahaka (USA) 712
Waheed (Kwt) 318
Wahoo (USA) 640
Wahpeton (USA) 712
Waikato (NZ) 349
Wainwright (USA) 660
Wakagumo (Jap) 296
Wakanami (Jap) 296
Wakashio (Jap) 278
Wakataka (Jap) 284
Wakeful (UK) 596
Walchensee (GFR) 196
Walkerton (UK) 585
Walnut (USA) 731
Walrus (UK) 567
Walter (GFR) 198
Walter E. Foster (Can) 84
Walther Hertwig (GFR) 201
Walther Von Ledebur (GFR) 200
Walvisbaai (SA) 413
Wamandai (Nld) 348
Wambrau (Nld) 348
Wan Shou (RoC) 458
Wanamassa (USA) 712
Wandenkolk (Brz) 63
Wandelaar (Bel) 50
Wangerooge (GFR) 199
Wannalancet (USA) 712
Wapakoneta (USA) 712
Wapato (USA) 712
Warmingham (UK) 601
Warnemünde (GDR) 183
Warspite (UK) 566
Warszawa (Pol) 390
Warta (Pol) 393
Washtucna (USA) 712
Wasperton (UK) 589
Wate (GFR) 198
Waterford (USA) 708
Watercourse (UK) 597
Waterfall (UK) 597
Waterfowl (UK) 597
Waterman (UK) 597
Watershed (UK) 597
Waterside (UK) 597
Waterspout (UK) 597
Waterwitch (UK) 591
Wathah (Kwt) 317
Wathena (USA) 712
Waubansee (USA) 712
Wauwatosa (USA) 712
Waxahatchie (USA) 712
Wedge (USA) 733
Wee Bong (RoK) 314
Weehawken (USA) 712
Weeraya (Sri) 433
Wega (GFR) 194, 201
Weilheim (GFR) 193
Weisswasser (GDR) 183
Welch (USA) 683
Wels (GFR) 193
Wen Shan (RoC) 454
Wenatchee (USA) 712
Werra (GFR) 195
Wesp (Bel) 52
West Milton (USA) 708
Westdiep (Bel) 50
Westensee (GFR) 196
Western Samar (Plp) 387
Westerwald (GFR) 197
Westgat (Nld) 348
Westhinder (Bel) 50
Westra (UK) 601
Westwind (GFR) 198
Westwind (USA) 725
Wetzlar (GFR) 193
Wewak (Aust) 44
Whale (USA) 633
Wheeling (USA) 714
Whimbrel (UK) 596
Whipple (USA) 680
White Bush (USA) 732
White Heath (USA) 732
White Holly (USA) 732
White Lupine (USA) 732
White Pine (USA) 732
White Plains (USA) 697
White Sage (USA) 732
White Sumac (USA) 732
Whitehead (UK) 595
Whitehorse (Can) 79
Whiting (USA) 735
Wichita (USA) 701
Widder (GFR) 194
Wielingen (Bel) 50
Wielingen (Nld) 348
Wiernier (USSR) 539
Wiesel (GFR) 193
Wiking (GFR) 198
Wildwood (Can) 79
Wilhelm Bauer (GFR) 188

Name	Page
Wilhelm Pieck (GDR)	184
Wilhelm Pieckstadt (GDR)	183
Wilhelm Pullwer (GFR)	200
Wilkes (USA)	717
Will Rogers (USA)	627
Willem van der Zaan (Nld)	344
Willemoes (Den)	117
Willemstad (Nld)	345
Willi Bansch (GDR)	181
William C. Lawe (USA)	675
William H. Bates (USA)	633
William H. Standley (USA)	660
William R. Rush (USA)	675
William V. Pratt (USA)	670
Wilton (UK)	584
Winamac (USA)	712
Windhoek (SA)	413
Wingina (USA)	712
Winnemucca (USA)	712
Wire (USA)	735
Wisconsin (USA)	655
Wismar (GDR)	181, 185
Wiston (UK)	585
Witte de With (Nld)	344
Wittensee (GFR)	196
Witthayaklom (Tld)	462
Wittigo (GFR)	198
Wittstock (GDR)	183
Wodnik (Pol)	393
Woerden (Nld)	346
Wol Mi (RoK)	315
Wolf (Nld)	345
Wolfe (Can)	83
Wolfsburg (GFR)	193
Wolgast (GDR)	183
Wolverton (UK)	589
Wood County (USA)	690
Woodlark (UK)	591
Woodrow Wilson (USA)	627
Woodrush (USA)	731
Worden (USA)	661
Wotan (GFR)	195
Wotton (UK)	585
Wu Chang (CPR)	99
Wu Kang (RoC)	458
Wu Sheng (RoC)	454
Wu Tai (RoC)	458
Wyaconda (USA)	733
Wyandot (USA)	717
Wyman (USA)	717

X

Name	Page
Xucuxuy (Gua)	214

Y

Name	Page
Yacuma (Bol)	53
Yaegumo (Jap)	292
Yaeshio (Jap)	278
Yaeyama (Jap)	292
Yaffo (Isr)	251
Yahagi (Jap)	293
Yakhroma (USSR)	549
Yakov Gakkel (USSR)	539
Yakov Smirnitsky (USSR)	539
Yama (Isr)	254
Yamadori (Jap)	284
Yamagumo (Jap)	280
Yamal (USSR)	544
Yamana (Arg)	28
Yamayuki (Jap)	296
Yan Gyi Aung (Bur)	67
Yan Lon Aung (Bur)	68
Yan Myo Aung (Bur)	67
Yan Taing Aung (Bur)	67
Yana (USSR)	547
Yanaba (USA)	712
Yanegua (USA)	712
Yankton (USA)	735
Yarden (Isr)	254
Yarhisar (Tur)	476
Yarkon (Isr)	251
Yarmouk (Syr)	450
Yarmouth (UK)	578
Yarmouth Navigator (UK)	601
Yarnton (UK)	589
Yarra (Aust)	40
Yashima (Jap)	288
Yashiro (Jap)	290
Yatanocas (USA)	712
Yavdezan (Alg)	22
Yavza (USSR)	551
Yay Bo (Bur)	68
Yedekci (Tur)	482
Yegorlik (USSR)	548
Yelcho (Chi)	93
Yellowknife (Can)	79
Yellowstone (USA)	696
Yelnya (USSR)	548
Yemelyan Pugatchev (USSR)	555
Yen Lun (CPR)	103
Yermak (USSR)	553
Yerofei Khabarov (USSR)	555
Yildiray (Tur)	472
Yildirim (Tur)	475
Yildiz (Tur)	475
Ymer (Swe)	445
Yocona (USA)	734
Yodo (Jap)	297
Yokose (Jap)	286
Yola (Nig)	354
Yon-Go (Jap)	290
Yong Dong (RoK)	314
Yong Mun (RoK)	316
Yosemite (USA)	697
Yoshino (Jap)	283, 293
Youville (Can)	79
Ystad (Swe)	440
Yu (Mly)	326
Yu Shan (RoC)	454
Yu Tai (RoC)	458
Yubari (Jap)	293
Yudachi (Jap)	282
Yuen Yang (RoC)	453
Yukikaze (Jap)	283
Yukon (Can)	74
Yukon (USA)	721
Yuma (USA)	712
Yung An (RoC)	456
Yung Cheng (RoC)	456
Yung Chi (RoC)	456
Yung Ching (RoC)	456
Yung Chou (RoC)	456
Yung Fu (RoC)	456
Yung Hsin (RoC)	456
Yung Jen (RoC)	456
Yung Ju (RoC)	456
Yung Kang (RoC)	459
Yung Lo (RoC)	456
Yung Nien (RoC)	456
Yung Ping (RoC)	456
Yung Shan (RoC)	456
Yung Sui (RoC)	456
Yupiter (USSR)	536
Yuri Lisyanskiy (USSR)	555
Yuri M. Shokalsky (USSR)	544
Yurij Godin (USSR)	540
Yuugumo (Jap)	280
Yuzbasi Tolunay (Tur)	480

Z

Name	Page
Z2-Z5	190
Z. Jovanovic-Spanac (Yug)	754
Zaal (Iran)	242
Zabaikalye (USSR)	535
Zacatecas (Mex)	335
Zafer (Tur)	473
Zafona (Isr)	254
Zaire (Por)	397
Zaire (Zai)	758
Zakarpatye (USSR)	535
Zambales (Plp)	386
Zambeze (Por)	397
Zamboanga del Norte (Plp)	386
Zander (GFR)	193
Zarti (Pan)	369
Zaporozhiye (USSR)	535
Zapoylara (USSR)	538
Zarya (USSR)	540
Zbik (Pol)	392
Zeefakkel (Nld)	348
Zeehond (Nld)	341
Zeeland (Nld)	343
Zeisig (GFR)	198
Zeitz (GDR)	183
Zeltin (Lby)	320
Zenit (USSR)	538, 546
Zenobe Gramme (Bel)	52
Zerbst (GDR)	183
Zeus (Gre)	213
Zeya (USSR)	547
Zharki (USSR)	511
Zhdanov (USSR)	509
Zhguchy (USSR)	514
Zhiguili (USSR)	550
Zingahar (YPDR)	751
Zingst (GDR)	183
Zinnia (Bel)	52
Zleiten (Lby)	323
Zobel (GFR)	193
Zolotoy Rog (USSR)	549
Zomer (Nld)	346
Zond (USSR)	537
Zorky (USSR)	514
Zorritos (Per)	380
Zoubin (Iran)	243
Zubr (Pol)	392
Zuiderkruis (Nld)	347
Zulfiquar (Pak)	368
Zulia (Ven)	741
Zulu (UK)	577
Zum Zum (Pak)	369
Zurara (UAE)	557
Zuraw (Pol)	392
Zvezda (USSR)	541
Zwaardvis (Nld)	341

CLASSES

A

A 17 (Swe) 437
A 69 (Fra) 163
A 69 (SA) 413
Abeking (Nig) 354
Aberdovey (UK) 600
Abhay (Ind, Mrt) 228, 331
Abhay (improved) (Ind) 228
Ability (USA) 698
Abkhasia class (USSR) 541
Abnaki (USA) 705
Abtao (Per) 374
Achelous (Indo, RoK, Plp, RoC, USA, Ven) 238, 315, 387, 458, 702, 744
Acme (USA) 694
Active (USA) 730
AD 41 (USA) 696
Adjutant (Fra, Gre, Ita, RoC, Tun, Tur, Uru) 168, 176, 211, 268, 456, 469, 477, 737
Admirable (Bur, DR, Mex, Plp, RoC, Vtn) 67, 123, 333, 334, 384, 388, 459, 746
Aegis Type (USA) 667
Aeolus (USA) 722
Agave (Ita) 268
Agdleq (Den) 118
Aggressive (Fra, Spn, USA, Uru) 167, 428, 694, 737
Agile (Ita) 268
Agosta (Fra, SA, Spn) 150, 412, 418
Aguilucho (Spn) 432
Aist (USSR) 532
Ajax (USA) 702
Akademik Krilov (USSR) 541
Akademik Kurchatov (USSR) 543
Akademik L. Orbeli class (USSR) 540
Akashi (Jap) 289, 299
Akizuki (Jap) 281, 296
Akshay (Ban) 49
Alatna (USA) 722
Alava (Spn) 424
Albacore (USA) 641
Albany (USA) 663
Albatros (Ita) 265
Albatroz (Por) 397
Alesha (USSR) 534
Alfa (USSR) 495
Alfange (Ang) 23
Algerine (Bur, Gre, Tld) 67, 213, 466
Alicudi (Ita) 271
Alkmaar class (Nld) 345
Allen M. Sumner (Arg, Brz, Gre, RoC, Ven) 27, 58, 205, 453, 742
Allen M. Sumner Fram II (Brz, Chi, Col, Iran, RoK, Tur, USA, Ven) 58, 90, 106, 242, 311, 473, 676, 742
Alligator (USSR) 529
Almirante (Chi) 90
Almirante Clemente (Ven) 743
Almirante Pereira da Silva (Por) 396
Aloe (Ecu) 129
Alpino (Ita) 264
Altay (USSR) 548
Alvin Type (USA) 643
Alvin Type (modified) (USA) 643
Alvsborg (Swe) 442
Amatsukaze (Jap) 281
Amazon (UK) 575
American Explorer (USA) 720
Amga (USSR) 533
Amphion (Iran, RoC) 245, 458
Amur (USSR) 534
Anchorage (USA) 689
Anchova (Brz) 60
Andizhan class (USSR) 542
Andrea Doria (Ita) 260
Andromeda (Spn) 426
Andromeda (converted) (USA) 717
Ane (Swe) 445
Angeln (Tur) 481
An Ju (DPRK) 308
Annapolis (Can) 74
Anshan (CPR) 97
An Tung (CPR) 104
AO 177 (USA) 700
APD 37 (RoC) 454
APD 87 (RoC) 454
Ape (Ita) 266
Aragosta (Ita) 269
Aragua (Ven) 741
Arauca (Col) 108
ARD 12 (Ecu) 129
Aréthuse (Fra) 151
Argo class (DR) 123
Argos (Ang) 22
Argus (Brz) 61
Ariadne (GFR) 194
Aristaeus (Col, GFR) 109, 195
Ark Royal (UK) 568
Arktika class (USSR) 553
Arko (Swe) 443
Artillerist (DPRK) 305
Asagumo (Jap) 297
Asashimo class (Jap) 297
Ash (Isr) 253
Asheville (Col, Gre, RoK, Tur, USA) 107, 208, 312, 475, 683
Ashland (RoC) 456
Atlandtida (DR) 124
Atrek (Indo, USSR) 237, 535
Atrevida (Spn) 424
Atsumi (Jap) 285
Attack (Aust, Indo, PNG) 41, 235, 370
Audace (Ita) 261
Audaz (Spn) 423
Auk (RoK, Mex, Per, Plp, RoC, Tur, Uru) 312, 333, 334, 381, 383, 454, 479, 737
Austin (USA) 688
Avon class (UK) 583
AVR Type (Kam) 301
Ayanami (Jap) 282
Azteca (Mex) 334
Azueta (Mex) 334

B

Baglietto Type (Alg) 21
Baikal (USSR) 551
Bainbridge (USA) 662
Balao (Chi, Gre, Spn) 88, 205, 419
Balder (Nld) 345
Baleares (Spn) 423
Balsam (Plp, USA) 389, 731
Baltimore (USA) 666
Bangrachan (Tld) 464
Bar (CPR, Tur) 104, 481
Barbel (USA) 638
Barcelo (Mtn) 330
"Barcelo (P 10)" (Spn) 425
Barnegat (Eth, Gre, Ita, Vtn) 136, 212, 270, 746
Barranquilla (Col) 108
Barrosa Pereira (Brz) 62
Barsø (Den) 119
Baskunchak (GDR) 184
Bathurst (CPR) 99
Batral (Fra, Mor) 164, 338
Batram (Mad) 323
Bat Sheva (Isr) 254
Battle (Iran, Pak) 242, 366
Bat Yam Type (Isr) 254
Bay (Can) 78
Belknap (USA) 660
Bellatrix (Ang, DR, Per) 22, 124, 379
Benewah (USA) 709
Benjamin Franklin (USA) 627
Bergamini (Ita) 264
Berk (Tur) 474
Berneval (Fra) 169
Bertram Type (Jor) 301
Bezhitsa (USSR) 546
Bihoro (Jap) 293
Bird (UK) 589
Biya (USSR) 539
Black Swan (Egy, Ind) 131, 227
Blackwood (Ind, UK) 227, 580
Blue Ridge (USA) 685
Bodensee (GFR) 196
Bolster (USA) 702
Bombarda (Por) 398
Boris Chilikin (USSR) 547
Bouchard (Arg, Par) 28, 371
Bowditch (USA) 717
Brave (Gre) 209
Bravo (USSR) 497
Briza (Pol) 394
Broadsword (Gua, UK) 214, 575
Bronstein (USA) 682
Brooke (USA) 678
Brooke PCF 420 (Aust) 41
Brooklyn (Arg, Chi) 26, 89
Bulldog (UK) 590
Bustler (UK) 598
Buyskes (Nld) 347
Byblos (Leb) 318

C

C/Kaibokan I (CPR) 99
C 65 (Fra) 161
C 70 (Fra) 156
C 80 (SAr) 405
Cabildo (Gre, Spn) 210, 427
Cacine (Por) 397
California (USA) 658
Callaghan (USA) 718
Campbell (USA) 727
Canberra (USA) 666
Cannon (Gre, Per, Plp, Tld, Uru) 207, 376, 383, 462, 736
Cape (Can, Eth, Hai, Iran, RoK, Tld, Tur, USA) 76, 137, 216, 243, 245, 313, 464, 478, 729
Carpenter (Fram I) (USA) 676
Cartmel (UK) 600
Casa Grande (RoC) 456
Casco (Plp, USA) 383, 727
Castle (CPR) 99
Castor (Spn) 429
Centauro (Ita) 265
Ceylon (Per) 375
CGC (Bur) 68
CH (Pak) 366
Chaho (DPRK) 307
Chan Tou (CPR) 104
Chanticleer (Tur, USA) 480, 705
Chapaev (USSR) 510
Charles F. Adams (GFR, USA) 189, 673
Charles Lawrence (Chi, Ecu, RoK, Mex) 91, 127, 311, 333
Charleston (USA) 691
Charlie (USSR) 491
Charlie II (USSR) 491
Chauvenet (USA) 717
Chayka (Indo) 238
Ch'eng Tu (CPR) 98
Cherokee (Arg, Chi, Col, DR, Ecu, Indo, Pak, Per, RoC, USA) 28, 91, 93, 107 125, 129, 238, 369, 380, 459, 705, 734
Cheverton Type (Bhr, Omn) 47, 362
Chifuri (Jap) 294
Chikugo (Jap) 283
Chiyokaze class (Jap) 297
Chodo (DPRK) 306
Chong-Jin class (DPRK) 307
Chulym (USSR) 551
Cimarron (jumboised) (USA) 700, 721
Circe (Fra) 167
Circe (modified) (Fra) 167
Claud Jones (Indo) 233
Clemenceau (Fra) 152
Cleveland (converted) (USA) 664
Cohoes (DR, Uru, Ven) 123, 739, 745
Colossus (Arg, Brz) 25, 56
Columbia (USA) 720
Comandante Joao Belo (Por) 396
Combattante IIG (Lby) 321
Combattante IIIB (Nig) 353
Comet (USA) 719
Commandant Rivière (Fra) 161
Compass Island (USA) 698
Confiance (UK) 598
Conrad (Brz) 61
Coontz (USA) 670
Costa Sur (Arg) 31
County (UK) 573
Courtney (Col) 107
CR (Pak) 366
Crosley (RoK, Mex) 311, 333
Currituck (USA) 706

D

D/Kaibokan II (CPR) 99
D 20 (Spn) 421
D 60 (Spn) 421
Dabur (Isr) 252
Daio (Jap) 292
Daphne (Den) 118
Daphné (Fra, Pak, Por, SA) 151, 365, 396, 412
Daring (Aust, Per) 39, 375
Darter (USA) 640
DD 280 73
DD 993 (Iran) 241
Dash (USA) 694
Dealey (Uru) 736
De Cristofaro (Ita) 265
De Ruyter (Per) 374
De Soto County (Ita, USA) 267, 690
Delfinen (Den) 115
Delta (USA) 702
Delta I (USSR) 487
Delta II (USSR) 487
Delta III (USSR) 487
Des Moines (USA) 665
Descubierta (modified) (Mor) 336
Detachment (Can) 79
Deutschland (GFR) 198
Dhafeer (UAE) 557
Dido (modified) (Pak) 365
Director (UK) 598
Diver (USA) 702, 734
Dixie (USA) 697
DKN Type (Indo) 239
Dmitri Ovtsyn (USSR) 539
Dnepr (USSR) 535, 537
Dog (UK) 598
Dokkum (Nld) 346
Dolfijn (Nld) 341
Dolphin (USA) 641
Dom Aleixo (Por) 397
Don (Indo, USSR) 237, 533
Draken (Swe) 438
Dreadnought (UK) 566
DTK 221 (Sud) 435
DTM 231 (Sud) 435
Dubna (USSR) 548
Improved Dubna class (USSR) 548
Dun (Can) 76
Durance class (Fra) 170
Durango (Mex) 332
Dvora (Isr) 252

E

E (UK) 590
E 50 (Fra) 162
E 52 (Fra) 162
E 52B (Fra) 162
E-71 class (Bel) 50
Eagle (USA) 730
Echo I (USSR) 496
Echo II (USSR) 492
Eddy (UK) 593
Edenton (USA) 706
Edsall (Mex) 332
Eko (Jap) 300
Elk River (RoK) 314
Elk River (converted) (USA) 709
Elk River (modified) (Pan) 370
Eltanin (USA) 716, 718
Emory S. Land (USA) 703
Enterprise (USA) 647
Erimo (Jap) 292
Essex (USA) 654
Ethan Allen (USA) 629
Etorofu (CPR) 99
Evgenya (USSR) 528

F

F 30 (Spn) 422
F 60 (Spn) 424
F 67 (Fra) 158
F 70 (Spn) 423
Fabian Wrede (Fin) 142
Fabius (Mex) 335
Falcon (Nor, USA) 359
Falster (Den) 120
Felicity (UK) 599
Ferocity (Gre) 209
Ferrel (USA) 667
FFG 7 (Aust, Spn) 40, 422
Fiji (Ind) 224
500 Ton (Jap) 284
Flagstaff (Isr, USA) 252, 729
Fletcher (Arg, Brz, Chi, GFR, RoK, Mex, Per, RoC, Tur, USA) 27, 58, 89, 190, 206, 310, 332, 376, 453, 474, 676
Flower (CPR, DR, Tld) 99, 104, 123, 466
Ford (Gha, Nig, Sin, SA, UK) 202, 353, 409, 413, 589
Fort (Can) 78
Forrestal (USA) 650
Forrest Sherman (USA) 672, 674
Foxtrot (Ind, Lby, USSR) 224, 320, 498
Frauenlob (GFR) 194
Freccia (Ita) 266
Fresh (UK) 597
Friesland (Nld) 343
Frösch (GDR) 182
Fu Chou (CPR) 104
Fukae (Jap) 299
Fukien (CPR) 102
Fulton (USA) 704
FW (GFR) 197

G

Gagarin (USSR) 545
Galeb (Yug) 756
Galati (CPR) 104, 105
Garcia (USA) 679
Garian (Lby) 322
Gässten (Nor) 359
Gdansk (Pol) 392
Gearing Fram I (Brz, Ecu, Gre, RoK, Pak, RoC, Tur, USA) 58, 126, 206, 310, 365, 452, 473, 675
Gearing Fram II (Arg, Gre, RoK, RoC, Tur) 27, 206, 310, 452, 473
George Washington (USA) 630
Girl (UK) 599
Girl (modified) (UK) 599
Glacier (USA) 724
Glavkos (Gre) 204
Glen (Can) 79
Glenard P. Lipscomb (USA) 632
Glover (USA) 699
Golf (CPR) 96
Golf I and II (USSR) 490
Gordy (CPR) 97
Gota Lejon (Chi) 89
Grayback (USA) 639
Greenville Victory (USA) 719
Grisha I, II & III (USSR) 521
Gromovoy (CPR) 104
Guadiaro (Spn) 429
Guardian (Bar) 49
Guppy IA (Arg, Per) 25, 374
Guppy II (Arg, Brz, Ven) 25, 55, 741
Guppy IIA (Gre, Tur) 205, 472
Guppy III (Brz, Gre, Ita, Tur) 55, 205, 259, 472
Gus (USSR) 532
Gyre (USA) 715

H

H (Fin) 142
Ha T'se (CPR) 103
Hai (GDR) 181
Hai Dau class (CPR) 99
Hai Kou (CPR) 100
Hai Nan class (DPRK, Pak) 305, 367
Hai Ping (CPR) 105
Hainan (CPR) 100
Häjen (Swe) 438
Halibut (USA) 636
Halland (Col, Swe) 106, 439
Ham (Fra, Ind, UK, YPDR, Yug) 166, 177, 229, 586, 591, 596, 600, 601, 751, 756
Hamakaze class (Jap) 297
Hamashio class (Jap) 299
Hamburg (GFR) 190
Hamilton (USA) 726
Han (CPR) 96
Hanayuki (Jap) 297
Hanchon (DPRK) 309
Hancock (USA) 653
Hano (Swe) 443
Harukaze (Jap) 283
Haruna (Jap) 279
Haruna (improved) (Jap) 280
Hashidate (CPR) 99
Hashima class (Jap) 299
Haskell (Spn) 426
Haskell (converted) (USA) 714
Hauk (Nor) 358
Haven (USA) 700
Hayabusa (Jap) 290
Hayase (Jap) 286
Hayashio (Jap) 278
Hayes (USA) 715
Head (UK) 586
Hecla (UK) 590
Hecla (improved) (UK) 590
Hercules (DR) 125
Hero (USA) 726
Heroj (Yug) 752
Heroj (improved) (Yug) 752
Herstal (Bel) 51
Hidaka (Jap) 295
Higgins (Arg, Ita) 30, 267
High Point (USA) 683
Hiryu (Jap) 297
Hoku (Alb, CPR) 19, 100
Hola (CPR) 99
Holland (Nld) 343
Hollyhock (USA) 731
Hotel II and III (USSR) 489
Hu Chwan (Alb, CPR, Pak, Rom, Tan) 19, 101, 367, 401, 460
Hugin class (Swe) 440
Hull (USA) 674
Humaita (Par) 371
Hunley (USA) 703
Hunt (Ecu, Egy, Ind, UK) 127, 132, 227, 584
Huntress (SAr, Sen) 405, 407
Huntsman (Ana) 23
Hvidbjørnen (Den) 117
Hvidbjørnen (modified) (Den) 116

I

Ikl/Vickers Type 206 (Isr) 251
Ilo (Per) 379
Iltis (GDR) 182
Ilyusha (USSR) 528
Impavido (Ita) 262

812 INDEX / CLASS

Imperial Marinheiro (Brz) 59
Impetuoso (Ita) 263
Independence (Spn) 420
Ingul (USSR) 556
Insect (UK) 599
Interceptor (Cmn, Qat, UAE, YPDR) 69, 400, 558, 751
Intrepid (USA) 653
Iowa (USA) 655
Ishim class (USSR) 551
Island (UK) 588
Isles (GFR, UK) 199, 601
Isuzu (Jap) 284
Iwo Jima (USA) 687
Iwon (DPRK) 308
Izu (Jap) 291

J

Jaguar (Gre, SAr, Tur) 208, 404, 475
Jerong (Mly) 326
Joao Coutinho (Col, Por) 107, 397
John F. Kennedy (USA) 648
Juliett (USSR) 493
Jupiter (Ang) 22
Jura (UK) 601

K

K (Fin) 142
K 8 (Egy, Pol, USSR) 134, 392, 529
K 48 (DPRK) 307
KB 123 (GDR) 182
Kala (Fin) 142
Kalar class (USSR) 547
Kaman (Iran) 243
Kamchatka (USSR) 551
Kamenka (GDR, USSR) 184, 539
Kamishima (CPR) 99
Kampela class (Fin) 142
Kan-Chu class (CPR) 104
Kanin (USSR) 514
Kapitan Belousoy (USSR) 554
Kapitan Chechkin (USSR) 555
Kapitan Izmaylov (USSR) 555
Kapitan Sorokin (USSR) 554
Kara (USSR) 505
Karhu (Fin) 141
Kartal (Tur) 475
Kasado (Jap) 287, 290
Kashin (USSR) 512
Kashin (modified) (USSR) 512
Katun (USSR) 556
Kave (Fin) 142
Kazbek (USSR) 548
Kedah (Mly) 326
Kedma (Isr) 254
Keila class (USSR) 552
Kelabang (Indo) 236
Kellar (Por) 398
Kenneth Whiting (Ita) 267
Khabarov (USSR) 552
Khobi (Alb, Indo, USSR) 20, 238, 549
Kiang Hu (CPR) 98
Kiang Nan (CPR) 98
Kiang Tung (CPR) 98
Kiev (USSR) 502
Kilauea (USA) 697
Kildin (USSR) 513
Kin (UK) 594
King (Arg) 28
Kitty Hawk (USA) 648
Klasma (USSR) 547
Klondike (USA) 696
Klongyai (Tld) 463
KM-4 (DPRK) 309
Knox (USA) 680
Kola (USSR) 520
Köln (GFR) 191
Kolomna class (USSR) 540
Komar (Alg, CPR, Cub, Egy, Indo, DPRK, Syr, Vtn) 21, 100, 112, 132, 235, 306, 450, 747
Komarov (USSR) 545
Konda (USSR) 549
Kondor I (GDR) 183, 184
Kondor II (GDR) 183
Koni class (USSR) 518
Korolev (USSR) 545
Kortenaer (Nld) 344
Koskelo (Fin) 143
Kosong (DPRK) 309
Kotlin (USSR) 516
Kouzu (Jap) 287
Krake (GDR) 185
Kraljevica (Ban, Eth, Indo, Sud, Yug) 49, 137, 236, 434, 755
Kresta I (USSR) 507
Kresta II (USSR) 506
KR 3 (Fin) 143
Kris (Mly) 326
Krivak I (USSR) 511
Krivak II (USSR) 511
Krogulec (Pol) 392
Kromantse (Gha) 201
Kronshtadt (Alb, CPR, Cub, Indo, Rom) 19, 100, 112, 234, 400
Kuckitat (Arg) 32
Kuha (Fin) 140
Kümo (GDR) 184
Kunashiri (Jap) 293
Kvalsund (Nor) 359
KW (Gre) 209
Kynda (USSR) 508

L

L (Fin) 142
L 51 (Swe) 445
L. Y. Spear (USA) 703
La Combattante (Fra) 165
La Combattante II (Gre) 207
La Combattante III (Gre) 207
La Dunkerquoise (Fra) 166
Labo (GDR) 183
Lafayette (USA) 627
Lake (NZ) 350
Lama (USSR) 533
Lampo (Ita) 266
Lance (Gam, Sen) 179, 407
Langeland (Den) 121
Lay (UK) 595
Lazaga (Mor) 337
Lazaga (P-00) (Spn) 425
LCM 3 (Bur) 68
LCM-6 (Plp, Sen, Uru) 387, 407, 739
LCM-8 (Pan, Plp) 370, 378
LCT (8) class (Com) 110
LCU (Tld) 466
LCU (DR, Indo, Plp) 124, 236, 387
LCU 501 (Gre, Kam, RoK, Par, RoC, Tur) 211, 302, 315, 372, 457, 479
LCU 1466 (Kam, Leb, RoC) 302, 318, 457
LCVP (Arg, Indo, Plp) 29, 236, 387
LDM 100 & 400 (Por) 398
LDP 200 (Por) 398
Le Fougueux (Fra, Tun, Yug) 166, 469, 754
Leahy (USA) 661
Leander (Chi, Ind, NZ, UK) 91, 225, 349, 576
Leander, Broad-Beamed (NZ, UK) 349
Lebed class (USSR) 531
Lebedev (USSR) 543
Lei Chou (CPR) 104
Lentra (USSR) 537, 539, 552
Leopard (Ban, Ind, UK) 48, 226, 579
Ley (UK) 586
Libau (USSR) 547
Libelle (GDR) 181
Lindau (GFR) 193
Lindormen (Den) 120
Liulom (Tld) 463
Loadmaster (Bhr, Bru, Omn) 47, 64, 363
Long Beach (USA) 662
Loreto (Per) 377
Los Angeles (USA) 631
Loyal (UK) 600
LPI (Spn) 425
LSIL (Plp) 387
LSIL 351 (RoC) 458
LSM-1 (Ecu, Gre, Isr, RoK, Par, Per, Plp, RoC, Ven, Vtn) 128, 210, 253, 315, 372, 378, 387 457, 744, 748
LSM 1 (modified) (Tur) 477
LSSL-1 (Plp, Vtn) 387, 748
LST 1 (Per) 378
LST (3) (Ind) 229
LST 1-511 (Indo) 236
LST 1-510 (Chi, Gre, RoK, RoC) 92, 210, 314, 415
LST 511 (Per) 378
LST 511-1152 (Ecu, Gre, Indo, RoK, Mly, Mex, Sin, RoC, Tur, Vtn) 128, 210, 236, 314, 327, 335, 409, 457, 478, 748
Lüneburg (GFR) 197
Lupo (Ita, Ven) 264, 742
Lupo (modified) (Per) 376
Lürssen TNC 45 (Indo) 235
Lürssen (Chi, Ecu) 92, 128
Lürssen S-143 (Nig) 353
Luta (CPR) 97
Luza class (USSR) 552
Lynch (Arg) 30

M

M 3 (Aus) 46
M 15 (Swe) 444
M 31 (Swe) 444
M 40 (Rom) 402
M 44 (Swe) 444
M 47 (Swe) 444
M 117 (Yug) 755
M 301 (Yug) 756
Maagen (Den) 118
Machete class (Gua) 214
Mackenzie (Can) 74
Mackinaw (USA) 725
Maestrale (Ita) 263
Majestic (Ind) 224
Majestic (modified) (Aust) 37
Mala (Yug) 753
Malaspina (Spn) 429
Manta (Ecu) 128
Manych (USSR) 548
Maranon (Per) 377
Mark (RoC) 459
Mark (converted) (USA) 709
Markab (USA) 629
Mars (USA) 697
Matsuura (Jap) 293
Matsuyuki (Jap) 296
Mattawee (CPR) 104
Maumee (USA) 721
Mayak (USSR) 536, 552
Mayakovsky (modified) (USSR) 544
Melitopol (USSR) 540
Melville (USA) 716
Meteor (USA) 719
MHV 70 (Den) 120
MHV 80 (Den) 120
MHV 90 (Den) 119
Midway (USA) 652
Mikhail Kalinin (USSR) 552
Minegumo (Jap) 281
Miner (UK) 595
Ming (CPR) 96
Mirka I & II (USSR) 518
Mirny (Mtn, USSR) 330, 536
Mispillion (jumboised) (USA) 721
Mission (Pak) (USA) 368, 714
Mitscher (USA) 671
Miura (Jap) 285
Miyake (Jap) 292
Mizutori (Jap) 284
Mol (Som, Sri) 410, 433
Moma (Bul, Pol, USSR) 66, 393, 536, 538
Mornar (Yug) 753
Moskva (USSR) 504, 554
MO IV (DPRK) 307
MO VI (Gn, USSR) 215, 525
MP 4 (Egy, USSR) 134, 531
MP 6 (USSR) 552
MP 10 (USSR) 531
Mrowka (Pol) 394
MSC 292 & 268 (Iran) 244
MSC 268 & 294 (RoK, Tur) 314, 477
MSC Type 60 (Bel, Den) 51, 121
MSC 294 (Gre) 211
MSC 322 (SAr) 404
MSO 498 (Bel, Fra) 51, 167
Muna class (USSR) 552
Murasame (Jap) 282

N

Näcken (Swe) 437
Najin (DPRK) 304
Nalon (Spn) 428
Nampo class (DPRK) 309
Nana-Go (Jap) 287
Nanuchka (Ind, USSR) 228, 522
Narhvalen (Den) 115
Narval (Fra) 151
Narwhal (USA) 632
Nasty (Gre, Tur) 208, 475
Natsushio (Jap) 278
Natya (USSR) 526
Nautilus (USA) 638
Nawarat (Bur) 67
Neosho (USA) 700
Nepa class (USSR) 551
Neptun (USSR) 550
Neptune (USA) 722
Nercha (USSR) 549
Nestin (Yug) 756
Nevelskoy (USSR) 542
Newport (USA) 690
Nikolai Zubov (USSR) 535, 538
Nils Juel (Den) 116
Nimitz (USA) 645
Niobe (GFR) 195
Niteroi (Brz) 57
Nitro (USA) 697
Nagekaze class (Jap) 297
Nojima (Jap) 292
Norton (Can) 79
Norwalk (USA) 718
November (USSR) 496
Nunobiki (Jap) 297
Nuoli (Fin) 139
NV 11 (Fin) 143
NV 13 (Fin) 143
NV 15 (Fin) 143
NV 24 (Fin) 143
NV 30 (Fin) 143
NV 101 (Fin) 143
Nyryat (Alb, Cub, Egy, Syr) 20, 113, 135, 450
Nyryat I (USSR) 552
Nyryat II (Iraq) 248

O

Oberon (Brz, Can, Chi, UK) 55, 72, 88, 567
Obluze (Pol) 391
Obluze (modified) (Pol) 391
Observation Island (USA) 713
October 6 (Egy) 133
Ohio (USA) 626
Oilpress (UK) 595
Okean (USSR) 537
Okhtensky (Egy, Indo, USSR) 135, 239, 556
Oksywie (Pol) 392
Oland (Swe) 439
OL Class (UK) 591
Olekma class (USSR) 549
Oliver Hazard Perry (USA) 677
Olya (USSR) 528
Onega (USSR) 539
Onversaagd (Nld) 346
Ooshio (Jap) 278
Oquendo (Spn) 422
Orel (USSR) 556
Osa (CPR, Iraq, Pol, Rom, Yug) 99, 247, 391, 401, 754
Osa I (Alg, Bul, Cub, Egy, GDR, Ind, DPRK, Syr, USSR) 21, 66, 112, 132, 181, 228, 306, 450, 523
Osa II (Alg, Cub, GDR, Ind, Lby, Som, USSR) 21, 112, 181, 228, 321, 410, 523
Oskol (USSR) 535
Oslo (Nor) 356
Osprey (USA) 683
Oxley (Aust) 36

P

P 4 (Alb, Bul, CPR, Cub, Egy, DPRK, Rom, Syr, Tan, Vtn, YAR, Zai) 20, 66, 101, 113, 133, 308, 401 450, 460, 747, 751, 758
P 6 (Alg, CPR, Cub, Egy, EqG, GDR, Gn, GB, Iraq, DPRK, Pol, Som, Tan, USSR, Vtn, YPDR) 21, 101, 113, 133, 135, 182, 215, 248, 308, 391, 410, 460, 525, 747, 751
P 48 (Sen, Tun) 406, 470
PA 75 (Fra) 153
Pabna (Ban) 48
Pajak (Pol) 394
Pamir (USSR) 536, 556
Papa (USSR) 491
Parinas (Per) 379
Passat (USSR) 543
Pat (Indo) 239
Patapsco (Chi, Col, Gre, RoC) 94, 109, 212, 459
Patra Type (IC) 273
Pattimura (Indo) 234
Paul Revere (USA) 691
PC 173 (Tur) 472
PC-461 (Indo, Plp, RoC) 234, 384, 459
PC 1638 (Chi, Tur) 92, 476
PCE 827 (Bur, Ecu, RoK, Plp) 67, 127, 312, 384
Pchela (USSR) 524
Peconic (USA) 722
Peder Skram (Den) 116
Pedro Teixeira (Brz) 59
Perdana (Mly) 325
Perth (Aust) 38
Perwira (Bru) 64
Petya I (Syr, USSR) 449, 518
Petya I Mod (USSR) 519
Petya II (Ind, USSR) 226, 518
PF 103 (Iran, Tld) 243, 461
PGM (Bur) 68
PGM-9 (Gre) 209
PGM 39 (Indo, Plp) 235, 385
PGM-53 (Eth) 137
PGM 59 (Vtn) 747
PGM-71 (DR, Ecu, Lbr, Per, Plp, Tld, Tur, Vtn) 124, 127, 319, 385, 463, 476, 747
PGM-71 (improved) (Iran) 243
Pigeon (USA) 704
Pilica (Pol) 392
Piratini (Brz) 60
Pirttisaari (Fin) 142
Pizarro (modernised) (Spn) 424
Plainview (USA) 699
Plejad (Swe) 441
PO 2 (Alb, Bul, Iraq) 20, 66, 248
Podzharny (Indo) 238
Point (USA, Vtn) 730, 748
Polar Star (USA) 724
Polimar (Mex) 334
Polnochniy (USSR) 530
Polnocny (Alg, Egy, Ind, Iraq, Lby, Pol, Som, YPDR) 21, 134, 229, 247, 323, 393, 410, 751
Poluchat (Alg, EqG, Ind, Tan, YAR, YPDR) 22, 135, 228, 460, 751, 751
Poluchat I (Alb, Gn, Iraq, Som, USSR) 20, 215, 248, 410, 552
Poluchat II class (Egy) 135
Poolster (Nld) 347
Porpoise (UK) 567
Porte (Can) 78
Poti (Bul, Rom, USSR) 65, 400, 522
Potomac (USA) 720
Potvis (Nld) 341
Povenets class (USSR) 546
Powhatan (USA) 722
Pozharny I (USSR) 552
PR 72 (Mor) 337
PR-72P (Per) 377
President (SA) 412
Primorye (USSR) 535
Private Leonard C. Brostrom (USA) 719
Proteus (USA) 704
PS 700 (Lby) 322
Pukkio (Fin) 142
Purga (USSR) 554
PV 1 (Fin) 143
PV 11 (Fin) 143
PV 21 (Fin) 143
PV 27 (Fin) 143
PV 32 (Fin) 143
PV 51 (Fin) 143
PX class (Mly) 327
PX class (improved) (Mly) 328

Q

Quebec (USSR) 501
Quilmes (Arg) 33

R

R (Indo) 237
Rade Koncar (Yug) 754
Raleigh (USA) 688
Raleigh (converted) (USA) 699
Rapier (SAr) 405
Rasmussen (Nig) 354
Rebun (Jap) 294
Red (USA) 731
Redwing (Fij, Sin) 137, 408
Reinøysund (Nor) 359
Reshef (Isr, SA) 251, 413
Resolution (UK) 564
Restigouche (Can) 74
Restigouche (improved) (Can) 75
Rhein (GFR) 195
Rhin (Fra) 171
Riga (Bul, CPR, Fin, GDR, Indo, USSR) 65, 98, 138, 180, 233, 520
Rigel (USA) 713
Rihtniemi (Fin) 140
Rio (Ven) 745
Rio Doce (Brz) 62
Rio Orinoco (Ven) 743
River (Aust, Bur, DR, Egy, Ind, Sri) 40, 67, 122, 132, 227, 432
Robbe (GDR) 182
Robert D. Conrad (USA) 715
Robert H. Smith (Tur) 473
Roger de Lauria (Spn) 420
Romeo (Bul, CPR, Egy, DPRK, USSR) 65, 96, 130, 304, 499
Ropucha (USSR) 530
Roraima (Brz) 60
Roslavl (CPR, Rom) 105, 402
Rothesay (UK) 578
Rover (UK) 592
Rudderow (RoK, RoC) 311, 454
Rude (USA) 667
Ruissalo (Fin) 140
RV 1 (Fin) 143
RV 4 (Fin) 143
RV 6 (Fin) 143
RV 8 (Fin) 143
RV 9 (Fin) 143
RV 10 (Fin) 143
RV 30 (Fin) 143
RV 41 (Fin) 143
RV 97 (Fin) 143

S

Name	Page
S 1 (CPR)	96
S 1 Sante Fe (Arg)	25
S 30 (Spn)	419
S 60 (Spn)	418
S 70 (Spn)	418
Saam (Iran)	242
Saar (Isr)	252
Sabah (Mly)	326
Sachsenwald (GFR)	197
Sacramento (USA)	701
Sagami (Jap)	288
Sailfish (USA)	640
Saint (Can)	79
St. Laurent (Can)	75
Salisbury (Ban, UK)	48, 579
Salta (Arg)	25
Samara (USSR)	538
Sam Kotlin (Pol)	390
Sam Kotlin I & II (USSR)	515
Samson (UK)	598
Samuel Gompers (USA)	696
San Giorgio (Ita)	262
Sao Roque (Por)	398
Sarancha (USSR)	523
Sariwan (DPRK)	305
Sasha (USSR)	528
Sauro (Ita)	258
Savage (Plp, Tun, Vtn)	383, 469, 746
Schoolboy (RoK)	313
Schütze (Brz, GFR)	60, 194
Schuyler Otis Bland (USA)	718
Schwalbe (Tan)	460
Sealift (USA)	720
Seal (UK)	602
Seawolf (USA)	637
Sechura (Per)	380
Siko (Jap)	300
Sekstan (Alb, Alg, Egy)	20, 22, 135
Sewart (Eth, RoK, Nic)	136, 137, 313, 351
Shanghai (Cmn, CPR, Con, DPRK, Rom, Tan, Vtn)	69, 100, 111, 306, 401, 460, 747
Shanghai II (Alb, CPR, Gn, Pak, SL)	20, 101, 215, 367, 407
Shantung (CPR)	102
Sharada (Ind)	228
Sheffield (UK)	574
Shenandoah (Indo, USA)	238, 696
Shenandoah (converted) (USA)	701
Shershen (Bul, Egy, GDR, DPRK, USSR, Yug)	66, 133, 181, 307, 524, 754
Shih Jian (CPR)	103
Shikinami (Jap)	296
Shmel (USSR)	525
Shu Kuang (CPR)	104
Sibir (USSR)	544
Silas Bent (USA)	717
Silbermöwe (Gre)	208
Simon Lake (USA)	703
Sin Hung (DPRK)	309
Sirius (Brz, Fra, Mor)	61, 166, 168, 338
Sithole (Indo)	239
Sjöormen (Swe)	437
Skate (USA)	637
Skipjack (USA)	635
Skory (Egy, USSR)	131, 517
Sleipner (Nor)	357
SM 165 (Rom)	402
SMB I (Egy, USSR)	134, 531
Smolny (USSR)	546
Smuggler 21SS (Ice)	221
SNA 72 (Fra)	150
Snogg (Nor)	358
Södermanland (Swe)	438
Sofia (USSR)	548
SO-I (Alg, Bul, Cub, Egy, GDR, Iraq, DPRK, USSR, Vtn, YPDR)	21, 66, 112, 133, 180, 247, 305, 523, 747, 751
Søløven (Den)	118
Sonya (USSR)	527
Sooraya (Sri)	433
Sorum (USSR)	556
Sotoyomo (Arg, Brz, Chi, DR, RoK, Per, RoC, USA)	28, 33, 63, 91, 125, 316, 378, 458, 459, 705, 734
Souya (Jap)	286
Spa (UK)	597
Sparviero (Ita)	266
Spear (Bhr, Indo, Mlw, Qat, StK, Sen, UAE, YPDR)	47, 236, 324, 400, 403, 407, 558, 751
Spica (Swe)	440
Spica-M (Mly)	325
Spitfire (UK)	601
Split (Yug)	753
Spruance (USA)	668
Spruance (improved) (USA)	668
Stenka (USSR)	524
Storis (USA)	725
Storm (Nor)	357
Sturgeon (USA)	633
Suamico (USA)	721
Suffren (Fra)	157
Sura (USSR)	550
Surapati (Indo)	234
Suribachi (USA)	697
Surveyor (USA)	666
Susa (Liby)	322
Sutjeska (Yug)	752
Sutlej (Ind)	230
Sverdlov (USSR)	509
Swatow (CPR, DPRK Vtn)	101, 306, 747
Swift (Hon, Kam, Mlt, Tld, Vtn)	217, 301, 329, 464, 749
Swiftsure (UK)	565
SX 404 (Pak)	365
SX 506 (Col)	106

T

Name	Page
T 4 (Cub, Som, USSR)	113, 410, 531
T 42 (Swe)	441
T 43 (Alb, Alg, Bul, CPR, Egy, Indo, Iraq, Pol, Syr, USSR)	20, 22, 66, 102, 134, 237, 249, 392, 450, 527, 551
T 43/AGR (USSR)	527
T 47 (Fra)	160
T 53 (Fra)	159
T 58 (USSR)	526
T 58 (Mod) (Ind)	230
T 301 (Alb, Egy, Rom)	20, 134, 402
Tachikaze (Jap)	279
Tacoma (DR, RoK, Tld)	122, 312, 462
Taechong (DPRK)	305
Tai Shan (CPR)	102
Takami (Jap)	286
Takatsuki (Jap)	280
Talara (Per)	379
Tan Lin (CPR)	104
Tang (Iran, Ita, USA)	241, 258, 640
Tango (USSR)	497
Tarawa (USA)	686
Tarmo (Fin)	141
Taucher (GDR)	184
Tejsten (Den)	119
Telkka (Fin)	143
Telnovsk (USSR)	538, 552
Tenko (Jap)	300
Terrebonne Parish (Gre, Spn, Tur, Ven)	210, 427, 478, 744
Thetis (GFR)	191
Thomaston (USA)	689
Thresher (USA)	634
Tide (Aus)	29
Tide (later) (UK)	591
Tiger (UK)	571
Ting Hai (CPR)	105
Tisza (Indo)	238
Tjeld (Nor)	358
TM (CPR)	104
TNC 48 (Sin)	408
Tokachi (Jap)	294
Tomba (USSR)	534
Ton (Arg, Gha, Ind, Ire, Mly, SA, UK)	30, 202, 229, 250, 326, 327, 413, 585
Ton (modified) (Aust, UK)	41, 589
Toplivo I (Alb)	20
Toplivo 3 (Alb)	20
Toti (Ita)	258
Town (Pak)	368
Tracker (Bhr, SA)	47, 415
Trad (Tld)	463
TR 40 (Rom, USSR)	402, 528
Trafalgar (UK)	565
Tral (DPRK)	305
Tree (CPR)	104
Tribal (UK)	577
Trident (Fra)	165
Trieste Type (USA)	643
Triton (Den, UK, USA)	117, 599, 636
Tromp (Nld)	342
Tropik (USSR)	544
Truxtun (USA)	659
Tugur (Indo)	239
Tuima (Fin)	139
Tulare (USA)	691
Tullibee (USA)	634
Turunmaa (Fin)	138
Turya (USSR)	524
Tydeman (Nld)	347
Type A (Sin)	408
Type B (Sin)	408
Type XXI (converted) (GFR)	188
Type 82 (UK)	572
Type 122 (GFR)	191
Type 142 (GFR)	193
Type 143 (GFR)	192
Type 148 (GFR)	192
Type 162 (GFR)	192
Type 205 (GFR)	188
Type 206 (GFR)	188
Type 210 (GFR)	188
Type 520 (GFR)	193
Type 521 (GFR)	193
Type 207 (Nor)	356
Type 209 (Col)	105
Type 209 (Indo)	232
Type 209 (Per)	373
Type 209 (Tur)	472
Type 209 (Ven)	741
Type 210 (Nor)	356

U

Name	Page
Uda (Indo, USSR)	238, 549
Ugra (Ind, USSR)	230, 532
Ukuru (CPR)	99
Umitaka (Jap)	284
Ural (USSR)	534
Urho (Fin, Swe)	141, 445
Usedom (USSR)	549
Uzushio (Jap)	278
Uzushio (improved) (Jap)	278

V

Name	Page
V 01 (Swe)	441
V 4 (Mex)	335
Vadso (Nor)	357
Valday (USSR)	551
Valerian Uryuaev (USSR)	539, 544
Valiant (UK)	566
Van Speijk (Nld)	344
Van Straelen (Nld)	346
Vanya (Bul, Syr, USSR)	66, 450, 528
Vasama (Fin)	139
Vasily Pronchishtchev (USSR)	555
Vasily Pronchishtchev (modified) (USSR)	542, 555
VC (Spn)	432
Vegesack (GFR, Tur)	201, 478
VG (Rom)	402
Victor (USSR)	495
Victor II (USSR)	495
Victory (USA)	714
Victory (converted) (USA)	713
Ville (Can)	79
Virginia (USA)	657
Visby (Swe)	439
Voda (USSR)	552
Voima (Fin)	141
Vukovklanac (Yug)	755
Vydra (Bul, Egy, USSR)	66, 134, 531
Vytegrales (USSR)	544, 546

W

Name	Page
W (SA)	412
Wako (Jap)	300
Walchensee (GFR)	196
Water (UK)	597
Wellington (Iran)	244
Westerwald (GFR)	197
Whampoa (CPR)	102
Whiskey (Alb, CPR, Egy, Indo, DPRK, Pol, USSR)	19, 96, 130, 232, 304, 390, 500
Whiskey Canvas Bag (USSR)	501
Whiskey Long-Bin (USSR)	494
Whiskey Twin Cylinder (USSR)	494
Whitby (Ind, NZ, UK)	226, 350, 580
White Sumac (USA)	732
Wichita (USA)	701
Wild Duck (UK)	594
Wild Duck (improved) (UK)	594
Wild Duck (later) (UK)	594
Wildervank (Eth, Omn)	136, 362
Wilhelm Bauer (USSR)	534
Wilkes (USA)	717
Willemoes (Den)	117
Winchester (Iran)	244
Wind (USA)	725
Wisla (Pol)	391
Wodnik (Pol)	393
Wolf (Nld)	345
Wood (Can)	79
Wu Hsi Pei Hai (CPR)	102

Y

Name	Page
Y (Fin)	142
Y 301 (Bur)	67
Yaezakura (Jap)	297
Yahagi (Jap)	293
Yakaze (Jap)	297
Yamagumo (Jap)	280
Yankee (USSR)	488
Yar (Isr)	254
Yarrow Type (Mly)	325
Yavza (USSR)	551
Yen Hsi (CPR)	103
Yen Lai class (CPR)	104
Yen Lun (CPR)	103
Yen Teng class (CPR)	105
Yermak (USSR)	553
Yevgenya (Iraq)	249
Ying Kou (CPR)	102
YLT 422 (RoC)	459
YM 1 (Fin)	142
YM 4 (Fin)	142
YM 22 (Fin)	142
YM 55 (Fin)	142
YMS-1 (RoK)	316
Yoko (Jap)	300
YTL 422 (Plp) (Tld)	389, 467
Yu Lin (CPR, Kam, Tan)	102, 302, 460
Yu Ling (CPR)	103
Yukikaze class (Jap)	297
Yuko (Jap)	300
Yunnan class (CPR)	103
Yurka (Egy, USSR)	134, 526
YW (Ecu)	129
YW 83 (Iran, USA)	246, 710

Z

Name	Page
Z (Egy, YPDR)	131, 751
Zhenya (USSR)	528
Zobel (GFR)	193
Zhuk (Cub, Iraq, USSR, YPDR)	113, 248, 525, 751
Zuiko (Jap)	300
Zulu IV (USSR)	499
Zwaardvis (Nld)	341
101 (Sud)	435
701 (Par)	371